Contents

Guide to the Dictionary

If the plural of a noun is irregular, it is shown like this.

hand·y·man /'hændimæn/ *n* [C] *plural* **handy-men** /-men/ someone who is good at making and repairing things.

Active words are marked and show you which words are important to learn and remember.

hang¹ /hæŋ/ *v* **hung** /hʌŋ/, hung, hanging
1 [I,T] to put something somewhere so that its top part is fixed but its bottom part is free to move, or to be in this position: *He hung his coat on the back of the door.* | **+ from/on etc** *Her portrait was hanging on the wall.* **2** [I,T], *past tense and past participle* **hanged** to kill someone by dropping them with a rope around their neck, or to die in this way: *Corey hanged himself in his prison cell.* **3** [I always + adv/prep] to stay in the air in the same place for a long time: *Dark clouds hung over the valley.* **4 hang your head** to look ashamed and embarrassed: *Lewis hung his head and refused to answer.* **5 hang in the balance** to be in a situation in which the result is not certain, and something bad may happen: *Our whole future is hanging in the balance.* **6 leave sb/sth hanging** to not finish something or not tell someone your decision about something: *The investigation should not be left hanging.*

Verbs which have irregular past tenses or past participles are shown like this.

The words in dark type show you some other words which are often used with this word.

Many words have more than one meaning. The most common meaning is shown first.

Phrasal verbs are shown after the main verb entry, in alphabetical order.

hang around (also **hang about** *BrE*) *phr v* [I,T] *informal* **1** to stay in one place without doing very much, often because you are waiting for someone: *We hung around for about an hour and then left.* **2 hang around with sb** to spend a lot of time with someone: *I don't like the people she hangs around with.*
hang back *phr v* [I] to not want to move forward or speak, often because you are shy: *Joe tends to hang back and let the others do the talking.*

Words and phrases which are mostly used in speech are shown like this.

hang on *phr v* **1 hang on!** *spoken* used to tell someone to wait for you: *Hang on, I'll be with you in a minute!* **2** [I] *informal* to hold something tightly: *Hang on everybody, the road's pretty bumpy.*
hang onto sb/sth *phr v* [T] *informal* to keep something: *Hang onto that letter – you might need it later.*

These letters tell you whether a verb is transitive or intransitive. [T] means it is transitive, so must have a direct object; [I] means it is intransitive, so cannot have a direct object.

hang out *phr v* [I] *informal* to spend a lot of time at a particular place or with particular people: *They hang around together.*
hang round *phr v* [I] *BrE* HANG AROUND
hang up *phr v* **1** [I] to finish a telephone conversation by putting the telephone down: *She said good night and hung up.* | **hang up on sb** (=put the phone down during a conversation because you are angry): *Don't hang up on me!* **2** [T **hang** sth ↔ **up**] to put something such as clothes on a hook or hange

The dictionary tells you if a word is formal (mostly used in writing or formal speech) or informal (mostly used with friends).

The meanings of words are explained simply, using a limited Defining Vocabulary of 2000 basic words.

hang² *n* **get the hang of (doing) sth** *informal* to learn how to do something: *You'll soon get the hang of using the computer.*

har·bour [1] *BrE*, **harbor** *AmE* /ˈhɑːbə‖-ˈhɑːrbər/ *n* [C] an area of water next to the land where ships can stay safely →see colour picture on page 697

British and American spellings are both shown.

harbour [2] *BrE*, **harbor** *AmE* — *v* [T] **1** to keep feelings or thoughts in your mind for a long time: **harbour doubts/suspicions etc** *Several of Wilson's colleagues harboured suspicions about him.* **2** to protect someone by hiding them from the police: *She was accused of harbouring deserters.*

These letters tell you whether a word is a noun, verb, adverb, adjective etc.

hard [1] /hɑːd‖hɑːrd/ *adj* **1** firm and stiff, and difficult to cut, press down, or break: *a hard mattress.* | *The plums are still too hard to eat,* →opposite SOFT **2** difficult to do or understand: *The interviewer asked some very hard questions.* | *it's hard (for sb) to do sth It's hard to say when Glen will be back.* →opposite EASY[1] **3** involving a lot of physical or mental effort or suffering: *a long hard climb to the top of the hill* | *Poor May, she's had a hard life.* | **hard work** *Bringing up children on your own is hard work.* **4** showing no kindness or sympathy: *Mr. Katz is a hard man to work for, but he's fair.* | **be hard on sb** *She's too hard on those kids.* **5** **give sb a hard time** *informal* to criticize someone or make jokes about them, so that they feel embarrassed or uncomfortable: *The guys were giving him a hard time about missing the ball.* **6** **do/learn sth the hard way** to make a lot of mistakes or have a lot of difficulty before learning something **7** **no hard feelings** *spoken* used to tell someone that you do not feel angry with them any more **8** **hard facts/evidence** facts etc that are true and can be proved **9** **a hard winter** a very cold winter — **hardness** *n* [U]

Words with the opposite meaning are shown after the examples.

Sentence patterns in dark type show you how this word is typically used in a sentence.

Idioms and fixed phrases are shown in dark type and have a definition which explains the whole phrase.

Words which are part of the same word family but which have different parts of speech like this are shown.

hard [2] *adv* **1** using a lot of effort or force: *She'd been working hard all day.* | *Come on, push harder!* **2** **be hard pressed/put/pushed to do sth** to have difficulty doing something: *They'll be hard pushed to pay back the money.* **3** **take sth hard** to feel very upset about something: *I didn't think that Joe would take the news so hard.*

Examples show you how you can use the word.

Usage notes give you extra information about a word, and help you avoid making mistakes.

USAGE NOTE: hard and hardly

Hard is an adverb used to say that something is done using a lot of effort or force: *We studied hard for two weeks.* **Hardly** means 'almost not': *I could hardly believe what she said.*

hard-and-fast /ˌ. . '. ◂/ *adj* **hard-and-fast rules** a rule that cannot be changed

This letter tells you that the noun is countable.

hard·back /ˈhɑːdbæk‖ˈhɑːrd-/ *n* [C] a book that has a strong stiff cover →compare PAPERBACK

Words which are related or which might also be useful are shown.

hard·ball /ˈhɑːbɔːl‖ˈhɑːrdbɒːl/ *n* **play hardball** *informal* to do everything you can to prevent someone from succeeding, even if this includes doing bad or unfair things

Pronunciation is shown after each word, like this.

hard·board /ˈhɑːdbɔːd‖ˈhɑːrdbɔːrd/ *n* [U] a kind of wood made out of smaller pieces of wood that have been pressed together

This letter tells you that the noun is uncountable.

Workbook

This workbook section contains information and exercises to help you use the dictionary. The easy exercises are marked *. Start with these exercises and then move on to the ones marked **. The answers to the exercises are on pages 793–796.

This dictionary tells you a lot about English words and how to use them – in writing and speaking English, as well as in reading and listening to English.

You can use this dictionary to:
• check the spelling of a word
• find the meaning of a word
• find how to use a word in a sentence
• find when and where to use a word correctly
• find the correct pronunciation of a word

The dictionary contains a lot of information in a very small space. You need to be able to find the information you want quickly and easily.

Finding a word quickly

Spelling

There are about 45,000 words and phrases explained in this dictionary, listed in alphabetical order. The English alphabet has 26 letters. The order of the letters is this:

A B C D E F G H I J K L M N O P Q R S T U V W X Y Z
a b c d e f g h i j k l m n o p q r s t u v w x y z

Exercise 1 * **Write these words in alphabetical order.**

| actor | world | hour | celebrate | job | quick |

1 .*actor*.. 2 .... 3 ....

4 .... 5 .... 6 ....

If two words start with the same letter, you must look at the second letter, then the third letter and so on.

Exercise 2 * **Write these words in alphabetical order.**

| where | white | wrong | wife | weight | which |

1 **weight**. 2 .... 3 ....

4 .... 5 .... 6 ....

Opening the dictionary at the right place

Close your dictionary and look at the side. There are some marks on the edge of the pages. These marks help you to open the dictionary in about the right place. Remember that words beginning:

A–D are in the first quarter of the dictionary
E–L are in the second quarter of the dictionary
M–R are in the third quarter of the dictionary
S–Z are in the last quarter of the dictionary

Finding the right page

Open the dictionary and you see a word in dark print at the top of
each page. The word at the top of the left hand page is the first word
on that page, and the word at the top of the right hand page is the
last word on that page. If you know the order of the alphabet, you
will be able to see easily whether you need to go forwards or
backwards to find the word you need.

Finding a word when you don't know the spelling

If you don't know the spelling of a word, think about the sound of
how the word starts. The spelling of English words is sometimes
difficult. This dictionary has special 'Spelling Notes' to help you.

Look at this chart:

Sound	Possible spellings	Sound	Possible spellings
/k/	cut, key, queen	/aɪ/	island, eye, aisle
/s/	city, soon, psychology	/dʒ/	January, general
/ʒ/	shop, chauffeur	/n/	never, know, pneumonia
/f/	foot, photograph	/r/	right, write

Exercise 3* **The words below are all spelt incorrectly. Find and write
the correct spelling.**

1 kamera **camera**   2 sycle   3 jeneral
4 kwestion   5 nife   6 fisical

Finding related words

Some words are made from other words. For example, the noun
acceleration comes from the verb **accelerate**, so it is given at the
same entry. In the same way, the noun **enjoyment** is in the entry for
the verb **enjoy**.

Exercise 4* **These words do not have separate entries in the
dictionary. Where can you find them?**

1 abdication _____   2 brutally _____

3 carnivorous _____   4 dissemination _____

5 explicitly _____   6 fantastically _____

Alternative spellings

Some words have different spellings in British and American
English – for example **colour** *BrE*, **color** *AmE*.

Exercise 5* **Write the British English spellings of these American English words:**

1 tire _tyre_   2 center _____   3 traveled _____

4 millimeter _____   5 defense _____   6 catalog _____

7 theater _____   8 maneuver _____   9 honor _____

The dictionary shows the standard spellings of all the words. Some words like **adaptor/adapter** have more than one standard spelling. Where this happens, both possibilities are shown in the dictionary.

Two word entries

Sometimes words are joined together with a hyphen, like **old-fashioned,** and sometimes they are written as two words, like **ice cream**. All these expressions are listed alphabetically.

Exercise 6** **Find these two word entries below in your dictionary. Write the word which comes after each one.**

1 Adam's apple _____ adapt   2 amusement park _____

3 bad-tempered _____   4 bank holiday _____

5 close-up _____   6 conveyor belt _____

Phrasal verbs

In English there are many verbs which are made up of two or three words. These are called 'phrasal verbs' (See Study Note on page 779). Phrasal verbs may have a completely different meaning from the main verb. They can be found after the entry for the main verb, like this:

> **dry**² *v* [I,T] to become dry, or to make something dry: *It'll only take me a few minutes to dry my hair.* —**dried** *adj: dried fruit*
>
> **dry off** *phr v* [I,T **dry sth ↔ off**] to become dry or make the surface of something dry: *The kids played in the pool and then dried off in the sun.*
>
> **dry out** *phr v* [I,T **dry sth ↔ out**] to dry completely, or to dry something completely: *Put your coat on the radiator to dry out.*
>
> **dry up** *phr v* **1** [I,T **dry sth ↔ up**] if a river or lake dries up, the water in it dissapears **2** [I] if a supply of something dries up, there is no more of it: *Our research project was cancelled when the money dried up.* **3** [I,T **dry sth ↔ up**] to dry dishes that have been washed, using a cloth

Exercise 7** **Find the meanings of the phrasal verbs. Write the phrasal verb in the correct form in the sentences below.**

come from   cut off   fill in   fill up   look after   look out for

1 Do you _____ Buenos Aires?

2 My mother is _____ the children.

3 Can you _____ the car please?

4 I'll _____ some unusual stamps while I'm in Chile.

5 I've _____ the membership form.

6 They'll _____ your telephone if you don't pay the bill.

Idioms

An idiom is an expression which means something different from the meanings of the separate words. This dictionary lists idioms under the first important word.

*Exercise 8*** **Look at these idioms. The words in dark print show you where you can find the idiom.**

1 the **acid** test

2 be **alive** and well

3 a different **ball game**

4 **add** insult to injury

5 behind sb's **back**

6 give someone a **hand**

Which idioms can be used in the sentences below? Write the number in the box at the end of the sentence.

a) This box is really heavy – could you _____ with it? ☑6

b) She told my boss I was late this morning. I don't like people saying things _____. ☐

c) Yes, the company had a very difficult time, but now we're _____. ☐

d) Moving from working to studying is difficult, as it's a whole _____. ☐

e) When you have installed the computer program, try it out. That's the _____. ☐

f) When George left his wife, he _____ by taking all her jewellery with him! ☐

Understanding the meaning

This dictionary shows the meanings of words in definitions, examples, and sometimes 'usage notes'.

Definitions

Start by looking at the definition of a word. The definitions have all been written using a limited defining vocabulary of 2,000 common words. This means that even definitions of difficult words are easy to understand.

*Exercise 9** **Look up the definitions of the words below:**

sunbathe   sunburn   sundial   sunlight   sunlit   sunrise
sunscreen   sunset   suntan

Now complete the sentences with the correct word.

1 She looked at the _____ and saw it was nearly 4 o'clock.

2 David got a beautiful _____ in Brazil. He's really brown.

3 If you _____ in this climate, you will get _____ if you

don't use a _____.

4 This room gets a lot of _____ in the mornings.

5 Today _____ is at 04.30 and _____ is at 20.30.

6 The house had a beautiful _____ sitting room.

Examples

The dictionary gives many examples of words in use. The examples show how the word is used.

Exercise 10 **Look at the definitions and examples for the words written in dark print in the questions below. Then try to answer the questions.**

1 Which medicine do you take to **alleviate** pain?

2 What is the best **antidote** to stress?

3 What might you **carry out**?

4 What might you **dislocate**?

5 What could a teacher use to **enliven** her lesson?

6 Why might you get the **jitters**?

More than one meaning

Many words in English have more than one meaning. The dictionary shows the different meanings in order of frequency: the meaning which is used most often is shown first. Each meaning has a number: **1** is always the most frequent meaning, but read all the meanings to make sure you have found the right one.

Exercise 11 * **Look at the dictionary entry for** light² *adj.* **and look at the sentences below. The adjective**
light **has a different meaning in each sentence. Write the number of the meaning as it is given in the dictionary.**

1 John doesn't have any homework tonight so his school bag is quite light. ☑2

2 I arrived early because the traffic was fairly light. ☐

3 I don't want very much to eat, just a light snack. ☐

4 It's quite warm in Guyana, even in the winter, so bring light clothes. ☐

5 Rosie always made light of all her problems. ☐

6 Mrs Dixon was sitting in a light blue car. ☐

7 Sit in a light place if you want to read a book. ☐

8 The film was a light comedy which we all enjoyed. ☐

9 We started talking at midnight and did not go to bed until it was light. ☐

10 Windsurfing was difficult because there was only a light wind. ☐

Exercise 12 **Look up the words in dark print in these sentences. Is this meaning the most frequent meaning? Write the number of the meaning at the end of the sentence.**

1 There has been a **wave** of thefts from the school. ☐

2 Keith wasn't wearing a **tie** on Friday. ☐
3 The food was awful so we didn't leave a **tip**. ☐
4 Did you hear the **report** from the gun? ☐
5 Mom got really **mad** when she heard what we'd done. ☐

Choosing the right form

Irregular plurals

Most nouns make their plural forms by adding **-s** or **-es**. If a word has an irregular plural the dictionary shows you the correct form.

Exercise 13* **Write the correct plural form of these words:**

1 knife *Knives*	2 sheep	3 tooth
4 man	5 child	6 foot

Comparative and superlative forms of adjectives

Most adjectives with one syllable make comparative and superlative forms by adding **-er** and **-est** (**rich, richer, richest**). Many adjectives with two or more syllables make the comparative form with **more** and **less** (**more comfortable, less expensive**). The superlative forms are made with **the most** and **the least** (**the most beautiful flower, the least expensive hotel**). Some adjectives do not follow this pattern. The dictionary tells you the comparative and superlative forms of these words. See the Study Note on page 783.

Parts of verbs

Most regular verbs add **-ed** to make the past tense form and the past participle (**I work/I worked/I have worked**). They make the present participle by adding **-ing** (**I am working**). Irregular verbs make their past tense, past participle and present participle in a different way. This dictionary shows you the past tense form, past participle and present participle of all irregular verbs at the entry for the infinitive.

You can find the past tense and past participle forms of verbs listed in the dictionary with a reference to the main verb.

Exercise 14* **Complete this chart of irregular verbs**

(1) INFINITIVE	(2) PAST TENSE	(3) PAST PARTICIPLE	(4) PRESENT PARTICIPLE
go	went	gone	going
	made	made	
drive			driving
	gave		giving
take		taken	
	wrote		
		taught	

This dictionary tells you a lot about the grammar of words and how to use them in sentences.

Word classes or 'parts of speech'

Words in English have different grammatical functions in a sentence. These grammatical functions are called 'word classes' or 'parts of speech'.

Look at this sentence:

My mother and father slept quietly in the new bed.

My mother and father slept quietly in the new bed.

Possessive pronoun / noun / conjunction / noun / verb / adverb / preposition / definite article / adjective / noun

Look at these two entries for the word **fly**. **Fly**^{1} is a verb and **fly**^{2} is a noun.

fly^1 /flaɪ/ *v* **flew** /fluː/ , **flown** /fləʊn‖floʊn/ , **flying 1** [I] to travel somewhere by plane: *they flew to Paris for their honeymoon.* | *We flew over the North Pole.* **2** [I] to move through the air: *A flock of seagulls flew overhead.* **3** [T] to take something somewhere by plane: *Medical supplies are being flown into the area.* **4** [I,T] to be the pilot of a plane: *Bill's learning to fly.* **5** [I,] to suddenly move very quickly: **+ down/up** *Timmy flew down the stairs and out of the door.* | **+ open** *The door suddenly flew open.* **6** [I] if time flies, it seems to pass quickly: *Is it 5:30 already? Boy, time sure does fly!* | **+ by/past** :*Last week just flew by.* **7 fly into a rage** also **fly off the handle** *spoken* to suddenly become very angry. **8** [I,T] to move into the air: *The French flag was flying over the Embassy.* | *Tommy was in the park, flying his new kite.* **9 go flying/send sb flying** to fall over or make someone fall over

fly^2 *n* [C] **1** a common small insect with two wings: *There were flies all over the food.* **2** also **flies** *BrE* the ZIP or row of buttons at the front of a pair of trousers: *Your fly is unzipped.* →see also **sb wouldn't hurt a fly** (HURT^1), **let fly** (LET)

Sometimes the same word may belong to more than one word class. There is an entry for each part of speech. If you see a small raised number after a word, this means it has more than one entry, and you will need to look at all of them to be sure you have found the one you want.

Exercise 15* **Look up the words. How many different grammatical forms does each word have? Write the number and the form, as in the example.**

1 clean *clean^1 adj, clean^2 v, clean^3 adv*

2 jump
3 murder
4 photograph
5 exercise
6 heat

Countable [C] and uncountable [U] nouns

If you look up a noun, the dictionary shows you whether it can have a plural form or not. Most nouns (like **car, shoe** and **hand**) in English have a plural form (**cars, shoes, hands**). They are countable [C] nouns. Nouns that don't have plurals (**rice, hydrogen, happiness**) are uncountable nouns, and are shown with the grammar code [U].

Exercise 16 **Look up the nouns in dark print below. Write [C] beside the countable nouns and [U] beside the uncountable nouns.**

   1 Where did you buy that **book**? $\boxed{C}$
   2 **Love** makes the world go round. $\square$
   3 Please give me some **money**. $\square$
   4 I need some **information** $\square$
   5 Table salt contains a lot of **sodium**. $\square$
   6 I've got a **letter** for you. $\square$

Some nouns are countable in some meanings and uncountable in other meanings. Look at the entry for **tea** below.

> **tea** /tiː/ *n* [C,U] **1** a drink made by pouring boiling water onto dried leaves, or the leaves that are used to make this drink: *a cup of tea* | *herbal teas* **2** *BrE* a small afternoon meal of tea with SANDWICHES or cakes **3** *BrE informal* a meal you eat in the evening; DINNER

It is marked [C, U]. This means that it is countable [C] in one meaning but uncountable [U] in its other meaning. For example, in the sentence: *Is there any tea in the pot?* tea is uncountable because we are thinking about the quantity of tea in the pot. In the sentence: *Sales of herbal teas have increased, tea* is countable because we are thinking about different kinds of tea. See the Study Note on page 775.

Transitive [T] and intransitive [I] verbs

If the word you look up is a verb, this dictionary tells you a lot about how to use it. First it tells you if the verb is transitive [T] or intransitive [I] (see the Study Note on page 777). Transitive [T] verbs (like **avoid**) are followed by a noun or noun phrase as a direct object.

Subject	Verb	Direct Object
The car	*avoided*	*the accident.*

Intransitive [I] verbs (like **arrive**) are never followed by a noun or noun phrase as a direct object. They may be followed by a complement.

Subject	Verb	Complement
My friends	arrived	at the hotel.

Sometimes, as with the verb **laugh**, there is no complement.

Subject	Verb	No Complement
The audience	laughed.	

Some verbs, like **smell**, can be intransitive [I] in one meaning and transitive [T] in another.
I can smell smoke! [T + direct object]
That flower smells very nice. [I + complement]

Exercise 17* **Look up the verbs in the sentences below. Are they used correctly or incorrectly? Mark each sentence with either a tick ☑ or a cross ☒.**

1 They arrived the station. ☐
2 She arrived at half past ten. ☐
3 The bell rang. ☐
4 They opened. ☐
5 I enjoyed in the evening. ☐
6 The rain stopped. ☐

Verbs like *be* and *seem*

A few verbs are not marked with [T] or [I]. Instead they are marked [linking verb]. This means they must be followed by a complement which is usually an adjective, a noun, or an adverb – as in these sentences.
She became President.
They appeared tired.
The rain was heavier.
(Read the Study Note on page 777 for more information about these verbs.)

Verbs followed by a clause beginning with 'that'

The sentences below show verbs which are often followed by a clause beginning with *that*.
I read that Steve had won the prize.
She said that she didn't see me.

This is shown in the dictionary by the code + **that** or + (**that**). If *that* is in brackets, it means you can leave it out.
She said she didn't see me.
David believed he had won the prize.

Using words together

In English, and most other languages, some words are often found near each other. For example, the verb **commit** is often used with the noun **crime**. You can see how the dictionary shows these word combinations in dark print in the entry below:

Exercise 18** **Look up the words in dark print. Then choose a word from the box and use it in the correct form to complete these sentences.**

> strike   have   make   take   commit   reach

1 Men ***commit*** more **crime**s than women.
2 I think you must have _____ a **mistake** in your calculations.
3 Eventually, they managed to _____ a **decision**.
4 We _____ lots of **photo**s of the scenery.
5 What? You think they're _____ an **affair**?
6 We need to _____ a **balance** between traditional thinking and new ideas.

Words which are often confused

Usage Notes give you more information about words and how to use them, and words which are often confused. They often show alternative words too. Look at this Usage Note about the word **affect**.

> **af·fect** /ə'fekt/ *v* [T] **1** to cause a change in someone or something or to change the situation they are in: *a disease that affects the heart and lungs* | *Help is beingsent to areas affected by the floods.* **2** to make someone feel strong emo·tions: *She was deeply affected by the news of Pauls death.* →compare EFFECT²

> **USAGE NOTE: affect and effect**
>
> **Affect** is always a verb, used to talk about the way one thing changes or influences another: *How will the new law affect young people?* **Effect** is a noun, meaning what happens as a result of a change or influence: *What effect will the new law have?* **Effect**, however, is sometimes used as a verb in formal English, meaning to make something happen: *efforts to effect a peaceful solution to the conflict.*

Exercise 19* **Look at the Usage Notes for the words in brackets ( ), and write the correct word to complete each sentence.**

1 Bad weather will _____ the north of the country. (affect)
2 The _____ of the hurricane were devastating. (affect)
3 She is _____ U. N. expert on food and agriculture. (an)
4 I bought ___ I.B.M. computer from my brother. (an)
5 Charles Manson was a _____ murderer. (famous)
6 Dustin Hoffman is a _____ actor. (famous)
7 What is the _____ of this CD player? (cost)
8 The _____ of owning a car is getting higher and higher. (cost)
9 John is an _____ engineer. (electric)
10 Laura drives an _____ car. (electric)

Pronunciation

Stress

If a word has two or more syllables, we put a stress on one of the syllables – we say it louder.
Look at the entry for **advantage**.

> **ad·van·tage** /əd'vɑːntɪdʒ‖əd'væn/ *n* [C,U]
> **1** something that helps you to be better or more successful *than other people:* **+ of** *the advantages of good education* | **+ over** *Her computer training gave her an advantage over the other students.* **2** a way in which something is good or useful: *Good public transport is just one of the advantages of living in a big city.*

/'/ this mark comes immediately before the second syllable and shows that we put the stress on the second syllable — we say ad<u>VANT</u>age.

Exercise 20 * **Now look at the stress patterns of these words and circle the correct stress.**

1 <u>A</u>bove   a<u>BOVE</u>
2 <u>PRO</u>fuse   pro<u>FUSE</u>
3 <u>BI</u>cycle   bi<u>CY</u>cle
4 <u>COM</u>parison   com<u>PAR</u>ison
5 <u>EC</u>onomic   eco<u>NOM</u>ic
6 <u>IM</u>agination   i<u>MAG</u>ination

Nouns and verbs with different stress

Read these sentences aloud:
That is a new Olympic record!
Did you record the TV programme on video?

Did you say **record** correctly in the two sentences? In the dictionary you can see that the noun **record**[1] is pronounced <u>RE</u>cord, but the verb **record**[2] is pronounced re<u>CORD</u>.

Exercise 21 * **Many words like** record **can be stressed in different ways. Look up the words** increase **and** permit **in the dictionary, and circle the correct stress.**

1 Global warming will <u>IN</u>crease/in<u>CREASE</u> in the next fifty years.
2 There has been a 50% <u>IN</u>crease/in<u>CREASE</u> in traffic in the capital.
3 You need a <u>PER</u>mit/per<u>MIT</u> to have a speedboat in Venice.
4 The regulations don't <u>PER</u>mit/per<u>MIT</u> you to enter the security area.

British and American pronunciations

This dictionary shows the standard British English pronunciation, then the standard American English pronunciation after two lines (like this ‖). Look at the British and American pronunciations of these words: **magazine, borough, tomato, bottle**.
Some words are stressed in different ways in British English and American English. Look at the entry for **address**[1].

ad·dress[1] /ə'dres‖ə'dres, 'ædres/ *n* [C] **1** the details of where someone lives or works, including the number of the building, name of the street, town etc: *I forgot to give Damien my new address.* **2** a formal speech: *the Gettysburg Address*

Speakers of American English often say <u>AD</u>Dress, whereas speakers of British English always say add<u>RESS</u>.

Consonants and vowels

The dictionary uses a phonetic alphabet (the International Phonetic Alphabet or IPA) to show pronunciation. The phonetic alphabet is explained on the inside back cover of the dictionary. Each dictionary entry is followed by a phonetic representation between slashes, like this: **apple** /'æpəl/. It isn't difficult to learn the phonetic alphabet. Start by learning the consonant symbols and then the vowel symbols.

*Exercise 22*** **Try to guess these words. They are all parts of the body.**

1 /æːm ‖ ɑːrm/	*arm*
2 /fʊt/	_____
3 /hed/	_____
4 /heə ‖ her/	_____
5 /feɪs/	_____
6 /niː/	_____
7 /leg/	_____
8 /maʊθ/	_____
9 /'ʃəʊldə ‖ 'ʃoʊldər/	_____

Parts of words

Syllables

*Exercise 23** **Look at the definition of** syllable **in the dictionary. Now write these words in the correct column.**

chocolate cheek chemistry children coin cinema

1 syllable	2 syllables	3 syllables
cheek	*children*	*cinema*

Learning vocabulary

There are more than 45,000 words in this dictionary. You cannot learn all these words, so you need to know which words are the most important. If you look in the dictionary some words are marked like this:

> **de·cide** /dɪˈsaɪd/ v 1 [I,T] to make a choice or judgement about something: **decide to do sth** *They decided to sell the house.* | **+ (that)** *She decided that the dress was too expensive.* | **+ what/how/when etc** *Have you decided when you are going to get married?* | **decide against sth** (=decide not to do something): *Marlowe thought about using his gun, but decided against it.* **2 deciding factor** the reason you finally make a particular decision: *Firman's testimony was the deciding factor in the case.* **3** [T] to be the reason why something has a particular result: *One punch decided the fight.*
> **decide on** sth *phr v* [T] to choose one thing from among many: *Have you decided on a name for a baby?*

Words which are marked like this are very frequent in English, and so it is important to learn them.

Strategies for learning and remembering vocabulary

Try these different ways of learning vocabulary:

1 Say the words aloud and try to make pictures in your head.
2 Write sentences about your friends and family using the words you have to learn.
3 Try learning families of words: **study** *n* **study** *v*, **student** *n*, **studious** *adj*, **studio** *n*, **studies** *n*.
4 Learn words about a particular subject: **music** *n*, **note** *n*, **key** *n*, **chord** *n*, **instrument** *n*, **play** *v*.
5 Try making word webs like this:

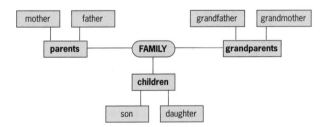

Aa

A, a /eɪ/ the letter 'a'

a *[box]* /ə; *strong* eɪ/ *also* **an** *(before a vowel sound) determiner* **1** used before a noun to show that you are talking about a general type of thing, not a specific thing: *Do you have a car?* | *Her boyfriend is an artist.* → compare THE¹ **2** one: *a thousand pounds* | *a dozen eggs* **3** used in some phrases that say how much of something there is: *a few weeks from now* | *a lot of people* **4** every or each: *A square has 4 sides.* | *once a week/$100 a day etc* (=one time each week, $100 each day etc): *He gets paid $100,000 a year.* **5** used before two nouns that are frequently mentioned together: *a knife and fork* **6** used before some singular nouns that are actions: *Have a look at this.*

USAGE NOTE: a or an

You use **an** before a word that starts with a vowel sound: *an apple* | *an hour* | *an MBA*. Use **a** for words that do not begin with a vowel sound: *a house* | *a useful tool* | *a CD player*. Note that you make this choice according to what the words sound like, not whether the first letter actually is a vowel or not. For example although the letter 'h' in 'hour' is not a vowel, **an** is used because it is pronounced like a vowel in this word.

---

a- /eɪ, æ, ə/ *prefix* used at the beginning of some words to mean 'not': *atypical* | *amoral*.

a·back /ə'bæk/ *adv* **be taken aback** to be very surprised or shocked: *I was taken aback by Linda's rudeness.*

ab·a·cus /'æbəkəs/ *n* [C] a wooden frame with small balls which can be moved along wires, used for counting

a·ban·don /ə'bændən/ *v* [T] **1** to leave someone or something for a long time or FOREVER, without intending to go back and get them: *The baby had been abandoned outside a hospital in Liverpool.* **2** to stop doing or using something because of problems: *The new policy had to be abandoned.* —**abandonment** *n* [U]

a·ban·doned /ə'bændənd/ *adj* not being used or looked after any more: *an abandoned building*

a·bashed /ə'bæʃt/ *adj* embarrassed or ashamed: *When he saw Ruth, he looked slightly abashed.*

a·bate /ə'beɪt/ *v* [I] *formal* to become less strong: *Our ship could not sail until the storm abated.*

ab·at·toir /'æbətwɑː‖-ɑːr/ *n* [C] *BrE* a place where animals are killed for their meat; SLAUGHTERHOUSE

ab·bess /'æbəs, 'æbes/ *n* [C] a woman who is in charge of a CONVENT and the NUNS who live there

ab·bey /'æbi/ *n* [C] a large church, especially one with buildings next to it where MONKS or NUNS live or used to live

ab·bot /'æbət/ *n* [C] a man who is in charge of a MONASTERY and the MONKS who live there

ab·bre·vi·ate /ə'briːvieɪt/ *v* [T] *formal* to make a word, story etc shorter

ab·bre·vi·a·tion /ə,briːvi'eɪʃən/ *n* [C] a shorter form of a word, which is used in writing. For example, Dr is the abbreviation of Doctor

ABC /,eɪ biː 'siː/ *n* [singular] *BrE*, **ABC's** *n* [plural] *AmE* the letters of the English alphabet as taught to children

ab·di·cate /'æbdɪkeɪt/ *v* **1** [I] to officially give up the position of being king or queen **2 abdicate responsibility** *formal* to refuse to be responsible for something any longer —**abdication** /,æbdɪ'keɪʃən/ *n* [C,U]

ab·do·men /'æbdəmən, æb'dəʊ-‖-'doʊ-/ *n* [C] *technical* the part of the body between the chest and the legs, which includes the stomach —**abdominal** /æb'dɒmɪnəl‖-'dɑː-/ *adj*

ab·duct /əb'dʌkt, æb-/ *v* [T] to take someone away illegally and by using force: *Police believe that the woman has been abducted.* —**abduction** /-'dʌkʃən/ *n* [U]

ab·er·ra·tion /,æbə'reɪʃən/ *n* [C,U] an action, event, or type of behaviour that is different from what usually happens: *a man of good character whose crime was regarded as just a temporary aberration*

a·bet /ə'bet/ *v* [T] → see **aid and abet** (AID²)

ab·hor /əb'hɔː‖ab'hɔːr, æb-/ *v* [T] **-rring, -rred** *formal* to hate something because it seems morally wrong: *He abhorred violence in any form.*

ab·hor·rent /əb'hɒrənt‖-'hɔːr-/ *adj formal* behaviour or beliefs that are abhorrent seem very bad and morally wrong —**abhorrence** *n* [U]

a·bide /ə'baɪd/ *v* [T] **can't abide sb/sth** to hate someone or something very much: *I can't abide his stupid jokes.*

abide by sth *phr v* [T] to obey a law, agreement etc: *You have to abide by the rules of the game.*

a·bid·ing /ə'baɪdɪŋ/ *adj* [only before noun] *literary* an abiding feeling or belief continues for a long time: *her abiding love of the English countryside* → see also LAW-ABIDING

a·bil·i·ty *[box]* /ə'bɪlɪti/ *n* [C,U] the mental skill or physical power to do something: *a young girl with great musical ability* | *ability to do sth A manager must have the ability to communicate well.*

USAGE NOTE: ability, skill, talent, and knack

Use these words about how well someone can do things. Your **ability** is what you can do mentally or physically: *artistic ability* | *athletic ability*. You can lose your ability to do something: *He lost his ability to walk after the accident.* A **skill** is something you can do well because you have learned and practised it: *a class to improve writing skills.* **Talent** is a natural ability to do something particularly well: *She has considerable musical talent.* A **knack** is a more informal word for something you do particularly well: *a knack for decorating.*

---

ab·ject /'æbdʒekt/ *adj* **1 abject poverty/misery/failure** when you are extremely poor, unhappy, or unsuccessful **2** abject behaviour shows that you are ashamed of what has happened: *an abject apology*

a·blaze /ə'bleɪz/ *adj* [not before noun] **1** burning with a lot of flames: *The old house was quickly ablaze.* | *set sth ablaze* (=make something burn with a lot of flames): *The ship was set ablaze by the explosion.* **2** very bright with colour or light: + **with** *a garden ablaze with summer flowers*

a·ble /ˈeɪbəl/ *adj* **1 able to do sth** having the power, skill, time, money etc to do something: *Will you be able to come tonight?*|*I was just able to reach the handle.* →opposite UNABLE **2** intelligent or good at doing something: *a very able student*

a·bly /ˈeɪbli/ *adv* skilfully or well: *The director was ably assisted by his team of experts.*

ab·norm·al /æbˈnɔːməl‖-ˈnɔːr-/ *adj* different from what is normal, especially in a way that is strange, worrying, or dangerous: *abnormal behaviour*|*abnormal levels of chlorine in the water* —**abnormally** *adv* —**abnormality** /ˌæbnɔːˈmælɪ̩ti‖-nər-/ *n* [C,U]

a·board /əˈbɔːd‖-ɔːrd/ *adv, prep* on or onto a ship, plane, or train: *I swam out to the yacht and climbed aboard.*

a·bode /əˈbəʊd‖əˈboʊd/ *n* [C] *formal* the place where you live: **right of abode** (=the right to live in a country)

a·bol·ish /əˈbɒlɪʃ‖əˈbɑː-/ *v* [T] to officially end a law, system etc: *unfair laws that should be abolished* —**abolition** /ˌæbəˈlɪʃən/ *n* [U] *the abolition of slavery*

a·bom·i·na·ble /əˈbɒmɪnəbəl, -mənə-‖əˈbɑː-/ *adj* extremely unpleasant or bad: *an abominable noise* —**abominably** *adv*

ab·o·rig·i·ne /ˌæbəˈrɪdʒɪ̩ni/ *n* [C] a member of the people who have lived in Australia from the earliest times

a·bort /əˈbɔːt‖-ɔːrt/ *v* **1** [T] to end a process or plan before it has finished because it would be too difficult or dangerous to continue: *The space flight had to be aborted because of computer problems.* **2** [T] to deliberately end a PREGNANCY when the baby is still too small to live

a·bor·tion /əˈbɔːʃən‖əˈbɔːr-/ *n* [C,U] when a PREGNANCY is deliberately ended while the baby is still too small to live: **have an abortion** *She was told about the dangers of having an abortion.*

a·bor·tive /əˈbɔːtɪv‖əˈbɔːr-/ *adj* an abortive action or attempt to do something is not successful

a·bound /əˈbaʊnd/ *v* [I] *literary* to exist in large numbers: *a river where fish abound*
  abound in/with sth *phr v* to contain a lot of something: *The park abounds with wildlife.*

a·bout /əˈbaʊt/ *prep* **1** concerning or dealing with a particular subject or person: *a book about how the universe began*|**all about** (=everything about): *Tell me all about it.* **2** *BrE* in many different directions or in different parts of a place; AROUND: *Clothes were scattered about the room.* **3 what about/how about** *spoken* **a)** used to make a suggestion: *How about coming to my house for a barbecue?*|*What about bringing a bottle of wine?* **b)** used to ask someone's opinion concerning something: *What about Jack? We can't just leave him here.*

a·bout /əˈbaʊt/ *adv* **1** a little more or less than a number or amount; APPROXIMATELY: *I live about 10 miles from here.* **2 be about to do sth** to be ready to start doing something: *We were about to leave when Jerry arrived.* **3 just about** almost: *Dinner's just about ready.* **4** *BrE* in many

different directions or in different parts of a place; AROUND: *People were lying about on the floor.* **5** *BrE* near you in the place you are now; AROUND: *Is Patrick about? There's a phone call for him.*

a·bove /əˈbʌv/ *prep* **1** in or to a higher position than something else: *Raise your arm above your head.*|*There's a light above the entrance.* →see colour picture on page 474 **2** more than a number, amount, or level: *Temperatures rose above zero today.* **3** louder than other sounds: *He couldn't hear her voice above the noise.* **4 above all** *formal* most importantly: *Above all, I would like to thank my parents.* **5 above suspicion/criticism etc** so honest or good that no one can think that you have done something wrong or criticize you **6** higher in rank or more powerful than someone else: *officers above the rank of lieutenant*

a·bove /əˈbʌv/ *adv* **1** in a higher position than something else: *The sound came from the room above.* **2** more than a number, amount, or level: *children aged 7 and above* **3** in an earlier part of something you are reading: *Write to the address given above for more information.*

a·bove board /ˌ‥ ˈ‥, ‥ˈ‥ ‥/ *adj* something such as a business deal that is above board is honest and legal: *Everything seems to be above board.*

a·bra·sive /əˈbreɪsɪv/ *adj* **1** someone who is abrasive talks to people in a rude and unkind way: *His abrasive manner offends some people.* **2** having a rough surface that can be used to rub things off other surfaces

a·breast /əˈbrest/ *adv* **1 keep abreast of sth** to know the most recent facts about a subject: *I listen to the radio to keep abreast of the news.* **2 two/three/four abreast** if people move forward two, three, or four abreast, they are all next to each other in a line: *The cyclists were riding three abreast, so no one could pass them.*

a·bridged /əˈbrɪdʒd/ *adj* a book, play etc that has been abridged has been made shorter: *the abridged version of the novel* —**abridge** *v* [T] →compare UNABRIDGED

a·broad /əˈbrɔːd‖əˈbrɒːd/ *adv* in or to a foreign country: *Did you enjoy living abroad?*|**go abroad** *He often has to go abroad on business.*

a·brupt /əˈbrʌpt/ *adj* **1** sudden and unexpected: *an abrupt change in the attitudes of voters* **2** not polite or friendly, especially because you do not want to waste time: *She was abrupt on the phone the first time we talked.* —**abruptly** *adv* —**abruptness** *n* [U]

ab·scess /ˈæbses/ *n* [C] a place on your body that is swollen and contains a yellow liquid because of infection

ab·scond /əbˈskɒnd, æb-‖æbˈskɑːnd/ *v* [I] *formal* to leave a place without permission, or leave somewhere after stealing something: *The firm's accountant had absconded with all the money.*

ab·sence /ˈæbsəns/ *n* **1** [C,U] when you are away from a place: *How do you explain your absence?*|+ **from** *frequent absences from work*|**in sb's absence** (=while they are away): *The vice president will handle things in my absence.* **2** [U] the lack of something: *the absence of evidence in the murder case*

ab·sent /ˈæbsənt/ *adj* **1** not at work, at school, at a meeting etc: *Most of the class was absent with flu today.* | + **from** *absent from school* **2** absent look/smile/expression a look etc that shows you are not thinking about what is happening

ab·sen·tee /ˌæbsənˈtiː◂/ *n* [C] **1** *formal* someone who is supposed to be in a place but is absent **2** absentee landlord/owner the owner of a building or piece of land who lives far away

ab·sen·tee·is·m /ˌæbsənˈtiːɪzəm/ *n* [U] regular absence from work or school without a good reason

ab·sent·ly /ˈæbsəntli/ *adv* in a way that shows you are not interested or not thinking about what is happening: *Rachel smiled absently and went on with her work.*

absent-mind·ed /ˌ ˈ ◂ / *adj* often forgetting or not noticing things because you are thinking of something else — **absent-mindedness** *n* [U] — **absent-mindedly** *adv*

ab·so·lute /ˈæbsəluːt/ *adj* **1** complete and total: *The show was an absolute disaster.* | *a ruler with absolute power* **2** definite and not likely to change: *I can't give you any absolute promises.*

ab·so·lute·ly /ˈæbsəluːtli, ˌæbsəˈluːtli/ *adv* **1** completely or totally: *Are you absolutely sure?* | absolutely no/nothing (=none or nothing at all): *It was the school holiday and the children had absolutely nothing to do.* **2** Absolutely! *spoken* used to tell someone that you agree completely, or to emphasize that you mean "yes": *"Do you really think so?" "Absolutely."* **3** Absolutely not! *spoken* used to tell someone that you disagree completely, or to emphasize that you mean "no"

ab·solve /əbˈzɒlv‖-ˈɑːlv/ *v* [T] *formal* to formally say that someone should not be blamed for something, or to forgive them

ab·sorb /əbˈsɔːb, əbˈzɔːb‖-ɔːrb/ *v* [T] **1** if something absorbs liquid, heat etc it takes in the liquid, heat etc through its surface: *The towel absorbed most of the water.* **2** be absorbed in sth to be very interested in something that you are doing, watching, reading etc: *I was completely absorbed in the book.* **3** if something is absorbed into something else, it becomes part of that other thing or becomes mixed with it: *the rate at which alcohol is absorbed into the blood* | *countries that had become absorbed into the Soviet Union* **4** to hear, read, or learn information and understand it: *She's a good student who absorbs information quickly.* — **absorption** /-ˈɔːpʃən‖-ɔːr-/ *n* [U]

ab·sor·bent /əbˈsɔːbənt, -ˈzɔː-‖-ɔːr-/ *adj* something that is absorbent can take in liquids through its surface: *absorbent sponges*

ab·sorb·ing /əbˈsɔːbɪŋ, -ˈzɔː-‖-ɔːr-/ *adj* so interesting that you do not notice or think about other things: *an absorbing article about space travel*

ab·stain /əbˈsteɪn/ *v* [I] **1** *formal* to not do something that you would normally enjoy doing: + **from** *Patients were advised to abstain from*

alcohol. **2** to deliberately not vote when something is being decided in a committee, parliament etc — **abstention** /əbˈstenʃən/ *n* [C,U]

ab·sti·nence /ˈæbstɪnəns/ *n* [U] when someone stops doing something that they would normally enjoy doing, especially for religious reasons

ab·stract /ˈæbstrækt/ *adj* **1** based on ideas rather than specific examples or real events: *Beauty is an abstract idea.* | *abstract arguments about justice* **2** abstract art consists of shapes and patterns that do not look like real things or people — **abstraction** /əbˈstrækʃən, æb-/ *n* [C,U]

ab·surd /əbˈsɜːd, -ˈzɜːd‖-ɜːrd/ *adj* seeming completely unreasonable or silly: *an absurd situation* | *an absurd hat* — **absurdly** *adv* — **absurdity** *n* [C,U]

a·bun·dance /əˈbʌndəns/ *n* [singular, U] *formal* a very large quantity of something: *There is an abundance of creative talent.* | in abundance (=in large numbers or quantities): *Wild flowers grew in abundance on the hillside.*

a·bun·dant /əˈbʌndənt/ *adj* existing in large quantities: *an abundant supply of fresh fruit*

a·bun·dant·ly /əˈbʌndəntli/ *adv* **1** very: *He made it abundantly clear that he was dissatisfied.* **2** in large quantities: *Poppies grew abundantly in the fields.*

a·buse¹ /əˈbjuːs/ *n* **1** [C,U] the wrong or bad use of something: + **of** *The newspapers are calling the President's action an abuse of power.* | drug/alcohol abuse (=when people take illegal drugs or drink too much) **2** [U] cruel or violent treatment of someone, usually by a person who should look after them: child abuse *a police investigation into reports of child abuse* | sexual abuse *victims of sexual abuse* **3** [U] rude and insulting things that someone says to another person

a·buse² /əˈbjuːz/ *v* [T] **1** to do cruel or violent things to someone: *Each year more than 700,000 children are abused or neglected.* **2** to use something too much or in the wrong way: *Garton had abused his position as mayor by offering jobs to his friends.* **3** to say cruel or unkind things to someone

a·bu·sive /əˈbjuːsɪv/ *adj* using words that are rude and insulting: *an abusive letter*

a·bys·mal /əˈbɪzməl/ *adj* very bad: *your son's abysmal performance in the examinations* — **abysmally** *adv*

a·byss /əˈbɪs/ *n* [C] **1** a very dangerous, frightening, or unhappy situation: *the abyss of nuclear war* **2** *literary* a very deep hole or space that seems to have no bottom

ac·a·dem·ic¹ /ˌækəˈdemɪk◂/ *adj* **1** connected with education, especially in a college or university: *students' academic achievements* | the academic year (=the period of the year when there are school or university classes) **2** something that is academic is not important because it is not likely to happen or have any effect: *We don't have any money, so the question of where to go on holiday is purely academic.*

GRAMMAR NOTE: a or **the (1)**
Use **a** or **an** before a noun when you are mentioning a person or thing for the first time, but use **the** when you mention that same person or thing again: *A man and a woman were sitting at the next table. The woman was much younger than the man.*

3 good at studying: *teaching the more academic children*

academic² *n* [C] a teacher in a college or university

a·cad·e·my /ə'kædəmi/ *n* [C] **1** a school or college that trains students in a special subject or skill: *a military academy* **2** an official organization whose purpose is to encourage the development of art, science, or literature

ac·cel·e·rate /ək'seləreɪt/ *v* **1** [I] if a car driver accelerates, they start to go faster: *Melissa accelerated as she drove onto the highway.* **2** [I,T] if a process accelerates or if you accelerate it, it starts to happen more quickly: *a plan to accelerate economic growth* —**acceleration** /ək,selə'reɪʃən/ *n* [U]

ac·cel·e·ra·tor /ək'seləreɪtəll-ər/ *n* [C] the thing that you press with your foot in a car to make it go faster

ac·cent /'æksəntll'æksent/ *n* [C] **1** a way of pronouncing words that someone has because of where they were born or live: *a strong northern accent* **2** the accent the importance given to something: + on *a training programme with the accent on safety* **3** when you emphasize part of a word: + on *The accent in the word 'important' is on the second syllable.* **4** a mark written above some letters, for example é or â

ac·cen·tu·ate /ək'sentʃueɪt/ *v* [T] to emphasize something or make it easier to notice

ac·cept /ək'sept/ *v* **1** [I,T] to take something or say yes to something that someone offers you: *Please accept this small gift.* | *He's been offered the job but can't decide whether to accept.* | **accept an invitation** *We would be happy to accept your invitation.* **2** [I,T] to agree to do something or to allow something to happen: *The manager would not accept her resignation.* | **accept advice/suggestions** *Jackie won't accept any advice.* **3** [T] to agree or admit or believe that something is true, especially an unpleasant fact: *The teacher would not accept any excuses.* | + that *I accept that we've made mistakes, but it's nothing we can't fix.* **4** [T] to let someone join an organization, university course etc: *I've been accepted at Harvard.* **5** [T] to let someone new become part of a group or society and treat them in the same way as other members: *It was a long time before the other kids at school accepted him.* **6** [T] to decide that there is nothing you can do to change an unpleasant situation: *Even when he was imprisoned, the Emperor would not accept defeat.* **7** [T] to let customers pay for something in a particular way: *We don't accept credit cards.* **8** **accept responsibility/blame** *formal* to admit that you are responsible for something bad that has happened: *The company have accepted responsibility for the accident.*

ac·cep·ta·ble /ək'septəbəl/ *adj* **1** good enough: *The essay was acceptable, but it wasn't her best work.* **2** if a kind of behaviour is acceptable, people approve of it and think that it should be allowed: *Smoking is no longer an acceptable habit.* —**acceptably** *adv* —**acceptability** /ək,septə'bɪlɪti/ *n* [U]

ac·cept·ance /ək'septəns/ *n* [U] **1** when you agree to accept someone's offer or invitation: *I was surprised at her acceptance of my offer.* **2** when people agree that something is right or true or should be allowed to happen: + of *After*

the revolution there was widespread acceptance of Marxist ideas. **3** when you decide that there is nothing you can do to change an unpleasant situation: *The general mood was one of acceptance.* **4** when someone is allowed to become part of a group or society: + into *the immigrants' gradual acceptance into the community* **5** **gain/find acceptance** to become popular or liked

ac·cept·ed /ək'septɪd/ *adj* an accepted idea or way of doing something is one that most people think is right or reasonable

ac·cess¹ /'ækses/ *n* [U] **1** the chance or right to see or use something: **have access to** *Students need to have access to the computer system.* **2** the way in which you can enter a building or get to a place: + to *The only access to the farm is along a muddy track.* | **gain access** *formal* (=enter): *The thieves gained access through the upstairs window.*

access² *v* [T] to find and use information, especially on a computer: *I couldn't access the file.*

ac·ces·si·ble /ək'sesɪbəl/ *adj* **1** easy to reach, find, or use: *The national park is not accessible by road.* | *the wide range of information that is accessible on the Internet* **2** easy to understand and enjoy: + to *Buchan succeeds in making a difficult subject accessible to the ordinary reader.* —**accessibility** /ək,sesɪ'bɪlɪti/ *n* [U] →opposite INACCESSIBLE

ac·ces·so·ry /ək'sesəri/ *n* [C] **1** [usually plural] something such as a bag, belt, or jewellery that you wear or carry because they are attractive: *a dress with matching accessories* **2** something that you can add to a machine, tool, car etc, which is useful or attractive **3** *law* someone who helps a criminal

accident

ac·ci·dent /'æksɪdənt/ *n* [C] **1** a situation in which someone is hurt or something is damaged without anyone intending it to happen: *Her parents were killed in a car accident.* | *I'm afraid he's been involved in a serious accident.* | **it was an accident** (=used to say that someone did not do something deliberately): *I didn't do it on purpose, it was an accident.* **2** **by accident** in a way that is not intended or planned: *I discovered by accident that he'd lied to me.*

ac·ci·den·tal /,æksɪ'dentl◂/ *adj* happening without being planned or intended: *accidental damage*

ac·ci·den·tal·ly /,æksɪ'dentl-i/ *adv* if you accidentally do something, you do it without intending to do it: *I accidentally set off the alarm.*

accident-prone /'... ,./ *adj* likely to have accidents: *an accident-prone child*

ac·claim[1] /əˈkleɪm/ v [T] to praise something a lot

acclaim[2] n [U] a lot of public praise for someone or something: *His first novel received widespread acclaim.*

ac·claimed /əˈkleɪmd/ adj praised by a lot of people: **highly/widely acclaimed** *Spielberg's highly acclaimed movie, 'Schindler's List'*

ac·cli·ma·tize (also **-ise** BrE) /əˈklaɪmətaɪz/ also **acclimate** AmE /əˈklaɪmət‖ˈækləmeɪt, ə-ˈklaɪmət/ v [I,T] to become used to the weather, way of living etc in a new place, or to make someone do this: **get acclimatized** *It takes the astronauts a few days to get acclimatized to conditions in space.* —**acclimatization** /ə,klaɪmətaɪˈzeɪʃən‖-tə-/ n [U]

ac·co·lade /ˈækəleɪd/ n [C] a prize or praise given to someone or something because people think they are very good

ac·com·mo·date /əˈkɒmədeɪt‖əˈkɑː-/ v [T] **1** to have enough space for a particular number of people or things: *The hall can accommodate 300 people.* **2** to give someone a place to stay, live, or work: *A new hostel was built to accommodate the students.* **3** formal to do what someone wants or provide them with what they need: *If you need more time, we'll try to accommodate you.*

ac·com·mo·dat·ing /əˈkɒmədeɪtɪŋ‖əˈkɑː-/ adj helpful and willing to do what someone else wants

ac·com·mo·da·tion /ə,kɒməˈdeɪʃən‖ə,kɑː-/ n [U] also **accommodations** [plural] AmE a place to live, stay, or work in: *The college will provide accommodation for all new students.*

ac·com·pa·ni·ment /əˈkʌmpənimənt/ n [C] **1** music played at the same time as someone sings or plays another instrument: *a tune with a simple guitar accompaniment* **2** formal something that is served or that happens at the same time as something else: *White wine is an excellent accompaniment to fish.*

ac·com·pa·ny /əˈkʌmpəni/ v [T] **1** formal to go somewhere with someone, especially in order to help or look after them: *Children under 12 must be accompanied by an adult.* **2** to play a musical instrument with someone who is playing or singing the main tune **3** to happen or exist at the same time as something else: *Any increase in costs is always accompanied by a rise in prices.*

ac·com·plice /əˈkʌmplɪs‖əˈkɑːm-, əˈkʌm-/ n [C] someone who helps a criminal to do something wrong or illegal

ac·com·plish /əˈkʌmplɪʃ‖əˈkɑːm-, əˈkʌm-/ v [T] to succeed in doing something; achieve: *The new government has accomplished a great deal.*

ac·com·plished /əˈkʌmplɪʃt‖əˈkɑːm-, əˈkʌm-/ adj very skilful: *an accomplished poet*

ac·com·plish·ment /əˈkʌmplɪʃmənt‖əˈkɑːm-, əˈkʌm-/ n **1** [C] formal something you have achieved or are able to do well: *Playing the piano is one of her many accomplishments.* **2** [U] when you succeed in accomplishing something: *the accomplishment of a lifelong ambition*

ac·cord[1] /əˈkɔːd‖-ɔːrd/ n **1 of your own accord** without being asked or forced to do something: *No one forced him to go. He left of his own accord.* **2 in accord (with sb/sth)** formal agreeing with someone or something, or not

different from something: *The committee's report is completely in accord with our suggestions.* **3** [C] an official agreement

accord[2] v [T] formal to treat someone or something in a special way, or give them special attention: *On his return Gagarin was accorded a hero's welcome.*

ac·cord·ance /əˈkɔːdəns‖əˈkɔːr-/ n **in accordance with** formal done in a way that follows a particular system or rule: *Safety checks were made in accordance with the rules.*

ac·cord·ing·ly /əˈkɔːdɪŋli‖əˈkɔːr-/ adv **1** in a way that is suitable for a particular situation: *If you work extra hours, you will be paid accordingly.* **2** formal as a result of something that has just been mentioned; therefore: *We have noticed that the books are slightly damaged, and accordingly, we have reduced the price.*

according to /.ˈ.. ./ prep **1** as shown by something or as said by someone: *According to our records she never paid her bill.* | *According to Angela, he's a great teacher.* **2** in the way that has been planned, or in a way that obeys the rules: *Everything went according to plan and we arrived on time.* **3** based on a particular amount or system: *You will be paid according to the amount of work you do.*

ac·cor·di·on /əˈkɔːdiən‖əˈkɔːr-/ n [C] a musical instrument like a box that you play by pulling the sides in and out while pushing buttons to produce different notes

ac·cost /əˈkɒst‖əˈkɔːst, əˈkɑːst/ v [T] if someone you do not know accosts you, they come up to you, and speak to you especially in a threatening way

account[1] /əˈkaʊnt/ n [C] **1** a written or spoken description of an event or situation: **give an account of** *Can you give us an account of what happened?* | **by/from all accounts** (=according to what everyone says): *By all accounts Frank was once a great player.* **2** an arrangement that allows you to keep your money in a bank and take amounts from it when you want to: *He couldn't remember his account number.* | *I'd like to withdraw £250 from my account.* → see also BANK ACCOUNT, CHECKING ACCOUNT, CURRENT ACCOUNT, DEPOSIT ACCOUNT **3 take into account/take account of** to consider or include particular facts when making a decision about something: *They should have taken into account the needs of foreign students.* **4** an arrangement with a shop that allows you to buy goods and pay for them later: *Here are the books you ordered. Shall I charge them to your account?* **5** a statement of money that you owe for things you have bought from a shop: **settle your account** (=pay what you owe): *Accounts must be settled within 30 days.* **6 on account of** because of: *Several people are late on account of the train strike.* **7 not on my/his etc account** spoken used to tell someone that they need not do something if they are only doing it to please you: *Don't stay up late on my account.* **8 on no account/not on any account** formal used to emphasize that someone must not do something for any reason: *On no account should anyone go near this man – he's dangerous.* → see also ACCOUNTS

account[2] v

account for sth phr v [T] **1** to be a particular amount or part of something: *Oil and gas* *account for 60% of the country's exports.* **2** to give a reason for something that has happened: *How do you account for this sudden change of policy?* **3** to be the reason for something: *If he really is taking drugs, that would account for his behaviour.*

ac·count·a·ble /ə'kaʊntəbəl/ *adj* [not before noun] responsible for the effects of your actions and willing to explain to or criticized for them: **+ for** *Managers must be accountable for their decisions.* | **hold sb accountable** (=consider that someone is responsible for something): *If students fail their exams, should their teachers be held accountable?* —**accountability** /ə,kaʊntə'bɪlɪti/ *n* [U]

ac·coun·tan·cy /ə'kaʊntənsi/ *BrE*, **ac·count·-ing** /ə'kaʊntɪŋ/ *AmE n* [U] the job of being an accountant

ac·coun·tant /ə'kaʊntənt/ *n* [C] someone whose job is to keep or check financial records

ac·counts /ə'kaʊnts/ *n* [plural] a record of the money that a company or person has received and spent: *the company's accounts from last year* → see also ACCOUNT¹

ac·cred·it·ed /ə'kredɨtɨd/ *adj* having official approval

ac·cu·mu·late /ə'kju:mjɨleɪt/ *v* [I,T] **1** to gradually increase in quantity until there is a large quantity in one place: *The dirt and dust had accumulated in the corners of the room.* **2** [T] to gradually get more and more possessions, money, knowledge etc: *By the time he died Methuen had accumulated a vast collection of paintings.* —**accumulation** /ə,kju:mjɨ'leɪʃən/ *n* [C,U]

ac·cu·ra·cy /'ækjɨrəsi/ *n* [U] exactness or correctness: *The bombs can be aimed with amazing accuracy.* → opposite INACCURACY

ac·cu·rate /'ækjɨrət/ *adj* exactly correct: *an accurate report of what happened* → opposite IN-ACCURATE —**accurately** *adv*

ac·cu·sa·tion /,ækjɨ'zeɪʃən/ *n* [C] a statement saying that someone has done something wrong or illegal: **make an accusation against sb** *Serious accusations have been made against him.*

ac·cuse /ə'kju:z/ *v* [T] to say that someone has done something wrong or illegal: **accuse sb of doing sth** *Are you accusing me of stealing?* —**ac-cuser** *n* [C]

ac·cused /ə'kju:zd/ *n* **the accused** [singular or plural] the person or people who are being accused of a crime in a court of law

ac·cus·ing /ə'kju:zɪŋ/ *adj* showing that you think someone has done something wrong: *She gave him an accusing look.* —**accusingly** *adv*

ac·cus·tom /ə'kʌstəm/ *v* [T] **accustom yourself to (doing) sth** to make yourself become used to something: *They'll have to accustom themselves to working long hours.*

ac·cus·tomed /ə'kʌstəmd/ *adj formal* **be accustomed to (doing) sth** to be used to something: *She was accustomed to a life of luxury.* | **become/get/grow accustomed to** *Ed's eyes quickly grew accustomed to the dark room.*

ace¹ /eɪs/ *n* [C] **1** a playing card with one SYMBOL on it, that has the highest or lowest value: *the ace of spades* **2** a first hit in tennis

or VOLLEYBALL that is too good for your opponent to hit back

ace² *adj* **ace pilot/player** *informal* someone who is an extremely good pilot, player etc —**ace** *n* [singular] *motorcycle ace Barry Sheene*

ache¹ /eɪk/ *v* [I] **1** if part of your body aches, it feels painful: *My legs are aching.* | *I ache all over.* **2** **be aching to do sth** to want to do something very much: *Jenny was aching to go home.*

ache² *n* [C] a continuous pain: **headache/backache/toothache** (=a continuous pain in your head, back, tooth etc) —**achy** *adj*: *My arm feels all achy.*

a·chieve /ə'tʃi:v/ *v* [T] to succeed in doing something good or getting the result you want: *He will never achieve anything if he doesn't work harder.* | *On the test drive Segrave achieved speeds of over 200 mph.* —**achiever** *n* [C] *a high achiever* (=someone who is very successful in their work or studies) —**achievable** *adj*

a·chieve·ment /ə'tʃi:vmənt/ *n* **1** [C] something important that you achieve: *Winning the championship is quite an achievement.* **2** [U] when you succeed in doing or getting what you have worked for: *the achievement of a lifetime's ambition*

ac·id¹ /'æsɨd/ *n* **1** [C,U] a type of liquid chemical substance. A strong acid can burn holes in the things it touches: *hydrochloric acid* **2** **the acid test** a situation that proves whether something is true or as good as it is supposed to be: *It looks good, but will it work? That's the acid test.* —**acidic** *adj* —**acidity** /ə'sɪdɨti/ *n* [U]

acid² *adj* **1** having a very sour or BITTER taste **2** **acid remark/comment** something you say that uses humour in an unkind way

acid rain /,.. './ *n* [U] rain that damages the environment because it contains acid, especially from factory smoke → see colour picture on page 278

ac·knowl·edge /ək'nɒlɪdʒ‖-'nɑ:-/ *v* [T] **1** to accept or admit that something is true or that a situation exists: **+ that** *Angie has acknowledged that she made a mistake.* | **acknowledge sth as** *These beaches are generally acknowledged as the best in Europe.* **2** to officially accept that a government, court, leader etc has legal authority: *They are refusing to acknowledge the court's decision.* **3** to write to someone telling them that you have received something they sent you: *We must acknowledge her letter.* **4** to show someone that you have seen them or heard what they have said: *Tina walked straight past without acknowledging us.*

ac·knowl·edge·ment, acknowledgment /ək-'nɒlɪdʒmənt‖-'nɑ:-/ *n* [C] **1** something that someone says, writes, or does to thank someone or to show that they have received something: *I haven't received an acknowledgement of my letter yet.* **2** something that shows you admit or accept that something is true or that a situation exists: *an acknowledgement of defeat*

ac·ne /'ækni/ *n* [U] a skin problem which is common among young people and causes small spots to appear on the face

a·corn /'eɪkɔ:n‖-ɔ:rn, -ərn/ *n* [C] the nut of an OAK tree

a·cous·tic /ə'ku:stɪk/ *adj* **1** relating to sound and the way people hear things **2** an acoustic musical instrument does not have its sound made louder electronically: *an acoustic guitar*

a·cous·tics /ə'ku:stɪks/ *n* **1** [plural] the way in which the shape and size of a room make it good or bad for hearing music or speeches **2** [U] the scientific study of sound

ac·quaint·ance /ə'kweɪntəns/ *n* **1** [C] someone you know, but not very well **2** [U] when you know someone and have met them: **make sb's acquaintance** (=meet someone): *I've never made his acquaintance.*

ac·quaint·ed /ə'kweɪntɪd/ *adj formal* **1 be acquainted with sb** to know someone, but not well: *Roger and I are already acquainted.* | **get/ become acquainted** (=meet someone and start to know them): *I'll leave you two to get acquainted.* **2 be acquainted with sth** to know about something: *My lawyer is already acquainted with the facts.*

ac·qui·esce /ˌækwi'es/ *v* [I] *formal* to agree to do what someone wants or to let them do what they want, without arguing or complaining, even though you do not like it —**acquiescence** *n* [U]

ac·quire /ə'kwaɪə‖ə'kwaɪr/ *v* [T] **1** to get something, especially by buying it: *The Getty Museum acquired the painting for £6.8 million.* **2** to learn knowledge or skills: *Think about how you can use the skills you have acquired.*

ac·qui·si·tion /ˌækwɪ'zɪʃən/ *n* **1** [U] the process of getting something: **+ of** *the acquisition of wealth* **2** [C] something that someone has obtained, especially by buying it: *a new acquisition*

ac·quit /ə'kwɪt/ *v* [T] decide in a court of law that someone is not guilty of a crime: *Simons was acquitted of murder.*

ac·quit·tal /ə'kwɪtl/ *n* [C,U] an official announcement in a court of law that someone is not guilty

a·cre /'eɪkəǁ-ər/ *n* [C] a unit for measuring an area of land, equal to 4840 square yards or about 4047 square metres

a·cre·age /'eɪkərɪdʒ/ *n* [U] the area of a piece of land measured in acres

ac·rid /'ækrɪd/ *adj* having a very strong and unpleasant smell that hurts your nose or throat: *a cloud of acrid smoke*

ac·ri·mo·ni·ous /ˌækrɪ'məʊniəs‖-'moʊ-/ *adj* an acrimonious argument, meeting etc is one in which people feel very angry and speak angrily to each other: *an acrimonious divorce* —**acrimoniously** *adv*

ac·ri·mo·ny /'ækrɪmənǁ-moʊni/ *n* [U] *formal* very angry feelings between people, often strongly expressed

ac·ro·bat /'ækrəbæt/ *n* [C] someone who entertains people by doing difficult physical actions, for example balancing on a high rope, especially in a CIRCUS —**acrobatic** /ˌækrə-'bætɪk/ *adj*

ac·ro·bat·ics /ˌækrə'bætɪks/ *n* [plural] movements or tricks like those of an acrobat

ac·ro·nym /'ækrənɪm/ *n* [C] a word that is made from the first letters of a group of words. For example, NATO is an acronym for the North Atlantic Treaty Organization.

a·cross /ə'krɒsǁə'krɔːs/ *adv, prep* **1** from one side of something to the other side: *The farmer was walking across the field towards us.* | *Vince looked out across the valley.* | *At its widest point, the river is two miles across.* → see colour picture on page 474 **2** reaching or spreading from one side of an area to the other: *the only bridge across the river* | *The rain will spread slowly across southern England.* **3** on or towards the opposite side of something: *Andy lives across the road from us.* **4 across the board** affecting everyone in an organization: *a pay increase of 8% across the board*

a·cryl·ic /ə'krɪlɪk/ *adj* acrylic paints or cloth are made from a chemical substance

act[1] /ækt/ *v* **1** [I] to do something: *Unless the government acts soon, more people will die.* | **act on advice/orders/instructions** (=do what sb says): *We're acting on the advice of our lawyer.* **2** [I] to behave in a particular way: *Nick's been acting very strangely recently.* **3** [I,T] to perform as a character in a play or film: *Mike got an acting job on TV.* **4 act as sb** to do a job which is not your usual one: *My brother speaks French – he will act as interpreter.* **5** [I] to have a particular effect: **act as sth** *Salt acts as a preservative.*

act sth ↔ out *phr v* [T] to show how an event happened by performing it like a play

---

USAGE NOTE: act and action

You can use **action** as a countable noun when it means the same as act: *a kind act* | *a kind action.* **Act** is also used in some fixed phrases when it means a particular type of action: *an act of friendship* | *an act of war* | *He was caught in the act* (=caught doing something bad). **Act** is always countable, but **action** can be uncountable: *We must take action immediately.* | *What we need is immediate action.*

---

act[2] *n* **1** [C] something that someone has done: *an act of kindness* | *a criminal act* **2** [C] also **Act** a law that has been officially passed by the government: *The Criminal Justice Act* **3** [C] also **Act** one of the main parts into which a play, OPERA etc is divided: *Hamlet kills the king in Act 5.* **4** [C] one of the short pieces of entertainment in a television or theatre show: *a comedy act* **5** [singular] when someone pretends to have feelings that they do not have: *He doesn't care, Laura – it's just an act.* **6 get your act together** *informal* to start to do things in a more organized or effective way: *If Julie doesn't get her act together, she'll never graduate.* **7 get in on the act** *informal* to try to get advantages from an activity that someone else has started

act·ing[1] /'æktɪŋ/ *adj* **acting manager/director etc** someone who does the job of the manager etc

---

GRAMMAR NOTE: a or the (2)
Use **the** before a thing or person when it is clear which one you are talking about: **the** *old man who lives next door.* Use **a** or **an** to talk about a person or thing when it is not important to say which one: *I went out to buy* **a** *newspaper.* | **A** *girl in my class told me about it.*

while the person who usually does it is not there, or until a new manager etc is chosen

acting² *n* [U] the job or skill of performing in plays or films

ac·tion /'ækʃən/ *n* **1** [U] when you do something in order to deal with a situation or for a particular purpose: *We've talked enough. Now is the time for action.* | **take action** (=do something to deal with a problem): *The government must take action before it's too late.* | **course of action** (=something you could do to deal with a situation): *The best course of action would be to tell her the whole story.* | **put sth into action** (=do things to make something happen): *When will you start putting your plan into action?* **2** [C] something that you do: *You shouldn't be blamed for other people's actions.* | *Tanya's prompt action saved his life.* **3** **be out of action** if someone or something is out of action, they cannot move or work because they are injured or broken: *My car's out of action again.* | **put sb/sth out of action** *The accident has put Jim out of action for two weeks.* **4** [U] the effect that a natural or chemical process has on something: *cliffs worn away by the action of the waves* **5** **the action** *informal* exciting and important things that are happening: *New York's where the action is.* **6** **in action** doing a particular job, activity, or sport: *a chance to see top ski jumpers in action* **7** [C,U] fighting during a war: **in action** *Ann's husband was killed in action.*

action-packed /ˌ.. '. / *adj* an action-packed film or story has a lot of exciting things happening

action re·play /ˌ.. '../ *n* [C] *BrE* when an interesting part of a sports event is shown again on film or television immediately after it happens; INSTANT REPLAY *AmE*

ac·ti·vate /'æktɪveɪt/ *v* [T] *formal* to make something start working: *This switch activates the alarm.* —**activation** /ˌæktɪ'veɪʃən/ *n* [U]

ac·tive¹ /'æktɪv/ *adj* **1** always doing things, or always ready or able to do things: *Grandpa's very active for his age.* | *an active member of the Labour Party* **2** *technical* an electronic system that is active is ready to work: *The alarm is now active.* **3** an active VOLCANO is likely to send up fire and smoke **4** if a verb or sentence is active, the person or thing doing the action is the SUBJECT of the verb. In the sentence 'The boy kicked the ball', the verb 'kick' is active. → compare PASSIVE¹

active² *n* **the active (voice)** the active form of a verb → compare PASSIVE²

ac·tive·ly /'æktɪvli/ *adv* in a way that involves doing things to try to make something happen: *The government has actively encouraged immigration.*

ac·tiv·ist /'æktɪvɪst/ *n* [C] someone who works to achieve social or political change

ac·tiv·i·ty /æk'tɪvɪti/ *n* **1** [C,U] things that someone does, especially for pleasure or to try to achieve something: *after-school activities* | *an increase in terrorist activity* **2** [U] a situation in which a lot of things are happening and people are moving around: *There's been a lot of activity on the stock exchange.* → opposite INACTIVITY

ac·tor /'æktəl-ər/ *n* [C] someone who performs in a play or film

ac·tress /'æktrɪs/ *n* [C] a woman who performs in a play or film

ac·tu·al /'æktʃuəl/ *adj* real, especially when compared with what you believed, expected, or intended: *Were those his actual words?* | *The actual cost is a lot higher than we'd thought.*

ac·tu·al·ly /'æktʃuəli, -tʃəli/ *adv especially spoken* **1** used when you want to say what really happens or is really true: *Did she actually say that in the letter?* | *the people who actually run the country* **2** used when you want to say something that may seem strange or surprising or is different from what people imagine: *He may look young, but actually he's 45.* **3** used in order to be polite when you are disagreeing with someone: *"Great! I love French coffee!" "It's German actually."*

ac·u·men /'ækjʊmən, ə'kjuːmən/ *n* [U] the ability to think quickly and make good decisions: *business acumen*

ac·u·punc·ture /'ækjʊˌpʌŋktʃəl-ər/ *n* [U] a way of stopping pain or treating an illness by putting thin needles into someone's body

a·cute /ə'kjuːt/ *adj* **1** very serious or severe: *acute pain* | *an acute shortage of medical staff* **2** good at understanding things quickly and clearly: *Simon's manner concealed an agile and acute mind.* **3** good at noticing small differences in sound or smell **4** *technical* an acute disease or illness becomes dangerous very quickly: *acute tuberculosis* → compare CHRONIC **5** *technical* an acute angle is less than 90 degrees

a·cute·ly /ə'kjuːtli/ *adv* very strongly or painfully: *She was acutely embarrassed when she realized her mistake.*

ad /æd/ *n* [C] *informal* an advertisement

AD /ˌeɪ 'diː/ Anno Domini; used to show that a date is a particular number of years after the birth of Christ: *Attila died in 453 AD.* → compare BC

ad·age /'ædɪdʒ/ *n* [C] a well-known phrase that says something wise; PROVERB

ad·a·mant /'ædəmənt/ *adj formal* determined not to change your opinion, decision etc: *Taylor is adamant that he is not going to quit.* —**adamantly** *adv*

Ad·am's ap·ple /ˌædəmz 'æpll'ædəmz ˌæpl/ *n* [C] the part of your body at the front of your neck that sticks out slightly and moves when you talk or swallow

a·dapt /ə'dæpt/ *v* **1** [I] to change your behaviour or ideas to fit a new situation: **+ to** *Old people find it hard to adapt to life in a foreign country.* **2** [T] to change something so that it is suitable for a new need or purpose: *The car's engine had been adapted to take unleaded fuel.* **3** [T] to change a book or play so that it can be made into a film or television programme **4** **be well adapted to sth** to be especially suitable for something: *Alpine flowers are well adapted to the cold winters.*

a·dapt·a·ble /əˈdæptəbəl/ *adj* able to change and be suitable or successful in new and different situations —**adaptability** /əˌdæptəˈbɪlɪti/ *n* [U]

ad·ap·ta·tion /ˌædæpˈteɪʃən/ *n* **1** [C] a play or film that is based on a book: *a film adaptation of Zola's novel* **2** [U] when something changes or is changed to make it suitable for a new situation: *adaptation to the environment*

a·dapt·er, adaptor /əˈdæptəll-ər/ *n* [C] **1** something used to connect two pieces of equipment that are of different sizes **2** *BrE* a special PLUG that makes it possible to connect more than one piece of equipment to the electricity supply

add /æd/ *v* **1** [T] to put something with something else or with a group of other things: **add sth to sth** *Do you want to add your name to the mailing list?* | *Add one egg to the mixture.* **2** [T] to put numbers or amounts together to calculate the total: *If you add 5 and 3 you get 8.* **3** [I,T] to increase the amount, cost, or degree of something by putting something more with it: *Sales tax adds 15% to the bill.* | **+ to** *Darkness just adds to the spooky atmosphere.* **4** [I,T] to say more about something when you are speaking: **+ that** *The judge added that this case was one of the worst she had ever seen.* **5 add insult to injury** to make a situation even worse for someone who has already been badly or unfairly treated

add sth ↔ **on** *phr v* [T] to increase the size or amount of something by adding another part or amount: *They're going to add on another bedroom at the back.* | **+ to** *VAT at 17.5% will be added on to your bill.*

add up *phr v* **1** [I,T **add** sth ↔ **up**] to put numbers or amounts together and then calculate the total: *Add your scores up and we'll see who won.* **2 not add up** to not seem true or reasonable: *His story just doesn't add up.*

ad·der /ˈædəll-ər/ *n* [C] a small poisonous snake

ad·dict /ˈædɪkt/ *n* [C] **1** someone who is unable to stop taking drugs: *a heroin addict* **2** *informal* someone who likes something very much and does it a lot: *game-show addicts*

ad·dic·ted /əˈdɪktɪd/ *adj* **1** unable to stop taking a drug: **+ to** *Marvin soon became addicted to sleeping pills.* **2** *informal* doing something a lot because you like it very much: *My children are completely addicted to computer games.*

ad·dic·tion /əˈdɪkʃən/ *n* [C,U] when you need to have alcohol or drugs regularly because you are addicted to them

ad·dic·tive /əˈdɪktɪv/ *adj* making you addicted to something: *a highly addictive drug*

ad·di·tion /əˈdɪʃən/ *n* **1 in addition** used to add another fact to what has already been mentioned: *The school has 12 classrooms.* | *In addition there is a large office that could be used for meetings.* | **+ to** *In addition to her teaching job, she plays in a band.* **2** [U] the process of adding together several numbers or amounts to get a total **3** [C] something that is added: *The tower is a later addition to the cathedral.*

ad·di·tion·al /əˈdɪʃənəl/ *adj* added to what is already there: *There's an additional charge for baggage over the weight limit.* —**additionally** *adv*

ad·di·tive /ˈædɪtɪv/ *n* [C] a chemical that is added to a food or drink to improve its taste or colour, or to keep it fresh

ad·dress [1] /əˈdresll-ˈdres, ˈædres/ *n* [C] **1** the details of where someone lives or works, including the number of the building, name of the street and town etc: *I forgot to give Damien my new address.* **2** a formal speech: *the Gettysburg Address*

ad·dress [2] /əˈdres/ *v* [T] **1** *formal* to speak directly to a person or a group: *A guest speaker then addressed the audience.* | **address sth to sb** *You should address your question to the chairman.* **2** to write a name and address on an envelope, package etc: **address sth to sb** *There's a letter here addressed to you.* **3** *formal* to pay attention to a problem and try to deal with it: *an education policy that fails to address the needs of disabled students* **4** to use a particular name or title when speaking or writing to someone: **address sb as** *The President should be addressed as "Mr. President."*

ad·ept /ˈædept, əˈdeptll-ˈdept/ *adj* good at doing something that needs care or skill: **+ at** *He became adept at cooking her favourite Polish dishes.* —**adeptly** *adv*

ad·e·quate /ˈædɪkwɪt/ *adj* **1** enough for a particular purpose: *Her income is hardly adequate to pay the bills.* **2** fairly good, but not excellent: *The critics described his performance as "barely adequate".* →opposite INADEQUATE —**adequacy** *n* [U] —**adequately** *adv*

ad·here /ədˈhɪəll-ˈhɪr/ *v* [I] to stick firmly to something: **+ to** *Make sure the paper adheres firmly to the wall.*

adhere to sth *phr v* [T] to continue to behave according to a particular rule, agreement, or belief: *Not all the countries adhered to the treaty.*

ad·her·ence /ədˈhɪərənsll-ˈhɪr-/ *n* [U] when you behave according to particular rules, ideas, or beliefs

ad·her·ent /ədˈhɪərəntll-ˈhɪr-/ *n* [C] someone who agrees with and supports a particular idea, opinion, or political party

ad·he·sion /ədˈhiːʒən/ *n* [U] when one thing sticks to another thing

ad·he·sive /ədˈhiːsɪv/ *n* [C] a substance such as glue that can stick things together —**adhesive** *adj*: *adhesive tape*

ad hoc /ˌæd ˈhɒkll-ˈhɑːk, -ˈhoʊk/ *adj* done or arranged only when a situation makes it necessary, and without any previous planning: *I'd been working for him on an ad hoc basis.* —**ad hoc** *adv*

ad·ja·cent /əˈdʒeɪsənt/ *adj formal* next to something: *a door leading to the adjacent room* | **+ to** *buildings adjacent to the palace*

ad·jec·tive /ˈædʒɪktɪv/ *n* [C] a word that describes a noun or PRONOUN. In the sentence 'I bought a new car', 'new' is an adjective. —**adjectival** /ˌædʒɪkˈtaɪvəl◂/ *adj*: *an adjectival phrase*

ad·join·ing /əˈdʒɔɪnɪŋ/ *adj* next to something, and connected to it: *an adjoining office* —**adjoin** *v* [T]

ad·journ /əˈdʒɜːnll-ˈdʒɜːrn/ *v* [I,T] to stop a meeting for a short time or until a later date: *The* *committee adjourned for an hour.* —**adjourn-ment** *n* [C,U]

ad·ju·di·cate /ə'dʒuːdɪkeɪt/ *v* [I,T] *formal* to be the judge in a competition or make an official de-cision about a problem or argument: *The European Court was asked to adjudicate in the dispute.* —**adjudicator** *n* [C] —**adjudication** /ə-ˌdʒuːdɪ'keɪʃən/ *n* [U]

ad·just /ə'dʒʌst/ *v* **1** [T] to change or move something slightly so that it is in the right posi-tion: *Where's the lever for adjusting the car seat?* **2** [I] to make small changes to the way you do things in order to get used to a new situation or condition: + **to** *We're gradually adjusting to the new way of working.* —**adjustable** *adj*: *an adjustable lamp*

ad·just·ment /ə'dʒʌstmənt/ *n* [C,U] **1** a small change made to a machine, plan, or system: **make adjustments to sth** *I've made a few adjust-ments to our original calculations.* **2** a change in the way you behave or think: **make adjust-ments** *You have to make some adjustments when you live abroad.*

ad·lib /ˌæd 'lɪb/ *v* [I,T] to say something in a speech or a performance without preparing or planning it: *She forgot her lines and had to ad-lib.* —**ad lib** *adj, adv* —**ad-lib** *n* [C]

ad·min·is·ter /əd'mɪnɪstəll-ər/ *v* [T] **1** to manage the affairs of a company, government etc: *officials who administer the transport system* **2** to organize the way a test or punishment is given, or the way a law is used **3** *formal* to give someone a drug or medical treatment: *The medicine was administered in regular doses.*

ad·min·is·tra·tion /ədˌmɪnɪ'streɪʃən/ *n* [U] **1** the work of managing the affairs of a com-pany, government etc: *Have you any experience in administration?* **2** the administration *espe-cially AmE* the part of the national, state, or city government that is controlled by the pres-ident, GOVERNOR, or MAYOR: *the Kennedy Admin-istration*

ad·min·is·tra·tive /əd'mɪnɪstrətɪvll-streɪtɪv/ *adj* connected with managing a company, coun-try etc: *The job is mainly administrative.* —**ad-ministratively** *adv*

ad·min·is·tra·tor /əd'mɪnɪstreɪtəll-ər/ *n* [C] someone who manages the affairs of a govern-ment department, organization etc

ad·mi·ra·ble /'ædmərəbəl/ *adj* something that is admirable deserves to be praised and admired: *an admirable achievement* —**ad-mirably** *adv*

ad·mi·ral /'ædmərəl/ *n* [C] an officer who has a very high rank in the Navy

ad·mi·ra·tion /ˌædmə'reɪʃən/ *n* [U] when you respect and admire something or someone: + **for** *Dylan had a deep admiration for Picasso's later work.*

ad·mire /əd'maɪəll-'maɪr/ *v* [T] **1** to have a very good opinion of someone because of their good qualities or their achievements: **admire sb for sth** *I always admired my mother for her cour-age and patience.* **2** to look at someone or some-thing and think how beautiful or impressive they are: *We stopped halfway up the hill to admire the view.* —**admirer** *n* [C] *My teacher was a great admirer of Shakespeare.*

ad·mis·si·ble /əd'mɪsəbəl/ *adj formal* accept-able or allowed, especially in a court of law: *admissible evidence* → opposite INADMISSIBLE

ad·mis·sion /əd'mɪʃən/ *n* **1** [C] when you admit that something bad or unpleasant is true: + **of** *If he resigns, it will be an admission of guilt.* **2** [C,U] permission that is given to someone to study at a college, be treated in a hospital, join a club etc: + **to** *Tom has applied for admission to Oxford next year.* **3** [U] the price charged when you go to a film, sports event, concert etc: *Admis-sion $6.50*

ad·mit /əd'mɪt/ *v* **1** [I,T] to agree or say that something is true, although you do not want to: *He was wrong, but he won't admit it.* | + **(that)** *You may not like her, but you have to admit that Sheila is good at her job.* | + **to** *He'll never admit to the murder.* **2** [T] to let someone or some-thing enter a place or join a club or organiza-tion: *Only ticket holders will be admitted into the stadium.* **3 be admitted** to be taken into hos-pital because you are ill

ad·mit·tance /əd'mɪtəns/ *n* [U] permission to enter a place: *Journalists were refused admit-tance to the meeting.*

ad·mit·ted·ly /əd'mɪtɪdli/ *adv* used when you are admitting that something is true: *Admit-tedly, it's not a very good photograph, but you can recognize who it is.*

ad·mon·ish /əd'mɒnɪʃll-'maː-/ *v* [T] *literary* to tell or warn someone that they have done some-thing wrong —**admonishment** *n* [C,U]

a·do /ə'duː/ *n* **without more/further ado** with-out any more delay

ad·o·les·cence /ˌædə'lesəns/ *n* [U] the period when a young person is developing into an adult, usually between the ages of 12 and 17

ad·o·les·cent /ˌædə'lesəntₑ/ *n* [C] a young person who is developing into an adult —**ado-lescent** *adj*

a·dopt /ə'dɒptll-'daːpt/ *v* [T] **1** to let someone else's child become a part of your family and make him or her legally your daughter or son: *Melissa was adopted by the Simpsons when she was only two.* **2** to begin to use a particular plan or way of doing something: *The police are adopting more forceful methods.* **3** to formally approve a suggestion: *The committee voted to adopt our proposals.* —**adopted** *adj*: *their adopted daughter*

a·dop·tion /ə'dɒpʃənllə'daːp-/ *n* **1** [U] when you decide to use a particular plan or method: *improvements that followed the adoption of new technology* **2** [C,U] when someone adopts some-one else's child: *Children of parents who had died were offered for adoption.*

a·dor·a·ble /ə'dɔːrəbəl/ *adj* very attractive: *an adorable little puppy*

ad·o·ra·tion /ˌædə'reɪʃən/ *n* [U] great love and admiration

a·dore /ə'dɔːllə'dɔːr/ *v* [T] **1** to love and admire someone very much: *Tim absolutely adores his older brother.* **2** to like something very much: *I adore this place. It's so peaceful here.*

a·dorn /ə'dɔːnll-ɔːrn/ *v* [T] *formal* to decorate something and make it more attractive: *The church walls were adorned with beautiful carv-ings.* —**adornment** /ə'dɔːnməntll-ɔːr-/ *n* [C,U]

a·dren·a·lin /əˈdrenəl-ˌn/ *n* [U] a chemical produced by your body that gives you more energy when you are frightened, excited, or angry

a·drift /əˈdrɪft/ *adv* **1** a boat that is adrift is not tied to anything, and is moved around by the ocean or wind **2 come adrift** if something comes adrift, it becomes separated from the thing it should be fastened to

a·droit /əˈdrɔɪt/ *adj* able to use your hands skilfully or to think and use words quickly: *an adroit negotiator* — **adroitly** *adv*

ad·u·la·tion /ˌædʒʊˈleɪʃən/ *n* [U] when someone receives more praise and admiration than they deserve

ad·ult[1] /ˈædʌlt, əˈdʌlt/ *n* [C] a fully grown person or animal

adult[2] *adj* **1** fully grown: *an adult male frog* **2** typical of an adult: *an adult view of the world* **3** adult films, magazines etc are about sex and are not suitable for children

a·dul·ter·y /əˈdʌltəri/ *n* [U] when someone who is married has sex with someone who is not their husband or wife — **adulterous** *adj*

ad·vance[1] /ədˈvɑːns‖ədˈvæns/ *n* **1 in advance** if you do something in advance, you do it so that something is ready or available at the time in the future when it will be needed: *a delicious dish that can be prepared in advance* **2** [C,U] when something is discovered, invented, or improved, with the result that there is progress: *effective drugs and other advances in medicine* **3** [C] a movement forward to a new position, especially by an army: *Napoleon's advance towards Moscow* **4** [C, usually singular] money paid to someone before the usual time: + **on** *Could I have a small advance on my salary?* → see also ADVANCES

advance[2] *v* **1** [I,T] if scientific knowledge advances, or if it is advanced, it develops and improves: *research to advance our understanding of genetics* **2** [I] to move forward to a new position: + **on** *Viet Cong forces were advancing on Saigon.* **3** [T] to suggest a plan or idea so that people can consider it: *new proposals advanced by the Spanish delegation* — **advancement** *n* [C,U] *the advancement of science*

advance[3] *adj* done or given before an event: **advance warning/notice/booking** *advance warning of a hurricane* | *You can make an advance booking with your credit card.* (=buy a ticket before a performance, journey etc)

ad·vanced /ədˈvɑːnst‖ədˈvænst/ *adj* **1** using the most modern ideas, equipment, and methods: *the most advanced computer on the market* **2 advanced Physics/Mathematics/Chemistry etc** Physics, Mathematics etc at a high level: *a course in Advanced Computer Studies*

ad·van·ces /ədˈvɑːnsəz‖ədˈvæn-/ *n* [plural] attempts to start a sexual relationship with someone: *He became violent when the girl rejected his advances.*

ad·van·tage[1] /ədˈvɑːntɪdʒ‖ədˈvæn-/ *n* [C,U] **1** something that helps you to be better or more successful than other people: + **of** *the advantages of a good education* | + **over** *Her computer training gave her an advantage over the other students.* **2** a way in which something is good or useful: *Good public transport is just one of the advantages of living in a big city.* **3 take advantage of sth/sb a)** to use a situation to help you do or get something you want: *We took advantage of the good weather by going for a picnic.* **b)** to unfairly use a person in order to get something for yourself: *I don't mind helping, but I resent being taken advantage of.* **4 to your advantage** helpful and likely to make you richer or more successful

ad·van·ta·geous /ˌædvənˈteɪdʒəs, ˌædvæn-/ *adj* helpful and likely to make you more successful

ad·vent /ˈædvent/ *n* **the advent of sth** when something important first starts to exist or to be used by a lot of people: *the advent of television* | *the advent of communism*

ad·ven·ture /ədˈventʃə‖-ər/ *n* [C,U] an exciting experience in which dangerous or unusual things happen: *a book about her adventures in South America*

ad·ven·tur·er /ədˈventʃərə‖-ər/ *n* [C] someone who travels to new places, doing exciting things

ad·ven·tur·ous /ədˈventʃərəs/ *adj* **1** also **adventuresome** *AmE* wanting to do new, exciting, dangerous things **2** exciting and involving danger: *an adventurous expedition up the Amazon* — **adventurously** *adv*

ad·verb /ˈædvɜːb‖-vɜːrb/ *n* [C] a word that describes or adds to the meaning of a verb, an adjective, another adverb, or a sentence. For example, 'slowly' in 'He walked slowly' and 'very' in 'It was a very good book' are adverbs — **adverbial** /ˈædvɜːbiəl‖-ɜːr-/ *adj*

ad·ver·sa·ry /ˈædvəsəri‖ˈædvərseri/ *n* [C] *formal* an enemy or someone you are competing against

ad·verse /ˈædvɜːs‖-ɜːrs/ *adj* *formal* **1 adverse conditions/effects** conditions or effects that are bad and cause problems: *adverse weather conditions* **2 adverse publicity/comment etc** when people criticize something or someone and say that they are not very good — **adversely** *adv*

ad·ver·si·ty /ədˈvɜːsɪti‖-ɜːr-/ *n* [C,U] difficulties or problems in your life: *showing courage in times of adversity*

ad·vert /ˈædvɜːt‖-ɜːrt/ *n* [C] *BrE* an advertisement

ad·ver·tise /ˈædvətaɪz‖-ər-/ *v* **1** [I,T] to tell people about a product, or service in order to persuade them to buy it or use it: *a poster advertising sportswear* | *I saw your car advertised in the evening paper.* **2** [I] to make an announcement in a newspaper, asking for someone to work for you or for something that you need: + **for** *RCA is advertising for an accountant.* — **advertiser** *n* [C]

ad·ver·tise·ment /ədˈvɜːtɪsmənt‖ˌædvər-ˈtaɪz-/ *n* [C] a set of words or pictures in a newspaper, magazine etc, or a short film on television

---

GRAMMAR NOTE: countable and uncountable (1)
If you can put numbers in front of a noun (*one horse, two tickets* etc) and make it plural, that noun is **countable**: *n* [C]. A substance (e.g. *butter, air*), or an idea or quality (e.g. *beauty, information*) cannot be made plural or used with **a** or **an**. These are **uncountable**: *n* [U].

that advertises a product → compare COMMER-CIAL[2]

ad·ver·tis·ing /'ædvətaɪzɪŋǁ-ər-/ n [U] the business of advertising things on television, in newspapers etc

ad·vice /əd'vaɪs/ n [U] what you say to someone when you tell them what you think they should do: **+ on/about** *a book that's full of advice on babycare* | **give (sb) advice** *Let me give you some advice. Don't write so fast.* | **ask sb's advice** (=ask them what to do): *Beth decided to ask her doctor's advice.* | **take/follow sb's advice** (=do what they advise you to do): *Did you take your father's advice?* | **piece of advice** *He offered me one piece of advice that I've never forgotten.*

ad·vis·a·ble /əd'vaɪzəbəl/ adj [not before noun] something that is advisable should be done in order to avoid problems or risks: *It is advisable to wear a safety belt at all times.* → opposite IN-ADVISABLE — **advisability** /əd,vaɪzə'bɪlǁti/ n [U]

ad·vise /əd'vaɪz/ v **1** [I,T] to tell someone what you think they should do: **advise sb to do sth** *The doctor advised me to take more exercise.* | **advise (sb) against doing sth** (=tell someone not to do something): *His lawyers had advised against making a statement to the press.* | **advise (sb) on sth** *Franklin advises us on financial matters.* **2** [T] *formal* to officially tell someone something: *You will be advised when the work is completed.*

ad·vis·er, advisor /əd'vaɪzəǁ-ər/ n [C] someone whose job is to give advice about a subject: **+ on** *the President's adviser on foreign affairs*

ad·vi·so·ry /əd'vaɪzəri/ adj having the purpose of giving advice: *an advisory committee*

ad·vo·cate[1] /'ædvəkeɪt/ v [T] to suggest or say that you strongly support a particular way of doing things: *Buchanan advocates tougher trade policies.* — **advocacy** /-kəsi/ n [U]

ad·vo·cate[2] /'ædvəkǝt, -keɪt/ n [C] **1** someone who strongly supports a particular way of doing things: **+ of** *an advocate of prison reform* **2** *law* a lawyer who speaks for someone in a court of law and tries to prove they are not guilty

aer·i·al[1] /'eəriəlǁ'er-/ adj from a plane or happening in the air: *aerial photographs* (=taken from the air) | *aerial attacks*

aerial[2] n [C] *BrE* a piece of metal or wire used for receiving radio or television SIGNALS; ANTEN-NA *AmE* → see picture at CAR

ae·ro·bic /eə'rəʊbɪkǁe'rəʊ-/ adj aerobic exercise makes your heart and lungs stronger

aer·o·bics /eə'rəʊbɪksǁe'rəʊ-/ n [U] active physical exercise done to music, usually in a class: *Are you going to aerobics tonight?* (=to an aerobics class)

aer·o·dy·nam·ics /,eərəʊdaɪ'næmɪksǁ,erəʊ-/ n [U] the scientific study of how objects move through the air — **aerodynamic** adj

aer·o·plane /'eərəpleɪnǁ'erə-/ *BrE* n [C] a flying vehicle with wings and an engine; AIR-PLANE *AmE* → see colour picture on page 669

aer·o·sol /'eərəsɒlǁ'erəsɑːl/ n [C] a small metal container from which a liquid can be forced out by pressing a button: *an aerosol hairspray* → see picture at SPRAY

aer·o·space /'eərəʊspeɪsǁ'erəʊ-/ n [U] the design and production of aircraft and space vehicles: *the aerospace industry*

aes·thet·ic also **esthetic** *AmE* /iːs'θetɪk, es-ǁes-/ adj relating to beauty and the study of beauty: *the aesthetic qualities of literature* — **aesthetically** /-kliǁ/ adv: *aesthetically pleasing*

aes·thet·ics also **esthetics** *AmE* /iːs'θetɪks, es-ǁes-/ n [U] the study of beauty, especially beauty in art

a·far /ə'fɑːǁə'fɑːr/ adv **from afar** *literary* from a long distance away

af·fa·ble /'æfəbəl/ adj friendly and easy to talk to: *an affable guy* — **affably** adv

af·fair /ə'feəǁə'fer/ n [C] **1** an event or a set of related events, especially unpleasant ones: *The Watergate affair brought down the Nixon administration.* **2** a secret sexual relationship between two people, when at least one of them is married to someone else: **have an affair** *Ed's having an affair with his boss's wife.* **3 be sb's affair** if something is your affair, you do not want other people to know about it or become involved in it

af·fairs /ə'feəzǁə'ferz/ n [plural] situations or subjects that a person, business, or government has to deal with: *the company's financial affairs* | **affairs of state** (=government business)

af·fect /ə'fekt/ v [T] **1** to cause a change in someone or something, or to change the situation they are in: *a disease that affects the heart and lungs* | *Help is being sent to areas affected by the floods.* **2** to make someone feel strong emotions: *She was deeply affected by the news of Paul's death.* → compare EFFECT[2]

USAGE NOTE: affect and effect

Affect is always a verb, used to talk about the way one thing changes or influences another: *How will the new law affect young people?* **Effect** is a noun, meaning what happens as the result of a change or influence: *What effect will the new law have?* **Effect**, however, is sometimes used as a verb in formal English, meaning to make something happen: *efforts to effect a peaceful solution to the conflict.*

---

af·fec·ta·tion /,æfek'teɪʃən/ n [C,U] unnatural or insincere behaviour

af·fect·ed /ə'fektɪd/ adj speaking or behaving in a way that is not sincere or natural: *Olivia spoke in a high, affected voice.*

af·fec·tion /ə'fekʃən/ n [C,U] a feeling of gentle love: **+ for** *Barry felt a great affection for her.*

af·fec·tion·ate /ə'fekʃənǝt/ adj behaving in a way that shows you love someone: *an affectionate child* — **affectionately** adv

af·fil·i·ate /ə'fɪlieɪt/ v **be affiliated with/to** to be officially connected with, or controlled by a larger organization: *a TV station affiliated to CBS* — **affiliation** /ə,fɪli'eɪʃən/ n [C,U] *What are the group's political affiliations?*

af·fin·i·ty /ə'fɪnǝti/ n **1** [singular] a feeling that you like and understand someone because you are similar: **+ for/with/between** *She felt a natural affinity for these people.* **2** [C,U] when two things are very similar or closely related to each other

af·firm /ə'fɜːmǁ-ɜːrm/ v [T] *formal* to say definitely that something is true: *The President affirmed his intention to reduce taxes.* — **affirmation** /,æfə'meɪʃənǁ,æfər-/ n [C,U]

af·fir·ma·tive /ə'fɜːmətɪv‖-ɜːr-/ adj formal meaning "yes": an affirmative answer | **answer in the affirmative** (=say "yes") —**affirmatively** adv

af·fix /ə'fɪks/ v [T] formal to fasten or stick something to something else: A recent photograph should be affixed to your form.

af·flict /ə'flɪkt/ v [T] formal if you are afflicted by a disease or problem, it affects you badly: Towards the end of his life he was afflicted with blindness. | a country afflicted by famine

af·flic·tion /ə'flɪkʃən/ n [C,U] formal something that causes suffering or pain

af·flu·ent /'æfluənt/ adj rich: an affluent suburb of Paris —**affluence** n [U]

af·ford /ə'fɔːd‖-ɔːrd/ v [T] **1 can afford a)** to have enough money to pay for something: I wish we could afford a new computer. | I can't afford to buy a new car. **b)** if you cannot afford to do something or let something happen, you must not do it or let it happen because it will cause problems: We can't afford to offend our regular customers. **2** formal to provide something: The walls afforded some protection from the wind.

af·ford·a·ble /ə'fɔːdəbəl‖-ɔːr-/ adj something that is affordable is not too expensive, and ordinary people are able to pay for it: a list of good affordable hotels

af·front /ə'frʌnt/ n [singular] something that makes you feel offended or insulted: **+ to** The accusation was an affront to his pride.

a·field /ə'fiːld/ adv **far/further afield** far or further away: As he grew more confident, he started to wander further afield.

a·float /ə'fləʊt‖ə'floʊt/ adj **1** floating on water **2 keep/stay afloat** to have enough money to pay your debts and continue in business: She had to borrow more money just to keep the company afloat.

a·fraid /ə'freɪd/ adj [not before noun] **1 I'm afraid** spoken used when you are politely telling someone something that may annoy, upset, or disappoint them: I won't be able to come with you, I'm afraid. | **+ (that)** I'm afraid this is a no smoking area. | "Are we late?" "I'm afraid so." (=yes) | "Are there any tickets left?" "I'm afraid not." (=no) **2** frightened because you think someone or something is unpleasant or will hurt you: I could see by the look in his eyes that he was afraid. | **+ of** Small children are often afraid of the dark. **3** frightened or worried that something bad may happen: **afraid of doing sth** A lot of people are afraid of losing their jobs. | **+ (that)** I didn't say anything because I was afraid the other kids would laugh at me. | **afraid for sb/sth** (=worried that something bad will happen to someone): I thought you were in danger and I was afraid for you.

a·fresh /ə'freʃ/ adv **start afresh** to start again from the beginning: We decided to move to Sydney and start afresh.

af·ter[1] /'ɑːftə‖'æftər/ prep **1** when a particular time or event has happened: What are you doing after class? | **after that** (=used to say what happens next): Then we went to the museum. After that, we had lunch. | **an hour/2 weeks etc after sth** We left an hour after daybreak. **2** following someone or something in a set or list of things: Whose name is after mine on the list? **3 after 10 minutes/3 hours etc** when 10 minutes etc have passed: After a while, the woman returned. **4** AmE used to say how many minutes past the hour it is when saying the time: It's 10 after five. **5 day after day/year after year etc** continuing for a very long time: Day after day we waited, hoping she'd call. **6 one after the other** when each one immediately follows the one before: We led the horses one after the other out of the barn. **7** because of something that has happened: I'm surprised he came, after the way you treated him. **8** in spite of something: After all the trouble I had, Reese didn't even say thank you. **9 be after sb** to be looking for someone: The FBI is after him for fraud. **10 be after sth** to be trying to get something that belongs to someone else: You're just after my money! **11 after all a)** in spite of what you thought was true or expected to happen: Rita didn't have my pictures after all. Jake did. | It didn't rain after all. **b)** used when you are saying something that shows that what you have just said is right: Don't shout at him – he's only a baby, after all. **12 be called/named after sb** to be given the same name as someone else: She was named Sarah, after my grandmother. → compare BEFORE[1], SINCE[2]

af·ter[2] linking word at a later time than the time something happens: Voitek left Poland after the war. | **10 days/2 weeks after** He discovered the jewel was a fake a month after he bought it.

USAGE NOTE: after an hour and in an hour

Use these phrases to talk about the time in the future when you are going to do something. However, compare the sentences: We'll leave after an hour and We'll leave in an hour. In the first sentence, the speaker is planning how long to stay in a place before they get there. In the second, the speaker is already at a place, and is deciding how much longer to stay there.

---

af·ter[3] adv later than someone or something else: Gina came on Monday; I got here the day after.

af·ter·ef·fect /'ɑːftərɪˌfekt‖'æf-/ n [C usually plural] an unpleasant effect that remains after the condition or event that caused it: **+ of** the after-effects of his illness

af·ter·life /'ɑːftəlaɪf‖'æftər-/ n [singular] the life that some people believe you have after you die

af·ter·math /'ɑːftəmæθ‖'æftər-/ n [singular] the situation after an accident, storm, war etc when people are still dealing with what happened: **in the aftermath of** the refugee crisis in the aftermath of the civil war

af·ter·noon /ˌɑːftə'nuːn‹ ‖ˌæftər-/ n [C,U] the period of time between 12 o'clock and the evening: We should get there at about three in the afternoon. | There are no afternoon classes today. | **this afternoon** (=today in the afternoon): Can you go swimming this afternoon?

af·ter·shave /'ɑːftəʃeɪv‖'æftər-/ n [C,U] a liquid with a pleasant smell that a man puts on his face after he SHAVEs

af·ter·taste /'ɑːftəteɪst‖'æftər-/ n [singular] a taste that stays in your mouth after you eat or drink something: a drink with a sour aftertaste

af·ter·thought /'ɑːftəθɔːt‖'æftərθɔːt/ n [C usually singular] something that you think of and mention or add later

A

af·ter·wards /ˈɑːftəwədz‖ˈæftərwərdz/ also **afterward** *AmE adv* later, after something else has happened: **2 days/5 weeks etc afterwards** *We met at school but didn't get married until two years afterwards.*

a·gain /əˈgen, əˈgeɪn‖əˈgen/ *adv* **1** one more time: *Could you say that again? I can't hear.* | *I'll never go there again.* | *I'm sorry, Mr Kay is busy. Could you call again later?* | **once again** (=again, for at least the third time): *Once again the Americans are the Olympic champions.* **2** in the same condition, situation, or place as before: *I can't wait for Jamie to be well again.* | *Susan's home again, after studying in France.* **3 again and again** many times: *Say it again and again until you learn it.* **4 all over again** repeating something from the beginning: *The tape broke, so we had to record the programme all over again.* **5 then/there again** *spoken* used to add a fact or opinion to what you have just said: *Carol's always had nice clothes – but then again she earns a lot.*

a·gainst /əˈgenst, əˈgeɪnst‖əˈgenst/ *prep* **1** opposed to or disagreeing with an idea, plan, system etc: *Most people are against fox-hunting.* **2** fighting or competing with someone or something: *Sampras is playing against Becker in the final.* | *the battle against inflation* **3 against the law/the rules** not allowed by the law or the rules: *It is against the law to sell alcohol to children.* **4 against sb's wishes/advice/orders etc** if you do something against someone's wishes etc, you do it even though they tell you not to do it: *She got married to him against her parents' wishes.* **5** touching a surface: *The cat's fur felt soft against her hand.* | *Sheldon leaned lazily back against the wall.* → see colour picture on page 474 **6 have sth against sb/sth** to dislike or disapprove of someone or something: *I have nothing against people making money, but they ought to pay taxes on it.* **7** in the opposite direction to the movement or flow of something: *sailing against the wind* **8** protecting you from harm or damage: *a cream to protect against sunburn*

age¹ /eɪdʒ/ *n* **1** [C,U] the number of years that someone has lived or that something has existed: *games for children of all ages* | *Patrick is about my age.* (=he is about the same age as me) | **at the age of** *12/50 etc Jamie won his first tournament at the age of 15.* | **4/15 etc years of age** *formal* (=4, 15 etc years old) | **for his/her age** (=compared with other people the same age): *Judy's very tall for her age.* **2 under age** not old enough to be legally allowed to do something: *I can't buy you a drink, you're under age.* **3** [U] when something is old: *a letter that was brown with age* **4** [C] a particular period of history: *the computer age* | *the history of painting through the ages* **5 come of age** to reach the age at which you are legally considered to be an adult **6 age group** the people who are a particular age, considered as a group: *a book for children in the 8–12 age group* → see also AGES, OLD AGE

age² *v* [I,T] to become older and weaker, or make someone seem older and weaker: *He has aged a lot since his wife died.* —**ageing** *BrE* **aging** *AmE adj*: *an aging rock star*

a·ged¹ /eɪdʒd/ *adj* **aged 5/15 etc** 5, 15 etc years old: *a class for children aged 12 and over*

a·ged² /ˈeɪdʒɪd/ *adj* **1** very old: *his aged parents* **2 the aged** old people: *the cost of caring for the sick and aged*

age·less /ˈeɪdʒləs/ *adj* never seeming old or old-fashioned: *ageless fashions*

a·gen·cy /ˈeɪdʒənsi/ *n* [C] **1** a business that arranges services for people: *I got this job through an employment agency.* **2** an international organization or government department that does a particular job: *the UN agency responsible for helping refugees*

a·gen·da /əˈdʒendə/ *n* [C] **1** a list of the subjects to be discussed at a meeting: **on the agenda** *The next item on the agenda is finances.* **2 be on the agenda** if something is on the agenda, there is a plan to do something about it: **sth is high on the agenda** (=people think something is very important and plan to deal with it soon): *Health care reforms are high on the President's agenda.*

a·gent /ˈeɪdʒənt/ *n* [C] **1** a person or company whose job is to deal with someone else's business for them: *Our agent in Rome handles all our Italian contracts.* **2** someone who works for a government and tries to get secret information about another country or organization: *a secret agent*

age-old /ˌ. ˈ.◂/ *adj* hundreds of years old: *age-old customs and traditions*

a·ges /ˈeɪdʒɪz/ *n* [plural] *informal* a long time: **for ages** *I haven't seen Lorna for ages.*

ag·gra·vate /ˈægrəveɪt/ *v* [T] **1** to make a bad situation worse: *The doctors say her condition is aggravated by stress.* **2** to annoy someone: *He really aggravates me sometimes.* —**aggravating** *adj* —**aggravation** /ˌægrəˈveɪʃən/ *n* [C,U]

ag·gre·gate /ˈægrɪgɪt/ *n* [C,U] a total —**aggregate** *adj*

ag·gres·sion /əˈgreʃən/ *n* [U] angry or threatening behaviour or feelings that often result in fighting: *The bombing was an unprovoked act of aggression.*

ag·gres·sive /əˈgresɪv/ *adj* **1** behaving in an angry or threatening way, as if you want to fight or attack someone: *After a few drinks he became very aggressive.* **2** very determined to succeed: *aggressive sales techniques* —**aggressively** *adv* —**aggressiveness** *n* [U]

ag·gres·sor /əˈgresə‖-ər/ *n* [C] a person or country that begins a fight or war with another person or country

ag·grieved /əˈgriːvd/ *adj* feeling angry or unhappy because you think you have been unfairly treated

a·ghast /əˈgɑːst‖əˈgæst/ *adj* [not before noun] suddenly feeling or looking shocked: *She stared at him aghast.*

a·gile /ˈædʒaɪl‖ˈædʒəl/ *adj* **1** able to move quickly and easily: *as agile as a monkey* **2** able to think quickly and intelligently: *old people who are still mentally agile* —**agility** /əˈdʒɪləti/ *n* [U]

a·gi·tate /ˈædʒɪteɪt/ *v* [I] to protest in order to achieve social or political changes: *workers agitating for higher pay* —**agitator** *n* [C]

a·gi·ta·ted /ˈædʒɪteɪtɪd/ *adj* very anxious, nervous, or upset: *You really shouldn't get so agitated.* —**agitation** /ˌædʒɪˈteɪʃən/ *n* [U]

ag·nos·tic /ægˈnɒstɪk, əg-‖-ˈnɑː-/ *n* [C] someone who believes that it is not possible to know whether God exists → compare ATHEIST —**ag-nostic** *adj* —**agnosticism** /-t₁'sızəm/ *n* [U]

a·go /ə'gəʊllə'goʊ/ *adj* used to say how far back in the past something happened: **10 years/a moment/a long time ago** *Jeff left an hour ago.* | *We went there a long time ago.*

ag·o·nize (also **-ise** *BrE*) /'ægənaız/ *v* [I] to think and worry for a long time about a decision that you have to make: **+ about/over** *Jane had been agonizing all day about what to wear.*

ag·o·niz·ing (also **-sing** *BrE*) /'ægənaızıŋ/ *adj* extremely painful or difficult: *an agonizing decision* —**agonizingly** *adv*

ag·o·ny /'ægəni/ *n* [C,U] very severe pain or suffering: **in agony** *The poor man was in agony.*

a·gree /ə'griː/ *v* **1** [I,T] to have the same opinion about something: **+ with** *I agree with Karen. It's much too expensive.* | **+ that** *Everyone agreed that the new rules were stupid.* | **+ about/ on** *My first husband and I never agreed about anything.* → opposite DISAGREE **2** [I,T] to make a decision together after discussing something: **agree to do sth** *They agreed to share the cost of the party.* | **on** *We're still trying to agree on a date for the wedding.* | **+ that** *It was agreed that Mr Rollins should sign the contract on May 1st.* **3** [I,T] to say yes when someone suggests a plan or asks you to do something: **agree to do sth** *She agreed to stay at home with Charles.* | **+ to** *The boss would never agree to such a plan.* **4** [I] if two pieces of information agree, they say the same thing: **+ with** *Your story doesn't agree with what the police have said.*

agree with sb/sth *phr v* [T] **1** to believe that something is right: **agree with sb** *I don't agree with hitting children.* **2** **not agree with sb** to make someone ill: *Some dairy products don't agree with me.*

a·gree·a·ble /ə'griːəbəl/ *adj* **1** pleasant or enjoyable: *very agreeable weather* **2** **be agreeable to sth** *formal* to be willing to do something or to let it be done: *Are you sure Johnson is agreeable to the idea?* —**agreeably** *adv*: *I was agreeably surprised.*

a·greed /ə'griːd/ *adj* **1** an agreed price, method, arrangement etc is one that people have discussed and accepted **2** **be agreed** if people are agreed, they have decided together what to do: *Are we all agreed on the date for our next meeting?*

a·gree·ment /ə'griːmənt/ *n* **1** [C] an arrangement or promise to do something, made by two or more people, countries, organizations etc: *a trade agreement* | **come to/reach an agreement** *Lawyers on both sides finally reached an agreement today.* **2** [U] when two or more people have the same opinion as each other: **in agreement** *Not all scientists are in agreement with this theory.* → opposite DISAGREEMENT

ag·ri·cul·ture /'ægrı,kʌltʃər/ *n* [U] the work of growing crops and keeping animals on farms for food, and the methods that are used —**agricultural** /,ægrı'kʌltʃərəl/ *adj*

a·ground /ə'graʊnd/ *adv* if a ship runs aground, it gets stuck in water that is not very deep

ah /ɑː/ *interjection* used when you feel surprise, sympathy, dislike, pleasure etc: *Ah, what a lovely baby!*

a·ha /ɑː'hɑː/ *interjection* used when you suddenly understand or realize something: *Aha! So that's where you've been hiding!*

a·head /ə'hed/ *adv* **1** in front of someone or something: *Joe ran ahead to see what was happening.* | **+ of** *Do you see that red car ahead of us?* | **up ahead** *Just up ahead on the right is my old school.* **2** in or into the future: **look/plan ahead** *In this type of business it's important to plan ahead.* **3** before someone arrives or finishes: **+ of** *There were five people ahead of me at the doctor's.* **4** **go ahead** *spoken* used to tell someone they can do something: *Go ahead – help yourself to a drink.* **5** making more progress than other people or things: **+ of** *Jane is well ahead of the rest of her class.* **6** more successful than another player or team in a game, competition etc **7** to be successful in your job or in what you are doing **8** **ahead of schedule/time** before the time that was planned or arranged: *The building was completed ahead of schedule.*

aid[1] /eıd/ *n* **1** [U] money, food, or services that are given by an organization to help people: *The UN is sending aid to the earthquake victims.* | *overseas aid* **2** **with the aid of** using something to help you do something: *bacteria viewed with the aid of a microscope* **3** **in aid of** in order to collect money for a group of people who need help **4** [C] a thing that helps you do something: *notebooks and study aids* **5** **come/ go to the aid of** sb to help someone: *She went to the aid of an injured man.*

aid[2] *v* [T] **1** to help or give support to someone **2** **aid and abet** *law* to help someone do something illegal

aide also **aid** *AmE* /eıd/ *n* [C] someone whose job is to help someone in a more important position, especially a politician: *a White House aide to President Nixon*

AIDS /eıdz/ *n* [U] Acquired Immune Deficiency Syndrome; a very serious disease that stops your body from defending itself against infection

ai·ling /'eılıŋ/ *adj* weak or ill, and not getting stronger or better: *the country's ailing economy* | *his ailing mother*

ail·ment /'eɪlmənt/ n [C] an illness that is not very serious: *people suffering from minor ailments*

aim[1] /eɪm/ v **1** [I] to plan or intend to achieve something: **+ for/at** *We're aiming for a gold medal in the Olympics.* | **aim to do sth** *If you're aiming to become a doctor, you'll have to study hard.* **2 be aimed at sb** if something is aimed at someone, it is made or done so that certain people will like it or be influenced by it: *a TV commercial aimed at teenagers* | *Was that criticism aimed at me?* **3** [I,T] to point a weapon at someone or something that you want to hit: **+ at** *The gun was aimed at his head.* **4 be aimed at doing sth** to be intended to achieve something: *a program aimed at creating more jobs*

aim[2] n **1** [C] a purpose that you are hoping to achieve: *The main aim of the course is to improve your spoken English.* | *I flew to California with the aim of finding a job.* **2 take aim** to point a weapon at someone or something: **+ at** *He took aim at the pigeon and fired.* **3** [U] someone's ability to hit something by throwing or shooting something at it: *Mark's aim wasn't very good.*

aim·less /'eɪmləs/ adj without a clear purpose or reason —**aimlessly** adv: *The boys had been wandering around aimlessly.*

ain't /eɪnt/ spoken a short form of 'am not', 'is not', 'are not', 'has not', or 'have not' that many people think is not correct: *Ain't that the truth!*

air[1] /eəʳ/ n **1** [U] the mixture of gases which we breathe and which surrounds the Earth: **fresh air** (=clean air): *Let's go outside and get some fresh air.* **2 the air** the space above the ground or around things: *David threw the ball up into the air.* **3 by air** travelling by plane: *Most people travel to the islands by air.* **4 air travel/safety etc** involving planes or connected with flying: *the world's worst air disaster* **5** [singular] a general appearance or feeling: **+ of** *There was an air of mystery about her.* **6 be on/off the air** to be broadcasting or not broadcasting on the radio or on television **7 it's up in the air** spoken used to say that something has not been decided yet, and no one is certain about what will happen → see also **thin air** (THIN[1]), AIRS

air[2] v **1** [I,T] also **air out** AmE if clothes air, or if you air them, you dry them in a warm place where there is plenty of fresh air: *Hang your sweater up to air.* **2** [T] also **air sth ↔ out** to make a room smell fresh by letting air from outdoors flow through it **3** [T] to make your opinions, ideas, complaints etc known to other people: *Everyone will get a chance to air their views.* **4** [T] to broadcast a programme on television or radio: *Star Trek was first aired in 1966.* —**airing** n [singular]

air·bag /'eəbæg‖'er-/ n [C] a bag in a car that fills with air to protect people in an accident

air·borne /'eəbɔːn‖'erbɔːrn/ adj flying or floating in the air

air con·di·tion·er /'. .‚.../ n [C] a machine that makes the air in a room, car etc stay COOL

air con·di·tion·ing /'. .‚.../ n [U] a system that makes the air in a room, building etc stay COOL —**air conditioned** adj

air·craft /'eəkrɑːft‖'erkræft/ n [C], plural **aircraft** a plane or any vehicle that can fly

aircraft car·ri·er /'.. ‚.../ n [C] a type of ship that has a large flat surface that planes fly from

air·fare /'eəfeə‖'erfer/ n [C] the price of a plane trip

air·field /'eəfiːld‖'er-/ n [C] a place that military planes or small planes fly from

air force /'. ./ n [C] the military organization of a country that uses planes when fighting a war

air·head /'eəhed‖'er-/ n [C] informal an insulting word for someone who seems stupid

air host·ess /'. ‚../ n [C] BrE a woman who looks after the passengers in a plane

air·i·ly /'eərʲli‖'er-/ adv in a way that shows you do not care very much about something: *"Oh, just do whatever you want,"* she said airily.

airing cup·board /'.. ‚../ n [C] BrE a warm cupboard where sheets and clean clothes are kept

air·less /'eələs‖'er-/ adj without fresh air

air·lift /'eə‚lɪft‖'er-/ n [C] when people or things are taken to a place by plane, because it is too difficult or dangerous to get there by road —**airlift** v [T] *Thirty villagers were airlifted to safety.*

air·line /'eəlaɪn‖'er-/ n [C] a company that provides a regular service to carry passengers to different places by plane

air·lin·er /'eə‚laɪnə‖'er‚laɪnər/ n [C] a large plane for passengers

air·mail /'eəmeɪl‖'er-/ n [U] the system of sending letters, packages etc by plane: *Did you send Grandma's present by airmail?*

air·man /'eəmən‖'er-/ n [C], plural **airmen** someone who has a low rank in a country's AIR FORCE

air·plane /'eəpleɪn‖'er-/ n [C] AmE a vehicle that flies by using wings and one or more engines; AEROPLANE BrE → see colour picture on page 669

air·port /'eəpɔːt‖'erpɔːrt/ n [C] a place that you arrive at or leave from when travelling by plane → see colour picture on page 669

air raid /'. ./ n [C] an attack by enemy planes

airs /eəz‖erz/ n [plural] a way of behaving and talking that someone has because they want to seem more important than they really are: **put on airs** *Monica has been putting on airs ever since she moved to Beverly Hills.*

air·ship /'eə‚ʃɪp‖'er-/ n [C] an old type of aircraft consisting of a large BALLOON filled with gas and an engine below

air·space /'eəspeɪs‖'er-/ n [U] the sky above a particular country, which is controlled by that country

air strike /'. ./ n [C] an attack by military planes against an enemy

air·strip /'eə‚strɪp‖'er-/ n [C] a long narrow piece of land that planes can fly to and from

air·tight /'eətaɪt‖'er-/ adj completely closed so that air cannot get in or out: *airtight containers*

air time /'. ./ n [U] the amount of time that a radio or television station allows for a particular song, advertisement etc to be broadcast

air·y /'eərʲi/ adj an airy room, building etc has a lot of space and fresh air

airy-fai·ry /‚.. '..◂/ adj BrE informal airy-fairy ideas are not at all clear or practical

aisle /aɪl/ *n* [C] a long space where you can walk between rows of seats in a theatre, church, bus, plane etc

a·jar /əˈdʒɑːꟾꟾəˈdʒɑːr/ *adj* a door or window that is ajar is not completely closed

a.k.a. /ˌeɪ keɪ ˈeɪ, ˈækə/ *adv* the written abbreviation of 'also known as'; used when giving someone's real name together with the name they are known by: *John Phillips, a.k.a. The Mississippi Mauler*

a·kin /əˈkɪn/ *adj formal* **akin to sth** similar to something: *His music is much more akin to jazz than rock.*

à la carte /ˌæ lə ˈkɑːt, ˌɑː lɑːꟾꟾˈkɑːrt/ *adj, adv* French if food in a restaurant is à la carte, each dish has its own separate price

a·lac·ri·ty /əˈlækr‚ti/ *n* **with alacrity** *literary* quickly and eagerly

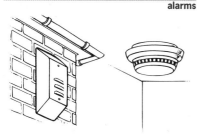

alarms

a·larm¹ /əˈlɑːmꟾꟾəˈlɑːrm/ *n* **1** [U] a feeling of fear or anxiety because something dangerous might happen: *Calm down! There's no cause for alarm.* **2** [C] something such as a bell, loud noise, or light that warns people of danger: *a fire alarm | a car alarm* (=one protecting your car) **3** [C] *informal* an alarm clock **4 raise/sound the alarm** to warn everyone about something bad or dangerous that is happening: *They first sounded the alarm about the problem of nuclear waste in 1955.* **5 false alarm** when people think something dangerous is going to happen, but this is a mistake

alarm² *v* [T] to make someone feel very worried or anxious —**alarmed** *adj*: *There's no need to look so alarmed.*

alarm clock /.ˈ. ./ *n* [C] a clock that makes a noise at a particular time to wake you up

a·larm·ing /əˈlɑːmɪŋꟾꟾ-ɑːr-/ *adj* very frightening or worrying: *an alarming increase in violent crime*

a·larm·ist /əˈlɑːm‚stꟾꟾ-ɑːr-/ *adj* making people worried about dangers that do not exist: *alarmist reports about communist spies* —**alarmist** *n* [C]

a·las /əˈlæs/ *interjection literary* used when you are very sad about something

al·ba·tross /ˈælbətrɒsꟾꟾ-trɔːs, -trɑːs/ *n* [C] a very large sea bird

al·be·it /ɔːlˈbiː‚tꟾꟾɒl-/ *linking word formal* although

al·bi·no /ælˈbiːnəʊꟾꟾælˈbaɪnoʊ/ *n* [C] a person or animal born with very white skin, white hair, and pink eyes

al·bum /ˈælbəm/ *n* [C] **1** a group of songs recorded by a particular performer or group on a record, CD or TAPE: *Do you have the Clash's first album?* **2** a book in which you put photographs, stamps etc

al·co·hol /ˈælkəhɒlꟾꟾ-hɔːl/ *n* [U] **1** drinks such as beer, wine, WHISKY etc that can make you drunk: *We do not serve alcohol to people under 21.* **2** a colourless liquid contained in drinks that make you drunk

al·co·hol·ic¹ /ˌælkəˈhɒlɪk‹ꟾꟾ-ˈhɔː-/ *adj* **1** containing alcohol: *an alcoholic drink* →opposite NON-ALCOHOLIC **2** unable to stop the habit of drinking too much alcohol: *She divorced her alcoholic husband.*

alcoholic² *n* [C] someone who cannot stop the habit of drinking too much alcohol: *His father was an alcoholic.*

al·co·hol·is·m /ˈælkəhɒlɪzəmꟾꟾ-hɔː-/ *n* [U] the medical condition of being an alcoholic

al·cove /ˈælkəʊvꟾꟾ-koʊv/ *n* [C] a small place in a wall of a room that is built further back than the rest of the wall

ale /eɪl/ *n* [U] a type of beer

a·lert¹ /əˈlɜːtꟾꟾ-ɜːrt/ *adj* **1** always watching and ready to notice anything strange, unusual, dangerous etc: **+ to** *Cyclists must always be alert to the dangers of overtaking parked cars.* **2** able to think quickly and clearly: *I knew that I had to remain wide awake and alert.*

alert² *v* [T] to warn someone of a problem or of possible danger: *As soon as we suspected it was a bomb, we alerted the police.*

alert³ *n* **1 be on the alert** to be ready to notice and deal with a problem: *Police are on the alert for trouble.* **2** [C] a warning to be ready for possible danger: *a flood alert*

A lev·el /ˈeɪ ˌlevəl/ *n* [C] an examination in a particular subject taken in England and Wales, usually at the age of 18

al·gae /ˈældʒiː,-giː/ *n* [U] a plant without stems or leaves that lives in or near water

al·ge·bra /ˈældʒ‚brə/ *n* [U] a type of mathematics that uses letters and signs to show numbers, amounts etc —**algebraic** /ˌældʒ‚-ˈbreɪ·ɪk‹/ *adj: algebraic formulae*

a·li·as¹ /ˈeɪliəs/ *prep* used to talk about someone's real name together with another name they use: *the spy Margaret Zelle, alias Mata Hari*

alias² *n* [C] a false name, usually used by a criminal

al·i·bi /ˈæl‚baɪ/ *n* [C] proof that someone was not where a crime happened and is therefore not guilty of the crime

a·li·en¹ /ˈeɪliən/ *adj* **1** very different and strange: **+ to** *Her way of life is totally alien to me.* **2** relating to creatures from other worlds: *alien life-forms*

alien² *n* [C] **1** *formal* a foreigner who is not a citizen of the country where he or she is living **2** a creature that comes from another world: *a film about aliens from Mars*

a·li·en·ate /ˈeɪliəneɪt/ *v* [T] **1** to make someone stop supporting you **2** to make someone feel they no longer belong to your group: *We don't want to alienate kids who already have problems at school.* —**alienation** /ˌeɪliəˈneɪʃən/ *n* [U] *a feeling of alienation from society*

a·light¹ /əˈlaɪt/ *adj* [not before noun] **1** burning: **set sth alight** (=make something burn): *Several cars were set alight by rioters.*

A

2 someone whose face or eyes are alight is happy or excited

alight² v [I] formal **1** if a bird, insect etc alights on something, it stops flying and comes down on to it **2** to step out of a vehicle at the end of a journey: *She alighted from the train.*

a·lign /əˈlaɪn/ v [I,T] **1 align yourself with sb** to support another political group or country because you have the same aims: *Five Democrats have aligned themselves with the Republicans on this issue.* | **be aligned with sb** *a country politically aligned with the West* **2** to arrange something so that it is in the same line as something else — **alignment** n [C,U]

a·like¹ /əˈlaɪk/ adj [not before noun] almost exactly the same; similar: *All the new cars look alike to me.*

alike² adv **1** in a similar way, or in the same way: *When we were younger we dressed alike.* **2** used to say that two people or groups both do something: *The new rule was criticized by teachers and students alike.*

al·i·mo·ny /ˈælɪˌmənɪ‖-moʊni/ n [singular] money that someone has to pay regularly to their former wife or husband after a DIVORCE

a·live /əˈlaɪv/ adj [not before noun] **1** living and not dead: *They didn't expect to find anyone alive after the explosion.* **2** continuing to exist: **keep sth alive** *ancient traditions that are kept alive in country villages* **3** if a place is alive, there is a lot of movement, activity, or excitement there: **+ with** *The stadium was alive with excitement.* | **come alive** *The streets come alive after ten o'clock.* **4 be alive and well** to be healthy or successful: *The British novel is still alive and well in the 1990s.*

all¹ /ɔːl‖ɒːl/ determiner, pron **1** the whole of an amount or period of time: *Have we spent all the money?* | *I've been waiting all day for him to call.* | *He was wearing a black leather jacket. That's all I can remember.* (=it is the only thing I remember) | **+ of** *All of this land belongs to me.* | **all the time** (=continuously or very often): *Bill talks about work all the time.* **2** every person or thing in a group of people or things: *Did you answer all twenty questions.* | *We all wanted to go home.* | **+ of** *Listen, all of you, I have an important announcement.* **3** very many different types of things, people, or places: *You can buy all kinds of things in the bazaar.* **4 (not) at all** used to say that something is not even slightly true, or to ask if something is even slightly true: *The place hasn't changed at all.* | *Was anyone at all interested in my idea?* **5 for all …** in spite of something: *For all his faults, he was a good father.* **6 all told** including every person or thing: *There were seventeen of us, all told.* ➡ see also **after all** (AFTER¹), **all the same** (SAME), **in all** (IN¹)

USAGE NOTE: all

All is used with a singular verb with uncountable nouns: *All the money had gone.* | *All my work had been ruined.* It is also used with a plural verb with countable nouns: *All her friends are rich.* | *All the people had gone.*

---

all² adv **1** completely: *Ruth was sitting all alone.* | *The judges were dressed all in black.* **2 all over a)** in every part of a place: *We've*

been looking all over for you.* | *There were papers all over the floor.* | *I'm just glad it's all over.* **3 5 all/20 all etc** used to say that the two players or teams in a game both have the same number of points: *The score was 2 all at half-time.* **4 all but** almost completely: *It was all but impossible to find anywhere to park.* **5 all along** during all of a period of time: *I knew all along that I couldn't trust him.* **6 all in all** used when you are giving your opinion about the whole of a situation, event, book, film etc: *All in all, I think the festival was a big success.* **7 all the better/easier etc** used to emphasize that something was better or easier etc because of the situation: *The job was made all the easier by having the right tools.* ➡ see also ALL RIGHT¹

Al·lah /ˈælə/ n the Muslim name for God

all-a·round /ˌ. ˈ. ◂/ adj [only before noun] AmE good at doing many different things, especially in sports; ALL-ROUND BrE: *the best all-around player*

al·lay /əˈleɪ/ v [T] formal **allay sb's worries/ fears/suspicions etc** to make someone feel less worried, frightened etc: *I did my best to allay her fears.*

all clear /ˌ. ˈ./ n **the all clear** permission to begin doing something: *We have to wait for the all clear from the safety committee before we can start.*

al·le·ga·tion /ˌælɪˈɡeɪʃən/ n [C] a statement that someone has done something bad or illegal, which is not supported by proof: *allegations that the police had tortured prisoners*

al·lege /əˈledʒ/ v [T] to say that something is true without showing proof: *Baldwin is alleged to have killed two people.*

al·leged /əˈledʒd/ adj supposed to be true, but not proved: *the group's alleged connections with organized crime* — **allegedly** /əˈledʒɪdli/ adv

al·le·giance /əˈliːdʒəns/ n [C] loyalty or support given to a leader, country, belief etc: *allegiance to the flag*

al·le·go·ry /ˈælɪɡərɪ‖-ɡɔːri/ n [C,U] a story, poem, painting etc in which a moral lesson is taught by showing goodness, evil, hope etc as people, places, or events — **allegorical** /ˌælɪˈɡɒrɪkəl‖-ˈɡɔːr-/ adj

al·ler·gic /əˈlɜːdʒɪk‖-ɜːr-/ adj **1** having an allergy: **+ to** *Are you allergic to anything?* **2** caused by an allergy: *an allergic reaction to the bee sting*

al·ler·gy /ˈælədʒɪ‖-ər-/ n [C] a condition that makes you ill when you eat, touch, or breathe a particular thing: **+ to** *an allergy to peanuts*

al·le·vi·ate /əˈliːvɪeɪt/ v [T] formal to make something less bad or severe: *Aspirin should alleviate the pain.* | *The road was built to alleviate traffic problems.*

al·ley /ˈælɪ/ also **al·ley·way** /ˈælɪweɪ/ n [C] a narrow street between buildings

al·li·ance /əˈlaɪəns/ n [C] an agreement between countries or groups of people to work together or support each other: **+ between** *the alliance between students and factory workers in 1968* | **+ with** *Britain's alliance with its NATO partners*

al·lied /ˈælaɪd, əˈlaɪd/ adj **1 Allied** belonging to the countries that fought together against Germany in the First or Second World War:

attacks by Allied armies **2 be allied to/with sth** to be joined or connected with something: *a science that is closely allied to sociology*

al·li·ga·tor /ˈælɪɡeɪtəl-ər/ *n* [C] a large animal like a CROCODILE that lives in the US and China

al·lit·er·a·tion /əˌlɪtəˈreɪʃən/ *n* [U] the use of a series of words that begin with the same sound in order to make a special effect, for example in 'Round the rocks runs the river'

al·lo·cate /ˈæləkeɪt/ *v* [T] to decide to allow a particular amount of money, time etc to be used for a particular purpose: **allocate sth for sth** *The hospital has allocated $500,000 for AIDS research.*

al·lo·ca·tion /ˌæləˈkeɪʃən/ *n* **1** an amount of something that is allocated **2** [U] the decision to allocate something: *the allocation of state funds to the university*

al·lot /əˈlɒtlləˈlɑːt/ *v* **-tted, -tting** [T] to give something to someone as their share. or to allow an amount of time for something: *Each person was allotted two tickets.*

al·lot·ment /əˈlɒtməntlləˈlɑːt-/ *n* **1** [C,U] when an amount of something is given to someone as their share: *the allotment of funds* **2** [C] a small area of land that people in Britain can rent for growing vegetables

all out /ˌ. ˈ.◂/ *adv* **go all out** to try with a lot of effort and determination: *We'll be going all out to win.* —**all-out** *adj*: *an all-out effort*

al·low /əˈlaʊ/ *v* [T] **1** to give someone permission to do something or have something: **be allowed** *Smoking is not allowed in the library.* | **allow sb sth** *We're allowed four weeks holiday a year.* | **allow sb to do sth** *My parents would never allow me to stay out late.* | **allow sb in/out/up etc** *You're not allowed in here.* **2** to make it possible for something to happen or for someone to do something, especially by not trying to stop it: **allow sb/sth to do sth** *We mustn't allow the situation to get any worse.* **3** to plan that a particular amount of time, money etc will be needed for a particular purpose: *Allow 14 days for delivery.* | **allow yourself sth** *Allow yourself two hours to get to the airport.* —**allowable** /əˈlaʊəbəl/ *adj*

allow for sth *phr v* [T] to include the possible effects of something in your plans so that you can deal with them: *Even allowing for delays, we should finish early.*

al·low·ance /əˈlaʊəns/ *n* **1** [C] money that you are given regularly or for a special reason: *His father gives him a small monthly allowance.* | *a travel allowance* **2 make allowances for** to consider someone's behaviour or work in a sympathetic way because they have a problem or disadvantage

al·loy /ˈælɔɪllˈælɔɪ, əˈlɔɪ/ *n* [C] a metal made by mixing two or more different metals

all right[1] /ˌ. ˈ./ *adj, adv* [not before noun] *spoken* **1** good enough, but not excellent: *"How's the food?" "It's all right, but I've had better."* **2** not hurt, not upset, or not having problems: *Kate was looking very pale – I hope she's all right.* **3 that's all right a)** used to reply when

someone thanks you: *"Thanks for your help!" "That's all right."* **b)** used to tell someone you are not angry when they say they are sorry: *"Sorry I'm late!" "That's all right!"* **4** suitable: *We need to fix a time for our meeting. Would Thursday afternoon be all right?* **5 is it all right if...?** used to ask for someone's permission to do something: *Is it all right if I close the window?* **6 be doing/going all right** to be successful in your job or life: *"How's your new restaurant?" "Oh, it's doing all right, thanks."*

USAGE NOTE: all right and alright

The usual way of writing this is **all right**. *Don't worry about me – I'm all right.* | *All right, let's go.* Some people consider the spelling *alright* to be incorrect, and it is best to avoid it in formal writing.

---

all right[2] *interjection* used to say "yes" when someone asks you to do something or suggests something: *"Let's go now." "All right."*

all-round /ˈ. ./ *adj* [only before noun] *BrE* good at doing many different things, especially in sports; ALL-AROUND *AmE*: *an all-round athlete* —**all-rounder** /ˌ. ˈ./ *n* [C]

al·lude /əˈluːd/ *v*

allude to sb/sth *phr v* [T] *formal* to mention something or someone in an indirect way

al·lure /əˈljʊəllˈlʊr/ *n* [U] an exciting quality that attracts people: *the allure of travel* —**allure** *v* [T]

al·lur·ing /əˈljʊərɪŋllˈlʊr-/ *adj* very attractive: *an alluring smile*

al·lu·sion /əˈluːʒən/ *n* [C,U] *formal* when you mention something or someone in an indirect way: *His poetry is full of historical allusions.*

al·ly[1] /ˈælaɪllˈælaɪ, əˈlaɪ/ *n* [C] **1** a country that helps another country, especially in war: *the US and its European allies* **2** a person who supports you in a difficult situation

ally[2] *v* [I,T] **ally yourself to/with** to join with another person, organization, or country and support them

al·might·y /ɔːlˈmaɪtillˈ-/ *adj* **1** having the power to do anything: *Almighty God* | **the Almighty** (=God) **2** very big or loud: *The box hit the ground with an almighty crash.*

al·mond /ˈɑːməndllˈɑː-, ˈæ-, ˈæl-/ *n* [C] a flat white nut with a slightly sweet taste

al·most /ˈɔːlməʊstllˈɒːlmoʊst, ɒːlˈmoʊst/ *adv* nearly but not completely: *Are we almost there?* | *Almost all children like to read.* | *I'm sorry, I almost forgot to call you.*

alms /ɑːmzllɑːmz, ɑːlmz/ *n* [plural] *old-fashioned* money, food etc given to poor people

a·loft /əˈlɒftlləˈlɔːft/ *adv literary* high up in the air: *They held the banner aloft for everyone to see.*

a·lone /əˈləʊnlləˈloʊn/ *adj, adv* **1** not with other people: *Do you like living alone?* | **all alone** (=completely alone): *I was all alone in a strange city.* | **alone with/together** (=when there is no one else except the two of you): *Suddenly they*

GRAMMAR NOTE: much and many
You can only use **much, how much** and **a little** with <u>uncountable</u> nouns: *How much information do you have?* You can only use **many, how many** and **a few** with plural <u>countable</u> nouns: *How many people are coming to the party?* | *I've invited a few friends.*

found themselves alone together in the same room. **2 she/you alone** only her, you etc: *He alone can do the job.* **3 leave/let sb alone** to stop annoying someone **4 leave/let sth alone** to stop touching or changing something: *Leave that clock alone or you'll break it.*

a·long[1] /ə'lɒŋ‖ə'lɔːŋ/ *prep* **1** from one place on a line, road, river etc to another place on it: *We took a walk along the river.* | *She looked anxiously along the line of faces.* **2** in a line next to or on something long: *They've put up a fence along the road.* | *photographs arranged along the shelf* **3** at a particular place on a line, road, river etc: *The house is somewhere along this road.*

along[2] *adv* **1** going forward: *I was driving along, listening to the radio.* **2 go/come/be along** to go or come to a place: *The next bus should be along in a minute.* **3 go/come along** to go somewhere with someone else: *We're going out – you're welcome to come along!* **4 take/bring sb along** to take or bring someone with you somewhere: *Do you mind if I bring a friend along?* **5 along with** in addition to and at the same time: *Dunne was murdered along with three RUC men near Amargh.* **6 get/come along** to develop or make progress: *How are you getting along in your new job?* | *Kurt's English is coming along fine – he's obviously good at languages.* → see also **all along** (ALL[2])

a·long·side /ə,lɒŋ'saɪd‖ə,lɔːŋ-/ *adv, prep* close to and along the edge of something: *a boat tied up alongside the dock*

a·loof /ə'luːf/ *adj* **1** deliberately staying away from other people or not talking to them, especially because you think you are better than they are: *She seemed cold and aloof.* **2** if you are aloof from something, especially a difficult situation, you avoid becoming involved in it

a·loud /ə'laʊd/ *adv* **1** in a voice that people can hear: *Will you please read the poem aloud?* | *He cried aloud with pain.* **2 think aloud** to say your thoughts as they come into your mind

al·pha·bet /'ælfəbet/ *n* [C] a set of letters that are used when writing a language: *the Greek alphabet*

al·pha·bet·i·cal /,ælfə'betɪkəl◂/ *adj* arranged according to the letters of the alphabet: *The names are listed in alphabetical order.* —**alphabetically** /-klɪ/ *adv*

al·pine /'ælpaɪn/ *adj* belonging to or relating to the Alps or other high mountains: *alpine flowers*

al·read·y /ɔːl'redi‖ɒːl-/ *adv* **1** before now or before a particular time: *By the time he arrived, the room was already crowded.* **2** used to say that something has been done before and does not need to be done again: *We've been there already.* | *"Would you like some lunch?" "No, thank you, I've already eaten."* **3** sooner than expected: *I've forgotten the number already.* | *Is he leaving already?*

al·right /ɔːl'raɪt‖ɒːl-/ *adv* another spelling of ALL RIGHT that some people consider to be incorrect

al·so /'ɔːlsəʊ‖'ɒːlsoʊ/ *adv* in addition to something you have mentioned: *We specialize in shoes, but we also sell handbags.*

al·tar /'ɔːltə‖'ɒːltər/ *n* [C] a kind of holy table,

especially used in a church for religious ceremonies

al·ter /'ɔːltə‖'ɒːltər/ *v* [I,T] to change or make something or someone change: *When she went back to her hometown, she found it had hardly altered.* | *They had to alter their plans.*

al·ter·a·tion /,ɔːltə'reɪʃən‖,ɒːl-/ *n* [C,U] a change in something, or the process of changing it: *Alterations to clothes can be expensive.*

al·ter·ca·tion /,ɔːltə'keɪʃən‖,ɒːltər-/ *n* [C] *formal* a noisy argument

al·ter·nate[1] /ɔːl'tɜːnɪt‖'ɒːltər-/ *adj* **1** happening in a regular way, first one thing, then the other thing, then the first one again: *alternate rain and sunshine* **2 alternate days/weeks/Mondays etc** every second day, week etc: *My ex-husband has the children alternate weekends.* **3** *AmE* available to be used instead of something or someone else; ALTERNATIVE —**alternately** *adv*

al·ter·nate[2] /'ɔːltəneɪt‖'ɒːltər-/ *v* **1** [I] if two things alternate, first one thing happens, then the other, then the first one again, and this process continues: **+ between** *Her moods alternated between joy and sadness.* **2** [T] to do or use first one thing and then the other and then the first thing again: **alternate sth with sth** *In some plays Shakespeare alternated prose with verse.* —**alternating** *adj: alternating layers of sand and stone*

al·ter·na·tive[1] /ɔːl'tɜːnətɪv‖ɒːl'tɜːr-, æl-/ *adj* **1** an alternative plan, idea etc can be used instead of another one: *The main road is blocked, so drivers should choose an alternative route.* **2** different from what is usual or accepted: *an alternative lifestyle* | *alternative medicine*

alternative[2] *n* [C] something you can choose to do or use instead of something else: *Before you spend a lot of money on gas central heating, consider the alternatives.* | **+ to** *Many farmers are now growing maize as an alternative to wheat.* | **have no alternative but to do sth** (=when you cannot choose to do anything else): *I have no alternative but to report you to the police.*

al·ter·na·tive·ly /ɔːl'tɜːnətɪvli‖ɒːl'tɜːr-, æl-/ *adv* used to suggest an alternative to your first suggestion: *I could come to your house, or alternatively we could meet in town.*

al·though /ɔːl'ðəʊ‖ɒːl'ðoʊ/ *linking word* **1** in spite of the fact that something is true: *Although it was raining we decided to go for a walk.* **2** but: *We only spent $800, although that doesn't include the hotel bill.*

al·ti·tude /'æltɪtjuːd‖-tuːd/ *n* [C,U] the height of something above sea level: **high/low altitude** *Breathing becomes more difficult at high altitudes.*

al·to /'æltəʊ‖-toʊ/ *n* [C,U] a female singer with a low voice, or a male singer with a high voice

al·to·geth·er /ˌɔːltə'geðə‹ ‖ˌɒːltə'geðər‹ / *adv*
1 completely: *Bradley seems to have disappeared altogether.* | *I'm not altogether sure what this word means.* | *an altogether different type of problem* **2** considering everything or including the whole amount: *There were five of us altogether.* | *It did rain a lot, but altogether I'd say it was a good trip.*

USAGE NOTE: altogether and all together

Use **altogether** to talk about a whole amount or number: *There were 50 people there altogether.* | *Your shopping comes to £39 altogether.* Use **all together** as an adjective phrase to say that people or things are together as a group: *Try to keep your school records all together.*

---

al·tru·is·tic /ˌæltru'ɪstɪk‹ / *adj* actions or aims that are altruistic show that you care more about other people's needs and happiness than about your own — **altruism** /'æltruɪzəm/ *n* [U]

al·u·min·i·um /ˌæljʊ'mɪniəm‹, ˌælə-/ *BrE*, **a·lu·mi·num** /ə'luːmɪ̩nəm/ *AmE* — *n* [U] a silver-white metal that is light and easy to bend

al·ways /'ɔːlwĭz, -weɪz‖'ɒːl-/ *adv* **1** at all times, or every time: *Always lock your car.* **2** for ever, or for as long as you can remember: *We're always ready to help you.* | *He said he'd always love her.* | *I've always wanted to go to China.* **3** happening continuously, especially in an annoying way: *The stupid car is always breaking down!* **4 you could always...** *spoken* used to make a polite suggestion: *You could always try calling her.*

USAGE NOTE: always

Use **always** between the auxiliary verb or modal verb and the main verb: *I can always tell when he's lying.* Use **always** after the verb 'to be' when it is the main verb in a sentence: *He's always late.* | *They are always arguing.*

---

am /m, əm; *strong* æm/ the first person singular present tense of the verb BE

am, a.m. /ˌeɪ 'em/ used in times from MIDNIGHT until just before NOON: *I start work at 9:00 a.m.* → compare PM

a·mal·ga·mate /ə'mælgəmeɪt/ *v* [I,T] to join together or join two organizations together to become a bigger organization: *The two companies are amalgamating to form a huge multi-national corporation.* — **amalgamation** /əˌmælgə'meɪʃən/ *n* [C,U]

a·mass /ə'mæs/ *v* [T] to gradually get a lot of money or information: *merchants who had been amassing wealth and property*

am·a·teur¹ /'æmətə, -tʃʊə, -tʃə, ˌæmə't3ː‖-'æmətʃur, -tər/ *adj* doing something because you enjoy it and not as a job: *an amateur boxer* | *amateur football*

amateur² *n* [C] **1** someone who does something because they enjoy it and not as a job → compare PROFESSIONAL² **2** someone who does not have experience or skill in doing something: *It looked as if the building had been decorated by a bunch of amateurs.*

am·a·teur·ish /'æmətərɪʃ, ˌæmə'tjʊərɪʃ, -'t3ːrɪʃ‖ˌæmə'tʊr-, -'t3ːr-/ *adj* not very skilfully done: *his amateurish attempts at painting*

a·maze /ə'meɪz/ *v* [T] to make someone feel very surprised: *Kay amazed her friends by saying she was getting married.*

a·mazed /ə'meɪzd/ *adj* [not before noun] very surprised: **+ at** *We were amazed at how quickly the kids learned the song.* | **+ (that)** *I'm amazed that you remember him.*

a·maze·ment /ə'meɪzmənt/ *n* [U] when you feel very surprised: **in amazement** *I stared at him in amazement.*

a·maz·ing /ə'meɪzɪŋ/ *adj* making someone feel very surprised: *What an amazing story!* — **amazingly** *adv*: *an amazingly generous offer*

am·bas·sa·dor /æm'bæsədə‖-dər/ *n* [C] an important official that a government sends to another country to manage its relations with that country: *the Mexican ambassador to Canada* — **ambassadorial** /æmˌbæsə'dɔːriəl/ *adj*

am·ber /'æmbə‖-ər/ *n* [U] **1** a hard yellowish-brown clear substance used for making jewellery: *an amber necklace* **2** a yellowish-brown colour: *The traffic lights turned to amber.* — **amber** *adj*

am·bi·dex·trous /ˌæmbɪ'dekstrəs‹ / *adj* able to use either hand equally skilfully

am·bi·ence also **ambiance** *AmE* /'æmbiəns/ *n* [U] *literary* the way a place makes you feel: *the restaurant's friendly ambience*

am·bi·gu·i·ty /ˌæmbɪ̩'gjuː̩ti/ *n* [C,U] when what someone has said or written can have more than one possible meaning: *There were several ambiguities in the letter.*

am·big·u·ous /æm'bɪgjuəs/ *adj* if what someone says or writes is ambiguous, it can have more than one possible meaning

am·bi·tion /æm'bɪʃən/ *n* **1** [C] something that you have been wanting to achieve for a long time: *Her ambition is to climb Mount Everest* **2** [U] a strong determination to become successful or powerful: *Ambition drove Macbeth to kill the king and seize power.*

am·bi·tious /æm'bɪʃəs/ *adj* **1** determined to be successful or powerful: *He is young and very ambitious.* **2** an ambitious plan aims to achieve something very great but very difficult: *the most ambitious engineering project of modern times*

am·biv·a·lent /æm'bɪvələnt/ *adj* not sure whether you like something or whether you want it: **+ about** *I think Carla's ambivalent about getting married.* — **ambivalence** *n* [U]

am·ble /'æmbəl/ *v* [I] to walk slowly in a relaxed way: *He ambled down the street, smoking a cigarette.*

am·bu·lance /'æmbjə̩ləns/ *n* [C] a special vehicle for taking ill or injured people to hospital

ambulance

am·bush¹ /'æmbʊʃ/ *n* [C] a sudden attack by people who have been waiting and hiding: *Two soldiers were killed in an ambush near the border.*

ambush² *v* [T] to attack someone from a place where you have been hiding

a·me·li·o·rate /ə'miːliəreɪt/ *v* [T] *formal* to make something better

a·men /ɑː'men, eɪ-/ *interjection* used at the end of a Christian or Jewish prayer

a·me·na·ble /ə'miːnəbəl, ə'men-/ *adj* willing to listen or do something: **+ to** *I'm sure they'll be amenable to your suggestions.*

a·mend /ə'mend/ *v* [T] to make small changes or improvements to something that has been written: *The law has been amended several times.*

a·mend·ment /ə'mendmənt/ *n* **1** [C,U] a change made in the words of a law or document: **+ to** *an amendment to the new Finance Bill* **2** [C] one of the laws in the US Constitution: *the Fifth Amendment*

a·mends /ə'mendz/ *n* **make amends** to do something to show that you are sorry for the harm you have caused: *I tried to make amends by inviting him to lunch.*

a·me·ni·ty /ə'miːnɪ̥tiǁə'me-/ *n* [C usually plural] something that is available for you to use or visit in a place, which makes living there enjoyable and pleasant: *The hotel's amenities include a pool and two bars.*

A·mer·i·can[1] /ə'merɪ̥kən/ *adj* **1** from or connected with the United States: *American cars | American foreign policy* **2** North American/South American from or connected with one of the countries in North America or South America

American[2] *n* [C] someone from the United States

American foot·ball /.ˌ... '../ *n* [U] *BrE* an American game in which two teams wearing HELMETS and special protective clothing carry, kick, or throw an OVAL ball; FOOTBALL *AmE* → see colour picture on page 636

American In·di·an /.ˌ... '.../ *n* [C] NATIVE AMERICAN

A·mer·i·can·is·m /ə'merɪ̥kənɪzəm/ *n* [C] an American word or phrase, especially one that someone uses when speaking or writing in British English

am·e·thyst /'æmɪ̩θɪ̩st/ *n* [C,U] a purple stone used in jewellery

a·mi·a·ble /'eɪmiəbəl/ *adj* friendly and pleasant: *an amiable child* —**amiably** *adv* —**amiability** /ˌeɪmiə'bɪlɪ̥ti/ *n* [U]

am·i·ca·ble /'æmɪkəbəl/ *adj* friendly and without arguments: *an amicable divorce* —**amicably** *adv*

a·mid /ə'mɪd/ also **a·midst** /ə'mɪdst/ *prep formal* among something, or while something is happening: *surviving amid the horrors of war*

a·miss[1] /ə'mɪs/ *adj* **be amiss** if something is amiss, there is a problem: *She sensed something was amiss.*

amiss[2] *adv* **take sth amiss** to feel offended or upset about something someone has said or done because you have understood it wrongly

am·mo·ni·a /ə'məʊniəǁ-'moʊ-/ *n* [U] a gas or liquid with a strong unpleasant smell, used in cleaning substances

am·mu·ni·tion /ˌæmjʊ̩'nɪʃən/ *n* [U] **1** things such as bullets, bombs etc that are fired from guns **2** information that can be used to criticize someone

am·ne·si·a /æm'niːziəǁ-ʒə/ *n* [U] the medical condition of not being able to remember anything

am·nes·ty /'æmnəsti/ *n* [C,U] **1** an official order by a government that allows prisoners to be free **2** a period of time when you can admit

to doing something illegal or give up weapons without being punished

a·moe·ba /ə'miːbə/ *n* [C] a very small creature that has only one cell

a·mok /ə'mɒkǁə'mɑːk/ *adv* **run amok** to behave in a very violent and uncontrolled way: *The gunman ran amok in a shopping mall.*

a·mong /ə'mʌŋ/ also **amongst** /ə'mʌŋst/ *prep* **1** in a particular group of people or things: *a decision that has caused a lot of anger among women | among friends* (=with people who are your friends): *Relax, you're among friends here. | talk/fight/argue etc among yourselves* (=talk, fight etc with each other) **2** in the middle of: *We found him hiding among the bushes. | Rescue teams searched among the wreckage for survivors.* **3** share/divide/distribute sth among to give each person in a group a part of something: *His money will be divided among his three children.* **4** used when you are mentioning one or two people or things from a larger group: *Swimming and diving are among the most popular Olympic events. | among other things We discussed, among other things, ways to raise money.*

a·mor·al /eɪ'mɒrəl, æ-ǁeɪ'mɔː-, -'mɑː-/ *adj* behaving in a way that shows you do not care if what you are doing is wrong

am·o·rous /'æmərəs/ *adj* full of sexual desire or feelings of love

a·mor·phous /ə'mɔːfəsǁ-ɔːr-/ *adj* without a definite shape

a·mount[1] /ə'maʊnt/ *n* [C] how much of something there is: *Please pay the full amount. | + of I was surprised at the amount of work I had to do.*

amount[2] *v*

amount to sth *phr v* [T] **1** to have the same meaning or effect as something, without saying it directly: *What he said amounted to an apology.* **2** to add up to a total of a particular amount: *Jenny's debts amount to $1000.*

amp /æmp/ also **am·pere** /'æmpeəǁ-pɪr/ *n* [C] a unit for measuring an electric current

am·phet·a·mine /æm'fetəmiːn, -mɪ̩n/ *n* [C,U] an illegal drug that gives people more energy and makes them feel excited

am·phib·i·an /æm'fɪbiən/ *n* [C] an animal such as a FROG that can live on land and in water

am·phib·i·ous /æm'fɪbiəs/ *adj* living, travelling, or happening on both land and water: *an amphibious vehicle*

am·phi·thea·tre *BrE*, **amphitheater** *AmE* /'æmfɪ̩ˌθɪətəǁ-tər/ *n* [C] a large circular building without a roof and with many rows of seats around a central space, used for performances

am·ple /'æmpəl/ *adj* **1** more than enough: *There's ample room in here for everyone.*

2 ample belly/bosom etc a part of someone's body that is large —**amply** *adv*

am·pli·fi·er /'æmplɪ̩faɪəǁ-faɪr/ *n* [C] a piece of electronic equipment used to make music and other sounds louder

am·pli·fy /'æmplɪ̩faɪ/ *v* [T] **1** to make sounds louder using electronic equipment **2** to make something such as a feeling stronger —**amplification** /ˌæmplɪ̩fɪ̩'keɪʃən/ *n* [U]

am·pu·tate /'æmpjʊ̩teɪt/ *v* [I,T] to cut off a part of someone's body for medical reasons: *After the accident, the doctors had to amputate her leg.* —**amputation** /ˌæmpjʊ̩'teɪʃən/ *n* [C,U]

am·pu·tee /ˌæmpjʊ̩'tiː/ *n* [C] someone who has had a part of their body amputated

a·muse /ə'mjuːz/ *v* [T] **1** to make someone laugh or smile: *Harry's jokes always amused me.* **2** to entertain someone and help them to spend their time enjoyably: *some games to amuse the children on long car journeys* | **amuse yourself** *The kids amused themselves playing hide-and-seek.*

a·mused /ə'mjuːzd/ *adj* **1** smiling or laughing because something is funny: *an amused grin* | **+ at/by** *Rod was highly amused by my attempts at cooking.* **2 keep someone amused** to entertain someone and help them to spend their time enjoyably: *It's hard work trying to keep the kids amused on rainy days.*

a·muse·ment /ə'mjuːzmənt/ *n* **1** [U] the feeling you have when you think that something is funny: **in/with amusement** *I listened in amusement as Bobby tried to explain.* **2** [C,U] ways of enjoying yourself: **for amusement** (=in order to enjoy yourself): *What do you do for amusement in this town?*

amusement ar·cade /ˌ.. ..ˌ./ *n* [C] *BrE* a place where people can play games on machines by putting coins in them

amusement park /ˌ.. ..ˌ./ *n* [C] a large park where people can have fun riding on big machines, for example ROLLER COASTERS

a·mus·ing /ə'mjuːzɪŋ/ *adj* funny and entertaining: *a highly amusing story* | **find sth amusing** (=think something is funny): *I didn't find your comment amusing.*

an /ən; *strong* æn/ *determiner* used instead of 'a' when the following word begins with a vowel sound: *an orange* | *an X-ray* | *an hour*

a·nach·ro·nis·m /ə'nækrənɪzəm/ *n* [C] something that seems unsuitable because it is in the wrong historical period: *The royal family seems something of an anachronism nowadays.* —**anachronistic** /əˌnækrə'nɪstɪk/ *adj*

a·nae·mi·a *BrE*, **anemia** *AmE* /ə'niːmiə/ *n* [U] a medical condition in which you do not have enough red cells in your blood —**anaemic** *BrE*, **anemic** *AmE adj*

an·aes·thet·ic *BrE*, **anesthetic** *AmE* /ˌænɪs-**θet·ɪk** / *n* [C,U] a drug that stops you feeling pain, used during a medical operation

a·naes·the·tist *BrE*, **anesthetist** *AmE* /ə-'niːsθɪ̩tɪstǁə'nes-/ *n* [C] someone whose job is to give anaesthetics to people in hospitals

a·naes·the·tize (also **-ise** *BrE*), **anesthetize** *AmE* /ə'niːsθɪ̩taɪzǁə'nes-/ *v* [T] to make someone unable to feel pain by giving them an anaesthetic

an·a·gram /'ænəgræm/ *n* [C] a word or phrase made by changing the order of the letters in another word or phrase: *'Silent' is an anagram of 'listen'.*

a·nal /'eɪnl/ *adj* relating to the ANUS

a·nal·o·gous /ə'næləgəs/ *adj formal* similar to another situation or thing: **+ to** *Operating the system is analogous to driving a car.*

a·nal·o·gy /ə'nælədʒi/ *n* [C,U] a comparison between two situations, processes etc that seem similar: **draw an analogy** (=make a comparison): *We can draw an analogy between the brain and a computer.*

an·a·lyse *BrE*, **analyze** *AmE* /'ænəl-aɪz/ *v* [T] to examine or think about something carefully in order to understand it: *We're trying to analyse what went wrong.* | *The patient's blood is tested and analyzed.*

a·nal·y·sis /ə'nælɪ̩sɪ̩s/ *n, plural* **analyses** /-siːz/ [C,U] careful examination of something in order to understand it better or find out what it consists of: *The team are carrying out a detailed analysis of the test results.* | *analysis of the rock samples*

an·a·lyst /'ænəl-ɪ̩st/ *n* [C] **1** someone whose job is to analyse a subject and give opinions about it: *a financial analyst* **2** a PSYCHOANALYST

an·a·lyt·i·cal /ˌænəl'ɪtɪkəl/, **an·a·lyt·ic** /-'lɪtɪk/ *adj* using methods that help you examine things carefully: *an analytical mind*

an·a·lyze /'ænəl-aɪz/ the American spelling of ANALYSE

an·ar·chist /'ænəkɪ̩stǁ-ər-/ *n* [C] someone who believes that there should be no government or laws, but ordinary people should work together to improve society —**anarchism** *n* [U]

an·ar·chy /'ænəkiǁ-ər-/ *n* [U] a situation in which no one obeys rules or laws and there is no control or government: *efforts to prevent the country from sliding into anarchy* —**anarchic** /æ'nɑːkɪkǁ-ɑːr-/ *adj*

a·nath·e·ma /ə'næθɪ̩mə/ *n* [singular, U] *formal* something that you hate: **+ to** *Darwin's ideas were anathema to Church leaders*

a·nat·o·my /ə'nætəmi/ *n* **1** [U] the scientific study of the structure of the body **2** [singular] the structure of a living thing, organization, or social group, and how it works: *the anatomy of modern society* —**anatomical** /ˌænə'tɒmɪkəlǁ-'tɑː-/ *adj* —**anatomically** /-kli/ *adv*

an·ces·tor /'ænsəstə, -ses-ǁ-sestər/ *n* [C] a member of your family who lived a long time ago, before your grandparents: *His ancestors*

GRAMMAR NOTE: comparatives and superlatives
For short adjectives of one syllable, add **-er** or **-est** to the word: e.g. *old - older - oldest*. (Sometimes you must double the last letter: e.g. *big - bigger - biggest*). For long adjectives put **more** or **the most** before the word: e.g. *more comfortable - the most interesting*.

came from Italy. → compare DESCENDANT —**an·cestral** /æn'sestrəl/ *adj*

an·ces·try /'ænsəstri, -ses-‖-ses-/ *n* [C,U] your ancestors, or the origin of your family: *people of Scottish ancestry*

an·chor¹ /'æŋkəll-ər/ *n* [C] **1** a heavy metal object that is lowered into the water to prevent a ship or boat from moving **2** *AmE* someone who reads the news on television or radio and is in charge of the programme; NEWSREADER *BrE*

anchor

anchor

anchor² *v* [I,T] **1** to lower the anchor of a ship or boat to prevent it from moving: *Three tankers were anchored in the bay.* **2** to fasten something firmly so that it cannot move: *We anchored the tent with strong ropes.*

an·cho·vy /'ænt∫əvi‖'ænt∫ouvi/ *n* [C,U] a small fish that tastes very salty

an·cient /'ein∫ənt/ *adj* **1** happening or existing many hundreds of years ago: *ancient Rome* **2** *humorous* very old: *I look absolutely ancient in that photograph!*

and /ənd, ən; *strong* ænd/ *linking word* **1** used to join two words or parts of sentences: *a knife and fork* | *They started shouting and screaming.* | *Martha was going to the store, and Tom said he'd go with her.* **2** used to say that one thing happens after another: *Grant knocked and went in.* **3** *especially spoken* used instead of 'to' after certain verbs such as 'come', 'go', 'try': *Try and finish your homework before dinner.* **4** used in numbers and when adding numbers: *Six and four make ten.* | *three and a half* **5** used to say that one thing is caused by something else: *I missed lunch and I'm starving!* **6** used between words that you are repeating, to emphasize what you are saying: *Crime just gets worse and worse.*

an·droid /'ændrɔid/ *n* [C] a ROBOT that looks completely human

an·ec·dot·al /ˌænik'dəʊtḷ‖-'doʊ-/ *adj* consisting of stories based on someone's personal experience: *The report is based on anecdotal evidence. It can't be called scientific!*

an·ec·dote /'ænikdəʊt‖-doʊt/ *n* [C] a short amusing or interesting story about something that really happened to you or someone else

a·ne·mi·a /ə'ni:miə/ *n* the American spelling of ANAEMIA —**anemic** *adj*

a·nem·o·ne /ə'neməni/ *n* [C] a garden plant with red, white, or blue flowers

an·es·thet·ic /ˌænəs'θetɪkˌ/ *n* [C,U] the American spelling of ANAESTHETIC

a·nes·the·tist /ə'ni:sθɪtɪst‖ə'nes-/ *n* [C] the American spelling of ANAESTHETIST

a·nes·the·tize /ə'ni:sθətaɪz‖ə'nes-/ *v* [T] the American spelling of ANAESTHETIZE

a·new /ə'nju:‖ə'nu:/ *adv literary* in a new or different way: *She started life anew in New York.*

an·gel /'eɪndʒəl/ *n* [C] **1** a spirit, especially with wings and dressed in white, who is believed to live with God in HEAVEN **2** *spoken* a very kind person: *Oh, thanks! You're an angel!* —**angelic** /æn'dʒəlɪk/ *adj*

an·ger¹ /'æŋgəll-ər/ *n* [U] a strong violent feeling that you have when someone has behaved badly or been unkind to you: *insults that aroused his anger* | **in anger** (=when you are angry): *You should never hit a child in anger.*

anger² *v* [T] to make someone feel angry: *The court's decision angered environmentalists.*

an·gle¹ /'æŋgəl/ *n* [C] **1** the space between two lines or surfaces that meet or cross each other, measured in degrees: *an angle of 45°* → see also RIGHT ANGLE **2** **at an angle** sloping, not upright or level: *The tree was growing at an angle.* **3** a way of considering a problem or situation: *Let's try to look at the problem from a different angle.* **4** the direction from which you look at something: *From that angle we should be able to see a little better.*

angle² *v* [T] to turn or move something so that it is not straight or upright

angle for sth *phr v* [T] to try to make someone offer you something without asking for it directly: *I think she's angling for an invitation to the party.*

An·gli·can /'æŋglikən/ *adj* relating to the Church of England —**Anglican** *n* [C] —**Anglicanism** *n* [U]

an·gli·cize (also -**ise** *BrE*) /'æŋglɪsaɪz/ *v* [T] to make something more English

an·gling /'æŋglɪŋ/ *n* [U] the activity of fishing with a hook and a line —**angler** *n* [C]

an·gry /'æŋgri/ *adj* if you are angry, you feel a strong emotion because someone has behaved badly to you or a situation is wrong or unfair: *She was angry with him because he had lied to her.* | *The roads were blocked by angry French farmers.* | **+ about** *Don't you feel angry about the way you've been treated?* | **+ that** *Local people are angry that they weren't consulted about plans to expand the airport.* —**angrily** *adv* → see colour picture on page 277

an·guish /'æŋgwɪ∫/ *n* [U] very great pain or worry: *the anguish of not knowing the truth* —**anguished** *adj*: *anguished cries for help*

an·gu·lar /'æŋgjɑlɑ‖-ər/ *adj* **1** having sharp corners **2** very thin, and without much flesh on your bones: *a tall, angular young man*

an·i·mal¹ /'ænɪməl/ *n* [C] **1** a living thing that can move around and is not a plant, bird, insect, fish, or person: *farm animals* | *wild animals* **2** any living thing that can move around and is not a plant, including people: *Humans are highly intelligent animals.* **3** *informal* someone who behaves in a cruel, violent, or unpleasant way

animal² *adj* **1** connected with or made from animals: *animal fats* **2** **animal urges/instincts etc** human feelings, desires etc that are connected with sex, food, and other basic needs

an·i·mate /'ænɪmɪt/ *adj formal* living → opposite INANIMATE

an·i·mat·ed /'ænɪmeɪtɪd/ *adj* **1** showing a lot of interest and energy: *an animated debate* **2** **animated cartoon/film etc** a film in which pictures and MODELS seem to move and talk —**animatedly** *adv*

an·i·ma·tion /ˌænɪ'meɪ∫ən/ *n* **1** [U] the process of making animated films **2** [C] an animated film **3** [U] energy and excitement

an·i·mos·i·ty /ˌænɪˈmɒsɪti ||-ˈmɑː-/ *n* [C,U] *formal* when someone strongly dislikes another person or group, and often feels very angry towards them: *There was a lot of animosity between the two leaders.*

an·i·seed /ˈænɪsiːd/ *n* [U] the strong-tasting seeds of a plant used in alcoholic drinks and in sweets

an·kle /ˈæŋkəl/ *n* [C] the part of your body where your foot joins your leg

an·nals /ˈænlz/ *n* **in the annals of sth** *formal* in the whole history of a particular subject: *Never, in the annals of modern warfare, has there been such a famous victory.*

an·nex /əˈneks||əˈneks, ˈæneks/ *v* [T] to take control of a country or area next to your own, especially by using force — **annexation** /ˌænekˈseɪʃən/ *n* [C,U]

an·nexe *BrE*, **annex** *AmE* /ˈæneks/ *n* [C] a sep- arate building that has been added to a larger one: *a hospital annexe*

an·ni·hi·late /əˈnaɪəleɪt/ *v* [T] to destroy something or defeat someone completely: *The champion annihilated his opponent in the third round.* — **annihilation** /əˌnaɪəˈleɪʃən/ *n* [U]

an·ni·ver·sa·ry /ˌænɪˈvɜːsəri||-ɜːr-/ *n* [C] a date which is remembered because something important happened on that date in a previous year: *our wedding anniversary | the 50th anniversary of India's independence* → compare BIRTHDAY

An·no Dom·i·ni /ˌænəʊ ˈdɒmɪnaɪ||-noʊ ˈdɑː-/ *formal* AD

an·nounce /əˈnaʊns/ *v* [T] **1** to officially tell people about something so that everyone knows: *The winner of the competition will be announced shortly.* | **+ (that)** *A police spokesman announced that a man had been arrested.* **2** to say something in a loud or angry way: **+ (that)** *Liam suddenly announced that he was leaving the band.*

an·nounce·ment /əˈnaʊnsmənt/ *n* **1** [C] an important official statement about something that has happened or will happen: **make an announcement** *Listen everyone, I have an important announcement to make.* **2** [singular] when someone tells a lot of people about something: **+ of** *the announcement of the election results*

an·nounc·er /əˈnaʊnsə||-ər/ *n* [C] someone who gives information or introduces people on television or radio

an·noy /əˈnɔɪ/ *v* [T] to make someone feel a little angry: *Jane wouldn't stop complaining and it was beginning to annoy me.*

an·noy·ance /əˈnɔɪəns/ *n* **1** [U] the feeling of being annoyed: *Mia's annoyance never showed.* **2** [C] something that annoys you: *The dog next door is a constant annoyance.*

an·noyed /əˈnɔɪd/ *adj* a little angry: **+ with** *Are you annoyed with me just because I'm a bit late?* | **+ at/about** *She was really annoyed at the way ˌhe just ignored her.* | **+ that** *My sister's annoyed that we didn't call.*

an·noy·ing /əˈnɔɪ-ɪŋ/ *adj* making you feel annoyed: *an annoying habit of interrupting* — **annoyingly** *adv*

an·nu·al /ˈænjuəl/ *adj* **1** happening once every year: *the annual conference* **2** calculated

over a period of one year: *He has an annual income of around $500,000.* — **annually** *adv*

an·nul /əˈnʌl/ *v* [T] **-lled, -lling** *formal* to officially state that a marriage or legal agreement no longer exists — **annulment** *n* [C,U]

a·nom·a·ly /əˈnɒməli||əˈnɑː-/ *n* [C,U] *formal* something that is different from what you would normally expect, and which seems incorrect or unfair: *anomalies in the tax system*

a·non /əˈnɒn||əˈnɑːn/ the written abbreviation of 'anonymous', used especially to show that the writer of a poem or song is not known

an·o·nym·i·ty /ˌænəˈnɪmɪti||-ti/ *n* [U] when the name of a person who has done something is kept secret: *The author prefers anonymity.*

a·non·y·mous /əˈnɒnɪməs||əˈnɑː-/ *adj* **1** someone who is anonymous does not let you know what their name is: *The person concerned wishes to remain anonymous.* **2** done, made, or given by someone whose name is not known: *an anonymous letter* — **anonymously** *adv*

a·no·rak /ˈænəræk/ *n* [C] *BrE* a short coat with a part that covers your head

an·o·rex·i·a /ˌænəˈreksiə/ also **anorexia ner·vo·sa** /ˌænəˌreksiə nɜːˈvəʊsə||-nər'voʊ-/ *n* [U] a mental illness that makes people stop eating, so that they become dangerously thin

an·o·rex·ic /ˌænəˈreksɪk◂/ *adj* someone who is anorexic is very thin and ill because they have a mental illness that makes them stop eating

an·oth·er /əˈnʌðə||-ər/ *determiner, pron* **1** one more person or thing of the same kind: *Do you want another beer? | Buy one CD and we'll give you another, completely free.* **2** a different person or thing: *You'll just have to find another job.* | *She lives in another part of the country.*

an·swer[1] /ˈɑːnsə||ˈænsər/ *v* [I,T] **1** to say something to someone when they have asked you a question or spoken to you: *"I don't know," she answered.* | **answer a question** *I had to answer a lot of questions about my previous job.* | **answer sb** *Why don't you answer me?* | **+ that** *Clare answered that she was not interested in their offer.* **2** **answer the telephone/door** to pick up the telephone when it rings or go to the door when someone knocks or rings the bell **3** **answer a letter/advertisement** to reply to a letter or advertisement **4** to reply to a question in a test, competition etc: *Please answer as many questions as you can.*

answer back *phr v* [I,T **answer sb back**] if someone, especially a child, answers back, he or she replies to an adult in a rude way: *Don't answer me back, young man!*

answer for sth *phr v* [T] to have to explain to someone about something wrong you have done, or to be punished for it: *One day you'll have to answer for this.*

answer[2] *n* **1** [C,U] a reply to something that someone asks or writes: *I told you before, the answer is no!* | **+ to** *Mark never got an answer to his letter.* | **in answer to** (=as a reply to something): *In answer to your question, I think Paul's right.* | **give sb an answer** *Give me an answer as soon as possible.* **2** [C] a reply to a question in a test, competition etc: *What was the answer to question 7?* **3** [C] the result obtained from calculating numbers **4** [C] something that solves a problem: **+ to** *A bit more money would be the answer to all our problems.*

answering ma·chine /'... .,./ also **an·swer·phone** *BrE* /'ɑːnsəfəʊn‖'ænsərfoʊn/ *n* [C] a machine that records your telephone calls when you cannot answer them

ant /ænt/ *n* [C] a common small red or black insect that lives in large groups

an·tag·o·nis·m /æn'tægənɪzəm/ *n* [U] when people strongly dislike or oppose someone or something: **+ between** *There has always been a lot of antagonism between the two families.* | **+ towards** *There's a lot of antagonism towards city people who move into the area.*

an·tag·o·nis·tic /æn,tægə'nɪstɪk‹/ *adj* opposing an idea or plan, or showing that you dislike someone: *an antagonistic attitude to foreigners*

an·tag·o·nize (also **-ise** *BrE*) /æn'tægənaɪz/ *v* [T] to make someone feel angry with you: *We really need his help, so don't antagonize him.*

An·tarc·tic /æn'tɑːktɪk‖-ɑːr-/ *n* **the Antarctic** the very cold, most southern part of the world → compare ARCTIC —**Antarctic** *adj*

an·te·lope /'æntɪləʊp‖'æntəl-oʊp/ *n* [C] an animal like a DEER that has long horns and can run very fast

an·te·na·tal /,æntɪ'neɪtl‹/ *adj BrE* connected with the medical care given to a woman who is PREGNANT; PRENATAL: *an antenatal clinic* → compare POSTNATAL

an·ten·na /æn'tenə/ *n* [C] **1** *plural* **antennae** one of two long thin parts on an insect's head, that it uses to feel things **2** *AmE* a piece of equipment on a television, car, roof etc for receiving radio or television broadcasts; AERIAL *BrE* → see picture at CAR

an·them /'ænθəm/ *n* [C] a song that is sung at special religious, sports, or political ceremonies → see also NATIONAL ANTHEM

ant·hill /'ænt,hɪl/ *n* [C] a pile of earth on the ground over the place where ANTS live

an·thol·o·gy /æn'θɒlədʒi‖æn'θɑː-/ *n* [C] a set of stories, poems etc collected together in one book: *an anthology of American Literature*

an·thro·pol·o·gy /,ænθrə'pɒlədʒi‖-'pɑː-/ *n* [U] the scientific study of people, their customs, beliefs etc —**anthropologist** *n* [C] —**anthropological** /,ænθrəpə'lɒdʒɪkəl‖-'lɑː-/ *adj*

an·ti- /'æntɪ‖'æntaɪ/ *prefix* **1** opposed to something, or strongly disliking a particular group of people: *antinuclear protests* | *anti-American feeling* **2** used to prevent something: *antifreeze* (=a substance used to prevent a car's engine from freezing) **3** used at the beginning of some words to mean 'not': *antisocial*

an·ti·bi·ot·ic /,æntɪbaɪ'ɒtɪk‹‖-'ɑː-/ *n* [C] usually *plural* a drug, such as PENICILLIN, that is used to cure infections —**antibiotic** *adj*

an·ti·bod·y /'æntɪ,bɒdi‖-,bɑː-/ *n* [C] a substance produced in the body to fight disease

an·tic·i·pate /æn'tɪsɪpeɪt/ *v* [T] **1** to expect something to happen: *The police are anticipating trouble when the factory closes.* | **+ that** *It's anticipated that the campaign will raise over $100,000.* **2** to think about what will happen and do something to prepare for it: *Try to anticipate what kind of questions you'll be asked.*

an·tic·i·pa·tion /æn,tɪsɪ'peɪʃən/ *n* [U] **1** a hopeful feeling that something good is going to happen: *I was full of excitement and anticipation as I started off on my journey.* **2 in anticipation**

of if you do something in anticipation of something happening, you prepare for it before it happens

an·ti·cli·max /,æntɪ'klaɪmæks/ *n* [C,U] something that seems disappointing because it happens after something that was much better: *Coming home after our trip was rather an anticlimax.*

an·ti·clock·wise /,æntɪ'klɒkwaɪz‹‖-'klɑːk-/ *adj adv BrE* moving in the opposite direction to the hands of a clock; COUNTERCLOCKWISE *AmE*: *Turn the handle anticlockwise.* → opposite CLOCKWISE

an·tics /'æntɪks/ *n* [plural] funny, silly, or annoying behaviour: *The band are famous for their antics both on and off the stage.*

an·ti·dote /'æntɪdəʊt‖-doʊt/ *n* [C] **1** something that makes an unpleasant situation better: **+ to** *Laughter is one of the best antidotes to stress.* **2** a substance that stops the effects of a poison: *The snake's bite is deadly, and there's no known antidote.*

an·ti·freeze /'æntɪfriːz/ *n* [U] a chemical that is put in the water in car engines to stop it from freezing

an·tip·a·thy /æn'tɪpəθi/ *n* [U] *formal* when people dislike someone or something or are opposed to them: *growing antipathy towards American multinational companies*

an·ti·quat·ed /'æntɪkweɪtɪd/ *adj* old-fashioned and not suitable for modern needs or conditions: *antiquated laws*

an·tique /æn'tiːk‹/ *n* [C] a piece of furniture, jewellery etc that is old and usually valuable: *priceless antiques* | *an antique shop* (=one that sells antiques) —**antique** *adj*: *an antique table* → compare ANCIENT

an·tiq·ui·ty /æn'tɪkwɪti/ *n* **1** [U] ancient times: *a tradition that stretches back into antiquity* **2** [C usually plural] a building or object made in ancient times: *Roman antiquities* **3** [U] the fact of being very old: *a building of great antiquity*

anti-sem·i·tis·m /,ænti 'semɪtɪzəm/ *n* [U] when people hate Jewish people and behave towards them in an unfair and unpleasant way —**anti-semitic** /,ænti sɪ'mɪtɪk‹/ *adj*

an·ti·sep·tic /,æntɪ'septɪk‹/ *n* [C,U] a chemical substance that kills harmful BACTERIA, especially on wounds or infected parts of the body —**antiseptic** *adj*: *antiseptic cream*

an·ti·so·cial /,æntɪ'səʊʃəl‹‖-'soʊ-/ *adj* **1** antisocial behaviour upsets, harms, or annoys other people: *Kids as young as eight are turning to vandalism, petty crime, and other forms of antisocial behaviour.* **2** unwilling to meet other people and talk to them: *I hope you won't think I'm antisocial, but I can't come out tonight.*

an·tith·e·sis /æn'tɪθɪsɪs/ *n* [C] *formal* the exact opposite of something: *His radical socialist opinions are the antithesis of his father's political beliefs.*

ant·ler /'æntlə‖-ər/ *n* [C] one of the two horns on the head of male DEER

an·to·nym /'æntənɪm/ *n* [C] *technical* a word that means the opposite of another word: *'War' is the antonym of 'peace'.* → compare SYNONYM

a·nus /'eɪnəs/ *n* [C] *technical* the part of the body from which FAECES leave the body

an·vil /'ænvɪl/ *n* [C] an iron block on which pieces of hot metal are shaped using a hammer

anx·i·e·ty /æŋˈzaɪəti/ n **1** [C,U] a strong feeling of worry about something that may happen: **+ about** *Her anxiety about the children grew as the hours passed.* **2** [U] a strong feeling of wanting to do something but being worried that you will not succeed: **anxiety to do sth** *The soldiers had thrown away their guns and packs in their anxiety to get to the boats.*

anx·ious /ˈæŋkʃəs/ adj **1** very worried about something that may happen: *an anxious look.* **+ about** *June's anxious about going such a long way on her own.* | **anxious time/moment** *There were one or two anxious moments as the plane seemed to lose height.* **2** feeling strongly that you want to do something or want something to happen: **anxious to do sth** *Ralph is anxious to prove that he can do the job.* | **+ that** *We're very anxious that no-one else finds out about this.* —**anxiously** adv: *"What's wrong?" he asked anxiously.*

an·y[1] /ˈeni/ determiner, pron **1** used in negative statements and questions to mean 'some': *Is there any coffee left?* | *I don't think that will make any difference.* | **+ of** *Are any of Nina's relatives coming for Christmas?* **2** used to mean 'every' or 'every kind of', when it does not matter which one or which kind it is: *a question that any child could answer* | *Any help would be welcome.* → see also **in any case** (CASE), **at any rate** (RATE[1])

any[2] adv used in negative statements or questions to mean 'at all': *I don't see how things could be any worse.* | *She couldn't walk any further without a rest.* | *Society is never going to get any better.*

an·y·bod·y /ˈeniˌbɒdi, ˈenibədi‖-ˌbɑːdi/ pron ANYONE

an·y·how /ˈenihaʊ/ adv informal ANYWAY

an·y more, anymore /ˌeniˈmɔː‖-ɔːr/ adv **not anymore** if something does not happen any more, it used to happen in the past but it does not happen now: *Frank doesn't live here any more.*

an·y·one /ˈeniwʌn/ also **anybody** pron **1** used in questions and negative statements to mean a person: *Is there anyone at home?* | *She'd just moved and didn't know anyone.* **2** any person or any people, when it does not matter exactly who: *Anyone can learn to swim.*

an·y·place /ˈenipleɪs/ adv AmE ANYWHERE

an·y·thing /ˈeniθɪŋ/ pron **1** used in questions and negative statements to mean 'something': *Do you need anything from the store?* | *Her father didn't know anything about it.* | **or anything** spoken (=or anything similar): *Would you like a Coke or anything?* **2** any thing, event, situation etc, when it is not important which one: *That cat will eat anything.* | *I could have told him almost anything and he would have believed me.* **3 anything like** used in questions and negative statements to mean 'similar to': *Carrie doesn't look anything like her sister.* **4 anything but** not at all: *No, when I told him, he seemed anything but pleased.*

an·y·way /ˈeniweɪ/ also **anyhow** informal adv **1** in spite of something: *The bride's mother was ill, but they had the wedding anyway.* **2** used to continue what you are saying or to change the subject of a conversation: *I think she's the same age as Lori, but anyway she's just had a baby.* | *Anyway, where do you want to go for lunch?* **3** used when you are adding something to support what you have just said: *He decided to sell his bike – he never used it anyway.* **4** used to ask the reason for something: *So, why were you there anyway?*

an·y·where /ˈeniweə‖-wer/ also **anyplace** AmE – adv **1** in or to any place, when it is not important where: *Fly anywhere in Europe for £150.* **2** used in questions and negative statements to mean 'somewhere' or 'nowhere': *I can't find my keys anywhere.* | *Did you go anywhere last night?* **3 not anywhere near** spoken used to emphasize that something is not true: *We don't have anywhere near enough money to buy a new car.* **4 not get anywhere** to not be successful at something you have been trying to do: *I've been trying to get my dad to lend me the car, but I'm not getting anywhere.*

a·part /əˈpɑːt‖-ɑːrt/ adv **1** separated by a distance or period of time: *Our birthdays are only two days apart.* | *My husband and I are living apart at the moment.* | **+ from** *She was standing a little apart from the others.* **2** separated into different parts: *He had to take the camera apart to fix it.* | **come/fall apart** (=break into many pieces): *The old book just fell apart in my hands.* **3 apart from** especially BrE **a)** except for: *Apart from a couple of spelling mistakes, your essay is excellent.* **b)** in addition to: *Who was at the party? Apart from you and Jim, I mean.* **4 tell sb/sth apart** if you cannot tell someone or something apart, you think they look exactly the same

a·part·heid /əˈpɑːtheɪt, -teɪt, -taɪt, -taɪd‖-ɑːr-/ n [U] a system, formerly used in South Africa, in which white people ruled and black people were not allowed the same political and legal rights as them

a·part·ment /əˈpɑːtmənt‖-ɑːr-/ n [C] a set of rooms on one floor of a large building, where someone lives; FLAT BrE

apartment build·ing /.ˈ.. ˌ../ also **apartment house** /.ˈ.. ˌ./ n [C] AmE a building that is divided into separate apartments → see colour picture on page 79

ap·a·thet·ic /ˌæpəˈθetɪk◂/ adj not interested in anything and unwilling to make any effort: *Too many of our students are apathetic about learning.* —**apathetically** /-kli/ adv

ap·a·thy /ˈæpəθi/ n [U] the feeling of not being interested in anything and being unwilling to make any effort to change things: *public apathy about the coming election*

ape /eɪp/ n [C] a large monkey without a tail or with a very short tail, such as a GORILLA

a·per·i·tif /əˌperɪˈtiːf/ n [C] a small alcoholic drink that you have before a meal

---

GRAMMAR NOTE: transitive and intransitive (1)
Transitive verbs have an object: *I like your dress.* | *Did you find the key?* These verbs are shown like this: v [T]. **Intransitive** verbs do not have an object: *He laughed.* | *I'll wait in the car.* These verbs are shown like this: v [I].

ap·er·ture /ˈæpətʃə‖ˈæpərtʃur/ n [C] a small hole, especially one that lets light into a camera

a·pex /ˈeɪpeks/ n [C] **1** the highest or most important part of something: *the apex of a pyramid* **2** the most successful part of something: *the apex of his career*

aph·ro·dis·i·ac /ˌæfrəˈdɪziæk/ n [C] a food or drug that makes someone want to have sex

a·piece /əˈpiːs/ adv each: *Red roses cost £1 apiece.* (=for each one)

a·poc·a·lypse /əˈpɒkəlɪps‖əˈpɑː-/ n **the Apocalypse** the destruction and end of the world, according to some religions

a·poc·a·lyp·tic /əˌpɒkəˈlɪptɪk ‖ə,pɑː-/ adj about terrible events that may happen in the future

a·po·lit·i·cal /ˌeɪpəˈlɪtɪkəl‖/ adj not having any interest in or connection with politics

a·pol·o·get·ic /əˌpɒləˈdʒetɪk‖ə,pɑː-/ adj saying that you are sorry about something: *He was really apologetic about forgetting my birthday.* —**apologetically** /-kli/ adv

ap·ol·o·gize (also **-ise** BrE) /əˈpɒlədʒaɪz‖əˈpɑː-/ v [I] to say that you are sorry about something that you have done or said: **+ for** *He apologized for being so late.* **|+ to** *Apologize to your sister now!*

a·pol·o·gy /əˈpɒlədʒi‖əˈpɑː-/ n [C] something that you say or write to show that you are sorry: *I hope you will accept my apology for any trouble I may have caused.*

a·pos·tle /əˈpɒsl‖əˈpɑː-/ n [C] one of the 12 men chosen by Christ to teach people about Christianity —**apostolic** /ˌæpəˈstɒlɪk ‖-ˈstɑː-/ adj

a·pos·tro·phe /əˈpɒstrəfi‖əˈpɑː-/ n [C] **a)** the sign (') used to show that one or more letters or figures are missing, such as in the word 'don't' (=do not) or in the date '96 (=1896/1996 etc) **b)** the sign (') used before or after the letter 's' to show that something belongs or relates to someone: *Mandy's coat | We need to protect both countries' borders* **c)** the sign (') used before 's' to show the plural of letters and numbers: *2 A's and 4 B's on my school report*

ap·pal BrE, **appall** AmE /əˈpɔːl‖əˈpɒːl/ v [T] **-lled, -lling** if something appals you, it shocks you a lot because it is very unpleasant: *The idea of killing animals for fur appals me.* —**appalled** adj

ap·pal·ling /əˈpɔːlɪŋ‖əˈpɒː-/ adj **1** shocking or terrible: *children living in appalling conditions* **2** informal very bad: *an appalling movie* —**appallingly** adv

ap·pa·ra·tus /ˌæpəˈreɪtəs‖-ˈræ-/ n, plural **apparatus**, or **apparatuses** [C,U] a set of equipment etc used for a particular purpose: *firemen wearing breathing apparatus*

ap·par·el /əˈpærəl/ n [U] formal clothes: *men's apparel*

ap·par·ent /əˈpærənt/ adj **1** easily seen or understood: *It soon became apparent that we had one major problem – Edward.* **|for no apparent reason** (=without a reason): *For no apparent reason he began to shout at her.* **2** seeming to be true or real: *We were reassured by his apparent lack of concern.*

ap·par·ent·ly /əˈpærəntli/ adv **1** according to what you have heard is true, although you are not completely sure: *She apparently caught him in bed with another woman.* | *Apparently, Susan's living in Madrid now.* **2** according to the way something seems, even though it may not really be true: *They were still chatting, apparently unaware that the train had left.*

ap·pa·ri·tion /ˌæpəˈrɪʃən/ n [C] a GHOST

ap·peal¹ /əˈpiːl/ v **1** [I] to ask people for money, information etc, especially publicly: **+ to** *Police are appealing to the public for information.* **|+ for** *Local authorities have appealed for volunteers.* **2** **appeal to sb** to seem attractive or interesting to someone: *The new programme should appeal to our younger viewers.* **3** [I] to formally ask a higher court to change the decision of a lower court: *Atkins is certain to appeal against the conviction.*

ap·peal² n **1** [C] when a person or group appeals for money, information etc: **launch an appeal** *UNICEF is launching an appeal for the flood victims.* **2** [U] the appeal of something is the quality that makes you like it or want it: *The traditional rural lifestyle has lost none of its appeal.* **3** [C,U] when someone appeals to a higher court to change the decision of a lower court: **+ to** *an appeal to the Supreme Court*

ap·peal·ing /əˈpiːlɪŋ/ adj attractive or interesting —**appealingly** adv

ap·pear /əˈpɪə‖əˈpɪr/ v **1** [linking verb] to seem: *Sandra appeared relaxed and confident at the interview.* | *The noise appeared to come from the bedroom.* **2** [I] to begin to be seen: *Suddenly a face appeared at the window.* **3 appear on television/on stage/in the news etc** to act or be shown on television, in a play etc: *John Thaw appears regularly on television.* **4** [I] to happen, exist, or become available for the first time: *Irving's novel is soon to appear in paperback.*

ap·pear·ance /əˈpɪərəns‖əˈpɪr-/ n **1** [C,U] the way that someone or something looks or seems to other people: *The Christmas lights gave the house a festive appearance.* | *six ways to improve your personal appearance* **2** [C usually singular] when someone or something arrives: *the sudden appearance of several reporters at the hospital* **3** [singular] the point at which something begins to exist or starts being used: *Viewing has increased since the appearance of cable TV.* **4** [C] a public performance in a film, play, concert etc: *his first appearance on stage in 1953* **5 put in an appearance** informal to go somewhere, usually for only a short time: *I wouldn't be surprised if Lewis put in an appearance tonight.*

ap·pease /əˈpiːz/ v [T] to do something to make someone less angry: *This is seen as a move to appease left-wingers in the party.* —**appeasement** n

ap·pend /əˈpend/ v [T] formal to add something to a piece of writing

ap·pend·age /əˈpendɪdʒ/ n [C] something that is added to something bigger or more important

ap·pen·di·ci·tis /əˌpendɪˈsaɪtɪs/ n [U] an illness in which your appendix swells and becomes painful

ap·pen·dix /əˈpendɪks/ n [C] **1** a small organ in your body near your stomach **2** plural **appendixes** or **appendices** /-dɪsiːz/ a part at the end of a book that has additional information

ap·pe·tite /'æpɪˌtaɪt/ n [C,U] **1** the feeling that makes you want to eat: *Don't eat now, you'll spoil your appetite.* **2 appetite for success/travel/ knowledge etc** the desire to be successful, to travel etc

ap·pe·tiz·er (also **-tiser** *BrE*) /'æpɪˌtaɪzəl-ər/ n [C] a small dish of food served at the beginning of a meal

ap·pe·tiz·ing (also **-tising** *BrE*) /'æpɪˌtaɪzɪŋ/ adj food that is appetizing looks or smells very good

ap·plaud /ə'plɔːdǁə'plɔːd/ v [T] **1** to hit your open hands together to show that you have enjoyed a play, concert, speaker etc; CLAP **2** *formal* to say that an idea, plan etc is very good

ap·plause /ə'plɔːzǁə'plɔːz/ n [U] the sound of people hitting their hands together to show that they have enjoyed a play, concert, speaker etc: *The thunderous applause continued for over a minute.*

ap·ple /'æpəl/ n [C] a hard round red or green fruit that is white inside → see picture at FRUIT and colour plate on page 439

ap·pli·ance /ə'plaɪəns/ n [C] a piece of electrical equipment such as a REFRIGERATOR or a DISHWASHER that is used in people's homes

ap·plic·a·ble /'plɪkəbəl, 'æplɪkəbəl/ adj affecting or suitable for a particular person, group, or situation: **+ to** *The tax laws are not applicable to foreign visitors.*

ap·pli·cant /'æplɪkənt/ n [C] someone who has formally asked for a job, a place at a college etc, especially by writing a letter

ap·pli·ca·tion /ˌæplɪ'keɪʃən/ n **1** [C] an official, usually written, REQUEST for a job, place at a college etc **2** [C,U] a way in which something can be used, for example a new idea, drug, or piece of equipment: *The new technology could have military applications.* **3** [C] a PROGRAM on a computer **4** [C,U] when you spread a liquid or cream onto a surface

application form /ˌ..'.. ./ n [C] a printed piece of paper on which you write the answers to questions about why you should get a job, a place in college etc: *It took hours to fill in the application form.*

ap·plied /ə'plaɪd/ adj **applied maths/science/ linguistics etc** a subject that is studied for a practical purpose — compare PURE

ap·ply /ə'plaɪ/ v **1** [I] to officially ask to be considered for a job, place at a college etc, especially by writing a letter: **+ for** *Kevin's applied for a management job in Atlanta.* **2** [I,T] to affect or be suitable for a particular person, group, or situation: **+ to** *The 20% discount only applies to club members.* **3** [T] to use something such as a method or law: *You can apply good teaching methods to any subject.* **4** [T] to spread something such as paint or a cream on a surface: *Apply an antiseptic cream to the affected area.* **5** [T] **apply yourself (to sth)** to work very hard and carefully, especially for a long time: *I wish John would apply himself a little more!*

ap·point /ə'pɔɪnt/ v [T] **1** to choose someone for a job etc: *They've appointed a new principal at the school.* **2** *formal* to say officially when or where something will happen: *Judge Bailey appointed a day in July for the trial.*

ap·point·ed /ə'pɔɪntɪd/ adj **the appointed time/date/place etc** the time, date etc that has been decided

ap·point·ment /ə'pɔɪntmənt/ n **1** [C] a meeting that has been arranged for a particular time and place: **make an appointment** *I'd like to make an appointment with Dr. Hanson.* | **miss an appointment** *I'm sorry I missed our appointment.* **2** [C,U] when you choose someone for an important job: *the appointment of a new Supreme Court Justice* **3 by appointment** if something can only be done by appointment, you have to arrange it before you go: *Dr. Sutton will only see you by appointment.*

ap·por·tion /ə'pɔːʃənǁ-ɔːr-/ v *formal* **1** [T] to decide how something should be divided and given to people **2 apportion blame** to say who should be blamed

ap·prais·al /ə'preɪzəl/ n [C,U] an official description of how valuable, effective, or successful someone or something is: *an annual appraisal of employees' work*

ap·praise /ə'preɪz/ v [T] *formal* to carefully decide how valuable, important etc something is: *We are still appraising the situation.*

ap·pre·cia·ble /ə'priːʃəbəl/ adj *formal* noticeable or important: *There's been no appreciable change in the patient's condition.* —**appreciably** adv

ap·pre·ci·ate /ə'priːʃieɪt/ v **1** [T] to understand and enjoy the good qualities or value of something: *All the bad weather here makes me appreciate home.* **2** [T] to be grateful for something: *Lyn greatly appreciated the flowers you sent.* **3 I would appreciate it if** used to politely ask someone to do something: *I'd really appreciate it if you could drive Kathy to school today.* **4** [T] to understand a difficult situation or problem: *You don't seem to appreciate how hard this is for us.*

ap·pre·ci·a·tion /əˌpriːʃi'eɪʃən/ n [U] **1** a feeling of being grateful to someone: **show your appreciation** *a small gift to show our appreciation for all your hard work* **2** an understanding of a difficult situation or problem: *You just have no appreciation of how serious this all is!* **3** the enjoyment you feel when you recognize the good qualities of something: *As he grew older, his appreciation for his home town grew.*

ap·pre·cia·tive /ə'priːʃətɪv/ adj showing that you have enjoyed something or feel grateful for it — **appreciatively** adv

ap·pre·hend /ˌæprɪ'hend/ v [T] *formal* to find a criminal and take them away, usually to a police station; ARREST

ap·pre·hen·sion /ˌæprɪ'henʃən/ n [U] a feeling of anxiety or fear about something in the future: *News of the plane crash increased Tim's apprehension about flying.*

ap·pre·hen·sive /ˌæprɪ'hensɪv◂/ adj worried or anxious about something in the future — **apprehensively** adv

ap·pren·tice /ə'prentɪs/ n [C] someone who works for an employer for an agreed amount of time in order to learn a skill

ap·pren·tice·ship /ə'prentɪsʃɪp/ n [C,U] when someone learns a job or skill while working for an employer, especially for a fixed period of time

ap·proach¹ /ə'prəʊtʃ‖ə'prəʊtʃ/ v **1** [I,T] to move closer to someone or something: *We watched as their car approached.* | *A man approached me, asking if I'd seen a little girl.* **2** [T] to ask someone for something when you are not sure if they will do what you want: *She's been approached by two schools about a teaching job.* **3** [I,T] to almost be a particular time, age, temperature etc: *It's now approaching 7 o'clock.* **4** [T] to begin to deal with something

approach² n **1** [C] a way of doing something or dealing with a problem: **+ to** *a creative approach to teaching science* **2** [U] when something gets closer: **the approach of** *The air got colder with the approach of winter.* **3** [C] a road or path leading to a place: *The easiest approach to the beach is down the cliff path.*

ap·proach·a·ble /ə'prəʊtʃəbəl‖ə'prəʊtʃ-/ adj friendly and easy to talk to: *Dr. Grieg seems very approachable.* → opposite UNAPPROACHABLE

ap·pro·ba·tion /ˌæprə'beɪʃən/ n [U] formal praise or approval

ap·pro·pri·ate¹ /ə'prəʊpri-ɪt‖ə'prəʊ-/ adj suitable for a particular time, situation, or purpose: *That sort of language just isn't appropriate in an interview.* → opposite INAPPROPRIATE — **appropriately** adv — **appropriateness** n [U]

ap·pro·pri·ate² /ə'prəʊprieɪt‖ə'prəʊ-/ v [T] **1** formal to take or steal something **2** to officially take money for a particular purpose

ap·prov·al /ə'pruːvəl/ n [U] **1** official permission: *We have to get approval from the Chief of Police.* **2** the opinion that someone or something is good: *I was always trying to get my father's approval.*

ap·prove /ə'pruːv/ v **1** [T] to officially agree to something: *We are waiting for our proposals to be approved.* **2** [I] to believe that someone or something is good or acceptable: **+ of** *I don't approve of taking drugs.*

ap·prov·ing /ə'pruːvɪŋ/ adj showing that you approve of someone or something: *an approving nod* — **approvingly** adv

ap·prox /ə'prɒks‖ə'prɑːks/ adv the written abbreviation of 'approximately'

ap·prox·i·mate¹ /ə'prɒksɪmɪt‖ə'prɑːk-/ adj an approximate amount, time, measurement etc is not exact but is nearly right: *They think it's worth £10,000, but that's only an approximate figure.*

ap·prox·i·mate² /ə'prɒksɪmeɪt‖ə'prɑːk-/ v formal to be similar to but not exactly the same as something else — **approximation** /ə'prɒksɪ-'meɪʃən‖-prɑːk-/ n [C,U]

ap·prox·i·mate·ly /ə'prɒksɪmɪtli‖ə'prɑːk-/ adv a little more or less than an exact number, amount etc; about: *Approximately 35% of the students come from Japan.*

a·pri·cot /'eɪprɪkɒt‖'æprɪkɑːt/ n [C] a small soft yellow fruit with one large seed

A·pril /'eɪprəl/ written abbreviation **Apr** n [C,U] the fourth month of the year → see Usage Note at MONTH

April Fool's Day /ˌ.. '. ./ n [singular] April 1, a day for playing tricks on people

a·pron /'eɪprən/ n [C] a piece of clothing that you wear to protect your clothes when you cook

apt /æpt/ adj **1** apt to likely to do something: *They're good kids but apt to get into trouble.* **2** exactly right for a particular situation or purpose: *an apt remark* — **aptly** adv

ap·ti·tude /'æptɪtjuːd‖-tuːd/ n [C,U] a natural ability to do something well or to learn it quickly: *Ginny seems to have a real aptitude for painting.*

a·quar·i·um /ə'kweəriəm‖ə'kwer-/ n [C] **1** a clear glass container for fish or other water animals to live in **2** a building where people go to look at fish or other water animals

A·quar·i·us /ə'kweəriəs‖ə'kwer-/ n [C,U] the sign of the Zodiac of people who are born between January 20th and February 18th, or someone who belongs to this sign

a·quat·ic /ə'kwætɪk, ə'kwɒt-‖ə'kwæ-, ə'kwɑː-/ adj living or happening in water: *aquatic plants* | *aquatic sports*

aq·ue·duct /'ækwɪdʌkt/ n [C] a structure like a bridge that takes water across a valley

Ar·ab /'ærəb/ n [C] someone whose language is Arabic and whose family come from the Middle East or North Africa

Ar·a·bic /'ærəbɪk/ n [singular] the language of Arab people or the religious language of Islam

ar·a·ble /'ærəbəl/ adj arable land is suitable for growing crops

ar·bi·ter /'ɑːbɪtə‖'ɑːrbətər/ n [C] **1** someone who helps two people or groups to agree, or who judges who is correct **2** arbiter of style/fashion/taste etc someone who influences people's opinions about what is fashionable etc

ar·bi·tra·ry /'ɑːbɪtrəri, -trɪl‖'ɑːrbɪtreri/ adj arbitrary actions or rules seem unfair because they are not based on any practical or good reasons: *I don't see why they have this arbitrary age-limit.* — **arbitrariness** n [U] — **arbitrarily** /'ɑːbɪtrərɪli‖ˌɑːrbɪ'trerɪli/ adv

ar·bi·trate /'ɑːbɪtreɪt‖'ɑːr-/ v [I,T] to officially help two people or groups to agree — **arbitrator** n [C]

ar·bi·tra·tion /ˌɑːbɪ'treɪʃən‖ˌɑːr-/ n [U] the process in which someone tries to help two people or groups to agree

arc /ɑːk‖ɑːrk/ n [C] part of a circle or any curved line

ar·cade /ɑː'keɪd‖ɑːr-/ n [C] **1** a place where people go to play VIDEO GAMES etc; AMUSEMENT ARCADE **2** a covered path with shops on each side of it **3** also **shopping arcade** BrE a large building or group of buildings where there are many shops

arch¹ /ɑːtʃ‖ɑːrtʃ/ n [C], plural **arches** **1** a curved structure at the top of a door, window, bridge etc, or something that has this curved shape **2** the curved middle part of the bottom of your foot — **arched** adj: *an arched doorway*

arch

arch² v [I,T] to form a curved shape, or make something have a curved shape: *The cat arched her back and hissed.*

ar·chae·ol·o·gist also **archeologist** AmE /ˌɑːki'ɒlədʒɪst‖ˌɑːrki'ɑː-/ n [C] someone who studies ancient societies by digging up and examining what remains of their buildings, graves, tools etc

ar·chae·ol·o·gy also **archeology** AmE /-ˌɑːkiˈɒlədʒiǁˌɑːrkiˈɑː-/ n [U] the study of ancient societies by digging up and examining what remains of their buildings, graves, tools etc — **archaeological** /ˌɑːkiəˈlɒdʒɪkəlǁˌɑːrkiəˈlɑː-/ adj — **archaeologically** /-kli/ adv

ar·cha·ic /ɑːˈkeɪ-ɪkǁɑːr-/ adj archaic language, ideas etc seem very old-fashioned: the archaic language of the Bible

arch·bish·op /ˌɑːtʃˈbɪʃəpǁˌɑːrtʃ-/ n [C] the most important priest within a country, in some Christian religions

ar·che·ol·o·gist /ˌɑːkiˈɒlədʒɪstǁˌɑːrkiˈɑː-/ n [C] the American spelling of ARCHAEOLOGIST

ar·che·ol·o·gy /ˌɑːkiˈɒlədʒiǁˌɑːrkiˈɑː-/ the American spelling of ARCHAEOLOGY

ar·cher /ˈɑːtʃəǁˈɑːrtʃər/ n [C] someone who fires ARROWS from a BOW

ar·cher·y /ˈɑːtʃəriǁˈɑːr-/ n [U] the sport of shooting ARROWS from a BOW

ar·chi·tect /ˈɑːkɪˌtektǁˈɑːr-/ n [C] someone whose job is to design buildings

ar·chi·tec·ture /ˈɑːkɪˌtektʃəǁˈɑːrkɪˌtektʃər/ n [U] **1** the style and design of buildings: medieval architecture **2** the skill and process of designing buildings — **architectural** /ˌɑːkɪˈtektʃərəlǁˌɑːr-/ adj — **architecturally** adv

ar·chives /ˈɑːkaɪvzǁˈɑːr-/ n [plural] information about the history of a country, organization, family etc, or the place where this is kept

arch·way /ˈɑːtʃweɪǁˈɑːrtʃ-/ n [C] the place where you can walk under an ARCH

Arc·tic /ˈɑːktɪkǁˈɑːrk-/ n **the Arctic** [singular] the very cold part of the world around the North Pole → compare ANTARCTIC — **arctic** adj

ar·dent /ˈɑːdəntǁˈɑːr-/ adj having strong feelings of admiration or determination: an ardent football supporter | an ardent desire to win — **ardently** adv

ar·dour BrE, **ardor** AmE /ˈɑːdəǁˈɑːrdər/ n [U] formal very strong feelings of admiration, excitement, or love

ar·du·ous /ˈɑːdjuəsǁˈɑːrdʒuəs/ adj needing a lot of effort and hard work: an arduous task | an arduous climb

are /ə; strong ɑːǁər; strong ɑːr/ the present tense plural of BE

ar·e·a /ˈeəriəǁˈeriə/ n [C] **1** a particular part of a place, city, country etc: Dad grew up in the Portland area. **2** a part of a house, office, park etc that is used for a particular purpose: Their apartment has a large kitchen area. **3** a particular subject or type of activity: I have experience in software marketing and related areas. **4** the size of a flat surface, calculated by multiplying its length by its width

area code /ˈ... ˌ./ n [C] AmE the part of a telephone number that you have to add for a different town or country; CODE BrE

a·re·na /əˈriːnə/ n **1** [C] a building with a large flat central area surrounded by raised

seats, used for sports or entertainment: Wembley arena **2** **the political/public/academic etc arena** all the people and activities connected with politics, government etc: Feminism has played a prominent role in the political arena since the 1960s.

aren't /ɑːntǁˈɑːrənt/ **a)** the short form of 'are not': Things aren't the same since you left. **b)** the short form of 'am not', used in asking questions: I'm in big trouble, aren't I?

ar·gu·a·ble /ˈɑːgjuəbəlǁˈɑːr-/ adj **1** **it is arguable that** used to give good reasons why something might be true: It's arguable that the new law will make things better. **2** not definitely true or correct; DEBATABLE: Whether we'll get our money back is arguable.

ar·gu·a·bly /ˈɑːgjuəbliǁˈɑːr-/ adv used to give your opinion about something: San Francisco, arguably the most beautiful city in the USA

ar·gue /ˈɑːgjuːǁˈɑːr-/ v **1** [I,T] to clearly explain why you think something is true or should be done: + **that** Smith argued that most teachers are underpaid. | + **for/against** They are arguing for a change in the law. **2** [I] to disagree with someone, usually by talking or shouting in an angry way: + **about/over** Paul and Rachel always seem to be arguing about money. | + **with** They are always arguing with each other.

ar·gu·ment /ˈɑːgjʊməntǁˈɑːr-/ n [C] **1** a disagreement, especially one in which people talk loudly and angrily: **have an argument** My parents had a big argument last night. | + **about** It was the usual argument about what to watch on television. **2** the reasons that you give to try and prove that something is right or wrong, true or false etc: + **for/against** She put forward several arguments for becoming a vegetarian.

ar·gu·men·ta·tive /ˌɑːgjʊˈmentətɪvǁˌɑːr-/ adj liking to argue

a·ri·a /ˈɑːriə/ n [C] a song that is sung by only one person in an OPERA

ar·id /ˈærɪd/ adj formal getting very little rain, and therefore very dry: arid land | an arid climate

Ar·ies /ˈeəriːz, ˈeəri-iːzǁˈeriːz/ n [C,U] the sign of the Zodiac of people who are born between March 21st and April 19th, or someone who belongs to this sign

a·rise /əˈraɪz/ v [I] **arose, arisen, arising 1** if a problem or difficult situation arises, it begins to happen: the problems that arise from rushing things too much. **2** literary to stand up **3** literary to get out of bed in the morning

ar·is·toc·ra·cy /ˌærɪˈstɒkrəsiǁ-ˈstɑː-/ n [C] the people in the highest social class, who traditionally have a lot of land, money, and power, especially in Europe in past times

ar·is·to·crat /ˈærɪstəkræt, əˈrɪ-ǁ-ərɪ-/ n [C] someone who belongs to the highest social class, especially in Europe in past times — **aristocratic** /ˌærɪstəˈkrætɪk, əˌrɪ-ǁ-ərɪ-/ adj

a·rith·me·tic /əˈrɪθmətɪk/ n [U] the skill of working with numbers by adding, dividing,

---

A

multiplying etc → compare MATHEMATICS —**a-rithmetic** /ˌærɪθ'metɪk◂/ adj —**arithmetically** / -kli/ adv

arm[1] /ɑːm‖ɑːrm/ n [C] **1** the long part of your body between your shoulder and your hand: *I was carrying a pile of books under my arm.*|*He put his arm around my shoulders.*|**arms crossed/folded** (=crossed in a relaxed way in front of your chest) **2** a part of something that is shaped like an arm: *The cutting wheel is on the end of a steel arm.* **3** the part of a piece of clothing that covers your arm; SLEEVE **4 be up in arms** *informal* to be very angry: *The whole town is up in arms about the closure of the hospital.* → see also ARMS

arm[2] v [T] to give someone weapons

ar·ma·dil·lo /ˌɑːmə'dɪləʊ‖ˌɑːrmə'dɪloʊ/ n [C] a small animal with a pointed nose and a hard shell that lives in hot dry parts of North and South America

ar·ma·ments /'ɑːməmənts‖'ɑːr-/ n [plural] weapons and military equipment: *nuclear armaments*

arm·band /'ɑːmbænd‖'ɑːrm-/ n [C] a band of material that you wear around the top part of your arm

arm·chair /'ɑːmtʃeə, ˌɑːm'tʃeə‖'ɑːrmtʃer, ˌɑːrm'tʃer/ n [C] a comfortable chair with sides that you can rest your arms on → see picture at CHAIR and colour picture on page 474

armed /ɑːmd‖ɑːrmd/ adj carrying weapons: *an armed guard*|**+ with** *The suspect is armed with a shotgun.*|**armed robbery** (=using a weapon): *He got ten years in prison for armed robbery.* **2** having or knowing something useful: *I went into the meeting armed with a copy of the report.*

armed forc·es /ˌ. '../ n **the armed forces** a country's military organizations

ar·mi·stice /'ɑːmₐstₐs‖'ɑːrm-/ n [C] an agreement to stop fighting

ar·mour BrE, **armor** AmE /'ɑːmə‖'ɑːrmər/ n [U] **1** metal or leather clothing worn in past times by men in battle: *a suit of armour* **2** a layer of strong material that protects something

ar·moured BrE, **armored** AmE /'ɑːməd‖ 'ɑːrmərd/ adj protected against bullets or other weapons by a strong layer of metal: *an armoured car*

ar·mour·y BrE, **armory** AmE /'ɑːməri‖'ɑːr-/ n [C] a place where weapons are stored

arm·pit /'ɑːm,pɪt‖'ɑːrm-/ n [C] the hollow place under your arm where it joins your body

arms /ɑːmz‖ɑːrmz/ n [plural] weapons: *supplying arms to the rebels*|*an international arms dealer*

arms con·trol /'. .,./ n [U] when powerful countries try to limit the number of war weapons that exist

arms race /'. ./ n **the arms race** when two or more countries try to produce more effective weapons than each other

ar·my /'ɑːmi‖'ɑːr-/ n [C] **1** the part of a country's military force that is trained to fight on land: *a British army officer*|**the army** *Our son is in the army.* **2** a large group of people or animals involved in the same activity: *an army of ants*

a·ro·ma /ə'rəʊmə‖ə'roʊ-/ n [C] a strong pleasant smell: *the aroma of fresh coffee* —**aromatic** / ˌærə'mætɪk◂/ adj: *aromatic oils*

a·ro·ma·ther·a·py /ə,rəʊmə'θerəpi‖ə,roʊ-/ n [U] the use of pleasant smelling plant oils to make you feel healthy and relaxed —**aromatherapist** n [C]

a·rose /ə'rəʊz‖ə'roʊz/ v the past tense of ARISE

a·round /ə'raʊnd/ adv, prep **1** also **round** BrE on all sides of something, so that it is surrounded: *We put a fence around the yard.*|*Mario put his arms around her.* → see colour picture on page 474 **2** also **round** BrE in a circular movement: *Water pushes the wheel around.* **3** also **round** BrE to or in many parts of a place: *Stan showed me around the office.*|**all around** (=in all parts of): *an international company with offices all around the world* **4** also **round** BrE in or near a particular place: *Is there a bank around here?* **5** also **round** BrE along the outside of a place, instead of through it: *We had to go around to the back of the house.* **6 be around a)** to be in the same place as you are: *It was 11:30 at night, and nobody was around.* **b)** to exist or be available to use: *That joke's been around for years.* **7 turn/move/spin etc sth around** to move something so it is facing the opposite direction: *I'll turn the car around and pick you up at the door.* **8 around 10/6/200 etc** also **about** *especially BrE* used when you do not know an exact number to give a number that is close to it; APPROXIMATELY: *Dodger Stadium seats around 50,000 people.* **9 around and around** continuing to move in circles: *We drove around and around the town, looking for her house.* → see also ROUND[2]

a·rous·al /ə'raʊzəl/ n [U] excitement, especially sexual excitement

a·rouse /ə'raʊz/ v [T] **1** to make someone have a particular feeling: *Her behaviour aroused the suspicions of the police.* **2** to make someone feel sexually excited

ar·range /ə'reɪndʒ/ v [T] **1** to make plans for something to happen: *I've arranged a meeting with Jim.*|**arrange (for sb) to do sth** *Have you arranged to play football on Sunday?* **2** to put a group of things or people in a particular order or position: *She arranged the flowers carefully in a vase.*

ar·range·ment /ə'reɪndʒmənt/ n **1** [C usually plural] the things that you must organize for something to happen: *travel arrangements*|**make arrangements for** *Lee's still making arrangements for the wedding.* **2** [C,U] something that has been agreed between two people or groups: *We have a special arrangement with the bank.* **3** [C] a group of things in a particular position or order: *a flower arrangement*

ar·ray[1] /ə'reɪ/ n [C usually singular] a large group of different things, especially one that seems very impressive or surprising: *a dazzling array of acting talent*

array[2] v [T usually passive] *formal* to arrange something in an attractive way

ar·rears /ə'rɪəz‖ə'rɪrz/ n [plural] **1 be in arrears** to owe someone more money than you should because your payment is late: *We're six weeks in arrears with the rent money.* **2** money that is owed and should already have been paid

ar·rest[1] /əˈrest/ v [T] **1** if a police officer arrests someone, he or she takes them away because they are believed to be guilty of a crime: **arrest sb for sth** *The police arrested Eric for shoplifting.* **2** *formal* to stop something happening or make it happen more slowly: *The drug is used to arrest the spread of the disease.*

arrest[2] n [C,U] when a police officer takes someone away and guards them because they may have done something illegal: **make an arrest** *The police expect to make an arrest soon.* | **be under arrest** (=have just been arrested): *Don't move, you're under arrest!*

ar·riv·al /əˈraɪvəl/ n **1** [U] when you arrive somewhere: *Shortly after our arrival in Florida, Lottie got robbed.* **2** **the arrival of** the time when a new idea, method, product etc is first used or discovered: *The arrival of the personal computer changed the way we work.* **3** [C] a person or thing that has arrived: *a new arrival*

ar·rive /əˈraɪv/ v [I] **1** to get to a place: *Your letter arrived yesterday.* | *The train finally arrived in New York at 8.30 pm.* **2** to happen: *At last the big day arrived!* **3** **arrive at a conclusion/decision** to decide what to do about something after a lot of effort **4** to begin to exist or to start being used: *Our sales have doubled since computer games arrived.* | *It was just past midnight when the baby arrived.* (=was born)

ar·ro·gant /ˈærəɡənt/ adj believing that you are more important than anyone else: *an arrogant, selfish man* — **arrogantly** adv — **arrogance** n [U]

ar·row /ˈærəʊ ˈæroʊ/ n [C] **1** a thin straight weapon with a point at one end that you shoot from a BOW **2** a sign (→), used to show the direction or position of something

arrows

arse /ɑːs ˈɑːrs/ BrE, **ass** AmE — n [C] **1** a rude word for the part of your body that you sit on **2** *spoken* a rude word for a stupid and annoying person **3** **shift/move your arse** *spoken* an impolite way of telling someone to hurry up

ar·se·nal /ˈɑːsənəl ˈɑːr-/ n [C] a large number of weapons, or the building where they are stored

ar·se·nic /ˈɑːsənɪk ˈɑːr-/ n [U] a very strong poison

ar·son /ˈɑːsən ˈɑːr-/ n [U] the crime of deliberately making something burn, especially a building — **arsonist** n [C]

art /ɑːt ɑːrt/ n **1** [U] the use of drawing, painting etc to make beautiful things or to express ideas: *Steve's studying art at college.* **2** [U] things that are produced by art, such as drawings and paintings: *modern art* | *an art exhibition* | **work of art** *Some important works of art were stolen.* **3** [C,U] the skill involved in making or doing something: *the art of writing*

ar·te·fact /ˈɑːtɪfækt ˈɑːr-/ n [C] → see ARTIFACT

ar·te·ry /ˈɑːtəri ˈɑːr-/ n [C] **1** one of the tubes that takes blood from your heart to the rest of your body → compare VEIN **2** *formal* a main road, railway line, or river — **arterial** /ɑːˈtɪəriəl ɑːrˈtɪr-/ adj

art·ful /ˈɑːtfəl ˈɑːrt-/ adj good at deceiving people — **artfully** adv

art gal·le·ry /ˈ. ˌ.../ n [C] a room or building where people can look at famous paintings and other types of art; GALLERY AmE

ar·thri·tis /ɑːˈθraɪtɪs ɑːr-/ n [U] a disease that causes pain and swelling in the joints of your body — **arthritic** /-ˈθrɪtɪk/ adj: *arthritic fingers*

ar·ti·choke /ˈɑːtɪtʃəʊk ˈɑːrtɪtʃoʊk/ n [C] a round green vegetable with thick pointed leaves and a firm base → see picture at VEGETABLE

ar·ti·cle /ˈɑːtɪkəl ˈɑːr-/ n [C] **1** a piece of writing in a newspaper, magazine etc: *Did you read that article on the space shuttle?* **2** a thing, especially one of a group of things: *an article of clothing* **3** in grammar, the word 'the' (=the definite article), or the word 'a' or 'an' (=the indefinite article)

ar·tic·u·late[1] /ɑːˈtɪkjələt ɑːr-/ adj able to express your thoughts and feelings clearly: *a bright and articulate child* — **articulately** adv

ar·tic·u·late[2] /ɑːˈtɪkjəleɪt ɑːr-/ v [T] to put your thoughts or feelings into words: *Children's worries about divorce are not always clearly articulated.* — **articulation** /ɑːˌtɪkjəˈleɪʃən ɑːr-/ n [U]

ar·tic·u·la·ted /ɑːˈtɪkjəleɪtɪd ɑːr-/ adj especially BrE a vehicle that is articulated is made as two joined parts that can bend to go around corners: *an articulated lorry*

ar·ti·fact also **artefact** BrE /ˈɑːtɪfækt ˈɑːr-/ n [C] an object that was made and used a long time ago, especially one that is studied by ARCHAEOLOGISTS: *Egyptian artefacts*

ar·ti·fi·cial /ˌɑːtɪˈfɪʃəl ˌɑːr-/ adj **1** not natural, but made by people: *artificial sweeteners* | *an artificial leg* **2** not natural or sincere: *an artificial smile* — **artificially** adv

artificial in·tel·li·gence /ˌ.... .ˈ.../ n [U] the science of how to make computers do things that people can do, such as make decisions and understand language

artificial res·pi·ra·tion /ˌ.... ..ˈ../ n [U] a method of helping an unconscious person to start breathing again by blowing air into their mouth

ar·til·le·ry /ɑːˈtɪləri ɑːr-/ n [U] big guns, either on wheels or fixed in one place

ar·ti·san /ˌɑːtɪˈzæn ˈɑːrtɪzən/ n [C] *formal* someone who does skilled work with their hands; CRAFTSMAN

art·ist /ˈɑːtɪst ˈɑːr-/ n [C] someone who produces or performs any kind of art, including painting, drawing, music, and dance

ar·tiste /ɑːˈtiːst ɑːr-/ n [C] *formal* someone such as a singer or actor who performs in a theatre, club etc

ar·tis·tic /ɑːˈtɪstɪk ɑːr-/ adj **1** showing skill or imagination in painting, drawing etc: *I never knew you were so artistic.* **2** connected with art or with being an artist: *artistic freedom* — **artistically** /-kli/ adv

art·ist·ry /ˈɑːtɪstri ˈɑːr-/ n [U] a very high level of skill in sport, art, cooking etc: *the magnificent artistry of the great tennis players*

arts /ɑːts ɑːrts/ n **1** **the arts** art, music, theatre, film, literature etc, all considered together: *government funding for the arts* **2** [plural] school or college subjects such as

A

History or French that are not connected with science: *an arts degree*

art·work /'ɑːtwɜːk‖'ɑːrtwɜːrk/ *n* **1** [U] the pictures or decorations that are included in a book, magazine etc: *Some of the artwork is absolutely brilliant.* **2** [C,U] *especially AmE* paintings and other pieces of art: *His private collection includes artworks by Dufy and Miro.*

art·y /'ɑːti‖'ɑːrti-/ *BrE,* **art·sy** /'ɑːtsi‖'ɑːr-/ *AmE* — *adj* a person, place, or style that is arty shows an interest in art in a fashionable, but perhaps insincere, way: *an arty film student*

as /əz; *strong* æz/ *adv, prep, linking word* **1** used when you are comparing things, or saying that they are like each other: *These houses aren't as old as the ones near the river.* | *He was as surprised as anyone when they offered him the job.* **2** used when you are describing what job, use, or appearance of something is: *In the past, women were mainly employed as secretaries or teachers.* | *The kids dressed up as animals.* | *John used an old blanket as a tent.* **3** used when you are describing the way that people think of something: *Settlers saw the wilderness as dangerous rather than beautiful.* **4** in the same way: *Leave things as they are until the police come.* | *As I said earlier, this research has only just started.* **5** while something is happening: *The phone rang just as I was leaving.* **6 as if/as though** in a way that makes you think that something is true: *They all looked as if they were used to working outdoors.* **7 as to** about: *She offered no explanation as to why she'd left so suddenly.* **8 as of today/December 12th/next spring etc** starting at a particular time and continuing from that time: *The pay raise will come into effect as of January 1st.* **9 as for sb/sth** used to start talking about a subject or person that someone has already mentioned: *As for racism, much progress has been made.* **10** because: *James decided not to go out as he was still really tired.* → see also **as long as** (LONG²), **as a matter of fact** (MATTER¹), **such as** (SUCH), **as well as** (WELL¹), **as yet** (YET¹), **as well** (WELL¹), **so as** (SO¹)

USAGE NOTE: as and like

Use **as** and **like** to compare people or things: *She sings like a professional.* | *She sings as well as a professional.* | *She's as good as a professional.* However, if you say: *She sings as a professional* you mean that she sings as a professional job.

---

asap /ˌeɪ es eɪ'piː‖ˌeɪsæp/ *adv* the abbreviation of 'as soon as possible': *Please reply asap.*

as·bes·tos /æs'bestəs/ *n* [U] a substance that does not burn easily, that was often used as a building material

as·cend /ə'send/ *v* [I,T] *formal* to move up or move to the top of something: *The plane ascended rapidly.* → opposite DESCEND

as·cen·dan·cy /ə-'sendənsi/ also **ascendency** /ə-'sendənsi/ *n* [U] a position of power, influence, or control: *the ascendancy of Japanese companies in the electronics market*

as·cent /ə'sent/ *n* **1** [C, usually singular] the activity of moving or climbing up: *a successful ascent of Mount Everest* **2** [C,] the process of becoming more important or successful **3** [C, usually singular] a path or road that goes gradu-

ally up: *a steep ascent up the mountain* → opposite DESCENT

as·cer·tain /ˌæsə'teɪn‖ˌæsər-/ *v* [T] *formal* to discover or find out something: *School officials are trying to ascertain the facts.*

as·cet·ic /ə'setɪk/ *adj* living a simple strict life, usually for religious reasons —**ascetic** *n* [C] —**asceticism** *n* [U]

as·cribe /ə'skraɪb/ *v* **ascribe sth to sb/sth** *phr v* [T] *formal* to believe that something happens or exists because of someone or something else: *Carter ascribed his problems to a lack of money.*

a·sex·u·al /eɪ'sekʃuəl/ *adj technical* without sex, sex organs, or sexual activity: *asexual reproduction in some plants* —**asexually** *adv*

ash /æʃ/ *n* [C,U] **1** the soft grey powder that is left after something has been burned: *cigarette ash* | **sb's ashes** (=the grey powder that is left after a dead body has been burned) **2** a type of forest tree, or the hard wood from this tree

a·shamed /ə'ʃeɪmd/ *adj* **1** feeling embarrassed or guilty about something: **+ of** *Mike felt ashamed of his old clothes.* | **ashamed of yourself** *You should be ashamed of yourself, acting like that!* **2 be ashamed of sb** uncomfortable or angry because someone has done something to embarrass you: *Helen felt ashamed of her parents.*

ash·en /'æʃən/ *adj* very pale because of shock or fear: *Her face was ashen.*

a·shore /ə'ʃɔː‖ə'ʃɔːr/ *adv* onto or towards the side of a lake, river, sea, or ocean: *Brian pulled the boat ashore.*

ash·tray /'æʃtreɪ/ *n* [C] a small dish where you put used cigarettes

a·side¹ /ə'saɪd/ *adv* **1 move/step etc aside** to move, step etc to the side: *Bob stepped aside to let me pass.* **2 put/set/leave sth aside (for sth)** to keep or save something so that it can be used later: *I'm trying to put aside £20 a week for my trip to Italy.* | *A room was set aside for the tests.* **3 aside from** apart from

aside² *n* [C] something you say in a quiet voice so that only a few people can hear

ask /ɑːsk‖æsk/ *v* [I,T] **1** to say to someone that you want them to tell you something: *"What's your name?" she asked quietly.* | **ask sb a question** *Can I ask a question?* | **ask (sb) about sth** *Did they ask you about your qualifications?* | **ask (sb) whether/if/why/what etc** *Helen asked him if he was married.* **2** to say to someone that you want them to do something for you, give you something, help you, advise you etc: *Sarah wants to ask your advice.* | *If you need anything, just ask.* | **ask (sb) for** *Some people don't like to ask for help.* | **ask sb to do sth** *Ask Paula to post the letters.* **3** to say to someone that you want to know if you can be allowed to do something: **ask (sb) if/whether** *Why don't you ask your dad if you can borrow his boat?* | **ask to do sth** *Susie's asked to go home early.* **4** to invite someone to go somewhere: **ask sb out** (=ask someone to go with you for a meal, drink etc): *Mark would like to ask her out, but he's too shy.* | **ask sb in** (=ask someone to come into your house, room etc) **5** to want a particular amount of money for something you are selling: *He's asking $2000 for that old car!* **6 If you ask me** used to emphasize your own opinion: *If you* *ask me, he's crazy.* **7 ask yourself** used to say that someone should think very carefully about something: *Ask yourself, who is going to benefit from the changes?* **8 Don't ask me!** *spoken* used when you do not know the answer to a question and are annoyed that someone has asked: *"When will Vicky get home?" "Don't ask me!"* **9 be asking for trouble** *informal* to be behaving in a way that will probably cause trouble: *Leaving your car here is just asking for trouble.*

Usage note: ask, inquire/enquire, demand, and request

Ask is the usual verb you use for questions or for when you want information: *Why don't you ask Dave?* | *Would anyone like to ask any questions?* **Inquire/enquire** is more formal than **ask**: *I would like to inquire about job openings.* If you **demand** something, you expect to get what you want: *I demand an explanation.* Use **request** to ask for something formally or officially: *He requested permission to return home.*

---

a·skew /əˈskjuː/ *adv* not completely straight or level: *His tie was askew and he smelt of brandy.*

a·sleep /əˈsliːp/ *adj* **1** sleeping: *Be quiet. The baby is asleep.* | **fast/sound asleep** (=sleeping very deeply): *Look at Tom. He's fast asleep.* **2 fall asleep** to begin to sleep: *I always fall asleep watching TV.*

as·par·a·gus /əˈspærəgəs/ *n* [U] a long thin green vegetable shaped like a small stick

as·pect /ˈæspekt/ *n* [C] one of the parts of a situation or subject that can be considered separately: *The committee discussed several aspects of the traffic problem.*

as·phalt /ˈæsfælt‖ˈæsfɔːlt/ *n* [U] a hard black substance used for making the surface of roads or paths

as·phyx·i·ate /æsˈfɪksieɪt, əs-/ *v* [T] *formal* to make someone unable to breathe, so that they may die —**asphyxiation** /æs,fɪksiˈeɪʃən, əs-/ *n* [U]

as·pi·ra·tion /ˌæspɪˈreɪʃən/ *n* [C usually plural] a strong desire to have or to achieve something: *the aspirations of ordinary men and women*

as·pire /əˈspaɪə‖əˈspaɪr/ *v* [I] to have a strong desire to achieve something: **+ to** *people who work hard and aspire to a better way of life*

as·pir·in /ˈæsprɪn/ *n* [C,U] a drug that reduces pain and fever

as·pir·ing /əˈspaɪərɪŋ‖əˈspaɪr-/ *adj* **aspiring politician/writer/painter etc** someone who wants to become a politician, writer, painter etc

ass /æs/ *n* [C] **1** *AmE* a rude word for the part of your body that you sit on: *Jamie fell right on his ass.* **2** *informal* someone who is behaving stupidly: *Don't be such an ass!* **3** *especially literary* a DONKEY

as·sail·ant /əˈseɪlənt/ *n* [C] *formal* someone who attacks another person

as·sas·sin /əˈsæsɪn/ *n* [C] someone who murders an important person

as·sas·sin·ate /əˈsæsɪneɪt‖-səneɪt/ *v* [T] to murder an important person: *a plot to assassinate the President* —**assassination** /ə,sæs-ɪˈneɪʃən‖-sənˈeɪ-/ *n* [C,U] *an assassination attempt*

as·sault¹ /əˈsɔːlt‖əˈsɒːlt/ *n* [C,U] a violent attack on a person or place: **+ on** *an increase in the number of sexual assaults on women*

assault² *v* [T] to attack someone violently: *McGillis claimed he had been assaulted by a gang of youths.*

as·sem·ble /əˈsembəl/ *v* **1** [I,T] to come together or gather people together in the same place: *A crowd had assembled in front of the White House.* **2** [T] to put the different parts of something together: *The bookcase is fairly easy to assemble.*

as·sem·bly /əˈsembli/ *n* **1** [C,U] a regular meeting of all the students and teachers in a school: *School assembly begins at 9 o'clock.* **2** [C] a group of people who have come together for a particular purpose: *the United Nations General Assembly*

as·sent /əˈsent/ *n* [U] *formal* official agreement or approval: *The directors have given their assent to the proposals.* —**assent** *v* [I]

as·sert /əˈsɜːt‖-ɜːrt/ *v* **1** [T] to say firmly that something is true: *men who assert that everything can be explained scientifically* **2 assert your rights/independence/authority etc** to show that you are determined to have your rights etc: *Teenagers are always looking for ways to assert their independence.* **3 assert yourself** to behave or speak in a confident and determined way so that other people notice you

as·ser·tion /əˈsɜːʃən‖-ɜːr-/ *n* [C,U] a confident statement: *Davis repeated his assertion that he was innocent.*

as·ser·tive /əˈsɜːtɪv‖-ɜːr-/ *adj* behaving in a confident and determined way: *You must be more assertive if you want people to listen to you.* —**assertiveness** *n* [U] —**assertively** *adv*

as·sess /əˈses/ *v* [T] to examine something and make a decision about it, especially about its quality, amount, or value: *First we must assess the cost of repairing the damage.* —**assessment** *n* [C,U] *I agree entirely with your assessment of the situation.*

as·set /ˈæset/ *n* **1** [C] something or someone that helps you to succeed: *Her knowledge of computers was a real asset.* | **+ to** *You're an asset to the company, George.* **2** [C, usually plural] something that a company owns, that can be sold to pay debts

as·sid·u·ous /əˈsɪdjuəs‖-dʒuəs/ *adj* working with a lot of effort and care —**assiduously** *adv*

as·sign /əˈsaɪn/ *v* [T] **1** to give someone a job to do: **assign sth to sb** *Specific tasks will be assigned to each member of the team.* | **assign sb to** *doctors who were assigned to military hospitals* **2** to give something to someone for them to use: *Each department is assigned a budget.*

as·sign·ment /əˈsaɪnmənt/ *n* [C] a piece of work that you are given to do: *a homework*

GRAMMAR NOTE: the passive (1)

You use a verb in the **passive** to say that something happens to the subject of the sentence. You form the passive using **be/is/was** and the past participle.

ACTIVE: *They* **chose** *a new leader.* → PASSIVE: *A new leader* **was chosen**.

assignment | *Nichol was sent on a dangerous and difficult assignment to Bosnia.*

as·sim·i·late /ə'sɪmɪleɪt/ v **1** [T] to learn and understand facts and ideas and be able to use them: *Children can usually assimilate new information more quickly than adults.* **2 be assimilated (into)** to become part of a group and be accepted by it: *New immigrants from Asia were gradually assimilated into Canadian society.* —**assimilation** /ə'sɪmɪ'leɪʃən/ n [U]

as·sist /ə'sɪst/ v [I,T] to help someone to do something: **assist sb in/with** *Two nurses assisted Dr Bernard in performing the operation.*

as·sist·ance /ə'sɪstəns/ n [U] *formal* help and support: *Students receive very little financial assistance from the government.* | **be of assistance** (=help someone): *Can I be of any assistance, madam?* | **come to sb's assistance** (=help someone who is in danger or difficulty)

as·sis·tant /ə'sɪstənt/ n [C] **1** someone who helps someone else to do their work by doing the less important jobs: *Meet Jane Lansdowne, my new assistant.* **assistant manager/director/ editor** *Tom's assistant editor on the local newspaper.* **2** someone whose job is to help customers in a shop: *a shop assistant*

as·so·ci·ate¹ /ə'səʊʃieɪt, ə'səʊsi-llə'sou-/ v **1 be associated with sth** to be connected with something: *the health problems that are associated with smoking* **2** [T] to make a connection in your mind between one thing or person and another: **associate sth with sth** *Most people associate Florida with sunshine and long sandy beaches.*

  associate with sb *phr* v [T] *formal* to spend time with someone: *I don't like the kind of people she associates with.*

as·so·ci·ate² /ə'səʊʃiɪt, ə'səʊ-llə'sou-/ n [C] someone that you work or do business with: *a business associate*

as·so·ci·a·tion /ə,səʊsi'eɪʃən, ə,səʊʃi-llə,sou-/ n **1** also **Association** [C] an organization for people who have the same aims or interests, or who do the same kind of work: *the Association of University Teachers* **2 in association with** working with another organization or person: *concerts sponsored by the Arts Council in association with local businesses* **3** [C, usually plural] a memory or feeling that you have when you think about a place: *Los Angeles has happy associations for me.*

as·sort·ed /ə'sɔːtɪdll-ɔːr-/ adj of various different types: *a box of assorted cookies*

as·sort·ment /ə'sɔːtməntll-ɔːr-/ n [C] a mixture of various things or of different types of the same thing: *an assortment of chocolates*

as·sume /ə'sjuːmllə'suːm/ v [T] **1** to think that something is true although you have no proof: **+ (that)** *Your light wasn't on so I assumed you were out.* | **assuming (that)** (=if we accept that something is true): *Assuming the picture is a Van Gogh, how much do you think it is worth?* **2 assume power/control/responsibility etc** *formal* to begin to control people, events etc or become responsible for them: *The Chinese Communists assumed power in 1949.* **3 assume an air/expression/manner** *formal* to pretend to have a particular feeling or attitude: *Andy assumed an air of innocence as the teacher walked past.* **4** to do something to hide what

your name is, what you look like, where you live etc: *He assumed a false identity.*

as·sumed /ə'sjuːmdllə'suːmd/ adj **under an assumed name** using a false name

as·sump·tion /ə'sʌmpʃən/ n [C] **1** something that you think is true although you have no proof: **+ that** *the assumption that computers can solve all our problems* | **on the assumption that** *We're working on the assumption that prices will continue to rise.* **2 assumption of** when someone starts to take power, starts an important job etc: *On its assumption of power, the new government promised an end to the war.*

as·sur·ance /ə'ʃʊərənsllə'ʃʊr-/ n **1** [C] a definite statement or promise: **+ that** *He gave me a firm assurance that there would be no further delays.* **2** [U] confidence in your own abilities; SELF-ASSURANCE: *Cindy answered their questions with quiet assurance.*

as·sure /ə'ʃʊəllə'ʃʊr/ v [T] *spoken* to tell someone that something will definitely happen or is definitely true, so that they are less worried: *The document is genuine, I can assure you.* | **assure sb (that)** *The doctor assured me that I wouldn't feel any pain.*

as·sured /ə'ʃʊədllə'ʃʊrd/ adj **1** confident about your abilities: *Kurt seems older now and more assured.* **2** certain to be achieved: *A Republican victory seemed assured.* **3 be/feel assured of sth** to feel certain that something will happen or will be achieved: *People can no longer feel assured of regular employment.* —**assuredly** /ə'ʃʊərɪdllə'ʃʊr-/ adv

as·te·risk /'æstərɪsk/ n [C] a mark like a star (*) used to show that there is a note about a particular word or phrase

asth·ma /'æsməll'æzmə/ n [U] an illness that causes difficulties in breathing —**asthmatic** /æs'mætɪkllæz-/ adj

as·ton·ish /ə'stɒnɪʃllə'stɑː-/ v [T] to surprise someone very much: *Martina's speed and agility astonished her opponent.*

as·ton·ished /ə'stɒnɪʃtllə'stɑː-/ adj very surprised: **+ at/by** *We were quite astonished at her ignorance.*

as·ton·ish·ing /ə'stɒnɪʃɪŋllə'stɑː-/ adj very surprising: *an astonishing £5 million profit* —**astonishingly** adv

as·ton·ish·ment /ə'stɒnɪʃməntllə'stɑː-/ n [U] complete surprise: **to sb's astonishment** *To our astonishment, Sue won the race.* | **in astonishment** *"What are you doing here?" she cried in astonishment.*

as·tound /ə'staʊnd/ v [T] to make someone feel extremely surprised or shocked: *Berger's fans were astounded by his decision to quit.*

as·tound·ing /ə'staʊndɪŋ/ adj extremely surprising or shocking: *astounding news* —**astoundingly** adv

a·stray /ə'streɪ/ adv **1 go astray** to become lost: *One of the documents we sent them has gone astray.* **2 lead sb astray** *often humorous* to encourage someone to do bad or immoral things: *Mom worried that I'd be led astray by the older girls.*

a·stride /ə'straɪd/ adv, prep with one leg on each side of something: *She was sitting astride her bicycle.*

as·trol·o·gy /ə'strɒlədʒi‖ə'strɑː-/ n [U] the study of the movements of the planets and stars based on the belief that they influence people's lives —**astrologer** n [C] —**astrological** /ˌæstrə-'lɒdʒɪkəl ‖-'lɑː-/ adj

as·tro·naut /'æstrənɔːt‖-nɒːt, -nɑːt/ n [C] someone who travels in a SPACECRAFT

as·tro·nom·i·cal /ˌæstrə'nɒmɪkəl ‖-'nɑː-/ adj **1** especially spoken astronomical prices or costs are extremely high **2** connected with the study of the stars —**astronomically** /-kli/ adv

as·tron·o·my /ə'strɒnəmi‖ə'strɑː-/ n [U] the scientific study of the stars and planets —**astronomer** n [C]

as·tute /ə'stjuːt‖ə'stuːt/ adj clever and quick to understand how to get an advantage from a situation —**astuteness** n [U] —**astutely** adv

a·sy·lum /ə'saɪləm/ n **1** [U] protection that a government gives to people who have left their own country for political reasons **2** [C] old-fashioned a hospital for people with mental illnesses

at /ət; strong æt/ prep **1** used to say where someone or something is: Meet me at my house. ➡ see colour picture on page 474 **2** used to say when something happens: The movie starts at 8:00. | A lot of people get lonely at Christmas. **3** used to say that an action is directed towards someone or something: Jake shot at the deer but missed. | Stop shouting at me! **4** because of someone or something: None of the kids laughed at his joke. | Jenny, I'm surprised at you! **5** good/bad at able or not able to do something well: Debbie's always been good at learning languages. **6** used to say what the price, speed, level etc of something is: Gas is selling at about $1.25 a gallon. ➡ see also **at all** (ALL[1]), **at first** (FIRST[1]), **at least** (LEAST[1])

ate /et,eɪt/ v the past tense of EAT

a·the·ist /'eɪθi-ɪst/ n [C] someone who does not believe in God ➡ compare AGNOSTIC —**atheism** n [U]

ath·lete /'æθliːt/ n [C] someone who is good at sports, especially running

ath·let·ic /æθ'letɪk, əθ-/ adj **1** physically strong and good at sport **2** connected with athletes or athletics: He has plenty of athletic ability.

ath·let·ics /æθ'letɪks, əθ-/ n [U] **1** BrE sports such as running races and jumping; TRACK AND FIELD AmE **2** AmE sports and physical exercise in general: high school athletics ➡ see colour picture on page 636

at·las /'ætləs/ n [C] a book of maps

ATM /ˌeɪ tiː 'em/ n [C] especially AmE Automated Teller Machine; a machine that you get money from; CASHPOINT BrE

at·mo·sphere /'ætməsfɪə‖-fɪr/ n **1** [singular] the kind of feeling or quality that a place or situation seems to have: a hotel with a relaxed, friendly atmosphere **2** **the atmosphere** the mixture of gases that surrounds the Earth **3** [singular] the air inside a room: a smoky atmosphere

at·mo·spher·ic /ˌætməs'ferɪk/ adj **1** beautiful and mysterious: atmospheric music **2** relating to the Earth's atmosphere: atmospheric temperature

at·om /'ætəm/ n [C] the smallest part that a substance can be divided into

a·tom·ic /ə'tɒmɪk‖ə'tɑː-/ adj **1** relating to atoms: atomic structure **2** using the power that is produced by splitting atoms: atomic weapons

atomic bomb /ˌ.ˌ '.ˌ/ also **atom bomb** /'.. ../ n [C] a very powerful bomb that uses the power made by splitting atoms

atomic en·er·gy /ˌ.ˌ '.../ n [U] the power made by splitting atoms, often used to make electricity

a·tro·cious /ə'trəʊʃəs‖ə'trou-/ adj extremely bad: Your spelling is atrocious! —**atrociously** adv

a·troc·i·ty /ə'trɒsɪti‖ə'trɑː-/ n [C,U] an extremely cruel or violent action: the atrocities of war

at·tach /ə'tætʃ/ v **1** [T] to fasten or join one thing to another: attach sth to sth Please attach a photograph to your application form. | There's a health club attached to the hotel. **2** **attach importance/value/blame etc to sth** to decide that something is important, valuable etc: Don't attach too much importance to what Nick says. **3** **be attached to sth** to join another group or organization especially for a short time: Bowen was attached to the 3rd Army Corps while serving in Northern Ireland.

at·tached /ə'tætʃt/ adj **be attached to** to like someone or something very much: We had become very attached to each other over the years.

at·tach·ment /ə'tætʃmənt/ n **1** [C,U] formal a strong feeling of loyalty, love, or friendship: + to the boy's close emotional attachment to his sister **2** [C] a part that you fasten to a piece of equipment to make it do different things: an electric drill with a screwdriver attachment

at·tack[1] /ə'tæk/ v **1** [I,T] to use violence against a person or place: Police are hunting a man who attacked a 15-year-old girl. | The town was attacked by the rebel army. **2** [T] to criticize someone or something strongly: attack sb for doing sth Several newspapers attacked the President for not doing enough. **3** [T] if a disease attacks something it damages it: The AIDS virus attacks the body's immune system. **4** [I,T] to kick or throw a ball forward during a game in order to get a GOAL or point —**attacker** n [C]

attack[2] n **1** [C,U] a violent action that is intended to harm someone or something: Coleman was the victim of a vicious attack. | + on a terrorist attack on a British army base | **be/come under attack** (=be attacked) **2** [C,U] strong criticism: + on an attack on the government's welfare policy **3** [C] a sudden short period of illness or nervousness: + of a severe attack of fever **4** [C] the players in a game such as football who try to get points ➡ see also HEART ATTACK

at·tack·er /ə'tækə‖-ər/ n [C] someone who physically attacks someone else: She was able to give the police a good description of her attacker. | a sex attacker

at·tain /ə'teɪn/ v [T] to achieve something after trying for a long time: More women are attaining high positions in business. —**attainment** n [C,U] the attainment of our objectives —**attainable** adj

at·tempt[1] /ə'tempt/ v [T] to try to do something that is difficult or dangerous: The second question was so difficult I didn't even attempt it. | **attempt to do sth** Marsh was accused of attempting to import the drugs illegally.

attempt² n [C] when you try to do something: **attempt to do sth** So far, all attempts to resolve the problem have failed. | **make no attempt** (=not try): He made no attempt to hide his anger. | + **at** It was an attempt at humour, but nobody laughed.

at·tend /ə'tend/ v [I,T] formal to go to a meeting, school, church etc: More than 2000 people are expected to attend this year's conference. | All students must attend classes regularly.

attend to sb/sth phr v [T] formal to deal with something or someone: I have some urgent business to attend to.

at·tend·ance /ə'tendəns/ n [C,U] **1** the number of people who attend an event, such as a meeting, concert etc: Church attendances have fallen in recent years. **2** when someone goes regularly to a school, church etc: + **at** A child's attendance at school is required by law.

at·tend·ant /ə'tendənt/ n [C] someone whose job is to take care of a public place and deal with customers: a parking lot attendant

at·ten·tion /ə'tenʃən/ n [U] **1** when you watch, listen to, or think about something: Can I have your attention, please. (=please listen) | + **to** Her work shows great attention to detail. | **pay attention (to sth)** (=listen, watch etc): I wish you'd pay attention when I'm giving instructions. | **attract/get sb's attention** (=make someone notice you): Phil was trying to attract the waiter's attention. | **draw attention to sth** (=make people notice it): a report that drew attention to the problem of water pollution → see also **undivided attention** (UNDIVIDED) **2** the interest that people show in someone or something: **attract attention** Rohmer's latest movie has attracted considerable attention from the critics. | **the centre of attention** (=the person that everyone is interested in): Johnny enjoyed being the centre of attention. **3** special care or treatment: patients requiring urgent medical attention **4** **stand at/to attention** to stand up straight like a soldier

at·ten·tive /ə'tentɪv/ adj **1** listening or watching carefully: an attentive audience **2** making sure that someone has everything they need: an attentive host — **attentively** adv

at·tic /'ætɪk/ n [C] a room at the top of a house → see colour picture on page 79

at·ti·tude /'ætɪ̩tjuːd‖-tuːd/ n **1** [C,U] what you think and feel about something: I don't understand your attitude. Why don't you trust her? | + **to/towards** He has a very old-fashioned attitude towards women. **2** [U] informal if someone or something has attitude, they seem exciting and unusual and full of confidence, and do not seem to care what other people think about them: a band with attitude

at·tor·ney /ə'tɜːni‖-ɜːr-/ n [C] AmE a lawyer

at·tract /ə'trækt/ v [T] **1** to make someone like something or feel interested in it: I was attracted by the idea of living on a desert island. | **attract sb to sth** What was it that attracted you to the job? | **attract attention** Diana's visit to Washington attracted massive media attention. **2** **be attracted to sb** to like someone in a sexual way: I've always been attracted to blondes. **3** if something attracts people or things it makes them move towards it: Left-over food attracts flies.

at·trac·tion /ə'trækʃən/ n **1** [C] something that attracts people because it is interesting or enjoyable: Elvis Presley's home has become a major tourist attraction. | One of the attractions of being single is that you can go out with whoever you like. **2** [C,U] when one person is attracted to another because they like them very much: sexual attraction

at·trac·tive /ə'træktɪv/ adj **1** pretty or pleasant to look at: an attractive young woman **2** good enough to make people interested: an attractive salary — **attractively** adv

at·tri·bute¹ /ə'trɪbjuːt‖-bjət/ v

attribute sth to sb/sth phr v [T] **1** to say that a situation or event was caused by something: The increase in crime can be attributed to social changes. **2** to say that something was written, said, or made by a particular person: a painting attributed to Rembrandt — **attributable** adj

at·tri·bute² /'ætrɪ̩bjuːt/ n [C] a good or useful quality: What attributes should a good manager possess?

au·ber·gine /'əʊbəʒiːn‖'oʊbər-/ n [C] BrE a large dark purple vegetable; EGGPLANT AmE → see picture at VEGETABLE

au·burn /'ɔːbən‖'ɔːbərn/ adj auburn hair is a reddish brown colour → see colour picture on page 244

auc·tion /'ɔːkʃən‖'ɒːk-/ n [C] an event at which things are sold to the person who offers the most money — **auction** v [T]

auc·tio·neer /ˌɔːkʃə'nɪə‖ˌɒːkʃə'nɪr/ n [C] someone who is in charge of an auction

au·dac·i·ty /ɔː'dæsɪ̩ti‖ɒː-/ n [U] brave or shocking behaviour: **have the audacity to do sth** (=do something that seems shocking, especially something very annoying that you should not do): I can't believe he had the audacity to ask for more money. — **audacious** /ɔː'deɪʃəs‖ɒː-/ adj

au·di·ble /'ɔːdɪ̩bəl‖'ɒː-/ adj loud enough to be heard: Her voice was barely audible. — **audibly** adv — opposite INAUDIBLE

au·di·ence /'ɔːdiəns‖'ɒː-, 'ɑː-/ n [C] **1** the people who watch or listen to a performance: The audience began clapping and cheering. **2** a formal meeting with someone who is very important: an audience with the Pope

au·di·o /'ɔːdiəʊ‖'ɒːdioʊ/ adj for recording and broadcasting sound: audio tapes

au·di·o·vis·u·al /ˌɔːdiəʊ'vɪʒuəl‖ˌɒːdioʊ-/ adj using recorded pictures and sound: audiovisual equipment for language teaching

au·dit /'ɔːdɪt‖'ɒː-/ n [C] when someone officially examines a company's financial records to check that they are correct — **audit** v [T] — **auditor** n [C]

au·di·tion /ɔː'dɪʃən‖ɒː-/ n [C] a short performance by an actor, singer etc to test whether he or she is good enough to perform in a play, concert etc — **audition** v [I,T]

au·di·to·ri·um /ˌɔːdɪ̩'tɔːriəm‖ˌɒː-/ n [C] the part of a theatre where people sit to watch a performance

aug·ment /ɔːg'ment‖ɒːg-/ v [T] formal to increase something by adding to it

au·gur /'ɔːgə‖'ɒːgər/ v **augur well/ill** formal to be a sign that something good or bad will happen in the future

Au·gust /ˈɔːgəstǁˈɔː-/ written abbreviation **Aug** n [C,U] the eighth month of the year → see Usage Note at MONTH

aunt /ɑːntǁænt/ also **aunt·ie** /ˈɑːntiǁˈæn-/ informal — n [C] the sister of your father or mother, or the wife of your UNCLE → see picture at FAMILY

au pair /əʊ ˈpeəǁoʊ ˈper/ n [C] a young woman who stays with a family in a foreign country and looks after their children

au·ra /ˈɔːrə/ n [C] a quality or feeling that seems to come from a person or place: *Inside the church there was an aura of complete tranquillity.*

au·ral /ˈɔːrəl/ adj relating to the sense of hearing: *aural skills* → compare ORAL[1]

aus·pic·es /ˈɔːspɪsəzǁˈɔː-/ **under the auspices of** formal with the help and support of an organization: *The research was done under the auspices of Harvard Medical School.*

aus·pi·cious /ɔːˈspɪʃəsǁɒː-/ adj formal an auspicious time or event makes you expect success in the future → opposite INAUSPICIOUS

aus·tere /ɔːˈstɪə, ɒ-ǁɒːˈstɪr/ adj **1** plain and simple and without decoration: *an austere style of painting* **2** very strict and serious: *a cold, austere woman* **3** without comfort or enjoyment: *Life in the monastery was austere.*

aus·ter·i·ty /ɔːˈsterɪti, ɒ-ǁɒː-/ n [U] bad economic conditions in which people do not have enough money to live: *the austerity of the postwar years*

au·then·tic /ɔːˈθentɪkǁɒː-/ adj something that is authentic really is what it seems to be: *authentic Indian food | an authentic Picasso painting* —**authentically** /-kli/ adj —**authenticity** /ˌɔːθenˈtɪsɪti/ n [U]

au·thor /ˈɔːθəǁˈɒːθər/ n [C] someone who writes a book, article etc: *Robert Louis Stevenson, the author of 'Treasure Island'*

au·thor·i·tar·i·an /ɔːˌθɒrɪˈteəriənǁɒːˌθɑːrɪˈter-, ə,θɒːˈ-/ adj forcing people to obey strict rules or laws and not allowing any freedom: *an authoritarian regime*

au·thor·i·ta·tive /ɔːˈθɒrɪtətɪv, ə-ǁəˈθɑːrəteɪtɪv, əˈθɒː-/ adj **1** an authoritative book, statement etc is trusted because it is written by someone who knows a lot about a subject: *an authoritative textbook on European history* **2** seeming confident and able to control a situation: *The captain spoke in a calm and authoritative voice.* —**authoritatively** adv

au·thor·i·ty /ɔːˈθɒrɪti, ə-ǁəˈθɑː-, əˈθɒː-/ n **1** [U] the power or right to make important decisions and control people: **the authority to do sth** *Every manager has the authority to dismiss employees.* **|+ over** *Some parents appear to have no authority over their children.* **|in authority** (=in a powerful position): *You should write and complain to someone in authority.* **2** [C] an organization or government department that makes official decisions and controls public services: *the local education authority | the author-*

ities British police are co-operating with the Malaysian authorities. **3** [C] someone who is respected because of their knowledge about a subject: **+ on** *Dr Ballard is an authority on tropical diseases.*

au·thor·ize (also **-ise** BrE) /ˈɔːθəraɪzǁˈɒː-/ v [T] to give official permission to do something: *Who authorized the payments into Maclean's account? | Only senior officers were authorized to handle secret documents.* —**authorization** (also **-isation** BrE) /ˌɔːθəraɪˈzeɪʃənǁˌɒːθərə-/ n [C,U]

au·tis·tic /ɔːˈtɪstɪkǁɒː-/ adj autistic children have a mental illness that prevents them communicating with other people

au·to·bi·og·ra·phy /ˌɔːtəbaɪˈɒgrəfiǁˌɒːtəbaɪˈɑː-/ n [C] a book that someone writes about their own life —**autobiographical** /ˌɔːtəbaɪəˈgræfɪkəlǁˌɒː-/ adj

au·to·graph /ˈɔːtəgrɑːfǁˈɒːtəgræf/ n [C] if a famous person gives you their autograph, they sign their name on something for you —**autograph** v [T] *an autographed picture*

au·to·ma·ted /ˈɔːtəmeɪtɪdǁˈɒː-/ adj an automated system, process, factory etc uses machines: *a fully automated telephone system* —**automation** /ˌɔːtəˈmeɪʃənǁɒː-/ n [U]

au·to·mat·ic[1] /ˌɔːtəˈmætɪkǁˌɒː-/ adj **1** an automatic machine is designed to work by itself without much human control: *an automatic camera* **2** certain to happen because of a rule or system: *We get an automatic pay increase every year.* **3** done without thinking: *an automatic reaction* —**automatically** /-kli/ adv: *You shouldn't automatically assume that your teacher is right.*

automatic[2] n [C] **1** a car with a system of GEARS that operate themselves **2** a gun that shoots bullets continuously

au·to·ma·tion /ˌɔːtəˈmeɪʃənǁɒː-/ n [U] the use of machines to do work, instead of people —**automated** /ˈɔːtəmeɪtɪdǁˈɒː-/ adj

au·to·mo·bile /ˈɔːtəməbiːlǁˈɒːtəmoʊ-/ n [C] AmE a car

au·ton·o·mous /ɔːˈtɒnəməsǁɒːˈtɑː-/ adj having the power to make independent decisions or rules: *an autonomous state* —**autonomy** n [U] *political autonomy*

au·top·sy /ˈɔːtɒpsiǁˈɒːtɑːp-/ n [C] an official examination of a dead body to discover why the person has died

au·tumn /ˈɔːtəmǁˈɒː-/ n [C,U] the season when the leaves fall off the trees; FALL AmE —**autumnal** /ɔːˈtʌmnəlǁɒː-/ adj

aux·il·ia·ry /ɔːgˈzɪljəri, ɔːk-ǁɒːgˈzɪljəri, -ˈzɪləri/ adj giving additional help or support: *auxiliary nurses* —**auxiliary** n [C]

auxiliary verb /ˌ...ˈ.../ n [C] a verb used with another verb to form questions, negative sentences, and tenses. In English the auxiliary verbs are 'be', 'do', 'have'.

a·vail[1] /əˈveɪl/ n **to no avail/of no avail** formal without success: *They had searched everywhere, but to no avail.*

GRAMMAR NOTE: the passive (1)

You use a verb in the **passive** to say that something happens to the subject of the sentence. You form the passive using **be/is/was** and the past participle.

ACTIVE: *They **chose** a new leader.* → PASSIVE: *A new leader **was chosen**.*

avail² v **avail yourself of sth** formal to accept an offer or use an opportunity: Students should avail themselves of every opportunity to improve their English.

a·vai·la·ble /ə'veɪləbəl/ adj **1** if something is available, you can get it, buy it, or use it: 'The Lion King' is available now on video for only £12.99! | **+ for** land available for development **2** if someone is available, you can go and talk to them because they are not busy: Dr Wright is not available at the moment. —**availability** /ə,veɪlə'bɪlɪti/ n [U]

av·a·lanche /'ævəlɑːnʃ‖-læntʃ/ n [C] **1** a large amount of snow that falls down the side of a mountain **2 an avalanche of** a very large number of things that happen or arrive at the same time: An avalanche of letters came in from admiring fans.

av·ant garde /,ævɒːŋ 'gɑːd‖,ævɑːŋ 'gɑːrd◂/ adj avant-garde literature, music, art etc is very modern and different from existing styles: an avant-garde film

av·a·rice /'ævərɪs/ n [U] formal an extreme desire for wealth; GREED —**avaricious** /,ævə'rɪʃəs◂/ adj

a·venge /ə'vendʒ/ v [T] literary to punish someone because they have harmed you or your family: He wanted to avenge his brother's death.

av·e·nue /'ævɪnjuː‖-nuː/ n [C] **1** also **Avenue** a road in a town: Fifth Avenue **2** a possible way of achieving something: We need to explore every avenue if we want to find a solution.

av·er·age¹ /'ævərɪdʒ/ adj **1** [only before noun] the average amount is the amount you get by adding several quantities together and then dividing the result by the number of quantities: The average temperature in July is around 35°C. **2** [only before noun] an average person or thing is a typical example of a person or of a type of thing: What does the average worker in Britain earn a month? **3** not very good but not very bad: I didn't think it was a great movie — just average really.

average² n **1** [C] the amount that you get by adding several quantities together and then dividing the result by the number of quantities: **+ of** House prices have risen by an average of 2%. **2 on average** based on a calculation of what usually happens: We spend, on average, around £40 a week on food. **3 above/below average** higher or lower than the usual level or amount: students of above average ability

average³ v [T] to be or do a particular amount as an average: The train travelled at speeds averaging 125 mph.
average out phr v [I] to result in a particular average amount: Our weekly profits average out at about $750.

a·verse /ə'vɜːs‖-ɜːrs/ adj **not be averse to** formal or humorous willing to do or enjoy something: Charles was not averse to the occasional cigar.

a·ver·sion /ə'vɜːʃən‖ə'vɜːrʒən/ n **have an aversion to sth** to not like something: She has an aversion to cats.

a·vert /ə'vɜːt‖-ɜːrt/ v [T] **1** to prevent something unpleasant from happening: negotiations aimed at averting a crisis **2 avert your eyes/gaze** to look away from something

a·vi·a·ry /'eɪviərɪ‖'eɪvieri/ n [C] a large CAGE where birds are kept

a·vi·a·tion /,eɪvi'eɪʃən‖,eɪ-, ,æ-/ n [U] the activity of flying or making aircraft

av·id /'ævɪd/ adj eager: an avid reader of romantic novels —**avidly** adv

av·o·ca·do /,ævə'kɑːdəʊ‖-doʊ/ n [C,U] a fruit with a thick green or dark purple skin that is green inside and has a large seed in the middle

a·void /ə'vɔɪd/ v [T] **1** to make sure that something bad does not happen: You can avoid a lot of problems by using traveller's cheques. **2** to deliberately stay away from someone or something: I have the impression John's trying to avoid us. **3 avoid doing sth** to deliberately not do something: It's best to avoid going out in the strong midday sun. —**avoidance** n [U] —**avoidable** adj

a·wait /ə'weɪt/ v [T] formal **1** to wait for something: Briggs is awaiting trial for murder. **2** if a situation or event awaits someone, it is going to happen to them: A warm welcome awaits you.

a·wake¹ /ə'weɪk/ adj **be/lie/stay etc awake** to not be sleeping: I lay awake, worrying about my exams. | **keep sb awake** The storm kept us awake all night. | **wide awake** (=completely awake)

awake² v awoke /ə'wəʊk‖ə'woʊk/, awoken /ə'wəʊkən‖ə'woʊ-/, awaking [I,T] literary to wake up or to make someone wake up: She awoke the following morning feeling refreshed.

a·wak·en /ə'weɪkən/ v formal **1** [T] to make someone have a sudden feeling: Several strange events had already occurred to awaken our suspicions. **2** [I,T] to wake up or make someone wake up
awaken to sth phr v [T] formal to begin to realize something: People were awakening to the fact that the communist system was failing.

a·wak·en·ing /ə'weɪkənɪŋ/ n [singular, U] when you suddenly start to realize a fact or experience a feeling: the awakening of her mind to social realities

a·ward¹ /ə'wɔːd‖-ɔːrd/ v [T] to officially give someone a prize or money: **be awarded sth** Einstein was awarded the Nobel Prize for his work in physics.

award² n [C] **1** a prize that someone gets for something that they have achieved: Susan Sarandon won the 'Best Actress' award. **2** an amount of money that is given to someone because of a judge's decision: Hemmings received an award of $300,000 in compensation.

a·ware /ə'weə‖ə'wer/ adj **1** knowing about or realizing something: **+ of** Most smokers are aware of the dangers of smoking. | **+ that** I suddenly became aware that someone was moving around downstairs. **2** knowing about and interested in something: This class isn't really politically aware. ➔ opposite UNAWARE —**awareness** n [U]

a·wash /ə'wɒʃ‖ə'wɔːʃ, ə'wɑːʃ/ adj **1** covered with water: streets awash with flood water **2 awash with** having too much of something: Hollywood is awash with rumours.

a·way¹ /ə'weɪ/ adv **1** moving further from a place, or staying far from a place: Go away! | Diane drove away quickly. | **+ from** away from the fire! ➔ see colour picture on page 474 **2** at a particular distance from a place: The *sea is only five miles away.* **3** into a safe place: *Put all your toys away now, please.* **4** not at home or in your usual place of work: *Will you look after the house while I'm away?* **5 2 days/ 3 weeks etc away** at a particular time in the future: *Christmas is only a month away.* **6** used to say that something gradually disappears: *All the water had boiled away.* **7** without stopping: *He's been working away on the patio all day.* **8** if a team plays away, they play at their opponent's STADIUM → see also **right away** (RIGHT²)

away² *adj* **away game/match** a sports game that is played at your opponent's STADIUM → opposite HOME¹

awe /ɔːr/ *n* [U] a feeling of great admiration and sometimes fear: **in/with awe** *She gazed with awe at the breathtaking landscape.* | **be in awe of sb** (=respect someone and be slightly afraid of them)

awe·in·spir·ing /ˈ. .ˌ../ *adj* very impressive and making you feel a lot of respect or admiration: *an awe-inspiring achievement*

awe·some /ˈɔːsəmǁˈɔː-/ *adj* very impressive, often in a way that is frightening: *an awesome responsibility*

aw·ful /ˈɔːfəlǁˈɒː-/ *adj* **1** very bad or unpleasant: *What awful weather!* | *This soup tastes awful!* **2 an awful lot (of)** *spoken* very much or very many: *It's going to cost an awful lot of money.*

aw·ful·ly /ˈɔːfəliǁˈɒː-/ *adv spoken* very: *I'm awfully sorry – I didn't mean to disturb you.*

awk·ward /ˈɔːkwədǁˈɒːkwərd/ *adj* **1** difficult to deal with: *Let's hope they don't ask too many awkward questions.* **2** embarrassed and shy: *He*

stood in a corner, looking awkward and self-conscious.* **3** deliberately unhelpful: *I wish you'd stop being so awkward!* **4** difficult to use, hold, or carry: *This camera's rather awkward to use.* —**awkwardly** *adv* —**awkwardness** *n* [U]

a·woke /əˈwəʊkǁəˈwoʊk/ *v* the past tense of AWAKE

a·wok·en /əˈwəʊkənǁəˈwoʊ-/ *v* the past participle of AWAKE

a·wry /əˈraɪ/ *adj, adv* **1 go awry** to not happen in the way that was planned: *All their plans had gone awry.* **2** not in the correct place or position: *He was walking unsteadily, with his hat awry.*

axe¹ also **ax** *AmE* /æks/ *n* [C] a tool used for cutting wood, with a wooden handle and a metal blade

axe² also **ax** *AmE v* [T] *informal* to suddenly get rid of or reduce jobs, services, or costs: *The company has announced it's decision to axe 700 jobs.*

ax·is /ˈæksɪs/ *n* [C], *plural* **axes** /ˈæksiːz/ **1** the imaginary line or pole around which something turns, for example the Earth **2** a line at the side or bottom of a GRAPH, used for marking measurements

ax·le /ˈæksəl/ *n* [C] the bar that connects two wheels on a vehicle

aye /aɪ/ *adv spoken informal* a word meaning 'yes', used especially in Scotland and the North of England

az·ure /ˈæʒə, ˈæʒjʊə, ˈæzjʊəlǁˈæʒər/ *adj, n* [U] bright blue

Bb

B, b /biː/ *n* [C] the letter 'b'

B&B /ˌbiː ənd 'biː/ *n* [C] the abbreviation of BED AND BREAKFAST

BA, B.A. /ˌbiː 'eɪ/ *n* [C] Bachelor of Arts; a university degree in a subject such as history or literature → see also BSC

baa /baː/ *v* [I] if a sheep baas, it makes a long loud sound —**baa** *n* [C]

bab·ble /'bæbəl/ *v* [I] to talk quickly in a way that is stupid or difficult to understand: *What are you babbling on about?* —**babble** *n* [U]

babe /beɪb/ *n* [C] *literary* a baby

ba·boon /bə'buːn‖bæ-/ *n* [C] a large monkey

ba·by /'beɪbi/ *n* **1** [C] a very young child who has not yet learned to talk: *A baby was crying upstairs.* | *a baby girl* | **have a baby** (=give birth to a baby): *Has Sue had her baby yet?* **2** *AmE spoken* a way of speaking to someone you love: *Bye, baby. I'll be back by six.* **3** **a baby bird/rabbit/elephant etc** a very young animal

baby car·riage /'... ˌ../ also **baby bug·gy** /'.. ˌ../ *n* [C] *AmE* a thing on wheels that you put a baby in and push along; PRAM *BrE*

ba·by·ish /'beɪbi-ɪʃ/ *adj* silly, unsuitable and like something a baby would do, use etc: *We were taught that it was babyish for a boy to cry.*

ba·by·sitter /'beɪbiˌsɪtəl-ər/ *n* [C] someone who looks after children while their parents go out for a short time —**babysitting** *n* [U] *I earn some extra money from babysitting.* —**babysit** *v* [I,T]

bach·e·lor /'bætʃələl-ər/ *n* **1** [C] a man who is not married **2** **Bachelor of Arts/Science/Education etc** the title of a first university degree

bachelor's de·gree /'... ˌ../ *n* [C] a first university degree

back

John's shirt is on back to front *BrE* / backwards *AmE*

They stood back to back

back¹ /bæk/ *n* **1** [C] **a)** the part of your body between the back of your shoulders and your bottom: *My back was really aching.* **b)** the bones that go from your neck to your bottom: *He broke his back in a motorcycle accident.* **2** [C,

usually singular] the part of something that is furthest from or behind the direction that it faces: **the back of** *We climbed into the back of the truck.* | *Joe's somewhere at the back of the hall.* | **in back of** *AmE* (=where the back of something is): *The pool's in back of the house.* | **out back** *AmE* (=behind a building): *Tom's working on the car out back.* → opposite FRONT¹ **3** the part of a seat that you rest your back against when you are sitting: **the back of** *He rested his arm on the back of the sofa.* **4** **back to front** *BrE* in a position so that the front is where the back should be: *You've got your sweater on back to front.* **5** **behind sb's back** without someone knowing, especially about something unkind you are saying about them: *They're always talking about her behind her back.* **6** **be at/in the back of your mind** if something is at the back of your mind, you are always thinking about it a little: *There was always a slight fear in the back of his mind.* **7** **get off my back!** *spoken* said when you want someone to stop telling you to do something: *I'll do it in a minute. Just get off my back!* **8** **be on sb's back** *spoken* to keep telling someone to do something, or to keep criticizing them, so they get annoyed: *The boss has been on my back about being late.* **9** **have your back to/against the wall** *informal* to be in a very difficult situation → see also **turn your back on** (TURN¹)

back² *adv* **1** where someone or something was before: *Put the milk back in the refrigerator.* | *Roger said he'd be back in an hour.* **2** in or into the condition that someone or something was in before: *I woke up at 5 a.m. and couldn't get back to sleep.* **3** in the direction that is behind you: *Harry looked back to see if he was still being followed.* **4** as a reply or reaction to what someone has done: *Can you call me back later?* | *Gina smiled, and the boy smiled back.* **5** away from the front of something or away from a person or thing: *Her hair was pulled back in a ponytail.* **6** in or towards an earlier time: *This all happened about three years back.* **7** **back and forth** in one direction and then in the opposite direction: *He walked back and forth across the floor.*

back³ *v* **1** [T] to support someone or something, especially by using your money or power: *The bill is backed by several environmental groups.* **2** [I,T] to move in the direction that is behind you, or to make a vehicle move in this way: *We slowly backed away from the snake.* | *Teresa backed the car down the driveway.* **3** [T] to BET that a horse, team etc will win something so that you get money if they do: *Who did you back to win the Superbowl?*

back down *phr v* [I] to accept that you have lost or to admit that you are wrong: *Rosen backed down when he saw how big the other guy was.*

back off *phr v* [I] **1** to move away from something: *Back off a little, you're too close.* **2** *spoken, especially AmE* used to tell someone to stop annoying you: *Back off! I don't need your advice.*

back onto sth *phr v* [T] if a building backs onto a place, the back of the building is near it: *The houses back onto a busy road.*

back out *phr v* [I] to decide not to do something that you had promised to do: *They backed out of the deal at the last minute.*

back up *phr v* **1** [T **back** sb/sth ↔ **up**] to support what someone is doing or saying, or show that it is true: *He had evidence on video to back up his claim.* **2** [I,T **back** sth ↔ **up**] to make a copy of information on a computer **3** [I,T **back** sth ↔ **up**] to make a car go backwards

back [4] *adj* **1** in the back or behind something: *the back door | in the back garden* **2 back street/road** a street or road that is away from the main streets of a town or area **3 back rent/taxes/pay** money that someone owes from an earlier date: *We owe £350 in back rent.*

back·ache /'bækeɪk/ *n* [C,U] pain in your back

back·bone /'bækbəʊnǁ-boʊn/ *n* **1 the backbone of** the most important part of something: *The cocoa industry is the backbone of Ghana's economy.* **2** [C] the bone down the middle of your back; SPINE **3** [U] courage and determination

back·break·ing /'. ,../ *adj* backbreaking work is very difficult and tiring

back·date /,bæk'deɪtǁ'bækdeɪt/ *v* [T] to make something have its effect from an earlier date: *a pay increase backdated to January*

back·drop /'bækdrɒpǁ-drɑːp/ *n* [C] **1** the conditions or situation in which something happens, which help to explain it: *The Spanish Civil War was the backdrop for Orwell's novel.* **2** also **backcloth** the painted cloth behind a stage

back·er /'bækəǁ-ər/ *n* [C] someone who supports a plan, organization etc, especially by providing money: *We need backers for the festival.*

back·fire /,bæk'faɪəǁ'bækfaɪr/ *v* [I] if something you do backfires, it has an effect that is the opposite of what you wanted

back·gam·mon /'bækgæmən/ *n* [U] a game for two players, using flat round pieces and DICE on a board

back·ground /'bækgraʊnd/ *n* **1** [C] the type of education, experience, and family that someone has: *The kids here have very different backgrounds. | He has a background in Computer Science.* **2 in the background a)** sounds, people, things etc that are in the background are not the main ones that you can see or hear: *In the background you can see the school. | the sound of traffic in the background* **b)** someone who stays in the background tries not to be noticed: *A waiter stood quietly in the background.* **3** [singular, U] a BACKDROP —**background** *adj*

back·ing /'bækɪŋ/ *n* **1** [U] support or help, especially by providing money: *financial backing for the project* **2** material used for the back surface of an object

back·lash /'bæklæʃ/ *n* [C] when people start to oppose something that was previously becoming stronger or more popular: *the backlash against feminist ideas*

back·log /'bæklɒgǁ-lɒːg, -lɑːg/ *n* [C, usually singular] work that still needs to be done and should have been done earlier: *a huge backlog of orders from customers*

back·pack[1] /'bækpæk/ *n* [C] a large bag that you carry on your back when you go walking or camping ➜ see picture at BAG

backpack[2] *v* [I] to go walking and camping carrying a backpack —**backpacker** *n* [C] —**backpacking** *n* [U]

back seat /,. '. / *n* [C] **1** the seat in the back of a car **2 take a back seat** to be less involved in an activity than you used to be

back·side /'bæksaɪd/ *n* [C] *informal* the part of your body that you sit on

back·stage /,bæk'steɪdʒ◂/ *adv* in the area behind the stage in a theatre: *There was great excitement backstage.* —**backstage** *adj: a backstage pass* (=that allows you to go backstage in a theatre)

back·stroke /'bækstrəʊkǁ-stroʊk/ *n* [singular] a style of swimming on your back

back-to-back /,. .'. / *adj, adv* **1** happening one after the other: *We played two concerts back-to-back.* **2** with the backs of two things or people facing or connected with each other: *They stood back-to-back. | back-to-back houses*

back·track /'bæktræk/ *v* [I] to say something in a less definite way than you did before: *The minister denied that he was backtracking.*

back·up /'bækʌp/ *n* **1** [C] a copy of something that you can use if the original thing is lost or does not work: *Always make backup files at the end of the day.* **2** [C,U] someone or something that provides help or support when it is needed: *Four more police cars provided backup.*

back·ward /'bækwədǁ-wərd/ *adj* **1** towards the direction that is behind you: *a backward glance.* **2** developing more slowly and less successfully than is usual: *a backward child*

backwards /'bækwədzǁ-wərdz/ also **backward** *especially AmE adv* **1** in the direction that is behind you: *She took a step backwards in surprise.* ➜ opposite FORWARD *BrE* **2** in the opposite way to the ususal way: *Can you say the alphabet backwards?* **3** with the front part pointing towards the back: *Your T-shirt is on backwards.* **4 backwards and forwards** first in one direction, then in the opposite direction, many times **5** towards the past ➜ opposite FORWARD *BrE*

back·wa·ter /'bækwɔːtəǁ-wɒːtər, -wɑː-/ *n* [C] a town or place far away from the main cities

back·woods /'bækwʊdz/ *n* [plural] an area in the forest that is far from any towns

back·yard /,bæk'jɑːd◂ǁ-'jɑːrd◂/ *n* [C] **1** *BrE* a small enclosed area behind a house **2** *AmE* an area of grass behind a house

ba·con /'beɪkən/ *n* [U] meat from a pig, often cut into long thin pieces

bac·te·ri·a /bæk'tɪəriəǁ-'tɪr-/ *n* [plural] very small living things, some of which cause disease —**bacterial** *adj*

bad[1] /bæd/ *adj* **worse, worst 1** not good or pleasant: *a bad smell | I'm afraid I have some bad news for you.* **2** low in quality or below an acceptable standard: *He was the worst teacher I*

GRAMMAR NOTE: the progressive
You form the **present progressive** by using **be/is/was** + present participle: *They are coming.*
You form the **past progressive** by using **was/were** + present participle: *He was lying.*

ever had. | **+ at** *Brian is really bad at sports.*
3 be bad for to be harmful: *Too many sweets are bad for your teeth.* | *Smoking is bad for you.*
4 serious or severe: *a bad cold* | *The political situation is getting worse.* **5 not bad** *spoken* used to say that something is fairly good, acceptable, or better than you expected: "*How are you?*" "*Oh, not bad.*" | *The film wasn't bad, actually.*
6 not morally good or not behaving well: *He's not really a bad boy.* **7 too bad** *spoken* **a)** *BrE* used to say that you do not care how someone feels about something: "*I'm late for work!*" "*Too bad, you should have got up earlier!*" **b)** used to say that you are sorry that something unpleasant has happened to someone: *It's too bad she missed all the fun.* **8** *spoken informal* very good or exciting: "*How was the concert?*" "*It was bad!*" **9** food that is bad is not safe to eat because it is not fresh: *The milk has gone bad.*
10 feel bad to feel ashamed or sorry about something: *I felt really bad about missing your birthday.* **11 a bad heart/back/leg etc** permanently injured or not working correctly: *The fever left him with a bad heart.* **12 bad language** swearing or rude words

bad² *adv spoken nonstandard* BADLY

bad debt / ˌ. ˈ. / *n* [C] a debt that is unlikely to ever be paid

bade /bæd, beɪd/ the past tense and past participle of BID

badge /bædʒ/ *n* [C] **a)** a piece of metal, plastic etc that you wear on your clothes that shows which organization you work for: *a sheriff's badge* **b)** *BrE* a piece of metal, plastic etc that you wear on your clothes that has writing or a picture on it; BUTTON *AmE*: *She was wearing a badge that said "I am 4 today!"*

bad·ger /ˈbædʒə‖-ər/ *n* [C] an animal with black and white fur that lives under the ground

bad·ly /ˈbædli/ *adv* **worse** /wɜːs‖wɜːrs/, **worst** /wɜːst‖wɜːrst/ **1** in a way that is not done well: *a badly written book* → opposite WELL² **2** very much or very seriously: *The refugees badly need clean water.* | *badly injured*

bad·min·ton /ˈbædmɪntən/ *n* [U] a game similar to tennis, played by hitting a small object with feathers on it over a net

bad·mouth /ˈbædmaʊθ/ *v* [T] *informal* a disapproving word meaning to say bad things about someone and complain about them: *Emma's always badmouthing him behind his back.*

bad-tem·pered / ˌ. ˈ.. / *adj* easily annoyed: *George seems bad-tempered this morning.*

baf·fle /ˈbæfəl/ *v* [T] if something baffles you, you cannot understand why it happens —**baffling** *adj*

baf·fled /ˈbæfəld/ *adj* unable to understand something at all: *Scientists are completely baffled by the results.*

bag¹ /bæg/ *n* [C] **1** a container made of paper, plastic, cloth etc that opens at the top: *a shopping bag* | *packing a bag for the weekend* **2** *BrE* a bag used by women to carry money and personal things; HANDBAG **3** the amount a bag can hold: *two bags of rice per family* **4 bags of** *spoken, especially BrE* a lot of something: *We've got bags of time. There's no need to rush.* **5 bags under your eyes** dark circles or loose skin under your eyes **6 old bag** an insulting

expression for an unpleasant or unattractive woman

bags

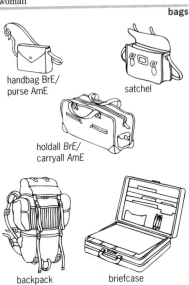

handbag *BrE*/ purse *AmE*

satchel

holdall *BrE*/ carryall *AmE*

backpack

briefcase

bag² *v* [T] **1** to put things in a bag **2** *informal* to manage to get something that a lot of people want: *Try to bag a couple of seats at the front.*

ba·gel /ˈbeɪgəl/ *n* [C] a type of bread that is shaped like a ring

bag·ful /ˈbægful/ *n* [C] the amount a bag can hold

bag·gage /ˈbægɪdʒ/ *n* [U] **1** the bags that you carry when you are travelling; LUGGAGE **2** *informal* the beliefs, opinions, and experiences from your past, that affect the way you think now: *emotional baggage*

bag·gy /ˈbægi/ *adj* baggy clothes are big and loose: *a baggy t-shirt*

bag la·dy / ˈ. ˌ.. / *n* [C] *informal* an offensive word for a woman who has no home and lives in the streets

bag·pipes /ˈbægpaɪps/ *n* [plural] a Scottish musical instrument which is played by forcing air out of a bag through pipes

bail¹ /beɪl/ *n* [U] money paid so that someone can leave prison until their TRIAL: **release sb on bail/grant sb bail** (=let someone out of prison when bail is paid): *Hamilton was released on bail of $50,000.*

bail² *v*

bail out *phr v* **1** [T **bail** sb ↔ **out**] to leave money with a court of law so that someone can leave prison until their TRIAL **2** [T **bail** sb/sth **out**] to do something to help someone out of trouble, especially by giving them money: *You can't expect your parents to bail you out every time you're in debt.* **3** [T **bail** sth ↔ **out**] to remove water from the bottom of a boat **4** *AmE* [I] to escape from a plane using a PARACHUTE; BALE OUT *BrE*

bai·liff /ˈbeɪlɪf/ n [C] **1** BrE someone whose job is to take people's property when they owe money **2** AmE someone whose job is to guard the prisoners in a court of law

bait[1] /beɪt/ n [singular, U] **1** food used to attract fish or animals so that you can catch them **2** something that is given or offered to make someone interested in a product, idea etc

bait[2] v [T] **1** to put food on a hook to catch fish or in a trap to catch animals **2** to laugh at someone or make jokes about them in order to upset them

bake /beɪk/ v [I,T] to make things such as bread and cakes: I'm baking a cake for Laurie.

baked beans /ˌ. ˈ./ n [U] white beans cooked with TOMATO and sold in TINS

bak·er /ˈbeɪkəll-ər/ n [C] **1** someone whose job is to make bread, cakes etc **2** baker's BrE a shop that sells bread, cakes etc

bak·er·y /ˈbeɪkəri/ n [C] a place where bread, cakes etc are made or sold

bal·ance[1] /ˈbæləns/ n **1** [U] when your weight is evenly spread so that you are steady: **lose your balance** (=be unable to stay steady): Billy lost his balance and fell. | **off balance** (=unable to stay steady): I was still off balance when he hit me again. **2** [singular, U] when two equal or opposite things are treated as though they are equally important: We need more balance in political reporting. | **strike a balance between** (=make sure that two things have equal importance): Parents have to strike a balance between protecting their children and allowing them to be independent. **3** [singular, U] when different things can exist together without one part affecting the other too much: the balance between the separate branches of government | the balance of nature **4** **the balance** the amount of something such as money that remains after some has been used or spent: What's the balance on my credit card? **5** **be/hang in the balance** to be in a situation where the result of something could be good or bad: The whole future of Bosnia hangs in the balance. **6** [C] technical a piece of equipment for weighing things **7** **on balance** used to tell someone your opinion after considering all the facts: I think on balance I prefer the new system.

bal·ance[2] v **1** [T] to give the right amount of importance to two or more things: A working parent has to balance family life and career. **2** [I,T] to get into a steady position, without falling to one side or the other, or to put something in this position: You have to learn to balance when you ride a bicycle. **3** [I,T] **balance the books/budget** to make sure that you do not spend more than you have available: Congress is attempting to balance the budget. **4** [T] to consider one thing in relation to something else: **balance sth against** Our rights have to be balanced against our responsibilities.

bal·anced /ˈbælənst/ adj **1** giving equal and fair attention to all sides: a balanced picture of the issues **2** including a good mixture of all the things that are needed: a balanced diet

balance of pay·ments /ˌ... ˈ../ also **balance of trade** /ˌ... ˈ./ n [singular] especially BrE the amount of money that a country earns from selling goods and services abroad, compared to the amount that it spends

balance of pow·er /ˌ... ˈ../ n **the balance of power** the way in which power is divided between the members of a group of people, countries, or organizations: a shift in the balance of power

balance sheet /ˈ.. ./ n [C] a written statement of everything that a company spends, owes, or owns

bal·co·ny /ˈbælkəni/ n [C] **1** a small area outside an upstairs window, where you can sit or stand → see colour picture on page 79 **2** the seats upstairs in a theatre

bald /bɔːldllbɔːld/ adj **1** having little or no hair on your head → see colour picture on page 244 **2** not having enough of the substance that normally covers the surface of something: bald tyres —**baldness** n [U]

bald·ing /ˈbɔːldɪŋllˈbɔːl-/ adj losing hair on your head

bald·ly /ˈbɔːldlillˈbɔːld-/ adv if you say something baldly, you show no emotion when you say it: "I want you to leave," she said baldly.

bale[1] /beɪl/ n [C] a large amount of something such as paper or HAY that is tied tightly together

bale[2] v

bale out phr v [I] to escape from a plane using a PARACHUTE; BAIL OUT AmE

bale·ful /ˈbeɪlfəl/ adj looking angry: She gave me a baleful stare. —**balefully** adv

balk /bɔːk, bɔːlkllbɔːk, bɔːlk/ the American spelling of BAULK

ball /bɔːlllbɔːl/ n [C] **1** a round object that you throw, hit, kick etc in a game, or any object shaped like this: yellow tennis balls | a ball of wool → see colour picture on page 636 **2** **be on the ball** informal to be able to think or deal with something quickly: If we had been on the ball, this might not have happened. **3** **have a ball** informal to enjoy something very much: We had a ball last night! **4** **set/start the ball rolling** informal to begin an activity or event **5** a large formal occasion where people dance **6** **the ball of the foot/hand/thumb** the rounded part at the base of your largest toe or at the base or top of your thumb → see also BALLS. **play ball** (PLAY[1])

bal·lad /ˈbæləd/ n [C] a song that tells a story or describes a situation, especially about love

bal·le·ri·na /ˌbæləˈriːnə/ n [C] a female ballet dancer

bal·let /ˈbæleɪllbæˈleɪ, ˈbæleɪ/ n **1** [U] a type of dancing done on a stage in a theatre, in which a story is told with music but no words **2** [C] a dance done in this style: the ballet 'Swan Lake' **3** [C] a group of ballet dancers who work together: the Bolshoi ballet

ball game /ˈ.. ./ n [C] **1** AmE a game of BASEBALL, BASKETBALL, or football **2** informal **a whole new ball game/a different ball game** a situation that is very different from the one you were in before: I've used word processors before, but this is a whole new ball game!

bal·lis·tic /bəˈlɪstɪk/ adj **go ballistic** spoken to suddenly become very angry

bal·loon[1] /bəˈluːn/ n [C] a small coloured rubber bag that is filled with air to use as a toy or decoration

balloon[2] v [I] to become much larger in size or amount: skirts ballooning in the wind | The deficit ballooned to $350 billion.

bal·lot¹ /'bælət/ n **1 ballot paper** BrE a piece of paper that you use to vote **2** [C,U] a system of voting in secret

ballot² v [T] especially BrE to find out what people think by letting them vote: All members will be balloted before any action is taken.

ballot box /'.. ../ n **1 the ballot box** the process of voting or the time when voting happens: The voters will give their opinion of the Governor at the ballot box. **2** [C] the box where you put the papers that you use to vote

ball·park /'bɔːlpɑːk‖'bɔːlpɑːrk/ n **1** [C] AmE a field for playing BASEBALL, with seats for people to watch the game **2 a ballpark figure/estimate** a number or amount that is not exactly correct but is close enough: a ballpark figure of, say, $2 million.

ball·point pen /ˌbɔːlpɔɪnt 'pen‖ˌbɔːl-/ also **ballpoint** n [C] a kind of pen with a very small ball in the end that controls the flow of ink

ball·room /'bɔːlrʊm, -ruːm‖'bɔːl-/ n [C] a large room where formal dances take place

balls /bɔːlz‖bɔːlz/ n [plural] **1** spoken an impolite word for TESTICLES **2** spoken informal courage and determination: It took balls to be that tough with Mr Dozier.

balm /bɑːm‖bɑːm, bɑːlm/ n [U] a liquid that you rub onto your skin to reduce pain

balm·y /'bɑːmi‖'bɑːmi, 'bɑːlmi/ adj balmy weather or air is warm and pleasant

ba·lo·ney /bə'ləʊni‖-'loʊ-/ n [U] informal something that is silly or not true: What a load of old baloney!

bal·us·trade /ˌbæləˈstreɪd‖ˈbæləstreɪd/ n [C] a stone wall around the roof of a large building or around the edge of a BALCONY

bam·boo /ˌbæmˈbuː◂/ n [U] a tall plant with hard hollow stems, often used for making furniture

ban¹ /bæn/ n [C] an official order that says that something must not be used or done: a global ban on nuclear testing

ban² v [T] -nned, -nning to officially say that something must not be done, used etc: Smoking inside the building is banned.| **ban sb from doing sth** Chappel was banned from contacting his ex-wife.

ba·nal /bə'nɑːl, bə'næl/ adj ordinary and not interesting —**banality** /bə'nælˌti/ n [C,U]

ba·na·na /bə'nɑːnə‖-'næ-/ n [C] a long curved yellow fruit → see picture at FRUIT

band¹ /bænd/ n [C] **1** a group of musicians who play together → compare ORCHESTRA **2** a group of people who work together to achieve the same aims: a small band of terrorists **3** a circular piece of something: a rubber band **4** a line of colour: STRIPE: a fish with a black band along its back **5** one of the parts or groups that something is divided into: Above £20,000, you are in a higher tax band.

band² v

band together phr v [I] to start working with other people in order to achieve something: 150 families have banded together to fight the drug dealers.

ban·dage¹ /'bændɪdʒ/ n [C] a long piece of cloth that you wrap around a wound or an injury

bandage² v [T] to put a bandage onto a wound or around an injury

Band-Aid /'. ./ n [C] AmE trademark a small piece of material that sticks to your skin to cover small wounds; a PLASTER BrE

ban·dan·na also **bandana** /bæn'dænə/ n [C] a large brightly coloured piece of cloth that you wear around your head or neck

B and B /ˌbiː ənd 'biː/ the abbreviation of BED AND BREAKFAST

ban·dit /'bændˌt/ n [C] someone who robs people, especially people who are travelling

band·stand /'bændstænd/ n [C] a small building in a park that has a roof but no walls, used for musical performances

band·wag·on /'bænd,wægən/ n **jump/climb on the bandwagon** to start doing something because a lot of other people are doing it: Many celebrities are jumping on the health bandwagon and producing exercise videos.

ban·dy /'bændi/ v **be bandied about/around** if names or facts are bandied about, people often mention them when talking about something

bane /beɪn/ n **be the bane of sb's life/existence** humourous to cause a lot of problems for you: That car! It's the bane of my life!

bang¹ /bæŋ/ v **1** [I,T] to make a loud noise, especially by hitting something against something hard: He started banging his dish on the table. → see colour picture on page 635 **2** [T] to accidentally hit a part of your body against something hard and hurt yourself: I banged my knee on the corner of the bed.

bang² n **1** [C] a sudden loud noise, usually made by something hard hitting something else or by something exploding: There was a loud bang, followed by the sound of breaking glass. → see colour picture on page 635 **2 with a bang** informal in a way that is very exciting, noticeable, or successful: The New Year's Party went with a bang. **3** when part of your body hits something: a nasty bang on the head

bang³ adv informal directly or exactly: They've built a parking lot bang in the middle of town.| **bang on** (=exactly correct): Yes, your answer's bang on!

bang⁴ interjection used to make the sound of a gun or bomb: "Bang! Bang! You're dead!" Tommy shouted.

bang·er /'bæŋə‖-ər/ n **1** [C] BrE informal a SAUSAGE **2 old banger** an old car in bad condition

ban·gle /'bæŋgəl/ n [C] a solid band of metal, wood etc that you wear around your wrist

bangs /bæŋz/ n [plural] AmE hair that is cut straight across your FOREHEAD; FRINGE BrE → see colour picture on page 244

ban·ish /'bænɪʃ/ v [T] **1** to get rid of a feeling, problem etc: I decided to banish all thoughts of ever marrying him. **2** to punish someone by making them leave an event, job, country etc: He was banished from the Olympics after a failed drugs test. —**banishment** n [U] → compare EXILE²

ban·is·ter /'bænˌstə‖-ər/ n [C] the piece of wood that you hold onto at the side of stairs

ban·jo /'bændʒəʊ‖-dʒoʊ/ n [C] a musical instrument with four or more strings and a circular body

bank[1] /bæŋk/ n [C] **1** the company or place where you can borrow money, save money etc: *I went to the bank at lunchtime to pay in my salary.* **2** land along the side of a river or lake: *trees lining the river bank* **3** a place where a type of thing is stored until someone needs it: *a blood bank* **4** a large pile of snow, sand etc **5 cloud/fog etc bank** a large area of cloud, FOG etc

bank[2] v **1** [I,T] to put or keep money in a bank **2** [I,T] to make a plane slope to one side when it is turning: *The plane banked and turned toward Honolulu.*

bank on sb/sth phr v [T] to depend on something happening: *We were banking on Jesse being here to help.*

bank ac·count /'. .,./ n [C] an arrangement that allows you to keep your money in a bank and take it out when you want to

bank·er /'bæŋkəll-ər/ n [C] someone who works in a bank in an important position

bank hol·i·day /ˌ. '.../ n [C] BrE an official holiday when banks and most companies are closed

bank·ing /'bæŋkɪŋ/ n [U] the business of a bank

bank·note /'bæŋknəʊtll-noʊt/ n [C] especially BrE a piece of paper money; BILL AmE

bank·rupt[1] /'bæŋkrʌpt/ adj unable to pay your debts and therefore unable to continue in business: **go bankrupt** *Many small businesses went bankrupt during the recession.*

bankrupt[2] v [T] to make someone become bankrupt

bank·rupt·cy /'bæŋkrʌptsi/ n [C,U] a situation in which you become bankrupt: *a sharp increase in bankruptcies last year*

bank tel·ler /'. ,../ n [C] a TELLER

ban·ner /'bænəll-ər/ n [C] **1** a long piece of cloth on which something is written, often carried between two poles: *crowds waving banners that read "Welcome Home"* **2** a flag **3** a belief or principle: **under the banner of** (=supporting a particular belief or principle): *an election fought under the banner of 'social justice'*

ban·quet /'bæŋkwɪt/ n [C] a formal meal for a lot of people

ban·ter /'bæntəll-ər/ n [U] conversation that has a lot of jokes in it —**banter** v [I]

bap /bæp/ n [C] BrE a round soft bread ROLL

bap·tis·m /'bæptɪzəm/ n [C,U] a religious ceremony in which someone is touched or covered with water to make them a member of the Christian faith —**baptismal** /bæp'tɪzməl/ adj

Bap·tist /'bæptɪst/ n [C] a member of a Christian group that believes baptism should only be for those old enough to understand its meaning

bap·tize (also **-ise** BrE) /bæp'taɪz/ v [T] to do a baptism

bar[1] /baːllbaːr/ n [C] **1 a)** a place that sells alcoholic drinks →compare PUB **b)** BrE one of the rooms inside a PUB **2** the long wooden surface in a bar where alcoholic drinks are sold and served: *O'Keefe stood at the bar.* **3** a small block

of something solid: *a bar of chocolate* →see colour picture on page 440 **4** a long piece of metal or wood: *A lot of houses had bars across the windows.* →see picture at CAGE **5** something that prevents you from making progress or succeeding: *Lack of money should not be a bar to educational opportunity.* **6** a group of notes in music: *She sang the first three bars of the song.* **7 behind bars** in prison **8 the bar** the profession of being a lawyer, or lawyers considered as a group →see also SNACK BAR

bar[2] v [T] **-rred, -rring 1** to officially prevent someone from doing something: **bar sb from** *We're barred from taking pictures inside the courtroom.* **2 bar sb's way** to stand in front of someone so that they cannot go somewhere: *He stood in the doorway, barring my way.* **3** if a door is barred it has been closed and locked

bar[3] prep **1** except: *It was a great performance, bar one little mistake.* **2 bar none** used to emphasize that something is the best: *Stone is the sexiest actress in the world, bar none.*

bar·bar·i·an /baː'beəriənllbaːr'ber-/ n [C] someone who behaves badly or cruelly, and does not respect normal ideas of what is good, valuable, beautiful etc —**barbarian** adj

bar·bar·ic /baː'bærɪkllbaːr-/ adj violent and cruel: *a barbaric act of terrorism* —**barbarically** /-kli/ adv

bar·bar·ous /'baːbərəsllbaːr-/ adj cruel and stupid: *a barbarous regime* —**barbarously** adv

barbecue

bar·be·cue[1] /'baːbɪkjuːllbaːr-/ n [C] **1** a party at which you cook and eat food outdoors: *Let's have a barbecue on the beach.* **2** a structure on which you cook food over a fire outdoors

barbecue[2] v [T] to cook food on a barbecue outdoors

barbed wire /ˌ. '.◄/ n [U] wire with short sharp points on it, used to stop people getting over fences, walls etc

bar·ber /'baːbəll baːr bər/ n [C] a man whose job is to cut men's hair

bar·bi·tu·rate /baː'bɪtʃʊrɪtllbaːr'bɪtʃʊrɪt, -reɪt/ n [C] a drug that makes people calm or makes them sleep

bar code /'. ./ n [C] a row of black lines on products for sale that a computer reads when you buy them

---

GRAMMAR NOTE: the present (1)
Use the **present progressive** to say what is happening now, at the time you are speaking: *Dad's working at home today.* | *We're waiting for a bus.* Use the **simple present** to talk about what normally happens: *He works from 9 to 5.* | *We usually go to school by bus.*

bard /bɑːd‖bɑːrd/ n [C] literary a poet

bare¹ /beə‖ber/ adj **1** not covered by clothes: Her feet were bare and her dress was dirty. → compare NAKED **2** empty, or not covered by anything: The room looked very bare. | a bare hillside **3** including only the smallest amount of something that you need: a report giving just the bare facts | **the bare necessities/essentials** (=the basic things that you need): The refugees took only the bare essentials with them. **4** **with your bare hands** without using a weapon or tools: Smith killed her with his bare hands. —**bareness** n [U]

bare² v [T] to let something be seen by uncovering it: The dog bared its teeth and growled.

bare-bones /'. ./ adj AmE informal having only the most basic things that are needed: a bare-bones military operation

bare-foot /ˌbeəˈfʊtˌd‖ˈberfʊtˌd/ adj, adv not wearing any shoes or socks: walking barefoot in the sand

bare-ly /'beəli‖'berli/ adv **1** only just: She was barely 17 when she had her first child. | I could barely stay awake. **2** used to emphasize that something happens immediately after something else: He'd barely sat down when she started asking questions.

barf /bɑːf‖bɑːrf/ v [I] AmE spoken informal to VOMIT —**barf** n [U]

bar-gain¹ /'bɑːgɪn‖'bɑːr-/ n [C] **1** something you buy for less than its usual price: At £2,500 this car is a real bargain. **2** when you agree to do something because someone else has agreed to do something: **make/strike a bargain** (=agree to do something): We've made a bargain that Paul does the shopping and I cook. **3** **into the bargain** especially BrE as well as everything else: Myrtle has two jobs, three children, and looks after her sick mother into the bargain.

bargain² v [I] to discuss the conditions of a sale, agreement etc: bargaining for better pay

bargain for sth phr v [T] to expect that something will happen: I hadn't bargained for the next difficulty. | **get more than you bargained for** (=get more than you expected, or find that something is much more difficult than you expected)

barge¹ /bɑːdʒ‖bɑːrdʒ/ n [C] a long narrow boat with a flat bottom, used to carry goods

barge² v [I] informal to walk somewhere quickly, pushing past people or things: **+ through/past** Ferguson barged past the guards at the door.

barge into sth phr v [I] to go into a place when you were not invited: What do you mean, barging into my house!

bar-i-tone /'bærɪtəʊn‖-toʊn/ n [C] a male singing voice that is fairly low, but not the lowest

bark¹ /bɑːk‖bɑːrk/ v **1** [I] if a dog barks, it makes several short loud sounds **2** [T] also **bark out** to say something quickly in a loud voice: "Name?" barked a fierce-looking soldier. **3** **be barking up the wrong tree** spoken to be asking the wrong questions or doing the wrong things when you are trying to find out about something: Colin didn't do it. You're barking up the wrong tree.

bark² n **1** [C] the sound a dog makes **2** [U] the material that forms the surface of the wood of a tree

bar-ley /'bɑːli‖'bɑːrli/ n [U] a grain used in making food and alcohol

bar-maid /'bɑːmeɪd‖'bɑːr-/ n [C] BrE a woman who serves drinks in a bar; BARTENDER AmE

bar-man /'bɑːmən‖'bɑːr-/ n [C] BrE a man who serves drinks in a bar; BARTENDER AmE

barm-y /'bɑːmi‖'bɑːrmi/ adj BrE spoken informal slightly crazy

barn /bɑːn‖bɑːrn/ n [C] a large building on a farm for keeping crops and sometimes animals

barn-yard /'bɑːnjɑːd‖'bɑːrnjɑːrd/ n [C] the area on a farm around a barn

ba-rom-e-ter /bəˈrɒmɪtə‖-ˈrɑːmɪtər/ n [C] **1** **a barometer of public opinion/business/confidence etc** something that shows you what people think, what is going to happen etc: Universities became a barometer of political currents. **2** an instrument for measuring changes in air pressure and weather —**barometric** /ˌbærəˈmetrɪk/ adj

ba-roque /bəˈrɒk, bəˈrəʊk‖bəˈroʊk, -ˈrɑːk/ adj made in the very decorated style that was common in Europe in the 17th century

bar-racks /'bærəks/ n [plural] a group of buildings in which soldiers live

bar-rage /'bærɑːʒ‖bəˈrɑːʒ/ n **1** [singular] when there are a lot of complaints, questions, sounds etc that happen very quickly after each other: **+ of** Despite a barrage of criticism, the trial went ahead. **2** [C usually singular] the continuous shooting of guns

barred /bɑːd‖bɑːrd/ adj a barred window has bars across it to stop people getting through it: stone walls with high barred windows

bar-rel /'bærəl/ n [C] **1** a large container for liquids such as beer → see picture at CONTAINER **2** the part of a gun that the bullets are shot through

bar-ren /'bærən/ adj **1** if land is barren, plants cannot grow on it **2** old-fashioned if a woman is barren, she cannot have children —**barrenness** n [U]

bar-ri-cade¹ /'bærɪkeɪd, ˌbærɪˈkeɪd/ n [C] something that is temporarily built across a road, door etc to prevent people from going through

barricade² v [T] to build a barricade: Johnstone barricaded the door with the bookcase.

bar-ri-er /'bæriə‖-ər/ n [C] **1** something such as a rule, situation, or problem that prevents or limits what people can do: an attempt to reduce trade barriers **2** a type of fence that prevents people from entering an area: barriers to hold back the crowds **3** an object that separates two places, groups of people etc: The Alps form a natural barrier across Europe.

bar-ring /'bɑːrɪŋ/ prep unless there are: Barring any last minute problems, we should finish on Friday.

bar-ris-ter /'bærɪstə‖-ər/ n [C] a lawyer in Britain who can work in the higher law courts

bar-tend-er /'bɑːˌtendə‖'bɑːr,tendər/ n [C] AmE someone whose job is to make and serve drinks in a bar; BARMAN, BARMAID BrE

bar-ter /'bɑːtə‖-rtər/ v [I,T] to exchange goods, work, or services without using money —**barter** n [U]

base¹ /beɪs/ v [T] to use somewhere as your

main place of business or activities: **be based in** *a law firm based in Denver*

base sth **on/upon** sth *phr v* [T] to use particular information or facts as a point from which to develop an idea, plan etc: *The play was loosely based on Amelia Earhart's life.*

base² *n* **1** [C] A place where people in the army, navy etc live and work **2** [C] the lowest part or surface of something: *a black vase with a round base | the base of the skull* **3** [C] the main place from which you work or do other activities: *The village provides an excellent base from which to explore the surrounding countryside.* **4** [C, usually singular] the people, money, groups etc from which a lot of support or power comes: *Mandela had a broad base of political support.* **5** [C] the main place where the work of a company or organization is done: *Microsoft's base is in Redmond.* **6** [U] the most important part of something from which new ideas develop: *Both French and Spanish come from a Latin base.* **7 be off base** *AmE informal* be completely wrong: *The estimate he gave was way off base.* **8 touch/cover all the bases** *AmE* to do or think about something thoroughly, so that all possible problems are dealt with **9** [C] the main substance in a mixture, to which other things can be added: *paints with a water base* **10** [C] one of the four places that a player must run to in order to get a point in baseball

base³ *adj formal* morally bad: *man's baser instincts*

base·ball /'beɪsbɔːl‖-bɒːl/ *n* **1** [U] a game in which two teams try to get points by hitting a ball and running around four BASES → see colour picture on page 636 **2** [C] the ball used in the game of baseball

base·ment /'beɪsmənt/ *n* [C] a room or rooms in a building that are under the level of the ground → see colour picture on page 79

bas·es /'beɪsiːz/ *n* the plural of BASIS

bash¹ /bæʃ/ *v* [T] **1** to hit something or someone hard: *He bashed his toe on the coffee table.* **2 union-bashing/Democrat-bashing/EU-bashing etc** *informal* when people criticize a group or organization, especially in newspapers or on television

bash² *n* [C] *informal* a large party: *They're having a big bash over at the club tonight.*

bash·ful /'bæʃfəl/ *adj* easily embarrassed; shy —**bashfully** *adv*

ba·sic /'beɪsɪk/ *adj* **1** forming the main or most necessary part of something: *the basic principles of mathematics | There are two basic problems here.* **2** simple or not fully developed: *basic health care for children*

ba·sic·al·ly /'beɪsɪkli/ *adv* **1** *spoken* used to introduce a simple explanation of something: *Well, basically the teacher said he'll need extra help with French.* **2** in the most important ways: *Norwegian and Danish are basically the same.*

ba·sics /'beɪsɪks/ *n* **the basics** the most important skills or facts connected with a subject: **the basics of** *a class that teaches you the basics of first aid*

bas·il /'bæzəl/ *n* [U] a sweet-smelling HERB

ba·sin /'beɪsən/ *n* [C] **1** *BrE* a bowl for liquids or food: *Pour the hot water into a basin.* **2** *BrE* the round container in a bathroom which you

use to wash your hands and face; SINK **3** *technical* a large area of land that is lower than the land around it: *the Amazon basin*

ba·sis /'beɪsɪs/ *n* [C], *plural* **bases** /-siːz/ **1 on the basis of** because of a particular fact or reason: *Some planning decisions were taken on the basis of very poor evidence.* **2 on a weekly/ informal/freelance etc basis** happening regularly at a particular time or happening in a particular way: *Meetings are held on a monthly basis.* **3** the information or ideas from which something develops: **+ for** *The video will provide a basis for class discussion.*

bask /bɑːsk‖bæsk/ *v* [I] **1** to lie somewhere warm and enjoy doing this: **+ in** *a cat basking in the sun* **2** to be enjoying people liking you or praising you: **+ in** *basking in the glory of his early success*

baskets

shopping basket   picnic basket

bas·ket /'bɑːskɪt‖'bæ-/ *n* [C] **1** a container made from thin pieces of wood, plastic, wire etc, woven together: *a basket full of fruit* **2** when a player gets the ball into the net in basketball

bas·ket·ball /'bɑːskɪtbɔːl‖'bæskɪtbɒːl/ *n* **1** [U] a game in which two teams try to win points by throwing a ball through a net → see colour picture on page 636 **2** [C] the ball used in this game

bass¹ /beɪs/ *n* **1** [C] a man who sings in a very low voice **2** [U] the lower half of the whole RANGE of musical notes **3** [C] a DOUBLE BASS —**bass** *adj*: *a bass guitar*

bass² /bæs/ *n* [C,U] a fish that can be eaten

bas·soon /bə'suːn/ *n* [C] a long wooden musical instrument that produces a low sound

bas·tard /'bɑːstəd, 'bæ-‖'bæstərd/ *n* [C] **1** *spoken* an offensive word for a man you do not like or are angry with: *You stupid bastard!* **2** *spoken* an insulting or joking word for a man: *You lucky bastard!* **3** *old-fashioned* someone whose parents are not married to each other

bas·ti·on /'bæstiən‖-tʃən/ *n* [C] an organization, place, profession etc that protects old beliefs or old ways of doing things: *the Academie Française, bastion of French culture*

bat¹ /bæt/ *n* [C] **1** a piece of wood used to hit the ball in games such as BASEBALL, CRICKET, and TABLE TENNIS etc → see colour picture on page 636 **2** a small animal that flies around at night

bat² *v* **-tted, -tting** **1** [I] to be trying to hit the ball with a bat in CRICKET or BASEBALL **2 not bat an eyelid/eye** *BrE* **not bat an eye** *AmE informal* to seem not to be upset or surprised by something that happens: *The boss didn't bat an eye when I said I was leaving.*

batch /bætʃ/ *n* [C] a group of things or people that arrive together, are made together etc: *the latest batch of student essays*

bat·ed /'beɪtɪd/ *adj* **with bated breath** in a very excited and anxious way: *I waited for her answer with bated breath.*

bath[1] /bɑːθ‖bæθ/ *n* [C] **1 a)** water that you sit or lie in to wash yourself: *I love to sit and soak in a hot bath.* | **run a bath** *Sandy went upstairs to run a bath.* **b)** *BrE* the long container that you sit or lie in to wash yourself; BATHTUB *AmE* **2** when you sit and wash yourself in a bath: **have a bath** *BrE*/**take a bath** *AmE I'll have a quick bath before we go out.*

USAGE NOTE: bath

When you are talking about washing your body in a large container of water indoors, say **have a bath** or **take a bath**: *Will I have time to take a bath before we go out?* When you are talking about swimming in the sea or in a river, use the verb **bathe** or the phrase **go for a bathe**: *It was hot, so we decided to go for a bathe in the river.* | *There were people bathing down by the rocks.* (Don't use **have/take a bath** in this meaning.) When you are talking about lying in the sun, use the verb **sunbathe**: *They spent the afternoon sunbathing on the roof,* not the phrase **have/ take a bath.**

---

bath[2] *v* [T] *BrE* to wash someone in a bath: *I'm just going to bath the baby.*

bathe /beɪð/ *v* **1** [I] to wash yourself in a bath: *Water was scarce, and we only bathed once a week.* **2** [T] to wash someone, usually in a bath: *Dad bathed Johnny and put him to bed.* **3** [T] to wash or cover part of your body with a liquid, especially as a medical treatment **4** [I] *old-fashioned* to swim for enjoyment **5 be bathed in light** to look beautiful in the light: *a beach bathed in the clear light of morning*

bathing suit /'beɪðɪŋ suːt, -sjuːt‖-suːt/ *n* [C] a piece of clothing that you wear for swimming; SWIMSUIT

bath·robe /'bɑːrəʊb‖'bæθroʊb/ *n* [C] a long loose piece of clothing made of thick soft cloth, that you wear before or after you have a bath

bath·room /'bɑːθrʊm, -ruːm‖'bæθ-/ *n* [C] **1** a room where there is a bath, a SHOWER etc, and usually a toilet **2** *AmE* **go to the bathroom** to use the toilet

bath·tub /'bɑːθtʌb‖'bæθ-/ *n* [C] *especially AmE* a long large container that you fill with water to sit in and wash yourself; BATH *BrE*

bat·on /'bætɒn, -tn‖bæ'tɑːn, bə-/ *n* [C] **1** a stick used to direct a group of musicians **2** a stick that a police officer uses as a weapon

bats·man /'bætsmən/ *n* [C] *plural* **batsmen** /-mən/ the person who is trying to hit the ball in CRICKET

bat·tal·ion /bə'tæljən/ *n* [C] a large group of soldiers consisting of several smaller groups

bat·ter[1] /'bætəll-ər/ *n* **1** [U] a liquid mixture of flour, milk, eggs etc, used in cooking: *fish in batter or breadcrumbs* **2** [U] *AmE* a thick mixture of flour, eggs, milk etc used for making cakes **3** [C] the person who is trying to hit the ball in BASEBALL

bat·ter[2] *v* [I,T] to hit someone or something many times, usually in a way that causes injury or damage: **batter against** *Waves battered against the rocks.* —**battering** *n* [C,U]

bat·tered /'bætədll-ərd/ *adj* **1** old and slightly damaged: *a battered old paperback book* **2 battered wives/women** women who have been attacked by the man that they live with

bat·ter·y /'bætəri/ *n* **1** [C] an object that provides the electrical power for a toy, machine, car etc: *I need some new batteries for my Walkman.* | **flat battery** (=a battery with no power): *If you leave the car lights on, you'll get a flat battery.* **2** [C] several large guns used together **3** [U] *law* the crime of hitting someone

bat·tle[1] /'bætl/ *n* **1** [C,U] when two armies fight each other in one place: *the battle of Trafalgar* | *Thousands of soldiers were killed in battle.* **2** [C] a situation in which two people or groups compete or argue with each other: **+ for** *a battle for power* **3** [C] an attempt to solve a difficult problem: **+ against** *the battle against AIDS*

battle[2] *v* [I,T] to try very hard to achieve something when this is very difficult: *My mother battled bravely against breast cancer for years.*

bat·tle·field /'bætlfiːld/, **bat·tle·ground** /'bætlgraʊnd/ *n* [C] a place where a battle has been fought

bat·tle·ments /'bætlmənts/ *n* [plural] a low wall around the top of a castle

bat·tle·ship /'bætl,ʃɪp/ *n* [C] a very large ship used in wars

baulk *BrE*, **balk** *AmE* /bɔːk,bɔːlk/ *v* [I] to refuse to do something unpleasant or difficult: **+ at** *They baulked at paying so much.*

bawl /bɔːl‖bɒːl/ *v* [I,T] *informal* to shout or cry loudly: *"Fares please!" bawled the bus conductor.*

bay /beɪ/ *n* **1** [C] a place where a curve in the coast partly surrounds an area of sea: *a beautiful sandy bay* **2 keep/hold sth at bay** to prevent something dangerous or unpleasant from coming too close: *Use your hands or feet to keep your attacker at bay.* **3 loading bay/cargo bay/sick bay etc** a part of a building or vehicle that is used for one particular purpose

bay leaf /'. ./ *n* [C] a sweet-smelling leaf used in cooking

bay·o·net /'beɪənɪt, -net/ *n* [C] a long knife fixed to the end of a long gun

ba·zaar /bə'zɑːll-'zɑːr/ *n* [C] **1** a market or a group of shops, especially in the Middle East **2** a sale to collect money for an organization such as a church or school: *the annual church bazaar*

BBC /,biː biː 'siːᵇ/ *n* **the BBC** the British Broadcasting Corporation; the British radio and television company that is paid for by the state

BBQ a written abbreviation of BARBECUE

BC /,biː 'siː/ *adv* used after a date to show that it was before the birth of Christ: *The Great Pyramid dates from around 2600 BC* → compare AD

be[1] /bi; *strong* biː/ *auxiliary verb* **1** used with a present participle to form the CONTINUOUS tenses of verbs: *Jane was reading by the fire.* | *Don't disturb me while I'm working.* **2** used with a past participle to form the PASSIVE: *Smoking is not permitted on this flight.*

3 used to show what might happen in the future, in CONDITIONAL sentences: *If I were rich, I'd buy myself a Rolls Royce.* **4** used to show what you expect will happen in the future: *I'll be leaving tomorrow.* → see also BEEN

be[2] *v* **1** [linking verb] used to give the name, date, or position of something or someone, or to describe it: *January is the first month of the year.* | *The concert was last night.* | *Julie wants to be a doctor.* | *Where is Sara?* | *You're very cheerful today!* | *I'm hungry.* **2 there is/there are/there were etc** used in order to show that something or someone exists: *There's a hole in the knee of your jeans.* | *Last night there were only eight people at the cinema.*

beach /biːtʃ/ *n* [C] an area of sand or small stones at the edge of the sea → see colour picture on page 243

bea·con /ˈbiːkən/ *n* [C] a flashing light, used as a sign to warn or guide boats, planes etc

bead /biːd/ *n* [C] **1** a small round ball of plastic, glass etc, usually used for making jewellery **2** a small drop of liquid such as water or blood: *beads of sweat*

bead·y /ˈbiːdi/ *adj* beady eyes are small, dark and shiny

beak /biːk/ *n* [C] the hard pointed mouth of a bird

bea·ker /ˈbiːkəⁿ-ər/ *n* [C] *BrE* a cup with straight sides

beam[1] /biːm/ *n* **1 a)** a line of light shining from the sun, a lamp etc: *The beam of the flashlight flickered and went out.* **b)** a line of energy such as RADIATION or MICROWAVES **2** a long heavy piece of wood or metal used in building houses, bridges etc **3** a big happy smile

beam[2] *v* **1** [I] to smile or look at someone very happily: **+ at** *Uncle Willie beamed at us proudly.* **2** [I,T] to send out energy, light, radio or television SIGNALS: *The signal was beamed up to a satellite.*

bean /biːn/ *n* [C] **1 a)** the seed of one of many types of climbing plants that is cooked as a food **b)** a seed case from one of these plants that is eaten as a vegetable → see picture at VEGETABLE **2** a seed used in making some types of food or drinks: *coffee beans* → see also **be full of beans** (FULL[1])

bean·sprout /ˈbiːnspraʊt/ *n* [C] the small white stem from a bean seed that is eaten as a vegetable

bear[1] /beəⁿber/ *v* **bore** /bɔːⁿbɔːr/, **borne** /bɔːnⁿbɔːrn/, **bearing** [T] **1 bear sth in mind** to not forget an important fact while you are deciding or judging something: **bear in mind that** *Bear in mind that this method does not always work.* **2 can't bear** to dislike something very much: *I can't bear it when you cry.* | **can't bear to do sth** *It was so horrible I couldn't bear to watch.* **3** to bravely accept or deal with a painful or unpleasant situation: *The pain was almost more than she could bear.* **4 bear a resemblance/relation etc to sth** to be similar to or connected with someone or something: *The murder bears a*

remarkable resemblance to another case five years ago. **5 bear the blame/cost/responsibility etc** to be responsible for something, agree to pay for something etc: *You must bear some of the blame yourself.* **6** *formal* to have a particular name or mark: *a briefcase bearing the initials 'WSJ'P* **7 bear the brunt of** to experience the worst part of a bad situation: *It's the poor who bear the brunt of an economic recession.* **8 bear fruit** if a plan or decision bears fruit, it is successful **9 bear witness** *formal* to show that something is true or exists: *Campion's latest film bears witness to her skill as a director.* **10** to support the weight of something: *The weight of the building is borne by thick stone pillars.* **11** to have a particular feeling towards someone: **bear a grudge** (=feel angry with someone for a long time because of something they have done) **12 bear with me** *spoken* used to ask someone politely to wait while you do something: *If you'll bear with me for a minute, I'll just check if he's here.* **13 bear right/left** to turn right or left: *Bear left at the lights.* **14** *formal* to give birth to a baby: *She'll never be able to bear children.* **15** *formal* to carry something from one place to another: *Jane arrived bearing trays of food.* → see also **bring sth to bear** (BRING)

bear down on sb/sth *phr v* [T] to move quickly towards someone or something in a threatening way: *People ran out of the way as the truck bore down on them.*

bear sb/sth **out** *phr v* [T] to show that something is true: *Our fears about the radiation levels were borne out by the research.*

> **USAGE NOTE: bear, stand, tolerate**, and **put up with**
>
> Use these words to talk about accepting or dealing with a bad situation. **Bear** means that someone is being brave: *The pain was almost too much to bear.* **Stand** is usually used in the phrase **can't stand**: *I can't stand all this noise!* **Tolerate** and **put up with** mean the same thing, but **tolerate** is more formal: *Why do you put up with him being so rude?* | *I'm surprised you tolerate his behaviour.*

bear[2] *n* [C] a large strong animal with thick fur

bear·a·ble /ˈbeərəbəlⁿˈber-/ *adj* a situation that is bearable is difficult or unpleasant but you can deal with it: *His letters made her loneliness bearable.*

beard /bɪədⁿbɪrd/ *n* [C] the hair that grows on a man's chin → see colour picture on page 244 —**bearded** *adj*

bear·er /ˈbeərəⁿˈberər/ *n* [C] **1** someone who brings you something such as a message or letter: *the bearer of bad news* **2** someone who carries something: *a flag bearer*

bear·ing /ˈbeərɪŋⁿˈber-/ *n* **1 have a bearing on sth** to have a connection with or an influence on something: *Leigh's comments have no bearing on the subject.* **2 lose your bearings** to become confused about where you are: *Apparently the*

GRAMMAR NOTE: the present (2)
Use the **simple present** to talk about things that are true in general: *Carlos lives in Madrid.* | *She works in a bank.* | *Water boils at 100°C.* But use the **present progressive** to talk about what you are studying: *I'm learning English.* | *She's studying history.*

boat lost its bearings in the fog. **3 get your bearings** to find out where you are or feel confident that you know what you are doing: *It takes time to get your bearings in a new job.*

beast /biːst/ *n* [C] **1** *literary* an animal, especially a wild or dangerous one **2** *old-fashioned* used to say that someone is cruel or unpleasant: *You horrible beast!*

beat[1] /biːt/ *v* **beat, beaten** /'biːtn/, **beating**
1 [T] to be more successful than other people in a game or competition: *Spain beat Italy 3–1.*
2 [T] to hit someone many times with your hand, a stick etc: **beat sb to death/beat sb unconscious** (=beat them until they die or are unconscious) **3** [I,T] to hit something regularly or continuously: *The rain beat loudly on the tin roof.* **4** [T] to mix food together quickly using a fork or a kitchen tool: *Beat the eggs and add them to the sugar mixture.* **5** [I] if your heart beats, it makes a regular movement and sound: *My heart seemed to be beating much too fast.*
6 not beat about/around the bush to talk about something honestly, even though it is unpleasant or embarrassing: *I won't beat about the bush, Alex. I'm leaving you.* **7** [T] *spoken* to be better than something: **it beats working/studying** etc *spoken: It's not the greatest job, but it beats cleaning houses.* **8 you can't beat** *spoken* used to say that something is the best: *You can't beat St Tropez for good weather.* **9 it beats me** *spoken* used to say that you do not understand or know the answer to something: *"Where does this piece go?" "It beats me!"* → see also **off the beaten track/path** (BEATEN)

beat down *phr v* [I] **1** if the sun beats down, it shines brightly and the weather is hot **2** if the rain beats down, it rains very hard

beat sb/sth ↔ **off** *phr v* [T] to hit someone who is attacking you until they go away

beat sb **to** sth *phr v* [T] to get or do something before someone else is able to: *I called to ask about buying the car, but someone had beaten me to it.*

beat sb ↔ **up** *phr v* [T] to hit someone until they are badly hurt: *Her husband went crazy and beat her up.*

beat up on sb *phr v* [T] *AmE* to attack someone younger or weaker than you until they are badly hurt

beat[2] *n* **1** [C] one of a series of regular movements, sounds, or hitting actions: *a heart beat | the slow beat of a drum* **2 a)** [singular] the pattern of strong-sounding musical notes that are repeated in a piece of music: *The song has a beat you can dance to.* **b)** [C] one of the notes in this pattern **3** [singular] the area of a town or city etc that a police officer is responsible for: **on the beat** *We need more police on the beat.*

beat[3] *adj informal* very tired: *You look dead beat!*

beat·en /'biːtn/ *adj* **off the beaten track/path** far away from places that people usually visit: *a little hotel off the beaten track*

beat·ing /'biːtɪŋ/ *n informal* **take a beating** to be harmed or criticized very badly: *Tourism has taken a beating since the bombings started.*

beat-up /'. ./ *adj informal* old and in bad condition: *a beat-up old car*

beau·ti·cian /bjuː'tɪʃən/ *n* [C] someone whose job is to give beauty treatment to your skin, hair etc

beau·ti·ful /'bjuːtɪfəl/ *adj* **1** a woman, girl, or child who is beautiful is very attractive: *the most beautiful woman in the world* **2** very attractive or good to listen to: *a beautiful pink dress | beautiful music | a beautiful view*

USAGE NOTE: beautiful, pretty, handsome, good-looking, cute

These words are all used to say that someone is attractive. **Beautiful** is a strong word meaning extremely attractive in a way that is quite rare: *the most beautiful actress in Hollywood.* **Pretty**, **handsome**, and **good-looking** are less strong ways of describing someone who is attractive. Use **pretty** about younger women and girls: *She's the prettiest girl I ever met.* **Handsome** is usually used to describe men: *a tall, dark, handsome stranger.* However, it can be used about attractive older women. Use **good-looking** about both men and women: *That guy you were with last night was very good-looking!* **Cute** is used about babies and children, but can also be used about young men and women, especially in American English: *Her kids are really cute!*

---

beau·ty /'bjuːti/ *n* **1** [U] the quality of being beautiful: *a woman of great beauty | the beauty of the Swiss Alps* **2** also **beaut** [C] *informal* something that is very good: *His new car's a beaut.* **3** beauty treatments, products etc are intended to make people look more beautiful, especially women: *Do you use beauty creams?* **4 the beauty of** a good quality that makes something especially suitable or useful: *The beauty of this type of exercise is that you can do it anywhere.* **5** [C] *old-fashioned* a woman who is very beautiful

beauty sal·on *BrE* /'. .,..ll'.. .,./, **beauty par·lor** *AmE* /'. .,../ *n* [C] a place where you can have beauty treatments for your skin, hair etc

beauty spot /'.. ./ *n* [C] a beautiful place in the countryside

bea·ver /'biːvəll-ər/ *n* [C] a North American animal with thick fur and a wide flat tail

be·bop /'biːbɒpll-baːp/ *n* [U] a style of JAZZ music

be·came /bɪ'keɪm/ *v* the past tense of BECOME

be·cause /bɪ'kɒz, bɪkəzllbɪ'kɔːz, bɪkəz/ *linking word* **1** for the reason that: *You can't go because you're too young.* **2 because of** as a result of something or someone: *We weren't able to have the picnic because of the rain.* **3 just because ...** *spoken* used to say that although one thing is true, it does not mean that something else is true: *Just because you're older it doesn't mean you can boss me around.*

beck /bek/ *n* **be at sb's beck and call** to always be ready to do what someone wants

beck·on /'bekən/ *v* [I,T] **1** to move your hand or arm to show that you want someone to move towards you: *He beckoned her to join him.* **2** if a place or situation beckons, it seems likely that you will go there: *The summer was here and the coast beckoned.*

be·come /bɪ'kʌm/ *v* **became** /bɪ'keɪm/, **become, becoming 1** [linking verb] if something becomes warmer, harder etc it was not warm in the past but now it is: *The weather had become warmer.* | *Kennedy became the first Catholic president.* | *It is becoming harder to find good staff.* **2 what/whatever became of...?** used in order to ask what happened to someone or something: *Whatever became of Nigel and Denise?* **3** [T] *formal* to be suitable for someone: *Such aggressive behaviour does not become you.*

USAGE NOTE: become, get and go

Use these words about something that develops or changes. They mean the same, but **become** is more formal than **get**: *He's becoming very successful.* | *Prague is becoming more popular with tourists.* **Get** is the word you would usually choose, especially in spoken English: *It's getting dark outside.* | *By now I was getting very tired.* **Go** is used in some fixed phrases: *Have you gone crazy?* | *Everything suddenly went quiet.*

---

beds

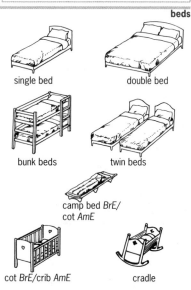

single bed

double bed

bunk beds

twin beds

camp bed *BrE*/ cot *AmE*

cot *BrE*/crib *AmE*

cradle

bed /bed/ *n* **1** [C,U] a piece of furniture for sleeping on: *a double bed* | *in bed I lay in bed reading.* | *go to bed Jamie usually goes to bed at about 7 o'clock.* | *get out of bed She looked like she had just got out of bed.* | *make the bed* (=tidy the bed covers) **2 go to bed with sb** to have sex with someone **3** [C] the ground at the bottom of the ocean, a river, or a lake: *the sea bed* **4** [C] an area of ground that has been prepared for plants to grow in: *flower beds* **5** [singular] a layer of something that is a base for something else: *prawns on a bed of lettuce*

bed and break·fast /ˌ. . '../ **B&B** *n* [C] someone's house or a small hotel where you pay to sleep and have breakfast; B AND B

bed·clothes /'bedkləʊðz, -kləʊz‖-kloʊðz, -kloʊz/ *n* [plural] BEDDING¹

bed·ding /'bedɪŋ/ *n* [U] **1** the sheets, BLAN-

KETS etc that you put on a bed **2** something soft that an animal sleeps on, such as dried grass

be·drag·gled /bɪ'dræɡəld/ *adj* looking dirty, wet, and untidy

bed·rid·den /'bed,rɪdn/ *adj* unable to get out of bed because you are old or ill

bed·room /'bedrʊm, -ruːm/ *n* [C] a room for sleeping in

bed·side /'bedsaɪd/ *n* [C] the area around a bed: *His family has been at his bedside all night.*

bed·sit /ˌbed'sɪt/ **bed·sit·ter** /ˌbed'sɪtə‖-ər/ **bed-sitting room** /ˌ. '.. ./ *n* [C] *BrE* a rented room used for both living and sleeping in

bed·spread /'bedspred/ *n* [C] a large cloth cover that goes on top of a bed

bed·time /'bedtaɪm/ *n* [C,U] the time when you usually go to bed: *It's way past your bedtime!*

bee /biː/ *n* [C] a black and yellow flying insect that makes HONEY

beech /biːtʃ/ *n* [C,U] a kind of tree that produces nuts, and has a smooth grey surface

beef¹ /biːf/ *n* **1** [U] meat from a cow **2** [C] *informal* a complaint: *What's the beef about this time?*

beef² *v*
beef sth ↔ **up** *phr v* [T] *informal* to improve something, especially by making it stronger: *Security around the palace has been beefed up since the attack.*

beef·bur·ger /'biːfˌbɜːɡə‖-bɜːrɡər/ *n* [C] *BrE* beef that is cut up into very small pieces and cooked in a flat round shape; BURGER

beef·y /'biːfi/ *adj* a beefy man is big, strong, and often fat

bee·hive /'biːhaɪv/ *n* [C] a place where BEES are kept to produce HONEY; HIVE

been /biːn, bɪn‖bɪn/ *v* **1** the past participle of BE **2 have been to** used to say that someone has gone to a place and come back: *Kate has just been to Japan.*

beep /biːp/ *v* **1** [I] if a machine beeps, it makes a short high sound: *The computer beeps when you make a mistake.* **2** [I,T] if a horn beeps, or you beep it, it makes a loud noise
—**beep** *n* [C]

beep·er /'biːpə‖-ər/ *n* [C] a small machine that you carry with you which makes a sound to tell you to telephone someone; PAGER

beer /bɪə‖bɪr/ *n* [C,U] an alcoholic drink made from grain, or a glass, can, or bottle of this drink: *a pint of beer* | *Do you fancy a beer?*

bees·wax /'biːzwæks/ *n* [U] a substance produced by BEES, used in making CANDLES

beet /biːt/ *n* [C,U] **1** also **sugar beet** a vegetable that sugar is made from **2** *AmE* a dark red vegetable that is the root of a plant; BEETROOT *BrE*

bee·tle /'biːtl/ *n* [C] an insect with a hard round black back

beet·root /'biːtruːt/ *BrE n* [C] a dark red vegetable that is the root of a plant; BEET *AmE*

be·fall /bɪ'fɔːl‖-'fɔːl/ *v* [I,T] *formal* if something unpleasant or dangerous befalls you, it happens to you: *She died of smallpox, a fate that befell many emigrants.*

be·fit /bɪ'fɪt/ *v* [T] *formal* to seem suitable or good enough for someone: *a funeral befitting a national hero* —**befitting** *adj*

be·fore¹ /bɪ'fɔːll-'fɔːr/ *prep* **1** earlier than something: *I usually shower before having breakfast.*|*Denise got there before me.* **2** in front of: *The priest knelt before the altar.* **3** in a more important position than someone or something: *His wife and children come before his job.* **4** at a particular distance in front of a place as you travel towards it: *Turn right just before the station.*

before² *adv* at an earlier time: *They'd met before, at one of Sally's parties.*

before³ *linking word* **1** earlier than the time when something happens: *John wants to talk to you before you go.* **2** so that something bad does not happen: *You'd better lock your bike before it gets stolen.* **3 before you know it** *spoken* used in order to say that something will happen very soon: *You'd better get going – it'll be dark before you know it.*

be·fore·hand /bɪ'fɔːhændll-'fɔːr-/ *adv* before something happens or is done: *When you give a speech, it's natural to feel nervous beforehand.*

be·friend /bɪ'frend/ *v* [T] to become someone's friend, especially someone who needs your help

be·fud·dled /bɪ'fʌdəld/ *adj* completely confused: *Annie looked a little befuddled.*

beg /beg/ *v* **-gged, -gging 1** [I,T] to ask for something in an urgent or anxious way: **beg sb to do sth** *I begged her to stay, but she wouldn't.* **2** [I] to ask someone for food, money etc because you are very poor: *children begging in the streets* **3 I beg your pardon** *spoken* **a)** *formal* used to say sorry for something you have said or done: *Oh, I beg your pardon, did I step on your toe?* **b)** *formal* used to show that you strongly disagree: *"New York's a terrible place." "I beg your pardon, that's my home town!"* **c)** used to ask someone politely to repeat something: *"It's 7 o'clock" "I beg your pardon?" "I said it's 7 o'clock."*

beg·gar /'begəll-ər/ *n* [C] **1** someone who lives by asking people for food and money **2** *BrE informal* used when you feel sorry for someone, feel angry with someone etc: *The poor beggar broke both his legs!*

be·gin /bɪ'gɪn/ *v* **began** /bɪ'gæn/, **begun** /bɪ'gʌn/, **beginning 1** [I,T] to start doing or feeling something, or to start to happen or exist: *The meeting will begin at 10:00.*|**begin to do sth** *It's beginning to rain.*|**begin doing sth** *Nicola began learning English last year.*|**begin with** *Let's begin with exercise 5.*|**begin by doing sth** *May I begin by thanking you all for coming.* **2 to begin with a)** used to introduce the first or most important point: *To begin with, you mustn't take the car without asking.* **b)** used to say what something was like at the start: *I didn't break it! It was like that to begin with.* **c)** in the first part of an activity or process: *The children helped me to begin with, but they soon got bored.* **3 begin with** if a book, speech, word etc begins with something, that is how it starts: *It begins with a description of the author's home.*

be·gin·ner /bɪ'gɪnəll-ər/ *n* [C] someone who has just started to do or learn something

be·gin·ning /bɪ'gɪnɪŋ/ *n* [C, usually singular] the start or first part of something: *the beginning of the film*

be·grudge /bɪ'grʌdʒ/ *v* [T] to feel upset because someone else has something you would like: *Honestly, I don't begrudge him his success.*

be·guile /bɪ'gaɪl/ *v* [T] *formal* to persuade or trick someone into doing something, especially by saying nice things to them

be·gun /bɪ'gʌn/ *v* the past participle of BEGIN

be·half /bɪ'hɑːfllbɪ'hæf/ *n* **on behalf of sb/on sb's behalf** instead of someone: *He agreed to speak on my behalf.*

be·have /bɪ'heɪv/ *v* **1** [I] to do or say things in a particular way: *You behaved bravely in a very difficult situation.* **2** [I,T] to be polite and not cause trouble: *Tom was quieter than his brother and knew how to behave.*|**behave yourself** *If you behave yourself you can have an ice-cream.*

be·hav·iour *BrE*, **behavior** *AmE* /bɪ'heɪvjəll-ər/ *n* [U] **1** the way that a person or animal behaves: *Can TV shows affect children's behaviour?* **2** *technical* what an object, substance etc normally does: *the behaviour of cancer cells*

be·head /bɪ'hed/ *v* [T] to cut someone's head off

be·hind¹ /bɪ'haɪnd/ *prep* **1** at or towards the back of something: *I was driving behind a Rolls Royce.*|**right behind** (=just behind): *The car park is right behind the supermarket.* ➔ see colour picture on page 474 **2** not as successful or ADVANCED as someone or something else: *We're three points behind the other team.*|**behind schedule** *Work on the new building is three months behind schedule.* **3** responsible for something or causing it to happen: *The police believe a local gang is behind the robberies.* **4** supporting a person, idea etc: *Whatever you decide to do, I'll be right behind you.* **5 behind the times** not modern; old-fashioned

behind² *adv* **1** at or towards the back of something: *Several other runners were following close behind.* **2** in the place where someone or something was before: *When I got there I realized I'd left the tickets behind.* **3 be/get behind** to be late or slow in doing something: *We are three months behind with the rent.*

behind³ *n* [C] *informal* the part of your body that you sit on

be·hold /bɪ'həʊldll-'hoʊld/ *v* [T] *literary* to see something —**beholder** *n* [C]

beige /beɪʒ/ *n* [U] a pale brown colour ➔ see colour picture on page 114 —**beige** *adj*

be·ing /'biːɪŋ/ *n* **1** [C] a living person, either imaginary or real: *strange beings from outer space* **2 come into being** to begin to exist: *Their political system came into being in the early 1900s.*

be·lat·ed /bɪ'leɪtɪd/ *adj* happening or arriving late: *a belated birthday card* —**belatedly** *adv*

belch /beltʃ/ *v* **1** [I] to let air come noisily out through your mouth from your stomach **2** [T] to produce a lot of smoke, fire etc: *factory chimneys belching black smoke*

be·lea·guered /bɪ'liːgədll-ərd/ *adj* having a lot of problems: *the beleaguered president of the troubled computer company*

bel·fry /'belfri/ *n* [C] a tower for a bell, especially on a church

be·lie /bɪ'laɪ/ *v* [T] *formal* to give you a wrong idea about something: *He has an energy that belies his 85 years.*

be·lief /bɪ'liːf/ *n* **1** [U, singular] the feeling that something is true or exists: **+ that** *the belief* *that children learn best through playing* | **+ in** *belief in magic* | **contrary to popular belief** (=not what most people believe): *Contrary to popular belief, drinking coffee does not make you less drunk.* **2 beyond belief** used to emphasize that something is very bad, good, strange etc: *Tired beyond belief, we kept on walking.* **3** [singular] the feeling that someone or something is good and can be trusted: **+ in** *a strong belief in the importance of education* **4** [C, usually plural] an idea that you think is true: *religious beliefs*

be·liev·a·ble /bɪ'liːvəbəl/ *adj* something that is believable can easily be believed and seems likely to be true: *a believable love story* —**believably** *adv* → opposite UNBELIEVABLE

be·lieve /bɪ'liːv/ *v* **1** [T] to think that something is true or that someone is telling the truth: *He said Kevin started the fight, but no one believed him.* | **+ (that)** *I can't believe he's only 25!* | **believe sb to be sth** *The jury believed Jones to be innocent.* **2** [T] to have a particular opinion about something, without being completely sure: **+ (that)** *I believe she'll be back on Monday.* **3 I can't/don't believe** used when you are very surprised or shocked: *I can't believe you lied to me!* **4 would you believe it!** used when you are surprised or slightly angry about something: *Would you believe it, he even remembered my birthday!* **5 could not believe your eyes** used to say that you were very surprised by something **6 believe it or not** *spoken* used when something is true but surprising: *Believe it or not, I don't actually dislike him.* **7** [I] to have religious faith

believe in sth *phr v* [T] **1** to be sure that something or someone definitely exists: *Do you believe in ghosts?* **2** to think that someone or something is good, or able to be trusted: *We believe in democracy.*

be·liev·er /bɪ'liːvəl-ər/ *n* [C] **1** someone who believes that a particular idea or thing is very good: **a firm/great believer in** *I'm a great believer in healthy eating.* **2** someone who believes in a particular religion

be·lit·tle /bɪ'lɪtl/ *v* [T] *formal* to say that something is less important than it really is: *Why do they always try to belittle our efforts!*

bell /bel/ *n* [C] a metal object that makes a ringing sound when it is hit: *The bell rang for school to start.* → see also **ring a bell** (RING²)

bel·lig·er·ent /bɪ'lɪdʒərənt/ *adj* willing to fight or argue: *a belligerent attitude* —**belligerence** *n* [U]

bel·low /'beləʊl-loʊ/ *v* [I,T] to shout something in a very loud low voice

bell pep·per /'. ‚../ *n* [C] *AmE* a hollow red, green, or yellow vegetable; PEPPER *BrE*

bel·ly /'beli/ *n* [C] *informal* your stomach, or the part of your body between your chest and the top of your legs

belly but·ton /'.. ‚../ *n* [C] *informal* the small hole just below your waist on the front of your body; NAVEL

be·long /bɪ'lɒŋǁbɪ'lɔːŋ/ *v* [I] **1** to be in the right place or situation: **belong in/on/at/here** etc *Books like that don't belong in the classroom.* | *Please put the chair back where it belongs.* **2** to feel happy and comfortable in a place or with a group of people: *I'm going back to Scotland, where I belong.*

belong to sb/sth *phr v* [T] **1** to be a member of a group or organization: *Mary and her husband belong to the yacht club.* **2** to be owned by someone: *Who does this umbrella belong to?*

be·long·ings /bɪ'lɒŋɪŋzǁbɪ'lɔːŋ-/ *n* [plural] the things that you own, especially the ones that you carry with you

be·lov·ed /bɪ'lʌvɪd/ *adj literary* loved very much: *my beloved wife, Fiona* —**beloved** *n* [singular]

be·low /bɪ'ləʊǁ-'loʊ/ *adv, prep* **1** in a lower place or position, or on a lower level: *Jake lives in the apartment below.* | *A corporal is below a captain in rank.* → see colour picture on page 474 **2** less than a particular number: *Anything below £500 would be a good price.* **3** on a later page or lower on the same page: **see below** *For more information, see below.* → compare UNDER

belt¹ /belt/ *n* [C] **1** a band of leather, cloth etc that you wear around your waist → see colour picture on page 113 **2** a circular band of material such as rubber that moves parts of a machine: *The car's fan belt is loose.* **3** a large area of one type of land: *America's farming belt* **4 have sth under your belt** to have already done something useful or important: *They already have three hit records under their belts.* → see also SEAT BELT

belt² *v* [T] *informal* to hit someone or something hard

belt sth ↔ **out** *phr v* [T] to sing a song very loudly

be·mused /bɪ'mjuːzd/ *adj* slightly confused

bench /bentʃ/ *n* **1** [C] a long seat for two or more people, used especially outdoors **2 the bench** *law* the judges who work in a court: *He was appointed to the bench in 1974.*

bench·mark /'bentʃmɑːkǁ-mɑːrk/ *n* [C] something used for comparing and measuring another number, rate, level etc: *The test results provide a benchmark for measuring student achievement.*

bend¹ /bend/ *v* **bent** /bent/, **bent, bending** [I,T] **1** to move a part of your body so that it is no longer straight or so that you are no longer standing upright: *Bend your knees slightly.* | **bend down/over** *He bent down to tie his shoelace.* → see colour picture on page 670 **2** to be curved or to make something be curved: *You've bent the handle.* **3 bend over backwards** to try very hard to help someone: *Our new neighbours bent over backwards to help us when we moved house.* → see also **bend/stretch the rules** (RULE¹)

bend² *n* [C] a curve in something, especially a road or river: *The river goes around a bend by the farm.*

GRAMMAR NOTE

Don't forget to add **-s** or **-es** to verbs in the **simple present** when the subject is third person singular (**he, she, it** or another singular person or thing): *I teach French and Alan teach**es** English.* | *Jo drives to work.*

be·neath /bɪˈniːθ/ adv, prep **1** under or below something: *the warm sand beneath her feet* \ *He stood on the bridge, looking at the water beneath.* **2** if someone or something is beneath you, you think that they are not good enough for you: *She seemed to think that talking to us was beneath her.*

ben·e·fac·tor /ˈbenɪˌfæktəl-ər/ n [C] *formal* someone who gives money or help to someone else

ben·e·fi·cial /ˌbenɪˈfɪʃəl◂/ adj helpful or useful: **+ to** *The agreement will be beneficial to both groups.* —**beneficially** adv

ben·e·fi·cia·ry /ˌbenɪˈfɪʃəriǁ-ˈfɪʃieri/ n [C] *formal* someone who is helped by an event: *Businesses were the main beneficiaries of the tax cuts.*

ben·e·fit[1] /ˈbenɪfɪt/ n **1** [C,U] money that you get from the government when you are ill or when you do not have a job: *All his family are on benefits.* (=receiving benefits) \ *social security benefits* **2** [C,U] an advantage or improvement that you get from something: *There are obvious benefits for the computer users.* \ **for sb's benefit** (=in order to help them): *Liu Han translated what he had said for my benefit.* **3** [C] a performance, concert etc that makes money for a CHARITY **4** **give sb the benefit of the doubt** to believe or trust someone even though it is possible that they are lying or are wrong

benefit[2] v **-fited, -fiting,** also **-fitted, -fitting 1** [T] if something benefits someone, it helps them: *The new policy changes mainly benefit small companies.* **2** [I] to be helped by something: **+ from/by** *Most of these children would benefit from an extra year at school.*

be·nev·o·lent /bɪˈnevələnt/ adj *formal* kind and generous —**benevolence** n [U]

be·nign /bɪˈnaɪn/ adj **1** *technical* not likely to seriously hurt you or to cause CANCER: *a benign tumour* **2** *formal* kind and unlikely to harm anyone → compare MALIGNANT

bent[1] /bent/ v the past tense and past participle of BEND

bent[2] adj **1** curved and no longer flat or straight: *His bike lay in the grass, its front wheel all bent.* **2** **be bent on** to be determined to do something or have something: *Mendoza was bent on getting a better job.* **3** *BrE* a bent policeman or other person in an official position is dishonest: *a bent cop* **4** *BrE spoken informal* an offensive word meaning HOMOSEXUAL

bent[3] n [singular] a natural skill or way of thinking: *writers of a more philosophical bent*

be·queath /bɪˈkwiːð, bɪˈkwiːθ/ v [T] *formal* to arrange that someone will get something you own after you die

be·quest /bɪˈkwest/ n [C] *formal* something that you arrange to give to someone after you have died

be·reaved /bɪˈriːvd/ adj *formal* **1** if someone is bereaved, someone they love has died **2** **the bereaved** people whose friends or family members have died —**bereavement** n [C,U]

be·reft /bɪˈreft/ adj *formal* **1** **bereft of sth** completely without something: *bereft of all hope* **2** feeling sad and alone

be·ret /ˈbereɪǁbəˈreɪ/ n [C] a soft round flat hat that has a tight band around the head

ber·ry /ˈberi/ n [C] a small soft fruit with very small seeds

ber·serk /bɜːˈsɜːk, bə-ǁbɜːrˈsɜːrk, ˈbɜːrsɜːrk/ adj **go berserk** *informal* to become very angry and violent in a crazy way: *The guy went berserk and started hitting Paul.*

berth /bɜːθǁbɜːrθ/ n [C] **1** a place to sleep on a train or boat **2** the place where a ship comes to land

be·set /bɪˈset/ v **beset, beset, besetting** [T] *formal* to cause trouble for someone: *The family was beset by financial difficulties.*

be·side /bɪˈsaɪd/ prep **1** next to or very close to someone or something: *Gary sat down beside me.* \ *a cabin beside the lake* → see colour picture on page 474 **2** used to compare two people or things: *This year's sales figures don't look very good beside last year's.* **3** **be beside the point** to not be important: *"I'm not hungry." "That's beside the point, you need to eat!"* **4** **be beside yourself (with anger/fear/grief/joy etc)** to feel a particular emotion very strongly: *The boy was beside himself with fury.*

be·sides[1] /bɪˈsaɪdz/ adv **1** *spoken* said when you are giving another reason for something: *I wanted to help her out. Besides, I needed the money.* **2** used to say that something is also true: *Besides going to college, she works fifteen hours a week.*

USAGE NOTE: besides and except

Use **besides** to mean 'in addition to someone or something else': *Is there anything to drink besides coffee?* \ *Who's coming besides your parents?* **Except** means that someone or something is not included: *I remembered everything except my toothbrush.*

---

besides[2] prep in addition to something or someone: *Who's going to be there besides David and me?*

be·siege /bɪˈsiːdʒ/ v **1** **be besieged by people/worries/thoughts etc** to be surrounded by a lot of people or to be very worried etc: *a rock star besieged by fans* **2** **be besieged with letters/questions/demands etc** to receive a lot of letters, be asked a lot of questions etc: *The radio station was besieged with letters of complaint.* **3** [T] if an army besieges a place, soldiers surround it

best[1] /best/ adj [the superlative of 'good'] better than anyone or anything else: *the best player on the team* \ *What's the best way to get to El Paso?* \ **my best friend** (=the one I know and like the most)

best[2] adv [the superlative of 'well'] **1** more than anyone else or anything else: *Helen knows him best.* \ *Which song do you like best?* **2** in a way that is better than any other: *It works best if you oil it thoroughly first.* **3** **as best you can** as well as you can: *She would have to manage as best she could.*

best[3] n **1** **the best** someone or something that is better than any others: *Which stereo is the best?* **2** **want/deserve etc the best** to want, deserve etc a situation or result that is better than any other you could achieve: *All parents want the best for their children.* **3** **do/try your best** to try very hard to achieve something: *I did my best, but I still didn't pass.* **4** **at best** used to emphasize that something is not very good, even when you consider it in the best possible way: *You should get 10 or, at best, 11 thousand dollars pension.* **5 at your/its etc best** doing something as well as you are, it is etc able to: *The movie shows Hollywood at its best.* **6 make the best of sth/make the best of a bad job** to accept a bad situation and do what you can to make it better: *It's not going to be easy, but we'll just have to make the best of it.* **7 be (all) for the best** to have a good result, even though at first this seemed unlikely: *"She didn't get that job." "Well maybe it's for the best – she wouldn't have enjoyed it."*

best man /ˌ. ˈ./ n [singular] the man who helps at a wedding and stands next to the man who is getting married

be·stow /bɪˈstəʊ‖-ˈstoʊ/ v [T] *formal* to give someone something, especially something important

best·sel·ler /ˌbestˈselə‖-ər/ n [C] a book that a lot of people have bought —**best-selling** *adj*: *best-selling author, Tom Clancy*

bet[1] /bet/ v **bet, bet, betting 1 I/I'll bet** *spoken* **a)** said when you think that something is probably true or will probably happen: *I'll bet that made her mad!|I bet it'll rain tomorrow.* **b)** used to show that you agree with someone or understand how they feel: *"I was furious." "I bet you were!"* **c)** used to show that you do not believe someone: *"I was really worried about you." "Yeah, I'll bet."* **2 you bet (your life)!** *spoken* used to agree with someone or to say that you are definitely going to do something: *"Are you coming along?" "You bet!"* **3** [I,T] to try to win money by guessing the result of a race, game etc: **bet sth on sth** *Brad bet fifty bucks on the Bears to win.|*bet sb $5/£10 etc (that)* *Sue bet £5 that I wouldn't pass my driving test.*

bet[2] n [C] **1 a)** when you try to win money by guessing the result of a race, game etc: **have a bet on sth** *Higgins had a bet on the World Series.* **b)** the money that you GAMBLE with in order to try to win more money: *a $10 bet* **2 your best bet** *spoken* used when you are telling someone what is the best thing to do: *Your best bet would be to avoid the motorway.* **3 a good bet** something that is likely to be useful or successful: *The earrings seemed like a good bet for a birthday present.* ➞ see also **hedge your bets** (HEDGE[2])

be·tray /bɪˈtreɪ/ v [T] **1** to behave dishonestly towards someone who loves you, trusts you, or supports you, or do something that will cause problems for them: *We all feel that Charles has betrayed us.* **2** to tell people secrets that harm your country, party, company etc **3** to let people see an emotion that you were trying to hide: *Her face betrayed no hint of her nervousness.*

be·tray·al /bɪˈtreɪəl/ n [C,U] the act of betraying someone

bet·ter[1] /ˈbetə‖-ər/ *adj* **1** [the comparative of 'good'] more useful, suitable, interesting etc than something or someone else: *He's applying for a better job.|*better than* *The weather is a lot better than it was last week.|*much better* *The Mexican place across the street has much better food.|*feel better* *I'd feel better if I could talk to someone about this.* **2 a)** less ill or less painful than before: *Eve had the flu, but she's much*

better now.|*get better* *I hope your sore throat gets better soon.|*feel better* *David's feeling a little better since he started taking the penicillin.* **b)** completely well again after being ill: *I don't think you should go swimming until you're better.* **3 it would be better (to do sth)** used to give advice about what someone should do: *It would be better to employ a qualified electrician.* **4 get better** to improve: *Her tennis is getting a lot better.* **5 the sooner the better/the bigger the better etc** used in order to emphasize that something should happen as soon as possible, that it should be as big as possible etc: *She liked hot baths, the hotter the better.* **6 have seen better days** *informal* to be in a bad condition: *The sofa had definitely seen better days.*

USAGE NOTE: better

Had better or **'d better** are used to firmly advise someone about what they should do, especially in order for them to avoid something bad happening: *You'd better go now or you'll be late. | She'd better phone to say she won't be coming.* **You'd better** is a very direct way of giving advice, and can also be used to tell someone what to do: *You'd better get out of here now! | You'd better not do that again.* For this reason, do not use **you'd better** when you want to make a polite suggestion. Instead, use phrases such as **why don't you..., why not...,** or **it might be a good idea to...**

---

better[2] *adv* [the comparative of 'well'] **1** to a higher degree; more: *Which one do you like better?|*better than* *Marilyn knows New York a lot better than I do.* **2** in a better way: *better than* *Tina speaks French better than her sister.* **3 had better (do sth)** *spoken* **a)** used to tell someone they ought to be something: *It's getting late, you'd better get changed.* **b)** used when you are warning someone that they should or should not do something: *You'd better not tell Dad about this.* ➞ see also BETTER OFF

better[3] *n* **1 get the better of sb a)** if a feeling gets the better of you, you do not control it when you should: *Finally, his curiosity got the better of him and he read Dee's letter.* **b)** to defeat someone **2 for the better** in a way that improves the situation: **a change for the better** *Smaller classes are definitely a change for the better.*

better[4] *v* [T] *formal* to achieve something that is better than something else: *No team has ever bettered our record.*

better off /ˌ.. ˈ. ◂/ *adj* **1** more successful, richer, or having more advantages than you did before: *Most businesses in the area are better off than they were 10 years ago.* **2 be better off (doing sth)** *spoken* used to give advice about what someone should do: *Honestly, you're better off without him.*

be·tween[1] /bɪˈtwiːn/ *prep* **1** in or into the space or time that separates two things, people, or events: *Judy was sitting between Kate and me.|Try not to eat between meals.* ➞ see also IN-BETWEEN and see colour picture on page 474 **2** used to show the highest and lowest price, age, temperature etc, or the greatest and smallest amount, distance etc: *The project will cost between 10 and 12 million dollars.* **3** used to show that something is divided or shared by two people, places, or things: *We had about two loads of laundry between us.* **4** used to show a relationship or comparison between two people, things, events etc: *What's the difference between the two computers?* **5** used to show how two places are connected: *a regular train service between London and Paris*

USAGE NOTE: between and among

Use **between** to talk about being in the middle of two people, things, times etc: *They arrived between two-thirty and three.* Use **among** when someone or something is in the middle of three or more people, things etc: *They wandered among the crowds in the marketplace.*

between[2] also **in between** *adv* **a)** in or into the space that separates two things, people etc: *two houses with a fence between* **b)** in or into the time that separates two events: *periods of frantic activity with brief pauses in between* → see also IN-BETWEEN

bev·er·age /ˈbevərɪdʒ/ *n* [C] *formal* a drink: *alcoholic beverages*

be·ware /bɪˈweəǁ-ˈwer/ *v* [I only in imperative and infinitive] used to warn someone to be careful: **beware of (doing) sth** *Beware of the dog!* | *Please beware of signing anything without reading it carefully.*

be·wil·dered /bɪˈwɪldədǁ-ərd/ *adj* very confused and not sure what to do or think: *a bewildered old woman wandering in the street* — **bewilderment** *n* [U]

be·wil·der·ing /bɪˈwɪldərɪŋ/ *adj* making you feel very confused: *a bewildering range of choices*

be·witched /bɪˈwɪtʃt/ *adj* so interested in or attracted by someone or something that you cannot think clearly

be·yond[1] /bɪˈjɒndǁbɪˈjɑːnd/ *prep* **1** on or to the far side of something: *Beyond the river, cattle were grazing.* **2** **beyond repair/control/belief** etc used to say that something cannot be repaired, controlled, believed etc: *It's no good. It's broken beyond repair.* | *Due to circumstances beyond our control, the performance is cancelled.* **3** more than a particular amount or limit: *continuing to work beyond retirement age* **4** later than a particular time, date etc: *The ban has been extended beyond 1998.* **5** **it's beyond me (why/what etc)** *spoken* used to say that you do not understand something: *It's beyond me why they ever got married at all.* **6** except for: *The island doesn't have much industry beyond tourism.*

beyond[2] *adv* **1** on or to the far side of something: *a view from the mountains to the plains beyond* **2** later than a particular time, date etc: *planning for the year 2000 and beyond*

bi- /baɪ/ *prefix* used at the beginning of some words to mean including two of something, or doing something twice: *bilingual* (=speaking two languages perfectly, or written using two languages) | *bimonthly* (=every two months, or twice a month)

bi·as[1] /ˈbaɪəs/ *n* [C,U] an opinion about whether something is good or bad that unfairly influences how you deal with it: **+ against/in favour of** *The judge's decision definitely shows a bias against women.*

bias[2] *v* [T] to make something less fair

bi·ased /ˈbaɪəst/ *adj* judging something unfairly because of your personal opinions: *Most newspapers reporting are pretty biased.* | **in favour of/against/towards** *He's pretty biased against anyone who didn't go to university.*

bib /bɪb/ *n* [C] a piece of cloth or plastic that you tie under a baby's chin to protect its clothes while it eats

bi·ble /ˈbaɪbəl/ *n* [C] **1 the Bible** the holy book of the Christian religion **2** a copy of this book **3** a useful and important book on a particular subject: *a textbook that is the medical student's bible*

bib·li·og·ra·phy /ˌbɪbliˈɒɡrəfiǁ-ˈɑːɡ-/ *n* [C] a list of all the books and articles connected with a particular subject

bi·cen·te·na·ry /ˌbaɪsenˈtiːnəriǁ-ˈtenəri, -ˈsentəneri/ *BrE,* **bi·cen·ten·ni·al** *AmE* /ˌbaɪsenˈteniəl/ *n* [C] the day or year exactly 200 years after an important event: *the bicentenary of Mozart's death*

bi·ceps /ˈbaɪseps/ *n* [C], *plural* **biceps** the large muscle on the front of your upper arm

bick·er /ˈbɪkəǁ-ər/ *v* [I] to argue about something that is not very important: **+ about/over** *The kids were bickering about who would sleep in the top bunk.*

bi·cy·cle /ˈbaɪsɪkəl/ *n* [C] a vehicle with two wheels that you ride by pushing the PEDALs with your feet → see colour picture on page 669

bid[1] /bɪd/ *n* [C] **1** an attempt to achieve or get something: **+ for** *Clinton's successful bid for the presidency in 1992* | **bid to do sth** *$5000 has been offered in a bid to catch the killer.* **2** an offer to pay a particular price for something: *a bid of $50 for the plate* **3** an offer to do work for someone at a particular price: **+ for** *The company accepted the lowest bid for the contract.*

bid[2] *v* **bid, bid, bidding** **1** [I,T] to offer to pay a particular price for something in an AUCTION: **+ for** *Freeman bid £50,000 for an antique table.* **2** **bid to do sth** *informal* to try to do something **3** [I] to offer to do some work for someone at a particular price

bid[3] *v* **bade** /bæd, beɪd/, *or* **bid, bid,** *or* **bidden** /ˈbɪdn/, **bidding** [T] *literary* **bid sb good morning/goodbye etc** to say good morning, goodbye etc to someone

bid·ding /ˈbɪdɪŋ/ *n* [U] **1** when people in an AUCTION say how much they are willing to pay for something **2** **do sb's bidding** *literary* to do what someone tells you to do

bide /baɪd/ *v* **bide your time** to wait until the right time to do something

bi·en·ni·al /baɪˈeniəl/ *adj* happening once every two years

big /bɪɡ/ *adj* **1** of more than average size or amount; large: *a big red balloon* | *There's a big age difference between them.* | *How big is their new house?* **2** important or serious: *The big game is on Friday.* | *The company lost another big contract this year.* **3** **your big sister/big brother** *informal* a sister or brother who is older than you: *This is my big sister.* **4** *informal* successful or popular: *Microsoft is big in the software market.* | **make it big** (=become very successful): *I knew I'd never make it big as a professional golfer.* **5** **big deal!** used when you do not think something is as important as someone else thinks it is: *His idea of a pay rise is to give me another £5 a month! Big deal!*

Big Ap·ple /ˌ. '../ *n informal* **the Big Apple** New York City

Big Broth·er /ˌ. '../ *n* [singular] a person, organization, or government that seems to control people's lives and limit their freedom

big busi·ness /ˌ. '../ *n* [U] very large companies considered as a group that has a big influence on society

big·head·ed /ˌbɪg 'hedⁱd◂/ *adj* someone who is bigheaded thinks they are better than other people

big name /ˌ. '.◂/ *n* [C] a famous actor, singer, company etc: *big names like IBM, Hewlett-Packard and Digital* —**big-name** *adj*: *big-name Broadway entertainers*

big·ot /'bɪgət/ *n* [C] someone who is bigoted

big·ot·ed /'bɪgətⁱd/ *adj* someone who is bigoted has very strong and unreasonable opinions about people who belong to a different race, religion, or political group, and refuses to change their opinions

big·ot·ry /'bɪgətri/ *n* [U] bigoted behaviour or beliefs

big shot /'. ./ *n* [C] *informal* someone who has an important or powerful job

big-tick·et /'. ../ *adj AmE informal* very expensive: *big-ticket items like CD players and videos*

big time¹ /'. ./ *adv informal, especially AmE* used to emphasize something that has just been said: *"So I'm in trouble, huh?" "Yeah, big time!"*

big time² *n* **the big time** *informal* when someone is very famous or important, for example in politics or sports: *She first hit the big time in the musical 'Evita'.* —**big-time** *adj*: *big-time drug dealers*

bike¹ /baɪk/ *n* [C] *informal* **1** a bicycle: *kids riding their bikes in the street* **2** *especially AmE* a MOTORCYCLE

bike² *v* [I] to travel on a bicycle

bik·er /'baɪkəll-ər/ *n* [C] someone who rides a MOTORCYCLE, especially as part of a group

bi·ki·ni /bᵻ'ki:ni/ *n* [C] a piece of clothing in two parts that women wear for swimming

bi·lat·er·al /baɪ'lætərəl/ *adj* **bilateral agreement/treaty etc** an agreement between two groups or countries: *bilateral Middle East peace talks* —**bilaterally** *adv*

bile /baɪl/ *n* [U] **1** a liquid produced by your LIVER to help your body DIGEST food **2** *literary* strong anger and hate

bi·lin·gual /baɪ'lɪŋgwəl/ *adj* **1** able to speak two languages **2** spoken or written in two languages: *a bilingual dictionary*

bill¹ /bɪl/ *n* [C] **1** a list of things you have bought or services you have used and the amount you have to pay for them: **pay a bill** *I have to remember to pay the phone bill this week.* **2** a plan for a new law, written down for a government to decide on: *a Senate tax bill* **3** *AmE* a piece of paper money; NOTE, BANK-NOTE *BrE*: *a ten-dollar bill* **4** a bird's beak → see also **foot the bill** (FOOT²)

bill² *v* [T] **1** to send a bill to someone: *They've billed me for things I didn't buy.* **2** **bill sth as** to advertise something in a particular way: *The boxing match was billed as "the fight of the century".*

bill·board /'bɪlbɔːdll-bɔːrd/ *n* [C] a big sign used for advertising, especially next to a road; HOARDING *BrE*

bil·let /'bɪlⁱt/ *v* [T] to put soldiers in people's houses to live for a short time —**billet** *n* [C]

bill·fold /'bɪlfəʊldll-foʊld/ *n* [C] *AmE* a small flat leather folding case for putting paper money in; WALLET

bil·liards /'bɪljədzll-ərdz/ *n* [U] a game played on a cloth-covered table, in which balls are hit against each other into pockets at the edge of the table

bil·lion /'bɪljən/ *number, plural* **billion** or **billions** 1,000,000,000 —**billionth** *number*

bill of rights /ˌ. . './ *n* [C] an official written list of the most important rights of the citizens of a country

bil·low /'bɪləʊll-loʊ/ *v* [I] if smoke billows, a lot of it rises into the air: *Smoke came billowing out of the building.* —**billow** *n* [C]

bil·ly goat /'bɪli gəʊtll-goʊt/ *n* [C] *informal* a male goat

bim·bo /'bɪmbəʊll-boʊ/ *n* [C] *informal* an offensive word meaning an attractive but stupid woman

bi·month·ly /baɪ'mʌnθli/ *adj, adv* happening or being done every two months or twice each month: *a bimonthly magazine* | *The magazine is published bimonthly.*

bin /bɪn/ *n* [C] a large container for storing things or for putting waste in → see picture at KITCHEN

bi·na·ry /'baɪnəri/ *adj technical* **1** **the binary system** a system of counting, used in computers, in which numbers are shown using a system that only includes the numbers 0 and 1 **2** consisting of two things or parts

bind¹ /baɪnd/ *bound* /baʊnd/, *bound, binding* *v* **1** [T] to tie something together firmly, with string or rope: *His legs were bound with rope.* **2** *also* **bind together** [T] *formal* to form a strong connection between two people, countries etc: *We are bound together by history and language.*

3 [T] to make someone obey something such as a law or promise: *Each country is bound by the treaty.* **4** [T] to fasten the pages of a book together and put them in a cover **5** [I,T] to make substances stick together in a mass: *Use a beaten egg to bind the hamburger together.*

bind sb over *phr v* [T] *BrE law* to order someone to cause no more trouble for a period of time

bind² *n* **a bind** *informal* an annoying or difficult situation: *It's such a bind having to walk everywhere.*

bind·ing¹ /ˈbaɪndɪŋ/ *adj* a contract, agreement etc that is binding must be obeyed: *The contract isn't binding until you sign it.*

binding² *n* [C] the cover of a book

binge¹ /bɪndʒ/ *n* [C] *informal* a short period of time when you drink too much alcohol, eat too much food etc: **go on a binge** *He's gone out on a binge with his mates.*

binge² *v* [I] to eat a lot of food in a very short time

bin·go /ˈbɪŋɡəʊ‖-ɡoʊ/ *n* [U] a game in which you win if a set of numbers chosen by chance are the same as a line of numbers on your card

bi·noc·u·lars /bɪˈnɒkjʊ̈ləz, baɪ-‖-ˈnɑːkjʊ̈lərz/ *n* [plural] a pair of glasses like short TELESCOPES used for looking at distant objects

bi·o·chem·is·try /ˌbaɪəʊˈkemɪstri‖ˌbaɪoʊ-/ *n* [U] the scientific study of the chemistry of living things —**biochemist** *n* [C] —**biochemical** *adj*

bi·o·de·gra·da·ble /ˌbaɪəʊdɪˈɡreɪdəbəl◂ ˌbaɪoʊ-/ *adj* a material that is biodegradable is able to decay naturally so that it does not harm the environment: *Most plastic is not biodegradable.*

bi·og·ra·pher /baɪˈɒɡrəfə‖-ˈɑːɡrəfər/ *n* [C] someone who writes a biography

bi·og·ra·phy /baɪˈɒɡrəfi‖-ˈɑːɡ-/ *n* [C,U] a book about a person's life, or all books like this considered as a group —**biographical** /ˌbaɪəˈɡræfɪkəl◂/ *adj*

bi·o·lo·gi·cal /ˌbaɪəˈlɒdʒɪkəl◂ ‖-ˈlɑː-/ *adj* connected with biology: *a biological process* —**biologically** /-kli/ *adv*

bi·ol·o·gy /baɪˈɒlədʒi‖-ˈɑːl-/ *n* [U] the scientific study of living things —**biologist** *n* [C]

bi·op·sy /ˈbaɪɒpsi‖-ɑːp-/ *n* [C] when cells, skin etc are removed from someone who is ill, in order to learn more about a disease they may have

bi·o·tech·nol·o·gy /ˌbaɪəʊtekˈnɒlədʒi‖ˌbaɪoʊtekˈnɑː-/ *n* [U] the use of living things such as cells and BACTERIA in science and industry to make drugs, chemicals etc

bi·par·ti·san /ˌbaɪpɑːtɪ̈ˈzæn‖baɪˈpɑːrtɪ̈zən/ *adj* consisting of two political parties: *a bipartisan committee*

bi·plane /ˈbaɪpleɪn/ *n* [C] an old-fashioned type of plane with two sets of wings

birch /bɜːtʃ‖bɜːrtʃ/ *n* [C,U] a tree with smooth thin branches and BARK that comes off easily

bird /bɜːd‖bɜːrd/ *n* [C] an animal with wings and feathers that produces eggs and can usually fly → see also **kill two birds with one stone** (KILL¹)

bird·ie /ˈbɜːdi‖ˈbɜːrdi/ *n* [C] *AmE* a small light object with feathers that you hit across a net in BADMINTON; SHUTTLECOCK

bird of prey /ˌ. . ˈ./ *n* [C] a bird that kills other birds and small animals to eat them

bird·seed /ˈbɜːdsiːd‖ˈbɜːrd-/ *n* [U] a mixture of seeds for feeding birds

bi·ro /ˈbaɪərəʊ‖ˈbaɪroʊ/ *n* [C] *BrE trademark* a type of pen

birth /bɜːθ‖bɜːrθ/ *n* **1 give birth (to)** if a woman gives birth, she produces a baby from her body: *Jo gave birth to a baby girl at 6:20 a.m.* **2** [C,U] the time when a baby comes out of its mother's body: **at birth** (=when someone is born): *Joel weighed 7 pounds at birth.* **3** [U] someone's family origin: **by birth** *Her grandfather was French by birth.* **4 the birth of sth** the time when something begins to exist: *the birth of the new democracy*

birth cer·tif·i·cate /ˈ. .ˌ..../ *n* [C] an official document that shows when and where you were born

birth con·trol /ˈ. .ˌ./ *n* [U] when you use methods to control whether you have a baby or not: *advice on birth control*

birth·day /ˈbɜːθdeɪ‖ˈbɜːrθ-/ *n* [C] the date on which you were born, when you celebrate each year: *a birthday card* | *When is your birthday?* | *Happy Birthday!* (=what you say to someone on their birthday)

birth·mark /ˈbɜːθmɑːk‖ˈbɜːrθmɑːrk/ *n* [C] an unusual mark on someone's skin that is there when they are born

birth·place /ˈbɜːθpleɪs‖ˈbɜːrθ-/ *n* [C] the place where someone was born

birth·rate /ˈbɜːθreɪt‖ˈbɜːrθ-/ *n* [C] the average number of births during a particular period of time

bis·cuit /ˈbɪskɪ̈t/ *n* [C] **1** *BrE* a thin dry usually sweet cake; COOKIE *AmE*: *chocolate biscuits* → see colour picture on page 440 **2** *AmE* a kind of bread that is baked in small round shapes

bi·sex·u·al¹ /baɪˈsekʃuəl/ *adj* sexually attracted to both men and women —**bisexuality** /ˌbaɪsekʃuˈæli̇ti/ *n* [U]

bisexual² *n* [C] someone who is sexually attracted to both men and women

bish·op /ˈbɪʃəp/ *n* [C] a priest with a high rank who is in charge of the churches and priests in a large area

bi·son /ˈbaɪsən/ *n* [C] a wild animal like a large cow with long hair; BUFFALO

bit¹ /bɪt/ *n* **1 a** (little) bit slightly, but not very much; a little: *Can you turn the radio down a little bit?* | **a bit** upset/stupid/cold etc *I'm a little bit tired this morning.* | **not a bit** (=not at all): *He didn't seem a bit embarrassed.* **2 quite a bit** a fairly large amount: *He'd probably be willing to pay her quite a bit of money.* **3** [C] a small amount or piece of something: **+ of** *The floor was covered in tiny bits of glass.* | **to bits** (=into small pieces): *I tore the letter to bits and burned it.* **4** [C] a unit for measuring the amount of information a computer can use **5** [singular] *informal* a short amount of time: **in a bit** (=a short time from now): *We'll talk about the Civil War in just a bit.* | **bit by bit** (=gradually): *I could see that she was learning, bit by bit.* | **for a bit** *BrE* (=for a short time): *Could you look after the baby for a bit?* **6 every bit as** used to emphasize that someone or something is as good, surprising etc as someone or something else: *Ray was every bit* as good-looking as his brother. **7 a bit of a problem/surprise/fool etc** *BrE spoken* a problem etc but not a very big or serious one: *I'm sorry, I can't stop, I'm in a bit of a hurry.* **8** [C] a part of a tool for cutting or making holes **9** [C] a metal bar that is put in the mouth of a horse and used to control its movements

bit² *v* the past tense of BITE

bitch¹ /bɪtʃ/ *n* **1** [C] an offensive word for a woman that you dislike: *She's such a bitch!* **2 be a bitch** *spoken informal* to cause problems or be difficult: *I love this sweater but it's a bitch to wash.* **3** [C] a female dog

bitch² *v* [I] *informal* to complain or say unkind things about someone or something, especially when they are not there: **+ about** *He's been bitching all day about the fact that Jimmy owes him money.*

bitch·y /ˈbɪtʃi/ *adj informal* often saying unkind things about people —**bitchily** *adv* —**bitchiness** *n* [U]

bite¹ /baɪt/ *v* **bit, bitten, biting** **1** [I,T] to cut or crush something with your teeth: *Be careful of the dog. Jerry said he bites. | She bites her fingernails. | Marta got bitten by a snake. | **+ into** I had just bitten into the apple.* **2 bite the dust** *informal* to die, fail, be defeated, or stop working: *Government plans to increase VAT finally bit the dust yesterday.* **3 bite the bullet** to decide to do something even though it is unpleasant: *The company had to bite the bullet and repair the fault in their product.* **4** [I] to start to have a serious effect on something: *The new tobacco taxes have begun to bite.*

bite

bite² *n* **1** [C] the act of cutting or crushing something with your teeth, or the piece of food that is cut: *Can I have a bite of your pizza? | **take a bite** He took a bite of the cheese.* **2** [C] a wound made when an animal or insect bites you: *I'm covered in mosquito bites!* **3 a bite (to eat)** *informal* a quick meal: *Let's have a bite to eat before we go.* **4** [C] when a fish takes the food from a hook

bite-size /ˈ. ./ also **bite-sized** *adj* the right size to fit in your mouth easily: *bite-size pieces of chicken*

bit·ing /ˈbaɪtɪŋ/ *adj* **1** a biting wind is unpleasantly cold **2** biting criticisms or remarks are very unkind —**bitingly** *adv*

bit·ten /ˈbɪtn/ *v* the past participle of BITE

bit·ter¹ /ˈbɪtəl-ər/ *adj* **1** angry for a long time because you feel that something bad or unfair has happened to you: *She feels very bitter about the way the courts treated her.* **2** making you feel very unhappy: *The judge's decision was a bitter blow to her.* **3** full of hate and anger: *bitter enemies* **4** having a strong taste, like coffee without sugar **5** air or weather that is bitter is unpleasantly cold: *a bitter wind* **6 to/until the bitter end** to the end, even though unpleasant things happen: *The UN stayed in the war zone until the bitter end.* —**bitterness** *n* [U]

bitter² *n* [C,U] *BrE* beer with a bitter taste, or a glass of this: *A pint of bitter, please.*

bit·ter·ly /ˈbɪtəlil-ər/ *adv* **1** in a way that makes you very unhappy, or that shows that you are very unhappy: *bitterly disappointed | "She doesn't care," he said bitterly.* **2 bitterly cold** very cold **3** in a way that is full of hate and anger: *a bitterly fought battle*

bi·tu·men /ˈbɪtʃʊmɪn‖bɪˈtuː-/ *n* [U] a thick black sticky substance used for covering roads and roofs

bi·zarre /bɪˈzɑː‖-ˈzɑːr/ *adj* very unusual and strange: *a bizarre coincidence* —**bizarrely** *adv*

black¹ /blæk/ *adj* **1** having the darkest colour, like the colour of the night sky or of coal: *a black dress | The mountains looked black against the sky.* → see colour picture on page 244 **2** belonging to a race of people with dark skin: *Over half the students here are black.* **3** black coffee or tea does not have milk in it **4** a situation that is black seems very bad: *Things were looking very black for the British steel industry.* **5 black humour/comedy** humour that makes unpleasant subjects seem funny **6 black and blue** *informal* having a lot of BRUISES on your body **7** angry or disapproving: *black looks* —**blackness** *n* [U]

black² *n* **1** [U] the colour of the night sky or of coal → see colour picture on page 114 **2** [C] also **Black** someone belonging to a race of people with dark skin **3 in black and white** written or printed: *The rules are there in black and white for everybody to see.* **4 be in the black** to have money in your bank account: *We're in the black for the first time in three years.* → opposite **be in the red** (RED²)

black³ *v*

black out *phr v* [I] to suddenly become unconscious: *Sharon blacked out and fell to the floor.*

black belt /ˌ. ˈ./ *n* [C] a high rank in JUDO and KARATE, or someone who has this rank

black·ber·ry /ˈblækbəril-beri/ *n* [C] a very sweet black or dark purple BERRY

black·bird /ˈblækbɜːd‖-bɜːrd/ *n* [C] a common bird, the male of which is completely black

black·board /ˈblækbɔːd‖-bɔːrd/ *n* [C] a dark smooth board that you write on with CHALK in schools → see colour picture on page 80

black·cur·rant /ˌblækˈkʌrənt‖-ˈkɜːr-/ *n* [C] a small blue-black BERRY eaten as a fruit

black·en /ˈblækən/ *v* [I,T] to become black, or make something black: *Smoke had blackened the kitchen walls.*

black eye /ˌ. ˈ./ *n* [C] an area of dark skin around someone's eye that is the result of them being hit

black hole /ˌ. ˈ./ *n* [C] an area in space that pulls everything near it into it

black·list /ˈblækˌlɪst/ *v* [T] to put someone or something on a list of people or things that are considered bad or dangerous: *Members of the Communist Party have been blacklisted and are unable to find work.*

black mag·ic /ˌ. ˈ../ *n* [U] evil magic connected with the Devil

black·mail /ˈblækmeɪl/ *n* [U] when someone makes you pay them money or do what they want by threatening to tell secrets about you —**blackmail** *v* [T] —**blackmailer** *n* [C]

black mar·ket /ˌ. ˈ../ *n* [C] when things are bought or sold illegally: **on the black market**

drugs that were only available on the black market

black·out /ˈblækaʊt/ *n* [C] **1** a period during a war when lights must be turned off or covered at night **2** when you suddenly become unconscious: *He's suffered from blackouts since the accident.*

black sheep /ˌ. ˈ./ *n* [C] someone who is considered to be bad or embarrassing by the rest of their family or group

black·smith /ˈblæk,smɪθ/ *n* [C] someone who makes and repairs things made of iron, especially HORSESHOEs

black·top /ˈblæktɒpǁ-tɑːp/ *n* [U] *AmE* the thick black substance used to cover roads; TARMAC *BrE*

blad·der /ˈblædəǁ-ər/ *n* [C] the part of your body where URINE is stored before it leaves your body

blade /bleɪd/ *n* [C] **1** the flat sharp cutting part of a knife, tool, or weapon: *The blade needs to be kept sharp.* | *razor blades* **2** a leaf of grass or a similar plant **3** the flat wide part of an OAR, PROPELLER etc

blame[1] /bleɪm/ *v* [T] **1** to say or think that someone is responsible for something bad: *It's not fair to blame Charlie. He didn't know anything.* | **blame sb for sth** *Mothers often blame themselves for their children's problems.* | **blame sth on sb** *Don't try to blame this on me!* | **be to blame** (=be responsible for something bad): *Hospital staff were not in any way to blame for the baby's death.* **2** **I don't blame you/them etc** *spoken* used to say that you think it was reasonable for someone to do what they did: *"I lost my temper with Ann." "I don't blame you – she's very annoying."*

USAGE NOTE: blame

Compare the way the nouns **blame** and **fault** are used in the following sentences: *They were not to blame for the accident.* | *The accident was not their fault.* **Blame** is used in a few fixed ways, especially **be to blame**, **get the blame** and **put the blame on sb**, but **fault** is usually used in the phrase **be sb's fault**: *It was all your fault! Why do I always get the blame?*

---

blame[2] *n* [U] when other people say you are responsible for a mistake or something bad: **get the blame (for sth)** (=be blamed): *I don't know why I always get the blame for other people's mistakes.* | **take the blame** (=say that you are responsible): *You shouldn't have to take the blame if you didn't do it.*

blame·less /ˈbleɪmləs/ *adj* not guilty of anything bad: *a blameless life*

blanch /blɑːntʃǁblæntʃ/ *v* [I] to become pale because you are afraid or shocked: **+ at** *Nick glanced at Jeff, who had blanched at the news.*

bland /blænd/ *adj* **1** not interesting and not exciting: *bland TV quiz shows* **2** bland food has very little taste: *a very bland white sauce* —**blandly** *adv* —**blandness** *n* [U]

blank[1] /blæŋk/ *adj* **1** a blank sheet of paper, CASSETTE etc has nothing written or recorded on it **2** **go blank** if your mind goes blank, you are suddenly unable to remember something: *When she saw the exam questions, her mind went*

blank. **3** a blank expression or look shows no feelings —**blankness** *n* [U]

blank[2] *n* [C] an empty space on a piece of paper, for you to write a word or letter in: *Fill in the blanks on the application form.* ➡ see also **draw a blank** (DRAW[1])

blan·ket[1] /ˈblæŋkɪt/ *n* [C] **1** a thick warm cover for a bed **2** *literary* a thick layer of something that covers something: *a blanket of snow on the mountains*

blanket[2] *adj* **a blanket statement/rule/ban** a statement, rule etc that affects everyone or includes all possible kinds of something: *a blanket ban on all types of hunting*

blanket[3] *v* [T] to cover something completely: *The coast was blanketed in fog.*

blank·ly /ˈblæŋkli/ *adv* without showing any emotion or understanding: *When I spoke to him in Russian, he stared at me blankly.*

blare /bleəǁbler/ also **blare out** *v* [I,T] to make a very loud unpleasant noise: *blaring horns* | *music blaring out from her car* —**blare** *n* [singular]

blas·phe·my /ˈblæsfi̩mi/ *n* [C,U] something you say or do that insults God or insults people's religious beliefs —**blasphemous** *adj*: *blasphemous talk* —**blaspheme** /blæsˈfiːm/ *v* [I]

blast[1] /blɑːstǁblæst/ *n* **1** [C] an explosion: *The blast knocked him forward.* **2** [C] a sudden strong movement of wind or air: *a blast of icy air* **3** **full blast** as strongly or loudly as possible: *When I got home, she had the TV on full blast.* **4** [C] a sudden very loud noise: *a trumpet blast* **5** [singular] *AmE spoken* an enjoyable and exciting experience: *We had a blast at Mitch's party.*

blast[2] *v* **1** [I,T] to break rock into pieces using explosives: *They blasted a tunnel through the side of the mountain.* **2** also **blast out** [I,T] to produce a lot of loud noise, especially music: *a radio blasting out pop music* **3** [T] to attack a place or person with bombs or large guns: *Two gunmen blasted their way into the building.*

blast[3] *interjection BrE spoken* used when you are annoyed about something: *Blast! I've lost my keys!*

blast fur·nace /ˈ. ,../ *n* [C] a large industrial structure where heat is used to separate iron from the rock that contains it

blast-off /ˈ. ./ *n* [singular] when a SPACECRAFT leaves the ground: *10 seconds to blast-off!*

bla·tant /ˈbleɪtənt/ *adj* very noticeable and offensive: *a blatant lie* —**blatantly** *adv*

blaze[1] /bleɪz/ *n* **1** [C] a large fire: *Fire officials continued searching for the cause of the blaze.* **2** **a blaze of light/colour** a very bright light or colour: *a blaze of sunshine* **3** **in a blaze of glory/publicity** receiving a lot of praise or public attention: *In a blaze of publicity, Maxwell launched a new newspaper.*

blaze[2] *v* [I] to burn or shine very brightly and strongly: *a huge log fire blazing in the hearth*

blaz·er /ˈbleɪzəǁ-ər/ *n* [C] a kind of JACKET with a special sign of a school or club on it: *a school blazer*

blaz·ing /ˈbleɪzɪŋ/ *adj* **1** extremely hot: *a blazing summer day* **2** very angry: *a blazing row*

bleach[1] /bliːtʃ/ *n* [U] a chemical used to clean things or make them whiter

bleach² *v* [T] to make something white or lighter in colour by using chemicals or sunlight: *bleached hair*

bleach·ers /ˈbliːtʃəzǁ-ərz/ *n* [plural] *AmE* rows of seats where people sit to watch sports games

bleak /bliːk/ *adj* **1** a bleak situation seems very bad and unlikely to improve: *Without a job, the future seemed bleak.* **2** cold and unattractive: *a bleak November day* | *the bleak landscape of the northern hills* —**bleakness** *n* [U]

blear·y /ˈblɪəriǁˈblɪri/ *adj* if you have bleary eyes you cannot see clearly because you are tired or have been crying: **bleary-eyed** *Sam came down to breakfast looking bleary-eyed.* —**blearily** *adv*

bleat /bliːt/ *v* [I] **1** to make the sound that a sheep or goat makes **2** *BrE informal* to complain in a silly or annoying way: *Stop bleating!* —**bleat** *n* [C]

bled /bled/ *v* the past tense and past participle of bleed

bleed /bliːd/ *v* **bled** /bled/, **bled, bleeding** [I] if you bleed, blood comes out of a cut on your body: *The cut on his forehead was bleeding again.*

bleed·ing /ˈbliːdɪŋ/ *n* [U] the flow of blood from a wound

bleep¹ /bliːp/ *n* [C] a high electronic sound: *the shrill bleep of the alarm clock*

bleep² *v* [I] to make a high electronic sound

bleep·er /ˈbliːpəǁ-ər/ *n* [C] *BrE* a small electronic machine you carry with you, that makes a high sound when it receives a message for you; PAGER

blem·ish /ˈblemɪʃ/ *n* [C] a mark that spoils something: *a blemish on her cheek* —**blemished** *adj*

blend¹ /blend/ *v* **1** [T] to mix two or more things together thoroughly: *Blend the butter and sugar.* **2** [I,T] to combine two different features: *a story that blends fact and fiction*

blend in *phr v* [I] if something blends in, it looks suitably similar to everything around it: **+ with** *We chose curtains that blended in with the wallpaper.* | **blend into sth** *old stone cottages that blend into the landscape*

blend² *n* [C] a mixture of two or more things: *a unique blend of Brazilian and Colombian coffee* | *the right blend of sunshine and soil for growing grapes*

blend·er /ˈblendəǁ-ər/ *n* [C] a small electric machine that you use to mix food → see picture at KITCHEN

bless /bles/ *v* **blessed, or blest** /blest/, **blessed, or blest, blessing** [T] **1** to ask God to protect someone or something: *Their mission had been blessed by the Pope.* **2** **be blessed with sth** to be lucky enough to have something: *George was blessed with good looks.* **3** to ask God to make something holy: *The priest blessed the bread and wine.* **4** **bless you** *spoken* said when someone SNEEZES

bless·ed /ˈblesɪd/ *adj* **1** enjoyable or desirable: *a moment of blessed silence* **2** *BrE spoken*

used to show that you are annoyed: *I've cleaned every blessed room in the house.* **3** *formal* holy and loved by God: *the Blessed Virgin Mary*

bless·ing /ˈblesɪŋ/ *n* **1** [C] something good that improves your life or makes you happy: *The rain was a real blessing after all that heat.* **2** [U] someone's approval or encouragement: *They were determined to marry, with or without their parents' blessing.* **3** **a mixed blessing** something that is both good and bad: *Living close to the office turned out to be a mixed blessing.* **4** **a blessing in disguise** something that seems to be bad but that you later realize is good: *The lack of tourism on the island could be a blessing in disguise.* **5** [singular, U] protection and help from God, or the prayer in which you ask for this

blew /bluː/ *v* the past tense of BLOW

blight¹ /blaɪt/ *n* [singular, U] something which damages or spoils things: *the poverty that is a blight on our nation*

blight² *v* [T] to damage or spoil something: *an area blighted by unemployment*

blind¹ /blaɪnd/ *adj* **1** unable to see: *She was born blind.* **2** **the blind** people who cannot see **3** **blind faith/loyalty/panic etc** strong feelings that make you do things without thinking: *blind faith in their military leaders* **4** **blind to sth** unable or unwilling to notice something: *blind to their own weaknesses* **5** **turn a blind eye to sth** to pretend not to notice something bad that is happening **6** **blind corner/bend** a blind bend on a road is dangerous because you cannot see cars coming around it until they are in front of you —**blindness** *n* [U]

blind² *v* [T] **1** to make someone unable to see, either permanently or for a short time: *The deer was blinded by our headlights.* **2** to make someone unable to notice or realize the truth about something: **blind sb to sth** *Being in love blinded me to his faults.*

blind³ *n* [C] a piece of cloth or other material that you pull down to cover a window → see picture at KITCHEN → see also VENETIAN BLIND

blind·fold¹ /ˈblaɪndfəʊldǁ-foʊld/ *v* [T] to cover someone's eyes with a piece of cloth so that they cannot see: *The hostages were blindfolded and led to the cellar.*

blind·fold² *n* [C] a piece of cloth or other material that is put over someone's eyes to prevent them from being able to see

blind·ing /ˈblaɪndɪŋ/ *adj* **blinding light/flash** a very bright light

blind·ly /ˈblaɪndli/ *adv* **1** not seeing or not noticing what is around you: *She sat staring blindly out of the window.* **2** without thinking or understanding: *Don't blindly accept what they tell you.*

blind spot /ˈ. ./ *n* [C] a particular difficulty in accepting or understanding the facts about something: *He has a blind spot when it comes to his daughter's faults.*

blink¹ /blɪŋk/ *v* **1** [I,T] to open and close your eyes quickly: *He blinked as he stepped out into*

GRAMMAR NOTE: the present perfect progressive
You use the **present perfect progressive** to say how long you have been doing something: *I **have been learning** English for two years.* Remember that some verbs are not usually used in the progressive: *I **have known** Richard for 4 years.* not *I have been knowing Richard for 4 years.*

the sunlight. **2** if a light blinks, it goes on and off

blink² *n* **1** [C] the action of blinking **2 on the blink** *BrE informal* not working properly: *The phone's been on the blink all week*

blink·er /'blɪŋkəll-ər/ *n* [C] *AmE informal* TURN SIGNAL

blink·ered /'blɪŋkədll-ərd/ *adj* refusing to accept ideas about a subject that are new or different: *a blinkered attitude to life*

blip /blɪp/ *n* [C] **1** *informal* a sudden and temporary change from what usually happens: *This month's rise in prices could be just a blip.* **2** a flashing light on the screen of a piece of electronic equipment

bliss /blɪs/ *n* [U] complete happiness: *Two weeks lazing on a Greek island – what perfect bliss!*

bliss·ful /'blɪsfəl/ *adj* very happy: *the first blissful weeks after we married* **—blissfully** *adv*: *blissfully unaware of the problems ahead*

blis·ter¹ /'blɪstəll-ər/ *n* [C] a small area of skin that is swollen and full of liquid because it has been rubbed or burned

blister² *v* [I,T] to get blisters or cause blisters on skin or on a surface **—blistered** *adj*: *blistered hands*

blis·ter·ing /'blɪstərɪŋ/ *adj* **1** criticizing someone very strongly: *a blistering attack on the government* **2** extremely hot: *blistering heat*

blithe·ly /'blaɪðli/ *adv* without serious or careful thought: *They blithely ignored the danger.* **—blithe** *adj*

blitz /blɪts/ *n* **1 the Blitz** the attack on British cities from the air during the Second World War **2** [C] when you use a lot of effort to achieve something in a short time: *The campaign starts next month with a TV advertising blitz.* **—blitz** *v* [T]

bliz·zard /'blɪzədll-ərd/ *n* [C] a storm with a lot of wind and snow

bloat·ed /'bləʊtˌɪdll'bloʊ-/ *adj* **1** a body that is bloated is unpleasantly swollen because of gas or liquid forming inside it: *bloated corpses floating in the river.* **2** feeling very full and uncomfortable

blob /blɒbllblɑːb/ *n* [C] a small drop of a thick liquid: *blobs of paint*

bloc /blɒkllblɑːk/ *n* [C] a group of countries with the same political aims, working together: *the former Soviet bloc*

block¹ /blɒkllblɑːk/ *n* [C] **1** a piece of a solid material with straight sides: *a block of concrete | wooden blocks* **2** a square area of houses or buildings formed by four streets: *Let's walk around the block.* **3** *AmE* the distance along a city street from where one street crosses it to the next: *We're just two blocks from the bus stop.* **4** *BrE* a large building with many homes or offices in it: *a block of flats* **5** something that makes it difficult or impossible to move or progress: *a road block* **6** a single amount of something: *To delete a block of text, highlight it, then press 'Del'.*

block² *v* [T] **1** also **block up** to prevent anything from passing through a narrow space: *My nose is blocked up. | Whose car is blocking the driveway?* **2** to stop something from being done: *The council blocked the plan.* **3** to be in front of a light, a view, a window etc so that

other people cannot see properly: *You're blocking my view.*

block sth ↔ **off** *phr v* [T] to completely close a road or path: *The freeway exit's blocked off.*

block sth ↔ **out** *phr v* [T] **1** to stop light passing through something: *Thick smoke had completely blocked out the light.* **2** to try to stop yourself thinking about something: *She had managed to block memories of her unhappy childhood.*

block·ade /blɒ'keɪdllblɑː-/ *n* [C] when an army surrounds a place to prevent people, food, weapons etc from getting in or coming out: *a naval blockade* **—blockade** *v* [T]

block·age /'blɒkɪdʒll'blɑː-/ *n* [C] something that blocks a tube, road etc: *a blockage in the drain*

block·bust·er /'blɒk,bʌstəll'blɑːk,bʌstər/ *n* [C] *informal* a book or film that is very successful: *Spielberg's new blockbuster*

block cap·i·tals /ˌ. '../ also **block let·ters** /ˌ. '.../ *n* [plural] letters in their large form, for example A, B, C, instead of a, b, c

bloke /bləʊkllbloʊk/ *n* [C] *BrE informal* a man

blonde¹ also **blond** /blɒndllblɑːnd/ *adj* **1** blonde hair is pale or yellow **→** see colour picture on page 244 **2** someone who is blonde has pale or yellow hair

blonde² *n* [C] *informal* a woman who has pale or yellow hair: *a good-looking blonde*

blood /blʌd/ *n* **1** [U] the red liquid that your heart pumps around your body: *blood flowing from an open wound* **2** [U] the family or race that you come from: *a woman of royal blood* **3 new blood** new members in an organization who bring new ideas: *We need some new blood in the department.* **4 bad blood** angry feelings between people: *There was a long history of bad blood between Jose and Arriola.* **→** see also **in cold blood** (COLD¹)

blood bank /'. ./ *n* [C] a place where blood is stored to be used in hospitals

blood·bath /'blʌdbɑːθll-bæθ/ *n* [singular] when a lot of people are violently killed in one place

blood·cur·dling /'blʌd,kɜːdlɪŋll-ɜːr-/ *adj* very frightening: *bloodcurdling screams*

blood do·nor /'. ,../ *n* [C] someone who gives their blood for doctors to use in treating other people

blood group /'. ./ *n* [C] *BrE* one of the types into which human blood can be divided

blood·hound /'blʌdhaʊnd/ *n* [C] a large dog with a very good sense of smell

blood·less /'blʌdləs/ *adj* without killing or violence: *a bloodless revolution*

blood pres·sure /'. ,../ *n* [U] the force with which the blood moves around your body: *a special diet for people with high blood pressure*

blood·shed /'blʌdʃed/ *n* [U] when people are killed in fighting or in a war

blood·shot /'blʌdʃɒtll-ʃɑːt/ *adj* bloodshot eyes look slightly red

blood·sport /'blʌd,spɔːtll-,spɔːrt/ *n* [C] a sport such as hunting, that involves killing animals

blood·stained /'blʌdsteɪnd/ *adj* something that is bloodstained has marks of blood on it

blood·stream /'blʌdstriːm/ *n* [singular] the

blood as it flows around your body: *drugs injected into the bloodstream*

blood·thirst·y /ˈblʌdˌθɜːstɪ‖-ɜːr-/ *adj* someone who is bloodthirsty enjoys doing violent things or watching violence: *bloodthirsty bandits*

blood type /ˈ. ./ *n* [C] *AmE* one of the groups into which human blood can be divided

blood ves·sel /ˈ. ˌ../ *n* [C] one of the tubes in your body that blood flows through

blood·y¹ /ˈblʌdi/ *adj* **1** covered in blood: *a bloody nose* **2** involving actions that kill or wound a lot of people: *the bloody struggle for independence*

bloody² *adj, adv BrE spoken* used to emphasize what you are saying, in a slightly rude way, especially when you are annoyed: *Don't be a bloody fool!* | *It was a bloody stupid thing to do.*

bloom¹ /bluːm/ *n* [C] **1** a flower: *lovely yellow blooms* **2** **in (full) bloom** with the flowers fully open: *The lilies are in bloom.*

bloom² *v* [I] **1** if flowers bloom they open: *lilacs blooming in the spring* **2** to look happy and healthy or successful

blos·som¹ /ˈblɒsəm‖ˈblɑː-/ *n* [C,U] a flower or the flowers on a tree or bush: *peach blossoms*

blossom² *v* [I] **1** if trees blossom, they produce flowers **2** also **blossom out** to develop in a beautiful, happy, or successful way: *She has blossomed out into a beautiful young woman.*

blot¹ /blɒt‖blɑːt/ *v* [T] **-tted, -tting** to dry spots of liquid on a surface using a cloth or soft paper

blot sth ↔ **out** *phr v* [T] **1** to stop yourself from thinking about something: *He tried to blot out his memory of Marcia.* **2** to make it impossible to see something: *clouds blotting out the sun*

blot² *n* [C] **1** a mark on paper made by a spot of ink falling on it **2** **a blot on the landscape** something that spoils the appearance of a place

blotch /blɒtʃ‖blɑːtʃ/ *n* [C] a pink or red mark on the skin or a coloured mark on something —**blotchy** *adj: blotchy skin* —**blotched** *adj*

blotting pa·per /ˈ. ˌ../ *n* [U] soft thick paper used for drying wet ink on a page after writing

blouse /blaʊz‖blaʊs/ *n* [C] a shirt for women: *a white satin blouse* → see colour picture on page 113

blow¹ /bləʊ‖bloʊ/ *v* **blew** /bluː/, **blown** /bləʊn‖bloʊn/, **blowing** **1** [I] if the wind or a current of air blows, it moves: *A cold wind blew from the east.* **2 a)** [T] if the wind blows something somewhere, it moves it in that direction: *The wind blew leaves across the path.* | *Trees had been blown down.* **b)** [I] to be moved by the wind: *curtains blowing in the breeze* **3 a)** [I] to send air out through your mouth: *Renee blew on her soup.* **b)** [T] to make or shape something by sending air out of your mouth: *blowing bubbles* **4 blow your nose** to force air through your nose and into a HANDKERCHIEF **5** [I,T] to make a sound by sending air through a musical instrument, whistle etc: *The referee's whistle blew.* **6 blow sth off/away/out** to violently remove or destroy something with an explosion or by shooting: *an explosion that blew the ship right out of the water.* **7** [T] *spoken* to lose a good opportunity by making a mistake: *I've blown my chances of getting into university.* **8** [T] *informal* to spend a lot of money quickly in a care-

less way: *He got a big insurance payment, but he blew it all on a new stereo.* **9 blow your top** *informal* to suddenly become extremely angry: *If you tell Dad, he'll blow his top.* **10** [I,T] to suddenly stop working because too much electricity has passed through: *The fuse blew.* | *The hairdryer's blown a fuse.*

blow sb **away** *phr v* [T] *spoken* to completely surprise someone, especially with something they admire

blow sth ↔ **out** *phr v* to blow air on to a flame and make it stop burning: *Blow out all the candles.*

blow over *phr v* [I] if an argument or storm blows over it ends: *They've been quarrelling again, but it'll soon blow over.*

blow up *phr v* **1** [I,T **blow** sth ↔ **up**] to destroy something, or be destroyed, by an explosion: *The bridge was blown up by terrorists.* **2** [T **blow** sth ↔ **up**] to fill something with air or gas: *Come and help me blow up the balloons.*

blow² *n* [C] **1** a hard hit with a hand, tool, or weapon: *a blow to the head* **2** an event that makes you very unhappy or shocks you: *Her mother's death was a terrible blow.* **3 come to blows** if two people come to blows, they get so angry that they start hitting each other

blow-by-blow /ˌ. . ˈ.◂/ *adj* **a blow-by-blow account** a detailed description of an event, describing everything that happened in the correct order

blow dry /ˈ. ./ *v* [T] to dry hair using an electric HAIRDRYER that you hold in your hand

blown /bləʊn‖bloʊn/ *v* the past participle of BLOW

blow·out /ˈbləʊaʊt‖ˈbloʊ-/ *n* [C] *informal* **1** when a tyre suddenly BURSTS **2** a big expensive meal or a large party

blow·pipe /ˈbləʊpaɪp‖ˈbloʊ-/ *n* [C] a tube that is used as a weapon for firing small objects

blow-up /ˈ. ./ *n* [C] a photograph, or part of a photograph, that has been made larger

blub·ber¹ /ˈblʌbə‖-ər/ also **blub** /blʌb/ *BrE v* [I] *informal* to cry noisily

blubber² *n* [U] the fat of sea animals, especially WHALES

blud·geon /ˈblʌdʒən/ *v* [T] to hit someone several times with something heavy

blue¹ /bluː/ *adj* **1** having the colour of a clear sky on a fine day: *the blue lake* | *a dark blue dress* → see colour picture on page 114 **2** *informal* sad: *I've been feeling kind of blue lately.* **3 blue joke/movie** a joke or film about sex → see also **once in a blue moon** (ONCE¹) —**bluish** *adj*

blue² *n* [U] **1** a blue colour: *The curtains were a beautiful dark blue.* → see colour picture on page 114 **2 out of the blue** *informal* unexpectedly: *Mandy's phonecall came out of the blue.* → see also BLUES

blue·bell /ˈbluːbel/ *n* [C] a small plant with blue flowers that grows in the forest

blue·ber·ry /ˈbluːbəri‖-beri/ *n* [C] a small dark blue round fruit: *blueberry pie*

blue-chip /ˌ. ˈ.◂/ *adj* a blue-chip company or INVESTMENT is safe, and unlikely to lose money: *a blue-chip investment*

blue-col·lar /ˌ. ˈ.◂/ *adj* blue-collar workers do jobs such as repairing machines and making things in factories

blue·print /'blu:ˌprɪnt/ *n* [C] **1** a plan for describing how to achieve something: *a blueprint for health care reform* **2** a plan for making a machine or building a house

blue rib·bon /ˌ. '../ *n* [C] *especially AmE* a small piece of blue material given to the first prize winner of a competition —**blue-ribbon** *adj*: *a blue-ribbon recipe*

blues /blu:z/ *n* [plural] **1** a slow, sad style of music that came from the southern US: *a blues singer* **2** **have/get the blues** *informal* to be or become sad

bluff¹ /blʌf/ *v* [I,T] to pretend that you are going to do something or that you know about something, when this is not true: *Don't believe her – she's bluffing!*

bluff² *n* **1** [C,U] an attempt to make someone believe that you are going to do something when you have no intention of doing it: *He even threatened to resign, but I'm sure it's all bluff.* **2** **call sb's bluff** to tell someone to do what they are threatening to do because you do not believe they will do it

blun·der¹ /'blʌndə‖-ər/ *n* [C] a careless or stupid mistake that causes serious problems: *a terrible political blunder*

blunder² *v* [I] **1** to make a careless or stupid mistake **2** to move in an unsteady way as if you cannot see well: *Jo blundered into the kitchen, still sleepy.*

blunt¹ /blʌnt/ *adj* **1** not sharp: *blunt scissors | a blunt pencil* → see picture at SHARP **2** saying exactly what you think, even if it upsets people: *Visitors are often shocked by Maria's blunt manner.* —**bluntness** *n* [U]

blunt² *v* [T] to make someone's feelings or senses less strong: *Too much alcohol had blunted my reactions.*

blunt·ly /'blʌntli/ *adv* speaking in a direct, honest way that sometimes upsets people: *To put it bluntly, there's no way you're going to pass.*

blur¹ /blɜː‖blɜːr/ *n* [singular] something that you cannot see clearly or cannot remember clearly: *a blur of horses running past | The crash is all a blur in my mind.*

blur² *v* **-rred, -rring** [I,T] **1** to make the difference between two things less clear: *a type of movie that blurs the lines between reality and imagination* **2** to become difficult to see clearly, or to make something difficult to see: *a mist blurring the outline of the distant hills*

blurb /blɜːb‖blɜːrb/ *n* [singular] a short description giving information about a new book, new product etc

blurred /blɜːd‖blɜːrd/ also **blur·ry** /'blɜːri/ *adj* blurred shapes, pictures, or thoughts are unclear: *blurred vision | blurry photos*

blurt /blɜːt‖blɜːrt/ also **blurt out** *v* [T] to say something suddenly and without thinking: *Peter blurted out the news before we could stop him.*

blush /blʌʃ/ *v* [I] to become red in the face, usually because you are embarrassed: *She's so shy she blushes whenever I speak to her.* | **+ with** *Toby blushed with pride.* —**blush** *n* [C] *remarks that brought a blush to my cheeks*

blus·ter /'blʌstə‖-ər/ *v* [I] to speak in a loud, angry way —**bluster** *n* [U]

blus·ter·y /'blʌstəri/ *adj* blustery weather is very windy: *a blustery winter day*

BO /ˌbiː 'əʊl-'oʊ/ *n* [U] *informal* an unpleasant smell from a person's body

bo·a con·strict·or /'bəʊə kənˌstrɪktə‖'boʊə kənˌstrɪktər/ *n* [C] a large snake that kills animals by crushing them

boar /bɔː‖bɔːr/ *n* [C] **1** a male pig **2** a wild pig

board¹ /bɔːd‖bɔːrd/ *n* **1** [C] a flat piece of wood, plastic etc, that is used for a particular purpose: *a chopping board | a chess board* **2** [C] the group of people in a company or organization who make the rules and important decisions: *the school's board of governors* **3** [C] a flat piece of wood or plastic on a wall where you put information for someone to see: *Can I put this notice on the board? | The teacher had written some examples up on the board.* → see also BLACKBOARD, BULLETIN BOARD, NOTICEBOARD **4** [C] a long thin flat piece of wood used for making floors, fences etc **5** **on board** on a plane, ship, train etc: *all the passengers on board* **6** **take sth on board** to listen to and consider a suggestion, idea etc: *We'll try to take some of your suggestions on board.* **7** **across the board** affecting all groups or all the members of a group: *increases in pay across the board* **8** [U] the meals that are provided when you pay to stay somewhere, for example in a hotel: *Room and board is $350 per month.*

board² *n* [U] meals that are provided for you when you stay somewhere: **board and lodging** *BrE*/**room and board** *AmE* (=a room to sleep in and food)

board³ *v* **1** [I,T] to get on a plane, ship, train etc, in order to travel somewhere: *Passengers in rows 15 to 25 may now board the plane.* **2** [I] if a plane or ship is boarding, passengers are getting onto it: *Flight 503 for Lisbon is now boarding.*

board sth ↔ **up** *phr v* [T] to cover a window or door with wooden boards: *The house next door has been boarded up for months.*

board·er /'bɔːdə‖'bɔːrdər/ *n* [C] **1** a student who lives at his or her school **2** someone who pays to live in someone else's house and has meals there; LODGER *BrE*

board game /'. ./ *n* [C] an indoor game played on a specially designed board

boarding house /'.. ./ *n* [C] a private house, not a hotel, where you pay to sleep and eat

boarding school /'.. ./ *n* [C] a school where students live as well as study

board·room /'bɔːdruːm, -rʊm‖'bɔːrd-/ *n* [C] a room where the DIRECTORS of a company have meetings

board·walk /'bɔːdwɔːk‖'bɔːrdwɒːk/ *n* [C] *AmE* a raised path made of wood, usually built next to the sea

boast¹ /bəʊst‖boʊst/ *v* **1** [I] to talk too proudly about something that you have or something that you have done: *He enjoyed boasting about his wealth.* **2** [T] to have something that is very good or useful: *The new health club boasts an Olympic-sized swimming pool.*

boast² *n* [C] something that you like telling people because you are proud of it

boast·ful /'bəʊstfəl‖'boʊst-/ *adj* talking too proudly about yourself: *When he was drunk, he became loud and boastful.* —**boastfully** *adv*

boat /bəʊt‖boʊt/ n [C] **1** something that you sail in to travel across water: *fishing boats* | **by boat** (=in a boat): *You can only get to the island by boat.* → compare SHIP¹ **2 be in the same boat (as)** *informal* to be in the same unpleasant situation as someone else: *We're all in the same boat, so stop complaining.* → see also **miss the boat/bus** (MISS¹), **rock the boat** (ROCK²)

USAGE NOTE: boat and ship

A **boat** is usually smaller than a **ship** or travels shorter distances: *a fishing boat* | *We rented a rowing boat for the day.* | *a boat race.* But in spoken English, the word **boat** is sometimes used to talk about a big ship that travels a long distance: *The boat with its 400 passengers finally reached Cape Cod on May 6th.*

---

bob¹ /bɒb‖bɑːb/ v **-bbed, -bbing** [I] to move up and down in water: *a small boat bobbing up and down*

bob² n [C] **1** *plural* **bob** *BrE informal* a SHILLING **2** a way of cutting hair so that it is the same length all the way around your head → see colour picture on page 244

bob·bin /ˈbɒbɪn‖ˈbɑː-/ n [C] a small round object that you wind thread onto, for example in a SEWING MACHINE

bob·by /ˈbɒbi‖ˈbɑːbi/ n [C] *BrE informal* a policeman

bobby pin /ˈ.. ./ n [C] *AmE* a small thin metal thing used to hold a woman's hair in place; HAIRGRIP *BrE*

bode /bəʊd‖boʊd/ v **bode well/ill** *literary* to be a good or bad sign for the future

bod·ice /ˈbɒdɪs‖ˈbɑː-/ n [C] the part of a woman's dress above her waist

bod·i·ly¹ /ˈbɒdɪli‖ˈbɑː-/ adj relating to the human body: *bodily changes*

bodily² adv if you move someone bodily you push them or lift them: *I had to lift him bodily onto the bed.*

bod·y /ˈbɒdi‖ˈbɑːdi/ n **1** [C] **a)** the physical structure of a person or animal: *a strong healthy body* **b)** the central part of a person or animal's body, not including the arms or legs: *Keep your arms close to your body.* **c)** the dead body of a person: *Several bodies have been found near the crash site.* **2** [C] an official group of people who work together: *the governing body of the university* **3** [singular] a large amount of information, writing etc: **+ of** *A growing body of evidence suggests that exercise may reduce the risk of cancer.* **4** [C] the main part of something: *the body of the report* **5** [C] the main structure of a car or aircraft, not including the wheels or engine

body build·ing /ˈ.. ˌ../ n [U] the activity of doing physical exercises to make your muscles bigger and stronger — **body builder** n [C]

bod·y·guard /ˈbɒdiɡɑːd‖ˈbɑːdiɡɑːrd/ n [C] someone whose job is to protect an important person

body lan·guage /ˈ.. ˌ../ n [U] the movements of your body that show what you are really feeling or thinking

bod·y·work /ˈbɒdiwɜːk‖ˈbɑːdiwɜːrk/ n [U] the main metal structure of a car, including the doors but not including the engine, wheels etc: *The bodywork's beginning to rust.*

bog¹ /bɒɡ, bɔːɡ/ n [C,U] an area of soft wet muddy ground

bog² v **get/be bogged down** to be unable to make any progress because you have become too involved in dealing with a particular problem: *Let's not get bogged down with minor details.*

bo·gey /ˈbəʊɡi‖ˈboʊɡi/ n [C] *BrE* a piece of the soft substance from inside your nose

bo·gey·man /ˈbəʊɡimæn‖ˈboʊ-/ n [C] an evil spirit, especially in children's imagination or stories

bog·gle /ˈbɒɡəl‖ˈbɑː-/ v **the mind boggles** *spoken* used to say that something is difficult to imagine or believe: *When you think how much they must spend on clothes – well, the mind fairly boggles.*

bog·gy /ˈbɒɡi‖ˈbɑː-/ adj boggy ground is soft, wet, and muddy

bo·gus /ˈbəʊɡəs‖ˈboʊ-/ adj *informal* false, but pretending to be real: *a bogus police officer*

bo·he·mi·an /bəʊˈhiːmiən, bə-‖boʊ-, bə-/ adj a bohemian way of living is typical of artists, writers etc who want to be different from the rest of society — **bohemian** n [C]

boil¹ /bɔɪl/ v **1** [I,T] if you boil liquid, or it boils, it becomes so hot that BUBBLES rise to the surface and the liquid changes to gas: *Drop the noodles into boiling salted water.* **2** [I,T] if something containing liquid boils, the liquid inside it is boiling: *Ben, the kettle's boiling.* **3** also **boil up** [I,T] to cook food in boiling water: *Boil the eggs for five minutes.* **4** to feel very angry: *I was boiling with rage.*

boil down to sth *phr v* **it (all) boils down to** used to say that one fact or question is more important than any other: *It all boils down to how much money you have.*

boil over *phr v* [I] to boil and flow over the sides of a pan

boil² n **1 bring sth to the boil** to heat something in a pan until it boils: *Bring the soup to the boil and cook for another 5 minutes.* **2** [C] a painful infected SWELLING under your skin

boil·er /ˈbɔɪlə-ər/ n [C] **1** a piece of equipment that heats water for people to use in their house, for example for washing or for heating the rooms **2** a large container for boiling water to provide steam for an engine

boil·ing /ˈbɔɪlɪŋ/ adj **boiling hot** extremely hot

boiling point /ˈ.. ./ n [singular] the temperature at which a liquid boils

bois·ter·ous /ˈbɔɪstərəs/ adj noisy, cheerful and full of energy: *a group of boisterous children* — **boisterously** adv

bold /bəʊld‖boʊld/ adj **1** confident and willing to take risks: *Yamamoto's plan was bold and ori-*

GRAMMAR NOTE: for and since

Use **for** with periods of time: *I've been waiting here for 25 minutes.* | *We've lived here for 6 years.*
Use **since** with the date or time when something started: *I've been waiting here since 7 o'clock.* | *We've lived here since 1992.*

B

ginal. **2** writing, shapes, or colours that are bold are very clear and strong or bright: *wallpaper with bold stripes* —**boldly** *adv* —**boldness** *n* [U]

bol·lard /ˈbɒləd, -lɑːdǁˈbɑːlərd/ *n* [C] *BrE* a short thick upright post in the street

bol·locks /ˈbɒləksǁˈbɑː-/ *BrE interjection* a very rude word used when you are angry or disagree strongly with someone

bol·ster /ˈbəʊlstəǁˈboʊlstər/ also **bolster up** *v* [T] to improve something by giving support and encouragement: *Roy's promotion seems to have bolstered his confidence.*

bolt¹ /bəʊltǁboʊlt/ *n* [C] **1** a metal bar that slides across to fasten a door or window **2** a screw with no point, which is used with a NUT to hold two pieces of metal or wood together

bolt² *v* **1** [I] to run away suddenly, especially because you are afraid: *He bolted across the street as soon as he saw them.* **2** [T] to close or lock a door or window with a bolt **3** also **bolt down** [T] to eat something very quickly: *Don't bolt your food.* **4** [T] to fasten two things together using a bolt: *The shelves are bolted to a metal frame.*

bolt³ *adv* **sit/stand bolt upright** to sit or stand with your back very straight: *Suddenly Dennis sat bolt upright in bed.*

bomb¹ /bɒmǁbɑːm/ *n* **1** [C] a container filled with a substance that will explode: *bombs dropping on the city* **2** **the bomb** NUCLEAR weapons

bomb² *v* **1** [T] to attack a place with bombs: *Terrorists have bombed the central railway station.* **2** [I] *informal* if a play, film etc bombs, it is unsuccessful: *His latest play bombed on Broadway.* **3** **bomb along/down etc** *BrE informal* to move very quickly

bom·bard /bɒmˈbɑːdǁbɑːmˈbɑːrd/ *v* [T] **1** to continuously attack a place with guns and bombs: *Sarajevo was bombarded from all sides.* **2** **bombard sb with questions/information/letters etc** to ask someone so many questions, give them so much information etc, that it is difficult for them to deal with everything: *Both leaders were bombarded with questions from the press.* —**bombardment** *n* [C,U]

bomb dis·pos·al /ˈ. .ˌ.. ./ *n* [U] the job of making bombs safe or removing them safely from an area

bomb·er /ˈbɒməǁˈbɑːmər/ *n* [C] **1** a plane that drops bombs **2** someone who puts a bomb somewhere

bomb·shell /ˈbɒmʃelǁˈbɑːm-/ *n* [C] *informal* a shocking piece of news: *Then she dropped a bombshell, "I'm pregnant."*

bo·na fi·de /ˌbəʊnə ˈfaɪdiǁˈboʊnə faɪd/ *adj* real and not pretending to be something else: *The swimming pool is for bona fide members of the club only.*

bo·nan·za /bəˈnænzə, bəʊ-ǁbə-, boʊ-/ *n* [C] a situation in which a lot of people or companies are successful and make a lot of money or get what they want: *the oil bonanza of the 80s*

bond¹ /bɒndǁbɑːnd/ *n* [C] **1** a shared feeling or interest that unites people: **+ between** *the natural bond between mother and child* **2** an official document promising that a government or company will pay back money that it has

borrowed, often with INTEREST: *government bonds*

bond² *v* [I,T] **1** when one thing bonds with another, or if something bonds them together, they become joined or firmly glued together **2** to develop a special relationship with someone: **+ with** *The players are finally bonding with each other as a team.*

bond·age /ˈbɒndɪdʒǁˈbɑːn-/ *n* [U] **1** when someone is tied up for sexual pleasure **2** a situation in which people have no freedom

bond·ing /ˈbɒndɪŋǁˈbɑːn-/ *n* [U] when a special relationship develops between people

bone¹ /bəʊnǁboʊn/ *n* **1** [C,U] one of the hard parts in the frame of the body: *Sam broke a bone in his foot.* | *fragments of bone* **2** **have a bone to pick with sb** *spoken* used to tell someone that you want to talk to them because you are annoyed about something they have done **3** **make no bones about (doing) sth** to not feel nervous or ashamed about doing or saying something: *She makes no bones about her ambitions.* **4** **a bone of contention** something that causes arguments

bone² *v* [T] to remove the bones from fish or meat

bone dry /ˌ. ˈ.◂/ *adj* completely dry

bon·fire /ˈbɒnfaɪəǁˈbɑːnfaɪr/ *n* [C] a large outdoor fire, used especially for burning RUBBISH

bon·net /ˈbɒnɪtǁˈbɑː-/ *n* [C] **1** *BrE* the part at the front of a car that covers the engine HOOD *AmE* → see picture at CAR **2** a hat that ties under the chin, worn especially by babies **3** a hat worn by women in past times

bo·nus /ˈbəʊnəsǁˈboʊ-/ *n* [C] **1** money added to someone's usual pay for example because they have worked hard or their company has been very successful: *a Christmas bonus* **2** something good that you had not expected to get from a situation: *The fact that our house is so close to the school is an added bonus.*

bon·y /ˈbəʊniǁˈboʊ-/ *adj* very thin: *bony fingers*

boo /buː/ *v* [I,T] to shout 'boo' to show that you do not like someone's performance, speech etc —**boo** *n* [C]

boob /buːb/ *n* [C] **1** [usually plural] *informal* one of a woman's breasts **2** a mistake

boo·by prize /ˈbuːbi praɪz/ *n* [C] a prize given as a joke to the person who finishes last in a competition

booby trap /ˈ.. ./ *n* [C] a bomb or other dangerous thing that is hidden in something that seems harmless —**booby-trapped** *adj*

book¹ /bʊk/ *n* [C] **1** a set of printed pages fastened together in a cover so that you can read them: *a book by Charles Dickens* | *Have you read 'The Wasp Factory'? It's a fantastic book.* **2** sheets of paper fastened together in a cover that you can write on: *an address book* | *a cheque book* **3** a set of things such as stamps or tickets fastened together inside a paper cover **4** **by the book** exactly according to the rules **5** **be in sb's good/bad books** *informal* if you are in someone's good books, they are pleased with you. If you are in their bad books, they are annoyed with you

book² *v* **1** [I,T] *BrE* to arrange to have or do something at a particular time in the future: *The train was very crowded and I wished I'd booked a* seat. | **booked up/fully booked** (=no seats, rooms etc left): *I'm sorry, we're fully booked for the 14th February.* **2** [T] *AmE informal* to ARREST someone **3** [T] *BrE* if a football REFEREE books a player who has broken the rules, they write down the player's name in an official book

book in/into *phr v* **1** *BrE* [I] to arrive at a hotel, sign your name, collect your key etc; CHECK IN: *I'll call you as soon as I've booked in.* **2** [T **book** sb ↔ **in/into**] to arrange for someone to stay at a hotel: *She's booked you in at the Hilton.*

book·case /'bʊk-keɪs/ *n* [C] a piece of furniture with shelves to hold books → see colour picture on page 474

book·ie /'bʊki/ *n* [C] *informal* someone who makes money by taking BETS on the result of horse races, sports games etc; BOOKMAKER

book·ing /'bʊkɪŋ/ *n* [C] *BrE* an arrangement that you make to use a hotel room, have seats at the theatre etc, at a particular time in the future: **make a booking** *Can I make a booking for tonight?*

booking of·fice /'.. ,../ *n* [C] *BrE* a place where people buy train or bus tickets

book·keep·ing /'bʊk,ki:pɪŋ/ *n* [U] the job or activity of recording the financial accounts of a business or organization —**bookkeeper** *n* [C]

book·let /'bʊklɪt/ *n* [C] a small book that gives information: *a booklet that gives advice to patients with the disease*

book·mak·er /'bʊk,meɪkəl-ər/ *n* [C] *formal* a BOOKIE

book·mark /'bʊkmɑ:kǁ-mɑ:rk/ *n* [C] a piece of paper that you put in a book so that you can find the page you want

books /bʊks/ *n* [plural] written records of the financial accounts of a business

book·shop /'bʊkʃɒpǁ-ʃɑ:p/ *BrE,* **bookstore** /'bʊkstɔ:ǁ-stɔ:r/ *AmE — n* [C] a shop that sells books

book·stall /'bʊkstɔ:lǁ-stɒːl/ *n* [C] *BrE* a small shop with an open front that sells books and magazines, especially at a railway station

book·worm /'bʊkwɜ:mǁ-wɜːrm/ *n* [C] someone who likes reading very much

boom¹ /bu:m/ *n* [C] **1** a period when there is a big increase in a particular kind of activity or something is suddenly very popular: *a boom in sales* | *the building boom in the 1980s* **2** [C,U] a time when a country's ECONOMY is very successful

boom² *v* [I] **1** if business or a country's ECONOMY is booming, there is a lot of business activity and companies are very successful **2** if an activity is booming, it is becoming very popular **3** if prices are booming, they are increasing quickly **4** to make a loud deep sound: *Hector's voice boomed above the others.* —**booming** *adj*

boo·me·rang /'bu:məræŋ/ *n* [C] a curved stick that comes back to you when you throw it

boon /bu:n/ *n* [C] something that is useful and makes your life easier or better

boost¹ /bu:st/ *n* [C] **1** [usually singular] something that helps you become more successful and feel more confident and happy: **+ to** *Princess Diana's visit gave a big boost to patients.* **2** an increase in the amount of something

boost² *v* [T] to increase the value or amount of something: *Christmas boosts sales by 30%.* | *Winning really boosts your confidence.*

boost·er /'bu:stəl-ər/ *n* **1 confidence/ego/ morale etc booster** something that increases someone's confidence etc **2** [C] an engine that provides additional power for a SPACECRAFT **3** [C] a small quantity of a drug that increases the effect of one that was given before: *a booster vaccination*

boot¹ /bu:t/ *n* [C] **1** a type of strong heavy shoe that covers your whole foot and the lower part of your leg: *hiking boots* → see picture at SHOE **2** *BrE* a covered space in the back of a car, used for carrying bags, boxes etc; TRUNK *AmE* → see picture at CAR **3 put the boot in** *BrE informal* **a)** to be unkind to someone who is already upset **b)** to kick someone when they are on the ground **4 get the boot/be given the boot** *informal* to be forced to leave your job: *"What happened to Sandra?" "Oh, she got the boot."* **5 the boot's on the other foot** *BrE spoken* used to say that the situation has changed, and you now have power over someone who used to have power over you

boot² *v* [T] *informal* to kick someone or something hard: *Joe booted the ball across the field.*

booth /bu:ðǁbu:θ/ *n* [C] **1** a small enclosed area, often used for doing something privately: *a telephone booth* | *a voting booth* | *a ticket booth* **2** a table that is partly enclosed by tall seats in a restaurant

boot·leg /'bu:tleg/ *adj* bootleg products are made and sold illegally: *bootleg cassette tapes* —**bootlegging** *n* [U] —**bootlegger** *n* [C]

boot·y /'bu:ti/ *n* [U] *literary* valuable things taken by the winners in a war: *Caesar's armies returned home loaded with booty.*

booze¹ /bu:z/ *n* [U] *informal* alcoholic drink

booze² *v* [I] *informal* to drink a lot of alcohol

booz·er /'bu:zəl-ər/ *n* [C] **1** *BrE informal* a PUB **2** someone who drinks a lot of alcohol

booze-up /'.. ./ *n* [C] *BrE informal* an occasion when people drink a lot of alcohol together

bor·der¹ /'bɔ:dəlǁ'bɔ:rdər/ *n* [C] **1** the official line that separates two countries: **+ between** *the border between India and Pakistan* **2** a band around the edge of something, often for decoration: *a skirt with a red border*

border² *v* [T] **1** to be in a line around the edge of something: *willow trees bordering the river* **2** to share a border with another country: *the Arab States bordering Israel*

border on sth *phr v* [T] to be very nearly a particular kind of behaviour, attitude, feeling etc: *Her behaviour often borders on insanity.*

bor·der·line¹ /'bɔ:dəlaɪnǁ'bɔ:rdər-/ *adj* used to say that someone or something has almost or only just reached a particular level, so you are not sure about them: *In borderline cases we may ask candidates to come for a second interview.*

borderline² *n* [singular] the point at which one quality, condition etc ends and another begins: *the borderline between sleep and being awake*

bore¹ /bɔ:ǁbɔ:r/ *v* **1** [T] to make someone feel bored: *Am I boring you?* **2** [I,T] to make a deep round hole in a hard surface

bore² *n* **1** [C] someone who talks too much

about uninteresting things **2** [singular] something dull and uninteresting you have to do

bore³ v the past tense of BEAR

bored /bɔːd‖bɔːrd/ adj tired and impatient because something is uninteresting or you have nothing to do: *He looked bored and kept yawning loudly.* | **+ with** *We got bored with lying on the beach and went off to explore the town.* | **bored stiff/bored to tears** (=extremely bored) → see colour picture on page 277

bore·dom /ˈbɔːdəm‖ˈbɔːr-/ n [U] the feeling you have when you are bored

boring

The lesson is boring. The students are bored.

bor·ing /ˈbɔːrɪŋ/ adj not interesting in any way: *This book's so boring – I don't think I'll ever get to the end of it.* | *She was forced to spend the evening with Helen and her boring new boyfriend.*

born¹ /bɔːn‖bɔːrn/ v **be born a)** when a person or animal is born, it comes out of its mother's body or an egg and begins its life: *I was born in Tehran.* | *Our eldest son was born on Christmas Day.* | **be born into** (=be a member of that family): *Grace was born into a wealthy family.* **b)** when something such as an idea is born, it starts to exist

born² adj **a born leader/teacher etc** someone who has a natural ability to lead, teach etc

borne /bɔːn‖bɔːrn/ v the past participle of BEAR → see also AIRBORNE

bo·rough /ˈbʌrə‖-roʊ/ n [C] a town or part of a large city that is responsible for managing its own schools, hospitals, roads etc: *the New York borough of Queens*

bor·row /ˈbɒrəʊ‖ˈbɑːroʊ, ˈbɔː-/ v **1** [T] to use something that belongs to someone else and give it back to them later: *Could I borrow your dictionary for a moment?* → see picture at LEND **2** [I,T] to take money from a bank or other financial organization and pay it back over a period of time, usually with INTEREST: *The company has had to borrow heavily to stay in business.* → opposite LEND **3** [T] to take or copy ideas or words: *English has borrowed many words from French.*

bos·om /ˈbʊzəm/ n **1** [singular] the front part of someone's chest, especially a woman **2** [C, usually plural] a woman's breast **3** **bosom friend/buddy** *informal* a very close friend

boss¹ /bɒs‖bɔːs/ n [C] someone who is in charge of people and tells them what to do, espe-

cially at work: *She asked her boss if she could have some time off.* | *Who's the boss around here?*

boss² v [T] also **boss around** to tell people to do things, especially when you have no authority to do it: *Stop bossing me around!*

boss·y /ˈbɒsi‖ˈbɔːsi/ adj always telling other people what to do, in a way that is annoying: *Stop being so bossy!* — **bossily** adv — **bossiness** n [U]

bot·a·ny /ˈbɒtənil‖ˈbɑː-/ n [U] the scientific study of plants — **botanist** n [C] — **botanical** /bəˈtænɪkəl/ adj: *botanical gardens*

botch /bɒtʃ‖bɑːtʃ/ v [T] *informal* also **botch up** to do something badly and carelessly: *Louise really botched my haircut last time.*

both /bəʊθ‖boʊθ/ determiner, quantifier, pronoun **1** used to talk about two people or things together: *Anne and John are both scientists.* | *They both have good jobs.* | *Hold it in both hands.* | **both of** *Both of my grandfathers were farmers.* → compare NEITHER¹ **2** **both... and...** used to emphasize that the two things you mention are both true: *Dave felt both excited and nervous before his speech.*

both·er¹ /ˈbɒðə‖ˈbɑːðər/ v **1** [T] to annoy someone, especially by interrupting what they are doing: *"Why didn't you ask me for help?" "I didn't want to bother you."* **2** [I,T] to make someone feel slightly worried or upset: *Mandy hates walking home alone at night but it doesn't bother me.* **3** [I,T] to make the effort to do something: *Tom failed mainly because he did not bother to complete his course work.* **4** **can't be bothered (to do sth)** *BrE* used to say that you do not have enough interest or energy to do something: *I ought to clean the car, but I can't be bothered.* **5** **not bothered** *spoken, especially BrE* if you are not bothered about something, it is not important to you: *"What time do you want to leave?" "I'm not bothered – you decide."*

both·er² n [U] problems or trouble that someone has to spend time dealing with, worries about etc: **it's no bother** (=used to say you are happy to help someone): *"Thanks for all your help." "That's okay; it's no bother at all."*

both·er³ *interjection BrE* used when you are annoyed about something: *Oh bother! I've forgotten my wallet.*

bot·tle¹ /ˈbɒtl‖ˈbɑːtl/ n [C] **1** a glass or plastic container with a narrow top, used for keeping liquids in: *a wine bottle* **2** **hit the bottle** *informal* to start drinking a lot of alcohol regularly

bot·tle² v [T] to put a liquid into a bottle: *This wine is bottled in Burgundy.* — **bottled** adj: *bottled water*
 bottle sth **↔ up** phr v [T] to not allow yourself to show strong feelings: *Don't bottle up your anger. Let it out.*

bottle bank /ˈ.. ./ n [C] a large container in a public place where you leave empty bottles so that the glass can be used again → see colour picture on page 278

bot·tle·neck /ˈbɒtlnek‖ˈbɑː-/ n [C] **1** a part of a process that causes delays **2** a place where a road becomes narrow, making the traffic slow down

bot·tom¹ /ˈbɒtəm‖ˈbɑː-/ n **1** [C, usually singular] the lowest part of something: **at the bottom of** *Print your name at the bottom of the* *letter.* ➡ opposite TOP[1] **2** [singular] the lowest position in an organization or company: **at the bottom** *Lewis started at the bottom and now he runs the company.* **3** [C, usually singular] the flat surface on the lowest side of an object: **on the bottom of** *What's that on the bottom of your shoe?* **4** [C] *informal* the part of your body that you sit on **5** [singular] the ground under an ocean, river, valley etc: **+ of** *The bottom of the river is very rocky.* **6** **get to the bottom of sth** *informal* to find the real cause of a problem or situation: *Dad swore that he would get to the bottom of all this.* **7** **be at the bottom of sth** to be the basic cause of a problem or situation ➡ see also ROCK BOTTOM

bottom[2] *adj* in the lowest place or position: *The papers are in the bottom drawer.*

bot·tom·less /ˈbɒtəmləs‖ˈbɑː-/ *adj* **1** seeming to have no limit: *There is no bottomless pit of money in any organization.* **2** extremely deep: *the bottomless depths of the ocean*

bottom line /ˌ.. ˈ./ **the bottom line** the most basic and important fact about a situation: *The bottom line is that we have to finish the project on time.*

bough /baʊ/ *n* [C] a large tree branch

bought /bɔːt‖bɒːt/ *v* the past tense and past participle of BUY

boul·der /ˈbəʊldə‖ˈboʊldər/ *n* [C] a large round rock ➡ see colour picture on page 243

boule·vard /ˈbuːlvɑːd‖ˈbʊləvɑːrd, ˈbuː-/ *n* [C] a wide road in a town or city, usually with trees along the sides

bounce[1] /baʊns/ *v*
1 [I,T] to hit a surface and then move away from it, or make an object do this: **+ off** *The ball bounced off the garage into the road.* **2** [I] to jump up and down on a soft surface: **+ on** *Don't bounce on the bed.* **3** [I,T] if a cheque bounces, or a bank bounces a cheque, the bank will not pay the amount because there is not enough money in the account of the person who wrote it **4** [I] to move somewhere in a happy ENERGETIC way: **into/along etc** *The children came bouncing into the room.*

bounce back *phr v* [I] to feel better quickly or become successful again after having a lot of problems: *The team bounced back after a series of defeats.*

bounce[2] *n* [C,U] when something bounces, or the quality that makes things able to bounce, or a movement of bouncing: *Catch the ball on the first bounce.*

bounc·er /ˈbaʊnsə‖-ər/ *n* [C] someone whose job is to keep people who behave badly out of a club, bar etc

bounc·ing /ˈbaʊnsɪŋ/ *adj* healthy and active, used especially about babies: *a bouncing baby boy*

bounc·y /ˈbaʊnsi/ *adj* **1** able to BOUNCE easily: *a bouncy ball* | *a bouncy bed* **2** happy and full of energy

bound[1] /baʊnd/ *v* the past tense and past participle of BIND

bound[2] *adj* [not before noun] **1** **be bound to do sth** used to say someone is certain to do something or something is certain to happen: *Madeleine's such a nice girl – she's bound to make friends.* | *Interest rates are bound to go up this year.* **2** having a legal or moral duty to do something: **+ by** *The company is bound by law to provide us with safety equipment.* **3** **be bound up with sth** to be closely connected with something: *His problems are mainly bound up with his mother's death.* **4** intending to go in a particular direction or to a particular place: **+ for** *a plane bound for Thailand*

bound[3] *v* **1** [I] to move quickly and with large steps or jumps: *Grace came bounding down the stairs.* **2** **be bounded by** if a place is bounded by a wall, border, river etc, it has the wall etc around its edge: *a village bounded by trees*

bound[4] *n* [C] a long or high jump

bound·a·ry /ˈbaʊndəri/ *n* [C] **1** the line that marks the edge of a surface, space, or area of land: **+ between** *The Mississippi forms a natural boundary between Tennessee and Arkansas.* ➡ compare BORDER[1] **2** the highest limit that something can reach: **+ of** *the boundaries of human knowledge*

bound·less /ˈbaʊndləs/ *adj* without limits: *boundless energy*

bounds /baʊndz/ *n* [plural] **1** legal or social limits or rules: *That sort of behaviour is beyond the bounds of decency.* **2** **out of bounds** if somewhere is out of bounds to someone, they are not allowed to enter it

boun·ti·ful /ˈbaʊntɪfəl/ *adj literary* **1** existing in large amounts: *a bountiful supply of fresh food* **2** giving very generously

boun·ty /ˈbaʊnti/ *n* **1** [C] money that is given as a reward for catching a criminal **2** [U] *literary* something that is supplied in large or generous amounts: *nature's bounty*

bou·quet /bəʊˈkeɪ, buː-‖boʊ-, buː-/ *n* **1** [C] an arrangement of flowers that you give to someone **2** [C,U] the smell of a wine

bour·bon /ˈbʊəbən‖ˈbɜːr-/ *n* [U] a type of American WHISKY

bour·geois /ˈbʊəʒwɑː‖bʊrˈʒwɑː/ *adj* typical of people who are too concerned with money, property, and correct social behaviour

bour·geoi·sie /ˌbʊəʒwɑːˈziː‖ˌbʊr-/ *n* **the bourgeoisie** the social class that owns most of the wealth ➡ compare MIDDLE CLASS

bout /baʊt/ *n* [C] **1** a short period of illness or activity: **+ of** *a bout of coughing* **2** a BOXING or WRESTLING competition

bou·tique /buːˈtiːk/ *n* [C] a small shop that sells fashionable clothes

bo·vine /ˈbəʊvaɪn‖ˈboʊ-/ *adj technical* relating to cows

bounce

GRAMMAR NOTE: the past progressive

You use the **past progressive** to describe a situation or action that continued for a limited period in the past: *People were shouting and screaming.* You use the **simple past** to say that something happened in the middle of an activity: *They **arrived** while we **were having** dinner.*

bow¹ /baʊ/ v **1** [I,T] to bend your head or the top part of your body forward, often as a sign of respect: *He bowed respectfully to the king.* | *The actors bowed and left the stage.* **2** [I] to bend or curve: *trees bowing in the wind*

bow

bow out *phr v* [I] to decide not to do something any longer: **+ of** *Gunnell is bowing out of athletics at the end of the year.*

bow to sb/sth *phr v* [T] to finally agree to do something that other people want you to do: *Once again, the government has had to bow to the wishes of the people.*

bow² /baʊ/ n [C] **1** the action of bowing **2** the front part of a ship → compare STERN²

bow³ /bəʊ||boʊ/ n [C] **1** a band of cloth or string tied in two circles, used as a decoration or when tying shoes: *Jenny had a big red bow in her hair.* **2** a weapon used for shooting ARROWS, made of a long curved piece of wood held by a tight string **3** a thing that you use for playing instruments such as the VIOLIN, which consists of a piece of wood with horsehair attached to it

bow·el /ˈbaʊəl/ n [C usually plural] the tube-like part of the body which carries solid waste food that has been DIGESTed from the stomach out of the body

bowl¹ /bəʊl||boʊl/ n [C] **1** a round container that is open at the top, used to hold food, liquids etc: *a bowl of soup* **2** also **bowlful** the amount that a bowl will hold: **+ of** *a bowl of rice*

bowl² v [I,T] **1** *BrE* to play a game of BOWLS **2** to throw a ball to the BATSMAN in cricket **3** *AmE* to play the game of BOWLING

bowl sb ↔ **over** *phr v* [T] to make someone very pleased, excited, or surprised: *When Tony met Angela, he was completely bowled over.*

bow-legged /ˈbəʊˌlegd, -ˌlegɪd||ˈboʊ-/ adj having legs that curve outwards at the knee

bowl·er /ˈbəʊlə||ˈboʊlər/ n [C] a player who throws the ball at the BATSMAN in CRICKET

bowler hat /ˌ.. ˈ./ especially BrE a hard round black hat worn by businessmen in past times

bowl·ing /ˈbəʊlɪŋ||ˈboʊ-/ n [U] an indoor game in which a heavy ball is rolled along a wooden track in order to knock over SKITTLES

bowls /bəʊlz||boʊlz/ n [U] *BrE* an outdoor game in which you roll heavy balls towards a small ball

bow tie /ˌbəʊ ˈtaɪ||ˌboʊ-/ n [C] a man's tie fastened in the shape of a BOW → see colour picture on page 113

box¹ /bɒks/ n [C] **1** a container for putting things in, especially one with four straight sides: *a cardboard box* → see picture at CONTAINER **2** also **boxful** the amount that a box can hold: **+ of** *Mary ate a whole box of chocolates.* **3** a small room or enclosed space, especially in a theatre or a law court: *the jury box* **4** a PO BOX **5** **the box** *BrE informal* the television

box² v [T] also **box up** to put things in boxes: *It took us a day to box up everything in the study.* **2** to take part in the sport of BOXING

box sb/sth ↔ **in** *phr v* [T] to surround someone so that they cannot get out or get away

box·er /ˈbɒksə||ˈbɑːksər/ n [C] someone who does boxing as a sport, especially when this is their job: *a heavyweight boxer*

boxer shorts /ˈ.. ./ n [plural] loose cotton underwear for men

box·ing /ˈbɒksɪŋ||ˈbɑːk-/ n [U] a game in which two men fight by hitting each other wearing big leather GLOVES → see colour picture on page 636

Boxing Day /ˈ.. ./ n [C,U] *BrE* the 26th December, the day after Christmas Day, which is a national holiday in the UK

box of·fice /ˈ. ˌ../ n [C] a place in a theatre, concert HALL etc where tickets are sold

boy /bɔɪ/ n **1** [C] a male child or a young man: *a school for boys* **2** [C] a young son: *How old is your little boy now?* **3** **the boys** *informal* a man's male friends: *Friday's his night out with the boys.* **4** also **oh boy** used when you are excited, pleased, or angry about something: *Boy, those were great times!*

boy·cott /ˈbɔɪkɒt||-kɑːt/ v [T] to refuse to buy, use, or do something because you think something is wrong or unfair: *Our family boycotts all products tested on animals.* —**boycott** n [C]

boy·friend /ˈbɔɪfrend/ n [C] a boy or man with whom you have a romantic relationship

boy·hood /ˈbɔɪhʊd/ n [U] the time when someone is a boy

boy·ish /ˈbɔɪ-ɪʃ/ adj looking or behaving like an attractive young man: *his slim, boyish figure*

Boy Scout /ˌ. ˈ.||ˈ. ./ n **1** **The Boy Scouts** an organisation for boys that teaches them practical skills **2** [C] a member of this organization → compare GIRL SCOUT, GUIDE

bra /brɑː/ n [C] a piece of underwear that a woman wears to support her breasts

brace¹ /breɪs/ v [T] to prepare for something unpleasant: **brace yourself for** *Sandra braced herself for an argument.*

brace² n [C] something you use or wear in order to support something else: *Jill had to wear a neck brace for six weeks.*

brace·let /ˈbreɪslɪt/ n [C] a band or chain that you wear around your wrist or arm as jewellery → see picture at JEWELLERY

bra·ces /ˈbreɪsɪz/ n [plural] **1** *BrE* two narrow bands, usually made of ELASTIC, that you wear over your shoulders and fasten to your trousers to hold them up; SUSPENDERS *AmE* → see colour picture on page 113 **2** also **brace** *BrE* a wire frame that some children wear to make their teeth straight

brac·ing /ˈbreɪsɪŋ/ adj bracing weather is cold and makes you feel healthy: *a bracing sea breeze*

brack·et¹ /ˈbrækɪt/ n [C] **1** **income/tax/age etc bracket** a group of people who have a similar income, tax level etc: *Price's new job puts him in the highest tax bracket.* **2** one of the pairs of signs [] or () put around words to show additional information: **in brackets** *All grammar information is given in brackets.* **3** a piece of metal or wood fixed to a wall to support something, such as a shelf

bracket² v [T] **1** to put brackets around a word **2** to consider a group of people or things as similar: *Don't bracket us with those idiots.*

brag /bræg/ v [I] **-gged, -gging** to talk too proudly about what you have done, what you own etc: **brag about** *Ray likes to brag about his success with women.*

braid¹ /breɪd/ n **1** [U] threads woven together and used to decorate clothes: *gold braid* **2** [C] *AmE* a length of something, especially hair, made by twisting three pieces together; PLAIT *BrE* → see colour picture on page 244 —**braided** *adj*

braid² v [T] *AmE* to twist three long pieces of hair, rope etc over and under each other to make one long piece; PLAIT *BrE*

braille /breɪl/ n [U] a type of printing with raised round marks that blind people can read by touching

brain¹ /breɪn/ n **1** [C] the organ inside your head that controls how you think, feel, and move: *Jorge suffered brain damage in the accident.* **2 brains** the ability to think clearly and learn quickly: *If you had any brains, you'd know what I mean.* **3** [C, usually plural] *informal* someone who is very intelligent: *Some of the best brains in the country are here tonight.* **4 the brains behind sth** the person who thought of or started a successful plan, system, organization etc: *Bill Gates, the brains behind Microsoft* **5 have sth on the brain** *informal* to be unable to stop thinking about something → see also **pick sb's brains** (PICK¹), **rack your brains** (RACK²)

brain² v [T] *informal* to hit someone on the head very hard: *I'll brain you if you don't be quiet!*

brain·child /ˈbreɪntʃaɪld/ n [singular] *informal* one person's successful idea or INVENTION: **+ of** *The personal computer was the brainchild of Steve Jobs.*

brain·storm /ˈbreɪnstɔːm‖-stɔːrm/ n [singular] *informal* **1** *AmE* a sudden very good idea; BRAINWAVE *BrE* **2** *BrE* when you are suddenly unable to think clearly

brain·stor·ming /ˈbreɪnstɔːmɪŋ‖-ɔːr-/ n [U] when you develop ideas or solve problems in a group

brain·wash /ˈbreɪnwɒʃ‖-wɒːʃ, -wɑːʃ/ v [T] to force someone to change their beliefs by telling them something that is completely wrong many times: *People are brainwashed into believing that being fat is some kind of crime.* —**brainwashing** n [U]

brain·wave /ˈbreɪnweɪv/ n [C] *BrE* a sudden very good idea; BRAINSTORM *AmE*

brain·y /ˈbreɪni/ adj *informal* intelligent

brake¹ /breɪk/ n [C] the part of a vehicle that makes it go more slowly or stop

brake² v [I] to make a vehicle go more slowly or stop, using its brake: *Jed had to brake to avoid hitting the car in front.*

bran /bræn/ n [U] the crushed skin of wheat and other grain. Eating bran every day is supposed to help the bowels work efficiently

branch¹ /brɑːntʃ‖bræntʃ/ n [C] **1** a part of a tree that grows out from the TRUNK → see picture at TREE **2** one part of an organization, a subject of study, or a family group: *The bank has branches all over the country.* | *Which branch of science are you studying?* | *the New Zealand branch of the family* **3** a smaller, less important part of something that leads away from the main part of it: *a branch of the River Nile*

branch² v [I] also **branch off** to divide into two or more smaller, narrower, or less important parts, or be divided in this way: *When you reach Germain Street, the road branches into two.*

branch out *phr* v [I] to do something new in addition to what you usually do: **+ into** *Our local shop has decided to branch out into renting videos.*

brand¹ /brænd/ n [C] **1** a product made by a particular company: *different brands of washing powder* **2** a particular quality or way of doing something: *Nat's special brand of humour* **3** a mark burned into an animal's skin that shows who it belongs to

brand² v [T] **1** to describe someone as a very bad type of person: **brand sb as sth** *All English football supporters get branded as hooligans.* **2** to make a mark on an animal in order to show who it belongs to

bran·dish /ˈbrændɪʃ/ v [T] to wave something around in a dangerous and threatening way: *Chisholm burst into the office brandishing a knife.*

brand name /ˈ. ./ n [C] the name a company gives to a product it makes

brand-new /ˌ. ˈ.◂/ adj new and not used at all: *a brand-new car*

bran·dy /ˈbrændi/ n [C,U] a strong alcoholic drink made from wine, or a glass of this drink

brash /bræʃ/ adj behaving too confidently and speaking too loudly: *a brash young salesperson*

brass /brɑːs‖bræs/ n **1** [U] a shiny yellow metal that is a mixture of COPPER and ZINC: *a pine chest with brass handles* **2 the brass (section)** a group of musical instruments made of brass, such as TRUMPETs, in an ORCHESTRA or band

bras·si·ere /ˈbræziə‖brəˈzɪr/ n [C] *old-fashioned* a BRA

brat /bræt/ n [C] *informal* a badly behaved child: *a spoiled brat*

bra·va·do /brəˈvɑːdəʊ‖-dəʊ/ n [U] behaviour that is intended to show that you are brave and confident, even when you are not

brave¹ /breɪv/ adj dealing with danger, pain, or difficult situations with courage: *brave soldiers* | *Marti's brave fight against cancer* —**bravely** adv —**bravery** n [U]

brave² v [T] to deal with a difficult, dangerous, or unpleasant situation: *The crowd braved icy wind and rain to see the procession.*

bra·vo /ˈbrɑːvəʊ, brɑːˈvəʊ‖-vəʊ/ interjection a word you shout to show that you like or approve of something

brawl /brɔːl‖brɒːl/ n [C] a noisy fight, especially in a public place: *a drunken brawl* —**brawl** v [I]

brawn /brɔːn‖brɒːn/ n [U] physical strength —**brawny** adj: *brawny arms*

bra·zen¹ /ˈbreɪzən/ adj feeling no shame about your bad behaviour: *a brazen lie* —**brazenly** adv

brazen² v

brazen sth ↔ out *phr* v [T] to pretend that you do not feel guilty about something bad you have done or not admit that you have done it

bra·zi·er /ˈbreɪziəll-ʒər/ *n* [C] a metal container used for burning coal, wood etc outside

breach /briːtʃ/ *n* [C,U] when you break a law, rule, agreement etc: *The publication of this book would be a serious breach of trust.* | **in breach of** *You are in breach of your contract.* —**breach** *v* [T]

bread /bred/ *n* **1** [U] a common food made from FLOUR, water, and YEAST: *a loaf of bread* | *granary bread* | *a slice of bread* → see colour pictures on pages 439 and 440 **2** [U] *slang* money

bread·crumbs /ˈbredkrʌmz/ *n* [plural] very small pieces of bread used in cooking

breadth /bredθ, bretθ/ *n* **1** [C,U] the distance from one side of something to the other; WIDTH **2** [U] the wide variety of something, for example someone's experience or knowledge: + **of** *No one could equal Dr Brenninger's breadth of knowledge.*

bread·win·ner /ˈbred,wɪnəll-ər/ *n* [C] the person who earns most of the money needed to support a family

break[1] /breɪk/ *v* **broke** /brəʊkllbrouk/, **broken** /ˈbrəʊkənllˈbrou-/, **breaking 1** [I,T] if something breaks, or someone breaks it, it separates into two or more pieces, especially because it has been hit or dropped: *The kids broke a window while they were playing ball.* | *Careful, those glasses break easily.* | **break your leg, arm etc** *Sharon broke her leg skiing.* **2** [I,T] if you break a tool or a machine, or it breaks, it is damaged and no longer working properly: *Someone's broken the TV.* **3** [T] to disobey a law or rule: *He didn't realize that he was breaking the law.* **4** **break a promise/an agreement/your word** to not do what you promised to do: *politicians who break their election promises* **5** **break for lunch/coffee etc** to stop working in order to eat or drink something: *We broke for lunch at about 12:30.* **6** [T] to stop something from continuing: *The silence was broken by the sound of gunfire.* | **break the habit** (=stop wanting to do something) | **break sb's concentration** (=stop someone from being able to think about their work) **7** **break your journey** to stop travelling for a short time to rest **8** **break sb's heart** to make someone very unhappy by ending a relationship with them or by doing something that they do not want **9** **break a record** to do something faster or better than it has ever been done before **10** **break the news to sb** to tell someone about something bad that has happened **11** **break loose/free** to escape: *The cattle had broken loose during the night.* **12** [I] if news about an important event breaks, it becomes known by everyone: *The next morning, the news broke that Monroe was dead.* **13** **break even** to neither make a profit nor lose money: *We broke even in our first year of business.* **14** **break the ice** to make people who have just met each other feel less nervous and start to have a conversation **15** [I] if day breaks, light begins to show in the sky as the sun rises **16** [I] if a wave breaks, it begins to look white on top because it is coming close to the shore **17** [I] if a boy's voice breaks, it becomes lower and starts to sound like a man's voice **18** [I] if a storm breaks, it suddenly begins **19** [I] if the weather breaks, it suddenly changes

break away *phr v* [I] **1** to escape from someone **2** to change what you have been doing because it limits your freedom, is boring etc: + **from** *Duchamp wanted to break away from old established traditions in art.*

break down *phr v* **1** [I] if a car or a machine breaks down, it stops working **2** [I] if something breaks down, it cannot continue because there are too many problems: *His marriage broke down and his wife left him.* **3** [I] to start crying because you are very upset: *Imelda broke down in tears at the funeral.* **4** [T **break sth ↔ down**] to hit something such as a door so hard that it falls down: *The police had to break down the door to get in.* **5** [I,T] to change something or separate it into different parts: *enzymes which break down food in the stomach*

break in *phr v* **1** [I] to enter a building using force to steal something: *Thieves broke in during the night and took the hi-fi.* **2** [I] to interrupt someone while they are speaking: *The operator broke in saying, "You need another 75p to continue the call."*

break into sth *phr v* [T] **1** to enter a building using force to steal something: *They broke into the room through the back window.* **2** **break into a run/dance etc** to suddenly start running, dancing etc **3** to start being involved in doing something: *American companies are trying to break into Eastern European markets.*

break off *phr v* **1** [T] to remove a piece from the main part of something: *She broke off a piece of cheese.* **2** [T] to end a relationship: *The US has broken off diplomatic relations with Iran.* **3** [I,T] to suddenly stop doing something or talking to someone

break out *phr v* [I] **1** if a disease, fire, or war breaks out, it starts to happen: *Nine months later, war broke out in Korea.* **2** to escape from prison **3** **break out in a sweat** to start sweating (SWEAT)

break through *phr v* **1** [T **break through** sth] to go through something, using force: *Demonstrators tried to break through police lines.* **2** [I,T] if the sun breaks through, you can see it through the clouds

break up *phr v* **1** [T **break** sth ↔ **up**] to separate something into smaller parts: *One day his business empire will be broken up.* **2** [I,T **break** sth ↔ **up**] to break, or break something into small pieces: *The ship broke up on the rocks.* | *We used shovels to break up the soil.* **3** [I] to end a relationship: *Troy and I broke up last month.* **4** [T] to stop people fighting, arguing etc **5** [I] if a meeting, party etc breaks up, it ends and people start to leave

break with sb/sth *phr v* [T] to end a relationship or association with someone or something

---

USAGE NOTE: break, tear, cut, smash, crack, burst

You cannot **break** something soft such as cloth or paper, but you can **tear** it (=pull it apart, leaving rough edges where the parts have separated) or **cut** it (=divide it using a knife, scissors etc): *He angrily tore the letter into pieces.* | *She cut the paper into squares.* Things made of glass, CHINA etc can **break** (or **get broken**) or **smash** (=break suddenly into many small pieces): *The plate smashed on the stone floor.* If something hard

cracks, it breaks but the parts do not get separated: *His windshield cracked, but it didn't break.* If something suddenly breaks because of pressure from inside, it **bursts**: *She blew up the paper bag until it burst.*

break [2] *n* **1** [C] a short time when you stop what you are doing in order to rest or eat: **take a break** *We're all getting tired. Let's take a break for ten minutes.* | **lunch/coffee/tea break** (=when you stop to have lunch, coffee etc): *What time is your lunch break?* **2** [C] a short holiday: *Are you going anywhere over the Easter break?* **3** [C] a pause or space in the middle of something: *a break in the conversation* | *a break in the clouds* **4** [C] a chance to become successful: *The band's big break came when they sang on a local TV show.* **5** [singular] a change that ends a relationship or TRADITION: **+ with** *a break with the past* **6** [C] a place where something has been broken: *It's a nasty break – the bone has splintered.* **7 break of day** *literary* the time when it first becomes light at the beginning of the day

break·age /ˈbreɪkɪdʒ/ *n* [C] something that has been broken: *All breakages must be paid for.*

break·a·way /ˈbreɪkəweɪ/ *adj* a breakaway group is a group that is formed by people who left a larger group because of a disagreement

break·down /ˈbreɪkdaʊn/ *n* **1** [C,U] when a relationship or process stops working successfully: *Gail blames me for the breakdown of our marriage.* | *a breakdown in the peace talks* **2** [C,U] when a car or a piece of machinery stops working **3** [C] a NERVOUS BREAKDOWN **4** [C] a statement explaining the details of something: *I'd like a breakdown of these figures, please.*

break·fast /ˈbrekfəst/ *n* [C,U] the meal you have when you get up in the morning: **have breakfast** *Have you had breakfast yet?*

break-in /ˈ. ./ *n* [C] when someone breaks a door or window to enter a building and steal things: *There was a break-in at the college last night.*

breaking point /ˈ. ˌ./ *n* [U] if someone or something has reached breaking point, they can no longer deal with problems or work well: *His nerves were strained to breaking point.*

break·neck /ˈbreɪknek/ *adj* **at breakneck speed/pace** dangerously fast: *She was driving at breakneck speed.*

break·through /ˈbreɪkθruː/ *n* [C] an important new discovery or development: *a technological breakthrough*

break·up /ˈbreɪkʌp/ *n* [C] **1** when a marriage or romantic relationship ends **2** when an organization or country separates into smaller parts: *the breakup of the Soviet Union*

break·wa·ter /ˈbreɪkˌwɔːtəll-ˌwɔːtər, -ˌwɑː-/ *n* [C] a strong wall built out into the sea to protect the SHORE from the force of the waves

breast /brest/ *n* **1** [C] one of the two round raised parts on a woman's chest that can pro-

duce milk for her babies **2** [C,U] the front of a bird's body, or the meat from this: *turkey breast* **3** [C] *literary* your chest or heart → see also DOUBLE-BREASTED

breast-feed /ˈ. ./ *v* [I,T] if a woman breast-feeds, she feeds a baby with milk from her breasts

breast·stroke /ˈbrest-strəʊkll-strəʊk/ *n* [U] a way of swimming on your front in which you push your arms forward and then pull them outwards and back

breath /breθ/ *n* **1** [U] the air that comes out of your lungs when you breathe: *I can smell alcohol on your breath.* | **bad breath** (=it smells bad) **2 take a breath** to take air into your lungs: *He took a deep breath and dived into the water.* **3 be out of breath** to have difficulty breathing, for example because you have been running **4 hold your breath a)** to stop breathing for a short time while keeping air in your lungs: *Can you hold your breath under water?* **b)** to wait anxiously to see what is going to happen: *We were all holding our breath, waiting for the winner to be announced.* **5 get your breath back/catch your breath** to rest after running, climbing etc until you can breathe normally again **6 a breath of fresh air a)** a chance to breathe clean pure air: *I think I'll just step outside for a breath of fresh air.* **b)** something that is new, different, and enjoyable: *an exciting young designer who has brought a breath of fresh air to the fashion world* **7 don't hold your breath** *spoken* used to tell someone that something will probably not happen or will take a long time **8 take your breath away** if something takes your breath away, it is very surprising, especially because it is very beautiful or exciting: *a view that will take your breath away* → see also BREATHTAKING **9 under your breath** in a quiet voice, so that other people cannot hear: *"I hate you," he muttered under his breath.*

breath·a·lys·er *BrE*, **breathalyzer** *AmE* /ˈbreθəl-aɪzəll-ər/ *n* [C] *trademark* a piece of equipment used by the police to test whether car drivers have drunk too much alcohol — **breathalyse** *v* [T] *BrE*

breathe /briːð/ *v* **1** [I,T] to take air into your lungs and let it out again: *Is he still breathing?* | *Try not to breathe the fumes.* | **breathe in/out** (=take air in or let it out): *They stood on the cliff breathing in the fresh sea air.* | **breathe deeply** (=take in a lot of air): *Relax and breathe deeply.* **2 breathe down sb's neck** *informal* to watch someone so carefully that it makes them feel nervous or annoyed: *I can't work with you breathing down my neck.* **3 not breathe a word** to not say anything at all about something that is secret: *Promise not to breathe a word to anyone.* — **breathing** *n* [U]

breath·er /ˈbriːðəll-ər/ *n* [C] *informal* a short rest: *Let's take a breather.*

breathing space /ˈ. ../ *n* [U, singular] a short period before you need to start working or worrying about a situation again

B

GRAMMAR NOTE: the past perfect
You form the **past perfect** using **had** and the past participle. Use the past perfect to talk about something that happened in the past before another past action: *Kay stayed behind after everyone else **had gone** home.* | *She told me what she **had done**.*

breath·less /'breθləs/ *adj* having difficulty in breathing normally —**breathlessly** *adv*

breath·tak·ing /'breθ͟teɪkɪŋ/ *adj* extremely impressive, exciting, or surprising: *a breathtaking view* —**breathtakingly** *adv*

breed[1] /briːd/ *v* **bred** /bred/, **bred, breeding** **1** [I] if animals breed, they have babies: *Rats can breed every six weeks.* **2** [T] to keep animals or plants in order to produce young animals or develop new plants: *He breeds cattle.* **3** [T] to cause a bad feeling or situation, which develops and gets worse: *crowded living conditions that breed violence and crime*

breed[2] *n* [C] **1** a particular type of dog, horse etc **2 a new breed** a new type of person or thing: *the first of a new breed of home computers*

breed·er /'briːdəll-ər/ *n* [C] someone who breeds animals or plants: *a racehorse breeder*

breed·ing /'briːdɪŋ/ *n* [U] **1** the process of animals producing babies: *the breeding season* **2** the activity of keeping animals in order to produce young animals or to develop new types: *They usually just keep one bull for breeding.* **3** *old-fashioned* good MANNERS as a result of coming from an upper class family

breeding ground /'... ./ *n* [C] **1** a place or situation where something bad grows or develops: *a potential breeding ground for crime* **2** a place where animals or birds go to breed

breeze[1] /briːz/ *n* [C] a light gentle wind → see also **shoot the breeze** (SHOOT[1])

breeze[2] *v* **breeze in/out/along etc** *informal* to walk somewhere in a relaxed, confident way: *She just breezed into my office and asked for a job.*

breez·y /'briːzi/ *adj* **1** cheerful and relaxed: *a breezy manner* **2** breezy weather is when the wind blows fairly strongly but in a pleasant way: *a breezy but sunny day* —**breezily** *adv*

breth·ren /'breðrən/ *n* [plural] *old-fashioned* the members of an organization, especially a religious group

brev·i·ty /'brevₜti/ *n* [U] *formal* **1** when something is expressed in very few words: *He was commended for the sharpness and brevity of his speech.* **2** when something continues for a short amount of time

brew[1] /bruː/ *v* **1 be brewing** if something bad is brewing, it will happen soon: *There's a storm brewing.* **2** [T] to make beer **3** [I,T] to make a drink of tea or coffee

brew[2] *n* [C] *informal* a drink that is brewed, such as tea or beer

brew·er /'bruːəll-ər/ *n* [C] a person or company that makes beer

brew·er·y /'bruːəri/ *n* [C] a place where beer is made, or a company that makes beer

bribe[1] /braɪb/ *n* [C] money or a gift that someone gives to a person in an official position to persuade them to do something dishonest: *The judge admitted that he had accepted bribes.*

bribe[2] *v* [T] to pay money to someone to persuade them to help you by doing something dishonest: **bribe sb to do sth** *Sykes had bribed two police officers to give false evidence.*

brib·er·y /'braɪbəri/ *n* [U] when someone offers or accepts bribes

bric-a-brac /'brɪk ə ˌbræk/ *n* [U] small cheap objects that you have in your house for decoration

brick[1] /brɪk/ *n* [C,U] a hard block of baked clay used for building walls, houses etc: *a brick wall*

brick[2] *v*
brick sth ↔ up *phr v* [T] to fill or close a space by building a wall of bricks in it: *They've bricked up the windows in the old house.*

brick·lay·er /'brɪk͟leɪəll-ər/ *n* [C] someone whose job is to build walls with bricks —**bricklaying** *n* [U]

brid·al /'braɪdl/ *adj* relating to a bride or a wedding: *a bridal gown*

bride /braɪd/ *n* [C] a woman who is getting married

bride·groom /'braɪdgruːm, -grʊm/ *n* [C] a man who is getting married

brides·maid /'braɪdzmeɪd/ *n* [C] a woman or girl who helps the BRIDE on the day of her wedding

bridge[1] /brɪdʒ/ *n* **1** [C] a structure built over a river, road etc so that people or vehicles can cross it: *the bridge over the Mississippi* → see colour picture on page 243 **2** [C] something that provides a connection between two things: *The training programme is seen as a bridge between school and work.* **3 the bridge** the high part of a ship where people stand when they are controlling the ship **4** [U] a card game for four players **5 the bridge of your nose** the upper part of your nose between your eyes

bridge[2] *v* [T] **1 bridge the gap (between)** to reduce the difference between two things or people: *an attempt to bridge the gap between rich and poor* **2** to build or form a bridge over something: *We used a log to bridge the stream.*

bri·dle[1] /'braɪdl/ *n* [C] a set of leather bands that you put over a horse's head to control its movements

bridle[2] *v* [T] to put a bridle on a horse
bridle at sth *phr v* [T] if you bridle at something, you do not agree with it or it makes you annoyed

brief[1] /briːf/ *adj* **1** continuing for only a short time: *a brief visit* **2** using only a few words: *a brief letter* | **in brief** (=in as few words as possible): *Here is the sports news, in brief.* —**briefly** *adv* → see also **BREVITY**

brief[2] *n* [C] a set of instructions explaining someone's duties or jobs: *My brief is to increase our sales.*

brief[3] *v* [T] to give instructions or necessary information to someone: **brief sb on sth** *Before the interview we had been briefed on what to say.*

brief·case /'briːfkeɪs/ *n* [C] a flat case used for carrying papers or books for work → see picture at BAG

brief·ing /'briːfɪŋ/ *n* [C,U] when people are given information or instructions: *a press briefing*

briefs /briːfs/ *n* [plural] underwear worn between your waist and the top of your legs

bri·gade /brɪ'geɪd/ *n* [C] a large unit of soldiers, forming part of an army → see also **FIRE BRIGADE**

brig·a·dier /ˌbrɪɡə'dɪəll-'dɪr/ *n* [C] an officer who has a high rank in the British army

bright /braɪt/ *adj* **1** shining strongly or full of light: *a bright sunny day* | *bright lights*

2 bright colours are strong and easy to see: *Her dress was bright red.* **3** intelligent: *Vicky is a very bright child.* **4** cheerful: *a bright smile* **5** a bright future is likely to be successful: *You have a bright future ahead of you!* —**brightly** *adv*: *brightly coloured balloons* —**brightness** *n* [U]

bright·en /ˈbraɪtn/ also **brighten up** *v* **1** [I,T] to become brighter or more pleasant, or to make something brighter: *Flowers would brighten up this room.* | *The weather should brighten in the afternoon.* **2** [I,T] to become more cheerful, or to make someone more cheerful: *She brightened up when she saw us coming.*

bril·liant /ˈbrɪljənt/ *adj* **1** brilliant light or colour is very bright and strong: *brilliant sunshine* **2** very good, intelligent or skilful: *a brilliant scientist* **3** BrE spoken used to say that you like or enjoy something very much: *"How was your holiday?" "It was brilliant!"* —**brilliance** *n* [U] —**brilliantly** *adv*

brim¹ /brɪm/ *n* [C] **1** the bottom part of a hat that turns outwards **2** **filled/full to the brim** as full as possible: *The glass was full to the brim.*

brim² *v* **-mmed, -mming** [I] to be very full of something: **+ with** *Clive was brimming with confidence at the start of the race.*

brim over *phr v* [I] **1** **brim over with excitement/confidence etc** to be very excited, confident etc **2** if a bowl, glass etc is brimming over, it is so full that liquid is flowing out over the top

brine /braɪn/ *n* [U] salty water, often used for preserving food

bring /brɪŋ/ *v* [T] **brought** /brɔːt‖brɒːt/, **brought, bringing 1** to take something or someone with you when you come to a place or person: *I brought these pictures to show you.* | **bring sb/sth with you** *She brought her children with her to the party.* | **bring sb sth** (=bring it for them): *Rob brought her a glass of water.* **2** **bring sth out/up/down etc** to move something somewhere: *He put his hand in his pocket and brought out a knife.* **3** to make something happen or cause a reaction: *an enthusiastic welcome that brought a smile to her face* **4** **can't bring yourself to do sth** to not be able to do something, especially because it is unpleasant: *I couldn't bring myself to kill the poor creature.* **5** **bring sth to an end** to make something stop or finish: *We hope that the peace process will bring this violence to an end.* **6** **bring sth to sb's attention** *formal* to tell someone about something: *Thank you for bringing the problem to our attention.* **7** **bring sth to bear** *formal* to use your power, influence etc to try to persuade people to do something or change a situation: *The US and Britain brought pressure to bear on Iraq to allow UN inspections.* **8** to make someone come to a place: *The fair brings a lot of people to the town.*

bring sth ↔ **about** *phr v* [T] to make something happen: *The war brought about huge social and political changes.*

bring sb/sth **around/round** *phr v* [T] **1 bring the conversation round/around to** to deliberately and gradually change the subject of a conversation: *Helen tried to bring the conversation around to the subject of marriage.* **2** to make someone conscious again

bring sth/sb ↔ **back** *phr v* [T] **1** to return from somewhere with something or someone: *These are a few souvenirs I brought back from India.* **2** to start using something again that was used in the past: *Many states have voted to bring back the death penalty.* **3** to make someone remember something: *The smell of cut grass brought back memories of the summer.*

bring sb/sth **down** *phr v* [T] **1** to make something or someone fall: *An enemy plane was brought down by rocket launchers.* **2** to reduce the number or amount of something: *Improved farming methods have brought down the price of food.* **3** **bring down a government/president etc** to force a government etc to stop governing a country

bring sth ↔ **forward** *phr v* [T] **1** to arrange for something to happen at an earlier time than was originally planned: *The meeting had been brought forward to Wednesday.* **2** to suggest a new plan or idea: *Mayor Daley brought forward a plan to fight urban crime.*

bring sb/sth ↔ **in** *phr v* [T] **1** to ask someone to take part in something in order to help with a problem: *The police had to bring in the FBI to help with their search.* **2** to earn or produce an amount of money: *sales that will bring in more than £2 million* **3** to officially start a new system, method, or rule for the first time: *The city council will bring in new regulations to restrict parking.*

bring sth ↔ **off** *phr v* [T] to succeed in doing something difficult: *She'll get a promotion if she brings off this deal.*

bring sth ↔ **on** *phr v* [T] to cause a pain or illness: *a bad cold brought on by going out in the rain*

bring sth ↔ **out** *phr v* [T] **1** to produce and begin to sell a new product: *The National Tourist Organization has just brought out a new guide book.* **2** **bring out the best/worst in sb** to make someone show the best or worst part of their character: *Becoming a father has brought out the best in Dan.* **3** to make something easier to notice: *a new shampoo that really brings out the highlights in your hair*

bring sb/sth **round** *phr v* BRING AROUND

bring sb/sth ↔ **up** *phr v* [T] **1** to look after children until they are adults: *Rachel had been brought up by her grandmother.* | **well/badly brought up** (=behaving well or badly because of the way you were brought up) **2** to start to talk about something: *She wished she'd never brought up the subject of money.*

brink /brɪŋk/ *n* **be on the brink of** if you are on the brink of something exciting or terrible, you will experience it soon: *two nations on the brink of war*

brisk /brɪsk/ *adj* **1** quick and full of energy: *a brisk walk* **2** **brisk trade/business etc** when things are being sold very quickly: *The ice-cream man was doing a brisk trade.* —**briskly** *adv* —**briskness** *n* [U]

bris·tle¹ /ˈbrɪsəl/ *n* [C,U] short stiff hair, wire etc: *a brush with short bristles* —**bristly** *adj*

bristle² *v* [I] **1** if an animal's hair bristles, it stands up stiffly because of fear or anger **2** to behave in a way that shows you are very annoyed: *She bristled with indignation.*

bristle with sth *phr v* [T] to have a lot of something: *a battleship bristling with guns*

Brit /brɪt/ *n* [C] *informal* someone from Great Britain

Brit·ish[1] /'brɪtɪʃ/ *adj* from or connected with Great Britain

British[2] *n* [plural] **the British** the people of Great Britain

Brit·on /'brɪtn/ *n* [C] someone from Great Britain

brit·tle /'brɪtl/ *adj* hard but easily broken: *The twigs were dry and brittle, and cracked beneath their feet.*

broach /brəʊtʃ‖broʊtʃ/ *v* **broach the subject/ question etc** to mention a subject that may be embarrassing or unpleasant: *At last he broached the subject of her divorce.*

broad /brɔːd‖brɒːd/ *adj* **1** very wide: *broad shoulders* **2** including many different kinds of things or people: *a broad range of interests* **3** general, and without a lot of details: *a broad outline of the plan* **4** **in broad daylight** during the day, when it is light: *He was attacked in the street in broad daylight.* **5** a broad ACCENT (=way of speaking) clearly shows where you come from: *a broad Scottish accent*

broad·cast[1] /'brɔːdkɑːst‖'brɒːdkæst/ *n* [C] a programme on radio or television: *a news broadcast*

broadcast[2] *v* broadcast, broadcast, broadcasting **1** [I,T] to send out a radio or television programme: *Channel 5 will broadcast the game at 6 o'clock.* **2** [T] to tell something to a lot of people: *If I tell you, don't go broadcasting it all over the place.* —**broadcasting** *n* [U]

broad·cast·er /'brɔːdkɑːstə‖'brɒːdkæstər/ *n* [C] someone who speaks on radio and television programmes

broad·en /'brɔːdn‖'brɒːdn/ *v* [I,T] **1** to include or make something include more different kinds of things or people: *training designed to broaden your knowledge of practical medicine* **2** also **broaden out** to make something wider, or to become wider: *The river broadens out here.*

broad·ly /'brɔːdli‖'brɒːd-/ *adv* **1** in a general way: *I know broadly what to expect.* **2** **smile/ grin broadly** to have a big smile on your face

broad·mind·ed /ˌbrɔːd'maɪndɪd◂‖ˌbrɒːd-/ *adj* willing to accept behaviour or opinions that are very different from your own

broad·side /'brɔːdsaɪd‖'brɒːd-/ *n* [C] a strong spoken or written attack: *an angry editorial broadside in today's paper*

bro·cade /brə'keɪd‖broʊ-/ *n* [U] thick cloth that has a pattern of gold and silver threads —**brocaded** *adj*

broc·co·li /'brɒkəli‖'brɑː-/ *n* [U] a green vegetable

bro·chure /'brəʊʃə, -ʃʊə‖broʊ'ʃʊr/ *n* [C] a thin book that gives information or advertises something: *a travel brochure*

broil /brɔɪl/ *v* [T] *AmE* to cook something under or over direct heat; GRILL *BrE*: *broiled chicken*

broil·er /'brɔɪlə‖-ər/ *n* [C] *AmE* an open metal shelf in a COOKER, used for cooking food under direct heat

broke[1] /brəʊk‖broʊk/ *adj informal* **1** having no money at all: *I can't pay you now – I'm broke.*

Buildings

Exercise 1

Look at the words in the picture. Find the words which match these definitions.

1 a small area outside an upstairs window, where you can sit or stand **balcony**

2 an outdoor area with a stone floor near a house _____

3 a room or rooms in a building that are under the level of the ground _____

4 a room at the top of a house _____

5 a pipe or hole that waste liquids go down to be carried away _____

6 a passage inside a building for smoke from a fire to go up and out through the roof _____

7 a line of upright wooden posts with wire between, used to divide or enclose an area of land _____

8 a hole in a door through which letters are delivered _____

9 a building where you keep your car _____

10 the path you walk on at the side of a road _____

11 a large circular piece of metal that receives signals for satellite television _____

12 a very tall building in a city _____

Exercise 2

Play 'What's the difference?' with your friends.
Ask 'What's the difference between:

patio / garden
attic / basement
house / flat
chimney / drain
fence / hedge*

*Look at the picture of 'Countryside' to see a hedge.

first floor *BrE*/ second floor *AmE*

skyscraper

second floor *BrE*/ third floor *AmE*

block of flats *BrE*/ apartment building *AmE*

...d floor *BrE*/ ...floor *AmE*

balcony

fire escape

...rraced houses *BrE*/ row houses *AmE*

roof

bungalow

satellite dish

semi-detached house *BrE*/ duplex *AmE*

chimney

patio

clothesline

basement

phone box *BrE* / phone booth *AmE*

detached house *BrE*

streetlight

attic

window

windowsill

lamp-post

garage

shutter

garden *BrE*/ yard *AmE*

letter box *BrE*/ mail slot *AmE*

drive *BrE*/ driveway

pavement *BrE*/ sidewalk *AmE*

drain

gate

fence *BrE*/ picket fence *AmE*

road

blackboard

whiteboard

map

noticeboard *BrE*/
bulletin board *AmE*

TIMETABLE

timetable *BrE*/
schedule *AmE*

blackboard rubber *BrE*/
eraser *AmE*

a) Guam Sas power

b) Swing plums (is

c)

marker

teacher

photocopier *BrE*/
copier *AmE*

bin *BrE*/
wastebasket *AmE*

pen

pe

pupil *BrE*/ student *AmE*

textbook

Sellotape *BrE*/ Scotch tape *AmE*

exercise book *BrE*/
notebook *AmE*

glue

stapler

diary *BrE*/
agenda *AmE*

desk

ch

fol

scissors

ring binder

screen

com

printout

CD-ROM drive

printer

disk drive

keyboard

mouse mat

mouse pad

cacul

chair

pencil
sharpener

mouse
floppy disk

schoolbag

CD-ROM

2 go broke to lose so much money that you have to close your business: *The company went broke last year.*

broke² *v* the past tense of BREAK

bro·ken¹ /'brəukən‖'brou-/ *adj* **1** damaged or in small pieces because of being hit, dropped etc: *a broken leg* | *a broken plate* → see picture at CRACKED **2** a broken machine or piece of equipment does not work: *a broken clock* **3** interrupted by spaces, not continuous: *a broken white line* **4 broken marriage** a marriage that has ended, and the husband and wife no longer live together **5 broken home** a family in which the children's parents no longer live together: *Are children from broken homes more likely to do badly at school?* **6 broken agreement/promise etc** when someone did not do what they promised to **7 broken English/French etc** English, French etc that is spoken slowly, with a lot of mistakes

broken² *v* the past participle of BREAK

broken-down /ˌ.. '.◂/ *adj* in bad condition: *a broken-down old barn*

broken-heart·ed /ˌ.. '..◂/ *adj* very sad, especially because someone you love has died or left you

bro·ker¹ /'brəukə‖'broukər/ *n* [C] someone whose job is to buy and sell property, insurance etc for someone else → see also STOCKBROKER

broker² *v* [T] to arrange the details of a deal, plan etc so that everyone can agree to it: *an agreement brokered by the UN*

bron·chi·tis /brɒŋ'kaɪtɪs‖brɑːŋ-/ *n* [U] an illness that affects your breathing and makes you cough

bronze /brɒnz‖brɑːnz/ *n* [U] **1** a hard metal that is a mixture of COPPER and TIN **2** a dark red-brown colour —**bronze** *adj*

bronze med·al /ˌ. '../ *n* [C] the prize that you get for coming third in a race or competition

brooch /brəutʃ‖broutʃ/ *n* [C] a piece of jewellery that you fasten to your clothes with a pin → see picture at JEWELLERY

brood¹ /bruːd/ *v* [I] to think about something angrily or sadly for a long time: *You can't just sit there brooding over your problems.*

brood² *n* [C] a family of young birds

brook /brʊk/ *n* [C] a small stream

broom /bruːm, brʊm/ *n* [C] a brush with a long handle, used for sweeping floors

broom·stick /'bruːm,stɪk, 'brʊm-/ *n* [C] the long thin handle of a broom

broth /brɒθ‖brɔːθ/ *n* [U] thick soup

broth·el /'brɒθəl‖'brɑː-, 'brɔː-/ *n* [C] a house where men pay to have sex with women

broth·er /'brʌðə‖-ər/ *n* [C] **1** a man or boy who has the same parents as you: *older/younger/big/little brother Isn't that your little brother?* (=younger than you) → see picture at FAMILY **2** a man who belongs to the same group or race as you: *We must support our African brothers in their struggle.* **3** a male member of a religious group, especially a MONK

Classroom

Exercise 1

Look at your classroom. Look at the picture. Tick [✓] the objects which are in your classroom.

blackboard ☐   glue ☐   pencil ☐

scissors ☐   calculator ☐   keyboard ☐

pencil sharpener ☐   screen ☐

CD-ROM ☐   map ☐   photocopier ☐

student ☑   CD-ROM drive ☐   marker ☐

teacher ☐   chair ☐   mouse ☐   printer ☐

text book ☐   desk ☐   mouse mat ☐

printout ☐   wastebin ☐   disk drive ☐

noticeboard ☐   whiteboard ☐   exercise

book ☐   pen ☐   schoolbag ☐

Exercise 2

Complete these pairs of words.

1 chair + *desk*

2 chalk + b _ _ _ _ _ _ _ _

3 floppy disk + d _ _ _ d _ _ _ _

4 pencil + p _ _ _ _ _ s _ _ _ _ _ _ _ _

5 marker + w _ _ _ _ _ _ _ _ _

6 printer + p _ _ _ _ _ _ _

7 student + t _ _ _ _ _ _

8 mouse mat + m _ _ _ _

Exercise 3

Look at the picture. There are five things we use for writing. What are they?

1 pne = *pen*

3 khalc =

5 clinep =

2 yekbroad =

4 rekmra =

broth·er·hood /ˈbrʌðəhʊdǁ-ər-/ n **1** [U] a friendly loyal relationship that unites many people: *peace and human brotherhood* **2** [C] an organization of people who share the same political aims or religious beliefs

brother-in-law /ˈ... ... ,. / n [C] **1** the brother of your husband or wife **2** the husband of your sister → see picture at FAMILY

broth·er·ly /ˈbrʌðəliǁ-ər-/ adj **brotherly love/feeling** the kind of love or feeling you would expect a brother to show

brought /brɔːtǁbrɒːt/ v the past tense and past participle of BRING

brow /braʊ/ n [C] **1** the part of your face above your eyes and below your hair; FOREHEAD **2** the line of hairs above each of your eyes; EYEBROW **3** **the brow of a hill** *BrE* the top part of a hill

brow·beat /ˈbraʊbiːt/ v [T] to try to force someone to do something, especially in a threatening way: *Don't let them browbeat you into doing all the work.*

brown¹ /braʊn/ adj having the same colour as chocolate or wood: *brown shoes* —**brown** n [U] → see colour pictures on page 114 and page 244

brown² v [I,T] if food browns, or if you brown it, you cook the food until it is brown

browse /braʊz/ v [I] **1** to look at the goods in a shop without buying anything: *"Can I help you?" "No thanks. I'm just browsing."* **2** to look through a book or magazine without any particular purpose: *I was browsing through the catalogue.*

bruise¹ /bruːz/ n [C] a mark on the skin of a person or piece of fruit where it has been damaged by a hit or a fall: *That's a nasty bruise you've got.*

bruise² v [T] to cause a bruise on the skin of someone or something: *He fell and bruised his knee.* —**bruising** n [U]

bru·nette /bruːˈnet/ n [C] a woman with dark brown hair

brunt /brʌnt/ n **bear/take the brunt of** to suffer the worst part of something unpleasant: *I had to bear the brunt of his anger.*

brushes

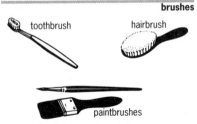

toothbrush

hairbrush

paintbrushes

brush¹ /brʌʃ/ n **1** [C] a thing that you use for cleaning, painting etc, consisting of hairs fastened on to a handle → see also HAIRBRUSH, PAINTBRUSH, TOOTHBRUSH **2** [singular] a movement of brushing something: *I'll just give my hair a quick brush.* **3** **a brush with** when something unpleasant almost happens to you: *a brush with death*

brush² v **1** [T] to clean, sweep, or tidy something with a brush: *Go brush your teeth.* **2** [T] to remove something with a brush or with your hand: **brush sth off/away** *She brushed the*

crumbs off her lap. **3** [I,T] to touch someone or something lightly as you go past them: **+ against** *Her hair brushed against my arm.*

brush sb/sth ↔ aside phr v [T] to refuse to listen to or consider someone's opinion: *He brushed aside all criticisms.*

brush up (on) sth phr v [I] to quickly practise and improve your skills or knowledge: *I have to brush up on my French before I go to Paris.*

brush-off /ˈ. ./ n informal **give sb the brush-off** to show someone that you do not want to be friendly with them: *I wanted to ask her out to dinner, but she gave me the brush-off.*

brush·wood /ˈbrʌʃwʊd/ n [U] small branches of trees and bushes

brusque /bruːsk, brʊskǁbrʌsk/ adj using very few words when you speak, in a way that seems rude: *a brusque manner* —**brusquely** adv

brus·sels sprout /ˌbrʌsəlz ˈspraʊt/ n [C] a small round green vegetable

bru·tal /ˈbruːtl/ adj **1** very cruel and violent: *a brutal attack* **2** saying something unpleasant without caring about people's feelings: *She needs to be told what she is doing wrong, but you don't need to be brutal about it.* —**brutally** adv: *brutally honest remarks* —**brutality** /bruːˈtæləti/ n [C,U]

bru·tal·ize (also **-ise** *BrE*) /ˈbruːtəl-aɪz/ v [T] **1** to make someone violent, cruel, and unable to feel sympathy: *the brutalizing effects of war* **2** to treat someone in a cruel and violent way —**brutalization** /ˌbruːtəl-aɪˈzeɪʃənǁ-tələ-/ n [U]

brute¹ /bruːt/ n [C] **1** a cruel violent man **2** a large strong animal: *a great brute of a dog*

brute² adj **brute force/strength** physical strength that is used instead of gentle clever methods: *In the end I had to use brute force to open the box.*

brut·ish /ˈbruːtɪʃ/ adj without human feelings or intelligence: *brutish behaviour*

BSc /ˌbiː es ˈsiː/ *BrE*, **B.S.** /ˌbiː ˈes/ *AmE* — n [C] Bachelor of Science; a university degree in a science subject

BSE /ˌbiː es ˈiː/ n [U] a disease that kills cattle by destroying the brain and NERVOUS SYSTEM

bub·ble¹ /ˈbʌbəl/ n [C] a ball of air in a liquid: *soap bubbles*

bubble² v [I] **1** if a liquid bubbles, it produces bubbles, especially when it boils **2** **bubble (over) with joy/excitement etc** to show that you feel very happy, excited etc

bubble gum /ˈ.. ./ n [U] a type of CHEWING GUM that you can blow into a bubble

bub·bly /ˈbʌbli/ adj **1** full of bubbles **2** cheerful and full of energy: *a bubbly personality*

buck¹ /bʌk/ n [C] **1** *AmE, AustrE spoken* a dollar: *Could you lend me 20 bucks?* **2** **pass the buck** to try to make someone else responsible for something that you should deal with: *You can't keep passing the buck!* **3** the male of some animals, for example DEER and rabbits **4** **buck naked** *AmE spoken* wearing no clothes: *Sean was standing outside, buck naked.*

buck² v [I, T] if a horse bucks, or bucks its rider, it kicks its back feet up in the air, making its rider fall off

buck·et /ˈbʌkɪt/ n [C] **1** a large round container with a handle over the top, used for carrying liquids **2** the amount that a bucket will hold: **+ of** *a bucket of water*

buck·le¹ /ˈbʌkəl/ v **1** [I,T] also **buckle up** to fasten a buckle, or be fastened with a buckle: *The strap buckles at the side.* **2** [I] if your knees buckle, they become weak and bend **3** [I,T] to bend because of heat or pressure, or to make a substance bend in this way: *The bridge had buckled over the years.*

buckle down *phr v* [I] *informal* to start working seriously: *You'd better buckle down or you'll never pass your exams.*

buckle² *n* [C] a thing made of metal used for fastening a belt, shoe, bag etc → see picture at FASTENER

bud¹ /bʌd/ *n* [C] **1** a young flower or leaf before it opens **2** *AmE spoken* BUDDY

bud² *v* [I] **-dded, -dding** to produce buds

Bud·dhis·m /ˈbʊdɪzəm‖ˈbuː-, ˈbʊ-/ *n* [U] the belief and religion based on the teachings of Buddha —**Buddhist** *n* [C] —**Buddhist** *adj*

bud·ding /ˈbʌdɪŋ/ *adj* beginning to develop: *a budding relationship*

bud·dy /ˈbʌdi/ *n* [C] **1** *informal* a friend: *We're good buddies.* **2** *AmE spoken* used to address a man or boy you do not know: *Hey buddy! Leave her alone!*

budge /bʌdʒ/ *v* [I,T] *informal* **1** to move, or to move someone or something from one place to another: *The car won't budge.* | **+ from** *Mark hasn't budged from his room all day.* **2** to change your opinion, or to make someone change theirs: *Once Dad's made up his mind, he won't budge.*

bud·ge·ri·gar /ˈbʌdʒərɪgɑː‖-gɑːr/ *n* [C] a small brightly coloured bird, often kept in a cage as a pet

bud·get¹ /ˈbʌdʒɪt/ *n* [C] a careful plan of how to spend the money that is available for you to spend, or the money itself: **+ of** *They have a budget of £1.5 million for the project.* | **cut/trim the budget** (=spend less) | **balance the budget** (=make the money that is spent equal to the money that is received)

budget² *v* [I] to carefully plan and control how much you will spend: **budget for** (=save money for something): *We didn't budget for any travel costs.*

budget³ *adj* very low in price: *a budget flight*

bud·get·a·ry /ˈbʌdʒɪtəri‖-teri/ *adj* relating to a budget: *budgetary limits*

bud·gie /ˈbʌdʒi/ *n* [C] *BrE* a BUDGERIGAR

buff¹ /bʌf/ *n* [C] **wine/computer/opera etc buff** someone who is interested in and knows a lot about wine, computers etc

buff² *v* [T] to make a surface shine by polishing (POLISH) it with something soft

buff³ *adj* pale brown

buf·fa·lo /ˈbʌfələʊ‖-loʊ/ *n* [C], *plural* **buffalos, buffaloes,** or **buffalo 1** a type of cattle with long curved horns that lives in Africa and Asia **2** a BISON

buff·er /ˈbʌfəl-ər/ *n* [C] **1** something or someone that reduces the unpleasant effects of something else: **+ against** *The trees act as a buffer against strong winds.* | *Support from friends can provide a buffer against stress.* **2** one of the two pieces of metal on springs, on the front or back of a train, that protects the train from damage if it hits anything —**buffer** *v* [T]

buf·fet¹ /ˈbʊfeɪ‖bəˈfeɪ/ *n* [C] a meal in which people serve themselves at a table and then move away to eat

buf·fet² /ˈbʌfɪt/ *v* [T] if wind, rain, or the sea buffets something, it hits it with a lot of force: *Chicago was buffeted by storms last night.*

buffet car /ˈ.. .‖ˈ. ./ *n* [C] *BrE* the part of a train where you can buy food and drink

buf·foon /bəˈfuːn/ *n* [C] *old-fashioned* someone who does silly and stupid things

bug¹ /bʌg/ *n* [C] **1** *informal* a small insect **2** *informal* a GERM that causes an illness: *a flu bug* **3** **get the bug/be bitten by the bug** *informal* have a sudden strong interest in doing something: *They've all been bitten by the football bug.* **4** a small mistake in a computer PROGRAM that stops it from working correctly: *There's a bug in the system.* **5** a small piece of electronic equipment for listening secretly to other people's conversations

bug² *v* [T] **-gged, -gging 1** to use electronic equipment to listen secretly to other people's conversations: *Are you sure this room isn't bugged?* **2** *spoken* to annoy someone: *Stop bugging me!*

bug·ger /ˈbʌgəl-ər/ *interjection BrE* a rude word used when you are annoyed with someone or something

bug·gy /ˈbʌgi/ *n* [C] a light folding chair on wheels that you push small children in; STROLLER *AmE*

bu·gle /ˈbjuːgəl/ *n* [C] a musical instrument like a TRUMPET which is used in the army to call soldiers —**bugler** *n* [C]

build¹ /bɪld/ *v* **built** /bɪlt/, **built, building 1** [I,T] to make a building or large structure, for example a house, bridge, or ship: *More homes are being built near the lake.* **2** [T] to develop something slowly: *We are working to build a more peaceful world.*

build sth ↔ **into** *phr v* [T] to make something a permanent part of something else: *A physical training program is built into the course.*

build on sth *phr v* [T] to use something you have done to continue your success: *We hope to build on what we learned last year.*

build up *phr v* **1** [I,T **build** sth ↔ **up**] if something builds up, or you build it up, it gradually increases or grows: *You need to build your strength up after your illness.* | *They've built up the business over a number of years.* **2 build up sb's hopes** to make someone think they will get what they want, when in fact it is unlikely: *Don't build your hopes up.*

build up to sth *phr v* [T] to gradually prepare

GRAMMAR NOTE: 'if' clauses (1)
Use the simple present to talk about the future in clauses beginning **if...** : *I will hit you* **if** *you* **do** *that again*. *not* 'if you will do that again'. **If** *you* **take** *a taxi, you'll be OK. not* 'if you will take a taxi...'
Use 'will' in the other part of the sentence.

for an important or exciting event: *What's all this activity building up to?*

build² *n* [U, singular] the shape and size of someone's body: *Maggie is tall with a slim build.* → see colour picture on page 244

build·er /'bɪldəll-ər/ *n* [C] *especially BrE* a person or a company that builds or repairs buildings

build·ing /'bɪldɪŋ/ *n* [C] **1** a place such as a house, church, or factory that has a roof and walls: *The old church was surrounded by tall buildings.* **2** [U] the process or business of building things

building block /'.. ./ *n* [C] **1** [C, usually plural] one of the pieces or parts that make it possible for something big or important to exist: *Reading and writing are the building blocks of our education.* **2** one of a set of CUBES that young children play with

building site /'... ./ *n* [C] a place where houses, factories etc are being built

building so·ci·e·ty /'... ..,.../ *n* [C] *BrE* a type of bank where you can save money or borrow money to buy a house; SAVINGS AND LOAN ASSOCIATION *AmE*

build-up /'. ./ *n* [C, usually singular] a gradual increase: *The build-up of traffic is causing major problems in cities.*

built /bɪlt/ *the* past tense and past participle of BUILD

built-in /,. '.◂/ *adj* features, attitudes etc that are built-in are a permanent part of something: *built-in wardrobes | There is a built-in unfairness in the system.*

bulb /bʌlb/ *n* [C] **1** the central glass part of an electric light, where the light shines from: *We need a new bulb in the kitchen.* **2** a round root that grows into a plant: *tulip bulbs*

bul·bous /'bʌlbəs/ *adj* fat and round: *a bulbous nose*

bulge¹ /bʌldʒ/ *n* [C] a curved shape caused by something pressing against a flat surface: *What's that bulge in the carpet?*

bulge² *v* also **bulge out** [I] to stick out in a rounded shape: *Jeffrey's stomach bulged over his trousers.*

bu·lim·i·a /bju:'lɪmɪə, bʊ-/ *n* [U] an illness that makes someone eat too much and then VOMIT because they are afraid of being fat —**bulimic** *adj*

bulk /bʌlk/ *n* **1** the bulk of sth the main or largest part of something: *The bulk of the work has already been done.* **2** [singular] the size of something or someone, especially a large size: *His bulk made it difficult for him to move quickly enough.* **3 in bulk** in large quantities: *It's cheaper to buy things in bulk.*

bulk·y /'bʌlki/ *adj* big and difficult to move: *a bulky package*

bull /bʊl/ *n* **1** [C] a male cow, or the male of some other large animals such as an ELEPHANT or WHALE **2** [U] *informal* BULLSHIT **3 take the bull by the horns** *informal* to confidently deal with a difficult or dangerous situation

bull·dog /'bʊldɒgll-dɔːg/ *n* [C] a powerful dog with a short neck and short thick legs

bull·doze /'bʊldəʊzll-doʊz/ *v* [T] to destroy buildings etc with a bulldozer

bull·doz·er /'bʊldəʊzəll-doʊzər/ *n* [C] a large

powerful vehicle that can push over buildings and move rocks

bul·let /'bʊlɪt/ *n* [C] a small rounded or pointed piece of metal that is fired from a gun

bul·le·tin /'bʊlətɪn/ *n* [C] **1** a short news report: *Our next bulletin is at 6 o'clock.* **2** a regular letter or report that an organization produces to help people its news

bulletin board /'... ,./ *n* [C] **1** *especially AmE* a board on a wall where you can put information for people to see; NOTICEBOARD *BrE* → see colour picture on page 80 **2** a place in a computer system where a group of people can leave or read messages

bull·fight /'bʊlfaɪt/ *n* [C] an outdoor entertainment in Spain, Portugal etc in which a man fights a BULL —**bullfighter** *n* [C] —**bullfighting** *n* [U]

bull·horn /'bʊlhɔːnll-hɔːrn/ *n* [C] *AmE* an object in the shape of a CONE that you talk through to make your voice louder; MEGAPHONE

bul·lion /'bʊljən/ *n* [U] blocks of gold or silver

bul·lock /'bʊlək/ *n* [C] a young BULL

bull's-eye /'. ./ *n* [C] the centre of the round board that you aim at in SHOOTING, DARTS etc

bull·shit¹ /'bʊl,ʃɪt/ *interjection* a rude word used when you do not agree with or believe what someone has said

bullshit² *v* [I,T] a rude word meaning to say something that is stupid or untrue —**bullshitter** *n* [C]

bul·ly¹ /'bʊli/ *v* [T] to frighten someone or threaten to hurt them, especially if they are weaker or smaller than you —**bullying** *n* [U]

bully² *n* [C] someone who uses their strength or power to frighten or hurt others

bum¹ /bʌm/ *n* [C] *informal* **1** *BrE* the part of your body that you sit on **2** *especially AmE* someone who is very lazy: *Get out of bed, you bum!* **3** *AmE* someone who has no home or job

bum² *v* [T] -**mmed, -mming** *informal* to ask someone if you can borrow or have something: *Can I bum a cigarette?*

bum around *phr v* [I,T] *informal* to spend time travelling for pleasure, not spending much money and not doing very much: *I spent the summer bumming around Europe.*

bum·ble·bee /'bʌmblbiː/ *n* [C] a large BEE

bum·bling /'bʌmblɪŋ/ *adj* [only before noun] confused and CLUMSY and making a lot of mistakes

bum·mer /'bʌməll-ər/ *n* [singular] *spoken informal* a situation that is disappointing or annoying: **a bummer** *You can't go? What a bummer.*

bump¹ /bʌmp/ *v* **1** [I,T] to hit or knock against something, especially by accident: *Mind you don't bump your head! | + into/against It was so dark I bumped into a tree.* **2** [I] to move in an uneven way because the ground is not smooth: **+ along** *The truck bumped along the rough track.*

bump into sb *phr v* [T] *informal* to meet someone when you were not expecting to: *Guess who I bumped into this morning?*

bump sb ↔ off *phr v* [T] *informal* to kill someone

bump sth ↔ up *phr v* [T] *BrE informal* to increase something: *In the summer they bump up the prices by 10 per cent.*

bump² n [C] **1** an area of skin that is hard and raised because you have hit it on something: **+ on** *Derek's got a nasty bump on his head.* **2** a small raised area on a surface: **+ in** *a bump in the road* **3** a sudden movement in which one thing hits against another thing, or the sound that this makes: *Danny sat down with a bump.*

bump·er¹ /ˈbʌmpəll-ər/ n [C] the part across the front and back of a car that protects it if it hits anything → see picture at CAR

bumper² adj [only before noun] larger than usual: *a bumper crop*

bumper stick·er /ˈ.. ,../ n [C] a small sign with a message on it on the bumper of a car

bump·y /ˈbʌmpi/ adj **1** a bumpy surface has a lot of raised parts on it: *a bumpy road* **2** a bumpy journey in a car or plane is uncomfortable because the road or weather is bad

bun /bʌn/ n [C] **1** BrE a small round sweet cake: *a currant bun* **2** bread that is made in a small round shape: *a hamburger bun* **3** a way of arranging long hair by fastening it in a small round shape

bunch¹ /bʌntʃ/ n [C] **1** a group of similar things that are fastened, held, or growing together at one point: **+ of** *a bunch of grapes* | *a beautiful bunch of violets* → see colour picture on page 440 **2** [singular] *informal* **a)** a group of people: *My class are a really nice bunch.* | **+ of** *a bunch of idiots* **b)** AmE informal a large amount: **+ of** *The doctor asked me a bunch of questions.*

bunch² v [I,T] also **bunch together** to stay close together in a group, or to make a group: *The children were bunched together by the door.*

bunch up phr v [I,T **bunch** sth ↔ **up**] if material bunches up, or if you bunch it up, it goes into tight folds: *My skirt got all bunched up in the car.*

bun·dle¹ /ˈbʌndl/ n [C] **1** a group of things such as papers, clothes, or sticks that are fastened or tied together: **+ of** *a bundle of newspapers* **2** **be a bundle of nerves/fun etc** informal to be very nervous, a lot of fun etc

bundle² v [I,T] **1** to move someone or something quickly and roughly into a place, or to move quickly into a place with a lot of other people: **+ into/through/out of etc** *The police bundled Jason into the back of the van.* | *A dozen kids bundled out of the classroom.* **2** [T] to include other things with something someone buys: **+ with** *The computer comes bundled with word-processing software.*

bundle sth ↔ **up** phr v [T] to collect things into a bundle: *Bundle up the newspapers and we'll take them to be recycled.*

bung¹ /bʌŋ/ n [C] **1** BrE a round piece of rubber, wood etc used to close the top of a container **2** BrE informal a BRIBE

bung² v [T] BrE informal to put something somewhere: **bung sth in/on etc** *Bung the butter in the fridge, will you?*

bung sth ↔ **up** phr v [T] informal **1** to block a hole by putting something in it **2** **be bunged up** to be unable to breathe through your nose because you have a cold

bun·ga·low /ˈbʌŋɡələʊll-loʊ/ n [C] a house that is built on one level → see colour picture on page 79

bun·gle /ˈbʌŋɡəl/ v [T] to do something badly:

The builders bungled the job completely. —**bungling** n [U]

bun·ion /ˈbʌnjən/ n [C] a painful swollen place on the side of your toe

bunk /bʌŋk/ n [C] **1** a narrow bed on a train, or ship, which is joined to the wall **2** **bunk beds** two beds that are one on top of the other → see picture at BED **3** **do a bunk** BrE informal to suddenly leave a place without telling anyone

bun·ker /ˈbʌŋkəll-ər/ n [C] **1** a strongly built SHELTER, usually under the ground, built for protection against bombs **2** BrE a wide hole on a GOLF COURSE filled with sand; SANDTRAP AmE

bun·ny /ˈbʌni/ also **bunny rab·bit** /ˈ.. ,../ n [C] a rabbit – used especially by children or when you are talking to children

buoy¹ /bɔɪllˈbuːi, bɔɪ/ n [C] an object that floats on the water to show safe and dangerous areas

buoy² v also **buoy up** [T] to make someone feel happier, more confident etc: *Jill was buoyed up by success.*

buoy·ant /ˈbɔɪəntllˈbɔɪənt, ˈbuːjənt/ adj **1** cheerful and confident: *Bob was in a buoyant mood.* **2** buoyant prices, profits etc stay at a high level **3** able to float —**buoyancy** n [U]

bur·den¹ /ˈbɜːdnllˈbɜːrdn/ n [C] *formal* **1** something difficult or worrying that you are responsible for: **+ on** *I don't want to be a burden on my children when I'm old.* **2** **the burden of proof** formal the duty to prove something **3** *literary* something heavy that you have to carry

burden² v [T] **1** to cause a lot of problems for someone: *We won't burden her with any more responsibility.* **2** also **burden down** to make someone have to carry something very heavy: *She struggled up the hill, burdened down by shopping.*

bu·reau /ˈbjʊərəʊllˈbjʊroʊ/ n [C] **1** an office or organization that collects or provides information: *an employment bureau* **2** *especially AmE* a government department, or part of one: *the Federal Bureau of Investigation* **3** BrE a piece of furniture with drawers and a sloping lid that you can open and use as a desk **4** AmE a piece of furniture with drawers, used for keeping clothes in; CHEST OF DRAWERS

bu·reauc·ra·cy /bjʊəˈrɒkrəsi, lbjʊˈrɑː-/ n **1** [U] an official system that is annoying or confusing because it has too many rules, long processes etc **2** [C,U] the officials in a government or business who are employed and not elected

bu·reau·crat /ˈbjʊərəkrætllˈbjʊr-/ n [C] someone who works in a government organization and uses official rules very strictly

bu·reau·crat·ic /ˌbjʊərəˈkrætɪk◄ll,bjʊr-/ adj involving a lot of official rules and processes

burg·er /ˈbɜːɡəllˈbɜːrɡər/ n [C] a HAMBURGER

bur·glar /ˈbɜːɡləllˈbɜːrɡlər/ n [C] someone who goes into buildings in order to steal things

burglar a·larm /ˈ.. ,../ n [C] a piece of equipment that makes a loud noise when a burglar gets into a building → see picture at ALARM

bur·glar·ize /ˈbɜːɡləraɪzllˈbɜːr-/ v [T] AmE to burgle a place

bur·glar·y /ˈbɜːɡlərillˈbɜːr-/ n [C,U] the crime of going into a building to steal things

bur·gle /ˈbɜːɡəlllˈbɜːr-/ BrE, **burglarize** AmE

— *v* [T] to go into a building and steal things from it

bur·i·al /'beriəl/ *n* [C,U] the act or ceremony of putting a dead body into a grave

bur·ly /'bɜːli‖'bɜːrli/ *adj* a burly man is big and strong

burn[1] /bɜːn‖bɜːrn/ *v* **burned** *or* **burnt** /bɜːnt ‖bɜːrnt/, **burned** *or* **burnt**, **burning** **1** [I,T] to damage something or hurt someone with fire or heat, or to be hurt or damaged in this way: *Be careful with that cigarette, you don't want to burn a hole in the carpet.* | **burn sth on sth** *Dave burnt his hand on the iron.* **2** [I] to produce heat and flames: *Is the fire still burning?* **3** [I,T] if something burns a FUEL, or if it burns, it is used to produce power, heat or light: *Cars burn gasoline.* **4** [I] also **burn up** to feel unpleasantly hot: *My face is burning up.* **5** **get burned** *especially AmE spoken* **a)** to have your feelings hurt **b)** to lose a lot of money, especially in a business deal **6** [I] *literary* if a light burns, it shines —**burned** *adj*

burn sth ↔ **down** *phr v* [I,T] if a building burns down or is burned down, it is destroyed by fire

burn sth ↔ **off** *phr v* [T] **burn off energy/fat/calories** to use up energy etc by doing physical exercise

burn out *phr v* [I,T **burn** sth ↔ **out**] if a fire burns out, or burns itself out, it stops burning because there is no coal, wood etc left

burn up *phr v* **1** [I,T **burn** sth ↔ **up**] if something burns up or is burned up, it is completely destroyed by fire **2** [T **burn** sb **up**] *AmE informal* to make someone angry: *The way he treats her really burns me up.*

burn[2] *n* [C] an injury or mark caused by fire or heat: *Many of the victims suffered severe burns.*

burned out /ˌ. '.‹/ also **burnt out** *adj* **1** tired or ill because you have been working too hard: *I was completely burned out after my exams.* **2** a burned out building, car etc has had the inside of it destroyed by fire

burn·er /'bɜːnə‖'bɜːrnər/ *n* **1** [C] the part of a COOKER that produces heat or a flame **2** **put sth on the back burner** *informal* to delay dealing with something until a later time

burn·ing /'bɜːnɪŋ‖'bɜːr-/ *adj* [only before noun] **1** on fire: *a burning house* **2** feeling very hot: *burning cheeks* **3** **burning ambition/need etc** a very strong AMBITION, need etc **4** **burning question/issue** a very important question that must be dealt with

bur·nished /'bɜːnɪʃt‖'bɜːr-/ *adj* burnished metal has been POLISHed until it shines —**burnish** *v* [T]

burnt[1] /bɜːnt‖bɜːrnt/ *v* a past tense and past participle of BURN

burnt[2] *adj* damaged or hurt by burning: *Sorry the toast is a little burnt.*

burnt out /ˌ. '.‹/ BURNED OUT

burp /bɜːp‖bɜːrp/ *v informal* [I] if you burp, gas comes up from your stomach and makes a noise —**burp** *n* [C]

bur·row[1] /'bʌrəʊ‖'bɜːroʊ/ *v* [I,T] to make a hole or small TUNNEL in the ground: + **under** *Rabbits had burrowed under the wall.*

burrow[2] *n* [C] a hole in the ground made by a rabbit, FOX etc

bur·sar /'bɜːsə‖'bɜːrsər/ *n* [C] someone at a college or school who is responsible for money that is paid or received

bur·sa·ry /'bɜːsəri‖'bɜːr-/ *n* [C] money given to a student to help them pay for their university studies; SCHOLARSHIP

burst

The balloon burst.

burst[1] /bɜːst‖bɜːrst/ *v* **burst, burst, bursting** **1** [I,T] to break open or apart suddenly and violently, or to make something do this: *The kids burst all the balloons with pins.* **2** **be bursting** to be very full of something: + **with** *Florence is always bursting with tourists.* | **be bursting at the seams** (=be too full): *Classrooms are bursting at the seams.* **3** [I] to move suddenly and with a lot of energy or violence: + **into/through etc** *Jenna burst into the room.* | **burst open** *The door burst open and 20 or 30 policemen rushed in.* **4** **be bursting to do sth** extremely keen to do something: *Becky's just bursting to tell you her news.* **5** **be bursting with pride/confidence etc** to be extremely proud, confident etc

burst in on sb/sth *phr v* [T] to interrupt someone suddenly and noisily: *I'm sorry to burst in on you like this.*

burst into sth *phr v* [T] **burst into tears/flames/song etc** to suddenly start crying, burning, singing etc: *The car hit a tree and burst into flames.*

burst out *phr v* **1** **burst out laughing/crying** to suddenly start to laugh or cry **2** [I] to say something suddenly and loudly: *"I don't believe it!" Duncan burst out.*

burst[2] *n* [C] a short sudden period of activity or noise: + **of** *In a sudden burst of energy Denise cleaned the whole house.*

burst[3] *adj* broken or torn apart violently: *a burst pipe* | *burst blood vessels*

bur·y /'beri/ *v* [T] **1** to put a dead body into a grave: *Auntie Jo was buried in Woodlawn Cemetery.* **2** to cover something so that it cannot be seen: *The dog was burying a bone.* | + **under** *Dad's glasses were buried under a pile of newspapers.* **3** **bury the hatchet** to become friends with someone again after an argument **4** **bury your face/head in sth** to press your face into something soft, usually when you are upset

bus[1] /bʌs/ *n* [C], *plural* **buses** a large vehicle that people pay to travel on: *There were only three people on the bus.* | **by bus** *I usually go to school by bus.* → see colour picture on page 669

bus[2] *v* [T] **-ssed, -ssing** *BrE* **-sed, -sing** to take a group of people somewhere in a bus: *Many children are being bussed to schools in other areas.*

bush /bʊʃ/ *n* **1** [C] a plant like a small tree with a lot of branches: *a rose bush* → see colour picture on page 243 **2** **the bush** areas of Australia or Africa that are still in a wild state

bush·y /'bʊʃi/ *adj* bushy hair or fur grows thickly: *a bushy tail*

bus·i·ly /'bɪzɪli/ *adv* in a busy way: *The class were all busily writing.*

busi·ness /'bɪznɪs/ *n* **1** [U] the activity of producing, buying, or selling goods or services: **do business with** *We do a lot of business with people in Rome.* **2 go into business/go out of business** to start a new company, or to close a company because it is not making enough money: *Pam's going into business with her sister.|Many small companies have recently gone out of business.* **3** [U] the work that you do as your job to earn money: **on business** (=because of your job): *Al's gone to Japan on business.* **4** [U] the amount of work a company is doing, or the amount of money a company is making: **business is good/bad/slow etc** *Business is always slow during the winter.* **5** [C] an organization that produces or sells goods or services: **run a business** *Graham runs a printing business.* **6** [U] *spoken* something about your life that you do not think other people have the right to know: *"Are you going out with Ben tonight?" "That's my business."|**none of your business** It's none of your business how much I earn.|**mind your own business** (=used to tell someone in a direct way that something is private) **7** [singular] a subject, event, or activity that you have a particular opinion of: *Rock climbing can be a risky business.* **8 get down to business** to start dealing with an important subject **9 mean business** *informal* to be determined to do something **10 have no business doing sth** if someone has no business doing something, they should not do it

busi·ness·like /'bɪznɪs-laɪk/ *adj* sensible and practical in the way you do things: *a businesslike manner*

busi·ness·man /'bɪznɪsmən/ *n* [C] **1** a man who works at a fairly high level in a company **2** be a good businessman to be good at dealing with money or running a company

busi·ness·wom·an /'bɪznɪs,wʊmən/ *n* [C] **1** a woman who works at a fairly high level in a company **2** be a good businesswoman to be good at dealing with money or running a company

busk /bʌsk/ *v* [I] *BrE* to play music in a public place to earn money —**busker** *n* [C]

bus pass /'. ./ *n* [C] a special ticket that gives you cheap or free bus travel

bus stop /'. ./ *n* [C] a place at the side of a road, marked with a sign, where buses stop for passengers → see colour picture on page 669

bust[1] /bʌst/ *v* [T] **bust** or **busted, bust** or **busted, busting** *informal* **1** to break something: *Someone bust his door down while he was away.* **2** if the police bust someone, they catch them for a crime: *He got busted for possession of drugs.*

bust[2] *n* [C] **1** a woman's breasts, or the measurement around a woman's breasts and back: *a 34 inch bust* **2** *informal* a situation where the police force their way into a place looking for illegal activities; RAID: *a major drugs bust* **3** a MODEL of someone's head, shoulders, and upper chest: **+ of** *a bust of Shakespeare*

bust[3] *adj informal* **1 go bust** a business that goes bust has to close because it has lost so much money: *More and more small businesses are going bust each year.* **2** broken: *the TV's bust again.*

bus·tle[1] /'bʌsəl/ *n* [singular] busy and noisy activity: **+ of** *the bustle of the big city* —**bustling** *adj*

bustle[2] *v* [I] to move around and do things in a quick, busy way: **+ about/around** *Linda was bustling around in the kitchen.*

bust-up /'. ./ *n* [C] *informal* a fight or argument

bus·y[1] /'bɪzi/ *adj* **1** working or spending a lot of time doing something: *Alex is busy studying for his exams.|+ with I'm busy with a customer at the moment. Can I call you back?* **2** full of people, vehicles etc: *a busy airport|The roads were very busy this morning.* **3** *especially AmE* a telephone line that is busy is being used; ENGAGED *BrE: I got a busy signal.* —**busily** *adv*

busy[2] *v* **busy yourself with** to do something in order to make time seem to go faster: *Josh busied himself with cleaning the house.*

bus·y·bod·y /'bɪzi,bɒdɪ‖-,bɑːdi/ *n* [C] someone who is too interested in other people's private lives

but[1] /bət; *strong* bʌt/ *linking word* **1** used before you say something that is different or the opposite from what you have just said: *Grandma didn't like the song, but we loved it.|Learning Chinese was difficult, but it meant that I got this job.* **2** used before you give the reason why something did not happen or is not true: *Carla was supposed to come tonight, but her husband took the car.* **3** *spoken* used to show surprise at what has just been said: *"I have to go tomorrow." "But you only just arrived!"* **4** *spoken* **but then (again)** ... used to add some information that makes what you have just said less surprising: *I didn't understand the film at all. But then I was really tired.* **5** *spoken* used after phrases such as "excuse me" and "I'm sorry": *Excuse me, but haven't we met before?*

but[2] *prep* except: *Joe can come any day but Monday.|Nobody but Liz knows the truth.|**the last/next but one** *I was the last but one to arrive.*

USAGE NOTE: but and except

Use **but** and **except** to talk about someone or something that is not included in a particular group: *Everyone was there except John. | He eats anything but pork.* **But** can be used after "none", "all", "no-one", "anywhere", "everything" or "none": *There was no-one there but John.| They looked everywhere but in the shed.*

---

butch /bʊtʃ/ *adj informal* a woman who is butch looks, dresses, or behaves like a man

butch·er[1] /'bʊtʃəll-ər/ *n* [C] **1** someone that owns or works in a shop that sells meat

---

GRAMMAR NOTE: 'if' clauses (2)
When you imagine a present situation that is not real, or a future situation that is very unlikely, use **if + simple past**: *If he really loved you, he wouldn't treat you like this.* (=he does not love you). | *If I won a million dollars on the lottery, I would buy a yacht.* Use **would** in the other part of the sentence.

2 butcher's a shop that sells meat **3** someone who has killed a lot of people cruelly and without reason

butcher² v [T] **1** to kill animals and prepare their meat as food **2** to kill people in a cruel way: *Thousands were butchered.*

but·ler /ˈbʌtlə‖-ər/ n [C] the most important male servant in a big house

butt¹ /bʌt/ n [C] **1** the person that other people often make jokes about: **the butt of** *John is always the butt of the class's jokes.* **2** *informal, especially AmE* the part of your body that you sit on; BUTTOCKS **3** the end of a cigarette after it has been smoked **4** the end of the handle of a gun

butt² v [I,T] to hit or push someone or something with the head

butt in phr v [I] *informal* to interrupt a conversation: *Sorry, I didn't mean to butt in.*

but·ter¹ /ˈbʌtə‖-ər/ n [U] **1** a solid yellow food made from cream that you spread on bread or use in cooking: *a slice of bread and butter* → see colour pictures on pages 439 and 440 **2 butter wouldn't melt in sb's mouth** *spoken informal* used to say that someone looks as if they would never do anything wrong, but this is not really true

butter² v [T] to spread butter on something: *hot buttered toast*

butter sb ↔ **up** phr v [T] *informal* to say nice things to someone so that they will do what you want

but·ter·cup /ˈbʌtəkʌp‖-ər-/ n [C] a small shiny yellow wild flower

but·ter·fly /ˈbʌtəflaɪ‖-ər-/ n [C] **1** an insect with large coloured wings **2 have butterflies (in your stomach)** *informal* to feel very nervous

butterfly

but·tock /ˈbʌtək/ n [C, usually plural] one of the two parts of your body that you sit on

but·ton¹ /ˈbʌtn/ n [C] **1** one of the small round things sewn on a shirt, a pair of trousers etc that you put through a hole in order to fasten it: *Do your buttons up, Sam.* → see picture at FASTENER **2** a small part on a machine that you press to make it start, stop etc: **push/press a button** *Just press the 'on' button.* **3** *AmE* a small piece of metal or plastic with a message or picture on it that you can fasten to your clothes; BADGE *BrE*

button² v also **button up** [I,T] to fasten something with buttons, or to be fastened with buttons: *Button up your coat.*

but·ton·hole /ˈbʌtnhəʊl‖-hoʊl/ n [C] a hole for a button to be put through to fasten a shirt etc

but·tress /ˈbʌtrəs/ v [T] *formal* to do something to support a system, argument etc: *They tried to buttress their argument with quotations.*

bux·om /ˈbʌksəm/ adj a buxom woman has large breasts

buy¹ /baɪ/ v bought /bɔːt‖bɒːt/, bought, buying **1** [I,T] to get something by paying money for it: *Have you bought Bobby a birthday present yet?* | **buy sth from sb** *I'm buying a car from a friend.* | **buy sth for** *She bought those shoes for £15.* **2** [T] *informal* to believe an explanation or

reason for something: *I just don't buy that story.* **3 buy time** *informal* to delay something because you do not want it to happen or are not ready for it: *Keep him talking, just to buy us more time.*

buy into sth phr v [T] **1** to buy part of a business **2** *informal* to believe in an idea: *Don't buy into this idea that women must have perfect bodies.*

buy sb ↔ **off** phr v [T] to pay someone to stop causing you trouble

buy sb/sth ↔ **out** phr v [T] to get control of a business by buying all the SHARES in it

buy sth ↔ **up** phr v [T] to quickly buy as much as you can of something: *A road-building firm is buying up all the properties in the area.*

buy² n **be a good buy** to be good value for money: *The Brazilian white wine is a good buy.*

buy·er /ˈbaɪə‖-ər/ n [C] **1** someone who is buying something, especially something expensive: *We've found a buyer for our house.* **2** someone whose job is to choose and buy the goods that a shop or company will sell

buzz¹ /bʌz/ v **1** [I] to make a continuous noise like the sound of a BEE: *Why's the TV buzzing like that?* → see colour picture on page 635 **2** [I] to be full of people talking in an excited way: + **with** *The whole building was buzzing with news of the fire.*

buzz² n **1** [C] a continuous noise like the sound of a BEE → see colour picture on page 635 **2** [singular] *informal* a feeling of excitement or success: *I get a real buzz from living in New York.*

buz·zard /ˈbʌzəd‖-ərd/ n [C] **1** *BrE* a large hunting bird **2** *AmE* a large bird that eats dead animals

buzz·er /ˈbʌzə‖-ər/ n [C] a piece of electrical equipment that makes a buzzing sound, used as a SIGNAL: *I pressed the buzzer.*

by¹ /baɪ/ prep **1** used with passive forms of verbs to show who did something or what caused something: *a film made by Steven Spielberg* | *a play by Shakespeare* | *Sylvie was hit by a car.* **2** next to or very close to something: *I'll meet you by the bank.* → see colour picture on page 474 **3** holding, using, or doing a particular thing: *I grabbed the hammer by the handle.* | *Send it by airmail.* | **by car/plane/train/bus** etc *We travelled across India by train.* | **by doing sth** *Carol earns extra money by babysitting.* **4** no later than a particular time: *Your report has to be done by 5:00.* **5 by mistake/accident/chance** without intending to do something: *Hugh locked the door by mistake.* **6** according to: *By law, you must be over 16 to marry.* | *It's 9.30 by my watch.* **7** past: *Sophie ran by me on her way to the bus stop.* **8** used in measurements and numbers: *The room is 14 feet by 12 feet.* | *What's 7 multiplied by 8?* | *Anne gets paid by the hour.* | *You have to buy this material by the metre.* **9** by day/bit by bit/one by one in units of **10 by day/by night** in the daytime or at night: *Bats sleep by day and hunt by night.* **11 by the way** *spoken* used to begin talking about a subject that is not related to the one you were talking about: *By the way, Cheryl called while you were out.* **12 (all) by yourself** completely alone: *They left the boy by himself for two days!*

B

by[2] *adv* **1** past: *Two cars went by, but nobody stopped.* | *Three hours went by before we heard any news.* **2 by and large** used when you are talking generally about something: *By and large, I agree.*

bye /baɪ/ also **bye-bye** /ˌ. '.||'. ./ *interjection* goodbye: *Bye Sandy! See you later.*

by-e·lec·tion /'. .ˌ../ *n* [C] *BrE* an election to replace a politician who has left Parliament or died

by·gone /'baɪgɒn||-gɔːn/ *adj* **bygone days/ age/era etc** a period of time in the past

by·gones /'baɪgɒnz||-gɔːnz/ *n* **let bygones be bygones** used to say that you forgive someone for something bad they have done

by·pass[1] /'baɪpɑːs||-pæs/ *n* [C] **1** a road that takes traffic around the outside of a town or city **2 heart bypass/bypass surgery** a way of directing blood through new tubes to avoid the part of someone's heart that is not working properly

bypass[2] *v* [T] to make what you are doing easier by avoiding something: *The road bypasses the town.* | *I bypassed the paperwork by phoning the owner of the company.*

by-prod·uct /'. ˌ../ *n* [C] **1** something that is made during the process of making something else: *Plutonium is a by-product of nuclear processing.* **2** an unplanned or unexpected result of a situation or event: *His lack of respect for authority was a by-product of his upbringing.*

by·stand·er /'baɪˌstændə||-ər/ *n* [C] someone who watches what is happening without taking part: **innocent bystander** *Several innocent bystanders were killed by the explosion.*

byte /baɪt/ *n* [C] a unit for measuring the amount of information a computer can use, equal to eight BITS

by·way /'baɪweɪ/ *n* [C] a small road or path that is not used very much

by·word /'baɪwɜːd||-wɜːrd/ *n* [C] the name of someone or something that has become known for having a particular quality: **+ for** *His name has become a byword for honesty.*

B

Cc

C, c /siː/ the letter 'c'

C the written abbreviation of CELSIUS or CENTI-GRADE

cab /kæb/ n [C] **1** a car in which you pay the driver to take you somewhere; taxi → see colour picture on page 669 **2** the part of a TRUCK or train where the driver sits

cab·a·ret /ˈkæbəreɪ‖ˌkæbəˈreɪ/ n [C,U] entertainment such as music and dancing performed in a restaurant or club while customers eat and drink

cab·bage /ˈkæbɪdʒ/ n [C,U] a large round vegetable with thick leaves that is usually cooked → see picture at VEGETABLE

cab·bie /ˈkæbi/ n [C] *informal* a taxi driver

cab·in /ˈkæbɪn/ n [C] **1** a small room on a ship where you sleep **2** a small house made of wood, usually in a forest or the mountains: *a log cabin* **3** the area inside a plane where the passengers or the pilots sit

cab·i·net /ˈkæbɪnɪt/ n **1** [C] a piece of furniture with doors and shelves, used for storing or showing things: *a drinks cabinet* **2 the Cabinet** an important group of politicians who make decisions or advise the leader of a government

ca·ble¹ /ˈkeɪbəl/ n **1** [C,U] a plastic or rubber tube containing wires that carry electronic SIGNALS, telephone messages etc: *an underground telephone cable* **2** [U] CABLE TELEVISION: **on cable** *I'll wait for the movie to come out on cable.* **3** [C,U] a thick strong metal rope **4** [C] a message sent by electrical or radio SIGNALS; TELEGRAM

cable² v [I,T] to send someone a cable

cable car /ˈ.. ./ n [C] a vehicle that hangs from a cable and carries people up mountains

cable tel·e·vi·sion /ˌ. ˈ...., ˌ. ..ˈ../ also **cable TV** /ˌ.. ˈ./ n [U] a system of broadcasting television by sending SIGNALS through cables under the ground

cache /kæʃ/ n [C] a number of things that are hidden, or the place where they are hidden: **+ of** *Police found a cache of weapons in the house.*

cack·le /ˈkækəl/ v [I] to laugh in an unpleasant loud high voice —**cackle** n [C]

cac·tus /ˈkæktəs/ n [C], *plural* **cacti** /-taɪ/, *or* **cactuses** a desert plant covered with small sharp points

ca·dence /ˈkeɪdəns/ n [C] a regular pattern of sound, especially the sound of someone's voice rising or falling

ca·det /kəˈdet/ n [C] someone who is training to become an officer in the army, navy, AIR FORCE, or police

cadge /kædʒ/ v [T] *BrE informal* to ask someone for money, food, cigarettes etc because you do not have any: **cadge sth from/off sb** *I managed to cadge ten quid off dad.*

cae·sar·e·an, cesarean /sɪˈzeəriən‖-ˈzer-/ also **caesarean sec·tion** /ˌ.... ˈ../ n [C] an operation in which a woman's body is cut open to allow a baby to be born

ca·fe also **café** /ˈkæfeɪ‖kæˈfeɪ, kə-/ n [C] a small restaurant

caf·e·te·ri·a /ˌkæfɪˈtɪəriəl‖-ˈtɪr-/ n [C] a restaurant where people get their own food and take it to a table to eat it: *the college cafeteria*

caf·feine /ˈkæfiːn‖kæˈfiːn/ n [U] a chemical substance in coffee, tea, and some other drinks that makes people feel more active

cage

bar

cage /keɪdʒ/ n [C] a structure made of wires or bars in which birds or animals can be kept

caged /keɪdʒd/ adj in a cage: *He walked up and down like a caged lion.*

cag·ey /ˈkeɪdʒi/ adj *informal* not willing to talk about your plans, intentions, past life etc: **+ about** *He's being very cagey about what he's going to do with the money.*

ca·goule /kəˈɡuːl/ n [C] *BrE* a thin plastic coat with a HOOD

ca·hoots /kəˈhuːts/ n *informal* **be in cahoots (with)** to be working secretly with others, usually to do something dishonest: *The soldiers were in cahoots with the drug smugglers.*

ca·jole /kəˈdʒəʊl‖-ˈdʒoʊl/ v [T] to persuade someone to do something by praising them or making promises to them: *He tried to cajole her into having something to eat.*

cake /keɪk/ n **1** [C,U] a sweet food made by baking a mixture of flour, butter, sugar etc: *a birthday cake* | *Would you like a piece of cake?* → see colour picture on page 440 **2** [C] a small piece of something, made into a flat shape: *fish cakes* **3 have your cake and eat it** to have all the advantages of a situation without any of its disadvantages

caked /keɪkt/ adj [not before noun] **caked in/ with** covered with a thick layer of something: *Paul's boots were soon caked with mud.*

ca·lam·i·ty /kəˈlæmɪti/ n [C,U] an unexpected event that causes a lot of damage or suffering: *The government was determined to avoid yet another political calamity.* | *The area has been plagued by calamity.*

cal·ci·um /ˈkælsiəm/ n [U] a silver-white ELEMENT that helps form teeth, bones, and CHALK

cal·cu·late /ˈkælkjʊleɪt/ v **1** [T] to find out something or measure something by using numbers: *The price is calculated in US dollars.* **2** to guess something or make a decision about something based on information you have: *It's difficult to calculate what effect these changes will have on the company.* **3 be calculated to do sth** to be intended to have a particular effect: *The ads are calculated to attract women voters.*

cal·cu·lat·ed /ˈkælkjʊleɪtɪd/ adj **1 calculated risk/gamble** something you do after thinking carefully, although you know it may have bad results **2** deliberately and carefully planned to have a particular effect: *It was a calculated attempt to deceive the public.*

cal·cu·lat·ing /ˈkælkjɵleɪtɪŋ/ *adj* someone who is calculating makes careful plans to get what they want, without caring about how this affects other people: *a cold and calculating man*

cal·cu·la·tion /ˌkælkjɵˈleɪʃən/ *n* [C,U] when you add, multiply, or divide numbers to find out an amount, price etc: *According to the Institute's calculations, nearly 80% of teenagers have tried drugs.*

cal·cu·la·tor /ˈkælkjɵleɪtəll-ər/ *n* [C] a small electronic machine that can calculate numbers → see colour picture on page 80

cal·en·dar /ˈkælɪndəll-ər/ *n* **1** [C] a set of pages showing the days and months of a year **2** [C] all the things that you plan to do in the next few days, months etc: *The President's calendar is completely full at the moment.* **3** [C] a system that divides and measures time in a particular way: *the Jewish calendar* **4 calendar year/month** a period of time that begins on the first day of the month or year and ends on the last day of the month or year

calf /kɑːfllkæf/ *n* [C], *plural* **calves** /kɑːvz llkævz/ **1** the back of your leg between your knee and foot **2** the baby of a cow, or of some other large animal such as an ELEPHANT

cal·i·bre *BrE*, **caliber** *AmE* /ˈkælɪbəll-ər/ *n* **1** [U] someone's level of ability or quality: *players of the highest calibre* **2** [C] the width of a bullet or the inside part of a gun

call¹ /kɔːllkɒːl/ *v* **1 be called** to have a particular name: *What was that movie called again?* **2** [T] to give someone a name: *They finally decided to call the baby Joel.* **3** [T] to describe someone or something in a particular way, or to say that they have a particular quality: *News reports have called it the worst disaster of this century.* **4** [I,T] to telephone someone: *I called about six o'clock but no one was home.* | *He said he'd call me tomorrow.* **5** [T] to ask or order someone to come to you: *I can hear Mom calling me. I'd better go.* | *The headmaster called me into his office.* **6** [T] to arrange for something to happen: **call a meeting/strike/election etc** *A meeting was called for 3 pm Wednesday.* **7** also **call out** [I,T] to say or shout something because you want someone to hear you: *"I'm coming!" Paula called down the stairs.* | *A little voice called out my name.* **8** also **call by** [I] *BrE* to visit somewhere for a short time to see someone: *Your friend Alex called earlier.* **9** if a train, bus etc calls at a place, it stops there to let passengers get on or off **10 call it a day** *informal* to stop working, usually because you are tired: *Come on, guys, let's call it a day.* **11 call the shots** if someone calls the shots, that person makes the important decisions about what should be done

call back *phr v* **1** [I,T **call** sb **back**] to telephone someone again, or to telephone someone who tried to telephone you earlier: *Okay, I'll call back around three.* | *Ms. Brinston is on*

another line. *Can she call you back later?* **2** [I] *BrE* to return to a house or shop that you went to earlier for a short time: *I'll call back tonight with my car to pick it up.*

call for *phr v* **1** [T **call for** sth] to demand or need something: *Congressmen are calling for an investigation into the scandal.* **2** [T **call for** sb] *BrE* to go to someone's home before you go somewhere together: *I'll call for you at about eight.*

call in *phr v* **1** [T **call** sb ↔ **in**] to ask someone to come and help you with a difficult situation: *Police have been called in to help with the hunt for the missing child.* **2** [I] to telephone the place where you work, especially to report something **3** [I] *BrE* to visit a person or place while you are on your way to somewhere else: *Nick often calls in on his way home from work.*

call sth ↔ **off** *phr v* [T] to decide that a planned event will not happen: *The game was called off due to bad weather.*

call on sb/sth *phr v* [T] **1** also **call upon** to formally ask someone to do something: *The UN has called on both sides to start peace talks.* **2** to visit someone for a short time: *a salesman calling on customers*

call out *phr v* **1** [I,T **call** sth ↔ **out**] to say something loudly: *"Hey!" she called out to him.* **2** [T **call** sb/sth ↔ **out**] to ask someone to come and deal with something: *"Where's Dr. Cook?" "She's been called out."*

call up *phr v* **1** [I,T **call** sb ↔ **up**] *especially AmE* to telephone someone: *Why don't you call Suzie up and see if she wants to come over?* **2** [T **call** sth ↔ **up**] to make information appear on a computer screen **3** [T **call** sb ↔ **up**] *BrE* to officially order someone to join the army, navy, or AIR FORCE; DRAFT *AmE*

call² *n* **1** [C] a conversation on the telephone, or an attempt to talk to someone by telephone: *She's expecting a call from the office soon.* | **get a call** *I got a call from Teresa yesterday; she's fine.* | **give sb a call** *Just give me a call from the airport when you arrive.* | **make a call** *Sorry, I have to make a telephone call.* | **return sb's call** (=telephone someone back): *Ask him to return my call when he comes home.* **2 be on call** ready to go to work if you are needed: *Heart surgeons are on call 24 hours a day.* **3** [C] a shout or cry: *a call for help* **4 no call for/no call to do sth** *spoken* used to tell someone that their behaviour is wrong or that something is unnecessary: *She had no call to talk to you like that.* **5** [C] a short visit: **pay a call on sb** *Should we pay a call on Nadia while we're in Paris?* **6** [C] when people say publicly that they want something to happen: **+ for** *the call for a new constitution for Britain* **7** [C] the sound an animal or bird makes: *the mating call of the bald eagle*

call·er /ˈkɔːləll ˈkɒːlər/ *n* [C] **1** someone who makes a telephone call: *Didn't the caller say who she was?* **2** *BrE* someone who visits your house: *Be very careful about letting unknown callers into your home.*

SPELLING NOTE

Words with the sound /k/, like **cut**, may be spelt **k-**, like **key**, or **qu-**, like **queen**.
Words with the sound /s/, like **city**, may be spelt **s-**, like **soon**, or **ps-**, like **psychology**.

cal·lig·ra·phy /kəˈlɪgrəfi/ n [U] the art of producing beautiful HANDWRITING

call-in /ˈ. ./ n [C] AmE a radio or television programme in which people telephone to give their opinions; PHONE-IN BrE

call·ing /ˈkɔːlɪŋ||ˈkɒː-/ n [C] a strong desire or feeling that you should do a particular kind of work, especially work that helps other people: **+ to** a calling for the priesthood

cal·lous /ˈkæləs/ adj unkind and not caring that other people are suffering —**callously** adv —**callousness** n [U]

calm[1] /kɑːm||kɑːm, kɑːlm/ adj **1** relaxed and not angry or upset: **keep calm** Please, everyone, try to keep calm! **2** completely still, or not moving very much: The water was much calmer in the bay. **3** not windy: a calm clear day — **calmly** adv —**calmness** n [U]

calm[2] v [T] to make someone quiet after they have been angry, excited, or upset: Matt was trying to calm the baby.

calm down phr v [I,T] to become quiet after you have been angry, excited, or upset, or to make someone become quiet: Calm down and tell me what happened. | It took a while to calm the kids down.

calm[3] n [singular, U] a time when it is peaceful and quiet, and there is not much activity or excitement: The police appealed for calm following the shooting of a teenager.

cal·o·rie /ˈkæləri/ n [C] **1** a unit for measuring the amount of energy a particular food can produce: An average potato has about 90 calories. **2** technical a unit for measuring heat

calves /kɑːvz||kævz/ n the plural of CALF

cam·cor·der /ˈkæm-,kɔːdə||-,kɔːrdər/ n [C] a small VIDEO camera that you can carry around with you

camcorder

came /keɪm/ v the past tense of COME

cam·el /ˈkæməl/ n [C] a large desert animal with a long neck and one or two HUMPs

cam·e·o /ˈkæmi-əu||-ou/ n [C] **1** a small part in a film or play acted by a famous actor: Whoopi Goldberg makes a cameo appearance in the movie. **2** a piece of jewellery with a raised shape, usually of a person's face, on a dark background

cam·e·ra /ˈkæmərə/ n [C] a piece of equipment used for taking photographs, making films, or producing television pictures

cam·e·ra·man /ˈkæmərəmæn/ n [C] someone who operates a camera for a television or film company

cam·ou·flage[1] /ˈkæməflɑːʒ/ n [C,U] clothes or colours that hide you by making you look the same as the things around you: a soldier in camouflage | The Arctic fox's white fur is an excellent winter camouflage.

camouflage[2] v [T] to hide something by making it look like the things around it: Hunters camouflage the traps with leaves and branches.

camp[1] /kæmp/ n [C,U] **1** a place where people stay in tents for a short time: After hiking all morning, we returned to camp. **2** a place where children go to stay for a short time and do special activities: summer camp | scout camp

3 prison/labour/refugee camp a place where people are kept, usually in unpleasant conditions

camp[2] v [I] **1** also **camp out** to set up a tent and stay there for a short time: Where should we camp tonight? **2** **go camping** to take a holiday in which you sleep in tents —**camping** n [U] camping equipment

cam·paign[1] /kæmˈpeɪn/ n [C] a series of things that you plan and do in order to achieve a particular result, especially in business or politics: an election campaign | **+ for/against** a campaign for equal rights for homosexuals

campaign[2] v [I] to do things publicly to try to achieve a particular result, especially in politics: **+ for/against** We're campaigning for the right to smoke in public places. —**campaigner** n [C]

camp bed /ˌ. ˈ.||ˈ. ./ n [C] BrE a light narrow bed that folds flat and is easy to carry; COT AmE → see picture at BED

camp·er /ˈkæmpə||-ər/ n [C] **1** someone who is staying in a tent for a short time **2** a vehicle that has beds and cooking equipment so that you can stay in it while you are on holiday

camp·site /ˈkæmpsaɪt/ BrE, **camp·ground** /ˈkæmpgraund/ AmE — n [C] a place where you can stay in a tent

cam·pus /ˈkæmpəs/ n [C,U] the land or buildings of a college: **on campus** Most first-year students live on campus.

can[1] /kən; strong kæn/ modal verb could **1** to be able to do something: I can't swim! | Jess can speak French fluently. | We couldn't afford a vacation last year. | Can you smell smoke? **2** to be allowed to do something: You can go out when you've finished your homework. **3** spoken used to ask someone to give you something or to do something: Can I have a chocolate biscuit? | Can you help me take the clothes off the line? **4** used to offer to do something: Can I help you with those bags? **5** used to show your surprise that something is true, or that someone believes that something is true: Can things really be that bad? | You can't be serious. **6** used to show what is possible or likely: We are confident that the missing climbers can be found. **7** used to show what often happens or how someone often behaves: It can get pretty cold here at night.

USAGE NOTE: can

Can is used with many verbs relating to physical or mental ability: I can smell something burning. | Can you believe that? Don't say "I am smelling something burning" or "Are you believing that".

---

can[2] /kæn/ n [C] **1** a metal container in which food or liquid is kept without air: **+ of** a can of tuna fish → see picture at CONTAINER **2** a **(whole) can of worms** a complicated situation that causes a lot of problems when you start to deal with it

can[3] v [T] **-nned, -nning** to preserve food by putting it in a closed metal container with no air: The fish is canned within 24 hours at the port.

ca·nal /kəˈnæl/ n [C] a long narrow area of water made for ships or boats to travel along

ca·nar·y /kəˈneəri||-ˈneri/ n [C] a small yellow bird that sings and is often kept as a pet

can·cel /ˈkænsəl/ v [T] **-lled, -lling** BrE **-led, -ling** AmE **1** to decide that something you have planned will not happen: *I had to cancel my trip to Rome.* **2** to tell someone that you no longer want something: *I'd like to cancel my subscription to 'Time' magazine.*

cancel sth ↔ **out** phr v [T] if one thing cancels out another, it makes it have no effect: *The huge meal I ate cancelled out all the exercise I had done.*

can·cel·la·tion /ˌkænsəˈleɪʃən/ n [C,U] when someone decides they will not do something or something will not happen: *The plane is full right now, but sometimes there are cancellations.* | **+ of** *the cancellation of our order*

cancer n [C,U] a serious disease in which cells in someone's body grow in a way that is not normal: *lung cancer* | *He died of cancer at the age of 63.* —**cancerous** adj

Can·cer /ˈkænsəll-ər/ n [C,U] the sign of the Zodiac of people who are born between June 21st and July 22nd, or someone who belongs to this sign

can·did /ˈkændɪd/ adj honest, even when the truth may be unpleasant or embarrassing: *a candid article about his drug addiction* —**candidly** adv

can·di·da·cy /ˈkændɪdəsi/ n [C,U] when someone is a candidate, usually for a political position: *She announced her candidacy at the convention.*

can·di·date /ˈkændɪdɪt, -deɪt, -dɪt/ n [C] **1** someone who tries to get elected to a political position or who tries to get a good job: *Which candidate are you voting for?* | **+ for** *Sara seems to be a likely candidate for the job.* **2** BrE someone who takes an examination

can·dle /ˈkændl/ n [C] a stick of WAX that you burn to produce light → see picture at LIGHT¹

can·dle·light /ˈkændl-laɪt/ n [U] the light that a candle makes

can·dle·stick /ˈkændl-stɪk/ n [C] an object used to hold a candle

can·dour BrE, **candor** AmE /ˈkændəll-ər/ n [U] the quality of being honest, even when the truth may be unpleasant or embarrassing

can·dy /ˈkændi/ n [C,U] especially AmE a sweet food made of sugar or chocolate; SWEET BrE

can·dy·floss /ˈkændiflɒsll-flɑːs, -flɒːs/ n [U] BrE a soft mass of pink sugar on a stick; COTTON CANDY AmE

cane¹ /keɪn/ n **1** [C,U] the hard smooth stem of some plants, used to make furniture or to support plants in the garden: *a cane chair* | *Support the tomato plants with garden canes.* **2** [C] a long thin stick used to help you walk **3** [C] a long thin stick used for hitting people as a punishment, especially children in schools: *Most European countries have abolished the cane.*

cane² v [T] to punish someone by hitting them with a cane

ca·nine /ˈkeɪnaɪn, ˈkæ-ll-ˈkeɪ-/ adj relating to dogs

can·is·ter /ˈkænɪstəll-ər/ n [C] a metal container for storing a gas or dry food: *a canister of tear gas*

can·na·bis /ˈkænəbɪs/ n [U] an illegal drug that is smoked

canned /kænd/ adj canned food is sold in small metal containers; TINNED BrE: *canned pineapple chunks*

can·ni·bal /ˈkænɪbəl/ n [C] someone who eats human flesh —**cannibalism** n [U] —**cannibalistic** /ˌkænɪbəˈlɪstɪk/ adj

can·non /ˈkænən/ n [C] a large gun, fixed to the ground or on wheels

cannon ball /ˈ.. ./ n [C] a heavy iron ball fired from a cannon

can·not /ˈkænət, -nɒtll-nɑːt/ modal verb the negative of CAN: *I cannot accept your offer.*

can·ny /ˈkæni/ adj clever, careful, and not easily deceived

ca·noe /kəˈnuː/ n [C] a long light narrow boat that is pointed at both ends, which you move using a PADDLE

ca·noe·ing /kəˈnuːɪŋ/ n [U] the sport or activity of using a canoe: *go canoeing* *We used to go canoeing every Saturday.*

can·on /ˈkænən/ n [C] a Christian priest who works in a CATHEDRAL

can o·pen·er /ˈ. ˌ.../ n [C] a tool for opening cans of food; TIN OPENER BrE → see picture at KITCHEN

can·o·py /ˈkænəpi/ n [C] a cover above a bed or seat, usually used as a decoration

can't /kɑːntllkænt/ the short form of CANNOT: *I can't go with you today.*

can·tan·ker·ous /kænˈtæŋkərəs/ adj often angry and always complaining: *a cantankerous old man*

can·teen /kænˈtiːn/ n [C] a place in a factory, school, or office where people go to eat and drink

can·ter /ˈkæntəll-ər/ v [I,T] if a horse canters, it GALLOPs slowly —**canter** n [singular]

can·vas /ˈkænvəs/ n **1** [U] a type of strong cloth that is used to make bags, tents, shoes etc **2** [C] a piece of canvas on which a picture is painted

can·vass /ˈkænvəs/ v **1** [I,T] to ask people who they will be voting for in an election, and try to persuade them to vote for your party: *Someone was here canvassing for the Green Party.* **2** [T] to find out people's opinions about something: *The company canvassed 600 people who used their product.*

can·yon /ˈkænjən/ n [C] a deep narrow valley with steep sides: *the Grand Canyon*

cap¹ /kæp/ n [C] **1** a soft hat with a curved part sticking out at the front: *a baseball cap* → see colour pictures on pages 113 and 636 **2** something that covers and protects the end or top of something: *a bottle cap* | *Put the cap back on that pen!*

cap² v [T] **1** to do or say something that is better, worse, funnier etc than the thing that someone else has said or done: *Lewis capped a brilliant season by beating the world record.* **2** to limit the amount of money, that can be used, spent, or demanded

ca·pa·bil·i·ty /ˌkeɪpəˈbɪlɪti/ n [C,U] the ability of a machine, person, or organization to do something, especially something difficult: *What you can do depends on your computer's graphics capability.* | **+ to** *The country has the capability to produce nuclear weapons.*

ca·pa·ble /ˈkeɪpəbəl/ adj **1 capable of (doing) sth** having the power, skill, or other qualities that are needed to do something: *Do you think he's capable of murder?* → opposite IN-CAPABLE **2** skilful and effective: *Sue is an extremely capable lawyer.*

ca·pac·i·ty /kə'pæsˌti/ *n* **1** [U, singular] the amount that a container, space, building etc can hold: **+ of** *The fuel tank has a capacity of 12 gallons.* | *The stadium was filled to capacity last night* (=completely filled). **2** [C,U] your ability to do something: **+ for** *Jan has a real capacity for hard work.* **3** [C, usually singular] if you do something in a particular capacity, you do it as part of your job or official position: *She has travelled a lot in her capacity as a journalist.* **4** [U, singular] the amount that a factory or machine can produce: *The factory is finally working to full capacity.*

cape /keɪp/ *n* [C] **1** a loose piece of clothing without SLEEVES that fastens around your neck and hangs from your shoulders **2** a large piece of land surrounded on three sides by water: *Cape Cod*

ca·pil·la·ry /kə'pɪlərill'kæpəleri/ *n* [C] a very small narrow tube that carries blood around your body → compare ARTERY, VEIN

cap·i·tal[1] /'kæpˌtl/ *n* **1** [C] the city where the central government of a country or state is: *What's the capital of Poland?* **2** [U] money you use to start a business or to make more money **3** [C] a letter of the alphabet that is printed in its large form, used at the beginning of a name or sentence: *Write your name in capitals.* **4** [C] a place that is important for a particular activity: *Hollywood is the capital of the movie industry.*

capital[2] *adj* [only before noun] **1** relating to money that is used to make more wealth: *We need a bigger capital investment to improve our schools.* **2 capital offence/crime** a crime that is bad enough to be punished by death

cap·i·tal·ise /'kæpˌtl-aɪz/ a British spelling of CAPITALIZE

cap·i·tal·is·m /'kæpˌtl-ɪzəm/ *n* [U] an economic system in which business and industry is owned privately, and money is made from the profits of these → compare COMMUNISM, SOCIALISM — **capitalist** *n* [C] — **capitalistic** /ˌkæpˌtl'ɪstɪk◂/ *adj*

cap·i·tal·ize (also **-ise** *BrE*) /'kæpˌtl-aɪz/ *v* [T] **capitalize on** sth *phr v* [T] to use something in order to get an advantage: *She capitalized on his mistake and won the game.*

capital pun·ish·ment /ˌ... '.../ *n* [U] when someone is legally killed as a punishment for a crime

ca·pit·u·late /kə'pɪtʃʊleɪt/ *v* [I] to stop fighting or arguing with someone and accept their demands — **capitulation** /kə,pɪtʃʊ'leɪʃən/ *n* [C,U]

cap·puc·ci·no /ˌkæpʊ'tʃiːnəʊll-noʊ/ *n* [C,U] coffee made with hot FROTHY milk

ca·price /kə'priːs/ *n* [C,U] *formal* a sudden and unreasonable change in someone's opinion or behaviour

ca·pri·cious /kə'prɪʃəs/ *adj* likely to suddenly change without any warning: *Helen's just as capricious as her mother was.* | *capricious spring weather* — **capriciously** *adv*

Cap·ri·corn /'kæprɪkɔːnll-kɔːrn/ *n* [C,U] the sign of the Zodiac of people who are born between December 22nd and January 19th, or someone who belongs to this sign

cap·size /kæp'saɪzll'kæpsaɪz/ *v* [I,T] if a boat capsizes or you capsize it, it turns over in the water

cap·sule /'kæpsjuːlll-səl/ *n* [C] **1** a small rounded container **2** the part of a SPACESHIP in which people live and work

cap·tain[1] /'kæptˌn/ *n* [C] **1** also **Captain** someone who is in charge of a ship or plane **2** also **Captain** an officer who has a middle rank in an army, AIR FORCE, or navy **3** someone who leads a team or group

captain[2] *v* [T] to lead a team or group of people as their captain

cap·tain·cy /'kæptˌnsi/ *n* [U] the position of being captain of a team

car

bumper
bonnet *BrE*/ hood *AmE*
tax disc
door handle
rear window
headlight
windscreen wiper *BrE*/ windshield wiper *AmE*
windscreen *BrE*/ windshield *AmE*
sunroof
boot *BrE*/ trunk *AmE*
rear light/ taillight
sidelight *BrE*/ parking light *AmE*
tyre *BrE*/ tire *AmE*
wing mirror *BrE*/ side mirror *AmE*
hubcap
mudflap *BrE*/ splash guard *AmE*
numberplate *BrE*/ license plate *AmE*
indicator
wing *BrE*/ fender *AmE*
petrol cap *BrE*/ gas tank door *AmE*
aerial *BrE*/ antenna *AmE*

cap·tion /ˈkæpʃən/ n [C] a few words written above or below a picture that explain what it is about

cap·ti·vate /ˈkæptɪˌveɪt/ v [T] to attract and interest you very much: *Alex was captivated by her beauty.* —**captivating** adj: *She had a captivating smile.*

cap·tive¹ /ˈkæptɪv/ adj **1** kept as a prisoner or in a small space: *captive animals* **2 captive audience** people who listen to or watch someone or something because they have to, not because they want to **3 take/hold sb captive** to make someone become a prisoner, or to keep someone as a prisoner

captive² n [C] someone who is kept as a prisoner, especially in a war

cap·tiv·i·ty /kæpˈtɪvəti/ n [U] when someone is kept as a prisoner or in a small space: **in captivity** *Many animals won't breed in captivity.*

cap·tor /ˈkæptəl-ər/ n [C] *formal* someone who keeps another person as a prisoner

cap·ture¹ /ˈkæptʃəl-ər/ v [T] **1** to catch someone in order to keep them as a prisoner: *He was captured at the airport.* **2** to get control of a place, especially during a war: *The town was captured by enemy troops after 10 days' fighting.* **3** to get control of money, companies, business etc **4** to succeed in showing or describing something by using pictures or words: *His new book really captures what the 1920s were like.* **5 capture sb's imagination/attention** to make someone feel very interested in what you are saying or showing

capture² n [U] **1** when someone captures a person or animal: *Higgins avoided capture by hiding in the woods.* **2** when someone takes control of something or somewhere

car /kɑːǁkɑːr/ n [C] **1** a vehicle with four wheels and an engine, designed to be used by a small number of people: *Joe got into the car.* | *You can't park your car there!* | *the problem of pollution caused by car exhausts* | *Did you come by car?* → see colour picture on page 669 **2** one of the connected parts of a train: *a restaurant car*

ca·rafe /kəˈræf, kəˈrɑːf/ n [C] a glass bottle with a wide top, used for serving wine and water at meals

car·at also **karat** *AmE* /ˈkærət/ n [C] a unit for measuring how pure gold is, or how heavy jewels are

car·a·van /ˈkærəvæn/ n [C] **1** *BrE* a vehicle that a car pulls behind it, that you can cook and sleep in on holiday → see colour picture on page 669 **2** *BrE* a covered vehicle that is pulled by a horse and that some people live and travel in; **WAGON** *AmE*: *a gypsy caravan* **3** a group of people with animals or vehicles who travel together

car·bo·hy·drate /ˌkɑːbəʊˈhaɪdreɪt, -drətǁˌkɑːrbou-/ n [C,U] a substance in some foods that provides your body with heat and energy

car·bon /ˈkɑːbənǁˈkɑːr-/ n [U] a chemical **ELEMENT** found in coal, **DIAMOND**s and petrol

car·bon·at·ed /ˈkɑːbəneɪtɪdǁˈkɑːr-/ adj carbonated drinks have a lot of **BUBBLE**s in them

carbon cop·y /ˌ.. ˈ../ n [C] **1** something or someone that is very similar to another thing or person: *The robbery is a carbon copy of one that took place last year.* **2** a copy of a page of writing made using **CARBON PAPER**

carbon di·ox·ide /ˌkɑːbən daɪˈɒksaɪdǁˌkɑːrbən daɪˈɑːk-/ n [U] the gas produced when animals breathe out or when **CARBON** is burned in air

carbon mo·nox·ide /ˌkɑːbən məˈnɒksaɪdǁˌkɑːrbən məˈnɑːk-/ n [U] a poisonous gas produced when engines burn petrol

carbon pa·per /ˈ.. ˌ../ n [C,U] thin paper, with a blue or black substance on one side, that you use to make a copy of something you write

car boot sale /ˌ. ˈ. ˌ./ n [C] a sale where people sell things from the back of their cars

car·bu·ret·tor *BrE*, **carburetor** *AmE* /ˌkɑːbjʊˈretə, -bə-ǁˈkɑːrbəreɪtər/ n [C] the part of a car engine where air and petrol mix

car·cass /ˈkɑːkəsǁˈkɑːr-/ n [C] the body of a dead animal

car·cin·o·gen /kɑːˈsɪnədʒənǁkɑːr-/ n [C] a substance that causes **CANCER**

cards

credit card

birthday card

playing cards

postcards

card /kɑːdǁkɑːrd/ n **1** [C] a small piece of plastic or stiff paper that shows information about someone or something: *an identity card* | *a credit card* **2** [C] a piece of folded stiff paper, with a picture on the front and a message inside that you send to people on special occasions: *a birthday card* **3** [C] one of a set of 52 small pieces of stiff paper with pictures or numbers on them that are used to play games: *Pick any card from the pack.* | **play cards** *Every Sunday afternoon they would play cards.* **4** [C] a **POSTCARD** **5** [U] *BrE* thick stiff paper **6 put/lay your cards on the table** to be completely honest about your plans and intentions **7 be on the cards** *BrE*, **be in the cards** *AmE* to seem likely to happen: *I've left Brenda. It's been on the cards for a long time.*

card·board /ˈkɑːdbɔːdǁˈkɑːrdbɔːrd/ n [U] very stiff thick paper, used especially for making boxes

car·di·ac /ˈkɑːdi-ækǁˈkɑːr-/ *adj technical* relating to the heart: **cardiac arrest** (=when the heart stops working)

car·di·gan /ˈkɑːdiǁˈkɑːr-/ *n* [C] a piece of woollen clothing that covers the top half of your body and is fastened down the front with buttons → see colour picture on page 113

car·di·nal¹ /ˈkɑːdənəlǁˈkɑːr-/ *n* [C] a priest who has a high rank in the Roman Catholic church

cardinal² *adj* very important or basic: *a cardinal rule*

cardinal num·ber /ˌ... ˈ.../ *n* [C] a number such as 1, 2 or 3, that shows how many of something there are → compare ORDINAL NUMBER

care¹ /keəǁker/ *v* **1** [I,T] to be concerned about or interested in someone or something: **+ about** *He doesn't care about anybody but himself.* | **care what/who/how etc** *I don't care what you do.* **2 who cares?** *spoken* used to say that you do not care about something because you do not think it is important **3 I/he/they etc couldn't care less** *spoken* used to say that someone does not care at all about something, especially about what other people think or do **4 would you care for sth?/would you care to do sth?** *formal* used to ask someone if they want something or want to do something: *Would you care for a drink?*

care for sb/sth *phr v* [T] to look after someone or something: *Angie gave up her job to care for her mother.* | *instructions on caring for your new car*

care² *n* **1** [U] the process of looking after someone or something: *Your father will need constant medical care.* | *workers responsible for the care of young children* | *With proper care, your washing machine should last for years.* **2 take care of a)** to look after someone or something: *Who's taking care of the baby?* | *Karl will take care of the house while we're on vacation.* **b)** to do the work or make the arrangements that are necessary for something to happen: *I'll take care of making the reservations.* **3** [U] when you are careful to avoid damaging something, making a mistake etc: *You need to put more care into your work.* | *Fragile! Handle with care.* **4** [C,U] something that makes you feel worried or sad: *Forget all your cares.* | **not have a care in the world** (=not have any problems or worries) **5 take care a)** *spoken, informal* used to say goodbye to family or friends **b)** to be careful: *It's very icy, so take care driving home.* **6 in care** *BrE* a child who is in care is being looked after in a local council home, not by their parents: **take sb into care** *After their mother died, the children were taken into care.*

ca·reer¹ /kəˈrɪəǁ-ˈrɪr/ *n* [C] **1** a job or profession that you have been trained for and intend to do for a long time: **+ in** *a career in law* **2** the period of time in your life that you spend working: *Ted spent most of his career as a teacher.*

career² *BrE v* [I] to move quickly forwards in a way that is not controlled: **+ down/through/across etc** *A couple of boys on bikes careered down the hill.*

care·free /ˈkeəfriːǁˈker-/ *adj* without any problems or worries: *a carefree childhood*

care·ful /ˈkeəfəlǁˈker-/ *adj* **1** trying very hard to avoid doing anything wrong or damaging something: *a careful driver* | *Anna was care-*

ful not to upset Steven. **2 (be) careful!** *spoken* used to tell someone to think about what they are doing so that something bad does not happen: *Be careful with that ladder!* — **carefully** *adv*

care·less /ˈkeələsǁˈker-/ *adj* not paying attention to what you are doing: *It was very careless of you to leave your keys in the car.* — **carelessly** *adv* — **carelessness** *n* [U]

car·er /ˈkeərəǁkerər/ *n* [C] someone who takes care of a child or of someone who is old or ill

ca·ress /kəˈres/ *v* [T] to gently touch or kiss someone in a way that shows you love them — **caress** *n* [C]

care·tak·er /ˈkeəˌteɪkəǁˈkerˌteɪkər/ *n* [C] *BrE* someone whose job is to take care of a building, especially a school

car·go /ˈkɑːgəʊǁˈkɑːrgoʊ/ *n* [C,U] *plural* **cargoes** the goods being carried in a ship, plane etc: *a cargo of oil*

car·i·ca·ture /ˈkærɪkətʃʊəl-tʃʊr/ *n* [C,U] a funny picture or description of someone that makes them seem more silly or amusing than they really are — **caricature** *v* [T]

car·ing /ˈkeərɪŋǁˈker-/ *adj* providing care and support for others: *a warm and caring person*

car·jack·ing /ˈkɑːˌdʒækɪŋǁˈkɑːr-/ *n* [U] the crime of attacking and robbing someone, or forcing them to drive somewhere, while they are driving their car

car·nage /ˈkɑːnɪdʒǁˈkɑːr-/ *n* [U] *formal* when a lot of people are killed or wounded

car·nal /ˈkɑːnlǁˈkɑːrnl/ *adj formal* carnal desires and feelings are sexual and physical

car·na·tion /kɑːˈneɪʃənǁkɑːr-/ *n* [C] a sweet-smelling white, pink, or red flower

car·ni·val /ˈkɑːnɪvəlǁˈkɑːr-/ *n* [C,U] a public celebration with dancing, drinking, and entertainment: *carnival time in Rio*

car·ni·vore /ˈkɑːnɪˌvɔːǁˈkɑːrnɪˌvɔːr/ *n* [C] an animal that eats meat — **carnivorous** /kɑːˈnɪvərəs ǁkɑːr-/ *adj*

car·ol /ˈkærəl/ *n* [C] a song that people sing at Christmas

car·ou·sel /ˌkærəˈsel/ *n* [C] **1** the circular moving belt that you collect your bags and SUITCASES from at an airport **2** *especially AmE* a machine with wooden horses that turns around and around and that people ride on for fun

carp¹ /kɑːpǁkɑːrp/ *n* [C,U] *plural* **carp** a large fish that lives in lakes or rivers, or this fish eaten as food

carp² *v* [I] to complain a lot about something or criticize someone in an annoying way: *I wish you'd stop carping about the way I dress.*

car park /ˈ. ./ *n* [C] *BrE* a place where cars can park; PARKING LOT *AmE*

car·pen·ter /ˈkɑːpʲntəǁˈkɑːrpʲntər/ *n* [C] someone whose job is making and repairing wooden objects

car·pen·try /ˈkɑːpʲntriǁˈkɑːr-/ *n* [U] the work of a carpenter

car·pet /ˈkɑːpʲtǁˈkɑːr-/ *n* **1** [C,U] a heavy woollen material for covering a floor, or a piece of this material → compare RUG **2 carpet of leaves/flowers etc** *literary* a thick layer of leaves etc — **carpet** *v* [T]

car·port /ˈkɑːpɔːtǁˈkɑːrpɔːrt/ *n* [C] a small

covered area where you park a car, usually beside a house → compare GARAGE

car·riage /ˈkærɪdʒ/ *n* [C] **1** a vehicle with wheels that is pulled by a horse **2** *BrE* one of the connected parts of a train where passengers sit; CAR *AmE: a non-smoking carriage* → see colour picture on page 669

car·ri·er /ˈkæriəll-ər/ *n* [C] **1** a person, vehicle, or machine that moves goods or passengers from one place to another **2** someone who passes a disease to other people without having it themselves

carrier bag /ˈ... ˌ./ *n* [C] *BrE* a bag that you are given in a shop to carry the things you have bought

car·rot /ˈkærət/ *n* **1** [C,U] a long thick orange vegetable → see picture at VEGETABLE **2** [C] something that is offered to someone to persuade them to do something: **carrot and stick approach/method etc** (=using a mixture of promises and threats to persuade someone to do something)

car·ry /ˈkæri/ *v* **1** [T] to hold someone or something in your hands or on your back and take them from one place to another: *Can you carry that suitcase for me? | The bus was carrying 25 passengers. | **carry sth into/across/back etc** pipes for carrying oil across the desert* → see colour picture on page 670 **2** [T] to have a disease which can be passed to others: *Many diseases are carried by insects.* **3** [T] to have something with you in your pocket, bag etc: *Larry always carries a gun.* **4** [T] to contain a particular piece of information, story, or advertisement: *All the newspapers carried articles about the plane crash.* **5** [I] if a sound carries, it can be heard a long way away: *The sound carried as far as the lake.* **6** [T] to have a particular result: *Murder carries a life sentence in this state.* **7 be carried** to be approved by the people voting at a meeting: *The motion was carried by 20 votes to 12.* **8 carry sth too far** to do or say something too much or for too long: *It was funny at first, but you've carried the joke too far.* **9 be/get carried away** to be or become so excited that you are no longer in control of what you do or say: *I got carried away and bought three pairs of shoes!* **10 carry weight** if some-one's opinions carry weight, other people think they are important and may be persuaded by them: *My views don't seem to carry much weight around here.*

carry sth ↔ **off** *phr v* [T] to do something successfully: *It's a difficult thing to do, but I'm sure she'll be able to carry it off.*

carry on *phr v* [I,T] to continue doing something: *You'll make yourself ill if you carry on working like that.*

carry sth ↔ **out** *phr v* [T] **1** to do something that needs to be organized and planned: *Teenagers carried out a survey on attitudes to drugs.* **2** to do something that someone has told you to do or that you have said you will do: *I'm supposed to carry out her instructions and report back. | Soldiers are trained to carry out orders without question.*

carry through *phr v* **1** [T **carry** sth ↔ **through**] to complete or finish something successfully: *Once he starts a project, he always carries it through.* **2** [T **carry** sb **through** (sth)] to help someone to get through an illness

or a difficult time: *Her sense of humour usually carries her through.*

car·ry·all /ˈkæri-ɔːll-ɒːl/ *n* [C] *AmE* HOLDALL *BrE* → see picture at BAG

car·ry·cot /ˈkærikɒtll-kɑːt/ *n* [C] *BrE* a small thing like a bed used for carrying a baby → see picture at BED

carry-out /ˈ... ./ *n* [C] a meal that you buy from a restaurant to eat somewhere else, or a restaurant that sells this food; TAKEOUT *AmE*; TAKE-AWAY *BrE*

car·sick /ˈkɑːˌsɪkll-kɑːr-/ *adj* [not before noun] feeling sick when you are travelling in a car —**carsickness** *n* [U]

cart¹ /kɑːtll-kɑːrt/ *n* [C] **1** a vehicle with two or four wheels, that is pulled: *a wooden cart drawn by a horse* **2** *AmE* a large wire basket on wheels used in a SUPERMARKET; TROLLEY *BrE*

cart² *v* [T] *informal* to carry or take something or someone somewhere: *I'm sick of carting this suitcase around.*

carte blanche /ˌkɑːt ˈblɑːnʃll,kɑːrt-/ *n* [U] the freedom to do exactly what you want in a situation: **give sb carte blanche** *Her parents gave her carte blanche to organize the party.*

car·tel /kɑːˈtelll-kɑːr-/ *n* [C,U] a group of companies that work together to control prices on a particular product

car·ti·lage /ˈkɑːtˌlɪdʒll-kɑːrtəlɪdʒ/ *n* [C,U] the strong substance that can stretch, and that surrounds the JOINTS in your body

car·tog·ra·phy /kɑːˈtɒɡrəfill-kɑːrˈtɑː-/ *n* [U] the skill or work of making maps —**cartographer** *n* [C]

car·ton /ˈkɑːtnll-kɑːrtn/ *n* [C] a box made from stiff paper or plastic that contains food or drink: *a milk carton* → see picture at CONTAINER

car·toon /kɑːˈtuːnll-kɑːr-/ *n* [C] **1** a film made using characters that are drawn and not real **2** a funny drawing or set of drawings that makes a joke, usually in a newspaper —**cartoonist** *n* [C] *He was a skilled cartoonist.*

car·tridge /ˈkɑːtrɪdʒll-kɑːr-/ *n* [C] **1** a small piece of equipment that contains something that you put inside a machine to make it work: *an ink cartridge* **2** a tube containing explosive material and a bullet for a gun

cart·wheel /ˈkɑːt-wiːll ˈkɑːrt-/ *n* [C] a movement in which you throw yourself sideways onto your hands and bring your legs over your head —**cartwheel** *v* [I]

cartwheel

carve /kɑːvllkɑːrv/ *v* **1** [T] to cut something, especially wood or stone, into a particular shape: *All the figures are carved from a single tree.* **2** [I,T] to cut cooked meat into smaller pieces with a large knife: *Dad always carves the turkey.*

carve sth ↔ **out** *phr v* [T] **carve out a career/niche/role etc** to become successful by working hard, especially in business: *She carved out a career for herself in the competitive world of advertising.*

carve sth ↔ **up** *phr v* [T] to divide something into different parts in a way that people think is bad: *The government is carving up the area into new electoral districts.*

carv·ing /ˈkɑːvɪŋ‖ˈkɑːr-/ *n* **1** [C] an object made by cutting wood, stone etc **2** [U] the activity or skill of cutting wood, stone etc

cas·cade /kæˈskeɪd/ *n* [C] *literary* something that flows or hangs down in large amounts: **+ of** *Her hair was a cascade of soft curls.* —**cascade** *v* [I] *Flowering plants cascaded over the balcony.*

case /keɪs/ *n* **1** [C] a situation or problem that exists, or an example of that situation or problem: *In some cases, it may be necessary to talk to the child's parents.* | **+ of** *a case of mistaken identity* | **be the case** *People working together can do great things, and this was certainly the case in Maria's neighbourhood.* | **in sb's case** *No one should be here after 6 o'clock, but in your case I'll make an exception.* **2** **in that case** because of the fact that has just been mentioned: *"I'll be home late tonight." "Well, in that case, I won't cook dinner."* **3** **in any case** *spoken* used to say that a fact or situation remains the same even if other things change: *Of course we'll take you home – we're going that way in any case.* **4** **in case of sth** *formal* if or when something happens: *In case of fire, break the glass.* **5** **(just) in case** **a)** used to say that someone should do something because something else might happen or be true: *Take your umbrella in case it rains.* **b)** used to mean "if": *In case you missed the first episode, here is the story so far.* **6** [C] something that must be decided in a court of law: *a court case dealing with cruelty to animals* **7** [C] an event or set of events that the police deal with: *a murder case* **8** [C, usually singular] all the facts or reasons that can be used to prove that something is right or wrong: **+ for/against** *There is a good case for changing the rule.* **9** [C] an illness or someone who is being treated by a doctor for an illness: *In serious cases, the patient loses their ability to work.* **10** [C] a container for storing something: *a jewelry case* **11** [C] *BrE* a SUITCASE **12** [C,U] *technical* the form of a word, usually a noun, that shows its relationship to other words in a sentence **13** **be on sb's case** *informal* to criticize someone a lot and keep checking that they are not doing anything wrong, especially in a way that seems unfair and unkind → see also LOWER CASE, UPPER CASE

case stud·y /ˈ. ˌ../ *n* [C] a detailed study of a particular person, group, or situation over a period of time

cash[1] /kæʃ/ *n* [U] **1** money in the form of coins and notes: **pay cash** *"Are you paying by credit card?" "No, I'll pay cash."* | **in cash** *He had about £200 in cash in his wallet.* **2** *informal* money in any form: *I'm short of cash at the moment.*

cash[2] *v* [T] to exchange a cheque for money: *Do you cash traveller's cheques?*

cash in on sth *phr v* [T] to get advantages from a situation: *The suggestion that they are cashing in on the tragedy is completely untrue.*

cash card /ˈ. ./ *n* [C] a plastic card used for getting money from a machine at a bank

cash crop /ˈ. ./ *n* [C] a crop that is grown to be sold rather than to be used by the people growing it

ca·shew /ˈkæʃuː, kəˈʃuː/ *n* [C] a small curved nut that you can eat, or the tree on which these nuts grow

cash flow /ˈ. ./ *n* [U] the movement of money into and out of a company: *cashflow problems*

cash·ier /kæˈʃɪə‖-ˈʃɪr/ *n* [C] someone whose job is to receive and pay out money in a bank, shop etc

cash·mere /ˈkæʃmɪə‖ˈkæʒmɪr, ˈkæʃ-/ *n* [U] a type of fine soft wool: *an expensive cashmere sweater*

cash·point /ˈkæʃpɔɪnt/ *n* [C] *BrE* a machine that you can get money from: ATM *AmE*

cash re·gis·ter /ˈ. ˌ.../ *n* [C] a machine used in shops to keep money in and record the amount of money received each time something is sold; TILL

cas·ing /ˈkeɪsɪŋ/ *n* [C] a layer of rubber, metal etc that covers and protects something inside it

ca·si·no /kəˈsiːnəʊ‖-noʊ/ *n* [C], *plural* **casinos** a place where people try to win money by gambling (GAMBLE)

cask /kɑːsk‖kæsk/ *n* [C] a round wooden container used for holding wine

cas·ket /ˈkɑːskɪt‖ˈkæs-/ *n* [C] **1** a small decorated box for keeping valuable things in **2** *AmE* the box a dead person is buried in; COFFIN *BrE*

cas·se·role /ˈkæsərəʊl‖-roʊl/ *n* [C,U] a mixture of meat and vegetables that are cooked together slowly

cas·sette /kəˈset/ *n* [C] a small flat plastic case with TAPE inside, used for playing or recording sound or pictures

cassette player /ˈ. ˌ../ *n* [C] a machine used for playing cassettes

cast[1] /kɑːst‖kæst/ *v* [T] **cast, cast, casting** **1** to give an actor a part in a film, play etc: *Rickman was cast as the Sheriff of Nottingham.* **2** *literary* to throw something somewhere: *fishermen casting their nets into the sea* **3** **cast light on/onto** **a)** to explain or give new information about something: *Can you cast any light on the meaning of these figures?* **b)** *literary* to send light onto a surface **4** **cast a shadow** **a)** to make people feel less happy or hopeful about something and make them feel worried: *The bad news cast a shadow over his visit.* **b)** to make a shadow appear on something: *trees casting a shadow across the lawn* **5** **cast a spell on/over** **a)** to get someone's attention or admiration, and keep it for a long time: *Sinatra's voice soon cast its spell over the audience.* **b)** to say magic words to make something happen **6** **cast doubt on** to make someone feel less certain about something: *I didn't mean to cast doubt on Bobby's version of the story.* **7** **cast an eye over sth** to check or look at something quickly: *Can you cast an eye over these figures and tell me what you think?* **8** to make something in a particular shape by pouring hot metal into a special container: *a statue cast in bronze* **9** **cast a vote** to vote in an election

cast sb/sth ↔ **aside** *phr v* [T] to get rid of something or someone: *When he became President, he cast aside all his former friends.*

cast off *phr v* **1** [I] to untie the rope that keeps a boat fastened to a post on the land, so that the boat can sail away **2** [T **cast** sb/sth ↔ **off**] *literary* to get rid of something or someone: *a country that has cast off Communist rule*

cast² n [C] **1** all of the actors in a film: *an all-star cast* **2** a hard cover fitted over your arm, leg etc to support a broken bone: *a plaster cast*

cast·a·way /ˈkɑːstəweɪlˈkæst-/ n [C] someone who is alone on an island after their ship has sunk

caste /kɑːstlkæst/ n [C,U] one of the social classes in India into which people are born

cast·er also **castor** BrE /ˈkɑːstəlˈkæstər/ n [C] a small wheel fixed to the bottom of a piece of furniture so that it can be easily moved

cas·ti·gate /ˈkæstɪɡeɪt/ v [T] *formal* to criticize or punish someone severely —**castigation** /ˌkæstɪˈɡeɪʃən/ n [U]

casting vote /ˈ.. ˌ./ n [C] the vote of the person in charge of a meeting, that can be used to make a decision when both sides have an equal number of votes

cast i·ron /ˌ. ˈ./ n [U] a type of iron that is very hard but breaks easily

cast-iron /ˌ. ˈ.ˌ/ adj **1 cast-iron excuse/alibi/guarantee etc** an excuse etc that is very certain and cannot fail **2** made of cast iron: *a cast-iron pan*

cas·tle /ˈkɑːsəllˈkæ-/ n [C] a very large strong building built in the past to protect the people inside from attack

cast-offs /ˈ. ./ n [plural] clothes or other things that you do not want any more, that you give to someone else —**cast-off** adj

cast·or /ˈkɑːstəlˈkæstər/ n a British spelling of CASTER

cas·trate /kæˈstreɪtlˈkæstreɪt/ v [T] to remove the sexual organs of a male animal or a man —**castration** /kæˈstreɪʃən/ n [C,U]

cas·u·al /ˈkæʒuəl/ adj **1** relaxed and not worried about things: *His casual attitude toward work irritates me.* **2** casual clothes are comfortable and are worn in informal situations **3** [only before noun] without any clear aim or serious interest: *a casual glance at the newspapers | She wanted something more than a casual relationship.* **4** temporary or used for a short time: *casual employment* —**casually** adv

cas·u·al·ty /ˈkæʒuəlti/ n **1** [C] someone who is hurt in an accident or a battle: *There were no casualties in today's accident on the M10.* | **heavy casualties** (=a lot of people hurt or killed) **2 be a casualty of** to suffer because of a particular situation: *The city library is the latest casualty of the cutbacks.* **3** [U] BrE the part of a hospital that people are taken to when they need urgent treatment; EMERGENCY ROOM AmE: *An ambulance rushed her to casualty.*

cat /kæt/ n [C] **1** a small animal that is often kept as a pet or used for catching mice (MOUSE) **2** a large animal that is related to this animal for example a lion **3 let the cat out of the bag** *informal* to tell a secret without intending to

cat·a·clys·m /ˈkætəklɪzəm/ n [C] *literary* a sudden violent event or change: *the cataclysm of*

the First World War —**cataclysmic** /ˌkætə-ˈklɪzmɪk◂/ adj

cat·a·logue¹ (also **catalog** AmE) /ˈkætəlɒg ‖-lɒːɡ, -lɑːɡ/ n **1** [C] a book with information about goods that you can buy from a particular shop **2** [C] a list of all the objects, paintings, books etc in a place **3 a catalogue of disasters/errors** a set of bad events that happen one after another

catalogue² (also **catalog** AmE) v [T] to put a list of things into a particular order and write it in a catalogue

cat·a·lyst /ˈkætl-ɪst/ n [C] **1** someone or something that results in important changes: **+ for** *The women's movement became a catalyst for change in the workplace.* **2** a substance that makes a chemical reaction happen more quickly, without being changed itself

cat·a·ma·ran /ˌkætəməˈræn/ n [C] a sailing boat with two separate HULLS

cat·a·pult¹ /ˈkætəpʌlt/ v **1** [T] to make someone or something move through the air extremely quickly: **+ across/through/into etc** *The force of the explosion catapulted him into the air.* **2 catapult (sb) to fame/stardom** to suddenly become famous or successful. or to make someone suddenly famous or successful: *The character of "Rocky" catapulted Stallone to stardom.*

catapult² n [C] BrE a small stick in the shape of a Y with a band of rubber between the ends, that children use to throw stones

cat·a·ract /ˈkætərækt/ n [C] a medical condition affecting the LENS in someone's eye, that makes them slowly lose their sight

ca·tas·tro·phe /kəˈtæstrəfi/ n [C] a terrible event that causes a lot of destruction or suffering

cat·as·troph·ic /ˌkætəˈstrɒfɪk ‖-ˈstrɑː-/ adj causing a lot of destruction or suffering: *the catastrophic effects of the flooding*

catch¹ /kætʃ/ v **caught** /kɔːtlkɒːt/, **catching** **1** [T] if the police catch someone who has done something illegal, they find them and stop them from escaping: *The police have caught the man suspected of the murder.* **2** [T] to stop someone from escaping by running after them and holding them: *He was too fat and slow to catch the little boy.* **3** [T] to get hold of and stop something that is moving through the air: *Throw the ball to Tom and see if he can catch it.* **→** see colour picture on page 670 **4** [T] if a moving object catches you, it hits you **5** [I,T] to become accidentally stuck to something, or to make something do this: *His shirt caught on the fence and tore.* **6 be caught in/without etc** to be unable to avoid an unpleasant situation: *We were caught in the rain.* **7** [T] to see someone doing something wrong: **catch sb doing sth** *I caught him looking through my files.* | **catch sb red-handed** (=to see someone at the moment they are doing something wrong) **8** to suddenly see someone or something for a moment: *I caught sight of Luisa in the crowd.* **9 catch sb's eye** to make someone notice some-

C

GRAMMAR NOTE: 'if' clauses (3)
When you imagine a past situation that did not really happen, use **if + past perfect**: *If they had offered me the job, I would have taken it.* (=but they did not offer me it). Use **would have + past participle** in the other part of the sentence.

thing: *bright colours that catch the eye*
10 [T] to get an illness: *Put your coat on! You don't want to catch a cold!* **11 catch a bus/ train etc** to get on a bus, train etc: *I catch the 7.30 train every morning.* **12** [T] to not be too late to do something, talk to someone etc: *If you hurry you might catch her before she leaves.* **13** [T] if the light catches an object or if the object catches the light, light shines on it and makes it look bright **14 catch fire** to start burning, especially accidentally **15 not catch sth** to not hear or understand something clearly: *I'm sorry, I didn't catch your name.* **16 catch the sun** if someone has caught the sun, their skin looks a little red or brown because of the effect of the sun's light

catch on *phr v* [I] **1** to begin to understand something: *Explain the rules to Zoë – she catches on fast.* **2** if an activity or style catches on, it becomes popular

catch sb ↔ out *phr v* [T] *BrE* to make someone make a mistake, especially by asking them a question they cannot answer: *She tried to catch me out by asking me where I'd first met her husband.*

catch up *phr v* [I,T **catch sb/sth up**] **1** to come up from behind someone or something and reach the same point: **+ with** *I had to run to catch up with her.* **2** to reach the same standard or level as someone or something else: **+ with** *At first he was bottom of the class, but he soon caught up.*

catch up on sth *phr v* [T] to do something that you have not yet had time to do: *I need to catch up on some sleep this weekend.*

catch² *n* [C] **1** the act of catching something that has been thrown or hit: *That was a great catch!* **2** *informal* a hidden problem or difficulty: *The rent is so low there must be a catch.* **3** a quantity of something that has been caught, usually fish: *a large catch of tuna fish* **4** a hook for fastening something and holding it shut

Catch-22 /ˌkætʃ twenti 'tuː/ *n* [singular] a situation that you cannot escape from because of something that is part of the situation itself: *You can't get a job without experience, and you can't get experience without a job. It's a Catch-22.*

catch·ing /'kætʃɪŋ/ *adj* [not before noun] an illness that is catching is easily passed from one person to another

catch·ment ar·e·a /'kætʃmənt ˌeəriəl-ˌeriə/ *n* [C] the area that a school takes its students from

catch phrase /'. ./ *n* [C] a word or phrase that is easy to remember and is often repeated by an entertainer, or political party, or newspaper

catch·y /'kætʃi/ *adj* a catchy song or tune is pleasant and easy to remember

cat·e·chis·m /'kætɪˌkɪzəm/ *n* [singular] a set of questions and answers about the Christian religion that people learn before becoming members of a church

cat·e·gor·i·cal /ˌkætɪˈɡɒrɪkəl‖-'ɡɔː-, -'ɡɑː-/ *adj* clearly stating that something is completely certain: *Fox gave a categorical denial of his guilt.* —**categorically** /-kli/ *adv*

cat·e·go·rize (also **-ise** *BrE*) /'kætɪɡəraɪz/ *v* [T] to put people or things into groups according to what type they are: *We've categorized the students by age.*

cat·e·go·ry /'kætɪɡərill-ɡɔːri/ *n* [C] a group of people or things that have the same qualities or features: **fall into a category** (=belong to a category): *Voters fall into one of three categories.*

ca·ter /'keɪtəll-ər/ *v* [I,T] *especially AmE* to provide and serve food and drinks at a party, meeting etc: *Who's catering your daughter's wedding?* —**caterer** *n* [C]

cater for sb/sth *phr v* [T] *BrE* to provide a particular group of people with what they need or want: *a holiday company catering for the elderly*

cater to sb *phr v* [T] **1** to provide a particular group of people with what they need or want: *a small shabby hotel catering to foreign visitors* **2** *BrE* to provide something that someone wants, but think is bad: *I was really spoilt – Mum used to cater to my every whim.*

cat·er·pil·lar /'kætəˌpɪləll-tər,pɪlər/ *n* [C] a small creature with a long body and a lot of legs, that eats leaves

ca·thar·tic /kə'θɑːtɪk, kæ-‖kə'θɑːr-/ *adj* a cathartic experience helps you to deal with difficult emotions and get rid of them — **catharsis** *n* [C,U]

ca·the·dral /kə'θiːdrəl/ *n* [C] a very large church that is the main church in a particular area

Cath·o·lic /'kæθəlɪk/ *adj* connected with the Roman Catholic church —**Catholic** *n* [C] — **Catholicism** /kə'θɒlɪsɪzəm‖kə'θɑː-/ *n* [U]

catholic *adj formal* **have catholic tastes** to like a wide variety of things: *Susan has catholic tastes in music.*

cat's eye /'. ./ *n* [C] one of a line of small flat objects fixed down the middle of a road, that shines when it is lit by car lights

cat·sup /'kætsəp/ *n* [U] *AmE* KETCHUP

cat·tle /'kætl/ *n* [plural] cows and BULLs kept on a farm

cat·ty /'kæti/ *adj informal* deliberately saying unkind things about someone —**cattiness** *n* [U] —**cattily** *adv*

cat·walk /'kætwɔːk‖-wɔːk/ *n* [C] the long raised path that MODELs walk on in a fashion show

Cau·ca·sian /kɔːˈkeɪziənll kɔːˈkeɪʒən/ *adj* someone who is Caucasian belongs to a race that has white or pale skin —**Caucasian** *n* [C]

caught /kɔːtll kɔːt/ *v* the past tense and past participle of CATCH

caul·dron also **caldron** /'kɔːldrənll kɔːl-/ *n* [C] a large round metal pot for boiling liquids over a fire: *a witch's cauldron*

cau·li·flow·er /'kɒlɪˌflaʊəll kɔːliˌflaʊər, 'kɑː-/ *n* [C,U] a vegetable with green leaves around a large firm white centre ➡ see picture at VEGETABLE

'cause /kɒz, kəzll kɒz, kəz/ *linking word spoken* BECAUSE

cause¹ /kɔːzll kɔːz/ *n* **1** [C] a person, event, or thing that makes something happen: **+ of** *What was the cause of the accident?* **2** [U] reasons for feeling or behaving in a particular way: **+ for** *She had no cause for complaint.* **3** [C] a principle or aim that a group of people support or fight for: **for a good cause** *I don't mind giving money if it's for a good cause.*

cause² *v* [T] to make something happen: *Heavy traffic is causing long delays on the free-*

way. | **cause sb sth** *Tom's behaviour is causing me a lot of problems.* | **cause sb/sth to do sth** *We still don't know what caused the computer to crash.*

cause·way /ˈkɔːzweɪǁ-kɒz-/ *n* [C] a raised road or path across wet ground or through water

caus·tic /ˈkɔːstɪkǁˈkɒs-/ *adj* **1 a caustic remark/comment etc** something you say that is extremely unkind or criticizes someone very severely **2** a caustic substance contains chemicals that can burn through things: *caustic soda*

cau·tion¹ /ˈkɔːʃənǁˈkɒː-/ *n* **1** [U] when someone does something carefully, not taking any risks, and avoiding danger: **with caution** *Sick animals should be handled with great caution.* **2 word/note of caution** a warning to be careful: *One note of caution: never try this trick at home.* **3** [C] *BrE* a spoken warning given by a policeman when you have done something wrong

caution² *v* [T] *formal* to warn someone that something might be dangerous or difficult: **caution sb against sth** *The children were cautioned against talking to strangers.*

cau·tion·ar·y /ˈkɔːʃənəriǁˈkɒːʃəneri/ *adj* giving advice or warning: **a cautionary tale** (=a story that is intended to warn people)

cau·tious /ˈkɔːʃəsǁˈkɒː-/ *adj* careful to avoid danger: *a cautious driver* —**cautiously** *adv*: *He looked cautiously out from behind the door.*

cav·al·cade /ˌkævəlˈkeɪd, ˈkævəlkeɪd/ *n* [C] a line of people on horses or in cars or carriages moving along in a ceremony

cav·a·lier /ˌkævəˈlɪəǁ-ˈlɪr‹/ *adj* not caring or thinking about other people or about things that are important: *a cavalier attitude towards safety*

cav·al·ry /ˈkævəlri/ *n* [U] soldiers who fight while riding on horses

cave¹ /keɪv/ *n* [C] a large natural hole in the side of a cliff or under the ground ➜ see colour picture on page 243

cave² *v*

cave in *phr v* [I] **1** to fall down or inwards: *The roof just caved in.* **2** to stop opposing something because you have been persuaded or threatened: **+ to** *He finally caved in to our demands.*

cave·man /ˈkeɪvmæn/ *n* [C] someone who lived many thousands of years ago, when people lived in caves

cav·ern /ˈkævənǁ-ərn/ *n* [C] a large deep cave

cav·i·ar also **caviare** /ˈkæviɑːǁ-ɑːr/ *n* [U] an expensive food consisting of fish eggs

cav·i·ty /ˈkævɪti/ *n* [C] **1** a hole or space inside something solid **2** a hole in a tooth where it has decayed

ca·vort /kəˈvɔːtǁ-ɔːrt/ *v* [I] to behave in a noisy, excited, or sexual way, often by moving around a lot: *pictures of the two of them cavorting on a beach*

CC 1 the abbreviation of "carbon copy", used to show you are sending copies of a letter to other people **2** the abbreviation of "cubic centimetre": *a 2000 cc engine*

CD /ˌsiː ˈdiː‹/ *n* [C,U] Compact Disc; a small circular piece of hard plastic on which music or information is recorded: *Have you heard their latest CD?*

CD play·er /ˈ. ../ *n* [C] a piece of equipment used to play music CDs

CD-ROM /ˌsiː diː ˈrɒmǁ-ˈrɑːm/ *n* [C,U] Compact Disc Read-Only Memory; a CD on which large quantities of information can be stored to be used by a computer ➜ see colour picture on page 80

cease /siːs/ *v* [I,T] *formal* to stop doing something or stop happening: *By noon the rain had ceased.* | **cease doing sth** *The company ceased trading on 31st October.* | **cease to do sth** *He never ceases to amaze me.*

cease·fire /ˈsiːsfaɪəǁ-faɪr/ *n* [C] an agreement for both sides in a war to stop fighting

cease·less /ˈsiːsləs/ *adj formal* continuing for a long time without stopping: *his parents' ceaseless arguing* —**ceaselessly** *adv*

ce·dar /ˈsiːdəǁ-ər/ *n* [C,U] a tall CONIFEROUS tree, or the red sweet-smelling wood of this tree

cede /siːd/ *v* [T] *formal* to give something, usually land, to another country or person

cei·ling /ˈsiːlɪŋ/ *n* [C] **1** the inside surface of the top part of a room **2** a limit which is set to stop prices, wages etc getting too high

cel·e·brate /ˈseləbreɪt/ *v* [I,T] to do something special because it is a special occasion, or because something good has happened: *You got the job? Let's celebrate!* | *How do you want to celebrate your birthday?*

cel·e·brat·ed /ˈseləbreɪtɪd/ *adj* famous or talked about a lot: *a celebrated musician* | **+ for** *Florence is celebrated for its architecture.*

cel·e·bra·tion /ˌseləˈbreɪʃən/ *n* **1** [C] an occasion or party when you celebrate something: *New Year's celebrations* **2** [U] when something is celebrated: **in celebration of** *a party in celebration of his promotion*

ce·leb·ri·ty /sɪˈlebrɪti/ *n* [C] a famous person, especially an actor or entertainer

cel·e·ry /ˈseləri/ *n* [U] a vegetable with long firm pale green stems ➜ see picture at VEGETABLE

ce·les·ti·al /sɪˈlestiəlǁ-tʃəl/ *adj literary* relating to the sky or HEAVEN

cel·i·bate /ˈseləbət/ *adj* someone who is celibate does not have sex —**celibacy** *n* [U]

cell /sel/ *n* [C] **1** a small room in a police station or prison where prisoners are kept **2** the smallest part of an animal or plant that can exist on its own: *red blood cells*

cel·lar /ˈseləǁ-ər/ *n* [C] a room under a house: *a wine cellar*

cel·list /ˈtʃelɪst/ *n* [C] someone who plays the cello

cel·lo /ˈtʃeləʊǁ-loʊ/ *n* [C] a large wooden musical instrument, shaped like a VIOLIN, that you hold between your knees and play by pulling a BOW across the strings

cel·lo·phane /ˈseləfeɪn/ *n* [U] *trademark* a thin transparent material used for wrapping things

cel·lu·lar /ˈseljələǁ-ər/ *adj* relating to the cells in a plant or animal

cellular phone /ˌ... ˈ./ also **cell·phone** /ˈselfəʊnǁ-foʊn/ *n* [C] a telephone that you can carry with you and use anywhere; MOBILE PHONE

cel·lu·lite /ˈseljəlaɪt/ *n* [U] fat that is just below someone's skin and that makes it look uneven and unattractive

cel·lu·loid /ˈselj‿ɔɪd/ *n* [U] *trademark* a substance like plastic, used in the past to make film: **on celluloid** (=on cinema film): *Chaplin's comic genius is preserved on celluloid.*

cel·lu·lose /ˈselj‿ɔusll‿ous/ *n* [U] the material that the cell walls of plants are made of and that is used to make plastics, paper etc

Cel·si·us /ˈselsiəs/ *n* [U] a SCALE of temperature in which water freezes at 0° and boils at 100°

ce·ment¹ /sɪˈment/ *n* [U] a grey powder used in building that becomes hard when it is mixed with water and allowed to dry

cement² *v* [T] **1** to cover something with cement **2** to make a relationship stronger: *The country has cemented its trade connections with the US.*

cem·e·tery /ˈsemɪtrill‿teri/ *n* [C] a place where dead people are buried

cen·sor /ˈsensəl‿ər/ *v* [T] to examine books, films etc in order to remove anything that is offensive, politically dangerous etc —**censor** *n* [C]

cen·sor·ship /ˈsensəʃɪpll‿ər-/ *n* [U] the practice of censoring something

cen·sure /ˈsenʃəl‿ər/ *v* [T] *formal* to officially criticize someone for something they have done wrong —**censure** *n* [U]

cen·sus /ˈsensəs/ *n* [C] an occasion on which official information is gathered about the number of people in a country, their ages, jobs etc

cent /sent/ *n* [C] written sign ¢; a unit of money worth 1/100 of a dollar; PENNY

cen·te·na·ry /senˈtiːnərill‿ˈten-, ˈsentəneri/ *BrE*
cen·ten·ni·al /senˈteniəl/ *AmE* — *n* [C] the day or year exactly one hundred years after an important event

cen·ter /ˈsentəl‿ər/ *n, v* the American spelling of CENTRE

Cen·ti·grade /ˈsentɪɡreɪd/ *n* [U] a SCALE of temperature in which water freezes at 0° and boils at 100°; CELSIUS

cen·ti·me·tre *BrE*, **centimeter** *AmE* /ˈsentɪˌmiːtəll‿ər/ *n* [C] written abbreviation **cm**; a unit for measuring length, equal to 1/100 of a meter or 0.39 inches

cen·tral /ˈsentrəl/ *adj* **1** [only before noun] in the middle of an object or area: *Central Asia* | *The prison is built around a central courtyard.* **2** [only before noun] making all the important decisions about how a country or company is managed and organized: *central government* (=government of a whole country, at a national rather than local level) **3** more important than anything else: *Owen played a central role in the negotiations.* **4** convenient because of being near the centre of a town or area —**centrally** *adv*: *The beach is a long walk, but at least the hotel's centrally located.*

central heat·ing /ˌ‿ ˈ‿/ *n* [U] a system of heating buildings in which heat is produced in one place and is taken to the rest of the building by pipes

Central In·tel·li·gence A·gen·cy /ˌ‿ ˈ‿ ‿ ˌ‿/ *n* [singular] CIA

cen·tral·ize (*also* **-ise** *BrE*) /ˈsentrəlaɪz/ *v* [T] to change the way a country or organization is controlled so that it is governed or organized by

one group of people in one place —**centralization** /ˌsentrəlaɪˈzeɪʃənll‿lə-/ *n* [U]

cen·tre¹ *BrE*, **center** *AmE* /ˈsentəl‿ər/ *n* [C] **1** the middle part or point of something: *The carpet had a flower pattern at the centre.* | **+ of** *Draw a line through the centre of the circle.* **2** a place or building used for a particular purpose: *a shopping centre* **3** a place where most of the important things happen that are related to a business or activity: *a major financial centre* **4** the part in the middle of a city or town where most of the shops, restaurants, clubs etc are **5** **the centre** a political position which does not support extreme views **6** **be the centre of attention** to be the person that people give the most attention to: *Ginny always wants to be the centre of attention.*

centre² *BrE*, **center** *AmE* *v* [T] to move something to a position at the centre of something else

centre on/around sth *phr v* [I,T] to treat something as the most important feature or part of something: *The film centres on the hunt for a serial killer.* | *His whole life centres around his job.*

centre of grav·i·ty /ˌ‿ ‿ ‿ ˈ‿/ *n* [singular] point in an object at which it can balance

cen·tre·piece *BrE*, **centerpiece** *AmE* /ˈsentəpiːsll‿ər-/ *n* [C] **1** a decoration in the middle of a table **2** the most important, attractive, or noticeable part of something: **+ of** *The glass staircase is the centrepiece of the new store.*

cen·tu·ry /ˈsentʃəri/ *n* [C] a period of 100 years, used especially in giving dates: *These trees have been here for several centuries.* | *a building dating from the 19th century*

ce·ram·ics /sɪˈræmɪks/ *n* **1** [U] the art of making pots, bowls, TILES etc from clay **2** [plural] artistic objects made from clay: *an exhibition of ceramics* —**ceramic** *adj*

ce·re·al /ˈsɪəriəll‿ˈsɪr-/ *n* **1** [C,U] breakfast food that is made from grain and usually eaten with milk **2** [C] a plant grown to produce grain for food, for example wheat or rice

cer·e·bral /ˈserᵻbrəll‿səˈriː-, ˈserᵻ-/ *adj technical* relating to or affecting the brain

cerebral pal·sy /ˌ‿‿‿ ‿ ll‿ ‿‿, ‿‿ ˈ‿/ *n* [C] an illness caused by damage to the brain before or during birth, which makes people have difficulty speaking or moving

cer·e·mo·ni·al /ˌserᵻˈməuniəl‿ ll‿ˈmou-/ *adj* used in a ceremony —**ceremonially** *adv*

cer·e·mo·ny /ˈserᵻmənill‿mouni/ *n* **1** [C] a formal public or religious event, for example when people get married or a new building is opened: *the marriage ceremony* **2** [U] the formal words and actions that are said or done on special occasions

cer·tain¹ /ˈsɜːtnll‿ˈsɜːrtn/ *adj* **1** completely sure and without any doubts: **+ (that)** *I'm certain that he's telling the truth.* | **+ about** *Are you certain about that?* | **+ what/how/whether etc** *It's not completely certain why this process happens.* **2** **know/say for certain** to know something without any doubt: *We can't say for certain when the plane will arrive.* **3** sure to happen or be true: **+ that** *It now seems certain that the President will win the election.* **4** **make certain (that)** to do something in order to be sure that something happens or is done: *Employers must make* *certain that all employees are treated fairly.* → see also UNCERTAIN

certain² *determiner, pron* **1** also **certain of** *formal* a word used to talk about a person or thing without saying exactly who or what they are: *It seems that certain people have been using my computer while I was away.* | *There are certain things I just can't talk about with her.* **2 a certain amount** some: *You might experience a certain amount of discomfort.*

cer·tain·ly /'sɜːtnli‖'sɜːr-/ *adv* **1** without any doubt: *Chris certainly spends a lot of money on clothes.* **2** *spoken* used when agreeing to let someone do something or have something; of course: *"Can I have a look at your paper?" "Certainly!"* **certainly not!** (used when refusing to let someone do or have something)

cer·tain·ty /'sɜːtnti‖'sɜːr-/ *n* **1** [U] when you are completely sure about something: **with certainty** *It is difficult to say with absolute certainty what time the crime took place.* **2** [C] something that is definitely true or will definitely happen: *It's a certainty that prices will continue to rise.*

cer·tif·i·cate /sə'tɪfɪkət‖sər-/ *n* [C] a document that officially states that something is true: **birth/marriage/death certificate** (=giving details of someone's birth etc)

cer·ti·fy /'sɜːtɪfaɪ‖'sɜːr-/ *v* [T] **1** to officially state that something is correct or true: *A doctor certified the passenger dead at the scene.* | **+ (that)** *Doctors have certified that Pask is unfit to continue with his trial.* **2** to be given an official paper which states that you have completed a course of training: *He has been certified as a mechanic.* **3** to officially state that someone is mentally ill

cer·ti·tude /'sɜːtɪtjuːd‖'sɜːrtɪtuːd/ *n* [U] *formal* the state of being or feeling certain about something

cer·vix /'sɜːvɪks‖'sɜːr-/ *n* [C] the narrow opening into a woman's UTERUS — **cervical** /'sɜːvɪkəl, sə'vaɪkəl‖'sɜːrvɪkəl/ *adj*

ce·sar·e·an /sɪ'zeəriən‖-'zer-/ another spelling of CAESAREAN

ces·sa·tion /se'seɪʃən/ *n* [C,U] *formal* when something stops, especially fighting: *a cessation of hostilities*

cess·pool /'sespuːl/ also **cess·pit** /'sespɪt/ *BrE n* [C] an underground container or hole where waste water from a house is collected

cf used in writing to tell the reader to compare the item or subject being mentioned with something else

CFC /ˌsiː ef 'siː/ *n* chlorofluorocarbon; a type of gas that is used in REFRIGERATORS, AEROSOLS etc, which causes damage to the OZONE around the Earth

chafe /tʃeɪf/ *v* [I,T] if you chafe part of your body, or if something chafes against it, the skin becomes sore because something is rubbing against it

chag·rin /'ʃægrɪn‖ʃə'grɪn/ *n* [U] *formal* when you feel disappointed and annoyed because

something has not happened the way you hoped

chain

link

chain¹ /tʃeɪn/ *n* **1** [C,U] a series of metal rings connected together in a line: *a delicate gold chain* | *The chandelier was suspended by a heavy chain.* **2** [C] a group of shops, hotels etc that are owned by the same person or company **3** [C] a series of similar things in a line: *a mountain chain* **4 chain of events** related events that happen one after the other: *the chain of events that caused World War I* **5 in chains** someone who is in chains has chains fastened around their legs or arms to prevent them from escaping → see also FOOD CHAIN

chain² *v* [T] to fasten one thing or person to another, using a chain: *John chained his bicycle to the fence.*

chain let·ter /'. ˌ../ *n* [C] a letter that is sent to several people who are asked to send copies to more people

chain re·ac·tion /ˌ. .'../ *n* [C] a number of related events or chemical changes which happen one after the other, each one causing the next one

chain-smoke /'. ./ *v* [I,T] to smoke cigarettes one after the other — **chain-smoker** *n* [C]

chain store /'../ *n* [C] one of a group of shops that are all owned by the same company

chairs

armchair

rocking chair

stool

wheelchair

deckchair

chair [1] /tʃeə‖tʃer/ n **1** [C] a piece of furniture for one person to sit on, which has a back, a seat, and four legs → see colour pictures on pages 80 and 474 **2** [singular] someone who is in charge of a meeting or a committee **3** [singular] **a)** BrE the position of being a PROFESSOR at a university **b)** AmE the person in charge of a department in a university

chair [2] v [T] to be the chairperson of a meeting or committee

chair·per·son /'tʃeə,pɜːsən‖'tʃer,pɜːrsən/ **chair·man** /-mən/ **chair·wom·an** /-,wumən/ n [C] **1** someone who is in charge of a meeting or committee **2** someone who is in charge of a large company or organization

USAGE NOTE: chairperson

Chairman can be used for both men and women, but many people prefer to use **chairperson** or **chair**, especially if the sex of the person is not known. **Chairwoman** can be used if the person is a woman.

chal·et /'ʃæleɪ‖ʃæ'leɪ/ n [C] a small wooden house with a steeply sloping roof

chalk [1] /tʃɔːk‖tʃɒːk/ n **1** [U] soft white rock **2** [C,U] small sticks of soft white rock used for writing or drawing → see colour picture on page 80 **3** like **chalk and cheese** BrE completely different from each other

chalk [2] v [I,T] to write or draw with chalk **chalk sth ↔ up** phr v [T] informal to succeed in winning or getting something: Yesterday they chalked up their third win of the season.

chalk·board /'tʃɔːkbɔːd‖'tʃɔːkbɔːrd/ n [C] a BLACKBOARD

chalk·y /'tʃɔːki‖'tʃɒː-/ adj similar to chalk, or containing chalk

chal·lenge [1] /'tʃælɪndʒ/ n **1** [C,U] something new, exciting, or difficult that needs a lot of skill and effort to do: the challenge of a new job | **meet a challenge** Let's work together to meet the challenge. **2** [C] an invitation from someone to compete or fight: **face a challenge** He faces another challenge for his WBO super-middleweight crown. **3** [C] when someone refuses to accept another person's authority, position, or ideas: **+ to** a direct challenge to Hague's leadership

challenge [2] v [T] **1** to say that you doubt whether something is right, fair, or legal, and try to persuade people to change it: She is challenging the decision made by the court. **2** to invite someone to compete against you or to test their ability to do something: We were challenged to a game of tennis. —**challenger** n [C]

chal·leng·ing /'tʃælɪndʒɪŋ/ adj a challenging job or activity is difficult to do, but is interesting and enjoyable because you have to use a lot of skill or effort: Teaching young children is a challenging and rewarding job.

cham·ber /'tʃeɪmbə‖-ər/ n [C] **1** a room used for a special purpose: We wanted to hear her speech but the council chamber was full. **2** a hollow space inside something such as your body or a machine: a gun with six chambers **3** one of the two parts of a parliament which is split into two different groups: The Senate is the upper chamber of Congress. **4** old-fashioned a bedroom or private room

cham·ber·maid /'tʃeɪmbəmeɪd‖-ər-/ n [C] a woman whose job is to clean and tidy bedrooms in a hotel

chamber mu·sic /'.. ,../ n [U] CLASSICAL music written for a small group of performers

cham·bers /'tʃeɪmbəz‖-ərz/ n [plural] the offices used by a judge or a BARRISTER

cha·me·le·on /kə'miːliən/ n [C] a small LIZARD whose skin changes and becomes the same colour as the things around it

champ /tʃæmp/ n [C] informal a CHAMPION

cham·pagne /ʃæm'peɪn/ n [U] a French white wine that has a lot of BUBBLES and is often drunk on special occasions

cham·pi·on [1] /'tʃæmpiən/ n [C] **1** a person, team etc that wins a competition, especially in sport **2** **champion of** someone who publicly fights for and defends an aim or principle: a champion of civil rights

champion [2] v [T] to publicly fight for the rights and aims of a group of people: He had championed the cause of the poor for many years.

cham·pi·on·ship /'tʃæmpiənʃɪp/ n **1** [C] a competition to find the best player or team in a particular sport: the US basketball championships **2** [singular] the position or title of being a champion

chance [1] /tʃɑːns‖tʃæns/ n **1** [C] a time or situation that you can use to do something that you want to do; OPPORTUNITY: **have/get a chance** Visitors will have a chance to look round the factory. | **give sb a chance** (=let them do sth): If you'll just give me a chance, I'll tell you what happened. | **+ of** That's our only chance of escape! **2** [U] when things happen without being planned: **by chance** We met by chance at a friend's party. **3** [C,U] the possibility that something will happen or that someone will succeed: **there's a chance (that)** There's a chance that we won't go anyway. | **have a chance** (=be likely to succeed): I don't have a chance of passing the test tomorrow. | **chances are** spoken (=it is likely): Chances are they're stuck in traffic. | **sb's chances** (=how likely someone is to succeed): What are Rachel's chances of getting the job? **4** **take a chance** to do something that involves a risk: I'm moving – I'm not taking any chances when the next earthquake hits. **5** **by any chance** spoken used in order to ask politely whether something is true: Are you Ms Sampson's daughter, by any chance? **6** **no chance!** spoken especially BrE used to emphasize that something will definitely not happen: "Perhaps Dad will lend us the car." "No chance!" → see also **stand a chance** (STAND [1])

USAGE NOTE: chance and opportunity

Use these words to talk about something you are able to do because of the situation you are in or because of luck: I had the opportunity to meet the leading actors. | He never had the chance to go to university. **Chance** can also mean a possibility: There's a chance I'll see him at the party.

chance [2] v **1** [T] informal to do something that involves a risk: **chance it** (=take a risk): We can chance it and try to get tickets there. **2** [I] literary to do something without intending or expecting to do it: He chanced to find the key under the mat.

chance³ *adj* not planned; accidental: *a chance meeting*

chan·cel·lor /ˈtʃɑːnsələ‖ˈtʃænsələr/ *n* [C]
1 the head of a university: *the Chancellor of UCLA* **2** the head of the government in some countries **3** also **Chancellor of the Exchequer** the British government minister in charge of taxes and government spending

chanc·y /ˈtʃɑːnsi‖ˈtʃænsi/ *adj informal* uncertain or involving risks

chan·de·lier /ˌʃændəˈlɪə‖-ˈlɪr/ *n* [C] a large decoration made of pieces of glass that hold lights or candles, which hangs from the ceiling

change¹ /tʃeɪndʒ/ *v* **1** [I,T] to become different, or make someone or something become different: *Susan has changed a lot since I last saw her.* | *The club has recently changed its rules.* | **change from sth to sth** *The traffic lights changed from green to red.* | **into** *Winter has finally changed into spring.* **2** [I,T] to stop having or doing one thing and start having or doing something else instead: *You'll have to change planes in Denver.* | **change (from sth) to sth** *it will be hard at first when we change to the new system, but it will be worth it.* | **change the subject** (=start talking about something else): *I'm sick of politics – let's change the subject.* **3 change your mind** to change your decision, plan, or opinion: *If you change your mind, let me know.* **4 a)** [I,T] to take off your clothes and put on different ones: *I'll just change my shoes, then we can go.* | **into/out of** *She changed into her old shabby jeans.* | **get changed** *It won't take me a minute to get changed.* **b)** [T] if you change a baby or change its NAPPY, you put clean dry clothes on it **5** [T] **a)** to exchange money from one country for money from another: *I want to change my dollars into pesos.* **b)** to exchange a larger unit of money for smaller units that add up to the same value: *Can you change a £20 note?* **6** [T] to take something back to the shop where you bought it and exchange it for something else **7** [T] if you change a bed, you put clean sheets on it **8 change hands** to become someone else's property: *The car has changed hands several times.*

change sth ↔ **around** *phr v* [T] to move things into different positions: *The room looks bigger since we changed the furniture around.*

change over *phr v* [I] to stop doing or using one thing and start doing or using something different: *Will the US ever change over to the metric system?*

USAGE NOTE: change

If you want to say that one thing replaces another, use **change of**: *There's been a change of plan.* | *There could be a change of government in the next election.* If you want to talk about changes that happen to someone or something, use **change in**: *recent changes in the law* | *There haven't been many changes in my father's attitude towards women.*

---

change² *n* **1** [C,U] the process by which something or someone becomes different, or the result of that process: **+ in** *a change in the weather* | **+ of** *a change of government* | **change of heart** (=a change in your opinion or attitude) **2** [C] something new that you have or use instead of something else: *Take a change of clothes with you.* **3** [C usually singular] something that is interesting or enjoyable because it is different from what is usual: **for a change** *Why don't we just stay home for a change?* | **make a change** *I'm nervous about flying, but it will make a change.* **4** [U] **a)** the money you get back when you have paid more than the price of something: *I got 50p change.* **b)** money in the form of coins: **in change** (=in coins) | **have change for** (=give someone coins in exchange for a note): *Do you have change for £5?*

change·a·ble /ˈtʃeɪndʒəbəl/ *adj* likely to change, or changing often: *changeable weather*

change·o·ver /ˈtʃeɪndʒˌəʊvə‖-ˌoʊvər/ *n* [C] a change from one activity or system to another: *the changeover from manual to computerised records*

chan·nel¹ /ˈtʃænl/ *n* [C] **1** a television station: *What's on Channel 4?* → compare STATION¹ **2** a long narrow area that water or other liquids can flow along: *an irrigation channel* **3** a deep part of a river, sea etc that ships can sail through **4** [usually plural] a system for obtaining information or communicating with people, or an official way for getting something done

channel² *v* [T] **-lled, -lling** *BrE*, **-led, -ling** *AmE*
1 to use something such as money or energy for a particular purpose: **+ into** *Roger needs to channel his creativity into something useful.* **2** to cut a channel into something, or to make a liquid go somewhere through a channel: *a device for channelling away the water*

channel hop·ping /ˈ.. ˌ../, also **channel surfing** *n* [U] when you change from one television channel to another several times to see what programmes are being shown

chant¹ /tʃɑːnt‖tʃænt/ *n* [C] **1** words or phrases that are repeated again and again: *a football chant* **2** a religious song with a regularly repeated tune, with many words sung on one note: *Gregorian chants*

chant² *v* **1** [I,T] to repeat a word or phrase again and again: *an angry crowd chanting slogans* **2** to sing or say a religious song or prayer in a way that involves singing phrases on one note

Cha·nu·kah /ˈhɑːnʊkə‖ˈkɑːnəkə, ˈhɑː-/ *n* [U] HANUKKAH

cha·os /ˈkeɪ-ɒs‖-ɑːs/ *n* [U] a state of complete disorganization and confusion: **in chaos** *The game ended in chaos with fans invading the field.*

cha·ot·ic /keɪˈɒtɪk‖-ˈɑːtɪk/ *adj* a situation that is chaotic is very disorganized and seems very confusing: *The classroom was chaotic, with kids shouting and throwing things.*

chap /tʃæp/ *n* [C] *BrE informal* a man, especially one you know and like: *a decent sort of chap*

chap·el /ˈtʃæpəl/ *n* [C] a small Christian church

chap·e·rone¹ /ˈʃæpərəʊn‖-roʊn/ *n* [C] an older person who in the past went to places with a young person, especially an unmarried woman, to take care of them and make sure that they behaved properly

chaperone² *v* [T] to go somewhere with someone as their chaperone

chap·lain /ˈtʃæplɪn/ *n* [C] a priest who works for the army, a hospital, a college etc

chapped /tʃæpt/ *adj* skin that is chapped is sore and cracked as a result of cold weather or wind: *chapped lips*

chap·ter /'tʃæptəll-ər/ *n* [C] **1** one of the parts a book is divided into **2** a particular period or event in someone's life or in history: + **in/of** *a remarkable chapter in human history*

char·ac·ter /'kærɪktəll-ər/ *n* **1** [C,U] all of the qualities that make a person, place, or thing different from any other: *There's a very serious side to her character.* **2** [U] the good qualities that make someone or something special and interesting: *an old house with a lot of character* **3** [C] a person in a book, play, film etc **4** [C] a particular kind of person: *Dan's a strange character.* **5** [C] an unusual and humorous person: *Charlie's such a character!* **6** [C] a letter, mark, or sign used in writing, printing, or COMPUTING: *Chinese characters*

char·ac·ter·is·tic[1] /ˌkærɪktə'rɪstɪk/ *n* [C] a quality or feature that someone or something typically has: *the characteristics of a good manager* | *Each wine has particular characteristics.*

characteristic[2] *adj* typical of a particular person or thing: *Mark, with characteristic kindness, offered to help.* —**characteristically** /-kli/ *adv*

char·ac·ter·ize (also **-ise** *BrE*) /'kærɪktəraɪz/ *v* [T] **1** to be a typical quality or feature of someone or something: *What kind of behaviour characterizes the criminal mind?* **2** to describe the character of someone or something in a particular way: + **as** *He has often been characterised as a born leader.* —**characterization** /ˌkærɪktəraɪ'zeɪʃənll-tərə-/ *n* [C,U]

cha·rade /ʃə'rɑːdllʃə'reɪd/ *n* [C] a situation in which people pretend that something is true or serious, but that everyone knows is not: *Their marriage is just a charade.*

char·coal /'tʃɑːkəʊll'tʃɑːrkoʊl/ *n* [U] a black substance made of burned wood, used for burning as FUEL or for drawing

charge[1] /tʃɑːdʒlltʃɑːrdʒ/ *n* **1** [C,U] the amount of money you have to pay for something: *There is a minimum charge of £2 for the service.* | **free of charge** (=at no cost): *We give it free of charge.* **2** be in charge to be the person who controls or is responsible for someone or something: *Rodriguez is in charge of the LA office.* **3** take charge to take control of someone or something: + **of** *Mrs Williams will take charge of the first lesson after lunch.* **4** [C] an official police statement saying that someone might be guilty of a crime: **on charges of** *George was being held on charges of second-degree murder.* | **bring/press charges** (=make an official statement saying that you think someone is guilty of a crime, with the result that they may have to go to a court of law): *Some women decide not to press charges because they do not want the pressure of a long court case.* **5** [C] an attack in which people or animals move forward quickly **6** [C] the amount of electricity in a BATTERY etc

charge[2] *v* **1** [I,T] to ask someone to pay a particular amount of money for something: *The lawyer only charged us £50.* | + **for** *How much do you charge for a haircut?* **2** [T] to record the cost of something on someone's bill, so that they can pay for it later: *Charge the room to my*

account. | **charge sth** *AmE* (=pay with a credit card): *"Would you like to pay in cash?" "No, I'll charge it."* **3** [T] to state officially that someone might be guilty of a crime: + **with** *Ron's been charged with assault.* **4** [I,T] to run towards someone or something to attack them: *When the soldiers charged, the protesters ran away.* **5** [I,T] to put electricity into a piece of electrical equipment such as a BATTERY

charge card /'. ./ *n* [C] **1** *BrE* a plastic card that you can use to buy things in one particular shop and pay for them later **2** a CREDIT CARD

charged /tʃɑːdʒdlltʃɑːrdʒd/ *adj* a charged situation is filled with strong emotions: *Funerals are emotionally charged events.*

char·i·ot /'tʃæriət/ *n* [C] a vehicle with two wheels pulled by a horse, used in ancient times in battles and races

cha·ris·ma /kə'rɪzmə/ *n* [U] the natural ability to attract and influence other people —**charismatic** /ˌkærɪz'mætɪk/ *adj*

char·i·ta·ble /'tʃærɪtəbəl/ *adj* **1** charitable organizations give money or help to people who need them **2** kind and generous —**charitably** *adv*

char·i·ty /'tʃærɪti/ *n* **1** [C,U] an organization or the organizations that give money or help to people who need them: *Several charities sent aid to the flood victims.* | *All profits from the book will go to charity.* **2** [U] money or gifts given to people who need help: *Many homeless people depend on charity to survive.*

charity shop /'... ,./ *n* [C] *BrE* a shop that sells used things, especially clothes, at a cheap price, in order to make money for a charity, a church etc; THRIFT SHOP *AmE*

char·la·tan /'ʃɑːlətənll'ʃɑːr-/ *n* [C] someone who pretends to have special skills or knowledge

charm[1] /tʃɑːmlltʃɑːrm/ *n* **1** [C,U] the special quality someone or something has that makes people like them: *This town has a charm you couldn't find in a big city.* **2** [C] an object, phrase, or action believed to have special magic powers: *a lucky charm* **3** work like a charm to work exactly as you had hoped

charm[2] *v* [T] to make someone like you: *He was absolutely charmed by her dazzling smile.* —**charmer** *n* [C]

charmed /tʃɑːmdlltʃɑːrmd/ *adj* lucky because good things happen to you: **a charmed life/existence** *Why was she so unhappy when she had such a charmed life?*

charm·ing /'tʃɑːmɪŋll'tʃɑːr-/ *adj* very pleasing or attractive: *What a charming house!* —**charmingly** *adv*

charred /tʃɑːdlltʃɑːrd/ *adj* black from having been burned: *Firemen had to drag the charred bodies out of the wreck.* —**char** *v* [I,T]

chart[1] /tʃɑːtlltʃɑːrt/ *n* [C] **1** information that is shown in the form of a picture, GRAPH etc: *a weather chart* **2** the charts a list of the most popular records: *That song has been at the top of the charts for over 6 weeks.* **3** a detailed map of the sea or stars

chart[2] *v* [T] **1** to record information about a situation or set of events over a period of time: *Teachers are attempting to chart each student's progress through the year.* **2** to make a map of an area of land, sea, or sky

char·ter¹ /ˈtʃɑːtəǁˈtʃɑːrtər/ n [C] a statement of the principles, duties, and purposes of an organization: *the charter of the United Nations*

charter² v [T] to pay a company for the use of a boat, plane etc: *We'll have to charter a bus for the trip.*

chase¹ /tʃeɪs/ v **1** [I,T] to run after someone or something to catch them: *He chased after her to return her bag.* | *a cat chasing a mouse* **2** to make someone or something leave: **+ away** *I chased the dog away from the rose bushes.* **3** [I] to rush or hurry somewhere: **+ in/around/up etc** *Those kids are always chasing in and out!* **4** [I,T] to try very hard to get something you want: *There are too many people chasing a limited number of jobs.*

chase² n **1** [C] the act of following someone or something quickly to catch them: *a car chase* **2 give chase** *literary* to chase someone or something

chas·m /ˈkæzəm/ n **1** [singular] a big difference between different ideas or groups of people: **+ between** *the chasm between rich and poor people* **2** a very deep hole between two areas of rock or ice

chas·sis /ˈʃæsi/ n [C] *plural* **chassis** /ˈʃæsiːz/ the frame on which the body of a vehicle is built

chaste /tʃeɪst/ *adj old-fashioned* morally pure, especially by not having sex — **chastely** *adv*

chas·ten /ˈtʃeɪsən/ v [T] *formal* to make someone realize that their behaviour is wrong: *The experience had clearly chastened her.*

chas·tise /tʃæˈstaɪz/ v [T] *formal* to criticize or punish someone severely

chas·ti·ty /ˈtʃæstɨ̥ti/ n [U] when someone does not have sex and does not behave in a sexually immoral way: *Catholic priests must take a vow of chastity.*

chat¹ /tʃæt/ v [I] **-tted, -tting** to talk in a friendly and informal way
chat sb up *phr v* [T] *BrE informal* to talk to someone in a way that shows you think they are sexually attractive

chat² n [C,U] a friendly informal conversation

chât·eau /ˈʃætəuǁʃæˈtou/ n [C], *plural* **châteaux** or **châteaus** a castle or large country house in France

chat show /ˈ. ./ n [C] *BrE* a television or radio show on which people are asked questions and talk about themselves; TALK SHOW

chat·ter /ˈtʃætəǁ-ər/ v [I] **1** to talk a lot about things that are not important: *Anna chattered on and on.* **2** if your teeth chatter, they knock together because you are cold or afraid — **chatter** n [U]

chat·ty /ˈtʃæti/ *adj informal* **1** liking to talk a lot **2** having a friendly informal style: *a chatty letter*

chauf·feur /ˈʃəufə, ʃəuˈfɜːǁˈʃoufər, ʃouˈfɜːr/ n [C] someone whose job is to drive a car for someone else — **chauffeur** v [T]

chau·vin·ist /ˈʃəuvɨ̥nɨ̥stǁˈʃou-/ n [C] **1** someone who believes that their country is better than other countries **2** a man who thinks that men are better than women — **chauvinism** n [U] — **chauvinistic** /ˌʃəuvɨ̥ˈnɪstɪkǁˌʃou-/ *adj*

cheap¹ /tʃiːp/ *adj* **1** not expensive, or less expensive than you expect: *The fruit there is really cheap.* | *a car that's cheap to run* **2** low in price and of bad quality: *a cheap plastic handbag* **3** *AmE* not liking to spend money; MEAN *BrE*: *He's so cheap we didn't even go out on my birthday.* — **cheaply** *adv* — **cheapness** n [U]

cheap² *adv informal* at a low price: *I was lucky to get it so cheap.* | **be/going cheap** (=selling for a lower price than normal)

cheap·en /ˈtʃiːpən/ v **1** [T] to do something that makes you feel ashamed: *Don't cheapen yourself by answering his insults.* **2** [T] to become or make something become lower in value or price: *The dollar's rise in value has cheapened imports.*

cheap·skate /ˈtʃiːpskeɪt/ n [C] *informal* someone who does not like spending money or giving gifts

cheat

Mike was cheating in the Spanish test.

cheat¹ /tʃiːt/ v **1** [I] to behave in a dishonest way in order to win or get something: *He always cheats when we play cards.* | *Dana was caught cheating in her history test.* **2** [T] to trick or deceive someone: **cheat sb out of sth** *Miller cheated the old woman out of all her money.* **3 feel cheated** to feel that you have been treated wrongly or unfairly
cheat on sb *phr v* [T] if you cheat on your husband, girlfriend etc, you have sex with someone else: *I think Dan's cheating on Debbie again.*

cheat² n [C] someone who cheats: *You're a liar and a cheat!*

check¹ /tʃek/ v **1** [I,T] to do something in order to make sure that everything is correct or the way you expect it : *"Did Barry lock the back door?" "I don't know, I'll check."* | **+ (that)** *Please check that you have handed in your homework before you leave.* | **+ for** *Check the eggs for cracks before you buy them.* | **+ whether/if** *Can you check whether we have any milk?* | **double check** (=check something twice) **2** [I] to ask permission to do something or to ask whether something is possible: **+ with** *I'll just check with Mom to see if I can come over to your house.* | **+ whether/if** *You'll have to check if there's room in*

GRAMMAR NOTE: direct and indirect speech
There are two ways of reporting what someone said:
DIRECT SPEECH (using "..."): **"I forgot** to phone you," she said, **"I am** really sorry."
INDIRECT SPEECH: She said that she **had forgotten** to phone me and she **was** really sorry.

the car for you first. **3** [T] to stop something bad from getting worse: *We hope the new drug will help check the spread of the disease.* **4** [T] *AmE* to put someone's bags, coat etc in a special place where they can be kept safe: *Can I check that for you, sir?*

check in *phr v* [I,T] to go to the desk at a hotel, airport etc and say that you have arrived: *Passengers should check in an hour before departure.*

check sth ↔ **off** *phr v* [T] to put a mark next to something on a list to show that you have finished dealing with it: *Check their names off the list as they arrive.*

check on sb/sth ↔ *phr v* [T] also **check up on** to make sure that someone is doing what they are supposed to be doing, or that something is how it should be: *I'll just go check on dinner.* | *Mom is always checking up on me.*

check out *phr v* **1** [T **check** sth ↔ **out**] *informal* to make sure that something is true, correct, or acceptable: *You should check out his story before you print it.* **2** [I] to pay the bill and leave a hotel: *We have to check out by 12 o'clock.* **3** [T **check** sth ↔ **out**] *especially AmE* to borrow books from a library

check² *n* **1** [C] an examination to find out if something is correct, true, or safe: *a security check* | **do/run a check** (=find out information about): *I'll have them run a check on this blood sample.* **2** [C] the American spelling of CHEQUE **3** [C,U] something that controls something else and prevents it from becoming too large or getting worse: **hold/keep sth in check** *I was barely able to hold my temper in check.* **4** [C] *AmE* a list that you are given in a restaurant that shows how much you have to pay for your meal; BILL **5** [C,U] a pattern of coloured squares: *a tablecloth with red and white checks* **6** [C] *AmE* a mark (✓) that you put next to an answer to show that it is correct or next to something on a list etc to show that you have noticed it; TICK *BrE* **7** [U] the position of the KING in a game of CHESS when it can be directly attacked by the other player's pieces

check·book /ˈtʃekbʊk/ *n* [C] the American spelling of CHEQUEBOOK *BrE*

checked /tʃekt/ *adj* having a regular pattern of different coloured squares: *a checked shirt* → see colour picture on page 114

check·ered also **chequered** *BrE* /ˈtʃekəd‖-ərd/ *adj* marked with squares of two different colours: *a checkered flag*

check·ers /ˈtʃekəz‖-ərz/ *n* [U] *AmE* a game for two players, using 12 flat round pieces each and a special board with 64 squares; DRAUGHTS *BrE*

checking ac·count /ˈ.. .,./ *n* [C] *AmE* a bank account that you can take money out of at any time; CURRENT ACCOUNT *BrE*

check·list /ˈtʃek,lɪst/ *n* [C] a list that helps to remind you of all the things you have to do for a particular job or activity

check·mate /ˈtʃekmeɪt/ *n* [U] the final move in a game of CHESS when the KING is directly attacked and cannot escape

check·out /ˈtʃek-aʊt/ also **checkout coun·ter** /ˈ.. ,./ *AmE* — *n* [C] the place in a SUPERMARKET where you pay for goods

check·point /ˈtʃekpɔɪnt/ *n* [C] a place where

an official person stops people and vehicles to examine them

check·up, check-up /ˈtʃek-ʌp/ *n* [C] an occasion when a doctor or DENTIST examines you to see if you are healthy: *Dentists recommend regular check-ups to help prevent tooth decay.*

ched·dar /ˈtʃedəʲ-ər/ *n* [U] a firm smooth yellow or orange cheese

cheek /tʃiːk/ *n* **1** [C] one of the two soft round parts of your face below your eyes: *He kissed her lightly on the cheek.* → see picture at HEAD¹ **2** [singular, U] *BrE* rude and annoying behaviour that shows a lack of respect for someone: **have the cheek to do sth** (=do something that seems rude and surprising): *He had the cheek to ask me for more money.*

cheek·bone /ˈtʃiːkbəʊn‖-boʊn/ *n* [C] the bone just below your eye

cheek·y /ˈtʃiːki/ *adj BrE* behaving in a way that seems a little rude, or doing something that you should not do, especially when this seems amusing: *a chubby little boy with a cheeky grin*

cheer¹ /tʃɪəʲ-ɪr/ *v* [I,T] to shout approval, encouragement etc: *The audience cheered as the band began to play.*

cheer sb/sth ↔ **on** *phr v* [T] to encourage a person or a team by cheering for them: *Highbury Stadium was packed with fans cheering on the home team.*

cheer sb **up** *phr v* [I,T] to become happier, or to make someone feel happier: *She took him out to dinner to cheer him up.*

cheer² *n* [C] a shout of approval, happiness, or encouragement

cheer·ful /ˈtʃɪəfəl‖-ˈtʃɪr-/ *adj* **1** happy and showing this by your behaviour: *Pat is keeping remarkably cheerful despite being in a lot of pain.* **2** bright, pleasant, and making you feel happy: *a cheerful kitchen* —**cheerfully** *adv* —**cheerfulness** *n* [U]

cheer·lead·er /ˈtʃɪə,liːdəʲ-ˈtʃɪr,liːdər/ *n* [C] a member of a team of young women that encourages a crowd to cheer at a sports event

cheer·less /ˈtʃɪələs‖-ˈtʃɪr-/ *adj* cheerless weather, places, or times make you feel sad and bored: *a cheerless winter day*

cheers /tʃɪəz‖tʃɪrz/ *interjection* **1** what you say just before you drink a glass of alcohol with someone, to show friendly feelings towards them **2** *BrE informal* thank you

cheer·y /ˈtʃɪəri‖-ˈtʃɪri/ *adj* smiling and cheerful: *a little boy with a cheery smile* —**cheerily** *adv*

cheese /tʃiːz/ *n* [C,U] a solid food made from milk, that is usually white or yellow → see colour picture on page 440

cheese·cake /ˈtʃiːzkeɪk/ *n* [C,U] a sweet cake made with soft white cheese

chees·y /ˈtʃiːzi/ *adj AmE informal* cheap and not of good quality, or not sincere: *a really cheesy movie*

chee·tah /ˈtʃiːtə/ *n* [C] an African wild cat that has black spots and is able to run very fast

chef /ʃef/ *n* [C] the chief cook in a restaurant

chem·i·cal¹ /ˈkemɪkəl/ *adj* related to substances used in chemistry, or involving the changes that happen when two substances combine: *a chemical reaction* —**chemically** /-kli/ *adv*

chemical² n [C] a substance used in or produced by a chemical process

chem·ist /'kemɪst/ n [C] **1** a scientist who does work related to chemistry: *a research chemist* **2** BrE someone who is trained to prepare drugs and medicines for sale in a shop → compare PHARMACIST

chem·is·try /'kemɪstri/ n [U] **1** the science of studying chemicals and what happens to them when they change or combine with each other **2** the way substances combine in a process, thing, person etc: *This drug causes changes to the body's chemistry.*

chem·ist's /'kemɪsts/ n [C] BrE a shop where you can buy medicines, beauty products etc: DRUGSTORE AmE → compare PHARMACY

cheque /tʃek/ n [C] BrE a printed piece of paper that you sign and use to pay for things; CHECK AmE: **+ for** *a cheque for £350* | **pay by cheque** (=with a cheque): *Can I pay by cheque?*

cheque·book /'tʃekbʊk/ n [C] BrE a small book of cheques; CHECKBOOK AmE

chequ·ered /'tʃekədǁ-ərd/ a British spelling of CHECKERED

cher·ish /'tʃerɪʃ/ v [T] **1** to take care of someone or something you love very much **2** to be very important to someone: **cherished hopes/ dreams etc** *cherished memories of family Christmases*

cher·ry /'tʃeri/ n **1** [C] a small round soft red fruit with a large seed → see picture at FRUIT **2** [C,U] a tree that produces cherries, or the wood from this tree

cher·ub /'tʃerəb/ n [C] an ANGEL shown in paintings as a small child with wings

chess /tʃes/ n [U] a board game for two players in which you must trap your opponent's KING in order to win

chest /tʃest/ n **1** [C] the front part of your body between your neck and stomach **2** [C] a large strong box with a lid, that you use to keep things in: *We keep our blankets in a cedar chest.* **3 get sth off your chest** to tell someone about something that has worried or annoyed you for a long time

chest·nut /'tʃesnʌt/ n **1** [C] a smooth red-brown nut you can eat **2** [C] the tree on which these nuts grow **3** [U] a dark red-brown colour — **chestnut** adj

chest of drawers /ˌ. . './ n [C] a piece of furniture with drawers, used for keeping clothes in; BUREAU AmE:

chest of drawers

chew /tʃuː/ v [I,T] **1** to crush food with your teeth before swallowing it: *The dentist said I wouldn't be able to chew anything for a while.* **2** to bite something several times without eating it: *Stop chewing on your pencil!*

chew sb out phr v [T] AmE informal to speak angrily to someone who has done something wrong: *My boss chewed me out for being late.*

chew sth ↔ over phr v [T] to think carefully about a problem, idea etc

chewing gum /'. . ./ n [U] also **gum** a type of sweet that you chew for a long time, but do not swallow

chew·y /'tʃuːi/ adj needing to be chewed a lot before it can be swallowed: *chewy toffee*

chic /ʃiːk/ adj fashionable and showing good style

chick /tʃɪk/ n [C] a baby bird, especially a baby chicken

chick·a·dee /ˌtʃɪkə'diː/ n [C] a small North American bird with a black head

chick·en¹ /'tʃɪkɪn/ n **1** [C] a farm bird that is kept for its meat and eggs **2** [U] the meat from a chicken: *roast chicken*

chicken² adj informal not brave enough to do something: *Are you chicken? Is that why you won't come with us?*

chicken³ v

chicken out phr v [I] informal to decide not to do something because you are not brave enough: *He wanted to try a parachute jump, but he chickened out at the last minute.*

chicken pox /'tʃɪkɪn ˌpɒksǁ-ˌpɑːks/ n [U] a common illness that children get, that causes a fever and red spots on the skin

chic·o·ry /'tʃɪkəri/ n [C] a plant with leaves that are eaten without being cooked

chide /tʃaɪd/ v [T] literary to speak angrily to someone because they have done something wrong

chief¹ /tʃiːf/ adj [only before noun] **1** more important than anything else: *Our chief concern is for the safety of the children.* **2** highest in rank: *the chief political reporter for the Washington Post*

chief² n [C] the leader of a group or organization: **+ of** *the chief of police*

chief·ly /'tʃiːfli/ adv mainly: *a book that is intended chiefly for students of art*

chief·tain /'tʃiːftən/ n [C] the leader of a tribe

chif·fon /'ʃɪfɒnǁʃɪ'fɑːn/ n [U] soft very thin cloth used for making women's clothing

chil·blain /'tʃɪlbleɪn/ n [C] a painful red area on the skin, that is caused by being cold

child /tʃaɪld/ n [C] plural **children** /'tʃɪldrən/ **1** a young person who is not yet fully grown: *There are over 30 children in each class.* | *a five-year-old child* **2** a son or daughter: *Both our children are married now.* | **an only child** (=someone with no sisters or brothers) → see picture at FAMILY **3 be child's play** to be very easy to do: *Learning French had been child's play compared with learning Arabic.*

child·bear·ing /'tʃaɪld,beərɪŋǁ-,ber-/ n [U] **1** the process of giving birth to children **2 childbearing age** the period of a woman's life during which she can have babies

child ben·e·fit /ˌ. '.../ n [U] money that the British government gives every week to families with children

child·birth /'tʃaɪldbɜːθǁ-bɜːrθ/ n [U] the process in which a baby is born

child·care /'tʃaɪldkeəǁ-ker/ n [U] an arrangement in which someone looks after children whose parents are at work

child·hood /'tʃaɪldhʊd/ n [C,U] the time when you are a child: *Sara had a very happy childhood.*

child·ish /'tʃaɪldɪʃ/ adj **1** an adult who is childish behaves in a silly way, like a small child: *Stop being so childish.* **2** typical of a child: *a childish voice* —**childishly** *adv* —**childishness** *n* [U]

child·less /'tʃaɪldləs/ *adj* having no children: *childless couples*

child·like /'tʃaɪldlaɪk/ *adj* having the good qualities of a child, such as natural or trusting behaviour: *childlike innocence*

child·min·der /'tʃaɪld,maɪndəll-ər/ *n* [C] *BrE* someone who looks after young children while their parents are at work —**childminding** *n* [U]

child·proof /'tʃaɪldpruːf/ *adj* designed to prevent a child from being hurt: *All medicine bottles should have childproof caps.*

chil·dren /'tʃɪldrən/ *n* the plural of CHILD

> **USAGE NOTE: child, baby, infant, toddler, teenager,** and **kid**
>
> **Baby** and **infant** are both words for a very young child who was born not long ago, but the word **infant** is much more formal. A child who has just learned to walk is a **toddler**. Children aged 13 to 19 are **teenagers**. **Kid** is an informal word meaning a child or young person.

child sup·port /'. .,./ *n* [U] money that someone pays regularly to their former wife or husband in order to help look after their children; MAINTENANCE *BrE*

chill[1] /tʃɪl/ *v* **1** [T] to make something or someone cold: *Champagne should be chilled before serving* . **2** [I] *informal* also **chill out** to relax instead of feeling angry or nervous: *Chill out, Dave, it doesn't matter.*

chill[2] *n* **1** [singular] a feeling of coldness: *There was a chill in the early morning air.* **2** [C] a sudden feeling of fear: *a threatening look in his eyes that sent a chill down my spine* **3** [C] a slight illness like a cold

chil·li *BrE*, **chili** *AmE* /'tʃɪli/ *n* **1** [C,U] a small thin red or green vegetable with a very hot taste: *chilli sauce* **2** [U] a dish made with beans, meat, and chillies

chil·ling /'tʃɪlɪŋ/ *adj* making you feel frightened: *a chilling report about the spread of a terrible new disease*

chill·y /'tʃɪli/ *adj* **1** cold enough to make you feel uncomfortable: *a chilly morning*|*the chilly waiting-room* **2** behaving in an unfriendly way: *She was polite but chilly and formal.*

chime /tʃaɪm/ *v* [I,T] if a clock or bell chimes, it makes a ringing sound: *The clock chimed six.* —**chime** *n* [C]

chime *phr v* [I] to say something in order to add your opinion to a conversation: *"The kids could go too," Maria chimed in.*

chim·ney /'tʃɪmni/ *n* [C] a wide pipe that takes smoke up from a fire and out through the roof: *factory chimneys* → see colour picture on page 79

chimney sweep /'.. ./ *n* [C] someone whose job is to clean the inside of chimneys

chim·pan·zee /,tʃɪmpæn'ziː, -pən-/ also **chimp** /tʃɪmp/ *informal n* [C] an African animal like a monkey

chin /tʃɪn/ *n* [C] the front part of your face below your mouth → see picture at HEAD[1]

chi·na /'tʃaɪnə/ *n* [U] **1** a hard white substance used for making plates, cups etc

2 plates, cups, and dishes made from china: *the cupboard where we keep our best china*

chink /tʃɪŋk/ *n* [C] **1** a narrow crack or hole in something: *I could see light through a chink in the wall.* **2** a short ringing sound made by objects touching each other: *the chink of glasses*

chin·os /'tʃiːnəʊzll-noʊz/ *n* [plural] loose trousers made from cotton

chintz /tʃɪnts/ *n* [U] smooth cotton cloth with flower patterns on it: *chintz covers on the chairs*

chip[1] /tʃɪp/ *n* [C] **1** *BrE* a long thin piece of potato cooked in oil; FRENCH FRY *AmE*: *fish and chips* **2** *AmE* a thin dry piece of fried (FRY) potato eaten cold; CRISP *BrE*: *barbecue flavor potato chips* **3** a small piece of SILICON with electronic parts on it, that is used in computers; MICROCHIP **4** a small piece of wood, stone etc that has broken off something: *a path of limestone chips* **5** a crack or mark left when a small piece is broken off something: *Look, this vase has a chip in it* **6 have a chip on your shoulder** *informal* to have an angry attitude to life because you think you have been treated unfairly in the past: *He's always had a chip on his shoulder about not going to college.* **7** a small flat coloured piece of plastic used in GAMBLING games instead of money **8 be a chip off the old block** *informal* to be like one of your parents in the way that you look or behave **9 when the chips are down** *informal* when there is a serious situation → see also BLUE-CHIP

chip[2] *v* [T] to break a small piece off something: *She chipped a tooth on an olive stone.* —**chipped** *adj*: *a chipped cup*

chip sth ↔ **away** *phr v* [T] to break small pieces off something: *Sandy chipped away the plaster covering the tiles.*

chip away at sth *phr v* [T] **1** to gradually reduce or damage something: *Government policies were chipping away at the rights of workers.* **2** to break small pieces off something

chip in *phr v* **1** [I] to interrupt a conversation by saying something: *The whole family chipped in with suggestions.* **2** [I,T **chip in** sth] to give some money to add to what other people are giving: *Clare's classmates have chipped in more than $100 to help her buy the wheelchair.*

chip·munk /'tʃɪpmʌŋk/ *n* [C] a small brown North American animal like a SQUIRREL, that has black and white lines on its fur

chip·per /'tʃɪpəll-ər/ *adj especially AmE* happy and healthy

chi·rop·o·dist /kɪ'rɒpədɪst, ʃɪ-ll-'rɑː-/ *n* [C] *BrE* someone whose job is to treat and care for people's feet; PODIATRIST *AmE* —**chiropody** *n* [U]

chirp /tʃɜːplltʃɜːrp/ *v* [I] if a bird or insect chirps, it makes short high sounds: *sparrows chirping in the trees* —**chirp** *n* [C]

chirp·y /'tʃɜːpillltʃɜːrpi/ *adj BrE informal* cheerful: *You seem very chirpy this morning,*

chis·el /'tʃɪzəl/ *n* [C] a metal tool with a sharp end, used for cutting into wood or stone → see picture at TOOLS

chit /tʃɪt/ *n* [C] a short note that shows how much money someone owes or has paid

chit-chat /'. ./ *n* [U] *informal* informal conversation about unimportant things

chiv·al·rous /'ʃɪvəlrəs/ *adj formal* a man who

is chivalrous behaves politely and kindly to women —**chivalry** n [U]

chives /tʃaɪvz/ n [plural] a plant with long thin leaves that taste like onion, used in cooking

chlo·rine /'klɔːriːn/ n [U] a yellow-green gas that is used to keep swimming pools clean

chlo·ro·fluo·ro·car·bon /ˌklɔːrəʊˌfluərəʊ-'kɑːbən‖ˌklɔːrəʊˌflʊərəʊ'kɑːr-/ n [C] technical a CFC

chlor·o·form /'klɒrəfɔːm,'klɔː-‖'klɔːrəfɔːrm/ n [U] a liquid with a strong smell that was used by doctors in the past to make a person unconscious

chock-a-block /ˌtʃɒk ə 'blɒk‖'tʃɑːk ə ˌblɑːk/ adj **be chock-a-block (with sth)** to be full of people or things that are very close together

chock-full /ˌ. '.‹/ adj informal completely full or containing a very large amount of something: + **of** a fruit drink that is chock-full of vitamins

choco·late /'tʃɒklət‖'tʃɑːkələt, 'tʃɔːk-/ n **1** [U] a sweet brown food often sold in a block: a chocolate bar | chocolate ice cream → see colour picture on page 440 **2** [C] a small piece of sweet food covered with chocolate: a box of chocolates **3** [U] a drink made from hot milk and chocolate

choice[1] /tʃɔɪs/ n **1** [singular, U] the right to choose or the chance to choose between two or more things: If you had a choice, where would you want to live? | The prizewinner was given a choice between £10,000 and a cruise. | **have no choice** He had no choice but to move back into his parents' house. **2** [C] a decision to choose one thing or person rather than another: It was a difficult choice, but we finally decided Hannah was the best. | **make a choice** I hope I've made the right choice. **3** [singular, U] all the different things or people you can choose from: + **of** The supermarket offers a choice of different foods. | **have a choice** You will have a choice of five questions in the test. | **a wide choice** (=a lot of things to choose from): There is a wide choice of hotels. **4** [C usually singular] the person or thing that someone has chosen: **first choice** (=the thing you wanted most): Going to Hawaii was our first choice, but we couldn't really afford it. **5** **by choice** if you do something by choice, you do it because you want to: Do you really believe that people are homeless by choice?

choice[2] adj of high quality: choice plums

choir /kwaɪə‖kwaɪr/ n [C] a group of people who sing together, especially in a church or school: Susan sings in the school choir.

choke[1] /tʃəʊk‖tʃoʊk/ v **1** [I,T] to prevent someone from breathing or be prevented from breathing, because the throat is blocked or because there is not enough air: The fumes were choking me. | + **on** Leila nearly choked on a fish bone. **2** [T] to fill a road, pipe etc completely and block it: **be choked with** The roads were choked with traffic.

choke sth ↔ **back** phr v [T] to control yourself so that you do not show how angry, sad etc you are: Anna choked back the tears as she tried to speak.

choke up phr v [I] **be choked up** to feel such strong emotions about something that you are almost crying: Bill wanted to thank him, but he was too choked up to speak.

choke[2] n [C] **1** a part of a car that controls the amount of air going into the engine **2** the act or sound of choking

chok·er /'tʃəʊkə‖'tʃoʊkər/ n [C] a piece of jewellery or narrow cloth that fits closely around your neck

chol·e·ra /'kɒlərə‖'kɑː-/ n [U] a serious disease that affects the stomach and BOWELS

cho·les·te·rol /kə'lestərɒl‖-roʊl/ n [U] a substance in your body which doctors think may cause heart disease

choose /tʃuːz/ v chose /tʃəʊz‖tʃoʊz/, chosen /'tʃəʊzən‖'tʃoʊ-/, choosing [I,T] **1** to decide which one of several things or possibilities you want: Will you help me choose a present for Dad? | + **what/which/whether etc** We were free to choose whatever we wanted. | **choose sb to do sth** They chose Roy to be the team captain. | + **between/from** The students had to choose between doing geography or studying another language. **2** to decide to do something: **choose to do sth** Donna chose to stop working after she had the baby. **3** **there is little/nothing to choose between** used to say that two or more things are equally good

choos·y /'tʃuːzi/ adj difficult to please: Jean's very choosy about what she eats.

chop[1] /tʃɒp‖tʃɑːp/ v -pped, -pping [T] **1** also **chop** sth ↔ **up** to cut something, especially food, into small pieces: Shall I chop these onions up? | **chop** sth **into** Chop the tomatoes into fairly large pieces. → see colour picture on page 439 **2** [T] to cut wood into pieces using a tool with a long handle and a sharp blade: Greta was out chopping wood for the fire. **3** **chop and change** BrE informal to keep changing your opinion

chop sth ↔ **down** phr v [T] to make a tree fall down by chopping it

chop sth ↔ **off** phr v [T] to cut part of something away from the rest of it by hitting it with a sharp tool: Be careful you don't chop your fingers off.

chop[2] n [C] **1** a small flat piece of meat on a bone: a pork chop **2** a quick hard hit with the side of your hand or with a heavy sharp tool: a karate chop

chop·per /'tʃɒpə‖'tʃɑːpər/ n [C] **1** informal a HELICOPTER **2** a heavy tool with a sharp blade used for cutting meat, wood etc

chop·py /'tʃɒpi‖'tʃɑːpi/ adj choppy water has a lot of waves, especially because the weather is windy

chop·sticks /'tʃɒpstɪks‖'tʃɑːp-/ n [plural] a pair of thin sticks used for eating food in China, Japan etc

cho·ral /'kɔːrəl/ adj choral music is intended to be sung by a CHOIR

chord /kɔːd‖kɔːrd/ n [C] a combination of two or more musical notes played at the same time

---

chore /tʃɔːlltʃɔːr/ *n* [C] a job that you have to do, especially one that is boring: *household chores*

chor·e·og·ra·phy /ˌkɒriˈɒgrəfi, ˌkɔːllˌkɔːriˈɑːg-/ *n* [U] the art of arranging how dancers should move during a performance —**choreographer** *n* [C] —**choreograph** /ˈkɒriəgrɑːf, ˈkɔːllˈkɔːriəgræf/ *v* [I,T]

chor·tle /ˈtʃɔːtlllˈtʃɔːrtl/ *v* [I] to laugh in a low voice —**chortle** *n* [C]

cho·rus /ˈkɔːrəs/ *n* [C] **1** the part of a song that is repeated after each VERSE **2** a group of people who sing together **3** a piece of music written to be sung by a large group of people: *the Hallelujah Chorus* **4 the chorus** the group of singers and dancers in a show, who do not have the main parts **5 a chorus of thanks/ disapproval/criticism etc** something said or expressed by a lot of people at the same time

chose /tʃəʊzlltʃoʊz/ *v* the past tense of CHOOSE

cho·sen /ˈtʃəʊzənllˈtʃoʊ-/ *v* the past participle of CHOOSE

Christ¹ /kraɪst/ *n* Jesus Christ, the man on whose life, death, and teaching the Christian religion is based

Christ² *interjection informal* used to express anger or surprise: *Christ! Can't you leave me alone?*

chris·ten /ˈkrɪsən/ *v* [T] **be christened** to be given your name at a Christian religious ceremony soon after you are born: *She was christened Elizabeth Ann.*

chris·ten·ing /ˈkrɪsənɪŋ/ *n* [C] a Christian ceremony in which a baby is given a name

Chris·tian¹ /ˈkrɪstʃən, -tiən/ *adj* based on Christianity, or believing in it: *Christian beliefs | the Christian Church*

Christian² *n* [C] someone whose religion is Christianity

Chris·ti·an·i·ty /ˌkrɪstiˈænᵻti/ *n* [U] the religion that is based on the life and teaching of Jesus Christ

Christian name /ˈ.. ./ *n* [C] your first name

Christ·mas /ˈkrɪsməs/ *n* [C,U] **1** a Christian holiday on December 25th that celebrates the birth of Christ, when people give and receive gifts **2** the period of a few days just before, after, and including this day: *What did you do over Christmas?*

Christmas car·ol /ˌ.. ˈ../ *n* [C] a Christian song sung at Christmas

Christmas Day /ˌ.. ˈ./ *n* [C,U] December 25th, the day on which Christians celebrate the birth of Christ

Christmas Eve /ˌ.. ˈ./ *n* [C,U] the day before Christmas Day

Christmas tree /ˈ.. ./ *n* [C] a tree that you put inside your house and decorate for Christmas

chrome /krəʊmllkroʊm/ also **chro·mi·um** /ˈkrəʊmiəmllˈkroʊ-/ *n* [U] a hard metal substance used for covering objects with a shiny surface: *doors with chrome handles*

chro·mo·some /ˈkrəʊməsəʊmllˈkroʊməsoʊm/ *n* [C] *technical* a part of every living cell, which

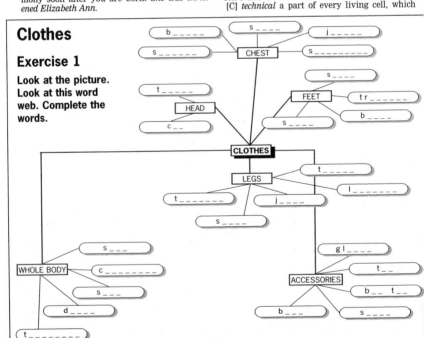

Clothes

Exercise 1

Look at the picture. Look at this word web. Complete the words.

CHEST — b _ _ _ _ _, s _ _ _ _, j _ _ _ _ _, s _ _ _ _ _ _, s _ _ _ _ _ _ _ _

HEAD — t _ _ _ _ _, c _ _

FEET — s _ _ _ _, t r _ _ _ _ _ _, b _ _ _, s _ _ _ _

CLOTHES

LEGS — t _ _ _ _ _, l _ _ _, t _ _ _ _ _ _, j _ _ _ _, s _ _ _

WHOLE BODY — s _ _ _, c _ _ _ _ _ _ _, s _ _, d _ _ _, t _ _ _ _ _ _ _

ACCESSORIES — g l _ _ _ _, t _ _, b _ _ t _ _, b _ _ _, s _ _ _

y Sports

SWIMMING POOL

OPEN

CLOSED

Loren'z RESTAU

TOWNS

cap

sweatband

overalls *BrE*/ coveralls *AmE*

turban

collar

tie

blouse

shirt

bow tie

waistcoat *BrE*/ vest *AmE*

T-shirt

sweatshirt

tracksuit *BrE*/ sweats *AmE*

suit

gloves

coat

skirt

jacket

trousers *BrE*/ pants *AmE*

shoes

rts

s

ers *BrE*/ akers *AmE*

ari

braces *BrE*/ suspenders *AmE*

scarf   cardigan

sweater/jumper *BrE*

belt

handkerchief

n jacket

jeans

dungarees *BrE*/ overalls *AmE*

pocket

s

tights *BrE*/ pantyhose *AmE*

dress

leggings

ces

yellow

white

mauve

green

navy

black

red

ora

purple

blue

khaki

maroon

tar

pink

be

brown

stripy *BrE*/
striped *AmE*

flowery *BrE*/
flowered *AmE*

checked

spotted / spotty *BrE*
polka-dotted *AmE*

plain *BrE*
solid *AmE*

magen

patterned

grey *BrE*/ gray *AmE*

controls the character, shape etc that a plant or animal has

chron·ic /'krɒnɪk‖'krɑː-/ adj a chronic illness or problem continues for a long time and is usually serious: *chronic lung disease|a chronic shortage of teachers* —**chronically** /-kli/ adv: *chronically sick patients*

chron·i·cle /'krɒnɪkəl‖'krɑː-/ n [C] a written record of historical events, arranged in the order in which they happened —**chronicle** v [T] *a TV series chronicling the development of medical science*

chron·o·log·i·cal /ˌkrɒnə'lɒdʒɪkəl‖ˌkrɑːnə-'lɑː-/ adj arranged according to the order in which events happened: **in chronological order** *a list of World Cup winners in chronological order* —**chronologically** /-kli/ adv

chrys·a·lis /'krɪsəlɪs/ n [C] a MOTH or BUTTERFLY at the stage of development when it has a hard outside covering, before becoming a LARVA and then an adult → compare COCOON[1]

chry·san·the·mum /krɪ'sænθɪməm/ n [C] a garden plant that has large brightly coloured flowers

chub·by /'tʃʌbi/ adj slightly fat —**chubbiness** n [U]

chuck /tʃʌk/ v [T] *informal* to throw something: *Chuck that magazine over here, would you?*

chuck sth ↔ away/out phr v [T] *informal* to throw something away: *We had to chuck out a lot of stuff when we moved.*

chuck sth ↔ in phr v [T] *BrE informal* to stop doing a job or activity that is boring or annoying: *If you hate the job so much, why don't you chuck it in?*

chuck sb ↔ out phr v [T] *informal* to force someone to leave a place: *There was a fight, and some guys got chucked out of the bar.*

chuck·le /'tʃʌkəl/ v [I] to laugh quietly: *Terry chuckled to himself as he read his book.* —**chuckle** n [C]

chug /tʃʌg/ v -gged, -gging [I] if the engine of a vehicle or boat chugs, it makes a repeated low sound while moving: *The little boat chugged slowly along the canal.* —**chug** n [C]

chum /tʃʌm/ n [C] *old-fashioned* a good friend —**chummy** adj

chunk /tʃʌŋk/ n [C] **1** a large piece of something: **+ of** *a chunk of cheese* → see colour picture on page 440 **2** a large part or amount of something: *The hospital bills took a big chunk out of her savings.*

Colours and Patterns

Exercise 1

We mix colours and make new colours. Complete the sentences below.

1 If you mix brown and white, you make

 beige.

2 _____ is a mixture of white and black.

3 If you mix yellow and brown, you can make

 _____.

4 Mix white and _____ and make cream.

5 Orange is made by mixing _____ and yellow.

6 Red and _____ together make maroon.

7 Dark blue is a mixture of blue and

 _____.

8 A mixture of white and _____ makes light blue.

Exercise 2

We make patterns with lines and shapes. Look at the names of the patterns. Which lines or shapes can you see in each pattern?

1 checked

2 spotted / spotty / polka dot

3 flowery / floral

4 striped / stripy / stripey

5 tartan

 a circles of colour

 b flower shapes

 c parallel lines

 d lines crossing other lines

 e squares of different colours

Exercise 3

Look at the room you are in. Which colours can you see? Which patterns can you see?

chunk·y /ˈtʃʌŋki/ *adj* **1** thick and heavy: *chunky jewellery* **2** someone who is chunky has a broad heavy body

church /tʃɜːtʃ‖tʃɜːrtʃ/ *n* **1** [C,U] a building where Christians go to pray: *How often do you go to church?* **2** also **Church** [C] one of the separate groups within the Christian religion: *the Catholic Church*

church·go·er /ˈtʃɜːtʃˌɡəʊə‖ˈtʃɜːrtʃˌɡoʊər/ *n* [C] someone who goes to church regularly

church·yard /ˈtʃɜːtʃjɑːd‖ˈtʃɜːrtʃjɑːrd/ *n* [C] a piece of land around a church where dead people are buried

churl·ish /ˈtʃɜːlɪʃ‖ˈtʃɜːr-/ *adj* not polite or friendly: *It seemed churlish to refuse her invitation.*

churn¹ /tʃɜːn‖tʃɜːrn/ *v* **1** also **churn up** [T] to make water or mud move around violently, throwing up the surface of it: *Cars had churned up the muddy track.* **2** [I] if your stomach is churning, you feel sick because you are nervous **3** [T] to make butter in a churn

churn sth ↔ **out** *phr v* [T] *informal* to produce large quantities of something quickly: *She churns out about three new books every year.*

churn² *n* [C] **1** a container that is filled with milk and shaken to make butter **2** *BrE* a large metal container used to store milk: *milk churns*

chute /ʃuːt/ *n* [C] **1** a long narrow structure that slopes down, so that things or people can slide down it: *a water chute* **2** *informal* a PARACHUTE

chut·ney /ˈtʃʌtni/ *n* [U] a mixture of fruit, sugar, and SPICES, that is eaten with cheese or meat

CIA /ˌsiː aɪ ˈeɪ/ *n* **the CIA** Central Intelligence Agency; the department of the US government that collects secret information about other countries

CID /ˌsiː aɪ ˈdiː/ *n* [U] Criminal Investigation Department; the department of the British police that deals with serious crimes

ci·der /ˈsaɪdə‖-ər/ *n* [C,U] **1** *BrE* an alcoholic drink made from apples **2** *AmE* a non-alcoholic drink made from apples

ci·gar /sɪˈɡɑː‖-ˈɡɑːr/ *n* [C] something that people smoke, made from tobacco leaves that have been rolled into a thick tube

cig·a·rette /ˌsɪɡəˈret‖ˌsɪɡəˈret, ˈsɪɡəˌret/ *n* [C] a paper tube filled with tobacco that people smoke

ci·lan·tro /sɪˈlæntrəʊ‖sɪˈlɑːntroʊ, -ˈlæn-/ *n* [U] *AmE* a plant used to give a special taste to food; CORIANDER *BrE*

cinch /sɪntʃ/ *n* **be a cinch** *informal* to be very easy to do: *The written test was a cinch.*

cin·der /ˈsɪndə‖-ər/ *n* [C] a very small piece of burnt wood, coal etc

cin·e·ma /ˈsɪnəmə/ *n* **1** [C] *BrE* a building where you go to see films; MOVIE THEATER *AmE*: *I haven't been to the cinema for ages.* **2** [U] the art or industry of making films: *the influence of Hollywood on Indian cinema*

cin·na·mon /ˈsɪnəmən/ *n* [U] a brown SPICE that is used especially in sweet food

cir·ca /ˈsɜːkə‖ˈsɜːr-/ *prep formal* used before a date to show that something happened around that year, but you cannot know exactly: *He was born circa 1100.*

cir·cle¹ /ˈsɜːkəl‖ˈsɜːr-/ *n* **1** [C] a completely round flat shape, like the letter O, or a group arranged in this shape: *The children were dancing in a circle.* | *a circle of chairs* ➡ see picture at SHAPES **2** [C] a group of people who know each other or share the same interest: *Myers' new book has been praised in literary circles.* | **+ of** *her large circle of friends* **3** [singular] *BrE* an area of seats upstairs in a theatre; BALCONY **4 go around in circles** to travel or to discuss something without making any progress because you keep coming back to the same point ➡ see also VICIOUS CIRCLE

circle² *v* **1** [I,T] to move in a circle around something: *Our plane circled the airport several times.* **2** [T] to draw a circle around something: *Circle the correct answer.*

cir·cuit /ˈsɜːkɪt‖ˈsɜːr-/ *n* **1** [C] a circular track or journey: *a racing circuit* **2** [C] the complete circle that an electric current flows around **3** [singular] all the places that are usually visited by someone who is doing a particular activity: *a well known speaker on the international lecture circuit*

cir·cu·i·tous /sɜːˈkjuːɪtəs‖sɜːr-/ *adj formal* going from one place to another in a way that is not the most direct way: *We travelled by a circuitous route to avoid the town centre.*

cir·cuit·ry /ˈsɜːkɪtri‖ˈsɜːr-/ *n* [U] a system of electric circuits

cir·cu·lar¹ /ˈsɜːkjələ‖ˈsɜːrkjələr/ *adj* **1** shaped like a circle: *a circular table* **2** going around to different places and coming back to where you started: *a circular journey*

circular² *n* [C] a printed advertisement or notice that is sent to a lot of people at the same time: *a circular from the school to all parents*

cir·cu·late /ˈsɜːkjəleɪt‖ˈsɜːr-/ *v* **1** [I] if information or ideas circulate, they become known by many people: *There's a rumour circulating about Mandy.* **2** [T] to send or give information, facts etc to a group of people: *I'll circulate the report at the meeting.* **3** [I,T] to move around within a system, or to make something do this: *Blood circulates around the body.*

cir·cu·la·tion /ˌsɜːkjəˈleɪʃən‖ˌsɜːr-/ *n* **1** [U] the movement of blood around your body: *Exercise can improve circulation.* **2** [singular] the number of copies of a newspaper or magazine that are usually sold: *a magazine with a circulation of 400,000* **3 in circulation** used by people and passing from one person to another: *The government has reduced the number of $100 bills in circulation.*

cir·cum·cise /ˈsɜːkəmsaɪz‖ˈsɜːr-/ *v* [T] to cut off the skin at the end of a boy's or man's PENIS, or to cut off part of a girl's sex organs —**circumcision** /ˌsɜːkəmˈsɪʒən‖ˌsɜːr-/ *n* [C,U]

cir·cum·fer·ence /səˈkʌmfərəns‖sər-/ *n* [C,U] the distance around the outside of a circle or round object: *The earth's circumference is nearly 25,000 miles.*

cir·cum·spect /ˈsɜːkəmspekt‖ˈsɜːr-/ *adj formal* thinking carefully about things before doing them; CAUTIOUS: *I advise you to be more circumspect about what you say in public.*

cir·cum·stance /ˈsɜːkəmstæns, -stəns‖ˈsɜːr-/ *n* **1** [C usually plural, U] a fact or condition that affects what happens in a situation: *Under normal circumstances she would never have left* *her child with a stranger.* **2 under/in the circumstances** used to say that because of a particular situation you think that something is necessary, right, acceptable etc: *I think we did the best we could in the circumstances.* **3 under/in no circumstances** used to emphasize that something must never happen: *Under no circumstances should you leave this house!* **4 sb's circumstances** the amount of money someone has: *Everyone will be taxed according to their circumstances.*

cir·cum·stan·tial /ˌsɜːkəmˈstænʃəl‖ˌsɜːr-/ *adj* **circumstantial evidence** facts, especially relating to a crime, that make you believe that something happened but do not definitely prove it: *The circumstantial evidence strongly suggested that he was guilty.*

cir·cum·vent /ˌsɜːkəmˈvent‖ˌsɜːr-/ *v* [T] *formal* to avoid having to obey a rule or law: *The company has opened an office abroad in order to circumvent the tax laws.* —**circumvention** /-ˈvenʃən/ *n* [U]

cir·cus /ˈsɜːkəs‖ˈsɜːr-/ *n* [C] a group of people and animals that travels to different places performing tricks and entertainments

cis·tern /ˈsɪstən‖-ərn/ *n* [C] a container in which water is stored inside a building

cit·a·del /ˈsɪtədəl, -del/ *n* [C] a strong castle where people in the past could be safe if their city was attacked

ci·ta·tion /saɪˈteɪʃən/ *n* [C] **1** an official statement publicly praising someone's actions or achievements: *a citation for bravery* **2** a phrase or sentence taken from a book, speech etc

cite /saɪt/ *v* [T] **1** to mention something as an example or proof of something else: *The mayor cited the latest crime figures as proof of the need for more police.* **2** *AmE law* to order someone to come to a court of law because they have done something wrong: *He was cited for speeding.*

cit·i·zen /ˈsɪtɪˌzən/ *n* [C] **1** someone who lives in a particular town, state, or country: *the citizens of Moscow* **2** someone who legally belongs to a particular country, whether they live there or not: *The US government was advising all American citizens to leave Liberia.*

cit·i·zen·ship /ˈsɪtɪˌzənʃɪp/ *n* [U] **French/ Japanese etc citizenship** the legal right of being a French, Japanese etc citizen: *She married him to get Swiss citizenship.*

cit·rus /ˈsɪtrəs/ *adj* **1** a citrus fruit is a fruit such as an orange or lemon **2** a citrus tree grows citrus fruit

cit·y /ˈsɪti/ *n* [C] **1** a large important town: *New York City* **2** the people who live in a city: *The city has been living in fear since last week's earthquake.*

civ·ic /ˈsɪvɪk/ *adj* relating to a town or city and its citizens: *civic pride* (=pride in your town or city) | *civic duties* (=relating to the government or organization of a city)

civ·ics /ˈsɪvɪks/ *n* [U] *AmE* a school subject dealing with the rights and duties of citizens and the way government works

civ·il /ˈsɪvəl/ *adj* **1** relating to the people or things in a country that are not part of military or religious organizations: *the civil aircraft industry* | *We were married in a civil ceremony, not in church.* **2** relating to the laws about the pri-

vate business, rights, property etc of people, not laws about crime: *civil law and criminal law* **3** polite but not very friendly: *I know you don't like him, but just try to be civil.*

civil en·gi·neer·ing /ˌ... ...ˈ../ *n* [U] the planning, building, and repair of roads, bridges, large buildings etc

ci·vil·ian /sɨˈvɪljən/ *n* [C] anyone who is not a member of a military organization or the police: *Many innocent civilians were killed.* —**civilian** *adj*: *civilian clothes*

civ·i·li·za·tion (also **-isation** *BrE*) /ˌsɪvəl-aɪ-ˈzeɪʃən‖-vələˈzeɪ-/ *n* **1** [C,U] a society that is well organized and developed: *contemporary European civilization* | *the ancient civilizations of Greece and Rome* **2** [U] when people live in a well organized society and have a comfortable way of life: *all the benefits of modern civilization*

civ·i·lize (also **-ise** *BrE*) /ˈsɪvəl-aɪz/ *v* [T] to educate and improve a society so that it is more organized and developed: *The Romans hoped to civilize all the tribes of Europe.*

civ·i·lized (also **-ised** *BrE*) /ˈsɪvəl-aɪzd/ *adj* **1** a civilized society is well organized and has highly developed laws and customs: *Care for the elderly is essential in a civilized society.* **2** behaving politely and sensibly: *Let's sit around the table and discuss this in a civilized way.*

civil rights /ˌ... ˈ./ *n* [plural] the legal rights that every citizen of a country has, such as the right to be treated equally whatever their race or religion

civil ser·vant /ˌ... ˈ../ *n* [C] someone who works in the civil service

civil ser·vice /ˌ... ˈ../ *n* **the civil service** all the government departments and the people who work in them

civil war /ˌ... ˈ./ *n* [C,U] a war between groups of people from the same country

clack /klæk/ *v* [I] to make a repeated short hard sound: *the sound of high-heeled shoes clacking along the corridor* —**clack** *n* [singular]

clad /klæd/ *adj literary* dressed or covered in something: *a lady clad in silk and lace* | *snow-clad mountains*

claim[1] /kleɪm/ *v* **1** [T] to say that something is true, even though it has not been proved: + **(that)** *Evans went to the police claiming that someone had tried to murder him.* | **claim to be sth** *Ask Louie, he claims to be an expert.* **2** [I,T] to ask for something because you have a right to it or because it belongs to you: *Elderly people can claim £10 a week heating allowance.* | *This jacket was left behind after the party – but no one's been back to claim it.* **3** [T] if an accident, war etc claims lives, people die because of it

claim[2] *n* **1** [C] a demand for something that you have a right to receive: *insurance claims* | + **for** *She put in a claim for accommodation expenses.* **2** [C] a statement that something is true, even though it has not been proved: + **that** *Cardoza denied claims that he was involved in drug smuggling.* **3** [C] a right to have something: + **to** *Surely they have a rightful claim to their father's land?* **4 claim to fame** *humorous* the one important or interesting fact about someone or something: *The town's claim to fame is that it has the largest car park in the country.*

clair·voy·ant /kleə'vɔɪənt‖kler-/ n [C] someone who says they can see what will happen in the future —**clairvoyance** n [U] —**clairvoyant** adj

clam[1] /klæm/ n [C,U] a small sea animal with a shell, that people eat

clam[2] v -mmed, -mming
clam up phr v [I] informal to suddenly stop talking and refuse to say anything more: *Tom always clams up if you ask him about his girlfriend.*

clam·ber /'klæmbəl-ər/ v [I] to climb over something with difficulty, using your hands and feet: **+ over/out/up etc** *He clambered over the rocks.*

clam·my /'klæmi/ adj wet and sticky in an unpleasant way: *clammy hands*

clam·our[1] BrE, **clamor** AmE /'klæməl-ər/ n [singular] **1** a loud continuous noise of people talking and shouting: *a clamour of voices in the next room* **2** a complaint or a demand for something made by a lot of people: **+ for** *the clamour for lower taxes*

clamour[2] BrE, **clamor** AmE — v [I] to demand something loudly: **+ for** *All the kids were clamouring for attention.*

clamp[1] /klæmp/ v [T] **1** to hold something tightly in a particular position so that it does not move: **clamp sth over/between/around sth** *He clamped his hand over her mouth.* **2** BrE to fasten a piece of equipment onto the wheel of a car that has been parked illegally, so that it cannot be moved; BOOT AmE
clamp down phr v [I] to become very strict in order to stop or limit something, especially criminal activity: **+ on** *The police are clamping down on drunk drivers.*

clamp[2] n [C] **1** a tool used to fasten or hold things together tightly **2** BrE a piece of equipment that can be fastened onto the wheel of a car that is illegally parked, so that it cannot move; DENVER BOOT AmE

clamp·down /'klæmpdaʊn/ n [singular] a sudden official action to stop or reduce an illegal activity: **+ on** *a clampdown on illegal immigration*

clan /klæn/ n [C] **1** informal a large family: *The whole clan will be coming over for Christmas.* **2** a large group of Scottish families that are all related to each other: *the Campbell clan*

clan·des·tine /klæn'destɪn/ adj secret and usually illegal

clang /klæŋ/ v [I,T] to make a loud ringing sound like metal being hit: *The prison gate clanged shut behind him.* —**clang** n [C]

clank /klæŋk/ v [I] to make the loud noise made when one heavy metal object hits another: *clanking chains* —**clank** n [C] *the clank of machinery*

clap[1] /klæp/ v -pped, -pping **1** [I,T] to hit your hands together several times to show that you enjoyed something or approve of something: *The audience was clapping and cheering.* | **clap your hands** *The coach clapped his hands and yelled, "OK, listen!"* ➡ see colour picture on page 473 **2 clap sb on the back/shoulder** to hit someone on the back or shoulder with your hand in a friendly way **3 clap your hand over/to** to suddenly put your hand over a part of your face: *She clapped her hand over her mouth,*

realizing she had said too much. —**clapping** n [U]

clap[2] n [C] **clap of thunder** a very loud sound made by THUNDER

clar·i·fy /'klærɪfaɪ/ v [T] to make something easier to understand by explaining it in more detail: *The discussion helped us to clarify our aims and ideas.* —**clarification** /ˌklærɪfɪˈkeɪʃən/ n [C,U]

clar·i·net /ˌklærɪˈnet/ n [C] a musical instrument like a long black tube, which you play by blowing into it —**clarinettist** n [C]

clar·i·ty /'klærəti/ n [U] clearness in the way you speak, write, or think: *the clarity of Irving's writing style*

clash[1] /klæʃ/ v **1** [I] to fight, argue, or disagree: **+ with** *Demonstrators clashed with police on the streets of Paris.* **2** [I] if two colours or styles clash, they do not look nice together: **+ with** *That red tie clashes with your jacket.* **3** [I] if two events clash, they happen at the same time: **+ with** *Unfortunately, the concert clashes with my evening class.* **4** [I,T] to make a loud sound by hitting two metal objects together

clash[2] n [C] **1** a fight, argument, or disagreement: **+ between** *a clash between the President and Republicans in the Senate* **2** when ideas, opinions, or feelings are very different and go against each other: *a clash of loyalties* **3** a loud sound made by two metal objects hitting together: *the clash of the cymbals*

clasp[1] /klɑːsp‖klæsp/ n **1** [C] a small metal object used to fasten a bag, belt, piece of jewellery etc **2** [singular] a tight firm hold; GRIP: *the firm clasp of her hand*

clasp[2] v [T] to hold someone or something tightly in your hands or arms: *She clasped the baby in her arms.*

class[1] /klɑːs‖klæs/ n **1** [C] a group of students who are taught together: *We were in the same class at school.* | **class of '96/'74/'88 etc** AmE (=students who finished school that year) **2** [C,U] a period of time during which students are taught: *When's your next class?* | *No talking in class.* **3** [C] a series of lessons in one subject: *a class in computer design* | *an evening class* **4** [C,U] the social group that you belong to: *the professional classes* | *Success in their country seems to be based on class rather than ability.* | *a working class family* **5** [C] a type of people or things that are considered to be better or worse than other groups: *You get a nicer class of people living in this area.* | **not in the same class** (=not as good as someone or something): *As a tennis player, he's not in the same class as his brother.* **6** [C] a group of plants, animals, words etc that can be studied together because they are similar: *There are four main word classes: nouns, verbs, adjectives, and adverbs.* **7** [U] the kind of style, skill, or beauty that people admire: *The team showed real class in this afternoon's game.*

class[2] v **class sb/sth as sth** to decide that someone or something belongs in a particular group: *Heroin and cocaine are classed as hard drugs.*

clas·sic[1] /'klæsɪk/ adj **1** a classic book, film etc has been popular for a long time and is considered to be important: *the classic film 'Casablanca'* **2** a **classic example/mistake/symptom etc** a very typical example, mistake etc: *Tiredness and loss of appetite are classic* *symptoms of depression.* **3** a classic style or design is attractive in a simple and traditional way: *a classic dark grey suit*

classic² *n* [C] a book, film etc that has been popular for a long time and is considered to be important: *'Moby Dick' is one of the classics of American literature.*

clas·si·cal /ˈklæsɪkəl/ *adj* **1** based on a traditional set of ideas: *classical Indian dance* **2** belonging to the CULTURE of ancient Greece and Rome: *classical architecture* **3** classical music music by people such as Beethoven and Mozart that is considered to be serious and important

clas·sics /ˈklæsɪks/ *n* [U] the study of the language, literature, and history of ancient Greece and Rome

clas·si·fied /ˈklæsɪfaɪd/ *adj* classified information, documents etc are officially secret

clas·si·fy /ˈklæsɪfaɪ/ *v* [T] to put things or people into groups according to their type, size, age etc: **classify sb/sth as sth** *Whales are classified as mammals, not fish.* —**classification** /ˌklæsɪfɪˈkeɪʃən/ *n* [C,U]

class·mate /ˈklɑːsmeɪt‖ˈklæs-/ *n* [C] someone who is in the same class as you at school or college: *Discuss the question with your classmates.*

class·room /ˈklɑːs-rʊm, -ruːm‖ˈklæs-/ *n* [C] a room in a school where students are taught

class·work /ˈklɑːswɜːk‖ˈklæswɜːrk/ *n* [U] school work that you do in class rather than at home → compare HOMEWORK

class·y /ˈklɑːsi‖ˈklæsi/ *adj informal* expensive and fashionable: *a classy sports car*

clat·ter /ˈklætə‖-ər/ *v* [I] if hard objects clatter, they make a loud unpleasant noise when they hit against each other: *The pots clattered to the floor.* —**clatter** *n* [singular] *the clatter of dishes*

clause /klɔːz‖klɒːz/ *n* [C] **1** a part of a legal document: *A clause in the contract states when payment must be made.* **2** a group of words that contains a subject and a verb, which may be only part of a sentence

claus·tro·pho·bi·a /ˌklɔːstrəˈfəʊbiə‖ˌklɒːstrə-ˈfoʊ-/ *n* [U] fear of being in a small space or in a crowd —**claustrophobic** *adj*: *I won't go in lifts – I'm claustrophobic.*

claw¹ /klɔː‖klɒː/ *n* [C] a sharp curved hard part on the toe of an animal or bird → see picture at CRAB

claw² *v* [I,T] if a person or animal claws something, they tear or pull at it using their nails or claws: *Her fingers clawed his back.* | + **at** *The kitten was clawing at my trouser leg.*
　claw sth ↔ back *phr v* [T] to try hard to get something back, especially money

clay /kleɪ/ *n* [U] a type of heavy soil that is used for making pots, bricks etc

clean¹ /kliːn/ *adj* **1** not dirty: *Are your hands clean?* | *All work surfaces must be kept spotlessly clean.* **2** not offensive or about sex: *good clean fun* **3** honest and fair: *a clean fight* **4** without

any record of crimes or mistakes: *a clean driving licence* **5** come clean *informal* to admit that you have not told the truth about something: *You should come clean and tell her who really did it.* **6** clean slate if you start doing something with a clean slate, you start doing it without problems or mistakes from the past preventing you from being successful → see also CLEANLINESS

clean² *v* [I,T] to remove dirt from something: *It took me ages to clean the stove.* —**clean** *n* [singular] *The car needs a good clean.* —**cleaning** *n* [U]
　clean out *phr v* [T] **1** [clean sth ↔ out] to make a building, room etc clean and tidy by removing things from it: *We spent the whole of Sunday cleaning out the garage.* **2** [clean sb out] if something expensive cleans you out, you spend all your money on it
　clean up *phr v* **1** [I,T clean sb/sth ↔ up] to make something that is very dirty clean and tidy: *A lot of money has been spent on cleaning up the region's beaches.* **2** [T clean sth ↔ up] to get rid of crime or dishonest behaviour in an area or organization → see also CLEANUP

clean³ *adv* used to emphasize that an action or movement is done completely: *The bullet went clean through his leg.*

clean-cut /ˌ. ˈ.◂/ *adj* neat and tidy in your appearance

clean·er /ˈkliːnə‖-ər/ *n* **1** [C] someone whose job is to clean offices, houses etc **2** toilet/kitchen/oven etc cleaner a substance used to clean toilets, kitchens etc **3** the cleaner's the DRY CLEANER'S

clean·li·ness /ˈklenlinɪs/ *n* [U] the practice of being clean or keeping things clean: *poor standards of cleanliness*

clean·ly /ˈkliːnli/ *adv* quickly and smoothly, with one movement: *The knife cut cleanly through the cake.*

cleanse /klenz/ *v* [T] to make something such as a wound or your skin completely clean: *Cleanse the wound with antiseptic.*

cleans·er /ˈklenzə‖-ər/ *n* [C,U] a substance used for cleaning your face

clean-shav·en /ˌ. ˈ.◂/ *adj* a man who is clean-shaven does not have a BEARD

clean-up /ˈkliːnʌp/ also **clean-up** *n* [singular] **1** a process in which you remove dirt, waste, or harmful substances from a place: *The cleanup of the oil spill took months.* **2** the process of getting rid of crime or dishonest behaviour in an area or organization

clear¹ /klɪə‖klɪr/ *adj* **1** easy to understand, see, read, or hear: *The instructions aren't clear at all.* | *She gave the police a clear description of her attacker.* **2** impossible to doubt: *a clear admission of guilt* | *Hugh made it quite clear that he was not interested.* **3** be clear (about sth) to be certain about something: *Is everyone clearer now about what they're supposed to be doing?* **4** a clear substance or liquid is transparent: *clear glass bottles* **5** not blocked: + **of** *All major*

SPELLING NOTE
Words with the sound /k/, like **cut**, may be spelt **k-**, like **key**, or **qu-**, like **queen**.
Words with the sound /s/, like **city**, may be spelt **s-**, like **soon**, or **ps-**, like **psychology**.

roads are now clear of snow. **6** a clear sky has no clouds: *On a clear day you can see for miles.* **7 a clear conscience** the feeling you have when you know that you have behaved in the right way **8 a clear head** the ability to think quickly and well: *You need a clear head to do any kind of job that involves driving.*

clear² *v* **1** [T] to make an area or surface tidy by removing things from it: *I'll just clear these papers off the desk.* | **clear the table** *After meals, I clear the table and dad does the dishes.* **2** [T] to remove something or someone from a place because they are blocking it: *I was out at 6.30 clearing snow.* | **clear sb/sth from sth** *Trucks have just finished clearing the fallen trees from the road.* **3** [I] if the weather or sky clears, it becomes brighter **4 clear your throat** to cough a little in order to make it easier for you to speak **5** [T] to prove that someone is not guilty of something: **clear sb of (doing) sth** *Johnson was cleared of murdering his wife.* **6** [T] to give or get official permission to do something: *Has the plane been cleared to land?* **7** [T] to go over something such as a fence or wall without touching it: *The horse cleared the first fence easily.* **8** [I] if a cheque clears, the money goes from the bank account of the person who wrote it into the bank account of the person they wrote it to **9 clear the air** to discuss a problem with someone because you do not want a disagreement

clear sth ↔ **away** *phr v* [I,T] to make a room or place tidy by removing things from it or putting them where they should stay: *Jamie, will you clear your toys away!*

clear off *phr v* [I] *BrE informal* to leave a place quickly: *The landlord told them to clear off.* —**clear off!** *interjection: Oi! You kids! Clear off!*

clear out *phr v* [T **clear** sth ↔ **out**] to tidy a place by removing things that you no longer want from it: *I need to clear out that dresser.*

clear up *phr v* **1** [I,T **clear** sth ↔ **up**] to make a place tidy by removing things from it or putting them where they should be: *We should clear up the basement before your parents visit.* **2** [T **clear** sth ↔ **up**] to explain something that is confusing or mysterious: *There are one or two points I'd like to clear up before we begin.* **3** [I] if the weather clears up, it becomes brighter **4** [I] if an infection clears up, it gets better

clear³ *adv* away from something or someone: **+ of** *Firemen pulled the driver clear of the wreckage.*

clear⁴ *n* **in the clear a)** not guilty of something **b)** no longer having problems or difficulties: *The debt is being paid off but we're not in the clear yet.*

clear·ance /ˈklɪərəns‖ˈklɪr-/ *n* **1** [C,U] official permission to do something: *We're waiting for clearance to unload the ship.* **2 slum/snow/ land clearance** a process in which something is removed from a place because it is not wanted

clear-cut /ˌ. ˈ.◂/ *adj* certain or definite: *There is no clear-cut solution.*

clear·ing /ˈklɪərɪŋ‖ˈklɪr-/ *n* [C] a small area in a forest where there are no trees

clear·ly /ˈklɪəli‖ˈklɪrli/ *adv* **1** in a way that is impossible to doubt: *Clearly, the situation is more serious than we first thought.* **2** in a way

that is easy to see, hear etc: *Remember to speak slowly and clearly.* | *The footpaths were all clearly marked.* **3** if you think clearly, you are not at all confused

clear-sight·ed /ˌ. ˈ.◂/ *adj* good at understanding situations and making decisions about what should be done: *a clear-sighted analysis of the problem*

cleav·age /ˈkliːvɪdʒ/ *n* [C,U] the space between a woman's breasts

cleav·er /ˈkliːvəl-ər/ *n* [C] a knife with a large square blade used for cutting meat

clef /klef/ *n* [C] a sign at the beginning of a line of written music that shows the PITCH of the notes: *the bass clef*

clem·en·cy /ˈklemənsi/ *n* [U] *formal* when someone is not punished severely for a serious crime, in a way that shows kindness and FOR-GIVENESS by the judge or person who decides what punishment to give

clench /klentʃ/ *v* [T] **clench your fists/teeth/ hands** to close your hands or your mouth tightly, especially because you are angry: *Hal began beating on the door with clenched fists.* | *"Go away!" she muttered, clenching her teeth.*

cler·gy /ˈklɜːdʒi‖ˈklɜːr-/ *n* [plural] priests and religious leaders, considered as a group: *The clergy have much less power than they used to have.*

cler·gy·man /ˈklɜːdʒimən‖ˈklɜːr-/ *n* [C] *plural* **clergymen** /-mən/ a male member of the clergy

cler·ic /ˈklerɪk/ *n* [C] a member of the clergy

cler·i·cal /ˈklerɪkəl/ *adj* **1** relating to office work: *a clerical worker* **2** relating to the CLERGY

clerk /klɑːk‖klɜːrk/ *n* [C] **1** someone whose job is to keep the records or accounts in an office, law court etc: *a bank clerk* **2** *AmE* someone who deals with people arriving at a hotel: *Please return your keys to the desk clerk.*

clev·er /ˈklevəl-ər/ *adj* **1** *especially BrE* able to learn and understand things quickly; intelligent: *I wasn't clever enough to go to university.* **2** using your intelligence to get what you want, especially in a slightly dishonest way: *a clever lawyer* **3** designed in an unusual and effective way: *What a clever little gadget!* —**cleverly** *adv* —**cleverness** *n* [U]

cli·ché /ˈkliːʃeɪ‖kliːˈʃeɪ/ *n* [C] an expression that is used too often and no longer has any real meaning: *all the usual political clichés*

click¹ /klɪk/ *v* **1** [I,T] to make a short hard sound, or to make something produce this sound: *Her high heels clicked across the wooden floor.* **2 click your fingers** make a short hard sound by moving your thumb quickly across your second finger **3** [I] *informal* to suddenly understand something: *It suddenly clicked – the woman I had met the day before was Jim's wife.* **4** [I] *informal* if two people click, they like each other as soon as they meet **5** [I,T] to press a button on a computer MOUSE to make the computer do something: **+ on** *Double click on 'OK'.*

click² *n* [C,U] a short hard sound: *The door shut with a click.* ➡ see colour picture on page 635

cli·ent /ˈklaɪənt/ *n* [C] someone who pays a person or organization for services or advice: *I have a meeting with an important client.*

cli·en·tele /ˌkliːənˈtel‖ˌklaɪənˈtel, ˌkliː-/ *n* [singular] the people who regularly go to a shop, restaurant etc: *Our clientele consists mainly of single people.*

cliff /klɪf/ *n* [C] a high steep rock or piece of land: *She was standing near the edge of the cliff.*
→ see colour picture on page 243

cli·mac·tic /klaɪˈmæktɪk/ *adj* a climactic event or period of time is one in which very important or exciting things happen

cli·mate /ˈklaɪmᵻt/ *n* **1** [C] the typical weather conditions in an area: *a hot and humid climate* **2** [C usually singular] the kind of situation or the general feelings and opinions that exist at a particular time: **political/economic/intellectual etc climate** *Small businesses are finding life difficult in the present economic climate.* —**climatic** /klaɪˈmætɪk/ *adj*

cli·max /ˈklaɪmæks/ *n* [C] **1** the most important or exciting part of a situation, book, film etc: **+ of** *Competing in the Olympic Games was the climax of his career.* | **reach a climax** *The revolution reached its climax in 1921.* **2** an ORGASM —**climax** *v* [I,T]

climb /klaɪm/ *v* **1** [I,T] to move up or down towards the top of something: *Kids love climbing trees.* | *She slowly climbed up to the top of the hill.* → see colour picture on page 670 **2** to move somewhere using your hands and feet: **+ out of/ into/over etc** *Bob climbed into the back of the truck.* **3** [I] to go up mountains for sport or enjoyment: **go climbing** *We went climbing in the Himalayas last year.* **4** [I] to move gradually to a higher position: *Flight 104 climbed into the night sky.* **5** [I] if a number or amount climbs, it increases: *The temperature was climbing steadily.* —**climb** *n* [C]
  climb down *phr v* [I] to admit that you were wrong about something after being sure that you were right: *Management have refused to climb down over the issue of wage increases.*

climb·down /ˈklaɪmdaʊn/ *n* [C, usually singular] when someone admits that they are wrong, especially because they are forced to: *The Prime Minister denied that the new policy was a climbdown.*

climb·er /ˈklaɪmə‖-ər/ *n* [C] someone who climbs rocks or mountains as a sport

climb·ing /ˈklaɪmɪŋ/ *n* [U] the sport of climbing mountains or rocks: *climbing boots* | *Her hobbies include riding and mountain climbing.*

climb·ing frame /ˈ.. ˌ./ *n* [C] *BrE* a structure for children to climb on; JUNGLE GYM *AmE*

clinch /klɪntʃ/ *v* [T] *informal* to finally succeed in getting or winning something after trying very hard: *They clinched the championship after scoring in the final minute.*

cling /klɪŋ/ *v* clung /klʌŋ/, clung, clinging [I] **1** to hold someone or something tightly, especially because you do not feel safe: **+ to/on/ together** *The little girl was clinging to her mother, crying.* **2** to stick to something: *Sand clung to her arms and legs.* **3** to keep something you have, although this is very difficult: **+ to/on/onto** *He is still clinging on to power.*
  cling to sb/sth *phr v* [T] to continue to believe or hope for something, even though there is no real reason to: *She still clung to the hope that he loved her.*

cling·film /ˈklɪŋfɪlm/ *n* [U] *BrE trademark* thin transparent plastic used for wrapping food; SARAN WRAP *AmE trademark*

cling·ing /ˈklɪŋɪŋ/ *adj* **1** a clinging piece of clothing fits tightly to your body: *a clinging pair of satin jeans* **2** clingy

cling·y /ˈklɪŋi/ *adj* needing someone too much and frightened of doing things alone: *a clingy child*

clin·ic /ˈklɪnɪk/ *n* [C] **1** a place where people go for medical treatment and advice: *a dental clinic* **2** *AmE* a small hospital in an area far away from large cities

clin·i·cal /ˈklɪnɪkəl/ *adj* **1** relating to medical treatment and tests rather than medical ideas: *The drug has undergone a number of clinical trials.* **2** not influenced by feelings and only considering facts: *Her attitude to our relationship was cold and clinical.* —**clinically** /-kli/ *adv*

cli·ni·cian /klɪˈnɪʃən/ *n* [C] *technical* a doctor who studies diseases by examining people

clink /klɪŋk/ *v* [I,T] if pieces of glass or metal clink, or if you clink them, they make a short ringing sound when they touch each other —**clink** *n* [C,U]

clip[1] /klɪp/ *n* **1** [C] a small metal or plastic object used to hold things together **2** [C] a short part of a film or television programme that is shown especially in order to advertise it: *a clip from Robert De Niro's latest movie*

clip[2] *v* -pped, -pping **1** [I,T] to fasten things together using a clip, or to become fastened in this way: **+ to/onto** *The lamp clips onto the front of the bicycle.* **2** to cut something, making small quick cuts with your scissors: *Walt stood in front of the mirror, clipping his moustache.*

clipped /klɪpt/ *adj* a clipped voice has short quick sounds and is not very friendly: *a clipped military accent*

clip·pers /ˈklɪpəz‖-ərz/ *n* [plural] a tool used for cutting small pieces off something: *nail clippers*

clip·ping /ˈklɪpɪŋ/ *n* **1** [C] a piece that has been cut out of a newspaper or magazine: *a newspaper clipping* **2** [C usually plural] a small piece that has been cut away from something: *a pile of grass clippings*

clique /kliːk/ *n* [C] a small group of people who know each other well and are often unfriendly to other people

clit·o·ris /ˈklɪtərˌɪs/ *n* [C] a part of a woman's sex organs which gives her pleasure

cloak /kləʊk‖kloʊk/ *n* [C] a warm piece of clothing like a coat without SLEEVES that hangs from your shoulders

cloak-and-dag·ger /ˌ.. '..◂/ *adj* secret and mysterious: *cloak-and-dagger methods of obtaining information*

cloak·room /ˈkləʊkrʊm, -ruːm‖ˈkloʊk-/ *n* [C] **1** a room in a public building where you can leave your coat, bag etc **2** *BrE* the toilets in a public building

clob·ber /ˈklɒbə‖ˈklɑːbər/ *v* [T] *spoken informal* **1** to hit someone hard: *I'll clobber that boy when I find him!* **2** to defeat someone easily in a game or competition

clock[1] /klɒk‖klɑːk/ *n* **1** [C] an instrument that shows the time: *She glanced at the clock.* | *The room was silent except for the ticking of the clock.* → see colour picture on page

474 **2 around the clock** all day and all night without stopping: *Volunteers had to work around the clock to get everything ready.* **3 against the clock** as fast as possible, because you are competing in something or do not have much time in which to finish something **4 turn/put/ set the clock back** to go back to old and worse ways of doing things: *Women's groups warned that the new law would turn the clock back fifty years.* **5** [C] an instrument in a car that tells you how far it has travelled **6 around/round the clock** all day and all night

clock[2] *v* [T] to measure the speed at which some-one travels or moves, or to travel at a particular speed: *The police clocked him at 160 kilometres an hour.*

clock up sth *phr v* [T] to reach a number or amount: *We clocked up 125,000 miles on our old car.*

clock·wise / ˈklɒk-waɪz‖ˈklɑ:k-/ *adv* in the same direction as the moving parts on the face of a clock: *Turn the dial clockwise.* —**clockwise** *adj* → opposite ANTICLOCKWISE *BrE* COUNTERCLOCK-WISE *AmE*

clock·work / ˈklɒk-wɜ:k‖ˈklɑ:k-wɜ:rk/ *n* **1 like clockwork** in exactly the way that you planned: *Production at the factory has been going like clockwork.* **2 (as) regular as clockwork** very regularly: *My grandparents used to take me to the park every Sunday, regular as clockwork.* **3** [U] a type of machinery that starts when you turn a key: *clockwork toy soldiers*

clog[1] / klɒg‖klɑ:g/ also **clog up** *v* [I,T] to block something or to become blocked: *potato peelings clogging the drain.*

clog[2] *n* [C] a shoe made of wood or with a wood-en SOLE → see picture at SHOE

clois·ter / ˈklɔɪstə‖-ər/ *n* [C] a covered area around the edges of a garden in a church, MON-ASTERY etc

clone[1] / kləʊn‖kloʊn/ *n* [C] **1** *technical* an exact GENETIC copy of a plant or animal de-veloped from one of its cells by a scientist **2** *informal* someone or something that is almost exactly like another person or thing

clone[2] *v* [T] to produce a plant or an animal that is a clone

close[1] / kləʊz‖kloʊz/ *v* [I,T] **1** if you close something such as a door or window, or if it closes, it shuts: *Do you mind if I close the window?* | *Close your eyes and go to sleep.* | *The door closed quietly behind her.* **2** if a shop, road, school etc closes, or if someone closes it, it shuts for a short time: *What time does the library close tonight?* **3** to end something, or to end: *Pro-fessor Schmidt closed his speech with a quote from Tolstoy.* **4** also **close down** to stop existing as a business, factory, shop etc, or to make some-thing stop existing: *Hundreds of coal mines have closed since World War II.*

close down *phr v* [I,T **close** sth ↔ **down**] to stop existing as a business or industry, or to make a business or industry stop existing

close in *phr v* [I] **1** to move closer to someone or something, especially in order to attack them: + **on** *Rebel soldiers are closing in on the town.* **2** if the night closes in, it starts to get darker

close sth ↔ **off** *phr v* [T] to separate part of a

road or place from the area that surrounds it so that people cannot go there

close[2] / kləʊs‖kloʊs/ *adj, adv* **1** near in space: *The shops are quite close – only five minutes walk.* | + **to** *They rented a villa close to the beach* **2** near in time: + **to** *By the time we left it was close to midnight.* **3 be close to** to be almost something: *Inflation is now close to 6%.* | **come close to (doing) sth** *Their lead guitarist came close to leaving the band.* **4** [only before noun] giving careful attention to something: *I want you to pay close attention to what I am about to say.* **5** if two people are close, they like or love each other very much: *We were close friends when we were at high school.* | + **to** *Are you close to your sister?* **6** a close association, relationship etc is one in which people talk or work together a lot: *British companies should be trying to establish closer links with Europe.* **7** a close competition, game, or race is won or lost by only a few points **8** close **relation/relative** a member of your family, such as parent, brother, or sister **9** close weather is warm and uncomfortable —**closely** *adv* —**closeness** *n* [U]

close[3] / kləʊz‖kloʊz/ *n* [singular] the end of an activity or period of time: *The summer was drawing to a close.* | *It's time to bring the meeting to a close.*

closed / kləʊzd‖kloʊzd/ *adj* **1** not open to the public: *Most of the shops are closed on Sunday.* **2** not open: *Keep your eyes closed.* **3** a closed society or group is unwilling to accept new ideas or influences

closed cir·cuit tel·e·vi·sion / ˌ.. ˈ... ˌ.. ...ˈ./ also **CCTV** / ˌsiː siː tiː ˈviː/ *n* [C,U] a system in which hidden television cameras film what is happening in a public place in order to help pre-vent crime

close-knit / ˌ.. ˈ.◂/ also **closely-knit** / ˌ.. ˈ.◂/ *adj* a close-knit family or group have good rela-tionships with each other and support and help each other

close-set / ˌkləʊs ˈset◂‖ˌkloʊs-/ *adj* close-set eyes are very near to each other

clos·et[1] / ˈklɒzɪt‖ˈklɑː-, ˈklɒː-/ *n* [C] *especially AmE* a tall cupboard where you keep your clothes, built into the wall of a room; WARDROBE *BrE*

closet[2] *adj* **a closet liberal/Christian/ Republican etc** someone who keeps their true opinions, way of life etc a secret: *He accused me of being a closet fascist.*

close-up / ˈkləʊs ʌp‖ˈkloʊs-/ *n* [C] a photograph of someone or something that is taken from very near to them: *a close-up of an old woman's face*

clos·ing / ˈkləʊzɪŋ‖ˈkloʊ-/ *adj* the closing part of something such as a speech, book, or race is the final part: *the closing paragraph of the article*

clo·sure / ˈkləʊʒə‖ˈkloʊʒər/ *n* [C,U] when a factory, company, school etc is closed permanently: *Unemployment is high because of several recent factory closures.* | + **of** *the closure of the hospital*

clot / klɒt‖klɑ:t/ *n* [C] a place where blood or another liquid has become almost solid: *a blood clot in his leg* —**clot** *v* [T,S]

cloth / klɒθ‖klɔ:θ/ *n* **1** [U] material made from cotton, wool etc that is used for making clothes, sheets etc: *a suit made of grey cloth* → see picture at CLOTHES **2** [C] a piece of material that is used for cleaning, drying, or covering something: *Rub the stain gently with a damp cloth.*

USAGE NOTE: cloth, fabric, and material

Use **cloth** to talk about the cotton, wool etc that is used for making clothes, sheets, curtains etc: *red silk cloth | a bag made of thick cotton cloth.* **Fabric** can be countable or uncountable and is used to talk about cloth generally, or different types of cloth: *fine Italian fabrics | What kind of fabric are your sofa covers made of?* When **material** is an uncountable noun, it can be used for any type of cloth or fabric: *There isn't enough material to make curtains.* Do not use **cloth** or **cloths** to mean 'the things that people wear'. The correct word is **clothes**: *a clothes shop | She spends a lot of money on clothes.*

---

clothe /kləʊð‖kloʊð/ v [T] to provide clothes for someone: *She earns barely enough to feed and clothe her children.*

clothed /kləʊðd‖kloʊðd/ adj **be clothed** *formal* to be dressed in particular clothes: *He was clothed in a white robe.* | **fully/partly etc clothed** *I found him in bed, fully clothed.*

clothes

clothes

cloth/material

clothes /kləʊz, kləʊz‖kloʊðz, kloʊz/ n [plural] the things such as shirts, skirts, or trousers that people wear: *Remember to bring some clean clothes.*

USAGE NOTE: clothes, piece of clothing, and garment

Clothes is a plural noun and cannot be used in the singular. Use it to talk generally about the things that people wear: *It might be cold, so bring some warm clothes.* | *I don't have any formal clothes.* If you are talking about something such as a shirt, skirt etc, say **a piece of clothing** or, more formally, a **garment**: *Customers may take two pieces of clothing/garments into the fitting room.* Usually, however, you can use a more exact word for a piece of clothing: *Someone spilled red wine all over my dress.* | *That's a nice shirt.*

---

clothes·line /'kləʊzlaɪn, 'kləʊz-‖'kloʊðz-, 'kloʊz-/ n [C] a rope that you hang clothes on so

---

that they will dry → see colour picture on page 79

clothes peg /'. ./ *BrE*, **clothes·pin** /'kləʊðzpɪn, 'kləʊz-‖'kloʊðz-, 'kloʊz-/ *AmE* — n [C] a small wooden or plastic object used to fasten clothes to a clothesline

cloth·ing /'kləʊðɪŋ‖'kloʊ-/ n [U] *formal* clothes in general – use this to talk about a particular type of clothes, or a large quantity of clothes: *Supplies of food and clothing were taken to the refugee camps.* | *protective clothing*

cloud[1] /klaʊd/ n **1** [C,U] a white or grey mass in the sky that consists of very small drops of water: *Storm clouds moved closer overhead.* **2** [C] a mass of smoke or dust, or a large number of things all moving together in the air: *He drove out of the driveway in a cloud of dust.* **3 be under a cloud** to be in a situation in which a lot of people disapprove of you: *Ryder resigned under a cloud of suspicion.* **4 on cloud nine** *informal* very happy

cloud[2] v **1** [T] to make something less easy to understand, or make someone less able to think clearly: *Don't allow personal feelings to cloud your judgment.* **2** [T] to make something less pleasant or enjoyable: *Terrorist threats clouded the opening ceremony.* **3** [I,T] also **cloud up** if glass or a liquid clouds, or if something clouds it, it becomes difficult to see through: *Steam had clouded up the windows.*

cloud over phr v [I] if the sky clouds over, it becomes dark and full of clouds

cloud·less /'klaʊdləs/ adj a cloudless sky is clear and bright

cloud·y /'klaʊdi/ adj **1** cloudy weather is dark or grey because the sky is full of clouds **2** a cloudy liquid is not clear or transparent

clout /klaʊt/ n *informal* **1** [U] power or influence: *Trade unions now have less political clout than they used to.* **2** [singular] *BrE* when you hit someone hard: *You'll get a clout round the ear if you're not careful!*

clove /kləʊv‖kloʊv/ n **1** [C] a small sweet strong-smelling dried black flower, used in cooking **2 a clove of garlic** one of the parts that a GARLIC plant is made up of

clo·ver /'kləʊvə‖'kloʊvər/ n [C] a small plant with white or purple flowers and three round leaves on each stem

clown[1] /klaʊn/ n [C] **1** someone who entertains people by dressing in strange clothes, painting their face, and doing funny things, especially in a CIRCUS **2** someone who is always making jokes and behaving in a funny way: *Len was always a real clown at school.*

clown[2] also **clown around/about** v [I] to behave in a funny or stupid way: *Stop clowning around you two!*

club[1] /klʌb/ n [C] **1** an organization for people who share an interest or enjoy similar activities, or the building where they meet: *She's a member of a local drama club.* **2** a NIGHTCLUB **3** a special stick used to hit the ball in GOLF: *a set of golf clubs* → see colour picture on

---

GRAMMAR NOTE: a or the (1)

Use **a** or **an** before a noun when you are mentioning a person or thing for the first time, but use **the** when you mention that same person or thing again: *A man and a woman were sitting at the next table. The woman was much younger than the man.*

page 636 **4** a heavy stick that is used as a weapon **5 clubs** a group of playing cards with a black shape with three leaves printed on them: *the King of clubs*

club² *v* [T] **-bbed, -bbing** to hit someone with a large heavy object

club together *phr v* [I] if a group of people club together, they all share the cost of something: *They clubbed together to buy her some flowers.*

club·house / ˈklʌbhaʊs / *n* [C] the main building of a sports club where people can meet and talk

cluck / klʌk / *v* [I] if a chicken clucks, it makes a short, low sound —**cluck** *n* [C]

clue / kluː / *n* **1** [C] an object or piece of information that helps to solve a crime or something you do not know the answer to: **+ to** *Police are searching for clues to the identity of the murderer.* | **give (sb) a clue** *The title of the book should give you a clue as to what it's about.* **2 not have a clue** *informal* to not know or understand something at all: *"Do you know where Karen is?" "I haven't got a clue."*

clued-up / ˌ. ˈ. / *BrE*, **clued-in** *AmE* — *adj* knowing a lot about something: *You need to keep yourself clued-up about all the latest developments.*

clump¹ / klʌmp / *n* [C] a group of trees, bushes, plants etc that are close together: **+ of** *a clump of grass*

clump² *v* [I] to walk with slow noisy steps: *I heard Grandpa clumping down the stairs in his heavy boots.*

clum·sy / ˈklʌmzi / *adj* **1** a clumsy person often knocks against things, damages things by accident, or does things in a way that is not skilful: *At 13, she was clumsy and shy.* **2** something that is clumsy is large, heavy, and often difficult to use: *big clumsy shoes* **3** said or done in a way that is careless, without considering other people's feelings: *a clumsy apology* —**clumsily** *adv* —**clumsiness** *n* [U]

clung / klʌŋ / *v* the past tense and past participle of CLING

clunk / klʌŋk / *v* [I,T] to make a loud heavy sound: *The door clunked shut.* —**clunk** *n* [C]

clus·ter¹ / ˈklʌstəl-ər / *n* [C] a group of things of the same kind that are very close together: **+ of** *a cluster of small houses*

cluster² *v* [I,T] to form a group of people or things: **+ around/round/together** *A small group of students clustered around the noticeboard.*

clutch¹ / klʌtʃ / *v* [T] to hold something tightly: *Amy had to clutch the railing to keep her balance.*

clutch² *n* **1** [C] the part of a car that you press with your foot when you change GEAR **2 be in sb's clutches** if you are in the clutches of someone powerful or dangerous, they control or influence you

clut·ter¹ / ˈklʌtəl-ər / also **clutter up** *v* [T] to make something untidy by covering or filling it with things: *Piles of books and papers were cluttering up his desk.*

clutter² *n* [U] a lot of things scattered in an untidy way: *I can't stand all this clutter!*

cm *n* the written abbreviation of CENTIMETRE

c/o the written abbreviation of 'care of'; used when you are sending a letter to someone who will give it to the person you are writing to:

Send the letter c/o Anne Miller, 8 Brown St., Peoria, IL

Co. / kəʊlˈkoʊ / **1** the abbreviation of 'company': *Hilton, Brooks & Co.* **2** the written abbreviation of COUNTY: *Co. Durham*

co- / kəʊlˈkoʊ / *prefix* used to form words that are about doing something together or with someone else: *We co-wrote a book on India.*

coach¹ / kəʊtʃlˈkoʊtʃ / *n* [C] **1** someone who trains a person or team in a sport: *a basketball coach* **2** *BrE* a bus with comfortable seats used for long journeys; bus *AmE*: *a coach tour of Europe* **3** a closed vehicle with four wheels pulled by horses that people in past times travelled in: *a coach and horses*

coach² *v* [I,T] **1** to train a person or team in a sport: *Hal coaches the local football team.* **2** to give someone additional private lessons in a subject: *He was coached in most subjects for the first two terms.* —**coaching** *n* [U]

coal / kəʊllˈkoʊl / *n* **1** [U] a hard black substance that is burnt to produce heat: *a coal fire* **2 coals** [plural] burning pieces of coal

co·a·li·tion / ˌkəʊəˈlɪʃənlˌkoʊə- / *n* [C,U] when two or more political parties combine to form a government or to win an election: *a coalition government*

coarse / kɔːslˈkɔːrs / *adj* **1** rough and thick, not smooth or fine: *a coarse woollen blanket* **2** rude and offensive: *The guys were making coarse jokes about the women at the bar.* —**coarsely** *adv* —**coarseness** *n* [U]

coast¹ / kəʊstlˈkoʊst / *n* [C] the land next to the sea: *the Pacific coast* | *They've rented a cottage on the South Coast.* ➡ see colour picture on page 243 —**coastal** *adj*

coast² *v* [I] **1** to keep moving in a vehicle or on a bicycle without using power from the engine or without using your legs: *We coasted downhill.* **2** to achieve something very easily: *Wilson coasted to victory in the election.*

coast guard / ˈ. . / *n* [C] a person or group that helps boats and swimmers that are in danger

coast·line / ˈkəʊstlaɪnlˈkoʊst- / *n* [C,U] the edge of the coast: *a rocky coastline*

coat¹ / kəʊtlˈkoʊt / *n* [C] **1** a piece of clothing with long SLEEVEs that you wear over your other clothes: *a heavy winter coat* | *a lab coat* ➡ see colour picture on page 113 **2** a layer of a substance such as paint that covers a surface: **+ of** *I'll give the walls a fresh coat of paint.* **3** an animal's fur, wool, or hair: *The dog had a thick glossy coat.*

coat² *v* [T] to cover a surface with a thin layer of something: **coat sth with sth** *The books were thickly coated with dust.*

coat·ing / ˈkəʊtɪŋlˈkoʊ- / *n* [C] a thin layer of something that covers a surface: *There was just a light coating of snow.*

coat of arms / ˌ. . ˈ. / *n* [C] a set of pictures or patterns that are used as the special design of a family, town, university etc

coax / kəʊkslˈkoʊks / *v* [T] to persuade someone to do something by talking to them gently and kindly: **coax sb into doing sth/coax sb to do sth** *We managed to coax him into eating a little supper.*

cob·ble / ˈkɒbəllˈkɑː- / also **cob·ble·stone** / ˈkɒbəlstəʊnlˈkɑːbəlstoʊn / *n* [C usually plural] round stone used in the past for making road surfaces —**cobbled** *adj: cobbled streets*

cob·bler /ˈkɒblə‖ˈkɑːblər/ *n* [C,U] *old-fashioned* someone whose job is to make or repair shoes

co·bra /ˈkəʊbrə‖ˈkoʊ-/ *n* [C] an African or Asian poisonous snake

cob·web /ˈkɒbweb‖ˈkɑːb-/ *n* [C] a structure consisting of fine threads made by SPIDERS to catch insects

cobweb

Coca-Co·la /ˌkəʊkə ˈkəʊlə‖ˌkoʊkə ˈkoʊlə/ also- **Coke** *n* [C,U] *trademark* a sweet brown non-alcoholic drink

co·caine /kəʊˈkeɪn, kə-‖koʊ-/ *n* [U] a drug that prevents pain, or that is taken illegally for pleasure

cock¹ /kɒk‖kɑːk/ *n* **1** *BrE* a male chicken; ROOSTER *AmE* **2** a rude word for a PENIS

cock² *v* [T] to raise or move part of your head or face to one side: *Jeremy cocked his head to one side, listening carefully.*

  cock sth ↔ up *phr v* [T] *BrE spoken informal* to spoil a plan or arrangement by making a stupid mistake: *These last-minute changes have really cocked up the schedule.* → see also COCK-UP

cock·e·rel /ˈkɒkərəl‖ˈkɑː-/ *n* [C] a young male chicken

cock-eyed /ˌ ˈ ◂/ *adj informal* **1** not sensible or practical: *I don't know how you get these cockeyed ideas!* **2** not straight or level: *His hat was on at a cockeyed angle.*

cock·ney /ˈkɒkni‖ˈkɑːk-/ *n* **1** [C] someone, especially a WORKING CLASS person, who comes from the east part of London **2** [U] the way of speaking English that is typical of someone from this area

cock·pit /ˈkɒkˌpɪt‖ˈkɑːk-/ *n* [C] the part of a plane or racing car in which the pilot or driver sits

cock·roach /ˈkɒk-rəʊtʃ‖ˈkɑːk-roʊtʃ/ *n* [C] a large black or brown insect that often lives where food is kept

cock·sure /ˌkɒkˈʃʊə◂‖ˌkɑːkˈʃʊr◂/ *adj informal* too confident about your own abilities

cock·tail /ˈkɒkteɪl‖ˈkɑːk-/ *n* **1** [C] an alcoholic drink made from a mixture of different drinks **2** [C,U] a mixture of small pieces of food: *fruit cocktail*

cock-up /ˈ ˌ ./ *n* [C] *BrE informal* when your plans are completely spoiled because of mistakes: *I'm afraid there's been a cock-up over the hotel reservations.*

cock·y /ˈkɒki‖ˈkɑːki/ *adj informal* too confident about yourself, in a way that annoys other people: *He's very talented, but far too cocky.* —**cockiness** *n* [U]

co·coa /ˈkəʊkəʊ‖ˈkoʊkoʊ/ *n* [U] **1** a dark brown powder used to make chocolate and to make food taste of chocolate **2** a hot drink made from this powder: *a cup of cocoa*

co·co·nut /ˈkəʊkənʌt‖ˈkoʊ-/ *n* [C,U] a large brown nut with white flesh, which is filled with a liquid

co·coon¹ /kəˈkuːn/ *n* [C] a bag of silky threads around a young insect, that protects it while it is growing

co·coon² *v* **be cocooned** to be protected or surrounded by comfort: *What a relief to be cocooned in the warmth of my bed.*

cod /kɒd‖kɑːd/ *n* [C,U] a large sea fish that lives in the North Atlantic, or this fish as food

code /kəʊd‖koʊd/ *n* **1** [C] a set of rules or laws: *The restaurant was fined for ignoring the Health and Safety Code.* | **code of conduct/ ethics/practice** (=rules of correct behaviour in a particular profession): *a code of medical ethics* **2** [U] a system of words, letters, or signs that are used instead of ordinary writing or speech, in order to send secret messages: **in code**: *messages written in code* **3** [C] *BrE* the part of a telephone number that you have to add for a different town or country; AREA CODE *AmE*: *The code for Manchester is 0161.* → see also BAR CODE, POSTCODE, ZIP CODE

cod·ed /ˈkəʊdʒd‖ˈkoʊ-/ *adj* a coded message uses a system of words, letters or signs, instead of ordinary writing or speech, to keep its meaning secret

co-ed /ˌkəʊˈed◂‖ˈkoʊed/ *adj* co-ed schools and colleges are ones where male and female students study together

co·erce /kəʊˈɜːs‖ˈkoʊɜːrs/ *v* [T] *formal* to force someone to do something by threatening them: *He claimed that he had been coerced into confessing.* —**coercion** /kəʊˈɜːʃən‖koʊˈɜːrʒən/ *n* [U]

co·ex·ist /ˌkəʊɪɡˈzɪst‖ˌkoʊ-/ *v* [I] to exist together in spite of having different opinions, needs, or political systems: *Can the two countries coexist after the war?* —**coexistence** *n* [U]

cof·fee /ˈkɒfi‖ˈkɒːfi, ˈkɑːfi/ *n* **1** [U] a brown powder that is made by crushing the beans of the coffee tree **2** [U] a hot brown drink made from this powder: *Want a cup of coffee?* **3** [C] *BrE* a cup of coffee: *Two coffees, please.*

coffee ta·ble /ˈ.. ˌ../ *n* [C] a low table in a LIVING ROOM

cof·fers /ˈkɒfəz‖ˈkɒːfərz, ˈkɑː-/ *n* [plural] the money that an organization has available to spend: *It will all be paid for out of the city's coffers.*

cof·fin /ˈkɒfɪn‖ˈkɒː-, ˈkɑː-/ *n* [C] the box in which a dead person is buried

cog /kɒɡ‖kɑːɡ/ *n* [C] a wheel in a machine with bits like teeth around the edge that fit into bits on another cog, so that when one cog turns, it makes the other turn

co·gent /ˈkəʊdʒənt‖ˈkoʊ-/ *adj formal* a cogent reason is strong enough to persuade people that something is correct: *There were cogent reasons for a nuclear test ban.* —**cogently** *adv*

co·gnac /ˈkɒnjæk‖-, ˈkɑː-/ *n* [C,U] a type of BRANDY (=strong alcoholic drink) made in France

co·hab·it /ˌkəʊˈhæbʒt‖ˌkoʊ-/ *v* [I] *formal* if two unmarried people cohabit, they live together as though they were married —**cohabitation** /kəʊ-ˌhæbʒˈteɪʃən‖koʊ-/ *n*

co·her·ent /kəʊˈhɪərənt‖koʊˈhɪr-/ *adj* clear and easy to understand: *a coherent answer* —**coherently** *adv* —**coherence** *n* [U]

co·he·sion /kəʊˈhiːʒən‖koʊ-/ *n* [U] when a group of people are closely united: *What the country needs is a sense of national cohesion.*

coil¹ /kɔɪl/ also **coil up** *v* [I,T] to wind or twist into a round shape, or to make something do this: *The snake coiled around the tree.* —**coiled** *adj*

coil[2] *n* [C] **1** a piece of wire, rope etc that has been wound into a circular shape: *a coil of rope* **2** a type of CONTRACEPTIVE

coin[1] /kɔɪn/ *n* **1** [C] a piece of money made of metal: *He collects foreign coins.* **2 toss/flip a coin** to decide something by throwing a coin into the air and guessing which side will show when it falls: *Let's flip a coin to see who goes first.*

coin[2] *v* [T] to invent a new word or phrase that many people start to use: *I wonder who coined the word "cyberpunk".*

co·in·cide /ˌkəʊɪnˈsaɪd‖ˌkoʊ-/ *v* [I] **1** to happen by chance at the same time or in the same place as something else: **+ with** *Their wedding anniversary coincides with my birthday.* **2** if two people's ideas or opinions coincide, they are the same

co·in·ci·dence /kəʊˈɪnsɪdəns‖koʊ-/ *n* [C,U] a surprising situation in which two similar events happen by chance at the same time or to the same people: *What a coincidence! I hadn't expected to meet you here.* | **by coincidence** *By an odd coincidence, my husband and my father have the same first name.* —**coincidental** /kəʊˌɪnsɪˈdentl‖koʊ-/ *adj* —**coincidentally** *adv*

col·an·der /ˈkʌləndə, ˈkɒl-‖ˈkʌləndər, ˈkɑː-/ *n* [C] a metal or plastic bowl with holes in it, used for separating liquid from food

cold[1] /kəʊld‖koʊld/ *adj* **1** having a low temperature: *I'm really cold – can you turn on the heater?* | *It's cold outside.* | **go/get cold** (=become cold): *My coffee's gone cold.* | **ice-cold/freezing cold** (=very cold): *The water was freezing cold.* **2** without friendly feelings: *a polite but cold greeting* **3** cold food is cooked, but is not eaten while it is hot: *a lunch of cold chicken and salad* **4 get/have cold feet** *informal* to start to feel that you are not brave enough to do something: *She was getting cold feet about getting married.* **5 give sb the cold shoulder** to deliberately ignore someone or be unfriendly to them **6 in cold blood** in a cruel deliberate way without any emotion: *innocent civilians murdered in cold blood* —**coldness** *n* [U] ➡ see also COLDLY

cold[2] *n* **1** [C] a common illness that makes it difficult to breathe through your nose: **have a cold** *You sound as if you have a cold.* | **catch a cold** *Keep your feet dry so you don't catch a cold.* **2** [U] **the cold** a very low temperature, especially outside: *Come in out of the cold.* | *She was wrapped in a thick woollen shawl, to protect her from the cold.* **3 to be left out in the cold** *informal* to not be included in an activity: *Anyone who didn't join the gang was left out in the cold.*

cold[3] *adv* suddenly and completely: *In the middle of his speech, he stopped cold.*

cold-blood·ed /ˌ ˈ...◂/ *adj* **1** cruel and showing no feelings: *a cold-blooded killer* **2** having a body temperature that changes according to the temperature of the air or ground around: *Snakes are cold-blooded animals.*

cold-heart·ed /ˌ ˈ...◂/ *adj* showing no sympathy: *a cold-hearted man*

cold·ly /ˈkəʊldli‖ˈkoʊld-/ *adv* in an unfriendly way: *"I'm busy," said Sarah coldly.*

cold tur·key /ˌ ˈ../ *n* [U] if you go cold turkey, you suddenly stop taking an illegal drug or stop

smoking, and experience unpleasant effects because of this

cole·slaw /ˈkəʊlslɔː‖ˈkoʊlslɔː/ *n* [U] a SALAD made with thinly cut RAW CABBAGE

col·ic /ˈkɒlɪk‖ˈkɑː-/ *n* [U] pain in the stomach that babies often get

col·lab·o·rate /kəˈlæbəreɪt/ *v* [I] **1** to work together to produce or achieve something: **+ on/with** *The two authors collaborated on the translation of the novel.* **2** to help an enemy army or government that controls your country: *There are rumours that he collaborated with the secret police.* —**collaborator** *n* [C]

col·lab·o·ra·tion /kəˌlæbəˈreɪʃən/ *n* [U] **1** when you work together with someone to produce something: *The two companies worked in close collaboration on the project.* **2** help given to an enemy during a war

col·lage /ˈkɒlɑːʒ‖kəˈlɑːʒ/ *n* **1** [C] a picture made by sticking pieces of paper, cloth etc onto a surface **2** [U] the art of making pictures in this way

col·lapse[1] /kəˈlæps/ *v* [I] **1** to fall down or inwards suddenly: *Many buildings collapsed during the earthquake.* **2** to suddenly fall down or become unconscious because you are ill or very weak: *He collapsed with a dangerously high fever.* **3** to fail suddenly and completely: *Thousands were made unemployed after the country's mining industry collapsed.*

collapse[2] *n* [C,U] **1** the sudden failure of a business, process, plan etc: *the stock market collapse of 1987* **2** when something falls down or inwards: *Floods caused the collapse of the bridge.* **3** when you are so weak that you almost fall down unconscious: *The prisoner was in a state of nervous collapse.*

col·lap·si·ble /kəˈlæpsɪbəl/ *adj* something that is collapsible can be folded up into a smaller size: *a collapsible table*

collars

col·lar[1] /ˈkɒlə‖ˈkɑːlər/ *n* [C] **1** the part of a shirt, coat, dress etc that fits around your neck ➡ see colour picture on page 113 **2** a leather band fastened around an animal's neck

collar[2] *v* [T] *informal* to catch and hold someone: *Two policemen collared him before he could get away.*

col·lar·bone /ˈkɒləbəʊn‖ˈkɑːlərboʊn/ *n* [C] one of a pair of bones that go from the base of your neck to your shoulders ➡ see picture at SKELETON

col·lat·e·ral /kəˈlætərəl/ *n* [U] *technical* property or money that you promise to give to someone if you cannot pay back a debt: *He offered his house as collateral for the loan.*

col·league /ˈkɒliːgǁˈkɑː-/ n [C] someone you work with: *my colleague at the university*

col·lect[1] /kəˈlekt/ v **1** [T] to get things and bring them together: *I'll collect everyone's papers at the end of the test.* **2** [T] to get and keep things that interest you: *I started collecting foreign coins when I was eight years old.* **3** [I,T] to ask a lot of people to give money for a particular purpose: *We're collecting money for the Red Cross.* **4** [I] to come together in a place: *A crowd of people had collected at the scene of the accident.* **5** [T] *BrE* to go to a particular place and bring someone or something away: **collect sb from** *Can you collect the kids from school?* **6 collect yourself/your thoughts** to make yourself calmer and able to think more clearly

collect[2] *adj,adv AmE* **1 call sb collect** if you call someone collect, the person who gets the telephone call pays for it **2 collect call** a telephone call that is paid for by the person who gets it

col·lect·ed /kəˈlektɪd/ adj **1 collected poems/stories etc** all the poems, stories etc of a particular writer included together in one book: *the collected works of Shakespeare* **2** calm and in control of yourself and your thoughts, feelings etc

col·lec·tion /kəˈlekʃən/ n **1** [C] a set of similar things that you keep together, especially because they are interesting or attractive: *your CD collection* | **+ of** *a fine collection of modern paintings* **2** [U] when you bring together things of the same type from different places: **+ of** *the collection of reliable information* **3** [C,U] when you ask people for money for a particular purpose: *We're planning to have a collection for UNICEF.* **4** [C,U] when something is taken away from a place: *Garbage collections are made every Tuesday morning.* **5** [singular] *informal* a group of people or things that are together in the same place: *There was an odd collection of people at the party.*

col·lec·tive[1] /kəˈlektɪv/ adj [only before noun] shared or done by all the members of a group together: **collective decision/effort etc** *It's our collective responsibility to see that everything is done right.* —**collectively** adv

collective[2] n [C] a business owned and controlled by the people who work in it

col·lec·tor /kəˈlektəǁ-tər/ n [C] **1 rent/tax/ ticket collector** someone whose job is to collect money or tickets from people **2** someone who collects interesting or beautiful things for pleasure: *a stamp collector*

col·lege /ˈkɒlɪdʒǁˈkɑː-/ n **1** [C,U] a place where students study after they leave school: *an art college* **2** [C] a part of a university: *King's College, Cambridge*

col·lide /kəˈlaɪd/ v [I] to crash violently into something or someone: *The two trains collided* (=hit each other) *in a tunnel.* | **+ with** *In the thick fog, her car collided with a lorry.*

col·lie·ry /ˈkɒljəriǁˈkɑː-/ n [C] *BrE* a coal mine

and the buildings and machinery connected with it

col·li·sion /kəˈlɪʒən/ n [C,U] a violent crash in which one vehicle hits another: **head-on collision** (=between vehicles going in opposite directions): *a head-on collision between two trains*

col·lo·qui·al /kəˈləʊkwiəlǁ-ˈloʊ-/ adj colloquial language is the kind of language used in informal conversations: *colloquial expressions* —**colloquially** adv —**colloquialism** n [C]

col·lu·sion /kəˈluːʒən/ n [U] *formal* when someone secretly agrees with someone else to do something dishonest or illegal: *collusion between politicians and Mafia leaders*

co·lon /ˈkəʊlɒnǁˈkoʊ-/ n [C] the mark (:), used in writing to introduce a list, examples etc

colo·nel /ˈkɜːnlǁˈkɜːr-/ n [C] an officer with a high rank in the Army, Marines, or the US Air Force

co·lo·ni·al /kəˈləʊniəlǁ-ˈloʊ-/ adj relating to colonialism or a colony: *Ghana became independent in 1986 after 85 years of colonial rule.*

co·lo·ni·al·is·m /kəˈləʊniəlɪzəmǁ-ˈloʊ-/ n [U] the system by which a powerful country rules another less powerful country —**colonialist** adj, n [C]

col·o·nize (also **-ise** *BrE*) /ˈkɒlənaɪzǁˈkɑː-/ v [T] to get control of another country or area and send your own people to live there: *Australia was colonized in the 18th century.* —**colonization** /ˌkɒlənaɪˈzeɪʃənǁˌkɑːlənə-/ n [U]

col·o·ny /ˈkɒləniǁˈkɑː-/ n [C] **1** a country or area that is controlled by a more powerful country: *Algeria was formerly a French colony.* **2** a group of people with the same interests who live together: *an artists' colony* **3** a group of the same kind of animals living together: *an ant colony*

col·or /ˈkʌlərǁ-ər/ the American spelling of COLOUR ➞ see colour picture on page 114

color-blind /ˈ.. ./ the American spelling of COLOUR BLIND

col·or·ful /ˈkʌləfəlǁ-lər-/ the American spelling of COLOURFUL

col·or·less /ˈkʌlələsǁˈkʌlər-/ the American spelling of COLOURLESS

co·los·sal /kəˈlɒsəlǁkəˈlɑː-/ adj extremely large: *They've run up colossal debts.*

colour[1] *BrE*, **color** *AmE* /ˈkʌlərǁ-ər/ n **1** [C,U] red, blue, yellow etc: *"What colour is your new car?" "Blue."* | *the colors of the rainbow* | *houses painted in bright colours* | **in colour** *The meat should be pale pink in colour.* ➞ see colour picture on page 114 **2** [U] the quality of having colours: *flowers that will add colour to your garden* **3 colour photograph/film/television** a photograph, film etc that shows all the different colours, not just black and white **4** [C,U] how dark or light someone's skin is: *people of all colors* **5** [U] the appearance of someone's skin, that shows how healthy they are: *The fresh air has brought some colour to her cheeks.* **6** [U]

---

interesting or exciting qualities: *a story full of life, colour, and adventure* → see also COLOURS, OFF COLOUR

colour in *BrE*/**color in** *AmE*

colour² *BrE*, **color** *AmE* — *v* **1** [T] to make something a different colour: *Do you colour your hair or is it natural?* **2** also **colour in** [T] to put colour onto a drawing or picture using coloured pencils: *Can you trace the picture and colour it in?* **3** **colour sb's judgment/opinion etc** to influence your opinion about something: *Personal feelings coloured his judgment.*

colour-blind *BrE*, **color-blind** *AmE* /'...'./ *adj* not able to see the difference between particular colours — **colour blindness** *n* [U]

col·oured *BrE*, **colored** *AmE* /'kʌləd‖-ərd/ *adj* **1** having a colour, or colours such as blue, red, yellow etc: *coloured glass* **2** an offensive word used about someone who belongs to a race that does not have white skin

col·our·ful *BrE*, **colorful** *AmE* /'kʌləfəl‖-lər-/ *adj* **1** having a lot of bright colours: *a garden full of colourful flowers* **2** interesting, exciting, and full of variety: *You might say he's led a colourful life.*

col·our·ing *BrE*, **coloring** *AmE* /'kʌlərɪŋ/ *n* **1** [U] the colour of something, especially someone's hair, skin, eyes etc: *Mandy had her mother's dark coloring.* **2** [C,U] a substance used to give a particular colour to something, especially food: *Use food colouring to tint the icing.*

col·our·less *BrE*, **colorless** *AmE* /'kʌlələs‖'kʌlər-/ *adj* **1** not having any colour: *a colorless liquid* **2** not interesting or exciting: *a colourless little man*

col·ours *BrE*, **colors** *AmE* /'kʌləz‖-lərz/ *n* [plural] the colours that are used to show that you belong to or support a team, school, club etc: *UCLA's colors are blue and gold.*

colt /kəʊlt‖koʊlt/ *n* [C] a young male horse

col·umn /'kɒləm‖'kɑ:-/ *n* [C] **1** a tall upright stone structure like a thick pole, that supports a roof or reminds people of an event, PILLAR: *the marble columns of a Greek temple* **2** an article on a particular subject that appears regularly in a newspaper or magazine: *an advice column* **3** something with a narrow shape: + *of a column of smoke* **4** numbers or words written under each other down a page: *Pick a number from the first column.* **5** a long moving line of people, vehicles etc: + *of a column of soldiers on the march*

col·umn·ist /'kɒləmɪst, -ləmnɪst‖'kɑ:-/ *n* [C]

someone who regularly writes articles for a newspaper or magazine

co·ma /'kəʊmə‖'koʊ-/ *n* [C] a state in which someone is not conscious for a long time, usually as a result of an accident or illness: **be in a coma** *Ben was in a coma for six days.*

comb¹ /kəʊm‖koʊm/ *n* [C] a piece of plastic or metal with a row of thin teeth, that you use to make your hair tidy

comb² *v* [T] **1** to make your hair tidy with a comb: *Run upstairs and comb your hair!* **2** to search a place thoroughly: **comb sth for sth** *Police are combing the area for more bombs.*

com·bat¹ /'kɒmbæt‖'kɑ:m-/ *n* [C,U] fighting during a war: *men with little experience of armed combat* | **in combat** *Her husband was killed in combat.*

com·bat² /'kɒmbæt, kəm'bæt‖kəm'bæt, 'kɑ:m-bæt/ *v* [T] **-ated, -ating** also **-tted, -tting** to try to stop something bad from happening or getting worse: *The police are using new technology to combat crime.*

com·ba·tant /'kɒmbətənt‖kəm'bætnt/ *n* [C] someone who fights in a war

com·ba·tive /'kɒmbətɪv‖kəm'bætɪv/ *adj* ready to fight or argue: *Paul was in a combative mood.*

com·bi·na·tion /ˌkɒmbɪ'neɪʃən‖ˌkɑ:m-/ *n* [C] **1** two or more different things that are used or put together: + *of a combination of bad management and inexperience* **2** a set of numbers or letters you need to open a combination lock

combination lock /...'. ./ *n* [C] a lock that is opened by using a special set of numbers or letters

com·bine¹ /kəm'baɪn/ *v* **1** [I,T] to join together, or join two or more things together: *The two chemicals combine to produce a powerful explosive.* | **combined with** *The heat combined with the loud music was beginning to make her feel ill.* **2** [T] to do two very different activities at the same time: **combine sth with sth** *She manages to combine family life with a career.*

com·bine² /'kɒmbaɪn‖'kɑ:m-/ *n* [C] **1** also **combine harvester** a large machine used on a farm to cut a crop and separate the grain **2** a group of businesses that work together

com·bus·ti·ble /kəm'bʌstɪbəl/ *adj* technical starting to burn easily: *Gasoline is highly combustible.*

com·bus·tion /kəm'bʌstʃən/ *n* [U] the process of burning

come /kʌm/ *v* [I] **came** /keɪm/, **come, coming** **1** if someone or something comes, they move to the place where you are or to the place where you are going: *Did you come by train?* | + **to/towards/here etc** *Come here, right now!* | *Is Susan coming to the wedding?* | **come and do sth** *Come and have dinner with us.* | **come to do sth** *She comes to see us every summer.* **2** to arrive somewhere or reach a place: *When Bert came home from work, he looked tired.* | *The phone bill has come at a bad time.* | + **to** *At last we came to a small village.* | **here comes** spoken (=used to say that someone is arriving now): *Here comes Karen now.* **3** if a time or event comes, it arrives or starts to happen: *Spring came early that year.* | *The time has come to make some changes.* **4** to have a particular position in a list, race, or competition: *What letter comes after 'u'?* | *come*

first/last/next etc *I came last in the cycle race.*
5 to reach a particular height or length: **+ to/ up to/down to** *The water only came up to my knees.* **6** to be produced or sold in a particular form: *The sweaters come in four sizes.* **7 come loose/undone/open etc** to become loose, untied etc: *Your shoelace has come undone.* **8** to be available: **+ in** *Do these shoes come in black?* **9 come as a surprise/shock etc** to make someone feel surprised etc: *Her death came as a shock to everyone.* **10 come to do sth** to begin to do something: *That's the kind of behaviour I've come to expect from him.* **11 come naturally/easily** to be easy for someone to do: **+ to** *Acting came naturally to Rae.* **12 in the years/days to come** in the future: *I think we shall regret this decision in the years to come.* **13 come to think of it** *spoken* used to say that you have just remembered something: *Come to think of it, Cooper did mention it to me.* **14 come and go** to exist for only a short time and then disappear: *Fashions come and go.* → see also **how come** (HOW¹), **come to mind** (MIND¹), **come to life** (LIFE), **come clean** (CLEAN¹), **come unstuck** (UNSTUCK)

come about *phr v* [I] to happen or develop: *How did this extraordinary situation come about?*

come across *phr v* **1** [T **come across** sth] to meet someone or discover something by chance: *I came across this photograph among some old newspapers.* **2** [I] if someone or something comes across in a particular way, that is how they seem to people: **+ as** *He comes across as a nice guy.*

come along *phr v* [I] **1** to appear or arrive: *I'm ready to take any job that comes along.* **2** to develop or improve: *Terry's work has really come along this year.* **3** to follow someone or go with them: *Can I come along too?*

come apart *phr v* [I] *especially BrE* to break into pieces without anyone using force: *The book just came apart in my hands.*

come around *phr v* [I] *AmE* to COME ROUND

come at sb *phr v* [T] to move towards someone in a threatening way: *She came at him with a knife.*

come away *phr v* [T] *BrE* to become unfastened or separated from something: **+ from** *I pulled, and the handle came away from the door.*

come back *phr v* [I] **1** to return: *When is your sister coming back from Europe?* **2 come back to sb** to suddenly be remembered: *Then, everything William had said came back to me.* **3** to become fashionable again: *Long skirts are coming back.* → see also COMEBACK

come between sb *phr v* [T] to cause trouble between people: *I didn't want the question of money to come between us.*

come by *phr v* **1** [T **come by** sth] to get something that is rare or difficult to find: **be hard to come by** *Jobs are very hard to come by in the summer months.* **2** [I,T] *AmE* to visit someone for a short time: *Veronica came by to see me today.*

come down *phr v* [I] **1** if a price, level etc comes down, it becomes lower: *Wait until prices come down before you buy.* **2** if a building or tree comes down, it falls or is made to fall: *This old wall will have to come down.*

come down on sb/sth *phr v* [T] **1** to punish someone severely: *The school came down hard on any students who were caught drinking.* **2 come down on the side of** to decide to support something or someone: *The court came down on the side of the boy's father.*

come down to sth *phr v* [T] if a problem or decision comes down to a particular point, that is the most important point involved in it: *It all comes down to money in the end.*

come down with sth *phr v* [T] to get an illness: *I think I'm coming down with flu.*

come forward *phr v* [I] to offer to help: *Witnesses are asked to come forward with information about the robbery.*

come from *phr v* [T] to have first lived in a particular place or existed in a particular form: *His mother came from Texas.* | *The word 'video' comes from the Latin word meaning 'I see'.*

come in *phr v* [I] **1** to enter a room or house: *Come in and sit down.* **2** to arrive: *Reports are coming in of an earthquake in Japan.* **3 come in first/second etc** to finish first, second etc in a race or competition **4** to become fashionable or popular: *I remember when miniskirts first came in.* **5 come in useful/handy** to be useful: *Bring some rope – it might come in handy.* **6** when the TIDE comes in, it moves towards the land

come in for sth *phr v* **come in for criticism/ blame** to be criticized or blamed: *After the riots the police came in for a lot of criticism.*

come into sth *phr v* [T] **1** to be involved in something: *How exactly does her husband come into the story?* **2** to receive money from someone who has died: *I came into some money when my grandfather died.*

come of sth *phr v* [T] **1** to result from something: *We wanted to start a pop group, but nothing ever came of it.* **2 come of age** to reach the age when you are legally considered to be an adult

come off *phr v* **1** [I,T **come off** sth] to become removed from something: *A button had come off his coat.* **2** [I] to succeed: *a $4 million deal that didn't come off* **3 come off well/ badly** to get into a good or bad situation as a result of something: *If we have an argument, I always come off worst.* **4 come off it!** *spoken* used to tell someone that you think they are lying or saying something stupid: *Oh, come off it! Don't pretend you didn't know.*

come on *phr v* **1** [I] to start working: *The lights suddenly came on in the cinema.* **2 come on!** *spoken* **a)** used to tell someone to hurry, or to encourage them to do something: *Come on, it's not that hard.* **b)** used to tell someone that you do not believe them: *Oh come on, don't lie to me!*

come out *phr v* [I] **1** to become known: *The truth will come out eventually.* **2** to become available for people to buy: *When does his new book come out?* **3** to state your opinions clearly and directly: *Why don't you just come out and say what you really think?* **4** if something you say comes out in a particular way, that is how it sounds or how it is understood: *I tried to explain, but it came out all wrong.* **5** if dirt or a mark comes out, it is removed by washing or cleaning it **6 not come out** if a photograph does not come out, you do not get a clear picture: *Some of our wedding photos didn't come out.* **7** when the sun, moon, or stars come out, they appear in the sky

come out in sth *phr v* **come out in spots/a rash** *BrE* to become covered in spots because you are ill

come out with sth *phr v* [T] to say something, especially in a way that is not expected: *Tanya comes out with some stupid remarks.*

come over *phr v* **1** [I] to come to a place: *Can I come over to your place tonight?* **2** [T **come over** sb] if a feeling comes over you, it affects you strongly: *A wave of sleepiness came over her.* | *I'm sorry I was so rude – I don't know what came over me!* **3** [I] if someone or something comes over in a particular way, that is how they seem to people: **+ as** *Mrs Robins comes over as a cold, strict woman.*

come round *BrE*, **come around** *especially AmE phr v* [I] **1** to visit someone: *Paul is coming round to my house for tea.* **2** to change your opinion so that you now agree with someone: **+ to** *I'm sure he'll come round to our way of thinking.* **3** to become conscious again: *He must have been drugged – we'll have to wait till he comes round.* **4** to happen as a regular event: *Christmas will soon be coming round again.*

come through *phr v* **1** [T **come through** sth] to continue to exist or succeed after a difficult or dangerous time: *We've come through all kinds of trouble together.* **2** [I] if a piece of news or a result comes through, it becomes known or arrives: *His divorce should come through next month.*

come to *phr v* **1** [T **come to** sth] to reach a particular result: *After a long discussion, we finally came to a decision.* **2** **come to £20/$3 etc** to be a total amount of £20, $3 etc: *That comes to $24.67 ma'am.* **3** [T **come to** sb] if an idea or memory comes to you, you suddenly realize or remember it: *I can't remember her name just now, but it'll come to me.* **4** [I] to become conscious again: *When I came to, I was lying on the grass.*

come under sth *phr v* [T] **1** **come under attack/fire/pressure etc** to be attacked, criticized, threatened etc: *The students have come under pressure to report their friends.* **2** to be controlled by something: *These schools come under the control of the Department of Education.* **3** to be in a particular part of a book or information system: *Skiing? That'll come under 'Sport'.*

come up *phr v* [I] **1** to be mentioned or suggested: *The subject didn't come up at the meeting.* **2** **be coming up** to be happening soon: *Isn't your birthday coming up?* **3** if a problem comes up, it suddenly happens: *Something's come up, so I won't be able to go with you.* **4** when the sun or moon comes up, it rises

come up against sb/sth *phr v* [T] to have to deal with problems, opposition etc: *when black politicians come up against racist attitudes*

come upon sb/sth *phr v* [T] *literary* to COME ACROSS someone or something

come up to sth *phr v* [T] to be as good as something: *This work doesn't come up to your usual standards.*

come up with sth *phr v* [T] to think of an idea, plan, reply etc: *They still haven't come up with a name for the baby.*

come·back /'kʌmbæk/ *n* **1** **make a comeback** to return after a long time and become popular or successful again: *a fashion that made a brief comeback in the 1980s* **2** [C] a quick reply that is clever or funny: *I can never think of a good comeback.*

co·me·di·an /kə'mi:diən/ *n* [C] someone whose job is to tell jokes and make people laugh

come·down /'kʌmdaʊn/ *n* [singular] *informal* a situation that is not as good as something that you had before: *From boxing champion to prison cook – what a comedown!*

com·e·dy /'kɒmɪdi||'kɑː-/ *n* [C, U] a funny film, play etc or entertainment of that type: *We saw the new Robin Williams comedy last night.*

com·et /'kɒmɪt||'kɑː-/ *n* [C] a very bright object in the sky like a star with a tail

come·up·pance /kʌm'ʌpəns/ *n* **get your comeuppance** *informal* to be punished or suffer because you have done something bad: *He gets his comeuppance at the end of the play.*

com·fort[1] /'kʌmfət||-ərt/ *n* **1** [U] a feeling of being physically relaxed and satisfied without any pain: *shoes designed for comfort* | *Now you can sit in comfort and watch the show.* **2** [U] a feeling of being calm or hopeful after having been worried or sad: *Your letter brought me great comfort after Henry died.* **3** [U] a way of living in which you have all the things you need: **in comfort** *They had saved enough money to spend their old age in comfort.* **4** **be a comfort to** to help someone feel calm or less worried: *She was a great comfort to me while I was in hospital.* **5** [C, usually plural] something that makes your life more comfortable: *the comforts of modern civilization* | *home comforts* → opposite DISCOMFORT

comfort[2] *v* [T] to make someone feel happier or less worried by being kind to them: *Jean was terribly upset, and we all tried to comfort her.* —**comforting** *adj* —**comfortingly** *adv*

com·for·ta·ble /'kʌmftəbəl, 'kʌmfət-||'kʌmfərt-, 'kʌmft-/ *adj* **1** making you feel physically relaxed and satisfied: *The hotel room was small, clean and comfortable.* | *a comfortable chair* **2** emotionally relaxed and not worried: *I'm much more comfortable knowing you're around.* **3** having enough money to live on without worrying: *We're not rich, but we are comfortable.* —**comfortably** *adv* → opposite UNCOMFORTABLE

com·fort·er /'kʌmfətə||-fərtər/ *n* [C] *AmE* a cover for a bed that is filled with soft warm material; QUILT

com·fy /'kʌmfi/ *adj informal* comfortable

com·ic[1] /'kɒmɪk||'kɑː-/ *adj* funny or amusing: *a comic character*

comic[2] *n* [C] **1** someone whose job is to tell jokes and make people laugh; COMEDIAN **2** also **comic book** *especially AmE* a magazine that tells a story using sets of pictures

com·i·cal /'kɒmɪkəl||'kɑː-/ *adj* funny in a strange or unexpected way: *He looked comical, his hands waving in the air.* —**comically** /-kli/ *adv*

comic book /'.. ./ *n* [C] *especially AmE* a COMIC

comic strip /ˈ.. ./ *n* [C] a set of pictures that tell a short funny story

com·ing[1] /ˈkʌmɪŋ/ *n* **1** **the coming of** when something new begins: *With the coming of the railroad, the population grew quickly.* **2 comings and goings** *informal* the movements of people as they arrive and leave a particular place: *She watches the comings and goings of all their visitors.*

coming[2] *adj* [only before noun] happening soon: *animals preparing for the coming winter* → see also UP-AND-COMING

com·ma /ˈkɒməǁˈkɑːmə/ *n* [C] the mark (,) used in writing or printing to show a short pause

com·mand[1] /kəˈmɑːndǁkəˈmænd/ *n* **1** [C] an order that must be obeyed: *Don't shoot until your officer gives the command.* **2** [U] control of a group of people or a situation: **in command** *Who is in command here?* **3** [C] an instruction to a computer to do something **4** [singular] a thorough knowledge of something, especially a language: **have (a) command of** *have a good command of English*

command[2] *v* **1** [I,T] to order someone to do something: **command sb to do sth** *The king commanded his men to guard the palace.* **2** to control something: *Admiral Douglas commands a fleet of 200 ships in the Pacific.* **3** [T] to get attention, respect etc because you are important or popular: *a teacher who commands a great deal of respect*

com·man·dant /ˌkɒmənˈdæntǁˈkɑːməndænt/ *n* [C] the chief officer in charge of a military organization

com·man·deer /ˌkɒmənˈdɪəǁˌkɑːmənˈdɪr/ *v* [T] to take someone's property for military use: *The hotel was commandeered for use as a hospital.*

com·mand·er /kəˈmɑːndəǁkəˈmændər/ *n* [C] **1** an officer who is in charge of a military organization or group **2** an officer who has a middle rank in a navy

com·mand·ing /kəˈmɑːndɪŋǁkəˈmæn-/ *adj* [only before noun] making people respect you: *He has a commanding manner and voice.*

com·mand·ment /kəˈmɑːndməntǁkəˈmænd-/ *n* [C] one of a set of ten rules given by God in the Bible that tell people how they should behave

com·man·do /kəˈmɑːndəʊǁkəˈmændoʊ/ *n* [C] a soldier who is specially trained to make surprise attacks into enemy areas

com·mem·o·rate /kəˈmeməreɪt/ *v* [T] to show that an event or person is remembered with respect: *a monument commemorating those who died in the war* —**commemorative** *adj* —**commemoration** /kəˌmeməˈreɪʃən/ *n* [U]

com·mence /kəˈmens/ *v* [I,T] *formal* to begin: *Work on the building will commence immediately.*

com·mence·ment /kəˈmensmənt/ *n* [C,U] *formal* the beginning of something: *Fees must be paid prior to commencement of the course.*

com·mend /kəˈmend/ *v* [T] to formally praise someone or something: *She was commended for*

her years of service to the community. —**commendation** /ˌkɒmənˈdeɪʃənǁˌkɑː-/ *n* [C,U]

com·men·da·ble /kəˈmendəbəl/ *adj* deserving praise: *a commendable effort* —**commendably** *adv*

com·men·su·rate /kəˈmenʃərɨt/ *adj* *formal* equal to or suitable for a particular amount, size, level etc: **+ with** *The salary will be commensurate with age and experience.*

com·ment[1] /ˈkɒməntǁˈkɑː-/ *n* **1** [C,U] an opinion that you give about someone or something: **make a comment** *He kept making rude comments about the other guests.* **2 no comment** *spoken* used to say that you do not want to answer a question

comment[2] *v* [I,T] to give an opinion about someone or something: **+ on** *People were always commenting on my sister's looks.* | **+ that** *Lee commented that the film was very violent.*

com·men·ta·ry /ˈkɒməntərɨǁˈkɑːmənteri/ *n* **1** [C,U] a description of an event that is broadcast on the television or radio, while the event is happening: *live commentary on the race* **2** [C,U] written explanations and opinions about a subject, book, or idea: *political commentary*

com·men·ta·tor /ˈkɒmənteɪtəǁˈkɑːmənteɪtər/ *n* [C] **1** someone who describes an event on television or radio **2** someone who knows a lot about a subject and writes about it or discusses it: *political commentators* —**commentate** /ˈkɒmənteɪtǁˈkɑː-/ *v* [I]

com·merce /ˈkɒmɜːsǁˈkɑːmɜːrs/ *n* [U] the buying and selling of goods and services

com·mer·cial[1] /kəˈmɜːʃəlǁ-ɜːr-/ *adj* connected with the buying and selling of things and with making money: *The film was a huge commercial success.* —**commercially** *adv*

commercial[2] *n* [C] an advertisement on television or radio: *soft drinks commercials* —**commercialism** *n* [U]

com·mer·cial·ized (also **-ised** *BrE*) /kəˈmɜːʃəlaɪzdǁ-ɜːr-/ *adj* too concerned with making money: *Christmas is getting so commercialized.*

com·mis·e·rate /kəˈmɪzəreɪt/ *v* [I] to say you feel sympathy for someone who is unhappy about something —**commiseration** /kəˌmɪzəˈreɪʃən/ *n* [C,U]

com·mis·sion[1] /kəˈmɪʃən/ *n* **1** [C] an official group whose job is to find out about or control an activity: *the Equal Opportunities Commission* **2** [C,U] money paid to someone when they sell something: **+ on** *He earns 30% commission on each car.* **3** [C,U] when people ask someone to do a piece of work for them, for example to write a play or paint a picture

commission[2] *v* [T] to ask for a piece of work to be done by someone, especially by a writer, artist, or musician: *a report commissioned by the government* | **commission sb to do sth** *Renshaw has been commissioned to design a new bridge.*

com·mis·sion·er /kəˈmɪʃənəǁ-ər/ *n* [C] someone who has an important position in an official organization: *a police commissioner*

GRAMMAR NOTE: a or the (2)
Use **the** before a thing or person when it is clear which one you are talking about: *the old man who lives next door.* Use **a** or **an** to talk about a person or thing when it is not important to say which one: *I went out to buy* **a** *newspaper.* | **A** *girl in my class told me about it.*

com·mit /kə'mɪt/ v **-tted, -tting 1** [T] to do something wrong or illegal: *Brady committed a series of brutal murders.* | **commit a crime** *The crime was committed around 7.30 pm.* | **commit suicide** (=kill yourself) **2** [T] to say that you will definitely do something: *The city has committed itself to cleaning up the environment.* | *Bill's contract commits him to working at weekends.* **3** [T] to use money, time, energy etc in order to achieve something: **commit sb/sth to sth** *Her whole life was committed to politics.* **4 commit sth to memory** to learn and remember something **5 not commit yourself** to refuse to say what you think or feel about something: *McCarthy wouldn't commit himself on his future plans.*

com·mit·ment /kə'mɪtmənt/ n **1** [C,U] a promise to do something or to behave in a particular way: **commitment to (doing) sth** *We have a commitment to providing quality service.* **2** [U] determination and loyalty: *The team showed great commitment.* | **+ to** *Her commitment to her job is beyond doubt.* **3** [C] something that you have arranged to do which prevents you from doing anything else: *Mr Williams will be unable to attend due to prior commitments.*

com·mit·ted /kə'mɪt‚d/ adj willing to work very hard at your job or at an activity: *a committed teacher*

com·mit·tee /kə'mɪti/ n [C] a group of people who meet regularly and have been chosen to do a particular job or make decisions: *the Highways Committee* | *a committee meeting* | **be on a committee** (=be a member of it): *He's on the finance committee of a mental health charity.*

com·mod·i·ty /kə'mɒd‚ti||kə'mɑː-/ n [C] a product that is bought and sold: *a valuable commodity*

com·mon[1] /'kɒmən||'kɑː-/ adj **1** existing in large numbers or happening often: *Foxes are quite common in this country.* | *a common spelling mistake* | **it is common (for sb) to do sth** *It's common for new fathers to feel jealous of their babies.* | **common practice** (=a usual way of doing something): *Working from home is common practice.* | **+ among** *a disease common among young children* **2** belonging to or shared by two or more people or things: *a common goal* | *We both had a common interest.* | **+ to** *problems that are common to all big cities* | **common ground** (=things that people or groups agree about or are interested in): *There was little common ground between the two sides.* | **the common good** (=what is best for everyone): *We need to work together for the common good.* **3 common knowledge** if something is common knowledge a lot of people know about it, even though it is supposed to be a secret: *It's common knowledge that Sam's an alcoholic.* **4** [only before noun] ordinary and not special in any way: *the common people* (=ordinary people) **5** *BrE* from a low social class: *She's so common!*

common[2] n **1 have sth in common** to have the same interests or features as another person or thing: *The two computers have several features in common.* | **+ with** *I found I had a lot in common with Mary.* **2 in common with** in the same way as someone or something else: *In common with many other schools, we suffer from overcrowded classrooms.* **3** [C] a large area of grass in a

village or town that people walk or play sport on: *a walk on the common*

common-law /ˌ.. './ adj **common-law husband/wife** someone who you have lived with for a long time as if they were your husband or wife

com·mon·ly /'kɒmənli||'kɑː-/ adv usually or often: *a bird commonly found in Malaysia*

com·mon·place /'kɒmənpleɪs||'kɑː-/ adj very common or ordinary: *Divorce has become increasingly commonplace.*

common sense /ˌ.. '.◂/ n [U] the ability to behave in a sensible way and make practical decisions: *Just use your common sense.*

com·mo·tion /kə'məʊʃən||-'moʊ-/ n [singular, U] sudden noise or activity: *What's all this commotion?*

com·mu·nal /'kɒmjʊnəl, kə'mjuːnl||'kɑː-/ adj shared by a group of people: *a communal bathroom*

com·mune[1] /'kɒmjuːn||'kɑː-, kə'mjuːn/ n [C] a group of people who live and work together and share their possessions

com·mune[2] /kə'mjuːn/ v [I] *literary* **commune with sb/sth** to share your thoughts and feelings without using words: *communing with nature*

com·mu·ni·cate /kə'mjuːn‚keɪt/ v **1** [I,T] to exchange information with other people using words, letters, telephones etc: *Anna has problems communicating in English.* | **+ with** *They communicated with each other using sign language.* **2** [I,T] to talk about your thoughts and feelings so that other people can understand them clearly: **+ with** *Teenagers often find it difficult to communicate with their parents.* | **communicate sth to sb** *He doesn't communicate his ideas very clearly to the students.*

com·mu·ni·ca·tion /kə‚mjuːn‚'keɪʃən/ n **1** [U] the process of exchanging information or ideas by speaking or writing: **+ between** *There seems to be a lack of communication between the different departments.* | **be in communication with** *The pilot stayed in constant communication with the control tower.* | **means of communication** *Radio and television are important means of communication.* **2** [C] *formal* a letter, message, or telephone call

com·mu·ni·ca·tions /kə‚mjuːn‚'keɪʃənz/ n [plural] the different ways of sending and receiving information using computers, telephones, radios etc: *The power failure disrupted communications.*

com·mu·ni·ca·tive /kə'mjuːn‚kətɪv||-keɪtɪv/ adj willing to talk to other people or give them information: *Customers complained that the sales clerks were not very communicative.*

com·mu·nion /kə'mjuːnjən/ n [U] **1** *formal* a feeling of sharing thoughts and emotions with someone **2** a Christian ceremony in which bread and sometimes wine is shared

Com·mun·ism, communism /'kɒmjʊn‚nɪzəm|| 'kɑː-/ n [U] a political system based on the idea that people are equal and that things should not be privately owned

Com·mu·nist, communist /'kɒmjʊn‚st||'kɑː-/ n [C] someone who supports or believes in communism —**Communist** adj: *the Communist Party*

com·mu·ni·ty /kəˈmjuːnˌti/ n **1** [C] a small area or town and the people who live in it: *a farming community* | *She does a lot of volunteer work in the local community.* **2** [C] a group of people with the same NATIONALITY, religion, or interests: *a large Asian community* | *the international business community.*

community ser·vice /.,... '../ n [U] work that someone does to help other people without being paid, especially as a punishment for a crime

com·mute /kəˈmjuːt/ v **1** [I] to regularly travel to work, especially a long distance: + **to/from** *Jerry commutes from Scarsdale to New York.* **2** [T] *formal* to make a punishment given to a criminal less severe: *Her sentence was commuted to life imprisonment.*

commuters

com·mut·er /kəˈmjuːtəll-ər/ n [C] someone who regularly travels to work, especially a long distance: *In the rush-hour the trains are full of commuters.*

com·pact¹ /kəmˈpækt, ˈkɒmpæktllkəmˈpækt/ adj small and taking up very little space: *the compact design of modern computers*

com·pact² /kəmˈpækt/ v [T] to press something soft together so that it becomes smaller or more solid —**compacted** adj

compact disc /,.. './ n [C] a CD

com·pan·ion /kəmˈpænjən/ n [C] someone who you spend a lot of time with, or who you go somewhere with: *She became his close friend and constant companion.* | *a travelling companion*

com·pan·ion·ship /kəmˈpænjənʃɪp/ n [U] friendship from people who you spend time with: *I missed the companionship of work.*

com·pa·ny /ˈkʌmpəni/ n **1** [C] an organization that makes or sells goods or services: *Ian works for a big insurance company.* | *the Ford Motor Company* **2** [U] when someone is with you: *They obviously enjoy each other's company.* | *All I have for company is the dog.* | **in the company of/in sb's company** *He never felt very relaxed in the company of women.* | **keep sb company** (=be with someone so that they do not feel lonely): *I'm going to keep Mum company till Dad gets back.* | **be good company** (=be someone you enjoy being with): *Anna's a nice girl and very good company.* **3** [C] a group of actors, dancers etc who work together: *the Royal Ballet Company*

com·pa·ra·ble /ˈkɒmpərəbəllˈkɑːm-/ adj similar to something else in size, number, quality etc: *The surveys showed comparable results.* | + **to/with** *Is the pay rate comparable to that of other companies?*

com·par·a·tive¹ /kəmˈpærətɪv/ adj **1** considering what is similar and different about things of the same kind: *a comparative study of European languages* **2** **comparative calm/ safety/ease etc** calm, safety, ease etc when compared to something else or to what is usual: *Pierce beat her opponent with comparative ease.* (=fairly easily)

comparative² n [C] the form of an adjective or adverb that you use when comparing two things or people, or when comparing how someone or something used to be with how they are now. For example, 'taller' is the comparative of 'tall', and 'better' is the comparative of 'good'

com·par·a·tive·ly /kəmˈpærətˌvli/ adv compared to something else or to what happened before: *The children were comparatively well-behaved today.*

com·pare /kəmˈpeəll-ˈper/ v **1** [T] to examine two or more things in order to find out how they are similar or different : *Compare these wines and tell us what you think.* **compare sth with/to sth** *The report compares pollution levels in London with those in other cities.* **2** [I,T] to say that something or someone is like someone or something else: **compare sb/sth to sb/sth** *He has been compared to John F. Kennedy.* **3** **compared to/with** used to say how two people or things are different: *You're slim compared to her!* | *The company has made a profit of £24m, compared with £12m last year.* **4** [I] to be as good as someone or something else: + **with** *Nothing compares with the taste of good home cooking.* **5** **compare notes** if people compare notes, they talk about something they have done in order to see if they share the same opinion about it: *I'll call you after the exams, and we can compare notes.*

com·pa·ri·son /kəmˈpærˌsən/ n **1** [C,U] when someone compares two different things or people: + **of** *a comparison of crime figures in Chicago and Detroit* | **make/draw a comparison** (=consider how similar two people or things are): *Many people have drawn a comparison between her and her mother.* **2** **in/by comparison** when you are comparing two people or things: *We were wealthy in comparison with a lot of families.* **3** **there's no comparison** used to say that someone or something is much better than someone or something else: *There's just no comparison between home-made and shop-bought bread.*

com·part·ment /kəmˈpɑːtməntll-ɑːr-/ n [C] **1** a small enclosed space inside something where you can put things: *a luggage compartment* **2** one of the separate areas of a train in which passengers sit: *a no-smoking compartment*

com·pass /ˈkʌmpəs/ n [C] an instrument that shows what direction you are travelling in

com·pas·ses /ˈkʌmpəsˌz/ n **a pair of compasses** an instrument that you use for drawing circles

com·pas·sion /kəmˈpæʃən/ n [U] sympathy for someone who is suffering: + **towards** *Diana appealed for greater compassion for AIDS sufferers.*

com·pas·sion·ate /kəmˈpæʃənˌt/ adj feeling sympathy for people who are suffering: *a caring, compassionate man*

com·pat·i·ble /kəm'pæt¦bəl/ *adj* **1** able to exist or be used together without problems: **+ with** *First make sure that the software is compatible with your machine.* | *Some people think that science is not compatible with religion.* **2** two people who are compatible are able to have a good relationship, because they have the same interests, opinions etc —**compatibility** / kəm,pæt¦'bil¦ti / *n* [U] → opposite INCOMPATIBLE

com·pat·ri·ot /kəm'pætriət‖-'peɪt-/ *n* [C] someone who is from the same country as you

com·pel /kəm'pel/ *v* -**lled, -lling** [T] to force someone to do something: **compel sb to do sth** *She was compelled to resign because of bad health.* → see also COMPULSION

com·pel·ling /kəm'pelɪŋ/ *adj* **1** extremely interesting or exciting : *a compelling TV drama* **2** a compelling argument, reason etc is very strong and makes you accept or believe it: *a compelling reason for getting rid of the death penalty*

com·pen·sate /'kɒmpənseɪt‖'kɑːm-/ *v* **1** [I] to have a good effect which makes the bad effect of something else much less important: **+ for** *Her intelligence more than compensates for her lack of experience.* **2** [I,T] to pay someone money because they have been injured, have lost money, possessions etc: **compensate sb for sth** *You will be compensated for any loss of wages.*

com·pen·sa·tion /,kɒmpən'seɪʃən‖,kɑːm-/ *n* **1** [U] money that is paid to someone because they have been injured or lost money, possessions etc: **+ for** *Farmers are demanding compensation for loss of income.* | **in compensation** *Dr Hawkins received £15,000 in compensation.* **2** [C,U] something that makes a bad situation seem better: *One of the compensations of being ill was that I saw more of my family.*

com·père /'kɒmpeə‖'kɑːmper/ *n* [C] *BrE* someone who introduces the performers on a television programme, theatre show etc

com·pete /kəm'piːt/ *v* [I] to try to win something or to be more successful than someone else: *How many runners will compete?* | **+ with/against** *We've had to cut our prices in order to compete with the big supermarkets.*

com·pe·tent /'kɒmp¦tənt‖'kɑːm-/ *adj* good at your job or at something else you do: *Olive's a very competent teacher.* —**competence** *n* [U] —**competently** *adv* → opposite INCOMPETENT

com·pe·ti·tion /,kɒmp¦'tɪʃən‖,kɑːm-/ *n* **1** [U] a situation in which people or organizations compete with each other: **+ between/among** *Competition between travel companies has never been stronger.* | **+ for** *There was fierce competition for the few jobs available.* | **be in competition with** *Judy is in competition with four others for the role.* **2** [singular, U] the people or groups that compete against you, especially in business: **the competition** *Our aim is simple – to be better than the competition.* **3** [C] an organized event in which people or teams compete against each other: *At the age of only 13, he won an international piano competition.* | **enter a competition** *Teams from 10 different schools entered the competition.*

com·pet·i·tive /kəm'pet¦tɪv/ *adj* **1** a competitive situation is one in which people or organizations try to be more successful than others: *Advertising is a highly competitive indus-*

try. | *competitive sports* **2** competitive prices or products are fairly cheap: *Our rates are very competitive.* **3** determined to be more successful than other people, companies etc: *He's always so competitive.* —**competitiveness** *n* [U]

com·pet·i·tor /kəm'pet¦tə‖-ər/ *n* [C] a person, team, company etc that competes with another: *We sell twice as many computers as our competitors.*

com·pi·la·tion /,kɒmp¦'leɪʃən‖,kɑːm-/ *n* [C] a record, TAPE, book etc that contains many different songs, programmes, poems etc from other records: *Beatles compilation*

com·pile /kəm'paɪl/ *v* [T] to make a book, list etc using different pieces of information

com·pla·cent /kəm'pleɪsənt/ *adj* too pleased with what you have achieved so that you no longer try to improve: *We've been playing well, but we mustn't get too complacent.* —**complacency** *n* [U] —**complacently** *adv*

com·plain /kəm'pleɪn/ *v* [I,T] to say that you are annoyed or not satisfied about something: *"No one ever tells me anything!" Rosie complained.* | **+ about** *The neighbours have been complaining about the noise.* | **+ (that)** *Local kids complained that there was nowhere for them to play.* | **+ to** *I'm going to complain to the manager!*

complain of sth *phr v* [T] to say that you feel ill or have a pain in part of your body: *Tom's been complaining of chest pains.*

com·plaint /kəm'pleɪnt/ *n* **1** [C,U] something that you say or write when you are annoyed or unhappy about something: **+ about** *an increase in the number of complaints about rail services* | **+ against** *complaints against police officers* | **make a complaint** *You can make a formal complaint to the Health Authority.* **2** [C] something that you complain about: *My main complaint is the prices they charge.* **3** [C] an illness that affects part of your body: *a stomach complaint*

com·ple·ment[1] /'kɒmpl¦ment‖'kɑːm-/ *v* [T] to help to show the good qualities of another person or thing: *The pink curtains complement the carpet perfectly.*

com·ple·ment[2] /'kɒmpl¦mənt‖'kɑːm-/ *n* [C] **1** something that makes another thing seem good: **+ to** *The wine was the perfect complement to the meal.* **2** the number or quantity needed to make a group complete: **a full complement** *The English department already has its full complement of teachers.* **3** a word used in grammar for the word or phrase which follows the verb and describes its subject → compare COMPLIMENT[1]

com·plete[1] /kəm'pliːt/ *adj* **1** having all the parts, details etc that are necessary or usual: *the complete works of Shakespeare* | *a complete sentence* → opposite INCOMPLETE **2** [only before noun] *informal* used before a noun to emphasize what you are saying, TOTAL: *Bart's a complete idiot!* | *The news came as a complete surprise.* **3** **be complete** to be finished: *The work should be complete by now.* **4** **complete with** including or containing something additional: *a luxury villa complete with swimming pool* —**completeness** *n* [U]

complete[2] *v* [T] **1** to finish doing or making something: *He never completed the course due to problems at home.* **2** to add what is needed to make a full set or group

com·plete·ly /kəmˈpliːtli/ *adv* in every way; TOTALLY: *I completely forgot about your birthday.* | *Geoff's a completely different person since he retired.*

com·ple·tion /kəmˈpliːʃən/ *n* [U] when something such as a piece of work is finished: *Repair work is scheduled for completion in April.* | + of *the completion of the $80 million project*

com·plex[1] /ˈkɒmpleks‖ˌkɑːmˈpleks-/ *adj* consisting of many connected parts, especially in a way that is difficult to understand or explain: *the complex nature of the human mind* | *a highly complex issue* —**complexity** /kəmˈpleksɪti/ *n* [U,C]

com·plex[2] /ˈkɒmpleks‖ˈkɑːm-/ *n* [C] **1** a group of buildings or one large building used for a particular purpose: *a vast new shopping complex* **2** an emotional problem in which someone is anxious about something : *an inferiority complex*

com·plex·ion /kəmˈplekʃən/ *n* **1** [C,U] the natural colour and appearance of the skin on your face: *a pale complexion* **2** [singular] the way something appears to be: *This puts an entirely new complexion on things* (=makes them seem completely different).

com·pli·ance /kəmˈplaɪəns/ *n* [U] *formal* when people obey a rule or law: + with *compliance with company regulations*

com·pli·ant /kəmˈplaɪənt/ *adj* willing to obey other people's wishes and demands: *You're too compliant.*

com·pli·cate /ˈkɒmplɪkeɪt‖ˈkɑːm-/ *v* [T] to make something difficult to understand or deal with: *Don't tell Michael about this. It'll only complicate matters.*

com·pli·cat·ed /ˈkɒmplɪkeɪtɪd‖ˈkɑːm-/ *adj* something that is complicated is difficult to understand or deal with because it contains many different parts or details: *The instructions are much too complicated.* → opposite SIMPLE

com·pli·ca·tion /ˌkɒmplɪˈkeɪʃən‖ˌkɑːm-/ *n* **1** [C,U] a problem that makes a situation more difficult to understand or deal with: *I hope there aren't any added complications.* (=any other complications) **2** [C usually plural] another medical problem or illness that happens when someone is already ill: *There were complications following surgery.*

com·plic·i·ty /kəmˈplɪsɪti/ *n* [U] when someone allows another person to do something bad or illegal

com·pli·ment[1] /ˈkɒmplɪmənt‖ˈkɑːm-/ *n* **1** [C] something that you say or do in order to praise someone or to show that you admire them: **pay sb a compliment** *He was always paying her compliments and telling her how pretty she looked.* | **take sth as a compliment** (=consider it as a compliment) **2** **with the compliments of/ with sb's compliments** used by an organization when they send or give something to you: *Please accept these tickets with our compliments.* → compare COMPLEMENT[2]

com·pli·ment[2] /ˈkɒmplɪment‖ˈkɑːm-/ *v* [T] to say something nice to someone in order to praise them, for example about their appearance or how well they have done something: **compliment sb on sth** *They complimented Jamie on his excellent English.*

com·pli·men·ta·ry /ˌkɒmplɪˈmentəri‖ˌkɑːm-/ *adj* **1** given free to someone: *We got two complimentary tickets for the game.* **2** saying that you like something and think it is good: *He wasn't very complimentary about the food.*

com·ply /kəmˈplaɪ/ *v* [I] *formal* to obey an order or request: + with *Anyone who fails to comply with the law will have to pay a £100 fine.*

com·po·nent /kəmˈpəʊnənt‖-ˈpoʊ-/ *n* [C] one of the different parts of a machine or system: *car components*

com·pose /kəmˈpəʊz‖-ˈpoʊz/ *v* **1** [T] if something is composed of a group of things or people, it consist of them: **be composed of** *The workforce is composed largely of women.* **2** [I,T] to write a piece of music: *Nyman composed the music for the film 'The Piano'.* **3 compose yourself** to become calm after feeling angry, upset, or excited **4** [T] to write the words of a letter or speech after thinking carefully about them

com·posed /kəmˈpəʊzd‖-ˈpoʊzd/ *adj* calm and not upset or angry: *She remained composed throughout the interview.* → see also COMPOSE

com·pos·er /kəmˈpəʊzə‖-ˈpoʊzər/ *n* [C] someone who writes music

com·po·site /ˈkɒmpəzɪt‖kɑːmˈpɑː-/ *adj* made up of different parts: *a composite image* —**composite** *n* [C]

com·po·si·tion /ˌkɒmpəˈzɪʃən‖ˌkɑːm-/ *n* **1** [U] the substances, parts, members etc that something consists of: + of *the chemical composition of soil* | *the composition of the jury in the O. J. Simpson case* **2 a)** [C] a piece of music that someone has written: *one of Beethoven's early compositions* **b)** [U] the art or process of writing music or poetry **3** [U] the way in which the different parts of a painting or photograph are arranged: *The composition is excellent.* **4** [C,U] a short piece of writing about a subject by a student; ESSAY

com·post /ˈkɒmpɒst‖ˈkɑːmpoʊst/ *n* [U] a mixture of decayed leaves, plants etc that you add to the soil to help plants grow

com·po·sure /kəmˈpəʊʒə‖-ˈpoʊʒər/ *n* [singular, U] the appearance or feeling of being calm and confident: *We kept our composure even when we were losing 4 – 0.*

com·pound[1] /ˈkɒmpaʊnd‖ˈkɑːm-/ *n* [C] **1** a chemical compound is a substance that consists of two or more ELEMENTS (=basic substances such as OXYGEN or CARBON) **2** an area that contains a group of buildings and is surrounded by a wall or fence: *a prison compound* **3** also **compound noun/adjective/verb** two or more words that are used together as a noun, adjective, or verb

com·pound[2] /kəmˈpaʊnd/ *v* [T] to make a difficult situation worse: *Our problems were compounded by appalling weather conditions.*

SPELLING NOTE

Words with the sound /k/, like **cut**, may be spelt **k-**, like **key**, or **qu-**, like **queen**.
Words with the sound /s/, like **city**, may be spelt **s-**, like **soon**, or **ps-**, like **psychology**.

com·pre·hend /ˌkɒmprɪ'hend‖ˌkɑːm-/ v [I,T] *formal* if someone does not comprehend something, they do not understand or realize it: *They don't seem to comprehend how serious this is.*

com·pre·hen·si·ble /ˌkɒmprɪ'hensɪbəl‖ˌkɑːm-/ adj easy to understand: **+ to** *language that is comprehensible to the average reader* → opposite INCOMPREHENSIBLE

com·pre·hen·sion /ˌkɒmprɪ'henʃən‖ˌkɑːm-/ n
1 [C,U] a test of how well students understand written or spoken language: *a listening comprehension* **2** [U] the ability to understand something: *The whole situation is completely beyond my comprehension.* (=it is impossible for me to understand)

com·pre·hen·sive /ˌkɒmprɪ'hensɪv◂‖ˌkɑːm-/ adj including everything that is needed: *a comprehensive account of the war* —**comprehensively** adv

comprehensive school /ˌ..'.. ˌ./ also **comprehensive** n [C] a school in Britain for students aged between 11 and 18, who are of all levels of ability

com·press /kəm'pres/ v [I,T] to press something or make something smaller so that it takes up less space or takes less time: *compressed air* —**compression** /kəm'preʃən/ n [U]

com·prise /kəm'praɪz/ v *formal* **1** [T] also **be comprised of** to consist of particular parts, groups, or people: *The committee is comprised of 8 members.* **2** [T] to form part of a larger group: *Women comprise over 75% of our staff.*

com·pro·mise¹ /'kɒmprəmaɪz‖'kɑːm-/ n [C,U] when people or groups accept less than they really want, especially in order to make an agreement: *Neither side was willing to compromise.* | **make/reach a compromise** *Talks will continue until a compromise is reached.*

compromise² v **1** [I] if two people or groups compromise, they end an argument by accepting something that is not exactly what they want: *President Chirac has said that he would be ready to compromise.* **2 compromise your principles/beliefs etc** to do something that is against your principles, beliefs etc **3 compromise yourself** to do or say something dishonest or embarrassing so that other people no longer respect you **4** [T] to have a harmful effect on something: *fears that spending cuts could compromise passenger safety*

com·pro·mis·ing /'kɒmprəmaɪzɪŋ‖'kɑːm-/ adj a compromising situation is difficult and embarrassing because people think that you have done something dishonest or wrong: *The photographs have put the Senator in a compromising position.*

com·pul·sion /kəm'pʌlʃən/ n **1** [C usually singular] a strong desire to do something, usually something wrong or stupid: *I had a sudden compulsion to hit her.* **2** [U] when someone is forced to do something that they do not want to do: *You don't have to go to the meeting. There's no compulsion.* → see also COMPEL

com·pul·sive /kəm'pʌlsɪv/ adj **1** doing something a lot because you have a strong desire to do it which you cannot control and makes you unable to stop: *compulsive eating* **2 a compulsive liar/gambler etc** someone who cannot stop lying, gambling (GAMBLE) etc —**compulsively** adv

com·pul·so·ry /kəm'pʌlsəri/ adj something that is compulsory must be done because of a rule or law: *compulsory military service*

com·punc·tion /kəm'pʌŋkʃən/ n **have no compunction about** to not feel guilty about doing something, even though other people may think that it is wrong: *They have no compunction about killing animals.*

com·put·er /kəm'pjuːtəl-ər/ n [C] an electronic machine that can store and arrange large quantities of information, which can be used to do many different things: *All our data is kept on computer.* | *sales of home computers* | **computer program/system/game etc** *The new computer system at work is always going down.* → see colour picture on page 80

com·put·er·ize (also **- ise** *BrE*) /kəm'pjuːtəraɪz/ v [T] to use a computer to store information or to control the way something is done: *a computerized filing system* —**computerization** /kəm,pjuːtəraɪ'zeɪʃən‖-rə-/ n [U]

com·put·ing /kəm'pjuːtɪŋ/ n [U] the use or study of computers

com·rade /'kɒmrɪd, -reɪd‖'kɑːmræd/ n [C]
1 *literary* a friend, especially someone who fights together with you in a war **2 Comrade** used to talk to or about another person in some LEFT-WING countries or organizations —**comradeship** n [U]

con¹ /kɒn‖kɑːn/ v [T] *informal* to trick someone in order to get something that you want: **con sb into (doing) sth/out of sth** *She was conned out of her life savings.*

con² n *informal* [C usually singular] a trick to get someone's money or to make someone do something: *The advertisement says they're offering free holidays, but it's all a big con.* → see also **the pros and cons** (PRO)

con·cave /kɒn'keɪv◂, kən-‖kɑːn'keɪv◂, kən-/ adj having a surface that curves inwards : *a concave mirror* → opposite CONVEX

con·ceal /kən'siːl/ v [T] to hide something carefully: *Cannabis was found concealed in the suitcase.* | **conceal sth from sb** *Sue tried hard to conceal her disappointment from the others.* —**concealment** n [U]

con·cede /kən'siːd/ v **1** [T] to admit that something is true, although you do not want to: **+ (that)** *She reluctantly conceded that I was right.* **2** [T] to let someone have something although you do not want to: **concede sth to sb** *Japan was forced to concede the islands to Russia.* | **concede to sb's demands** (=agree to do what they demand): *In the end the government conceded to the terrorists' demands.* **3** [I,T] to admit that you are not going to win a game, argument etc: **concede defeat** (=accept you have lost): *Perot conceded defeat in the election.*

con·ceit /kən'siːt/ n [U] an attitude that shows that you are too proud of what you can do, how you look etc

con·ceit·ed /kən'siːtɪd/ adj behaving in a way that shows you are too proud of what you can do, how you look etc: *I don't want to seem conceited, but I know I'll win.* —**conceitedly** adv

con·cei·va·ble /kən'siːvəbəl/ adj something that is conceivable could happen or be true: **+ that** *It is conceivable that the experts are wrong.* —**conceivably** adv → opposite INCONCEIVABLE

con·ceive /kən'siːv/ v **1** [I,T] to be able to imagine a situation: + **of** *It is impossible to conceive of the size of the universe.* **2** [T] to think of a new idea or plan: *The show was originally conceived by American film star Richard Gere.* **3** [I,T] to become PREGNANT

con·cen·trate /ˈkɒnsəntreɪt‖ˈkɑːn-/ v **1** [I] to think very carefully about something you are doing: *With all this noise, it's hard to concentrate.* | *He will have to concentrate his mind on the job we're doing now.* **2 be concentrated on/ in/around etc** to exist in large numbers or amounts in a particular place: *Most of New Zealand's population is concentrated in the north island.*

> **concentrate on** sth ↔ *phr v* [T] to give most of your attention to one thing: *I want to concentrate on my career for a while before I have kids.*

con·cen·trat·ed /ˈkɒnsəntreɪtⁱd‖ˈkɑːn-/ adj **1** [only before noun] using a lot of effort or determination on one particular job, attempt etc: *He made a concentrated effort to improve his French.* **2** a concentrated liquid is thick and strong because most of the water has been removed from it: *concentrated orange juice*

con·cen·tra·tion /ˌkɒnsən'treɪʃən‖ˌkɑːn-/ n **1** [U] the ability to think very carefully about something for a long time: **lose concentration** *The moment they lose concentration they forget everything I have told them to do.* **2** [C,U] a large amount of something in the same place

concentration camp /ˌ‥'‥ ‥/ n [C] a prison where large numbers of people are kept in very bad conditions, usually during a war

con·cen·tric /kən'sentrɪk/ adj concentric circles are of different sizes and have the same centre

con·cept /ˈkɒnsept‖ˈkɑːn-/ n [C] a general idea or principle: + **of** *the concept of freedom for all* —**conceptual** /kən'septʃuəl/ adj —**conceptually** adv

con·cep·tion /kən'sepʃən/ n **1** [C] a general idea about what something is like, or a way of understanding what something is like: + **of** *the Romantics' conception of the world* **2** [U] when a woman or female animal becomes PREGNANT

con·cern¹ /kən'sɜːn‖-ɜːrn/ n **1** [C,U] a feeling of worry about something important, or the thing that worries you: + **about** *There is growing concern about the pollution in our cities.* **2** [C,U] something that is important to you or that involves you: *Our main concern is for the children's safety.* **3 be of concern (to sb)** to be important to you and make you feel worried: *The destruction of the rainforests is of concern to us all.* **4** [C] a company or business: *The restaurant is a family concern.*

concern² v [T] **1** to affect or involve someone: *What we're planning doesn't concern you.* **2** to make someone feel worried or upset: *The teenage drug problem concerns most parents.* **3** to be about something or someone: *Many of Woody Allen's movies are concerned with life in New York.* **4 concern yourself (with sth)** to become involved in something that interests or worries you: *You don't need to concern yourself with this, Jan.*

con·cerned /kən'sɜːnd‖-ɜːrn/ adj **1** involved in something or affected by it: *Divorce is always painful, especially when children are concerned.* **2** worried about something important: + **about** *I am concerned about his eyesight.* **3 as far as sb's concerned** used to show someone's opinion: *As far as I'm concerned, the whole idea is crazy.* **4 as far as sth is concerned** used to show which subject or thing you are talking about : *As far as money is concerned, the club is doing fairly well.*

con·cern·ing /kən'sɜːnɪŋ‖-ɜːr-/ prep about, or relating to, something: *Police are asking for information concerning the incident.*

con·cert /ˈkɒnsət‖ˈkɑːnsərt/ n [C] a performance given by musicians or singers: *I've managed to get tickets for the Oasis concert.*

con·cert·ed /kən'sɜːtⁱd‖-ɜːr-/ adj a concerted effort or attempt is made by working in a very determined way, often with other people: *We should all make a concerted effort to raise this money.*

con·cer·to /kən'tʃɜːtəʊ‖-'tʃertoʊ/ n [C] a piece of CLASSICAL music, usually for one instrument and an ORCHESTRA

con·ces·sion /kən'seʃən/ n [C] **1** something that you agree to in order to end an argument: **make concessions** *The government will never make concessions to terrorists.* **2** a special right given to someone by the government, an employer etc: *tax concessions for married people* **3** [C] BrE a reduction in the price of tickets, FARES etc for certain groups of people, for example students

con·cil·i·a·tion /kənˌsɪli'eɪʃən/ n [U] formal the process of trying to end an argument between people

con·cil·i·a·tory /kən'sɪliətəri‖-tɔːri/ adj formal intended to make someone stop being angry

con·cise /kən'saɪs/ adj short and clear, without using too many words: *a concise answer* —**concisely** adv —**conciseness** n [U]

con·clude /kən'kluːd/ v **1** [T] to decide something after considering all the information you have: + **that** *Doctors have concluded that sunburn can lead to skin cancer.* **2** [I,T] formal to complete something that you have been doing: *The study was concluded last month.* | **conclude an agreement/treaty/deal etc** (=to complete a political or business agreement successfully) **3** [I,T] to end a meeting, speech, or piece of writing by doing or saying one final thing: + **with** *The seminar concluded with a question and answer session.* —**concluding** adj: *concluding remarks*

con·clu·sion /kən'kluːʒən/ n [C] **1** something that you decide after considering all the information you have: + **that** *I've come to the conclusion that she's lying.* **2** the end or final part of something: *Your essay's fine, but the conclusion needs more work.* **3** [U] when a political or business agreement is completed: *the conclusion of trade talks*

con·clu·sive /kən'kluːsɪv/ adj proving that something is true: **conclusive evidence** *There is no conclusive evidence connecting him with the crime.* —**conclusively** adv

con·coct /kən'kɒkt‖-'kɑːkt/ v [T] **1** to invent a story, plan, or excuse, especially to deceive someone: *She concocted a story about her mother being sick.* **2** to make something unusual by mixing different things together —**concoction** /kən'kɒkʃən‖-'kɑːk-/ n [C, U]

con·course /ˈkɒŋkɔːsǁˈkɑːŋkɔːrs/ n [C] a large HALL or open place in a public building such as an airport

con·crete[1] /ˈkɒŋkriːtǁˈkɑːŋ-/ n [U] a substance used for building that is made by mixing sand, water, small stones, and CEMENT —**concrete** v [T]

con·crete[2] /ˈkɒŋkriːtǁkɑːnˈkriːt/ adj **1** made of concrete: *a concrete floor* **2** clearly based on facts, not on beliefs or guesses: **concrete information/evidence/facts etc** *We need concrete information about the man's identity.*

con·cur /kənˈkɜːǁ-ˈkɜːr/ v [I] *formal* to agree with someone: + **with** *Dr. Hastings concurs with our decision.* —**concurrence** /kənˈkʌrənsǁ -ˈkɜːr-/ n [U]

con·cur·rent /kənˈkʌrəntǁ-ˈkɜːr-/ adj existing or happening at the same time: *He is serving two concurrent prison sentences.* —**concurrently** adv

con·cus·sion /kənˈkʌʃən/ n [C,U] slight damage to your brain that makes you become unconscious or feel sick —**concuss** /kənˈkʌs/ v [T]

con·demn /kənˈdem/ v [T] **1** to say very strongly that you do not approve of someone or something: *Politicians were quick to condemn the bombing.* **2** to give a severe punishment to someone who is guilty of a crime: **condemn sb to death** *The murderer was condemned to death.* **3** to force someone to live in an unpleasant way or to suffer: **condemn sb to sth** *These orphans have been condemned to a life of poverty.* **4** to say officially that a building is not safe enough to be used

con·dem·na·tion /ˌkɒndəmˈneɪʃən, -demǁ ˌkɑːn-/ n [C,U] a statement of very strong disapproval: + **of** *Condemnation of the plans came from all political parties.*

con·den·sa·tion /ˌkɒndenˈseɪʃən, -dən-ǁˌkɑːn-/ n [U] small drops of water that appear when steam or hot air touches a cold surface, for example glass

con·dense /kənˈdens/ v **1** [I,T] if gas or hot air condenses, it becomes a liquid as it becomes colder **2** [T] to make a speech or piece of writing shorter by using fewer words to say the same thing **3** [T] to make a liquid thicker by removing some of the water from it: *condensed soup*

con·de·scend /ˌkɒndɪˈsendǁˌkɑːn-/ v [I] **1** *often humorous* to agree to do something even though you think that you should not have to do it: **condescend to do sth** *Do you think you could condescend to help your sister?* **2** **condescend to sb** to behave as if you are better or more important than someone else —**condescension** /-ˈsenʃən/ n [U]

con·de·scend·ing /ˌkɒndɪˈsendɪŋ◂ǁˌkɑːn-/ adj showing that you think you are better or more important than other people: *He was laughing at her in that condescending way he had.*

con·di·tion[1] /kənˈdɪʃən/ n **1** [C,U] the state that someone or something is in: *I'm not buying the car until I see what condition it's in.* | **be in good/bad/terrible condition** *The VCR is still in pretty good condition.* **2** [plural] **conditions a)** the situation in which people live or work, especially the physical things that affect them: **living/working conditions** *Poor working conditions were part of their daily lives.* **b)** the weather at a particular time: *Icy conditions on the*

roads are making it difficult to drive. **3** [C] something that must happen or be done before something else can happen or be done: + **for** *a set of conditions for getting into college* | **on condition that/on one condition** (=only if a particular thing happens) **4** [U] the state of health of a person or animal: **in no condition to do sth** (=too ill, drunk, upset etc to do something): *Molly is in no condition to return to work.* **5** [C] an illness: *a heart condition*

con·di·tion[2] v [T] **1** to make a person or animal behave in a particular way by training or influencing them over a period of time: **condition sb/sth to do sth** *Pavlov conditioned the dogs to expect food when they heard a bell.* **2** to add a special liquid to your skin or hair to keep it healthy —**conditioning** n [U]

con·di·tion·al /kənˈdɪʃənəl/ adj **1** if an offer, agreement etc is conditional, it will only happen if something else happens: + **on** *His college place is conditional on his exam results.* **2** a conditional sentence is one that usually begins with 'if' or 'unless', and states something that must be true or must happen before something else can be true or happen

con·di·tion·er /kənˈdɪʃənəl-ər/ n [C,U] a liquid that you put on your hair after washing it to keep it in good condition

con·do /ˈkɒndəʊǁˈkɑːndoʊ/ n [C], *plural* **condos** *AmE informal* a condominium

con·do·lence /kənˈdəʊlənsǁ-ˈdoʊ-/ n [C usually plural, U] sympathy for someone when someone they love has died: *Please offer my condolences to your mother.*

con·dom /ˈkɒndəmǁˈkɑːn-, ˈkʌn-/ n [C] a thin piece of rubber that a man wears over his PENIS during sex to stop a woman becoming PREGNANT, or to protect against disease

con·do·min·i·um /ˌkɒndəˈmɪniəmǁˌkɑːn-/ n [C] *AmE* a building that consists of separate apartments which are owned by the people living in them, or one of these apartments

con·done /kənˈdəʊnǁ-ˈdoʊn/ v [T] to approve of or allow behaviour that most people think is wrong: *I cannot condone the use of violence.*

con·du·cive /kənˈdjuːsɪvǁ-ˈduː-/ adj *formal* **be conducive to** if a situation is conducive to something, it makes that thing possible or likely to happen: *The sunny climate is conducive to outdoor activities.*

con·duct[1] /kənˈdʌkt/ v **1** [T] to carry out or organize something: *The children are conducting an experiment with two magnets.* | *The group conducted a guerrilla campaign against the president in the 1970s.* **2** [I,T] to stand in front of musicians or singers and direct their playing or singing **3** [T] if something conducts electricity or heat, it allows the electricity or heat to travel along or through it **4** **conduct yourself** the way that you conduct yourself is the way that you behave: *Public figures have a duty to conduct themselves correctly.*

con·duct[2] /ˈkɒndʌkt, -dəktǁˈkɑːn-/ n [U] **1** the way someone behaves **2** the way an activity is organized and done: + **of** *The mayor was not satisfied with the conduct of the meeting.*

con·duc·tor /kənˈdʌktəǁ-ər/ n [C] **1** someone who conducts a group of musicians or singers **2** *BrE* someone whose job is to collect payments from passengers on a bus or train

3 *AmE* someone who is in charge of a train or the workers on it **4** something that allows heat or electricity to travel along or through it

cone /kəʊn‖koʊn/ *n* [C] **1** a hollow or solid object with a round base and a point at the top: *an orange traffic cone* **2** **ice cream cone** a container that you can eat, which has ICE CREAM inside it and on top, and which has a pointed bottom; CORNET *BrE* **3** a thing that grows on the branches of PINE and FIR trees, which contains the seeds of the tree; PINECONE

con·fec·tion·e·ry /kən'fekʃənəri/ *n* [U] sweets, cakes etc

con·fed·e·ra·tion /kən,fedə'reɪʃən/ also **con·fed·e·ra·cy** /kən'fedərəsi/ *n* [C] a group of people, political parties, or organizations that have united to achieve an aim — **confederate** /kən'fedərⱨt/ *adj*

con·fer /kən'fɜː‖-'fɜːr/ *v* -**rred, -rring** **1** [I] to discuss something with other people so that everyone can express their opinion: + **with** *You may confer with the other team members.* **2 confer a degree/honour etc on sb** to officially give someone a degree etc

con·fe·rence /'kɒnfərəns‖'kɑːn-/ *n* [C] a large formal meeting in which people exchange ideas about business, politics etc: *a sales conference*

con·fess /kən'fes/ *v* [I,T] **1** to admit that you have done something wrong or illegal: *It didn't take long for her to confess.* | **confess to (doing) sth** *James wouldn't confess to the robbery.* **2** to admit something that you feel embarrassed about: + **that** *Lyn confessed that she had fallen asleep in class.* **3** to tell a priest or God about the bad things you have done — **confessed** *adj*: *a confessed killer*

con·fes·sion /kən'feʃən/ *n* **1** [C] a statement that you have done something wrong or illegal: **make a confession** *He's made a full confession to the police.* **2** [C,U] the act of confessing what you have done wrong to a priest or God

con·fet·ti /kən'feti/ *n* [U] small pieces of coloured paper that you throw over a man and woman who have just married

con·fide /kən'faɪd/ *v* [I,T] to tell a secret to someone you trust: **confide to sb that** *Joel confided to her that he was going to leave his wife.* **confide in** sb *phr v* [T] to tell someone about something that is very private: *I don't trust her enough to confide in her.*

con·fi·dence /'kɒnfⱨdəns‖'kɑːn-/ *n* **1** [U] belief in your own ability to do things well: *Her problem is that she lacks confidence.* | **give sb confidence** *Living in another country gave me more confidence.* **2** [U] the feeling that something is true, or that it will good results: *We're looking forward to Saturday's match with confidence.* **3** [U] a feeling of trust that someone will not tell your secrets to other people: **gain sb's confidence** (=make someone feel that they can trust you): *It took a long time to gain the little boy's confidence.* **4 in confidence** if you tell someone something in confidence, you tell them in secret and they must not tell anyone

else **5** [C] a secret or a piece of personal information that you tell someone: *After a couple of days they were already exchanging confidences.*

con·fi·dent /'kɒnfⱨdənt‖'kɑːn-/ *adj* **1** sure that you can do something well: + **about** *We won't continue until you feel confident about using the equipment.* | **confident of doing sth** *She seems very confident of winning.* → compare SELF-CONFIDENT **2** very sure that something is going to happen: + **(that)** *I'm confident that he's the right man for the job.* — **confidently** *adv*

con·fi·den·tial /,kɒnfⱨ'denʃəl‖,kɑːn-/ *adj* intended to be kept secret: *confidential information* — **confidentially** *adv* — **confidentiality** /,kɒnfⱨdenʃi'ælⱨti‖,kɑːn-/ *n* [U]

con·fine /kən'faɪn/ *v* [T] **1 be confined to a)** to happen in only one place or time, or affect only one group of people: *The fire was confined to the ground floor of the building.* **2** to keep someone or something within the limits of a particular subject or activity: **confine yourself to** *Try to confine yourself to spending $120 a week.* **3** to make someone stay in a place they cannot leave, for example a prison: *They were confined in a dark, narrow room for several months.*

con·fined /kən'faɪnd/ *adj* a confined space or area is very small

con·fine·ment /kən'faɪnmənt/ *n* [U] when someone is made to stay in a room or area: *They were held in confinement for three weeks.*

con·fines /'kɒnfaɪnz‖'kɑːn-/ *n* [plural] the walls, limits, or borders of something: **within/ beyond the confines of sth** *Some of the work should be carried out beyond the confines of the school.*

con·firm /kən'fɜːm‖-ɜːrm/ *v* [T] **1** to say or prove that something is definitely true: *Dr. Martin confirmed the diagnosis of cancer.* | + **that** *Can you confirm that the money has been paid?* **2** to tell someone that an arrangement that was possible is now definite: *Please confirm your reservations 72 hours in advance.* **3 be confirmed** to be made a full member of the Christian church at a special ceremony

con·fir·ma·tion /,kɒnfə'meɪʃən‖,kɑːnfər-/ *n* [C,U] **1** a statement that something is definitely true, or that something will definitely happen: *We're waiting for confirmation of the report.* **2** a religious ceremony in which someone is made a full member of the Christian church

con·firmed /kən'fɜːmd‖-ɜːr-/ *adj* **a confirmed bachelor/smoker/atheist** someone who has been something for a long time and is unlikely to change: *Charlie was a confirmed bachelor, until he met Helen.*

con·fis·cate /'kɒnfⱨskeɪt‖'kɑːn-/ *v* [T] to take something away from someone, either because they are not allowed to have it or as a punishment: *The police confiscated his gun.* — **confiscation** /,kɒnfⱨ'skeɪʃən‖,kɑːn-/ *n* [C,U]

con·flict[1] /'kɒnflɪkt‖'kɑːn-/ *n* [C,U] **1** a disagreement or fighting between people, groups, or countries: + **between** *a conflict between*

GRAMMAR NOTE: a or the (3)
You can use a noun without **a/an** or **the** if: **1.** it is a singular proper noun: *How far is it to* **Oxford**? **2.** it is an uncountable noun: *What kind of* **music** *do you like?* **3.** it is a plural noun: *Cats can see in the dark.* (=cats in general)

neighbouring states | **in conflict with** *As a teenager she was always in conflict with her father.*
2 a situation in which you have to choose between opposing things: **+ between** *In a conflict between work and family, I would always choose family.*

con·flict² /kən'flɪkt/ *v* [I] if two ideas, beliefs, or opinions conflict, they cannot both be true: **+ with** *Surely that conflicts with what you said before?* | *conflicting legal advice*

con·form /kən'fɔːmǁ-ɔːrm/ *v* [I] **1** to behave in the way that most other people behave: *There's always pressure on kids to conform.* **2** to obey or follow an established rule, pattern etc: **+ to** *Seatbelts must conform to official safety standards.* —**conformity** *n* [U]

con·form·ist /kən'fɔːmɪstǁ-ɔːr-/ *n* [C] someone who behaves or thinks too much like everyone else —**conformist** *adj*

con·found /kən'faʊnd/ *v* [T] if something confounds someone, it is impossible to explain or understand it and they feel very surprised and shocked: *Her illness confounded the doctors.*

con·front /kən'frʌnt/ *v* [T] **1** to try to make someone admit they have done something wrong: **confront sb about sth** *I just can't confront her about her drinking.* | **confront sb with sth** *Confronted with the video evidence, she had to admit she had been involved.* **2** to deal with something difficult or unpleasant, usually in a brave way: *We want to help you to confront your problems.* **3** to stand in front of someone, so that they feel threatened: *Opening the door, I was confronted by two men demanding money.*

con·fron·ta·tion /ˌkɒnfrən'teɪʃənǁ,kɑːn-/ *n* [C,U] a situation in which there is a lot of angry disagreement: *Stan always avoids confrontations.*

con·fuse /kən'fjuːz/ *v* [T] **1** to make someone feel unable to think clearly or understand something: *His directions really confused me.* **2** to think wrongly that one person, thing, or idea is someone or something else: **confuse sb/sth with** *It's easy to confuse Sue with her sister. They look so much alike.*

con·fused /kən'fjuːzd/ *adj* **1** unable to understand something clearly: *I'm totally confused.* | **+ about** *If you're confused about anything, call me.* → see colour picture on page 277 **2** not clear or not easy to understand: *a confused answer*

con·fus·ing /kən'fjuːzɪŋ/ *adj* difficult to understand: *This map is really confusing.*

con·fu·sion /kən'fjuːʒən/ *n* **1** [C,U] when people do not understand what is happening or what something means: **+ about/over** *There's a lot of confusion about the new rules.* **2** when you wrongly think that one person or thing is someone or something else: *To avoid confusion, the teams wore different colours.* **3** [U] when a situation is confusing because there is a lot of noise and activity: *After the explosion the airport was a scene of total confusion.*

con·geal /kən'dʒiːl/ *v* [I] if a liquid such as blood congeals, it becomes thick or solid

con·ge·ni·al /kən'dʒiːniəl/ *adj formal* pleasant in a way that makes you feel comfortable and relaxed: *a congenial host*

con·gen·i·tal /kən'dʒenɪtl/ *adj* affecting someone from the time they are born: *a congenital heart problem*

con·ges·ted /kən'dʒestɪd/ *adj* full or blocked, for example because there are too many vehicles or people: *congested motorways* —**congestion** /-'dʒestʃən/ *n* [U]

con·glom·e·rate /kən'glɒmərɪtǁ-'glɑː-/ *n* [C] a large company made up of many different smaller companies

con·glom·e·ra·tion /kən,glɒmə'reɪʃənǁ-,glɑː-/ *n* [C] *formal* a group of many different things gathered together

con·grat·u·late /kən'grætʃʊleɪt/ *v* [T] to tell someone that you are happy because they achieved something, or because something good has happened to them: **congratulate sb on sth** *I want to congratulate you on your exam results.*

con·grat·u·la·tions /kən,grætʃʊ'leɪʃənz/ *n* [plural] *spoken* used to congratulate someone: *You won? Congratulations!* | **+ on** *Congratulations on your engagement!*

con·gre·gate /'kɒngrɪgeɪtǁ'kɑːŋ-/ *v* [I] to come together in a group: *Birds congregate here in the autumn.*

con·gre·ga·tion /ˌkɒngrɪ'geɪʃənǁ,kɑːŋ-/ *n* [C] a group of people gathered in a church for a religious service, or the people who usually go to a particular church

con·gress /'kɒngresǁ'kɑːŋgrɪs/ *n* **1 Congress** the group of people elected to make laws for the US, consisting of the Senate and the House of Representatives **2** a large meeting of members of an organization, or members of several different organizations —**congressional** /kən'greʃənəl/ *adj*

con·gress·man /'kɒngrɪsmənǁ'kɑːŋ-/ *n* [C] a man who is elected to be in Congress

con·gress·wo·man /'kɒngrɪs,wʊmənǁ'kɑːŋ-/ *n* [C] a woman who is elected to be in Congress

con·i·cal /'kɒnɪkəlǁ'kɑː-/ *adj* shaped like a CONE

co·ni·fer /'kəʊnɪfə, 'kɒ-ǁ'kɑːnɪfər/ *n* [C] a tree for example a PINE or FIR tree, which has CONEs (=hard brown woody fruit which contain seeds) on its branches and usually does not lose its leaves in winter

co·nif·e·rous /kə'nɪfərəsǁkoʊ-, kə-/ *adj* coniferous trees have CONEs (=hard brown woody fruit which contain seeds) and do not usually lose their leaves in winter:

con·jec·ture /kən'dʒektʃəǁ-ər/ *n* [C,U] *formal* when you guess something because you do not have enough information to be certain about it: *I'm afraid the report is pure conjecture.* —**conjecture** *v* [I,T]

con·ju·gal /'kɒndʒʊgəlǁ'kɑː-/ *adj formal* relating to marriage: *conjugal bliss*

con·ju·gate /'kɒndʒʊgeɪtǁ'kɑː-/ *v* [T] *technical* to give all the parts of a verb in a fixed order —**conjugation** /ˌkɒndʒʊ'geɪʃənǁ,kɑː-/ *n* [C,U]

con·junc·tion /kən'dʒʌŋkʃən/ *n* **1 in conjunction** with working, happening, or being used with someone or something else: *The worksheets should be used in conjunction with the video.* **2** [C] a word such as 'but', 'and', or 'while', that connects phrases or parts of sentences; LINKING WORD

con·jure /'kʌndʒəǁ'kɑːndʒər, 'kʌn-/ *v*

conjure sth **up** *phr v* [T] **1** to make an idea, picture, or memory very clear and strong in someone's mind: *She lay back, trying to conjure up a vision of a tropical island.* **2** to cleverly make something appear: *Pete can conjure up a meal out of whatever's in the fridge.*

con·jur·er also **conjuror** /ˈkʌndʒərəlˈkɑːndʒərər, ˈkʌn-/ *n* [C] someone who performs magic tricks

con·jur·ing /ˈkʌndʒərɪŋllˈkɑːn-, ˈkʌn-/ *n* [U] when someone performs clever tricks, making things appear, disappear etc as if by magic

con·man /ˈkɒnmænllˈkɑːn-/ *n* [C] *informal* someone who tries to get money or valuable things by tricking people

con·nect /kəˈnekt/ *v* **1** [I,T] to join two places or things together: *The M11 connects London and Cambridge.* | *I can't see how these pipes connect.* → opposite DISCONNECT **2** [T] to realize that two facts, events, or people are related to each other: **connect sb/sth with** *I never connected her with Sam.* **3** [T] to join something to a supply of electricity, gas, water, or the telephone network: *The phone isn't connected yet.* → opposite DISCONNECT **4** [T] to join two telephone lines, allowing two people to speak to each other: *Hold the line, I'm trying to connect you.* **5** [I] to be planned so that passengers can continue their journey on a different plane, train, bus etc: *a connecting flight to Rio*

con·nect·ed /kəˈnektɪd/ *adj* **1** if two things are connected with each other, there is a relationship between them: **+ with** *Police think the killings may be connected with each other in some way.* | **closely connected** *The two ideas are closely connected.* **2** if two things are connected to each other, they are joined together: **+ to** *The computer is connected to a laser printer.*

con·nec·tion /kəˈnekʃən/ *n* **1** [C,U] a relationship between things, people, ideas etc: **+ between** *the connection between smoking and lung cancer* | **+ with** *Does this have any connection with our conversation yesterday?* **2** [C, U] the joining together of two or more things, especially by electricity, telephone, or computer: *Connection to the Internet usually takes only seconds.* **3** [C] a connecting plane, train, bus etc: *If we don't get there soon I'm going to miss my connection.* **4** **in connection with** concerning something: *Police are questioning a man in connection with the crime.*

con·nec·tions /kəˈnekʃənz/ *n* [plural] important people you know, who you can ask to help you or do something for you: *Ramsey has connections; let's ask him.*

con·nive /kəˈnaɪv/ *v* [I] to secretly work to achieve something wrong or illegal, or allow something wrong or illegal to happen: **connive (with sb) to do sth** *She's conniving with Tony to get Grandma's money.* — **connivance** *n* [C,U]

con·nois·seur /ˌkɒnəˈsɜːlˌkɑːnəˈsɜːr/ *n* [C] someone who knows a lot about something such as art, good food, or music: **+ of** *a true connoisseur of fine wines*

con·no·ta·tion /ˌkɒnəˈteɪʃənlˌkɑː-/ *n* [C] an idea or a feeling that a word makes you have in addition to what it actually means: *a word with negative connotations*

con·quer /ˈkɒŋkəllˈkɑːŋkər/ *v* **1** [I,T] to win control of a country or defeat an enemy by fighting a war: *Egypt was conquered by the Ottoman Empire in 1517.* **2** [T] to get control over a feeling or a problem that you have, using a lot of effort: *I didn't think I'd ever conquer my fear of heights.* — **conqueror** *n* [C]

con·quest /ˈkɒŋkwestllˈkɑːn-/ *n* [C,U] when someone gets control of a group of people, an area, or a situation: **+ of** *the Spanish conquest of the Incas* | *man's conquest of space*

con·science /ˈkɒnʃənsllˈkɑːn-/ *n* [C,U] **1** the set of feelings that tell you whether what you are doing is morally right or wrong: **a guilty conscience** (=when you feel guilty because you have done something wrong): *She still had a guilty conscience about not offering to help.* | **a clear conscience** (=when you know that you have done nothing wrong): *I've finished all my work, so I can go out tonight with a clear conscience.* **2** **on sb's conscience** making someone feel guilty about something: *Tim's suicide is always going to be on his mother's conscience.*

con·sci·en·tious /ˌkɒnʃiˈenʃəsllˌkɑːn-/ *adj* showing a lot of care and attention: *a conscientious worker* — **conscientiously** *adv*

conscientious ob·jec·tor /ˌ.... ˈ..../ *n* [C] someone who refuses to fight in a war because of their moral or religious beliefs

con·scious /ˈkɒnʃəsllˈkɑːn-/ *adj* **1** **be conscious of/that** to notice or realize something: *Jodie was very conscious of the fact that he was watching her.* **2** awake and able to understand what is happening: *Owen was still conscious when they arrived.* **3** **conscious effort/attempt** etc when someone deliberately tries to do something or makes a firm decision to do something: *Her voice was so boring that I had to make a conscious effort to listen to her.* **4** **safety-conscious/fashion conscious/health conscious** etc thinking that safety, fashion etc is very important — **consciously** *adv* → opposite UNCONSCIOUS[1]

> **USAGE NOTE: conscious**
>
> The usual opposite word for the adjective **conscious** is **unconscious**: *The driver is still unconscious following the accident earlier this afternoon.* However, the opposite of the noun **conscious** in psychology can either be **subconscious** or **unconscious**. Don't confuse **conscious** with **conscientious**. **Conscious** means 'awake and able to think': *She is still not conscious after the operation.* **Conscientious** means 'very careful and hard-working in the way you do your work': *a quiet conscientious student*

con·scious·ness /ˈkɒnʃəsn‚sllˈkɑːn-/ *n* **1** [U] the condition of being awake and understanding what is happening: **lose consciousness** *She lost consciousness at 6 o'clock and died two hours later.* **2** [U] the opinions and ideas that a group of people have: *her political consciousness* **3** [U] your mind and your thoughts **4** [singular] the state of knowing that something exists: *There's a growing consciousness amongst athletes about the dangers of steroids.*

cons·cript[1] /ˈkɒnskrɪptllˈkɑːn-/ *n* [U] someone who has been made to join the army, navy etc

con·script[2] /kənˈskrɪpt/ *v* [T] to make someone join the army, navy etc — **conscription** /-ˈskrɪpʃən/ *n* [U]

consecrate

con·se·crate /ˈkɒnsɪkreɪt‖ˈkɑːn-/ v [T] to have a special ceremony that makes a place or object holy —**consecration** /ˌkɒnsɪˈkreɪʃən‖ˌkɑːn-/ n [U]

con·sec·u·tive /kənˈsekjʊtɪv/ adj happening one after the other: *It rained for three consecutive days.* —**consecutively** adv

con·sen·sus /kənˈsensəs/ n [singular,U] general agreement between everyone in a group: *The consensus of opinion is that Miller should resign.*

con·sent¹ /kənˈsent/ n [U] permission to do something: *He had taken the vehicle without the owner's consent.*

consent² v [I] to give your permission for something or to agree to something: + **to** *Father consented to the marriage.*

con·se·quence /ˈkɒnsɪkwəns‖ˈkɑːnsɪkwens/ n **1** [C] something that happens as a result of something else: *The safety procedure had been ignored, with tragic consequences.* **2 of little/no consequence** *formal* not important

con·se·quent·ly /ˈkɒnsɪkwəntli‖ˈkɑːnsɪ-kwentli/ adv as a result: *We talked all night and consequently overslept the next morning.*

con·ser·va·tion /ˌkɒnsəˈveɪʃən‖ˌkɑːnsər-/ n [U] **1** the protection of natural things such as wild animals, forests, or beaches **2** the controlled use of a supply of water, gas etc to prevent it from being wasted —**conservationist** n [C]

con·ser·va·tis·m /kənˈsɜːvətɪzəm‖-ɜːr-/ n [U] the belief that any changes to the way things are done must happen slowly and have very good reasons: *political conservatism*

con·ser·va·tive¹ /kənˈsɜːvətɪv‖-ɜːr-/ adj **1 Conservative** belonging to or concerned with the Conservative Party in Britain: *a Conservative MP* **2** preferring not to make any changes: *a very conservative attitude to education* **3** a conservative estimate is a guess that is deliberately low, and perhaps lower than the real amount

conservative² n [C] **1 Conservative** a member or supporter of the Conservative Party in Britain **2** someone who does not like changes

con·ser·va·to·ry /kənˈsɜːvətərɪ‖-ˈsɜːrvətɔːri/ n [C] a room with glass walls and a glass roof, usually joined to the side of a house

con·serve /kənˈsɜːv‖-ɜːrv/ v [T] to prevent something from being wasted, damaged, or destroyed: *We can offer advice on conserving electricity.*

con·sid·er /kənˈsɪdə‖-ər/ v **1** [I,T] to think very carefully about something: *My client needs time to consider your offer.* | **consider doing sth** *Have you every considered living abroad?* **2** [T] to remember particular facts or details when making a decision: *You should consider the effect the move will have on your family.* | + **how/what/who etc** *Have you considered how hard life is for these refugees?* **3** [T] to think of someone or something in a particular way: **consider sb (to be) sth** *Mrs. Gillan was considered to be an excellent teacher.* | **consider sth (to be) sth** *We consider your support absolutely essential.*

con·sid·e·ra·ble /kənˈsɪdərəbəl/ adj large enough to be important or to have an effect: *a considerable amount of money* —**considerably** adv

con·sid·er·ate /kənˈsɪdərɪt/ adj a considerate person thinks about other people's feelings and needs: +**of** *Try to be more considerate of your neighbours.* —**considerately** adv → opposite INCONSIDERATE

con·sid·e·ra·tion /kənˌsɪdəˈreɪʃən/ n **1** [C] a fact or detail that you need to think about when deciding something: *Financial considerations have to be taken into account.* **2** [U] attention to other people's feelings and needs **3** [U] careful thought and attention: *After further consideration, he decided not to take the job.* | **under consideration** (=being discussed and thought about) **4 take sth into consideration** to remember a particular fact or detail when making a decision: *We'll take into consideration the fact that you were ill.*

con·sid·ered /kənˈsɪdəd‖-ərd/ adj **1 all things considered** used when you are saying what you believe after thinking about all the facts: *All things considered, I think the day went well.* **2** a considered opinion or action is based on careful thought

con·sid·er·ing /kənˈsɪdərɪŋ/ prep, linking word used before stating a fact that you know has had an effect on a particular situation: + **(that)** *Considering we missed the bus, we're actually not too late.*

con·sign /kənˈsaɪn/ v [T] to put someone or something somewhere, especially to get rid of them: **consign sb/sth to** *I'm not ready to be consigned to an old folks' home yet!*

con·sign·ment /kənˈsaɪnmənt/ n [C] a quantity of goods that is sent somewhere: + **of** *a new consignment of toys*

con·sist /kənˈsɪst/ v **consist of** sth phr v [T] to be made of or contain a number of different things: *The exhibition consists of over 30 paintings.*

con·sis·ten·cy /kənˈsɪstənsi/ n **1** [U] the quality of always happening or behaving in the same way: + **in** *There's no consistency in the way they apply the rules.* → opposite INCONSISTENCY **2** [C,U] how thick or firm a mixture is: *a dessert with a nice, creamy consistency*

con·sis·tent /kənˈsɪstənt/ adj **1** always happening or behaving in the same way: *Joe's work has shown consistent improvement this term.* **2 be consistent with** to say the same thing or follow the same principles as something else: *His story is not consistent with the facts.* —**consistently** adv: *consistently high sales* → opposite INCONSISTENT

con·so·la·tion /ˌkɒnsəˈleɪʃən‖ˌkɑːn-/ n [C,U] someone or something that makes you feel better when you are sad or disappointed: *They were still together, and at least that was one consolation.*

con·sole /kənˈsəʊl‖-ˈsoʊl/ v [T] to help to make someone who is sad or disappointed feel better: *No one could console her when her first child died.*

con·sol·i·date /kənˈsɒlɪdeɪt‖-ˈsɑː-/ v [I,T] **1** to combine two or more things such as organizations, jobs, or large amounts of money to form a single thing that is more effective: *In the 1950s several small school systems were consolidated into one large one.* **2** to make your power stronger or make sure that you continue to be successful: *I felt that it was time to consolidate* *my position in the company.* —**consolidation** /kənˌsɒlɪˈdeɪʃən‖-ˌsɑː-/ *n* [C,U]

con·so·nant /ˈkɒnsənənt‖ˈkɑːn-/ *n* [C] any letter of the English alphabet except a, e, i, o, and u → compare VOWEL

con·sort /kənˈsɔːt‖-ˈsɔːrt/ *v*
consort with sb *phr v* [T] to spend time with someone, especially someone who is bad: *She was accused of consorting with the enemy.*

con·sor·ti·um /kənˈsɔːtiəm‖-ɔːr-/ *n* [C], *plural* **consortia** /-tiə/ or **consortiums** a number of companies, organizations etc working together: *a consortium of banks*

con·spic·u·ous /kənˈspɪkjuəs/ *adj* very easy to notice because of being different from other people or things: *Being so tall makes him very conspicuous.* —**conspicuously** *adv* → opposite INCONSPICUOUS

con·spir·a·cy /kənˈspɪrəsi/ *n* [C,U] a secret plan made by two or more people to do something harmful or illegal: *a conspiracy to overthrow the king*

con·spir·a·tor /kənˈspɪrətəl-tər/ *n* [C] someone who is part of a group that is secretly planning to do something harmful or illegal —**conspiratorial** /kənˌspɪrəˈtɔːriəl/ *adj*

con·spire /kənˈspaɪəl-spaɪr/ *v* [I] **1** to secretly plan with other people to do something harmful or illegal: *The four men had conspired to rob a bank.* **2** *formal* to happen at the same time and have a bad result: **conspire to do sth** *Events conspired to make sure he lost the election.*

con·sta·ble /ˈkʌnstəbəl‖ˈkɑːn-/ *n* [C] a British police officer of the lowest rank

con·stant /ˈkɒnstənt‖ˈkɑːn-/ *adj* **1** happening regularly or all the time: *The children must be kept under constant supervision.* **2** staying the same for a period of time: *driving at a constant speed* —**constancy** *n* [U]

con·stant·ly /ˈkɒnstəntli‖ˈkɑːn-/ *adv* all the time or regularly: *Her teenage daughter is constantly on the phone.*

con·stel·la·tion /ˌkɒnstɪˈleɪʃən‖ˌkɑːn-/ *n* [C] a group of stars that forms a particular pattern and has a name

con·ster·na·tion /ˌkɒnstəˈneɪʃən‖ˌkɑːnstər-/ *n* [U] a feeling of shock or worry: *She stared at him in consternation.*

con·sti·pa·tion /ˌkɒnstɪˈpeɪʃən‖ˌkɑːn-/ *n* [U] when someone is unable to empty their BOWELS —**constipated** /ˈkɒnstɪpeɪtɪd‖ˈkɑːn-/ *adj*

con·stit·u·en·cy /kənˈstɪtʃuənsi/ *n* [C] an area of the country that elects someone to a parliament, or all the people who live and vote there

con·stit·u·ent /kənˈstɪtʃuənt/ *n* [C] **1** someone who votes and lives in a particular constituency **2** one of the parts that form something: *the constituents of a bomb* —**constituent** *adj*

con·sti·tute /ˈkɒnstɪtjuːt‖ˈkɑːnstɪtuːt/ *v* **1** if several parts constitute something, they form it together: *the 50 states that constitute the USA*
2 to be considered to be something: *According to Marx, money "constitutes true power".*

con·sti·tu·tion /ˌkɒnstɪˈtjuːʃən‖ˌkɑːnstɪˈtuː-/ *n* [C] **1** also **Constitution** a set of laws and principles that describes the power and the purpose of a government, organization etc: *the Constitution of the United States* **2** someone's health and strength: **a strong/weak constitution** *She'll get better – she's got a strong constitution.*

con·sti·tu·tion·al /ˌkɒnstɪˈtjuːʃənəl‖ˌkɑːnstɪˈtuː-/ *adj* **1** allowed or limited by a constitution: *constitutional limits on the Queen's power* **2** relating to a constitution: *a constitutional amendment* (=change to the original set of laws) —**constitutionally** *adv*

con·strain /kənˈstreɪn/ *v* [T] to limit what someone or something can do or become, often by force: *Our work has been constrained by a lack of money.*

con·strained /kənˈstreɪnd/ *adj* **feel constrained to do sth** to feel that you must do something: *Ernie felt constrained to explain further.*

con·straint /kənˈstreɪnt/ *n* [C,U] something that limits your freedom to do what you want: *Financial constraints limited our choice of housing.*

con·strict /kənˈstrɪkt/ *v* [T] **1** to make something smaller, tighter, or narrower: *Her throat constricted.* **2** to limit someone's freedom to do what they want —**constriction** /-ˈstrɪkʃən/ *n* [C,U]

con·struct /kənˈstrʌkt/ *v* [T] to build something large such as a house, bridge, or road: *The Empire State Building was constructed in 1931.*

con·struc·tion /kənˈstrʌkʃən/ *n* **1** [U] the process of building something large such as a house, bridge, or road: **under construction** (=being built): *Several new offices are under construction.* **2** [C] something that is built: *a large wooden construction* **3** [C] the way in which words are put together in a sentence: *complex grammatical constructions*

con·struc·tive /kənˈstrʌktɪv/ *adj* intended to be helpful, or likely to produce good results: *constructive criticism* —**constructively** *adv*

con·strue /kənˈstruː/ *v* [T] to understand a remark or an action in a particular way: **construe sth as** *Your behaviour might be construed as aggression.*

con·sul /ˈkɒnsəl‖ˈkɑːn-/ *n* [C] an official who lives in a foreign city and whose job is to help citizens of his or her own country who are there —**consular** /ˈkɒnsjʊləl‖ˈkɑːnsələr/ *adj*

con·su·late /ˈkɒnsjʊlət‖ˈkɑːnsələt/ *n* [C] the official building where a consul lives and works

con·sult /kənˈsʌlt/ *v* **1** [T] to ask someone for advice or information, or to look for it in a book, map etc: *Consult your doctor if the headaches continue.* **2** [I,T] to ask for someone's opinion or permission before deciding something: *I can't believe you sold the car without consulting me!*

con·sul·tan·cy /kənˈsʌltənsi/ *n* [C] a company that advises and trains people in other companies

containers

a packet *BrE*/pack *AmE*/ bag of sugar/peas

a packet *BrE*/pack *AmE* of cigarettes/gum

tube

a box of eggs/matches

tube of toothpaste

carton

sachet *BrE*/packet *AmE*

barrel   drum

can/tin *BrE*

crate

con·sul·tant /kən'sʌltənt/ *n* [C] **1** someone with a lot of experience in a particular subject whose job is to give advice about it: *a marketing consultant* **2** *BrE* a SENIOR hospital doctor who knows a lot about a particular kind of medical treatment

con·sul·ta·tion /ˌkɒnsəl'teɪʃən‖ˌkɑːn-/ *n* **1** [C,U] a discussion in which people who are affected by a decision can say what they think should be done: *It was all done completely without consultation.* | **in consultation with** (=with the agreement and help of someone): *The plan was drawn up in consultation with the mayor.* **2** [C,U] a meeting in which you get advice from someone such as a doctor, or the advice they give: *The school counsellor is always available for consultation.* **3** [U] when you look for information in a book: *There are old examination papers available for consultation.*

con·sume /kən'sjuːm‖-'suːm/ *v* [T] **1** to use energy, goods, time etc: *The country consumes far more than it produces.* **2** *formal* to eat or drink something **3 be consumed with passion/guilt/rage** etc to have a very strong feeling that you cannot ignore **4** if fire consumes something, it destroys it completely

con·sum·er /kən'sjuːməǁ-'suːmər/ *n* [C] someone who buys or uses goods and services: *laws to protect consumers*

con·sum·ing /kən'sjuːmɪŋ‖-'suː-/ *adj* [only before noun] a consuming feeling or interest is so strong that it controls you: *Her consuming ambition is to be an opera singer.*

con·sum·mate¹ /'kɒnsəmeɪt‖'kɑːn-/ *v* [T] to make a marriage or a relationship complete by having sex —**consummation** /ˌkɒnsə'meɪʃən‖ˌkɑːn-/ *n* [U]

con·sum·mate² /kən'sʌmɪt/ *adj formal* showing great skill: *a consummate politician*

con·sump·tion /kən'sʌmpʃən/ *n* [U] **1** the amount of electricity, gas etc that someone or something uses: *a car with low fuel consumption* **2** *formal* the act of eating or drinking

con·tact¹ /'kɒntækt‖'kɑːn-/ *n* **1** [U] communication with a person, organization, or country: **+ with** *We don't have much contact with my husband's family.* | **keep/stay in contact with** *Have you kept in contact with any of your school friends?* **2** [U] when two people or things touch against each other: **come into contact (with)** *Kids come into contact with all kinds of germs at school.* **3** [C] someone you know who may be able to help you or give you advice

contact² *v* [T] to telephone or write to someone: *Who can we contact in an emergency?*

contact lens /'.. ./ *n* [C] a small round piece of plastic you put on your eye to help you see clearly

con·ta·gious /kən'teɪdʒəs/ *adj* **1** a contagious disease can be passed from person to person by touch **2** someone who is contagious has a disease like this **3** if a feeling, attitude, or action is contagious, other people quickly begin to feel it or do it: *contagious laughter*

con·tain /kən'teɪn/ *v* [T] **1** to have something inside, or have something as a part: *We also found a wallet containing $45.* | *a report that contained some shocking information* **2** to control the emotions you feel: *Nina was trying hard to contain her amusement.* | **contain yourself** *Greg was so excited he could hardly contain himself.* **3** to stop something from spreading or escaping: *Doctors are making every effort to contain the disease.*

con·tain·er /kən'teɪnəǁ-ər/ *n* [C] something such as a box or bottle that can be filled with something

con·tam·i·nate /kən'tæmɪneɪt/ *v* [T] to make something dirty or dangerous by adding something such as chemicals or poison to it: *Chemical waste had contaminated the water supply.* —**contamination** /kənˌtæmɪ'neɪʃən/ *n* [U]

con·tem·plate /'kɒntəmpleɪt‖'kɑːn-/ *v* [T] to think about something, especially in a serious way or for a long time: **contemplate doing sth** *Have you ever contemplated leaving him?* —**contemplation** /ˌkɒntəm'pleɪʃən‖ˌkɑːn-/ *n* [U]

con·tem·po·ra·ry[1] /kən'tempərəri, -pəri‖ -pəreri/ *adj* **1** belonging to the present time: *contemporary art* **2** happening or existing in the same period of time: *contemporary accounts of the war*

contemporary[2] *n* [C] a person living or working at the same time as someone else: *Mozart was greatly admired by his contemporaries.*

con·tempt /kən'tempt/ *n* [U] **1** a feeling that someone or something does not deserve any respect: *Stuart treated his wife with utter contempt.*|+ **for** *Their contempt for foreigners was obvious.* **2** contempt of court *law* when someone does not do what a judge or court of law has ordered

con·temp·ti·ble /kən'temptⱼbəl/ *adj* used to emphasize that you think someone or something is completely immoral, dishonest, unfair etc, and should not be respected: *a contemptible piece of legislation*|*contemptible behaviour* —**contemptibly** *adv*

con·temp·tu·ous /kən'temptʃuəs/ *adj* showing that you dislike someone or something and have no respect for them: *the guard's contemptuous attitude towards his prisoners* —**contemptuously** *adv*

con·tend /kən'tend/ *v* **1** [T] *formal* to state or argue that something is true: + **that** *Democrats contend that the new tax is unfair.* **2** [I] to compete against someone to get something: + **for** *Twelve teams contended for the title.*

   contend with sth *phr v* [T] to have a problem that you must deal with, which makes it difficult for you to do something: *The builders had to contend with severe weather conditions.*

con·tend·er /kən'tendə‖-ər/ *n* [C] someone who is competing in a competition

con·tent[1] /kən'tent/ *adj* [not before noun] satisfied and happy: **content to do sth** *Gary seems content to sit at home and watch TV all day.*| + **with** *I'd say she's fairly content with her life at the moment.* —**contentment** *n* [U] → see also to **your heart's content** (HEART)

con·tent[2] /'kɒntent‖'kɑːn-/ *n* [singular] **1** the amount of a substance that something contains: *Peanut butter has a high fat content.* **2** the ideas or information in a book, programme etc: + **of** *Is the content of such a magazine suitable for 13-year-olds?* → see also CONTENTS

con·tent[3] /kən'tent/ *v* **content yourself with sth** to accept something, even though it is not what you really wanted: *Jack's driving, so he'll have to content himself with a soft drink.*

con·tent·ed /kən'tentⱼd/ *adj* satisfied and happy: *a contented cat curled up by the fire* —**contentedly** *adv* → opposite DISCONTENTED

con·ten·tion /kən'tenʃən/ *n* **1** [C] *formal* an opinion that someone expresses **2** [U] arguments and disagreements between people: **bone of contention** (=a subject that people argue about): *The children's education soon became a bone of contention between Ralph and his wife.*

con·ten·tious /kən'tenʃəs/ *adj formal* likely to cause an argument

con·tents /'kɒntents‖'kɑːn-/ *n* [plural] **1** the things that are inside a box, bag, house etc: *the contents of his luggage* **2** the words or ideas that are written in a book, letter etc: *The contents of the report are still unknown.* **3** the list

at the beginning of a book, showing what the different parts of the book are about

con·test[1] /'kɒntest‖'kɑːn-/ *n* [C] a competition: *a beauty contest*

con·test[2] /kən'test/ *v* [T] **1** to try to change an official decision because you disagree with it: *We intend to contest the judge's decision.* **2** to try to win something, especially an election: *The 1984 elections were contested by a large number of parties.*

con·tes·tant /kən'testənt/ *n* [C] someone who takes part in a competition

con·text /'kɒntekst‖'kɑːn-/ *n* [C,U] **1** the situation within which something happens: *You need to consider these events in their historical context.* **2** the words that come before and after a word or phrase, that help you understand its meaning: *Can you guess the meaning of this word from its context?*

con·ti·nent /'kɒntⱼnənt‖'kɑːn-/ *n* [C] **1** one of the main areas of land in the world, such as Africa, Asia, or Europe **2** the Continent *BrE* Western Europe, not including Britain

con·ti·nen·tal /ˌkɒntⱼ'nentl‖ˌkɑːn-/ *adj* **1** belonging to or consisting of a continent ,and not any of the islands around it: *flights across the continental US* **2** *BrE* on or belonging to the continent of Europe, not including Britain

con·tin·gen·cy /kən'tɪndʒənsi/ *n* [C] something that may possibly happen and cause problems: **contingency plans** *We have contingency plans to deal with any computer failures.*

con·tin·gent[1] /kən'tɪndʒənt/ *adj formal* **contingent on** depending on whether something happens: *Further payment will be contingent on whether the work is completed on time.*

contingent[2] *n* [C] **1** a group of people at an event who all come from the same area or organization: *Has the Scottish contingent arrived?* **2** a group of soldiers or police that forms part of a larger group

con·tin·u·al /kən'tɪnjuəl/ *adj* repeated often or happening continuously over a long period of time: *I get fed up with their continual arguing.*|*continual pain* —**continually** *adv*

USAGE NOTE: continual and continuous

Use these words to talk about the way something happens and how long it continues. Use **continual** when something is repeated often over a long time: *continual interruptions* | *The phone's been ringing continually all day.* When something continues without stopping, use **continuous**: *several days of continuous rain* | *Education is a continuous process.*

---

con·tin·u·a·tion /kənˌtɪnju'eɪʃən/ *n* **1** [C] something that follows or is joined to something else and seems a part of it: *Bogarde's second book is a continuation of his autobiography.* **2** [singular, U] when something continues for a long time without stopping: *the continuation of family traditions*

con·tin·ue /kən'tɪnjuː/ *v* **1** [I,T] to keep happening, existing, or doing something without stopping: *The fighting continued for two days.*|**continue to do sth** *The city's population will continue to grow.* **2** [I,T] to start again after a pause: *The story continues on page*

27. | *Can we continue this discussion later?* **3** [I] to go further in the same direction: + **on/up/along** etc *We said goodbye and continued on our way.* —**continued** *adj: We are grateful for your continued support.*

con·ti·nu·i·ty /ˌkɒntɪˈnjuːətiˌl, ˌkɑːntɪˈnuː-/ *n* [U] when something continues over a long period of time without being interrupted or changed: *Changing doctors is likely to affect the continuity of your treatment.*

con·tin·u·ous /kənˈtɪnjuəs/ *adj* **1** continuing without stopping: *These plants need a continuous supply of fresh water.* **2** the continuous form of a verb in grammar is used to show that an action is continuing to happen. In the sentence 'She is watching TV', 'is watching' is in the continuous form —**continuously** *adv*

con·tort /kənˈtɔːt‖-ɔːrt/ *v* [I,T] if your face or body contorts, or is contorted, it is twisted into an unnatural shape: *Shelby's face was contorted with pain.* —**contortion** /-ˈtɔːʃən‖-ɔːr-/ *n* [C,U]

con·tour /ˈkɒntʊəl‖ˈkɑːntʊr/ *n* [C] **1** the shape around the edge or surface of something: *the pale contours of his face* **2** also **contour line** a line on a map joining points of equal height

con·tra·band /ˈkɒntrəbænd‖ˈkɑːn-/ *n* [U] goods that are brought into or taken out of a country illegally

con·tra·cep·tion /ˌkɒntrəˈsepʃən‖ˌkɑːn-/ *n* [U] methods of preventing a woman becoming PREGNANT; BIRTH CONTROL

con·tra·cep·tive /ˌkɒntrəˈseptɪv‖ˌkɑːn-/ *n* [C] something that prevents a woman becoming PREGNANT —**contraceptive** *adj: the contraceptive pill*

con·tract[1] /ˈkɒntræktl‖ˈkɑːn-/ *n* [C] a formal written agreement between two people, companies etc: *Stacy signed a three year contract with a small record company.* —**contractual** /kənˈtræktʃuəl/ *adj: a contractual arrangement*

con·tract[2] /kənˈtrækt/ *v* **1** [I] to become smaller: *Metal contracts as it becomes cooler.* ➔opposite EXPAND **2** [T] *formal* to get a serious illness: *Sharon contracted AIDS from a dirty needle.*

con·trac·tion /kənˈtrækʃən/ *n* **1** [U] the process of becoming smaller: *the contraction of our manufacturing industry* ➔opposite EXPANSION **2** [C] *technical* when a muscle suddenly and painfully gets tighter, especially during the birth of a baby **3** [C] *technical* a word that has been made shorter. For example, 'don't' is a contraction of 'do not'.

con·trac·tor /kənˈtræktəl‖ˈkɑːntræktər/ *n* [C] a person or company that does work or supplies goods for another company: *a building contractor*

con·tra·dict /ˌkɒntrəˈdɪktl‖ˌkɑːn-/ *v* **1** [T] if one statement, story, fact etc contradicts another, they are different or opposite, and so they cannot both be true: *The witnesses' reports contradict each other.* **2** [I,T] to say that what someone else has just said is wrong or not true: *Susan thought I was a teacher and I didn't contradict her.*

con·tra·dic·tion /ˌkɒntrəˈdɪkʃən‖ˌkɑːn-/ *n* **1** [C] a difference between two statements, facts etc which means they cannot both be true: + **between** *There's a contradiction between what*

the company claims to do and what it actually does. **2** [U] when you say that a statement or opinion made by someone else is wrong or not true: *He could say whatever he liked without fear of contradiction.* **3** **a contradiction in terms** words used together that have opposite meanings: *To call him an honest thief seems like a contradiction in terms.*

con·tra·dic·to·ry /ˌkɒntrəˈdɪktəriˌ‖ˌkɑːn-/ *adj* if two statements are contradictory, they are different from each other, and cannot both be true

con·trap·tion /kənˈtræpʃən/ *n* [C] *informal* a strange-looking machine or piece of equipment

con·tra·ry[1] /ˈkɒntrəriˌl‖ˈkɑːntreri/ *n* *formal* **1** **on the contrary** used to emphasize that the opposite of what someone has just said is actually true: *We didn't start the fire. On the contrary, we helped put it out.* **2** **to the contrary** saying or showing the opposite of something else: *Despite rumours to the contrary, their relationship is very good.* **3** **the contrary** *formal* the opposite: *She was not disappointed. Quite the contrary – she was pleased.*

USAGE NOTE: contrary

Compare **on the contrary**, **on the other hand**, and **in contrast**. Use **on the contrary** to show that what has just been said is completely wrong: *"Tom is a good student, isn't he?" "On the contrary, he's lazy and stupid."* Use **on the other hand** to add an idea or opinion which is different, but does not mean the first idea is wrong: *He's not very good in class, but on the other hand he's very good at sports.* **In contrast** is used to show that something is completely and surprisingly different: *He's very mean to his wife, but in contrast gives his kids anything they want.*

---

contrary[2] *adj* **1** **contrary to** **a)** used to say that something is true and the opposite is false: *Contrary to popular belief* (=although most people think the opposite), *gorillas are shy and gentle creatures.* **b)** breaking a law or rule: *actions that are contrary to International Law* **2** completely different or opposite to each other: *contrary opinions*

con·trast[1] /ˈkɒntrɑːstl‖ˈkɑːntræst/ *n* **1** [C,U] a big difference between people, situations, ideas etc that are being compared: + **between** *the contrast between life in the city and life on the farm* **2** **in contrast/by contrast** used to compare objects or situations that are completely different: *By contrast, the second exam was very difficult.*

con·trast[2] /kənˈtrɑːstl‖-ˈtræst/ *v* **1** [T] to compare two people, ideas, objects etc and show how they are different from each other: **contrast sth with sth** *In this programme Chinese music is contrasted with Western classical music.* **2** [I] if two things contrast, they are very different from each other: + **with** *His views on religion contrast sharply with my own.* —**contrasting** *adj: contrasting colours*

con·tra·vene /ˌkɒntrəˈviːnl‖ˌkɑːn-/ *v* [T] *formal* to do something that is not allowed by a law or a rule: *The sale of alcohol to children under 18 contravenes the licensing laws.* —**contravention** /-ˈvenʃən/ *n* [C,U]

con·trib·ute /kənˈtrɪbjuːt/ *v* [I,T] **1** to join with other people in giving money, help, or ideas for a particular purpose: + **towards** *We all contributed towards a present for Jack.* **2 contribute** to to be one of the causes of something: *All this worry almost certainly contributed to his ill health.* **3** to write for a newspaper or magazine — **contributor** *n* [C]

con·tri·bu·tion /ˌkɒntrɪ'bjuːʃən||ˌkɑːn-/ *n* [C] **1** something that you give or do to help make something successful: + **to** *Einstein's enormous contribution to science* | *The UN has made an important contribution to world peace.* **2** money that you give to help pay for something

con·trib·u·to·ry /kən'trɪbjʊtəri||-tɔːri/ *adj* [only before noun] helping to cause or produce something: *Smoking is a contributory cause of heart disease.*

con·trive /kən'traɪv/ *v* [T] **1** *formal* to succeed in doing something difficult: **contrive to do sth** *Somehow she contrived to escape.* **2** to succeed in making something happen: *It was Richard who had contrived the prince's murder.* **3** to make or invent something: *The programs had been hastily contrived.*

con·trived /kən'traɪvd/ *adj* seeming false and not natural: *Lauren spoke with a contrived southern accent.*

con·trol[1] /kən'trəʊl||-'troʊl/ *n* **1** [U] the power or authority to make someone or something do what you want: **have control over** *Peter and Rachel have no control over their son.* | **out of control** (=impossible to control): *The car went out of control and hit a tree.* | **under control** (=being controlled): *It's all right – the situation is now completely under control.* **2** [U] the power to decide what will happen in an organization or place: **take control of** *Rioters took control of the prison.* | **in control** (=having the power to control): *The government is no longer in control of the country.* **3** [C,U] when you limit the amount or growth of something: *the control of inflation* | *import controls* **4** [U] the ability to remain calm, even when you are angry or excited; SELF-CONTROL: **lose control** *I just lost control and punched him!* **5** [C] one of the parts of a machine, television etc that you use to make it work: *the volume control on the television* **6** [C,U] the place where something is officially checked: *passport control*

control[2] *v* [T] **-lled, -lled, -lling 1** to make someone or something do what you want, or make them work in a particular way: *a teacher who can't control the kids* **2** to have the power to decide what will happen in an organization or place: *Rebels control all the roads into the capital.* **3** to limit the amount or growth of something **4** to make yourself behave calmly, even if you feel angry, excited, or upset: *I find it very difficult to control my temper sometimes.*

con·tro·ver·sial /ˌkɒntrə'vɜːʃəl||ˌkɑːntrə-'vɜːrʃəl/ *adj* causing a lot of disagreement and argument: *the controversial subject of abortion* — **controversially** *adv*

con·tro·ver·sy /'kɒntrəvɜːsi, kən'trɒvəsi||'kɑːntrəvɜːrsi/ *n* [C,U] a lot of disagreement and

argument about something: + **over/about** *The controversy over the nuclear energy program is likely to continue.*

con·ur·ba·tion /ˌkɒnɜː'beɪʃən||ˌkɑːnɜːr-/ *n* [C] a group of towns that have spread and become joined together

con·va·lesce /ˌkɒnvə'les||ˌkɑːn-/ *v* [I] to spend time getting well after an illness — **convalescence** *n* [U] *a long period of convalescence*

con·vec·tion /kən'vekʃən/ *n* [U] the movement caused by warm gas or liquid rising, and cold gas or liquid sinking

con·vene /kən'viːn/ *v* [I,T] *formal* to come together or bring people together for a meeting

con·ve·ni·ence /kən'viːniəns/ *n* [U] the quality of being convenient: *I like the convenience of living close to where I work.* → opposite INCONVENIENCE[1]

con·ve·ni·ent /kən'viːniənt/ *adj* **1** helpful, useful, or suitable when doing something and not causing problems: *Would 10:30 be a convenient time to meet?* | + **for** *It's more convenient for me to pay by credit card.* **2** near and easy to get to: *a convenient place to shop* — **conveniently** *adv* → opposite INCONVENIENT

con·vent /'kɒnvənt||'kɑːnvent/ *n* [C] a place where NUNS live and work

con·ven·tion /kən'venʃən/ *n* **1** [C,U] the normal and traditional way of behaving and thinking in a society: *She shocked her neighbours by ignoring every social convention.* **2** [C] a large formal meeting of people who belong to the same profession, organization etc: *a teachers' convention* **3** [C] a formal agreement between countries: *the Geneva Convention on Human Rights*

con·ven·tion·al /kən'venʃənəl/ *adj* **1** thinking and behaving in the normal and traditional way: *My parents have very conventional attitudes about sex.* → opposite UNCONVENTIONAL **2** of the usual type that has been used for a long time: *The microwave is much faster than the conventional oven.* **3** [only before noun] conventional weapons and wars do not use NUCLEAR power — **conventionally** *adv*

con·verge /kən'vɜːdʒ||-'vɜːrdʒ/ *v* [I] to come from different directions and meet at the same place: *The place where two streams converge to form a river.* | + **on** *Thousands of fans converged on the stadium.*

con·ver·sa·tion /ˌkɒnvə'seɪʃən||ˌkɑːnvər-/ *n* [C,U] an informal talk between two or more people: *a telephone conversation* | **have a conversation** *Please don't interrupt. We're having a conversation.* | **make conversation** (=to talk to someone in order to be polite) — **conversational** *adj*

con·verse /kən'vɜːs||-'vɜːrs/ *v* [I] *formal* to have a conversation with someone

con·ver·sion /kən'vɜːʃən||-'vɜːrʒən/ *n* [C,U] **1** a change from one system or purpose to another: + **to/into** *Canada's conversion to the metric system* **2** when someone changes and

C

SPELLING NOTE
Words with the sound /k/, like **cut**, may be spelt **k-**, like **key**, or **qu-**, like **queen**.
Words with the sound /s/, like **city**, may be spelt **s-**, like **soon**, or **ps-**, like **psychology**.

convert

accepts a religion or set of ideas: **+ to** *Tyson's conversion to Islam surprised the media.*

con·vert¹ /kən'vɜːt‖-'vɜːrt/ *v* [I,T] **1** to change from one system or purpose to another, or to change something in this way: **+ into** *a sofa that converts into a bed | We're going to convert the garage into a workshop.* **2** to accept a different religion, opinion etc, or to make someone do this: **convert sb to sth** *Steven has converted to Islam.*

con·vert² /'kɒnvɜːt‖'kɑːnvɜːrt/ *n* [C] someone who has been persuaded to accept a particular religion or belief

con·ver·ti·ble /kən'vɜːt̬əbəl‖-ɜːr-/ *n* [C] a car with a roof that you can fold back or remove

con·vex /ˌkɒn'veks◂, kən-,'kɒnveks‖ˌkɑːn'veks◂, kən-,'kɑːnveks/ *adj* curved outwards, like the outside edge of a circle **→ opposite** CONCAVE

con·vey /kən'veɪ/ *v* [T] *formal* to express your feelings, ideas, or thoughts to other people: *Mark's eyes clearly conveyed his disappointment.*

conveyor belt /.'... ./ *n* [C] a long moving band of rubber or metal, used to move things from one place to another

con·vict¹ /kən'vɪkt/ *v* [T] to officially decide in a court of law that someone is guilty of a crime: **be convicted of** *Both men were convicted of murder. | a convicted terrorist* **→ opposite** ACQUIT

con·vict² /'kɒnvɪkt‖'kɑːn-/ *n* [C] someone who has been proved guilty of a crime and sent to prison

con·vic·tion /kən'vɪkʃən/ *n* **1** [C] when someone is convicted of a crime: *Bradley had two previous convictions for drug offences.* **2** [C,U] a very strong belief or opinion: *religious convictions* **→ opposite** ACQUITTAL

con·vince /kən'vɪns/ *v* [T] **1** to make someone feel certain that something is true: **convince sb that** *I managed to convince them that our story was true. | convince sb of sth Shaw had convinced the jury of his innocence.* **2** a word used to mean "persuade", which some people think is incorrect: *Can you convince her to come with you?* **→ compare** PERSUADE

con·vinced /kən'vɪnst/ *adj* **be convinced (that)** to feel certain that something is true: *Maud's parents were convinced she was taking drugs.*

con·vinc·ing /kən'vɪnsɪŋ/ *adj* making you believe that something is true or right: *a convincing argument* **—convincingly** *adv*

con·viv·i·al /kən'vɪviəl/ *adj formal* friendly and pleasantly cheerful: *a convivial atmosphere*

con·vo·lut·ed /'kɒnvəluːt̬d‖'kɑːn-/ *adj formal* complicated and difficult to understand: *convoluted legal language*

con·voy /'kɒnvɔɪ‖'kɑːn-/ *n* [C] a group of vehicles or ships travelling together

con·vulse /kən'vʌls/ *v* [I,T] if your body convulses, it starts to shake violently: *We were convulsed with laughter.* (=we laughed a lot)

con·vul·sion /kən'vʌlʃən/ *n* [C] a sudden violent movement of your body, caused by illness

coo /kuː/ *v* [I] **1** to make a sound like that of a DOVE or a PIGEON **2** to make soft, loving noises

cook¹ /kʊk/ *v* [I,T] to prepare food for eating by using heat: *Whose turn is it to cook supper tonight? | Grandma's cooking for the whole family this weekend.* **2** [I] if food cooks, it is heated until it is ready to eat: *While the potatoes are cooking, prepare a salad.*

cook sth ↔ up *phr v* [T] *informal* to invent an excuse or to plan something dishonest: *a plan cooked up by the two brothers to make more money*

cook² *n* [C] someone who cooks and prepares food

cook·book /'kʊkbʊk/ also **cookery book** /'.../ *BrE n* [C] a book that tells you how to prepare and cook food

cook·er /'kʊkə‖-ər/ *n* [C] *BrE* a large piece of kitchen equipment used for cooking food; STOVE *AmE* **→ see picture at** KITCHEN

cook·e·ry /'kʊkəri/ *n* [U] *BrE* the skill and methods of preparing food and cooking it; COOKING

cook·ie /'kʊki/ *n* [C] *especially AmE* a type of thin hard cake; BISCUIT *BrE*: *chocolate chip cookies* **→ see colour picture on page 440**

cook·ing /'kʊkɪŋ/ *n* [U] **1** the activity of preparing food and cooking it: *Cooking is fun. | Who does the cooking?* **2** food made in a particular way or by a particular person: *Indian cooking | I prefer Mum's cooking.*

cool¹ /kuːl/ *adj* **1** fairly cold, but not too cold: *a cool refreshing drink | a cool breeze* **2** calm and not nervous or excited: *Now, stay cool — everything is OK.* **3** not as friendly as usual: *The boss didn't actually criticize me, but he was very cool towards me.* **4** *spoken informal* used about something or someone that you like or admire: *Bart's a real cool guy.* **—coolness** *n* [U]

cool² *v* **1** also **cool down** [I,T] to become a little colder, or to make something a little colder: *Allow the cake to cool before cutting it.* **2** [I] if feelings or relationships cool, they become less strong

cool down *phr v* **1** [I, T **cool** sth ↔ **down**] to become a little colder, or to make something a little colder: *Let the engine cool down* **2** [I] to become calm after being angry: *The long walk home helped me cool down.*

cool off *phr v* [I] **1** to return to a normal temperature after being hot: *We went for a swim to cool off.* **2** to become calm after being angry

cool³ *n* **1** **keep your cool** to stay calm in a difficult situation: *Rick was starting to annoy her, but she kept her cool.* **2** **lose your cool** to stop being calm in a difficult situation: *Nick lost his cool when Ryan yelled at him.* **3** **the cool** a temperature that is cool: *the cool of the evening*

cool·ly /'kuːl-li/ *adv* **1** in a way that seems unfriendly or not interested **2** calmly: *Bond coolly told him to put down the gun.*

coop¹ /kuːp/ *n* [C] a CAGE for chickens

coop² *v* **be cooped up** to be kept in a place that is too small, or to be made to stay indoors: *We were glad to be out in the fresh air after being cooped up all morning.*

co·op·e·rate also **co-operate** *BrE* /kəʊ'ɒpəreɪt‖koʊ'ɑːp-/ *v* [I] **1** to work with someone else in order to achieve something that you both want: **+ with** *Local police are cooperating with the army in the search for the missing teenager.* **2** to help someone willingly when they ask you to help: *We can deal with this problem, if you're willing to cooperate.* **—cooperation** /kəʊ,ɒp-'reɪʃən‖koʊ,ɑːp-/ *n* [U]

co·op·e·ra·tive¹ also **co-operative** *BrE* /
kəʊˈɒpərətɪvǁkoʊˈɑːp-/ *adj* **1** willing to help:
Ned has always been very cooperative in the past.
2 done by people working together: *The play
was a cooperative effort between the two schools.*
— **cooperatively** *adv*

cooperative² also **co-operative** *BrE* *n* [C] a
business, farm, shop etc that is owned and managed by a group of people working together

co·or·di·nate¹ also **co-ordinate** *BrE* /kəʊ-
ˈɔːdɪneɪtǁkoʊˈɔːr-/ *v* [T] **1** to organize people or
things so that they work together effectively:
The project is being coordinated by Dr Ken Pease.
2 to make the parts of your body move well together: *Small children often find it difficult co-
ordinate their movements.*

co·or·di·nate² also **co-ordinate** *BrE* /kəʊ-
ˈɔːdɪnɪtǁkoʊˈɔːr-/ *n* [C] *technical* one of a set of
numbers or letters that give the exact position of
a point on a map

co·or·di·na·tion also **co-ordination** *BrE* /
kəʊˌɔːdɪˈneɪʃənǁkoʊˌɔːr-/ *n* [U] **1** when people or
things are organized so that they work together
effectively: **of** *the coordination of all military activities* **2** the way in which the parts of your body
move together to do something: *Computer games
can help develop hand-to-eye coordination.*

co·or·di·na·tor also **co-ordinator** *BrE* /kəʊ-
ˈɔːdɪneɪtəǁkoʊˈɔːrdɪneɪtər/ *n* [C] someone who
organizes the way people work together

cop /kɒpǁkɑːp/ *n* [C] *informal especially AmE* a
police officer

cope /kəʊpǁkoʊp/ *v* [I] to deal with something
successfully: **with** *How do you cope with all this
work?*

cop·i·er /ˈkɒpiəǁ-ər/ *n* [C] *AmE* a PHOTOCOPIER

co·pi·ous /ˈkəʊpiəsǁˈkoʊ-/ *adj* in large quantities: *Adrian always takes copious notes at
lectures.* — **copiously** *adv*

cop·per /ˈkɒpəǁˈkɑːpər/ *n* **1** [U] an orange-
brown metal **2** [C] *BrE informal* a coin with a
low value, made of brown metal: *Can you lend
me a few coppers?* **3** [C] *BrE informal* a police
officer

copse /kɒpsǁkɑːps/ *n* [C] a small group of trees
or bushes

cop·u·late /ˈkɒpjʊleɪtǁˈkɑːp-/ *v* [I] *formal* to
have sex — **copulation** /ˌkɒpjʊˈleɪʃənǁˌkɑːp-/ *n*
[U]

copy¹ /ˈkɒpiǁˈkɑːpi/ *n* [C] **1** something that
is made to look exactly like something else:
make a copy of *Please would you make me a
copy of this letter?* **2** a book, magazine, or newspaper which is one of many that are all the
same: *Have you seen my copy of 'The Times'?*

copy² *v* **1** [T] to make something that looks
exactly like something else: *Could you copy the
report and send it out to everyone?* **2** [T] to do
something that someone else has done, or behave like someone else: *The system has been copied by other organizations, and has worked well.*
3 [I,T] to cheat by writing what someone else
has written, especially in school work or a test
copy sth ↔ **out** *phr v* [T] *BrE* to write something exactly as it is written somewhere else:
Copy out the poem into your exercise books.

cop·y·right /ˈkɒpiraɪtǁˈkɑː-/ *n* [C,U] the legal
right to be the only person or company that can
produce a book, or perform a play, song etc

cor·al /ˈkɒrəlǁˈkɔː-, ˈkɑː-/ *n* [U] a hard pink,
white, or red substance that is formed from the
bones of very small sea animals

cord /kɔːdǁkɔːrd/ *n* [C,U] **1** a piece of thick
string or thin rope **2** wire covered with plastic
for connecting equipment to a supply of electricity; CABLE; FLEX *BrE*

cor·di·al /ˈkɔːdiəlǁˈkɔːrdʒəl/ *adj formal* friendly
and polite: *We received a cordial welcome.* — **cor-
dially** *adv*

cord·less /ˈkɔːdləsǁˈkɔːrd-/ *adj* a cordless telephone or piece of electrical equipment uses a
BATTERY and is not connected to an electricity
supply

cor·don¹ /ˈkɔːdnǁˈkɔːrdn/ *n* [C] a line of police
or soldiers around an area, preventing people
from entering or leaving it: *Several protesters
tried to push through the police cordon.*

cordon² *v*
cordon sth ↔ **off** *phr v* [T] to surround an area
with police or soldiers, preventing people from
entering or leaving it: *Police have cordoned off
the building where the bomb was found.*

cords /kɔːdzǁkɔːrdz/ *n* [plural] *informal* cordu-
roy trousers

cor·du·roy /ˈkɔːdʒərɔɪ, -dʒʊ-ǁˈkɔːrdə-/ *n* [U]
thick strong cotton cloth with raised lines on
one side

core /kɔːǁkɔːr/ *n* **1** [singular] the central or
most important part of something: **of** *the core
of the problem* **core beliefs/vocabulary/
subjects etc** (=the most important beliefs,
words, subjects etc): *Students have to study five
core subjects.* **2** [C] the hard central part of an
apple or PEAR **3** **to the core** completely or very
much: *His words shocked me to the core.* **4** [C]
the central part of the earth or any other PLANET
➜ see also HARD-CORE

co·ri·an·der /ˌkɒriˈændəǁˌkɔːriˈændər/ *n* [U]
BrE a plant used to give a special taste to food;
CILANTRO *AmE*

cork /kɔːkǁkɔːrk/ *n* **1** [U] the soft light BARK
(=skin) of a Mediterranean tree that is used for
making things: *cork floor tiles* **2** [C] a round
piece of this substance that is pushed into the
top of a bottle to close it

cork·screw /ˈkɔːkskruːǁˈkɔːrk-/ *n* [C] the tool
you use to pull a cork out of a bottle

corn /kɔːnǁkɔːrn/ *n* **1** [U] *BrE* the grain or
seeds of crops such as wheat **2** [U] *AmE* a tall
plant with large yellow seeds, or these seeds
cooked and eaten as a vegetable; MAIZE, SWEET-
CORN *BrE* **3** [C] a painful area of thick hard
skin on your foot

cor·ner¹ /ˈkɔːnəǁˈkɔːrnər/ *n* [C] **1** the point at
which two lines, edges, or walls meet: **in the
corner** *Two men were sitting in the corner of the
room.* | *Write your address in the top right-hand
corner of the page.* ➜ see picture at EDGE **2** the
place where two roads or streets meet: **on/at the
corner** *children playing on street
corners* | **round/around the corner** (=on the
other side of the corner): *There's a bus stop just
around the corner from where I live.* **3** a place
that is far away or difficult to get to: *a remote
corner of Scotland* **4** **out of the corner of your
eye** if you see something out of the corner of
your eye, you notice it without turning your
head **5** also **corner kick** a kick from the corner

of the field in a game of football → see also **cut corners** (CUT[1])

corner[2] v [T] **1** to force a person or an animal into a position from which they cannot easily escape: *Gibbs cornered Cassetti in the hallway and asked for his decision.* **2 corner the market** to get total control of the supply of a particular type of goods

cor·ner·stone /ˈkɔːnəstəʊn‖ˈkɔːrnərstoʊn/ n [C] something that is very important because everything else depends on it: + **of** *Trust and respect are the cornerstones of any relationship.*

cor·net /ˈkɔːnɪt‖kɔːrˈnet/ n [C] **1** a musical instrument like a TRUMPET **2** a container that you can eat, which has ICE CREAM inside it and on top, and which has a pointed bottom

corn·flakes /ˈkɔːnfleɪks‖ˈkɔːrn-/ n [plural] a type of breakfast food made from corn

corn·flour /ˈkɔːnflaʊə‖ˈkɔːrnflaʊr/ n [U] *BrE* a fine white flour made from corn, used in cooking; CORNSTARCH *AmE*

corn·starch /ˈkɔːnstɑːtʃ‖ˈkɔːrnstɑːrtʃ/ n [U] *AmE* cornflour

corn·y /ˈkɔːni‖ˈkɔːrni/ adj informal too familiar, ordinary, or old-fashioned to be funny or interesting: *a corny joke*

cor·o·na·ry[1] /ˈkɒrənəri‖ˈkɔːrəneri, ˈkɑː-/ n [C] a type of HEART ATTACK

coronary[2] adj [only before noun] technical relating to the heart: *coronary disease*

cor·o·na·tion /ˌkɒrəˈneɪʃən‖ˌkɔː-, ˌkɑː-/ n [C] a ceremony in which someone officially becomes a king or queen

cor·o·ner /ˈkɒrənə‖ˈkɔːrənər, ˈkɑː-/ n [C] someone whose job is to officially find out the causes of sudden or accidental deaths

cor·po·ral /ˈkɔːpərəl‖ˈkɔːr-/ n [C] a soldier who has a low rank in the army or AIR FORCE

corporal pun·ish·ment /ˌ... ˈ.../ n [U] a way of punishing someone by hitting them

cor·po·rate /ˈkɔːpərɪt‖ˈkɔːr-/ adj [only before noun] **1** relating to a corporation **2** shared by all the people in a group: *corporate responsibilities*

cor·po·ra·tion /ˌkɔːpəˈreɪʃən‖ˌkɔːr-/ n [C] **1** a large business organization: *a multinational corporation* **2** *BrE* a group of people elected to govern a town

corps /kɔː‖kɔːr/ n [singular] **1** a group in the army, especially one with special duties: *the medical corps* **2** a group of people who do a particular job: *the press corps*

corpse /kɔːps‖kɔːrps/ n [C] a dead body

cor·pus /ˈkɔːpəs‖ˈkɔːr-/ n [C] plural **corpuses** or **corpora** /-pərə/ technical a large amount of written or spoken language collected together to be studied: *a corpus of spoken English*

cor·pus·cle /ˈkɔːpəsəl, kɔːˈpʌ-‖ˈkɔːrpə-/ n [C] one of the red or white blood cells in your body

cor·ral /kəˈrɑːl‖kəˈræl/ n [C] an enclosed area where cattle or horses are kept, especially in the US

cor·rect[1] /kəˈrekt/ adj **1** right or without any mistakes: *the correct answers* | *"Your name is Ives?" "Yes, that's correct."* **2** suitable for a particular situation or use: *correct behaviour* —**correctly** adv: *Have you spelled it correctly?* —**correctness** n [U] → opposite INCORRECT

cor·rect[2] v [T] **1** to show someone that something is wrong, and make it right: *Correct my pronunciation if it's wrong.* | *She spent all evening correcting exam papers* (=marking the mistakes). **2** to make something work the way it should: *Eyesight problems can usually be corrected with glasses.*

cor·rec·tion /kəˈrekʃən/ n [C,U] a change in something that makes it correct or better, or when you change something in this way

cor·rec·tive /kəˈrektɪv/ adj formal intended to correct something which has a fault: *corrective lenses for the eyes*

cor·re·la·tion /ˌkɒrɪˈleɪʃən‖ˌkɔː-, ˌkɑː-/ n [C,U] when two things are connected in some way, and one has an effect on the other: + **between** *There is a correlation between unemployment and crime.* —**correlate** /ˈkɒrəleɪt‖ˈkɔː-, ˈkɑː-/ v [I,T]

cor·re·spond /ˌkɒrɪˈspɒnd‖ˌkɔːrɪˈspɑːnd, ˌkɑː-/ v [I] **1** to be the same or to have the same effect or value as something else: + **with/to** *The French 'baccalauréat' roughly corresponds to British 'A-levels'.* **2** if two people correspond, they write letters to each other

cor·re·spon·dence /ˌkɒrɪˈspɒndəns‖ˌkɔːrɪˈspɑːn-, ˌkɑː-/ n **1** [U] letters that people write: *I try to type all my correspondence.* **2** [U] the activity of writing letters: + **with** *His correspondence with Hemingway continued for years.* **3** [C] when two facts or statements are similar or the same: *the close correspondence between the French and German reports of these events*

cor·re·spon·dent /ˌkɒrɪˈspɒndənt‖ˌkɔːrɪˈspɑːn-, ˌkɑː-/ n [C] someone whose job is to report news from a distant place or write about a particular subject: *the political correspondent for 'The Times'*

cor·re·spon·ding /ˌkɒrɪˈspɒndɪŋ‖ˌkɔːrɪˈspɑːn-, ˌkɑː-/ adj [only before noun] having the same position, effect, or importance as something else: *Profits are higher than in the corresponding period last year.* —**correspondingly** adv

cor·ri·dor /ˈkɒrɪdɔː‖ˈkɔːrɪdər, ˈkɑː-/ n [C] a long narrow area between two rows of rooms

cor·rob·o·rate /kəˈrɒbəreɪt‖kəˈrɑː-/ v [T] formal to provide information that supports or proves someone's statement: *Heywood's account of the attack was corroborated by a security video.* —**corroboration** /kəˌrɒbəˈreɪʃən‖kəˌrɑː-/ n [U] —**corroborative** /kəˈrɒbərətɪv‖-ˈrɑːbəreɪtɪv/ adj law: *corroborative evidence*

cor·rode /kəˈrəʊd‖-ˈroʊd/ v [I,T] if metal corrodes, or if water, chemicals etc corrode it, it is slowly destroyed: *Many of the electrical wires have corroded.*

cor·ro·sion /kəˈrəʊʒən‖-ˈroʊ-/ n [U] the gradual destruction of metal by water, chemicals etc —**corrosive** /-sɪv/ adj

cor·ru·gated /ˈkɒrəgeɪtɪd‖ˈkɔː-, ˈkɑː-/ adj corrugated metal or CARDBOARD is made in rows of curved FOLDs that look like waves: *a corrugated iron roof*

cor·rupt[1] /kəˈrʌpt/ adj dishonest or immoral: *a corrupt judge* | *a corrupt political system*

corrupt[2] v [T] to make someone dishonest or immoral: *Proctor has been corrupted by power.* | *films that corrupt our children's minds* —**corruptible** adj

cor·rup·tion /kəˈrʌpʃən/ n [U] **1** dishonest or immoral behaviour by politicians or people who work for the government: *The police are being investigated for corruption.* **2** when someone is influenced in a way that makes them dishonest or immoral: *the corruption of today's youth by drugs*

cor·set /ˈkɔːsɪt‖ˈkɔːr-/ n [C] a piece of tight-fitting women's underwear worn in order to make them look thinner, especially in past times

cos·met·ic¹ /kozˈmetɪk‖kɑːz-/ adj [only before noun] **1** intended to make your skin or body more beautiful: *cosmetic surgery* **2** improving the appearance of something but not making the important changes it needs: *cosmetic changes to the law*

cosmetic² n [C usually plural] products such as creams and powders, used to make your face and skin more attractive

cos·mic /ˈkozmɪk‖ˈkɑːz-/ adj relating to the whole universe, or happening in OUTER SPACE: *cosmic radiation*

cos·mo·pol·i·tan /ˌkozməˈpolɪtən‖ˌkɑːzmə-ˈpɑː-/ adj **1** consisting of people from many different parts of the world: *a cosmopolitan city like New York* **2** showing wide experience of different people and places: *cosmopolitan tastes*

cos·mos /ˈkozmos‖ˈkɑːzməs/ n **the cosmos** the whole universe

cost¹ /kost‖kɔːst/ n **1** [C,U] the amount of money that you have to spend on something: *the high cost of educating children* | **cover the cost** (=be enough to pay for something): *Will £100 cover the cost of books?* | **the cost of living** (=the cost of all the food, clothes etc that you need): *a 4% increase in the cost of living* → compare PRICE¹ **2** [singular] something that you must give or lose in order to get something else: *War is never worth its cost in human life.* | **at the cost of** *Bernard saved his family at the cost of his own life.* **3** **at all costs/at any cost** whatever effort is needed: *They will try to win the next election at any cost.* **4** **at cost price** *BrE*, **at cost** *AmE* if you sell something at cost price, you sell it for the same price that you paid **5** **find/know/learn etc sth to your cost** to know or find out about something from your own unpleasant experience: *Mountain climbing can be very dangerous, as Heidi discovered to her cost.*

USAGE NOTE: cost, price, charge, value, and expense

Use **cost** to talk about how much you have to pay for something: *How much did your CD player cost?* | *the total cost of the vacation.* Use **price** about the amount of money you have to pay for something in a shop, restaurant etc: *Their prices seem pretty high.* Use **charge** (noun and verb) about the amount of money someone makes you pay: *They charged me $45 for delivering the goods.* | *an additional delivery charge of $45.* **Value** is used about how much something such as jewellery or furniture is worth: *He sold the house for much less than its real value.* If you want to talk about something that costs a lot of money, use **expense**: *the expense of living in a city like London*

---

cost² v cost, cost, costing [T] **1** to have a particular price: *This dress cost $75.* | **cost sb sth** *How much did the repairs cost you?* | **it costs sth to do sth** *It costs more to travel by air.* **2** to make someone lose something important: **cost sb sth** *a mistake that cost him his life*

cost³ v [T] costed, costed, costing to calculate how much money will be needed to pay for something: *A building company costed the job at £2000.*

co-star¹ /ˈkəʊ stɑː‖ˈkoʊ stɑːr/ n [C] one of the two or more famous actors that work together in a film or play

co-star² v **1** [I] to be working in a film or play with other famous actors: *Meryl Streep co-stars with Clint Eastwood in The Bridges of Madison County.* **2** [T] if a film or play co-stars two or more famous actors, they are in it

cost ef·fec·tive /ˌ. ˈ.../ adj producing the best profits or advantages at the lowest cost: *the most cost-effective method of advertising*

cost·ly /ˈkostli‖ˈkɔːstli/ adj **1** costing a lot of money; expensive: *Replacing all the windows would be too costly.* **2** causing a lot of problems, especially by making you lose something important: *a costly political scandal*

costume /ˈkostjuːm‖ˈkɑːstuːm/ n [C,U] **1** a set of clothes worn by actors when they are performing in a play or film: *He designed the costumes for 'Swan Lake'.* **2** clothes that are typical of a particular country or period of history: *the Maltese national costume*

co·sy *BrE*, **cozy** *AmE* /ˈkəʊzi‖ˈkoʊzi/ adj warm and comfortable: *a cosy room*

cot /kot‖kɑːt/ n [C] **1** *BrE* a small bed with high sides for a young child; CRIB *AmE* → see picture at BED **2** *AmE* a light narrow bed that folds up; CAMP BED *BrE* → see picture at BED

cot·tage /ˈkotɪdʒ‖ˈkɑː-/ n [C] a small house, especially in the country → see colour picture on page 243

cottage cheese /ˌ. ˈ.‖. ./ n [U] soft white cheese

cot·ton¹ /ˈkotn‖ˈkɑːtn/ n [U] **1** cloth or thread made from the cotton plant: *a cotton shirt* | *a reel of black cotton* **2** a plant producing soft white hair that is used for making cloth and thread **3** *AmE* a soft mass of cotton used for cleaning wounds or your skin; COTTON WOOL *BrE*

cotton² v

cotton on *phr v* [I] *informal* to realize what something means: *It was a long time before I cottoned on to what he was talking about.*

cotton can·dy /ˌ. ˈ../ n [U] *AmE* a soft mass of pink sugar on a stick; CANDYFLOSS *BrE*

cotton wool /ˌ. ˈ.◂/ n [U] *BrE* a soft mass of cotton, used especially for cleaning your skin

couch¹ /kautʃ/ n [C] a long comfortable piece of furniture that you can sit on

---

GRAMMAR NOTE: countable and uncountable (2)
Some nouns can be **countable** or **uncountable**. For example: **chicken** n [C,U].
● Countable: *A fox had killed some of the chickens.* (=birds)
● Uncountable: *chicken cooked in red wine* (=meat)

couch² *v* **be couched in** to be expressed in a particular way: *His refusal was couched in polite terms.*

couch po·ta·to /ˈ. ..,../ *n* [C] *informal* someone who spends a lot of time sitting and watching television

cough¹ /kɒf‖kɒːf/ *v* [I] if you cough you make air come out of your throat with a sudden short sound: *He was awake coughing all night.*

cough up *phr v* [I,T] *informal* to pay someone money although you do not want to: *I had to cough up £200 for a new printer.*

cough² *n* [C] **1** when someone coughs, or the sound of someone coughing: *I heard a loud cough behind me.* **2** an illness that makes you cough: **have a cough** *Amy has a bad cough.*

could /kəd; *strong* kʊd/ *modal verb* **1** the past tense of CAN: *Could you understand what he was saying?* | *She said she couldn't find it.* **2** used to say that something is possible or may be true: *Most accidents in the home could easily be prevented.* | *You could be right, I suppose.* | *How could anyone be so cruel?* (=how is it possible?) | *If you could live anywhere in the world, where would it be?* | **could have** (=used to say that something might have happened, especially when it did not happen): *She could have been killed.* **3** **could you/could I etc** *spoken* used to politely ask someone to do something, or ask permission to do something: *Could I ask you a couple of questions?* | *Could you open the window?* **4** used to suggest doing something: *You could try calling his office.* | **could always** *We could always stop and ask directions.* **5** **I could** *spoken* used to say that you feel angry, sad, hungry etc enough to do something: *I could have killed him when he said that!*

could·n't /ˈkʊdnt/ the short form of COULD NOT

could·ve /ˈkʊdəv/ the short form of COULD HAVE

coun·cil , **Council** /ˈkaʊnsəl/ *n* [C] **1** a group of people elected to control a town or area: *Los Angeles City Council* **2** a group of people elected by an organization to make decisions or give advice: *the UN Security Council* **3** **council house/flat** a house or apartment in Britain provided by a local council for a low rent

coun·cil·lor *BrE,* **councilor** *AmE* /ˈkaʊnsələ‖ -ər/ *n* [C] a member of a council

counsel¹ /ˈkaʊnsəl/ *v* [T] **-lled, -lling** *BrE* **-led, -ling** *AmE* to advise someone about their problems: *Dr Wengers counsels teenagers with drug problems.*

coun·sel² *n* **1** [singular] a lawyer who speaks for someone in court: *counsel for the prosecution* **2** [U] *literary* advice

coun·sel·ling *BrE,* **counseling** *AmE* /ˈkaʊnsəlɪŋ/ *n* [U] when people are given advice and help about their problems: *a counselling service for drug users*

coun·sel·lor *BrE,* **counselor** *AmE* /ˈkaʊnsələ‖ -ər/ *n* [C] someone whose job is to advise people who have problems: *a marriage counsellor*

count¹ /kaʊnt/ *v* **1** [T] also **count up** to calculate the total number of people or things in a group: *It took hours to count all the votes.* **2** [I] to say numbers in the correct order: *Can you count in Japanese?* **3** [T] to think of someone or something in a particular way: **count sb/sth as** *I've always counted Rob as one of my best friends.* | **count yourself lucky** (=think that you have been lucky) **4** [I] to be important and have an important effect: *First impressions count for a lot.* (=are very important) **5** [I] to be officially allowed or accepted: *You cheated, so your score doesn't count.* **6** [T] to include something in a total: **counting** *There are five in our family, counting me.* **7** **don't count your chickens** *spoken* used to tell someone not to be too sure that they will get what they want

count against sb *phr v* [T] if something counts against you, it makes people less likely to choose you, or more likely to punish you: *Her age was likely to count against her.*

count sb **in** *phr v* **count me in** *spoken* to say that you want to be involved in something that has been suggested: *"We're thinking of having a barbecue." "Count me in."*

count on sb/sth *phr v* [T] **1** to depend on someone or something: *You can always count on Doug in a crisis.* **2** **not count on** to not expect something: *We hadn't counted on so many people coming.*

count sth ↔ **out** *phr v* [T] to put things down one by one as you count them: *He counted out ten $50 bills.*

count² *n* **1** [C, usually singular] the process of counting, or the total that you get when you count things: *The final count showed that Larson had won by 110 votes.* **2** **lose count (of)** to forget how many: *"How many girlfriends have you had?" "Oh, I've lost count."* **3** **on both/all/several etc counts** in both ways, in every way etc: *We were proved wrong on both counts.* **4** [C] also **Count** a man who has a high social rank in Europe because of the family he comes from **5** [C] one of the crimes that the police say someone is guilty of: *Davis was found not guilty on all counts.*

count·a·ble /ˈkaʊntəbəl/ *adj* a countable noun has a singular and a plural form, for example 'table'/'tables' and 'apple'/'apples' → opposite UNCOUNTABLE

count·down /ˈkaʊntdaʊn/ *n* [C, usually singular] **1** when numbers are counted backwards to zero before something happens: *countdown to take-off* **2** the period before an important event happens when it gets closer and closer: *the countdown to the millennium*

coun·te·nance¹ /ˈkaʊntɪnəns/ *n* [C] *literary* someone's face or expression

countenance² *v* [T] *formal* to accept or approve of something

coun·ter¹ /ˈkaʊntəl-ər/ *n* **1** [C] the place in a shop, bank etc where you go to be served: *There was a long queue and only two girls working behind the counter.* **2** [C] *AmE* a flat surface in the kitchen where you prepare food → see picture at KITCHEN **3** [C] a small round object used in some games that are played on a board

counter² *v* [T] **1** to prevent something or reduce its effect: *efforts to counter inflation* **2** to say something in order to try to prove that what someone said is not true: *"That's not what the statistics show," she countered.*

counter³ *adv* **run/be counter to** sth *formal* to have an effect that is opposite to an opinion, belief etc: *ideas that run counter to the Church's traditional view of marriage*

counter- /ˈkaʊntəll-tər/ *prefix* opposite or opposing: *counter-productive* (=the opposite of productive)

coun·ter·act /ˌkaʊntərˈækt/ *v* [T] to reduce the bad effect of something by doing something that has the opposite effect: *new laws intended to counteract the effects of pollution*

coun·ter·at·tack /ˈkaʊntərəˌtæk/ *n* [C] an attack on an enemy that has attacked you — **counterattack** *v* [I,T]

coun·ter·bal·ance /ˌkaʊntəˈbæləns‖-tər-/ *v* [T] to have an equal and opposite effect to something else: *Falling sales in Europe have been counterbalanced by rising sales in the US* — **counterbalance** /ˈkaʊntəˌbæləns‖-tər-/ *n* [C]

coun·ter·clock·wise /ˌkaʊntəˈklɒkwaɪz‖-tər-ˈklɑːk-/ *adj, adv AmE* moving in the opposite direction to the HANDs on a clock; ANTICLOCKWISE *BrE* → opposite CLOCKWISE

coun·ter·feit /ˈkaʊntəfɪt‖-tər-/ *adj* made to look exactly like the real thing to deceive people: *counterfeit money* — **counterfeit** *v* [T]

coun·ter·part /ˈkaʊntəpɑːt‖-tərpɑːrt/ *n* [C] someone or something that has the same job or purpose as someone else in a different organization, country, or place: *The Saudi Foreign Minister met his French counterpart for talks.*

coun·ter·pro·duc·tive /ˌkaʊntəprəˈdʌktɪv‖-tər-/ *adj* causing the opposite result to the one you want: *Punishing children can be counterproductive.*

coun·ter·sign /ˈkaʊntəsaɪn‖-ər-/ *v* [T] to SIGN something that someone else has already signed: *Your doctor should countersign the form.*

coun·tess /ˈkaʊntɪ̥s/ *n* [C] a woman with a high social rank

count·less /ˈkaʊntləs/ *adj* very many: *a drug that has saved countless lives*

coun·try[1] /ˈkʌntri/ *n* **1** [C] an area of land that has its own government, leader, army etc, for example France, China or the USA: *Bahrain became an independent country in 1971.* **2** the **country a)** the land that is away from towns and cities; countryside: *I've always lived in the country.* **b)** all the people who live in a country: *a government that has the support of the country*

country[2] *adj* in or relating to towns and areas away from cities: *country people | country roads*

country house /ˌ.. ˈ./ *n* [C] *BrE* a large house in the country which has a lot of land and has often been owned by the same family for hundreds of years

coun·try·man /ˈkʌntrimən/ *n* [C] *plural* **countrymen** /-mən/ someone from your own country

country mu·sic /ˈ.. ˌ../ **country and western** /ˌ.. . ˈ../ *n* [U] a type of music from the southern and western US

coun·try·side /ˈkʌntrisaɪd/ *n* [U] land that is away from towns and cities and has farms, areas of trees etc in it: *the beauty of the English countryside*

coun·ty /ˈkaʊnti/ *n* [C] an area in Britain, Ireland, or the US with its own local government

coup /kuː/ *n* [C] **1** also **coup d'état** /ˌkuː deɪˈtɑː‖-deˈtɑː/ when a group of people suddenly take control of a country, especially by using force **2** [usually singular] an impressive achievement: *Winning that contract was a real coup.*

cou·ple[1] /ˈkʌpəl/ *n* **1** **a couple (of)** *especially spoken* two or a few: *There were a couple of kids in the back of the car.* | *I'll be ready in a couple of minutes.* **2** [C] two people who are married or have a romantic relationship: *Do you know the couple living next door? | married couples*

USAGE NOTE: couple and pair

Use **couple** to talk about any two things of the same type: *There are a couple of guys waiting outside.* Use **pair** to talk about two things that are used together: *a pair of shoes | a pair of scissors.* However in informal British English, **couple** can also be used to mean a small number of things or people, though not exactly two: *I'll be ready in a couple of minutes.*

---

couple[2] *v formal* **1** [T] to join two things together, especially two vehicles **2 coupled with** together with: *Low rainfall coupled with high temperatures destroyed the crops.*

cou·pon /ˈkuːpɒn‖-pɑːn/ *n* [C] **1** a small piece of paper that you exchange for goods or use to pay less money for them: *a coupon for ten cents off a jar of coffee* **2** a printed form, for example in a newspaper, used to order goods, enter a competition etc

cour·age /ˈkʌrɪdʒ‖ˈkɜːr-/ *n* [U] the abilities to behave bravely in a difficult situation, or to do something that seems very difficult or frightening: *She showed great courage throughout her long illness.* | **have the courage (to do sth)** *Martin wanted to ask her to marry him, but he didn't have the courage to do it.* → see also **pluck up the courage** (PLUCK[1])

cou·ra·geous /kəˈreɪdʒəs/ *adj* very brave: *a courageous decision* — **courageously** *adv*

cour·gette /kʊəˈʒet‖kʊr-/ *n* [C] *BrE* a long vegetable with a dark green skin; ZUCCHINI *AmE* → see picture at VEGETABLE

cou·ri·er /ˈkʊriəll-ər/ *n* [C] **1** someone whose job is to deliver documents and packages **2** *BrE* someone who is employed by a travel company to help people who are on holiday

course[1] /kɔːs‖kɔːrs/ *n* **1 of course a)** *spoken* used to answer "yes" when you want to emphasize your answer, or when you are surprised or annoyed: *"Can I borrow your notes?" "Of course you can." | "Are you going to invite Phil to the party?" "Of course I am."* **b)** used when you are mentioning something that you think most people know: *The insurance has to be renewed every year, of course.* **2 of course not** *spoken* used to answer "no" when you want to emphasize your answer, or when you are surprised or annoyed: *"Do you mind if I'm a bit late?" "Of course not."* **3** [C] a series of lessons about a subject : *a three-day training course* | **+ in/on** *a course in computing* **4** [C] one of the parts of a meal: *a three-course meal | the main course* **5** a course of tablets/injections/ treatment etc *especially BrE* medicine or medical treatment that someone has regularly for a period of time **6** [C] an area where races happen or GOLF is played: *a race course* **7** [C,U] the direction in which something moves: *The plane changed course and headed for Rome.* | **on/ off course** (=going in the right or wrong direction): *Larsen's ship had been blown off course.* **8** [singular] the way in which events develop:

in the course of time (=gradually over a period of time): *The situation will improve in the course of time.* | **+ of** *events that changed the course of history* | **run/take its course** (=develop in the usual way): *You'll just have to let things take their course.* **9** [C] something that you can do to deal with a situation: **course of action** *The best course of action would be to speak to her privately.* **10 in/during the course of** during a process or period of time: *During the course of our conversation, I found out that he had worked in France.* **11 be on course for sth/to do sth** to be likely to achieve something: *Hodson is on course to break the world record.* → see also in **due course** (DUE[1]), **as a matter of course** (MATTER[1])

course[2] *v* [I] *literary* to flow quickly: *Tears coursed down her cheeks.*

course-book /ˈ. ./ *n* [C] a book written to be used by students as part of a particular course of study

court[1] /kɔːt‖kɔːrt/ *n* **1** [C,U] a place where a judge or a group of people decide whether someone is guilty of a crime: *the European Court of Justice* | *Wilkins had to appear in court as a witness.* | **take sb to court** (=make someone be judged in a court): *If they don't pay, we'll take them to court.* **2 the court** the judge and other people who decide whether someone is guilty of a crime: *The court decided that West was guilty.* **3** [C,U] an area where sports such as tennis and BASKETBALL are played: *Sampras and Becker are playing on No 1 court.* **4** [C] the place where a king or queen spends their time, or the people with them: *the court of Louis XIV*

court[2] *v* **1** [I,T] *old-fashioned* to have a romantic relationship with someone **2** [T] to try to please someone so that they will support you: *politicans busy courting voters* **3 court disaster** to do something that is likely to have very unpleasant results

cour·te·ous /ˈkɜːtiəs‖ˈkɜːr-/ *adj formal* very polite: *a very courteous young man* — **courteously** *adv*

cour·te·sy /ˈkɜːtˌsi‖ˈkɜːr-/ *n* **1** [U] polite behaviour: *She didn't even have the courtesy to apologize.* **2 courtesies** [plural] things that you say or do to be polite: *The President was exchanging courtesies with his guests.*

court·house /ˈkɔːthaʊs‖ˈkɔːrt-/ *n* [C] *especially AmE* a building containing courts of law and government offices

court·ier /ˈkɔːtiə‖ˈkɔːrtɪr/ *n* [C] someone who had an important position at a royal COURT in past times

court mar·tial /ˌ. ˈ..‖ˌ. ˌ../ *n* [C] a military court or an occasion when a soldier is judged by a military court — **court-martial** *v* [T]

court·room /ˈkɔːtruːm, -rʊm‖ˈkɔːrt-/ *n* [C] the room where someone is judged in a court of law

court·ship /ˈkɔːtʃɪp‖ˈkɔːrt-/ *n* [C,U] *old-fashioned* when a man and a woman have a romantic relationship

court·yard /ˈkɔːtjaːd‖ˈkɔːrtjaːrd/ *n* [C] an open space surrounded by walls or buildings

cous·in /ˈkʌzən/ *n* [C] the child of your AUNT or UNCLE → see picture at FAMILY

cove /kəʊv‖koʊv/ *n* [C] a place on a coast where the land bends inwards, making a small area of sea that is protected from wind, storms etc

cov·e·nant /ˈkʌvənənt/ *n* [C] a formal written agreement

cov·er[1] /ˈkʌvəl-ər/ *v* [T] **1** also **cover up** to put something over the top of something else to protect, close, or hide it: *Cover the pan and let the sauce simmer.* | *tables covered with clean white cloths* **2** to be on top of something and form a layer on its surface: *Snow covered the ground.* | **be covered in/with** (=there is a lot of a substance on the surface of something): *Your boots are covered in mud!* **3** to include or deal with something: *The course covers all aspects of business.* **4** to be enough money to pay for something: *Will $100 cover the cost of textbooks?* **5** to travel a distance: *We had covered 20 kilometres by lunchtime.* **6** used to say the size of the area of something: *The city covers an area of 20 square kilometres.* **7** if an insurance agreement covers someone or something, it promises to pay money if they are injured, damaged, stolen etc: *This policy covers you against accident or injury.* **8** to report the details of an event for a newspaper, television, or radio: *She was sent to Harare to cover the crisis in Rwanda.* **9** to aim a gun somewhere to protect someone from being attacked or to prevent someone from escaping: *Police officers covered the back entrance.*

cover for sb *phr v* [T] to do someone else's work because they are ill or are somewhere else: *I'll be covering for Sandra next week.*

cover sth ↔ **up** *phr v* [T] **1** to put something over the top of something else: *Cover the furniture up before you start painting.* **2** to prevent people from finding out the truth about something, especially a bad situation that you are responsible for: *Nixon's officials tried to cover up the Watergate affair.*

cover[2] *n* **1** [C] something that covers and protects something else : *a cushion cover* **2** [C] the front or back of a book, magazine etc: *His picture was on the front cover of Newsweek.* **3** [U] insurance against being lost or stolen, or against being injured or ill: *The policy provided £100,000 of medical cover.* **4** [U] protection from bad weather or attack: *Everyone ran for cover when the shooting started.* | **take cover** (=go somewhere to be protected from the weather or from being attacked): *We took cover under a tree.* **5** something that is used to hide someone's illegal activities: *The company is just a cover for the Mafia.* → see also COVERS, UNDERCOVER

cov·er·age /ˈkʌvərɪdʒ/ *n* [U] the amount of attention given to a news story by television, radio, or the newspapers: *Her death attracted widespread media coverage.*

cover

cov·er·alls /ˈkʌvərɔːlz‖-ɒːlz/ n [plural] AmE a piece of clothing that you wear over all your clothes to protect them; OVERALLS BrE

cov·er·ing /ˈkʌvərɪŋ/ n [C] something that covers something else: a light covering of snow

covering let·ter /ˌ... ˈ../ BrE, **cover let·ter** /ˈ.. ˌ../ AmE — n [C] a letter sent with a document or package, explaining what it is or giving more information about it

cov·ers /ˈkʌvəz‖-ərz/ n [plural] the sheets, BLANKETs etc on a bed

cov·ert /ˈkʌvət, ˈkəʊvɜːt‖ˈkoʊvərt/ adj done secretly: covert operations — **covertly** adv

cover-up /ˈ.. ./ n [C] when a government tries to prevent people from finding out the truth about something: CIA officials denied there had been a cover-up.

cov·et /ˈkʌvɪt/ v [T] literary to want something that someone else has

cow[1] /kaʊ/ n **1** [C] a large animal that is kept on farms for milk **2** [singular] BrE spoken an insulting word for a woman

cow[2] v [T] **be cowed** to be so frightened by someone that you will obey them: The children were cowed into obedience.

cow·ard /ˈkaʊədll-ərd/ n [C] someone who is not brave enough to do something that they ought to do: They kept calling me a coward because I didn't want to fight. — **cowardly** adj: a cowardly thing to do

cow·ard·ice /ˈkaʊədɪsll-ərd-/ n [U] behaviour that shows you are not brave enough to do something you ought to do

cow·boy /ˈkaʊbɔɪ/ n [C] **1** a man whose job is to look after cattle, especially in North America **2** BrE informal someone whose work is bad or who is dishonest in business

cow·er /ˈkaʊəll-ər/ v [I] to move back or bend down low because you are afraid: The hostages were cowering in a corner.

coy /kɔɪ/ adj **1** pretending to be quiet or shy: a coy smile **2** not wanting to tell people about something: Tania was always coy about her age. — **coyly** adv

coy·ote /ˈkɔɪ-əʊt, kɔɪˈəʊtɪllˈkaɪ-oʊt, kaɪˈoʊti/ n [C] a wild animal like a dog, which lives in America

co·zy /ˈkəʊzillˈkoʊzi/ the American spelling of COSY — **cozily** adv — **coziness** n [U]

crab /kræb/ n [C,U] a sea animal with a round flat shell and ten legs, the front two of which have PINCERs on them, or the meat from this animal

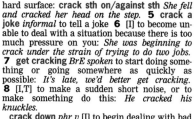

crab

pincer/claw

crack[1] /kræk/ v **1** [I,T] if something cracks, or if you crack it, it starts to break so that a line appears on its surface: The ice was starting to crack. **2** [T] to break the shell of an egg or nut **3** [T] informal to find the answer to a difficult problem: Yes! I've finally cracked it! **4** [I,T] to accidentally hit part of your body against a

hard surface: crack sth on/against sth She fell and cracked her head on the step. **5** crack a joke informal to tell a joke **6** [I] to become unable to deal with a situation because there is too much pressure on you: She was beginning to crack under the strain of trying to do two jobs. **7** **get cracking** BrE spoken to start doing something or going somewhere as quickly as possible: It's late, we'd better get cracking. **8** [I,T] to make a sudden short noise, or to make something do this: He cracked his knuckles.

crack down phr v [I] to begin dealing with bad or illegal behaviour very strictly: + on The government plans to crack down on child pornography on the Internet.

crack up phr v informal **1** [I] to become mentally ill because you have a lot of problems: I'm worried about Lisa – I think she's cracking up. **2** **not all it's cracked up to be** not as good as people think: Life as a model isn't all it's cracked up to be.

crack[2] n **1** [C] a thin line on something where it is damaged: A huge crack had appeared in the ceiling. **2** [C] a very narrow space between two things or two parts of something: a crack in the curtains **3** [C] an unkind joke: **make a crack (about)** Stop making cracks about my sister! **4** **have/take a crack at sth** informal to try to do something: Okay let's have a crack at fixing this bike. **5** [C] a sudden short noise that sounds like a stick breaking: The firework exploded with a loud crack. **6** [U] a very dangerous illegal drug **7** **at the crack of dawn** very early in the morning: We had to get up at the crack of dawn.

crack[3] adj very skilful or well trained: crack troops‖a **crack shot** (=someone who is very good at shooting)

crack·down /ˈkrækdaʊn/ n [singular] when a crime or kind of bad behaviour is dealt with very strictly in order to try to stop it from happening: a crackdown on drunk driving

cracked

broken

cracked

cracked /krækt/ adj something that is cracked is damaged with thin lines on its surface: a cracked mirror

crack·er /ˈkrækəll-ər/ n **1** [C] a thin BISCUIT often eaten with cheese **2** [C] a brightly coloured paper tube containing a small present, which people pull open at Christmas

3 [singular] *BrE informal* something that is very good: *Thompson's goal was a real cracker!*

crack·ers /'krækəz‖-ərz/ *adj BrE informal* crazy: *You're crackers!*

crack·le /'krækəl/ *v* [I] to make a lot of short noises that sound like wood burning in a fire: *This radio's crackling.* —**crackle** *n* [singular] → see colour picture on page 635

crack·pot /'krækpɒt‖-pɑːt/ *adj* slightly crazy or strange: *Whose crackpot idea was this?*

cra·dle¹ /'kreɪdl/ *n* **1** [C] a small bed for a baby → see picture at BED **2 the cradle of** the place where something began: *Athens, the cradle of western democracy*

cradle² *v* [T] to hold something gently: *Tony cradled the baby in his arms.*

craft¹ /krɑːft‖kræft/ *n* [C] an activity for which you need skill, especially with your hands

craft² *n* [C], *plural* **craft** a boat

crafts·man /'krɑːftsmən‖'kræfts-/ *n* [C] *plural* **craftsmen** /-mən/ someone who is skilled at making things and does this as a job: *furniture made by the finest craftsmen*

crafts·man·ship /'krɑːftsmənʃɪp‖'kræfts-/ *n* [U] the skill of making something beautiful with your hands: *high standards of craftsmanship*

craft·y /'krɑːfti‖'kræf-/ *adj* good at getting what you want by cleverly deceiving people: *You crafty devil!* —**craftily** *adv*

crag /kræg/ *n* [C] a high rough rock

crag·gy /'krægi/ *adj* **1** very steep and covered with large rocks **2** a craggy face has a lot of lines

cram /kræm/ *v* **-mmed, -mming 1** [T] to force a lot of things into a small space: *She managed to cram all her clothes into one suitcase.* **2 be crammed with** to be full of people or things: *The streets were crammed with tourists.* **3** [I] to prepare for a test by studying very hard just before the test: *Julia stayed up all night cramming for her final.*

cramp /kræmp/ *n* [C,U] a bad pain in your muscles that makes it difficult to move: *I've got cramp in my leg!*

cramped /kræmpt/ *adj* a cramped house or office is uncomfortable because there is not enough space

cran·ber·ry /'krænbəri‖-beri/ *n* [C] a small red BERRY: *cranberry sauce*

crane¹ /kreɪn/ *n* [C] **1** a large machine with a long metal arm used to lift heavy things **2** a water bird with very long legs

crane² *v* [I,T] to stretch your neck forward to see something: *He craned to get a better view of the stage.*

cra·ni·um /'kreɪniəm/ *n* [C] *technical* the part of your head that covers your brain

crank /kræŋk/ *n* [C] **1** someone who has strange ideas: *a religious crank* **2** a handle on a piece of equipment, which you turn to move something

cran·ny /'kræni/ *n* [C] a small hole → see also **every nook and cranny** (NOOK)

crap /kræp/ *n* [U] *informal* an impolite word for something that you think is very bad quality, wrong, or untrue: *There's so much crap on TV nowadays!* —**crap** *adj*

craps /kræps/ *n* [U] a game played with DICE for money in the US

crash¹ /kræʃ/ *v* **1** [I,T] to have an accident in a car, plane etc by hitting something: **+ into/ through etc** *We crashed straight into the car in front.* **2** [I] to make a loud noise, usually by falling or moving suddenly: **+ into/through/ against etc** *the sound of waves crashing against the rocks.* → see colour picture on page 635 **3** [I] if a computer crashes, it suddenly stops working **4** [I] if a STOCK MARKET crashes, prices suddenly fall by a large amount

crash² *n* [C] **1** a bad accident involving cars, planes etc: *Six vehicles were involved in the crash.* | *car/plane/train etc crash All 265 passengers were killed in the plane crash.* **2** a sudden loud noise made when something breaks or hits something else: *We were woken by the sound of a loud crash downstairs.* | **with a crash** *The tray fell to the floor with a crash.* → see colour picture on page 635 **3** when a computer suddenly stops working **4** when prices on a STOCK MARKET suddenly fall by a large amount: *fears of another stock market crash*

crash bar·ri·er /'. ‚.../ *n* [C] a fence that divides the two sides of a road or that prevents a crowd from moving forward

crash course /'. ./ *n* [C] a short course in which you study the most basic and important things about a subject very quickly

crash hel·met /'. ‚../ *n* [C] a hard hat worn by MOTORCYCLISTS, racing drivers etc to protect their heads

crash-land /'. ./ *v* [I,T] to land a damaged plane

crass /kræs/ *adj* behaving in a way that seems stupid because you do not seem to care about upsetting or offending people: *crass remarks*

crate /kreɪt/ *n* [C] a large box used for carrying fruit, bottles etc: *a crate of beer* → see picture at CONTAINER

cra·ter /'kreɪtə‖-ər/ *n* [C] **1** the round open top of a VOLCANO **2** a large hole in the ground, especially caused by an explosion

cra·vat /krə'væt/ *n* [C] a piece of cloth or silk that a man ties loosely around his neck under the collar of his shirt → compare TIE², SCARF

crave /kreɪv/ *v* [T] to want something very much: *He craved affection.*

crav·ing /'kreɪvɪŋ/ *n* [C] a very strong desire for something: *a craving for chocolate*

crawl¹ /krɔːl‖krɒːl/ *v* [I] **1** to move on your hands and knees: **+ through/into/along etc** *We crawled through a hole in the fence.* → see colour picture on page 670 **2** if an insect crawls, it moves using its legs: *Flies were crawling all over the food.* **3** if a vehicle crawls, it moves very slowly: *We crawled all the way into town.* **4** [I] to be too pleasant to someone because they are important or can help you: *He's always crawling to the boss.* **5 be crawling with** to contain a lot of insects or people, especially in a way that seems unpleasant: *The tent was crawling with ants!*

crawl² *n* **1** [singular] a very slow speed: *cars moving along at a crawl* **2 the crawl** a way of swimming in which you move one arm and then the other over your head while kicking your feet up and down

cray·fish /ˈkreɪˌfɪʃ/ n [C,U] a small animal like a LOBSTER that can be eaten

cray·on /ˈkreɪən, -ɒnǁ-ɑːn, -ən/ n [C] a stick of coloured WAX used by children for drawing: *brightly coloured children's crayons.*

craze /kreɪz/ n [C] a game or style of clothes, music etc that is very popular for a short time: *the latest craze to hit New York*

cra·zy /ˈkreɪzi/ adj **1** very strange or not very sensible: *Our friends all think we're crazy.* **2** angry or annoyed: **drive sb crazy** (=make someone very annoyed): *Stop it, you're driving me crazy!* **3** **be crazy about** to like someone or something very much: *Lee's crazy about cats.* **4** mentally ill: *a crazy old woman* | **go crazy** *Sometimes I feel as if I'm going crazy.* **5** if a group of people go crazy, they become very excited: *Gascoigne scored and the fans went crazy.* —**crazily** adv —**craziness** n [U]

creak /kriːk/ v [I] if something such as a door or wooden floor creaks, it makes a long high noise when it moves: *The door creaked shut behind him.* —**creak** n [C] → see colour picture on page 635 —**creaky** adj

cream[1] /kriːm/ n **1** [U] a thick white liquid obtained from milk: *strawberries and cream* **2** [C,U] a thick smooth substance that you put on your skin to make it softer or less painful: LOTION: *face cream* **3** **the cream** of the best people or things in a group: *the cream of Europe's footballers*

cream[2] adj having a yellowish-white colour

cream cheese /ˌ. ˈ.ǁ. ./ n [U] soft white smooth cheese

cream·y /ˈkriːmi/ adj containing cream or looking like cream: *The sauce was smooth and creamy.*

crease[1] /kriːs/ n [C] a line on cloth, paper etc where it has been folded

crease[2] v [I,T] if a piece of cloth, paper etc creases, or you crease it, it becomes marked with a line after it has been folded: *Try not to crease your jacket.* —**creased** adj

cre·ate /kriˈeɪt/ v [T] to make something new exist or happen: *The new factory should create 450 jobs.* | *the problems created by the increase in traffic*

cre·a·tion /kriˈeɪʃən/ n **1** [U] when someone makes something new exist or happen: *the creation of a United Europe* **2** [C] something new that someone makes, especially using their imagination or skill: *the artist's latest creation* **3** **Creation** when God made the universe and everything in it

cre·a·tive /kriˈeɪtɪv/ adj **1** a creative person is good at thinking of new ideas or way of doing things: *one of Japan's most talented and creative film directors* **2** using your imagination to think of new ideas or ways of doing things: *the creative part of my work* —**creatively** adv

cre·a·tiv·i·ty /ˌkriːeɪˈtɪvǝti/ n [U] the ability to use your skill or imagination to produce new ideas or things

cre·a·tor /kriˈeɪtǝlǝr/ n [C] someone who makes or invents something: *Walt Disney, the creator of Mickey Mouse*

crea·ture /ˈkriːtʃǝl-ǝr/ n [C] **1** an animal, fish, or insect: *We should respect all living creatures.* | *a mythical creature* **2** **charming/**

ungrateful etc creature someone who is CHARMING, UNGRATEFUL etc

creature com·forts /ˌ.. ˈ.. / n [plural] things that make people's lives more comfortable: *The hotel had all the creature comforts of his home in London.*

crè·che /kreʃǁkreʃ, kreɪʃ/ n [C] *BrE* a place where babies are looked after while their parents are at work

cre·dence /ˈkriːdəns/ n [U] **give/lend credence to sth** to believe something, or make something seem likely to be true: *Recent discoveries give credence to the theory that the illness is caused by stress.*

cre·den·tials /krɪˈdenʃəlz/ n [plural] **1** things that show that someone has the ability to do something, for example their previous training or experience: *She has excellent academic credentials.* **2** an official document that shows that you are who you say you are

cred·i·bil·i·ty /ˌkredɪˈbɪlǝti/ n [U] when someone is believed and trusted: *The scandal has damaged the government's credibility.*

cred·i·ble /ˈkredɪbəl/ adj able to be believed or trusted: *a credible witness*

cred·it[1] /ˈkredɪt/ n **1** [U] a way of buying goods in which you arrange to pay for them later: **on credit** *The TV and the washing machine were bought on credit.* **2** [U] praise given to someone for doing something: *It's not fair – I do all the work and he gets all the credit!* | **give sb credit for sth** *You've got to give him credit for trying.* **3** **be a credit to sb/sth** also **do sb/sth credit** to be so good that everyone who is connected with you can be proud of you: *You're a credit to the school!* **4** [C] a successfully completed part of a college course **5** a payment made into a bank account **6** **be in credit** to have money in your bank account → see also CREDITS

cred·it[2] v [T] **1** to add money to a bank account: *The cheque will be credited to your account.* → opposite DEBIT[2] **2** to believe that something surprising is true: **would you credit it** (=used when you think something is surprising): *Would you credit it! He's won!*
credit sb with sth *phr v* [T] to admit that someone has a quality: *Credit me with some intelligence, please!*
credit sb/sth with sth also **credit sth to sb/sth** *phr v* [T] to say that someone or something is responsible for inventing something or making something good happen: *Daguere was originally credited with the idea.*

cred·it·a·ble /ˈkredɪtəbəl/ adj good, especially considering how difficult it is to do something: *The French team finished a creditable second.* —**creditably** adv

credit card /ˈ... ./ n [C] a small plastic card that you use to buy goods or services and pay for them later → see picture at CARD

credit lim·it /ˈ.. ˌ../ n [C] the amount of money that you are allowed to borrow or spend using your credit card

cred·i·tor /ˈkredɪtǝl-ǝr/ n [C] a person or organization that you owe money to → compare DEBTOR

cred·its /ˈkredɪts/ n **the credits** a list of the people who made a television programme or film

cre·do /ˈkriːdəʊ, ˈkreɪ-‖-doʊ/ n [C] a short statement that expresses a belief or rule

creed /kriːd/ n [C] a set of beliefs or principles, especially someone's religious or political beliefs: *there were people of every creed* (=belonging to every religion)

creek /kriːk/ n [C] **1** BrE a narrow area of water where the sea or a river flows into the land **2** AmE a small narrow stream or river **3 be up the creek** spoken to be in a difficult situation: *I'll really be up the creek if I don't get my passport by Friday.*

creep[1] /kriːp/ v [I] **crept** /krept/, **crept, creeping 1** to move very carefully and quietly so that no one will notice you: *She crept downstairs in the dark.* **2** to gradually begin to appear: + **in/into/over** *A note of panic had crept into his voice.* **3** to move very slowly: *A thick mist was creeping down the hillside.*

creep up phr v [I] to gradually increase: *The total number of people out of work crept up to 5 million.*

creep up on sb/sth phr v [T] **1** to surprise someone by walking up behind them quickly: *I wish you wouldn't creep up on me like that!* **2** to happen sooner than you expect, or when you are not expecting something to happen: *Old age tends to creep up on you.*

creep up to sb phr v [T] BrE informal to be nice to someone in authority in an insincere way in order to get advantages for yourself

creep[2] n [C usually singular] someone who you dislike a lot: *Go away, you little creep!*

creep·er /ˈkriːpə‖-ər/ n [C] a plant that grows up walls or along the ground

creeps /kriːps/ n **give sb the creeps** informal to make someone feel nervous or frightened: *That guy gives me the creeps!*

creep·y /ˈkriːpi/ adj slightly frightening: *a creepy movie*

cre·mate /krɪˈmeɪt‖ˈkriːmeɪt/ v [T] to burn the body of a dead person —**cremation** /krɪˈmeɪʃən/ n [C,U]

crem·a·to·ri·um /ˌkreməˈtɔːriəm‖ˌkriː-/ n [C] a building in which the bodies of dead people are burned

crepe also **crêpe** /kreɪp/ n **1** [U] thin light cloth with a slightly rough surface **2** [C] a very thin PANCAKE **3** [U] a type of rubber used for making the bottoms of shoes

crepe pa·per /ˌ. ˈ..‖ˈ. ˌ../ n [U] thin brightly coloured paper, used especially to make decorations

crept /krept/ v the past tense and past participle of CREEP

cre·scen·do /krɪˈʃendəʊ‖-doʊ/ n [C] when a piece of music becomes gradually louder

cres·cent /ˈkresənt/ n [C] **1** a curved shape that is wider in the middle and pointed at the ends: *a crescent moon* ➡ see picture at SHAPES **2 Crescent** used in the names of small streets in towns and cities: *Turn left into Woodford Crescent.*

crest /krest/ n [C] **1** the top of a hill or wave **2** an upright group of feathers on a bird's head **3** a special picture used as the sign of a school, town, important family etc

crest·fal·len /ˈkrest,fɔːlən‖-,fɔːl-/ adj especially literary very sad or disappointed

cre·vasse /krɪˈvæs/ n [C] a deep wide crack, especially in thick ice

crev·ice /ˈkrevɪs/ n [C] a narrow crack, especially in rock

crew /kruː/ n [C] **1** the people that work together on a ship, plane etc **2** a group of people who work together on something: *the movie's cast and crew*

crib /krɪb/ n [C] AmE a baby's bed with bars around the sides; COT BrE ➡ see picture at BED

crick /krɪk/ n [C] a sudden painful stiffness of the muscles in your neck or back

crick·et /ˈkrɪkɪt/ n **1** [U] a game in which two teams try to get points by hitting a ball and running between two WICKETS (=sets of three sticks) ➡ see colour picture on page 636 **2** [C] an insect that makes a short loud noise by rubbing its wings together

crime /kraɪm/ n **1** [U] illegal activity: *There was very little crime when we moved here.* | **crime prevention** (=work done to stop crime from happening) | **petty crime** (=crime that is not very serious) **2** [C] an illegal action that can be punished by law: **commit a crime** *He committed a number of crimes in the area.* **3 it is a crime** used to say that something is morally wrong: *It's a crime to waste food.*

crim·i·nal[1] /ˈkrɪmɪnəl/ adj **1** [only before noun] relating to crime: *criminal behaviour* | **criminal record** (=an official record of crimes someone has committed): *He doesn't have a criminal record.* **2** used to say that you think it is wrong to do something: *It's criminal to charge so much for popcorn at the movies!* —**criminally** adv

criminal[2] n [C] someone who is proved guilty of a crime

crimp /krɪmp/ v [T] AmE to prevent something from developing or growing

crim·son /ˈkrɪmzən/ n [U] a dark red colour —**crimson** adj

cringe /krɪndʒ/ v [I] **1** to feel embarrassed by something: **cringe at sth** *I just cringe at the thought of some of the things we used to wear.* **2** to move back or away from something because you are afraid

crin·kle /ˈkrɪŋkəl/ also **crinkle up** v [I,T] to become covered with very small folds, or to make something do this: *Mandy crinkled her nose in disgust.* —**crinkled** adj —**crinkly** adj

crip·ple[1] /ˈkrɪpəl/ n [C] a word for someone who cannot walk properly that is now considered to be offensive

cripple[2] v [T] **1** to hurt someone so they can no longer walk: *Many people are crippled by car accidents.* **2** to seriously damage something or make it much weaker: *The country's economy has been crippled by drought.* —**crippled** adj —**crippling** adj

cri·sis /ˈkraɪsɪs/ n [C,U] plural **crises** /ˈkraɪsiːz/ a time when a problem or situation is very bad or dangerous: *the Cuban missile crisis*

crisp[1] /krɪsp/ adj **1** pleasantly dry, firm, and easily broken: *a nice crisp pastry* **2** fresh and firm: *a nice crisp salad* **3** weather that is crisp is cold and dry: *a crisp winter morning* **4** clean and having no lines or folds: *crisp clean sheets* —**crisply** adv

crisp[2] n [C] BrE a thin, flat round piece of potato cooked in very hot oil and eaten cold as a SNACK; CHIP AmE: a packet of crisps

crisp·y /'krıspi/ adj food that is crispy is pleasantly hard and breaks easily: crispy bacon

criss·cross /'krıskrɒs‖-krɔːs/ v [I,T] to make a pattern of straight lines that cross over each other, or to make this pattern on something: flyovers crisscrossing the city —**crisscross** adj

cri·te·ri·on /kraı'tıərıən‖-'tır-/ n [C usually plural], **plural criteria** a fact or standard used to help you decide something: + **for** What are the criteria for selecting the winner?

crit·ic /'krıtık/ n [C] **1** someone whose job is to give their opinion of a film, book etc: a literary critic for the Times **2** someone who says that a person, idea etc is bad or wrong: an outspoken critic of military spending

crit·i·cal /'krıtıkəl/ adj **1** saying that you think a person or thing is bad or wrong: + **of** Degas was critical of the plan. **2** something that is critical is very important, because what happens in the future depends on it: + **to** This next phase is critical to the project's success. **3** very serious or dangerous : **critical condition/illness** The driver is still in a critical condition in hospital. **4** describing the good and bad qualities of something: a critical analysis of Macbeth —**critically** /-kli/ adv

crit·i·cis·m /'krıtⱼsızəm/ n **1** [C,U] when you say what you think is bad about someone or something, or the things that you say: Kate doesn't take criticism very well/‖She made several criticisms of my argument.‖**constructive criticism** (=that helps someone or something to improve) **2** [U] writing or speech that describes the good and bad qualities of something: literary criticism

crit·i·cize (also **-ise** BrE) /'krıtⱼsaız/ v [I,T] to say what you think is bad about someone or something: She always criticizes my cooking.‖**criticize sb for (doing) sth** The regime was criticized for its disregard of human rights.

cri·tique /krı'tiːk/ n [C] a piece of writing that describes the good and bad qualities of something

crit·ter /'krıtəll-ər/ n [C] AmE informal an animal, fish, or insect; CREATURE

croak /krəʊk‖krouk/ v **1** [I] to make a deep low sound like the sound a FROG makes **2** [I,T] to speak in a low rough voice as if you have a sore throat **3** [I] informal to die —**croak** n [C]

cro·chet /'krəʊʃeı‖krou'ʃeı/ v [I,T] to make clothes, BLANKETS etc from WOOL, using a special needle with a hook at one end —**crochet** n [U]

crock /krɒk‖krɑːk/ n **1** [C] old-fashioned a clay pot **2** [singular] AmE informal something that is not true or not believable

crock·e·ry /'krɒkəri‖'krɑː-/ n [U] cups, plates, dishes etc

croc·o·dile /'krɒkədaıl‖'krɑː-/ n [C] a large tropical REPTILE that has a long body and a long mouth with sharp teeth, and lives in lakes and rivers

cro·cus /'krəʊkəs‖'krou-/ n [C] a small purple, yellow, or white flower that grows in early spring

crois·sant /'krwɑːsɒŋ‖ krwɑː'sɑːnt/ n [C] a soft piece of bread shaped in a curve and eaten for breakfast

croissant

cro·ny /'krəʊni‖'krouni/ n [C] informal one of a group of friends

crook[1] /krʊk/ n **1** [C] informal a criminal, or someone who is not honest: They're a bunch of crooks. **2** the **crook of your arm** the inside part of your arm where it bends at the elbow

crook[2] v [T] to bend a part of your body, especially your finger or arm

crook·ed /'krʊkⱼd/ adj **1** twisted, bent, or not straight: a crooked mouth **2** informal not honest: a crooked cop —**crookedly** adv

croon /kruːn/ v [I,T] to sing in a soft gentle voice —**crooner** n [C] famous crooners like Bing Crosby

crop[1] /krɒp‖krɑːp/ n [C] **1** a plant such as wheat, rice, or fruit that is grown to be eaten **2** the amount of wheat, rice etc that is produced in a single season **3 a crop of** a number of people or things that are together at the same time: I've got a whole crop of essays to read.

crop[2] v **1** [T] to make something shorter by cutting it: He cropped his hair short. **2** [T] if an animal crops grass, it makes it shorter by eating it **3** [I] if a plant crops, it produces fruit etc
crop up phr v [I] to appear or happen suddenly and unexpectedly: Let me know if any problems crop up.

crop·per /'krɒpəll'krɑː-pər/ **come a cropper** BrE informal **a)** to fall over **b)** to fail in an embarrassing way

cro·quet /'krəʊkeı, -kill'krou'keı/ n [U] a game played on grass in which you hit balls under curved wires using a wooden hammer

cross[1] /krɒs‖krɔːs/ v **1** [I,T] to go from one side of a road, river, place etc to the other: Look both ways before crossing the road. **2** [T] if two or more roads, lines etc cross, they go across each other: The road crosses the railway at this point. **3** [T] if you cross a line, you go over and beyond it: The crowd roared as the first runner crossed the finish line. **4** [T] if you cross your arms or legs, you put one on top of the other **5 cross your mind** if an idea or thought crosses your mind, you think about it for a short time: It never crossed my mind that she might be right. **6** [T] to mix two BREEDS of animal or plant to form a new breed: + **with** A mule is produced by crossing a horse with a donkey. **7** [T] to make someone angry by opposing their wishes
cross sth ↔ **off** phr v [I,T] to draw a line through something on a list to show that it has been dealt with: Cross off their names as they arrive.

SPELLING NOTE
Words with the sound /k/, like **cut**, may be spelt **k-**, like **key**, or **qu-**, like **queen**.
Words with the sound /s/, like **city**, may be spelt **s-**, like **soon**, or **ps-**, like **psychology**.

cross sth ↔ **out** *phr v* [T] to draw a line through something that you have written, especially because it is wrong: *Just cross out the old number and write in the new one.*

cross² *n* [C] **1** a wooden post with another post crossing it near the top, where people were left to die as a punishment in ancient times: *Jesus died on the cross.* **2** an object in the shape of a cross that is used as a sign of the Christian faith **3** a mixture of two things: **a cross between sth and sth** *It looks like a cross between a dog and a rat!* **4** *BrE* a mark (x) on paper, used to show where something is or that something that has been written is not correct

cross³ *adj BrE* annoyed or angry: **+ with** *Are you cross with me?*

cross·bar /ˈkrɒsbɑː‖ˈkrɔːsbɑːr/ *n* [C] **1** a bar that joins two upright posts, especially two GOALPOSTS **2** the top bar of a bicycle frame

cross·bow /ˈkrɒsbəʊ‖ˈkrɔːsboʊ/ *n* [C] a weapon used to shoot ARROWS with a lot of force

cross-coun·try /ˌ. ˈ..◂/ *adj* [only before noun] **1** across fields and not along roads: *cross-country running* **2** from one side of a country to the other: *a cross-country flight*

cross-ex·am·ine /ˌ. .ˈ..../ *v* [I,T] to ask someone questions about something they have just said to see if they are telling the truth, especially in a court of law —**cross-examination** /ˌ. ...ˈ../ *n* [C,U]

cross-eyed /ˌ. ˈ.◂ ‖ˈ. ./ *adj* if someone is cross-eyed, their eyes look in towards their nose

cross·fire, **cross-fire** /ˈkrɒsfaɪə‖ˈkrɔːsfaɪr/ *n* [U] **1 be caught in the crossfire** to be involved in a situation in which other people are arguing **2** when bullets from two or more different directions pass through the same area

cross·ing /ˈkrɒsɪŋ‖ˈkrɔː-/ *n* [C] **1** a place where you can safely cross a road, river etc **2** a place where two roads, lines etc cross **3** a journey across the sea

cross-legged

Tony is sitting cross-legged.

Kara is sitting with her legs crossed.

cross-legged /ˌkrɒs ˈlegd◂‖ˌkrɔːs ˈlegɪd◂/ *adv, adj* in a sitting position with your knees wide apart and your ANKLES crossed: *Children sat cross-legged on the floor.*

cross-pur·pos·es /ˌ. ˈ.../ *n* [plural] **at cross-purposes** two people who are at cross-purposes do not understand each other because they are talking about different things but do not realize it

cross-ref·er·ence /ˌ. ˈ...‖ˈ. .ˌ../ *n* [C] a note in a book that tells you to look in a different place in the same book for more information

cross·roads /ˈkrɒsrəʊdz‖ˈkrɔːsroʊdz/ *n, plural* **crossroads** [C] **1** a place where two roads

meet and cross each other ➞ see colour picture on page 669 **2** a time in your life when you have to make an important decision that will affect your future: **at a crossroads** *Neale's career was at a crossroads.*

cross sec·tion, **cross-section** /ˈ. ˌ../ *n* [C] **1** something that has been cut in half so that you can look at the inside, or a drawing of this: *a cross section of the brain* **2** a group of people or things that is typical of a larger group: *a cross-section of the American public*

cross·walk /ˈkrɒswɔːk‖ˈkrɔːswɔːk/ *n* [C] *AmE* a specially marked place for people to cross a road; PEDESTRIAN CROSSING *BrE*

cross·word /ˈkrɒswɜːd‖ ˈkrɔːswɜːrd/ also **cross-word puz·zle** /ˈ. ˌ../ *n* [C] a game in which you write the answers to questions in a pattern of numbered boxes

crossword

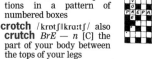

crotch /krɒtʃ‖krɑːtʃ/ also **crutch** *BrE* — *n* [C] the part of your body between the tops of your legs

crouch /kraʊtʃ/ also **crouch down** *v* [I] to lower your body close to the ground by bending your knees and back: *We crouched behind the wall.*

crow¹ /krəʊ‖kroʊ/ *n* **1** [C] a large shiny black bird that makes a loud sound **2 as the crow flies** measured in a straight line: *Cheyenne is 90 miles from here as the crow flies.*

crow² *v* [I] **1** if a COCK crows, it makes a loud high sound **2** to talk about something you have done in a very proud and annoying way: **+ about/over** *She keeps crowing about her exam results.*

crow·bar /ˈkrəʊbɑː‖ˈkroʊbɑːr/ *n* [C] a strong iron bar used for lifting or opening things

crowd¹ /kraʊd/ *n* **1** [C] a large group of people in one place: *A crowd gathered to watch the parade.*| **+ of** *a crowd of fans* **2** [singular] a group of friends or people who have similar interests

crowd² *v* **1** [I,T] to gather together in large numbers: *Shoppers crowded the streets.*| **+ around/into etc** *People crowded around the scene of the accident.* **2** [T] to move too close to someone: *Move back – you're crowding me!*
   crowd sb/sth ↔ **out** *phr v* [T] to force someone or something out of a place or situation: *The big supermarkets have been crowding out small grocery stores for years.*

crowd·ed /ˈkraʊdɪd/ *adj* too full of people or things: *a crowded room*

crown¹ /kraʊn/ *n* [C] **1** a circle made of gold and jewels worn by kings or queens on their heads **2 the crown** the position of being king or queen, or the government of a country ruled by a king or queen: *land which belongs to the crown* **3** the top part of a hat, head, or hill: *a hat with a high crown* **4** an artificial top for a damaged tooth

crown² *v* [T,I] **1** to place a crown on someone's head, so that they officially become king or queen: *She was crowned nearly fifty years ago.* **2 be crowned with** *literary* having something covering the top: *mountains crowned with snow*

crown·ing /'kraʊnɪŋ/ adj more valuable, important, or beautiful than anything else you have or have done: **crowning glory/ achievement etc** *The hotel's crowning glory is a stunning rooftop garden.*

cru·cial /'kruːʃəl/ adj extremely important: *crucial decisions involving millions of dollars* —**crucially** adv: *Education is crucially important.*

cru·ci·fix /'kruːsɪ̬fɪks/ n [C] a cross with a figure of Christ on it

cru·ci·fix·ion /ˌkruːsɪ̬'fɪkʃən/ n **1** [C,U] the act of killing someone by fastening them to a cross and leaving them to die **2** **the Crucifixion** the death of Christ in this way

cru·ci·fy /'kruːsɪ̬faɪ/ v [T] **1** to kill someone by fastening them to a cross **2** *informal* to criticize someone severely and cruelly

crude /kruːd/ adj **1** offensive or rude, especially about sex: *a crude joke* **2** in a natural condition: *crude oil* **3** not developed to a high standard or made with great skill: *a crude shelter* —**crudely** adv

cru·el /'kruːəl/ adj **1** deliberately making people or animals feel pain or sadness: **+ to** *Children can be very cruel to each other.* **2** a cruel event causes a lot of sadness: *Her husband's death was a cruel blow.* —**cruelly** adv

cru·el·ty /'kruːəlti/ n **1** [U] behaviour that is cruel: *Would you like to sign a petition against cruelty to animals?* **2** [C] a cruel action

cruise[1] /kruːz/ v [I] **1** to sail along slowly: *boats cruising on Lake Michigan* **2** to move at a steady speed in a car, plane etc: *We cruised along at 55 miles per hour.*

cruise[2] n [C] a holiday on a large ship

cruis·er /'kruːzə‖-ər/ n [C] a large fast WARSHIP

cruise ship /'. ./ n [C] a large ship with restaurants, bars etc that people have holidays on

crumb /krʌm/ n [C] **1** a very small piece of dry food, especially bread or cake →see colour picture on page 440 **2** a very small amount of something: **+ of** *I managed to pick up a few crumbs of information at the meeting.*

crum·ble /'krʌmbəl/ v **1** [I,T] to break apart into small pieces, or make something do this: *an old stone wall, crumbling with age* **2** [I] to lose power, become weak, or fail: *The entire economy was crumbling.*

crum·my /'krʌmi/ adj spoken bad or unpleasant: *What a crummy movie!*

crum·ple /'krʌmpəl/ v [I,T] to crush something, especially paper or cloth: *Crumpling the envelope in her hand, she tossed it into the fire.* —**crumpled** adj

crunch[1] /krʌntʃ/ v **1** [I] to make a noise like something being crushed: *The snow crunched as we walked.* →see colour picture on page 635 **2** [I,T] to eat hard food in a way that makes a noise: **+ on** *The dog was crunching on a bone.*

crunch[2] n [singular] **1** a noise like the sound of something being crushed: *I could hear the crunch of their footsteps on the gravel.* →see colour picture on page 635 **2** **the crunch** *informal* the moment during a difficult situation when you need to make an important decision: *When it comes to the crunch, you have to do what's best for yourself.*

crunch·y /'krʌntʃi/ adj food that is crunchy is pleasantly hard and makes a noise when you eat it: *crunchy carrots*

cru·sade /kruː'seɪd/ n [C] a determined attempt to change something that you feel very strongly about: *a crusade against violence* —**crusade** v [I] —**crusader** n [C]

crush[1] /krʌʃ/ v [T] **1** to press something so hard it breaks or is damaged: *Wine is made by crushing grapes.* **2** to completely defeat someone or something: *The rebellion was crushed by the government.*

crush[2] n **1** [C] a feeling of love for someone, especially someone older than you: **have a crush on sb** *Ben has a crush on his teacher.* **2** [singular] a crowd of people pressed so close together that it is difficult for them to move: *We forced our way through the crush towards the stage.*

crust /krʌst/ n [C,U] **1** the hard brown surface of bread **2** the baked outside part of foods such as PIES **3** a thin, hard, dry layer on the surface of something: *the earth's crust*

crust·y /'krʌsti/ adj **1** having a pleasantly hard crust: *crusty bread* **2** *informal* unfriendly and easily annoyed: *a crusty old man*

crutch /krʌtʃ/ n [C] **1** [usually plural] a special stick that you put under your arm to help you walk when you have hurt your leg **2** something that someone needs to support or help them: *Tom uses those pills as a crutch.* **3** *BrE* CROTCH

crux /krʌks/ n **the crux** the most important part of a problem, question, argument etc: **+ of** *The crux of the matter is whether murder was his intention.*

cry[1] /kraɪ/ v **cried, cried, crying 1** [I] to produce tears from your eyes, usually because you are sad or hurt: *The baby was crying upstairs.* | *I always cry at sad movies.* **2** [I,T] to say something loudly: *"Stop!" she cried.* **3** **cry over spilt milk** *informal* to waste time worrying about something that cannot be changed **4** **cry on sb's shoulder** *informal* to tell someone why you are unhappy or worried

cry out *phr v* **1** [I,T] to make a loud sound of fear, shock, pain etc, or to say something loudly: *He cried out in pain.* | *Marie cried out sharply, "Don't touch it!"* **2** **be crying out for sth** to need something urgently: *This country is crying out for science teachers.*

cry[2] n **1** [C] a loud sound or shout showing fear, pain, shock etc: *We heard a terrible cry in the next room.* | **+ of** *We woke to cries of "Fire!".* **2** [C] a sound made by a particular animal or bird: *the cry of the eagle* **3** **a cry** when someone cries: *You'll feel better after you've had a good cry.* **4** **be a far cry from** to be very different from something else: *It was a far cry from the tiny office she was used to.*

cry·ing /'kraɪ-ɪŋ/ adj **1** **a crying need for sth** an urgent need for something: *There is a crying need for better public transport.* **2** **it's a crying shame** *spoken* used to say that you are angry and upset about something: *It's a crying shame the way she treats that child.*

crypt /krɪpt/ n [C] a room under a church

cryp·tic /'krɪptɪk/ adj mysterious or having a hidden meaning: *a cryptic message* —**cryptically** /-kli/ adv

crys·tal /ˈkrɪstl/ *n* **1** [C,U] a type of rock that is transparent **2** [U] high quality glass: *crystal wine glasses* **3** [C] a regular shape that forms naturally when some MINERAL substances become solid: *crystals of ice | salt crystals*

crystal ball /ˌ.. ˈ./ *n* [C] a glass ball that some people believe you can look into to see the future

crys·tal·lize (also -**ise** *BrE*) /ˈkrɪstəlaɪz/ *v* [I,T] **1** to form crystals: *At what temperature does sugar crystallize?* **2** to make an idea, plan etc become clear or fixed: *Writing things down helps to crystallize your thoughts* —**crystallization** /ˌkrɪstəlaɪˈzeɪʃən‖-lə-/ *n* [U]

cub /kʌb/ *n* [C] a young bear, lion etc

cub·by·hole /ˈkʌbi həʊl‖-hoʊl/ *n* [C] a small space for storing things in

cube¹ /kjuːb/ *n* [C] **1** a solid object with six equal square sides: *a sugar cube | an ice cube* → see picture at SHAPES and colour picture on page 440 **2** the cube of sth the number you get when you multiply a number by itself twice

cube² *v* [T] **1** to multiply a number by itself twice: *4 cubed is 64.* **2** to cut food into cubes

cu·bic /ˈkjuːbɪk/ *adj* **cubic centimetre/inch/metre etc** a measurement of space in which the length, width, and height are all equal

cu·bi·cle /ˈkjuːbɪkəl/ *n* [C] a small enclosed part of a room: *cubicles in the library for studying*

cuck·oo /ˈkʊkuː‖ˈkuːkuː, ˈkʊ-/ *n* [C] a bird that puts its eggs in other birds' NESTS

cu·cum·ber /ˈkjuːkʌmbə‖-ər/ *n* [C] a long thin rounded vegetable with a dark green skin, usually eaten RAW → see picture at VEGETABLE

cud·dle /ˈkʌdl/ *v* [I,T] to put your arms around someone or something as a sign of love: *Danny cuddled the puppy.* —**cuddle** *n* [C] *Come and give me a cuddle.*

cuddle up *phr v* [I] to lie or sit very close to someone or something: **+ to** *Rebecca cuddled up to Mum on the couch.*

cud·dly /ˈkʌdli/ *adj* someone or something that is cuddly makes you want to cuddle them: *a cuddly baby*

cue /kjuː/ *n* [C] **1** a word or action that tells someone to speak or act in a play, film etc: *Tony stood by the stage, waiting for his cue.* **2** an action or event that is a sign for something else to happen: **+ for** *I think that was a cue for us to leave.* **3** **(right) on cue** happening or done at exactly the right moment: *I was just asking where you were when you walked in, right on cue.* **4** **take your cue from** to copy what someone else does, especially to behave in the right way **5** a long straight wooden stick used for hitting the ball in games such as POOL

cuff¹ /kʌf/ *n* [C] **1** the end part of a SLEEVE **2** **off the cuff** not prepared for or thought about earlier: *an off the cuff remark*

cuff

cuff² *v* [T] **1** to put HANDCUFFS on someone: *Cuff him!* **2** *BrE* to hit someone lightly with your open hand

cuff link /ˈ. ./ *n* [C] a small piece of jewellery used to hold the cuff on a shirt together

cuffs /kʌfs/ *n* [plural] *informal* HANDCUFFS

cui·sine /kwɪˈziːn/ *n* [U] a particular style of cooking: *French cuisine*

cul-de-sac /ˈkʌl də ˌsæk, ˈkʊl-‖ˌkʌl də ˈsæk, ˌkʊl-/ *n* [C] a street which is closed at one end

cu·li·na·ry /ˈkʌlɪnəri‖ˈkʌlɪneri, ˈkjuːl-/ *adj* [only before noun] connected with cooking: *culinary skills*

cull /kʌl/ *v* *formal* **1** [T] to collect information from many different places: **+ from** *photographs culled from various sources* **2** [I,T] to kill the weakest animals in a group, reducing their numbers —**cull** *n* [C]

cul·mi·nate /ˈkʌlmɪneɪt/ *v* [T] *formal* **culminate in sth** to have something as an important final result: *a series of arguments that culminated in a divorce*

cul·mi·na·tion /ˌkʌlmɪˈneɪʃən/ *n* [singular] the final or highest point of something, reached after a long period of effort or development: *That discovery was the culmination of his life's work.*

cul·pa·ble /ˈkʌlpəbəl/ *adj* *formal* deserving blame —**culpability** /ˌkʌlpəˈbɪlɪti/ *n* [U]

cul·prit /ˈkʌlprɪt/ *n* [C] **1** someone who is guilty of a crime or of doing something wrong **2** *informal* the reason for a particular problem or difficulty: *High production costs are the main culprit.*

cult /kʌlt/ *n* [C] **1** a religious group that is not part of an established religion **2** a fashion, film etc that has become very popular among a particular group of people: *cult film director John Waters*

cul·ti·vate /ˈkʌltɪveɪt/ *v* [T] **1** to prepare and use land for growing crops **2** to develop a particular skill or quality in yourself: *I've cultivated a knowledge of art.* **3** to develop a friendship with someone, especially someone who can help you: *You need to cultivate useful contacts.* —**cultivation** /ˌkʌltɪˈveɪʃən/ *n* [U]

cul·ti·vat·ed /ˈkʌltɪveɪtɪd/ *adj* **1** someone who is cultivated is intelligent and knows a lot about art, literature etc: *a cultivated man* **2** used for growing crops: *cultivated land*

cul·tu·ral /ˈkʌltʃərəl/ *adj* **1** relating to a particular society and its way of life: *England has a rich cultural heritage.* **2** relating to art, literature, music etc: *The city is trying to promote cultural activities.* —**culturally** *adv*

cul·ture /ˈkʌltʃə‖-ər/ *n* **1** [C,U] the art, beliefs, behaviour, ideas etc of a particular society or group of people: *youth culture | students learning about American culture* **2** [U] activities that are connected to art, literature, music etc: *New York City is a good place for anyone who is interested in culture.* **3** [C,U] the process of growing BACTERIA for scientific use, or the bacteria produced by this process

cul·tured /ˈkʌltʃəd‖-ərd/ *adj* someone who is cultured is well educated and knows a lot about art, literature, music etc: *a handsome, cultured man*

cum·ber·some /ˈkʌmbəsəm‖-bər-/ *adj* **1** slow and difficult: *Getting a passport can be a cumbersome process.* **2** heavy and difficult to move or use: *cumbersome camping equipment*

cum·in /ˈkʌmɪn/ *n* [U] a strong-smelling seed or the brown powder made from this seed, used in cooking

cu·mu·la·tive /ˈkjuːmjʊlətɪv‖-leɪtɪv/ *adj* increasing gradually as more of something is added or happens: *The effects of the drug are cumulative.* —**cumulatively** *adv*

cun·ning /ˈkʌnɪŋ/ *adj* clever and good at deceiving people: *a cunning criminal* —**cunning** *n* [U] —**cunningly** *adv*

cup   mug   glass

cup¹ /kʌp/ *n* [C] **1** a small round container with a handle, that you use to drink from, or the drink that it contains: *a cup and saucer* | *a cup of coffee* **2** a specially shaped container that is given as a prize in a competition **3 the (...) cup** a sports competition in which the prize is a special cup: *the 3rd round of the FA cup* **4** *AmE* an exact measure of quantity used in cooking: *Stir in a cup of flour.*

cup² *v* [T] **-pped, -pping** to form your hands into the shape of a cup: *She cupped her hands around the mug.*

cup·board /ˈkʌbəd‖-ərd/ *n* [C] a piece of furniture with doors and shelves for storing clothes, plates, food etc → see picture at KITCHEN

cu·ra·ble /ˈkjʊərəbəl‖ˈkjʊr-/ *adj* an illness that is curable can be cured → opposite INCURABLE

cu·rate /ˈkjʊərɪt‖ˈkjʊr-/ *n* [C] a priest whose job is to help the priest in an area

cu·ra·tor /kjʊˈreɪtə-ər/ *n* [C] someone who is in charge of a MUSEUM

curb¹ /kɜːb‖kɜːrb/ *n* [C] **1** something which helps to control or limit something: **+ on** *curbs on public spending* **2** *AmE* the edge of the part of a road where people can walk; KERB *BrE*: *Larry tripped on the curb.*

curb² *v* [T] to control or limit something: *Max tried hard to curb his temper.*

cur·dle /ˈkɜːdl‖ˈkɜːrdl/ *v* [I,T] to become thicker, or to make a liquid do this: *Add a little flour to stop the mix from curdling.*

cure¹ /kjʊə‖kjʊr/ *v* [T] **1** to make an injury or illness better, so that the person who was ill is well: *Penicillin will cure most infections.* | *She's hoping this new doctor can cure her back pain.* → compare HEAL **2** to solve a problem or improve a bad situation: *government action to cure unemployment* **3** to preserve food, leather etc by drying it, hanging it in smoke, or covering it with salt: *cured ham*

cure² *n* [C] **1** a medicine or treatment that can cure an illness **+ for** *a cure for AIDS* **2** something that solves a problem or improves a bad situation **+ for** *There's no easy cure for poverty.*

cur·few /ˈkɜːfjuː‖ˈkɜːr-/ *n* [C] a time during which everyone must stay indoors: *The government imposed a curfew from sunset to sunrise.*

cu·ri·o /ˈkjʊəriəʊ‖ˈkjʊrioʊ/ *n* [C] a small object that is valuable because it is old, beautiful, or rare

cu·ri·os·i·ty /ˌkjʊəriˈɒsɪ̩ti‖ˌkjʊriˈɑːs-/ *n* [U, singular] the desire to know something or to learn about something: **+ about** *Children have a natural curiosity about the world around them.* | **out of curiosity** *Just out of curiosity, how old are you?*

cu·ri·ous /ˈkjʊəriəs‖ˈkjʊr-/ *adj* **1** wanting to know or learn about something: *The accident attracted a few curious looks.* | **+ about** *Aren't you curious about what happened to her?* **2** strange or unusual: *a curious noise* | **+ that** *It's curious that she left without saying goodbye.* —**curiously** *adv*

curl¹ /kɜːl‖kɜːrl/ *n* [C] a small piece of something, especially hair, that forms a curved shape: *a little girl with blonde curls* | *a curl of smoke* —**curly** *adj* → see colour picture on page 244

curl² *v* [I,T] to form a curved shape, or to make something do this: *Should I curl my hair?* | *Smoke curled from the chimney.*

   curl up *phr v* [I] **1** to lie or sit with your arms and legs bent close to your body: *Phoebe curled up on the bed and fell asleep.* **2** if paper, leaves etc curl up, the edges become curved and point upwards

curl·er /ˈkɜːlə‖ˈkɜːrlər/ *n* [C, usually plural] a small metal or plastic tube that is used to make hair curl

cur·rant /ˈkʌrənt‖ˈkɜːr-/ *n* [C] a small dried fruit, often used in cakes

cur·ren·cy /ˈkʌrənsi‖ˈkɜːr-/ *n* **1** [C,U] the type of money that a country uses: *foreign currency* | *The local currency is francs.* **2** [U] when something is generally accepted or used: *The idea enjoys wide currency in academic circles.*

cur·rent¹ /ˈkʌrənt‖ˈkɜːr-/ *adj* [only before noun] happening or existing at the present time: *Denise's current boyfriend* —**currently** *adv*

current² *n* **1** [C] a continuous movement of water or air in a particular direction: *There's a strong current in the river.* **2** [C,U] a flow of electricity through a wire

current ac·count /ˈ.. ..ˌ./ *n* [C] *BrE* a bank account that you can take money out of at any time; CHECKING ACCOUNT *AmE*

cur·ric·u·lum /kəˈrɪkjʊ̩ləm/ *n, plural* **curricula** /-lə/ *or* **curriculums** [C] all of the subjects that are taught at a school, college etc

cur·ry /ˈkʌri‖ˈkɜːri/ *n* [C,U] a type of food from India with meat or vegetables cooked with hot SPICES

curse¹ /kɜːs‖kɜːrs/ *v* **1** [I] to swear: *Ralph cursed loudly.* **2** [T] to say or think bad things about someone or something because they have made you angry: **curse sb/sth for (doing) sth** *I cursed myself for not buying the car insurance sooner.*

GRAMMAR NOTE: comparatives and superlatives
For short adjectives of one syllable, add **-er** or **-est** to the word: e.g. *old - older - oldest.* (Sometimes you must double the last letter: e.g. *big - bigger - biggest*). For long adjectives put **more** or **the most** before the word: e.g. *more comfortable - the most interesting.*

curse² *n* [C] **1** a word or words that you use when you swear, or when you are angry **2** magical words that are intended to bring someone bad luck: *a witch's curse* **3** something that causes trouble, harm etc: *Car crime is a curse on our society.*

cur·sor /'kɜːsəll'kɜːrsər/ *n* [C] a mark on a computer screen that moves to show where you are writing

cur·so·ry /'kɜːsərill'kɜːr-/ *adj* done quickly without much attention to detail: **a cursory glance/examination etc** *After a cursory look at the menu, Grant ordered a burger.*

curt /kɜːtllkɜːrt/ *adj* using few words when you speak to someone, in a way that seems rude: *He gave a curt reply.* —**curtly** *adv* —**curtness** *n* [U]

cur·tail /kɜː'teɪllkɜːr-/ *v* [T] *formal* to reduce or limit something: *new laws to curtail immigration* —**curtailment** *n* [U]

cur·tain /'kɜːtnll'kɜːrtn/ *n* [C] a piece of hanging cloth that can be pulled across a window, stage etc: **draw the curtains** (=close or open the curtains)

curt·sy, curtsey /'kɜːtsill'kɜːr-/ *n* [C] a movement a woman makes by bending her knees with one foot behind the other, as a sign of respect to a more important person —**curtsy** *v* [I]

curve¹ /kɜːvllkɜːrv/ *n* [C] a line or shape which gradually bends like part of a circle: *a curve on a graph* | *a sharp curve in the road*

curve² *v* [I,T] to bend or move in the shape of a curve, or to make something do this: *a golf ball curving through the air* —**curved** *adj* —**curvy** *adj*

cush·ion¹ /'kʊʃən/ *n* [C] **1** a cloth bag filled with soft material that you sit or lie on to make yourself more comfortable ➡ see colour picture on page 474 **2** something that stops one thing from hitting another thing: *The hovercraft rides on a cushion of air.*

cushion² *v* [T] **1** to reduce the effects of something unpleasant **2** to protect something with something soft: *A good running shoe will help to cushion your feet.*

cush·y /'kʊʃi/ *adj informal* a cushy job or situation is very easy

cuss /kʌs/ *v* [I] *AmE informal* to swear

cus·tard /'kʌstədll-ərd/ *n* **1** [C,U] a soft baked mixture of milk, eggs, and sugar **2** [U] *BrE* a thick sauce that is poured over sweet foods

cus·to·di·an /kʌ'stəʊdiənll-'stoʊ-/ *n* [C] someone whose job is to take care of a public building or a valuable object

cus·to·dy /'kʌstədi/ *n* [U] **1** the right to take care of a child, given by a court when the child's parents are legally separated: *My ex-wife has custody of the kids.* **2** **in custody** being kept in prison until you go to court

cus·tom /'kʌstəm/ *n* **1** [C,U] something that people do in a society because it is traditional: *the custom of throwing rice at weddings* **2** [U] all people who use a particular shop or business: *We lost a lot of custom when the new supermarket opened.* ➡ see also CUSTOMS

cus·tom·a·ry /'kʌstəmərill-meri/ *adj* usual or normal: *It is customary to cover your head in the temple.* —**customarily** /'kʌstəmər̩lill,kʌstə'mer-̩li/ *adv*

custom-built /ˌ.. '.◂/ *adj* a custom-built car, machine etc has been specially built for the person buying it

cus·tom·er /'kʌstəməll-ər/ *n* [C] someone who buys goods or services from a shop or company: *IBM is one of our biggest customers.*

USAGE NOTE: customer, shopper, client, patient, and **guest**

These words all mean someone who buys or receives goods or services. If you go out and buy things, you are a **shopper**, but if you buy something in a particular shop, you are that shop's **customer:** *The mall was full of shoppers.* | *We don't get many customers in the evening.* If you are paying someone such as a lawyer for professional services, you are a **client,** but if you are seeing a doctor, you are a **patient.** If you are staying in a hotel, you are a **guest.**

cus·tom·ize (also **-ise** *BrE*) /'kʌstəmaɪz/ *v* [T] to change something to make it just right for you

cus·toms /'kʌstəmz/ *n* [plural] the place where your bags are checked for illegal goods when you go into a country

cut¹ /kʌt/ *v* **cut, cut, cutting 1** [I,T] to use a knife or scissors to divide something, to remove a piece from something etc: *I cut the string around the package.* | *Cut the cheese into cubes.* | *Bob used a saw to cut a hole in the ice.* **2** [T] to reduce the amount of time, money etc that you spend: **cut costs** *The company has closed several factories to cut costs.* **3** [T] to injure yourself with a sharp object: *Sam fell and cut his head.* **4** [T] to remove part of a film or speech because it might offend people: *The sex scenes had been cut from the film.* **5** **cut corners** *informal* to do something less well than you should do, because you are trying to save time, money etc **6** **cut class/school** *AmE* to not go to a class or to school when you should go

cut across sth *phr v* [T] **1** to go across an area rather than around it: *Shane cut across three lanes of traffic to the exit.* **2** if a problem or feeling cuts across different groups of people, they are all affected by it: *The drug problem cuts across all social classes.*

cut back *phr v* [I,T **cut** sth ↔ **back**] to reduce the amount, size, or cost of something: *Oil production is being cut back.*

cut down *phr v* **1** [I,T **cut** sth ↔ **down**] to reduce the amount of something you do or use: *I'm trying to cut down on my drinking.* **2** [T **cut** sth ↔ **down**] to cut a tree so that it all falls to the ground: *All the beautiful old oaks had been cut down to build houses.*

cut in *phr v* [I] to interrupt someone who is speaking: *Mark cut in to ask if I'd seen his keys.*

cut off *phr v* [T] **1** [**cut** sth ↔ **off**] to remove a piece from something using a sharp tool such as a knife: *Cut the top off the pineapple.* **2** [**cut** sth ↔ **off**] to stop supplying electricity, gas, water etc to someone: *They'll cut off your electricity if you don't pay the bill.* **3** **be/get cut off** to be unable to finish talking to someone because something is wrong with the telephone connection **4** [**cut** sb/sth ↔ **off**] to separate someone or something from other people or things, or to prevent them from going somewhere: *A heavy snowfall cut us off from the town.*

cut out *phr v* **1** [T **cut** sth ↔ **out**] to remove a piece from something, using a knife or scissors: *Cut a circle out of the piece of card.* **2** [I] if a motor cuts out, it stops working suddenly **3** **cut it/that out!** *spoken* used to tell someone to stop doing something that is annoying you **4** **not be cut out for/not be cut out to be** to not have the qualities that would make you suitable for a job or activity: *I wasn't really cut out to be a teacher.*

cut short *phr v* [T **cut** sth ↔ **short**] to make something finish earlier than it should have done: *His career was cut short by a back injury.*

cut sth ↔ **up** *phr v* [T] to cut something into small pieces: *Cut up two carrots.*

cut² *n* [C] **1** a wound that you get when something sharp cuts your skin: *Luckily, I only got a few cuts and bruises.* **2** a reduction in the size, number, or amount of something: + **in** *a huge cut in the education budget* **3** a hole or mark made by something sharp: *a small cut in the side of the tyre* **4** a HAIRCUT **5** *informal* someone's share of something, especially money: *Everyone's taking a cut of the profits.* **6** **be a cut above (the rest)** *informal* to be better than someone or something else: *The movie is a cut above most made-for-TV films.*

cut and dried /ˌ.. ˈ. ◂/ *adj* a decision or result that is cut and dried will definitely happen and cannot be changed

cut·back /ˈkʌtbæk/ *n* [C, usually plural] a reduction in something such as the amount of money spent by a government: + **in** *cutbacks in funding*

cute /kjuːt/ *adj* **1** very pretty or attractive: *What a cute baby!* **2** *AmE* confident, but in a way that seems rude: *Ignore him – he's just trying to be cute.* —**cutely** *adv* —**cuteness** *n* [U]

cutlery

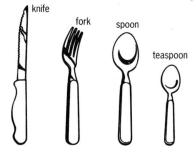

knife
fork
spoon
teaspoon

cut·le·ry /ˈkʌtləri/ *n* [U] knives, forks, and spoons; SILVERWARE *AmE*

cut·let /ˈkʌtl̩t/ *n* [C] a small piece of meat with a bone in it: *lamb cutlets*

cut-off /ˈkʌtɒf‖-ɒːf/ *n* [C] a limit or level at which you must stop doing something: *The cut-off date for applying was June 3rd.*

cut-price also **cut-rate** /ˌ. ˈ. ◂/ *adj* cheaper than the normal price: *cut-price petrol*

cut·ter /ˈkʌtə‖-ər/ *n* [C] a tool that cuts things: *wire cutters*

cut·throat /ˈkʌtθrəʊt‖-θroʊt/ *adj* willing to do anything to succeed: *the cutthroat competition between computer companies*

cut·ting¹ /ˈkʌtɪŋ/ *n* [C] **1** a stem or leaf that is cut from a plant to be grown into a new plant **2** *BrE* a piece of writing that is cut from a newspaper or magazine; CLIPPING

cutting² *adj* a cutting remark is unkind and intended to upset someone

cutting edge /ˌ.. ˈ./ *n* **be at/on the cutting edge** to be at the most ADVANCED or newest stage of something —**cutting-edge** *adj*: *cutting-edge technology*

CV /ˌsiː ˈviː/ *n* [C] *BrE* a document that describes your education and the jobs that you have done, used when you are trying to get a new job; RESUMÉ *AmE*

cwt *n* [C] the written abbreviation of HUNDRED-WEIGHT

cy·a·nide /ˈsaɪənaɪd/ *n* [U] a very strong poison

cy·ber- /ˈsaɪbə‖-ər/ *prefix* relating to computers, especially using computers to send messages on the Internet: *cybersex | cybertechnology*

cy·ber·ca·fé /ˈsaɪbəkæfeɪ‖-ər/ *n* [C] a place where you can use computers that are connected to the Internet, and also buy cups of coffee

cy·ber·space /ˈsaɪbəspeɪs‖-ər-/ *n* [U] all the connections between computers around the world, considered as a real place where information, messages etc can exist

cy·cle¹ /ˈsaɪkəl/ *n* [C] **1** a number of connected events that happen many times in the same order: *the life cycle of the frog* **2** a bicycle or MOTORCYCLE

cycle² *v* [I] *especially BrE* to ride a bicycle: *John goes cycling every Sunday.* —**cyclist** *n* [C] —**cycling** *n* [U] → see colour picture on page 636

cy·clic /ˈsaɪklɪk/ also **cyc·li·cal** /ˈsɪklɪkəl, ˈsaɪ-/ *adj* happening many times in a regular pattern

cy·clone /ˈsaɪkləʊn‖-kloʊn/ *n* [C] a very strong wind that moves in a circle

cyg·net /ˈsɪɡn̩t/ *n* [C] a young SWAN

cyl·in·der /ˈsɪlɪndə‖-ər/ *n* [C] **1** a shape, object, or container with circular ends and straight sides → see picture at SHAPES **2** the part in a car engine, in which the PISTON moves up and down: *a six-cylinder engine*

cy·lin·dri·cal /sɪˈlɪndrɪkəl/ *adj* in the shape of a cylinder

cym·bal /ˈsɪmbəl/ *n* [C] a musical instrument like a round metal plate, played by hitting it with a stick

cyn·ic /ˈsɪnɪk/ *n* [C] someone who believes that people do things only to help themselves: *Working in politics has made Sheila a cynic.* —**cynicism** /ˈsɪnɪsɪzəm/ *n* [U]

cyn·i·cal /ˈsɪnɪkəl/ *adj* unwilling to believe that anyone has good or honest reasons for doing something: *Since her divorce she's become very cynical about men.* —**cynically** /-kli/ *adv*

cyst /sɪst/ *n* [C] a small LUMP containing liquid that can grow in your body

czar /zɑː‖zɑːr/ *n* [C] another spelling of TSAR

Dd

D, d the letter 'd'

-'d the short form of WOULD or HAD: *Ask her if she'd like to go with us.* | *If I'd only known!*

D.A. /ˌdiː ˈeɪ/ *n* [C] the abbreviation of DISTRICT ATTORNEY

dab¹ /dæb/ *v* [I,T] **-bbed, -bbing** to lightly touch something several times in order to dry it or put something on it: *Emily dabbed at her eyes with a handkerchief.* | **dab sth on/over etc** *I'll just dab some suntan lotion on your shoulders.*

dab² *n* [C] a small amount of a substance: *a dab of paint*

dab·ble /ˈdæbəl/ *v* [I] to do something or be involved in something in a way that is not serious: **+ in** *As a teenager she had dabbled in drugs.*

dad /dæd/ also **dad·dy** /ˈdædi/ *n* [C] *informal* father: *Run and tell your daddy I'm home.*

daf·fo·dil /ˈdæfədɪl/ *n* [C] a tall yellow flower that grows in early spring

daft /dɑːft‖dæft/ *adj BrE spoken informal* silly: *What a daft thing to do!*

dag·ger /ˈdæɡə‖-ər/ *n* [C] a short pointed knife, used as a weapon

dai·ly /ˈdeɪli/ *adj* **1** happening, done, or produced every day: *a daily newspaper* **2** relating to a single day: *a daily rate of pay* **3** **daily life** the things you do every day —**daily** *adv*

dain·ty /ˈdeɪnti/ *adj* small, pretty, and delicate: *a dainty little girl* —**daintily** *adv*

dai·ry /ˈdeəri‖ˈderi/ *n* **1** [C] a farm where milk, butter, and cheese are produced **2** [C] a company that buys and sells milk, butter etc **3** **dairy products** milk and foods made from milk, such as butter and cheese

dai·sy /ˈdeɪzi/ *n* [C] a white flower with a bright yellow centre

dale /deɪl/ *n* [C] *literary* a valley

dal·ma·tian /dælˈmeɪʃən/ *n* [C] a dog with white hair and black spots

dam¹ /dæm/ *n* [C] a wall built across a river to make a lake

dam² *v* [T] **-mmed, -mming** to build a dam across a river

dam·age¹ /ˈdæmɪdʒ/ *n* [U] **1** physical harm done to something, so that it is broken or spoiled: *We went up on the roof to have a look at the damage.* | **+ to** *Was there any damage to your car?* | **do/cause damage** *Don't worry, the kids can't do any damage.* **2** a bad effect on someone or something: **+ to** *the damage to Simon's reputation*

damage² *v* [T] **1** to physically harm something: *The storm damaged the tobacco crop.* **2** to have a bad effect on someone or something: *The latest shooting has damaged the chances of a ceasefire.* —**damaging** *adj*

dam·a·ges /ˈdæmɪdʒɪz/ *n* [plural] *law* money that someone must pay to someone else for harming that person or their property: *The court ordered her to pay £500 in damages.*

dame /deɪm/ *n* [C] **1** a woman who has been

given the British title Dame: *Dame Judi Dench* **2** *AmE old-fashioned* a woman

dam·mit /ˈdæmɪt/ *interjection* used when you are annoyed or angry: *Hurry up, dammit!*

damn¹ /dæm/ also **damned** *adv spoken* **1** used to emphasize something: *We're damn lucky we got here before the storm.* **2** **damn well** used to emphasize how determined or sure you are about something: *She can do whatever she damn well wants.*

damn² *n spoken* **not give a damn** to not care at all about something: *I don't give a damn what he thinks.*

damn³ *interjection* used when you are annoyed or disappointed: *Damn! I forgot to bring my wallet!* —**damn** *adj*: *Turn off that damn TV.*

damn⁴ *v* [T] **damn it/you/sb etc** *spoken* said when you are very angry: *Damn those kids!*

damned /dæmd/ *adj* **1** *spoken* used when you are angry about something: *That damned fool, Hodges!* **2** **I'll be damned** *spoken* used when you are surprised: *Well, I'll be damned! It's Tom!* **3** **be damned** to be punished by God after your death by being sent to HELL

damn·ing /ˈdæmɪŋ/ *adj* criticising someone or something very severely and showing that they are very bad: *a damning indictment of US foreign policy*

damp /dæmp/ *adj* slightly wet, usually in a cold and unpleasant way: *The basement was cold and damp.* —**damp, dampness** *n* [U] —**damply** *adv*

damp·en /ˈdæmpən/ *v* [T] **1** to make something slightly wet: *Dampen the shirt slightly before ironing it.* **2** **dampen sb's enthusiasm/ spirits** to make someone feel less excited or interested

damp·er /ˈdæmpə‖-ər/ *n* **put a damper on sth** to stop something from being enjoyable: *His sad news put a real damper on the party.*

dam·sel /ˈdæmzəl/ *n* [C] **damsel in distress** *humorous* a young woman who needs help

dance¹ /dɑːns‖dæns/ *v* **1** [I] to move your body at the same speed as music: *Who's that dancing with Tom?* **2** **dance the waltz/tango etc** to do a particular kind of dance —**dancing** *n* [U] —**dancer** *n* [C]

dance² *n* **1** [C] when you dance with someone: *Let's have one more dance.* **2** [C] a particular set of movements that you perform with music: *The only dance I know is the waltz.* **3** [C] when a lot of people go somewhere to dance: *a school dance* **4** [U] the art or activity of dancing: *dance lessons*

dan·de·li·on /ˈdændɪlaɪən/ *n* [C] a small bright yellow wild flower

dan·druff /ˈdændrəf, -drʌf/ *n* [U] small white pieces of dead skin from your head

dan·ger /ˈdeɪndʒə‖-ər/ *n* **1** [U] the possibility that someone or something will be harmed: **+ of** *Is there any danger of infection?* | **in danger** (=in a dangerous situation): *I had a sudden feeling that Ben was in danger.* **2** [C] something or someone that may harm you: *He's a danger to others.* | **+ of** *the dangers of smoking* **3** [C,U] the possibility that something unpleasant will happen: **in danger of doing sth** *Maggie is in serious danger of getting fired.*

dan·ger·ous /ˈdeɪndʒərəs/ *adj* able or likely to harm you: *a dangerous criminal* | *It's dangerous to walk alone at night around here.* —**dangerously** *adv*

dan·gle /ˈdæŋɡəl/ *v* [I,T] to hang or swing loosely, or to make something do this: **+ from** *The keys were dangling from his belt.*

dank /dæŋk/ *adj* unpleasantly wet and cold: *a cold, dank cellar*

dap·pled /ˈdæpəld/ *adj* marked with spots of colour, light, or shade: *the dappled shade*

dare¹ /deə‖der/ *v* **1** [I] to be brave enough to do something, used especially in negative sentences: **dare (to) do sth** *Robbins wouldn't dare argue with the boss.* **2 how dare you/he etc** spoken used when you are very angry about what someone has said or done: *How dare you call me a liar!* **3 don't you dare** spoken used to tell someone that they must not do something: *Don't you dare talk to me like that!* **4 dare sb to do sth** to try to persuade someone to do something dangerous: *I dare you to jump!*

dare² *n* [C] when you ask someone to do something dangerous to prove that they are not afraid

dare·dev·il /ˈdeədevəl‖ˈder-/ *n* [C] someone who likes doing dangerous things —**daredevil** *adj*

daren't /deənt‖dernt/ the short form of "dare not": *I daren't tell him. He'd be furious!*

dar·ing¹ /ˈdeərɪŋ‖ˈder-/ *adj* **1** willing to do dangerous things: *a daring rescue attempt* **2** new or unusual in a slightly shocking way: *a daring evening dress* —**daringly** *adv*

daring² *n* [U] the courage to do dangerous things

dark¹ /dɑːk‖dɑːrk/ *adj* **1** a dark place is one where there is little or no light: *Turn on the light; it's dark in here.* ➡ opposite LIGHT² **2** closer to black than to white in colour: *dark hair* | *dark green* ➡ opposite LIGHT² **3** a dark person has black hair, brown skin etc: *a small, dark man* ➡ see colour picture on page 244 ➡ opposite FAIR¹ **4** mysterious or frightening: *a dark side to his character* **5** a period of time that is unhappy or without hope: *the dark days of the war*

dark² *n* **1** **the dark** when there is no light: *My son is afraid of the dark.* **2 after/before dark** at night or before night begins: *I don't like walking home after dark.* **3 in the dark** informal not knowing about something important because no one has told you about it: *Watson had kept us in the dark about selling the club.*

dark·en /ˈdɑːkən‖ˈdɑːr-/ *v* [I,T] to become darker, or to make something darker: *The sky darkened and rain began to fall.* | *a darkened room*

dark horse /ˌ. ˈ./ *n* [C] someone who is not well known and who surprises people by doing something or achieving something

dark·ly /ˈdɑːkli‖ˈdɑːrk-/ *adv* in a way that makes people feel frightened: *The police warned darkly of 'further charges' against us.*

dark·ness /ˈdɑːknəs‖ˈdɑːrk-/ *n* [U] when there is no light: *the darkness of a winter morning* | *in* **darkness** (=without any light): *The whole room was in darkness.*

dark·room /ˈdɑːkruːm, -rʊm‖ˈdɑːrk-/ *n* [C] a room with a red light or no light, used for developing photographic film

dar·ling¹ /ˈdɑːlɪŋ‖ˈdɑːr-/ *n* [C] used to address someone that you love: *Come here, darling.*

darling² *adj* [only before noun] much loved: *my darling daughter*

darn¹ /dɑːn‖dɑːrn/ *v* [T] to repair a hole in clothes by sewing thread across it: *darning socks*

darn² also **darned** /dɑːnd‖dɑːrnd/ *adv* spoken AmE used to emphasize what you are saying: *darned good*

dart¹ /dɑːt‖dɑːrt/ *n* [C] **1** a small pointed object like an ARROW that you can aim and throw in the game of darts **2** a small pointed object thrown or shot as a weapon **3** a small fold stitched into a piece of clothing to make it fit

dart² *v* [I] to move suddenly and quickly in a particular direction: *A little girl had darted out into the road.*

darts /dɑːts‖dɑːrts/ *n* [U] a game in which you throw darts at a circular board

dash¹ /dæʃ/ *v* **1** [I] to go somewhere very quickly: **+ into/across/out etc** *She dashed into the room.* **2 dash sb's hopes** to destroy someone's hopes completely: *Hopes of peace were dashed as riots broke out.* **3** [T] to make something hit violently against something else: **dash sth against/to etc** *Strong winds dashed the ship against the rocks.*

dash off *phr v* [I] to leave somewhere very quickly: *Tim had to dash off after class.*

dash² *n* **1** **make a dash for** to run very quickly towards something: *One of the prisoners made a dash for the open gate.* **2** [singular] a small amount of a liquid: *a dash of lemon* **3** [C] a mark (–) used in writing or printing, to separate parts of a sentence **4** [C] informal a dashboard

dash·board /ˈdæʃbɔːd‖-bɔːrd/ *n* [C] the part at the front of a car that has the controls on it

da·ta /ˈdeɪtə, ˈdɑːtə/ *n* [U, plural] information or facts: *He's collecting data for his report.*

da·ta·base /ˈdeɪtəbeɪs/ *n* [C] a large amount of information stored in a computer system

data pro·cess·ing /ˌ.. ˈ.../ *n* [U] the use of computers to store and organize information

date¹ /deɪt/ *n* [C] **1** a particular day of the month or of the year, shown by a number: *"What's today's date?" "It's August 11th."* | **date of birth** (=the day you were born) | **set/fix a date** (=choose a date): *Have you set a date for the wedding?* **2** when you go to a bar, restaurant, film etc with someone you like in a romantic way: *Mike's got a date tonight.* **3** AmE someone you go on a date with: *My date's taking me out to dinner.* **4** a time when something has been arranged to happen: **make a date** (=arrange a time): *Let's make a date to see that new play.* | **later date** (=a time in the future) **5 to date** until now: *This is the best research on the subject to date.* **6** a sweet sticky brown fruit with a single long seed → see also OUT-OF-DATE, UP-TO-DATE

date² *v* **1** [T] to write the date on something: *a letter dated May 1st, 1923* **2** [T] to find out when something old was made or how long it has existed: *Geologists can date the rocks by examining fossils in the same layer.* **3** [I,T] to seem old-fashioned, or to make something seem old-fashioned: *The 1960s slang in the film dates it.* **4** [I,T] *AmE* to have a romantic relationship with someone: *How long have you been dating Monica?*

date from sth also **date back to** sth *phr v* [T] to have existed since a particular time: *The cathedral dates from the 13th century.*

dat·ed /'deɪt̬ɪd/ *adj* no longer fashionable: *The big Cadillac now seemed a little dated.*

daub /dɔːb‖dɒːb/ *v* [T] to paint or write words or pictures on a surface in a careless, untidy and sometimes shocking way: *Someone had daubed graffiti all over her door.*

daugh·ter /'dɔːtə‖'dɒːtər/ *n* [C] your female child → see picture at FAMILY

daughter-in-law /'.. ., ./ *n* [C] your son's wife → see picture at FAMILY

daunt·ed /'dɔːntɪd‖'dɒːn-/ *adj* feeling afraid or worried: *He was a bit daunted by the prospect of meeting her parents.*

daunt·ing /'dɔːntɪŋ‖'dɒːn-/ *adj* frightening or worrying: *a daunting task*

daw·dle /'dɔːdl‖'dɒː-/ *v* [I] to waste time by doing things too slowly: *Stop dawdling – we'll be late.*

dawn¹ /dɔːn‖dɒːn/ *n* **1** [U] the time of day when light first appears: *We talked until dawn.* **2** the dawn of civilization/time etc the time when something began or first appeared

dawn² *v* [I] **1** if a day or morning dawns, it begins: *The morning dawned fresh and clear.* | **2** it/the truth dawns on sb used to say that someone realises something: *It suddenly dawned on me that we might be looking in the wrong place.*

day /deɪ/ *n* **1** [C] a period of time equal to 24 hours: *I'll be back in ten days.* **2** [C,U] the period of time between when it becomes light in the morning and when it becomes dark in the evening: *The days begin to get longer in the spring.* | **all day** *It's rained all day.* **3** [C usually singular] the time during the day when you are usually awake: *My day usually begins at six o'clock.* | **long day** (=a day when you had to get up early and were busy all day) **4** [C] the hours you work in a day: *Jean works an eight-hour day.* **5** one day on a particular day in the past: *She just walked in here one day.* **6** these days used to talk about the way something is now, which is different from how it was in the past: *It isn't safe to walk the streets these days.* **7** one day/some day at some time in the future: *We'll buy that dream house some day.* **8** in my/his/Shakespeare's etc day at a time in the past when someone was young or when someone was alive **9** to this day even now: *To this day we don't know what really happened.* **10** the other day *spoken* a few days ago: *I saw Roy the other day.* **11** make someone's day *informal* to make someone very happy: *That card really made my day.* **12** have had its day to no longer be popular or successful: *I think the royal family*

has had its day. **13** day after day/day in day out used to emphasize that something boring or unpleasant continues to happen: *I'm sick of sitting at the same desk day after day.* **14** day by day slowly and gradually: *She was getting stronger day by day.* → see also DAILY, DAYS

USAGE NOTE: talking about days

Use **on** to talk about a particular day in the week: *It's her birthday on Friday.* If you are talking about a day in the week before this one, use **last**: *I had lunch with Barry last Monday.* Use **next** with the name of a day in the week after this one: *See you next Thursday!* Don't say 'on next Thursday'. Only use **the** in front of the name of a day if you are talking about a particular day of a particular week: *We're going on vacation on the Monday after Christmas.*

day·break /'deɪbreɪk/ *n* [U] the time of day when light first appears: *We set off at daybreak.*

day·care /'deɪkeə‖-ker/ *n* [U] *AmE* care of young children while their parents are at work: *Earning just $100 a week, she can't afford daycare.*

daycare cen·ter /'.. ,../ *n* [C] *AmE* a place where babies are looked after while their parents are at work; CRECHE *BrE*

daycare cen·tre /'.. ,../ *n* [C] *BrE* a place where people who are old or ill can be looked after during the day

day·dream¹ /'deɪdriːm/ *v* [I] to think about pleasant things so that you forget what you should be doing: *Jessica sat at her desk, daydreaming about Tom.* —daydreamer *n* [C]

daydream² *n* [C] pleasant thoughts you have while you are awake, that make you forget what you should be doing

day·light /'deɪlaɪt/ *n* [U] the light produced by the sun during the day: *The children could see daylight through a small window in the roof.* | in broad daylight (=during the day when everyone can see) *The young girl was attacked on a main road in broad daylight.*

day·lights /'deɪlaɪts/ *n* [plural] *informal* **1** scare/frighten the living daylights out of sb *informal* to frighten someone a lot **2** beat the living daylights out of sb to hit someone many times and hurt them badly

day re·turn /, . .'. ./ *n* [C] *BrE* a train or bus ticket for travelling somewhere and returning on the same day: *a day return to Oxford*

days /deɪz/ *n literary* **1** sb's days the time when someone is alive: *He went home to Iowa to end his days in peace.* **2** a period in time or in the past: these days (=now) *Kids are much more relaxed with their parents these days.* | the old/olden days (=in the past) *In the old days we had to wash in freezing cold water.*

day·time /'deɪtaɪm/ *n* [U] the period between the time it gets light in the morning and the time it gets dark in the evening

day-to-day /, . .'. ./ *adj* [only before noun] happening every day as a regular part of your life: *our day-to-day routine*

daze /deɪz/ *n* in a daze unable to think clearly: *He wandered around in a daze.*

dazed /deɪzd/ *adj* unable to think clearly, usually because you are shocked or have been in an accident: *The news left him feeling dazed.*

daz·zle /'dæzəl/ *v* [T] **1** if a strong light dazzles you, it is so strong that you cannot see for a short time **2** if someone or something dazzles you, you think they are very impressive: *They were clearly dazzled by her talent and charm.*

daz·zling /'dæzəlɪŋ/ *adj* **1** a dazzling light is so bright that you cannot see for a short time after you look at it **2** very impressive, exciting, or interesting: *a dazzling performance*

de- /di:, dɪ/ *prefix* used at the beginning of some words to mean to remove something or make it less: *decaffeinated coffee* (=coffee which has had the caffeine removed)| *devalue* (=make the value of something less, especially a country's money)

dea·con /'di:kən/ *n* [C] an official in some Christian churches

dea·con·ess /'di:kənəs/ *n* [C] a female official in some Christian churches

dead[1] /ded/ *adj* **1** no longer alive: *Her mother's been dead for two years.*| *I think that plant's dead.* **2** an engine, telephone etc that is dead is not working because there is no power: *Is the battery dead?*| **go dead** *The phones went dead in the storm.* **3** a place that is dead does not have anything interesting happening in it: *The bar is usually dead until about 10 o'clock.* **4** a part of your body that is dead has no feeling in it for a short time: **go dead** *I'd been sitting down for so long my leg went dead.* **5 over my dead body** *spoken* used when you are determined not to allow something to happen: *You'll marry him over my dead body!* **6** complete or exact: *We all stood waiting in dead silence.*| *in the dead centre of the circle* **7** a dead language is no longer used by people

---

USAGE NOTE: dead and died

Use **dead** to talk about things or people who are no longer alive: *I think this plant's dead.* | *He's been dead for 20 years.* **Died** is the past tense and past participle of the verb 'to die': *She died of a heart attack.*

---

dead[2] *adv informal* **1** completely: **dead tired** *I've been dead tired all day.*| **stop dead** *She stopped dead when she saw us.* **2** directly or exactly: *You can't miss it – it's dead ahead at the lights.*| **dead on time/midnight/3 o'clock etc** *The plane landed dead on time.* **3** *BrE spoken* very or extremely: *Who was that boy you were with last night? He was dead good-looking.*

dead[3] *n* **1 the dead** people who are dead **2 in the dead of night/winter** in the middle of the night or of winter

dead·en /'dedn/ *v* [T] to make a feeling or sound less strong: *drugs to deaden the pain*

dead end /ˌ. '.∢/ *n* [C] **1** a street with no way out at one end **2** a situation from which no progress is possible

dead heat /ˌ. './ *n* [C] the result of a race in which two people finish at exactly the same time

dead·line /'dedlaɪn/ *n* [C] a date or time by which you must finish something: *Friday's deadline is going to be very difficult to meet.*

dead·lock /'dedlɒk‖-lɑːk/ *n* [singular, U] when people, organizations, or countries cannot agree:

break the deadlock (=end it): *The UN is trying to break the deadlock between the two countries.*

dead·ly[1] /'dedli/ *adj* very dangerous and likely to cause death: *deadly weapons*

deadly[2] *adv* **deadly serious/boring/dull etc** very serious, boring etc: *I'm deadly serious. This isn't a game!*

dead·pan /'dedpæn/ *adj* sounding and looking completely serious when you are not

deaf[1] /def/ *adj* **1** unable to hear: *I'm deaf in my right ear.* **2 the deaf** people who are deaf **3 deaf to sth** unwilling to listen to something: *The guards were deaf to the prisoners' complaints.* —**deafness** *n* [U]

deaf·en /'defən/ *v* [T] to make it difficult for you to hear anything: *We were deafened by the noise of the engines.* —**deafening** *adj: deafening music*

deal[1] /di:l/ *n* **1** [C] an agreement or arrangement, especially in business or politics: *They've just signed a new deal with their record company.*| **strike/do/make a deal** *Carter agreed to do a deal with the police.* **2 get a good deal** to buy something at a cheap or fair price: *You can get some good deals on flights to Florida.* **3 a great/good deal** a large quantity of something: **+ of** *She does a great deal of work for charity.*| **a great deal more/less/longer etc** *He knows a good deal more than I do about computers.* **4** [C usually singular] the way someone is treated in a situation: **a raw deal** (=unfair treatment): *Women often get a raw deal from their employers.* ➤ see also **big deal** (BIG)

deal[2] *v* [I,T] dealt, dealt, dealing **1** also **deal out** to give out playing cards to players in a game: *Whose turn is it to deal?* **2** to buy and sell illegal drugs: *He had started to deal to pay for his own drug habit.* **3 deal a blow (to sb)** to harm or shock someone: *The party has been dealt another blow by the latest scandals.* —**dealing** *n* [U]

deal in sth *phr v* [T] to buy and sell a particular type of product: *a business dealing in wedding requirements*

deal with sb/sth *phr v* [T] **1** to take the correct action to find an answer to a problem or complete a piece of work: *Who's dealing with the new account?* **2** to do business with a company or person: *We've been dealing with their company for ten years.* **3** to be about a particular subject: *a book dealing with the history of Ireland*

deal·er /'di:lə‖-ər/ *n* [C] **1** someone who buys and sells a particular product: *a car dealer* **2** the person who gives out the cards in a card game

deal·er·ship /'di:ləʃɪp‖-ər-/ *n* [C] a business that sells the products of a particular company, especially cars: *a Ford dealership*

deal·ings /'di:lɪŋz/ *n* [plural] personal or business relations with someone: **+ with** *Have you had any dealings with Microsoft?*

dean /di:n/ *n* [C] **1** an official with a high rank in some universities: *Dean of Arts* **2** a priest with a high rank in the Anglican church

dear[1] /dɪə‖dɪr/ *interjection* **oh dear** used when you are disappointed, annoyed, or upset: *Oh dear! I forgot to phone Ben.*

dear[2] *n* [C] *spoken* used to address someone you like or love: *How was your day, dear?*

D

dear³ *adj* **1** used before a name at the beginning of a letter: *Dear Dr. Ward, ...* **2** *BrE* expensive: *I'd love to buy it but it's too dear.* **3** used to show that you like someone or something: **dear old/little** *dear old Aunt Agatha* **4** **be dear to you/your heart** if something is dear to you, it is important to you and you care about it a lot: *Money was a subject that was dear to his heart.*

dear·ly /'dɪəlɪ‖'dɪrli/ *adv* very much: *Jamie loved his sister dearly.* | *I'd dearly love to go to Hawaii.*

dearth /dɜːθ‖dɜːrθ/ *n* [singular] *formal* a lack of something: + **of** *a dearth of trained staff*

death /deθ/ *n* **1** [C,U] the end of someone's life: *Marioni lived in Miami until his death.* | *The number of deaths from AIDS is increasing.* | **starve/bleed etc to death** (=die in this way) *He choked to death on a fish bone.* **2** **scared/bored/worried etc to death** *informal* very frightened, bored, worried **3** [singular] the end of something: *the death of Communism* **4** **put sb to death** to kill someone, usually as a punishment: *Fifty villagers were put to death.*

death·bed /'deθbed/ *n* **on his/her deathbed** when someone is dying

death·ly /'deθli/ *adj* extreme in an unpleasant, worrying, or shocking way: **deathly silence/hush/quiet etc** (=completely silent), in a way that makes you a little frightened): *A deathly silence fell on the room.* | **deathly pale/cold** (=extremely pale or cold)

death pen·al·ty /'. ,.../ *n* [C] when someone is killed as a legal punishment for a crime → compare CAPITAL PUNISHMENT

death row /,deθ 'rəʊl‖-'roʊ/ *n* [U] the part of a prison where prisoners are kept waiting to be killed as a punishment: *He's been on death row for three years.*

death trap /'. ./ *n* [C] *informal* a vehicle or building that is in such a bad condition that it is dangerous

de·base /dɪ'beɪs/ *v* [T] *formal* to reduce the quality or value of something: *a society debased by corruption* —**debasement** *n* [C,U]

de·ba·ta·ble /dɪ'beɪtəbəl/ *adj* an idea, fact, or decision that is debatable may be right but it could easily be wrong: *It is debatable whether nuclear weapons actually prevent war.*

de·bate¹ /dɪ'beɪt/ *n* **1** [C] an organized discussion on an important subject: *a debate on crime and punishment* **2** [U] the process of discussing a subject or question: *After much debate, the committee decided to close the hospital.*

debate² *v* **1** [I,T] to discuss a subject formally so that you can make a decision or solve a problem: *The plan has been thoroughly debated in Parliament.* **2** [T] to think about whether or not to do something: *While I was debating whether or not to call him, the phone rang.*

de·bauched /dɪ'bɔːtʃt‖-'bɔːtʃt,-'bɑːtʃt/ *adj* behaving in an immoral way —**debauchery** *n* [U]

de·bil·i·tat·ing /dɪ'bɪlɪteɪtɪŋ/ *adj formal* a debilitating illness, problem etc has a very serious effect on someone making them weak

deb·it¹ /'debɪt/ *n* [C] an amount of money that you take out of your bank account → opposite CREDIT¹

debit² *v* [T] to take money out of a bank account: *The sum of £50 has been debited from your account.* → opposite CREDIT²

deb·o·nair /,debə'neə‖-'ner/ *adj* a man who is debonair is fashionable and confident

de·brief /,diː'briːf/ *v* [T] to ask someone questions in order to get information about a job they have just done for you → opposite BRIEF³ —**debriefing** *n* [C,U]

deb·ris /'debriː, 'deɪ-‖dəˈbriː, deɪ-/ *n* [U] the pieces of something that are left after the rest has been destroyed: *debris from the explosion*

debt /det/ *n* **1** [C] money that you owe to someone: *He finally has enough money to pay off his debts.* **2** [U] when you owe money to someone: **in debt** *The company was heavily in debt.* **3** [singular] a feeling of being grateful to someone who has helped you or done something for you: **be in sb's debt** *I'll be forever in your debt for the way you've supported me.*

debt·or /'detə‖-ər/ *n* [C] someone who owes money

de·but /'deɪbjuː, 'debjuː‖deɪ'bjuː, dɪ-/ *n* [C] the first time that a performer or sports player performs in public: *the band's debut album*

dec·ade /'dekeɪd, de'keɪd/ *n* [C] a period of ten years

dec·a·dent /'dekədənt/ *adj* having low moral standards and being more interested in pleasure than anything else —**decadence** *n* [U]

de·caf /'diːkæf/ *n* [C,U] decaffeinated coffee

de·caf·fein·a·ted /diː'kæfɪneɪtɪd/ *adj* a drink that is decaffeinated has had the CAFFEINE removed

de·cay¹ /dɪ'keɪ/ *n* [U] when something decays: *Brushing your teeth regularly protects against decay.* | *The building has fallen into decay.*

decay² *v* **1** [I,T] to be slowly destroyed, usually by natural processes: *the decaying remains of a dead sheep* **2** [I] to become weaker or less important: *a feudal system which had decayed but not died* —**decayed** *adj*

de·ceased /dɪ'siːst/ *n formal* **the deceased** someone who has died —**deceased** *adj*

de·ceit /dɪ'siːt/ *n* [U] when someone tries to make people believe something that is not true: *The government had a history of deceit.* —**deceitful** *adj*

de·ceive /dɪ'siːv/ *v* [T] to make someone believe something that is not true: *Campbell tried to deceive the police.*

De·cem·ber /dɪ'sembə‖-ər/ *written abbreviation* **Dec** *n* [C,U] the twelfth month of the year

de·cen·cy /'diːsənsi/ *n* [U] **1** morally correct behaviour: *old-fashioned notions of courtesy and decency* **2** **have the decency to do sth** to do something that you should do: *You could at least have had the decency to tell me that you would be late.*

de·cent /'diːsənt/ *adj* **1** good enough or fairly good: *a decent salary* | *Don't you have a decent pair of shoes?* **2** honest and good: *Her parents are decent hard-working people.* **3** not showing too much of your body: *Don't come in, I'm not decent!* —**decently** *adv*

de·cen·tral·ize (also **-ise** *BrE*) /,diː'sentrəlaɪz/ *v* [T] to change a government or organization so that decisions are made in a lot of different places, instead of only one place —**decentralization** /diːˌsentrəlaɪˈzeɪʃən‖-lə-/ n [U]

de·cep·tion /dɪˈsepʃən/ n [C,U] when someone deliberately makes another person believe something that is not true: *They obtained the money by deception.*

de·cep·tive /dɪˈseptɪv/ adj something that is deceptive seems very different from how it really is: *She seems very calm, but appearances can be deceptive.* —**deceptively** adj

dec·i·bel /ˈdesɪˌbel,-bəl/ n [C] a unit for measuring how loud a sound is

de·cide /dɪˈsaɪd/ v **1** [I,T] to make a choice or judgement about something: **decide to do sth** *They decided to sell the house.* | **+ (that)** *She decided that the dress was too expensive.* | **+ what/how/when** etc *Have you decided when you're going to get married?* | **decide against sth** (=decide not to do something): *Marlowe thought about using his gun, but decided against it.* **2 deciding factor** the reason you finally make a particular decision: *Firman's testimony was the deciding factor in the case.* **3** [T] to be the reason why something has a particular result: *One punch decided the fight.*
decide on sth *phr v* [T] to choose one thing from among many: *Have you decided on a name for the baby?*

de·cid·ed·ly /dɪˈsaɪdɪdli/ adv very much, in a way that is easy to notice: *Her boss was decidedly unsympathetic.*

de·cid·u·ous /dɪˈsɪdʒuəs/ adj deciduous trees have leaves that fall off in autumn →compare EVERGREEN

dec·i·mal¹ /ˈdesɪˌməl/ adj based on the number ten: *the decimal system*

decimal² n [C] a number, for example 0.1 or 0.25, which is less than one and is shown by a mark (.) followed by the number of TENTHS, then HUNDREDTHS etc

decimal point /ˌ... './ n [C] the mark (.) in a decimal

dec·i·mate /ˈdesɪˌmeɪt/ v [T] *formal* to destroy a large part of something: *The population has been decimated by war.*

de·ci·pher /dɪˈsaɪfəl-ər/ v [T] to find the meaning of something that is difficult to read or understand

de·ci·sion /dɪˈsɪʒən/ n [C] a choice or judgement that you make: **make/take/reach/come to a decision** *I hope I've made the right decision.* | *The jury took three days to reach a decision.* | **decision to do sth** *Brett's sudden decision to join the army surprised everyone.*

de·ci·sive /dɪˈsaɪsɪv/ adj **1** having an important effect on the result of something: *a decisive moment in his career* **2** good at making decisions quickly and clearly: *a strong, decisive leader* **3** a decisive victory, result etc is very definite and clear: *The US team won a decisive victory.* —**decisively** adv —**decisiveness** n [U]

deck¹ /dek/ n [C] **1 a)** the flat top part of a ship, that you can walk on: *Let's go up on deck.*

b) one of the levels on a ship, plane, or bus: *the lower deck* **2** *AmE* a set of playing cards; PACK *BrE*

deck² v
deck sth/sb ↔ out *phr v* [T] to put decorations or special clothes on something or someone: *The street was decked out with flags.*

deck·chair /ˈdektʃeəl-tʃer/ n [C] a folding chair with a long seat made of cloth →see picture at CHAIR

dec·la·ra·tion /ˌdekləˈreɪʃən/ n [C,U] an official statement about something: *a declaration of war*

de·clare /dɪˈkleəl-ˈkler/ v [T] **1** to say officially and publicly that something is happening or that something is true: *Jones was declared the winner.* | *The US declared war on Britain in 1812.* **2** to say clearly and publicly what you think or feel: **+ that** *Jack declared that he knew nothing about the robbery.* **3** to state the value of things that you have bought or own, because you may have to pay tax on them

de·cline¹ /dɪˈklaɪn/ v **1** [I] to become weaker, smaller, less important, or less good: *As his health has declined, so has his influence.* **2** [I,T] *formal* to refuse something, usually politely: *We asked them to come, but they declined our invitation.*

decline² n [C,U] when something declines: *a decline in profits* | **be on the decline** (=be declining)

de·code /ˌdiːˈkəʊd‖-ˈkoʊd/ v [T] to discover the meaning of a secret or complicated message

de·com·pose /ˌdiːkəmˈpəʊz‖-ˈpoʊz/ v [I] to be slowly destroyed by a natural process: *The body had already started to decompose.*

de·cor /ˈdeɪkɔːl-kɔːr/ n [C,U] the way that a room or the inside of a building looks, and the kind of furniture, CARPETS etc that are in it: *The hotel has 1930's decor.*

decorate

dec·o·rate /ˈdekəreɪt/ v [T] **1** to make something look more attractive by adding things to it: **decorate sth with sth** *The cake was decorated with icing.* **2** to paint or put paper onto the walls of a room or building: *I spent the weekend decorating the bathroom.* **3** to give someone a MEDAL to officially honour them: *He was decorated for bravery in the war.*

dec·o·ra·tion /ˌdekəˈreɪʃən/ n **1** [C] something that you add in order to make something look more attractive: *Christmas decorations*

D

---

2 [U] the activity of decorating something: *The berries are mainly used for decoration.* **3** [C] a MEDAL that is given to someone to officially honour them

dec·o·ra·tive /ˈdekərətɪv‖ˈdekərə-, ˈdekəreɪ-/ *adj* pretty and used as a decoration: *a decorative pot* —**decoratively** *adv*

dec·o·ra·tor /ˈdekəreɪtəll-ər/ *n* [C] *BrE* someone whose job is to decorate buildings

de·co·rum /dɪˈkɔːrəm/ *n* [U] *formal* behaviour that is polite and suitable for a particular occasion

de·coy /ˈdiːkɔɪ/ *n* [C] something that is used to lead a person or animal into a trap —**decoy** /dɪˈkɔɪ/ *v* [T]

de·crease /dɪˈkriːs/ *v* [I,T] to become less, or to make something do this: *The number of people who smoke has continued to decrease.* → opposite INCREASE[1] —**decrease** /ˈdiːkriːs/ *n* [C,U] *a decrease in sales*

de·cree /dɪˈkriː/ *n* [C] an official order or decision —**decree** *v* [T]

de·crep·it /dɪˈkrepɪt/ *adj* old and in bad condition: *a decrepit old car*

de·crim·in·a·lize (also **-ise** *BrE*) /diːˈkrɪmɪnəlaɪz/ *v* [T] to change the law so that something is not illegal any more —**decriminalization** /ˌdiːkrɪmɪnəlaɪˈzeɪʃənll-lə-/ *n* [U]

ded·i·cate /ˈdedɪkeɪt/ *v* [T] **1** to say that a book, film, song etc has been written or made for someone, to show that you respect or love them: *The book is dedicated to his mother.* **2** **dedicate yourself/your life to sth** to spend all your time trying to do something: *She dedicated her life to helping the poor.*

ded·i·cat·ed /ˈdedɪkeɪtɪd/ *adj* working very hard at doing something because you think it is important: *The teachers are all very dedicated.*

ded·i·ca·tion /ˌdedɪˈkeɪʃən/ *n* **1** [U] when you work very hard because you believe that what you are doing is important: *Getting to the top of any sport requires tremendous dedication.* **2** [U] when something is given in someone's name in order to honour them: *a dedication ceremony* **3** [C] the words used when dedicating a book to someone

de·duce /dɪˈdjuːsll·ˈduːs/ *v* [T] *formal* to decide that something is true using the information that you have

de·duct /dɪˈdʌkt/ *v* [T] to take away an amount from a total: *Taxes are deducted from your pay.* —**deductible** *adj*

de·duc·tion /dɪˈdʌkʃən/ *n* **1** [C] an amount that is taken away from a total: *My salary is about $2000 a month, after deductions.* **2** [C,U] when you decide that something is likely to be true, using the information that you have: *his formidable powers of deduction*

deed /diːd/ *n* [C] **1** *literary* something that someone does: *good deeds* **2** *law* an official document which shows that something has been agreed, especially one showing that someone owns something

deem /diːm/ *v* [T] *formal* to decide officially that something is true: *The judge deemed several of the questions inappropriate.*

deep[1] /diːp/ *adj* **1** if something is deep, there is a long distance from the surface to the bottom: *The water's not very deep.* | *Terry had a deep cut*

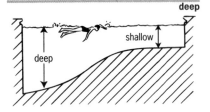

deep

shallow

deep

in his forehead. **2** a deep feeling or belief is felt very strongly: *a deep love of classical music* **3** a deep sound or voice is very low **4** a deep colour is dark and strong **5** if something is 2cm, 4 metres etc deep, it measures 2cm, 4 metres etc from the surface to the bottom: *The pool was 5 metres deep.* **6** serious and often difficult to understand: *a deep novel* **7** **deep sleep** if someone is in a deep sleep, it is difficult to wake them up **8** **take a deep breath** to breathe a lot of air into your lungs, especially before doing something difficult or frightening: *I took a deep breath and walked into the director's office.* **9** **deep in debt** owing a lot of money **10** **deep in thought/conversation** thinking so hard or talking so much that you do not notice anything else → see also DEPTH

deep[2] *adv* **1** far into something: *Leopards live deep in the jungle.* **2** **deep down a)** if you feel or know something deep down, you are sure about it: *Deep down, I knew she was right.* **b)** if someone is kind, cruel etc deep down, that is what they are really like, even though they seem not to be **3** **run/go deep** if a feeling runs or goes deep, people feel it very strongly: *Resentment against the police in this area runs deep.* **4** **two/three etc deep** rows or layers of two, three etc people or things

deep·en /ˈdiːpən/ *v* [I,T] to become worse, or make something become worse: *The crisis deepened.*

deep fried /ˌ. ˈ. ◂/ *adj* cooked in a lot of hot oil

deep·ly /ˈdiːpli/ *adv* extremely or very much: *She was deeply upset.*

deep-seat·ed, deep-rooted /ˌ. ˈ. ◂/ *adj* a deep-seated feeling or idea is strong and very difficult to change

deer /dɪəll·dɪr/ *n* [C] a large wild animal that lives in forests, some of which has long horns that look like tree branches

de·face /dɪˈfeɪs/ *v* [T] to spoil the appearance of something by writing or making marks on it: *The gravestone had been defaced by vandals.*

de·fault[1] /dɪˈfɔːltll·ˈfɔːlt/ *v* [I] to not do something that you have legally agreed to do: **+ on** *He defaulted on his loan payments.*

default[2] *n* **by default** if something happens by default, it happens because something else fails to happen: *The other team never arrived, so we won by default.*

default[3] *adj* [only before noun] the default way of doing something is the usual way of doing it unless you decide to change it: *The default page size is A4.*

de·feat[1] /dɪˈfiːt/ *v* [T] **1** to win a game, battle, or election against someone; BEAT: *Michigan defeated USC in Saturday's game.* **2** to make something or someone fail: *The plan was defeated by a lack of money.*

defeat² *n* **1** [C,U] when someone loses a game, battle, or election: *Becker suffered a surprising defeat.* | *She'll never admit defeat.* **2** [singular] victory over someone or something: *the defeat of fascism*

de·feat·ist / dɪˈfiːtɪst / *adj* behaving in a way that shows you expect to fail: *defeatist attitudes* —**defeatism** *n* [U] —**defeatist** *n* [C]

de·fect¹ / ˈdiːfekt, dɪˈfekt / *n* [C] a fault in the way something is made or the way it works: *There is a defect in the braking system.* —**defective** / dɪˈfektɪv / *adj*: *defective machinery*

de·fect² / dɪˈfekt / *v* [I] to leave your own country or organization and go to an enemy country or organization —**defector** *n* [C] —**defection** / -ˈfekʃən / *n* [C,U]

de·fence *BrE*, **defense** *AmE* / dɪˈfens / *n* **1** [U] the weapons, soldiers etc that a country uses to protect itself from attack: *Each year the US spends billions of dollars on defense.* **2** [C,U] something that you do or say to protect someone or something from being attacked or criticized: *the defence of Stalingrad in World War Two* | **come to sb's defence** *The famous writer Emile Zola came to Dreyfus's defence.* **3** [singular] the people in a court who try to show that someone is not guilty of a crime: *Is the defence ready to call their first witness?* **4** [singular] something that you say to show that you are not guilty of a crime or of doing something wrong: *Her defence was that she had not intended to kill him.* **5** [C,U] the players in a game such as football who try to stop the other team from getting points

de·fence·less *BrE*, **defenseless** *AmE* / dɪˈfensləs / *adj* unable to protect yourself: *a defenceless old woman*

de·fend / dɪˈfend / *v* **1** [T] to protect someone or something from being attacked: **defend sth against/from** *Missiles were brought in to defend the town from possible attack.* | **defend yourself** *He said he used the knife to defend himself.* **2** [T] to protect something or someone from criticism: *How can you defend the use of animals for testing cosmetics?* **3** [I,T] to try to prevent another team's players from getting goals **4** [T] to try to win a sports competition again, so that you remain CHAMPION: *Germany are defending World Cup champions.* **5** [T] to be the lawyer who tries to show in court that someone is not guilty of a crime —**defender** *n* [C]

de·fen·dant / dɪˈfendənt / *n* [C] *law* the person in a court who has been ACCUSED of a crime

de·fense¹ / dɪˈfens / the American spelling of DEFENCE

de·fense² / ˈdiːfens / *n* [C,U] *AmE* the players in a game such as football who try to stop the other team from getting points

de·fense·less / dɪˈfensləs / the American spelling of DEFENCELESS

de·fen·sive¹ / dɪˈfensɪv / *adj* **1** used for protection against attack: *defensive weapons* **2** behaving in a way that shows you think someone is criticizing you: *She got really defensive when I asked her why she hadn't finished.* —**defensively** *adv* —**defensiveness** *n* [U]

defensive² *n* **on the defensive** ready to defend yourself because someone is criticizing or attacking you: *The President's speech has put the Republicans on the defensive.*

de·fer / dɪˈfɜːll-ˈfɜːr / *v* -**rred**, -**rring** [T] to officially delay something until a later date: *His military service was deferred until he finished college.*

def·er·ence / ˈdefərəns / *n* [U] *formal* behaviour that shows that you respect someone and think that they know more than you or they are more important than you —**deferential** / ˌdefəˈrenʃəl◂ / *adj*

de·fi·ance / dɪˈfaɪəns / *n* [U] when you refuse to obey someone in authority or a rule, law etc

de·fi·ant / dɪˈfaɪənt / *adj* refusing to obey someone in authority or a rule, law etc —**defiantly** *adv*

de·fi·cien·cy / dɪˈfɪʃənsi / *n* [C,U] **1** a lack of something: *a vitamin deficiency* **2** a fault that makes something not good enough: *the deficiencies of the public transportation system*

de·fi·cient / dɪˈfɪʃənt / *adj* **1** something that is deficient in a particular thing does not have enough of it: *a diet that is deficient in iron* **2** not good enough

def·i·cit / ˈdefɪsɪt / *n* [C] the amount by which the money that a company or country receives is less than the money that it spends

de·file / dɪˈfaɪl / *v* [T] *formal* to do something which spoils a pure or holy thing: *graves defiled by racist graffiti* —**defilement** *n* [U]

de·fine / dɪˈfaɪn / *v* [T] **1** to say exactly what something means or describe exactly what something is like: *It's hard to define what makes a good manager.* **2** to clearly show the limits or shape of something: *a clearly defined budget*

def·i·nite / ˈdefɪnɪt, ˈdefənɪt / *adj* **1** completely certain and not likely to be changed: *We don't have a definite arrangement yet.* **2** very clear and easy to notice: *She shows definite signs of improvement.*

definite ar·ti·cle / ˌ... ˈ... / *n* [singular] a phrase used in grammar meaning 'the' → compare INDEFINITE ARTICLE

def·i·nite·ly / ˈdefɪnɪtli, ˈdefənɪtli / *adv* certainly and without any doubt: *That was definitely the best movie I've seen all year.*

def·i·ni·tion / ˌdefɪˈnɪʃən / *n* [C] a phrase or sentence that says exactly what a word, phrase, or idea means

de·fin·i·tive / dɪˈfɪnɪtɪv / *adj* **1** the definitive book, film etc about something is the one that is thought to be the best and cannot be improved **2** a definitive statement, answer etc is certain and will not be changed: *There is no definitive answer to the problem.* —**definitively** *adv*

de·flate / ˌdiːˈfleɪt, dɪ- / *v* **1** [T] to make someone feel less important or confident **2** [I,T] if something deflates, or if you deflate it, the air or gas inside it comes out —**deflated** *adj*: *He looked somewhat deflated by the news.*

de·flect / dɪˈflekt / *v* **1** [I,T] to make something turn in a different direction, or to be turned in this way: *The bullet deflected off the wall.* **2 deflect criticism/anger etc** to stop people criticizing someone or something, being angry etc —**deflection** / -ˈflekʃən / *n* [C,U]

de·for·es·ta·tion / diːˌfɒrɪˈsteɪʃənll-ˌfɔːr-,-ˌfɑː- / *n* [singular,U] when all the trees in an area are cut down or destroyed

de·formed /dɪ'fɔːmdǁ-ɔːrmd/ *adj* something that is deformed has the wrong shape, especially because it has grown or developed wrongly: *Her left leg was deformed.* —**deform** *v* [I,T]

de·for·mi·ty /dɪ'fɔːmɪtiǁ-ɔːr-/ *n* [C,U] when part of someone's body is not the normal shape

de·fraud /dɪ'frɔːdǁ-'frɒːd/ *v* [T] to get money from a company or organization dishonestly: *He attempted to defraud the bank of thousands of dollars.*

de·frost /ˌdiː'frɒstǁ-'frɒːst/ *v* [I,T] **1** if frozen food defrosts, or if you defrost it, it becomes warmer and stops being frozen **2** if a FREEZER or REFRIGERATOR defrosts, or if you defrost it, it is turned off so that the ice inside it melts

deft /deft/ *adj* quick and skilful: *a deft catch* —**deftly** *adv*

de·funct /dɪ'fʌŋkt/ *adj* not existing any more, or not working any more: *the now defunct Bureau of State Security*

de·fuse /ˌdiː'fjuːz/ *v* [T] **1** to stop a bomb from exploding by removing the FUSE **2** to make people calmer in an worrying or dangerous situation: *Tim tried to defuse the tension.*

de·fy /dɪ'faɪ/ *v* [T] **1** to refuse to obey someone or something: *He defied his father's wishes and joined the army.* **2 defy description/belief/ logic etc** to be impossible to describe, believe, explain etc: *The place just defies description.*

de·gen·e·rate¹ /dɪ'dʒenəreɪt/ *v* [I] to become worse: *The party soon degenerated into a drunken brawl.* —**degeneration** /dɪ,dʒenə'reɪʃən/ *n* [U]

de·gen·e·rate² /dɪ'dʒenərɪt/ *adj* having very low moral standards —**degenerate** *n* [C]

de·grade /dɪ'greɪd/ *v* [T] if something degrades someone, it makes people lose their respect for that person: *Pornography degrades women.* —**degrading** *adj* —**degradation** /ˌdegrə'deɪʃən/ *n* [U]

de·gree /dɪ'griː/ *n* [C] **1** a unit for measuring temperature **2** a course at a university, or the QUALIFICATION given to someone who has successfully finished the course: *a law degree* | *a degree in history* **3** the level or amount of something: *students with different degrees of ability* | *The operation involves a high degree of risk.* **4 to a degree/to a certain degree/to some degree** used to say that something is partly true: *To a degree he's right.*

de·hy·drat·ed /ˌdiːhaɪ'dreɪtɪdǁdiː'haɪdreɪ-/ *adj* ill or weak because you do not have enough water in your body —**dehydrate** *v* [I,U] —**dehydration** /ˌdiːhaɪ'dreɪʃən/ *n* [U]

de·i·ty /'diːɪti, 'deɪ-/ *n* [C] a god or GODDESS

dé·jà vu /ˌdeɪʒɑː 'vjuː/ *n* [U] the feeling that what is happening now has happened before

de·ject·ed /dɪ'dʒektɪd/ *adj* sad and disappointed: *a dejected look* —**dejectedly** *adv* —**dejection** /-'dʒekʃən/ *n* [U]

de·lay¹ /dɪ'leɪ/ *v* **1** [I,T] to wait until a later time to do something: *We've decided to delay the trip until next month.* **2** [T] to make someone or something late: *Our flight was delayed by bad weather.*

delay² *n* [C,U] a situation in which someone or something is made to wait, or the length of the waiting time: *An accident is causing long delays on Route 95.*

de·lec·ta·ble /dɪ'lektəbəl/ *adj formal* very pleasant, especially to taste: *delectable handmade chocolates*

del·e·gate¹ /'delɪgɪt/ *n* [C] someone chosen by a group or organization to do something for the whole group, such as speak or vote for them at a meeting

del·e·gate² /'delɪgeɪt/ *v* [I,T] to give part of your work or responsibilities to someone in a lower position than you: *You must learn to delegate more.*

del·e·ga·tion /ˌdelɪ'geɪʃən/ *n* **1** [C] a small group of people that a group or organization sends to a meeting to explain their opinions, vote for them etc: *A UN delegation was sent to the peace talks.* **2** [U] the process of giving someone part of your work, power, responsibilities etc: *the delegation of authority*

de·lete /dɪ'liːt/ *v* [T] to remove a letter, word etc from a piece of writing or from a computer's MEMORY —**deletion** /-'liːʃən/ *n* [C,U]

de·lib·e·rate¹ /dɪ'lɪbərɪt/ *adj* **1** intended or planned, and not happening accidentally: *a deliberate attempt to deceive the public* **2** slow and careful: *His steps were slow and deliberate.*

de·lib·e·rate² /dɪ'lɪbəreɪt/ *v* [I,T] to think about something carefully, before making an important decision: *The jury deliberated for 3 days before finding them guilty.*

de·lib·er·ate·ly /dɪ'lɪbərɪtli/ *adv* if you do something deliberately, you do it because you intend or want to do it: *The police think the fire was started deliberately.* ➔ opposite ACCIDENTALLY

de·lib·e·ra·tion /dɪ,lɪbə'reɪʃən/ *n* [C,U] careful thought or discussion about a problem: *The committee will finish its deliberations today.*

del·i·ca·cy /'delɪkəsi/ *n* **1** [U] the quality of being delicate: *the delicacy of the petals* | *a situation that needs to be handled with great delicacy* **2** [C] a rare or expensive kind of food, thought to be especially nice to eat: *In France, snails are considered a delicacy.*

del·i·cate /'delɪkɪt/ *adj* **1** something that is delicate is easily damaged or broken: *a delicate piece of lace* **2** a delicate situation needs to be dealt with very carefully: *The negotiations are at a very delicate stage.* **3** delicate hands, fingers etc are attractive and graceful: *long delicate fingers* **4** someone who is delicate becomes ill very easily: *a delicate child* **5** a delicate colour, taste, or smell is pleasant and not very bright or strong: *a delicate shade of pink* —**delicately** *adv*

del·i·ca·tes·sen /ˌdelɪkə'tesən/ *n* [C] a small shop that sells cheese, cooked meat, SALADS, bread etc

de·li·cious /dɪ'lɪʃəs/ *adj* delicious food tastes very good

de·light¹ /dɪ'laɪt/ *n* **1** [U] the feeling you have when you are very pleased and excited: *Krystal laughed with delight.* **2** [C] something that makes you happy or satisfied: *the delights of owning your own home*

delight² *v* [T] to give someone a feeling of pleasure and enjoyment: *She delighted her fans with her performance.*

delight in sth *phr v* [T] to enjoy something very much: *She delights in shocking people.*

de·light·ed /dɪˈlaɪtˌɪd/ *adj* very pleased and excited about something: **be delighted to do sth** *Thank you for your invitation. I'd be delighted to come.* | **+ with/by** *Helen was clearly delighted with her presents.*

de·light·ful /dɪˈlaɪtfəl/ *adj* very nice or enjoyable: *a delightful book for children*

de·lin·quen·cy /dɪˈlɪŋkwənsi/ *n* [U] *formal* criminal behaviour, especially by young people ➡ see also JUVENILE DELINQUENT — **delinquent** *adj*

de·lir·i·ous /dɪˈlɪriəs/ *adj* **1** confused and unable to think clearly because you are very ill **2** *literary* extremely happy and excited: *She was delirious with joy.* — **deliriously** *adv*

de·liv·er /dɪˈlɪvəl-ər/ *v* **1** [I,T] to take something such as a letter or a package to a place: *I used to deliver newspapers when I was a kid.* | *I'm having some flowers delivered for her birthday.* **2** [T] to make a speech: *The priest delivered a sermon about forgiveness.* **3** [I,T] to do the things that you have promised: **+ on** *Voters are angry that politicians haven't delivered on their promises.* | **deliver the goods** (=do what you have said you will do) **4 deliver a baby** to help a mother with the birth of her baby

de·liv·er·y /dɪˈlɪvəri/ *n* [C,U] **1** the act of taking something to someone's house, office etc: *Pizza Mondo offers free delivery for any pizza over $10.* **2** the process of a baby being born

del·ta /ˈdeltə/ *n* [C] a low area of land where a river separates into many smaller rivers flowing towards the sea: *the Mississippi Delta*

de·lude /dɪˈluːd/ *v* [T] to make someone believe something that is not true; DECEIVE: *He's deluding himself if he thinks he'll get the job.* — **deluded** *adj*

del·uge /ˈdeljuːdʒ/ *n* [C] **1** a large flood, or a period of time when it rains continuously **2** a large amount of something such as letters, questions etc that someone gets all at the same time — **deluge** *v* [T] *We were deluged with mail.*

de·lu·sion /dɪˈluːʒən/ *n* [C,U] a false belief about something: *Kevin's still under the delusion that his wife loves him.*

de·luxe /dɪˈlʌksǁ-ˈlʊks/ *adj* deluxe goods are of better quality and are more expensive than ordinary goods of the same kind: *a deluxe queen-sized bed*

delve /delv/ *v* [I] to put your hand deep inside a bag, box etc in order to try and find something: **+ into/inside** *She delved inside her handbag.*
delve into sth *phr v* [T] to search for information about someone or something: *Reporters are always delving into TV stars' private lives.*

de·mand[1] /dɪˈmɑːndǁdɪˈmænd/ *n* **1** [singular, U] if there is a demand for something, people want to buy it: **a big/huge demand for sth** (=a lot of people want to buy it): *There's been a big demand for Oasis's new record.* **2** [C] something that you ask for very firmly: *Union members will be on strike until the company agrees to their demands.* **3 be in demand** to be wanted by a lot

of people: *She's been in great demand ever since her book was published.* ➡ see also DEMANDS

de·mand[2] *v* [T] **1** to ask for something very firmly: *The President demanded the release of all the hostages.* **2** to order someone to tell you something: *"What are you doing here?" she demanded.* **3** to make you use a lot of time, effort, skill etc: *Learning a language demands a great deal of time and effort.*

de·mand·ing /dɪˈmɑːndɪŋǁdɪˈmæn-/ *adj* someone or something that is demanding uses a lot of your time, effort, skill etc: *a very demanding job*

de·mands /dɪˈmɑːndzǁ-ˈmændz/ *n* [plural] the effort and time that a job, situation, person etc needs you to spend on them: *Homework makes heavy demands on children nowadays.*

de·mean·ing /dɪˈmiːnɪŋ/ *adj* making you feel that you are not important or respected: *a demeaning job* — **demean** *v* [T]

de·mea·nour *BrE*, **demeanor** *AmE* /dɪˈmiːnə ǁ-ər/ *n* [U] *formal* the way someone behaves, dresses, speaks etc, which shows what their character is like

de·men·ted /dɪˈmentˌɪd/ *adj* crazy or strange

de·mise /dɪˈmaɪz/ *n* [U] **1** the failure of someone or something that used to be successful: *the demise of the steel industry* **2** *formal* someone's death

dem·o /ˈdeməʊǁ-moʊ/ *n* [C] *informal* **1** a piece of recorded music or SOFTWARE that you play or show to someone you hope will buy it **2** *BrE* a DEMONSTRATION: *an anti-war demo*

de·moc·ra·cy /dɪˈmɒkrəsiǁdɪˈmɑː-/ *n* [C,U] the system in which everyone in a country can vote to choose the government, or a country that has this system: *the struggle for democracy* | *Britain is the world's oldest democracy.*

dem·o·crat /ˈdeməkræt/ *n* [C] **1 Democrat** someone who supports or is a member of the Democratic Party in the US **2** someone who supports the idea of democracy

dem·o·crat·ic /ˌdeməˈkrætɪk ◂/ *adj* **1** a democratic country, government, or system is one in which all the people can vote to choose the government: *democratic elections* **2** a democratic way of doing something is one in which everyone can take part in making decisions — **democratically** /-kli/ *adv*

Democratic Par·ty /ˌ.ˈ.. ˌ../ *n* [singular] one of the two main political parties in the US

de·mol·ish /dɪˈmɒlɪʃǁdɪˈmɑː-/ *v* [T] **1** to completely destroy a building **2** to prove that an idea or opinion is completely wrong: *He demolished my argument in minutes.* — **demolition** /ˌdeməˈlɪʃən/ *n* [C,U]

de·mon /ˈdiːmən/ *n* [C] an evil spirit — **demonic** /dɪˈmɒnɪkǁ-ˈmɑː-/ *adj*

dem·on·strate /ˈdemənstreɪt/ *v* [T] **1** to show that something is true: *The survey demonstrates that fewer college graduates are finding jobs.* **2** to show someone how to do something by doing it yourself: *Our ski instructor began by demonstrating the correct way to turn.* **3** to

---

GRAMMAR NOTE: the present (1)
Use the **present progressive** to say what is happening now, at the time you are speaking: *Dad's working at home today.* | *We're waiting for a bus.* Use the **simple present** to talk about what normally happens: *He works from 9 to 5.* | *We usually go to school by bus.*

show that you have a particular skill, quality, or feeling: *She hasn't demonstrated much interest in her schoolwork.*

dem·on·stra·tion /ˌdemənˈstreɪʃən/ *n* **1** [C] when a large group of people meet to protest against something or show support for something **2** [C,U] if you give a demonstration you show a group of people how to do something: *cookery demonstrations* **3** [C] proof that someone or something has a particular skill, quality, feeling etc: *a powerful demonstration of his talents*

de·mon·stra·tive /dɪˈmɒnstrətɪv/ *adj* willing to show how much you love someone, for example by touching or kissing them

dem·on·stra·tor /ˈdemənstreɪtə‖-ər/ *n* [C] someone who takes part in a demonstration

de·mor·a·lized (also **-ised** *BrE*) /dɪˈmɒrəlaɪzd‖-ˈmɔː-, -ˈmɑː-/ *adj* if you feel demoralized, you lose confidence and feel that you cannot succeed: *I came out of the interview feeling totally demoralized.*

de·mor·a·li·zing (also **-ising** *BrE*) /dɪˈmɒrəlaɪzɪŋ‖-ˈmɔː-, -ˈmɑː-/ *adj* something that is demoralizing makes you less confident and hopeful: *a demoralising 7-0 defeat* —**demoralize** also **-ise** *BrE* v [T]

de·mote /dɪˈməʊt‖-ˈmoʊt/ *v* [T] give someone a less important job → opposite PROMOTE — **demotion** /-ˈməʊʃən‖-ˈmoʊ-/ *n* [C,U]

de·mure /dɪˈmjʊə‖-ˈmjʊr/ *adj* shy, quiet, and well-behaved

den /den/ *n* [C] **1** *AmE* a room in a house where people relax, read, watch television etc **2** a place where people meet to do something secret or immoral: *opium dens* **3** the home of some types of animals such as lions and FOXes

de·ni·al /dɪˈnaɪəl/ *n* **1** [C,U] a statement saying that something is not true: *Despite his denials, the jury found him guilty.* **2** [U] when someone is not allowed to have something or do something: *the denial of basic human rights* → see also DENY

den·i·grate /ˈdenɪɡreɪt/ *v* [T] *formal* to criticize someone or something unfairly and make them seem less good or important than they really are: *I'm not trying to denigrate his achievements.*

den·im /ˈdenɪm/ *n* [U] a type of strong cotton cloth used for making JEANS

de·nom·i·na·tion /dɪˌnɒmɪˈneɪʃən‖dɪˌnɑː-/ *n* [C,U] **1** a religious group that is part of a larger religious organization **2** the value of coins or pieces of paper that are used as money: *bills in denominations of $1 and $5*

de·note /dɪˈnəʊt‖-ˈnoʊt/ *v* [T] to mean something or be used as a sign for something: *Each X on the map denotes 500 people.*

de·nounce /dɪˈnaʊns/ *v* [T] to say publicly that you think that someone or something is very bad: *The bishop denounced the film as being immoral.*

dense /dens/ *adj* **1** containing a lot of things or people close together: *dense pine forests* **2** dense smoke, cloud etc is difficult to see through —**densely** *adv*

den·si·ty /ˈdensɪti/ *n* [C,U] **1** how many people or things there are in an area, in relation to its size: *Taiwan has a high population density.*

2 *technical* the relationship between an object's weight and the amount of space it fills

dent¹ /dent/ *n* [C] a hollow place in the surface of something where it has been hit or pressed: *a big dent in the car*

dent² *v* [T] **1** to make someone less confident or less proud: *The experience had dented his confidence.* **2** to hit or press something, making a hollow place in its surface —**dented** *adj*

den·tal /ˈdentl/ *adj* relating to teeth: *dental health*

dental floss /ˌ.. ˈ./ *n* [U] a kind of thin string that you use for cleaning between your teeth

den·tist /ˈdentɪst/ *n* [C] someone whose job is to treat people's teeth —**dentistry** *n* [U]

den·tures /ˈdentʃəz‖-ərz/ *n* [plural] a set of artificial teeth

de·nun·ci·a·tion /dɪˌnʌnsiˈeɪʃən/ *n* [C,U] a public statement in which you criticize someone or something

de·ny /dɪˈnaɪ/ *v* [T] **1** to say that something is not true: *In court they denied all the charges against them.* | + **(that)** *Charlie denied that he had lied about the money.* | **deny doing sth** *She denies cheating in the test.* **2** to not let someone have something: *Smokers are being denied medical treatment unless they stop smoking.* → see also DENIAL

de·o·do·rant /diːˈəʊdərənt‖-ˈoʊ-/ *n* [C,U] a substance that people put on their skins to stop bad smells

de·part /dɪˈpɑːt‖-ɑːrt/ *v* [I] *formal* to leave: *The next train for Paris will depart from Platform 2.*

de·part·ment /dɪˈpɑːtmənt‖-ɑːr-/ *n* [C] one of the parts of a large organization such as a college, government, or company: *She works in the design department of a large company.*

department store /.ˈ.. ./ *n* [C] a large shop that sells many different products such as clothes, kitchen equipment etc

de·par·ture /dɪˈpɑːtʃə‖-ˈpɑːrtʃər/ *n* **1** [C,U] when a person, plane, train etc leaves a place: *Check in at the airport an hour before departure.* **2** [C] *formal* a change from what is usual or expected: *a departure from her normal routine*

de·pend /dɪˈpend/ *v* **it/that depends** *spoken* used to say that you cannot give a definite answer, because you do not know what will happen: *"Are you coming to my house later?" "It depends. I might have to work."*

depend on/upon *phr v* [T] **1** to need someone or something's help in order to live or to continue: *patients who depend on regular blood transfusions* **2** to change according to something else: *Ticket prices may vary, depending on the time of day.* **3** to trust someone or something: *You can always depend on me.*

de·pen·da·ble /dɪˈpendəbəl/ *adj* able to be trusted: *a dependable employee*

de·pen·dant *BrE*, **dependent** *AmE* — /dɪˈpendənt/ *n* [C] someone, especially a child, who needs the help of another person to pay for their food, clothes etc: *Did she have any dependants?*

de·pen·dent /dɪˈpendənt/ *adj* **1** needing someone's or something's help in order to live or to continue: *Children of that age are still very dependent on their mothers.* **2** **be dependent on/ upon** *formal* to change according to something else: *Starting salary is dependent on experience.* —**dependence** n [U]

de·pict /dɪˈpɪkt/ v [T] show someone or something in a story or picture: *Shakespeare depicts him as a ruthless tyrant.* —**depiction** /-ˈpɪkʃən/ n [C,U]

de·plete /dɪˈpliːt/ v [T] to reduce the amount of something: *Many of our forests have been depleted by acid rain.* —**depletion** /-ˈpliːʃən/ n [U] *the depletion of the ozone layer*

de·plore /dɪˈplɔːǁ-ˈplɔːr/ v [T] *formal* to say that you think something is very bad and that you strongly disapprove of it: *a statement deploring the use of chemical weapons* —**deplorable** adj

de·ploy /dɪˈplɔɪ/ v [T] to move soldiers and military equipment to a place so that they can be used if necessary

de·port /dɪˈpɔːtǁ-ɔːrt/ v [T] to force someone to leave a country and go back to the country where they came from —**deportation** /ˌdiːpɔːˈteɪʃənǁ-ɔːr-/ n [C,U]

de·pose /dɪˈpəʊzǁ-ˈpoʊz/ v [T] to make a leader give up his or her position —**deposed** adj: *the deposed dictator*

de·pos·it[1] /dɪˈpɒzɪtǁdɪˈpɑː-/ n [C] **1** a part of the price of a house, car etc that you pay first so that it will not be sold to anyone else: *We put down a deposit on the house yesterday.* **2** an amount of money that is paid into someone's bank account: *I'd like to make a deposit please.* **3** an amount or layer of a substance in a particular place: *huge deposits of gold*

deposit[2] v [T] **1** to put money into a bank account: *How much would you like to deposit?* **2** *formal* to put something down

deposit ac·count /.ˈ.. .,./ n [C] a bank account that you use for saving money, which pays INTEREST on the money you have in it

dep·ot /ˈdepəʊǁˈdiːpoʊ/ n [C] **1** a place where goods are stored **2** *AmE* a small train or bus station

de·praved /dɪˈpreɪvd/ adj morally bad or evil: *They said his pictures were sexually depraved.* —**depravity** /dɪˈprævɪti/ n [U]

de·pre·ci·ate /dɪˈpriːʃieɪt/ v [I] to become less valuable: *A new car depreciates as soon as it is driven.* —**depreciation** /dɪˌpriːʃiˈeɪʃən/ n [U]

de·press /dɪˈpres/ v [T] **1** to make someone feel very sad or not hopeful about the future: *I can't watch the news anymore – it depresses me too much.* **2** to reduce the amount or value of something: *The bad weather has depressed sales.*

de·pressed /dɪˈprest/ adj **1** very sad: *She felt lonely and depressed.* **2** not having enough jobs or business activity

de·press·ing /dɪˈpresɪŋ/ adj making you feel sad or not hopeful about the future: *a depressing TV programme*

de·pres·sion /dɪˈpreʃən/ n [C,U] **1** a feeling of sadness and a loss of hope, or a mental illness that makes you feel this feeling: *The patient is suffering from depression.* **2** a long period when there is not a lot of business activity: *the Depression of the 1930s*

de·prive /dɪˈpraɪv/ v

deprive sb **of** sth *phr v* [T] to take something away from someone: *Prisoners were deprived of sleep for up to three days.*

de·prived /dɪˈpraɪvd/ adj not having enough of the things that are necessary for a normal, happy life: *a deprived childhood.*

depth /depθ/ n **1** [C,U] **a)** the distance from the top to the bottom of something: *Plant the seeds at a depth of about 2cm.* **b)** the distance from the front of an object to the back of it **2** [U] how serious someone's feelings are, or how much they know about something **3 in depth** including all the details: *We need to explore the problem in more depth.* **4 be out of your depth** to be in a situation that is too difficult for you to deal with: *She felt out of her depth amongst all these famous people.*

depths /depθs/ n **be in the depths of despair/ depression** to be very unhappy

dep·u·ty /ˈdepjɵti/ n [C] someone who has the second most powerful position in an organization: *My deputy will be in charge while I'm away.*

de·ranged /dɪˈreɪndʒd/ adj behaving in a crazy and often dangerous way: *a deranged criminal*

der·e·lict /ˈderɪlɪkt/ adj a derelict building or piece of land is in very bad condition because it has not been used for a long time: *a derelict house*

de·ride /dɪˈraɪd/ v [T] *formal* to say or show that you think that something is silly or unimportant —**derision** /dɪˈrɪʒən/ n [U] —**derisive** adj

de·ri·so·ry /dɪˈraɪsəri/ adj **1** too small to be considered seriously: *a derisory pay increase* **2** unkind and intended to make someone feel stupid: *derisory laughter*

der·i·va·tion /ˌderɪˈveɪʃən/ n [C,U] what something developed from, especially a word or phrase

de·rive /dɪˈraɪv/ v [T] **derive pleasure/ satisfaction/comfort etc from sth** to get pleasure, satisfaction etc from someone or something

der·ma·ti·tis /ˌdɜːməˈtaɪtɪsǁˌdɜːr-/ n [U] a disease of the skin

de·rog·a·to·ry /dɪˈrɒgətəriǁdɪˈrɑːgətɔːri/ adj speaking about someone in an insulting or strongly disapproving way: *He made some rather derogatory remarks about my work.*

de·scend /dɪˈsend/ v [I,T] *formal* to go down: *He slowly descended the steps of the plane.* → opposite ASCEND

descend from sb *phr v* [T] **be descended from** sb to be related to someone who lived a long time ago: *She is descended from a family of French aristocrats.*

de·scen·dant /dɪˈsendənt/ n [C] someone who is related to a person who lived long ago: *a descendant of an African king* → compare ANCESTOR

de·scent /dɪˈsent/ n **1** [C,U] the process of going down: *The plane began its descent.* → opposite ASCENT **2** [U] your family origins, especially the country that you came from: **be of Russian/Irish/German etc descent** *Tara's family is of Irish descent.*

de·scribe /dɪˈskraɪb/ v [T] to say what someone or something is like by giving details: *Police asked the woman to describe her attacker.* | *Conditions in the camps have been described as atrocious.* |**+ how/what/why etc** *It's hard to describe how I felt.*

de·scrip·tion /dɪ'skrɪpʃən/ n [C,U]
1 something that you say or write that describes someone or something: + of *a description of life in the Middle Ages* | give a description *Police have given a detailed description of the missing child.* **2** of some description of one kind or another: *I think it's a weapon of some description.* —**descriptive** /-tɪv/ *adj*

des·e·crate /'desɪkreɪt/ v [T] to damage something holy —**desecration** /ˌdesɪ'kreɪʃən/ n [singular, U]

de·seg·re·ga·tion /ˌdiːsegrɪ'geɪʃən‖ˌdiː,seg-/ n [U] a process in which people of different races are no longer kept separate: *the desegregation of schools* —**desegregated** /diː'segrɪgeɪtɪd/ *adj* —**desegregate** v [T]

des·ert[1] /'dezət‖-ərt/ n [C,U] a large area of hot, dry land where not much grows: *the Sahara desert*

de·sert[2] /dɪ'zɜːt‖-ɜːrt/ v **1** [T] to leave someone and not help them any more: *Her boyfriend deserted her when she got pregnant.* **2** [T] to leave a place so that it is empty: *People have deserted the villages and gone to work in the cities.* **3** [I] to leave the army without permission —**desertion** /-'zɜːʃən‖-ɜːr-/ n [C,U]

de·sert·ed /dɪ'zɜːtɪd‖-ɜːr-/ *adj* empty and quiet because people have gone away: *At night the streets are deserted.*

de·sert·er /dɪ'zɜːtə‖-'zɜːrtər/ n [C] a soldier who leaves the army without permission

des·ert i·sland /ˌ.. '../ n [C] a small tropical island with no-one living on it, which is far from other places

de·serve /dɪ'zɜːv‖-ɜːrv/ v [T] **1** if someone deserves something, they should get it because of the way they have behaved: *After all that work you deserve a rest.* | deserve to do sth *To be honest, we didn't really deserve to win.* **2** to be important enough to be considered or treated in a particular way: *The story didn't deserve all the attention it got.* —**deserved** *adj* —**deservedly** /dɪ'zɜːvɪdli‖-ɜːr-/ *adv*

de·serv·ing /dɪ'zɜːvɪŋ‖-ɜːr-/ *adj* [only before noun] deserving help and support

de·sign[1] /dɪ'zaɪn/ n **1** [U] the way that something has been planned or made: *We've made one or two changes to the computer's original design.* **2** [C] a pattern used to decorate something: *curtains with a floral design* **3** [C] a drawing or plan that shows how something will be made or what it will look like **4** [U] the process of making drawings or plans for something

design[2] v [I,T] to draw or plan something that will be made, done, or built: *The palace was designed by an Italian architect.*

des·ig·nate /'dezɪgneɪt/ v [T] to choose someone or something for a particular job or purpose: *The building was designated as a temporary hospital.* —**designation** /ˌdezɪg'neɪʃən/ n [C,U]

de·sign·er /dɪ'zaɪnə‖-ər/ n [C] **1** someone whose job is to think of and plan how something will be made: *a fashion designer* **2** designer jeans/sportswear/sunglasses clothes etc made by a fashionable designer

de·sir·a·ble /dɪ'zaɪərəbəl‖-'zaɪr-/ *adj* something that is desirable is something you want because it is good: *a desirable job with a big law firm* —**desirability** /dɪ,zaɪərə'bɪlɪti‖-,zaɪr-/ n [U]

de·sire[1] /dɪ'zaɪə‖-'zaɪr/ n **1** [C,U] a strong feeling that you want something very much: + for *the desire for knowledge* | desire to do sth *She had no desire to marry.* **2** [U] *formal* a strong feeling that you want to have sex with someone

desire[2] v **1** [T] *formal* to want or hope for something : *He desires only to be left alone.* **2** leave a lot to be desired *especially spoken* to not be very good: *The standard of teaching in many schools leaves a lot to be desired.*

de·sired /dɪ'zaɪəd‖-'zaɪrd/ *adj* have the desired effect/result to have the effect or result you wanted: *She wanted to make me look stupid, and her remarks had the desired effect.*

de·sist /dɪ'zɪst, dɪ'sɪst/ v [I] *formal* to stop doing something

desk /desk/ n [C] a table that you sit at to write and work ➡ see colour picture on page 80

des·o·late /'desələt/ *adj* a place that is desolate is empty and seems sad: *a desolate landscape* —**desolation** /ˌdesə'leɪʃən/ n [U]

de·spair[1] /dɪ'speə‖-'sper/ n [U] a feeling of being very unhappy and without hope: in despair *Anne buried her head in her hands in despair.*

despair[2] v [I] to feel that there is no hope at all: *Don't despair – I think we can help you.* | + of *They were beginning to despair of ever hearing from their son again.* —**despairing** *adj*

de·spatch /dɪ'spætʃ/ a British spelling of DIS-PATCH

des·per·ate /'despərɪt/ *adj* **1** willing to do anything to change a bad situation, even if it is dangerous or unpleasant: *Joe had been unemployed for over a year and was getting desperate.* | a desperate attempt to escape **2** a desperate situation is very bad or serious: *a desperate shortage of food* —**desperately** *adv* —**desperation** /ˌdespə'reɪʃən/ n [U]

de·spic·a·ble /dɪ'spɪkəbəl, 'despɪ-/ *adj* extremely unpleasant or cruel: *You're a despicable liar!* —**despicably** *adv*

de·spise /dɪ'spaɪz/ v [T] to strongly dislike someone or something, for example because you think they are stupid, cruel, or have behaved very badly

de·spite /dɪ'spaɪt/ *prep* **1** used to say that something is true, although something else you say seems to make it unlikely; in spite of (SPITE): *She still loved him despite the way he had treated her.* **2** despite yourself although you did not intend to: *He smiled at the little girl despite himself.*

de·spon·dent /dɪ'spɒndənt‖dɪ'spɑːn-/ *adj* unhappy and without hope: *Sue came out of the boss's office looking very despondent.* —**despondency** n [U] —**despondently** *adv*

des·pot /'despɒt, -ət‖'despət, -ɑːt/ n [C] someone, especially the ruler of a country, who uses power in a cruel and unfair way —**despotic** /dɪ'spɒtɪk‖-'spɑː-/ *adj*

des·sert /dɪ'zɜːt‖-ɜːrt/ n [C,U] sweet food eaten after the main part of a meal

de·sta·bil·ize (also -ise *BrE*) /diː'steɪbɪlaɪz/ v [T] to have a bad effect on something, especially the political or economic system in a country, and make it likely to have serious problems

des·ti·na·tion /ˌdestɪ'neɪʃən/ n [C] the place that someone or something is going to

des·tined /ˈdestɪnd/ *adj* certain to do or become something in the future: **destined to do sth** *She was destined to become her country's first woman Prime Minister.*

des·ti·ny /ˈdestɪni/ *n* [C,U] the things that will happen to someone in the future, or the power that controls this; FATE: *a nation fighting to control its own destiny*

des·ti·tute /ˈdestɪtjuːt/ *adj* having no money, no home, no food etc: *The floods left thousands of people destitute.* —**destitution** /ˌdestɪˈtjuːʃən/ *n* [U]

de·stroy /dɪˈstrɔɪ/ *v* [T] to damage something very badly, so that it cannot be repaired: *The building was completely destroyed by fire.*

de·struc·tion /dɪˈstrʌkʃən/ *n* [U] when something is destroyed: + **of** *the destruction of the ozone layer* —**destructive** /-tɪv/ *adj*

de·tach /dɪˈtætʃ/ *v* [T] to remove a part of something, especially a part that is designed to be removed —**detachable** *adj*

de·tached /dɪˈtætʃt/ *adj* **1** not reacting to something in an emotional way: *Smith remained cold and detached throughout his trial.* **2** *BrE* a detached house is not joined to another house →see colour picture on page 79 —**detachment** *n* [C,U]

de·tail[1] /ˈdiːteɪl‖dɪˈteɪl/ *n* [C,U] a small fact or piece of information about something: *The documentary included a lot of historical detail.* | **in detail** (=thoroughly): *He describes the events in great detail.*

detail[2] *v* [T] to give all the facts or information about something: *The list detailed everything we would need for our trip.*

de·tailed /ˈdiːteɪld‖dɪˈteɪld/ *adj* including a lot of information or facts: *a detailed analysis of the text*

de·tain /dɪˈteɪn/ *v* [T] if the police detain someone, they do not allow them to leave

de·tect /dɪˈtekt/ *v* [T] to notice something that is not easy to see, hear etc: *Paul detected a note of disappointment in his mother's voice.* —**detectable** *adj* —**detection** /-ˈtekʃən/ *n* [U]

de·tec·tive /dɪˈtektɪv/ *n* [C] a police officer whose job is to discover the person who is responsible for a crime

de·tec·tor /dɪˈtektər/ *n* [C] a piece of equipment that finds or measures something: *a metal detector*

de·ten·tion /dɪˈtenʃən/ *n* **1** [U] when someone is kept in prison because the police think that they have done something illegal **2** [C,U] a punishment in which students stay at school after the other students have left

de·ter /dɪˈtɜː‖-ˈtɜːr/ *v* [T] **-rred, -rring** to make someone less likely to do something bad by making it difficult or by punishing them: *security measures aimed at deterring shoplifters*

de·ter·gent /dɪˈtɜːdʒənt‖-ˈtɜːr-/ *n* [C,U] a liquid or powder containing soap, used for washing clothes, dishes etc

de·te·ri·o·rate /dɪˈtɪəriəreɪt‖-ˈtɪr-/ *v* [I] to become worse: *David's health deteriorated rapidly.* —**deterioration** /dɪˌtɪəriəˈreɪʃən‖-ˌtɪr-/ *n* [U]

de·ter·mi·na·tion /dɪˌtɜːmɪˈneɪʃən‖-ɜːr-/ *n* [U] the ability to continue trying to do something even when it is difficult

de·ter·mine /dɪˈtɜːmɪn‖-ɜːr-/ *v* [T] **1** *formal* to find out the facts about something: *Experts have been unable to determine the cause of the explosion.* **2** to officially decide something

de·ter·mined /dɪˈtɜːmɪnd‖-ɜːr-/ *adj* wanting to do something very much so that you will not let anyone or anything stop you: *He was determined to become an artist.* | + **(that)** *I'm determined that my children should have the best education possible.*

de·ter·min·er /dɪˈtɜːmɪnəl‖-ˈtɜːrmɪnər/ *n* [C] a word used before a noun or an adjective to show which thing you mean. In the phrases "the car" and "some new cars", "the" and "some" are determiners.

de·ter·rent /dɪˈterənt‖-ˈtɜːr-/ *n* [C] something that makes people less likely to do something: *an effective deterrent to car thieves*

de·test /dɪˈtest/ *v* [T] to hate someone or something: *I was going out with a boy my mother detested.*

det·o·nate /ˈdetəneɪt/ *v* [I,T] to explode or to make something explode: *Nuclear bombs were detonated in tests in the desert.* —**detonation** /ˌdetəˈneɪʃən/ *n* [C,U]

det·o·na·tor /ˈdetəneɪtəl-ər/ *n* [C] a piece of equipment used to make a bomb explode

de·tour /ˈdiːtʊəl-tʊr/ *n* [C] a way of going from one place to another that is longer than the usual way

de·tox /ˈdiːtɒks‖-tɑːks/ *n* [U] *informal* a treatment that helps ADDICTs stop drinking alcohol or taking drugs

de·tract /dɪˈtrækt/ *v*
detract from *phr v* [T] to make something seem worse than it really is: *One small mistake isn't going to detract from your achievements.* —**detraction** /-ˈtrækʃən/ *n* [C,U]

det·ri·ment /ˈdetrɪmənt/ *n* **to the detriment of** having a harmful effect on something: *He started working longer hours, to the detriment of his health.* —**detrimental** /ˌdetrɪˈmentl‖/ *adj*

de·val·ue /diːˈvæljuː/ *v* **1** [T] to make someone or something seem less important or valuable: *The skills of women were often devalued.* **2** [I,T] to reduce the value of a country's money —**devaluation** /diːˌvæljuˈeɪʃən/ *n* [C,U]

dev·a·state /ˈdevəsteɪt/ *v* [T] to damage a place very badly: *Bombing raids devastated the city of Dresden.* —**devastation** /ˌdevəˈsteɪʃən/ *n* [U]

dev·a·stat·ed /ˈdevəsteɪtɪd/ *adj* extremely sad and shocked: *Ellen was devastated when we told her what had happened.*

dev·a·stat·ing /ˈdevəsteɪtɪŋ/ *adj* **1** causing a lot of damage: *Chemical pollution has had a devastating effect on the environment.* **2** making

---

GRAMMAR NOTE: the present (2)
Use the **simple present** to talk about things that are true in general: *Carlos lives in Madrid.* | *She works in a bank.* | *Water boils at 100°C.* But use the **present progressive** to talk about what you are studying: *I'm learning English.* | *She's studying history.*

someone feel extremely sad and shocked: *Losing your job can be a devastating experience.*

de·vel·op /dɪ'veləp/ *v* **1** [I,T] to grow or change into something bigger or more important, or to make something do this: *plans to develop the local economy* | **+ into** *Wright is fast developing into one of this country's most talented players.* **2** [T] to make a new product or idea successful: *scientists developing new drugs to fight AIDS* **3** [T] to begin to have an illness or feeling: *Her baby developed a fever during the night.* **4** [I] to begin to happen or exist: *A crisis seems to be developing within the Conservative Party.* **5** [T] to use special chemicals on photographic film to make the pictures **6** [T] to build houses, offices etc on a piece of land — **developed** *adj*

de·vel·op·er /dɪ'veləpəl-ər/ *n* [C] someone who makes money by buying land and building houses, factories etc on it

de·vel·op·ment /dɪ'veləpmənt/ *n* **1** [C, U] the process of becoming bigger, better, more important etc, or the result of this process: *Vitamins are necessary for a child's growth and development.* | **+ of** *the development of computer technology* **2** [C] a new event that changes a situation: *Our reporter has news of the latest developments in Moscow.* **3** [U] the process of building new houses, factories etc **4** [C] a group of new houses or other buildings: *a new housing development*

de·vi·ant /'diːviənt/ also **de·vi·ate** /'diːviˌʲt/ *AmE adj formal* different from what is normal in a strange or bad way: *deviant behaviour* — **deviant** *n* [C]

de·vi·ate /'diːvieɪt/ *v* [I] to be or become different from what is normal or acceptable: **+ from** *The results of the survey deviate from what we might have expected.* — **deviation** /ˌdiːviˈeɪʃən/ *n* [C,U]

de·vice /dɪ'vaɪs/ *n* [C] a machine or tool used for a particular purpose: *labour-saving devices such as washing machines and dishwashers*

dev·il /'devəl/ *n* **1 the Devil** the most powerful evil spirit, according to some religions **2** [C] any evil spirit **3 speak/talk of the devil** *spoken* used when you suddenly see someone that you have just been talking about

dev·il·ish /'devəlɪʃ/ *adj* evil and cruel: *a devilish smile* — **devilishly** *adv*

devil's ad·vo·cate /ˌ... '.../ *n* **play/be devil's advocate** to pretend to disagree with someone in order to have a good discussion with them

de·vi·ous /'diːviəs/ *adj* dishonest in a clever way: *a devious scheme for making money* — **deviously** *adv* — **deviousness** *n* [U]

de·vise /dɪ'vaɪz/ *v* [T] to plan or think of a new way of doing something: *software that allows you to devise your own computer games*

de·void /dɪ'vɔɪd/ *adj* **devoid of sth** not having a particular quality: *The area is completely devoid of charm.*

de·vote /dɪ'vəʊtǁ-'vout/ *v* **1** [T] **devote time/effort/energy etc to sth** to use your time, effort etc to do something: *She devoted most of her spare time to tennis.* **2** [T] to deal with one main subject or activity: *a whole chapter is devoted to the question of the environment*

de·vot·ed /dɪ'vəʊt̪dǁ-'vou-/ *adj* very loyal or

loving: *I'm one of your most devoted admirers!* | **+ to** *She's devoted to her cats.* — **devotedly** *adv*

de·vo·tion /dɪ'vəʊʃənǁ-'vou-/ *n* [U] **1** great love and loyalty: *Their devotion to each other grew stronger over the years.* **2** a strong interest in or willingness to do something: *devotion to duty* **3** strong religious feeling

de·vour /dɪ'vaʊəl-'vaʊr/ *v* [T] **1** to eat something quickly because you are very hungry: *She devoured three burgers and a pile of fries.* **2** if you devour information, books etc, you read a lot very eagerly

de·vout /dɪ'vaʊt/ *adj* very religious: *a devout Catholic* — **devoutly** *adv*

dew /djuːǁduː/ *n* [U] small drops of water that form on outdoor surfaces during the night

dex·ter·i·ty /dek'sterˌti/ *n* [U] skill in using your hands to make or do things — **dexterous** /'dekstərəs/, **dextrous** /'dekstrəs/ *adj*

di·a·be·tes /ˌdaɪə'biːtiːz, -tˌs/ *n* [U] a disease in which there is too much sugar in your blood — **diabetic** /-'betɪk◂/ *adj*

di·a·bol·i·cal /ˌdaɪə'bɒlɪkəl◂ǁ-'bɑː-/ *adj* **1** evil or cruel: *a diabolical killer* **2** *BrE, spoken* very bad: *The hotel we stayed in was diabolical.*

di·ag·nose /'daɪəgnəʊzǁ-nous/ *v* [T] to find out what illness a person has: *He was diagnosed HIV positive in 1982.*

di·ag·no·sis /ˌdaɪəg'nəʊsˌsǁ-'nou-/ *n* [C,U] plural **diagnoses** when a doctor says what illness someone has

di·ag·nos·tic /ˌdaɪəg'nɒstɪk◂ǁ-'nɑː-/ *adj* **diagnostic methods/tests etc** methods, tests etc that are used to help make a diagnosis

di·ag·o·nal /daɪ'ægənəl/ *adj* **1** a diagonal line is straight and slopes up or down **2** going from one corner of a square shape to the opposite corner — **diagonal** *n* [C] — **diagonally** *adv*: *Tony was sitting diagonally opposite me.*

di·a·gram /'daɪəgræm/ *n* [C] a drawing that uses simple lines to show what something looks like, where something is, how something works etc: **+ of** *a diagram of a car engine*

dial¹ /daɪəl/ *v* [I,T] **-lled, -lling** *BrE* **-led, -ling** *AmE* to press the buttons or turn the dial on a telephone: *Sorry, I must have dialled the wrong number.*

dial² *n* [C] **1** the round part of a clock, watch, machine etc that has numbers that show you the time or a measurement **2** part of a telephone that you turn in order to dial a number

di·a·lect /'daɪəlekt/ *n* [C,U] a form of a language that is spoken in one part of a country: *a regional dialect*

di·a·logue (also **dialog** *AmE*) /'daɪəlɒgǁ-lɔːg, -lɑːg/ *n* [C,U] **1** a conversation in a book, play, or film: *The dialogue in the movie didn't seem natural.* **2** a formal discussion between countries or groups: **+ between/with** *an opportunity for dialogue between the opposing sides*

di·am·e·ter /daɪ'æmˌtəl-ər/ *n* [C,U] a line that goes from one side of a circle to the other and passes through the centre: *The wheel was about two feet in diameter.*

di·a·met·ri·cally /ˌdaɪə'metrɪkli/ *adv* **diametrically opposed** completely different or opposite

di·a·mond /'daɪəmənd/ *n* **1** [C,U] a very valuable clear hard stone, used in jewellery and in industry: *a diamond ring* **2** [C] a shape with four straight sides of equal length that stands on one of its points → see picture at SHAPES **3 diamonds** a group of playing cards with a diamond shape printed on them **4** [C] the field where people play BASEBALL

di·a·per /ˈdaɪəpəlˈdaɪpər/ *n* [C] *AmE* a piece of cloth or thick soft paper you put on a baby's bottom to hold liquid and solid waste; NAPPY *BrE*

di·a·phragm /ˈdaɪəfræm/ *n* [C] **1** the muscle between your lungs and your stomach that controls your breathing **2** a round flat rubber object that a woman uses as a CONTRACEPTIVE

di·ar·rhoea *BrE*, **diarrhea** *AmE* /ˌdaɪəˈrɪə/ *n* [U] an illness in which waste from the BOWELS is not solid and comes out often

di·a·ry /ˈdaɪəriˈdaɪri/ *n* [C] **1** a book in which you write down things that have happened to you **2** a book in which you write down things that you must do

dice¹ /daɪs/ *n* [C] *plural*
dice [C] a small CUBE with a different number of spots on each side, used in games: **throw/roll the dice** *Throw the dice to start the game.*

dice

dice² *v* [T] to cut food into small square pieces: *diced carrots* —**diced** *adj*

dic·ey /ˈdaɪsi/ *adj informal* used to say that you cannot be sure about something, because there is a risk that something bad or dangerous may happen: *Making films with wild animals is always a dicey business.*

di·chot·o·my /daɪˈkɒtəmiˈka:-/ *n* [C] *formal* the difference that exists between two opposite things or ideas

dic·tate /dɪkˈteɪtˈdɪkteɪt/ *v* **1** [I,T] to say words for someone else to write down: **dictate sth to sb** *She dictated the letter to her secretary.* **2** [T] to influence or control something: *The weather will dictate whether we can go.*

dic·ta·tion /dɪkˈteɪʃən/ *n* **1** [U] when someone says words for someone else to write down **2** [C,U] sentences that a teacher reads out to test a student's ability to understand and write a language correctly: *French dictation*

dic·ta·tor /dɪkˈteɪtəlˈdɪkteɪtər/ *n* [C] a leader who has complete power —**dictatorial** /ˌdɪktəˈtɔːriəl◂/ *adj*

dic·ta·tor·ship /dɪkˈteɪtəʃɪplˈ-ər-/ *n* [C,U] a system in which a dictator controls a country

dic·tion /ˈdɪkʃən/ *n* [U] *formal* the way someone pronounces words

dic·tion·a·ry /ˈdɪkʃənəriˈ-neri/ *n* [C] a book that gives a list of words in alphabetical order, with their meanings in the same or another language

did /dɪd/ *v* the past tense of DO

did·n't /ˈdɪdnt/ the short form of "did not"

die /daɪ/ *v* died, died, dying **1** [I,T] to stop living: *Hector's upset because his dog's just died.* | *He died a natural death.* | + **of/from** *She died of breast cancer.* **2 be dying for something/be dying to do sth** *spoken* to want to have or to do something very much: *I'm dying to meet her.* **3 old habits/old traditions/old customs die hard** used to say that it takes a long time to change to a new way of doing something

die away *phr v* [I] if a sound, wind, or light dies away, it becomes weaker and stops: *The footsteps died away.*

die down *phr v* [I] to become less strong or violent: *The wind finally died down this morning.*

die out *phr v* [I] to disappear completely or no longer exist: *The last wolves in this area died out 100 years ago.*

die·hard /ˈdaɪhɑːdlˈ-hɑːrd/ *n* [C] *informal* someone who does not like change and refuses to accept new ideas: *a group of diehard Marxists*

die·sel /ˈdiːzəl/ *n* [U] a type of oil used in the engines of some vehicles

di·et¹ /ˈdaɪət/ *n* **1** [C,U] the kind of food that you eat each day: *A healthy diet and exercise are important for good health.* **2** [C] a plan to eat only certain kinds or amounts of food: *a low-fat diet* | **be on a/go on a diet** (=eat certain kinds or amounts of food in order to become thinner)

diet² *v* [I] to eat less in order to become thinner

dif·fer /ˈdɪfər/ *v* [I] **1** to be different: + **from** *The new system differs from the old in several important ways.* **2** to have different opinions

dif·fe·rence /ˈdɪfərəns/ *n* **1** [C] the way in which one person or thing is different from another: + **between** *There are many differences between public and private schools.* **2** [singular] an amount by which one thing is different from another: **difference in age/price/size etc** *The two jackets might look the same, but there's a huge difference in price.* | + **between** *There's an age difference of 12 years between me and my wife.* **3 make a big difference/make all the difference** to have a good effect on a situation or person: *Swimming twice a week can make a big difference to the way you feel.* **4 make no difference** to have no effect on a situation or person: *It makes no difference to me what you do.* **5 difference of opinion** a disagreement **6 have your differences** to have disagreements with someone or different opinions from them: *We've had our differences, but we're still friends.*

dif·fe·rent /ˈdɪfərənt/ *adj* **1** not similar to something or someone, or not the same as before: *Have you had a haircut? You look different.* | + **from** *New York and Chicago are very different from each other.* | + **to** *BrE/* + **than** *AmE Life in Russia is totally different to life in Britain.* **2** [only before noun] used when talking about people or things that are of the same type but are separate from each other: *I asked three different doctors, and they all said the same thing.* | *She visited his office on three different occasions.* —**differently** *adv*

---

dif·fe·ren·tial /ˌdɪfəˈrenʃəl◂/ *n* [C] the degree of difference between two things: *wage differentials*

dif·fe·ren·ti·ate /ˌdɪfəˈrenʃieɪt/ *v* [I,T] to notice or understand the difference between things or people: + **between** *Most people couldn't differentiate between the two drinks.* —**differentiation** /ˌdɪfərenʃiˈeɪʃən/ *n* [U]

dif·fi·cult /ˈdɪfɪkəlt/ *adj* **1** not easy to understand, do, or deal with: *She finds English very difficult* | *it is difficult to do sth It was difficult to concentrate because of all the noise.* **2** not friendly, helpful, or easy to please: *Simon was often moody and difficult.*

dif·fi·cul·ty /ˈdɪfɪkəlti/ *n* **1** [U] when something is not easy to do: **have difficulty (in) doing sth** *David's having difficulty finding a job.* | **with difficulty** *She got out of her chair with difficulty.* **2** [C,U] a problem: *a country with economic difficulties*

dif·fi·dent /ˈdɪfɪdənt/ *adj* not behaving or speaking in a confident way: *a shy diffident boy* —**diffidence** *n* [U]

dif·fuse¹ /dɪˈfjuːz/ *v* **1** [I,T] to make ideas, information etc available to a lot of people **2** [I,T] to make heat, light etc spread over a large area **3** [T] to make a bad feeling less strong: *Maria tried to diffuse the tension by telling jokes.*

dif·fuse² /dɪˈfjuːs/ *adj formal* spread over a large area: *a large and diffuse organization*

dig¹ /dɪg/ *v* **dug** /dʌg/, **dug, digging 1** [I,T] to move earth or make a hole in it using a tool, your hands, or a machine: *The kids had dug a huge hole in the sand.* **2** **dig your heels in** to be determined to do something or to refuse to change your ideas about something

dig

dig into *phr v* [I,T **dig sth into** sth] to push hard into something, or to make something do this: *The cat kept digging its claws into my leg.*

dig sth ↔ **out** *phr v* [T] to find something that you have not seen or used for a long time: *Remind me to dig out that book for you.*

dig sth ↔ **up** *phr v* [T] **1** to remove something from under the earth using a tool or your hands: *Beth was in the garden digging up weeds.* **2** to find hidden or forgotten information by searching carefully: *See if there's anything you can dig up on the guy.*

dig² *n* [C] **1** *informal* an unkind thing you say to annoy someone: **have a dig at sb** *He's always having a dig at me about my weight.* **2** the process of digging in a place to find ancient objects to study: *an archaeological dig*

di·gest /daɪˈdʒest, dɪ-/ *v* [T] **1** to change food in the stomach into a form your body can use: *Some babies can't digest cow's milk.* **2** to understand new information after thinking about it carefully: *It took us a while to digest the news.* —**digestible** *adj*

di·ges·tion /daɪˈdʒestʃən, dɪ-/ *n* [C,U] the process of digesting food

di·git /ˈdɪdʒɪt/ *n* [C] **1** a single number: *a seven-digit phone number* **2** *technical* a finger or toe

dig·i·tal /ˈdɪdʒɪtl/ *adj* **1** a **digital watch/clock** a watch or clock that shows the time in the form of numbers **2** using a system in which information is shown in the form of changing electrical SIGNALS: *a digital recording*

dig·ni·fied /ˈdɪgnɪfaɪd/ *adj* calm, serious, and proud in a way that makes other people respect you: *a dignified leader*

dig·ni·ta·ry /ˈdɪgnɪtəri‖-teri/ *n* [C] someone who has an important official position: *foreign dignitaries*

dig·ni·ty /ˈdɪgnɪti/ *n* [U] calm, serious behaviour, even in difficult situations, that makes people respect you: *a woman of compassion and dignity*

di·gress /daɪˈgres/ *v* [I] to begin talking about something that is not related to the subject you were talking about before —**digression** /-ˈgreʃən/ *n* [C,U]

digs /dɪgz/ *n* [plural] *BrE informal* a room that you rent in someone's house

dike /daɪk/ *n* [C] another spelling of DYKE

di·lap·i·dat·ed /dɪˈlæpɪdeɪtɪd/ *adj* a dilapidated building or vehicle is old and in very bad condition —**dilapidation** /dɪˌlæpɪˈdeɪʃən/ *n* [U]

di·late /daɪˈleɪt/ *v* [I,T] to become wider or more open or to make something do this —**dilation** /-ˈleɪʃən/ *n* [U]

di·lem·ma /dɪˈlemə, daɪ-/ *n* [C] a situation in which you have to make a difficult choice between two possible actions: **be in a dilemma** *He's in a dilemma about whether to accept the job or not.*

dil·i·gent /ˈdɪlɪdʒənt/ *adj* working very hard: *a diligent student* —**diligently** *adv* —**diligence** *n* [U]

di·lute /daɪˈluːt/ *v* [T] to make a liquid weaker or thinner by mixing another liquid with it: *diluted fruit juice* —**dilute** /ˌdaɪˈluːt◄/ *adj* —**dilution** /daɪˈluːʃən/ *n* [C,U]

dim¹ /dɪm/ *adj* **1** not bright or easy to see: *the dim light of a winter evening* **2** **dim memory/awareness** etc something that you do not remember or understand well: *I had only a dim memory of my grandparents.* **3** *informal, especially BrE* stupid: *She can be really dim at times!* —**dimly** *adv*

dim² *v* [I,T] to become less bright, or make something less bright: *Could you dim the lights a little?*

dime /daɪm/ *n* **1** [C] a coin worth 10 CENTS **2** **a dime a dozen** *informal* very common and therefore not special: *Jobs like his are a dime a dozen.*

di·men·sion /daɪˈmenʃən, dɪ-/ *n* **1** [C] a part of a situation that affects the way you think about it: **new/different dimension** *The baby has added a whole new dimension to their life.* **2** [plural] the size of something, including its length, width, and height: *What are the dimensions of the room?*

dime store /ˈ. ./ *n* [C] *AmE* a shop that sells different kinds of cheap things

di·min·ish /dɪˈmɪnɪʃ/ *v* [I,T] to become smaller or less important or to make something smaller or less important: *the country's diminishing political influence*

di·min·u·tive /dɪˈmɪnjʊtɪv/ *adj formal* very small

dim·ple /ˈdɪmpəl/ *n* [C] a small hollow place on your cheek or chin

din /dɪn/ *n* [singular] a loud continuous unpleasant noise

dine /daɪn/ *v* [I] *formal* to eat dinner

dine out *phr v* [I] *formal* to eat in a restaurant

din·er /ˈdaɪnə‖-ər/ *n* [C] **1** *especially AmE* a

small restaurant that serves cheap meals **2** someone who eats in a restaurant

din·ghy /'dɪŋgi, 'dɪŋi/ *n* [C] a small boat often used for taking people between a ship and the land

din·gy /'dɪndʒi/ *adj* dirty and dull: *a small dingy room*

dining room /'.. ./ *n* [C] a room where you eat meals in a house or hotel

din·ner /'dɪnəǁ-ər/ *n* [C,U] the main meal of the day, usually eaten in the evening: *What time's dinner?*

dinner jack·et /'.. ,../ *n* [C] *BrE* a black or white JACKET worn by men on formal occasions; TUXEDO *AmE*

di·no·saur /'daɪnəsɔːǁ-sɔːr/ *n* [C] a large animal that lived in very ancient times and no longer exists: *fossilized dinosaur bones*

dip[1] /dɪp/ *v* **1** [T] to put something into a liquid and quickly lift it out again: **dip sth in/into sth** *Janet dipped her feet into the water.* **2** [I] *informal* to become lower or go down: *Temperatures dipped below freezing.*

dip into *phr v* [T] **1** to use some of an amount of money: *Medical bills forced her to dip into her savings.* **2** to read parts of a book but not all of it

dip[2] *n* **1** [C,U] a thick SAUCE that you dip food into before you eat it: *a sour cream dip* **2** [C] a place where the surface of something goes down suddenly: *a dip in the road* **3** [C] when the level or amount of something becomes lower: *a dip in prices* **4** [singular] *informal* a quick swim: *Is there time for a dip before lunch?*

diph·ther·i·a /dɪf'θɪəriə, dɪp-ǁ-'θɪr-/ *n* [U] a serious infectious disease of the throat

di·plo·ma /dɪ'pləʊməǁ-'ploʊ-/ *n* [C] an official document showing that someone has successfully finished a course of study

di·plo·ma·cy /dɪ'pləʊməsiǁ-'ploʊ-/ *n* [U] **1** the activity of dealing with political relations between countries: *an expert at international diplomacy* **2** skill in dealing with people and difficult situations: *He handled the problem with great diplomacy.*

dip·lo·mat /'dɪpləmæt/ *n* [C] someone who is employed by a government to live in another country and make sure that their own country is listened to, its citizens are treated correctly etc

dip·lo·mat·ic /ˌdɪplə'mætɪk◂/ *adj* **1** relating to political relations between countries: *Feingold plans to join the diplomatic service.* **2** good at dealing with people in a way that does not offend them: *He won't give you a thing unless you're very diplomatic.* —**diplomatically** /-kli/ *adv*

dire /daɪəǁdaɪr/ *adj* extremely serious or terrible: *the dire consequences of war*

direct[1] /dɪ'rekt, ˌdaɪ'rekt◂/ *adj* **1** without any other places, people, actions, or processes coming in between: *the most direct route to Madrid* | *Over 100 people have died as a direct result of the fighting.* **2** saying exactly what you mean

in an honest way: *It's best to be direct with children when someone in the family dies.* **3** exact or complete: *Weight increases in direct proportion to mass.* —**directness** *n* [U] → opposite INDIRECT

direct[2] *v* [T] **1** to be in charge of something: *Hanley was asked to direct the investigation.* **2** to give actors in a play, film etc instructions about what to do: *Barbra Streisand both starred in and directed the movie.* **3** to tell someone which way to go: *Can you direct me to the airport?* **4** to say things to or about a particular person: **+ at/towards/against etc** *My criticisms were directed at Ken, not at you.* **5** if you direct something such as money, help, or effort at a person, problem etc, you want them to receive it: *an aid effort directed at Rwandan refugees* **6** to aim something in a particular direction: *He directed the light towards the house.*

direct[3] *adv* **1** without stopping or changing direction: *You can fly direct from London to Nashville.* **2** without dealing with anyone else first: *You'll have to contact the manager direct.*

di·rec·tion /dɪ'rekʃən, daɪ-/ *n* **1** [C] the place or point towards which someone or something moves, faces, or is aimed: **in the direction of sth/in sth's direction** *We walked off in the direction of the hotel.* | **in the opposite direction** *Jeff stepped forward, hailing a taxi that was going in the opposite direction.* **2** [C] the general way in which someone or something happens or develops: *Suddenly the conversation changed direction.* **3** [U] the control, guidance, or instructions of a particular person: **under sb's direction** *The company has become very successful under Martini's direction.* **4** [U] a general purpose or aim: *I sometimes feel that my life lacks direction.* **5** **sense of direction** the ability to know which way to go: *Bill's always getting lost – he has no sense of direction.*

di·rec·tions /dɪ'rekʃənz, daɪ-/ *n* [plural] instructions about how to get somewhere or about how to do something: *Could you give me directions to the bus station?*

di·rec·tive /dɪ'rektɪv, daɪ-/ *n* [C] an official order or instruction

di·rect·ly /dɪ'rektli, daɪ-/ *adv* **1** with no other person, process etc between: *It's easier if you order the book directly from the publisher.* **2** **directly opposite/in front/behind etc** exactly opposite, in front etc: *Lucas sat directly behind us.* **3** **speak/ask/answer etc directly** to say exactly what you mean

di·rec·tor /dɪ'rektə, daɪ-ǁ-ər/ *n* [C] **1** someone who controls or manages a company, organization, or activity: *Her new job is marketing director.* **2** someone who gives instructions to actors and other people in a film or play: *film director Ken Russell*

di·rec·to·ry /daɪ'rektəri, dɪ-/ *n* [C] a book or list of names, facts etc, arranged in alphabetical order: *the telephone directory*

dirt /dɜːtǁdɜːrt/ *n* [U] **1** something such as dust or mud, that makes things dirty: *The walls were black with age and dirt.* **2** especially *AmE*

---

earth or soil: *He dug another spadeful of dirt.* | **dirt track/road** (=one that consists of soil, mud and stones) **3** *informal* information about someone that could harm them if other people knew about it: **dig up (the) dirt on sb** (=try to find out damaging things about someone) **4** **dirt cheap** extremely cheap: *We got the couch dirt cheap in a sale.*

dirt·y[1] / ˈdɜːtiǁˈdɜːr- / *adj* **1** not clean: *There's a stack of dirty dishes in the sink.* **2** about sex in a way that is a little unpleasant and unacceptable: *dirty jokes* **3** unfair or dishonest: *a dirty fighter* | *That was a dirty trick.* **4** **do sb's dirty work** to do an unpleasant or dishonest job for someone: *I told them to do their own dirty work.*

dirty[2] *v* [T] to make something dirty

dis- / dɪs / *prefix* **1** used at the beginning of some words to mean 'not': *disrespectful* | *dishonesty* (=behaviour that is not honest) **2** used at the beginning of some words to mean to remove or stop something: *disconnect a plug* | *disinfect a wound*

dis·a·bil·i·ty / ˌdɪsəˈbɪlɪti / *n* [C,U] a physical or mental condition that makes it difficult for someone to do things in the way most people do: *She's never let her disability hold back her career in politics.*

dis·a·bled / dɪsˈeɪbəld / *adj* **1** someone who is disabled cannot use a part of their body in the way most people are able to: *a disabled worker* **2** **the disabled** people who are disabled

dis·ad·van·tage / ˌdɪsədˈvɑːntɪdʒǁ-ˈvæn- / *n* [C] something that makes your progress or success difficult: *Your main disadvantage is lack of experience.* | **be at a disadvantage** *I was at a disadvantage because I didn't speak French.* —**disadvantageous** / ˌdɪsædvənˈteɪdʒəs, -væn- / *adj*

dis·ad·van·taged / ˌdɪsədˈvɑːntɪdʒdǁ-ˈvæn- / *adj* having social disadvantages, for example not much money or very little education: *disadvantaged kids from the inner cities*

dis·af·fec·ted / ˌdɪsəˈfektɪd / *adj* no longer supporting the leader, ruler, political party etc that you supported before: *disaffected Communists*

dis·a·gree / ˌdɪsəˈɡriː / *v* [I] **1** to have a different opinion from someone else: **+ with** *Roth doesn't like anybody who disagrees with them.* | **+ about/on** *Those two disagree about everything.* **2** if statements or reports about the same thing disagree, they are different from each other

dis·a·gree·a·ble / ˌdɪsəˈɡriːəbəl / *adj* unpleasant and not enjoyable: *a disagreeable experience* —**disagreeably** *adv*

dis·a·gree·ment / ˌdɪsəˈɡriːmənt / *n* **1** [C,U] when you do not agree with someone: **+ over/about etc** *She left the company after a disagreement over contracts.* **2** [U] differences between two statements, reports etc that should be the same: **+ between** *There is considerable disagreement between the statements of the two witnesses.*

dis·al·low / ˌdɪsəˈlaʊ / *v* [T] *formal* to officially refuse to allow something because a rule has been broken: *The referee disallowed the goal.*

dis·ap·pear[■] / ˌdɪsəˈpɪəlǁ-ˈpɪr / *v* [I] **1** to become impossible to see or find: *She turned around, but the man had disappeared.* **2** to stop existing: *Many species of plants and animals disappear every year.* **3** **disappearance** *n* [C,U]

dis·ap·point / ˌdɪsəˈpɔɪnt / *v* [T] to make someone unhappy because something good that they hoped for or expected did not happen: *I'm sorry to disappoint you, but we won't be going on holiday this year.*

dis·ap·point·ed[■] / ˌdɪsəˈpɔɪntɪd / *adj* unhappy because something you hoped for did not happen, or was not as good as you expected: **+ (that)** *He was really disappointed that Kerry couldn't come.* | **bitterly disappointed** (=very disappointed): *If we lose, I'll be bitterly disappointed.*

dis·ap·point·ing / ˌdɪsəˈpɔɪntɪŋ / *adj* not as good as you expected or hoped: *The game ended with a disappointing score of 2-2.* —**disappointingly** *adv*

dis·ap·point·ment / ˌdɪsəˈpɔɪntmənt / *n* **1** [U] a feeling of sadness that something is not as good as you expected, or has not happened: **+ at** *Brian's disappointment at not being chosen was obvious.* **2** [C] someone or something that is not as good as you hoped or expected: *What a disappointment that movie was!* | *Kate feels as if she's a disappointment to her family.*

dis·ap·prove[■] / ˌdɪsəˈpruːv / *v* [I] to not approve of someone or something: **+ of** *Her parents disapprove of her lifestyle.* —**disapproval** *n* [U]

dis·arm / dɪsˈɑːmǁ-ˈɑːrm / *v* **1** [I] if a country disarms, it reduces the size of its army, navy etc and the number of weapons it has: *Both sides must disarm before the peace talks can begin.* **2** [T] to make someone less angry and more friendly: *Susie's reply disarmed him.* **3** [T] to take away someone's weapons: *Police managed to disarm the man.*

dis·ar·ma·ment / dɪsˈɑːməməntǁ-ˈɑːr- / *n* [U] the reduction of the size of a country's army, navy etc, and the number of weapons it has: *nuclear disarmament*

dis·arm·ing / dɪsˈɑːmɪŋǁ-ˈɑːr- / *adj* behaving in a way that stops you from feeling unfriendly, angry, or criticizing someone: *He gave her his most disarming smile.*

dis·ar·ray / ˌdɪsəˈreɪ / *n* **be in disarray** to be very untidy, disorganized, or confused: *By 1985, the party was in complete disarray.*

dis·as·ter[■] / dɪˈzɑːstəǁdɪˈzæstər / *n* [C,U] **1** an event such as an accident, flood, or storm that causes a lot of harm: *an air disaster in which 329 people died* **2** a complete failure: *As a career move, his latest job was a disaster.*

di·sas·trous / dɪˈzɑːstrəsǁdɪˈzæ- / *adj* very bad or ending in complete failure: *It was a disastrous trip from the beginning.*

dis·band / dɪsˈbænd / *v* [I,T] *formal* to stop existing as an organization, or to make an organization officially stop existing

dis·be·lief / ˌdɪsbɪˈliːf / *n* [U] a feeling that something is not true or does not exist: **in disbelief** *I looked at him in disbelief.*

dis·be·lieve / ˌdɪsbɪˈliːv / *v* [T] to not believe someone or not believe that something is true, because you think there are good reasons for not believing them —**disbelieving** *adj*: *"Really?" said Simon in a disbelieving tone of voice.*

disc also **disk** *AmE* / dɪsk / *n* [C] **1** a round flat shape or object: *a revolving metal disc* **2** a record or CD → see also COMPACT DISC **3** a flat piece of CARTILAGE between the bones of your back → see also DISK

dis·card /dɪsˈkɑːd‖-ɑːrd/ v [T] to get rid of something or throw it away: *River birds are often hurt by discarded fishing hooks.*

di·scern /dɪˈsɜːn‖-ɜːrn/ v [T] *formal* to see, notice, or understand something: *I could just discern the outline of the bridge in the fog.* —**discernible** *adj*

di·scern·ing /dɪˈsɜːnɪŋ‖-ɜːr-/ *adj* able to make good judgements, especially about art, style etc: *a superb hotel for the discerning traveller* —**discernment** *n* [U]

dis·charge[1] /dɪsˈtʃɑːdʒ‖-ɑːr-/ v **1** [T] to officially allow someone to leave an organization such as the army, or a place such as a hospital or prison: + **from** *Blanton was discharged from hospital last night.* **2** [I,T] to send, pour, or let out liquids or gases **3** [T] *formal* to perform a duty or promise

dis·charge[2] /ˈdɪstʃɑːdʒ‖-tʃɑːrdʒ/ n **1** [U] official permission to leave an organization such as an army, or a place such as a hospital or prison: *He got married shortly after his discharge from the army.* **2** [C,U] a substance that comes out of something: *a discharge of toxic waste*

di·sci·ple /dɪˈsaɪpəl/ n [C] someone who believes in the ideas of a great leader or teacher

dis·ci·pli·nar·i·an /ˌdɪsɪplɪˈneəriən‖-ˈner-/ n [C] someone who makes people obey strict rules: *Dad was always the disciplinarian in the family.*

dis·ci·pline[1] /ˈdɪsɪplɪn/ n [U] **1** the practice of making people obey rules and orders, or the situation that results from this: *The school has very high standards of discipline.* **2** a way of training your mind and body, or of learning to control your behaviour: *It took him a lot of hard work and discipline to make the Olympic team.*

discipline[2] v [T] **1** to teach someone to obey rules and control their own behaviour: *The Parkers are not very good at disciplining their children.* **2** to punish someone who has disobeyed an organization's rules.

disc jock·ey /ˈ. ,../ n [C] a DJ

dis·claim /dɪsˈkleɪm/ v [T] *formal* to say that you are not responsible for or do not know anything about something

dis·claim·er /dɪsˈkleɪməl-ər/ n [C] an official statement that you are not responsible for, or are not connected with, something that may be considered bad.

dis·close /dɪsˈkləʊz‖-ˈkloʊz/ v [T] to tell someone something that was previously a secret: *The newspaper refused to disclose where their information came from.*

dis·clo·sure /dɪsˈkləʊʒə‖-ˈkloʊʒər/ n [C,U] a secret that someone tells people, or the act of telling this secret: *a disclosure of corruption in the mayor's office*

dis·co /ˈdɪskəʊ‖-koʊ/ n [C] a place or event where people dance to popular music

dis·col·our *BrE*, **discolor** *AmE* /dɪsˈkʌlə‖-ər/ v [I,T] to change colour, or to make something change colour, so that it looks unattractive: *Use lemon juice to stop sliced apples from discolouring.* —**discoloration** /dɪsˌkʌləˈreɪʃən/ n [C,U]

dis·com·fort /dɪsˈkʌmfət‖-ərt/ n **1** [U] slight pain, or a feeling of being physically uncomfortable: *Your injury isn't serious, but it may cause some discomfort.* **2** [C] something that makes you uncomfortable: *the discomforts of long distance travel*

dis·con·cert·ing /ˌdɪskənˈsɜːtɪŋ◂‖-ɜːr-/ *adj* making you feel slightly embarrassed, confused, or worried: *The old man was staring at her in a most disconcerting way.* —**disconcert** v [T] —**disconcerted** *adj*

dis·con·nect /ˌdɪskəˈnekt/ v [T] to take out the wire, pipe etc that connects a machine or piece of equipment to something: *Disconnect the cables before you try to move the computer.*

dis·con·nect·ed /ˌdɪskəˈnektʃd◂/ *adj* disconnected thoughts or ideas do not seem to be related to each other

dis·con·tent·ed /ˌdɪskənˈtentʃd◂/ *adj* unhappy or not satisfied: + **with** *After two years, I became discontented with my job.* —**discontent** n [U]

dis·con·tin·ue /ˌdɪskənˈtɪnjuː/ v [T] to stop doing or providing something: *My favourite lipstick has been discontinued!*

dis·cord /ˈdɪskɔːd‖-ɔːrd/ n **1** [U] *formal* disagreement between people: *marital discord* **2** [C,U] an unpleasant sound produced by musical notes that do not go together well —**discordant** /dɪsˈkɔːdənt‖-ɔːr-/ *adj*

dis·count[1] /ˈdɪskaʊnt/ n [C] a reduction in the usual price of something: *Sales start Monday, with discounts of up to 50%.*

dis·count[2] /dɪsˈkaʊnt‖ˈdɪskaʊnt/ v [T] **1** to consider something unlikely to be true or important: *Larry tends to discount any suggestion I ever make.* **2** to reduce the price of something

dis·cour·age /dɪsˈkʌrɪdʒ‖-ˈkɜːr-/ v [T] **1** to try to make someone less likely to do something: **discourage sb from doing sth** *They're trying to discourage staff from smoking at work.* **2** to make someone less confident or less willing to do something: *Don't be discouraged by your results.* —**discouragement** n [C,U] → opposite ENCOURAGE

dis·cour·aged /dɪsˈkʌrɪdʒd‖-ˈkɜːr-/ *adj* no longer having the confidence you need to continue doing something: *Students may get discouraged if they are criticized too often.* —**discouraging** *adj*

dis·cour·te·ous /dɪsˈkɜːtiəs‖-ɜːr-/ *adj formal* not polite —**discourteously** *adv*

dis·cov·er /dɪsˈkʌvə‖-ər/ v [T] **1** to find something that was hidden, or that people did not know about before: *Columbus discovered America in 1492.* **2** to find out a fact, or the answer to a question: + **who/what/how etc** *Did you ever discover who sent you the flowers?* —**discoverer** n [C]

dis·cov·e·ry /dɪsˈkʌvəri/ n **1** [C] a fact, piece of knowledge, or an answer to a question that was not known before: **make a discovery** *Astronomers have made significant discoveries about our galaxy.* **2** [U] when someone finds something that was hidden or not known about before: *the discovery of oil in Texas*

dis·cred·it /dɪsˈkredʃt/ v [T] to make people stop trusting or respecting someone or something: *The defense lawyer will try to discredit our witnesses.* —**discredit** n [U]

di·screet /dɪˈskriːt/ *adj* careful about what you say or do so that you do not embarrass or upset people: *It wasn't very discreet of you to call me at the office.* —**discreetly** *adv*

di·screp·an·cy /dɪ'skrepənsi/ *n* [C,U] a difference between two things that should be the same: **+ between** *If there is any discrepancy between the two reports, make a note of it.*

di·scre·tion /dɪ'skreʃən/ *n* [U] **1** the authority to decide what is the right thing to do in a situation: *Promotions are left to the discretion of the manager.* | **at sb's discretion** *Tipping is entirely at the customer's discretion.* **2** when you are careful about what you say or do, so that you do not upset or embarrass people: *This situation must be handled with discretion.*

di·scrim·i·nate /dɪ'skrɪmɪneɪt/ *v* **1** [I] to unfairly treat one person or group differently from another: **+ against** *She claims that she has been discriminated against on the grounds of sex.* **2** [I,T] to recognize a difference between things: **+ between** *The child must first learn to discriminate between letters of similar shape.*

di·scrim·i·nat·ing /dɪ'skrɪmɪneɪtɪŋ/ *adj* able to know what is of good quality and what is not

di·scrim·i·na·tion /dɪ,skrɪmɪ'neɪʃən/ *n* [U] **1** when one group of people is unfairly treated differently from another: *sex discrimination* | **+ against** *discrimination against disabled people in employment* **2** the ability to know what is of good quality and what is not

dis·cus /'dɪskəs/ *n* [C, singular] a sport in which you throw a heavy plate-shaped object as far as you can, or the object that you throw

di·scuss /dɪ'skʌs/ *v* [T] to talk about something with someone in order to exchange ideas or decide something: *We're meeting today to discuss our science project.* | **discuss sth with sb** *I'd like to discuss this with my father first.*

di·scus·sion /dɪ'skʌʃən/ *n* [C,U] a conversation in which people discuss something: **have a discussion (about sth)** *In class that day that had a discussion about the political parties.* | **under discussion** (=being discussed)

dis·dain /dɪs'deɪn/ *n* [U] *formal* a lack of respect for someone or something, because you think they are not important or good enough: **+ for** *Mason could not conceal his disdain for uneducated people.* —**disdainful** *adj* —**disdainfully** *adv*

dis·ease /dɪ'ziːz/ *n* [C,U] an illness or serious medical condition: *heart disease* —**diseased** *adj*

> **USAGE NOTE: disease, illness, sickness**
>
> Although **disease** and **illness** are often used to mean the same thing, it is the **disease** that actually makes you ill: *He suffers from heart disease.* An **illness** is the condition of being ill, which may be caused by a **disease**: *She missed a lot of school because of her illness.* **Sickness** is a particular type of illness: *radiation sickness* | *travel sickness*

dis·em·bark /,dɪsɪm'bɑːk‖-ɑːrk/ *v* [I] to get off a ship or plane —**disembarkation** /,dɪsembɑː-'keɪʃən‖-bɑːr-/ *n* [U]

dis·em·bod·ied /,dɪsɪm'bɒdid‖-'bɑː-/ *adj* a disembodied sound or voice comes from someone who cannot be seen

dis·en·chant·ed /,dɪsɪn'tʃɑːntɪd‖-'tʃænt-/ *adj* disappointed because you no longer believe that

something is good or important: **+ with** *Anne was becoming disenchanted with her marriage.* —**disenchantment** *n* [U]

dis·en·gage /,dɪsɪn'geɪdʒ/ *v* [I,T] to separate something from something else that was connected to it: *Disengage the gears when you park the car.* —**disengagement** *n* [U]

dis·en·tan·gle /,dɪsɪn'tæŋgəl/ *v* **1 disentangle yourself (from)** to escape from a difficult situation that you are involved in **2** to untie ropes, strings etc that have become twisted or tied together

dis·fig·ure /dɪs'fɪgə‖-'fɪgjər/ *v* [T] to spoil the appearance of someone or something: *His face was badly disfigured in the accident.* —**disfigurement** *n* [C,U]

dis·grace¹ /dɪs'greɪs/ *n* **1 be a disgrace** to be very bad and unacceptable: *The food in that place is a disgrace.* | **+ to sb/sth** *Doctors like you are a disgrace to the medical profession.* **2 in disgrace** when people disapprove of you because you have done something wrong: *Harry left the school in disgrace.*

disgrace² *v* [T] to do something so bad that people lose respect for you, your family, or your group: *How could you disgrace us all like that?*

dis·grace·ful /dɪs'greɪsfəl/ *adj* extremely bad or unacceptable: *Your manners are disgraceful!* —**disgracefully** *adv*

dis·grun·tled /dɪs'grʌntld/ *adj* annoyed, disappointed, and not satisfied: *disgruntled employees*

dis·guise¹ /dɪs'gaɪz/ *v* [T] **1** to change your usual appearance, voice etc so that people will not recognize you: **disguise yourself as sb/sth** *She disguised herself as a man.* **2** if you disguise your feelings or opinions, you do not let people know what they really are: *Dan couldn't disguise his feelings for Katie.*

disguise² *n* [C,U] things that you wear to change your appearance and hide who you really are: *The glasses were part of his disguise.* | **in disguise** (=wearing a disguise): *He travelled around in disguise.*

dis·gust¹ /dɪs'gʌst, dɪz-/ *n* [U] when you feel very strongly that you do not like someone or something, or do not approve of them: **with disgust** *Everybody looked at me with disgust.* | **in disgust** *We waited an hour before leaving in disgust.*

disgust² *v* [T] if something or someone disgusts you, you feel very strongly that you dislike or disapprove of them —**disgusted** *adj*: *We felt disgusted by the way we'd been treated.*

dis·gust·ing /dɪs'gʌstɪŋ, dɪz-/ *adj* very unpleasant: *What is that disgusting smell?* —**disgustingly** *adv*

dish¹ /dɪʃ/ *n* [C] **1** a round container with low sides, used for holding food: *a serving dish* **2** food cooked or prepared in a particular way: *a wonderful pasta dish* → see also DISHES

dish² *v*

dish sth ↔ out *phr v* [T] *informal* to give something to people: *He's always dishing out unwanted advice.*

dis·heart·ened /dɪs'hɑːtnd‖-ɑːrtn/ *adj* disappointed because you do not think you will achieve something you have been hoping for —**dishearten** *v* [T]

dis·heart·en·ing /dɪsˈhɑːtn̩ɪŋ‖-ɑːr-/ *adj* making you lose hope and confidence: *It was disheartening to see how little had been done.* —**dishearteningly** *adv*

dish·es /ˈdɪʃ̩z/ *n* [plural] all the plates, cups, bowls etc that are used during a meal: **do the dishes** (=wash them)

di·shev·elled *BrE*, **disheveled** *AmE* /dɪˈʃevəld/ *adj* dishevelled clothes, hair etc are very untidy: *She looked tired and dishevelled.*

dis·hon·est /dɪsˈɒnɪst‖-ˈɑː-/ *adj* likely to lie, steal, or cheat: *a dishonest politician* —**dishonesty** *n* [U] —**dishonestly** *adv*

dis·hon·our[1] *BrE*, **dishonor** *AmE* /dɪsˈɒnə‖-ˈɑːnər/ *n* [U] *formal* when people no longer respect you or approve of you because you have done something dishonest or immoral: **bring dishonour on sb/sth** *His behaviour brought dishonour on the family.*

dishonour[2] *BrE*, **dishonor** *AmE* — *v* [T] *formal* to do something so bad that other people stop respecting you

dis·hon·ou·ra·ble *BrE*, **dishonorable** *AmE* /dɪsˈɒnərəbəl‖-ˈɑː-/ *adj* not morally correct or acceptable —**dishonourably** *adv*

dish·tow·el /ˈdɪʃˌtaʊəl/ *n* [C] *AmE* a cloth used for drying dishes; TEA TOWEL *BrE* → see picture at KITCHEN

dish·wash·er /ˈdɪʃˌwɒʃə‖-ˌwɒːʃər, -ˌwɑː-/ *n* [C] a machine that washes dishes → see picture at KITCHEN

dis·il·lu·sion /ˌdɪsɪˈluːʒən/ *v* [T] to make someone realize that something they thought was true or good is not: *I hate to disillusion you, but she's never coming back.* —**disillusionment** *n* [U]

dis·il·lu·sioned /ˌdɪsɪˈluːʒənd◂/ *adj* unhappy because you have lost your belief that someone or something is good or right

dis·in·fect /ˌdɪsɪnˈfekt/ *v* [T] to clean something with a chemical that destroys BACTERIA —**disinfection** /-ˈfekʃən/ *n* [U]

dis·in·fec·tant /ˌdɪsɪnˈfektənt/ *n* [C,U] a chemical that destroys BACTERIA

dis·in·her·it /ˌdɪsɪnˈherɪt/ *v* [T] to prevent someone from receiving any of your money or property after your death

dis·in·te·grate /dɪsˈɪntɪɡreɪt/ *v* [I] **1** to break up into small pieces: *The whole plane just disintegrated in mid-air.* **2** to become weaker and be gradually destroyed: *Pam kept the kids when the marriage disintegrated.* —**disintegration** /dɪsˌɪntɪˈɡreɪʃən/ *n* [U]

dis·in·terest·ed /dɪsˈɪntrɪstɪd/ *adj* able to judge a situation fairly because you will not get any advantages for yourself from it: *disinterested advice* —**disinterest** *n* [U]

USAGE NOTE: disinterested and uninterested

People sometimes use **disinterested** to mean 'not interested in something', although it really means that someone is not personally involved in a situation so they can judge it fairly: *a group of*

---

disinterested investigators. If you want to say that someone is not interested in something, use **uninterested**: *She seemed totally uninterested in what we had to say.*

dis·joint·ed /dɪsˈdʒɔɪntɪd/ *adj* a disjointed speech or piece of writing is not easy to understand because the words or ideas are not arranged in a clear order —**disjointedly** *adv*

disk /dɪsk/ *n* [C] **1** a small flat piece of plastic or metal used for storing information in a computer **2** the American spelling of DISC → see also HARD DISK, FLOPPY DISK

disk drive /ˈ. ./ *n* [C] a piece of equipment in a computer that is used to pass information to or from a disk → see colour picture on page 80

dis·kette /dɪsˈket‖ˈdɪskət/ *n* [C] a FLOPPY DISK

disk jock·ey /ˈ. ˌ.. / *n* [C] *AmE* a DJ

dis·like[1] /dɪsˈlaɪk/ *v* [T] to not like someone or something: *Why do you dislike her so much?*

dis·like[2] /dɪsˈlaɪk, ˈdɪslaɪk/ *n* [C,U] a feeling of not liking someone or something: + **of/for** *She shared her mother's dislike of housework.* | **take a dislike to sb/sth** *They took an instant dislike to each other.*

dis·lo·cate /ˈdɪsləkeɪt‖-loʊ-/ *v* [T] to make a bone come out of its normal place: *I dislocated my shoulder playing football.* —**dislocation** /ˌdɪsləˈkeɪʃən‖-loʊ-/ *n* [C,U]

dis·lodge /dɪsˈlɒdʒ‖-ˈlɑːdʒ/ *v* [T] to force something out of its position: *Lee dislodged a few stones as he climbed over the old wall.*

dis·loy·al /dɪsˈlɔɪəl/ *adj* not supporting your friends, family, country etc, or doing things that may harm them: *He was accused of being disloyal to his country.* —**disloyalty** *n* [U]

dis·mal /ˈdɪzməl/ *adj* making you feel unhappy and without hope: *dismal weather* —**dismally** *adv*

dis·man·tle /dɪsˈmæntl/ *v* [I,T] **1** to take something apart so that it is in separate pieces: *Chris dismantled the bike in five minutes.* **2** to gradually get rid of a system or organization: *the dismantling of the Communist system*

dis·may[1] /dɪsˈmeɪ/ *n* [U] the strong feeling of worry, disappointment, and unhappiness that you have when something unpleasant happens

dismay[2] *v* [T] to make someone feel worried, disappointed, and unhappy: *I was dismayed to hear that you were leaving.*

dis·mem·ber /dɪsˈmembə-ər/ *v* [T] *formal* to cut or tear a body into pieces: *The driver was dismembered in a horrible accident.*

dis·miss /dɪsˈmɪs/ *v* [T] **1** to refuse to consider someone's ideas, opinions etc: **dismiss sth as** *He dismissed the idea as impossible.* **2** *formal* to make someone leave their job: *If you're late again you'll be dismissed!* **3** to send someone away or allow them to go: *Classes will be dismissed early tomorrow.* —**dismissal** *n* [C,U]

dis·miss·ive /dɪsˈmɪsɪv/ *adj* refusing to consider someone or something seriously: + **of** *She*

GRAMMAR NOTE: the present perfect (2)
You use the **present perfect**: **1** to talk about something that happened in the past, but which still affects the situation now: *I've lost my passport.* **2** to talk about something that happened in the past, and continues to happen now: *I have lived in London for many years.* (=I still live there now).

tends to be dismissive of anyone who complains.
—**dismissively** *adv*

dis·mount /dɪsˈmaʊnt/ *v* [I] to get off a horse, bicycle, or MOTORCYCLE

dis·o·be·di·ent /ˌdɪsəˈbiːdiənt, ˌdɪsəʊ-‖ ˌdɪsə-, ˌdɪsoʊ-/ *adj* deliberately not doing what you are told to do: *a disobedient child* —**disobediently** *adv* —**disobedience** *n* [U]

dis·o·bey /ˌdɪsəˈbeɪ, ˌdɪsəʊ-‖ˌdɪsə-, ˌdɪsoʊ-/ *v* [I,T] to refuse to do what you are told to do: *She would never disobey her parents.*

dis·or·der /dɪsˈɔːdə‖-ˈɔːrdər/ *n* **1** [U] when things or people are very untidy or disorganized: *The house was in a state of complete disorder.* **2** civil/public disorder when a lot of people in a country do not obey the law and cannot be controlled **3** [C] an illness that prevents part of your body from working properly: *a rare liver disorder* —**disordered** *adj*

dis·or·der·ly /dɪsˈɔːdəli‖-ˈɔːrdər-/ *adj* **1** untidy: *clothes left in a disorderly heap* **2** noisy or violent, especially in a public place: *Jerry was charged with being drunk and disorderly.* —**disorderliness** *n* [U]

dis·or·gan·ized (also **-ised** *BrE*) /dɪsˈɔːɡənaɪzd‖-ˈɔːr-/ *adj* not arranged or planned very well: *The whole meeting was completely disorganized.* —**disorganization** /dɪsˌɔːɡənaɪˈseɪʃən‖-ˌɔːrɡənə-/ *n* [U]

dis·or·i·ent·ed /dɪsˈɔːrientɪd/ *also* **dis·or·ien·tat·ed** /dɪsˈɔːrienteɪtɪd/ *BrE adj* confused and not really able to understand what is happening or where you are: *After the long flight, I was tired and disoriented for a week.* —**disorienting, disorientating** *adj* —**disorientation** /dɪsˌɔːriənˈteɪʃən/ *n* [U]

dis·own /dɪsˈəʊn‖-ˈoʊn/ *v* [T] to say that you no longer have any connection with someone or something: *His family disowned him when he decided to marry an actress.*

di·spar·a·ging /dɪˈspærədʒɪŋ/ *adj* disparaging remarks, looks etc show that you do not think someone or something is very good or important: *Her mother was always making disparaging comments about her choice of boyfriends.* —**disparage** *v* [T]

dis·pa·rate /ˈdɪspərɪt/ *adj formal* disparate things are very different and not connected with each other: *She uses a range of disparate materials in her artwork.* —**disparately** *adv*

di·spar·i·ty /dɪˈspærɪti/ *n* [C,U] *formal* a difference between things, especially an unfair difference: + **in/between** *the disparities between rich and poor*

dis·pas·sion·ate /dɪsˈpæʃənɪt/ *adj* not influenced by personal feelings: *a dispassionate opinion* —**dispassionately** *adv*

di·spatch¹ (also **despatch** *BrE*) /dɪˈspætʃ/ *v* [T] to send someone or something to a place: *The packages were dispatched yesterday.*

dispatch² (also **despatch** *BrE*) *n* [C] a message sent between government or military OFFICIALS, or sent to a newspaper by one of its writers

di·spel /dɪˈspel/ *v* -**lled**, -**lling** [T] *formal* to stop someone believing or feeling something: *Mark's calm words dispelled our fears.*

di·spen·sa·ry /dɪˈspensəri/ *n* [C] a place where medicines are prepared and given out

dis·pen·sa·tion /ˌdɪspənˈseɪʃən, -pen-/ *n* [C,U] permission to do something that is not usually allowed

di·spense /dɪˈspens/ *v* [T] **1** to give or provide people with something: *The machines in the hall dispense drinks.* **2** to prepare and give medicines to people
dispense with sth *phr v* [T] to not use or do something because it is no longer necessary: *Your new computer dispenses with the need for a secretary.*

di·spens·er /dɪˈspensə‖-ər/ *n* [C] a machine that you can get things such as drinks or money from: *a cash dispenser*

di·sperse /dɪˈspɜːs‖-ɜːrs/ *v* [I,T] to scatter in different directions, or to make something do this: *Police used tear gas to disperse the crowd.* —**dispersal** *n* [U]

di·spir·it·ed /dɪˈspɪrɪtɪd/ *adj* sad and without hope —**dispiritedly** *adv*

dis·place /dɪsˈpleɪs/ *v* [T] **1** to take the place of someone or something: *Coal has been displaced by natural gas as a major source of energy.* **2** to make a group of people leave the place where they normally live: *Over a million people had been displaced by the war.* —**displacement** *n* [U] —**displaced** *adj*

di·splay¹ /dɪˈspleɪ/ *n* **1** [C,U] an attractive arrangement of things for people to look at: **be on display** (=being displayed): *A collection of African masks will be on display till the end of the month.* **2** a display of affection/temper etc when someone clearly shows a particular feeling, attitude, or quality: *an impressive display of skill* **3** a public event in which something is shown: *a military display* | *a firework display*

display² *v* [T] **1** to put things where people can see them easily: *tables displaying pottery* **2** to clearly show a feeling, attitude, or quality: *He displayed no emotion at Helen's funeral.*

dis·pleased /dɪsˈpliːzd/ *adj formal* annoyed: *His Majesty was very displeased.* —**displease** *v* [T] —**displeasure** /dɪsˈpleʒə‖-ər/ *n* [U]

dis·po·sa·ble /dɪˈspəʊzəbəl‖-ˈspoʊ-/ *adj* intended to be used once or for a short time and then thrown away: *a disposable toothbrush*

disposable in·come /.ˌ... ˈ../ *n* [U] the amount of money you have after paying all your bills, taxes etc

dis·pos·al /dɪˈspəʊzəl‖-ˈspoʊ-/ *n* **1** [U] when you get rid of something: + **of** *the safe disposal of radioactive waste* **2** be at sb's disposal to be available for someone to use: *My car and driver are at your disposal.*

dis·pose /dɪˈspəʊz‖-ˈspoʊz/ *v*
dispose of sth *phr v* [T] **1** to get rid of something: *How did the killer dispose of his victims' bodies?* **2** to deal with something such as a problem or question successfully: *The court quickly disposed of the case.*

dis·posed /dɪˈspəʊzd‖-ˈspoʊzd/ *adj formal* **1** be disposed to do sth to be willing to do something: *I don't feel disposed to interfere.* **2** well/favourably/kindly disposed (to) liking or approving of something: *He had always been kindly disposed towards his stepdaughter.*

dis·po·si·tion /ˌdɪspəˈzɪʃən/ *n* [C] *formal* someone's usual character: *a warm and friendly disposition*

dis·pro·por·tion·ate /ˌdɪsprə'pɔːʃənʲtᵻ ‖-ɔːr-/ *adj* too much or too little in relation to something: *The movie has received a disproportionate amount of publicity.* —**disproportionately** *adv*

dis·prove /dɪs'pruːv/ *v* [T] to show that something is false: *Lane was unable to disprove the accusation.*

di·spute[1] /dɪ'spjuːt,'dɪspjuːt/ *n* [C,U] **1** a serious argument or disagreement: *a pay dispute* | **be in dispute (with sb)** *Some of the players are in dispute with club owners.* **2** **be open to dispute** to not be completely certain: *The results of this research are still open to dispute.*

dis·pute[2] /dɪ'spjuːt/ *v* [T] to say that you think something is not correct or true: *The main facts of Morton's book have never been disputed.*

dis·qual·i·fy /dɪs'kwɒlʲfaɪ‖-'kwɑː-/ *v* [T] to stop someone from taking part in an activity or competition, usually because they have done something wrong: + **from** *Schumacher was disqualified from the race.* —**disqualification** /dɪsˌkwɒlʲfʲ'keɪʃən‖-ˌkwɑː-/ *n* [C,U]

dis·qui·et /dɪs'kwaɪət/ *n* [U] *formal* the feeling of being anxious or not satisfied about something: *public disquiet about animal testing*

dis·re·gard /ˌdɪsrɪ'gɑːd‖-ɑːrd/ *v* [T] to ignore something: *The judge ordered us to disregard the witness's last statement.* —**disregard** *n* [U]

dis·re·pair /ˌdɪsrɪ'peə‖-'per/ *n* [U] when something is in a bad condition and needs to be repaired: **fall into disrepair** *The old house has been allowed to fall into disrepair.*

dis·rep·u·ta·ble /dɪs'repjʲtəbəl/ *adj* thought to be involved in dishonest activities: *a slightly disreputable establishment*

dis·re·pute /ˌdɪsrɪ'pjuːt/ *n* [U] *formal* **bring sb/sth into disrepute** to make people stop trusting or respecting someone or something: *Beth had brought the family name into disrepute.*

dis·re·spect /ˌdɪsrɪ'spekt/ *n* [U] a lack of respect or politeness

dis·re·spect·ful /ˌdɪsrɪ'spektfəl/ *adj* not behaving in a polite way that shows respect for someone or something —**disrespectfully** *adv*

dis·rupt /dɪs'rʌpt/ *v* [T] to stop a situation, event etc from continuing normally: *Traffic will be severely disrupted by road works.* —**disruptive** *adj* —**disruption** /-'rʌpʃən/ *n* [C,U]

dis·sat·is·fied /dɪ'sætʲsfaɪd, dɪs'sæ-/ *adj* not satisfied, especially because something is not as good as you had expected: + **with** *If you are dissatisfied with this product, please return it for a full refund.* —**dissatisfaction** /dɪˌsætʲs'fækʃən, dɪsˌsæ-/ *n* [U]

dis·sect /dɪ'sekt, daɪ-/ *v* [T] to cut up the body of a plant or animal in order to study it —**dissection** /-'sekʃən/ *n* [C,U]

dis·sem·i·nate /dɪ'semʲneɪt/ *v* [T] to spread information, ideas etc to as many people as possible: *a system to disseminate information on the health care available* —**dissemination** /dɪˌsemʲ'neɪʃən/ *n* [U]

dis·sent /dɪ'sent/ *n* [U] when someone strongly disagrees with an opinion, especially a political or religious one, that most people accept: *political dissent* —**dissent** *v* [I] —**dissenter** *n* [C]

dis·ser·ta·tion /ˌdɪsə'teɪʃən‖ˌdɪsər-/ *n* [C] a long piece of writing about a subject, especially one that you write as part of a university degree

dis·ser·vice /dɪ'sɜːvʲs, dɪs'sɜː-‖-ɜːr-/ *n* [singular, U] something that harms someone or something: **do sb a disservice** *The new laws have done young people a great disservice.*

dis·si·dent /'dɪsʲdənt/ *n* [C] someone who publicly criticizes their government or political party —**dissident** *adj* —**dissidence** *n* [U]

dis·sim·i·lar /dɪ'sɪmʲlə, dɪs'sɪ-‖-ər/ *adj* not the same —**dissimilarity** /dɪˌsɪmʲ'lærʲti, dɪs,sɪ-/ *n* [C,U]

dis·si·pate /'dɪsʲpeɪt/ *v* [I,T] *formal* to disappear, or to make something do this: *The smoke gradually dissipated into the air.*

dis·so·ci·ate /dɪ'səʊʃieɪt, -sɪeɪt‖-'soʊ-/ also **dis·as·so·ci·ate** /ˌdɪsə'səʊʃieɪt, -sɪeɪt‖-'soʊ-/ *v* [T] to say that you have no connection with or are not responsible for someone or something: *The company dissociated itself from the comments made by Mr Hoffman.* —**dissociation** /dɪˌsəʊʃi'eɪʃən, -sɪeɪ-‖-,soʊ-/ *n* [U]

dissolve

dis·solve /dɪ'zɒlv‖dɪ'zɑːlv/ *v* **1** [I,T] if something solid dissolves, or if you dissolve it, it is mixed with a liquid so that it becomes liquid itself: *Dissolve the tablets in warm water.* **2** [T] to formally or legally end a marriage, business arrangement etc: *All trade unions were dissolved.* **3** [I] to become weaker and disappear: *Our fears gradually dissolved.* **4** **dissolve into tears/laughter etc** to start to cry, laugh etc so much that you cannot control yourself

dis·suade /dɪ'sweɪd/ *v* [T] *formal* to persuade someone not to do something: *I wish I could have dissuaded Rob from his plan.*

dis·tance[1] /'dɪstəns/ *n* **1** [C,U] the amount of space between two places or things: **short/long distance** *It's just a short distance from here to the restaurant.* **2** [singular] a point or place that is far away, but close enough to be seen or heard: **in the distance** *I glimpsed George's red shirt in the distance.* | **at/from a distance** *The detective followed him at a distance.* **3** **within walking/ driving distance** near enough to walk or drive to: *The lake is within walking distance of my house.* **4** **keep your distance a)** to avoid becoming too friendly or involved with someone or something: *Managers should keep their distance from employees.* **b)** to stay away from someone or something

distance[2] *v* **distance yourself** to say that you have little or no connection with someone or something: *The party is distancing itself from its violent past.*

dis·tant /'dɪstənt/ *adj* **1** far away from where you are now, or a long time from now: *the distant hills* | *in the distant past* **2** not very closely related to you: *a distant cousin* **3** not very friendly with or interested in other people: *a very formal and distant man* — **distantly** *adv*

dis·taste /dɪs'teɪst/ *n* [singular, U] the feeling you have when you strongly dislike or disapprove of something and it seems very unpleasant: + **for** *a distaste for modern art*

dis·taste·ful /dɪs'teɪstfəl/ *adj* very unpleasant or offensive: *I just want to forget the whole distasteful episode.*

dis·til *BrE*, **distill** *AmE* /dɪ'stɪl/ *v* [T] **-lled, -lling** to turn a liquid into gas and then turn the gas into liquid again, in order to make it purer or stronger: *distilled water* — **distillation** /ˌdɪstɪ'leɪʃən/ *n* [C,U]

dis·til·le·ry /dɪ'stɪləri/ *n* [C] a factory where alcoholic drinks such as WHISKY are produced by distilling

dis·tinct /dɪ'stɪŋkt/ *adj* **1** clearly different or separate: *Two entirely distinct languages are spoken in the region.* **2** clearly seen, heard, or understood: *A distinct smell of burning came from the kitchen.* **3** **as distinct from** used to emphasize that you are talking about one thing and not another: *childhood as distinct from adolescence* — **distinctly** *adv*

dis·tinc·tion /dɪ'stɪŋkʃən/ *n* **1** [C] a clear difference between things: + **between** *the distinction between fiction and reality* | **make/draw a distinction** *The author draws a distinction between "crime" and "sin".* **2** [C] a special honour given to someone: *Sol had the distinction of leading the delegation.* **3** of distinction unusually good: *an artist of great distinction*

dis·tinc·tive /dɪ'stɪŋktɪv/ *adj* showing a person or thing to be different from others: *Chris has a very distinctive laugh.* — **distinctiveness** *n* [U] — **distinctively** *adv*

dis·tin·guish /dɪ'stɪŋgwɪʃ/ *v* **1** [I,T] to recognize or understand the difference between similar things or people: + **between** *Young children often can't distinguish between TV programs and commercials.* **2** [T] to be able to see or hear something, even if it is difficult: *The light was too dim for me to distinguish anything clearly.* **3** [T] to be the thing that makes someone or something different from other people or things: *Brightly coloured feathers distinguish the male peacock from the female.* **4** **distinguish yourself** to do something so well that people notice and remember you — **distinguishable** *adj*

dis·tin·guished /dɪ'stɪŋgwɪʃt/ *adj* very successful and therefore respected: *a distinguished medical career*

dis·tort /dɪ'stɔːtǁ-ɔːrt/ *v* [T] **1** to tell people about a fact, statement etc in a way that changes its meaning: *Journalists distorted what he actually said.* **2** to change the shape or sound of something so it is strange or unclear: *Her thick glasses seemed to distort her eyes.* — **distorted** *adj* — **distortion** /-'stɔːʃənǁ-ɔːr-/ *n* [C,U]

dis·tract /dɪ'strækt/ *v* [T] to take someone's attention away from what they are doing: *Don't distract me while I'm driving!* | + **from** *Charles is easily distracted from his studies.*

dis·tract·ed /dɪ'stræktɪd/ *adj* anxious and unable to think clearly about what is happening around you: *She seemed nervous and distracted.*

dis·trac·tion /dɪ'strækʃən/ *n* **1** [C,U] something that takes your attention away from what you are doing: *I can't study at home – there are*

too many distractions. **2** [C] a pleasant and not very serious activity that you do for amusement **3** **drive sb to distraction** to annoy someone

dis·traught /dɪ'strɔːtǁ-'strɔːt/ *adj* extremely anxious or upset: *A policewoman was trying to calm the boy's distraught mother.*

dis·tress¹ /dɪ'stres/ *n* [U] **1** a feeling of extreme worry and unhappiness: *Children suffer emotional distress when their parents divorce.* **2** when someone or something is in great danger or difficulty: **in distress** *charities that aid families in distress*

distress² *v* [T] to make someone feel extremely worried or upset: *She had been badly distressed by his visit.* — **distressed** *adj*

dis·tress·ing /dɪ'stresɪŋ/ *adj* making you feel extremely upset and anxious: *a distressing experience* — **distressingly** *adv*

dis·trib·ute /dɪ'strɪbjuːt/ *v* [T] **1** to give something to each person in a group: *Can you distribute copies of the report to everyone?* **2** to supply goods to shops and companies in a particular area: *The tape costs $19.95 and is distributed by American Video.* — **distribution** /ˌdɪstrɪ'bjuːʃən/ *n* [U]

dis·trib·u·tor /dɪ'strɪbjʊtəǁ-ər/ *n* [C] a company or person that supplies goods to shops or companies

dis·trict /'dɪstrɪkt/ *n* [C] an area of a city or country: *a pleasant suburban district*

district at·tor·ney /ˌ... '...../ *n* [C] *AmE* a lawyer who works for the government in a particular area and brings criminals to court

dis·trust¹ /dɪs'trʌst/ *n* [U] a feeling that you cannot trust someone: + **of** *There's a certain distrust of technology among older people.* — **distrustful** *adj*

distrust² *v* [T] to not trust someone or something: *Meg had always distrusted banks.*

dis·turb /dɪ'stɜːbǁ-ɜːrb/ *v* [T] **1** to interrupt what someone is doing by making a noise, asking a question etc: *Josh told me not to disturb him before ten.* **2** to make someone feel worried or slightly nervous: *There were several things about the situation that disturbed him.*

dis·turb·ance /dɪ'stɜːbənsǁ-ɜːr-/ *n* **1** [C,U] something that interrupts you or stops you doing something you would normally do: *People are complaining about the disturbance caused by the roadworks.* **2** [C] when people are fighting, behaving noisily etc in public: *The police arrested three men for creating a disturbance at the bar.*

dis·turbed /dɪ'stɜːbdǁ-ɜːrbd/ *adj* not behaving in a normal way because of mental or emotional problems

dis·turb·ing /dɪ'stɜːbɪŋǁ-ɜːr-/ *adj* making you feel worried or nervous: *a disturbing increase in violent crime*

dis·use /dɪs'juːs/ *n* [U] when something is no longer used: *The building eventually fell into disuse.*

ditch¹ /dɪtʃ/ *n* [C] a long narrow hole cut into the ground at the side of a field, road etc

ditch² *v* [T] *informal* to get rid of someone or something: *The team ditched their latest coach.*

dith·er /'dɪðəǁ-ər/ *v* [I] to be unable to make a decision: *She dithered over what to wear.*

dit·to¹ /ˈdɪtəʊ‖-toʊ/ *adv* used when you agree with what someone has just said, or to avoid repeating a word or phrase: *"I love pizza!" "Ditto!"* | *There's a meeting on March 2nd, ditto on April 6th.*

ditto² *n* [C] a mark (″) that you write under a word in a list so that you do not have to write the same word again

dit·ty /ˈdɪti/ *n* [C] *humorous* a short simple song or poem

di·van /dɪˈvæn‖ˈdaɪvæn/ *n* [C] **1** a bed with a thick base **2** a long low soft seat with no arms or back

dive¹ /daɪv/ *v* [I] **dived** (also **dove** /dəʊv‖doʊv/ *AmE*) **diving** **1** to jump into the water with your head and arms first: **+ into** *Harry dived into the swimming pool.* **2** to swim under water using breathing equipment **3** if a bird or aircraft dives, it moves down through the air very quickly **4** to jump forward or to one side in order to catch or avoid something: *Richard dived to his left for the ball.*

dive
diving board

dive² *n* [C] **1** a jump into the water with your head and arms going in first **2** *informal* a place such as a bar or a hotel that is cheap and dirty: *We ate an some dive out by the airport.*

div·er /ˈdaɪvəʳ-ər/ *n* [C] someone who swims under water with breathing equipment: *a scuba diver*

di·verge /daɪˈvɜːdʒ, dɪ̩-‖-ɜːrdʒ-/ *v* [I] to be different or to develop in different ways: *At this point the two explanations diverge.* — **divergence** *n* [C,U] — **divergent** *adj*

di·verse /daɪˈvɜːs‖dɪ̩ˈvɜːrs, daɪ-/ *adj formal* very different from each other: *London is home to people of many diverse cultures.* — **diversity** *n* [U]

di·ver·si·fy /daɪˈvɜːsɪ̩faɪ‖dɪ̩ˈvɜːr-, daɪ-/ *v* [I,T] to begin to make different products or get involved in new areas of business: **+ into** *a computer company that is diversifying into the software market* — **diversification** /daɪˌvɜːsɪ̩fɪ̩ˈkeɪʃən‖dɪ̩-ˌvɜːr-, daɪ-/ *n* [U]

di·ver·sion /daɪˈvɜːʃən, dɪ̩-‖-ɜːrʒ-ən/ *n* **1** [C] something that takes your attention away from something else: **create a diversion** *The prisoners created a diversion so the others could escape.* **2** [C,U] a change in the direction or purpose of something: **+ of** *the diversion of resources into education* **3** [C] *BrE* when traffic has to use a different road because the usual way is blocked

di·vert /daɪˈvɜːt, dɪ̩-‖-ɜːrt/ *v* [T] **1** to change the direction or purpose of something: *Traffic is being diverted to avoid the accident.* | *Huge salaries for managers divert money from patient care.* **2 divert (sb's) attention from** to stop someone from giving their attention to something: *Tax cuts diverted people's attention from the real economic problems.*

di·vest /daɪˈvest, dɪ̩-/ *v*

divest sb of sth *phr v* [T] *formal* to take something away from someone: *a leader divested of power*

di·vide¹ /dɪ̩ˈvaɪd/ *v* **1** [I,T] to separate something, or to become separated, into two or more parts: **divide sth into** *The teacher divided the class into groups.* | **divide sth between/among** *Divide the fruit mixture among four glasses.* **2** [T] to keep two areas separate from each other: **divide sth from** *A curtain divided his sleeping area from the rest of the room.* **3** also **divide up** [T] to separate something into two or more parts and share it among two or more people: **divide sth between/among** *How do you divide your time between work and family?* **4** [I,T] to calculate how many times one number is contained in a larger number: *15 divided by five is three.* **5** [T] to make people disagree and form groups with different opinions: **be divided over** *Experts are bitterly divided over what to do.*

divide² *n* [C usually singular] a difference between two groups: *They're on opposite sides of the political divide.*

div·i·dend /ˈdɪvɪ̩dɒnd, -dend/ *n* [C] **1** a part of a company's profit that is paid to people who have SHARES in the company **2 pay dividends** if something you do will pay dividends, it will give you an advantage in the future

di·vine /dɪ̩ˈvaɪn/ *adj* having the qualities of God, or coming from God: *praying for divine guidance*

div·ing /ˈdaɪvɪŋ/ *n* [U] **1** the activity of swimming under water using breathing equipment **2** the activity of jumping into water with your head and arms first

diving board /ˈ.. ./ *n* [C] a board above a SWIMMING POOL from which you can jump into the water → see picture at DIVE

di·vin·i·ty /dɪ̩ˈvɪnɪ̩ti/ *n* [U] **1** the study of God and religious beliefs; THEOLOGY **2** the quality of being like God

di·vis·i·ble /dɪ̩ˈvɪzɪ̩bəl/ *adj* able to be divided, especially by another number: **+ by** *15 is divisible by three and five.*

di·vi·sion /dɪ̩ˈvɪʒən/ *n* **1** [C,U] when something is divided into two or more parts or groups, or the way that it is divided: **+ between** *a division between public and private life* **2** [C,U] a disagreement among members of a group: *deep divisions in the Socialist party* **3** [U] the process of calculating how many times a small number will go into a larger number → compare MULTIPLICATION **4** [C] a group within a large company, army, organization etc: *the financial division of the company*

di·vi·sive /dɪ̩ˈvaɪsɪv/ *adj* causing a lot of disagreement among people: *This action would be extremely divisive.*

di·vorce¹ /dɪ̩ˈvɔːs‖-ɔːrs/ *n* [C,U] the legal ending of a marriage: *In Britain, one in three marriages ends in divorce.*

divorce² *v* **1** [I,T] to legally end a marriage: *Sue divorced Malcolm for cruelty.* | **get divorced**

D

Ben's parents got divorced when he was nine.
2 [T] *formal* to separate one thing from another: **divorce sth from** *His ideas are completely divorced from reality.* —**divorced** *adj: Her parents are divorced*

di·vor·cée /dʒ,vɔː'siːǁdə,vɔːr'seɪ/ *n* [C] someone, usually a woman, who is divorced

di·vulge /daɪ'vʌldʒ, dʒ-/ *v* [T] to give someone information, especially about something that is secret: *Doctors should never divulge confidential information.*

DIY /,diː aɪ 'waɪ/ *n* [U] *BrE* DO-IT-YOURSELF; the activity of building, repairing, or decorating parts of your house yourself

diz·zy /'dɪzi/ *adj* feeling that you are losing your balance, for example because you have been spinning round or you are ill: *She feels dizzy when she stands up.* —**dizziness** *n* [U]

dizzy

DJ /,diː 'dʒeɪ/ *n* [C] someone who introduces popular music on radio or television; an abbreviation for DISK JOCKEY

DNA /,diː en 'eɪ/ *n* [U] a substance that carries GENETIC information in a cell

do¹ /duː/ *auxiliary verb* **did** /dɪd/, **done** /dʌn/, **doing** **1** used with another verb to form questions or negatives: *What did you say?|Mark doesn't work here any more.* **2** *spoken* used to form QUESTION TAGS: *You went to London at the weekend, didn't you?|Her dress looks great, doesn't it?* **3** used to emphasize the main verb: *I did tell you – you obviously forgot!|He really did enjoy the trip.* **4** used to avoid repeating another verb: *She eats a lot more than I do.|so/neither do I She feels really angry and so do I.* (=I feel angry too)*|Paul didn't like the play and neither did I.* (=I did not like it either)

do² *v* **did, done, doing** **1** [T] to perform an action or job: *What are you doing?|Have you done your homework yet?* **2 do well/badly etc** to make good, bad etc progress: *Neil has done much better at school this year.* **3 do sb good** to make someone feel better or happier: *Let's go to the beach. Come on, it will do you good.* **4 do a lot for/not do much for** to have a good or bad effect on something: *The publicity surrounding the affair won't do much for his chances in the election.* **5 do something** to take action to solve a problem: *Don't just stand there – do something!* **6 do your hair/nails/make up etc** to make your hair etc look nice **7 what do you do?** *spoken* used to ask someone what their job is **8 will/would do** *especially spoken* to be suitable or good enough: *The recipe says to use butter but vegetable oil will do.* **9** [T] used to say how fast a car etc travels: *That idiot must be doing at least 100 miles an hour!* **10 do drugs** to take illegal drugs

do away with *phr v* [T] *informal* **1** [**do away with** sth] to make something unnecessary: *One disk will do away with the need for all those files.* **2** [**do away with** sb] to kill someone
do sb in *phr v* [T] *informal* to kill someone
do sth over *phr v* [T] **do it over** *AmE* to do

something again, especially because you did it wrong the first time
do up *phr v* [I,T **do** sth ↔ **up**] **1** to fasten or tie something: *The skirt does up at the back.|Robbie can't do his shoelaces up yet.* **2** to repair and improve a building, car etc: *They've done up the old house beautifully.*
do with sth *phr v* **1 be/have to do with** to be about something or related to something: *The lecture is to do with new theories in physics.|Jack's job is something to do with television.* **2 could do with** to need or want something: *I could do with a drink.*
do without *phr v* **1** [I,T **do without** sth] to not have something: *We couldn't do without the car.* **2 could do without** *spoken* used to say that something is annoying you or making things difficult for you: *I could do without all this hassle at work.*

do³ *n* **1** [C] *informal* a party or other social event: *Jodie's having a big do for her birthday.* **2 dos and don'ts** things that you must or must not do: *I'm still learning all the dos and don'ts of the job.*

do·cile /'dəʊsaɪlǁ'dɑːsəl/ *adj* quiet and easy to control: *a docile animal* —**docility** /dəʊ'sɪlʒti ǁdɑː-/ *n* [U]

dock¹ /dɒkǁdɑːk/ *n* **1** [C] a place where goods are taken on and off ships **2 the dock** *BrE* the place in a court of law where the prisoner stands; THE STAND *AmE*

dock² *v* **1** [I,T] when a ship docks, it arrives at a dock **2 dock sb's pay** to reduce the amount of money that you pay someone, because they have done something wrong: *If you come in late again, we'll have to dock your pay.*

dock work·er /'. ,../ also **dock·er** /'dɒkǁ'dɑːkər/ *BrE* — *n* [C] a person whose job is to move goods on and off ships

doc·tor¹ /'dɒktǁ'dɑːktər/ *n* [C] **1** someone whose job is to treat people who are ill: *You should see a doctor about that cough.* **2** someone who has a doctorate: *a Doctor of Philosophy*

cians. Someone who is trained to treat animals is a **vet**, or **veterinarian** in American English.

doctor² *v* [T] to change something, especially in a way that is not honest: *Do you think the police doctored the evidence?*

doc·tor·ate /ˈdɒktərɪt‖ˈdɑːk-/ *n* [C] a university degree at the highest level

doc·trine /ˈdɒktrɪn‖ˈdɑːk-/ *n* [C,U] a belief or set of beliefs, especially religious or political ones

doc·u·ment¹ /ˈdɒkjɐmənt‖ˈdɑːk-/ *n* [C] **1** a piece of paper that has official information written on it: *legal documents* **2** a piece of work that you write and keep on a computer

doc·u·ment² /ˈdɒkjɐment‖ˈdɑːk-/ *v* [T] to record information about something by writing about it, photographing it etc: *The programme documents the life of a teenage mother.*

doc·u·men·ta·ry /ˌdɒkjɐˈmentəri‖ˌdɑːk-/ *n* [C] a serious film or television programme that gives facts and information about something: *a documentary about homeless people*

doc·u·men·ta·tion /ˌdɒkjɐmənˈteɪʃən, -menˈ-‖ˌdɑːk-/ *n* [U] documents that provide a record of something

dod·dle /ˈdɒdl‖ˈdɑːdl/ *n BrE informal* **be a doddle** to be extremely easy: *The exam was a doddle.*

dodge¹ /dɒdʒ‖dɑːdʒ/ *v* **1** [I,T] to move suddenly to the side in order to avoid someone or something: *He managed to dodge the other man's fists.* **2** [T] to avoid talking about something or doing something: *The President was accused of deliberately dodging the issue.*

dodge² *n* [C] *informal* a way of avoiding something that you should do: *a tax dodge*

dodg·y /ˈdɒdʒi‖ˈdɑː-/ *adj BrE informal* **1** someone or something that is dodgy cannot be trusted or depended on: *Joe's a really dodgy character.* **2** a dodgy activity is probably illegal: *a dodgy deal*

doe /dəʊ‖doʊ/ *n* [C] a female DEER

does /dəz; *strong* dʌz/ *v* the 3rd person singular of the present tense of DO

does·n't /ˈdʌznt/ *v* the short form of "does not"

dog¹ /dɒg‖dɔːg/ *n* [C] a very common animal that is often kept as a pet or as a working animal: *a guard dog* | *I'm just off to walk the dog.*

dog² *v* [T] **-gged, -gging** if a problem or bad luck dogs you, it causes trouble for a long time

dog-eared /ˈ. ./ *adj* dog-eared books have the corners of their pages folded or torn

dog·ged /ˈdɒgɪd‖ˈdɔː-/ *adj* [only before noun] determined to do something even though it is difficult: *his dogged determination to learn English* — **doggedly** *adv*

dog·house /ˈdɒghaʊs‖ˈdɔːg-/ *n* **1 be in the doghouse** *informal* to have annoyed or made someone angry with you **2** [C] *AmE* a little building for a dog to sleep in; KENNEL *BrE*

dog·ma /ˈdɒgmə‖ˈdɔːgmə, ˈdɑːgmə/ *n* [C,U] beliefs that people are expected to accept as true without having any doubts or without asking for any explanation: *religious dogma*

dog·mat·ic /dɒgˈmætɪk‖dɔːg-, dɑːg-/ *adj* someone who is dogmatic has very strong beliefs which they are not willing to change, even when

it would be reasonable to do so — **dogmatically** /-kli/ *adv*

do-good·er /ˌ. ˈ..‖ˈ.. ˌ./ *n* [C] *informal* someone who thinks they are helping others, but who often gets involved when they are not wanted

dogs·bod·y /ˈdɒgzˌbɒdi‖ˈdɔːgzˌbɑːdi/ *n* [C] *BrE informal* someone who has to do all the ordinary boring jobs in a place: *I'm just the office dogsbody.*

do·ing¹ /ˈduːɪŋ/ *n* **1 be sb's (own) doing** to be someone's fault: *His bad luck was all his own doing.* **2 take some doing** to be hard work: *Getting the place clean is going to take some doing.*

doing² the present participle of DO

do-it-your·self /ˌ. .ˈ. ‹/ *n* [U] DIY

dol·drums /ˈdɒldrəmz‖ˈdoʊl-, ˈdɑːl-, ˈdɔːl-/ *n* **be in the doldrums** if an activity or situation is in the doldrums, nothing new or exciting is happening or there is no improvement: *Sales have been in the doldrums for most of the year.*

dole¹ /dəʊl‖doʊl/ *n* [U] *BrE* money that the government gives to people who are unemployed: **be on the dole** (=be receiving government money)

dole² *v*

dole sth ↔ **out** *phr v* [T] to give money, food, advice etc in small amounts to a lot of people: *Dad began doling out porridge from the saucepan.*

dole·ful /ˈdəʊlfəl‖ˈdoʊl-/ *adj written* someone who has a doleful expression looks sad: *Tim gave me a doleful look.* — **dolefully** *adv*

doll /dɒl‖dɑːl, dɔːl/ *n* [C] a toy that looks like a small child or person

dol·lar /ˈdɒlə‖ˈdɑːlər/ *n* [C] **1** written sign $; the standard unit of money in the US, Australia, Canada, New Zealand etc: *The company has a $7 million debt.* **2** a piece of paper or a coin worth this amount

dol·lop /ˈdɒləp‖ˈdɑː-/ *n* [C] a small amount of thick liquid or soft food, that is dropped onto or into something: *Serve the pudding hot with a dollop of cream.*

dol·phin /ˈdɒlfɪn‖ˈdɑːl-, ˈdɔːl-/ *n* [C] a sea MAMMAL like a large grey fish, which is very intelligent

dolphin

do·main /dəˈmeɪn, dəʊ-‖də-, doʊ-/ *n* [C] *formal* **1** if something is someone's domain, they control it, are responsible for it, or their group usually does it: *Politics has traditionally been a male domain.* **2** all the things that are included in a subject or activity: *The problem is outside the domain of medical science.* **3** an area that is controlled by someone in past times

dome /dəʊm‖doʊm/ *n* [C] a round curved roof — **domed** *adj*

dome

do·mes·tic /dəˈmestɪk/ *adj* **1** happening within one country and not involving any others: *Canada's domestic affairs* **2** relating to family relationships and life at home: *a victim of domestic violence* **3** enjoying spending time at home, doing things such as cooking **4** a domestic animal is kept as a pet

do·mes·ti·cat·ed /dəˈmestɪˌkeɪtɪd/ *adj* domesticated animals live with people as pets or on a farm

do·mes·tic·i·ty /ˌdəʊmesˈtɪsˌtɪ, ˌdɒ-/ *n* [U] life at home with your family

dom·i·nant /ˈdɒmɪnənt ǁ ˈdɑː-/ *adj* **1** strongest, most important, or most noticeable: *TV news is the dominant source of information in our society.* **2** wanting to control people or events: *a dominant personality* —**dominance** *n* [U]

dom·i·nate /ˈdɒmɪneɪt ǁ ˈdɑː-/ *v* [I,T] to have power and control over someone or something: *For sixty years France had dominated Europe.* **2** [I,T] to be the strongest, most important, or most noticeable feature of something: *The murder trial has been dominating the news this week.* —**domination** /ˌdɒmɪˈneɪʃən ǁ ˌdɑː-/ *n* [U]

dom·i·neer·ing /ˌdɒmɪˈnɪərɪŋ ǁ ˌdɑːmɪˈnɪr-/ *adj* trying to control other people without considering their feelings: *a domineering father*

do·min·ion /dəˈmɪnjən/ *n* [U] **1** *literary* the power or right to rule people **2** [C] *formal* the land owned or controlled by a ruler or government: *the king's dominion*

dom·i·no /ˈdɒmɪnəʊ ǁ ˈdɑːmɪnoʊ/ *n plural* **dominoes 1** [C] one of a set of small pieces of wood or plastic with spots on, used for playing a game **2** **dominoes** [U] the game played using dominoes

don[1] /dɒn ǁ dɑːn/ *v* [T] **-nned, -nning** *formal* to put on a hat, coat etc

don[2] *n* [C] *BrE* a teacher at a university, especially at Oxford or Cambridge

do·nate /dəʊˈneɪt ǁ ˈdoʊneɪt/ *v* [T] to give something useful to a person or organization that needs help: *Our school donated £500 to the Red Cross.*

do·na·tion /dəʊˈneɪʃən ǁ doʊ-/ *n* [C,U] something, especially money, that you give to help a person or organization: **make a donation** *Please make a donation to UNICEF.*

done[1] /dʌn/ *v* the past participle of DO

done[2] *adj* **1** finished or completed: *The job's nearly done.* **2** cooked enough to be eaten: *I think the hamburgers are done.* **3** **done!** *spoken* used to accept a deal that someone offers you: *"I'll give you £15 for it ." "Done!"* **4** **be done for** *spoken informal* to be in serious trouble or likely to fail: *If we get caught, we're done for.*

don·key /ˈdɒŋki ǁ ˈdɑːŋki/ *n* **1** [C] a grey or brown animal like a small horse with long ears **2** **for donkey's years** *BrE informal* for a very long time: *I've known Kevin for donkey's years.*

donkey work /ˈ.. ./ *n* *BrE informal* **do the donkey work** to do the hard or boring part of an activity or job

do·nor /ˈdəʊnə ǁ ˈdoʊnər/ *n* [C] **1** a person, group etc that gives something, especially money, to an organization in order to help people: *The Museum received $10,000 from an anonymous donor.* **2** someone who gives some of their blood or part of their body to help a person who is ill

don't /dəʊnt ǁ doʊnt/ the short form of "do not": *I don't know.*

do·nut /ˈdəʊnʌt ǁ ˈdoʊ-/ *n* [C] a DOUGHNUT

doo·dle /ˈduːdl/ *v* [I,T] to draw shapes, patterns etc while you are thinking about something else: *I spent most of the class doodling in my notebook.* —**doodle** *n* [C]

doom[1] /duːm/ *n* **1** [U] a terrible situation in the future that you are unable to avoid: *a sense of impending doom* (=something bad that will soon happen) **2** **doom and gloom** *humorous* a feeling that the future will be terrible: *Barry's always full of doom and gloom.*

doom[2] *v* [T] to make something terrible certain to happen: **be doomed to (do) sth** *They were doomed to repeat the mistakes of the past.* —**doomed** *adj: The mission was doomed from the start.*

door /dɔː ǁ dɔːr/ *n* **1** [C] the thing that you open and close to get in or out of a house, room, car etc: *Will you shut the door please.* | *I'll lock the back door on my way out.* **2** [C] the space made by an open door: **out of/through the door** *Lisa ran through the door into the garden.* **3** **next door** in the room, house etc next to where you are: *the people who live next door* **4** **at the door** if there is someone at the door, there is someone waiting for you to open it **5** **answer/get the door** to open the door to see who is there **6** **door to door** **a)** between one place and another: *If you drive it should only take you 20 minutes door to door.* **b)** going to each house on a street to sell something, collect money etc: *The police questioned the neighbourhood door to door.* | *a door-to-door salesman*

door·bell /ˈdɔːbel ǁ ˈdɔːr-/ *n* [C] a button by the door of a house that you press to let the people inside know you are there

door·knob /ˈdɔːnɒb ǁ ˈdɔːrnɑːb/ *n* [C] a round handle on a door

door·man /ˈdɔːmæn, -mən ǁ ˈdɔːr-/ *n* [C] a man who works at the door of a hotel, theatre etc, helping people who are coming in and out

door·step /ˈdɔːstep ǁ ˈdɔːr-/ *n* **1** [C] a step just outside a door to a building **2** **on your doorstep** very near to where you live or are staying: *Wow! The beach is right on your doorstep!*

door·way /ˈdɔːweɪ ǁ ˈdɔːr-/ *n* [C] the space where the door opens into a room or building

dope[1] /dəʊp ǁ doʊp/ *n* [U] *informal* an illegal drug, especially MARIJUANA

dope[2] also **dope up** *v* [T] *informal* to give a drug to a person or animal to change their behaviour: *They have to dope the lions before they can catch them.*

dork /dɔːk ǁ dɔːrk/ *n* [C] *informal, especially AmE* someone that you think is stupid because they behave strangely or wear strange clothes: *He's such a dork!* —**dorky** *adj*

dor·mant /ˈdɔːmənt ǁ ˈdɔːr-/ *adj* not active now, but able to be active at a later time: *a dormant volcano*

dor·mi·to·ry /ˈdɔːmɪtəri ǁ ˈdɔːrmɪˌtɔːri/ also **dorm** /dɔːm ǁ dɔːrm/ *informal n* [C] **1** a large room where a lot of people sleep **2** *AmE* a large building at a school or college where students live; HALL OF RESIDENCE *BrE*

dor·sal /ˈdɔːsəl ǁ ˈdɔːr-/ *adj* [only before noun] *technical* relating to the back of a fish or animal: *a whale's dorsal fin*

DOS /dɒs ǁ dɑːs/ *n* [U] *trademark* Disk Operating System; SOFTWARE that is put onto a computer system to make all the different parts work together

dos·age /ˈdəʊsɪdʒ‖ˈdoʊ-/ n [C] the amount of a medicine that you should take: *Do not exceed the stated dosage.*

dose¹ /dəʊs‖doʊs/ n [C] **1** a measured amount of medicine: *One dose of this should get rid of the problem.* **2** the amount of something that you experience at one time: **in small doses** (=for short amounts of time) *She's OK in small doses, but I wouldn't like to live with her.*

dose² also **dose up** v [T] to give someone some medicine: *Dose yourself up with vitamin C if you think you're getting a cold.*

doss /dɒs‖dɑːs/ also **doss down** v [I] *BrE informal* to sleep somewhere uncomfortable, usually because you have no choice: *homeless people dossing in doorways*

dos·si·er /ˈdɒsieɪ‖ˈdɔːsjeɪ, ˈdɑː-/ n [C] a set of papers that include detailed information about someone or something: *The police keep dossiers on all suspected criminals.*

dot¹ /dɒt‖dɑːt/ n **1** [C] a small round mark or spot: *The stars look like small dots of light in the sky.* **2 on the dot** *informal* exactly at a particular time: *Penny arrived at nine o'clock on the dot.*

dot² v [T] **-tted, -tting** **1** to mark something by putting a dot on it or above it **2** to spread things out within an area: **+ around** *The company now has over 20 stores dotted around the country.*

dote /dəʊt‖doʊt/ v

dote on sb/sth *phr v* [T] to love someone very much, especially in a way that seems silly to other people: *Steve dotes on his son.*

dot·ing /ˈdəʊtɪŋ‖ˈdoʊ-/ adj [only before noun] a doting husband, mother etc dotes on his or her wife, child etc: *He was spoiled by his doting mother.*

dot·ted line /ˌ.. ˈ./ n **1** [C] a line of printed DOTS: *Cut along the dotted lines.* **2 sign on the dotted line** *informal* to officially agree to something, especially by writing your name to show that you agree on a contract

dot·ty /ˈdɒti‖ˈdɑːti/ adj *informal, especially BrE* slightly crazy

double¹ /ˈdʌbəl/ adj **1** twice the usual amount, size, or number: *I'll have a double whiskey, please.* | *a double helping of ice-cream* **2** made to be used by two people: *a double room* | *a double bed* **3** having two parts that are similar or the same: *double doors* | *a double garage* → see picture at BED

double² v [I,T] [I] to become twice as large or twice as much, or to make something do this: *They offered to double my salary if I stayed with the company.* | **+ in** *Our puppy has doubled in size since we bought it.*

double as sb/sth also **double up as** sb/sth *phr v* [T] to have a second use, job, or purpose: *The sofa doubles as a bed.* | *The bar owner doubles up as the town sheriff.*

double back *phr v* [I] to turn around and go back the way you have just come: *I doubled back and headed south again.*

double up also **double over** *phr v* [I,T **be doubled up/over**] to bend at the waist because you are in pain or laughing: *The whole audience was doubled up with laughter.*

double³ n **1** [C,U] something that is twice the size, quantity, value, or strength of something else: *I sold my old bike for £50 but I should have asked for double.* **2 sb's double** someone who looks very similar to someone else

double⁴ determiner twice as much or twice as many: *The necklace is worth double the amount we paid for it.*

double-bar·relled *BrE*, **double-barreled** *AmE* /ˌ.. ˈ.. ◂/ adj **1** a double-barrelled gun has two places where the bullets come out **2** *BrE* a double-barrelled family name has two parts

double bass /ˌdʌbəl ˈbeɪs/ n [C] a very large STRINGED INSTRUMENT, shaped like a VIOLIN, that you play while standing up

double-breast·ed /ˌ.. ˈ.. ◂/ adj a double breasted JACKET or coat has two rows of buttons down the front

double-check /ˌ.. ˈ./ v [I,T] to check something again so that you are completely sure: *I think I turned off the oven, but I'll double-check.*

double-cross /ˌ.. ˈ./ v [T] to cheat someone, usually after you have agreed to do something dishonest with them — **double cross** n [C]

double-deck·er /ˌ.. ˈ.. ◂/ n [C] a bus with two levels

double glaz·ing /ˌ.. ˈ../ n [U] *especially BrE* two layers of glass in windows or doors, that help keep a room warmer and quieter — **double glaze** v [T]

double life /ˌ.. ˈ./ n [C] a secret part of your life which is very different from the life that other people know about: *a double life as a spy*

doub·les /ˈdʌbəlz/ n [U] a game, especially of tennis, played by two pairs of people

double stand·ard /ˌ.. ˈ../ n [C usually plural] a rule or principle that is unfair because it treats one person or group differently from another: *The black community are accusing the police of double standards.*

double take /ˌ.. ˈ./ n **do a double take** to quickly look at someone or something again because you are surprised by what you just saw or heard

doub·ly /ˈdʌbli/ adv **1** twice as much: *doubly painful* **2** in two ways: *Rita was doubly distrusted, as a woman and as a foreigner.*

doubt¹ /daʊt/ n **1** [C,U] the feeling that something is not true or that someone cannot be trusted: **+ about** *Dad's always had serious doubts about my boyfriend.* | **there is/l have no doubt that** *There was no doubt that the witness was telling the truth.* **2 be in doubt** to be uncertain: *Sonia was in doubt about what to do.* **3 no doubt** *especially spoken* used to say that you think something is likely: *No doubt he's married by*

GRAMMAR NOTE: for and since

Use **for** with periods of time: *I've been waiting here for 25 minutes.* | *We've lived here for 6 years.*
Use **since** with the date or time when something started: *I've been waiting here since 7 o'clock.* |
We've lived here since 1992.

doubt

now. **4 no doubt about it** *spoken* used to show that you are certain about something: *Tommy's a great manager – no doubt about it.* **5 without doubt** used to say that something is definitely true: *He is, without doubt, the most annoying person I know!* **6 show/prove sth beyond doubt** to show or prove that something is definitely true

doubt² *v* [T] **1** to think that something may not be true or that it is unlikely: *Do you doubt her story?* | + (that) *I doubt it will make any difference.* **2** *formal* to not trust or believe someone or something: *I sometimes doubt her motives for being so friendly.*

> ### USAGE NOTE: doubt
>
> When you use the word **doubt** in a simple statement, it can be followed by 'that', 'if', or 'whether': *I doubt that the mail has arrived yet.* | *I doubt whether he's coming.* However, if the statement is negative, it can only be followed by 'that': *We don't doubt that she can do the job.* When you use the noun **doubt** after 'no' or 'not', it is always followed by 'that': *There's no doubt that he is guilty.*

doubt·ful /'daʊtfəl/ *adj* **1** unlikely to happen: + that *It's doubtful that we'll go abroad this year.* **2** not certain about something: *Jules looked doubtful about the suggestion.* **3** unlikely to be true: *a doubtful claim* —**doubtfully** *adv*

doubt·less /'daʊtləs/ *adv* very likely to happen or be true: *There will doubtless be someone at the party that you know.*

dough /dəʊ‖doʊ/ *n* [U] a soft mixture containing flour that you use to bake bread, PASTRY etc

dough·nut also **donut** /'dəʊnʌt‖-doʊ-/ *n* [C] a small cake that is usually shaped like a ring

dour /dʊə,'daʊə‖'daʊər, dʊr/ *adj* looking unfriendly and serious: *a dour expression* —**dourly** *adv*

douse also **dowse** /daʊs/ *v* [T] **1** to stop something burning by throwing water on it: *Firefighters quickly doused the blaze.* **2** to pour liquid over something

dove¹ /dʌv/ *n* [C] a type of small white bird often used as a sign of peace

dove² /dəʊv‖doʊv/ *v AmE* a past tense of DIVE

dow·dy /'daʊdi/ *adj* unattractive or unfashionable

down¹ /daʊn/ *adv, prep* **1** towards or in a lower place or position: *Lorraine bent down to kiss the little boy.* | *Several trees were blown down in the storm.* | *We ran down the hill.* | *James is down in the cellar.* → see colour picture on page 474 **2** to or at a lower rate, amount etc: *Slow down! You're going too fast.* | *Exports are down this year by 10%.* **3** towards the south or in a place that is further south than you are: *Gail's driving down to London to see her brother.* **4** in a direction away from where you are: *Could you go down to the baker's and get some bread?* | *They live down the road.* **5 write/note/take etc sth down** to write something on paper: *Write down your answers on a separate sheet.* | *Can I take down the details please?* **6 down the road/line** *spoken* at some time in the future: *We'd like to have children, but that's still a long way down the*

road. **7 be down to sb** to be for someone to decide or be responsible for: *If you want to take risks, that's down to you.*

down² *adj* [not before noun] **1** unhappy: *I've never seen Brett looking so down.* **2** behind in a game by a particular number of points: *We were down by 6 points at half-time.* **3** a computer that is down is not working

down³ *v* [T] to drink something quickly: *Matt downed his coffee and left.*

down⁴ *n* [U] thin soft feathers or hair

down-and-out /ˌ. . '. ‹/ *n* [C] someone who has no home, job, or money —**down-and-out** *adj*

down·cast /'daʊnkɑːst‖-kæst/ *adj* sad or disappointed: *The team were understandably downcast after their 4-0 defeat.*

down·er /'daʊnə‖-ər/ *n informal* **1** [singular] an experience that makes you feel unhappy: *a movie that ends on a real downer* **2** [C] a drug that makes you feel very relaxed

down·fall /'daʊnfɔːl‖-fɔːl/ *n* [singular] a situation in which you suddenly stop being successful, rich, important: *Greed will be his downfall.*

down·grade /'daʊngreɪd/ *v* [T] to give someone a less important job or make something seem less important: *Scott may be downgraded to assistant manager.*

down·heart·ed /ˌdaʊnˈhɑːtɪd‖-ɑːr-/ *adj* **be downhearted** to feel sad about something

down·hill /ˌdaʊnˈhɪl‹/ *adv, adj* **1** towards the bottom of a hill, or on a slope that goes down: *The truck's brakes failed and it rolled downhill.* | *downhill skiing* **2 go downhill** to become worse: *After Bob lost his job, things went downhill rapidly.* **3 be all downhill/be downhill all the way** to become easier: *The worst is over. It's all downhill from here.* → opposite UPHILL

Dow·ning Street /'daʊnɪŋ striːt/ *n* [U] the government of Great Britain: *talks between Dublin and Downing Street*

down·load /ˌdaʊnˈləʊd‖-ˈloʊd/ *v* [T] to move information from one part of a computer system to another using a MODEM

down pay·ment /ˌ. '. ./ *n* [C] the first payment you make on something expensive that you will pay for over a long period: *We've made a down payment on a new car.*

down·play /ˌdaʊnˈpleɪ/ *v* [T] to make something seem less important than it really is: *The police downplayed the seriousness of the situation.*

down·pour /'daʊnpɔː‖-pɔːr/ *n* [C usually singular] a lot of rain that falls in a short time

down·right /'daʊnraɪt/ *adv* thoroughly and completely: *The plan wasn't just risky – it was downright dangerous!*

down·shift·ing /'daʊnˌʃɪftɪŋ/ *n* [U] when people give up highly-paid successful jobs in order to have more time to do what they want, even though they earn less money —**downshifter** *n* [C] —**downshift** *v* [I]

down·side /'daʊnsaɪd/ *n* **the downside** the negative side of something: *The downside of the plan is the cost.*

down·size /'daʊnsaɪz/ *v* [I,T] to reduce the number of people working in a company in order to cut costs —**downsizing** *n* [U]

Down's Syn·drome /'. ,. ./ also **Downs** *n* [U] a condition that someone is born with that stops them from developing normally both mentally and physically: *a Downs baby*

down·stairs /ˌdaʊnˈsteəz◂ ‖-ˈsterz/ *adv, adj* on or towards a lower level of a building, especially a house: *Run downstairs and answer the door.* | *the downstairs rooms* → opposite UPSTAIRS

down·stream /ˌdaʊnˈstriːm◂/ *adv* in the same direction that a river or stream is flowing

down-to-earth /ˌ. . ˈ.◂/ *adj* someone who is down-to-earth is sensible and practical

down·town /ˌdaʊnˈtaʊn◂/ *adv, adj* especially *AmE* to or in the centre of a city or town: *Do you work downtown?* | *downtown Los Angeles*

down·trod·den /ˈdaʊnˌtrɒdn‖-ˌtrɑːdn/ *adj* treated badly or without respect by people who have power over you

down·turn /ˈdaʊntɜːn‖-tɜːrn/ *n* [C usually singular] a time when there is less business activity and conditions become worse: + *in a downturn in the economy*

down·wards /ˈdaʊnwədz‖-wərdz/ *especially BrE*, **downward** *especially AmE adv* **1** moving or pointing towards a lower position: *The balloon drifted slowly downwards.* **2** decreasing to a lower level: *The Dollar moved downwards against the Deutschmark.* → opposite UPWARDS — **downward** *adj*

down·wind /ˌdaʊnˈwɪnd/ *adj, adv* in the same DIRECTION that the wind is moving

down·y /ˈdaʊni/ *adj* covered in thin soft feathers or hair: *a downy chick*

dow·ry /ˈdaʊəri‖ˈdaʊri/ *n* [C] money or property that a woman's family gives to her new husband in some societies

dowse /daʊs/ *v* to DOUSE

doze /dəʊz‖doʊz/ *v* [I] to sleep lightly, usually for a short time: *Graham dozed for an hour.*
    doze off *phr v* [I] to fall asleep: *I was just dozing off when they arrived.*

doz·en /ˈdʌzən/ *determiner, n* **1** a group of 12 things: *two dozen eggs* **2** **dozens (of)** *informal* a lot of something: *We tried dozens of times.*

Dr the written abbreviation of "Doctor"

drab /dræb/ *adj* dull or uninteresting: *a drab grey coat* — **drabness** *n* [U]

draft¹ /drɑːft‖dræft/ *n* **1** [C] a piece of writing, a drawing, or a plan that is not yet finished: **first draft** *I've made a first draft of my speech for Friday.* **2** [C] a written order for money to be paid by a bank **3 the draft** *AmE* a system in which people must fight for their country during a war

draft² *v* [T] **1** to write a plan, letter, report etc that you will need to change before it is finished: *The House plans to draft a bill on education.* **2** *AmE* to order someone to fight during a war: **draft sb into** *Brad's been drafted into the army.*

draft³ *adj* the American spelling of DRAUGHT

drafts·man /ˈdrɑːftsmən‖ˈdræfts-/ *n* the American spelling of DRAUGHTSMAN

draft·y /ˈdrɑːfti‖ˈdræfti/ *adj* the American spelling of DRAUGHTY

drag¹ /dræg/ *v* **-gged, -gging 1** [T] to pull someone or something heavy along the ground: **drag sth away/along/through etc** *Ben dragged his sledge through the snow.* → see colour picture on page 670 **2** [T] to make someone go somewhere that they do not want to go: *My mother used to drag me out to church every week.*

3 drag yourself away (from) to stop doing something, although you do not want to: *Can't you drag yourself away from the TV for five minutes?* **4** [I] if time or an event drags, it is boring and seems to go very slowly: *History lessons always seemed to drag.* **5** [I] if something is dragging along the ground, part of it is touching the ground as you move: *Your coat's dragging in the mud.* **6 drag your feet** *informal* to take too much time to do something: *The police are being accused of dragging their feet on this case.*
    drag sb/sth **into** sth *phr v* [T] to make someone get involved in a situation even though they do not want to: *I'm sorry to drag you into this mess.*
    drag on *phr v* [I] to continue for too long: *The meeting dragged on all afternoon.*
    drag sth **out** *phr v* [T] to make a situation or event last longer than necessary: *How much longer are you going to drag this argument out?*
    drag sth **out of** sb *phr v* [T] to force someone to tell you something, especially by trying hard to persuade them

drag² *n* **1 a drag** *informal* something or someone that is boring or unexciting: *"I'd have to stay in tonight." "What a drag."* **2** [C] when someone breathes in smoke from their cigarette: **take a drag on** *Al took a drag on his cigarette.* **3 in drag** *informal* a man in drag is wearing women's clothes

drag·on /ˈdrægən/ *n* [C] a large imaginary animal that has wings and a long tail, and can breathe fire

drag·on·fly /ˈdrægənflaɪ/ *n* [C] a flying insect with a long brightly coloured body

drain¹ /dreɪn/ *v* **1 a)** [T] to make a liquid flow away from something: *Drain the water from the peas.* **b)** [I] if something drains, the liquid in it or on it flows away: *Let the pasta drain.* **c)** [I] if a liquid drains, it flows away: *The bath water slowly drained away.* **2** [T] to make you very tired: *a draining experience*

drain² *n* **1** [C] a pipe or hole that waste liquids go down to be carried away → see colour picture on page 79 **2 a drain on** sth something that uses too much time, money, or strength: *Paying for her course has been a real drain on her savings.* **3 down the drain** *informal* wasted or not having any result: *He's failed his driving test again! All that money down the drain.*

drain·age /ˈdreɪnɪdʒ/ *n* [U] the system or process by which water or waste liquids can flow away from a place

drained /dreɪnd/ *adj* very tired: *I felt completely drained after they had all gone home.*

drain·pipe /ˈdreɪnpaɪp/ *n* [C] *BrE* a pipe that carries rain water down from the roof of a building

drake /dreɪk/ *n* [C] a male duck

dra·ma /ˈdrɑːmə‖ˈdrɑːmə, ˈdræmə/ *n* **1** [C,U] a serious play for the theatre, television, or radio, or plays in general **2** [U] the study of performing in plays: *drama classes* **3** [C,U] exciting or unusual things that happen: *a life full of drama*

dra·mat·ic /drəˈmætɪk/ *adj* **1** sudden and surprising: *a dramatic change in temperature* **2** exciting and impressive: *a dramatic speech* **3** related to the theatre or plays: *Miller's dramatic works* **4** showing your feelings in a way that makes other people notice you: *Tristan*

dramatics

threw up his hands in a dramatic gesture. —
dramatically /-kli/ *adv*

dra·mat·ics /drə'mætıks/ *n* **1** amateur dramatics when a group of people practice and perform plays for enjoyment and do not receive money for their performance **2** [plural] behaviour that is intended to get attention and is not sincere: *I'm sick and tired of her dramatics.*

dram·a·tist /'dræmətˌɪst/ *n* [C] someone who writes plays

dram·a·tize (also **-ise** *BrE*) /'dræmətaız/ (also **-ise** **1** [T] to make a book or event into a play: *a novel dramatized for TV* **2** [I,T] to make an event seem more exciting than it really is: *Do you always have to dramatize everything?* — **dramatization** /ˌdræmətaı'zeıʃən‖-tə-/ *n* [C,U]

drank /dræŋk/ *v* the past tense of DRINK

drape /dreıp/ *v* [T] to put cloth, clothing etc loosely over or around something: **drape sth over/across/around** *Mina's scarf was draped elegantly over her shoulders.* | **be draped in sth** *The coffin was draped in black.*

drapes /dreıps/ *n* [plural] *AmE* heavy curtains

dras·tic /'dræstık/ *adj* drastic actions or changes are strong, sudden, and often severe: *The President promised drastic changes in health care.* — **drastically** /-kli/ *adv*: *Prices have been drastically reduced.*

draught *BrE*, **draft** *AmE* /drɑːft‖dræft/ *n* **1** [C] a current of air blowing through a room **2** **on draught** beer that is on draught is kept in a BARREL and pumped out to be served

draughts /drɑːfts‖dræfts/ *n* [U] *BrE* a game played by two people each with 12 round pieces, on a board of 64 squares; CHECKERS *AmE*

draughts·man *BrE* **draftsman** *AmE* /'drɑːftsmən‖'dræfts-/ someone who draws all the parts of a new building or machine that is being planned

draugh·ty *BrE*, **drafty** *AmE* /'drɑːfti‖'dræfti/ *adj* a draughty room has cold air blowing through it

draw¹ /drɔː‖drɔː/ *v* **drew** /druː/, **drawn** /drɔːn ‖drɒːn/, **drawing 1** [I,T] to make a picture of something with a pencil or a pen: *He's good at drawing animals.* | **draw sb sth** *Could you draw me a map?* **2** [T] to move something or someone by pulling them gently: *I drew my chair closer to the TV set.* **3** [T] if a carriage is drawn by horses, they pull it along **4** [I,T] *especially BrE* if two teams or players draw, they both win the same number of points: *Inter drew with Juventus last night.* **5** **draw the curtains** to open or close the curtains **6** [T] to choose the winning numbers or tickets in a competition such as a LOTTERY: *The winning numbers are drawn on Saturday evening.* **7** **draw lots** to use chance to decide who should do something, especially by taking pieces of paper with people's names on our of a container: *We drew lots to see who would go first.* **8** **draw a gun/knife/sword etc** to take a weapon from its container or from your pocket **9** [T] to take money from your bank account: *I'd just drawn £50 out of the bank.* **10** [I] to move in a particular direction: **into/out of/past** *A police car drew into our drive.* **11** **draw near** *literary* to move closer in time or space: *The summer holidays are drawing near.* **12** **draw to an end/a close/a halt etc** to

end or stop: *Another year was drawing to an end.* **13** **draw (sb's) attention to sth** to make someone notice something or show them something: *I'd like to draw your attention to the last paragraph.* **14** [T] to attract or interest someone: **draw sb to** *What first drew you to film-making?* **15** **draw the line (at sth)** to refuse to do something because you do not approve of it, although you are willing to do other things: *I don't mind helping you, but I draw the line at telling lies.* **16** **draw a distinction/comparison/parallel** to say that two things are different or similar in some way **17** **draw a blank** to be unable to find something or think of something: *Police searching for the missing nine-year old have drawn a blank.* **18** **draw breath** to take air into your lungs **19** [T] to make people have a particular reaction, for example to make them angry or interested: *The new law drew a storm of protest.*

draw in *phr v* [I] if the days or nights are drawing in, it is getting dark earlier in the evening

draw sb ↔ into sth *phr v* [T] to involve someone in something that they do not want to do: *Keith refused to be drawn into our argument.*

draw on sth *phr v* [T] to use your money, experience etc to help you do something: *A good writer draws on his own experience.*

draw up *phr v* **1** [T **draw sth ↔ up**] to think of and write a list, plan etc: *We drew up a list of possible options.* **2** [I] if a vehicle draws up, it stops: *A silver Rolls Royce drew up outside the bank.*

draw² *n* [C] **1** *especially BrE* a game that ends with both teams or players having the same number of points **2** when someone chooses the winning number in a competition such as a LOTTERY

draw·back /'drɔːbæk‖'drɒː-/ *n* [C] something that might be a problem or disadvantage: *The only drawback to a holiday in Scotland is the weather.*

drawer /drɔː‖drɔːr/ *n* [C] a part of a piece of furniture that slides in and out and is used for keeping things in: *the top drawer of the desk* → see picture at KITCHEN

draw·ing /'drɔːɪŋ‖'drɒː-/ *n* **1** [C] a picture you make with a pen or pencil: *She showed us a drawing of the house.* **2** [U] the art or skill of making pictures with a pen or pencil: *I've never been good at drawing.*

drawing board /'.. ./ *n* **(go) back to the drawing board** to start working on a new plan or idea after one you have tried has failed: *Our proposal wasn't accepted, so it's back to the drawing board.*

drawing pin /'.. ./ *n* [C] *BrE* a short pin with a wide flat top, used for fastening paper to a board; THUMBTACK *AmE*

drawing room /'.. ./ *n* [C] *old-fashioned* a large room in a house where people can sit and talk and meet visitors

drawl /drɔːl‖drɒːl/ *v* [I,T] to speak slowly with long vowel sounds —**drawl** *n* [singular] *a slow Texas drawl*

drawn¹ /drɔːn‖drɒːn/ *v* the past participle of DRAW

drawn² *adj* someone who looks drawn has a thin pale face because they are ill, tired, or worried

drawn-out /ˌ. '. ◂/ *adj* seeming to continue for a

very long time: *long drawn-out a long drawn-out process*

dread[1] /dred/ *v* **1** [T] to feel very worried about something that is going to happen: *Phil's really dreading his interview tomorrow.* | *dread doing sth I always used to dread going to the dentist's.* **2** **I dread to think** *spoken* used when you think a situation is very worrying: *I dread to think what might happen if she finds out.*

dread[2] *n* [U] a feeling of worry or fear: *dread of the unknown*

dread·ful /'dredfəl/ *adj* very bad or unpleasant: *What dreadful weather!* —**dreadfully** *adv*

dread·locks /'dredlɒks‖-lɑːks/ *n* [plural] hair which hangs in long thick pieces like rope

dream[1] /driːm/ [C] **1** a series of thoughts, images, and experiences that come into your mind when you are asleep: **have a dream** *I had a funny dream last night.* | **bad dream** (=frightening or unpleasant dream) **2** something that you hope will happen: *It was his dream to play football for his country.* **3** **beyond your wildest dreams** better than anything you imagined or hoped for **4** **in a dream** someone who is in a dream does not pay attention to what is happening around them because they are thinking a lot about something else

USAGE NOTE: dream

Both **dreamed** and **dreamt** are used as the past tense and past participle of **dream** in British English, but Americans usually use **dreamed**.

dream[2] *v* **dreamed** or **dreamt** /dremt/, **dreamed** or **dreamt, dreaming 1** [I,T] to have a dream while you are asleep: **+ (that)** *I often dream that I'm falling.* **2** [I,T] to think about something that you would like to happen: **+ of** *We dream of having our own home.* | **+ (that)** *Cath never dreamt she'd be offered the job.* (=she never expected it would happen) **3** **wouldn't dream of (doing) sth** *spoken* used to say that you would never do something because you think it is wrong: *I wouldn't dream of letting my daughter go out on her own at night.*

dream sth ↔ up *phr v* [T] to think of a plan or idea, especially an unusual one: *Who dreams up these TV commercials?*

dream[3] *adj* **dream car/house/team etc** the best car, house etc that you can imagine: *a dream team to send to the Olympics*

dream·er /'driːmə‖-ər/ *n* [C] someone who has plans or ideas that are not practical

dream·y /'driːmi/ *adj* **1** imagining pleasant things and not paying attention: *a bright but dreamy child* | *a dreamy look* **2** pleasant, peaceful, and relaxing: *dreamy music* —**dreamily** *adv*

drear·y /'drɪəri‖'drɪri/ *adj* dull and uninteresting: *the same old dreary jobs* —**drearily** *adv*

dredge /dredʒ/ *v* [I,T] to remove mud or sand from the bottom of a river, or to search the bottom of a river or lake for something: *Police*

are dredging the lake in their search for the missing teenager.

dredge sth ↔ up *phr v* [T] *informal* to start talking about something bad or unpleasant that happened a long time ago: *Why do the papers have to dredge up that old story?*

dregs /dregz/ *n* [plural] **1** the last remaining parts of a liquid, especially coffee or wine, including any solid pieces that have sunk to the bottom: *coffee dregs* **2** **the dregs of society** an offensive expression used to describe people that you think are not important or useful

drench /drentʃ/ *v* [T] to make something completely wet —**drenched** *adj*: *Look at you, you're drenched!*

dress[1] /dres/ *v* **1** [I,T] to put clothes on someone or on yourself: *Can you dress the kids for me?* | **get dressed** *Hurry up and get dressed!* **2** **be dressed** to be wearing clothes: *Are you dressed yet?* | **be dressed in** (=be wearing a particular type of clothes): *She was dressed all in black.* **3** **well-dressed/badly-dressed** wearing SMART clothes, untidy clothes etc **4** [I] to wear a particular type of clothes: *Dress warmly – it's cold out.* **5** **dress a wound/cut etc** to clean and cover a wound to protect it

dress up *phr v* **1** [I] to wear clothes that are more formal than the ones you usually wear: *It's only a small party. You don't need to dress up.* **2** [I,T **dress sb ↔ up**] to wear special clothes, shoes etc for fun: **+ as** (=so you look like someone else): *She dressed up as a witch for Halloween.* | **+ in** *old clothes for the kids to dress up in*

USAGE NOTE: dress, put on and wear

Dress means 'to put on clothes' or 'to wear a particular type of clothes': *David got up and dressed quickly.* | *She always dresses fashionably.* If you **put on** a piece of clothing, you dress yourself in that thing: *You'd better put your coat on before you go out.* Use **wear** to say that you have a piece of clothing on your body: *She was wearing a pink jacket.* | *Is that a new shirt you're wearing?*

dress[2] *n* **1** [C] a piece of clothing worn by a woman or girl, which covers the top of her body and some or all of her legs →see colour picture on page 113 **2** [U] clothing of a particular type: *casual/informal/evening dress It's casual dress for dinner tonight.*

dress·er /'dresə‖-ər/ *n* [C] **1** *BrE* a large piece of furniture with shelves for holding dishes and plates **2** *AmE* a piece of furniture with drawers for holding clothes; CHEST OF DRAWERS →see picture at CHEST OF DRAWERS

dress·ing /'dresɪŋ/ *n* **1** [C,U] a mixture of oil and other things that you pour over SALAD **2** [C] a piece of material for covering and protecting a wound: *The nurse will change your dressing.*

dressing gown /'...' / *n* [C] *BrE* a piece of cloth-

GRAMMAR NOTE: the past progressive
You use the **past progressive** to describe a situation or action that continued for a limited period in the past: *People were shouting and screaming.* You use the **simple past** to say that something happened in the middle of an activity: *They **arrived** while we **were having** dinner.*

ing like a long loose coat that you wear before you get dressed; ROBE *AmE*

dressing room /'.. ./ *n* [C] a room where an actor or actors gets ready before going on stage or on television

dressing ta·ble /'.. ,../ *n* [C] *BrE* a piece of BEDROOM furniture like a table with a mirror on top

dress re·hears·al /'. .,../ *n* [C] the last time actors practise a play before they perform it

dress·y /'dresi/ *adj* dressy clothes are suitable for formal occasions

drew /dru:/ *v* the past tense of DRAW

drib·ble /'drɪbəl/ *v* **1** [I] *BrE* if you dribble, the liquid in your mouth runs out onto your chin; DROOL *AmE*: *The baby's dribbling on your jacket.* **2** [I,T] to flow slowly in irregular drops, or to make a liquid flow in this way: + from/down/out etc *Dribble a little olive oil onto the salad.* **3** [I,T] to move a ball forward by repeatedly kicking or bouncing (BOUNCE) it in football or BASKETBALL —**dribble** *n* [C,U]

dribs and drabs /ˌdrɪbz ən 'dræbz/ *n* in dribs and drabs in small irregular amounts or numbers: *The guests arrived in dribs and drabs.*

dried /draɪd/ *v* the past tense and past participle of DRY

dri·er /'draɪəll-ər/ *n* [C] another spelling of DRYER

drift¹ /drɪft/ *v* [I] **1** to be moved along by the air or by the movement of the water: *The boat drifted down the river.* | + out/towards/along etc *We watched the boat drift slowly out to sea.* **2** to move somewhere slowly or gradually, without hurrying: + towards/across/in etc *People were drifting into the stadium.* **3** to get into a situation in a way that is not planned or intended: *I just drifted into teaching as a career.* **4** if snow or sand drifts, the wind moves it into large piles

drift apart *phr v* [I] if people drift apart, they gradually stop being friends

drift² *n* [C] **1** a large pile of snow or sand that has been blown by the wind: *massive snow drifts* **2** catch/get sb's drift to understand the general meaning of what someone says: *I don't speak Spanish very well but I think I got her drift.* **3** a very slow movement: *the drift of the continents away from each other*

drill¹ /drɪl/ *n* **1** [C] a tool or machine used for making holes in something hard: *an electric drill* | *a dentist's drill* **2** [C,U] a method of teaching something by making people repeat the same thing many times **3** fire/emergency drill when you practise what you should do in a dangerous situation: *We had a fire drill at school yesterday.* **4** [U] when soldiers practice marching

drill² *v* **1** [I,T] to make a hole with a drill: *He was drilling holes for the shelves.* | drill for oil/gas *drilling for oil in Texas* **2** [T] to teach someone by making them repeat the same thing many times

dri·ly /'draɪli/ *adv* another spelling of DRYLY

drink¹ /drɪŋk/ *v* drank /dræŋk/, drunk /drʌŋk/, drinking **1** [I,T] to take liquid into your mouth and swallow it: *What would you like to drink?* | *I drink far too much coffee.* **2** to drink alcohol, especially regularly: *"Whisky?" "No, thanks, I don't drink."* —**drinking** *n* [U]

drink to sb/sth *phr v* [T] to wish someone success, good health etc and have an alcoholic drink: *Let's drink to Patrick's success in his new job.*

drink² *n* [C,U] **1** liquid that you can drink, or an amount of liquid that you drink: *Can I have a drink of water please?* | food and drink **2** alcohol or an alcoholic drink: *Have we got plenty of drink for the party?*

drink·er /'drɪŋkəll-ər/ *n* [C] someone who often drinks alcohol: **heavy drinker** (=someone who drinks a lot)

drip¹ /drɪp/ *v* -pped -pping **1** [I] to produce small drops of liquid: *That tap's still dripping.* **2** [I,T] to fall in small drops, or to make small drops fall from something: drip from/off/through etc *Water was dripping through the ceiling.*

drip

drop

tap *BrE/* faucet *AmE*

drip² *n* **1** [C] one of the small drops of liquid that falls from something: *She put a bucket on the floor to catch the drips.* **2** [singular] the action or sound of a liquid falling in small drops: *the steady drip of rain from the roof* **3** [C] *BrE* a piece of hospital equipment used for putting liquids directly into your blood; IV *AmE*: *She was put on a drip after the operation.* **4** [C] *informal* someone who is boring and weak

drip·ping /'drɪpɪŋ/ also **dripping wet** /ˌ.. '. ◂/ *adj* very wet: *Take off your coat – it's dripping wet.*

drive¹ /draɪv/ *v* drove /drəʊvlldroʊv/, driven /'drɪvən/, driving **1** [I,T] to control a vehicle and make it move: *I can't drive.* | *Fiona drives a red Honda.* | + up/down/over etc *They're driving down to Rome next week.* **2** [T] if you drive someone somewhere, you take them there in a car + to/back/home etc *Can I drive you to the station?* | *Our neighbour's going to drive us to the airport.* **3** [T] to force people to move to a different place or do something in a different place: *The recent crime wave has driven business away from the area.* **4** [T] to provide the power for something **5** [T] to make someone very angry, unhappy, excited etc, or make them do something bad or unpleasant: drive sb crazy/mad etc *I wish they'd stop that noise! It's driving me crazy.* | drive sb to sth *Problems with her marriage drove her to attempt suicide.* **6** [T] to hit a stick or nail very hard into a surface: *She drove the post into the ground.* **7** [T] to make a person or organization work very hard

drive at sth *phr v* [T] what sb is driving at the thing that someone is really trying to say: *Look, just what are you driving at?*

drive sb ↔ **away** *phr v* [T] to behave in a way that makes someone want to leave you: *Her husband's violence finally drove her away.*

drive off *phr v* **1** [I] if a car drives off, it leaves **2** [I,T drive sb ↔ off] to force someone to go away: *A man with a gun drove them off the farm.*

drive² *n* **1** [C] a trip in a car: *It's a three day drive to Vienna.* **2** also **driveway** [C] the road or area for cars between a house and the street →see colour picture on page 79 **3** [C] a strong natural need: *the male sex drive* **4** [C] a planned effort to achieve a particular result: **economy drive** (=effort to save money) **5** [U] determination and energy to succeed: *Mel's got tremendous drive.* **6** [C, singular] a system in a computer that can read or store information → see colour picture on page 80

drive-by /ˈ. ./ *adj* **drive-by shootings/killings etc** when someone is shot from a moving car

drive-in /ˈ. ./ *adj* **drive-in restaurant/cinema/ movie** a restaurant, cinema etc where you can buy food or watch a film without leaving your car — **drive-in** *n* [C]

driv·el /ˈdrɪvəl/ *n* [U] nonsense: **talk drivel** *He talks such drivel sometimes!*

driv·en /ˈdrɪvən/ *v* the past participle of DRIVE

driv·er /ˈdraɪvəl-ər/ *n* [C] someone who drives: *a taxi driver*

driv·er's li·cense /ˈ.. ˌ../ *n* [C] *AmE* a DRIVING LICENCE

drive-through /ˈ. ./ *adj* a drive-through restaurant, bank etc can be used without getting out of your car

drive·way /ˈdraɪvweɪ/ also **drive** *n* [C] the road or area for cars between your house and the street → see colour picture on page 79

driv·ing [1] /ˈdraɪvɪŋ/ *adj* **1 driving rain/snow** rain or snow that is falling very heavily and fast **2 the driving force (behind sth)** the person, organization who is mainly responsible for making something happen: *Masters has been the driving force behind the company's success.*

driving [2] *n* [U] the act of driving a car, or the way someone drives: *His driving is terrible.*

driving li·cence /ˈ.. ˌ../ *BrE*, **driver's li·cense** *AmE* — *n* [C] an official card that says that you are legally allowed to drive a car

driz·zle [1] /ˈdrɪzəl/ *n* [U] very light rain

drizzle [2] *v* [I] to rain very lightly: *Come on, it's only drizzling.*

drone /drəʊn‖droʊn/ *v* [I] to make a low continuous noise: *A plane droned overhead.* —**drone** *n* [singular]

drone on *phr v* [I] to talk in a boring way for a long time: **+ about** *Joe kept droning on about his problems at work.*

drool /druːl/ *v* [I] **1** if you drool, the liquid in your mouth runs out onto your chin: *At the sight of food the dog began to drool.* **2** to show in a silly way that you like someone or something a lot: **+ over** *Sarah was drooling over the lead singer through the whole concert!*

droop /druːp/ *v* [I] to hang or bend down often because of being weak or tired: *Can you water the plants? They're starting to droop.*

drop [1] /drɒp‖drɑːp/ *v* **-pped, -pping 1** [T] to let something you are holding fall to the ground: *The dog ran up and dropped a stick at my feet.* → see colour picture on page 670 **2** [I] to fall: **+ from/off/onto etc** *The bottle rolled off the table and dropped onto the floor.* | *He dropped into his chair with a sigh.* **3** [T] also **drop off** to take someone to a place in a car, before continuing to somewhere else: *She drops the kids off at school on her way to work.* **4 drop in/by** to visit someone when you have not arranged to come at a particular time: *Imran dropped in on his way home from work.* **5** [I] to fall to a lower level or amount: *The temperature dropped to -15° overnight.* **6** [T] to stop doing something or stop

planning to do something: *We've dropped the idea of going by plane.* | **drop everything** (=stop what you are doing) **7** [T] to decide not to include someone or something in a group: **drop sb from sth** *Morris has been dropped from the team.* **8** [T] to stop talking about something, especially because it is upsetting someone: **let it drop/let the matter drop** *I wish you'd let the matter drop.* | **drop it/drop the subject** *Just drop it, will you? I don't want to argue.* **9 drop dead** to die suddenly and unexpectedly **10 drop sb a line** *informal* to write a letter to someone **11 drop a hint** to give someone some advice, a suggestion, or a warning in a way that is not direct: *I've dropped a few hints about what I want for my birthday.*

drop off *phr v* **1** [I] *informal* to begin to sleep: *Just as I was dropping off, I heard a noise downstairs.* **2** [I] to become lower in level or amount: *The demand for leaded petrol dropped off in the 1970s.* **3** [T **drop** sb/sth ↔ **off**] to take someone or something to a place in a car, before continuing to somewhere else

drop out *phr v* [I] to stop going to university or stop an activity before you have finished it: **+ of** *Too many students drop out of college in the first year*

drop [2] *n* **1** [C] a very small amount of liquid that falls in a round shape: *a tear drop* | **+ of** *Add a few drops of lemon juice.* **2** [singular] a distance from something down to the ground: *It's a twenty foot drop from this cliff.* **3** [singular] when the amount, level, or number of something becomes much less or much lower: **+ in** *a sudden drop in temperature* **4 a drop in the ocean** *BrE* / **a drop in the bucket** *AmE* an amount of something that is too small to have any effect

drop·out /ˈdrɒpaʊt‖ˈdrɑːp-/ *n* [C] **1** someone who leaves school or college without completing their course **2** someone who does not want a CAREER or possessions because they do not want to work or live in a CONVENTIONAL way

drop·pings /ˈdrɒpɪŋz‖ˈdrɑː-/ *n* [plural] solid waste from animals or birds

drought /draʊt/ *n* [C,U] a long period of dry weather when there is not enough water

drove [1] /drəʊv‖droʊv/ *v* the past tense of DRIVE

drove [2] *n* [C] a large group of animals or people that move together: *a drove of cattle* | **in droves** *Tourists come in droves to see the White House.*

drown [ ] /draʊn/ *v* **1** [I,T] to die by being under water too long, or to kill someone in this way: *Two swimmers drowned near Santa Cruz yesterday.* | *Over a hundred people were drowned when the ferry sank.* **2** [T] also **drown out** to prevent a sound from being heard by making a louder noise: *We put on some music to drown out their yelling.*

drown·ing /ˈdraʊnɪŋ/ *n* [C,U] death caused by being under water too long: *a fear of drowning*

drow·sy /ˈdraʊzi/ *adj* tired and almost asleep: *The tablets might make you feel drowsy.* — **drowsiness** *n* [U] — **drowsily** *adv*

drudg·e·ry /ˈdrʌdʒəri/ *n* [U] boring work: *the drudgery of housework*

drug [1] /drʌg/ *n* [C] **1** [usually plural] an illegal substance that people smoke, swallow etc to make them feel happy: **take/use drugs** *Many people admit that they took drugs in their twenties.* | **be on drugs** (=use drugs regularly):

She looks as though she's on drugs. | **soft drugs** (=illegal drugs such as marijuana that are not considered to be very harmful) | **hard drugs** (=dangerous very strong illegal drugs, for example cocaine and heroin) | **drug addict** (=someone who cannot stop taking drugs) **2** a medicine or a substance for making medicines: *a drug to treat depression*

drug[2] *v* [T] **-gged, -gging** **1** to give someone drugs, usually to stop them feeling pain or to make them sleep **2** to put a drug into food or drink

drug·store /ˈdrʌgstɔː‖-stɔːr/ *n* [C] *AmE* a shop where you can buy medicines, beauty products etc; CHEMIST'S *BrE*

drum[1] /drʌm/ *n* [C] **1** a round musical instrument which you play by hitting it with your hand or a stick: **the drums** (=a set of drums): *Jason's learning to play the drums.* **2** a large round container for storing liquids such as oil or chemicals → see picture at CONTAINERS

drum[2] *v* [I,T] **-mmed, -mming** to hit the surface of something many times in a way that sounds like drums: *The rain was drumming on the roof.*

drum sth into sb *phr v* [T] to say something to someone so often that they cannot forget it: *The dangers of tobacco were drummed into us at school.*

drum sth ↔ **up** *phr v* [T] to try to get help, money etc by asking a lot of people: *Mike's out trying to drum up some more business.*

drum·mer /ˈdrʌmə‖-ər/ *n* [C] someone who plays the drums

drum·stick /ˈdrʌmˌstɪk/ *n* [C] **1** the leg of a chicken, TURKEY etc, cooked as food **2** a stick that you use to play a drum

drunk[1] /drʌŋk/ *v* the past participle of DRINK

drunk[2] *adj* unable to control your behaviour, speech etc because you have drunk too much alcohol: **get drunk** *Bill got really drunk at Sue's party.*

drunk[3] also **drunk·ard** /ˈdrʌŋkəd‖-ərd/ *n* [C] someone who is drunk or who often gets drunk

drunk·en /ˈdrʌŋkən/ *adj* [only before noun] drunk or behaving in a way that shows that you are drunk: *a drunken crowd* | *drunken shouting* — **drunkenness** *n* [U] — **drunkenly** *adv*

dry[1] /draɪ/ *adj* **1** having no water or other liquid inside or on the surface: *Can you check if the washing's dry yet?* → opposite WET[1] **2** dry weather does not have rain: *The weather tomorrow will be cold and dry.* **3** if your mouth, throat, or skin is dry, it does not have enough of the natural liquid that is usually in it **4** someone who has a dry sense of humour seems serious when they are making a joke **5** not interesting or exciting to read of listen to: *dry political debates* — **dryness** *n* [U]

dry[2] *v* [I,T] to become dry, or to make something dry: *It'll only take me a few minutes to dry my hair.* — **dried** *adj*: *dried fruit*

dry off *phr v* [I,T **dry sth** ↔ **off**] to become dry or make the surface of something dry: *The kids played in the pool and then dried off in the sun.*

dry out *phr v* [I,T **dry sth** ↔ **out**] to dry completely, or to dry something completely: *Put your coat on the radiator to dry out.*

dry up *phr v* **1** [I,T **dry sth** ↔ **up**] if a river or lake dries up, the water in it disappears **2** [I] if a supply of something dries up, there is no

more of it: *Our research project was cancelled when the money dried up.* **3** [I,T **dry sth** ↔ **up**] to dry dishes that have been washed, using a cloth

dry-clean /ˌ. ˈ./ *v* [I,T] to clean clothes with chemicals instead of water

dry clean·er's /ˌ. ˈ../ *n* [C] a shop where you take clothes to be dry-cleaned

dry·er, drier /ˈdraɪə‖-ər/ *n* [C] a machine that dries things, especially clothes or hair: *a hair dryer*

dry·ly, drily /ˈdraɪli/ *adv* if you say something dryly, you speak in a serious way although you are really making a joke

du·al /ˈdjuːəl‖ˈduːəl/ *adj* [only before noun] having two of something, or two parts: *My wife has dual nationality. Her parents are Brazilian but she was born in the US.*

dub /dʌb/ *v* [T] **-bbed, -bbing** **1** to change the original spoken language of a film or television programme into another language: **dub sth into** sth *an Italian film dubbed into English* **2** to give someone or something a humorous name that describes them or their character: *They immediately dubbed him 'Fatty'.*

du·bi·ous /ˈdjuːbiəs‖ˈduː-/ *adj* **1** **be dubious** to have doubts about whether something is good or true: **+ about** *I'm very dubious about the quality of food in this café.* **2** not seeming honest, safe, or valuable: *a dubious character* — **dubiously** *adv*

duch·ess /ˈdʌtʃɪs/ *n* [C] a woman with the highest social rank below a PRINCESS, or the wife of a DUKE: *the Duchess of York*

duck[1] /dʌk/ *v* **1** [I,T] to lower your body or head very quickly to avoid being hit or seen: *She had to duck her head to get through the doorway.* **2** [T] *informal* to avoid something that is difficult or unpleasant: *His speech ducked all the real issues.* **3** [T] *BrE* to push someone under water for a short time as a joke; DUNK *AmE*: *kids ducking each other in the pool*

duck[2] *n* [C,U] a common water bird with short legs and a wide beak, or the meat from this bird: *roast duck*

duck·ling /ˈdʌklɪŋ/ *n* [C] a baby duck

duct /dʌkt/ *n* [C] **1** a tube in a building for carrying liquids, air, electric wires etc **2** a thin narrow tube inside your body that liquid or air goes through: *a tear duct*

dud /dʌd/ *adj informal* useless or not working: *a dud cheque* — **dud** *n* [C] *This battery's a dud.*

due[1] /djuː‖duː/ *adj* **1** **be due** to be expected to happen or arrive at a particular time: *The flight from Munich was due at 7:48 pm.* | **+ back/in/out etc** *My library books are due back tomorrow.* | **be due to do sth** *The film isn't due to start until 10.30.* **2** **be due for** if someone is due for something it is the time that they should have it: *The baby's due for a feed.* **3** **due to** if one thing is due to another, it happens as a result of it: *Our bus was late due to heavy traffic.* **4** **be due** needing to be paid: *The first payment of £25 is now due.* **5** deserved by someone or owed to someone: **be due (to sb)** *He never got the recognition he was due.* **6** **in due course/time** at a more suitable time in the future: *Your complaints will be answered in due course.* **7** *formal* suitable or right in that situation

due[2] *adv* **due north/south/east/west** directly or exactly north, south etc

due[3] *n* **give sb his/her etc due** to admit that someone has good qualities even though you are criticizing them: *I don't like the man, but to give him his due, he is good at his job.*

du·el /'dju:əl‖'du:əl/ *n* [C] a fight between two people with guns or swords —**duel** *v* [I]

dues /dju:z‖du:z/ *n* [plural] the money that you pay to be a member of an organization: *union dues*

du·et /dju'et‖du'et/ *n* [C] a piece of music for two performers

duffel bag, duffle bag /'dʌfəl bæg/ *n* [C] a bag made of strong cloth, with a round bottom and a string around the top

duffel coat, duffle coat /'dʌfəl kəut‖-kout/ *n* [C] *especially BrE* a coat of rough heavy cloth, which has a HOOD

dug /dʌg/ *v* the past tense and past participle of DIG

duke, Duke /dju:k‖du:k/ *n* a man with the highest social rank below a prince

dull[1] /dʌl/ *adj* **1** not interesting or exciting: *What a dull party.* **2** not bright or shiny: *a dull grey sky* **3** a dull sound is not clear or loud: *I heard a dull thud.* **4** a dull pain is not severe: *a dull ache in my shoulder* —**dully** *adv* —**dullness** *n* [U]

dull[2] *v* [T] to make something become less severe or less clear: *a drug to dull the pain*

du·ly /'dju:li‖'du:li/ *adv formal* at the correct time or in the correct way: *The taxi she had ordered duly arrived.*

dumb[1] /dʌm/ *adj* **1** *old-fashioned* unable to speak. Some people consider this to be offensive **2** *informal, especially AmE* stupid: *What a dumb idea.* —**dumbly** *adv*

dumb[2]

dumb down *phr v* [T] to change something in a way that has a very bad effect, by making it much too simple or much less effective: *the dumbing down of TV news*

dumb·found·ed /dʌm'faʊndɪd/ *adj* so surprised that you cannot speak: *He stared at me, absolutely dumbfounded.*

dum·my /'dʌmi/ *n* [C] **1** a figure of a person: *a dressmaker's dummy* **2** a copy of a weapon, tool, vehicle etc that you cannot use: *It wasn't a real gun, it was a dummy.* **3** *BrE* a rubber object that you put into a baby's mouth for it to suck; PACIFIER *AmE*

dump[1] /dʌmp/ *v* [T] **1** to drop or put something somewhere in a careless way: **dump sth in/on/down etc** *They dumped their bags on the floor and left.* **2** To get rid of something that you do not want: *Illegal chemicals had been dumped in the river.*

dump[2] *n* [C] **1** a place where unwanted waste is taken and left: *the town's main rubbish dump.* **2** *informal* a place that is unpleasant because it is dirty, ugly, or boring: *This town's a real dump.* **3** **be down in the dumps** *informal* to feel very unhappy

dump·ling /'dʌmplɪŋ/ *n* [C] a round mixture of flour and fat cooked in boiling liquid: *stew with herb dumplings*

dump·ster /'dʌmpstəl-ər/ *n* [C] *trademark AmE* a large metal container used for holding waste; SKIP *BrE*

dump·y /'dʌmpi/ *adj informal* short and fat: *a dumpy little woman*

dune /dju:n‖du:n/ *n* [C] a hill made of sand shaped by the wind: *sand dunes* →see colour picture on page 243

dung /dʌŋ/ *n* [U] solid waste from animals, especially large animals

dun·ga·rees /ˌdʌŋgə'ri:z/ *n* [plural] *BrE* trousers with a square piece of cloth that covers your chest; OVERALLS *AmE* →see colour picture on page 113

dun·geon /'dʌndʒən/ *n* [C] a dark prison under the ground, used in past times

dunk /dʌŋk/ *v* [T] **1** to quickly put something into a liquid and then take it out again before you eat it: *Don't dunk your biscuit in your tea!* **2** to push someone under water for a short time as a joke; DUCK *BrE* —**dunk** *n* [C]

dun·no /dʌnəʊ/ *spoken nonstandard* I **dunno** a short form of "I do not know"

du·o /'dju:əʊ‖'du:oʊ/ *n* [C] two people who sing or do something else together

dupe /dju:p‖du:p/ *v* [T] to deceive someone: *He was duped into paying $300 to a man who said he was a lawyer.* —**dupe** *n* [C]

duplex /'du:pleks/ *n* [C] *AmE* a type of house which is joined to another house by one shared wall →see colour picture on page 79

du·pli·cate[1] /'dju:plɪkɪt‖'du:-/ *adj* a duplicate copy of something is made to be exactly the same as something else: *a duplicate key* —**duplicate** *n* [C]

du·pli·cate[2] /'dju:plɪkeɪt‖'du:-/ *v* [T] to copy or repeat something exactly: *duplicated notes* | *Scientists have tried to duplicate the effects in the lab.* —**duplication** *n* [U]

dur·a·ble /'djʊərəbəl‖'dʊr-/ *adj* staying in good condition for a long time: *durable clothing* —**durability** /ˌdjʊərə'bɪlɪtil‖dʊr-/ *n* [U]

du·ra·tion /dju'reɪʃən‖dʊ-/ *n* [U] *formal* the length of time that something continues: *Food was rationed for the duration of the war*

du·ress /dju'res‖dʊ-/ *n* [U] *formal* **under duress** if you do something under duress, you are forced to do it: *Her confession was made under duress.*

dur·ing /'djʊərɪŋ‖'dʊr-/ *prep* **1** all through a period of time: *I try to swim every day during the summer.* **2** at some point in a period of time: *Henry died during the night.*

USAGE NOTE: during and for

During answers the question 'when': *She learned Italian during her stay in Milan.* **For** answers the question 'how long?': *He studied in the US for five years.*

GRAMMAR NOTE: the past perfect

You form the **past perfect** using **had** and the past participle. Use the past perfect to talk about something that happened in the past before another past action: *Kay stayed behind after everyone else **had gone** home.* | *She told me what she **had done**.*

dusk /dʌsk/ n [U] when it is starting to get dark at the end of the day → compare DAWN[1]

dust[1] /dʌst/ n [U] very small bits of dirt or soil that you can see like a powder in the air, as a layer on furniture etc: *The truck drove off in a cloud of dust.* | *The furniture was covered in dust!*

dust[2] v [I,T] to clean the dust from something: *Did you dust the living room?*

dust sth ↔ **off** phr v [T] to clean something by brushing dust etc off it: *She dusted the snow off Billy's coat.*

dust·bin /'dʌstbɪn/ n [C] BrE a large container outside your home where you put waste so that it can be taken away; GARBAGE CAN AmE

dust·er /'dʌstəll-ər/ n [C] a cloth for removing dust from furniture

dust·man /'dʌstmən/ n [C] BrE, plural **dustmen** /-mən/ someone whose job is to take away waste material left in containers outside people's houses; GARBAGE COLLECTOR AmE

dust·pan /'dʌstpæn/ n [C] a flat container with a handle and a brush, used to remove dust and dirt from the floor

dust·y /'dʌsti/ adj covered or filled with dust: *a dusty room*

du·ti·ful /'djuːtɪfəll'duː-/ adj a dutiful person is loyal and always does what they are told: *a dutiful daughter* —**dutifully** adv

du·ty /'djuːtill'duː-/ n **1** [C,U] something that you have to do because it is right or it is part of your job: *The government has a duty to provide education.* | *He was carrying out his official duties as ambassador.* **2** **be on/off duty** a doctor, nurse, police officer etc who is on or off duty, they are either working or not working **3** [C] a tax you pay on something you buy

duty-free /ˌ.. '. ◂/ adj duty-free goods can be brought into a country without paying tax on them: *duty-free cigarettes* —**duty-free** adv

du·vet /'duːveɪ, 'djuː-ll duː'veɪ/ n [C] especially BrE a thick warm cover that you cover yourself with in bed; COMFORTER AmE

dwarf[1] /dwɔːfll dwɔːrf/ n [C] **1** an imaginary creature in stories that looks like a small man: *Snow White and the Seven Dwarfs* **2** an offensive word for a person who is very short

dwarf[3] v [T] something that dwarfs other things is so big that is makes the others seem very small: *The church is dwarfed by skyscrapers.*

dwell /dwel/ v [I] **dwelt** /dwelt/ or **dwelled**, **dwelt** or **dwelled**, **dwelling** literary to live some-

where: *strange creatures that dwell in the forest*

dwell on/upon sth phr v [T] to think or talk for too long about something bad or unpleasant: *You shouldn't dwell on the past.*

dwel·ler /'dweləll-ər/ n [C] **city/town/cave dweller** someone that lives in a city, town etc

dwell·ing /'dwelɪŋ/ n [C] formal a house, apartment etc where people live

dwin·dle /'dwɪndl/ v [I] to gradually become less or smaller: *Their stores of food had dwindled away to almost nothing.* —**dwindling** adj: *a dwindling population*

dye[1] /daɪ/ n [C,U] a substance used to change the colour of hair, cloth etc

dye[2] v [T] **dyed, dyed, dyeing** to change the colour of something using a dye: *Sam's dyed his hair green.*

dy·ing /'daɪ-ɪŋ/ v the present participle of DIE

dyke, dike /daɪk/ n [C] **1** a wall or bank of earth built to prevent water from flooding a place **2** BrE a long narrow hole cut in the ground to take water away

dy·nam·ic /daɪ'næmɪk/ adj **1** full of energy and ideas: *a dynamic young businesswoman* **2** technical a dynamic force causes movement: *dynamic energy* —**dynamically** /-kli/ adv

dy·nam·ics /daɪ'næmɪks/ n **1** [plural] the way in which systems or people behave and affect each other: *the dynamics of power in large businesses* **2** [U] the science of the movement of objects

dy·na·mite /'daɪnəmaɪt/ n [U] **1** a powerful explosive **2** informal something or someone that is dynamite is exciting or likely to cause trouble: *That band is dynamite!*

dy·na·mo /'daɪnəməʊll-moʊ/ n [C], plural **dynamos** a machine that changes some form of power into electricity

dyn·as·ty /'dɪnəstill'daɪ-/ n [C] a family of rulers who have controlled a country for a long time: *The Habsburg dynasty ruled in Austria from 1278 to 1918.* —**dynastic** /dɪ'næstɪklldaɪ-/ adj

dys·en·te·ry /'dɪsəntərill-teri/ n [U] a serious disease that causes severe DIARRHOEA

dys·func·tion·al /dɪs'fʌŋkʃənəl/ adj not working or behaving normally

dys·lex·i·a /dɪs'leksiə/ n [U] a condition which causes people to have difficulty with reading and writing —**dyslexic** adj

Ee

E, e the letter 'e'

E /iː/ **1** the written abbreviation of EAST or EASTERN **2** the abbreviation of Ecstasy, an illegal drug that gives people a lot of energy and makes them able to dance for long periods of time

each /iːtʃ/ *determiner, pron* every one of two or more things, considered separately: *Each bedroom has its own shower.* | *I gave a toy to each of the children.* | **three/half/a piece etc each** *Mum says we can have two cookies each.*

USAGE NOTE: each, every, all and **both**

Use **each** with a singular countable noun to mean 'every person or thing in the group considered separately': *Each child at the party was given a present.* Use **every** with a singular countable noun to mean 'every person or thing in a group, considered together': *Every child in the class passed the test.* Use **all** with a plural countable noun to mean 'every one of a group of things or people': *All the children enjoyed the trip.* Use **both** with a plural countable noun to mean 'two people or things, considered together': *Both our children are in college.*

---

each oth·er /. '../ *pron* used to show that each of two or more people does something to the other or others: *They kissed each other passionately.* → see also ONE ANOTHER

ea·ger /ˈiːɡəll-ər/ *adj* wanting to do something very much, or waiting with excitement for something to happen: *We were all eager to get started.* — **eagerly** *adv* — **eagerness** *n* [U]

ea·gle /ˈiːɡəl/ *n* [C] a big wild bird with a large curved beak that eats small animals

eagle-eyed /ˌ.. '..</ *adj* very good at seeing or noticing things: *An eagle-eyed customer spotted the mistake.*

ear /ɪəllɪr/ *n* **1** [C] one of the two things either side of your head that you hear with: *She turned and whispered something in his ear.* → see picture at HEAD[1] **2 have an ear for music/languages etc** to be good at hearing, recognizing, and copying sounds **3 be all ears** *informal* if you are all ears, you are very interested to hear what someone is going to say: *Go ahead, I'm all ears.* **4 play it by ear** to do what seems sensible when things happen, instead of planning **5** [C] an ear of corn or wheat is the top part of the plant that produces the grain

ear·drum /ˈɪədrʌmll-ɪr-/ *n* [C] a tight thin skin inside your ear that allows you to hear sound

earl, Earl /ɜːlllɜːrl/ *n* [C] a man with a high social rank in Britain

earlobe /ˈɪələʊbll-ɪr-/ *n* [C] the soft piece at the bottom of your ear → see picture at HEAD[1]

ear·ly[1] /ˈɜːlillˈɜːrli/ *adj* **1** near to the beginning of a day, year, someone's life etc: *We're going to the early evening performance.* | *the early part of the 20th century* **2** before the usual or expected time: *You're early! It's only five o'clock!* **3** [only before noun] one of the first people,

events, machines etc: *early settlers in New England* | *an early model Ford* **4 at the earliest** used to say that something will not happen before the time mentioned, and it might happen later: *He'll arrive on Monday at the earliest.* **5 the early hours** the time between MIDNIGHT and morning **6 it's early days** used to say that it is too soon to know what the result of something will be: *She's had a few problems with her new school, but it's early days yet.* **7 early night** if you have an early night, you go to bed earlier than usual → opposite LATE

ear·ly[2] *adv* **1** before the usual or expected time: *Try to arrive early if you want a good seat.* **2** near the beginning of a period of time: *We'll have to leave early tomorrow morning.* **3** near the beginning of an event, story, process etc: *a scene that takes place early in the film* | **early on** (=at an early stage): *I realized early on that this relationship wasn't going to work.* → opposite LATE

ear·mark /ˈɪəmɑːkllˈɪrmɑːrk/ *v* [T] to decide that something will be used for a particular purpose: *The money was earmarked for a new school building.*

ear·muffs /ˈɪəmʌfsll-ɪr-/ *n* [plural] two pieces of material joined by a band over your head, worn to keep your ears warm

earn /ɜːnllɜːrn/ *v* [I,T] **1** to get money by working: *She earns nearly £30,000 a year.* | *You won't earn much as a waitress!* **2** to get something that you deserve: *I think we've earned a rest after all that work!* **3 earn a living** to work to get enough money to pay for the things you need: *He earned his living as a writer.* — **earner** *n* [C]

ear·nest /ˈɜːnˌstllˈɜːr-/ *adj* **1** very serious and believing that what you say is important: *an earnest young man* **2 in earnest** if something starts happening in earnest, it starts happening properly or seriously: *On Monday your training begins in earnest.* **3 be in earnest** to really mean what you are saying — **earnestly** *adv* — **earnestness** *n* [U]

earn·ings /ˈɜːnɪŋzllˈɜːr-/ *n* [plural] money that you earn by working: *Average earnings in Europe have risen by 3%.*

ear·phones /ˈɪəfəʊnzllˈɪrfoʊnz/ *n* [plural] electrical equipment that you put over your ears to listen to a radio, PERSONAL STEREO etc

ear·plug /ˈɪəplʌgll-ɪr-/ *n* [C usually plural] a small piece of rubber that you put into your ear to keep out noise

ear·ring /ˈɪərɪŋll-ɪr-/ *n* [C usually plural] a piece of jewellery that you fasten to your ear → see picture at JEWELLERY

ear·shot /ˈɪəʃɒtllˈɪrʃɑːt/ *n* **within earshot/out of earshot** near enough or not near enough to hear what someone is saying: *Make sure the kids are out of earshot before you tell her.*

ear-split·ting /ˈ. ../ *adj* very loud: *an ear-splitting scream*

earth /ɜːθllɜːrθ/ *n* **1** also **the Earth** [singular] the PLANET that we live on: *The space shuttle will return to earth next week.* | *the planet Earth* | *the most beautiful place on earth* → compare WORLD **2** [U] the substance that plants, trees etc grow in; soil: *footprints in the wet earth* **3 what/why/how etc on earth...?** *spoken* used to ask a question about something that you are very

E

surprised or annoyed about: *What on earth made you say such a stupid thing?* **4** cost/pay/ charge the earth *informal* to cost, pay etc a very large amount of money: *That holiday must have cost the earth!* **5** come down to earth (with a bump) to realize that life has returned to normal and that there are problems you must deal with **6** [C usually singular] *BrE* a wire that makes electrical equipment safe by connecting it to the ground; GROUND *AmE*

> **USAGE NOTE: earth, world and land**
>
> The **earth** is the planet we live on: *The earth moves around the sun every 365 days.* The **world** is the earth and all its people, countries etc: *It's one of the largest countries in the world.* You can also use **earth** to mean 'the world': *It's the highest mountain on earth.* When you compare the earth's surface to the sea, use **land**: *After weeks at sea, the sailors saw land.* When you compare it to the sky, use **earth**: *The spacecraft returned to earth safely.*

earth·en·ware / ˈɜːθənweə, -ðən-‖ˈɜːrθənwer, -ðən-/ *adj* made of baked clay — **earthenware** *n* [U]

earth·ly / ˈɜːθli‖ˈɜːrθli/ *adj* no earthly reason/ use/chance etc no reason, use etc at all: *There's no earthly reason for me to go.*

earth·quake / ˈɜːθkweɪk‖ˈɜːrθ-/ *n* [C] a sudden shaking of the earth's surface that often causes a lot of damage

earth-shat·ter·ing / ˈ. ˌ.../ *adj* surprising or shocking and very important: *earth-shattering news*

earth·worm / ˈɜːθwɜːm‖ˈɜːrθwɜːrm/ *n* [C] a long brown WORM that lives in the soil

earth·y / ˈɜːθi‖ˈɜːrθi/ *adj* **1** earthy humour is about sex and the human body: *her earthy sense of humour* **2** tasting or smelling like soil: *mushrooms with an earthy flavour* — **earthiness** *n* [U]

ear·wig / ˈɪəwɪg‖ˈɪr-/ *n* [C] a long brown insect that moves quickly and has two curved pointed parts at the back of its body

ease¹ /iːz/ *n* [U] **1** with ease if you do something with ease, it is very easy: *It's the ease with which thieves can break in that worries me.* **2** at your ease feeling comfortable and confident: *Nurses do try to make patients feel at ease.* | ill at ease (=not relaxed): *He looks so ill at ease in a suit.*

ease² *v* **1** [I,T] to make something less severe or difficult, or to become less severe or difficult: *The drugs will ease the pain.* **2** [T] to move something slowly and carefully into another place: *Ease the patient on to the bed.*
ease off also **ease up** *phr v* [I] if something eases off, it gets less or gets better: *I'll wait until the rain eases off before I go out.*
ease up *phr v* [I] **1** to do something more slowly than before or work less hard: *You should ease up or you'll make yourself ill!* **2** to ease off

ea·sel / ˈiːzəl/ *n* [C] a frame that you put a painting on while you paint it

eas·i·ly / ˈiːzəli/ *adv* **1** without difficulty: *This recipe can be made quickly and easily.* **2** easily the best/biggest/most stupid etc definitely the

best, biggest etc: *She is easily the most intelligent girl in the class.* **3** could/can/might easily used to say that something is very likely to happen: *Teenage parties can easily get out of control.*

east¹, East /iːst/ *n* **1** [singular, U] the direction from which the sun rises: *Which way is east?* | *The new road will pass to the east of the village.* **2** the east the eastern part of a country or area: *Rain will spread to the east later today.* **3** the East **a)** the countries in Asia, especially China and Japan: *more open trading between the East and the West* **b)** the countries in the eastern part of Europe, especially the ones that had Communist governments

east², East *adj* **1** in the east or facing east: *the east coast of the island* **2** east wind a wind that comes from the east

east³ *adv* towards the east: *The garden faces east.*

east·bound / ˈiːstbaʊnd/ *adj* travelling or leading towards the east: *An accident on the east-bound side of the freeway is blocking traffic.*

Eas·ter / ˈiːstə‖-ər/ *n* [C,U] a holiday in March or April when Christians remember the death of Christ and his return to life: *We went skiing in Vermont at Easter.*

Easter egg / ˈ.. ./ *n* [C] a chocolate egg given at Easter

eas·ter·ly / ˈiːstəli‖-ərli/ *adj* **1** towards the east or in the east: *sailing in an easterly direction* **2** easterly winds come from the east

east·ern, Eastern / ˈiːstən‖-ərn/ *adj* **1** in or from the east part of a country or area: *the largest city in eastern Iowa* | *Eastern Europe* **2** Eastern in or from the countries in Asia, especially China and Japan: *Eastern religions*

east·ern·most / ˈiːstənməʊst‖-ərnmoʊst/ *adj* furthest east: *the easternmost part of the island*

east·ward, eastwards / ˈiːstwəd, -ədz‖-wərd, -ərdz/ *adj, adv* going or facing towards the east: *on the eastward slope of the hillside* | *ships moving eastward*

eas·y¹ / ˈiːzi/ *adj* **1** not difficult: *I can answer all these questions – they're easy!* | *Having a computer will make things a lot easier.* **2** comfortable and not feeling worried: *If it'll make you feel easier, I'll phone when I get there.* | *He'll do anything for an easy life.*

easy² *adv* **1** take it/things easy to relax and not let things worry or upset you: *The doctor says I must take things easy for a while.* **2** go easy on/with sth *informal* to not use too much of something: *Go easy on the wine if you're driving.* **3** go easy on sb *informal* to be gentle or less strict with someone: *Go easy on Peter – he's having a hard time at school.* **4** easier said than done *spoken* used to say that it would be difficult to do what has been suggested: *I should just tell her to leave me alone, but that's easier said than done.*

easy chair / ˈ.. ˈ. , ˈ.. ./ *n* [C] a large comfortable chair

easy·go·ing / ˌ.. ˈ.. / *adj* not strict and not easily upset or worried: *Her parents are pretty easy-going.*

easy lis·ten·ing / ˌ.. ˈ../ *n* [U] music with a nice tune that makes you feel relaxed

eat /iːt/ *v* ate /et, eɪt‖eɪt/, eaten / ˈiːtn/, eating **1** [I,T] to put food in your mouth and swallow it: *Eat your dinner!* | *You won't get better if you don't eat.* | **something to eat** (=some food): *Would you like something to eat?* **2** [I] to have a meal: *We usually eat at seven.*

eat sth ↔ away, eat away at sth *phr v* [T] to gradually remove or reduce the amount of something: *Rust had eaten away at the metal frame.*

eat into sth *phr v* [T] **1** to gradually reduce the amount of time, money etc that is available: *All these reports are really eating into our savings.* **2** to damage something: *Acid eats into the metal, damaging the surface.*

eat out *phr v* [I] to eat in a restaurant, not at home: *I don't feel like cooking – let's eat out tonight.*

eat sth ↔ up *phr v* [I,T] *spoken* to eat all of something: *Come on, Kaylee, eat up!*

eat·er /ˈiːtəll-ər/ *n* [C] **big/light/fussy etc eater** someone who eats a lot, not much, only particular things etc

eating dis·or·der /ˈ.. .,../ *n* [C] a medical condition in which someone does not eat normal amounts, especially when they are frightened of getting fat → see also ANOREXIA, BULIMIA

eaves /iːvz/ *n* [plural] the edges of a roof that stick out beyond the walls: *birds nesting under the eaves*

eaves·drop /ˈiːvzdrɒp ll-drɑːp/ *v* [I] **-pped, -pping** to listen secretly to other people's conversations — **eavesdropper** *n* [C] → compare OVERHEAR

eavesdrop

ebb¹ /eb/ *n* **1** also **ebb tide** [singular] the flow of the sea away from the land, when the TIDE goes out **2** **be at low ebb** to be in a bad state: *By March 1933, the economy was at its lowest ebb.* **3** **ebb and flow** when something increases and decreases in a regular pattern: *the ebb and flow of consumer demand* → opposite FLOW¹

ebb² *v* [I] **1** also **ebb away** to gradually decrease: *His courage slowly ebbed away.* **2** if the TIDE ebbs, it flows away from the land

eb·o·ny /ˈebəni/ *n* [C,U] a tree with hard black wood, or the wood itself — **ebony** *adj*

e·bul·li·ent /ɪˈbʌliənt, ɪˈbʊ-/ *adj formal* very happy and excited: *an ebullient mood* — **ebullience** *n* [U]

EC /ˌiː ˈsiːↄ/ *n* **the EC** the European Community; a political organization of European countries that encourages trade and friendship between countries that are members; the EU

ec·cen·tric¹ /ɪkˈsentrɪk/ *adj* behaving in a way that is unusual and strange: *an eccentric old woman* | *students dressed in eccentric clothing* — **eccentrically** /-kli/ *adv* — **eccentricity** /ˌeksen-ˈtrɪsəti, -sən-/ *n* [C,U]

eccentric² *n* [C] someone who always behaves in an unusual but amusing way

ec·cle·si·as·ti·cal /ɪˌkliːziˈæstɪkəl/ also **ec·cle·si·as·tic** /-ˈæstɪkↄ/ *adj* ecclesiastical activities, buildings etc involve or belong to the Christian church: *ecclesiastical history*

ech·o¹ /ˈekəʊll ˈekoʊ/ *n* [C] *plural* **echoes 1** a sound that you hear again because it was made, for example, in a large empty room or a valley **2** something that is very similar to what has happened or been said before: *a murder which has echoes of Kennedy's assassination*

echo² *v* **echoed, echoed, echoing 1** [I] if a sound or place echoes, you hear sounds repeated because you are in, for example, a large empty room or a valley: *voices echoing around the cave* | *The theatre echoed with laughter and applause.* **2** [T] to repeat and agree with what someone else has said: *This report echoes what I said two weeks ago.*

e·clipse¹ /ɪˈklɪps/ *n* [C] when the sun or the moon seems to disappear, because one of them is passing between the other one and the Earth

eclipse² *v* [T] **1** to become more powerful, famous, or important than someone or something else so that they are no longer noticed: *His achievement was eclipsed by his sister's success in the final.* **2** to make the sun or moon disappear in an eclipse

e·co- /ˈiːkəʊ/ *prefix* relating to the environment: *ecofriendly* | *ecosystem*

e·co-friend·ly /ˈiːkəʊˌfrendlill ˈiːkoʊ-/ *adj* not harmful to the environment: *ecofriendly products*

e·co·lo·gi·cal /ˌiːkəˈlɒdʒɪkəl ll-ˈlɑː-/ *adj* concerning the way that plants, animals, and people affect their environment and how the environment can be kept healthy: *ecological problems caused by the huge oil spill* | *an ecological study* — **ecologically** /-kli/ *adv*

e·col·o·gy /ɪˈkɒlədʒill ɪˈkɑː-/ *n* [singular, U] the way in which plants, animals, and people are related to each other and to their environment, or the study of this — **ecologist** *n* [C]

ec·o·nom·ic /ˌekəˈnɒmɪkↄ, ˌiː-ll-ˈnɑː-/ *adj* concerning the trade, industry, and the making of money within a country: *criticism of the government's economic policy* | *economic links with South America* — **economically** /-kli/ *adv*: *an economically undeveloped area*

ec·o·nom·i·cal /ˌekəˈnɒmɪkəl, ˌiː-ll-ˈnɑː-/ *adj* using money, time, products, etc carefully and without wasting any: *an economical method of heating* — **economically** /-kli/ *adv*

ec·o·nom·ics /ˌekəˈnɒmɪks, ˌiː-ll-ˈnɑː-/ *n* [U] the study of the way in which money, goods, and services are produced and used

e·con·o·mist /ɪˈkɒnəmɪstll ɪˈkɑː-/ *n* [C] someone who studies economics

e·con·o·mize (also **-ise** *BrE*) /ɪˈkɒnəmaɪzll ɪ-ˈkɑː-/ *v* [I] to reduce the amount of money or time that you spend on something: *We're trying to economize on heating.*

e·con·o·my¹ /ɪˈkɒnəmill ɪˈkɑː-/ *n* **1** [C] the way that money, businesses, and products are organized in a country or area: *a capitalist economy* | *the growing economies of southeast*

GRAMMAR NOTE: the future

To talk about the **future** you can use: 1. **will +** basic form of verb: *I'll* (=I will) *see you tomorrow.* 2. **be going to** (used to say that something will happen soon): *I think it's going to rain.* 3. the **present progressive** (used to say what is planned or intended): *We're having a party on Saturday.*

Asia | *the global economy* (=the economy of the whole world) **2** [C,U] the careful use of things so that nothing is wasted and less money is spent: *If you can't afford the rent, you'll have to make some economies.*

economy² *adj* cheap or intended to save money: *an economy class air ticket*

e·co·sys·tem /ˈiːkəʊˌsɪstɪ̈m‖-koʊ-/ *n* [C] all the animals and plants in an area, and their relation to each other and their environment

eco-war·ri·or /ˈiːkəʊ ˌwɒriə‖ˈiːkoʊ ˌwɒːriər, -ˌwɑː-/ *n* [C] someone who tries to prevent damage to the environment by protesting against new roads, nuclear power etc

ec·sta·sy¹ /ˈekstəsi/ *n* [C,U] a feeling of great happiness: *an expression of pure ecstasy*

Ecstasy² *n* [U] an illegal drug used especially by young people to give a feeling of happiness and energy

ec·stat·ic /ɪkˈstætɪk, ek-/ *adj* feeling very happy and excited: *an ecstatic welcome from thousands of people* —**ecstatically** /-kli/ *adv*

ECU, ecu /ˈekjuː‖eɪˈkuː/ *n* [C] European Currency Unit; the official unit of money of the European Union

ec·ze·ma /ˈeksɪ̈mə‖ˈeksɪ̈mə, ˈegzɪ̈mə, ɪgˈziːmə/ *n* [U] a condition in which skin becomes dry, red, and uncomfortable

ed·dy /ˈedi/ *n* [C] a circular movement of water, wind, dust, etc —**eddy** *v* [I]

edge

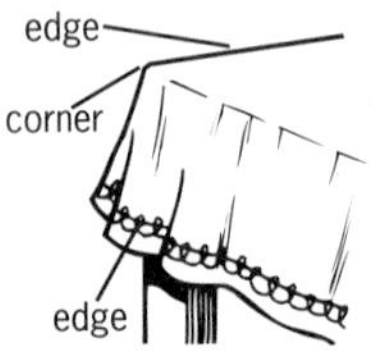

edge¹ /edʒ/ *n* [C] **1** the part of something that is furthest from the centre: *Just leave it on the edge of your plate.* | *She was standing at the water's edge, looking out to sea.* **2** the thin, sharp part of a tool used for cutting: *Careful – that knife's got a very sharp edge!* **3 have the edge on/over** to be slightly better than someone or something else: *This word processor certainly has the edge over the others we have reviewed.* **4 be on edge** to feel nervous: *He's waiting for his exam results, so he's a bit on edge.*

edge² *v* **1** [I,T] to move slowly and gradually, or to make something do this: *The car edged forwards through the crowds.* **2** [T] to put something along the edge of something to decorate it: *sleeves edged with lace*

edge·ways also **edge·wise** *AmE* /ˈedʒweɪz, -waɪz/ *adv* **1 not get a word in edgeways** to not be able to say anything because someone else is talking too much: *When Ann's mother is here I can't get a word in edgeways.* **2** with the edge or thinnest part forward; sideways: *Slide the table in edgeways.*

edg·y /ˈedʒi/ *adj* feeling worried and likely to get upset easily: *You seem a little edgy – what's the matter?*

ed·i·ble /ˈedɪ̈bəl/ *adj* something that is edible can be eaten → opposite INEDIBLE

e·dict /ˈiːdɪkt/ *n* [C] *formal* an official public order made by someone in a position of power

ed·i·fice /ˈedɪ̈fɪ̈s/ *n* [C] *formal* a large building: *a photo of their Head Office, a grand Victorian edifice*

ed·it /ˈedɪ̈t/ *v* [T] to prepare a book, film etc by correcting mistakes and deciding which parts to keep

e·di·tion /ɪˈdɪʃən/ *n* [C] **1** the copies of a book, newspaper etc that are all the same: *a new edition of a dictionary* | *in today's edition of The Times* **2** one of a group of television or radio programmes broadcast regularly with the same name: *last week's edition of "Friends"*

ed·i·tor /ˈedɪ̈tə‖-ər/ *n* [C] the person who decides what should be included and checks for mistakes in a book, newspaper, magazine etc —**editorial** /ˌedɪ̈ˈtɔːriəl/ *adj*

ed·i·to·ri·al /ˌedɪ̈ˈtɔːriəl◂/ *n* [C] a piece of writing in a newspaper that gives the editor's opinion: *an editorial on gun control laws*

ed·u·cate /ˈedjʊkeɪt‖ˈedʒə-/ *v* [T] to teach someone, especially in a school or college: *The country should spend more money on educating our children.* | **+ about** *a campaign to educate teenagers about the dangers of smoking* —**educator** *n* [C] *especially AmE*

ed·u·cat·ed /ˈedjʊkeɪtɪ̈d‖ˈedʒə-/ *adj* **1** an educated person has a high standard of knowledge and education: *a well-educated young woman* **2 educated guess** a guess that is likely to be correct because you have enough information

ed·u·ca·tion /ˌedjʊˈkeɪʃən‖ˌedʒə-/ *n* [singular, U] the process of learning or the knowledge that you get at school or college: *They had worked hard to give their son a good education.* → see also FURTHER EDUCATION, HIGHER EDUCATION

ed·u·ca·tion·al /ˌedjʊˈkeɪʃənəl◂‖ˌedʒə-/ *adj* **1** educational organizations, standards etc are involved with teaching and learning: *how to improve standards in our educational institutions* **2** teaching you something that you did not know: *It was an educational visit, not a holiday.* —**educationally** *adv*

ed·u·tain·ment /ˌedjʊˈteɪnmənt‖ˌedʒə-/ *n* [U] television programmes, computer games etc that are intended to teach people and entertain them at the same time

EEC /ˌiː iː ˈsiː/ *n* **the EEC** the European Economic Community; the former name for the EU

eel /iːl/ *n* [C] a long thin fish that looks like a snake

ee·rie /ˈɪəri‖ˈɪri/ *adj* strange and frightening: *an eerie sound* —**eerily** *adv* —**eeriness** *n* [U]

ef·fect¹ /ɪˈfekt/ *n* **1** [C,U] the way something is affected, changed, or influenced by something else: *What effect would a new road have on the village?* **2** [C,U] an idea or feeling that an artist, writer etc tries to make you have: *The paintings give an effect of light.* | *a word used just for effect* **3 put sth into effect** to make a plan or idea happen: *Nothing had been done to put the changes into effect.* **4 come into effect/take effect** to start being used or start to have results: *The new law comes into effect from January.* **5 in effect** used when you are describing what the real situation is, when this was not expected or intended: *It's called a pay rise, but in effect wages will fall.* **6 to this/that effect** used to say that you are giving the general meaning of what someone said, not their exact words: *The report says he's no good at his job, or words to that effect.*

effect² *v* [T] *formal* to make something happen: *We are hopeful of effecting a cure for this disease very soon.*

ef·fec·tive /ɪ'fektɪv/ *adj* **1** producing the result that was wanted: *a very effective treatment for headaches* | *an effective advertising campaign* → opposite INEFFECTIVE **2** be/become effective to start being used officially: *These prices are effective from April 1.* —**effectiveness** *n* [U]

ef·fec·tive·ly /ɪ'fektɪvli/ *adv* **1** in a way that produces the result that you want: *He didn't deal with the problem very effectively.* **2** used to describe what the real situation is, when this is not what was expected or intended: *By parking here you effectively prevented everyone from leaving.*

ef·fects /ɪ'fekts/ *n* [plural] *formal* the things that you own; → see also SOUND EFFECTS, SPECIAL EFFECTS

ef·fem·i·nate /ɪ'femɪnət/ *adj* a man who is effeminate looks or behaves like a woman —**effeminately** *adv*

ef·fer·vesc·ent /,efə'vesənt◄ ||,efər-/ *adj* a liquid that is effervescent has BUBBLES of gas rising in it —**effervescence** *n* [U]

ef·fi·cient /ɪ'fɪʃənt/ *adj* working well, quickly, and without wasting time or energy: *a very efficient secretary* | *an efficient heating system* → opposite INEFFICIENT —**efficiency** *n* [U] **efficiently** *adv*

ef·fi·gy /'efɪdʒi/ *n* [C] a figure of a person that makes them look ugly or funny, often burned as part of a ceremony

ef·flu·ent /'efluənt/ *n* [C,U] *formal* liquid waste → see colour picture on page 278

ef·fort /'efət||'efərt/ *n* **1** [U] the physical or mental energy needed to do something: *It takes a lot of time and effort to organize a concert.* | *I put a lot of effort into this project.* (=I worked very hard) **2** [C,U] an attempt to do something: *All my efforts at convincing him failed miserably.* | **make an effort (to do sth)** *You could at least make an effort to be polite!* | **in an effort to do sth** *We've been working night and day in an effort to finish this on time.* | **be an effort** (=be difficult or painful): *I was so weak, even eating was an effort.*

ef·fort·less /'efətləs||'efərt-/ *adj* done skilfully in a way that seems easy: *She swam with smooth effortless strokes.* —**effortlessly** *adv*

ef·fu·sive /ɪ'fjuːsɪv/ *adj* showing strong feelings of thanks, admiration, or friendliness: *effusive greetings* —**effusively** *adv* —**effusiveness** *n* [U]

EFL /,i: ef 'el/ English as a Foreign Language; the way English is taught to people who speak a different language

eg, e.g. /,i: 'dʒiː/ a written abbreviation that means "for example": *citrus fruit, e.g. oranges and grapefruit*

e·gal·i·tar·i·an /ɪ,gælɪ'teəriən||-'ter-/ *adj* believing that everyone should have the same rights and opportunities —**egalitarian** *n* [C] — **egalitarianism** *n* [U]

egg¹ /eg/ *n* **1** [C] a round object with a hard surface that contains a baby bird, insect, snake etc: *When do blackbirds lay their eggs?* **2** [C,U] an egg, especially from a chicken, used as food: *bacon and eggs for breakfast* **3** [C] a cell produced inside a woman or female animal that can develop into a baby

egg² *v*

egg sb ↔ on *phr v* [T] to encourage someone to do something that they should not do: *He was scared to jump, but his friends kept egging him on.*

egg·plant /'egplɑːnt||-plænt/ *n* [C,U] *especially AmE* a large vegetable with a smooth shiny purple skin; AUBERGINE *BrE* → see picture at VEGETABLE

egg·shell /'egʃel/ *n* [C,U] the hard outside part of a bird's egg

e·go /'iːgəʊ, 'egəʊ||-goʊ/ *n* [C] **1** the opinion that you have about yourself: *That award was a real boost for my ego.* | **have a big ego** (=think that you are very clever or important): *politicians with big egos* **2** **ego trip** *informal* something that someone does because it makes them feel important

e·go·cen·tric /,iːgəʊ'sentrɪk◄, ,e-||-goʊ-/ *adj* believing that you are more important, interesting etc than other people

e·go·tis·m /'iːgətɪzəm, 'e-/ **e·go·is·m** /'iːgəʊ ɪzəm, 'e-||-goʊ-/ *n* [U] the belief that you are more interesting or important than other people —**egotist** *n* [C] —**egotistic** /,iːgə'tɪstɪk◄, ,e-/, **egotistical** *adj*

eh /eɪ/ *interjection BrE spoken* used to ask someone to say something again: *"It'll cost £500." "Eh? How much?"*

ei·der·down /'aɪdədaʊn||-dər-/ *n* [C] a warm cover used on top of BLANKETS on a bed → compare QUILT, DUVET

eight /eɪt/ *number* **1** 8 **2** eight o'clock: *Dinner will be at eight.*

eigh·teen /,eɪ'tiːn◄/ *number* 18 —**eighteenth** *number*

eighth /eɪtθ/ *number* **1** 8th **2** 1/8

eigh·ty /'eɪti/ *number* 80 —**eightieth** *number*

ei·ther¹ /'aɪðə||'iːðər/ *conjunction* either ... or used to give a list of possibilities or choices: *You can have either tea, coffee, or fruit juice.* | *Either say you're sorry, or get out!*

USAGE NOTE: either ... or and neither ... nor

Use a singular verb with these words when you are writing if the second noun is singular: *If either Doris or Meg calls, please take a message.* | *Neither Theo nor Garth is very tall.* If the second noun is plural, use a plural verb: *If either my sister or my parents come, please let them in.* However, in informal speech, people usually use a plural verb, whether the noun is singular or plural.

---

either² *determiner, pron* **1** one of two things or people when it is not important which: *Can either of you lend me £5?* | *I've lived in New York and Chicago, but I don't like either city very much.* | **either way** *You can get there by train or plane, but either way it's very expensive.* **2** **on either side/at either end etc** on both sides, at both ends etc: *He sat in the back of the car with a policeman on either side.* → compare BOTH

either³ *adv* used in negative sentences to mean also: *"I can't swim." "I can't either."*

e·jac·u·late /ɪˈdʒækjɨleɪt/ *v* [I,T] when a male ejaculates, SPERM comes out of his PENIS —**ejaculation** /ɪˌdʒækjɨˈleɪʃən/ *n* [C,U]

e·ject /ɪˈdʒekt/ *v* **1** [T] *formal* to push or throw something out with force: *Any trouble-makers will be ejected from the meeting.* **2** [I] to jump out of a plane that is going to crash **3** [T] to make something come out of a machine by pressing a button: *How do I eject the CD?* —**ejection** /ɪˈdʒekʃən/ *n* [C,U]

eke /iːk/ *v*
  eke sth ↔ **out** *phr v* [T] **1** to make something such as food or money last a long time by using small amounts of it **2** **eke out a living/existence** to get just enough food or money to live on

e·lab·o·rate¹ /ɪˈlæbərɨt/ *adj* having a lot of small details or parts that are connected in a complicated way: *fabric with an elaborate design | an elaborate plan* —**elaborately** *adv*

e·lab·o·rate² /ɪˈlæbəreɪt/ *v* [I,T] to give more details about something you have said or written: *You say you disagree – would you like to elaborate on that?* —**elaboration** /ɪˌlæbəˈreɪʃən/ *n* [U]

e·lapse /ɪˈlæps/ *v* [I] *formal* if a period of time elapses, it passes

e·las·tic /ɪˈlæstɪk/ *adj* a material that is elastic can stretch and then go back to its usual shape or size: *an elastic waistband* —**elastic** *n* [U] —**elasticity** /ˌiːlæˈstɪsɨti/ *n* [U]

elastic band /.ˌ. ˈ./ *n* [C] *BrE* a thin circle of rubber that stretches, used for fastening things together; RUBBER BAND

e·lat·ed /ɪˈleɪtɨd/ *adj* extremely happy and excited: *I was elated when Mary told me she was pregnant.* —**elation** /ɪˈleɪʃən/ *n* [U]

el·bow¹ /ˈelbəʊ‖-boʊ/ *n* [C] **1** the joint where your arm bends **2** **elbow-room** if you have enough elbow-room, there is enough space for you to move or work easily: *Will you stand back and give me some elbow-room, please?*

elbow² *v* [T] to push someone with your elbow, especially in order to move past them: *She elbowed her way through the crowd.*

el·der¹ /ˈeldə‖-ər/ *adj* **1** **elder brother/sister/daughter/son** an older brother, sister etc: *My elder sister is a nurse.* **2** **the elder** the older one of two people: *Sarah is the elder of the two sisters.*

elder² *n* [C usually plural] **1** someone who is older than you are: *Young people should have respect for their elders.* **2** an older person who is important and respected: *a meeting of the village elders*

USAGE NOTE: elder and older

Use **elder** to talk about the members of a family: *Nick is my elder brother.* Use **older** to compare the age of people or things: *My sister is two years older than I am.*

el·der·ly /ˈeldəli‖ˈeldərli/ *adj* **1** old or becoming old: *an elderly woman with white hair* **2** **the elderly** people who are old: *a home that provides care for the elderly* → compare OLD, ANCIENT

el·dest /ˈeldɨst/ *adj* **eldest son/daughter/brother/sister** the oldest son etc

e·lect /ɪˈlekt/ *v* [T] **1** to choose someone for an official position by voting: *Clinton was elected President in 1992.* **2** **elect to do sth** *formal* to choose to do something: *Hanley elected to take early retirement.*

e·lec·tion /ɪˈlekʃən/ *n* [C] an occasion when people vote to choose someone for an official position: *The party must win the next election!* —**electoral** /ɪˈlektərəl/ *adj*

e·lec·to·rate /ɪˈlektərɨt/ *n* [singular] all the people in a country who are allowed to vote: *We have to convince the electorate that we will not raise taxes.*

e·lec·tric /ɪˈlektrɪk/ *adj* **1** an electric light, HEATER etc works using electricity: *an electric oven | an electric guitar* **2** extremely exciting: *The atmosphere in the courtroom was electric.*

USAGE NOTE: electric and electrical

Use **electric** as an adjective before the names of things that need electricity in order to work: *an electric clock | electric lights.* Use **electrical** as a more general word to talk about people and their work, or about things that use or produce electricity: *an electrical engineer | My dad's company imports electrical goods.*

e·lec·tri·cal /ɪˈlektrɪkəl/ *adj* using or concerned with electricity: *electrical goods | an electrical engineer*

electric chair /.ˌ.. ˈ./ *n* **the electric chair** a chair in which criminals are killed as a punishment using electricity

el·ec·tri·cian /ɪˌlekˈtrɪʃən, ˌelɪk-/ *n* [C] someone whose job is to fit and repair electrical equipment

e·lec·tri·ci·ty /ɪˌlekˈtrɪsɨti, ˌelɪk-/ *n* [U] the power that is carried by wires and used to provide light or make machines work: *The electricity will be cut off if you don't pay your bill.*

electric shock /.ˌ.. ˈ./ *n* [C] a sudden painful shock caused when you accidentally touch electricity

e·lec·tri·fy /ɪˈlektrɨfaɪ/ *v* [T] **1** to change a railway so that the trains use electrical power, or to provide electricity in an area **2** if a performance electrifies the people who are watching it, it makes them very excited —**electrified** *adj* —**electrifying** *adj*: *Her words had an electrifying effect.*

e·lec·tro·cute /ɪˈlektrəkjuːt/ *v* [T] to kill someone by passing electricity through their body —**electrocution** /ɪˌlektrəˈkjuːʃən/ *n* [U]

e·lec·trode /ɪˈlektrəʊd‖-troʊd/ *n* [C] a point at which electricity enters or leaves something such as a BATTERY

e·lec·tron /ɪˈlektrɒn‖-trɑːn/ *n* [C] one of the parts of an atom, that has a NEGATIVE electric charge → compare NEUTRON, PROTON

e·lec·tron·ic /ɪˌlekˈtrɒnɪk, ˌelɪk-‖-ˈtrɑː-/ *adj* **1** using electrical power and MICROCHIPS to operate machines such as computers, radios and CALCULATORS **2** using electronic equipment: *electronic music* —**electronically** /-kli/ *adv*

e·lec·tron·ics /ɪˌlekˈtrɒnɪks, ˌelɪk-‖-ˈtrɑː-/ *n* [U] the study or the process of making electronic equipment, such as computers or televisions: *the electronics industry*

el·e·gant /'elɪ̯gənt/ *adj* having a graceful and attractive style or appearance: *a tall, elegant woman* —**elegance** *n* [U] —**elegantly** *adv*

el·e·ment /'elɪ̯mənt/ *n* [C] **1** a simple chemical substance that consists of only one kind of atom → compare COMPOUND[1] **2 an element of surprise/truth/risk etc** a small amount of surprise, truth, risk etc: *There's an element of truth in what he says.* **3** one part of a plan, system, piece of writing etc: *a movie with all the elements of a great love story* **4** a group of people of a particular type: *a small criminal element within the club* **5 be in your element** to be happy doing something, because you are good at it **6** the metal part of a piece of electrical equipment that is used for heating → see also ELEMENTS

el·e·men·tal /ˌelɪ̯'mentl̩/ *adj* an elemental emotion is simple, basic, and strong

el·e·men·ta·ry /ˌelɪ̯'mentəri/ *adj* **1** simple or basic: *an elementary mistake* **2** relating to the first and easiest part of a subject: *a book of elementary chemistry* **3** AmE relating to the first six or eight years of a child's education; PRIMARY BrE: *an elementary school*

elementary school /ˌ..ˈ.. ./ also **grade school** *n* [C] AmE a school for the first six or eight years of a child's education: PRIMARY SCHOOL BrE

el·e·ments /'elɪ̯mənts/ *n* **the elements** weather, especially wind and rain: *A cave provided shelter from the elements.*

el·e·phant /'elɪ̯fənt/ *n* [C] a very large grey animal with big ears, and a TRUNK

el·e·vate /'elɪ̯veɪt/ *v* [T] *formal* to give someone or something a more important rank or position: *In the 1920s he was elevated to Secretary of State.*

el·e·vat·ed /'elɪ̯veɪtɪd/ *adj formal* in a high position or at a high level

el·e·vat·ing /'elɪ̯veɪtɪŋ/ *adj* educating or improving your mind: *an elevating experience*

el·e·va·tion /ˌelɪ̯'veɪʃən/ *n* **1** [C] a height above the level of the sea: *The observatory is located at an elevation of 2600m.* **2** [U] *formal* when someone is given a more important position or rank: *the judge's elevation to the Supreme Court*

el·e·va·tor /'elɪ̯veɪtəl-ər/ *n* [C] AmE a machine in a building that takes people up or down from one level to another; LIFT BrE

el·ev·en /ɪ'levən/ *number* number[1] 11 —**eleventh** *number*

elf /elf/ *n* [C], *plural* **elves** /elvz/ a small imaginary person with pointed ears

e·li·cit /ɪ'lɪsɪt/ *v* [T] *formal* to get information or a reaction from someone: *Short questions are more likely to elicit a response.*

el·i·gi·ble /'elɪ̯dʒɪbəl/ *adj* **1** having the right to do or receive something: **+ for** *Students are eligible for financial support.* | **eligible to do sth** *Are you eligible to vote?* **2** rich, attractive, not yet married, and therefore desirable as a hus-

band: *an eligible bachelor* —**eligibility** /ˌelɪdʒə-'bɪlɪti/ *n* [U]

e·lim·i·nate /ɪ'lɪmɪneɪt/ *v* [T] **1** to completely get rid of something or someone: *Electronic banking eliminates the need for cash or cheques.* **2 be eliminated** to be defeated in a sports competition, so that you can no longer take part in it: *Our team was eliminated in the third round.*

e·lim·i·na·tion /ɪˌlɪmɪ'neɪʃən/ *n* [U] **1** when something is got rid of completely or completely destroyed: *the control and elimination of nuclear weapons* **2 process of elimination** a way of finding the right answer to something by proving all the other answers wrong until only the right one is left

e·lite /eɪ'liːt, ɪ-/ *n* [singular] a small group of people who have a lot of power or influence because of their wealth, knowledge etc

e·lit·ist /eɪ'liːtɪst, ɪ-/ *adj* an elitist system is one in which a small group of people have much more power than other people —**elitism** *n* [U]

el·lip·ti·cal /ɪ'lɪptɪkəl/ also **el·lip·tic** /-tɪk/ *adj* shaped like a long circle but with slightly flat sides; OVAL

elm /elm/ *n* [C,U] a large tall tree with broad leaves.

el·o·cu·tion /ˌelə'kjuːʃən/ *n* [U] the art of speaking well and clearly

e·lon·gat·ed /'iːlɒŋgeɪtɪdlɪ'lɔːŋ-/ *adj* long and thin: *elongated shadows* —**elongate** *v* [I,T]

e·lope /ɪ'ləʊplɪ'loʊp/ *v* [I] to go away secretly with someone to get married

el·o·quent /'eləkwənt/ *adj* able to express your ideas and opinions clearly in a way that influences other people: *an eloquent speaker* —**eloquently** *adv* —**eloquence** *n* [U]

else /els/ *adv* **1** a word meaning "in addition", used after words beginning with "any-", "no-", "some-", and after question words: *Clayton needs someone else to help him.* | *What else can I get you?* **2** a word meaning "different" or "other", used after words beginning with "any-", "no-", "some-", "every-" and after question words: *everyone else* (=all the others) | *Is there anything else to eat?* | *She was wearing someone else's coat.* **3 or else** used to say that if something does not happen, another thing will happen, usually something bad: *She'd have to pay, or else she'd go to prison.*

else·where /els'weəˌ 'elsweəlɪelswer/ *adv* in or to another place: *Snow is expected elsewhere in the region.*

ELT /ˌiː el 'tiː/ *n* [U] *especially BrE* English Language Teaching; the teaching of the English language to people whose first language is not English

e·lu·ci·date /ɪ'luːsɪdeɪt/ *v* [I,T] *formal* to explain something very clearly and make it easy to understand

e·lude /ɪ'luːd/ *v* [T] **1** to avoid being found or caught by someone, especially by tricking them: *Jones eluded the police for six weeks.* **2** if something that you want eludes you, you do not find

---

GRAMMAR NOTE: 'if' clauses (1)

Use the simple present to talk about the future in clauses beginning with **if...** : *I will hit you* **if** *you* **do** *that again.* not 'if you will do that again'. **If** *you* **take** *a taxi, you'll be OK.* not 'if you will take a taxi...'
Use 'will' in the other part of the sentence.

it or achieve it: *Success has eluded him so far.*
3 if a fact eludes you, you cannot remember it:
Her name eludes me at the moment.

e·lu·sive /ɪ'luːsɪv/ *adj* difficult to find, or remember: *The fox was elusive and clever.* —**elu-
sively** *adv*

elves /elvz/ the plural of ELF

'em /əm/ *pron spoken nonstandard* short for
'them': *Tell the kids I'll pick 'em up after school.*

e·ma·ci·a·ted /ɪ'meɪʃieɪtɪd, -si-/ *adj* extremely
thin because of illness or lack of food

e-mail, **email** /'iː meɪl/ *n* [U] electronic mail;
a system for sending messages by computer —
e-mail *v* [T]

em·a·nate /'emǝneɪt/ *v*
emanate from sth *phr v* [T] to come from or
out of something: *Wonderful smells emanated
from the kitchen.* —**emanation** /ˌemǝ'neɪʃǝn/ *n*
[U]

e·man·ci·pate /ɪ'mænsɪpeɪt/ *v* [T] *formal* to
give people the same legal, political, and social
rights as other people —**emancipated** *adj*
—**emancipation** /ɪˌmænsɪ'peɪʃǝn/ *n* [U]

em·balm /ɪm'bɑːm‖-'bɑːm, -'bɑːlm/ *v* [T] to preserve a dead body by using chemicals and oils

em·bank·ment /ɪm'bæŋkmǝnt/ *n* [C] a wide
wall of earth or stones built to stop water from
flooding an area, or to support a road or railway

em·bar·go /ɪm'bɑːgǝʊ‖-'bɑːrgǝʊ/ *n* [C], *plural*
embargoes an official order to stop trade with
another country: *The UN is considering lifting
the oil embargo* (=ending it). —**embargo** *v* [T]

em·bark /ɪm'bɑːk‖-ɑːrk/ *v* [I] to get on a ship
—**embarkation** /ˌembɑː'keɪʃǝn‖-bɑːr-/ *n* [C,U]
→ opposite DISEMBARK
embark on/upon sth *phr v* [T] to start something new, difficult, or exciting: *Hal is leaving
the band to embark on a solo career.*

em·bar·rass /ɪm'bærǝs/ *v* [T] to make someone feel ashamed, stupid, or uncomfortable: *I
hope I didn't embarrass you.*

em·bar·rassed /ɪm'bærǝst/ *adj* feeling ashamed, stupid, or uncomfortable, especially when
other people are watching or listening: *Everyone
was staring at me and I felt really embarrassed.*
→ see also picture on page 277

em·bar·ras·sing /ɪm'bærǝsɪŋ/ *adj* making
you feel embarrassed: *embarrassing questions*

em·bar·rass·ment /ɪm'bærǝsmǝnt/ *n* **1** [U]
the feeling you have when you are embarrassed:
*Billy looked down and tried to hide his
embarrassment.* **2** [C] something or someone
that makes you feel embarrassed: *His mother's
boasting was a constant embarrassment to him.*

em·bas·sy /'embǝsi/ *n* [C] a group of OFFICIALS
who deal with their country's affairs in a foreign
country, or the building they work in

em·bed·ded /ɪm'bedɪd/ *adj* firmly and deeply
stuck in the surface or an object: + **in** *Small
stones had become embedded in the ice.*

em·bel·lish /ɪm'belɪʃ/ *v* [T] **1** to make a story
more interesting by adding details to it that are
not true **2** to make something more beautiful
by adding decorations to it —**embellishment** *n*
[C,U]

em·ber /'embǝr/ *n* [C usually plural] a piece
of wood or coal that stays red and very hot after
a fire has stopped burning

em·bez·zle /ɪm'bezǝl/ *v* [I,T] to steal money
that your employer has made you responsible
for —**embezzlement** *n* [U]

em·bit·tered /ɪm'bɪtǝd‖-ǝrd/ *adj* feeling very
angry, and hating people, because of unpleasant
or unfair things that they have done —**embitter**
v [T]

em·bla·zon /ɪm'bleɪzǝn/ *v* [T] to put a name,
design etc on something so that it can be seen
clearly

em·blem /'emblǝm/ *n* [C] a picture, shape, or
object that is the sign of something

em·bod·i·ment /ɪm'bɒdɪmǝnt‖ɪm'bɑː-/ *n* **the
embodiment of** someone or something that is a
very typical example of an idea or quality: *He is
the embodiment of evil.*

em·bod·y /ɪm'bɒdi‖ɪm'bɑːdi/ *v* [T] to be the perfect example of an idea or quality: *Mrs. Miller
embodies everything I admire in a teacher.*

em·boss /ɪm'bɒs‖ɪm'bɑːs, -'bɔːs/ *v* [T] to decorate the surface of metal, leather, paper etc with a
raised pattern —**embossed** *adj*

em·brace /ɪm'breɪs/ *v* [T] *formal* **1** to put
your arms around someone and hold them in a
loving way: *Rob reached out to embrace her.*
2 to eagerly accept an idea, opinion, religion
etc: *Many Romans had embraced the Christian
religion.* **3** *formal* to include something: *a
study that embraces every aspect of the subject*
—**embrace** *n* [C]

em·broi·der /ɪm'brɔɪdǝr‖-ǝr/ *v* **1** [I,T] to decorate cloth by sewing a picture or pattern on it
2 [T] to make a story more interesting by adding details to it that are not true

em·broi·der·y /ɪm'brɔɪdǝri/ *n* [U] a decoration
or pattern made by sewing cloth, or the act of
making this

em·broil /ɪm'brɔɪl/ *v* **be embroiled in** to be involved in a fight, an argument, or a difficult situation: *I don't want to get embroiled in a long
argument about money.*

em·bry·o /'embriǝʊ‖-briǝʊ/ *n* [C] an animal or
human that has just begun to develop inside its
mother's body → compare FOETUS

em·e·rald /'emǝrǝld/ *n* [C] a bright green jewel

e·merge /ɪ'mɜːdʒ‖-ɜːrdʒ/ *v* [I] **1** to appear or
come out from somewhere: + **from** *He emerged
from his hiding place.* **2** to become known: *New
evidence has emerged.*|+ **that** *It later emerged
that she had been seeing him secretly.* **3** to come
to the end of a difficult situation: *They emerged
triumphant from the battle.* —**emergence** *n* [U]

e·mer·gen·cy /ɪ'mɜːdʒǝnsi‖-ɜːr-/ *n* [C] an unexpected and dangerous situation that must be
dealt with immediately: *Quick! Call an ambulance! This is an emergency!* —**emergency** *adj*:
emergency exit (=the door used in an emergency)

emergency brake /.'.. ,./ *n* [C] *AmE* a thing
in a car that you pull up with your hand to stop
the car from moving; HANDBRAKE *BrE*

emergency room /.'... ,./ *n* [C] *AmE* the part
of a hospital where you go if you have been injured in an accident; CASUALTY *BrE*

e·mer·ging /ɪ'mɜːdʒɪŋ‖-ɜːr-/ *also* **e·mer·gent**
/-dʒǝnt/ *adj* just starting to develop: *the emer-
ging nations of the world*

em·i·grant /'emɪgrǝnt/ *n* [C] someone who
leaves their own country to live in another
→ compare IMMIGRANT

em·i·grate /ˈemɪɡreɪt/ v [I] to leave your own country to go and live in another: *The Remingtons emigrated to Australia.* — **emigration** /ˌemɪˈɡreɪʃən/ n [U]

> **USAGE NOTE: emigrate, immigrate and migrate**
>
> Use **emigrate** to talk about people who leave their country to live in another one: *My grandparents emigrated from Italy.* Use **immigrate** to talk about people who enter a country in order to live there: *Yuko immigrated to the US last year.* Use **migrate** to talk about birds that go to another part of the world in the autumn and the spring.

em·i·nent /ˈemɪnənt/ adj famous and important: *a team of eminent scientists*

em·i·nent·ly /ˈemɪnəntli/ adv formal very: *He's eminently qualified to do the job.*

e·mis·sion /ɪˈmɪʃən/ n [C,U] when gas, heat, light, sound etc is sent out, or the gas, heat etc that is sent out: *attempts to reduce emissions from cars*

e·mit /ɪˈmɪt/ v [T] **-tted, -tting** to send out gas, heat, light, sound etc: *The kettle emitted a shrill whistle.*

e·mo·tion /ɪˈməʊʃən‖ɪˈmoʊ-/ n [C,U] a strong feeling such as love or hate: *Her voice was trembling with emotion.* | *Women tend to express their emotions more easily than men.*

e·mo·tion·al /ɪˈməʊʃənəl‖ɪˈmoʊ-/ adj **1** showing your emotions to other people, especially by crying: *He became very emotional when I mentioned his first wife.* **2** making people have strong feelings: *the emotional impact of the film* **3** connected with your feelings: *emotional problems* — **emotionally** adv

e·mo·tive /ɪˈməʊtɪv‖ɪˈmoʊ-/ adj making people have strong feelings: *Abortion is an emotive issue.*

em·pa·thy /ˈempəθi/ n [U] the ability to understand someone's feelings and problems — **empathize** v [I] → compare SYMPATHY

em·pe·ror /ˈempərə‖-ər/ n [C] the ruler of an EMPIRE

em·pha·sis /ˈemfəsɪs/ n [C,U], plural **emphases** /-siːz/ **1** the special importance that you give to something: *place/put emphasis on Most schools do not place enough emphasis on health education.* **2** if you put emphasis on a particular word, you say it louder to show that it is important

em·pha·size (also **-ise** BrE) /ˈemfəsaɪz/ v [T] to show that an opinion, idea, quality etc is important: *My teacher always emphasized the importance of grammar.*

em·phat·ic /ɪmˈfætɪk/ adj expressing your meaning strongly: *Dale's answer was an emphatic "No!"* — **emphatically** /-kli/ adv

em·pire /ˈempaɪə‖-paɪr/ n [C] **1** a group of countries that are controlled by one ruler or government **2** a group of organizations that are all controlled by one person or company: *a media empire*

em·pir·i·cal /ɪmˈpɪrɪkəl/ adj based on scientific methods or practical experience, not on ideas: *Empirical evidence is needed to support their theory.*

em·ploy /ɪmˈplɔɪ/ v [T] **1** to pay someone to work for you: *The factory employs over 2,000 people.* | **be employed as sth** *He was employed as a language teacher.* **2** to use a particular object, method, or skill: *They employed new photographic techniques.*

em·ploy·ee /ɪmˈplɔɪ-iː, ˌemplɔɪˈiː/ n [C] someone who is paid to work for someone else: *a government employee*

em·ploy·er /ɪmˈplɔɪə‖-ər/ n [C] a person or company that pays people to work for them: *a reference from your employer*

em·ploy·ment /ɪmˈplɔɪmənt/ n [U] **1** work that you do to earn money: *Students start looking for employment when they leave college.* **2** when people are employed: *a government report on training and employment* | **full employment** (=when everyone has a job) → see also UNEMPLOYMENT **3** formal the use of an object, method, or skill to achieve something: *the employment of military force to gain control of the area*

em·pow·er /ɪmˈpaʊə‖-ər/ v **1** [T] to give someone more control over their own life: *Information and education empower people.* **2** **be empowered to do sth** formal to have the power or right to do something: *The college is empowered to grant degrees.*

em·press /ˈemprɪs/ n [C] the female ruler of an EMPIRE, or the wife of an EMPEROR

emp·ty¹ /ˈempti/ adj **1** having nothing or no one inside: *an empty box* | *empty spaces* **2** without meaning, value, or importance: *empty promises* — **emptiness** n [U]

empty

empty

full

empty² v **1** also **empty out** [T] to remove everything that is inside a container, cupboard etc: *I found your umbrella when I was emptying out the wardrobe.* | *Rachel emptied the soup into a pan.* **2** [I] to become empty: *The room emptied very quickly.*

empty-hand·ed /ˌ...ˈ.../ adj without getting anything: *The thieves fled the building empty-handed.*

em·u·late /ˈemjʊleɪt/ v [T] formal to try to be like someone because you admire them: *Children naturally emulate their heroes.*

en·a·ble /ɪˈneɪbəl/ v [T] to make it possible for someone to do something or for something to happen: **enable sb to do sth** *The money from her aunt enabled Jan to buy the house.*

en·act /ɪˈnækt/ v [T] **1** to make something a law: *Congress refused to enact the bill.* **2** formal to perform a story as a play

e·nam·el /ɪˈnæməl/ n [U] **1** a substance like glass that is put on metal, clay etc for decoration or for protection **2** the hard smooth surface of your teeth

en·am·oured BrE, **enamored** AmE /ɪˈnæməd‖-ərd/ adj formal **be enamoured of/with** to like someone or something very much: *You don't seem very enamoured with your new job.*

en·case /ɪnˈkeɪs/ v **be encased in** to be completely covered by something: *Lisa's broken leg was encased in plaster.*

en·chant·ed /ɪnˈtʃɑːntᵻd‖ɪnˈtʃæn-/ *adj*
1 made to feel very happy, interested, and excited: *You'll be enchanted by the beauty of the city.* **2** changed by magic: *an enchanted forest*

en·chant·ing /ɪnˈtʃɑːntɪŋ‖ɪnˈtʃæn-/ *adj* very attractive: *an enchanting smile*

en·cir·cle /ɪnˈsɜːkəl‖-ɜːr-/ *v* [T] to surround someone or something : *an ancient city encircled by high walls*

en·clave /ˈenkleɪv, ˈeŋ-/ *n* [C] a place or group of people surrounded by other areas or groups that are different from it: *a Spanish enclave on the Moroccan coast*

en·close /ɪnˈkləʊz‖-ˈkloʊz/ *v* [T] **1** to put something inside an envelope with a letter: *Please enclose a stamped addressed envelope.* **2** to surround an area, especially with a fence or wall: *A high wall enclosed the garden.* —**enclosed** *adj*

en·clo·sure /ɪnˈkləʊʒə‖-ˈkloʊʒər/ *n* [C] an area that is surrounded by something such as a wall or fence: *The animals are kept in a large enclosure.*

en·com·pass /ɪnˈkʌmpəs/ *v* [T] to include a lot of ideas, subjects etc, or a large area: *a national park encompassing 400 square miles*

en·core /ˈɒŋkɔː‖ˈɑːŋkɔːr/ *n* [C] a short piece of music that a performer adds or repeats at the end of a performance because people ask for it

en·coun·ter[1] /ɪnˈkaʊntəl-ər/ *v* [T] **1** to experience something that causes difficulty: *The engineers encountered more problems when the rainy season began.* **2** *literary* to meet someone or something: *I was just twelve years old when I first encountered him.*

encounter[2] *n* [C] when two people or groups meet, especially in a way that is dangerous or not expected: *a chance encounter with the famous actor, Wilfred Lawson*

en·cour·age /ɪnˈkʌrɪdʒ‖ɪnˈkɜːr-/ *v* [T] **1** to try to persuade someone to do something, especially by making them more confident **2** to make it easier for something to happen: *Cheaper tickets might encourage people to use public transport.* —**encouragement** *n* [C,U] → opposite DISCOURAGE

en·cour·ag·ing /ɪnˈkʌrᵻdʒɪŋ‖ɪnˈkɜːr-/ *adj* giving you hope and confidence: *This time, the news is more encouraging.* —**encouragingly** *adv*

en·croach /ɪnˈkrəʊtʃ‖-ˈkroʊtʃ/ *v*
encroach on/upon sth *phr v* [T] **1** to take away more and more of someone's time, power, rights etc: *I don't let my work encroach on my private life.* **2** to cover more and more of an area or space that is intended for something else: *Long grass is starting to encroach onto the highway.*

en·crust·ed /ɪnˈkrʌstᵻd/ *adj* covered with something hard, such as jewels, ice, or dried mud: *a bracelet encrusted with diamonds*

en·cy·clo·pe·di·a also **encyclopaedia** *BrE* /ɪnˌsaɪkləˈpiːdiə/ *n* [C] a book that contains facts about many subjects

end[1] /end/ *n* [C] **1** the last part of a period of time, activity, book, film etc: + *of the end of the story* | *at the end Rob's moving to Maine at the end of September.* **2** the farthest point of a place

or thing: *We walked to the end of the road.* | *the deep end of the pool* **3** when something is finished or no longer exists: **be at an end** *His political career was at an end.* | **come to an end** *Their relationship had come to an end.* | **put an end to** *a peace agreement that will put an end to the fighting* **4** **in the end** after a lot of time or discussion; finally: *In the end, we decided to go to Florida.* **5** a purpose or aim: *She'll use any method to achieve her own ends.* **6** (for) **days/ hours etc on end** for many days, hours etc without stopping: *It rained for days on end.* **7** **no end** *spoken* very much or very many: *That used car I bought has given me no end of trouble.* **8** **make ends meet** to get just enough money to buy what you need: *It's been hard to make ends meet since Ray lost his job.* **9** **at the end of your tether** *BrE*/**at the end of your rope** *AmE* extremely annoyed, upset, and impatient → see also ODDS AND ENDS, **get (hold of) the wrong end of the stick** (WRONG[1])

end[2] *v* [I,T] to finish or stop, or to make something finish: *World War II ended in 1945.* | *Lucy decided to end her relationship with Jeff.*
end in sth *phr v* [T] to finish in a particular way: *Their marriage ended in divorce.*
end up *phr v* [I] to finally be in a particular place, situation, or state that you did not intend: *I always end up paying the bill.*

en·dan·ger /ɪnˈdeɪndʒəl-ər/ *v* [T] to put someone or something in a dangerous or harmful situation: *Smoking seriously endangers your health.*

endangered spe·cies /.ˌ.. ˈ../ *n* [C] a type of animal or plant that may soon no longer exist

en·dear /ɪnˈdɪə‖ɪnˈdɪr/ *v*
endear sb **to** sb *phr v* [T] to make someone popular and liked by other people: *His remarks did not endear him to the audience.* —**endearing** *adj*: *an endearing smile*

en·dear·ment /ɪnˈdɪəmənt‖ɪnˈdɪr-/ *n* [C,U] something you say that expresses your love for someone

en·deav·our[1] *BrE*, **endeavor** *AmE* /ɪnˈdevə‖-ər/ *n* [C,U] *formal* an attempt or effort to do something: *We wish you well in your future endeavours.*

endeavour[2] *BrE*, **endeavor** *AmE* — *v* [I] *formal* to try very hard

en·dem·ic /enˈdemɪk, ɪn-/ *adj* happening all the time in a particular place or among a particular group of people: *Violent crime is now endemic in the city.*

end·ing /ˈendɪŋ/ *n* [C] **1** the end of a story, film, etc: *a happy ending* **2** the last part of a word: *Present participles have the ending '-ing'.*

en·dive /ˈendɪv‖ˈendaɪv/ *n* [C,U] *AmE* a vegetable with BITTER-tasting leaves that are eaten RAW IN SALADS

end·less /ˈendləs/ *adj* continuing for a very long time, especially in an annoying way: *I'm tired of his endless complaining.* —**endlessly** *adv*

en·dorse /ɪnˈdɔːs‖-ɔːrs/ *v* [T] to officially say that you support or approve of someone or something: *The president refuses to endorse military action.* —**endorsement** *n* [C,U]

en·dow /ɪnˈdaʊ/ *v* [T] **1** to give a college, hospital etc a large sum of money that will provide it with an income **2** **be endowed with** *formal* to naturally have a good quality, feature, or ability: *a woman endowed with both beauty and intelligence*

en·dow·ment /ɪn'daʊmənt/ *n* [C,U] a large amount of money that is given to a college, hospital etc so that it has an income

end-pro·duct /'. ,../ *n* [C] the thing that is produced at the end of a process

en·dur·ance /ɪn'djʊərəns‖ɪn'dʊr-/ *n* [U] the ability to suffer pain or deal with difficulties for a long time: *The marathon really tested his endurance.*

en·dure /ɪn'djʊəl‖ɪn'dʊr/ *v* [T] to patiently suffer pain or deal with a difficult situation for a long time: *The prisoners had to endure months of hunger.*

en·dur·ing /ɪ'djʊərɪŋ‖-'dʊr-/ *adj* continuing to exist for a long time: *an enduring friendship*

en·e·my /'enəmi/ *n* **1** [C] someone who hates you or wants to harm you: *The judge was assassinated by his political enemies.* | **make enemies** *He'd made many enemies during his career.* **2 the enemy** the country or army that you are fighting against in a war: *territory controlled by the enemy*

en·er·get·ic /ˌenə'dʒetɪk◂‖-ər-/ *adj* very active and able to work hard: *America needs a young, strong, energetic leader.* —**energetically** /-kli/ *adv*

en·er·gy /'enədʒi‖-ər-/ *n* [C,U] **1** the ability to do a lot of work or activities without feeling tired: *She came back from her trip full of energy and enthusiasm.* **2** power from oil, coal etc that produces heat and makes machines work: *atomic energy*

en·force /ɪn'fɔːs‖-ɔːrs/ *v* [T] **1** to make people obey a rule or law: *The police are determined to enforce the speed limit.* **2** to force something to happen: *an enforced silence* —**enforcement** *n* [U] —**enforceable** *adj*

en·gage /ɪn'geɪdʒ/ *v* [T] *formal* **1** to attract someone and keep them interested: *a film that engages both mind and eye* **2** to employ someone: *We'll have to engage a tutor for Eric.*

engage in *phr v* **1 engage in sth/be engaged in sth** to involve yourself in an activity: *men who had often engaged in criminal activities* **2 engage sb in conversation** to begin talking to someone

en·gaged /ɪn'geɪdʒd/ *adj* **1** having agreed to get married: **get engaged** *Viv and Tony got engaged last month.* | **+ to** *Have you met the man she's engaged to?* **2** *BrE* if a telephone line is engaged, it is already being used by someone; **BUSY** *AmE*

en·gage·ment /ɪn'geɪdʒmənt/ *n* [C] **1** an agreement to get married: *They announced their engagement at Christmas.* **2** an arrangement to do something or meet someone: *Professor Blake has an engagement already on Tuesday.*

en·gag·ing /ɪn'geɪdʒɪŋ/ *adj* attractive and interesting: *an engaging personality*

en·gen·der /ɪn'dʒendə‖-ər/ *v* [T] *formal* to be the cause of a situation or feeling: *Racial in-*

equality will always engender conflict and violence.

en·gine /'endʒɪn/ *n* [C] **1** the part of a car, plane etc that makes it move by producing power from oil, steam, or electricity → compare MOTOR[1] **2** a vehicle that pulls a railway train → see colour picture on page 669

engine driv·er /'.. ,../ *n* [C] *BrE* a train driver

en·gi·neer[1] /ˌendʒ‖'nɪə‖-'nɪr/ *n* [C] **1** someone who designs the way roads, bridges, machines etc are built **2** *BrE* someone who repairs machines or electrical equipment **3** someone who controls the engines on a ship **4** *AmE* someone who drives a train; **ENGINE DRIVER** *BrE*

engineer[2] *v* [T] to secretly and effectively arrange something: *He had powerful enemies who engineered his downfall.*

en·gi·neer·ing /ˌendʒ‖'nɪərɪŋ‖-'nɪr-/ *n* [U] the work of designing the way roads, bridges, machines etc are built

En·glish[1] /'ɪŋglɪʃ/ *n* **1** [U] the language that is spoken in Great Britain, the US, Australia etc **2 the English** [plural] the people of England:

English[2] *adj* **1** connected with the English language **2** connected with or coming from England

en·grave /ɪn'greɪv/ *v* [T] to cut words or pictures into the surface of metal, wood, glass etc: *a gold pen engraved with his initials*

en·grav·ing /ɪn'greɪvɪŋ/ *n* [C] a picture printed from an engraved piece of metal

en·grossed /ɪn'grəʊst‖-'groʊst/ *adj* so interested in something that you do not think of anything else: **+in** *He was so engrossed in his work that he forgot about lunch.*

en·gulf /ɪn'gʌlf/ *v* [T] **1** to have a very strong effect on a person, place, or thing: *a war that engulfed the whole of Europe* **2** to completely surround or cover something: **be engulfed in** *The building was engulfed in flames.*

en·hance /ɪn'hɑːns‖ɪn'hæns/ *v* [T] to improve something: *Adding lemon juice will enhance the flavour.* —**enhancement** *n* [C,U]

e·nig·ma /ɪ'nɪgmə/ *n* [C] someone or something that is strange, mysterious, and difficult to understand: *That man will always be an enigma to me.* —**enigmatic** /ˌenɪg'mætɪk◂/ *adj*: *an enigmatic smile*

en·joy /ɪn'dʒɔɪ/ *v* [T] **1** to get pleasure from something: *Did you enjoy the movie?* | **enjoy doing sth** *My wife really enjoys playing golf.* **2 enjoy yourself** to be happy and have fun: *It was a wonderful party, and we all enjoyed ourselves enormously.* **3** to have something good, such as success or a particular right or advantage: *The team enjoyed unexpected success this season.* —**enjoyment** *n* [U] *We hope the bad weather didn't spoil your enjoyment.*

en·joy·a·ble /ɪn'dʒɔɪəbəl/ *adj* giving you pleasure: *We all had an enjoyable afternoon.*

en·large /ɪn'lɑːdʒ‖-ɑːrdʒ/ *v* [T] to make some-

E

GRAMMAR NOTE: 'if' clauses (2)

When you imagine a present situation that is not real, or a future situation that is very unlikely, use **if + simple past**: *If he really loved you, he wouldn't treat you like this.* (=he does not love you). | *If I won a million dollars on the lottery, I would buy a yacht.* Use **would** in the other part of the sentence.

thing bigger: *I'm going to get some of these pictures enlarged.*

enlarge on sth *phr v* [T] to give more details or facts about something you have already mentioned: *Mrs Bye did not enlarge on what she meant by 'unsuitable'.*

en·large·ment /ɪnˈlɑːdʒməntǁ-ɑːr-/ *n* [C] a photograph that has been printed again in a larger size

en·light·en /ɪnˈlaɪtn/ *v* [T] *formal* to give someone information or explain something to them: *Would you kindly enlighten me as to what you are doing here?* —**enlightening** *adj*

en·light·ened /ɪnˈlaɪtənd/ *adj* sensible and with a modern attitude to life: *a country with an enlightened approach to women's education*

en·list /ɪnˈlɪst/ *v* **1** **enlist the help/services etc of sb** to persuade someone to help you: *I enlisted the help of a friend to make the costumes.* **2** [I] to join the army, navy etc: *My grandfather enlisted when he was 18.*

en·liv·en /ɪnˈlaɪvən/ *v* [T] to make something more interesting or exciting: *The teacher used songs and stories to enliven her lesson.*

en masse /ˌɒn ˈmæsǁˌɑːn-/ *adv* together as a group: *City councillors threatened to resign en masse.*

en·mi·ty /ˈenmɪti/ *n* [U] *formal* a strong feeling of hate and anger towards someone: *the causes of enmity between the two nations*

e·nor·mi·ty /ɪˈnɔːmɪtiǁ-ɔːr-/ *n* **the enormity of** how big, serious, or terrible something is: *He could not understand the enormity of his crime.*

e·nor·mous /ɪˈnɔːməsǁ-ɔːr-/ *adj* extremely big: *You should see their house – it's enormous!* | *There's an enormous amount of work to finish.*

e·nor·mous·ly /ɪˈnɔːməsliǁ-ɔːr-/ *adv* extremely or very much: *an enormously popular writer*

e·nough[1] /ɪˈnʌf/ *adv* **1** as much as is necessary: *I've studied the subject enough to know the basic facts.* | **big/good/old etc enough** *This bag isn't big enough to hold all my stuff.* **2** **nice/happy/busy enough** fairly nice, happy etc: *She's nice enough, but I don't think she likes me.* **3** **sth is bad/difficult/hard etc enough...** *spoken* used to say that the existing situation is bad, but something else will make it worse: *It's bad enough that I have to work late – then you make jokes about it!* **4** **strangely/oddly/funnily enough** used to say that something is strange: *Funnily enough, the same thing happened to me yesterday.* ➞ see also **sure enough** (SURE[2])

USAGE NOTE: enough

Enough is used after adjectives or adverbs, but it is usually used before a noun: *They're rich enough to have three cars.* | *I can't walk fast enough to keep up with you.* | *Do we have enough money for the tickets?* In sentences with "there" as the subject, **enough** can also be used after a noun: *There's room enough for everyone.*

enough[2] *quantifier* **1** as much or as many as necessary: *Do we have enough food for everybody?* | *I think we've done enough for one day.* | **enough to do sth** *He doesn't earn enough to pay the rent.* **2** **have had enough (of)** *spoken* to want something to stop because it annoys you:

enough

Joel wasn't tall enough to play

There wasn't enough cake for everyone

I'd had enough of the neighbours' noise, so I called the police. **3** **that's enough** *spoken* used to tell a child to stop behaving badly

en·quire /ɪnˈkwaɪəǁ-ˈkwaɪr/ *BrE* another spelling of INQUIRE

en·qui·ry /ɪnˈkwaɪəriǁˈɪŋkwaɪri, ˈɪŋkwǝri/ *BrE* another spelling of INQUIRY

en·rage /ɪnˈreɪdʒ/ *v* [T] to make someone very angry: *a newspaper report that has enraged local residents* —**enraged** *adj*

en·rich /ɪnˈrɪtʃ/ *v* [T] to improve the quality of something: *Education can enrich your life.* —**enrichment** *n* [U]

en·rol *BrE*, **enroll** *AmE* /ɪnˈrəʊlǁ-ˈrəʊl/ *v* [I,T] **-lled, -lling** to become or make someone officially a member of a course, school etc: *30 students have enrolled on the cookery course.* —**enrolment** *n* [C,U]

en route /ˌɒn ˈruːtǁˌɑːn-/ *adv* on the way: **+ to** *We passed through St Louis en route to Dallas.*

en·sconce /ɪnˈskɒnsǁ-skɑːns/ *v* **be ensconced** to be in a safe or comfortable place without any intention of moving: *Martha was firmly ensconced in a large chair by the fire.*

en·sem·ble /ɒnˈsɒmbəlǁɑːnˈsɑːm-/ *n* [C] a small group of musicians or actors who perform together regularly

en·shrine /ɪnˈʃraɪn/ *v* [T] *formal* to preserve a law, TRADITION, or right, especially writing it down: *civil rights enshrined in the Constitution*

en·sign /ˈensaɪn, -sənǁˈensən/ *n* [C] a flag on a ship that shows what country the ship belongs to

en·slave /ɪnˈsleɪv/ *v* [T] *formal* **1** to trap someone in a situation from which they cannot escape **2** to make someone a SLAVE

en·sue /ɪnˈsjuːǁɪnˈsuː/ *v* [I] *formal* to happen after something, often as a result of it: *A long silence ensued.* —**ensuing** *adj*: *The ensuing battle was fierce.*

en·sure /ɪnˈʃʊəl-ˈʃʊr/ v [T] *especially BrE* to make certain that something happens or is done: **+ (that)** *You must ensure that this door remains locked.*

en·tail /ɪnˈteɪl/ v [T] to involve something or make it necessary: *Does your new job entail much travelling?*

en·tan·gle /ɪnˈtæŋɡəl/ v **be entangled 1** to be involved with someone or something in a way that causes problems: **+ with** *Jay became romantically entangled with a work colleague.* **2** to be caught and trapped in a net or mass of ropes, hair etc: *a fish entangled in the net* — **entanglement** n [C,U]

en·ter /ˈentəl-ər/ v **1** [I,T] to go or come into a place: *Everyone stopped talking when he entered.* | *The police tried to stop the marchers from entering the square.* **2** [T] to start working in a particular profession or organization: *She's hoping to enter the medical profession.* **3** [T] to start to take part in an activity: *America entered the war in 1917.* **4** [I,T] to arrange to take part in a competition, race, or examination, or to arrange for someone to do this: *She entered the competition and won.* **5** [T] to put information into a computer, or to write information on a special paper or in a book: *Enter your name on the form.* **6** [T] to begin a period of time: *The talks are now entering their third week.*

enter into sth *phr v* [T] **1** to start something: *Both sides must enter into negotiations.* **2** to affect or influence something that is being considered: *Money didn't enter into my decision to leave.* **3 enter into an agreement/contract etc** *formal* to officially make an agreement

en·ter·prise /ˈentəpraɪzl-ər-/ n **1** [C] a company or business: *The farm is a family enterprise.* **2** [C] a large and complicated piece of work that you plan and do with other people: *The film festival is a huge enterprise.* **3** [U] the ability and willingness to start new businesses or activities in spite of difficulties and risks: *the spirit of enterprise and adventure that built America's new industries* → see also FREE ENTERPRISE

en·ter·pris·ing /ˈentəpraɪzɪŋl-tər-/ adj able and willing to do things that are new or difficult: *One enterprising young man started his own radio station.*

en·ter·tain /ˌentəˈteɪnl-tər-/ v **1** [T] to do something that interests and amuses people: *He spent the next hour entertaining us with jokes.* **2** [I,T] to treat someone as a guest by providing food and drink for them: *Mike is entertaining clients at that new restaurant.* **3** [T] *formal* to consider or think about an idea, doubt, suggestion etc: *I would never entertain such an idea.*

en·ter·tain·er /ˌentəˈteɪnəl-tərˈteɪnər/ n [C] someone who tells jokes, sings etc to amuse people: *a circus entertainer*

en·ter·tain·ing /ˌentəˈteɪnɪŋ‹ l-tər-/ adj amusing and interesting: *an entertaining book*

en·ter·tain·ment /ˌentəˈteɪnməntl-tər-/ n **1** [U] things such as television, films etc that amuse or interest people: *the entertainment industry* **2** [C] a performance or show: *a musical entertainment*

en·thral *BrE*, **enthrall** *AmE* /ɪnˈθrɔːll-ˈθrɒːl/ v [T] **-lled, -lling** to keep someone's attention and

interest completely: *The kids were absolutely enthralled by the stories.* — **enthralling** adj

en·thuse /ɪnˈθjuːzll ɪnˈθuːz/ v [I] to talk about something with excitement and admiration: **+ about/over** *She spent the whole evening enthusing about her new job.*

en·thu·si·as·m /ɪnˈθjuːziæzəmllɪnˈθuː-/ n [U] a strong feeling of interest, excitement, or admiration about something: **+for** *The boys all share an enthusiasm for sports.* — **enthusiast** n [C]

en·thu·si·as·tic /ɪnˌθjuːziˈæstɪk‹ ll-ˌθuː-/ adj showing a lot of interest and excitement about something: *An enthusiastic crowd cheered the winners.* — **enthusiastically** /-kli/ adv

en·tice /ɪnˈtaɪs/ v [T] to persuade someone to do something by offering them something pleasant: *Goods are attractively displayed to entice the customer.* — **enticing** adj: *an enticing menu*

en·tire /ɪnˈtaɪəl-ˈtaɪr/ adj whole or complete: *I've spent the entire day cooking.*

en·tire·ly /ɪnˈtaɪəlill-ˈtaɪr-/ adv completely: *She had entirely forgotten about Alexander.*

en·tir·e·ty /ɪnˈtaɪərˌtill-ˈtaɪr-/ n **in its/their entirety** *formal* as a whole and including every part: *The judge must look at the case in its entirety.*

en·ti·tle /ɪnˈtaɪtl/ v [T] **1** to give someone the right to have or do something: **be entitled to sth** *Citizens of EU countries are entitled to free medical treatment.* **2** to give a title to a book, song etc: *a short poem entitled "Pride of Youth"* — **entitlement** n [C,U]

en·ti·ty /ˈentˌti/ n [C] *formal* something that exists as a single and complete unit: *East and West Germany became once more a single political entity.*

en·tou·rage /ˈɒntʊrɑːʒll ˈɑːn-/ n [C] a group of people who travel with an important person: *The president's entourage followed in six limousines.*

en·trance /ˈentrəns/ n **1** [C] a door or gate that you go through to enter a place: *Meet me at the front entrance to the building.* **2** [U] the right to enter a place, or become a member of a profession, university etc: *There will be an entrance fee of $30.* **3 make an/your entrance** to come into a place, especially in a way that makes people notice you: *Sheila waited for the right moment to make her dramatic entrance.* → compare ENTRY

USAGE NOTE: entrance and entry

Compare **entrance** and **entry**. The usual word for when someone enters a place or organization is **entry**: *Entry to the building is by a side door.* | *Ireland's entry into the EC.* **Entrance** is used to talk about when someone enters a place during a public ceremony or performance: *The crowd was wild by the time Noel finally made his entrance*, or to talk about the right to enter somewhere: *You'll have to pay an entrance fee.* | *a college entrance examination*

---

en·tranced /ɪnˈtrɑːnstll-ˈtrænst/ adj feeling great pleasure because of something very beautiful which has taken all your attention: *Li Yuan sat there, entranced by the beauty of the music.* — **entrance** v [T]

en·trant /ˈentrənt/ n [C] *formal* someone who enters a competition, university, or profession

en·treat /ɪnˈtriːt/ v [T] *formal* to ask someone to do something for you, showing that you will be very upset if they do not do it: *She entreated me to forgive her.* —**entreaty** n [C,U]

en·trenched /ɪnˈtrentʃt/ adj strongly established and not likely to change: *entrenched attitudes*

en·tre·pre·neur /ˌɒntrəprəˈnɜːǁˌɑːntrəprəˈnɜːr/ n [C] someone who starts a company and arranges business deals —**entrepreneurial** adj

en·trust /ɪnˈtrʌst/ v [T] to make someone responsible for something: **entrust sb with sth** *I was entrusted with the task of looking after the money.*

en·try /ˈentri/ n **1** [U] when you go into a place: *The thieves gained entry through an open window.* **2** [C] a piece of work or a set of answers which someone sends to be judged in a competition: *The closing date for entries is January 6.* **3** [U] when someone becomes a member of a group or profession: + **into** *Britain's entry into the European Community* **4** [U] the right to enter a place: *When reporters arrived at the gate, they were refused entry.* **5** [C] a short piece of writing in a book, a list etc: *a dictionary entry* **6** [U] when information is written onto a computer: *data entry*

en·twine /ɪnˈtwaɪn/ v [T] **1** to twist something around something else: *flowers entwined in her hair* **2** **be entwined** to be closely connected: *The two sisters' lives were deeply entwined.*

e·nu·me·rate /ɪˈnjuːməreɪtǁɪˈnuː-/ v [T] *formal* to name all the things on a list one after another

en·vel·op /ɪnˈveləp/ v [T] to cover or surround something completely: *The building was soon enveloped in flames.*

en·ve·lope /ˈenvələup ǁ-loup/ n [C] a flat folded paper cover that you put a letter in before you post it

en·vi·a·ble /ˈenviəbəl/ adj an enviable situation or quality is good and other people wish they could have it: *He's in the enviable position of only having to work six months a year.* —**enviably** adv

envelope

en·vi·ous /ˈenviəs/ adj wishing that you had something that someone else has: + **of** *Tom was deeply envious of his brother's success.* —**enviously** adv

en·vi·ron·ment /ɪnˈvaɪərənməntǁ-ˈvaɪr-/ n **1** **the environment** the land, water, and air that people, animals, and plants live in: *laws to protect the environment* → see colour picture on page 278 **2** [C,U] the conditions in which you live and work, that affect your life: *a pleasant working environment*

USAGE NOTE: environment

Compare **environment** and **surroundings**. Your **environment** is all the people, things, and ideas that you live among and which influence your life: *She grew up in a very liberal environment.* | *a depressing environment.* Your **surroundings** are the physical things around you, for example buildings, hills, and trees: *a small friendly hotel in pleasant surroundings*

en·vi·ron·ment·al /ɪnˌvaɪərənˈmentlǁ-ˌvaɪr-/ adj relating to the air, land, or water on Earth: *environmental damage caused by pollution* —**environmentally** adv

en·vi·ron·men·tal·ist /ɪnˌvaɪərənˈmentəlɪ̈stǁ-ˌvaɪr-/ n [C] someone who tries to protect the environment

environmentally friend·ly /ˌ.ˌ... ˈ../ adj products that are environmentally friendly do not contain things that will harm the environment

en·vis·age /ɪnˈvɪzɪdʒ/ also **en·vi·sion** /ɪnˈvɪʒən/ v [T] to think that something is likely to happen in the future: *I don't envisage any major problems.*

en·voy /ˈenvɔɪ/ n [C] someone who is sent by their government to a foreign country to deal with situations that affect their own country

en·vy[1] /ˈenvi/ v [T] to wish you had something that someone else has, or that you could do something they do: *I envy Colin – he travels all over the world in his job!* | **envy sb (for) sth** *The other boys envied and admired him for his success with girls.*

envy[2] n **1** [U] the feeling of wanting something that someone else has: *He was looking with envy at Al's new car.* **2** **be the envy of** to be something very good that other people admire and want: *Our facilities are the envy of most schools.*

en·zyme /ˈenzaɪm/ n [C] a chemical substance produced by living cells in plants and animals, that causes changes in other chemical substances

e·phem·e·ral /ɪˈfemərəl/ adj *formal* existing only for a short time: *the ephemeral nature of human existence*

ep·ic[1] /ˈepɪk/ adj **1** very big or impressive: *an epic voyage around the world* **2** an epic story or poem is long and describes exciting events and brave actions: *an epic novel about the French Revolution*

epic[2] n [C] a long book, poem, or film containing exciting adventures: *Homer's epic, 'The Odyssey'*

ep·i·dem·ic /ˌepɪˈdemɪk/ n **1** [C] when a disease spreads quickly among a lot of people: *a flu epidemic* **2** [singular] when something bad suddenly starts to happen a lot: *a car crime epidemic*

ep·i·lep·sy /ˈepɪ̈lepsi/ n [U] a disease of the brain that can make someone suddenly unconscious and unable to control their movements —**epileptic** /ˌepɪ̈ˈleptɪk/ adj: *an epileptic fit*

ep·i·lep·tic /ˌepɪ̈ˈleptɪk/ n [C] someone who has epilepsy

ep·i·logue /ˈepɪ̈lɒgǁ-lɔːg, -lɑːg/ n [C] a speech or piece of writing added to the end of a book, film, or play

ep·i·sode /ˈepɪ̈səudǁ-soud/ n [C] **1** one of the parts of a television or radio story that are broadcast separately: *an episode of "Star Trek"* **2** an important event or period in history, in a story or in someone's life: *one of the most exciting episodes in Nureyev's career*

ep·i·taph /ˈepɪ̈tɑːfǁ-tæf/ n [C] something written about a dead person, on the stone over their grave

e·pit·o·me /ɪˈpɪtəmi/ n **be the epitome of** to be a very typical example of something: *Lord Soames was the epitome of a true gentleman.*

E

e·pit·o·mize (also **-ise** *BrE*) /ɪˈpɪtəmaɪz/ *v* [T] to be the most typical example of something: *The recent crisis seems to epitomize the problems in British industry.*

e·poch /ˈiːpɒk‖ˈepək/ *n* [C] A period in history

e·qual¹ /ˈiːkwəl/ *adj* **1** the same in size, value, amount etc: *Divide the cake mixture into two equal parts.* | **be equal to** *One inch is equal to 2.54 centimetres.* **2** having the same rights, chances etc as everyone else: *Democracy is based on the idea that all people are equal.* | **equal rights/opportunities** (=the same rights to employment, pay etc for everyone): *equal rights for women* | **on an equal footing/on equal terms** (=with neither having an advantage over the other): *Small businesses can't compete on equal terms with large organizations.*

equal² *v* [T] **-lled, -lling** *BrE* **-led, -ling** *AmE* **1** to be the same as something else in size, number, amount etc: *Four plus four equals eight.* **2** to be as good as something or someone else: *Johnson has equalled the Olympic record.*

equal³ *n* [C] **1** someone who has the same ability, rights, or position in society as someone else: *Men and women should be treated as equals.* **2** **without equal** better than any other: *a medical service without equal in the whole of Europe*

e·qual·i·ty /ɪˈkwɒlɪti‖ˈkwɑː-/ *n* [U] when people have the same rights and advantages: *racial equality* → opposite INEQUALITY

e·qual·ize (also **-ise** *BrE*) /ˈiːkwəlaɪz/ *v* **1** [T] to make two or more things equal in size, value etc: *equalizing pay rates in the steel industry* **2** [I] *BrE* to get a point or goal in a game so that you have the same number of points or goals as your opponents: *Spain equalized in the 75th minute.*

e·qual·ly /ˈiːkwəli/ *adv* **1** just as much: *Both teams are equally capable of winning.* **2** in equal parts or amounts: *We'll divide the work equally.* **3** *spoken* used before saying something that is as important as what you have just said: *A teacher who tries to be popular will lose respect. Equally, it is unwise to be too strict.* **4** in a way that is fair: *We have to try to treat everyone equally.*

eq·ua·nim·i·ty /ˌiːkwəˈnɪmɪti, ˌekwə-/ *n* [U] *formal* calmness in a difficult situation: *He received this terrible news with equanimity.*

e·quate /ɪˈkweɪt/ *v* [T] *formal* to consider that one thing is the same as something else: *Don't equate criticism with blame.*

e·qua·tion /ɪˈkweɪʒən/ *n* [C] a statement in mathematics showing that two quantities are equal, for example 2y + 4 = 10

e·qua·tor /ɪˈkweɪtə‖-ər/ *n* **the equator** the imaginary line around the Earth that divides it equally into its northern and southern halves — **equatorial** /ˌekwəˈtɔːriəl/ *adj*

e·ques·tri·an /ɪˈkwestriən/ *adj* connected with horse riding

e·qui·lib·ri·um /ˌiːkwɪˈlɪbriəm/ *n* [U] **1** [singular, U] a balance between opposing forces,

influences etc: *The supply and the demand for money must be kept in equilibrium.* **2** [U] a calm state of mind

e·quip /ɪˈkwɪp/ *v* [T] **-pped, -pping** **1** to provide someone or something with the things that are needed for a particular purpose: *The boys had equipped themselves with ropes and torches before entering the cave.* | **be equipped with sth** *All their soldiers were equipped with assault rifles.* **2** to prepare someone for something by giving them the necessary skills: **equip sb to do sth** *His training had not equipped him to deal with this kind of emergency.* — **equipped** *adj*: *a well-equipped hospital*

e·quip·ment /ɪˈkwɪpmənt/ *n* [U] the things that are used for a particular activity: *camping equipment* | **piece of equipment** *an expensive piece of electronic equipment*

eq·ui·ta·ble /ˈekwɪtəbəl/ *adj* *formal* fair and equal for everyone: *an equitable distribution of resources* — **equitably** *adv*

eq·ui·ty /ˈekwɪti/ *n* [U] *formal* when everyone is fairly treated: *the principles of justice and equity*

e·quiv·a·lent¹ /ɪˈkwɪvələnt/ *adj* equal in amount, value, or rank to something or someone else: **+ to** *The workers received a bonus equivalent to two months' pay.*

equivalent² *n* [C] something that has the same value, size, meaning etc as something else: *Some French words have no equivalents in English.*

er /ɜː, ə‖ɜːr, ər/ *interjection* a sound you make when you are not sure what to say next: *Well, er, thanks for all your help.*

ER /ˌiː ˈɑː‖-ˈɑːr/ *n* EMERGENCY ROOM

e·ra /ˈɪərə‖ˈɪrə/ *n* [C] a period of time in history that is different from other periods: *the Reagan era* | **+ of** *a new era of peace and international cooperation*

e·rad·i·cate /ɪˈrædɪkeɪt/ *v* [T] to get rid of something such as an illness or social problem completely: *attempts to eradicate prejudice* — **eradication** /ɪˌrædɪˈkeɪʃən/ *n* [U]

e·rase /ɪˈreɪz‖ɪˈreɪs/ *v* [T] to completely remove written or recorded information: *All his records had been erased.*

e·ras·er /ɪˈreɪzə‖-sər/ *n* [C] *especially AmE* a piece of rubber used for removing pencil marks from paper; RUBBER *BrE*

e·rect¹ /ɪˈrekt/ *adj* in a straight, upright position: *The dog stopped and listened with its ears erect.*

erect² *v* [T] **1** *formal* to build something: *This ancient church was erected in 1121.* **2** to put something in an upright position: *Security barriers were erected to hold the crowd back.*

e·rec·tion /ɪˈrekʃən/ *n* **1** [C,U] when a man's PENIS becomes stiff and increases in size because of sexual excitement **2** [U] when something is built or put in an upright position: **+ of** *the erection of a war memorial*

e·rode /ɪˈrəʊd‖ɪˈroʊd/ *v* **1** [I,T] if land, rocks etc are eroded or if they erode, they are gradu-

E

GRAMMAR NOTE: 'if' clauses (3)
When you imagine a past situation that did not really happen, use **if + past perfect**: *If they had offered me the job, I would have taken it.* (=but they did not offer me it). Use **would have + past participle** in the other part of the sentence.

ally destroyed, by the wind, rain, or sea: *The coastline is being eroded by the sea.* **2** [T] to gradually destroy someone's power, confidence, rights etc: *Her confidence has been eroded by recent criticism.* — **erosion** /ɪˈrəʊʒən‖ɪˈrəʊ-/ *n* [U]

e·rot·ic /ɪˈrɒtɪk‖ɪˈrɑː-/ *adj* involving sexual love or causing feelings of sexual desire: *an erotic dream* — **erotically** /-kli/ *adv*

err /ɜː‖ɜːr/ *v* **1** [I] *formal* to make a mistake **2** **err on the side of caution** to be too careful rather than risk making mistakes

er·rand /ˈerənd/ *n* [C] a short trip that you make to buy something or do something for someone: **run an errand** *Could you run an errand for Grandma?*

er·rant /ˈerənt/ *adj humorous* behaving badly: *an errant husband*

er·rat·ic /ɪˈrætɪk/ *adj* changing often without any reason, or moving in an irregular way: *the England team's rather erratic performance in the World Cup* — **erratically** /-kli/ *adv*

er·ro·ne·ous /ɪˈrəʊniəs‖ɪˈroʊ-/ *adj formal* incorrect: *erroneous statements* — **erroneously** *adv*

er·ror /ˈerə‖ˈerər/ *n* [C,U] a mistake, especially one that causes problems: *a computer error* | **make an error** *The police admitted that several errors had been made.* | *a serious error of judgement* | **in error** (=because of a mistake): *The letter was opened in error.* | **human error** (=a mistake caused by a person not a machine): *an accident caused by human error*

USAGE NOTE: error and mistake

A **mistake** is something that you do by accident, or is the result of a bad judgement: *I'm sorry; I took your pen by mistake.* | *We made a mistake in buying this car.* An **error** is a mistake you make in something you are doing, that can cause problems: *You've made a serious error in calculating your taxes.*

---

e·rupt /ɪˈrʌpt/ *v* [I] **1** to happen suddenly or violently: *Fighting erupted after the demonstrations.* **2** if a VOLCANO erupts, it sends out smoke and fire into the sky **3** to suddenly become angry or start to shout: *The crowd erupted when Henning scored the winning goal.* — **eruption** /ɪˈrʌpʃən/ *n* [C,U] *a volcanic eruption*

es·ca·late /ˈeskəleɪt/ *v* **1** [I,T] if violence or a war escalates or is escalated, it quickly becomes worse: *Fighting has escalated in several areas.* **2** [I] if prices escalate, they increase: *escalating interest rates* — **escalation** /ˌeskəˈleɪʃən/ *n* [C,U]

es·ca·la·tor /ˈeskəleɪtə ‖-ər/ *n* [C] moving stairs that carry people from one level of a building to another

es·ca·pade /ˈeskəpeɪd/ *n* [C] an exciting adventure that may be dangerous

es·cape¹ /ɪˈskeɪp/ *v* **1** [I] to succeed in getting away from a place, especially when someone is trying to catch you or stop you from leaving: **+ from/through etc** *Two men escaped from the prison.* **2** [I,T] to avoid a

dangerous or unpleasant situation: **+ from** *Watching television was his way of escaping from reality.* | **escape death/injury/punishment etc** *The driver and his two passengers only narrowly escaped death.* **3** [T] if something escapes you, you cannot remember it: *Her name escapes me at the moment.* **4** [T] if something escapes your notice or attention, you do not notice it: *Nothing escapes Bill's attention.* **5** [I] if gas, liquid etc escapes from somewhere, it gets out when you do not want it to — **escaped** *adj*: *escaped prisoners*

es·cape² *n* **1** [C,U] when someone escapes from a place or from an unpleasant or dangerous situation: *There's no chance of escape.* | *The family had a narrow escape* (=they were almost killed). **2** [singular, U] a way to forget about a worrying or boring situation: *Reading poetry is one form of escape.* → see also FIRE ESCAPE

es·cap·is·m /ɪˈskeɪpɪzəm/ *n* [U] entertainment or activity that helps you to forget about your work or worries and think of something more enjoyable: *Those old Hollywood movies are pure escapism.* — **escapist** *adj*

es·cort¹ /ɪˈskɔːt‖-ɔːrt/ *v* [T] to go somewhere with someone, for example to protect or guard them: *Armed guards escorted the prisoners into the courthouse.* | *David offered to escort us to the theatre.*

es·cort² /ˈeskɔːt‖-ɔːrt/ *n* **1** [C,U] a person or people who go somewhere with someone in order to protect or guard them: *a police escort* | **under escort** (=with an escort): *The prisoners will be transported under military escort.* **2** [C] someone who goes with another person to a social event, usually a man who goes with a woman

Es·ki·mo /ˈeskɪməʊ‖-moʊ/ *n* [C] a word meaning a member of one of the groups of people who live in the far north of Canada, Alaska etc, that some people consider offensive — **Eskimo** *adj* → compare INUIT

ESL /ˌiː es ˈel/ *n* [U] English as a Second Language; the teaching of English to students whose first language is not English, but are living in an English-speaking country

es·o·ter·ic /ˌesəˈterɪk, ˌiːsə-/ *adj* known or understood only by a few people who have special knowledge: *esoteric teachings*

es·pe·cial·ly /ɪˈspeʃəli/ *adv* **1** much more than usual, or much more than other people or things: *These chairs are especially suitable for people with back problems.* | *The kids really enjoyed the holiday, especially the trip to Disneyland.* **2** for a particular person, reason etc: **+ for** *I made this card especially for you.* → compare SPECIALLY

es·pi·o·nage /ˈespiənɑːʒ/ *n* [U] the activity of finding out the secrets of a country or company that is fighting or competing against you; spying (SPY)

es·pouse /ɪˈspaʊz/ *v* [T] *formal* to support an idea or belief

es·pres·so /eˈspresəʊ, ɪˈspre-‖-soʊ/ *n* [C,U] very strong black coffee, usually served in a small cup

es·say /ˈeseɪ/ *n* [C] a short piece of writing about a particular subject, especially by a student

es·sence /'esəns/ n **1** [singular, U] the most basic and important idea or quality: + of *There is no leadership – that's the essence of the problem.* | in essence (=basically): *The choice is, in essence, quite simple.* **2** [U] a liquid used in cooking that has a strong smell or taste and is obtained from a plant, flower etc: *vanilla essence*

es·sen·tial /ɪ'senʃəl/ adj **1** important and necessary: + for/to *A balanced diet is essential for good health.* | it is essential to do sth *It is essential to check the oil level regularly.* | it is essential that *It is essential that we don't give up.* **2** the most basic and important: *He failed to understand the essential difference between the two theories.*

es·sen·tial·ly /ɪ'senʃəli/ adv used when you are stating the most basic facts about something: *Your analysis is essentially correct.*

es·sen·tials /ɪ'senʃəlz/ n [plural] things that are important and necessary: *We only have enough money for essentials like food and clothing.*

es·tab·lish /ɪ'stæblɪʃ/ v [T] **1** to start a company, organization etc that will exist for a long time: *The school was established in 1922.* **2** to decide something: *We need to establish our main priorities.* **3** to achieve or give someone a respected position in society or in an organization: *She worked hard to establish her position within the party.* | establish sb/sth as sth *Guterson's novel established him as one of America's most exciting writers.* **4** establish relations/contacts/links etc to start having a relationship or communicating with someone: *In recent months they have established contacts with companies abroad.* **5** to find out facts or prove that something is true: *We have been unable to establish the cause of the accident.* | + that *Doctors established that death was due to poisoning.* — established adj

es·tab·lish·ment /ɪ'stæblɪʃmənt/ n **1** [C] *formal* an organization such as a company, shop, or school: *an educational establishment* (=a school or college) **2** [U] when someone starts a company, organization, system etc: + of *the establishment of NATO in 1949* **3** the Establishment the organizations and groups in a society that have had a lot of power and influence for a long time: *a political scandal that shocked the Establishment*

es·tate /ɪ'steɪt/ n [C] **1** a large area of land in the countryside, usually with one large house on it **2** *BrE* an area where a lot of houses of the same kind have been built together: *a housing estate* **3** all of someone's property and money that is left after they die: *She left her entire estate to me.* **4** an estate car

estate a·gent /.'. ,../ n [C] *BrE* someone whose job is to buy and sell houses and land for people; REAL ESTATE AGENT or REALTOR *AmE*

estate car /.'. ./ n [C] *BrE* a car with a door at the back, and a lot of space for boxes, cases etc; STATION WAGON *AmE*

es·teem[1] /ɪ'stiːm/ n [U] *formal* respect and admiration for someone: hold sb in high esteem (=respect someone very much): *She was held in high esteem by everyone she knew.* ➡ see also SELF-ESTEEM

esteem[2] v [T] *formal* to respect and admire someone: highly esteemed (=greatly respected): *a highly esteemed artist*

es·thet·ic /iːs'θetɪk||es-/ an American spelling of AESTHETIC

es·ti·mate[1] /'estɪmeɪt/ v [T] to decide what you think the value, size etc of something is, partly by guessing and partly by calculating: + that *We estimate that 75% of our customers are teenagers.* | estimate sth at *The cost of repairs has been estimated at $1500.* — estimated adj: *An estimated 10,000 people took part in the demonstration.*

es·ti·mate[2] /'estɪmɪt/ n [C] **1** what you think the value, size etc of something is, after calculating it quickly: *According to some estimates, two thirds of the city was destroyed.* | a rough estimate (=not exact): *At a rough estimate, I'd say it's 300 years old.* **2** a statement of how much it will probably cost to build or repair something: *I got three estimates so I could pick the cheapest.*

es·ti·ma·tion /,estɪ'meɪʃən/ n [U] your judgement or opinion about someone or something: *Philip has really gone down in my estimation* (=I respect him less).

es·tranged /ɪ'streɪndʒd/ adj *formal* **1** no longer living with your husband or wife: *Jim is Sarah's estranged husband.* **2** no longer communicating with your family or friends because of an argument — estrangement n [C,U]

es·tro·gen /'iːstrədʒən||'es-/ the American spelling of OESTROGEN

es·tu·a·ry /'estʃuəri, -tʃəri/ n [C] the wide part of a river where it joins the sea

etc /et 'setərə/ adv the written abbreviation of 'et cetera'; used after a list to show that there are other similar things or people that could be added: *cars, ships, planes etc*

etch /etʃ/ v [I,T] to cut lines on a metal, glass, or stone surface in order to make a picture

e·ter·nal /ɪ'tɜːnəl||-ɜːr-/ adj continuing for ever: *eternal love* — eternally adv

e·ter·ni·ty /ɪ'tɜːnɪti||-ɜːr-/ n **1** [U] time without end, especially the time after death that some people believe continues for ever **2** an eternity *informal* a period of time that seems very long because you are bored, anxious etc: *We waited for what seemed like an eternity.*

e·the·re·al /ɪ'θɪəriəl||ɪ'θɪr-/ adj very delicate and light, in a way that does not seem real: *ethereal beauty* — ethereally adv

eth·ic /'eθɪk/ n [singular] an idea or belief that influences people's behaviour and attitudes: *the Christian ethic*

eth·i·cal /'eθɪkəl/ adj **1** connected with principles of what is right and wrong: *Research on animals raises difficult ethical questions.* **2** morally good and correct: *It would not be ethical for doctors to talk publicly about their patients.* — ethically /-kli/ adv

eth·ics /'eθɪks/ n [plural] rules or principles of behaviour used to decide what is right and wrong: *the ethics of scientific research*

eth·nic /'eθnɪk/ adj relating to a particular race of people: *an ethnic minority*

e·thos /'iːθɒs||'iːθɑːs/ n [singular] the typical ideas and moral attitudes that a person or group of people have: *The whole ethos of our society has changed.*

et·i·quette /'etɪket||-kət/ n [U] the rules of polite behaviour

E

et·y·mol·o·gy /ˌetɪˈmɒlədʒiⅡ-ˈmɑː-/ n [U] the study of the origins and changing meanings of words —**etymological** /ˌetɪməˈlɒdʒɪkəⅡ-ˈlɑː-/ adj —**etymologically** /-kli/ adv

EU /ˌiː ˈjuː/ n [singular] European Union; a European political and economic organization that encourages trade and friendship between the countries that are members

eu·phe·mis·m /ˈjuːfɪˌmɪzəm/ n [C,U] a polite and more pleasant word or phrase used to avoid saying something that may be shocking or embarrassing —**euphemistic** /ˌjuːfəˈmɪstɪk⊲/ adj —**euphemistically** /-kli/ adv

eu·pho·ri·a /juːˈfɔːriəⅡjuː-/ n [U] extreme happiness and excitement —**euphoric** /-ˈfɒrɪkⅡ-ˈfɔː-, -ˈfɑː-/ adj

Eu·ro also **euro** /ˈjʊərəʊⅡˈjʊroʊ/ n [C singular] a unit of money intended to be used by all the countries in the European Union: *The Euro is expected to replace the British pound within a few years.*

Eu·ro- /ˈjʊərəʊⅡˈjʊroʊ/ prefix connected with Europe or the EU: *Euro-MPs.* (=members of the European Parliament)

Eu·ro·pe·an /ˌjʊərəˈpiːən⊲ Ⅱˌjʊrə-/ adj from or connected with Europe: *the European Parliament* —**European** n [C]

European U·nion /ˌ.... ˈ../ n [singular] the EU

eu·tha·na·si·a /ˌjuːθəˈneɪziəⅡ-ˈneɪʒə/ n [U] the practice of killing people who are old or very ill in order to stop them suffering

e·vac·u·ate /ɪˈvækjueɪt/ v [T] to move people from a dangerous place to a safer place: *Children were evacuated from London to country areas.* —**evacuation** /ɪˌvækjuˈeɪʃən/ n [C,U]

e·vac·u·ee /ɪˌvækjuˈiː/ n [C] someone who has been evacuated from somewhere

e·vade /ɪˈveɪd/ v [T] **1** to avoid doing something you should do, or avoid talking about something: *Briggs evaded the interviewer's question.* **2** to escape from someone who is trying to catch you: *He evaded capture by hiding in a cave.*

e·val·u·ate /ɪˈvæljueɪt/ v [T] formal to carefully consider something or someone in order to decide how good or bad they are: *Teachers meet regularly to evaluate the progress of each student.* —**evaluation** /ɪˌvæljuˈeɪʃən/ n [C, U]

e·van·gel·i·cal /ˌiːvænˈdʒelɪkəl⊲/ adj an evangelical Christian believes that Christian faith and studying the Bible are more important than religious ceremonies

e·vap·o·rate /ɪˈvæpəreɪt/ v **1** [I,T] if a liquid evaporates or if something evaporates it, it changes into steam: *Boil the sauce until most of the liquid has evaporated.* **2** [I] to slowly disappear: *Support for the idea has evaporated.* —**evaporation** /ɪˌvæpəˈreɪʃən/ n [U]

e·va·sion /ɪˈveɪʒən/ n [C,U] when you avoid doing something that you should do: *tax evasion*

e·va·sive /ɪˈveɪsɪv/ adj **1** trying to avoid answering questions directly: *an evasive answer* **2** evasive action something that you do to avoid being injured or harmed —**evasively** adv —**evasiveness** n [U]

eve /iːv/ n **1** Christmas Eve/New Year's Eve the night or day before Christmas or New Year **2** the eve of the time just before an important event: *There were widespread demonstrations on the eve of the election.*

e·ven[1] /ˈiːvən/ adv **1** used in order to emphasize that something is surprising or unexpected: *Even the youngest children enjoyed the concert.* | *He hadn't even remembered it was my birthday!* **2** even bigger/better/more etc used to emphasize that something is bigger, better etc: *She knows even less about it then I do.* | *If you could finish it today, that would be even better.* **3** even if used to emphasize that if something happens it will not change what you have just said: *I'll never speak to her again, even if she apologizes.* **4** even though although: *She wouldn't go onto the ski slope, even though Tom offered to help her.* **5** even so in spite of this: *They made lots of money that year, but even so the business failed.*

even[2] adj **1** flat, level, or smooth: *You need an even surface to work on.* **2** an even rate, temperature etc does not change much: *an even body temperature* **3** an even number can be divided by two. For example 2, 4, 6, and 8 are even numbers. → opposite ODD **4** an even competition is one in which both players or teams have an equal chance of winning **5** be even informal to no longer owe someone money: *If you give me $5 we'll be even.* **6** get even informal to harm someone as much as they have harmed you: + with *I'll get even with you one day!* → see also break even (BREAK[1])

even[3] v

even out phr v [I,T **even** sth ↔ **out**] if differences even out or if you even them out they become less: *The differences in class sizes will even out over a period of time.*

eve·ning /ˈiːvnɪŋ/ n **1** [C,U] the end of the day and the early part of the night: *I have a class on Thursday evenings.* | *We spent a very pleasant evening with Ray and his girlfriend.* **2** (good) evening spoken used to greet someone when you meet them in the evening: *Evening, Rick.*

e·ven·ly /ˈiːvənli/ adv **1** with equal amounts or numbers of something spread over all parts of an area or divided among a group of people: *We divided the money evenly.* | *Spread the glue evenly over the surface.* **2** if two teams or opponents are evenly matched, they have an equal chance of winning

e·vent /ɪˈvent/ n [C] **1** something that happens, especially something important, interesting, or unusual: *the most important events of the 1990s* | course of events (=the way things happen): *Nothing you could have done would have changed the course of events.* **2** a performance, competition, party etc that has been arranged for a particular date and time: *a major sporting event* **3** in any event/at all events whatever happens: *In any event, it seems likely that prices will continue to rise.* **4** in the event of rain/fire/an accident etc formal if there is rain, a fire etc: *Britain agreed to support the US in the event of war.* **5** in the event used to emphasize that you are saying what actually happened rather than what you thought would happen: *In the event we didn't have to wait long for the results of the test.*

e·vent·ful /ɪˈventfəl/ adj full of interesting or important events: *an eventful life*

e·ven·tu·al /ɪˈventʃuəl/ adj [only before noun] happening at the end of a process: *China's eventual control of Hong Kong*

e·ven·tu·al·i·ty /ɪˌventʃuˈælɨti/ *n* [C] *formal* a possible event or result, especially an unpleasant one: *We must be prepared for any eventuality.*

e·ven·tu·al·ly /ɪˈventʃuəli, -tʃəli/ *adv* after a long time: *He worked so hard that eventually he made himself ill.*

ev·er /ˈevəll'evər/ *adv* **1** at any time – a word used mostly in questions, negative sentences, or sentences with 'if': *Nothing ever makes Paula angry.* | *If you're ever in Wilmington, give us a call.* | *Have you ever eaten snails?* | **the best/ biggest etc ever** *That was the best meal I've ever had.* | **hotter/thinner/better etc than ever** (=hotter, thinner etc than before): *I woke up the following morning feeling worse than ever.* | **hardly ever** (=almost never): *Jim's parents hardly ever watch TV.* | **as popular/bad/happy etc as ever** (=as popular, bad etc as in the past): *I saw Liz the other day looking as cheerful as ever.* **2** used to say that something continues to happen: **ever since** (=continuously since): *He started teaching here when he was 20, and he's been here ever since.* | **ever-growing/ever- increasing etc** (=continuing to grow, increase etc all the time): *the ever-growing population problem* | **for ever** (=always in the future): *His name will live for ever* **3** **ever so/ever such a** *BrE* used to emphasize what you are saying: *It's ever so cold in here.* → see also FOREVER

ev·er·green /ˈevəɡriːnll-ər-/ *adj* an evergreen tree or plant has leaves that do not fall off in winter — **evergreen** *n* [C] → compare DECIDUOUS

ev·er·last·ing /ˌevəˈlɑːstɪŋˌllˌevərˈlæ-/ *adj* continuing for ever: *everlasting peace* — **everlastingly** *adv*

ev·er·more /ˌevəˈmɔːllˌevərˈmɔːr/ *adv literary* always in the future

ev·ery /ˈevri/ *determiner* **1** each one of a group of people or things: *Every student* (=all the students) *will take the test.* | **every single** (=used to emphasize that you mean all): *He told Jan every single thing I said.* **2** used to say how often something happens: *We get the newspaper every day.* | **every now and then/every so often** (=sometimes, but not often): *I still see her every now and then.* **3** **one in every hundred/two in every thousand etc** used to show how many people or things in a group are affected by something: *a disease that will kill one in every thousand babies* **4** as much as possible; a lot: *I'll make every effort to get there on time.* | *He comes round to see Jenny at every opportunity.* **5** **every which way** *informal* in every direction: *People were running every which way.*

USAGE NOTE: every one and everyone

Every one means 'each single person or thing in a group': *Every one of the books had a torn page.* **Everyone** means 'all the people in a group': *Everyone is waiting for you.*

---

ev·ery·bod·y /ˈevribɒdɪll-bɑːdi/ *pron* EVERY- ONE

ev·ery·day /ˈevrideɪ/ *adj* [only before noun] ordinary, usual, or happening every day: *Worries are just part of everyday life.*

ev·ery·one /ˈevriwʌn/ also **everybody** *pron* every person: *Is everyone ready to go?* | *Everyone agreed that the concert had been a success.* | **everyone else** (=all the other people): *I was still awake but everyone else had gone to bed.*

ev·ery·place /ˈevripleɪs/ *adv AmE spoken* EVERYWHERE

ev·ery·thing /ˈevriθɪŋ/ *pron* **1** each thing or all things: *She criticizes everything I do.* | *You look upset. Is everything all right?* | **everything else** (=all the other things): *Jim does the dishes, but I do everything else.* **2** **and everything** *spoken* used to mean all the other things like the thing you have just mentioned: *Make sure the kids brush their teeth and everything before they go to bed.* **3** **be/mean everything** to be the thing that is more important than anything else: *Money isn't everything.* → compare NOTHING[1]

ev·ery·where /ˈevriweəll-wer/ *adv* in or to every place: *I've looked everywhere for my keys.* → compare NOWHERE

e·vict /ɪˈvɪkt/ *v* [T] to legally force someone to leave the house they are renting from you: *Higson was evicted for non-payment of rent.* — **eviction** /ɪˈvɪkʃən/ *n* [C,U]

ev·i·dence /ˈevɨdəns/ *n* [U] **1** facts, statements, or signs that make you believe that something exists or is true: *What evidence do you have to support your theory?* | **+ of** *scientists looking for evidence of life on other planets* | **+ that** *There is evidence that the drug may be harmful to pregnant women.* **2** facts given or objects shown in a court of law to help prove whether or not someone is guilty of a crime: *A vital piece of evidence was missing.* | **give evidence** (=tell a court what you know): *Delaney had to give evidence at his brother's trial.* **3** **be in evidence** *formal* to be easily seen or noticed: *The police were very much in evidence around the factory gate.*

ev·i·dent /ˈevɨdənt/ *adj formal* easily noticed or understood; OBVIOUS: **it is evident that** *It was evident that Bill and his wife weren't happy.*

ev·i·dent·ly /ˈevɨdəntli/ *adv* **1** used to say that a fact can easily be noticed: *The President was evidently unwell.* **2** used to say that you think something is probably true because of information that you have: *Evidently burglars had got into the office.*

e·vil[1] /ˈiːvəl/ *adj* very cruel or harmful: *an evil dictator* | *the evil effects of drug abuse*

evil[2] *n formal* [C,U] something that is very bad and has a very cruel or harmful effect: *the evils of racism*

e·voc·a·tive /ɪˈvɒkətɪvllɪˈvɑː-/ *adj* making you remember or imagine something pleasant: **+ of** *The smell of bread baking is evocative of my childhood.*

e·voke /ɪˈvəʊkllɪˈvoʊk/ *v* [T] to make someone feel or remember something: *The film evoked*

GRAMMAR NOTE: direct and indirect speech

There are two ways of reporting what someone said:

DIRECT SPEECH (using "..."): **"I forgot** to phone you," she said, **"I am** really sorry."

INDIRECT SPEECH: She said that she **had forgotten** to phone me and she **was** really sorry.

memories of the time I lived in France. —**evocation** /ˌevəˈkeɪʃən, ˌiːvəʊ-‖-ˌiːvoʊ-/ *n* [C,U]

ev·o·lu·tion /ˌiːvəˈluːʃən, ˌevə-‖ˌevə-/ *n* [U] **1** the gradual development of plants and animals that happens over millions of years: *Darwin's theory of evolution* **2** the gradual change and development: **+ of** *the evolution of computer technology* —**evolutionary** *adj*

e·volve /ɪˈvɒlv‖ɪˈvɑːlv/ *v* [I,T] to develop or make something develop gradually: *a political system that has evolved over several centuries*

ewe /juː/ *n* [C] a female sheep

ex- /eks/ *prefix* **ex-husband/ex-wife/ex-prime minister** someone who was someone's husband, wife etc previously

ex·a·cer·bate /ɪɡˈzæsəbeɪt‖-ər-/ *v* [T] to make a bad situation worse: *The drugs they gave her only exacerbated the pain.*

ex·act[1] /ɪɡˈzækt/ *adj* **1** correct in every detail: *an exact description* | *I can't remember the exact date.* | **to be exact** *spoken* (=used to give an exact number or amount): *They're here for two weeks, well 13 days, to be exact.* **2** **the exact opposite** someone or something that is as different as possible from another person or thing: *Leonard's shy and quiet – the exact opposite of his brother.* —**exactness** *n* [U]

exact[2] *v* [T] *formal* to demand and get something from someone by using threats, force etc: *The Mafia had exacted a high price for their protection.*

ex·act·ing /ɪɡˈzæktɪŋ/ *adj* needing a lot of care, effort, and attention: *an exacting task*

ex·act·ly /ɪɡˈzæktli/ *adv* **1** used to say an amount or number is completely correct: *We got home at exactly six o'clock.* | *I don't know exactly where she lives.* **2** used to emphasize what you are saying: *They were wearing exactly the same dress.* **3** *spoken* used to show that you agree completely with someone: *"We should spend more on education." "Exactly!"* **4** **not exactly** *spoken* **a)** used to say that something is not at all true: *Why is Tim on a diet? I mean, he's not exactly fat!* **b)** used to reply that something is not completely true: *"Sheila's ill, is she?" "Not exactly, she's just tired."*

ex·ag·ge·rate /ɪɡˈzædʒəreɪt/ *v* [I,T] to make something seem bigger, larger, worse etc than it really is: *Charlie says that everyone in New York has a gun, but I'm sure he's exaggerating.* —**exaggerated** *adj* —**exaggeration** /ɪɡˌzædʒəˈreɪʃən/ *n* [C,U]

ex·alt·ed /ɪɡˈzɔːltd‖-ˈzɔːl-/ *adj formal* of a very high rank or highly respected: *Jenkins was promoted to an exalted position within the company.*

ex·am /ɪɡˈzæm/ *n* [C] **1** an official test of knowledge or ability in a particular subject: *a chemistry exam* | **pass/fail an exam** *If he passes these exams he'll go to university.* | **take/sit an exam** (=do an exam): *When do you take your final exams?* **2** *AmE* A set of medical tests: *an eye exam*

ex·am·i·na·tion /ɪɡˌzæmˈneɪʃən/ *n* **1** [C,U] when someone looks at or considers something carefully: *Every astronaut is given a thorough medical examination.* | *On closer examination, the painting was found to be a forgery.* **2** [C] *formal* an official test of knowledge or ability in a particular subject: *The examination results will be announced in September.*

ex·am·ine /ɪɡˈzæmn̩/ *v* [T] **1** to look at something carefully in order to find out something: *The doctor examined her shoulder and sent her for an X-ray.* **2** to consider an idea or plan carefully: *The finance committee will examine your proposals.* **3** *formal* to ask someone questions to find out what they know about something: *You will be examined on American history.*

ex·am·in·er /ɪɡˈzæmn̩əll-ər/ *n* [C] someone who tests a student's knowledge in an examination

ex·am·ple /ɪɡˈzɑːmpl‖ɪɡˈzæm-/ *n* **1** [C] something that you mention because it is typical of the kind of thing you are talking about: **+ of** *Amiens cathedral is a good example of Gothic architecture.* | **give sb an example of** *Can anyone give me an example of a transitive verb?* **2** **for example** used when you are giving an example to show what you mean: *There's been a big increase in food prices this year. For example, the price of meat has doubled.* **3** [C] someone whose behaviour is very good and should be copied by other people: **set an example** (=behave in a way that other people should follow): *A good captain should set an example for the rest of the team.*

ex·as·pe·rat·ed /ɪɡˈzɑːspəretd‖-ˈzæs-/ *adj* very annoyed: *Bella gave an exasperated sigh and turned away.* —**exasperate** *v* [T] —**exasperation** /ɪɡˌzɑːspəˈreɪʃən‖-ˌzæs-/ *n* [U]

ex·as·pe·rat·ing /ɪɡˈzɑːspəretɪŋ‖-ˈzæs-/ *adj* very annoying: *It's so exasperating when you're in a hurry and your computer breaks down.*

ex·ca·vate /ˈekskəveɪt/ *v* [I,T] to dig up the ground, especially in order to find things from the past: *archeologists excavating an ancient city* —**excavation** /ˌekskəˈveɪʃən/ *n* [C,U]

ex·ceed /ɪkˈsiːd/ *v* [T] **1** to be more than a particular number or amount: *The cost must not exceed $150.* **2** to go beyond an official or legal limit: *She was fined for exceeding the speed limit.*

ex·ceed·ing·ly /ɪkˈsiːdɪŋli/ *adv formal* extremely: *an exceedingly difficult task*

ex·cel /ɪkˈsel/ *v* [I] **-lled, -lling** *formal* **1** to do something very well, or much better than most people: **+ at/in** *I never excelled at sport.* **2** **excel yourself** to do something even better than usual

ex·cel·lent /ˈeksələnt/ *adj* extremely good or of very high quality: *What an excellent idea!* —**excellently** *adv* —**excellence** *n* [U]

ex·cept /ɪkˈsept/ *linking word, prep* not including a particular thing, person, or fact: *We're open every day except Monday.* | **+ for** *Everyone went to the show, except for Scott.* | **+ what/when** etc *I don't know anything about it, except what I've read in the newspaper.* | **+ (that)** *I have earrings just like those, except they're silver.*

ex·cept·ed /ɪkˈseptd/ *adj formal* not included: *He doesn't have many interests, politics excepted.*

ex·cept·ing /ɪkˈseptɪŋ/ *prep* not including; except: *All the students, excepting three or four, spoke fluent English.*

ex·cep·tion /ɪkˈsepʃən/ *n* **1** [C,U] someone or something that is not included in a general statement: *There's always an exception to every rule.* | **be no exception** (=not be different from the others): *Bill was usually in a bad mood on Mondays and today was no exception.* | **with the exception of** *Everyone came to the party, with the exception of Mary, who wasn't feeling well.* | **without exception** *All Spielberg's films,* *without exception, have been tremendously successful.* **2 make an exception** to treat someone or something differently by not including them in a rule: *We don't normally accept credit cards, but we'll make an exception in your case.* **3 take exception to** *formal* to be offended by something: *I take great exception to your remarks.*

ex·cep·tion·al /ık'sepʃənəl/ *adj* **1** unusually good: *an exceptional student* **2** unusual and not likely to happen often: *The teachers were doing their best under exceptional circumstances.* — **exceptionally** *adv*

ex·cerpt /'eksɜːpt‖-ɜːrpt/ *n* [C] a short piece taken from a book, piece of music etc

ex·cess[1] /ık'ses, 'ekses/ *n* **1** [singular, U] a larger amount of something than is usual or is needed: **an excess of** *Tests showed an excess of calcium in the blood.* **2 in excess of** more than an amount or level: *Our profits were in excess of $5 million.* **3 do sth to excess** to do something too much: *Brody smoked and drank to excess.*

ex·cess[2] /'ekses/ *adj* [only before noun] more than is usual or allowed: *a charge of £75 for excess baggage*

ex·cess·es /ık'sesⁱz/ *n* [plural] actions that are immoral or harmful: *the worst excesses of the rockstar's lifestyle*

ex·ces·sive /ık'sesɪv/ *adj* too much or too great: *Don's wife left him because of his excessive drinking.* — **excessively** *adv*

ex·change[1] /ıks'tʃeɪndʒ/ *n* **1** [C,U] when you give something to someone who gives you something else: **+ of** *an exchange of information* | **in exchange for** *The Europeans traded weapons in exchange for gold.* **2** [C] a short conversation or argument: *angry exchanges between our lawyer and the judge* | **exchange of views/ideas** (=a discussion) **3** [C] an arrangement in which students or teachers visit each other's country to work or study: *Sophie's gone on an exchange to Germany.* **4** [U] money that can be used to buy things from another country: *foreign exchange* **5** [C] a TELEPHONE EXCHANGE **6** [C] a STOCK EXCHANGE

exchange[2] *v* **1** [T] to give something to someone who gives you something else: *The two armies exchanged prisoners.* | **exchange sth for sth** *I'd like to exchange this shirt for a smaller one.* **2 exchange glances/greetings/words etc** if two people exchange GLANCEs, greetings etc, they look at each other, greet each other etc — **exchangeable** *adj*

exchange rate /.'. ./ *n* [C] the amount of another country's money that you get when you exchange your own country's money for it: *The exchange rate is 5.12 francs to the US dollar.*

ex·cise /'eksaız/ *n* [C,U] the government tax on goods produced and used inside a country

ex·ci·ta·ble /ık'saıtəbəl/ *adj* becoming excited too easily: *She's a very excitable child.*

ex·cite /ık'saıt/ *v* [T] **1** to make someone feel excited or nervous: *Agassi is the kind of player who really excites the crowd.* **2** *formal* to cause a particular feeling or reaction: *Rumours of the couple's divorce have excited a lot of public curiosity.*

ex·cit·ed /ık'saıtⁱd/ *adj* happy, interested, or hopeful because something good has happened or is expected: *I'm so excited – Steve's coming*

home tomorrow. | **+ about** *The kids are getting really excited about our trip to California.* — **excitedly** *adv*

ex·cite·ment /ık'saıtmənt/ *n* [U] the feeling of being excited: *Gerry couldn't sleep after all the excitement of the day.*

ex·cit·ing /ık'saıtıŋ/ *adj* making you feel excited: *Their trip to Australia sounded really exciting.*

ex·claim /ık'skleɪm/ *v* [I,T] to say something suddenly and loudly because you are surprised, excited, or angry: *"Wow!" exclaimed Bobby, "Look at that car!"*

ex·cla·ma·tion /ˌeksklə'meɪʃən/ *n* [C] a sound, word, or phrase that you say suddenly and loudly to express surprise, anger, or excitement

exclamation mark /.'.. ./ *especially BrE* also **exclamation point** *AmE* — *n* [C] the mark (!) that is written after an exclamation

ex·clude /ık'skluːd/ *v* [T] **1** to not allow someone to take part in something or enter a place: **exclude sb from (doing) sth** *Until 1994 the black population was excluded from voting.* **2** to deliberately not include something: **exclude sth from sth** *Some of the data had been excluded from the report.* **3** to decide that something is not a possibility: *Police have excluded the possibility that Barkin killed herself.*

ex·clud·ing /ık'skluːdıŋ/ *prep* not including: *The cost of hiring a car is £180 a week, excluding insurance.*

ex·clu·sion /ık'skluːʒən/ *n* **1** [U] when someone is not allowed to take part in something: *the exclusion of professional athletes from the Olympics* **2 do sth to the exclusion of** to do something so much that you do not do or think about anything else: *She's been studying hard to the exclusion of everything else.*

ex·clu·sive[1] /ık'skluːsıv/ *adj* **1** expensive and only for people who have a lot of money: *an exclusive Manhattan hotel* **2** used or done by only one person or group, and not shared: *an exclusive interview with President Mandela* **3 exclusive of** not including: *The price of a trip is $450, exclusive of meals.* — **exclusiveness** *n* [U]

exclusive[2] *n* [C] an important news story that is only in one newspaper, magazine etc

ex·clu·sive·ly /ık'skluːsıvli/ *adv* only: *This offer is available exclusively to club members.*

ex·cre·ment /'ekskrⁱmənt/ *n* [U] *formal* solid waste from a person's or animal's body

ex·crete /ık'skriːt/ *v* [I,T] *technical* to get rid of waste from the body — **excretion** /ık'skriːʃən/ *n* [C,U]

ex·cru·ci·at·ing /ık'skruːʃieıtıŋ/ *adj* extremely painful: *The pain in my knee was excruciating.* — **excruciatingly** *adv*

ex·cur·sion /ık'skɜːʃən‖ık'skɜːrʒən/ *n* [C] a short trip, usually made by a group of people for pleasure: **+ to** *an excursion to the island of Burano*

ex·cu·sa·ble /ık'skjuːzəbəl/ *adj* behaviour that is excusable is easy to forgive → compare INEXCUSABLE

ex·cuse[1] /ık'skjuːz/ *v* [T] **1 excuse me** *spoken* **a)** used to politely get someone's attention or to say you are sorry for accidentally doing something: *Excuse me, is this the right bus for the* airport?| Oh, *excuse me, I didn't mean to step on your foot.* **b)** used to politely tell someone that you are leaving a place: *Excuse me a moment, there's someone at the door.* **2** to forgive someone, usually for something that is not very serious: *Please excuse my bad handwriting.* **3** to allow someone not to do something that they should do: **excuse sb from (doing) sth** *You are excused classes for the rest of the week.* **4** to provide a reason for someone's bad behaviour so that it does not seem so bad: *Nothing can excuse lying to your parents.*

ex·cuse[2] /ɪkˈskjuːs/ *n* [C] **1** a reason that you give to explain why you did something wrong: **+ for** *What's your excuse for being late?* **2** a false reason that you give to explain why you are doing something: *The party was so awful Karl was glad of an excuse to leave.*

USAGE NOTE: excuse and reason

An **excuse** is the explanation that you give when you have not done something that you should have done, or when you have done something wrong: *What's your excuse for not doing your homework?* A **reason** is a fact that explains why something happens, exists, or is true: *There are several reasons why he can't be here tonight.*

---

ex·e·cute /ˈeksɪkjuːt/ *v* [T] **1** to kill someone, especially as a legal punishment for a crime **2** *formal* to do something that has been planned or ordered: *a carefully executed plan* —**execution** /ˌeksɪˈkjuːʃən/ *n* [U]

ex·e·cu·tion·er /ˌeksɪˈkjuːʃənəll-nər/ *n* [C] someone whose job is to kill criminals as a legal punishment

ex·ec·u·tive[1] /ɪgˈzekjʊtɪv/ *n* [C] **1** an important manager in a company: *a sales executive* **2** **the executive** the committee in an organization that has the power to make decisions

executive[2] *adj* **1** connected with making decisions, especially in a company or business: *an executive committee* **2** expensive and suitable for people who have important jobs: *executive homes*

ex·em·pla·ry /ɪgˈzempləri/ *adj formal* exemplary behaviour is excellent and can be used as an example for people to copy: *He led an exemplary life.*

ex·em·pli·fy /ɪgˈzemplɪfaɪ/ *v* [T] *formal* to be a very typical example of something, or to give an example of something that is typical: *Stuart exemplifies the kind of student we like at our school.*

ex·empt[1] /ɪgˈzempt/ *adj* having special permission not to do a duty, not to pay for something etc: **+ from** *Medical products are exempt from state taxes.*

exempt[2] *v* [T] to give someone official permission not to do something, not to pay for something etc: **exempt sb from sth** *Anyone who is mentally ill is exempted from military service.* —**exemption** /ɪgˈzempʃən/ *n* [C,U]

ex·er·cise[1] /ˈeksəsaɪzll-ər-/ *n* **1** [C,U] physical activity that you do in order to stay strong and healthy: **do exercises** *You can do special exercises to strengthen your back.*| **take exercise** *The doctor said I need to take more exercise.* **2** [C] a piece of written work or a set of written

questions that is intended to help you learn something: *For homework, do exercises 1 and 2.* **3** [C] a set of military actions for soldiers to practise their skills **4** [U] *formal* the use of a power or right: *the exercise of our right to vote*

exercise[2] *v* **1** [I,T] to do physical activities so that you stay strong and healthy: *It is important to exercise regularly.* **2** *formal* to use a power, ability, or right that you have: *She exercised her influence to get Rigby the job.*

ex·ert /ɪgˈzɜːtll-ɜːrt/ *v* [T] **1 exert authority/influence/pressure etc** to use your authority or influence in order to make something happen: **+ on** *The UN is exerting pressure on the two countries to stop the war.* **2 exert yourself** to make a strong physical or mental effort

ex·er·tion /ɪgˈzɜːʃənll-ɜːr-/ *n* [C,U] when you make a lot of physical or mental effort: *Paul's face was red with exertion.*

ex·hale /eksˈheɪl/ *v* [I,T] to breathe out: *Take a deep breath, then exhale slowly.* → opposite IN-HALE

ex·haust[1] /ɪgˈzɔːstll-ˈzɒːst/ *v* [T] **1** to use all of something: *Eventually, the world's oil supply will be exhausted.* **2** to make someone very tired: *The trip totally exhausted us.*

exhaust[2] *n* **1** [C] also **exhaust pipe** a pipe on a car that waste gas comes out of **2** [U] the waste gas that is produced when an engine is working: *Car exhaust is the main reason for pollution in the city.*

ex·haust·ed /ɪgˈzɔːstɪdll-ˈzɒːs-/ *adj* extremely tired: *Jill lay in the grass, exhausted after her long run.* —**exhaustion** *n* [U]

ex·haust·ing /ɪgˈzɔːstɪŋll-ˈzɒːs-/ *adj* making you feel extremely tired: *It was a long and exhausting journey.*

ex·haus·tive /ɪgˈzɔːstɪvll-ˈzɒːs-/ *adj* thorough and complete: *an exhaustive search of the area* —**exhaustively** *adv*

exhaust pipe /.ˈ. ./ *n* [C] an EXHAUST

ex·hib·it[1] /ɪgˈzɪbɪt/ *v* **1** [I,T] to put something in a public place so people can see it: *His paintings will be exhibited in the National Gallery.* **2** [T] *formal* to show a quality, ability, emotion etc: *The prisoner exhibited no signs of remorse for what he had done.*

exhibit[2] *n* [C] an object that is shown in a MUSEUM or other public place

ex·hi·bi·tion /ˌeksɪˈbɪʃən/ *n* [C,U] **1** a public show where people can go and see paintings, photographs etc: **+ of** *an exhibition of historical photographs* **2** when someone shows their skill, or a particular kind of behaviour, in public: *an impressive exhibition of athletic skill*

ex·hil·a·rat·ed /ɪgˈzɪləreɪtɪd/ *adj* feeling extremely happy and excited: *When she was with Charles she felt young and exhilarated.* —**exhilarate** *v* [T] —**exhilaration** /ɪgˌzɪləˈreɪʃən/ *n* [U]

ex·hil·a·rat·ing /ɪgˈzɪləreɪtɪŋ/ *adj* making you feel extremely happy and excited: *The balloon ride was exhilarating.*

ex·hort /ɪgˈzɔːtll-ɔːrt/ *v* [T] *formal* to try to persuade someone to do something —**exhortation** /ˌeksɔːˈteɪʃənll-ɔːr-/ *n* [C,U]

ex·ile[1] /ˈeksaɪl, ˈegzaɪl/ *n* **1** [U] when someone is forced to leave their country and live somewhere else, usually for political reasons: **in exile**

a writer who lives in exile **2** [C] someone who has been exiled: *Cuban exiles living in the US*

exile[2] *v* [T] to force someone to leave their country and live somewhere else usually for political reasons: *He was exiled from Russia in the 1930s.* —**exiled** *adj*

ex·ist /ɪgˈzɪst/ *v* [I] to be real, present, or alive: *Do ghosts really exist?* | *a custom that still exists*

ex·ist·ence /ɪgˈzɪstəns/ *n* **1** [U] when something exists: + **of** *Do you believe in the existence of God?* | **in existence** *Mammals have been in existence for many millions of years.* **2** [C] the type of life that someone has: *a terrible existence*

ex·ist·ing /ɪgˈzɪstɪŋ/ *adj* existing systems, situations etc are the ones that people use or that exist now: *We need new computers to replace the existing ones.*

ex·it[1] /ˈegzɪ̩t, ˈeksɪ̩t/ *n* [C] **1** a door that you go through to leave a place: *There are two exits at the back of the plane.* **2** when you leave a room, theatre, stage etc: **make an exit** *The President made a quick exit after his speech.* **3** the place where you leave a MOTORWAY or FREEWAY: *Take exit 23 for the city.*

exit[2] *v* **1** [I,T] to finish using a computer PROGRAM: *Press f3 to exit.* **2** [I] *formal* to leave a place: *The band exited through a door behind the stage.*

ex·o·dus /ˈeksədəs/ *n* [singular] when a lot of people leave a place at the same time: *the exodus of Russian scientists to America*

ex·on·e·rate /ɪgˈzɒnəreɪt‖ɪgˈzɑː-/ *v* [T] *formal* to officially say that someone is not guilty after they have been blamed for something: *Ross was exonerated from all blame.* —**exoneration** /ɪgˌzɒnəˈreɪʃən‖-ˌzɑː-/ *n* [U]

ex·or·bi·tant /ɪgˈzɔːbɪ̩tənt‖-ɔːr-/ *adj* an exorbitant price is much higher than it should be —**exorbitantly** *adv*

ex·or·cize (also **-ise** *BrE*) /ˈeksɔːsaɪz‖-ɔːr-/ *v* [T] to force evil spirits to leave a place or someone's body by using special prayers and ceremonies —**exor·cism** /-sɪzəm/ *n* [C,U] —**exorcist** *n* [C]

ex·ot·ic /ɪgˈzɒtɪk‖ɪgˈzɑː-/ *adj* unusual and exciting, especially because of a connection with a distant country: *an exotic flower from Africa* —**exotically** /-kli/ *adv*

ex·pand /ɪkˈspænd/ *v* [I,T] to become larger in size or number, or to make something larger: *The population of Texas expanded rapidly in the '60s.* | *We're planning to expand our recycling services.* —**expandable** *adj*

  expand on/upon sth *phr v* [T] *formal* to add more details or information to something that you have already said: *Could you expand on your last comment, please?*

ex·panse /ɪkˈspæns/ *n* [C] a very large area of land, sea, sky etc: + **of** *the vast expanse of the Pacific Ocean*

ex·pan·sion /ɪkˈspænʃən/ *n* [U] when something increases in size, number, or amount: *a period of economic expansion*

ex·pan·sive /ɪkˈspænsɪv/ *adj* very friendly and willing to talk a lot: *After dinner, Mr. Woods relaxed and became more expansive.* —**expansively** *adv*

ex·pat·ri·ate /eksˈpætriət, -trieɪt‖eksˈpeɪ-/ also **ex·pat** /ˌeksˈpæt/ *n* [C] someone who lives in a foreign country —**expatriate** *adj*

ex·pect /ɪkˈspekt/ *v* **1** [T] to think that something will happen: **expect (to) do sth** *Do you expect to travel a lot this year?* | *You surely don't expect me to drive you home?* | + **(that)** *We expect the meeting will finish about 5 o'clock.* **2** [T] to believe that someone must do something because it is their duty: *The officer expects absolute obedience from his men.* | **expect sb to do sth** *We're expected to work late sometimes.* **3** | **expect** *spoken especially BrE* used to say that you think something is probably true: *You've had a busy day. I expect you're tired.* | **I expect so** *"Do you think Andreas will pass his exam?" "Yes, I expect so."* **4** **be expecting sb/sth** to be waiting for someone or something to arrive: *I'm expecting a letter from Japan.* **5** **be expecting** *informal* to be PREGNANT

ex·pec·tan·cy /ɪkˈspektənsi/ *n* [U] the feeling that something exciting or interesting is going to happen: *a look of expectancy* → see also LIFE EXPECTANCY

ex·pec·tant /ɪkˈspektənt/ *adj* **1** hopeful that something good or exciting will happen: *An expectant crowd gathered at the movie premiere.* **2 expectant mother** a PREGNANT woman —**expectantly** *adv*

ex·pec·ta·tion /ˌekspekˈteɪʃən/ *n* **1** [C,U] a strong belief or hope that something will happen: + **of** *O'Leary entered the competition without much expectation of success.* | + **that** *Our decision was based on the expectation that prices would rise.* **2** [C usually plural] a belief that something will be good in the future: **high expectations** (=a belief that things will be good): *Many refugees arrive in the country with high expectations.*

ex·pe·di·ent[1] /ɪkˈspiːdiənt/ *adj* helpful or useful, sometimes in a way that is morally wrong: *She thought it would be expedient to use a false name.* —**expediency** also **expedience** *n* [U] *an act of political expediency*

expedient[2] *n* [C] a clever way of dealing with a situation

ex·pe·di·tion /ˌekspɪ̩ˈdɪʃən/ *n* [C] **1** a long and carefully organized journey, especially to a dangerous place: *an expedition to the North Pole* **2** a short trip made for a particular purpose: *a shopping expedition*

ex·pel /ɪkˈspel/ *v* [T] **-lled, -lling 1** to officially order someone to leave a school, organization, or country: **expel sb from** *Jake was expelled from school for smoking.* **2** *formal* to force air, water, or gas out of something

ex·pend /ɪkˈspend/ *v* [T] *formal* to use money, time, energy etc: *A lot of effort has already been expended on the education of their children.*

---

ex·pen·da·ble /ɪkˈspendəbəl/ adj not needed enough to be kept or saved: *generals who regarded the lives of soldiers as expendable*

ex·pen·di·ture /ɪkˈspendɪtʃəll-ər/ n [U] formal **1** the total amount of money that a government, organization, or person spends: **+ on** *The expenditure on medical care has doubled in the last 20 years.* **2** when someone spends or uses money, time, or effort: *the wasteful expenditure of time*

ex·pense /ɪkˈspens/ n **1** [C,U] the amount of money you spend on something: **household/ medical/living expenses** (=money that you spend for a particular purpose)|**at great expense** (=costing a lot of money): *We were wined and dined at great expense by Kate's boss.* **2 expenses** [plural] money that you spend on travel, hotels etc when you are working, and then get back from your employer: *a claim for travel expenses* **3 at the expense of** achieved by harming someone or something: *The asbestos industry continued to expand at the expense of public health.* **4 at sb's expense a)** if you do something at someone's expense, they pay for you to do it: *Guy spent a year in Canada at his parents' expense.* **b)** in a way that makes someone seem stupid: *Louis kept making jokes at his wife's expense.*

ex·pen·sive /ɪkˈspensɪv/ adj costing a lot of money: *an expensive suit* → opposite INEXPENSIVE

ex·pe·ri·ence[1] /ɪkˈspɪərɪənsll-ˈspɪr-/ n **1** [U] knowledge or skill that you get from doing a job or activity or from being in different situations: **have experience** in *Do you have any experience in marketing?*|**in my experience** *In my experience, a credit card is always useful.* **2** [C] something that happens to you and has an effect on how you feel or what you think: *Visiting Paris was a wonderful experience.*|**+ of** *Write about your first experience of travelling abroad.*

experience[2] v [T] to be affected by something: *The company is experiencing problems with its computer system.*|*The patient is experiencing a lot of pain.*

ex·pe·ri·enced /ɪkˈspɪərɪənstll-ˈspɪr-/ adj having a lot of skill or knowledge because you have done something often or for a long time: *a very experienced pilot* → opposite INEXPERIENCED

ex·per·i·ment[1] /ɪkˈsperɪmənt/ n [C] **1** a scientific test done to find out or prove something: **do/perform experiments (on)** *They did experiments on rats to test the drug.* **2** a process in which you try to find out if a new idea of method is effective: *St. Mary's School is an experiment in bilingual education.* —**experimental** /ɪkˌsperɪˈmentl̩/ adj —**experimentally** adv

ex·per·i·ment[2] /ɪkˈsperɪment/ v [I] **1** to try using various ideas, methods, materials etc in order to find out what effect they have: **+ with** *Many teenagers experiment with drugs.* **2** to do a scientific test in order to find out or prove something: **+ on/with** *Do you think it's right to experiment on animals?* —**experimentation** /ɪkˌsperɪmenˈteɪʃən/ n [U]

ex·pert[1] /ˈekspɜːtll-ɜːrt/ n [C] someone with special skills or knowledge of a subject: **+ on/in** *Dr Higgs is an expert on ancient Egyptian art.* —**expert** adj: *expert advice* —**expertly** adv

ex·per·tise /ˌekspɜːˈtiːzll-ɜːr-/ n [U] special skills or knowledge that you learn by experience or training: *medical expertise*

ex·pir·a·tion /ˌeksp^əˈreɪʃən/ n [U] the end of a period of time in which an official document or agreement can be used; EXPIRY BrE: *the expiration of the treaty*

ex·pire /ɪkˈspaɪəll-ˈspaɪr/ v [I] if a document or legal agreement expires, the period of time in which you can use it ends

ex·pir·y /ɪkˈspaɪərill-ˈspaɪri/ n [U] BrE the end of a period of time in which an official document or agreement can be used; EXPIRATION

ex·plain /ɪkˈspleɪn/ v [I,T] **1** to make something clear or easy to understand by talking or writing about it: *Can someone explain how this thing works?*|**explain (sth) to sb** *I explained the rules to Sara.* **2** to give or be the reason for something: **+ why** *Brad never explained why he was late.*|**+ that** *I explained that I'd missed the bus.*

explain sth ↔ **away** phr v [T] to make something seem to be unimportant or not your fault: *Claire tried to explain away the bruises on her arm.*

ex·pla·na·tion /ˌekspləˈneɪʃən/ n **1** [C] what you say or write to make something easier to understand: **+ of** *Dr Ewing gave a detailed explanation of how to use the program.* **2** [C,U] the reason why something happens or exists: **+ for** *Is there any explanation for his behaviour?*

ex·plan·a·to·ry /ɪkˈsplænətərill-tɔːri/ adj giving information about something or explaining how something works: *an explanatory booklet* → see also SELF-EXPLANATORY

ex·ple·tive /ɪkˈspliːtɪvll-ˈsplətɪv/ n [C] formal a swear word

ex·pli·ca·ble /ekˈsplɪkəbəl/ adj something that is explicable can be easily understood or explained: *For no explicable reason, Judy always remembered his phone number.* → opposite INEXPLICABLE

ex·pli·cit /ɪkˈsplɪs^ɪt/ adj **1** very clear and easy to understand: *Could you be more explicit?* **2** showing or describing all the details of sex or violence: *explicit love scenes* —**explicitly** adv

ex·plode /ɪkˈspləʊdll-ˈsploud/ v **1** [I,T] to BURST suddenly and violently, making a loud noise and causing damage, or to make something do this: *The car bomb exploded at 6:16.* **2** [I] to suddenly become very angry: *Susie exploded when I told her I'd wrecked her car.* → see also EXPLOSION

ex·ploit[1] /ɪkˈsplɔɪt/ v [T] **1** to pay or give someone much less than they value of the work they do for you or the goods they sell to you: *It's important that students doing work experience should not be exploited by employers.* **2** to use something effectively so that you get as much advantage as possible from it: *We must exploit the country's mineral resources.* —**exploitation** /ˌeksplɔɪˈteɪʃən/ n [U]

ex·ploit[2] /ˈeksplɔɪt/ n [C usually plural] something brave or interesting that someone has done: *a book about Annie Oakley's exploits*

ex·plor·a·to·ry /ɪkˈsplɔːrətərillɪkˈsplɔːrətɔːri/ adj done in order to find out more about something: *exploratory surgery*

ex·plore /ɪkˈsplɔːｌｌ-ˈsplɔːr/ v **1** [I,T] to travel through an unfamiliar area to find out what it is like: *We spent a week exploring the Oregon coastline.* **2** [T] to discuss or think about something carefully: *Explore all the possibilities before you make a decision.* —**exploration** /ˌekspləˈreɪʃən/ n [C,U] *a voyage of exploration*

ex·plor·er /ɪkˈsplɔːrəｌ-ər/ n [C] someone who travels to places that people have not visited before

ex·plo·sion /ɪkˈspləʊʒənｌｌ-ˈsploʊ-/ n **1** [C,U] when something such as a bomb explodes, or the loud noise it causes: *The force of the explosion shook the building.* **2** a sudden large increase: *the population explosion*

ex·plo·sive¹ /ɪkˈspləʊsɪvｌ-ˈsploʊ-/ adj **1** something that is explosive can cause an explosion: *an explosive mixture of gases* **2** likely to make people become violent or angry: *an explosive situation* | *Abortion is an explosive issue.*

explosive² n [C] a substance that can cause an explosion

ex·po·nent /ɪkˈspəʊnəntｌｌ-ˈspoʊ-/ n [C] someone who supports a particular idea or belief and tries to persuade other people that it is good: *an exponent of socialism*

ex·port¹ /ˈekspɔːtｌｌ-ɔːrt/ n **1** [U] the business of selling products to another country: + *of* the *export of live animals* **2** [C] a product that is sold to another country: *Oil is now one of Malaysia's main exports.* → compare IMPORT¹

ex·port² /ɪkˈspɔːtｌｌ-ɔːrt/ v [I,T] to send and sell goods to another country: *Japan exports electronic equipment to dozens of countries.* → compare IMPORT²

ex·port·er /ɪkˈspɔːtəｌｌ-ˈspɔːrtər/ n [C] a person, company, or country that sells goods to other countries

ex·pose /ɪkˈspəʊzｌｌ-ˈspoʊz/ v [T] **1** to remove the cover from something that is usually covered: **expose sth to sth** *When a wound is exposed to the air, it heals more quickly.* **2** to put someone in a situation, place etc that may be harmful or dangerous: **be exposed to** *Workers in the nuclear industry were exposed to high levels of radiation.* **3** to tell people the truth about something bad or dishonest: *His criminal activities were finally exposed in 'The Daily Mirror'.* **4** to give someone experience of different ideas, TRADITIONS etc: **be exposed to** *Children who have been exposed to different cultures are less likely to be prejudiced.* **5** to allow light onto a piece of film in a camera in order to produce a photograph

ex·posed /ɪkˈspəʊzdｌｌ-ˈspoʊzd/ adj not protected from the weather: *an exposed hillside*

ex·po·sure /ɪkˈspəʊʒəｌｌ-ˈspoʊʒər/ n **1** [C,U] when someone or something is put into a harmful situation without any protection: + *to Skin cancer is often caused by too much exposure to the sun.* **2** [C,U] when the newspapers, television etc tell people the true facts about the bad behaviour of an important or respected person: *the exposure of a high-ranking official as a Mafia boss* **3** [U] the harmful effects of staying outside for a long time when the weather is extremely cold: *Three climbers died of exposure.* **4** [C] the amount of film that is used each time you take a photograph: *This roll has 36 exposures.*

ex·press¹ /ɪkˈspres/ v [T] **1** to tell people what you think or feel: *A number of people expressed their concern.* | **express yourself** (=clearly say what you think or feel) **2** to show your thoughts and feelings by your behaviour or through art, music etc: *The look on Paul's face expressed utter despair.*

express² adj **1** an express wish, aim, command etc is very specific and clearly stated: *It was her express wish that you should inherit her house.* **2** an express service is very fast

express³ also **express train** /.ˈ. ./ n [C] a fast train which stops at only a few stations

ex·pres·sion /ɪkˈspreʃən/ n **1** [C] a word or phrase that has a particular meaning: *"Mustn't grumble," my father said. It was an expression he often used.* **2** [C] a look on someone's face: *He came back with a cheerful expression on his face.* **3** [C,U] when you say, write, or do something: + *of I'm sending these flowers as an expression of my gratitude.*

ex·pres·sion·less /ɪkˈspreʃənləs/ adj an expressionless face or voice does not show what someone feels or thinks

ex·pres·sive /ɪkˈspresɪv/ adj showing what someone thinks or feels: *expressive eyes* — **expressively** adv

ex·press·ly /ɪkˈspresli/ adv formal **1** in a clear and definite way: *Students had been expressly forbidden to enter that part of the building.* **2** if you expressly do something, you do it for one particular purpose or reason: *The building is expressly designed for disabled people.*

ex·press·way /ɪkˈspreswei/ n [C] AmE a very wide road in a city on which cars can travel fast → see also MOTORWAY

ex·pul·sion /ɪkˈspʌlʃən/ n [C,U] when someone is officially ordered to leave a country, school, or organization: *the expulsion of Communists from the government*

ex·qui·site /ɪkˈskwɪzɪ̪t, ˈekskwɪ-/ adj extremely beautiful and delicate: *an exquisite diamond ring* — **exquisitely** adv

ex·tend /ɪkˈstend/ v **1** [I] to continue over a particular distance or period of time: + *for/ through/into* etc *The forest extended for miles in all directions.* **2** [T] to increase something or make it larger: *The club is being extended to make space for a new dance area* **3** [T] to make an agreed arrangement continue for a longer period: *The authorities have extended her visa for another six months.* **4** [T] to include or affect a particular group of people, things, or activities: *The ban on imports does not extend to medical supplies.* **5** **extend thanks/sympathy/a welcome** formal to offer someone thanks, sympathy etc **6** [T] to stretch out a part of your body: *Perry extended his arms in a welcoming gesture.*

ex·ten·sion /ɪkˈstenʃən/ n **1** [singular, U] when something is increased to include more: + *of* the *extension of Soviet power in Eastern Europe* **2** [C] a new room or part that is added to a building: *We're building an extension at the back of the house.* **3** [C] a telephone that is connected to the central telephone system of a large building or company: *My extension number is 3821.* **4** [C] an additional period of time that someone is officially given: *When his visa ran out, they granted him an extension.*

ex·ten·sive /ık'stensıv/ *adj* large in amount or area: *Doctors have done extensive research into the effects of stress.*

ex·tent /ık'stent/ *n* **1** [singular] how big, important, or serious something is: *What's the extent of the damage?* | *Violence has increased to such an extent that people are afraid to leave their homes.* **2** **to some extent/to a certain extent** partly but not completely: *To some extent, it was my fault.*

ex·ten·u·a·ting cir·cum·stan·ces /ık-ˌstenjueıtıŋ 'sɜːkəm,stænsɪz, -stənsˌɪz‖-'sɜːr-/ *n* [plural] facts which partly explain or excuse bad behaviour

ex·te·ri·or /ık'stıəriəll-'tıriər/ *n* [C usually singular] the appearance or outside surface of something: *repairs to the exterior of the building* | *Her calm exterior hid her intense anger.* —**exterior** *adj* → opposite INTERIOR

ex·ter·mi·nate /ık'stɜːmɪneıt‖-ɜːr-/ *v* [T] to kill all of a particular group of people or animals —**extermination** /ık,stɜːmɪ'neıʃən‖-ɜːr-/ *n* [C,U]

ex·ter·nal /ık'stɜːnl‖-ɜːr-/ *adj* **1** relating to the outside of something: *There are no external signs of injury* (=on the outside of someone's body) **2** coming from outside an organization or country: *external examiners* → opposite INTERNAL

ex·tinct /ık'stıŋkt/ *adj* **1** a type of animal or plant that is extinct no longer exists **2** an extinct VOLCANO is no longer active

ex·tinc·tion /ık'stıŋkʃən/ *n* [U] when a type of animal or plant no longer exists: *Greenpeace believes that whales are in danger of extinction.*

ex·tin·guish /ık'stıŋgwıʃ/ *v* [T] **1** *formal* to make a fire or light stop burning or shining: *Please extinguish all cigarettes.* **2** *literary* to destroy an idea or feeling: *The news extinguished all hope of his return.*

ex·tin·guish·er /ık'stıŋgwıʃəll-ər/ *n* [C] FIRE EXTINGUISHER

ex·tol /ık'stəull-'stoul/ *v* [T] **-lled, -lling** to praise something very much: *Jamie was extolling the virtues of the single life.*

ex·tort /ık'stɔːt‖-ɔːrt/ *v* [T] to force someone to give you money by threatening them: *He was accused of trying to extort money from business associates.* —**extortion** /-'stɔːʃənll-ɔːr-/ *n* [U]

ex·tor·tion·ate /ık'stɔːʃənˌtll-ɔːr-/ *adj* extortionate prices are much too high

ex·tra [1] /'ekstrə/ *adj, adv* **1** more than the usual amount: *a large mushroom pizza with extra cheese* **2** especially: *If you're extra good I'll buy you an ice cream.*

extra [2] *n* [C] **1** something that is added to a product or service and costs more: *The price of the car includes extras such as a sun roof and CD player.* **2** an actor in a film who does not say anything

extra- /ekstrə/ *prefix* outside: *extramarital sex* (=sex outside marriage with someone who is not your husband or wife)

ex·tract [1] /ık'strækt/ *v* [T] **1** to make someone give you information, money etc that they do not want to give: *The police failed to extract any information from him.* **2** *formal* to remove something: *gaps in her mouth where teeth had been extracted*

ex·tract [2] /'ekstrækt/ *n* **1** [C] a small part of a story, poem, song etc: *an extract from "A Midsummer Night's Dream"* **2** [C,U] a substance that is taken from a plant by a special process: *vanilla extract*

ex·trac·tion /ık'strækʃən/ *n* **1** [C,U] the process of removing an object or substance from something else: *the extraction of salt from sea water* **2** **of French/Irish etc extraction** having family members who come from France, Ireland etc even though you were not born in that country

ex·tra·cur·ric·u·lar /ˌekstrəkə'rıkjʊlə ‖-ər‹/ *adj* extracurricular activities are not part of your usual schoolwork

ex·tra·dite /'ekstrədaıt/ *v* [T] to send someone who may be guilty of a crime back to the country where the crime happened for their TRIAL in a law court —**extradition** /,ekstrə'dıʃən/ *n* [C,U]

ex·tra·ne·ous /ık'streınıəs/ *adj formal* not directly related to a particular subject: *His report contains too many extraneous details.*

ex·tra·or·di·na·ry /ık'strɔːdənərill‖k'strɔːr-dn-eri, ,ekstrə'ɔːr-/ *adj* **1** unusually good or special: *Ellington had an extraordinary musical talent.* **2** strange, unusual, or surprising: *What an extraordinary idea!* —**extraordinarily** *adv*

ex·trav·a·gant /ık'strævəgənt/ *adj* **1** spending or costing too much money: *You've been terribly extravagant, buying all these presents.* | *wild extravagant parties* **2** unlikely to be true or really happen: *extravagant claims that the drug cures AIDS* —**extravagantly, extravagance** *n* [C,U]

ex·trav·a·gan·za /ık,strævə'gænzə/ *n* [C] a large and expensive show

ex·treme [1] /ık'striːm/ *adj* **1** very great: *extreme heat* **2** extreme opinions, behaviour, situations etc are unusual and different from what most people consider to be reasonable: *In one extreme case a child of ten was imprisoned.* **3** the extreme farthest parts of something, farthest in a particular direction, or farthest from the centre: *in the extreme north of the country*

extreme [2] *n* **1** [C] one of the two opposite limits of temperature, behaviour etc: *folk who have learned to survive the extremes of their climate* **2** **go to extremes/carry sth to extremes** to do something to an unreasonable degree: *Caution is sensible, but not when it's carried to extremes.* **3** **in the extreme** extremely: *a man who was selfish in the extreme*

ex·treme·ly /ık'striːmli/ *adv* to a very great degree: *I'm extremely sorry.*

ex·trem·ist /ık'striːmˌıst/ *n* [C] someone who has extreme opinions, especially about politics or religion: *left-wing extremists* —**extremist** *adj* —**extremism** *n* [U]

ex·trem·i·ty /ık'stremˌti/ *n* [C] *formal* the area furthest from the centre of something: *the city's northern extremity*

ex·tri·cate /'ekstrˌkeıt/ *v* **extricate yourself from sth** to escape from a difficult situation: *Perrault could not extricate himself from the relationship once it had started*

ex·tro·vert, extravert /'ekstrəvɜːtll-ɜːrt/ *n* [C] someone who is confident and enjoys being with other people —**extrovert, extroverted** *adj* → compare INTROVERTED

ex·u·be·rant /ɪɡˈzjuːbərənt‖ɪɡˈzuː-/ *adj* very happy, excited, and full of energy: *Judith was in an exuberant mood.* —**exuberance** *n* [U]

ex·ude /ɪɡˈzjuːd‖ɪɡˈzuːd/ *v* **1** [T] to show a lot of a feeling or quality: *a young man who exuded charm* **2** [I,T] to flow out slowly, or to make something do this

eye[1] /aɪ/ *n* [C] **1** one of the two organs in your face that you see with: *Gina has blue eyes.* | *Close your eyes.* → see picture at HEAD[1] **2 blue-eyed/one-eyed/bright-eyed etc** having blue eyes, one eye etc **3 keep an eye on** to watch what someone or something does in order to prevent something bad from happening: *Can you keep an eye on the baby while I make a phone call?* **4 keep an eye out for** to be ready to notice someone or something that you are looking for: *Can you keep an eye out for my keys?* **5 keep your eyes open/peeled** to watch carefully: *Keep your eyes peeled – he must be hiding around here somewhere.* **6 in the eyes of/in sb's eyes** according to someone's opinion: *Divorce is a sin in the eyes of the Church.* **7 have your eye on** to have noticed something that you want to buy or have: *I've got my eye on a nice little sports car.* **8 have an eye for** to be good at noticing what is valuable or attractive: *Gail has a good eye for colour.* **9 cannot take your eyes off** to be unable to stop looking at someone or something: *He was so gorgeous, I couldn't take my eyes off him.* **10 set/lay eyes on** to see someone or something, especially for the first time: *The first time I set eyes on him I knew I liked him.* **11 with your eyes open** knowing what all the problems of a situation might be: *I went into the business with my eyes open so it's no use complaining now.* **12 be up to your eyes in** *spoken* to have a lot of things to deal with: *I'm up to my eyes in paperwork.* **13** the hole in a needle that you put thread through → see picture at NEEDLE → see also **could not believe your eyes** (BELIEVE), **catch sb's eye** (CATCH[1]), **look sb in the eye** (LOOK[1]), **see eye to eye (with sb)** (SEE), **turn a blind eye** (TURN[1]), **cast an eye over sth** (CAST[1]), **to the naked eye** (NAKED)

eye[2] *v* [T] **eyed, eyed, eyeing** or **eying** to look at someone or something with interest, especially because you do not trust them or because you want something: *The child eyed me with curiosity.*

eye·ball /ˈaɪbɔːl‖-bɒːl/ *n* [C] the whole of your eye, including the part that is hidden inside your head

eye·brow /ˈaɪbraʊ/ *n* [C] the line of short hairs above your eye → see picture at HEAD[1]

eye·catch·ing /ˈ. ˌ../ *adj* something that is eye-catching is so unusual or attractive that you notice it: *eye-catching advertisements*

eye·lash /ˈaɪlæʃ/ *n* [C] one of the small hairs that grow on the edge of your eyelids → see picture at HEAD[1]

eye·lid /ˈaɪlɪd/ *n* [C] the piece of skin that covers your eye when it is closed

eye·o·pen·er /ˈ. ˌ.../ *n* [singular] an event, situation etc that makes you realize some surprising facts: *Visiting Russia was a real eye-opener for me.*

eye·shad·ow /ˈ. ˌ../ *n* [U] a coloured substance that women put on their eyelids as MAKE-UP

eye·sight /ˈaɪsaɪt/ *n* [U] the ability to see: *You need perfect eyesight to be a pilot.*

eye·sore /ˈaɪsɔː‖-sɔːr/ *n* [C] a building or area that is very ugly: *The glass factory is a real eyesore.*

eye·wit·ness /ˈaɪˌwɪtn̩s/ *n* [C] someone who sees an event and is able to describe it afterwards: *According to eyewitnesses the robbery was carried out by four men.*

E

GRAMMAR NOTE: a or the (1)
Use **a** or **an** before a noun when you are mentioning a person or thing for the first time, but use **the** when you mention that same person or thing again: *A man and a woman were sitting at the next table. The woman was much younger than the man.*

Ff

F, f the letter 'f'

F /ef/ the written abbreviation of FAHRENHEIT: *Water boils at 212° F.*

fa·ble /'feɪbəl/ *n* [C] a short story that teaches a moral lesson

fab·ric /'fæbrɪk/ *n* **1** [C,U] cloth: *heavy woollen fabric* **2** [singular] the walls and roof of a building **3** [singular] the basic structure and customs of society: *The family is the most important unit in the social fabric.*

fab·ri·cate /'fæbrɪkeɪt/ *v* [T] to make up a story or a piece of information in order to deceive someone: *The police were accused of fabricating evidence.* —**fabrication** /ˌfæbrɪ'keɪʃən/ *n* [C,U]

fab·u·lous /'fæbjʊləs/ *adj* **1** extremely good: *You look fabulous!* **2** unusually large: *The painting was sold for a fabulous sum.*

fab·u·lous·ly /'fæbjʊləsli/ *adv* extremely: *a fabulously rich woman*

fa·cade, façade /fə'sɑːd, fæ-/ *n* [C] **1** a way of behaving that hides your real feelings or character: *Behind that cheerful facade she's really quite a lonely person.* **2** the front of a building

face[1] /feɪs/ *n* **1** [C] the front part of your head, where your eyes, nose, and mouth are: *a girl with a round, pretty face* | *He had a surprised look on his face.* → see picture at HEAD[1] **2** [C] an expression on someone's face: **sb's face fell** (=they started to look disappointed): *Lynn's face fell when I said Sean already had a girlfriend.* | **make/pull a face** (=twist your face into a funny or rude expression) | **keep a straight face** (=stop yourself from laughing): *When I saw what he was wearing, I could hardly keep a straight face.* | **sb's face lights up** (=they suddenly look happy) **3 face to face (with) a)** looking directly at someone: *I'd rather talk to him face to face than on the phone.* **b)** in a situation where you may have to experience something unpleasant: *It was the first time he had ever come face to face with death.* **4 in the face of** when having to accept a difficult or dangerous situation: *Marie was very brave, even in the face of great suffering.* **5 new/familiar face** someone you have not seen before, or someone you already know: *In the middle of the crowd I recognized a familiar face.* **6** [C] an outside surface of an object, usually its front: *a clock face* | *the north face of Mount Rainier* **7 on the face of it** when you first consider something, before you know the details: *On the face of it, this seems like a perfectly good idea.* **8 lose/save face** to lose or avoid losing the respect of other people: *If I win, Lee will lose face and hate me even more.* **9 to sb's face** if you say something to someone's face, you say it when they are with you: *They'd never dare say that to his face.*

face[2] *v* [T] **1** to have to accept or deal with a bad situation or problem: *He faced a lot of problems in his short life.* | **face the fact that** *You're going to have to face the fact that John loves someone else.* | **let's face it** *spoken* (=used to say that someone has to accept an unpleasant fact): *Let's face it – you're never going to be a star player.* **2** if a person, building, object etc faces someone or something they have their front turned towards them: *Dean turned to face me.* | *Rita's apartment faces the sea.* **3 be faced with** to be in a situation where you have to deal with something difficult: *She's going to be faced with some very tough choices.* **4 can't face doing sth** to feel that you cannot do something because it is too unpleasant: *I can't face seeing Ben again.* **5** to deal with someone, or talk to someone, when this is difficult: *You're going to have to face him sooner or later.* **6** to play against an opponent or team: *Sampras faces Becker in the men's final tomorrow.*

face up to sth *phr v* [T] to accept and deal with something difficult or unpleasant instead of ignoring it: *You'll have to face up to your responsibilities.*

face·less /'feɪsləs/ *adj* a faceless official, organization etc does not seem to be interested in your personally, but only as someone they have to deal with officially: *faceless bureaucrats*

face·lift /'feɪslɪft/ *n* **1** [C] a medical operation to make your face look younger by removing loose skin **2 give sth a facelift** to make something look newer or better by repairing it, painting it etc: *We're going to give the reception area a facelift.*

fac·et /'fæsɪt/ *n* [C] one of several parts of someone's character, a situation etc: *Social life is an important facet of university education.*

fa·ce·tious /fə'siːʃəs/ *adj* saying things that are intended to be funny and clever but which annoy people: *facetious comments* —**facetiously** *adv* —**facetiousness** *n* [U]

face val·ue /ˌ. '../ *n* **1 take sth at face value** to accept something without thinking that it might not be as good or true as it seems **2** [singular] the value that is written on something such as a coin, ticket etc

fa·cial[1] /'feɪʃəl/ *adj* on your face, or relating to your face: *facial hair* —**facially** *adv*

facial[2] *n* [C] a process in which your face is specially cleaned: *I'm going to have a facial at that new beauty salon.*

fa·cil·i·tate /fə'sɪlɪteɪt/ *v* [T] *formal* to make it easier for something to happen: *We've employed temporary staff to facilitate the enrolment of new students.* —**facilitation** /fəˌsɪlɪ'teɪʃən/ *n* [U]

fa·cil·i·ties /fə'sɪlɪtiz/ *n* [plural] rooms, equipment, or services that are provided for a purpose: *The hotel has excellent conference facilities.*

fa·cil·i·ty /fə'sɪlɪti/ *n* [C] a service or feature that a machine or system has: *The program has a search facility.*

fac·sim·i·le /fæk'sɪmɪli/ *n* [C] an exact copy of a picture, piece of writing etc

fact /fækt/ *n* **1** [C] something that you know is true, or that has definitely happened: *We can't comment until we know all the facts.* | **the fact that** *She's just ignoring the fact that he's already married.* | **I know for a fact (that)** *spoken* (=used to say that you definitely know something is true) **2 in fact/as a matter of fact/in actual fact** used when you are adding a piece of information or when you are saying what the real truth of a situation is: *I know her really well, in fact I had dinner with her last week.* **3** [U] things that really happen or exist: *It is often* *difficult to separate fact from fiction.* **4 the fact (of the matter) is** *spoken* used when you are telling someone what the real truth of a situation is **5 sth is a fact of life** used to say that a bad situation exists and must be accepted: *Violent crime seems to have become a fact of life.* **6 the facts of life** information about sex and how babies are born

fac·tion /ˈfækʃən/ *n* [C] a small group of people within a larger group, who have different ideas from the other members: *The President hopes to unite the warring factions within his Party.* —**factional** *adj*

fac·tor /ˈfæktəl-ər/ *n* [C] **1** one of several things that influence or cause a situation: **+** *The weather could be an important factor in tomorrow's game.* **2** *technical* a number that a larger number can be divided by exactly. For example 3 is a factor of 15.

fac·to·ry /ˈfæktəri/ *n* [C] a building where goods are produced in large quantities: *a shoe factory* ➡ see colour picture on page 278

fac·tu·al /ˈfæktʃuəl/ *adj* based on facts: *factual information* —**factually** *adv*

fac·ul·ty /ˈfækəlti/ *n* **1** [C] *formal* a natural ability, such as the ability to see, hear, or think: *At the age of 95 he was still in possession of all his faculties.* **2** [C] a group of university departments: *the Faculty of Arts* **3 the faculty** *AmE* all the teachers in a school or college

fad /fæd/ *n* [C] something that you are interested in for a short time or a fashion that is popular for a short time: *His interest in photography was just a passing fad.*

fade /feɪd/ *v* **1** also **fade away** [I] to gradually disappear or become weaker: *Her memories of Egypt soon faded.* **2** [I,T] if clothes or coloured objects fade, or if light fades them, they lose their colour or brightness: *faded blue jeans*

fae·ces also **feces** *AmE* /ˈfiːsiːz/ *n* [plural] *technical* solid waste material that is passed out of the body

fag /fæg/ *n* [C] *BrE informal* a cigarette

Fah·ren·heit /ˈfærənhaɪt/ *n* [U] a SCALE of temperature in which water freezes at 32° and boils at 212°

fail¹ /feɪl/ *v* **1** [I,T] to be unsuccessful in doing something: *I failed my biology test.* | **fail to do sth** *Doctors failed to save the girl's life.* **2** [I] to not do what is expected or needed: **fail to do sth** *Her invitation failed to arrive.* **3** [T] to decide that someone has not passed a test or examination: *The examiner told me he was going to fail me.* **4 I fail to see/understand** used when you are annoyed by something that you do not accept or understand: *I fail to see why you think it's so funny.* **5** [I] if a bank or company fails, it cannot continue because it has no money **6** [I] if a machine or a part of someone's body fails, it stops working: *The engine failed just after the plane took off.* **7** [I] if a crop fails, it does not grow **8 failing health/sight/ memory etc** when your health, sight etc is becoming worse

fail² **without fail a)** if you do something without fail, you always do it: *Barry comes over every Friday without fail.* **b)** used to tell someone firmly that they must do something: *I want that work finished by tomorrow, without fail!*

fail·ing¹ /ˈfeɪlɪŋ/ *n* [C] a fault or weakness: *He loved her in spite of her failings.*

failing² *prep* **failing that** used to say that if one thing is not possible or available, there is another one you could try: *You could try phoning, but failing that, a letter only takes a few days.*

fail·ure /ˈfeɪljəl-ər/ *n* **1** [C,U] a lack of success in achieving or doing something: **end in failure** *All his plans ended in failure.* **2** [C] someone or something that is not successful: *I feel like such a failure.* **3** [C,U] when a machine or part of your body stops working properly: *the failure of the computer system* | **heart/kidney/ liver failure** (=when your heart etc stops working) **4 failure to do sth** the fact that someone has not done something they should have done: *We were worried about his failure to contact us.*

faint¹ /feɪnt/ *adj* **1** difficult to see, hear, or smell: *a faint sound* **2 a faint possibility/ chance/hope etc** a very small possibility etc: *There's still a faint hope that they might be alive.* **3** feeling weak and as if you are about to become unconscious: **+ with** *He was faint with hunger.* **4 not have the faintest idea** to not know anything at all about something: *I don't have the faintest idea what you are talking about.* —**faintly** *adv*

faint² *v* [I] to become unconscious for a short time —**faint** *n* [C]

fair¹ /feəlfer/ *adj* **1** reasonable and acceptable, according to what people usually think is right: *a fair wage for the job* | *It's not fair! You always agree with Sally!* **2 fair enough** *BrE spoken* used to say that you think something is reasonable: *"I'll come if I can bring my sister with me." "Fair enough."* **3** treating everyone in an equal or just way: *a fair trial* **4** neither particularly good nor particularly bad: *Her written work is excellent but her spoken French is only fair.* **5 a fair size/number/amount etc** *BrE* a fairly large size, number etc: *By lunchtime we had travelled a fair distance.* **6** fair hair or skin is light in colour **7** weather that is fair is pleasant and not windy or rainy —**fairness** *n* [U]

fair² *adv* **1 fair and square** in a fair and honest way: *They won fair and square.* **2 play fair** to play or behave in a fair and honest way

fair³ *n* [C] **1** an outdoor event, at which there are large machines to ride on and games to play **2** a regular event where companies show and advertise their products: *a trade fair*

fair·ground /ˈfeəgraʊnd||-fer-/ *n* [C] an open area of land on which a fair takes place

fair·ly /ˈfeəlil-ˈferli/ *adv* **1** more than a little, but much less than very; QUITE *BrE*: *She speaks English fairly well.* | *a fairly large garden* **2** in a way that is just or reasonable: *I felt that I hadn't been treated fairly.*

fai·ry /ˈfeəril-ˈferi/ *n* [C] an imaginary creature with magic powers, that looks like a small person with wings

fairy tale /ˈ.. ./ *n* [C] a story for children in which magical things happen

faith /feɪθ/ *n* **1** [U] a strong belief that you can trust someone or something to be right or to do the right thing: **+ in** *I have great faith in her ability.* **2 in good faith** if you do something in good faith, you do it believing it to be the honest or right thing to do **3** [U] belief and trust in God: **+ in** *a strong faith in God* **4** [C] a religion: *the Jewish faith*

faith·ful /ˈfeɪθfəl/ *adj* **1** remaining loyal to someone or something and continuing to support them: *a faithful friend* **2** describing an event or copying an image exactly: *a faithful account of what happened* **3** loyal to your wife, BOYFRIEND etc by not having a sexual relationship with anyone else: **+ to** *Have you always been faithful to your husband?* —**faithfulness** *n* [U]

faith·ful·ly /ˈfeɪθfəl-i/ *adv* **1** in a faithful way: *Bessie had served the family faithfully for 30 years.* **2** Yours faithfully *especially BrE* the usual polite way of ending a formal letter which begins Dear Sir or Dear Madam

faith·less /ˈfeɪθləs/ *adj formal* someone who is faithless cannot be trusted: *a faithless friend*

fake¹ /feɪk/ *n* [C] a copy of something valuable that is intended to deceive people: *We thought it was a Picasso, but it was a fake.*

fake² *adj* made to look like a real material or object in order to deceive people: *fake fur*

fake³ *v* **1** [I,T] to pretend to be ill, interested, pleased etc when you are not: **fake it** *I thought he was really hurt but he was just faking it.* **2** [T] to make an exact copy of something, or make up figures or results, in order to deceive people: *He faked his uncle's signature on the note.*

fal·con /ˈfɔːlkən‖ˈfæl-/ *n* [C] a large bird that hunts small animals or is trained to hunt them

fall¹ /fɔːl‖fɔːl/ *v* [I] **fell** /fel/, **fallen** /ˈfɔːlən‖ˈfɔːl-/, **falling** **1** to drop down towards the ground: *Snow began to fall as we left the building.* **| + over/from/out etc** *Our big apple tree fell over in the storm.* **2** to move accidentally down onto the ground when you are standing, walking, running etc: *Don't worry, I'll catch you if you fall.* **| + down/into/onto etc** *I slipped and fell down the stairs.* ➔ see colour picture on page 670 **3** to go down to a lower level or amount: *Temperatures may fall below zero tonight.* **| fall sharply** (=fall by a large amount): *The number of robberies fell sharply last year.* **4** fall asleep/ ill/silent etc to start to sleep, be ill etc: *I'm always tired; I even fall asleep in my chair.* | *Everyone fell silent as Beth walked in.* **5** fall in love to begin to love someone or something: **+ with** *I fell in love with her the moment I saw her.* **6** fall into a group/category etc to be part of a group of similar people or things: *Both of these novels fall into the category of literary fiction.* **7** fall short of to fail to achieve the result or standard you wanted: *The company fell short of its sales target this year.* **8** night/ darkness falls *literary* to become dark **9** if a leader or a government falls, they lose their power: *The government fell after only six months.* **10** be falling to pieces/bits to be in a very bad condition because of being very old **11** fall flat if something you say falls flat, people do not think it is funny, amusing, interesting etc: *Most of his jokes seemed to fall flat.* **12** to hang loosely: *Maria's hair fell in loose curls.* **13** *literary* to be killed in a war: *a monument to the soldiers who fell in the war* **14** fall on to happen on a particular day or date: *Christmas falls on a Friday this year.*

fall apart *phr v* [I] **1** to separate into small pieces: *The old book just fell apart in my hands.* **2** to stop working effectively: *The country's economy was falling apart.*

fall back on sth *phr v* [T] to use something that you have used before after something new has failed to work: *Theatres are falling back on old favourites rather than risking money on new plays.*

fall behind *phr v* [I,T **fall behind** sth] to not finish something by the time you are supposed to: *Work on the new sports stadium has fallen behind schedule.*

fall for sb/sth *phr v* [T] **1** [fall for sth] to be tricked into believing something that is not true: *We told him we were Italian and he fell for it!* **2** [fall for sb] to start to love someone you think is attractive: *Samantha fell for a man half her age.*

fall off *phr v* [I] to become less: *Demand for records has fallen off recently.*

fall out *phr v* [I] to have a quarrel: **+ with** *Nina's fallen out with her brother.*

fall through *phr v* [I] to fail to happen or be completed: *Our holiday plans fell through at the last minute.*

fall² *n* **1** [C] the act of falling: *He had a bad fall from a horse.* **2** [C] the amount of something that has fallen: *a heavy fall of snow* **3** [C] a decrease in the amount, level, or price of something: **+ in** *a sudden fall in temperature* ➔ opposite RISE¹ **4** [singular] *AmE* the season between summer and winter, when the weather becomes colder; AUTUMN: *Brad's going to Georgia Tech in the fall.* **5** [singular] a situation when someone or something is defeated or loses power: *the fall of Rome* ➔ see also FALLS

fal·la·cy /ˈfæləsi/ *n* [C] a false idea or belief: *the fallacy that money brings happiness*

fall·en /ˈfɔːlən‖ˈfɔːl-/ *v* the past participle of FALL

fall guy /ˈ. ./ *n* [C] *informal, especially AmE* someone who is punished for someone else's crime or mistake

fal·li·ble /ˈfæləbəl/ *adj* able to make a mistake: *We're all fallible, you know.* ➔ opposite INFALLIBLE

fall·out /ˈfɔːlaʊt‖ˈfɔːl-/ *adj* the RADIOACTIVE dust that is left in the air after a NUCLEAR explosion

fal·low /ˈfæləʊ‖-loʊ/ *adj* fallow land is left without any crops or farm animals on it

falls /fɔːlz‖fɔːlz/ *n* [plural] a WATERFALL in a large river

false /fɔːls‖fɒːls/ *adj* **1** not true or correct: *He gave the police false information.* **2** not real, but intended to seem real: *false eyelashes | false teeth* **3** not sincere or honest: *Her welcoming smile seemed false.* **4** false alarm a warning of something bad that does not happen: *We thought there was a fire, but it was a false alarm.* **5** false start an unsuccessful attempt to begin a process or event: *After several false starts, the show finally began.* **6** under false pretences if you get something under false PRETENCES, you get it by deceiving people —**falsely** *adv*

false·hood /ˈfɔːlshʊd‖ˈfɒːls-/ *n* [C] *formal* a statement that is not true

fal·set·to /fɔːlˈsetəʊ‖fɒːlˈsetoʊ/ *n* [C] a very high male voice —**falsetto** *adj, adv*

family

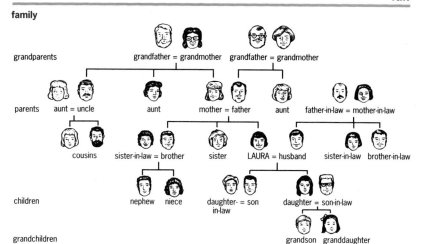

grandparents — grandfather = grandmother — grandfather = grandmother

parents — aunt = uncle — aunt — mother = father — aunt — father-in-law = mother-in-law

cousins — sister-in-law = brother — sister — LAURA = husband — sister-in-law — brother-in-law

children — nephew — niece — daughter-in-law = son — daughter = son-in-law

grandchildren — grandson — granddaughter

fal·si·fy / ˈfɔːlsɪˌfaɪ‖ˈfɔːl-/ *v* [T] to change a document, report etc so that it contains false information: *He was accused of falsifying the company's accounts.*

fal·ter / ˈfɔːltəl‖ˈfɔːltər/ *v* [I] **1** to become less confident or less determined: *His determination to succeed never faltered.* **2** to speak or move in a way that seems weak or uncertain: *She faltered for a moment.*

fame / feɪm/ *n* [U] when a lot of people know about you because of what you have achieved: *rise to fame Schiffer rose to fame as a model when she was only 17.* → see also **claim to fame** (CLAIM²)

famed / feɪmd/ *adj* known about by a lot of people: + **for** *mountains famed for their beauty*

fa·mil·i·ar / fəˈmɪliəl-ər/ *adj* **1** easy to recognize because you have seen or heard them before: *a familiar face*|**look/sound familiar** *The voice on the phone sounded very familiar.* **2 be familiar with sth** to know something well: *Are you familiar with this type of computer?* **3** being too friendly or informal towards someone: *I didn't like the familiar way he was talking to me.* —**familiarly** *adv*

fa·mil·i·ar·i·ty / fəˌmɪliˈærɪti/ *n* [U] **1** a good knowledge of something: + **with** *a familiarity with Russian poetry* **2** a feeling of being relaxed and comfortable because you are with people you know well

fa·mil·i·ar·ize (also **-ise** *BrE*) / fəˈmɪliəraɪz/ *v* **familiarize yourself with sth/familiarize someone with sth** to learn about or teach someone about something so that they know it well: *Familiarize yourself with the office routine.*

fam·i·ly / ˈfæməli/ *n* **1** [C] a group of people who are related to each other, especially parents and their children: *Do you know the family next*

door?|**run in the family** (=be common in a particular family): *Heart disease runs in our family.* **2** [C] children: **start a family** (=have children)|**bring up/raise a family** *the problems of bringing up a family of five* **3** [C] a group of things, especially animals or plants, that are related: *tigers and other members of the cat family*

family plan·ning / ˌ... ˈ../ *n* [U] when you use CONTRACEPTIVES to control the number of children you want

fam·ine / ˈfæmɪn/ *n* [C,U] a situation in which a large number of people have little or no food for a long time

fa·mous / ˈfeɪməs/ *adj* known about by a lot of people: *a famous actor*|+ **for** *France is famous for its wine.*

USAGE NOTE: famous

Compare **famous**, **well-known**, **notorious** and **infamous**. **Famous** is a stronger word than **well-known**, and it means that a great many people over a very wide area know who you are, what you do etc: *a famous movie star* | *She always wanted to be rich and famous.* You can be **well-known** within a smaller area: *a well-known figure in the town* | *He wants to go into local politics, but he's not very well-known.* **Notorious** means "famous for something bad": *a notorious drinker and gambler.* **Infamous** means the same as **notorious** when it is used before a noun: *an infamous criminal,* but it can also simply mean "evil or wicked": *his infamous cruelty.*

---

fa·mous·ly / ˈfeɪməsli/ *adv* **get on/along famously** to have a friendly relationship with someone

fan¹ / fæn/ *n* [C] **1** someone who likes a particular sport, kind of music etc very much, or

---

SPELLING NOTE
Words with the sound /f/ may be spelt **ph-**, like photograph.

who admires a famous person: *a football fan* | *He was a big fan of Elvis Presley.* **2** a machine, or a thing that you wave with your hand, that makes the air move so that you become less hot

fans

fan² *v* **-nned, -nning** [T] to make air move around by waving a fan, piece of paper etc: *She sat back, fanning herself with a newspaper.*
fan out *phr v* [I] if a group of people fan out, they move out from a central point in different directions: *The soldiers fanned out across the moor.*

fa·nat·ic /fə'nætɪk/ *n* [C] someone whose beliefs and behaviour are extreme, especially concerning religion or politics: *religious fanatics* | *a golf fanatic* —**fanatical** *adj* —**fanatically** /-kli/ *adv* —**fanaticism** /-t₁'sɪzəm/ *n* [U]

fan·cy¹ /'fænsi/ *adj* **1** special, unusual or having a lot of decoration **2** very expensive or high quality: *We can't afford such a fancy hotel.*

fancy² *v* [T] **1** *especially BrE* to like or want something: *Do you fancy a drink, Les?* **2** *BrE informal* to feel sexually attracted to someone: *I really fancy that guy.* **3** *literary* to believe that something is true: + **(that)** *Henry fancied he'd met her before somewhere.* **4** **fancy/fancy that!** *BrE spoken* used when you are surprised or shocked about something: *Fancy meeting you here!*

fancy³ *n* **1** [singular] a feeling that you would like something or someone: **take a fancy to** *I think Grant's taken a fancy to you!* **2** **take sb's fancy** *especially BrE* if something takes your fancy, you want to have it: *None of the cakes took my fancy.*

fancy dress /ˌ.. './ *n* [U] *BrE* unusual clothes that you wear for fun or for a party, that make you look like a different person

fan·fare /'fænfeə‖-fer/ *n* [C] a short piece of music played loudly on a TRUMPET to introduce an important person or event

fang /fæŋ/ *n* [C] a long sharp tooth of an animal such as a snake or dog

fan·ny /'fæni/ *n* [C] *AmE informal* the part of your body that you sit on; BOTTOM

fan·ta·size (also **-ise** *BrE*) /'fæntəsaɪz/ *v* [I,T] to imagine something strange or pleasant happening to you: + **(that)** *I used to fantasize that I was a famous dancer.* | + **about** *We all fantasize about winning the lottery.*

fan·tas·tic /fæn'tæstɪk/ *adj* **1** *informal* extremely good, attractive, enjoyable etc: *You look fantastic!* | *We had a fantastic holiday in New Orleans.* **2** *informal* a fantastic amount is very large: *She spends a fantastic amount on clothes.* **3** strange or unreal: *fantastic tales of knights and dragons* —**fantastically** /-kli/ *adv*

fan·ta·sy /'fæntəsi/ *n* [C,U] an experience or situation that you imagine but is not real: *I had fantasies about becoming a racing driver.*

FAQ /ˌef eɪ 'kjuː/ *n* [C] frequently asked questions; a list of answers to the questions that are most often asked by members of a group of people who discuss a subject together on the Internet

far¹ /fɑː‖fɑːr/ *adv* **farther** /'fɑːðə‖'fɑːrðər/, **farthest** /'fɑːðɪst‖'fɑːr-/, *or* **further** /'fɜːðə‖ 'fɜːrðər/, **furthest** /'fɜːðɪst‖'fɜːr-/ **1** a long distance: *I don't want to drive very far.* | *Let's see who can swim the farthest.* | **how far** (=what is the distance): *How far is it to the station?* | **far away** *I don't see my brother very often – he lives too far away.* **2** very much: **far better/far more intelligent etc** *Our new car is far better than the old one.* | **far too much/fat/early etc** *You can't carry that box – it's far too heavy.* | **by far** *The girls' exam results were better by far than the boys'.* **3** a long time: *stories from far back in the past* | *We worked far into the night.* **4 as far as I know** *spoken* used to say that you think something is true, but you may be wrong because you do not know all the facts: *As far as I know, Fran intends to come to the party.* **5 far from a)** instead of: **far from doing sth** *Far from helping the situation, you've made it worse.* **b)** not at all: **far from happy/pleased etc** *Peter looked far from happy.* | **far from it** *"Did you enjoy the film?" "Far from it – I went to sleep!"* **6 so far** until now: *We haven't had any problems so far.* **7 how far** used to talk about the degree to which something is true: *How far is violent crime caused by violence on TV?* **8 so far so good** *spoken* used to say that you are satisfied with the way a situation or activity has been happening or developing: *"How's your new job?" "So far so good."* **9 sb will/should go far** used to say that you think someone will be successful: *She's a good dancer and should go far.* **10 as far as possible** as much as possible: *We try to buy from local businesses as far as possible.* **11 go so far as to do sth** to do something that seems surprising or extreme: *He even went so far as to call her a liar.* **12 go too far** to do something so much that you annoy or upset people: *He's always been rude, but this time he went too far.* **13 not go (very) far** if something, especially money, does not go far, there is not enough of it for your needs : *A dollar doesn't go very far these days.*
➝ see also **as far as sb is concerned** (CONCERNED)

USAGE NOTE: far

You can use **far** to talk about distances in questions and negatives: *How far is the hotel?* | *It's not very far.* You can also use **far** after **too**, **as** and **so**: *We won't get there in a day – it's too far.* | *I carried it as far as I could.* | *He swam out so far that the others started to get worried.* Don't use **far** with ordinary statements, however – ie, don't say "It is far to the hotel". Instead use **a long way** or **a long distance**: *He walked a long way.* | *It's a long way from the station to the gallery.* | *My house is quite a long distance from the stadium.*

---

far² *adj* **farther, farthest,** *or* **further, furthest**
1 a long way away from something else: *We can walk if it's not far.* ➝ see picture at NEAR **2** [only before noun] most distant from where

you are: *the far side of the room* **3 the far left/ right** people who have political opinions that are much more extreme than those of most people **4 be a far cry from** to be very different from something else: *Europe was a far cry from what Tom had expected.*

far·a·way /ˈfɑːrəweɪ/ *adj* **1** [only before noun] *literary* distant: *faraway places* **2 faraway look** an expression on your face that shows that you are not thinking about what is around you

farce /fɑːs‖fɑːrs/ *n* **1** [singular] an event or situation that is badly organized: *I'm telling you, the trial was a total farce.* **2** [C] a humorous play in which a lot of silly things happen —**farcical** *adj*

fare[1] /feə‖fer/ *n* [C] the price you pay to travel by train, plane, bus etc: *Train fares are going up again.*

fare[2] *v* [I] *formal* **fare well/badly etc** to be successful, unsuccessful etc in a particular situation: *Women are now faring better in politics.*

fare·well /feəˈwel‖fer-/ *n* [C] *formal* goodbye: *We made our farewells and left.* | *a farewell party*

far-fetched /ˌ. ˈ.◂/ *adj* not likely to be true: *I thought her story was pretty far-fetched.*

farm[1] /fɑːm‖fɑːrm/ *n* [C] an area of land used for keeping animals or growing food: *The farm is about 4000 acres.*

farm[2] *v* [I,T] to use land for growing crops and keeping animals: *Our family has farmed here for years.*

farm·er /ˈfɑːmə‖ˈfɑːrmər/ *n* [C] someone who owns or manages a farm

farm·hand /ˈfɑːmhænd‖ˈfɑːrm-/ *n* [C] someone who is employed to work on a farm

farm·house /ˈfɑːmhaʊs‖ˈfɑːrm-/ *n* [C] the main house on a farm, where the farmer lives

farm·ing /ˈfɑːmɪŋ‖ˈfɑːrmɪŋ/ *n* [U] the practice or business of keeping animals or growing crops on a farm

farm·yard /ˈfɑːmjɑːd‖ˈfɑːrmjɑːrd/ *n* [C] the area next to or around farm buildings

far-off /ˌ. ˈ.◂/ *adj literary* a long distance away or a long time ago: *a far-off land*

far-reach·ing /ˌ. ˈ.◂/ *adj* having a big influence or effect: *far-reaching tax reforms*

far·sight·ed /ˌfɑːˈsaɪtɪd◂‖ˌfɑːr-/ *adj* **1** able to understand how a situation will develop and therefore skilful at making wise decisions: *a farsighted economic plan* **2** *AmE* able to see or read things clearly only when they are far from your eyes; LONGSIGHTED *BrE*

fart /fɑːt‖fɑːrt/ *v* [I] *informal* an impolite word meaning to make air come out of your BOWELS —**fart** *n* [C]

far·ther /ˈfɑːðə‖ˈfɑːrðər/ *adj, adv* the COMPARATIVE form of FAR → compare FURTHER[1]

USAGE NOTE: farther and further

Use **farther** to talk about distances: *The bar's just a little farther down the street.* Use **further** to talk about time, quantities, or degrees: *House prices will probably drop further next year.* | *I don't want to discuss this any further.* People often use **further** about distance, although sometimes this is considered to be incorrect.

---

far·thest /ˈfɑːðɪst‖ˈfɑːr-/ *adv, adj* the SUPERLATIVE form of FAR

fas·ci·nate /ˈfæsɪneɪt/ *v* [T] to attract or interest someone very much: *Mechanical things have always fascinated me.*

fas·ci·nat·ing /ˈfæsɪneɪtɪŋ/ *adj* extremely interesting, especially because you are learning something new: *a fascinating subject*

fas·ci·na·tion /ˌfæsɪˈneɪʃən/ *n* [singular, U] the state of being very interested in something: + **with** *a fascination with the supernatural*

fas·cis·m /ˈfæʃɪzəm/ *n* [U] an extreme RIGHTWING political system in which people's lives are completely controlled by the state

fas·cist /ˈfæʃɪst/ *n* [C] **1** someone who supports fascism **2** someone who is cruel and unfair: *My headteacher was a real fascist.* —**fascist** *adj*

fash·ion[1] /ˈfæʃən/ *n* **1** [C,U] the style of clothes, hair, behaviour etc that is popular at a particular time: **be in fashion** *Hats are in fashion again.* | **go out of fashion** (=stop being popular): *Shoes like that went out of fashion years ago.* | **the latest fashion** *Gabi always buys all the latest fashions.* **2** [U] the activity of making or selling clothes **3 in a ... fashion** *formal* in a particular way: *Leave the building in an orderly fashion.*

fashion[2] *v* [T] *formal* to shape or make something with your hands or a few tools: *He fashioned a turban out of a torn piece of cloth.*

fash·ion·a·ble /ˈfæʃənəbəl/ *adj* something that is fashionable is popular or thought to be good at a particular time: *Long skirts are fashionable now.* | *In Japan it's fashionable to give products English names.* | **fashionable restaurant/shop/ area etc** (=one that a lot of people go to) → opposite UNFASHIONABLE, OLD-FASHIONED —**fashionably** *adv*

fast[1] /fɑːst‖fæst/ *adj* **1** moving, happening, or done quickly: *a fast runner* | *a fast car* | *The metro is the fastest way to get around.* **2** [not before noun] a clock that is fast shows a time that is later than the real time: *Is it really 5 o'clock, or is your watch fast?* **3 fast track** a way of achieving something more quickly than it is normally done: **on the fast track (for)** *young professionals on the fast track for promotion* **4 make sth fast** to tie something such as a boat or tent firmly to something else

fast[2] *adv* **1** moving or happening quickly: *Stop driving so fast!* | *You're learning fast.* **2 fast asleep** completely asleep **3** firmly or tightly: **be stuck fast** *The boat's stuck fast in the mud.* | **hold sb/sth fast** *Rudi began to fall, but the rope held him fast.*

fast[3] *v* [I] to eat nothing or less than usual for a period of time, especially for religious reasons: *Many Christians fast during Lent.* —**fast** *n* [C]

fas·ten /ˈfɑːsən‖ˈfæ-/ *v* **1** [I,T] to join together the two sides of something so that it is closed, or to become joined together: *Fasten your seat belts.* | *Can you fasten my necklace for me?* | *I'm too fat. My skirt won't fasten.* **2** [T] to attach something firmly to another object or surface: **fasten sth to/onto sth** *Fasten those ladders onto the roof before you climb up there.* **3** [T] to close and lock a window, gate etc

fas·ten·er /ˈfɑːsənə‖ˈfæsənər/ *n* [C] *BrE* something such as a button, pin, or ZIP that you use to join two parts of something together

F

fasteners

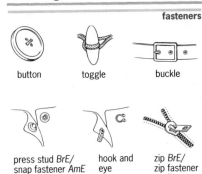

button   toggle   buckle

press stud *BrE*/   hook and   zip *BrE*/
snap fastener *AmE*   eye   zip fastener
   AmE

fas·ten·ing /ˈfɑːsənɪŋ‖ˈfæ-/ *n* [C] something
you use to hold another thing shut

fast food /ˈ. ./ *n* [U] hot food such as
HAMBURGERS, that a restaurant cooks and serves
quickly to customers

fast-for·ward /ˌ. ˈ../ *v* [I,T] if you fast-forward a
TAPE or VIDEO TAPE, you wind it forward quickly
without playing it —**fast forward** *n* [U]

fas·tid·i·ous /fæˈstɪdiəs/ *adj* careful or paying
a lot of attention to small details, especially in
your appearance or work —**fastidiousness** *n* [U]
—**fastidiously** *adv*

fat¹ /fæt/ *adj* **1** weighing too much: *Chris is
worried about getting fat.* **2** thick or wide: *a big
fat cigar* **3** **fat chance** *spoken* used to say that
something is very unlikely to happen: *What,
Max get a job? Fat chance!* **4** **a fat lot of good/
use etc** *BrE spoken* not at all useful or helpful:
Well, you've been a fat lot of help.

USAGE NOTE: fat

If you want to be polite about someone, do not
say that they are **fat**. **(A little) overweight** or
large is a more polite way of saying the same
thing. In American English, you can also use **heavy**. **Plump** is most often used about women and
children, and means 'pleasantly fat'. If someone is
fat in a way that badly affects their health, the
word is **obese**, which is the word most often
used by doctors to describe the condition of
being fat.

---

fat² *n* **1** [U] the substance under the skin of
people and animals which helps to keep them
warm **2** [C,U] a substance contained in foods
such as milk, cheese, butter etc **3** [C,U] a thick
oily substance taken from animals or plants and
used in cooking: *Fry the potatoes in oil or vegetable fat.*

fa·tal /ˈfeɪtl/ *adj* **1** resulting in someone's
death: *Meningitis can often be fatal.* | **fatal
accident/injury/illness etc** *a fatal heart attack*
2 having a very bad effect: *fatal mistake Her
fatal mistake was to marry the wrong man.* —**fa-
tally** *adv*

fa·tal·i·ty /fəˈtælɨti/ *n* [C] a death caused by an
accident or violent attack

fate /feɪt/ *n* **1** [C singular] the things, usually
bad or serious things, that happen to someone :
No one knows what the fate of the refugees will

be. **2** [U] a power that is believed to control
what happens in people's lives: *Fate brought us
together.* | **by a twist of fate** (=in an unexpected
way): *By a strange twist of fate, we were on the
same plane.*

fat·ed /ˈfeɪtɨd/ *adj* [not before noun] certain to
happen or to do something because a mysterious
force is controlling events: **fated to do sth** *We
were fated to meet.*

fate·ful /ˈfeɪtfəl/ *adj* having an important, usually bad, effect on future events: *a fateful decision* —**fatefully** *adv*

fat-free /ˌ. ˈ./ *adj* containing no fat: *a fat-free
diet*

fa·ther¹ /ˈfɑːðə‖-ər/ *n* [C] **1** your male parent
➔ see picture at FAMILY **2** **Father** a title given
to a priest, especially in the Roman Catholic
Church: *Do you know Father Vernon?*

father² *v* [T] to become a male parent: *his desire
to father a child*

Father Christ·mas /ˌ.. ˈ../ *n* [singular] *BrE* an
old man with a red coat and white BEARD who,
children believe, brings them presents at Christmas; SANTA CLAUS

father fig·ure /ˈ.. ˌ../ *n* [C] an older man who
you trust and respect

fa·ther·hood /ˈfɑːðəhʊd‖-ðər-/ *n* [U] the state
of being a father

father-in-law /ˈ.. . ˌ./ *n* [C] the father of your
husband or wife ➔ see picture at FAMILY

fa·ther·ly /ˈfɑːðəli‖-ðər-/ *adj* typical of a kind
or concerned father: *He put a fatherly arm
around her shoulders.*

fath·om¹ /ˈfæðəm/ *v* [T] also **fathom out** to
understand what something means after thinking about it carefully: *I just couldn't fathom out
what she meant.*

fathom² *n* [C] a unit for measuring how deep
water is, equal to 1.83 metres

fa·tigue /fəˈtiːɡ/ *n* [U] **1** extreme tiredness:
They were cold, and weak with fatigue.
2 *technical* weakness in a substance such as
metal that may cause it to break

fat·ten /ˈfætn/ *v* [T] to make an animal become
fatter so that it is ready to eat
   fatten sb/sth up *phr v* [T] to make a thin
person or animal fatter: *Grandma always
thinks I need to be fattened up.*

fat·ten·ing /ˈfætn-ɪŋ/ *adj* likely to make you
fat: *Avoid fattening foods like cakes and chocolate.*

fat·ty /ˈfæti/ *adj* containing a lot of fat: *fatty
food*

fat·u·ous /ˈfætʃuəs/ *adj* very silly or stupid: *a
fatuous remark*

fau·cet /ˈfɔːsɨt‖ˈfɒː-/ *n* [C] *AmE* something
that you turn on or off in order to control the
flow of water from a pipe; TAP *BrE*

fault¹ /fɔːlt‖fɒːlt/ *n* **1** **be sb's fault** to be responsible for a mistake or for something bad
that has happened: *It's not my fault we missed the
bus.* | **it's sb's own fault** *It was her own fault she
failed the exam. She didn't do any work.* | **be at
fault** *It was the other driver who was at fault.*
2 [C] a problem with something that stops it
working correctly: *an electrical fault* **3** **find
fault with** to look for things that are wrong with
something or someone in order to complain
about them: *Why do you always have to find fault*

with my work? **4** [C] something that is wrong or not perfect in someone's character: *His only fault is that he has no sense of humour.* **5** [C] a large crack in the rocks that form the Earth's surface: *the San Andreas fault*

fault² *v* [T] to find a mistake in something: *Her performance couldn't be faulted.*

fault·less /'fɔːltləs‖'fɒːlt-/ *adj* having no mistakes; perfect: *Yasmin spoke faultless French.*

fault·y /'fɔːltiɪ‖'fɒːlti/ *adj* **1** not working properly: *faulty wiring* **2** not correct: *faulty reasoning*

fau·na /'fɔːnəl‖'fɒː-/ *n* [C,U] technical all the animals living in a particular place → compare FLORA

faux pas /ˌfəʊ 'pɑː, ˌfəʊ pɑː‖ˌfoʊ-/ *n* [C] something you say or do which offends people because it is socially unacceptable

fa·vour¹ *BrE*, **favor** *AmE* /'feɪvəll-ər/ *n* **1** [C] something you do for someone to help them or be kind to them: **do sb a favour** *Could you do me a favour and look after the kids for an hour?* | **ask sb a favour/ask a favour of sb** (=ask someone to do something for you) **2** **be in favour of sth** to agree with and support a plan, idea, or system: *Are you in favour of the death penalty?* **3** [U] **in favour/out of favour** if someone or something is in favour, people like them and approve of them. If someone or something is out of favour, people do not like them or approve of them: *Traditional teaching methods are back in favour.* **4** **in sb's/sth's favour a)** if something is in someone's favour, it is likely to help them win or succeed: *The conditions are in our favour.* **b)** if a game, vote etc ends in someone's favour, they win: *The vote was 60-40 in his favour.* **c)** if a court or official group decision is in someone's favour, it decides that they are right: *The Supreme Court decided in his favour.* **5** **in favour of sth** if you refuse one thing in favour of something else, you decide to use the second thing: *Plans for a tunnel were rejected in favour of the bridge.*

favour² *BrE*, **favor** *AmE* — *v* [T] **1** to prefer one thing more than other choices: *Congress favors financial help to universities.* **2** to unfairly treat one person or group better than another: *tax cuts that favour the rich*

fa·vou·ra·ble *BrE*, **favorable** *AmE* /'feɪvərəbəl/ *adj* **1** showing that you like or approve of someone or something: *I've heard favourable reports about your work.* | **make a favourable impression** *Try to make a favourable impression on my mother.* **2** likely to make something happen or succeed: *a favourable economic climate* — **favourably** *adv* → opposite UN-FAVOURABLE

fa·vou·rite¹ *BrE*, **favorite** *AmE* /'feɪvərɪt/ *adj* [only before noun] liked more than others of the same kind: *Who's your favourite actor?*

favourite² *BrE*, **favorite** *AmE* — *n* [C] **1** someone or something that you like more than any other one of its kind: *I like all her books, but this one is my favourite.* **2** someone

who receives more attention and approval than is fair: *Teachers shouldn't have favourites.* **3** the team, runner etc that is expected to win a competition: *The Yankees are favorites to win the World Series.*

fa·vou·ri·tis·m *BrE*, **favoritism** *AmE* /'feɪvərɪtɪzəm/ *n* [U] when one person or group is unfairly treated better than another

fawn¹ /fɔːn‖fɒːn/ *v*
fawn on/over sb *phr v* [T] to praise someone and be friendly to them because you want something

fawn² *n* **1** [C] a young DEER **2** [U] a light yellow brown colour

fax machine

fax /fæks/ *n* **1 a)** [C] a document that is sent down a telephone line and then printed using a special machine: *Did you get my fax?* **b)** [U] the system of sending documents this way: *a letter sent by fax* **2** [C] also **fax machine** a machine used for sending and receiving faxes —**fax** *v* [T]

FBI /ˌef biː 'aɪ/ *n* **the FBI** the Federal Bureau of Investigation; the US police department that is controlled by the government and is concerned with FEDERAL law

fear¹ /fɪəll fɪr/ *n* **1** [C,U] the feeling you get when you are afraid or worried that something bad will happen: **+ of** *a fear of flying* | **in fear of** *The citizens of the town live in fear of enemy attack.* | **+ that** *fears that the rapist might strike again* | **+ for** *fears for our children's safety* **2** **for fear of/for fear that** because you are worried that you will make something happen: *She kept quiet, for fear of saying the wrong thing.* **3 No fear!** *spoken* used when answering someone's question, to say that you are definitely not going to do something or definitely do not want something to happen

fear² *v* **1** [T] to feel afraid or worried that something bad will happen: *Fearing a snowstorm, many people stayed home.* | **(that)** *Experts fear there may be more cases of the disease.* **2** [T] to be afraid of someone: *a dictator feared by his country* **3 fear for** to be worried about someone who may be in danger: *We left the country because we feared for our lives.*

GRAMMAR NOTE: a or the (2)
Use **the** before a thing or person when it is clear which one you are talking about: *the old man who lives next door.* Use **a** or **an** to talk about a person or thing when it is not important to say which one: *I went out to buy a newspaper.* | *A girl in my class told me about it.*

fear·ful /ˈfɪəfəl‖ˈfɪr-/ *adj formal* **1** afraid: *fearful of doing sth He said no more, fearful of upsetting her.* **2** *BrE* very bad: *The small kitchen was in a fearful mess.* —**fearfully** *adv*

fear·less /ˈfɪələs‖ˈfɪr-/ *adj* not afraid of anything: *a fearless soldier* —**fearlessly** *adv* —**fearlessness** *n* [U]

fear·some /ˈfɪəsəm‖ˈfɪr-/ *adj* very frightening: *a fearsome sight*

fea·si·ble /ˈfiːzɪbəl/ *adj* possible, and likely to work: *Your plan sounds quite feasible.*

feast¹ /fiːst/ *n* [C] **1** a large meal for a lot of people to celebrate a special occasion: *a wedding feast* **2** *informal* a big meal: *That was a real feast!* **3** a religious holiday

feast² *v* **1** [I] to eat a large meal to celebrate something **2** **feast your eyes on** to look at something for a long time because you like it

feat /fiːt/ *n* [C] something that someone does that shows a lot of strength or skill: *an amazing feat of engineering* | **be no mean feat** (=be difficult to do): *Getting a doctorate is no mean feat!*

fea·ther¹ /ˈfeðə‖-ər/ *n* [C] one of the light soft things that covers a bird's body

feather

feather² *v* [T] **feather your nest** to make yourself rich by dishonest methods

feath·er·y /ˈfeðəri/ *adj* soft and light like feathers: *a fern with delicate feathery leaves*

fea·ture¹ /ˈfiːtʃə‖-ər/ *n* [C] **1** an important, interesting, or typical part of something: *a report that compares the safety features of new cars* **2** [usually plural] a part of someone's face, such as their eyes, nose etc: *a portrait showing her fine delicate features* **3** a piece of writing in a newspaper or a programme about someone or something: *Have you read the feature on Johnny Depp in today's paper?*

feature² *v* **1** [T] if a film, magazine, show etc features someone, they have an important part in it: *a new movie featuring Meryl Streep* **2** [I] to be an important part of something: + *in Violence seems to feature heavily in all his stories.*

feature film /ˈ.. ˌ./ *n* [C] a film made for the cinema, not a television programme or a short film

Feb·ru·a·ry /ˈfebruəri, ˈfebjuri‖ˈfebjueri/ *written abbreviation* **Feb** *n* [C,U] the second month of the year

fe·ces /ˈfiːsiːz/ the American spelling of FAECES

fed /fed/ *v* the past tense and past participle of FEED

fed·e·ral /ˈfedərəl/ *adj* **1** relating to the national government of a country, such as the US, which consists of several states: *federal laws* **2** consisting of a group of states that are controlled by a central government: *the Federal Republic of Germany*

Federal Bu·reau of In·ves·ti·ga·tion /ˌ... ˌ.. ˌ...ˈ../ *n* [singular] the FBI

fed·e·ra·tion /ˌfedəˈreɪʃən/ *n* [C] a large organization that consists of countries or smaller organizations: *the International Boxing Federation*

fed up /ˌ. ˈ./ *adj* [not before noun] *informal* annoyed, bored, or unhappy: + **with** *She was fed up with being treated like a servant.*

fee /fiː/ *n* [C] an amount of money that you pay for professional services or that you pay to do something: *medical fees | college fees | an entrance fee* (=payment to enter a place)

fee·ble /ˈfiːbəl/ *adj* **1** extremely weak: *His voice sounded feeble.* **2** a feeble joke, excuse etc is not very good and is not funny or believable

feed¹ /fiːd/ *v* **fed** /fed/, **fed, feeding 1** [T] to give food to a person or animal: *Have you fed the cats?* **2** [I] if animals or babies feed, they eat: + **on** *Hippos feed mainly on grass.* **3** [T] to provide enough food for a group of people: *How can you feed a family on $50 a week?* **4** [T] to put information into a computer **5** [T] to give someone false information: *People get fed all kinds of lies by the media.*

feed² *n* **1** [U] food for animals: *cattle feed* **2** [C] *BrE* milk or food that you give to a baby: *Has he had his feed yet?*

feed·back /ˈfiːdbæk/ *n* [U] advice or criticism about something you have done or made telling you how good or useful it is: *The teacher's been giving us helpful feedback.*

feel¹ /fiːl/ *v* **felt** /felt/, **felt, feeling 1** [linking verb] to have a feeling or emotion, for example when you are happy, hungry, cold etc: *I feel really hot – can someone open the window? | Neal felt sad when she'd gone. | We were feeling tired after the long journey.* | + **as if/as though** *I felt as though I'd won a million dollars.* **2** [linking verb] used to say how something seems to you: **it feels** *It feels great to be back home. | How does it feel to be married?* | **it feels like** *I was only there for a couple of hours, but it felt like a week.* | **sth feels** *Her skin felt cold.* **3** [I,T] to have an opinion based on your feelings rather than on facts: + **(that)** *I feel that I should do more to help.* | + **about** *What does Michael feel about the idea?* | **feel sure/certain** *We felt certain that something terrible would happen* | **feel strongly about** (=have strong opinions): *A lot of people feel very strongly about the issue of abortion.* **4** [T] to touch something with your fingers in order to find out what it is like: *Feel my forehead. Does it seem hot?* **5** **feel around/inside etc (for sth)** to try to find something by using your fingers: *He felt around in his pocket for his keys.* **6** [T] to notice something touching you: *She felt something crawling up her leg.* **7** **feel like** sth to want to eat, drink, or do something: *Do you feel like anything more to eat?* **8** to experience the good or bad results of something: *Companies are starting to feel the effects of the strike.* **9** **feel your way a)** to move carefully with your hands out in front of you because you cannot see well: *He felt his way along the dark passage.* **b)** to do things slowly and carefully, because you are unsure about a new situation ➔ see also **be/feel sorry for sb** (SORRY)

feel for sb/sth *phr v* [T] to feel sympathy for someone: *I really feel for you, Joel, but I don't know what to suggest.*

feel² *n* [singular] **1** the way something feels when you touch it: *the feel of the sand under our feet* **2** the way that something seems to people: *The music has a sort of jazzy feel to it.* **3** **have a feel for** *informal* to have a natural ability to do something: *Pete has a real feel for languages.* **4 get the feel of sth** *informal* to start to feel confident about using something or doing something: *a car that's easy to drive, once you get the feel of it*

feel·ers /ˈfiːləz‖-ərz/ *n* [plural] the two long things on an insect's head that it uses to feel or touch things

feel·ing /ˈfiːlɪŋ/ *n* **1** [C] something that you feel in your mind or body: *feelings of shame and guilt | a sudden feeling of tiredness | It was a wonderful feeling to be home again. | Don't try to hide your feelings.* **2** [C] your opinion or attitude: *My own feeling is that we should wait. | +* **about** *Have you asked Carol what her feelings are about having children?* **3 have/get a feeling (that)** to think that something is probably true or will probably happen: *I had a feeling that he'd refuse. | Do you ever get the feeling that you are being watched?* **4** [U] the ability to feel pain, heat, cold etc in your body: *He lost all feeling in his legs.* **5 bad/ill feeling** anger or lack of trust between people: *The divorce caused a lot of bad feeling between them,* **6** [U] sympathy or an ability to understand the emotion expressed in music, poetry etc: *She plays the violin with great feeling.* ➜ see also **gut feeling** (GUT[1]), **hurt sb's feelings** (HURT[1])

feet /fiːt/ *n* the plural of FOOT

feign /feɪn/ *v* [T] *literary* to pretend: *Feigning a headache, I went upstairs to my room.*

feist·y /ˈfaɪsti/ *adj* having a strong determined character and a lot of energy: *a big feisty woman with short red hair*

fe·line /ˈfiːlaɪn/ *adj* like a cat or relating to a cat

fell[1] /fel/ *v* the past tense of FALL

fell[2] *v* [T] **1** to cut down a tree **2** to knock someone down

fel·low[1] /ˈfeləʊ‖-loʊ/ *n* [C] **1** *old-fashioned* a man: *What a strange fellow he is!* **2** *BrE* a member of an important society or college: *a Fellow of the Royal College of Surgeons*

fellow[2] *adj* **fellow workers/students/ passengers etc** people who work, study, travel etc with you

fel·low·ship /ˈfeləʊʃɪp‖-loʊ-/ *n* **1** [U] a feeling of friendship that people have because they share the same interests **2** [C] a group of people with the same beliefs or interests, who have meetings together: *a Christian youth fellowship* **3** [C] a job in a university that includes detailed study of a subject and teaching

fel·on /ˈfelən/ *n* [C] *law* a criminal who is guilty of a serious crime : *a convicted felon*

fel·o·ny /ˈfeləni/ *n* [C,U] *law* a serious crime such as murder

felt[1] /felt/ *v* the past tense and past participle of FEEL

felt[2] *n* [U] a soft thick cloth made from wool or other material that has been pressed flat

felt tip pen /ˌ. ˈ. ./ also **felt tip** /ˈ. ./ *BrE n* [C] a pen that has a hard piece of felt at the end that the ink comes through

fe·male[1] /ˈfiːmeɪl/ *adj* **1** belonging to the sex that can have babies or produce eggs: *a female monkey | female workers | the female sex* **2** a female plant or flower produces fruit

female[2] *n* [C] a person or animal that belongs to the sex that can have babies or produce eggs

fem·i·nine /ˈfemɪnˑn/ *adj* **1** having qualities that are thought to be typical of women: *feminine clothes* **2** belonging to a group of nouns, adjectives etc in some languages that is different from the MASCULINE and NEUTER groups. In English grammar, feminine nouns and PRONOUNS are ones that mean female people or animals. ➜ compare MASCULINE

fem·i·nin·i·ty /ˌfemɪˈnɪnˑti/ *n* [U] qualities that are thought to be typical of women

fem·i·nis·m /ˈfemɪnɪzəm/ *n* [U] the belief that women should have the same rights and opportunities as men —**feminist** *n, adj: a feminist writer | militant feminists*

fe·mur /ˈfiːməⁱ-ər/ *n* [C] *technical* the large bone in the top part of your leg; THIGH bone

fence[1] /fens/ *n* [C] **1** a line of upright wooden posts with wire or wood between, used to divide or enclose an area of land: *the garden fence* ➜ see colour picture on page 79 **2** *informal* someone who buys and sells stolen goods

fence[2] *v* [I] to fight with a sword as a sport

fence sth ↔ in *phr v* [T] to surround a place with a fence

fence sb/sth ↔ off *phr v* [T] to separate one area from another with a fence: *We fenced off part of the field.*

fenc·ing /ˈfensɪŋ/ *n* [U] **1** a sport in which people fight with long thin swords **2** fences, or the material used to make them

fend /fend/ *v* **fend for yourself** to look after yourself without help from other people: *Now that the kids are old enough to fend for themselves, we're free to travel more.*

fend sb/sth ↔ off *phr v* [T] **1** to defend yourself from an attack: *She managed to fend off her attacker.* **2** to avoid criticism or a difficult question: *Henry did his best to fend off questions about his private life.*

fend·er /ˈfendə‖-ər/ *n* [C] **1** *AmE* the part of a car that covers the wheels ➜ see picture at CAR **2** *BrE* a low wall or bar around a FIREPLACE to prevent wood or coal from falling out

fer·ment[1] /fəˈment‖fər-/ *v* [I,T] if fruit, wine etc ferments or is fermented, the sugar in it changes to alcohol —**fermentation** /ˌfɜːmenˈteɪʃən‖ˌfɜːrmən-/ *n* [U]

fer·ment[2] /ˈfɜːment‖ˈfɜːr-/ *n* [U] excitement or trouble in a country, caused especially by political change: *Russia was in a state of political ferment.*

fern /fɜːn‖fɜːrn/ *n* [C] a plant with green leaves shaped like large feathers, but no flowers

fe·ro·cious /fəˈrəʊʃəs‖-ˈroʊ-/ *adj* extremely violent and angry: *a ferocious-looking dog | a ferocious battle* —**ferociously** *adv*

fe·ro·ci·ty /fəˈrɒsˑti‖fəˈrɑː-/ *n* [U] extreme violence: *Felipe was shocked by the ferocity of her anger.*

fer·ret[1] /ˈferˑt/ *v*

ferret sth ↔ out *phr v* [T] *informal* to succeed in finding something, especially information: *She finally managed to ferret out the truth.*

ferret[2] *n* [C] a small animal, used for hunting rats and rabbits

fer·rous /ˈferəs/ *adj* *technical* containing iron: *ferrous metals*

fer·ry[1] /ˈferi/ *n* [C] a boat that regularly carries people, often with their cars, across a narrow area of water → see colour picture on page 669

ferry² v [T] to regularly carry people or goods a short distance from one place to another: *a bus that ferries tourists from the hotel to the beach*

fer·tile /ˈfɜːtaɪlǁˈfɜːrtl/ *adj* **1** fertile land or soil produces plenty of good crops **2** someone who is fertile is able to produce babies → opposite INFERTILE **3 fertile imagination** *often humorous* someone who has a fertile imagination is good at thinking of original and unusual ideas —**fertility** /fɜːˈtɪlɪtiǁfɜːr-/ *n* [U]

fer·ti·lize (also **-ise** *BrE*) /ˈfɜːtɪlaɪzǁˈfɜːrtl-aɪz/ *v* [T] **1** *technical* if an egg is fertilized, the egg and a SPERM join together so that a new animal or baby can start to develop: *a fertilized embryo* **2** to put fertilizer on the soil to help plants grow —**fertilization** /ˌfɜːtɪlaɪˈzeɪʃənǁˌfɜːrtl-ə-/ *n* [U]

fer·ti·liz·er /ˈfɜːtɪlaɪzəǁˈfɜːrtl-aɪzər/ *n* [C,U] a chemical or natural substance that you put on the soil to help plants grow

fer·vent /ˈfɜːvəntǁˈfɜːr-/ *adj* believing or feeling something very strongly: *a fervent anti-communist* —**fervently** *adv*

fer·vour *BrE*, **fervor** *AmE* /ˈfɜːvəǁˈfɜːrvər/ *n* [U] very strong belief or feeling: *religious fervour*

fest /fest/ *n* **beer/song/food fest etc** *AmE* an informal occasion when a lot of people drink, sing, or eat together

fes·ter /ˈfestəǁ-ər/ *v* [I] **1** if a bad situation or a problem festers, it continues to get worse and become more unpleasant over a long period: *centuries of festering anger and bitterness* **2** if a wound festers, it becomes infected

fes·ti·val /ˈfestɪvəl/ *n* [C] **1** a time when people celebrate something, especially a religious holiday: *The main Christian festivals are Christmas and Easter.* **2** an occasion when there are a lot of concerts, films, or performances, which happens in the same place every year: *the Cannes film festival*

fes·tive /ˈfestɪv/ *adj* happy or cheerful because people are celebrating something: *Christmas is often called "the festive season".*

fes·tiv·i·ty /feˈstɪvɪti/ *n* **1 festivities** [plural] things that people do to celebrate such as dancing, eating, and drinking **2** [U] when people are celebrating happily: *The town enjoyed five days of festivities.*

fes·toon /feˈstuːn/ *v* [T] to cover something with long pieces of cloth, flowers etc as a decoration: *The streets were festooned with flags.*

fe·tal /ˈfiːtl/ the American spelling of FOETAL (FOETUS)

fetch /fetʃ/ *v* [T] **1** to go and get something or someone and bring them back: *Can you go and fetch the doctor?* | *Quick, fetch the ladder.* **2** to be sold for a particular amount of money: *The painting is expected to fetch over $1 million.*

fetch·ing /ˈfetʃɪŋ/ *adj* attractive: *She looks very fetching in that dress.*

fête¹ /feɪt/ *n* [C] **1** *BrE* an outdoor event with games, competitions, and things for sale, to collect money for a special purpose **2** *AmE* a special occasion to celebrate something

---

Countryside

Exercise 1

Think about these things. Which things move and which are still? Which things can you pick up? Which things can you enter? Which things grow? Which things can you hear and smell? Mark the chart below like the examples.

	waterfall	hedge	pebble	stream	beach	sand	sea	wave	grass	river	bush	cottage	valley	forest
pick up	✗	✗												
enter		✗												
grow	✗													
move		✗												
hear		✗												
smell	✗	✗												

Exercise 2

Look at the picture for five minutes. Close your eyes and imagine a walk in part of the countryside. Look at the things around you. Which things are colourful? Listen to the sounds. Which things are noisy? Touch things. How do they feel? Which things are cold? Which things are rough? Which are smooth? Think of the smells. Which smells are nice?
Tell your friends about your experiences.

HEIGHT

tall

medium height

small

short

1 2 3 4 5 6 7 8 9 10

BUILD slim overweight petite plump thin well-b

long curly hair

ponytail

short curly hair

short hair

stubble

straight dark hair

parting *BrE*/ part *AmE*

bobbed hair

fringe *BrE*/ bangs *AmE*

receding hair

spiky hair

plait *BrE*/ braid *AmE*

white hair

shoulder length wavy hair

moustache *BrE*/ mustache *AmE*

beard

bald

HAIR

fête² v [T] to welcome someone by having a public celebration for them: *The champions were fêted from coast to coast.*

fet·ish /'fetɪʃ, 'fiː-ll'fetɪʃ/ n [C] **1** something unusual that someone gets sexual pleasure from: *a leather fetish* **2** something that someone does too much or thinks about too much: *Suzie had a real fetish about exercise.*

fe·tus /'fiːtəs/ the American spelling of FOETUS

feud /fjuːd/ n [C] an angry argument between two people or groups that continues for a long time: *a bitter feud between the two neighbours* —**feud** v [I]

feud·al /'fjuːdl/ adj the feudal system was a social system in the Middle Ages, in which people lived and worked on land that was owned by a LORD —**feudalism** n [U]

fe·ver /'fiːvəll-ər/ n **1** [C,U] an illness in which you have a very high temperature: *Drink a lot of fluids, it'll help your fever go down.* **2** [singular, U] when people are very excited: *election fever in Brazil* | **fever pitch** *Our excitement had reached fever pitch.* —**fevered** adj → see also HAY FEVER

fe·ver·ish /'fiːvərɪʃ/ adj **1** someone who is feverish has a fever: *She looked hot and feverish.* **2** done extremely quickly because the situation is urgent: *They worked at a feverish pace.* **3** very excited or worried: *feverish anxiety* —**feverishly** adv

few /fjuː/ $quantifier$ **1** a small number of things, people etc: **a few** *Let's wait a few minutes.* | *There are a few more things I'd like to talk about.* | **+ of** *Why not invite a few of your friends?* | the next few/the last few *The next few days are going to be very busy.* **2** **quite a few/a good few** a fairly large number of things or people: *Quite a few people came to the meeting.* **3** not many: *In the 1950s few people had televisions.* | **very few** *Very few companies have women directors.* | **+ of** *The people were friendly, but few of them spoke English.* **4** **be few and far between** not happening or found very often: *Good jobs are few and far between these days.*

USAGE NOTE: few, a few, little and a little

Use **few** with plural countable nouns to mean 'not many': *Few people said they'd help.* Use **a few** with plural countable nouns to mean 'some': *A few people arrived late.* Use **little** in more formal English with uncountable nouns to mean 'not much': *There's usually little traffic early in the morning.* Use **a little** with uncountable nouns to mean 'a small amount of something': *There was only a little ice cream left.*

---

fi·an·cé /fi'ɒnseɪll‚fiːɑːn'seɪ/ n [C] the man you have said officially you are going to marry

fi·an·cée /fi'ɒnseɪll‚fiːɑːn'seɪ/ n [C] the woman you have said officially you are going to marry

fi·as·co /fi'æskəʊll-koʊ/ n [C], *plural* **fiascoes**, or **fiascos** an event that is so unsuccessful that people feel embarrassed about it: *The evening was a total fiasco from start to finish.*

fib /fɪb/ n [C] *informal* a small, unimportant lie:

Describing People

Exercise 1

Look at the picture. Read the descriptions of the people. Find the people in the picture. Write the number after the description.

a Sunhila Makan is 53. She is petite, and wears her hair in a plait. _4_

b Polly Deacon is a young black woman. She is slim. Her curly black hair is quite short. _____

c Peter Pearson is 23 years old. He is very tall and has spiky, blond hair. _____

d Nick Baggio is bald, but he has a beard. He is fairly well-built. _____

e Mandy Simpson is 32. She has beautiful wavy auburn hair. _____

f Kylie Deacon is 5 years old. She has long curly hair and a ponytail. _____

g George Denton is going to be 68 next year. He is quite plump. His hair is now grey and receding. _____

h Frank Perkins is about thirty years old. He has mousy hair and stubble. He is rather overweight. _____

i Eve Mammet is short and has red hair and a fringe. _____

j Arthur Jenkins has white hair and a white moustache. He is medium height and about 70 years old. _____

Exercise 2

Write a short description of yourself. Describe your height, your build and your hair.

You shouldn't tell fibs. It's not nice. —**fibber** *n*
—**fib** *v* [I] *He's always fibbing.*

fi·bre *BrE*, **fiber** *AmE* /'faɪbəll-ər/ *n* **1** a material such as cotton or NYLON, which consists of thin threads: *man-made fibre* **2** [C] one of the threads that form this material **3** [U] parts of plants that you eat but do not DIGEST, which help food to move through your body: *The doctor said I need more fibre in my diet.* —**fibrous** *adj*

fi·bre·glass *BrE*, **fiberglass** *AmE* /'faɪbəglɑːs ‖-bərglæs/ *n* [U] a light material made from glass or plastic threads, used for making racing cars, small boats etc

fibre op·tics *BrE*, **fiber optics** *AmE* /ˌ.. '../ *n* [U] the use of long thin threads of glass or plastic to carry information in the form of light, especially on telephone lines —**fibre optic** *adj*

fick·le /'fɪkəl/ *adj* **1** someone who is fickle often changes their opinion about what they want or like: *Every politician knows that voters are fickle.* **2** something that is fickle, such as the weather, often changes suddenly

fic·tion /'fɪkʃən/ *n* **1** [U] books and stories about imaginary people and events: *A. A. Milne was a popular writer of children's fiction.* → compare NONFICTION **2** [singular, U] something that is not true: *The story turned out to be a complete fiction.*

fic·tion·al /'fɪkʃənəl/ *adj* fictional people or events are from a book or story, and are not real

fic·ti·tious /fɪk'tɪʃəs/ *adj* something that is fictitious has been made up and is not real: *He uses a fictitious name.*

fid·dle[1] /'fɪdl/ *v BrE informal* to dishonestly get money out of an organization by cheating it in small ways: *His boss found out that he'd been fiddling his expenses.*

fiddle with sth also **fiddle around/about with** sth *phr v* [T] **1** to keep moving something around with your hands, especially because you are bored or nervous: *I wish he'd stop fiddling with his keys.* **2** to move parts of a machine in order to make it work, but without knowing what you should do: *I spent hours fiddling with the radio trying to get the BBC.*

fiddle[2] *n* [C] **1** a VIOLIN **2** *BrE* a dishonest way of getting money: *an insurance fiddle*

fid·dler /'fɪdləll-ər/ *n* [C] someone who plays the VIOLIN

fid·dly /'fɪdli/ *adj* difficult to use or do because you have to move very small objects: *a fiddly little switch*

fi·del·i·ty /fɪ'deldₜti/ *n* [U] *formal* loyalty, especially to your wife or husband by not having sex with other people → opposite INFIDELITY

fid·get /'fɪdʒₜt/ *v* [I] to keep moving your hands or feet, because you are bored or nervous: *The children were fidgeting in their seats.* —**fidgety** *adj*

field[1] /'fiːld/ *n* **1** [C] an area of land that is used for growing crops, keeping animals, or playing a sport: *fields of wheat | playing fields* → see colour picture on page 243 **2** [C] a subject that people study: *Professor Kramer is an expert in the field of radio astronomy.* **3** **oil/gas/coal field** an area where there is a lot of oil, gas, or coal under the ground **4** **the field** all the people or companies that are competing against each other: *lead the field* (=be the most success-

ful person or company): *They now lead the field in computer graphics.* **5** **field of view/vision** the area that someone can see **6** **magnetic/ gravitational field** an area where there is a strong natural force **7** **have a field day** to have a chance to do a lot of something that you enjoy, especially by criticizing someone: *Any time there's a scandal in politics, the media have a field day with it.*

field[2] *v* [T] **1** to catch or stop a ball after it has been hit in a game of BASEBALL or CRICKET **2** **field a question** to answer a difficult question: *The Mayor fielded a lot of tricky questions from the reporters.*

field·er /'fiːldəll-ər/ *n* [C] one of the players who tries to catch the ball in BASEBALL or CRICKET

field hock·ey /'. ,../ *n* [U] *AmE* a game played on grass by two teams with long curved sticks and a ball; HOCKEY *BrE*

field mar·shal /ˌ. '..◂/ *n* [C] an officer with the highest rank in the British Army

field test /'. ./ *n* [C] a test of a new product or system that is done outside the LABORATORY in real conditions —**field-test** *v* [T]

field trip /'. ./ *n* [C] a trip in which students go somewhere to learn about a subject: *a geography field trip*

field·work /'fiːldwɜːkll-wɜːrk/ *n* [U] the study of subjects outside the CLASSROOM or LABORATORY: *I'll be doing archaeological fieldwork over the summer.*

fiend /fiːnd/ *n* [C] **1** an evil person: *Sex fiend strikes again!* **2** someone who is very interested in something and does it a lot: *a crossword fiend*

fiend·ish /'fiːndɪʃ/ *adj* **1** very clever in an unpleasant way: *a fiendish plot* **2** very difficult: *a fiendish puzzle* —**fiendishly** *adv*

fierce /fɪəsllfɪrs/ *adj* **1** a fierce person or animal looks very violent or angry and ready to attack: *fierce dogs* **2** done with a lot of energy and determination: *Competition for jobs is very fierce.* **3** fierce heat, cold, weather etc is extreme: *a fierce storm* —**fiercely** *adv* —**fierceness** *n* [U]

fi·er·y /'faɪərɪllfaɪri/ *adj* **1** full of strong or angry emotion: *a fiery speech | She has a fiery temper.* **2** looking like fire: *a fiery sunset*

fi·es·ta /fi'estə/ *n* [C] a holiday in Spain or Latin America, when people dance, play music etc

fif·teen /ˌfɪf'tiːn◂/ *number* **15** —**fifteenth** *number*

fifth[1] /fɪfθ, fɪftθ/ *number* 5th

fifth[2] *n* [C] one of five equal parts of something

fif·ty /'fɪfti/ *number* **1** 50 **2** **the fifties a)** the years from 1950 to 1959 **b)** the numbers from 50 to 59 —**fiftieth** *number*

fifty-fif·ty /ˌ.. '..◂/ *adj, adv spoken* **1** divided or shared equally between two people: *I think we should divide the profits fifty-fifty.* **2** **a fifty-fifty chance** an equal chance that something will happen or will not happen: *The operation has a fifty-fifty chance of success.*

fig /fɪg/ *n* [C] a small soft sweet fruit that is often eaten dried, or the tree on which this grows → see picture at FRUIT

fig. the abbreviation for FIGURE

fight[1] /faɪt/ *v* **fought** /fɔːtllfɔːt/, **fought**, **fighting 1** [I,T] if people fight, they hit or kick each other: *Two boys were fighting in the school playground.*|*Bruno fought Tyson for the World Heavyweight Championship.* **2** [I,T] to take part in a war: *My dad fought in Vietnam.*| **+ for** *He fought for the Russians.*| **fight a war/battle** *They were fighting a war of independence against a powerful enemy.* **3** [I,T] to try hard to stop something bad from happening or make something good happen: **fight to do sth** *Local people have been fighting to save the school.*|**fight for sth** (=fight to achieve something): *Women fought for the right to vote.*|**fight sth/fight against sth** (=fight to stop something from happening): *new laws aimed at fighting crime*|*He fought against racism all his life.* **4** [I] to argue: *They're always fighting – I don't know why they stay together.*| **+ over/about** *Let's try not to fight over money.* **5** [T] to try to win an election or a court CASE: *Some people say he's too old to fight another election.* **6** **fight your way through/across etc** to move through a group of people by pushing past them: *They had to fight their way through the crowd.*

fight back *phr v* **1** [I] to fight or argue with someone who has attacked you or criticized you: *There didn't seem to be any point in trying to fight back.* **2** [T **fight back** sth] to try hard not to show your feelings: *"Just go away," she said, fighting back her tears.*

fight sb/sth ↔ **off** *phr v* [T] **1** to fight someone who is attacking you and make them go away: *They managed to fight off their attackers.* **2** to get rid of a feeling or illness: *I can't seem to fight off this cold.*

fight sth **out** *phr v* [T] to fight or argue until one person wins: *We left them alone to fight it out themselves.*

fight² *n* **1** [singular] a determined attempt to achieve something or stop something from happening: **fight to do sth** *the fight to save the rainforests*| **+** *Mandela's fight for freedom.*| **+ against** *She lost her fight against cancer.* (=she died) **2** [C] when two people or groups try to hurt or kill each other by hitting, kicking, or shooting each other: *Tyson lost the fight.*|*He's always getting into fights at school.* **3** [C] a battle between two armies: *the fight for Bunker Hill* **4** [C] an argument: **have a fight with sb** *They've had a fight with the neighbours.*

fight·er /ˈfaɪtəl-ər/ *n* [C] **1** also **fighter plane** /ˈ.. ./ a small fast military plane that can destroy other planes **2** someone who fights in a war: *Serb fighters* **3** a BOXER **4** someone who continues to try to do something although it is difficult ➙ see also FIREFIGHTER

fight·ing /ˈfaɪtɪŋ/ *n* [U] when soldiers fight during a war or battle: *There has been more fighting on the streets of the capital.*

fig·ment /ˈfɪgmənt/ *n* **a figment of sb's imagination** something that you imagine to be real, which does not exist: *All this nonsense about ghosts is just a figment of your imagination.*

fig·u·ra·tive /ˈfɪgjˈ ̣rətɪv, -gə-/ *adj* using words to mean something different from their ordinary meaning in order to emphasize an idea. For example 'a mountain of debt' is a figurative phrase meaning a very large amount of debt —**figuratively** *adv* ➙ compare LITERAL

fig·ure¹ /ˈfɪgə‖ˈfɪgjər/ *n* [C] **1** a number that shows an amount, especially in an official report: *The crime figures have gone down again.* **2** a number between from 0 to 9, written as a sign, not as a word: *Write the amount in words and figures.*|**double figures** (=more than 9 and less than 100): *Temperatures reached double figures – over 14°C.* **3** an amount of money: *an estimated figure of $200 million* **4** **good at figures** good at ARITHMETIC **5** a word meaning the shape of a woman's body, used especially to say how attractive it is: *She has a great figure.* **6** a word meaning a person, used to say what kind of person someone is: *an important political figure*|*a sad lonely figure* **7** a person seen in a picture or from a distance: *I could see a dark figure on the horizon.* **8** a numbered drawing in a book **9** a shape in mathematics: *a six-sided figure*

figure² *v* **1** [I] to be included as an important part of something: *Marriage didn't really figure in their plans.* **2** [T] *AmE spoken* to have a particular opinion after thinking about a situation: **+ that** *I figured that it was time to leave.* **3** **that figures/it figures** *spoken* used to say that you expected that something would happen: *"I forgot to bring my checkbook again." "That figures."*

figure sth/sb ↔ **out** *phr v* [T] to understand something or someone after thinking about them: *Detectives are still trying to figure out what happened.*|*She's an odd character – I really can't figure her out.*

fig·ure·head /ˈfɪgəhed‖ˈfɪgjər-/ *n* [C] a leader who has no real power

figure of speech /ˌ.. . ˈ./ *n* [C] a word or phrase used with a different meaning from the ordinary one, in order to give you a picture in your mind or to emphasize an idea: *When I said they'll be 'in the firing line', it was just a figure of speech – I meant they'll get blamed.*

fil·a·ment /ˈfɪləmənt/ *n* [C] a very thin thread, especially the thin wire in a LIGHT BULB

file¹ /faɪl/ *n* [C] **1** a set of papers containing information about a particular person or thing: *The school keeps files on each student.* **2** an amount of information in a computer that is stored under a particular name: *If you want to delete a file, just click on this icon.* **3** a box or folded piece of heavy paper that is used to keep papers in: *He took a file down from the shelf.* **4** **on file** if something is on file, it is kept in an official file so that it can be used later: *We'll keep your application on file.* **5** a metal tool with a rough surface that is used to make something smooth ➙ see picture at TOOLS ➙ see also SINGLE FILE

file² *v* **1** [T] to store papers or information in a particular order or in a particular place: *The letters are filed alphabetically.* **2** [I] if people file somewhere, they walk in a line, one behind the

F

other: *The jury filed into the courtroom.* **3** [I,T] *law* make an official statement saying that you are going to do something, especially in a court: *Ted Danson's wife has filed for divorce.* **4** [T] to rub something with a metal tool to make it smooth or cut it: *She sat filing her nails.*

fil·et /ˈfɪlɪtǁˈfɪlɪt, -leɪ, fɪˈleɪ/ the usual American spelling of FILLET

fil·i·bus·ter /ˈfɪlɪbʌstəl-ər/ *n* [C] a long speech that is intended to delay voting in parliament or Congress —**filibuster** *v* [I]

filing cab·i·net /ˈ.. ˌ.../ (also **file cabinet** /ˈ. ˌ.../ *AmE*) *n* [C] a piece of office furniture with drawers for storing important papers

fil·ings /ˈfaɪlɪŋz/ *n* [plural] very small pieces that come off a piece of metal when it is filed (FILE²)

---

fill in/fill out

form

---

fill¹ /fɪl/ *v* **1** [T] also **fill up** to make something full: *He began filling the tank with water.* | *Crowds of people soon filled the streets.* **2** also **fill up** [I] to become full: + **with** *The trench was filling up with water.* **3** [T] also **fill in** to put something in a hole or crack in order to make a smooth surface: *Fill any cracks in the wall before you paint it.* | *teeth that need filling* **4** [T] if a sound, smell, or light fills a place, you notice it because it is strong or loud: *The smell of fresh bread filled the kitchen.* **5** **fill a job/position/vacancy etc** to get or take a job that has been offered: *I'm sorry, but the position has already been filled.* **6** **be filled with joy/sadness etc** to have a strong feeling of JOY, sadness etc **7** **fill a need/demand** to give people something they want or need: *A cheap bus service that fills a need for elderly people.*

fill sb/sth ↔ in *phr v* **1** to write information in special spaces on a printed piece of paper: *He asked me to fill in a tax form.* **2** to put something in a hole or crack to make the surface smooth **3** to tell someone about things that have happened recently: *I'll fill you in on all the news later.*

fill out *phr v* **1** [T **fill** sth ↔ **out**] to write information in special spaces on a printed piece of paper: *You'll have to fill out a membership form before you can use the gym.* **2** [I] to get fatter: *Her face is beginning to fill out.*

fill up *phr v* [I,T **fill** sth ↔ **up**] to become full or make something full: *Can I fill up your glass?* | *The train was starting to fill up.*

fill² *n* **your fill** as much of something as you want, or can deal with: *I've had my fill of screaming kids today!*

fil·let¹ /ˈfɪlɪtǁˈfɪlɪt, -leɪ, fɪˈleɪ/ *v* [T] to remove the bones from a piece of meat or fish

fillet² also **filet** *AmE n* [C,U] a piece of meat or fish without any bones

fill·ing¹ /ˈfɪlɪŋ/ *n* **1** [C] a small amount of metal that is put into a hole in your tooth **2** [C,U] the food that is put inside a PIE, SANDWICH etc: *apple pie filling*

filling² *adj* food that is filling makes your stomach feel full

filling sta·tion /ˈ.. ˌ../ *n* [C] a place where you can buy petrol for your car

film¹ /fɪlm/ *n* **1** [C] a story that is told using moving pictures; MOVIE *AmE*: *Have you seen any good films recently?* | *the film industry* (=the business of making films) **2** [C, U] the roll of thin plastic that you use in a camera for taking photographs or recording moving pictures: *35mm colour film* **3** [singular, U] a very thin layer of a substance spread on a surface: *a film of oil on the lake*

film² *v* [I,T] to make a film of something for the cinema or television: *The movie was filmed in China.* → compare RECORD²

film-mak·er /ˈ. ˌ../ *n* [C] someone who makes films for the cinema or television

film star /ˈ. ./ *n* [C] a famous film actor or actress; MOVIE STAR

film·y /ˈfɪlmi/ *adj* made of very thin material: *a filmy nightgown*

fil·ter¹ /ˈfɪltəl-ər/ *n* [C] a thing that gas or liquid is put through to remove solid substances that are not wanted: *a water filter*

filter² *v* **1** [T] to clean a liquid or gas using a filter: *filtered drinking water* **2** [I] to gradually move into a place: *The audience began to filter into the hall.* **3** [I] if information filters somewhere, people gradually hear about it: *The news slowly filtered through to everyone in the office.*

filter sth ↔ **out** *phr v* [T] to remove something by using a filter

filth /fɪlθ/ *n* [U] **1** very unpleasant dirt: *Wash that filth off your shoes.* **2** very rude or offensive words, stories, pictures etc connected with sex

filth·y /ˈfɪlθi/ *adj* **1** extremely dirty: *Doesn't he ever wash that jacket? It's filthy.* **2** very rude or offensive, especially about sex: *filthy language*

fin /fɪn/ *n* [C] **1** a part of a fish's body shaped like a small wing that helps it to swim **2** a part shaped like this on a car or a plane

fi·nal¹ /ˈfaɪnl/ *adj* **1** [only before noun] last in a series or happening at the end of something: *the final chapter of the book* **2** if a decision, offer, or agreement is final, it cannot be changed: *Is that your final decision?*

final² *n* [C] the last and most important game, race etc in a competition: *the World Cup Final* | **the finals** the finals of the NBA championship

fi·na·le /fɪˈnɑːliǁfɪˈnæli/ *n* [C] the last part of a concert, entertainment, or piece of music: *the grand finale* (=the last and most exciting part)

fi·nal·ist /ˈfaɪnəl-ɪst/ *n* [C] one of the people or teams that reaches the last part of a competition

fi·nal·i·ty /faɪˈnæləti/ *n* [U] the fact or the feeling that something has ended or been decided and cannot be changed: *the finality of death*

fi·nal·ize (also **-ise** *BrE*) /ˈfaɪnəl-aɪz/ *v* [T] to finish the last part of a plan, business agreement etc: *Can we finalize the details of the deal?*

fi·nal·ly /ˈfaɪnəl-i/ adv **1** after a long time: *After several delays, the plane finally took off at 6:00.* **2** used when you are saying the last of a series of things: *And finally, I'd like to thank my teachers.* **3** in a way that will not be changed: *It's not finally settled yet.*

fi·nals /ˈfaɪnlz/ n [plural] **1** BrE the examinations that students take at the end of their last year at university **2** AmE the examinations that students take at the end of each class in high school and college

fi·nance[1] /ˈfaɪnæns, fɪˈnænsǁfɪˈnæns, ˈfaɪnæns/ n **1** [U] the control of how money should be spent, especially in a company or government: *the finance department* **2** [U] money that you borrow or receive in order to pay for something important: *How will you get the finance to start your business?* **3** finances [plural] the money that a person, company etc has: *The school's finances are limited.*

finance[2] v [T] to provide money for something: *publicly financed services*

fi·nan·cial /fɪˈnænʃəl, faɪ-/ adj connected with money: *a financial adviser*ǀ*financial aid* —**financially** adv

fi·nan·cier /fɪˈnænsɪə, faɪˈnæn-ǁˌfɪnənˈsɪr/ n [C] someone who controls or lends large sums of money

finch /fɪntʃ/ n [C] a small wild bird with a short beak

find[1] /faɪnd/ v [T] found /faʊnd/, found, finding **1** to discover, see, or get something that you have been looking for: *I can't find my keys.*ǀ*Scientists are still trying to find a cure for AIDS.*ǀ**find sb sth** (=find something for someone): *I think we can find you a job.* **2** to discover something by chance: *She found $100 in the street.* **3** to see or realize that something is happening or has happened: **find sb doing sth** *When the police arrived, they found him lying on the floor.*ǀ**+ that** *Michael woke up to find that the bedroom was flooded.* **4** to have a particular opinion or feeling about someone or something: *I don't find his jokes at all funny.*ǀ**find it hard/easy etc to do sth** *I found it hard to understand her.* (=it was difficult for me to understand her) **5** to learn or know something by experience: **+ that** *I soon found that it was quicker to go by bus.* **6** **be found** to live or exist somewhere: *a type of cactus that is found only in Arizona* **7** to have enough time, money, energy etc to be able to do what you want to do: *When do you find the time to read?* **8** **find your way** to arrive at a place by discovering the way to get there: *Can you find your way, or do you need a map?* **9** **find yourself somewhere/doing sth** to realize that you have arrived somewhere or are doing something, without intending to: *Suddenly I found myself back at the hotel.* **10** **find sb guilty/find sb not guilty** law to officially decide that someone is guilty or not guilty of a crime **11** **find fault with** to criticize someone or something: *The teacher would always find fault with my work.* **12** **find your feet** to become confident in a new situation: *Matt's only been at the school two weeks and he hasn't found his feet yet.* ➡ see also **find a home for** (HOME[1])

find out phr v **1** [I,T **find** sth ↔ **out**] to get information about something or someone: *We never found out her name.*ǀ**+ what/how/where** etc *He hurried off to find out what the problem was.*ǀ**+ about** *If Dad finds out about this, he'll go crazy.* **2** [T **find** sb **out**] informal to discover that someone has been doing something dishonest or illegal: *What happens if we're found out?*

find[2] n [C] something good or valuable that you discover by chance: *That little Greek restaurant was a real find.*

find·ings /ˈfaɪndɪŋz/ n [plural] something that has been learnt or decided as the result of an official study: *The Commission's findings are presented in a report.*

fine[1] /faɪn/ adj **1** very good or of a very high quality: *fine wine*ǀ*a fine performance by William Hurt* **2** very thin, or in very small pieces or drops: *a fine layer of dust*ǀ*fine rain* **3** spoken good enough: *"What do you want for lunch?" "A sandwich would be fine."* **4** spoken healthy or reasonably happy: *"How are you?" "I'm fine, thanks."* **5** fine details or differences are small or exact and difficult to see: *I didn't understand some of the finer points in the argument.* **6** fine weather is bright and sunny **7** **it's fine (by me)** spoken used to say that you agree to something: *"How about seeing a film?" "That's fine by me."*

fine[2] adv spoken in a very satisfactory way, without any problems; well: *"How's everything going?" "Fine."*ǀ*The car's working fine now.*

fine[3] n [C] money that you have to pay as a punishment: *a parking fine*

fine[4] v [T] to make someone pay money as a punishment: **fine sb for sth** *He was fined $50 for speeding.*

fine·ly /ˈfaɪnli/ adv **1** in very small pieces: *finely chopped onion* **2** very exactly: *finely tuned instruments*

fine print /ˌ. ˈ./ n [U] SMALL PRINT

fi·nesse /fɪˈnes/ n [U] a clever and delicate way of dealing with people and things

fin·ger[1] /ˈfɪŋgəǁ-ər/ n **1** [C] one of the five parts at the end of your hand, including your thumb **2** **keep your fingers crossed** spoken to hope that something will happen in the way you want it to: *I had a job interview today. I'm just keeping my fingers crossed!* **3** **not lift a finger** spoken to not make any effort to help someone with their work: *I do all the work – Frank never lifts a finger.* **4** **put your finger on** to realize exactly what is wrong, different, or unusual about something: *There's something strange about him, but I can't put my finger on it.*

finger[2] v [T] to touch or feel something with your fingers

fin·ger·nail /ˈfɪŋgəneɪlǁ-gər-/ n [C] the hard flat part that covers the top end of your finger

fin·ger·print /ˈfɪŋgəprɪntǁ-gər-/ n [C] the mark made by the pattern of lines at the end of someone's finger

fingerprint

fin·ger·tip /ˈfɪŋgətɪpǁ-gər-/ n **1** [C] the end of a finger **2** **have sth at your fingertips** to have information easily available and ready to use

fin·i·cky /ˈfɪnɪki/ adj difficult to please: *a finicky eater*

fin·ish¹ /'fɪnɪʃ/ v **1** [I,T] to come to the end of doing or making something, so that it is complete: *Have you finished your homework?*|**finish doing sth** *Let me just finish typing this report.* → opposite START¹ **2** [I] *especially BrE* to end: *What time does the concert finish?* **3** also **finish up/finish off** [T] to eat, drink, or use all the rest of something: *Finish your breakfast before it gets cold, Tom.* **4 finish second/third etc** to be in second, third etc position at the end of a race, competition etc

finish sth ↔ off *phr v* [T] **1** to do the last part of something to make it complete: *I've done most of the work – I'll finish it off tomorrow.* **2** to eat, drink, or use all of something: *Who finished off the cake?*

finish up *phr v* **1** [T **finish** sth ↔ **up**] to eat or drink all the rest of something: *Why don't you finish up the pie?* **2** [I] *BrE* to finally be in a particular place or situation after a lot of other things have happened: *We finished up in Rome after a three week tour.*

finish with sb/sth *phr v* [T] **1 have finished with sth** *BrE* also **be finished with sth** *especially AmE* to no longer need something that you have been using: *Have you finished with the scissors?* **2** *BrE* to end a relationship with someone: *He's finished with Elise after all these years.*

finish² *n* **1** [singular] the end of something, especially a race: **close finish** (=when a race ends with the competitors close together): *It was a close finish but Jarrett won.* **2** [C] the appearance of the surface of an object after it has been painted, POLISHed etc: *a table with a glossy finish*

fin·ished /'fɪnɪʃt/ *adj* **1** [only before noun] completed: *the finished product* **2 be finished** *spoken* to have finished doing something: *Wait I'm not quite finished.* **3** [not before noun] no longer able to continue successfully: *If the bank doesn't lend us the money, we're finished.*

fi·nite /'faɪnaɪt/ *adj* having an end or a limit: *Earth's finite resources*

fir /fɜː‖fɜːr/ also **fir·tree** /'fɜːtriː‖'fɜːr-/ *n* [C] a tree with leaves shaped like needles that do not fall off in winter

fire¹ /faɪə‖faɪr/ *n* **1** [C,U] the flames, light, and heat produced when something burns: *Fire destroyed part of the building.*|*forest fires*|**on fire** (=burning): *The house is on fire!*|**catch fire** (=start to burn): *Two farmworkers died when a barn caught fire.*|**set sth on fire/set fire to sth** (=make something start to burn): *An angry crowd set fire to stores.*|**put out a fire** (=stop it burning): *It took firefighters two days to put out the fire.* **2** [C] a pile of burning wood or coal used to heat a room or cook food: *a camp fire* **3** [U] when guns are fired: *enemy fire*|**open fire** (=start shooting) **4** [C] *BrE* a piece of equipment that uses gas or electricity to heat a room: *Could you turn the fire on, please?*

fire² *v* **1** [I,T] to shoot bullets from a gun: *Several shots were fired at the President's car.* **2** [T] to make someone leave their job; SACK *BrE*: *The boss threatened to fire anyone who was late.* **3** also **fire up** [T] to make someone very excited or interested in something: *exciting stories that fired our imagination* **4 fire questions (at)** to ask someone a lot of questions very quickly: *The reporters fired non-stop questions at*

him. **5 oil/gas-fired** *BrE* made to work by using oil, gas etc: *a coal-fired power station*

fire a·larm /'. .,./ *n* [C] a piece of equipment that makes a loud noise to warn people of a fire in a building

fire·arm /'faɪərɑːm‖'faɪrɑːrm/ *n* [C] *formal* a gun

fire bri·gade /'. .,./ *BrE*, **fire de·part·ment** /'. .,../ *AmE n* [C] an organization of people whose job is to stop fires

fire en·gine /'. .,./ *n* [C] a large vehicle that carries firefighters and their equipment

fire es·cape /'. .,./ *n* [C] metal stairs on the outside of a building, that people can use to escape if there is a fire → see colour picture on page 79

fire ex·tin·guish·er /'. .,.../ *n* [C] a piece of equipment used for stopping small fires

fire extinguisher

fire·fight·er /'faɪə,faɪtə‖'faɪr,faɪtər/ *n* [C] someone whose job is to stop fires

fire hydrant /'. .,./ *n* [C] a water pipe in the street used to get water for stopping fires burning

fire·man /'faɪəmən‖'faɪr-/ *n* [C] a man whose job is to stop fires

fire·place /'faɪəpleɪs‖'faɪr-/ *n* [C] the open place in the wall of a room where you can burn wood or coal to heat the room

fire·proof /'faɪəpruːf‖'faɪr-/ *adj* something that is fireproof cannot be damaged by fire: *a fireproof door*

fire ser·vice /'. .,../ *n* [C] an organization that works to stop fires

fire·side /'faɪəsaɪd‖'faɪr-/ *n* [singular] the area around a fireplace or small fire: *sitting by the fireside*

fire sta·tion /'. .,./ *n* [C] a building for FIRE-FIGHTERs and their equipment and vehicles

fire truck /'. ./ *n* [C] *AmE* a FIRE ENGINE

fire·wood /'faɪəwʊd‖'faɪr-/ *n* [U] wood for burning on fires

fire·work /'faɪəwɜːk‖'faɪrwɜːrk/ *n* [C usually plural] a small object that explodes or burns with a coloured light, used for celebrating special events: *a Fourth of July fireworks display*

firing squad /'. .,./ *n* [C] a group of soldiers whose duty is to shoot a prisoner

firm¹ /fɜːm‖fɜːrm/ *adj* **1** something that is firm is not soft when you press it, but it is not completely hard: *a bed with a firm mattress*|*Choose the firmest tomatoes.* **2** [only before noun] definite and not likely to change: *No firm decision has been reached.*|*They remained firm friends.* **3** not allowing anyone to disobey you and determined not to change your decisions: **+ with** *You need to be firm with children.* **4 a firm grip/grasp/hold** a tight, strong way of holding on something: *Joe took her hand in his firm grip.* —**firmly** *adv* —**firmness** *n* [U]

firm² *n* [C] a business or company: *an engineering firm*

first¹ /fɜːst‖fɜːrst/ *number, adv, pron, adj* **1** before anyone or anything else; 1st: *the first* *name on the list* | *My sister said I'd be the first to get married.* | **come/finish first** (=win a race or competition): *Jane came first in the 100 metres race.* **2** before anything else happens, or before doing anything else: *I always read the sports page first.* | *Do your homework first, then you can go out.* **3** happening or done before other similar events or actions: *Welles made his first film at the age of 25.* | *Is this the first time you been to England?* **4 first prize** the prize for the person who wins a competition **5 at first** in the beginning: *At first he seemed very strict, but now I really like him.* **6** at the beginning of a period, situation, or activity: *When I first started learning English, I couldn't pronounce the words.* **7 in the first place a)** used when you are giving the first of several reasons or facts to prove what you are saying: *Quinn couldn't have committed the crime. In the first place he's not a violent man.* **b)** at the start of the situation: *If you'd done the right thing in the first place, we wouldn't have problems now.* **8** more important than anything else: *Our first priority must be to restore peace.* | **come first** (=be most important): *Ron's kids always come first.* **9 first of all a)** before doing anything else: *First of all, let's get all the equipment together.* **b)** used at the beginning of a sentence to talk about the first or most important thing or reason in a series: *I don't think Helen should go — first of all she's too young.* **10 first thing** as soon as you wake up or start work in the morning: *I'll call you first thing tomorrow, okay?* **11 at first glance/sight** when you first see someone or something, especially before you are able to look at them more carefully: *At first glance there didn't seem to be much wrong with her.* **12 your first choice** the thing or person you like best when you are choosing something or someone

first² *n* **1 a first** something that has never happened before: *"Dad actually washed the dishes tonight." "That's a first."* **2** [C] the highest level of university degree you can get in Britain

first aid /ˌ. '. / *n* [U] simple medical treatment that you give to an injured person before the doctor arrives

first-class /ˌ. '. ◂ / *adj* **1** excellent: *Eric has proved himself a first-class performer.* **2** in or using the best and most expensive part of a train, ship, or plane: *two first-class tickets* —**first-class** *adv*: *passengers travelling first class*

first floor /ˌ. '. ◂ / *n* [singular] **1** *BrE* the floor of a building just above the one at the bottom level **2** *AmE* the floor of a building at the bottom level → compare GROUND FLOOR

first·hand /ˌ. '. ◂ / *adj* learned, seen or known directly, not from other people: *officers with firsthand experience of tank warfare* —**firsthand** *adv*: *suffering that I have seen firsthand*

first la·dy /ˌ. '../ *n* [C] the wife of the President of the US

first·ly /ˈfɜːstli‖-ɜːr-/ *adv* used to say that the thing you are going to mention is the first one and will be followed by others: *The building is unsuitable, firstly because it is too small, and secondly because it is in the wrong place.*

first name /'. ./ *n* [C] the name that comes before your family name: *My teacher's first name is Caroline.* → compare LAST NAME, MIDDLE NAME

first per·son /ˌ. '.. ◂ / *n* [singular] **the first person** the form of the verb that you use with 'I' and 'we'

first-rate /ˌ. '. ◂ / *adj* excellent: *a first-rate show*

fis·cal /ˈfɪskəl/ *adj* connected with government taxes, debts, and spending: *the city's fiscal policies*

fish¹ /fɪʃ/ *n, plural* fish, *or* fishes **1** [C] a type of creature that lives in water and uses its FINs and tail to swim: *How many fish did you catch?* **2** [U] the flesh of a fish used as food

fish² *v* [I] to try to catch fish: + **for** *Dad's fishing for salmon.*

fish around also **fish about** *phr v* [I] to search for something in a bag, pocket etc: *He fished around in his pocket for a penny.*

fish sth ↔ out *phr v* [T] to take or pull something out: *Sally opened her briefcase and fished out a small card.*

fish·er·man /ˈfɪʃəmən‖-ʃər-/ *n* [C] a man who catches fish as a job or a sport

fish·ing /ˈfɪʃɪŋ/ *n* [U] the sport or job of catching fish: **go fishing** *Do you want to go fishing?*

fishing rod /'.. ./ also **fishing pole** *AmE* — *n* [C] a long thin stick with a long string and a hook tied to it, used for catching fish

fish·mon·ger /ˈfɪʃmʌŋgə‖-maːŋgər, -mʌŋ-/ *n* [C] *especially BrE* someone who sells fish

fish·y /ˈfɪʃi/ *adj* **1** *informal* seeming bad or dishonest: *There's something fishy about this business.* **2** tasting or smelling like fish

fist /fɪst/ n [C] a hand closed with all the fingers curled inwards: *She shook her fist angrily.*

fit[1] /fɪt/ v **fitted, fitted, fitting** also **fit, fit, fitting** *AmE* **1** [I,T] to be the right size and shape for someone or something: *I wonder if my wedding dress still fits me? | This lid doesn't fit very well.* **2** [I,T] to put something, such as a piece of equipment, in the place where it will be used: **fit sth on/in etc** *We're having new locks fitted on all the main doors.* **3** [I, T] if something fits in a container, room, or vehicle, or if you can fit it in, there is enough room for it: *Will the cases fit in the back of your car? | I can't fit anything else into this suitcase.* **4** [T] to be suitable for something: *The music fits the words perfectly.*

fit in *phr v* **1** [I] to be accepted by other people in a group so that you can easily live or work with them: *The new students all had a hard time fitting in.* **2** [T **fit sb/sth ↔ in**] to have just enough time to do something or meet someone although you are busy: *Dr. Tyler can fit you in on Monday at 3:30.* **3** [T] to happen or do things in a time that does not affect other arrangements: **+ with** *Your training course doesn't fit in with our holiday plans.*

fit sb/sth ↔ out *phr v* [T] to provide someone or something with all the things necessary for a particular purpose: *Tommy was fitted out with a new suit for the awards ceremony.*

USAGE NOTE: fit

Although both **fit** and **fitted** can be used in the past tense, **fit** is the usual word: *The shoes fit perfectly.*

---

fit[2] *adj* **1** suitable and good enough: *After the party he was not in a fit state to drive.* **2** *especially BrE* healthy and strong, especially because you exercise regularly: *Jogging helps me keep fit.* → opposite UNFIT **3 see/think fit to do sth** to decide that it is right to do something, even though other people may disagree: *Do whatever you think fit.*

fit[3] *n* **1 have/throw a fit** *informal* to become very angry and shout a lot: *Dad's going to have a fit when he sees what you've done.* **2** [C] a sudden feeling or attack of something that you cannot control: *a coughing fit | a fit of rage* **3** [C] when someone suddenly becomes unconscious for a short time and cannot control their body movements: *an epileptic fit* **4 be a good/tight/perfect etc fit** to fit a person or a particular space well, tightly, perfectly etc: *The skirt's a perfect fit.*

fit·ful /ˈfɪtfəl/ *adj* happening for short periods of time, not continuously or regularly: *Thunder woke her out of a fitful sleep.*

fit·ness /ˈfɪtnəs/ *n* [U] **1** when you are healthy or strong enough to do hard work or sports: *exercises to improve physical fitness* **2** the quality of being suitable for something, especially a job: *They were still unsure of his fitness for the priesthood.*

fit·ted /ˈfɪtɪd/ *adj* **1 be fitted with** to have something as a permanent part: *The car is fitted with an electronic alarm system.* **2** [only before noun] *BrE* made or cut to fit a particular space: *fitted cupboards*

fit·ting /ˈfɪtɪŋ/ *adj formal* right or suitable: *The music was a fitting end to this grand ceremony.*

fit·tings /ˈfɪtɪŋz/ *n* [plural] *especially BrE* **1** parts of a piece of furniture or equipment: *a sink with chrome fittings* **2** things that are fastened inside a house, but that can be moved: *The price of the house includes standard fittings.*

five /faɪv/ *number* 5

fiv·er /ˈfaɪvə-ər/ *n* [C] *BrE informal* £5 or a five pound note

fix[1] /fɪks/ *v* [T] **1** to repair something: *Do you know anyone who can fix the sewing machine?* **2** to arrange an exact time, place, price, or limit: *We haven't fixed a day for the party yet.* **3** *BrE* to fasten something firmly to something else: *We fixed the shelves to the wall using screws.* **4** to prepare a meal or drinks: *Can you set the table while I finish fixing dinner?* **5** *especially AmE* to make your hair and face look neat and attractive: *Let me fix my hair before we go.* **6** to make dishonest arrangements so that an election, competition etc has the result you want: *If you ask me, the whole election was fixed.*

fix up *phr v* **1** [I,T **fix sth ↔ up**] *BrE* to arrange a meeting, trip, event etc: *They'd already fixed up to go to Majorca.* **2** [T **fix sth ↔ up**] to improve something or make it more suitable: *We're trying to get the house fixed up before my parents come to visit.* **3 fix sb up with sth** *BrE* to provide someone with something they want: *Can you fix me up with a bed for the night?*

fix[2] *n* **1 be in a fix** to be in a difficult situation: *We're going to be in a real fix if we miss the last bus.* **2** [singular] an amount of an illegal drug such as HEROIN **3 quick fix** an easy way of dealing with a problem: *There is no quick fix to defeat terrorism.*

fix·a·tion /fɪkˈseɪʃən/ *n* [C] a strong and unnatural interest in a particular thing or person: *Brian has a fixation with guns.* — **fixated** *adj*

fixed /fɪkst/ *adj* **1** already decided and impossible to change: *The date of the exam is fixed now. | Lloyd has fixed ideas about religion.* **2** impossible to move: *The table is fixed to the wall.*

fix·ed·ly /ˈfɪksɪdli/ *adv* looking at or thinking about only one thing: *As he talked, he was staring fixedly at her.*

fix·ture /ˈfɪkstʃə-ər/ *n* [C] **1** [usually plural] a piece of furniture or equipment that is fastened inside a house and is sold as part of the house: *bathroom fixtures* **2** *BrE* a sports event that has been arranged

fizz /fɪz/ *n* [singular] the BUBBLES of gas in some types of drinks, or the sound they make: *The mineral water has lost its fizz.* → see colour picture on page 635 — **fizz** *v* [I]

fiz·zle /ˈfɪzəl/ *v*

fizzle out *phr v* [I] to gradually end in a weak or disappointing way: *The party fizzled out before midnight.*

fiz·zy /ˈfɪzi/ *adj* a fizzy drink contains BUBBLES of gas

fjord /ˈfiːɔːd, fjɔːdlˈfiːˈɔːrd, fjɔːrd/ *n* [C] a long narrow area of sea between high cliffs

flab / flæb / *n* [U] *informal* soft, loose fat on a person's body: *I need to get rid of some of this flab!*

flab·ber·gas·ted / ˈflæbəˌgɑːstɪdllˈbər.gæs- / *adj informal* extremely surprised or shocked

flab·by / ˈflæbi / *adj* having too much soft loose fat: *I'm getting all flabby since I stopped swimming.*

flag¹ / flæg / *n* [C] a piece of cloth with a coloured picture or pattern on it used as the sign of a country or as a SIGNAL: *The crowd was cheering and waving flags.* | *the American flag*

flag

flag² *v* [I] **-gged, -gging** to become tired or less interested: *By ten o'clock everyone was beginning to flag.* —**flagging** *adj*

flag sb/sth ↔ down *phr v* [T] to make the driver of a vehicle stop by waving at them: *Rhoda flagged down a cab.*

flag·pole / ˈflæɡpəʊll-poʊl / *n* [C] a tall pole for a flag

fla·grant / ˈfleɪɡrənt / *adj* done in a very noticeable and shocking way: *a flagrant abuse of authority* —**flagrantly** *adv*

flag·ship / ˈflæɡʃɪp / *n* [C] the best and most important product or service that a company has: *the flagship of the new Ford range*

flail / fleɪl / *v* [I,T] to wave or swing around in a way that is not controlled: *She slipped on the icy road, arms and legs flailing.*

flair / fleəllfler / *n* **1** [singular] a natural ability to do something very well: *Carla's always had a flair for languages.* **2** [U] the exciting quality that someone has who does things in an interesting way: *Bates' advertising campaigns showed flair and imagination.*

flak / flæk / *n* [U] *informal* criticism: *Melissa knew she'd get a lot of flak for dating her boss.*

flake¹ / fleɪk / *n* [C] **1** a small flat thin piece of something: *Flakes of paint fell from the ceiling.* **2** *AmE spoken* someone who seems slightly crazy —**flaky** *adj*

flake² *v* [I] to break off in small thin pieces: *The paint on the door is starting to flake off.*

flake out *phr v* [I] **1** *informal* to go to sleep because you are very tired: *I flaked out on the couch with the TV on.* **2** *AmE spoken* to stop thinking clearly and forget things because you are too busy or nervous

flam·boy·ant / flæmˈbɔɪənt / *adj* **1** behaving in a very confident way that makes people notice you: *a flamboyant stage personality* **2** brightly coloured and noticeable: *a flamboyant purple suit*

flame¹ / fleɪm / *n* **1** [C,U] hot bright burning gas that you see when something is on fire: *a candle flame* **2** **in flames** burning strongly: *By the time the firemen arrived, the house was in flames.*

flame² *v* [T] to send someone a message on the Internet that is insulting or shows you are angry by being written only in CAPITAL letters

fla·men·co / fləˈmeŋkəʊll-koʊ / *n* [C, U] a type of fast, exciting Spanish dancing or music

flam·ing / ˈfleɪmɪŋ / *adj* [only before noun] **1** very bright: *flaming red hair* **2** burning brightly: *flaming torches* **3** *spoken informal* used to show that you are annoyed: *I wish that flaming dog would stop barking!*

fla·min·go / fləˈmɪŋɡəʊll-ɡoʊ / *n* [C] a tall pink tropical water bird

flam·ma·ble / ˈflæməbəl / *adj* something that is flammable burns very easily ➡ opposite NON-FLAMMABLE ➡ compare INFLAMMABLE

USAGE NOTE: flammable, inflammable

Both **flammable** and **inflammable** mean 'able to burn easily': *A truck carrying highly flammable materials overturned on a highway this morning.* However, **flammable** is the most usual word. The opposite of both of these words is **non-flammable**.

flan / flæn / *n* [C] a round open PIE filled with fruit, cheese etc

flank¹ / flæŋk / *n* [C] **1** the side of a person's or animal's body **2** the side of an army in a battle

flank² *v* **be flanked by** to have someone or something on one or both sides: *a marble entrance flanked by fountains*

flan·nel / ˈflænl / *n* **1** [U] soft cloth that is used for making warm clothes: *a flannel nightgown* **2** [C] *BrE* a piece of cloth you use to wash yourself

flap¹ / flæp / *n* **1** [C] a flat piece of material, that is fastened by one edge to a surface and hangs down loosely over something **2** **be/get in a flap** *informal* to be very excited and worried about something: *She's in a bit of a flap over moving house.*

flap² *v* **-pped, -pping** **1** [T] if a bird flaps its wings, it moves them up and down **2** [I] if a piece of cloth, paper etc flaps, it moves around quickly and makes a noise: *The ship's sails flapped in the wind.* **3** [I] *BrE informal* to behave in an anxious and excited way: *There's no need to flap.*

flare¹ / fleəllfler / *v* **1** also **flare up** [I] to suddenly begin to burn very brightly: *Lightning flared and flickered.* **2** [I] also **flare up** to suddenly become worse, very angry, or violent: *Violence has flared up again in the region.*

flare² *n* [C] **1** a thing that produces a bright flame when it is shot into the air, especially as a sign that help is needed **2** a sudden bright flame

flared / fleədllflerd / *adj* trousers or skirts that are flared become wider towards the bottom

flare-up / ˈ. ./ *n* [C] when a situation or illness suddenly becomes very bad or violent: *an angry flare-up which brought renewed fighting*

flash¹ / flæʃ / *v* **1** [I,T] to shine brightly for a moment, or to make a light do this: *Why is that driver flashing his headlights?* **2** [I] to move or happen very quickly: + **by/past/through** *A police car flashed by, sirens wailing.* | *A sudden thought flashed through my mind.* **3** **flash a smile/glance/look** to smile or look at someone quickly

flash² *n* **1** [C] a sudden quick bright light: *a flash of lightning* **2** [C] a sudden idea or feeling: *a flash of inspiration* **3** [C,U] a bright light on a camera that you use to take photographs when there is not enough light **4 in a flash/ like a flash** very quickly: *Wait right here. I'll be back in a flash.* **5 a flash in the pan** a sudden success that ends quickly

flash·back /ˈflæʃbæk/ *n* [C] **1** a scene in a film, play, book etc that shows something that happened earlier in the story **2** a sudden clear memory of an event that happened in the past

flash·light /ˈflæʃlaɪt/ *n* [C] *AmE* a small electric light that you can carry in your hand; TORCH *BrE*

flash·y /ˈflæʃi/ *adj* too big, bright, or expensive, in a way that you disapprove of: *a flashy new sports car*

flask /flɑːsk‖flæsk/ *n* [C] **1** a small flat bottle used for carrying alcohol **2** *BrE* a special type of bottle used for keeping liquids either hot or cold: *a thermos flask* **3** a glass bottle with a narrow top used by scientists

flat[1] /flæt/ *adj* **1** smooth and level, without any raised, curved, or hollow parts: *lay the paper on a flat surface* | *the flat landscape of Holland* **2** a flat object has two side surfaces and is not thick or deep: *a flat bottle* **3** a tyre that is flat does not have enough air inside it **4** a drink that is flat does not taste fresh because it has no more BUBBLES of gas **5** *BrE* a BATTERY that is flat has lost its electrical power **6 E flat/B flat** etc the musical note that is halfway between E, B etc and the note below **7** a musical note that is flat is played or sung slightly lower than it should be → compare SHARP[1] **8** dull and uninteresting: *Life seems very flat since you left.* **9 flat rate/fee** etc a price that is the same for every occasion and never changes: *They charge a flat rate for delivery.* **10** a flat shoe has a low heel

flat[2] *n* **1** [C] *BrE* a set of rooms for someone to live in, that is part of a larger building; APARTMENT *AmE*: *They live in a flat just off Russell Square.* | **a block of flats** (=a large building with many flats in it) → see colour picture on page 79 **2** [C] a tyre that does not have enough air inside it **3 the flat of** the flat part or side of something: *David hit the desk with the flat of his hand.*

flat[3] *adv* **1** in a straight position along a flat surface: **lie flat** (=on your back): *Lie flat on the floor and bend your knees.* **2 in 10 seconds/ two minutes etc flat** *informal* in exactly 10 seconds, two minutes etc : *I was dressed and out of the house in ten minutes flat.* **3 flat out a)** spoken as fast as possible: *We've been working flat out to get everything ready.* **b)** *AmE* spoken in a definite way: *Dean flat out refused to go.* → see also **fall flat** (FALL[1])

flat·ly /ˈflætli/ *adv* **1 flatly refuse/deny etc** to say something in a definite way that is not likely to change: *She flatly refused to tell us where he was.* **2** without showing any emotion: *"It's hopeless," he said flatly.*

flat·mate /ˈflætmeɪt/ *n* [C] *BrE* someone who shares a flat with one or more other people; ROOMMATE *AmE*

flats /flæts/ *n* [plural] an area of land that is at a low level, especially near water: *mud flats*

flat·ten /ˈflætn/ *v* [I,T] to make something flat or to become flat: *Their crops had been flattened by the heavy rain.*

flat·ter /ˈflætər/ *v* [T] **1** to praise someone in order to please them, sometimes when you do not really mean it: *I know I'm not beautiful, so don't try to flatter me!* **2 be/feel flattered** to be pleased because someone has shown you that they like or admire you: *I felt very flattered to be offered such an important job.* **3** to make someone look more attractive than they really are: *She wore a dress that flattered her plump figure.* **4 flatter yourself** to believe that something good about yourself is true: *I flatter myself that I know a good wine when I taste one.* —**flatterer** *n* [C] —**flattering** *adj: a flattering photograph*

flat·ter·y /ˈflætəri/ *n* [U] praise that you do not really mean: *She uses flattery to get what she wants.*

flaunt /flɔːnt‖flɒːnt, flɑːnt/ *v* [T] to show your wealth, success, beauty etc in order to make other people admire you: *Pam was flaunting her diamonds at Jake's party.*

flau·tist /ˈflɔːtɪst‖ˈflɔː-/ *n* [C] *BrE* someone who plays the FLUTE; FLUTIST *AmE*

fla·vour[1] *BrE*, **flavor** *AmE* /ˈfleɪvər/ *n* **1** [C] the particular taste of a food or drink: *Which flavour do you want – chocolate or vanilla?* **2 orange-flavoured/chocolate-flavoured etc** tasting like oranges, chocolate etc: *almond-flavored cookies* **3** [U] the quality of tasting good: *For extra flavour, add some red wine.* **4** [singular] a particular quality that something has: *San Francisco has a very European flavour.*

flavour[2] *BrE*, **flavor** *AmE* — *v* [T] to give something a particular taste: *The rice is flavoured with onion.*

fla·vour·ing /ˈfleɪvərɪŋ/ *n* [C,U] something used to give food or drink a particular flavour

flaw /flɔː‖flɒː/ *n* [C] a mistake, mark, or weakness that stops something from being perfect: *The cups have a small flaw in the pattern.*

flawed /flɔːd‖flɒːd/ *adj* not perfect because of mistakes, marks, or weaknesses: *a flawed experiment*

flaw·less /ˈflɔːləs‖ˈflɒː-/ *adj* perfect, without any mistakes, marks, or weaknesses: *Burton's flawless performance as Hamlet* —**flawlessly** *adv*

flea /fliː/ *n* [C] a very small jumping insect that bites animals to feed on their blood

flea mar·ket /ˈ. ˌ../ *n* [C] a market where old or used goods are sold

fleck /flek/ *n* [C] a small mark or spot: *The bird is dark brown with flecks of yellow.*

flecked /flekt/ *adj* having small marks or spots: *large red flowers flecked with white*

fledg·ling /ˈfledʒlɪŋ/ *adj* a fledgling country, organization etc is new and still developing: *a fledgling democracy*

flee /fliː/ *v* [I,T] **fled** /fled/, **fled, fleeing** to leave a place very quickly, in order to escape from danger: *The president was forced to flee the country after the revolution.*

fleece[1] /fliːs/ *n* **1** [C,U] the woolly coat of a sheep **2** [U] an artificial soft material used to make warm clothes —**fleecy** *adj*

fleece[2] *v* [T] *informal* to make someone pay too much money for something

fleet /fliːt/ *n* [C] **1** a group of ships, or all the ships in a navy **2** a group of vehicles controlled or owned by one company: *a fleet of trucks*

fleet·ing / 'fliːtɪŋ / *adj* happening for only a moment: *a fleeting glance*

flesh[1] / fleʃ / *n* [U] **1** the soft part of the body of a person or animal, between the skin and the bones **2** the soft part of a fruit or vegetable that you can eat **3 in the flesh** if you see someone in the flesh, you see the real person, not just a picture of them: *He's even more handsome in the flesh than on television.* **4 your own flesh and blood** someone who is part of your family: *What a shocking way to treat your own flesh and blood!*

flesh[2] *v*

flesh sth ↔ **out** *phr v* [T] to add more details to something: *Try to flesh out your essay with a few more examples.*

flesh·y / 'fleʃi / *adj* consisting of a lot of flesh: *the fleshy part of your hand*

flew / fluː / the past tense of FLY

flex[1] / fleks / *v* [T] to bend or move part of your body so that your muscles stretch

flex[2] *n* [C, U] *BrE* wire covered with plastic for connecting electrical equipment to the supply of electricity; CORD *AmE*

flex·i·ble / 'fleksɪbəl / *adj* **1** able to change or be changed easily: *flexible working hours* → opposite INFLEXIBLE **2** easy to bend: *shoes with flexible rubber soles* — **flexibility** / ˌfleksɪ'bɪlɪti / *n* [U]

flick / flɪk / *v* **1** [T] to make something small and light go through the air with a quick movement of your hand, a whip etc: **flick sth from/off etc** *Barry flicked the ash from his cigarette.* → see colour picture on page 473 **2** [I,T] to move with a sudden, quick movement or to make something do this: *The horse's tail flicked from side to side* *especially BrE* to press a SWITCH in order to start or stop electrical equipment: *Sandra flicked on the light.* — **flick** *n* [C] *a flick of the wrist*

flick through sth *phr v* [T] *BrE* to look at a book, magazine etc quickly: *I flicked through the journal looking for his article.*

flick·er[1] / 'flɪkər / *v* [I] **1** to burn or shine with an unsteady light: *flickering candles* **2** to appear for a moment: *A look of anger flickered across Andrea's face.*

flick·er[2] *n* [singular] **1** an unsteady light or quick sudden movement: *the flicker of the old gas lamp* **2** a feeling or an expression on your face that passes quickly: *A flicker of a smile crossed his face.*

fli·er / 'flaɪər / *n* [C] another spelling of FLYER

flies / flaɪz / *n* [plural] *BrE* the ZIP or row of buttons at the front of a pair of trousers

flight / flaɪt / *n* **1** [C] a journey in a plane, or the plane making a particular journey: *What time is the next flight to Miami?* | *BA flight 242* **2** [U] when something flies through the air: **in flight** *a bird in flight* **3** **flight of stairs/steps** a set of stairs between one floor and the next: *She fell down a whole flight of stairs.* **4** [U] when

someone runs away or escapes: *the flight of refugees from the war zone*

flight at·tend·ant / '. .ˌ.. / *n* [C] *AmE* someone whose job is to look after passengers on a plane and serve them meals; STEWARD

flight deck / '. . / *n* [C] the place where a pilot sits to control a plane

flight·less / 'flaɪtləs / *adj* a flightless bird is unable to fly

flim·sy / 'flɪmzi / *adj* **1** thin and light, or not strong: *flimsy cloth* | *a flimsy table* **2** a flimsy argument, excuse etc is not good or strong enough for you to believe: *The evidence against him is very flimsy.*

flinch / flɪntʃ / *v* [I] **1** to make a sudden small backward movement because you are afraid, hurt or shocked: *He raised his hand, and the child flinched.* **2** to avoid doing something because it is unpleasant: **+ from** *She never flinches from the truth, no matter how painful.*

fling[1] / flɪŋ / *v* [T] **flung** / flʌŋ /, **flung**, **flinging** to throw or move something quickly and with a lot of force: **fling sth at/into/on etc** *Gina pulled off her coat and flung it on the chair.* | *Val flung her arms around my neck.* | **fling yourself down/ through etc** *He sighed and flung himself down on the chair.*

fling[2] *n* [C] **1** a short and not very serious sexual relationship **2** a short period of time when you really enjoy yourself

flint / flɪnt / *n* [C,U] a type of very hard stone that makes a small flame when you strike it with steel

flip / flɪp / *v* **-pped, -pping** **1** [T] to turn something over or into a different position with a quick, sudden movement: **flip sth ↔ over** *He started flipping over the pages.* **2** [T] to throw something flat up into the air so that it turns over: **flip a coin** (=in order to decide something): *Let's flip a coin to see who goes first.* **3** [I] also **flip out** *informal* to suddenly become very angry or crazy: *Harry flipped when he found out that I had damaged his motorcycle.* **4** [T] to press a SWITCH in order to start or stop electrical equipment: *You just flip a switch and the machine does everything for you.*

flip through sth *phr v* [T] to look at a book, magazine etc quickly

flip chart / '. . / *n* [C] large sheets of paper which are joined a the top so that you can turn them over, and are used to write down informaiton in front of groups of people in meetings, classes etc

flip-flop / '. . / *n* [C] *BrE* a light open shoe that has only a v-shaped band to hold your foot; THONG *AmE*: *He was dressed for the beach, in shorts and flip-flops.*

flip·pant / 'flɪpənt / *adj* not serious enough about something, in a way that shows a lack of respect: *Don't get flippant with me, young man!* — **flippantly** *adv* — **flippancy** *n* [U]

flip·per / 'flɪpər / *n* [C] **1** a flat part of the body that some sea animals, for example SEALS, use for swimming **2** a large flat rubber shoe that you use for swimming under water

---

GRAMMAR NOTE: countable and uncountable (2)
Some nouns can be **countable** or **uncountable**. For example: **chicken** *n* [C,U].
• Countable: *A fox had killed some of the chickens.* (=birds)
• Uncountable: *chicken cooked in red wine* (=meat)

flip·ping / ˈflɪpɪŋ / *adj BrE spoken informal* used to emphasize that you are annoyed: *Where's my flipping pen?*

flip side / ˈ. ./ *n* [singular] *informal* the bad side or effects of something rather than its good side or effects: *The flip side is that the medicine may cause hair loss.*

flirt¹ /flɜːt‖flɜːrt/ *v* [I] to behave as if you are sexually attracted to someone, but not in a very serious way: **+ with** *He's always flirting with the women in the office.*

flirt with sth *phr v* [T] **1** to think about doing something, but not be very serious about it: *I've been flirting with the idea of moving to Greece.* **2** **flirt with danger/disaster** to do something that might be dangerous or have a very bad effect

flirt² *n* [C] someone who flirts: *Dave is such a flirt!*

flir·ta·tion /flɜːˈteɪʃən‖flɜːr-/ *n* **1** [C] when someone is interested in something for a short time: *the artist's brief flirtation with photography* **2** [U] when you behave as if you are sexually attracted to someone, but not in a serious way

flir·ta·tious /flɜːˈteɪʃəs‖flɜːr-/ *adj* behaving as if you are sexually attracted to someone, but not in a serious way —**flirtatiously** *adv* —**flirtatiousness** *n* [U]

flit /flɪt/ *v* [I] **-tted, -tting** to move quickly and quietly from one place to another: *birds flitting from branch to branch*

float¹ /fləʊt‖floʊt/ *v* **1 a)** [I] to stay or move on the surface of a liquid without sinking: *oil floats on water* | *Someone had seen a body floating near the shore.* **b)** [T] to make something float: *The logs are floated down the river.* **2** [I] to stay in the air or move slowly through the air: *The balloon floated up into the sky.* **3** [T] to sell SHARES or BONDS to people for the first time

float² *n* [C] a large vehicle that is decorated to be part of a PARADE

flock¹ /flɒk‖flɑːk/ *n* [C] **1** a group of sheep, goats, or birds: *a flock of geese* **2** a large group of people: *a flock of tourists*

flock² *v* [I] if people flock to a place, a lot of them go there: *People have been flocking to see the play.*

flog /flɒg‖flɑːg/ *v* [T] to beat someone with a whip or stick as a punishment —**flogging** *n* [C,U]

flood¹ /flʌd/ *v* **1** [I,T] to cover a place with water, or to become covered with water: *The river floods the valley every spring.* | *The basement flooded and everything got soaked.* **2** [I,T] to arrive or go somewhere in large numbers: **+ in/into/across** *Offers of help came flooding in.* **3** **be flooded with** to receive so many letters, complaints etc, that you cannot deal with them all: *After the show, the station was flooded with calls from angry viewers.* **4** **flood the market** to sell something in very large quantities, so that the price goes down

flood back *phr v* [I] if a memory floods back, you suddenly remember it very clearly: *I saw her picture the other day, and it all came flooding back.*

flood² *n* [C] **1** a very large amount of water that covers an area that is usually dry: *homes washed away by floods* **2** **flood of** a very large

number of things or people that arrive at the same time: *We've had a flood of inquiries.*

flood·gate /ˈflʌdgeɪt/ *n* **open the floodgates** to suddenly make it possible for a lot of people to do something: *The case could open the floodgates for thousands of other similar claims.*

flood·ing /ˈflʌdɪŋ/ *n* [U] when an area that is usually dry becomes covered with water: *The heavy rain has caused more flooding.*

flood·light /ˈflʌdlaɪt/ *n* [C] a large bright light, used for lighting sports fields, public buildings etc

flood·lit /ˈflʌdlɪt/ *adj* lit by floodlights

floor¹ /flɔː‖flɔːr/ *n* [C] **1** the surface that you stand on when you are inside a building: *She was sweeping the kitchen floor.* ➔ see colour picture on page 474 **2** one of the levels in a building: *My office is on the third floor.* ➔ see colour picture on page 79 **3** **ocean/forest floor** the ground at the bottom of the ocean or in a forest: *creatures that live on the ocean floor* **4** **the floor** the people who are at a public meeting, apart from the main speakers: *Are there any questions from the floor?*

floor² *v* [T] **1** to surprise or shock someone so much that they do not know what to say: *At first she was completely floored by his question.* **2** *AmE* to make a car go very fast

floor·board /ˈflɔːbɔːd‖ˈflɔːrbɔːrd/ *n* [C] a board in a wooden floor

floor·ing /ˈflɔːrɪŋ/ *n* [U] a material used to make or cover floors

floor plan / ˈ. ./ *n* [C] a drawing of a room or the inside of a building, as seen from above

flop¹ /flɒp‖flɑːp/ *v* [I] **-pped, -pping 1** to sit or fall down quickly because you are tired: **+ into/onto etc** *Sarah flopped down into an armchair.* **2** if a film, play, plan etc flops, it is not successful: *The musical flopped on Broadway.* **3** to hang down loosely: *Her hair flopped across her face.*

flop² *n* [C] **1** something that is not successful: *The show's first series was a complete flop.* **2** the noise or movement that something makes when it falls down: *He fell with a flop into the water.*

flop·py /ˈflɒpi‖ˈflɑːpi/ *adj* soft and hanging loosely down: *a floppy hat*

floppy disk / ˌ.. ˈ./ also **floppy** *n* [C] a small flat piece of plastic, used for storing information from a computer; DISKETTE ➔ see colour picture on page 80

flo·ra /ˈflɔːrə/ *n* [U] all the plants that grow in a particular place

flo·ral /ˈflɔːrəl/ *adj* made of flowers or decorated with flowers: *floral patterns*

flor·id /ˈflɒrɪd‖ˈflɔː-, ˈflɑː-/ *adj literary* **1** florid skin is red: *florid cheeks* **2** containing too much decoration or too many difficult and unusual words: *florid language*

flor·ist /ˈflɒrɪst‖ˈflɔː-/ *n* [C] **1** also **florist's** a shop that sells flowers **2** someone who works in a shop that sells flowers

floss /flɒs‖flɑːs, flɔːs/ *v* [I,T] to clean between your teeth with DENTAL FLOSS

flo·til·la /fləˈtɪlə‖floʊ-/ *n* [C] a group of small ships

flounce /flaʊns/ *v* [I] to walk in a way that shows you are angry: **+out/off** *She frowned and flounced out of the room.*

floun·der[1] /ˈflaʊndəll-ər/ v [I] **1** to have great difficulty saying or doing something, especially because you do not know what to do: *She floundered helplessly, unable to think of a reply.* **2** to move with difficulty in water, mud etc, especially because you are trying not to sink

flounder[2] n [C,U] a flat fish that lives in the sea

flour /flaʊəllflaʊr/ n [U] powder made from grain, used especially for making bread

flour·ish[1] /ˈflʌrɪʃllˈflɜːrɪʃ/ v **1** [I] to develop and be successful, or to grow well: *conditions in which businesses can flourish* | *Herbs flourished in her tiny garden.* **2** [T] to wave something in your hand to make people notice it: *Henry came out flourishing a $100 bill.* —**flourishing** adj: *Manchester's flourishing music scene*

flourish[2] n **with a flourish** with a large confident movement that makes people notice you: *He opened the door with a flourish.*

flout /flaʊt/ v [T] *formal* to deliberately disobey a rule or law: *Drivers regularly flout the speed limits.*

flow[1] /fləʊllfloʊ/ n **1** [C usually singular] a steady continuous movement of something, for example a liquid: *They tried to stop the flow of blood.* | *the constant flow of refugees across the border* **2** [C usually singular] a supply of something: + **of** *efforts to control the flow of drugs into the US* **3** [U] when ideas or a conversation can continue without being interrupted: *Sorry, I didn't mean to interrupt your flow.* **4 go with the flow** *spoken* to decide to do the same as other people, and not try to do something different → see also CASH FLOW

flow[2] v [I] **1** if something such as a river flows, it moves in a steady continuous way: *The River Elbe flows through the Czech Republic.* | *A steady stream of cars flowed past her window.* **2** if words or ideas flow, they continue without stopping: *He picked up his pen, but the words wouldn't flow.* **3** to hang down loosely in an attractive way: *Her hair flowed down over her shoulders.*

flow chart /ˈ. ˌ./ n [C] a drawing that uses shapes and ARROWS to show how a series of actions or parts of a system are connected with each other

flow·er[1] /ˈflaʊəll-ər/ n [C] **1** the coloured part of a plant or tree that produces the seeds or fruit: *The tree has beautiful pink flowers in early spring.* **2** a plant which is grown for its flowers

flower[2] v [I] if a plant or tree flowers, it produces flowers

flow·er·bed /ˈflaʊəbedll-ər-/ n [C] an area of ground in which flowers are grown

flow·ered /ˈflaʊədll-ərd/ adj decorated with pictures of flowers: *a flowered dress* → see colour picture on page 114

flow·er·pot /ˈflaʊəpɒtll-ərpaːt/ n [C] a pot in which you grow plants → see picture at POT

flow·er·y /ˈflaʊəri/ adj **1** decorated with pictures of flowers: *a flowery pattern* → see colour picture on page 114 **2** flowery speech or writing uses complicated and unusual words instead of simple clear language

flown /fləʊnllfloʊn/ the past participle of FLY

fl. oz. n the written abbreviation of FLUID OUNCE

flu /fluː/ n [U] a common disease which is like a bad cold but is more serious: *The whole team has got flu.*

fluc·tu·ate /ˈflʌktʃueɪt/ v [I] to change very often, especially from a high level to a low one and back again: *The price of copper fluctuated wildly.*

fluc·tu·a·tion /ˌflʌktʃuˈeɪʃən/ n [C] when something fluctuates: *Plants are easily affected by fluctuations in temperature.*

flue /fluː/ n [C] a pipe through which smoke or heat from a fire can pass out of a building

flu·en·cy /ˈfluːənsi/ n [U] the ability to speak or write a language well, without stopping or making mistakes

flu·ent /ˈfluːənt/ adj able to speak or write a language very well, without stopping or making mistakes: *Jem can speak fluent Japanese.* | + **in** *Candidates must be fluent in two European languages.* —**fluently** adv

fluff[1] /flʌf/ n [U] **1** small light pieces of waste wool, thread etc: *She picked the fluff off her sweater.* **2** soft fur or feathers, especially from a young animal or bird

fluff[2] v [T] **1** also **fluff up/out** to make something soft appear larger by shaking or brushing it: *a bird fluffing out its feathers* **2** *informal* to make a mistake or do something badly: *Ricky fluffed the catch and we lost the game.*

fluff·y /ˈflʌfi/ adj made of or covered with something soft and light: *a fluffy kitten* —**fluffiness** n [U]

flu·id[1] /ˈfluːɪd/ n [C,U] *technical* a liquid: *My doctor told me to rest and drink plenty of fluids.*

fluid[2] adj **1** likely to change: *The situation is still very fluid.* **2** moving in a smooth and graceful way: *the tiger's powerful fluid movements* —**fluidity** /fluˈɪdɪti/ n [U]

fluid ounce /ˌ. ˈ./ written abbreviation **fl. oz.** n [C] a unit for measuring liquid. There are 20 fluid ounces in a British pint, and 16 in an American pint.

fluke /fluːk/ n [C] something that only happens because of luck: *The goal was a fluke.*

flung /flʌŋ/ the past tense and past participle of FLING

flunk /flʌŋk/ v [I,T] *AmE informal* to fail a test or course: *I flunked my history exam.*

flunk out phr v [I] *AmE informal* to be forced to leave a school or college because your work is not good enough: *Tim flunked out of Yale.*

flun·key, flunky /ˈflʌŋki/ n [C] someone who is always with an important person and always does what they want, agrees with what they say etc

flu·o·res·cent /fluəˈresəntllfluˈ-, flɔː-/ adj **1** a fluorescent light consists of a long white glass tube, which contains a special gas **2** fluorescent colours shine very brightly

flu·o·ride /ˈfluəraɪdllˈfluraɪd/ n [U] a chemical that helps to protect teeth against decay

flur·ry /ˈflʌrillˈflɜːri/ n **1** [C usually singular] when there is suddenly a lot of activity for a short time: *There was a sudden flurry of excitement when the band appeared.* **2** [C] when it snows for a short time: *flurries of snow*

flush[1] /flʌʃ/ v **1** [I,T] if you flush a toilet, of it flushes, you make water go through it to clean it **2** [T] to get rid of something by pouring water onto it **3** [I] to become red in the face, especially because you are embarrassed or angry: *Billy flushed and looked down.* → see also FLUSHED

flush sb ↔ out *phr v* [T] to make someone leave the place where they are hiding: *Indian police managed to flush out the terrorists using tear gas.*

flush² *n* **1** [C, usually singular] the red colour that appears on your face when you are very embarrassed etc **2 a flush of pride/excitement etc** a sudden feeling of pride, excitement etc

flush³ *adj* [not before noun] **1** if two surfaces are flush with each other, they are at exactly the same level: *Is that cupboard flush with the wall?* **2** *informal* someone who is flush has plenty of money: *I'll buy dinner. I'm feeling flush at the moment.*

flushed /flʌʃt/ *adj* **1** red in the face: *Her face was a little flushed.* **2 flushed with excitement/success** excited or pleased in a way that is easy to notice: *Jill ran in, flushed with excitement.*

flus·tered /ˈflʌstəd‖-ərd/ *adj* feeling nervous and confused: *Jay got flustered and forgot what he was supposed to say.*

flute /fluːt/ *n* [C] a musical instrument shaped like a pipe, which you play by holding it across your lips and blowing into it

flut·ist /ˈfluːtˌst/ *n* [C] *AmE* someone who plays the flute: FLAUTIST *BrE*

flut·ter¹ /ˈflʌtə‖-ər/ *v* **1** [I] to wave or move gently in the air: *flags fluttering in the wind* **2** [I,T] if a bird or insect flutters its wings, it moves them quickly up and down **3** [I] if your heart or your stomach flutters, you feel very excited or nervous

flutter² *n* [C usually singular] **1** *BrE informal* if you have a flutter, you try to win money by GAMBLING **2** a fluttering movement

flux /flʌks/ *n* **be in (a state of) flux** to be changing a lot, so that you cannot be sure what will happen: *The fashion world is in a state of constant flux.*

fly¹ /flaɪ/ *v* **flew** /fluː/, **flown** /fləʊn‖floʊn/, **flying 1** [I] to travel somewhere by plane: *they flew to Paris for their honeymoon.* | *We flew over the North Pole.* **2** [I] to move through the air: *A flock of seagulls flew overhead.* **3** [T] to take something somewhere by plane: *Medical supplies are being flown into the area.* **4** [I,T] to be the pilot of a plane: *Bill's learning to fly.* **5** [I] to suddenly move very quickly: + **down/up** *Timmy flew down the stairs and out of the door.* | + **open** *The door suddenly flew open.* **6** [I] if time flies, it seems to pass quickly: *Is it 5:30 already? Boy, time sure does fly!* | + **by/past** *Last week just flew by.* **7 fly into a rage** also **fly off the handle** *spoken* to suddenly become very angry **8** [I,T] to move in the air, or to make something move in the air: *The French flag was flying over the Embassy.* | *Tommy was in the park, flying his new kite.* **9 go flying/send sb flying** to fall over or make someone fall over

fly² *n* [C] **1** a common small insect with two wings: *There were flies all over the food.* **2** also **flies** *BrE* the ZIP or row of buttons at the front of a pair of trousers: *Your fly is unzipped.* → see also **sb wouldn't hurt a fly** (HURT¹), **let fly** (LET)

fly-by-night /ˈ. ., ./ *adj* a fly-by-night company cannot be trusted and is not likely to exist for very long: *a fly-by-night insurance company*

fly·er, flier /ˈflaɪə‖-ər/ *n* [C] **1** a piece of paper that advertises something **2** *informal* a pilot

fly fish·ing /ˈ. ,../ *n* [U] fishing using a special hook shaped like a fly

fly·ing¹ /ˈflaɪ-ɪŋ/ *n* [U] the activity of travelling by plane or being a pilot: *fear of flying.*

flying² *adj* **1** able to fly: *a type of flying insect* **2 with flying colours** if you pass a test with flying colours, you are very successful in it **3 get off to a flying start** to begin something such as a job or a race very well

flying sau·cer /ˌ.. ˈ../ *n* [C] an object that some people say they have seen in the sky, which carries creatures from space; UFO

fly·o·ver /ˈflaɪ-əʊvə‖-oʊvər/ *n BrE* a bridge that carries one road over another road; OVERPASS *AmE*

FM /ˌef ˈem‹/ *n* [U] a system used for broadcasting radio programmes

foal /fəʊl‖foʊl/ *n* [C] a very young horse

foam¹ /fəʊm‖foʊm/ *n* [U] **1** a mass of very small BUBBLES on the surface of something: *white foam on the tops of the waves* **2** a thick substance like this that you use to clean something, or to help you SHAVE —**foamy** *adj*

foam² *v* [I] **1** to produce foam **2 be foaming at the mouth** to be very angry

foam rub·ber /ˌ. ˈ..‹/ *n* [U] soft rubber that is used to fill CUSHIONS

focal point /ˈfəʊkəl pɔɪnt‖ˈfoʊ-/ *n* [C] the thing that people pay the most attention to: *the focal point of the picture.*

fo·cus¹ /ˈfəʊkəs‖ˈfoʊ-/ *v* **1** [I,T] to give all your attention to a particular thing: + **on** *In his speech he focused on the economy.* | **focus attention on sth** (=make people pay special attention to something) **2** [T] to turn the LENS on a camera, TELESCOPE etc, so you can see something clearly **3** [I,T] if you focus your eyes, or if your eyes focus, you are able to see clearly

focus² *n* **1** [U] special attention that you give to a particular person or subject: *traditional education, with its focus on basic reading and writing skills* **2 be the focus of attention** to be the person or thing that people pay most attention to: *She loves being the focus of attention.* **3 out of focus** if a photograph is out of focus, the edges of the things you see are not clear **4 in focus** if a photograph is in focus, the edges of the things you see are clear —**focused** *adj*

fod·der /ˈfɒdə‖ˈfɑːdər/ *n* [U] food for farm animals

foe /fəʊ‖foʊ/ *n* [C] *literary* an enemy

foe·tus *BrE*, **fetus** *AmE* /ˈfiːtəs/ *n* [C] a young human or animal before it has been born — **foetal** *adj*: *foetal abnormalities*

fog /fɒɡ‖fɑːɡ, fɔːɡ/ *n* [C,U] thick cloudy air near the ground, which is difficult to see through

fo·gey, fogy /ˈfəʊɡi‖ˈfoʊ-/ *n* [C] *informal, plural* **-eys**, *or* **-ies** someone who has old-fashioned ideas and does not like change: *old fogey Don't be such an old fogey!*

fog·gy /ˈfɒɡi‖ˈfɑːɡi, ˈfɔːɡi/ *adj* **1** not clear because of fog: *a damp and foggy morning* **2 I don't have the foggiest (idea)** *spoken* used to emphasize that you do not know something: *"When's Barry coming back?" "I don't have the foggiest."*

fog·horn /ˈfɒghɔːn‖ˈfɑːghɔːrn, ˈfɒːg-/ n [C] a loud horn used by ships

foi·ble /ˈfɔɪbəl/ n [C] a habit that is slightly strange or silly: *It's just one of his little foibles.*

foil¹ /fɔɪl/ n [U] metal sheets that are thin like paper, used for wrapping food

foil² v [T] if you foil someone's plans, you stop them from succeeding

foist /fɔɪst/ v

foist sth **on/upon** sb phr v [T] to make someone accept something that they do not want: *People are fed up with having rules and regulations foisted on them.*

fold

fold¹ /fəʊld‖foʊld/ v **1** [T] to bend a piece of paper, cloth etc so that one part covers another part: *She folded her clothes and put them on a chair.* | **fold** sth **in two/in half** (=fold it across the middle): *Fold the paper in two.* **2** also **fold up** [I,T] to make something, for example a table or chair, smaller by bending it or closing it, so that it can be stored: *Be sure to fold up the ironing board when you're finished.* | *a folding chair* **3 fold your arms** to bend your arms, so that they are resting across your chest **4** [I] also **fold up** if a company folds, it is unsuccessful and cannot continue

fold² n [C] **1** a line made in paper, cloth etc when you fold one part of it over another **2** [usually plural] a loose piece of material or skin that hangs down: *She adjusted the folds of her dress.* **3 return/come back to the fold** to come back to the group or political party that you used to belong to: *a former Republican who has returned to the fold* **4** a small area where sheep are kept for safety

fold·er /ˈfəʊldə‖ˈfoʊldər/ n [C] **1** a large folded piece of hard paper, in which you keep loose papers → see colour picture on page 80 **2** a picture on a computer screen that shows you where a FILE is kept

fo·li·age /ˈfəʊli-ɪdʒ‖ˈfoʊ-/ n [U] the leaves of a plant

folk¹ /fəʊk‖foʊk/ adj folk music, art, dancing etc is traditional and typical of the ordinary people who live in a particular area

folk² n [U]FOLK MUSIC

folk he·ro /ˈ. ˌ../ n [C] someone who people in a particular area admire because of what they have done: *'Swampy' is now a local folk hero.*

folk·lore /ˈfəʊklɔː‖ˈfoʊklɔːr/ n [U] the tradi-

tional stories, customs etc of the people who live in a particular area

folk mu·sic /ˈ. ˌ../ n [U] traditional music from a particular area, especially the countryside

folks /fəʊks‖foʊks/ n [plural] **1** informal your parents or family: *I need to call my folks sometime this weekend.* **2** spoken used to talk to a group of people in a friendly way: *Howdy folks, it's good to see everyone here tonight!*

folk·sy /ˈfəʊksi‖ˈfoʊ-/ adj informal friendly and informal, especially in a way that is typical of people and places in the countryside

fol·li·cle /ˈfɒlɪkəl‖ˈfɑː-/ n [C] one of the small holes in the skin that hair grows from

fol·low /ˈfɒləʊ‖ˈfɑːloʊ/ v **1 a)** [I,T] to walk or drive behind someone: *If you follow me, I'll show you to your room.* | **followed by** *A woman came into the office, followed by three young children.* **b)** [T] to secretly go closely behind someone else, to find out where they are going: *Marlowe looked over his shoulder to make sure no one was following him.* **2** [I,T] to happen immediately after something else: *In the weeks that followed Angie tried to forget about Sam.* | **followed by** *There was a shout from the garage followed by a loud crash.* **3** [T] to do what someone says you should do, or obey rules or instructions: *She followed her mother's advice.* | *Did you follow the instructions on the box?* **4** [I,T] to do the same thing as someone else, after they have done it: **follow suit** (=when someone does the same thing that someone else has done): *When Allied Stores reduced prices, other companies were forced to follow suit.* | **follow** sb's **example/lead** (=to do the same thing because you think it is a good thing to do) **5 follow (in)** sb's **footsteps** to do the same job that someone else did before you: *Toshi followed in his father's footsteps and started his own business.* **6 as follows** used to introduce a list of names, instructions etc: *The winners are as follows: first place, Tony Gwynn; second place,...* **7** [T] to be interested in what happens in a sport or in a subject: *Do you follow baseball at all?* **8** [T] to go in the same direction as something else: *The road follows the river for the next six miles.* **9** [I,T] spoken to understand something such as an explanation or story: *Sorry, I don't quite follow you* **10 it follows (that)** used to say that something must be true because something else is true: *Of course she drinks, but it doesn't necessarily follow that she's an alcoholic.*

follow sb **around** phr v [T] to follow someone everywhere they go: *My little brother is always following me around.*

follow sth ↔ **through** phr v [I,T] to do what needs to be done to complete something or make it successful: *Harry started training as an actor, but he never followed it through.*

follow sth ↔ **up** phr v [I,T] to find out more about something, or do more about something: *I saw an ad in the paper and I decided to follow it up.*

fol·low·er /ˈfɒləʊə‖ˈfɑːloʊər/ n [C] someone who believes in or supports someone or something such as a set of ideas or a religion: *a follower of Karl Marx*

fol·low·ing[1] /ˈfɒləʊɪŋ‖ˈfɑːloʊ-/ *adj* **the following day/year/chapter etc** the day, year etc after the one you have just mentioned: *Neil arrived on Friday, and his wife came the following day.*

following[2] *n* **1** [singular] a group of people who support or admire someone such as a performer: *The band has a huge following in the States.* **2** **the following** the people or things that you are going to mention next

following[3] *prep* immediately after something, or as a result of something: *Following the success of his latest movie, he has had several offers from Hollywood.*

follow-up /ˈ.. ./ **1** [C,U] something that is done after something else to check it, or make sure that it is successful: **follow-up visit/question/ treatment etc** *It's a long term illness and regular follow-up appointments are required.* **2** [C] a film, book, record etc that is made after another one, especially one that has the same subject or characters: *The follow-up wasn't as good as the original film.*

fol·ly /ˈfɒli‖ˈfɑːli/ *n* [C,U] *formal* if something is folly, it is very stupid: *an act of sheer folly*

fo·ment /fəʊˈment/ *v* [T] *formal* to cause trouble and encourage people to start fighting each other or opposing the government: *National Front candidates are accused of fomenting violence against ethnic minorities.*

fond /fɒnd‖fɑːnd/ *adj* **1** **be fond of** to like someone or something very much: *Mrs Winters is very fond of her grandchildren.* **2** **be fond of doing sth** to enjoy doing something, or to do something often: *They're fond of using legal jargon.* **3** **fond memories** if you have fond memories of something, it makes you happy when you think of it: *I have fond memories of my time at Oxford.* **4** **fond hope/belief/wish** something you hope or wish were true, but probably is not **5** a fond look is kind and gentle and shows that you like someone very much —**fondness** *n* [U]

fon·dle /ˈfɒndl‖ˈfɑːndl/ *v* [T] to touch someone's body in a gentle or sexual way: *Max saw his girlfriend fondling a man's bottom in a pub.*

fond·ly /ˈfɒndli‖ˈfɑːndli/ *adv* **1** in a way that shows you like someone or something very much: *Greta smiled fondly at him.* **2** **fondly imagine/hope** to wrongly think that something is true or that something will happen: *people who fondly imagine that Britain is still a world power*

font /fɒnt‖fɑːnt/ *n* [C] **1** *technical* a set of printed letters which are a particular shape and size **2** a container for water in a church, used for BAPTISMS

food /fuːd/ *n* **1** [U] things that people and animals eat: *How much do you spend on food?* **2** [C,U] a kind of food: *I love Chinese food.* **3** **food for thought** something that makes you think carefully → see also HEALTH FOOD, JUNK FOOD, SEAFOOD

food bank /ˈ. ./ *n* [C] *AmE* a place that gives food to people who need it

food chain /ˈ. ./ *n* [singular] animals and plants considered as a group, in which one animal is eaten by another animal, which is eaten by another, etc

food poi·son·ing /ˈ. ˌ.../ *n* [U] an illness caused by eating food that contains harmful BACTERIA

food pro·cess·or /ˈ. ˌ.../ *n* [C] a piece of electrical equipment for preparing food, that cuts or mixes it very quickly

food stamp /ˈ. ./ *n* [C usually plural] *AmE* an official piece of paper that poor people can use instead of money to buy food

fool[1] /fuːl/ *n* [C] **1** a stupid person: *I felt such a fool, locking my keys in the car like that.* **2** **make a fool of yourself** to do something stupid, which you feel embarrassed about later: *She realized she'd made a complete fool of herself over him.* **3** **make a fool (out) of sb** to deliberately try to make someone seem stupid: *Darren thought she was trying to make a fool out of him in front of his friends.*

fool[2] *v* **1** [T] to trick or deceive someone: **fool sb into doing sth** *Don't be fooled into buying more insurance than you need.* **2** **you could have fooled me** *spoken* used when you do not believe what someone has told you: *"Your dad's upset about this too, you know." "Well, you could have fooled me!"*

fool around *phr v* [I] **1** to spend time playing games or behaving in a silly way: *Stop fooling around you two!* **2** to have a sexual relationship with someone else's wife, boyfriend etc

fool with sb/sth *phr v* [T] *especially AmE* to use something in a dangerous or silly way: *A hacker had been fooling with the hospital computers.*

fool·har·dy /ˈfuːlˌhɑːdi‖-ɑːr-/ *adj* taking risks that are not necessary —**foolhardiness** *n* [U]

fool·ish /ˈfuːlɪʃ/ *adj* not sensible or wise: *It was a very foolish thing to do. | The king was a vain, foolish man.* —**foolishly** *adv* —**foolishness** *n* [U]

fool·proof /ˈfuːlpruːf/ *adj* a foolproof plan or method etc is certain to be successful

foot[1] /fʊt/ *n* [C] **1** *plural* **feet** /fiːt/ your feet are the parts of your body at the end of your legs that you stand on **2** written abbreviation **ft.**, *plural* **feet**, *or* **foot** a unit for measuring length, equal to 12 inches or 0.3048 meters **3** **on foot** if you go somewhere on foot, you walk there: *We set out on foot to explore the city.* **4** **the foot of** the bottom of something such as a mountain, tree, or page, or the end of a bed **5** **be on your feet** a) to be standing for a long time without sitting down: *On this job we're on our feet all day.* b) to be healthy again after being ill: *It's good to see you on your feet again!* **6** **get/rise/ jump etc to your feet** to stand or jump up after you have been sitting: *The fans cheered and rose to their feet.* **7** **set foot in** to go to or into a place: *If that woman ever sets foot in this house, I'm leaving!* **8** **put your foot down** a) to say very firmly that someone must do something: *Brett didn't want to go, but Dad put his foot down.* b) to make a car go faster **9** **put your feet up** to rest and relax **10** **put your foot in it** to say something that is embarrassing, or that upsets someone **11** **have/keep your feet on the ground** to be sensible and practical in the way you do things **12** **get your foot in the door** to get your first opportunity to work in a particular organization **13** **-footed** having a particular number or kind of feet: *a four-footed animal* → see also **the boot's on the other foot**

(BOOT¹), **get cold feet** (COLD¹), **drag your feet** (DRAG¹)

foot² *v* **foot the bill** *informal* to pay for something: *The insurance company should foot the bill for the damage.*

foot·age /'fʊtɪdʒ/ *n* [U] film that shows a particular event: *footage of the 1936 Olympics*

foot·ball /'fʊtbɔːlǁ-bɒːl/ *n* **1** [U] **a)** *BrE* a game in which two teams try to kick a ball between two posts at either end of a field; SOCCER; : *Does anyone want a game of football?* | *a football match* → see colour picture on page 636 **b)** *AmE* an American game in which two teams wearing HELMETs and special protective clothes carry, kick, or throw an oval ball into an area at the end of a field to win points; AMERICAN FOOTBALL *BrE*: *Are you going to the football game on Saturday?* → see colour picture on page 636 **2** [C] the ball used in these games → see colour picture on page 636 —**footballer** *n* [C]

foot·bridge /'fʊt,brɪdʒ/ *n* [C] a narrow bridge for people to walk over

foot·hill /'fʊt,hɪl/ *n* [C usually plural] one of the low hills at the bottom of a group of mountains: *the foothills of the Rockies*

foot·hold /'fʊthəʊldǁ-hoʊld/ *n* [C] **1** a position from which you can start trying to get what you want: *Republicans gained a foothold during the last elections.* **2** a space where you can safely put your foot when you are climbing a rock

foot·ing /'fʊtɪŋ/ *n* [U] **1** the conditions or arrangements under which people do something, or under which something is done: *Women can compete on an equal footing with men.* (=they have the same advantages and disadvantages) **2** a firm hold with your feet on a surface: *A local boy lost his footing and fell 200 feet down a steep bank.*

foot·lights /'fʊtlaɪts/ *n* [plural] a row of lights along the front of the stage in a theatre

foot lock·er /'. ,../ *n* [C] *AmE* a large strong plain box for keeping your possessions in

foot·loose /'fʊtluːs/ *adj* **footloose and fancy free** not married and able to do what you want because you do not have responsibilities

foot·note /'fʊtnəʊtǁ-noʊt/ *n* [C] a note at the bottom of a page in a book, that gives more information about something on that page

foot·path /'fʊtpɑːθǁ-pæθ/ *n* [C] a path for people to walk along, especially in the countryside

foot·print /'fʊt,prɪnt/ *n* [C] a mark made by a foot or shoe: *footprints in the snow*

footprints

foot·sie /'fʊtsi/ *n* **play footsie** *informal* to secretly touch someone's feet with your feet under a table, in a way that shows you are sexually attracted to them

foot·step /'fʊtstep/ *n* [C] the sound of each step when someone is walking: *He heard footsteps in the hall.* → see also **follow in sb's footsteps** (FOLLOW)

foot·stool /'fʊtstuːl/ *n* [C] a low piece of furniture used for supporting your feet when you are sitting down

foot·wear /'fʊtweəǁ-wer/ *n* [U] things you wear on your feet, such as shoes or boots

for¹ /fə; *strong* fɔːǁfər; *strong* fɔːr/ *prep*
1 intended to be given to or used by a particular person or group: *Save a piece of cake for Noah.* | *I've got some good news for you.* | *Leave those chairs out – they're for the concert.* **2** used to show the purpose of an object, action, etc: *a knife for cutting bread* | *What did you do that for?* (=why did you do it?) | *What's this gadget for?* (=what is its purpose?) | *a space just large enough for the bed to fit into* | *The house is for sale.* (=available to be sold) **3** in order to get or do something: *Alison is looking for a job.* | *We were waiting for the bus.* | *Let's go for a walk.* **4** used in order to show the time when something is planned to happen: *an appointment for 3:00* | *It's time for dinner.* **5** in order to help someone: *Let me lift that box for you.* | *What can I do for you?* (=can I help you?) **6** used to talk about a particular length of time: *I've known Kim for a long time.* | *Bake the cake for 40 minutes.* **7** because of or as a result of: *I got a ticket for going through a red light.* | *The award for the highest sales goes to Pete McGregor.* **8** used to show where a person, vehicle etc is going: *The plane for Las Vegas took off an hour late.* | *I was just leaving church when the phone rang.* **9** used to talk about a particular distance: *We walked for miles.* **10** used to show a price or amount: *a check for $100* | *an order for 200 copies* | *I'm not working for nothing.* (=without being paid) **11 for breakfast/lunch/dinner** used to say what you ate or will eat at breakfast, dinner etc: *"What's for lunch?" "Hamburgers."* | *We had steak for dinner last night.* **12 for sb/sth to do sth** used when you are discussing what is happening, what may happen, or what can happen: *It's unusual for it to be this cold in June.* | *The plan is for us to leave on Friday morning and pick up Joe.* **13** if you are happy, sad etc for someone, you feel happy, sad etc because something has happened to them: *I'm really happy for you.* **14 for now** used to say that a situation can be changed later: *Just put the pictures in a box for now.* **15 work for/play for etc** to play a sport in a particular team, work at particular company etc: *She worked for Exxon until last year.* | *He plays for the Boston Red Sox.* **16** supporting, or agreeing with someone or something; IN FAVOUR OF: *How many people voted for Mulhoney?* | *I'm for getting a pizza, what about you?* **17 for all a)** considering how little: *For all the good I did, I shouldn't have tried to help.* **b)** considering how much or many: *For all the plays she's seen, she's never seen "Hamlet".* **18 for all I know/care** *spoken* used to say that you really do not know or care: *He could be in Canada by now for all I know.* **19 for Christmas/for sb's birthday etc** in order to celebrate Christmas, someone's BIRTHDAY etc: *What did you get for your birthday?* | *We went to my grandmother's for Thanksgiving last year.* **20** having the same meaning as another word, sign etc: *What's the Spanish word for dish?* **21** when you consider a particular fact: *Libby's very tall for her age.* **22 be (in) for it** *informal* to be in trouble for something that you have done: *You'll be for it when she finds out you've ruined her best dress.*

F

for[2] *conjunction literary* because: *Please leave, for I am too sad to talk.*

for·age /ˈfɒrɪdʒ‖ˈfɑː-, ˈfɔː-/ *v* [I] to search for food or other things you need, especially outdoors

for·ay /ˈfɒreɪ‖ˈfɔː-, ˈfɑː-/ *n* [C] when someone tries to do something for a short time, or goes somewhere for a short time: *a brief foray into politics*

for·bear·ance /fɔːˈbeərəns‖fɔːrˈber-/ *n* [U] *formal* when you are patient and do not get angry or upset

for·bid /fəˈbɪd‖fər-/ *v* **forbade** /-ˈbeɪd‖-ˈbæd/, *or* **forbid, forbidden** /-ˈbɪdn/, **forbidding** [T] **1** *formal* to order someone not to do something: *forbid sb to do sth I forbid you to see that man again.* **2 God/Heaven forbid** *spoken* used to say that you hope very much that something will not happen: *"He's not coming back, is he?" "God forbid!"*

for·bid·den /fəˈbɪdn‖fər-/ *adj* not allowed, especially because of an official rule: **it is forbidden to do sth** *It's forbidden to smoke in the hospital.*

for·bid·ding /fəˈbɪdɪŋ‖fər-/ *adj* something that is forbidding looks frightening, unfriendly, or dangerous: *The mountains looked more forbidding as we got closer.*

force[1] /fɔːs‖fɔːrs/ *n* **1** [C] a group of people who have been trained to do military or police work: *the Air Force* | *forces that are loyal to the rebels* | **the forces** (=the army, navy, and air force considered together) **2** [U] the use of violence or physical strength to do something: *The police used force to break up the demonstration.* **3** [U] a strong effect that something has: *The force of the explosion threw her backwards.* | **with great force** *The waves were hitting the rocks with great force* **4** [C] something or someone that has a very powerful effect: *The US is probably the most important force in the world economy.* | *the forces of nature* **5 join/combine forces** to work together to do or achieve something: *Companies from several countries joined forces to produce the satellite.* **6** [C usually singular] a measure of wind strength **7 in force a)** when there are a lot of a particular kind of people or things: *The mosquitoes are going to be out in force tonight.* **b)** if a law or rule is in force, it must be obeyed **8 force of habit** when you do something because you have always done it: *I still get up at 6.30 everyday. Force of habit, I suppose.*

USAGE NOTE: force, power, strength

Force is the natural power that something has: *The force of the wind knocked the fence down.* **Power** is the ability and authority that you have to do something, or the energy that is used to make something work: *Congress was the power to make laws.* | *Their home is heated by solar power.* **Strength** is the physical quality that makes you strong: *He didn't have the strength to walk any further.*

---

force[2] *v* [T] **1** to make someone do something they do not want to do: *Bad health forced him into early retirement.* | **force sb to do sth** *I had to force myself to get up this morning.* **2** to use physical strength to move something or go somewhere: *Firefighters had to force the door.* (=open

it using force) | **force your way through/into etc** *Burglars had forced their way into the garage.*

force sth on/upon sb *phr v* [T] to make someone accept something that they do not want

forced /fɔːst‖fɔːrst/ *adj* **1 forced smile/laugh/interest etc** a smile etc you make because you feel you have to, and not because you really want to: *Anne gave a forced smile.* **2** done suddenly because a situation makes it necessary: *The plane had to make a forced landing in a field.* **3** done using force: *a forced entry*

force·ful /ˈfɔːsfəl‖ˈfɔːrs-/ *adj* powerful and strong: *a forceful personality* | *forceful arguments* —**forcefully** *adv* —**forcefulness** *n* [U]

for·ceps /ˈfɔːseps, -sɪps‖ˈfɔːr-/ *n* [plural] a medical instrument for picking up, holding, or pulling things

for·ci·ble /ˈfɔːsɪbəl‖ˈfɔːr-/ *adj* using physical force: *the forcible repatriation of refugees* —**forcibly** *adv*: *The demonstrators were forcibly removed from the embassy.*

ford[1] /fɔːd‖fɔːrd/ *n* [C] a place in a river where the water is not deep and you can walk or drive across

ford[2] *v* [T] to walk or drive across a river where the water is not too deep

fore /fɔː‖fɔːr/ *n* **come to the fore** to become important: *Environmental issues came to the fore in the 1980s.*

fore·arm /ˈfɔːrɑːm‖-ɑːrm/ *n* [C] the part of your arm between your hand and your elbow

fore·bod·ing /fɔːˈbəʊdɪŋ‖fɔːrˈboʊ-/ *n* [C,U] a feeling that something bad will happen: *We waited for news with a sense of foreboding.*

fore·cast[1] /ˈfɔːkɑːst‖ˈfɔːrkæst/ *n* [C] a description of what is likely to happen: *the weather forecast*

forecast[2] *v* [T] **forecast**, *or* **forecasted**, **forecasting** to say what is likely to happen: *Warm weather has been forecast for the weekend.* —**forecaster** *n* [C]

fore·close /fɔːˈkləʊz‖fɔːrˈkloʊz/ *v* [I,T] to take away someone's property because they cannot pay the money that they borrowed to buy it —**foreclosure** /-ˈkləʊʒə‖-ˈkloʊʒər/ *n* [U]

fore·court /ˈfɔːkɔːt‖ˈfɔːrkɔːrt/ *n* [C] a large open area in front of a building

fore·fa·ther /ˈfɔːˌfɑːðə‖ˈfɔːrˌfɑːðər/ *n* [C, usually plural] *literary* someone who was part of your family a long time ago; ANCESTORS

fore·fin·ger /ˈfɔːˌfɪŋgə‖ˈfɔːrˌfɪŋgər/ *n* [C] the finger next to your thumb; INDEX FINGER

fore·front /ˈfɔːfrʌnt‖ˈfɔːr-/ *n* **be in/at the forefront of sth** to have an important and leading part in developing a new idea: *The Institute has been at the forefront of research into AIDS.*

fore·go, forgo /fɔːˈgəʊ‖fɔːrˈgoʊ-/ *v* [T] *formal* to say you do not need to have something: *We're asking our employees to forego a wage rise this year.*

fore·gone con·clu·sion /ˌ.. ˈ.../ *n* if something is a foregone conclusion, the result of it is certain: *The election result was a foregone conclusion.*

fore·ground /ˈfɔːgraʊnd‖ˈfɔːr-/ *n* **the foreground** the part of a picture, photograph etc nearest to you

fore·head /ˈfɒrɪd, ˈfɔːhed‖ˈfɔːrɪd, ˈfɑːr-,

'fɔːrhed/ *n* [C] the part of your face above your eyes → see picture at HEAD¹

for·eign /'fɒrɪn‖'fɔː-, 'faː-/ *adj* **1** not from your own country: *She spoke with a slightly foreign accent.* \ *foreign workers* **2** involving or dealing with other countries: *the Minister for Foreign Affairs* **3** **be foreign to** to be strange or difficult for someone to understand: *Their way of life was completely foreign to her.* **4** **foreign body/matter** something that has got into a place where it does not belong: *Tears serve the function of washing away any foreign body in the eye.*

for·eign·er /'fɒrɪnər‖'fɔːrɪnər, 'faː-/ *n* [C] someone who is from a country that is not your own

foreign ex·change /ˌ.. ./ *n* [U] the system of buying and selling foreign money, or foreign money itself

fore·leg /'fɔːleg‖'fɔːr-/ *n* [C] a front leg of an animal

fore·man /'fɔːmən‖'fɔːr-/ *n* [C] the person in charge of a group of workers

fore·most /'fɔːməʊst‖'fɔːrmoʊst/ *adj* [only before noun] the most famous or important: *the foremost writer of her time*

fo·ren·sic /fə'rensɪk, -zɪk/ *adj* using scientific methods to solve crimes

fore·run·ner /'fɔːˌrʌnə‖-ər/ *n* [C] a type of something that existed at an earlier time: *It is now seen as the forerunner of the modern computer.*

fore·see /fɔː'siː‖fɔːr-/ *v* [T] **foresaw** /-'sɔː-‖-'sɒː/, **foreseen** /-'siːn/, **foreseeing** to expect that something will happen in the future: *No one could have foreseen such a disaster.*

fore·see·a·ble /fɔː'siːəbəl‖fɔːr-/ *adj* **for/in the foreseeable future** continuing for as long as you can imagine: *Leila will be staying here for the foreseeable future.*

fore·shad·ow /fɔː'ʃædəʊ‖fɔːr'ʃædoʊ/ *v* [T] *literary* to be a sign of something that will happen

fore·sight /'fɔːsaɪt‖'fɔːr-/ *n* [singular, U] the ability to imagine what might happen in the future, and consider this in your plans

fore·skin /'fɔːˌskɪn‖'fɔːr-/ *n* [C] the loose skin covering the end of a man's PENIS

for·est /'fɒrɪst‖'fɔː-, 'faː-/ *n* [C,U] a large area of land covered with trees → see colour picture on page 243

fore·stall /fɔː'stɔːl‖fɔːr'stɒːl/ *v* [T] to prevent something from happening by doing something first: *The Army was sent in to forestall trouble.*

for·est·ry /'fɒrɪstri‖'fɔː-, 'faː-/ *n* [U] the job of planting and taking care of trees in forests

fore·taste /'fɔːteɪst‖'fɔːr-/ *n* **be a foretaste of** to be a sign of what something will be like in the future: *The riots in the city were only a foretaste of what was to come.*

fore·tell /fɔː'tel‖fɔːr-/ *v* [T] **foretold** /-'təʊld‖ -'toʊld/, **foretold, foretelling** to say what will happen in the future

for·ev·er /fər'evə‖-vər/ *adv* **1** for all future time; always: *I'll remember you forever.* **2** *spoken* used to emphasize that something

lasts for a long time or takes a long time: *It seemed to take forever to get to the airport.*

fore·warn /fɔː'wɔːn‖fɔːr'wɔːrn/ *v* [T] to warn someone about something that might happen: *We'd been forewarned about the dangers of travelling at night.*

fore·went /fɔː'went‖fɔːr-/ *v* the past tense of FOREGO

fore·word /'fɔːwɜːd‖'fɔːrwɜːrd/ *n* [C] a short piece of writing at the beginning of a book about the book or its writer

for·feit /'fɔːfɪt‖'fɔːr-/ *v* [T] to give something up or have it taken away from you, usually because you have broken a rule: *criminals who have forfeited their right to freedom* —**forfeit** *n* [C]

for·gave /fə'geɪv‖fər-/ *v* the past tense of FORGIVE

forge¹ /fɔːdʒ‖fɔːrdʒ/ *v* [T] **1** to illegally copy something to make people think it is real: *a forged passport* **2** to develop a strong relationship with other groups: *A special alliance has been forged between the US and Canada.*

forge ahead *phr v* [I] to do something successfully and confidently: *a team that has forged ahead in the league*

forge² *n* [C] a place where metal objects or goods are made by heating and shaping them

forg·er /'fɔːdʒə‖'fɔːrdʒər/ *n* [C] someone who illegally copies documents, paintings etc, to make people think they are real

for·ge·ry /'fɔːdʒəri‖'fɔːr-/ *n* **1** [C] something such as a document or painting that has been illegally copied; FAKE **2** [U] the crime of illegally copying something

for·get /fə'get‖fər-/ *v* [I,T] **forgot** /-'gɒt ‖-'gɑːt/, **forgotten** /-'gɒtn‖-'gɑːtn/, **forgetting** **1** to be unable to remember information, something that happened, or how to do something: *I'll never forget the look on her face when I told her I was leaving.* \ + **(that)** *Don't forget that Linda's birthday is Friday.* \ + *You haven't forgotten about today's meeting?* \ + **what/how/where etc** *I've forgotten what I was going to say!* **2** to fail to remember to do something that you should do: *I'm sorry – I've forgotten your book.* \ **forget to do sth** *Someone's forgotten to turn off the lights.* \ + **(that)** *Dan forgot he was supposed to pick us up from school.* **3** to stop thinking about someone or something: *She had never forgotten Sam, even after all these years.* \ + **about** *Just forget about work and relax.* **4** **forget it** used to tell someone that something is not important: *"I'm sorry I broke your mug." "Forget it."* **5** **I forget** *spoken* used instead of "I have forgotten": *Sandra's bringing her boyfriend – I forget his name now.* **6** **...and don't you forget it!** used to remind someone angrily about something that should make them behave differently: *This is my house, and don't you forget it!* **7** **forget yourself** *formal* to do or say something you should not in a social situation or when you are talking to someone in authority: *Beth forgot herself and suddenly burst out laughing.*

F

GRAMMAR NOTE: comparatives and superlatives
For short adjectives of one syllable, add **-er** or **-est** to the word: e.g. *old - older - oldest.* (Sometimes you must double the last letter: e.g. *big - bigger - biggest*). For long adjectives put **more** or **the most** before the word: e.g. *more comfortable - the most interesting.*

USAGE NOTE: forget

If you want to talk about the place where you have left something, use the verb **leave**, not the verb **forget**. Compare: *I've left my book at home.* | *I've forgotten my book and I've forgotten my keys.* | *I've left my keys in the car.* Don't say "I've forgotten my keys in the car".

for·get·ful /fəˈgetfəl‖fər-/ *adj* often forgetting things: *Grandpa's getting forgetful in his old age!* —**forgetfulness** *n* [U] —**forgetfully** *adv*

for·give /fəˈgɪv‖fər-/ *v* [I,T] **forgave** /-ˈgeɪv/, **forgiven** /-ˈgɪvən/, **forgiving 1** to decide not to be angry or punish someone who has done something wrong: *I knew that my mother would forgive me.* | *If anything happened to the kids, she'd never forgive herself.* | **forgive sb for (doing) sth** *She never forgave him for embarrassing her in front of her colleagues.* **2 forgive me** *spoken* used before you say or ask something that might seem rude: *Forgive me for asking, but how much did you pay for your computer?* **3 sb could be forgiven for sth** used to say that you understand why someone would think or do something: *You could be forgiven for thinking that nobody lives here.*

for·give·ness /fəˈgɪvnɪs‖fər-/ *n* [U] when someone forgives another person for something they have done wrong

for·giv·ing /fəˈgɪvɪŋ‖fər-/ *adj* willing to forgive: *a kind and forgiving man*

for·go /fɔːˈgəʊ‖fɔːrˈgoʊ/ FOREGO

for·got /fəˈgɒt‖fərˈgɑːt/ *v* the past tense of FORGET

for·got·ten /fəˈgɒtn‖fərˈgɑːtn/ *v* the past participle of FORGET

fork¹ /fɔːk‖fɔːrk/ *n* [C] **1** a small tool used for picking up and eating food, with a handle and three or four points → see picture at CUTLERY **2** a tool used for digging and breaking up soil, with a handle and three or four points → see picture at GARDENING EQUIPMENT **3** a place where a road or river divides into two parts: *Turn left at the fork in the road.*

fork² *v* [I] if a road or river forks, it divides into two parts

fork sth out (also **fork sth ↔ over** *AmE*) *phr v* [I,T] *informal* to spend a lot of money on something because you have to: *We'll have to fork out nearly £1,000 for tuition fees.*

forked /fɔːkt‖fɔːrkt/ *adj* with one end that divides into two parts: *a forked tongue*

for·lorn /fəˈlɔːn‖fərˈlɔːrn/ *adj* sad and lonely: *a forlorn figure sitting on a park bench* —**forlornly** *adv*

form¹ /fɔːm‖fɔːrm/ *n* [C] **1** one type of something: *a cleaner, safer form of public transport* **take the form of** happen or exist in a particular way **2** [C] an official document with spaces where you give information **fill in/fill out a form**: *an application form* | *Fill in the form using black ink.* **3** [C] *BrE* a class in school: *the fifth form* **4** [C] a shape that you cannot see clearly: *A dark form emerged from the bushes.* **5** [C] a way of showing or saying a word, for example one that shows it is in the past or the plural: *'Was' is the past form of the verb 'to be'.* **6** [U] *BrE* how well or badly someone is performing or playing **in/on form** (=playing well)

form² *v* **1** [I,T] to start to exist, or to make something start to exist: *Ice had begun to form on the inside of the windows.* | *These rocks were formed over 4000 million years ago.* **2** [I,T] to make or become a particular shape: *Fold the paper in two to form a triangle.* | *A queue quickly began to form.* **3** [T] to make something by combining two or more parts: *In English the past tense is usually formed by adding "-ed".* **4** [T] to be the thing mentioned, or one part of it: *The Rio Grande forms the boundary between Texas and Mexico.* | *Rice forms the main part of their diet.* **5** [T] to start an organization or business: *The United Nations was formed in 1945.* **6 form an opinion/impression** to begin to have an opinion etc based on the information you have

form·al /ˈfɔːməl‖ˈfɔːr-/ *adj* **1** suitable for official or serious occasions: *I've got a suit that I wear on formal occasions.* | *"How do you do" is a formal expression, used when you meet someone for the first time.* | *We made a formal complaint.* **2 formal** **education/training/qualifications** education, training etc that you get in a school or college —**formally** *adv*

for·mal·de·hyde /fɔːˈmældɪhaɪd‖fɔːr-/ *n* [U] a strong-smelling gas that is mixed with water and used for preserving things

for·mal·i·ty /fɔːˈmæləˌti‖fɔːr-/ *n* **1** [C] a formal or official part of a process that must be done: *There are a few legal formalities to complete before the agreement is finalized.* **2** [U] very polite, formal behaviour: *He greeted his guests with great formality.*

for·mal·ize (also **-ise** *BrE*) /ˈfɔːməlaɪz‖ˈfɔːr-/ *v* [T] to make a plan or decision official, including all its details: *The contracts must be formalized within one month.*

for·mat¹ /ˈfɔːmæt‖ˈfɔːr-/ *n* [C] the way something is organized or designed: *I'd like to try a new format for next week's meeting.*

format² *v* [T] **-tted**, **-tting 1** to organize the space on a computer DISK so that information can be stored on it **2** to arrange the words and pictures on a document, page etc —**formatting** *n* [U] —**formatted** *adj*

for·ma·tion /fɔːˈmeɪʃən‖fɔːr-/ *n* **1** [U] when something develops in a particular thing, organization, or shape: + of *Damp air encourages the formation of mould.* | *the formation of a democratic government* **2** [C,U] when something forms a particular shape, or the shape in which it is formed: *rock formations* | *soldiers marching in formation* (=marching together in a pattern)

for·ma·tive /ˈfɔːmətɪv‖ˈfɔːr-/ *adj* **formative years/period etc** the time when you are young and your character is developing

for·mer¹ /ˈfɔːmə‖ˈfɔːrmər/ *adj* [only before noun] happening, existing, or true in the past, but not now: *former US president, Jimmy Carter*

former² *n* **the former** *formal* the first of two things that you have just mentioned: *Of the two theories, the former seems more likely.* → compare LATTER¹

for·mer·ly /ˈfɔːməli‖ˈfɔːrmərli/ *adv* in the past: *Sri Lanka was formerly called Ceylon.*

for·mi·da·ble /ˈfɔːmɪdəbəl, fəˈmɪd-‖ˈfɔːr-, fər-/ *adj* **1** a formidable person is powerful and slightly frightening: *a formidable opponent*

2 difficult and needing a lot of hard work, careful thought etc: *We have to cut pollution by 50% – a formidable task.* —**formidably** *adv*

form·less /ˈfɔːmləs‖ˈfɔːrm-/ *adj* lacking a definite shape or structure: *models wearing thin formless garments*

for·mu·la /ˈfɔːmjʊlə‖ˈfɔːrm-/ *n* [C], *plural* **formulas,** *or* **formulae** /-liː/ **1** a group of numbers or letters that show a mathematical or scientific rule **2** a method used to make something successful: + **for** *There's no magic formula for a happy marriage.* **3** a list of the different substances in a mixture

for·mu·late /ˈfɔːmjʊleɪt‖ˈfɔːrm-/ *v* [T] **1** to develop a plan and decide all the details: *We are trying to formulate policies that suit the needs of the people.* **2** to express your thoughts, feelings, or ideas, choosing your words carefully: *The interviewer barely gave Higgs time to formulate a reply.* —**formulation** /ˌfɔːmjʊˈleɪʃən‖ˌfɔːr-/ *n* [C,U]

for·sake /fəˈseɪk‖fər-/ *v* **forsook** /-ˈsʊk/, **forsaken** /-ˈseɪkən/, **forsaking** [T] *literary* **1** to leave someone when they need you **2** to stop doing, using, or having something: *I won't forsake my principles.*

fort /fɔːt‖fɔːrt/ *n* [C] a strong building used by soldiers for defending a place

for·te /ˈfɔːteɪ‖fɔːrt/ *n* [singular] if an activity is your forte, you are good at doing it: *Cooking isn't really my forte.*

forth /fɔːθ‖fɔːrθ/ *adv literary* out or away from a place: *He went forth into the desert.* → see also **back and forth** (BACK[2]) **and so on/forth** (SO[1])

forth·com·ing /ˌfɔːθˈkʌmɪŋ‖ˌfɔːrθ-/ *adj* **1** [only before noun] *formal* happening soon: *the forthcoming election* **2** [not before noun] if something is forthcoming, it is given or offered to someone: *If more money is not forthcoming, we'll have to close the theatre.* **3** [not before noun] willing to give information: *Michael wasn't very forthcoming about his plans.*

forth·right /ˈfɔːθraɪt‖ˈfɔːrθ-/ *adj* saying what you think honestly and directly: *Bill answered in his usual forthright manner.*

forth·with /fɔːθˈwɪθ, -ˈwɪð‖fɔːrθ-/ *adv formal* immediately: *All leave is to be cancelled forthwith.*

for·ti·fi·ca·tions /ˌfɔːtɪfɪˈkeɪʃənz‖ˌfɔːr-/ *n* [plural] towers, walls etc built to protect a place

for·ti·fy /ˈfɔːtɪfaɪ‖ˈfɔːr-/ *v* [T] **1** to build towers, walls etc around a place to defend it: *a fortified city* **2** to make someone feel physically or mentally stronger: *We fortified ourselves with a beer before we started.* —**fortification** /ˌfɔːtɪfɪˈkeɪʃən‖ˌfɔːr-/ *n* [U]

for·ti·tude /ˈfɔːtɪtjuːd‖ˈfɔːrtɪtuːd/ *n* [U] *formal* courage

fort·night /ˈfɔːtnaɪt‖ˈfɔːrt-/ *n* [C usually singular] *BrE* two weeks: *The meetings take place once a fortnight.* | *a fortnight's holiday*

for·tress /ˈfɔːtrɪs‖ˈfɔːr-/ *n* [C] a big strong building used for defending a place

for·tu·i·tous /fɔːˈtjuːɪtəs‖fɔːrˈtuː-/ *adj formal* lucky, and happening by chance to be good: *a fortuitous discovery*

for·tu·nate /ˈfɔːtʃənət‖ˈfɔːr-/ *adj* lucky: **be fortunate to do sth** *We were fortunate enough to get tickets for the last show.* | + **(that)** *It was fortu-nate that the ambulance arrived so quickly.* → opposite UNFORTUNATE

for·tu·nate·ly /ˈfɔːtʃənətli‖ˈfɔːr-/ *adv* **1** used to say that it is a good thing that something happens, is true, or exists: *Fortunately I had a good job at the time.* **2** happening because of good luck: *We were late getting to the airport, but fortunately our plane was delayed.*

for·tune /ˈfɔːtʃən‖ˈfɔːr-/ *n* **1** [C] a lot of money: *Julia must have spent a fortune on her wedding dress!* | *He made a fortune on that deal.* **2** [C usually plural, U] chance, or the good and bad things that happen to you: *a win that marked a change in the team's fortunes* **3** **tell sb's fortune** to tell someone what will happen to them in the future

fortune tel·ler /ˈ.. ˌ../ *n* [C] someone who tells you what will happen to you in the future

for·ty /ˈfɔːti‖ˈfɔːrti/ *number* 40 —**fortieth** *number*

for·um /ˈfɔːrəm/ *n* [C] a meeting or situation in which people can discuss an important subject: *a forum for debate on bullying in schools*

for·ward[1] /ˈfɔːwəd‖ˈfɔːrwərd/ *adv* **1** also **forwards** towards a place in front of you: *He leaned forward to hear what they were saying.* | *Could you move your chair forwards a little?* **2** used to say that something is making progress or improving: *NASA's space project cannot go forward without more money.* **3** towards the future: *We must look forward and invest in new technology.* → see also FAST FORWARD, **look forward to sth** (LOOK[1]) → opposite BACKWARD

forward[2] *adj* **1** forward planning/thinking etc when you make plans for the future: *Forward planning is essential if the campaign is to succeed.* **2** [only before noun] closer to a place that is in front of you: *Roadblocks prevented further forward movement.* **3** too confident and friendly with people you do not know very well

forward[3] *v* [T] to send letters, packages, or E-mail messages to someone at another address

forward[4] *n* [C] an attacking player in a sport such as football

forwarding ad·dress /ˈ... ˌ.‖ˈ... ˌ./ *n* [C] a new address to which your mail is sent

forward-look·ing /ˈ.. ˌ../ *adj* planning for the future by trying new ideas: *Forward-looking schools are already exploring these possibilities.*

for·wards /ˈfɔːwədz‖ˈfɔːrwərdz/ *adv* FORWARD

fos·sil /ˈfɒsəl‖ˈfɑː-/ *n* [C] part of an animal or plant that lived thousands of years ago, or its shape preserved in rock —**fossil** *adj*

fos·ter[1] /ˈfɒstəl‖ˈfɑːstər/ *v* [T] **1** to encourage a feeling or skill to develop: *Our weekly meetings help to foster team spirit.* **2** to take care of someone else's child for a period of time, without becoming their legal parent → compare ADOPT

foster[2] *adj* **1** foster parents/family/home etc the people who foster a child, or the child's temporary home **2** foster child a child who is fostered

fought /fɔːt‖fɑːt/ *v* the past tense and past participle of FIGHT

foul[1] /faʊl/ *adj* **1** very dirty or having a very unpleasant smell: *foul-smelling water* **2** *especially BrE* very unpleasant: *The weather's been foul all week.* | **in a foul mood/temper** *She*

came home from work in a foul mood. **3 foul
language** rude and offensive words

foul² *v* [T] **1** if a sports player fouls another
player, they do something that is against the
rules: *Berger was fouled in the penalty area.*
2 to make something very dirty
  foul sth ↔ **up** *phr v* [I,T] *informal* to spoil
  something completely: *I was ill and it really
  fouled up the holiday.*

foul³ *n* [C] something someone does in a sports
game that is against the rules

foul play /ˌ. './ *n* [U] if the police think someone's death was caused by foul play, they think
the person was murdered: *Police have found a
body, but they don't suspect foul play.*

found¹ /faʊnd/ *v* the past tense and past participle of FIND

found² *v* [T] **1** to start an organization: *The
Academy was founded in 1666.* **2 be founded
on/upon** to be based on a set of ideas or beliefs:
*The US was founded on the idea of religious free-
dom.*

foun·da·tion /faʊnˈdeɪʃən/ *n* **1** [C] a basic
idea or belief that something is based on: **+ of**
*Justice and equality are the foundation of any de-
mocracy.* ‖ **lay the foundation for sth** *an agreement that will lay the foundations for peace*
2 [C] an organization that gives money for
special purposes: *the National Foundation for the
Arts* **3** [C] *AmE* (also **foundations** *plural
especially BrE*) the solid base under the ground
that supports a building **4** [singular] when an
organization is established **5 be without
foundation/have no foundation** if a story etc is
without foundation, there is no proof that it is
true: *These accusations are completely without
foundation.*

found·er /ˈfaʊndə‖-ər/ *n* [C] someone who
starts an organization

foun·dry /ˈfaʊndri/ *n* [C] a place where metals
are melted and made into things

foun·tain /ˈfaʊntɪn‖ˈfaʊntn/ *n* [C] a structure
that sends water up into the air

fountain pen /ˈ.. ./ *n* [C] a pen that you fill
with ink

four /fɔː‖fɔːr/ *number* **1** 4 **2 on all fours** on
your hands and knees: *crawling around on all
fours*

four·some /ˈfɔːsəm‖ˈfɔːr-/ *n* [C] a group of four
people doing something together: *I'll invite Jo
for dinner to make up a foursome.*

four·teen /ˌfɔːˈtiːn◂‖ˌfɔːr-/ *number* 14 —**four-
teenth** *number*

fourth /fɔːθ‖fɔːrθ/ *number* **1** 4th **2** *AmE*
¼ quarter

Fourth of Ju·ly /ˌ. .. ./ *n AmE* [singular] a national holiday in the US

fowl /faʊl/ *n* [C], *plural* **fowl** or **fowls** a bird such
as a chicken that is kept for its meat and eggs
→ see also WILDFOWL

fox¹ /fɒks‖fɑːks/ *n* [C] a wild animal like a dog
with red-brown fur, a pointed face, and a thick
tail

fox² *v* [T] *BrE* to be difficult to do or understand

foy·er /ˈfɔɪeɪ‖ˈfɔɪər/ *n* [C] a room at the entrance to a hotel, theatre etc

frac·as /ˈfrækɑː‖ˈfreɪkəs/ *n* [singular] a short
noisy fight or argument

frac·tion /ˈfrækʃən/ *n* **1** [C] a number that is
smaller than 1, for example ¾ and ½ **2** [singular]
a very small amount of something: **+ of** *We paid
only a fraction of the original price.* —**fractional**
adj —**fractionally** *adv*

frac·ture¹ /ˈfræktʃəl-ər/ *n* [C] a crack in something hard such as a bone or rock

fracture² *v* [T] to crack or break something
hard such as a bone or rock: *Your arm isn't
fractured, just badly bruised.*

fra·gile /ˈfrædʒaɪl‖-dʒəl/ *adj* **1** easily broken
or destroyed: *fragile glassware*‖*a fragile peace
agreement* **2** not strong: *a fragile old lady* —**fra-
gility** /frəˈdʒɪləti/ *n* [U]

frag·ment¹ /ˈfrægmənt/ *n* [C] a small piece of
something: **+ of** *fragments of glass*

frag·ment² /fræɡˈment‖ˈfræɡment, ˈfræɡˈment/
v [I,T] to break something, or be broken, into
many small parts: *a day fragmented by interrup-
tions and phone calls* —**fragmented** *adj*

fra·grance /ˈfreɪɡrəns/ *n* [C,U] a pleasant
smell: *a delicate fragrance*

fra·grant /ˈfreɪɡrənt/ *adj* smelling pleasant: *a
fragrant rose*

frail /freɪl/ *adj* thin and weak: *a frail old man*

frail·ty /ˈfreɪlti/ *n* [C,U] a physical or moral
weakness: *human frailty*

frame¹ /freɪm/ *n* [C] **1** a wood, metal, or
plastic structure that surrounds something such
as a picture, door, or window: *a gilt picture
frame* → see colour picture on page 474 **2** the
main structure of a building, vehicle, or piece of
furniture: *a bicycle frame* **3** the shape of someone's body: *her small slender frame* **4 frame of
mind** the way you feel about something: *I don't
think you'll be able to convince him while he's in
that frame of mind.*

frame² *v* [T] **1** to put a picture or photograph
into a frame: *a framed portrait of the Queen*
2 to deliberately make someone seem guilty of
a crime: *Murphy claims he was framed by his
partner.* **3** *formal* to express something carefully: *Jack hesitated, unsure how to frame his request.*

frames /freɪmz/ *n* [plural] the part of a pair of
GLASSES that surrounds the LENSes

frame·work /ˈfreɪmwɜːk‖-wɜːrk/ *n* [C] **1** a set
of rules, facts, or beliefs that people use to make
plans or decisions: *We must work within the fra-
mework of the existing budget.* **2** the main
structure that supports something such as a
building or vehicle

fran·chise /ˈfræntʃaɪz/ *n* **1** [C] permission given to another business person to sell a company's products or services **2** [U] the legal right
to vote in an election

frank /fræŋk/ *adj* **1** speaking in an honest and
direct way, and not trying to hide the truth or
your true feelings: *a frank exchange of opinions*‖*I'll be perfectly frank with you – he may
not recover.* **2 to be frank** *spoken* used when
you are saying what you really think: *To be
frank, I don't think it will work.* —**frankly** *adv*
—**frankness** *n* [U]

frank·fur·ter /ˈfræŋkfɜːtəl-fɜːrtər/ *n* [C] a long
SAUSAGE; HOT DOG

fran·tic /ˈfræntɪk/ *adj* **1** hurrying in an
anxious and disorganized way: *a frantic rush for
the last remaining tickets* **2** very anxious or

upset: *The girl's parents were frantic with worry.*
—**frantically** /-kli/ *adv*

fra·ter·nal /frə'tɜːnl‖-ɜːr-/ *adj* relating to or between brothers: *fraternal love*

fra·ter·ni·ty /frə'tɜːnɪti‖-ɜːr-/ *n* **1** [C] a club of male students in the US **2** [U] *formal* a feeling of friendship among a group of people

frat·er·nize (also **-ise** *BrE*) /'frætənaɪz‖-ər-/ *v* [I] to be friendly with someone, especially someone who you should not be friendly with: **+ with** *Soldiers who fraternize with the enemy will be shot.*

fraud /frɔːd‖frɒːd/ *n* **1** [C,U] when someone deceives people to get money: *The police arrested him for tax fraud.* **2** [C] someone who deliberately deceives people to get an advantage: *She realized that the salesman had been a fraud.*

fraud·u·lent /'frɔːdjʊlənt‖'frɒːdʒə-/ *adj* dishonest and illegal: *fraudulent business deals*
—**fraudulently** *adv*

fraught /frɔːt‖frɒːt/ *adj* **1 fraught with problems/difficulty/danger** full of problems, difficulty, danger etc: *a situation fraught with difficulties* **2** *informal* very anxious or worried

fray¹ /freɪ/ *v* **1** [I,T] if cloth frays, or if something frays it, its threads become loose at the edge **2** [I] if your temper frays you become annoyed: *As the temperature rose, tempers began to fray.*

fray² *n* **enter/join the fray** to take part in a fight or argument: *More protesters arrived and joined in the fray.*

freak¹ /friːk/ *n* [C] **1** *informal* someone who has a very strong interest in something: *Carrot juice is a favourite with health freaks.* **2** someone or something that is very strange: *He looked at me as if I were some kind of freak.*

freak² *adj* **freak accident/storm etc** a very unusual accident, storm etc

freak³ *v* [I,T] *spoken* also **freak out** to suddenly become very angry, frightened, or anxious, or to make someone do this: *I was an hour late and Dad totally freaked!* | *Horror films always freak me out.*

freck·le /'frekəl/ *n* [C usually plural] a small brown spot on someone's skin: *a little girl with red hair and freckles* —**freckled** *adj*

-free /friː/ *suffix* **fat-free/rent-free/trouble-free etc** without fat, rent, trouble etc: *a fat-free diet* | *duty-free cigarettes*

free¹ /friː/ *adj* **1** allowed to live, exist, or happen without being controlled: *free competition between airline companies* | *a free and fair election* | **be free to do sth** *The children are free to choose any of the activities.* **2** not costing any money: *We got two free tickets for the game.* | *Entrance to the gallery is free.* | **free of charge** *Pregnant women can get dental treatment free of charge.* **3** not a prisoner: **set sb free** (=let someone leave a prison): *The UN demanded that the hostages be set free.* **4** not busy doing other things: *Let's go out for a meal – when are you free?* | **free time** (=when you are not busy) **5** not being used by anyone else: *Excuse me, is*

this seat free? **6 a free hand** permission to do something the way you want to **7 feel free** *spoken* used to tell someone that they are allowed to do something: *Feel free to ask questions.* **8 free of/from** without something harmful or unpleasant: *Keep the garden free of weeds.*

free² *v* [T] **1** to allow someone to leave a prison or somewhere they have been forced to stay: *Atkins was freed from jail yesterday.* **2** to help someone by removing something unpleasant: **free sb from** *an attempt to free himself from drug addiction* **3** to make someone or something no longer trapped or kept prisoner somewhere: *Firefighters freed two men trapped in the burning building.* **4** also **free up** to make something available so that it can be used: *Hiring an assistant will free up your time to do other things.*
→ see also FREELY

free³ *adv* **1** without having to pay any money: *Children under 12 travel free.* | **for free** *Kylie's fixing my car for free.* **2** to escape from a place or situation: **break free** *Lucille finally broke free and started a new life.* **3** not fixed or held in a place or position: *She undid her hair, letting it fall free.*

free·bie, freebee /'friːbiː/ *n* [C] *informal* something you are given that you do not have to pay for

free·dom /'friːdəm/ *n* **1** [C,U] the right to live your life the way you want to, make your own decisions, express your own opinions etc, without being prevented or controlled: *Kids have too much freedom nowadays.* | **freedom of speech/choice etc** (=the right to say or choose what you want) | **freedom to do sth** *People should have the freedom to vote for whoever they choose.* **2** [U] when someone is no longer in prison **3 freedom from sth** when you are not affected by something harmful: *freedom from fear and oppression*

freedom fight·er /'.. ,../ *n* [C] someone who fights in a war against a bad government or army → compare TERRORIST

free en·ter·prise /,. '.../ *n* [U] when companies are allowed to operate without much government control

free-for-all /,. . '.'/ *n* [C usually singular] *informal* a fight or noisy argument involving a lot of people

free kick /,. './ *n* [C] a kick by a football player after a player of the other team has broken the rules

free·lance /'friːlɑːns‖-læns/ *adj, adv* working independently for several different organizations: *a freelance journalist* | *How long have you been working freelance?* —**freelancer** *n* [C]

free·ly /'friːli/ *adv* **1** without anyone trying to control you or prevent you doing something: *We encourage our students to speak freely.* | *People can now travel freely across the border.* | *countries where abortion is freely available* **2 freely admit/acknowledge** to agree that something is true: *I freely admit I made a bad choice.* **3** in large amounts: *He gives freely to local charities.*

free mar·ket /ˌ. '../ n [singular] when prices and trade are not controlled by the government

Free·ma·son /ˈfriːˌmeɪsən, ˌfriːˈmeɪsən/ n [C] a man who belongs to a secret society in which members help other members to be successful

free-range /ˌ. '.◂/ adj coming from or relating to farm animals that are allowed to live outside and are not kept in small rooms or cages: *free-range eggs*

free speech /ˌ. './ n [U] the right to express your opinions: *Americans are guaranteed the right to free speech in the Constitution.*

free-way /ˈfriːweɪ/ n [C] *AmE* a wide road on which cars can travel at a fast speed; MOTORWAY *BrE*

free will /ˌ. '../ n **1** when people control their own lives by the choices and decisions they make **2 do sth of your own free will** to do something because you want to, not because you have to: *She went of her own free will.*

freeze[1] /friːz/ v **froze** /frəʊz‖frouz/, **frozen** /ˈfrəʊzən‖ˈfrou-/, **freezing 1** [I,T] to become solid and hard, or to make something solid and hard because the temperature is very cold: *The water pipes may freeze if you don't leave your heating on.* **2** [T] to preserve food for a long time by keeping it very cold: *I'm going to freeze some of this bread.* **3** [I] if you freeze, you feel very cold: *You'll freeze if you don't wear a coat.* **4** [I] to suddenly stop moving and stay very still: *Hugh froze when he saw the snake.* **5** [T] to officially prevent money from being spent, or stop prices, wages etc from increasing: *Our budget for next year has been frozen.*

freeze[2] n **1 price/wage freeze** when prices or wages are not allowed to increase **2** [C usually singular] when an activity or process is stopped for a period of time: *There's a freeze on recruitment at the moment.*

freez·er /ˈfriːzəl-ər/ n [C] a container where food is kept frozen so that it can be stored, which is operated by electricity ➡ compare FRIDGE ➡ see picture at KITCHEN

freez·ing[1] /ˈfriːzɪŋ/ adj *informal* very cold: *It's freezing outside! | Shut the door! I'm freezing!*

freezing[2] n **above/below freezing** above or below 32°F or 0°C

freez·ing point /'.. ./ n [C,U] the temperature at which a liquid freezes

freight /freɪt/ n [U] goods carried by road, trains, planes, or ships

freight·er /ˈfreɪtəl-ər/ n [C] a plane or ship that carries goods

French fry /ˌ. './ n [C usually plural] *AmE* long thin piece of potato cooked in fat; CHIP *BrE*

French win·dow /ˌ. '../ n [C usually plural] large glass doors

fre·net·ic /frɪˈnetɪk/ adj fast and exciting, but sometimes making you feel tired or confused: *the frenetic pace of life in New York* —**frenetically** /-kli/ adv

fren·zied /ˈfrenzid/ adj wild, uncontrolled, and excited: *the sound of frenzied shouts and applause* —**frenziedly** adv

fren·zy /ˈfrenzi/ n **1** [singular, U] when you are so anxious or excited that you are unable to control your behaviour: **in a frenzy** *In a frenzy, Brady began kicking and punching the police officers* **2 a frenzy of activity** when people are

suddenly very busy: *The house was a frenzy of activity as we got ready for the party.*

fre·quen·cy /ˈfriːkwənsi/ n **1** [U] the number of times that something happens, or the fact that it happens a lot: **+ of** *the frequency of bacterial infections in AIDS patients* **2** [C,U] the rate at which a sound or light wave is repeated: *The human ear cannot hear sounds of very high frequency.*

fre·quent[1] /ˈfriːkwənt/ adj happening often: *Her teacher is worried about her frequent absences from class.* ➡ opposite INFREQUENT

fre·quent[2] /frɪˈkwent‖frɪˈkwent, ˈfriːkwənt/ v [T] to go to a place often: *a café frequented by artists and intellectuals*

fre·quent·ly /ˈfrikwəntli/ adv *formal* often: *Passengers complain that trains are frequently cancelled.*

fres·co /ˈfreskəʊ‖-koʊ/ n [C], *plural* **frescoes** a picture painted on wet PLASTER on a wall

fresh /freʃ/ adj **1** new and different from the previous ones: *We need to try a fresh approach. | I've put some fresh sheets on your bed.* | **make a fresh start** (=start living or working in a new way): *They decided to move to Australia and make a fresh start.* **2** fresh food and flowers are in good condition because they have been produced or picked recently: *fresh strawberries* **3** pleasantly COOL or clean: *a fresh breeze | a fresh minty taste* | **fresh air** (=air from outside a building): *It's nice to get some fresh air.* **4 fresh water** water that contains no salt and comes from rivers and lakes **5 fresh from/out of** having just left a place: *a new teacher fresh from university* **6 fresh in your mind/memory** etc if something is fresh in your mind, you remember it clearly, because it happened recently: *You might want to write about your trip while it's still fresh in your mind.* **7** not tired, and having plenty of energy: *Lucy woke up feeling fresh and relaxed.* **8** healthy-looking: *a fresh complexion* —**freshness** n [U]

fresh·en /ˈfreʃən/ v
freshen up *phr* v [I] *especially spoken* to wash your hands and face, so that you feel clean and comfortable: *Would you like to freshen up before dinner?*

fresh·ly /ˈfreʃli/ adv very recently: *freshly mown grass*

fresh·man /ˈfreʃmən/ n [C] *AmE* a student in the first year of HIGH SCHOOL or college

fresh·wa·ter /ˈfreʃwɔːtəl-wɔːtər, -wɑː-/ adj a freshwater fish lives in rivers or lakes

fret /fret/ v [I] to worry

fret·ful /ˈfretfəl/ adj old-fashioned worried and complaining about unimportant things: *a fretful child* —**fretfully** adv

Fri. the written abbreviation of Friday

fri·ar /ˈfraɪəl-ər/ n [C] a kind of MONK

fric·tion /ˈfrɪkʃən/ n [U] **1** when people disagree with each other and argue in an unfriendly way: *friction between parents and their teenage children* **2** when one surface rubs against another: *the heat produce by friction*

Fri·day /ˈfraɪdi/ written abbreviation **Fri.** n [C,U] the day of the week between Thursday and Saturday

fridge /frɪdʒ/ n [C] a metal container where food is kept cold and fresh by electricity, but not frozen → compare FREEZER → see picture at KITCHEN

fried /fraɪd/ adj cooked in hot oil

friend /frend/ n [C] someone that you know well and enjoy spending time with: *Martha went to London with some friends.* |**best friend** *Even my best friend didn't know my secret.* |**old friend** (=one you have known a long time): *Lee's an old friend of mine.* |**make friends** (=start a friendly relationship): *He's very shy, and finds it difficult to make friends with people.* |**be friends with sb** (=have a friendly relationship with someone)

USAGE NOTE: friend

Remember to use a possessive noun or pronoun in phrases such as: *He's a friend of mine.* | *A friend of ours told us ...* | *my mother's best friend* | *Is Chris a friend of yours?*

---

friend·ly /'frendli/ adj behaving towards other people in a way that shows that you like them: *a friendly smile* |**+ to/towards** *The local people are very friendly towards tourists.* —**friendliness** n [U] → see also ENVIRONMENTALLY FRIENDLY, USER-FRIENDLY

friend·ship /'frendʃɪp/ n [C,U] a relationship in which two people are friends: *Their friendship began in college.* |*a close friendship*

fries /fraɪz/ n [plural] *especially AmE* potatoes cut into long thin pieces and cooked in hot oil; CHIPS *BrE*

frieze /friːz/ n [C] a decorated border along the top of a wall

frig·ate /'frɪgɪt/ n [C] a small fast ship used by the navy to protect other ships

fright /fraɪt/ n [singular, U] a sudden feeling of fear: **give sb a fright** (=make someone frightened): *Sorry, I didn't mean to give you a fright.* |**in fright** (=because of fright): *They both ran off in fright*

fright·en /'fraɪtn/ v [T] to make someone feel afraid: *Don't shout like that – you'll frighten the baby.* |**frighten sb into doing sth** (=force someone to do something by frightening them)
frighten sb ↔ **away/off** *phr v* [T] to make a person or animal afraid or nervous so that they go away or stop doing something: *loud noises that frightened the birds away*

fright·ened /'fraɪtnd/ adj feeling afraid, because you think something bad is going to happen: *Don't be frightened. No one's going to hurt you.* |**+ of** *When I was a child, I was frightened of the dark.* |**+ that** *She was frightened that there was someone outside her room.* → see colour picture on page 277

fright·en·ing /'fraɪtn-ɪŋ/ adj making you feel afraid: *a frightening experience* —**frighteningly** adv

fright·ful /'fraɪtfəl/ adj *BrE spoken* very bad: *The house was in a frightful mess.*

fright·ful·ly /'fraɪtfəli/ adv *BrE old-fashioned* very: *I'm frightfully sorry.*

fri·gid /'frɪdʒ₃d/ adj **1** a woman who is frigid does not like having sex **2** *literary* not friendly

frill /frɪl/ n [C] **1** a decoration on the edge of a piece of cloth, made from another piece of cloth with many small folds in it **2** [usually plural] an additional feature which is nice, but not nec-

essary: *a cheap straightforward insurance service with no frills*

frill·y /'frɪli/ adj decorated with many folds of cloth around the edges: *a frilly blouse*

fringe¹ /frɪndʒ/ n [C] **1** *BrE* the part of your hair that hangs over your FOREHEAD; BANGS *AmE* → see colour picture on page 244 **2** the outside edge of something: *He was standing on the fringe of the crowd.* |*the fringes of the town* **3** a decoration on a curtain etc, which consists of hanging threads along the edge: *a cowboy jacket with a leather fringe* **4** a small part of a group, organization, or activity that is very different from the main part and is not at all typical: *the fascist fringe of British politics*

fringe² adj [only before noun] not belonging to the main part of a subject, activity, or group: *fringe issues*

fringe³ v [T] to form a border along the edge of something: *a line of palm trees fringing the shore*

fringe ben·e·fit /'. ,.../ n [C usually plural] something that you get from your employer in addition to your wages, for example a car or free travel

frisk /frɪsk/ v [T] to put your hands on someone's body, searching in their pockets etc, to check that they do not have any hidden weapons or drugs

frisk·y /'frɪski/ adj full of energy and fun: *frisky lambs*

frit·ter /'frɪtəl-ər/
fritter sth ↔ **away** *phr v* [T] to waste money or time on unimportant things

fri·vol·i·ty /frɪ'vɒlətil-'vɑː-/ n [C,U] when people behave in a way that is not serious or sensible: *childish frivolity*

friv·o·lous /'frɪvələs/ adj **1** behaving in a silly way when you should be sensible: *a frivolous remark* **2** wasting money or time on unimportant things: *a frivolous pastime*

frizz·y /'frɪzi/ adj frizzy hair is very tightly curled

fro /frəʊlfroʊ/ adv → see **to and fro** (TO³)

frog /frɒglfrɑːg, frɔːg/ n [C] a small green animal that lives near water and has long legs for jumping

frog

frog·man /'frɒgmənl 'frɑːg-, 'frɔːg-/ n [C] someone whose job is to swim and work under water wearing a rubber suit and special equipment for breathing

frol·ic /'frɒlɪkl'frɑː-/ v [I] **frolicked, frolicked, frolicking** *literary* to play happily —**frolic** n [C]

from /frəm; *strong* frɒmlfrəm; *strong* frɑm, frɑːm/ *prep* **1** starting at a particular place, time, or level: *He drove all the way from Colorado.* |*The morning class is from 9.00 to 11.00.* |*Prices range from $80 to $250.* |**from now on** (=starting now and continuing into the future): *From now on Mr Collins will be teaching this class.* **2** used to say where someone was born, or where they usually live or work: *"Where are you from?" "I'm from South Africa."* |*Our speaker today is from the University of Montana.* **3** used when you are saying how far a distance is: *We live about five miles from the airport.* **4** used to say who gave or sent something: *Who is the present from?* |*I got a phone call* *from Ernie today.* **5** if something is taken from a place, person, or amount, it is removed or taken away: *He pulled his shoes out from under the bed.* | *Subtract $40.00 from the total.* **6** used to say where something was made or produced: *food from local farms* **7** used to say where you are when you see something: *We could see the house from the road.* **8** used to give the reason for an opinion: *From what I've read, the company seems to be in difficulties.* **9 a week/2 months etc from now** one week, two months etc after the time when you are speaking: *One month from now we'll be in Mexico!* **10** used to state the substance that is used to make something: *Beer is made from hops.* **11** used after words such as 'stop', 'protect', or 'keep', to introduce the thing that is stopped or avoided: *This will stop you from feeling sick.* **12** used to state the cause of something: *death rates from accidents* | **suffer from** (=be affected by): *My sister suffers from asthma.* **13** used when you are comparing things: *He's quite different from his brother.*

frond /frɒnd‖frɑːnd/ *n* [C] a leaf of a FERN or PALM

front¹ /frʌnt/ *n* **1 the front a)** the part of something that is furthest forward: *Let's sit at the front of the bus.* **b)** the most important side or surface of something, which you look at first: *The magazine had a picture of Princess Diana on the front.* | **+ of** *The front of the house was painted yellow.* → opposite BACK¹ **2 in front of a)** facing something: *Kelly sat down in front of the mirror.* → see colour picture on page 474 **b)** near the entrance to a building facing the street: *He parked in front of a small hotel.* **c)** where someone can see or hear you: *Don't say anything in front of the children.* → opposite BEHIND¹ **3 in front a)** further forward than someone or something else; ahead: *The car in front braked suddenly.* | **+ of** *There was a tall man sitting in front of me, so I couldn't see the screen.* **b)** winning in a game or competition: *The Germans were in front at half-time.* **4** a line along which fighting takes place during a war: *More troops were sent to the Western Front.* **5 a front a)** when someone pretends to have a feeling or quality that they do not really have: *I know it's worrying, but we must try to put on a brave front.* **b)** an organization or activity that seems to be legal but which is secretly being used for an illegal purpose: *The drug dealers were using the travel company as a front for their operations.* **6 on the political/business/sporting etc front** *especially spoken* used to say that you are talking about politics, business etc: *We've had some good news on the business front.* **7** *technical* a line where two masses of air that have different temperatures meet each other: *a cold front moving across the country*

USAGE NOTE: front

Use **in front of** when one thing is separate from the other: *A child ran into the road in front of us.* Use **in/at the front (of)** when one thing is inside or is a part of another: *The emergency exit is at/in the front of the plane.* | *Our seats were in/at the front of the hall.*

---

front² *adj* at or in the front of something: *the front door* | *tickets for front row seats*

front³ *v* [T] to face something: *The building fronts Lake Michigan.*

front·al /ˈfrʌntl/ *adj* towards, or at the front of something: *a frontal attack* | *the frontal lobe of the brain*

fron·tier /ˈfrʌntɪə‖frʌnˈtɪr/ *n* [C] **1** the border of a country: *a town on the frontier between France and Spain* **2 the frontiers of** the limits of what is known about something: *the frontiers of science*

front line /ˌ. ˈ.◂/ *n* **the front line** the place where fighting happens in a war —**front-line** *adj*: *front-line soldiers*

front-page /ˌ. ˈ.◂/ *adj* **front-page news/story etc** news that is important enough to be on the front page of a newspaper

front-run·ner /ˌ. ˈ../ *n* [C] the person, company etc that is most likely to win or succeed: *the front-runner in the race for the Republican nomination*

frost¹ /frɒst‖frɒːst/ *n* **1** [U] a white powder of ice, which forms on surfaces outside when the temperature is very cold: *trees covered with frost* **2** [C] very cold weather, when water freezes: *an early frost* | *a hard frost* (=extremely cold weather)

frost² *v* [T] *AmE* to cover a cake with FROSTING; ICE *BrE*

frost·bite /ˈfrɒstbaɪt‖ˈfrɒːst-/ *n* [U] when your fingers, toes etc become frozen and are badly damaged —**frostbitten** /-bɪtn/ *adj*

frost·ing /ˈfrɒstɪŋ‖ˈfrɒːstɪŋ/ *n* [U] *AmE* a sweet substance that you put on cakes, made from sugar and liquid; ICING

frost·y /ˈfrɒsti‖ˈfrɒːsti/ *adj* **1** very cold or covered with FROST: *a frosty morning* | *frosty ground* **2** unfriendly: *a frosty greeting*

froth¹ /frɒθ‖frɒːθ/ *n* [singular, U] a white mass of BUBBLES that forms on top of a liquid

froth² *v* [I] to produce a lot of froth

froth·y /ˈfrɒθi‖ˈfrɒːθi/ *adj* a liquid that is frothy has lots of small BUBBLES on top: *a cup of hot frothy capuccino*

frown¹ /fraʊn/ *v* [I] to make an angry or unhappy expression by moving your EYEBROWS together, so that lines appear on your FOREHEAD: *Mel frowned and pretended to ignore me.*

frown on/upon sth *phr v* [T] to disapprove of something: *In the 1930s divorce was frowned upon.*

frown² *n* [C] the expression on your face when you frown: *He looked at her with a puzzled frown.*

froze /frəʊz‖froʊz/ *v* the past tense of FREEZE

fro·zen¹ /ˈfrəʊzən‖ˈfroʊ-/ *v* the past participle of FREEZE

frozen² *adj* **1** frozen food has been stored at very low temperatures to preserve it: *frozen peas* **2** *spoken* feeling very cold: *Can you turn up the heating? I'm frozen.* **3** changed into ice or made very hard because of the very cold weather: *The ground was frozen.* | *the frozen lake*

fru·gal /ˈfruːɡəl/ *adj* **1** careful to only buy what is necessary: *As children we were taught to be frugal and hard-working.* **2** a frugal meal is small and does not cost much —**frugally** *adv*

fruit /fruːt/ *n*, *plural* **fruit** or **fruits** **1** [C,U] something such as an apple, orange, or STRAWBERRY which grows on a plant, tree or bush, and

fruits

flesh
stone BrE/ pit AmE — peach — skin
pear
plum
apple
cherries
pip BrE/ seed AmE — peel
bananas
seeds BrE/ pips AmE
melon
pineapple
mango
papaya
figs
grapes
olives
lychees

F

contains seeds: *a bowl of fruit* | **fruit salad** (=a mixture of pieces of several different kinds of fruit) **2 the fruits of sth** the good results from something that you have worked hard to achieve: *They can now enjoy the fruits of their labours.* → see also **bear fruit** (BEAR¹)

fruit·ful /ˈfruːtfəl/ *adj* producing good results: *a fruitful meeting*

fru·i·tion /fruˈɪʃən/ *n* **come to fruition** *formal* if a plan comes to fruition, it starts to be successful: *In 1969 their plans finally came to fruition.*

fruit·less /ˈfruːtləs/ *adj* failing to produce good results, especially after much effort: *Brad spent*

three fruitless months in Chicago, trying to find a job. —**fruitlessly** *adv*

fruit·y /ˈfruːti/ *adj* tasting or smelling strongly of fruit: *a fruity wine*

frus·trate /frʌˈstreɪt‖ˈfrʌstreɪt/ *v* [T] **1** if something frustrates you, it makes you feel impatient or angry because you are unable to do what you want to do: *If you try to teach children too much too quickly, you will only confuse and frustrate them.* **2** to prevent someone's plans or efforts from succeeding: *Their plans were frustrated by a disastrous fire.*

frus·trat·ed /frʌˈstreɪtⁱd‖ˈfrʌstreɪtⁱd/ *adj* feeling impatient or angry because you are unable to do what you want to do: **+ with** *She's getting really frustrated with her computer. It's always crashing.*

frus·trat·ing /frʌˈstreɪtɪŋ‖ˈfrʌstreɪtɪŋ/ *adj* making you feel impatient or angry because you cannot do what you want to do: *They keep sending me the wrong forms – it's very frustrating.*

frus·tra·tion /frʌˈstreɪʃən/ *n* [C,U] the feeling of being impatient or angry because you are unable to do what you want to do: *There is a deep sense of frustration among many high school teachers.*

fry /fraɪ/ *v* [I,T] **fried, fried, frying** to cook something in hot oil, or be cooked in hot oil: *Do you want me to fry some eggs?*

frying pan /ˈ.. ./ *n* [C] a round flat pan with a long handle, used for frying food

ft. the written abbreviation of FOOT or FEET

fudge¹ /fʌdʒ/ *n* [U] a soft creamy sweet food

fudge² *v* [T] to avoid giving exact details or a clear answer about something: *Clinton tried to fudge the tax issue.*

fuel¹ /ˈfjuːəl/ *n* [C,U] a substance such as coal, gas, or oil, which can be burned to produce heat or power

fuel² *v* [T] **-lled, -lling** BrE, **-led, -ling** AmE to make a situation worse, or make someone's feelings stronger: *high inflation, fuelled by high government spending*

fu·gi·tive /ˈfjuːdʒⁱtɪv/ *n* [C] someone who has escaped and is trying to avoid being caught, especially by the police: *a fugitive from justice*

ful·fil BrE, **fulfill** AmE /fʊlˈfɪl/ *v* [T] **-lled, -lling 1 fulfil a promise/duty/obligation etc** to do something that you have promised to do, or do something that you should do: *The government hasn't fulfilled its promise to cut taxes.* **2 fulfil a dream/wish/ambition** to do something that you have always wanted to do: *Bruce had finally fulfilled his dream of becoming a racing driver.* **3 fulfil a role/function/need** to do something that is useful or needed for a particular purpose: *The church fulfils an important role in the local community.* **4 fulfil sb's expectations/hopes** to be as good as someone had expected or hoped: *I knew that I could never fulfil my parents' expectations of me.*

ful·filled /fʊlˈfɪld/ *adj* completely satisfied with your life or your job

---

GRAMMAR NOTE: transitive and intransitive (2)
Some verbs can be used **transitive** or **intransitive**. For example: **read** *v* [T,I]
• Transitive: *I can't read your handwriting.*
• Intransitive: *Tom learned to read at the age of four.*

ful·fil·ling /fʊlˈfɪlɪŋ/ adj a job, relationship etc that is fulfilling makes you feel satisfied

ful·fil·ment BrE, **fulfillment** AmE /fʊl-ˈfɪlmənt/ n [U] **1** the feeling of being satisfied, especially in your work because you feel you are using all your abilities: Ann's work gives her a real sense of fulfilment. **2** when someone does what they have promised to do, what they should do, or what they have always wanted to do: His trip to Europe was the fulfilment of a lifelong ambition.

full /fʊl/ adj **1** if a container, room, space etc is full, no more things or people can go into it: The train was full, so we had to wait for the next one. | Check the fuel tank is full. | + of We found a box full of old letters. | **full up** We arrived late, and the hotel was already full up. → see picture at EMPTY **2** complete and including all of something: Please write down your full name and address. | You have our full support. | the full cost of repairs **3** be full of **a)** to contain a lot of a particular kind of thing or person: In summer the town is full of tourists. | Eric's essay is full of mistakes. **b)** if you are full of excitement, confidence, GUILT etc, you feel very excited, confident, guilty etc: Her heart was full of joy. **c)** if you are full of ideas, suggestions etc you have a lot of ideas etc to suggest **4** full size/speed/ volume etc as large, fast, loud etc. as possible: The car was approaching at full speed. **5** also **full up** BrE informal having eaten so much food that you do not want to eat any more: "Would you like some more cake?" "No thanks. I'm full." **6** a full life/day etc a life or day in which you are very busy or active: Even though she's disabled she leads a very full life. **7** be full of yourself spoken to talk a lot about yourself in a proud and annoying way **8** in full view of sb in a place where someone can easily see you: He took off his clothes in full view of the neighbours. **9** be in full swing if a party, meeting etc is in full swing, it has started and everyone is taking part in it **10** be full of beans to be happy and have a lot of energy **11** full marks BrE the highest possible number of points that you can get for schoolwork **12** a full face or figure is round or large **13** made with a lot of material and fitting loosely: a full skirt

full² n in full if you pay an amount of money in full, you pay the whole amount → see also **live life to the full** (LIVE¹)

full³ adv **1** literary directly: The sun shone full on her face. **2** full on working at the greatest possible power: The spotlights were full on.

full-blown /ˌ. ˈ.◂/ adj fully developed: full-blown AIDS

full-fledged /ˌ. ˈ.◂/ adj AmE completely developed, trained, or established; FULLY-FLEDGED BrE

full-grown /ˌ. ˈ.◂/ adj a full-grown animal, plant, or person has developed to their full size and will not grow any bigger

full house /ˌ. ˈ./ n [C] when a theatre, cinema etc is completely full of people

full-length /ˌ. ˈ.◂/ adj **1** full-length play/ novel/film etc a play etc that is not shorter than the normal length **2** full-length skirt/dress a skirt etc that reaches the ground **3** full-length mirror/photograph etc a mirror or picture that shows all of a person

full moon /ˌ. ˈ./ n [singular] the moon when it looks completely round

full-scale /ˌ. ˈ.◂/ adj [only before noun] **1** using all possible powers or forces: a full-scale nuclear war | a full-scale inquiry into the disaster **2** a full-scale MODEL, copy, picture etc. is the same size as the real thing

full stop /ˌ. ˈ./ n [C] BrE a mark (.) that you use to show the end of a sentence, or after the shortened form of a word; PERIOD AmE

full-time /ˌ. ˈ.◂/ adv if you work or study full-time, you work or study during the whole week, especially from Monday to Friday —**full-time** adj: a full-time job → compare PART-TIME

ful·ly /ˈfʊli/ adv completely: a fully trained nurse

fully-fledged /ˌ.. ˈ.◂/ adj completely developed, trained, or established; FULL-FLEDGED AmE: Noel and Liam were now fully-fledged superstars.

fum·ble /ˈfʌmbəl/ v [I] to try to hold or find something with difficulty, using your hands in a nervous or careless way: Gary fumbled for the light switch in the dark.

fume /fjuːm/ v [I] to be very angry: She had been waiting for over an hour, and she was fuming.

fumes /fjuːmz/ n [plural] strong-smelling gas or smoke, which is unpleasant to breathe in: gasoline fumes → see colour picture on page 278

fu·mi·gate /ˈfjuːmɪˌɡeɪt/ v [T] to get rid of infection or insects. from a place by using special chemicals —**fumigation** /ˌfjuːmɪˈɡeɪʃən/ n [U]

fun¹ /fʌn/ n [U] **1** enjoyment, or something that is enjoyable: **have fun** The children all had a lot of fun. | **it's no fun** (=it is not at all enjoyable) spoken: It's no fun being alone in a big city. | **for fun/for the fun of it** (=because you enjoy it, not for any other reason): Tina's started doing art classes, just for fun! **2** **make fun of** to try to make someone or something seem stupid by making jokes about them: At school the other children used to make fun of him because he was fat.

USAGE NOTE: fun and funny

Use **fun** to talk about events and activities that are enjoyable, such as games and parties: Let's go to the beach and have some fun. **Funny** is an adjective that describes someone or something that makes you laugh: Bob's jokes are really funny.

---

fun² adj **1** [only before noun] enjoyable: It'll be a fun day out. **2** enjoyable to be with: Terry is a fun person.

func·tion¹ /ˈfʌŋkʃən/ n [C] **1** the purpose that something is made for, or the purpose of someone's job: What's the exact function of this program? | The function of a chairman is to lead and control meetings. **2** an important party, ceremony, or other official event: The mayor has to attend all kinds of official functions.

function² v [I] **1** to work in a particular way: Can you explain exactly how this new system will function? **2** if a machine is functioning, it is working in the way that it should work

function as sth phr v [T] to be used in a particular way: a noun functioning as an adjective

func·tion·al /ˈfʌŋkʃənəl/ *adj* designed to be useful rather than attractive: *office furniture that is purely functional*

fund[1] /fʌnd/ *n* [C] **1** an amount of money that is kept for a particular purpose: *the school sports fund* **2** funds [plural] the money that you need to do something: **raise funds** (=collect funds): *We're trying to raise funds for a new swimming pool.*

fund[2] *v* [T] to provide money for an activity, organization, event etc: *a project funded by the World Health Organization*

fun·da·men·tal /ˌfʌndəˈmentl◂/ *adj* relating to the most basic and important parts of something: *fundamental changes to the education system* —**fundamentally** *adv*: *Marxism and capitalism are fundamentally opposed to each other.*

fun·da·men·tal·ist /ˌfʌndəˈmentəlˌɪst/ *n* [C] someone who has a strong belief that the rules of their religion must be obeyed very strictly. —**fundamentalist** *adj* —**fundamentalism** *n* [U]

fun·da·men·tals /ˌfʌndəˈmentlz/ *n* [plural] the most important ideas, rules etc that something is based on: *the fundamentals of computer programming*

fund·ing /ˈfʌndɪŋ/ *n* [U] money provided by the government or an official organization for particular work or activities: *funding for universities*

fund·rais·ing /ˈ. ˌ../ *n* [U] the activity of collecting money for a particular purpose —**fundraising** *adj*: *fund-raising activities*

fu·ne·ral[ ] /ˈfjuːnərəl/ *n* [C] a ceremony for someone who has just died: *The funeral will be held on Thursday at St Patrick's church.*

funeral di·rec·tor /ˈ... .ˌ../ *n* [C] an UNDER-TAKER

funeral home /ˈ... .ˌ./ also **funeral par·lour** /ˈ... .ˌ./ *n* [C] the place where a body is kept before a funeral

fun·fair /ˈfʌnfeəll-fer/ *n* [C] *BrE* a noisy outdoor event where you can ride on machines or play games to win prizes; FAIR

fungus

fun·gus /ˈfʌŋgəs/ *n* [C,U], *plural* **fungi** or **funguses** a plant such as a MUSHROOM, which has a flat top and a stem. Another type of fungus is like a powder which grows on wood, food etc: *The walls were covered with some kind of fungus.*

funk /fʌŋk/ *n* [U] a type of popular music with a strong beat that is based on JAZZ and African music

funk·y /ˈfʌŋki/ *adj informal* **1** music that is funky has a good strong beat and is enjoyable to listen to **2** *AmE* modern, fashionable, and interesting: *a funky Mexican restaurant that serves surprisingly good food*

fun·nel /ˈfʌnl/ *n* [C] **1** an object with a wide top and a narrow tube at the bottom, used for pouring liquids into a container **2** *BrE* a round metal CHIMNEY on top of a ship or train

fun·ni·ly /ˈfʌnˌli/ *adv* **funnily enough** *spoken* used when you are going to tell someone an interesting and surprising fact: *Funnily enough, I was just going to call you when you called me.*

fun·ny[ ] /ˈfʌni/ *adj* **1** amusing and making you laugh: *She looks really funny in that hat.* | *a funny story* **2** strange or unusual: *What's that funny noise?* | *That's funny! I'm sure I left my keys in this drawer, but they aren't here now.* **3** slightly ill: *I've been feeling funny ever since I bumped my head.* **4** *informal* involving tricks or dishonest behaviour: *We don't want any funny business.*

fur[ ] /fɜːllfɜːr/ *n* **1** [U] the thick soft hair that covers the bodies of some animals such as dogs and cats **2** [C,U] the fur-covered skin of an animal, used especially for making clothes, or a piece of clothing made from furs: *a fur coat*

fu·ri·ous /ˈfjʊəriəsllˈfjʊr-/ *adj* **1** very angry: *Her daughter was furious when she found out they'd been reading her private letters.* ➞ see colour picture on page 277 **2** done with a lot of speed, violence, or effort: *The horseman rode off at a furious gallop.* —**furiously** *adv*

furl /fɜːllfɜːrl/ *v* [T] to roll or fold something such as an UMBRELLA or sail

fur·long /ˈfɜːlɒŋllˈfɜːrlɒːŋ/ *n* [C] a unit for measuring distance, equal to 1/8 of a mile or 201 metres

fur·nace /ˈfɜːnɪsllˈfɜːr-/ *n* [C] an enclosed space with a very hot fire in it, used for melting metals or producing power or heat

fur·nish /ˈfɜːnɪʃllˈfɜːr-/ *v* [T] **1** to put furniture into a house or room: *They had furnished their home with costly antiques.* **2** to provide someone with something that they need: *Her bank manager was able to furnish her with the necessary information*

fur·nished /ˈfɜːnɪʃtllˈfɜːr-/ *adj* a furnished room, house, etc has furniture in it

fur·nish·ings /ˈfɜːnɪʃɪŋzllˈfɜːr-/ *n* [plural] the furniture, CARPETS, curtains, decorations etc in a room

fur·ni·ture[ ] /ˈfɜːnɪtʃəllˈfɜːrnɪtʃər/ *n* [U] objects such as chairs, tables, and beds, that you use in a room, office etc: *antique furniture* | *office furniture*

fu·ro·re *BrE*, **furor** *AmE* /ˈfjʊərɔːllˈfjʊrɔːr/ *n* [singular] *formal* when a lot of people are very angry about something that has happened: *Darwin's theories caused a furore at the time.*

fur·row[1] /ˈfʌrəʊllˈfɜːroʊ/ *n* [C] **1** one of the deep lines cut into the soil by a farmer's PLOUGH, so that seeds can be planted **2** a deep line on the surface of someone's face

furrow[2] *v* [I,T] *literary* to make lines appear on someone's face or FOREHEAD: *A frown furrowed her brow.* —**furrowed** *adj*

fur·ry /ˈfɜːri/ *adj* covered with fur, or with something that feels like fur: *small furry animals*

fur·ther[1] /ˈfɜːðəllˈfɜːrðər/ *adv* **1** more: *I have nothing further to say.* | *Their discussions had not progressed any further.* **2** at or to a longer distance away: *Their home is further down the street.* **3** at a later or earlier time: *further back* *in history* **4 not get any further** to not achieve any more progress: *Police say they have not got any further with their investigations.*

further[2] *adj* [only before noun] additional: *Are there any further questions?*

further[3] *v* [T] *formal* to help something to succeed: *efforts to further the cause of peace*

further ed·u·ca·tion /ˌ.. ..ˈ../ *n* [U] *BrE* education for people who have finished school but are not at a university

fur·ther·more /ˌfɜːðəˈmɔː‖ˈfɜːrðərmɔːr/ *adv formal* in addition to what has already been said

fur·thest /ˈfɜːðɪst‖ˈfɜːr-/ *adj, adv* as far away as possible from a particular place: *the furthest corner of the room*

fur·tive /ˈfɜːtɪv‖ˈfɜːr-/ *adj* behaving as if you want to keep something secret: *a furtive glance* —**furtively** *adv*

fu·ry /ˈfjʊəri‖ˈfjʊri/ *n* [singular U] **1** extreme anger: *I saw the look of fury on his face.* **2** *literary* the violent force of something: *the fury of the storm*

fuse[1] /fjuːz/ *n* [C] **1** a short wire inside a piece of electrical equipment that melts if too much electricity passes through it: *The fuse has blown.* (=it has melted and stopped the electrical equipment from working) **2** a part that is connected to a bomb, FIREWORK etc, that delays or starts the explosion

fuse[2] *v* [I,T] **1** to join together and become one thing, or to join two things together: *The bones of the spine had become fused together.* **2** *BrE* if an electrical system fuses, or if you fuse it, it stops working because the fuse has melted: *The lights had fused.*

fu·se·lage /ˈfjuːzəlɑːʒ‖-sə-/ *n* [C] the main part of a plane

fu·sion /ˈfjuːʒən/ *n* [C,U] when two things are joined together or combined

fuss[1] /fʌs/ *n* **1** [singular U] when people become very excited, angry, upset etc, especially about something that is not very serious or important: *I didn't understand what all the fuss was about.* (=why people are so excited, angry etc) **2 make a fuss/kick up a fuss** to complain angrily or noisily about something: *The man at the next table was making a fuss because his food was cold.* **3 make a fuss of sb** *BrE*/**over sb** *AmE* to look after someone very well and pay a lot of attention to them: *My grandparents always make a fuss of me when I go and see them.*

fuss[2] *v* [I] to behave in a nervous, anxious way,

worrying over unimportant things: *Stop fussing! We'll be home soon!*

fuss over sb *phr v* [T] to pay too much attention to making someone comfortable or safe because you are worried about them

fuss·y /ˈfʌsi/ *adj* **1** someone who is fussy is very careful about which things they choose, and only likes a few things: **+ about** *He's very fussy about his food.* **2** too worried about unimportant details: *a fussy old woman*

fu·tile /ˈfjuːtaɪl‖-tl/ *adj* certain to be unsuccessful: *Janet ran after the thief in a futile attempt to get her purse back.* —**futility** /fjuːˈtɪləti/ *n* [U] *the futility of war*

fu·ton /ˈfuːtɒn‖-tɑːn/ *n* C a soft flat MATTRESS that can be used as a bed or folded into a seat

fu·ture[1] /ˈfjuːtʃə‖-ər/ *n* **1 the future** the time after now: *Do you have any plans for the future?* | *In the future, people will be able to travel to other planets.* | **in the near future** (=soon): *I'm hoping to go to Atlanta in the near future.* **2** [C] what will happen to someone or something: *My parents have already planned out my whole future.* **3 in future a)** always in the future starting from now: *I'll be more careful in future.* **b)** at some time in the future: *In future these techniques may be used to treat a wide range of illnesses.* **4** [singular, U] if someone or something has a future, they are likely to be successful or to be able to continue: *Do you think the team has a future without their best player?* | *a talented musician with a brilliant future in front of her*

fu·ture[2] *adj* [only before noun] **1** happening or existing in the future: *preserving the countryside for future generations* | **future wife/husband/ president** (=someone who will be your wife etc in the future): *the future president of the United States* **2 the future tense** the form of a verb that is used to show a future action or state

future per·fect /ˌ.. ˈ../ *n* **the future perfect** the form of a verb that is used to show that an action will be completed before a particular time in the future

fu·tur·is·tic /ˌfjuːtʃəˈrɪstɪk◂/ *adj* something that is futuristic is very modern and unusual and looks the way things may look in the future: *a futuristic sports car design by Alfa Romeo*

fuzz /fʌz/ *n* [U] short soft hair, or material like hair

fuzz·y /ˈfʌzi/ *adj* **1** unclear: *Unfortunately all the photographs are a little fuzzy.* **2** fuzzy hair is soft and curly

Gg

G, g /dʒiː/ the letter 'g'

gab·ble /ˈgæbəl/ v [I,T] to talk so quickly that people cannot understand what you are saying

ga·ble /ˈgeɪbəl/ n [C] the top part of a wall of a house where it joins a roof, making a shape like a TRIANGLE

gad /gæd/ v **-dded, -dding**
gad about/around phr v [I] to go out to different places and enjoy yourself

gad·get /ˈgædʒɪt/ n [C] a small tool or machine that helps you do something: a useful little gadget for cutting tomatoes

gaffe /gæf/ n [C] an embarrassing mistake

gag[1] /gæg/ v **-gged, -gging 1** [T] to cover someone's mouth with a piece of cloth so that they cannot make any noise: The robbers had tied her up and gagged her. **2** [I] to feel that you are going to be sick and bring up food from your stomach **3** [T] to prevent people from reporting information about something, or telling other people about it: the government's attempt to gag the press

gag[2] n [C] **1** informal a joke or funny story **2** a piece of cloth used to gag someone

ga·ga /ˈgɑːgɑː/ adj informal confused in your mind because you are old

gag·gle /ˈgægəl/ n [C] **1** a group of GEESE **2** a noisy group of people: a gaggle of school-children

gai·e·ty /ˈgeɪ‿ti/ n [U] old-fashioned a feeling of fun and happiness

gai·ly /ˈgeɪli/ adv old-fashioned in a happy, cheerful way

gain[1] /geɪn/ v **1** [I,T] to get or achieve something that is important, useful, or valuable: You can gain a lot of computer experience doing this job. | The army gained control of enemy territory. ➔ opposite LOSE **2** [T] to increase in something: Bea has gained a lot of weight since Christmas. **3** [I] if a clock or watch gains, it works too fast **4 gain ground** to become more popular or stronger: The Democrats are gaining ground on their rivals.
gain on sb/sth phr v [T] to start getting closer to the person, car etc that you are chasing

---

USAGE NOTE: gain, earn, and win

Use **gain** to talk about getting more of something such as an ability or quality: You'll gain a lot of experience working here. Use **earn** to talk about getting money by working: She earns about $50,000 a year. Use **win** to say that someone gets a prize in a game or competition: Brian won first prize in the skating competition.

---

gain[2] n **1** [C,U] an increase in the amount or level of something: Try to avoid too much weight gain. | + **in** There were steady gains in wage levels through the decade. **2** [C] an advantage or an improvement: gains in medical science

gait /geɪt/ n [singular] the way that someone walks: He had a slow ambling gait.

ga·la /ˈgɑːlə‖ˈgeɪlə, ˈgælə/ n [C] a special public performance or celebration: a gala night at the opera to raise money for charity

gal·ax·y /ˈgæləksi/ n [C] one of the large groups of stars that make up the universe —**galactic** /gəˈlæktɪk/ adj

gale /geɪl/ n [C] a very strong wind: Our fence blew down in the gale.

gall /gɔːl‖gɒːl/ n **have the gall to do sth** to be rude without caring what other people think: She had the gall to say that I looked fat!

gal·lant /ˈgælənt/ adj old-fashioned **1** brave: a gallant soldier **2** kind, especially to women —**gallantly** adv —**gallantry** n [U]

gal·le·ry /ˈgæləri/ n [C] **1** a room or building where you can look at famous paintings and other types of art: the Uffizzi gallery in Florence **2** an upper floor like a BALCONY inside a HALL, church, or theatre, where you can sit

gal·ley /ˈgæli/ n [C] **1** a kitchen on a ship or a plane **2** an ancient war ship that was rowed by SLAVES

gal·lon /ˈgælən/ n [C] a unit for measuring liquid, equal to 4.5435 litres in Britian or 3.785 litres in the US

gal·lop /ˈgæləp/ v [I] if a horse gallops, it runs very quickly —**gallop** n [singular]

gal·lows /ˈgæləʊz‖-loʊz/ n [C], plural **gallows** a structure used in the past for killing criminals by hanging (HANG) them

ga·lore /gəˈlɔː‖-ˈlɔːr/ adj [only after noun] in large amounts: He was a rich kid, with toys galore.

gal·va·nize (also **-ise** BrE) /ˈgælvənaɪz/ v [T] to make someone suddenly realize that they must do something: **galvanize sb into action** The urgency of his voice galvanized them into action.

gal·va·nized (also **-ised** BrE) /ˈgælvənaɪzd/ adj galvanized metal has been treated in a special way so that it does not RUST

gam·bit /ˈgæmbɪt/ n [C] something you say to get an advantage in an argument, or to start a conversation: "You don't like Jamie very much," she said as an opening gambit.

gam·ble[1] /ˈgæmbəl/ v [I] to try to win money by guessing the result of a horse race, by playing cards etc: Jack lost over $7000 gambling in Las Vegas. —**gambling** n [U] Gambling is illegal in some states. —**gambler** n [C]

gamble[2] n **be a gamble** if something you do is a gamble, you cannot be sure if it will be successful or if you will lose money: Buying an old car can be a real gamble.

game[1] /geɪm/ n **1** [C] a kind of activity or sport in which people or teams compete with each other, that is played according to a set of

---

GRAMMAR NOTE: the passive (2)

Most transitive verbs can be made **passive**. If you want to say who or what did the action in a passive sentence, use **by**. ACTIVE: An American millionaire **bought** the picture. PASSIVE: The picture **was bought by** an American millionaire.

rules: *Do you know any good card games?* | *The game of golf first started in Scotland.* **2** [C] an occasion when people play a game: *Did you watch the baseball game last night?* | *Italy won their first game 4-0.* **3** **play games** to behave in a silly annoying way, for example by not saying what you really think, or not treating a situation seriously enough: *I wish you'd stop playing games with me!* **4** [U] wild animals and birds that are hunted for food or as a sport **5** **give the game away** to accidentally say something that lets someone guess a secret **6** **what's your game?** *spoken* used when you think someone is secretly doing something that they should not do

game² *adj* [not before noun] willing to do something: *I'm game if you are.*

gamekeep·er /'. ../ *n* [C] someone whose job is to look after wild animals and birds that will be hunted

games /geɪmz/ *n* [plural] an event at which a lot of different sports are played: *the Olympic Games*

game show /'. ./ *n* [C] a television programme in which people play games in order to win prizes

gam·mon /'gæmən/ *n* [U] *BrE* meat from a pig that has been preserved using salt

gam·ut /'gæmət/ *n* [singular] all of the possible types of different things of the same kind: *In the weeks after she left, she experienced the whole gamut of emotions.*

gang¹ /gæŋ/ *n* [C] **1** a group of young people, especially a group that often causes trouble and fights: *A gang of kids were standing on the corner of the street.* **2** a group of criminals who work together: *a gang of international drug smugglers* **3** *informal* a group of friends **4** a group of workers

gang² *v*

gang up on sb *phr v* [T] if a group of people gang up on someone, they join together in order to criticize or attack that person: *Helen thinks they're all ganging up on her.*

gang·land /'gæŋlænd, -lənd/ *adj* gangland murders or violence are connected with organized groups of criminals: *gangland killings*

gan·gling /'gæŋglɪŋ/, also **gan·gly** /'gæŋgli/ *adj* unusually tall and thin and not graceful: *a gangly teenager*

gang·plank /'gæŋplæŋk/ *n* [C] a board you walk on between a ship and the land

gan·grene /'gæŋgriːn/ *n* [U] a medical condition in which someone's flesh starts to decay

gang·ster /'gæŋstəll-ər/ *n* [C] a member of a group of violent criminals: *Al Capone was a Chicago gangster.*

gang·way /'gæŋweɪ/ *n* [C] **1** a board or stairs you walk on to go onto a ship or plane **2** *BrE* the space between two rows of seats in a theatre, bus, train etc

gaol /dʒeɪl/ a British spelling of JAIL

gaol·er /'dʒeɪləll-ər/ *n* [C] a British spelling of JAILER

G

Feelings

Exercise 1

Look at the pictures. Read the words for the emotions. Now complete the following sentences.

1 I went to the party in jeans and a T-shirt. All the other people were wearing smart suits and dresses. I felt very e_____ .

2 Mrs Relkin is very a_____ with the people who live above her. They like rock music and make a lot of noise.

3 Cathy waited for two hours to see the doctor. She had nothing to read and there was nothing to do. She felt b_____ .

4 The engineer came to repair her washing machine three times last week, but now it isn't working again. Belinda is f_____ .

5 Liam is very s_____ . He doesn't like meeting new people.

6 I was very s_____ when I saw her green hair.

7 Alan is w_____ about his daughter. She is climbing in Colorado and she hasn't phoned for a week.

8 Keith was very h_____ when he got the prize.

9 When they arrived at the top of the mountain, they were very t_____ .

10 She was very s_____ when her cat died.

11 Martin was alone in the dark house. He heard strange noises. He was f_____ .

12 The policeman told Jenny to turn right, but the sign said 'No right turn.' She felt very c_____ .

sad

happy

surprised

bored

tired

confused/puzzled

embarrassed

shy

worried

angry

furious

scared/frightened

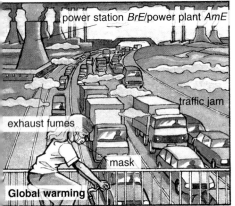

Global warming

Air pollution stops heat leaving the atmosphere. The gradual warming of the Earth is called global warming.

Travel

Cars cause pollution and congestion. Other ways travelling are less harmful to the environment.

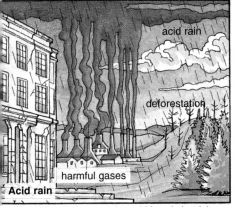

Acid rain

Acid rain is rain that contains acid from industrial pollution. It is harmful to trees and buildings.

Energy

Energy that comes from wind, water or solar pow better for the environment.

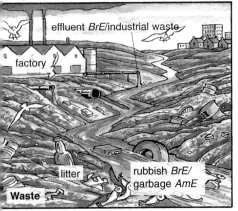

Waste

Harmful chemicals from factories and waste from houses pollute fields and rivers.

Recycling

Some things like paper, plastic, cans and glass c be collected and used again. This is called recyc

gap

Ken squeezed through a gap in the fence.

gap /gæp/ *n* [C] **1** a difference between two situations, groups, amounts etc: **+ between** *the widening gap between rich and poor* | *There's a big age gap between them.* **2** a space between two things or two parts of something: **+ in/between** *The cat escaped through a gap in the fence.* | *Dave has a big gap between his two front teeth.* **3** something that is missing in a situation, which makes it not seem complete or stops you from feeling satisfied: **+ in** *When my wife left me, it left a big gap in my life.* **4** a period of time in which nothing happens or nothing is

said: **+ in** *an uncomfortable gap in the conversation*

gape /geɪp/ *v* [I] to look at something or someone in surprise, with your mouth open: **+ at** *Anna gaped at him in horror.*

gap·ing /'geɪpɪŋ/ *adj* [only before noun] a gaping hole, wound, or mouth is open very wide

gar·age /'gærɑːʒ, -rɪdʒ‖gə'rɑːʒ/ *n* [C] **1** a building where you keep your car ➡ see colour picture on page 79 **2** a place where cars are repaired **3** *BrE* a place where you buy petrol; a GAS STATION *AmE*

garb /gɑːb‖gɑːrb/ *n* [U] *literary* a particular style of clothing

gar·bage /'gɑːbɪdʒ‖'gɑːr-/ *n* [singular, U] *especially AmE* waste material such as old food, dirty paper, and empty bags, or the container this is put in; RUBBISH *BrE*: *Can somebody take out the garbage?*

garbage can /'.. ,./ *n* [C] *AmE* a container that you put waste in; DUSTBIN *BrE* ➡ see picture at KITCHEN

garbage col·lec·tor /'.. .,../ *n* [C] *AmE* someone whose job is to take away waste material left in containers outside people's houses; DUSTMAN *BrE*

The Environment

Exercise 1

Look at the pictures and read the words about the environment. Tick ☑ the things which are good for the environment and put a cross ☒ by the things which are bad.

pollution ☐   effluent ☐   harmful gases ☐

solar panel ☐   acid rain ☐

wind turbine ☐   bottle bank ☑

traffic jam ☐   litter ☐   recycled paper ☐

exhaust fumes ☒   bicycle ☐

public transport ☐   global warming ☐

Exercise 2

Read about these activities. Match them to the words and phrases underneath. Write the number beside the word or phrase.

1 Smoke and harmful gases mix with water in the clouds and make rain that damages trees and buildings.

2 Some buildings have special panels in the roof, which use energy from the sun to make electricity.

3 Philip usually buys chips on his way home, and drops the bag on the ground.

4 Rachel takes her old bottles to the bottle bank. New bottles are made from old glass.

5 Stella says there are always traffic jams and she can't find a place to park her car.

6 The Earth is getting warmer, because of air pollution which stops heat from leaving the atmosphere.

recycling __4__

acid rain ____

litter ____

global warming ____

congestion ____

solar power ____

G

rake hoe fork spade lawn mowers

shears

trowel

secateurs/
pruning shears

hose

sprinkler

watering
can

hover mower

gar·bled /ˈgɑːbəld‖ˈgɑːr-/ *adj* a garbled message or garbled information is confusing and very difficult to understand: *The train announcements were too garbled to understand.*

gar·den /ˈgɑːdn‖ˈgɑːr-/ *n* [C] **1** a piece of land next to your house where there is grass and you can grow flowers; YARD *AmE*: *We want a house with a big garden for the kids.* → see colour picture on page 79 **2 gardens** a public park where a lot of flowers and unusual plants are grown

gar·den·er /ˈgɑːdnə‖ˈgɑːrdnər/ *n* [C] someone who works in a garden, as a job or for pleasure

gar·den·ing /ˈgɑːdnɪŋ‖ˈgɑːr-/ *n* [U] the activity or job of working in a garden etc: *I'm hoping to do some gardening this weekend.*

gar·gle /ˈgɑːgəl‖ˈgɑːr-/ *v* [I] to clean or DISINFECT your throat with water or a special liquid that you do not swallow

gar·ish /ˈgeərɪʃ‖ˈger-/ *adj* very brightly coloured and unpleasant to look at: *a garish carpet* —**garishly** *adv* —**garishness** *n* [U]

gar·land /ˈgɑːlənd‖ˈgɑːr-/ *n* [C] a ring of flowers or leaves, worn for decoration

gar·lic /ˈgɑːlɪk‖ˈgɑːr-/ *n* [U] a small plant like an onion with a very strong taste, used in cooking

gar·ment /ˈgɑːmənt‖ˈgɑːr-/ *n* [C] *formal* a piece of clothing: *Wash delicate garments by hand.*

gar·nish /ˈgɑːnɪʃ‖ˈgɑːr-/ *v* [T] to decorate food with a small piece of a fruit or vegetable —**garnish** *n* [C]

gar·ret /ˈgærɪt/ *n* [C] *literary* a small room at the top of a house: *a penniless artist starving in a garret*

gar·ri·son /ˈgærɪsən/ *n* [C] a group of soldiers who live in and defend a particular building or town —**garrison** *v* [T]

gar·ter /ˈgɑːtəl‖ˈgɑːrtər/ *n* [C] a band used for holding up SOCKS or STOCKINGS

gas /gæs/ *n* **1** [C,U] a substance in a form like air, that you usually cannot see or feel: *gases such as hydrogen and nitrogen* → see colour picture on page 278 **2** [U] a clear substance like air that is burned and used for cooking and heating: *a gas stove* **3** [U] *AmE* also **gasoline** a liquid made from PETROLEUM, used for producing power in car engines; petrol *BrE*: *We need to stop for gas before we drive into the city.* **4 step on the gas** *especially AmE* to make a car move faster by pressing the ACCELERATOR

gas² *v* [T] **-ssed, -ssing** to poison or kill someone with gas

gas cham·ber /ˈ. ˌ../ *n* [C] a room that is filled with poisonous gas, used for killing people

gas·e·ous /ˈgæsiəs/ *adj* like gas or in the form of gas

gash /gæʃ/ *n* [C] a deep cut in something —**gash** *v* [T]

gas·ket /ˈgæskɪt/ *n* [C] a flat piece of rubber which is placed between two surfaces in a piece of machinery to prevent steam, oil etc from escaping

gas mask /ˈ. ./ *n* [C] a piece of equipment worn over your face to protect you from breathing poisonous gases

gas·o·line /ˈgæsəliːn/ *n* [U] *AmE* also **gas** — [U] *AmE* a liquid used for producting power in car engines; petrol *BrE*

gasp /gɑːsp‖gæsp/ *v* **1** [I] to make a short sudden noise when you breathe in, usually because you are surprised or shocked: *As the flames reached the roof, the crowd gasped in alarm.* **2** [I,T] to quickly breathe in a lot of air because you are having difficulty breathing normally: *"Wait for me!" he gasped.* (=he said while breathing a lot of air very quickly) | **gasp for breath/air** *Kim crawled out of the pool, gasping for air.* —**gasp** *n* [C] *a gasp of surprise*

gas sta·tion /ˈ. ˌ../ *n* [C] *AmE* a place that sells petrol; PETROL STATION *BrE*

gas·tric /ˈgæstrɪk/ *adj* *technical* relating to the stomach: *gastric ulcers*

gas·tro·nom·ic /ˌgæstrəˈnɒmɪk‖-ˈnɑː-/ *adj* connected with cooking and eating good food

gate /geɪt/ *n* [C] **1** the part of a fence or outside wall that you can open and close like a door: *Who left the gate open?* → see colour picture on page 79 **2** the part of an airport where you get on the plane

gat·eau /ˈgætəʊ‖gɑːˈtoʊ/ n [C,U] BrE, plural **gateaux** /-təʊz‖-toʊz/ a large cake often filled and decorated with cream and fruit

gate·crash /ˈgeɪtkræʃ/ v [I,T] to go to a party or event that you have not been invited to — **gate-crasher** n [C]

gate·way /ˈgeɪt-weɪ/ n **1** [C] an opening in a fence or outside wall that can be closed with a gate **2 the gateway to** a place, especially a city, that you go through in order to reach a much larger place: St. Louis was once the gateway to the West.

gath·er /ˈgæðə‖-ər/ v **1** [I,T] if people gather, or if someone gathers them somewhere, they come together in the same place: Dozens of photographers gathered outside Jackson's hotel. | If you gather the kids, I'll start the car. | **+ around/round** A crowd gathered around to watch the fight. **2** [T] also **gather up** to collect things into one pile or place: "Wait for me," said Anna, gathering up her books. **3** [T] to get information, ideas etc over a period of time: I'm trying to gather new ideas for my next novel. **4** [T] to believe that something is true based on the information you have: **+ (that)** I gather you've not been well recently. **5 gather force/ speed/intensity etc** to become stronger, faster etc: The car gathered speed quickly as it rolled down the hill.

gath·er·ing /ˈgæðərɪŋ/ n [C] a group of people meeting together for a particular purpose: a family gathering

gau·dy /ˈgɔːdi‖ˈgɒːdi/ adj clothes, decorations etc that are gaudy are too bright and look cheap — **gaudily** adv

gauge¹ /geɪdʒ/ n [C] **1** an instrument that measures the amount or size of something: a fuel gauge **2** a standard that you use to decide what a situation is like: **+ of** Money is not the only gauge of success. **3** the thickness of something such as a piece of metal

gauge² v [T] **1** to decide what someone's feelings, intentions etc probably are: a study to gauge public reaction to the proposed changes | **+ whether/how etc** I couldn't gauge how he felt from the look on his face. **2** to measure something using a particular instrument or method

gaunt /gɔːnt‖gɒːnt/ adj very thin and pale, especially because of illness

gaunt·let /ˈgɔːntlət‖ˈgɒːnt-/ n **1 run the gauntlet** to be criticized or attacked by a lot of people: There was no way to avoid running the gauntlet of media attention. **2 throw down the gauntlet** to invite someone to fight, argue, or compete with you **3** [C] a long thick GLOVE that you wear for protection

gauze /gɔːz‖gɒːz/ n [U] thin light cloth with small holes in it, often used for covering wounds — **gauzy** adj

gave /geɪv/ v the past tense of GIVE

gawk /gɔːk‖gɒːk/ v [I] to look at someone or something for a long time, in a way that looks stupid: **+ at** Don't just stand there gawking at those girls.

gawk·y /ˈgɔːki‖ˈgɒːki/ adj someone who is gawky is tall and does not move GRACEFULLY: a gawky teenager — **gawkiness** n [U]

gawp /gɔːp‖gɒːp/ v [I] BrE to look at something for a long time, especially with your mouth open because you are surprised: What are you gawping at?

gay¹ /geɪ/ adj **1** a gay person is sexually attracted to people of the same sex; HOMOSEXUAL: My son's just told me he's gay. | gay rights protestors → compare LESBIAN **2** old-fashioned happy and cheerful: gay laughter **3** old-fashioned bright and attractive: gay ribbons → see also GAIETY, GAILY

gay² n [C] someone, especially a man, who is sexually attracted to people of the same sex; HOMOSEXUAL

gaze /geɪz/ v [I] to look at someone or something for a long time: **+ at/into etc** She sat gazing out of the window. — **gaze** n [singular] Judith tried to avoid his gaze.

GCSE /ˌdʒiː siː es ˈiː/ n [C] General Certificate of Secondary Education; an examination that is taken by students aged 15 or 16 in Britain

gear¹ /ɡɪə‖ɡɪr/ n **1** [C,U] the gears are the equipment in a car or other vehicle that turns power from the engine into movement: The car has five gears. | **change gear** (=change to a different gear): Every time I change gear the car makes a horrible noise. **2** [U] special equipment, clothing etc that you need for a particular activity: camping gear

gear² v [T] **1 be geared to** to be organized in order to achieve a particular purpose: All his training was geared to winning an Olympic gold medal. **2 be geared up** to be prepared for a situation or to do a particular activity: He arrived all geared up for trouble.

gear·box /ˈɡɪəbɒks‖ˈɡɪrbɑːks/ n [C] a metal box that contains the gears of a car

gear stick /ˈ. ./ BrE also **gear le·ver** /ˈ. ˌ../ BrE, **gear shift** /ˈ. ./ AmE — n [C] a long stick with a handle that you move to change gears in a car

GED /ˌdʒiː iː ˈdiː/ n the **GED** General Equivalency Diploma; a DIPLOMA in the US that can be studied for at any time by people who did not finish their HIGH SCHOOL education

geese /ɡiːs/ n the plural of GOOSE

gee·zer /ˈɡiːzə‖-ər/ n [C] spoken informal a man: Bill's a funny old geezer.

gel¹ /dʒel/ n [C,U] a thick wet substance like JELLY, used especially to keep your hair in a particular style

gel² v [I] **-lled, -lling 1** if a liquid gels, it becomes thicker and sets **2** if an idea or plan gels, it becomes clearer or more definite: They were going to make a movie together, but the project never gelled. **3** if people gel, they begin to work together well as a group

gel·a·tine /ˈdʒelətiːn‖-tn/ BrE, **gel·a·tin** /-tn‖-tn/ AmE n [U] a clear substance that is used to make liquid food more solid

gel·ig·nite /ˈdʒelɪɡnaɪt/ n [U] a very powerful explosive

gem /dʒem/ n [C] **1** a jewel that is cut into a particular shape **2** informal someone or something that is very special: My granddaughter's a real gem.

Gem·i·ni /ˈdʒemɪˌnaɪ‖-ni/ n [C,U] the sign of the Zodiac of people who are born between May 21st and June 21st, or someone who belongs to this sign

gen /dʒen/ *n* [U] *BrE spoken* information about something: *I'll try and get the gen on what happened at the party.*

gen·der /'dʒendəll-ər/ *n* [C,U] **1** *formal* the fact of being male or female: *You can't be denied a job simply on the grounds of gender.* **2** [U] the system in some languages of dividing nouns, PRONOUNS and adjectives into MASCULINE, FEMININE, or NEUTER or one of these types of words

gene /dʒiːn/ *n* [C] a part of a CELL of a living thing which controls what it will be like and how it will develop, which is passed from parent to child

gen·er·al[1] /'dʒenərəl/ *adj* **1** including only the main features of something, not the details: *a general introduction to computers* | *I think I've got the general idea now.* (=I understand the main points) **2 in general** usually, or in most situations: *In general women are less well paid than men.* **3** considering the whole of a thing, group, or situation, rather than its parts: *The general condition of the house is good, but it does need decorating.* | **in general** *We want to raise awareness of the environment in general.* **4** involving or affecting everyone or most people: *How soon will the drug be available for general use?* **5** not limited to one subject or type of thing: *Her general knowledge is good.* **6 as a general rule** usually, or in most situations: *As a general rule, you should phone before visiting someone.* **7 the general public** the ordinary people in society

general[2], **General** *n* [C] an officer with a very high rank in an army, AIR FORCE, or navy

general e·lec·tion /ˌ... .'../ *n* [C] an election in which all the voters in a country choose a government

gen·er·al·i·za·tion (also **-isation** *BrE*) /ˌdʒenərəlaɪ'zeɪʃənll-lə-/ *n* [C] a statement that may be true in most situations, but is not true in every situation: *sweeping generalization* (=one that is definitely not true about all the people or things that you are talking about)

gen·er·al·ize (also **-ise** *BrE*) /'dʒenərəlaɪz/ *v* [I] **1** to make a statement about something without mentioning any details: *It's impossible to generalize about such a complicated subject.* | *It would be a mistake to generalize from only a few examples.* **2** to form an opinion based on only very little information: *It's stupid to generalize and say that all young people are rude.* | *It's not fair to generalize from a few cases that all politicians are dishonest.*

gen·er·al·ly /'dʒenərəli/ *adv* **1** usually: *Meg an generally works late on Fridays.* **2** by or to most people: *It's generally believed that the story is true.* **3** considering something as a whole: *The new arrangements have generally worked very well.*

general prac·ti·tion·er /ˌ... .'.../ *n* [C] a GP

gen·e·rate /'dʒenəreɪt/ *v* [T] **1** to make something happen or start to exist: *Our discussion generated a lot of new ideas.* **2** to produce electricity, power, heat etc

gen·e·ra·tion /ˌdʒenə'reɪʃən/ *n* **1** [C] all the people who are about the same age: *Three generations of Monroes have lived in this house.* | *the younger generation* (=young people) **2** [C] the

average period of time between your birth and the birth of your children: *A generation ago, no one had home computers.* **3** [C] machines or other products which are all at a similar stage of development: *the next generation of computers* **4** [U] the production of energy, for example electricity

generation gap /..'.. ,./ *n* [singular] a lack of understanding between two generations of people caused by their different way of thinking

gen·e·ra·tor /'dʒenəreɪtəll-ər/ *n* [C] a machine that produces electricity

ge·ner·ic /dʒɪ'nerɪk/ *adj* describing or relating to a whole group of similar things —**generically** /-kli/ *adv*

gen·e·ros·i·ty /ˌdʒenə'rɒsɪtill-'rɑː-/ *n* [C,U] when you are happy to give money, time etc to help someone, or something you do that shows this: *Thank you for your generosity.*

gen·e·rous /'dʒenərəs/ *adj* **1** someone who is generous is kind because they often give people money, presents etc: *Judith's always been very generous to me.* **2** larger than the usual amount: *a generous slice of cake* —**generously** *adv*: *Ann has generously offered to pay for the tickets.*

gen·e·sis /'dʒenɪsɪs/ *n* [singular] *formal* the beginning of something

ge·net·ic /dʒɪ'netɪk/ *adj* relating to GENES or genetics: *genetic engineering* —**genetically** /-kli/ *adv*

ge·net·ics /dʒɪ'netɪks/ *n* [plural] the study of how the development and form of living things is affected by their GENES —**geneticist** /-tɪsɪst/ *n* [C]

ge·ni·al /'dʒiːniəl/ *adj* cheerful, kind and friendly —**geniality** /ˌdʒiːni'ælɪti/ *n* [U]

gen·i·tals /'dʒenɪtlz/, **gen·i·ta·li·a** /ˌdʒenɪ'teɪliə/ *n* [plural] *technical* the outer sex organs —**genital** *adj*

ge·ni·us /'dʒiːniəs/ *n* **1** someone who has an extremely high level of intelligence, artistic ability, or skill at a particular activity, for example Einstein or Picasso **2** [U] great and unusual ability: *a work of pure genius*

gen·o·cide /'dʒenəsaɪd/ *n* [U] the murder of a very large number of people who belong to the same race or group

gen·re /'ʒɒnrəll'ʒɑːnrə/ *n* [C] *formal* a class of art, music, literature etc that shares a particular style or subject: *the science fiction genre*

gent /dʒent/ *n* [C] *informal* **1** a gentleman **2 the Gents** *BrE* a public toilet for men

gen·teel /dʒen'tiːl/ *adj* extremely polite, used about someone from a high social class —**gentility** /-'tɪlɪti/ *n* [U]

gen·tle /'dʒentl/ *adj* **1** careful not to hurt or damage anyone or anything: *Mia's such a gentle person!* **2** not strong or loud or extreme: *a gentle voice* | *a gentle breeze* —**gentleness** *n* [U] —**gently** *adv*

gen·tle·man /'dʒentlmən/ *n* [C], *plural* **gentlemen** /-mən/ **1** a man who is polite and behaves well towards other people: *Roland is a perfect gentleman.* **2** a polite word that you can use when talking about to a man: *Can you show this gentleman to his seat?* —**gentlemanly** *adj*

USAGE NOTE: gentleman

Gentleman and **lady** are often used as a respectful way to talk to or about a man or woman, especially when the person is there and you do not know their name: *It isn't my turn – this gentleman/lady was here before me.* The phrase **Ladies and gentlemen** is also used at the beginning of a speech: *Ladies and gentlemen, I'd like to introduce tonight's guest speaker.* At other times, the usual word is just **man** or **woman**: *There's a man/woman at the door. | I was talking to the man/woman who runs the local store today.*

gen·try /ˈdʒentri/ *n* [plural] *old-fashioned* the gentry people who belong to a high social class

gen·u·ine /ˈdʒenjuⁱn/ *adj* **1** a genuine feeling or desire is one that you really feel, not one that you pretend to feel: *Mrs Lee showed a genuine concern for Lisa's well-being.* **2** something genuine is exactly what it seems to be; real: *a genuine diamond* — **genuinely** *adv*

ge·nus /ˈdʒiːnəs, ˈdʒen-/ *n* [C], *plural* **genera** /ˈdʒenərə/ *technical* a group of animals or plants of the same general types or SPECIES

ge·og·ra·phy /dʒiˈɒɡrəfi, ˈdʒɒɡrəfi‖dʒiˈɑːɡ-/ *n* [U] the study of the countries of the world, including their rivers, mountains, cities etc — **geog·rapher** *n* [C] — **geographic** /ˌdʒiːəˈɡræfɪk◂/ **geographical** *adj*

ge·ol·o·gy /dʒiˈɒlədʒi‖-ˈɑːl-/ *n* [U] the study of materials such as rocks, soil, and minerals, and the way they have changed since the Earth was formed — **geologist** *n* [C] — **geological** /ˌdʒiːə-ˈlɒdʒɪkəl◂‖-ˈlɑː-/ *adj*

ge·o·met·ric /ˌdʒiːəˈmetrɪk◂/, also **ge·o·met·ric·al** /-trɪkəl/ *adj* **1** a geometric shape or pattern has regular shapes and lines **2** relating to geometry

ge·om·e·try /dʒiˈɒmᵻtri‖-ˈɑːm-/ *n* [U] the study in mathematics of the form and relationships of angles, lines, curves etc

ge·ri·at·ric /ˌdʒeriˈætrɪk◂/ *adj* connected with the medical care of old people: *a geriatric hospital*

ge·ri·at·rics /ˌdʒeriˈætrɪks/ *n* [U] the medical treatment and care of old people

germ /dʒɜːm‖dʒɜːrm/ *n* [C] **1** a very small living thing that can make you ill **2** **the germ of an idea/hope etc** the beginning of an idea, feeling etc that may develop and grow

German mea·sles /ˌdʒɜːmən ˈmiːzəlz‖ˌdʒɜːr-/ *n* [U] a disease that causes red spots on your body; RUBELLA

ger·mi·nate /ˈdʒɜːmᵻneɪt‖ˈdʒɜːr-/ *v* [I,T] if a seed germinates, or is germinated, it begins to grow — **germination** /ˌdʒɜːmᵻˈneɪʃən‖ˌdʒɜːr-/ *n* [U]

ger·und /ˈdʒerənd/ *n* [C] a noun formed from the PRESENT PARTICIPLE of a verb, for example 'reading' in the sentence 'He enjoys reading.'

ges·ta·tion /dʒeˈsteɪʃən/ *n* [U] **1** *technical* the period when a baby develops in its mother's body **2** the period when an idea develops

ges·tic·u·late /dʒeˈstɪkjᵿleɪt/ *v* [I] to move your arms and hands because you are very excited, angry, or want to tell someone something: *Jane gesticulated wildly and shouted "Stop! Stop!"*

ges·ture¹ /ˈdʒestʃəl-ər/ *n* [C] **1** a movement of your head, arm, or hand that shows what you mean or how you feel: *a rude gesture* **2** something you do or say to show that you care about someone or something: *It would be a nice gesture if we sent some flowers.*

gesture² *v* [I] to tell someone something by moving your arms, hands, or head: *Tom gestured for me to move out of the way.*

get /ɡet/ *v* **got** /ɡɒt‖ɡɑːt/, **got** *or* **gotten** /ˈɡɒtn‖ˈɡɑːtn/ *AmE*, **getting** **1** [T] to buy or obtain something: **get sb sth** *I got him a watch for his birthday.* | **get sth for sb** *Would you like me to get some bread for you while I'm out?* | **get sth for £5/$9 etc** *My Aunt got these earrings for $3.* **2** [T] to receive or be given something: *I didn't get your letter. | Did you get the job?* | **get sth from/off sb** *How much money did you get from grandma?* **3** **have got to** have something: *I've got a lot of work to do. | I've got three sisters. | Clare's got blue eyes.* **4** **get angry/worse/ill etc** to become angry, worse, ill etc: *Children get bored very easily. | The weather had suddenly gotten cold.* **5** [I] to move or arrive somewhere: *How did he manage to get into their house?* | **+ to** *When you get to the end of the road, turn left.* **6** [T] to move something somewhere: *I hurt my shoulder when I was getting my suitcase down from the rack.* **7** [T] to bring someone or something to a place: **get sb/sth** *Carrie, can you go and get the doctor?* **8** **get sb/sth to do sth** to make someone or something do something, or persuade someone to do something: *I tried to get Jill to come out tonight, but she was too tired.* **9** **get to do sth** *informal* to have an opportunity to do something: *Tom got to drive a Porsche today.* **10** **get sth fixed/done etc** to fix, finish something etc or pay someone to do this: *We'll have to get this room painted.* **11** [T] to earn an amount of money, or receive an amount of money for something you sell: *Tim gets about $50,000 a year. | They got £95,000 for their house.* **12** **get the bus/a flight etc** to travel somewhere on a bus, plane etc **13** [T] to understand something: *Tracey didn't get the joke.* **14** [T] to catch a disease: *People usually get measles when they're young.* **15** **get going/moving** *spoken* to make yourself do something more quickly: *We have to get going, or we'll be late!* **16** **get to know/like etc** to gradually begin to know, like etc someone or something: *As you get to know the city, I'm sure you'll like it better.* **17** **get the door/phone** *spoken* to answer the door or the telephone: *Val, can you get the phone, please – I'm making dinner.*

get about *BrE* also **get around** *phr v* [I] **1** to be able to move or travel to different places: *My Gran can't get about much anymore.* **2** if news or information gets about, a lot of people hear about it: *I'm pregnant but I don't want it getting about just yet.*

G

GRAMMAR NOTE: phrasal verbs (1)
Phrasal verbs are verbs with more than one part. They consist of **verb + adverb** or **verb + preposition** (e.g. *look after, turn out, put off*). Some phrasal verbs have three parts: **verb + adverb + preposition** (e.g. *look forward to, put up with*).

get sth ↔ **across** *phr v* [T] to be able to make someone understand an idea or piece of information: *It was difficult to get my ideas across in such a short interview.*

get along also **get on** *phr v* [I] **1** to have a friendly relationship with someone or a group of people: **+ with** *We get on really well with each other.* **2** to make progress with something you are doing: *How are you getting along at school?*

get around (also **get round** *BrE*) *phr v* **1** [T **get around** sth] to find a way of dealing with a problem, usually by avoiding it: *Businesses are looking for ways to get around the tax laws* **2** [I] to be able to move or travel to different places **3** also **get about** *BrE* [I] if news or information gets around, a lot of people hear about it: *If this news gets around, we'll have reporters calling us all day.* **4** [T **get around** sb] to persuade someone to do what you want by being nice to them : *My Dad might drive us to the party. I'll see if I can get around him.*

get around to sth *phr v* [T] to do something you have been intending to do for a long time: *I need to go to the library but I haven't got around to it yet.*

get at *phr v* [T] **1 what sb is getting at** used when you are asking someone to explain what they mean: *Did you understand what he was getting at?* **2** [T **get at** sth] to be able to reach something easily: *I could see the ring stuck under there, but I couldn't get at it.* **3** [T **get at** sb] *informal* to criticize someone continuously especially in a way that annoys and upsets them **4 get at the meaning/truth etc** to discover the meaning or truth etc of something

get away *phr v* [I] **1** to leave a place, especially when this is difficult: *Barney had to work late, and couldn't get away.* **2** to escape from someone who is chasing you: *The two men got away in a red Volkswagen.* **3** to go on holiday: *Will you get away this summer?*

get away with sth *phr v* [T] to do something wrong and not be punished for it: *The kid was kicking me, and his mother just let him get away with it!*

get back *phr v* **1** [I] to return, especially to the place where you live: *What time do you think you'll get back?* **2** [T **get** sth **back**] to have something that you had lent or lost returned to you: *Did you get your purse back?* **3** [T **get** sb **back** also **get back at** sb] to do something to hurt or embarrass someone who has hurt or embarrassed you: *Jerry's trying to think of ways to get back at her for leaving him.*

get back to *phr v* **1** [T **get back to** sth] to start doing something again after not doing it for a long time: *She found it hard to get back to work after having the baby.* **2** [T **get back to** sb] to talk or write to someone at a later time: *I'll try to get back to you later today.*

get by *phr v* [I] to have enough money to buy the things you need, but not more: *He only earns just enough to get by.* | **get by on £10/$200 etc** *I don't know how she manages to get by on £50 a week.*

get down *phr v* **1** [T **get** sb **down**] *informal* to make someone feel unhappy: *The weather's really getting me down.* **2** [T **get** sth ↔ **down**] to write something down, especially quickly: *Let me get your address down before I forget it.* **3** [T **get** sth **down**] to swallow food or drink, often with difficulty: *Get this medicine down and you'll soon feel better.* **4** [I] to lower your body towards or onto the ground

get down to sth *phr v* [T] to finally start doing something that you have to do: *By the time we finally got down to work it was already 10:00.*

get in *phr v* **1** [I] to be allowed or able to enter a place: *You can't get in to the club without an I.D. card.* **2** [I] when a train, bus etc gets in, it arrives: *My train gets in at 20.00.* **3** [I] to arrive home: *I didn't get in until 10 o'clock last night.* **4** [I] if a politician or political party gets in, they win an election: *Do you think the Conservatives will get in again?*

get in on sth *phr v* [T] *informal* to become involved in something that other people are doing: **get in on the act** *One supermarket started a banking service and now they're all trying to get in on the act.*

get into sth *phr v* [T] **1** to be accepted by a college or university: *You'll have to work harder if you want to get into college.* **2** *informal* to begin to be interested in an activity or subject: *When I was in high school I got into rap music.* **3 what's got into sb** *spoken* used to say that someone is behaving very differently from normal: *I don't know what's got into William. He's not normally so rude.* ➔ see also **get into the habit** (HABIT)

get off *phr v* **1** [I,T **get off** sth] to climb down from something you were on, such as a bus, train or horse **2** [I,T **get** sb **off**] to receive little or no punishment for a crime, or to help someone escape punishment: *I can't believe his lawyers managed to get him off.* **3** [I,T] to finish working: *What time do you get off work ?* **4 where does sb get off doing sth** *AmE spoken* used to say that you are angry with someone because of something they have done, for example telling you to do something: *Where does he get off telling me how to live my life?* **5 get off!** *spoken* used to tell someone to stop touching you or to keep away from something

get off on sth *phr v* [T] *spoken informal* to be excited by something or feel physical pleasure from it, especially sexually

get off to sth *phr v* [T] **get off to a good/bad start** (START²)

get off with sb *phr v* [T] *informal* to start a sexual relationship with someone: *Chris got off with Sally at the Christmas party.*

get on *phr v* **1** [I,T **get on** sth] also **get onto** to walk onto a vehicle such as a bus or climb onto an animal such as a horse **2 get on with** sth to continue doing something, especially after you have stopped for a short time: *Stop talking and get on with your work.* **3** [I] *especially BrE* to have a friendly relationship with someone: **+ with** *She doesn't get on with her mother at all.* **4** [I] to succeed in your job or make progress with a job you are doing **5 be getting on** *informal* to be getting old

get onto sb/sth *phr v* [T] **1** to start talking about a particular subject: *Then we got onto the subject of women, and Craig wouldn't shut up.* **2** to write or speak to someone who you want to help you: *I'd better get onto the landlord about the leaking pipe.*

G

get out *phr v* [I] **1** to escape from a place: + **of** *How did the dog get out of the yard?* **2** if information gets out, a lot of people know about it even though it is supposed to be secret: *The minister had to resign when news of his affair got out.*

get out of sth *phr v* **1** [T **get out of** sth] to avoid doing something you ought to do: *She couldn't get out of the meeting, so she cancelled our dinner.* **2** [T **get** sth **out of** sb] to persuade someone to tell you something or to give you something: *I'll see if I can get some money out of my Dad.*

get over *phr v* **1** [T **get over** sth] to become healthy again after being ill, or to feel better after a bad experience: *The doctor said it will take a couple of weeks to get over the infection.* **2 get** sth **over with** to finish doing something as quickly as possible because you find it unpleasant: *"It should only hurt a little." "OK. Just get it over with."*

get round *phr v* [I,T] *BrE* to get around

get round to sth *BrE phr v* [T] to get around to doing something

get through *phr v* **1** [T **get through** sth] to manage to deal with or live through an unpleasant experience: *I don't know how I got through the weeks after my husband died.* **2** [I] to succeed in reaching someone on the telephone: *It took her 20 minutes to get through to the ticket office.*

get through to sb *phr v* [T] to be able to make someone understand something difficult: *Ben tried to apologize a few times, but he couldn't get through to her.*

get to sb *phr v* [T] *informal* to upset or annoy someone: *Don't let him get to you. He's just teasing you.*

get together *phr v* **1** [I] to meet with other people: *We must get together for a drink sometime.* **2. get yourself together/get it together** to begin to be in control of your life and your emotions: *It took a year for me to get myself together after she left.*

get up *phr v* **1** [I,T **get** sb **up**] to wake up and get out of bed, or make someone do this: *I have to get up at 6:00 tomorrow.* **2** [I] to stand up: *Corrinne got up slowly and went to the window.*

get up to sth *phr v* [T] to do something bad: *Go and see what the kids are getting up to.*

get·a·way /ˈɡetəweɪ/ *n* **make a getaway** to escape quickly from a place, especially after doing something illegal

get-to·geth·er /ˈ. .,../ *n* [C] a friendly, informal meeting or party: *a small get-together with friends*

gey·ser /ˈɡiːzəllˈɡaɪzər/ *n* [C] a hole in the earth from which hot water and steam can suddenly rise

ghast·ly /ˈɡɑːstliIIˈɡæstli/ *adj* extremely bad or unpleasant: *What ghastly weather! | It's that ghastly woman again.*

ghet·to /ˈɡetəʊIl-toʊ/ *n* [C], *plural* **ghettos**, *or* **ghettoes** a part of a city where people of a particular race or class live, usually in bad conditions

ghost /ɡəʊstIlɡoʊst/ *n* [C] the spirit of a dead person that some people believe they can see or feel: *They say the captain's ghost still walks the waterfront at night.* —**ghostly** *adj*

ghost

ghost town /ˈ. ./ *n* [C] a town that is empty because most of the people have left

ghoul /ɡuːl/ *n* [C] an evil spirit in stories that takes dead bodies from graves and eats them —**ghoulish** *adj*

GI /ˌdʒiː ˈaɪ/ *n* [C] a soldier in the US army

gi·ant[1] /ˈdʒaɪənt/ *adj* much larger than other things of the same type: *a giant TV screen*

giant[2] *n* [C] **1** an extremely tall strong man in children's stories **2** a very successful or important person or company: *a giant of the music industry*

gib·ber·ish /ˈdʒɪbərɪʃ/ *n* [U] things someone says or writes that have no meaning or are difficult to understand

gibe /dʒaɪb/ *n* [C] another spelling of JIBE

gid·dy /ˈɡɪdi/ *adj* feeling slightly sick and unable to balance; DIZZY

gift /ɡɪft/ *n* [C] **1** something that you give to someone as a present **2** a natural ability to do something: + **for** *Gary has a real gift for telling stories.*

gift·ed /ˈɡɪftɪd/ *adj* **1** having a natural ability to do something very well, for example painting, playing music, or playing a sport: *one of the most gifted players in the game* **2** a gifted child is very intelligent

gift to·ken /ˈ. ,../ *BrE*, **gift cer·tif·i·cate** /ˈ. ,.../ *AmE n* [C] a piece of paper that you can exchange for a book, record, etc in a shop, given to someone as a present

gift wrap /ˈ. ./ *v* [T] to wrap a present with attractive coloured paper

gig /ɡɪɡ/ *n* [C] a popular music or JAZZ concert

gi·gan·tic /dʒaɪˈɡæntɪk/ *adj* extremely big: *a gigantic phone bill*

gig·gle /ˈɡɪɡəl/ *v* [I] to laugh in a silly way, especially because you are nervous or embarrassed —**giggle** *n* [C]

gild /ɡɪld/ *v* [T] to cover the surface of something with a thin layer of gold or gold paint

gill /ɡɪl/ *n* [C] one of the organs on the sides of a fish through which it breathes

gilt /ɡɪlt/ *adj* covered with a thin layer of gold or gold-coloured paint: *a gilt chair* —**gilt** *n* [U]

gim·mick /ˈɡɪmɪk/ *n* [C] something unusual that is used to attract people's attention: *advertising gimmicks* —**gimmicky** *adj*

gin /dʒɪn/ *n* [C,U] a strong clear alcoholic drink made from grain

gin·ger[1] /ˈdʒɪndʒəll-ər/ *n* [U] a light brown root with a strong, hot taste that is used in cooking

ginger[2] *adj* *BrE* hair or fur that is ginger is bright orange brown in colour: *a ginger cat*

gin·ger·ly /ˈdʒɪndʒəliIl-ər-/ *adv* very slowly, carefully, and gently: *Jack lowered himself gingerly onto the old chair.*

gip·sy /ˈdʒɪpsi/ a British spelling of GYPSY

G

gi·raffe /dʒɪˈrɑːfǁ-ˈræf/ *n* [C] a tall animal that has a very long neck, dark spots on its fur, and lives in Africa

gir·der /ˈgɜːdəǁˈgɜːrdər/ *n* [C] an iron or steel beam, used in building bridges or large buildings

gir·dle /ˈgɜːdlǁˈgɜːr-/ *n* [C] a type of tight-fitting underwear for women

girl /gɜːlǁgɜːrl/ *n* [C] **1** a female child: *She's tall for a girl of her age.* **2** a daughter: *Karen has two boys and a girl.* **3** a word meaning a young woman, which is considered offensive by some women: *A nice girl like you needs a boyfriend.* **4** **the girls** *informal* a woman's female friends: *I'm going out with the girls tonight.*

girl·friend /ˈgɜːlfrendǁˈgɜːrl-/ *n* [C] **1** a girl or woman with whom you have a romantic relationship **2** a woman's female friend

girl·hood /ˈgɜːlhʊdǁˈgɜːrl-/ *n* [U] the period of time in a woman's life when she is a girl

girth /gɜːθǁgɜːrθ/ *n* [C,U] the distance around the middle of something: *the girth of the tree's trunk*

gist /dʒɪst/ *n* **the gist** [singular] the main points or general meaning of what someone has said or written: **+ of** *Those aren't his exact words, but that's the gist of what he said.*

give¹ /gɪv/ *v* **gave** /geɪv/, **given** /ˈgɪvən/, **giving** **1** [T] to provide someone with something they can have or use: **give sb sth** *Can you give me a ride to school tomorrow?* | *I gave Jen a CD for Christmas.* | **give sth to sb** *They gave the job to that guy from Texas.* **2** [T] to put something near someone, or in their hand, so that they can use it, hold it etc: **give sth to sb** *He gave the books to Carl.* | **give sb sth** *Here, give me your coat. I'll hang it up for you.* **3** [T] to perform an action: *Gus gave her a long look.* | **give sb a call/ring** (=phone someone): *Give me a call around 8:00.* | **give a speech/performance etc** *The President will be giving a speech at the ceremony.* **4** [T] to tell someone information or details about something: *The brochure gives all the details.* | **give sb sth** *Would you give Kim a message for me?* **5** to make someone have or feel something: *Your letter gave me hope.* | *The noise is giving me a headache.* | **give sb trouble/problems etc** *My back has been giving me trouble lately.* **6** **give sb/sth time** to allow a person or situation to have time to do something or develop in a particular way: *Give her some time. She'll make the right decision.* **7** [T] to make someone or something have a particular quality or appearance: *Dark clothes will give you a slimmer look.* **8** **give (sb) the impression/sense etc** to make someone have a particular idea or feeling about someone or something: *The room gives the impression of being much larger than it is.* **9** **give (sth) thought/attention/consideration etc** to spend some time thinking about something carefully **10** [T] to offer to pay an amount of money for something: *I'll give you $75 for the oak desk.* **11** [I] to bend, stretch, or break when pressure or weight is put on something: *The leather will give slightly as you wear the boots.* **12** **give or take** *spoken* used to say that the number mentioned is not exact: *The show lasts about an hour, give or take five minutes.* → see also GIVE AND TAKE **13** **give sb your**

word to promise to do something **14** **give a party** to organize and have a party **15** **give way a)** if a bridge, roof, wall etc gives way, it falls down because it cannot support the weight of something **b)** *BrE* to allow traffic on a bigger road to go first; YIELD *AmE*: *a give way sign* **c)** if something gives way to something else, it is replaced by it: *Sadness soon gave way to joy and relief.* **d)** to stop arguing or disagreeing and allow someone to do something, or admit that you are wrong: *Neither of them was willing to give way.*

give away *phr v* **1** [T **give** sth ↔ **away**] to give something you own to someone without selling it to them: *I gave my old clothes away to charity.* | *We're giving away a bottle of wine with every purchase.* **2** [T **give** sb/sth ↔ **away**] to do or say something which allows other people to guess your secret: *He said he hadn't told her, but his face gave him away.* (=showed that he had told her) | **give the game away** (=accidentally let someone know about a secret) → see also GIVEAWAY

give sth ↔ **back** *phr v* [T] to return something to its owner: *Give me back my pencils!* | *I have to give Rick his car back by 3.00.*

give in *phr v* **1** [I] to agree to do something that you were unwilling to do: *Andy had been asking her out for months, so she finally gave in.* | **give in to sth** *If you feel the need for a cigarette, try not to give in to it.* **2** to accept that you have lost a fight, game etc **3** [T **give** sth ↔ **in**] *BrE* to give something such as an official paper or a piece of work to someone: *Can you give in your exams now, please?*

give off *phr v* [T] to produce a smell, light, heat, etc: *The old mattress gave off a faint smell of damp.*

give out *phr v* **1** [T **give** sth ↔ **out**] to give something to each of several people: *Give out the leaflets as they're leaving the club.* **2** [I] to stop working correctly: *My voice gave out half way through the song.*

give up *phr v* **1** [I,T **give** sth ↔ **up**] to admit that you cannot do something and stop trying to finish it: *Vlad has given up trying to teach me Russian.* **2** [T **give** sth ↔ **up**] to stop doing or having something: *She gave up her job, and started writing.* | *I gave up smoking a year ago.* **3** **give yourself/sb up** to allow yourself or someone else to be caught by the police or enemy soldiers: *He gave himself up after police surrounded the property.*

give up on sb *phr v* [T] to stop hoping that someone will do something, or that something will happen: *The doctors had almost given up on her when she came out of the coma.*

give² *n* [U] the ability of a material to bend or stretch when it is under pressure, rather than break

give and take /ˌ. . ˈ./ *n* [U] if there is give and take between two people, each person agrees to do some of the things that the other person wants: *In every successful marriage there is a certain amount of give and take.*

give·a·way /ˈgɪvəweɪ/ *n* [singular] **be a (dead) giveaway** to make it very easy for someone to guess something: *Vince was lying. His red face was a dead giveaway.*

given¹ *v* the past participle of GIVE

giv·en² /ˈɡɪvən/ *adj* [only before noun] **1** a given time, date etc is one that has been previously arranged: *All claims have to be made by a given date.* **2 any given .../a given ...** a particular time or thing that can be used as an example of what you are talking about: *There are thousands of homeless people in London at any given time.*

given³ *prep* if you consider: *Given the circumstances, you've coped well.*

given name /ˈ... ./ *n* [C] *AmE* FIRST NAME

gla·cial /ˈɡleɪʃəl/ *adj* connected with ice or glaciers: *glacial streams*

gla·ci·er /ˈɡlæsiəǁˈɡleɪʃər/ *n* [C] a large mass of ice that moves slowly down a mountain valley

glad /ɡlæd/ *adj* **1** [not before noun] pleased and happy about something: **+ (that)** *We're so glad that you decided to stay.* | **glad to know/ see/hear** *I'm glad to hear you're feeling better.* **2 be glad to do sth** to be willing and eager to do something: *He said he'd be glad to help me.* **3 be glad of sth** to be grateful for something: *Aunt Meg will be glad of the company.* **4** making people feel happy: *a glad day for everyone*

glade /ɡleɪd/ *n literary* a space without trees in a forest

glad·i·a·tor /ˈɡlædieɪtəǁ-ər/ *n* [C] a man who had to fight other men or animals at a public event in ancient Rome

glad·ly /ˈɡlædli/ *adv* willingly or happily: *She said she'd gladly pay for any damages.*

glam·o·rize (also **-ise** *BrE*) /ˈɡlæmərɑɪz/ *v* [T] to make something appear more attractive than it really is: *Hollywood always glamorizes gangsters.*

glam·or·ous /ˈɡlæmərəs/ *adj* attractive and exciting, especially because of being connected with wealth or success

glam·our *BrE*, **glamor** *AmE* /ˈɡlæməǁ-ər/ *n* [U] when something is attractive and exciting because it is connected with wealth or success: *the glamour of a Caribbean cruise*

glance¹ /ɡlɑːnsǁɡlæns/ *v* [I] **1** to look at someone or something for a short time: *He didn't even glance in her direction.* | **+ at/down/towards etc** *Lucy glanced at the clock.* **2** to read something quickly but not carefully: **+ through/at** *Paul glanced through the menu and ordered a hamburger.*

glance² *n* **1** [C] a quick short look at someone or something: *Doug and Jean exchanged a glance.* **2 at a glance** immediately: *I knew at a glance that something was wrong.*

glanc·ing /ˈɡlɑːnsɪŋǁˈɡlæn-/ *adj* [only before noun] hitting something at an angle from the side and not hitting it directly

gland /ɡlænd/ *n* [C] an organ in the body that produces a liquid substance, such as SWEAT or SALIVA — **glandular** /ˈɡlændjʊ̇ləǁ-dʒələr/ *adj*

glandular fe·ver /ˌ... ˈ../ *n BrE* a serious infectious illness that makes you feel weak and tired for a long time afterwards; MONO *AmE*

glare¹ /ɡleəǁɡler/ *v* [I] **1** to look at someone or something in an angry way, usually for a long time: **+ at** *They glared at each other across the table.* **2** if light glares, it shines so strongly that it hurts your eyes: *Sunlight glared off the brilliant snow.*

glare² *n* **1** [singular] a strong bright light which hurts your eyes: *the glare of the sun* **2** [C] a long angry look: *She gave him an icy glare.*

glar·ing /ˈɡleərɪŋǁˈɡler-/ *adj* **1** too bright to look at: *a glaring light* **2** bad and very noticeable: *glaring mistakes*

glass /ɡlɑːsǁɡlæs/ *n* **1** [U] a hard transparent material that is used for making windows and bottles: *Don't cut yourself on the broken glass!* | *a glass vase* **2** [C] a container made of glass used for drinking, or the drink in it: *Did you put the wine glasses on the table?* **a glass of sth** *Would you like a glass of water?* → see picture at CUP **3** [U] objects made of glass: *an impressive collection of Venetian glass*

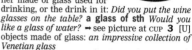
glass

glass cei·ling /ˌ. ˈ../ *n* [U] an imaginary limit which prevents women from reaching the highest level in a company, even though there are no rules or laws to prevent them from doing this

glasses

lens

frame

glass·es /ˈɡlɑːsɪzǁˈɡlæ-/ *n* [plural] two pieces of special glass surrounded by plastic, metal etc which you wear in front of your eyes in order to see better; SPECTACLES: *I can't find my glasses.* | **a pair of glasses** (=one set of glasses)

glass fi·bre /ˌ. ˈ.../ *n* [U] *BrE* FIBREGLASS

glass·house /ˈɡlɑːshaʊsǁˈɡlæs-/ *n* [C] *BrE* a glass building used for growing plants; GREENHOUSE

glass·ware /ˈɡlɑːsweəǁˈɡlæswer/ *n* [U] glass objects, especially ones used for drinking and decoration

glass·y /ˈɡlɑːsiǁˈɡlæsi/ *adj* **1** smooth and shining, like glass: *the glassy surface of the lake* **2** glassy eyes show no expression, interest, or emotion

glaze¹ /ɡleɪz/ *v* **1** [I] also **glaze over** if your eyes glaze over, they show no expression because you are bored or tired **2** [T] to cover clay pots, bowls etc with a liquid that gives them a

glaze

GRAMMAR NOTE: the progressive
You form the **present progressive** by using **be/is/was** + present participle: *They are coming.*
You form the **past progressive** by using **was/were** + present participle: *He was lying.*

G

hard shiny surface **3** [T] to put glass into a window frame — **glazed** adj

glaze² n **1** [C] a liquid that is put on clay pots, bowls etc to give them a shiny surface **2** [U] a liquid put on fruit, cake, or meat to give it an shiny surface

gleam¹ /gliːm/ v [I] **1** to shine softly: *The Rolls Royce gleamed in the moonlight.* **2** **gleam with happiness/joy etc** to show a particular feeling in your eyes or face: *His green eyes gleamed with pleasure.*

gleam² n **1** [C] the brightness of something that shines: *The table shone with the gleam of silver and glass.* **2** [singular] a sudden expression that appears for a moment on someone's face or in their eyes: *A gleam of humour lit up her eyes.*

glean /gliːn/ v [T] to find out information slowly and with difficulty: **glean sth from** *I've managed to glean a few details about him from his friends.*

glee /gliː/ n [U] happiness or excitement you feel when something good happens to you: *The children laughed with glee.* — **gleeful** adj — **gleefully** adv

glen /glen/ n [C] a deep narrow valley

glib /glɪb/ adj said in a way that makes something sound simple, easy, or true when it is not: *She was careful not to let her answer sound too glib.* — **glibly** adv

glide /glaɪd/ v [I] to move smoothly, quietly, and without effort: *We watched the sailboats glide across the lake.* — **glide** n [C]

glid·er /ˈglaɪdər/ n [C] a light plane without an engine

glid·ing /ˈglaɪdɪŋ/ n [U] the sport of flying a glider

glim·mer¹ /ˈglɪmər/ n [C] **1** **a glimmer of hope/doubt etc** a small amount of hope, doubt etc **2** a weak unsteady light

glimmer² v [I] to shine with a light that is not very bright or steady: *Faint starlight glimmered on the rooftops.*

glimpse¹ /glɪmps/ n [C] **1** when you see someone or something very quickly for a short time: **get/catch a glimpse of** *Dad only caught a glimpse of the guy who stole our car.* **2** a short experience of something that helps you to understand it: *a glimpse into the future*

glimpse² v [T] to see someone or something very quickly for a short time: *For a second I glimpsed her face, then she was gone.*

glint /glɪnt/ v [I] **1** to give out small flashes of light: *I saw something glinting in the darkness.* **2** if your eyes glint with pleasure, anger etc, they show pleasure, anger etc — **glint** n [C]

glis·ten /ˈglɪsən/ v [I] to shine because of being wet or oily: **glisten with sth** *His back was glistening with sweat.*

glitch /glɪtʃ/ n [C] a small problem that prevents something from working correctly: *a computer glitch.*

glit·ter¹ /ˈglɪtər/ v [I] to shine with a lot of small flashes of light: *Snow was glittering in the morning light.* — **glittering** adj

glitter² n [U] **1** brightness made up of many flashing points of light: *the glitter of her diamond ring* **2** the attractiveness and excitement connected with rich and famous people or places: *the glitter of Las Vegas*

gloat /gləʊt‖gloʊt/ v [I] to show in an annoying way that you are happy about your success or about someone else's failure: *Dick was still gloating over his team's win.*

glo·bal /ˈgləʊbəl‖ˈgloʊ-/ adj affecting or including the whole world: *global environmental issues* — **globally** adv

global warm·ing /ˌ.. ˈ../ n [U] an increase in world temperatures, caused by an increase of CARBON DIOXIDE around the Earth

globe /gləʊb‖gloʊb/ n **1** **the globe** the world: *Our company has offices all over the globe.* **2** [C] an object shaped like a ball **3** [C] a round object with a map of the earth drawn on it

glob·u·lar /ˈglɒbjələr‖ˈglɑːbjələr/ adj shaped like a ball or drop of liquid

glob·ule /ˈglɒbjuːl‖ˈglɑː-/ n [C] a small drop of liquid or a melted substance: *small globules of oil*

gloom /gluːm/ n [singular,U] **1** almost complete darkness **2** a strong feeling of sadness and having no hope

gloom·y /ˈgluːmi/ adj **1** making you feel that a situation will not improve: *a gloomy sales forecast* **2** feeling sad because you do not have a lot of hope: *the gloomy faces of the rescue workers* **3** dark, especially in a way that seems sad: *They were led through the gloomy church by an old priest.* — **gloomily** adv

glo·ri·fied /ˈglɔːrɪfaɪd/ adj [only before noun] made to seem like something more important: *Many people still think of computers as glorified typewriters.*

glo·ri·fy /ˈglɔːrɪfaɪ/ v [T] **1** to make something seem more important or better than it really is: *We must avoid glorifying war.* **2** to praise someone, especially God — **glorification** /ˌglɔːrɪfɪˈkeɪʃən/ n [U]

glo·ri·ous /ˈglɔːriəs/ adj **1** having or deserving praise or honour: *a glorious achievement* **2** extremely enjoyable or beautiful: *What a glorious day!* — **gloriously** adv

glo·ry¹ /ˈglɔːri/ n **1** [U] praise and honour given to someone: *The team finished the season covered in glory.* **2** [C] the things about a place or way of life which are beautiful or make people feel proud: *the glories of ancient Greece*

glory² v

glory in sth phr v [T] to enjoy something very much: *They gloried in their newfound freedom.*

gloss¹ /glɒs‖glɔːs, glɑːs/ n [singular,U] the shiny appearance of something: *a new hair gel that adds gloss to your hair*

gloss² v [T] to give a short explanation for a difficult word or idea

gloss over sth phr v [T] to deliberately not mention the details of something such as a mistake, so that people do not notice it

glos·sa·ry /ˈglɒsəri‖ˈglɔː-, ˈglɑː-/ n [C] a list of explanations of technical or unusual words, printed at the end of a book

gloss·y /ˈglɒsi‖ˈglɔːsi, ˈglɑːsi/ adj **1** shiny and smooth: *glossy, healthy hair* **2** glossy magazines, photographs etc are printed on shiny good quality paper

glove /glʌv/ n [C] a piece of clothing worn on

your hand, with separate parts for the thumb and each finger ➡ see colour picture on page 113

glow¹ /gləʊ‖gloʊ/ n [singular] **1** a gentle steady light, especially from something that is burning without flames: *The sky was filled with an orange glow.* **2** the bright colour your face has when you exercise or are healthy **3 a glow of pleasure/pride/satisfaction etc** a strong feeling of pleasure, pride etc

glow² v [I] **1** to shine with a gentle steady light: *My new watch glows in the dark.* **2** to produce a red light and heat without flames: *A fire was glowing in the grate.* **3** if your face glows, it is red or hot because of exercise or strong feelings: *Standing there in his new suit, he positively glowed.* **4 glow with happiness/pride/pleasure etc** to show in your expression that you are very happy, proud etc: *She glowed with happiness.* | *Their young faces glowed with interest.*

glow·er /ˈglaʊəl-ər/ v [I] to look at someone in an angry way: + **at** *Jill glowered at her husband but said nothing.*

glow·ing /ˈgləʊɪŋ‖ˈgloʊ-/ adj **glowing report/ description etc** a report etc that praises someone or something

glu·cose /ˈgluːkəʊs‖-koʊs/ n [U] a natural form of sugar that exists in fruits

glue¹ /gluː/ n [C,U] a sticky substance used for joining things together ➡ see colour picture on page 80

glue² v [T] **glued, gluing** or **glueing 1** to join things together, using glue: *Cut out the pieces and glue the edges together.* **2 be glued to** *informal* to be looking at something with all your attention: *All eyes were glued to the clock on the wall.*

glum /glʌm/ adj sad or disappointed —**glumly** adv

glut¹ /glʌt/ n [C usually singular] a bigger supply of something than is necessary: *a glut of violent video games*

glut² v [T] **be glutted with** to be supplied with too much of something: *The world market is glutted with oil.*

glu·ti·nous /ˈgluːtɪ̣nəs‖-tn-əs/ adj thick and sticky: *The spaghetti had turned into a glutinous mass.*

glut·ton /ˈglʌtn/ n **1** [C] someone who eats too much **2 a glutton for punishment** someone who seems to enjoy working very hard or doing something unpleasant

glut·ton·y /ˈglʌtəni/ n [U] when someone eats much more than they need to

gm a written abbreviation for GRAM

GMT /ˌdʒiː em ˈtiː/ n [U] Greenwich Mean Time; the time as measured at Greenwich in London, used as an international standard for measuring time

gnarled /nɑːld‖nɑːrld/ adj rough and twisted: *a gnarled branch* | *gnarled fingers*

gnat /næt/ n [C] a small flying insect that bites

gnaw /nɔː‖nɒ/ v [I,T] to keep biting something: *The animal began to gnaw at the ropes holding her.*

gnaw at sb phr v [T] if a feeling or thought gnaws at you, it makes you feel worried or anxious: *Guilt had been gnawing at me all day.*

gnaw·ing /ˈnɔːɪŋ‖ˈnɒ-/ adj [only before noun]

worrying or painful, over a long period of time: *gnawing doubts*

gnome /nəʊm‖noʊm/ n [C] a creature in children's stories like a little old man with a pointed hat and a BEARD

GNP /ˌdʒiː en ˈpiː/ n [singular] Gross National Product; the total value of all the goods and services produced in a country, usually in a single year

go¹ /gəʊ‖goʊ/ v **went** /went/, **gone** /gɒn‖gɔːn/, **going 1** [I] to leave a place in order to go somewhere else: *I wanted to go, but Craig insisted we stay.* | **be/get going** (=leave): *It's late – I must be going.* **2** [I] to move towards a place: *Mom went into the kitchen.* | *Let's go home.* **3** [I] to visit a place: *Nancy has gone to Paris.* (=she is in Paris now) | *Nancy has been to Paris.* (=she has visited Paris in the past) **4** [I] to travel on a bus, plane etc: *You take the train and we will go by car.* **5** [I] to travel somewhere in order to do something: *They've gone shopping.* | *Mick's gone to buy a paper.* | *Let's go for a walk.* **6 be going to do sth** used to say that something will happen or is supposed to happen: *It looks like it's going to rain.* | *He's going to marry Ann.* ➡ compare GONNA **7** [I] to reach as far as a particular place, or lead to a particular place: *The roots of the tree go very deep.* **8** [I] to belong or fit in a particular place or position: *"Where do the plates go?" "On the shelf."* **9** [linking verb] to become: *I think this milk's gone sour.* | *My hair's going grey.* **10** [linking verb] to be or remain in a particular state: *All her complaints went unheard.* (=no one listened to them) | **go hungry** (=not have anything to eat) **11 go to church/ school etc** to regularly attend a church, school etc: *Is Brett going to college next year?* **12** [linking verb] to happen or develop in a particular way: *How did your interview go?* | **go well/fine/wrong etc** *Everything started to go wrong all of a sudden.* **13** [I] *informal* if a machine goes, it works: *My car wouldn't go this morning.* **14** [I] to disappear: *Has your headache gone yet?* **15** [I] if money goes, it is spent **16** [I] if time goes, it passes: *I just don't know where the time goes.* | *The hours go so slowly at work.* **17** [I] to get worse or not work correctly: *Dad's hearing is starting to go.* **18** [I] to have particular words or music or a particular sound: *How does the song go?* **19** [I] to look or taste good together: + **together** *Those colours don't go together very well.* | **go with sth** *Does red wine go with chicken?* **20 to go a)** still remaining before something happens: *Only two weeks to go before we leave for South America!* **b)** *AmE* food that is bought from a restaurant and taken away to be eaten: *I'll have a large order of fries to go, please.* **21 How's it going?/How are things going?/How goes it?** *spoken* used to ask someone how they are: *"Hey Jimmy, how's it going?" "All right, I guess."*

go about sth phr v [T] to do something or begin doing something: *Perhaps I'm going about this the wrong way.*

go after sb/sth phr v [T] to try to get something or catch someone: *Karr hesitated a moment, then went after her.*

go against sb/sth phr v **1** [T **go against** sth] to do the opposite of what someone wants you to do: *You've really angered him by going* *against his wishes.* **2** [T **go against** sb] if a decision such as a vote goes against you, you do not get the decision or result that you wanted

go ahead *phr v* [I] **1** to begin or continue: *The railway strike looks likely to go ahead tomorrow.* | **+ with** *They plan to go ahead with their wedding later this year.* **2** to take place: *The sale went ahead as planned.*

go along *phr v* [I] to continue doing a particular activity: *You'll learn how to do it as you go along*

go along with sb/sth *phr v* [T] to agree with or support someone or something: *They were happy to go along with our suggestions.*

go around (also **go round** *BrE*) *phr v* [I] **1 go around doing sth** to do something, especially something that other people do not approve of: *You can't go around saying things like that.* | *She always goes around barefoot.* **2** if an illness or a piece of news is going around, it is being passed from one person to another **3** to be enough for everyone: *Are there enough glasses to go around?*

go at sb/sth *phr v* [T] to start to do something, especially fighting or arguing, with a lot of energy: *The boys went at each other until the teacher pulled them apart.*

go away *phr v* [I] **1** to leave a place or a person: *Go away! Leave me alone!* **2** to spend some time away from home, especially on holiday: *We're going away for the weekend.* **3** to disappear or not happen anymore: *My headache still hasn't gone away.*

go back *phr v* [I] to return to a place: **+ to** *I'll never go back to my old school.*

go back on sth *phr v* [T] if you go back on a promise or agreement, you do not do what you promised to do

go back to sth *phr v* [T] **1** to start doing an activity again after you have stopped doing it: *I can't study any more – I'll go back to it later.* **2** to have its origin in a particular time in the past: *The company's history goes back to 1925.*

go by *phr v* **1** [I] if time goes by, it passes: *Two months went by before Tony called.* **2** [T **go by** sth] to use information, rules etc to help you decide what to do: *Don't go by that map. It's really old.* | *We'll have to go by the referee's decision.*

go down *phr v* [I] **1** to become less in level, amount, size, quality etc: *The temperature went down to freezing last night.* | *The swelling in her knee didn't go down for days.* **2** when the sun goes down, it goes below the HORIZON at the end of the day **3** if a ship goes down, it sinks **4** if a plane does down, it crashes **5** if a computer goes down, it stops working **6 go down well/badly etc** used to say that something is accepted or not accepted by people: *Robbie's jokes didn't go down very well with her parents.*

go down with sth *phr v* [T] *informal* to catch an illness: *Ron's gone down with flu.*

go for sb/sth *phr v* [T] **1** to choose a particular thing **2** to like someone or something: *Shane always goes for blondes.* **3** [**go for** sb] to attack someone: *She went for him with a knife.* **4** to try to get or win something: *We're going for the gold medal.* **5** *spoken* to also be true about someone or something else:

I told him to work harder, and that goes for you too.

go in for sth *phr v* [T] to like doing something: *I've never gone in for modern art.*

go into sth *phr v* [T] **1** to start working in a particular profession: *Vivian wants to go into teaching.* **2** to describe or explain something thoroughly: *I don't want to go into details right now, but it was horrible.*

go off *phr v* **1** [I] to explode: *The bomb went off without warning.* **2** [I] to make a loud noise: *My alarm clock didn't go off!* **3 go off well/badly etc** to happen in a particular way: *The ceremony went off perfectly.* **4** *BrE* [I] if food goes off, it goes bad **5** [T] *BrE informal* to stop liking someone or something: *I've gone off coffee.*

go off with sth *phr v* [T] to take away something that belongs to someone else: *She's gone off with my pen.*

go on *phr v* [I] **1** to continue without stopping or changing: *We can't go on fighting like this!* | *The meeting went on longer than I expected.* **2** to happen: *What's going on down there?* **3** to do something new when you have finished something else: *Shall we go on to the next item on the agenda?* **4** to continue speaking, after you have stopped for a while: **+ with** *After a short pause, Maria went on with her story.* **5** if time goes on, it passes: *As time went on, he became more friendly.* **6** *spoken* used to encourage someone to do something: *Go on, have some more cake.*

go out *phr v* [I] **1** to leave your house, especially in order to do something you enjoy: *Are you going out tonight?* | **go out for dinner/lunch etc** *We went out for brunch on Sunday.* **2** to have a romantic relationship with someone: *How long have you two been going out?* | **go out with** sb *Lisa used to go out with my brother.* **3** if a light or fire goes out, it stops shining or burning **4** if the tide goes out, it moves back from the land **5** to stop being fashionable or used: *I thought flared trousers went out years ago.*

go over *phr v* **1** [T] to look at or think about something carefully: *I've gone over the budget and I don't think we can afford a new computer.* **2** [T] to repeat something in order to learn it or to understand it: *Once again I went over exactly what I needed to say.*

go round *phr v* [I] *BrE* to go around

go through *phr v* **1** [T **go through** sth] to have a very upsetting or difficult experience: *She's just been through a divorce.* **2** [I] if a deal, agreement or law goes through, it is officially accepted: *My car loan application has finally gone through.* **3** [T **go through** sth] to use all of something: *Jeremy goes through at least a litre of milk every day!* **4** [T **go through** sth] to look at, read, or explain something carefully: *Have you been going through my handbag again?*

go through with sth *phr v* [T] to do something you had planned or promised to do: *I'm not sure if I can go through with the wedding.*

go under *phr v* [I] *informal* if a business goes under, it has serious problems and fails

go up *phr v* [I] **1** to increase in number or amount: *Our rent has gone up by almost 20%.* **2** to be built: *All of those houses have gone up in the past 6 months.* **3** to explode or be destroyed by fire: *The factory went up in flames before the firemen got there.*

go with sb/sth *phr v* [T] **1** to be included as part of something: *The car goes with the job.* | *the responsibilities that go with having a family* **2** to accept someone's idea or plan: *Let's go with John's original idea.*

go without sth *phr v* [T] to be able to manage without something: *We're out of milk – I'm afraid you'll have to go without.* | *She had gone without food to feed the children.*

USAGE NOTE: go, gone and been

Gone is the usual past participle of **go**: *George has gone to Denver.* (=he is there now) Use **been** as the past participle with the sense of go that means 'visit': *George has been to Denver.* (=he has visited Denver in the past, but is not there now)

---

go² *n, plural* **goes 1** [C] an attempt to do something: **have a go (at sth)** *We thought we'd have a go at making our own Easter eggs.* **2** [C] *especially BrE* someone's turn in a game etc: *Whose go is it?* **3 make a go of sth** to make something such as a business or a marriage successful **4 on the go** very busy or working all the time

goad /gəʊd‖goʊd/ *v* [T] to make someone do something by annoying them until they do it: **goad sb into (doing) sth** *Troy's friends goaded him into asking Susan for a date.*

go-a·head /ˈ. .,./ *n* **give sb the go-ahead** *informal* to officially give someone permission to start doing something

goal /gəʊl‖goʊl/ *n* [C] **1** when you make the ball go into the goal to win a point, or the point won by doing this: *Ramos scored two goals for the US.* **2** in sports such as football, the area into which a player tries to put the ball in order to win a point **3** something that you hope to achieve in the future: *My goal is to study law at Harvard.*

goal·ie /ˈgəʊli‖ˈgoʊ-/ *n* [C] *informal* a GOAL-KEEPER

goal·keep·er /ˈgəʊl,ki:pə‖ˈgoʊl,ki:pər/- also **goal·tend·er** /ˈgəʊl,tendə‖ˈgoʊl,tendər/ *AmE* — *n* [C] the player on a sports team who tries to stop the ball from going into the goal

goal·post /ˈgəʊlpəʊst‖ˈgoʊlpoʊst/ *n* [C usually plural] one of the two posts with a bar between them, which form the sides of a GOAL in games such as football or HOCKEY

goat /gəʊt‖goʊt/ *n* [C] a common farm animal with horns and with long hair under its chin

goat

gob·ble /ˈgɒbəl‖ˈgɑ:-/ *v* [T] **-bbled, -bbling** *informal* also **gobble up** to eat something very quickly

gob·ble·dy·gook, **gob·bledegook** /ˈgɒbəldɪguːk‖ ˈgɑ:bəldiguk, -guːk/ *n* [U] *informal* complicated

language, especially in official documents, that ordinary people cannot understand

go-be·tween /ˈ. .,./ *n* [C] someone who takes messages between people who are not able or willing to meet each other

gob·let /ˈgɒblɪt‖ˈgɑ:b-/ *n* [C] a cup made of glass or metal, with a base and a stem but no handles

gob·lin /ˈgɒblɪn‖ˈgɑ:b-/ *n* [C] a small ugly creature in children's stories who tricks people

gobs /gɒbz‖gɑ:bz/ *n* [plural] *informal* a large amount of something: *pecan pie with gobs of ice cream*

go-cart /ˈ. ./ the usual American spelling of GO-KART

God /gɒd‖gɑ:d/ *n* [singular] **1** the BEING who Christians, Jews, and Muslims pray to **2 God/ oh God/my God** *spoken* used to express strong feelings of surprise, anger etc **3 I swear/ hope/wish to God** *spoken* used to emphasize that you promise, hope, or wish that something is true **4 God (only) knows** *spoken* used to show that you are annoyed because you do not know or understand something: *God only knows where those kids are now!* **5 what/how/where/who in God's name** *spoken* used to ask a question when you are surprised or angry: *Where in God's name have you been?* **6 God forbid** *spoken* used to say that you hope that something does not happen: *God forbid that your father finds out about this.*

USAGE NOTE: God

The word **God** is used in a non-religious way in many expressions to show surprise, fear, anger etc. Note, however, that some people find these uses offensive.

---

god *n* [C] **1** a male BEING who is believed to have power over some part of nature or the world: *the god Krishna* **2** someone or something that is given too much importance: *Science became their god.*

god·child /ˈgɒdtʃaɪld‖ˈgɑ:d-/ *n* [C] *plural* **godchildren** /-,tʃɪldrən/ a child whose religious education a GODPARENT has promised to be responsible for at a religious ceremony

god·dam·mit /gɒˈdæmɪt‖,gɑ:d'dæm-/ *interjection AmE* DAMMIT

god·damn /ˈgɒdæm‖,gɑ:d'dæm / **god·damned** /-dæmd/ *adj AmE spoken* DAMN

god·dess /ˈgɒdɪs‖ˈgɑ:-/ *n* [C] a female BEING who is believed to have power over some part of nature or the world: *Venus, the goddess of love*

god·fa·ther /ˈgɒd,fɑ:ðə‖ˈgɑ:d,fɑ:ðər/ *n* [C] a man who promises at a religious ceremony to be responsible for a child's religious education

god-fear·ing /ˈ. .,./ *adj old-fashioned* behaving according to the rules of a religion

god-for·sak·en /ˈgɒdfəseɪkən‖ˈgɑ:dfər-/ *adj* a godforsaken place has nothing interesting or cheerful in it

god·less /ˈgɒdləs‖ˈgɑ:d-/ *adj* not showing any respect for or belief in God

G

GRAMMAR NOTE: the present (1)

Use the **present progressive** to say what is happening <u>now</u>, at the time you are speaking: *Dad's working at home today.* | *We're waiting for a bus.* Use the **simple present** to talk about what normally happens: *He works from 9 to 5.* | *We usually go to school by bus.*

god·like /ˈgɒdlaɪk‖-aːd-/ adj having a quality like God or a god: a godlike chief | godlike status

god·moth·er /ˈgɒd,mʌðə‖ˈgaːd,mʌðər/ n [C] a woman who promises at a religious ceremony to be responsible for a child's religious education

god·pa·rent /ˈgɒd,peərənt‖ˈgaːd,per-/ n [C] someone who promises at a religious ceremony to be responsible for a child's religious education

god·send /ˈgɒdsend‖ˈgaːd-/ n [singular] something good that happens at a time when you really need it: Being able to drive has been a godsend since we moved here.

goes /gəʊz‖goʊz/ v the third person singular present of GO

go-get·ter /ˌ. ˈ.., ˈ. ‖..ˈ. ‖‖. ./ n [C] informal someone who is likely to be successful because they are very determined

gog·gle-eyed /ˌgɒgəl ˈaɪd‖ ‖,gaː-/ adj informal with your eyes wide open and a surprised expression on your face

gog·gles /ˈgɒgəlz‖ˈgaː-/ n [plural] large round glasses with an edge that fits closely to your face, used to protect your eyes: a pair of swimming goggles → see colour picture on page 636

go·ing[1] /ˈgəʊɪŋ‖ˈgoʊ-/ n [U] **1** informal the speed at which you travel or work: **good/hard/ slow etc going** We got there in four hours, which wasn't bad going. **2** **while the going's good** BrE while a situation is good, an before it gets worse: You should get out while the going's good.

going[2] adj **1** **the going rate** the usual cost of a service, or the usual pay for a job: £25 an hour is the going rate for private lessons. **2** [not before noun] available: Are there any jobs going where you work? | **the best/biggest/nicest etc ... going** We think we make the best computers going. **3** **a going concern** a successful business: The restaurant is being offered for sale as a going concern.

going-o·ver /ˌ. ˈ../ n [singular] a thorough examination: My car needs a good going-over.

goings-on /ˌ. ˈ./ n [plural] informal strange or interesting events or activities

go-kart especially BrE, **go-cart** especially AmE /ˈgəʊ kaːt‖ˈgoʊ kaːrt/ n [C] a small vehicle that people use in races for fun, which has an open frame and a small engine

gold[1] /gəʊld‖goʊld/ n **1** [U] a valuable soft yellow metal that is used to make jewellery, coins etc **2** [C,U] the colour of this metal

gold[2] adj **1** made of gold: a gold necklace **2** having the colour of gold: a gold dress

gold·en /ˈgəʊldən‖ˈgoʊl-/ adj **1** having a bright yellow colour: golden hair **2** made of gold: a golden crown **3** **a golden opportunity** a rare chance to get something valuable or to be very successful **4** **golden age** a time when you were very happy, or when great things were being achieved: the golden age of film **5** **golden wedding** BrE the date that is exactly 50 years after a wedding

gold·fish /ˈgəʊld,fɪʃ‖ˈgoʊld-/ n [C] a small orange fish often kept as a pet

gold med·al /ˌ. ˈ../ n [C] a round flat piece of gold that is given to someone who wins a race or competition

gold·mine /ˈgəʊldmaɪn‖ˈgoʊld-/ n [C] **1** a business or activity that produces a lot of

money: That pub's an absolute goldmine. **2** a place where gold is taken out of the ground

golf /gɒlf‖gɑːlf, gɔːlf/ n [U] a game in which you try to hit a small white ball into holes in the ground with a CLUB (=a kind of long stick) → see colour picture on page 636 — **golfer** n [C]

golf club /ˈ. ./ n [C] **1** a long stick used for hitting the ball in golf → see colour picture on page 636 **2** a place where a group of people pay to play golf

golf course /ˈ. ./ n [C] an area of land on which you play golf

gol·ly /ˈgɒli‖ˈgaːli/ interjection old-fashioned used when you are surprised

gone[1] /gɒn‖gɔːn/ v the past participle of GO

gone[2] prep BrE informal later than a particular time or older than a particular age: It was gone midnight when we got back.

gong /gɒŋ‖gɑːŋ, gɔːŋ/ n [C] a round piece of metal that hangs in a frame and is hit with a stick to make a loud sound

gon·na /ˈgɒnə, gənə‖ˈgɔːnə, gɑːnə/ nonstandard a way of saying or writing 'going to': This isn't gonna be as quick as we thought.

goo /guː/ n [U] a thick, sticky substance; GOOP AmE: What's that goo in your hair?

good[1] /gʊd/ adj **better** /ˈbetə‖-ər/, **best** /best/ **1** of a high standard: Peter's exam results were good, but Sue's were even better. **2** useful or suitable for a particular purpose: It's a good day for going to the beach. **3** clever or skilful: a good swimmer | + **at** Andrea is very good at languages. **4** enjoyable and pleasant; nice: good weather | It's good to see you again. **5** **be good for sb** to be healthy for your body or your mind: Watching so much TV isn't good for you. **6** able to be used, and not broken or damaged: You need good strong boots for walking. | **(as) good as new** The car looks as good as new again. | **be good for two days/five years etc** (=can be used in that time): The guarantee on my new watch is good for five years. **7** a good child behaves well: Sit here and be a good girl. **8** kind and helpful: **good of sb (to do sth)** It's good of you to come at such short notice. **9** **as good as** nearly: The work is as good as finished. **10** morally right: He had always tried to lead a good life. **11** [only before noun] large in size, amount, or degree: **a good while** (=a long time): They've been gone a good while, haven't they? | **a good many/few** (=quite a lot): There were a good few people at church this morning. | **a good 10 minutes/3 miles etc** (=at least 10 minutes etc) **12** complete or thorough: The car needs a good wash. | Have a good look at this picture. **13** **in good time** early: I want to get to the airport in good time. **14** **good/oh good** spoken used when you are pleased about something or agree with something: "I've finished." "Good, that was quick." **15** **good luck** spoken used to say that you hope that someone is successful **16** **good God/grief/heavens etc** spoken used when you are angry, surprised etc: Good grief! Is it 12 o'clock already? **17** **it's a good thing** spoken also **it's a good job** BrE used when you are glad that something has happened: It's a good job I brought the map.

USAGE NOTE: good and well

Use **good** as an adjective to talk about the quality of someone or something: *She's a good singer.* Use **well** as an adverb to talk about the way that something is done: *She sings very well.*

good[2] *n* **1** [U] something that improves a situation or gives you an advantage: **be no good/do no good** (=not have any use or effect): *It's no good crying now.* | *You can talk to her, but it won't do any good.* | **do sb good** (=make someone feel better): *It'll do you good to have a holiday.* | **for sb's own good** (=to help someone): *Take your medicine – it's for your own good.* **2** **be no good/not be any good/not be much good** to be of a low quality or standard: *This radio's no good.* | *The film wasn't much good, was it?* **3** [U] the idea of what is morally right: *the battle between good and evil* | **be up to no good** *informal* (=to be doing or planning something that is wrong or bad) **4** **for good** permanently: *We moved out of the city for good in 1989.*

good af·ter·noon /ˌ. ˌ..'./ *interjection* used to say hello to someone in the afternoon

good·bye /ɡʊdˈbaɪ/ *interjection* used when you are leaving or being left by someone: *Goodbye, Mrs. Anderson.* | **say goodbye (to sb)** *I just want to say goodbye to Erica.*

good eve·ning /ˌ. '../ *interjection* used to say hello to someone in the evening: *Good evening, ladies and gentlemen!* → compare GOOD NIGHT

good-for-noth·ing /ˌ. '..ˌ. / *n* [C] someone who is lazy or has no skills — **good-for-nothing** *adj*

good-hu·moured *BrE*, **good-humored** *AmE* /ˌ. '.. / *adj* cheerful and friendly

good·ies /ˈɡʊdiz/ *n* [plural] *informal* things that are attractive and pleasant, especially things that are good to eat: *a bag of goodies*

good-look·ing /ˌ. '..< / *adj* with an attractive face

good mor·ning /ˌ. '../ *interjection* used to say hello to someone in the morning: *Good morning! Did you sleep well?*

good-na·tured /ˌ. '..< / *adj* kind and cheerful, and not easily made angry — **good-naturedly** *adv*

good·ness /ˈɡʊdn¹s/ *n* **1** also **my goodness** *spoken* said when you are surprised: *My goodness, you've lost a lot of weight!* **2** [U] the quality of being good: *Anne believed in the basic goodness of people.*

good night /ˌ. './ *interjection* said when you are leaving or being left by someone at night, especially late at night: *Good night, Sandy. Sleep well!* → compare GOOD EVENING

goods /ɡʊdz/ *n* [plural] things that are produced in order to be sold: *electrical goods*

good·will /ˌɡʊdˈwɪl/ *n* [U] kind feelings between people: *Christmas should be a time of peace and goodwill.*

goody-good·y /ˌ.. ˌ../ also **goody-two-shoes** /ˌ.. '. ./ *n* [C] someone who tries too hard to seem very good and helpful in order to please their parents, teachers etc

goo·ey /ˈɡuːi/ *adj informal* sticky, soft, and usually sweet: *gooey cakes*

goof[1] /ɡuːf/ *v* [I] *AmE informal* to make a silly mistake: *Oops! I goofed again.*

goof around *phr v* [I] *AmE informal* to spend

time doing silly things; MESS ABOUT *BrE*: *We were just goofing around at the mall.*

goof off *phr v* [I] *AmE informal* to waste time or avoid doing any work: *Jason's been goofing off in class lately.*

goof[2] *n* [C] *informal especially AmE* **1** someone who is silly: *You big goof!* **2** a silly mistake

goof·y /ˈɡuːfi/ *adj informal* stupid or silly: *a goofy smile*

goop /ɡuːp/ *n* [U] *AmE informal* a thick sticky substance; GOO

goose /ɡuːs/ *n* [C,U], *plural* **geese** /ɡiːs/ a common water bird that is similar to a duck but bigger

goose·ber·ry /ˈɡʊzbəri, ˈɡuːz-, ˈɡuːs-‖ˈɡuːsberi/ *n* [C] **1** a small round green fruit with a sour taste: *gooseberry pie* **2** **play gooseberry** *BrE informal* to be with two people who love each other and want to be alone

goose pim·ples *especially BrE* /ˈ. ˌ../, **goose bumps** /ˈ. ./ *especially AmE* — *n* [plural] a condition in which your skin comes up in small points because you are cold or afraid

go·pher /ˈɡəʊfəl‖ˈɡoʊfər/ *n* [C] a North and Central American animal like a large rat with no tail, that lives in holes in the ground

gore[1] /ɡɔː‖ɡɔːr/ *v* [T] if an animal gores someone, it wounds them with its horns

gore[2] *n* [U] blood from a wound

gorge[1] /ɡɔːdʒ‖ɡɔːrdʒ/ *n* [C] a deep narrow valley with steep sides

gorge[2] *v* **gorge yourself on sth** to eat until you are too full: *The kids have gorged themselves on chocolate bars all afternoon.*

gor·geous /ˈɡɔːdʒəs‖ˈɡɔːr-/ *adj informal* very beautiful or pleasant: *What a gorgeous sunny day!* | *I think Lizzie is gorgeous.*

go·ril·la /ɡəˈrɪlə/ *n* [C] the largest kind of APE (=animal like a monkey)

gorse /ɡɔːs‖ɡɔːrs/ *n* [U] a bush with many sharp points and yellow flowers that grows wild in the countryside

gor·y /ˈɡɔːri/ *adj* involving a lot of violence and blood: *a gory film*

gosh /ɡɒʃ‖ɡɑːʃ/ *interjection* used when you are surprised: *Gosh! I never knew that!*

gos·ling /ˈɡɒzlɪŋ‖ˈɡɑːz-, ˈɡɒːz-/ *n* [C] a baby GOOSE

gos·pel /ˈɡɒspəl‖ˈɡɑːs-/ *n* **1** [C] one of the four stories of Christ's life in the Bible **2** [U] also **gospel truth** something that is completely true: *You can't take what she says as gospel.* **3** [U] also **gospel music** a type of Christian music usually performed by black singers

gos·sip[1] /ˈɡɒsₗp‖ˈɡɑː-/ *n* **1** [C,U] conversation or writing about other people's behaviour and private lives, often including unkind or untrue remarks: *People love hearing gossip about film stars.* **2** [C] someone who likes talking about other people's private lives

gossip[2] *v* [I] to talk or write about other people's behaviour and private lives: **+ about** *What are you two gossiping about?*

got /ɡɒt‖ɡɑːt/ *v* the past tense and a past participle of GET

got·ta /ˈɡɒtə‖ˈɡɑːtə/ *v nonstandard* a way of saying or writing 'got to': *I gotta go now – see you tomorrow.*

got·ten /'gɒtn‖'gɑːtn/ *v* the usual American past participle of GET

> **USAGE NOTE: got, gotten, have got,** and **have**
>
> The usual past participle of **get** is **gotten** in American English and **got** in British English.

gouge /gaʊdʒ/ *v* [T] to make a deep hole or cut in the surface of something — **gouge** *n* [C]
> **gouge** sth ↔ **out** *phr v* [T] to make a deep hole in something by removing part of its surface: *Glaciers had gouged out the valley during the Ice Age.*

gourd /gʊəd‖gɔːrd, gʊrd/ *n* [C] a large fruit with a hard shell that is sometimes used as a con-tainer

gour·met[1] /'gʊəmeɪ‖'gʊr-, gʊr'meɪ/ *adj* [only before noun] relating to good food and drink: *a gourmet restaurant*

gourmet[2] *n* [C] someone who enjoys and knows a lot about good food and drink

gout /gaʊt/ *n* [U] a painful condition that makes your toes, knees, and fingers hurt and swell

gov·ern /'gʌvən‖-ərn/ *v* **1** [I,T] to officially control a country or state and make all the decisions about taxes, laws etc: *The Socialist Party governed for thirty years.* **2** [T] to control the way a system or situation works: *the laws governing the universe*

gov·ern·ess /'gʌvən¦s‖-ər-/ *n* [C] a woman who lives with a family and teaches their children at home, especially in past times

gov·ern·ment /'gʌvəmənt, 'gʌvənmənt‖ 'gʌvərn-/ *n* **1** [C] also **Government** the group of people who govern a country or state: *The government has promised to improve standards in education.* **2** [U] the process of governing or the system used for governing: *democratic government*

gov·er·nor, Governor /'gʌvənə‖-ər/ *n* [C] the person in charge of an organization or place: *the Governor of California* — **governorship** *n* [U]

gown /gaʊn/ *n* [C] **1** a long dress worn by a woman for a formal occasion: *a black silk evening gown* **2** a long loose piece of clothing worn for a particular activity or ceremony: *his graduation gown*

GP /ˌdʒiː 'piː/ *n* [C] *BrE* general practitioner; a doctor who is trained in general medicine: *If the headaches continue, contact your GP.*

GPA /ˌdʒiː piː 'eɪ/ *n* [C] *AmE* grade point average; the average of a student's marks over a period of time in the US education system

grab[1] /græb/ *v* [T] **-bbed, -bbing 1** to take hold of someone or something suddenly or roughly: *He grabbed my bag and ran off.* **2 grab sb/someone's attention** *informal* attract someone's attention: *The film grabs your attention from the start.* **3 grab some food/ sleep etc** *informal* to eat something quickly or sleep for a very short time: *I'll just grab a sandwich for lunch.* **4 grab a chance/opportunity** to quickly take advantage of an opportunity: *Grab the opportunity to travel while you can.*

> **grab at** sth/sb *phr v* [T] to quickly put out your hand in order to try to take hold of something or someone

grab[2] *n* **1 make a grab for/at** to suddenly try to take hold of something: *Parker made a grab for the knife.* **2 be up for grabs** *informal* if a job, prize, or opportunity is up for grabs, it is available for anyone who wants to try to get it

grace[1] /greɪs/ *n* [U] **1** a smooth way of moving that appears natural, relaxed, and attractive: *She moved with the grace of a dancer.* **2** polite and pleasant behaviour: **have the grace to do sth** *At least he had the grace to apologize.* | **with good grace** (=willingly and cheerfully): *Kevin accepted his defeat with good grace.* **3** additional time that you are allowed for finishing a piece of work, paying a debt etc: a **week's/month's etc grace** *I couldn't pay, so they have given me a week's grace.* **4** a short prayer before a meal: *Who will say grace?* **5 Your/His etc Grace** used as a title for talking to or about a DUKE, DUCHESS, or ARCHBISHOP

grace[2] *v* **1 grace sb/sth with your presence** *humorous* used when someone arrives late, or when someone who does not often come to meetings or events arrives: *I'm so glad you've decided to grace us with your presence!* **2** [T] *formal* to make a place or an object look more attractive: *His new painting now graces the wall of the dining-room.*

grace·ful /'greɪsfəl/ *adj* **1** moving in a smooth and attractive way, or having an attractive shape: *a graceful dancer* | *an arch supported by graceful columns* **2** polite and pleasant: *a graceful apology* — **gracefully** *adv*

gra·cious /'greɪʃəs/ *adj* **1** behaving in a polite, kind, and generous way: *a gracious host* **2** having the kind of expensive comfort and beauty that only rich people can afford: *gracious living* **3 (goodness) gracious!** *spoken old-fashioned* used to express surprise — **graciously** *adv*

gra·da·tion /grəˈdeɪʃən/ *n* [C] *formal* a small change in a set of changes: *gradations of colour from dark red to pink*

grade[1] /greɪd/ *n* **1** [C,U] a level of quality or importance: *Grade A eggs* | *After five years she's still only on the basic salary grade.* **2** [C] a number or letter that shows how well you have done in your school work: *Betsy always gets good grades.* **3 make the grade** to succeed or reach the necessary standard: *Very few kids make the grade as professional footballers.* **4** [C] one of the 12 years you are in school in the US: *He's just finished third grade.*

grade[2] *v* [T] **1** to arrange things according to their quality or importance: *potatoes graded according to size* **2** *AmE* to give a mark to an examination paper or to a piece of school work. MARK *BrE*: *I spent the weekend grading tests.*

grade cross·ing /'. ˌ../ *n* [C] *AmE* a place where a road and railway cross each other; LEVEL CROSSING *BrE* ➡ see colour picture on page 669

grade point av·e·rage /'. . ˌ.../ *n* [C] GPA

grade school /'. ˌ./ *n* [C] *AmE* an ELEMENTARY SCHOOL

gra·di·ent /'greɪdiənt/ *n* [C] a degree of slope, especially of a road or railway: *a steep gradient*

grad·u·al /'grædʒuəl/ *adj* happening, developing, or changing slowly over a long time: *a gradual increase in the number of jobs available*

grad·u·al·ly /ˈgrædʒuəli/ *adv* if something happens or changes gradually, it happens slowly over a long time: *Gradually, their marriage got better.*

grad·u·ate[1] /ˈgrædʒuˌit/ *n* [C] **1** someone who has completed a course at a university: + **of** *a graduate of Oxford university* **2** *AmE* someone who has completed a course at a school, college, or university: *a high-school graduate*

grad·u·ate[2] /ˈgrædʒueit/ *v* [I] **1** to obtain a degree from a college or university: + **from** *Ruth has just graduated from Princeton.* **2** *AmE* to complete your education at HIGH SCHOOL **3 graduate (from sth) to sth** to start doing something that is more important or more difficult: *You start by repeating the sentences, then graduate to making up your own.*

grad·u·ate[3] /ˈgrædʒuˌit/ *adj* [only before noun] *AmE* a graduate student is studying for a MASTER'S DEGREE or a PHD after receiving their first degree; POSTGRADUATE *BrE*

grad·u·at·ed /ˈgrædʒueitˌd/ *adj* divided into different levels or sizes: *graduated rates of pay*

grad·u·a·tion /ˌgrædʒuˈeiʃən/ *n* [U] when you complete a university degree or an American HIGH SCHOOL education: *After graduation, Sally trained as a teacher.*

graf·fi·ti /græˈfiːti, grə-/ *n* [U] writing and pictures that are drawn on the walls of buildings, usually illegally

graft[1] /grɑːft‖græft/ *n* **1** [C] a piece of healthy skin or bone taken from someone's body and put on a damaged part of their body: *skin grafts* **2** [U] *AmE* the practice of dishonestly using your position to get money or advantages: *politicians accused of graft* **3** [U] *informal especially BrE* hard work: *a hard day's graft* **4** [C] a piece cut from one plant and joined to another plant so that it grows there

graft[2] *v* [I,T] **1** to put a piece of skin or bone from one part of someone's body onto another part that has been damaged **2** to join a part of a plant or tree onto another plant or tree to produce a new one

grain /grein/ *n* **1** [C,U] a seed or seeds of crops such as corn, wheat, or rice: *All they had left were a few grains of rice.* **2** [C] a very small piece or amount of something: *grains of sand‖There's not a grain of truth in what she said.* **3 the grain** the lines or patterns you can see in things such as wood, rock, or cloth: *Split the wood along the grain.* **4 go against the grain** if something that you must do goes against the grain, you do not like doing it because it is not what you would normally do: *It really went against the grain to throw all that food away.*

gram , **gramme** /græm/ *n* [C] written abbreviation **g** or **gm**; a unit for measuring weight, equal to 1/1000 of a kilogram or 0.035 ounces

gram·mar /ˈgræməl-ər/ *n* **1** [U] the rules by which words change their form and are combined into sentences: *She always corrects my*

grammar. **2** [C] a book that describes grammar rules: *a good English grammar*

grammar school /ˈ.. ˌ./ *n* [C] a school in Britain for children over the age of 11, who have to pass an examination to go there

gram·mat·i·cal /grəˈmætɪkəl/ *adj* **1** [only before noun] relating to the use of grammar: *You're still making grammatical errors.* **2** correct according to the rules of grammar: *a grammatical sentence* —**grammatically** /-kli/ *adv* → opposite UNGRAMMATICAL

gran /græn/ *n* [C] *BrE informal* a GRANDMOTHER

gra·na·ry /ˈgrænəri‖ˈgrei-, ˈgræ-/ *n* [C] a place where grain, especially wheat, is stored

grand[1] /grænd/ *adj* **1** a grand building, occasion etc is very impressive, big, or important: *a grand ceremony at the Palace* **2 grand total** the final total you get when you add up several numbers or amounts **3** rich and important but too proud: *He thinks he's too grand to talk to us.* **4** *informal* very good, pleasant, or enjoyable: *a grand day out* —**grandly** *adv*

grand[2] *n* [C] *informal, plural* **grand** 1000 pounds or dollars: *Bill only paid five grand for that car.*

grand·child /ˈgræntʃaild/ *n* [C] the child of your son or daughter → see picture at FAMILY

grand·dad /ˈgrændæd/ *n* [C] *informal* a GRANDFATHER

grand·daugh·ter /ˈgrænˌdɔːtəl-ˌdɔːtər/ *n* [C] the daughter of your son or daughter → see picture at FAMILY

gran·deur /ˈgrændʒəl-ər/ *n* [U] impressive beauty, power, or size: *the grandeur of the mountains*

grand·fa·ther /ˈgrændˌfɑːðəl-ər/ *n* [C] the father of your mother or father → see picture at FAMILY

grandfather clock /ˈ... ˌ./ *n* [C] a tall clock in a wooden case that stands on the floor

gran·di·ose /ˈgrændiəus‖-ous/ *adj* grandiose plans sound very important but are really not practical

grand ju·ry /ˌ. ˈ../ *n* [C] a group of people in the US who decide whether someone who may be guilty of a crime should be judged in a court of law

grand·ma /ˈgrænmɑː/ *n* [C] *informal* a GRANDMOTHER

grand·moth·er /ˈgrænˌmʌðəl-ər/ *n* [C] the mother of your mother or father → see picture at FAMILY

grand·pa /ˈgrænpɑː/ *n* [C] *informal* a GRANDFATHER

grand·par·ent /ˈgrænˌpeərənt‖-ˌper-/ *n* [C] the parent of your mother or father → see picture at FAMILY

grand pi·an·o /ˌ. ˈ.../ *n* [C] a large expensive piano that is often used at concerts

grand slam /ˌ. ˈ./ *n* [C] the winning position in all of a set of important sports competitions in the same year

G

GRAMMAR NOTE: the present (2)
Use the **simple present** to talk about things that are true in general: *Carlos lives in Madrid.* | *She works in a bank.* | *Water boils at 100°C.* But use the **present progressive** to talk about what you are studying: *I'm learning English.* | *She's studying history.*

grand·son /ˈgrænsʌn/ n [C] the son of your son or daughter → see picture at FAMILY

grand·stand /ˈgrændstænd/ n [C] a large structure with rows of seats and a roof, where people sit to watch sports

grange /greɪndʒ/ n [C] a large country house with farm buildings

gran·ite /ˈgrænɪt/ n [U] a very hard grey or pink rock, often used for building

gran·ny /ˈgræni/ n [C] informal a GRAND-MOTHER

gra·no·la /grəˈnəʊlə‖-ˈnoʊ-/ n [U] AmE a breakfast food made from nuts, grains, and seeds

grant¹ /grɑːnt‖grænt/ v **1** **take it for granted (that)** to believe that something is true without making sure: You can't take it for granted that your parents will pay for college. **2** **take sb for granted** to expect that someone will always be there when you need them, and never thank them: He spends all his time at work and takes his family for granted. **3** [T] formal to give someone something that they have asked for, especially official permission to do something: Ms. Chung was granted American citizenship last year. **4** [T] to admit that something is true although it does not make much difference to your opinion: He's not an intellectual, I grant you, but he does work hard.

grant² n [C] an amount of money given to someone by an organization for a particular purpose: a research grant

gran·ule /ˈgrænjuːl/ n [C] a very small hard piece of something: instant coffee granules — **granular** /-jʊlə‖-lər/ adj

grape /greɪp/ n [C] a small round juicy green or purple fruit that grows on a VINE and is often used to make wine → see picture at FRUIT and see colour picture on page 440

grape·fruit /ˈgreɪpfruːt/ n [C] a yellow fruit with a BITTER taste and thick skin like an orange

grape·vine /ˈgreɪpvaɪn/ n **hear sth on/through the grapevine** to hear news because it has been passed from one person to another in conversation: I heard it through the grapevine that Julie's getting married.

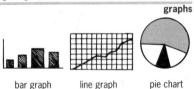

bar graph   line graph   pie chart

graph /græf, grɑːf‖græf/ n [C] a drawing that shows how two or more sets of measurements are related to each other: a graph showing population growth over 50 years

graph·ic /ˈgræfɪk/ adj **a graphic account/ description etc** a very clear description of an event that gives a lot of details: a graphic account of her unhappy childhood — **graphically** /-kli/ adv: She described the scene graphically.

graphic de·sign /ˌ. .ˈ./ n [U] the art of combining pictures and words in the production of books, magazines etc — **graphic designer** n [C]

graph·ics /ˈgræfɪks/ n [plural] drawings or images, especially produced on a computer

graph·ite /ˈgræfaɪt/ n [U] a soft black substance that is a type of CARBON and is used in pencils

grap·ple /ˈgræpəl/ v [I] to fight or struggle with someone, holding them tightly: + **with** A young man was grappling with the guard.
grapple with sth phr v [T] to try hard to deal with a difficult problem: I've been grappling with this essay question all morning.

grasp¹ /grɑːsp‖græsp/ v [T] **1** to take and hold something firmly in your hands: Grasp the rope with both hands. **2** to completely understand a complicated fact or idea: At the time I didn't fully grasp what he meant.
grasp at sth phr v [T] to quickly try to reach and take hold of something

grasp² n [singular] **1** the ability to understand a complicated idea or situation: **a good/poor grasp of** a good grasp of spoken English | **beyond sb's grasp** (=too difficult for them to understand) **2** the possibility of being able to achieve or get something: **within/beyond sb's grasp** Eve felt that success was finally within her grasp. **3** when someone holds something: The bottle slipped out of his grasp and smashed on the floor.

grasp·ing /ˈgrɑːspɪŋ‖ˈgræs-/ adj too keen to get money: a hard, grasping man

grass /grɑːs‖græs/ n **1** [U] a very common plant with thin green leaves that grows across fields, parks, etc: Please keep off the grass. | a blade of grass → see colour picture on page 243 **2** [C,U] a particular kind of grass: mountain grasses — **grassy** adj: a grassy bank

grass·hop·per /ˈgrɑːsˌhɒpə‖ˈgræsˌhɑːpər/ n [C] an insect that jumps with its long back legs and makes short loud noises

grass·land /ˈgrɑːslænd‖ˈgræs-/ also **grasslands** [plural] n [U] a large area of land covered with wild grass

grass roots /ˌ. ˈ./ n **the grass roots** the ordinary people in an organization, not the leaders — **grass-roots** adj: grass-roots support

grate¹ /greɪt/ v **1** [T] to rub food such as cheese or vegetables using a tool with a rough surface, in order to break it into small pieces: grated carrot → see colour picture on page 439 **2** [I] to make an unpleasant sound by rubbing against something else: + **on/against** The chalk grated on the blackboard. **3** **grate on sb/grate on sb's nerves** informal to make someone feel annoyed: Her voice really grates on my nerves.

grate² n [C] the metal frame that holds wood, coal etc in a FIREPLACE

grate·ful /ˈgreɪtfəl/ adj **1** feeling that you want to thank someone because of something kind that they have done: **be grateful (to sb) for sth** Mona was very grateful to Peter for his advice. → opposite UNGRATEFUL **2** **I would be grateful if you could/would ...** used to ask something in a formal situation or a letter: I would be grateful if you would allow me to visit your school. — **gratefully** adv: We gratefully accepted their offer of help.

grat·er /ˈgreɪtə‖-ər/ n [C] a tool used for grating food

grat·i·fy /ˈgrætɪfaɪ/ v [T] formal to make someone pleased or satisfied: She was gratified by the *result.* —**gratified** *adj* —**gratifying** *adj*: *It was gratifying to know that I had won.* —**gratification** /ˌgrætɪfɪˈkeɪʃən/ *n* [U]

grat·ing[1] /ˈgreɪtɪŋ/ *n* [C] a metal frame with bars across it, used to cover a window or a hole in the ground

grating[2] *adj* a grating sound is unpleasant and annoying: *a loud grating laugh*

grat·is /ˈgrætɪs, ˈgreɪtɪs/ *adj, adv formal* without any payment being asked for; free

grat·i·tude /ˈgrætɪtjuːd‖-tuːd/ *n* [U] the feeling of being grateful: *I would like to express my gratitude to everyone who helped us.* ➔ opposite INGRATITUDE

gra·tu·i·tous /grəˈtjuːɪtəs‖-ˈtuː-/ *adj* said or done without a good reason in a way that offends someone: *gratuitous violence in films*

gra·tu·i·ty /grəˈtjuːɪti‖-ˈtuː-/ *n* [C] *formal* a small additional amount of money given to someone for a service they have provided; TIP

grave[1] /greɪv/ *n* [C] the place where a dead body is buried: *We visited my grandfather's grave.*

grave[2] *adj* **1** very serious and worrying: *I have grave doubts about her ability as a teacher.* **2** looking or sounding very serious: *Dr. Fry looked grave. "I have some bad news," he said.* —**gravely** *adv*

grav·el /ˈgrævəl/ *n* [U] small stones used to make a surface for paths or roads —**gravelled** *BrE* **graveled** *AmE adj*: *a gravelled driveway*

grav·el·ly /ˈgrævəli/ *adj* a gravelly voice sounds low and rough

grave·stone /ˈgreɪvstəʊn‖-stoʊn/ *n* [C] a stone on a grave that shows the name of the person buried there and the dates when they were alive

grave·yard /ˈgreɪvjɑːd‖-jɑːrd/ *n* [C] an area of ground where people are buried, often near a church ➔ compare CEMETERY

grav·i·tate /ˈgrævɪteɪt/ *v* [I] **gravitate to/ towards** to be attracted to something and move towards it or become involved with it: *Students gravitate towards others with similar interests.*

grav·i·ta·tion·al /ˌgrævɪˈteɪʃənəl/ *adj* technical relating to gravity: *the Earth's gravitational pull*

grav·i·ty /ˈgrævɪti/ *n* [U] **1** the force that makes objects fall to the ground: *the laws of gravity* **2** *formal* seriousness: + *of We were soon made aware of the gravity of the situation.*

gra·vy /ˈgreɪvi/ *n* [U] SAUCE made from the juices that come from meat as it cooks

gray[1] /greɪ/ *adj* the usual American spelling of GREY —**grayness** *n* [U]

gray[2] *n* [U] the usual American spelling of GREY

graze[1] /greɪz/ *v* **1** [I,T] if an animal grazes, it eats grass: *cattle grazing in the field* **2** [T] to break the surface of your skin by accidentally rubbing against something rough: *Billy grazed his knee when he fell.* **3** [T] to touch something lightly while passing it: *A bullet grazed his cheek.*

graze[2] *n* [C] a break in the surface of your skin caused by rubbing against something rough: *cuts and grazes*

grease[1] /griːs/ *n* [U] **1** soft fat from animals or vegetables **2** a thick oily substance that is put on the moving parts of a car or machine to make it run smoothly

grease[2] *v* [T] to put grease on something: *Grease the tin lightly with butter.*

greas·y /ˈgriːsi, -zi/ *adj* covered in grease or oil, or full of grease: *greasy food* | *greasy hair*

great /greɪt/ *adj* **1** *spoken* very good; excellent: *It's great to see you again!* | *We had a great time in Rio.* **2** *informal* very useful or suitable for something: + *for Our holiday villas are great for families with children.* **3** very large in size, amount, or degree: *a great pile of newspapers* | **great big** (=very big): *Will caught a great big fish!* | **a great many** (=a large number): *A great many people died in the flood.* | **great friend** (=a very close friend) **4** [only before noun] very important, successful, or famous: *the great civilizations of the past* | *the greatest movie star of them all* **5** *spoken* used when you are annoyed and think that something is not good at all: *"Your car won't be ready until next week." "Oh, great!"* **6** **great-grandfather/great-aunt etc** the grandfather, AUNT etc of one of your parents **7** **great-nephew/great-granddaughter etc** the NEPHEW, GRANDDAUGHTER etc of your child —**greatness** *n* [U]

great·ly /ˈgreɪtli/ *adv formal* extremely or very much: *Your chances of getting cancer are greatly increased if you smoke.*

greed /griːd/ *n* [U] when you want to have more money, food, power etc than you need: *Burning the rainforest is motivated by greed.*

greed·y /ˈgriːdi/ *adj* wanting more money, food, power etc than you need: *Don't be so greedy – leave some cake for the rest of us!* —**greedily** *adv* —**greediness** *n* [U]

green[1] /griːn/ *adj* **1** having the colour of grass: *green eyes* **2** covered with grass, trees, bushes etc: *We must preserve green areas of the town.* **3** connected with protecting the environment: *green issues* **4** **be green with envy** to be very jealous, wishing you had something that someone else has **5** *informal* young and lacking experience: *The trainees are still pretty green.* **6** **have green fingers** *BrE*/**have a green thumb** *AmE* to be good at making plants grow

green[2] *n* **1** [C,U] the colour of grass ➔ see colour picture on page 114 **2** [C] the smooth flat area of grass around a hole on a GOLF COURSE **3** [C] *BrE* an area of grass in the middle of a village

green·back /ˈgriːnbæk/ *n* [C] *AmE informal* a dollar BILL

green belt /ˈ. ./ *n* [C,U] an area of land around a city where building is not allowed

green card /ˌ. ˈ./ *n* [C] a document that shows that a foreigner can live and work in the US

green·e·ry /ˈgriːnəri/ *n* [U] green leaves and plants

green·gro·cer /ˈgriːnˌgrəʊsə‖-ˌgroʊsər/ *n* [C] *BrE* **1** **greengrocer's** a shop that sells fruit and vegetables **2** someone who owns a shop that sells fruit and vegetables

green·house /ˈgriːnhaʊs/ *n* [C] a glass building used for growing plants that need to be protected from the weather

greenhouse ef·fect /ˈ.. ˌ../ *n* **the greenhouse effect** the warming of the air around the Earth as a result of the sun's heat being trapped by POLLUTION ➔ see colour picture on page 278

green·ing /ˈgriːnɪŋ/ *n* [U] when people's opinions change and they become more interested in protecting the environment: *the greening of British politics*

greens /griːnz/ *n* [plural] vegetables with large green leaves

Green·wich Mean Time /ˌgrenɪtʃ ˈmiːn taɪm, ˌgrɪ-, -nɪdʒ-/ *n* [U] GMT

greet /griːt/ *v* [T] **1** to welcome someone, for example by saying 'hello': *The children came rushing out to greet me.* **2** to react to something in a particular way: **be greeted with** *The first speech was greeted with cheers and laughter.*

greet·ing /ˈgriːtɪŋ/ *n* [C,U] something that you say or do when you meet someone, write to them, or telephone them: **exchange greetings** (=say hello to each other)

gre·gar·i·ous /grɪˈɡeəriəs‖-ˈger-/ *adj* someone who is gregarious enjoys being with other people; SOCIABLE

gre·nade /grɪ¦ˈneɪd/ *n* [C] a small bomb that can be thrown, or fired from a gun

grew /gruː/ *v* the past tense of GROW

grey¹ usually **gray** *AmE* /greɪ/ *adj* **1** having the colour of black mixed with white: *grey rain clouds* **2** having grey hair: **go grey** *My father went grey in his forties.* → see colour picture on page 244 **3** weather that is grey is dull and cloudy weather: *It was a grey Sunday morning.* **4** boring or unattractive: *grey businessmen* **5 grey area** a part of a subject such as law or science that is hard to deal with because the rules are not clear

grey² usually **gray** *AmE n* [C,U] the colour of black mixed with white → see colour picture on page 114

grey·hound /ˈgreɪhaʊnd/ *n* [C] a thin dog with long legs that can run very fast, often in races

grey·ing /ˈgreɪ-ɪŋ/ *BrE*, **graying** *AmE adj* greying hair is starting to become grey

grid /grɪd/ *n* [C] **1** a pattern of straight lines that cross each other and form squares **2** the system of numbered squares printed on a map that helps you find exactly where something is **3** *BrE* a network of CABLES that supply an area with electricity

grid·lock /ˈgrɪdlɒk‖-lɑːk/ *n* [U] when the streets are so full of cars that the cars cannot move: *The city suffers from constant traffic gridlock.* —**gridlocked** *adj*

grief /griːf/ *n* [U] **1** extreme sadness, especially because someone you love has died: *His grief was obvious from the way he spoke.* **2 Good grief!** *spoken* said when you are slightly surprised or annoyed **3 come to grief a)** to be unsuccessful: *Their business came to grief after only six months.* **b)** to be hurt or damaged in an accident: *The expedition came to grief on Vanikoro Reef.*

griev·ance /ˈgriːvəns/ *n* [C,U] something that you complain about because you think it is unfair, or a feeling of being treated unfairly: **+ against** *He has a grievance against his former employer.*

grieve /griːv/ *v* **1** [I] to feel extremely sad, especially because someone you love has died: *Sue's grieving over the death of her mother.* **2** [T] **be grieved by sth** to be made to feel unhappy by something: *it grieves me to think/*

see/say etc *It grieves me to see him wasting his talents.*

griev·ous /ˈgriːvəs/ *adj formal* very serious and likely to be harmful: *a grievous error* —**grievously** *adv*

grill¹ /grɪl/ *v* **1** [I,T] if you grill food, or if food grills, you cook it by putting it close to a strong heat; BROIL *AmE* **2** [T] *informal* to ask someone a lot of difficult questions over a long period of time: *They let the man go after grilling him for several hours.*

grill² *n* [C] **1** *BrE* a part of a COOKER which cooks food on a metal shelf, using strong heat → see picture at KITCHEN **2** a metal frame on which food can be cooked over a fire **3** also **grille** a frame of metal bars which protects people or things, for example around machinery or windows

grim /grɪm/ **grimmer, grimmest** *adj* **1** making you feel worried and unhappy: *grim economic news* **2** very serious and determined: *a grim-faced judge* **3** a grim place is unattractive and unpleasant: *grim industrial towns* —**grimly** *adv* —**grimness** *n* [U]

gri·mace /grɪˈmeɪs, ˈgrɪməs/ *v* [I] to twist your face in an ugly way because you feel pain or do not like something: **+ with** *Theo rolled around on the floor grimacing with pain.* —**grimace** *n* [C]

grime /graɪm/ *n* [U] thick black dirt that forms a layer on surfaces

grim·y /ˈgraɪmi/ *adj* covered in thick black dirt: *grimy windows*

grin¹ /grɪn/ *v* [I] **-nned, -nning** to smile with a very wide smile: **+ at** *Sally was grinning at Martin from across the room.*

grin² *n* [C] a wide smile: *"I'm getting married," said Clare, with a big grin.*

grind¹ /graɪnd/ *v* [T] **ground** /graʊnd/, **ground, grinding 1** to crush something such as coffee beans into small pieces or powder **2** to make something such as a knife sharp by rubbing it against a rough hard surface **3** if you grind your teeth, you rub them together **4 grind to a halt** if something grinds to a HALT, it stops moving or making progress: *Traffic slowly ground to a halt.*

grind down *phr v* [T **grind** sb ↔ **down**] to treat someone cruelly or unfairly for a long time, so that they lose all their courage and hope: *She had been ground down by years of poverty and hardship.*

grind on *phr v* [I] to continue for an unpleasantly long time: *The morning seemed to be grinding on.*

grind² *n* [singular] *informal* hard or boring work that takes a lot of your time: *It's Monday again – back to the grind.*

grind·er /ˈgraɪndə‖-ər/ *n* [C] a machine that grinds something: *a coffee grinder*

grind·ing /ˈgraɪndɪŋ/ *adj* **grinding poverty** extreme POVERTY

grip¹ /grɪp/ *n* **1** [singular] a tight hold on something, or your ability to hold it: **+ on** *Get a firm grip on the rope.* **2** [singular] the control you have over a person, a situation, or your emotions: **get a grip on yourself** (=try to control your emotions) **3 come/get to grips with sth** to start dealing with a situation effectively: *Have you got to grips with your new job yet?* **4** [U] the ability of something to stay on a surface without sliding: *I want some tennis shoes with a good grip.*

grip² *v* [T] **-pped, -pping 1** to hold something very tightly: *I gripped his hand in fear.* **2** to have a strong effect: *Unusually cold weather has gripped the northwest.* **3** to keep your attention completely: *The nation was gripped by the trial of OJ Simpson.* **4** [T] if something grips a surface, it stays on without sliding

gripe /graɪp/ *v* [I] *informal* to complain continuously — **gripe** *n* [C]

grip·ping /ˈgrɪpɪŋ/ *adj* very exciting and interesting: *a gripping story*

gris·ly /ˈgrɪzli/ *adj* extremely unpleasant because death or violence is involved: *the grisly discovery of a body in the cellar*

gris·tle /ˈgrɪsəl/ *n* [U] the part of a piece of meat that is not soft enough to eat — **gristly** *adj*

grit¹ /grɪt/ *n* [U] **1** very small pieces of stone or sand **2** *informal* determination and courage — **gritty** *adj*

grit² *v* [T] **-tted, -tting 1 grit your teeth** to use all your determination to keep going in a difficult or painful situation **2** to put grit on a frozen road to make it less SLIPPERY

groan /grəʊn‖groʊn/ *v* [I] to make a long deep sound because you are in pain, or are not happy about something: *Captain Marsh was holding his arm and groaning.|Go clean your room, and don't groan.* — **groan** *n* [C]

gro·cer /ˈgrəʊsə‖ˈgroʊsər/ *n* [C] **1 the grocer's** *BrE* a small shop that sells food, cleaning products etc **2** someone who owns a small shop that sells food, cleaning products etc

gro·cer·ies /ˈgrəʊsəriz‖ˈgroʊ-/ *n* [plural] things that you buy in a grocer's shop or a SUPERMARKET

grocery store /ˈ... ˌ./ *AmE* also **gro·ce·ry** /ˈgrəʊsəri‖ˈgroʊ-/ *n* [C] a shop that sells food, cleaning products etc

grog·gy /ˈgrɒgi‖ˈgrɑːgi/ *adj* feeling weak and ill — **groggily** *adv*

groin /grɔɪn/ *n* [C] where your legs join at the front of your body

groom¹ /gruːm, grʊm/ *v* **1** [T] to train someone for an important job: **+ for** *Chris is clearly being groomed for the job of manager.* **2** [T] to clean and brush an animal — **grooming** *n* [U] → see also WELL-GROOMED

groom² *n* [C] **1** also **bridegroom** a man who is getting married, or has just been married **2** someone whose job is to take care of horses

groove /gruːv/ *n* **1** [C] a long deep line cut into a surface **2** [singular] *AmE informal* the way things should be done, so that it seems easy and natural: **get back in the groove** *It will take the players a while to get back in the groove.*

grope /grəʊp‖groʊp/ *v* **1** [I] to try to find something you cannot see, using your hands: **+ for/around** *Ginny groped for the light switch.* **2 grope your way along/across/to** etc to go somewhere by feeling the way with your hands

because you cannot see: *I got up and groped my way to the bathroom.* **3 grope for sth** to try hard to find the right words to say or the right solution to a problem

gross¹ /grəʊs‖groʊs/ *adj* **1** *spoken* very unpleasant to look at or think about: *There was one really gross part in the movie.* **2** a gross amount is the total amount of money before taxes or costs have been taken away: *Our gross profit was £50,000.* → compare NET³ **3** [only before noun] wrong and unacceptable: *There are some gross inequalities in pay between men and women.* **4** a gross weight is the total weight of something, including its wrapping — **grossly** *adv* — **grossness** *n* [U]

gross² *v* [T] if you gross a particular amount of money, you earn that amount before tax is taken away

gross sb ↔ **out** *phr v* [T] *spoken* to say or do something that makes someone feel sick: *Don't talk about your operation! It grosses me out.*

gross na·tion·al prod·uct /ˌ. ... ˈ../ *n* [singular] GNP

gro·tesque /grəʊˈtesk‖groʊ-/ *adj* ugly or strange in a way that is unpleasant or frightening — **grotesquely** *adv*

grot·to /ˈgrɒtəʊ‖ˈgrɑːtoʊ/ *n* [C] a small CAVE

grouch¹ /graʊtʃ/ *n* [C] *informal* **1** someone who is always complaining **2** something unimportant that you complain about: *My main grouch is that they didn't tell me what was going on.*

grouch² *v* [I] *informal* to complain in a slightly angry way

grouch·y /ˈgraʊtʃi/ *adj* feeling annoyed and complaining a lot — **grouchiness** *n* [U]

ground¹ /graʊnd/ *n* **1 the ground** the surface of the earth: *The ground was covered in autumn leaves.* **2** [singular, U] the soil on and under the surface of the earth: *The ground's too hard to plant trees now.* **3 sports/football/parade etc ground** a piece of land used for a special purpose **4** [U] an area of knowledge, ideas, experience etc: *I think the book tries to cover too much ground.* **5 hold/stand your ground** to refuse to change your opinion even though people disagree with you **6 get off the ground** to start being successful: *His company hasn't really got off the ground yet.* **7 gain/lose ground** to become more or less successful or popular: *Republicans have been gaining ground in recent months.* **8** [singular] *AmE* a wire that connects a piece of electrical equipment to the ground for safety; EARTH *BrE* → see also GROUNDS

USAGE NOTE: ground, floor, earth, and **soil**

The **ground** is the surface of the land when you are outdoors: *The leaves fell gently to the ground.* The **floor** is the surface you walk on inside a building: *She was sweeping the kitchen floor.* You grow things outdoors in the **earth** or **soil**.

ground² *v* **1** [T] *informal* to stop a child from going out with their friends as a punishment: *If* you stay out that late again, you'll be grounded for a week. **2** [T] to stop an aircraft or pilot from flying: *All planes are grounded due to snow.* **3 be grounded in sth** to be based on something: *Base your work on principles grounded in research.* **4** [T] *AmE* to make a piece of electrical equipment safe by connecting it to the ground with a wire; EARTH *BrE*

ground³ *v* the past tense and past participle of GRIND

ground beef /ˌ. './ *n* [U] *AmE* BEEF that has been cut into very small pieces; MINCE *BrE*

ground·break·ing /'graʊndˌbreɪkɪŋ/ *adj* involving important new discoveries or methods that change the way something is done: *groundbreaking research in physics*

ground floor /ˌ. 'ˈ./ *n* [C] the part of a building that is on the same level as the ground

ground·ing /'graʊndɪŋ/ *n* [singular] training in the basic parts of a subject or skill: *You need a good grounding in mathematics to do this course.*

ground·less /'graʊndləs/ *adj* **groundless fears/suspicions etc** fears, etc that are not based on facts or reason

ground rule /'. ../ *n* [C] a rule or principle that behaviour or actions should be based on: *There are a few ground rules you should follow.*

grounds /graʊndz/ *n* [plural] **1** reasons for doing something: **on the grounds of/that** *You can't fire a woman on the grounds that she's pregnant.* | **+ for** *Snoring! That should be grounds for divorce!* **2** the land or gardens around a large building: *They walked around the hospital grounds.*

ground·swell /'graʊndswel/ *n* **a groundswell of support/opinion/enthusiasm** a sudden increase in how strongly people feel about something: *There has been a groundswell of support for change.*

ground·work /'graʊndwɜːk‖-wɜːrk/ *n* [U] work that has to be done to prepare for something: *The revolution laid the groundwork for progress.*

group¹ /gruːp/ *n* [C] **1** several people or things that are all together in the same place, or that are connected in some way: **+ of** *Everyone please get into groups of four.* | *a group of teachers* **2** musicians or singers who perform together, usually playing popular music: *a rock group*

group² *v* [I,T] to form a group, or to arrange people or things in a group: **be grouped around sth** *The village was made up of houses grouped around the church.* | **be grouped into** *Birds can be grouped into several classes.*

group·ing /'gruːpɪŋ/ *n* [C] a set of people or things that have the same aims, qualities, or features: *political groupings*

grouse /graʊs/ *n* [C] **1** a small fat bird that is hunted for food **2** a small complaint about something: *My one grouse is that the screen is too small.* — **grouse** *v* [I]

grove /grəʊv‖groʊv/ *n* [C] an area of land where a particular type of tree grows: *a lemon grove*

grov·el /'grɒvəl‖'grɑː-, 'grʌ-/ *v* [I] **-lled, -lling** *BrE*, **-led, -ling** *AmE* **1** to try too hard to please someone or to keep telling them you are sorry: *Never grovel to your boss.* **2** to move around on your hands and knees because you are looking

for something: *I saw him grovelling in the road for his hat.*

grow

Sunflowers can grow to a height of ten feet.

grow /grəʊ‖groʊ/ *v* **grew** /gruː/, **grown** /grəʊn‖groʊn/, **growing 1** [I] to develop and become bigger or longer over a period of time: *Jamie's grown two inches this year.* **2** [I,T] if plants grow, or you grow them, they develop and become bigger: *Not many plants can grow in the far north.* | *We're trying to grow roses this year.* **3** [I] to increase: *a growing business* | *The number of students grew by 5% last year.* | **growing number** *A growing number of people are working from home.* **4 grow old/bored/strong etc** to become old, bored etc over a period of time **5** [T] to let your hair or nails get longer

grow into sb/sth *v* [T] **1** to develop and become a particular kind of person or thing: *Gene's grown into a handsome young man.* **2** if a child grows into clothes, he or she becomes big enough to wear them

grow on sb *phr v* [T] if someone or something grows on you, you gradually start to like them: *After a while their music grows on you.*

grow out of sth *phr v* [T] **1** if children grow out of clothes, they become too big to wear them **2** to stop doing something as you get older: *Sarah still sucks her thumb, but she'll grow out of it.*

grow up *phr v* [I] **1** to develop from being a child to being an adult: *I grew up in Glasgow.* **2** to start to exist and become bigger: *Villages grew up along the river.*

grow·er /'grəʊə‖'groʊər/ *n* [C] a person or company that grows fruit, vegetables etc in order to sell them

growl /graʊl/ *v* [I] if an animal growls, it makes a deep angry sound: *Our dog always growls at visitors.* — **growl** *n* [C]

grown¹ /grəʊn‖groʊn/ *v* the past participle of GROW

grown² *adj* **grown man/woman** an adult, especially one who is not behaving in an adult way: *It was sad to see grown men fighting over a woman.*

grown-up¹ /ˌ. 'ˈ./ *n* [C] a word meaning an adult, used especially by or to children: *Ask a grown-up to help you.*

grown-up² *adj* fully developed as an adult: *She has two grown-up sons.*

growth /grəʊθ‖groʊθ/ n **1** [singular, U] when something develops in size or amount: *Vitamins are necessary for healthy growth.*|*rapid population growth* **2** [singular,U] when something becomes more important or more people do it, like it etc: *a growth of interest in African music*|+ **of** *the growth of fascism* **3** [U] the development of someone's character: *The job will provide opportunities for personal growth.* **4** [C] something that grows in your body or on your skin, caused by a disease

grub /grʌb/ n **1** [U] *informal* food **2** [C] a young insect in the form of a small white worm

grub·by /ˈgrʌbi/ adj dirty: *grubby hands*

grudge[1] /grʌdʒ/ n [C] a feeling that you dislike someone because of something they have done: + **against** *John's got a grudge against his sister.*

grudge[2] also **begrudge** v [T] to be unwilling to give something to someone, or do something for someone etc: *grudge sb sth He grudged Mary every penny he paid in alimony.*

grudg·ing /ˈgrʌdʒɪŋ/ adj done in a way that shows you do not really want to do something: *a grudging apology* — **grudgingly** adv: *Rob grudgingly offered to drive us to the airport.*

gru·el·ling *BrE*, **grueling** *AmE* /ˈgruːəlɪŋ/ adj very tiring: *a gruelling 25 mile walk*

grue·some /ˈgruːsəm/ adj very unpleasant and usually connected with violent death or injury: *a gruesome murder*

gruff /grʌf/ adj sounding unfriendly or annoyed: *"I'm not interested," said a gruff voice.* — **gruffly** adj

grum·ble /ˈgrʌmbəl/ v [I] to complain in a quiet but slightly angry way: + **about** *Amy's always grumbling about how expensive things are.* — **grumble** n [C]

grump·y /ˈgrʌmpi/ adj having a bad temper and complaining a lot: *You're grumpy today. What's wrong?* — **grumpily** adv — **grumpiness** n [U]

grunge /grʌndʒ/ n [U] *AmE informal* oily dirt; GRIME — **grungy** adj

grunt /grʌnt/ v **1** [I,T] to make short sounds, especially because you do not want to talk: *She just grunted hello and kept walking.* **2** [I] if a pig grunts, it makes short low sounds — **grunt** n [C]

guar·an·tee[1] /ˌgærənˈtiː/ v [T] **1** to promise that something will happen or be done: *We guarantee delivery within 48 hours.*|+ **(that)** *Can you guarantee that it will arrive tomorrow?*|**guarantee to do sth** *We guarantee to refund your money if you are not satisfied.* **2** to give a written promise to repair or replace a product that has a fault

guarantee[2] n [C] **1** a written promise from a company to repair or replace a product that has a fault: *a two-year guarantee*|**be under guarantee** (=be protected by a guarantee): *Is the microwave still under guarantee?* **2** a promise that something will be done or will happen: + **(that)** *There's no guarantee that the books will be delivered this week.*

guard[1] /gɑːd‖gɑːrd/ n **1** [C] someone whose job is to protect a person or place, or to make sure that a person does not escape: *security guards*|*prison guards* **2** **be on guard/stand guard** to be responsible for protecting a place or

person: *Hogan was on guard until midnight.* **3** [singular] a group of soldiers or police officers who guard something: *The changing of the guard.* **4** [C] *BrE* someone who is in charge of a train **5** [C] something that covers and protects someone or something: *a hockey player's face guard* **6** **be under (armed) guard** to be protected or kept prisoner by a group of people with weapons **7** **be on your guard** to be ready to deal with a bad situation: *Be on your guard against pickpockets.* **8** **catch sb off guard** to surprise someone by doing something that they were not ready to deal with

guard[2] v [T] to protect someone or something from being attacked or stolen, or to prevent a prisoner from escaping

guard against sth *phr* v [T] to try to prevent something from happening by being careful: *Exercise can help guard against a number of serious illnesses.*

guard·ed /ˈgɑːdɪd‖ˈgɑːr-/ adj careful not to show your emotions or give away information: *a guarded welcome*

guard·i·an /ˈgɑːdiən‖ˈgɑːr-/ n [C] **1** someone who is legally responsible for someone else's child **2** *formal* a person or organization that tries to protect laws, moral principles etc: *The UN is the guardian of peace in the area.* — **guardianship** n [U]

guer·ril·la /gəˈrɪlə/ n [C] a member of an unofficial military group that is fighting for political reasons: *guerrilla warfare*

guess[1] /ges/ v **1** [I,T] **a)** to try to answer a question or make a judgement without knowing all the facts: *"How old is Ginny's son?" "I'd say 25, but I'm just guessing."* **b)** to get the right answer to something in this way: *"Don't tell me, you got the job." "How did you guess?"*|*I guessed his age just by looking at him.*|+ **(that)** *I'd never have guessed you two were sisters.* **2** **I guess** *spoken* **a)** used when you suppose that something is true or likely: *His light's on, so I guess he's still up.* **3** **I guess so/not** *spoken* used in order to say yes or no when you are not very sure: *"She wasn't happy?" "I guess not."* **4** **guess what** *spoken* used when you want to tell someone some surprising news: *Guess what! Alan's asked me to marry him!*

guess[2] n [C] **1** an attempt to guess something: **make/have/take a guess** *Make a guess if you don't know the answer.*|*Have a guess where we're going tonight!*|**at a guess** *spoken* (=used to say that what you are saying is just a guess): *He's about 50 at a guess.* **2** an opinion about something you are guessing: **my guess is (that)** *My guess is that there won't be many people at the party.* **3** **be anybody's guess** *informal* to be something that no one can possibly know: *Where he disappeared to was anybody's guess.*

guess·work /ˈgeswɜːk‖-wɜːrk/ n [U] when you try to find the answer to something by guessing

guest /gest/ n [C] **1** someone who you invite to stay in your home, be at your party etc: *We're having guests this weekend.* **2** someone who is staying in a hotel **3** someone famous who is invited to take part in a television programme, concert etc: *My guest this evening is Tina Turner.*|*Michael Foot is the guest speaker at this year's conference.* **4** **be my guest** *spoken* used to

G

give someone permission to use something of yours: *"Could I use your phone?" "Be my guest."*

guid·ance /ˈgaɪdəns/ n [U] helpful advice

guide[1] /gaɪd/ n [C] **1** someone whose job is to show a place to tourists: *a tour guide* **2** a book that provides information or explains how to do something: *a guide for new parents* **3** something or someone that helps you decide what you should do or how you should do it: *A friend's experience isn't always the best guide.* **4 Guide** *BrE* also **Girl Guide** a girl or woman who belongs to an organization that teaches girls practical skills such as camping, and teaches them to be good members of society → compare SCOUT **5 the Guides** *BrE* an organization that teaches girls practical skills such as camping, and teaches them to be good members of society → compare **the Scouts** (SCOUT)

guide[2] v [T] **1** to help someone go somewhere: *Taking her arm, Andrew guided her to their table.* | *We were guided through the mountains by a local villager.* **2** to show or tell someone what they should do: *You should be guided by your doctor on your diet.*

guide·book /ˈgaɪdbʊk/ n [C] a book that gives tourists information about a place

guide dog /ˈ. ./ n [C] *BrE* a dog that is specially trained to guide a blind person; SEEING EYE DOG *AmE*

guide·lines /ˈgaɪdlaɪnz/ n [plural] official advice about the way to do something: + **on/for** *guidelines on health and safety at work*

guild /gɪld/ n [C] an organization of people who share the same interests or profession: *the Writers' Guild*

guile /gaɪl/ n [U] *formal* the use of clever but dishonest methods to deceive people

guil·lo·tine /ˈgɪlətiːn/ n [C] a piece of equipment that was used in the past to cut off the heads of criminals — **guillotine** v [T]

guilt /gɪlt/ n **1** [U] a strong feeling of shame and sadness that you have when you have done something wrong: **feeling/sense of guilt** *Martha felt a great sense of guilt about ending the relationship.* **2** when someone has broken a law: *The jury was sure of the defendant's guilt.* **3** when someone is responsible for something bad that has happened; FAULT → opposite INNOCENCE

guilt-rid·den /ˈ. ../ adj feeling extremely guilty about something

guilt·y /ˈgɪlti/ adj **1** ashamed because you have done something that you know is wrong: **feel guilty about sth** *I feel guilty about not inviting her to the party.* **2** having broken a law or a rule: + **of** *These men are guilty of promoting murder.* | **find sb guilty** (=decide that someone is officially guilty of a crime): *The jury found him not guilty of murder.* — **guiltily** adv — **guiltiness** n [U] → opposite INNOCENT

> **USAGE NOTE: guilty, ashamed,** and **embarrassed**
>
> Use **guilty** to say that someone is unhappy because they have done something that has harmed someone else: *He felt guilty about being away from home so often.* Use **ashamed** about someone who feels very sorry about something bad they have done: *She was ashamed of having told her mother a lie.* Use **embarrassed** to say that someone is upset be-

cause they have done something that makes them seem silly to other people: *He was embarrassed about the way he behaved at the party.*

guin·ea pig /ˈgɪni pɪg/ n [C] **1** a small furry animal with no tail, that is often kept as a pet **2** *informal* someone who is used in a test, for example to find out whether a new medicine or product works properly

guise /gaɪz/ n [C] *formal* the thing something seems to be, even though it is not: **in/under the guise of** *The deal was made under the guise of friendship.*

gui·tar /gɪˈtɑːr/ n [C] a musical instrument with strings, a long neck and a wooden body, which you play by pulling the strings — **guitarist** n [C]

gulf /gʌlf/ n [C] **1** a serious and important difference between two groups of people, where neither understands or is concerned about the other: + **between** *There is a widening gulf between the rich and the poor.* **2** a large area of sea partly surrounded by land: *the Gulf of Mexico*

gull /gʌl/ n [C] a SEAGULL

gul·li·ble /ˈgʌlɪbəl/ adj easily tricked as a result of always trusting other people — **guillibility** /ˌgʌlɪˈbɪlɪti/ n [U]

gul·ly /ˈgʌli/ n [C] a small narrow valley with steep sides

gulp /gʌlp/ v **1** [T] also **gulp down** to swallow a drink quickly: *She gulped her tea and ran to catch the bus.* **2** [T] also **gulp in** to breathe large amounts of air quickly: *Steve leaned on the car and gulped in the night air.* **3** [I] to swallow suddenly because you are surprised or nervous: *Shula read the test questions, and gulped.* — **gulp** n [C]

gum[1] /gʌm/ n **1** [C usually plural] the pink part inside your mouth that holds your teeth **2** [U] a sweet substance that you CHEW for a long time but do not swallow; CHEWING GUM

gum[2] v [T+adv/prep] **-mmed, -mming** *BrE* to stick two things together, using glue

gump·tion /ˈgʌmpʃən/ n [U] *informal* the ability and determination to decide what needs to be done and to do it: *I like Kathy because she's got gumption.*

gun[1] /gʌn/ n [C] a weapon from which bullets are fired → see also **jump the gun** (JUMP[1]) **stick to your guns** (STICK[1])

gun[2] v **1** [T] *AmE informal* to make a car go very fast by pressing the ACCELERATOR very hard **2 be gunning for sb** to be looking for a way to harm someone or cause them trouble

gun sb ↔ down *phr v* [T] to shoot someone and kill or badly injure them: *Bobby Kennedy was gunned down in a hotel.*

gun·boat /ˈgʌnbəʊt/ n [C] a small military ship

gun·fire /ˈgʌnfaɪər/ n [U] the repeated firing of guns, or the noise made by this: *The sound of gunfire shattered the peace of this normally quiet town.*

gun·man /ˈgʌnmən/ n [C] a criminal who uses a gun

gun·ner /ˈgʌnər/ n [C] a soldier, sailor etc whose job is to aim or fire a large gun

gun·point /ˈɡʌnpɔɪnt/ n [U] **at gunpoint** when someone threatens people with a gun, or when someone is threatened with a gun: *We were held at gunpoint throughout the robbery.*

gun·pow·der /ˈɡʌnˌpaʊdəǁ-ər/ n [U] an explosive powder

gun·run·ning /ˈɡʌnˌrʌnɪŋ/ n [U] when guns are taken into a country illegally — **gunrunner** n [C]

gun·shot /ˈɡʌnʃɒtǁ-ʃɑːt/ n **1** [C] the sound made when a gun is fired: *We heard three gunshots.* **2** [U] the bullets fired from a gun: *a gunshot wound*

gur·gle /ˈɡɜːɡəlǁˈɡɜːr-/ v [I] to make a sound like flowing water: *The baby lay gurgling on the bed.* — **gurgle** n [C]

gu·ru /ˈɡʊruː/ n [C] **1** *informal* someone who is famous and very respected because they know a lot about, or are very skilled in, a particular subject: *football guru Terry Venables* **2** a Hindu religious teacher or leader

gush¹ /ɡʌʃ/ v [I,T] **1** if liquid gushes from something, it comes out quickly in large quantities: **+ out of/ from etc** *Water was gushing out of the pipe. | Blood was gushing from the wound.* **2** to praise someone or something so much that people think you are not sincere: *"I absolutely adore your dress," she gushed.*

gush² n [C] **1** a large quantity of liquid that suddenly flows from somewhere: *a gush of warm water* **2** a gush of anxiety/relief etc when you suddenly feel anxious etc: *I felt a gush of relief that the children were safe.*

gust¹ /ɡʌst/ n [C] a sudden strong wind: *A gust of wind blew our tent over. | gust of air/rain/ snow etc* (=air, rain, snow etc blown forcefully by the wind) — **gusty** adj

gust² v [I] if wind gusts, it blows strongly and suddenly: *Winds gusting up to 70 mph have been reported in the North.*

gus·to /ˈɡʌstəʊǁ-toʊ/ n [U] **with gusto** with a lot of energy and enjoyment: *The band were playing with great gusto.*

gut¹ /ɡʌt/ n *informal* **1** gut reaction/feeling etc when you are sure that a feeling is right, although you cannot give a reason for it: *I had a gut feeling that he was a dangerous man.* **2** [C] the tube in your body that food passes through → see also GUTS

gut² v [T] **-tted, -tting 1** to destroy the inside of a building completely: *The school was completely*

gutted by fire. **2** to remove the organs from inside a fish or animal in order to prepare it for cooking → see also GUTTED

guts /ɡʌts/ n [plural] *informal* **1** courage and determination that you need in order to do something difficult or unpleasant: *It takes guts to leave a violent relationship.* **2** the organs inside your body **3** hate sb's guts *informal* to hate someone very much

guts·y /ˈɡʌtsi/ adj *informal* brave and determined: *The team gave a gutsy performance.*

gut·ted /ˈɡʌtɪd/ adj [not before noun] *BrE spoken* **1** very disappointed or shocked: *She'll be gutted when she finds out she's not going.* **2** seriously damaged or completely destroyed: *The building was gutted by fire.*

gut·ter /ˈɡʌtəǁ-ər/ n [C] **1** the low place along the edge of a road where water flows away **2** an open pipe that is fixed to a roof and carries away rain water

gut·tur·al /ˈɡʌtərəl/ adj a guttural sound is produced deep in the throat

guy /ɡaɪ/ n *informal* [C] **1** a man: *He's a really nice guy.* **2** you guys/those guys *spoken, especially AmE* used to talk to or about two or more people: *We'll see you guys Sunday, okay?*

guz·zle /ˈɡʌzəl/ v [I,T] *informal* to eat or drink a lot of something quickly

gym /dʒɪm/ n **1** [C] a special HALL or room that has equipment for doing physical exercise **2** [U] sports and exercises done indoors, especially as a school subject: *a gym class*

gym·na·si·um /dʒɪmˈneɪziəm/ n [C] a GYM

gym·nas·tics /dʒɪmˈnæstɪks/ n [U] a sport in which skilful physical exercises and movements are performed, often in competitions — **gymnast** /ˈdʒɪmnæst, -nəst/ n [C] *She's an Olympic gymnast.*

gy·nae·col·o·gy *BrE*, **gynecology** *AmE* /ˌɡaɪnɪˈkɒlədʒiǁ-ˈkɑː-/ n [U] the study and treatment of medical conditions that affect women — **gynaecologist** n [C] — **gynaecological** /ˌɡaɪnɪˌkəˈlɒdʒɪkəlǁ-ˈlɑː-/ adj

gyp·sy also **gipsy** *BrE* /ˈdʒɪpsi/ — n [C] a member of a group of people who live and travel around in CARAVANs

gy·rate /dʒaɪˈreɪtǁˈdʒaɪreɪt/ v [I] to turn around fast in circles: *dancers gyrating wildly*

G

GRAMMAR NOTE: the present perfect (2)
You use the **present perfect**: **1** to talk about something that happened in the past, but which still affects the situation now: *I've lost my passport.* **2** to talk about something that happened in the past, and continues to happen now: *I have lived in London for many years.* (=I still live there now).

Hh

H, h /eɪtʃ/ the letter 'h'

ha /hɑː/ *interjection spoken* used to show that you are surprised or pleased about something: *Ha! I knew I was right.* → see also HA HA

hab·it /'hæbɪt/ *n* **1** [C,U] something that you do regularly, and usually without thinking: **be in the habit of doing sth** *Jeff was in the habit of taking a walk after dinner.* | **get into/in the habit of doing sth** *Try to get into the habit of taking regular exercise.* | **out of habit/from habit** *After he left home, I was still cleaning his room out of habit.* **2** [C] something that you do regularly that is annoying or bad for your health: *Biting your nails is a very bad habit.* | **have a habit of doing sth** *She has a habit of never finishing her sentences.* | **break/kick the habit** *Brad's been smoking for 20 years and just can't kick the habit.* **3** [C] a set of long, loose clothes worn by members of some religious groups

---

USAGE NOTE: habit, custom, and tradition

A **habit** is something that someone does often, usually without thinking about it, because they have done it so many times before: *Smoking is a dangerous habit.* A **custom** is a way of doing something that people in a particular society normally do: *The custom here is to shake hands when you meet.* A **tradition** is a belief or way of doing something that has existed among a group of people for a very long time: *It's a family tradition to put real candles on the Christmas tree.*

---

hab·i·ta·ble /'hæbɪtəbəl/ *adj* suitable for people to live in → opposite UNINHABITABLE

hab·i·tat /'hæbɪtæt/ *n* [C] the natural environment in which a plant or animal lives

hab·i·ta·tion /ˌhæbɪ'teɪʃən/ *n* [U] when people live in a place: *There was no sign of habitation on the island.*

ha·bit·u·al /hə'bɪtʃuəl/ *adj* **1** usual or typical: *Jane was in her habitual bad temper this morning.* **2** happening as a habit, or often doing something because it is a habit: *a habitual smoker* —**habitually** *adv*

hack¹ /hæk/ *v* [I+adv/prep, T] to cut something into pieces roughly or violently: *All of the victims had been hacked to death.*
hack into sth *phr v* [T] to use a computer to enter someone else's computer system: *Morris managed to hack into a federal computer network.* —**hacker** *n* [C]

hack² *n* [C] someone who writes low quality books, newspaper articles etc

hack·neyed /'hæknɪd/ *adj* a hackneyed phrase is boring and does not have much meaning because it has been used too often

hack·saw /'hæksɔː/ *n* [C] a small SAW used especially to cut metal

had /d, əd, həd; *strong* hæd/ *v* **2 be had** to be tricked or made to look stupid: *She had the feeling she'd been had.* → see also ·'D

had·dock /'hædək/ *n* [C,U] a fish that lives in northern oceans, and is caught for food

had·n't /'hædnt/ the short form of 'had not'

hae·mo·phil·i·a *BrE*, **hemophilia** *AmE* /ˌhiːmə'fɪliə/ *n* [U] a serious disease in which the flow of blood cannot be stopped when someone is injured —**haemophiliac** /-liæk/ *n* [C]

hae·mor·rhage *BrE*, **hemorrhage** *AmE* /'hemərɪdʒ/ *n* [C,U] when someone suddenly loses a lot of blood

hae·mor·rhoids *BrE*, **hemorrhoids** *AmE* /'hemərɔɪdz/ *n* [plural] *technical* painful swollen BLOOD VESSELS near the ANUS

hag /hæg/ *n* [C] an ugly or unpleasant old woman

hag·gard /'hægəd‖-ərd/ *adj* having a thin face and dark marks around your eyes because you are tired or ill: *She arrived home looking pale and haggard.*

hag·gle /'hægəl/ *v* [I] to argue about the amount that you will pay for something: **+ over** *We were haggling over the price for an hour.*

hah /hɑː/ *interjection* HA

ha ha /ˌ. './ *interjection* used in writing to show that someone is laughing

hail¹ /heɪl/ *v* **1** [T] to call or wave to someone: **hail a cab/taxi** (=wave at a taxi to make it stop) **2** [I] if it hails, frozen rain falls from the sky
hail sb/sth **as** sth *phr v* [T] to say how good someone or something is, especially in newspapers, magazines etc: *Davos was hailed as a national hero.*
hail from *phr v* [I] to come from a particular place: *Dr Starkey hails from Massachusetts.*

hail² *n* **1** [U] small hard drops of frozen rain that fall from the sky **2** a hail of bullets/stones etc a lot of bullets, stones etc that are shot or thrown at someone

hail·stone /'heɪlstəʊn‖-stoʊn/ *n* [C usually plural] a small drop of hard frozen rain

hail·storm /'heɪlstɔːm‖-ɔːrm/ *n* [C] a storm when a lot of hail falls

hair /heə‖her/ *n* **1** [U] the things like thin threads that grow on your head: *Mike's the guy with the blond curly hair.* | *I want to grow my hair.* → see colour picture on page 244 **2** [C,U] one of the things like thin threads that grow on a person's or animal's skin: *The sofa was covered in dog hairs.* → compare FUR **3** short-haired/dark-haired etc having a particular type of hair or fur: *a long-haired cat* **4 let your hair down** *informal* to stop being serious and enjoy yourself

hair·brush /'heəbrʌʃ‖'her-/ *n* [C] a brush used to make your hair tidy → see picture at BRUSH

hair·cut /'heəkʌt‖'her-/ *n* **1** [C usually singular] when you have your hair cut by someone: *You need a haircut.* **2** [C] the style in which your hair has been cut: *a short haircut*

hair·do /'heəduː‖'her-/ *n* [C], *plural* **hairdos** *informal* the style into which a woman's hair has been cut

hair·dress·er /'heəˌdresə‖'her-ˌdresər/ *n* [C] someone who washes, cuts, and arranges people's hair: *I have an appointment at the hairdresser's.*

hair·dry·er /'heəˌdraɪə‖'her-ˌdraɪər/ *n* [C] a machine for drying hair

hair·grip /'heəgrɪp‖'her-/ *n* [C] *BrE* a small thin

metal thing used to hold a woman's hair in place; **BOBBY PIN** *AmE*

hair·line /ˈheəlaɪnǁˈher-/ *n* **1** [C] the place at the front of your head where your hair starts growing **2** a hairline **crack/fracture** a very thin crack in something hard such as glass or a bone

hair·pin /ˈheə‚pɪnǁˈher-/ *n* [C] a U-shaped piece of metal that holds a woman's hair in place

hairpin bend /ˌ‥ ˈ‥/ *BrE*, **hairpin turn** *AmE* — *n* [C] a U-shaped bend on a steep road

hair-rais·ing /ˈ‥ ‚‥/ *adj* frightening in an exciting way: *hair-raising adventures*

hair·style /ˈheəstaɪlǁˈher-/ *n* [C] the style of your hair after it has been cut, brushed etc

hair·y /ˈheəriǁˈheri/ *adj* **1** having a lot of body hair: *a hairy chest* **2** *spoken* dangerous or frightening — **hairiness** *n* [U]

hale /heɪl/ *adj* **hale and hearty** *humorous* healthy and full of energy

half[1] /hɑːfǁhæf/ *n, determiner, plural* **halves** /hɑːvzǁhævz/ **1** one of two equal parts of something: *The wall is half a mile long.* | *Over half the people in this area are unemployed.* | *Their son is two and a half.* | **+ of** *I only saw the first half of the film.* | **cut/reduce sth by half** (=make it 50% smaller) **2** half **the fun/time/reason etc** *spoken* a large part of the fun, the time etc: *Half the time we don't really know what we're doing.* **3** **not half as good/bad/surprised etc** much less good, surprised etc than someone or something else, or much less than you expected: *The movie wasn't half as good as the book.* **4** half **past one/two/three etc** *especially BrE* thirty minutes after one o'clock, two o'clock etc: *We're meeting at half past seven.* **5** half **one/two/three etc** *BrE spoken* thirty minutes after one o'clock, two o'clock etc: *"What time do you usually leave?" "About half five."*

half[2] *adv* partly but not completely: *He shouldn't be allowed to drive – he's half blind!* | *I half expected her to yell at me.* | *a half-empty bottle*

half a doz·en /ˌ‥ ˈ‥‥/ *number* also **a half dozen** six: *half a dozen donuts*

half-baked /ˌ‥ ˈ‥◂/ *adj informal* a half-baked idea, plan etc has not been thought about at all carefully or sensibly

half board /ˌ‥ ˈ‥/ *n* [U] *especially BrE* the price of a room in a hotel including breakfast and dinner

half-broth·er /ˈ‥ ‚‥/ *n* [C] a brother who is the child of only one of your parents

half-heart·ed /ˌ‥ ˈ‥‥ ǁ‥ ‚‥/ *adj* a half-hearted attempt is done without any real effort or interest: *He made a half-hearted attempt to tidy his room.*

half-mast /ˌ‥ ˈ‥/ *adj* **fly/be at half-mast** if a flag flies or is at half-mast, it is lowered to the middle of its pole because someone important has died

half·pen·ny /ˈheɪpni/ *n* [C] a small coin worth half of one **PENNY**, used in Britain in the past

half-sis·ter /ˈ‥ ‚‥/ *n* [C] a sister who is the child of only one of your parents

half term /ˌ‥ ˈ‥/ *n* [C,U] *BrE* a short holiday in the middle of a school **TERM**

half time /ˌ‥ ˈ‥ ǁ‥ ‚‥/ *n* [U] a period of rest between two parts of a game such as football

half·way /ˌhɑːfˈweɪ◂ ǁˌhæf-/ *adj, adv* at a middle point between two places, or in the middle of a

period of time: *We had reached the halfway mark of the trail.* | **+ through/down/up etc** *Halfway through the meal, Dan got up.*

half-wit /ˈ‥ ‚‥/ *n* [C] a stupid person — **half-witted** *adj*

hal·i·but /ˈhæl‚bət/ *n* [C,U] a large flat sea fish

hall /hɔːlǁhɒːl/ *n* **1** [C] the area just inside the door of a building that leads to other rooms: *The bathroom's just down the hall on the right.* **2** [C] a building or large room that is used for important events such as meetings, concerts etc: *a dance hall* | *Carnegie Hall*

hall·mark /ˈhɔːlmɑːkǁˈhɒːlmɑːrk/ *n* [C] **1** a quality, idea, or method that is typical of a person or thing: **+ of** *Discipline is the hallmark of any successful organization.* **2** an official mark put on silver, gold etc to prove that it is real

hal·lo /həˈləʊ, he-, hæ-ǁˈloʊ/ *interjection BrE* **HELLO**

hall of res·i·dence /ˌ‥ ‥ ˈ‥‥/ *n* [C] *BrE* a college or university building where students live; **DORMITORY** *AmE*

hal·lowed /ˈhæləʊdǁ-loʊd/ *adj* **1** respected and important: *the hallowed memories of our war heroes* **2** made holy: *hallowed ground*

Hal·low·een /ˌhæləʊˈiːn◂ ǁ-loʊ-/ *n* [U] the night of October 31, when children dress as **WITCH**es, **GHOST**s etc

hal·lu·ci·nate /həˈluːs‚neɪt/ *v* [I] to see, feel, or hear something that is not really there

hal·lu·ci·na·tion /hə‚luːs‚ˈneɪʃən/ *n* [C,U] something you see, feel, or hear that is not really there — **hallucinatory** /həˈluːs‚nətɒrilⁱ-tɔːri/ *adj*

hall·way /ˈhɔːlweɪǁˈhɒːl-/ *n* [C] the area just inside the door of a building that leads to other rooms

ha·lo /ˈheɪləʊǁ-loʊ/ *n, plural* **halos** a golden circle that is shown in paintings above the head of a holy person

halt[1] /hɔːltǁhɒːlt/ *v* [I,T] *formal* to stop or make something stop: *The city council has halted repair work on the subways.*

halt[2] *n* [singular] when something stops happening or moving for a period of time: **come/grind to a halt** *The bus slowly ground to a halt.* | **bring sth to a halt** *Yesterday's strike brought production to a halt.* | **call a halt** (=officially stop an activity from continuing): *It's time that we called a halt to these corrupt practices.*

hal·ter /ˈhɔːltəǁˈhɒːltər/ *n* [C] a piece of rope or leather fastened around a horse's head in order to lead it

halt·ing /ˈhɔːltɪŋǁˈhɒːl-/ *adj* stopping a lot when you move or speak, especially because you are nervous: *She spoke in a halting voice.*

halve /hɑːvǁhæv/ *v* [T] **1** to reduce the amount of something by half: *Food production was almost halved during the war.* **2** to cut something into two equal pieces: *Wash and halve the mushrooms.*

halves /hɑːvzǁhævz/ *n* the plural of **HALF**

ham[1] /hæm/ *n* [C,U] preserved meat from the upper part of a pig's leg: *a slice of ham* ➡ see colour picture on page 440

ham[2] *v informal* **ham it up** to perform or behave with too much false emotion

ham·burg·er /ˈhæmbɜːgəǁ-bɜːrgər/ *n* **1** [C] small pieces of **BEEF** that are pressed together, cooked in a flat round shape and eaten between pieces of round bread **2** [U] *AmE* BEEF that is cut into very small pieces; MINCE *BrE*

ham·let /ˈhæmlɪt/ *n* [C] a very small village

ham·mer[1] /ˈhæməll-ər/ *n* [C] a tool used for hitting nails into wood → see picture at TOOLS

hammer[2] *v* **1** [I,T] to hit something with a hammer **2** [I] to hit something several times, making a lot of noise: *Mike was hammering on the door with his fists.*

hammer sth into sb *phr v* [T] to continue repeating something in order to force people to remember it: *Mom hammered the message into us: don't talk to strangers!*

hammer out sth *phr v* [T] to finally agree on a solution, contract etc after arguing about details for a long time: *It took several days to hammer out an agreement.*

ham·mock /ˈhæmək/ *n* [C] a large net or piece of material used for sleeping on, that hangs between two trees or poles

ham·per[1] /ˈhæmpəll-ər/ *v* [T] to make it difficult for someone to move, do, or achieve something: *The search was hampered by bad weather.*

hamper[2] *n* [C] a large basket with a lid

ham·ster /ˈhæmstəll-ər/ *n* [C] a small animal with soft fur and no tail that is often kept as a pet

ham·string[1] /ˈhæmˌstrɪŋ/ *n* [C] a TENDON behind your knee

hamstring[2] *v* [T] **hamstrung** /-ˌstrʌŋ/, **hamstring, hamstringing** to make it difficult for a person or group to do or achieve something: *a government hamstrung by student protests*

hand[1] /hænd/ *n* **1** [C] the body part at the end of a person's arm that includes the fingers and thumb: *She writes with her left hand.*| *Tom stood in the doorway with his hands in his pockets.*| **take** sb's **hand/take** sb **by the hand** *I took her hand and helped her down the stairs.*| **hold hands (with** sb**)** *They sat there holding hands through the entire film.* → see colour picture on page 473 **2 right-handed/left-handed** always using the right hand or left hand to do things such as write, use tools etc **3 on the one hand... on the other hand** used when you are comparing two different facts or ideas: *On the one hand, they work slowly, but on the other hand they always finish the job.* **4 on hand/to hand** close and ready to be used when needed: *Keep a supply of candles on hand in case of power cuts.* **5 at hand** near in time or space: **close/near at hand** *Nurses are always close at hand in case of emergency.* **6 by hand** by a person and not by a machine: *She does all her washing by hand.* **7 a hand** help, especially to do physical work: **give/lend** sb **a hand** *Can you give me a hand moving this box?*| **need a hand** *Do you need a hand with the cooking?* **8 in** sb's **hands/in the hands of** sb controlled by someone or taken care of by someone: *Responsibility for the schedule is entirely in your hands.* **9 at the hands of** if you suffer at the hands of someone, they treat you badly **10 get/lay your hands on** sth to find or obtain something: *I read every book I could get my hands on.* **11 get out of hand** to become impossible to control: *Todd's behaviour is getting totally out of hand.* **12 hand in hand a)** holding each other's hands: *They walked hand in hand through the park.* **b) go hand in** hand to happen together: *Wealth and power go hand in hand.* **13 in hand** being dealt with now: *We need to discuss the most suitable working methods for the job in hand.* **14 have your hands full** to be very busy or too busy: *You're going to have your hands full once you have the baby!* **15 hands off** *spoken* used to warn someone not to touch something that is yours: *Hands off my cookies!* **16** [C] one of the long things that point to the numbers on a clock **17** [C] a set of playing cards held by one person in a game **18 all hands on deck!** used to tell people that they all have to help

hand[2] *v* [T] **1** to give something to someone: **hand** sb sth *Can you hand me a towel?* **2 you have to hand it to** sb *spoken* used to show admiration for someone: *You have to hand it to Liz – she's a great cook!*

hand sth ↔ **around** (also **hand** sth ↔ **round** *BrE*) *phr v* [T] to offer something to all the people in a group: *Could you hand the sandwiches around please, Mike?*

hand sth ↔ **back** *phr v* [T] to give something back to the person who gave it to you: *Mr Evans handed back our essays today.*

hand sth ↔ **down** *phr v* [T] to give something to a younger relation, or to people who live after you: *traditions that were handed down from generation to generation*

hand sth ↔ **in** *phr v* [T] to give something to someone in a position of authority: *Please hand in your application by September 30.*

hand sth ↔ **out** *phr v* [T] to give something to everyone in a group: *They were handing out free T-shirts at the club.*

hand over *phr v* [T **hand** sb/sth ↔ **over**] to give someone or something to the person who wants to deal with them: *The thief was caught and handed over to the police.*

hand·bag /ˈhændbæg/ *n* [C] *especially BrE* a small bag used by women to carry money and personal things; PURSE *AmE* → see picture at BAG

hand·book /ˈhændbʊk/ *n* [C] a small book with instructions and information about a particular subject: *an employee handbook*

hand·brake /ˈhændbreɪk/ *n* [C] *BrE* a thing in a car that you pull up with your hand to stop the car from moving; EMERGENCY BRAKE *AmE*

hand·cuffs /ˈhændkʌfs/ *n* [plural] two metal rings joined by a chain, used for holding a prisoner's wrists together —**handcuff** *v* [T]

hand·ful /ˈhændfʊl/ *n* **1** [C] an amount that you can hold in your hand: **+ of** *a handful of nuts* **2 a handful of** a small number of people or things: *Only a handful of people came to the meeting.*

hand·gun /ˈhændgʌn/ *n* [C] a small gun you hold in one hand when you shoot

hand·i·cap /ˈhændikæp/ *n* [C] **1** something permanently wrong with a person's mind or body: *a severe physical handicap* **2** something that makes it difficult for you to do or achieve something: *Not being able to speak French was a real handicap.*

hand·i·capped /ˈhændikæpt/ *adj* not able to use a part of your body or mind normally because it has been damaged: **mentally/physically handicapped** *schools for mentally handicapped children*

H

hand·i·work /ˈhændiwɜːk‖-wɜːrk/ n [U] something that someone does or makes: *Both films are the handiwork of respected directors.*

hand·ker·chief /ˈhæŋkətʃɪf‖-kər-/ n [C] a small piece of cloth or paper used for drying your nose or eyes

han·dle[1] /ˈhændl/ v [T] **1** to deal with or organize something: *The job was so stressful, he couldn't handle it any longer.* | *Ms Lee handled all of our travel arrangements.* **2** to pick up, hold, or touch something: *Handle all packages with care.* **3** to buy, sell, or deal with products or services: *Upton was charged with handling stolen goods.*

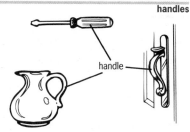

handles

handle

han·dle[2] n [C] the part of something that is used for holding or opening it: *a door handle*

han·dle·bars /ˈhændlbɑːz‖-bɑːrz/ n [plural] the bars above the front wheel of a bicycle or MOTORCYCLE, that control the direction you go in

han·dler /ˈhændlə‖-ər/ n [C] someone whose job is to deal with or be in charge of a particular kind of thing: *baggage handlers* | *a police dog and its handler*

hand lug·gage /ˈ. ˌ../ n [U] small bags that you carry with you when you travel on a plane

hand·made /ˌhændˈmeɪd◂/ adj made by a person and not a machine: *handmade shoes*

hand·out /ˈhændaʊt/ n [C] **1** money or food that is given to someone, usually because they are poor **2** a piece of paper with printed information on it, that is given to people in a class, meeting etc

hand·picked /ˌhændˈpɪkt◂/ adj carefully chosen for a particular purpose: *Daly had been handpicked for the job.*

hand·shake /ˈhændʃeɪk/ n [C] an action in which two people take each other's right hand when they meet or leave each other: *a firm handshake*

hand·some /ˈhænsəm/ adj **1** a man who is handsome is attractive: *a tall handsome young officer* **2** handsome profit/sum/offer etc a large amount of money

hands-on /ˈ. ./ adj hands-on experience/training etc experience, training etc that you get by doing something rather than studying it

hand·writ·ing /ˈhænd͵raɪtɪŋ/ n [U] the way that someone writes with a pen or pencil: *She has very neat handwriting.*

hand·y /ˈhændi/ adj **1** useful, or simple to use: *a handy little gadget* | **come in handy** (=be useful in the future): *The extra key may come in handy.* **2** *informal* near and easy to reach: *Make sure you have your passport handy.* **3** **be handy with sth** to be good at using something, especially a tool: *Terry's very handy with a needle and thread.*

hand·y·man /ˈhændimæn/ n [C], *plural* **handymen** /-men/ someone who is good at making and repairing things

hang[1] /hæŋ/ v **hung** /hʌŋ/, **hung**, **hanging** **1** [I,T] to put something somewhere so that its top part is fixed but its bottom part is free to move, or to be in this position: *He hung his coat on the back of the door.* | **+ from/on etc** *Her portrait was hanging on the wall.* **2** [I,T], *past tense and past participle* **hanged** to kill someone by dropping them with a rope around their neck, or to die in this way: *Corey hanged himself in his prison cell.* **3** [I always + adv/prep] to stay in the air in the same place for a long time: *Dark clouds hung over the valley.* **4** **hang your head** to look ashamed or embarrassed: *Lewis hung his head and refused to answer.* **5** **hang in the balance** to be in a situation in which the result is not certain, and something bad may happen: *Our whole future is hanging in the balance.* **6** **leave sb/sth hanging** to not finish something or not tell someone your decision about something: *The investigation should not be left hanging.*

He hung his jacket up.

hang around (also **hang about** *BrE*) *phr v* [I,T] *informal* **1** to stay in one place without doing very much, often because you are waiting for someone: *We hung around for about an hour and then left.* **2** **hang around with sb** to spend a lot of time with someone: *I don't like the people she hangs around with.*

hang back *phr v* [I] to not want to move forward or speak, often because you are shy: *Joe tends to hang back and let the others do the talking.*

hang on *phr v* **1** **hang on!** *spoken* used to tell someone to wait for you: *Hang on, I'll be with you in a minute!* **2** [I] *informal* to hold something tightly: *Hang on everybody, the road's pretty bumpy.*

hang onto sb/sth *phr v* [T] *informal* to keep something: *Hang onto that letter – you might need it later.*

hang out *phr v* [I] *informal* to spend a lot of time at a particular place or with particular people: *They hang out together.*

hang round *phr v* [I] *BrE* HANG AROUND

hang up *phr v* **1** [I] to finish a telephone conversation by putting the telephone down: *She said good night and hung up.* | **hang up on sb** (=put the phone down during a conversation

H

---

because you are angry): *Don't hang up on me!*
2 [T **hang** sth ↔ **up**] to put something such as clothes on a hook or hanger

hang² *n* **get the hang of (doing) sth** *informal* to learn how to do something: *You'll soon get the hang of using the computer.*

hang·ar /ˈhæŋəll-ər/ *n* [C] a very large building where aircraft are kept → see colour picture on page 669

hang·er /ˈhæŋəll-ər/ *n* [C] a thing for hanging clothes on, made of a curved piece of metal or wood with a hook

hanger-on /ˌ.. ˈ./ *n* [C], *plural* **hangers-on** someone who spends a lot of time with important or rich people for their own advantage

hang glid·ing /ˈ. ˌ../ *n* [U] the sport of flying using a large frame covered with cloth that you hold on to —**hang glider** *n* [C]

hang·out /ˈhæŋaʊt/ *n* [C] *informal* a place that you like to go to often, such as a bar

hang·o·ver /ˈhæŋəʊvəll-oʊvər/ *n* [C] when someone feels ill because they have drunk too much alcohol the evening before

hang-up /ˈ. ./ *n* [C] **have a hang-up about sth** *informal* to feel anxious or embarrassed about something: *Cindy has a hang-up about her nose.*

han·ker /ˈhæŋkəll-ər/ *v informal*
hanker after/for sth *phr v* [T] to feel that you want something very much: *She's always hankered after a place of her own.*

han·kie also **hanky** /ˈhæŋki/ *n* [C] *informal* a HANDKERCHIEF

hap·haz·ard /ˌhæpˈhæzəd‹ ‖-ərd‹/ *adj* happening or done in a way that is not planned is not organized according to any system: *a haphazard way of working* —**haphazardly** *adv*

hap·less /ˈhæpləs/ *adj literary* unlucky

hap·pen /ˈhæpən/ *v* [I] **1** if an event or situation happens, it exists and continues for a period of time, usually without being planned: *We must do all we can to prevent such a disaster ever happening again.* | *Did anything exciting happen while I was away?* | **happen to sb/sth** *Strange things have been happening to me lately.* **2** to be the result of something you do: *When I try to turn on the motor, nothing happens.* | **what happens if...?/what would happen if...?** *What happens if your parents find out?* **3 happen to do sth** to do or to have something by chance: *I happened to see Hannah at the store today.* **4 as it happens/it (just) so happens** used to say that something happens by chance, especially when this is surprising: *It just so happened that Mike and I had been to the same school.*
happen on/upon sb/sth *phr v* [T] to find something or meet someone by chance: *We just happened on the cabin when we were hiking one day.*

USAGE NOTE: happen, occur, take place, and happen to

Use **happen** especially to talk about past or future events that are accidents or are not planned: *A funny thing happened on my way to school.* | *What will happen if you have to change jobs?* **Occur** is more formal, and is used to talk about an event that has already happened: *The explosion occurred about 5:30 a.m.* Use **take place** to talk about a planned event: *Their wedding will* take place on Saturday. Use **happen to** to say that a person or thing is affected by an event: *What happened to your car?* | *This is the second time this has happened to him.*

hap·pen·ing /ˈhæpənɪŋ/ *n* [C] something that happens, especially a strange event

hap·pi·ly /ˈhæpɪli/ *adv* **1** in a happy way: *They're very happily married.* **2** fortunately: *Happily, no one was hurt in the fire.* **3** very willingly: *I'll happily look after the kids while you're away.*

hap·pi·ness /ˈhæpɪnɪs/ *n* [U] when someone is happy

hap·py /ˈhæpi/ *adj* **1** feeling pleased and cheerful, often because something good has happened to you: *Sam's been looking a lot happier recently.* | *Congratulations! I'm very happy for you.* → opposite UNHAPPY → see colour picture on page 277 **2 be happy to do sth** to be willing to do something, especially to help someone else: *Our team of experts will be happy to answer any questions.* **3** making you feel pleased or happy: *a happy marriage* | *Those were the happiest years of my life.* **4** satisfied and not worried: **+ with/about** *Are you happy with their decision?* **5 Happy Birthday/Happy New Year etc** used as a way of greeting someone on a special occasion

USAGE NOTE: happy, content, glad, and ecstatic

There are several different words to describe being happy. Someone who is **content** is feeling happy because they are satisfied: *They're content to lead a simple life.* Someone who is **glad** is pleased about something that has happened: *I'm so glad you were able to come.* If someone is very excited as well as happy they are **ecstatic**: *An ecstatic crowd cheered as the players ran onto the field.*

happy-go-luck·y /ˌ.. ˈ..‹ / *adj* not caring or worrying about what happens

ha·rangue /həˈræŋ/ *v* [T] to speak angrily to someone, often for a long time, to try to persuade them that you are right —**harangue** *n* [C]

har·ass /ˈhærəs, həˈræs/ *v* [T] to deliberately annoy or threaten someone, often over a long period of time: *They claim that they are being harassed by the police.*

har·assed /ˈhærəst, həˈræst/ *adj* anxious and tired: *Val looked very harassed when I saw her.*

har·ass·ment /ˈhærəsmənt, həˈræsmənt/ *n* [U] threatening or offensive behaviour: **sexual/racial harassment** *Tina accused her boss of sexual harassment.*

har·bour¹ *BrE*, **harbor** *AmE* /ˈhɑːbəll-ˈhɑːrbər/ *n* [C] an area of water next to the land where ships can stay safely → see colour picture on page 669

harbour² *BrE*, **harbor** *AmE* —*v* [T] **1** to keep feelings or thoughts in your mind for a long time: **harbour doubts/suspicions etc** *Several of Wilson's colleagues harboured suspicions about him.* **2** to protect someone by hiding them from the police: *She was accused of harbouring deserters.*

H

hard[1] /hɑːd‖hɑːrd/ *adj* **1** firm and stiff, and difficult to cut, press down, or break: *a hard mattress.* | *The plums are still too hard to eat.* → opposite SOFT **2** difficult to do or understand: *The interviewer asked some very hard questions.* | **it's hard (for sb) to do sth** *It's hard to say when Glenn will be back.* → opposite EASY[1] **3** involving a lot of physical or mental effort or suffering: *a long hard climb to the top of the hill* | *Poor May, she's had a hard life.* | **hard work** *Bringing up children on your own is hard work.* **4** showing no kindness or sympathy: *Mr. Katz is a hard man to work for, but he's fair.* | **be hard on sb** *She's too hard on those kids.* **5** **give sb a hard time** *informal* to criticize someone or make jokes about them, so that they feel embarrassed or uncomfortable: *The guys were giving him a hard time about missing the ball.* **6** **do/learn sth the hard way** to make a lot of mistakes or have a lot of difficulty before learning something **7** **no hard feelings** *spoken* used to tell someone that you do not feel angry with them any more **8** **hard facts/evidence** facts etc that are true and can be proved **9** **a hard winter** a very cold winter — **hardness** *n* [U]

hard[2] *adv* **1** using a lot of effort or force: *She'd been working hard all day.* | *Come on, push harder!* **2** **be hard pressed/put/pushed to do sth** to have difficulty doing something: *They'll be hard pushed to pay back the money.* **3** **take sth hard** to feel very upset about something: *I didn't think that Joe would take the news so hard.*

USAGE NOTE: hard and hardly

Hard is an adverb used to say that something is done using a lot of effort or force: *We studied hard for two weeks.* **Hardly** means 'almost not': *I could hardly believe what she said.*

---

hard-and-fast /ˌ. . '.◂/ *adj* **hard-and-fast rules** a rule that cannot be changed

hard·back /'hɑːdbæk‖'hɑːrd-/ *n* [C] a book that has a strong stiff cover → compare PAPERBACK

hard·ball /'hɑːdbɔːl‖'hɑːrdbɔːl/ *n* **play hardball** *informal* to do everything you can to prevent someone from succeeding, even if this includes doing bad or unfair things

hard·board /'hɑːdbɔːd‖'hɑːrdbɔːrd/ *n* [U] a kind of hard wood made out of smaller pieces of wood that have been pressed together

hard-boiled /ˌ. '.◂/ *adj* a hard-boiled egg has been boiled until the yellow part becomes solid

hard cash /ˌ. './ *n* [U] money in the form of coins and NOTES

hard cop·y /'. ˌ../ *n* [U] information from a computer that is printed onto paper

hard core /ˌ. './ *n* [singular] *BrE* **1** the small group of people in an organization who are its most active and determined members: *the hard core of the Communist Party* **2** a small group of people who refuse to change their behaviour or beliefs: *the hard core of drunk drivers who carry on drinking and driving*

hard·core, hard-core /ˌ. '.◂/ *adj* [only before noun] **1** having very strong beliefs or opinions that are unlikely to change: *hardcore opposition to abortion* **2** **hard-core pornography** pictures, films etc that show details of sexual behaviour, often in a very unpleasant way

hard disk /ˌ. './ *n* [C] A part that is fixed inside a computer, used for permanently keeping information

hard·en /'hɑːdn‖'hɑːrdn/ *v* **1** [I,T] to become firm or stiff, or to make something firm or stiff: *The pottery has to harden before it's painted.* **2** [I,T] to become less kind, less afraid, and more determined, or to make someone feel like this: *Ged's expression hardened when he saw her.*

hard-head·ed /ˌ. '.◂/ *adj* able to make difficult decisions without being influenced by your emotions

hard-heart·ed /ˌ. '.◂/ *adj* not caring about other people's feelings

hard-hit·ting /ˌ. '.◂/ *adj* criticizing someone or something in a strong and effective way: *a hard-hitting TV documentary*

hard-line /ˌ. '.◂/ *adj* unwilling to change your extreme opinions: *hard-line conservatives* — **hard-liner** *n* [C]

hard·ly /'hɑːdli‖'hɑːrdli/ *adv* **1** almost not: *I hardly know the people I'm working with.* (=do not know them very well) | **can/could hardly do sth** *I could hardly wait to see him again.* | **hardly any/anything/anyone** (=almost nothing or no one): *She'd eaten hardly anything all day.* | **hardly ever** *We hardly ever go out in the evening.* **2** used to say that something is not at all true, possible, surprising etc: *This is hardly the ideal time to buy a house.* → compare BARELY

hard-nosed /ˌ. './ *adj* not affected by your emotions, and determined to get what you want: *a hard-nosed negotiator*

hard of hear·ing /ˌ. . '../ *adj* unable to hear well

hard-pressed /ˌ. '.◂/ *adj* **1** having a lot of problems and not much money or time: *help for hard-pressed families* **2** **sb will/would be hard-pressed to do sth** used to say that it will or would be difficult for someone to do something: *We'll be hard-pressed to finish on time.*

hard sell /ˌ. './ *n* [singular] a way of selling in which someone tries very hard to persuade you to buy something

hard·ship /'hɑːdʃɪp‖'hɑːrd-/ *n* [C,U] something that makes your life difficult, especially not having enough money: *Many families were suffering economic hardship.* | *the hardships of daily life*

hard shoul·der /ˌ. '../ *n* [singular] *BrE* the area at the side of a big road where you are allowed to stop if you have a problem with your car; SHOULDER *AmE*

hard up /ˌ. '.◂/ *adj* *informal* not having enough of something, especially money

hard·ware /'hɑːdweə‖'hɑːrdwer/ *n* [U] **1** computer machinery and equipment → compare SOFTWARE **2** equipment and tools you use in your home and garden: *a hardware store*

hard-wear·ing /ˌ. '.◂/ *adj* *BrE* clothes, materials etc that are hard-wearing will stay in good condition for a long time; LONGWEARING *AmE*

hard·wood /'hɑːdwʊd‖'hɑːrd-/ *n* [C,U] strong heavy wood used for making furniture

hard-work·ing /ˌ. '.◂/ *adj* working with a lot of effort: *a hard-working student*

har·dy /'hɑːdi‖'hɑːrdi/ *adj* strong and able to exist in difficult conditions: *hardy plants*

hare /heə‖her/ *n* [C] an animal like a rabbit that has long ears and is able to run very fast

hare·brained /ˈheəbreɪnd‖ˈher-/ *adj* not sensible or practical: *a harebrained scheme*

har·em /ˈhɑːriːm, hɑːˈriːm‖ˈhærəm,ˈher-/ *n* [C] the group of wives or women living with a rich or powerful man in some Muslim societies in the past

hark /hɑːk‖hɑːrk/ *v*
hark back to *phr v* [T] to keep talking about things that happened in the past: *He's always harking back to his days in Hollywood.*

har·lot /ˈhɑːlət‖ˈhɑːr-/ *n* [C] *literary* a PROSTITUTE

harm[1] /hɑːm‖hɑːrm/ *n* **1** [U] damage or hurt: **do harm** *Modern farming methods do a lot of harm to the environment.* | **do sb harm** *I don't think a little wine does you any harm.* | **come to no harm** (=not be hurt or damaged): *They got lost in the fog, but luckily they came to no harm.* **2 there's no harm in doing sth** used to suggest that it might be useful to do something: *There's no harm in asking.* **3 not mean any harm** to have no intention of hurting or upsetting anyone: *I was only kidding – I didn't mean any harm.* **4 no harm done** *spoken* used to tell someone that you are not upset by what they have done or said: *"I'm sorry." "That's okay. No harm done."* **5 out of harm's way** in a safe place: *She was glad the children were at home, out of harm's way.*

harm[2] *v* [T] to damage or hurt something or someone: *Too much sun can harm your skin.*

harm·ful /ˈhɑːmfəl‖ˈhɑːrm-/ *adj* causing harm: *the harmful effects of pollution*

harm·less /ˈhɑːmləs‖ˈhɑːrm-/ *adj* **1** not dangerous or likely to cause any harm: *Their dog barks a lot but it's harmless.* **2** not likely to upset or offend anyone: *harmless fun* —**harmlessly** *adv*

har·mon·i·ca /hɑːˈmɒnɪkə‖hɑːrˈmɑː-/ *n* [C] a small musical instrument that you hold to your mouth and blow into, moving it from side to side

har·mon·ize (also **-ise** *BrE*) /ˈhɑːmənaɪz‖ˈhɑːr-/ *v* **1** [I,T] to work well or look good together, or to make something do this: *Every effort should be made to harmonize the new buildings with the landscape.* **2** [I,T] to sing or play musical notes that make a pleasant sound with the main tune

har·mo·ny /ˈhɑːməni‖ˈhɑːr-/ *n* **1** [U] when people are not arguing, fighting, or disagreeing: *People of many races live here in harmony.* **2** [C,U] combinations of musical notes that sound good together —**harmonious** /hɑːˈməʊniəs‖hɑːrˈmoʊ-/ *adj* —**harmoniously** *adv*

har·ness[1] /ˈhɑːnəs‖ˈhɑːr-/ *n* **1** [C,U] a set of leather bands fastened with metal that is used to control a horse **2** [C] a set of bands that is used to hold someone in a place or to stop them from falling: *a safety harness*

harness[2] *v* [T] **1** to control and use the natural power of something: *harnessing the wind to generate electricity* **2** to fasten two animals together, or to fasten an animal to something, using a harness

harp[1] /hɑːp‖hɑːrp/ *n* [C] a large musical instrument with strings stretched on a frame with three corners —**harpist** *n* [C]

harp[2] *v*

harp on *phr v* [I] *informal* also **harp on about** *BrE* [I,T] to talk about something all the time, in a way that is annoying or boring: *I wish they'd stop harping on about the fact they're vegetarians.*

har·poon /hɑːˈpuːn‖hɑːr-/ *n* [C] a weapon like a SPEAR used for hunting WHALES

harp·si·chord /ˈhɑːpsɪkɔːd‖ˈhɑːrpsɪkɔːrd/ *n* [C] a musical instrument like a piano, used especially in CLASSICAL music

har·row·ing /ˈhærəʊɪŋ‖-roʊ-/ *adj* very shocking and upsetting: *harrowing pictures of the prison camps*

harsh /hɑːʃ‖hɑːrʃ/ *adj* **1** harsh conditions are difficult to live in and are very uncomfortable: *harsh Canadian winters* **2** unpleasantly bright, loud, or rough: *harsh lighting* **3** unkind, cruel, or strict: *harsher laws to deal with drunk drivers* —**harshly** *adv* —**harshness** *n* [U]

har·vest[1] /ˈhɑːvɪst‖ˈhɑːr-/ *n* [C,U] **1** the time when crops are gathered from the fields, or the act of gathering them: *the wheat harvest* **2** the size or quality of crops: *a good harvest*

harvest[2] *v* [T] to gather crops from the fields

has /z, əz, həz; *strong* hæz/ *v* the third person singular of the present tense of HAVE

has-been /ˈ. ./ *n* [C] *informal* someone who was once important or popular but is not any more

hash /hæʃ/ *n* **1 make a hash of** *informal* to do something very badly **2** hashish

hash·ish /ˈhæʃiːʃ, -iːʃ/ *n* [U] an illegal drug that is smoked

has·n't /ˈhæznt/ *v* the short form of 'has not'

has·sle[1] /ˈhæsəl/ *n* [C,U] *spoken* something that is annoying because it causes problems or is difficult to do: *It's such a hassle not having a washing machine.*

hassle[2] *v* [T] *informal* to continuously ask someone to do something, in a way that is annoying: *Just stop hassling me, will you?*

haste /heɪst/ *n* [U] when you hurry to do something, because you do not have enough time: *In her haste, Pam forgot the tickets.*

has·ten /ˈheɪsən/ *v* **1** [T] to make something happen sooner: *Resting will hasten recovery.* **2 hasten to do sth** to do or say something quickly: *Gina hastened to assure him that everything was fine.*

hast·y /ˈheɪsti/ *adj* done quickly, especially too quickly and without thinking carefully: *a hasty decision* —**hastily** *adv*: *A meeting was hastily organized.*

hat /hæt/ *n* [C] something that you wear to cover or protect your head: *a big straw hat* ➔ see also **old hat** (OLD)

hatch[1] /hætʃ/ *v* [I,T] **1** if an egg hatches or is hatched, it breaks and a baby bird, fish, or insect is born **2** also **hatch out** to break though an egg in order to be born **3 hatch a plot/plan** to plan something secretly: *The group hatched a plot to kidnap the President's daughter.*

hatch[2] *n* [C] a hole in a ship, plane, or wall, that people or things can pass through, or the door that covers it

hatch·et /ˈhætʃɪt/ *n* **1** [C] a small AXE with a short handle **2 do a hatchet job on sb** *informal* to criticize someone severely and often unfairly ➔ see also **bury the hatchet** (BURY)

hate[1] /heɪt/ v [T] **1** to dislike someone or something very much: *Bill really hates his father.* | *I've always hated tomatoes.* | **hate doing sth** *Pam hates having her photo taken.* **2 I hate to think what/how** spoken used when you feel sure that something would have a bad result: *I hate to think what Dad would say about this!* — **hated** adj: *a hated dictator*

hate[2] n [U] an angry feeling of wanting to harm someone you dislike: *a look of hate*

hate·ful /ˈheɪtfəl/ adj very unpleasant or unkind: *What a hateful thing to say!*

ha·tred /ˈheɪtrɪd/ n [U] formal a feeling of hate: *eyes full of hatred* | **+ of** *an intense hatred of authority*

hat trick /ˈ. ./ n [C] three successes coming one after the other, for example three GOALs by one player

haugh·ty /ˈhɔːtiǁˈhɒː-/ adj proud and behaving as if other people are not as good as you are: *a haughty smile* — **haughtily** adv

haul[1] /hɔːlǁhɒːl/ v [I,T] to pull something heavy or to pull hard: *We managed to haul him out of the water.*

haul[2] n **1** [C] a large amount of things that have been stolen or found by the police: *a big drugs haul* **2 a long haul** something that takes a lot of time and effort: *the long haul back to fitness* **3** [C] the amount of fish caught in a net

haul·age /ˈhɔːlɪdʒǁˈhɒːl-/ n [U] the business of carrying things by road or railway

haunch·es /ˈhɔːntʃɪzǁˈhɒːn-/ n [plural] the part of your body that you sit on, and the tops of your legs

haunt[1] /hɔːntǁhɒːnt/ v [T] **1** if the spirit of a dead person haunts a place, it appears there often: *a ship haunted by ghosts of sea captains* **2** if something unpleasant haunts you, you keep remembering it or being affected by it: *ex-soldiers still haunted by memories of the war*

haunt[2] n [C] a place that someone likes to go to often: *The café was a favourite haunt of artists.*

haunt·ed /ˈhɔːntɪdǁˈhɒːn-/ adj a haunted place is one where people believe that the spirits of dead people live: *a haunted house*

haunt·ing /ˈhɔːntɪŋǁˈhɒːn-/ adj beautiful, sad, and staying in your thoughts for a long time: *haunting landscapes* — **hauntingly** adv: *hauntingly beautiful music*

have[1] /v, əv, həv; strong hæv/ auxiliary verb **had** /d, əd, həd/; strong /hæd/, **had, having** **1** used with the past participle of a verb to make the perfect tenses: *Have you seen the new Disney movie?* | *She had lived in Peru for thirty years.* **2** used with some modal verbs and a past participle to make a past modal: *Carrie should have been nicer.* | *I must've left my wallet at home.* **3 had better** used to say what is the best thing to do: *You'd better take the cake out of the oven.* | *I'd better phone and say we'll be late.*

4 have had it spoken used to say that something or someone is in a very bad state and will not be able to continue: *I think the car's had it.*

5 I've had it with spoken used when you are annoyed by someone or something and do not want to deal with them any more: *I've had it with this job. I'm leaving!* **6 here and there** in several different places or parts of something: *Here and there you can see a few scratches, but generally the car's in good condition.*

have[2] v [T not in passive] **had, had, having** **1** also **have got** used to say what someone or something looks like, or what features they possess: *He's got brown eyes and dark hair.* | *Japan has a population of over 120 million.* **2** also **have got** to own something, or be able to use something: *Kurt had a nice bike, but it got stolen.* | **have a CD player?** | **have the money/time etc** (=have enough money, time etc): *I'd like to help, but I don't have the time.* **3** to eat, drink, or smoke something: *Let's go and have a beer.* | *We're having steak tonight.* | **have lunch/breakfast/dinner etc** *What time do you usually have lunch?* **4** to experience or do something: **have problems/trouble etc** *I'm having problems using this fax machine.* | **have fun** *The kids had great fun at the theme park.* | **have a meeting/party** *Let's have a party!* | **have a holiday/bath/wash etc** *I'll just have a quick wash before we leave.* **5** BrE also **have got** to receive something such as a letter, information, or advice: *Have you had any news from Michael?* **6** also **have got** to keep something in a particular position or state: *He had his eyes closed.* | *You've always got the TV on so loud.* **7 may I have/can I have/I'll have** spoken used when you are asking for something: *I'll have two hot dogs, please.* **8 have a friend/sister/uncle etc** also **have got** BrE to know or be related to someone: *Julie had six brothers.* **9** also **have got** to be allowed a particular amount of time to do something: *You have 30 minutes to finish the test.* **10** also **have got** to become ill or be injured in a particular way: *Sheila's had the flu for a week.* | *He's got a broken leg.* **11** also **have got** to be carrying something with you: *Watch out! He's got a gun!* | **have sth on you** *How much money have you on you?* **12** also **have got** to think of something: *Wait, I've got an idea.* | *She had many happy memories of her time in Japan.* **13 have sth ready/done etc** to make something ready, or finish something: *They promised to have the job done by Friday.* **14 have a baby** if a woman has a baby, it is born from her body: *Sasha's had twins!* **15 have your hair cut/have your house painted etc** to pay someone to cut your hair, paint your house etc **16** also **have sb especially** BrE to be with someone, or be visited by someone: *Sorry, I didn't realize you had guests.* | *We're having people to dinner.* **17 have (got) it in for sb** spoken to want to harm someone: *Dean's teacher has really got it in for him.* **18 have nothing against** used to say that you do not dislike someone or something: *I have nothing against hard work, but this is ridiculous.* → see also **be had** (HAD)

have sth/sb on phr v [T] **1** [**have sth ↔ on**] also **have got sth on** BrE to be wearing some-

[H]

GRAMMAR NOTE: for and **since**
Use **for** with periods of time: *I've been waiting here for 25 minutes.* | *We've lived here for 6 years.*
Use **since** with the date or time when something started: *I've been waiting here since 7 o'clock.* | *We've lived here since 1992.*

thing: *Mark had on a denim jacket.* **2 be having sb on** *BrE* to make someone believe something that is not true: *He said he was the Managing Director? He was having you on!*

have sth **out** *phr v* [T] **1** [**have** sth **out**] to have something removed from your body, usually by a medical operation: *She had her appendix out last year.* **2 have it out with sb** *informal* to talk to someone directly and honestly about something bad they have done or a problem they have caused: *I think it's time you had it out with Richard.*

have³ **have to do sth** also **have got to do sth** *modal verb* **1** if you have to do something, you must do it because someone makes you do it, or a situation makes it necessary: *You don't have to answer all the questions.* | *Susan hates having to get up early.* **2** used to say that it is important that something happens: *You have to believe me!* | *There has to be an end to all this violence.* **3** used to tell someone how to do something: *First you have to take the wheel off.* **4** used to say that you are sure that something will happen or is true: *He has to be lying – there's no other explanation.*

USAGE NOTE: have to, have got to, and must

Use all of these to talk about what it is necessary to do. Use **have to** to say that something is necessary, and you do not have a choice about it: *I'm sorry – I have to go now.* | *He has to work late tonight.* Use **must** to say that something is necessary, and that you know it is a good idea: *I really must study harder.* | *We must visit Grandma sometime soon.* Use **have got** instead of **have to** or **must** in order to emphasize how important something is: *I've got to talk to him.* The past tense of **have to**, **have got to**, and **must** is **had to**: *I had to talk to him.*

---

ha·ven /'heɪvən/ *n* [C,U] a place where people feel safe and happy

have·n't /'hævnt/ *v* the short form of 'have not'

hav·oc /'hævək/ *n* [U] a very confused situation in which there is a lot of damage: **cause havoc** *The storm caused havoc everywhere.* | **wreak havoc (on)** *The war will wreak havoc on the country's economy.*

hawk /hɔːk‖hɒːk/ *n* [C] a large wild bird that eats small birds and animals

haw·thorn /'hɔːθɔːn‖'hɒːθɔːrn/ *n* [C,U] a small tree that has small white flowers and red berries (BERRY)

hay /heɪ/ *n* [U] grass that has been cut and dried and is used as food for animals

hay fe·ver /'. ,../ *n* [U] a medical condition like a bad COLD, caused by breathing in dust from plants

hay·stack /'heɪstæk/ *n* [C] a large pile of stored hay

hay·wire /'heɪwaɪəll-waɪr/ *adj* **go haywire** *informal* to start working in completely the wrong way: *My computer's going haywire again.*

haz·ard¹ /'hæzədll-ərd/ *n* [C] something that may be dangerous or cause accidents: *a health hazard* —**hazardous** *adj*: *hazardous waste*

hazard² *v* **hazard a guess** to say something that is only a suggestion or guess: *I don't know how much he earns, but I could hazard a guess.*

haze /heɪz/ *n* [singular,U] smoke, dust, or mist in the air: *a heat haze*

ha·zel¹ /'heɪzəl/ *adj* hazel eyes are light greenish-brown

hazel² *n* [C,U] a small tree that produces nuts

haz·y /'heɪzi/ *adj* **1** air that is hazy is not clear because there is smoke, dust, or mist in it: *a hazy summer morning* **2** not clear or exact: *My memories of that night are a little hazy.*

he /i, hi; *strong* hiː/ *pron* [used as the subject of a verb] used to talk about a male person or animal that has already been mentioned: *"How's Josh?" "Oh, he's fine."*

head

forehead
eyebrow
ear
eye
cheek
nose
nostrils
dimple
mouth
lip
neck
chin

head¹ /hed/ *n* **1** [C] the top part of your body that has your eyes, mouth, brain etc in it: *He turned his head to look at her.* **2** [C] your mind: *Terry's head is filled with strange ideas.* | **do sth in your head** (=calculate something in your mind): *You have to work out the answer in your head.* **3** [C] the leader or most important person in a group or organization: *the head waiter* | **+ of** *the former head of the FBI* | **the head(teacher)** *BrE* (=the teacher who is in charge of a school): *Any student caught smoking will have to see the head.* **4** [singular] the top or front of something, or the most important part of it: *Write your name at the head of the page.* **5 go over sb's head a)** to be too difficult for someone to understand: *I could see that the discussion was going over their heads.* **b)** to ask a more important person to deal with something than the person you would normally ask: *I annoyed her by going over her head to the director.* **6 get sth into your head** *informal* to understand and realize something: *I wish he'd get it into his head that school is important.* **7 keep/lose your head** to behave sensibly or stupidly in a difficult situation **8 keep your head above water** to succeed in continuing, even though you have a lot of problems with money **9 go to sb's head** to have a strong effect on someone, so that they do silly things: *She promised that she wouldn't let success go to her head.* **10 I can't make head nor tail of** used when you are completely unable to understand something: *I can't make head or tail of these instructions.* **11 come to a head** if a problem comes to a head, it becomes worse and you have to do something about it immediately:

The situation came to a head when the workers went on strike. **12 a head/per head** for each person: *The meal worked out at £15 a head.* **13 laugh/shout/scream your head off** *informal* to laugh, shout etc a lot

head² *v* **1** [I,T] to go or make something go in a particular direction: **+ for/towards/up etc** *a boat heading for the shore* **2** [T] to be in charge of a government, organization, or group: *Most one-parent families are headed by women.* **3 be heading for** also **be headed for** *AmE* if you are heading for a situation, it is likely to happen: *The company was heading for disaster.* **4** [T] to be at the top of a list, a page, or a group of words: *The longest list was headed "Problems."*

head sb/sth ↔ **off** *phr v* [T] to stop someone moving in a particular direction by moving in front of them: *The police headed them off at the crossroads.*

head·ache /ˈhedeɪk/ *n* [C] **1** a pain in your head: *I've got a headache.* **2** a serious problem that you worry about

head·dress /ˈhed-dres/ *n* [C] something that someone wears on their head for decoration at a ceremony or special occasion: *a feathered head-dress*

head·gear /ˈhedgɪəll-gɪr/ *n* [U] hats and other things that you wear on your head

head·ing /ˈhedɪŋ/ *n* [C] the title at the top of a piece of writing

head·lamp /ˈhedlæmp/ *n* [C] *BrE* a HEADLIGHT

head·land /ˈhedlənd/ *n* [C] an area of land that sticks out into the sea

head·light /ˈhedlaɪt/ *n* [C] one of the large lights at the front of a vehicle ➡ see picture at CAR

head·line /ˈhedlaɪn/ *n* **1** [C] the title of a newspaper report, printed in large letters **2 the headlines** the important points of the main news stories

head·long /ˈhedlɒŋll-lɔːŋ/ *adv* **1 rush headlong into sth** to do something important without thinking carefully about it first: *Fran isn't the type to rush headlong into marriage.* **2** with your head going first: *Ben went tumbling headlong down the hill.*

head·mas·ter /ˌhedˈmɑːstəllˈhedˌmæstər/ *n* [C] *BrE* a male teacher who is in charge of a school; PRINCIPAL *AmE*

head·mis·tress /ˌhedˈmɪstrɪsllˈhedˌmɪs-/ *n* [C] *BrE* a female teacher who is in charge of a school; PRINCIPAL *AmE*

head·on /ˌ. ˈ.◂/ *adv* **1 meet/crash/hit head-on** if two vehicles meet head-on, the front part of one vehicle hits the front part of the other: *A car and a truck had collided head-on.* **2** in a direct and determined way: *She decided to face her difficulties head-on.* —**head-on** *adj*: *a head-on collision*

head·phones /ˈhedfəʊnzll-foʊnz/ *n* [plural] a piece of equipment that you wear over your ears to listen to a radio or recording

head·quar·ters /ˈhedˌkwɔːtəz, ˌhedˈkwɔːtəzll-ɔːrtərz/ *n* [plural] also **HQ** the place from which a company, organization, or military action is controlled

head·room /ˈhed-rʊm, -ruːm/ *n* [U] the amount of space above your head inside a car, or above a car when it is under a bridge

head start /ˌ. ˈ./ *n* [C] an advantage that helps you to be successful: *His education gave him a head start.*

head·stone /ˈhedstəʊnll-stoʊn/ *n* [C] a piece of stone on a grave, that has the dead person's name on it

head·strong /ˈhedstrɒŋll-strɔːŋ/ *adj* very determined to do what you want: *a headstrong child*

head·way /ˈhedweɪ/ *n* **make headway** to come closer to achieving something: **+ towards/with/in etc** *We have made little headway towards a solution.*

head·y /ˈhedi/ *adj* making you feel excited, or as if you are drunk: *the heady days of their youth*

heal /hiːl/ *v* [I,T] also **heal up** if a wound or broken bone heals, or if someone heals it, it becomes healthy again: *The scratch on her finger healed quickly.* —**healer** *n* [C]

health /helθ/ *n* [U] **1** the general condition of your body, and how healthy you are: *Smoking can damage your health* | **in good/poor etc health** *Elsie's not in very good health.* **2** how successful an economic system or organization is: *the health of the economy*

health centre /ˈ. ˌ../ *n* [C] *BrE* a place where there are several doctors and nurses, where you can get medical advice and treatment

health club /ˈ. ./ *n* [C] a place where you pay to use a GYM, exercise equipment etc

health food /ˈ. ./ *n* [C,U] food that contains only natural substances: *a health food shop*

health·ful /ˈhelθfəl/ *adj* *AmE* good for your body: *healthful eating habits*

health·y /ˈhelθi/ *adj* **1** strong and not likely to become ill: *a healthy baby girl* ➡ opposite UNHEALTHY **2** good for your body or your mind: *a healthy diet* | *It's not healthy for her to depend on him like that.* **3** strong and successful —**healthily** *adv*

heap¹ /hiːp/ *n* [C] a large untidy pile of things: **+ of** *a heap of newspapers* | **in a heap** *His clothes lay in a heap by the bed.* ➡ see picture at PILE

heap² *v* **1** [T] also **heap up** to put a lot of things on top of each other in an untidy way: **be heaped with** *plates heaped with food* **2 heap praise/criticism/insults on** to praise, criticize etc someone a lot

hear

Mike didn't hear the phone because
he was listening to music.

hear /hɪəllhɪr/ *v* **heard** /hɜːdllhɜːrd/, **heard**, **hearing** **1** [I,T] if you hear something, a sound comes into your ears: *Can you hear that noise?* | *She called his name but he didn't hear.* | **hear sb doing sth** *I thought I heard someone knocking.* **2** [I,T] to be told or find out some

H

information: **+ (that)** *We were sorry to hear that you were ill.* | **+ about** *Where did you hear about the job, Miss Blair?* **3 (do) you hear (me)?** *spoken* said when you are giving someone an order and want to be certain that they will obey you: *Be home by ten, you hear?* **4 I won't hear of sth** *spoken* used to say that you will not allow something, especially because you want to help someone: *I offered to pay, but he wouldn't hear of it.* **5 hear a case** if a case is heard, a court listens to the EVIDENCE, and decides whether or not someone is guilty: *The case will be heard on July 16th.* **6 hear! hear!** *especially BrE* used in a meeting or discussion to say that you agree with the person who is speaking

hear from sb *phr v* [T] to get news or information from someone, usually in a letter or by phone: *Have you heard from Jane?*

hear of sb/sth *phr v* [T] **have heard of** to know that someone or something exists because you have been told about them: *Phil Merton? I've never heard of him.*

hear sb **out** *phr v* [T] to listen to someone's explanation for something, without interrupting: *I know you're angry, but just hear me out.*

hear·ing /ˈhɪərɪŋ‖ˈhɪr-/ *n* **1** [U] the sense that you use to hear sounds: *My hearing's not as good as it used to be.* **2** [C] a meeting of a court or committee to find out the facts about something **3 a (fair) hearing** an opportunity for someone to explain their actions or ideas: *The company can't get rid of you without giving you a fair hearing.*

hearing aid /ˈ.. ./ *n* [C] a small thing to make sounds louder, that you put in your ear if you cannot hear well

hearing im·paired /ˈ.. .,./ *adj* unable to hear well or to hear at all

hear·say /ˈhɪəseɪ‖ˈhɪr-/ *n* [U] something that other people have told you but which may not be true: *It's just hearsay, but they tell me he's leaving.*

hearse /hɜːs‖hɜːrs/ *n* [C] a large car for carrying a dead body in a COFFIN at a funeral

heart /hɑːt‖hɑːrt/ *n* **1** [C] the organ inside your chest that pumps blood around your body: *Tom could feel his heart beating faster.* **2** [C,U] your strongest emotions and your most true feelings: *He's strict, but he has a kind heart.* | **in your heart** *I knew in my heart that he was right.* | **with all your heart** *She wished with all her heart that she had never met him.* | **at heart** (=used to say what someone's character is really like) *I'm just a kid at heart.* **3** [C] a shape used to mean a heart or love → see picture at SHAPES **4 the heart of sth** the centre or most important part of something: *deep in the heart of the countryside* | **the heart of the matter/problem/question etc** *Let's get to the heart of the matter.* **5 know/learn sth by heart** to correctly remember all of something: *Learn this tune by heart before next week's lesson.* **6 hearts** a group of playing cards with a red heart shape printed on them: *the queen of hearts* **7 sb's heart sank** used to say that someone suddenly became very sad or disappointed: *Bert's heart sank when he saw the mess.* **8 to your heart's content** as much as you want to: *You can run around here to your heart's content.* **9 kind-hearted/cold-hearted/hard-hearted etc** having a kind, unkind, cruel etc character **10 take/lose heart** to begin to have

more hope or to stop having hope: *I've failed my driving test so many times I'm beginning to lose heart.* **11 not have the heart to do sth** *spoken* to be unable to do something because you do not want to make someone unhappy: *I didn't have the heart to tell her the truth.* **12 sb's heart isn't in it** *spoken* if someone's heart is not in something, they do not really want to do it because they are worrying about something else: *He tried to work, but his heart wasn't in it.* **13 sb's heart goes out to sb** to feel a lot of sympathy for someone

heart·ache /ˈhɑːteɪk‖ˈhɑːrt-/ *n* [U] a feeling of great sadness: *the heartache felt by children when their parents divorce*

heart at·tack /ˈ. .,./ *n* [C] a serious medical condition in which a person's heart suddenly stops beating normally or regularly

heart·beat /ˈhɑːtbiːt‖ˈhɑːrt-/ *n* [C,U] the action or the sound of a heart pushing blood through the body: *The doctor listened to the baby's heartbeat.*

heart·break /ˈhɑːtbreɪk‖ˈhɑːrt-/ *n* [U] a strong feeling of sadness, especially about a person you love

heart·break·ing /ˈhɑːtˌbreɪkɪŋ‖ˈhɑːrt-/ *adj* making you feel very sad: *heartbreaking pictures of starving children*

heart·brok·en /ˈhɑːtˌbrəʊkən‖ˈhɑːrt.broʊ-/ *adj* very sad because of something that has happened: *I don't know how to tell him about the accident – he'll be heartbroken.*

heart dis·ease /ˈ. .,./ *n* [U] a medical condition which prevents someone's heart from working normally

heart·ened /ˈhɑːtnd‖ˈhɑːr-/ *adj* feeling happier and more hopeful —**hearten** *v* [T] → opposite DISHEARTENED

heart·en·ing /ˈhɑːtnɪŋ‖ˈhɑːr-/ *adj* making you feel happier and more hopeful: *heartening news* → opposite DISHEARTENING

heart fail·ure /ˈ. .,./ *n* [U] a serious medical condition in which someone's heart stops working, usually resulting in death

heart·felt /ˈhɑːtfelt‖ˈhɑːrt-/ *adj* felt very strongly and sincerely: *heartfelt thanks*

hearth /hɑːθ‖hɑːrθ/ *n* [C] the part of the floor around a FIREPLACE

heart·i·ly /ˈhɑːtɪli‖ˈhɑːr-/ *adv* **1** loudly and cheerfully: *He laughed heartily.* **2** very much or completely: *I'm heartily sick of hearing about her problems.*

heart·land /ˈhɑːtlənd‖ˈhɑːrt-/ *n* [C] the part of a country where an activity or belief is based or is strongest: *the industrial heartland of England*

heart·less /ˈhɑːtləs‖ˈhɑːrt-/ *adj* cruel or not feeling any sympathy: *This was a heartless and insensitive way to treat an elderly woman.* —**heartlessly** *adv*

heart·rend·ing /ˈhɑːtˌrendɪŋ‖ˈhɑːrt-/ *adj* literary making you feel very sympathetic towards someone: *heartrending sobs*

heart·strings /ˈhɑːtˌstrɪŋz‖ˈhɑːrt-/ *n* **tug/pull on sb's heartstrings** to make someone feel a lot of sympathy or sorrow

heart-to-heart /ˌ.. .ˈ. ◂/ *n* [C] a conversation in which two people say honestly what they think or feel: *It's time you and I had a heart-to-heart.* —**heart-to-heart** *adj*

heart·warm·ing /ˈhɑːtˌwɔːmɪŋ‖ˈhɑːrt,wɔːr-/ adj making you feel happy and hopeful: a heart-warming story

heart·y /ˈhɑːtɪ‖ˈhɑːrti/ adj **1** very cheerful and friendly: We were given a hearty welcome. **2** a hearty meal or APPETITE is very large

heat¹ /hiːt/ n **1** [U] the temperature of something when it is warm or hot: the heat of the sun **2 the heat a)** very hot weather: the heat a constantly complaining about the heat. **b)** AmE the system in a house that keeps it warm; HEAT-ING BrE **3 in the heat of the moment** if you do something in the heat of the moment, you do it without thinking, especially because you are excited or angry: In the heat of the moment, I said some things I didn't mean. **4** [C] a part of a race or competition. The winners of each heat compete against each other in the next part.

heat² v [I,T] also **heat up** to become warm or hot, or to make something warm or hot: This house is very expensive to heat.

heat·ed /ˈhiːtɪd/ adj **1** kept warm by using a heater: a heated swimming pool **2 heated argument/discussion/debate** an argument etc in which people become very angry and excited

heat·er /ˈhiːtəll-ər/ n [C] a machine used for heating air or water

heath /hiːθ/ n [C] an area of land where rough grass and small plants grow

hea·then /ˈhiːðən/ n [C] old-fashioned someone who does not belong to your religion —**heathen** adj

heath·er /ˈheðəll-ər/ n [C,U] a small bush with purple flowers that grows on hills

heat·ing /ˈhiːtɪŋ/ n [U] BrE the system in a house that keeps it warm; HEAT AmE

heatwave /ˈ..../ n [C] a period of unusually hot weather

heave /hiːv/ v **1** [I,T] to pull, throw, or lift something heavy with a lot of effort: She heaved the box onto the back of the truck. **2 heave a sigh** to breathe out loudly, because you have stopped worrying about something: We can all heave a sigh of relief now that it's over. —**heave** n [C]

heav·en /ˈhevən/ n [U] **1** also **Heaven** the place where many people believe God lives and good people go after they die → compare HELL **2** informal something that you like very much: It was heaven to lie back in a nice hot bath. **3 for heaven's sake** spoken used when you are annoyed or angry: For heaven's sake, shut up! **4 heaven forbid** spoken used to emphasize that you hope something will not happen: And if, heaven forbid, he has an accident, what should I do then?

heav·en·ly /ˈhevənli/ adj **1** [only before noun] relating to heaven: a heavenly choir of angels **2** spoken very good or pleasant: Isn't this weather heavenly?

heavenly bod·y /ˌ... ˈ.../ n [C] a star, PLANET, or moon

heav·ens /ˈhevənz/ n **1 (Good) Heavens!** spoken used when you are surprised or slightly annoyed: Good Heavens! Where have you been? **2 the heavens** literary the sky

heav·i·ly /ˈhevɪli/ adv very much or a lot: **drink/smoke heavily** He's been drinking heavily since the accident. | **rain/snow heavily** It had rained heavily all night. | **heavily dependent/reliant/influenced** Our work is heavily dependent on computers.

heav·y /ˈhevi/ adj

heavy

1 weighing a lot: I can't lift this box – it's too heavy. | How heavy are you? (=how much do you weigh?) **2** large in amount: Traffic is heavy on the A19. | **heavy rain/snow** Heavy snowfalls closed roads in the area. | a heavy smoker/drinker I like wine, but I'm not a heavy drinker. **3 heavy day/schedule/timetable** one that is very busy and full of activities **4** very serious or complicated: It got a bit heavy when she started talking about death. | **heavy going** (=difficult): I find her novels pretty heavy going. **5** heavy food or a heavy meal makes your stomach feel too full: a heavy lunch **6 with a heavy heart** feeling very sad —**heaviness** n [U]

heavy bags

heavy-du·ty /ˌ.. ˈ../ adj strong enough to be used often or for hard work: heavy-duty plastic gloves

heavy-hand·ed /ˌ.. ˈ.·◂/ adj dealing with people in a way that does not consider their feelings: heavy-handed police tactics

heavy met·al /ˌ.. ˈ.·◂/ n [U] a type of very loud ROCK music with a strong beat

heav·y·weight /ˈheviweit/ n [C] **1** someone who has a lot of power and importance: one of the heavyweights of the movie industry **2** a BOXER from the heaviest weight group —**heavyweight** adj: the heavyweight champion of the world

heck /hek/ interjection used to emphasize what you are saying when you are annoyed: Oh, heck! I've lost my glasses.

heck·le /ˈhekəl/ v [I,T] to interrupt someone who is making a speech or performing —**heckler** n [C] —**heckling** n [U]

hec·tare /ˈhektɑː, -teəll-ter/ n [C] a unit for measuring an area of land, equal to 10,000 square metres

hec·tic /ˈhektɪk/ adj very busy or full of activity: It's been a really hectic week.

he'd /id, hid; strong hiːd/ the short form of 'he would' or 'he had': I'm sure he'd drive you there. | He'd never been a good dancer.

hedge¹ /hedʒ/ n [C] a row of bushes used to separate one field or garden from another → see colour picture on page 243

GRAMMAR NOTE: the past progressive
You use the **past progressive** to describe a situation or action that continued for a limited period in the past: People were shouting and screaming. You use the **simple past** to say that something happened in the middle of an activity: They **arrived** while we **were having** dinner.

hedge² /v/ **1** [I] to avoid giving a direct answer: *I got the feeling he was hedging.* **2 hedge your bets** to reduce your chances of failing by trying several different possibilities instead of one

hedge·hog /ˈhedʒhɒg‖-hɔːg, -hɑːg/ *n* [C] a small animal whose body is covered in stiff sharp points

hedge·row /ˈhedʒrəʊ‖-roʊ/ *n* [C] *especially BrE* a line of bushes and small trees growing along the edge of a field or road

he·don·is·m /ˈhiːdənɪzəm/ *n* [U] the belief that pleasure is the most important thing in life —**hedonist** *n* [C] —**hedonistic** /ˌhiːdənˈɪstɪk◂/ *adj*

heed¹ /hiːd/ *v* [T] *formal* to pay attention to advice or a warning

heed² *n* [U] **take heed of/pay heed to** *formal* to pay attention to something important: *Roy paid no heed to her warning.*

heed·less /ˈhiːdləs/ *adj literary* **heedless of** not paying attention to something important: *Blake rode on, heedless of the dangers ahead.*

heel /hiːl/ *n* **1** [C] the back part of your foot **2** [C] the bottom part of a shoe that is under your heel, which is usually thicker than the other parts: *boots with three inch heels* ➝ see picture at SHOE

hef·ty /ˈhefti/ *adj* **1** big, heavy, or strong: *a hefty punch* **2 a hefty price/sum etc** a large amount of money: *Parking on the pavement could get you a hefty fine.*

heif·er /ˈhefə‖-ər/ *n* [C] a young female cow

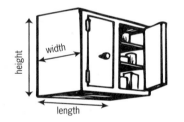

height

height /haɪt/ *n* **1** [C,U] how tall or high someone or something is: *Howard and Ben are about the same height.* ➝ see colour picture on page 244 **2 the height of** when something is the strongest, busiest, best etc it can ever be: *Mini skirts were the height of fashion.* | *the height of the tourist season*

height·en /ˈhaɪtn/ *v* [I,T] to increase or make something increase: *The movie has heightened public awareness of AIDS.*

heights /haɪts/ *n* [plural] **1** a high position or place: *I've always been afraid of heights.* **2 to new heights** to a higher or more successful level: *Prices jumped to new heights on Wednesday.*

hei·nous /ˈheɪnəs/ *adj formal* extremely shocking and bad: *a heinous crime*

heir /eə‖er/ *n* [C] someone who has the legal right to receive the money, property, or title of a person who has died

heir·ess /ˈeərɪs, ˈeəres‖-er-/ *n* [C] a woman who

has the legal right to receive the money, property, or title of a person who has died

heir·loom /ˈeəluːm‖ˈer-/ *n* [C] a valuable object that has been owned by the same family for many years: *Carrie's ring is a family heirloom.*

held /held/ the past tense and past participle of HOLD

hel·i·cop·ter /ˈhelɪkɒptə‖-kɑːptər/ *n* [C] an aircraft with long thin metal parts on top which spin very fast to make it fly ➝ see colour picture on page 669

he·li·um /ˈhiːliəm/ *n* [U] a gas that is lighter than air

he'll /il, hil; *strong* hiːl/ the short form of 'he will' or 'he shall'

hell /hel/ *n* **1** also **Hell** [singular] the place where, according to some religions, bad people are punished after death **2** [U] a situation, experience, or place that is very difficult or unpleasant: **be hell** *My schooldays were absolute hell.* | **go through hell/put sb through hell** *My mother went through hell with my father's drinking.* **3** [singular] *spoken* an impolite way to emphasize a question or statement: *Get the hell out of here!* | **what/why/where etc the hell?** *Where the hell have you been?* **4 a/one hell of a** *spoken* used to emphasize the idea that something is very big, very good etc: *He's a hell of a salesman.* | *a hell of a lot of money* **5 for the hell of it** *spoken* for no particular reason or purpose: *We threw a party, just for the hell of it.* **6 all hell broke loose** *informal* used to say that a situation suddenly became very noisy or violent **7 from hell** used to say that someone or something is the worst possible example of that kind of person or thing: *the teenager from hell* **8 like hell** *informal* doing something a lot or using a lot of effort: *We had to work like hell to get the job done on time.*

hel·lo also **hallo** *BrE,* **hullo** *BrE* /həˈləʊ, he-‖-ˈloʊ-/ *interjection* **1** used when you meet or greet someone: *Hello, my name is Betty.* **2** used when you answer the telephone or start a telephone conversation: *"Hello?" "Hello, is Chad there?"* **3 say hello** to have a quick conversation with someone: *Joy stopped by to say hello today.*

helm /helm/ *n* **at the helm** in charge of a group, team, or organization: *With Davies at the helm, the team is bound to succeed.*

hel·met /ˈhelmɪt/ *n* [C] a hard hat that covers and protects your head: *a motorcycle helmet* ➝ see colour picture on page 636

help¹ /help/ *v* **1** [I,T] to make it possible or easier for someone to do something: **help sb (to) do sth** *Is there anything I can do to help?* | *Do you want me to help you move that table?* | **help sb with sth** *Dad, can you help me with my homework?* **2** [I,T] to improve a situation: *It might help to talk to someone about your problems.* | *Brushing your teeth helps prevent cavities.* **3 can't/couldn't help** to be unable to stop yourself from doing something: *I just couldn't help laughing.* **4 I can't help it** *spoken* said when you think you should not be blamed for something: *I can't help it if she lost the stupid book!* **5 help yourself (to sth)** to take something that you want, such as food, without asking: *Help yourself to anything in the fridge.*

6 help! *spoken* used to call someone to help you because you are in danger

help out *phr v* [I,T **help** sb **out**] to help someone because they are very busy, have a lot of problems etc: *Sarah's going to help out with the cooking tonight.*

help[2] *n* **1** [U] when you help someone: *Do you need any help with that?* **2 with the help of** using: *I opened the can with the help of a knife.* **3 be a lot of help/be a real help** to be useful: *The instructions weren't a lot of help.* **4** [U] something that saves you from danger: *Go get help, quickly!*

help·er /'helpǝll-ǝr/ *n* [C] someone who helps another person

help·ful /'helpfǝl/ *adj* **1** useful: *The map was really helpful.* **2** willing to help: *Everyone was so helpful.* —**helpfully** *adv* —**helpfulness** *n* [U]

help·ing /'helpɪŋ/ *n* [C] an amount of a particular food; SERVING: *a huge helping of potatoes*

helping verb /'.. ,./ *n* [C] *AmE* an AUXILIARY VERB

help·less /'helplǝs/ *adj* unable to look after yourself or protect yourself: *I lay helpless in my hospital bed.* —**helplessly** *adv* —**helplessness** *n* [U]

hem /hem/ *n* [C] the edge of a piece of clothing that is turned under and stitched down

hem sb ↔ **in** *phr v* [T] to completely surround someone so that they cannot get away: *Police gathered around the protesters, hemming them in.*

hem·i·sphere /'hemɪˌsfɪǝll-fɪr/ *n* [C] one of the two halves of the earth: *the northern hemisphere*

he·mo·phil·i·a /ˌhiːmǝ'fɪliǝ/ the American spelling of HAEMOPHILIA

hem·or·rhage /'hemǝrɪdʒ/ the American spelling of HAEMORRHAGE

hem·or·rhoids /'hemǝrɔɪdz/ the American spelling of HAEMORRHOIDS

hemp /hemp/ *n* [U] a plant used for making rope, cloth, and the drug CANNABIS

hen /hen/ *n* [C] a fully grown female bird, especially a female chicken

hence /hens/ *adv formal* **1** for this reason: *The sugar from the grapes remains in the wine, hence the sweet taste.* **2 two weeks/six months etc hence** two weeks, six months etc from now

hence·forth /ˌhens'fɔːθll-'fɔːrθ/ also **hence·for·ward** /-'fɔːwǝdll'fɔːrwǝrd/ *adv formal* from now on: *The Great Hall will henceforth be known as "Phillips Hall".*

hench·man /'hentʃmǝn/ *n* [C] someone who supports a politician or a criminal by doing unpleasant things for them

hen·pecked /'henpekt/ *adj* a henpecked husband is controlled by his wife and always obeys her

hep·a·ti·tis /ˌhepǝ'taɪtɪs◂/ *n* [U] a disease of the LIVER that makes your skin turn yellow

her /ǝ, hǝ; *strong* hɜːllǝr, hǝr; *strong* hɜːr/ *determiner, pron* **1** belonging to or concerning a female person or animal that has already been mentioned: *That's her new car.* **2** the object form of 'she': *Chris saw her last week.* **3** used to talk about a country or ship that has already been mentioned

her·ald[1] /'herǝld/ *v* [T] **1** to be a sign that something is going to happen soon: *Familiar music heralded another news bulletin.* **2** to publicly praise someone or something: *He was heralded as the poet of his generation.*

herald[2] *n* [C] **herald of** a sign that something will soon happen: *daffodils, the first bright heralds of spring*

herb /hɜːbllɜːrb, hɜːrb/ *n* [C] a plant added to food to improve its taste, or used to make medicine —**herbal** *adj*: *herbal remedies*

her·bi·vore /'hɜːbɪˌvɔːll'hɜːrbɪˌvɔːr, 'ɜːr-/ *n* [C] an animal that only eats plants —**herbivorous** /hɜː'bɪvǝrǝsllhɜːr-, ɜːr-/ *adj* →compare CARNIVORE

herd[1] /hɜːdllhɜːrd/ *n* [C] a group of animals of the same kind that lives and feeds together: *a herd of cattle*

herd[2] *v* [I,T] to form a group, or to make people or animals move together as a group: *The tour guide herded us onto the bus.*

here /hɪǝllhɪr/ *adv* **1** in or to this place: *I'm going to stay here with Kim.* | *We came here on Dad's birthday.* **2** if a period of time is here, it has begun: *Spring is here!* **3** at this point in a discussion or piece of writing: *The subject is too difficult to explain here.* **4** used when you give someone something: **here's** *Here's a spade – get digging!* | **here you are** (=used when giving someone something they have asked for): *"Could you bring me a glass of water, please?" "Here you are, sir."* **5** used to say that you have arrived somewhere, or that someone you have been waiting for or looking for has arrived: *Here comes the bus.* | **here's ...** *Here's the restaurant I was telling you about.* | **here you are/here he is etc** *Here you are – we've been looking everywhere for you.* **6** used when you are talking about someone or something that is with you: *Laura here is a great cook.* **7 here goes** said before you do something exciting, dangerous, or new: *Are you ready? OK, here goes.*

here·a·bouts /ˌhɪǝrǝ'baʊts, 'hɪǝrǝbaʊtsllˌhɪr-, 'hɪr-/ *adv* around or near the place where you are: *There aren't many shops hereabouts.*

here·af·ter /ˌhɪǝr'ɑːftǝllhɪr'æftǝr/ *adv formal* from this time: *two groups hereafter referred to as groups A and B*

here·by /ˌhɪǝ'baɪ, 'hɪǝbaɪllˌhɪr-, 'hɪr-/ *adv formal* as a result of this statement: *I hereby pronounce you man and wife.*

he·red·i·ta·ry /hɪ'redɪˌtǝrill-teri/ *adj* a hereditary quality, ability, or disease is passed to a child by its parents: *Heart disease is often hereditary.*

he·red·i·ty /hɪ'redɪti/ *n* [U] the process by which physical or mental qualities pass from a parent to a child

here·in /ˌhɪǝr'ɪnllˌhɪr-/ *adv formal* in this place, situation, document etc: *the conditions stated herein*

her·e·sy /'herǝsi/ *n* [C,U] a belief that a religious or political group considers to be wrong or evil

her·e·tic /'herǝtɪk/ *n* [C] someone whose beliefs are considered to be wrong or evil —**heretical** /hɪ'retɪkǝl/ *adj*

her·i·tage /'herɪtɪdʒ/ *n* [C,U] the traditional be-

H

liefs, customs etc that have been in a society for a long time: *Ireland's musical heritage*

her·mit /ˈhɜːmɪt‖ˈhɜːr-/ *n* [C] someone who prefers to live away from other people

her·ni·a /ˈhɜːniə‖ˈhɜːr-/ *n* [C] a medical condition in which an organ pushes through the skin or muscle that covers it; RUPTURE

he·ro /ˈhɪərəʊ‖ˈhɪroʊ/ *n* [C], *plural* **heroes**
1 someone who is admired for doing something very brave or good: *He became a local hero after saving a boy's life.* **2** the man who is the main character in a book, film, or play ➡ see also HEROINE

he·ro·ic /hɪˈrəʊɪk‖-ˈroʊ-/ *adj* extremely brave, strong, or determined: *a heroic act of bravery | It was a heroic effort.*

he·ro·ics /hɪˈrəʊɪks‖-ˈroʊ-/ *n* [plural] language or behaviour that seems brave but is really silly or dangerous: *Don't try any heroics.*

her·o·in /ˈherəʊɪn‖-roʊ-/ *n* [U] a very strong illegal drug made from MORPHINE

her·o·ine /ˈherəʊɪn‖-roʊ-/ *n* [C] **1** the woman who is the main character in a book, film, or play **2** a woman who is admired for doing something very brave or good

her·o·is·m /ˈherəʊɪzəm‖-roʊ-/ *n* [U] great courage: *stories of heroism and daring*

her·on /ˈherən/ *n* [C] a large wild bird with very long legs and a long beak, that lives near water

her·ring /ˈherɪŋ/ *n* [C,U] a long thin silver sea fish

hers /hɜːz‖hɜːrz/ *pron* the possessive form of 'she'; belonging to or concerning a female person or animal that has already been mentioned: *That's my car. This is hers. | Angela is a friend of hers.*

her·self /əˈself, hə-; *strong* hɜː-‖ərˈself, hər-; *strong* hɜːr-/ *pron* **1** the REFLEXIVE form of 'she': *She made herself a cup of coffee. | Julie hurt herself.* **2** the strong form of 'she', used to emphasize the subject or object of a sentence: *It's true! Vicky told me so herself.* **3 (all) by herself** alone or without help from anyone else: *She went to the concert by herself. | Lynn made dinner all by herself.* **4 (all) to herself** for her own use: *Alison had the whole place to herself that night.* **5 be/feel yourself** to feel well and in a normal state

he's /ɪz, hɪz; *strong* hiːz/ the short form of 'he is' or 'he has': *He's my brother. | He's lost his keys.*

hes·i·tant /ˈhezɪtənt/ *adj* slow to do something because you are nervous or uncertain: *a hesitant smile*

hes·i·tate /ˈhezɪteɪt/ *v* **1** [I] to pause for a moment before doing or saying something: *She hesitated before answering his question.* **2 don't hesitate to do sth** used to tell someone that you are very willing for them to do something: *Don't hesitate to call me if you need any help.*

hes·i·ta·tion /ˌhezɪˈteɪʃən/ *n* [C,U] when you hesitate: *There was a slight hesitation before he answered. | have no hesitation in doing sth* (=be very willing): *I have no hesitation in recommending him for the job.*

het·e·ro·ge·ne·ous /ˌhetərəʊˈdʒiːniəs‖-roʊ-/ also **het·e·ro·ge·nous** /ˌhetəˈrɒdʒənəs‖ -ˈrɑː-/ *adj formal* having parts or members that

are very different from each other: *a heterogeneous group of pictures* ➡ compare HOMOGENEOUS

het·e·ro·sex·u·al /ˌhetərəˈsekʃuəl/ *adj* sexually attracted to people of the opposite sex —**heterosexual** *n* [C] ➡ compare BISEXUAL[1], HOMOSEXUAL

het up /ˌhet ˈʌp/ *adj BrE* anxious: *You get het up over really silly things.*

hex·a·gon /ˈheksəgən‖-gɑːn/ *n* [C] a flat shape with six sides —**hexagonal** /hekˈsægənəl/ *adj*

hey /heɪ/ *interjection* used to get someone's attention or to show someone you are surprised or annoyed: *Hey! Look who's here!*

hey·day /ˈheɪdeɪ/ *n* [C] the time when someone or something was most popular, successful, or powerful: **sb's/sth's heyday** *In its heyday, the mill produced flour for the whole area.*

hi /haɪ/ *interjection informal* hello: *Hi! How are you?*

hi·a·tus /haɪˈeɪtəs/ *n* [singular] *formal* a pause in an activity

hi·ber·nate /ˈhaɪbəneɪt‖-ər-/ *v* [I] if an animal hibernates, it sleeps all the time during winter —**hibernation** /ˌhaɪbəˈneɪʃən‖-bər-/ *n* [U]

hic·cup also **hiccough** /ˈhɪkʌp, -kəp/ *n* [C] **1** when your throat makes repeated short sounds that you cannot control: **have/get (the) hiccups** *The baby always gets hiccups after feeding.* **2** a small problem: *The trip was a complete success, despite a few hiccups.*

hiccup² *v* [I] **-pped, -pping** to have hiccups

hid·den /ˈhɪdn/ *adj* difficult to see, find, or notice: *hidden cameras | There may have been a hidden meaning in what he said.*

hide¹ /haɪd/ **hid** /hɪd/, **hiding, hidden** /ˈhɪdn/ *v* **1** [T] to put something in a place where no one else can see or find it: *Suzy's gone and hidden my keys again.* | **hide sth in/under etc** *Jane hid the presents in the cupboard.* **2** [I] to go or stay in a place where no one can see or find you: *Quick! She's coming – we'd better hide.* **3** [T] to not show your feelings: *Matt looked down, anxious to hide his confusion.* **4** [T] to deliberately not tell someone something: *I have nothing to hide.*

hide² *n* [C,U] an animal's skin, especially when it is removed to be used for making leather

hide-and-seek /ˌ. . ˈ./ *n* [U] a children's game in which a child tries to find other children who are hiding

hide·a·way /ˈhaɪdəweɪ/ *n* [C] a place where you can go when you want to be alone

hid·e·ous /ˈhɪdiəs/ *adj* extremely ugly or unpleasant: *a hideous new building* —**hideously** *adv*

hide·out /ˈ. ./ *n* [C] a place where you can hide

hid·ing /ˈhaɪdɪŋ/ *n* **be in hiding/go into hiding** to hide somewhere because you have done something illegal or are in danger

hi·er·ar·chy /ˈhaɪrɑːki‖-ɑːr-/ *n* **1** [C,U] a system of organization in which people are arranged into ranks of importance and authority **2** [C] the most important and powerful members of an organization: *All policy decisions are made by the party hierarchy.* —**hierarchical** /haɪˈrɑːkɪkəl‖-ɑːr-/ *adj*

hi·e·ro·glyph·ics /ˌhaɪrəˈglɪfɪks/ *n* [plural] a system of writing that uses pictures instead of words —**hieroglyphic** *adj*

hi-fi /ˈhaɪ faɪ, ˌhaɪ ˈfaɪ/ *n* [C] a piece of electronic equipment for playing recorded music ➙ see colour picture on page 474

high

a high shelf

a tall building

high¹ /haɪ/ *adj* **1** something that is high has a long distance between its bottom and its top: *the highest mountain in Colorado* ➙ opposite LOW¹ — compare TALL **2** a long way above the ground: *a high window* | **high up** *Look how high up the kite has gone.* **3** used in questions and statements about height: **how high?** *How high is the Eiffel Tower?* | **knee-high/shoulder-high etc** *The grass was knee-high.* **4** greater than usual in amount or number: *Temperatures will remain high today.* | *The cost of living is higher in the capital city than in the rest of the country.* **5** having an important or powerful position in an organization: *What's the highest rank in the Navy?* **6** very good: **have a high opinion of** *I have a very high opinion of his work.* | **high quality/standards etc** *We insist on high standards of quality and efficiency.* **7** behaving in an unusual way because of taking illegal drugs: **be high on sth** *They were high on cocaine.* **8** containing a lot of a particular substance: **high in fat/sugar/salt etc** *Spinach is very high in iron.* **9** near the top of the set of sounds that humans can hear: *I can't sing the high notes.*

high² *adv* **1** at or to a level high above the ground: *seagulls flying high in the sky* **2** at or to a high value, amount, level etc: *Jenkins has risen high in the company.* **3** **look/search high and low** to look everywhere for someone or something

high³ *n* [C] **1** the highest price, temperature etc: *Temperatures today will reach an all-time high of 48°.* **2** a feeling of pleasure or excite-

ment caused by success, drugs, or good luck: *She's been on a real high ever since she met Joe.*

high·brow /ˈhaɪbraʊ/ *adj* a highbrow book, film etc is serious and often difficult to understand

high-class /ˌ. ˈ.◂/ *adj* of good quality and style, and usually expensive: *a high-class restaurant*

higher ed·u·ca·tion /ˌ... ...ˈ.../ *n* [U] education at a college or university rather than a school ➙ compare FURTHER EDUCATION

high-hand·ed /ˌ. ˈ.◂/ *adj* using your authority or power in an unreasonable way — **high-handedness** *n* [U]

high heels /ˌ. ˈ./ *n* [plural] women's shoes with a high HEEL — **high-heeled** /ˌ. ˈ.◂/ *adj*

high jump /ˈ. ./ *n* **the high jump** a sport in which you run and jump over a bar that is raised higher after each successful jump — **high jumper** *n* [C]

high·lands /ˈhaɪləndz/ *n* [plural] an area with a lot of mountains: *the Scottish highlands*

high·light¹ /ˈhaɪlaɪt/ *v* [T] **1** to make something the main subject or problem that people pay attention to: *Our newsletter highlights issues of interest to students.* **2** to cover written words with a line or block of colour, so that you can see them more easily

highlight² *n* [C] the most important, interesting, or enjoyable part of something: *You can see highlights of today's game after the news.*

high·light·er /ˈhaɪlaɪtəⅼ-ər/ *n* [C] a brightly coloured pen used for highlighting words in a book, article etc

high·ly /ˈhaɪli/ *adv* **1** very: *Rachel is a highly intelligent girl.* **2** **highly respected/regarded/thought of** very much respected or admired

highly-strung /ˌ.. ˈ.◂/ *especially BrE*, **high strung** /ˌ. ˈ.◂/ *AmE* — *adj* nervous, and easily upset or excited

High·ness /ˈhaɪnɪs/ *n* **Her/His/Your Highness** used when you are talking to a member of a royal family who is not the king or queen

high-pitched /ˌ. ˈ.◂/ *adj* a high-pitched sound is high and sharp

high-pow·ered /ˌ. ˈ.◂/ *adj* **1** a high-powered machine is very powerful: *a high-powered speedboat* **2** having an important job with a lot of responsibility: *a high-powered businessman*

high-pres·sure /ˌ. ˈ.◂/ *adj* **1** a high-pressure job or situation is one in which you need to work very hard to be successful **2** having or using a lot of pressure: *a high-pressure water hose*

high-pro·file /ˌ. ˈ.◂/ *adj* attracting a lot of attention: *a high-profile court case*

high-rise /ˈ. ./ *adj* a high-rise building is very tall — **high-rise** *n* [C]

high school /ˈ. ./ *n* [C,U] **1** a school in the US and Canada for students from 14 to 18 years old **2** used in the names of some schools in Britain for students from 11 to 18 years old: *Manchester High School for Girls*

high-spir·it·ed /ˌ. ˈ...◂/ *adj* having a lot of en-

H

GRAMMAR NOTE: the past perfect
You form the **past perfect** using **had** and the past participle. Use the past perfect to talk about something that happened in the past before another past action: *Kay stayed behind after everyone else **had gone** home.* | *She told me what she **had done**.*

ergy and enjoying having fun: *a high-spirited little boy*

high street /ˈ. ./ *n* [C] *BrE* the main street in a town, where all the shops and businesses are: *Kensington High Street*

high-strung /ˌ. ˈ.◂/ *adj* an American form of HIGHLY-STRUNG

high-tech /ˌhaɪ ˈtek◂/ *adj* using the most modern machines, equipment, and methods: *a new high-tech camera*

high tide /ˌ. ˈ./ *n* [C,U] the time when the sea reaches its highest level

high-way /ˈhaɪweɪ/ *n* [C] *AmE* a wide main road that joins one city to another; MOTORWAY *BrE*

hi-jack /ˈhaɪdʒæk/ *v* [T] to use violence or threats to take control of a plane, vehicle etc —**hijacker** *n* [C] —**hijacking** *n* [C,U]

hike /haɪk/ *v* **1** [I,T] to take a long walk in the countryside or mountains: **go hiking** *The Lake District is a great place to go hiking.* **2** [T] also **hike** sth ↔ **up** to increase prices, taxes etc by a large amount: *Banks are likely to hike interest rates again.* —**hike** *n* [C]

hi-lar-i-ous /hɪˈleəriəs‖-ˈler-/ *adj* extremely funny: *She thinks his jokes are hilarious.*

hi-lar-i-ty /hɪˈlærˌti/ *n* [U] a situation in which people are very cheerful and laugh a lot

hill /hɪl/ *n* **1** [C] an area of high land, like a small mountain: *a little cottage on a hill* | *The sun set behind the blue hills.* → see colour picture on page 243 **2 over the hill** *informal* no longer young, or too old to do a job well

hill-side /ˈhɪlsaɪd/ *n* [C] the sloping part of a hill

hill-y /ˈhɪli/ *adj* with a lot of hills: *hilly terrain* (=land)

hilt /hɪlt/ *n* **to the hilt** completely, or as much as possible: *She's prepared to defend him to the hilt.*

him /ɪm; *strong* hɪm/ *pron* the object form of 'he': *Have you sent him an invitation?* | *I'll look for him downstairs.*

him-self /ɪmˈself; *strong* hɪm-/ *pron* **1** the RE-FLEXIVE form of 'he': *Bill looked at himself in the mirror.* | *He seemed to enjoy himself last night.* **2** the strong form of 'he', used to emphasize the subject or object of a sentence: *Mr Wexford himself came down to greet us.* **3 (all) by himself** alone or without help: *He tried to fix the car by himself.* **4 (all) to himself** for his own use: *Ben had the house to himself.* **5 be/feel himself** to feel well and in a normal state

hind /haɪnd/ *adj* **hind legs/feet** the back legs or feet of an animal

hin-der /ˈhɪndə‖-ər/ *v* [T] to make it difficult for someone to do something, or for something to happen: *The bad weather is hindering rescue efforts.*

hin-drance /ˈhɪndrəns/ *n* [C] someone or something that makes it difficult for you to do something: **be a hindrance to** *Marie feels marriage would be a hindrance to her career.*

hind-sight /ˈhaɪndsaɪt/ *n* [U] the ability to understand something only after it has happened: **with hindsight** *With hindsight, we'd all do things differently.*

Hin-du /ˈhɪnduː, ˌhɪnˈduː◂/ *n* [C] someone who believes in Hinduism

Hin-du-is-m /ˈhɪnduː-ɪzəm/ *n* [U] the main reli-

gion in India, which includes belief in many gods and in REINCARNATION

hinge¹ /hɪndʒ/ *n* [C] a metal part used to fasten a door to its frame, a lid to a box etc, so that it can swing open and shut —**hinged** *adj*

hinge² *v*
hinge on/upon sth *phr v* [T] to depend on something: *Suddenly, his whole future hinged on Luisa's decision.*

hint¹ /hɪnt/ *n* [C] **1** something you say in a very indirect way, but wanting other people to know what you mean: **drop hints** *Sue has been dropping hints about what she wants for her birthday.* | **take a/the hint** (=understand what someone really wants): *I kept looking at my watch, but she wouldn't take the hint.* **2** a small amount of something: *There was a hint of perfume in the air.* **3** a useful piece of advice: *cookery hints*

hint² *v* [I,T] to say something in an indirect way so that someone can guess what you mean: **+ (that)** *Peg has been hinting that she wants a baby.*

hip¹ /hɪp/ *n* [C] one of the two parts on the sides of your body, where your legs join your body

hip² *adj informal* modern and fashionable: *The coffee shop was the hip place to hang out.*

hip-pie, also **hippy** /ˈhɪpi/ *n* [C] someone who is opposed to the usual standards of society, who wears colourful clothes and has long hair. People first started becoming hippies in the 1960s: *She joined a hippie commune in the '60s.*

hip-po /ˈhɪpəʊ‖-poʊ/ *n* [C] *informal* a hippopotamus

hip-po-pot-a-mus /ˌhɪpəˈpɒtəməs‖-ˈpɑː-/ *n* [C], *plural* **hippopotamuses, hippopotami** /-maɪ/ a large African animal with a big head, fat body, and thick grey skin, that lives in or near water

hire¹ /haɪə‖haɪr/ *v* [T] **1** *BrE* to pay money to borrow something for a short time; RENT *AmE*: *Let's hire a car and drive down to Cornwall.* **2** to employ someone to work for you: *We've decided to hire a nanny for baby Carolyn.*
hire sth ↔ **out** *phr v* [T] *BrE* to allow someone to use something for a short time in exchange for money: *Do you know of any place that hires out costumes?*

hire² *n* [U] *BrE* an arrangement that you make to borrow something for a short time in exchange for money: *a car hire company* | **for hire** *fishing boats for hire*

his /ɪz; *strong* hɪz/ *determiner, pron* belonging to or concerning a male person or animal that has already been mentioned: *Leo hates cleaning his room.* | *I think I picked up his suitcase by mistake.*

His-pan-ic /hɪˈspænɪk/ *adj* from or relating to a country where Spanish or Portuguese is spoken —**Hispanic** *n* [C]

hiss /hɪs/ *v* [I] **1** to make a noise that sounds like 'ssss': *I could hear steam hissing from the pipe.* **2** to say something in a hissing voice: *"Just keep quiet!" he hissed.* → see colour picture on page 635 —**hiss** *n* [C]

his-to-ri-an /hɪˈstɔːriən/ *n* [C] someone who studies or writes about history

his-tor-ic /hɪˈstɒrɪk‖-ˈstɔː-, -ˈstɑː-/ *adj* a historic place or event is important because it will be remembered as a part of history: *a historic moment*

his·tor·i·cal /hɪˈstɒrɪkəl‖-ˈstɔː-, -ˈstɑː-/ *adj*
1 connected with the study of history: *historical research* **2** historical events, people etc happened or existed in the past: *The novel blends historical fact with fiction.* —**historically** /-kli/ *adv*

his·to·ry /ˈhɪstəri/ *n* **1** [U] all the things that happened in the past, especially the political, social, and economic development of a country: *The Civil War was a turning point in American history.* **2** [U] the study of history, especially as a subject in school or university: *a class in European history* **3** [singular] the development of something since it started: *one of the finest performers in the history of opera* **4** **have a history of sth** to have had a particular illness, problem etc in the past: *Paul has a history of heart trouble.*

his·tri·on·ics /ˌhɪstriˈɒnɪks‖-ˈɑːn-/ *n* [plural] extremely emotional behaviour that is intended to get people's sympathy or attention —**histrionic** *adj*

hit[1] /hɪt/ *v* **hit, hit, hitting** **1** [T] to swing your hand, or something held in your hand, hard against someone or something: *He hit the ball right into the crowd.* | *It felt like someone had hit me in the stomach.* **2** [T] to crash into someone or something quickly and hard: *The speeding car swerved and hit the wall.* | *I fainted and hit my head on the table.* **3** [T] to reach a particular number, position etc: *Unemployment has hit 11.3%.* **4** [T] to have a bad effect on someone or something: *In 1977, the area was hit by massive floods.* | **be hard hit** (=be very badly affected): *The company has been hard hit by decreasing sales.* **5** [T] to wound someone or damage something with a bullet or bomb: *He was hit in the chest and died instantly.* **6** [T] if a fact or a thought hits you, you suddenly realize its importance: *It suddenly hit me that he was just lonely.* **7** **hit it off (with sb)** *informal* to like someone as soon as you meet them **8** **hit the roof/ceiling** *informal* to become very angry: *Dad's going to hit the roof when he sees this mess!* **9** **hit the nail on the head** *spoken* used to say that what someone has said is exactly right

hit back *phr v* [I] to attack or criticize someone who has attacked or criticized you: *Yesterday Clinton hit back at his critics.*

hit on *phr v* [T **hit on/upon** sth] to have a good idea about something, usually by chance: *Phil hit upon an ingenious way to raise money for the club.*

hit out at/against sb/sth *phr v* [T] *BrE* to say or show that you disapprove of someone or something: *The bishop has hit out at the government's policy on homelessness.*

hit[2] *n* **1** [C] a film, song, play etc that is very successful: *She had a big hit with her first album.* **2** [C] when you successfully hit something you are aiming at: *I scored a hit with my first shot.* **3** **be a hit (with sb)** to be liked very much: *Your cousin was a big hit at the party.* **4** [C] when you hit something with your hand or with something in your hand

hit-and-miss also **hit-or-miss** /ˌ. . ˈ./ *adj* *informal* done in a way that is not planned or organized

hit-and-run /ˌ. . ˈ.◂/ *adj* a hit-and-run accident is one in which a driver hits someone or some-

thing and then drives away without stopping to help

hitch[1] /hɪtʃ/ *v* **1** [I,T] *informal* to travel by asking for free rides in other people's cars: **hitch a ride/lift** *We tried to hitch a ride into Perth.* **2** [T] to fasten one thing to another: *Dad hitched the boat to the back of the car.*

hitch sth ↔ **up** *phr v* [T] to pull a piece of clothing up: *She hitched up her skirt and stepped over the wall.*

hitch[2] *n* [C] a small problem that causes a delay: *a technical hitch* | **without a hitch** *Dinner went off without a hitch.*

hitch·hike /ˈhɪtʃhaɪk/ *v* [I] to travel by asking for free rides in other people's cars —**hitchhiker** *n* [C] —**hitchhiking** *n* [U]

hi-tech *adj* another spelling of HIGH-TECH

hith·er·to /ˌhɪðəˈtuː‖-ər-/ *adv formal* until now

hit list /ˈ. ./ *n* [C] *informal* the people or things that you plan to do something bad to

hit man /ˈ. ./ *n* [C] *informal* a criminal who has been paid to kill someone

HIV /ˌeɪtʃ aɪ ˈviː◂/ *n* [U] a kind of VIRUS that enters the body through blood or sexual activity and can cause AIDS: **be HIV positive** *She's been HIV positive for 11 years.*

hive /haɪv/ also **beehive** *n* **1** [C] a type of box that BEES are kept in **2** **a hive of activity** a place where everyone is very busy

h'm, hmm /m, hm/ *interjection* a sound that you make when you are in doubt, or when you pause to think about something

HMS /ˌeɪtʃ em ˈes/ *n* [C] His/Her Majesty's Ship; a title for a ship in the British navy: *the HMS Bounty*

hoard[1] /hɔːd‖hɔːrd/ *n* [C] a group of things that someone keeps hidden, or that are found buried somewhere: *a hoard of gold coins*

hoard[2] also **hoard up** *v* [T] to collect large amounts of food, money etc and keep them in a secret place: *squirrels hoarding nuts for the winter* —**hoarder** *n* [C]

hoard·ing /ˈhɔːdɪŋ‖ˈhɔːr-/ *n* [C] *BrE* a board on which large advertisements are stuck; BILLBOARD

hoarse /hɔːs‖hɔːrs/ *adj* a hoarse voice sounds rough, as if the person speaking has a sore throat —**hoarsely** *adv* —**hoarseness** *n* [U]

hoax /həʊks‖hoʊks/ *n* [C] an attempt to make people believe something that is not true: *The bomb threat turned out to be a hoax.*

hob /hɒb‖hɑːb/ *n* [C] *BrE* the flat top of a COOKER where you cook food in pans

hob·ble /ˈhɒbəl‖ˈhɑː-/ *v* [I] to walk with difficulty, taking small steps, because you are injured

hob·by /ˈhɒbi‖ˈhɑː-/ *n* [C] an activity that you enjoy doing in your free time: *Tricia's hobby is gardening.*

ho·bo /ˈhəʊbəʊ‖ˈhoʊboʊ/ *n* [C] *AmE informal* someone who travels around and has no home or job; TRAMP

hock·ey /ˈhɒki‖ˈhɑːki/ *n* [U] **1** *BrE* a game played on grass, in which two teams of players use long curved sticks to hit a ball; FIELD HOCKEY *AmE* **2** *AmE* a game played on ice in which two teams of players use long curved sticks to hit a hard flat object; ICE HOCKEY *BrE* ➡ see colour picture on page 636

hodge·podge /'hɒdʒ pɒdʒ‖'hɑːdʒ pɑːdʒ/ *n* [singular] the American form of the word HOTCHPOTCH

hoe /həʊ‖hoʊ/ *n* [C] a garden tool with a long handle, used for making the soil loose —**hoe** *v* [I,T] ➡ see picture at GARDENING EQUIPMENT

hog¹ /hɒg‖hɒːg, hɑːg/ *n* 1 [C] *especially AmE* a large pig that is kept for its meat 2 **go the whole hog** *informal* to do something thoroughly or completely: *Why don't we go the whole hog and get champagne?*

hog² *v* [T] **-gged, -gging** *informal* to keep or use all of something for yourself: *Katie hogged the whole box of chocolates!*

hoist¹ /hɔɪst/ *v* [T] to lift something heavy, especially using ropes or a machine

hoist² *n* [C] a piece of equipment used for lifting heavy things

hold¹ /həʊld‖hoʊld/ *v* **held** /held/, **held, holding** 1 [T] to have something in your hands or arms: *Can you hold my bag for a minute?* | **hold hands** (=when two people hold each other's hands): *lovers holding hands* ➡ see colour pictures on pages 473 and 670 2 [T] to keep something in a particular position: **hold sth up** (=in a high position): *She held the piece of paper up so we could see it.* | **hold sth open** *Do you want me to hold the door open for you?* | **hold sth in place** (=prevent it from moving): *The cupboard was held in place by four large screws.* 3 [T] to have a meeting, ceremony, election, concert etc: *Elections are usually held every five years.* 4 [T] to have enough space for an amount of people or things: *a brand new stadium which can hold up to 80,000 people* 5 [T] to keep someone or something in a particular place: *All our files are held on computer.* | *The hostages were held in a secret location.* 6 [T] to have a job, position, or QUALIFICATION: *Men still hold most of the top managerial posts.* 7 [I,T] *spoken* to wait or stop doing something: **hold it!** *Hold it a minute! I need to talk to you.* | **hold the line** (=used to tell someone to wait for another person to come to the telephone): *Mr Penrose is busy. Can you hold the line?* 8 **hold an opinion/belief/view** *formal* to think or believe that something is true 9 **hold sb's interest/attention** to make someone continue to be interested: *She knows how to hold her students' interest.* 10 **hold a conversation** to have a conversation: *He can hold a conversation in several European languages.* 11 **hold your own** to be as good at doing something as other people: *Pakistan's batsmen can hold their own with the best in the world.* 12 **hold your breath** to wait to find out what happens, in a nervous and excited way: *We held our breath while the results were read out.* 13 [T] to stop a plane, train etc from moving so that someone can get on, or save a room, seat, or ticket for someone to use: *They held the plane for me at the airport.* 14 [T] if an army holds a place, they control it: *The islands were held by the Germans throughout World War II.* 15 **hold shares** to own SHARES in a company 16 [I,T] if something holds, or holds something's weight, it does not break 17 **not hold water** to not seem true or reasonable: *His argument doesn't hold water.* 18 **hold true/good** *formal* to be true: *I think her state-*ment holds true for older women. ➡ see also **hold sb to ransom** (RANSOM)

hold sth against sb *phr v* [T] to blame someone for something they have done: *If you can't come, I won't hold it against you.*

hold back *phr v* 1 [T **hold** sth ↔ **back**] to prevent a group of people or things from moving forward: *The police couldn't hold back the crowds.* 2 [I,T **hold back** sth] to stop yourself from showing a particular feeling or saying something: *She held back her tears.* | *I wanted to tell him what I thought of him, but I held back.* 3 [T **hold** sb ↔ **back**] to prevent someone being successful or from doing what they want to do: *Firms are being held back because of lack of money.*

hold down *phr v* [T] 1 to keep something at a low level: *BA say they'll hold down ticket prices until the New Year.* 2 **hold down a job** to keep your job: *He's never been able to hold down a job for more than a month.*

hold off *phr v* [I,T] to delay doing something: *We held off making the decision for a month.*

hold on *phr v* [I] 1 *spoken* used to tell someone to wait or stop talking, for example during a phone call: *Yeah, hold on, Mike is right here.* 2 to continue to do something difficult until it gets better: *The Rangers held on to win the final game in the final period.*

hold onto sth *phr v* [T] 1 to hold something tightly: *She held onto his jacket.* 2 to keep something and not sell it or give it to someone: *You should hold onto the painting. It might be worth a lot of money.*

hold out *phr v* 1 [T] to move something towards someone, especially in order to offer it to them: *Jean held out a small envelope.* 2 [I] to continue fighting to defend yourself, or keep refusing to do something: *The rebels are holding out in the south.* 3 [I] if a supply of something holds out, there is still some of it left: *Supplies of food are expected to hold out for another couple of weeks.* 4 **hold out hope** to think that something might happen: *The doctors don't hold out much hope of a recovery.*

hold out for sth *phr v* [T] to refuse to accept less than you have asked for: *The union are holding out for more money.*

hold sth **over** sb *phr v* [T] to use information about someone to control or threaten them

hold sb **to** sth *phr v* [T] to make someone do what they have promised to do: *"He said he would do it." "Well, you'd better hold him to it."*

hold together *phr v* [I,T **hold** sth **together**] to continue to be united or joined together, or make something do this: *The children are the only thing holding their marriage together.*

hold up *phr v* 1 [T **hold** sb/sth ↔ **up**] to make someone or something late: *Sorry, I didn't mean to hold everybody up.* 2 [T **hold up** sth] to try to steal money from a shop, bank etc, using a gun

hold² *n* 1 [singular] when someone holds something: **take hold of sth** (=start to hold something): *Warren took hold of her hand.* 2 **get hold of** to find someone or obtain something: *I need to get hold of him quickly.* | *Drugs are easy to get hold of.* 3 **keep hold of a)** to continue to hold something: *He struggled to keep hold of the dog.* **b)** to keep something and not lose it, give it to someone, or sell it: *It was a lovely watch – I* *wish I'd kept hold of it.* **4 put sth on hold** to decide something at a later time, rather than now: *The tunnel project has been put on hold.* **5 put sb on hold** to make someone wait on the telephone: *I will have to put you on hold.* **6 have a hold on/over** to have power or control over someone **7 take hold** to start to have an effect on someone or something: *Once the disease takes hold, it's very difficult to get rid of.* **8** [C] the part of a ship where goods are stored

hold·all / 'həʊld-ɔːl‖'hoʊld-ɒːl/ *n* [C] *BrE* a bag used for carrying clothes, tools etc; CARRYALL *AmE* ➙ see picture at BAG

hold·er / 'həʊldə‖'hoʊldər/ *n* [C] **1** someone who has something: *the Olympic record holder | UK passport holders* **2** something that holds or contains something else: *a red candle holder*

hold·ing / 'həʊldɪŋ‖'hoʊl-/ *n* [C] a part of a company that someone owns

hold·o·ver / 'həʊld,əʊvə‖'hoʊld,oʊvər/ *n* [C] *AmE* an idea, fashion, method etc from the past that has continued to the present: *styles that are a holdover from the '60s*

hold·up also **hold-up** *BrE* / 'həʊldʌp‖'hoʊld-/ *n* [C] **1** a delay, especially one caused by traffic: *long hold-ups on the M25* **2** when people try to steal money from a bank, shop etc, using a gun: *This is a holdup. Everyone get down on the floor.*

hole[1] / 'həʊl‖'hoʊl/ *n* [C] **1** an empty space in the surface of something solid: *Someone had drilled a hole in the wall. | There's a hole in my sock.* **2** one of the small holes in the ground that you try to hit the ball into when you are playing GOLF **3** something wrong in an idea, plan, or story: **be full of holes** (=have a lot of things that are wrong): *The witness's testimony was full of holes.* **4** *informal* an unpleasant place: *I have to get out of this hole.* **5 be in a hole** *spoken* to be in a difficult situation and have a lot of problems **6 make a big hole in** *informal* to use a lot of an amount of money so that there is not much left ➙ see also BLACK HOLE

hole[2] *v*

hole up also **be holed up** *phr v* [I] to hide somewhere for a period of time: *Journalists Swain and Schonberg were holed up in the US embassy.*

hol·i·day[1] / 'hɒlədɪ‖'hɑːlɪˌdeɪ/ *n* [C] **1** a day when you do not have to go to work, school etc: **national/public holiday** also **bank holiday** *BrE* (=when everyone in a country has a holiday): *Labor Day is a national holiday in the US.* **2** *BrE* a period of time when you rest and do not go to work or school, especially when you go to another place for enjoyment; VACATION *AmE: We went to Italy for our holidays last year. | **be on holiday** (=be having a holiday): "Where's Bridget?" "She's on holiday this week."*

holiday-mak·er / '... ,../ *n* [C] *BrE* someone who goes to a place for a holiday

hol·i·ness / 'həʊlinəs‖'hoʊ-/ *n* **1** [U] the quality of being holy **2 Your/His Holiness** used to talk to or about an important religious leader

ho·lis·tic / həʊ'lɪstɪk‖hoʊ-/ *adj* dealing with or examining the whole of something, not just parts of it: *a holistic approach to medicine*

hol·ler / 'hɒlə‖'hɑːlər/ *v* [I,T] *AmE informal* to shout loudly: *Dad hollered at me to hurry up.* —**holler** *n* [C]

hol·low[1] / 'hɒləʊ‖'hɑː-/ *adj* **1** something that is hollow has an empty space inside: *a hollow tree* **2** hollow promises, threats, or words are not sincere or are about something that is not really going to happen: *the hollow promises of politicians* **3 hollow laugh/voice** a laugh or voice that has a low sound, and shows no emotion —**hollowness** *n* [U] —**hollowly** *adv*

hollow[2] *n* [C] an area that is lower than the surrounding surface

hollow[3] *v*

hollow sth ↔ **out** *phr v* [T] to remove the inside of something

hol·ly / 'hɒli‖'hɑːli/ *n* [U] a tree with green leaves and red berries (BERRY), used as a decoration at Christmas

hol·o·caust / 'hɒləkɔːst‖'hɑːləkɒːst/ *n* [C] when a very large number of people are killed and a lot of things are destroyed: *a nuclear holocaust*

hol·o·gram / 'hɒləgræm‖'hoʊl-,'hɑːl-/ *n* [C] a special picture made with a LASER which looks as if it is real, because you can see the sides as well as the front of the image

hol·ster / 'həʊlstə‖'hoʊlstər/ *n* [C] a leather container, used for carrying a gun

ho·ly / 'həʊli‖'hoʊ-/ *adj* **1** connected with God or religion; SACRED: *the holy city of Jerusalem* **2** very religious: *a holy man*

hom·age / 'hɒmɪdʒ‖'hɑː-/ *n* [U] something you say or do to show respect for an important person or for something they have achieved: **pay homage to** *The President paid homage to all who had fought or died in the war.*

home[1] / həʊm‖hoʊm/ *n* **1** [C,U] the place where you usually live, especially with your family: *I stayed at home and watched television. | a housing estate with over 100 new homes | He left home (=stopped living with his family) when he was 15.* **2 be/feel at home** feel comfortable somewhere, or feel confident doing something: *They always try to make their guests feel at home.* **3 the home of** the place where something comes from, or which is famous for something: *Chicago is known as the home of the blues.* **4 make yourself at home** *spoken* used to tell someone to relax when they are visiting your home **5** a place where a particular group of people are looked after, for example old people or children who have no parents: *He dreaded getting old and having to go into a home.* **6 at home** at the place where a team usually plays: *Barcelona lost 2-0 at home.* **7 find a home for** *BrE* to find a place where something can be kept: *Can you find a home for these glasses?*

home[2] *adv* **1** to or at the place where you live: *What time does Mike get home? | Hi, honey, I'm home.* **2 take home** to earn an amount of money after tax has been taken away: *I take home about $200 a week.* **3 drive/bring sth home** to make someone realize something, by showing it or talking about it in a very clear way: *McCullin's photographs brought home to people the horrors of war.*

home³ *adj* **1** connected with or belonging to your home or family: *What's your home address?* | *I'm looking forward to some home cooking* (=meals cooked by your family) *over Christmas.* **2** playing on your own sports team or field rather than on an opponent's: *The home team is ahead by four runs.* → opposite AWAY² **3 home truths** unpleasant facts about someone or something **4** connected with your own particular country, not foreign countries: *home affairs*

home⁴ *v*

home in on *phr v* [T] **1** to move directly towards something: *A Tomahawk missile homed in on the ship.* **2** to give all your attention to something, especially a mistake or a problem

home·com·ing /ˈhəʊmˌkʌmɪŋ‖ˈhoʊm-/ *n* [C] when someone goes back to their home after being away for a long time

home e·co·nom·ics /ˌ. .ˈ..ˈ./ *n* [U] the study of cooking, SEWING and other skills used at home, taught as a subject at school

home·land /ˈhəʊmlænd, -lənd‖ˈhoʊm-/ *n* [C] the country where someone was born

home·less /ˈhəʊmləs‖ˈhoʊm-/ *adj* **1** a homeless person does not have a place to live: *The war left a lot of people homeless.* **2 the homeless** people who do not have a place to live —**homelessness** *n* [U]

home·ly /ˈhəʊmli‖ˈhoʊm-/ *adj* **1** *BrE* simple and ordinary in a way that makes you feel comfortable: *a small hotel with a warm, homely atmosphere* **2** *AmE* a homely person is not very attractive: *a rather homely face* —**homeliness** *n* [U]

home·made /ˌhəʊmˈmeɪd‖ˌhoʊm-/ *adj* made at home and not bought from a shop: *homemade jam*

home·mak·er /ˈhəʊmˌmeɪkə‖ˈhoʊmˌmeɪkər/ *n* [C] *especially AmE* someone who works at home, cooking and cleaning; a HOUSEWIFE

ho·me·op·a·thy /ˌhəʊmiˈɒpəθi‖ˌhoʊmiˈɑːp-/ *n* [U] medical treatment in which someone who is ill is given very small amounts of a substance that has the same effects as the disease —**homeopathic** /ˌhəʊmiəˈpæθɪk‖ˌhoʊ-/ *adj* —**homeopath** /ˈhəʊmiəˌpæθ‖ˈhoʊ-/ *n* [C]

home·page /ˈ. ./ *n* [C] a place on the INTERNET where you can find information about a person, company etc

home run /ˌ. ˈ./ *n* [C] a long hit in BASEBALL, which lets the player run around all the bases (BASE) and get a point

home·sick /ˈhəʊmˌsɪk‖ˈhoʊm-/ *adj* feeling sad because you are a long way from your home: *On her first night at camp, Sheila felt very homesick.* —**homesickness** *n* [U]

home·stead /ˈhəʊmsted, -stɪd‖ˈhoʊm-/ *n* [C] a farm and the area of land and buildings around it

home town /ˌ. ˈ./ also **home·town** /ˈhəʊmtaʊn‖ˈhoʊm-/ *n* [C] the place where someone was born, or where they have spent most of their life: *Mike Tyson's hometown of Brownsville*

home·ward /ˈhəʊmwəd‖ˈhoʊmwərd/ *adj* going towards home: *my homeward journey* —**homeward** *adv*

home·work /ˈhəʊmwɜːk‖ˈhoʊmwɜːrk/ *n* [U] **1** work for school that a student does at home **2 sb has done his/her homework** used to say that someone has prepared well for something → compare HOUSEWORK

hom·i·cid·al /ˌhɒmɪˈsaɪdl◂‖ˌhɑː-/ *adj* likely to murder someone

hom·i·cide /ˈhɒmɪsaɪd‖ˈhɑː-/ *n* [C,U] the crime of murder

ho·mo·ge·ne·ous /ˌhəʊməˈdʒiːniəs‖ˌhoʊ-/ also **ho·mo·ge·nous** /həˈmɒdʒɪnəs‖-ˈmɑː-/ *adj formal* consisting of parts or members that are all the same

ho·mo·pho·bia /ˌhəʊməˈfəʊbiə‖ˌhoʊməˈfoʊ-/ *n* [U] hatred and fear of homosexuals —**homophobic** *adj*

ho·mo·sex·u·al /ˌhəʊməˈsekʃuəl◂, ˌhɒ-‖ˌhoʊ-/ *n* [C] someone who is sexually attracted to people of the same sex; GAY —**homosexual** *adj* —**homosexuality** /ˌhəʊməsekʃuˈæləti, ˌhɒ-‖ˌhoʊ-/ *n* [U]

hone /həʊn‖hoʊn/ *v* [T] **1** to improve a skill **2** to make a knife, sword etc sharp

hon·est /ˈɒnɪst‖ˈɑːn-/ *adj* **1** someone who is honest does not lie, cheat, or steal: *He seems a good, honest man.* → opposite DISHONEST **2** sincere and telling the true facts about something: *Give me an honest answer.* **3 to be honest** *spoken* used when you are saying what you really think: *To be honest, I don't think she has much chance of winning.*

hon·est·ly /ˈɒnɪstli‖ˈɑːn-/ *adv* **1** *spoken* used to say what you really think, or to emphasize that you are telling the truth: *I honestly don't know what's the best thing to do.* **2** *spoken* used when you are surprised and annoyed: *Well honestly! What an idiotic thing to say!* **3** in an honest way: *Walters spoke honestly about her problems.*

hon·es·ty /ˈɒnɪsti‖ˈɑːn-/ *n* [U] **1** the quality of being honest: *We never doubted Frank's honesty.* **2 in all honesty** *spoken* used to tell someone what you really think is true: *In all honesty, we made a lot of mistakes.*

hon·ey /ˈhʌni/ *n* [U] **1** a sweet substance made by BEES, used as food **2** *spoken especially AmE* a name that you call someone you love

hon·ey·comb /ˈhʌnikəʊm‖-koʊm/ *n* [C,U] something that BEES make to store HONEY in, which has six-sided cells

hon·ey·moon /ˈhʌnimuːn/ *n* [C] a holiday that people have after their wedding: *Jen and Dave are going to Alaska on their honeymoon.* —**honeymooner** *n* [C]

hon·ey·suck·le /ˈhʌniˌsʌkəl/ *n* [C] a sweet-smelling plant that grows on walls and fences

honk /hɒŋk‖hɑːŋk, hɔːŋk/ *v* [I,T] to make a loud noise using a car HORN: *A taxi driver honked his horn behind her.* —**honk** *n* [C]

hon·or /ˈɒnə‖ˈɑːnər/ *n* the American spelling of honour

hon·or·a·ble /ˈɒnərəbəl‖ˈɑːn-/ *adj* the American spelling of honourable

hon·or·ar·y /ˈɒnərəri‖ˈɑːnəreri/ *adj* an honorary job, TITLE etc is given to someone because of their achievements: *an honorary degree*

hon·our[1] *BrE*, **honor** *AmE* /ˈɒnəlˈɑːnər/ *n*
1 [U] strong moral beliefs and standards of behaviour that make people respect and trust you: *He's a man of honor.* **2** [U] **in honour of sb/in sb's honour** when people do something to show respect to someone, for example by having a special ceremony: *a ceremony in honour of the soldiers who died* **3 be an honour** to be something that makes you feel proud and glad: *It's a great honour to receive this award.* **4** [C] something such as a special title or MEDAL that is officially given to someone because of their achievements: *Churchill received many of his country's highest honours.* **5 Your Honour** used to speak to a judge

honour[2] *BrE*, **honor** *AmE* — *v* [T] **1** to treat someone with special respect, because you admire them: *J.F.K. was honored as a national hero.* | **honour sb with sth** (=give someone a special title or award for their achievements): *In 1966 he was honoured with the Nobel Prize for Medicine.* **2 be/feel honoured** to feel very proud and glad: *I'm deeply honoured to be here.* **3 honour a contract/agreement etc** to do what you have agreed to do in a contract etc

hon·our·a·ble *BrE*, **honorable** *AmE* /ˈɒnərəbəlˈɑːn-/ *adj* behaving in a way that is morally right, which makes people respect you: *an honourable man* **—honourably** *adv*

hood /hʊd/ *n* **1** [C] a part of a coat or JACKET that you can pull up to cover your head **2** *AmE* the metal cover over the engine on a car; BONNET *BrE* → see picture at CAR **3** *informal* a violent criminal who attacks people and causes trouble

hood·ed /ˈhʊdɪd/ *adj* having a hood: *a hooded jacket*

hood·lum /ˈhuːdləm/ *n* [C] *old-fashioned* a criminal who attacks people or causes trouble

hood·wink /ˈhʊdˌwɪŋk/ *v* [T] to trick someone in a clever way: *She managed to hoodwink him into lending her the money.*

hoof /huːfⅡhʊf, huːf/ *n* [C], *plural* **hoofs** or **hooves** /huːvzⅡhʊvs, huːvz/ the foot of an animal such as a horse

hook[1] /hʊk/ *n* [C] **1** a curved piece of metal or plastic, used for hanging things on, or catching fish: *a coat hook* **2 let/get sb off the hook** to help someone to avoid a difficult situation, especially when they have caused this situation by their own actions: *"Jo says she'll tell him." "That lets me off the hook."* **3 off the hook** when the part of the telephone that you speak into is not in its usual place, so no one can call you **4 left/right hook** a kind of PUNCH

hook[2] *v* [T] to fasten or hang something onto or around something else: *He hooked his umbrella around the handle.*

hook sth ↔ up *phr v* [T] to connect a computer, television etc to another piece of equipment or to a system: *Millions of people are now hooked up to the Internet.*

hooked /hʊkt/ *adj* **1** if you are hooked on something, you like it a lot and want to continue doing it: **+ on** *It's easy to get hooked on computer games.* **2** if you are hooked on a drug, you feel that you must keep taking it and cannot stop: *You only have to smoke crack once, and then you're hooked* **3** shaped like a hook: *a hooked nose*

hook·er /ˈhʊkəⅡ-ər/ *n* [C] *informal, especially AmE* a PROSTITUTE

hook·y /ˈhʊki/ *n* **play hooky** *AmE informal* to stay away from school without permission: *The kids were caught playing hooky at the mall.*

hoo·li·gan /ˈhuːlɪgən/ *n* [C] a noisy violent person who causes trouble in public places: *football hooligans* **—hooliganism** *n* [U]

hoop /huːpⅡhuːp, hʊp/ *n* [C] a circular piece of metal, plastic etc: *Throw the ball through the hoop.*

hoo·ray /hʊˈreɪ, ˌhuːˈreɪ/ *interjection* something that people shout when they are very glad about something

hoot[1] /huːt/ *n* [C] the sound made by an OWL, or a ship or car's HORN

hoot[2] *v* [I,T] **1** if an OWL hoots, it makes a loud noise **2** if a ship or car hoots, it makes a loud noise, using its HORN

hoo·ver /ˈhuːvəⅡ-ər/ *v* [I,T] *BrE* to clean the floor using a VACUUM CLEANER (=a machine that sucks up dirt)

Hoover *n* [C] *trademark BrE* a VACUUM CLEANER

hooves /huːvzⅡhʊvz, huːvz/ *n* the plural of HOOF

hop[1] /hɒpⅡhɑːp/ *v* [I] **-pped, -pping 1** *informal* to go somewhere quickly, especially into a car, plane, bus etc: **+ in/on etc** *Hop in and I'll give you a ride.* **2 a)** to move by jumping on one leg: *Willie hopped on one leg, and then the other.* → see colour picture on page 670 **b)** to move by making short quick jumps: *rabbits hopping along*

hop[2] *n* [C] a short jump → see also HOPS

hope[1] /həʊpⅡhoʊp/ *v* [I,T] to want something to happen or be true: **+ (that)** *I hope you feel better soon.* | **hope to do sth** *He's hoping to take a trip to Africa next year.* | **I hope so** *spoken* (=when you hope something will happen): *"Will Grandma be there?" "I hope so."* | **I hope not** *spoken* (=when you hope something will not happen): *"Do you think it's going to rain?" "I hope not!"*

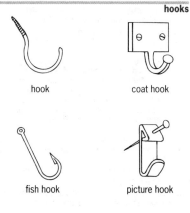

hook   coat hook

fish hook   picture hook

hooks

USAGE NOTE: hope to and hope that

Use **hope to** to talk about something that you or someone else wants to do, and **hope that** to talk about what you hope will happen: *Michelle hopes* to go to college. | I hope that Michelle will go to college.

hope[2] n [C,U] **1** the feeling that something good will happen: *Her voice sounded full of hope.* | + **of** *hopes of an early end to the war* | **give sb hope** *a new treatment that gives hope to cancer patients* | **lose/give up hope** (=when you think something you want will definitely not happen): *Ben's parents had lost all hope of seeing him again.* | **raise sb's hopes** (=make someone feel that something they want is more likely to happen) | **have high hopes** (=when you think that someone is very likely to succeed): *Damon Hill had high hopes at the start of the competition.* **2** a chance that something will happen in the way that you want: **no/not much/little hope** *There's no hope of getting the money back.* **3 in the hope that/of** because you hope that something will happen: *She stayed on in the hope that she would be able to speak to him.* **4 be sb's only/last/best hope** to be the only, last etc person or thing that can help you to succeed: *You must help me! You're my last hope.*

hope·ful /'həupfəl‖'houp-/ adj **1** if you are hopeful about a situation, you think that something good will probably happen: *We're hopeful about our chances of winning.* **2** something that is hopeful makes you feel that what you want is likely to happen: *There are hopeful signs that an agreement will be reached.* —**hopefulness** n [U]

hope·ful·ly /'həupfəli‖'houp-/ adv **1** a word used at the beginning of a sentence when you are saying what you hope will happen: *Hopefully, the letter will be here by Monday.* **2** in a hopeful way: *"Can we go to the zoo tomorrow?" he asked hopefully.*

hope·less /'həupləs‖'houp-/ adj **1** very bad and not likely to get better: *a hopeless situation* **2** very bad at doing something: *I'm hopeless at spelling.* **3** if something you try to do is hopeless, it is certain to fail: *a hopeless task* **4** feeling that you have no hope: *a hopeless look on her face* —**hopelessly** adv —**hopelessness** n [U]

hops /hɒps‖hɑːps/ n [plural] the flowers of a plant that are used for making beer

horde /hɔːd‖hɔːrd/ n [C] a very large crowd or group of people: *hordes of tourists*

ho·ri·zon /həˈraɪzən/ n **1 the horizon** the place where the land or sea seems to meet the sky: *The sun dropped below the horizon.* **2 be on the horizon** if something is on the horizon, it seems likely to happen soon: *Another 1930s style Depression is on the horizon.*

ho·ri·zons /həˈraɪzənz/ n [plural] the limit of your ideas, knowledge, and experience: *The good thing about university is that it broadens your horizons.*

hor·i·zon·tal /ˌhɒrɪˈzɒntl ‖ˌhɑːrɪˈzɑːntl / adj completely flat or level: *a horizontal surface* —**horizontally** adv → compare VERTICAL

hor·mone /ˈhɔːməun‖ˈhɔːrmoun/ n [C] a substance produced by your body, which helps it to develop or grow —**hormonal** /hɔːˈməunl‖hɔːr-ˈmou-/ adj

horn /hɔːn‖hɔːrn/ n **1** [C,U] one of the two hard pointed parts that grows on the heads of cows, goats etc, or the substance this is made of **2** [C] the thing in a car that you push to make a sound as a warning: *Ernie stopped and blew his*

horn. **3** [C] a metal musical instrument that is wide at one end, which you play by blowing: *the French horn*

hor·o·scope /ˈhɒrəskəup‖ˈhɑːrəskoup, ˈhɔː-/ n [C] a description of your character and things that will happen to you, based on the position of the stars and PLANETS when you were born

hor·ren·dous /hɒˈrendəs, hə-‖hɑː-, hɔː-/ adj *especially spoken* very bad: *The traffic was horrendous.* —**horrendously** adv

hor·ri·ble /ˈhɒrɪbəl‖ˈhɔː-, ˈhɑː-/ adj very unpleasant or unkind: *What a horrible smell!* | *a horrible old man* —**horribly** adv

hor·rid /ˈhɒrɪd‖ˈhɔː-, ˈhɑː-/ adj *informal* a word meaning horrible, used especially by children: *Don't be so horrid to your sister.*

hor·rif·ic /hɒˈrɪfɪk, hə-‖hɑː-, hɔː-/ adj very bad and very shocking: *a horrific accident* —**horrifically** /-kli/ adv

hor·ri·fy /ˈhɒrɪfaɪ‖ˈhɔː-, ˈhɑː-/ v [T] to shock someone very much: *I was horrified when I found out how much the repairs were going to cost.* —**horrifying** adj

hor·ror /ˈhɒrə‖ˈhɔːrər, ˈhɑː-/ n **1** [C,U] a strong feeling of shock and fear, or something that makes you feel this: *She stared at him in horror.* | *the horrors of war* **2 horror movie/film/story** a film or story in which strange or frightening things happen

horse /hɔːs‖hɔːrs/ n [C] a large animal with four legs that people ride on: *She trotted up to them on her horse.* → see also DARK HORSE

horse·back /ˈhɔːsbæk‖ˈhɔːrs-/ n **1 on horseback** riding a horse **2 horseback riding** *AmE* the activity of riding a horse; HORSE-RIDING *BrE*

horse chest·nut /ˌ. ˈ..‖ˈ. ,.-/ n [C] a large tree that produces brown nuts, or a nut from this tree

horse-drawn /ˈ. ./ adj pulled by a horse

horse·man /ˈhɔːsmən‖ˈhɔːrs-/ n [C], *plural* **horsemen** /-mən/ someone who rides horses

horse·play /ˈhɔːspleɪ‖ˈhɔːrs-/ n [U] when people play in a rough way by pushing and hitting each other

horse·pow·er /ˈhɔːs.pauə‖ˈhɔːrs.paur/ written abbreviation **hp** n [C], *plural* **horsepower** a unit for measuring the power of an engine

horse·rid·ing /ˈ. ..-/ n [U] *BrE* the activity of riding a horse; HORSEBACK RIDING *AmE*

horse·shoe /ˈhɔːʃ.ʃuː, ˈhɔːs-‖ˈhɔːr-/ n [C] a curved piece of iron that is put on to the bottom of a horse's foot

hor·ti·cul·ture /ˈhɔːtɪ.kʌltʃə‖ˈhɔːrtɪ.kʌltʃər/ n [U] the study or practice of growing plants —**horticultural** /ˌhɔːtɪˈkʌltʃərəl‖ˌhɔːr-/ adj

hose[1] /həuz‖houz/ n **1** also **hose-pipe** /ˈ. ./ [C,U] a long tube that can bend, through which air or water flows → see picture at GARDENING EQUIPMENT **2** [plural] *AmE* PANTYHOSE

hose[2] v

hose sth ↔ down *phr v* [T] to use a hose to put water on something, for example in order to clean it

ho·sier·y /ˈhəuzjəri‖ˈhouʒəri/ n [U] things such as socks and STOCKINGS

hos·pice /ˈhɒspɪs‖ˈhɑː-/ n [C] a special hospital where people who are dying are looked after

hos·pi·ta·ble / 'hɒspɪtəbəl, hɒ'spɪ-‖hɑː'spɪ-, 'hɑːspɪ-/ *adj* friendly and generous to someone who is visiting you or staying with you: *The local people are very hospitable.* —**hospitably** *adv*

hos·pi·tal / 'hɒspɪtl‖'hɑː-/ *n* [C,U] a building where sick or injured people receive medical treatment: **in hospital** *BrE*/**in the hospital** *AmE Rick's dad is still in the hospital.*

hos·pi·tal·i·ty / ˌhɒspɔ̩'tælɔ̩tïli‖ˌhɑː-/ *n* [U] friendly and kind behaviour towards visitors

hos·pi·tal·ized (also **-ised** *BrE*) / 'hɒspɪtl-aɪzd‖'hɑː-/ **be hospitalized** when someone has to go to hospital for medical treatment

host[1] / həʊst‖hoʊst/ *n* [C] **1** the person at a party who invited the guests and organized the party **2** someone who introduces the guests on a television or radio show: *a game show host* **3** a country, city, or organization that provides the space, equipment etc for a special event: *the host city for the next Olympic Games* **4** a (whole) host of a large number of: *a host of possibilities*

host[2] *v* [T] to be the host of an event: *Which country is hosting the next World Cup?*

hos·tage / 'hɒstɪdʒ‖'hɑː-/ *n* [C] someone who is kept as a prisoner in order to force people to do something: **take sb hostage** (=catch someone and use them as a hostage): *Three nurses were taken hostage by the terrorists.*

hos·tel / 'hɒstl‖'hɑː-/ *n* [C] a cheap place for people to stay when they are away from home, or a place for people who have no home: *a youth hostel*

host·ess / 'həʊstɪs‖'hoʊ-/ *n* [C] **1** the woman at a party who invited the guests and organized the party **2** *AmE* a woman who takes people to their seats in a restaurant

hos·tile / 'hɒstaɪl‖'hɑːstl, 'hɑːstaɪl/ *adj* **1** very unfriendly and likely to attack or argue with someone: *a hostile crowd* **2** opposing something very strongly: *Public opinion was hostile to the war.* **3** belonging to an enemy: *hostile territory*

hos·til·i·ties / hɒ'stɪlɔ̩tiz‖hɑː-/ *n* [plural] *formal* when people fight with each other: *efforts to end the hostilities in the region*

hos·til·i·ty / hɒ'stɪlɔ̩ti‖hɑː-/ *n* [U] **1** unfriendly and angry feelings or behaviour: *hostility between staff and students* **2** when people are strongly opposed to something: *hostility to the idea of a united Europe*

hot[1] / hɒt‖hɑːt/ *adj* **-tter, -ttest 1** high in temperature: *The soup's really hot.* | *the hottest day of the year* **2** having a burning taste; SPICY: *hot salsa* **3** *informal* very good, popular, or exciting: *a hot new band* **4** likely to cause trouble or arguments: **hot topic/issue** (=a subject that people disagree a lot about): *Abortion is a hot topic in the US.* **5** **be in the hot seat** to have to deal with a lot of difficult questions or problems **6** **hot favourite** *BrE*, **hot favorite** *AmE* the person, party etc that most people expect to win **7** **in hot pursuit** following someone very quickly and closely, to catch them

8 **hot potato** a subject that is difficult to deal with, because any decision could make a lot of people angry: *The airport project has become a political hot potato.*

hot[2] *v* **hotted, hotting**
hot up *phr v* [I] *especially BrE* if something is hotting up, there is a lot of excitement and activity: *The election campaign is hotting up.*

hot air / ˌ. './ *n* [U] things someone says that sound important, but really are not

hot air bal·loon / ˌ. '. ˌ.,./ *n* [C] a very large BALLOON that can carry people in the air

hot·bed / 'hɒtbed‖'hɑːt-/ *n* [C] a place where a lot of a particular kind of activity happens: *Berkeley was a hotbed of leftist politics in the '60s.*

hotch·potch / 'hɒtʃpɒtʃ‖'hɑːtʃpɑːtʃ/ *especially BrE*, **hodgepodge** *AmE* — *n* [singular] a strange mixture of different things

hot dog / ˌ. '.‖'. ./ *n* [C] a long SAUSAGE, eaten in a long piece of bread

hot dog

ho·tel / həʊ'tel‖hoʊ-/ *n* [C] a building where people pay to stay

hot·head·ed / ˌhɒt'hed-ɔ̩d◂‖ˌhɑːt-/ *adj* a hotheaded person becomes angry or excited easily, and does things too quickly, without thinking carefully first —**hothead** / 'hɒthed ‖'hɑːt-/ *n* [C]

hot·house / 'hɒthaʊs‖'hɑːt-/ *n* [C] a heated glass building, used for growing tropical plants

hot·line / '. ./ *n* [C] a special telephone number that people can call for information or advice

hot·ly / 'hɒtli‖'hɑːtli/ *adv* **1** **hotly debated/disputed** when people discuss or argue about something a lot, because they have strong feelings about it: *a hotly debated issue* **2** **hotly contested/fought** when people try very hard to win an election, competition etc: *the hotly contested race for governor*

hot·plate / 'hɒtpleɪt‖'hɑːt-/ *n* [C] a metal surface that is heated and used for cooking food

hot·shot / 'hɒtʃɒt‖'hɑːtʃɑːt/ *n* [C] *informal* someone who is very successful and confident —**hotshot** *adj*: *a hotshot lawyer*

hot·spot / '. ./ *n* [C] **1** a place where there is likely to be trouble, fighting etc: *Soldiers were moved to hotspots along the border.* **2** an area on a computer screen that you CLICK on to make pictures, information etc

hot-tem·pered / ˌ. '..◂/ *adj* a hot-tempered person becomes angry very easily

hot-wa·ter bot·tle / ˌ. '. ˌ../ *n* [C] a rubber container filled with hot water, used to keep your body warm

hound[1] / haʊnd/ *n* [C] a dog used for hunting

hound[2] *v* [T] to keep following someone and asking them questions in an annoying or threatening way: *She's constantly hounded by reporters.*

hour / aʊə‖aʊr/ *n* **1** [C] a period of 60 minutes: *The meeting lasted an hour and a half.* | *I'll be home in about an hour.* (=an hour from

---

GRAMMAR NOTE: the future
To talk about the **future** you can use: 1. **will +** basic form of verb: *I'll* (=I will) *see you tomorrow.*
2. **be going to** (used to say that something will happen soon): *I think it's going to rain.* 3. the
present progressive (used to say what is planned or intended): *We're having a party on Saturday.*

now) | *The lake is an hour from Hartford.* (=it takes an hour to go there from Hartford) **2** [C] a period of time in the day when something happens: **opening hours** (=when a shop is open): *Opening hours are from 9:00 a.m. to 8:00 p.m.* | **lunch hour** (=the time when you stop working and have lunch) **3 hours** *informal* a long time: *She spends hours on the phone.* **4** [singular] the time of day when a new hour starts, for example 1 o'clock, 2 o'clock etc: **on the hour** *Classes begin on the hour.* **5** [C] a particular time during the day or night: *The subway doesn't run at this hour of the night.* | **at all hours** (=at any time, even very late at night): *The baby keeps them awake at all hours.* **6 after hours** after the time when a company, shop etc is usually open: *The key is usually kept with the caretaker after hours.* **7** [C] an important time in history or in your life: *You were there in my hour of need.* (=when I needed help)

hour·glass /ˈaʊəɡlɑːsǁˈaʊrɡlæs/ *n* [C] a glass container for measuring time, in which sand moves to the bottom in exactly one hour

hour·ly /ˈaʊəliǁˈaʊrli/ *adj* happening every hour: *an hourly news bulletin*

house[1] /haʊs/ *n, plural* **houses** /ˈhaʊzɪz/ **1** [C] a building that you live in, especially one that is used by a family: *I'm going over to Dean's house.* **2** [singular] all the people who live in a house: *Be quiet or you'll wake the whole house!* **3** [C] a building used for a particular purpose: *the Opera House* | *a hen house* **4** [C] a group of people who make the laws of a country: *The President will speak to both Houses of Congress on Thursday.* **5 be on the house** *spoken* if drinks or meals in a restaurant are on the house, they are free **6** *BrE* [C] one of the groups into which the children in a school are divided, for the purposes of competing in sports etc → see also FULL HOUSE, IN-HOUSE

USAGE NOTE: house

A **house** is a building for people to live in, and usually has more than one level (storey). A **cottage** is usually a small, old house, especially in the country. A **bungalow** is a fairly modern house built on only one level. A set of rooms (including a kitchen and a bathroom) inside a larger building is called an **apartment** or a **flat** in British English. A small one-room apartment is sometimes called a **bedsitter** or **bedsit** in British English.

house[2] /haʊz/ *v* [T] **1** to provide someone with a place to live: *a program to house the homeless* **2** if a building houses something, it is kept there: *The new building will house the college's art collection.*

house ar·rest /ˈ. ˌ./ *n* **be under house arrest** to have been ordered not to leave your house by the government

house·boat /ˈhaʊsbəʊtǁ-boʊt/ *n* [C] a special boat that you can live in

house·bound /ˈhaʊsbaʊnd/ *adj* unable to leave your house, because you are ill or old

house·hold[1] /ˈhaʊshəʊldǁ-hoʊld/ *adj* **1** [only before noun] belonging to, used in, or connected with your home: *household goods* | *household chores* **2 be a household name/word** someone

or something that is famous or known about by many people

household[2] *n* [C] all the people who live together in one house: *The average household spends $200 a week on food.*

house hus·band /ˈ. ˌ./ *n* [C] a married man who works at home doing the cooking, cleaning etc

house·keep·er /ˈhaʊsˌkiːpəǁ-ər/ *n* [C] someone whose job is to do the cooking, cleaning etc in a house or hotel

house·keep·ing /ˈhaʊsˌkiːpɪŋ/ *n* [U] the work that you do at home, such as cooking and cleaning

house·man /ˈhaʊsmən/ *n* [C] *BrE, plural* **housemen** /-mən/ a young doctor who has almost finished training and is working in a hospital; INTERN *AmE*

House of Com·mons /ˌ. . ˈ../ *n* [singular] the part of the British parliament whose members are elected by the people

House of Lords /ˌ. . ˈ./ *n* [singular] the part of the British parliament whose members are not elected

House of Rep·re·sen·ta·tives /ˌ. . ˌ.ˈ.../ *n* [singular] the larger of the two groups of people who make the laws in countries such as the US and Australia → compare SENATE

house·plant /ˈhaʊsplɑːntǁ-plænt/ *n* [C] a plant that is grown indoors for decoration

house·proud /ˈhaʊspraʊd/ *adj* someone who is houseproud spends a lot of time cleaning and taking care of their home

Houses of Par·lia·ment /ˌ.. ˈ.../ *n* [singular] the British parliament

house-to-house /ˌ. . ˈ. ◂/ *adj* **house-to-house search/inquiries/visits etc** when people go to all the houses in an area to find out about something

house·wares /ˈhaʊsweəzǁ-werz/ *n* [plural] *AmE* things used in the home, such as plates and lamps

house·warm·ing /ˈ. ˌ./ *n* [C] a party to celebrate moving into a new house

house·wife /ˈhaʊswaɪf/ *n* [C] *plural* **housewives** /-waɪvz/ a woman who works at home doing the cooking, cleaning etc for her family → see also HOMEMAKER

house·work /ˈhaʊswɜːkǁ-wɜːrk/ *n* [U] the work that you do to take care of a house such as cleaning, washing etc

hous·ing /ˈhaʊzɪŋ/ *n* **1** [U] houses for people to live in: *a shortage of good housing* **2** [C] a cover for a machine: *the engine housing*

housing es·tate /ˈ.. ˌ./ *BrE*, **housing de·vel·op·ment** /ˈ. ˌ.../ *AmE* — *n* [C] a group of houses that have been built together in the same area

hov·el /ˈhɒvəlǁˈhʌ-, ˈhɑː-/ *n* [C] *literary* a small dirty place where someone lives

hov·er /ˈhɒvəǁˈhʌvər, ˈhɑː-/ *v* [I] **1** to stay in one place in the air while flying: *A helicopter hovered above the crowd.* **2** to stay around one place, especially because you are waiting for something: *Richard was hovering by the door, hoping to talk to me.*

hov·er·craft /ˈhɒvəkrɑːftǁˈhʌvərkræft, ˈhɑː-/ *n* [C] a vehicle that travels just above the surface of land or water by means of a strong current of air which is forced out of it → see colour picture on page 669

how[1] /haʊ/ *adv* **1** used to ask about the way to do something or the way something happens: *How do you spell your name?* | *How did you hear about the job?* **2** used to ask about the amount, size, or degree of something: *How old is Debbie?* | *How many children do you have?* | **how much** (=used to ask the price of something): *How much are those peaches?* **3** used to ask about someone's health: *How are you feeling?* **4** used to ask someone their opinion: *"How do I look?"* *"Great!"* **5** used before an adjective or adverb to make it stronger: *I was amazed at how small she was.* **6 how are you (doing)?/how's it going?** *spoken* used to ask if someone is well and happy: *"Hi, Kelly. How are you?"* *"Fine, thanks."* **7 how about...?** *spoken* used to suggest doing something: *How about a drink after work?* **8 how come?** *spoken* used to ask why, especially when you are surprised about something: *"I can't come to the dance." "How come?"* **9 how do you do?** *spoken formal* used when you meet someone for the first time

how[2] *linking word* used to explain about the way to do something or the way something happens: *I'm sorry, but that's how we do things in this house.* | **how to do sth** *Will you show me how to use the fax machine?*

how·ev·er[1] /haʊ'evəl-ər/ *adv* **1** used to add an idea or fact that is surprising or unexpected after what you have just said: *Normally he is an excellent student. His recent behaviour, however, has been terrible.* **2 however long/serious/ slowly etc** used to show that it makes no difference how long, serious etc something is or how slowly strangely etc it happens: *I want that car, however much it costs.*

however[2] *linking word* in any way: *You can do it however you like.*

howl /haʊl/ *v* [I] **1** if a dog or a WOLF howls, it makes a long loud crying sound **2** if the wind howls, it makes a loud high sound **3** to cry very loudly: *The baby just howled when I held him* —**howl** *n* [C]

HQ /ˌeɪtʃ 'kjuː/ *n* [C,U] the abbreviation of HEAD-QUARTERS

hr the written abbreviation of HOUR

HRH the abbreviation of His Royal Highness or Her Royal Highness

hub /hʌb/ *n* [C] **1** the central part of an area, system etc that all the other parts are connected to: *the hub of the country's rail network* **2** the central part of a wheel

hub·bub /'hʌbʌb/ *n* [singular] many noises heard at the same time: *the hubbub of the crowd*

hud·dle[1] /'hʌdl/ *also* **huddle together/up** *v* [I] if a group of people huddle together, they stand or sit closely together because they are cold or frightened: *homeless people huddled around the fire to keep warm*

huddle[2] *n* [C] a group of people or things that are close together

hue /hjuː/ *n* [C] *literary* a colour: *a golden hue*

huff[1] /hʌf/ *n* **in a huff** angry because someone has offended you: *Ray lost his temper and walked out in a huff.*

huff[2] *v* **huff and puff** to breathe in a noisy way, especially because you are doing something tir-ing: *When we got to the top of the hill, we were all huffing and puffing.*

hug[1] /hʌg/ *v* [T] **-gged, -gging 1** to put your arms around someone in a friendly way and hold them tightly: *We hugged and said goodnight.* **2** if a path or road hugs a cliff, the coast etc, it stays very close to the edge of it

hug

hug[2] *n* [C] the action of hugging someone: *Give me a hug before you go.*

huge /hjuːdʒ/ *adj* extremely large: *huge sums of money*

huge·ly /'hjuːdʒli/ *adv* extremely: *a hugely talented musician*

huh /hʌh,hʌ/ *interjection* used when you are asking a question or when you are slightly annoyed about something: *Not a bad restaurant, huh?*

hulk /hʌlk/ *n* [C] **1** an old ship, plane, or ve-hicle that is not used any more **2** a large heavy person or thing

hull /hʌl/ *n* [C] the main part of a ship

hul·la·ba·loo /ˌhʌləbə'luː, 'hʌləbəluː/ *n* [singu-lar] *informal* a lot of noise or excitement, especially about something surprising or shock-ing: *There's been a huge hullabaloo over his new book.*

hul·lo /hʌ'ləʊll-'loʊ/ *interjection* a British spell-ing of hello

hum /hʌm/ *v* **-mmed, -mming 1** [I,T] to make a tune by making a continuous sound with your lips closed: *If you don't know the words, just hum.* **2** [I] to make a low continuous sound: *in-sects humming in the sunshine* **3 be humming** if a place is humming, it is very busy and there is a lot of activity —**hum** *n* [singular] *the hum of traffic*

hu·man[1] /'hjuːmən/ *adj* **1** belonging to or re-lating to people: *the human voice* | **human error** (=a mistake made by a person and not a machine): *NASA said the accident was a result of human error.* **2 human nature** behaviour, faults, qualities etc that are typical of ordinary people **3 sb is only human** used to say that someone should not be blamed for what they have done: *She's only human – she makes mis-takes like everyone else.*

human[2] *also* **human be·ing** /ˌ.. '../ *n* [C] a man, woman, or child

hu·mane /hjuː'meɪn/ *adj* kind, not cruel, espe-cially to people or animals who are suffering —**humanely** *adv* → opposite INHUMANE

hu·man·is·m /'hjuːmənɪzəm/ *n* [U] a system of beliefs concerned with people's needs rather than religious ideas —**humanist** *n* [C] —**hu·manistic** /ˌhjuːmə'nɪstɪk◂/ *adj*

hu·man·i·tar·i·an /hjuːˌmænɪ'teəriənll-'ter-/ *adj* concerned with improving people's living conditions and preventing unfair treatment —**humanitarian** *n* [C] —**humanitarianism** *n* [U]

hu·man·i·ties /hjuː'mænətiz/ *n* **the humanities** subjects such as literature, history, and languages rather than mathematics and sciences

hu·man·i·ty /hjuː'mænəti/ *n* [U] **1** kindness, respect, and sympathy towards other people: *a man of great humanity* → opposite INHUMANITY

H

2 people in general: *the danger to humanity of pollution* **3** the state of being human

hu·man·kind /ˌhjuːmənˈkaɪnd/ *n* [U] people in general

hu·man·ly /ˈhjuːmənli/ *adv* **humanly possible** possible if you use all your skills, knowledge, and time: *It's not humanly possible to finish the building by next week.*

human race /ˌ.. ˈ./ *n* **the human race** all people

human re·sourc·es /ˌ.. .ˈ..ǁ.. ˈ.../ *n* [plural] the department in a company that deals with employing new people, keeps records about people who work for the company, and helps them with problems they may have; PERSONNEL

human rights /ˌ..ˈ./ *n* [plural] the basic rights that everyone has to be treated fairly, especially by their government

hum·ble¹ /ˈhʌmbəl/ *adj* **1** believing that you are not any better or more important than other people **2** relating to a low social class or position: *the senator's humble beginnings on a farm in Iowa* —**humbly** *adv*

humble² *v* [T] to make someone realize that they are not as important, good, kind etc as they thought: *their mighty leader who humbled the enemy* —**humbling** *adj*

hum·drum /ˈhʌmdrʌm/ *adj* boring, ordinary, and never changing very much: *a humdrum job*

hu·mid /ˈhjuːmɪd/ *adj* air that is humid feels warm and wet

hu·mid·i·ty /hjuːˈmɪdɪti/ *n* [U] the amount of water that is contained in the air

hu·mil·i·ate /hjuːˈmɪlieɪt/ *v* [T] to make someone seem stupid or weak: *Mrs. Banks humiliated me in front of the whole class.* —**humiliated** *adj* —**humiliation** /hjuːˌmɪliˈeɪʃən/ *n* [C,U]

hu·mil·i·at·ing /hjuːˈmɪlieɪtɪŋ/ *adj* making you feel humiliated: *It's humiliating to be beaten by a child.*

hu·mil·i·ty /hjuːˈmɪlɪti/ *n* [U] the quality of believing that you are not any better or more important than other people

hu·mor·ous /ˈhjuːmərəsǁˈhjuː-, ˈjuː-/ *adj* funny and enjoyable: *a humorous account of her trip to Egypt* —**humorously** *adv*

hu·mour¹ *BrE*, **humor** *AmE* /ˈhjuːməǁ-ˈhjuːmər, ˈjuː-/ *n* [U] **1 sense of humour** the ability to laugh at things and think that they are funny: *I don't like her – she's got no sense of humour.* **2** the quality in something that makes it funny: *There's a lot of humour in his songs.* **3 good humour** a cheerful friendly attitude

humour² *BrE*, **humor** *AmE* — *v* [T] to do what someone wants so that they will not become angry or upset: *Just humour me and listen, please.*

hu·mour·less *BrE*, **humorless** *AmE* /ˈhjuːmələsǁˈhjuːmər-, ˈjuː-/ *adj* too serious and not able to laugh at things that are funny

hump¹ /hʌmp/ *n* **1** [C] a small hill or raised part on a road **2** [C] a raised part on the back of a person or animal: *a camel's hump*

hump² *v* [T] *BrE informal* to carry something heavy somewhere: *I managed to hump the suitcase upstairs.*

hunch¹ /hʌntʃ/ *n* **have a hunch** to think that something is true or that something will happen, even if you have no information about it: *I had a hunch that you'd call today.*

hunch² *v* [I] to bend down and forward so that your back forms a curve: *He was sitting in his study, hunched over his books.* —**hunched** *adj*: *hunched shoulders*

hunch·back /ˈhʌntʃbæk/ *n* [C] an offensive word for someone who has a large raised part on their back

hun·dred /ˈhʌndrɪd/ *number* **1** 100: *a hundred years* | *two hundred miles* **2 hundreds of sth** a very large number of something: *Hundreds of people joined in the march.* —**hundredth** *number*

> **USAGE NOTE: hundred**
>
> British people say **hundred and** in numbers like this: *326 = three hundred and twenty-six.* Americans usually miss out **and**: *326 = three hundred twenty-six.* Plural forms like **hundreds** and **thousands** can be used when they are not part of another number: *Hundreds of people attended the concert.* | *Thousands of pounds have been spent on the new hospital.*

hun·dred·weight /ˈhʌndrɪdweɪt/ *written abbreviation* **cwt** *n* [C] a measure of weight equal to 112 pounds or 50.8 kilograms in Britain and 100 pounds or 45.36 kilograms in the US

hung /hʌŋ/ *v* the past tense and past participle of HANG

hun·ger /ˈhʌŋɡəǁ-ər/ *n* [U] **1** the feeling you have when you want or need to eat: *The baby was crying with hunger.* **2** a severe lack of food, especially for a long period of time: *Hundreds of people are dying of hunger every day.*

hunger strike /ˈ.. ./ *n* [C] when someone refuses to eat as a way of protesting about something

hung·o·ver /hʌŋˈəʊvəǁ-ˈoʊvər/ *adj* feeling ill because you drank too much alcohol the previous day

hun·gry /ˈhʌŋɡri/ *adj* **1** wanting to eat something: *I'm hungry, let's eat!* **2 go hungry** to not have enough food to eat: *Many people in our city go hungry every day.* **3 be hungry for sth** to want something very much: *Rick was hungry for a chance to work.* —**hungrily** *adv*

hung-up /ˌ. ˈ./ *adj informal* worrying too much about someone or something: *You shouldn't get all hung-up about him, he isn't worth it!*

hunk /hʌŋk/ *n* [C] **1** a thick piece of something: *a hunk of bread* ➜ see colour picture on page 440 **2** *informal* an attractive man who has a strong body

hun·ker /ˈhʌŋkəǁ-ər/ *v* **hunker down** *phr v* [I] to sit on your heels with your knees bent in front of you; SQUAT

hunt¹ /hʌnt/ *v* [I,T] **1** to chase animals in order to catch and kill them: *These dogs have been trained to hunt.* **2** to look for someone or something very carefully: **+ for** *Police are still hunting for the murderer.*

hunt sb/sth ↔ down *phr v* [T] to find an enemy or criminal after searching very carefully: *a plan to hunt down people owing money*

hunt² *n* [C] **1** a careful search for someone or something: **+ for** *The hunt for the missing child continues today.* **2** an occasion when people chase animals in order to catch and kill them

hunt·er /ˈhʌntəǁ-ər/ *n* [C] someone who hunts wild animals

hunt·ing /'hʌntɪŋ/ n [U] **1** the activity of chasing animals in order to catch and kill them **2 job-hunting/house-hunting etc** a search for a job, a house to live in etc

hur·dle¹ /'hɜːdl‖'hɜːr-/ n [C] **1** a problem or difficulty that you must deal with before you can do something else: *The interview with the director was the final hurdle in getting the job.* **2** a small fence that a person or a horse jumps over during a race

hurdle² v [I,T] to jump over something while you are running —**hurdler** n [C]

hurl /hɜːl‖hɜːrl/ v [T] **1** to throw something using a lot of strength: **hurl sth through/across/out etc** *Someone hurled a brick through the window.* **2 hurl insults/abuse etc at sb** to shout angrily at someone

hur·ray /hʊˈreɪ/ also **hooray** interjection used to show that you are pleased about something

hur·ri·cane /'hʌrɪkən‖'hɜːrɪˌkeɪn/ n [C] a violent storm with very strong fast winds → compare TORNADO

hur·ried /'hʌrɪd‖'hɜːrɪd/ adj quicker than usual —**hurriedly** adv

hur·ry¹ /'hʌri‖'hɜːri/ v [I,T] to do something or go somewhere more quickly than usual, or to make someone do this: *You'll catch the train if you hurry.* |+ **along/across/down etc** *We hurried home to watch the football game.*
hurry up phr v **1 hurry up!** spoken used to tell someone to do something more quickly: *Hurry up! We're late.* **2** [**hurry sb/sth up**] to make someone do something more quickly or make something happen more quickly : *Try to hurry the kids up or they'll be late for school.*

hurry² n **1 be in a hurry** to need to do something, go somewhere etc more quickly than usual: *I can't talk now – I'm in a hurry.* **2 (there's) no hurry** spoken used to tell someone that they do not have to do something immediately: *You can pay me back next week – there's no hurry.* **3 not be in any hurry/be in no hurry** to be able to wait because you have a lot of time in which to do something: *Take your time, I'm not in any hurry.*

hurt¹ /hɜːt‖hɜːrt/ v **hurt, hurt, hurting 1** [T] to make yourself or someone else feel pain: *She hurt her shoulder playing baseball.* | *Careful you don't hurt yourself with that knife.* **2** [I,T] if part of your body hurts, you feel pain in it: *My feet really hurt after all that walking!* **3** [I,T] to make someone feel upset or unhappy: *His comments weren't true, but they hurt.* | **hurt sb's feelings** *I'm sorry, I didn't mean to hurt your feelings.* **4 it won't/doesn't hurt (sb) to do sth** spoken used to say that there is no reason why someone should not do something: *It won't hurt him to make his own dinner for once.* **5 sb wouldn't hurt a fly** spoken used to say that someone is very gentle and is not likely to hurt anyone

hurt² adj **1** injured: **badly/seriously/slightly hurt** *Kerry was badly hurt in a skiing accident.*

2 very upset or unhappy: *I was very hurt by what you said.*

USAGE NOTE: hurt

When **hurt** is used to talk about damage to your body, you may be **slightly/badly/seriously hurt**. However, do not use these adverbs to talk about being made unhappy by someone's behaviour. Compare: *She was badly/slightly hurt when she fell off the ladder*, and *She was very deeply/very hurt by his unkind words.* → see also Usage Note at WOUND

---

hurt·ful /'hɜːtfəl‖'hɜːrt-/ adj making you feel upset or unhappy: *a hurtful remark*

hur·tle /'hɜːtl‖'hɜːr-/ v [I] to move or fall very fast: + **down/along/across etc** *A huge rock came hurtling down the mountainside.*

hus·band /'hʌzbənd/ n [C] the man that a woman is married to → see picture at FAMILY

hush¹ /hʌʃ/ v **hush** spoken used to tell someone to be quiet, or to comfort a child who is crying
hush sth **up** phr v [T] to prevent people from knowing about something dishonest: *The bank tried to hush the whole thing up.*

hush² n [singular] a peaceful silence

hushed /hʌʃt/ adj quiet, or speaking quietly, especially because you are excited or do not want other people to hear you: *people speaking in hushed voices*

hush-hush /ˌ. ˈ. ◂ ‖ˌ. ./ adj informal secret: *a hush-hush military project*

husk /hʌsk/ n [C,U] the dry part that covers some grains or seeds

hus·ky¹ /'hʌski/ adj **1** a husky voice is deep and sounds rough but attractive **2** *AmE* a husky man is big and strong —**huskily** adv —**huskiness** n [U]

husky² n [C] a dog with thick hair, often used for pulling SLEDGES over snow

hus·tle¹ /'hʌsəl/ v **1** [T] to make someone move quickly, often by pushing them: **hustle sb into/out/through sth** *Jackson was hustled into his car by bodyguards.* **2** [I] *AmE* to hurry in doing something or going somewhere: *We've got to hustle or we'll be late!* **3** [I,T] *AmE informal* to sell or obtain things illegally: *Young boys were hustling stolen goods on the street.*

hustle² n **hustle and bustle** busy and noisy activity

hus·tler /'hʌslə‖-ər/ n [C] *especially AmE* someone who gets money in illegal and dishonest ways

hut /hʌt/ n [C] a small building with only one or two rooms: *a wooden hut*

hutch /hʌtʃ/ n [C] a wooden box that pet rabbits are kept in

hy·a·cinth /'haɪəsɪnθ/ n [C] a garden plant with small flowers shaped like bells and a sweet smell

hy·brid /'haɪbrɪd/ n [C] **1** an animal or plant that is produced from two different types of animal or plant **2** something that is a mixture of two or more things —**hybrid** adj

---

GRAMMAR NOTE: 'if' clauses (1)
Use the simple present to talk about the future in clauses beginning **if...** : *I will hit you* **if** *you* **do** *that again. not* 'if you will do that again'. **If** *you* **take** *a taxi, you'll be OK. not* 'if you will take a taxi...'
Use 'will' in the other part of the sentence.

hy·drant /ˈhaɪdrənt/ n see FIRE HYDRANT

hy·draul·ic /haɪˈdrɒlɪk, -ˈdrɔː-ǁ-ˈdrɒː-/ adj moved or operated by the pressure of water or other liquids: *hydraulic brakes* —**hydraulically** /-kli/ adv

hy·dro·e·lec·tric /ˌhaɪdrəʊ-ɪˈlektrɪk◂ ǁ-droʊ-/ adj using water power to produce electricity: *a hydroelectric dam*

hy·dro·gen /ˈhaɪdrədʒən/ n [U] a gas that is lighter than air, and that becomes water when it combines with OXYGEN

hy·e·na /haɪˈiːnə/ n [C] a wild animal like a dog that makes a loud laughing sound

hy·giene /ˈhaɪdʒiːn/ n [U] the practice of keeping yourself and the things around you clean in order to prevent diseases: *Hygiene is very important when preparing a baby's food.*

hy·gien·ic /haɪˈdʒiːnɪkǁ-ˈdʒe-, -ˈdʒiː-/ adj clean and likely to prevent diseases from spreading

hymn /hɪm/ n [C] a song sung in Christian churches

hype¹ /haɪp/ n [U] when something is talked about a lot on television, in the newspapers etc, to make it seem good or important: *the media hype surrounding Spielberg's new movie*

hype² v [T] also **hype** sth ↔ **up** to try to make people think something is good or important by advertising it or talking about it a lot on television, in the newspapers etc: *The insurance industry is usually quick to hype its products.*

hyped up /ˌ. ˈ.◂/ adj informal very anxious or excited about something: *Try not to get too hyped up about the test.*

hy·per /ˈhaɪpəǁ-ər/ adj informal very excited or with a lot of energy

hyper- /haɪpəǁ-ər/ prefix used at the beginning of some words to mean 'much more than usual' or 'much bigger than usual': *hypersensitive* | *hypermarket* (=a very large supermarket)

hy·per·ac·tive /ˌhaɪpərˈæktɪv◂/ adj a hyperactive child cannot keep still or quiet for very long —**hyperactivity** /ˌhaɪpərækˈtɪvᵻti/ n [U]

hy·per·bo·le /haɪˈpɜːbəliǁ-ɜːr-/ n [U] a way of describing something by saying that it is much bigger, smaller, heavier etc than it really is

hy·per·mar·ket /ˈhaɪpəˌmɑːkᵻtǁ-pərˌmɑːr-/ n [C] BrE a very large SUPERMARKET outside a town

hy·per·sen·si·tive /ˌhaɪpəˈsensᵻtɪv◂ ǁ-pər-/ adj becoming annoyed or upset very easily

hy·per·ten·sion /ˌhaɪpəˈtenʃənǁ-pər-/ n [U] technical a medical condition in which someone's BLOOD PRESSURE is too high

hy·phen /ˈhaɪfən/ n [C] a short line (-) that joins words or parts of words

---

USAGE NOTE: hyphens

Use a **hyphen** (-) to join two or more words that are used as an adjective in front of a noun: *a two-car family* | *a ten-year-old boy*. You can also say: *a family with two cars* | *a boy who is ten years old*.

---

hy·phen·ate /ˈhaɪfəneɪt/ v [T] to join words or parts of words with a hyphen —**hyphenated** adj —**hyphenation** /ˌhaɪfəˈneɪʃən/ n [U]

hyp·no·sis /hɪpˈnəʊsᵻsǁ-ˈnoʊ-/ n [U] when someone is put into a state in which their thoughts and actions can be influenced: *under hypnosis He remembered details of his childhood under hypnosis.*

hyp·not·ic /hɪpˈnɒtɪkǁ-ˈnɑː-/ adj 1 hypnotic sounds or images make you feel sleepy, especially because sounds or movements are repeated: *hypnotic music* 2 relating to hypnosis: *a hypnotic trance* —**hypnotically** /-kli/ adv

hyp·no·tist /ˈhɪpnətᵻst/ n [C] someone who hypnotizes people

hyp·no·tize (also **-ise** BrE) /ˈhɪpnətaɪz/ v [T] to make someone go into a state in which they feel they are asleep, so that you can influence what they think or do —**hypnotism** n [U]

hy·po·chon·dri·ac /ˌhaɪpəˈkɒndriækǁ-ˈkɑːn-/ n [C] someone who worries all the time about their health, even when they are not ill —**hypochondriac** adj —**hypochondria** /-driə/ n [U]

hy·poc·ri·sy /hɪˈpɒkrᵻsiǁ-ˈpɑː-/ n [U] when someone pretends to be a good person, or to believe something that they do not really believe

hyp·o·crite /ˈhɪpəkrɪt/ n [C] someone who pretends to be a good person, or to believe something that they do not really believe

hyp·o·crit·i·cal /ˌhɪpəˈkrɪtɪkəl◂/ adj pretending to be a good person or to believe something you do not really believe: *It would be hypocritical to get married in church when we don't believe in God.* —**hypocritically** /-kli/ adv

hy·po·der·mic /ˌhaɪpəˈdɜːmɪk◂ ǁ-ɜːr-/ n [C] a piece of medical equipment with a hollow needle used for putting drugs into someone's body through the skin; SYRINGE —**hypodermic** adj

hy·po·ther·mi·a /ˌhaɪpəʊˈθɜːmiəǁ-poʊˈθɜːr-/ n [U] technical a serious medical condition in which someone's body becomes very cold

hy·poth·e·sis /haɪˈpɒθᵻsᵻsǁ-ˈpɑː-/ n [C], plural **hypotheses** /-siːz/ an idea that someone suggests as an explanation of something, but that they have not proved to be true

hy·po·thet·i·cal /ˌhaɪpəˈθetɪkəl◂/ adj based on a situation that is not real but might happen: *Students were given a hypothetical law case to discuss.* —**hypothetically** /-kli/ adv

hys·ter·ec·to·my /ˌhɪstəˈrektəmi/ n [C,U] a medical operation to remove a woman's UTERUS

hys·te·ri·a /hɪˈstɪəriəǁ-ˈsteriə/ n [U] extreme excitement, anger, fear etc that you cannot control: *The incident provoked mass hysteria.*

hys·ter·i·cal /hɪˈsterɪkəl/ adj 1 informal extremely funny: *a hysterical new comedy* 2 unable to control your behaviour or emotions because you are very upset, afraid, excited etc —**hysterically** /-kli/ adv

hys·ter·ics /hɪˈsterɪks/ n [plural] 1 when you cannot control your behaviour or emotions because you are very upset, afraid, excited etc 2 **be in hysterics** informal to be laughing and not able to stop

Ii

I, i /aɪ/ the letter 'i'

I *pron* used when the person who is speaking is the subject of a verb: *I saw Mike yesterday.* | *My husband and I are going to Mexico.*

ice¹ /aɪs/ *n* **1** [U] water that has frozen and become solid: *Do you want some ice in your drink?* **2 break the ice** to make people who do not know each other feel relaxed, by starting to talk to them

ice / ice cubes

ice² *v* [T] *BrE* to cover a cake with ICING; FROST *AmE*
ice over/up *phr v* [I] to become covered with ice: *The lake iced over during the night.*

ice·berg /'aɪsbɜːg‖-bɜːrg/ *n* [C] a very large piece of ice floating in the sea

ice cap /'. ./ *n* [C] an area of thick ice that always covers the land at the North Pole and South Pole

ice-cold /ˌ. '.◂ / *adj* extremely cold: *ice-cold drinks*

ice cream /ˌ. '.◂ ‖'. ./ *n* [C,U] a frozen sweet food made of milk or cream and sugar

ice cube /'. ./ *n* [C] a small block of ice that you put in a drink ➡ see picture at ICE

ice hock·ey /'. ˌ../ *n* [U] *BrE* a game played on ice in which two teams of players use long curved sticks to hit a hard flat object; HOCKEY *AmE* ➡ see colour picture on page 636

ice lol·ly /'. ˌ../ *n* [C] *BrE* a piece of sweet tasting ice on a stick; POPSICLE *AmE*

ice pack /'. ./ *n* [C] a bag of ice

ice rink /'. ./ *n* [C] a specially prepared area of ice, used for skating (SKATE) on, usually inside a building

ice skate¹ /'. ./ *v* [I] to slide on ice wearing boots with a metal part on the bottom ➡ see colour picture on page 636 —**ice skating** *n* [U] —**ice skater** *n* [C]

ice skate² *n* [C] a boot with a metal part on the bottom, used for ice skating ➡ see colour picture on page 636

i·ci·cle /'aɪsɪkəl/ *n* [C] a thin pointed piece of ice that hangs down ➡ see picture at ICE

ic·ing /'aɪsɪŋ/ *n* [U] a mixture made from sugar and water or sugar and butter, used to cover cakes; FROSTING *AmE*

i·con /'aɪkɒn‖-kɑːn/ *n* [C] **1** someone or something that many people admire and connect with an important idea: *a feminist icon* **2** a small picture on a computer screen that makes the computer do something when you choose it: *To send a fax, click on the telephone icon.* **3** also **ikon** a picture or figure of a holy person —**iconic** /aɪˈkɒnɪk‖-ˈkɑː-/ *adj*

ic·y /'aɪsi/ *adj* **1** extremely cold: *an icy wind* **2** covered in ice: *an icy road*

I'd /aɪd/ the short form of 'I had' or 'I would'

ID /ˌaɪ 'diː/ *n* [C,U] a document that shows your name, address etc, usually with a photograph: *May I see some ID please?*

i·dea /aɪˈdɪə/ *n* **1** [C] a plan or suggestion, especially one you think of suddenly: *What a good idea!* | **+ for** *Where did you get the idea for the book?* | **have an idea** *I have an idea – let's go to the beach.* **2** [singular, U] understanding or knowledge of something: **+ of** *This book gives you an idea of what life was like during the war.* | **a rough idea** (=not exact): *Give me a rough idea of how much it will cost.* | **have no idea** (=not know at all): *Richard had no idea where Celia had gone.* **3** [singular] the aim or purpose of doing something: **+ of** *The idea of the game is to hit the ball into the holes.* **4** [C] an opinion or belief: **+ about** *Bill has some strange ideas about women.*

i·deal¹ /aɪˈdɪəl◂ / *adj* **1** the best that something could possibly be: *an ideal place for a picnic* **2** perfect, but not likely to exist: *In an ideal world there would be no war.*

ideal² *n* [C] **1** a principle or belief that seems good: *democratic ideals* **2** a perfect example of something: *the ideal of beauty*

i·deal·is·m /aɪˈdɪəlɪzəm/ *n* [U] the belief that you should live according to high standards or principles, even if it is difficult —**idealist** *n* [C]

i·deal·is·tic /aɪˌdɪəˈlɪstɪk◂ / *adj* believing in principles and high standards, even if they cannot be achieved in real life —**idealistically** /-kli/ *adv*

i·deal·ize (also **-ise** *BrE*) /aɪˈdɪəlaɪz/ *v* [T] to imagine that something is perfect or better than it really is —**idealization** /aɪˌdɪəlaɪˈzeɪʃən‖-lə-/ *n* [C,U]

i·deal·ly /aɪˈdɪəli/ *adv* **1** used to say how you would like things to be, even if it is not possible: *Ideally I'd like to live in the country.* **2** perfectly: *Barry is ideally suited for the job.*

i·den·ti·cal /aɪˈdentɪkəl/ *adj* exactly the same: **+ to** *Your shoes are identical to mine.* | **identical twins** (=two babies that are born together and look the same) —**identically** /-kli/ *adv*

i·den·ti·fi·a·ble /aɪˈdentɪfaɪəbəl/ *adj* easy to recognize

i·den·ti·fi·ca·tion /aɪˌdentɪfɪˈkeɪʃən/ *n* [U] **1** something official that shows your name, address etc, usually with a photograph, used: *You can use a passport as identification.* **2** when you say that you recognize someone or something: *The bodies are awaiting identification.*

i·den·ti·fy /aɪˈdentɪfaɪ/ *v* [T] to recognize and name someone or something: *Can you identify the man who robbed you?*
identify with sb *phr v* [T] to be able to understand someone's feelings because you have those feelings too: *It was easy to identify with the novel's main character.*

i·den·ti·ty /aɪˈdentɪti/ *n* **1** [C,U] who someone is: *The identity of the killer is still unknown.* **2** [U] the qualities that someone has that make them different from other people: *our cultural identity* | **sense of identity** *Many people's sense of identity comes from their job.*

i·de·o·lo·gic·al /ˌaɪdɪəˈlɒdʒɪkəl◂ ‖-ˈlɑː-/ *adj* based on a particular set of beliefs or ideas: *ideo-*

logical objections to the changes —**ideologically** /-kli/ *adv*

i·de·ol·o·gy /ˌaɪdi'ɒlədʒil-'ɑːl-/ *n* [C,U] a set of beliefs or ideas, especially political beliefs: *Marxist ideology*

id·i·o·cy /'ɪdiəsi/ *n* [C,U] extremely stupid behaviour

id·i·om /'ɪdiəm/ *n* [C] a group of words that have a different meaning from the usual meaning of the separate words: *'To kick the bucket' is an idiom meaning 'to die'.*

id·i·o·mat·ic /ˌɪdiə'mætɪk◂/ *adj* **1** idiomatic language is typical of the way people usually talk and write **2** idiomatic expression/phrase an idiom —**idiomatically** /-kli/ *adv*

id·i·o·syn·cra·sy /ˌɪdiə'sɪŋkrəsi/ *n* [C] an unusual habit or way of behaving —**idiosyncratic** /ˌɪdiəsɪn'krætɪk◂/ *adj*

id·i·ot /'ɪdiət/ *n* [C] a stupid person: *Some idiot drove into the back of my car.* —**idiotic** /ˌɪdi-'ɒtɪk◂ ll-'ɑːt-/ *adj* —**idiotically** /-kli/ *adv*

i·dle /'aɪdl/ *adj* **1** lazy **2** not working or being used: *machines lying idle in our factories* **3** having no useful purpose or reason: *This is just idle gossip.* —**idleness** *n* [U] —**idly** *adv*

i·dol /'aɪdl/ *n* [C] **1** someone or something that you admire very much **2** a picture or object that is worshipped (WORSHIP) as a god

i·dol·ize (also **-ise** *BrE*) /'aɪdəl-aɪz/ *v* [T] to admire someone so much that you think they are perfect: *They idolize their little boy.*

i·dyl·lic /ɪ'dɪlɪk, aɪ-llaɪ-/ *adj* very pleasant and peaceful: *an idyllic country scene* —**idyllically** /-kli/ *adv*

i.e. /ˌaɪ 'iː◂/ used when you want to explain the exact meaning of something: *The movie is only for adults, i.e. those over 18.*

if /ɪf/ *linking word* **1** used to talk about something that might happen: *If you get the right answer, you win a prize.* | *What will you do if you don't get into college?* **2** used to mean 'whether', when you are asking or deciding something: *I wonder if John's home yet.* **3** used when you are talking about something that always happens: *If I don't go to bed by 11, I feel terrible the next day.* **4** used to ask or suggest something politely: *If I might ask one question...*

if·fy /'ɪfi/ *adj informal* **1** something that seems iffy does not seem good, suitable, or honest: *The weather looks a bit iffy today.* **2** not sure about whether you want to do something or if you think something should happen: *Carol sounded a bit iffy about the party.*

ig·loo /'ɪgluː/ *n* [C] a house made from blocks of hard snow and ice

ig·nite /ɪg'naɪt/ *v formal* **1** [I,T] to start burning, or to make something start burning **2** [T] to start a dangerous situation, angry argument etc: *actions that could ignite a civil war*

ig·ni·tion /ɪg'nɪʃən/ *n* **1** [singular] the electrical part of a car engine that makes it start working: *Turn the key in the ignition.* **2** [U] *formal* the act of making something start to burn

ig·no·min·i·ous /ˌɪgnə'mɪniəs/ *adj formal* making you feel ashamed or embarrassed: *an ignominious defeat* —**ignominiously** *adv*

ig·no·rance /'ɪgnərəns/ *n* [U] lack of knowledge or information about something: *people's fear and ignorance about AIDS*

ig·no·rant /'ɪgnərənt/ *adj* **1** not knowing facts or information that you should know: + **of** *We went on, ignorant of the dangers.* **2** *BrE* rude or impolite

ig·nore /ɪg'nɔːll-'nɔːr/ *v* [T] to not pay any attention to someone or something: *Don't just ignore me when I'm speaking to you.*

USAGE NOTE: ignore

Compare **ignore** and **be ignorant of**. If you **ignore** something you know about it but pay no attention to it: *Many drivers simply ignore speed limits.* If you **are ignorant** of something, you do not know about it: *Most passengers were totally ignorant of the safety procedures.*

---

i·gua·na /ɪ'gwɑːnə/ *n* [C] a large tropical American LIZARD

i·kon /'aɪkɒnll-kɑːn/ *n* [C] ICON

il- /ɪl/ *prefix* used at the beginning of some words to mean 'not': *illogical* | *illegal*

I'll /aɪl/ the short form of 'I will' or 'I shall'

ill¹ /ɪl/ *adj* **1** suffering from a disease or not feeling well; SICK: *Jenny can't come – she's ill.* | **seriously/critically ill**(=extremely ill) **2** bad or harmful: *the ill effects of alcohol*

ill² *adv* **1** badly or unpleasantly: *We were ill prepared for the cold weather.* **2** can ill afford (to do) sth to not be able to do something because it would make your situation more difficult

ill³ *n* [C usually plural] a bad thing, especially a problem or something that makes you worry: *the social ills caused by poverty*

ill-ad·vised /ˌ. .'.◂/ *adj* not sensible —**ill-advisedly** *adv*

il·le·gal /ɪ'liːgəl/ *adj* not allowed by law: *It is illegal to park your car here.* —**illegally** *adv* → opposite LEGAL

illegal im·mi·grant /ˌ...'.../ also **illegal a·li·en** /ˌ...'.../ *AmE* — *n* [C] someone who comes into a country to live or work without official permission

il·le·gi·ble /ɪ'ledʒ¦bəl/ *adj* difficult or impossible to read: *illegible handwriting* —**illegibly** *adv*

il·le·git·i·mate /ˌɪl¦'dʒɪt¦m¦t◂/ *adj* **1** an illegitimate child has parents who are not married **2** not allowed by the rules: *an illegitimate use of public money* —**illegitimately** *adv* —**illegitimacy** *n* [U]

ill-e·quipped /ˌ. .'.◂/ *adj* not having the necessary equipment or skills: *Too many hospitals are dirty and ill-equipped.*

ill-fat·ed /ˌ. '.◂/ *adj* unlucky because a lot of bad things happen: *an ill-fated attempt to climb Everest*

il·li·cit /ɪ'lɪs¦t/ *adj* illegal or not approved of by society: *an illicit love affair* —**illicitly** *adv*

il·lit·e·rate /ɪ'lɪtər¦t/ *adj* unable to read or write —**illiteracy** *n* [U]

ill-man·nered /ˌ. '.◂/ *adj formal* not polite

ill·ness /'ɪln¦s/ *n* [C,U] a disease of your body or mind, or the state of having a disease: *mental illness*

il·lo·gi·cal /ɪ'lɒdʒɪk∂llɪ'lɑː-/ *adj* not sensible or reasonable: *illogical behaviour* —**illogically** /-kli/ *adv*

ill-treat /ˌ. '. / *v* [T] to be cruel to someone, especially to a child or an animal: *The prisoners were beaten and ill-treated.* —**ill-treatment** *n* [U]

il·lu·mi·nate /ɪˈluːmɪneɪt, ɪˈljuː-ǁ-ˈluː-/ *v* [T] **1** to make light shine on something: *The room was illuminated by candles.* **2** to make something easier to understand —**illumination** /ɪˌluːmɪˈneɪʃən, ɪˌljuː-ǁ-ˌluː-/ *n* [U]

il·lu·mi·nat·ing /ɪˈluːmɪneɪtɪŋ, ɪˈljuː-ǁ-ˈluː-/ *adj* making something easier to understand: *an illuminating piece of research*

il·lu·sion /ɪˈluːʒən/ *n* [C] **1** something that seems to be different from the way it really is: *The mirrors in the room gave an illusion of space.* **2** a false idea or belief: **be under an illusion** (=believe something that is not true): *Terry is under the illusion all women love him.* | **have no illusions about** (=realize how difficult or unpleasant something is): *We have no illusions about the hard work that lies ahead.*

il·lus·trate /ˈɪləstreɪt/ *v* [T] **1** to explain or make something clear by giving examples: *A chart might help to illustrate this point.* **2** to draw or paint pictures for a book: *a children's book illustrated by Dr. Seuss*

il·lus·tra·tion /ˌɪləˈstreɪʃən/ *n* **1** [C] a picture in a book **2** [C,U] an example that helps you understand something: **+ of** *a striking illustration of what I mean*

il·lus·tra·tor /ˈɪləstreɪtəǁ-tər/ *n* [C] someone who draws pictures for books or magazines, as their job

il·lus·tri·ous /ɪˈlʌstriəs/ *adj formal* very famous and admired by a lot of people: *our illustrious guest, Professor Williams*

ill will /ˌ. ˈ./ *n* [U] an extremely unfriendly attitude towards someone

I'm /aɪm/ the short form of 'I am'

im- /ɪm/ *prefix* used at the beginning of some words to mean 'not': *impossible* | *impractical*

im·age /ˈɪmɪdʒ/ *n* [C] **1** the way that people consider someone or something to be: **improve your image** *The party is trying to improve its image with women voters.* **2** a picture that you can see through a camera, on a television, or in a mirror **3** a picture that you have in your mind: *She had a clear image of how he would look in twenty years' time.* **4** a word, picture, or phrase that describes an idea in a poem, book, or film

im·ag·e·ry /ˈɪmɪdʒəri/ *n* [U] the use of words, pictures, or phrases to describe ideas or actions in poems, books, films etc: *the disturbing imagery of Bosch's paintings*

i·ma·gi·na·ry /ɪˈmædʒɪnəriǁ-neri/ *adj* not real, but imagined: *Many children have imaginary friends.*

i·ma·gi·na·tion /ɪˌmædʒɪˈneɪʃən/ *n* [C,U] the ability to form pictures or ideas in your mind: *Art is all about using your imagination*

i·ma·gi·na·tive /ɪˈmædʒɪnətɪv/ *adj* **1** able to think of new and interesting ideas: *an imaginative writer* **2** containing new and interesting ideas: *an imaginative story* —**imaginatively** *adv*

i·ma·gine /ɪˈmædʒɪn/ *v* [T] **1** to think of what something would be like if it happened: **+ (that)** *Imagine you're lying on a beach somewhere.* | **imagine sb doing sth** *I can't imagine you being a father!* **2** to think that something is true when it is not: *No one is out there, you're imagining things.* **3** to think that something is probably true: **+ (that)** *I imagine Kathy will be there.*

im·bal·ance /ɪmˈbæləns/ *n* [C,U] when two things are not equal in size, or not the right size in relation to each other: *The condition is caused by a hormonal imbalance.*

im·be·cile /ˈɪmbəsiːlǁ-səl/ *n* [C] a stupid person

im·bibe /ɪmˈbaɪb/ *v* [I,T] *formal* to drink something, especially alcohol

im·bue /ɪmˈbjuː/ *v* **be imbued with sth** *formal* to be filled with a feeling or quality: *His songs were imbued with a romantic tenderness.*

im·i·tate /ˈɪmɪteɪt/ *v* [T] to copy the way someone does something: *Children often imitate their parents' behaviour.* —**imitative** *adj* —**imitator** *n* [C] → compare COPY[2]

im·i·ta·tion[1] /ˌɪmɪˈteɪʃən/ *n* **1** [C,U] when you copy the way someone talks, behaves etc: *Harry can do an excellent imitation of Elvis.* | *Children learn by imitation.* **2** [C] something that is a cheaper copy of something expensive

imitation[2] *adj* imitation leather/wood/ivory etc something that looks like leather, wood etc, but is not

im·mac·u·late /ɪˈmækjʊlɪt/ *adj* very clean and neat: *The house looked immaculate.* —**immaculately** *adv*

im·ma·te·ri·al /ˌɪməˈtɪəriəl ǁ-ˈtɪr-/ *adj formal* not important: *The difference in our ages is immaterial.*

im·ma·ture /ˌɪməˈtʃʊəǁ-ˈtʃʊr/ *adj* **1** behaving in a way that is not sensible enough for your age: *Stop being so childish and immature!* **2** not fully formed or developed —**immaturity** *n* [U] —**immaturely** *adv*

im·mea·su·ra·ble /ɪˈmeʒərəbəl/ *adj* extremely large or extreme: *His comments have caused immeasurable damage.* —**immeasurably** *adv*

im·me·di·ate /ɪˈmiːdiət/ *adj* **1** happening or done now with no delay: *Campaigners have called for an immediate end to the road building plan.* **2** needing to be dealt with quickly: *Our immediate concern was to stop the fire from spreading.* **3** [only before noun] next to or nearest to a place: *Police want to question anyone who was in the immediate area.* **4** happening just after or just before something: *plans for the immediate future* **5** **immediate family** your parents, children, brothers, and sisters

im·me·di·ate·ly /ɪˈmiːdiətli/ *adv* **1** without any delay: *Open this door immediately!* **2** next to something in position, or just before or after something in time: *They live immediately above us.*

USAGE NOTE: immediately

If you use **immediately** it can sound as if you are ordering someone to do something, so try to avoid it if you want to be polite. It is better to use the phrase **as soon as possible**: *I would be grateful if you could send me the information as soon as possible.* | *Could you let me know as soon as possible?*

im·mense /ɪˈmens/ *adj* used to emphasize how big or important something is: *An immense amount of money has been spent on research.* —**immensity** *n* [U]

im·mense·ly /ɪˈmensli/ *adv* very much: *I enjoyed the course immensely.*

im·merse /ɪˈmɜːs‖-ɜːrs/ *v* [T] **1** **be immersed in/immerse yourself in** to be completely involved in something: *Grant is completely immersed in his work.* **2** to put something completely in a liquid —**immersion** /ɪˈmɜːʃən, -ʒən‖ ɪˈmɜːrʒən/ *n* [U]

im·mi·grant /ˈɪmɪɡrənt/ *n* [C] someone who comes to live in a country from another country: *immigrant workers* → compare EMIGRANT

im·mi·gra·tion /ˌɪmɪˈɡreɪʃən/ *n* [U] **1** when people come to a country in order to live there **2** the place in an airport, at a border etc where your PASSPORT and other documents are checked

im·mi·nent /ˈɪmɪnənt/ *adj* going to happen very soon: *The building is in imminent danger of collapse.* —**imminence** *n* [U] —**imminently** *adv*

im·mo·bile /ɪˈməʊbaɪl‖ɪˈmoʊbəl/ *adj* not moving, or not able to move: *Marcus remained immobile.* —**immobility** /ˌɪməˈbɪlɪti/ *n* [U]

im·mo·bi·lize (also **-ise** *BrE*) /ɪˈməʊbɪlaɪz‖ ɪˈmoʊ-/ *v* [T] to stop someone or something from moving: *He was immobilized by a broken leg for several weeks.*

im·mor·al /ɪˈmɒrəl‖ɪˈmɔː-/ *adj* morally wrong: *Exploiting people is immoral.* —**immorally** *adv* —**immorality** /ˌɪməˈrælɪti/ *n* [U]

im·mor·tal /ɪˈmɔːtl‖-ɔːr-/ *adj* **1** living or continuing for ever: *Nobody is immortal.* **2** an immortal poem, song etc is old and famous: *the immortal words of Shakespeare* —**immortality** /ˌɪmɔːˈtælɪtl‖-ɔːr-/ *n* [U]

im·mor·tal·ize (also **-ise** *BrE*) /ɪˈmɔːtəlaɪz‖ -ɔːr-/ *v* [T] to make someone or something famous for a long time by writing about them, painting them etc: *The scene has been immortalized by many artists.*

im·mov·a·ble /ɪˈmuːvəbəl/ *adj* impossible to move or change

im·mune /ɪˈmjuːn/ *adj* **1** someone who is immune to an illness cannot get it: **+ to** *You're immune to chickenpox if you've had it once.* **2** not affected by problems, criticisms etc that affect other people: **+ to** *Their business seems to be immune to economic pressures.* —**immunity** *n* [U]

immune sys·tem /.ˈ. ˌ../ *n* [C] the system in your body that protects it against illness

im·mu·nize (also **-ise** *BrE*) /ˈɪmjʊnaɪz/ *v* [T] to give someone a drug to prevent them from getting a disease: **immunize sb against sth** *Get your baby immunized against measles.* —**immunization** /ˌɪmjʊnaɪˈzeɪʃən‖-nə-/ *n* [C,U]

im·mu·ta·ble /ɪˈmjuːtəbəl/ *adj formal* never

changing or impossible to change —**immutability** /ɪˌmjuːtəˈbɪlɪti/ *n* [U]

imp /ɪmp/ *n* [C] a small creature in stories who has magic powers and behaves badly

im·pact[1] /ˈɪmpækt/ *n* **1** [C] the effect something or someone has: *the environmental impact of car use* | **have/make an impact on sth** *He had a big impact on my life.* **2** [singular, U] the force of one object hitting another: *The impact of the crash made her car turn over.* | **on impact** *missiles that explode on impact*

impact[2] /ɪmˈpækt/ also **impact on** *especially AmE* — *v* [I,T] to have a noticeable effect on someone or something: *The closure of the airport will seriously impact on the city's economy.*

im·pair /ɪmˈpeə‖-ˈper/ *v* [T] to make something less good: *Boiling the soup will impair its flavour.* —**impairment** *n* [U]

im·paired /ɪmˈpeəd‖-ˈperd/ *adj* **1** damaged or made weaker: *Radio reception had been impaired by the storm.* **2** **visually impaired/sb's hearing is impaired** unable to see or hear very well

im·pale /ɪmˈpeɪl/ *v* [T] to violently push a sharp object through something or someone: *He was impaled on railings.*

im·part /ɪmˈpaːt‖-aːrt/ *v* [T] *formal* **1** to give information, knowledge etc to someone **2** to give a particular quality to something: *Garlic imparts a delicious flavour to the sauce.*

im·par·tial /ɪmˈpaːʃəl‖-aːr-/ *adj* not supporting or preferring one person, group, or opinion rather than another: *We offer impartial help and advice.* —**impartially** *adv* —**impartiality** /ɪmˌpaːʃiˈælɪti‖-aːr-/ *n* [U]

im·pass·a·ble /ɪmˈpaːsəbəl‖ɪmˈpæ-/ *adj* impossible to travel along: *Some streets are impassable due to snow.*

im·passe /æmˈpaːs‖ˈɪmpæs/ *n* [singular] a situation in which it is impossible to continue because people cannot agree: **reach an impasse** *Discussions about pay have reached an impasse.*

im·pas·sioned /ɪmˈpæʃənd/ *adj* an impassioned speech, argument etc is full of strong feelings and emotion

im·pas·sive /ɪmˈpæsɪv/ *adj* not showing any emotions: *His face was impassive as the judge spoke.* —**impassively** *adv*

im·pa·tient /ɪmˈpeɪʃənt/ *adj* **1** annoyed because of delays or mistakes that make you wait: *After an hour's delay, the passengers were becoming impatient.* | **+ with** *He gets impatient with the slower kids.* **2** if you are impatient to do something, you want to do it as soon as possible and do not want to wait: **impatient to do sth** *Gary was impatient to leave.* —**impatience** *n* [U] —**impatiently** *adv*

im·peach /ɪmˈpiːtʃ/ *v* [T] *law* if a president, MAYOR etc is impeached, he or she is officially charged with a serious crime —**impeachment** *n* [U]

im·pec·ca·ble /ɪmˈpekəbəl/ *adj* perfect and without any mistakes: *She has impeccable taste in clothes.* —**impeccably** *adv*

im·pede /ɪmˈpiːd/ *v* [T] *formal* to make it difficult for someone or something to make progress: *Rescue attempts were impeded by storms.*

im·ped·i·ment /ɪmˈpedɪmənt/ *n* [C] **1** a fact or event that makes it difficult or impossible for something to happen: **+ to** *The country's debt has* *been an impediment to development.* **2** a physical problem that makes speaking, hearing, or moving difficult: *a speech impediment*

im·pel /ɪmˈpel/ *v* [T] **-elled, -elling** *formal* to make you feel very strongly that you must do something: **feel impelled to do sth** *She felt impelled to speak.*

im·pend·ing /ɪmˈpendɪŋ/ *adj* an impending event or situation, especially an unpleasant one, is going to happen very soon: *an impending divorce*

im·pen·e·tra·ble /ɪmˈpenɪtrəbəl/ *adj* **1** impossible to get through or see through: *impenetrable fog* **2** very difficult or impossible to understand: *impenetrable legal jargon*

im·per·a·tive¹ /ɪmˈperətɪv/ *adj* **1** *formal* extremely important and urgent **2** in grammar an imperative verb expresses a command

imperative² *n* [C] **1** something that must be done urgently: *Reducing pollution has become an imperative.* **2** the form of a verb that expresses a command. In "Do it now!" the verb 'do' is in the imperative.

im·per·cep·ti·ble /ˌɪmpəˈseptɪbəl‖-pər-/ *adj* impossible to notice: *His hesitation was almost imperceptible.* **—imperceptibly** *adv*

im·per·fect¹ /ɪmˈpɜːfɪkt‖-ɜːr-/ *adj formal* not completely perfect: *It's an imperfect world.* **—imperfection** /ˌɪmpəˈfekʃənll-pər-/ *n* [C,U]

imperfect² *n* [singular] the form of a verb that shows an incomplete action in the past. In 'We were walking down the road' the verb 'were walking' is in the imperfect.

im·pe·ri·al /ɪmˈpɪəriəl‖-ˈpɪr-/ *adj* **1** relating to an EMPIRE or to the person who rules it **2** related to the system of weights and measurements based on INCHes, YARDs, MILEs etc

im·per·son·al /ɪmˈpɜːsənəl‖-ɜːr-/ *adj* not showing any feelings of sympathy, friendliness etc: *an impersonal letter* **—impersonally** *adv*

im·per·so·nate /ɪmˈpɜːsəneɪt‖-ɜːr-/ *v* [T] to copy the way someone talks, behaves etc in order to pretend that you are that person, or to make people laugh: *They were arrested for impersonating police officers.* | *She's quite good at impersonating politicians.* **—impersonator** *n* [C] **—impersonation** /ɪmˌpɜːsəˈneɪʃən‖-ɜːr-/ *n* [U]

im·per·ti·nent /ɪmˈpɜːtɪnənt‖-ɜːr-/ *adj* rude and not showing respect: *Don't be impertinent, young man.* **—impertinently** *adv* **—impertinence** *n* [U]

im·per·vi·ous /ɪmˈpɜːviəs‖-ɜːr-/ *adj* **1** not affected or influenced by something: **+ to** *He seemed impervious to criticism.* **2** not allowing liquid to pass through: *impervious rock*

im·pet·u·ous /ɪmˈpetʃuəs/ *adj* someone who is impetuous does things quickly, without thinking: *She was very impetuous in her youth.* **—impetuously** *adv*

im·pe·tus /ˈɪmpɪtəs/ *n* [U] **1** an influence that makes something happen or happen more quickly: *Public protest has provided the impetus for reform.* **2** *technical* a force that makes an object start moving, or keeps it moving

im·pinge /ɪmˈpɪndʒ/ *v*
impinge on/upon sth *phr v* [T] *formal* to have an effect on something or someone: *conditions which impinge on students' exam success*

imp·ish /ˈɪmpɪʃ/ *adj* behaving in a bad but funny way: *an impish grin* **—impishly** *adv*

im·plac·a·ble /ɪmˈplækəbəl/ *adj* very determined to continue opposing someone or something: *her implacable hostility to the plan* **—implacably** *adv*

im·plant¹ /ɪmˈplɑːnt‖ɪmˈplænt/ *v* [T] **1** to fix an idea or image in someone's mind so that they cannot forget it: *Her beauty remained implanted in Raymond's mind.* **2** to put something into someone's body by a medical operation: *Doctors implanted a new lens in her eye.* **—implantation** /ˌɪmplɑːnˈteɪʃən‖-plæn-/ *n* [U]

im·plant² /ˈɪmplɑːnt‖-plænt/ *n* [C] something that has been put into someone's body in a medical operation: *silicon breast implants*

im·plau·si·ble /ɪmˈplɔːzɪbəl‖-ˈplɔː-/ *adj* not likely to be true: *an implausible excuse* **—implausibly** *adv*

im·ple·ment¹ /ˈɪmplɪment/ *v* [T] if you implement a plan, process etc, you begin to make it happen: *Airlines have until 2002 to implement the new safety recommendations.* **—implementation** /ˌɪmplɪmenˈteɪʃən/ *n* [U]

im·ple·ment² /ˈɪmplɪmənt/ *n* [C] a tool: *farming implements*

im·pli·cate /ˈɪmplɪkeɪt/ *v* [T] to suggest or show that someone or something is involved in something bad or illegal: **implicate sb in sth** *Two other people have been implicated in the robbery.*

im·pli·ca·tion /ˌɪmplɪˈkeɪʃən/ *n* **1** [C] a possible result of a plan, action etc: **+ of** *What are the implications of the decision?* | **have implications for** *This ruling will have implications for many other people.* **2** [C,U] something that you suggest is true, without saying it directly: **+ that** *I resent your implication that I was lying.*

im·pli·cit /ɪmˈplɪsɪt/ *adj* **1** suggested or understood but not stated directly: *There was implicit criticism in what she said.* **2** **implicit faith/trust etc** faith, trust etc that is complete and with no doubts: *I have implicit faith in your abilities.* **—implicitly** *adv* → compare EXPLICIT

im·plode /ɪmˈpləʊd‖-ˈploʊd/ *v* [I] *formal* to explode inwards **—implosion** /ɪmˈpləʊʒən‖ -ˈploʊ-/ *n* [C,U]

im·plore /ɪmˈplɔː‖-ɔːr/ *v* [T] *formal* to ask for something in an emotional way; BEG: **implore sb to do sth** *Joan implored him not to leave.*

im·ply /ɪmˈplaɪ/ *v* [T] to suggest that something is true without saying or showing it directly: **+ (that)** *He implied that the money hadn't been lost, but was stolen.* → compare INFER

im·po·lite /ˌɪmpəˈlaɪt◂/ *adj formal* not polite; rude: *She worried that her questions would seem impolite.*

im·port¹ /ˈɪmpɔːt‖-ɔːrt/ *n* [C,U] something that is brought into a country in order to be sold, or the process of doing this: *Car imports have risen recently.* | *There has been a ban on the import of tropical animals.* → opposite EXPORT¹

im·port² /ɪmˈpɔːt‖-ɔːrt/ *v* [T] to bring something into a country from abroad in order to sell it: *oil imported from the Middle East* **—importer** *n* [C] **—importation** /ˌɪmpɔːˈteɪʃən‖-ɔːr-/ *n* [U]

im·por·tance /ɪmˈpɔːtəns‖-ɔːr-/ *n* [U] the quality of being important: *Doctors are stressing the importance of regular exercise.* | *Environmental issues are of great importance.*

im·por·tant /ɪmˈpɔːtənt‖-ɔːr-/ adj **1** having a big effect or influence: *important questions* | **it is important to do sth** *It's important to explain things to the patient.* **2** having a lot of power or influence: *an important senator* —**importantly** adv

im·pose /ɪmˈpəʊz‖-ˈpoʊz/ v **1** [T] to force people to accept a rule, a tax, your beliefs etc: **impose sth on sb** *You shouldn't try and impose your views on your children.* **2** [I] to unreasonably ask someone to do something for you that may cause them a lot of work or trouble: **+ on/upon** *We could ask the neighbours to help again, but I don't want to impose on them.*

im·pos·ing /ɪmˈpəʊzɪŋ‖-ˈpoʊ-/ adj large and impressive: *an imposing building*

im·po·si·tion /ˌɪmpəˈzɪʃən/ n **1** [C] something that someone unreasonably expects or asks you to do for them: *They stayed a month? What an imposition!* **2** [U] when you introduce something such as a rule, tax, or punishment: *the imposition of taxes on cigarettes*

im·pos·si·ble /ɪmˈpɒsḁbəl‖ɪmˈpɑː-/ adj **1** not able to be done or to happen: *It's impossible to sleep with all this noise.* **2** extremely difficult to deal with: *an impossible situation* —**impossibly** adv —**impossibility** /ɪmˌpɒsḁˈbɪlḁti‖-ˌpɑː-/ n [C,U]

im·pos·tor also **imposter** /ɪmˈpɒstə‖-ˈpɑːstər/ n [C] someone who pretends to be someone else in order to trick people

im·po·tent /ˈɪmpətənt/ adj **1** unable to do things well because you do not have enough power, strength, or control: *an impotent city government* **2** a man who is impotent is unable to have sex because he cannot get an ERECTION —**impotently** adv —**impotence** n [U]

im·pound /ɪmˈpaʊnd/ v [T] *law* if the police or law courts impound your possessions, they take them and keep them until you pay some money: *Illegally parked vehicles will be impounded.*

im·pov·e·rished /ɪmˈpɒvərɪʃt‖-ˈpɑː-/ adj *formal* very poor: *an impoverished country*

im·prac·ti·cal /ɪmˈpræktɪkəl/ adj an impractical plan, suggestion etc is not sensible because it would be too expensive or difficult —**impractically** /-kli/ adv —**impracticality** /ɪmˌpræktɪˈkælḁti/ n [U]

im·pre·cise /ˌɪmprɪˈsaɪs◂/ adj not exact: *The directions were imprecise and confusing.* —**imprecisely** adv —**imprecision** /-ˈsɪʒən/ n [U]

im·preg·nate /ˈɪmpregneɪt‖ɪmˈpreg-/ v [T] *formal* **1** to make a substance spread completely through something: *paper impregnated with perfume* **2** to make a woman or female animal PREGNANT

im·press /ɪmˈpres/ v [T] **1** to make someone admire something or someone: *She dresses like that to impress people.* **2** **impress sth on sb** to make someone realize that something is very important: *My parents impressed on me the value of education.* —**impressed** adj

im·pres·sion /ɪmˈpreʃən/ n [C] **1** your impression of someone or something is the way that they seem to you: **+ of** *What was your first impression of Richard?* | **have/get the impression (that)** *I got the impression that Rob didn't like me.* | **give the impression (that)** (=make people think something is true): *She gives the im-*

pression that she's very rich. | **make a good/bad impression** *She made a good impression at her interview.* **2** when someone copies the way a famous person talks or behaves, in order to make people laugh: *He did a brilliant impression of Prince Charles.* **3** the mark left by pressing something into a soft surface

im·pres·sion·a·ble /ɪmˈpreʃənəbəl/ adj easy to influence: *The children are at an impressionable age.*

im·pres·sion·is·tic /ɪmˌpreʃəˈnɪstɪk◂/ adj based on a general feeling of what something is like: *She gave an impressionistic account of the events* —**impressionistically** /-kli/ adv

im·pres·sive /ɪmˈpresɪv/ adj making you admire something: *Anna gave an impressive performance on the piano.* —**impressively** adv

im·print¹ /ˈɪmprɪnt/ n [C] the mark left by an object that has been pressed onto something: *the imprint of his hand on the clay*

im·print² /ɪmˈprɪnt/ v **1** **be imprinted on your mind/memory** if something is imprinted on your mind or memory, you can never forget it **2** [T] to print or press a mark on something

im·pris·on /ɪmˈprɪzən/ v [T] to put someone in prison or to keep them in a place they cannot escape from: *People used to be imprisoned in the Tower of London.* —**imprisonment** n [U]

im·prob·a·ble /ɪmˈprɒbəbəl‖-ˈprɑː-/ adj not likely to happen or be true: **+ that** *It seems improbable that humans have ever lived here.* —**improbably** adv —**improbability** /ɪmˌprɒbəˈbɪlḁti ˌprɑː-/ n [C,U]

im·promp·tu /ɪmˈprɒmptjuː‖ɪmˈprɑːmptuː/ adj done or said without any preparation or planning: *an impromptu party* —**impromptu** adv

im·prop·er /ɪmˈprɒpə‖-ˈprɑːpər/ adj **1** not correct according to moral, social, or professional rules: *Many students failed due to improper use of punctuation.* **2** illegal or dishonest: *This was an improper use of company funds.* —**improperly** adv: *improperly dressed*

im·pro·pri·e·ty /ˌɪmprəˈpraɪəti/ n [C,U] *formal* something that is unacceptable according to moral, social, or professional standards

im·prove /ɪmˈpruːv/ v [I,T] to become better, or to make something better: *Her English is improving.* | *Swimming can improve your muscle tone.* —**improved** adj

improve on/upon sth *phr v* [T] to do something better than before or make it better: *No one's been able to improve on her Olympic record.*

im·prove·ment /ɪmˈpruːvmənt/ n [C,U] when something becomes better than it was: **+ in** *There's certainly been an improvement in Danny's schoolwork.* | **be an improvement on sth** (=be better than something else): *This job is an improvement on my last one.* | **there's room for improvement** *His playing has made progress, but there's still room for improvement.*

USAGE NOTE: improvement

Use **improvement in** to talk about something that has got better: *There has been a great improvement in his work.* Use **improvement on** to compare two things, when one of them is better than the other: *Today's weather is a definite improvement on yesterday's.*

im·pro·vise /ˈɪmprəvaɪz/ v [I,T] to make or do something without any preparation, using what you have: *I left my lesson plans at home, so I'll have to improvise.* —**improvisation** /ˌɪmprəvaɪˈzeɪʃən‖ɪm prɑːvə-/ n [C,U]

im·pu·dent /ˈɪmpjɐd̑ənt/ adj formal rude and not showing respect: *an impudent child* —**impudence** n [U] —**impudently** adv

im·pulse /ˈɪmpʌls/ n [C] **1** a sudden desire to do something before thinking about whether it is sensible: **impulse to do sth** *I managed to resist the impulse to hit him.* | **on impulse** (=because of an impulse): *I bought this dress on impulse, and I'm not sure if I like it now.* **2** technical a single push or force moving for a short time in one direction along a wire or NERVE

im·pul·sive /ɪmˈpʌlsɪv/ adj tending to do things without thinking about the results: *It was rather an impulsive decision.* —**impulsively** adv —**impulsiveness** n [U]

im·pu·ni·ty /ɪmˈpjuːn̑ɨti/ n [U] **with impunity** without risk of punishment: *We cannot let them break laws with impunity.*

im·pure /ˌɪmˈpjʊə‖-ˈpjʊr/ adj mixed with other substances: *impure drugs*

im·pu·ri·ty /ɪmˈpjʊəȓɨti‖-ˈpjʊr-/ n [C] a part of an almost pure substance that is of a lower quality: *minerals containing impurities*

in[1] /ɪn/ prep **1** used with the name of a container, place, or area to show where something is: *The paper is in the top drawer.* | *He lived in Spain for 15 years.* | *We swam in the sea.* ➡ see colour picture on page 474 **2** used with the names of months, years, seasons etc to say when something happened: *I was born in May 1969.* | *In the winter, we use a wood stove.* **3** during or at the end of a period of time: *We finished the whole project in a week.* | *Gerry should be home in an hour.* **4** included as part of something: *One of the people in the story is a young doctor.* | *In the first part of the speech, he talked about the environment.* **5** used to describe the condition or attitude of something or someone: *The company was in trouble.* | *She looked up in surprise.* **6** wearing something: *men in grey suits* **7** using a particular way of speaking or writing: *"I'm afraid," said Violet in a quiet voice.* | *I wrote to him in Italian.* **8** involved with a particular kind of job: *She's in advertising.* | *new developments in medicine* **9** arranged in a particular way: *We stood in a line.* | *Put the words in alphabetical order* **10 in all** used to say what the total amount of something is: *There were 25 of us in all.*

in[2] adj, adv **1** so that something is contained inside or surrounded by something: *He opened the washing machine and bundled his clothes in.* **2** inside a building or room, especially the one where you live or work: *You're never in when I call.* **3** if a plane, bus etc is in, it has arrived at the airport, station etc: *His flight won't be in for four hours.* **4** given or sent to a person in order to be read or looked at: *Your homework has to be in by Friday.* **5** if you write, paint, or draw

something in, you write it etc in the correct place: *I drew in the eyes and mouth.* **6** if clothes, colours, etc are in, they are fashionable: *Long hair is in again.* **7 be in for sth** if someone is in for a surprise or shock, it is going to happen to them: *She's in for a shock if she thinks we're going to pay.* **8 be in on sth** to be involved in doing, talking about, or planning something: *Were you in on my birthday surprise?* **9 have (got) it in for sb** informal if someone has got it in for you, they do not like you and try to cause problems for you

in- /ɪn/ prefix used at the beginning of some words to mean 'not': *insensitive* | *inappropriate* | *inconvenience* (=when something is not convenient for someone and causes problems for them)

in·a·bil·i·ty /ˌɪnəˈbɪl̑ɨti/ n [singular] when you are unable to do something: *his inability to make friends*

in·ac·ces·si·ble /ˌɪnəkˈsesɨbəl/ adj impossible to reach: *The village is often inaccessible in winter.*

in·ac·cu·ra·cy /ɪnˈækjɐrəsi/ n [C,U] a written or spoken mistake, or when something contains mistakes: *There were several inaccuracies in the report.* | *The inaccuracy of her description meant that the man could not be arrested.*

in·ac·cu·rate /ɪnˈækjɐȓɨt/ adj not correct: *Many of the figures quoted in the article were inaccurate.* —**inaccurately** adv

in·ac·tion /ɪnˈækʃən/ n [U] when someone fails to deal with a problem or difficult situation: *The city council was criticized for its inaction on the problem.*

in·ac·tive /ɪnˈæktɪv/ adj not doing anything or not working.

in·ac·tiv·i·ty /ˌɪnækˈtɪv̑ɨti/ n [U] when people do not do anything or do not do any work: *long periods of inactivity*

in·ad·e·qua·cy /ɪnˈædɨkwəsi/ n **1** [U] a feeling that you are unable to deal with situations because you are not as good as other people: *Unemployment can cause feelings of inadequacy.* **2** [C,U] when something is not good enough in quality, ability etc for a particular purpose: *the inadequacy of safety standards in the coal mines* | *He pointed out the inadequacies in the voting system.*

in·ad·e·quate /ɪnˈædɨkwɨt/ adj not enough, big enough etc for a particular purpose: *inadequate health care services* —**inadequately** adv

in·ad·mis·si·ble /ˌɪnədˈmɪsɨbəl/ adj formal inadmissible EVIDENCE cannot be used in a court of law: *The judge ruled that the secretly-taped conversations were inadmissible.*

in·ad·ver·tent·ly /ˌɪnədˈvɜːtəntli‖-ɜːr-/ adv without intending to do something: *She inadvertently knocked his arm.* —**inadvertent** adj

in·ad·vis·a·ble /ˌɪnədˈvaɪzəbəl/ adj not sensible: *It's inadvisable to take medicine without asking your doctor.*

in·a·li·en·a·ble /ɪnˈeɪliənəbəl/ adj formal an inalienable right cannot be taken away from you

---

GRAMMAR NOTE: 'if' clauses (2)
When you imagine a present situation that is not real, or a future situation that is very unlikely, use **if + simple past**: *If he really loved you, he wouldn't treat you like this.* (=he does not love you). | *If I won a million dollars on the lottery, I would buy a yacht.* Use **would** in the other part of the sentence.

i·nane /ɪˈneɪn/ adj extremely stupid or without much meaning: *inane jokes*

in·an·i·mate /ɪnˈænɪmɪt/ adj not living: *He paints inanimate objects like rocks and furniture.*

in·ap·pro·pri·ate /ˌɪnəˈprəʊpriɪt/ adj not suitable or correct: *The clothes they brought were totally inappropriate.* —**inappropriately** adv

in·ar·tic·u·late /ˌɪnɑːˈtɪkjələt ǁ-ɑːr-/ adj not able to express yourself well when you speak: *inarticulate youths* —**inarticulately** adv

in·as·much as /ˌɪnəzˈmʌtʃ əz/ linking words formal used in order to begin a phrase that explains the first part of your sentence: *She's guilty, inasmuch as she knew what the others were planning.*

in·au·di·ble /ɪnˈɔːdɪbəlǁ-ˈɒː-/ adj too quiet to be heard: *Her reply was inaudible.* —**inaudibly** adv

in·au·gu·rate /ɪˈnɔːgjʊreɪtǁɪˈnɒː-/ v [T] **1** to have a formal ceremony in order to show that someone new has an important job, or that a new building is open: *The President was inaugurated in January.* **2** to open a new building or start a new service with a ceremony —**inaugural** adj —**inauguration** /ɪˌnɔːgjʊˈreɪʃənǁɪˈnɒː-/ n [C,U]

in·aus·pi·cious /ˌɪnɔːˈspɪʃəsǁˌɪnɒː-/ adj formal seeming to show that the future will be unlucky: *an inauspicious start to our trip*

in·born /ˌɪnˈbɔːnǁ-ɔːrn/ adj an inborn quality is one that you have had since birth: *an inborn talent for languages*

Inc. the written abbreviation of INCORPORATED, used after names of companies in the US: *General Motors Inc.*

in·cal·cu·la·ble /ɪnˈkælkjʊləbəl/ adj too great to be measured: *The scandal has done incalculable damage to the college's reputation.* —**incalculably** adv

in·can·des·cent /ˌɪnkænˈdesənt ǁ-kən-/ adj **1** giving a bright light when heated **2** extremely angry —**incandescence** n [U]

in·can·ta·tion /ˌɪnkænˈteɪʃən/ n [C] a set of special words that someone uses in magic

in·ca·pa·ble /ɪnˈkeɪpəbəl/ adj unable to do something or to feel a particular emotion: **be incapable of doing sth** *He seems to be incapable of sitting still.* —**incapably** adv

in·ca·pa·ci·tate /ˌɪnkəˈpæsɪteɪt/ v [T] to make someone too ill or weak to live normally: *He was incapacitated by the illness for several months.*

in·ca·pa·ci·ty /ˌɪnkəˈpæsɪti/ n [U] lack of ability or strength to do something, especially because you are ill

in·car·ce·rate /ɪnˈkɑːsəreɪtǁ-ɑːr-/ v [T] formal to put someone in prison —**incarceration** /ɪnˌkɑːsəˈreɪʃənǁ-ɑːr-/ n [U]

in·car·nate /ɪnˈkɑːnɪtǁ-ɑːr-/ adj evil/the devil etc incarnate someone who people think is the human form of evil etc

in·car·na·tion /ˌɪnkɑːˈneɪʃənǁ-ɑːr-/ n **1** [C] the time during which someone is alive in the form of a particular person or animal: *He believes he was a cat in a previous incarnation.* **2** be the incarnation of goodness/evil etc to be the perfect example of goodness etc

in·cen·di·a·ry /ɪnˈsendiəriǁ-dieri/ adj incendiary bomb/device etc a bomb etc designed to cause a fire

in·cense /ˈɪnsens/ n [U] a substance that has a pleasant smell when you burn it

in·censed /ɪnˈsenst/ adj very angry

in·cen·tive /ɪnˈsentɪv/ n [C,U] something that encourages you to work harder, or to start something new: **incentive (for sb) to do sth** *The government provides incentives for businesses to invest.*

in·cep·tion /ɪnˈsepʃən/ n [singular] formal the start of an organization: *He has been chairman of the Society since its inception.*

in·ces·sant /ɪnˈsesənt/ adj never stopping: *incessant noise from the road* —**incessantly** adv

in·cest /ˈɪnsest/ n [U] illegal sex between people who are closely related, for example between brother and sister —**incestuous** /ɪnˈsestʃuəs/ adj

inch¹ /ɪntʃ/ n, plural **inches** **1** [C] a unit for measuring length, equal to 2.54 centimetres **2** not give/budge an inch to refuse to change your opinions at all: *It's not worth arguing – he won't give an inch.*

inch² v [I] to move very slowly and carefully, or to move something this way: *Paul inched his way forward to get a better view.*

in·ci·dence /ˈɪnsɪdəns/ n [singular] formal how often something happens: *an unusually high incidence of childhood cancer*

in·ci·dent /ˈɪnsɪdənt/ n [C] something unusual, serious, or violent that happens: *Anyone who saw the incident should contact the police.*

in·ci·den·tal /ˌɪnsɪˈdentl/ adj happening or existing in connection with something else that is more important: *Where the story is set is incidental to the plot.*

in·ci·den·tal·ly /ˌɪnsɪˈdentli/ adv used when you are giving additional information, or changing the subject of a conversation: *Incidentally, Jenny's coming over tonight.*

in·cin·e·rate /ɪnˈsɪnəreɪt/ v [T] to burn something in order to destroy it —**incinerator** n [C] —**incineration** /ɪnˌsɪnəˈreɪʃən/ n [U]

in·cip·i·ent /ɪnˈsɪpiənt/ adj [only before noun] formal starting to happen or exist: *incipient panic*

in·ci·sion /ɪnˈsɪʒən/ n [C] technical a cut that a doctor makes in someone's body during an operation

in·ci·sive /ɪnˈsaɪsɪv/ adj incisive remarks are very clear and firm, and deal with the most important part of a subject

in·cite /ɪnˈsaɪt/ v [T] to deliberately make someone feel so angry or excited that they do something bad: *One man was jailed for inciting a riot.* —**incitement** n [C,U]

in·clem·ent /ɪnˈklemənt/ adj formal inclement weather is unpleasantly cold, wet etc

in·cli·na·tion /ˌɪnklɪˈneɪʃən/ n [C,U] the desire to do something: **inclination to do sth** *I didn't have the time or inclination to go with them.*

in·cline¹ /ɪnˈklaɪn/ v formal **1** [T] to think that a particular belief or opinion is probably right: **+ to** *I incline to the view that the child was telling the truth.* **2** [I,T] to slope at a particular angle, or make something do this: *She inclined her head towards him.*

in·cline² /ˈɪnklaɪn/ n [C] a slope: *a steep incline*

in·clined /ɪnˈklaɪnd/ adj **1** [not before noun] likely or tending to do something: **+ to** *Children*

are inclined to get lost. **2 be inclined to agree/
believe/think etc** to have a particular opinion,
but not express it very strongly: *I'm inclined to
think Ed is right.*

in·clude /ɪnˈkluːd/ *v* [T] **1** if a group or set includes something or someone, it has that person
or thing as one of its parts: *The price includes car
rental.* **2** to make someone or something part
of a larger group or set: **include sth in/on sth**
Try to include Rosie more in your games, Sam.
→ opposite EXCLUDE

in·clud·ing /ɪnˈkluːdɪŋ/ *prep* used to show that
someone or something is part of a larger group
or set that you are talking about: *There were 20
people in the room, including the teacher.*
→ opposite EXCLUDING

in·clu·sion /ɪnˈkluːʒən/ *n* [C,U] when you include someone or something in a larger group or
set, or someone or something that is included:
*Are there any new inclusions on the list?|Are
there any doubts about her inclusion in the team?*

in·clu·sive /ɪnˈkluːsɪv/ *adj* **1** an inclusive
price or cost includes everything: **+ of** *The cost is
£600 inclusive of insurance.* **2 Monday to Friday
inclusive/15-20 inclusive etc** including Monday
and Friday and all the days between them, 15
and 20 and all the numbers between them etc: *He
will be away from 22-24 March inclusive.*

in·cog·ni·to /ˌɪnkɒgˈniːtəʊ, ɪnˌkɑːgˈniːtoʊ/ *adv*
hiding who you really are: *The princess was
travelling incognito.*

in·co·her·ent /ˌɪnkəʊˈhɪərənt◂ ‖-koʊˈhɪr-/ *adj*
confused and not clear: *a rambling incoherent
speech* **—incoherently** *adv* **—incoherence** *n* [U]

in·come /ˈɪŋkʌm, ˈɪn-/ *n* [C,U] the money that
you earn: *people on a low income*

income tax /ˈ.. ./ *n* [U] tax paid on the money
you earn

in·com·ing /ˈɪnkʌmɪŋ/ *adj* [only before noun]
coming into or towards a place, or going to
arrive soon: *Incoming flights are delayed.|The
phone will only take incoming calls.*

in·com·mu·ni·ca·do /ˌɪnkəmjuːnɪˈkɑːdəʊ‖
-doʊ/ *adj, adv* not allowed or not wanting to
communicate with anyone

in·com·pa·ra·ble /ɪnˈkɒmpərəbəl‖-ˈkɑːm-/ *adj*
so impressive, beautiful etc that nothing or no
one is better: *There was an incomparable view of
San Marco from the Piazza.* **—incomparably**
adv

in·com·pat·i·ble /ˌɪnkəmˈpætʃbəl◂/ *adj* too
different to be able to exist or live together: *Tony
and I have always been incompatible.|* **+ with** *be-
haviour incompatible with his responsibilities*
—incompatibility /ˌɪnkəmpætʃˈbɪlʃti/ *n* [U]

in·com·pe·tence /ɪnˈkɒmpʃtəns‖-ˈkɑːm-/ *n* [U]
when someone does not have the ability to do
their job properly

in·com·pe·tent /ɪnˈkɒmpʃtənt‖-ˈkɑːm-/ *adj* not
having the ability or skill to do your job: *As a
teacher, he was completely incompetent.* **—incom-
petently** *adv* **—incompetent** *n* [C]

in·com·plete /ˌɪnkəmˈpliːt◂/ *adj* not having all
its parts, or not finished: *an incomplete
sentence | The report is still incomplete.* **—incom-
pletely** *adv* **—incompleteness** *n* [U]

in·com·pre·hen·si·ble /ˌɪnkɒmprɪˈhensʃbəl‖
-ˈkɑːm-/ *adj* impossible to understand: *incom-

prehensible legal language* **—incomprehensibly**
adv

in·com·pre·hen·sion /ˌɪnkɒmprɪˈhenʃən‖
-ˈkɑːm-/ *n* [U] *formal* when you do not understand something: *She watched with complete in-
comprehension.*

in·con·ceiv·a·ble /ˌɪnkənˈsiːvəbəl/ *adj* too
strange to seem possible: **+ that** *It was inconceivable that such a pleasant man could be violent.*
—inconceivably *adj*

in·con·clu·sive /ˌɪnkənˈkluːsɪv◂/ *adj* not leading to any decision or result: *The evidence is in-
conclusive.*

in·con·gru·ous /ɪnˈkɒŋgruəs‖-ˈkɑːŋ-/ *adj* seeming to be wrong or strange in a particular situation: *He looked incongruous in his new suit.*
—incongruously *adv* **—incongruity** /ˌɪnkən-
ˈgruːʃti/ *n* [C,U]

in·con·se·quen·tial /ˌɪnkɒnsʃˈkwenʃəl◂ ‖
-ˈkɑːn-/ *adj formal* not important: *He can remember the most inconsequential things.*

in·con·sid·er·ate /ˌɪnkənˈsɪdərʃt◂/ *adj* not caring about other people's needs or feelings: *It was
inconsiderate of you not to call.* → opposite CON-
SIDERATE

in·con·sis·ten·cy /ˌɪnkənˈsɪstənsi/ *n* **1** [C,U]
something in a report, argument etc that cannot
be true if something else in the report or argument is true: *the inconsistencies in her statement*
2 [U] when you change your ideas too often or
do something differently each time, so that
people do not know what you think or want:
*There's too much inconsistency in the way the
rules are applied.* → opposite CONSISTENCY

in·con·sis·tent /ˌɪnkənˈsɪstənt◂/ *adj* **1** two
ideas or statements that are inconsistent are
different and cannot both be true: *His story was
inconsistent with the evidence.* **2** not doing
things in the same way each time, or not following an expected principle: *Children get confused
if parents are inconsistent.* **—inconsistently** *adv*
→ opposite CONSISTENT

in·con·sol·a·ble /ˌɪnkənˈsəʊləbəl‖-ˈsoʊ-/ *adj*
so sad that you cannot be comforted: *His widow
was inconsolable.* **—inconsolably** *adv*

in·con·spic·u·ous /ˌɪnkənˈspɪkjuəs◂/ *adj* not
easily noticed: *I sat in the corner, trying to be as
inconspicuous as possible.* **—inconspicuously**
adv → opposite CONSPICUOUS

in·con·ti·nent /ɪnˈkɒntʃnənt‖-ˈkɑːn-/ *adj* unable to control your BLADDER or BOWELS **—incon-
tinence** *n* [U]

in·con·tro·vert·i·ble /ˌɪnkɒntrəˈvɜːtʃbəl‖ɪn-
ˌkɑːntrəˈvɜːr-/ *adj* an incontrovertible fact
cannot be proved to be false: *We have incontrovertible evidence that he was there when the crime
was committed.* **—incontrovertibly** *adv*

in·con·ve·ni·ence[1] /ˌɪnkənˈviːniəns/ *n* [C,U]
something that causes you problems or
difficulties, or when someone has problems or
difficulties: *We apologize for any inconvenience
caused by the delay.*

inconvenience[2] *v* [T] to cause problems or
difficulties for someone: *"I'll drive you home."
"Are you sure? I don't want to inconvenience you."*

in·con·ve·ni·ent /ˌɪnkənˈviːniənt◂/ *adj* causing
problems or difficulties: *Is this an inconvenient
time?* **—inconveniently** *adv*

in·cor·po·rate /ɪnˈkɔːpəreɪt‖-ɔːr-/ v [T] to include something as part of a group, system etc: *incorporate sth into sth Several safety features have been incorporated into the car's design.* —**incorporation** /ɪnˌkɔːpəˈreɪʃən‖-ɔːr-/ n [U]

In·cor·po·rat·ed /ɪnˈkɔːpəreɪtɪdn‖-ɔːr-/ written abbreviation **Inc.** adj used after the name of a company to show that it is a CORPORATION

in·cor·rect /ˌɪnkəˈrekt◂/ adj not correct; wrong: *incorrect spelling* —**incorrectly** adv

in·cor·ri·gi·ble /ɪnˈkɒrɪdʒəbəl‖-ˈkɔː-/ adj someone who is incorrigible is bad in some way and cannot be changed: *That man's an incorrigible liar.*

in·cor·rup·ti·ble /ˌɪnkəˈrʌptəbəl◂/ adj too honest to be persuaded to do anything wrong: *an incorruptible judge*

in·crease[1] /ɪnˈkriːs/ v [I,T] to become larger or to make something larger in number or amount: *Regular exercise increases your chances of living longer.*|+ **by** *The price of oil has increased by 4%.* —**increasing** adj: *increasing concern about job security* —**increased** adj
➔ opposite DECREASE

increase

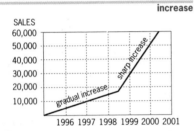

in·crease[2] /ˈɪŋkriːs/ n [C,U] a rise in amount or level: + **in** *a huge increase in profits*| **be on the increase** (=increasing): *Crime in the city is on the increase.* ➔ opposite DECREASE

in·creas·ing·ly /ɪnˈkriːsɪŋli/ adv more and more: *It's becoming increasingly difficult to find employment.*

in·cred·i·ble /ɪnˈkredəbəl/ adj **1** too strange to be believed: *It's incredible how much you remind me of your father.* **2** extremely good, large, or impressive: *They serve the most incredible food.*

in·cred·i·bly /ɪnˈkredəbli/ adv **1** extremely: *It's incredibly beautiful here in the spring.* **2** in a way that is difficult to believe: *Incredibly, he was not injured.*

in·cred·u·lous /ɪnˈkredjɣləs‖-dʒə-/ adj showing that you are unwilling to believe something: *"They don't have a TV?" asked one incredulous woman.* —**incredulously** adv —**incredulity** /ˌɪnkrɪˈdjuːlɪtill-ˈduː-/ n [U]

in·cre·ment /ˈɪŋkrɪmənt/ n [C] a regular increase in an amount: *an annual salary increment of 2%* —**incremental** /ˌɪŋkrɪˈmentl◂/ adj: *incremental growth in spending*

in·crim·i·nate /ɪnˈkrɪmɪneɪt/ v [T] to make someone seem guilty of a crime: *He refused to incriminate himself by answering questions.* —**incriminating** adj: *highly incriminating evidence*

in·cu·bate /ˈɪŋkjɣbeɪt/ v [I,T] if a bird incubates its egg or if an egg incubates, it is kept warm until it HATCHes —**incubation** /ˌɪŋkjɣˈbeɪʃən/ n [U]

in·cu·ba·tor /ˈɪŋkjɣbeɪtə‖-ər/ n [C] **1** a machine used in hospitals for keeping weak babies alive **2** a machine for keeping eggs warm until the young birds come out

in·cul·cate /ˈɪŋkʌlkeɪt‖ɪnˈkʌl-/ v [T] formal to make someone accept an idea by repeating it to them often

in·cum·bent[1] /ɪnˈkʌmbənt/ n [C] someone who has an elected position: *The council election will be tough for the incumbents.*

incumbent[2] adj formal **it is incumbent on/ upon sb to do sth** it is the duty or responsibility of someone to do something

in·cur /ɪnˈkɜː‖-ˈkɜːr/ v [T] **-rred, -rring** if you incur a debt, a punishment etc, you do something that means you own money, will get that punishment etc: *The oil company incurred a debt of $5 billion last year.*

in·cur·a·ble /ɪnˈkjʊərəbəl‖-ˈkjʊr-/ adj impossible to cure: *an incurable disease* —**incurably** adv ➔ opposite CURABLE

in·cur·sion /ɪnˈkɜːʃən, -ʒən‖ɪnˈkɜːrʒən/ n [C] formal a sudden attack or arrival into an area that belongs to other people

in·debt·ed /ɪnˈdetɪd/ adj **be indebted to sb** formal to be very grateful to someone: *I am indebted to you for your help.* —**indebtedness** n [U]

in·de·cent /ɪnˈdiːsənt/ adj likely to morally offend or shock people: *indecent photographs* —**indecency** n [C,U] ➔ compare DECENT

in·de·ci·sion /ˌɪndɪˈsɪʒən/ n [U] when you are unable to make a decision: *After a week of indecision, the jury finally gave its verdict.*

in·de·ci·sive /ˌɪndɪˈsaɪsɪv◂/ adj unable to make decisions: *a weak, indecisive leader* —**indecisiveness** n [U]

in·deed /ɪnˈdiːd/ adv **1** used to add more information to support a statement: *Most of the people were illiterate. Indeed, only 8% of the population could read.* **2** used to emphasize a statement or an answer: *I enjoyed the concert very much indeed.*|*"Vernon is one of the best pilots around." "Oh, yes, indeed."*

in·de·fen·si·ble /ˌɪndɪˈfensəbəl◂/ adj extremely bad or morally wrong, and therefore impossible to excuse or explain: *indefensible behaviour*

in·de·fin·a·ble /ˌɪndɪˈfaɪnəbəl◂/ adj difficult to describe or explain: *For some indefinable reason she felt afraid.* —**indefinably** adv

in·def·i·nite /ɪnˈdefənɪt/ adj an indefinite action or period of time has no definite end arranged for it: *He was away in Alaska for an indefinite period.*

indefinite ar·ti·cle /ˌ...ˈ...,/ n [C] the word 'a' or 'an' in the English language or a word in another language that is used like 'a' and 'an' ➔ compare DEFINITE ARTICLE

in·def·i·nite·ly /ɪnˈdefənɪtli/ adv for a period of time without an arranged end: *It's been postponed indefinitely.*

in·del·i·ble /ɪnˈdeləbəl/ adj impossible to forget or remove: *The film left an indelible impression on me.*| *indelible ink* —**indelibly** adv

in·del·i·cate /ɪnˈdelɪkɪt/ *adj formal* slightly rude or offensive: *an indelicate question*

in·dem·ni·fy /ɪnˈdemnɪfaɪ/ *v* [T] *law* to promise to pay someone if something they own becomes lost or damaged, or if they are injured

in·dem·ni·ty /ɪnˈdemnɪti/ *n law* **1** [U] protection in the form of a promise to pay for any damage or loss **2** [C] money that is paid to someone for any damage, loss, or injury

in·dent /ɪnˈdent/ *v* [T] to leave more space at the beginning of a line of writing than you leave on the other lines

in·den·ta·tion /ˌɪndenˈteɪʃən/ *n* [C] a cut or small hole in the surface of something

in·de·pen·dence /ˌɪndɪˈpendəns/ *n* [U] **1** the freedom and ability to make your own decisions and take care of yourself, without having to ask other people for help, money, or permission: *Teenagers must be allowed some degree of independence.* **2** political freedom from control by another country: *The United States declared its independence in 1776.*

in·de·pen·dent /ˌɪndɪˈpendənt◂/ *adj* **1** confident, free, and not needing to ask other people for help, money, or permission to do something: *He had always been more independent than his other brothers.* **2** not controlled by another government or organization: *India became an independent nation in 1947.* **3** not influenced by other people: *an independent report on the experiment* —**independently** *adv*

in-depth /ˈ. ./ *adj* **in-depth study/report etc** a study or report that is very thorough and considers all the details

in·de·scrib·a·ble /ˌɪndɪsˈkraɪbəbəl/ *adj* something that is indescribable is so good, strange, frightening etc that it is hard to describe: *My joy at seeing him was indescribable.* —**indescribably** *adv*

in·de·struc·ti·ble /ˌɪndɪsˈtrʌktɪbəl◂/ *adj* too strong to destroy: *denim clothes that are nearly indestructible* —**indestructibility** /ˌɪndɪstrʌktɪˈbɪlɪti/ *n* [U]

in·de·ter·mi·nate /ˌɪndɪˈtɜːmɪnɪt◂ ‖-ɜːr-/ *adj* impossible to know exactly: *a woman of indeterminate age*

in·dex¹ /ˈɪndeks/ *n* [C], *plural* **indexes** or **indices 1** an alphabetical list at the end of a book, that contains all the names, subjects etc in the book and the pages where you can find them **2** a set of cards or a DATABASE with information in alphabetical order **3** something you can use to compare prices, costs etc or to measure changes: *an index of economic growth*

index² *v* [T] to make an index for something

index fin·ger /ˈ.. ˌ../ *n* [C] the finger next to your thumb; FOREFINGER

In·di·an /ˈɪndiən/ *n* [C] **1** NATIVE AMERICAN **2** someone from India —**Indian** *adj*

Indian sum·mer /ˌ... ˈ../ *n* [C] a period of warm weather in the autumn

in·di·cate /ˈɪndɪkeɪt/ *v* **1** [T] if facts indicate something, they show that it exists or is likely to be true: **+ that** *Research indicates that women live longer than men.* **2** [T] to point at something: *Indicating a chair, he said, "Please, sit down."* **3** [T] to say or do something that shows what you want or intend to do: **+ that** *He indicated that he had no desire to come with us.* **4** [I,T] *BrE* to show which way you are going to turn when you are driving; SIGNAL: *I indicated left.*

in·di·ca·tion /ˌɪndɪˈkeɪʃən/ *n* [C,U] a sign that something exists or is likely to be true: *Did Rick ever give any indication that he was unhappy?*

in·dic·a·tive /ɪnˈdɪkətɪv/ *adj* **1** **be indicative of** to show that something exists or is likely to be true: *His reaction is indicative of how frightened he is.* **2** in grammar, an indicative verb expresses a fact or action

in·di·ca·tor /ˈɪndɪkeɪtəl-ər/ *n* [C] **1** an event, fact etc that shows that something exists or shows you the way something is developing: *All the main economic indicators suggest that business is improving.* **2** *BrE* one of the lights on a car which show which way it is going to turn; TURN SIGNAL *AmE* → see picture at CAR

in·di·ces /ˈɪndɪsiːz/ *n* a plural of INDEX

in·dict /ɪnˈdaɪt/ *v* [I,T] to officially charge someone with a crime —**indictment** *n* [C,U] —**indictable** *adj*: *an indictable offense*

in·dif·fer·ence /ɪnˈdɪfərəns/ *n* [U] when someone is not interested in or does not care about something: *her husband's indifference to how unhappy she was*

in·dif·fer·ent /ɪnˈdɪfərənt/ *adj* not interested and not caring: **+ to** *an industry that seems indifferent to environmental concerns*

in·di·ge·nous /ɪnˈdɪdʒənəs/ *adj* indigenous plants, animals etc have always lived or grown naturally in the place where they are now

in·di·gest·i·ble /ˌɪndɪˈdʒestɪbəl◂/ *adj* food that is indigestible is difficult for your stomach to deal with → see also DIGEST

in·di·ges·tion /ˌɪndɪˈdʒestʃən/ *n* [U] the uncomfortable stomach pain that you get when you eat too much or too fast

in·dig·nant /ɪnˈdɪgnənt/ *adj* angry because you feel you have been insulted or unfairly treated: *Indignant parents said the school cared more about money than education.* —**indignantly** *adv* —**indignation** /ˌɪndɪgˈneɪʃən/ *n* [U]

in·dig·ni·ty /ɪnˈdɪgnɪti/ *n* [C,U] a situation that makes you feel very ashamed, unimportant, and not respected: *I suffered the final indignity of being taken to the police station.*

in·di·rect /ˌɪndɪˈrekt◂/ *adj* **1** not directly caused by something or not directly connected with it: *The accident was an indirect result of the heavy rain.* **2** not using the straightest or most direct way: *an indirect route* —**indirectly** *adv*

indirect speech /ˌ... ˈ./ *n* REPORTED SPEECH

in·dis·creet /ˌɪndɪˈskriːt◂/ *adj* careless about what you say or do, especially by talking about a secret: *Try to stop him from saying something indiscreet.* —**indiscreetly** *adv*

SPELLING NOTE
Words with the sound /aɪ/ may be spelt **e-**, like **eye**, or **ai-**, **aisle**.

in·dis·cre·tion /ˌɪndɪˈskreʃən/ n [C,U] unwise behaviour that shows a lack of careful thought and often seems immoral to other people: *sexual indiscretions | youthful indiscretion*

in·dis·crim·i·nate /ˌɪndɪˈskrɪmɪnɪt◂/ adj indiscriminate actions are done without considering who will be affected or harmed: *indiscriminate killings by teenage gangs* —**indiscriminately** adv

in·di·spens·a·ble /ˌɪndɪˈspensəbəl◂/ adj someone or something that is indispensable is so important or useful that you cannot manage without them: *The information he provided was indispensable to our research.*

in·dis·put·a·ble /ˌɪndɪˈspjuːtəbəl/ adj a fact that is indisputable is definitely true: *an indisputable link between smoking and cancer.* —**indisputably** adv

in·dis·tinct /ˌɪndɪˈstɪŋkt◂/ adj difficult to see, hear, or remember clearly: *indistinct voices in the next room* —**indistinctly** adv

in·dis·tin·guish·a·ble /ˌɪndɪˈstɪŋgwɪʃəbəl/ adj so similar that you cannot see any difference: *This material is indistinguishable from real silk.*

in·di·vid·u·al[1] /ˌɪndɪˈvɪdʒuəl◂/ adj **1** considered separately from other people or things in the same group: *Each individual drawing is slightly different.* **2** belonging to or intended for one person rather than a group: *Individual attention must be given to every student.*

individual[2] n [C] one person, considered separately from the rest of the group or society that they live in: *the rights of the individual*

in·di·vid·u·al·ist /ˌɪndɪˈvɪdʒuəlɪst/ n [C] someone who does things in their own way, without being influenced by other people —**individualism** n [U] —**individualistic** /ˌɪndɪˌvɪdʒuəˈlɪstɪk◂/ adj

in·di·vid·u·al·i·ty /ˌɪndɪˌvɪdʒuˈæləti/ n [U] the quality that makes someone different from everyone else: *work that allows children to express their individuality*

in·di·vid·u·al·ly /ˌɪndɪˈvɪdʒuəli/ adv separately, not together in a group: *The teacher met everyone individually.*

in·doc·tri·nate /ɪnˈdɒktrɪneɪt‖ɪnˈdɑːk-/ v [T] to teach someone to accept a particular set of beliefs and not consider any others: *indoctrinated by the whole military training process* —**indoctrination** /ɪnˌdɒktrɪˈneɪʃən/ n [U]

in·do·lent /ˈɪndələnt/ adj formal lazy —**indolently** adv —**indolence** n [U]

in·dom·i·ta·ble /ɪnˈdɒmɪtəbəl‖ɪnˈdɑː-/ adj formal **indomitable spirit/courage etc** determination, courage etc that is very strong —**indomitably** adv

in·door /ˈɪndɔː‖-ɔːr/ adj covered by a building, or happening inside a building: *an indoor swimming pool* → opposite OUTDOOR

in·doors /ˌɪnˈdɔːz‖-ˈɔːrz◂/ adv into or inside a building: *It's raining – let's go indoors. | He stayed indoors all morning.* → opposite OUTDOORS

in·duce /ɪnˈdjuːs‖ɪnˈduːs/ v [T] **1** formal to make someone decide to do something: **induce sb to do sth** *Whatever induced you to spend so much money on a car?* **2** to cause a particular physical condition: *This drug may induce drowsiness.* **3** to make a woman give birth to her baby by giving her a special drug

in·duce·ment /ɪnˈdjuːsmənt‖ɪnˈduːs-/ n [C,U] formal something that you are offered to persuade you to do something

in·duct /ɪnˈdʌkt/ v [T] to officially introduce someone into a group or organization

in·duc·tion /ɪnˈdʌkʃən/ n [C,U] the process of officially introducing someone into a group or organization: *We run regular induction courses for new employees.*

in·dulge /ɪnˈdʌldʒ/ v **1** [I,T] to let yourself do or have something that you enjoy, especially something that is considered bad for you: **+ in** *I sometimes indulge in a cigarette at a party. |* **indulge yourself** *Go on, indulge yourself for a change!* **2** [T] to let someone do or have whatever they want, even if it is bad for them: *Ralph indulges his children terribly.*

in·dul·gence /ɪnˈdʌldʒəns/ n **1** [U] the habit of eating too much, drinking too much etc: *a life of indulgence* **2** [C] something that you do or have for pleasure, not because you need it: *Chocolate is my only indulgence.*

in·dul·gent /ɪnˈdʌldʒənt/ adj willing to let someone have whatever they want, even if it is bad for them: *indulgent parents* —**indulgently** adv

in·dus·tri·al /ɪnˈdʌstriəl/ adj **1** connected with industry or with the people working in industry: *industrial pollution* **2** having a lot of factories: *an industrial region* —**industrially** adv

in·dus·tri·al·ist /ɪnˈdʌstriəlɪst/ n [C] the owner of a factory, industrial company etc

in·dus·tri·al·ized (also **-ised** *BrE*) /ɪnˈdʌstriəlaɪzd/ adj an industrialized country or area has a lot of industry —**industrialization** /ɪnˌdʌstriəlaɪˈzeɪʃən‖-lə-/ n [U]

industrial park /ˌ...ˈ./ also **industrial es·tate** /ˌ....ˈ./ *BrE* — n [C] an area of land that has offices, businesses, small factories etc on it

in·dus·tri·ous /ɪnˈdʌstriəs/ adj formal always working hard: *industrious young women* —**industriously** adv

in·dus·try /ˈɪndəstri/ n **1** [U] the production of goods, especially in factories: *The country's economy is supported by industry.* **2** [C] all the companies that work in one particular type of trade or service: *the clothing industry*

in·ed·i·ble /ɪnˈedɪbəl/ adj not suitable for eating: *inedible mushrooms*

in·ef·fec·tive /ˌɪnɪˈfektɪv◂/ adj not achieving the correct effect or result: *the treatment was completely ineffective* —**ineffectively** adv —**ineffectiveness** n [U]

in·ef·fec·tu·al /ˌɪnɪˈfektʃuəl◂/ adj not good enough, strong enough, or confident enough to do what you should do: *an ineffectual leader* —**ineffectually** adv

in·ef·fi·cient /ˌɪnɪˈfɪʃənt◂/ adj not working well, and wasting time, money, or energy: *an inefficient use of good farm land* —**inefficiently** adv —**inefficiency** n [C,U]

in·el·e·gant /ɪnˈeləgənt/ adj not graceful or attractive: *writing that is sloppy and inelegant* —**inelegantly** adv —**inelegance** n [U]

in·el·i·gi·ble /ɪnˈelɪdʒəbəl/ adj not allowed to do or to have something: *Non-citizens are ineligible to vote in the election.* —**ineligibility** /ɪnˌelɪdʒəˈbɪləti/ n [U]

in·ept /ɪˈnept/ adj not good at doing something: *an inept driver* —**ineptly** adv —**ineptitude** n [U]

in·e·qual·i·ty /ˌɪnɪˈkwɒlɪtɪ‖-ˈkwɑː-/ n [C,U] an unfair situation, in which some groups in society have less money, fewer opportunities etc than others: *the many inequalities in our legal system*

in·eq·ui·ty /ɪnˈekwɪti/ n [C,U] formal unfairness, or something that is unfair

in·ert /ɪˈnɜːt‖-ɜːrt/ adj **1** technical not producing a chemical reaction when combined with other substances: *inert gases* **2** formal not moving: *He checked her inert body for signs of life.*

in·er·tia /ɪˈnɜːʃəǁ-ɜːr-/ n [U] **1** when a situation does not change, or changes too slowly: *the problem of inertia in large government departments* **2** technical the force that keeps an object in the same position until it is moved or that keeps it moving until it is stopped **3** a feeling that you do not want to move or do anything to change the situation you are in

in·es·cap·a·ble /ˌɪnɪˈskeɪpəbəl/ adj formal a fact that is inescapable cannot be ignored: *The inescapable conclusion is that Reynolds killed himself.* —**inescapably** adv

in·es·ti·ma·ble /ɪnˈestɪməbəl/ adj formal used to emphasize how good, useful, or valuable something is: *The records are of inestimable value to historians.* —**inestimably** adv

in·ev·i·ta·ble /ɪˈnevɪtəbəl/ adj **1** something that is inevitable will definitely happen and you cannot avoid it: *Death is inevitable.* **2 the inevitable** something that will definitely happen: *Finally, the inevitable happened and he lost his job.* —**inevitably** adv: *Inevitably, his alcohol problem affected his work.* —**inevitability** /ɪnˌevɪtəˈbɪlɪti/ n [U]

in·ex·act /ˌɪnɪɡˈzækt/ adj formal not exact: *Psychology is an inexact science.*

in·ex·cus·a·ble /ˌɪnɪkˈskjuːzəbəl/ adj inexcusable behaviour is too bad or too rude to be excused —**inexcusably** adv

in·ex·haust·i·ble /ˌɪnɪɡˈzɔːstɪbəl‖-ˈzɒːs-/ adj existing in large amounts that can never be finished or used up: *Nuclear fusion could provide an inexhaustible supply of energy.*

in·ex·o·ra·ble /ɪnˈeksərəbəl/ adj formal an inexorable process cannot be stopped —**inexorably** adv: *Slowly, inexorably, the cliff is being washed away.*

in·ex·pen·sive /ˌɪnɪkˈspensɪv/ adj cheap but good: *an inexpensive vacation* —**inexpensively** adv

in·ex·pe·ri·enced /ˌɪnɪkˈspɪərɪənst‖-ˈspɪr-/ adj not having much experience or knowledge: *an inexperienced driver* —**inexperience** n [U]

in·ex·plic·a·ble /ˌɪnɪkˈsplɪkəbəl‖ɪnˈeksplɪkəbəl, ˌɪnɪkˈsplɪk-/ adj too unusual or strange to be explained or understood: *the inexplicable disappearance of a young woman* —**inexplicably** adv

in·ex·tric·a·bly /ˌɪnɪkˈstrɪkəbli, ɪnˈekstrɪk-/ adv formal things that are inextricably connected cannot be separated from each other: *Poverty and bad health are inextricably linked.* —**inextricable** adj

in·fal·li·ble /ɪnˈfæləbəl/ adj **1** something that is infallible always works correctly: *an infallible cure for hiccups* **2** someone who is infallible is never wrong: *Many small children believe their parents are infallible.* —**infallibly** adv —**infallibility** /ɪnˌfæləˈbɪlɪti/ n [U]

in·fa·mous /ˈɪnfəməs/ adj well known for being bad or evil: *an infamous criminal* —**infamously** adv → compare FAMOUS

in·fan·cy /ˈɪnfənsi/ n [U] **1** the period in a child's life before he or she can walk or talk: *Their son died in infancy.* **2 in its infancy** something that is in its infancy is just starting to be developed: *In the 1930s air travel was still in its infancy.*

in·fant /ˈɪnfənt/ n [C] formal a baby or very young child

in·fan·tile /ˈɪnfəntaɪl/ adj infantile behaviour seems silly in an adult because it is more suitable to a child: *his stupid infantile jokes*

in·fan·try /ˈɪnfəntri/ n [U] soldiers who fight on foot

in·fat·u·at·ed /ɪnˈfætʃueɪtɪd/ adj having unreasonably strong feelings of romantic or sexual love for someone: **+ with** *He's infatuated with her.* —**infatuation** /ɪnˌfætʃuˈeɪʃən/ n [C,U]

in·fect /ɪnˈfekt/ v [T] **1** to give someone a disease: *The number of people who have been infected has already reached 10,000.* **2** to make food, water etc dangerous and likely to spread disease: *a bacteria that can infect fruit* **3** if a feeling that you have infects other people, it makes them begin to feel the same way: *His cynicism seems to have infected the whole team.*

in·fect·ed /ɪnˈfektɪd/ adj **1** someone who is infected with a disease has the disease **2** a wound that is infected has harmful BACTERIA in it which prevent it from getting better **3** food, water etc that is infected contains BACTERIA that spread disease

in·fec·tion /ɪnˈfekʃən/ n [C,U] a disease in part of your body, caused by BACTERIA or a VIRUS: *Wash the cut thoroughly to protect against infection.* | *an ear infection*

in·fec·tious /ɪnˈfekʃəs/ adj **1** an infectious disease can be passed from one person to another **2** someone who is infectious has a disease that could be passed to other people **3** infectious feelings or laughter spread quickly from one person to another

in·fer /ɪnˈfɜː‖-ɜːr/ v [T] **-rred, -rring** formal to decide that particular facts must be true because of other information that you already have: *What can you infer from the high level of radiation in the water?* → compare IMPLY

USAGE NOTE: infer and imply

Compare **infer** and **imply**. As a listener you **infer** something (=take a particular meaning from) the words of the speaker: *I inferred from his remarks that he hadn't enjoyed the visit.* As a speaker, your words **imply** something (=suggest a particular meaning indirectly): *He implied that he hadn't enjoyed the visit.*

---

in·fer·ence /ˈɪnfərəns/ n [C] formal a fact that you decide must be true, based on information that you already know, or the process of doing this

in·fe·ri·or¹ /ɪnˈfɪərɪə‖-ˈfɪrɪər/ adj not good, or not as good as someone or something else: *Larry always makes me feel inferior.* | **+ to** *His work is* *inferior to mine.* — **inferiority** /ɪnˌfɪəriˈɒrɪtiǁɪnˌfɪriˈɔːr-/ *n* [U] → compare SUPERIOR¹

in·fer·ior² *n* [C] someone who has a lower position or rank than you in an organization → compare SUPERIOR²

in·fer·no /ɪnˈfɜːnəʊǁ-ɜːrnoʊ/ *n* [C] *literary* a very large and dangerous fire: *a raging inferno*

in·fer·tile /ɪnˈfɜːtaɪlǁ-ˈfɜːrtl/ *adj* **1** an infertile person or animal cannot have babies **2** infertile land is not good enough to grow plants in — **infertility** /ˌɪnfəˈtɪlɪtiǁ-fər-/ *n* [U]

in·fest /ɪnˈfest/ *v* [T] if insects, rats etc infest a place, they are there in large numbers and usually cause damage: **be infested with** *an old carpet infested with fleas* — **infestation** /ˌɪnfeˈsteɪʃən/ *n* [C,U]

in·fi·del /ˈɪnfɪdəl/ *n* [C] *old-fashioned* an insulting word for someone who does not believe in what you consider to be the true religion

in·fi·del·i·ty /ˌɪnfɪˈdelɪti/ *n* [C,U] when someone is unfaithful to their wife or husband by having sex with someone else

in·fight·ing /ˈɪnˌfaɪtɪŋ/ *n* [U] unfriendly disagreement between members of the same group or organization: *political infighting*

in·fil·trate /ˈɪnfɪltreɪtǁɪnˈfɪltreɪt, ˈɪnfɪl-/ *v* [I,T] to secretly join an organization or enter a place to find out information about it or harm it: *The police have made several attempts to infiltrate the Mafia.* — **infiltrator** *n* [C] — **infiltration** /ˌɪnfɪlˈtreɪʃən/ *n* [U]

in·fi·nite /ˈɪnfɪnɪt/ *adj* **1** used to emphasize how strong something is or how much there is of it: *a teacher with infinite patience* **2** continuing for ever: *an infinite universe* — **infinitely** *adv*

in·fin·i·tes·i·mal /ˌɪnfɪnɪˈtesɪməl◂/ *adj* extremely small: *infinitesimal changes in temperature*

in·fin·i·tive /ɪnˈfɪnɪtɪv/ *n* [C] the basic form of a verb, used with 'to'. In the sentence 'I forgot to buy milk', 'to buy' is an infinitive.

in·fin·i·ty /ɪnˈfɪnɪti/ *n* **1** [U] a space or distance without limits or without an end **2** *technical* a number that is larger than any other

in·firm /ɪnˈfɜːmǁ-ɜːrm/ *adj formal* weak or ill, especially because of being old

in·fir·ma·ry /ɪnˈfɜːməriǁ-ɜːr-/ *n* [C] *formal* **1** *BrE* a hospital **2** *especially AmE* a place, especially in a school, where you go if you are ill

in·fir·mi·ty /ɪnˈfɜːmɪtiǁ-ɜːr-/ *n* [C,U] *formal* bad health or a particular illness

in·flame /ɪnˈfleɪm/ *v* [T] *literary* to make someone have strong feelings of anger, excitement etc

in·flamed /ɪnˈfleɪmd/ *adj* a part of your body that is inflamed is red and painful

in·flam·ma·ble /ɪnˈflæməbəl/ *adj* inflammable materials or substances burn very easily: *Butane is highly inflammable.* → opposite NON-FLAMMABLE

in·flam·ma·tion /ˌɪnfləˈmeɪʃən/ *n* [C,U] swelling and soreness on or in a part of your body, which is often red and painful

in·flam·ma·to·ry /ɪnˈflæmətəriǁ-tɔːri/ *adj formal* an inflammatory speech, piece of writing etc is likely to cause feelings such as anger or hatred

in·flat·a·ble /ɪnˈfleɪtəbəl/ *adj* an inflatable object has to be filled with air before you can use it: *an inflatable mattress*

in·flate /ɪnˈfleɪt/ *v* **1** [I,T] if you inflate something or it is inflated, it fills with air or gas and becomes larger: *The machine quickly inflates the tires.* **2** [T] to make a number bigger, a cost higher etc: *a policy that has inflated land prices by nearly 50%* → opposite DEFLATE

in·flat·ed /ɪnˈfleɪtɪd/ *adj* **1** inflated prices, rents, figures etc are higher than is reasonable: *Inflated land prices prevented local companies from expanding.* **2** filled with air or gas: *an inflated balloon*

in·fla·tion /ɪnˈfleɪʃən/ *n* [U] **1** a continuing increase in prices or the rate at which prices increase: *the Mexican government's efforts to control inflation* **2** the process of filling something with air or gas

in·fla·tion·a·ry /ɪnˈfleɪʃənəriǁ-ʃəneri/ *adj* likely to cause an increase in prices: *inflationary wage increases*

in·flec·tion also **inflexion** /ɪnˈflekʃən/ *n* [C,U] **1** the way the ending of a word changes to show that it is plural, in the past tense etc **2** the way in which someone's voice changes when they ask a question, say yes or no etc: *"Well Hello!" he said with a mocking inflection.*

in·flex·i·ble /ɪnˈfleksɪbəl/ *adj* **1** inflexible rules, opinions etc cannot be changed easily: *a school with inflexible rules* **2** inflexible material is stiff and will not bend — **inflexibly** *adv* — **inflexibility** /ɪnˌfleksɪˈbɪlɪti/ *n* [U]

in·flict /ɪnˈflɪkt/ *v* [T] to make someone suffer something unpleasant: **inflict sth on/upon sb** *the damage inflicted on the enemy* — **infliction** /-ˈflɪkʃən/ *n* [U]

in·flu·ence¹ /ˈɪnfluəns/ *n* **1** [C,U] the power to have an effect on the way that someone or something develops, behaves, or thinks: *Vince used his influence with the union to get his nephew a job.* **2** [C] someone or something that has an effect on other people or things: *Alex's parents always thought that I was a bad influence on him.* **3** **under the influence (of drink/drugs/alcohol)** *informal* drunk or feeling the effects of a drug

influence² *v* [T] to have an effect on the way someone or something develops, behaves, or thinks: *I don't want to influence your decision.*

in·flu·en·tial /ˌɪnfluˈenʃəl◂/ *adj* having a lot of influence: *an influential politician* — **influentially** *adv*

in·flu·en·za /ˌɪnfluˈenzə/ *n* [U] *formal* FLU

in·flux /ˈɪnflʌks/ *n* [C usually singular] the arrival of large numbers of people or things: *an influx of cheap imported cars*

in·fo /ˈɪnfəʊǁ-foʊ/ *n* [U] *informal* INFORMATION

in·fo·mer·cial /ˈɪnfəʊˌmɜːˈʃəl‖-foʊˌmɜːr-/ n [C] a short television programme that gives information about something, but is really intended to persuade you to buy something

in·form /ɪnˈfɔːm‖-ɔːrm/ v [T] to formally tell someone about something: *There was a note informing us that Charles had left.*

inform against/on sb *phr v* [T] to tell the police, an enemy etc about what someone has done

in·for·mal /ɪnˈfɔːməl‖-ɔːr-/ adj **1** relaxed and friendly: *an informal meeting* **2** suitable for ordinary situations or conversations: *an informal letter to your family* —**informally** adv —**informality** /ˌɪnfɔːˈmælɪti‖-fɔːr-/ n [U]

in·for·mant /ɪnˈfɔːmənt‖-ɔːr-/ n [C] someone who gives information to another person

in·for·ma·tion /ˌɪnfəˈmeɪʃən‖-fər-/ n [U] facts or details about a situation, person, event etc: + **about/on** *I need some more information about this machine.* | **piece of information** *a useful piece of information*

information su·per·high·way /ˌɪnfəmeɪʃən ˌsuːpəˈhaɪweɪ, -ˌsjuː-‖-fərmeɪʃən ˌsuːpər-/ n [singular] the **INTERNET**

information tech·nol·o·gy /ˌ..ˈ.. ˌ.../ n [U] the use of electronic processes, especially computers, for gathering information, storing it; **IT**

in·form·a·tive /ɪnˈfɔːmətɪv‖-ɔːr-/ adj providing useful facts or ideas: *a very informative book* —**informatively** adv

in·formed /ɪnˈfɔːmd‖-ɔːr-/ adj having a lot of knowledge or information about a particular subject or situation: *Women should be able to make an informed choice about contraception.* | *well-informed voters*

in·form·er /ɪnˈfɔːmə‖-ɔːrmər/ n [C] someone who secretly gives information to the police or other government organizations about people who are involved in illegal activities

in·frac·tion /ɪnˈfrækʃən/ n [C,U] formal an act of breaking a rule or law

in·fra·red /ˌɪnfrəˈred◂/ adj infrared light produces heat but cannot be seen

in·fra·struc·ture /ˈɪnfrəˌstrʌktʃə‖-tʃər/ n [C usually singular] the basic systems that a country or organization needs in order to work properly: *Japan's economic infrastructure*

in·fu·ri·ate /ɪnˈfjʊərieɪt‖-fjʊr-/ v [T] to make someone very angry: *He really infuriates me!*

in·fu·ri·a·ting /ɪnˈfjʊərieɪtɪŋ‖-fjʊr-/ adj very annoying: *an infuriating two hour delay* —**infuriatingly** adv

in·fuse /ɪnˈfjuːz/ v formal **1** [T] to fill someone or something with a particular feeling or quality: *the coach's attempts to infuse some enthusiasm into the team* **2** [I,T] to put a substance such as tea into very hot water, so that its taste passes into the water —**infusion** /-ˈfjuːʒən/ n [C,U]

in·ge·ni·ous /ɪnˈdʒiːniəs/ adj **1** an ingenious plan, machine, idea etc is the result of intelligent thinking and new ideas **2** an ingenious person is very good at inventing things, thinking of how to solve problems etc —**ingeniously** adv

in·ge·nu·i·ty /ˌɪndʒəˈnjuːɪti‖-ˈnuː-/ n [U] skill at inventing things, thinking of how to solve problems etc

in·gest /ɪnˈdʒest/ v [T] formal to eat something —**ingestion** /-ˈdʒestʃən/ n [U]

in·grained /ˌɪnˈɡreɪnd◂/ adj **1** ingrained attitudes or behaviour have existed for a long time and are difficult to change **2** ingrained dirt is under the surface of something and is difficult to remove

in·gra·ti·ate /ɪnˈɡreɪʃieɪt/ v **ingratiate yourself (with)** to try to make people like you by praising them or being nice to them: *a politician trying to ingratiate himself with the voters* —**ingratiating** adj —**ingratiatingly** adv

in·grat·i·tude /ɪnˈɡrætɪˌtjuːd‖-tuːd/ n [U] when someone is not grateful for something

in·gre·di·ent /ɪnˈɡriːdiənt/ n [C] **1** one of the things from which a type of food is made: *Flour, water, and eggs are the most important ingredients.* **2** one of the qualities that makes something successful: *all the ingredients of a good romantic novel*

in·hab·it /ɪnˈhæbɪt/ v [T] formal to live in a particular place: *a forest inhabited by bears and moose* —**inhabitable** adj

in·hab·i·tant /ɪnˈhæbɪtənt/ n [C] one of the people who live in a particular place

in·hale /ɪnˈheɪl/ v [I,T] formal to breathe air, smoke, or gas into your lungs: *Try not to inhale the fumes from the glue.* → opposite **EXHALE** —**inhalation** /ˌɪnhəˈleɪʃən/ n [C,U]

in·hal·er /ɪnˈheɪlə‖-ər/ n [C] a small plastic tube from which you can breathe a special medicine if you have difficulty breathing

in·her·ent /ɪnˈhɪərənt, -ˈher‖-ˈhɪr-, -ˈher-/ adj a quality that is inherent in something is a natural part of it: *a problem that is inherent in the system* —**inherently** adv

in·her·it /ɪnˈherɪt/ v **1** [I,T] to receive money, a house etc from someone who has died: *I inherited the house from my uncle.* **2** [T] to have a particular physical appearance or character that one of your parents had: *Her stubbornness she had inherited from her mother.* **3** to have a belief, problem etc that someone else had before you: *economic difficulties inherited from the previous government*

in·her·i·tance /ɪnˈherɪtəns/ n [C,U] money, property etc that you receive from someone who has died

---

in·hib·it /ɪnˈhɪbɪ̇t/ *v* [T] **1** to prevent something from growing or developing: *new treatments to inhibit the spread of the disease* **2** *formal* to make it harder for someone to do something

in·hib·it·ed /ɪnˈhɪbɪ̇tɪ̇d/ *adj* too nervous or worried to say or do what you really want —**inhibitedly** *adv*

in·hi·bi·tion /ˌɪnhɪ̇ˈbɪʃən/ *n* [C,U] a feeling of worry or embarrassment that makes it hard for you to say what you really think or what you really want to do: *She soon loses her inhibitions when she's had a few glasses of wine.*

in·hos·pi·ta·ble /ˌɪnhɒˈspɪtəbəl‖ˌɪnhɑːˈspɪt-/ *adj* **1** an inhospitable place is difficult to live in because it is very hot, very cold etc **2** unfriendly to people who are visiting you —**inhospitably** *adv*

in-house /ˌ. ˈ.◂/ *adj, adv* within a company or organization rather than outside it: *an in-house training department*

in·hu·man /ɪnˈhjuːmən/ *adj* **1** very cruel: *inhuman treatment* **2** lacking any human qualities in a way that seems strange or frightening: *an inhuman scream*

in·hu·mane /ˌɪnhjuːˈmeɪn◂/ *adj* treating people or animals in a cruel and unacceptable way: *inhumane living conditions* —**inhumanely** *adv*

in·hu·man·i·ty /ˌɪnhjuːˈmænɪ̇ti/ *n* [U] extreme cruelty: *the inhumanity and injustice of the apartheid regime*

in·im·i·ta·ble /ɪˈnɪmɪ̇təbəl/ *adj* very different from the way that most people do something: *Jerry gave the speech in his own inimitable style.* —**inimitably** *adv*

in·iq·ui·ty /ɪˈnɪkwɪ̇ti/ *n* [C,U] *formal* a situation or fact that is very unfair or very wrong: *the iniquity of locking up all mental patients* —**iniquitous** *adj*

i·ni·tial[1] /ɪˈnɪʃəl/ *adj* happening at the beginning; first: *the initial stages of the disease* —**initially** *adv*: *I was employed initially as a temporary worker.*

initial[2] *n* [C usually plural] the first letter of a name: *a suitcase with the initials S.H. on it*

initial[3] *v* [T] to write your initials on a document: *Could you initial this form for me, please?*

i·ni·ti·ate /ɪˈnɪʃieɪt/ *v* [T] **1** to arrange for something important to start: *The prison has recently initiated new security procedures.* **2** to let someone join an organization or to show them an activity for the first time —**initiation** /ɪˌnɪʃiˈeɪʃən/ *n* [C,U]

i·ni·tia·tive /ɪˈnɪʃətɪv/ *n* **1** [U] the ability to make decisions and take action without waiting for someone to tell you what to do: *I was impressed by the initiative she showed.* **2** [C] a plan or process that has been started to solve a particular problem: *state initiatives to reduce spending* **3 take the initiative** to be the first person to do something to solve a particular problem

in·ject /ɪnˈdʒekt/ *v* [T] **1** to put a drug into your body, using a special needle: *Both patients have been injected with a new drug.* **2** to improve something by adding a particular quality to it: *remarks that injected some humour into the situation*

in·jec·tion /ɪnˈdʒekʃən/ *n* **1** [C,U] an act of putting a drug into your body, using a special needle **2** [C] the act of putting money into an organization, plan etc: *The business received a cash injection of $6 million.*

in·junc·tion /ɪnˈdʒʌŋkʃən/ *n* [C] *law* an official order given by a court that stops someone from being allowed to do something

in·jure /ˈɪndʒə‖-ər/ *v* [T] to hurt a person or animal: *She was badly injured in the accident.*

in·jured /ˈɪndʒəd‖-ərd/ *adj* an injured person or animal has been hurt: *We helped the injured rider to the waiting ambulance.*

in·ju·ry /ˈɪndʒəri/ *n* [C,U] physical harm that someone suffers in an accident or attack, or a particular example of this: *serious head injuries*

in·jus·tice /ɪnˈdʒʌstɪ̇s/ *n* [C,U] a situation in which people are treated badly and unfairly: *the violence and injustice of the plantation system*

ink /ɪŋk/ *n* [C,U] a coloured liquid used for writing, printing etc

ink·ling /ˈɪŋklɪŋ/ **have an inkling** to think that something may possibly happen, may be true etc: *We had no inkling that he was leaving.*

in·land[1] /ˈɪnlənd/ *adj* an inland area, city etc is not near the coast

in·land[2] /ɪnˈlænd/ *adv* in a direction away from the coast and towards the centre of a country: *driving inland*

in-laws /ˈ. ./ *n* [plural] *informal* the mother and father of your husband or wife, or other members of their family

in·let /ˈɪnlet, ˈɪnlɪ̇t/ *n* [C] **1** a narrow area of water formed by a sharp bend in the coast or in the edge of a lake **2** the part of a machine where liquid or gas flows in

in·mate /ˈɪnmeɪt/ *n* [C] someone who is kept in a prison or in a hospital for people with mental illnesses

inn /ɪn/ *n* [C] a small hotel, especially one in the countryside

in·nards /ˈɪnədz‖-ərdz/ *n* [plural] the parts inside your body, especially your stomach

in·nate /ˌɪˈneɪt◂/ *adj* an innate quality has been part of your character since you were born: *an innate sense of fun* —**innately** *adv*

in·ner /ˈɪnə‖-ər/ *adj* **1** on the inside or close to the centre of something: *the inner ear* → opposite OUTER **2** inner feelings, thoughts, meanings etc are secret and not expressed **3 inner circle** the few people in an organization, political party etc who control it or share power with its leader

inner cit·y /ˌ.. ˈ..◂/ *n* [C] the part of a city that is near the centre, especially the part where the buildings are in a bad condition and the people are poor: *Crime in our inner cities seems to be getting worse.* —**inner city** *adj*

in·ner·most /ˈɪnəməʊst‖-nərmoʊst/ *adj* **1** your innermost feelings, desires etc are the ones you feel most strongly and keep private **2** *formal* furthest inside → opposite OUTERMOST

in·ning /ˈɪnɪŋ/ *n* [C] one of the nine playing periods in a game of BASEBALL

in·nings /ˈɪnɪŋz/ *n* [C], *plural* **innings** one of the playing periods in a game of CRICKET

inn·keep·er /ˈɪnˌkiːpə‖-ər/ *n* [C] *old-fashioned* someone who owns or manages an INN

in·no·cence /ˈɪnəsəns/ n [U] **1** the fact of not being guilty of a crime: *How did they prove her innocence?* **2** when someone has not had much experience of life, especially with the result that they do not understand that people can be bad, cruel, dishonest etc: *a child's innocence*

in·no·cent /ˈɪnəsənt/ adj **1** not guilty of a crime: *Nobody would believe that I was innocent.* | *innocent of murder* **2** not having much experience of life, especially not knowing that people can be bad, cruel, dishonest etc: *I was thirteen years old and very innocent.* **3** used to emphasize that someone who was hurt or harmed had not done anything wrong: *the innocent victims of a drunk driver* **4** done or said without intending to harm or offend anyone: *an innocent remark* —**innocently** adv

in·noc·u·ous /ɪˈnɒkjuəs‖ɪˈnɑːk-/ adj not likely to harm anyone or cause trouble: *At first, his questions seemed innocuous enough.* —**innocuously** adv —**innocuousness** n [U]

in·no·va·tion /ˌɪnəˈveɪʃən/ n [C,U] a new idea, method etc that is used for the first time, or the use of new ideas, methods etc: *recent innovations in computing* —**innovate** /ˈɪnəveɪt/ v [I] —**innovative** adj —**innovator** n [C]

in·nu·en·do /ˌɪnjuˈendəʊ‖-doʊ/ n [C,U], plural **innuendoes**, or **innuendos** a remark suggesting something about sex, or that someone has done something wrong, that is deliberate but is not stated directly: *nasty innuendoes about Laurie and the boss*

in·nu·me·ra·ble /ɪˈnjuːmərəbəl‖ɪˈnjuː-, ɪˈnuː-/ adj very many

in·of·fen·sive /ˌɪnəˈfensɪv◂/ adj unlikely to offend anyone: *a quiet, inoffensive man* —**inoffensively** adv

in·or·di·nate /ɪˈnɔːdənət‖-ɔːr-/ adj much more than is reasonable: *an inordinate amount of time* —**inordinately** adv

in·or·gan·ic /ˌɪnɔːˈɡænɪk◂‖-ɔːr-/ adj not consisting of or produced from living things: *inorganic fertilizers*

in·pa·tient /ˈɪnpeɪʃənt/ n [C] someone who stays in a hospital at least one night to get medical treatment → compare OUTPATIENT

in·put /ˈɪnpʊt/ n **1** [U] ideas, advice, money, or effort that you put into a job, meeting etc in order to help it succeed: *Students have an important input into what the class covers.* **2** electrical power that is put into a machine for it to use **3** information that is put into a computer → compare OUTPUT

in·quest /ˈɪnkwest/ n [C] an official legal process to find out the cause of a sudden or unexpected death

in·quire also **enquire** BrE /ɪnˈkwaɪə‖-ˈkwaɪr/ v [I,T] formal to ask someone for information: **+ about** *I am writing to inquire about your advertisement in the New York Post.* —**inquirer** n [C]

   inquire into sth phr v [T] to collect information to find out why something happened: *The investigation will inquire into the reasons for the fire.*

in·quir·ing also **enquiring** BrE /ɪnˈkwaɪərɪŋ‖-ˈkwaɪr-/ adj **1** always wanting to find out new things: *Young children have such inquiring minds.* **2** an inquiring glance/look etc when

the expression on your face shows that you want to ask a question —**inquiringly** adv

in·quir·y also **enquiry** BrE /ɪnˈkwaɪəri‖ɪnˈkwaɪri, ˈɪŋkwəri/ n [C] **1** a question you ask in order to get information: *We're getting a lot of inquiries about our new bus service.* **2** [C,U] official process of finding out why something happened, especially something bad: *There will be an official inquiry into the incident.*

> **USAGE NOTE: enquiry and inquiry**
>
> **Enquiry** and **inquiry** are almost the same, but **enquiry** is more often used for a simple request for information, and **inquiry** for a long serious study: *Several people have made enquiries about the job.* | *a government inquiry into the disaster*

in·qui·si·tion /ˌɪŋkwəˈzɪʃən/ n [C] formal a series of questions that someone asks you in a threatening or unpleasant way

in·quis·i·tive /ɪnˈkwɪzətɪv/ adj interested in a lot of different things and wanting to find out more about them: *a cheerful, inquisitive little boy* —**inquisitively** adv —**inquisitiveness** n [U]

in·roads /ˈɪnrəʊdz‖-roʊdz/ n **make inroads into/on** to take away power, trade, votes etc from someone or something by becoming more successful than them: *Their new soft drink is already making huge inroads into the market.*

ins and outs /ˌ. . ˈ./ n [plural] all the exact details of a complicated situation, system, problem etc: *I'm still learning the ins and outs of my new job.*

in·sane /ɪnˈseɪn/ adj **1** informal completely stupid, often in a way that is dangerous: *You must've been totally insane to go with him!* | *an insane idea* **2** seriously mentally ill —**insanely** adv

in·san·i·ty /ɪnˈsænəti/ n [U] **1** the condition of being seriously mentally ill **2** an extremely stupid and possibly dangerous thing to do

in·sa·tia·ble /ɪnˈseɪʃəbəl/ adj always wanting more and more of something: *an insatiable appetite for cheap romantic novels* —**insatiably** adv

in·scribe /ɪnˈskraɪb/ v [T] to cut or write words on something, especially on the surface of a stone or coin: *a medal inscribed with the initials J.S.* —**inscription** /-ˈskrɪpʃən/ n [C]

in·scru·ta·ble /ɪnˈskruːtəbəl/ adj difficult to understand because you are not sure what someone is thinking or feeling: *an inscrutable smile* —**inscrutably** adv —**inscrutability** /ˌɪnˌskruːtəˈbɪlˌti/ n [U]

in·sect /ˈɪnsekt/ n [C] a small creature such as an ANT or a fly, with six legs and a body divided into three parts

in·sec·ti·cide /ɪnˈsektˌsaɪd/ n [U] a chemical used for killing insects

in·se·cure /ˌɪnsɪˈkjʊə◂‖-ˈkjʊr◂/ adj **1** not feeling confident about yourself, your abilities, your relationships etc: *I was young, very shy and insecure.* **2** not safe or not protected: *The future of the company is still insecure.* —**insecurity** n [U] —**insecurely** adv

in·sem·i·na·tion /ɪnˌsemˌˈneɪʃən/ n [U] technical the act of putting SPERM into a woman's or female animal's body to make her have a baby: *artificial insemination* (=done by medical treatment, not sex)

in·sen·si·tive /ɪnˈsensɪtɪv/ *adj* not noticing other people's feelings, and not realizing that something that you do will upset them: *insensitive questions about her divorce* —**insensitively** *adv* —**insensitivity** /ɪnˌsensɪˈtɪvɪti/ *n* [U]

in·sep·a·ra·ble /ɪnˈsepərəbəl/ *adj* **1** people who are inseparable are always together and are very friendly with each other **2** *formal* two things that are inseparable cannot be considered separately: *In poetry, meaning is often inseparable from form.* —**inseparably** *adv*

in·sert¹ /ɪnˈsɜːt‖-ɜːrt/ *v* [T] to put something inside or into something else: *Insert the key in the lock.* —**insertion** /-ˈsɜːʃən‖-ɜːr-/ *n* [C,U]

in·sert² /ˈɪnsɜːt‖-ɜːr-/ *n* [C] something that is designed to be put inside or into something else: *special inserts to protect your heels*

in·side¹ /ɪnˈsaɪd/ *prep, adv* **1** in or into a container, room, building etc: *He opened the box to find two kittens inside.* | *We pushed open the door and stepped inside.* → see colour picture on page 474 → opposite OUTSIDE **2** if you have a feeling or thought inside, you feel or think it without telling anyone: *Inside, I felt confident and calm.* | *Don't keep the anger inside.* **3** used in order to emphasize that what is happening in a country or organization is only known by people who belong to it: *People inside the company have told us about the changes.* **4** in less time than: *We'll be there inside an hour.*

in·side² /ɪnˈsaɪd, ˈɪnsaɪd/ *n* **1** the inside the part of something that is inside: *The inside of the car was filthy.* **2** inside out with the usual outside parts on the inside: *Your shirt is inside out.* **3** know/learn sth inside out to know everything about a subject: *She knows the business inside out.*

in·side³ /ˈɪnsaɪd/ *adj* **1** on or facing the inside of something: *the inside pages of a magazine* **2** inside information/the inside story information that is known only by people who are part of an organization, company etc.

in·sid·er /ɪnˈsaɪdə‖-ər/ *n* [C] someone who has a special knowledge of a particular organization because they are part of it: *Insiders have confirmed that Regan has been sacked.*

in·sides /ɪnˈsaɪdz, ˈɪnsaɪdz/ *n* [plural] the parts inside your body, especially your stomach

in·sid·i·ous /ɪnˈsɪdiəs/ *adj* happening gradually without being noticed, but causing a lot of harm: *the insidious effects of breathing polluted air* —**insidiously** *adv* —**insidiousness** *n* [U]

in·sight /ˈɪnsaɪt/ *n* [C,U] the ability to understand something clearly, or an example of this: + into *The article gives us a real insight into Chinese culture.*

in·sig·ni·a /ɪnˈsɪɡniə/ *n* [C], *plural* insignia a BADGE or other object that shows someone's military or official position

in·sig·nif·i·cant /ˌɪnsɪɡˈnɪfɪkənt◂/ *adj* too small or unimportant to consider or worry about: *an insignificant change in the unemployment rate* —**insignificantly** *adv* —**insignificance** *n* [U]

in·sin·cere /ˌɪnsɪnˈsɪə‖-ˈsɪr◂/ *adj* pretending to be pleased, sympathetic etc, but not really meaning what you say: *an insincere smile* —**insincerely** *adv* —**insincerity** /-ˈserɪti/ *n* [U]

in·sin·u·ate /ɪnˈsɪnjueɪt/ *v* [T] to make people think that something bad is true, without directly saying that it is: *Are you insinuating that she didn't deserve the promotion?* —**insinuation** /ɪnˌsɪnjuˈeɪʃən/ *n* [C,U]

in·sip·id /ɪnˈsɪpɪd/ *adj* not interesting, exciting, or attractive: *I was expecting the food to be spicy, but it was kind of insipid.* —**insipidly** *adv*

in·sist /ɪnˈsɪst/ *v* [I,T] **1** to say firmly that something is true, especially when other people think it may not be true: + **(that)** *Mike insisted that Joelle would never have gone by herself.* | + **on** *She always insisted on her innocence.* **2** to demand that something should be done: + **on** *They're insisting on your resignation.* | + **(that)** *I insisted that he leave.*

in·sis·tence /ɪnˈsɪstəns/ *n* [U] the act of demanding that something should be done: *Kennedy's insistence that the missiles be sent back to Russia*

in·sis·tent /ɪnˈsɪstənt/ *adj* firmly saying that something should be done: *She's very insistent that we should all be on time.* —**insistently** *adv*

in·so·far as, in so far as /ɪnsəʊˈfɑːr əz‖-soʊ-/ linking word *formal* to the degree that one thing affects something else: *Insofar as sales are concerned, the company is doing very well.*

in·so·lent /ˈɪnsələnt/ *adj* rude and not showing any respect to someone in authority: *She just stared back with an insolent grin.* —**insolence** *n* [U] —**insolently** *adv*

in·sol·u·ble /ɪnˈsɒljəbəl‖ɪnˈsɑːl-/ also **in·solv·a·ble** /ɪnˈsɒlvəbəl‖-ˈsɑːl-/ *AmE* — *adj* impossible to solve: *insoluble problems*

in·sol·vent /ɪnˈsɒlvənt‖ɪnˈsɑːl-/ *adj* informal not having enough money to pay what you owe; BANKRUPT

in·som·ni·a /ɪnˈsɒmniə‖-ˈsɑːm-/ *n* [U] when you cannot sleep —**insomniac** /-niæk/ *n* [C]

in·spect /ɪnˈspekt/ *v* [T] **1** to make an official visit to a building or organization to check that everything is of a good enough standard: *All schools are inspected once a year.* **2** to examine something carefully: *Sara inspected her reflection in the mirror.* —**inspection** /-ˈspekʃən/ *n* [C,U]

in·spec·tor /ɪnˈspektə‖-ər/ *n* [C] **1** someone whose job is to check that something is of a good enough standard and that rules are being obeyed: *a health inspector* **2** a police officer of middle rank

in·spi·ra·tion /ˌɪnspɪˈreɪʃən/ *n* [C,U] **1** someone or something that gives you the idea to do something: + **for** *My trip to Mexico was the inspiration for the novel.* **2** be an inspiration to sb to encourage someone to be as good, successful etc as possible: *Her hard work and imagination are an inspiration to us all.* —**inspirational** *adj*

in·spire /ɪnˈspaɪə‖-ˈspaɪr/ *v* [T] **1** to make someone want to do or achieve something: *inspire sb to (do) sth Encouragement will inspire children to try even harder.* **2** to make other people work harder, try harder etc: *inspire sth in sb/inspire sb with sth A good captain should inspire confidence in his men.* —**inspiring** *adj*

in·spired /ɪnˈspaɪəd‖-ˈspaɪrd/ *adj* very skilful and special: *It was an inspired piece of public relations.*

in·sta·bil·i·ty /ˌɪnstəˈbɪləti/ n [U] when a situation or someone's behaviour changes a lot so that you are never sure what will happen next: *a period of economic and political instability | emotional instability* → see also UNSTABLE

in·stall /ɪnˈstɔːl‖-ˈstɒːl/ v [T] to put a piece of equipment somewhere and connect it so that it is ready to be used: *Companies spend thousands of dollars installing security cameras.* —**installation** /ˌɪnstəˈleɪʃən/ n [C,U]

in·stal·ment BrE, **installment** AmE /ɪnˈstɔːlmənt/ n [C] **1** a payment that you make every week, month etc in order to pay for something: *We're paying for the car in monthly instalments.* **2** one of the parts of a story that appears separately each day or week in a magazine or newspaper

in·stance /ˈɪnstəns/ n **1 for instance** for example: *She's totally unreliable – for instance, she often leaves the children alone in the house.* **2** [C] an example of a particular kind of situation or behaviour: + **of** *instances of police brutality*

in·stant[1] /ˈɪnstənt/ adj **1** happening immediately: *The movie was an instant success.* **2** instant food is in the form of powder and is prepared by adding hot water: *instant coffee* —**instantly** adv

instant[2] n [singular] a moment: *He paused for an instant before replying.*

in·stan·ta·ne·ous /ˌɪnstənˈteɪniəs◂/ adj happening immediately: *Wilson's remarks provoked an instantaneous response.* —**instantaneously** adv

instant re·play /ˌ.. ˈ../ n [C] AmE when a part of a sports game on television is shown again immediately after it happens; ACTION REPLAY BrE

in·stead /ɪnˈsted/ adv in the place of someone or something else: *If Lily can't go, I'll go instead.* | + **of** *Why don't you do something, instead of just talking about it?*

in·sti·gate /ˈɪnstɪɡeɪt/ v [T] formal to make something start to happen: *Gang leaders are accused of instigating the riot.* —**instigator** n [C] —**instigation** /ˌɪnstɪˈɡeɪʃən/ n [U]

in·stil BrE, **instill** AmE /ɪnˈstɪl/ v [T] -lled, -lling to make someone think, feel, or behave in a particular way: **instil sth in/into sb** *General Hartson had instilled a sense of pride into all his men.*

in·stinct /ˈɪnstɪŋkt/ n [C,U] a natural way of reacting or behaving that is not learnt or deliberate: *Instinct told me that something was wrong.* —**instinctive** /ɪnˈstɪŋktɪv/ adj —**instinctively** adv

in·sti·tute[1] /ˈɪnstɪtjuːt‖-tuːt/ n [C] an organization that does scientific or educational work: *the California Institute of Technology*

institute[2] v [T] formal to start or establish a system, rule, legal process etc: *He has threatened to institute legal proceedings against the company.*

in·sti·tu·tion /ˌɪnstɪˈtjuːʃən‖-ˈtuː-/ n [C] **1** a large important organization such as a university, church, or bank: *higher education institutions* **2** a place such as a hospital or prison where people are looked after **3** a custom accepted by most people in a society: *the institution of marriage* —**institutional** adj

in·struct /ɪnˈstrʌkt/ v [T] **1** to officially tell someone to do something **instruct sb to do sth** *Police officers were instructed to search the house.* **2** to teach someone how to do something: *We instruct the children in basic reading skills.*

in·struc·tion /ɪnˈstrʌkʃən/ n **1** [C usually plural] information or advice that tells you how to do or use something: **follow instructions** *Follow the instructions on the back of the packet.* **2** [C usually plural] an order: *Wait here until I give you further instructions.* **3** [U] formal training in a particular skill or subject: *instruction in basic computer skills* —**instructional** adj

in·struc·tive /ɪnˈstrʌktɪv/ adj giving useful information: *an instructive tour of the area* —**instructively** adv

in·struc·tor /ɪnˈstrʌktəl-ər/ n [C] someone who teaches a particular subject, sport etc: *a ski instructor*

in·stru·ment /ˈɪnstrʊmənt/ n [C] **1** a small tool used especially by scientists and doctors: *medical instruments* **2** something such as a piano or VIOLIN used for producing musical sounds **3** a piece of equipment for measuring and showing distance, speed etc

in·stru·men·tal /ˌɪnstrʊˈmentl◂/ adj **1** be instrumental in (doing) sth to be the thing or person that makes something happen: *a clue that was instrumental in solving the mystery* **2** instrumental music is for instruments, not voices —**instrumentally** adv

in·sub·or·di·nate /ˌɪnsəˈbɔːdənət◂‖-ɔːr-/ adj refusing to obey someone who has a higher rank than you —**insubordination** /ˌɪnsəbɔːdɪˈneɪʃən‖-ɔːr-/ n [U]

in·sub·stan·tial /ˌɪnsəbˈstænʃəl◂/ adj not strong, large, or good enough: *The evidence against him was insubstantial.*

in·suf·fi·cient /ˌɪnsəˈfɪʃənt◂/ adj not enough: *insufficient medical supplies* —**insufficiently** adv —**insufficiency** n [singular, U]

in·su·lar /ˈɪnsjʊlə‖ˈɪnsələr, ˈɪnʃə-/ adj not interested in anything except your own group, country, way of life etc: *The British have a reputation for being rather insular.* —**insularity** /ˌɪnsjʊˈlærəti‖-sə-, -ʃə-/ n [U]

in·su·late /ˈɪnsjʊleɪt‖ˈɪnsə-, ˈɪnʃə-/ v [T] to cover or protect something so that electricity, sound, heat etc cannot get in or out: *The pipes should be insulated so they don't freeze.* —**insulation** /ˌɪnsjʊˈleɪʃən‖ˌɪnsə-/ n [U]

in·su·lin /ˈɪnsjʊlɪn‖ˈɪnsə-/ n [U] a substance produced naturally by your body that allows sugar to be used for energy

in·sult /ɪnˈsʌlt/ v [T] to say or do something that offends someone: *How dare you insult my* *wife like that!* —**insulting** *adj* —**insult** /ˈɪnsʌlt/ *n* [C]

in·sur·ance /ɪnˈʃʊərəns‖-ˈʃʊr-/ *n* [U] when you pay a company money and they pay the costs if you are ill, have a car accident etc: *an insurance policy* | *Does your insurance cover things stolen from your car?* | *We claimed £1000 back from our insurance company after the burglary.* | *travel insurance*

in·sure /ɪnˈʃʊə‖-ˈʃʊr/ *v* **1** [I,T] to buy or provide insurance: *Many companies won't insure young drivers.* | *Are these paintings insured?* **2** an American spelling of ENSURE —**insurable** *adj*

in·sur·mount·a·ble /ˌɪnsəˈmaʊntəbəl‖-sər-/ *adj* an insurmountable problem is too difficult to deal with

in·sur·rec·tion /ˌɪnsəˈrekʃən/ *n* [C,U] an attempt by a group of people within a country to take control using force: *an armed insurrection*

in·tact /ɪnˈtækt/ *adj* not broken or damaged: *The package arrived intact.*

in·take /ˈɪnteɪk/ *n* [singular] **1** the amount of food, liquid etc that you eat or drink: *Reducing your alcohol intake will help you lose weight.* **2** the number of people allowed to enter a school, profession etc: *a yearly intake of 300 students*

in·tan·gi·ble /ɪnˈtændʒɪbəl/ *adj* an intangible quality or feeling is difficult to describe or understand although you know it exists: *There was an intangible quality of mystery about the place.* —**intangibly** *adv* —**intangibility** /ɪnˌtændʒɪˈbɪlti/ *n* [U]

in·te·gral /ˈɪntɪɡrəl, ɪnˈteɡrəl/ *adj* forming a necessary part of something: *Training is an integral part of any team's preparation.* —**integrally** *adv*

in·te·grate /ˈɪntɪɡreɪt/ *v* **1** [I,T] to join in the life and customs of a group or society, or to help someone do this: *teachers helping shy students to integrate into the class* **2** [T] to combine two or more things in order to make an effective system: *This software integrates moving pictures with sound.* —**integrated** *adj* —**integration** /ˌɪntɪˈɡreɪʃən/ *n* [U]

in·teg·ri·ty /ɪnˈteɡrɪti/ *n* [U] the quality of being honest and having high moral standards: *a man of integrity*

in·tel·lect /ˈɪntɪlekt/ *n* [C,U] the ability to understand things and think intelligently: *a woman of superior intellect*

in·tel·lec·tual /ˌɪntɪˈlektʃuəl/ *adj* **1** concerning the ability to think and understand ideas and information: *the intellectual development of children* **2** intelligent and often thinking about complicated ideas: *one of those trendy intellectual doctors* —**intellectual** *n* [C] —**intellectually** *adv*

in·tel·li·gence /ɪnˈtelɪdʒəns/ *n* [U] **1** the ability to learn and understand things: *a child of average intelligence* **2** information about the secret activities of other governments: *foreign intelligence services*

in·tel·li·gent /ɪnˈtelɪdʒənt/ *adj* good at learning and understanding things; clever —**intelligently** *adv*

gent is an adjective. An **intelligent** person is good at learning and understanding things. **Intellectual** can be an adjective or a noun. An **intellectual** is someone who is well educated and interested in subjects which need long periods of study. A small child, or even a dog, can be **intelligent** but cannot be called an **intellectual**.

in·tel·li·gi·ble /ɪnˈtelɪdʒəbəl/ *adj* easy to understand —**intelligibly** *adv*

in·tend /ɪnˈtend/ *v* **1** [T] to have something in your mind as a plan or purpose: **intend to do sth** *Hughes intends to resign soon.* | **intend doing sth** *intend contacting them as soon as possible.* **2** **be intended for** to be provided or designed for someone or something: *The facilities are intended solely for the use of company employees*

in·tense /ɪnˈtens/ *adj* **1** felt or affecting someone very strongly: *He watched the woman with intense interest.* **2** involving a lot of thought, work, effort etc in a short period of time: *a period of intense activity* **3** serious, with strong feelings and opinions: *an intense young man* —**intensely** *adv* —**intensity** *n* [U]

in·ten·si·fy /ɪnˈtensɪfaɪ/ *v* [I,T] to increase in strength, size, or amount, or to make something do this: *The campaign has intensified in recent weeks.* —**intensification** /ɪnˌtensɪfɪˈkeɪʃən/ *n* [U]

in·ten·sive /ɪnˈtensɪv/ *adj* involving a lot of work, learning, or effort within a short time: *an intensive driving course* —**intensively** *adv*

intensive care /ˌ... ˈ./ *n* [U] a hospital department for people who are seriously ill or badly injured

in·tent¹ /ɪnˈtent/ *n* [singular,U] *formal* something that you intend to do: *The jury has to decide whether the woman had any intent to injure her baby.*

intent² *adj* **1** **be intent on (doing) sth** to be determined to do something: *She was intent on making a good impression.* **2** giving careful attention to something: *She listened with an intent expression.*

in·ten·tion /ɪnˈtenʃən/ *n* [C,U] something that you plan to do: *His intention is to become World Champion by the time he is 21.* | **have no intention of doing sth** (=definitely not intend to do something): *I have no intention of getting married.* | **with the intention of doing sth** *Peter went to the US with the intention of getting a job at a university.*

in·ten·tion·al /ɪnˈtenʃənəl/ *adj* done deliberately in order to get a particular result: *I'm sorry if I upset you – it wasn't intentional.* —**intentionally** *adv*

inter- /ɪntəl-tər/ *prefix* used at the beginning of some words to mean 'between': *intermarriage* (=marriage between people of different races, religions etc)

in·ter·act /ˌɪntərˈækt/ *v* [I] **1** to talk to people and make relationships with them: + **with** *It's interesting how members of the group interact with each other.* **2** if things interact, they have an effect on each other —**interaction** /-ˈækʃən/ *n* [C,U]

in·ter·ac·tive /ˌɪntərˈæktɪv/ *adj* **1** involving communication between a computer and the person using it: *an interactive software program* *for children* **2** involving communication with other people — **interactively** *adv*

in·ter·cept /ˌɪntəˈsept‖-ər-/ *v* [T] to stop someone or something that is going from one place to another: *Shearer ran back and intercepted the ball.* —**interception** /-ˈsepʃən/ *n* [C,U]

in·ter·change·a·ble /ˌɪntəˈtʃeɪndʒəbəl‖-tər-/ *adj* things that are interchangeable can be used instead of each other: *Sometimes the words 'of' and 'from' are interchangeable in English, for example after the verb 'to die'.* —**interchangeably** *adv*

in·ter·com /ˈɪntəkɒm‖ˈɪntərkɑːm/ *n* [C] a system that people in different parts of a large building use to communicate with each other

in·ter·con·ti·nen·tal /ˌɪntəkɒntɪˈnentl‖-tərkɑːn-/ *adj* between CONTINENTS: *an intercontinental flight*

in·ter·course /ˈɪntəkɔːs‖ˈɪntərkɔːrs/ *n* [U] *formal* when two people have sex

in·ter·de·pen·dent /ˌɪntədɪˈpendənt‖-tər-/ *adj* interdependent people or things depend on each other: *a team of interdependent workers* —**interdependence** *n* [U] —**interdependently** *adv*

in·terest¹ /ˈɪntrɪst/ *n* **1** [singular, U] the feeling that you want to give your attention to something and find out more about it: + **in** *We both share an interest in music.* | **lose interest (in sth)** (=stop being interested): *Kelly lost interest halfway through the movie.* | **take an interest (in sb/sth)** *He's never taken much of an interest in me.* **2** [C] a subject or activity that you enjoy studying or doing when you are not working: *His main interests are reading and photography.* **3** [U] money charged or paid by a bank when you borrow or save money: *a 19% interest rate* **4** [U] a feature of a place or situation that makes you want to find out more about it: *local places of interest* | **be of interest to sb** *Your gossiping is of no interest to me.* **5** [C,U] something that gives you an advantage: *We're only thinking of your best interests.* | **be in sb's interest(s)/be in the interests of sb** *It's in everyone's interests to try to resolve this dispute as soon as possible.* **6** [C] *technical* a SHARE in a company: *He sold all his interests in the company.* **7** in the interest(s) of justice/safety/efficiency etc in order to make something fairer, safer etc: *A few changes were made to the car's design in the interests of safety.*

interest² *v* [T] to make someone want to give their attention to something and find out more about it: *Here are some books that might interest you.*

in·terest·ed /ˈɪntrɪstɪd/ *adj* **1** feeling that you want to give your attention to someone or something and find out more about them: + **in** *All she's interested in is boys!* | **be interested to hear/know/learn etc** *We'd be interested to know what you think of these proposals.* **2** eager to do or have something: **be interested in doing sth** *Lisa is interested in studying law.* **3** **interested parties/groups** the people or groups who will be affected by a situation

in·terest·ing /ˈɪntrɪstɪŋ/ *adj* unusual or exciting in a way that keeps your attention: *There were a lot of interesting people on the tour.* —**interestingly** *adv*

in·ter·fere /ˌɪntəˈfɪə‖-tərˈfɪr/ *v* [I] to deliberately become involved in a situation when you are not wanted or needed: *Stop interfering, will you!* | + **in** *It's better not to interfere in their arguments.*
 interfere with sth *phr v* [T] to prevent something from continuing or developing successfully: *Don't let sports interfere with your schoolwork.*

in·ter·fer·ence /ˌɪntəˈfɪərəns‖-tərˈfɪr-/ *n* [U] **1** when someone interferes in something: *I resented his interference in my personal life.* **2** when bad weather or an electrical problem causes noise on the radio or makes a television picture unclear

in·ter·im¹ /ˈɪntərɪm/ *adj* an interim arrangement, report etc is a temporary one, used until a final one is made

interim² *n* **in the interim** in the period of time between two events

in·te·ri·or /ɪnˈtɪəriə‖-ˈtɪriər/ *n* [C] the inside part of something: *a car with a brown leather interior* → opposite EXTERIOR

interior de·sign /ˌ...ˈ./ *n* [U] the job of choosing the colours, materials, furniture etc for the inside of people's houses — **interior designer** *n* [U]

in·ter·ject /ˌɪntəˈdʒekt‖-tər-/ *v* [I,T] *formal* to interrupt someone with a sudden remark: *"I'm sorry, I don't agree" Kim interjected.*

in·ter·jec·tion /ˌɪntəˈdʒekʃən‖-tər-/ *n* [C] a word or phrase that is used to express surprise, shock, pain etc. In the sentence "Ouch! That hurts!", 'ouch' is an interjection.

in·ter·lude /ˈɪntəluːd‖-ər-/ *n* [C] a period of time between activities or events: *a musical interlude*

in·ter·mar·ry /ˌɪntəˈmæri‖-ər-/ *v* [I] to marry someone from a different religion, social group etc — **intermarriage** *n* [U]

in·ter·me·di·a·ry /ˌɪntəˈmiːdiəri‖ˌɪntərˈmiːdieri/ *n* [C] someone who helps two people or groups to agree with each other: *Boyle acted as intermediary in the negotiations.*

in·ter·me·di·ate /ˌɪntəˈmiːdiət‖-tər-/ *adj* **1** an intermediate class, course etc is for students who are in the middle stages of learning something **2** between two stages

in·ter·mi·na·ble /ɪnˈtɜːmɪnəbəl‖-ɜːr-/ *adj* very boring and continuing for a long time: *interminable delays* — **interminably** *adv*

in·ter·mis·sion /ˌɪntəˈmɪʃən‖-tər-/ *n* [C] a pause between the parts of a play, concert, film etc; INTERVAL *BrE*

in·ter·mit·tent /ˌɪntəˈmɪtənt‖-tər-/ *adj* happening sometimes but not regularly or continuously: *intermittent rain showers* — **intermittently** *adv*

in·tern¹ /ɪnˈtɜːn‖-ɜːrn/ *v* [T] to put someone in prison, especially for political reasons — **internment** *n* [C,U]

in·tern² /ˈɪntɜːn‖-ɜːrn/ *n* [C] *AmE* someone who has almost finished training as a doctor and is working in a hospital; HOUSEMAN *BrE*

in·ter·nal /ɪnˈtɜːnl‖-ɜːr-/ *adj* **1** inside something such as your body or a country: *internal bleeding* | *an internal flight from Denver to Chicago* **2** within a particular country, organization, company etc — **internally** *adv* → opposite EXTERNAL

in·ter·na·tion·al /ˌɪntəˈnæʃənəl‖-tər-/ adj connected with or involving more than one country: *the International Law Association* —**internationally** adv

In·ter·net /ˈɪntənet‖-tər-/ n **the Internet** a system that allows people using computers around the world to exchange information: *Are you on the Internet yet?*

in·ter·per·son·al /ˌɪntəˈpɜːsənəl‖-tərˈpɜːr-/ adj involving relationships between people

in·ter·play /ˈɪntəpleɪ‖-tər-/ n [singular, U] the effect that two people or things have on each other: *the interplay of light and colour in her paintings*

in·ter·pret /ɪnˈtɜːprɪt‖-ɜːr-/ v **1** [I] to change words spoken in one language into another →compare TRANSLATE **2** [T] to explain or decide the meaning of an event, statement etc: **interpret sth as sth** *His silence was interpreted as guilt.*

in·ter·pre·ta·tion /ɪnˌtɜːprɪˈteɪʃən‖-ɜːr-/ n [C,U] **1** a way of explaining or understanding information, someone's actions etc: + **of** *Their interpretation of the evidence was very different from ours.* **2** the way someone performs a play, plays a piece of music etc: *Branagh's interpretation of Hamlet*

in·ter·pret·er /ɪnˈtɜːprɪtə‖-ˈtɜːrprɪtər/ n [C] someone who changes the spoken words of one language into another →compare TRANSLATOR

in·ter·re·lat·ed /ˌɪntərɪˈleɪtɪd‹/ adj things that are interrelated are connected and have an effect on each other

in·ter·ro·gate /ɪnˈterəgeɪt/ v [T] to ask someone a lot of questions, often in a threatening way: *Police interrogated the suspect for over two hours.* —**interrogator** n [C] —**interrogation** /ɪnˌterəˈgeɪʃən/ n [C,U]

in·ter·rog·a·tive /ˌɪntəˈrɒgətɪv‹‖-ˈrɑː-/ n [C] a word or sentence that asks a question —**interrogative** adj

in·ter·rupt /ˌɪntəˈrʌpt/ v **1** [I,T] to stop someone while they are speaking or doing something by suddenly saying or doing something yourself: *"What exactly do you mean?" Barker interrupted.* **2** [T] to stop a process or activity for a short time: *His career was interrupted by the war.* —**interruption** /-ˈrʌpʃən/ n [C,U]

in·ter·sect /ˌɪntəˈsekt‖-tər-/ v [I,T] if two lines, roads etc intersect, they go across each other

in·ter·sec·tion /ˌɪntəˈsekʃən, ˈɪntəsekʃən‖-tər-/ n [C] a place where two roads, lines etc meet, especially where they cross each other: *a busy intersection*

in·ter·spersed /ˌɪntəˈspɜːst‖-tərˈspɜːrst/ adj mixed with something: *sunny periods interspersed with showers*

in·ter·twined /ˌɪntəˈtwaɪnd‖-tər-/ adj twisted together or closely connected: *intertwined branches*

in·ter·val /ˈɪntəvəl‖-tər-/ n **1** [C] a period of time between two events or activities: *After a short interval there was a knock at the door.* **2 at regular intervals** happening regularly: *Visit your dentist at regular intervals for a check-up.* **3 at daily/weekly/monthly etc intervals** every day, week, month etc: *Your work will be assessed at three-monthly intervals.* **4** [C] BrE a short pause between the parts of a play, concert etc; INTERMISSION

in·ter·vene /ˌɪntəˈviːn‖-tər-/ v [I] **1** to do something to try to stop an argument, problem, war etc: + **in** *Police eventually had to intervene in the dispute.* **2** to happen between two events, especially in a way that interrupts or prevents something: *They had planned to get married, but the war intervened.* —**intervention** /-ˈvenʃən/ n [C,U]

in·ter·ven·ing /ˌɪntəˈviːnɪŋ‖-tər-/ adj **the intervening years/months/decades etc** the amount of time between two events: *I hadn't seen him since 1988 and he'd aged a lot in the intervening years.*

in·ter·view[1] /ˈɪntəvjuː‖-ər-/ n [C] **1** a formal meeting in which someone is asked questions, usually to find out if they are suitable for a job: *We would like to invite you to attend an interview on Tuesday.* + **for** *I've got an interview for a Saturday job.* **2** an occasion when someone famous is asked questions: + **with** *an exclusive interview with Mel Gibson* **give an interview** *Cantona refused to give any interviews after the incident.*

interview[2] v [T] to ask someone questions during an interview —**interviewer** n [C]

in·tes·tine /ɪnˈtestɪn/ n [C] a long tube in your body that takes food from your stomach, turns it into a form the body can use, and carries waste out —**intestinal** adj

in·ti·mate[1] /ˈɪntɪmɪt/ adj **1** having a very close relationship: *She only told a few intimate friends that she was pregnant.* **2** very private or personal: *a long and intimate conversation* **3 an intimate knowledge/understanding of sth** a knowledge or understanding of all the details or parts of something: *Ted has an intimate knowledge of the local area.* **4** a place that is intimate is small and quiet and makes you feel relaxed: *an intimate little bar* —**intimately** adv —**intimacy** n [U]

in·ti·mate[2] /ˈɪntɪmeɪt/ v [T] formal to make someone understand what you mean without saying it directly: + **that** *The manager intimated that they would not be renewing his contract.* —**intimation** /ˌɪntɪˈmeɪʃən/ n [C,U]

in·tim·i·date /ɪnˈtɪmɪdeɪt/ v [T] to frighten someone, especially so that they do what you want: *Ben seems to enjoy intimidating younger children.* —**intimidation** /ɪnˌtɪmɪˈdeɪʃən/ n [U]

in·tim·i·dat·ed /ɪnˈtɪmɪdeɪtɪd/ adj made to feel nervous or frightened: *She felt intimidated walking into the bar on her own.* —**intimidating** adj

in·to /ˈɪntə, before vowels ˈɪntʊ; strong ˈɪntuː/ prep **1** towards the inside of something or a place: *How did you get into the house?* *Don't fall into the water!* →see colour picture on page 474 **2** involved in a situation or activity: *I was always getting into trouble.* *I'd like to go into teaching.* **3 make/turn/shape etc sth into sth** make something become a different shape or form: *Make the dough into a ball.* **4** hitting someone or something in a sudden and violent way: *The car had run into a tree.* **5 be into sth** spoken to like and be interested in something: *Dave's really into windsurfing.* **6** in a particular direction: *She looked straight into my eyes.*

in·tol·e·ra·ble /ɪn'tɒlərəbəl‖-'tɑː-/ adj extremely bad, unpleasant, or painful: intolerable living conditions —**intolerably** adv

in·tol·e·rant /ɪn'tɒlərənt‖-'tɑː-/ adj not willing to accept ways of thinking and behaving that are different from your own —**intolerance** n [U] —**intolerantly** adv

in·to·na·tion /ˌɪntə'neɪʃən/ n [C,U] the way your voice goes up and down as you speak

in·tox·i·cat·ed /ɪn'tɒksɪ̩keɪtɪ̩d‖-'tɑːk-/ adj **1** formal suffering from the effects of too much alcohol; DRUNK **2** extremely happy and excited because of success, love, power etc —**intoxicating** adj —**intoxicate** v [T] —**intoxication** /ɪnˌtɒksɪ̩'keɪʃən‖-ˌtɑːk-/ n [U]

in·trac·ta·ble /ɪn'træktəbəl/ adj formal very difficult to control or solve: intractable problems

in·tra·net /'ɪntrənet/ n [C] a system for sending computer messages between people who work for the same company or organization, which is similar to the Internet but smaller

in·tran·si·gent /ɪn'trænsɪ̩dʒənt/ adj formal not willing to change your opinions or behaviour —**intransigence** n [U]

in·tran·si·tive /ɪn'trænsɪ̩tɪv/ n [C] a verb that does not have an object. In the sentence, 'She was crying,' 'cry' is an intransitive verb. → compare TRANSITIVE VERB

in·tra·ve·nous /ˌɪntrə'viːnəs‹/ adj intravenous drugs, INJECTIONs etc are put directly into one of your VEINs —**intravenously** adv

in·trep·id /ɪn'trepɪ̩d/ adj willing to go to dangerous or unknown places: intrepid explorers —**intrepidly** adv

in·tri·cate /'ɪntrɪkɪ̩t/ adj containing a lot of small parts or details: an intricate pattern in the rug —**intricacy** n [C,U] —**intricately** adv

in·trigue¹ /ɪn'triːg/ v [T] to interest someone a lot, especially by being strange or mysterious: He was intrigued by the dark-haired woman sitting opposite him. —**intriguing** adj —**intriguingly** adv

in·trigue² /'ɪntriːg/ n [C,U] secret plans to harm or deceive someone: political intrigue

in·trin·sic /ɪn'trɪnsɪk, -zɪk/ adj forming part of the basic character of something: the intrinsic beauty of the landscape —**intrinsically** /-kli/ adv

in·tro·duce /ˌɪntrə'djuːs‖-'duːs/ v [T] **1** to make a plan, plan etc happen or exist for the first time: The company introduced a no-smoking policy last year. **2** if you introduce people who are meeting for the first time, you tell them each other's names: **introduce sb to sb** Alice, may I introduce you to Megan. | **introduce yourself** (=formally tell someone who you are): The woman sitting next to me introduced herself as Dr Barbara Daly. **3** **introduce sb to sth** to tell or teach someone something about something for the first time: It was Mary who introduced us to Thai food. **4** to announce who is going to speak or perform at the beginning of a meeting, show etc: I'd like to introduce our speaker, Mr Gordon Brown. **5** to be the person who talks between

performances, INTERVIEWs etc on a television or radio show: the Eurovision Song Contest, introduced by Terry Wogan

in·tro·duc·tion /ˌɪntrə'dʌkʃən/ n **1** [U] when you make a change, plan etc happen or exist for the first time: **+ of** the introduction of personal computers into schools **2** [C] a written or spoken explanation at the beginning of a book or speech **3** [C] something that helps you become familiar with a subject, organization etc: The course is intended to provide a basic introduction to Art History. **4** [C usually plural] when you tell people who are meeting for the first time each other's names

in·tro·duc·to·ry /ˌɪntrə'dʌktəri‹/ adj **1** introductory chapter/paragraph/remark etc things that someone writes or says at the beginning of a book or speech in order to explain what it is about **2** introductory course/lesson/lecture etc a course, lesson etc intended for people who have never done an activity before: an introductory course in data processing

in·tro·spec·tive /ˌɪntrə'spektɪv‹/ adj thinking a lot about your own thoughts and feelings —**introspectively** adv —**introspection** /-'spekʃən/ n [U]

in·tro·vert /'ɪntrəvɜːt‖-ɜːrt/ n [C] someone who is quiet and shy and spends a lot of time thinking alone, and does not like to be with other people → opposite EXTROVERT

in·tro·vert·ed /'ɪntrəvɜːtɪ̩d‖-ɜːr-/ adj someone who is introverted is quiet and shy and spends a lot of time thinking alone, and does not like to be with other people → opposite EXTROVERTED

in·trude /ɪn'truːd/ v [I] to go into a place or become involved in a situation where you are not wanted: I'm sorry to intrude, but I need to talk to you. | **+ on/upon/into** journalists who intrude upon people's private lives —**intrusion** /-'truːʒən/ n [C,U] —**intrusive** /-sɪv/ adj

in·trud·er /ɪn'truːdə‖-ər/ n [C] someone who enters a building or area where they are not supposed to be

in·tu·i·tion /ˌɪntjuː'ɪʃən‖-tuː-, -tjuː-/ n [C,U] an ability to know or understand something that is based on your feelings rather than on facts: You should learn to trust your intuition.

in·tu·i·tive /ɪn'tjuːɪ̩tɪv‖-'tuː-, -'tjuː-/ adj based on feelings rather than facts: She seemed to have an intuitive understanding of the problem. —**intuitively** adv

In·u·it /'ɪnuːt, 'ɪnjuːt/ n the **Inuit** a group of people who live in the far north of Canada, Greenland, Alaska, and Siberia —**Inuit** adj

in·un·date /'ɪnəndeɪt/ v [T] to receive so much of something that you cannot deal with all of it: We were inundated with requests for tickets.

in·vade /ɪn'veɪd/ v **1** [I,T] to enter a country using military force in order to take control: The Romans invaded Britain in 54 BC. **2** [T] to go into a place in large numbers: Overjoyed fans invaded the sports field. —**invader** n [C] —**invasion** /-'veɪʒən/ n [C,U]

GRAMMAR NOTE: transitive and intransitive (1)
Transitive verbs have an object: I like *your dress*. | Did you find *the key*? These verbs are shown like this: v [T]. **Intransitive** verbs do not have an object: He laughed. | I'll wait in the car. These verbs are shown like this: v [I].

in·val·id[1] /ɪnˈvælɪd/ *adj* not acceptable because of a law or rule: *an invalid passport* —**invalidity** /ˌɪnvəˈlɪdɪti/ *n* [U]

in·va·lid[2] /ˈɪnvəlɪd, -lɪd‖-lɪd/ *n* [C] someone who is very ill or old and needs to be looked after

in·val·u·a·ble /ɪnˈvæljuəbəl, -jʊbəl‖-ˈvæljʊbəl/ *adj* extremely useful: *I'd like to thank our volunteers for their invaluable help.*

in·var·i·a·bly /ɪnˈveəriəbli‖-ˈver-/ *adv* almost always: *She invariably arrived home from work exhausted.* —**invariable** *adj*

in·vent /ɪnˈvent/ *v* [T] **1** to make, design, or produce something for the first time: *Who invented the light bulb?* **2** to think of an idea, excuse etc, usually in order to deceive someone: *You'll have to invent a better excuse than that!*

in·ven·tion /ɪnˈvenʃən/ *n* **1** [C] something that has been invented: *inventions such as fax machines and E-mail* **2** [U] when someone invents something: + *of the invention of television*

in·ven·tive /ɪnˈventɪv/ *adj* able to think of new and interesting ideas: *Ed's a very inventive cook.* —**inventiveness** *n* [U] —**inventively** *adv*

in·ven·tor /ɪnˈventəl-ər/ *n* [C] someone who makes, designs, or produces new things

in·ven·tory /ˈɪnvəntri‖-tɔːri/ *n* [C] a list of all the things in a place

in·vert /ɪnˈvɜːt‖-ɜːrt/ *v* [T] *formal* to turn something upside down or put it in the opposite position from its normal one —**inversion** /-ˈvɜːʃən‖ -ˈvɜːrʒən/ *n* [C,U]

inverted com·mas /ˌ..ˌ ˈ..ˌ/ *n* [plural] *BrE* signs (" ") or (' ') used at the beginning and end of a written word or sentence to show that someone said or wrote it; QUOTATION MARKS

in·vest /ɪnˈvest/ *v* **1** [I,T] to give money to a company or bank, or to buy something, in order to get a profit later: + **in** *$6 million has been invested in the construction of a new film studio.* **2** [T] to use a lot of time or effort to make something succeed: *She invests a lot of time and energy in her work.* —**investor** *n* [C]

invest in sth *phr v* [T] to buy something because you need it or because it will be useful: *I think it's time you invested in a new pair of jeans.*

in·ves·ti·gate /ɪnˈvestɪɡeɪt/ *v* [I,T] to try to find out about something, especially about a crime or accident: *Detectives are investigating a brutal murder.* —**investigator** *n* [C] —**investigative** /-ɡətɪv‖-ɡeɪtɪv/ *adj*: *investigative journalism*

in·ves·ti·ga·tion /ɪnˌvestɪˈɡeɪʃən/ *n* [C,U] an official attempt to find out about something, especially a crime or accident: + **into** *an investigation into police corruption* | **under investigation** (=being investigated): *Safety procedures at the airport are currently under investigation.*

in·vest·ment /ɪnˈvestmənt/ *n* **1** [C,U] the money that you give to a company or bank in order to get a profit later, or the act of doing this: *a £500,000 investment* | + **in** *US investment in foreign companies* **2** [C] something that you buy because it will be more valuable or useful later: *We bought the house as an investment.*

in·vet·e·rate /ɪnˈvetərɪt/ *adj* **inveterate liar/smoker/gambler** etc someone who lies a lot, smokes a lot etc and will not stop

in·vig·o·ra·ting /ɪnˈvɪɡəreɪtɪŋ/ *adj* making you feel more active and healthy: *an invigorating sea breeze* —**invigorate** *v* [T] —**invigorated** *adj*

in·vin·ci·ble /ɪnˈvɪnsɪbəl/ *adj* too strong to be defeated or destroyed —**invincibly** *adv*

in·vis·i·ble /ɪnˈvɪzɪbəl/ *adj* impossible to see: *The entrance to the cave was almost invisible.* —**invisibly** *adv* —**invisibility** /ɪnˌvɪzɪˈbɪlɪti/ *n* [U]

in·vi·ta·tion /ˌɪnvɪˈteɪʃən/ *n* **1** [C,U] when you invite someone to do something or go somewhere: **an invitation to (do) sth** *I'm waiting for an invitation to her house.* **2** [C] a card or piece of paper inviting someone to a party, wedding etc; INVITE *AmE*

in·vite[1] /ɪnˈvaɪt/ *v* [T] **1** to ask someone to go somewhere or do something: *"Are you going to Tim's party?" "No, we weren't even invited."* | **invite sb to (do) sth** *All local residents are invited to attend the meeting.* **2** **invite trouble/criticism** etc to do something that is likely to cause problems: *Going out and leaving the house unlocked is inviting trouble.*

invite sb **along** *phr v* [T] to ask someone to come with you when you go somewhere: *She invited some of her friends along to watch the game.*

invite sb **in** *phr v* [T] to ask someone to come into your home

invite sb **over** (also **invite** sb **round** *BrE*) *phr v* [T] to ask someone to come to your home: *Why don't you invite Jim and Katie over for a drink?*

> **USAGE NOTE: invite**
>
> **Invite** is usually used only to talk about the fact that you have been asked to go somewhere: *I've been invited to Barbara's party.* Do not use the word **invite** when you are actually inviting someone. Instead, say something like: *"Would you like to come to my party?"*

in·vite[2] /ˈɪnvaɪt/ *n* [C] *informal* an invitation

in·vit·ing /ɪnˈvaɪtɪŋ/ *adj* something that is inviting makes you want to have some of it, see more of it etc: *the inviting smell of freshly baked bread* —**invitingly** *adv*

in·voice /ˈɪnvɔɪs/ *n* [C] a list that shows how much you owe for goods or work that has been done —**invoice** *v* [T]

in·voke /ɪnˈvəʊk‖-ˈvoʊk/ *v* [T] *formal* to use a law, principle etc to support your opinions or actions: *Section 8.3 of the contract was invoked in support of the decision.*

in·vol·un·ta·ry /ɪnˈvɒləntəri‖ɪnˈvɑːləntəri/ *adj* an involuntary movement or reaction is one that you suddenly make or have without intending to: *an involuntary cry of pain* —**involuntarily** *adv*

in·volve /ɪnˈvɒlv‖ɪnˈvɑːlv/ *v* [T] **1** to include or affect someone or something: *a riot involving forty-five prisoners* **2** to include something as a necessary part of something else: *What exactly does the job involve?* | **involve doing sth** *Being a rock star involves giving lots of interviews.* **3** to make someone take part in something: **involve sb in sth** *Schools are trying to involve parents more in their children's education.*

in·volved /ɪnˈvɒlvd‖ɪnˈvɑːlvd/ *adj* **1** **be/get involved in** sth to take part in an activity or event: *How many people are involved in the decision-making process?|Al was reluctant to get involved in their dispute.* **2** complicated: *a long involved answer* —**involvement** *n* [U]

in·ward /ˈɪnwəd‖-wərd/ *adj* **1** felt or thought, but not expressed to other people: *Her calm expression hid an inward fear.* **2** on or towards the inside of something —**inwardly** *adv*

in·wards /ˈɪnwədz‖-wərdz/ *especially BrE*, **inward** *especially AmE* — *adv* towards the inside: *The door opened inwards.* → opposite OUTWARDS

in-your-face /ˈ. . ˌ./ *adj* doing something in a way that shows you do not care what other people think of you and which may shock some people: *Hollerbach's in-your-face style of comedy*

i·o·dine /ˈaɪədiːn‖-daɪn/ *n* [U] a chemical that is an ELEMENT and is often used on wounds to prevent infection

IOU /ˌaɪ əʊ ˈjuː‖-oʊ-/ *n* [C] *informal* an abbreviation of 'I owe you'; a piece of paper that shows that you owe someone money

IPA /ˌaɪ piː ˈeɪ‹/ *n* [singular] International Phonetic Alphabet; a system of signs showing the sounds made in speech

IQ /ˌaɪ ˈkjuː/ *n* [C] Intelligence Quotient; a method of measuring how intelligent someone is: *She has an IQ of 120.*

ir- /ɪr/ *prefix* used at the beginning of some words to mean 'not': *irregular|irrational*

i·rate /ˌaɪˈreɪt‹/ *adj formal* extremely angry: *complaints from irate customers*

i·ris /ˈaɪərɪs‖ˈaɪrɪs/ *n* [C] **1** a tall plant with purple, yellow, or white flowers and long thin leaves **2** the round coloured part of your eye

irk /ɜːk‖ɜːrk/ *v* [T] to annoy someone

i·ron /ˈaɪən‖ˈaɪərn/ *n* **1** [U] a common heavy metal that is an ELEMENT and used in making steel **2** [C] a piece of electrical equipment that you use for making clothes smooth

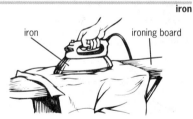

iron   ironing board

iron[2] *v* [I,T] to make clothes smooth using an iron: *Can you iron my shirt for me?* —**ironing** *n* [U] *I still haven't done the ironing.*
iron sth ↔ **out** *phr v* [T] to solve a small problem: *We'll need some time to iron out these difficulties.*

iron[3] *adj* **1** made of iron: *an iron gate* **2** an **iron fist/grip** very strict control: *He ruled the country with an iron fist.*

Iron Cur·tain /ˌ.. ˈ../ *n* **the Iron Curtain** the name that used to be used for the border between the Communist countries of eastern Europe and the rest of Europe

i·ron·ic /aɪˈrɒnɪk‖-ˈrɑː-/ *adj* **1** an ironic situation is strange or amusing because what happens is completely different from what you expected: *It's ironic that Bill was the only person to fail the examination.* **2** using words that are different from what you really mean in order to be amusing or show that you are annoyed —**ironically** /-kli/ *adv*

ironing board /ˈ... ./ *n* [C] a narrow table used for ironing (IRON) → see picture at IRON

i·ron·y /ˈaɪərəni‖ˈaɪrə-/ *n* [U] **1** the part of a situation that is strange or amusing because what happens is completely different from what you expected: *The irony is that the drug was supposed to save lives, but it killed him.* **2** the use of words that are different from what you really mean in order to be amusing or show that you are annoyed

ir·ra·tion·al /ɪˈræʃənəl/ *adj* not reasonable: *an irrational fear of spiders* —**irrationally** *adv* —**irrationality** /ɪˌræʃəˈnælɪti/ *n* [U]

ir·rec·on·cil·a·ble /ɪˌrekənˈsaɪləbəl‹/ *adj* irreconcilable attitudes, opinions etc are so different that it is impossible to reach an agreement: *irreconcilable differences of opinion* —**irreconcilably** *adv*

ir·reg·u·lar /ɪˈregjɡlə‖-ər/ *adj* **1** having a shape or surface that is not smooth or even: *a face with irregular features* **2** not happening at regular times or at the usual time: *an irregular heartbeat* **3** not following the usual rules in grammar: *irregular verbs* **4** *BrE formal* slightly dishonest or illegal: *This is all highly irregular.* —**irregularly** *adv* —**irregularity** /ɪˌregjɡˈlærɪti/ *n* [C,U]

ir·rel·e·vant /ɪˈreləvənt/ *adj* something that is irrelevant is not important because it has no effect in a particular situation: *His age is irrelevant if he can do the job.* —**irrelevantly** *adv* —**irrelevance** *n* [C,U]

ir·rep·a·ra·ble /ɪˈrepərəbəl/ *adj* impossible to repair —**irreparably** *adv*

ir·re·place·a·ble /ˌɪrɪˈpleɪsəbəl‹/ *adj* too valuable or rare to be replaced by anything else: *an irreplaceable work of art*

ir·re·pres·si·ble /ˌɪrɪˈpresɡbəl‹/ *adj* **1** an irrepressible feeling, attitude etc is very strong and cannot be controlled: *irrepressible excitement* **2** full of energy and always happy —**irrepressibly** *adv*

ir·re·proach·a·ble /ˌɪrɪˈprəʊtʃəbəl‹‖-ˈproʊtʃ-/ *adj* impossible to criticize or blame: *Her behaviour has always been irreproachable.* —**irreproachably** *adv*

ir·re·sist·i·ble /ˌɪrɪˈzɪstɡbəl‹/ *adj* **1** impossible not to want, like, enjoy etc: *There was masses of irresistible food at the wedding.* **2** too strong or powerful to control —**irresistibly** *adv*

ir·re·spec·tive /ˌɪrɪˈspektɪv/ *adv* **irrespective of** used to say that something does not affect a situation at all: *Anyone can participate, irrespective of age.*

ir·re·spon·si·ble /ˌɪrɪˈspɒnsɡbəl‹‖-ˈspɑːn-/ *adj* behaving in a careless way, without thinking of the bad results of what you do: *What an irresponsible attitude!* —**irresponsibly** *adv*

ir·rev·e·rent /ɪˈrevərənt/ *adj* not showing respect for religion, customs etc: *an irreverent sense of humour* —**irreverence** *n* [U] —**irreverently** *adv*

ir·re·vers·i·ble /ˌɪrɪ'vɜːsʲbəlǁ-ɜːr-/ *adj* something that is irreversible is impossible to change back to the way it was before: *irreversible brain damage*

ir·rev·o·ca·ble /ɪ'revəkəbəl/ *adj* impossible to change: *an irrevocable decision* —**irrevocably** *adv*

ir·ri·gate /'ɪrʲgeɪt/ *v* [T] to supply land or crops with water —**irrigation** /ˌɪrʲ'geɪʃən/ *n* [U]

ir·ri·ta·ble /'ɪrʲtəbəl/ *adj* easily annoyed: *He's always irritable in the morning.* —**irritably** *adv* —**irritability** /ˌɪrʲtə'bɪlʲti/ *n* [U]

ir·ri·tant /'ɪrʲtənt/ *n* [C] *formal* **1** something that makes you feel annoyed: *Bob's droning accent was a constant irritant.* **2** something that makes part of your body painful and sore

ir·ri·tate /'ɪrʲteɪt/ *v* [T] **1** to annoy someone: *Her attitude really irritated me.* **2** to make a part of your body painful and sore: *Wool irritates my skin.* —**irritating** *adj* —**irritatingly** *adv* —**irritation** /ˌɪrʲ'teɪʃən/ *n* [C,U]

is /s, z, əz; *strong* ɪz/ the 3rd person singular of the present tense of BE

Is·lam /'ɪslɑːm, 'ɪz-, ɪs'lɑːm/ *n* [U] the religion that was started by Muhammed and whose holy book is the Koran —**Islamic** /ɪz'læmɪk, ɪs-/ *adj*

is·land /'aɪlənd/ *n* [C] a piece of land completely surrounded by water: *the Canary Islands*

is·land·er /'aɪləndəǁ-ər/ *n* [C] someone who lives on an island

isle /aɪl/ *n* [C] *literary* an island

is·n't /'ɪzənt/ the short form of 'is not': *The essay isn't due until Friday.*

i·so·late /'aɪsəleɪt/ *v* [T] to make or keep one person or thing separate from others: *The new prisoner was isolated as soon as he arrived.*

i·so·lat·ed /'aɪsəleɪtʲd/ *adj* **1** far away from other places: *an isolated farmhouse* **2** feeling lonely because it is difficult for you to meet people and talk to them: *Mothers with young children often feel isolated.* **3** **an isolated case/example/incident** an event, action, example etc that is the only one

i·so·la·tion /ˌaɪsə'leɪʃən/ *n* **1** [U] when someone or something is alone and separate from other people or places: *Because of its isolation, the island developed its own culture.* **2** **in isolation** happening or existing separately from other things: *These events cannot be examined in isolation from one another.* **3** [U] a feeling of being lonely

is·sue¹ /'ɪʃuː, 'ɪsjuːǁ'ɪʃuː/ *n* **1** [C] a subject or problem: *Abortion was a key issue* (=very important) *in the 1989 elections.* **2** [C] a magazine or newspaper printed for a particular day, week, or month: *the latest issue of Vogue* **3** **take issue with** to disagree or argue with someone: *He took issue with Farrell's statement.* **4** **make an issue of sth** to argue about something although it is not important

issue² *v* [T] **1** to officially make a statement or give an order, a warning etc: *a statement issued by the White House* **2** to officially provide or produce something: **issue sb with** *All staff will be issued with protective clothing.*

it /ɪt/ *pron* **1** a thing, situation, person, or idea that has already been mentioned: *"Did you bring your umbrella?" "No, I left it at home."* | *"Where's the bread?" "It's on the shelf."* **2** the situation that someone is in now: *How's it going, Bob?* (=how are you?) | *I like it here in Caxford.* **3** used as the subject or object of a sentence when the real subject or object is later in the sentence: *It costs less to drive than to take the bus.* **4** used with the verb "be" to talk about the weather, time, distance etc: *It's raining again.* | *What time is it?* **5** used to emphasize one piece of information in a sentence: *I don't know who took your book, but it wasn't me.* **6** used as the subject of the words 'seem', 'appear', 'look', and 'happen': *It looks like Henry's not going to be able to come to lunch.* **7** **it's me/John/a pen etc** used to give the name of a person or thing when it is not already known: *"Who's on the phone?" "It's Jill."*

IT /ˌaɪ 'tiː/ *n* [U] the abbreviation of INFORMATION TECHNOLOGY

i·tal·ics /ɪ'tælɪks/ *n* [plural] a style of printed letters that slope to the right —**italic** *adj* —**italicize** /-lʲsaɪz/ *v* [T]

itch¹ /ɪtʃ/ *v* [I] to have an unpleasant feeling on your skin that makes you want to rub it with your fingernails

itch² *n* [C] **1** an unpleasant feeling on your skin that makes you want to rub it with your nails **2** *informal* a strong desire to do or have something —**itchy** *adj* —**itchiness** *n* [U]

it'd /'ɪtəd/ the short form of 'it would' or 'it had': *It'd be nice to go to the beach.* | *It'd been raining all day.*

i·tem /'aɪtəm/ *n* **1** [C] a single thing in a set, group, or list: *There are over twenty items on the menu.* **2** [C] a piece of news in a newspaper or magazine, or on television: *an item about the kidnapping in the paper*

i·tem·ize (also **-ise** *BrE*) /'aɪtəmaɪz/ *v* [T] to make a list with details about each thing on the list —**itemized** *adj*

i·tin·e·rant /aɪ'tɪnərənt/ *adj formal* travelling from place to place: *an itinerant musician*

i·tin·e·ra·ry /aɪ'tɪnərəriǁ-nəreri/ *n* [C] a plan or list of the places you will visit on a trip

it'll /'ɪtl/ the short form of 'it will': *It'll never work.*

it's /ɪts/ the short form of 'it is' or 'it has': *It's snowing!* | *It's been a great year.*

its /ɪts/ *determiner* the possessive form of 'it': *The tree has lost all of its leaves.*

it·self /ɪt'self/ *pron* **1** the REFLEXIVE form of 'it': *The cat was washing itself.* **2** **in itself** only the thing mentioned, and not including anything else: *We're proud you finished the race. That in itself is an accomplishment.*

IV /ˌaɪ 'viː/ *n* [C] *AmE* a piece of hospital equipment used for putting liquids directly into your blood; DRIP *BrE*

I've /aɪv/ the short form of 'I have': *I've seen you somewhere before.*

i·vo·ry /'aɪvəri/ *n* [U] **1** the hard smooth yellow-white substance from the TUSK of an ELEPHANT **2** a pale yellow-white colour —**ivory** *adj*

i·vy /'aɪvi/ *n* [U] a climbing plant with dark green shiny leaves

Jj

J, j /dʒeɪ/ the letter 'j'

jab ¹ /dʒæb/ v [I,T] to push something into or towards something else with short quick movements: *He angrily jabbed a finger into my chest.*

jab ² n [C] **1** a sudden hard push, especially with a pointed object **2** *BrE informal* an INJECTION: *a tetanus jab*

jab·ber /'dʒæbə‖-ər/ v [I] to talk quickly but not very clearly: *Franco jabbered away about football.*

jack ¹ /dʒæk/ n [C] **1** a piece of equipment used for lifting something heavy, such as a car **2** one of the picture cards used in card games

jack ² v

jack sth ↔ **in** *phr v* [T] *BrE informal* to stop doing something such as your job or a course of study: *I'd love to jack in my job.*

jack sth ↔ **up** *phr v* [T] **1** to lift something heavy using a jack: *Dad jacked the car up so I could change the tyre.* **2** to increase prices, sales etc by a large amount: *Airlines always jack up fares at Christmas.*

jack·al /'dʒækɔːl, -kəl‖-kəl/ n [C] a wild animal like a dog, that lives in Africa and Asia

jack·et /'dʒækɪ̩t/ n [C] a short light coat → see colour picture on page 113

jacket po·ta·to /ˌ.. .ˌ../ n [C] *BrE* a potato baked with its skin on

jack-in-the-box /'.. .ˌ./ n [C] a toy shaped like a box that a figure jumps out of when you open it

jack knife /'.. ./ n [C] a knife with a blade that folds into its handle

jack-knife v [I] if a large vehicle with two parts jack-knifes, the back part swings towards the front part because the driver cannot control it

jack·pot /'dʒækpɒt‖-pɑːt/ n **1** a large amount of money that you can win **2 hit the jackpot a)** to win a lot of money **b)** to be very successful or lucky: *The National Theatre hit the jackpot with its first musical, Guys and Dolls.*

Ja·cuz·zi /dʒə'kuːzi/ n [C] *trademark* a large bath for one or more people that produces BUBBLES

jade /dʒeɪd/ n [U] a hard green stone used for making jewellery

ja·ded /'dʒeɪdɪ̩d/ adj no longer feeling interested or excited: *She seemed jaded and in need of a break.*

jag·ged /'dʒægɪ̩d/ adj having a rough edge with sharp points: *jagged rocks*

jag·u·ar /'dʒægjuə‖'dʒægwɑːr/ n [C] a large wild cat with black spots, from Central and South America

jail ¹ also **gaol** *BrE* /dʒeɪl/ n [C,U] a place where a criminal is kept as a punishment; prison

jail ² also **gaol** *BrE* — v [T] to put someone in prison

jail·er also **gaoler** *BrE* /'dʒeɪlə‖-ər/ n [C] someone who guards prisoners in a prison

jam ¹ /dʒæm/ n **1** [C,U] a thick sticky sweet food made from fruit: *raspberry jam* → see colour picture on page 439 **2** [C] a situation in which it is difficult to move because there are too many people, cars etc: *Visitors were asked to arrive at different times, to avoid a jam.* → see also TRAFFIC JAM **3 be in a jam/get into a jam** to be or become involved in a difficult situation

jam ² v **-mmed, -mming 1** [T] to push someone or something using a lot of force, especially into a small place: *I managed to jam everything into one suitcase.* **2** [I,T] if a machine, door, gun etc jams, or if you jam it, it no longer works properly because something is stopping one of its parts from moving: *Every time I try to use the fax, it jams.* **3** [T] to fill a place with a lot of people or things, so that no one or nothing can move: *Excited football fans jammed the streets.* **4** [T] to deliberately block radio messages by broadcasting noise —**jammed** adj: *The door is jammed again.*

jam·bo·ree /ˌdʒæmbə'riː/ n [C] a big noisy party or celebration

jam-packed /ˌ. '.ˌ/ adj informal completely full of people or things: *The slopes were jam-packed with skiers.*

jan·gle /'dʒæŋgəl/ v [I,T] if small metal objects jangle, they make a ringing noise as they hit against each other: *Her jewellery jangled when she moved.* —**jangle** n [singular]

jan·i·tor /'dʒænɪ̩tə‖-ər/ n [C] *especially AmE* someone whose job is to clean and look after a large building; CARETAKER *BrE: the school janitor*

Jan·u·a·ry /'dʒænjuəri, -njuri‖-njueri/ written abbreviation **Jan** n [C,U] the first month of the year → see usage note at MONTH

jar ¹ /dʒɑː‖dʒɑːr/ n [C] a round glass container with a lid, used for storing food: *a jam jar*

jar ² v [I,T] **-rred, -rring 1** to damage something by a sudden shock or pressure: *Alice jarred her knee when she jumped off the wall.* **2** to make someone feel uncomfortable or annoyed: *The noise of the drill was starting to jar on my nerves.*

jar·gon /'dʒɑːgən‖'dʒɑːrgən, -gɑːn/ n [U] words and phrases used by people in the same profession that are difficult for people not in that profession to understand: *medical jargon*

jaun·dice /'dʒɔːndɪ̩s‖'dʒɒːn-, 'dʒɑː-/ n [U] an illness in which your skin becomes yellow

jaun·diced /'dʒɔːndɪ̩st‖'dʒɒːn-, 'dʒɑː-/ adj if you have a jaundiced attitude to something, you think it is probably bad because of your previous experience: *a jaundiced view of the world*

jaunt /dʒɔːnt‖dʒɒːnt, dʒɑːnt/ n [C] a short journey for pleasure

jaun·ty /'dʒɔːnti‖'dʒɒːnti, 'dʒɑːnti/ adj showing that you feel confident and cheerful: *With a jaunty step, he went upstairs.* —**jauntily** adv

---

GRAMMAR NOTE: transitive and **intransitive (2)**
Some verbs can be used **transitive** or **intransitive**. For example: **read** v [T,I]
• Transitive: *I can't read your handwriting.*
• Intransitive: *Tom learned to read at the age of four.*

jav·e·lin /ˈdʒævəlɪ̯n/ *n* **1** [C] a long pointed stick thrown as a sport **2** [U] a sport in which you throw a long pointed stick as far as you can

jaw /dʒɔːǁdʒɔː/ *n* **1** [C] one of the two bones in your face that contain your teeth **2** [C] the bottom part of your face, below your mouth **3** sb's jaw dropped used to say that someone looked very surprised or shocked → see picture at HEAD

jay·walk·ing /ˈdʒeɪˌwɔːkɪŋǁ-ˌwɒː-/ *n* [U] when you walk across a street in a careless or dangerous way

jazz¹ /dʒæz/ *n* [U] a type of music with a strong beat, which was originally played by black Americans, and often includes TRUMPET, SAXOPHONE, drums, and BASS¹ (3): *modern jazz* | *a singer in a jazz band*

jazz² *v*
jazz sth ↔ **up** *phr v* [T] to make something more exciting and interesting: *A few pictures will jazz up the walls.*

jeal·ous /ˈdʒeləs/ *adj* **1** feeling angry or unhappy because someone else has something that you wish you had: *Tara was jealous when she saw all the girls in their new dresses.* | **+ of** *You're just jealous of me because I got better grades.* **2** feeling angry or unhappy because someone you like or love is showing interest in another person: *My boyfriend always gets jealous when I talk to other guys.*

USAGE NOTE: jealous

Jealous has two meanings. It can be used about someone who is annoyed that another person has something that they would like but do not have: *Wait till she hears about my new job – she'll be really jealous!* **Jealous** can also mean angry and unhappy because you think your wife, boyfriend, girlfriend etc loves someone else more than they love you: *He would get jealous every time she went out.* You feel **envious** when someone has something nice or special and you wish you had it too: *She had always been envious of her sister's good looks.*

—**jealously** *adv* —**jealousy** *n* [C,U]

jeans /dʒiːnz/ *n* [plural] a popular type of trousers made from DENIM → see colour picture on page 113

Jeep /dʒiːp/ *n* [C] *trademark* a vehicle made for travelling over rough ground

jeer /dʒɪəǁdʒɪr/ *v* [I,T] to say rude things to someone or laugh at them: *Kids jeered and threw stones at us.* —**jeer** *n* [C]

Jell-O, jello /ˈdʒeləʊǁ-loʊ/ *n* [U] *AmE trademark* JELLY

jel·ly /ˈdʒeli/ *n* **1** [C,U] *BrE* a soft sweet solid food made with fruit juice that shakes when you move it; JELL-O *AmE* **2** [U] *especially AmE* a thick sweet food made from fruit, usually eaten on bread: *a peanut butter and jelly sandwich*

jel·ly·fish /ˈdʒelifɪʃ/ *n* [C] a transparent sea animal with long parts that hang down from its body: *She got stung by a jellyfish when she was out swimming.*

jem·my /ˈdʒemi/ *BrE*, **jimmy** *AmE* — *n* [C] a metal bar used especially by thieves to open locked doors, windows etc

jeop·ar·dize (also **-ise** *BrE*) /ˈdʒepədaɪzǁ-ər-/ *v* [T] to risk losing or destroying something valuable or important: *He didn't want to jeopardize his career by complaining about his boss.*

jeop·ar·dy /ˈdʒepədiǁ-ər-/ *n* [U] in jeopardy likely to be lost, destroyed, or ended because of something: *The peace talks are in jeopardy.*

jerk¹ /dʒɜːkǁdʒɜːrk/ *v* [I,T] to move with a sudden quick movement, or make something move this way: *Sara jerked her head up to look at him.* | *He turned away, jerking the blanket over his head.*

jerk² *n* [C] **1** a sudden quick movement: *She unplugged the iron with an angry jerk.* **2** *AmE informal* someone who is stupid or very annoying

jerk·y /ˈdʒɜːkiǁ-ɜːr-/ *adj* moving with sudden quick movements, not smoothly —**jerkily** *adv*

jer·sey /ˈdʒɜːziǁ-ɜːr-/ *n* **1** [C] a shirt made of soft material, worn for playing sports **2** [C] *BrE* a SWEATER **3** [U] a soft material made of cotton or wool

jest /dʒest/ *n* in jest something you say in jest is intended to be funny, not serious —**jest** *v* [I]

jest·er /ˈdʒestəǁ-ər/ *n* [C] a man employed in the past by a king or ruler to entertain people with jokes, stories etc

Je·sus¹ /ˈdʒiːzəs/ *n* Jesus Christ

Jesus² *interjection informal* used when you are very surprised or annoyed. Some people find this use offensive

jet¹ /dʒet/ *n* [C] **1** a very fast plane **2** a thin stream of gas, liquid etc that is forced out of a small hole: *a strong jet of water*

jet² *v* [I] *informal* to travel somewhere by plane: *You could be jetting off for a week in the Caribbean.*

jet-black /ˌ. ˈ. ◂/ *adj* very dark black: *jet-black hair*

jet en·gine /ˌ. ˈ../ *n* [C] a powerful engine used to make planes move

jet lag /ˈ. ./ *n* [U] the feeling of being very tired after a long journey in a plane —**jet-lagged** *adj*

jet-pro·pelled /ˌ. .ˈ. ◂/ *adj* using a jet engine for power —**jet propulsion** /ˌ. .ˈ../ *n* [U]

jet·ti·son /ˈdʒetɪ̯sən, -zən/ *v* [T] **1** to get rid of something that you do not need or want: *The company is trying jettison any unprofitable operations.* **2** to throw something away, from a plane or moving vehicle: *The pilot had to jettison some fuel.*

jet·ty /ˈdʒeti/ *n* [C] a wide stone or wooden structure used for getting on and off boats

Jew /dʒuː/ *n* [C] someone whose religion is Judaism: *The Jews originally lived in ancient Israel.*

jew·el /ˈdʒuːəl/ *n* [C] a valuable stone, such as a DIAMOND

jew·elled *BrE*, **jeweled** *AmE* /ˈdʒuːəld/ *adj* decorated with valuable stones

jew·el·ler *BrE*, **jeweler** *AmE* /ˈdʒuːələǁ-ər/ *n* [C] someone who sells, makes, or repairs jewellery

jew·el·lery *BrE*, **jewelry** *AmE* /ˈdʒuːəlri/ *n* [U] things that you wear for decoration, such as rings and NECKLACEs

Jew·ish /ˈdʒuːɪʃ/ *adj* belonging to a group of people whose religion is Judaism

jewellery *BrE* jewelry *AmE*

ring

earrings

bracelet

necklace

brooch

jibe¹ also **gibe** /dʒaɪb/ *n* [C] something that you say that makes someone else seem silly

jibe² *v* [I] *AmE informal* if two statements, actions etc jibe with each other, they agree or make sense together: *The driver told a lot of stories that didn't jibe.*

jif·fy /ˈdʒɪfi/ *n* **in a jiffy** *informal* very soon: *I'll be back in a jiffy.*

jig /dʒɪg/ *n* [C] a type of quick dance, or the music for this dance

jig·gle /ˈdʒɪgəl/ *v* [I,T] to move from side to side with short quick movements, or to make something move this way

jig·saw /ˈdʒɪgsɔ:ǁ-sɒ:/ also **jigsaw puz·zle** /ˈ.. ,../ *n* [C] a game consisting of a picture that has been cut up into many small pieces that you try to fit together again

jigsaw

jilt /dʒɪlt/ *v* [T] to suddenly end a romantic relationship with someone in a way that upsets them

jin·gle¹ /ˈdʒɪŋgəl/ *v* [I,T] to shake metal objects together so that they make a noise like small bells, or to make this noise: *Tom nervously jingled the coins in his pocket.*

jingle² *n* **1** [C] a short song used in television and radio advertisements **2** [singular] the sound of small metal objects being shaken together

jinx /dʒɪŋks/ *n* [singular] someone or something that brings bad luck: *There's some kind of jinx on the team.* —**jinxed** *adj* —**jinx** *v* [T]

jit·ters /ˈdʒɪtəzǁ-ərz/ *n* [plural] a feeling of being nervous and anxious: **get the jitters** *I get the jitters if I drink too much coffee.*

jit·ter·y /ˈdʒɪtəri/ *adj* worried and nervous: *She was so jittery about seeing him, she couldn't keep still.*

job /dʒɒbǁdʒɑ:b/ *n* [C] **1** work that you do regularly in order to earn money: **get/find a job** *I got a part-time job as a waitress.* |**apply for a job** (=try to get a job): *She applied for a job at a bank.* |**out of a job** (=unemployed) **2** a duty or responsibility: *Leave the dishes – that's my job.* **3** a piece of work that you must do, usually without being paid: *I always end up doing the unpleasant jobs around the house.* **4** **on the job** while doing work or at work: *All our employees get on the job training.* **5** **make a good/bad job of sth** *BrE* to do something well or badly: *Sarah made a good job of that presentation.* **6** **do a nice/great etc job** to do something very well: *Tina did a nice job on your hair.* **7** **it's a good job** *BrE spoken* used to say that it is lucky something happened: *It's a good job you were wearing your seat belt.* **8** **do the job** *informal* to make something have the result that you want or need: *A little more glue should do the job.* **9** **just the job** *BrE spoken* exactly what is needed or wanted: *That table you gave us was just the job!*

USAGE NOTE: job, work, occupation, career, and profession

Work is what you do to earn money: *I have to go to work now.* | *He can't find work.* Your **job** is the particular type of work that you do: *Jeff got a job as a waiter.* **Occupation** is a word used especially on official forms meaning the job that you do: *Please state your name, address, and occupation.* A **career** is a professional job that you do for most of your life: *Her political career began 20 years ago.* A **profession** is a job in an area of work such as law, medicine, or teaching, for which you need special training and education: *the medical profession* | *Not enough people are entering the teaching profession.* (=are entering teaching).

---

job·less /ˈdʒɒbləsǁˈdʒɑ:b-/ *adj* without a paid job: *10% of the town's workers are jobless.*

jock·ey /ˈdʒɒkiǁˈdʒɑ:ki/ *n* [C] someone who rides horses in races

joc·u·lar /ˈdʒɒkjʊləǁˈdʒɑ:kjʊlər/ *adj formal* cheerful and making jokes: *He seemed to be in a jocular mood.*

jog /dʒɒgǁdʒɑ:g/ *v* **1** [I,T] to run slowly, especially for exercise: *Julie jogs 3 miles every morning.* → see colour picture on page 670 **2** **jog sb's memory** to make someone remember something: *This photo might jog your memory.* **3** [T] to knock or push something lightly by mistake: *Someone's hand jogged her elbow, and she spilt her drink.* —**jog** *n* [singular]

jog·ging /ˈdʒɒgɪŋǁˈdʒɑ:-/ *n* [U] the activity of running for exercise: *I'm thinking of taking up jogging.* —**jogger** *n* [C]

join¹ /dʒɔɪn/ *v* **1** [T] to become a member of an organization, society, or group: *Trevor joined the BBC in 1969.* **2** [T] to connect or fasten things together: *Join the two pieces of wood with strong glue.* **3** [I,T] if two roads, rivers, or parts of something join, they come together and are connected at a particular place: *the point where the two rivers join* **4** [I,T] if two groups, countries etc join together, they become a single group, organization, country etc **5** [T] to do something together with someone else, or go somewhere to do something with someone else: *Other unions joined the strike.* |**join sb (for sth)** *Why don't you join us for dinner?* |**join (with) sb in doing sth** *Please join with me in welcoming tonight's speaker.* **6** **join hands** if two people join hands, they hold each other's hands **7** **join a queue/line** to go and stand in a line with other people who are waiting

join 362

join in *phr v* [I,T **join in** sth] to begin to take part in an activity that other people are involved in: *The other children wouldn't let Sam join in.* | *Everyone joined in the conversation.*

join up *phr v* [I] **1** to meet in order to do something: *We can all join up for a drink later.* **2** *BrE* to become a member of the army, navy etc

join² *n* [C] a place where two parts of an object are connected or fastened together

join·er /'dʒɔɪnəll-ər/ *n* [C] *BrE* someone who makes wooden doors, window frames etc → compare CARPENTER

joint¹ /dʒɔɪnt/ *adj* shared, owned by, or involving two or more people: *They have to reach a joint decision.* | *a joint bank account* | **joint effort** (=when two people work together): *The record was a joint effort between U2 and Pavarotti.* —**jointly** *adv*: *Sam and I are jointly responsible for the project.*

joint² *n* [C] **1** a part of the body where two bones meet: *the hip joint* **2** a place where two things or parts of an object are joined together: *One of the joints between the pipes was leaking.* **3** *BrE* a large piece of meat with a bone in it for cooking: *a joint of beef* **4** *informal* a place such as a bar, club, or restaurant: *a hamburger joint* **5** *informal* a cigarette that contains CANNABIS

joint ven·ture /ˌ. '../ *n* [C] a business arrangement in which two or more companies work together

joke¹ /dʒəʊklldʒoʊk/ *n* **1** [C] something funny that you say or do to make people laugh: *Don't get mad – it's only a joke.* | **tell a joke** (=tell a short funny story): *Ed loves telling jokes.* | **take a joke** (=be able to laugh at a joke about yourself): *Come on – can't you take a joke?* | **get/see the joke** (=understand why a joke is funny) | **play a joke on sb** (=trick someone to make people laugh) **2** [singular] *informal* a situation that is so silly or unreasonable that it makes you angry: *Those meetings are a joke!* **3** **make a joke (out) of sth** to treat something serious as if it were funny **4** **be no joke** used to emphasize that a situation is serious or difficult: *Looking after three kids on your own is no joke.* **5** **get beyond a joke** to become serious and worrying: *I haven't heard from her for weeks – it's getting beyond a joke.*

joke² *v* [I] **1** to say funny things **2** **be joking** to say something without meaning it: *Listen, I'm not joking – there is real danger.* **3** **you're joking/you must be joking** *spoken* used when you are surprised by what someone has just said because it seems strange or silly: *What? Buy a house on my salary? You must be joking!* —**jokingly** *adv*

jok·er /'dʒəʊkəll'dʒoʊkər/ *n* [C] **1** someone who likes to say or do funny things **2** a card used in some card games that has no fixed value

jol·ly¹ /'dʒɒlill'dʒɑːli/ *adj* happy and cheerful

jolly² *adv BrE spoken old-fashioned* very: *It's jolly cold outside!*

jolt¹ /dʒəʊltlldʒoʊlt/ *n* [C] **1** a sudden strong movement: *Sam woke with a jolt when the phone rang.* **2** a sudden shock: *It gave me a jolt to see her looking so ill.*

jolt² *v* [I,T] to move suddenly and strongly, or to make someone or something do this: *The train jolted to a halt.*

jos·tle /'dʒɒsəll'dʒɑː-/ *v* [I,T] to push against other people in a crowd: *Spectators jostled for a better view.*

jot /dʒɒtlldʒɑːt/ *v*
jot sth ↔ down *phr v* [T] to write something quickly on a piece of paper: *Let me just jot down your phone number.*

jour·nal /'dʒɜːnlll-ɜːr-/ *n* [C] **1** a magazine for people who are interested in a particular subject: *a scientific journal* **2** a written account of the things that happen to you each day

jour·nal·is·m /'dʒɜːnəl-ɪzəmll-ɜːr-/ *n* [U] the job of writing reports for newspapers, magazines, television, or radio

jour·nal·ist /'dʒɜːnəl-ɪ̯stll-ɜːr-/ *n* [C] someone who writes reports for newspapers, magazines, television, or radio

jour·ney /'dʒɜːnill-ɜːr-/ *n* [C] a trip from one place to another, especially over a long distance: *a long car journey* | *My journey to work usually takes about an hour.*

jo·vi·al /'dʒəʊviəll'dʒoʊ-/ *adj* friendly and cheerful: *a jovial laugh*

jowls /dʒaʊlz/ *n* [plural] the skin that covers your bottom jaw

joy /dʒɔɪ/ *n* **1** [C,U] a feeling of great happiness and pleasure, or something that gives you this feeling: *She cried with joy when she heard the news.* **2** [U] *BrE spoken* success in what you are trying to do: *I've looked everywhere for those keys but I haven't had any joy.* **3** **be a joy to watch/teach etc** *spoken* used to say that you enjoy watching, teaching etc someone or something very much

joy·ful /'dʒɔɪfəl/ *adj* very happy, or making people very happy: *a joyful reunion* —**joyfully** *adv*

joy·ous /'dʒɔɪəs/ *adj literary* very happy, or making people very happy: *a joyous song* —**joyously** *adv*

joy·rid·ing /'dʒɔɪˌraɪdɪŋ/ *n* [U] when someone steals and drives a car in a fast and dangerous way —**joyride** *v* [I] —**joyrider** *n* [C]

joy·stick /'dʒɔɪˌstɪk/ *n* [C] a handle used to control an aircraft or a computer game

JP /ˌdʒeɪ 'piː/ *n* [C] a Justice of the Peace

jr the written abbreviation of JUNIOR

jub·i·lant /'dʒuːbɪ̯lənt/ *adj* extremely happy because you have been successful: *a jubilant crowd* —**jubilation** /ˌdʒuːbɪ̯'leɪʃən/ *n* [U]

ju·bi·lee /'dʒuːbɪ̯liː, ˌdʒuːbɪ̯'liː/ *n* [C] a date that is celebrated when it is exactly 25 years, 50 years etc after an important event: *silver jubilee* (=25 years) | *golden jubilee* (=50 years)

Ju·da·is·m /'dʒuːdeɪ-ɪzəm, 'dʒuːdə-ll'dʒuːdə-, 'dʒuːdi-/ *n* [U] the Jewish religion

judge¹ /dʒʌdʒ/ *n* **1** [C] someone whose job is to decide how criminals should be punished in a court of law: *Judge Hart gave Scott an 18-month prison sentence.* **2** [C] someone who decides who has won a competition: *a panel of judges* **3** **a good/bad judge of sth** someone whose opinion about something is usually right or is usually wrong: *She's a good judge of character.*

judge² *v* **1** [I,T] to form an opinion about someone or something: *It's harder to judge distances when you're driving in the dark.* | **judge sb/sth on sth** *Employees should be judged on the quality of their work.* **2** **judging by/from** used when you are giving a reason for saying or thinking something: *Judging by the team's performance today, they have a good chance of winning the championship.* **3** [I,T] to decide who has won a competition: *Who's judging the talent contest?* **4** [I,T] to form an opinion about someone and decide what is wrong with their character or behaviour after thinking carefully about them: *You have no right to judge other people's lifestyles.* **5** [T] to decide in a court of law whether someone is guilty of a crime

judg·ment (also **judgement**) /'dʒʌdʒmənt/ *n*
1 [U] the ability to make sensible decisions about situations or people: *a serious error of judgement* **2** [C,U] a legal decision given by a judge in a court of law **3** [C,U] your opinion about something

judg·ment·al also **judgemental** *BrE* /dʒʌdʒ-'mentl/ *adj* too eager to criticize people

ju·di·cial /dʒuː'dɪʃəl/ *adj* relating to a court of law, judges etc: *the judicial system*

ju·di·cia·ry /dʒuː'dɪʃəri‖-ʃieri, -ʃəri/ *n* **the ju·diciary** *formal* all the judges in a country considered as forming part of the system of government

ju·di·cious /dʒuː'dɪʃəs/ *adj formal* sensible and careful: *a judicious use of resources*

ju·do /'dʒuːdəʊ‖-doʊ/ *n* [U] a sport from Japan in which you try to throw your opponent onto the ground

jug /dʒʌg/ *n* [C] a container used for pouring liquids

jug·gle /'dʒʌgəl/ *v* **1** [I,T] to keep objects moving through the air by throwing and catching them very quickly **2** [T] to try to fit two or more jobs, activities etc into your life: *It's hard work trying to juggle family life and a career.*

jug·gler /'dʒʌgləll-ər/ *n* [C] someone who juggles to entertain people

juice /dʒuːs/ *n* **1** [C,U] the liquid from fruit or vegetables, or a drink made from this: *orange juice* **2** [U] the liquid that comes out of meat when it is cooked

juic·y /'dʒuːsi/ *adj* **1** containing a lot of juice: *a juicy peach* **2** **juicy gossip/details etc** *informal* interesting or shocking information about someone or something —**juiciness** *n* [U]

juke box /'dʒuːk bɒks‖-baːks/ *n* [C] a machine, often in a bar, that plays music when you put money in

Ju·ly /dʒʊ'laɪ/ written abbreviation **Jul** *n* [C,U] the seventh month of the year → see usage note at MONTH

jum·ble¹ /'dʒʌmbəl/ *n* **1** [singular] an untidy group of things: *a jumble of pots and pans* **2** [U] *BrE* things that are sold at a jumble sale

jumble² also **jumble up** *v* [T] to mix things together so that they become untidy: *Don't jumble all my papers up.*

jumble sale /'.. ./ *n* [C] *BrE* a sale of used clothes, books etc in order to raise money; RUMMAGE SALE *AmE*

jum·bo /'dʒʌmbəʊ‖-boʊ/ *adj* [only before noun] larger than other things of the same type: *a jumbo sausage*

jumbo jet /'.. ./ also **jumbo** *n* [C] a very big plane that carries passengers

jump¹ /dʒʌmp/ *v* **1** [I,T] to push yourself off the ground using your legs, or to go over something doing this: *The fans started cheering and jumping up and down.* | *A horse could jump a five-foot fence.* | + **into/off/down etc** *Boys were diving and jumping off the bridge.* → see colour picture on page 670 **2** [I] to move quickly or suddenly in a particular direction: + **up/into/out** *Paul jumped up to answer the door.* **3** [I] to make a sudden movement because you are surprised or frightened: **make sb jump** *I didn't hear you come in – you made me jump!* **4** [I] to increase suddenly and by a large amount: *Profits have jumped by 20% in the last six months.* **5** [I] to change quickly from one subject to another: *The story jumps from Tom's childhood to his wartime adventures.* **6** **jump to conclusions** to form an opinion about something before you have all the facts **7** **jump the gun** to start doing something too soon without thinking about it carefully **8** **jump down sb's throat** to suddenly speak angrily to someone **9** **jump for joy** to be extremely happy **10** **jump the queue** to go ahead of other people who are waiting to do something without waiting for them to go first

jump at sth *phr v* [T] to eagerly accept the chance to do something: *Ruth jumped at the chance to study in Paris.*

jump² *n* **1** [C] when you push yourself off the ground using your legs: *the best jump of the competition* **2** [singular] a sudden increase in an amount or value: *a big jump in house prices*

jump·er /'dʒʌmpəll-ər/ *n* [C] **1** *BrE* a piece of clothing made of wool that covers the upper part of your body and your arms; SWEATER → see colour picture on page 113 **2** *AmE* a dress without SLEEVEs, usually worn over a BLOUSE

jump·y /'dʒʌmpi/ *adj informal* nervous or anxious

junc·tion /'dʒʌŋkʃən/ *n* [C] a place where roads or railway lines join: *a railroad junction*

junc·ture /'dʒʌŋktʃəll-ər/ *n* **at this juncture** *formal* at this point in an activity or period of time: *At this juncture, I suggest we take a short break.*

June /dʒuːn/ written abbreviation **Jun** *n* [C,U] the sixth month of the year → see usage note at MONTH

jun·gle /'dʒʌŋgəl/ *n* [C,U] a large tropical forest with trees and large plants growing very close together

jungle gym /'.. ,./ *n* [C] *AmE* a structure for children to climb on; CLIMBING FRAME *BrE*

ju·ni·or /'dʒuːniəll-ər/¹ *adj* having a low rank in an organization or profession: *a junior executive* → compare SENIOR¹

juggle

J

SPELLING NOTE
Words with the sound /dʒ/ may be spelt **g-**, like **general**.

junior² n [C] **1** AmE a student in the third year of HIGH SCHOOL or college **2** BrE a child who goes to a junior school **3** **be 10 years/6 months etc sb's junior** to be ten years, six months etc younger than someone: He married a woman ten years his junior. → compare SENIOR²

Junior written abbreviation **Jr.** AmE used after the name of a man who has the same name as his father: John J. Wallace Junior

junior col·lege /ˌ... '../ n [C,U] a college in the US and Canada where students do a course for two years

junior high school /ˌ... '. ./ also **junior high** /ˌ... '. ./ n [C,U] a school in the US and Canada for students between the ages of 12 and 14 or 12 and 15

junior school /'... ,./ n [C,U] a school in Britain for children between the ages of 7 and 11

junk /dʒʌŋk/ n [U] old things that have no use or value: The garage was filled with junk.

junk food /'. ./ n [U] food that is not healthy because it contains a lot of fat or sugar

junk·ie /'dʒʌŋki/ n [C] informal **1** a drug ADDICT **2** humorous someone who likes something so much that they cannot stop doing it: My dad's a TV junkie.

junk mail /'. ./ n [U] letters advertising goods and services

junk·yard /'dʒʌŋkjɑːdǁ-jɑːrd/ n [C] a place where old cars, machines etc are kept and the useful parts are saved

jun·ta /'dʒʌntə, 'hʊntə/ n [C] a military government that got its power by using force

Ju·pi·ter /'dʒuːpʲtəlǁ-ər/ n [singular] the fifth PLANET from the sun

jur·is·dic·tion /ˌdʒʊərʲs'dɪkʃənǁˌdʒʊr-/ n [U] the legal power to make decisions about something: a matter outside the court's jurisdiction

ju·ror /'dʒʊərəlǁ'dʒʊrər/ n [C] a member of a jury

ju·ry /'dʒʊərilǁ'dʒʊri/ n [C] **1** a group of twelve ordinary people in a court who decide whether someone is guilty **2** a group of people who choose the winner of a competition

just /dʒəst; strong dʒʌst/ adv **1** only: It happened just a few weeks ago. | "Who was there?" "Just me and Elaine." | I just want to go to bed. (=that is all I want to do) | "What's the letter?" "Oh it's just a bank statement." (=used to say that something is not very important, interesting, difficult, etc) **2** if something has just happened, it happened only a short time ago: She's just got married. | I've just had a really good idea. **3** just before/after/outside/over etc a little before, after, outside etc: Lucy got home just after us. | They live just outside Paris. **4** exactly: You look just like your dad. | **just as** (=at exactly the same time as): The phone rang just as we were leaving. **5** just as good/important/much etc equally as good, important etc: The $250 TV is just as good as the $300 one. **6** spoken used to emphasize something you are saying: I just couldn't believe the news. **7** spoken used to politely ask or tell someone something: Could I just use your phone for a minute? **8** just about almost: We're just about finished. **9** be just about to do sth to be going to do something very soon: We were just about to go riding when it

started raining. **10** be just doing sth used to emphasize that you are doing something now or at the time you are talking about: I'm just making dinner now. | She was just leaving. **11** (only) just if something just happens, it does happen, but it almost did not: They just got to the station in time. **12** just a minute/second spoken used to ask someone to wait for a short time: Just a second – I can't find my keys. **13** just now spoken **a)** a short time before now: He was here just now. **b)** at this time, although the situation will change very soon: I'm busy just now. Can I call you back later? **14** just in case spoken because you think you may need something, or that something may happen: I'll take my umbrella with me just in case. **15** it's just as well spoken used to say that it is lucky that something happened: It's just as well you were there to help. **16** just because ... doesn't mean used to say that although one thing is true, this does not mean that another thing is also true: Just because you're older than me doesn't mean you know better than I do.

just² /dʒʌst/ adj formal morally right and fair: a just punishment → opposite UNJUST

jus·tice /'dʒʌstʲs/ n [U] **1** fairness in the way people are treated: Children have a strong sense of justice. **2** the system by which people are judged in courts of law and criminals are punished: the criminal justice system **3** do sb/sth justice to show or talk about someone in a way that makes them seem as attractive, kind, intelligent etc as they really are: This picture doesn't do you justice.

Justice of the Peace /ˌ... . . './ abbreviation **JP** n [C] someone who has the power to decide whether a person is guilty of a crime in a small local court

jus·ti·fi·a·ble /'dʒʌstʲfaɪəbəl/ adj done for good reasons: a justifiable decision **—justifiably** adv: Local people are justifiably angry about the plan.

jus·ti·fi·ca·tion /ˌdʒʌstʲfʲ'keɪʃən/ n [C,U] a good reason for doing something: I can't see any possible justification for the attack.

jus·ti·fied /'dʒʌstʲfaɪd/ adj if something is justified, there are good reasons for it: Your complaints are certainly justified. → opposite UNJUSTIFIED

jus·ti·fy /'dʒʌstʲfaɪ/ v [T] to give a good enough reason for doing something that other people think is unreasonable: How can you justify spending so much money on a coat?

jut /dʒʌt/ also **jut out** v [I] to stick out further than the surrounding things: a point of land that juts out into the ocean

ju·ve·nile /'dʒuːvənaɪlǁ-nəl, -naɪl/ adj **1** used to talk about crime by young people: juvenile crime **2** behaving in an annoying way, which is more suitable for a child than an adult: a juvenile sense of humour **—juvenile** n [C]

juvenile de·lin·quent /ˌ... .'../ n [C] formal a child or young person who behaves in a criminal way

jux·ta·pose /ˌdʒʌkstə'pəʊzǁ'dʒʌkstəpoʊz/ v [T] formal to put together things that are very different **—juxtaposition** /ˌdʒʌkstəpə'zɪʃən/ n [C,U]

J

Kk

K, k /keɪ/ the letter 'k'

K /keɪ/ **1 K** *informal* the abbreviation of 1000 pounds or dollars: *He earns $50K.* **2 K** the abbreviation of KILOBYTE

ka·bob /kəˈbɑːb/ *n* [C] *AmE* for KEBAB

ka·lei·do·scope /kəˈlaɪdəskəʊpǁ-skoʊp/ *n* **1** [singular] used to emphasize that something contains a large number of very different things: *the city's kaleidoscope of cultures* **2** [C] a tube with mirrors and pieces of coloured glass at one end, that shows coloured patterns when you turn it

kan·ga·roo /ˌkæŋɡəˈruː/ *n* [C] a large Australian animal that jumps and carries its babies in a pocket on its stomach

kangaroo
pouch

ka·put /kəˈpʊt/ *adj spoken* broken: *The lawnmower's kaput.*

kar·at /ˈkærət/ *n* [C] *AmE* a unit for measuring how pure a piece of gold is; CARAT *BrE*

ka·ra·te /kəˈrɑːti/ *n* [U] a Japanese sport in which you fight using your hands and feet

kar·ma /ˈkɑːməǁ-ɑːr-/ *n* [U] the force that is produced by the things you do in your life and that will influence you in the future, according to some religions

kay·ak /ˈkaɪæk/ *n* [C] a small boat for one person

ke·bab /kɪˈbæbǁkɪˈbɑːb/ *n* [C] *BrE* small pieces of meat and vegetables, cooked on a stick; KABOB *AmE*

keel¹ /kiːl/ *n* [C] **1** the bottom part of a boat **2 on an even keel** continuing in the same way, without any sudden changes or problems: *The administration has managed to keep the economy on an even keel.*

keel² *v*
　　keel over *phr v* [I] to fall over

keen /kiːn/ *adj* **1** wanting to do something very much: *US companies are keen to enter the Chinese market.* **2** *especially BrE* if you are keen on someone or something, you like them very much or are very interested in them: *a keen golfer* | **+ on** *I'm not very keen on their music.* **3 a keen sense of sth** when someone is very good at doing something, or feels something very strongly: *He has a keen sense of humour.*
—**keenly** *adj*

keep¹ /kiːp/ *v* **kept** /kept/, **kept, keeping**
1 [I, linking verb] to continue to be in the same condition, state, or position and not change or move: *I wish you would keep still for a moment.* | *This blanket should help you keep warm.* **2** [T] to make someone or something continue to be in the same condition, state, or place: *Do you want me to keep the window open?* | *My work's been keeping me very busy.* | *They kept their plans secret for as long as possible.* **3 keep (on) doing sth** to continue doing something, or repeat an action many times: *If he keeps on growing like this, he'll be taller than his dad.* **4** [T] to continue to have something and not give it to someone, sell it etc: *You can keep the book. I don't need it now.* | *They're keeping the house in Colorado and selling this one.* **5** [T] to have something in a place, so that it is available to use: *We usually keep the bleach under the sink.* | *The information is kept on computer.* **6** [T] to prevent someone from leaving a place: *They kept him in jail for two weeks.* **7 keep sb waiting** to make someone have to wait **8** [T] to delay someone: *I don't know what's keeping her. It's 8:00 already.* **9 keep a promise/appointment** to do what you have promised or arranged to do **10 keep a secret** to not tell anyone about a secret **11 keep a record/diary etc** to regularly write down information about something: *Keep a record of the food you eat for one week.* **12 keep at it** to continue working hard in order to do something: *If you keep at it I'm sure you'll succeed.* **13 it'll keep** *spoken* used to say that you can talk about something later **14 keep (yourself) to yourself** to avoid spending time with other people, because you want to be alone **15** [I] if food keeps, it stays fresh: *That yoghurt won't keep much longer.* **16** [T] to provide enough money for someone to buy food, clothes etc: *You can't keep a family of five on $200 a week.* **17** [T] to have animals and look after them: *We used to keep chickens.*

keep away *phr v* [I **keep** sth/sb ↔ **away**] to not go near someone or something, or make someone do this: *Keep away from the windows.*

keep back *phr v* **1** [T **keep** sth ↔ **back**] to not tell someone about something: *I know she was keeping something back from me.* **2** [I,T **keep** sb ↔ **back**] to not go close to something, or make someone do this: *Police ordered the crowds to keep back.*

keep sth ↔ **down** *phr v* [T] to control something in order to prevent it from increasing: *They promised to keep the rents down.*

keep from *phr v* [T] **1** [**keep** sth **from** sb] to not tell someone about something: *He kept Angie's death from his family for 3 days.* **2 keep sb/sth from doing sth** to prevent someone from doing something or prevent something from happening: *Put foil over the pie to keep it from burning.*

keep sb **in** *phr v* [T] to prevent someone from leaving a place, as a punishment: *The whole class was kept in after school.*

keep off *phr v* [T] **1** [**keep** sth ↔ **off**] to prevent something from affecting or damaging something else: *A hat will keep the sun off your head.* **2** [**keep off** sth] to not go onto an area of land: *Keep off the grass!* **3** [**keep off** sth] to not talk about something: *Maud tried to keep off politics.*

keep on *phr v* **1 keep on doing sth** to continue doing something, or do something many times: *Why do you keep on going there?* **2 keep on at sb about sth** *informal* to tell someone to do something again and again until they do it **3** [T **keep** sb **on**] to continue to employ someone: *If he's good enough they might keep him on.*

keep out *phr v* **1 Keep Out!** used on signs to tell people that they are not allowed in a place **2** [T **keep** sb/sth **out**] to prevent someone or

K

something from getting into something: *a coat that keeps the rain out*

keep out of sth *phr v* [T] to not become involved with something: *You keep out of this, Campbell.*

keep to *phr v* **1** [T **keep to** sth] to do what you should do, especially because you have agreed to do it: *They failed to keep to their side of the agreement.* **2** [T **keep to** sth] to not leave something: *Keep to the main roads.* **3 keep sth to a minimum** to make something happen as little as possible **4 keep sth to yourself** to not tell anyone else about something: *Kim kept Gina's secret to herself.*

keep up *phr v* **1** [I,T **keep** sth ↔ **up**] to continue doing something, or make something continue: *The French team kept up the pressure right until the end of the game.* | *Keep up the good work.* | **keep it up** *She's working really hard. She's bound to go to college if she keeps it up.* **2** [I] to do something as well or as quickly as other people: + **with** *Davey isn't keeping up with the rest of the class in reading.* **3** [I] to move as quickly as someone: *Hey, slow down, I can't keep up!* **4** [I] to deal with or know about something which is changing or growing a lot: *It's hard to keep up with all the changes in computer technology.* **5** [T **keep** sb **up**] to prevent someone from sleeping: *The baby kept us up all night.*

keep² *n* **1 earn your keep** to do enough work to pay for your food, clothes etc **2 for keeps** *spoken informal* for ever: *He said the jewellery was mine for keeps.*

keep fit /ˌ. ˈ. ◂/ *n* [U] *BrE* classes or exercises to make yourself stay healthy

keep·ing /ˈkiːpɪŋ/ *n* **1 for safe keeping** in order to prevent something being lost or stolen: *I'll put the tickets here for safe keeping.* **2 in keeping/out of keeping** suitable or not suitable: *The modern furniture wasn't really in keeping with the rest of the house.*

keep·sake /ˈkiːpseɪk/ *n* [C] a small object that you keep to remind you of someone

keg /keg/ *n* [C] a large container used for storing beer

ken·nel /ˈkenl/ *n* [C] **1** a small outdoor house for a dog to sleep in **2 kennels** a place where dogs are looked after

kept /kept/ *v* the past tense and past participle of KEEP

kerb *BrE*, **curb** *AmE* /kɜːb‖kɜːrb/ *n* [C] the edge of the PAVEMENT, where it joins the road

ker·nel /ˈkɜːnl‖ˈkɜːr-/ *n* [C] the centre part of a nut or seed, usually the part you can eat

ker·o·sene /ˈkerəsiːn/ *n* [U] *AmE* a type of oil that is burned for heat and light

ketch·up /ˈketʃəp/ *n* [U] a thick liquid made from TOMATOes that you put on food

ket·tle /ˈketl/ *n* [C] a container used for boiling water in → see picture at KITCHEN

key¹ /kiː/ *n* **1** [C] something that you put into a lock in order to open a door, start a car etc **2** [C] one of the things that you press to produce letters and numbers on a computer, or sounds on a piano **3 the key** the most important thing that helps you to do something or helps something to happen: *Preparation is the key to success.* **4** [C] a set of musical notes that is based on one particular note **5** [singular] the

part of a map or drawing, that explains what the signs on it mean **6** [C] a set of answers to an exercise or PUZZLE

key² *adj* [only before noun] very important and necessary, especially in order for something to succeed: *a key witness*

key³ *v*

key sth ↔ **in** *phr v* [T] to put information into a computer

key·board /ˈkiːbɔːd‖-bɔːrd/ *n* [C] a set of keys on a computer, a TYPEWRITER, or a piano, which you press to produce letters or sounds → see colour picture on page 80

keyed up /ˌ. ˈ./ *adj* excited or nervous about something: *We were all keyed up to go on vacation when the news came.*

key·hole /ˈkiːhəʊl‖-hoʊl/ *n* [C] the hole where you put a key into a lock

key·note /ˈkiːnəʊt‖-noʊt/ *adj* **keynote speaker/speech/address** a speech made by an important person, especially a politician, describing his or her main principles or intentions

key ring /ˈ. ./ *n* [C] a metal ring that you keep keys on

kg the written abbreviation of KILOGRAM

kha·ki /ˈkɑːkiː‖ˈkæki, ˈkɑːki/ *n* [U] a pale green-brown or yellow-brown colour, like the colour often worn by soldiers → see colour picture on page 114 — **khaki** *adj*

kick¹ /kɪk/ *v* **1** [T] to hit or move something with your foot: *The video shows King being kicked by police officers.* | **kick** sth **into/down/across** etc *He kicked the ball into the back of the net.* → see colour picture on page 670 **2** [I,T] to move your foot quickly forwards or backwards: *a baby kicking its legs* **3 kick a habit** to stop doing something such as smoking **4 kick up a fuss** *informal* to complain a lot because you are annoyed about something

kick in *phr v* [I] *informal* to begin to have an effect: *Those pills should kick in any time now.*

kick off *phr v* [I,T **kick** sth ↔ **off**] *informal* to start, or make an event start: *The festivities will kick off with a barbecue dinner.*

kick sb ↔ **out** *phr v* [T] *informal* to make someone leave: *He was kicked out of college for taking cocaine.*

kick² *n* [C] **1** an action of hitting something with your foot: *If the gate won't open, just give it a good kick.* (=kick it hard) **2** *informal* a feeling of excitement or pleasure, especially from doing something dangerous or dishonest: **get a kick out of** sth *Alan gets a real kick out of skiing.* | **do** sth **for kicks** *She started stealing for kicks.*

kick·back /ˈkɪkbæk/ *n* [C,U] *informal* money that a person gets for secretly and dishonestly helping someone; BRIBE

kick·off /ˈkɪkɒf‖-ɒːf/ *n* [C,U] the time when a game of SOCCER starts, or the first kick that starts it: *Kickoff is at midday.*

kid¹ /kɪd/ *n* **1** [C] *informal* a child or young person: *How many kids do you have?* | *college kids* **2** [C,U] a young goat, or the leather made from its skin

kid² *v* **-dded, -dding** *informal* **1** [I,T] to say something that is not true, especially as a joke: **just kidding** *Don't worry, I was just kidding.* **2** [T] to make someone believe something that is untrue or unlikely: *He likes to kid everyone* *he's a tough macho guy.* **3 no kidding/you're kidding** *spoken informal* used when you are surprised by what someone has said: *"They've offered her $50,000 a year." "You're kidding!"*

kid³ *adj* **kid brother/sister** *informal* a younger brother or sister

kid·nap /ˈkɪdnæp/ *v* [T] **-pped, -pping** to take someone away by force and keep them as your prisoner until people give you money or things you want —**kidnapper** *n* [C] —**kidnapping** *n* [C,U]

kid·ney /ˈkɪdni/ *n* [C] one of the two organs in the body that separate waste liquid from blood

kill¹ /kɪl/ *v* **1** [I,T] to make someone die: *He's in jail for killing a policeman.* | *Three people were killed when a car bomb exploded in Bilbao.* | *The disease can kill.* **2** [T] to make something stop, or prevent it from happening: *They gave her drugs to kill the pain.* **3 sb will kill sb** *spoken* used to say that someone will be very angry with another person: *My wife will kill me if she finds out.* **4 my feet/legs etc are killing me** *spoken* used to say that part of your body is hurting a lot **5 kill time** *informal* to spend time doing something, while you are waiting for something else to happen **6 have time/an hour/an afternoon etc to kill** to have nothing particular to do for an hour, an afternoon etc **7 kill two birds with one stone** to save time or effort by doing one thing at the same time you do another: *While I was in town I decided to kill two birds with one stone and go and see Grandpa as well.*

kill sb/sth ↔ **off** *phr v* [T] to get rid of someone or something: *His character gets killed off ten minutes into the film.*

kill² *n* [singular] **1** when an animal is killed **2 move/close in for the kill** to move closer to someone or something and get ready to kill, destroy, or defeat them: *His opponent was moving in for the kill.*

kill·er /ˈkɪlə‖-ər/ *n* [C] someone who has killed another person, or something that kills people: *The police are still looking for the girl's killer.*

kill·ing /ˈkɪlɪŋ/ *n* [C] **1** a murder: *a series of brutal killings* **2 make a killing** *informal* to make a lot of money very quickly

kiln /kɪln/ *n* [C] a special OVEN for baking clay pots, bricks etc

ki·lo /ˈkiːləʊ‖-loʊ/ *n* [C] a kilogram

kil·o·byte /ˈkɪləbaɪt/ *n* [C] a unit for measuring computer information, equal to 1024 BYTES

kil·o·gram also **kilogramme** /ˈkɪləgræm/ abbreviation **kilo,** written abbreviation **kg** *n* [C] a unit for measuring weight, equal to 1000 grams

kil·o·me·tre *BrE*, **kilometer** *AmE* /ˈkɪlə-ˌmiːtə, kɪˈlɒmɪtə‖kɪˈlɑːmɪtər/ written abbreviation **km** *n* [C] a unit for measuring length, equal to 1000 metres

kil·o·watt /ˈkɪləwɒt‖-wɑːt/ *n* [C] a unit for measuring electrical power, equal to 1000 WATTS

kilt /kɪlt/ *n* [C] a skirt traditionally worn by Scottish men

ki·mo·no /kɪˈməʊnəʊ‖-ˈmoʊnoʊ/ *n* [C] a loose piece of clothing traditionally worn in Japan

kin /kɪn/ *n* **1 next of kin** *formal* the person in your family who you are most closely related to **2** [plural] *old-fashioned* your family

kind¹ /kaɪnd/ *n* [C] **1** a type of person or thing: **+ of** *What kind of pizza do you want?* | **all kinds of** (=many different kinds of): *We sell all kinds of hats.* | **some kind of** (=used when you are not sure what something is like): *I think they're having some kind of party upstairs.* | **of its kind** *the course is the only one of its kind.* **2 kind of** *spoken informal* used when you are describing or explaining what something is like. You sometimes use 'kind of' to mean 'a little' or 'rather', but often it has no real meaning: *He looks kind of weird to me.* **3 of a kind** of the same type: *Each vase is handmade and is one of a kind.* (=the only one of its type) **4 in kind** if you pay someone in kind, you give them goods or services instead of money

kind² *adj* someone who is kind tries to help other people and shows that they care about them: *Everyone's been so kind to me.* | *Thank you for those kind words.* | **it's kind of sb (to do sth)** *It was kind of him to offer to help.*

kind·a /ˈkaɪndə/ *AmE spoken nonstandard* a short form of 'kind of': *I'm kinda tired.*

K

kitchen

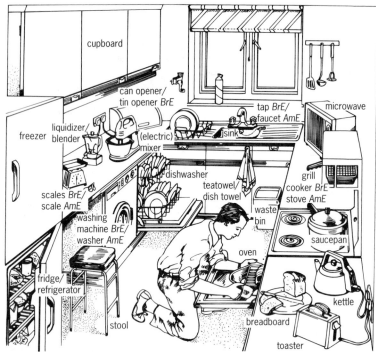

cupboard

can opener/
tin opener *BrE*

tap *BrE*/
faucet *AmE*

microwave

freezer

liquidizer/
blender

(electric)
mixer

sink

dishwasher

teatowel/
dish towel

grill

cooker *BrE*/
stove *AmE*

scales *BrE*/
scale *AmE*

washing
machine *BrE*/
washer *AmE*

waste
bin

oven

saucepan

fridge/
refrigerator

stool

breadboard

kettle

toaster

---

kin·der·gar·ten /ˈkɪndəɡɑːtn‖-dərɡɑːrtn/ *n* [C,U] **a)** *BrE* a school or part of a school for children aged two to five **b)** *AmE* a class for young children, usually aged five, that prepares them for school

kind-heart·ed /ˌ. ˈ..◂ ‖ˈ. ˌ..◂/ *adj* kind and generous: *a kind-hearted woman*

kin·dling /ˈkɪndlɪŋ/ *n* [U] small pieces of dry wood, leaves etc that you use for starting a fire

kind·ly¹ /ˈkaɪndli/ *adv* **1** used when someone has done something kind or generous: *Mr Thomas has kindly offered to let us use his car.* **2** in a kind way: *Miss Havisham looked kindly at Joe.* **3** *spoken formal* a word meaning 'please', often used when you are annoyed: *Kindly be brief. I have a number of calls to make.* **4 not take kindly to sth** to be annoyed or upset by something: *He didn't take kindly to being ordered around.*

kindly² *adj* [only before noun] kind and friendly: *a kindly old woman* —**kindliness** *n* [U]

kind·ness /ˈkaɪndn⅟s/ *n* [U] kind behaviour: *Sam never forgot her kindness.*

kin·dred /ˈkɪndr⅟d/ *adj* **a kindred spirit** someone who has the same ideas and feelings as you do

king /kɪŋ/ *n* [C] **1** a man from a royal family who rules a country: *the King of Spain | King Edward III* **2** the most important piece in a game of CHESS. If you lose your king you lose the game

king·dom /ˈkɪŋdəm/ *n* [C] **1** a country that has a king or queen: *the Kingdom of Nepal* **2 the animal kingdom** all animals considered together as a group

king·fish·er /ˈkɪŋˌfɪʃə‖-ər/ *n* [C] a small brightly coloured bird that lives near rivers

king-size /ˈ. ./ also **king-sized** *adj* very big: *a king-size bed*

kink /kɪŋk/ *n* [C] a twist in something that is normally straight: *The hose has a kink in it.*

kink·y /ˈkɪŋki/ *adj informal* kinky sexual activities are strange and unusual: *kinky sex videos*

ki·osk /ˈkiːɒsk‖-ɑːsk/ *n* [C] a small shop where you can buy things such as newspapers or tickets through a window

kip /kɪp/ *n* [singular, U] *BrE informal* if you have a kip, you sleep for a short time —**kip** *v* [T]

kip·per /ˈkɪpə‖-ər/ *n* [C] a type of fish that has been prepared using smoke and salt

kiss¹ /kɪs/ *v* [I,T] to touch someone with your lips: *She kissed me on the cheek. | Matt kissed her goodnight and left the room.*

kiss² *n* [C] **1** the action of touching someone with your lips: *Come here and give me a kiss.* **2 give sb the kiss of life** *BrE* to breathe air into someone's lungs in order to make them start breathing again

kit /kɪt/ *n* [C] **1** a set of things that you use for a particular purpose or activity: *a first-aid kit*

K

2 something that you buy in parts and put together yourself: *He made the model from a kit.*

kitch·en /'kɪtʃ³n/ *n* [C] the room where you prepare and cook food

kite /kaɪt/ *n* [C] a toy that you fly in the air on the end of a long string

kite

kitsch /kɪtʃ/ *n* [U] things such as decorations that amuse you because you think they show bad taste: *Her house was full of 1970s kitsch.* —**kitschy** *adj*

kit·ten /'kɪtn/ *n* [C] a young cat

kit·ty /'kɪti/ *n* [C usually singular] money that a group of people have collected and saved for a particular purpose

kitty-cor·ner /ˌ.. '../ *adv AmE informal* on the opposite corner of a street from a particular place: *His store is kitty-corner from the bank.*

ki·wi fruit /'kiːwiː fruːt/ *n* [C] a small sweet fruit with a brown skin, which is green inside

Kleen·ex /'kliːneks/ *n* [C,U] *trademark* a TISSUE

klutz /klʌts/ *n* [C] *AmE informal* someone who often drops things, or knocks things by mistake —**klutzy** *adj*

km *n* [C] the written abbreviation of KILOMETRE

knack /næk/ *n* [singular] *informal* the ability to do something well: *Harry has the knack of making friends wherever he goes.*

knack·ered /'nækəd‖-ərd/ *adj* [not before noun] *BrE spoken informal* very tired: *You look knackered.*

knap·sack /'næpsæk/ *n* [C] a bag that you carry on your back

knead /niːd/ *v* [T] to press a mixture of flour and water with your hands to make bread: *Knead the dough for three minutes.*

knee /niː/ *n* [C] **1** the middle part of your leg, where it bends **2** the part of your trousers that covers your knee: *His jeans had holes in both knees.* **3 bring sth to its knees** to make it impossible for a country, company etc to continue: *The country was brought to its knees by a wave of strikes.*

knee·cap /'niːkæp/ *n* [C] the bone at the front of your knee

knee-deep /ˌ. '.◂/ *adj* **1** deep enough to reach your knees: *The snow was almost knee-deep.* **2 knee-deep in sth** when you have a lot of something to deal with: *We ended up knee-deep in debt.*

knee-high /ˌ. '.◂/ *adj* tall enough to reach your knees: *knee-high grass*

knee-jerk /'. ./ *adj* **knee-jerk reaction/response** when someone immediately says or does something without thinking carefully enough: *knee-jerk reactions based on blind prejudice*

kneel /niːl/ **kneel down** *v* [I] **knelt** /nelt/ *or* **kneeled, knelt** *or* **kneeled, kneeling** to move down onto the floor so that the weight of your body is on your knees, or to be in this position: *She knelt down and began to pray.* → see colour picture on page 670

knew /njuː‖nuː/ *v* the past tense of KNOW

knick·ers /'nɪkəz‖-ərz/ *n* [plural] **1** *BrE* women's underwear that covers the area between the waist and the top of the legs;

PANTIES *AmE* **2** old-fashioned loose short trousers that fit tightly at the knees

knick-knacks /'nɪk næks/ *n* [plural] small objects used as a decoration

knife¹ /naɪf/ *n* [C], *plural* **knives** /naɪvz/ a tool used for cutting or as a weapon: *a knife and fork*│*gangs of young boys carrying knives* → see picture at CUTLERY

knife² *v* [T] to deliberately hurt someone using a knife

knight¹ /naɪt/ *n* [C] **1** a man with a high rank in the Middle Ages, who fought while riding a horse **2** in Britain, a man who is given a special HONOUR and can use the title 'Sir'

knight² *v* [T] to give someone a knighthood: *He was knighted in 1997.*

knight·hood /'naɪthʊd/ *n* [C,U] a special title that is given to someone by the King or Queen in Britain

knit /nɪt/ *v* [I,T] **knitted** *or* **knit, knitted** *or* **knit, knitting** to make clothes out of wool using long sticks to tie the wool together: *She's knitting me a sweater.*

knitting nee·dle /'.. ˌ../ *n* [C] one of the two sticks that you use to knit something

knit·wear /'nɪt-weə‖-wər/ *n* [U] knitted clothing

knives /naɪvz/ *n* the plural of KNIFE

knob /nɒb‖nɑːb/ *n* [C] a round handle that you turn or pull to open a door, turn on a radio etc

knob·bly /'nɒbli‖'nɑː-/ *BrE*, **knob·by** /'nɒbi‖ 'nɑːbi/ *AmE adj* not smooth, with hard parts sticking out from the surface: *knobbly knees*

knock

knock

knock over

knock¹ /nɒk‖nɑːk/ *v* **1** [I] to hit a door or window with your hand in order to attract someone's attention: **+ at/on** *There's someone knocking at the front door.* → see colour picture on page 473 **2** [I,T] to hit someone or something so that they move or fall down: *Careful you don't knock the camera.*│*They knocked him to the ground.* **3** [T] *informal* to criticize someone or something, especially unfairly: *"I hate this job." "Don't knock it – it could be worse!"* **4 knock some sense into sb** to make someone learn to behave in a more sensible way: *Maybe she can knock some sense into him.* **5 knock on wood** *AmE* something you say when you do not want your good luck to end; TOUCH WOOD *BrE*: *I haven't had a cold all winter, knock on wood.*

knock sth ↔ **back** *phr v* [T] to drink a large amount of alcohol very quickly: *We knocked back another bottle.*

knock down *phr v* **1** [T **knock** sth ↔ **down**] to destroy a building, wall etc: *Workers began knocking down sections of the wall.* **2 be/get knocked down** to be hit and injured by a car: *Tracy was knocked down by a car on her way*

K

home from school. **3** [T **knock** sth ↔ **down**] *informal* to reduce the price of something: *The stove was knocked down from $800 to $550.*

knock off *phr v informal* **1** [I] to stop working: *We knocked off at about 5 o'clock.* **2** [T **knock** sth ↔ **off**] to reduce the price of something by a particular amount: *I got him to knock $10 off the regular price.* **3 knock it off!** *spoken* used to tell someone to stop doing something annoying

knock out *phr v* [T] **1** [**knock** sb ↔ **out**] to make someone become unconscious, especially by hitting them: *Ali knocked out his opponent in the fifth round.* **2** [**knock** sb/sth ↔ **out**] to defeat a person or team so that they cannot continue in a competition: *Indiana got knocked out in the first round.*

knock sb/sth ↔ **over** *phr v* [T] to hit someone or something so hard that they fall down: *She nearly knocked over my drink.*

knock sth ↔ **up** *phr v* [T] *spoken informal* to quickly make something using the materials that you have available: *I'm sure I can knock up some pasta.*

knock² *n* [C] **1** the sound of someone or something hitting a hard surface: *There was a loud knock at the door.* **2** when something hits something else, especially in a way that causes damage or injury: *a knock on the head*

knock·er /ˈnɒkəˈnɑːkər/ *n* [C] a piece of metal on a door that you use to knock loudly

knock-on /ˌ. ˈ./ *adj* **have a knock-on effect** to cause something to happen, which makes something else happen etc: *The price rises will have a knock-on effect throughout the economy.*

knock·out /ˈnɒk-aʊtǁˈnɑːk-/ *n* [C] when a BOXER hits another boxer so hard that he cannot get up from the ground

knot

knot¹ /nɒtǁnɑːt/ *n* [C] **1** a place where two ends or pieces of rope, string etc have been tightly tied together **2** a unit for measuring the speed of a ship **3** a hard round place in a piece of wood where a branch once joined the tree **4 tie the knot** *informal* to get married

knot² *v* [T] **-tted, -tting** to tie together two ends or pieces of rope, string etc

know¹ /nəʊǁnoʊ/ *v* **knew** /njuːǁnuː/, **known** /nəʊnǁnoʊn/, **knowing** **1** [I,T] to have information about something in your mind: *"What time's the next bus?" "I don't know."* | + **about** *He knows a lot about cars.* | + **(that)** *Did you know that Bill Clinton has an Internet e-mail address?* | **know how/what/where etc** *Nobody knows where she's gone.* | **know how to do sth** (=be able to do something): *Do you know how to turn this thing off?* | **know the way** (=know how to go somewhere): *Luckily, Jo knew the way to the hospital.* **2** [T] to be familiar with a person, place, system etc because you have met them, been there, used it etc before: *I knew Hilary in high*

school. | **get to know** (=start to be familiar with someone or something and find out more about them): *a chance for students to get to know each other* | **know** sth **well** *Jean knows Paris well.* | **know** sth **inside out** (=be very familiar with something): *You should know the system inside out by now.* | **know** sth **like the back of your hand** (=be very familiar with a place) **3** be **known as** to be given a particular name or title: *Diana became known as 'the people's Princess'.* | *the Ministry of International Trade and Industry, better known as MITI* **4** [T] to have experience of something: **have never known** *I've never known a case quite like this one.* **5** [T] to realize or understand something: *I know exactly how you feel!* **6** [I,T] to be sure about something: *I just knew you'd say that!* **7 you know** *spoken* **a)** used when you are explaining or describing something, especially when you want the other person to imagine what it is like, or you are not sure which words to use: *She's very, you know, sophisticated.* **b)** used when you want to start talking about something: *You know, he's going to be taller than his dad.* **c)** used to emphasize that what you are saying is important: *She's really upset, you know.* **8 I know** *spoken* **a)** used to agree with someone: *"These shoes are so ugly!" "I know, aren't they awful?"* **b)** used when you suddenly think of an idea: *I know, let's ask Michael.* **9 let** sb **know** to tell someone about something: *Please let me know if you want to come.* **10 as far as I know** used to say that you think something is true, but you are not sure: *As far as I know, Gail left at 6.00.* **11 you never know** *spoken* used to say that something might happen, although it seems unlikely: *You never know. You might be lucky and win!* **12 Heaven/goodness/who knows** *spoken* used to emphasize that you do not know something: *Who knows how much it will cost.* (=it will cost a lot of money) **13 know better (than to do sth)** to realize that you should not do something: *Ben should have known better than to tell his mother.*

know of sb/sth *phr v* [T] to have been told about or have read about someone or something: *Do you know of any good restaurants around here?*

know² *n* **in the know** if someone is in the know, they know information about something which most people do not know: *Those in the know go to the beaches on the south of the island.*

know-all /ˈ. ./ *n* [C] *BrE* an annoying person who thinks he or she knows everything; KNOW-IT-ALL *AmE*

know-how /ˈ. ./ *n* [U] *informal* knowledge that you need to be able to do something: *technical know-how*

know·ing /ˈnəʊɪŋǁˈnoʊ-/ *adj* [only before noun] a knowing look, smile etc shows that you know what someone is thinking: *When I asked where her husband was, she gave me a knowing look.*

know·ing·ly /ˈnəʊɪŋliǁˈnoʊ-/ *adv* **1** deliberately: *He'd never knowingly hurt you.* **2** in a way that shows you know what someone is thinking: *Brenda smiled knowingly at me.*

know-it-all /ˈ. . ./ *n* [C] *AmE* a KNOW-ALL

knowl·edge /ˈnɒlɪdʒǁˈnɑː-/ *n* [U] **1** information that someone knows about something: *His knowledge of American history is im-*

pressive. | *our knowledge about the functioning of the brain* **2** **to (the best of) my knowledge** *spoken* used to say what you know about something, when there may be other facts that you do not know: *To my knowledge, no such agreement was made.* **3 without sb's knowledge** used to say that someone did not know that something was happening: *Someone had used his computer without his knowledge.* → see also **be common knowledge** (COMMON¹)

knowl·edge·a·ble /ˈnɒlɪdʒəbəl‖ˈnɑː-/ *adj* someone who is knowledgeable about something knows a lot about it: *Steve's very knowledgeable about politics.*

known¹ /nəʊn‖noʊn/ *v* the past participle of KNOW

known² *adj* known about, especially by many people: *a known criminal* | **be known for sth** (=be famous because of something): *Connery is known for his role in the James Bond films.* → see also WELL-KNOWN

knuck·le¹ /ˈnʌkəl/ *n* [C] one of the joints in your fingers

knuckle² *v*

knuckle down *phr v* [I] *informal* to start working hard

knuckle under *phr v* [I] *informal* to do what you are told to do, even though you do not want to

ko·a·la /kəʊˈɑːlə‖koʊ-/ also **koala bear** /ˌ.ˈ./ *n* [C] an Australian animal like a small bear that climbs trees

Ko·ran, Qur'an /kɔːˈrɑːn, kə-‖kəˈræn, -ˈrɑːn/ *n* **the Koran** the holy book of the Muslim religion

ko·sher /ˈkəʊʃə‖ˈkoʊʃər/ *adj* kosher food is prepared according to Jewish law

kow·tow /ˌkaʊˈtaʊ/ *v* [I] to do what a powerful person or group says you must do, in a way that makes other people not respect you: *I refuse to kowtow to that man.*

kph the written abbreviation of kilometres per hour

ku·dos /ˈkjuːdɒs‖ˈkuːdɑːs/ *n* [U] *informal* admiration and respect that you get for doing something important

kung fu /ˌkʌŋ ˈfuː/ *n* [U] a Chinese sport in which people fight with their feet and hands

kw *n* the written abbreviation of KILOWATT

K

GRAMMAR NOTE: direct and indirect speech
There are two ways of reporting what someone said:
DIRECT SPEECH (using "..."): *"**I forgot** to phone you," she said, "**I am** really sorry."*
INDIRECT SPEECH: *She said that she **had forgotten** to phone me and she **was** really sorry.*

L l

L, l /el/ the letter 'l'

lab /læb/ *n* [C] *informal* LABORATORY

la·bel¹ /'leɪbəl/ *n* [C]   **labels**
1 a piece of paper or other material with information on it that is stuck or tied to an object: *Always read the instructions on the label.* **2** also **record label** a company that makes records: *the EMI label* **3** a word or phrase that is used to describe someone or something: *The critics called the film an epic, and it certainly deserves that label.*

label

label

label² *v* [T] **-lled, -lling** *BrE* **-led, -ling** *AmE* **1** to fasten a label to something, or write information on something to show what it is: *Make sure all the bottles are clearly labelled.* **2** to use a word or phrase to describe someone: *He was labelled as a troublemaker.*

la·bor /'leɪbəll-ər/ *n* the American spelling of LABOUR

la·bor·a·tory /lə'bɒrətrill'læbrətɔːri/ also **lab** /læb/ *n* [C] a room or building in which scientists do tests and RESEARCH → see also LANGUAGE LABORATORY

labor camp /'.. ,./ *n* the American spelling of LABOUR CAMP

la·bor·er /'leɪbərəll-bərər/ *n* the American spelling of LABOURER

la·bo·ri·ous /lə'bɔːriəs/ *adj* needing a lot of time and effort to do: *the laborious process of examining all the data*

labor u·nion /'.. ,../ *n* [C] *AmE* a TRADE UNION

la·bour¹ *BrE,* **labor** *AmE* /'leɪbəll-ər/ *n* **1** [C,U] work, especially hard physical work: *The job involves a lot of manual labour.* **2** [U] the people who work in an industry or country, considered together as a group: *There is a shortage of skilled labour.* | *Labour is cheap.* **3** [singular, U] the process in which a baby is pushed out of its mother's body: **in labour** *Meg was in labour for six hours.* **4 Labour** the Labour Party **5 labour of love** work that you do because you enjoy it, not for money

labour² *BrE,* **labor** *AmE* — *v* **1** [I] to work very hard: *farmers laboring in the fields* | **over** *He laboured over the report for hours.* **2** to do something with difficulty: **labour to do something** *The group has spent ten years labouring to bring a ballet company to the city.*

labour camp *BrE,* **labor camp** *AmE* /'.. ,./ *n* [C] a place where prisoners are forced to do hard physical work

la·bour·er *BrE,* **laborer** *AmE* /'leɪbərəll-ər/ *n* [C] someone whose job involves a lot of physical work

Labour Par·ty /'.. ,../ *n* [singular] one of the main political parties in Britain — **Labour** *adj*: *a Labour MP*

lab·ra·dor /'læbrədɔːll-ɔːr/ *n* [C] a large dog, often used for guiding blind people

lab·y·rinth /'læbərɪnθ/ *n* [C] **1** a network of paths or PASSAGES from which it is difficult to find your way out: **+ of** *a labyrinth of narrow streets* **2** something that is very complicated and difficult to understand; MAZE: *a labyrinth of rules and regulations*

lace¹ /leɪs/ *n* [U] a delicate cloth made with patterns of very small holes: *lace curtains*

lace² *v* [T] also **lace up** to fasten clothes or shoes by tying the LACES: *Paul laced up his boots.*

la·ce·rate /'læsəreɪt/ *v* [T] *formal* to cut someone's skin badly and deeply: *His hand was badly lacerated by the broken glass.* — **laceration** /ˌlæsə'reɪʃən/ *n* [C]

lac·es /'leɪsɪz/ *n* [plural] strings that you tie together on shoes in order to fasten them → see picture at SHOE and colour picture on page 113

lack¹ /læk/ *n* [singular, U] when you do not have something or do not have enough of something: **+ of** *a lack of confidence*

lack² *v* [T] to not have something or not have enough of something: *The only thing she lacks is experience.*

lack·ing /'lækɪŋ/ *adj* **1 be lacking in sth** to not have something or not have enough of something: *His voice was completely lacking in emotion.* **2** [not before noun] not existing or available: *The information they need is lacking.*

lack·lus·tre /'læk,lʌstəll-ər/ *adj* not very good or exciting: *a lacklustre performance*

la·con·ic /lə'kɒnɪkll-'kɑː-/ *adj literary* using only a few words

lac·quer /'lækəll-ər/ *n* [U] a clear substance painted on wood or metal to give it a hard shiny surface — **laquered** *adj*

lac·y /'leɪsi/ *adj* decorated with LACE, or looking like lace

lad /læd/ *n* [C] *old-fashioned* a boy or young man

lad·der /'lædəll-ər/ *n* [C]   **ladder**
1 a piece of equipment used for climbing up to high places, consisting of two long bars connected with short bars **2** if you climb up the ladder in an organization, you move up to a higher position: *Stevens started on the bottom rung of the ladder.* **3** *BrE* a long hole in a woman's STOCKINGS or TIGHTS; RUN *AmE*

ladder

la·den /'leɪdn/ *adj* carrying a lot of heavy things: *Grandma walked in, laden with presents.*

la·dies /'leɪdiz/ *n* **the ladies** *BrE* a public toilet for women

ladies' room /'... ,/ *n* [C] *AmE* a room in a public building with toilets for women; THE LADIES *BrE*

la·dle /'leɪdl/ *n* [C] a large round deep spoon with a long handle, used for serving soup

la·dy /'leɪdi/ *n* [C] **1** a word meaning woman, used because people think it is more polite: *Good* *afternoon, ladies.* | *a little old lady with white hair* **2** a woman who is polite and behaves well: *A lady never swears.* **3** a woman from a high social class: *the lords and ladies of the French court* **4** **Lady** a title used before the name of a woman of high social rank: *Lady Helen Windsor* → see also LADIES

la·dy·bird BrE / 'leɪdibɜːd‖-bɜːrd /, **la·dy·bug** AmE / 'leɪdibʌg / *n* [C] a small round insect that is red with black spots

lag[1] /læg/ *v* **-gged, -gging**
lag behind *phr v* [I] to move more slowly than other people, or develop more slowly than other countries, organizations etc: *The country's economy has lagged far behind the economies of other countries in the region.*

lag[2] also **time lag** *n* [C] a delay between two events → see also JET LAG

la·ger / 'lɑːgə‖-ər / *n* [C,U] BrE a yellow beer, or a glass, bottle, or can of this beer

la·goon /lə'guːn/ *n* [C] an area of sea water that is separated from the sea by sand

laid /leɪd/ *v* the past tense and past participle of LAY

laid-back /ˌ. ˈ.◂ / *adj* relaxed and not seeming to worry about anything: *She's easy to talk to, and very laid-back.*

lain /leɪn/ *v* the past participle of LIE[1]

lair /leə‖ler/ *n* [C] the place where a wild animal hides and sleeps: *a wolf's lair*

lake /leɪk/ *n* [C] a large area of water surrounded by land: *Lake Michigan* → see colour picture on page 243

lamb /læm/ *n* [C,U] a young sheep, or the meat of a young sheep

lame /leɪm/ *adj* **1** unable to walk properly because your leg is injured or weak **2** *informal* a lame excuse is too silly to believe — **lamely** *adv*

la·ment /lə'ment/ *v* [I,T] *formal* to feel sad or disappointed about something, or say that you feel this — **lament** *n* [C]

lam·en·ta·ble / 'læməntəbəl, lə'mentəbəl/ *adj formal* very unsatisfactory or disappointing

lam·i·nat·ed / 'læmɪneɪtɪd/ *adj* laminated paper or wood is covered with a thin layer of plastic in order to protect it

lamp /læmp/ *n* [C] a thing that produces light by using electricity, oil, or gas: *a desk lamp* → see colour picture on page 474

lam·poon /læm'puːn/ *v* [T] to write about someone such as a politician in a funny way that makes them seem stupid

lamp-post /ˈ. ./ *n* [C] a tall pole with a lamp on top that stands by the side of a road → see colour picture on page 79

lamp·shade / 'læmpʃeɪd/ *n* [C] a cover over the top of a lamp

lance /lɑːns‖læns/ *n* [C] a pointed pole used as a weapon by soldiers on horses in past times

land[1] /lænd/ *n* **1** [U] an area of ground, especially when it is used for buildings or farming: *Who owns the land near the lake?* | *5000 acres of agricultural land* **2** [U] the solid dry part of the Earth's surface: **on land** *Frogs live on land and in the water.* **3** [C] *literary* a word meaning a country: *a faraway land*

land[2] *v* **1** [I,T] if a plane lands, or if a pilot lands a plane, the plane moves down until it is

safely on the ground: *Has her flight landed yet?* **2** [I] to fall or move down onto something after moving through the air: *Chris slipped and landed on his back.* **3** [I] to arrive somewhere in a boat, plane, etc: *The Pilgrims landed on Cape Cod in 1620.* **4** [T] to put goods or people onto the land after they have been carried by ship or by plane **5** [T] *informal* to finally succeed in getting a job, contract, or deal: *Kelly's landed a job with a big law firm.* **6** [T] to make someone be in a difficult situation in which they have a lot of problems or trouble: *He's managed to land himself in trouble again with the police.*

land·ing / 'lændɪŋ/ *n* [C] **1** the floor at the top of a set of stairs **2** when a plane comes down onto the ground after flying → compare TAKE-OFF

land·la·dy / 'lænd,leɪdi / *n* [C] **1** a woman that you rent a room or house from **2** a woman who owns or is in charge of a PUB or a small hotel

land·lord / 'lændlɔːd‖-lɔːrd/ *n* [C] **1** a man that you rent a room or house from **2** a man who owns or is in charge of a PUB

land·mark / 'lændmɑːk‖-mɑːrk / *n* [C] **1** something that helps you recognize where you are, such as a famous building **2** a very important event, change, or discovery in the development of something: *a landmark in the history of aviation*

land·mine / 'lændmaɪn/ *n* [C] a weapon that is put in or just under the surface of the ground, which explodes if someone or something touches it

land·own·er / 'lænd,əʊnə‖-,oʊnər/ *n* [C] someone who owns a large amount of land

land·scape / 'lændskeɪp/ *n* [C] **1** a view across an area of land: *an urban landscape* → compare SCENERY **2** a painting or a photograph of an area of land, especially in the countryside

land·slide / 'lændslaɪd/ *n* [C] **1** when a large amount of soil and rocks falls down the side of a hill, cliff, or mountain: *Part of the road is blocked by a landslide.* **2** when a person or political party wins a lot more votes than the others in an election: *a landslide victory* | *Blair won the 1997 election by a landslide.*

lane /leɪn/ *n* [C] **1** a narrow country road **2** used in the names of streets: *Turnpike Lane* **3** one of the parts that a road is divided into for one line of traffic: *the fast lane of the motorway* **4** one of the narrow areas of a sports track or swimming pool which is marked for each competing runner or swimmer: *Carl Lewis is running in lane eight.* **5** a ROUTE regularly used by ships and planes

language / 'læŋgwɪdʒ/ *n* **1** [C] a system of words, phrases, and grammar, used by people who live in a country or area to communicate with each other: *"Do you speak any foreign languages?" "Yes, I speak French."* | *language learning skills* | **sb's first language** (=the language you learn to speak as a child) **2** [U] the use of words, grammar etc to communicate with other people **3** [U] the kind of words that someone uses, or that are used when talking or writing about a particular subject: *the language of business* | *poetic language* | **bad language** (=rude words) **4** [C,U] a system of instructions used in computer PROGRAMS **5** [C,U] any

L

system of signs, movements, sounds etc that are used to express meanings or feelings: *the language of music*

language la·bor·a·tory /'.. .,...ll'.. ,..../ *n* [C] a room in a school or college where students can listen to TAPEs of a foreign language and practise speaking it

lan·guid /'læŋgwɪd/ *adj literary* moving or speaking slowly and with very little effort or energy

lan·guish /'læŋgwɪʃ/ *v* [I] to remain in a difficult situation for a long time: *United are currently languishing at the bottom of the league.*

lank·y /'læŋki/ *adj* very tall and thin

lan·tern /'læntən‖-ərn/ *n* [C] a type of lamp you can carry consisting of a glass or metal container with a light inside

lap [1] /læp/ *n* [C] **1** the flat area at the top of your legs when you are sitting down: *Go and sit on Grandad's lap.* **2** one journey around a race track: *Hill overtook Schumacher on the last lap.* **3** one part of a long journey **4 live in the lap of luxury** to have a comfortable life with a lot of money and possessions

lap [2] *v* -pped, -pping **1** [I] if water laps against something, it touches against it: *waves lapping against the shore* **2** [T] also **lap up** if an animal laps up a drink, it drinks it with quick movements of its tongue: *a cat lapping up milk*
lap sth ↔ up *phr v* [T] to accept something very eagerly in a way that shows you like it a lot: *He lapped up all the applause!*

la·pel /lə'pel/ *n* [C] the part at the front of a coat or JACKET that is joined to the collar and folds back on both sides

lapse [1] /læps/ *n* [C] **1** when someone forgets something or stops paying attention to something for a short time: *a lapse of concentration* **2** when someone makes a mistake or behaves badly, in a way that does not seem typical of them: *Apart from the occasional lapse her work seems quite good.* **3** [usually singular] a period of time between two events: *She returned to the stage after a lapse of several years.*

lapse [2] *v* [I] to end, especially because the official period when something is allowed to continue has ended: *Your membership of the tennis club has lapsed.*
lapse into sth *phr v* [T] **1** to become silent or asleep, or start to be in a particular state or condition: *They lapsed into silence.* **2** to start behaving or speaking in a different way: *Without thinking he lapsed into French.*

laptop

lap·top /'læptɒp‖-tɑːp/ *n* [C] a small computer you can carry with you

lard /lɑːd‖lɑːrd/ *n* [U] thick white fat used in cooking

lar·der /'lɑːdə‖'lɑːrdər/ *n* [C] a cupboard or small room used for storing food

large /lɑːdʒ‖lɑːrdʒ/ *adj* **1** big, or bigger than usual in size, number, or amount: *a large pizza | Birmingham is the second largest city in England. | large amounts of money* →opposite SMALL [1] **2 at large** in general: *facilities that are for the benefit of the community at large* **3 be at large** if a criminal or wild animal is at large, they have escaped from somewhere **4 by and large** used to say that something is generally true or usually happens: *By and large, the show was a success.* **5 larger than life** more exciting or interesting than other people or things

large·ly /'lɑːdʒli‖'lɑːr-/ *adv* mostly or mainly: *The delay was largely due to bad weather.*

large-scale /,. '.‖'. ,. / *adj* [only before noun] happening over a large area or involving a lot of people: *large-scale unemployment*

lark /lɑːk‖lɑːrk/ *n* [C] **1** a small wild brown bird that sings and has long pointed wings **2** *BrE informal* something that you do for amusement

lar·va /'lɑːvə‖'lɑːrvə/ *n* [C], *plural* **larvae** /-viː/ a young insect with a soft tube-shaped body, before it becomes an adult

lar·ynx /'lærɪŋks/ *n* [C] *technical* the part of your throat from which your voice is produced

la·sa·gne *BrE*, **lasagna** *AmE* /lə'sænjə, --'zæn-‖ -'zɑːn-/ *n* [C,U] a type of Italian food made with flat pieces of PASTA, meat or vegetables, cheese and a SAUCE made with milk

la·ser /'leɪzə‖-ər/ *n* [C] a piece of equipment that produces a powerful narrow beam of light, or the beam of light itself: *laser surgery*

lash [1] /læʃ/ *v* **1** [I,T] if rain, waves, or wind lash against something, they hit it hard or blow hard against it: *waves lashing against the rocks* **2** [T] to hit someone very hard with a whip or stick **3** [T] to tie something tightly to something else, using a rope
lash out *phr v* [I] to suddenly attack someone or speak angrily to them: + **at** *Georgie lashed out at him, screaming abuse.*

lash [2] *n* [C] when someone is hit with a whip as a punishment

lash·es /'læʃᵻz/ *n* [plural] eyelashes (EYELASH)

lass /læs/ *n* [C] *BrE* a word meaning a girl or young woman, used in Scotland and the North of England

las·so /lə'suː, 'læsəʊ‖-soʊ/ *n* [C] a rope with one end tied in a circle, used for catching cattle and horses —**lasso** *v* [T]

last [1] /lɑːst‖læst/ *determiner* **1** most recent: *When was the last time she was here? | last night/ week/Sunday etc Did you go out last night? | the last few months/10 years etc* (=the period until now): *The town has changed a lot in the last few years. | sb's last job/car/boyfriend etc* (=the one before your present job, car etc): *My last boyfriend was crazy about football.* **2** happening or coming at the end, after all the others: *What time does the last bus leave? | the last chapter of the book | last but one* (=the one before the last one) **3** the last person or thing is the only one that remains: *Is it all right if I have the last piece of cake?* **4 the last person/thing** the person or thing you did not expect at all, or the one that you want least of all: *Ella's the last person I wanted to see.* **5 have the last word** to say the last thing in a discussion or argument, or make the final decision about something

last² *adv* **1** most recently before now: *When did you last go shopping?* **2** after everything or everyone else: *The Rolling Stones came on stage last.* **3 last but not least** used before mentioning the last person or thing in a list to emphasize that they are still important: *Last but not least, I'd like to thank my mother.*

> **USAGE NOTE: last**
>
> 1 When your point of view is in the present, looking back to the past, say **last** night, **last** week etc: *I went to bed late last night.* | *I spoke to Sue last Monday.* But when your point of view is in the past, looking even further back into the past, use **previous**: *the previous night* | *the night before* | *the previous week* | *the week before* | *I told her I had spoken to Sue the previous Monday.* 2 Compare **latest** and **last**. Use **latest** when you mean 'new and most recent': *Have you heard the latest news?* Use **last** when you mean 'coming at the end' or 'coming before the latest one': *'The Magic Flute', was Mozart's last opera.* | *Have you read Bigg's latest novel? It's better than her last one.*

last³ *n, pron* **1 the last** the person or thing that comes after all the others: *Lee was the last to go to bed.* **2 at (long) last** after a long time: *She seems to have found happiness at last.* **3 the day/week/year before last** the day, week etc before the one that has just finished **4 the last of** the only part of something that remains: *Is this the last of the bread?*

last⁴ *v* [I,T] **1** to continue to happen or exist: *Jeff's operation lasted 3 hours.* **2** to continue to be effective: *The batteries will last for up to 8 hours.* **3** to continue to be in good condition and suitable for use: *This car will last for years if it's looked after.*

last-ditch /ˌ. ˈ.◂ / *adj* **a last-ditch effort/ attempt etc** a final attempt to achieve something before it becomes impossible: *a last-ditch effort to free the hostages*

last·ing /ˈlɑːstɪŋ‖ˈlæs-/ *adj* continuing for a long time: *a lasting impression*

last·ly /ˈlɑːstli‖ˈlæst-/ *adv* used to say that the next thing you mention will be the last thing: *And lastly, I'd like to thank my producer.*

> **USAGE NOTE: lastly**
>
> 1 Don't confuse **lastly** and **at last**. Use **lastly** when you are talking about several things in order and you want to show that you have reached the final thing on the list: *I'll start by asking you about your previous experience, then we can talk about your present employment, and lastly I'll tell you about the job here.* (Note that you can also use **finally** in the same way.) 2 Use **at last** when you want to show that something has happened after

a long time or after a lot of waiting: *She tried again and again until at last she succeeded.* | *When at last the rescuers found them, two people had already died.* | *"At last!"* she exclaimed as she managed to catch the waiter's eye.* (Note that you can also use **finally** in the same way.)

last-min·ute /ˌ. ˈ.◂ / *adj* happening or done very late within a period of time: *last-minute Christmas shopping*

last name /ˈ. ./ *n* [C] a SURNAME → compare FIRST NAME, MIDDLE NAME

latch¹ /lætʃ/ *n* [C] **1** a small metal bar used for fastening a door, gate, or window **2** a type of lock for a door, that needs a key when being opened from outside: **on the latch** (=closed but not locked)

latch² *v*

latch on *phr v* [I] *BrE informal* to understand or realize something

late /leɪt/ *adj, adv* **1** arriving, happening, or done after the expected time: *Sorry I'm late!* | *Our flight arrived two hours late.* | *We have a late breakfast.* | **+ for** *Peggy was late for school.* **2** near the end of a period of time: *St Mary's church was built in the late 18th century.* **3** near the end of the day: *It's getting late. We'd better go home.* **4** *formal* used to talk about someone who is dead: *the late Sir William Russell* **5 of late** *formal* recently: *The company has been having a difficult time of late.*

late·ly /ˈleɪtli/ *adv* recently: *I've been feeling very tired lately.*

> **USAGE NOTE: lately and recently**
>
> Use both of these words with the present perfect tenses to talk about something that began not long ago and is still continuing: *I haven't seen her lately.* | *She has seemed a little unhappy recently.* You can also use **recently** with the past tense to talk about something that happened not long ago: *She recently got married.*

la·tent /ˈleɪtənt/ *adj* something that is latent exists but remains hidden, and is likely to develop or become worse in the future: *latent hostility*

lat·er¹ /ˈleɪtəll-ər/ *adv* **1** after the present time or a time you are talking about: *I'll see you later.* | *Two years later he became President.* **2 later on** at some time in the future, or at some time after something else: *Later on in the movie the hero gets killed.*

later² *adj* **1** happening in the future, or after something else: *The decision will be made at a later date.* **2** more recent: *Later models of the car are much improved.*

lat·est¹ /ˈleɪtɪst/ *adj* the most recent or the newest: *What's the latest news?*

latest² *n* **1 the latest** the most recent news, fashion, or design: *Have you heard the latest?* **2 at the latest** used to tell someone the latest

L

> **GRAMMAR NOTE: a or the (2)**
>
> Use **the** before a thing or person when it is clear which one you are talking about: *the old man who lives next door.* Use **a** or **an** to talk about a person or thing when it is not important to say which one: *I went out to buy **a** newspaper.* | *A girl in my class told me about it.*

time at which something will or can happen: *I want you home by 11 at the latest.*

la·ther /ˈlɑːðə‖ˈlæðər/ *n* [singular, U] small white BUBBLEs produced by mixing soap with water

Lat·in¹ /ˈlætɪn‖ˈlætn/ *n* [U] the language used in ancient Rome

Latin² *adj* **1** written in Latin **2** relating to a country that speaks a language developed from Latin such as French or Italian

Latin A·mer·i·can /ˌ‥ ˈ‥‥ / *adj* relating to South or Central America

lat·i·tude /ˈlætɪtjuːd‖-tuːd/ *n* [C,U] the distance north or south of the EQUATOR, measured in degrees → compare LONGITUDE

lat·ter¹ /ˈlætə‖-ər/ *n* **the latter** *formal* the second of two people or things that are mentioned → compare FORMER²

latter² *adj* **1** the latter part of a period of time is the part that is nearest the end: *Neruda spent the latter part of his life in Italy.* **2** *formal* the latter one of two people or things that have been mentioned is the second one: *The latter option sounds more realistic.*

laud·a·ble /ˈlɔːdəbəl‖ˈlɔːd-/ *adj formal* deserving praise

laugh¹ /lɑːf‖læf/ *v* [I] to make a sound with your voice when you think something is funny: *Why are you all laughing?* | **+ at** *No one ever laughs at my jokes!* | **burst out laughing** (=suddenly start laughing)
  laugh at sb/sth *phr v* [T] to say unkind things about someone or something and make jokes about them: *Mommy, all the kids at school were laughing at me!*
  laugh sth ↔ **off** *phr v* [T] to pretend that something is not very serious or important by joking about it: *He laughed off suggestions that he was planning to resign.*

laugh² *n* **1** [C] the sound you make when you laugh: *a loud laugh* **2** **have the last laugh** to be successful, after other people have criticized you or thought that you could not succeed **3** **have a laugh** *BrE informal* to enjoy yourself: *She likes going out with her friends and having a laugh.* **4** **be a (good) laugh** *BrE informal* to be amusing **5** **do sth for a laugh** *BrE informal* to do something in order to enjoy yourself or as a joke

laugh·a·ble /ˈlɑːfəbəl‖ˈlæ-/ *adj* something that is laughable is so bad, silly etc, that you cannot treat it in a serious way

laughing stock /ˈ‥ ‿‿/ *n* [singular] someone or something that people think is silly and make jokes about because of something that has happened

laugh·ter /ˈlɑːftə‖ˈlæftər/ *n* [U] when you laugh, or the sound of people laughing: *a roar of laughter*

launch¹ /lɔːntʃ‖lɒːntʃ/ *v* [T] **1 launch an attack/inquiry/campaign etc** to start an attack etc: *The hospital is launching a campaign to raise money for new equipment.* **2** to make a new product or book available to be sold: *Jaguar is planning to launch a new sportscar.* **3** to send a SPACECRAFT into the sky or to put a boat into the water
  launch into sth *phr v* [T] to suddenly start talking about or criticizing something

launch² *n* [C] when something is launched

laun·der·ette /ˌlɔːndəˈret‖ˌlɒːn-/ *BrE*, **laun·dro·mat** /ˈlɔːndrəmæt‖ˈlɒːn-/ *AmE — n* [C] a place where you pay money to wash your clothes in a machine

laun·dry /ˈlɔːndri‖ˈlɒːn-/ *n* **1** [U] clothes, sheets etc that need to be washed, or that have been washed **2** [C] a place where clothes are washed

laur·el /ˈlɒrəl‖ˈlɔː-, ˈlɑː-/ *n* [C,U] a small tree with big smooth shiny leaves

la·va /ˈlɑːvə/ *n* [U] hot melted rock that flows from a VOLCANO

lav·a·to·ry /ˈlævətəri‖-tɔːri/ *n* [C] *formal* a toilet

lav·en·der /ˈlævɪndə‖-ər/ *n* [U] a plant with purple flowers that have a strong pleasant smell

lav·ish¹ /ˈlævɪʃ/ *adj* **1** big or impressive: *lavish dinner-parties* | *lavish presents* **2** giving something or someone a lot of praise and attention: **+ with** *The critics were lavish with their praise for his new novel.* —**lavishly** *adv*

lavish² *v*
  lavish sth **on** sb *phr v* [T] to give something to someone generously and in large amounts: *They lavish a lot of attention on their children.*

law /lɔː‖lɒː/ *n* **1** [U] the system of rules that people in a country or place must obey: **by law** (=according to the law): *Seatbelts must be worn by law.* | **against the law** (=illegal): *Drunk driving is against the law.* | **break the law** (=do something illegal) **2** [C] a rule that people in a country or place must obey: **+ against** *new laws against testing cosmetics on animals* | **+ on** *tough laws on immigration* **3** [U] the system of law studied as a subject **4** **the law** the police: *Is he in trouble with the law?* **5** **law and order** when people obey the law, and crime is controlled by the police and the courts of law **6** [C] a scientific rule that explains why something happens: *the law of gravity*

law·a·bid·ing /ˈ‥ ‿‿/ *adj* obeying laws: *law-abiding citizens*

law·ful /ˈlɔːfəl‖ˈlɒː-/ *adj formal* allowed by law: *lawful killing*

law·less /ˈlɔːləs‖ˈlɒː-/ *adj formal* not obeying the law, or not controlled by law

lawn /lɔːn‖lɒːn/ *n* [C] an area of grass that is kept cut short

lawn mow·er /ˈ‥ ‿‿/ *n* [C] a machine used for cutting grass → see picture at GARDENING EQUIPMENT

law·suit /ˈlɔːsuːt, -sjuːt‖ˈlɒːsuːt/ *n* [C] a claim or complaint against someone that is made in a court of law by a person or company

law·yer /ˈlɔːjə‖ˈlɒːjər/ *n* [C] someone whose job is to advise people about the law and speak for them in court

lax /læks/ *adj* not strict: *lax security*

lax·a·tive /ˈlæksətɪv/ *n* [C] a medicine or something that you eat that makes your BOWELs empty easily —**laxative** *adj*

lay¹ /leɪ/ *v* **laid** /leɪd/, **laid, laying 1** [T] to put something on a surface so that it is flat: **lay sth on/upon/down etc** *He laid his hand on her shoulder.* **2 lay bricks/carpet/cable etc** to put something in the correct place, especially on the ground or floor **3 lay eggs** if a bird, insect etc lays eggs, it produces them from its body **4 lay the blame etc on** *formal* to blame someone or something **5 lay (your) hands on sth** to find something: *I wish I could lay my hands on that book.* **6 lay claim to sth** *formal* to say officially that something belongs to you **7 lay the table** to put knives, forks etc on a table before a meal **8 lay yourself open to sth** to do something that makes it possible that you will be blamed, criticized etc **9 lay a finger/hand on sb** to hurt someone by hitting them: *If you lay a hand on her, I'll call the police.* **10 lay a trap** to prepare a trap to catch someone or something

lay sth ↔ **down** *phr v* [T] **1** to say officially what rules or methods must be obeyed or used: *strict safety regulations laid down by the government* **2 lay down the law** to tell other people what to do in an unpleasant way

lay into sb *phr v* [T] *informal* to attack someone or criticize them: *You should have heard Dad laying into Tommy!*

lay off *phr v* [T **lay** sb ↔ **off**] to stop employing a worker because there is not enough work to do

lay sth ↔ **on** *phr v* [T] to provide food, entertainment etc: *Lola really laid on a great meal for us.*

lay sth ↔ **out** *phr v* [T] **1** to spread something out: *Let's lay the map out on the table.* **2 be laid out** to be arranged in a particular way: *The gardens were attractively laid out.*

lay up *phr v* **be laid up (with)** to have to stay in bed because you are ill or injured: *She's laid up with flu.*

USAGE NOTE: lay, lie, and lie

Lay means to put something somewhere: *He laid the papers on the desk.* **Lie** has two different meanings. It can mean that someone or something is flat on a surface: *The cat was lying on the window ledge.* | *Don't leave your socks lying on the floor!* **Lie** also means 'to say something that is not true': *Are you lying to me?*

---

lay² *v* the past tense of LIE¹

lay³ *adj* **1** involved in church activities but not trained as a priest: *a lay preacher* **2** not having special training or knowledge: *It is difficult for the lay person to understand.*

lay-by /ˈ. ./ *n* [C] *BrE* an area at the side of a road where vehicles can stop

lay·er /ˈleɪə||-ər/ *n* [C] **1** an area of a substance that covers all of a surface: *a thick layer of dust* **2** one of several levels of different substances or materials that are on top of each other: *layers of rock*

lay·man /ˈleɪmən/ *n* [C] someone who is not trained in a particular subject or type of work

lay-off /ˈ. ./ *n* [C] **1** [usually plural] when workers' jobs are stopped because there is not enough work **2** [usually singular] when someone cannot do a sport because they are injured

lay·out /ˈleɪaʊt/ *n* [C] the way in which the rooms or objects in a place are arranged

laze /leɪz/ *v* [I] to relax and not do very much: *laze around/about They spent the afternoon lazing around on the beach.*

la·zy /ˈleɪzi/ *adj* **1** someone who is lazy does not like working or doing things that need effort: *Eva's the laziest girl in the class.* **2** a lazy period of time is spent relaxing: *lazy summer afternoons*

---

lb. *n* the written abbreviation of POUND

lead¹ /liːd/ *v* **led** /led/, **led, leading 1** [T] to take someone to a place by going with them or in front of them: **lead sb to/through/down etc** *Mrs Danvers led us down the corridor.* **2** [I,T] to go in front of a group of people or vehicles: *The school band is leading the parade.* **3** [I] if a door, road etc leads somewhere, you can get there by using it: **+ to/towards/into etc** *a quiet avenue leading to a busy main road* **4** [T] to be in charge of something: *Who's leading the investigation?* **5** [I,T] to be winning a game or competition: *At half-time, Green Bay was leading 12-0.* **6** [I,T] to be more successful than other people, companies, or countries: *The US leads the world in biotechnology.* **7 lead sb to do sth** to make someone do something or think something: *What led you to study geology?* | **lead sb to believe sth** (=make someone think that something is true when it is not): *Rod led us to believe he would pay us back immediately.* **8 lead the way a)** to go in front and show people how to go somewhere **b)** to be the first to do something: *Japanese companies led the way in using industrial robots.* **9 lead a busy/normal etc life** to have a particular kind of life

lead off sth *phr v* [T] if a road or room leads off somewhere, it is directly joined to that place: *A small track led off the main road.*

lead sb **on** *phr v* [T] to make someone believe that you want a romantic or sexual relationship with them when you do not

lead to sth *phr v* [T] to cause something to happen: *social problems that have led to an increase in the crime rate*

lead up to sth *phr v* [T] to come before something and often be a cause of it: *events leading up to the trial*

USAGE NOTE: lead, guide, and direct

Lead means to show people where to go by going first: *He led us down the mountain.* **Guide** means to show people where to go and explain things to them: *She guides tourists around the White House.* **Direct** means to explain to someone how to get somewhere: *Could you direct me to the station?*

---

lead² *n* **1** [singular] when a team, organization etc has more points or is more successful than everyone else in a race or competition: **be in the lead** *Lewis is still in the lead after the third lap.* | **take the lead** (=become the most successful person, team, country etc): *The US has taken the lead in space technology.* **2** [singular] the distance, number of points etc by which one team or player is ahead of another: *Italy has a 2-0 lead.* **3** [C] a piece of information that may help you to find the answer to a problem: *Do the police have any leads in the robbery?* **4** [C] the main acting part in a play or film: *The lead is played by Brad Pitt.* **5** [C] *BrE* a piece of rope, leather etc fastened to a dog's collar to control it **6** [C] *BrE* an electric wire used to connect a piece of electrical equipment to a power supply; CORD *AmE* **7 the lead (story)** the most important piece of news in a newspaper or news programme

lead³ /led/ *n* **1** [U] a heavy soft grey metal **2** [C,U] the dark grey substance in the centre of a pencil

lead·er /'li:dəll-ər/ n [C] **1** the person who is in charge of or controls a country, organization, team etc: + **of** *leaders of the world's most powerful nations* **2** the person, organization etc that is better than all the others in a race or competition

lead·er·ship /'li:dəʃɪpll-ər-/ n **1** [U] when someone is the leader of a team, organization etc: *Under his leadership China became an economic superpower.* **2** [U] the quality of being good at leading a team, organization, country etc: *America needs strong leadership.* **3** [singular] the people who lead a country, organization etc

lead·ing /'li:dɪŋ/ adj **1** best, most important, or most successful: *Julia Roberts plays the leading role in the film.* **2 a leading question** a question asked in a way that makes you give a particular answer

leaf¹ /li:f/ n [C], *plural* **leaves** /li:vz/ **1** one of the flat green parts of a plant that are joined to its stem or branches **2 take a leaf out of someone's book** to behave like someone else because you admire them **3 turn over a new leaf** to start to behave in a much better way

leaf² v

leaf through sth *phr v* [T] to turn the pages of a book or magazine quickly, without reading it carefully

leaf·let /'li:flɪ̩t/ n [C] a small piece of printed paper that gives information or advertises something

leaf·y /'li:fi/ adj **1** having a lot of leaves: *leafy vegetables* **2** having a lot of trees and plants: *a leafy suburb*

league /li:g/ n [C] **1** a group of sports teams or players who play games against each other: *Our team finished second in the league.* **2** a group of people or countries that join together because they have similar aims or beliefs **3 be in league (with)** to work together secretly to do something illegal or morally wrong: *Parry is suspected of being in league with terrorists.* **4** [usually singular] if you are in someone's league, you are as good or as successful as they are at doing something

leak¹ /li:k/ v **1** [I,T] if something leaks a liquid or gas, the liquid or gas comes out of a hole or crack in it: *The roof's leaking! | My car's leaking oil.* **2** [I] to pass through a hole or crack: + **out of/into** *Gas was leaking out of the pipes.* **3** [T] to deliberately give secret information to newspapers, television etc: *The letters were leaked to the press.* —**leakage** n [U]

leak out *phr v* [I] if secret information leaks out, a lot of people find out about it

leak² n [C] **1** a small hole that liquid or gas gets out through: *There's a leak in the water tank.* **2** gas or liquid that gets out through a hole: *an oil leak* **3** when secret information is deliberately given to newspapers, television etc: *security leaks*

leak·y /'li:ki/ adj having a hole or crack that liquid or gas can pass through: *a leaky roof*

lean¹ /li:n/ v **leaned** or **leant** /lent/ *BrE* **1** [I] to move or bend your body in a particular position: + **forward/back/across** etc *Celia leaned forward and kissed him.* **2** [I] to stand while resting part of your body against something: + **against/on** *Joe was leaning on the fence.* → see colour picture on page 670 **3** [T] to put something in a sloping position against something else: **lean** sth **on/against** sth *Lean the ladder against the wall.*

lean on sb/sth *phr v* [T] to get help and encouragement from someone: *I know I can always lean on my friends.*

lean² adj **1** thin in a healthy and attractive way: *Sven was lean and athletic.* **2** lean meat does not have much fat on it **3** not producing good results: *a lean year for small businesses*

lean·ing /'li:nɪŋ/ n [C] a tendency to agree with a particular set of ideas or beliefs: *socialist leanings*

leap¹ /li:p/ v [I] **leaped** or **leapt** /lept/, **leaped** or **leapt**, **leaping 1** to jump high into the air or over something: + **over/into/from** etc *Mendez leaped into the air after scoring a goal.* **2** to move very quickly and suddenly: + **up/out of** etc *Ben leapt up to answer the phone.* **3** to do something **leap at the opportunity/chance** to accept an opportunity very eagerly

leap² n [C] **1** a big jump **2** a large increase in number or amount: *a leap in oil prices*

leap·frog /'li:pfrɒgll-frɔːg, -frɑːg/ n [U] a children's game in which someone bends over and someone else jumps over them — **leapfrog** v [I,T]

leapfrog

leap year /'. ./ n [C] a year when February has 29 days instead of 28

learn /lɜːnll lɜːrn/ v **learned** or **learnt** /lɜːntll lɜːrnt/ *BrE*, **learned** or **learnt** *BrE*, **learning, learns 1** [I,T] to get knowledge of a subject or skill by studying or doing it: *Lisa's learning Spanish.* | **learn (how) to do** sth *I learned to drive when I was 18.* **2** [I,T] *formal* to find out information or news by hearing it from someone else: + **about** *We only learned about the accident later.* | + **(that)** *I was surprised to learn that Jack's left college.* **3** [I,T] to realize that something is important, and change the way you behave because of this: *She'll have to learn that she can't always get what she wants.* **4** [T] to get to know something so well that you can easily remember it: *Have you learned your lines for the play?* — **learner** n [C] *a slow learner*

USAGE NOTE: learn, teach, study

Learn means to study or practise something so that you know more about it or know how to do it: *She's learning to drive.* | *They're learning about the French Revolution.* **Teach** means to explain to someone how to do something or tell them more about something, especially over a period of time: *Who taught you to dance like that?* | *It's important to teach children about their history.* **Study** means to learn about something by reading books and going to classes at school, college etc: *She's studying English at London University.* | *John studies for three hours each night.*

---

learn·ed /'lɜːnɪ̩dll'lɜːr-/ adj *formal* having a lot of knowledge because you have read and studied a lot

learn·ing /'lɜːnɪŋll'lɜːr-/ n [U] knowledge that you get by reading and studying

learnt /lɜːnt‖lɜːrnt/ *v* the past tense and past participle of LEARN

lease /liːs/ *n* [C] a legal agreement in which you pay rent in order to use a building for a period of time: *a two-year lease on the apartment* —**lease** *v* [T]

leash /liːʃ/ *n* [C] a piece of rope or leather fastened to a dog's collar in order to control it

least¹ /liːst/ *adv* **1 at least a)** not less than a particular number or amount: *At least 150 people were killed in the earthquake.* **b)** *spoken* used to talk about something that shows a situation is not as bad as it could be: *Well, at least you got your money back.* **c)** *spoken* used before correcting or changing something that you have just said: *He's gone home, at least I think he has.* **d)** *spoken* used to tell someone that they should do something, even if they do not do anything else: *Will you at least say you're sorry?* **2** less than anything or anyone else: *She chose the least expensive ring.* | *the thing I least expected to happen* | **least of all** (=especially not): *I don't like any of them, least of all Debbie.* **3 not in the least/ not the least** not at all or none at all: *I wasn't in the least worried.* **4 to say the least** used to show that something is more serious than you are actually saying: *Mrs Lim was upset, to say the least.*

least² *quantifier* the smallest number or amount: *I get paid the least.* | *Even the least amount can kill you.*

leath·er /ˈleðə‖-ər/ *n* [U] animal skin used for making shoes, bags etc: *a leather belt*

leave¹ /liːv/ *v* **left** /left/, **left, leaving 1** [I,T] to go away from a place or person: *What time did you leave the office?* | *She left him watching the television.* **2** [I,T] to stop doing a job, going to a school, or being a member of an organization: *She left her job in order to have a baby.* **3** [I,T] to stop living somewhere and move to another place: *Nick doesn't want to leave California.* **4** [I,T] to end your relationship with your husband, a girlfriend etc: *His wife left him and he started drinking heavily.* | **+ for** *We're leaving for Paris tomorrow.* **5** [T] to put something somewhere: *Just leave those letters on my desk, please.* **6** [T] to let something stay in a particular state or condition: *Can we leave the dishes for later?* **7** [T] if you leave food or drink, you do not eat or drink all of it, often because you do not like it **8** [T] also **leave behind** to forget to take something with you when you leave a place: **leave sth on/at etc** *Oh no, I think I've left my keys in the front door.* **9 be left (over)** to remain after everything else has been taken away or used: *Is there any coffee left?* **10 leave sb alone** to stop annoying or upsetting someone: *Just go away and leave me alone.* **11 leave sth alone** *spoken* to stop touching something: *Leave that watch alone – you'll break it!* **12 leave sth to sb** to let someone decide something or be responsible for something: *I've always left financial decisions to my wife.* **13** [T] to give something to someone after you die: **leave sb sth** *My aunt left me this ring.*

leave sth behind *phr v* [T] to forget to take something with you when you leave a place

leave off *phr v* [I,T] *informal* to stop doing something: *Let's start from where we left off yesterday.*

leave sb/sth ↔ out *phr v* [T] to not include someone or something in a group, list, or activity: *She was upset about being left out of the team.*

leave² *n* [U] time that you are allowed to spend away from your job: *soldiers on leave* | **sick/ maternity leave** (=time away from work because you are ill or have had a baby)

leaves /liːvz/ *n* the plural of LEAF

lech·er·ous /ˈletʃərəs/ *adj* a lecherous man behaves towards women in a way that shows he is interested only in sex —**lechery** *n* [U] —**lecher** *n* [C]

lec·tern /ˈlektən‖-ərn/ *n* [C] a high desk that you stand behind when you make a speech

lec·ture¹ /ˈlektʃə‖-ər/ *n* [C] **1** a talk to a group of people about a subject: **+ on** *a lecture on Islamic art* | **give a lecture** *Dr. Hill gave a brilliant lecture.* **2** a long serious talk that criticizes someone or warns them about something: **+ on/ about** *I'm sick of Dad's lectures about my clothes.*

lecture² *v* **1** [T] to talk angrily to someone for a long time, especially in a way that is annoying or unfair: **lecture sb about sth** *They're always lecturing me about smoking.* **2** [I] to teach a group of people about a subject, especially at a college —**lecturer** *n* [C] *a history lecturer*

led /led/ *v* the past tense and past participle of LEAD

ledge /ledʒ/ *n* [C] a narrow flat surface like a shelf that sticks out from the side of a building or of a mountain

led·ger /ˈledʒə‖-ər/ *n* [C] a book in which the financial records of a company are kept

leech /liːtʃ/ *n* [C] a small soft creature that sticks to an animal's skin in order to drink its blood

leek /liːk/ *n* [C] a vegetable with long straight green leaves, that tastes like an onion → see picture at VEGETABLES

leer /lɪə‖lɪr/ *v* [I] to look at someone in an unpleasant way that shows you think they are sexually attractive —**leer** *n* [C]

lee·way /ˈliːweɪ/ *n* [U] freedom to do what you want: *Parents should give their children a certain amount of leeway.*

left¹ /left/ *adj* [only before noun] **1** on the side of your body that contains your heart: *Jim's broken his left leg.* **2** in the direction that is opposite to the right: *Take a left turn at the lights.*

left² *adv* towards the left side: *Turn left at the church.* → opposite RIGHT²

left³ *n* **1** [singular] the left side or direction: **on the/your left** *It's the second door on your left.* **2 the Left** political parties or groups that believe that wealth should be shared out more

L

Mark lent Julie £10. Julie borrowed £10 from Mark.   Julie paid Mark back the following week.

equally, for example Socialists → opposite RIGHT[3]

left[4] *v* the past tense and past participle of LEAVE

left-hand /ˌ. ˈ.◂/ *adj* [only before noun] on the left side of something: *the top left-hand drawer*

left-hand·ed /ˌ. ˈ..◂/ *adj* someone who is left-handed uses their left hand to do most things

left·o·vers /ˈleftəʊvəz‖-oʊvərz/ *n* [plural] food that has not been eaten during a meal

left wing /ˌ. ˈ./ *n* [singular] the group of people within a larger group whose ideas are more left-wing than those of everyone else

left-wing /ˌ. ˈ.◂/ *adj* supporting the political ideas of groups such as Socialists and Communists: *a left-wing newspaper* —**left-winger** *n* [C]

leg /leg/ *n* **1** [C] one of the two long parts of your body that you use for walking and standing, or a similar part on an animal: *She broke her leg skiing last year.* | *a boy with long skinny legs* **2** [C] one of the parts that support a table, chair etc **3** [C] the part of your trousers that covers your leg **4** [C] one of the parts of a long journey, a competition etc: *the second leg of the World Championship* **5 not have a leg to stand on** *informal* to be unable to prove that a statement you have made is true or right: *If you don't sign a contract, you won't have a leg to stand on.*

leg·a·cy /ˈlegəsi/ *n* [C] **1** a situation, especially a bad one, that exists as a result of things that happened before: *the legacy of the Vietnam war* **2** money or property that you receive from someone after they die

le·gal /ˈliːgəl/ *adj* **1** allowed or done according to the law: *a legal agreement* → opposite ILLEGAL **2** relating to the law: *the legal system* | **take legal action** (=when you ask a court to punish someone or force someone to do something) —**legally** *adv* —**legality** /lɪˈgælɪti/ *n* [U]

war. | *Her illness was a legitimate reason for being absent from work.*

le·gal·ize (also **-ise** *BrE*) /ˈliːgəlaɪz/ *v* [T] to change the law so that something is allowed: *a campaign to legalize cannabis* —**legalization** /ˌliːgəlaɪˈzeɪʃən‖-lə-/ *n* [U]

le·gend /ˈledʒənd/ *n* **1** [C,U] an old well-known story, often about brave people and their actions and adventures: *the legend of King Arthur* | *a figure from ancient legend* **2** [C] someone who is famous and admired for being very good at something: *rock'n'roll legend Buddy Holly*

le·gen·da·ry /ˈledʒəndəri‖-deri/ *adj* **1** very famous and admired: *the legendary baseball player Babe Ruth* **2** appearing in legends

leg·gings /ˈlegɪŋz/ *n* [plural] a piece of women's clothing that fits tightly around the legs: *She was wearing leggings and a baggy T-shirt.* → see colour picture on page 113

leg·gy /ˈlegi/ *adj* having long legs

le·gi·ble /ˈledʒɪbəl/ *adj* written clearly enough to be read: *His writing was barely legible.* —**legibly** *adv* → opposite ILLEGIBLE

le·gion /ˈliːdʒən/ *n* [C] a very large group of soldiers

le·gis·late /ˈledʒɪsleɪt/ *v* [I] to make a law about something: **+ against/for/on** *The government has no plans to legislate against smoking in public.* —**legislator** *n* [C]

le·gis·la·tion /ˌledʒɪsˈleɪʃən/ *n* [U] a law or set of laws: *European legislation on human rights*

le·gis·la·tive /ˈledʒɪslətɪv‖-leɪtɪv/ *adj* relating to laws or to making laws: *legislative powers*

le·gis·la·ture /ˈledʒɪsleɪtʃə, -lətʃ‖-ər/ *n* [C] a group of people that has the power to make laws: *the Ohio state legislature*

le·git·i·mate /lɪˈdʒɪtəmət/ *adj* **1** not illegal: *legitimate business activities* **2** fair and reasonable: *a legitimate question* —**legitimacy** *n* [U]

lei·sure /ˈleʒə‖ˈliːʒər/ *n* **1** [U] time when you are not working and can do things you enjoy: *leisure activities such as sailing and swimming* **2 at your leisure** as slowly as you want or when you want: *Read it at your leisure.*

leisure cen·tre /ˈ.. ˌ../ *n* [C] *BrE* a place where you can do sports, exercise classes etc

lei·sure·ly /ˈleʒəli‖ˈliːʒərli/ *adj* doing something in a relaxed way you do not have to hurry: *a leisurely walk around the park*

lem·on /'lemən/ *n* [C,U] a yellow fruit that tastes sour ➙ see colour picture on page 439

lem·on·ade /ˌleməˈneɪd/ *n* [U] **1** *BrE* a sweet colourless drink with a lot of BUBBLES **2** a drink made with lemon juice, sugar, and water

lend /lend/ *v* **lent** /lent/, **lent, lending 1** [T] to let someone borrow something that you own, which they will give back to you later: **lend sb sth** *Could you lend me £10?* | **lend sth to sb** *I've lent my bike to Tom.* **2** [I,T] if a bank lends money, it allows someone borrow it if they then pay it back with an additional amount of money **3** [T] *formal* to give something a particular quality: *The Prime Minister's presence lent a degree of importance to the occasion.* —**lender** *n* [C] —**lending** *n* [U]

USAGE NOTE: lend, borrow, and loan

Lend means to let someone use something of yours that they will give back later: *I can lend you a pen if you don't have one.* **Borrow** means to use something that belongs to someone else, which you will give back later: *Could I borrow your pen for a minute?* You can **lend** or **borrow** money, but an amount of money that you borrow from a bank is a **loan** [noun]: *a bank loan of £3,000.* In American English, the verb **loan** is often used informally instead of **lend**: *Could you loan me your pen?* This should be avoided in formal or written English, however.

---

length /leŋθ/ *n* **1** [C,U] how long something is from one end to another: *What's the length of the room?* | **in length** *The whale measured three metres in length.* ➙ see picture at HEIGHT **2** [C,U] the amount of time that something continues for: *I'm writing to complain about the length of time it's taken them to do the survey.* **3** **go to any/great lengths to do sth** to do everything you can to achieve something, or try very hard to do something: *She went to great lengths to help us.* **4** **at length a)** for a long time: *He spoke at length about the time he spent in Beirut.* **b)** *literary* after a long pause or period of time: *At length, Anna spoke: "What's your name?"* **5** [C] a piece of something that is long and thin: *two lengths of rope*

length·en /'leŋθən/ *v* [I,T] to become longer or make something longer: *The days lengthened as summer approached.*

length·ways /'leŋθweɪz/ also **length·wise** /-waɪz/ *adv* in the direction of the longest side: *Fold the cloth lengthwise.*

length·y /'leŋθi/ *adj* continuing for a long time: *a lengthy process*

le·ni·ent /'li:niənt/ *adj* not strict in the way you punish or deal with someone: *The judge was criticized for being too lenient.* —**leniency** *n* [U]

lens /lenz/ *n* [C] **1** a piece of curved glass or plastic that makes things look bigger or smaller: *glasses with thick lenses* ➙ see picture at GLASSES **2** the clear part inside your eye that helps you to see properly

lent /lent/ *v* the past tense and past participle of LEND

Lent *n* [U] the 40 days before Easter, when some Christians stop eating particular foods or doing other things which they enjoy

len·til /'lentl, -tɪl/ *n* [C usually plural] a small round seed which is dried and then cooked before being eaten

Le·o /'li:əʊ||'li:oʊ/ *n* [C,U] the sign of the Zodiac of people who are born between July 23rd and August 22nd, or someone who belongs to this sign

leop·ard /'lepəd||-ərd/ *n* [C] a large wild cat with yellow fur and black spots

le·o·tard /'li:ətɑːd||-ɑːrd/ *n* [C] a piece of women's clothing like a SWIMSUIT, used for dancing or exercising

lep·er /'lepə||-ər/ *n* [C] someone who has leprosy

lep·ro·sy /'leprəsi/ *n* [U] a serious infectious disease in which the flesh is gradually destroyed

les·bi·an /'lezbiən/ *n* [C] a woman who is sexually attracted to other women —**lesbian** *adj*

less[1] /les/ *adv* [comparative of **little**] **1** not so much, or to a smaller degree: *I definitely walk less since I've had the car.* ➙ opposite MORE[1] **2** **less and less** gradually becoming smaller in amount or degree: *Our trips became less and less frequent.*

USAGE NOTE: less

In informal English many people now use **less** and **least** with plural nouns, but this is still considered to be incorrect. **Fewer** and **fewest** are the generally accepted correct forms: *There were fewer people there than I expected.* | *Who has made the fewest mistakes?*

---

less[2] *quantifier* [comparative of **little**] **1** a smaller amount: *Most single parents earn £100 a week or less.* | **+ than** *I live less than a mile from here.* | **+ of** *She spends less of her time abroad now.* **2** **no less than** *spoken* used to emphasize that a number is surprisingly large: *It took no less than nine policemen to hold him down.*

USAGE NOTE: less and fewer

Use **less** before an uncountable noun: *You get more food for less money at Shop 'n' Save.* Use **fewer** before a countable noun: *Fewer students are studying science these days.*

---

less·en /'lesən/ *v* [I,T] to become less, or to make something become less: *A glass of wine a day can help lessen the risk of heart disease.* —**lessening** *n* [U]

less·er /'lesə||-ər/ *adj* [only before noun] **1** *formal* not as large or important as something else: *a lesser sum* **2** **the lesser of two evils** the less unpleasant or harmful of two bad choices **3** **lesser known** not as well known as others: *a lesser known French poet*

les·son /'lesən/ *n* [C] a period of time in which someone is taught a subject or skill: **take lessons** *Hannah is taking guitar lessons.*

let /let/ *v* [T] **let, let, letting 1** to give someone permission to do something: *I'll come if my dad lets me.* | **let sb do sth** *"Let him speak," said Ralph.* | **let sb go** (=to give permission for someone to leave a place) **2** to allow something to happen: *She let the handkerchief fall to the ground.* | *Let me through, I'm a doctor!* **3** **let's** *spoken* used to suggest to someone that you should do something together: *I'm hungry – let's*

L

eat. **4 let's see** *spoken* used when you are trying to remember or find something: *Now let's see, where did I put it?* **5 let go** to stop holding something: + **of** *"Let go of me!" Ben shouted.* **6 let sb know** to tell someone something: *Let me know when you're ready.* **7 let me do sth** *spoken* used when you are offering to help someone: *Let me carry that for you.* **8** to allow someone to use a room or building in return for money: *We're letting our spare room to a student.* **9 let alone** used to say that one thing is not true or does not happen, so another thing cannot possibly be true or happen: *Davey can't even crawl yet, let alone walk!* **10 let sth go/pass/ride** to not react to something annoying that someone has said or done: *We'll let it go this time, but don't be late again.* **11 let fly** to suddenly start shouting at someone or hitting them, especially because you feel angry

---

USAGE NOTE: let us

1 **Let us** is usually shortened to **let's** when it is used in conversation to make a suggestion that includes the person you are speaking to: *Come on, Jim, let's go and have lunch.* | *Let's have a party at the end of term.* 2 **Let's** can be used by itself to show that you agree with someone else's suggestion: *"Shall we go to the cinema tonight?" "Oh, yes, let's!"* 3 The negative of **let's** is **let's not:** *Let's not waste any more time on this.* (In British English **don't let's** is also possible.)

---

let sb **down** *phr v* [T] to disappoint someone, especially by not doing what you promised: *You won't let me down, will you?* → see also LETDOWN

let sb **in/into** *phr v* [T] to allow someone to enter a building or room

let sb **in on** sth *phr v* [T] to tell someone a secret

let sb **off** *phr v* [T] to not punish someone or not make them do something that they should have done: *I'll let you off this time, but don't do it again.*

let on *phr v* [I] to show that you know a secret: + **(that)** *I won't let on I know anything about it.*

let out *phr v* **1** [T **let** sb **out**] to allow someone to leave a building or room **2 let out a scream/cry etc** to make a sound, especially a loud one: *Suddenly, Ben let out a yell and jumped up.*

let up *phr v* [I] if rain or snow lets up, it stops or there is less of it → see also LETUP

let·down /'letdaʊn/ *n* [singular] *informal* something that disappoints you because it is not as good as you expected: *That movie was a real letdown.*

le·thal /'liːθəl/ *adj* something that is lethal can kill you: *a lethal dose of heroin*

le·thar·gic /lɪˈθɑːdʒɪk‖-ˈθɑːr-/ *adj* having no energy, so that you feel lazy or tired — **lethargy** /'leθədʒi‖-ər-/ *n* [U]

let's /lets/ the short form of 'let us'

let·ter /'letəl-ər/ *n* **1** [C] a written message that you put into an envelope and send to someone: *Could you post this letter for me?* **2** [C] one of the signs in writing that is used to mean a sound in speech: *the letter A* **3 do sth to the letter** to do exactly what you are told to do: *He followed their instructions to the letter.*

let·ter·box /'letəbɒks‖'letərbɑːks/ *n* [C] *BrE* **1** a hole in a door through which letters are delivered → see colour picture on page 79 **2** a box in a post office or in the street, where you post letters; MAILBOX *AmE*

let·tuce /'letɪs/ *n* [C,U] a round green SALAD vegetable with large thin leaves → see picture at VEGETABLES

let·up /'letʌp/ *n* [singular, U] a pause or reduction in a difficult or unpleasant activity: *There has been no letup in the fighting.*

leu·ke·mi·a also **leukaemia** *BrE* /luːˈkiːmiə/ *n* [U] a form of CANCER that affects the blood

lev·el[1] /'levəl/ *n* [C] **1** an amount, degree, or number of something: *A low fat diet will help cut your cholesterol level.* | *high levels of pollution* **2** the height or position of something in relation to the ground or another thing: *Check the water level in the radiator.* | **at eye level** (=at the same height as your eyes) **3** a standard of skill in a subject, sport etc: *an advanced level coursebook* **4** a position in a system that has different ranks: *lower level managers* **5** a floor in a building that has several floors: *Her office is on Level 3.*

level[2] *adj* **1** flat, with no part of the surface higher than the rest: *The floor must be completely level before you lay the tiles.* **2** at the same height or position as something else: + **with** *He bent down so that his face was level with the little boy's.*

level[3] *v* **-lled, -lling** *BrE* **-led, -ling** *AmE* **1** also **level off/out** [T] to make a surface flat **2** [T] to knock something down to the ground and destroy it: *An earthquake leveled several buildings in the city.* **3 level criticism/charges against sb** to say that you think someone has done something wrong

level off/out *phr v* [I] **1** to stop rising or falling, and continue at the same height or amount: *The plane began to level off at 30,000 feet.* **2** [T **level** sth ↔ **off/out**] to make a surface flat and smooth

level with sb *phr v* [T] *informal* to tell someone the truth or what you really think

level cross·ing /ˌ.. ˈ../ *n* [C] *BrE* a place where a road and railway cross; GRADE CROSSING *AmE* → see colour picture on page 669

level-head·ed /ˌ.. ˈ..◂/ *adj* calm and sensible

le·ver /'liːvəl'levər, 'liː-/ *n* [C] **1** a bar that you use to lift something heavy by putting one end under it and pushing the other end down **2** a stick or handle on a machine that you move to make the machine work — **lever** *v* [T]

le·ver·age /'liːvərɪdʒ‖'le-, 'liː-/ *n* [U] **1** influence that you have to make people do what you want: *Small businesses have less leverage when dealing with banks.* **2** the action, use, or power of a lever

lev·i·tate /'levɪteɪt/ *v* [I] to rise and float in the air as if by magic — **levitation** /ˌlevɪˈteɪʃən/ *n* [U]

lev·y[1] /'levi/ *v* **levy a tax/charge etc** to officially make someone pay a tax etc: + **on** *a tax levied on electrical goods*

levy[2] *n* [C] an amount of money, usually a tax, that you must pay

lewd /luːd/ *adj* using rude words or movements that make someone think of sex: *lewd comments*

lex·i·cal /ˈleksɪkəl/ *adj* relating to words

lex·i·con /ˈleksɪkənǁ-kɑːn, -kən/ *n* [singular] the words used in a language, or in a particular type of language

li·a·bil·i·ty /ˌlaɪəˈbɪlɪ̣ti/ *n* **1** [C,U] legal responsibility for something, especially for injury, damage, or a debt: + **for** *NorCo has admitted liability for the accident.* **2** [singular] something that causes serious problems or is likely to be dangerous: *That car of yours is a liability!*

li·a·ble /ˈlaɪəbəl/ *adj* **1** **be liable to do sth** to be likely to do something: *The car's liable to overheat on long trips.* **2** legally responsible for the cost of something

li·aise /liˈeɪz/ *v* [I] to exchange information, so that everyone involved in a job or activity knows what is happening: + **with** *Part of a librarian's job is to liaise with local schools.*

li·ai·son /liˈeɪzənǁˈliːəzɑːn, liˈeɪ-/ *n* [singular, U] the way two groups of people work together: + **between** *close liaison between the army and police*

li·ar /ˈlaɪəǁ-ər/ *n* [C] someone who tells lies

li·bel /ˈlaɪbəl/ *n* [C,U] the illegal action of writing or printing bad and untrue things about someone: *He is suing the magazine for libel.* —**libel** *v* [T] —**libellous** *BrE*, **libelous** *AmE adj* → compare SLANDER

lib·e·ral¹ /ˈlɪbərəl/ *adj* **1** willing to understand or respect other people's ideas and behaviour: *a liberal attitude towards sex* **2** supporting changes in political, social, or religious systems that give people more freedom **3** giving or using a lot of something: *Don't be too liberal with the salt.*

liberal² *n* [C] someone with liberal opinions or principles

lib·e·ral·ize (also **-ise** *BrE*) /ˈlɪbərəlaɪz/ *v* [T] to make a system, law, or moral attitude less strict —**liberalization** /ˌlɪbərəlaɪˈzeɪʃənǁ-lə-/ *n* [U]

lib·e·ral·ly /ˈlɪbərəli/ *adv* generously or in large amounts

lib·e·rate /ˈlɪbəreɪt/ *v* [T] **1** to free someone from a situation that makes their life difficult: *For the first time, she was liberated from her parents' strict rules.* **2** to free a place and the people in it from political or military control: *The city was liberated by the Allies in 1944.* —**liberating** *adj*: *a very liberating experience* —**liberator** *n* [C] —**liberation** /ˌlɪbəˈreɪʃən/ *n* [U]

lib·e·rat·ed /ˈlɪbəreɪtɪ̣d/ *adj* free to do the things you want, and not controlled by rules or other people

lib·er·ty /ˈlɪbətiǁ-ər-/ *n* **1** [C,U] when people have the same political and social rights as others, for example the right to vote or criticize the government: *principles of liberty and democracy* **2** [U] *formal* when someone is no longer being forced to stay somewhere or do something they do not want to do **3** **be at liberty to do sth** to have permission to do something: *I'm not at liberty to say where he is.* **4** **take the liberty of doing sth** to do something without asking permission, because you do not think it will upset anyone: *I took the liberty of helping myself to a drink.*

li·bi·do /lɪˈbiːdəʊǁ-doʊ/ *n* [C,U] sexual desire

Li·bra /ˈliːbrə/ *n* [C,U] the sign of the Zodiac of people who are born between September 23rd and October 23rd, or someone who belongs to this sign

li·brar·i·an /laɪˈbreəriənǁ-ˈbrer-/ *n* [C] someone who works in a library

li·bra·ry /ˈlaɪbrəri, -briǁ-breri/ *n* [C] a room or building containing books that you can read there or borrow: *a library book*

lice /laɪs/ *n* the plural of LOUSE

li·cence *BrE*, **license** *AmE* /ˈlaɪsəns/ *n* [C] **1** an official document that gives you permission to do something: *a licence to sell alcohol* **2** [U] *formal* freedom to do or say whatever you want

li·cense /ˈlaɪsəns/ *v* [T] to give official permission for someone to do something: **be licensed to do sth** *He is licensed to carry a gun.*

license plate /ˈ.. ./ *n* [C] *AmE* a sign with numbers and letters on it at the front and back of a car; NUMBER PLATE *BrE* → see picture at CAR

li·chen /ˈlaɪkən, ˈlɪtʃən/ *n* [C,U] a very small grey, green, or yellow plant that spreads over the surface of trees and stones

lick¹ /lɪk/ *v* [T] to move your tongue across the surface of something: *Judy's dog jumped up to lick her face.*

lick

lick² *n* **1** [C usually singular] an act of licking something: *Can I have a lick of your ice cream?* **2** a **lick of paint** *informal* a small amount of paint

lic·o·rice /ˈlɪkərɪs, -rɪʃ/ *n* [U] the American spelling of LIQUORICE

lid /lɪd/ *n* [C] a cover for a pot, box, or other container: *Where's the lid for this jar?*

lie¹ /laɪ/ *v* [I] **lay** /leɪ/, **lain** /leɪn/, **lying 1 a)** to be in a position in which your body is flat on the floor, a bed etc: + **on/in** *We lay on the beach all morning.* **b)** also **lie down** to put yourself in this position: *I'm going upstairs to lie down.* **2** to be in a particular place or position: *The town lies to the east of the lake.* | + **on/in/ below etc** *A pile of letters was lying on the doormat.* **3** if an idea or a problem lies in something, that is what causes it or is involved in it: + **in/with/between etc** *The fault appears to lie with the computer system.* **4** to remain in a particular condition or state: *A book lay open on her desk.* **5** **lie low** to remain hidden because someone is trying to find you **6** **lie ahead** to be going to happen in the future **7** **lie in wait (for sb/sth)** to remain hidden in order to attack someone or something

---

GRAMMAR NOTE: countable and uncountable (2)
Some nouns can be **countable** or **uncountable**. For example: **chicken** *n* [C,U].
● Countable: *A fox had killed some of the chickens.* (=birds)
● Uncountable: *chicken cooked in red wine* (=meat)

lie around also **lie about** BrE phr v **1** [I,T **lie around/about** sth] to be left in the wrong place, in an untidy way: *I wish you'd stop leaving your clothes lying around.* **2** to spend time relaxing, especially by lying down: *We just lay around on the beach the whole time.*

lie behind sth phr v [T] to be the true reason for an action: *I wonder what really lay behind her decision.*

lie down phr v **1** [I] to put yourself in a position in which your body is flat on the floor, a bed etc **2** **not take sth lying down** informal to refuse to accept bad treatment without complaining

lie in phr v [I] BrE to stay in bed longer than usual in the morning

lie² v [I] **lied, lied, lying** to tell someone something that you know is not true: + **to** *I would never lie to you.*

lie³ n [C] something that you say or write that you know is not true: **tell a lie** *I always know when she's telling lies.*

lie-down /'. ./ n [singular] BrE a short rest: *Why don't you have a lie-down?*

lie-in /'. ., . './ n [singular] BrE when you stay in bed longer than usual in the morning: *I usually have a lie-in on Sunday morning.*

lieu /lju:, lu:ǁlu:/ n **in lieu (of)** instead of: *time off in lieu of payment*

lieu·ten·ant /lef'tenəntǁlu:'ten-/ n [C] an officer who has a middle rank in the army, navy, or AIR FORCE

life /laɪf/ n, plural **lives** /laɪvz/ **1** [C,U] the period between someone's birth and death: *the happiest day of my life* | *He spent the rest of his life in France.* **2** [C,U] the state of being alive: *a baby's first moments of life* | *Wear a seatbelt – it could save your life.* **3** [C,U] all the experiences and activities that are typical of a particular way of living: *Life in New York is exciting.* | *family life* | *the American way of life* **4** **private/social/sex life** activities in your life that are private, done with friends, concerned with sex etc: *an active social life* **5** **way of life** the way someone chooses to live their life: *a traditional way of life* | *the American way of life* **6** [U] living things such as people, animals, or plants: *Is there life on other planets?* | *studying the island's plant life* **7** [U] activity or movement: *four years old and just so full of life* | *There were no signs of life in the house.* **8** **(in) real life** what really happens, rather than what happens in stories or in your imagination **9** [singular] the period of time that something continues to work or exist: *What's the average life of a family car?* **10** **that's life** spoken used when something bad has happened that you must accept **11** **bring sth to life/come to life** to make something more exciting, or to become more exciting: *The game really came to life in the second half.* **12** **not on your life!** spoken used to say that you will definitely not do something **13** [U] also **life imprisonment** when someone is put in prison for the rest of their life

life belt /'. ./ n [C] BrE a life buoy

life·boat /'laɪfbəʊtǁ-bəʊt/ n [C] a boat that is used to help people who are in danger at sea

life buoy /'. .ǁ'. ,.., '. ./ n [C] a large ring that you can throw to someone who is in danger in water, so that they will float

life ex·pec·tan·cy /,. .'...,/ n [C,U] the length of time that someone is likely to live

life guard /'. ./ n [C] someone whose job is to help swimmers who are in danger at the beach or a swimming pool

life in·sur·ance /'. .,./ n [U] a type of insurance that someone buys so that when they die their family will receive money

life jack·et /'. ,../ n [C] a piece of clothing that you wear around your chest so that you float if you fall into water

life·less /'laɪfləs/ adj **1** dead or seeming to be dead **2** lacking interest, excitement, or activity: *a lifeless performance*

life·like /'laɪflaɪk/ adj very much like a real person or thing: *a very lifelike statue*

life·line /'laɪflaɪn/ n [C] something that someone depends on completely: *The phone is her lifeline.*

life·long /'laɪflɒŋǁ-lɒːŋ/ adj [only before noun] continuing all through your life: *a lifelong friend*

life·sav·er /'laɪf,seɪvəǁ-ər/ n [C] someone or something that helps you in a very important way

life-size /'. ./ adj a life-size picture or STATUE is the same size as the thing or person that it is made to look like

life·style /'laɪfstaɪl/ n [C,U] the way that someone lives, including their work and activities, and what things they own: *Starting a family causes a major change in your lifestyle.*

life sup·port sys·tem /'. .. ,../ n [C] medical equipment that keeps someone alive when they are extremely ill

life-threat·en·ing /'. ,.../ adj a life-threatening illness can kill you

life·time /'laɪftaɪm/ n [C usually singular] the period of time during which someone is alive

life vest /'. ./ n [C] AmE a LIFE JACKET

lift¹ /lɪft/ v **1** [T] to move something or someone to a higher position: *Can you help me lift this box?* | *He lifted his hand to wave.* → see colour picture on page 670 **2** [T] to remove a rule or law that prevents someone from doing something: *The US has lifted trade restrictions with the country.* **3** [I] if cloud or MIST lifts, it disappears **4** [T] informal to steal something **5** **not lift a finger** informal to do nothing to help

lift off phr v [I] if a space vehicle lifts off, it leaves the ground and goes up into the air

lift² n **1** [C] BrE a machine that takes you up and down between floors in a building; ELEVATOR AmE **2** BrE [singular] a ride in a car; RIDE AmE: *Could anybody give Sue a lift home?* **3** [C] a movement in which something is lifted **4** **give sb a lift** to make someone more cheerful or confident

lift-off /'. ./ n [C,U] the moment when a space vehicle leaves the ground

lig·a·ment /'lɪgəmənt/ n [C] a band of strong material in your body that joins your bones together

light¹ /laɪt/ n **1** [U] the energy from the sun, a lamp etc that allows you to see things: *Light poured in through the window.* | *The light in here isn't very good.* **2** [C] something such as a lamp that produces light: *Can you turn the light on, please?* **3** [C usually plural] one of a set of red, green, and yellow lights that are used to control traffic: *Turn left at the lights.* **4 a light** a flame that starts a cigarette burning: *Excuse me, do you have a light ?* **5 bring sth to light/come to light** to make something known, or to become known: *New information about the case has come to light.* **6 in the light of sth** *BrE* **in light of sth** *AmE* after considering something: *In light of the low profits, we will have to make budget cuts.* **7 see sth in a new/different light** to understand something in a new or different way **8 shed/throw/cast light on sth** to provide new information about something so that it is easier to understand **9 a light at the end of the tunnel** something that gives you hope that a bad situation will end soon **10 see the light** to finally realize or understand something

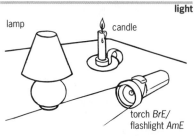

light

lamp

candle

torch *BrE*/
flashlight *AmE*

light² *adj* **1** pale and not dark: *a light blue dress* → opposite DARK¹ **2** not weighing much or weighing less than usual: *Your bag's lighter than mine.* → opposite HEAVY **3** not having much force or power: *a light wind* | *a light tap on the door* **4** thin and not very warm: *a light sweater* **5** a room that is light has plenty of light from the sun in it: *a light and airy studio* **6** food or drink that is light does not make you feel too full: *a light white wine* **7** not serious: *a light comedy on TV* **8 it is light** used to say that there is enough light to see by: *It was still light when we got home.* **9** small in amount or less than usual: *Traffic is much lighter on Sundays.* **10 light sleep** sleep from which you wake up easily **11 make light of sth** to joke about something or treat it as if it were not important

light³ *v* lit /lɪt/ or **lighted, lit** or **lighted, lighting 1** [I,T] to start burning, or to make something start burning: *I lit another cigarette.* | *The fire won't light* | *the wood's wet.* **2** [T] to produce light in a room etc: *The room was lit by two lamps.*

light up *phr v* **1** [I,T **light** sth ↔ **up**] to become bright or make something bright: *The fireworks lit up the night sky.* **2** [I] if someone's face or eyes light up, they suddenly look happy or excited **3** [I] *informal* to light a cigarette

USAGE NOTE: lit and lighted

Use **lit** as the past participle of the verb **light**: *Dean had already lit the candles.* Use **lighted** as an adjective before a noun: *a lighted candle.*

light⁴ *adv* **travel light** to travel without taking many things with you

light bulb /ˈ. ./ *n* [C] a round glass and metal object that produces light from electricity

light·ed /ˈlaɪtɪd/ *adj* **a lighted match/ cigarette/candle etc** a match etc that is burning

light·en /ˈlaɪtn/ *v* **1** [T] to reduce the amount of work, worry, debt etc that someone has: *The new computers should lighten our work load.* **2** [I,T] to become brighter, or make something become brighter: *As the sky lightened, we could see the full extent of the damage.* **3** [T] to reduce the weight of something

light·er /ˈlaɪtər/ *n* [C] a small object that produces a flame to light a cigarette

light-head·ed /ˌ. ˈ..◂/ *adj* not able to think clearly or move steadily because you are ill or have drunk too much alcohol

light-heart·ed /ˌ. ˈ...◂/ *adj* **1** cheerful and happy **2** not intended to be serious: *a light-hearted remark*

light·house /ˈlaɪthaʊs/ *n* [C] a tower with a bright light that warns ships of danger → see colour picture on page 669

light·ing /ˈlaɪtɪŋ/ *n* [U] the lights in a place, or the quality of the light: *Better street lighting might help prevent crime.*

light·ly /ˈlaɪtli/ *adv* **1** without using much force; GENTLY: *He touched her lightly on the shoulder.* **2** in small light amounts: *Sprinkle sugar lightly over the cake.* **3 not do sth lightly** to think very carefully and seriously about something before deciding to do it: *We did not make this decision lightly.* **4 escape lightly/get off lightly** to not be harmed or punished as much as you could have been

light·ning¹ /ˈlaɪtnɪŋ/ *n* [U] a bright flash of electrical light in the sky during a storm: *Several trees were struck (=hit) by lightning.*

lightning² *adj* extremely fast or sudden: *a lightning attack*

light·weight /ˈlaɪt-weɪt/ *adj* weighing very little: *a lightweight jacket*

lik·a·ble /ˈlaɪkəbəl/ LIKEABLE

like¹ /laɪk/ *prep* **1** similar to someone or something else: *His skin was brown and wrinkled, like leather.* | *Stop behaving like an idiot!* | *I'd love to have a car like yours.* | **look/ sound/feel etc like** *The building looked like a church.* → opposite UNLIKE **2** typical of a person or thing: *It's not like Dad to be late.* → opposite UNLIKE **3 what is sb/sth like?** used to ask someone to describe a person, place, or thing: *What's the new house like?* **4** such as: *Foods like spinach and broccoli contain a lot of iron.* **5 like this/that/so** *spoken* used to show someone the way in which something is or was done: *She had her arms around his neck, like this.* **6 something like** *spoken* not much more or less than a particular amount: *Seats cost something like $50 each.* **7 more like** *spoken* used to give a more correct figure or description than the one that has just been mentioned: *"He's been in there for 15 minutes!" "More like half an hour."*

like² *v* **1** [T] to enjoy something, or to think that someone or something is nice: *Do you like your job?* | *He likes Amy a lot.* | **like doing sth** *I really like swimming.* | **like to do sth** *Pam doesn't*

L

like to walk home late at night.|**like sth about sb/sth** The thing I like about Todd is that he's always cheerful. → opposite DISLIKE¹ **2** [T] to prefer that something is done in a particular way: How do you like your steak cooked?|**like (sb) to do sth** Jim likes to get to the airport early. **3 not like to do sth/not like doing sth** especially BrE not want to do something because you do not think it is fair, polite etc: I don't like disturbing her when she's busy. **4 I'd like ...** used to say what you want: I'd like a cheeseburger, please.|**I'd/he'd etc like to do sth** He'd like to know how much it will cost.|**I'd/he'd etc like sb to do sth** We'd like you to be there if you can. **5 would you like ...?** spoken used to ask someone if they want something: Would you like some more coffee?|**would you like to do sth?** Would you like to go to the cinema? **6 if you like** spoken, especially BrE **a)** used to suggest or offer something: We could watch a video this evening if you like. **b)** used to agree to something: "I'll come with you to the station." "Yes, if you like." **7 whatever/whenever/anything etc you like** spoken, especially BrE whatever, whenever etc you want: Come again whenever you like. **8 How do you like...?** spoken used to ask someone's opinion about something: "How do you like New York?" "It's great." **9 (whether you) like it or not** spoken used to say that something will happen or is true in spite of what someone wants or thinks: You're going to the dentist, like it or not!

USAGE NOTE: like

1 **Like** used on its own means 'to enjoy something or think that it is good': Do you like coffee? 2 When you are asking for something **I would like/I'd like** is more polite than **I want**: I'd like a cup of coffee please. 3 When you are offering something to someone, say **Would you like ...?**: Would you like a cup of coffee?

---

like³ n **1** sb's **likes and dislikes** the things someone likes and the things they do not like **2 and the like** and similar things: social problems such as poverty, unemployment and the like **3 the likes of** spoken used to talk about a particular type of person: He thinks he's too good for the likes of us.

like⁴ linking word spoken nonstandard **1** as if: He acted like he owned the place. **2 like I say/said** used to repeat something that you have already said: Like I said, we'll be away in August. **3** in the same way as: Do it like I told you to. **4** for example: Everything's so expensive. Like, last week I spent over £100 on shoes.

like⁵ adv spoken informal used when you pause when you are saying something: It was, like, 9 o'clock and she still wasn't home.

-like /laɪk/ suffix **cat-like/jelly-like etc** typical of or similar to a cat etc: She moved with cat-like grace.

like·a·ble also **likable** /ˈlaɪkəbəl/ adj likeable people are nice and easy to like: Greg's a very likeable chap.

like·li·hood /ˈlaɪklihʊd/ n **1** [singular, U] how likely something is to happen: **+ of/that** Even one drink can increase the likelihood of you having an accident. **2 in all likelihood** almost

certainly: The president will, in all likelihood, have to resign.

like·ly¹ /ˈlaɪkli/ adj probably true or probably going to happen: Snow showers are likely tomorrow.|**likely to do sth** She's likely to get upset if you ask her about it.|**it is likely that** It's likely that she knew the man who attacked her.

likely² adv **1** probably: I'd very likely have done the same thing as you did. **2 not likely** spoken, especially BrE used to say that you definitely will not do something: "Are you inviting Mary to the party?" "Not likely!"

like-mind·ed /ˌ. ˈ..◂/ adj **like-minded** people have similar interests and opinions

lik·en /ˈlaɪkən/ v

liken sb/sth to sb/sth phr v [T] to say that two people or things are similar: Critics likened the new theatre to a supermarket.

like·ness /ˈlaɪknɪs/ n **1** [singular, U] when someone or something is similar in appearance to someone or something else: a family likeness between the three sisters **2 a good/a remarkable/an excellent likeness of sb** a picture of someone that looks very like them

like·wise /ˈlaɪk-waɪz/ adv in the same way: The dinner was superb. Likewise, the concert.

lik·ing /ˈlaɪkɪŋ/ n **1 have a liking for sth** to like something: She has a liking for antiques. **2 take a liking to sb** to like someone you have just met **3 be to sb's liking** formal to be done in a way that someone likes or enjoys: I hope everything was to your liking, Sir. **4 too bright/strong/quiet etc for your liking** brighter, stronger etc than you like: This weather's a bit too hot for my liking.

li·lac /ˈlaɪlək/ n **1** [C,U] a small tree with pale purple or white flowers **2** [U] a pale purple colour —lilac adj

lilt /lɪlt/ n [singular] the pleasant way in which the sound of someone's voice or a tune changes

lil·y /ˈlɪli/ n [C] a plant with large white or coloured flowers

limb /lɪm/ n **1** [C] an arm or leg **2 out on a limb** alone and without help or support: By voting for Wiesner we'd gone out on a limb. **3** [C] a large branch of a tree

lim·bo /ˈlɪmbəʊ‖-boʊ/ n **be in limbo** to be in an uncertain situation because you are waiting for something: I'm in limbo until I get my examination results.

lime /laɪm/ n **1** [C,U] a bright green fruit with a sour taste, or the tree that this fruit grows on **2** [U] a white powdery substance used for making CEMENT

lime·light /ˈlaɪmlaɪt/ n **be in the limelight** to have the attention of a lot of people: Sanchez loves being in the limelight.

lim·e·rick /ˈlɪmərɪk/ n [C] a short humorous poem with five lines

lime·stone /ˈlaɪmstəʊn‖-stoʊn/ n [U] a type of rock that contains CALCIUM

lim·it¹ /ˈlɪmɪt/ n **1** [C, U] the greatest amount, number etc that is allowed or possible: a 65 mph speed limit|**to/on** There is a limit to what we can achieve in the time available.|**+ of** the limits of human endurance|**set a limit** (=say what a limit is): We need to set a limit on future wage increases. **2** [C] the border or edge of a place: **+ of** A fence marked the limit of the school fields.

3 within limits within the time, amount etc that is reasonable and acceptable: *People are free to choose, within limits, the hours that they work.* **4 off limits** if a place is off limits, you are not allowed to go there: *The beach is off limits after midnight.* **5 be over the limit** to have drunk more than the legal amount of alcohol for driving

limit[2] *v* [T] **1** to keep something within a particular point, amount, number etc: *The state tries to limit the number of children each family has.* | **limit sth to sth** *The economy will be limited to a 4% growth rate.* **2 be limited to** to exist or happen only in a particular place or at a particular time: *The damage was limited to the roof.* **3** to allow someone to have or use only a particular amount of something: **limit sb to sth** *He's been limited to one hour of TV a night.* — **limiting** *adj*

lim·i·ta·tion /ˌlɪmɪˈteɪʃən/ *n* **1** [C,U] when something is prevented from increasing to more than a particular level: **+ of/on** *the limitation of nuclear testing* **2 limitations** [plural] the limits of what someone or something is able to do: **have your limitations** *Computers have their limitations.*

lim·it·ed /ˈlɪmɪtᵻd/ *adj* not much or not many: *families living on limited incomes*

limited com·pa·ny /ˌ... ˈ.../ *n* [C] *BrE* a company whose owners only have to pay a limited amount of money if the company becomes BANK-RUPT

lim·ou·sine /ˈlɪməziːn, ˌlɪməˈziːn/ also **lim·o** /ˈlɪməʊll-moʊ/ *informal n* [C] a big expensive car, usually driven by a CHAUFFEUR

limp[1] /lɪmp/ *adj* not firm or strong: *a limp handshake* — **limply** *adv*

limp[2] *v* [I] to walk with difficulty because one leg is hurt: *He limped to the chair and sat down.* — **limp** *n* [singular] *Brody walks with a limp.*

linch·pin /ˈlɪntʃˌpɪn/ *n* **be the linchpin (of sth)** the most important person or thing on which a system or group depends: *My uncle was the linchpin of the family.*

line[1] /laɪn/ *n* **1** [C] a long thin mark on a surface, usually one that has been drawn or painted: *Draw a straight line from A to B.* | *It's forbidden to park on double yellow lines.* **2** [C] a row of people or things: **+ of** *a line of trees along the side of the road* **3** [C,U] *AmE* several people standing one behind another waiting to do something; QUEUE *BrE* **4** [C] a length of rope, string, or wire which has a particular purpose: *Could you hang the washing on the line?* | *a fishing line* **5** [C] a direction something travels in, or the imaginary path between two points in space: *Light travels in a straight line.* **6** [C] the connection between two telephones: **on the line** (=waiting to speak to someone on the telephone): *Don's on the line for you.* | **hold the line** *spoken* (=used to ask someone who is on the telephone to wait) **7** [C] *especially BrE* a track that a train travels along: *the main London to Glasgow line* **8** [C, usually plural] the shape of something

long or tall: *the long smooth lines of the train* **9** [C] a limit or border: **state/county line** (=the border between two states etc in the US) **10** [C] a way of thinking about or doing something: **along the lines of sth** (=in a particular way): *The meeting will be organized along the lines of the last one.* | **take a hard/tough line on sth** (=have a strict attitude towards something): *We take a tough line on drugs.* **11 in line** happening or behaving in the correct or expected way: **+ with** *The company's actions are in line with the state laws.* **12 be in line for sth** to be very likely to get or be given something: *He must be in line for promotion.* **13 on the line** if something such as your job is on the line, you may lose it **14 on line** connected to or using a computer system: *Most of us work on line.* **15** [C] a group of words in a poem, film, song etc: *the opening line of the song* **16** [C] a particular type of product made by a company: *a new line in sportswear* ➝ see also **somewhere along the line** (SOMEWHERE)

line[2] *v* [T] **1** to cover the inside of something with another material or substance: **be lined with sth** *The hood is lined with fur.* **2** to form rows along the edge of something: *Thousands of spectators lined the route.* | *a wide avenue lined with trees*

line up *phr v* **1** [I] to form or join a line of people: *OK class, line up by the door.* **2** [T **line sb/sth ↔ up**] to arrange people or things in a line: *The jars were lined up on the shelf.* **3** [T **line sb/sth ↔ up**] to organize an event or arrange for it to happen: *We've lined up some great guests for tonight's show.*

lin·e·ar /ˈlɪniəll-ər/ *adj* **1** consisting of lines, or in the form of a straight line: *a linear drawing* **2** a linear process is one in which one thing follows or develops from another, rather than happening at the same time

lined /laɪnd/ *adj* **1** a skirt, coat etc that is lined has a piece of material covering the inside: *a fur-lined coat* **2** lined paper has straight lines printed on it

lin·en /ˈlɪnᵻn/ *n* [U] **1** things made of cloth that you use in your home, for example sheets, TABLECLOTHS etc: *bed linen* **2** a high quality cloth like thick strong cotton

lin·er /ˈlaɪnəll-ər/ *n* [C] a large passenger ship that people travel long distances on: *a cruise liner*

lines·man /ˈlaɪnzmən/ *n* [C], *plural* **linesmen** /-mən/ someone who, in a sport, has the job of deciding whether the ball has gone out of the playing area

line-up /ˈ. ./ *n* [C usually singular] **1** the group of performers, players, or activities that will be part of an event **2** a group of people arranged in a row by the police so that a person who saw a crime can try to recognize the criminal

lin·ger /ˈlɪŋgəll-ər/ *v* [I] **1** to stay somewhere or continue something for longer than usual: *She lingered for a moment in the doorway.* | **linger**

L

over sth (=take a lot of time doing it): *They lingered over their coffee.* **2** also **linger on** if a smell, memory etc lingers, it does not disappear for a long time: *The memory of that day lingered on in her mind.*

lin·ge·rie /ˈlænʒəriː‖ˌlɑːnʒəˈreɪ, ˈlænʒəri/ *n* [U] a word meaning women's underwear, used especially by people selling or advertising it

lin·ger·ing /ˈlɪŋgərɪŋ/ *adj* continuing for a long time: *a long lingering kiss*

lin·go /ˈlɪŋgəʊ‖-goʊ/ *n informal* **1** [C usually singular] a language **2** [singular, U] the language and words used by people in a particular job or profession: *medical lingo*

lin·guist /ˈlɪŋgwɪst/ *n* [C] **1** someone who studies linguistics **2** someone who is good at languages

lin·guis·tic /lɪŋˈgwɪstɪk/ *adj* relating to language or linguistics: *a child's linguistic development*

lin·guis·tics /lɪŋˈgwɪstɪks/ *n* [U] the study of language

lin·ing /ˈlaɪnɪŋ/ *n* [C,U] a piece of material covering the inside of something such as a box, coat etc: *a jacket with a silk lining*

link¹ /lɪŋk/ *v* [T] **1** to make a connection between two or more situations, events, or people: **be linked to/with** *Lung cancer has been linked to smoking cigarettes.* **2** also **link up** to connect computers, communication systems etc so that information can be sent between them: **link sth to/with sth** *Our computers are linked to the central system.* **3** to join one place or thing to another: *a highway linking two major cities*

link² *n* [C] **1** a relationship or connection between two or more events, people, or ideas: **+ between** *The police do not think there is any link between this crime and last week's murder.* | **+ with** *Britain should be trying to develop closer links with the rest of Europe.* **2** one of the rings that makes up a chain ➔ see picture at CHAIN **3** a connection between two places that allows people to communicate or travel between them: *a satellite link*

link·age /ˈlɪŋkɪdʒ/ *n formal* [C,U] a connection or relationship between two things

linking verb /ˈ.. ˌ./ *n* [C] a verb that connects the subject of a sentence to its COMPLEMENT. In the sentence, 'She seems friendly', 'seems' is a linking verb.

linking word /ˈ.. ˌ./ *n* [C] a word such as 'but', 'and', or 'while', that connects phrases or parts of sentences; CONJUNCTION

li·no·le·um /lɪˈnəʊliəm‖-ˈnoʊ-/ also **li·no** /ˈlaɪnəʊ‖-noʊ/ *BrE* — *n* [U] smooth shiny material that is used for covering floors

lint /lɪnt/ *n* [U] *AmE* soft light pieces of thread or wool that come off cotton, wool, or other material: FLUFF *BrE*

li·on /ˈlaɪən/ *n* [C] a large African and Asian wild cat, the male of which has long thick hair around his neck

li·on·ess /ˈlaɪənes, -nɪs/ *n* [C] a female lion

lip /lɪp/ *n* [C] **1** one of the two edges of your mouth where the skin is redder or darker: *a kiss on the lips* ➔ see picture at HEAD **2** [usually singular] the edge of a container that you use to pour liquid from: *the lip of the jug*

lip-read /ˈlɪp riːd/ *v* [I,T] to watch someone's lips in order to understand what they are saying, because you cannot hear them — **lip-reading** *n* [U]

lip·stick /ˈlɪpˌstɪk/ *n* [C,U] a coloured substance that is put on the lips as MAKE-UP

liq·ue·fy /ˈlɪkwɪfaɪ/ *v* [I,T] if a gas or solid substance liquefies, it becomes a liquid

li·queur /lɪˈkjʊə‖lɪˈkɜːr/ *n* [C,U] a strong, usually sweet, alcoholic drink, usually drunk after a meal

liq·uid /ˈlɪkwɪd/ *n* [C,U] a substance such as water which flows, and is not solid or a gas — **liquid** *adj*: *liquid soap*

liq·ui·date /ˈlɪkwɪdeɪt/ *v* **1** [I,T] to close a business or company and sell its goods in order to pay a debt **2** [T] to kill someone — **liquidator** *n* [C] *The company is now in the hands of liquidators.* — **liquidation** /ˌlɪkwɪˈdeɪʃən/ *n* [C,U] *The company has gone into liquidation.*

liq·uid·iz·er also **liquidiser** /ˈlɪkwɪdaɪzə‖-ər/ *n* [C] *BrE* a small electric machine that you use for turning solid foods into liquids; BLENDER

liq·uor /ˈlɪkə‖-ər/ *n* [C,U] *AmE* a strong alcoholic drink such as WHISKY

liq·uo·rice *BrE*, **licorice** *AmE* /ˈlɪkərɪs, -rɪʃ/ *n* [C,U] a black substance with a strong taste, used especially for making SWEETS

liquor store /ˈ.. ./ *n* [C] *AmE* a shop where alcohol is sold; OFF-LICENCE *BrE*

lisp /lɪsp/ *v* [I,T] to pronounce the "s" sound like "th", for example so that the word "sing" sounds like "thing" — **lisp** *n* [C] *She speaks with a lisp.*

list¹ /lɪst/ *n* [C] a set of names, things, numbers etc written one below the other: *a shopping list* | **+ of** *Do you have a list of names and addresses?* | **on a list** *We have over 300 people on our waiting list.* | **make a list** *Make a list of all the equipment you'll need.*

list² *v* [T] to write a list, or to mention things one after the other: *All the players must be listed on the scoresheet.*

lis·ten /ˈlɪsən/ *v* [I] **1** to pay attention to what someone is saying or to something that you hear: *Everyone stopped what they were doing and listened.* | **+ to** *Have you listened to those tapes yet?* | *Are you listening to me?* ➔ compare HEAR **2** *spoken* used to get someone's attention before you say something: *Listen, if you need me, just ring.* **3** to seriously think about what someone tells you or advises you to do: *I told him it was dangerous, but he didn't listen.*

listen for sth/sb *phr v* [T] to pay attention so that you are sure you will hear a sound: *We listened for the sound of footsteps.*

listen in *phr v* [I] to listen to what someone is saying without them knowing it: *I think someone's listening in on the other phone.*

listen up *phr v* [I] *spoken* used to get people's attention so they listen to what you are going to say: *OK people, listen up!*

USAGE NOTE: listen and hear

If you **hear** something, you know that a sound has been made, and can often recognize what it is: *Did you hear that noise?* | *She could hear a phone ringing.* If you **listen** to something or someone, you pay attention to the words, sounds or music that they are making: *I'm sorry, could you repeat the question? I wasn't listening.* | *He* *only ever listens to music when he's driving. | The dog suddenly stood quite still, and listened intently.*

lis·ten·er /ˈlɪsənəlǁ-ər/ *n* **1** [C] someone who listens, especially to the radio **2 a good listener** someone who listens in a sympathetic way to other people

list·ing /ˈlɪstɪŋ/ *n* [C] **1** a printed list: *movie listings* **2** one of the names on a printed list

list·less /ˈlɪstləs/ *adj* tired, and not having the energy to do things: *The heat was making us feel listless.* —**listlessly** *adv*

lit /lɪt/ *v* the past tense and past participle of LIGHT

lit·a·ny /ˈlɪtəni/ *n* **a litany of sth** a long list of problems, questions, complaints etc: *a litany of economic problems*

li·ter /ˈliːtəlǁ-ər/ *n* the American spelling of LITRE

lit·e·ra·cy /ˈlɪtərəsi/ *n* [U] the ability to read and write

lit·e·ral /ˈlɪtərəl/ *adj* relating to the basic or original meaning of a words or statements: *a literal interpretation of the Bible* → compare FIGURATIVE

lit·e·ral·ly /ˈlɪtərəli/ *adv* **1** according to the basic or original meaning of a word or expression: *The word "melodrama" literally means a play with music. | She was literally shaking with fear.* **2** *spoken* used to emphasize what you are saying. Some people consider this meaning to be incorrect: *We've been working day and night, literally, to try to finish on time.* **3 take sb/sth literally** to not understand the real meaning of what someone says to you, because you are only thinking about the most simple meaning of the words they use: *When I told her to go and jump in the lake, I didn't think she'd take me literally!*

lit·e·ra·ry /ˈlɪtərəriǁˈlɪtəreri/ *adj* **1** relating to literature: *literary criticism* **2** typical of the style of writing used in literature: *literary language*

lit·e·rate /ˈlɪtərৠt/ *adj* **1** able to read and write **2** well educated → opposite ILLITERATE

lit·e·ra·ture /ˈlɪtərətʃəlǁ-tʃur/ *n* [U] **1** books, poems, plays etc that are considered to be very good and important: *the great classics of English literature* **2** printed information about something

lithe /laɪð/ *adj* able to move your body easily and gracefully

lit·i·ga·tion /ˌlɪtᵻˈɡeɪʃən/ *n* [U] the process of taking legal action in a court of law —**litigate** /ˈlɪtᵻɡeɪt/ *v* [I,T]

li·tre *BrE*, **liter** *AmE* /ˈliːtəlǁ-ər/ *n* [C] a unit for measuring liquid

lit·ter[1] /ˈlɪtəlǁ-ər/ *n* **1** [U] pieces of waste paper etc that people leave on the ground: *Anyone caught dropping litter will be fined.* → see colour picture on page 278 **2** [C] a group of baby animals born at the same time to one mother: *a litter of kittens*

litter[2] *v* [T] if a lot of things litter a place, they are spread all over it in an untidy way: **be littered with** *His desk was littered with books and papers.*

lit·tle[1] /ˈlɪtl/ *adj* **1** small in size: *a little house* **2 a little bit (of sth)** a small amount of something: *"Do you want some more wine?" "Just a little bit." | Add a little bit of milk to the sauce.* **3** short in time or distance: *I'll wait a little while and then call again. | Anna walked a little way down the road with him.* **4** young and small: *a little boy* | **little brother/sister** (=a younger brother or sister, who is still a child) **5** *especially spoken* used after another adjective to emphasize your feelings about someone or something that is small: *It's a nice little restaurant. | What a horrible little man!* **6** [only before noun] not important: *You worry too much about little things.*

little[2] *quantifier* **less** /les/, **least** /liːst/ **1** *formal* not very much: *Little is known about the disease. | I paid little attention to what they were saying.* | **very little** *I have very little money at the moment.* **2 a little** a small amount of something: *I know a little Spanish. | "More coffee?" "Just a little, thanks." | **a little** of I explained a little of the family's history.*

little[3] *adv* **1** not much: *She goes out very little.* **2 a little (bit)** slightly or to a small degree: *She trembled a little as she spoke. | Let's move the table a little bit closer to the wall.* **3 little by little** gradually: *Little by little she became more confident.* **4 little did sb think/realize etc** used to say that someone did not think or realize that something was true: *Little did they think that one day their son would be a famous musician.*

lit·ur·gy /ˈlɪtədʒiǁ-ər/ *n* [C,U] a fixed order of prayers, songs etc in a religious ceremony —**liturgical** /lɪˈtɜːdʒᵻkəlǁ-ɜːr-/ *adj*

live[1] /lɪv/ *v* **1 live in/at/near etc** to have your home in a particular place: *Matt lives in Boston. | Is your son still living at home?* **2** [I] to be alive or to continue to stay alive: *My grandmother lived to be 88. | Plants can't live without light.* **3** [I,T] to have a particular kind of life, or to live in a particular way: *She's always lived a quiet life. | Thousands of people in this country are living in poverty.* **4 live it up** *informal* to do things that you enjoy, usually spending a lot of money: *They spent the summer living it up in the South of France.* **5 live life to the full** to have an exciting and enjoyable life

live sth down *phr v* **not live sth down** to not be able to make people forget about something bad or embarrassing you have done: *I don't think we'll ever live this defeat down.*

live for sb/sth *phr v* [T] if someone lives for someone or something, they are the most important thing in that person's life: *She lives for ballet.*

live in *phr v* [I] to live in the same place where you work or study: *A lot of the students live in for their first year.*

live on *phr v* **1** *also* **live off** [T **live on/off** sth] to have only a small amount of money with which to buy things: *No one can live on £35 a week.* **2** *also* **live off** [T **live on/off** sth] to eat only a particular kind of food **3** [I] to continue to exist: *She will live on in our memories.*

live together *phr v* [I] to live with another person in a sexual relationship without being married: *Mark and I have been living together for two years.*

live up to sth *phr v* [T] to be as good as someone expects: **live up to sb's expectations** *I felt I could never live up to my father's expectations.*

live with sb/sth *phr v* [T] **1** [**live with** sb] to live with another person, especially in a sexual relationship without being married: *Tim's living with a girl he met at college.* **2** [**live with** sth] to accept a difficult situation even when it continues for a long time: *You just have to learn to live with these kinds of problems.*

live[2] /laɪv/ *adj* **1** not dead; LIVING: *He feeds his snake live rats.* **2** a live television or radio programme is broadcast at the same time as it happens or is performed: *a live broadcast of the World Cup Final* **3** performed for people who are watching: *The Dew Drop Inn has live music every weekend.* **4** with electricity flowing through it: *a live wire*

live[3] *adv* **1** being broadcast at the same time that it happens: *Don't miss tomorrow's final, live, on Sky Sports at 14.00.* **2** performing in front of people: *I'd love to see the band play live!*

live·li·hood /'laɪvlihʊd/ *n* [C,U] what you do to earn money in order to live: *Farming is their livelihood.*

live·ly /'laɪvli/ *adj* **1** cheerful and active: *a lively group of children* **2** interesting and exciting: *a lively debate* —**liveliness** *n* [U]

liv·en /'laɪvən/ *v*
liven up *phr v* [I,T **liven** sth ↔ **up**] to make something more exciting, or to become more exciting: *Better music might liven up the party up.*

liv·er /'lɪvəll-ər/ *n* **1** [C] a large organ in your body that cleans your blood **2** [U] the liver of an animal used as food

lives /laɪvz/ *n* the plural of LIFE

live·stock /'laɪvstɒkll-stɑːk/ *n* [U] animals that are kept on a farm

liv·id /'lɪvɪd/ *adj* extremely angry; FURIOUS: *Dad was livid when he heard what had happened.*

liv·ing[1] /'lɪvɪŋ/ *adj* **1** alive now: *Byatt is one of our greatest living writers.* **2** living things anything that lives, such as animals, plants, or people

living[2] *n* **1** [C usually singular] the way that you earn money in order to live: **earn/make a living** (=earn enough money): *It's hard to make a living as an actor.* **2** [U] the way that someone lives their life: *I've always believed in healthy living.* **3** the living all the people who are alive

living room /'.. ./ *n* [C] the main room in a house, where you relax, watch television etc

liz·ard /'lɪzədll-ərd/ *n* [C] a type of REPTILE that has four short legs and a long tail

lizard

'll the short form of WILL or SHALL: *He'll be here soon.*

lla·ma /'lɑːmə/ *n* [C] a large South American animal with thick woolly hair

load[1] /ləʊdllloʊd/ *n* **1** [C] a quantity of something that is carried by a vehicle, person etc: **+ of** *a ship carrying a full load of fuel and supplies* **2** a load of/loads of *spoken* a lot of something: *Don't worry, we still have loads of time.* **3** a load of rubbish/nonsense etc *spoken* used to say that something is completely wrong or very stupid: *I've never heard such a load of rubbish in my life!* **4** [C] the amount of work that a person or a machine has to do

load[2] *v* **1** also **load up** [I,T] to put a load of something on or into a vehicle: *The trucks were loading up with supplies of food and clothing.* | **load** sth **into/onto** sth *They loaded all their luggage into the car.* **2** [T] to put a PROGRAM into a computer: *Have you loaded that software yet?* **3** [T] to put bullets into a gun or film into a camera

load sb/sth ↔ **down** *phr v* [T] to make someone carry too many things or do too much work: **be loaded down with** sth *I was loaded down with groceries.*

load·ed /'ləʊdɪdll'loʊ-/ *adj* **1** containing bullets or film: *Is the camera loaded?* **2** carrying a load of something: *a loaded truck* **3** **loaded with** *informal* containing a lot of something: *The shelves were loaded with trophies.* **4** *spoken informal* very rich: *His grandmother's loaded.* **5 loaded question** a question that is unfair because it makes you give a particular answer

loaf /ləʊfllloʊf/ *n* [C], *plural* **loaves** /ləʊvzll loʊvz/ bread that has been baked in one large piece

loan[1] /ləʊnllloʊn/ *n* **1** [C] an amount of money that you borrow: *a $25,000 bank loan | We're repaying the loan over a 3-year period.* **2 on loan** being borrowed: *Most of the paintings are on loan from other galleries.* **3** [singular] when someone lends something to someone else: *Thanks for the loan of that book.*

loan[2] *v* [T] to lend someone something, especially money: **loan** sb sth/**loan** sth **to** sb *Can you loan me $20 until Friday?*

loan shark /'. ./ *n* [C] someone who lends money to people and charges a very high rate of INTEREST

loath /ləʊθllloʊθ/ *adj* **be loath to do** sth *formal* to be very unwilling to do something: *I was loath to leave her on her own.*

loathe /ləʊðllloʊð/ *v* [T] to hate someone or something very much —**loathing** *n* [C,U]

loath·some /'ləʊðsəmll'loʊð-/ *adj* very unpleasant; DISGUSTING

loaves /ləʊvzllloʊvz/ *n* the plural of LOAF

lob /lɒblllɑːb/ *v* [T] **-bbed, -bbing** to throw or hit something such as a ball so that it moves through the air in a high curve —**lob** *n* [C]

lob·by[1] /'lɒbill'lɑːbi/ *n* [C] **1** a large area inside the entrance of a building: *the hotel lobby* **2** a group of people who try to persuade the government to do something: *the anti-smoking lobby*

lobby[2] *v* [I,T] to try to persuade the government to do something: **+ for** *Demonstrators are lobbying for a change in the present laws.* —**lobbyist** *n* [C]

lobe /ləʊbllloʊb/ *n* [C] an EARLOBE

lob·ster /'lɒbstəll'lɑːbstər/ *n* [C,U] a sea animal with eight legs, a shell, and two large CLAWS, or this animal as food

lo·cal[1] /'ləʊkəll'loʊ-/ *adj* **1** relating to a particular place or area, especially the place you live in: *Our kids go to the local school.* | *the local newspaper* **2 local anaesthetic** an ANAESTHETIC that only affects part of your body

local[2] *n* **1** the locals the people who live in a place you are visiting: *I asked one of the locals for directions.* **2** sb's local *BrE informal* a PUB near someone's home where they often drink

lo·cal·i·ty /ləʊ'kælⱼ̩ti‖loʊ-/ *n* [C] *formal* a small area of a country, city etc

lo·cal·ized (also **-ised** *BrE*) /'ləʊkəlaɪzd‖'loʊ-/ *adj* only within a small area: *localized pain*

lo·cal·ly /'ləʊkəli‖'loʊ-/ *adv* in or near the area where you are or the area you are talking about: *Do you live locally?*

lo·cate /ləʊ'keɪt‖'loʊkeɪt/ *v* **1** [T] to find the exact position of something: *Divers have located the shipwreck.* **2 be located in/on/at etc** to be in a particular place or position: *The town is located on the shores of Lake Trasimeno.* **3** [I,T] if a company locates somewhere, it moves its offices there

lo·ca·tion /ləʊ'keɪʃən‖loʊ-/ *n* [C] **1** a particular place or position: + **of** *a map showing the location of the school* **2** [C,U] a place where part of a film is made, away from the STUDIO: **on location** *scenes shot on location in Montana*

lock[1] /lɒk‖lɑːk/ *v* **1** [I,T] to fasten something with a lock, or to be fastened with a lock: *Did you remember to lock the car? | The front door won't lock.* → opposite UNLOCK **2 lock sth in/away etc** to put something in a safe place and lock the door, lid etc: *He locked the money in a safe.* **3** [I] to become fixed in one position and unable to move: *The brakes locked and we skidded.*

lock sb in *phr v* [T] to prevent someone from leaving a place by locking the door

lock sb out *phr v* [T] to prevent someone from entering a place by locking the door

lock up *phr v* **1** [I,T **lock** sth ↔ **up**] to make a building safe by locking all the doors: *Would you mind locking up when you leave?* **2** also **lock away** [T **lock** sb ↔ **up/away**] to put someone in prison or in a hospital for people who are mentally ill: *Higgs was locked up for three years for his part in the robbery.*

lock[2] *n* [C] **1** the thing that is used to fasten a door, drawer etc and is usually opened with a key: *The doors and windows are fitted with safety locks.* **2** a part of a river or CANAL with gates where the water level can go up or down to raise or lower boats **3 lock, stock, and barrel** including every part of something: *They sold everything, lock, stock and barrel.* **4 under lock and key** kept safely in a place that is locked: *All her jewellery is kept under lock and key.* **5** a small number of hairs on your head that grow together: *She twisted a lock of hair between her fingers.*

lock·er /'lɒkə‖'lɑːkər/ *n* [C] a small cupboard where you leave books, clothes etc, for example at school

lock·et /'lɒkⱼ̩t‖'lɑː-/ *n* [C] a piece of jewellery like a small round box, worn on a chain around your neck

lock·smith /'lɒk,smɪθ‖'lɑːk-/ *n* [C] someone who makes and repairs locks

lo·co·mo·tive /ˌləʊkə'məʊtɪv‖ˌloʊkə'moʊ-/ *n* [C] a train engine

lo·cust /'ləʊkəst‖'loʊ-/ *n* [C] an insect similar to a large GRASSHOPPER that flies in large groups and often destroys crops: *a swarm of locusts*

lodge[1] /lɒdʒ‖lɑːdʒ/ *v* **1** [I] to become stuck somewhere: *A fish bone had lodged in his throat.* **2 lodge a complaint etc** to officially complain about something: *He has lodged a formal complaint with the club.* **3** [I] to live in someone else's house, paying rent: *She's lodging with friends at the moment.*

lodge[2] *n* [C] **1** a place in the country where people can stay for a short time, especially in order to do an outdoor activity: *a ski lodge* **2** a small house or room at the entrance to a bigger building: *the porter's lodge*

lodg·er /'lɒdʒə‖'lɑːdʒər/ *n* [C] *BrE* someone who lives in someone else's house, paying rent

lodg·ings /'lɒdʒɪŋz‖'lɑː-/ *n* [plural] *BrE* a room or rooms in someone's house that you pay rent to live in

loft /lɒft‖lɒːft/ *n* [C] *especially BrE* a room or space under the roof of a house; ATTIC

loft·y /'lɒftⱼ̩‖'lɒːfti/ *adj* **1** involving unusually high moral standards or aims: *lofty ideals* **2** *literary* high **3** behaving in a way that shows you think you are better than other people — **loftily** *adv*

log[1] /lɒg‖lɒːg, lɑːg/ *n* [C] **1** a thick piece of wood cut from a tree **2** an official record of events, for example on a ship or plane **3** a LOGARITHM

log[2] *v* [T] **-gged, -gging** to make an official record of events, facts etc, for example on a ship or plane

log off/out *phr v* [I] to do the things necessary for you to stop using a computer

log on/in *phr v* [I] to do the things necessary for you to be able to start using a computer

log·a·rith·m /'lɒgərɪðəm‖'lɒː-, 'lɑː-/ *n* [C] one of a set of numbers that you use to solve some mathematical problems

log cab·in /ˌ‿ '‿/ *n* [C] a small house made of logs

log·ger·heads /'lɒgəhedz‖'lɒːgər-, 'lɑː-/ *n* **be at loggerheads (with sb)** to disagree very strongly with someone: *The two families have been at loggerheads for years.*

log·ging /'lɒgɪŋ‖'lɒː-, 'lɑː-/ *n* [U] the activity of cutting down trees in order to sell the wood

lo·gic /'lɒdʒɪk‖'lɑː-/ *n* [U] **1** the science or study of thinking carefully about something using formal methods **2** a set of sensible and correct reasons: *There is no logic in releasing criminals just because prisons are crowded.*

lo·gic·al /'lɒdʒɪkəl‖'lɑː-/ *adj* **1** based on the rules of logic: *logical analysis* **2** reasonable and sensible: *He seems the logical choice for the job.* — **logically** /-kli/ *adv*

lo·gis·tics /lə'dʒɪstɪks‖loʊ-/ *n* **the logistics of sth** the practical arrangements that are necessary to make a complicated plan or activity succeed: *the logistics of organizing an international music festival* — **logistical** *adj* — **logistically** /-kli/ *adv*

L

GRAMMAR NOTE: comparatives and superlatives
For short adjectives of one syllable, add **-er** or **-est** to the word: e.g. *old - older - oldest.* (Sometimes you must double the last letter: e.g. *big - bigger - biggest*). For long adjectives put **more** or **the most** before the word: e.g. *more comfortable - the most interesting.*

lo·go /ˈləʊgəʊ‖ˈloʊgoʊ/ *n* [C] a design that is the official sign of a company or organization

loins /lɔɪnz/ *n* [plural] *literary* the part of the body below your waist, where the sex organs are

loi·ter /ˈlɔɪtəll-ər/ *v* [I] to stand in a public place with- out having a reason to be there —**loitering** *n* [U]

loll /lɒl‖lɑːl/ *v* [I] **1** also **loll around/about** *BrE* to sit or lie in a lazy or relaxed way: *He was lolling on a sunbed by the pool.* **2** if someone's head or tongue lolls, it hangs down: *The dog's tongue lolled out of its mouth.*

lol·li·pop /ˈlɒlipɒp‖ˈlɑːlipɑːp/ also **lol·ly** /ˈlɒli‖ˈlɑː-/ *BrE* — *n* [C] a SWEET made of boiled sugar or frozen juice on the end of a stick

lone /ləʊn‖loʊn/ *adj* [only before noun] *literary* being the only person or thing: *a lone figure standing in the snow | lone parents*

lone·ly /ˈləʊnli‖ˈloʊn-/ *adj* **1** unhappy because you are alone: *Aren't you lonely living on your own?* **2** [only before noun] *literary* a lonely place is a long way from where people live: *a lonely country road* —**loneliness** *n* [U]

lon·er /ˈləʊnə‖ˈloʊnər/ *n* [C] someone who prefers to be alone

lone·some /ˈləʊnsəm‖ˈloʊn-/ *adj AmE* LONELY

long[1] /lɒŋ‖lɔːŋ/ *adj* **1** measuring a great length from one end to the other: *long hair | It's a long walk home from here.* → see colour picture on page 244 → opposite SHORT[1] **2** continuing or seeming to continue for a great amount of time: *a long, boring meeting | take a long time It took a long time for the little girl to start to relax.* | *a long day/week* (=a boring or tiring day or week) | **long hours** (=more working hours than usual) **3** having a particular length: *The snake was at least 3 feet long.* **4** **in the long run** *informal* in the future, not immediately: *All our hard work will be worth it in the long run.* **5 a)** a long book has a lot of pages **b)** a long list has a lot of things on it

long[2] *adv* **1** a long time or for a long time: *Have you been waiting long? | Will you be long, or shall I wait?* | **for long** *Have you known the Garretts for long?* **2** **as long as** having the condition that; if: *You can go as long as you're back by four o'clock.* **3** at a time that is a long time before or after a particular time or event: **long before/after** *The farm was sold long before you were born.* **4 no longer** used in order to show that something happened in the past, but does not happen now: *Mr. Allen no longer works for the company.* **5 before long** soon: *It will be Christmas before long.*

long[3] *v* [I] *formal* to want something very much: + **for** *I used to long for a baby sister.* | **long to do sth** *The children longed to get outside.*

long-dis·tance /ˌ. ˈ..◂/ *adj* **1** travelling, running etc between places that are a long way away from each other: *long-distance flights* **2** a long-distance telephone call is to a place that is a long way away —**long-distance** *adv*

lon·gev·i·ty /lɒnˈdʒevɨtill‖lɑːn-, lɔːn-/ *n* [U] *formal* long life

long·hand /ˈlɒŋhænd‖ˈlɔːŋ-/ *n* [U] writing by hand rather than using a machine such as a computer

long·ing /ˈlɒŋɪŋ‖ˈlɔːŋɪŋ/ *n* [singular, U] when you want someone or something very much: *She*
had a great longing for her home country. —**longingly** *adv*

lon·gi·tude /ˈlɒndʒɨtjuːd‖ˈlɑːndʒɨtuːd/ *n* [C,U] a position on the Earth measured in degrees east or west of an imaginary line from the top of the Earth to the bottom —**longitudinal** /ˌlɒndʒ-ˈtjuːdɨnəl◂‖ˌlɑːndʒɨˈtuː-/ *adj* → compare LATI-TUDE

long jump /ˈ. ./ *n* [singular] a sport in which you jump as far as possible

long-lost /ˌ. ˈ.◂/ *adj* **long-lost friend/relative etc** a friend etc that you have not seen for a very long time: *He greeted me like a long-lost friend.*

long-range /ˌ. ˈ.◂/ *adj* [only before noun] **1** a long-range weapon can hit something that is a long way away: *a long-range missile* **2** long-range plans, decisions etc are concerned with the future

long shot /ˈ. ./ *n* [C] *informal* something that you try even though it is not likely to be successful

long·sight·ed /ˌlɒŋˈsaɪtɨd◂‖ˌlɔːŋ-/ *adj BrE* able to see or read things clearly only when they are far from your eyes: FARSIGHTED *AmE*

long-stand·ing /ˌ. ˈ..◂/ *adj* having continued or existed for a long time: *a long-standing agreement between the two countries*

long-suf·fer·ing /ˌ. ˈ...◂/ *adj* patient in spite of continuous problems or other people's annoying behaviour: *He leaves his long-suffering wife at home while he goes to the pub.*

long-term /ˌ. ˈ.◂/ *adj* continuing for a long period of time into the future: *the long-term effects of smoking* → compare SHORT-TERM → see also **in the long/short term** (TERM[1])

long-wear·ing /ˌlɒŋˈweərɪŋ◂‖ˌlɔːŋˈwer-/ *adj AmE* clothes, materials etc that are long wearing will stay in good condition for a long time; HARD-WEARING *BrE*

long-wind·ed /ˌlɒŋˈwɪndɨd◂‖ˌlɔːŋ-/ *adj* talking for too long in a way that is boring: *a long-winded speech*

loo /luː/ *n* [C] *BrE informal* a toilet

look[1] /lʊk/ *v* **1** [I] to turn your eyes towards something or someone so that you can see them: *I didn't see it. I wasn't looking.* | **at** *"It's time to go," said Patrick, looking at his watch.* | **down/away/over etc** *I looked down the road but she'd gone.* **2** [I] to try to find someone or something, using your eyes: + **for** *Brad was looking for you last night. | I've looked everywhere for my keys, but I can't find them. | Have you looked in here?* **3 be looking for trouble/a fight** *informal* to be behaving in a way that makes it likely that problems or a fight will happen **4** *linking verb* to seem to be something, especially by having a particular appearance: **look nice/tired/happy etc** *You look nice in that dress.* | **look like** *He looks like he hasn't slept for days.* **5 strange-/funny-/scruffy- etc looking** having a strange, funny etc appearance: *healthy-looking children* **6 look** *spoken* used when you are annoyed and want to emphasize what you are saying: *Look, I'm very serious about this.* **7** [T] *spoken* used to make someone notice something: *Dad, look what I made!* **8 look out!** *spoken* used to warn someone of danger: *Look out! There's a car coming.* **9 look sb in the eye** to look directly at someone when you are speaking to them, especially to show that you are not afraid of them or that you are telling the truth **10** [I] if a building looks in a particular direction, it faces that direction: *Our room looks over the harbour.*

look after sb/sth *phr v* [T] to take care of someone or something: *We look after Rodney's kids until he gets home from work.*

look ahead *phr v* [I] to think about what will happen in the future: *We need to look ahead and plan for next year.*

look around (also **look round** *BrE*) *phr v* [I,T] to look at different things in a particular place in order to buy something or learn about something: *We have 3 or 4 hours to look around the city.*

look at sb/sth *phr v* [T] **1** to read something quickly, but not thoroughly: *Jane was looking at a magazine while she waited.* **2** if someone such as a doctor looks at something or someone, they examine that thing or person: *The doctor looked at the cut on her head.* **3** to study and think carefully about something: *The government will look at the report this week.* **4 look at ...** *spoken* used to give someone or something as an example of a situation: *Of course you can get a good job without a degree – just look at your Uncle Ron.* **5** to consider something in a particular way: *It all depends how you look at the situation.*

look back *phr v* [I] to think about something that happened in the past: *Looking back on it, I think I was wrong to leave when I did.*

look down on sb/sth *phr v* [T] to think that you are better than someone or something else: *I'm sick of Ken looking down on me the whole time.*

look forward to sth *phr v* [T] to be excited and happy about something that is going to happen: **look forward to doing sth** *I'm really looking forward to going to Japan.*

look into sth *phr v* [T] to examine the facts about something: *We are looking into the cause of the fire.*

look on *phr v* **1** [I] to watch something, without being involved in it: *The crowd looked on as the two men fought.* **2** [T **look on** sb/sth] also **look upon** to think about someone or something in a particular way: *She always looked upon me as if I was stupid.*

look out for sb/sth *phr v* [T] to try and notice someone or something: *Look out for Jane at the conference.*

look sth/sb ⟷ **over** *phr v* [T] to examine something or someone quickly: *Can you look this letter over for me before I send it?*

look round *phr v* *BrE* LOOK AROUND

look through sth *phr v* [T] **1** to look for something in a pile of papers, a drawer, someone's pockets etc: *Look through your pockets and see if you can find the receipt.* **2** to read something carefully

look up *phr v* **1** [I] if a situation is looking up, it is getting better: *Things are looking up since I found a job.* **2** [T **look** sth ⟷ **up**] to find information in a book, on a computer etc: *If you don't know the word, look it up in the dictionary.* **3** [T **look** sb ⟷ **up**] to visit someone in the place where they live: *Look up my parents when you're in Boston.*

look up to sb *phr v* [T] to admire and respect someone: *He looks up to his older brother.*

look² *n* **1** [C usually singular] when you look at something: **have/take a look** *Let me take a look at that map again.* **2** [singular] when you search for something: *He's had a look for the file but he hasn't found it.* **3** [C] an expression in your eyes or face which shows how you feel: **give sb a look** *She gave me an angry look.* **4** [C usually singular] the appearance of someone or something: *I don't like the look of that cut.* **5** [singular] a particular fashion or style: *the grunge look* → see also LOOKS

look·a·like /ˈlʊkəlaɪk/ *n* [C] *informal* someone who looks very similar to a famous person: *a Madonna lookalike*

look·out /ˈlʊk-aʊt/ *n* **1 be on the lookout** to watch a place or pay attention to a situation because you are looking for someone or something: *Be on the lookout for snakes!* **2** [C] someone who watches carefully for danger, or the place where they do this

looks /lʊks/ *n* [plural] how attractive someone is: *Stop worrying about your looks.*

loom¹ /luːm/ *v* [I] **1** to appear as a large, unclear, threatening shape: **+ ahead/up etc** *The mountain loomed in front of us* **2** if a difficult situation looms, it is likely to happen soon: *My exams are looming.*

loom² *n* [C] a machine used for weaving cloth

loon·y /ˈluːni/ *n* [C] *informal* someone who behaves in a crazy or strange way —**loony** *adj*: *He's full of loony ideas.*

loop¹ /luːp/ *n* **1** [C] a shape like a curve or a circle, or a line, piece of wire, string etc that has this shape: *belt loops* (=cloth loops used for holding a belt on clothes) **2 be out of the loop** *AmE* to not be part of a group of people that make decisions: *Gaynor says he was out of the loop when the order was given.*

loop² *v* **1 loop** sth **over/round etc** to make something into a loop or to tie something with a loop **2** to go somewhere in a circular direction: *The storm is looping down through the Rockies.*

loop·hole /ˈluːphəʊl‖-hoʊl/ *n* [C] a small mistake in a law that makes it possible to legally avoid doing what the law says: *tax loopholes*

loose¹ /luːs/ *adj* **1** not firmly joined or fixed: *a loose tooth* | **come loose** (=become loose): *One of the buttons on your shirt is coming loose.* **2** not tied together or put together with anything else: *You can buy the chocolates loose or in a box.* **3** loose clothes are big and do not fit tightly **4** free to move around: **break loose** (=become loose): *Two of the prisoners broke loose from the guards.* **5** not exact: *My French isn't very good, but I can give you a loose translation.* **6 loose ends** parts of something such as an agreement that has not yet been completed: **tie up the loose ends** (=finish dealing with something) **7 be at a loose end** to have nothing to do **8** *old-fashioned* behaving in a sexually immoral way: *a loose woman* —**loosely** *adv*

loose² *n* **be on the loose** if a criminal or animal is on the loose, they have escaped

loose·can·non /ˌ. ˈ../ *n* [C usually singular] someone who is likely to cause trouble for the group or organization they are connected with by saying something publicly that is embarrassing for them

loos·en /ˈluːsən/ *v* [I,T] to become less tight or less firmly joined to something, or to make something do this: *The screws holding the shelf had loosened.* | *He loosened his tie.*

L

loosen up *phr v* [I] to become more relaxed and feel less worried: *Claire loosened up after a few drinks.*

loot¹ /luːt/ *v* [I,T] to steal things during a war or RIOT: *Shops were looted and burned down.* —**looting** *n* [U] —**looter** *n* [C]

loot² *n* [U] things that have been stolen

lop /lɒp‖lɑːp/ also **lop off** *v* [T] **-pped, -pping** to cut part of something off, especially a branch from a tree

lop·sid·ed /ˌ. '..◂/ *adj* having one side that is heavier or lower than the other: *a lop-sided grin*

lord /lɔːd‖lɔːrd/ *n* [C] **1** a man who has high social rank in Britain because of the family he comes from, the important job he does etc **2 Lord** the title used by a lord: *Lord Mountbatten*

Lord *n* **1** [singular] also **the Lord** a title for God or Jesus Christ **2 good/oh Lord!** *spoken* used when you are surprised, worried, or angry

lore /lɔː‖lɔːr/ *n* [U] traditional stories, history, or knowledge about magic, nature etc

lorry /ˈlɒri‖ˈlɔːri/ *n* [C] *BrE* a large vehicle used for carrying goods; TRUCK

lose /luːz/ *v* **lost** /lɒst‖lɒːst/, **lost, losing 1** [T] to no longer have something that is important to you or that you need: *Tom lost his job.* | *Drunk drivers should lose their licence.* **2** [T] to be unable to find someone or something: *Danny's always losing his keys.* **3** [I,T] to fail to win a game, argument, war etc: *Liverpool lost to AC Milan.* | *The Democrat candidate lost by 8000 votes.* **4** [T] to have less of something than before: *She's lost a lot of blood.* | **lose weight** (=become thinner) | **lose your memory/sight etc** (=when your memory, sight etc is failing) **5** [T] to no longer have a particular quality, belief, attitude etc: *The kids were losing interest in the game.* | **lose your temper/head** (=become angry) **6 lose an arm/leg etc** to have a serious injury in which your arm etc is cut off **7 lose your balance** to become unsteady and fall **8** if you lose your husband, wife, mother etc, that person dies **9 lose your life** to die: *5000 soldiers lost their lives.* **10** [T] to waste time or an opportunity: *You lost your chance!* **11** [T] if a clock or watch loses time, it runs too slowly: *My old watch loses about five minutes every day.* **12 have nothing to lose** to be in a situation in which you should try to do something because you may be successful, and you will not be in a worse situation if you fail **13 lose touch (with) a)** to no longer speak to, write to, or see someone: *I've lost touch with all my high school friends.* **b)** to not know the most recent information about something **14 lose your touch** to stop having an ability or skill **15 lose heart** to stop having hope and become disappointed: *The team lost heart after they lost their fifth game.* **16 lose sight of** to forget about the most important part of something: *We can't lose sight of our goals.*

lose out *phr v* [I] to be less likely to succeed, usually because someone else gets something important which you do not: + **to/in/on** *He lost out on a scholarship because his grades were low.*

los·er /ˈluːzəll-ər/ *n* [C] **1** someone who does not win a competition, game etc: **good/bad loser** (=someone who behaves well or badly

when they lose) **2** *informal* someone who is never successful in life, work, or relationships: *Pam's boyfriend is such a loser!*

loss /lɒs‖lɒːs/ *n* **1** [C,U] when you do not have something any longer, or when you have less of it: *The loss of their home was a shock to the family.* | **weight loss 2** [C,U] if a company makes a loss, it earns less money than it spends **3** [C] a game that you lose: *3 wins and 4 losses so far this season* **4** [U] a feeling of sadness because someone or something is not there any more: *She felt a great sense of loss when her son left home.* **5** [singular] a disadvantage caused by someone leaving or something being taken away: *If she leaves, it will be a great loss to the company.* **6** [C,U] the death of a person: *Troops suffered heavy losses in the first battle.* (=many deaths) **7 be at a loss** to not know what you should do or say: *Local people are at a loss to know how to start tackling such a rise in crime.*

lost¹ /lɒst‖lɒːst/ *adj* **1** not knowing where you are or how to find your way: **get lost** *We got lost driving around the city.* **2** if something is lost, you cannot find it: *My passport got lost in the post.* **3 be/feel lost** to not feel confident, usually because you are in a new or unusual situation **4 Get lost!** *spoken* used to tell someone rudely to go away **5 be lost on sb** if humour or advice is lost on someone, they cannot understand it: *The joke was lost on him.* **6** destroyed, ruined, or killed: *20 men were lost at sea.*

lost² *v* the past tense and past participle of LOSE

lot /lɒt‖lɑːt/ *n* **1 a lot** also **lots** *informal* a large amount, quantity, or number of something: **+ of** *There were a lot of people at the concert last night.* | *She's got lots of money.* | **a lot to do/see etc** *There's a lot to see in London.* **2 a lot quicker/easier/better etc** much quicker, easier etc: *You'll get there a lot faster if you drive.* **3** [singular] *BrE informal* a group of people or things: *I need to take this lot to the post office.* | *There's another lot of students starting next week.* **4 the lot** the whole of something: *He bought a huge bar of chocolate and ate the lot.* **5** [C] *AmE* an area of land used for a particular purpose: *a parking lot* **6** [C] something being sold at an AUCTION **7** [singular] the life you have and the things you experience: *Hers is not a happy lot.*

lo·tion /ˈləʊʃən‖ˈloʊ-/ *n* [C,U] a liquid that you put on your skin in order to make it soft or to protect it: *suntan lotion*

lot·te·ry /ˈlɒtəri‖ˈlɑː-/ *n* [C] a competition in which people win money if they choose the same numbers that the organizers choose

loud¹ /laʊd/ *adj* **1** making a lot of noise: *The TV's too loud!* | *a loud bang* **2** loud clothes are too brightly coloured —**loudly** *adv*

loud² *adv* **1** loudly: *You'll have to speak a bit louder.* **2 out loud** to speak so that people can hear you

loud·speak·er /ˌlaʊdˈspiːkə, ˈlaʊdˌspiːkə‖-ər/ *n* [C] a piece of equipment that makes sound louder

lounge¹ /laʊndʒ/ *n* [C] **1** a room in a hotel or airport, where people can sit and relax **2** *BrE* the room in your house where you sit and relax

lounge² *v* [I] to stand or sit somewhere in a relaxed way: *We were lounging by the pool.*

lounge about/around _phr v_ [I,T] _BrE_ to be lazy and waste your time doing nothing

louse /laʊs/ _n_ [C], _plural_ **lice** /laɪs/ a very small insect that lives on the skin and hair of animals and people

lou·sy /ˈlaʊzi/ _adj informal_ very bad: _I've had a lousy day!_

lov·a·ble, loveable /ˈlʌvəbəl/ _adj_ easy to love: _a lovable child_

love[1] /lʌv/ _v_ [T] **1** to like someone in a romantic or sexual way: _I love you._ | _the first boy I ever really loved_ **2** to like someone very much and care about them a lot, for example a member of your family: _I love my Mom._ **3** to like something very much, or enjoy doing something very much: _I love chocolate._ | **love doing sth** _Tom loves reading._ **4** **I'd love to (do sth)** _spoken_ used to say that you want to do something very much when someone asks you: _"Do you want to come for dinner sometime?" "I'd love to."_

love[2] _n_ **1** [U] a strong romantic feeling for someone: _He never told her about his love for her._ | **be in love (with sb)** (=have feelings of love for someone): _Lucy knew she was in love straightaway._ | **fall in love (with sb)** (=start to love someone): _I fell in love with her the first time we met._ | **love at first sight** (=when you love someone as soon as you meet them) **love story/song/letter** (=about love): _I've kept all his old love letters._ **2** [U] when you care very much about someone, for example a member of your family or a close friend: _My mother's love for me was never in doubt._ **3** [C] someone who you love: _You were my first love._ **4** [C,U] a strong feeling of liking or enjoying something very much, or something that gives you this feeling: _His greatest love is football._ | _She has a great love of music._ **5** **make love** to have sex with someone **6** **love from** used at the end of a letter to a friend or a member of your family: _Hope to see you soon. Love from Chris._ **7** **send/give sb your love** to send or give friendly greetings to someone: _Your father sends his love._ **8** _spoken_ used when talking to someone who you love: _Are you OK, love?_ **9** _BrE spoken informal_ used when talking in a friendly way to someone you do not know, especially a woman

love af·fair /ˈ. .,./ _n_ [C] a romantic sexual relationship

love·ly /ˈlʌvli/ _adj_ **1** beautiful: _You look lovely in that dress._ **2** _especially BrE_ very enjoyable: _Thanks for a lovely evening._

lov·er /ˈlʌvəl-ər/ _n_ [C] **1** someone you have a sexual relationship with, especially someone who you are not married to: _I think my wife has a lover._ **2** someone who enjoys something very much: _an art lover_

love·sick /ˈlʌv,sɪk/ _adj_ spending all your time thinking about someone you love

lov·ing /ˈlʌvɪŋ/ _adj_ behaving in a gentle, kind way that shows you love someone: _a wonderful, loving husband_ —**lovingly** _adv_

low[1] /ləʊlloʊ/ _adj_ **1** not high, or not far above the ground: _These shelves are a little too low for me._ | _a low ceiling_ | _low clouds_ **2** small, or smaller than usual in amount, value etc: _Temperatures in the west will be lower than yesterday._ | _Come and see our low prices!_ **3** below an acceptable standard: _She got a very low grade in English._ | _Cost-cutting has led to a lower quality of work._ **4** [not before noun] unhappy: _Kerry's been pretty low lately._ **5** a low voice, sound etc is quiet or deep **6** lights that are low are not bright **7** **low gear** first or second GEAR in a car → opposite HIGH[1]

low[2] _adv_ in a low position or at a low level: _The sun sank low on the horizon._ → opposite HIGH[2]

low[3] _n_ [C] a low price, level, degree etc: **all-time low** (=the lowest something has ever been): _Oil prices have dropped to an all-time low._ | _Tomorrow's low will be 8°C._

low·er[1] /ˈləʊəlˈloʊər/ _adj_ [only before noun] **1** being the bottom part of something, or at the bottom of something: _I injured my lower back._ | _the lower floors of the building_ **2** less important than other things of the same type: _lower levels of management_

lower[2] _v_ [T] **1** to become less, or to reduce something in amount, strength etc: _We're lowering prices on all our products!_ | **lower your voice** (=speak more quietly) **2** to move something down: _The flag was lowered at sunset._

lower case /,.. '.◂/ _n_ [U] letters written in their small form, for example a, b, c → compare CAPITAL[1], UPPER CASE

low-key /,. '.◂/ _adj_ done in a way that will not attract a lot of attention: _The reception was very low-key._

low-life /ˈ. ./ _n_ [C] _informal_ an unpleasant person such as a criminal

low·ly /ˈləʊlilˈloʊ-/ _adj especially literary_ low in rank or importance: _He had a very lowly job._

low-ly·ing /,. '.◂/ _adj_ low-lying land is not much higher than the level of the sea

loy·al /ˈlɔɪəl/ _adj_ always faithful to a person, set of beliefs, or country: _a loyal friend_

loy·al·ty /ˈlɔɪəlti/ _n_ **1** [U] the quality of being loyal: _The company demands loyalty from its workers._ **2** [C usually plural] a feeling of friendship and support towards someone or something: _political loyalties_ | _My loyalties lie with my family._

loyalty card /ˈ... ,./ _n_ [C] a card which you show every time you pay for goods at a particular shop, which allows you to have special advantages, for example to get some money back when you have spent a certain amount of money

loz·enge /ˈlɒz,ndʒlˈlɑː-/ _n_ [C] a small SWEET containing medicine

LP /,el 'piː/ _n_ [C] a long playing record; a record that plays for about 25 minutes on each side

L-plate /ˈel pleɪt/ _n_ [C] a red letter 'L' put on a car in Britain to show that the driver is learning to drive

LSD /,el es 'diː/ _n_ [U] an illegal drug that makes people HALLUCINATE

L

GRAMMAR NOTE: transitive and intransitive (1)
Transitive verbs have an object: _I like your dress._ | _Did you find the key?_ These verbs are shown like this: _v_ [T]. **Intransitive** verbs do not have an object: _He laughed._ | _I'll wait in the car._ These verbs are shown like this: _v_ [I].

Ltd the written abbreviation of LIMITED COMPANY used after the names of companies: *Process Supplies Ltd*

lu·bri·cant /'luːbrɪkənt/ *n* [C,U] a substance such as oil that is put on things that rub together, making them move more smoothly

lu·bri·cate /'luːbrɪkeɪt/ *v* [T] to put a lubricant on something —**lubrication** /ˌluːbrɪ'keɪʃən/ *n* [U]

lu·cid /'luːsɪd/ *adj* **1** clear and easy to understand: *a lucid and interesting article* **2** able to think clearly, especially while you are ill: *He was rarely lucid during his long illness.* —**lucidly** *adv*

luck /lʌk/ *n* [U] **1** something good that happens by chance: **have luck** *Have you had any luck finding a job?* **2** the way in which good or bad things happen to people by chance: *We seem to have had a lot of bad luck recently.* **3 be in luck/be out of luck** to get or not get something that you want: *You're in luck – there's one ticket left.* **4 Good luck/best of luck** used to say that you hope someone is successful **5 bad luck!/ hard luck!/tough luck!** *spoken* used to express sympathy for someone

luck out *phr v* [I] *AmE informal* to be lucky: *We lucked out and found someone who spoke English.*

USAGE NOTE: luck and lucky

If you use **luck** on its own, it usually means the good things that happen to you by chance: *That was a piece of luck!* | *Winning is just a matter of luck.* However, you can also have **good luck** or **bad luck**: *It was just bad luck that she arrived at that moment.* **Lucky** is an adjective used to describe a situation in which something good happens by chance, or someone who has good luck: *You were lucky Dad didn't see you do that!* | *That was lucky! The bike nearly knocked you over!*

---

luck·y /'lʌki/ *adj* having good luck; fortunate: *"I just got the last bus." "That was lucky!"* | *If you're lucky, you might still be able to get tickets.* | **be lucky to be/do/have sth** *You're lucky to have such a caring husband.* —**luckily** *adv*

lu·cra·tive /'luːkrətɪv/ *adj formal* a lucrative job or activity is one that you earn a lot of money from

lu·di·crous /'luːdɪkrəs/ *adj* stupid, wrong, and unreasonable: *It's ludicrous to spend so much on a car.* —**ludicrously** *adv*

lug /lʌg/ *v* [T] **-gged, -gging** *informal* to pull or carry something heavy with difficulty: *We lugged our suitcases up to our room.*

lug·gage /'lʌgɪdʒ/ *n* [U] the bags etc that you carry when you are travelling

lu·gu·bri·ous /luːˈguːbriəs/ *adj literary* very sad and serious —**lugubriously** *adv*

luke·warm /ˌluːkˈwɔːm‖-ˈwɔːrm/ *adj* **1** a liquid that is lukewarm is only slightly warm **2** not showing very much interest or excitement: *a lukewarm response*

lull¹ /lʌl/ *v* [T] **1** to make someone feel calm and sleepy: *Singing softly, she lulled us to sleep.* **2** to make someone feel safe so that they can easily be tricked: **lull sb into doing sth** *She was lulled into believing that there was no danger.*

lull² *n* [C] a short period when there is less activity or noise than usual: *a lull in the conversation*

lul·la·by /'lʌləbaɪ/ *n* [C] a song that you sing to children to make them sleep

lum·ber¹ /'lʌmbəl-ər/ *v* **1** [I] to move slowly and heavily: **+ along/towards etc** *The bear lumbered towards us.* **2 get/be lumbered with sth** to be given a job or responsibility that you do not want: *I got lumbered with babysitting my brother.*

lumber² *n* [U] *especially AmE* wood that is used for building

lu·mi·na·ry /'luːmɪnəril-neri/ *n* [C] someone who is famous and respected because of their knowledge or skills: *political luminaries*

lu·mi·nous /'luːmɪnəs/ *adj* able to shine in the dark

lump¹ /lʌmp/ *n* [C] **1** a small irregular piece of something solid: *a lump of clay* ➔ see colour picture on page 440 **2** a hard swelling on someone's skin or in their body **3 a lump in your throat** the tight feeling in your throat that you have when you want to cry

lump² *v* [T] to put two or more different people or things together and consider them as a single group: **lump sth together/with/into sth** *These symptoms are often lumped together under the general term depression.*

lump sum /ˌ. './ *n* [C] an amount of money given in a single payment: *When you retire, you'll receive a lump sum of £50,000.*

lump·y /'lʌmpi/ *adj* having lumps: *a lumpy mattress*

lu·na·cy /'luːnəsi/ *n* [U] behaviour that seems strange and unreasonable: *It would be sheer lunacy to give up college now.*

lu·nar /'luːnəl-ər/ *adj* relating to the moon: *a lunar eclipse*

lu·na·tic /'luːnətɪk/ *n* [C] someone who behaves in a stupid or very strange way that can be dangerous —**lunatic** *adj*

lunch¹ /lʌntʃ/ *n* [C,U] a meal that you eat in the middle of the day

lunch² *v* [I] *formal* to eat lunch

lunch·eon /'lʌntʃən/ *n* [C,U] *formal* lunch

lunch·time /'lʌntʃtaɪm/ *n* [C,U] the time in the middle of the day when people usually eat lunch

lung /lʌŋ/ *n* [C] one of two organs in your body that you use for breathing

lunge /lʌndʒ/ *v* [I] to make a sudden movement towards someone or something, often to attack them: **+ forward/at/towards** *Greg lunged forward to grab her arm.* —**lunge** *n* [C]

lurch¹ /lɜːtʃ‖lɜːrtʃ/ *v* [I] to move in an unsteady or uncontrolled way: **+ across/along etc** *He lurched drunkenly towards us.*

lurch² *n* **1 leave sb in the lurch** to leave someone in a very difficult situation, or result in someone being in a very difficult situation **2** [singular] when something or someone suddenly moves in an unsteady or uncontrolled way

lure¹ /lʊə, ljʊəl‖lʊr/ *v* [T] to persuade or trick someone into doing something by making it seem attractive, exciting etc: *The music and bright lights were luring people into the bar.*

lure² *n* [C] something that attracts people

lu·rid /ˈluərɪ̯d, ˈljuərɪ̯dǁˈlurɪ̯d/ *adj* **1** deliberately shocking and involving sex or violence: *a lurid description of the murder* **2** too brightly coloured: *a lurid green dress*

lurk /lɜːkǁlɜːrk/ *v* [I] to wait somewhere secretly, usually before doing something bad: *He was attacked by a man who had been lurking in the alley.*

lus·cious /ˈlʌʃəs/ *adj* extremely good to eat: *luscious ripe strawberries*

lush¹ /lʌʃ/ *adj* having a lot of green and healthy plants or leaves: *lush green fields*

lush² *n* [C] *AmE informal* someone who drinks too much alcohol

lust¹ /lʌst/ *n* [U] **1** a very strong feeling of sexual desire, or a strong desire **2** strong desire for something such as power or money —**lustful** *adj*: *a lustful look* **3** **lust for life** when someone has a lot of energy and seems to enjoy life very much

lust² *v* [I] **1** **lust after sb** to have a strong feeling of sexual desire for someone **2** **lust after/ for sth** to want something very much because you do not have it yet: *politicians lusting after power*

lus·tre *BrE*, **luster** *AmE* /ˈlʌstəǁ-ər/ *n* [singular, U] when something is attractive because it is shiny or bright: *the luster of her long dark hair* —**lustrous** *adj*

lust·y /ˈlʌsti/ *adj* strong and healthy: *The baby gave a lusty cry.* —**lustily** *adv*

lux·u·ri·ant /lʌgˈzjuəriənt, ləgˈʒuəriəntǁləgˈʒuriənt/ *adj* hair or plants that are luxuriant are healthy and growing thickly and strongly —**luxuriance** *n* [U]

lux·u·ri·ate /lʌgˈzjuərieɪt, ləgˈʒuəri-ǁləgˈʒuri-/ *v* **luxuriate in** sth *phr v* [T] to relax and enjoy the pleasure you feel: *She luxuriated in a hot bath.*

lux·u·ri·ous /lʌgˈzjuəriəs, ləgˈʒuəriəsǁləgˈʒuriəs/ *adj* very comfortable, beautiful, and expensive: *They stayed in a luxurious hotel.*

lux·u·ry /ˈlʌkʃəri/ *n* **1** [U] great comfort, especially resulting from beautiful or expensive things: *Caviar! I'm not used to such luxury!* **2** [C] something expensive that you want but do not need: *We can't afford luxuries like music lessons.*

ly·ing /ˈlaɪ-ɪŋ/ *v* the present participle of LIE

lynch /lɪntʃ/ *v* [T] if a crowd of people lynches someone they think is guilty of a crime, they hang that person without a TRIAL —**lynching** *n* [C]

lynch·pin /ˈlɪntʃpɪn/ *n* LINCHPIN

lyr·ic /ˈlɪrɪk/ *n* [C usually plural] the words of a song

lyr·i·cal /ˈlɪrɪkəl/ *adj* expressing feelings and emotions in a beautiful way: *lyrical poetry*

L

Mm

M, m /em/ the letter 'm'

MA, M.A. /ˌem ˈeɪ/ n Master of Arts, a higher university degree ➙ compare MSC

ma·am /mæm, mɑːm, məm/ ⟨em/ n AmE spoken a polite word you use to talk to a woman you do not know

mac /mæk/ n [C] BrE a coat worn to keep out the rain

ma·ca·bre /məˈkɑːbrə, -ˈbɑːblə̩rə, -bər/ adj strange and frightening

mac·a·ro·ni /ˌmækəˈrəʊni/ n [U] a type of PASTA in the shape of small tubes

ma·chet·e /məˈʃeti, məˈʃeti/ n [C] a large knife with a broad heavy blade

ma·chine¹ /məˈʃiːn/ n [C] a piece of equipment that uses power such as electricity to do a job: a sewing machine | Cutting the cloth is done by machine.

> USAGE NOTE: machine.
>
> Compare machine, appliance, tool, instrument, device, and gadget. A **machine** usually uses power, and you do not work it directly with your hands: the machines in the factory | Tickets are available from the machine on the platform. | a knitting machine. Electrical machines used in the home (such as washing machines) can also be called **appliances**: a shop selling household appliances. A **tool** is an object which you hold in your hand and which you use for making things from wood, metal, or other materials: carpenter's tools such as hammers, drills, and saws. An **instrument** is an object which you use to do very exact or careful work, usually by hand: medical/surgical instruments | A thermometer is an instrument for measuring temperature. **Device** is a general word for any object which has been produced for doing work, and is usually used when there is no particular word for that thing: an electronic device controls the opening of the doors. | I have no idea how this device works. **Gadget** is an informal word for a small and perhaps unusual device for doing a particular job: a clever little gadget for opening bottles.

machine² v [T] to make or shape something using a machine —**machinist** n [C]

machine gun /ˈ. ./ n [C] a gun that fires a lot of bullets very quickly

ma·chin·e·ry /məˈʃiːnəri/ n [U] 1 machines, especially large ones: agricultural machinery 2 an official system for organizing or achieving something: The machinery of the law works slowly.

mach·o /ˈmætʃəʊ‖ˈmɑːtʃoʊ/ adj informal having male qualities such as strength or courage but lacking qualities such as sympathy or understanding

mackintosh /ˈmækɪ̩ntɒʃ/ n [C] BrE old-fashioned a coat worn to keep out the rain

mad /mæd/ adj -dder, -ddest 1 informal angry: You make me so mad! | + at Lisa was really mad at me for telling Dad. | **go mad** BrE (=become very angry): Mum will go mad when she finds out what you've done. 2 BrE informal stupid: You're mad to get involved with someone like him! 3 **be mad about sb/sth** BrE informal to like someone or something very much: The kids are mad about football. 4 behaving in an excited or uncontrolled way: **go mad** The crowd went mad when Liverpool scored. 5 mentally ill

mad·am /ˈmædəm/ n 1 used to show respect when talking to a woman who is a customer in your shop, restaurant etc: Can I help you, madam? 2 **Dear Madam** used to begin a formal letter to a woman whose name you do not know

mad·den /ˈmædn/ v [T] to make someone very angry

mad·den·ing /ˈmædənɪŋ/ adj extremely annoying: The most maddening thing is that it's my own fault. —**maddeningly** adv

made¹ /meɪd/ v the past tense and past participle of MAKE

made² adj 1 **be made of** to be built from or consist of: The frame is made of silver. 2 **be made for** to be perfectly suitable for a particular person, group, or situation: I think Anna and Juan were made for each other. 3 **sb has got it made** spoken to have everything you need to be happy: When I was at university, I thought I'd got it made.

> USAGE NOTE: made
>
> **Made of** and **made from** have very similar meanings, but they are often used in slightly different ways. If the original material has been completely changed, use **made from**: Bread is made from flour and water. | luxury soap made from the finest ingredients. If the original materials can still be recognized, use **made of**: a statue made of the finest marble | a handbag made of cheap black plastic.

mad·house /ˈmædhaʊs/ n [C] a place that is very busy and noisy: It's a madhouse when the children are home.

mad·ly /ˈmædli/ adv 1 in a wild, uncontrolled way: Allen was beating madly on the door. 2 **madly in love** very much in love

mad·man /ˈmædmən/ n 1 a man who behaves in a very dangerous or stupid way: He drives like a madman. 2 old-fashioned a man who is mentally ill

mad·ness /ˈmædn̩s/ n [U] 1 very stupid and often dangerous behaviour: It would be madness to try to cross the desert on your own. 2 BrE severe mental illness; INSANITY

mael·strom /ˈmeɪlstrəm/ n [C] a confusing or frightening situation in which a lot of things happen very quickly

maes·tro /ˈmaɪstrəʊ‖-roʊ/ n [C] someone who can do something very well, especially a musician

maf·i·a /ˈmæfiə, ˈmɑːf-‖ˈmɑː-, ˈmæ-/ n **the Mafia** a large organization of criminals

mag·a·zine /ˌmæɡəˈziːn‖ˈmæɡəziːn/ n [C] 1 a large thin book with a paper cover, which is sold every week or every month: a fashion magazine 2 the part of a gun that holds the bullets

ma·gen·ta /məˈdʒentə/ n [U] a bright red-pink colour ➙ see colour picture on page 114 —**magenta** adj

M

mag·got /ˈmægət/ *n* [C] a young insect that looks like a WORM and grows into a FLY

ma·gic[1] /ˈmædʒɪk/ *n* [U] **1** a special power used to make strange or impossible things happen: *The witch cast a magic spell on the princess, making her sleep for 100 years.* **2** when someone does tricks which look like magic, for example to make things appear and disappear: *a magic show* **3** a special attractive quality: *the magic of the East* → see also BLACK MAGIC

magic² *adj* [only before noun] having magic powers or used in magic: *magic spells*

ma·gic·al /ˈmædʒɪkəl/ *adj* **1** very enjoyable and exciting, in a strange or special way: *a magical evening beneath the stars* **2** having magic powers or done using magic: *magical objects* —**magically** /-kli/ *adv*

ma·gi·cian /məˈdʒɪʃən/ *n* [C] **1** someone who does magic tricks to entertain people **2** a man in stories who has magic powers

ma·gis·trate /ˈmædʒɪˌstreɪt, -strɪt/ *n* [C] someone who decides if people are guilty of less serious crimes in a court of law

mag·nan·i·mous /mægˈnænɪməs/ *adj formal* kind and generous towards other people, especially someone you have just defeated —**magnanimity** /ˌmægnəˈnɪməti/ *n* [U]

mag·nate /ˈmægneɪt, -nɪt/ *n* [C] **steel/oil/ shipping etc magnate** a rich and powerful person who owns a company that produces steel, oil etc

mag·ne·si·um /mægˈniːziəm/ *n* [U] a light silver-white metal

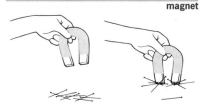

magnet

mag·net /ˈmægnɪt/ *n* [C] **1** a piece of iron or steel that makes other metal objects move towards it **2** a person or place that attracts many other people or things: *Darlington has become a magnet for new companies of all kinds.* —**magnetize** (also **-ise** *BrE*) *v* [T]

mag·net·ic /mægˈnetɪk/ *adj* **1** having the power of a magnet: *the Earth's magnetic field* **2** **magnetic tape/disk etc** special TAPE etc that contains electronic information which can be read by a computer or other machine **3** **magnetic personality/charm etc** a quality in someone's character that makes them very interesting, exciting, and attractive

mag·net·is·m /ˈmægnɪˌtɪzəm/ *n* [U] **1** the power that a magnet has to attract things **2** a quality that makes other people feel attracted to

you: *Cary Grant had an extraordinary magnetism which women found irresistible.*

mag·nif·i·cent /mægˈnɪfɪsənt/ *adj* very impressive because of being very big, beautiful etc: *a magnificent painting* —**magnificence** *n* [U]

mag·ni·fy /ˈmægnɪˌfaɪ/ *v* [T] **1** to make something look much bigger than it is by using a special glass LENS: *The image has been magnified 1000 times.* **2** to make something seem more important than it really is: *Differences between the parties were magnified by the press.* —**magnification** /ˌmægnɪfɪˈkeɪʃən/ *n* [C,U]

magnify

magnifying glass

magnifying glass /ˈ...ˌ./ *n* [C] a round piece of glass with a handle, that makes things look much bigger when you look through it → see picture at MAGNIFY

mag·ni·tude /ˈmægnɪtjuːdǁ-tuːd/ *n* [U] how large or important something is: *I hadn't realized the magnitude of the problem.*

mag·no·li·a /mægˈnəʊliəǁ-ˈnoʊ-/ *n* [C] a bush with large white or pink flowers

mag·pie /ˈmægpaɪ/ *n* [C] a black and white bird with a long tail

ma·hog·a·ny /məˈhɒgəniǁməˈhɑː-/ *n* [U] a hard dark wood, often used for making furniture

maid /meɪd/ *n* [C] **1** a female servant, especially in a large house **2** a maiden

maid·en¹ /ˈmeɪdn/ *also* **maid** *n* [C] *old-fashioned literary* a girl or young woman who is not married: *a fair maiden*

maiden² *adj* **maiden flight/voyage** the first trip that a plane or ship makes

maiden name /ˈ... ./ *n* [C] the family name that a woman had before she got married

mail¹ /meɪl/ *n* **1** **the mail** the system of collecting and delivering letters, packages etc; the POST *BrE*: *I just put the letter in the mail.* **2** [U] the letters, packages etc that are delivered to a particular person or at a particular time; POST *BrE*: *They sent my mail to the wrong address.* | *What time does the mail come?* → see also AIRMAIL, POST¹

mail² *v* [T] *especially AmE* to send a letter or package to someone; POST *BrE*: *I'll mail it to you tomorrow.*

mail·box /ˈmeɪlbɒksǁ-bɑːks/ *n* [C] a box where letters are delivered or collected

mailing list /ˈ... ./ *n* [C] a list of people's names

GRAMMAR NOTE: the passive (1)
You use a verb in the **passive** to say that something happens to the subject of the sentence. You form the passive using **be/is/was** and the past participle.
ACTIVE: *They **chose** a new leader.* → PASSIVE: *A new leader **was chosen**.*

M

and addresses that a company keeps in order to send customer or advertisements to them

mail·man /'meɪlmæn/ n [C] *AmE* a man who delivers letters and packages to people's houses; POSTMAN *BrE*

mail or·der /ˌ. '..◂/ n [U] when you buy goods from a company that sends them by POST

maim /meɪm/ v [T] to wound or injure someone very seriously and often permanently: *The accident left her maimed for life.*

main¹ /meɪn/ adj [only before noun] **1** bigger or more important than other things of the same kind: *the main meal of the day* | *Coffee is the country's main export.* **2 the main thing** *spoken* used to say that something is the most important thing in a situation: *You're both safe, that's the main thing.* **3 in the main** *spoken* generally: *The weather was very good in the main.*

main² n [C] also **the mains** a large pipe carrying water or gas, which is connected to people's houses by smaller pipes: *a broken water main*

main course /ˈ. ./ n [C] the main part of a meal

main·frame /'meɪnfreɪm/ n [C] a large computer that can work very fast and that a lot of people can use at the same time

main·land /'meɪnlənd, -lænd/ n **the mainland** the main part of an area of land, not the islands that are near it — **mainland** adj: *mainland Europe*

main line /ˌ. '.◂/ n [C] an important railway that connects two cities: *the main line between Belfast and Dublin*

main·ly /'meɪnli/ adv **1** used to say that something is true about most of a group of people or things: *The workforce consists mainly of women.* **2** used to say that something is generally true: *I bought the answering machine mainly for business reasons.*

main road /ˌ. './ n [C] a large and important road

main·stay /'meɪnsteɪ/ n [C] the most important part of something, which makes it possible for it to work correctly or to continue to exist: *Farming is still the mainstay of our country's economy.*

main·stream /'meɪnstriːm/ n **the mainstream** the most usual way of thinking about something or doing something, or the people who think or behave in this way — **mainstream** adj: *mainstream Japanese politics*

main·tain /meɪn'teɪn, mən-/ v [T] **1** to make something continue in the same way or at the same standard as before: *We need to maintain good relations with our customers.* **2** to keep something in good condition by taking care of it: *It costs a lot of money to maintain a big house.* **3 maintain that** to say that you are sure that something is true: *She has always maintained that her son is not dead.*

main·te·nance /'meɪntənəns/ n [U] **1** the work that is necessary to keep something in good condition: *car maintenance* **2** money that is paid to a former wife, husband, or to children, to support them after the marriage has ended

mai·son·ette /ˌmeɪzə'net/ n [C] *BrE* an apartment that is on two floors, which is part of a larger house

maize /meɪz/ n [U] *BrE* a tall plant with yellow seeds that are used for food; CORN *AmE*

ma·jes·tic /mə'dʒestɪk/ adj very big and impressive: *a majestic view of the lake* — **majestically** /-kli/ adv

maj·es·ty /'mædʒɪsti/ n **1** [U] when something is very impressive and beautiful: *the majesty of the Grand Canyon* **2 Your/Her/His Majesty** a formal title that is used to talk to or about a king or queen

ma·jor¹ /'meɪdʒəll-ər/ adj **1** very large or important, especially when compared to other things or people of a similar kind: *a major cause of heart disease* | *major changes in the Earth's climate* **2** a major key is one of the two main sets of musical notes: *a symphony in A major* → compare MINOR¹

major² n [C] **1** also **Major** an officer of middle rank in the army **2** *AmE* the main subject that you study at college or university: *His major is history.*

major³ v
major in sth *phr v* [T] *AmE* to study something as your main subject at a college or university: *I'm majoring in biology.*

ma·jor·i·ty /mə'dʒɒrɪtillmə'dʒɔː-, mə'dʒɑː-/ n **1** [singular] most of the people or things in a particular group: *The majority of adult smokers want to give up the habit.* **2** [C usually singular] the difference between the number of votes or places in parliament that the winner of an election gets and the number of votes or places that the next party or person gets: *Tony Blair won by a huge majority.* → compare MINORITY

make¹ /meɪk/ v **made** /meɪd/, **made, making**
1 [T] to produce or build something: *She makes all her own clothes.* | *The furniture was made by a Swedish firm.* | **make lunch/dinner etc** (=prepare lunch, dinner etc) **2** [T] **make a mistake/suggestion/promise etc** to do something wrong, suggest something, promise something etc: *They made a mistake on the electricity bill.* | *Roger made a good suggestion.* **3** [T] to cause someone to do something, or cause something to happen: *Sarah's really funny – she always makes me laugh.* | *Heavy rain is making the roads very slippery.* | **make sb sad/happy/excited etc** *Don't do that – you're making me nervous.* | **make it possible/difficult etc** *Computers are making it possible for more and more people to work from home.* **4** [T] to force someone to do something: *The police made them stand up against the wall.* **5** [T] to give someone a particular job or title: *They made her deputy manager.* **6** [T] to earn or get money: *Irene makes about $60,000 a year.* **7** [linking verb] to be a particular number or amount when added together: *2 and 2 make 4.* | *If you include us, that makes eight people for dinner.* **8 make it a)** to succeed in arriving somewhere: *We made it to the station just as the bus was leaving.* **b)** to be successful in a job or activity: *A lot of people want to be in films, but very few of them actually make it.* **9 make it Friday/10 o'clock etc** *spoken* used to arrange a day or time to meet someone: *Let's make it Saturday morning.* **10 make time** to leave enough time to do something: *Don't forget to make time to visit Grandpa this week.* **11** [T] to be suitable for a job or purpose, because you have the right qualities to do it: *John will make a good father.* **12 make the bed** to tidy the sheets on a bed so that it is ready to sleep in

M

13 that makes two of us *spoken informal* used to say that you feel the same as someone else: *"I'm so tired!" "Yeah, that makes two of us."*
14 make or break to make someone or something be very successful, or make them fail completely: *One of his reviews can make or break a play.* **15 make do** to do something using the things you have, when you do not have exactly what you want: *We'll have to make do with these old clothes.* → see also **be made of** (MADE[2]), **make sure** (SURE[1]), **make a difference** (DIFFERENCE), **make love** (LOVE[2]), **make sense** (SENSE[1]), **make the best of sth** (BEST[3]), **make friends** (FRIEND), **make up your mind** (MIND[1])

make for sth *phr v* [T] **1** to go towards a place: *They made for the nearest bar.* **2** to have a particular result or effect: *It should make for an interesting evening.* → see also **be made for** (MADE[2])

make sth **into** sth *phr v* [T] to change something into something else: *The opium is made into heroin.*

make sth **of** sb/sth *phr v* [T] **1 what do you make of sth** used to ask what someone's opinion is about something: *What do you make of this letter?* **2 not know what to make of sth** to be confused by something and not understand it **3 make too much of sth** to treat a situation as if it is more important than it really is: *He doesn't like us to make too much of his birthday.* → see also **make the most of sth** (MOST[2]), **make a mess sth** (MESS)

make off with *phr v* [T] to steal something: *The thieves made off with £3,000 worth of jeans.*

make out *phr v* **1** [T **make** ↔ **out**] to be able to hear, see, or understand something: *I can't make out what the sign says.* **2 make a cheque out to sb** to write a CHEQUE so that money is paid to a particular person **3 make out (that)** *informal* to say that something is true when it is not: *Brian was making out he had won.* **4** [I] *AmE informal* to kiss and touch in a sexual way

make up *phr v* **1** [T **make** sth ↔ **up**] to invent a story or an excuse: *Ron made up an excuse so his mother wouldn't be mad.* **2** [T **make up** sth] to combine together to form something: *the rocks and minerals that make up the Earth's outer layer* **3 make it up to sb** to do something good for someone because you feel responsible for something bad that happened to them: *I'm sorry I forgot your birthday! I promise I'll make it up to you.* **4** [I] to become friends with someone again, after an argument → see also **make up your mind** (MIND[1])

make up for sth *phr v* [T] **1** to REPLACE something that is lost or missing, or make a bad situation or event seem better: *He ate a big lunch, in order to make up for missing breakfast.* **2** to have so much of one quality that it does not matter that you do not have others: *Jay lacks experience, but he makes up for it with hard work.* **3 make up for lost time** to do something quickly because you started late or worked too slowly

make[2] *n* [C] **1** a type of product made by a company: *"What make is your car?" "It's a Honda."* **2 be on the make** to be secretly trying to get money or advantages for yourself in a dishonest or unfair way

make-be·lieve /'. .,./ *n* [U] when you imagine or pretend that something is real

make·o·ver /'meɪkəʊvəll-ouvər/ *n* [C] **1** when you change the way you look completely by buying new clothes, getting your hair cut etc **2** when you change the way a building, room etc looks

mak·er /'meɪkəll-ər/ *n* [C] a person or company that makes something: *the big three US car makers*|*film maker Steven Spielberg*

make·shift /'meɪkʃɪft/ *adj* [only before noun] made to last or be used for a short time, using the things that you have available: *a makeshift table made from boxes*

make-up, makeup /'meɪkʌp/ *n* [U] powder, creams, and LIPSTICK that people put on their faces to make themselves look more attractive: *Ginny put on her makeup.*

mak·ing /'meɪkɪŋ/ *n* **1** [U] the process or business of making something: *The making of the movie took four years.*|*the art of rug making* **2 in the making** used to say that someone is likely to be very successful at doing something, or something is likely to happen: *a new World Champion in the making*

mak·ings /'meɪkɪŋz/ *n* [plural] **have the makings of** to have the qualities or skills needed to become a particular kind of person or thing: *Sandy has the makings of a good doctor.*

mal·ad·just·ed /ˌmælə'dʒʌstɪd◂/ *adj* a maladjusted child has emotional problems and cannot form good relationships with other people

ma·laise /mə'leɪz, mæ-/ *n* [U] *formal* a situation in which a country, organization etc has problems that are difficult to deal with: *the general economic malaise*

ma·lar·i·a /mə'leəriəll-'ler-/ *n* [U] a serious disease that is common in hot countries and is spread by MOSQUITOes

male[1] /meɪl/ *adj* **1** belonging to the sex that cannot have babies: *a male lion* **2** typical of this sex: *a male voice*

male[2] *n* [C] a male person or animal

male chau·vin·ist /ˌmeɪl 'ʃəʊvₙn̩ɪst◂ ll-'ʃou-/ *n* a man who believes that men are better than women, and that men should not do work such as cooking, cleaning, looking after children etc: *He's a typical male chauvinist pig!* —**male chauvinism** *n* [U]

ma·lev·o·lent /mə'levələnt/ *adj* *formal* wanting to hurt or cause harm someone: *those dark malevolent eyes* —**malevolence** *n* [U]

mal·func·tion /mæl'fʌŋkʃən/ *n* [C] a fault in the way a machine works: *a malfunction in the computer system* —**malfunction** *v* [I]

mal·ice /'mælɪs/ *n* [U] when you want to hurt or harm someone: *Corran didn't do it out of malice.*

ma·li·cious /mə'lɪʃəs/ *adj* intended to hurt, upset, or embarrass someone: *malicious gossip* —**maliciously** *adv*

ma·lign /mə'laɪn/ *v* [T] *formal* to say or write unpleasant and untrue things about someone: *He's been much maligned by the press.*

ma·lig·nant /mə'lɪgnənt/ *adj* **1** containing CANCER cells: *a malignant tumour* → compare BENIGN **2** *formal* wanting to hurt or harm someone: *a malignant grin* —**malignancy** *n* [U]

M

ma·lin·ger /məˈlɪŋgəll-ər/ v [I] to avoid work by pretending to be ill —**malingerer** n [C]

mall /mɔːl, mæll|mɔːl/ n [C] a large covered area containing a lot of shops: *a shopping mall*

mal·lard /ˈmælədll-ərd/ n [C] a type of duck

mal·le·a·ble /ˈmæliəbəl/ adj **1** easy to press or bend into a new shape: *Gold is fairly malleable*. **2** *formal* if someone is malleable, it is easy to influence their ideas and opinions

mal·let /ˈmælɪt/ n [C] a wooden hammer → see picture at TOOLS

mal·nour·ished /ˌmælˈnʌrɪʃtll-ˈnɜː-, -ˈnʌ-/ adj ill or weak because of not eating enough food, or because of not eating good food

mal·nu·tri·tion /ˌmælnjʊˈtrɪʃənll-nʊ-/ n [U] a serious medical condition caused by not having enough food or not having enough good food: *80% of the children were suffering from malnutrition.*

mal·prac·tice /ˌmælˈpræktɪs/ n [C,U] when a doctor, lawyer etc fails to do his or her professional duty, or does something wrong: *evidence of serious malpractice*

malt /mɔːltllmɒːlt/ n **1** [U] grain, usually BARLEY, that is used for making beer, WHISKY etc **2** [C] *AmE* a type of non-alcoholic drink with ICE CREAM, chocolate etc added to it

mal·treat·ment /mælˈtriːtmənt/ n [U] *formal* cruel or unfair treatment: *daily maltreatment of prisoners* —**maltreat** v [T]

malt whis·ky /ˌ. ˈ../ n [U] high quality Scottish WHISKY

ma·ma /məˈmɑːllˈmɑːmə/ n [C] *AmE informal or BrE old-fashioned* mother

mam·mal /ˈmæməl/ n [C] a type of animal such as a human or a cow that gives birth to live babies and produces milk for them

mam·moth[1] /ˈmæməθ/ adj very big: *a mammoth job*

mammoth[2] n [C] a very big ELEPHANT that existed a long time ago

man[1] /mæn/ n, plural **men** /men/ **1** [C] an adult male person: *a middle-aged man* | *The man told us to wait.* | *a gambling man* (=a man who likes gambling) **2** [U] all people, both male and female, considered as a group: *one of the worst disasters in the history of man* **3** **the man in the street** an average or ordinary person: *The man in the street isn't interested in foreign policy issues.* → see also MEN

man[2] v [T] **-nned, -nning** to operate a machine, or be in charge of a place: *The checkpoint was manned by French UN soldiers.* —**manned** adj: *a manned rocket*

man[3] interjection *informal, especially AmE* used to emphasize what you are saying: *Man! Was she angry!*

man·a·cle /ˈmænəkəl/ n [C] an iron ring on a chain that is put around the hand or foot of a prisoner

man·age /ˈmænɪdʒ/ v **1** [I,T] to succeed in doing something difficult: *I don't know how we'll manage now that Keith's lost his job.* **2** [T] to be in charge of a company, shop etc, or the people who work there: *The hotel has been owned and managed by the Koidl family for 200 years.* **3** [T] *spoken humorous* to do something that causes problems: *The kids managed to spill paint all over the carpet.*

man·age·a·ble /ˈmænɪdʒəbəl/ adj easy to control or deal with: *My hair's more manageable since I had it cut.*

man·age·ment /ˈmænɪdʒmənt/ n **1** [U] the job of controlling and organizing the work of a company or organization and the people who work for it: *a management training course* | *problems caused by bad management* **2** [singular, U] the people who are in charge of controlling and organizing a company or organization: *The management has agreed to talk to the union.*

man·ag·er /ˈmænɪdʒəll-ər/ n [C] someone who is in charge of a bank, shop, sports team etc, or a group of people in a company: *That meal was terrible! I want to speak to the manager!* | *the manager of the Boston Red Sox*

man·ag·er·ess /ˌmænɪdʒəˈresll-ˈmænɪdʒərˌs/ n [C] *BrE old-fashioned* a woman who is in charge of a shop, restaurant, or hotel

man·a·ge·ri·al /ˌmænɪˈdʒɪəriəl ll-ˈdʒɪr-/ adj connected to the job of being a manager: *good managerial skills*

managing di·rec·tor /ˌ... .ˈ../ n [C] *BrE* a person who is in charge of a large company

man·date /ˈmændeɪt/ n [C] *formal* the official power to do something, because people have voted for it at an election: *The government could rightly claim a mandate for their reform programme.*

man·da·to·ry /ˈmændətərill-tɔːri/ adj something that is mandatory must be done because of a rule or law: *mandatory safety inspections*

mane /meɪn/ n [C] the long hair on the neck of a horse or lion

ma·neu·ver /məˈnuːvəll-ər/ n, v the American spelling of MANOEUVRE

ma·neu·ver·a·ble /məˈnuːvərəbəl/ adj the American spelling of MANOEUVRABLE

ma·neu·vers /məˈnuːvəzll-ərz/ n the American spelling of MANOEUVRES

mange /meɪndʒ/ n [U] a skin disease that makes animals lose their fur —**mangy** adj

man·ger /ˈmeɪndʒəll-ər/ n [C] a container for horses, cows etc to eat from

man·gle /ˈmæŋgəl/ v [T] to damage something badly by crushing or twisting it: *The car was badly mangled in the accident.*

man·go /ˈmæŋgəʊll-goʊ/ n [C] a sweet tropical fruit → see picture at FRUIT

man·grove /ˈmæŋgrəʊvll-groʊv/ n [C] a tropical tree that grows in or near water

man·han·dle /ˈmænhændl/ v [T] to move someone or something roughly, using force: *The report claimed that patients were manhandled and bullied.*

man·hole /ˈmænhəʊlll-hoʊl/ n [C] a covered hole on the surface of a road, which people go down to check pipes, wires etc

man·hood /ˈmænhʊd/ n [U] the fact of being a man, not a boy: *The tribe performs special ceremonies when the boys reach manhood.*

man·hunt /ˈmænhʌnt/ n [C] an organized search, especially for a criminal

ma·ni·a /ˈmeɪniə/ n [C,U] **1** a very strong feeling of interest, excitement, and liking for someone or something, especially shown by a lot of people at the same time: *Beatle mania*

2 *technical* a mental illness which makes some-one extremely excited or violent

ma·ni·ac /'meɪniæk/ *n* [C] *informal* someone who behaves in a stupid or dangerous way: *He drives like a maniac.* —**maniacal** /mə'naɪəkəl/ *adj*

man·ic /'mænɪk/ *adj* behaving in a very excited or extremely active way: *He seemed full of manic energy.*

manic de·pres·sive /ˌ.. .'../ *n* [C] someone who has a mental illness which makes them very sad or very excited —**manic depressive** *adj*

man·i·cure /'mænˌkjʊəl-kjʊr/ *n* [C,U] when someone cuts and polishes your FINGERNAILS —**manicure** *v* [T]

man·i·fest /'mænˌfest/ *v* **manifest itself** if something manifests itself, it can be seen or noticed: *The disease can manifest itself in many ways.* —**manifest** *adj formal*: *a manifest error of judgement* —**manifestly** *adv*

man·i·fes·ta·tion /ˌmænˌfe'steɪʃən‖-fə-/ *n* [C,U] *formal* something that happens, which shows clearly that a particular situation or feeling exists: *another manifestation of the greenhouse effect*

man·i·fes·to /ˌmænˌ'festəʊ‖-oʊ/ *n* [C] a written statement by a political group, saying what they want to do: *the Communist manifesto*

man·i·fold /'mænˌfəʊld‖-foʊld/ *adj formal* many, and of different kinds: *Their problems are manifold.*

ma·nip·u·late /mə'nɪpjʊleɪt/ *v* [T] **1** to make someone do what you want by secretly tricking them or influencing them: *He skilfully manipulated the media.* **2** to skilfully control or move something: *the computer's ability to manipulate large quantities of data* —**manipulation** /məˌnɪpjʊˈleɪʃən/ *n* [U]

ma·nip·u·la·tive /mə'nɪpjʊlətɪv‖-leɪ-/ *adj* good at secretly controlling or tricking people to get what you want: *Gina was charming, sly, and manipulative.*

man·kind /ˌmæn'kaɪnd/ *n* [U] all humans, considered as a group: *one of the most important events in the history of mankind*

man·ly /'mænli/ *adj* having qualities such as strength or courage that are considered to be typical of a man: *his strong manly shoulders* —**manliness** *n* [U]

man-made /ˌ. '.◂/ *adj* not made naturally, or not made of natural materials: *man-made fabrics* | *a man-made lake*

man·ne·quin /'mænɪkˌn/ *n* [C] a MODEL of a human body used for showing clothes

man·ner /'mænəl-ər/ *n* [singular] **1** the way in which someone behaves with other people: *She has a cheerful and friendly manner.* **2** *formal* the way in which something is done or happens: *the manner of his death* **3** **all manner of** *formal* many different kinds of things or people **4** **in a manner of speaking** *spoken* used to say that something is true in some ways, but

not completely true: *"Is she married?" "Yes, in a manner of speaking."* → see also MANNERS

man·nered /'mænəd‖-ərd/ *adj* **1** **mild mannered/well mannered/bad-mannered etc** behaving in a gentle, polite, impolite etc way **2** behaving in a way that does not seem natural or sincere: *He spoke in a highly mannered Oxford accent.*

man·ner·is·m /'mænərɪzəm/ *n* [C,U] a way of speaking or behaving that is typical of a particular person or group of people: *Eliot's ability to imitate Pound's mannerisms*

man·ners /'mænəz‖-ərz/ *n* [plural] the way you behave when you are with other people, and whether or not you are polite to them: **good/bad manners** *It's bad manners to talk while you're eating.*

ma·noeu·vra·ble *BrE*, **maneuverable** *AmE* /mə'nuːvərəbəl/ *adj* easy to move or turn

ma·noeu·vre¹ *BrE*, **maneuver** *AmE* /mə'nuːvəl/ *v* [I,T] to move or turn something into a different position: *Small boats are easier to manoeuvre.*

ma·noeu·vre² *BrE*, **maneuver** *AmE* /mə'nuːvəl -ər/ *n* [C] **1** a skilful or carefully planned movement: *a complicated manoeuvre* **2** [C,U] a carefully planned action in order to achieve something, especially by tricking people: *political maneuvers* → see also MANOEUVRES

ma·noeu·vres *BrE*, **maneuvers** *AmE* /mə'nuːvəz‖-ərz/ *n* [plural] when soldiers practise fighting a battle

man·or /'mænəl-ər/ *n* [C] a big country house with a large area of land around it

man·pow·er /'mænˌpaʊəl-ˌpaʊr/ *n* [U] all the workers that are needed to do a particular kind of work: *We don't have enough manpower right now to start a new project.*

man·ser·vant /'mænˌsɜːvəntl-sɜːr-/ *n* [C] a man who was someone's special servant, in past times

man·sion /'mænʃən/ *n* [C] a very large house

man·slaugh·ter /'mænˌslɔːtəl-ˌslɔːtər/ *n* [U] *law* the crime of killing someone without intending to → compare MURDER¹

man·tel·piece /'mæntlpiːs/ also **man·tel** /'mæntl/ *especially AmE* — *n* [C] the shelf above a FIREPLACE

man·tle /'mæntl/ *n* **1** **take on/assume/inherit the mantle** of *literary* to start to have an important job or position: *a star who will one day inherit the mantle of Marilyn Monroe* **2** a **mantle of snow/darkness etc** *literary* when an area is covered in snow, darkness etc

man·tra /'mæntrə/ *n* [C] a word or phrase that is repeated many times, for example while praying

man·u·al¹ /'mænjuəl/ *adj* **1** working using your hands, especially doing hard physical work: *manual work* | *manual workers* **2** not operated by a machine, or not using electricity: *a manual typewriter* —**manually** *adv*

GRAMMAR NOTE: the passive (1)
You use a verb in the **passive** to say that something happens to the subject of the sentence. You form the passive using **be/is/was** and the past participle.
ACTIVE: *They **chose** a new leader.* → PASSIVE: *A new leader **was chosen**.*

M

manual[2] n [C] a book that tells you how to use a machine: *a computer manual*

man·u·fac·ture[1] /ˌmænjʊˈfæktʃəllˌər/ v [T] to make large quantities of goods, using machines: *one of Europe's biggest paper manufacturing companies*

manufacture[2] n [U] *formal* the process of manufacturing goods, usually in large numbers

man·u·fac·tur·er /ˌmænjʊˈfæktʃərəllˌər/ n [C] a company that makes large quantities of goods, using machines: *the world's largest shoe manufacturer*

ma·nure /məˈnjʊəllməˈnʊr/ n [U] solid waste from animals which is put into the soil to make crops grow bigger, stronger etc

man·u·script /ˈmænjʊ̩skrɪpt/ n [C] **1** a book or piece of writing before it is printed: *a 350 page manuscript* **2** an old book written by hand before printing was invented: *an ancient Chinese manuscript*

man·y /ˈmeni/ *quantifier, pron* **more** /mɔːllmɔːr/, **most** /məʊstllmoʊst/ **1** of people or things – used especially in negative sentences or questions, or with 'too' or 'so': *There aren't many tickets left.* | *Were there many people at the concert?* | *You've eaten too many chocolates already.* | **+ of** *Many of us have had similar experiences.* | **a great many/a good many** (=a very large number): *I learned a great many things.* **2** used to ask or talk about the number of people or things: **how many** *How many bedrooms are there?* | **as many** (=the same number): *There weren't as many accidents as the previous year.* **3** **as many as** used before a number in order to emphasize that the number is surprisingly large: *As many as 60% of high school children say they have experimented with drugs.* **4** **many a time** *old-fashioned* often **5** **the many** most people: *Education for the many, not the few.*

map[1] /mæp/ n [C] a drawing of an area or country, showing rivers, roads, cities etc: *a map of Texas* ➡ see colour picture on page 80

map[2] v [T] **-pped, -pping** to make a map of an area

map sth ↔ out *phr v* [T] to plan something carefully: *Her parents had already mapped out her future.*

ma·ple /ˈmeɪpəl/ n [C,U] a type of tree whose leaves become a beautiful colour in autumn

mar /mɑːllmɑːr/ v [T] **-rred, -rring** to spoil something and make it seem less pleasant, attractive, or enjoyable: *The election campaign was marred by violence.*

Mar. the written abbreviation for MARCH

mar·a·thon[1] /ˈmærəθənllˌθɑːn/ n [C] a race in which people run just over 26 miles

marathon[2] *adj* [only before noun] continuing for a very long time: *a marathon session of Congress*

ma·raud·ing /məˈrɔːdɪŋllˌrɔː-/ *adj* searching for something to kill, steal, or destroy: *marauding soldiers*

mar·ble /ˈmɑːbəllˈmɑːr-/ n **1** [U] a hard rock that can be polished and used for making floors, STATUES etc **2** [C] a small coloured glass ball, used to play a children's game

march[1] /mɑːtʃllmɑːrtʃ/ v [I] **1** to walk together in a large group to protest about something: *Thousands of demonstrators marched*

through Rostock. **2** if soldiers march, they walk with regular steps: *The army marched past.* ➡ see colour picture on page 670 **3** to walk quickly because you are angry or determined: *She marched out of the room without looking at us.*

march[2] n [C] **1** an organized event in which people walk together to protest about something: *a civil rights march* **2** when soldiers walk together with regular steps **3** a piece of music with a regular beat for soldiers to march to

March written abbreviation **Mar.** n [C,U] the third month of the year ➡ see usage note at MONTH

marching band /ˈ.. ˌ./ n [C] a group of musicians who march while they play instruments

mare /meəllmer/ n [C] a female horse

mar·ga·rine /ˌmɑːdʒəˈriːn, ˌmɑːgə-llˈmɑːrdʒərɪ̩n/ n [U] a food used instead of butter, made from animal or vegetable fat

mar·gin /ˈmɑːdʒɪnllˈmɑːr-/ **margin** n [C] **1** the empty space at the side of a printed page: *I wrote some notes in the margin.* | *a wide/narrow margin* **2** the difference in the number of votes, points etc between the winners and the losers of an election or competition: *The Democrats won by a wide margin.* (=they had a lot more votes) **3** **margin of error** the amount by which a calculation can be wrong without affecting the final results **4** **profit margin** the amount of profit that a company makes

mar·gin·al /ˈmɑːdʒɪnəllˈmɑːr-/ *adj* very small or unimportant: *a marginal improvement*

mar·gin·al·ly /ˈmɑːdʒɪnəl-illˈmɑːr-/ *adv* very little or very slightly: *The other car was marginally cheaper.*

mar·i·jua·na /ˌmærɪ̩ˈwɑːnə, -ˈhwɑːnə/ n [U] an illegal drug that is smoked

ma·ri·na /məˈriːnə/ n [C] a small area of water where people pay to keep their boats

mar·i·nate /ˈmærɪ̩neɪt/ also **mar·i·nade** /ˌmærɪ̩ˈneɪd/ v [T] to put food into a mixture of oil, wine, SPICES etc before you cook it — **marinade** n [C,U]

ma·rine[1] /məˈriːn/ *adj* relating to the sea or living in the sea: *marine life*

marine[2] n [C] a soldier who is in the MARINES

mar·i·ner /ˈmærɪ̩nəllˌnər/ n [C] *literary* a sailor

Ma·rines /məˈriːnz/ also **Marine Corps** /ˈ. ./ *AmE* — n [U] a military organization that consists of soldiers who live and work on ships

mar·i·o·nette /ˌmæriəˈnet/ n [C] a toy that is moved by pulling strings which are connected to parts of its body ➡ compare PUPPET

mar·i·tal /ˈmærɪ̩tl/ *adj* connected with marriage: *marital problems* | *marital status* (=whether you are married or not)

mar·i·time /ˈmærɪ̩taɪm/ *adj* connected with the sea or ships: *Britain's traditional role as a maritime power.*

mark[1] /mɑːkllmɑːrk/ v [T] **1** to make a sign, shape, or word, using a pen or pencil: *Check the envelopes that are marked 'urgent' first.* **2** to show where something is: *The grave is marked* *by a stone cross.* **3** to check a test or students' work, and give a number or letter which shows how good it is: *Have you marked my essay yet?* **4** to show that something is happening, especially an important event or change: *The destruction of the Berlin wall marked the end of the Cold War.* **5** to celebrate an important event: *an exhibition to mark the anniversary of Picasso's birth* **6** to make a mark on something in a way that spoils or damages it: *The heels of his boots had marked the floor.* **7** to stay close to someone from the opposing team in a sports game to stop them playing well or getting the ball

mark sth ↔ **down** *phr v* [T] **1** to reduce the price of things that are being sold: *All the items in the store have been marked down for one week only.* **2** to write down details about something

mark sth ↔ **out** *phr v* [T] to show the shape or position of something by drawing lines, putting up signs etc: *The police had marked out the route for the race.*

mark sth ↔ **up** *phr v* [T] to increase the price of things that are being sold: *We could mark the prices up a little and still be competitive.*
→ see also MARK-UP

mark² *n* [C] **1** a spot, small dark area, cut etc on something, which spoils its appearance: *There were burn marks on the carpet.* **2** a sign or shape that is written or printed: *She made a mark on the map to show where her house was.* | *punctuation marks* **3** *BrE* a letter or number given by a teacher to show how good a student's work is; GRADE *AmE: I got the highest mark in the class.* | **pass mark** (=the mark needed to pass a test) **4** a level that something goes up or down to: *Sales have reached the $100 million mark.* **5** **make your mark** to become successful or famous: *a chance for him to make his mark in politics* **6** **a mark of** a sign that something is true or exists: *We'd like to give you this gift as a mark of our respect.* **7** **off the mark/wide of the mark** not correct: *This estimate was way off the mark.* (=completely wrong) **8** a type of car, machine etc: *a Lincoln Mark V*

mark·down /'mɑːkdaʊn‖'mɑːrk-/ *n* [C] a reduction in the price of something: *Huge markdowns on all stock!*

marked /mɑːkt‖mɑːrkt/ *adj* very easy to notice: *There has been a marked increase in crime in the last year.* —**markedly** /'mɑːkɪdli‖'mɑːr-/ *adv*

mark·er /'mɑːkə‖'mɑːrkər/ *n* [C] **1** an object, sign etc that shows the position of something: *a marker at the edge of the football field* **2** also **marker pen** a large pen with a thick point → see colour picture on page 80

mar·ket¹ /'mɑːkɪt‖'mɑːr-/ *n* **1** [C] an outside area where people buy and sell goods, food etc: *We buy all our vegetables from the market.* **2** [C] a STOCK MARKET **3** [C] a country or area where a company sells its goods: *China is our biggest market.* **4** **on the market** available for people to buy: *That house has been on the market for a year now.* **5** [singular] the number of people who want to buy something: *The market for used cars in the US seems to be getting smaller.* → see also BLACK MARKET, STOCK MARKET

market² *v* [T] to try to persuade someone to buy something by advertising it in a particular way: *The game is being marketed as a learning toy.*

mar·ket·a·ble /'mɑːkɪtəbəl‖'mɑːr-/ *adj* marketable goods or skills are easy to sell —**marketability** /ˌmɑːkɪtə'bɪlɪti‖ˌmɑːr-/ *n* [U]

market forc·es /ˌ.. '../ *n* [plural] the way that trade and business works without government controls, which results in particular levels of prices, wages etc

mar·ket·ing /'mɑːkɪtɪŋ‖'mɑːr-/ *n* [U] the activity of deciding how to advertise a product, what price to charge for it etc: *an effective marketing strategy* | *He works in marketing.*

mar·ket·place /'mɑːkɪtpleɪs‖'mɑːr-/ *n* [C] **1** an area in a town where there is a MARKET **2** **the marketplace** the business of buying and selling goods in competition with other companies

market re·search /ˌ.. '.., ˌ.. '../ *n* [U] when companies ask people about what kind of things they buy and why they buy them

mark·ing /'mɑːkɪŋ‖'mɑːr-/ *n* [C usually plural] the coloured shapes, patterns etc on something: *a cat with black and white markings*

marks·man /'mɑːksmən‖'mɑːrks-/ *n* [C] someone who can shoot a gun very well

mark-up /'. ./ *n* [C] the amount by which a shop increases the price of its goods from what they paid for them: *The usual markup is 20%.*

mar·ma·lade /'mɑːməleɪd‖'mɑːr-/ *n* [U] a kind of JAM made from oranges or LEMONS, usually eaten for breakfast

ma·roon¹ /mə'ruːn/ *n* [U] a dark red-brown colour → see colour picture on page 114 —**maroon** *adj*

maroon² *v* **be marooned** to be left in a place that you cannot escape from: *the story of a sailor who was marooned on a desert island*

mar·quee /mɑː'kiː‖mɑːr-/ *n* [C] **1** *BrE* a large tent, used especially for eating and drinking in **2** *AmE* a large sign outside a theatre or cinema, showing the name of the film or play that is being shown there

mar·riage /'mærɪdʒ/ *n* **1** [C,U] a relationship between two people who are married, or the state of being married: *a long and happy marriage* | *He is not interested in marriage.* **2** [C] a wedding ceremony: *The premises are not licensed for marriages.*

mar·ried /'mærid/ *adj* someone who is married has a husband or a wife: *Are you married or single?* | **+ to** *Harrison Ford is married to Melissa Mathison.*

mar·row /'mærəʊ‖-roʊ/ *n* **1** [U] the soft substance in the middle of bones **2** [C] *BrE* a large long green vegetable; SQUASH *AmE* → see picture at VEGETABLES

mar·ry /'mæri/ *v* [I,T] if two people get married, they become husband and wife: **get married** *When are you two going to get married?* | **marry sb** *She married a man who was half her age.*

Mars /mɑːz‖mɑːrz/ *n* [singular] a small red PLANET, fourth from the sun

marsh /mɑːʃ‖mɑːrʃ/ *n* [C,U] an area of soft wet land —**marshy** *adj*

mar·shal¹ /'mɑːʃəl‖'mɑːr-/ *n* [C] **1** someone who helps to organize or control a large public event: *race marshals* **2** *especially AmE* the officer in charge of a city's police or fire fighting department

M

marshal² /ˈmɑːʃəl‖ˈmɑːr-/ *v* [T] to organize something, so that you can use it in an effective way: *She paused and tried to marshal her thoughts.*

marsh·mal·low /ˌmɑːʃˈmæləʊ‖ˈmɑːrʃmeloʊ/ *n* [C,U] a soft white food made of sugar

mar·su·pi·al /mɑːˈsjuːpiəl‖mɑːrˈsuː-/ *n* [C] an animal such as a KANGAROO that carries its babies in a pocket of skin on its body

mart /mɑːt‖mɑːrt/ *n* an abbreviation of MARKET

mar·tial /ˈmɑːʃəl‖ˈmɑːr-/ *adj* connected with war or fighting

martial art /ˌ.. ˈ./ *n* [C] a sport such as KARATE in which you fight using your hands and feet

martial law /ˌ.. ˈ./ *n* [U] a situation in which the army governs a city, country etc

Mar·tian /ˈmɑːʃən‖ˈmɑːr-/ *n* [C] a creature that some people imagine lives on Mars

mar·tyr /ˈmɑːtəl‖ˈmɑːrtər/ *n* [C] **1** someone who dies for their religious or political beliefs **2** someone who tries to make people notice how much work they have to do or how many problems they have, in order to get sympathy —**martyred** *adj* —**martyrdom** *n* [U]

mar·vel¹ /ˈmɑːvəl‖ˈmɑːr-/ *v* [I,T] to admire something that is very impressive in a surprising way: + **at** *He marvelled at the technology involved in creating such a tiny computer.*

marvel² *n* [C] something or someone that is very impressive and that you admire: *Laser surgery is one of the marvels of modern medicine.*

mar·vel·lous *BrE*, **marvelous** *AmE* /-ˈmɑːvələs‖ˈmɑːr-/ *adj* extremely good or enjoyable: *a marvellous book*

Marx·is·m /ˈmɑːksɪzəm‖ˈmɑːr-/ *n* [U] a system of political ideas based on the writings of Karl Marx

Marx·ist /ˈmɑːksˌɪst‖ˈmɑːr-/ *adj* relating to Marxism —**Marxist** *n* [C]

mar·zi·pan /ˈmɑːzɪˌpæn‖ˈmɑːrts-, ˈmɑːrz-/ *n* [U] a sweet food made from ALMONDS, used for covering cakes

mas·ca·ra /mæˈskɑːrə‖mæˈskærə/ *n* [U] a dark substance that is used to colour the EYELASHes

mas·cot /ˈmæskət‖ˈmæskɑːt/ *n* [C] an animal, toy etc that a team or organization thinks will bring them good luck

mas·cu·line /ˈmæskjʊlən/ *adj* **1** having qualities that people think are typical of men: *a masculine voice* **2** belonging to a group of nouns, adjectives etc in some languages that is different from the FEMININE and the NEUTER groups. In English grammar, masculine nouns and pronouns are ones that mean male people or animals. → compare FEMININE

mas·cu·lin·i·ty /ˌmæskjʊˈlɪnɪti/ *n* [U] the qualities that are typical of a man → compare FEMININITY

mash /mæʃ/ *v* [T] to crush food until it is soft: *Mash the potatoes in a bowl.* → see colour picture on page 439 —**mashed** *adj*

mask¹ /mɑːsk‖mæsk/ *n* [C] something that covers all or part of your face in order to protect or hide it: *a ski mask | The doctor wore a mask over her mouth and nose.* → see colour picture on page 278

mask² *v* [T] to keep something from being seen, heard, or noticed: *The sugar masks the taste of the medicine.*

masked /mɑːskt‖mæskt/ *adj* wearing a mask

masking tape /ˈ.. ./ *n* [U] a kind of TAPE, used to protect part of something you are painting

mas·o·chis·m /ˈmæsəkɪzəm/ *n* [U] behaviour in which someone gets pleasure, for example sexual pleasure, from being hurt —**masochist** *n* [U] —**masochistic** /ˌmæsəˈkɪstɪk‹/ *adj*

ma·son /ˈmeɪsən/ *n* [C] **1** a STONEMASON **2** a FREEMASON

ma·son·ry /ˈmeɪsənri/ *n* [U] brick or stone that a building or wall is made from

mas·que·rade /ˌmæskəˈreɪd, ˌmɑːs-‖ˌmæs-/ *v* [I] to pretend to be someone or something else: + **as** *He masqueraded as a doctor.*

mass¹ /mæs/ *n* **1** [C] a large amount of something: *a mass of dark clouds* **2 masses** *BrE informal* a large number or amount of something: *I've got masses of homework.* **3 the masses** all the ordinary people in a society **4** [U] *technical* the amount of physical material in something: *the mass of a star*

mass² *adj* involving or intended for a large number of people: *mass communication*

mass³ *v* [I,T] to come together in a large group, or make people or things do this: *Troops are massing at the border.*

Mass *n* [C,U] the main religious ceremony in the Roman Catholic Church and some other Christian churches

mas·sa·cre /ˈmæsəkə‖-ər/ *n* [C] when a lot of people are killed, especially people who cannot defend themselves —**massacre** *v* [T] *The whole village was massacred by soldiers.*

mas·sage /ˈmæsɑːʒ‖məˈsɑːʒ/ *n* [C,U] the action of pressing and rubbing someone's body with your hands to reduce pain or make them relax: *He gave me a massage.* —**massage** *v* [T] *Massage my neck.*

mas·seur /mæˈsɜː, mə-‖-ˈsɜːr/ *n* [C] someone who gives massages

mas·seuse /mæˈsɜːz, mə-‖mæˈsuːz/ *n* [C] a woman who gives massages

mas·sive /ˈmæsɪv/ *adj* very big or causing a lot of damage: *a massive dog | Carl had a massive heart attack.* —**massively** *adv*

mass me·di·a /ˌ. ˈ.../ *n* **the mass media** all the people and organizations that provide information and news for the public

mass mur·der·er /ˌ. ˈ.../ *n* [C] someone who has murdered a lot of people

mass-pro·duced /ˌ. .ˈ./ *adj* made in large numbers using machinery so that each object can be sold cheaply: *mass-produced cars* —**mass production** *n* [C]

mast /mɑːst‖mæst/ *n* [C] a tall pole on which the sails of a ship are hung

mas·ter¹ /ˈmɑːstə‖ˈmæstər/ *n* [C] **1** old-fashioned the man who is in charge of an animal, a home, or a servant: *the dog's master* **2** someone who is very skilful at doing something: *a master of kung fu* **3** an original document, record etc from which copies are made **4** a male schoolteacher

master² *v* [T] **1** to learn a skill or language so well that you understand it completely and have no difficulty with it **2** to learn to control a feeling or situation: *I finally mastered my fear of water.*

master³ *adj* master copy/list/tape etc the original thing from which copies are made

mas·ter·ful /ˈmɑːstəfəl‖ˈmæstər-/ *adj* done with great skill: *a masterful performance*

master key /ˈ.. ../ *n* [C] a key that will open all the doors in a building

mas·ter·mind /ˈmɑːstəmaɪnd‖ˈmæstər-/ *n* [singular] someone who organizes a complicated plan, especially a criminal plan: *Corran was the mastermind behind the hijacking.* —**mastermind** *v* [T] *a robbery masterminded by terrorists*

mas·ter·piece /ˈmɑːstəpiːs‖ˈmæstər-/ *n* [C] a work of art, piece of writing etc that is of an excellent standard or is the best someone has produced

master's de·gree /ˈ.. ../, **master's** *n* [C] a university degree that you can get by studying for one or two years after your first degree

mas·ter·y /ˈmɑːstəri‖ˈmæ-/ *n* [U] **1** complete control of a person or a situation: + **of/over** *the champion's mastery over his opponent* **2** great skill or knowledge about something: + **of** *She has total mastery of the piano.*

mas·tur·bate /ˈmæstəbeɪt‖-tər-/ *v* [I,T] to rub your sexual organs in order to get sexual pleasure —**masturbation** /ˌmæstəˈbeɪʃən‖-tər-/ *n* [U]

mat¹ /mæt/ *n* [C] a piece of thick material which covers part of a floor, table etc

mat² *adj* another spelling of MATT

match¹ /mætʃ/ *n* **1** [C] a small wooden stick that produces a flame when you rub it against something: *a box of matches* | *He lit a match so we could see.* **2** [C] *especially BrE* a game or sports event: *a tennis match* **3** [singular] something that is the same colour or pattern as something else: *These shoes are a perfect match for the dress.* **4** **be no match for** to be much less strong, fast etc than an opponent: *Our team was no match for theirs.*

match² *v* **1** [I,T] if one thing matches another, or if two things match, they look good together because they have a similar colour, pattern etc: *The carpet matches the curtains.* **2** [I,T] to be the same or look the same as something else: *His socks don't match.* **3** also **match up** [T] to find something that is similar to or suitable for something else: *Match the words on the left with the meanings on the right.* **4** [T] to be equal to or as good as someone or something else: *No one can match Rogers' speed on the football field.*

match

These socks don't match.

match up *phr v* **1** [I] to be the same as or fit together with something: *The edges of the cloth don't match up.* **2** **match up to something** to be as good as you expected or as good as something else: *The CD didn't match up to the band's live performance.*

match·box /ˈmætʃbɒks‖-bɑːks/ *n* [C] a small box containing matches

match·ing /ˈmætʃɪŋ/ *adj* having the same colour, style, pattern etc as something else: *The twins wore matching T-shirts.*

match·less /ˈmætʃləs/ *adj formal* better than anything else that is similar: *her matchless beauty*

match·mak·er /ˈmætʃˌmeɪkəl‖-ər/ *n* [C] a person who tries to find a suitable person for someone else to marry

mate¹ /meɪt/ *n* **1** [C] *BrE informal* a friend: *my mate Dave* | *I went with some of my mates from work.* **2** *BrE and AustrE spoken* used as a friendly way to talk to someone else, especially a man: *How are you, mate?* **3** [C] the sexual PARTNER of an animal **4** an officer on a ship ➧ see also CLASSMATE, ROOMMATE

mate² *v* **1** [I] if animals mate, they have sex **2** [T] to put animals together so that they will have sex and produce babies

ma·te·ri·al¹ /məˈtɪəriəl‖-ˈtɪr-/ *n* **1** [C,U] cloth used for making clothes, curtains etc: *blue velvet material* ➧ see picture at CLOTHES **2** [C,U] a substance such as wood, plastic, paper etc from which things can be made: *building materials* **3** [U] information or ideas used in books, films etc: *The director wrote some new material for the play.* **4** **materials** [plural] the things you use for an activity: *art materials*

material² *adj* **1** relating to the real world or to physical objects and possessions, rather than religious or SPIRITUAL things: *the material comforts that money can buy* **2** *law* very important: *a material witness for the defence* ➧ compare IMMATERIAL

ma·te·ri·al·is·m /məˈtɪəriəlɪzəm‖-ˈtɪr-/ *n* [U] the belief that getting money and possessions is very important in life —**materialist** *adj* —**materialistic** /məˌtɪəriəˈlɪstɪk‖-ˌtɪr-/ *adj*

ma·te·ri·al·ize (also **-ise** *BrE*) /məˈtɪəriəlaɪz‖-ˈtɪr-/ *v* [I] if a possible event or plan materializes, it happens: *His dream failed to materialize.*

ma·ter·nal /məˈtɜːnl‖-ɜːr-/ *adj* **1** typical of the way a kind mother feels or acts: *maternal feelings* **2** **maternal grandfather/aunt etc** your mother's father, sister etc ➧ compare PATERNAL

ma·ter·ni·ty /məˈtɜːnɪti‖-ɜːr-/ *adj* [only before noun] used by or given to a woman who is going to have a baby or who has recently had a baby: *maternity clothes* | *maternity pay*

maternity leave /ˈ.... ./ *n* [U] time that a woman is allowed away from her job when she has a baby

math /mæθ/ *n* [U] *AmE* mathematics

math·e·mat·i·cal /ˌmæθɪˈmætɪkəl‖/ *adj* connected with or using mathematics: *a mathematical equation*

math·e·ma·ti·cian /ˌmæθɪməˈtɪʃən/ *n* [C] someone who studies or teaches mathematics

math·e·mat·ics /ˌmæθɪˈmætɪks/ *n* [U] the study or science of numbers or shapes

maths /mæθs/ *n* [U] *BrE* mathematics

GRAMMAR NOTE: phrasal verbs (1)
Phrasal verbs are verbs with more than one part. They consist of **verb + adverb** or **verb + preposition** (e.g. *look after, turn out, put off*). Some phrasal verbs have three parts: **verb + adverb + preposition** (e.g. *look forward to, put up with*).

M

mat·i·née /ˈmætɪˌneɪ‖ˌmætənˈeɪ/ n [C] a performance of a play or film in the afternoon

ma·tric·u·late /məˈtrɪkjˠleɪt/ v [I] formal to officially start a course of study at a university —**matriculation** /məˌtrɪkjˠˈleɪʃən/ n [U]

mat·ri·mo·ny /ˈmætrɪˌmənɪ‖-mouni/ n [U] formal the state of being married —**matrimonial** /ˌmætrɪˈməuniəl‖-ˈmou-/ adj

ma·tron /ˈmeɪtrən/ n BrE old-fashioned a nurse who is in charge of other nurses in a hospital

matt matte, mat /mæt/ adj a matt paint, colour, or photograph is not shiny

mat·ted /ˈmætˌd/ adj matted hair or fur is twisted and stuck together

mat·ter[1] /ˈmætəl-ər/ n **1** [C] a subject or situation that you have to think about or deal with, often one that causes problems: Several important matters were discussed. | He's busy with family matters. | **make matters worse** (=make a bad situation even more serious) **2 what's the matter?** especially spoken used to ask or talk about why someone is upset, angry etc: + **with** What's the matter with Ellie? **3 there's something/nothing the matter with** spoken used to say that there is or is not a problem with something: There's something the matter with the computer. | What's the matter with the phone? (=why is it not working normally?) **4 as a matter of fact** spoken used when you are giving a surprising or unexpected answer to a question or statement: "Do you know Liz?" "Yes, as a matter of fact we're cousins." **5 no matter how/where/what etc** spoken used to say that something remains the same whatever happens, or in spite of someone's efforts to change it: No matter how hard she tried, she couldn't get the door open. **6** [U] **a)** technical the material that everything in the universe is made of **b)** formal physical material of a particular kind: waste matter | vegetable matter **7 be a matter of practice/luck etc** to involve practice, luck etc: Learning to drive is a matter of using your common sense. **8 a matter of seconds/days/ inches etc** only a few seconds, days etc: We'll be in Singapore in a matter of hours. **9 it's only/ just a matter of time** used in order to say that something will definitely happen even though you cannot say exactly when: It's only a matter of time before a child is killed on that road. **10 be a matter of opinion** used to say that people have different opinions about something **11 a matter of life and death** a very dangerous or serious situation **12 for that matter** when what you have said about one thing is also true about another: I don't like him, or his sister for that matter! **13 as a matter of course/ routine** used to say that someone, especially in a company or official organization, does something because that is what is normally done in that situation

matter[2] v [I] to be important, or to have an effect on what happens: Money is the only thing that matters to him. | Will it matter if we're a few minutes late? | "Oh no, I forgot the camera!" "It doesn't matter."

matter-of-fact /ˌ...ˈ.◂/ adj showing no strong emotions when you are talking about something: We try to explain death to children in an understanding but matter-of-fact way.

mat·ting /ˈmætɪŋ/ n [U] strong rough material used for covering a floor

mat·tress /ˈmætrˌs/ n [C] the soft part of a bed that you lie on

ma·ture[1] /məˈtʃuəl-ˈtʃur/ adj **1** behaving in a reasonable way like an adult: She's very mature for her age. → opposite IMMATURE **2** fully grown or developed

mature[2] v **1** [I] to become fully grown or developed: The fly matures in only seven days. **2** [I] to begin to behave in a reasonable way like an adult: Pat's matured a lot since going to college.

mature stu·dent /ˌ.ˌ ˈ..◂/ n BrE a student at a university or college who is over 25 years old

ma·tu·ri·ty /məˈtʃuərˌtɪ‖-ˈtʃur-/ n [U] **1** the quality of behaving in a sensible way like an adult: His lack of maturity makes him unsuitable for such a responsible job. **2** the time when a person, animal, or plant is fully grown or developed: Rabbits reach maturity in only five weeks.

maud·lin /ˈmɔːdlɪn‖ˈmɔː-/ adj talking or behaving in a sad and silly way, especially when you are drunk

maul /mɔːl‖mɔːl/ v [T] **1** to injure someone by tearing their flesh: The hunter was mauled by a lion. **2** to touch or pull someone in a rough way, or in a way that they do not like: Stop mauling me!

mau·so·le·um /ˌmɔːsəˈliːəm‖ˌmɔː-/ n [C] a large stone building containing many graves or built over a grave

mauve /məuv‖mouv/ n [U] a pale purple colour —**mauve** adj → see colour picture on page 114

mav·e·rick /ˈmævərɪk/ n [C] someone who thinks or behaves in a way that is different from most people of their kind: a political maverick —**maverick** adj

mawk·ish /ˈmɔːkɪʃ‖ˈmɔː-/ adj showing too much emotion, in a way that is embarrassing —**mawkishly** adv

max /mæks/ n [U] **1** informal at the most: It'll cost $50 max. **2** the written abbreviation for maximum

max·im /ˈmæksˌm/ n [C] a well-known phrase that gives advice on how to behave

max·i·mize (also **-ise** BrE) /ˈmæksˌmaɪz/ v [T] to increase something as much as possible: We want to reduce costs and maximize profits. → opposite MINIMIZE

max·i·mum[1] /ˈmæksˌməm/ adj the maximum amount/number/speed etc the largest that is possible, allowed, or needed: The car has a maximum speed of 125 mph. —**maximum** n: Temperatures will reach a maximum of 30°C today. → opposite MINIMUM[1]

may /meɪ/ modal verb **1** used to say that there is a possibility that something is true or will happen: It may snow tonight. | We may not have enough money to go. **2 may I** spoken used to politely ask if you can do or have something: May I borrow your pen? **3** formal used to allow someone to do something: You may start writing now. → see also MIGHT[1], **may/might as well do sth** (WELL[1])

May n [C,U] the fifth month of the year → see usage note at MONTH

may·be /ˈmeɪbi/ adv **1** used to say that something may be true or may happen, but that you are not sure: Maybe Anna's already left. | There *were 300, maybe 400 people there.* **2** used to make a suggestion: *Maybe Jeff could help you.* → compare PERHAPS

may·day /ˈmeɪdeɪ/ *n* [singular] a radio SIGNAL used to ask for help when a ship or plane is in danger

may·hem /ˈmeɪhem/ *n* [U] an extremely confused situation in which people are very frightened or excited: *There was complete mayhem after the explosion.*

may·on·naise /ˌmeɪəˈneɪz‖ˈmeɪəneɪz/ *n* [U] a thick white SAUCE, often eaten with SALADs or cold food

mayor /meə‖ˈmeɪər/ *n* [C] **1** someone who is chosen to be the head of a local council in Britain **2** someone who is elected to lead the government of a town or city in the US

maze

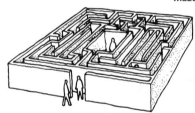

maze /meɪz/ *n* **1** [C] a system of paths that is difficult to find your way through, that has been specially designed as a game: *We got lost in the maze.* **2** [singular] a place that is difficult to find your way through: *a maze of dark hallways* **3** [singular] something that is complicated and difficult to understand: *a maze of government rules*

McCoy /məˈkɔɪ/ *n* **the real McCoy** *informal* something that is real and not a copy

me /mi; *strong* miː/ *pron* **1** the object form of 'I': *My sister is older than me. | He gave me a necklace.* **2** **me too** *spoken* said when you agree with someone: *"I'm hungry!" "Me too."* **3** **me neither** *spoken* said when you agree with a negative statement someone has just made: *"I don't like coffee." "Me neither."*

mead·ow /ˈmedəʊ‖-oʊ/ *n* [C] a field with wild grass and flowers

mea·gre *BrE*, **meager** *AmE* /ˈmiːgə‖-ər/ *adj* very small in amount: *a meagre breakfast*

meal /miːl/ *n* [C] a time when you eat food, or the food that is eaten then: **have a meal** *We always have a meal together in the evening.*

meal·time /ˈmiːltaɪm/ *n* [C] the usual time for eating a meal

mealy-mouthed /ˌ... ˈ.ˌ/ *adj* not brave or honest enough to say clearly what you think

mean¹ /miːn/ *v* **meant** /ment/, **meant**, **meaning** [T] **1** to have a particular meaning or message: *What does the word 'Konbanwa' mean? | The red light means 'stop'.* **2** to intend a particular meaning when you say something: *When I said 'soon', I meant in the next few weeks.* **3** to be sincere when you say something and say exactly what you think or feel: **mean it** *Did you really mean it when you said you loved me?* **4** to intend to do something or make something happen: *I've been meaning to call you for ages. |* **mean to do sth** *She didn't mean to upset you. |* **be meant to be sth** *It was meant to be a joke. |* **mean (for) sb to do sth** *I didn't mean her to find out.* **5** **be meant for sb/sth** to be intended for a particular person or purpose: *The flowers were meant for Mum. | These shoes aren't meant for walking.* **6** to have a particular result: *It's snowing, which means that it will take longer to get there.* **7** **be meant to do sth a)** to be generally believed to be something: *It's meant to be the best ice-cream in the world.* **b)** to be intended or allowed to do something: *You're not meant to look at the answers!* **8** **sb/sth means a lot (to sb)** used to say that someone or something is very important or special to someone: *It would mean a lot to Joe if you watched him play football.* **9** **mean business** be determined to do something: *She says she's going to beat him, and I think she means business.* **10** **mean well** if someone means well, they try to be helpful to other people, but often cause problems for them instead **11** **I mean** *spoken* **a)** used when you stop to think about what to say next: *She's just so nice. I mean, she's a really gentle person.* **b)** used when you want to change what you have just said: *She plays the violin, I mean the viola.* **12** **I mean it!** *spoken* used to emphasize what you are saying when you are very angry: *Don't ever say that word again – I mean it!* **13** **(Do) you mean ...?** *spoken* used when you want to check that you understand something: *You mean you want me to call you, or will you call me?* **14** **(Do) you know what I mean?** *spoken* used to ask someone if they understand you: *I feel disappointed. You know what I mean?* **15** **I know what you mean** *spoken* used to show that you understand someone or agree: *"There's nothing good on TV." "I know what you mean."* **16** **what do you mean?** *spoken* **a)** used when you do not understand someone **b)** used when you are very surprised and annoyed by something someone has done: *What do you mean, you sold your guitar?*

mean² *adj* **1** unkind or cruel: *Don't be so mean to your sister.* **2** *BrE* not willing to spend money: *He was too mean to buy me a present.* **3** *informal* very good: *Ray plays a mean game of tennis.* **4** **no mean** used to say that someone

M

or something is very good: *It was no mean achievement to win first prize.*

mean[3] *n* [usually singular] *technical* an average amount, figure, or value

me·an·der / mi'ændəll-ər/ *v* [I] to move in a slow or relaxed way not following any particular direction: *a meandering stream*

mean·ing / 'mi:nɪŋ/ *n* **1** [C,U] what you are supposed to understand from something you see, read, or hear: *I don't understand the meaning of this word.* | *Does the poem have any meaning?* **2** [U] the importance or purpose that something has: *the meaning of life*

mean·ing·ful / 'mi:nɪŋfəl/ *adj* **1** serious, useful, or important: *a meaningful relationship* **2** easy to understand: *The data isn't very meaningful to anyone but a scientist.* **3** **a meaningful look/smile etc** a look etc that clearly expresses the way someone feels — **meaningfully** *adv*

mean·ing·less / 'mi:nɪŋləs/ *adj* without any purpose or meaning: *Her whole life felt meaningless.*

means / mi:nz/ *n* **1** [C] a method, system, object etc that is used as a way of doing something: *We'll use any means we can to raise the money.* | *For many people, the car is their main means of transport.* **2** **by means of** using something to do something: *The oil is transported by means of a pipeline.* **3** **by all means** used to emphasize that someone should do or is allowed to do something: *By all means, come over and use the e-mail.* **4** **by no means** not at all: *The results are by no means certain.* **5** **a means to an end** something that you do or use only to achieve a result: *Bev always says her job is just a means to an end.* **6** [plural] the money or things that you have that make it possible for you to buy or do things: *They don't have the means to pay for private education.* | **a man of means** (=who has a lot of money)

meant / ment/ *v* the past tense and past participle of MEAN[1]

mean·time / 'mi:ntaɪm/ *n* **in the meantime** until something happens, or in the time between two events: *Dinner's nearly ready. In the meantime, who wants a drink?*

mean·while / 'mi:nwaɪl/ *adv* while something else is happening, or in the time between two events: *Mary was coming later. Meanwhile I did my homework.*

mea·sles / 'mi:zəlz/ *n* [U] also **the measles** an infectious illness in which you have a fever and small red spots on your face and body

meas·ly / 'mi:zli/ *adj informal* very small and disappointing in size or amount: *I only got a measly $5.*

mea·sur·a·ble / 'meʒərəbəl/ *adj* big enough to be measured or to have an effect: *measurable results* — **measurably** *adv*

mea·sure[1] / 'meʒəll-ər/ *v* **1** [I,T] to find out the size, length, or amount of something: *She measured the curtains.* | *He measured me for a new suit.* **2** [I] to be a particular size, length, or amount: *The table measures four feet by six feet.* **3** [T] to decide how important or great something is: *How do you measure success?*

measure sb/sth against sb/sth *phr v* [T] to decide how good, effective etc someone or something is by comparing them with another

person or thing: *All teachers should be measured against the same standard.*

measure up *phr v* [I] to be good enough to do a particular job or to reach a particular standard: + **to** *Does college measure up to your expectations?*

measure

tape measure

measure[2] *n* **1** [C, usually plural] an official action that is intended to deal with a problem: *government measures to cut air pollution* | **take measures** *They have to take drastic measures to save money.* **2** **a measure of sth** *formal* enough to be noticed, but not a large amount: *He achieved a measure of success.* **3** [C,U] a system for measuring the weight, length etc of something, or the unit of weight, length etc that is used: *An hour is a measure of time.* **4** **be a measure of sth** *formal* to be a sign of the importance, strength etc of something: *It's a measure of our trust that we let you go alone.* **5** **for good measure** in addition, so that what you do or give is enough: *Put in a bit more salt for good measure.*

mea·sure·ment / 'meʒəməntll-ʒər-/ *n* [C,U] the length, height, value etc of something, or the act of measuring this: *First of all, you'll need the exact measurements of the room.*

meat / mi:t/ *n* [U] the flesh of animals and birds eaten as food: *I don't eat much meat.* → see colour picture on page 440

USAGE NOTE: meat

The meat from some animals has a different name from the name of the animal it comes from. For example, the meat from a **cow** is called **beef**, the meat from a **pig** is called **pork** or **ham** or **bacon**, the meat from a **deer** is **venison**, and the meat from a **sheep** is **mutton**. But the meat from a **lamb** is **lamb**, and for birds the same word is used for both the meat and the bird it comes from: *Shall we have chicken or duck for dinner?*

meat·y / 'mi:ti/ *adj* containing a lot of meat or tasting strongly of meat

mec·ca / 'mekə/ *n* [singular] **1** a place that many people want to visit for a particular reason: *Florence is a mecca for art students.* **2** **Mecca** a city in Saudi Arabia which is a holy place for Muslims

me·chan·ic / mɪ'kænɪk/ *n* [C] someone whose job is to repair vehicles and machinery

me·chan·i·cal / mɪ'kænɪkəl/ *adj* **1** relating to machines, or using power from a machine: *mech-*

anical engineering | *a mechanical toy* **2** saying or doing something without thinking, because you have said or done it in the same way many times before: *a mechanical answer* —**mechanically** /-kli/ *adv*

me·chan·ics /mɪˈkænɪks/ *n* [U] **1** the science that deals with the effects of forces on objects **2 the mechanics of (doing) sth** the way in which something works or is done: *the mechanics of language*

mech·a·nis·m /ˈmekənɪzəm/ *n* [C] **1** the part of a machine that does a particular job: *a car's steering mechanism* **2** a way that something works or a process that makes it possible to perform an action: *The body has a mechanism for controlling temperature.*

mech·a·nize (also **-ise** *BrE*) /ˈmekənaɪz/ *v* [I,T] to change a process so that machines do work instead of people

mech·a·nized (also **-ised** *BrE*) /ˈmekənaɪzd/ *adj* done by machines, or using machines: *mechanized farming techniques*

med·al /ˈmedl/ *n* [C] a round, flat piece of metal given as a prize to someone who has won a competition or who has done something brave: *an Olympic gold medal*

me·dal·li·on /mɪˈdæliən/ *n* [C] a piece of metal like a large coin, worn as jewellery around the neck

med·al·list *BrE*, **medalist** *AmE* /ˈmedl-ɪst/ *n* [C] someone who has won a medal in a competition: *a silver medalist*

med·dle /ˈmedl/ *v* [I] to try to influence a situation that you do not understand and which someone else is responsible for: *He's meddling in other people's lives.*

me·di·a /ˈmiːdiə/ *n* **1 the media** television, radio, and newspapers: *reports in the media* | **media coverage/interest** (=the amount of attention paid to something by television programmes, newspaper stories etc): *The President's visit got a lot of media coverage.* **2** the plural of MEDIUM → see also MASS MEDIA

med·i·ae·val /ˌmediˈiːvəl, ˌmiː-/ a British spelling of MEDIEVAL

me·di·an /ˈmiːdiən/ *n* [C] *AmE* a narrow piece of land that divides a road and separates lines of traffic

me·di·ate /ˈmiːdieɪt/ *v* [I,T] to try to help two groups, countries etc to stop arguing and make an agreement: *The court had to mediate between Mr Hassel and his neighbours.* —**mediator** *n* [C] —**mediation** /ˌmiːdiˈeɪʃən/ *n* [U]

med·i·cal¹ /ˈmedɪkəl/ *adj* relating to medicine and the treatment of disease or injury: *medical school* | *She needs urgent medical treatment.* —**medically** /-kli/ *adv*

medical² *n* [C] *BrE* an examination of your body by a doctor to check that you are healthy; PHYSICAL² *AmE*

med·i·cated /ˈmedɪkeɪtɪd/ *adj* containing medicine: *medicated shampoo*

med·i·ca·tion /ˌmedɪˈkeɪʃən/ *n* [C,U] a drug given to people who are ill: *He's taking medication for his heart.*

me·di·ci·nal /mɪˈdɪsɪnəl/ *adj* a medicinal substance helps to cure illness or disease: *Cough syrup should be used for medicinal purposes only.*

med·i·cine /ˈmedsən, ˈmedɪsən/ *n* **1** [C,U] a substance for treating an illness, especially one that you drink: *Remember to take your medicine.* | *Medicines should be kept away from children.* **2** [U] the treatment and study of illnesses and injuries: *Sarah plans to study medicine.*

med·i·e·val also **mediaeval** *BrE* /ˌmediˈiːvəl/ *adj* produced in or connected with the MIDDLE AGES: *medieval poetry*

me·di·o·cre /ˌmiːdiˈəʊkə/ *adj* not very good in quality: *The food was mediocre.* —**mediocrity** /ˌmiːdiˈɒkrɪti/ *n* [U]

med·i·tate /ˈmedɪteɪt/ *v* [I] to make yourself very calm by relaxing completely, and thinking only about one thing such as a sound or a religious idea —**meditation** /ˌmedɪˈteɪʃən/ *n* [U]

me·di·um¹ /ˈmiːdiəm/ *adj* of middle size or amount: *What size drink do you want – small, medium or large?* | *a man of medium height*

medium² *n* [C] **1** *plural* **media** /-diə/ a way of communicating information or expressing ideas to people: *The Internet is a powerful advertising medium.* **2** *plural* **mediums** someone who says they are able to speak to dead people and receive messages from them

medium-sized /ˌ ˈ/ , **medium-size** *adj* not small or large: *medium-sized apples* | *medium-size business*

med·ley /ˈmedli/ *n* [C] tunes from different songs that are played one after the other as a single piece of music

meek /miːk/ *adj* very quiet and not willing to argue or ask for anything —**meekly** *adv* —**meekness** *n* [U]

meet /miːt/ *v* **met** /met/, **meeting 1** [I,T] to see and talk to someone for the first time, or to be introduced to someone: *Mike and Sara met at a party.* | *Haven't we met before?* **2** [I,T] to come to the same place as someone else because you have arranged it or by chance: *Let's meet for lunch tomorrow.* | *I'll meet you at the bus stop.* | *I met Joe while I was out shopping.* **3 (it's) nice to meet you** *spoken* said when you meet someone for the first time: *"Paul, this is Jack." "Nice to meet you."* **4** [T] to be at an airport, station etc when someone arrives: *I'm going to meet Anne's plane.* **5** [I,T] to join together at a particular place: *the place where the path meets the road* | *His eyebrows meet in the middle.* **6** [I] to come together with a group of people for a particular purpose or activity: *The chess club meets every Tuesday lunchtime.* **7** [T] to have enough or do enough of what is needed, or be good enough to reach a particular standard: *She didn't meet all of the requirements for the job.* **8 meet (sb) halfway** to do some of the things

GRAMMAR NOTE: the progressive
You form the **present progressive** by using **be/is/was** + present participle: *They are coming.*
You form the **past progressive** by using **was/were** + present participle: *He was lying.*

that someone wants, if they do some of the things that you want

meet up *phr v* [I] to meet someone informally in order to do something together: *Let's meet up later.*

meet with sb/sth *phr v* [T] **1** *especially AmE* to have a meeting with someone: *The President met with European leaders today in Paris.* **2** to get a particular reaction or result: *The new radio station has met with a lot of criticism.*

meet·ing / 'miːtɪŋ / *n* [C] an organized event where people meet to discuss something: *The teachers have a meeting this afternoon.* | *She's in a meeting – can you call back later?*

meg·a / 'megə / *adj informal* very big and impressive: *a mega party*

meg·a·byte / 'megəbaɪt / *n* [C] a unit for measuring computer information, that is equal to a million BYTEs

meg·a·lo·ma·ni·a / ˌmegələʊ'meɪniəl-loʊ- / *n* [U] the belief that you are more important and powerful than you really are —**megalomaniac** / -niæk / *n* [C]

meg·a·phone / 'megəfəʊnll-foʊn / *n* [C] a thing shaped like a big CONE, that you speak through to make your voice louder

mel·an·chol·y / 'melənkəlill-kɑːli / *n* [U] *literary* a feeling of great sadness —**melancholy** *adj*: *The song was quiet and a little melancholy.*

mel·ee / 'meleɪll'meɪleɪ, meɪ'leɪ / *n* [C] a confusing, noisy and sometimes violent situation: *Several people were hurt in the melee.*

mel·low[1] / 'meləʊll-loʊ / *adj* **1** pleasant and smooth: *mellow music* | *a mellow wine* **2** gentle or calm because of age or experience: *My dad's pretty mellow these days.* —**mellowness** *n* [U]

mellow[2] *v* [I,T] to become more relaxed and calm, or to make someone calmer: *She's mellowed over the years.*

me·lod·ic / mɪ'lɒdɪkllmɪ'lɑː- /, **me·lo·di·ous** / mɪ'ləʊdiəsll-loʊ- / *adj* having a pleasant tune or a pleasant sound like music: *a sweet melodic voice*

mel·o·dra·ma / 'melə,drɑːməll-,drɑːmə, -,dræmə / *n* [C,U] a story or play with many exciting events in which people's emotions are shown very clearly

mel·o·dra·mat·ic / ˌmelədrə'mætɪk◂ / *adj* showing strong emotions and behaving in a way that makes a situation seem more exciting or important than it really is: *He says he's going to run away but he's just being melodramatic.*

mel·o·dy / 'melədi / *n* [C,U] a song or tune

mel·on / 'melən / *n* [C,U] a large round fruit with a hard yellow, orange, or green skin and a lot of flat seeds ➡ see picture at FRUIT

melt / melt / *v* **1** [I,T] to change from solid to liquid, or to make something do this by heating it: *The snow's melting.* | *Melt the chocolate in a pan.* **2** [I] to suddenly feel love or sympathy: *Whenever I hear his voice, I just melt.*

melt

melt away *phr v* [I] to disappear quickly: *My anger melted away when she explained.*

melt·down / 'meltdaʊn / *n* [C,U] a very dangerous situation in which the material in a NU-CLEAR REACTOR melts and burns through its container

mem·ber / 'membəl-ər / *n* [C] **1** someone who has joined a club, group, or organization: *Are you a member of the tennis club?* | *Two band members quit yesterday.* **2** one of a group of similar people or things: *Cats and tigers are members of the same species.*

Member of Parliament / ˌ.. .. '... / abbreviation **MP** *n* [C] someone who has been elected by people in Britain and Northern Ireland to REPRESENT them in parliament

mem·ber·ship / 'membəʃɪpll-ər- / *n* **1** [U] when you are a member of a group or organization: *+ of BrE, + in AmE: I forgot to renew my membership in the sailing club.* **2** [singular, U] the members of an organization, or the total number of members: *The membership will vote for a chairman tonight.* | *an increase in membership*

mem·brane / 'membreɪn / *n* [C,U] a thin skin that covers or connects parts inside your body: *a membrane in the ear that helps us hear*

me·men·to / mɪ'mentəʊll-toʊ / *n* [C], *plural* **mementos** a small object that you keep to remind you of someone or something: *a memento of my college days*

mem·o / 'meməʊll-moʊ / *n* [C], *plural* **memos** a short official note written to another person in the same organization

mem·oirs / 'memwɑːzll-wɑːrz / *n* [plural] a book that someone has written about their own life and experiences

mem·o·ra·bil·i·a / ˌmemərə'bɪliə / *n* [plural] things that you keep or collect because they are connected with a famous person, event, or time: *Kennedy memorabilia*

mem·o·ra·ble / 'memərəbəl / *adj* very good and likely to be remembered: *Brando's memorable performances in 'On the Waterfront'* —**memorably** *adv*

mem·o·ran·dum / ˌmemə'rændəm / *n* [C], *plural* **memoranda** / -də / or **memorandums** *formal* a MEMO

me·mo·ri·al[1] / mɪ'mɔːriəl / *adj* [only before noun] made or done to remind people of someone who has died: **memorial service/ceremony/prize** *a memorial service for my grandfather*

memorial[2] *n* [C] a special structure that is built or made to remind people of someone who has died: *the Lincoln memorial* | *The wall was built as a memorial to soldiers who died in Vietnam.*

mem·o·rize (also **-ise** *BrE*) / 'meməraɪz / *v* [T] to learn and remember words, music, or other information

mem·o·ry / 'meməri / *n* **1** [C,U] the ability to remember things, places, experiences etc: *She's got a good memory for faces.* | *Could you draw the map from memory?* **2** [C usually plural] something that you remember from the past: *I have a lot of happy memories of that summer.* | **bring back memories** (=make you remember something): *That smell brings back memories of my childhood.* ➡ compare SOUVENIR **3** [C,U] the part of a computer which has an amount of space for storing information: *30 megabytes of memory* **4** **in memory of** for the purpose of remembering someone who has died: *a garden* *created in memory of the children killed in the attack* → see also **refresh sb's memory** (REFRESH)

men /men/ *n* the plural of MAN

men·ace¹ /'menɪs/ *n* [C] **1** something or someone that is dangerous or extremely annoying: *That man is a menace to society!* | *The mosquitoes are a real menace.* **2** [U] a threatening quality or feeling: *There was menace in her voice*

menace² *v* [T] *formal* to threaten someone or something

men·ac·ing /'menɪsɪŋ/ *adj* making you expect something dangerous or bad; THREATENING: *a menacing laugh*

mend¹ /mend/ *v* [T] to repair something that is broken, damaged, or torn: *You'd better mend that hole in the fence.*

mend² *n* **be on the mend** *informal* to be getting better after an illness

me·ni·al /'miːniəl/ *adj* menial work is boring and needs very little skill

men·in·gi·tis /ˌmenɪn'dʒaɪtɪs/ *n* [U] a serious infectious disease that affects the brain

men·o·pause /'menəpɔːz‖-pɒːz/ *n* [U] the time, usually around the age of 50, when a woman stops menstruating (MENSTRUATE)

men's room /'. ./ *n* [C] *AmE* men's toilet; GENTS *BrE*

men·stru·ate /'menstrueɪt/ *v* [I] *formal* when a woman menstruates every month, blood flows from her body —**menstrual** *adj* —**menstruation** /ˌmenstru'eɪʃən/ *n* [U]

men·tal /'mentl/ *adj* **1** [only before noun] relating to the mind, or happening in the mind: *a child's mental development* | *mental arithmetic* | **make a mental note** (=make an effort to remember): *I made a mental note to call Julie.* **2** [only before noun] relating to treatment of illnesses affecting the mind: *mental health* | *a mental institution* **3** [not before noun] *spoken informal* crazy: *That guy's mental!* —**mentally** *adv*: *mentally ill* | *mentally handicapped*

men·tal·i·ty /men'tælɪti/ *n* [C] a particular attitude or way of thinking: *an aggressive mentality*

men·tion¹ /'menʃən/ *v* [T] **1** to talk or write about something in a few words: *Cooper wasn't mentioned in the article.* | **mention sth to sb** *I'll mention the idea to her and see what she thinks.* | + **(that)** *He did mention that he was having problems.* **2 don't mention it** *spoken* used to say politely that there is no need for someone to thank you: *"Thanks for helping me out." "Don't mention it."* **3 not to mention** used when you are adding a piece of information that emphasizes what you have been saying: *He already has two houses and two cars, not to mention the boat.*

mention² *n* [singular, U] when you mention someone or something in a conversation or piece of writing: *Any mention of the accident upsets her.* | **no mention of** *There was no mention of any payment for the work.*

men·tor /'mentɔː‖-tɔːr/ *n* [C] an experienced person who advises and helps someone who is learning how to do a job —**mentoring** *n* [U]

men·u /'menjuː/ *n* [C], *plural* **menus 1** a list of all the food that is available for a meal in a restaurant: *Could we have the menu, please?* | *Do you have a vegetarian dish on the menu?* **2** a list

of things that you can ask a computer to do, that is shown on the screen

me·ow /mi'aʊ/ *n* a spelling of MIAOW, used especially in American English

MEP /ˌem iː 'piː/ *n* [C] Member of the European Parliament; someone who has been elected as a politician of the European Union

mer·ce·na·ry¹ /'mɜːsənəri‖'mɜːrsəneri/ *n* [C] a soldier who will fight for any country that will pay him or her

mercenary² *adj* only interested in making money

mer·chan·dise /'mɜːtʃəndaɪz, -daɪs‖'mɜːr-/ *n* [U] *formal* things that are for sale in shops

mer·chant¹ /'mɜːtʃənt‖'mɜːr-/ *n* [C] someone who buys and sells large quantities of goods: *a wine merchant*

merchant² *adj* [only before noun] merchant ships are used for trade, not for military purposes: **the merchant navy** *BrE*/**the merchant marine** *AmE My brother's in the merchant navy.*

mer·ci·ful /'mɜːsɪfəl‖'mɜːr-/ *adj* **1** a merciful death or end to something seems fortunate because it stops any more suffering: *The final whistle was a merciful release.* **2** likely to forgive people rather than punish them or be cruel to them

mer·ci·ful·ly /'mɜːsɪfəli‖'mɜːr-/ *adv* fortunately, because a situation could have been much worse: *At least her death was mercifully quick.*

mer·ci·less /'mɜːsɪləs‖'mɜːr-/ *adj* cruel and not caring if people suffer: *a merciless attack on innocent villagers*

mercury /'mɜːkjʊri‖'mɜːr-/ *n* [U] a liquid silver-white metal, used in THERMOMETERS

Mer·cu·ry *n* [singular] the smallest PLANET, closest to the sun

mer·cy /'mɜːsi‖'mɜːrsi/ *n* **1** [U] kindness and a willingness to forgive people: *The rebels showed no mercy.* **2 be at the mercy of** to be unable to do anything to protect yourself from someone or something: *In the open boat they were at the mercy of the wind and waves.*

mere /mɪə‖mɪr/ *adj* **1** used to emphasize how small or unimportant someone or something is: *He's a mere child – he can't understand.* | *She won by a mere two points.* **2** also **the merest** used to say that even though something is small or unimportant, it has a big effect: *The mere thought made her furious.*

mere·ly /'mɪəli‖'mɪrli/ *adv* **1** used to emphasize that something is exactly what you say, with no hidden meaning; just; only: *I'm not making criticisms, merely suggestions.* **2** used to emphasize that something or someone is very small or unimportant; only: *Education should be more than merely training to pass exams.*

merge /mɜːdʒ‖mɜːrdʒ/ *v* **1** [I,T] to combine or join together to form one thing: *a computer program that makes it easy to merge text and graphics* | + **with** *The company is planning to merge with a German motor manufacturer.* **2 merge into sth** to seem to disappear into something and become part of it: *a point where the sea merges into the sky*

merg·er /'mɜːdʒə‖'mɜːrdʒər/ *n* [C] when companies join to form one larger one

me·rid·i·an /məˈrɪdiən/ *n* [C] one of the imaginary lines drawn from the SOUTH POLE to the NORTH POLE on a map

me·ringue /məˈræŋ/ *n* [C,U] a light, sweet food made by baking a mixture of sugar and the white part of eggs

mer·it[1] /ˈmerɪt/ *n* [C,U] a good quality or feature: *Simplicity is one of the merits of this system.* | **have merit/be of merit** *a book of great merit*

merit[2] *v* [T] *formal* to deserve something: *The play certainly merits this award.*

mer·maid /ˈmɜːmeɪd‖ˈmɜːr-/ *n* [C] an imaginary creature with a woman's body and a fish's tail instead of legs

mer·ry /ˈmeri/ *adj* happy and having fun: **Merry Christmas!** (=used to greet someone at Christmas) —**merrily** *adv*

merry-go-round /ˈ.. ˌ./ *n* [C] a machine at a FAIR that turns around and around, and has MODEL animals and seats for children to sit on

mesh[1] /meʃ/ *n* [U] a piece of material made of threads or wires that have been woven together like a net: *A wire mesh screen covered the window.*

mesh[2] *v* [I] if two or more ideas or features mesh, they go well together: *Their different management styles never meshed successfully.*

mes·mer·ize (also **-ise** *BrE*) /ˈmezməraɪz/ *v* [T] to make someone feel that they cannot stop watching or listening to something because it is so interesting or attractive: *a video game that keeps kids mesmerized for hours* —**mesmerizing** *adj*

mess[1] /mes/ *n* **1** [singular, U] when a place looks dirty and untidy: *This house is a mess!* | *Don't make a mess of the kitchen, will you?* **2** [singular] *informal* a situation in which there are a lot of problems and difficulties: *His personal life was a mess.* **3** [C] a room where people in an army, navy etc eat and drink together

mess[2] *v*

mess around (also **mess about** *BrE*) *phr v informal* **1** [I] to play or do silly things when you should be working or paying attention: *Stop messing around and do your homework!* **2** [T **mess** sb **around/about**] to cause someone problems by behaving in an unreasonable way, or by not doing what they want: *Don't mess me around. Tell me where she went!*

mess around with (also **mess about with** *BrE*) *phr v* [T] *informal* **1** [**mess around with** sth] to play with something or make small changes to it; TINKER: *Who's been messing around with my camera?* **2** [**mess around with** sb] to have a sexual relationship with someone, especially someone who is involved in another relationship

mess up *phr v informal* **1** [T **mess** sth ↔ **up**] to spoil something: *I hope I haven't messed up your plans.* **2** [T **mess** sth ↔ **up**] to make something dirty or untidy: *Who messed up my clean kitchen?* **3** [I,T **mess** sth ↔ **up**] to make a mistake or do something badly: *"How did you do on the test?" "Oh, I really messed up."*

mess with sb/sth *phr v* [T] **don't mess with** spoken **a)** used to warn someone not to annoy another person: *Don't mess with me, buddy!* **b)** used to warn someone not to get involved with something dangerous: *Don't mess with drugs.*

mes·sage /ˈmesɪdʒ/ *n* [C] **1** a spoken or written piece of information that you send to another person: *"Janet just called." "Did she leave a message?"* | *Sorry, Tony's not home yet. Can I take a message?* **2** [usually singular] the main idea in a film, book, or speech: *The play has a clear message about the dangers of jealousy.* **3 get the message** *informal* to understand what someone wants you to do: *Hopefully he got the message and will stop bothering me!*

mes·sen·ger /ˈmesɪndʒə -sən-‖-ər/ *n* [C] someone who takes messages to other people

mes·si·ah /mɪˈsaɪə/ *n* **the Messiah a)** Jesus Christ according to the Christian religion **b)** the leader who will be sent by God to save the world, according to the Jewish religion

Mes·srs /ˈmesəz‖-ərz/ *formal* the written plural of Mr

mess·y /ˈmesi/ *adj* **1** dirty or untidy: *Sorry the house is so messy.* **2** a messy situation is complicated and unpleasant to deal with: *a messy divorce*

met /met/ *v* the past tense and past participle of MEET

me·tab·o·lis·m /mɪˈtæbəlɪzəm/ *n* [C,U] the chemical processes in your body that change food into the energy you need —**metabolic** /ˌmetəˈbɒlɪk‖-ˈbɑː-/ *adj*

met·al /ˈmetl/ *n* [C,U] a hard, usually shiny, substance such as iron, gold, or steel: *Is it made of metal or plastic?* | *We use metal cases for our computers.*

metal de·tec·tor /ˈ.. ˌ../ *n* [C] a machine used for finding metal buried under the ground, or one used at airports for finding metal weapons

me·tal·lic /mɪˈtælɪk/ *adj* made of metal, or similar to metal in appearance, sound, or taste: *a car painted metallic blue*

met·a·mor·pho·sis /ˌmetəˈmɔːfəsɪs‖-ˈmɔːr-/ *n* [C,U], *plural* **metamorphoses** /-siːz/ the process of changing into a completely different form: *a caterpillar's metamorphosis into a butterfly*

met·a·phor /ˈmetəfə, -fɔː‖-fɔːr/ *n* [C,U] a way of describing something by comparing it to something else that has similar qualities, without using the words 'like' or 'as': *"A river of tears" is a metaphor.* —**metaphorical** /ˌmetəˈfɒrɪkəl‖-ˈfɔː-, -faː-/ *adj* —**metaphorically** /-kli/ *adv* → compare SIMILE

mete /miːt/ *v*

mete sth ↔ **out** *phr v* [T] *formal* to do something to someone as a punishment

me·te·or /ˈmiːtiəl-ər/ *n* [C] a small piece of rock or metal that is moving through space and can be seen as a bright burning line in the sky

me·te·or·ic /ˌmiːtiˈɒrɪk‖-ˈɔːrɪk, -ˈɑːrɪk/ *adj* happening very suddenly, quickly, and successfully: *his meteoric rise to fame*

me·te·o·rite /ˈmiːtiəraɪt/ *n* [C] a small meteor that has landed on the Earth's surface

me·te·o·rol·o·gy /ˌmiːtiəˈrɒlədʒi‖-ˈrɑː-/ *n* [U] the scientific study of weather —**meteorologist** *n* [C]

me·ter /ˈmiːtə‖-ər/ *n* [C] **1** the American spelling of METRE **2** a piece of equipment that measures the amount of gas, electricity, time etc

M

you have used: *The cab driver looked at the meter and said, "$5.70, please".*

meth·a·done /ˈmeθədəʊn‖-doʊn/ *n* [U] *technical* a drug that is often given to people who are trying to stop taking HEROIN

me·thane /ˈmiːθeɪn‖ˈme-/ *n* [U] a gas with no colour or smell

meth·od /ˈmeθəd/ *n* [C] a way of doing something: *This is the simplest method of payment.* | *The school uses a variety of teaching methods.*

me·thod·i·cal /mɪˈθɒdɪkəl‖məˈθɑː-/ *adj* done in a careful and well organized way, or always doing things this way: *a methodical search* | *a methodical woman* —**methodically** /-kli/ *adv*

Meth·o·dist /ˈmeθədɪ̈st/ *adj* the Methodist Church is a Christian religious group that follows the ideas of John Wesley —**Methodist** *n* [C]

meth·o·dol·o·gy /ˌmeθəˈdɒlədʒi‖-ˈdɑː-/ *n* [C,U] the methods used to do a job or scientific study —**methodological** /ˌmeθədəˈlɒdʒɪkəl‖-ˈlɑː-/ *adj*

me·tic·u·lous /mɪˈtɪkjɵ̈ləs/ *adj* very careful about details, with everything done correctly: *They keep meticulous records.* —**meticulously** *adv*

me·tre *BrE*, **meter** *AmE* /ˈmiːtə‖-ər/ *n* **1** [C] written abbreviation **m**; a unit for measuring length equal to 100 centimetres or 39.37 inches **2** [C,U] the regular pattern of sounds made by the words of a poem

met·ric /ˈmetrɪk/ *adj* using the system of weights and measures based on the kilogram and the metre ➔ compare IMPERIAL

met·ro /ˈmetrəʊ‖-troʊ/ *n* [singular] a railway running under the ground in a city: *the Paris metro*

me·trop·o·lis /mɪˈtrɒpəlɪ̈s‖məˈtrɑː-/ *n* [C] a very large city, or the most important city of a country

met·ro·pol·i·tan /ˌmetrəˈpɒlɪ̈tən‖-ˈpɑː-/ *adj* [only before noun] in or part of a very large city

mg the written abbreviation of MILLIGRAM

mi·aow *BrE*, **meow** *especially AmE* /miˈaʊ/ *n* [C] the crying sound that a cat makes —**miaow** *v* [I]

mice /maɪs/ *n* the plural of MOUSE

mi·crobe /ˈmaɪkrəʊb‖-kroʊb/ *n* [C] an extremely small living creature that cannot be seen without a MICROSCOPE

mi·cro·bi·ol·o·gy /ˌmaɪkrəʊbaɪˈɒlədʒi‖-kroʊbaɪˈɑːl-/ *n* [U] the scientific study of very small living things —**microbiologist** *n* [C]

mi·cro·chip /ˈmaɪkrəʊˌtʃɪp‖-kroʊ-/ *n* [C] a very small piece of SILICON containing electronic parts, used in computers and machines

mi·cro·cos·m /ˈmaɪkrəʊˌkɒzəm‖-kroʊˌkɑː-/ *n* [C] a small group that has the same qualities or features as a much larger one: *San Jose has a good mix of people; it's a microcosm of America.*

mi·cro·fiche /ˈmaɪkrəʊfiːʃ‖-kroʊ-/ *n* [C,U] a sheet of film containing information printed in very small letters, which can be read using a special machine

mi·cro·or·gan·is·m /ˌmaɪkrəʊˈɔːɡənɪzəm‖-kroʊˈɔːr-/ *n* [C] an extremely small living creature that cannot be seen without a MICROSCOPE

mi·cro·phone /ˈmaɪkrəfəʊn‖-foʊn/ *n* [C] a piece of equipment that you speak into or play music into when you are recording it or making it louder

mi·cro·pro·ces·sor /ˈmaɪkrəʊˌprəʊsesəl‖-kroʊˌprɑːsesər/ *n* [C] the main MICROCHIP in a computer, which controls most of its operations

mi·cro·scope /ˈmaɪkrəskəʊp‖-skoʊp/ *n* [C] a scientific instrument that makes very small things look larger

mi·cro·scop·ic /ˌmaɪkrəˈskɒpɪk◂‖-ˈskɑː-/ *adj* extremely small: *microscopic organisms*

mi·cro·wave¹ /ˈmaɪkrəweɪv/ *n* [C] also **microwave oven** a machine that cooks food very quickly, using electric waves instead of heat ➔ see picture at KITCHEN

microwave² *v* [T] to cook food in a microwave oven

mid /mɪd/ *adj* [only before noun] in the middle of: *They moved to California in the mid 1960s.* | *She's in her mid-20s.* (=is about 25 years old) | *The match is in mid May.*

mid- /mɪd/ *prefix* middle: *a cold midwinter night* | *midlife crisis*

mid·air /ˌmɪdˈeə◂‖-ˈer◂/ *n* **in midair** in the air or sky: *The plane exploded in midair.* —**midair** *adj*: *a midair collision*

mid·day /ˌmɪdˈdeɪ◂‖ˈmɪd-deɪ/ *n* [U] twelve o'clock in the middle of the day; NOON ➔ compare MIDNIGHT

microscope

middle

Billy   Tom   Chris

Tom is in the middle.

mid·dle¹ /ˈmɪdl/ *n* **1 the middle a)** the centre part of something: *Why's your car parked in the middle of the road?* | *Look at this old photo – that's me in the middle.* **b)** the part that is between the beginning and the end of an

M

event, period, or story: *Someone fainted in the middle of the ceremony.* | *Go back to sleep – it's the middle of the night!* **2 be in the middle of (doing) sth** to be busy doing something: *Can I call you back later? I'm in the middle of cooking dinner.*

USAGE NOTE: middle and centre

The middle of something is the part that is farthest away from the sides or edges: *Someone left a toy in the middle of the floor.* The centre of something is exactly in the middle: *Put the vase in the centre of the table.*

---

middle² *adj* [only before noun] **1** nearest to the centre of something and furthest away from its edges or ends: *Shall we sit in the middle row?* | *The middle lane was blocked because of an accident.* **2** half of the way through an event or period of time: *We'll spend the middle part of the vacation in Florida.*

middle-aged /ˌ.. '.◂/ *adj* a middle-aged person is between about 40 and 60 years old —**middle age** *n* [U]

Middle Ag·es /ˌ.. '../ *n* **the Middle Ages** the period in European history between about 1100 and 1500 AD

middle class /ˌ.. '.◂/ *n* **the middle class** also **the middle classes** people such as teachers, doctors, or managers, who are neither very rich nor very poor

middle-class *adj* belonging to the middle class, or typical of such people: *children from middle-class families* | *middle-class attitudes*

Middle East /ˌ.. '.◂/ *n* **the Middle East** the area including Iran and Egypt and the countries between them

mid·dle·man /ˈmɪdlmæn/ *n* [C], *plural* **middlemen** /-men/ someone who buys things to sell to someone else, or who arranges a business deal between two other people

middle name /ˌ.. './ *n* [C] the name that comes between your first name and your family name

middle-of-the-road /ˌ.. . . '.◂/ *adj* middle-of-the-road opinions are not extreme, so most people agree with them: *a politician who appeals to middle-of-the-road voters*

middle school /ˈ.. ./ *n* [C] a school in Britain for children between the ages of 8 and 12, and in the US for children between 11 and 14

midg·et /ˈmɪdʒɪt/ *n* [C] a very small person. Some people consider this word to be offensive

Mid·lands /ˈmɪdləndz/ *n* **the Midlands** the central area of England, around Birmingham

mid·life cri·sis /ˌmɪdlaɪf ˈkraɪsɪs/ *n* [singular] when people of between about 40 and 50 years old have feelings of worry and doubt about themselves

mid·night /ˈmɪdnaɪt/ *n* [U] 12 o'clock at night: *We close at midnight.* ➔ compare MIDDAY

mid·riff /ˈmɪdrɪf/ *n* [C] the part of the body between your chest and your waist

midst /mɪdst/ *n* **in the midst of** in the middle of an event, situation, place, or group: *He was brought up in the midst of the '30s Depression.*

mid·sum·mer /ˌmɪdˈsʌmə◂ ‖-ər◂/ *n* [U] the middle of the summer: *a lovely midsummer day*

mid·term /ˌmɪdˈtɜːm◂ ‖-ˈtɜːrm◂/ *adj* [only before noun] in the middle of one of the main periods of the school year, or in the middle of an elected government's time in power: *midterm tests* | *midterm elections*

mid·way /ˌmɪdˈweɪ◂ ‖ˈmɪdweɪ/ *adj, adv* at the middle point between two places, or in the middle of a period of time: *There's a gas station midway between here and Fresno.* | *He collapsed midway through the performance.*

mid·week /ˌmɪdˈwiːk◂ ‖ˈmɪdwiːk/ *adj, adv* on one of the middle days of the week: *a midweek match against Liverpool* | *I'll be seeing him midweek.*

Mid·west /ˌmɪdˈwest/ *n* **the Midwest** the central area of the US —**Midwestern** *adj*

mid·wife /ˈmɪdwaɪf/ *n* [C], *plural* **midwives** /-waɪvz/ a nurse who has been trained to help when a woman has a baby

miffed /mɪft/ *adj informal* slightly annoyed

might¹ /maɪt/ *modal verb* **1** if something might happen or might be true, it is possible, but you are not certain: *I might be wrong, but I think he's French.* | *I might not be able to go.* | *What a stupid thing to do – you might have been killed!* **2** the past tense of 'may': *I thought it might rain, so I brought an umbrella.* ➔ see also **may/ might as well** (WELL¹)

might² *n* [U] *literary* strength and power: *She pushed with all her might.*

might·y¹ /ˈmaɪti/ *adj literary* strong and powerful, or big and impressive: *mighty warriors*

mighty² *adv AmE informal* very: *That chicken smells mighty good.*

mi·graine /ˈmiːɡreɪn, ˈmaɪ-‖ˈmaɪ-/ *n* [C] an extremely bad HEADACHE

mi·grant /ˈmaɪɡrənt/ *n* [C] a person, bird, or animal that regularly moves from one place to another: *migrant workers* ➔ compare EMIGRANT, IMMIGRANT

mi·grate /maɪˈɡreɪt‖ˈmaɪɡreɪt/ *v* [I] **1** birds or animals that migrate travel to a warmer part of the world in winter and come back in the spring **2** to go to live in another place, usually to find work: *farmworkers who migrate from state to state, harvesting crops* ➔ compare EMIGRATE

mi·gra·tion /maɪˈɡreɪʃən/ *n* [C,U] when a large group of birds, animals, or people move from one place to another: *the birds' annual migration to southern Europe* —**migratory** /maɪˈɡreɪtəri‖ˈmaɪɡrətɔːri/ *adj*

mike /maɪk/ *n* [C] *informal* a MICROPHONE

mil·age /ˈmaɪlɪdʒ/ *n* MILEAGE

mild /maɪld/ *adj* **1** not too severe, strong, or serious: *a mild case of flu* | *mild criticism* **2** not having a strong or hot taste: *mild cheddar cheese* | *a mild green chili* **3** mild weather is not too cold

mil·dew /ˈmɪldjuː‖-duː/ *n* [U] a white or grey substance that grows on walls, leather, and other surfaces in warm, slightly wet places —**mildewed** *adj*

mild·ly /ˈmaɪldli/ *adv* **1** slightly: *She seemed mildly amused.* **2 to put it mildly** *spoken* used to say that you could use much stronger words, but are being polite: *He's not very pleased with you, to put it mildly.*

mile /maɪl/ *n* **1** [C] written abbreviation **m**; a unit for measuring distance, equal to 1,760 yards

or 1,609 metres; *My house is about 15 miles north of here.* | *Mark walks at least five miles a day.*
2 miles *informal* a very long distance: *We walked for miles without seeing anyone.*

mile·age also **milage** / ˈmaɪlɪdʒ / *n* **1** [singular, U] the number of miles that a vehicle has travelled: *a used car with a low mileage* **2 get a lot of mileage out of sth** to get as much use or advantage from something as you possibly can: *The newspapers could get a lot of mileage out of that story.*

mile·stone / ˈmaɪlstəʊn‖-stoʊn / *n* [C] a very important event in the development of something: *Winning that medal was a milestone in her career.*

mil·i·tant / ˈmɪlɪtənt / *adj* willing to use force or violence to change politics or society: *a militant protest group* —**militant** *n* [C] —**militantly** *adv* —**militancy** *n* [U]

mil·i·ta·ris·m / ˈmɪlɪtərɪzəm / *n* [U] the belief that a country should increase its army, navy etc and use them to get what it wants —**militaristic** / ˌmɪlɪtəˈrɪstɪk◂ / *adj*

mil·i·ta·ry[1] / ˈmɪlɪtərɪ‖-teri / *adj* used by the army, navy etc, or relating to war: *military aircraft* | *All young men had to do military service.* —**militarily** *adv*

military[2] *n* **the military** the army, navy, and other military organizations of a country: *My father is in the military.*

mi·li·tia / mɪˈlɪʃə / *n* [C] an organized group of soldiers who are not members of a permanent or official army

milk[1] / mɪlk / *n* [U] a white liquid produced by female animals and humans to feed their babies: *People drink cows' and goats' milk.* | *a glass of milk* | *Would you like milk in your coffee?* → see colour picture on page 439

milk[2] *v* [T] **1** to take milk from a cow or goat **2 milk sb/sth for sth** *informal* to get all the money or advantages etc that you can from a person or situation: *I'm going to milk her for every penny she has.*

milk·man / ˈmɪlkmən / *n* [C], *plural* **milkmen** / -mən / someone who delivers milk to houses each morning

milk·shake / ˌ. ˈ.‖. ./ *n* [C,U] a drink made from milk mixed with fruit or chocolate

milk·y / ˈmɪlki / *adj* **1** a milky drink contains a lot of milk: *milky coffee* **2** a liquid that is milky is not clear and looks slightly white, like milk

mill[1] / mɪl / *n* [C] **1** a building containing a large machine for crushing grain, or the machine itself **2** a factory that produces paper, steel, or cloth

mill[2] *v* [T] to crush grain in a mill

mill around, mill about *phr v* [I] *informal* if a lot of people are milling around, they are moving around a place without a particular purpose: *Crowds of students were milling around in the streets.*

mil·len·ni·um / mɪˈleniəm / *n* [C], *plural* **millennia** **1** a period of 1000 years **2** the time when a new 1000-year period begins: *How will the country celebrate the millennium?*

mil·li·gram / ˈmɪlɪɡræm / written abbreviation **mg** *n* [C] a unit for measuring weight, equal to 1/1000th of a gram

mil·li·li·tre *BrE*, **milliliter** *AmE* / ˈmɪlɪˌliːtə‖-ər / written abbreviation **ml** *n* [C] a unit for measuring liquids, equal to 1/1000th of a litre

mil·li·me·tre *BrE*, **millimeter** *AmE* / ˈmɪlɪˌmiːtə‖ -ər / written abbreviation **mm** *n* [C] a unit for measuring length, equal to 1/1000th of a metre

mil·li·ne·ry / ˈmɪlɪnərɪ‖-neri / *n* [U] *old-fashioned* women's hats, or the activity of making these hats

mil·lion[1] / ˈmɪljən / *number* **1** 1,000,000: *$350 million* | *four million people* **2** also **millions** *spoken informal* an extremely large number of people or things: *It was a great party – there were millions of people there!* —**millionth** *number*

mil·lion·aire / ˌmɪljəˈneə‖-ˈner / *n* [C] someone who is very rich and has at least one million dollars or pounds

mime[1] / maɪm / *n* [C,U] the use of movements without words to tell a story

mime[2] *v* [I,T] to act something using movements without any words: *She stretched out her arms, miming a swimmer.*

mim·ic[1] / ˈmɪmɪk / *v* [T] **mimicked, mimicked, mimicking** to copy someone's behaviour or appearance: *Sally made us laugh by mimicking the teacher.* | *an insect that mimics the appearance of a wasp* —**mimicry** *n* [U]

mimic[2] *n* [C] a person or animal that is good at mimicking someone or something

min 1 the written abbreviation of 'minimum' **2** the written abbreviation of 'minute' or 'minutes'

mince[1] / mɪns / *v* **1** [T] to cut food into extremely small pieces, usually in a machine: *minced beef* **2 not mince (your) words** to say exactly what you think, even if this offends people: *He's always upsetting people – he certainly doesn't mince his words.*

mince[2] *n* [U] *BrE* meat that has been cut into very small pieces; GROUND BEEF, HAMBURGER *AmE*

mince·meat / ˈmɪnsmiːt / *n* [U] a sweet mixture of apples, dried fruit, and SPICES, but no meat

mince pie / ˌ. ˈ./ *n* [C] a small PIE filled with mincemeat, traditionally eaten at Christmas

mind[1] / maɪnd / *n* **1** [C,U] your thoughts, or the part of your brain used for thinking and imagining things: *I have a picture of him in my mind.* | *I keep going over the problem in my mind.* | *I can't think about that now, my mind is on other things.* (=I am thinking about something different) **2 change your mind** to change your opinion or decision about something: *If you change your mind and want to come, give us a call.* **3 make up your mind** to decide something, or become very determined to do something: *Have you made up your mind which college you want to go to?* **4 come/spring to mind** if something comes to mind, you suddenly think of it **5 cross/enter your mind** if something crosses your mind, you have a new thought or idea: *It never crossed my mind that she might be lying.* **6 have sth in mind** to be planning or intending to do something: *What changes do you have in mind?* **7 keep/bear sth in mind** to remember something because it will be useful in the future: *Keep in mind that the bank will be closed tomorrow.* **8 be on your mind** if some-

M

thing is on your mind, you keep worrying about it: *Her mother's ill and she's lost her job, so she's had a lot on her mind lately.* **9 take your mind off sth** to make you stop thinking about something: *Dad needs a vacation to take his mind off work.* **10 go/be out of your mind** *informal* to start to become mentally ill or to behave in a strange way: *I have so much to do – I feel like I'm going out of my mind.* | *She's going to marry him? – She must be out of her mind!* **11 put your mind to sth** to decide that you are definitely going to do something and try hard to achieve it: *I'm sure she'll pass her test if she puts her mind to it.* **12 have/keep an open mind** to be willing to accept other ideas and opinions **13 -minded** having a particular attitude or believing that a particular thing is important: *politically-minded students*

mind[2] *v* **1** [I,T] to feel annoyed or upset about something: *Do you think she'd mind if we didn't come?* | *It was raining, but we didn't mind.* **2 not mind doing sth** to be willing to do something: *I don't mind driving if you're tired.* **3 do you mind/would you mind** *spoken* used to ask politely if you can do something, or if someone will do something for you: *Do you mind if I use your phone?* | *Would you mind waiting here a minute?* **4 mind your own business** *spoken* used to say that someone should not ask questions about other people's lives: *"So did he kiss you?" "Mind your own business!"* **5 mind out** *spoken* used to warn someone to get out of the way or they might get hit or hurt themselves **6 never mind** *spoken* used to tell someone not to worry, or that something is not important: *"I'm sorry I'm so late." "Never mind – we haven't started yet anyway."*

mind·ful /ˈmaɪndfəl/ *adj* if you are mindful of a rule, fact, or warning you remember it and behave sensibly: *Mindful of the guide's warning, they returned before dark.*

mind·less /ˈmaɪndləs/ *adj* **1** stupid and without any real meaning or purpose: *mindless vandalism* **2** a mindless job is boring and you do not need much intelligence to do it —**mindlessness** *n* [U]

mind·set /ˈmaɪndset/ *n* [C] the attitude and way of thinking that someone has: *In recent years there has been something of a shift in the male mindset.* (=in the way men think)

mine[1] /maɪn/ *pron* the thing or things belonging to me: *"Whose coat is this?" "It's mine."* | *Can I borrow your radio? Mine's broken.* | *He's an old friend of mine.*

mine[2] *n* [C] **1** a deep hole or series of holes in the ground from which metal, coal etc is dug: *He's worked in the coal mines all his life.* **2** a type of bomb that is hidden below the ground or under water which explodes when it is touched

mine[3] *v* **1** [I,T] to dig into the ground to get gold, coal etc: *men mining for gold* **2** [T] to hide bombs under the ground or in the sea: *All the roads in the area had been mined.*

mine·field /ˈmaɪnfiːld/ *n* [C] **1** an area of land or sea where hidden bombs have been placed **2** a situation in which there are many hidden difficulties and dangers: *Getting a divorce is a dreadful business – it's a minefield!*

min·er /ˈmaɪnə‖-ər/ *n* [C] someone who works in a mine: *a coal miner*

min·e·ral /ˈmɪnərəl/ *n* [C] a natural substance such as iron or salt which is formed in the earth and present in some foods: *Milk is full of valuable vitamins and minerals.*

mineral wa·ter /ˈ... ˌ.../ *n* [C,U] water that comes from under the ground and contains MINERALS

min·gle /ˈmɪŋgəl/ *v* **1** [I,T] if smells, sounds, or feelings mingle, they combine with each other: *anger mingled with disappointment* **2** [I] to meet and talk with a lot of different people at a social event: *Reporters mingled with movie stars at the awards ceremony.*

min·i- /mɪni/ *prefix* very small or short: *a mini-break* (=a short holiday)

min·ia·ture[1] /ˈmɪnɪtʃə‖ˈmɪniətʃər/ *adj* [only before noun] much smaller than normal: *a theme park with a miniature railway*

miniature[2] *n* [C] **1** a very small painting, usually of a person **2 in miniature** exactly like someone or something else, but much smaller: *She's her mother in miniature.*

min·i·bus /ˈmɪnibʌs/ *n* [C] *BrE* a small bus for about 12 people

min·i·mal /ˈmɪnɪməl/ *adj* extremely small in amount or degree and therefore not worth worrying about: *The storm caused only minimal damage.* —**minimally** *adv*

min·i·mize (also **-ise** *BrE*) /ˈmɪnɪmaɪz/ *v* [T] **1** to make the degree or amount of something as small as possible: *To minimize the risk of getting heart disease, eat well and exercise daily.* **2** to make a computer document appear as a very small picture on the screen when you are not using it for a short time → opposite MAXIMIZE

min·i·mum[1] /ˈmɪnɪməm/ *adj* the minimum number or amount is the smallest that is possible or needed: *The minimum requirements for the job are a degree and two years' experience.* | *a minimum payment of $50 a month* → opposite MAXIMUM

minimum[2] *n* [singular] the smallest number or amount that is possible or needed: *Looking after a horse costs a minimum of £2000 a year.* | *Costs were kept to a minimum.* (=as small as possible) → opposite MAXIMUM

min·ing /ˈmaɪnɪŋ/ *n* [U] the job of digging gold, coal etc out of the ground: *coal mining in Oklahoma* | *mining companies*

min·is·cule /ˈmɪnəskjuːl/ *adj* another spelling of MINUSCULE

min·i·skirt /ˈmɪniskɜːt‖-skɜːrt/ *n* [C] a very short skirt

min·is·ter[1] /ˈmɪnɪstə‖-ər/ *n* [C] **1** a religious leader in some Christian churches → compare PRIEST **2** a politician who is in charge of a government department: *the Minister of Education*

minister[2] *v*
minister to sb/sth *phr v* [T] *formal* to give help to someone: *doctors ministering to the needs of their patients*

min·is·ter·i·al /ˌmɪnɪˈstɪəriəl‖-ˈstɪr-/ *adj* relating to a minister, or done by a minister: *ministerial decisions*

min·is·try /ˈmɪnɪstri/ *n* **1** [C] a government department: *the Defense Ministry* | *the Ministry of Agriculture* **2 the ministry** the profession of being a church leader, or the work done by a religious leader: *James wants to join the ministry*

min·i·van /'mɪnivæn/ *n* [C] *AmE* a large car with six to eight seats

mink /mɪŋk/ *n* [C,U] a small animal with soft brown fur, or the valuable fur from this animal: *a mink coat*

min·now /'mɪnəʊ‖-noʊ/ *n* [C] a very small fish

mi·nor¹ /'maɪnə‖-ər/ *adj* **1** small and not very important or serious: *We made a few minor changes to the plan.* | *minor* **illness/operation/ injury** *It's only a minor injury.* **2** a minor key is one of the two main sets of musical notes, often producing music that sounds sad → compare MAJOR¹

minor² *n* [C] *law* a child or young person who is not old enough to have adult rights or legal responsibilities

minor³ *v*

minor in sth *phr v* [T] *AmE* to study a second main subject as part of your degree: *I'm minoring in African Studies.*

mi·nor·i·ty /maɪ'nɒrɪtiǁmɪ'nɔː-, mɪ'nɑː-/ *n* **1** [singular] a small part of a larger group of people or things: *Only a minority of students get a first-class degree.* **2** [C usually plural] a group of people of a different race or religion than most people in a country: *people from ethnic minorities* | *minority* **group/language/interest** etc *language classes for minority groups* **3 be in the minority** to be fewer in number than any other group: *Boys are very much in the minority in the dance class.* → compare MAJORITY

mint¹ /mɪnt/ *n* **1** a sweet with the strong fresh taste of PEPPERMINT **2** [U] a plant with leaves that have a strong fresh taste, used in cooking **3** [C] a place where coins are officially made — **minty** *adj*: *a minty taste*

mint² *v* [T] to make a coin

mi·nus¹ /'maɪnəs/ *prep* **1** used in mathematics when you SUBTRACT one number from another: *17 minus 5 is 12 (17 – 5 = 12)* **2** a temperature of minus 5, minus 20 etc is 5 or 20 degrees below zero: *Temperatures tonight will fall to minus 8.* **3** without something that would normally be there: *He came back minus a couple of front teeth.* → opposite PLUS¹

minus² *n* [C] **1** also **minus sign** a sign (–) showing that a number is less than zero, or that the second of two numbers is to be subtracted (SUBTRACT) from the first **2** something bad about a situation: *There are pluses and minuses to living in a big city.* → opposite PLUS⁴

min·us·cule, miniscule /'mɪnɪˌskjuːl/ *adj* very small: *a minuscule amount of food*

min·ute¹ /'mɪnɪt/ *n* [C] **1** a period of time equal to 60 seconds: *Clare's train arrives in fifteen minutes.* | *It's three minutes to ten.* **2** a very short period of time: *It'll only take me a minute to do this.* | *He was there a minute ago.* **3 in a minute** very soon: *I'll do it in a minute.* **4 wait/just a minute** *spoken* **a)** used to ask someone to wait a short period of time: *"Are you coming with us?" "Yes, just a minute."* **b)** used

when you do not agree with someone: *Wait a minute – that can't be right!* **5 the minute (that)** as soon as: *I knew it was Jill the minute I heard her voice.* **6 last minute** at the last possible time, just before it is too late: *Frank changed his mind at the last minute and decided to come with us after all.* | *a few last-minute arrangements* **7 any minute** very soon: *She should get here any minute now.* **8 this minute** used to order someone to do something immediately: *Come here, this minute!* → see also MINUTES

mi·nute² /maɪ'njuːt‖-'nuːt/ *adj* **1** extremely small: *minute handwriting* **2** very careful and thorough: **in minute detail** *Johnson explained the plan in minute detail.*

min·utes /'mɪnɪts/ *n* [plural] an official written record of the things that were said during a meeting

mir·a·cle /'mɪrəkəl/ *n* [C] **1** something lucky that you did not expect to happen or did not think was possible: **it's a miracle (that)** *especially spoken: It's a miracle that no one was hurt.* | **work/perform miracles** (=do something very impressive): *The builders have worked miracles in finishing it so quickly.* **2** an action or event that seems impossible and is thought to be caused by God

mi·rac·u·lous /mɪ'rækjÿləs/ *adj* very lucky and completely unexpected: *a miraculous recovery* — **miraculously** *adv*

mi·rage /'mɪrɑːʒ‖mɪ'rɑːʒ/ *n* [C] when the hot air in a desert makes you see things that are not really there

mir·ror¹ /'mɪrə‖-ər/ *n* [C] a piece of special glass made so that when you look at it you see yourself or what is behind you: *He glanced at his reflection in the mirror.* | *Check your mirror before overtaking.*

mirror² *v* [T] to be very similar to something or to show clearly what it is like: *The excitement of the 1960s is mirrored in its music.*

mirth /mɜːθ‖mɜːrθ/ *n* [U] *formal* laughter and happiness

mis- /mɪs/ *prefix* used at the beginning of some words to mean 'bad' or 'badly', or 'wrong' or 'wrongly': *misbehave* | *mismanagement* | *misunderstand* | *miscalculation*

mis·ap·pre·hen·sion /ˌmɪsæprɪ'henʃən/ *n* [C,U] *formal* a wrong belief or opinion about something: **be under a misapprehension** (=believe that something is true when it is not): *I was under the misapprehension that Eric was still working in Germany.*

mis·ap·pro·pri·ate /ˌmɪsə'prəʊprieɪt‖-'proʊ-/ *v* [T] *formal* to dishonestly take something, especially money, that you are responsible for — **misappropriation** /ˌmɪsəprəʊpri'eɪʃən‖-proʊ-/ *n* [U] *misappropriation of funds*

mis·be·have /ˌmɪsbɪ'heɪv/ *v* [I] to behave badly

misbehaviour *BrE*, **misbehavior** *AmE* /ˌmɪsbɪ'heɪvjə‖-ər/ *n* [U] when someone behaves badly

mis·cal·cu·late /ˌmɪs'kælkjÿleɪt/ *v* [I,T] **1** to make a mistake when you are deciding how

M

much money you will need for something, how long it will take to do something etc: *We seriously miscalculated the cost of the project.* **2** to understand a situation wrongly and make a wrong decision about it: *The Government has miscalculated public opinion.* —**miscalculation** /ˌmɪsˌkælkjᵘˈleɪʃən/ *n* [C,U]

mis·car·riage /ˌmɪsˈkærɪdʒ, ˈmɪskærɪdʒ/ *n* **1** [C,U] if a woman has a miscarriage, her baby is born much too early to live → compare ABORTION **2 miscarriage of justice** when someone is wrongly punished by a court of law for something they did not do

mis·car·ry /mɪsˈkæri/ *v* **1** [I,T] to give birth to a baby too early for it to live **2** [I] *formal* to not be successful: *All our careful plans had miscarried.*

mis·cel·la·ne·ous /ˌmɪsəˈleɪniəs◂/ *adj* of many different kinds: *a miscellaneous assortment of books*

mis·chief /ˈmɪstʃɪf/ *n* [U] bad behaviour, especially by children, that is annoying but causes no serious harm: *He was a lively child, and full of mischief.*

mis·chie·vous /ˈmɪstʃɪvəs/ *adj* a mischievous child behaves badly, but in a way that makes people laugh rather than making them angry: *a mischievous little girl* —**mischievously** *adv*

mis·con·cep·tion /ˌmɪskənˈsepʃən/ *n* [C,U] an idea that is wrong or untrue, but which people still believe: **+ that** *the misconception that only gay people have AIDS*

mis·con·duct /ˌmɪsˈkɒndʌkt◂ˈ-ˈkɑːn-/ *n* [U] *formal* bad behaviour, especially by someone such as a doctor or lawyer: *Dr Patton was found guilty of serious professional misconduct.*

mis·deeds /ˈmɪsdiːdz/ *n* [plural] *literary* wrong or illegal actions

mis·de·mea·nour *BrE*, **misdemeanor** *AmE* /ˌmɪsdɪˈmiːnəˈ-ər/ *n* [C] *formal* a crime that is not very serious

mi·ser /ˈmaɪzəˈ-ər/ *n* [C] someone who hates spending money and likes to have a lot of it — **miserly** *adj* —**miserliness** *n* [U]

mis·e·ra·ble /ˈmɪzərəbəl/ *adj* **1** very unhappy: *Why are you looking so miserable?* **2** unpleasant: *The weather's been pretty miserable all summer.* **3** not at all good: *Nurses tend to earn a miserable salary.* —**miserably** *adv*

mis·e·ry /ˈmɪzəri/ *n* [U] **1** when someone is very unhappy: *the misery of life in the refugee camps* **2 put sb/sth out of their misery a)** *informal* to make someone stop feeling worried, especially by telling them something they are waiting to hear: *Come on, put us out of our misery and tell us what happened.* **b)** to kill an animal that is old or ill so that it does not suffer any more

mis·fire /ˌmɪsˈfaɪəˈ-ˈfaɪr/ *v* [I] **1** to not have the result that you intended: *Their plans misfired badly.* **2** if a gun misfires it does not fire properly

mis·fit /ˈmɪsˌfɪt/ *n* [C] someone who seems strange because they are different from the other people in a place: *I was always a bit of a misfit at our school.*

mis·for·tune /mɪsˈfɔːtʃənˈ-ɔːr-/ *n* [C,U] bad luck, or something that happens to you as a result of bad luck: **have the misfortune of doing**

sth/**have the misfortune to do** sth *He's the nastiest man I've ever had the misfortune to meet!*

mis·giv·ing /ˌmɪsˈgɪvɪŋ/ *n* [C,U] a feeling of doubt or worry about something: **have misgivings about sth** *I knew he had some misgivings about letting me use his car.*

mis·guid·ed /mɪsˈgaɪdᵻd/ *adj* based on a wrong idea or opinion: *the misguided belief that it would be easier to find work in London*

mis·han·dle /ˌmɪsˈhændl/ *v* [T] to deal with something in the wrong way: *The investigation was seriously mishandled by the police.*

mis·hap /ˈmɪshæp/ *n* [C,U] an accident or mistake: *We completed our journey without further mishap.*

mis·in·form /ˌmɪsɪnˈfɔːmˈ-ɔːrm/ *v* [T] to give someone information that is incorrect or untrue: *I'm afraid you've been misinformed – she doesn't live here any more.*

mis·in·ter·pret /ˌmɪsɪnˈtɜːprᵻtˈ-ɜːr-/ *v* [T] to not understand the real meaning of someone's words or behaviour: *I think she misinterpreted my offer of a ride home.* —**misinterpretation** /ˌmɪsɪntɜːprᵻˈteɪʃənˈ-ɜːr-/ *n* [C,U]

mis·judge /ˌmɪsˈdʒʌdʒ/ *v* [T] **1** to be wrong when you decide what someone or something is like: *The President had badly misjudged the mood of the voters.* **2** to make a wrong decision about how to do something: *Don misjudged the turn and crashed into the barrier.* —**misjudgment** *n* [C,U]

mis·lay /mɪsˈleɪ/ *v* [T] **mislaid** /-ˈleɪd/, **mislaid**, **mislaying** to put something somewhere and then forget where you put it: *I seem to have mislaid my gloves.*

mis·lead /mɪsˈliːd/ *v* [T] **misled** /-ˈled/, **misled**, **misleading** to deliberately make someone have the wrong idea or opinion about something: *Wiggins has admitted trying to mislead the police.*

mis·lead·ing /mɪsˈliːdɪŋ/ *adj* likely to make someone believe something that is not true: *Statistics can be very misleading.* —**misleadingly** *adv*

mis·man·age·ment /mɪsˈmænɪdʒmənt/ *n* [U] when someone manages a company or organization badly or illegally: *allegations of fraud and mismanagement* —**mismanage** *v* [T]

mis·match /ˈmɪsmætʃ/ *n* [C] a combination of things or people that do not work well together or are not suitable for each other: **+ between** *a mismatch between what's necessary and what's possible* —**mismatched** /ˌmɪsˈmætʃt◂/ *adj*

mis·no·mer /mɪsˈnəʊməˈ-ˈnoʊmər/ *n* [C] a name that does not seem suitable for the thing it describes: *As you can see, 'work room' is something of a misnomer!*

mi·so·gy·nist /mᵻˈsɒdʒᵻnᵻstˈmᵻˈsɑː-/ *n* [C] a man who hates women —**misogyny** *n* [U] — **misogynistic** /mᵻˌsɒdʒᵻˈnɪstɪk◂ˈ-ˌsɑː-/ *adj*

mis·placed /ˌmɪsˈpleɪst◂/ *adj* misplaced feelings of trust, love, confidence etc only exist because someone does not understand the real facts about something: *a misplaced sense of loyalty*

mis·print /ˈmɪsˌprɪnt/ *n* [C] a mistake in the way a word is spelt in a book, magazine etc

mis·quote /ˌmɪsˈkwəʊt◂ˈ-ˈkwoʊt/ *v* [T] to make a mistake when you are reporting what someone else has said or written: *They insisted that the Governor had been misquoted.*

mis·read /ˌmɪsˈriːd/ *v* [T] **misread** /-ˈred/, **misread** /-ˈred/, **misreading** **1** to understand a person or situation wrongly: *The UN misread the situation.* **2** to read something wrongly: *I must have misread the date on the letter.* —**misreading** *n* [C,U]

mis·rep·re·sent /ˌmɪsreprɪˈzent/ *v* [T] to deliberately give a wrong description of what is really happening or what someone really thinks — **misrepresentation** /ˌmɪsreprɪzenˈteɪʃən/ *n* [C,U]

miss¹ /mɪs/ *v* **1** [T] to feel sad because you cannot be with someone that you like, cannot do something that you enjoy etc: *I really missed Paula after she'd left.* | *What do you miss most about life in Canada?* **2** [T] to not do or not have something: *Vialli will miss tonight's game because of a knee injury.* | *Don't miss your free gift in next week's 'Q' magazine!* | **miss a chance/an opportunity** *I'd hate to miss the chance of meeting him.* **3** [T] to be too late for something: *By the time we got there, we'd missed the beginning of the movie.* | **miss a bus/train/plane etc** *Hurry up or we'll miss the train!* **4** **miss the boat/bus** *informal* to fail to use an opportunity to do something **5** [I,T] to not succeed in hitting or catching something: *She fired at the target but missed.* | *Jackson missed an easy catch.* **6** [T] to not see, hear, or notice something: *Jody found an error that everyone else had missed.* **7** **miss the point** to not understand the most important fact about something: *I'm sorry, I think you're missing the point completely.*

miss out *phr v* **1** [I] to not have the chance to do something enjoyable, interesting, or useful for you: *All my friends were having fun and going out to parties in the evenings, and I felt I was missing out.* **2** [T **miss** sth ↔ **out**] to forget to include a fact or detail: *I hope we haven't missed any names out from the list.*

miss² *n* **1** [C] when you do not succeed in hitting, catching, or holding something: *a penalty miss by McAteer in the second half* **2** **give sth a miss** *BrE spoken* to decide not to do something: *As the tickets were so expensive, we decided to give the concert a miss.*

Miss *n* **1** **Miss Smith/Jones etc** used in front of the name of a girl or woman who is not married **2** *spoken* used as a polite way of talking to a young woman when you do not know her name: *Excuse me Miss, you've dropped your umbrella.* **3** *BrE spoken* used by children when talking to a female teacher whether she is married or not: *Please Miss, can I leave the room?*

mis·shap·en /ˌmɪsˈʃeɪpən, mɪˈʃeɪ-/ *adj* something that is misshapen is not its normal or natural shape: *misshapen fingers*

mis·sile /ˈmɪsaɪl‖ˈmɪsəl/ *n* [C] **1** a weapon that can fly over long distances and that explodes when it hits the thing it has been aimed at: *nuclear missiles* **2** *formal* an object that is thrown in order to hurt someone

miss·ing /ˈmɪsɪŋ/ *adj* **1** someone or something that is missing is not in the place where you expect them to be: *Police are still searching for the missing child.* | **+ from** *There's a button missing from this shirt.* **2** not included: **+ from** *Why is my name missing from the list?*

mis·sion /ˈmɪʃən/ *n* [C] **1** an important job that someone has been given to do: *Our mission was to find out everything about their plans.* **2** a group of important people who are sent by their government to another country to discuss something or collect information: *a Canadian trade mission to Japan* **3** an important military job that someone is sent to do, especially an attack on the enemy: *a bombing mission* **4** the work of a missionary, or a building where they do their work

mis·sion·a·ry /ˈmɪʃənəriː‖-neriː/ *n* [C] someone who goes to a foreign country in order to teach people about Christianity

mis·spell /ˌmɪsˈspel/ *v* [T] **misspelled** *or* **misspelt** /-ˈspelt/, **misspelled** *or* **misspelt**, **misspelling** to spell a word wrongly — **misspelling** *n* [C,U]

mis·step /ˈmɪs-step/ *n* [C] *AmE* a mistake, especially one that offends or upsets people: *The senator has made several missteps recently.*

mist¹ /mɪst/ *n* [C,U] a layer of cloud close to the ground that makes it difficult for you to see very far: *mist over the river*

mist² *v* also **mist over/up** [I,T] to become covered with very small drops of water, or to make something do this: *All the windows had misted over.*

mis·take¹ /məˈsteɪk/ *n* **1** [C] something that is not correct, that you do, say, or write without intending to: *Ivan's work is full of spelling mistakes.* | **make a mistake** *I think you've made a mistake – I ordered fish, not beef.* **2** [C] something that you do that you later realize was not the right thing to do: *Marrying Julie was a big mistake.* | **it is a mistake to do sth** *It would be a mistake to underestimate Moya's ability.* | **make the mistake of doing sth** *I made the mistake of giving him my phone number.* **3** **by mistake** without intending to do something: *Someone must have left the door open by mistake.*

mistake² *v* [T] **mistook** /-ˈstʊk/, **mistaken** /-ˈsteɪkən/, **mistaking** **1** to understand something wrongly: *He'd mistaken the address.* **2** **there's no mistaking sb/sth** used to say that something is easy to recognize: *There was no mistaking the anger in her voice.*

mistake sb/sth **for** sb/sth *phr v* [T] to think that one person or thing is someone or something else: *I mistook him for his brother.*

mis·tak·en /məˈsteɪkən/ *adj* someone who is mistaken is wrong about something: *Look! If I'm not mistaken, there's your lost ring!* —**mistakenly** *adv*

mis·ter /ˈmɪstəl-ər/ *n* *AmE spoken informal* used to talk to a man whose name you do not know: *Hey mister, is this your wallet?*

Mis·ter *n* MR

mis·tle·toe /ˈmɪsəltəʊl-toʊ/ *n* [U] a plant with small round white fruit that is often used as a decoration at Christmas

mis·took /məˈstʊk/ *v* the past tense of MISTAKE

mis·treat /ˌmɪsˈtriːt/ *v* [T] to treat a person or animal cruelly: *The hostages said they had not been mistreated.* —**mistreatment** *n* [U]

mis·tress /ˈmɪstrɨs/ *n* [C] a woman that a married man has a sexual relationship with

mis·trust¹ /mɪsˈtrʌst/ *n* [singular, U] the feeling that you cannot trust someone: **+ of** *He had a deep mistrust of politicians.*

M

mistrust² v [T] to not trust someone —**mistrustful** adj —**mistrustfully** adv

mist·y /ˈmɪsti/ adj when the weather is misty there is a lot of mist: a misty November morning

mis·un·der·stand /ˌmɪsʌndəˈstændǁ-ər-/ v **misunderstand** /-ˈstʊd/, **misunderstood**, **misunderstanding** **1** [I,T] to not understand something correctly: I think you misunderstood my question. **2** be misunderstood if someone is misunderstood, people do not realize that they are actually good, kind, honest etc although they do not appear to be

mis·un·der·stand·ing /ˌmɪsʌndəˈstændɪŋǁ-ər-/ n **1** [C,U] when someone does not understand something correctly: widespread misunderstanding and confusion **2** [C] an argument that is not very serious

mis·use¹ /mɪsˈjuːs/ n [C,U] when something is used in the wrong way or for the wrong purpose: + of a misuse of power

mis·use² /ˌmɪsˈjuːz/ v [T] to use something in the wrong way or for the wrong purpose: The chairman was accused of misusing club funds.

mite /maɪt/ n [C] **1** a very small insect that lives in plants, animals' fur, stored food etc: dust mites **2** a small child, especially one you feel sorry for **3** a mite lonely/cold/unfriendly etc slightly lonely, cold etc

mit·i·gate /ˈmɪtɪɡeɪt/ v [T] formal to make something less harmful or less serious —**mitigation** /ˌmɪtɪˈɡeɪʃən/ n [U]

mit·i·gat·ing /ˈmɪtɪɡeɪtɪŋ/ adj **mitigating circumstances/factors etc** facts that make a crime or mistake seem less serious

mitt /mɪt/ n [C] **1** a type of leather GLOVE used for catching a ball in BASEBALL **2** a GLOVE made of thick material, worn to protect your hand: an oven mitt

mit·ten /ˈmɪtn/ n [C] a type of GLOVE that does not have separate parts for each finger

mix¹ /mɪks/ v **1** [I,T] if you mix two or more substances or if they mix, they combine to become a single substance: **mix sth and sth** You can make green by mixing blue and yellow paint. | **mix sth with sth** Shake the bottle well to mix the oil with the vinegar. **2** [I,T] to combine two or more different activities, ideas, styles etc: Glennie's latest CD mixes classical music and rock 'n' roll. **3** [I] to enjoy meeting and talking to other people, especially people you do not know very well: + with Charlie doesn't mix well with the other children.

mix sb/sth up phr v [T] **1** to think that one person or thing is someone or something else: I'm always mixing up the kids' names. **2** to change the order in which things have been arranged: Whatever you do, try not to mix those papers up. ➔ see also MIXED UP, MIX-UP

mix² n **1** [singular] all the different people or things contained in something, such as an organization or piece of writing: + of There was a good mix of people in the department. **2** [C,U] a powder that is added to liquid to make something: cake mix

mixed /mɪkst/ adj **1** consisting of a lot of different types of things, people, ideas etc: mixed herbs | **mixed feelings** (=feelings of happiness and sadness at the same time): We had mixed feelings about moving so far away. **2** be a **mixed blessing** to be partly good and partly bad:

Living so near my parents was a mixed blessing. **3** BrE for both males and females: a mixed school ➔ see also CO-ED

mixed mar·riage /ˌ. ˈ../ n [C] a marriage between people from different races or religions

mixed up /ˌ. ˈ. ◂/ adj **1** be mixed up in sth/be mixed up with sb to be involved in dishonest or illegal activities with someone who has a bad influence on you: He was only 14 when he got mixed up in drug-dealing and car theft. **2** confused and not confident: a lonely mixed-up adolescent **3** confused: I got a little mixed up and went to the wrong restaurant. ➔ see also mix up (MIX¹), MIX-UP

mix·er /ˈmɪksəǁ-ər/ n [C] **1** a piece of equipment used for mixing things together: a food mixer ➔ see picture at KITCHEN **2** a drink that can be mixed with alcohol: There are some mixers in the fridge.

mix·ture /ˈmɪkstʃəǁ-ər/ n **1** [C,U] something that is made by mixing two or more different substances together: cake mixture **2** [singular] when something contains two or more different feelings, ideas etc at the same time: Hal stared at her with a mixture of amusement and disbelief.

mix-up /ˈ. ./ n [C] informal a mistake or problem caused by people misunderstanding each other or getting confused about what should be done: There was a mix-up at the station and Eddie got on the wrong bus. ➔ see also mix up (MIX¹), MIXED UP

ml the written abbreviation of MILLILITRE

mm the written abbreviation of MILLIMETRE

moan¹ /məʊnǁmoʊn/ v [I] **1** to make a long low sound, especially because something hurts a lot: She lay on the bed moaning with pain. **2** to complain about something in an annoying way: I wish you'd stop moaning all the time.

moan² n [C] a long low sound made by someone who is in pain or very unhappy

moat /məʊtǁmoʊt/ n [C] a deep wide hole, usually filled with water, that is dug around a castle in order to defend it

mob¹ /mɒbǁmɑːb/ n **1** [C] a large, noisy crowd, especially one that is angry and violent **2** the Mob informal the MAFIA

mob² v [T] **-bbed, -bbing** if someone is mobbed, they are surrounded by a large excited crowd: Gallagher was mobbed by fans at the airport.

mo·bile¹ /ˈməʊbaɪlǁˈmoʊbəl, -baɪl/ adj **1** able to move or be moved quickly and easily: She's 83 now, and not really very mobile. **2** able to move easily from one job, place, or social class to another: Professional people have become increasingly mobile in recent years. **3** mobile library/shop/clinic etc BrE a library, shop etc that is in a vehicle and can be driven from one place to another

mo·bile² /ˈməʊbaɪlǁˈmoʊbiːl/ n [C] **1** a decoration made of small objects that is hung up and moves when air blows around it **2** a MOBILE PHONE

mobile home /ˌ.. ˈ./ n [C] a type of house that can be easily moved from one place to another

mobile phone /ˌ.. ˈ./ n [C] BrE a telephone that you can carry with you and use anywhere

mo·bil·i·ty /məʊˈbɪlətiǁmoʊ-/ n [U] **1** the ability to move from one job, place, or social class to another: *social mobility* **2** the ability to walk or to move part of your body

mo·bil·ize (also **-ise** BrE) /'məʊbl̩aɪz‖'moʊ-/ v [I,T] **1** to make large numbers of people get involved in doing something, especially something political: *mobilizing support among middle class voters* **2** to make an army ready for war —**mo·bilization** /,məʊbl̩laɪ'zeɪʃən‖,moʊbl̩lə-/ n [C,U]

mob·ster /'mɒbstəl‖'maːbstər/ n [C] *informal* a member of the MAFIA

mock¹ /mɒk‖maːk/ v [I,T] to laugh at someone or say unkind things about them in order to make them seem stupid: *Wilson was always mocking Joe's southern accent.* —**mockingly** adv

mock² adj [only before noun] **1** not real, but intended to be similar to a real situation so that you can practise what you would do in that situation: *a mock interview* **2** mock surprise/horror/seriousness surprise etc that you pretend to feel: *With mock seriousness he said: "I forgive you."*

mock·e·ry /'mɒkəri‖'maː-/ n **1** [U] when someone laughs at someone else or says unkind things about them in order to make them look stupid **2** make a mockery of sth to make a plan, system, organization etc seem useless or ineffective: *It makes a mockery of the whole legal system.*

mock·ing·bird /'mɒkɪŋbɜːd‖'maːkɪŋbɜːrd/ n [C] an American bird that copies the songs of other birds

mock-up /'. ./ n [C] a copy of a building, vehicle etc which is not real but looks real: *a mock-up of the space shuttle*

modal verb /,.. './ also **modal** n [C] *technical* a verb such as 'can', 'might', or 'must' that is used with other verbs to show ideas such as possibility, permission, or intention

mode /məʊd‖moʊd/ n [C] *formal* a particular way of behaving, living, or doing something: + of *a very efficient mode of transportation*

mod·el¹ /'mɒdl‖'maːdl/ n [C] **1** a small copy of something such as a car, plane, or building: *a model of the Space Shuttle* | *One of his hobbies is making models of famous buildings.* **2** someone whose job is to show clothes, hairstyles etc by wearing them and being photographed: *a fashion model* **3** someone or something that is a very good example or idea that other people copy: *The British electoral system has been used as a model by many new democracies.* **4** one type of car, machine etc made by a particular company: *the latest model from BMW* **5** someone who is employed to be painted or photographed by an artist or photographer

model² adj [only before noun] **1** model aeroplane/train/car etc a small copy of a plane, train etc **2** perfect: *he's been a model pupil*

model³ v **-lled, -lling** BrE **-led, -ling** AmE **1** [I,T] to wear and show new designs of clothes, hairstyles etc in order to advertise them: *Kate is modelling a black leather suit designed by Armani.* **2** [T] to copy a system or way of doing something: be modelled on sth *a*

constitution modelled on the French system **3** model yourself on to try to be like someone else: *She had modeled herself on her tennis idol, Steffi Graf.*

mod·el·ling BrE, **modeling** AmE /'mɒdl-ɪŋ‖ 'maː-/ n [U] the work of a fashion model: *a career in modelling*

mo·dem /'məʊdəm, -dem‖'moʊ-/ n [C] a piece of electronic equipment used for sending information from one computer to another down a telephone line

mod·e·rate¹ /'mɒdər̩t‖'maː-/ adj **1** neither very big nor very small, very hot nor very cold, very fast nor very slow etc: *a moderate rate of inflation* **2** having opinions or beliefs, especially about politics, that are not extreme: *a senator with moderate views*

mod·e·rate² /'mɒdəreɪt‖'maː-/ v [I,T] to make something less extreme or violent or to become less extreme or violent: *Drugs can help to moderate the symptoms.*

mod·e·rate³ /'mɒdər̩t‖'maː-/ n [C] someone whose opinions or beliefs, especially about politics, are not extreme —**moderately** adv

mod·e·ra·tion /,mɒdə'reɪʃən‖,maː-/ n **1** in moderation if you do something in moderation, you do not do it too much: *He only drinks in moderation.* **2** [U] *formal* sensible control of your behaviour

mod·ern /'mɒdn‖'maːdərn/ adj **1** using new methods, designs, or equipment: *a modern apartment block* | *modern technology* **2** using new styles or ways of thinking: *a modern approach to sex education* | *modern art/music/literature etc* (=art, music etc that uses new styles that are very different from traditional styles) **3** modern society/problems/life etc the ones that exist now, not the ones that existed in the past: *the pressures of modern living* —**modernity** /mɒ'dɜːnl̩ti‖məˈdɜːr-/ n [U]

mod·ern·ize (also **-ise** BrE) /'mɒdənaɪz‖ 'maː.dər-/ v [T] to change something so that it uses new equipment or new ideas: *a state program to modernize existing schools* —**modernization** /,mɒdənaɪ'zeɪʃən‖,maːdərnə-/ n [C,U]

modern lan·gua·ges /,.. '.../ n [plural] languages, such as French or German, that are spoken now

mod·est /'mɒdl̩st‖'maː-/ adj **1** not talking proudly about your achievements, abilities etc: *a quiet modest man* **2** not very big in size, amount, value etc: *a modest 2% pay increase* **3** shy and easily embarrassed about showing your body or about anything connected with sex —**modestly** adv

mod·es·ty /'mɒdl̩sti‖'maː-/ n [U] **1** the quality of not talking proudly about your achievements, abilities etc **2** when someone is not willing to show their body or talk about anything connected with sex

mod·i·cum /'mɒdɪkəm‖'maː-/ n a modicum of sth *formal* a small amount of something

mod·i·fi·ca·tion /,mɒdl̩fl̩'keɪʃən‖,maː-/ n [C,U] a small change that is made to something, or the

---

M

process of changing something: **+ to** *We've made a few modifications to the programme.*

mod·i·fi·er /'mɒdɪfaɪə‖'mɑːdɪfaɪr/ *n* [C] an adjective, adverb, or phrase that gives additional information about another word

mod·i·fy /'mɒdɪfaɪ‖'mɑː-/ *v* [T] **1** to make small changes to something in order to improve it: *Safety procedures have been modified since the fire.* **2** if one word modifies another, it gives more information about it

mod·u·lar /'mɒdjʊlə‖'mɑːdʒələr/ *adj* based on modules or made using modules: *modular furniture | The courses are arranged on a modular basis*

mod·ule /'mɒdjuːl‖'mɑːdʒuːl/ *n* [C] *technical* **1** one of several separate parts that can be combined to form a larger object, such as a machine or building **2** one part of a SPACE-CRAFT **3** *BrE* one of the parts that a course of study is divided into: *The syllabus comprises six modules.*

mo·hair /'məʊheə‖'məʊher/ *n* [U] expensive wool made from the hair of a goat

moist /mɔɪst/ *adj* slightly wet: *Make sure the soil is moist. | a moist chocolate cake* → compare DAMP

moist·en /'mɔɪsən/ *v* [I,T] to make something slightly wet, or to become slightly wet: *Moisten the clay with a little water.*

mois·ture /'mɔɪstʃə‖-ər/ *n* [U] small amounts of water in the air, on a surface etc: *The desert air contains hardly any moisture.*

mois·tur·iz·er (also **-iser** *BrE*) /'mɔɪstʃəraɪzə‖-ər/ *n* [C,U] a cream you put on your skin to keep it soft

mo·lar /'məʊlə‖'məʊlər/ *n* [C] one of the large teeth at the back of your mouth

mo·las·ses /məˈlæsɪz/ *n* [U] *especially AmE* a thick dark sweet liquid that is obtained from sugar plants

mold /məʊld‖moʊld/ the American spelling of MOULD

mold·ing /'məʊldɪŋ‖'moʊl-/ the American spelling of MOULDING

mold·y /'məʊldi‖'moʊl-/ the American spelling of MOULDY

mole /məʊl‖moʊl/ *n* [C] **1** a small animal with black fur that cannot see well and lives in holes in the ground **2** a small dark brown mark on your skin **3** someone who works for an organization, especially a government, while secretly giving information to an enemy or to a newspaper, television company etc

mol·e·cule /'mɒlɪkjuːl‖'mɑː-/ *n* [C] one or more connected atoms of a substance, which is the smallest amount of it that can exist —**molecular** /məˈlekjʊlə‖-ər/ *adj*

mo·lest /məˈlest/ *v* [T] to sexually attack or harm someone: *Harper was accused of molesting his 7-year-old stepdaughter.* —**molester** *n* [C] *a child molester* —**molestation** /ˌməʊleˈsteɪʃən‖ˌmoʊ-/ *n* [U]

mol·li·fy /'mɒlɪfaɪ‖'mɑː-/ *v* [T] *formal* to make someone feel less angry

mol·lusc *BrE*, **mollusk** *AmE* /'mɒləsk‖'mɑː-/ *n* [C] a type of sea or land animal, such as a SNAIL or CLAM, with a soft body covered by a hard shell

molt /məʊlt‖moʊlt/ the American spelling of MOULT

mol·ten /'məʊltən‖'moʊl-/ *adj* molten metal or rock is liquid because it is extremely hot

mom /mɒm‖mɑːm/ *n* [C] *AmE spoken informal* mother; MUM *BrE*: *Can I go to Barbara's, Mom?*

mo·ment /'məʊmənt‖'moʊ-/ *n* **1** [C] a very short period of time: *They stood in the lobby for a few moments talking. | in a moment I'll be back in a moment. | for a moment She paused for a moment before replying.* **2** [C] a particular point in time: **at that/this moment** *At that moment, the door opened and Danny walked in.* **3** **the moment (that)** as soon as: *The moment I heard your voice I knew something was wrong.* **4** **at the moment** now: *Gavin's working in Oakland at the moment.* **5** **for the moment** used to say that something is happening or is true now, but will probably change in the future: *Well, for the moment we're just considering the possibilities.* **6** **(at) any moment** used to say that something is likely to happen very soon: *The roof could collapse at any moment.* → compare MINUTE[1]

mo·men·tar·i·ly /'məʊməntərɪli‖ˌmoʊmən-'terɪli/ *adv* **1** for a very short time: *I was momentarily surprised by the question.* **2** *AmE* very soon: *I'll be with you momentarily.*

mo·men·ta·ry /'məʊməntəri‖'moʊmənteri/ *adj* continuing for a very short time: *There was a momentary silence before anyone dared to speak.*

mo·men·tous /məʊˈmentəs, mə-‖moʊ-, mə-/ *adj* a momentous event, occasion, decision etc is very important: *the momentous events in Central Europe*

mo·men·tum /məʊˈmentəm, mə-‖moʊ-, mə-/ *n* [U] **1** the force or energy that makes a moving object continue to move: **gain/gather momentum** (=move faster and faster): *The rock gained momentum as it rolled down the hill.* **2** the ability to keep increasing, developing, or being more successful: **gain/gather momentum** (=begin to increase or develop more quickly): *The election campaign is rapidly gathering momentum.*

mom·ma /'mɒmə‖'mɑːmə/ *n* [C] *AmE spoken informal* mother

mom·my /'mɒmi‖'mɑːmi/ *n* [C] *AmE* MUMMY

Mon. *n* the written abbreviation of Monday

mon·arch /'mɒnək‖'mɑːnərk, -ɑːrk/ *n* [C] a king or queen

mon·ar·chy /'mɒnəki‖'mɑːnərki/ *n* **1** [singular, U] the system in which a country is ruled by a king or queen **2** [C] a country that is ruled by a king or queen

mon·as·tery /'mɒnəstri‖'mɑːnəsteri/ *n* [C] a building in which MONKs live

mo·nas·tic /məˈnæstɪk/ *adj* connected with MONKs or a monastery

Mon·day /'mʌndi/ *n* written abbreviation **Mon** *n* [C,U] the day of the week between Sunday and Tuesday

mon·e·ta·ry /'mʌnɪtəri‖'mɑːnɪteri/ *adj* relating to money, especially all the money in a particular country: *monetary policy*

mon·ey /'mʌni/ *n* [U] **1** coins, paper notes etc that have a fixed value and are used for buying and selling things: *How much money do you have with you? | The boat must have cost a lot of*

money. | **spend money** *She spends a lot of money on clothes.* | **make money** (=earn money or make a profit): *John's business is making a lot of money.* | **save money** (=avoid spending): *You can save money by arranging your flight early.* **2** all the money that someone has: *Fred lost all his money when he was forced to close his business.* **3 get your money's worth** to get something that is really worth the price that you paid for it: *The concert only lasted an hour so we didn't really get our money's worth.* **4 that kind of money** *spoken* a lot of money or too much money: *People with that kind of money don't need to work.* | *They wanted $5000, and I just don't have that kind of money.* **5 have more money than sense** *spoken* to spend a lot of money on something that is not really worth it: *People who pay hundreds of pounds for trainers seem to have more money than sense.*

money mar·ket /'.. ,../ *n* [C] the banks and financial organizations that buy and sell BONDS, CURRENCY (=paper money) etc

mon·grel /'mʌŋgrəl‖'maːŋ-, 'mʌŋ-/ *n* [C] a dog that had parents that were two different kinds of dog

mon·i·tor¹ /'mɒnɪtə‖'maːnɪtər/ *n* [C] a piece of equipment with a screen that shows information or pictures, especially on a computer

monitor² *v* [T] to watch or measure something carefully for a period of time to see how it changes: *Doctors are monitoring the patient's condition carefully.*

monk /mʌŋk/ *n* [C] a member of a group of religious men who live together in a MONASTERY

mon·key /'mʌŋki/ *n* [C] a type of animal that lives in hot countries and uses its tail and hands to climb trees

monkey wrench /'.. ./ *n* [C] a tool used for holding or turning things

mon·o /'mɒnəʊ‖'maːnoʊ/ *n* [U] *informal AmE* a serious infectious illness that makes you feel weak and tired for a long time afterwards; GLANDULAR FEVER *BrE*

mono- /mɒnəʊ, -nəl-noʊ, -nə/ *prefix* used at the beginning of some words to mean having only one of something: *monolingual* (=using only one language)

mon·o·chrome /'mɒnəkrəʊm‖'maːnəkroʊm/ *adj* consisting only of the colours black, white, and grey: *a monochrome image*

mo·nog·a·my /mə'nɒgəmi‖mə'naː-/ *n* [U] when someone has a sexual relationship with one person and no one else, especially for their whole life — **monogamous** *adj*

mon·o·gram /'mɒnəgræm‖'maː-/ *n* [C] a design made from the first letters of someone's names, used on clothes, writing paper etc — **monogrammed** *adj*: *a monogrammed shirt*

mon·o·ling·ual /ˌmɒnəʊ'lɪŋgwəl‖ˌmaːnə-/ *adj* speaking or using only one language: *a monolingual dictionary*

mon·o·lith·ic /ˌmɒnə'lɪθɪk◂‖ˌmaː-/ *adj* a monolithic organization, political system etc is very large and powerful — **monolith** /'mɒnəlɪθ‖'maː-/ *n*

mon·o·logue also **monolog** *AmE* /'mɒnəlɒg‖ 'maːnl-ɒːg, -aːg/ *n* [C] **1** a long speech by one person in a play or film **2** a long period of one

person talking in a conversation, which prevents other people from talking

mo·nop·o·lize (also **-ise** *BrE*) /mə'nɒpəlaɪz‖mə- 'naː-/ *v* [T] to have complete control over something, especially a type of business, so that other people cannot share it: *The tobacco industry is monopolized by a few large companies.* — **monopolization** /məˌnɒpəlaɪ'zeɪʃən‖-ˌnaːpələ-/ *n* [U]

mo·nop·o·ly /mə'nɒpəli‖mə'naː-/ *n* **1** [C] the control of all or most of a business activity: **+ on/of** *Until recently, Bell Telephone had a monopoly on telephone services.* **2** [singular] when one person or organization has or controls something so that no one else can share it: *Adequate health care should not be the monopoly of the rich.* — **monopolistic** /məˌnɒpə'lɪstɪk◂‖məˌnaː-/ *adj*

Monopoly *n* [U] *trademark* a game using artificial money in which you try to get more money and property than your opponents

mon·o·syl·lab·ic /ˌmɒnəsɪ'læbɪk◂‖ˌmaː-/ *adj* someone who is monosyllabic seems rude because they do not say much or they give very short answers to questions

mon·o·syl·la·ble /'mɒnə,sɪləbəl‖'maː-/ *n* [C] a word that has only one SYLLABLE, for example 'no'

mon·o·tone /'mɒnətəʊn‖'maːnətoʊn/ *n* [singular] a way of speaking that continues on the same note without getting any louder or higher: *He continued talking in a slow monotone.*

mo·not·o·nous /mə'nɒtənəs‖mə'naː-/ *adj* boring and without any variety: *monotonous work* | *a flat monotonous landscape* — **monotony** *n* [U] — **monotonously** *adv*

mon·soon /ˌmɒn'suːn◂‖ˌmaːn-/ *n* [C] the time when it rains a lot in India and other southern Asian countries

mon·ster /'mɒnstə‖'maːnstər/ *n* [C] **1** a large ugly frightening creature in stories: *a sea monster* **2** someone who is extremely cruel and evil: *Only a monster could kill an innocent child.* **3** an object, animal etc that is extremely large: *That dog's a real monster!* — **monster** *adj*

mon·stros·i·ty /mɒn'strɒsɪti‖maːn'straː-/ *n* [C] something such as a building that is very large and ugly

mon·strous /'mɒnstrəs‖'maːn-/ *adj* very wrong, immoral, or unfair: *a monstrous crime* — **monstrously** *adv*

month /mʌnθ/ *n* [C] **1** one of the twelve periods of time that a year is divided into: *the month of May* | *The competition takes place at the end of this month.* **2** a period of time of about four weeks: *She had to wait over six months for her operation.*

> **USAGE NOTE: month**
>
> When you are talking about a month but not a particular date in that month, use 'in': *He was born in February.* | *She finishes school in July.* When you want to talk about a particular date in a month, use 'on': *He was born on February 20th.* | *She finishes school on the nineteenth of July.*

month·ly /'mʌnθli/ *adj* happening or done every month: *monthly team meetings* | *a monthly salary of $850* — **monthly** *adv*

M

mon·u·ment /ˈmɒnjʊ̯mənt‖ˈmɑ:-/ *n* [C] **1** a large structure that is built to remind people of an important event or famous person: **+ to** *a monument to Frederick the Great* **2** an old building or place that is very important: *ancient Roman monuments* **3** **be a monument to** to be a clear example of what can happen as a result of something else: *The squalid townships are a monument to the evils of the old apartheid system.*

mon·u·ment·al /ˌmɒnjʊ̯ˈmentl‖ˌmɑ:-/ *adj* **1** extremely large, bad, impressive etc: *Jeffries has admitted he made a monumental mistake.* **2** a monumental achievement, piece of work etc is very important and influences people in the future: *Darwin's monumental work on evolution* —**monumentally** *adv*

moo /mu:/ *v* [I] to make the sound that a cow makes —**moo** *n* [C]

mood /mu:d/ *n* **1** [C] the way that someone feels at a particular time, or the way a group of people feels: *His mood suddenly seemed to change.* | *Congress has misjudged the mood of the people.* | **be in a good/bad mood etc** (=be happy, annoyed etc): *You're certainly in a good mood today!* **2** **be in the mood (for)** to feel that you want to do something: *Are any of you in the mood for a game of cards?* | **be in no mood for/to do sth** (=not want to do something): *He was obviously in no mood for talking.* **3** **be in a mood** to be bad-tempered **4** [C] one of the sets of verb forms in grammar such as the INDICATIVE (=expressing a fact or action), the IMPERATIVE (=expressing a command) etc

mood·y /ˈmu:di/ *adj* **1** someone who is moody becomes upset or angry easily: *a moody teenager* **2** *especially AmE* having moods that change often and quickly: *moody music* —**moodily** *adv* —**moodiness** *n* [U]

moon /mu:n/ *n* **1** **the moon** the round object that moves around the Earth and shines in the sky at night **2** [singular] the shape of this object at a particular time of the month: *There's no moon tonight.* (=it cannot be seen) | **full moon** (=when the moon appears as a complete circle in the sky) **3** [C] a large round object that moves around a PLANET: *How many moons does Jupiter have?* **4** **over the moon** *BrE informal* very happy: *She's over the moon about her new job.* → see also **once in a blue moon** (ONCE[1])

moon·beam /ˈmu:nbi:m/ *n* [C] a beam of light from the moon

moon·light /ˈmu:nlaɪt/ *n* [U] the light of the moon

moon·lit /ˈmu:nˌlɪt/ *adj* made bright by the light of the moon: *a beautiful moonlit night*

moor[1] /mʊə‖mʊr/ *n* [C usually plural] *especially BrE* an area of high land covered with rough grass or low bushes: *the North Yorkshire Moors*

moor[2] *v* [I,T] to fasten a boat to land or to the bottom of the sea with a rope or chain

moor·ing /ˈmʊərɪŋ‖ˈmʊr-/ *n* **1** [C] the place where a ship or boat is fastened to land **2** **moorings** the ropes, chains etc used to fasten a ship or boat to the land

moose /mu:s/ *n* [C] a large wild animal with large flat horns and with a head like a horse

moot /mu:t/ *adj especially AmE* no longer likely to happen or exist, or no longer important: *The proposal is moot because there is no money to implement it.*

moot point /ˌ. ˈ./ *n* [C usually singular] something that has not yet been decided and that people have different opinions about: *Whether these laws will really reduce violent crime is a moot point.*

mop[1] /mɒp‖mɑ:p/ *n* **1** [C] a thing for washing floors consisting of a long stick with a SPONGE or pieces of thick string at the end **2** [singular] *informal* a mass of thick untidy hair: *a mop of black curly hair*

mop[2] *v* [T] **-pped, -pping** **1** to wash a floor with a mop **2** to remove liquid from a surface using a piece of soft material: *Earl mopped his face with a large handkerchief.*

mop sth ↔ up *phr v* [T] to clean liquid from a surface, using a piece of soft material: *Can you mop up the milk you've spilled?*

mope /məʊp‖moʊp/ also **mope around** *v* [I] to feel unhappy, often without making any effort to become cheerful again

mo·ped /ˈməʊped‖ˈmoʊ-/ *n* [C] a vehicle like a bicycle with a small engine → see colour picture on page 669

moral[1] /ˈmɒrəl‖ˈmɔ:-/ *adj* **1** [only before noun] based on the principles of what is right and wrong: *Terry refused to join the army for moral reasons.* | *I believe we have a moral duty to help the poor.* → opposite IMMORAL **2** **moral support** help and encouragement that you give to someone: *I offered to go with him to the dentist as moral support.* **3** **moral victory** when you show that your beliefs are right and fair even if you do not win the argument, game etc **4** a moral person has high standards of behaviour based on principles of what is right and wrong: *My grandfather was a very moral man* —**morally** *adv*

moral[2] *n* [C] something you learn from a story or from something that happens to you: *The moral of the story is that crime doesn't pay.* → see also MORALS

mo·rale /məˈrɑ:l‖məˈræl/ *n* [U] the level of confidence and hope for the future that a person or group feels: *Talk of job losses is bad for morale.*

mor·al·ist·ic /ˌmɒrəˈlɪstɪk◂‖ˌmɔ:-/ *adj* having very strong beliefs about what is right and wrong and about how people should behave —**moralist** /ˈmɒrəl̩st‖ˈmɔ:-/ *n* [C]

mo·ral·i·ty /məˈrælɪ̯ti/ *n* [U] principles or ideas about what is right and wrong: *declining standards of morality* | **+ of** *a discussion on the morality of abortion*

mor·al·ize (also **-ise** *BrE*) /ˈmɒrəlaɪz‖ˈmɔ:-/ *v* [I] to tell people what is the right or wrong way to behave, especially when you have not been asked for your opinion

mor·als /ˈmɒrəlz‖ˈmɔ:-/ *n* [plural] principles or standards of good behaviour, especially sexual behaviour: *His book reflects the values and morals of society at that time.*

mor·a·to·ri·um /ˌmɒrəˈtɔ:riəm‖ˌmɔ:-/ *n* [C usually singular] an official announcement stopping an activity for a period of time

mor·bid /ˈmɔ:bɪ̯d‖ˈmɔ:r-/ *adj* having too strong an interest in unpleasant subjects, especially death: *He has a morbid fascination with murder stories.*

more[1] /mɔ:‖mɔ:r/ *adv* **1** to a greater degree: **more interesting/expensive/quickly etc** *You'll* *have to be more careful next time.* | **more ... than** *My meal was more expensive than Dan's.* | **much/a lot/far more** *The students will feel much more confident if they work in groups.* → opposite LESS¹ **2** used to say that something happens a greater number of times or for longer than before: *I promised I'd help more with the housework.* | **more than** *We see our grandchildren more than we used to.* | **much/a lot/far more** *She goes out a lot more now that she has a car.* → opposite LESS¹ **3 not any more** no longer happening or true: *Sarah doesn't live here any more.* → see also ANY², ANY MORE, **once more** (ONCE¹)

USAGE NOTE: more

Use **more** as the opposite of both **less** and **fewer**: *I think I'll need more money.* | *There were more people there than yesterday.* **More** is also usually used to form the COMPARATIVE of an adjective with more than two syllables: *He's much more intelligent than me.* (NOT *He's much intelligenter than me.*)

more² *quantifier* **1** a greater amount or number than before: **more ... than** *There are more people without jobs than there used to be.* | **more than** *Orange juice costs more than beer in some bars.* **2** an additional number or amount: *Would you like some more coffee?* | **some/a few more** *I have to make a few more phone calls.* | **10/20 etc more** *We need five more chairs.* **3 more and more** an increasing number of something: *These days, more and more people travel long distances to work.* **4 more or less** almost: *The article says more or less the same thing as the other one.*

more·o·ver /mɔːrˈəʊvəl'-ˈoʊvər/ *adv formal* used when you give additional information which supports something that you have just said: *The new design is not acceptable. Moreover, it would delay the project even further.*

mo·res /ˈmɔːreɪz/ *n* [plural] *formal* the customs, social behaviour, and moral values of a particular group: *American social mores*

morgue /mɔːgllmɔːrg/ *n* [C] the place where dead bodies are kept before they are buried or burned

morn·ing /ˈmɔːnɪŋll'-ˈmɔːr-/ *n* [C,U] **1** the early part of the day, from when the sun rises until the middle of the day: *I got a letter from Wayne this morning.* | **in the morning** (=tomorrow morning): *I'll deal with it in the morning.* **2** the part of the night that is after MIDNIGHT: *The phone rang at three in the morning.* **3 (Good) Morning** *spoken* used when you meet someone in the morning: *Morning, Rick.*

mo·ron /ˈmɔːrɒnll'ˈmɔːrɑːn/ *n* [C] *informal* an offensive word for someone who has done something very stupid and annoying — **moronic** /məˈrɒnɪkllməˈrɑː-/ *adj*

mo·rose /məˈrəʊsll-ˈroʊs/ *adj* unhappy, bad-tempered, and silent — **morosely** *adv*

mor·phine /ˈmɔːfiːnll'ˈmɔːr-/ *n* [U] a powerful drug used to stop pain

mor·sel /ˈmɔːsəll'ˈmɔːr-/ *n* [C] *literary* a small piece of food: *a morsel of bread*

mor·tal¹ /ˈmɔːtlll'ˈmɔːrtl/ *adj* **1** not living for ever: *mortal creatures* → opposite IMMORTAL **2** causing death: *a mortal wound* **3 mortal fear/terror/danger etc** extreme fear, danger etc: *He lived in mortal fear of being attacked.* — **mortally** *adv*

mortal² *n* **1 lesser/ordinary/mere mortals** *humorous* ordinary people, when compared with people who are more important or more powerful **2** [C] *literary* a human being

mor·tal·i·ty /mɔːˈtælɪtillmɔːr-/ *n* [U] **1** also **mortality rate** the number of deaths during a particular period of time or from a particular cause: *infant mortality* (=the rate at which babies die) **2** the condition of being human and having to die: *After the heart attack, I became more aware of my own mortality.*

mor·tar /ˈmɔːtəll'ˈmɔːrtər/ *n* **1** [C] a heavy gun that fires EXPLOSIVEs in a high curve **2** [U] a mixture of CEMENT, sand, and water, used in building for joining bricks or stones together

mort·gage¹ /ˈmɔːgɪdʒll'ˈmɔːr-/ *n* [C] money you borrow in order to buy a house, and pay back over a number of years: *After he lost his job he couldn't pay his mortgage any more.*

mortgage² *v* [T] if you mortgage your house or land, you borrow money, agreeing to give a bank the house or land if you do not pay the money back

mor·ti·cian /mɔːˈtɪʃənllmɔːr-/ *n* [C] *AmE* someone whose job is to arrange funerals and prepare bodies to be buried; UNDERTAKER *BrE*

mor·ti·fy /ˈmɔːtɪfaɪll'ˈmɔːr-/ *v* [T] to feel extremely embarrassed or ashamed: **be mortified** *I was mortified to discover Sarah wearing the same dress as me at the party.* — **mortifying** *adj*

mor·tu·a·ry /ˈmɔːtʃuərill'ˈmɔːrtʃueri/ *n* [C] a building or room where dead bodies are kept before they are buried or burned

mo·sa·ic /məʊˈzeɪ-ɪkll moʊ-/ *n* [C,U] a pattern or picture made from small pieces of coloured stone, glass etc

mosque /mɒskllmɑːsk/ *n* [C] a building where Muslims go to pray

mos·qui·to /məˈskiːtəʊll-toʊ/ *n* [C] a small flying insect that bites and sucks blood, often causing diseases, especially MALARIA

moss /mɒsllmɔːs/ *n* [U] a small flat green or yellow plant that looks like fur and grows on trees and rocks — **mossy** *adj*

most¹ /məʊstllmoʊst/ *adv* **1** used before many adjectives and adverbs that have two or more SYLLABLEs in order to make the SUPERLATIVE form: *Anna is one of the most beautiful women I know.* | *I forgot to tell you the most important thing!* | *a virus most frequently found in stagnant water* **2** more than anything or anyone else: *She liked the dark beer most.* | **most of all** *I love all my family, but my Mum most of*

GRAMMAR NOTE: the future
To talk about the **future** you can use: 1. **will** + basic form of verb: *I'll* (=I will) *see you tomorrow.* 2. **be going to** (used to say that something will happen soon): *I think it's going to rain.* 3. the **present progressive** (used to say what is planned or intended): *We're having a party on Saturday.*

M

all. **3** *AmE spoken* almost: *We eat at Joe's most every weekend.* **4** *formal* very: *I was most surprised to discover we had been to the same school.*

most² *quantifier* **1** almost all of a particular group of people or things: *Most computers have a disk drive.* | **most of** *Most of the kids I know have parents who are divorced.* **2** more than anyone or anything else: **the most** *Ricardo's restaurant gives you the most food for your money.* | *Whoever scores most will win.* **3** the largest number or amount that is possible: **the most** *How can we get the most power from the engine?* | *I'm afraid the most I can give you is $100.* **4 at (the) most** used to say that a number or amount will not be larger than you say, and will probably be smaller: *The book should cost $10 at the most.* **5 make the most of sth** to take all the advantage you possibly can from a situation, especially because it will not last: *Go out and make the most of the sunshine.*

most·ly /ˈməʊstli‖ˈmoʊst-/ *adv* in most cases or most of the time: *Mostly, he travels by car or in his own plane.* | *The room was full of sports people, mostly football players.*

mo·tel /məʊˈtel‖moʊ-/ *n* [C] a hotel for people travelling by car

moth /mɒθ‖mɔːθ/ *n* [C] an insect similar to a BUTTERFLY that usually flies at night

moth·er¹ /ˈmʌðəʳ-ər/ *n* [C] **1 a)** your female parent: *My mother said I have to be home by 9:00.* | *Her mother once met President Kennedy.* ➔ see picture at FAMILY **b)** an animal's female parent **2 the mother of all** *informal* an extremely bad or severe example of something: *I woke up with the mother of all hangovers.*

mother² *v* [T] to take care of someone as if they were a child, especially when this is annoying: *Tom resented being constantly mothered by his wife.*

moth·er·hood /ˈmʌðəhʊd‖-ər-/ *n* [U] when someone is a mother

mother-in-law /ˈ... .,./ *n* [C] the mother of your husband or wife ➔ see picture at FAMILY

moth·er·ly /ˈmʌðəli‖-ər-/ *adj* similar to or typical of a kind mother: *a plump, motherly woman*

mother-of-pearl /,... .ˈ./ *n* [U] a smooth shiny substance on the inside of some shells, used for making buttons, jewellery etc

Mother's Day /ˈ.. ./ *n* [singular] a day when people give cards and gifts to their mothers

mother tongue /,.. ˈ./ *n* [C] the first language that you learn as a child

mo·tif /məʊˈtiːf‖moʊ-/ *n* [C] **1** an idea or subject that is regularly repeated and developed in a book, film etc **2** a small picture used to decorate something: *a T-shirt with a butterfly motif*

mo·tion¹ /ˈməʊʃən‖ˈmoʊ-/ *n* **1** [U] the process of moving, or the way that someone or something moves: *the gentle rolling motion of the ship* **2** [C] a single movement of your head or hand: *He made a motion with his hand, as if to tell me to keep back.* **3** [C] a suggestion that is made formally at a meeting and then decided on by voting: *I'd like to propose a motion to change working hours.* **4 (in) slow motion** when something is shown more slowly than usual on television or film so that all the actions can be clearly seen: *Let's look at that goal in slow motion.* | *The*

slow motion replay proved it was a foul. **5 go through the motions** to do something because you have to do it, rather than because you want to **6 put/set sth in motion** to start a process

motion² *v* [I,T] to tell someone to do something by moving your head or hand: **motion (for) sb to do sth** *She motioned for him to sit down.*

mo·tion·less /ˈməʊʃənləs‖ˈmoʊ-/ *adj* not moving at all: *He was standing motionless in the doorway.* —**motionlessly** *adv*

motion pic·ture /,.. ˈ...◂/ *n* [C] *AmE* a film made for cinema; MOVIE

mo·ti·vate /ˈməʊtɪˌveɪt‖ˈmoʊ-/ *v* [T] **1** to be the reason why someone does something: *The theft was motivated by greed.* **2** to make someone want to achieve something, especially by encouraging them to work harder —**motivated** *adj*: *Police believe the attack was racially motivated.* | *highly motivated students* (=students who are eager to work hard and succeed)

mo·ti·va·tion /,məʊtɪˈveɪʃən‖,moʊ-/ *n* **1** [U] when you are keen and willing to do something: *Jack is smart, but he lacks motivation.* **2** [C] the reason why you want to do something: **+ for** *What was your motivation for writing the book?*

mo·tive /ˈməʊtɪv‖ˈmoʊ-/ *n* [C] the reason why someone does something: **+ for** *Jealousy was the motive for the murder.*

mot·ley /ˈmɒtli‖ˈmɑːtli/ *adj* **a motley crew/ collection etc** a group of people or things that do not seem to belong together

mo·tor¹ /ˈməʊtəl‖ˈmoʊtər/ *n* [C] the part of a machine that uses electricity, petrol etc to make it move; ENGINE

motor² *adj* [only before noun] **1** using power provided by an engine: *a motor vehicle* **2** *BrE* relating to cars: *the motor industry*

mo·tor·bike /ˈməʊtəbaɪk‖ˈmoʊtər-/ *n* [C] *especially BrE* a MOTORCYCLE ➔ see colour picture on page 669

mo·tor·boat /ˈməʊtəbəʊt‖ˈmoʊtərboʊt/ *n* [C] a small fast boat with an engine

mo·tor·cade /ˈməʊtəkeɪd‖ˈmoʊtər-/ *n* [C] a group of cars that surround an important person's car to protect it

motor car /ˈ... ./ *n* [C] *formal* a car

mo·tor·cy·cle /ˈməʊtəˌsaɪkəl‖ˈmoʊtər-/ *n* [C] *especially AmE* a vehicle with two wheels and an engine —**motorcyclist** *n* [C]

mo·tor·ing /ˈməʊtərɪŋ‖ˈmoʊ-/ *adj* [only before noun] *BrE* relating to cars and driving: *a motoring holiday*

mo·tor·ist /ˈməʊtərˌɪst‖ˈmoʊ-/ *n* [C] someone who drives a car

mo·tor·ized (also **-ised** *BrE*) /ˈməʊtəraɪzd‖ˈmoʊ-/ *adj* having an engine: *a motorized wheelchair*

motor ve·hi·cle /ˈ.. ,.../ *n* [C] *formal* a car, bus etc

mo·tor·way /ˈməʊtəweɪ‖ˈmoʊtər-/ *n* [C] *BrE* a wide road for driving fast over long distances; FREEWAY *AmE*

mot·tled /ˈmɒtld‖ˈmɑː-/ *adj* covered with patterns of light and dark colours: *His skin looked mottled and unhealthy.*

mot·to /ˈmɒtəʊ‖ˈmɑːtoʊ/ *n* [C] a short statement that expresses the aims or principles of a person or organization

mould¹ *BrE*, **mold** *AmE* /məʊld‖moʊld/ *n*
1 [U] a green or black substance that grows on old food or on wet things: *There were dark patches of mould on the walls.* **2** [C] a container that you pour liquid into so that the liquid will take its shape when it becomes solid: *a jelly mould*

mould² *BrE*, **mold** *AmE* — *v* **1** [T] to shape a soft substance by pressing it or rolling it **2** [T] to influence the way someone's character or attitudes develop: *an attempt to mould public opinion*

mould·ing *BrE*, **molding** *AmE* /ˈməʊldɪŋ‖ˈmoʊl-/ *n* [C,U] a thin area of wood, stone etc around the edge of something as a decoration, for example around a picture frame or the edge of a wall

mould·y *BrE*, **moldy** *AmE* /ˈməʊldi‖ˈmoʊl-/ *adj* covered with mould: *mouldy cheese* | **go mouldy** *BrE* (=become mouldy)

moult *BrE*, **molt** *AmE* /məʊlt‖moʊlt/ *v* [I] when an animal or bird moults, it loses hair or feathers so that new ones can grow

mound /maʊnd/ *n* [C] **1** a pile of earth that looks like a small hill **2** a large pile of something: *a mound of papers*

mount¹ /maʊnt/ *v* **1** [I] also **mount up** to gradually increase: *His debts continued to mount up.* **2** [T] to organize and begin something, especially a plan or attack: *They are mounting a campaign to stop road building in the area.* **3** [I,T] to get on a horse or bicycle: *She mounted the horse and rode off.* **4** [T] *formal* to go up something such as stairs **5** [T] to fix something to or onto a surface: *The engine is mounted onto the chassis using special bolts.*

mount² *n* **1** Mount used in the names of mountains: *Mount Everest* **2** [C] *literary* a horse

moun·tain /ˈmaʊntˌn‖ˈmaʊntn/ *n* [C] **1** a very high hill: *the Swiss mountains* → see colour picture on page 243 **2** *informal* a large amount of something: *a mountain of ironing* **3** **make a mountain out of a molehill** to treat a small problem as if it were very serious

moun·tain·eer·ing /ˌmaʊntˌˈnɪərɪŋ‖ˌmaʊntn-ˈɪrɪŋ/ *n* [U] the activity of climbing mountains — **mountaineer** *n* [C]

moun·tain·ous /ˈmaʊntˌnəs‖ˈmaʊntnəs/ *adj* having a lot of mountains

mount·ing /ˈmaʊntɪŋ/ *adj* gradually increasing: *Chris read the letter with mounting anger.*

mourn /mɔːn‖mɔːrn/ *v* **1** [I,T] to feel very sad because someone has died: *After 10 years, she's still mourning her son's death.* **2** [T] to feel sad because something no longer exists: *Many old people mourn the loss of their youth and health.*

mourn·er /ˈmɔːnə‖ˈmɔːrnər/ *n* [C] someone who is at a funeral

mourn·ful /ˈmɔːnfəl‖ˈmɔːrn-/ *adj* very sad: *slow, mournful music* — **mournfully** *adv*

mourn·ing /ˈmɔːnɪŋ‖ˈmɔːr-/ *n* [U] feelings of great sadness because someone has died: *the outbreak of public mourning following Diana's death* | **be in mourning** (=be mourning someone)

mouse /maʊs/ *n* [C] **1** *plural* **mice** /maɪs/ a small animal with smooth fur, a long tail, and a pointed nose **2** *plural* **mouses** a small object connected to a computer, that you move with

your hand and press to give commands to the computer → see colour picture on page 80

mouse mat *BrE*, **mouse pad** *AmE* /ˈ. ./ *n* [C] a flat piece of rubber or plastic that you use the mouse of a computer on

mousse /muːs/ *n* [C,U] **1** a cold sweet food made from cream, eggs, and fruit or chocolate **2** a substance that you put in your hair to make it look thicker or to hold it in position

mous·tache also **mustache** *AmE* /məˈstɑːʃ‖ˈmʌstæʃ/ *n* [C] hair that a man grows on his upper lip → see colour picture on page 244

mous·y, mousey /ˈmaʊsi/ *adj* mousy hair is a light brown colour → see colour picture on page 244

mouth¹ /maʊθ/ *n* **1** [C] the part of your face that you use for speaking and eating → see picture at HEAD **2** **keep your mouth shut** *informal* to not talk about something, especially a secret: *The party's supposed to be a surprise, so keep your mouth shut about it.* **3** [C] the entrance to a CAVE or hole: *the mouth of a jar* **4** [C] the part of a river where it joins the sea **5** **big/loud mouth** *informal* someone who often says things that they should not say or who says things in a loud way **6** **make your mouth water** if food makes your mouth water, it looks so good you want to eat it immediately → see also MOUTH-WATERING

mouth² /maʊð/ *v* [T] to move your lips as if you are saying words, but without making any sound: *Karen was mouthing the answer to me behind the teacher's back.*

mouth off *phr v* [I] *informal* to talk angrily or rudely to someone: *Mick was suspended for mouthing off to teachers.*

mouth·ful /ˈmaʊθfʊl/ *n* **1** [C] an amount of food or drink that you put into your mouth at one time **2** **a mouthful** *informal* a long word or phrase that is difficult to say: *Her real name is quite a mouthful, so we just call her Dee.*

mouth·piece /ˈmaʊθpiːs/ *n* [C] **1** the part of a musical instrument, telephone etc that you put in your mouth or next to your mouth **2** [usually singular] a person, newspaper etc that a government or political organization uses to express its opinions: *Pravda used to be the mouthpiece of the Communist Party.*

mouth·wash /ˈmaʊθwɒʃ‖-wɒʃ, -wɑːʃ/ *n* [C,U] a liquid that you use to make your breath smell fresh or to get rid of a mouth infection

mouth-wa·ter·ing /ˈ. ˌ.../ *adj* mouth-watering food looks or smells extremely good

mov·a·ble /ˈmuːvəbəl/ *adj* something that is movable can be moved: *toy soldiers with movable arms and legs*

move¹ /muːv/ *v* **1** [I,T] to change from one place or position to another, or make something do this: *He moved the chair into the corner of the room.* | *I saw the dog's eyes move, so I knew he was alive.* | **+ about/around** *She could hear someone moving around in Gail's room.* **2** [I] also **move away** to go to a new place to live or work: *Henry moved away and we never saw him again.* | **+ to** *They moved to Birmingham in May.* | **move house** *BrE* (=go to live in a different house): *We're moving house next week.* **3** [T] to make someone feel a strong emotion, especially sadness or sympathy: *The story moved us to tears.* (=made us cry) **4** [I] to make progress, change,

M

or begin to achieve something: *Things are moving fast now we've got a new manager.* **5** [T] to change the time or order of something: *We'll have to move the party to another day.* **6 get moving** *spoken* used to tell someone they need to hurry: *If you don't get moving, you'll miss the bus.* **7** [I] *informal* to travel very fast: *That truck was really moving.*

move in *phr v* [I] **1** to start living in a new house: *When are you moving in?* **2** to start living with someone in the same house: **+ with/together** *Steve's moving in with his girlfriend.*

move off *phr v* [I] if a car, train etc moves off, it moves forward to start its journey: *The train began to move off slowly.*

move on *phr v* [I] **1** to leave a place where you have been staying so that you can continue on a trip: *After three days we decided it was time to move on.* **2** to start talking or writing about a new subject: *I'd like to move on now to the subject of education.* **3** to develop, improve, or become more modern: *Her ideas have hardly moved on since the thirties.*

move out *phr v* [I] to leave the house where you are living in order to go to live somewhere else: *We have to move out by next Friday.*

move over *phr v* [I] to change position so that there is more space for other people or things: *Move over so Jim can sit down.*

move up *phr v* **1** [I,T] to get a better job or move to a higher class in a school, or to make someone do this: *She's been moved up to the managerial level.* **2** [I] *BrE* to change position so that there is more space for other people or things: *Move up a bit – I'm squashed in the corner.*

move[2] *n* [C] **1** something that you decide to do to achieve something or make progress: *"I called Tom to say I don't want to see him again." "Good move!"* | *The White House says the talks are a definite move towards peace.* **2 make a move a)** to move in a particular direction: **+ towards/for** *Arnison made a move for the door.* **b)** *BrE spoken* to leave a place: *It's late, we'd better be making a move.* **3 be on the move** to be travelling to different places all the time **4 get a move on** *spoken* used to tell someone to hurry: *Get a move on, or we'll be late!* **5** when you go to live or work somewhere else: *The move to the new house took three days.* **6** when you change the position of one of the pieces in a game such as CHESS

move·ment /'mu:vmənt/ *n* **1** [C,U] a change in the place or position of something or someone: *I noticed a sudden movement behind the curtain.* **2** [C] a group of people who share the same aims or beliefs and work together to achieve them: *the anti-war movement* **3** [C] a gradual change in people's attitudes or behaviour: **+ away/towards** *a movement away from traditional values* **4** [C] one of the main parts that a piece of music, especially a SYMPHONY, is divided into **5 sb's movements** a person's activities during a period of time: *Police are trying to trace his movements over the last 48 hours.*

mov·er /'mu:vəll-ər/ *n* [C] *AmE* someone whose job is to help people move from one house to another

mov·ie /'mu:vi/ *n* [C] *especially AmE* **1** a FILM **2 the movies** *AmE* the CINEMA *BrE*: **go to**

the movies (=go to watch a movie): *How often do you go to the movies?*

movie star /'.. ./ *n* [C] a famous film actor or actress; FILM STAR *BrE*

movie thea·ter /'.. ,../ *n* [C] *AmE* a building where you go to see films; CINEMA *BrE*

mov·ing /'mu:vɪŋ/ *adj* **1** making you feel strong emotions, especially sadness or sympathy: *a deeply moving book* **2** [only before noun] able to move: *Oil the moving parts of this machine regularly.* — **movingly** *adv*: *He spoke movingly about his experiences in the war.*

mow /məʊll moʊ/ *v* **mowed, mowed** or **mown** /məʊnll moʊn/, **mowing** [I,T] to cut grass or crops with a machine: *When are you going to mow the lawn?*

mow sb ↔ down *phr v* [T] to deliberately kill a person or a lot of people with a gun, car etc, especially without caring who they are or whether they have done anything wrong: *Hundreds of protesters were mown down by the police.*

mow·er /'məʊəll moʊər/ *n* [C] a machine that you use to cut grass

MP /ˌem 'pi:/ *n* [C] Member of Parliament; someone who has been elected by people in Britain and Northern Ireland to REPRESENT them in parliament: *She's the MP for Liverpool North.*

mpg /ˌem pi: 'dʒi:/ the written abbreviation of 'miles per GALLON', used to say how much petrol a car uses

mph /ˌem pi: 'eɪtʃ/ the written abbreviation of "miles per hour"; used to say how fast a vehicle goes: *a car that can reach a speed of 180 mph*

Mr /'mɪstəll-ər/ *n* used in front of a man's family name when you are speaking or writing to him

Mrs /'mɪsɪz/ *n* used in front of a married woman's family name when you are speaking or writing to her

Ms /mɪz, məz/ *n written* used in front of the family name of a woman who does not think it is important that people know whether or not she is married

MSc, M.Sc. /ˌem es 'si:/ also **M.S.** /ˌem 'es/ *AmE* — *n* [C] Master of Science; a higher university degree in science → compare MA

Mt the written abbreviation of MOUNT: *Mt Everest*

much[1] /mʌtʃ/ *adv* **more** /mɔ:llmɔ:r/, **most** /məʊstllmoʊst/ **1** used before COMPARATIVES and SUPERLATIVES to mean 'a lot': *Dad's feeling much better now.* | *The fair this year was much more fun than last year.* **2 too much/so much/very much/how much etc** used to show the degree to which someone does something or something happens: *Thank you very much!* | *I know how much he likes Ann.* | *He was feeling so much better today that he went out for a walk.* **3 not much** not happening very often: *We don't go out much since the baby was born.* **4 much less** used to say that one thing is even less true or less possible than another: *He doesn't have enough money to buy new shoes, much less a new car.*

much[2] *quantifier* **1** used to mean a lot of something, especially in questions and negatives: *Was there much traffic?* | *We don't have much time.* **2** *formal or literary* a large amount: *There was much rejoicing when the travellers re-*

turned. |+ **of** *The storm is bringing rain to much of the country.* **3 how much** used to ask about the amount or cost of something: *How much is that green shirt?* | *She didn't know how much milk was left.* **4 so much/too much** used to talk about a large amount of something, especially one that is too large: *I have so much reading to do for tomorrow. I'll never get it done.* | *He says the government has spent too much money on weapons.* **5 be too much for sb** to be too difficult for someone: *Climbing stairs is too much for me since the operation.*

muck¹ /mʌk/ *n* [U] **1** something such as dirt or mud: *shoes covered in thick black muck* **2** *BrE* solid waste from animals: *dog muck*

muck² *v*

muck about/around *phr v BrE informal* **1** [I] to behave in a silly way and waste time: *Stop mucking about and get on with your homework.* **2** [T **muck** sb **about/around**] to cause trouble for someone by changing your mind a lot or not being honest: *Jim's really mucked me around – first he wants to go, then he doesn't.*

muck in *phr v* [I] *BrE informal* to work together with other people in order to get a job done: *When mom's busy, we all muck in and help with the housework.*

muck sth ↔ **up** *phr v* [T] *BrE informal* to spoil something, or do something badly: *Let me do that – you'll only muck it up.*

muck·y /ˈmʌki/ *adj BrE informal* dirty: *mucky windows*

mu·cus /ˈmjuːkəs/ *n* [U] a thick liquid produced in parts of your body, especially your nose

mud /mʌd/ *n* [U] wet earth that is soft and sticky: *His clothes and shoes were covered in mud.*

mud·dle¹ /ˈmʌdl/ *n* [C,U] when something is confusing so that mistakes are made: *The system for sending invoices is a complete muddle.* | *There is always a lot of confusion and muddle at the beginning of term.* | **be in a muddle** (=be confused)

muddle² *v especially BrE* **1** also **muddle up** [T] to put things in the wrong order: *The papers had all been muddled up.* **2 get (sth/sb) muddled up** to wrongly think that one person or thing is someone or something else: *I always get him and his brother muddled up.*

muddle through/on *phr v* [I] to continue doing something even though it is confusing or difficult: *We lost our equipment but muddled through anyway.*

mud·dy¹ /ˈmʌdi/ *adj* covered with mud or containing mud: *muddy boots* | *muddy water*

muddy² *v* [T] **1** to make a situation more complicated or more confusing than it was before: *We'll never reach a decision if they keep muddying the issue with religion.* **2** to make something dirty with mud

mues·li /ˈmjuːzli/ *n* [U] grain, nuts, and dried fruit that you eat with milk for breakfast

muff /mʌf/ *v* [T] *informal* to do something badly or make a mistake: *He muffed his last shot and finished second.*

muf·fin /ˈmʌfɪn/ *n* [C] **1** a small sweet cake: *a blueberry muffin* **2** *BrE* a small round type of bread that you eat hot with butter

muf·fle /ˈmʌfəl/ *v* [T] to make a sound less loud or clear: *Thick curtains muffled the traffic noise.*

muf·fled /ˈmʌfəld/ *adj* muffled voices or sounds cannot be heard clearly because something is in the way

muf·fler /ˈmʌflə‖-ər/ *n* [C] **1** *old-fashioned* SCARF **2** *AmE* a piece of equipment on a vehicle that makes the noise from the engine quieter; SILENCER *BrE*

mug¹ /mʌg/ *n* [C] **1** a large cup with straight sides used for drinking coffee, tea etc, or the amount contained in a mug → see picture at CUP **2** *BrE spoken* someone who is easily tricked: *You're a mug if you buy that car.*

mug² *v* [T] **-gged, -gging** to attack someone in a public place and take their money: *She was mugged and her purse was stolen.* —**mugger** *n* [C] —**mugging** *n* [U]

mug·gy /ˈmʌgi/ *adj informal* muggy weather is unpleasant because it is too warm and HUMID

mug·shot /ˈmʌgʃɒt‖-ʃɑːt/ *n* [C] *informal* a photograph of a criminal's face taken by the police

Mu·ham·mad /mʊˈhæmɪd, mə-/ *a* PROPHET who taught the ideas that Islam is based on

mulch /mʌltʃ/ *n* [singular, U] decaying leaves that you put on the soil to improve its quality

mule /mjuːl/ *n* [C] an animal that has a DONKEY and a horse as parents

mull /mʌl/ *v* [T]

mull sth ↔ **over** *phr v* [T] to think about something carefully: *Mull it over for a few days and let me know your decision.*

mul·lah /ˈmʌlə, ˈmʊlə/ *n* [C] a religious leader or teacher in Islam

multi- /ˈmʌltɪ/ *prefix* used at the beginning of some words to mean 'many': *a multicultural society* (=one that has people from many cultures) | *a multi-storey car park*

mul·ti·cul·tur·al /ˌmʌltiˈkʌltʃərəl◂/ *adj* involving people, customs, or ideas from many different countries, races, religions etc: *The US is a multicultural society.* —**multiculturalism** *n* [U]

mul·ti·lat·e·ral /ˌmʌltɪˈlætərəl◂/ *adj* involving several different countries, companies etc: *multilateral peace talks* —**multilaterally** *adv* → compare BILATERAL, UNILATERAL

mul·ti·me·di·a /ˌmʌltiˈmiːdiə◂/ *adj* [only before noun] using a mixture of sounds, pictures etc to give information, especially on a computer —**multimedia** *n* [U]

mul·ti·na·tion·al /ˌmʌltɪˈnæʃənəl◂/ *adj* **1** a multinational company has offices, factories etc in several different countries **2** involving people from several different countries: *a multinational peace-keeping force* —**multinationally** *adv*

mul·ti·ple¹ /ˈmʌltɪpəl/ *adj* including or involving many parts, people, events etc: *He suffered multiple injuries to his legs.*

M

multiple² n [C] a number that contains a smaller number an exact number of times: *20 is a multiple of 5.*

multiple choice /ˌ... '.ˌ/ adj a multiple choice test or question shows several different answers and you must choose the correct one

mul·ti·plex /'mʌltɪˌpleks/ n [C] a cinema that shows several different films at the same time on different screens

mul·ti·pli·ca·tion /ˌmʌltɪplɪˈkeɪʃən/ n [U] a method of calculating in which you add the same number to itself a particular number of times → compare DIVISION

mul·ti·pli·ci·ty /ˌmʌltɪˈplɪsˌti/ n [C,U] formal a large number or great variety of things: **+ of** *a machine with a multiplicity of parts*

mul·ti·ply /'mʌltɪˌplaɪ/ v [I,T] **1** to increase greatly, or to make something do this: *The number of asthma sufferers has multiplied over the last few years.* **2** to do a calculation in which you add one number to itself a particular number of times: *Four multiplied by five is 20.* → compare DIVIDE¹

mul·ti·pur·pose /ˌmʌltiˈpɜːpəsˌ ‖-ˈpɜːr-/ adj having many different uses: *a multipurpose knife*

mul·ti·ra·cial /ˌmʌltɪˈreɪʃəl/ adj including or involving many different races of people: *We live in a multiracial society.*

multi-sto·rey /ˌ... '..ˌ/ adj [only before noun] BrE a multi-storey building has a lot of levels: *a multi-storey car park*

mul·ti·tude /'mʌltɪˌtjuːd‖-tuːd/ n [C] literary a very large number of things or people: **+ of** *The garden was full of flowers in a multitude of colours.*

mum /mʌm/ n [C] BrE mother; **mom** AmE: *Mum, can I borrow some money?|My mum's a teacher.*

mum·ble /'mʌmbəl/ v [I,T] to say something too quietly, or not clearly enough for someone to understand you: *He mumbled something I did not hear.*

mum·bo-jum·bo /ˌmʌmbəʊ 'dʒʌmbəʊ‖-boʊ 'dʒʌmboʊ/ n [U] informal a belief that you think is nonsense, especially because it cannot be proved: *Surely you don't believe in astrology and all that mumbo-jumbo!*

mum·my /'mʌmi/ n [C] **1** BrE mother – used especially by or to young children; **mommy** AmE: *Go and ask Mummy if she'll help you.* **2** a dead body that has been preserved and wrapped in cloth, especially in ancient Egypt

mumps /mʌmps/ n [U] an infectious illness in which your throat and neck swell and become painful

munch /mʌntʃ/ v [I,T] to eat something with continuous movements of your mouth because you are enjoying it: *Anna sat munching her toast.*

munch·ies /'mʌntʃiz/ n [plural] AmE informal **1 have the munchies** to feel hungry **2** small pieces of food that you eat at a party

mun·dane /ˌmʌnˈdeɪnˌ/ adj ordinary and boring: *a mundane job* **—mundanely** adv

mu·ni·ci·pal /mjuːˈnɪsˌpəl‖mjuː-/ adj relating to the government of a town or city

mu·ni·tions /mjuːˈnɪʃənz‖mjuː-/ n [plural] military supplies such as bombs and guns

mu·ral /'mjʊərəl‖'mjʊrəl/ n [C] a picture painted on a wall

mur·der¹ /'mɜːdə‖'mɜːrdər/ n **1** [C,U] the crime of deliberately killing someone: *A man was yesterday charged with the murder of two young girls.*|**commit (a) murder** *4600 murders were committed in the US in 1975.* **2 get away with murder** informal used to say that someone is allowed to behave very badly and not be punished: *Those kids of theirs get away with murder!* **3 be murder** spoken be very difficult or unpleasant: *The traffic was murder this morning.*

murder² v [T] to kill someone deliberately and illegally: *He murdered his wife in a jealous rage.* **—murderer** n [C]

mur·der·ous /'mɜːdərəs‖'mɜːr-/ adj able or likely to violently kill someone: *murderous weapons of war* **—murderously** adv

murk·y /'mɜːki‖'mɜːr-/ adj dark and dirty: *murky water*

mur·mur /'mɜːmə‖'mɜːrmər/ n [C] a soft quiet sound made by someone's voice: *She answered in a low murmur.* **—murmur** v [I,T] *He softly murmured her name.*

mus·cle /'mʌsəl/ n **1** [C,U] one of the pieces of flesh inside your body that join bones together and make your body move: *Weight lifting will strengthen your arm muscles.*|**pull a muscle** (=injure a muscle) **2** [U] military, political, or financial influence

mus·cu·lar /'mʌskjʊlə‖-ər/ adj **1** having a lot of big muscles: *strong muscular arms* **2** related to or affecting the muscles: *a muscular disease*

muse /mjuːz/ v [I] formal to imagine or think a lot about something

mu·se·um /mjuːˈziːəm‖mjuː-/ n [C] a building where people can go and see important objects connected with history, science etc: *an art museum*

mush /mʌʃ/ n [singular, U] something unpleasantly soft, especially food: *The vegetables had been boiled to a mush.* **—mushy** adj

mush·room¹ /'mʌʃruːm, -rʊm/ n [C] a FUNGUS that has a stem and a round top, of which some types can be eaten and some are poisonous: *a chicken and mushroom pie*

mushroom² v [I] to increase or develop very quickly: *The city's population has mushroomed to over one million.*

mu·sic /'mjuːzɪk/ n [U] **1** a pattern of sounds made by people playing musical instruments or singing: *What kind of music do you like?*|**piece of music** *My favorite piece of music is Vivaldi's 'Four Seasons'.* **2** the art of writing or playing music: *music lessons* **3** a set of written marks that can be read as musical sounds: *Paul has never been able to read music.* (=understand written music) **4 face the music** to admit that you have done something wrong and accept your punishment

mu·sic·al¹ /'mjuːzɪkəl/ adj **1** relating to music: *musical instruments* **2** good at playing or singing music: *I'm not musical at all.* **—musically** /-kli/ adv

musical² n [C] a play or film that uses songs and music to tell a story

mu·si·cian /mjuːˈzɪʃən‖mjuː-/ n [C] someone who plays a musical instrument, especially as a job

mus·ket /ˈmʌskɪt/ *n* [C] a type of RIFLE used in the past

Mus·lim /ˈmʊzlɪm, ˈmʌz-, ˈmʊs-/ *n* [C] someone whose religion is Islam —**Muslim** *adj*

mus·lin /ˈmʌzlɪn/ *n* [U] a very thin cotton cloth

muss /mʌs/ also **muss up** *v* [T] *AmE informal* to make someone's hair, clothes etc untidy

mus·sel /ˈmʌsəl/ *n* [C] a small sea animal with a black shell and a soft body that you can eat

must[1] /məst; *strong* mʌst/ *modal verb*
1 used to say that something is necessary and has to be done: *All passengers must wear seatbelts.* | *You must not allow your dog out without a leash.* | *It's getting late, I really must go.*
➛ see also HAVE[3] **2** used to say that you think something is very likely to be true: *George must be almost eighty years old now.* | *That car must have been going at 90 miles an hour!* **3** used to suggest that someone should do something: *You must see Robin Williams' new movie. It's really funny.*

must[2] /mʌst/ *n* **a must** *informal* something that you must do or must have: *If you visit Florida, going to Disney World is a must.*

mus·tache /məˈstɑːʃ‖ˈmʌstæʃ/ *n* [C] *AmE* a MOUSTACHE ➛ see colour picture on page 244

mus·tang /ˈmʌstæŋ/ *n* [C] a small American wild horse

mus·tard /ˈmʌstəd‖-ərd/ *n* [U] **1** a hot-tasting yellow SAUCE usually eaten with meat **2** a plant whose seeds are used to make mustard

mus·ter /ˈmʌstə‖-ər/ *v* **1** **muster (up) courage/support etc** to find as much courage, support etc as you can in order to do something difficult: *I'm still trying to muster up the courage to speak to her.* **2** [T] to gather a group of soldiers into one place in order to fight an enemy

must·n't /ˈmʌsənt/ *v* the short form of MUST NOT

must·y /ˈmʌsti/ *adj* having a wet unpleasant smell: *musty old books* —**mustiness** *n* [U]

mu·tant /ˈmjuːtənt/ *n* [C] an animal or plant that is different from others of the same kind because of a change in its GENES —**mutant** *adj*

mu·tate /mjuːˈteɪt‖ˈmjuːteɪt/ *v* [I] if an animal or plant mutates, it becomes different from others of the same kind because of a change in its GENES —**mutation** /mjuːˈteɪʃən/ *n* [C,U]

mute[1] /mjuːt/ *adj* silent or not saying anything: *mute admiration*

mute[2] *n* [C] *old-fashioned* someone who cannot speak

mut·ed /ˈmjuːtɪd/ *adj* **1** not expressing strong feelings: *muted criticism* **2** quieter than usual: *the muted hum of London's traffic* **3** a muted colour is not very bright

mu·ti·late /ˈmjuːtɪleɪt/ *v* [T] to badly damage someone's body, especially by cutting off part of it: *the mutilated bodies of his victims* —**mutilation** /ˌmjuːtɪˈleɪʃən/ *n* [C,U]

mu·ti·neer /ˌmjuːtɪˈnɪə‖-ˈnɪr/ *n* [C] someone who takes part in a mutiny

mu·ti·nous /ˈmjuːtɪnəs‖-tn-əs/ *adj* refusing to obey or accept orders from someone in authority: *mutinous soldiers*

mu·ti·ny /ˈmjuːtɪni‖-tn-i/ *n* [C,U] when a group of people, especially soldiers or SAILORs, refuse to obey the person who is in charge of them, and take control for themselves —**mutiny** *v* [I]

mutt /mʌt/ *n* [C] *informal* a dog that is a mixture of different BREEDs

mut·ter /ˈmʌtə‖-ər/ *v* [I,T] to speak in a low quiet voice which is difficult to hear, especially when you are complaining about something: *"Stupid fool," he muttered.*

mut·ton /ˈmʌtn/ *n* [U] fairly low quality meat from a sheep

mu·tu·al /ˈmjuːtʃuəl/ *adj* **1** used when two people or groups both have the same feeling about each other, or both do the same thing to each other: *mutual respect* | *The feeling is mutual.* (=I feel the same way about someone as they feel about me) **2** shared by two or more people: *a mutual friend* —**mutually** *adj*: *a mutually beneficial arrangement* (=one that is good for both people, groups etc)

Mu·zak /ˈmjuːzæk/ *n* [U] *trademark* recorded music that is played in airports, shops etc, which many people think is boring

muz·zle[1] /ˈmʌzəl/ *n* [C]
1 the nose and mouth of an animal such as a dog
2 the end of a gun, where the bullets come out **3** something that you put over a dog's mouth so it cannot bite

muzzle

muz·zle[2] *v* [T] **1** to prevent someone, especially newspapers, television etc, from publicly giving their opinions, making facts known etc: *an attempt to muzzle the press* **2** to put a muzzle over a dog's mouth so that it cannot bite

my /maɪ/ *possessive pron* belonging to or about me: *That's my car over there.* | *I tried not to let my feelings show.*

myr·i·ad /ˈmɪriəd/ *n* [C] *literary* a very large number of something: *a myriad of colours* —**myriad** *adj*

my·self /maɪˈself/ *pron* **1** the REFLEXIVE form of 'me': *I burned myself on the stove.* | *I made myself a cup of coffee.* **2** used to emphasize the pronoun 'I': *I myself have the same problem.* **3** **(all) by myself** alone or without anyone else: *I went to the movie by myself.* | *I was all by myself in the house.* **4** **have sth (all) to myself** if you have a place to yourself, you are the only person there, and you can use it to do what you want: *I had the whole swimming pool to myself today.*

mys·te·ri·ous /mɪˈstɪəriəs‖-ˈstɪr-/ *adj* **1** strange and difficult to explain or understand: *a mysterious illness* **2** not saying much about something, because you want it to be a secret: *He's being very mysterious about his new girlfriend.* —**mysteriously** *adv*: *My money had mysteriously disappeared.*

mys·te·ry /ˈmɪstəri/ *n* **1** [C] something that is difficult to explain or understand: *The location of the stolen money remains a mystery.* | *It's a mystery to me how she got the job.* **2** [C] a story, especially about a murder, in which events are not explained until the end: *the Sherlock Holmes mystery stories* **3** [U] a quality that makes someone or something seem strange, interesting, and difficult to explain or understand: *The dark glasses gave her an air of mystery.*

mys·tic[1] /ˈmɪstɪk/ *n* [C] a religious teacher who tries to get knowledge about God and religious truth by praying and MEDITATION

mystic[2] *adj* mystical

M

mys·tic·al /ˈmɪstɪkəl/ also **mystic** adj connected with religious or magical powers that people cannot understand: *While he was in the desert, he had some kind of mystical experience.* —**mystically** /-kli/ adv

mys·ti·cis·m /ˈmɪstᵻsɪzəm/ n [U] when people try to get knowledge about God and religious truth by praying and MEDITATION

mys·ti·fy /ˈmɪstᵻfaɪ/ v [T] to make someone feel confused because they cannot explain or understand something: *a case that mystified the police* —**mystifying** adj

mys·tique /mɪˈstiːk/ n [U] the quality that makes something seem mysterious, special, and interesting: *the mystique of Hollywood*

myth /mɪθ/ n [C,U] **1** something that many people believe, but which is not true: *the myth that America is a free and open society* **2** an ancient story that explains a natural or historical event, or this kind of story in general: *Greek myths about the creation of the world*

myth·i·cal /ˈmɪθɪkəl/ adj **1** relating to myth: *mythical creatures such as the Minotaur* **2** not real or true, but only imagined: *the mythical Wild West of popular fiction*

my·thol·o·gy /mɪˈθɒlədʒi‖-ˈθɑː-/ n [C,U] ancient myths in general: *stories from Greek mythology* —**mythological** /ˌmɪθəˈlɒdʒɪkəl‖ -ˈlɑː-/ adj

Nn

N, n /en/ the letter 'n'

n the written abbreviation of NOUN

N the written abbreviation of NORTH or NORTH-ERN

'n' /ən/ a short written form of AND: *rock 'n' roll music*

N/A 1 the written abbreviation of 'not applicable'; used to show that you do not need to answer a particular question **2** the written abbreviation of 'not available'

nab /næb/ *v* [T] **-bbed, -bbing** *informal* to catch someone who has done something wrong: *The police nabbed him as he was coming out of the supermarket.*

naff /næf/ *adj BrE informal* silly and unfashionable: *a naff thing to say*

nag /næg/ *v* [I,T] **-gged, -gging** to keep asking someone to do something, especially in an annoying way: *My wife has been nagging me to fix the kitchen sink.*

nag·ging /'nægɪŋ/ *adj* making you worry or feel pain all the time: *a nagging headache*

nail[1] /neɪl/ *n* [C] **1** a thin pointed piece of metal with a flat end, that you hit with a hammer **2** the thin hard parts that grow on the top end of your fingers and toes: *Stop biting your nails!* → see also **hit the nail on the head** (HIT[1])

nail

nail[2] *v* [T] to fasten something to something else with a nail: *The windows were nailed shut.*

nail sb/sth ↔ **down** *phr v* [T] **1** to fasten something down with nails **2** to reach a final and definite decision about something: *After three weeks they finally nailed down the details of the deal.*

nail-bit·ing /'. ˌ../ *adj* very exciting because you do not know what will happen next: *a nail-biting finish*

nail·brush /'. ./ *n* [C] a small brush, used for cleaning your nails

nail file /'. ./ *n* [C] a thin piece of metal with a rough surface, used for shaping your nails

nail pol·ish also **nail varnish** *BrE* /'. ˌ../ *n* [U] liquid that women paint on their nails to make them look attractive

na·ive /naɪ'iːv/ *adj* lacking experience and always expecting that people will be nice and that things will happen easily: *I was young and naive.* **—naively** *adv* **—naivety** /naɪ'iːvəti/ *n* [U]

na·ked /'neɪkɪd/ *adj* **1** not wearing any clothes; NUDE: **stark naked** (=completely naked) **2** **with/to the naked eye** without using an instrument such as a MICROSCOPE to help you see

3 naked emotions are very strong and noticeable: *naked aggression* **—nakedness** *n* [U]

name[1] /neɪm/ *n* [C] **1** what someone or something is called: *Sorry, I've forgotten your name.* | **+ of** *What's the name of the street the school is on?* | **last name/family name** (=the name that all the people in your family have) | **first name** *His first name's Peter.* **2** **big/famous/household name** *informal* a famous person, company etc **3** [singular] the opinion that people have about a person, company etc, and whether they respect it etc; REPUTATION: *This kind of incident gives football a bad name.* **4** **be in sb's name** to legally belong to someone: *The house is in my name.* **5** **call sb names** to insult someone by using unpleasant words to describe them: *The other kids started calling me names.* **6** **make a name for yourself** to become well-known because of the work you do **7** **in the name of** because you believe that something is a good reason for doing something: *It was all done in the name of progress.* → see CHRISTIAN NAME, SURNAME

USAGE NOTE: first name

Your **first name** is your own name that people who know you use when they are speaking to you – this is also sometimes called your **Christian name**, especially in British English. Your **last name** is the one you share with all the members of your family – this is also called your **surname** in British English. Some people also have a **middle name** that comes between their other two names. This name is usually used only on official documents.

---

name[2] *v* [T] **1** to give someone or something a particular name: **name sb/sth after** also **name sth for** *AmE* (=give them the same name as another person or thing): *He was named after his grandfather.* **2** to say what the name of someone or something is: *Can you name this song?* **3** to officially choose someone for a job: *Mr Johnson was named as the new manager.* **4** to choose a date or price **5** **you name it** *spoken* used after a list of things to mean that there are many more that you could mention: *Beer, whisky, wine – you name it we've got it!*

name-drop·ping /'neɪmˌdrɒpɪŋ||-ˌdrɑː-/ *n* [U] when someone often mentions the names of famous people to make it seem that they know them personally **—namedropper** *n* [C]

name·less /'neɪmləs/ *adj* **1** **sb who shall remain nameless** used to say that you will not mention someone's name: *A certain film actor, who shall remain nameless, once had an affair with her.* **2** not known by a name: *pictures by a nameless photographer*

name·ly /'neɪmli/ *adv* used when you are going to give details of the people or things that you have been talking about: *The movie won two Oscars, namely 'Best Actor' and 'Best Director.'*

name·sake /'neɪmseɪk/ *n* **sb's namesake** the

GRAMMAR NOTE: 'if' clauses (2)

When you imagine a present situation that is not real, or a future situation that is very unlikely, use **if + simple past**: *If he really loved you, he wouldn't treat you like this.* (=he does not love you). | *If I won a million dollars on the lottery, I would buy a yacht.* Use **would** in the other part of the sentence.

N

person or thing that has the same name as someone or something else

nan·ny /ˈnæni/ n [C] a woman whose job is to take care of a family's children, usually in their own home

nap[1] /næp/ n [C] a short sleep during the day: *Dad usually takes a nap in the afternoon.*

nap[2] v [I] **-pped, -pping 1** to sleep for a short time during the day **2 be caught napping** *informal* to not be ready when something happens, although you should have been ready

na·palm /ˈneɪpɑːm‖-pɑːm, -pɑːlm/ n [U] a liquid that burns crops and people's skin, used as a weapon

nape /neɪp/ n [singular] the back of your neck

nap·kin /ˈnæpkɪn/ n [C] a small piece of cloth or paper, used for protecting your clothes and cleaning your hands when you are eating

nap·py /ˈnæpi/ n [C] *BrE* a piece of cloth or paper that you put between a baby's legs and fasten around its waist; DIAPER *AmE*: *I think his nappy needs changing.*

nar·cis·sis·m /ˈnɑːsɪsɪzəm‖ˈnɑːr-/ n [U] *formal* when someone spends a lot of time thinking about and admiring their own appearance and abilities —**narcissistic** /ˌnɑːsɪˈsɪstɪk‖ˌnɑːr-/ adj

nar·cot·ic /nɑːˈkɒtɪk‖nɑːrˈkɑː-/ n [C] a drug, especially one that is illegal: *He was arrested for possession of narcotics.* —**narcotic** adj

nar·rate /nəˈreɪt‖ˈnæreɪt, næˈreɪt, nə-/ v [T] to tell a story or explain what is happening in a film, television programme etc —**narration** /nəˈreɪʃən/ n [C,U]

nar·ra·tive /ˈnærətɪv/ n [C,U] the description of events in a story: *an exciting narrative* —**narrative** adj

nar·ra·tor /nəˈreɪtə‖ˈnæreɪtər, næˈreɪtər, nə-/ n [C] someone who tells the story in a film, book etc

narrow

a narrow street

a wide street

nar·row[1] /ˈnærəʊ‖-roʊ/ adj **1** measuring only a small distance from one side to the other: *the narrow streets of the old town | a narrow strip of water* **2 narrow victory/defeat etc** when someone wins or loses by only a small amount **3 a narrow escape** when you only just avoid danger or trouble —**narrowness** n [U] → see also NARROWLY

narrow[2] v [I,T] to become more narrow, or make something more narrow: *The road narrows here.*

narrow sth ↔ **down** *phr v* [T] to reduce the number of people or things that you can choose from, before making a final decision:

We've narrowed down the number of candidates to just two.

nar·row·ly /ˈnærəʊli‖-roʊ-/ adv only just, or only by a small amount: *The General narrowly avoided being killed in a car bomb attack.*

narrow-mind·ed /ˌ...ˈ...◄‖...ˌ.../ adj not willing to accept ideas that are new and different from your own

na·sal /ˈneɪzəl/ adj **1** a nasal sound or voice comes mostly through your nose: *a high nasal voice* **2** relating to the nose: *the nasal cavity*

nas·ty /ˈnɑːstɪ‖ˈnæsti/ adj very bad, unpleasant, or unkind: *a nasty shock | What a nasty thing to say!* —**nastiness** n [U] —**nastily** adv

na·tion /ˈneɪʃən/ n [C] a country and its people: *the richest nation in the world | The President will address the nation tomorrow.*

na·tion·al[1] /ˈnæʃənəl/ adj **1** relating to the whole of a country, rather than to part of it: *the national news | an issue of national importance* → compare INTERNATIONAL **2** owned or controlled by the government of a country: *the national bank of Peru* **3** typical of a particular country: *national dress*

national[2] n [C] *formal* a British, French etc national is a British, French etc person, especially one who is living in a different country

national an·them /ˌ... ˈ../ n [C] a country's official song

national hol·i·day /ˌ... ˈ.../ n [C] a day when people in a country do not work and the shops are closed; PUBLIC HOLIDAY

na·tion·al·ise /ˈnæʃənəlaɪz/ v a British spelling of NATIONALIZE

na·tion·al·is·m /ˈnæʃənəlɪzəm/ n [U] **1** when a group of people want to have their own government and be independent of another country: *Scottish nationalism* **2** the feeling of being proud of your country, especially when you believe that your country is much better than other countries: *the rise of German nationalism in the 1920s and 30s*

na·tion·al·ist /ˈnæʃənəlɪst/ n [C] someone who wants to form a separate country, or someone who thinks their country is better than any other country —**nationalist** adj: *nationalist leaders*

na·tion·al·is·tic /ˌnæʃənəˈlɪstɪk◄/ adj believing that your country is much better than other countries and their people: *a nationalistic speech*

na·tion·al·i·ty /ˌnæʃəˈnæləti/ n [C,U] if you have British, French etc nationality, you have the legal right to live in Britain, France etc: *Her husband has US nationality. | people of all nationalities* (=from many different countries)

na·tion·al·ize (also **-ise** *BrE*) /ˈnæʃənəlaɪz/ v [T] if a government nationalizes an organization, industry etc, it takes control of it → opposite PRIVATIZE —**nationalization** /ˌnæʃənəlaɪˈzeɪʃən‖-lə-/ n [U]

na·tion·al·ly /ˈnæʃənəli/ adv in all of a country: *Nationally, the jobless total rose to 2,606,602.*

national mon·u·ment /ˌ... ˈ.../ n [C] a building, area of land etc that is protected by the government for people to visit

national park /ˌ... ˈ./ n [C] a large area of beautiful land that is protected by the government for people to visit: *Yellowstone National Park*

na·tion·al se·cu·ri·ty /ˌ... .ˈ.../ n [U] the protection of a country from attack by other countries: *The information was kept secret in the interests of national security.*

na·tion·wide /ˌneɪʃənˈwaɪd◂, ˈneɪʃənwaɪd/ adj happening or existing in every part of a country: *a nationwide search* — **nationwide** adv

na·tive[1] /ˈneɪtɪv/ adj **1 native country/land etc** the country where you were born: *The football star returned to his native Belfast.* **2 native Californian/New Yorker etc** someone who was born in California, New York etc **3 sb's native language/tongue** the first language that you learned to speak when you were a child **4** growing or living in an area, not brought there from outside: *South Africa's native wildlife*

native[2] n **1 a native of** someone who was born in a particular place: *She's a native of southern Brazil.* **2** [C usually plural] *old-fashioned* someone who was living in Africa, South America etc when the Europeans arrived. Many people now consider this use to be offensive

Native A·mer·i·can /ˌ... .ˈ.../ n [C] someone who belongs to the groups of people who were living in North America before the Europeans arrived

native speak·er /ˌ.. ˈ../ n [C] someone who learned to speak a language when they were a baby, as their first language

NATO /ˈneɪtəʊ‖-toʊ/ n [singular] the North Atlantic Treaty Organization; a group of countries in North America and Europe that give military help to each other

nat·ter /ˈnætə‖-ər/ v [I] BrE informal to talk a lot about unimportant things — **natter** n [singular]

nat·u·ral[1] /ˈnætʃərəl/ adj **1** normal or usual: *Of course she's upset. It's a perfectly natural reaction.* | *It's not natural for a four-year-old to be so quiet.* **2** not made, caused, or controlled by humans: *earthquakes and other natural disasters* | *natural childbirth* (=without using drugs or special equipment) **3** having a particular skill or ability without being taught: *a natural athlete* — **naturalness** n [U]

natural[2] n **be a natural** to be very good at doing something without being taught: *Look how he swings that bat – he's a natural.*

natural gas /ˌ... ˈ./ n [U] gas used for cooking or heating, that is taken from under the ground

natural his·to·ry /ˌ... ˈ.../ n [U] the study of plants and animals

nat·u·ral·ist /ˈnætʃərəl¦st/ n [C] someone who studies plants and animals

nat·u·ral·ize (also **-ise** BrE) /ˈnætʃərəlaɪz/ **be naturalized** to be officially given the right to live in a country that you were not born in — **naturalization** /ˌnætʃərəlaɪˈzeɪʃən‖-lə-/ n [U]

nat·u·ral·ly[2] /ˈnætʃərəli‖-tʃərli, -tʃɑrli/ adv **1** used to say that something is what you would expect: *Naturally we're very disappointed.* **2** if something happens naturally, it happens without people trying to make it happen, or without using drugs, chemicals etc: *naturally curly hair* | *In the past, pests were controlled naturally.* | *Sodium chloride is found naturally in many foods.* (=exists in many foods) **3** used to talk about someone's usual character, or

about things that someone has always been good at doing: *He's naturally very shy.* | *a naturally gifted soccer player* | **sth comes naturally to sb** *Making money comes naturally to her.* **4** in a relaxed way, without trying to look or sound different from usual: *Try to speak as naturally as possible.*

natural re·sourc·es /ˌ... .ˈ.., ˌ... ˈ.../ n [plural] things such as oil, coal, gas, or metals that exist in a country and can be used by people: *Japan has few natural resources of its own.*

natural se·lec·tion /ˌ... .ˈ../ n [U] technical the process by which only the plants and animals that are suitable to their environment will continue to exist

na·ture /ˈneɪtʃə‖-ər/ n **1** [U] everything that exists in the world that is not made or controlled by humans, such as animals, plants, weather etc: *the forces of nature* **2** [C,U] someone's character, or what something is like: *Oswald's violent nature* | **the nature of** *changes in the nature of the job* | **by nature** (=used to say what someone's character is usually like): *By nature he's such a quiet boy.* | **not be in sb's nature** (=used to say that you do not think someone would behave in that way): *Patrick wouldn't say that. It's not in his nature.* ➡ see also GOOD-NATURED, **human nature** (HUMAN[1]), SECOND NATURE

nature re·serve /ˈ.. .ˌ./ n [C] an area of land where animals and plants are protected

naught /nɔːt‖nɒːt, nɑːt/ n [U] old-fashioned **1** nothing **2 come to naught** to fail

naugh·ty /ˈnɔːti‖ˈnɒːti, ˈnɑːti/ adj a naughty child behaves badly — **naughtiness** n [U] — **naughtily** adv

nau·se·a /ˈnɔːziə, -siəl‖ˈnɒːziə, -ʃə/ n [U] formal the feeling that you are going to VOMIT

nau·se·at·ed /ˈnɔːzieɪt¦d, -si-l‖ˈnɒːzi-, -ʃi-/ adj **1** *especially AmE* feeling that you are going to VOMIT **2** *informal* strongly disliking something because it is very unpleasant — **nauseate** v [T]

nau·se·at·ing /ˈnɔːzieɪtɪŋ, -si-l‖ˈnɒːzi-, -ʃi-/ adj **1** very unpleasant, or very annoying: *What a nauseating little person she is!* **2** very unpleasant and making you want to vomit: *the nauseating smell of rotting flesh* — **nauseatingly** adv

nau·ti·cal /ˈnɔːtɪkəl‖ˈnɒː-/ adj relating to ships or sailing — **nautically** /-kli/ adv

na·val /ˈneɪvəl/ adj relating to the navy: *a naval battle*

na·vel /ˈneɪvəl/ n [C] the small hole just below your waist, on the front of your body; BELLY BUTTON

nav·i·ga·ble /ˈnævɪɡəbəl/ adj deep and wide enough for ships to travel on: *Part of the St. Lawrence River is navigable.*

nav·i·gate /ˈnævɪɡeɪt/ v **1** [I] to find how to go to a place, especially by using maps: *Rick usually drives and I navigate.* **2** [I,T] to sail across or along an area of water

nav·i·ga·tion /ˌnævɪˈɡeɪʃən/ n [U] when you decide which direction to go in or which road to take when you are travelling somewhere: *sophisticated navigation equipment* — **navigational** adj

nav·i·ga·tor /ˈnævɪɡeɪtəl‖-ər/ n [C] the officer on a ship or plane who plans which direction it should be travelling in

na·vy /ˈneɪvi/ n [C] the people and ships that a country has for fighting a war at sea: *My dad was 20 when he joined the navy.*

navy blue /ˌ.. ˈ.◂/ also **navy** adj very dark blue —**navy blue** n [U] → see colour picture on page 114

Na·zi /ˈnɑːtsi/ n [C] a member of the main political party in Germany in the 1930s which was led by Adolf Hitler —**Nazism** n [U] —**Nazi** adj

nb or **NB** written to tell someone to pay attention to something important you have written

NBC /ˌen biː ˈsiː/ n [U] National Broadcasting Company; one of the main American television companies

NCO /ˌen siː ˈəʊl-ˈoʊ/ n [C] noncommissioned officer; a soldier such as a CORPORAL or SERGEANT

NE the abbreviation of NORTHEAST or NORTH-EASTERN

near

near   far

near¹ /nɪəllnɪr/ adv, prep **1** only a short dis-

tance from someone or something: *They live near Osaka.* | *Is there a bank near here?* → see colour picture on page 474   **2** close to a particular time: *She got more and more nervous as the wedding drew near.*   **3** close to having a particular quality or being a particular thing; almost: **near perfect/impossible etc** *a near perfect test score* | **near to tears/death** (=almost crying or dying) | **come/be near to doing sth** (=almost do something): *She came near to hitting him.*

USAGE NOTE: near and close

Near and **close** are both used to talk about short distances. **Close** is usually followed by the word **to**, but **near** is not: *There is a new supermarket near our house.* | *We live close to the bus stop.* **Close** is also used to talk about something that is not far away in time: *It was close to midnight.*

---

near² adj **1** only a short distance from someone or something: *It's very near.* | **the nearest** (=the closest): *The nearest town is 20 miles away.* **2 in the near future** soon: *We will have a new teacher joining us in the near future.* **3 near miss** a situation in which one thing almost hits something else: *Two planes had a near miss above the airport.* **4 nearest relative** the person who is most closely related to you, for example your father or mother

near·by /ˈnɪəbaɪllˈnɪr-/ adj [only before noun]

Food – Verbs

Exercise 1

Look at the pictures. Write the number of the definition beside the verb in the box.

chop ☐   grate ☐   mash ☐   peel ☐
pour ☐   slice ☑   spread ☐   squeeze ☐

1   to cut meat, bread etc. into thin flat pieces: Could you _____ the bread?

2   to put a soft substance onto a surface to cover it: _____ the remaining cream over the top of the cake.

3   to twist or press something in order to get liquid out of it: _____ some lemon juice onto the salad.

4   to rub food such as cheese or vegetables using a tool with a rough surface in order to break it into small pieces: _____d carrot

5   to make a liquid flow out of or into something: _____ the milk into the jug.

6   to remove the skin of a fruit or vegetable: Will you _____ the potatoes, please?

7   to cut something, especially food, into small pieces: Shall I _____ these onions up?

8   to crush food until it is soft: _____ the potatoes in a bowl.

Exercise 2

What can you do with these types of food? Tick [✓] the verbs you can use.

	chop	grate	mash	peel	pour	slice	spread	squeeze
apple								
bread								
cheese								
jam								
milk								
potato								
tomato								
water								

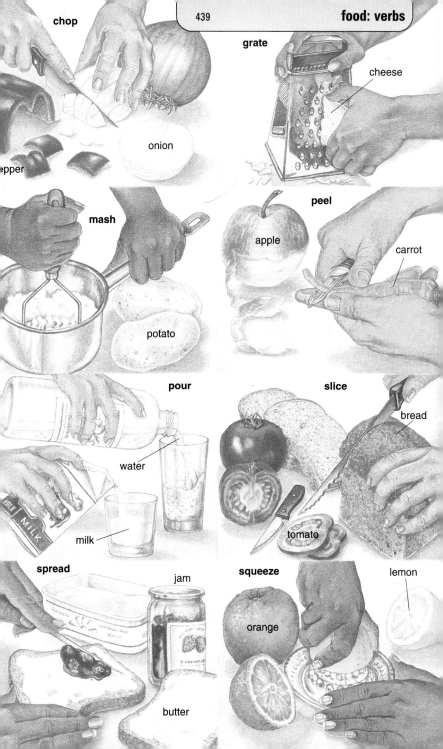

chop

onion

pper

grate

cheese

mash

potato

peel

apple

carrot

pour

water

milk

slice

bread

tomato

spread

jam

butter

squeeze

lemon

orange

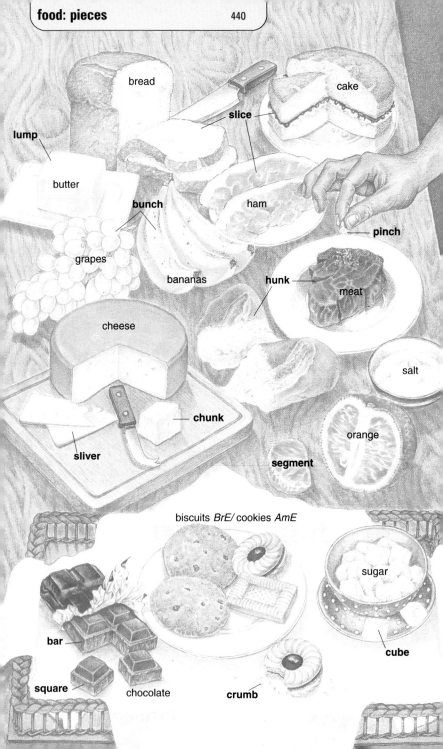

bread

cake

slice

lump

butter

bunch

ham

pinch

grapes

bananas

hunk

meat

cheese

salt

chunk

sliver

orange

segment

biscuits *BrE/* cookies *AmE*

sugar

bar

cube

square

chocolate

crumb

N

not far away: *They went swimming in a nearby lake.* —**nearby** /nɪəˈbaɪ‖ˈnɪr-/ *adv*

near·ly /ˈnɪəli‖ˈnɪrli/ *adv* almost, but not completely or not exactly: *We've nearly finished.* | *It's nearly seven years since I last saw him.*

near·sight·ed /ˌnɪəˈsaɪtɪd‖ˈnɪrsaɪtɪd/ *adj* unable to see things clearly unless they are close to you; SHORTSIGHTED *BrE* —**nearsightedness** *n* [U]

neat /niːt/ *adj* **1** arranged in a tidy or careful way: *He put his clothes in a neat pile on the bed.* | *They like to keep their house neat and tidy.* **2** *AmE informal* very good or enjoyable: *The fireworks were really neat!* **3** a neat person always arranges things in a tidy or careful way **4** simple and effective: *a neat solution to the problem* **5** if you drink alcohol neat, you drink it without adding any water, LEMONADE etc —**neatly** *adv* —**neatness** *n* [U]

ne·ces·sar·i·ly /ˈnesɪsərɪli, ˌnesɪˈserɪli‖ˌnesɪˈserɪli/ *adv* **1** **not necessarily** used to say that something may not be true, or may not always happen: *Expensive restaurants do not necessarily have the best food.* **2** used to say that something has to happen or be true; INEVITABLY: *Income tax laws are necessarily complicated.*

ne·ces·sa·ry /ˈnesɪsərɪ‖-seri/ *adj* if something is necessary, you need it in order to have something or do something: *"Should I bring my passport?" "No, that won't be necessary."* | *Will you make all the necessary arrangements?* | *The doctor says it may be necessary for me to have an operation.* | **if necessary** *They say they'll use force if*

necessary. | **a necessary evil** (=something bad or unpleasant that you have to accept because it is necessary): *Paying taxes is seen as a necessary evil.*

ne·ces·si·tate /nɪˈsesɪteɪt/ *v* [T] *formal* to make it necessary for you to do something: *His injuries may necessitate long-term treatment.*

ne·ces·si·ty /nɪˈsesɪti/ *n* **1** [C] something that you need to have or to use: *A car is a necessity for this job.* | *Election reforms are an absolute necessity.* **2** [U] when you must do something or something must be done: *There's no necessity to pay now.* (=you do not need to pay now) | **out of necessity** (=because you must do it): *They did it out of necessity.*

neck[1] /nek/ *n* [C] **1** the part of your body that joins your head to your shoulders: *a long, slender neck* → see picture at HEAD **2** the part of a piece of clothing that goes around your neck: *a V-neck sweater* (=one that has a neck shaped like a 'V') **3** the narrow part of a bottle **4** **be up to your neck in sth** *informal* **a)** to be in a very difficult situation: *Mason is up to his neck in debt.* **b)** to have too much work to do **5** **neck and neck** if two people, teams etc are neck and neck during a race or competition, they both have an equal chance of winning **6** **in this neck of the woods** *informal* in this area or part of the country: *What are you doing in this neck of the woods?*

neck[2] *v* **be necking** *old-fashioned* to be kissing in a sexual way

---

Food – Pieces

Exercise 1

Look at the pictures and read the words for pieces of food. Choose the right word in these sentences.

1 Can I have a cup of tea with milk and two slices/*lumps* of sugar?

2 I bought a new lump/bar of chocolate this morning but there are only two squares/lumps left.

3 Can you get me a bunch/cube of bananas when you go to the shop?

4 Put a small bar/lump of butter in the frying pan.

5 The farmer's lunch is two hunks/segments of bread and a bunch/chunk of cheese.

6 You've been eating biscuits, haven't you? There are crumbs/segments in the bed.

7 Put a piece/pinch of salt into the mixture when you make a cake.

8 I like to eat a big hunk/square of meat with a sliver/bar of cheese on top.

9 My girlfriend eats oranges when she is watching television. She always gives me a slice/segment during the advertisements.

10 Can I have a slice/hunk of cake, please?

Exercise 2

Look at the words for food. Complete these sentences. Find any words you don't know in the dictionary.

1 B_____, g_____ and o_____ are different types of fruit.

2 C_____ and b_____ are made from milk.

3 B_____, b_____ and c_____ are made from flour.

4 H____ is a type of m_____.

5 There is a lot of s_____ in a bar of c_____.

neck·lace /'nek-l₃s/ n [C] a piece of jewellery that you wear around your neck: *a pearl necklace* ➝ see picture at JEWELLERY

neck·line /'nek-laın/ n [C] the edge of a piece of woman's clothing around the neck

neck·tie /'nektaı/ n [C] AmE formal a TIE

nec·tar /'nektəll-tər/ n [U] **1** the sweet liquid that BEES collect from flowers **2** the drink of the gods, in ancient Greek stories

nec·ta·rine /'nektəriːn/ n [C] a juicy fruit like a PEACH

née /neɪ/ adj a word used before the family name that a woman had before she was married: *Lorna Brown née Wilson*

need[1] /niːd/ v [T] **1** if you need something, you must have it in order to live, or in order to do something: *I'm working on Sundays because I need the money.* | *You need a background in computer programming for this job.* | *You need to make reservations for Yosemite campgrounds.* **2 you don't need to/you needn't** used to give someone permission not to do something: *It's OK. You don't need to wait.* **3** used to say that someone should do something, or that something should be done: *She needs to see a doctor.* | **sth needs doing/cleaning/fixing etc** (=someone should do it, clean it etc): *The windows need cleaning.* **4 need sb to do sth** if you need someone to do something, you want them to do it for you: *We need you to stay here and answer the phone.*

need[2] n **1** [singular] when something must be done, especially to improve the situation: *an urgent need to improve teaching standards* | *the need for stricter safety regulations* | **if need be** (=if it is necessary): *I'll work all night if need be.* **2** [C usually plural] something you must have in order to have a normal life: *children's educational needs* **3 be in need of** to need something: *She was desperately in need of a vacation.* **4 in need** not having enough food or money: *families in need*

needles

needle   eye

needle   needle

nee·dle[1] /'niːdl/ n [C] **1** a small thin piece of steel used for sewing, that has a point at one end and a hole at the other end **2** a very thin metal tube used to put medicine into your body through your skin **3** a thin pointed piece of metal that moves around on an instrument that measures speed, weight, direction etc, which points to a particular number or direction **4** a small, thin pointed leaf, especially from a PINE tree **5** a long thin stick used in KNITTING **6** the part in a RECORD PLAYER that touches the record **7 like looking for a needle in a haystack** spoken used to say that something is almost impossible to find ➝ see also PINS AND NEEDLES

needle[2] v [T] informal to deliberately annoy someone, often in a joking way: *She's always needling Jim about his weight.*

need·less /'niːdləs/ adj **1 needless to say** used when you are telling someone about something that they probably already know or expect: *Needless to say, with four children we're always busy.* **2** not necessary, and often easily avoided: *needless suffering* —**needlessly** adv

nee·dle·work /'niːdlwɜːkll-wɜːrk/ n [U] sewing or things made by sewing

need·n't /'niːdnt/ spoken especially BrE the short form of 'do not need to'

need·y /'niːdi/ adj **1** having very little food or money: *a needy family* **2 the needy** people who do not have enough food or money

ne·gate /nɪ'geɪt/ v [T] formal to prevent something from having any effect: *The decision would effectively negate last year's Supreme Court ruling.* —**negation** /-'geɪʃən/ n [U]

neg·a·tive[1] /'negətɪv/ adj **1** having a bad or harmful effect: *Raising taxes could have a negative effect on the economy.* ➝ opposite POSITIVE **2** thinking only about the bad things about a situation, person etc: + **about** *She's been very negative about school lately.* ➝ opposite POSITIVE **3** saying no, or saying that you do not like something: *a negative answer* ➝ opposite AFFIRMATIVE **4** if a test is negative, it shows that someone does not have a disease, or that something does not exist ➝ opposite POSITIVE **5** less than zero: *a company experiencing negative growth* **6** a negative electrical current is of the type that is carried by ELECTRONS ➝ opposite POSITIVE —**negatively** adv

negative[2] n [C] **1** a word or phrase that means 'no' ➝ opposite AFFIRMATIVE **2** the film from which a photograph is printed, that shows dark areas as light, and light areas as dark

ne·glect[1] /nɪ'glekt/ v [T] **1** to not pay enough attention to someone or something, or not take care of them: *You mustn't neglect your family.* **2** to not do something that you should do: *The manufacturer had neglected to warn users about the possible health risks.* —**neglected** adj —**neglectful** adj

neglect[2] n [U] when something or someone is not looked after well: *children suffering from neglect*

neg·li·gence /'neglɪdʒəns/ n [U] when someone who is legally responsible for something does not do it properly with the result that something bad happens: *The boy's parents are suing the hospital for negligence.*

neg·li·gent /'neglɪdʒənt/ adj not doing something that you are responsible for, when this has caused something bad to happen

neg·li·gi·ble /'neglɪdʒ₃bəl/ adj very small and unimportant: *The damage was negligible.* —**negligibly** adv

ne·go·ti·a·ble /nɪ'gəʊʃiəbəl, -ʃə-ll-'goʊ-/ adj prices, amounts etc that are negotiable can be discussed and changed

ne·go·ti·ate /nɪ'gəʊʃieɪtll-'goʊ-/ v **1** [I,T] to discuss a political problem or business arrangement in order to reach an agreement: *UN representatives are trying to negotiate a ceasefire.* **2** [T] to succeed in going past or over a difficult place on a road, path etc: *old people carefully negotiating the steps*

ne·go·ti·a·tion /nɪˌgəʊʃiˈeɪʃənǁ-ˌgoʊ-/ n [C usually plural, U] official discussions between two groups who are trying to make an agreement: *Israel held secret negotiations with the PLO in Norway.*

Ne·gro /ˈniːgrəʊǁ-groʊ/ n [C] *old-fashioned* a word meaning a black person, which some people now consider offensive

neigh /neɪ/ v [I] if a horse neighs, it makes a loud noise —**neigh** n [C]

neigh·bour *BrE*, **neighbor** *AmE* /ˈneɪbə-ǁ-bər/ n [C] **1** someone who lives in a house or apartment very near you: *The Nelsons, our next-door neighbors, are always arguing.* (=the people who live in the house next to ours) **2** a person or country that is next to another person or country: *Write down your name and then pass the paper to your neighbor.* | *Germany's neighbours*

neigh·bour·hood *BrE*, **neighborhood** *AmE* /ˈneɪbəhʊdǁ-ər-/ n [C] a small area of a town, or the people who live there: *a neighborhood school* | *He grew up in a tough neighbourhood.*

neigh·bour·ing *BrE*, **neighboring** *AmE* /ˈneɪbərɪŋ/ adj [only before noun] near the place you are talking about: *neighbouring towns*

neigh·bour·ly *BrE*, **neighborly** *AmE* /ˈneɪbəliǁ-ər-/ adj friendly and helpful to the people who live near to you —**neighbourliness** n [U]

nei·ther[1] /ˈnaɪðəǁˈniːðər/ determiner, pron not one and not the other of two people or things: *The game wasn't very exciting, and neither team played well.* → compare EITHER[2], NONE[1]

neither[2] adv **1** used to agree with a negative statement: *"I don't like herb tea." "Neither do I."* | *"I haven't seen Greg in a long time." "Me neither."* (=I have not seen him either) **2** used to add more information to a negative statement: *She couldn't swim, and neither could her husband.* → compare ANY[1], EITHER[3]

neither[3] conjunction **neither ... nor ...** used to emphasize that something is not true about two people or things: *Neither his mother nor his father spoke English.*

neo- /niːəʊ, niːəǁniːoʊ, niːə/ prefix used at the beginning of a word to talk about styles, beliefs etc that are similar to ones that existed in the past: *a neoclassical palace*

ne·on /ˈniːɒnǁ-ɑːn/ n [U] a gas used in tubes in electric lights and signs: *neon light*

neph·ew /ˈnefjuː, ˈnev-ǁˈnef-/ n [C] the son of your brother or sister → see picture at FAMILY → compare NIECE

nep·o·tis·m /ˈnepətɪzəm/ n [U] when people use their power in an unfair way by giving the best jobs to their family, or friends

Nep·tune /ˈneptjuːnǁ-tuːn/ n [singular] the eighth PLANET from the sun

nerd /nɜːdǁnɜːrd/ n [C] *informal* a man who is boring and unfashionable, especially because he spends too much time using and talking about computers —**nerdish** adj —**nerdy** adj

nerve[1] /nɜːvǁnɜːrv/ n **1** [U] the ability to stay calm in a dangerous, difficult, or frightening situation: *It takes a lot of nerve to give a speech in front of so many people.* | **lose your nerve** *I was going to ask her for a pay-rise, but I lost my nerve.* **2** **have the nerve to do sth** *informal* used to say that someone does something very annoying: *And then he had the nerve to criticize my cooking!* **3** [C] a thing in your body that sends information to and from your brain, for example when you feel pain, or when you want to move your muscles

nerve-rack·ing, nerve-wrack·ing /ˈnɜːv-ˌrækɪŋǁ ˈnɜːrv-/ adj very worrying or frightening: *a nerve-racking experience*

nerves /nɜːvzǁnɜːrvz/ n [plural] *informal* **1** the feeling of being nervous because you are worried or a little frightened: *examination nerves* (=before an examination) | **be a bundle of nerves** (=when you are very nervous about something) **2** **get on sb's nerves** to annoy someone

ner·vous /ˈnɜːvəsǁˈnɜːr-/ adj **1** worried or frightened about something, and unable to relax: *Sam's very nervous about his driving test.* | *I wish you'd stop watching me. You're making me nervous.* **2** often worried or frightened, and easily upset: *a thin, rather nervous-looking man* | **be a nervous wreck** (=be very worried and frightened all the time) —**nervously** adv —**nervousness** n [U]

> **USAGE NOTE: nervous and annoyed**
>
> Do not confuse **nervous** (=worried and a little frightened about something) and **annoyed** (=a little angry about something): *He was quite nervous about having to speak in public.* | *I was getting more and more annoyed with his stupid questions.*

nervous break·down /ˌ.. ˈ../ n [C] a mental illness in which someone becomes very worried and unhappy, and cannot live a normal life

nervous sys·tem /ˈ.. ˌ../ n [C] the system of NERVES in your body, which you use to feel pain, heat etc, and to control your movements

nest[1] /nest/ n [C] **1** a place made by a bird to lay its eggs in **2** a place where insects or small animals live: *a hornets' nest*

nest[2] v [I] to make a nest somewhere

nest egg /ˈ. ./ n [C] an amount of money that you save

nes·tle /ˈnesəl/ v **1** [I,T] to move into a comfortable position, in which you are gently touching someone or something: *The little cat nestled in his arms.* **2** [I] to be in a position that is protected by a group of hills, trees, buildings etc: **+ among/between etc** *The village nestled among the Torridon hills.*

nets

fishing net

volleyball net

basketball net

net[1] /net/ n **1 a)** [U] a type of material made of pieces of string, wire etc, which are joined together with spaces between them **b)** [C] a piece of this material that you hit a ball into or over, that you use for catching fish etc: *a fishing net* | *He hit the ball into the net.* → see colour picture on page 636 **2 the Net** the INTERNET: *Businesses that do not have access to the Net are severely disadvantaged.* → see also SAFETY NET

net[2] v [T] **-tted, -tting 1** to get a particular amount of money as profit **2** to catch a fish in a net

net[3] also **nett** BrE /net/ adj **1** a net amount of money is the amount that remains after things such as taxes have been taken away: *a net profit of $500,000* → compare GROSS[1] **2 net weight** the weight of something without its container

net·ting /'netɪŋ/ n [U] material made from pieces of string, wire etc that are tied together with spaces between them

net·work[1] /'netwɜːk‖-wɜːrk/ n [C] **1** a group of radio or television companies that broadcast the same programmes in different parts of a country: *the three big TV networks* **2** a system of things or people that are connected with each other: *the freeway network* | *a network of friends* **3** a set of computers that are connected to each other so that they can share information

network[2] v **1** [I] to meet other people who do the same type of work in order to share information, help each other etc **2** [T] to connect several computers together so that they can share information — **networking** n [U]

neu·rol·o·gy /njʊˈrɒlədʒi‖nʊˈrɑː-/ n [U] the scientific study of the NERVOUS SYSTEM and the diseases relating to it — **neurologist** n [C] — **neurological** /ˌnjʊərəˈlɒdʒɪkəl ‖ˌnʊrəˈlɑː-/ adj

neu·ro·sis /njʊˈrəʊsɪs‖nʊˈroʊ-/ n [C,U], *plural* **neuroses** /-siːz/ a mental illness that makes someone very worried or frightened in a way that does not seem normal

neu·rot·ic /njʊˈrɒtɪk‖nʊˈrɑː-/ adj very worried or frightened about something in a way that does not seem normal: *She's neurotic about her health.* — **neurotic** n [C]

neu·ter[1] /'njuːtə‖'nuːtər/ adj belonging to a group of nouns, adjectives etc in some languages that is different from the FEMININE and the MASCULINE groups

neuter[2] v [T] to remove part of the sex organs of a male animal so that it cannot REPRODUCE

neu·tral[1] /'njuːtrəl‖'nuː-/ adj **1** not supporting any of the countries, groups, or people in a war, argument, election etc: *Switzerland was neutral during World War II.* | *neutral reporting* **2** a neutral colour is not strong or bright, for example grey

neutral[2] n [U] the position of the GEARs of a car when the engine does not turn the wheels: *Start the car in neutral.*

neu·tral·i·ty /njuːˈtrælɪti‖nuː-/ n [U] when a country or person does not support any of the countries or people in a war, argument etc

neu·tral·ize (also **-ise** BrE) /'njuːtrəlaɪz‖'nuː-/ v [T] to prevent something from having any effect: *The medicine neutralizes the acid in your stomach.* — **neutralization** /ˌnjuːtrəlaɪˈzeɪʃən ‖ˌnuːtrələ-/ n [U]

neu·tron /'njuːtrɒn‖'nuːtrɑːn/ n [C] a part of an atom that has no electrical CHARGE

nev·er /'nevə‖-ər/ adv **1** not at any time, or not once: *I've never been to Hawaii.* | *I never knew that you played the guitar!* (=I did not know until now) **2 never mind** *spoken* used to tell someone that something is not important, so they do not need to worry: *"We've missed the bus."* *"Never mind, there's another one in ten minutes."* **3 you never know** *spoken* used to say that something that seems unlikely could happen: *You never know, you might get the job.*

nev·er·the·less /ˌnevəðəˈles‖-vər-/ adv in spite of what has just been mentioned: *I think he's telling the truth. Nevertheless, I don't trust him.*

new /njuː‖nuː/ adj **1** recently made, built, or developed: *I want to see Madonna's new movie.* | *Can the new drugs help her?* **2** recently bought: *Do you like my new shoes?* **3** not used or owned by anyone before: *A used car costs a lot less than a new one.* | **brand new** (=completely new) **4** different, changed, or not known before: *Is your new teacher OK?* | **be new to sb** *a lifestyle that was completely new to me* **5** someone who is new in a place, job etc has recently arrived or started there: *Are you new here?* **6** recently discovered: *The police have found new evidence that suggests he's guilty.* — **newness** n [U]

USAGE NOTE: new, recent, modern, up-to-date, and latest

Use **new** to talk about something that has existed for only a short time: *Have you read Alice Walker's new book?* Use **recent** to talk about something, especially an event, that happened a short time ago: *He won a medal in the recent Olympics.* Use **modern** to describe things that exist now, especially to emphasize that they are different from earlier things of the same kind: *modern machinery* | *modern teaching methods.* Use **up-to-date** to describe the newest knowledge, information, way of doing things etc: *an up-to-date computer system.* Use **latest** to talk about the newest thing in a series of similar things: *the latest issue of Time magazine.*

new·born /ˈnjuːbɔːn‖ˈnuːbɔːrn/ adj a newborn

baby or animal has just been born —**newborn** *n* [C]

new·com·er /ˈnjuːˌkʌmə‖ˈnuːˌkʌmər/ *n* [C] someone who has recently arrived somewhere or recently started doing an activity: **+ to** *a newcomer to teaching*

new·fan·gled /ˌnjuːˈfæŋɡəld‖ˌnuː-/ *adj* newfangled ideas, machines etc have been recently invented but seem complicated or unnecessary: *newfangled ideas about raising children*

new·ly /ˈnjuːli‖ˈnuːli/ *adv* **newly built/married/ qualified etc** very recently built, married etc

new·ly·weds /ˈnjuːliwedz‖ˈnuː-/ *n* [plural] a man and a woman who have recently got married

news /njuːz‖nuːz/ *n* **1** [U] information about something that has happened recently: *an interesting piece of news* | **good/bad news** *I have some good news for you!* | **hear news** (=receive news): *Have you heard any news from Emma yet?* **piece of news** *an interesting piece of news* **2** [U] reports of recent events in the newspapers, on the radio or on television: *national and local news* | **+ of** *more news of an explosion in the city* | **news story/report** *a news report on the Middle East* **3 the news** a regular television or radio programme that gives you reports of recent events: *What time is the news on?* | **on the news** *I heard it on the news last night.* **4 that's news to me** *spoken* used when you are surprised or annoyed because you have not been told something earlier: *He's getting married? That's news to me.*

news a·gen·cy /ˈ. ˌ.../ *n* [C] a company that supplies reports on recent events to newspapers, radio, and television

news·a·gent /ˈnjuːzˌeɪdʒənt‖ˈnuːz-/ *n* [C] *BrE* **1 newsagent's** a shop that sells newspapers and magazines **2** someone who owns or works in a shop selling newspapers and magazines

news bul·le·tin /ˈ. ˌ.../ *n* [C] **1** *BrE* a short news programme on radio or television **2** *AmE* a short news programme about something important that has just happened, that is broadcast suddenly in the middle of a television or radio programme; NEWSFLASH *BrE*

news·cast /ˈnjuːzkɑːst‖ˈnuːzkæst/ *n* [C] *AmE* a news programme on the radio or television

news·cast·er /ˈnjuːzˌkɑːstə‖ˈnuːzˌkæstər/ *n* [C] someone who reads the news on television or radio

news·flash /ˈnjuːzflæʃ‖ˈnuːz-/ *n* [C] *BrE* a very short news programme about something important that has just happened, that is broadcast suddenly in the middle of a television or radio programme; NEWS BULLETIN *AmE*

news·let·ter /ˈnjuːzˌletə‖ˈnuːzˌletər/ *n* [C] a sheet of printed news about an organization that is sent regularly to its members: *our church newsletter*

news·pa·per /ˈnjuːsˌpeɪpə‖ˈnuːzˌpeɪpər/ *n* **1** also **paper** [C] a set of folded sheets of paper containing news, advertisements etc, that is sold daily or weekly: *the local newspaper* ➝ see colour picture on page 474 **2** [U] sheets of paper from old newspapers: *plates wrapped in newspaper*

USAGE NOTE: newspaper

Remember to use the preposition **in** for expressions such as: *I read it* **in the newspaper.** | *an*

---

advertisement **in the Evening Standard.**

news·print /ˈnjuːzˌprɪnt‖ˈnuːz-/ *n* [U] the paper and ink that is used to print newspapers

news·read·er /ˈnjuːzˌriːdə‖ˈnuːzˌriːdər/ *n* [C] *BrE* someone who reads the news on television or radio; ANCHOR *AmE*

news·stand /ˈnjuːzstænd‖ˈnuːz-/ *n* [C] a place on a street where newspapers are sold

news·wor·thy /ˈnjuːzˌwɜːði‖ˈnuːzˌwɜːrði/ *adj* important or interesting enough to be reported as news: *newsworthy events*

newt /njuːt‖nuːt/ *n* [C] a small animal with a long body, four legs, and a tail, that lives in water

New Tes·ta·ment /ˌ. ˈ.../ *n* **the New Testament** the part of the Bible that deals mainly with the life of Jesus Christ ➝ compare OLD TESTAMENT

new wave /ˌ. ˈ.◂/ *n* [U] people who are trying to introduce new ideas in music, films, art, politics etc: *the new wave of British cinema* —**new wave** *adj*

New World /ˌ. ˈ.◂/ *n* **the New World** North, Central, and South America: *Columbus' arrival in the New World*

New Year /ˌ. ˈ.◂/ *n* [U] the time when you celebrate the beginning of the year: *Happy New Year!*

new year *n* **the new year** the first few weeks of a year: *We're opening three new stores in the new year.*

New Year's Day /ˌ. ˈ./ *n* [singular, U] 1st January, the first day of the year in Western countries

New Year's Eve /ˌ. ˈ./ *n* [singular, U] 31st December, the last day of the year in Western countries

next¹ /nekst/ *adj* **1** the next day, time, event etc is the one that happens after the present one: *The next flight leaves in 45 minutes.* | *They returned to New York the next day.* | **next time** (=when this happens again): *Next time, be more careful!* | **next Monday/May/year etc** *See you next week.* **2** the next place is the one closest to where you are now: *Turn left at the next corner.* | *the people at the next table* **3** the next person or thing in a list, line etc is the one after the present one: *Who will be the next President?* | *Read the next chapter by Friday.* **4 the next best thing** the thing or situation that is almost as good as the one you really want: *Talking on the phone is the next best thing to being together.*

next² *adv* **1** immediately afterwards: *What shall we do next?* | *First, read the instructions. Next, write your name at the top of the page.* **2 next to** very close to someone or something, with nothing in between: *I sat next to a really nice lady on the plane.* | *Your glasses are there, next to the phone.* ➝ see colour picture on page 474 **3 next to nothing** very little: *I bought the car for next to nothing!*

next³ *pron* **1** the person or thing in a list, line etc that comes after the person or thing you are dealing with now: *Carrots. Milk. What's next on the list?* | *Who's next to see the doctor?* **2 the week/weekend/year etc after next** the week etc that follows the next one: *Let's meet some time the week after next.*

N

next door /ˌ. '.◂/ *adv* **1** in the room or building that is next to yours: *The Simpsons live next door.* **2 next door to** next to a building: *The baker's is right next door to the school.* —**next-door** *adj: my next-door neighbour*

next of kin /ˌ. . '. / *n* [C], *plural* **next of kin** the person who is your closest living relative: *Her next of kin was informed of her death.*

NHS /ˌen eɪtʃ 'es/ *n* **the NHS** the National Health Service; the British system that provides free medical treatment for everyone, paid for by taxes

nib /nɪb/ *n* [C] the part of a pen that puts the ink on the page

nib·ble /'nɪbəl/ *v* [I,T] to eat a small amount of food with very small bites: **+ on** *She was nibbling on a carrot.* —**nibble** *n* [C]

nice /naɪs/ *adj* **1** pleasant, attractive, or enjoyable: *Did you have a nice time at the beach?* | *That's a nice sweater.* | **nice and warm/cool/sweet etc** *It's nice and warm in here.* | **look/taste/smell nice** *You look nice in that suit.* | **it is nice to do sth** *It would be nice to go to Spain.* **2** friendly or kind: *They're all very nice people.* | **it is nice of sb (to do sth)** *It was nice of you to come.* | **be nice to sb** *Be nice to your little sister.* **3 (it's) nice to meet you/nice meeting you** spoken used when you meet someone for the first time —**niceness** *n* [U]

nice-look·ing /ˌ. '..◂/ *adj* attractive: *He's a nice-looking guy.*

nice·ly /'naɪsli/ *adv* **1** very well: *Belinda is always so nicely dressed.* | *His arm is healing nicely.* **2** in a polite or friendly way: *Ask nicely and I'll give you some chocolate.*

ni·ce·ty /'naɪsᵻti/ *n* [C] a small detail of how to behave: *She doesn't bother with the social niceties.*

niche /niːʃ, nɪtʃ/ *n* [C] **1** a job or activity that is perfect for someone's abilities and character: *She found her niche as a fashion designer.* **2** a hollow place in a wall, often made to hold STATUES

nick¹ /nɪk/ *n* **1 in the nick of time** just before it is too late or before something bad happens: *The doctor arrived in the nick of time.* **2** [C] a very small cut on the surface or edge of something **3 in good nick/in bad nick** *BrE informal* in good condition or in bad condition: *Our car's old but it's in good nick.*

nick² *v* [T] **1** to accidentally make a small cut on the surface or edge of something: *I nicked my chin when I was shaving.* **2** *BrE informal* to steal something: *Someone's nicked my bike!*

nick·el /'nɪkəl/ *n* **1** [C] a coin used in the US and Canada worth 5 cents **2** [U] a hard silver-white metal that is an ELEMENT and is used for making other metals

nickel-and-dime /ˌ.. . '.◂/ *adj AmE informal* not important or too concerned with saving small amounts of money: *We can't solve such problems with nickel-and-dime solutions.*

nick·name¹ /'nɪkneɪm/ *n* [C] a funny or unusual name, or a shorter form of someone's real name, that are often called by their friends or family: *His nickname was 'Curly' because of his hair.*

nickname² *v* [T] to give someone a nickname: *At school Robert was nicknamed Robbo.*

nic·o·tine /'nɪkətiːn/ *n* [U] the ADDICTIVE substance in tobacco

nicotine patch /'... ,. / *n* [C] a small piece of material containing nicotine that people wear on their skin to help them stop smoking

niece /niːs/ *n* [C] the daughter of your brother or sister, or the daughter of your husband's or wife's brother or sister ➡ see picture at FAMILY ➡ compare NEPHEW

nif·ty /'nɪfti/ *adj informal* very good, fast, or effective: *a nifty card trick*

nig·ger /'nɪgər/ *n* [C] a very offensive word for a black person

nig·gle /'nɪgəl/ *v* [T] **1** to complain about small details that are not important: **+ over** *She niggled over every detail of the bill.* **2** to annoy or worry someone slightly over a long time: *It niggled him that she had told him the wrong date.* —**niggle** *n* [C]

nig·gling /'nɪgəlɪŋ/ *adj* **niggling doubt/suspicion etc** a doubt etc that worries you slightly for a long time

nigh /naɪ/ *adv prep* **1** *literary* near **2** *well nigh/nigh on* *old-fashioned* almost

night /naɪt/ *n* **1** [C,U] the dark part of each 24-hour period, when people usually sleep: *I woke up in the middle of the night.* | **at night** *It's very cold here at night.* | **all night (long)** *Some supermarkets stay open all night.* | **a good night's sleep** (=when you sleep well all night): *What you need is a good night's sleep.* | **a late night** (=when you go to bed later than usual): *You look tired. Too many late nights!* **2** [C,U] the evening: **last night** *Did you go out last night?* | **tomorrow night** *Some friends are coming over tomorrow night.* | **Monday/Saturday etc night** *There's a party at Val's on Friday night.* | **a night out** (=when you go to a party, restaurant etc): *We had a really good night out.* **3 night and day/day and night** all the time: *The prisoners were guarded day and night.*

night·club /'naɪtklʌb/ *n* [C] a place where people can drink and dance, that is open late at night

night·dress /'naɪtdres/ *n* [C] a piece of loose clothing, like a dress, that women wear in bed

night·fall /'naɪtfɔːl‖-fɑːl/ *n* [U] *literary* the time in the evening when the sky becomes darker; DUSK

night·gown /'naɪtgaʊn/ *n* [C] a nightdress

night·ie /'naɪti/ *n* [C] *informal* a nightdress

nigh·tin·gale /'naɪtɪŋgeɪl/ *n* [C] a small European wild bird that sings beautifully, especially at night

night·life /'naɪtlaɪf/ *n* [U] entertainment in places where you can dance, drink alcohol etc in the evening: *Las Vegas is famous for its nightlife.*

night·ly /'naɪtli/ *adj, adv* happening every night: *a nightly news broadcast* | *The bar is open nightly.*

night·mare /'naɪtmeə‖-mer/ *n* [C] **1** a very frightening dream: *She still has nightmares about the accident.* **2** a very unpleasant experience: *It was a nightmare driving home in the snow.* —**nightmarish** *adj*

night owl /'. . / *n* [C] *informal* someone who enjoys being awake and feels most active late at night

night school /'. ./ n [U] classes taught in the evening: *I'm studying Spanish at night school.*

night shift /'. ./ n [C,U] a period of time at night during which people regularly work: **be on night shift** *Lee's on night shift at the hospital this week.*

night·stand /'naɪtstænd/ n [C] *AmE* a small table beside a bed

night·time /'naɪt-taɪm/ n [U] the time during the night when the sky is dark → opposite DAY-TIME

night watch·man /,. '../ n [C] someone whose job is to guard a building at night

nil /nɪl/ n [U] nothing or zero: *The score was seven nil.* | *His chances of winning are almost nil.*

nim·ble /'nɪmbəl/ adj able to move quickly and skilfully: *nimble fingers* | *a nimble climber* —**nimbly** adv

nin·com·poop /'nɪŋkəmpuːp/ n [C] *old-fashioned* a stupid person

nine /naɪn/ number **1** the number 9 **2** nine o'clock: *I have to be in the office by nine.*

nine·teen /,naɪn'tiːn◂/ number **1** the number 19 **2 talk nineteen to the dozen** to talk very quickly and without stopping —**nineteenth** number

nine-to-five /,. . './ adv work **nine-to-five** to work from nine o'clock until five o'clock, the hours that most people work in an office —**nine-to-five** adj: *a nine-to-five job*

nine·ty /'naɪnti/ number **1** the number 90 **2 the nineties a)** the years between 1990 and 1999 **b)** the numbers between 90 and 99: *The temperature was in the nineties.* **3 be in your nineties** to be aged between 90 and 99 —**ninetieth** number

ninth /naɪnθ/ number **1** 9th **2** one of nine equal parts

nip[1] /nɪp/ -**pped, -pping** v **1** [I,T] to bite someone or something with a small sharp bite: **+ at** *That stupid dog keeps nipping at my ankles.* **2** [I] *BrE informal* to go somewhere for a short time: *I've just got to nip out to the shops.* **3 nip something in the bud** to prevent something from becoming a problem by stopping it as soon as it starts

nip[2] n [C] a small sharp bite, or the action of biting someone or something

nip·ple /'nɪpəl/ n [C] **1** the dark raised circle in the middle of a woman's breast, which a baby sucks in order to get milk **2** one of the two dark raised circles on a man's chest **3** *AmE* the small piece of rubber on the end of a baby's bottle; TEAT *BrE*

nip·py /'nɪpi/ adj **1** weather that is nippy is cold **2** *BrE* able to move quickly: *a nippy little car*

nit /nɪt/ n [C] **1** the egg of a small insect that lives on people's heads **2** *BrE informal* a silly person

nit·pick·ing /'nɪt,pɪkɪŋ/ n [U] when someone criticizes small, unimportant details about another person's work, in a way that is very annoying —**nitpicking** adj: *nitpicking criticisms*

ni·trate /'naɪtreɪt, -trə̥t/ n [C,U] a chemical that is used to improve the soil that crops are grown in

ni·tro·gen /'naɪtrədʒən/ n [U] a gas that is an ELEMENT and is the main part of the Earth's air

nit·ty-grit·ty /,nɪti 'grɪti/ n **the nitty-gritty** *informal* the basic and practical facts and details: *Let's get down to the nitty-gritty and work out the cost.*

nit·wit /'nɪt-wɪt/ n [C] *informal* a silly person

no[1] /nəʊ‖noʊ/ adv **1** used to give a negative reply to a question, offer, or demand: *"Is she married?" "No, she's not."* | *"Do you want some more coffee?" "No, thanks."* | **say no** *I asked Dad if I could have a dog, but he said no.* **2** *spoken* used when you disagree with a statement: *"Gary's weird." "No, he's just shy."* **3** *spoken* used when you do not want someone to do something: *No, Jimmy, don't touch that.* → opposite YES[1]

no[2] determiner **1** not any or not at all: *I'm sorry, there are no tickets left.* | *He has no time to help.* **2** used on a sign to show that something is not allowed: *No smoking.* → see also **in no time** (TIME[1])

USAGE NOTE: no and not

Use **no** before nouns to mean 'not any', or to say that something is not allowed: *He has no job and no money.* | *a 'no smoking' sign.* You can also use **no** to agree with negative questions: *"It's not raining, is it?" "No, it isn't."* Use **not** to make a verb negative: *I'm not going camping.* When the word 'all' and words that begin with 'every-' are the subject of a sentence, use **not** to make it negative: *Not all the students finished the tests.* | *Not everyone likes horror movies.* You can also use **not** before names, pronouns, adverbs of frequency, and prepositions: *"Guess who's at the door?" "Not George, surely!"* | *"Do you watch sports on TV?" "Not very often."* | *It's open on Saturday, but not on Sunday.*

---

no[3] n [singular], plural **noes** a negative answer or decision: *Her answer was a definite no.*

no. plural **nos.** the written abbreviation of 'number'

no·bil·i·ty /nəʊ'bɪlɪ̥ti, nə-‖noʊ-, nə-/ n **1 the nobility** the group of people in some countries who have the highest social rank **2** [U] the quality of being noble

no·ble[1] /'nəʊbəl‖'noʊ-/ adj **1** morally good or generous: *a noble achievement* **2** belonging to the nobility: *noble families* —**nobly** adv

noble[2] **no·ble·man** /'nəʊbəlmən‖'noʊ-/ **no·ble·wom·an** /'nəʊbəl,wʊmən‖'noʊ-/ n [C] someone who belongs to the highest social rank

no·bod·y[1] /'nəʊbədi‖'noʊbɑːdi, -bədi/ pron no one

nobody[2] n [C] someone who is not important, successful, or famous: *I'm sick of being a nobody!*

noc·tur·nal /nɒk'tɜːnl‖nɑːk'tɜːr-/ adj **1** *technical* nocturnal animals are active at night and

---

GRAMMAR NOTE: the present perfect (2)
You use the **present perfect: 1** to talk about something that happened in the past, but which still affects the situation now: *I've lost my passport.* **2** to talk about something that happened in the past, and continues to happen now: *I have lived in London for many years.* (=I still live there now).

sleep during the day **2** *formal* happening at night

nod

The lady nodded her head. Sam shook his head.

nod /nɒd‖nɑːd/ *v* **-dded, -dding 1** [I,T] to move your head up and down, especially to say yes or to show that you understand something: *"Are you Jill?" he asked. She smiled and nodded.*|*Ben nodded his head sympathetically.* **2** to move your head up and down once in order to greet someone or to give them a sign: **+ to/at/towards** *I nodded to the waiter,*|*"Sally's in there," Jim said, nodding towards the kitchen.* —**nod** *n* [C]
  nod off *phr v* [I] *informal* to begin to sleep, often without intending to: *His speech was so boring I kept nodding off.*

no-frills /ˌ. ˈ.◂/ *adj* without any features that are not completely necessary; basic: *a no-frills airline*

no-go ar·e·a /ˌ. ˈ. ˌ.../ *n* [C] a place where there is a lot of crime and violence and where it is dangerous for people to go

noise /nɔɪz/ *n* [C,U] sound, or a sound, that is too loud, annoying, or not intended: *the noise of the traffic*|*Did you hear that clicking noise?*|**make (a) noise** *Stop making so much noise.*

> **USAGE NOTE: noise and sound**
>
> A **sound** is anything that you can hear: *the sound of the wind in the trees.* A **noise** is a sound, but is usually a loud, unexpected, or unpleasant one: *What's that noise?*|*the noise of the traffic*|*Those kids are making a lot of noise upstairs.*

noise·less·ly /ˈnɔɪzləsli/ *adv* without making any sound: *A waiter noiselessly entered the room.*

noise pol·lu·tion /ˈ. . ˌ.../ *n* [U] annoying loud continuous noise that has a harmful effect on people's lives: *noise pollution from nearby traffic*

nois·y /ˈnɔɪzi/ *adj* making a lot of noise, or full of noise: *noisy schoolkids*|*a noisy bar* —**noisily** *adv*

no·mad /ˈnəʊmæd‖ˈnoʊ-/ *n* [C] a member of a tribe that does not live in one fixed place, but travels around a country and stays in different areas: *the desert nomads of North Africa* —**nomadic** /nəʊˈmædɪk‖noʊ-/ *adj*

no-man's land /ˈ. . ˌ./ *n* [singular, U] land that no one owns or controls, especially an area between two opposing armies

nom·i·nal /ˈnɒmɪnəl‖ˈnɑː-/ *adj* **1 nominal leader/head etc** someone who has the title of leader etc although in fact no one person leads their organization or group **2 nominal amount/price/sum etc** a small amount of money: *I bought the house for a nominal sum in 1963.*

nom·i·nal·ly /ˈnɒmɪnəli‖ˈnɑː-/ *adv* officially described as something, when the description may not be true: *a nominally independent company*

nom·i·nate /ˈnɒmɪneɪt‖ˈnɑː-/ *v* [T] to officially suggest someone for a job or position: **nominate sb for/as sth** *I'd like to nominate Margaret as class representative.* —**nomination** /ˌnɒmɪˈneɪʃən‖ˌnɑː-/ *n* [C,U]

nom·i·nee /ˌnɒmɪˈniː‖ˌnɑː-/ *n* [C] someone who has been nominated for something: *Oscar nominee, Winona Ryder*

non- /nɒn‖nɑːn/ *prefix* used at the beginning of some words to mean 'not': *non-acoholic drinks*|*non-smokers*

non-ag·gres·sion /ˌ. .ˈ../ *n* [U] when a country or government does not use military force or threats against another: *a policy of non-aggression*

non-al·co·hol·ic /ˌ. . .ˈ.◂/ *adj* a non-alcoholic drink does not have any alcohol in it

non·cha·lant /ˈnɒnʃələnt‖ˌnɑːnʃəˈlɑːnt/ *adj* calm and not seeming worried or excited: *young men trying to look nonchalant* —**nonchalance** *n* [U] —**nonchalantly** *adv*

non-com·ba·tant /ˌ. ˈ...‖ˌ. .ˈ../ *n* [C] a member of an army who does not fight, for example an army doctor

non-com·mit·tal /ˌnɒnkəˈmɪtl◂‖ˌnɑːn-/ *adj* not giving a definite answer or opinion: *a non-committal reply* —**noncommitally** *adv*

non-con·form·ist /ˌnɒnkənˈfɔːmɪst‖ˌnɑːnkənˈfɔːr-/ *n* [C] someone who does not live or think in the way that most people do: *a political non-conformist* —**nonconformist** *adj*: *nonconformist views*

non·de·script /ˈnɒndɪˌskrɪpt‖ˌnɑːndɪˈskrɪpt◂/ *adj* not having any noticeable or interesting qualities: *a nondescript man in a grey suit*

none¹ /nʌn/ *pron* **1** not any of something: *"Can I have some more coffee?" "Sorry, there's none left."*|**+ of** *None of the money is mine.* **2** not one person or thing: **+ of** *None of my friends are here.*|**none at all** *Any car is better than none at all.*

none² *adv* **1 none the worse/wiser etc** not any worse than before, not knowing any more than before etc: *We were none the wiser for his explanation.* **2 none too soon/pleased/easy etc** not at all soon, happy etc: *Life was none too easy in those days.*

non·en·ti·ty /nɒˈnentɪti‖nɑː-/ *n* [C] someone who is not important or famous

none·the·less /ˌnʌnðəˈles◂/ *adv* *formal* in spite of what has just been mentioned; NEVERTHELESS: *The economy is improving, but people are losing jobs nonetheless.*

non-e·vent /ˌ. .ˈ./ *n* [C usually singular] *informal* an event that is much less exciting or interesting than you expected: *My 21st birthday was a complete non-event.*

non·ex·ist·ent /ˌnɒnɪɡˈzɪstənt◂‖ˌnɑːn-/ *adj* not

existing at all: *Industry is practically nonexistent in the area.*

non·fic·tion /ˌ. ˈ..ˌ/ *n* [U] books etc about real facts or events, not imagined ones —**nonfiction** *adj* → compare FICTION

non·flam·ma·ble /ˌnɒnˈflæməbəl‖ˌnɑːn-/ *adj* difficult or impossible to burn → opposite IN-FLAMMABLE, FLAMMABLE

non·in·ter·ven·tion /ˌ. ...ˈ..ˌ/ *n* [U] when a government refuses to become involved in the affairs of other countries

no-no /ˈ. ./ *n* [C] *informal* something that is not allowed, or not socially acceptable: *My parents think sex before marriage is a definite no-no.*

non-non·sense /ˌ. ˈ..ˌ/ *adj* [only before noun] very practical and direct: *a no-nonsense attitude to work*

non·pay·ment /ˌ. ˈ..ˌ/ *n* [U] when you do not pay money that you owe: + **of** *nonpayment of rent*

non·plussed /nɒnˈplʌst‖nɑːn-/ *adj* so surprised that you do not know what to say or do: *I was quite nonplussed at his news.*

non·prof·it-mak·ing /ˌnɒnˈprɒfɪ̣tmeɪkɪŋ‖ˌnɑːnˈprɑː-/ *BrE* **non-profit** *AmE* — *adj* a non-profitmaking organization uses the money it earns to help in its work instead of making a profit

non·pro·lif·e·ra·tion /ˌ. ...ˈ..ˌ/ *n* [U] the act of limiting the number of NUCLEAR or chemical weapons that are being made across the world

non-re·new·a·ble /ˌ.ˈ..⊲ / *adj* non-renewable types of energy such as coal or gas cannot be replaced after they have been used

non·sense /ˈnɒnsəns‖ˈnɑːnsens/ *n* [U] **1** statements or opinions that are not true or seem very stupid: *"This dress makes me look fat." "Nonsense, you look great!"* **2** stupid and annoying behaviour: *I'm not putting up with any more of your nonsense!* **3** speech or writing that has no real meaning or cannot be understood: *Children often make up nonsense songs.* —**nonsensical** /nɒnˈsensɪ̣kəl‖nɑːn-/ *adj*

non seq·ui·tur /ˌnɒn ˈsekwɪ̣tə‖ˌnɑːn ˈsekwɪ̣tər/ *n* [C] *formal* a statement that seems completely unrelated to the statements that were made before it

non-smok·er /ˌ. ˈ..ˌ/ *n* [C] someone who does not smoke

non-smok·ing /nɒnˈsməʊkɪŋ‖nɑːnˈsmoʊ-/ *adj* a nonsmoking area or building is one where smoking is not allowed

non·stan·dard /ˌ. ˈ.. ⊲ / *adj* nonstandard words, expressions, or pronunciations are sometimes considered to be incorrect by educated speakers → compare STANDARD[2]

non-start·er /ˌnɒnˈstɑːtə‖ˌnɑːnˈstɑːrtər/ *n* [C usually singular] *informal* an idea or plan that is very unlikely to succeed: *The whole idea sounds like a nonstarter to me.*

non-stick /ˌ. ˈ.⊲ / *adj* a nonstick pan has a special inside surface that food will not stick to

non-stop /ˌnɒnˈstɒp⊲‖ˌnɑːnˈstɑːp⊲ / *adv*, *adj* without stopping: *Dan worked nonstop for 12 hours. | a nonstop flight to New York*

non·vi·o·lence /ˌ. ˈ...ˌ/ *n* [U] when you oppose a government without fighting, for example by not obeying laws: *a policy of nonviolence* —**nonviolent** *adj*: *nonviolent protest*

noo·dle /ˈnuːdl/ *n* [C usually plural] long thin pieces of food made from flour, water, and eggs, which are cooked by boiling them: *chicken noodle soup*

nook /nʊk/ *n* **1** [C] a small quiet place: *a shady nook* **2 every nook and cranny** every part of a place: *We've searched every nook and cranny for that key.*

noon /nuːn/ *n* [U] 12 o'clock in the middle of the day; MIDDAY: *Lunch will be served at noon.*

no one /ˈ. ./ *pron* not anyone; NOBODY: *I called last night but no one was home.*

noose /nuːs/ *n* [C] a circle of a rope that becomes tighter as it is pulled

no·place /ˈ. ./ *adv* *AmE informal* nowhere: *There's noplace left to hide.*

nor /nɔː‖nɔːr/ *linking word* **1 neither ... nor** used to show that two facts, qualities, actions etc are both not true: *My mother's family were neither rich nor poor. | They can neither read nor write.* **2** *formal* used after a negative statement to make another negative statement: *He wasn't at the meeting, nor was he at work yesterday.*

norm /nɔːm‖nɔːrm/ *n* [C] **1 the norm** what is usual or average: *Unemployment is becoming the norm here.* **2** [C usually plural] the usual and acceptable way of behaving: *the values and norms of civilized society*

nor·mal /ˈnɔːməl‖ˈnɔːr-/ *adj* usual, typical, or expected: *Greg isn't acting like his normal self. | normal business hours* → opposite ABNORMAL

nor·mal·i·ty /nɔːˈmælɪ̣ti‖nɔːr-/ also **nor·mal·cy** /ˈnɔːməlsi‖ˈnɔːr-/ *AmE* — *n* [U] a situation in which everything happens in the usual way

nor·mal·ize (also **-ise** *BrE*) /ˈnɔːməlaɪz‖ˈnɔːr-/ *v* [I,T] to become normal again, or to make a situation become normal again: *In March 1944 Russia normalized relations with Italy.* —**normalization** /ˌnɔːməlaɪˈzeɪʃən‖ˌnɔːrmələ-/ *n* [U]

nor·mal·ly /ˈnɔːməli‖ˈnɔːr-/ *adv* **1** usually: *I normally go to bed around 11.* **2** in the usual or expected way: *Try to relax and breathe normally.*

north[1], **North** /nɔːθ‖nɔːrθ/ *n* [singular, U] **1** the direction towards the top of a map, the world, or to the left of someone facing the rising sun: *Which way is north?* **2 the north** the northern part of a country or area: *My grandparents came from the north.*

north[2], **North** *adj* **1** in the north or facing north: *the north end of the field* **2 north wind** a wind that comes from the north

north[3] *adv* **1** towards the north: *We headed north.* **2 up north** in the north or to the north: *The Simpsons are moving up north in May.*

USAGE NOTE: north/south/east/west of and **in the north/south/east/west of**

Use **north/south/east/west of** as an adjective phrase to describe where a place is in relation to another place: *Chicago is south of Milwaukee.* Use **in the north/south/east/west of** as a noun phrase to say which part of a place you are talking about: *The mountains are in the north of the province.*

---

north·bound /ˈnɔːθbaʊnd‖ˈnɔːrθ-/ *adj* travelling or leading towards the north: *northbound traffic*

north·east¹, **Northeast** /ˌnɔːθˈiːst◄ ‖ ˌnɔːrθ-/ *n*
1 [U] the direction that is between the north and the east **2** **the Northeast** the northeast part of a country —**northeastern** *adj*

northeast², **Northeast** *adj, adv* in, from, or towards the northeast: *a northeast wind | driving northeast*

nor·ther·ly /ˈnɔːðəli ‖ ˈnɔːrðərli/ *adj* **1** towards the north or in the north: *a northerly direction* **2** a northerly wind comes from the north

nor·thern , **Northern** /ˈnɔːðən ‖ ˈnɔːrðərn/ *adj* in or from the north part of a country or area: *northern California*

nor·thern·er , **Northerner** /ˈnɔːðənə ‖ ˈnɔːrðər-nər/ *n* [C] someone who comes from the north part of a country

nor·thern·most /ˈnɔːðənməʊst ‖ ˈnɔːrðərn-məʊst/ *adj* furthest north: *the northernmost tip of the island*

North Pole /ˌ. ˈ./ *n* [singular] the most north-ern point on the surface of the Earth, or the area around it

north·ward, **northwards** /ˈnɔːθwəd ‖ ˈnɔːrθwərd/ *adv* going or facing towards the north —**northward** *adj*

north·west¹, **Northwest** /ˌnɔːθˈwest◄ ‖ ˌnɔːrθ-/ *n* **1** [U] the direction that is between the north and the west **2** **the Northwest** the northwest part of a country —**northwestern** *adj*

northwest², **Northwest** *adj, adv* in, from, or to-wards the northwest: *a northwest wind | walking northwest*

nose¹ /nəʊz ‖ noʊz/ *n* **1** [C] the part of your face that you smell with and breathe through: *Someone punched him on the nose. | sb's nose is running* (=liquid is coming out of it because they have a cold) → see picture at HEAD **2** **(right) under sb's nose** so close to someone that they should notice, but do not: *The prisoner escaped right under our noses!* **3** **stick/poke your nose into** *informal* to ask questions about someone else's private life in a way that annoys them: *Jane's always sticking her nose into other people's business.* **4** **turn your nose up (at sth)** to refuse to accept something because you do not like it: *Most kids turn their noses up at fresh vegetables.* **5** [C] the front end of a plane, ROCKET etc **6** **look down your nose at sb** to think you are much better than someone else **7** **red-nosed/long-nosed etc** having a nose that is red, long etc → see also **blow your nose** (BLOW)

nose² *v* [I,T] move forward slowly and carefully: *The taxi nosed out into the traffic.*
nose around (also **nose about** *BrE*) *phr v* [I,T
nose around/about sth] to look at things that do not belong to you in order to find out pri-vate information: *Why were you nosing around in my room?*

nose·bleed /ˈnəʊzbliːd ‖ ˈnoʊz-/ *n* **have a nose-bleed** to have blood coming out of your nose

nose·dive /ˈnəʊzdaɪv ‖ ˈnoʊz-/ *n* **1** **take a nosedive** if amounts, prices etc take a nosedive, they suddenly fall: *Profits took a nosedive last year.* **2** [C] a sudden steep drop by a plane, with its front end pointing towards the ground —**nosedive** *v* [I]

nose job /ˈ. ./ *n* [C] *informal* a medical oper-ation on someone's nose in order to improve its shape

nosey *adj* another spelling of NOSY

nos·tal·gia /nɒˈstældʒə ‖ naː-/ *n* [U] the slightly sad feeling you have when you remember happy events from the past: **+ for** *nostalgia for his life on the farm* —**nostalgic** *adj* —**nostalgically** /-kli/ *adv*

nos·tril /ˈnɒstrɪl ‖ ˈnaː-/ *n* [C] one of the two holes at the bottom end of your nose, which you breathe through → see picture at HEAD

nos·y, **nosey** /ˈnəʊzi ‖ ˈnoʊ-/ *adj* always trying to find out private information about someone: *Our neighbours are really nosy.* —**nosiness** *n* [U]

not /nɒt ‖ naːt/ *adv* **1** used to make a word or statement have the opposite meaning: *Most stores are not open on Sundays. | He does not speak English. | not at all I was not at all surprised to see her. | not a lot/not much* (=little): *Not much is known about the disease.* **2** used in-stead of a whole phrase to mean the opposite of what has been mentioned before it: *No one knows if the story is true or not. | I hope not. "Is Mark still ill?" "I hope not." → compare SO¹* **3** **not only ... (but) also** used to say that in addi-tion to one thing being true, something else is also true: *She's not only funny, she's also clever.* **4** **not a/not one** not any person or thing; none: *Not one of the students knew the answer.* **5** **not bad!** *spoken* used to say that something is good: *"I got a B+ on my test!" "Not bad!"* **6** **not that ...** used to say that what you said before is not important to someone: *Sarah has a new boy-friend – not that I care.*

no·ta·ble /ˈnəʊtəbəl ‖ ˈnoʊ-/ *adj* important, interesting, or unusual enough to be noticed: *an area notable for its forests*

no·ta·bly /ˈnəʊtəbli/ *adv* especially; particu-larly: *Some politicians, most notably the Presi-dent, refused to comment.*

no·ta·tion /nəʊˈteɪʃən ‖ noʊ-/ *n* [C,U] a system of marks and signs to show musical sounds, numbers etc

notch¹ /nɒtʃ ‖ naːtʃ/ *n* [C] a V-shaped cut in a surface or edge: *He cut a notch into the stick.*

notch² *v* [T]
notch sth ↔ **up** *phr v* [T] to achieve a victory or a particular total: *He has notched up four goals in four games.*

note¹ /nəʊt ‖ noʊt/ *n* **1** [C] a short informal letter: *I wrote Jane a note to thank her.* **2** [C] something that you write down in order to re-member something: **make a note of** *I'll just make a note of your new address.* **3** [C] a particular musical sound or PITCH, or the sign in written music that means this: *He hummed a few notes of a tune.* **4** [C] *BrE* paper money; BILL *AmE: a ten-pound note* **5** **take note (of sth)** to pay careful attention to something: *We must always take note of our customers' views.* **6** **a note of anger/sadness etc** a slight quality or feeling of anger, sadness etc: *The movie ended on a note of hope.* **7** **of note** important: *a writer of note* → see also **compare notes** (COMPARE)

note² *v* [T] **1** to notice or pay careful attention to something: **+ that** *Please note that the museum is closed on Mondays.* **2** also **note down** to write something down so that you will remember it: *He noted down my name.*

note·book /ˈnəʊtbʊk ‖ ˈnoʊt-/ *n* [C] **1** a book in which you can write notes **2** a small computer that is about the size of a book

not·ed /ˈnəʊtɪd‖ˈnoʊ-/ *adj* well-known; famous: *a noted author* | **+ for** *an area noted for its cheeses*

note·pa·per /ˈnəʊtˌpeɪpə‖ˈnoʊtˌpeɪpər/ *n* [U] paper used for writing letters

notes /nəʊts‖noʊts/ *n* [plural] information that a student writes down in a lesson or from a book, in order to remember it: **take notes** *Did you take notes during the lecture?*

note·wor·thy /ˈnəʊtˌwɜːði‖ˈnoʊtˌwɜːr-/ *adj formal* important or interesting enough to deserve attention: *a noteworthy event*

noth·ing[1] /ˈnʌθɪŋ/ *pron* **1** not anything: *There's nothing in the bag.* | *Nothing you say will change what he thinks.* | **nothing else** (=nothing more): *I had nothing else to do, so I went to bed.* **2** not anything that you consider to be important or interesting: *I have nothing to wear!* | *"What did you say?" "Oh, nothing."* **3** zero: *The Red Sox won the game three nothing.* (=the Red Sox had 3; the other team had no points) **4 for nothing** without any result or payment: *I did all that work for nothing.* **5 have/be nothing to do with a)** if something has nothing to do with a fact or situation, it is not connected to that fact or situation: *The amount you earn has nothing to do with how hard you work.* **b)** if a situation has nothing to do with someone, they have no good reason to know about it: *What I said to Joe has nothing to do with you.* **6 nothing special** not particularly good: *The story was nothing special, but the pictures were nice.* **7 nothing but** only one thing, and not anything else: *We've had nothing but rain for two weeks.* **8 nothing much** *spoken* very little: *"What did he say?" "Oh, nothing much."* **9 there's nothing for it (but to do sth)** used when there is only one thing you can do in a situation: *There was nothing for it but to swim.* **10 (there's) nothing to it** *spoken* used when something is very easy to do **11 it was nothing** *spoken* used when someone thanks you for something you have done: *"Thanks a lot!" "It was nothing."*

nothing[2] *adv* **1 be nothing like** to have no qualities that are similar to someone or something: *We have hills at home, but they're nothing like this!* **2 be nothing short of** used to emphasize that something is particularly good, bad, unusual etc: *It was nothing short of a miracle that no-one was hurt.*

noth·ing·ness /ˈnʌθɪŋnəs/ *n* [U] a state of complete emptiness, where nothing exists

no·tice[1] /ˈnəʊtɪs‖ˈnoʊ-/ *v* [I,T] to see, feel, or hear someone or something: *I said "hello," but she didn't notice.* | **+ that** *Max noticed that I was getting nervous.*

notice[2] *n* **1** [C] a written or printed statement that gives information or a warning to people: *I put a notice up saying 'No Entry'.* **2** [U] information or a warning about something that will happen: **give sb notice** *You must give the bank three days' notice before closing your account.* **3 not take any notice/take no notice** to pay no attention to someone or something:

Don't take any notice of her, she's just annoyed. **4 at short notice/at a moment's notice** without much warning, so that you have only a short time to do something: *You can't expect us to leave at a moment's notice!* **5 until further notice** from now until another change is announced: *The store will be closed until further notice.* **6 hand/give in your notice** to tell your employer that you will soon be leaving your job

no·tice·a·ble /ˈnəʊtɪsəbəl‖ˈnoʊ-/ *adj* easy to notice: *There's been a noticeable improvement in your work.* —**noticeably** *adv*

no·tice·board /ˈnəʊtɪsˌbɔːd‖ˈnoʊtɪsˌbɔːrd/ *n* [C] *BrE* a board on a wall, that notices can be fixed to; BULLETIN BOARD *AmE* → see colour picture on page 80

no·ti·fi·ca·tion /ˌnəʊtɪfɪˈkeɪʃən‖ˌnoʊ-/ *n* [C,U] *formal* when someone is officially told about something

no·ti·fy /ˈnəʊtɪfaɪ‖ˈnoʊ-/ *v* [T] *formal* to tell someone something officially; INFORM: *Have you notified the police?*

no·tion /ˈnəʊʃən‖ˈnoʊ-/ *n* [C] an idea, belief, or opinion about something, especially one that is wrong: *Where did you get the notion that I was leaving?*

no·to·ri·e·ty /ˌnəʊtəˈraɪəti‖ˌnoʊ-/ *n* [U] when someone is famous for doing something bad

no·to·ri·ous /nəʊˈtɔːriəs, nə-‖noʊ-, nə-/ *adj* famous for something bad: **+ for** *The city is notorious for its rainy weather.* —**notoriously** *adv*

not·with·stand·ing /ˌnɒtwɪθˈstændɪŋ, -wɪð-‖ˌnɑːt-/ *prep, adv formal* in spite of something: *The team has continued to be successful notwithstanding recent criticism.*

nought /nɔːt‖nɒːt/ *n* [C] *BrE* the number 0; zero

noun /naʊn/ *n* [C] a word that is the name of a person, place, thing, or idea

nour·ish /ˈnʌrɪʃ‖ˈnɜːrɪʃ, ˈnʌ-/ *v* [T] **1** to give a person, animal, or plant the food they need in order to live and grow: *healthy well-nourished children* **2** to allow a feeling or belief to grow

nour·ish·ing /ˈnʌrɪʃɪŋ‖ˈnɜːr-, ˈnʌ-/ *adj* nourishing food makes you strong and healthy: *nourishing soup*

nour·ish·ment /ˈnʌrɪʃmənt‖ˈnɜːrɪʃ-, ˈnʌ-/ *n* [U] *formal* food that is needed to live, grow, and be healthy

nov·el[1] /ˈnɒvəl‖ˈnɑː-/ *n* [C] a long written story, usually about characters and events that are not real: *the novels of Jane Austen*

novel[2] *adj* new, different, and unusual: *What a novel idea!*

nov·el·ist /ˈnɒvəlɪst‖ˈnɑː-/ *n* [C] someone who writes novels

nov·el·ty /ˈnɒvəlti‖ˈnɑː-/ *n* **1** [C] something that is new and unusual: *at a time when television was still a novelty* **2** [U] the quality of being new, different, and unusual: *the novelty of using e-mail* **3** [C] a small cheap object often given as a present

No·vem·ber /nəʊˈvembə, nə-‖noʊˈvembər, nə-/

N

written abbreviation **Nov** n [C,U] the eleventh month of the year → see usage note at MONTH

nov·ice /ˈnɒvɪs‖ˈnɑː-/ n [C] someone who has just begun learning a skill or activity: *a novice at chess | novice drivers*

now[1] /naʊ/ adv **1** at the present time: *Jean and her husband are now living in Canada.* | **right now/just now** (=at the time of speaking): *Right now, we're not really ready to decide.* | **by/before now** (=before the present time): *Steve should be home by now.* | **from now on** (=starting now and continuing in the future): *Meetings will be held on Friday from now on.* | **for now** (=true at the present time but may change): *You're welcome to use my computer for now.* **2** immediately: *You'd better go now – you're late.* | **right now** spoken (=used to emphasize what you are saying): *Call her right now, before she leaves.* **3** spoken used when you pause or to get someone's attention: *Now...what did you say your name was?* **4** **(every) now and then/now and again** sometimes but not always: *He sees her every now and then at the college.*

now[2] also **now that** /ˈ. ./ linking word because of something or as a result of something: *Now that the kids have left home, the house feels empty.*

now·a·days /ˈnaʊədeɪz/ adv used to talk about what happens now, compared to the past: *People tend to live longer nowadays.*

no·where /ˈnoʊweə‖ˈnoʊwer/ adv **1** not in or to any place: *There's nowhere to put anything in our new apartment.* | **nowhere else** (=no other place): *If you have nowhere else to stay, you can sleep here.* **2** **get nowhere** to have no success, or to make no progress: *I feel I'm getting nowhere in this job.* **3** **nowhere near a)** not at all: *The food at Giorgio's is nowhere near as good as it used to be.* **b)** a long way from a particular place: *Buffalo is in New York State, but it's nowhere near New York City.*

nox·ious /ˈnɒkʃəs‖ˈnɑːk-/ adj formal harmful or poisonous: *noxious chemicals*

noz·zle /ˈnɒzəl‖ˈnɑː-/ n [C] a short tube on the end of a pipe or HOSE that controls the flow of liquid coming out

nr BrE the written abbreviation of 'near'

n't /ənt/ the short form of 'not': *He isn't* (=is not) *here.* | *She can't* (=cannot) *see him.* | *I didn't* (=did not) *do it.*

nu·ance /ˈnjuːɑːns‖ˈnuː-/ n [C,U] a very small difference in meaning, colour, or feeling

nu·cle·ar /ˈnjuːkliə‖ˈnuːkliər/ adj **1** using the energy that is produced when an atom is split or joined to another atom, which can produce great power, but also produces RADIATION which can be very dangerous: *a nuclear power station | nuclear weapons | a nuclear-free zone* (=a place where nuclear weapons and substances used for producing nuclear energy are not allowed) **2** relating to the use of nuclear weapons: *a full-scale nuclear war* **3** relating to the NUCLEUS (=central part) of an atom: *nuclear physics*

nuclear dis·ar·ma·ment /ˌ... ˈ.../ n [U] when a country or government gets rid of its NUCLEAR weapons

nuclear fam·i·ly /ˌ... ˈ.../ n [C] a family that consists of a father, mother, and children

nuclear re·ac·tor /ˌ... ˈ.../ n [C] a large machine that produces nuclear energy

nu·cle·us /ˈnjuːkliəs‖ˈnuː-/ n [C] plural **nuclei** /-klɪaɪ/ **1** the central part of an atom **2** the nucleus of sth the most important part of something: *Photographs by Weston form the nucleus of the collection.* **3** the central part of a cell

nude[1] /njuːd‖nuːd/ adj not wearing any clothes; NAKED —**nudity** n [U]

nude[2] n **1** **in the nude** not wearing any clothes **2** [C] a painting, photograph etc of someone who is not wearing any clothes

nudge /nʌdʒ/ v [T] to push someone or something gently with your elbow: *Ken nudged me and said, "Look!"* —**nudge** n [C]

nud·ist /ˈnjuːdɪst‖ˈnuː-/ n [C] someone who believes it is good for you to wear no clothes —**nudist** adj: *a nudist beach* —**nudism** n [U]

nug·get /ˈnʌgɪt/ n [C] a small rough piece of a valuable metal: *a gold nugget*

nui·sance /ˈnjuːsəns‖ˈnuː-/ n [C usually singular] someone or something that annoys you or causes problems: *Sorry to be a nuisance, but could I use your phone?* | **what a nuisance** spoken: *I've forgotten my keys. What a nuisance!*

nuke /njuːk‖nuːk/ v [T] informal to attack a place using nuclear weapons

null and void /ˌnʌl ənd ˈvɔɪd/ adj law having no legal authority: *The court declared the contract to be null and void.*

nul·li·fy /ˈnʌlɪfaɪ/ v [T] **1** law to state officially that something is not legally effective: *The Senate has voted to nullify the decree.* **2** especially BrE to make something less powerful or effective: *Recent wage increases have been nullified by inflation.*

numb[1] /nʌm/ adj **1** not able to feel anything: *My feet were numb with cold.* **2** very shocked and unable to think or speak: *We all felt numb when we heard the news.* —**numbness** n [U] —**numbly** adv

numb[2] v [T] to make a part of your body unable to feel anything: *The cold wind numbed my face.*

num·ber[1] /ˈnʌmbə‖-ər/ n **1** [C] a word or sign that shows an amount or quantity: *Add the numbers 7, 4, and 3.* **2** [C] a telephone number: *"Is Laura there?" "No, I'm afraid you have the wrong number."* **3** [C] a sign used to show the position of something in a set, list etc: *Look at question number five.* **4** [C] a set of numbers used to recognize something: *What's your credit card number?* **5** [C,U] an amount of something that can be counted: **the number of** *an increase in the number of cars on the roads* | **a large/great/small etc number of** also **large/great/small etc numbers of** *A large number of factories have closed in recent months.* | **a number of** (=several): *We received a number of complaints about the noise.* | **any number of** (=a lot of): *There could be any number of reasons why she's late.*

number[2] v [T] **1** to give a number to something that is part of a set or list: *Number the items from one to ten.* **2** if people or things number a particular amount, that is how many there are: *The crowd numbered around 20,000.* **3** **sb's/sth's days are numbered** someone or something cannot live or continue much longer: *Are the days of the British Royal Family numbered?*

number plate /ˈ... ./ n [C] BrE the sign on the front and back of a vehicle that shows its official

453 nymph

number; LICENSE PLATE *AmE* ➙ see picture at CAR

nu·me·ral /ˈnjuːmərəl‖ˈnuː-/ *n* [C] a written sign such as 5 or 22 used to show a number: *Roman numerals* —**numeral** *adj*

nu·me·rate /ˈnjuːmərɪt‖ˈnuː-/ *adj* able to understand basic mathematics

nu·mer·i·cal /njuːˈmerɪkəl‖nuː-/ *adj* expressed in numbers, or relating to numbers: **in numerical order** (=numbered 1, 2, 3 etc): *The pages should be in numerical order.* —**numerically** /-kli/ *adv*

nu·me·rous /ˈnjuːmərəs‖ˈnuː-/ *adj formal* many: *We've discussed this before on numerous occasions.*

nun /nʌn/ *n* [C] a member of a group of religious women that lives apart from other people in a CONVENT ➙ compare MONK

nurse[1] /nɜːs‖nɜːrs/ *n* [C] someone whose job is to look after people who are ill or injured, usually in a hospital

nurse[2] *v* [T] **1** to look after someone who is ill or injured **2** to try to cure an illness or injury by resting in bed: *Blake is in bed nursing an ankle injury.* **3** to have an idea or feeling in your mind for a long time: *Tom had always nursed an ambition to be a pilot.*

nur·se·ry /ˈnɜːsəri‖ˈnɜːr-/ *n* **1** [C,U] *especially BrE* a place where young children are looked after during the day; DAY CARE CENTER *AmE* **2** [C] a place where plants and trees are grown and sold **3** [C] *old-fashioned* a young child's room

nursery rhyme /ˈ... ./ *n* [C] a short song or poem for children

nursery school /ˈ... ./ *n* [C] a school for children between three and five years old

nurs·ing /ˈnɜːsɪŋ‖ˈnɜːr-/ *n* [U] the job of looking after people who are ill, injured, or very old: *What made you choose nursing as a career?*

nursing home /ˈ.. ./ *n* [C] a small hospital for people who are too old or ill to take care of themselves

nur·ture /ˈnɜːtʃəl‖ˈnɜːrtʃər/ *v* [T] *formal* **1** to feed and look after a child, plant etc while it is growing: *children nurtured by loving parents*

2 to help a plan, feeling etc develop: *We will nurture closer relationships with companies abroad.*

nut /nʌt/ *n* [C] **1** a large seed that you can eat, that usually grows in a hard brown shell: *a cashew nut* **2** a small piece of metal with a hole in the middle used for fastening things together **3** *informal* a crazy person ➙ see also NUTS

nut·crack·er /ˈnʌtˌkrækəl‖-ər/ *n* [C] also **nutcrackers** [plural] *BrE* the thing you use for cracking the shells of nuts

nu·tri·ent /ˈnjuːtriənt‖ˈnuː-/ *n* [C] a chemical or food that helps plants, animals, or people to live and grow: *Plants absorb nutrients from the soil.* —**nutrient** *adj*

nu·tri·tion /njuːˈtrɪʃən‖nuː-/ *n* [U] the kind of food you eat and the way it affects your health: *Good nutrition is vital.* —**nutritional** *adj*: *the nutritional content of foods* —**nutritionally** *adv*

nu·tri·tious /njuːˈtrɪʃəs‖nuː-/ *adj* food that is nutritious contains the substances that your body needs: *nutritious and cheap recipe ideas*

nuts /nʌts/ *adj spoken informal* crazy, silly, or angry: **go nuts** (=become crazy or angry): *I'll go nuts if I have to wait any longer.*|**drive sb nuts** *It's driving me nuts living with my parents.*

nut·shell /ˈnʌt-ʃel/ *n* **(to put it) in a nutshell** *spoken* used when you are explaining only the main facts or details about something: *The problem, in a nutshell, was money.*

nut·ter /ˈnʌtəl-ər/ *n* [C] *BrE informal* a crazy person: *That woman's a complete nutter!*

nut·ty /ˈnʌti/ *adj* **1** tasting like nuts: *The wine had a nice nutty flavour.* **2** *informal* crazy

nuz·zle /ˈnʌzəl/ *v* [I,T] to gently rub your head or nose against someone to show that you like them: *The dog nuzzled its head against her knees.*

NW the written abbreviation of NORTHWEST or NORTHWESTERN

ny·lon /ˈnaɪlɒn‖-lɑːn/ *n* [U] a strong artificial material used for making clothes, plastic, rope etc: *nylon stockings*|*a carpet made of 80% wool and 20% nylon*

nymph /nɪmf/ *n* [C] one of the spirits of nature who appears as a young girl in ancient Greek and Roman stories

Oo

O, o /əʊ‖oʊ/ the letter 'o'

O *spoken* zero – used when saying groups of numbers: *room 203*

oaf /əʊf‖oʊf/ *n* [C] a man or boy who is stupid or rude

oak /əʊk‖oʊk/ *n* [C,U] a large tree that is common in northern countries, or the hard wood of this tree

oar /ɔː‖ɔːr/ *n* [C] a long pole that is wide at one end, used for rowing a boat

o·a·sis /əʊ'eɪsɨs‖oʊ-/ *n* [C], *plural* **oases** /-siːz/ **1** a place in a desert where there are trees and water **2** somewhere that is more pleasant and peaceful than the area that surrounds it: *The park was an oasis of calm in the middle of the city.*

oath /əʊθ‖oʊθ/ *n* **1** [C] a formal promise; **swear/take an oath** *He swore an oath to support the Constitution.* **2** **be under oath** to have made an official promise to tell the truth in a court of law

oat·meal /'əʊtmiːl‖'oʊt-/ *n* [U] crushed oats used for making cakes or PORRIDGE

oats /əʊts‖oʊts/ *n* [plural] a grain that is eaten by people and animals

o·be·di·ence /ə'biːdiəns/ *n* [U] when someone does what a person, law, or rule tells them to do: **+ to** *obedience to her father's wishes*

o·be·di·ent /ə'biːdiənt/ *adj* someone who is obedient does what a person, law, or rule tells them to do: *a quiet and obedient child* —**obediently** *adv* → opposite DISOBEDIENT

o·bese /əʊ'biːs‖oʊ-/ *adj* much too fat, in a way that is dangerous to your health —**obesity** *n* [U]

o·bey /əʊ'beɪ, ə-‖oʊ-, ə-/ *v* [I,T] to do what a person, law, or rule tells you to do: *Most dogs will obey simple commands.* → opposite DISOBEY

o·bit·u·a·ry /ə'bɪtʃuəri‖-tʃueri/ *n* [C] a report of someone's death in a newspaper

ob·ject¹ /'ɒbdʒɪkt‖'aːb-/ *n* **1** [C] a thing that you can see, hold, or touch: *a small silver object* **2** [singular] the purpose of a plan, activity etc: **the object of sth** *The object of the game is to kick the ball into the goal.* **3** **an object of desire/ pity etc** someone or something that you want to have, feel sorry for etc **4** [C] the noun or phrase that describes the person or thing that is affected by the verb **5** **money/time etc is no object** used to say that the amount of money, time etc is not important and you can use as much as you want

ob·ject² /əb'dʒekt/ *v* [I,T] to say that you do not like or approve of something: *"Ron's too tired to drive,"* *Steve objected.* | **+ to** *I object to being called a 'foreigner'.* | **+ that** *Clare objected that it would cost too much.* → see also CONSCIENTIOUS OBJECTOR

ob·jec·tion /əb'dʒekʃən/ *n* [C] something that you say to show that you do not approve of an idea or plan: *I have no objection to her being invited.* | **have/make an objection** (=say that you do not approve of or agree with something)

ob·jec·tion·a·ble /əb'dʒekʃənəbəl/ *adj* unpleasant and likely to offend people; OFFENSIVE: *an objectionable remark*

ob·jec·tive¹ /əb'dʒektɪv/ *n* [C] an aim that you work hard to achieve: *Our main objective is to raise money.*

objective² *adj* not influenced by your own feelings or opinions: *We need an objective approach to the problem.* —**objectively** *adv* —**objectivity** /ˌɒbdʒek'tɪvɨti‖ˌaːb-/ *n* [U] → compare SUBJECTIVE

ob·li·gat·ed /'ɒblɨgeɪtɨd‖'aːb-/ *adj* **be/feel obligated to sb** *especially AmE* to feel that it is your duty to do something for someone

ob·li·ga·tion /ˌɒblɨ'geɪʃən‖ˌaːb-/ *n* [C,U] a moral or legal duty to do something: **an obligation to do sth** *Employers have an obligation to provide a safe working environment.* | **be under an obligation to do sth** *People entering the shop are under no obligation to buy.*

ob·lig·a·to·ry /ə'blɪgətəri‖-tɔːri/ *adj formal* something that is obligatory has to be done because of a law, rule etc; COMPULSORY: *obligatory school attendance*

o·blige /ə'blaɪdʒ/ *v* **1** [T] *formal* to make it necessary for someone to do something: **be obliged to do sth** *Doctors are obliged to keep all medical records secret.* **2** [I,T] to do something that someone has asked you to do: *Whenever we needed help, Ed was always happy to oblige.*

ob·liged /ə'blaɪdʒd/ *adj* **1** **feel obliged to do sth** to feel that you must do something: *I felt obliged to tell her the truth.* **2** **I'm very much obliged** *spoken* used to thank someone for their help and to say you are grateful to them

o·blig·ing /ə'blaɪdʒɪŋ/ *adj* always ready to help other people —**obligingly** *adv*

o·blique /ə'bliːk/ *adj* not said or written in a direct way: *oblique references to his drinking problem*

o·blit·er·ate /ə'blɪtəreɪt/ *v* [T] to destroy something completely: *Large areas of the city were obliterated.* —**obliteration** /əˌblɪtə'reɪʃən/ *n* [U]

o·bliv·i·on /ə'blɪviən/ *n* [U] **1** when someone is unconscious or does not notice what is happening around them: *He spent the night drinking himself into oblivion.* **2** when someone or something is completely forgotten: *old movie stars who have faded into oblivion*

o·bliv·i·ous /ə'blɪviəs/ *adj* not noticing or not knowing about something; UNAWARE: **+ to/of** *Max was fast asleep, completely oblivious to the noise outside.* —**obliviously** *adv*

ob·long /'ɒblɒŋ‖'aːblɔːŋ/ *adj* having a shape with four corners that is longer than it is wide: *an oblong box* —**oblong** *n* [C]

ob·nox·ious /əb'nɒkʃəs‖-'naːk-/ *adj* extremely unpleasant or rude: *What an obnoxious man!* —**obnoxiously** *adv*

o·boe /'əʊbəʊ‖'oʊboʊ/ *n* [C] a wooden musical instrument shaped like a narrow tube, which you play by blowing into it

ob·scene /əb'siːn/ *adj* **1** offensive and shocking in a sexual way: *obscene phone calls* **2** extremely immoral or unfair: *obscene pay increases* —**obscenely** *adv*

ob·scen·i·ty /əb'senɨti/ *n* **1** [C usually plural] a sexually offensive word or action: *kids shouting obscenities* **2** [U] sexually offensive behaviour or language, especially in a book, play etc: *laws against obscenity*

ob·scure[1] /əbˈskjʊəll-ˈskjʊr/ *adj* **1** difficult to understand: *Jarrett didn't like the plan, for some obscure reason.* **2** not famous: *an obscure poet*

obscure[2] *v* [T] **1** to prevent something from being seen: *The top of the hill was obscured by clouds.* **2** to make something difficult to learn about or understand: *legal language that obscures meaning*

ob·scu·ri·ty /əbˈskjʊərᵻtill-ˈskjʊr-/ *n* [U] when someone is no longer known or remembered: *O'Brien retired from politics and died in obscurity.*

ob·ser·vance /əbˈzɜːvənsll-ɜːr-/ *n* [U] *formal* the practice of obeying a law, or following a religious custom: + **of** *the observance of Ramadan*

ob·ser·vant /əbˈzɜːvəntll-ɜːr-/ *adj* good at noticing things: *an observant little girl*

ob·ser·va·tion /ˌɒbzəˈveɪʃənll,ɑːbzər-/ *n* **1** [U] the process of watching someone or something carefully: + **of** *Wilkins' book is based on his observation of wild birds.* | **be under observation** (=watched carefully): *He was kept under observation in the hospital.* **2** [C] a spoken or written remark: *The book contains some intelligent observations.* **3 powers of observation** a natural ability to notice what is happening around you

ob·ser·va·to·ry /əbˈzɜːvətərill əbˈzɜːrvətɔːri/ *n* [C] a special building from which scientists watch the sky

ob·serve /əbˈzɜːvll-ɜːrv/ *v* [T] **1** to watch someone or something carefully: *psychologists observing child behaviour* **2** *formal* to see or notice something: *I observed the suspect entering the house.* **3** *formal* to say something: *"We're already late," Hendry observed.* **4** to obey a law, agreement, or religious custom: *Both sides are observing the ceasefire.*

ob·serv·er /əbˈzɜːvəll-ɜːrvər/ *n* [C] **1** someone who attends meetings, classes etc to officially watch what is happening: *a group of UN observers in Bosnia* **2** someone who watches or notices something

ob·sess /əbˈses/ *v* [T] if you are obsessed with something or it obsesses you, you think about it all the time and cannot think of anything else: **be obsessed with/about** *William is obsessed with making money.*

ob·ses·sion /əbˈseʃən/ *n* [C] something that you cannot stop thinking about: + **with** *an obsession with sex* — **obsessional** *adj*: *obsessional behaviour*

ob·ses·sive /əbˈsesɪv/ *adj* thinking about someone or something all the time: *She's obsessive about her weight.* — **obsessively** *adv*

ob·so·lete /ˈɒbsəliːtll,ɑːbsəˈliːtᵻ/ *adj* no longer used or useful: *Our computer system will soon be obsolete.* — **obsolescence** /ˌɒbsəˈlesənsll,ɑːb-/ *n* [U]

ob·sta·cle /ˈɒbstəkəlll'ɑːb-/ *n* [C] **1** something that makes it difficult to do something: + **to** *Lack of confidence can be a big obstacle to success.* **2** something that blocks a road, path etc

ob·sti·nate /ˈɒbstᵻnᵻtll'ɑːb-/ *adj* refusing to change your opinions, or behaviour; STUBBORN: *an obstinate old man* — **obstinately** *adv* — **obstinacy** *n* [U]

ob·struct /əbˈstrʌkt/ *v* [T] **1** to block a road, path etc: *A van was obstructing traffic.* **2** to try to prevent something from happening by making it difficult: *Maya was charged with obstructing the investigation.* — **obstructive** *adj*: *obstructive behaviour*

ob·struc·tion /əbˈstrʌkʃən/ *n* **1 a)** [C] something that blocks a road, tube etc **b)** [singular, U] when a road, tube etc is blocked: *The accident caused an obstruction on the freeway.* **2** [U] when someone tries to prevent a legal or political process: *an obstruction of justice*

ob·tain /əbˈteɪn/ *v* [T] *formal* to get something: *Maps can be obtained at the tourist office.* — **obtainable** *adj*

ob·tuse /əbˈtjuːsll-ˈtuːs/ *adj* stupid or slow to understand something: *Am I being obtuse?*

ob·vi·ous /ˈɒbviəsll-ɑːb-/ *adj* easy to notice or understand: *an obvious mistake* | **it is obvious that** *It was obvious that Gina was lying.* — **obviously** *adv*: *She obviously didn't want to go.*

oc·ca·sion /əˈkeɪʒən/ *n* **1** [C] a time when something happens: *They had met on several occasions.* **2** [C] an important event or ceremony: **a special occasion** *We're saving the champagne for a special occasion.* **3** [singular] a suitable time, or reason to do something: *Christmas is an occasion to see old friends.* **4 on occasion(s)** sometimes but not often: *She can be very rude on occasion.*

oc·ca·sion·al /əˈkeɪʒənəl/ *adj* happening sometimes but not often: *Tomorrow will be warm with occasional showers.* — **occasionally** *adv*: *We occasionally meet for a drink.*

oc·cult /ˈɒkʌlt, əˈkʌltlləˈkʌlt, ˈɑːkʌlt/ *n* **the occult** the study of spirits and magic — **occult** *adj*: *occult practices*

oc·cu·pan·cy /ˈɒkjᵿpənsill'ɑːk-/ *n* [U] *formal* when someone uses a building or other space to live or work in

oc·cu·pant /ˈɒkjᵿpəntll'ɑːk-/ *n* [C] *formal* someone who lives in a building, room etc, or who is in it

oc·cu·pa·tion /ˌɒkjᵿˈpeɪʃənll,ɑːk-/ *n* **1** [C] *formal* a job or profession: *Please state your name and occupation.* **2** [U] when an army goes into another country and takes control of it using force: *the occupation of Poland* **3** [C] *formal* something that you enjoy doing: *His favourite occupation is fishing.*

oc·cu·pa·tion·al /ˌɒkjᵿˈpeɪʃənəl ll,ɑːk-/ *adj* connected with your job: **occupational hazard** (=a risk connected with a particular job)

oc·cu·pied /ˈɒkjᵿpaɪdll'ɑːk-/ *adj* **1** a room, bed, seat etc that is occupied is being used: *All the apartments on the first floor are occupied.* **2** busy doing or thinking about something:

GRAMMAR NOTE: the past perfect
You form the **past perfect** using **had** and the past participle. Use the past perfect to talk about something that happened in the past before another past action: *Kay stayed behind after everyone else **had gone** home.* | *She told me what she **had done**.*

keep sb occupied *I brought along some toys to keep the kids occupied.*

oc·cu·pi·er /ˈɒkjʊpaɪəlˈɑːkjʊpaɪr/ *n* [C] *BrE* someone who lives in or uses a place

oc·cu·py /ˈɒkjʊpaɪlˈɑːk-/ *v* [T] **1** to live, work etc in a particular place: *The seventh floor of the building is occupied by Salem Press.* **2** to fill a space or period of time: *A painting occupied the entire wall.|Sport occupies most of his spare time.* **3** to go into a place and take control of it, using military force: *Rebel forces occupied the city.* **4** *formal* to have a particular job or position: *people who occupy senior positions* **5** occupy yourself to be busy doing something so that you do not become bored: *How do you occupy yourself now that you're retired?*

oc·cur /əˈkɜːlləˈkɜːr/ *v* [I] **-rred, -rring** *formal* **1** to happen, especially without being planned first: *Major earthquakes like this occur very rarely.* **2** to exist or be present in a particular place or group: **+ in/among** *The disease occurs mainly in young children.*

occur to sb *phr v* [T] to come into your mind: *Did it never occur to you to phone?*

oc·cur·rence /əˈkʌrənslləˈkɜː-/ *n* [C] something that happens: *Stress-related illness is now a fairly common occurrence.*

o·cean /ˈəʊʃənllˈoʊ-/ *n* **1** the ocean the large area of salt water that covers most of the Earth's surface **2** [C] one of the five very large areas of water in the world: *the Indian Ocean* —oceanic /ˌəʊʃiˈænɪkˌˈoʊ-/ *adj*

o'clock /əˈklɒklləˈklɑːk/ *adv* one/two/three etc o'clock one of the times when the clock shows the exact hour as a number from 1 to 12: *We got up at six o'clock.*

oc·ta·gon /ˈɒktəɡənllˈɑːktəɡɑːn/ *n* [C] a flat shape that has eight sides —octagonal /ɒkˈtæɡənəllˈɑːk-/ *adj*

oc·tave /ˈɒktᵻv, -teɪvllˈɑːk-/ *n* [C] the set of eight musical notes between the first and last note of a SCALE

Oc·to·ber /ɒkˈtəʊbəllɑːkˈtoʊbər/ written abbreviation **Oct** *n* the tenth month of the year ➔ see usage note at MONTH

oc·to·pus /ˈɒktəpəsllˈɑːk-/ *n* [C], *plural* **octopuses** or **octopi** /-paɪ/ a sea creature with a soft body and eight TENTACLES (=arms)

odd /ɒdllɑːd/ *adj* **1** strange or different from what you expected: *Jake's an odd guy.|It's odd that she hasn't phoned.* **2** odd number a number that cannot be divided exactly by two ➔ compare EVEN² **3** odd jobs small practical jobs of different kinds **4** the odd drink/game/occasion etc *spoken, especially BrE* a few drinks, games etc, but not often and not regularly: *I still enjoy the odd game of tennis.* **5** 20-odd/30-odd etc *spoken* a little more than 20, 30 etc: *He must have worked here twenty odd years.* **6** separated from its pair or set: *an odd sock* **7** the odd man out/the odd one out someone or something that is different from the other people or things in a group

odd·i·ty /ˈɒdᵻtillˈɑː-/ *n* [C] a strange or unusual person or thing

odd·ly /ˈɒdlillˈɑːdli/ *adv* **1** in a strange or unusual way: *Roger's been behaving very oddly.* **2** oddly enough used when something seems

strange or surprising: *Oddly enough, she didn't seem offended.*

odds /ɒdzllɑːdz/ *n* [plural] **1** how likely it is that something will or will not happen, often expressed as a number: *The odds of winning the lottery are about 14 million to 1.* **2** at odds (with sb) disagreeing with someone: *Britain was at odds with France on the subject of nuclear testing.* **3** difficulties that make a good result seem very unlikely: **against all the odds** (=in spite of is seeming very unlikely): *He recovered from his injury against all the odds.*

odds and ends /ˌ. . ˈ./ *n* [plural] *informal* small things that are not important or valuable

ode /əʊdlloʊd/ *n* [C] a long poem written to or about a person or thing

o·dour *BrE*, **odor** *AmE* /ˈəʊdəllˈoʊdər/ *n* [C] a smell, especially an unpleasant one

o·dour·less *BrE*, **odorless** *AmE* /ˈəʊdələsllˈoʊdər-/ *adj* not having a smell: *an odorless gas*

oes·tro·gen *BrE*, **estrogen** *AmE* /ˈiːstrədʒənllˈes-/ *n* [C] a chemical substance produced by a woman's body

of /əv, ə; *strong* ɒvlləv, ə; *strong* ɑːv/ *prep* **1** belonging to, relating to, or part of something: *I love the colour of his shirt.|He's a friend of Sam's.|the first part of the story|members of a rock group* **2** used with words that show amounts or groups of people or things: *two kilos of sugar|a cup of coffee|a herd of elephants* **3** used to talk about a number or amount: *a pay rise of 9%|a child of eight* **4** used in dates: *the 23rd of January, 1998* **5** used to give the name of something: *the city of New Orleans* **6** used to show a reason or cause: *She died of cancer.* **7** used to say what something shows: *a photo of Paula's baby* **8** used to show direction: *I live just north of here.* **9** used after nouns describing actions to show who the action is done to or who did the action: *the testing of river water for chemicals* **10** written, made, produced etc by: *the novels of Charles Dickens* ➔ see also **of course** (COURSE¹)

off¹ /ɒfllɒːf/ *adv, prep* **1** away from or out of a place or position: *She waved goodbye as she drove off.|Keep off the grass!* ➔ see colour picture on page 474 **2** no longer connected or fastened to something: *A button has come off my shirt.|Take the lid off slowly.* **3** not working or being used: *All the lights were off.|Remember to switch the computer off.* **4** not at work or school because you are ill or on holiday: *Hal's been off work for six weeks.|I'm taking the day off tomorrow.* **5** lower in price: *You get 15% off if you buy $100 worth of groceries.* **6** far in distance or long in time: *mountains off in the distance|Spring is still a long way off.* **7** joined to a room, road, building, or area of land, or very near to it: *Oak Hills – isn't that off Route 290?|an island off the coast of Florida* (=a short distance from the coast) **8** be off to have started a journey: *At last, we're off!* **9** off and on/on and off for short periods of time, but not regularly: *I worked as a secretary off and on for three years.* ➔ see also BETTER OFF, WELL-OFF

off² *adj* **1** not correct or not good: *His calculations are off by 20%.* **2** an event that is off will not happen: *The wedding's off!* ➔ opposite ON³ **3** have an off day/week etc *spoken* to have a day, week etc when you are not doing something as well as you usually do **4 the off season** the time in the year when a place or business is not as busy as it usually is **5** *especially BrE* food or drink that is off is no longer fresh: *This milk smells off.*

of·fal /ˈɒfəl‖ˈɒː-, ˈɑː-/ *n* [U] the KIDNEYS, LIVER etc of an animal, used as food

off-chance /ˈ. ./ *n* **on the off-chance** hoping that something will happen, although it is unlikely: *He only went to the party on the off-chance that Pippa might be there.*

off·col·our /ˌ. ˈ.◂/ *adj BrE spoken* slightly ill

offence *BrE*, **offense** *AmE* /əˈfens/ *n* **1** [C] a crime: *a serious offence* | **commit an offence** *If you lie to the police, you are committing an offence.* **2 take/cause offence** to feel offended or to offend someone: *A lot of women took offence at Rawling's speech.*

offend /əˈfend/ *v* **1** [T] to make someone angry or upset: *I'm sorry, I didn't mean to offend you.* **2** [I] *formal* to do something that is a crime

of·fend·er /əˈfendə‖-ər/ *n* [C] someone who is guilty of a crime: *an institution for young offenders*

offense[1] /əˈfens/ *n* the American spelling of OFFENCE

offense[2] /ˈɒːfens, ˈɑː-/ *n* [C,U] *AmE* the players in a game such as football who try to get points; ATTACK *BrE*

of·fen·sive[1] /əˈfensɪv/ *adj* **1** used or intended for attacking: *an offensive weapon* → opposite DEFENSIVE[1] **2** likely to upset or offend people: *Some people found the song offensive.* — **offensively** *adv* — **offensiveness** *n* [U]

offensive[2] *n* **1** [C] an attack on a place by an army **2 be/go on the offensive** to attack or criticize people

offer[1] /ˈɒfəl‖ˈɒːfər, ˈɑː-/ *v* **1** [T] to say that you are willing to give something to someone: **offer sb sth** *Can I offer you a drink?* **2** [T] to say that you will pay a particular amount of money for something: *They've offered us £70,000 for the house.* **3** [T] to hold something out to someone, so that they can take it: *He offered me his handkerchief.* **4** [I,T] to say that you are willing to do something: **offer to do sth** *Carol didn't even offer to help.* **5** [T] to provide something that people want or need: *We offer a wide range of winter vacations.*

offer[2] *n* [C] **1** a statement that you will give something to someone or do something for them: *a 6.5% pay offer* | + **of** *Thanks for your offer of support.* **2** an amount of money that someone will pay for something: **make (sb) an offer of £10/$300 etc** *He made me an offer of $50 for the bike.* **3** a price that is lower than the usual price: *Don't miss our special offer – two videos for the price of one.* **4 on offer** *BrE* **a)** available to buy, use, or do: *Activities on offer include windsurfing and water-skiing.* **b)** being sold at a very cheap price: *Butter is on offer this week.*

of·fer·ing /ˈɒfərɪŋ‖ˈɒː-, ˈɑː-/ *n* [C] something that you give to someone, especially God

off·hand[1] /ˌɒfˈhænd◂ ‖ˌɒːf-/ *adj* not very friendly or polite: *"I'm going now," Piers said in an offhand voice.*

offhand[2] *adv* immediately, without time to

think: *I can't tell you offhand if I can come – I'll have to check my diary.*

office /ˈɒfɪs‖ˈɒː-, ˈɑː-/ *n* **1** [C] a building that belongs to an organization, where people work: *Are you going to the office today?* **2** [C] a room where you work that has a desk, telephone etc: *the manager's office* **3** [U] an important job or position: **in office** (=while having an important job or position): *The president died after only fifteen months in office.*

officer /ˈɒfɪsə‖ˈɒːfɪsər, ˈɑː-/ *n* [C] **1** someone who has a position of authority in the army, navy etc **2** someone who has a position of authority in an organization: *a local government officer* **3** a policeman or policewoman

> **USAGE NOTE: officer, official,** and **the authorities**
>
> An **officer** is someone in the police force or the military: *This club is for army officers and their wives.* An **official** is someone in a business or government organization who has a position of authority: *A factory official announced that 100 workers would be laid off.* **The authorities** are the people in an organization, especially in the government, who have the power to make decisions: *The authorities said the cause of the crash was unknown.*

official[1] /əˈfɪʃəl/ *adj* **1** approved of or done by someone in authority, especially the government: *an official inquiry into the plane crash* **2** connected with a position of authority: *Her official title is Public Safety Adviser.* **3** official reasons, information etc are what people are told, although they may not be true: *The official reason for his resignation was ill health.*

official[2] *n* [C] someone who has a position of authority in an organization, especially a government: *US Administration officials*

of·fi·cial·ly /əˈfɪʃəli/ *adv* **1** in an official or formal way: *The new bridge was officially opened this morning.* **2** according to the reason or information that has been given, which may not be true: *The meeting was cancelled, officially because of bad weather.*

of·fi·ci·ate /əˈfɪʃieɪt/ *v* [I] *formal* to do official duties at a ceremony or important event

off·ing /ˈɒfɪŋ‖ˈɒː-, ˈɑː-/ *n* **be in the offing** to be going to happen soon: *I heard that there might be a promotion in the offing.*

off·li·cence /ˈ. ../ *n* [C] *BrE* a shop that sells alcohol; LIQUOR STORE *AmE*

off·peak /ˌ. ˈ.◂/ *adj BrE* **a)** off-peak hours or periods of time are times when fewer people want to do or use something, for example travel, use their telephones etc **b)** off-peak travel, electricity etc is cheaper because it is done or used at these times: *off-peak rail services*

off-ramp /ˈ. ./ *n* [C] *AmE* a road for driving off a HIGHWAY or FREEWAY → opposite ON-RAMP

off·set /ˈɒfset, ˌɒfˈset‖ˈɒːfset, ˌɒːfˈset/ *v* [T] **off·set, offset, offsetting** to make a bad situation seem better by providing something good: *The cost of the flight was offset by the cheapness of the hotel.*

off·shoot /ˈɒfʃuːt‖ˈɒːf-/ *n* [C] something that has developed from something bigger: *The company was an offshoot of Bell Telephones.*

off·shore /ˌɒfˈʃɔːɹ ‖ ˌɒːfˈʃɔːr‹/ adj in the sea, at a distance from the coast: *America's offshore oil reserves* —**offshore** adv: *The boat is anchored offshore.*

off·side /ˌɒfˈsaɪd‹ ‖ ˌɒːf-/ adj, adv in a position where you are not allowed to touch the ball in games such as football

off·spring /ˈɒfˌsprɪŋ‖ˈɒːf-/ n, plural **offspring** someone's child or children

off·stage /ˌɒfˈsteɪdʒ‹ ‖ ˌɒːf-/ adv, adj just behind or at the side of a stage in a theatre: *There was a loud crash offstage.*

of·ten /ˈɒfən, ˈɒftən‖ˈɒː-/ adv **1** many times or regularly: *That was fun! We should do it more often.* | *How often do you see your parents?* | *All too often, victims of bullying are frightened to ask for help.* **2** in many situations or at many times: *Headaches are often caused by stress.* **3 every so often** sometimes but not very frequently: *We see each other every so often.*

o·gle /ˈəʊɡəl‖ˈoʊ-/ v [I,T] to look at someone in a way that shows clearly that you think they are sexually attractive

o·gre /ˈəʊɡə‖ˈoʊɡər/ n [C] **1** someone who is cruel and frightening **2** a large, ugly man in children's stories

oh /əʊ‖oʊ/ interjection **1** used to pause before saying something or replying to a question: *"What time are you going to lunch?" "Oh, I haven't decided yet."* **2** used to express strong emotions or to emphasize your opinion about something: *Oh, Sue, how lovely to see you!*

ohm /əʊm‖oʊm/ n [C] a unit for measuring electrical RESISTANCE

oil[1] /ɔɪl/ n [U] **1** a thick dark liquid from under the ground, used to make petrol: *the big oil companies* **2** a thick liquid used to make the parts of machines move more easily **3** a liquid made from plants or animal fat, used in cooking: *olive oil*

oil[2] v [T] to put oil into or onto something

oil paint·ing /ˈ. ˌ../ n [C,U] a picture painted with paint that contains oil, or the activity of doing this

oil rig /ˈ. ./ n [C] a large structure with equipment for getting oil out of the ground

oils /ɔɪlz/ n [plural] paints that contain oil: **in oils** (=using oil paints)

oil slick /ˈ. ./ n [C] a layer of oil floating on water, especially as the result of an accident involving a ship carrying oil

oil well /ˈ. ./ n [C] a deep hole made to get oil out of the ground

oil·y /ˈɔɪli/ adj **1** covered with oil, or containing a lot of oil: *an oily fish* **2** an oily substance is like oil: *an oily liquid*

oink /ɔɪŋk/ n [C] the sound that a pig makes —**oink** v [I]

oint·ment /ˈɔɪntmənt/ n [C,U] a substance that you rub into your skin, especially as a medical treatment

OJ /ˈəʊ dʒeɪ‖ˈoʊ-/ n [U] AmE informal orange juice

OK[1], **okay** /əʊˈkeɪ‖oʊ-/ adj spoken **1** healthy or happy, and not ill, injured, sad etc: *Do you feel OK now?* **2** good enough or acceptable: *Does my hair look OK?* **3** used to ask if you can do something, or to tell someone that they can do it: *Is it OK if I leave early?* —**OK okay** adv: *Is your computer working OK?*

OK[2], **okay** interjection **1** used when you start talking, or continue to talk after a pause: *OK, can we go now?* **2** used to say that you agree about something: *"We'd better be there by four." "Okay."*

OK[3], **okay** v [T] informal to officially agree to allow something to happen: *Has the bank okayed your loan?*

OK[4], **okay** n **the OK** informal if someone gives you the OK to do something, they give you permission to do it

old /əʊld‖oʊld/ adj **1** an old person or thing has lived or existed for a long time: *an old man* | *one of the oldest universities in the world* **2** old clothes, books etc have been used a lot before: *I give her all my old clothes.* **3** used to talk about the age of someone or something: *Our dog is three years old.* | *my ten-year-old daughter* | *How old is Kenny?* **4 your old house/job/teacher** etc the house, job etc that you had before, but do not have now: *I saw your old girlfriend last night.* **5 good old/poor old etc** spoken used to show that you like someone, feel sorry for them etc: *"Keith drove me home." "Good old Keith!"* **6 the same old ...** used to say that something has been repeated many times and is no longer interesting, useful etc: *They always ask the same old questions.* **7 an old friend/enemy etc** a friend, enemy etc that you have known for a long time **8 the old** old people **9 old boy/old girl** BrE **a)** someone who used to attend a particular school: *an old girls' reunion* **b)** old-fashioned spoken used to address someone in a friendly way: *What's the matter, old girl?* **c)** informal an old man or woman: *I was talking to the old boy next door this morning.* **10 old hat** old-fashioned and boring →compare ANCIENT ELDERLY

USAGE NOTE: old and elderly

Be careful about using **old** to talk about people. It is more polite to use the word **elderly**: *Elderly people often worry about crime.*

---

old age /ˌ. ˈ.‹/ n [U] the time in your life when you are old

old age pen·sion /ˌ. . ˈ../ n [C] BrE money paid by the government to old people who no longer work

old age pen·sion·er /ˌ. . ˈ.../ n [C] BrE someone who does not work any more, because they are old, and gets money from the government

old·en /ˈəʊldən‖ˈoʊld-/ adj **in the olden days/in olden times** a long time ago

old-fash·ioned /ˌ. ˈ..‹/ adj not modern and not fashionable any more: *old-fashioned ideas*

old flame /ˌ. ˈ./ n [C] informal your former boyfriend or girlfriend

old·ie /ˈəʊldi‖ˈoʊldi/ n [C] informal an old thing or person, especially a song or film

old man /. ˈ./ BrE spoken informal **1** your husband **2** your father

old peo·ple's home /ˌ. ˈ.. ˌ./ n [C] a place where old people live together and are looked after

Old Tes·ta·ment /ˌ. ˈ...‹/ n the Old Testament

the part of the Bible that is about the time before the birth of Christ → compare NEW TESTAMENT

old-tim·er /ˌ. ˈ../ n [C] AmE informal an old man

old-world /ˈ. ./ adj old in a pleasant or attractive way: the old-world charm of the village | old-world politeness

Old World /ˌ. ˈ.◂/ n the Old World Europe, and parts of Asia and Africa —**Old World** adj → compare NEW WORLD

ol·ive /ˈɒlᵻvᵻlˈɑː-/ n 1 [C] a small black or green fruit, eaten as a vegetable or used for making oil → see picture at FRUIT 2 [U] also **olive green** a pale green colour —**olive** adj

O·lym·pic Games /əˌlɪmpɪk ˈɡeɪmz/, **O·lym·pics** /əˈlɪmpɪks/ n the Olympic Games/the Olympics an international sports event held every four years —**Olympic** adj

ome·lette BrE, **omelet** AmE /ˈɒmlᵻtlˈɑːm-/ n [C] eggs beaten together and cooked, often with other foods added: a cheese omelette

o·men /ˈəʊmənlˈoʊ-/ n [C] a sign of what will happen in the future: a good omen

om·i·nous /ˈɒmᵻnəslˈɑː-/ adj making you feel that something bad is going to happen: ominous black clouds —**ominously** adv

o·mis·sion /əʊˈmɪʃən, ə-lloʊ-, ə-/ n [C,U] when someone is not included or something is not done: This report is full of mistakes and omissions.

o·mit /əʊˈmɪt, ə-lloʊ-, ə-/ v [T] **-tted, -tting** to not include someone or something: Several important details had been omitted.

om·ni·bus /ˈɒmnᵻbəs, -ˌbʌslˈɑːm-/ n [C] especially BrE a book that has a lot of stories, or a single programme that includes several separate programmes: the omnibus edition of Brookside

om·nip·o·tent /ɒmˈnɪpətəntllɑːm-/ adj formal very powerful and able to control everything —**omnipotence** n [U]

on¹ /ɒnlɑːn, ɔːn/ prep 1 on the surface of something: She was sitting on the bed. | the picture on the wall → see colour picture on page 474 2 in a place, or on a page: Henry grew up on a farm. | The answer is on page 44. 3 next to the side of a river, sea, road etc: a restaurant on the river 4 on the left/right on the left or right side of something 5 at some time during a particular day: See you on Monday. | He was killed on 22nd November 1963. 6 shown on television, or broadcast on the radio: There's a good comedy on TV tonight. 7 about a subject: a book on China 8 used to say that a person or thing is affected by something: a new tax on imported wine 9 using something to do something: Did you do these graphs on a computer? 10 travelling by bus, plane, train etc: Did you come here on the bus? 11 informal taking a medicine or drugs: She's on antibiotics. 12 **on a trip/vacation/holiday etc** during a trip, holiday etc: They met on a trip to Spain. 13 have/carry sth on you to have something with you now: Do you have a pen on you? 14 if you

spend money or time on something, you spend the money or time in order to do it or buy it 15 belonging to a team, committee, council etc: He's on the selection panel. 16 immediately after something happens: He was arrested on his return to Ireland. 17 spoken used to say that someone will pay for a meal, drink etc: Dinner's on me.

on² adv 1 used to say that someone continues to do something, or that something continues to happen: The peace talks dragged on (=continued slowly) for months. 2 operating or working: The lights are still on in her office. → opposite OFF¹ 3 if you have a piece of clothing on, you are wearing it: **put sth on** Put your coat on, it's cold out. 4 into a bus, plane, train, or ship: I got on at Vine Street. 5 **from then on/from that day on** after that time into the future: From that day on he hasn't drunk any alcohol. **on and off/off and on** (OFF¹) → see also HEAD-ON, **later on** (LATER¹)

on³ adj 1 if a film or television show is on, it is being shown or broadcast: The local news will be on in a minute. 2 if a machine is on, it is operating or working: The fax machine isn't on. → opposite OFF¹ 3 if an event is on, it will happen: There's a big pop festival on this weekend. 4 **it's not on** spoken used when you think someone should not do something

once¹ /wʌns/ adv 1 one time: "Have you been to Texas?" "Yes, but only once." | **once more/again** (=one more time): Say that once more. | **once a week/year etc** (=one time every week, year etc): She goes to the gym once a week. 2 **(every) once in a while** sometimes, but not often: My uncle sends us money every once in a while. 3 **at once a)** at the same time: I can't do two things at once! **b)** immediately: Everybody knew at once how serious the situation was. 4 **all at once** suddenly: All at once, the room went quiet. 5 in the past, but not now: This island once belonged to Portugal. 6 **for once** spoken used to say that something should happen more often: Will you just listen, for once? 7 **once and for all** definitely and finally: Let's settle this once and for all. 8 **once upon a time** a long time ago – used in children's stories 9 **once in a blue moon** very rarely: "How often do you see her?" "Only once in a blue moon."

once² linking word from the time something happens: Once he starts talking, it's difficult to shut him up.

once-o·ver /ˈ. ˌ../ n informal **give sb/sth the once-over** to quickly check something or someone: Ollie gave the car the once-over and decided not to buy it.

on·com·ing /ˈɒnˌkʌmɪŋllˈɑːn-, ˈɔːn-/ adj oncoming cars are coming towards you

one¹ /wʌn/ number 1 1 2 one o'clock: I have a meeting at one. 3 **one or two** a few: We've made one or two changes.

one² pron, plural **ones** 1 used when you are talking about someone or something that has already been mentioned: "Do you have a bike?"

GRAMMAR NOTE: the past perfect
You form the **past perfect** using **had** and the past participle. Use the past perfect to talk about something that happened in the past before another past action: Kay stayed behind after everyone else **had gone** home. | She told me what she **had done**.

"No, but I'm getting one for my birthday." | **the one** *Jane's the one with the red hair.* **2 one by one** if people do something one by one, first one person does it, then the next etc: *One by one, the passengers got off the bus.* **3 one after the other/one after another** if events or actions happen one after the other, they happen without much time between them: *He's had one problem after another this year.* **4 (all) in one** if something is many different things all in one, it is all of those things: *This is a TV, radio, and VCR all in one.* **5** *formal* used when you mean 'you', especially when you are talking about people in general: *One must be careful to keep exact records.*

one³ *determiner* **1** used to talk about a particular person or thing, especially when there are others of the same kind: *One reason I like the house is because of the big kitchen.* | **+ of** *One of the children is sick.* **2 one day/ afternoon etc a)** a particular day etc in the past: *I met him one day after school.* **b)** at some time in the future: *Let's go shopping one Saturday.* **3** only: *My one worry is that she will decide to leave college.* **4** *spoken* used to emphasize what you are saying about something or someone: *That is one cute kid!*

one an·oth·er /ˌ. .'../ *pron* each other: *They shook hands with one another.*

one-lin·er /ˌ. '../ *n* [C] a joke or funny remark that consists of one sentence

one-night stand /ˌ. . '. / *n* [C] *informal* when two people have sex, but do not intend to meet each other again

one-of-a-kind /ˌ. . '. / *adj* special and different from any other person or thing: *She's one of a kind.*

one-off /ˌ. '. ◂/ *adj* one-off things only happen once: *a one-off payment* — **one-off** *n* [C]

o·ner·ous /'ɒnərəs, 'əʊ-‖'ɑː-, 'oʊ-/ *adj formal* difficult and tiring: *onerous duties*

one·self /wʌn'self/ *pron formal* the REFLEXIVE form of 'one', used when you are talking about yourself or people in general

one-sid·ed /ˌ. '. ◂/ *adj* **1** only showing one opinion about a subject in a way that is unfair or makes people have the wrong idea: *a one-sided view of the problem* **2** a one-sided game or competition is one in which one person or team is much stronger than the other

one-time /'. . / *adj* former: *one-time bar-owner, Micky*

one-to-one /ˌ. . '. ◂/ *adj* between only two people: *tuition on a one-to-one basis*

one-track mind /ˌ. . '. / *n* **have a one-track mind** to always think about only one thing, usually sex

one-up·man·ship /wʌn 'ʌpmənʃɪp/ *n* [U] attempts to make yourself seem better than other people

one-way /ˌ. '. ◂/ *adj* **1** a one-way street is one on which cars can only travel in one direction **2** a one-way ticket is for travelling to a place, but not for coming back; SINGLE *BrE* → compare RETURN², ROUND TRIP

on·go·ing /'ɒn,gəʊɪŋ‖'ɑːn,goʊ-, 'ɔːn-/ *adj* continuing to happen: *ongoing discussions*

on·ion /'ʌnjən/ *n* [C,U] a round white vegetable, usually with brown skin, which has a

strong smell and taste: *a cheese and onion sandwich* → see picture at VEGETABLES

on·line, on-line /'ɒnlaɪn‖'ɑːn-, 'ɔːn-/ *adj, adv* **1** connected to other computers, especially computers that are on the INTERNET: *online banking facilities* (=available using the Internet) | **go online** (=start to be online): *All of our local schools will go online by the end of the year.* **2** directly connected to or controlled by a computer: *an online printer*

on·look·er /'ɒn,lʊkə‖'ɑːn,lʊkər, 'ɔːn-/ *n* [C] someone who watches something happening without being involved in it

on·ly¹ /'əʊnli‖'oʊnli/ *adv* **1** used to say that a number, price, or amount is surprisingly small: *Tammy was only 11 months old when she learned to walk.* | *A new TV for only £200!* **2** not more than: *It'll only take a few minutes.* | *You're only wearing a T-shirt.* **3** not anyone or anything else: *Parking is for customers only.* **4** not by any other method, or not for any other reason: *You can only get to the lake with a four-wheel-drive vehicle.* | *I only wanted to help.* **5** used to say that someone or something is not important: *It's only a piece of paper* **6** used to say that something happened very recently: *Congress passed the law only last year.* **7 only just a)** a very short time ago: *Lizzie's only just left.* **b)** almost not: *There's only just room for two people.* **8 if only** used to say that you wish you had done something: *If only I'd taken that job in Japan.* **9 not only...(but)** used to say that one thing is true, and another thing is also true, especially something that is surprising: *Not only is he a great footballer, he's also a poet.* **10 only too** very: **only too pleased/happy to do sth** *I'm sure he'll be only too pleased to see you.* | **know sth only too well** *He knew only too well the dangers he faced.*

USAGE NOTE: only

The meaning of a sentence can change depending on where you use **only**. Always put **only** just before the word it describes: *Only John saw the lion.* (=no one except John saw the lion) | *John only saw the lion.* (=he saw it, but he did not do anything else to it, such as take a photograph of it) | *John saw only the lion.* (=the lion was the only animal he saw)

---

only² *adj* **1** used to say that there are no other people or things of the same kind: *She's the only person I know who doesn't like chocolate.* **2 an only child** a child with no brothers or sisters **3 the only thing is...** *spoken* used when you want to talk about something that might be a problem: *I'd like to come see you – the only thing is my car's being fixed.*

only³ *linking word* but – used especially to talk about a problem that makes it difficult for you to do something: *We were going to go fishing, only it started raining.*

on-ramp /'. . / *n* [C] *AmE* a road for driving onto a HIGHWAY or FREEWAY → opposite OFF-RAMP

on·set /'ɒnset‖'ɑːn-, 'ɔːn-/ *n* **the onset of** the beginning of something: *the onset of the Cold War*

on·slaught /'ɒnslɔːt‖'ɑːnslɔːt, 'ɔːn-/ *n* [C] a very strong attack

on·to /'ɒntə; *before vowels* 'ɒntʊ‖'ɑːn-, 'ɒːn-/ *prep* **1** used with verbs showing movement to mean on a particular place: *The cat jumped onto the kitchen table.* → see colour picture on page 474 **2** **be onto sb** *informal* to know who did something wrong or illegal: *He knows we're onto him.* **3** **be onto something** *informal* to have an idea or information that may be very useful and important: *I think you may be onto something.*

o·nus /'əʊnəs‖'oʊ-/ *n* **the onus** the responsibility for doing something: *The onus is on the company to provide safety equipment.*

on·ward /'ɒnwəd‖'ɑːnward, 'ɒːn-/ *adj* moving forward or continuing: *the onward journey* —**onward, onwards** *adv*: *the history of Poland from 1919 onwards*

oo·dles /'uːdlz/ *n* **oodles of** *informal* a lot of

oops /ʊps/ *interjection* used when you have made a small mistake, dropped something etc: *Oops! I spilled the milk!*

ooze¹ /uːz/ *v* [I,T] **1** if a liquid oozes from something, or if something oozes a liquid, liquid flows from it slowly: *Blood oozed out of the wound.* **2** *informal* to show a lot of a particular quality: *His voice oozed confidence.*

ooze² *n* [U] very soft mud, especially at the bottom of a river

op /ɒp‖ɑːp/ *n* [C] *informal* a medical OPERATION

o·pal /'əʊpəl‖'oʊ-/ *n* [C,U] a white stone used in jewellery

o·paque /əʊ'peɪk‖oʊ-/ *adj* **1** not transparent **2** hard to understand → compare TRANSPARENT

open

open¹ /'əʊpən‖'oʊ-/ *adj* **1** not closed: *Who left the window open? | I could barely keep my eyes open. | A book lay open on the table.* **2** if a shop, bank etc is open, you can go into it and use it: *What time does the pharmacy open? | We're open until six.* **3** finished and ready for people to use: *When will the new library be open?* **4** available for anyone to do or take part in: **+ to** *Few jobs were open to women in those days.* **5** not surrounded by buildings, walls etc, or not covered: *walking across the open countryside | an open fire* **6** honest and not keeping anything secret: *We try to be open with each other.* **7** **keep/have an open mind** to not decide about something until you have heard what other people say about it **8** **keep your eyes/ears open** *spoken* to keep looking or listening carefully so that you notice anything that may be important **9** **open to criticism/discussion/misunderstanding etc** able to be criticized, discussed etc: *Her comments were open to misunderstanding.* **10** **be open to suggestions/new ideas** to want to hear other people's suggestions and ideas because you think they may be useful **11** not fastened: *His shirt was open.*

open² *v* **1** [T] to make something open: *Can you open the window? | She opened her eyes.* **2** [I] to become open: *The doors open automatically.* **3** [I] if a shop, bank etc opens at a particular time, people can use it after that time: *What time does the bookstore open on Sundays?* **4** [I] if a film, play, public building etc opens, people can start to see it or use it: *A new play opens next week on Broadway | The restaurant first opened in 1986.* **5** [I,T] to spread something out, or become spread out: *I can't open my umbrella. | The flowers are starting to open.* **6** [T] to make something officially available for people to use or visit: *Parts of the White House will be opened to the public.* **7** **open fire** to start shooting at someone or something: **+ on** *Troops opened fire on the protesters.* **8** [T] if you open a bank account, you arrange for it to start

open into/onto sth *phr v* [T] to lead directly into a place: *The kitchen opens onto the back yard.*

open up *phr v* **1** [I,T **open** sth ↔ **up**] to become available or possible, or to make something available or possible: *New business opportunities are opening up all the time.* **2** [I] to stop being shy and say what you really think: *It takes a long time for him to open up.*

USAGE NOTE: open, close, turn on, and **turn off**

Use **open** and **close** to talk about objects such as doors, windows, or boxes: *It's warm in here – could you open a window?* Use **turn on** and **turn off** to talk about water or gas, or about things that use electricity: *Turn on the TV; there's a good show on now.*

---

open³ *n* **in the open** **a)** outdoors: *It's fun to eat out in the open.* **b)** not hidden or secret: *The truth is finally out in the open.*

open-air /ˌ.. '.◂/ *adj* taking place outside, not in a building: *open-air concerts*

open-and-shut case /ˌ.. . '. / *n* [C] something that is very easy to prove

open day /'.. ./ *n* [C] *BrE* a day when a school or company lets people come in and see the work that is being done there

open-end·ed /ˌ.. '.◂/ *adj* without a fixed ending time: *an open-ended contract*

o·pen·er /'əʊpənə‖'oʊpənər/ *n* [C] **can/tin/bottle opener** something you use to open cans, bottles etc

open-heart sur·ge·ry /ˌ.. . '.../ *n* [U] when doctors cut open someone's chest to do an operation on their heart

open house /ˌ.. '. / *n* [C] *AmE* a time when a school, company etc lets people come in and see the work that is done there

o·pen·ing¹ /'əʊpənɪŋ‖'oʊ-/ *n* [C] **1** when a new business, building etc starts to be available for people to use: *the opening of the new art gallery* **2** the beginning of something: *a speech at the opening of the conference* **3** a job or opportunity that is available: *Are there any openings for gardeners?* **4** [C] a hole or space in something: *an opening in the fence*

opening² *adj* first or happening at the beginning: *the President's opening remarks | opening night* (=the first night of a new play, film etc)

O

o·pen·ly /ˈəʊpənli‖ˈoʊ-/ *adv* honestly and without keeping anything secret: *a chance to talk openly about your problems*

open-mind·ed /ˌ.. ˈ..◂/ *adj* interested in hearing about new ideas and using new ways of doing things: *My doctor isn't very open-minded about new treatments.* —**open-mindedness** *n* [U]

open-mouthed /ˌ.. ˈ.◂/ *adj, adv* with your mouth wide open, especially because you are surprised or shocked: *The children were staring open-mouthed at the television.*

o·pen·ness /ˈəʊpən-nɪs‖ˈoʊ-/ *n* [U] **1** when someone is honest and does not keep things secret **2** when someone is interested in hearing new ideas and suggestions from other people

open plan /ˌ.. ˈ./ *adj* an open plan office, school etc does not have walls dividing it into separate rooms

op·e·ra /ˈɒpərə‖ˈɑː-/ *n* [C,U] a musical play in which all of the words are sung — **operatic** /ˌɒpəˈrætɪk◂‖ˌɑːp-/ *adj* — **operatically** /-kli/ *adv* → see also SOAP OPERA

op·e·rate /ˈɒpəreɪt‖ˈɑː-/ *v* **1** [I,T] to work, or to make something work: *The machine seems to be operating smoothly.*|*He doesn't know how to operate the equipment.* **2** [I] to cut open someone's body in order to remove or repair a part that is damaged: *Surgeons operated on him for eight hours.* **3** [I,T] to take part in business activities, or to manage and control a business: *a large mining company, operating in Western Australia* **4** [I] to have a particular effect, or be used in a particular way: + **as** *These cells operate as a kind of early warning system.*

op·e·rat·ing room /ˈ.... ,./ *n* [C] *AmE* a part of a hospital where doctors do operations; OPERATING THEATRE *BrE*

operating sys·tem /ˈ.... ,../ *n* [C] a system in a computer that helps all the PROGRAMS to work

operating thea·tre /ˈ.... ,../ *n* [C] *BrE* a part of a hospital where doctors do operations; OPERATING ROOM *AmE*

op·e·ra·tion /ˌɒpəˈreɪʃən‖ˌɑː-/ *n* [C] **1** when doctors cut into someone's body to repair or remove a part that is damaged: *She's having an operation on her knee.* **2** [C] when people work together in a planned way in order to try and do something: *a rescue operation* **3** [C,U] part of a business or organization, or one of the parts of a company or organization: *GM has sold off its UK truck operation* **4** **be in operation** if a system or machine is in operation, it is working: *Video cameras were in operation.* **5** [U] the way in which something works, or when someone makes something work: *The job involves the operation of heavy machinery.*

op·e·ra·tion·al /ˌɒpəˈreɪʃənəl◂‖ˌɑː-/ *adj* **1** working and ready to be used: *The new airport will soon be operational.* **2** relating to the work of a business, government etc: *operational costs* — **operationally** *adv*

op·e·ra·tive /ˈɒpərətɪv‖ˈɑːpərə-, -ˈɑːpəreɪ-/ *adj* working or having an effect: *The law will become operative in a month.*

op·e·ra·tor /ˈɒpəreɪtə‖ˈɑːpəreɪtər/ *n* [C] **1** someone who works on a telephone SWITCHBOARD: *Ask the operator to help you with the call.* **2** someone whose job is to use a machine or piece of equipment: *a computer operator* **3** a company that does a particular type of business: *a tour operator*

oph·thal·mol·o·gy /ˌɒfθælˈmɒlədʒi‖ˌɑːfθæl-ˈmɑː-/ *n* [U] *technical* the study of eyes and eye diseases — **ophthalmologist** *n* [C]

o·pin·ion /əˈpɪnjən/ *n* **1** [C] what you think about a subject or situation: + **about/on** *Can I ask your opinion about something?*|**in my opinion** *spoken* (=used to say what you think about something): *In my opinion, he made the right decision.*|**public opinion** (=what most people in a country think): *Public opinion is against nuclear power.*|**get a second opinion** (=ask another person to advise you after you have already asked someone else) → see also **difference of opinion** (DIFFERENCE), **be a matter of opinion** (MATTER[1]) **2** **have a high/low/good etc opinion of** to think that someone or something is good, bad etc: *Her boss has a high opinion of her work.*

o·pin·ion·at·ed /əˈpɪnjəneɪtɪd/ *adj* having very strong opinions, in a way that annoys people: *an opinionated old fool*

opinion poll /ˈ... ./ *n* [C] when a lot of people are asked what they think about a subject, especially about politics

o·pi·um /ˈəʊpiəm‖ˈoʊ-/ *n* [U] a very strong illegal drug made from POPPY seeds

op·po·nent /əˈpəʊnənt‖əˈpoʊ-/ *n* [C] **1** someone who tries to defeat another person in a competition, game etc: *His opponent is twice as big as he is.* **2** someone who disagrees with a plan, idea etc: *opponents of Darwin's theory*

op·por·tune /ˈɒpətjuːn‖ˌɑːpərˈtuːn/ *adj formal* an opportune moment/time etc a good time for doing something

op·por·tun·ist /ˌɒpəˈtjuːnɪst‖ˌɑːpərˈtuː-/ *n* [C] someone who uses every chance to get power or advantages — **opportunism** *n* [U] — **opportunist, opportunistic** /ˌɒpətjuːˈnɪstɪk◂‖ˌɑːpərtuː-/ *adj*

op·por·tu·ni·ty /ˌɒpəˈtjuːnɪti‖ˌɑːpərˈtuː-/ *n* [C,U] a chance to do something: *I haven't had the opportunity to thank him yet.*|*job opportunities*

op·pose /əˈpəʊz‖əˈpoʊz/ *v* [T] to disagree with something and try to stop it: *They continue to oppose any changes to the present system.*

op·posed /əˈpəʊzd‖əˈpoʊzd/ *adj* **1** **be opposed to** to believe that something is wrong and should not be allowed: *Most people are opposed to the death penalty.* **2** **as opposed to** used to compare two different things or amounts: *The discount price is £25, as opposed to the usual price of £50.*

op·pos·ing /əˈpəʊzɪŋ‖əˈpoʊ-/ *adj* **1** opposing teams, groups etc are competing or arguing with each other **2** opposing ideas, opinions etc are completely different from each other

op·po·site[1] /ˈɒpəzɪt‖ˈɑː-/ *adj* **1** completely different: *I thought the music would relax me, but it had the opposite effect.* **2** facing something, or directly across from something: *a building on the opposite side of the river* **3** **the opposite sex** people who are of a different sex: *She finds it hard to talk to members of the opposite sex.* (=men)

opposite[2] *prep adv* if one thing or person is opposite another, they are facing each other: *Put the piano opposite the sofa.*|*He's moved into the house opposite.* → see colour picture on page 474

opposite³ *n* [C] something that is completely different from something else: *Everyone thought that the US would win easily. Instead, the opposite happened.*

opposite num·ber /ˌ... ˈ../ *n* [C usually singular] someone who does the same job as you for a different organization, a different country etc: *The British Foreign Secretary will meet his opposite number in the White House today.*

op·po·si·tion /ˌɒpəˈzɪʃən||ˌɑː-/ *n* [U] **1** when people disagree strongly with something: **+ to** *opposition to the war* **2** **the opposition** the person, team, company etc that you are trying to defeat or be more successful than **3** **the Opposition** *BrE* the second biggest political party in parliament, which is not in the government

op·press /əˈpres/ *v* [T] to treat people in an unfair and cruel way —**oppression** /əˈpreʃən/ *n* [U]

op·pressed /əˈprest/ *adj* treated unfairly or cruelly: *the oppressed minorities of Eastern Europe*

op·pres·sive /əˈpresɪv/ *adj* **1** cruel and unfair: *an oppressive military government* **2** making you feel uncomfortable: *oppressive heat*

op·pres·sor /əˈpresə||-ər/ *n* [C] a person or group that treats people in a cruel and unfair way

opt /ɒpt||ɑːpt/ *v* [I] to choose one thing instead of another: **+ for** *We've opted for a smaller car.* | **opt to do sth** *More high school students are opting to go to college.*

    opt out *phr v* [I] to choose not to join in a group or system: *Several countries may opt out of the agreement.*

op·tic /ˈɒptɪk||ˈɑːp-/ *adj* relating to the eyes: *the optic nerve* → see also OPTICS

op·ti·cal /ˈɒptɪkəl||ˈɑːp-/ *adj* **1** relating to the way light is seen, or relating to the eyes: *an optical instrument* **2** using light to record and store information, especially in computer systems —**optically** /-kli/ *adv*

optical il·lu·sion /ˌ... ·ˈ../ *n* [C] a picture or image that tricks your eyes and makes you see something that is not actually there

op·ti·cian /ɒpˈtɪʃən||ɑːp-/ *n* [C] **1** *BrE* someone who tests people's eyes and sells them GLASSES in a shop **2** *AmE* someone who makes GLASSES

op·tics /ˈɒptɪks||ˈɑːp-/ *n* [U] the scientific study of light → see also FIBRE OPTICS

op·ti·mis·m /ˈɒptɪmɪzəm||ˈɑːp-/ *n* [U] the belief that good things will happen: *optimism about the country's economic future* → opposite PESSIMISM

op·ti·mist /ˈɒptɪmɪst||ˈɑːp-/ *n* [C] someone who usually believes that good things will happen → opposite PESSIMIST

op·ti·mis·tic /ˌɒptɪˈmɪstɪk◄||ˌɑːp-/ *adj* believing that good things will happen in the future: **+ about** *Tom's optimistic about finding a job.* —**optimistically** /-kli/ *adv* → opposite PESSIMISTIC

op·ti·mum /ˈɒptɪməm||ˈɑːp-/ *adj formal* best or most suitable for a particular purpose: *optimum use of space*

op·tion /ˈɒpʃən||ˈɑːp-/ *n* [C] **1** something that you can choose to do: *It's the only option we have left.* **2** **have no option (but to do sth)** to have to do something, especially when you do not want to do it: *They had no option but to cut jobs.* **3** **keep/leave your options open** to not make a definite decision so that you have more possibilities to choose from: *Leave your options open until you have the results of the test.*

op·tion·al /ˈɒpʃənəl||ˈɑːp-/ *adj* if something is optional, you can choose to have it or do it, but do not have to: *The sunroof is optional.*

op·tom·e·trist /ɒpˈtɒmɪtrɪst||ɑːpˈtɑː-/ *n* [C] someone who examines people's eyes and orders GLASSES for them —**optometry** *n* [U]

op·u·lent /ˈɒpjʊlənt||ˈɑːp-/ *adj* decorated in an expensive way: *an opulent hotel* —**opulence** *n* [U] —**opulently** *adv*

or /ə; *strong* ɔː||ər; *strong* ɔːr/ *linking word* **1** used between two possibilities, or before the last in a series of possibilities: *Coffee or tea?* | *You can go by bus, by train, or by plane.* → compare EITHER¹ **2** used after a negative verb when you mean not one thing and not another thing: *They don't eat meat or fish.* **3** **also** **or else** used to warn someone that something bad will happen if they do not do something: *Hurry, or you'll miss your plane.* **4** **two or three/20 or 30 etc** used to say that you are not sure of the exact amount, but it is about two, three etc: *"How many people were there?" "About 30 or 40."* **5** **or so** used after a number, time, distance etc. to show that it is not exact: *There's a gas station a mile or so down the road.* **6** **or anything/something** *spoken* used to talk or ask about something similar to the thing you have just mentioned: *Do you want to go out for a drink or anything?* **7** used to further explain something that you have just said: *biology, or the study of living things*

o·ral¹ /ˈɔːrəl/ *adj* **1** spoken, not written: *an oral report* **2** relating to the mouth: *oral hygiene*

oral² *n* [C] a test in which questions and answers are spoken rather than written

or·ange¹ /ˈɒrɪndʒ||ˈɔː-, ˈɑː-/ *n* [C,U] **1** a round fruit with a thick skin, that is a colour between red and yellow, and contains a lot of juice → see picture at FRUIT **2** the colour of an orange → see colour picture on page 114

orange² *adj* having the colour between red and yellow: *an orange sweater*

o·rang·u·tang /ɔːˌræŋuːˈtæŋ||ɔːˈræŋətæŋ/ **also** **o·rang·u·tan** /-tæn/ *n* [C] a large animal like a monkey that has long arms and long orange hair

o·ra·tion /əˈreɪʃən, ɔː-/ *n* [C] *formal* a speech

or·a·tor /ˈɒrətə||ˈɔːrətər, ˈɑː-/ *n* [C] someone who is good at making political speeches

or·bit¹ /ˈɔːbɪt||ˈɔːr-/ *n* [C] the circle that something moves in when it is going around the Earth, the sun etc

---

GRAMMAR NOTE: the future
To talk about the **future** you can use: 1. **will** + basic form of verb: *I'll* (=I will) *see you tomorrow.* 2. **be going to** (used to say that something will happen soon): *I think it's going to rain.* 3. the **present progressive** (used to say what is planned or intended): *We're having a party on Saturday.*

orbit² *v* [I,T] to travel in space around a larger object such as the Earth, the sun etc: *a satellite that orbits the Earth*

or·chard /'ɔːtʃədll'ɔːrtʃərd/ *n* [C] a place where fruit trees are grown

or·ches·tra /'ɔːkɪstrəll'ɔːr-/ *n* [C] a large group of musicians who play CLASSICAL music together —**orchestral** /ɔː'kestrəllɔːr-/ *adj*

or·ches·trate /'ɔːkɪstreitll'ɔːr-/ *v* [T] to secretly organize the way something happens, especially something dishonest or unfair: *a carefully orchestrated propaganda campaign*

or·chid /'ɔːkɪdll'ɔːr-/ *n* [C] a tropical flower which is often very beautiful and unusual

or·dain /ɔː'deɪnllɔːr-/ *v* [T] to officially make someone a priest

or·deal /ɔː'diːl, 'ɔːdiːlllɔːr'diːl, 'ɔːrdiːl/ *n* [C] a very unpleasant experience: *School can be an ordeal for some children.*

or·der¹ /'ɔːdəll'ɔːrdər/ *n* **1** **in order to do sth** so that something can happen, or so that someone can do something: *Plants need light in order to live.* | *She had the operation in order to save her eyesight.* **2** [C,U] the way that several things are arranged, and which is first, which is second etc: *Can you keep the pictures in the same order?* | *The names were written in alphabetical order.* (=with 'a' first, then 'b' etc) **3** [C] when a customer asks for a particular kind of food or drink in a restaurant: **take sb's order** (=write down what someone wants to eat): *Can I take your order?* **4** [C] when a customer asks a company to make or send goods: *The school has just put in an order for 10 new computers.* **5** [C] an official instruction from someone in authority that must be obeyed: *Captain Marshall gave the order to advance.* **6** **out of order a)** if a machine is out of order, it has stopped working: *The photocopier is out of order again.* **b)** not arranged in the right order: *Don't let the files get out of order.* **7** **in order a)** legally or officially correct: *Your passport seems to be in order.* **b)** arranged in the right order: *Are all the slides in order?* **8** [U] when people obey laws or rules, and do not cause trouble: *Police are working hard to maintain law and order.* **9** [singular, U] the situation that exists in a country or area at a particular time: *a new world order*

order² *v* **1** [I,T] to ask for food or drink in a restaurant, bar etc: *He sat down and ordered a beer.* **2** [T] to ask a company to make or send something: *I've ordered a new table for the kitchen.* **3** [T] to officially tell someone that they must do something: *The judge ordered the jury not to discuss the trial.* **4** [T] to arrange something in a particular way: *The names are ordered alphabetically.*

USAGE NOTE: order and command

Order is used for most situations in which someone who is in a position of authority tells other people to do something: *The governor ordered an investigation into the shootings.* Use **command** when someone in the army, navy etc tells someone to do something: *The general commanded his troops to fire.*

---

or·der·ly¹ /'ɔːdəlill'ɔːrdərli/ *adj* **1** arranged or organized in a neat way: *an orderly desk* **2** well-behaved and not noisy: *an orderly crowd*

orderly² *n* [C] someone who does jobs in a hospital which do not need any special training

or·di·nal num·ber /ˌɔːdɪnəl 'nʌmbəllˌɔːrdɪnəl 'nʌmbər/ *n* [C] a number such as first, second, third etc →compare CARDINAL NUMBER

or·di·nance /'ɔːdɪnənsll'ɔːrdənəns/ *n* [C] especially AmE a law in a city or town, which states that something is not allowed or is limited: *parking ordinances*

or·di·na·ri·ly /'ɔːdənər‚lilˌɔːrdən'er‚li/ *adv* especially AmE usually: *I don't ordinarily go to movies in the afternoon.*

or·di·na·ry /'ɔːdənərill'ɔːrdəneri/ *adj* **1** not special, unusual, or different from other things: *It looks like an ordinary car, but it has a very special type of engine.* **2** ordinary people are not famous, rich, powerful, specially trained etc: *legal documents that are difficult for ordinary people to understand* **3** **out of the ordinary** very different from what usually happens

or·di·na·tion /ˌɔːdɪ'neɪʃənllˌɔːr-/ *n* [C,U] the ceremony in which someone is officially made a priest: *protests against the ordination of women* →see also ORDAIN

ore /ɔːllɔːr/ *n* [C,U] rock or earth from which metal can be obtained

or·gan /'ɔːgənll'ɔːr-/ *n* [C] **1** part of the body of a human, animal, or plant that has a particular purpose: *the liver and other internal organs* **2** a musical instrument like a piano, with large pipes to make the sound, played especially in churches **3** an electronic instrument with a KEYBOARD like a piano

or·gan·ic /ɔː'gænɪkllɔːr-/ *adj* **1** related to or produced by living things: *organic matter* →opposite INORGANIC **2** using farming methods that do not use chemicals that are harmful to the environment, or produced by these methods: *organic vegetables* —**organically** /-kli/ *adv*

or·gan·i·sa·tion /ˌɔːgənaɪ'zeɪʃənllˌɔːrgənə-/ a British spelling of ORGANIZATION

or·gan·ise /'ɔːgənaɪzll'ɔːr-/ a British spelling of ORGANIZE

or·gan·ised /'ɔːgənaɪzdll'ɔːr-/ a British spelling of ORGANIZED

or·gan·i·ser /'ɔːgənaɪzəll'ɔːrgənaɪzər/ a British spelling of ORGANIZER

or·gan·is·m /'ɔːgənɪzəmll'ɔːr-/ *n* [C] a living thing: *a microscopic organism*

or·gan·ist /'ɔːgən‚stll'ɔːr-/ *n* [C] someone who plays the ORGAN

or·gan·i·za·tion (also **-isation** BrE) /ˌɔːgənaɪ-'zeɪʃənllˌɔːrgənə-/ *n* **1** [C] a group that a lot of people, countries etc belong to, so that they can meet and do something together: *a charity organization* | *an organization of Christian students* **2** [U] the way in which something is organized, or the activity of organizing something: *He was responsible for the organization of the party's election campaign.* —**organizational** *adj*

or·gan·ize (also **-ise** BrE) /'ɔːgənaɪzll'ɔːr-/ *v* **1** [T] to plan or arrange something: *Who's organizing the New Year's party?* **2** [I,T] especially AmE to form an organization that protects workers' rights, or to persuade people to join one

or·gan·ized (also **-ised** BrE) /ˈɔːgənaɪzd‖ˈɔːr-/ adj **1 well organized/badly organized a)** planned and arranged well or badly: The exhibition wasn't very well organized. **b)** good or bad at organizing the things that you have to do: She's really badly organized. **2** an organized activity is arranged for and done by many people: organized sports

organized crime /ˌ... ˈ./ n [U] a large and powerful organization of criminals

or·gan·iz·er (also **-iser** BrE) /ˈɔːgənaɪzə‖ˈɔːrgənaɪzər/ n [C] someone who organizes an event: festival organizers

or·gas·m /ˈɔːgæzəm‖ˈɔːr-/ n [C,U] the moment when you have the greatest sexual pleasure during sex

or·gy /ˈɔːdʒi‖ˈɔːr-/ n [C] **1** a wild party, especially one in which people drink a lot of alcohol and have sex together **2 an orgy of** when people do something a lot, especially something bad: an orgy of violence

O·ri·ent /ˈɔːriənt, ˈɒ-‖ˈɔː-/ n **the Orient** old-fashioned the eastern part of the world, especially China and Japan

o·ri·en·tal /ˌɔːriˈentl‹, ˌɒ-‖ˌɔː-/ n [C] old-fashioned someone from Asia. Some people now consider this use of the word to be offensive

Oriental adj relating to Asia: Oriental culture

o·ri·en·ta·tion /ˌɔːriənˈteɪʃən, ˌɒ-‖ˌɔː-/ n **1** [C,U] the kind of beliefs and ideas that a group or person has: the group's right-wing political orientation **2** [U] training and preparation for a new job or activity: orientation week for new students **3 sexual orientation** whether someone is HETEROSEXUAL or HOMOSEXUAL

o·ri·ent·ed /ˈɔːrientɪd, ˈɒ-‖ˈɔː-/ also **orientated** BrE — adj mainly concerned with or aimed at a particular thing or group of people: complaints that the magazine has become too politically oriented

or·i·gin /ˈɒrɪdʒɪn‖ˈɔː-, ˈɑː-/ n [C,U] **1** the situation or place from which something comes, or where it began to exist: The word is of Latin origin. | the origin of life on Earth **2** the country, race, or class from which someone comes: He's proud of his Italian origins.

o·rig·i·nal[1] /əˈrɪdʒɪnəl, -dʒənəl/ adj **1** existing first, before any changes were made: The house still has its original stone floor. | Our original plan was too expensive. **2** the original painting, document etc is the one that existed first, and is not a copy: Is that an original Matisse? (=painting by Matisse) **3** completely new and different: a highly original style of painting

original[2] n [C] a painting, document etc that is not a copy

o·rig·i·nal·i·ty /əˌrɪdʒɪˈnælɪti/ n [U] the quality of being completely new and different: The design is good but lacks originality.

o·rig·i·nal·ly /əˈrɪdʒɪnəli, -dʒənəli/ adv in the beginning: Her family originally came from Thailand.

o·rig·i·nate /əˈrɪdʒɪneɪt/ v [I] formal to start to develop in a particular place or at a particular time: **+ in** The custom of having a Christmas tree originated in Germany.

or·na·ment /ˈɔːnəmənt‖ˈɔːr-/ n [C] an object that you keep in your house as a decoration: china ornaments

or·na·men·tal /ˌɔːnəˈmentl‹‖ˌɔːr-/ adj intended to be attractive rather than useful: ornamental plants

or·nate /ɔːˈneɪt‖ɔːr-/ adj having a lot of decoration: ornate furniture — **ornately** adv

or·ni·thol·o·gy /ˌɔːnɪˈθɒlədʒi‖ˌɔːrnɪˈθɑː-/ n [U] the study of birds — **ornithologist** n [C]

or·phan[1] /ˈɔːfən‖ˈɔːr-/ n [C] a child whose parents are dead

orphan[2] v [T] **be orphaned** to become an orphan when your parents die

or·phan·age /ˈɔːfənɪdʒ‖ˈɔːr-/ n [C] a place where orphans live, especially in past times

or·tho·dox /ˈɔːθədɒks‖ˈɔːrθədɑːks/ adj **1** believing in the traditional beliefs of a religion: an orthodox Jew **2** orthodox ideas or methods are the ones that most people think are the right or normal ones, especially because they have been used for a long time: orthodox methods of treating disease — **orthodoxy** n [C,U]

os·ten·si·ble /ɒˈstensɪbəl‖ɑː-/ adj [only before noun] an ostensible reason, aim etc is the one that is supposed to be true, but is not the real reason, aim etc: The ostensible reason for his dismissal was poor sales figures. — **ostensibly** adv

os·ten·ta·tious /ˌɒstənˈteɪʃəs, -ten-‖ˌɑː-/ adj done in order to make other people notice and admire you — **ostentatiously** adv — **ostentation** n [U]

os·tra·cize (also **-ise** BrE) /ˈɒstrəsaɪz‖ˈɑː-/ v [T] to be unfriendly towards someone, and not allow them to be part of your group: There was a time when criminals would be ostracized by the whole village. — **ostracism** /-sɪzəm/ n [U]

os·trich /ˈɒstrɪtʃ‖ˈɒː-, ˈɑː-/ n [C] a big African bird with long legs, that cannot fly

oth·er[1] /ˈʌðə‖ˈʌðər/ determiner adj **1** used when you have mentioned one person or thing from a group and want to talk about one or more of the rest: Anna has a job, but the other girls are still at school. | **the other one** Here's one sock, where's the other one? **2** used to talk about things or people that exist in addition to the person or thing you are talking about: The other students are about the same age as me. **3** used to talk about people or things that are different to the ones you are talking about: Can we meet some other time – I'm busy right now. | Their cottage is on the other side of the lake. **4 the other day/morning etc** spoken a few days ago; recently: I was talking to Ted the other day. **5 other than** except: She has no-one to talk to other than her family. **6 every other day/week etc** one day, week etc in every two: Her husband cooks dinner every other day. ➔ compare ANOTHER ➔ see also EACH OTHER

other[2] pron **1** used when you have mentioned one person or thing from a group and want to talk about one or more of the rest: We ate one of the pizzas and froze the other. **2** used to talk about things or people that exist in addition to the person or thing you are talking about: John's here – where are the others? **3 someone/something etc or other** used when you cannot be certain about what you are saying: We'll get the money somehow or other.

oth·er·wise /ˈʌðəwaɪz‖ˈʌðər-/ adv **1** used to say what will happen if something else does not happen first: You'd better go now, otherwise you'll be late. **2** except for what has just been mentioned: *The sleeves are a bit long, but otherwise the dress fits fine.* **3 think/decide etc otherwise** to think or decide the opposite of what someone else thinks or decides

ot·ter /ˈɒtə‖ˈɑːtər/ *n* [C] a small animal with brown fur, that swims and eats fish

ouch /aʊtʃ/ *interjection* something you say when you suddenly feel pain: *Ouch! That hurt!*

ought /ɔːt‖ɒːt/ *modal verb* **1** used to say someone should do something: **ought to (do sth)** *You ought to take a day off.* **2 ought to** used to say that you expect something to happen or be true: *The weather ought to be nice in August.* ➔ compare SHOULD

oughtn't /ˈɔːtnt‖ˈɒː-/ the short form of 'ought not'

ounce /aʊns/ *n* [C] **1** written abbreviation **oz**; a unit for measuring weight, equal to 1/16 of a pound or 28.35 grams **2 an ounce of truth/sense/ intelligence etc** a small amount of truth, sense etc: *If you had an ounce of sense, you'd leave him.*

our /aʊə‖aʊr/ *determiner* belonging to or relating to 'us': *Our daughter is at college.*

ours /aʊəz‖aʊrz/ *pron* the one or ones that belong to or are connected with us: *"Whose car is that?" "It's ours."* | *They have their tickets, but ours haven't come yet.*

our·selves /aʊəˈselvz‖aʊr-/ *pron* **1** the RE-FLEXIVE form of 'we': *It was strange seeing ourselves on television.* **2** used to emphasize the word 'we': *We started this business ourselves.* **3 (all) by ourselves** alone or without help: *We found our way here all by ourselves.* **4 to ourselves** not having to share with other people: *We'll have the house to ourselves next week.*

oust /aʊst/ *v* [T] to force someone out of a position of power: *an attempt to oust the communists from power*

out /aʊt/ *adj, adv* **1** away from the inside of a place or container: *Close the door on your way out.* | **+ of** *All his tools were out of their box on the floor.* ➔ see colour picture on page 474 **2** not in the place where you usually are, such as home or work: *Ms Jackson is out right now.* **3** outside: *Why don't you go out and play?* **4** a light or fire that is out is not shining or burning: *OK, kids. Put the lights out.* **5 out of** used to say how many people or things from a group something is true of: *Out of all the gifted footballers, only a few get to play for their country.* **6 be out of sth** to have none of something left: *We're almost out of gas.* **7** available to be bought: *Morrison has a new book out this month.* **8** *spoken* not possible: *Skiing's out because it costs too much.* **9 be out for sth/be out to do sth** *informal* to intend to do or get something: *He's just out to get attention.* **10** not allowed to continue playing a game, according to its rules **11** if the TIDE is out, the sea is at its lowest level

out-and-out /ˌ‥ ˈ‥◂/ *adj* [only before noun] used to emphasize that something or someone is a particular kind of thing or person: *an out-and-out lie*

out·back /ˈaʊtbæk/ *n* **the outback** the part of Australia far away from cities, where not many people live

out·break /ˈaʊtbreɪk/ *n* [C] when something

bad like a serious disease or war starts: *an outbreak of malaria*

out·burst /ˈaʊtbɜːst‖-bɜːrst/ *n* [C] when someone suddenly shows a strong emotion, especially anger: *an angry outburst*

out·cast /ˈaʊtkɑːst‖-kæst/ *n* [C] someone who is not accepted by other people: *a social outcast*

out·class /aʊtˈklɑːs‖-ˈklæs/ *v* [T] to be much better than someone at doing something

out·come /ˈaʊtkʌm/ *n* [singular] the final result of a meeting, process etc: *the outcome of the election*

out·cry /ˈaʊtkraɪ/ *n* [singular] an angry protest by a lot of people **+ against** *a public outcry against nuclear weapons testing*

out·dat·ed /ˌaʊtˈdeɪtᵻd◂/ *adj* no longer useful or modern: *factories full of outdated machinery*

out·do /aʊtˈduː/ *v* [T] **outdid** /-ˈdɪd/, **outdone** /-ˈdʌn/, **outdoing** to be better or more successful than someone else: *two brothers trying to outdo each other*

out·door /ˈaʊtdɔː‖-dɔːr/ *adj* [only before noun] not covered by a building, or happening outside any buildings: *an outdoor swimming pool* ➔ opposite INDOOR

out·doors /ˌaʊtˈdɔːz‖-ɔːrz/ *adv* not inside any buildings; outside: *I prefer working outdoors.* ➔ opposite INDOORS

out·er /ˈaʊtə‖-ər/ *adj* [only before noun] **1** on the outside of something: *Peel off the outer leaves away.* **2** from the middle of something: *an outer office* ➔ opposite INNER

out·er·most /ˈaʊtəməʊst‖-tərmoʊst/ *adj* [only before noun] furthest from the middle of something: *the outermost planets* ➔ opposite INNER-MOST

outer space /ˌ‥ ˈ‥/ *n* [U] the area outside the Earth's air where the stars and PLANETS are

out·fit /ˈaʊtfɪt/ *n* [C] a set of clothes that you wear together: *He arrived at the party in a cowboy outfit.*

out·go·ing /ˌaʊtˈgəʊɪŋ‖-ˈgoʊ-/ *adj* **1** enjoying meeting and talking to people **2** the **outgoing president/government etc** a person or group that is finishing a job as president, government etc **3** [only before noun] going away from a place: *outgoing phone calls*

out·go·ings /ˈaʊtˌgəʊɪŋz‖-ˌgoʊ-/ *n* [plural] *BrE* the amount of money that you spend on rent, food etc

out·grow /aʊtˈgrəʊ‖-ˈgroʊ/ *v* [T] **outgrew** /-ˈgruː/, **outgrown** /-ˈgrəʊn‖-ˈgroʊn/, **outgrowing** **1** to grow too big for something: *Kara's already outgrown her shoes.* **2** to change and develop so that you stop enjoying something: *I've outgrown the job really.*

out·ing /ˈaʊtɪŋ/ *n* [C] a short trip for a group of people: *We're going on a family outing.*

out·land·ish /aʊtˈlændɪʃ/ *adj* strange and unusual: *outlandish clothes* — **outlandishly** *adv*

out·last /aʊtˈlɑːst‖-ˈlæst/ *v* [T] to exist for longer than someone or something else or do something for longer than someone: *The whole point of the game is to outlast your opponent.*

out·law¹ /ˈaʊtlɔː‖-lɒː/ *v* [T] to officially say that something is illegal: *Gambling was outlawed here in 1980.*

outlaw² *n* [C] *old-fashioned* someone who is hiding from the police

out·lay /ˈaʊtleɪ/ n [C,U] an amount of money that you spend to start a new business, activity etc: *a huge initial outlay*

out·let /ˈaʊtlet, -lˌt/ n [C] **1** a place where gas, liquid etc can flow out of something **2** a shop or organization that sells a company's products **3** a way of expressing or getting rid of strong feelings: *I use judo as an outlet for stress.*

outline

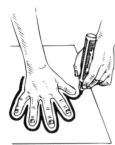

She is drawing an outline of her hand.

out·line¹ /ˈaʊtlaɪn/ n **1** [singular] the main ideas or facts about something: *an outline of the company's plan* **2** a line around the edge of something that shows its shape

outline² v [T] **1** to describe the main ideas or facts about something: *a speech outlining his work in refugee camps* **2** to draw a line around the edge of something to show its shape

out·live /aʊtˈlɪv/ v [T] to live longer than someone else: *She outlived her husband by 10 years.*

out·look /ˈaʊtlʊk/ n [C] **1** your general attitude to life and the world **+on** *Ann has a very positive outlook on life.* **2** what is expected to happen in the future **+ for** *The long-term outlook for the industry is worrying.*

out·ly·ing /ˈaʊtˌlaɪ-ɪŋ/ adj **outlying area/village/farm etc** a place that is a long way from other places

out·ma·noeu·vre *BrE*, **outmaneuver** *AmE* /ˌaʊtməˈnuːvəll-ər/ — v [T] to behave in a clever or skilful way so that you do better than someone

out·mod·ed /aʊtˈməʊdˌdll-ˈmoʊ-/ adj OUT-DATED

out·num·ber /aʊtˈnʌmbəll-ər/ v [T] to be greater in number than another group: *Women outnumber men in the nursing profession.*

out of bounds /ˌ. ˈ./ adj if a place is out of bounds, you are not allowed to go there: *The kitchen's out of bounds when I'm cooking.*

out-of-date /ˌ. ˈ.◂/ adj OUTDATED

out-of-the-way /ˌ. . ˈ.◂/ adj an out-of-the-way place is a long way from other places

out of work /ˌ. ˈ.◂/ adj without a paid job: *an out of work actor*

out·pa·tient /ˈaʊtˌpeɪʃənt/ n [C] someone who goes to a hospital for treatment but does not stay there all night

out·per·form /ˌaʊtpəˈfɔːmll-pərˈfɔːrm/ v [T] to do something better than other things or people: *Mart Stores continued to outperform other retailers.*

out·post /ˈaʊtpəʊstll-poʊst/ n [C] a small town or group of buildings a long way from other places

out·pour·ing /ˈaʊtpɔːrɪŋ/ n [C] when a lot of people suddenly start expressing an emotion: *the public outpouring of grief following the Princess's death*

out·put /ˈaʊtpʊt/ n [C,U] the amount of work, goods etc that someone or something produces: *Economic output is down by 10% this year.* ➔ compare INPUT

out·rage¹ /ˈaʊtreɪdʒ/ n [C,U] a feeling of extreme anger or shock, or something that causes this: *feelings of shock and outrage at such a brutal attack on a child* | *This is an outrage!*

outrage² v [T] to make someone feel very angry or shocked — **outraged** adj

out·ra·geous /aʊtˈreɪdʒəs/ adj very shocking and bad: *£200 for a hotel room – that's outrageous!* — **outrageously** adv

out·reach /ˈaʊtriːtʃ/ n [U] when an organization goes out to help people who have particular problems: *an outreach project for drug users*

out·right¹ /ˈaʊtraɪt/ adj [only before noun] **1** used to emphasize that something happens completely or someone does something completely: *outright victory* | *an outright ban on handguns* **2** saying something clearly and directly: *an outright refusal* | *an outright lie*

out·right² /aʊtˈraɪt/ adv **1** saying something clearly and directly: *You should have told him outright that you don't want to work there any more.* **2 be killed outright** to be killed immediately in an accident **3** completely: *They haven't rejected the plan outright.*

out·run /aʊtˈrʌn/ v [T] **outran** /-ˈræn/, **outrun**, **outrunning** **1** to run faster or further than someone **2** to develop more quickly than something: *The needs of the refugees have outrun the help available.*

out·set /ˈaʊtset/ n **at/from the outset** at or from the beginning of an event or process: *The rules were agreed at the outset of the game.*

out·shine /aʊtˈʃaɪn/ v [T] **outshone** /-ˈʃɒnll-ˈʃoʊn/, **outshone, outshining** to be much better at something than someone else

out·side¹ /aʊtˈsaɪd, ˈaʊtsaɪd/ also **outside of** especially AmE prep **1** out of a particular building or room, but still near it: *He left an envelope outside my door.* ➔ see colour picture on page 474 ➔ opposite INSIDE¹ **2** further than the edge of a city, town etc: *We live just outside Leeds.* **3** further than the limits of a situation, activity etc: *Teachers can't control what students do outside school.*

out·side² /aʊtˈsaɪd/ adv **1** not inside a building: *Can I go and play outside, Dad?* **2** not in a

GRAMMAR NOTE: 'if' clauses (1)
Use the simple present to talk about the future in clauses beginning **if...** : *I will hit you* **if** *you* **do** *that again.* *not* 'if you will do that again'. **If** *you* **take** *a taxi, you'll be OK. not* 'if you will take a taxi...'
Use 'will' in the other part of the sentence.

room or building, but close to it: *Wait outside, I want to talk to him alone.*

out·side³ /ˈaʊtˈsaɪd, ˈaʊtsaɪd/ *n* **1 the outside** the part of something that surrounds it: *The outside of the building is pink.* → opposite INSIDE² **2 on the outside** used to describe the way someone or something seems to be: *Their marriage seemed so perfect on the outside.*

out·side⁴ /ˈaʊtsaɪd/ *adj* [only before noun] **1 outside wall/toilet etc** a wall, toilet etc that is not inside a building **2 outside help/interest etc** help, interest etc from someone who does not belong to your group or organization

out·sid·er /aʊtˈsaɪdəll-ər/ *n* [C] someone who does not belong to a particular group, organization etc: *Sometimes I feel like an outsider in my own family.*

out·skirts /ˈaʊtskɜːtsll-skɜːrts/ *n* **the outskirts** the parts of a city or town that are furthest from the centre **on the outskirts** *They have an apartment on the outskirts of Geneva.*

out·spo·ken /aʊtˈspəʊkənll-ˈspoʊ-/ *adj* saying what you think even though it may shock or offend people: *an outspoken critic of the government's economic policy*

out·stand·ing /aʊtˈstændɪŋ/ *adj* **1** excellent and impressive: *an outstanding performance* **2** not yet done, paid, or solved: *an outstanding debt*

out·stand·ing·ly /aʊtˈstændɪŋli/ *adv* **outstandingly well/successful/beautiful etc** extremely well, successful etc: *The business has been outstandingly successful.*

out·stay /aʊtˈsteɪ/ *v* → see **outstay your welcome** (WELCOME)

out·stretched /ˌaʊtˈstretʃt◂/ *adj* outstretched arms, hands etc are stretched out as far as possible: *I took hold of his outstretched arm.*

out·strip /aʊtˈstrɪp/ *v* [T] **-pped, -pping** to be larger or better than someone or something else: *The pace of economic development far outstripped that of other countries.*

out·ward /ˈaʊtwədll-wərd/ *adj* **1 outward calm/control/composure etc** a feeling or quality that you seem to have, rather than one you really have: *Amy answered with outward composure.* **2** going away from a place or towards the outside: *an outward flight*

out·ward·ly /ˈaʊtwədlill-wərd-/ *adv* in the way people, things etc seem to be, rather than how they really are: *Outwardly he seems to be very happy.*

out·wards /ˈaʊtwədzll-wərdz/ *especially BrE* **outward** *especially AmE adv* towards the outside of something or away from the centre of something: *The universe is expanding outwards.* → opposite INWARDS

out·weigh /aʊtˈweɪ/ *v* [T] to be more important than something else: *The benefits outweigh the costs.*

out·wit /aʊtˈwɪt/ *v* [T] to use tricks or clever plans to do better than someone: *Our plan is to outwit the thieves.*

o·val /ˈaʊvəlll-oʊ-/ *n* [C] a shape like a circle, but which is longer than it is wide → see picture at SHAPES — **oval** *adj*

o·va·ry /ˈaʊvərill-oʊ-/ *n* [C] the part of a female person or animal that produces eggs

o·va·tion /aʊˈveɪʃənlloʊ-/ *n* [C] if people give someone an ovation, they CLAP their hands to show their approval: *standing ovation* (=when people stand and clap) → compare ENCORE

ov·en /ˈʌvən/ *n* [C] a piece of equipment that you cook food inside, shaped like a metal box with a door → see picture at KITCHEN

over¹ /ˈaʊvəllˈoʊvər/ *prep* **1** going from one side of something to the other, especially by jumping, climbing, flying, or crossing a bridge: *Can you jump over the stream?*|*the next bridge over the river* → compare ACROSS **2** above or higher than something: *The sign over the door said "No Exit."* → opposite UNDER¹ → compare ABOVE¹ ACROSS **3 over the road/street/river etc** on the opposite side of the road, street etc: *There's a supermarket over the road.* **4** on something or someone so that their hands or bodies are covered: *Put this blanket over him.* → see colour picture on page 474 → opposite UNDER¹ **5** more than a particular amount, number, or age: *It cost over £1000.* **6** during: *I saw Julie over the summer.* **7** down from the edge of something: *The car fell over a cliff.* **8 over here/there** used to direct someone to a place near to you, or near to a place you are looking at or talking about: *I'm over here!* **9 be/get over sth** to feel better after being ill or upset: *I still haven't got over this flu.* **10** about something: *They had an argument over who would take the car.* **11** using the telephone or a radio: *The salesman explained it to me over the phone.* → see also **all over** (ALL²), OVER-THE-COUNTER

over² *adv* **1** down from an upright position: *Kate fell over and hurt her ankle.*|*I saw him push the bike over.* **2** to a particular place: *Come over tomorrow and we'll go shopping.* **3** above or higher than something: *You can't hear anything when the planes fly over.* **4 (all) over again** once more from the beginning: *The computer lost all my work, and I had to do it all over again.* **5 over and over (again)** repeatedly: *He made us sing the some over and over until we got it right.* **6 start over** *AmE* to start doing something once more from the beginning **7 do it over** *AmE* to do something again, especially because you did it wrongly the first time **8 think/talk sth over** to think or talk about something carefully before deciding what to do: *Think it over, and give us your answer tomorrow.* **9 roll/turn/flip etc (sth) over** move something so that another side of it is showing: *He rolled over and went to sleep.* **10** more or higher than a particular amount, number, or age: *a game for children aged 6 and over*

over³ *adj* **1** [not before noun] finished: *The game's over.* **2 get sth over with** to do something unpleasant so that you do not have to worry about it any more: *Call her and get it over with.*

over- *prefix* used at the beginning of words to mean 'too much': *overeat*|*overpopulated*

o·ver·all¹ /ˌaʊvərˈɔːl ll,oʊvərˈɒːl◂/ *adj* considering or including everything: *The overall cost of the trip is $500.*

overall ² *adv* considering or including everything; generally: *Overall, the situation looks good.*

overall³ *n* [C] *BrE* a loose-fitting piece of clothing like a coat, that is worn over clothes to protect them

o·ver·alls /ˈəʊvərɔːlz‖ˈoʊvərɒːlz/ *n* [plural]
1 *BrE* a piece of clothing like a shirt and trousers joined together, that you wear over your clothes in order to protect them → see colour picture on page 113 **2** *AmE* trousers with a piece that covers your chest, held up by two bands that go over your shoulders; DUNGAREES *BrE* → see colour picture on page 113

o·ver·awed /ˌəʊvərˈɔːl‖ˌoʊvərˈɒː/ *adj* feeling respect or admiration, but slightly frightened, because someone or something is very impressive: *I felt overawed just looking at the stadium.*

o·ver·bear·ing /ˌəʊvəˈbeərɪŋ‖ˌoʊvərˈber-/ *adj* always trying to control other people without considering their feelings: *an overbearing father*

o·ver·board /ˈəʊvəbɔːd‖ˈoʊvərbɔːrd/ *adv*
1 over the side of a ship into the water: *He fell overboard into the icy water.* **2 go overboard** *informal* to do something too much, for example to praise or thank someone too much: *"That was absolutely amazing!" "OK, there's no need to go overboard."*

o·ver·bur·dened /ˌəʊvəˈbɜːdnd‖ˌoʊvərˈbɜːr-dnd/ *adj* having too much work to do: *over-burdened teachers*

o·ver·came /ˌəʊvəˈkeɪm‖ˌoʊvər-/ *v* the past tense of OVERCOME

o·ver·cast /ˌəʊvəˈkɑːst‖ˌoʊvərˈkæst◂/ *adj* dark and cloudy: *a grey, overcast sky*

o·ver·charge /ˌəʊvəˈtʃɑːdʒ‖ˌoʊvərˈtʃɑːrdʒ/ *v* [I,T] to charge someone too much money

o·ver·coat /ˈəʊvəkəʊt‖ˈoʊvərkoʊt/ *n* [C] a long thick warm coat

o·ver·come /ˌəʊvəˈkʌm‖ˌoʊvər-/ *v* [T] **overcame** /-ˈkeɪm/, **overcoming 1** to succeed in controlling a feeling or problem: *I'm trying to overcome my fear of flying.* **2 be overcome (by sth)** to be so strongly affected by something that you become weak or unable to control your feelings: *I was so overcome that I could hardly speak.* **3** to fight against someone or something and win

o·ver·com·pen·sate /ˌəʊvəˈkɒmpənseɪt, -pen-‖ˌoʊvərˈkɑːm-/ *v* [I] to try to correct a weakness or mistake by doing too much of the opposite thing —**overcompensation** /ˌəʊvəkɒmpənˈseɪʃən, -pen-‖ˌoʊvərkə-/ *n* [U]

o·ver·crowd·ed /ˌəʊvəˈkraʊdᵻd‖ˌoʊvər-/ *adj* filled with too many people: *overcrowded prisons* —**overcrowding** *n* [U]

o·ver·do /ˌəʊvəˈduː‖ˌoʊvər-/ *v* [T] **overdid** /-ˈdɪd/, **overdone** /-ˈdʌn/, **overdoing** to do or use too much of something: *overdo it Don't over-do the salt.*

o·ver·done /ˌəʊvəˈdʌn◂‖ˌoʊvər-/ *adj* cooked for too long

o·ver·dose /ˈəʊvədəʊs‖ˈoʊvərdoʊs/ *n* [C] too much of a drug taken at one time: *a heroin over-dose* —**overdose** *v* [I] *It's easy to overdose on paracetamol.*

o·ver·draft /ˈəʊvədrɑːft‖ˈoʊvərdræft/ *n* [C] an arrangement in which your bank allows you to spend more money than you have in your account: *a £200 overdraft*

o·ver·drawn /ˌəʊvəˈdrɔːn◂‖ˌoʊvərˈdrɒːn/ *adj* **be/go overdrawn** to have spent more money than the amount you have in your bank

o·ver·due /ˌəʊvəˈdjuː◂‖ˌoʊvərˈduː◂/ *adj* **1** not done or happening when expected; late: *Her baby's ten days overdue.* **2 be overdue (for sth)** if something is overdue, it should have happened a long time ago: *Salary increases are long overdue.*

o·ver·eat /ˌəʊvərˈiːt‖ˌoʊ-/ *v* [I] to eat too much —**overeating** *n* [U]

o·ver·es·ti·mate /ˌəʊvərˈestᵻmeɪt‖ˌoʊ-/ *v* [I,T] to think that someone or something is bigger, more important etc than they really are —**overestimate** /-tᵻmᵻt/ *n* [C] → opposite UNDERESTIMATE

o·ver·flow /ˌəʊvəˈfləʊ‖ˌoʊvərˈfloʊ/ *v* [I,T] **1** if a liquid overflows, it goes over the edges of its container: **+ with** *a sink overflowing with water* **2** if people or things overflow a place, there are too many of them to fit into it —**overflow** /ˈəʊvəfləʊ‖ˈoʊvərfloʊ/ *n* [C,U]

overflow

o·ver·grown /ˌəʊvəˈgrəʊn◂‖ˌoʊvərˈgroʊn◂/ *adj* covered with plants that have grown in an untidy way: *The garden was completely overgrown.*

o·ver·hang /ˌəʊvəˈhæŋ‖ˌoʊvər-/ *v* [I,T] **overhung** /-ˈhʌŋ/, **overhanging** to hang over something: *branches overhanging the path*

o·ver·haul /ˌəʊvəˈhɔːl‖ˌoʊvərˈhɒːl/ *v* [T] to repair or change all the parts of a machine, system etc —**overhaul** /ˈəʊvəhɔːl‖ˈoʊvərhɒːl/ *n* [C]

o·ver·head /ˌəʊvəˈhed◂‖ˌoʊvər-/ *adj, adv* above your head: *overhead cables | A plane flew over-head.*

o·ver·heads /ˈəʊvəhedz‖ˈoʊvər-/ *n* [plural] *especially BrE* money that a business has to spend on rent, electricity etc

o·ver·hear /ˌəʊvəˈhɪə‖ˌoʊvərˈhɪr/ *v* [T] **overheard** /-ˈhɜːd‖-ˈhɜːrd/, **overheard, overhearing** to hear what people are saying, not to you: *I overheard their conversation.* → compare EAVESDROP

o·ver·heat /ˌəʊvəˈhiːt‖ˌoʊvər-/ *v* [I,T] to become too hot

o·ver·hung /ˌəʊvəˈhʌŋ‖ˌoʊvər-/ *v* the past tense and past participle of OVERHANG

o·ver·joyed /ˌəʊvəˈdʒɔɪd‖ˌoʊvər-/ *adj* extremely happy because something good has happened

o·ver·kill /ˈəʊvəkɪl‖ˈoʊvər-/ *n* [U] *informal* when there is more of something than is necessary or more than you want: *the media overkill that afflicts all major sporting events*

o·ver·land /ˈəʊvəˈlænd◂‖ˌoʊvər-/ *adj, adv* across land, not by sea or air: *overland convoys of aid*

o·ver·lap /ˌəʊvəˈlæp‖ˌoʊvər-/ *v* [I,T] **-pped, -pping 1** if two things overlap, part of one thing covers part of the other: *a pattern of over-lapping circles* **2** if two subjects, activities, ideas etc overlap, they are similar in some ways, but not in others: *The case I'm working on over-laps with yours.* —**overlap** /ˈəʊvəlæp‖ˈoʊvər-/ *n* [C,U]

o·ver·leaf /ˌəʊvəˈliːf‖ˈoʊvərliːf/ *adv* used in writing to mention something on the other side of the page

o·ver·load /ˌəʊvəˈləʊd‖ˌoʊvərˈloʊd/ v [T] **1** to put too many people or things in a vehicle: *The boat was overloaded and began to sink.* **2** to give someone too much work to do

o·ver·look /ˌəʊvəˈlʊk‖ˌoʊvər-/ v [T] **1** to not notice something or to not realize how important it is: *It's easy to overlook mistakes when you're reading your own writing.* **2** if a building, room, window etc overlooks something, you can see that thing from the building, room etc: *a room overlooking the beach* **3** *formal* to forgive someone for a mistake, bad behaviour etc: *I am willing to overlook what you said this time.*

o·ver·ly /ˈəʊvəli‖ˈoʊvər-/ adv more than is normal or necessary: *We weren't overly impressed with the meal.*

o·ver·night[1] /ˌəʊvəˈnaɪt‖ˌoʊvər-/ adv **1** for or during the night: *She's staying overnight at a friend's house.* **2** quickly or suddenly: *You can't expect to lose weight overnight.*

o·ver·night[2] /ˈəʊvənaɪt‖ˈoʊvər-/ adj continuing all night: *an overnight flight to Japan*

o·ver·pass /ˈəʊvəpɑːs‖ˈoʊvərpæs/ n [C] *AmE* a structure like a bridge that allows one road to go over another road; FLYOVER *BrE*

o·ver·pop·u·lat·ed /ˌəʊvəˈpɒpjˈleɪtˈd‖ˌoʊvərˈpɑːp-/ adj a country or city that is overpopulated has too many people —**overpopulation** /ˌəʊvəpɒpjˈleɪʃən‖ˌoʊvərpɑːp-/ n [U]

o·ver·pow·er /ˌəʊvəˈpaʊəl‖ˌoʊvərˈpaʊər/ v [T] to defeat someone because you are stronger

o·ver·pow·er·ing /ˌəʊvəˈpaʊərɪŋ‖ˌoʊvər-ˈpaʊrɪŋ/ adj an overpowering feeling, need, smell etc is very strong: *an overpowering feeling of hopelessness*

o·ver·priced /ˌəʊvəˈpraɪst‖ˌoʊvər-/ adj too expensive

o·ver·ran /ˌəʊvəˈræn‖ˌoʊ-/ v the past tense of OVERRUN

o·ver·rat·ed /ˌəʊvəˈreɪtˈd‖ˌoʊ-/ adj not as good or important as some people think: *We thought the play was overrated.*

o·ver·re·act /ˌəʊvəriˈækt‖ˌoʊ-/ v [I] to be more angry, afraid, worried etc than you need to be —**overreaction** /-riˈækʃən/ n [C,U]

o·ver·ride /ˌəʊvəˈraɪd‖ˌoʊ-/ v [T] **overrode** /-ˈrəʊd‖-ˈroʊd/, **overridden** /-ˈrɪdn/, **overriding 1** to change a decision because you have the power to do so: *Congress has overridden the President's veto.* **2** to be more important than something: *The economy often seems to override other political issues.*

o·ver·rid·ing /ˌəʊvəˈraɪdɪŋ‖ˌoʊ-/ adj [only before noun] more important than anything else: *Security is of overriding importance.*

o·ver·rule /ˌəʊvəˈruːl‖ˌoʊ-/ v [T] to officially change an order or decision because you think that it is wrong: *"Objection overruled," said Judge Klein.*

o·ver·run /ˌəʊvəˈrʌn‖ˌoʊ-/ v **overran** /-ˈræn/, **overrun**, **overrunning 1** [T] if something bad overruns a place, it quickly spreads through it: *the town is being overrun by rats* **2** [I] if an event overruns, it continues for longer than planned: *The meeting overran by half an hour.*

o·ver·seas /ˌəʊvəˈsiːz‖ˌoʊvər-/ adj, adv to, in, or from a foreign country that is across the sea: *an overseas tour* | *I often get to travel overseas.*

o·ver·see /ˌəʊvəˈsiː‖ˌoʊvər-/ v [T] **oversaw** /-ˈsɔː‖-ˈsɒː/, **overseen** /-ˈsiːn/, **overseeing** to watch the progress of a group of workers to be sure that work is done correctly: *Bentley is overseeing the project.* —**overseer** /ˈəʊvəˌsiːə‖ˈoʊvər-ˌsiːər/ n [C]

o·ver·shad·ow /ˌəʊvəˈʃædəʊ‖ˌoʊvərˈʃædoʊ/ v [T] **1** to make an occasion or period of time less enjoyable and make people sad or worried: *The film festival was overshadowed by the news of the actor's death.* **2** to make someone seem less important by being more successful than they are: *He felt constantly overshadowed by his older brother.*

o·ver·shoot /ˌəʊvəˈʃuːt‖ˌoʊvər-/ v [I,T] **overshot** /-ˈʃɒt‖-ˈʃɑːt/, **overshot**, **overshooting** to miss a place where you wanted to stop or leave a road, by going too far past it: *I overshot the turn, and had to go back.*

o·ver·sight /ˈəʊvəsaɪt‖ˈoʊvər-/ n [C,U] a mistake that you make by not noticing something or by forgetting to do something

o·ver·sim·pli·fy /ˌəʊvəˈsɪmplˈfaɪ‖ˌoʊvər-/ v [I,T] to make a problem or situation seem more simple than it really is —**oversimplification** /ˌəʊvəsɪmplˈfˈkeɪʃən‖ˌoʊvər-/ n [C,U]

o·ver·sleep /ˌəʊvəˈsliːp‖ˌoʊvər-/ v [I] **overslept** /-ˈslept/, **overslept**, **oversleeping** to sleep for longer than you intended

o·ver·state /ˌəʊvəˈsteɪt‖ˌoʊvər-/ v [T] to talk about something in a way that makes it seem more important, serious etc than it really is; EXAGGERATE

o·ver·step /ˌəʊvəˈstep‖ˌoʊvər-/ v [T] **-pped**, **-pping 1** overstep rules/limits/authority etc to behave in a way that is not acceptable according to rules, limits etc: *Wilson has clearly overstepped his authority.* **2** overstep the mark to do or say more than you should, and offend people

o·vert /ˈəʊvɜːt, əʊˈvɜːt‖ˈoʊvərt, oʊˈvɜːrt/ adj done publicly without trying to hide anything: *overt discrimination* —**overtly** adv

o·ver·take /ˌəʊvəˈteɪk‖ˌoʊvər-/ v **overtook** /-ˈtʊk/, **overtaken** /-ˈteɪkən/, **overtaking 1** [I,T] to go past a moving vehicle because you are driving faster than it: *The accident happened as he was overtaking a bus.* **2** [T often passive] *literary* to have a sudden and unexpected effect on someone: *She was overtaken by exhaustion.* **3** [T] to develop or increase more quickly than someone or something: *Japan has overtaken many other countries in car production.*

over-the-coun·ter /ˌ.. ˈ..◂/ adj over-the-counter **drugs/medicines/tablets etc** drugs, medicines etc that can be bought without a PRESCRIPTION from a doctor

o·ver·throw /ˌəʊvəˈθrəʊ‖ˌoʊvərˈθroʊ/ v **overthrew** /-ˈθruː/, **overthrown** /-ˈθrəʊn‖-ˈθroʊn/, **overthrowing** [T] to use force to remove a leader or government from power

o·ver·time /ˈəʊvətaɪm‖ˈoʊvər-/ n [U] time that you work in addition to your usual working hours

o·ver·took /ˌəʊvəˈtʊk‖ˌoʊvər-/ v the past tense of OVERTAKE

o·ver·ture /ˈəʊvətjʊə, -tʃʊə, -tʃəl‖ˈoʊvərtjʊər, -tʃʊr, -tʃər/ n [C] **1** a piece of music that comes before a longer musical piece, especially an OPERA **2** *formal* also **overtures** an attempt to be friendly with a person or country: *The US began to make overtures to the new military government.*

o·ver·turn /ˌəʊvəˈtɜːn‖ˌoʊvərˈtɜːrn/ *v* **1** [I,T] if something overturns, or you overturn it, it turns upside down or falls over on its side: *The car overturned on a country road.* **2 overturn a ruling/verdict/law** to officially change a decision made by a court

o·ver·view /ˈəʊvəvjuː‖ˈoʊvər-/ *n* [C] a short description of a subject or situation giving its main features: *an overview of the history of the region*

o·ver·weight /ˌəʊvəˈweɪt‖ˌoʊvər-/ *adj* too heavy or too fat: *I'm ten pounds overweight.*
→ see colour picture on page 244

o·ver·whelm /ˌəʊvəˈwelm‖ˌoʊvər-/ *v* [T] if a feeling overwhelms you, you feel it very strongly: *Gary was overwhelmed with sadness.*

o·ver·whelm·ing /ˌəʊvəˈwelmɪŋ‖ˌoʊvər-/ *adj* **1** affecting you very strongly: *Shari felt an overwhelming urge to cry.* **2** very big in amount or number: *The Labour Party won by an overwhelming majority.* **—overwhelmingly** *adv*

o·ver·worked /ˌəʊvəˈwɜːkt‖ˌoʊvərˈwɜːrkt/ *adj* working too much: *overworked nurses* **—overwork** *n* [U]

o·ver·wrought /ˌəʊvəˈrɔːt‖ˌoʊvəˈrɔːt/ *adj* very upset, nervous, and worried

ow /aʊ/ *interjection* used when you suddenly feel pain: *Ow! That hurt!*

owe /əʊ‖oʊ/ *v* [T] **1** to have to pay someone because they have let you borrow money from them: *owe sb sth Bob owes me $20.* | *owe sth to sb We owe a lot of money to the bank.* **2** to feel that you should do something for someone because they deserve it: *I owe you an apology.* **3** to have something or achieve something because of someone's help: *"You must be pleased you've won." "I owe it all to you."*

owing to /ˈ.. ../ *prep* because of: *Work on the building has stopped, owing to lack of money.*

owl /aʊl/ *n* [C] a bird that hunts at night and has large eyes and a loud call
→ see also NIGHT OWL

owl

own¹ /əʊn‖oʊn/ *determiner pron* **1** belonging to or done by a particular person: *She wants her own room.* | *You have to learn to make your own decisions.* | *of sb's own He decided to start a business of his own.* **2 (all) on your own a)** alone: *Rick lives on his own.* **b)** without anyone's help: *Did you make that all on your own?* **3 get your own back (on sb)** *informal* to do something bad to someone because they have done something bad to you

own² *v* [T] to legally have something because you bought it or have been given it: *He owns two houses in Utah.*

own up *phr v* [I] to admit that you have done something wrong **own up to (doing sth)** *No one owned up to breaking the window.*

own·er /ˈəʊnə‖ˈoʊnər/ *n* [C] someone who owns something: *the owner of the dog* **—ownership** *n* [U]

ox /ɒks‖ɑːks/ *n* [C], *plural* **oxen** /ˈɒksən‖ˈɑːk-/ a large type of male cow, sometimes used to work on farms, to pull vehicles etc, especially in past times

ox·y·gen /ˈɒksɪdʒən‖ˈɑːk-/ *n* [U] a gas in the air that all living things need

oy·ster /ˈɔɪstə‖-ər/ *n* [C,U] a small sea animal that has a shell and produces a jewel called a PEARL

oz the written abbreviation of OUNCE or ounces

o·zone lay·er /ˈəʊzəʊn ˌleɪə‖ˈoʊzoʊn ˌleɪər/ *n* [singular] a layer of gases that stops harmful RADIATION from the sun reaching the Earth

---

GRAMMAR NOTE: 'if' clauses (2)
When you imagine a present situation that is not real, or a future situation that is very unlikely, use **if** + **simple past**: *If he really loved you, he wouldn't treat you like this.* (=he does not love you). | *If I won a million dollars on the lottery, I would buy a yacht.* Use **would** in the other part of the sentence.

Pp

P, p /piː/ the letter 'p'

p /piː/ *n* **1** *plural* **pp** the written abbreviation of 'page' **2** *BrE* the abbreviation of PENNY or PENCE

pa /pɑː/ *n* [C] *old-fashioned* father

PA /ˌpiː ˈeɪ/ *n* [C] **1** *BrE* PERSONAL ASSISTANT; a secretary who works for just one person **2** PUBLIC ADDRESS SYSTEM equipment that makes someone's voice louder when they are speaking to a crowd of people

pace¹ /peɪs/ *n* **1** [singular] the speed at which something happens or at which you do something such as move, work etc: *She heard someone behind her and quickened her pace.* | *the pace of change in Eastern Europe* **2** **keep pace (with)** to move or change as fast as something or someone else: *Supply has to keep pace with increasing demand.*

pace² *v* [I,T] **1** to walk around a lot when you are waiting or when you are worried about something **+around/up and down** *He paced up and down the hospital corridor.* **2** **pace yourself** to do something at a steady speed so you do not get tired quickly

pace·mak·er /ˈpeɪsˌmeɪkə‖-ər/ *n* [C] a small machine that is put in someone's heart to help it beat regularly

pac·i·fi·er /ˈpæsɪfaɪə‖-faɪər/ *n* [C] *AmE* a rubber object that a baby sucks on so that he or she does not cry; DUMMY *BrE*

pac·i·fist /ˈpæsɪfɪst/ *n* [C] someone who believes that all wars and violence are wrong —**pacifism** *n* [U]

pac·i·fy /ˈpæsɪfaɪ/ *v* [T] to make someone calm and quiet after they have been angry or upset

pack¹ /pæk/ *v* **1** [I,T] to put things into boxes, bags etc in order to take them somewhere: *I never pack until the night before a trip.* **2** [I,T] if a crowd of people packs a place, there are so many of them that the place is too full: *Thousands of people packed the stadium.* **3** [T] to cover or fill something closely with material to protect it: *Pack some newspaper around the bottles.*

pack sth ↔ **in** *phr v* [T] **1** also **pack** sth **into** sth to do a lot of things within a short period: *I don't know how we packed so much activity into one brief weekend.* **2** *BrE informal* to stop doing something, especially because you do not enjoy it: *Sometimes I just feel like packing my job in.*

pack sb/sth **off** *phr v* [T] *informal* to send someone away: *We were packed off to camp every summer.*

pack up *phr v* [I] **1** *informal* to finish work: *I think I'll pack up and go home early.* **2** *BrE informal* if a machine packs up, it stops working: *The television's packed up again.*

pack² *n* [C] **1** several things that have been wrapped or tied together in order to sell, carry,

---

Verbs of Movement 1 – Hands

Exercise 1

Look at the pictures. Read the definitions and write the verbs.

1 to make something small and light go through the air with a quick movement of your hand, a whip etc *flick*

2 to hit your hands together several times to show you enjoyed something or approve of something
_____

3 to hit a door or window with your hand in order to attract someone's attention _____

4 to press part of someone's flesh tightly between your finger and thumb _____

5 to move your finger in the direction of something in order to show someone _____

6 to rub your skin with your nails to stop it from itching _____

7 to twist or press something in order to get liquid out of it _____

8 to move your hand gently over something
_____

9 to hold someone's hand and move it up and down, as a greeting or when you have made an agreement _____

10 to gently touch part of someone's body with your fingers so that they want to laugh _____

Exercise 2

Complete the spaces in this text with the correct form of a verb from the picture.

Leo was painting when he fell off the ladder and hurt his arm. Leo's wife, Meg, phoned the doctor. The doctor kn**ocked** on the door and came into the room. Leo was lying on the floor and his wife was ho_____ his left hand and st_____ his arm. The doctor sh_____ hands with Meg and wa_____ at Leo. 'Where does it hurt?' Leo po_____ to his elbow. 'Can you feel this?' asked the doctor as he sc_____ Leo's hand. Leo nodded. The doctor put his finger in Leo's hand. 'Can you sq_____ my finger?' asked the doctor. 'No? Well, I think you must go to the hospital.'

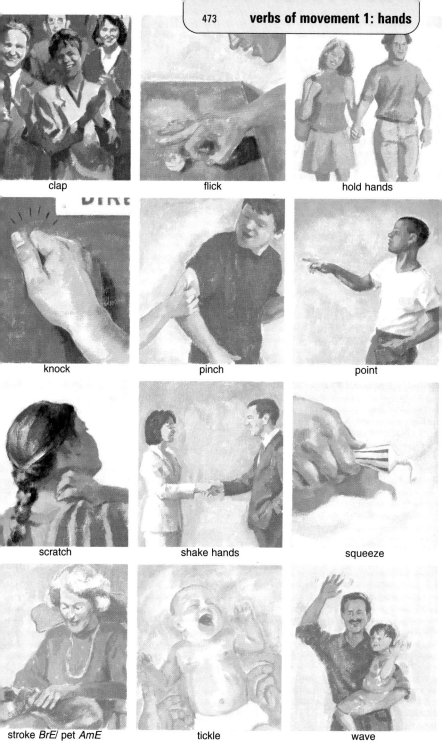

clap

flick

hold hands

knock

pinch

point

scratch

shake hands

squeeze

stroke *BrE*/ pet *AmE*

tickle

wave

clock
10
doorway
frame
door
18
mirror
ornaments
24
23
9
5
12
1
bookcase
6
picture
20
lamp
7
TV
shelf
8
speaker
video *BrE*/
VCR *AmE*
stereo
22
sofa
17
3
chair
floor
rug
2
box
13
remote control
cushion
11
vase
14
4
table
15
armchair
16
newspaper
21
chair

PREPOSITIONS

1. There are some books **above** the TV.

2. Helen is throwing the ball **across** the rug **to** the dog.

3. The sofa is **against** the wall.

4. Virginia is sitting **at** the table.

5. There is a mirror **behind** the lamp.

6. **Below** the stairs there is a shelf.

7. The shelf is **beside/next to** the bookcase.

8. The stereo is **between** the speakers.

9. There is a picture **by/near** the door.

10. Ashley is walking **down** the stairs **past** the clock **towards** the door.

11. There are some flowers **in** the vase.

12. The lamp is **in front of** the mirror.

13. There are some toys **inside** the box.

14. Virginia is pouring coffee **into** the mug.

15. The cat is jumping **off** the armchair **onto** the floor.

16. There is a book **on** the table.

17. The chair is **opposite** the sofa.

18. There are some trees **outside** the house.

19. There is a rug **over** the armchair.

20. Anna is going **through** the doorway **out of** the living room.

21. There is a newspaper **under** the table.

22. The cat is going **up** the stairs **away from** the living room.

23. There is a frame **around** the picture.

24. There are some ornaments **on top of** the bookcase.

P

Exercise 1

Look at the picture. Complete the answers to these questions.

1 Are the flowers under the vase? No, they're in the vase.

2 Is the lamp behind the mirror? No, it's i_ f_____ o__ the mirror.

3 Is the TV above the books? No, it's b_____ the books.

4 Is the sofa in the middle of the room? No it is a _____ the wall.

5 Are the ornaments under the bookcase? No, they're o__ t__ o__ the bookcase.

6 Are the trees inside the house? No, they're o_____ the house.

7 Are the toys on the floor? No, they're i_____ the box.

8 Is the newspaper on the table? No, it's u_____ the table.

9 Is the stereo opposite the speakers? No, it's b_____ the speakers.

Exercise 2

Look at the picture again. Complete the answers to these questions.

1 Is the cat jumping onto the armchair? No, it's jumping o_____ the armchair.

2 Is Virginia pouring coffee out of the mug? No, she's pouring coffee i_____ the mug.

3 Is the baby throwing the ball to the cat? No, she's throwing it t_____ the dog.

4 Is Ashley going up the stairs? No, he's coming d_____ the stairs.

5 Is Anna coming into the room? No, she's going i_____ the garden.

or send them: *Phone for your free information pack.* **2** *especially AmE* a small container that contains things of the same kind: *a pack of cigarettes* → see picture at CONTAINER **3** *BrE* a bag carried by soldiers or walkers on their shoulders **4** a group of wild animals that hunt together **5** a set of playing cards; DECK *AmE*

pack·age[1] /'pækɪdʒ/ *n* [C] **1** a set of products sold or offered together: *a new software package* **2** something that has been packed into a box or wrapped in paper, especially in order to send it; PARCEL **3** *AmE* the box, bag etc that food is put in for selling: *a package of cookies* → see picture at PARCEL

package[2] *v* [T] **1** to put something in a box, bag etc, especially to be sold: *food packaged in cartons* **2** to make something seem attractive so that people will become interested in it or buy it: *The band has been packaged to appeal to teenage girls.*

package tour /'.. ./ also **package hol·i·day** /'.. ,.../ *BrE* — *n* [C] a holiday arranged by a com- pany for a fixed price that includes your hotel and travel

pack·ag·ing /'pækɪdʒɪŋ/ *n* [U] the bags, boxes etc in which a product is sold

packed /pækt/ *adj* also **packed out** full of people: *a packed commuter train*

packed lunch /, '. / *n* [C] *BrE* food that you prepare at home and take to eat at work, on a trip etc

pack·et[1] /'pækɪt/ *n* [C] *especially BrE* a small container, usually made from paper, that contains things of the same kind: *a packet of biscuits* → see picture at CONTAINER

pack·ing /'pækɪŋ/ *n* [U] **1** when you put things into cases or boxes in order to send or take them somewhere: *I'll have to do my packing this evening.* **2** paper, plastic, cloth etc used to protect things when you pack them

pact /pækt/ *n* [C] a formal agreement be- tween two countries, groups, or people: *a peace pact*

pad[1] /pæd/ *n* [C] **1** a thick piece of soft ma- terial used to protect something or make it more comfortable: *knee pads* **2** a book of paper sheets, used for writing, drawing etc: *a sketch pad*

pad[2] *v* **1** [I] to walk somewhere softly and quietly: + **across/along etc** *The little cat padded across the floor towards me.* **2** [T] to protect something or make it more comfortable by covering or filling it with soft material

pad·ded /'pædɪd/ *adj* something that is padded is covered or filled with soft material, to make it more comfortable or thicker: *a padded envelope*

pad·ding /'pædɪŋ/ *n* [U] material used to make something softer or more comfortable

pad·dle[1] /'pædl/ *n* **1** [C] a short pole with a wide flat end, used for moving a small boat along → compare OAR **2** [C, usually singular] *BrE* when you walk in water that is not very deep: *Let's go for a paddle.*

paddle[2] *v* **1** [I,T] to move a small boat through water, using a paddle **2** [I] *BrE* to walk in water that is not very deep: *A group of children were paddling in the stream.*

pad·dock /'pædək/ *n* [C] a small field where horses are kept

pad·dy field /'pædi ,fiːld/ also **rice paddy**, **paddy** *n* [C] a field where rice is grown in water

pad·lock /'pædlɒk‖-lɑːk/ *n* [C] a small lock that you put on a door, bicycle etc — **padlock** *v* [T]

padlock

pae·di·a·tri·cian *BrE*, **pediatrician** *AmE* /,piːdiə'trɪʃən/ *n* [C] a doctor who treats children

pae·di·at·rics *BrE*, **pediatrics** *AmE* /,piːdi-'ætrɪks/ *n* [U] the area of medicine connected with children's illnesses

pa·gan /'peɪgən/ *adj* pagan religious beliefs and customs do not belong to any of the main world religions, and may come from a time be- fore these religions: *an ancient pagan festival* — **pagan** *n* [C]

page[1] /peɪdʒ/ *n* [C] a sheet of paper in a book, newspaper etc or one side of a sheet: *The book had several pages missing.*

page[2] *v* [T] **1** to call someone's name in a pub- lic place using a LOUDSPEAKER: *We couldn't find Jan at the airport, so we had her paged.* **2** to call someone using a small machine that receives messages

pag·eant /'pædʒənt/ *n* [C] a public show, espe- cially an outdoor one, that shows an event in history

pag·eant·ry /'pædʒəntri/ *n* [U] impressive cere- monies or events, that involve a lot of people wearing formal or special clothes

pag·er /'peɪdʒə‖-ər/ *n* [C] a small machine you carry with you that makes a noise when it receives a message

pa·go·da /pə'gəʊdə‖-'goʊ-/ *n* [C] an Asian TEMPLE that has several levels, with a decorated roof at each level

paid /peɪd/ *v* the past tense and past participle of PAY

pail /peɪl/ *n* [C] *old-fashioned* a container with a handle used for carrying liquids; BUCKET

pain[1] /peɪn/ *n* **1** [C,U] the feeling you have when part of your body hurts: *I woke up in the night with terrible stomach pains.* | **be in pain** (=feel pain): *Cassie lay groaning in pain on the bed.* **2** **a pain (in the neck)** *spoken* someone or something that is very annoying: *These pots and pans are a pain to wash.* **3** [C,U] a feeling of sadness: *the pain children feel when their parents divorce* → see also PAINS

pain[2] *v* [T] *formal* to make someone unhappy: *It pains me to see my mother growing old.*

pained /peɪnd/ *adj* worried and upset: *He had a pained expression on his face.*

pain·ful /'peɪnfəl/ *adj* **1** making you feel phy- sical pain: *Her ankle was swollen and painful.* **2** making you feel very unhappy: *painful memories of the war*

pain·ful·ly /'peɪnfəli/ *adv* **1** in a way that makes you feel physical pain or makes you un- happy: *She was painfully aware that she wasn't welcome.* **2** **painfully clear/obvious/apparent** easy to notice in a way that is unpleasant or embarrassing: *It was painfully obvious that he didn't like him.* **3** **painfully slow** extremely slow: *Re-building the bridge was a painfully slow process.*

pain·kill·er /ˈpeɪnˌkɪləll-ər/ *n* [C] a drug that reduces pain

pain·less /ˈpeɪnləs/ *adj* **1** not painful: *a painless death* **2** *informal* not involving much effort or hard work: *a painless way to learn Spanish*

pains /peɪnz/ *n* [plural] **be at pains to do sth/ take pains to do sth** to try very hard to do something: *He was at pains to emphasize the advantages of the new system.*

pains·tak·ing /ˈpeɪnzˌteɪkɪŋ/ *adj* very careful and thorough: *painstaking research* —**painstakingly** *adv*

paint[1] /peɪnt/ *n* [U] a liquid that you put on a surface to make it a particular colour: *a can of yellow paint* → see also PAINTS

paint[2] *v* [I,T] **1** to put paint on a surface: *What color are you painting the house?* **2** to make a picture of someone or something, using paint: *He's just finished painting his wife's portrait.*

paint·box /ˈpeɪntbɒksll-bɑːks/ *n* [C] a small box containing blocks of coloured paint

paint·brush /ˈpeɪntbrʌʃ/ *n* [C] a brush used to paint pictures or to paint walls → see picture at BRUSH

paint·er /ˈpeɪntəll-ər/ *n* [C] **1** someone who paints pictures; ARTIST: *a landscape painter* **2** someone whose job is painting houses, rooms etc: *a painter and decorator*

paint·ing /ˈpeɪntɪŋ/ *n* **1** [C] a painted picture: *an exhibition of paintings, drawings, and sculptures* **2** [U] the process of painting: *Van Gogh's style of painting*

paints /peɪnts/ *n* [plural] a set of small tubes or blocks of paint, used for painting pictures: *oil paints*

pair[1] /peəll-per/ *n* [C] **1** something made of two similar parts that are joined together: *a pair of scissors* **2** two things of the same kind that are used together: *a new pair of shoes* **3** two people who do something together or who know each other well: *a pair of dancers* | **in pairs** *Work in pairs on the next exercise.*

pair[2] *v*

  pair off *phr v* [I,T **pair** sb ↔ **off**] if two people pair off or are paired off, they do something together or start a relationship: *They are all hoping to pair their daughters off with rich men.*

  pair up *phr v* [I,T **pair** sb ↔ **up**] to form groups of two or to put things into groups of two: *I paired up with Mike for the quiz.*

pa·ja·mas /pəˈdʒɑːməzll-ˈdʒɑː-, -ˈdʒæ-/ the American spelling of PYJAMAS

pal /pæl/ *n* [C] *informal* a friend: *a college pal*

pal·ace /ˈpælɪs/ *n* [C] a large house where a king or queen lives: *Buckingham Palace*

pal·a·ta·ble /ˈpælətəbəl/ *adj* having a pleasant taste: *a palatable wine*

pal·ate /ˈpælɪt/ *n* [C] the top inside part of your mouth

pa·la·tial /pəˈleɪʃəl/ *adj* a palatial building is big and beautifully decorated: *a palatial five-star hotel*

pale[1] /peɪl/ *adj* **1** **pale blue/green/pink etc** light blue, green etc **2** having a white skin colour, especially because you are ill or frightened: *Jan looked tired and pale.*

pale[2] *v* **1** to seem less important, good etc when compared to something else: *Once you've experienced sailing, other sports pale in comparison.* **2** if you pale, your face becomes whiter: *Hettie paled when she heard what had happened.*

pal·ette /ˈpælɪt/ *n* [C] a board for mixing paints used by a painter who paints pictures

pall[1] /pɔːlllpɒːl/ *n* **a pall of smoke/dust etc** a dark cloud of smoke, dust etc

pall[2] *v* [T] to become less interesting or enjoyable: *The excitement of the new job began to pall after a while.*

pal·lid /ˈpælɪd/ *adj* pale and unhealthy: *a pallid complexion*

pal·lor /ˈpæləll-ər/ *n* [singular] a pale unhealthy colour of the skin or face: *Her skin had a deathly pallor.*

palm[1] /pɑːmllpɑːm, pɑːlm/ *n* [C] **1** the surface of the inside of your hand **2** a palm tree

palm[2]

  palm sb/sth ↔ **off** *phr v* [T] to persuade someone to accept something that is not what they really want: **palm sb off with sth** *I'm not going to be palmed off with excuses.* | **palm sth off on sb** *He tried to palm all his old clothes off on me.*

palm tree /ˈ. ./ *n* [C] a tall tree with large pointed leaves at the top, that grows near beaches or in deserts

pal·pa·ble /ˈpælpəbəl/ *adj* easy to notice: *a palpable sense of relief* —**palpably** *adv*

pal·pi·ta·tions /ˌpælpɪˈteɪʃənz/ *n* [plural] when your heart beats in a fast irregular way, especially because you are ill or very anxious

pal·try /ˈpɔːltrillpɒːl-/ *adj* too small to be useful or important: *a paltry 2.4% pay increase*

pam·per /ˈpæmpəll-ər/ *v* [T] to give someone a lot of care and attention: *You pamper that boy too much!*

pam·phlet /ˈpæmflɪt/ *n* [C] a thin paper book containing information about something

pan[1] /pæn/ *n* [C] **1** a round metal container used for cooking: *Melt the butter in a pan.* **2** *AmE* a metal container for baking things: *a 9-inch cake pan*

pan[2] *v* **-nned, -nning 1** [T] *informal* to strongly criticize a film, play etc in a newspaper or on television or radio: *Goldberg's latest movie has been panned by the critics.* **2** [I,T] to move a camera, especially a television camera, while filming or taking a photograph: **+ across/back** etc *The camera panned across the crowd.*

  pan out *phr v* [I] *informal* to happen or develop in a particular way: *Let's just wait and see how things pan out.*

pan·a·cea /ˌpænəˈsɪə/ *n* [C] something that people think will solve all their problems: *Money is not a panacea for the problems in our schools.*

pa·nache /pəˈnæʃ, pæ-/ *n* [U] a way of doing something that is exciting and makes it seem easy: *He played with skill and panache.*

pan·cake /ˈpænkeɪk/ *n* [C] a flat round food made from flour, milk, and eggs that is cooked in a pan

pan·da /ˈpændə/ *n* [C] a large black and white animal similar to a bear, that lives in China

pan·de·mo·ni·um /ˌpændɪˈməʊniəmll-ˈmoʊ-/ *n* [U] when there is a lot of noise and activity because people are angry, excited etc: *When Brazil scored, pandemonium broke out.*

pan·der /ˈpændəⅡ-ər/ *v*
pander to sb/sth *phr v* [T] to give someone what they want, even though you know it is not good for them: *newspapers that pander to people's prejudices*

pane /peɪn/ *n* [C] a piece of glass in a window or door

pan·el[1] /ˈpænl/ *n* **1** [C] a piece of wood, glass etc that is part of a door, wall, or ceiling **2** [C] a group of people who are chosen to discuss something or answer questions: *a panel of experts* **3** **instrument/control panel** the part inside a plane, boat etc where the controls are fixed

pan·elled *BrE*, **paneled** *AmE* /ˈpænld/ *adj* covered with flat pieces of wood: *a panelled door*

pan·el·ling *BrE*, **paneling** *AmE* /ˈpænəl-ɪŋ/ *n* [U] flat pieces of wood used to decorate walls, doors etc: *oak panelling*

pan·el·list *BrE*, **panelist** *AmE* /ˈpænəl-ₐst/ *n* [C] a member of a group of people who have been chosen to discuss something or answer questions

pang /pæŋ/ *n* [C] a sudden strong feeling of pain, sadness etc: *hunger pangs* | *She was having pangs of guilt about Pete.*

pan·han·dle /ˈpæn,hændl/ *v* [I] *AmE* to ask for money in the streets —**panhandler** *n* [C]

pan·ic[1] /ˈpænɪk/ *n* **1** [C,U] a sudden strong feeling of fear or anxiety that makes you unable to think clearly or behave sensibly: *His warning produced a wave of panic.* | **in (a) panic** *People ran into the streets in a panic after the explosion.* **2** [C] a situation in which there is a lot to do and not much time to do it in: *There was the usual last-minute panic just before the deadline.*

panic[2] *v* [I,T] **panicked, panicked, panicking** to feel so frightened that you do things without thinking clearly, or to make someone feel this way: *Stay where you are and don't panic!* —**panicky** *adj*

panic at·tack /ˈ.. ,./ *n* [C] when you are so frightened or anxious that you feel ill or cannot breathe easily: *She suffers from frequent panic attacks.*

panic-strick·en /ˈ.. ,../ *adj* extremely frightened

pan·o·ra·ma /,pænəˈrɑːməⅡ-ˈræmə/ *n* [C] a view over a wide area of land —**panoramic** /-ˈræmɪk◂/ *adj*: *a panoramic view of Hong Kong*

pan·sy /ˈpænzi/ *n* [C] a small flat brightly coloured garden flower

pant /pænt/ *v* [I] to breathe quickly with short noisy breaths, especially after exercising or because it is hot: *a dog panting in the heat*

pan·ther /ˈpænθəⅡ-ər/ *n* [C] a large black wild animal, that is a type of cat

pan·ties /ˈpæntiz/ *n* [plural] a piece of women's underwear that covers the area between the waist and the top of the legs; KNICKERS *BrE*

pan·to·mime /ˈpæntəmaɪm/ *n* [C,U] a funny play for children that is performed at Christmas in Britain

pan·try /ˈpæntri/ *n* [C] a small room near or in a kitchen where food and dishes are kept

pants /pænts/ *n* [plural] **1** *BrE* a piece of underwear that covers the area between the waist and the top of your legs; UNDERPANTS *AmE*

2 *especially AmE* a piece of clothing that covers you from your waist to your feet and has a separate part for each leg; TROUSERS *especially BrE* → see colour picture on page 113

pant·suit /ˈpæntsuːt, -sjuːtⅡ-suːt/ *n* [C] *AmE* a suit for women, which consists of a JACKET and trousers; TROUSER SUIT *BrE*

pan·ty·hose /ˈpæntihəʊzⅡ-hoʊz/ *n* [plural] *AmE* a piece of women's clothing that covers the legs from the feet to the waist, worn under dresses or skirts; TIGHTS *BrE* → see colour picture on page 113

pa·pa /pəˈpɑːⅡˈpɑːpə/ *n* [C] *old-fashioned* father

pa·pa·cy /ˈpeɪpəsi/ *n* **the papacy** the position and authority of the POPE

pa·pal /ˈpeɪpəl/ *adj* relating to the POPE

pa·per[1] /ˈpeɪpəⅡ-ər/ *n* **1** [U] thin material used for writing on, drawing on, wrapping things in etc: *He wrote her phone number down on a piece of paper.* | *a paper towel* **2** [C] a newspaper: *I read about it in yesterday's paper.* | *a local paper* **3** **papers** [plural] important or official documents or letters: *The papers are all ready for you to sign.* **4** [C] a piece of writing or a talk by someone who has studied a particular subject: *a paper on global warming.* **5** **on paper** if something seems true on paper, you think it is true but are not sure because it has not been tested in a real situation: *On paper, Barcelona seem the better team.* **6** [C] an examination or a piece of writing that is done as part of a course at school or university: *My history paper is due tomorrow.*

paper[2] *v* [T] to cover the walls of a room with WALLPAPER

pa·per·back /ˈpeɪpəbækⅡ-ər-/ *n* [C] a book with a soft paper cover → compare HARDBACK

pa·per·boy /ˈpeɪpəbɔɪⅡ-ər-/ *n* [C] a boy who delivers newspapers to people's houses

paper clip /ˈ.. ./ *n* [C] a small piece of curved wire used for holding sheets of paper together

pa·per·weight /ˈpeɪpəweɪtⅡ-ər-/ *n* [C] a small heavy object that is put on top of pieces of paper to keep them together

pa·per·work /ˈpeɪpəwɜːkⅡ-pərwɜːrk/ *n* [U] **1** work such as writing letters or reports, especially done as part of another job: *The job involves a lot of paperwork* **2** the documents that you need for a business deal, journey etc: *I've left all the paperwork in the office.*

par /pɑːⅡpɑːr/ *n* **1** **be on a par (with)** to be of the same standard as something or to be similar to it: *Technological developments in the US are now on a par with those in Japan.* **2** **be below par/not be up to par** to be not as good as the usual or expected standard: *Italy's performance in the Championships wasn't up to par.*

par·a·ble /ˈpærəbəl/ *n* [C] a short simple story, especially in the Bible, that teaches a moral or religious lesson

par·a·chute[1] /ˈpærəʃuːt/ *n* [C] a piece of equipment worn by people who jump out of planes, to make them fall through the air slowly

parachute

parachute² v [I] to jump from a plane using a parachute

pa·rade¹ /pə'reɪd/ n [C] **1** an event in which musical bands, decorated vehicles etc move down the street, especially as a celebration: *a May Day parade* **2** a military ceremony in which soldiers stand or march together in front of people of higher rank: **be on parade** (=be standing or marching in a military parade)

parade² v **1** [I] to march in a large group in order to celebrate or protest about something: **+ through/around** etc *Peace demonstrators paraded through the town.* **2** [I] to walk around in a way that shows that you want people to notice and admire you: **+ around/up/down** etc *Teenage girls were parading around the pool in their bikinis.* **3** [T] to show a particular quality or possession in order to make people admire you: *He loves parading his wealth in front of people.*

par·a·dise /'pærədaɪs/ n **1 Paradise** the place where some people think good people go after they die; HEAVEN **2** [singular, U] a place or situation that you like very much or that is very beautiful: *Hawaii is a paradise for wind surfers.*

par·a·dox /'pærədɒks‖-dɑːks/ n [C] a situation or statement that seems strange or impossible because it contains two opposing ideas, qualities etc: *It's a paradox that there are so many poor people living in such a rich country.* —**paradoxical** /ˌpærə'dɒksɪkəl‖-'dɑːk-/ adj —**paradoxically** /-kli/ adv

par·af·fin /'pærəfɪn/ n [U] **1** BrE oil used for heating and in lamps, made from PETROLEUM or coal; KEROSENE AmE **2** AmE a soft white substance used for making CANDLES

par·a·gon /'pærəgən‖-gɑːn/ n [C] someone who is extremely brave, good etc: *You can't expect politicians to be paragons of virtue.* (=perfectly good, honest etc)

par·a·graph /'pærəɡrɑːf‖-ɡræf/ n [C] a group of sentences in a piece of writing that starts on a new line

par·a·keet /'pærəkiːt/ n [C] a small brightly coloured bird with a long tail

parallel¹ adj **1** two lines that are parallel to each other are the same distance apart along their whole length: *The street runs parallel to the railroad.* **2** similar and happening at the same time: *The British and French police are conducting parallel investigations.*

par·al·lel² /'pærəlel/ n **1** [C] a connection or similarity between two things that happen or exist in different places or at different times: **+ between/with** *There are some interesting parallels between the two leaders.* | **draw a parallel between** (=show how two things are similar): *a parallel between ancient and modern theories of education* **2 in parallel** together with and at the same time as something else: *The two experiments were done in parallel.*

parallel³ v [T] *formal* to be similar to, or as good as something else: *Symptoms of depression often parallel those of more severe mental illnesses.*

par·a·lyse BrE, **paralyze** AmE /'pærəlaɪz/ v [T] **1** to make someone lose the ability to move their body or part of their body **2** to make something unable to work or continue normally: *Heavy snow has paralyzed transportation in several cities.*

par·a·lysed BrE, **paralyzed** AmE /'pærəlaɪzd/ adj **1** unable to move your body or part of your body because of an injury or illness: *He was paralyzed from the waist down after a motorcycle accident.* **2** unable to move, think clearly, or deal sensibly with a situation, especially because you are very frightened or shocked: *He stood in the doorway, paralysed by fear.*

pa·ral·y·sis /pə'ræləsˌs/ n [U] when you lose the ability to move your body or part of your body

par·a·med·ic /ˌpærə'medɪk/ n [C] someone who is trained to help people who are ill or injured but is not a doctor or nurse

pa·ram·e·ter /pə'ræmˌtəl-ər/ n [C usually plural] a limit on how much should be considered, discussed, included etc: *Congress will decide on parameters for the investigation.*

par·a·mil·i·ta·ry /ˌpærə'mɪlˌtəri‖-teri/ adj **1** a paramilitary organization fights and kills people illegally for political aims: *extremist paramilitary groups* **2** organized like an army, but not part of the official army of a country: *a paramilitary police operation* —**paramilitary** n [C]

par·a·mount /'pærəmaunt/ adj more important than anything else: *Safety is paramount.* | **of paramount importance** *Protecting the children's privacy is considered to be of paramount importance.*

par·a·noi·a /ˌpærə'nɔɪə/ n [U] **1** when you think that people are criticizing you or trying to harm you, when they are not **2** *technical* a mental illness that makes someone believe that other people want to harm or kill them —**paranoid** /'pærənɔɪd/ adj: *Stop being so paranoid!*

par·a·pher·na·li·a /ˌpærəfə'neɪliəl-fər-/ n [U] a group of different things that are used for an activity: *photographic paraphernalia*

par·a·phrase /'pærəfreɪz/ v [T] to express what someone says or writes in a shorter and clearer way —**paraphrase** n [C]

par·a·ple·gic /ˌpærə'pliːdʒɪk/ n [C] someone who is unable to move the lower part of their body —**paraplegic** adj

par·a·site /'pærəsaɪt/ n [C] **1** a plant or animal that lives on or in another plant or animal and gets food from it **2** someone who is lazy and expects other people to provide them with money, food etc —**parasitic** /ˌpærə'sɪtɪk/ adj

par·a·sol /'pærəsɒl‖-sɒːl, -sɑːl/ n [C] a thing you hold above your head to protect yourself from the sun → compare UMBRELLA

par·a·troop·er /'pærəˌtruːpəl-ər/ n [C] a

soldier who is trained to jump out of planes using a PARACHUTE

par·cel /ˈpɑːsəl‖ˈpɑːr-/ n [C] something that has been packed into a box or wrapped in paper, especially in order to send it; PACKAGE

parcel BrE/ package AmE

parched /pɑːtʃt‖pɑːrtʃt/ adj **1** spoken very thirsty **2** parched land is very dry

parch·ment /ˈpɑːtʃmənt‖ˈpɑːr-/ n [U] thick yellow-white writing paper used in past times

par·don[1] /ˈpɑːdn‖ˈpɑːrdn/ interjection **1** especially BrE (also **pardon me** AmE) used to politely ask someone to repeat something: "Your shoes are in the bedroom." "Pardon?" "I said your shoes are in the bedroom." **2 pardon me a)** used to say sorry politely : Pardon me – I hope I didn't hurt you. **b)** AmE used to politely get someone's attention; excuse me: Pardon me, is this the way to City Hall?

pardon[2] v [T] to officially decide not to punish someone for a crime: Over 250 political prisoners were pardoned by President Herzog.

pardon[3] n [C] when someone was officially forgiven for a crime: Tyler was later given a pardon. → see also **I beg your pardon** (BEG)

pare /peə‖per/ also **pare down** v [T] to gradually reduce the amount or number of something: We have had to pare costs down to a minimum.

par·ent /ˈpeərənt‖ˈper-/ n [C] someone's father or mother: My parents are coming to visit next week. → see picture at FAMILY —**parental** /pəˈrentl/ adj: parental duties

pa·ren·the·ses /pəˈrenθɨsiːz/ n [plural] the small curved lines (), used in writing to add information; BRACKETS: **in parentheses** The numbers in parentheses refer to page numbers.

par·ent·hood /ˈpeərənthʊd‖ˈper-/ n [U] when someone is a parent

par·ent·ing /ˈpeərəntɪŋ‖ˈper-/ n [U] the job or activity of being a parent: Does bad parenting always produce bad children?

par·ish /ˈpærɪʃ/ n [C] an area that has its own church

pa·rish·io·ner /pəˈrɪʃənə‖-ər/ n [C] someone who lives in a parish and regularly goes to church there

par·i·ty /ˈpærɨti/ n [U] the state of being equal with someone else, especially in your pay, rights, or power: **+ with** Prison officers are demanding pay parity with the police.

park[1] /pɑːk‖pɑːrk/ n [C] a large area with grass and trees in a town, where people walk, play games etc

park[2] v [I,T] to leave your car somewhere for a period of time: We managed to park near the entrance.

park·ing /ˈpɑːkɪŋ‖ˈpɑːr-/ n [U] **1** space where you can leave your car: Limited parking is available on Lemay Street. **2** the act of parking a car: The sign says "No Parking."

parking lot /ˈ.. ./ n [C] AmE a place for cars to park in; CAR PARK BrE

parking me·ter /ˈ.. ,../ n [C] a machine that you put money into when you park your car

parking tick·et /ˈ.. ,../ n [C] a piece of paper demanding money that is put on a vehicle that someone has parked illegally

par·lia·ment /ˈpɑːləmənt‖ˈpɑːr-/ n also **Parliament** [C,U] the group of people who are elected to make a country's laws and discuss important national and international affairs: The party could lose its majority in parliament. | the Hungarian parliament —**parliamentary** /ˌpɑːləˈmentəri‖ˌpɑːr-/ adj

par·lour BrE, **parlor** AmE /ˈpɑːlə‖ˈpɑːrlər/ n [C] **1** a type of shop that provides a particular service: a beauty parlour **2** a comfortable room in a house used especially for meeting guests, in past times

pa·ro·chi·al /pəˈrəʊkiəl‖-ˈroʊ-/ adj **1** only interested in the things that affect you and your local area: My parents lead very parochial lives. **2** relating to a PARISH

par·o·dy[1] /ˈpærədi/ n [C,U] a piece of writing, music etc that copies someone else's style in an amusing way: a parody of the Frankenstein movies

parody[2] v [T] to copy someone's style or behaviour in an amusing way

pa·role[1] /pəˈrəʊl‖-ˈroʊl/ n [U] when someone is allowed to leave prison but will have to return if they do not continue to behave well: **on parole** Williams was released on parole after 18 months.

parole[2] v [T] to allow someone to leave prison on parole

par·rot /ˈpærət/ n [C] a brightly coloured bird with a curved beak that can be taught to copy human speech

parrot

pars·ley /ˈpɑːsli‖ˈpɑːr-/ n [U] a plant with curled leaves and a fresh smell, used in cooking or as a decoration on food

pars·nip /ˈpɑːsnɨp‖ˈpɑːr-/ n [C,U] a large thick white or yellow root that is eaten as a vegetable

part[1] /pɑːt‖pɑːrt/ n **1** [C] a piece of something such as a film, object, area, or period of time: **+ of** Which part of town do you live in? | I studied Russian as part of my University course. **2** [C] one of the pieces that a machine or vehicle is made of: Do you sell parts for Ford cars? **3 play/have a part in** to be one of several things that makes something happen: Stress certainly plays a part in this kind of illness. **4 take part** to do something together with other people: Ten runners took part in the race. **5** [singular] what a particular person did in an activity that several people took part in: He was arrested for his part in the robbery. **6 on sb's part** done or caused by someone: It was a huge mistake on her part. **7** [C] the job of acting as a character in a play or film: **play the part of** Branagh played the part of Hamlet. **8** [C] AmE the line on your head made by separating your hair with a comb; PARTING BrE → see colour picture on page 244 **9 for the most part** for most of the time or usually: She is, for the most part, a fair person. **10 in part** partly: The accident was due in part to the bad weather. **11 be part and parcel of sth** included as part of something else: Stress is just part and parcel of everyday life. **12** [C] an equal part: Mix two parts sand to one *of cement.* **13 for my/his etc part** used to emphasize what someone's opinions or feelings are: *For my part, I wasn't convinced that she was telling the truth.* **14 the best/better part of sth** most of something: *We waited for the best part of an hour.*

part² *v* **1** also **part company** [I] *formal* to leave someone, or to end a relationship with them: **+ from** *Stephen parted from his wife last year.* **2** [I,T] to move two things apart or to be moved apart: *He parted the curtains and looked out into the street.* **3 be parted from** to be separated from someone or something that you love: *She couldn't bear to be parted from her children.* **4** [T] to separate your hair into two parts using a comb

part with sth *phr v* [T] to give or sell something to someone else, even though you do not really want to: *I hate to part with these boots, but they're worn out.*

part³ *adv* consisting partly of something: *The English test is part written, part spoken.*

par·tial /ˈpɑːʃəl‖ˈpɑːr-/ *adj* **1** not complete: *The advertising campaign was only a partial success.* **2 be partial to sth** to like something very much: *He's partial to a glass of whisky.*

par·tial·ly /ˈpɑːʃəli‖ˈpɑːr-/ *adv* partly but not completely: *She's partially deaf.*

par·tic·i·pant /pɑːˈtɪsɨpənt‖ˈpɑːr-/ *n* [C] someone who takes part in an activity or event

par·tic·i·pate /pɑːˈtɪsɨpeɪt‖ˈpɑːr-/ *v* [I] to take part in an activity or event: **+ in** *I'd like to thank everyone who participated in tonight's show.* —**participation** /pɑːˌtɪsɨˈpeɪʃən‖pɑːr-/ *n* [U] *They want more participation in the decision-making process.*

par·ti·ci·ple /ˈpɑːtɨsɪpəl‖ˈpɑːr-/ *n* [C] the form of a verb, usually ending in '-ing' or '-ed', that is used to form some verb tenses, or as an adjective ➔ see also PAST PARTICIPLE, PRESENT PARTICIPLE

par·ti·cle /ˈpɑːtɪkəl‖ˈpɑːr-/ *n* [C] a very small piece of something: *dust particles*

par·tic·u·lar¹ /pəˈtɪkjɨlə‖pərˈtɪkjɨlər/ *adj* **1** [only before noun] a particular thing or person is the one that you are talking about, and not any other: *On that particular occasion, we didn't really get an opportunity to talk.* **2** [only before noun] special or important enough to mention separately: *There was nothing in the letter of particular importance.* **3** [only before noun] belonging to one person or thing and not any other: *Each writer has his own particular style.* **4** very careful about choosing exactly what you like, and not easily satisfied: FUSSY: **+ about** *He's very particular about what he eats.*

particular² *n* **in particular** especially: *Old people in particular are often ill in winter.*

par·tic·u·lar·ly /pəˈtɪkjɨləli‖pərˈtɪkjɨlərli/ *adv* **1** much more than usual, or much more than other people or things; especially: *We're particularly worried about the increase in violent crime.* **2 not particularly** *spoken* used to say 'no' to a question or suggestion: *"Did you enjoy the movie?" "Not particularly."*

par·tic·u·lars /pəˈtɪkjɨləz‖pərˈtɪkjɨlərz/ *n* [plural] information or details about something: *I gave him all the particulars he needed.*

part·ing¹ /ˈpɑːtɪŋ‖ˈpɑːr-/ *n* **1** [C] *BrE* the line on your head made by separating your hair with a comb; PART *AmE* ➔ see colour picture on page 244 **2** [C,U] *formal* when two people leave each other or end a relationship

parting² *adj* **1 a parting kiss/gift/glance etc** something that you give someone as you leave **2 a parting shot** an unpleasant remark that you make to someone at the end of an argument

par·ti·san /ˌpɑːtɨˈzæn‖ˈpɑːrtɨzən, -sən/ *adj* supporting a political party, sports team etc and disliking all others: *A partisan crowd cheered the Bulls to victory.* —**partisan** *n* [C]

par·ti·tion¹ /pɑːˈtɪʃən‖pər-, pɑːr-/ *n* **1** [C] a thin wall that separates one part of a room from another **2** [U] when a country is divided into two or more separate countries: *the partition of India*

partition² *v* [T] **1** to divide a country or area into two or more parts **2** also **partition** sth ↔ **off** to divide a room into two parts by building a thin wall: *The Principal's office was partitioned off at one end of the room.*

part·ly /ˈpɑːtli‖ˈpɑːr-/ *adv* to some degree, but not completely: *I was partly to blame for the accident.*

part·ner¹ /ˈpɑːtnə‖ˈpɑːrtnər/ *n* [C] **1** someone that you dance with or play a game with: *Take your partners for the next dance.* **2** one of the people who owns a business: *a partner in a London law firm* **3** the person who you are married to or are having a relationship with **4** a country that your country has an agreement with: *Britain's EU partners*

partner² *v* [T] to be someone's partner in a dance or sport

part·ner·ship /ˈpɑːtnəʃɪp‖ˈpɑːrtnər-/ *n* **1** [C,U] a relationship between two people or organizations who work together to achieve something: **in partnership with** *a scheme organized by the business community in partnership with local colleges* **2** [U] when you are a partner in a business: **be in partnership** *We've been in partnership for five years.* **3** [C] a business owned by two or more people

part of speech /ˌ. . ˈ./ *n* [C] one of the groups into which words are divided, for example 'noun', 'verb', or 'adjective'

par·tridge /ˈpɑːtrɪdʒ‖ˈpɑːr-/ *n* [C,U] a small fat bird with a short tail that is hunted for food and sport

part-time /ˌ. ˈ.◂/ *adj, adv* working or studying for less than the usual number of hours: *Brenda works part-time.*｜*a part-time job* ➔ compare FULL-TIME

part·way also **part way** /ˈpɑːtweɪ‖ˈpɑːrt-/ *adv* some of the way into a place or into a period of time: *Eve got up and left partway through the lecture.*

par·ty¹ /ˈpɑːti‖ˈpɑːrti/ *n* [C] **1** a social occasion when people eat, drink, and enjoy themselves: *a birthday party*｜**have/give a party** *Nick and Jo are having a party on Saturday.* **2** an organization of people with the same political aims that tries to win elections: *the Democratic Party*｜*party members* **3** a group of people who do something together: *A search party was sent to look for the missing girl.* **4** one of the people or groups involved in a legal argument or agreement

party² *v* [I] *informal* to enjoy yourself with other people, especially by drinking alcohol, eating, and dancing: *We were out partying until 4 a.m.*

pass¹ /pɑːsǁpæs/ *v* **1** [I,T] also **pass by** to move or travel past someone or something: *Angie waved at me as she passed.* | *I pass his house every morning on the way to school.* **2** [I,T] to go across, through, around etc something else or to make something do this: **+ through/across/behind** etc *The new road passes right behind our house.* | *We passed through Texas on our way to Mexico.* **3** [T] to give something to someone by putting it in their hand: *Pass the salt please.* **4** [T] to kick, throw, or hit a ball to another player in your team during a game: *Johnson passes the ball quickly to Eliott, and Eliott scores!* **5** [I] if time passes, it goes by: *Several years had passed since I had last seen Jake.* **6** [T] to spend time in a particular way: *The security guards used to pass their time playing cards.* **7** [I,T] to succeed in a test or examination: *Gino's worried he's not going to pass his English exam.* **8** [T] to decide that someone has succeeded in a test or examination **9** [T] to officially accept a law or suggestion, especially by voting: *The new legislation was passed in 1996.* **10 pass sentence** to officially decide how a criminal will be punished **11 pass judgment** to give your opinion about something: *I'm here to listen – not to pass judgment.* **12** [I] to go from one person's control to someone else's: **+ to/into** etc *After he died, all his land passed to his children.* **13** [I] to end: *The storm soon passed.* **14 let sth pass** to deliberately not react when someone says or does something that you do not like: *It was an offensive remark, but I decided to let it pass.* **15 pass the buck** to say that someone else is responsible for something, instead of accepting blame or the problem yourself **16 pass water** to URINATE

pass sth ↔ **around** (also **pass** sth ↔ **round** *BrE*) *phr v* [T] to give something to each person in a group: *A list was passed around and we each had to sign our name.*

pass away *phr v* [I] a phrase meaning to die, used when you want to avoid upsetting someone by using the word 'die'

pass by *phr v* **1** [I,T **pass by** sth] to move to a place, person, or object and go past them: *If we pass by a post office, I'll get some stamps.* **2** [T **pass** sb **by**] if something passes you by, it exists or happens but you do not get any advantage from it: *She felt that life was passing her by.*

pass sth ↔ **down** *phr v* [T] to give or teach something to people who are younger than you or who live after you: *traditions that are passed down from one generation to another*

pass for sb/sth *phr v* [T] to be so similar to someone that people think that you are that person: *With her hair cut like that, she could pass for a boy.*

pass sb/sth **off** as sth *phr v* [T] to make people think that a person or thing is someone or something that they are not: *He managed to pass himself off as a doctor for three years!*

pass sth ↔ **on** *phr v* [T] **1** to tell someone something that someone else has told you: *OK, I'll pass the message on to Ms Chen.* **2** to give something to someone after you have finished

with it: *When you've read the report, pass it on to the others.*

pass out *phr v* [I] to suddenly become unconscious

pass up *phr v* [T] **pass up a chance/opportunity/offer** to not use a chance to do something: *You'd be crazy to pass up such an opportunity.*

pass² *n* [C] **1** when you kick, throw, or hit a ball to another member of your team: *a 30-yard pass* **2** an official document that shows you are allowed to enter a building, travel on a train or bus without paying etc: *a bus pass* **3** a successful result in an examination: *A pass is 50% or more.* **4** a road or path through or over mountains: *a narrow mountain pass*

pass·a·ble /ˈpɑːsəbəlǁˈpæ-/ *adj* **1** just good enough, but not very good: *He spoke passable French.* **2** a road or river that is passable is not blocked, so you can travel along or across it → opposite IMPASSABLE

pas·sage /ˈpæsɪdʒ/ *n* **1** [C] also **pas·sage·way** /ˈpæsɪdʒweɪ/ a narrow area with walls on each side, that connects one room or place to another: *up the stairs and along the passage* **2** [C] a short part of a book, speech, or piece of music: *Read the passage on page 32.* **3** [singular, U] movement from one place to another: *The bridge isn't strong enough to allow the passage of heavy vehicles.* **4** [C] a tube in your body that air or liquid can pass through: *nasal passages* **5 the passage of time** *literary* the passing of time **6** [C] a journey on a ship

pas·sé /ˈpæseɪ, ˈpɑː-ǁpæˈseɪ/ *adj* no longer modern or fashionable

pas·sen·ger /ˈpæsɪndʒə, -sən-ǁ-ər/ *n* [C] someone who is travelling in a car, plane, boat etc, but is not driving it

pass·er·by /ˌpɑːsəˈbaɪǁˌpæsər-/ *n* [C], *plural* **passersby** someone who is walking past a place, especially when something unexpected happens: *Several passersby saw the accident.*

pass·ing¹ /ˈpɑːsɪŋǁˈpæ-/ *adj* [only before noun] only continuing for a short period of time, and often not very important: *a passing thought*

passing² *n* **1 in passing** if you say something in passing, you mention it while you are mainly talking about something else: *The actress mentioned in passing that she had once worked in a factory.* **2 with the passing of time/of the years** used to say that something happens gradually: *With the passing of time, he began to enjoy living alone.*

pas·sion /ˈpæʃən/ *n* **1** [C,U] a very strong feeling of love or sexual desire: *a story of passion and revenge* **2** a strong belief in something, or when you have very strong feelings about something: *He spoke with great passion about his country.* **3 a passion for sth** a strong liking for something: *a passion for music*

pas·sion·ate /ˈpæʃənɨt/ *adj* **1** showing strong feelings about something or a strong belief in something: *a passionate speech* **2** showing strong feelings of love or sexual desire for someone: *a passionate kiss* —**passionately** *adv*

pas·sive¹ /ˈpæsɪv/ *adj* **1** tending to accept situations or things that other people do, without trying to change or influence them; **2** a passive activity is one in which you watch, look, or listen rather than do anything: *Watching TV is a largely passive activity.* **3** if a verb or sentence is passive, the subject of the verb or sentence is affected by the action of the verb. For example in the sentence 'Oranges are grown in California', the verb 'are grown' is passive — **passively** *adv* —**passivity** /pæˈsɪvɪti/ *n* [U] → compare ACTIVE¹, IMPASSIVE

passive² *n* **the passive (voice)** the passive form of a verb

passive smok·ing /ˌ.. ˈ../ *n* [U] when you breathe in smoke from a cigarette that someone else is smoking

Pass·o·ver /ˈpɑːsəʊvəˈpæsoʊvər/ *n* [singular,U] the Jewish holiday in the spring to remember when the Jews in ancient Egypt became free

pass·port /ˈpɑːspɔːtˈpæspɔːrt/ *n* [C] **1** a small official book that proves who you are and what country you are a citizen of **2 a passport to success/happiness etc** something that makes success, happiness etc possible: *Money is not necessarily a passport to happiness.*

pass·word /ˈpɑːswɜːdˈpæswɜːrd/ *n* [C] a secret word that you must use before being allowed to use a computer system or enter a place: *Please type in your password.*

past¹ /pɑːstˈpæst/ *adj* **1** [only before noun] having happened or existed in a time before now: *He has learned from past experience.* | *She was obviously trying to make up for past mistakes.* **2** [only before noun] used to talk about a period of time until now: *Tim's been in Spain for the past week.* **3** [not before noun] something that is past no longer exists or is finished: *Summer is past, winter is coming.* **4 past leader/president/champion etc** a leader, president etc in the past: *a past tennis champion* **5 past tense** also **the past** the form of a verb that is used to show a past action or state

past² *prep* **1** further than: *My house is a mile past the bridge.* **2** up to and beyond: *Tanya walked right past me!* → see colour picture on page 474 **3** later than a particular time: *It's ten past nine.* **4** older than a particular age: *She's past fifty.* **5** beyond a particular stage or limit: *This cheese is past its sell-by date.* **6 past it** too old to do something **7 I wouldn't put it past sb (to do sth)** *spoken* used to say that you would not be surprised if someone did something bad because it is typical of them: *I don't know if he stole the car, but I wouldn't put it past him!*

past³ *n* **1 the past a)** the time that existed before now: *People travel more now than they did in the past.* **b)** the form of a verb that is used to show a past action or state **2** [C, usually singular] all the things that have happened in

your life before now: *She doesn't talk about her past.*

past⁴ *adv* **1** up to and beyond a particular place: *Hal and his friends just drove past.* **2 go past** if a period of time goes past, it passes: *Several weeks went past without any news from home.*

pas·ta /ˈpæstəˈpɑː-/ *n* [U] food made from flour, eggs, and water and cut into various shapes and cooked

paste¹ /peɪst/ *n* [C,U] **1** a type of thick glue that is used for sticking paper **2** a soft thick mixture that can be easily shaped or spread: *Mix the water and the powder into a smooth paste.*

paste² *v* [T] to stick paper together or onto another surface with paste

pas·tel¹ /ˈpæstlˈpæˈstel/ *adj* [only before noun] a pastel colour is soft, pale, and light: *Her bedroom was painted in pastel pink.*

pastel² *n* [C,U] a small coloured stick, used for drawing, or a picture drawn in this way

pas·teur·ized (also **-ised** *BrE*) /ˈpɑːstʃəraɪzd, -stə-ˈpæs-/ *adj* pasteurized milk has been specially heated to kill any BACTERIA in it —**pasteurization** /ˌpɑːstʃəraɪˈzeɪʃənˌpæstʃərə-/ *n* [U]

pas·time /ˈpɑːstaɪmˈpæs-/ *n* [C] something that you enjoy doing when you are not working: *His pastimes include watching TV and reading.*

pas·tor /ˈpɑːstəˈpæstər/ *n* [C] a priest in some PROTESTANT churches

pas·tor·al /ˈpɑːstərəlˈpæ-/ *adj* **1** giving advice and looking after people's personal or religious happiness as part of your work: *There is always a pastoral side to a teacher's work.* **2** *literary* typical of peaceful country life: *pastoral scenes*

past par·ti·ci·ple /ˌ. ˈ..../ *n* [C] a PARTICIPLE that is usually formed by adding '-ed' to a REGULAR verb. It can be used in COMPOUND forms of a verb to make PERFECT tenses, or as an adjective. In the sentence 'Look what you have done', 'done' is the past participle.

past per·fect /ˌ. ˈ../ *n* **the past perfect** the tense of a verb that shows that an action was completed before another event or time in the past. In the sentence 'I had finished my breakfast before Rick called', 'had finished' is in the past perfect

pas·try /ˈpeɪstri/ *n* **1** [U] a mixture of flour, fat, and water that is baked used for making foods such as PIEs **2** [C] a small cake made with pastry

pas·ture /ˈpɑːstʃəˈpæstʃər/ *n* [C,U] land that is covered with grass which cattle, sheep etc feed on

past·y¹ /ˈpeɪsti/ *adj* looking very pale and unhealthy: *a pasty face*

pas·ty² /ˈpæsti/ *n* [C] *BrE* a small PIE filled with meat or vegetables

pat¹ /pæt/ *v* [T] **-tted, -tting** to touch someone or something lightly with your hand flat, especially in a friendly way: *Gill patted the dog.*

GRAMMAR NOTE: direct and indirect speech
There are two ways of reporting what someone said:
DIRECT SPEECH (using "..."): *"I forgot to phone you," she said, "I am really sorry."*
INDIRECT SPEECH: *She said that she had forgotten to phone me and she was really sorry.*

pat² n [C] **1** a way of touching someone or something lightly with your hand flat, especially in a friendly way: *He gave the dog a pat on the head.* **2 a pat on the back** when someone praises a person for something good they have done: *Alex deserves a pat on the back for all his hard work.*

pat³ adj a pat answer, explanation etc is said too quickly and sounds as if it has been used many times before —**pat** adv

patch¹ /pætʃ/ n [C] **1** a small piece of material used for covering a hole in your clothes: *an old sweater with patches on the elbows* **2** a part of an area that is different or looks different from the parts that surround it: *a damp patch on the ceiling* | *a bald patch* **3** a small piece of material to cover your eye **4** a small area of land: *a vegetable patch* **5** a bad patch BrE a difficult or unhappy time **6** not a patch on sb/sth not at all as good as someone or something: *The beaches here aren't a patch on the Caribbean.*

patch² v [T] to repair something by putting a small piece of material over a hole, especially in a piece of clothing
patch sth ↔ up phr v [T] **1** to end an argument and become friendly with someone again: *I've patched it up with my girlfriend.* **2** to repair something, often so it can be used for a short time and then replaired again properly at a later time: *They patched the car up enough to drive home.*

patch·work /ˈpætʃwɜːk‖-wɜːrk/ n [U] a type of sewing in which many different coloured pieces of cloth are sewn together: *a patchwork quilt*

patch·y /ˈpætʃi/ adj **1** happening or existing in a number of small separate areas: *patchy fog* **2** not complete or not all good: *My knowledge of biology is pretty patchy.*

pâ·té /ˈpæteɪ‖pɑːˈteɪ, pæ-/ n [U] a smooth mixture made from meat, fish, or vegetables, that you spread on bread

pa·tent¹ /ˈpeɪtnt, ˈpæ-‖ˈpæ-/ n [C] an official document that says that one person or company has the right to make or sell a new INVENTION or product and that no one else is allowed to copy it

patent² v [T] to obtain a patent for something

patent³ adj formal clear and easy to notice; OBVIOUS: *a patent lie*

patent leath·er /ˌpeɪtnt ˈleðə◂‖ˌpætnt ˈleðər/ n [U] very shiny leather, usually black: *patent leather shoes*

pa·tent·ly /ˈpeɪtntli‖ˈpæ-/ adv **patently obvious/false/unfair etc** completely clear, untrue, unfair etc, in a way that anyone can notice: *Helen's denial was immediate and patently untrue.*

pa·ter·nal /pəˈtɜːnl‖-ɜːr-/ adj **1** typical of the way a good father feels or acts **2 paternal grandfather/uncle etc** your father's father, brother etc —**paternally** adv → compare MATERNAL

pa·ter·ni·ty /pəˈtɜːnɪti‖-ɜːr-/ n [U] law the state of being a father

path /pɑːθ‖pæθ/ n [C], plural **paths** /pɑːðz‖pæðz/ **1** a track across an area of land that people walk along: *a path through the woods* → see colour picture on page 243 **2** the space in front of you as you move forward: *The police cleared a path through the crowd.* **3** the direction or line along which something moves: *the path of the moon*

pa·thet·ic /pəˈθetɪk/ adj **1** making you feel sadness or sympathy: *the pathetic sight of refugee children* | *Stop being so pathetic!* **2** informal very bad, useless, or weak: *Vicky made a pathetic attempt to apologize.* —**pathetically** /-kli/ adv

path·o·log·i·cal /ˌpæθəˈlɒdʒɪkəl◂‖-ˈlɑː-/ adj **1** pathological behaviour or feelings are extreme and unreasonable, and cannot be controlled: *a pathological liar* **2** technical connected with pathology

pa·thol·o·gist /pəˈθɒlədʒɪst‖-ˈθɑː-/ n [C] a doctor trained in pathology, especially one who finds out the cause of someone's death

pa·thol·o·gy /pəˈθɒlədʒi‖-ˈθɑː-/ n [U] the study of the causes and effects of diseases

pa·thos /ˈpeɪθɒs‖-θɑːs/ n [U] literary the quality in a person or a situation that makes you feel sympathy and sadness

path·way /ˈpɑːθweɪ‖ˈpæθ-/ n [C] a PATH

pa·tience /ˈpeɪʃəns/ n [U] **1** the ability to stay calm and not get angry when you have to wait for a long time or deal with a difficult situation: *After waiting for half an hour I ran out of patience.* | *I don't have the patience to be a teacher.* | **lose (your) patience** *One day she completely lost patience and shook the little girl.* **2** BrE a game of cards played by one person; SOLITAIRE AmE → opposite IMPATIENCE

pa·tient¹ /ˈpeɪʃənt/ n [C] someone who is being treated by a doctor, nurse etc

patient² adj able to wait calmly for a long time or to deal with difficult situations without becoming angry: *He was always patient, even with the slowest students.* —**patiently** adv → opposite IMPATIENT

pat·i·o /ˈpætiəʊ‖-oʊ/ n [C], plural **patios** an outdoor area with a stone floor next to a house, where people can sit outdoors → see colour picture on page 79

pa·tri·arch·al /ˌpeɪtriˈɑːkəl◂‖-ˈɑːr-/ adj ruled or controlled only by men: *a patriarchal society* —**patriarchy** /ˈpeɪtriɑːki‖-ɑːr-/ n [C,U]

pat·ri·ot /ˈpætriət, -trɒt, ˈpeɪ-‖ˈpeɪtriət, -triɑːt/ n [C] someone who loves their country

pat·ri·ot·ic /ˌpætriˈɒtɪk◂, ˌpeɪ-‖ˌpeɪtriˈɑːtɪk◂/ adj showing pride, loyalty, and love for your country: *patriotic song* —**patriotically** /-kli/ adv —**patriotism** /ˈpætriətɪzəm, ˈpeɪ-‖ˈpeɪ-/ n [U]

pa·trol¹ /pəˈtrəʊl‖-ˈtroʊl/ n **1** [C,U] when police, guards, soldiers etc go regularly around a building or part of a town to make sure there is no trouble there: **be on patrol** *Guards were on patrol all night.* **2** [C] a group of police, soldiers, planes etc that patrol a particular area: *the California Highway Patrol*

patrol² v [I,T] **-lled, -lling** to regularly go around a building or part of a town to make sure there is no trouble there: *Soldiers patrol the prison camp every hour.*

pa·trol·man /pəˈtrəʊlmən‖-ˈtroʊl-/ n [C] AmE a police officer who patrols a particular area

pa·tron /ˈpeɪtrən/ n [C] **1** someone who supports or gives money to an organization, artist, musical performer etc: *a patron of the arts* **2** formal someone who uses a particular shop, restaurant, theatre etc: *We ask patrons not to smoke.*

pat·ron·age /ˈpætrənɪdʒ/ n [U] the support that a patron gives to an organization, artist etc

pat·ron·ize (also **-ise** BrE) /ˈpætrənaɪz‖ˈpeɪ-, ˈpæ-/ v [T] **1** to behave or talk to someone in a way that shows you think they are less important or intelligent than you: Don't patronize me. **2** formal to regularly go to a particular shop, restaurant etc

pat·ro·niz·ing (also **-ising** BrE) /ˈpætrənaɪzɪŋ‖ˈpeɪ-, ˈpæ-/ adj someone who is patronizing talks to you in a way that shows they think you are less important or intelligent than them: He has such a patronizing attitude! —**patronizing** adv

patron saint /ˌ.. ˈ./ n [C] a SAINT (=Christian holy person) who is believed to give special protection to people who live in a particular place, people who do a particular activity etc

pat·ter /ˈpætə‖-ər/ n [singular] **1** the repeated sound of something lightly hitting a surface: + of the patter of raindrops on the path **2** very fast and continuous talk: a car salesman's patter —**patter** v [I] Outside the rain pattered lightly on the window.

pat·tern /ˈpætən‖ˈpætərn/ n [C] **1** a design made from shapes, colours, lines etc that are arranged in a regular way: a pattern of small red and white squares **2** the regular way in which something happens, develops, or is done: Romantic novels tend to follow a similar pattern. | the behaviour patterns of young children **3** a shape that you copy onto cloth, paper etc when you are making something, especially clothes: a skirt pattern

pat·terned /ˈpætənd‖-tərnd/ adj decorated with a pattern: patterned sheets → see colour picture on page 114

paunch /pɔːntʃ‖pɒːntʃ/ n [C] a man's fat stomach: I wish I could lose this paunch! —**paunchy** adj

pau·per /ˈpɔːpə‖ˈpɔːpər/ n [C] old-fashioned someone who is very poor

pause /pɔːz‖pɒːz/ v [I] to stop speaking or doing something for a short time before starting again: + for Tom paused for a moment, and then asked, "So what should I do?"

pause n [C] a short time when you stop speaking or doing something: There was a long pause in the conversation.

pave /peɪv/ v [T] **1** to cover a path, road etc with a surface of flat stones **2** **pave the way** to do something that will make something else possible in the future: The new law will pave the way for more rights for disabled people.

pave·ment /ˈpeɪvmənt/ n **1** [C] BrE the path you walk on at the side of a road; SIDEWALK AmE → see colour picture on page 79 **2** [U] AmE the hard surface of a road

pa·vil·ion /pəˈvɪljən/ n [C] **1** a temporary building used as a place for public entertainment, events etc **2** BrE a building at a sports field where players can change their clothes

paving stone /ˈ.. ./ n [C] a flat piece of stone used to make a surface for walking on

paw /pɔː‖pɒː/ n [C] the foot of an animal that has CLAWS, for example a lion or dog

paw v [I,T] if an animal paws something, it touches something with its paw: + at The dog was pawing at the door, trying to get out.

pawn /pɔːn‖pɒːn/ n [C] **1** one of the least powerful pieces in a game of CHESS **2** someone who has very little power, who is controlled by a much more powerful person or group

pawn v [T] to leave a valuable object with a pawnbroker so that you can borrow money: My grandmother had to pawn her wedding ring to buy food.

pawn·bro·ker /ˈpɔːnˌbrəʊkə‖ˈpɔːnˌbroʊkər/ n [C] someone who lends money to people in exchange for valuable objects

pay /peɪ/ v **paid** /peɪd/, **paid, paying 1** [I,T] to give someone money for something that you are buying from them, for work they have done etc: + for How much did you pay for that watch? | **be/get paid** Most people get paid monthly. | **well/highly paid** (=paid a lot of money for your work): a highly paid job in a law firm | **pay sb to do sth** Dad paid me £5 to wash the car. **2** [T] to give a person, company, or government etc money that you owe them: Do you have to pay tax when you are a student? **3** **pay attention** to listen to or watch someone or something carefully: Sorry, I wasn't paying attention. What did you say? **4** **pay a visit** to go to see a particular place or person: I was in New York and I thought I'd pay her a visit. **5** [I] to be worth doing because you get an advantage: Crime doesn't pay. **6** [I,T] if someone pays for what they have done, they are punished for it, or something bad happens to them because of it: + for One day I'll make you pay for this! | **pay the penalty/price** She committed a terrible crime, and now she must pay the penalty. **7** **pay sb a compliment** to tell someone that you think they are nice, attractive, intelligent etc **8** **pay your respects (to sb)** formal to visit or speak to someone in order to be polite, especially to say formally that you are sorry that someone has died: Sam came over to pay his respects to the family. **9** **pay tribute to** to publicly praise or thank someone or something **10** **pay lip service (to)** to say that you support or agree with something, without doing anything to prove it: Too many companies only pay lip service to customer service. **11** **pay your way** to pay for the things you want or use, without depending on someone else

pay sb/sth ↔ **back** phr v [T] to give someone the money that you owe them; REPAY: Can I borrow $10? I'll pay you back tomorrow.

pay sth ↔ **in/into** phr v [T] to put money into a bank account: She immediately paid the money into her savings account.

pay off phr v **1** [T **pay** sth ↔ **off**] to pay all the money that you owe **2** [I] if something that you do pays off, it is successful or helps you be successful: All that hard work finally paid off.

pay sth ↔ **out** phr v [I,T] to pay a lot of money for something: I paid out a lot of money for that car.

pay up phr v [I] informal to pay all the money that you owe, especially when you do not want to

pay n [U] money that you are given for working; SALARY: workers striking for higher pay | a big pay rise

P

pay·a·ble /ˈpeɪəbəl/ *adj* **1** a bill, debt etc that is payable must be paid: *A club fee of $30 is payable every year.* **2 payable to sb** a cheque etc that is payable to someone has that person's name written on it and should be paid to them

pay cheque *BrE*, **paycheck** *AmE* /ˈpeɪ-tʃek/ *n* [C] a cheque used for paying a worker his or her wages: *a monthly paycheck*

pay·day /ˈpeɪdeɪ/ *n* [U] the day when your wages are paid

pay·ee /peɪˈiː/ *n* [C] *technical* the person to whom money should be paid to

pay·ment /ˈpeɪmənt/ *n* **1** [C] an amount of money that should be paid or has been paid: *monthly payments* **2** [U] the act of paying: *Payment must be made within 30 days.*

pay·off /ˈpeɪɒfǁ-ɔːf/ *n* [singular] a good result from something that you do

pay phone /ˈ. ./ *n* [C] a public telephone that you pay to use

pay·roll /ˈpeɪrəʊlǁ-roʊl/ *n* [C] a list of people who are employed by a company, or the total amount of money that the company spends on their wages: **be on the payroll** (=be employed by a company)

PC[1] /ˌpiː ˈsiːʀ/ *n* [C] **1** personal computer; a small computer that is used by one person at a time **2** *BrE* police constable; a policeman of the lowest rank → see colour picture on page 80

PC[2] *adj* POLITICALLY CORRECT

PE /ˌpiː ˈiː/ *n* [U] physical education; sports and exercises that are taught as a school subject

pea /piː/ *n* [C] a round green seed that is cooked and eaten as a vegetable: *pie and peas* → see picture at VEGETABLES

peace /piːs/ *n* [U] **1** when there is no war or fighting: *There has been peace in the region for 6 years now. | a dangerous situation that threatens world peace |* **peace treaty** *Egypt and Israel signed a peace treaty in 1979. |* **peace talks** *The two sides will meet for peace talks in Geneva.* **2** when everything is very calm and quiet: **peace and quiet** *He went up to his room to get some peace and quiet. |* **in peace** *Mary, let your sister read in peace.* (=without being interrupted) **3** when you feel calm, happy, and not worried: **peace of mind** *Will you please call if you're going to be late, just for my peace of mind?* (=so I do not feel worried) **4 make (your) peace** to end an argument with someone, especially by telling them you are sorry: *He wanted to make peace with his father before he died.*

peace·a·ble /ˈpiːsəbəl/ *adj* peaceable people, activities etc are not angry or violent, and are not likely to cause arguments or fights — **peaceably** *adv*

peace·ful /ˈpiːsfəl/ *adv* **1** not using or intending violence: *a peaceful protest against nuclear weapons* **2** calm, quiet, and without any problems or excitement: *a peaceful day in the country* — **peacefully** *adv* — **peacefulness** *n* [U]

peace·keep·ing /ˈpiːsˌkiːpɪŋ/ *adj* **peacekeeping forces/operations etc** soldiers, military activities etc that are in a place where there is a war, to try to stop the fighting

peace·time /ˈpiːstaɪm/ *n* [U] when a country is not fighting a war → opposite WARTIME

peach /piːtʃ/ *n* [C] a soft round fruit with yellow and red skin and a large seed inside: *peaches and cream* → see picture at FRUIT

pea·cock /ˈpiːkɒkǁ-kɑːk/ *n* [C] a large male bird with long blue and green tail feathers that it can spread out

peak[1] /piːk/ *n* [C] **1** the time when someone or something is biggest, most successful, or strongest: *She is now at the peak of her career. | Traffic reaches a peak between four and six o'clock.* **2** a mountain or the pointed top of a mountain: *the snow-covered peaks of the Alps* → see colour picture on page 243 **3** the flat curved part of a hat that covers your eyes

peak[2] *v* [I] to reach the highest point or level: *Ice cream sales peak in July.*

peak[3] *adj* **1 peak level/value etc** the highest level, value etc that something can reach **2** *BrE* peak times are when the largest number of people are travelling, using a service etc: *peak traffic times*

peal /piːl/ *n* [C] a sudden loud repeated sound, such as laughter, THUNDER, or bells ringing: *Peals of laughter came from the audience.* — **peal** *v* [I]

pea·nut /ˈpiːnʌt/ *n* [C] a small nut with a soft light brown shell

peanut but·ter /ˌ...ˈ..ǁ..ˌ../ *n* [U] a soft food made from crushed peanuts, usually eaten on bread

pea·nuts /ˈpiːnʌts/ *n* [U] *informal* a very small amount of money: *He works for peanuts.*

pear /peəǁper/ *n* [C] a sweet juicy fruit that is round at the bottom and becomes thinner at the top → see picture at FRUIT

pearl /pɜːlǁpɜːrl/ *n* [C] a valuable small white round object, that forms inside an OYSTER and is used in jewellery: *a pearl necklace*

pear-shaped /ˈ. ./ *adj* **go pear-shaped** *informal* if something you are trying to do goes pear-shaped, it fails to happen in the way that you want; go wrong

peas·ant /ˈpezənt/ *n* [C] someone who does farm work on the piece of land where they live, especially in the past or in a poor country: *Most of the population were peasants – very few yet lived in the cities.*

peat /piːt/ *n* [U] a substance that is formed from decaying plants under the surface of the ground, used to help plants grow or burned instead of coal

peb·ble /ˈpebəl/ *n* [C] a small smooth stone that is usually found in a river or on a beach → see colour picture on page 243

peck[1] /pek/ *v* [I,T] if a bird pecks something, it hits or bites it with its beak: *birds pecking at breadcrumbs*

peck² /pek/ n [C] **1** **give sb a peck on the cheek** to kiss someone's cheek quickly and lightly **2** when a bird pecks something

pe·cu·li·ar /pɪˈkjuːliəll-liər/ adj **1** strange and a little surprising, especially in an unpleasant way: *The fish had a rather peculiar taste.* | *Kate's already gone? How peculiar!* **2** **be peculiar to** to be a quality that only one person, place, or thing has: *the strong flavour that is peculiar to garlic* —**peculiarly** adv: *There's something about his films that is peculiarly English.*

pe·cu·li·ar·i·ty /pɪˌkjuːliˈærˌti/ n **1** [C] an unusual or slightly strange habit or quality that only one person, group, place etc has: *Everyone has their little peculiarities* **2** [U] the quality of being strange or unusual

ped·a·go·gi·cal /ˌpedəˈɡɒdʒɪkəlll-ˈɡɑː-/ adj formal relating to teaching: *pedagogical methods*

ped·al¹ /ˈpedl/ n [C] **1** the part of a bicycle that you push round with your foot in order to make it move forward **2** the part of a car or machine that you press with your foot to control its movements

pedal² v [I,T] to ride a bicycle by pushing the pedals with your feet

pe·dan·tic /pɪˈdæntɪk/ adj paying too much attention to small details and wanting everything to be done exactly according to strict rules —**pedantically** /-kli/ adv

ped·dle /ˈpedl/ v [T] to sell illegal drugs or small cheap things

peddler /ˈpedləll-ər/ n [C] **1** AmE someone who used to go from place to place selling small things; PEDLAR BrE **2** **drug/dope peddler** oldfashioned someone who sells illegal drugs

ped·es·tal /ˈpedˌstəl/ n [C] **1** the base that you put a STATUE or a PILLAR on **2** **put sb on a pedestal** to admire someone so much that you think they are perfect

pe·des·tri·an¹ /pˌˈdestriən/ n [C] someone who is walking in the streets, rather than driving a car or riding a bicycle

pedestrian² adj **1** relating to pedestrians, or used by pedestrians: *a pedestrian crossing* (=where people can walk across the street) **2** ordinary, and not very interesting or exciting: *This year's cup final was a pedestrian affair.*

pedestrian cross·ing /ˌ...ˈ../ n [C] BrE a specially marked place for people to cross a road; CROSSWALK AmE

pe·di·a·tri·cian /ˌpiːdiəˈtrɪʃən/ n [C] the American spelling of PAEDIATRICIAN

pe·di·at·rics /ˌpiːdiˈætrɪks/ n [U] the American spelling of PAEDIATRICS

ped·i·gree¹ /ˈpedˌɡriː/ n [C,U] **1** the parents and other past family members of an animal, or the written record of them **2** the family history of a person, or what they have achieved in a particular skill or profession

pedigree² adj [only before noun] a pedigree animal has parents, grandparents etc from the same BREED of animals and is therefore of high quality

ped·lar /ˈpedləll-ər/ n [C] BrE someone who used to walk from place to place selling small things; PEDDLER AmE

pee /piː/ n [singular] informal when someone urinates (URINATE) —**pee** v [I]

peek¹ /piːk/ v [I] to look at something quickly and secretly: *The door was open, so I peeked into the room.*

peek² n [C] a quick look at something: **take a peek** *Take a peek in the oven and see if the cake's done.*

peel¹ /piːl/ v **1** [T] to remove the skin of a fruit or vegetable: *Will you peel the potatoes, please?* → see colour picture on page 439 **2** [I] also **peel off** if skin, paint, WALLPAPER etc peels, small pieces fall off its surface: *My skin always peels when I've been in the sun.*

peel off phr v **1** [T **peel** sth ↔ **off**] to remove something from the surface of something else: *Peel off the label.* **2** [I] to fall off the surface of something in small pieces: *The paint was beginning to peel off.*

peel² n [U] the skin of a fruit or vegetable that you remove before eating it: *orange peel* → see picture at FRUIT

peep¹ /piːp/ v [I] **1** to look at something quickly and secretly: **+ through/out/at etc** *I saw Joe peeping through the curtains.* **2** to appear: **+ out/above/through etc** *The sun finally peeped out from behind the clouds.*

peep² n **1** [C usually singular] a quick or secret look at something: *She took a peep at the answers in the back of the book.* **2** **not a peep** informal used to say that you have not heard someone make any noise or you have not seen them at all

peer¹ /pɪəllpɪr/ n **1** [C usually plural] your peers are people who are the same age as you or who have the same type of job or social position: *Teenagers usually prefer to spend their time with their peers.* | **peer group** *Kids often take drugs because of peer group pressure.* (=because they feel they must do the same things as other people of their age) **2** someone who belongs to a family of high social rank in Britain, for example a Lord

peer² v [I] to look very carefully, especially because you cannot see something well: **+ at/into/through etc** *Someone was peering through the window.*

peeve /piːv/ n [C] AmE **a pet peeve** (PET³)

peeved /piːvd/ adj informal annoyed: *Jim was rather peeved that his guest did not thank him for the meal.*

peg¹ /peɡ/ n [C] **1** a short piece of wood or metal that fits into a hole or is fastened to a wall, used for hanging things on etc: *a coat peg* **2** also **clothes peg** BrE a small plastic or wooden object used for fastening wet clothes to a WASHING line **3** also **tent peg** a pointed piece of wood or metal used for keeping a tent fastened to the ground

peg² v [T] **-gged, -gging** **1** to fasten something with pegs: *Peg the clothes on the washing line.*

P

GRAMMAR NOTE: a or the (1)
Use **a** or **an** before a noun when you are mentioning a person or thing for the first time, but use **the** when you mention that same person or thing again: *A man and a woman were sitting at the next table. The woman was much younger than the man.*

2 to keep prices, wages etc at a fixed level or value: *The exchange rate is pegged to the dollar.*

pel·i·can /ˈpelɪkən/ *n* [C] a bird with a very large beak that it uses for catching and holding fish

pel·let /ˈpelɪt/ *n* [C] a small hard ball made from paper, metal etc

pelt¹ /pelt/ *v* **1 pelt sb with sth** to attack someone by throwing a lot of things at them: *Two kids were pelting each other with snowballs.* **2 it's pelting down** it is raining very hard **3 pelt along/down etc** to run somewhere very fast

pelt² *n* **1** [C] the skin of a dead animal with the fur or hair still on it **2 at full pelt** as fast as possible

pel·vis /ˈpelvɪs/ *n* [C] the set of large wide curved bones at the base of your SPINE, to which your legs are joined ➝ see picture at SKELETON —**pelvic** *adj*

pen¹ /pen/ *n* [C] **1** a thing you use for writing and drawing in ink ➝ see colour picture on page 80 ➝ see also BALLPOINT PEN, FELT TIP PEN **2** a small area surrounded by a fence, used for keeping farm animals in

pen² *v* [T] **-nned, -nning** *literary* **1** to write a letter, note etc with a pen **2** to make a person or animal stay in a small area

pe·nal /ˈpiːnl/ *adj* relating to the punishment of criminals: *penal reforms*

pe·nal·ize (also **-ise** *BrE*) /ˈpiːnəlaɪz/ *v* [T] **1** to treat someone unfairly and make them have a disadvantage: *The current system penalizes people who live alone.* **2** to punish someone, for example a player or sports team by giving an advantage to the other team: *Our team was penalized for taking too much time.*

pen·al·ty /ˈpenlti/ *n* [C] **1** a punishment for not obeying a law, rule, or legal agreement: *a penalty of £50 for not paying your bus fare* | **the death penalty** (=the punishment of being killed) **2** a punishment against a team or player for breaking a rule in a game **3** in SOCCER a chance to kick the ball into the goal of the other team, because they have broken the rules

pen·ance /ˈpenəns/ *n* [C,U] a punishment that you accept, especially for religious reasons, to show that you are sorry for doing something bad

pence /pens/ abbreviation **p** *BrE* the plural of PENNY

pen·chant /ˈpɒnʃɒn, ˈpentʃənt/ *n* **a penchant for sth** when someone likes something particularly: *a penchant for fast cars*

pen·cil¹ /ˈpensəl/ *n* [C,U] a thing that you use for writing and drawing, which is made of wood and contains a stick made from a black or coloured substance: *The note was written in pencil.* ➝ see colour picture on page 80

pencil² *v* [T] to write or draw something using a pencil

pencil case /ˈ.. ./ *n* [C] a bag or box used for keeping pens, pencils etc in

pencil sharpener /ˈ.. ,../ *n* [C] a thing you use for making pencils sharp ➝ see colour picture on page 80

pen·dant /ˈpendənt/ *n* [C] a piece of jewellery that hangs from a chain around your neck

pend·ing¹ /ˈpendɪŋ/ *prep formal* until something happens, or while something happens: *The decision has been delayed pending further medical tests.*

pending² *adj formal* not yet officially decided, agreed on, or finished: *Their divorce is still pending.*

pen·du·lum /ˈpendjʊləm/ *n* [C] a long stick with a weight at the bottom that swings from side to side, used especially to make a large clock work

pen·e·trate /ˈpenɪtreɪt/ *v* **1** [I,T] to enter something or pass through it, especially when this is difficult: *bullets that can penetrate metal* | *The sun penetrated through the clouds.* **2** [T] to join an organization, company etc in order to find out secret information: *Government agents were able to penetrate the rebel army.* —**penetration** /ˌpenɪˈtreɪʃən/ *n* [U]

pen·e·trat·ing /ˈpenɪtreɪtɪŋ/ *adj* **1 penetrating look/stare etc** a look etc that makes you feel uncomfortable because the other person seems to know what you are thinking **2** showing an ability to understand things quickly and well: *They asked a number of penetrating questions.* **3** a penetrating sound is so loud that you hear it very clearly

pen friend /ˈ. ./ *BrE n* [C] a PEN PAL

pen·guin /ˈpeŋgwɪn/ *n* [C] a large black and white sea bird that cannot fly and uses its wings for swimming, and lives in Antarctica

pen·i·cil·lin /ˌpenɪˈsɪlɪn/ *n* [U] a substance used as a medicine to destroy BACTERIA

pe·nin·su·la /pɪˈnɪnsjʊlə/ *n* [C] a piece of land that is almost completely surrounded by water but is joined to a larger area of land

pe·nis /ˈpiːnɪs/ *n* [C] the male sex organ

pen·i·tent /ˈpenɪtənt/ *adj formal* feeling sorry about doing something bad, and showing you do not intend to do it again; REPENTANT —**penitence** *n* [U]

pen·i·ten·tia·ry /ˌpenɪˈtenʃəri/ *n* [C] a prison in the US: *the state penitentiary*

pen·knife /ˈpennaɪf/ *n* [C] a small knife with a blade that you can fold into its handle; a POCKET KNIFE

pen name /ˈ. ./ *n* [C] a name used by a writer instead of his or her real name

pen·nant /ˈpenənt/ *n* [C] a long pointed flag

pen·ni·less /ˈpenɪləs/ *adj* having no money

pen·ny /ˈpeni/ *n* [C] **1** *plural* **pence** /pens/ or **pennies**, abbreviation **p** a coin worth 1/100 of a pound **2** *plural* **pennies** a coin worth 1/100 of a dollar; CENT **3 every penny** all of an amount of money **4 not a penny** no money at all: *It won't cost you a penny!*

pen pal /ˈ. ./ *n* [C] someone living in another country who you write letters to and are friendly with, but who you do not meet

pen·sion /ˈpenʃən/ *n* [C] money that a company or the government pays regularly to someone after they have stopped working because they are old or ill

pen·sion·er /ˈpenʃənər/ *n* [C] *BrE* someone who is receiving a pension because they are old and have stopped working

pen·sive /ˈpensɪv/ *adj* thinking about something a lot and seeming slightly worried or sad: *He sat by the river, looking pensive.* —**pensively** *adv*

pen·ta·gon /ˈpentəgənǁ-gɑːn/ n [C] a flat shape with five sides and five angles

Pentagon n the Pentagon the US government building from which the army, navy etc are controlled, or the people who work there

pen·tath·lon /penˈtæθlənǁ-lən, -lɑːn/ n [C] a sports competition in which you have to do five different sports

pent·house /ˈpenthaʊs/ n [C] a very expensive and comfortable apartment on the top floor of a tall building

pent-up /ˌ.ˈ.◂/ adj pent-up emotions are emotions that you have stopped yourself from showing for a long time: *pent-up anger*

peo·ple[1] /ˈpiːpəl/ n **1** [plural] men, women, or children. 'People' is the usual plural of 'person': *I like the people I work with.| How many people were at the party?* **2** the people all the ordinary people in a country or place, who do not have important jobs or high social positions **3** [C] formal a race or nation: *the peoples of Asia* **4** of all people spoken used to emphasize that you are very surprised that a particular person did or could not do something: *It was Michael Jordan, of all people, who missed the shot.*

people[2] v be peopled with/by literary to be filled with people or things of a particular type

pep·per[1] /ˈpepəl-ər/ n **1** [U] a hot-tasting powder made from seeds that is used in cooking: *salt and pepper* **2** [C] a hollow red, yellow, or green vegetable with a sweet or hot taste: *green peppers* → see picture at VEGETABLES

pepper[2] v [T] be peppered with to contain a lot of a particular thing: *The article is peppered with quotations.*

pep·per·mint /ˈpepəˌmɪntǁ-ər-/ n **1** [U] a plant with a strong taste that is used in TOOTH-PASTE, medicine etc **2** [C] a SWEET with this taste

pep talk /ˈpep tɔːkǁ-tɔːk/ n [C] informal a talk that is intended to encourage people to work harder, win a game etc: *We had a pep talk from the coach before the game.*

per /pə; strong pɜːǁpər; strong pɜːr/ prep for each: *How much are bananas per pound?| He charges £20 per lesson.*

per cap·i·ta /pə ˈkæpⱼtəǁpər-/ adj, adv formal calculated by dividing the total amount of something by the number of people in a place

per·ceive /pəˈsiːvǁpər-/ v [T] formal **1** to understand or think about something in a particular way: *It is a difficult situation, but we don't perceive it as a major problem.* **2** to notice, hear, or see something that is not easy to notice: *It is difficult to perceive the difference between the two sounds.*

per·cent[1] also **per cent** BrE /pəˈsentǁpər-/ adj, adv **1** 5 percent (5%)/10 per cent (10%) etc equal to five, ten etc parts in every hundred: *There's a 10% service charge.| Inflation is down 2%.* **2** a/one hundred percent completely: *I agree with you a hundred percent.*

percent[2] also **per cent** BrE — n [C] 5 per cent (5%)/10 percent (10%) etc an amount that is equal to five, ten etc parts in every hundred: *70% of the people interviewed said they supported the President.*

per·cen·tage /pəˈsentɪdʒǁpər-/ n [C usually singular] an amount that is expressed as a part of a whole when the whole is considered as 100: *+ of A high percentage of Internet users are men.*

per·cep·ti·ble /pəˈseptⱼbəlǁpər-/ adj formal a perceptible change or difference can be seen or felt, although it is small: *perceptible changes in temperature* — **perceptibly** adv → opposite IMPER-CEPTIBLE

per·cep·tion /pəˈsepʃənǁpər-/ n [C] **1** your opinion of what something is and what it is like: *Young people have very different perceptions of marriage from their parents.* **2** [U] the way you notice things with your senses: *Drugs can change your perception of sounds.* **3** [U] the ability to understand or notice something quickly: *She shows unusual perception for a child of her age.*

per·cep·tive /pəˈseptɪvǁpər-/ adj good at noticing and understanding things or how someone is feeling: *a funny and perceptive novel about family life* — **perceptively** adv

perch[1] /pɜːtʃǁpɜːrtʃ/ n [C] a branch, stick etc where a bird sits

perch[2] v [I,T] **1** to be on the top or edge of something, or to put something there: *The hotel was perched high on a cliff above the bay.* **2** to sit on the edge of something: *She perched herself on the bar stool.*

per·co·la·tor /ˈpɜːkəleɪtəǁˈpɜːrkəleɪtər/ n [C] a pot in which coffee is made

per·cus·sion /pəˈkʌʃənǁpər-/ n [U] drums and other musical instruments that you hit

pe·ren·ni·al /pəˈreniəl/ adj a perennial problem happens often or continues for a long time: *the perennial problem of poverty*

per·fect[1] /ˈpɜːfɪktǁˈpɜːr-/ adj **1** of the best possible kind, without any faults or problems: *a car in perfect condition| Her Spanish is perfect.* → opposite IMPERFECT[1] **2** exactly right for a particular purpose: *This rug's perfect for the living room.* **3** used to emphasize what you are saying: *I felt a perfect fool!| It makes perfect sense.*

per·fect[2] /pəˈfektǁpər-/ v [T] to make something perfect: *The coach helps players to perfect their skills.*

per·fect[3] /ˈpɜːfɪktǁˈpɜːr-/ n the perfect (tense) the form of a verb showing time up to and including the present. In English this is usually formed with 'have' and the past participle, for example 'Someone has stolen my car.'; PRESENT PERFECT → see also FUTURE PERFECT, PAST PERFECT

per·fec·tion /pəˈfekʃənǁpər-/ n [U] when something is perfect: *I'll do my best, but don't expect perfection.*

per·fec·tion·ist /pəˈfekʃənⱼstǁpər-/ n [C] someone who is not satisfied with anything unless it is completely perfect

per·fect·ly /ˈpɜːfɪktliǁˈpɜːr-/ adv **1** in a perfect way: *She speaks English perfectly.* **2** used to emphasize what you are saying, especially when you are annoyed: *You know perfectly well what I'm talking about!*

per·fo·rat·ed /ˈpɜːfəreɪtⱼdǁˈpɜːr-/ adj perforated paper has a line of small holes in it so that a part of it can be torn off easily — **perforate** v [T] — **perforation** /ˌpɜːfəˈreɪʃənǁˌpɜːr-/ n [C,U]

per·form /pəˈfɔːm‖pərˈfɔːrm/ v **1** [I,T] to do something to entertain people, especially in public: *We performed 'Hamlet' last year.* **2** [T] to do something such as a job or piece of work: *an operation performed by surgeons at Guy's Hospital* **3** **perform well/badly** to work well or badly: *The car performs well on mountain roads.*

per·form·ance /pəˈfɔːməns‖pərˈfɔːr-/ n **1** [C] when a play or piece of music is performed: *a brilliant performance of Beethoven's Fifth Symphony* | *The next performance is at 8 o'clock.* **2** [C,U] how successful someone or something is, and how well they work: *The country's economic performance hasn't been good recently.* **3** [singular] when someone does a job or special activity: *Expenses will be paid for the performance of official duties.*

per·form·er /pəˈfɔːmə‖pərˈfɔːrmər/ n [C] an actor, musician etc who performs to entertain people: *a circus performer*

per·fume /ˈpɜːfjuːm‖ˈpɜːr-/ n [C,U] **1** a liquid with a strong pleasant smell, which you put on your skin: *She never wears perfume.* **2** *literary* a pleasant smell: *the rose's sweet perfume* —**perfumed** *adj*: *perfumed soap*

per·haps /pəˈhæps, præps‖pər-, præps/ *adv* **1** used to say that something may happen or may be true, but you are not sure; MAYBE: *Sarah's late – perhaps she missed the bus.* | **perhaps not** *"Maybe you shouldn't tell him." "Perhaps not."* **2** *spoken* used to politely ask or suggest something: *Perhaps you'd like to join us?*

> **USAGE NOTE: perhaps, maybe, and may be**
>
> Use **perhaps** or **maybe** to talk about something that is possible. **Maybe** is usually used at the beginning of a sentence or CLAUSE: *Maybe we can get together this weekend.* **Perhaps** is slightly more formal, and can be used in other places in a clause: *We can perhaps meet this weekend.* **May** is a modal verb that is sometimes used with the verb 'to be': *She may be here later.*

per·il /ˈperɪl/ n [C, U] *formal* great danger: *fears that our soldiers were in great peril* | *the perils of experimenting with drugs*

per·il·ous /ˈperɪləs/ *adj literary* very dangerous: *a perilous journey* —**perilously** *adv*

pe·rim·e·ter /pəˈrɪmɪtəl-ər/ n [C] the outside edges of a shape or area of land: *the perimeter of the airfield* | *the perimeter of a triangle* (=the total length of its sides)

pe·ri·od /ˈpɪəriəd‖ˈpɪr-/ n [C] **1** a length of time: *the period from Christmas Day until New Year's Day* | *a period of six weeks* | *We've been studying the Civil War period.* **2** a woman's period is the flow of blood from her body every month **3** *AmE* a DOT (.) in a piece of writing that shows the end of a sentence or an abbreviation; FULL STOP *BrE* **4** one of the equal parts that the school day is divided into: *The first period on Tuesday is history.*

period² *adj* **period costume/furniture** clothes or furniture in the style of a particular time in history

pe·ri·od·ic /ˌpɪəriˈɒdɪk ‖ˌpɪriˈɑː-/ also **period·ical** *adj* happening fairly regularly but not frequently: *periodic attacks of flu* —**periodically** / -kli/ *adv*: *The river floods the valley periodically.* | *Athletes are periodically tested for drugs.*

pe·ri·od·i·cal /ˌpɪəriˈɒdɪkəl‖ˌpɪriˈɑː-/ n [C] a magazine, especially one about a technical subject

pe·riph·e·ral¹ /pəˈrɪfərəl/ *adj* a peripheral idea, subject, or activity is related to the main one, but is less important

peripheral² n [C] a piece of equipment that is connected to a computer

pe·riph·e·ry /pəˈrɪfəri/ n [C] the outside area or edge of something: *an industrial site on the periphery of the city* → compare OUTSKIRTS

per·ish /ˈperɪʃ/ v [I] *literary* to die: *Hundreds perished when the ship sank.*

per·ish·a·ble /ˈperɪʃəbəl/ *adj* food that is perishable can become bad quickly: *milk and other perishable items*

per·ju·ry /ˈpɜːdʒəri‖ˈpɜːr-/ n [U] the crime of telling a lie in a law court

perk /pɜːk‖pɜːrk/ n [usually plural] something such as a car or free meals that you get from your work in addition to your pay: *Free travel is one of the perks of the job.*

perk up *phr v* [I,T **perk sb ↔ up**] to become more cheerful and interested in what is happening around you, or to make someone feel this way: *Meg soon perked up when his letter arrived.*

perm¹ /pɜːm‖pɜːrm/ n [C] a way of putting curls into straight hair by treating it with chemicals: *I've decided to have a perm.*

perm² v [T] to put curls into straight hair using chemicals: *Debbie's had her hair permed.*

per·ma·nent /ˈpɜːmənənt‖ˈpɜːr-/ *adj* continuing to exist for a long time or for all future time: *a permanent job* | *an illness that causes permanent loss of sight* —**permanence** n [U] → compare TEMPORARY

per·ma·nent·ly /ˈpɜːmənəntli‖ˈpɜːr-/ *adv* for all future time, or for a very long time: *The accident left him permanently disabled.*

per·me·ate /ˈpɜːmieɪt‖ˈpɜːr-/ v [I,T] to spread through every part of something: *Water had permeated through the wall.* | *A feeling of sadness permeates all his music.*

per·mis·si·ble /pəˈmɪsɪbəl‖pər-/ *adj formal* allowed by law or by the rules: *permissible levels of chemicals in drinking water*

per·mis·sion /pəˈmɪʃən‖pər-/ n [U] if you have permission to do something, someone in authority allows you to do it: *You have to ask permission if you want to leave early.* | *Did your father give you permission to use his car?*

per·mis·sive /pəˈmɪsɪv‖pər-/ *adj* allowing or not opposing behaviour that many people disapprove of: *the permissive society of the 1970s*

per·mit¹ /pəˈmɪt‖pər-/ v **-tted, -tting 1** *formal* [T] to allow something to happen, especially by a rule or law: *Smoking is not permitted inside the building.* | *The visa permits you to stay for three weeks.* **2** [I] to make it possible for something to happen: *We'll probably go to the beach, weather permitting.* (=if the weather is good enough)

per·mit² /ˈpɜːmɪt‖ˈpɜːrmɪt, pərˈmɪt/ n [C] an official written statement allowing you to do something: *You can't park here without a permit.* | *a work permit*

per·ni·cious /pəˈnɪʃəs‖pər-/ *adj formal* very harmful: *the pernicious effect of TV violence* | *a pernicious lie*

per·pen·dic·u·lar / ˌpɜːpənˈdɪkjˠlə◂ ‖ˌpɜːrpən-ˈdɪkjˠlər / *adj* exactly upright: *a perpendicular line* → compare HORIZONTAL, VERTICAL

per·pe·trate / ˈpɜːpˌtreɪt‖ˈpɜːr- / *v* [T] *formal* to do something that is wrong: *crimes perpetrated by young people* —**perpetrator** *n* [C]

per·pet·u·al / pəˈpetʃuəl‖pər- / *adj* continuing for ever or for a long time: *the perpetual noise of the machinery* —**perpetually** *adv*

per·pet·u·ate / pəˈpetʃueɪt‖pər- / *v* [T] *formal* to make something continue: *an education system that perpetuates divisions in society*

per·plexed / pəˈplekst‖pər- / *adj* confused by something that is difficult to understand: *He looked totally perplexed.* —**perplex** *v* [T]

per·se·cute / ˈpɜːsɪkjuːt‖ˈpɜːr- / *v* [T] to treat someone cruelly and unfairly, especially because of their beliefs: *a writer persecuted for criticizing the government* —**persecutor** *n* [C]

per·se·cu·tion / ˌpɜːsɪˈkjuːʃən‖ˌpɜːr- / *n* [U] when someone is treated cruelly or unfairly: *the persecution of Christians*

per·se·ver·ance / ˌpɜːsˌˈvɪərəns‖ˌpɜːrsˌˈvɪr- / *n* [U] determination to keep trying to do something difficult: *I admire her perseverance.*

per·se·vere / ˌpɜːsˌˈvɪə‖ˌpɜːrsˌˈvɪr / *v* [I] to continue trying to do something difficult in a determined way: *I'm not enjoying the course, but I'll persevere with it.*

per·sist / pəˈsɪst‖pər- / *v* [I] **1** to continue to do something, even though it is difficult or other people do not like it: **persist in (doing) sth** *At his trial for war crimes, he persisted in denying the charges.* **2** to continue to exist or happen: *Problems with the computer persist.*

per·sis·tent / pəˈsɪstənt‖pər- / *adj* **1** something unpleasant or annoying that is persistent continues to exist or happen for a long time: *the problem of persistent unemployment* **2** someone who is persistent continues to try to do something even though someone is opposing them: *She keeps saying 'no' but he's very persistent.* | *persistent attempts to bring down the government* —**persistently** *adv* —**persistence** *n* [U] *Eventually her persistence paid off and she got a job.*

per·son / ˈpɜːsən‖ˈpɜːr- / *n, plural* **people** / ˈpiː-pəl / **1** [C] a man, woman, or child: *Bert's a strange person.* | *a comedian who's good at making people laugh* | *a* **city/outdoor/cat etc person** (=someone who likes cities, outdoor activities, cats etc) **2 in person** if you do something in person, you do it by going somewhere yourself: *You'll have to apply for your passport in person.* → see also FIRST PERSON, SECOND PERSON, THIRD PERSON

USAGE NOTE: person, persons, people, and **peoples**

Person means one man, woman, or child: *She's a really generous person.* The plural of **person** is **persons**, but this is only used in more formal language. When you are talking about more than one person, the plural is **people**: *There were about 100 people at the wedding.* **People** is also a countable noun that means a particular race or group that live in a country. The plural is **peoples**: *the peoples of the Caribbean.*

per·so·na / pəˈsəʊnə‖pərˈsoʊ- / *n* [C] the way you behave when you are with other people: *the public persona of Hollywood's newest star*

per·son·al / ˈpɜːsənəl‖ˈpɜːr- / *adj* **1** [only before noun] belonging to you, done by you, or experienced by you, not other people: *books, clothes, and other personal belongings* | *I know from personal experience that it doesn't work.* | *The Mayor promised to give the matter his personal attention.* **2** involving someone's private life, their feelings, health, and relationships: *Can I ask you a personal question?* | *His personal problems are affecting his work.* | *personal hygiene* **3** criticizing someone in a rude or offensive way: *There's no need to make personal remarks.* | *It's nothing personal – I just don't agree with you.* (=I don't mean to be rude) **4** concerning your body or the way you look: *personal hygiene*

personal com·pu·ter / ˌ... .ˈ.. / *n* [C] a PC

personal i·den·ti·fi·ca·tion num·ber / ˌ... ....ˈ.. ˌ../ *n* a PIN

per·son·al·i·ty / ˌpɜːsəˈnælˌti‖ˌpɜːr- / *n* **1** [C,U] someone's character, especially the way they behave towards other people: *Alice has an outgoing personality.* **2** [C] a famous person, especially in sport, television, films, etc: *a TV personality*

per·son·al·ize (also **-ise** *BrE*) / ˈpɜːsənəlaɪz‖ˈpɜːr- / *v* [T] to change something so that it is suitable for what a particular person wants or needs: *It's pretty easy to personalize your PC.*

per·son·a·lized (also **-ise** *BrE*) / ˈpɜːsənəlaɪzd‖ˈpɜːr- / *adj* personalized objects have the name or INITIALS of the owner on them: *cars with personalized license plates*

per·son·al·ly / ˈpɜːsənəli‖ˈpɜːr- / *adv* **1** *spoken* used to emphasize that you are only giving your own opinion: *Personally, I think it's a bad idea.* **2** doing or having done something yourself: *He's personally responsible for all the arrangements.* **3** someone who you know personally is a friend or is someone who you have met: *I don't know her personally, but I like her books.*

personal or·ga·niz·er / ˌ... ˈ..../ *n* [C] a small book with loose sheets of paper, or a very small computer, for recording addresses, times of meetings etc

personal pro·noun / ˌ... ˈ.. / *n* [C] in grammar, a PRONOUN, such as 'I', 'you', and 'they', used for the person who is speaking, being spoken to, or being spoken about

per·son·i·fy / pəˈsɒnˌfaɪ‖pərˈsɑː- / *v* [T] **1** someone who personifies a quality is a typical example of it: *He is laziness personified!* **2** to describe or REPRESENT something as a person: *Time is often personified as an old man with a*

GRAMMAR NOTE: a or **the (2)**
Use **the** before a thing or person when it is clear which one you are talking about: *the old man who lives next door.* Use **a** or **an** to talk about a person or thing when it is not important to say which one: *I went out to buy a newspaper.* | *A girl in my class told me about it.*

beard. —**personification** /pə‚sɒnˌfˌ'keɪʃən‖pər-‚sɑː-/ *n* [C, U]

per·son·nel /‚pɜːsə'nel‖‚pɜːr-/ *n* **1** [plural] the people who work in an organization or for one kind of employer: *military personnel* **2** [U] the department in a company that deals with employing new people, keeps records about people who work for the company, and helps them with problems they may have; HUMAN RESOURCES: *a personnel manager*

per·spec·tive /pə'spektɪv‖pər-/ *n* **1** [C] a way of thinking about something: *Working abroad gives you a whole new perspective on life.* **2** [U] **keep/get sth in perspective** to think sensibly about something and not imagine that it is worse than it is **3** [U] a method of drawing a picture that makes objects look solid and shows depth and distance: *Children's drawings often have no perspective.*

per·spi·ra·tion /‚pɜːspə'reɪʃən‖‚pɜːr-/ *n* [U] *formal* SWEAT

per·spire /pə'spaɪə‖pər'spaɪr/ *v* [I] *formal* to SWEAT

per·suade /pə'sweɪd‖pər-/ *v* [T] **1** to make someone decide to do something by explaining to them why it is a good idea: *Ken finally persuaded Jo to apply for the job.* **2** to make someone believe something; CONVINCE: *He persuaded the jury that his client was not guilty.*

per·sua·sion /pə'sweɪʒən‖pər-/ *n* **1** [U] the act of persuading someone to do something: *With a little persuasion, Debbie agreed to come with us.* **2** [C] *formal* if you are of a particular persuasion, this is your belief or opinion: *arguments between people of different political persuasions*

per·sua·sive /pə'sweɪsɪv‖pər-/ *adj* good at influencing other people to believe or do what you want: *a persuasive argument* —**persuasively** *adv*

per·tain /pə'teɪn‖pər-/ *v*
pertain to *phr v* [T] *formal* to be directly connected with/to something: *information pertaining to next year's examinations*

per·ti·nent /'pɜːtˌnənt‖'pɜːr-/ *adj formal* pertinent remarks are directly related to the subject that is being considered; RELEVANT: *Reporters asked a few pertinent questions.*

per·turbed /pə'tɜːbd‖pər'tɜːrbd/ *adj* worried and upset: *He didn't seem at all perturbed by the news.* —**perturb** *v* [T]

pe·ruse /pə'ruːz/ *v* [T] *formal* to read something carefully: *an evening spent perusing the job advertisements*

per·vade /pə'veɪd‖pər-/ *v* [T] to spread throughout every part of a place: *A feeling of hopelessness pervaded the country.*

per·va·sive /pə'veɪsɪv‖pər-/ *adj* existing everywhere: *a pervasive fear of crime*

per·verse /pə'vɜːs‖pər'vɜːrs/ *adj* deliberately behaving in an unreasonable way: *He takes perverse pleasure in arguing with everyone.* —**perversely** *adv*

per·ver·sion /pə'vɜːʃən, -ʒən‖pər'vɜːrʒən/ *n* [C,U] **1** sexual behaviour that is considered unnatural and unacceptable **2** when something good or right is changed into something bad or wrong: *a perversion of the truth*

per·vert[1] /pə'vɜːt‖pər'vɜːrt/ *v* [T] to change

someone or something in a harmful way: *violent images that pervert the minds of young children*

per·vert[2] /'pɜːvɜːt‖'pɜːrvɜːrt/ *n* [C] someone whose sexual behaviour is considered unnatural and unacceptable

per·vert·ed /pə'vɜːtˌd‖pər'vɜːrt-/ *adj* unacceptable and considered to be unnatural or morally wrong: *a book written by someone with a perverted imagination*

pes·si·mis·m /'pesˌmɪzəm/ *n* [U] the feeling that things will be bad or unsuccessful → opposite OPTIMISM

pes·si·mist /'pesˌmɪst/ *n* [C] someone who always expects that things will be bad or unsuccessful: *Don't be such a pessimist – you're sure to pass.* → opposite OPTIMIST

pes·si·mis·tic /‚pesˌ'mɪstɪk‹/ *adj* expecting that things will be bad or unsuccessful: *Johnathan is pessimistic about his chances of winning.* → opposite OPTIMISTIC

pest /pest/ *n* [C] **1** a small animal or insect that destroys crops or food **2** *informal* an annoying person: *That kid next door is a real pest.*

pes·ter /'pestə‖-ər/ *v* [T] if you pester someone, you ask them for something so often that they get annoyed: *He keeps pestering me to buy him a new bike.*

pes·ti·cide /'pestˌsaɪd/ *n* [C] a chemical substance used to kill insects that damage crops

pet[1] /pet/ *n* [C] an animal that you keep at home → see also TEACHER'S PET

pet[2] *v* [T] **-tted, -tting 1** to move your hand over an animal's fur: *Our cat loves being petted.* **2** to kiss and touch someone in a sexual way

pet[3] *adj* **1 pet project/subject/theory etc** a plan, subject, or idea that you particularly like or are interested in: *congressmen looking for funding for their pet projects* **2 pet hate** *BrE/* **pet peeve** *AmE* something that particularly annoys you: *One of my pet peeves is people being late for meetings.*

pet·al /'petl/ *n* [C] one of the coloured parts that form the main part of a flower: *a blue flower with five petals* | *rose petals*

pet·er /'piːtə‖-ər/ *v* [I]
peter out *phr v* [I] to gradually become smaller and then come to an end: *The trail became narrower and eventually petered out altogether.*

pe·tite /pə'tiːt/ *adj* a woman who is petite is small and SLIM → see colour picture on page 244

pe·ti·tion[1] /pˌ'tɪʃən/ *v* [I,T] to formally ask someone in authority to do something: *Residents are petitioning against a new prison in the area.* | *We're going to London to petition our MP.*

petition[2] *n* [C] a piece of paper on which a lot of people have written their names, asking someone in authority to do something: *Will you sign a petition against experiments on animals?* | *Residents drew up a petition to protest the building of a new highway.*

pet·ri·fied /'petrˌfaɪd/ *adj* very frightened: *I thought the plane was going to crash – I was petrified!* —**petrify** *v* [T]

pet·rol /'petrəl/ *n* [U] *BrE* a liquid that you put in a vehicle to make the engine work; GAS, GASOLINE *AmE*

pe·tro·le·um /pˌ'trəʊliəm‖-'troʊ-/ *n* [U] oil that

is obtained from under the ground, used to make chemical substances: *petroleum-based products*

petrol sta·tion /ˈ.. ˌ../ *n* [C] *BrE* a place where you take your car to fill it up with petrol GAS STATION *AmE*

pet·ti·coat /ˈpetɪkəʊt‖-koʊt/ *n* [C] **1** *especially BrE* a piece of woman's underwear that is worn under a dress or skirt **2** a long skirt that was worn under a woman's dress or skirt in past times

pet·ty /ˈpeti/ *adj* **1** something that is petty is not serious or important: *a petty argument* | **petty crime** (=crime that is not very serious) **2** caring too much about small, unimportant rules or details: *She can be very petty about money.* —**pettiness** *n* [U]

pet·u·lant /ˈpetʃʊlənt/ *adj* behaving in an unreasonable impatient and angry way, like a child —**petulantly** *adv*: *The boy stamped his foot and frowned petulantly.*

pew /pjuː/ *n* [C] a long wooden seat in a church

pew·ter /ˈpjuːtə‖-ər/ *n* [U] a metal made by mixing LEAD and TIN

phan·tom[1] /ˈfæntəm/ *n* [C] *literary* a GHOST

phantom[2] *adj* [only before noun] imaginary and not real

pha·raoh /ˈfeərəʊ‖ˈferoʊ/ *n* [C] a ruler of ancient Egypt

phar·ma·ceu·ti·cal /ˌfɑːməˈsjuːtɪkəl‖ˌfɑːrməˈsuː-/ *adj* the pharmaceutical industry produces drugs and medicines: *large pharmaceutical companies*

phar·ma·cist /ˈfɑːməsɪst‖ˈfɑːr-/ *n* [C] someone whose job is to prepare drugs and medicines

phar·ma·cy /ˈfɑːməsi‖ˈfɑːr-/ *n* [C] **1** a store or a part of a store where medicines are prepared and sold → compare CHEMIST'S, DRUGSTORE **2** [C] the study and preparation of drugs and medicines

phase[1] /feɪz/ *n* [C] one part of a process in which something develops or grows: *the last phase of the project* | *Your child is just going through a 'naughty' phase.* → compare STAGE[1]

phase[2] *v* [T]
phase sth ↔ in *v* [T] to introduce something gradually: *New laws on smoking will be phased in over the next six months.*
phase sth ↔ out *phr v* [T] to gradually stop using or providing something: *Some manufacturers aim to phase out all tests on animals.*

PhD, Ph.D. /ˌpiː eɪtʃ ˈdiː/ *n* [C] Doctor of Philosophy, the highest university degree, or someone who has this degree

pheas·ant /ˈfezənt/ *n* [C] a large bird with a long tail, hunted for food and sport, or the meat from this bird

phe·nom·e·nal /fɪˈnɒmɪnəl‖-ˈnɑː-/ *adj* very unusual and impressive: *a phenomenal achievement* —**phenomenally** *adv*

phe·nom·e·non /fɪˈnɒmɪnən‖fɪˈnɑːmɪnɑːn, -nən/ *n* [C], *plural* **phenomena** /-nə/ something that happens or exists, especially something that is unusual or difficult to understand: *earthquakes, hurricanes, and other natural phenomena* | *Homelessness is not a new phenomenon.*

phew /fjuː/ *interjection* used when you feel tired, hot, or RELIEVED

phi·lan·thro·pist /fɪˈlænθrəpɪst/ *n* [C] someone who gives a lot of money and help to people who need it

phi·los·o·pher /fɪˈlɒsəfə‖-ˈlɑːsəfər/ *n* [C] someone who studies and develops ideas about philosophy: *ancient Greek philosophers*

phil·o·soph·i·cal /ˌfɪləˈsɒfɪkəl‖-ˈsɑː-/ **philosophic** /ˌfɪləˈsɒfɪk‖-ˈsɑː-/ *adj* **1** relating to philosophy: *a philosophical discussion* **2** someone who is philosophical accepts difficult or unpleasant things calmly: *Anderson is philosophical about his defeat.* —**philosophically** /-kli/ *adv*

phi·los·o·phy /fɪˈlɒsəfi‖-ˈlɑː-/ *n* [C, U] **1** the study of ideas about existence, thought, and behaviour, or one person's ideas on these things: *She's studying philosophy at university.* **2** [C] a set of beliefs about how you should live your life, do your job etc: *My philosophy is, enjoy life while you can!*

phlegm /flem/ *n* [U] a thick substance produced in your nose and throat, especially when you have a cold; MUCUS

phleg·mat·ic /flegˈmætɪk/ *adj formal* calm and not easily excited or worried

pho·bi·a /ˈfəʊbiə‖ˈfoʊ-/ *n* [C] a strong unreasonable fear of something: *Holly has a phobia about snakes.* —**phobic** *adj*

phone[1] /fəʊn‖foʊn/ *n* [C] **1** a telephone: *What's your phone number?* | *Could you answer the phone please?* | *You can book your tickets by phone.* **2 be on the phone a)** to be talking to someone else using a telephone: *Turn the TV down – I'm on the phone!* **b)** *BrE* to have a telephone: *Are you on the phone?*

phone[2] *v* also **phone up** [I,T] to speak to someone using a telephone; CALL: *Several people phoned the radio station to complain.* | *I'll phone up and find out when they're open.*

phone book /ˈ. ./ *n* [C] a book containing the names, addresses, and telephone numbers of people in an area; TELEPHONE DIRECTORY

phone booth /ˈ. ./ also **phone box** *BrE* — *n* [C] a structure containing a telephone that someone can use → see colour picture on page 79

phone call /ˈ. ./ *n* [C] when you speak to someone on the telephone, or try to speak to them on the telephone: *I need to make a quick phone call.* | *There's a phone call for you.*

phone card /ˈ. ./ *n* [C] a plastic card that can be used in some telephones instead of money

phone-in /ˈ. ./ *n* [C] a radio or television programme in which ordinary people give their opinions, ask questions etc over the telephone

pho·net·ic /fəˈnetɪk/ *adj* relating to the sounds of human speech: *a phonetic alphabet* (=that uses signs to represent the sounds) —**phonetically** /-kli/ *adv*

pho·net·ics /fəˈnetɪks/ *n* [U] the study of speech sounds

pho·ney[1] *BrE*, **phony** *AmE* /ˈfəʊni‖ˈfoʊ-/ *adj* false or not real, and intended to deceive someone; FAKE: *I gave the police a phony address.*

pho·ney[2] *BrE*, **phony** *AmE* — *n* [C] someone who pretends to be different from how they really are in order to deceive people

pho·no·graph /ˈfəʊnəgrɑːf‖ˈfoʊnəgræf/ *n* [C] *old-fashioned* a RECORD PLAYER

pho·ny /ˈfəʊni‖ˈfoʊ-/ *adj* the usual American spelling of phoney

phos·phate /ˈfɒsfeɪt‖ˈfɑːs-/ n [C,U] a chemical used in industry and farming

pho·to /ˈfəʊtəʊ‖ˈfoʊtoʊ/ n [C], plural **photos** informal a PHOTOGRAPH: I must take a photo of the hotel.

pho·to·cop·i·er /ˈfəʊtəʊˌkɒpiə‖ˈfoʊtəˌkɑːpiər/ n [C] especially BrE a machine that makes copies of documents by photographing them; COPIER AmE → see colour picture on page 80

pho·to·cop·y[1] /ˈfəʊtəʊˌkɒpi‖ˈfoʊtəˌkɑːpi/ n [C] a copy of a document made by a photocopier: Could you make a photocopy of this article, please.

photocopy[2] v [T] to make a copy of a document using a photocopier

photo fin·ish /ˌ.. ˈ../ n [C] when the leaders in a race finish so close together that a photograph has to be taken to show who won

pho·to·graph[1] /ˈfəʊtəɡrɑːf‖ˈfoʊtəɡræf/ also **photo** informal n [C] a picture that is made using a camera: an old photograph of my grandfather | **take a photograph**: Visitors are not allowed to take photographs. → compare PICTURE[1]

photograph[2] v [T] to make a picture of someone or something using a camera

pho·tog·ra·pher /fəˈtɒɡrəfə‖-ˈtɑːɡrəfər/ n [C] someone who takes photographs, especially as a job: a fashion photographer

pho·to·graph·ic /ˌfəʊtəˈɡræfɪk‖ˌfoʊ-/ adj connected with photographs and photography: photographic images | photographic equipment

pho·tog·ra·phy /fəˈtɒɡrəfi‖-ˈtɑː-/ n [U] the skill or process of taking photographs: Photography isn't just a matter of pointing the camera and pressing the button!

phrasal verb /ˌ.. ˈ./ n [C] in grammar, a verb with an adverb or preposition, which has a different meaning from the verb used alone. 'Set off', 'look after', and 'put up with' are all phrasal verbs.

phrase[1] /freɪz/ n [C] **1** a group of words that has its own meaning: Darwin's famous phrase, "the survival of the fittest" **2** a group of words without a main verb, that together form part of a sentence. In the sentence, 'I'll see you in the morning', 'in the morning' is a phrase → compare CLAUSE, SENTENCE[1]

phrase[2] v [T] to express something in a particular way, using words you have chosen: You will have to phrase your criticism very carefully. | He phrased his question politely. — **phrasing** n [U]

phys·i·cal[1] /ˈfɪzɪkəl/ adj **1** relating to someone's body rather than their mind: physical exercise | people with mental and physical disabilities **2** physical things are objects, buildings and other things that you can touch and see: attempts to improve the physical environment in our big cities **3** physical science is related to PHYSICS: physical chemistry → compare ORGANIC

physical[2] n [C] AmE an examination of your body by a doctor to check that you are healthy; MEDICAL[2] BrE

phys·i·cally /ˈfɪzɪkli/ adv in relation to the body rather than the mind: He's all right physically, but he's still very upset.

phy·si·cian /fɪˈzɪʃən/ n [C] AmE formal a doctor

phys·ics /ˈfɪzɪks/ n [U] the science that deals with the structure of objects and substances, and things such as light, heat, and movement — **physicist** n

phys·i·ol·o·gy /ˌfɪziˈɒlədʒi‖-ˈɑː-/ n [U] the science of how the bodies of living things work → compare ANATOMY — **physiological** /ˌfɪziəˈlɒdʒɪkəl‖-ˈlɑː-/ adj

phys·i·o·ther·a·py /ˌfɪziəʊˈθerəpi‖-zioʊ-/ n [U] medical treatment for muscles, using exercises, rubbing, heat etc — **physiotherapist** n [C]

phy·sique /fɪˈziːk/ n [C usually singular] a person's physique is the shape and size of their body: a man with a powerful physique

pi·a·nist /ˈpiːənɪst, ˈpjaː-‖ˈpiːænɪst, ˈpiːə-/ n [C] someone who plays the piano

pi·an·o /piˈænəʊ‖-noʊ/ n [C], plural **pianos** a large musical instrument that you play by pressing a row of narrow black and white bars

piano

pick[1] /pɪk/ v [T] **1** to choose something or someone: Students have to pick three courses. | Have you picked a date for the wedding yet? **2** to break off a flower or fruit from a plant: We've picked some flowers for you. | freshly picked strawberries **3** to pull off small pieces from something: She sat nervously picking bits of fluff off her sweater. **4** **pick a fight/argument/quarrel with sb** to deliberately begin to argue or fight with someone: Dean's always picking fights with the younger kids. **5** **pick your way** to move carefully, choosing exactly where to walk: She picked her way through the piles of rubbish and broken glass. **6** **pick sb's brain(s)** to ask someone for information or advice about something: I've got a problem with my computer – can I pick your brains? **7** to open a lock using something such as a piece of wire, not a key **8** **pick sb's pocket** to steal money etc from someone's pocket without them knowing

pick at phr v [T] if you pick at your food, you eat only a few small amounts of it, especially because you are worried or feeling ill: I was so nervous I could only pick at my lunch.

pick on phr v [T] to repeatedly criticize or upset someone unfairly: Greg, stop picking on your sister!

pick sb/sth ↔ **out** phr v [T] to recognize someone or something from among a group of people or things: She was able to pick out her attacker from a police lineup.

pick up phr v **1** [T **pick** sb/sth **up**] to lift someone or something: Pick me up, Daddy! | kids picking up shells at the beach | I picked up the phone just as it stopped ringing. → see colour picture on page 670 **2** [T **pick** sb/sth ↔ **up**] to collect someone or something, especially using a car: I'll pick up my stuff around six, okay? | What time should we pick you up at the airport? **3** [I] if business, your social life etc picks up, it improves: Sales should pick up before Christmas. **4** [I,T **pick up** sth] if someone's speed or the wind picks up, it gets faster or stronger: The car was gradually picking up speed. | The wind had picked up considerably. **5** [T **pick** sth ↔ **up**] to learn something without deliberately trying to: If *you go to live in another country you'll soon pick up the language.* **6** [T **pick** sth ↔ **up**] to get an illness from someone: *She's picked up a cold from a child at school.* **7** [T **pick** sth ↔ **up**] to notice, see, or hear something; DETECT: *The dogs were able to pick up the scent.* **8** [**pick** sth ↔ **up**] if a machine picks up a sound or a signal, it receives it: *We can pick up French radio stations from here.* | *The satellite failed to pick up the signal.* **9** [T **pick** sb ↔ **up**] if the police pick someone up, they arrest them or ask them questions **10** [T **pick** sb ↔ **up**] to talk to someone and try to begin a sexual relationship with them

pick² *n* **1 take your pick/have your pick** choose what you want from several things: *Would you like a chocolate? Here, take your pick.* | *At the height of her fame, she had her pick of all the eligible men in Hollywood.* **2 the pick of sth** *informal* the best thing or things in a group: *We'll be reviewing the pick of this month's new movies.* **3** [C] a PICKAXE

pick·axe *BrE*, **pickax** *AmE* /ˈpɪk-æks/ *n* [C] a large tool with a long handle and a curved iron bar, used for breaking up rocks, hard surfaces etc

pick·er /ˈpɪkəll-ər/ *n* [C] **cotton/fruit/grape etc picker** a person or machine that picks fruit etc

pick·et¹ /ˈpɪkɪ̩t/ *v* [I,T] if workers picket a factory or shop during a STRIKE, they stand in front of it and try to persuade other people not to go in as a protest

picket² also **picket line** /ˈ.. ./ *n* [C] a group of people who picket a factory, shop etc: *Two workers were hurt today trying to cross the picket line.*

picket fence /ˈ.. ˌ./ *n* [C] *AmE* a fence made of a line of pointed sticks fixed into the ground

pick·le¹ /ˈpɪkəl/ *n* **1** [C,U] pickles are vegetables that have been preserved in VINEGAR or SALT water **2** [U] *BrE* a thick cold SAUCE containing small pieces of vegetables preserved in VINEGAR

pickle² *v* [T] to preserve food in VINEGAR and salt

pick·led /ˈpɪkəld/ *adj* pickled vegetables, eggs etc have been preserved in VINEGAR

pick-me-up /ˈ. ˌ. ./ *n* [C] *informal* something that makes you feel cheerful or gives you more energy, especially a drink or medicine

pick·pock·et /ˈpɪkˌpɒkɪ̩tll-ˌpɑːk-/ *n* [C] someone who steals things from people's pockets in public places

pick·up /ˈpɪkʌp/ also **pickup truck** /ˈ.. ˌ. ./ *n* [C] a vehicle with a large open part at the back, used for carrying goods

pick·y /ˈpɪki/ *adj informal* someone who is picky only likes a small number of things: *a picky eater* | *Kelly's so picky about her clothes!*

pic·nic¹ /ˈpɪknɪk/ *n* [C] an occasion when people take food and eat it outdoors, away from their house, or the food they take with them: *We usually take a picnic when we go to the beach.*

picnic² *v* [I] **picnicked, picnicked, picnicking** to have a picnic

pic·to·ri·al /pɪkˈtɔːriəl/ *adj* relating to or using pictures

pic·ture¹ /ˈpɪktʃəll-ər/ *n* **1** [C] a painting, drawing, or photograph: *She keeps a picture of her boyfriend by her bed.* | **take a picture** (=take a photograph): *Do you mind if I take a picture of you?* | **sb's picture** (=a photograph of someone): *Leo's picture was in the paper yesterday.* ➝ see colour picture on page 474 **2** [singular] the general situation in a place, organization etc: *The political picture has changed greatly.* **3** [C usually singular] a description that gives you an idea of what something is like: **+ of** *The report gives a clear picture of life in the army.* **4 put/ keep sb in the picture** *informal* to give someone the information they need to understand a situation **5** [C] the image on a television or film screen **6 get the picture** *spoken* to understand something: *I don't want you around here any more, get the picture?* **7 the pictures** the cinema: *Do you want to go to the pictures on Saturday?* **8** [C] a FILM

picture² *v* [T] **1** to imagine something, especially by making an image of it in your mind: *I can still picture him standing there in his uniform.* **2** to show something or someone in a painting, drawing or photograph, especially a photograph in a newspaper or magazine: *The prince is pictured on nearly every front page today.*

pic·tur·esque /ˌpɪktʃəˈreskɑ/ *adj* a picturesque place is attractive, usually because it does not look modern

pid·gin /ˈpɪdʒɪn/ *n* [C,U] a language that is a mixture of two other languages

pie /paɪ/ *n* [C,U] **1** a food made with fruit or meat baked inside PASTRY: *an apple pie* **2** *BrE* a food made of meat, fish, or vegetables with potato on top **3 pie in the sky** *informal* a plan, idea, or promise that you do not thing will ever happen

piece¹ /piːs/ *n* [C] **1** [C] a part of something that has been separated or broken off from the rest of it: **+ of** *Do you want a piece of bread?* | **in pieces** (=broken into many pieces): *The vase lay in pieces on the floor.* | **smash/tear/rip sth to pieces** (=break something when you are angry) ➝ see colour picture on page 440 **2** one part of a set of things: *a chess piece* | *a beautiful piece of furniture* | *the pieces of a jigsaw puzzle* **3 a piece of** used with certain words to mean 'some' **a piece of advice/information/luck etc** *Let me give you a piece of advice. Don't get a job in publishing.* **4 go to pieces** to become so upset or nervous that you cannot think or behave normally **5 (all) in one piece** not damaged or injured: *I'm glad the china arrived in one piece.* **6 give sb a piece of your mind** *informal* to tell someone that you are very angry with them: *If I see her, I'll give her a piece of my mind!* **7 be a piece of cake** *informal* to be very easy to do **8** something that has been written or made by an artist, musician, or writer: *a beautiful piece of*

GRAMMAR NOTE: countable and uncountable (1)

If you can put numbers in front of a noun (*one horse, two tickets* etc) and make it plural, that noun is **countable**: *n* [C]. A substance (e.g. *butter, air*), or an idea or quality (e.g. *beauty, information*) cannot be made plural or used with **a** or **an**. These are **uncountable**: *n* [U].

music **9** a coin that is worth a particular amount: *a 50p piece*

piece² *v*

piece sth ↔ **together** *phr v* [T] **1** to discover the truth about something from different pieces of information: *Police are still trying to piece together a motive for the shooting.* **2** to put all the parts of something into their correct position

piece·meal /ˈpiːsmiːl/ *adj, adv* happening or done over a period of time in separate stages that are not connected: *The college developed in a piecemeal fashion over the years.*

piece·work /ˈpiːswɜːkǁ-wɜːrk/ *n* [U] when you are paid for the amount of work you do rather than for the number of hours you work

pier /pɪəǁpɪr/ *n* [C] a structure that is built out into the sea so that boats can stop next to it or people can walk along it: *a variety show at the end of the pier*

pierce /pɪəsǁpɪrs/ *v* [T] **1** to make a hole in or through something using an object with a sharp point: *I'm getting my ears pierced.* (=having holes in your ears to wear jewellery) *A bullet pierced his body.* **2** *literary* if a bright light or a loud sound pierces something, you can suddenly see it or hear it: *The lights from the boat pierced the fog.*

pierc·ing /ˈpɪəsɪŋǁˈpɪr-/ *adj* **1** a piercing sound is very loud or unpleasant: *a piercing scream* **2** a piercing wind is strong and cold **3** piercing eyes or looks show that someone is noticing everything: *He looked away from Mr. Darden's piercing eyes.*

pi·e·ty /ˈpaɪəti/ *n* [U] respect for God and religion

pig¹ /pɪg/ *n* [C] **1** a farm animal with short legs, a fat usually pink body, and a curled tail **2** an impolite word for someone who eats too much, or is dirty or unpleasant: *You ate all the pizza, you pig.*

pig² *v* **-gged, -gging**

pig out *phr v* [I] *informal* to eat too much of something: *We pigged out on ice cream last night.*

pi·geon /ˈpɪdʒ‹n/ *n* [C] a grey bird with short legs that is common in cities

pi·geon·hole /ˈpɪdʒ‹nhəʊlǁ-hoʊl/ *v* [T] to decide unfairly that someone or something belongs to a particular group or type: *People find out what you're good at and try to pigeonhole you.*

pigeon-toed /ˈ.. ./ *adj* having feet that point inwards

pig·gy·back /ˈpɪgibæk/ *n* [C] a way of carrying a child by putting him or her on your back — **piggyback** *adv*

piggy bank /ˈpɪgi bæŋk/ *n* [C] a small container in the shape of a pig, used by children for saving coins

pig·head·ed /ˌpɪgˈhedd̹‹ / *adj* determined to do things a particular way even when there are good reasons not to

pig·let /ˈpɪgl̹t/ *n* [C] a young pig

pig·ment /ˈpɪgmənt/ *n* [C,U] a substance that gives something its colour

pig·men·ta·tion /ˌpɪgmən'teɪʃ‹n/ *n* [U] the colouring of living things

pig·sty /ˈpɪgstaɪ/ also **pig·pen** /ˈpɪgpen/ *AmE* — *n* [C] **1** a place on a farm where pigs are kept **2** *informal* a room that is very dirty or untidy

pig·tail /ˈpɪgteɪl/ *n* [C] hair that has been pulled or twisted together and tied → compare BRAID¹, PONYTAIL

pike /paɪk/ *n* [C,U] a large fish that eats other fish and lives in rivers and lakes

pile

pile/stack   pile/heap

pile¹ /paɪl/ *n* **1** [C] a lot of similar things put one on top of the other: **+ of** *a pile of folded clothes* **2 piles of/a pile of** *informal* a lot of something: *I have piles of work to do tonight.*

pile² *v* **1** [I,T] also **pile up** to make a pile by collecting things together: *A lot of dirty pans piled up in the sink.* **2** [T] to fill or cover something with a lot of something: *a plate piled with spaghetti*

pile into/out of sth *phr v* [T] *informal* to go into or out of a place or vehicle in a disorganized way: *We all piled into the car.*

pile-up *phr v* [I,T] to become larger in quantity or amount: *Debts from the business were piling up quickly.*

pile-up /ˈ. ./ *n* [C] *informal* a traffic accident involving several vehicles: *a 16-car pile-up*

pil·fer /ˈpɪlfəǁ-ər/ *v* [I,T] to steal a small amount of something, or things that are not worth much

pil·grim /ˈpɪlgr‹m/ *n* [C] someone who travels to a holy place for a religious reason

pil·grim·age /ˈpɪlgr‹mɪdʒ/ *n* [C,U] a trip to a holy place for a religious reason

pill /pɪl/ *n* [C] **1** a small solid piece of medicine that you swallow **2 the Pill** a pill that some women take in order to prevent them from having a baby: **be on the pill** (=be taking birth control pills)

pil·lage /ˈpɪlɪdʒ/ *v* [I,T] if soldiers pillage a place, they steal things from it violently, especially during a war

pil·lar /ˈpɪləǁ-ər/ *n* **1** [C] a tall solid piece of stone, wood etc used to support part of a building **2 a pillar of the community/church etc** an active and important member of a group, organization etc

pil·lion /ˈpɪljən/ *n* [C] the seat for a passenger on a MOTORCYCLE — **pillion** *adv*

pil·low /ˈpɪləʊǁ-loʊ/ *n* [C] the soft object you put under your head when you sleep

pil·low·case /ˈpɪləʊkeɪsǁ-loʊ-/ *n* [C] a cover for a pillow

pi·lot /ˈpaɪlət/ *n* [C] **1** someone who flies a plane **2** someone who guides a ship through a difficult area of water **3 pilot study/programme etc** a study etc that is done to test whether people like an idea, product etc — **pilot** *v* [T]

pilot light /ˈ.. ./ n [C] a small gas flame that burns all the time in a gas OVEN, BOILER etc and is used to make it start

pimp /pɪmp/ n [C] a man who controls PROSTITUTES and takes the money that they earn

pim·ple /ˈpɪmpəl/ n [C] a small raised red spot on your skin — **pimply** adj

pin[1] /pɪn/ n [C] **1** a short thin piece of metal with a sharp point at one end, used especially for holding pieces of cloth together **2** AmE a piece of jewellery fastened to your clothes by a pin **3** a thin piece of metal used to fasten things together: He has to have pins put in his ankle. ➝ see also PINS AND NEEDLES, ROLLING PIN, SAFETY PIN

pin[2] v [T] **-nned, -nning 1** to fasten something or join things together with a pin: **pin sth together** Pin the back of the dress together first. | **pin sth to/onto etc** Have you seen the note pinned on the door? **2 pin your hopes on** to hope that something will happen, because all your plans depend on it: I hope she's not pinning all her hopes on winning. **3 pin the blame on sb** to blame someone for something, often unfairly **4** to press someone against something, stopping them from moving: He was pinned under the car.

　pin down phr v [T] **1** [pin sb down] to make someone decide something, or tell you what their decision is: I couldn't pin him down to a definite date. **2** [pin sth down] to discover exactly what something is: Scientists believe they have pinned down the cause of the illness.

PIN /pɪn/ n an abbreviation for personal identification number; a secret number you use to take out money from a cash machine at a bank etc

pin·a·fore /ˈpɪnəfɔː‖-fɔːr/ n [C] BrE a dress that does not cover your arms, usually worn over a shirt etc

pin·ball /ˈpɪnbɔːl‖-bɒːl/ n [U] a game played on a machine in which you push buttons to try to stop a ball rolling off a sloping board: a pinball machine

pin·cer /ˈpɪnsə‖-ər/ n [C] one of the pair of CLAWS (=sharp curved nails) that some insects and SHELLFISH have ➝ see picture at CRAB

pinch[1] /pɪntʃ/ v **1** [T] to press a part of someone's flesh tightly between your finger and thumb: He pinched her arm playfully. ➝ see colour picture on page 473 **2** [T] informal to steal something that is not worth much: Someone's pinched my pen!

pinch[2] n **1 pinch of salt/pepper etc** the amount of salt, pepper etc that you can hold between your finger and thumb ➝ see colour picture on page 440 **2** [C] an act of pressing someone's flesh between your finger and thumb **3 at a pinch** BrE **in a pinch** AmE only with difficulty or only if really necessary: I could get $300, maybe $400 dollars in a pinch. **4 feel the pinch** to have financial difficulties because you do not have enough money: Small businesses are feeling the pinch. **5 take sth with a pinch of salt** to not completely believe what someone says to you

pinched /pɪntʃt/ adj a pinched face looks thin and unhealthy

pin·cush·ion /ˈpɪnˌkʊʃən/ n [C] something soft that you stick pins into to hold them

pine[1] /paɪn/ n **1** also **pine tree** /ˈ. ./ [C,U] a tall tree with long leaves shaped like needles **2** [U] the pale wood from this tree

pine[2] also **pine away** v [I] to be sad and lonely and gradually become weaker because you cannot be with the person you love or have something you want: **+ for** Poor Charlie was clearly pining for his son.

pine·ap·ple /ˈpaɪnæpəl/ n [C,U] a large brown tropical fruit with pointed leaves that stick out of the top, or its sweet yellow flesh ➝ see picture at FRUIT

pine·cone /ˈpaɪnkəʊn‖-koʊn/ n [C] a thing that grows on the branches of pine trees, which contains the seeds of the pine tree

ping /pɪŋ/ v [I] if a bell or a metal object pings, it makes a short high ringing sound — **ping** n [C]

ping-pong /ˈ. ./ n [U] informal TABLE TENNIS

pin·ion /ˈpɪnjən/ v [T] formal to hold or tie up someone's arms or legs very tightly

pink /pɪŋk/ adj pale red: a pink dress — **pink** n [C,U] ➝ see colour picture on page 114

pink·ie, pinky /ˈpɪŋki/ n [C] informal the smallest finger on your hand

pin·na·cle /ˈpɪnəkəl/ n **1** [singular] the highest or most successful part of something: **of** She reached the pinnacle of success as a writer at the age of 45. **2** literary [C] a high mountain top

pin·point[1] /ˈpɪnpɔɪnt/ v [T] to say exactly where something is or what something is: I'm trying to pinpoint where we are on the map.

pinpoint[2] adj **with pinpoint accuracy** in exactly the right position: the plane's ability to drop bombs with pinpoint accuracy

pin·prick /ˈpɪnˌprɪk/ n [C] **1** a very small spot of something: pinpricks of light **2** a very small hole like one made by a pin

pins and nee·dles /ˌ. .ˈ. ./ n **1** [U] the uncomfortable feeling that you get when your blood returns to a part of your body, for example after sitting in an uncomfortable position **2** AmE **be on pins and needles** to be very nervous: Mom's been on pins and needles waiting to hear from you.

pin·stripe /ˈpɪnstraɪp/ n [U] dark-coloured cloth with thin light-coloured lines on it: a blue pinstripe suit — **pinstriped** adj

pint /paɪnt/ n [C] a unit for measuring liquid, equal to 0.473 litres in the US or 0.568 litres in Britain

pin-up /ˈpɪnʌp/ n [C] a picture of someone famous or attractive, often wearing hardly any clothes

pi·o·neer[1] /ˌpaɪəˈnɪə‖-ˈnɪr/ n [C] **1** one of the first people to do something that other people will continue to develop: the pioneers of modern space travel **2** one of the first people to travel to an unknown place and begin living there

pioneer[2] v [T] to be the first person to do, invent, or use something new: a new surgical technique pioneered by the Cambridge team

pi·ous /ˈpaɪəs/ adj having strong religious beliefs, and showing this in the way you behave — **piously** adv

pip[1] /pɪp/ n [C] BrE a small seed of a fruit such as an apple or orange ➝ see picture at FRUIT

pip² *v* [T] **-pped, -pping** *BrE* to beat someone by a small amount or at the last moment in a race or competition: *Jones pipped Hill by one point.*

pipe¹ / paɪp / *n* [C] **1** a tube that liquid or gas flows through: *a water pipe* **2** a thing used for smoking tobacco, consisting of a small tube with a container shaped like a bowl at one end **3** a musical instrument like a tube that you blow through **4 pipe dream** an idea, plan etc that will probably never happen: *Money and fame – isn't that all a pipe dream?*

pipe² *v* [T] to send a liquid or gas through a pipe to another place: *The oil is piped from Alaska.*
  pipe up *phr v* [I] *informal* to suddenly start speaking: *Then Dennis piped up, saying he didn't agree.*

pipe·line / paɪp-laɪn / *n* **1** [C] pipes used for carrying gas, oil etc over long distances **2 be in the pipeline** if a change, idea, or event is in the pipeline, it is being planned and will happen soon

pip·ing¹ / paɪpɪŋ / *n* [U] a system of pipes, used for carrying a liquid or gas: *lead piping*

piping² *adj* **piping hot** very hot: *piping hot soup*

pi·quant / ˈpiːkənt‖ˈpiːkənt, piːˈkɑːnt / *adj formal* having a pleasantly hot taste: *a piquant chili sauce* —**piquancy** *n* [U]

pique¹ / piːk / *v* [T] **pique sb's interest/curiosity** to make someone very interested in something

pique² *n* [U] *formal* when someone is annoyed or upset: *Greta left in a fit of pique.*

piqued / piːkt / *adj* annoyed or offended by something, often something not very important

pi·ra·cy / ˈpaɪərəsil‖ˈpaɪrə- / *n* [U] **1** the crime of attacking and stealing from ships **2** when someone illegally copies and sells other people's work: *software piracy*

pi·ra·nha / pɔ̍ˈrɑːnjə, -nə / *n* [C] a South American fish with sharp teeth that lives in rivers and eats flesh

pi·rate¹ / ˈpaɪərət‖ˈpaɪrət / *n* [C] **1** a SAILOR who attacks other boats and steals things from them **2** someone who illegally copies and sells someone else's work: *video pirates*

pirate² *v* [T] to illegally copy and sell someone else's work

Pis·ces / ˈpaɪsiːz / *n* [C,U] the sign of the zodiac of people who are born between February 19th and March 20th, or someone who belongs to this sign

piss¹ / pɪs / *v* [I] *spoken informal* an impolite word meaning to URINATE
  piss sb ↔ **off** *phr v* [T] *spoken* an impolite expression meaning to annoy someone very much: *Andy really pisses me off.*

piss² *n* *spoken* **1** [singular, U] an impolite word meaning URINE or when someone urinates (URINATE) **2 take the piss (out of sb/sth)** *BrE spoken informal* to make jokes about someone, especially about the way they do something: *If you keep taking the piss, I'm going to punch you.*

pissed / pɪst / *adj spoken informal* **1** *BrE* drunk: *Ian was really pissed last night.* **2** *AmE* an impolite word meaning very angry: *Karen is pissed at Andrea, she won't take her calls.* **3 pissed off** *BrE informal* an impolite expression meaning annoyed, unhappy, or disappointed

pis·ta·chi·o / pɔ̍ˈstɑːʃiəʊl‖pɔ̍ˈstæʃiou / *n* [C] a small green nut you can eat

pis·tol / ˈpɪstl / *n* [C] a small gun you hold in one hand

pis·ton / ˈpɪstən / *n* [C] a part of an engine that moves up and down to make the other parts move

pit¹ / pɪt / *n* [C] **1** a hole that has been dug in the ground **2** *spoken* a house or room that is untidy or dirty: *Erica's house is a total pit!* **3** a mine, especially a coal mine **4 be the pits** *spoken informal* to be very bad: *This place is the pits!* **5 in the pit of your stomach** if you feel a bad emotion in the pit of your stomach, it is so strong that you almost feel sick **6** *AmE* the large hard seed in some fruits: *a peach pit* → see picture at FRUIT **7 the pits** *BrE*, **the pit** *AmE* the place beside a race track where a race car gets petrol, changes tyres etc

pit² *v* [T] **-tted, -tting** *AmE* to take out the large hard seed inside some types of fruit
  pit sb/sth against sb/sth *phr v* [T] to test one person or thing against another: *This week's big game pits Houston against Miami.*

pit bull ter·ri·er / ˌ. . ˈ...ˌ / *n* [C] a small, extremely strong, and sometimes violent dog

pitch¹ / pɪtʃ / *v* **1** [T] to throw something with a lot of force: *pitch sth over/into etc Carl tore up her letter and pitched it into the fire.* **2** [I,T] to throw the ball to the BATTER in a game of BASEBALL: *Who's pitching for the Red Sox today?* **3** [I,T] to fall suddenly and heavily in a particular direction, or to make someone or something fall in this way: **+ into/forward etc** *He was so drunk he pitched head first over the wall.* **4** [T] to set something at a particular level: *He pitched the level of his lecture far too high.* **5** [T] to make sound at a particular level: *The song's pitched too high for me.* **6 pitch a tent** to put up a tent **7** [I,T] *informal especially AmE* to try to persuade someone to buy or do something: *The meeting is your chance to pitch your ideas to the boss.* **8** [I] if a ship or plane pitches, it moves violently up and down during stormy weather
  pitch in *phr v* [I] *informal* to work with a group of people so that you can complete an activity more quickly

pitch² *n* **1** [C] *BrE* an area of ground used for playing a sport: *a cricket pitch* **2** [singular U] how high or low a musical note or someone's voice is **3** [C] a throw of the ball in a game of BASEBALL, or a way it can be thrown **4** [singular, U] the strength of your feelings or opinions about something: **fever pitch** (=very excited feelings): *Their excitement rose to fever pitch.* **5** [U] a backward and forward movement of a ship or plane **6** [U] a black sticky substance that is used on roofs and ships to stop water coming through

pitch black / ˌ. ˈ. ˌ / also **pitch dark** *adj* completely black or dark: *It was pitch black in the basement.*

pitch·er / ˈpɪtʃəl-ər / *n* [C] **1** a container used for holding and pouring liquids: *a pitcher of beer* **2** the BASEBALL player who throws the ball to the BATTER

pitch·fork / ˈpɪtʃfɔːkl‖-fɔːrk / *n* [C] a tool with a long handle and two or three metal points, used especially for lifting dried cut grass

pit·e·ous /ˈpɪtiəs/ adj literary making you feel a lot of sympathy for someone: a piteous cry. —**piteously** adv

pit·fall /ˈpɪtfɔːl‖-fɔːl/ n [C] a problem or mistake that is likely to happen in a particular situation: the pitfalls of buying an old car

pith /pɪθ/ n [U] the white substance just under the skin of fruit such as oranges

pith·y /ˈpɪθi/ adj spoken or written in strong clear language: pithy comments

pit·i·ful /ˈpɪtɪfəl/ adj **1** making you feel sad and sympathetic: a pitiful sight **2** extremely bad: His performance last night was pitiful. —**pitifully** adv

pit·i·less /ˈpɪtɪləs/ adj showing no sympathy towards people who are suffering: a pitiless dictator

pit·tance /ˈpɪtəns/ n [C usually singular] a very small amount of money: She earns a pittance.

pit·ted /ˈpɪtɪd/ adj a pitted surface is covered in small marks or holes

pit·y [1] /ˈpɪti/ n **1 it's a pity (that)** [singular] used when you are disappointed about a situation and wish it was different: It's a pity you can't come. **2** [U] sympathy for someone who is suffering or unhappy: I don't need your pity!|**take/have pity on sb** (=feel sympathy for someone and try to help them)

pity [2] v [T] to feel sympathy for someone who is suffering or in a bad situation: I pity anyone who has to live with Sean.

piv·ot /ˈpɪvət/ n [C] **1** a fixed central point or pin that something balances or turns on **2** the most important thing about a situation which affects everything else —**pivot** v [I,T]

piv·ot·al /ˈpɪvətəl/ adj having a very important effect on the way something develops: A good education is pivotal to a successful career.

pix·el /ˈpɪksəl/ n [C] technical the smallest unit of an image on a computer screen

pix·ie /ˈpɪksi/ n [C] a very small imaginary creature that looks like a person and has magic powers

piz·za [ ] /ˈpiːtsə/ n [C,U] a thin flat round bread, baked with TOMATO, cheese, and usually vegetables or meat on top

plac·ard /ˈplækɑːd‖-kərd/ n [C] an advertisement on a wall or a large sign that people carry, usually one with a political statement on it

pla·cate /pləˈkeɪt‖ˈpleɪkeɪt/ v [T] formal to stop someone feeling angry by doing or saying things that will please them —**placatory** /pləˈkeɪtəri, ˈplækətəri‖ˈpleɪkətɔːri/ adj

place [1] /pleɪs/ n [C] **1** a particular area, point, or position: Keep your passport in a safe place.|a beautiful place surrounded by mountains|Paint is coming off the wall in places. (=in some places) **2** a building or area that is suitable for a particular purpose or activity: **place to eat/live etc** Are there any decent places to eat round here?|**+ for** This would be a great place for a party. **3** a particular building, town, country etc: She was born in a place called Black River Falls.|**sb's place** (=someone's house): I'm going over to Jeff's place for dinner. **4 take place** to happen: When did the robbery take place? **5 be in place/be out of place** to be in the correct or incorrect position or order: Put the CDs back in their place.|She didn't have a hair out of place. **6** an opportunity to study a particular subject, join a team etc: There are a few places left on the German course. **7** someone's or something's importance or position: No-one could ever take her place. (=be as important or good)|**friends in high places** (=important people you know): Carla has friends in high places. **8 put sb in his/her place** to show someone that they are not as important, intelligent etc as they think they are: I'd like to put her in her place, the little snob! **9 be going places** informal to start to become successful: Nick's the kind of guy who could really go places. **10 in place of** instead of: There's football on in place of the normal programmes. **11** the right occasion or situation for something: This isn't the place to discuss money. **12 in first/second/third etc place** first, second etc position in a race or competition: Jerry finished in third place. **13 in the first/second place** spoken used when you are giving your first, second etc reason in an argument or discussion: Well, in the first place, I can't afford it, and in the second place I'm not really interested. **14** a seat on a bus, train etc, or a position in a line of people **15 all over the place** informal everywhere: There were policemen all over the place! **16 out of place** not suitable for or comfortable in a particular situation: I felt really out of place at Cindy's wedding.

USAGE NOTE: place, space, and room

Use **place** to talk about an area or a part of an area: The best place to sit is right in front of the stage. Use both **space** and **room** to talk about empty areas. **Space** can mean the size of an area, or it can mean the area itself: There's a lot of space in the back of these cars. | I had trouble finding a parking space. **Room** means that there is enough space for a particular purpose: There's room in the back seat for all three of you. Don't say "There's enough place."

---

place [2] v [T] **1** to put something carefully somewhere: **place sth in/on etc** Seth placed his trophy on the top shelf. **2** to put someone or something in a particular situation: His resignation places the government in an embarrassing position. **3** to decide that someone or something is important or valuable: Society should place more emphasis on honesty. **4 can't place sb** to be unable to remember who someone is or where you have seen them before: I remember the name, but I can't place him. **5** formal to find a job for someone: The agency had placed her in a local firm. **6 place an order** to ask a shop or business to get something for you **7 place an advertisement** to arrange for an advertisement

---

GRAMMAR NOTE: countable and uncountable (2)

Some nouns can be **countable** or **uncountable**. For example: **chicken** n [C,U].
• Countable: A fox had killed some of the chickens. (=birds)
• Uncountable: chicken cooked in red wine (=meat)

placebo 500

to appear in a newspaper **8 place a bet** to risk money guessing the result of a future event

pla·ce·bo /plə'siːbəʊ‖-boʊ/ *n* [C] a substance given to someone instead of medicine, without telling them it is not real, that often still makes them feel better

place·ment /'pleɪsmənt/ *n* **1** [C] a job or position that is found for someone, especially to give them experience of work: *a work experience placement* **2** [singular, U] when you put something or someone in a particular place or position

plac·id /'plæsɪd/ *adj* not easily made angry or upset: *a placid baby* —**placidly** *adv*

pla·gia·ris·m /'pleɪdʒərɪzəm/ *n* [C,U] when someone copies another person's idea or work and pretends it is their own, or something that has been copied: *She was accused of plagiarism in her thesis.*

pla·gia·rize (also **-ise** *BrE*) /'pleɪdʒəraɪz/ *v* [I,T] to use someone else's ideas or work and pretend they are yours —**plagiarist** *n* [C]

plague¹ /pleɪɡ/ *n* **1** [C,U] a disease that spreads quickly, killing a lot of people **2** a **plague of rats/locusts etc** an uncontrollable and harmful number of rats etc

plague² *v* [T] **1** to make someone suffer continuously: *Renee had always been plagued by ill health.* **2** to annoy someone continuously

plaice /pleɪs/ *n* [C,U] a flat sea fish that people eat

plaid /plæd/ *n* [C,U] *AmE* material with a pattern of squares and lines or the pattern itself; TARTAN —**plaid** *adj*

plain¹ /pleɪn/ *adj* all one colour, with no pattern or design: *a plain carpet* → see colour picture on page 114 **1** easy to understand or recognize; CLEAR: **it's plain that** *It's plain that he doesn't agree.* **2** not complicated or unusual: *plain food* **3** a word meaning unattractive, used especially to describe a woman **4** showing clearly and honestly what you think about something: *Let's have some plain, truthful answers.*

plain² *n* [C] a large area of flat land: *the Spanish plains*

plain³ *adv* **plain stupid/wrong/rude etc** *informal* definitely stupid, wrong etc: *They're just plain lazy.*

plain·clothes /ˌ ˈ ˌ / *adj* plainclothes police wear ordinary clothes so that they can work without being recognized

plain·ly /'pleɪnli/ *adv* **1** in a way that is easy to see, hear, or understand: *He's plainly unhappy.* **2** simply or without decoration: *a plainly dressed young girl* **3** clearly and honestly: *He spoke plainly about the loss of his wife.*

plain·tiff /'pleɪntɪf/ *n* [C] *law* a person who takes someone to a law court to prove that they have done something wrong → compare DEFENDANT

plain·tive /'pleɪntɪv/ *adj* sounding sad: *the plaintive cry of the wolf*

plait¹ /plæt‖pleɪt/ *v* [T] *BrE* to twist three long pieces of hair, rope etc over and under each other to make one long piece; BRAID *AmE*

plait² *n* [C] *BrE* a length of something, especially hair, made by twisting three pieces together; BRAID *AmE*

plan¹ /plæn/ *n* [C] **1** an idea or arrangement for achieving something that will happen in the future: *Her plan is to finish school and then travel.* | *the Middle East peace plan* | **make plans** *Helen's busy making plans for her wedding.* | **go according to plan** (=happen in the way you expected): *If things go according to plan, we'll go on Monday.* **2** a drawing of a building, room etc, as it would be seen from above, showing its shape and measurements: *the plans for a new library*

plan² *v* **-nned, -nning 1** [I,T] to think about something you want to do, and how you will do it: *Grace began to plan what she would wear for the interview.* | *We've been planning our trip for months.* **2** [I,T] to intend to do something: **plan on doing sth/plan to do sth** *How long do you plan on staying?* | *Where do you plan to go next year?* **3** [T] to think about something you are going to make or build, and decide what it will look like: *We spend ages planning the garden.*

plane /pleɪn/ *n* [C] **1** a vehicle with wings and an engine, which can fly **2** a level or standard of conversation, intelligence etc: *Jill's work is on a higher artistic plane than mine.* **3** a tool used for making wooden surfaces smooth → see picture at TOOLS **4** *technical* a completely flat surface

plan·et /'plænɪt/ *n* [C] **1** a very large round object in space that moves around a star such as the sun: *Mercury is the smallest planet.* | *the planet Earth* **2 the planet** the world: *the environmental future of the planet* —**planetary** *adj*

plan·e·tar·i·um /ˌplænɪ'teəriəm‖-'ter-/ *n* [C] a building where lights on a curved ceiling show the movements of planets and stars

plank /plæŋk/ *n* [C] a long flat piece of wood: *a solid plank of wood*

plank·ton /'plæŋktən/ *n* [U] extremely small plants and animals that live in the sea and are eaten by fish

plan·ner /'plænə‖-ər/ *n* [C] someone whose job is to plan something, especially the way towns develop

plant¹ /plɑːnt‖plænt/ *n* [C] **1** a living thing that has leaves and roots and is usually smaller than a tree: *Don't forget to water the plants.* | *a tomato plant* **2** a factory and all its equipment: *a chemical plant*

plant² *v* [T] **1** to put plants or seeds in the ground to grow: *I planted the rose bush last year.* | *a hillside planted with pine trees* **2** *informal* to hide stolen or illegal goods in someone's bags, room etc in order to make that person seem guilty: **plant sth on sb** *Someone must have planted the drugs on her.* **3** to put something firmly somewhere: *Plant your feet firmly on the pedals, and then push.* **4** **plant an idea/doubt/suspicion** to mention something that makes someone begin to have an idea, doubt etc: *Their conversation had planted doubts in Yuri's mind.*

plan·ta·tion /plæn'teɪʃən, plɑːn-‖plæn-/ *n* [C] a large farm, especially in a hot country, where a single crop such as tea, cotton, or sugar is grown: *a rubber plantation*

plaque /plɑːk, plæk‖plæk/ *n* **1** [C] a piece of flat metal or stone on a wall with writing on it that reminds people of a famous person or event that is connected with that place: *The plaque* *read: Samuel Johnson was born here.* **2** [U] a harmful substance that forms on your teeth

plas·ma /ˈplæzmə/ *n* [U] the liquid part of your blood that carries blood cells

plas·ter¹ /ˈplɑːstəlˈplæstər/ *n* **1** [U] a substance used for covering walls and ceilings to give them a smooth surface **2** [C] *BrE* a piece of special material that you stick on your skin to cover small wounds; BAND-AID *AmE* **3 be in plaster** *BrE* if someone's leg, arm etc is in plaster, it is covered with a hard white substance to protect a broken bone

plaster² *v* [T] **1** to spread or stick something all over a surface so that it is thickly covered: **be plastered with sth** *a wall plastered with pictures* **2** to cover a wall or ceiling with PLASTER

plaster cast /ˌ.. ˈ., ˈ... / *n* [C] **1** a cover made from plaster of Paris, used to protect a broken bone **2** a copy of something made from plaster of Paris

plas·tered /ˈplɑːstədlˈplæstərd/ *adj informal* very drunk: *I got plastered last night.*

plaster of Par·is /ˌplɑːstər əv ˈpærₔsll̩ˌplæs-/ *n* [U] a white powder that you mix with water and which becomes very hard when it dries, used especially for making STATUEs

plas·tic¹ /ˈplæstɪk/ *n* [C,U] a cheap light material which is used for making different objects, and is produced by a chemical process: *toys made of plastic*

plastic² *adj* made of plastic: *a plastic bag | plastic spoons*

plas·tic·i·ty /plæˈstɪsₔti/ *n* [U] *technical* the quality of being easily made into any shape

plastic sur·ge·ry /ˌ.. ˈ... / *n* [U] medical treatment to improve the way someone's face or body looks

plate /pleɪt/ *n* [C] **1** a flat dish that you use for eating or serving food: *a china plate* **2** also **plateful** the amount of food that a plate will hold: *a plate of spaghetti* **3** a flat piece of metal or glass: *The drill is attached to the bench by a metal plate.* **4 gold/silver plate** metal with a thin covering of gold or silver **5** also **number/license/registration plate** one of the signs with numbers and letters on at the front and back of a car: *New Jersey plates* **6** [C] a picture in a book, printed on good quality paper

plat·eau /ˈplætəʊllplæˈtoʊ/ *n* [C] **1** a large area of flat land that is higher than the land around it **2** a period when the level of something does not change: *Inflation has reached a plateau.*

plat·ed /ˈpleɪtₔd/ *adj* covered with a thin layer of metal, especially gold or silver: *a silver-plated spoon*

plate glass /ˌ. ˈ.◂ / *n* [U] glass made in large thick sheets, used especially in shop windows

plat·form /ˈplætfɔːmll-fɔːrm/ *n* [C] **1** a raised structure for people to stand or work on: *He climbed on to the platform and began to address the crowd. | an oil platform in the Atlantic* **2** the raised place where you get on and off a train → see colour picture on page 669 **3** the main ideas and aims of a political party, especially those stated just before an election: *We were elected on a platform of reform.* **4** a chance for someone to express their opinions: *He used the TV interview as a platform for his views on education.*

plat·i·num /ˈplætₔnəm/ *n* [U] an expensive heavy silver-white metal that is often used to make jewellery

plat·i·tude /ˈplætₔtjuːdll-tuːd/ *n* [C] a statement that has been made so many times before that it is considered boring: *a speech full of platitudes*

pla·ton·ic /pləˈtɒnɪkll-ˈtɑː-/ *adj* a platonic relationship is friendly but not sexual

pla·toon /pləˈtuːn/ *n* [C] a small group of soldiers

plat·ter /ˈplætəll-ər/ *n* [C] *AmE* a large plate, used for serving food

plau·dit /ˈplɔːdₔtllˈplɔː-/ *n* [C usually plural] *formal* praise

plau·si·ble /ˈplɔːzₔbəllˈplɔː-/ *adj* something that is plausible seems likely to be true: *a plausible explanation* → opposite IMPLAUSIBLE

play¹ /pleɪ/ *v* **1** [I,T] to take part in a sport or game: *Do you know how to play chess? | The guys are playing basketball. |* **play against sb/play sb** *The 49ers are playing the Vikings on Saturday. |* **play for** (=play in a team): *Garcia plays for the Hornets.* **2** [I,T] to do things that you enjoy, for example using toys and taking part in games – use this especially about children: *He has lots of toys to play with. | Why don't you go out and play with your friends?* **3** [I,T] to use a musical instrument to produce music: *When I was at school I used to play the piano.* **4** [I,T] if you play a record, radio etc, or it plays, it produces music or sounds: *She always plays her radio really loud. | What's that song they're playing?* **5** [T] to take part in a film, programme, play etc as one of the characters in it: *The hero is played by Sean Penn.* **6 play a trick/joke on sb** to do something to surprise or trick someone **7** [I,T] to behave in a particular way: **play it cool** (=pretend to be calm) | **play the fool** (=behave in a silly way): *I wish he'd stop playing the fool.* **8 play safe/play it safe** to not take any risks or do anything that might cause problems **9 play games** to behave in a silly and annoying way which wastes times or causes problems for other people **10 play ball** *AmE* **a)** to play with a ball: *Don't play ball in the house.* **b)** *informal* to agree to do what someone wants you to do: *Do you think he'll play ball?* **11 play a part/role** to have an effect on something: *Genetic factors may also play a part.* **12 play it by ear** *informal* to not plan what you are going to do, but decide when you know what the situation is like: *I'm not sure what mood he'll be in, so we'll have to play it by ear.* **13 be playing with fire** to be doing something that could make something very bad happen: *If you invest in the stock market now, you're playing with fire.* **14 play on your mind** if something plays on your mind, you worry about it a lot **15 play for time** to try to make something happen more slowly, because you need more time, or you do not want it to happen → see also **play hooky** (HOOKY), **play truant** (TRUANT)

play around *phr v* [I] **1** *informal* to have a sexual relationship with someone who is not your husband or wife **2** to spend time playing games or behaving in a silly way: *I wish those kids would stop playing around outside our house.*

play around/about with sth *phr v* [T] → see PLAY WITH STH

play at sth *phr v* [T] **1** to pretend to do something, or not do it seriously or properly **2 what is he/she etc playing at?** *spoken* used when you are annoyed with someone, especially because they have not done what they said they would do

play sth ↔ **back** *phr v* [T] to let someone hear or see again something that has been recorded on a TAPE, VIDEO etc

play sth ↔ **down** *phr v* [T] to try to make something seem less important or bad than it really is: *The government was anxious to play down the latest economic figures.*

play sb **off against** sth *phr v* [T] to try to make two people or groups argue or compete with each other, in order to get advantages for yourself

play on sth *phr v* [T] to use someone's worries, fears, weaknesses etc to persuade them to believe something: *The film plays on people's fears and prejudices.*

play sth ↔ **up** *phr v* **1** [T **play** sth ↔ **up**] to make something seem better, more important etc than it really is: *Newspaper reports tried to play up the mystery surrounding Elvis's death.* **2** [I] if children play up, they behave badly

play with sth, **play around/about with** sth *phr v* [T] **1** to keep touching or moving something: *Stop playing with the remote control!* **2** to do something in different ways, in order to find the best way of doing it: *I've been playing around with different designs.* → see also PLAY AROUND

play² *n* **1** [C] a story that is written to be performed by actors, especially in a theatre: *We went to see a new play by Tom Stoppard at the National Theatre.* | **put on a play** (=perform a play): *the play was put on by a local school* **2** [U] the activity of playing a game or sport: *Rain stopped play.* **3** [U] things that people, especially children, do to enjoy themselves: *a play area with slides and swings* | **at play** (=playing) **4 come into play** to have an effect on a situation: *Luck comes into play quite a lot.* **5 bring/put sth into play** to use something or make it have an effect: *This is where you should bring your experience into play.* **6 play on words** when you use a word or phrase so that it can have two meanings, often as a joke → see also PUN

play·act·ing /ˈ. ../ *n* [U] when someone pretends to be serious or sincere, but is not

play·boy /ˈpleɪbɔɪ/ *n* [C] a rich man who does not work and spends time enjoying himself

play-by-play /ˌ. . ˈ. ˌ. / *adj AmE* a play-by-play description of a sports game describes what is happening on television or radio while the game is taking place: *play-by-play coverage of the California Angels' home game*

play·er /ˈpleɪəll-ər/ *n* [C] **1** someone who plays a game or sport: *a piano player* **2** someone who plays a musical instrument **3** one of the people, countries etc that are involved in a situation: *a major player in the UN peace talks*

play·ful /ˈpleɪfəl/ *adj* **1** done for fun, not because you are serious: *playful teasing* **2** very active and happy: *a playful little kitten* —**playfully** *adv* —**playfulness** *n* [U]

play·ground /ˈpleɪɡraʊnd/ *n* [C] an outdoor area where children can play, especially while they are at school

play·group /ˈpleɪɡruːp/ *n* [C] *BrE* an organized group where small children go to play, learn etc in the years before they go to school

play·house /ˈpleɪhaʊs/ *n* [C] **1** a theatre – used especially in the names of theatres: *the Harlow Playhouse* **2** a small house or tent that children can play in

playing card /ˈ.. ./ *n* [C] a CARD → see picture at CARD

playing field /ˈ.. ./ *n* [C] **1** an area used for playing football, BASEBALL etc **2 level playing field** when people, companies, countries etc can compete equally and fairly with each other because none of them have special advantages

play·mate /ˈpleɪmeɪt/ *n* [C] *old-fashioned* a friend that a child plays with

play-off, **playoff** /ˈ. ./ *n* [C] a game between the best teams or players in a competition, in order to choose the final winner

play·pen /ˈpleɪpen/ *n* [C] a piece of equipment with a net or wooden BARS around it, which young children can play in safely

play·room /ˈpleɪrʊm, -ruːm/ *n* [C] a room for children to play in

play·thing /ˈpleɪˌθɪŋ/ *n* [C] **1** someone who you use only for your own enjoyment, without caring about their feelings **2** *formal* a toy

play·time /ˈpleɪtaɪm/ *n* [C] a period of time when children at school can play

play·wright /ˈpleɪraɪt/ *n* [C] someone who writes plays

plc /ˌpiː el ˈsiː/ *n* [C] the abbreviation for Public Limited Company; used after the names of big companies in Britain that you can buy SHARES in: *British Telecom PLC*

plea /pliː/ *n* [C] **1** when someone asks for something urgently and anxiously: *Her mother ignored her pleas for help.* **2** *law* the answer that someone gives when they are asked if they are guilty or not guilty in a court of law

plea-bar·gain·ing /ˈ. ˌ.../ *n* [U] when someone is promised a less severe punishment after their TRIAL if they admit that they were guilty of a crime

plead /pliːd/ *v* **pleaded** *or* **pled** /pled/ **pleading 1** [I] to ask for something in an urgent and anxious way: **+ with** *Amy pleaded with the stranger to help her.* **2** [I,T] *law* to officially say in a court of law whether or not you are guilty of a crime: *"How do you plead?" "Not guilty."* —**pleadingly** *adv*: *She looked at him pleadingly.*

pleas·ant /ˈplezənt/ *adj* **1** enjoyable, nice, or good: *a pleasant surprise* | *They spent a pleasant evening together.* **2** polite and friendly: *a pleasant young man in a dark suit* —**pleasantly** *adv*: *The weather was pleasantly warm.* → opposite UNPLEASANT

pleas·an·tries /ˈplezəntriz/ *n* [plural] *formal* polite things that you say when you meet someone

please¹ /pliːz/ *interjection* **1** used when you are politely asking for something: *Please could I have a glass of water?* | *Can you all sit down, please?* **2 yes please** *spoken* used to politely say that you want something that someone offers you: *"More coffee?" "Yes please!"*

please[2] *v* **1** [I,T] to make someone feel happy or satisfied: *Mark has always been hard to please.* **2 whatever/however etc you please** used to say that someone can do anything they want, do something in any way they want etc: *He can do whatever he pleases. I don't care.* **3 if you please** *spoken formal* used when you are politely asking someone to do something: *Close the door, if you please.*

pleased /pliːzd/ *adj* **1** happy or satisfied: **+ with/about** *Are you pleased with the result?* | **pleased to do sth** *You'll be pleased to hear that your application has been successful.* | **pleased (that)** *I was very pleased that he agreed to see me.* **2 (I'm) pleased to meet you** *spoken* a polite expression used when you meet someone for the first time

plea·sur·a·ble /ˈpleʒərəbəl/ *adj formal* enjoyable: *a pleasurable experience*

pleasure /ˈpleʒəll-ər/ *n* **1** [U] a feeling of happiness, satisfaction, or enjoyment: **for pleasure** *I often read for pleasure.* **2 be a pleasure** if something is a pleasure, you enjoy it very much: *The latest model from Vauxhall is an absolute pleasure to drive.* **3 (it is) my pleasure** *spoken* used to say politely that you enjoyed something, or that you were glad to do something for someone: *"Thanks for coming." "My pleasure."* **4 take pleasure in doing sth** to enjoy doing something, especially something someone else does not want you to do: *She took great pleasure in telling him that he was wrong.*

pleat /pliːt/ *n* [C] a flat fold in a skirt, pair of trousers, dress etc

pleat·ed /ˈpliːtəd/ *adj* a pleated skirt, dress etc has a lot of narrow flat folds

pleb /pleb/ *n* [C] *humorous informal* someone who belongs to a low social class

pleb·is·cite /ˈplebəsɪtll-saɪt/ *n* [C,U] when everyone in a country votes about an important decision; REFERENDUM

pled /pled/ *v* the past tense and past participle of PLEAD

pledge[1] /pledʒ/ *n* [C] **1** a serious promise or agreement to do something or to give something to help someone: *Several countries made pledges of aid.* **2 take the pledge** *old-fashioned* to seriously promise that you will no longer drink alcohol

pledge[2] *v* [T] **1** to make a formal, usually public, promise to do something: *They have pledged to cut inflation.* **2** to make someone formally promise something: *We were all pledged to secrecy.*

plen·ti·ful /ˈplentɪfəl/ *adj* if something is plentiful, there is a lot of it available: *a plentiful supply of fresh fruit and vegetables* —**plentifully** *adv*

plen·ty[1] /ˈplenti/ *quantifier, n* [U] a lot – used to say that there is enough of something or more than enough: **+ of** *We have plenty of time to get to the airport.* | **plenty to do/eat etc** *There should be plenty to eat at the picnic.*

plenty[2] *adv* **plenty more** a lot more, so that there is enough or more than enough: *There's plenty more room in the car.*

pleth·o·ra /ˈpleθərə/ *n* **a plethora of** *formal* a very large number: *a plethora of complaints*

pli·a·ble /ˈplaɪəbəl/ *adj* **1** able to bend easily without breaking or cracking: *Roll the clay until it is soft and pliable.* **2** easily influenced by other people

pli·ers /ˈplaɪəzll-ərz/ *n* [plural] a tool for cutting wire or pulling nails out of wood: *a pair of pliers* → see picture at TOOLS

plight /plaɪt/ *n* [singular] a bad, serious, or sad situation that someone is in: *the plight of the homeless*

plim·soll /ˈplɪmsəl, -səʊll-səl, -soʊl/ *n* [C] a light shoe made of CANVAS

plod /plɒdllplɑːd/ *v* [I] **-dded, -dding** to move slowly or do something too slowly, because you are tired or bored: **+ on/along** *The old dog plodded along behind him.*

plonk /plɒŋkllplɑːŋk, plɔːŋk/ *n* [U] *BrE informal* cheap wine

plop[1] /plɒpllplɑːp/ *v* [T] **-pped, -pping** to sit down, fall down, or drop something somewhere suddenly: *She plopped down onto the sofa.*

plop[2] *n* [C] the sound made by something when it falls in or is dropped into liquid

plot[1] /plɒtllplɑːt/ *n* [C] **1** a secret plan to do something illegal or harmful: *a plot to kill General Zia* **2** the events that form the main story of a book, film, or play: *I didn't really understand the plot.* **3** a small piece of land for building or growing things on

plot[2] *v* **-tted, -tting** **1** [I,T] to make a secret plan to harm someone or do something illegal: *He denied plotting to kidnap the girl.* **2** [T] also **plot out** to mark information on a CHART or map: *The earthquakes are plotted on a map.*

plough[1] *BrE*, **plow** *AmE* /plaʊ/ *n* [C] a large piece of equipment used on farms to turn over the surface of the land so that seeds can be planted → see also SNOWPLOUGH

plough[2] *BrE*, **plow** *AmE* — *v* **1** [I,T] to cut long lines in the ground, so that seeds can be planted, using a plough: *newly plowed fields* **2** [I] to hit or move something with a lot of force: **+ into** *A truck plowed into the back of my car.* | **+ through** *The ship ploughed through the waves.*

plough sth ↔ **back** *phr v* [T] to spend a company's profits on improving the company, buying new equipment etc

plough on *phr v* [I] to continue doing something, even though it is difficult or boring

plough through sth *phr v* [T] to read all of something even though it is difficult, long, or boring

ploy /plɔɪ/ *n* [C] a clever way of getting an advantage, especially by deceiving someone: *He's not really ill – it's just a ploy to get us to feel sorry for him.*

pluck¹ /plʌk/ *v* **1** [T] to take something quickly from someone or something: *She plucked a handkerchief from her sleeve.* **2 pluck up the courage** to decide to do something difficult or unpleasant, which you were not brave enough to do before: *I finally plucked up the courage to ask for a raise.* **3** to pull the feathers off a bird before cooking it **4** to play a musical instrument by pulling the strings with your fingers

pluck² *n* [U] courage and determination to do something that is difficult or dangerous —**plucky** *adj*: *a plucky kid*

plugs

plug

plug

plug¹ /plʌg/ *n* [C] **1** the thing that you push into a wall to connect a piece of electrical equipment to the electricity supply **2** a round flat piece of rubber used for blocking the hole in a bath or SINK **3** *informal* when someone mentions their newest book, film etc in a television or radio programme in order to advertise it

plug² *v* [T] **-gged, -gging 1** also **plug up** to fill or block a hole **2** to mention the name of a book, film, etc on a radio or television programme to advertise it

plug away *phr v* [I] to continue working hard at something: *He's been plugging away at his essay all week.*

plug sth ↔ **in/into** *phr v* [T] to connect a piece of electrical equipment to the electricity supply, or to another piece of equipment: *Is the TV plugged in?* → opposite UNPLUG

plug·hole /ˈplʌghəʊl‖-hoʊl/ *n* [C] *BrE* a hole in a bath or SINK, where the water can flow out

plum /plʌm/ *n* [C] a soft, round fruit, which is purple, red, or yellow → see picture at FRUIT

plum·age /ˈpluːmɪdʒ/ *n* [U] a bird's feathers

plumb·er /ˈplʌmə‖-ər/ *n* [C] someone whose job is to repair water pipes, TAPS, toilets etc

plumb·ing /ˈplʌmɪŋ/ *n* [U] the system of water pipes in a building

plume /pluːm/ *n* [C] **1** a small cloud of smoke, dust, gas etc that rises upwards: *We could see a* plume of smoke coming from the chimney. **2** a large feather

plum·met /ˈplʌmɪt/ *v* [I] to suddenly and quickly fall or become less in value: *House prices have plummeted over the past year.*

plump¹ /plʌmp/ *adj* **1** slightly fat in an attractive way: *a sweet, plump little girl* → see colour picture on page 244 **2** attractively round and full: *plump juicy strawberries* | *plump cushions*

plump² *v*

plump for sth *v* [T] *informal* to choose one out of several things, after thinking carefully: *In the end I plumped for the tuna steak.*

plump sth ↔ **up** *phr v* [T] to make a PILLOW or CUSHION bigger and softer by shaking and hitting it

plun·der¹ /ˈplʌndə‖-ər/ *v* [I,T] to steal or take large amounts of money or things from somewhere: *The city was first captured and plundered in 1793.* | *We cannot go on plundering the Earth's resources.*

plunder² *n* [U] *literary* the act of stealing things, or the things that someone steals

plunge¹ /plʌndʒ/ *v* **1** [I] to fall downwards, especially into water: *The van plunged into the river.* **2** [T] to push something into another thing using a lot of force: *He plunged the knife into the man's chest.* **3** [I] to suddenly become lower in value: *The price of gas plunged to 99 cents a gallon.*

plunge sb/sth **into** sth *phr v* [T] to cause someone or something to be in a bad, difficult or dangerous situation: *America was suddenly plunged into war.*

plunge² *n* **1 take the plunge** to decide to do something that may involve risks, after thinking about it carefully, for example to get married **2** [singular] when something suddenly becomes lower in value: *a plunge in share values*

plung·er /ˈplʌndʒə‖-ər/ *n* [C] a thing you use for unblocking a pipe in a SINK or bath, which consists of a straight handle with a large rubber cup

plu·per·fect /pluːˈpɜːfɪkt‖-ɜːr-/ *n* **the pluperfect** the PAST PERFECT

plu·ral /ˈplʊərəl‖ˈplʊr-/ *n* [C] the form of a word that shows you are talking about more than one person, thing, etc, which is usually formed by adding 's'. For example, 'dogs' is the plural of 'dog', and 'children' is the plural of 'child'.

plus¹ /plʌs/ *prep* used when one number or amount is added to another. In calculations, plus is written as +: *Three plus six equals nine. (3+6=9)* | *The jacket costs $49.95 plus tax.*

plus² *linking word informal* and also: *I had to carry her cases, plus all her other things.*

plus³ *adj* **1** more than a particular amount: *She makes $50,000 a year plus.* | *a temperature of plus 12° (=12 degrees above zero)* **2 plus or minus** used to say how much an amount can vary: *The results are accurate plus or minus 3 percentage points.* → compare MINUS³

plus⁴ *n* [C] **1** something that is good about something: *The restaurant's location is a real plus.* **2** a plus sign

plush /plʌʃ/ *adj* comfortable, expensive, and of good quality: *a large plush office*

plus sign /ˈ. ./ *n* [C] the sign (+)

Plu·to /ˈpluːtəʊ‖-toʊ/ *n* [singular] a small PLA-NET, ninth from the sun

plu·to·ni·um /pluːˈtəʊniəm‖-ˈtoʊ-/ *n* [U] a metal used for producing NUCLEAR power

ply /plaɪ/ *v* [I,T] **plied**, **plied**, **plying 1 ply your trade** *literary* to do your usual work, especially by trying to sell things to people **2** *old-fashioned* to travel regularly between two places in a boat, taxi etc
ply sb with sth *phr v* [T] to keep giving someone large amounts of food and drink

ply·wood /ˈplaɪwʊd/ *n* [U] a board made from thin sheets of wood stuck together

pm, p.m. /ˌpiː ˈem/ used in times from NOON until just before MIDNIGHT: *I get off work at 5:30 p.m.* → compare AM

PMT /ˌpiː em ˈtiː/ also **PMS** /ˌpiː em ˈes/ *n* [U] Premenstrual Tension; feelings of anger, sadness, tiredness etc, or physical pain that some women have before their PERIOD

pneu·mat·ic /njuːˈmætɪk‖nʊ-/ *adj* **1** technical filled with air: *a pneumatic tyre* **2** using air pressure: *a pneumatic drill* —**pneumatically** /-kli/ *adv*

pneu·mo·ni·a /njuːˈməʊniə‖nʊˈmoʊ-/ *n* [U] a serious disease of the lungs

poach /pəʊtʃ‖poʊtʃ/ *v* **1** [T] to gently cook food such as eggs or fish in boiling liquid **2** [I,T] to illegally catch or hunt animals or fish on someone else's private land

poach·er /ˈpəʊtʃə‖ˈpoʊtʃər/ *n* [C] someone who illegally hunts or catches animals or fish on another person's private land

PO Box /ˌpiː əʊ ˈbɒks‖-oʊ ˈbɑːks/ *n* [C] Post Office Box; a box with a number in a post office, which you can have mail sent to instead of your home

pock·et[1] /ˈpɒkɪt‖ˈpɑːkɪt/ *n* [C] **1** a small flat cloth bag sewn into or onto a piece of clothing, for keeping small things in: *There's some money in my jacket pocket.* | *Julie took her hands out of her pockets.* → see colour picture on page 113 **2** a container made from a flat piece of material fixed to the inside of a car door, the back of a plane seat etc, for putting things in **3** the money that you have to spend: *The bridge was paid for out of the pockets of the local people.* (=they had to pay for it) **4** a small area or group of people: *pockets of resistance* | *an airpocket* **5** **out of pocket** if you are out of pocket, you have less money than you should have because you have had to pay for something → see also **pick sb's pocket** (PICK[1])

pocket[2] *v* [T] **1** to keep money for yourself, especially money that you got secretly and dishonestly: *An employee was arrested for pocketing $4 million of the company's profits.* **2** to put something in your pocket: *He pocketed the keys of the safe.*

pocket[3], **pocket-sized** /ˌ...ˈ.◂/ *adj* small enough to fit into a pocket: *a pocket calendar* | *a pocket-sized notebook*

pock·et·book /ˈpɒkɪtbʊk‖ˈpɑː-/ *n* [C] *AmE* **1** a WALLET, or PURSE **2** a small notebook

pock·et·ful /ˈpɒkɪtfʊl‖ˈpɑː-/ *n* [C] the amount that will fill a pocket: *She always carried a pocketful of pills.*

pocket knife /ˈ... ./ *n* [C] a small knife with a blade that you can fold into its handle

pock·mark /ˈpɒkmɑːk‖ˈpɑːkmɑːrk/ *n* [C] a small hollow mark on someone's skin, made by a skin disease —**pockmarked** *adj*

pod /pɒd‖pɑːd/ *n* [C] the long green part of plants such as beans and PEAS, which the seeds grow in: *a pea pod*

po·di·a·trist /pəˈdaɪətrɪst/ *n* [C] *AmE* a doctor who takes care of people's feet and treats foot diseases; CHIROPODIST *BrE* —**podiatry** *n* [U]

po·di·um /ˈpəʊdiəm‖ˈpoʊ-/ *n* [C] **1** a tall desk that you stand behind to give a speech **2** a small raised area for a performer, speaker etc to stand on, sometimes with a tall desk in front of it

po·em /ˈpəʊəm‖ˈpoʊ-/ *n* [C] a piece of writing that is written in short lines, especially using words that RHYME (=have similar sounds at the end): *a famous poem by William Wordsworth*

po·et /ˈpəʊɪt‖ˈpoʊ-/ *n* [C] someone who writes poems

po·et·ic /pəʊˈetɪk‖poʊ-/ *adj* **1** relating to poetry or typical of poetry: *poetic language* **2** beautifully written, painted etc and affecting your emotions: *the poetic quality of some of his photographs* —**poetically** /-kli/ *adv*

poetic jus·tice /ˌ... ˈ../ *n* [U] when something bad happens to someone who did something bad before, in a way that seems like a suitable punishment

poetic li·cence *BrE*, **poetic license** *AmE* /ˌ... ˈ../ *n* [U] the freedom to change facts, not obey grammar rules etc because you are writing an imaginary story or a poem

po·et·ry /ˈpəʊɪtri‖ˈpoʊ-/ *n* [U] **1** poems in general: *Emily Dickinson's poetry* → compare PROSE **2** the art of writing poems: *a poetry class*

poi·gnant /ˈpɔɪnjənt/ *adj* making you have strong feelings of sadness or sympathy: *a poignant scene near the end of the film* —**poignancy** *n* [U] —**poignantly** *adv*

point[1] /pɔɪnt/ *n* **1** [C] a fact or idea that someone talks or writes about: **make a point** (=mention a fact or idea): *I agreed with several of the points he made.* | **that's a point** *spoken* (=used when someone has mentioned something important which needs to be considered): *"Have you spoken to Alan?" "That's a point! I completely forgot to tell him."* **2 the point** the most important idea or part of something: **the point is** *spoken*: *The point is we just don't have enough money.* | **get to the point** (=start talking about the most important part of something): *I wish she'd hurry up and get to the point.* | **that's not the point** *spoken* (=used to say that what someone has mentioned is much less important than something else): *"But I gave you the money back." "That's not the point: you shouldn't have taken it."* **3** [C] a time or part of a process when something happens: *At that point I began to get seriously worried.* | **high/low point** (=the best or worst part of something): *the high point of his career* | **reach/get to the point** *It got to the point where we both wanted a divorce.* **4** [C] an exact position or place: *the point where two lines cross each other* **5** [U] the purpose or reason for doing something: *The whole point of travelling is to experience new things.* | **there's no point/ what's the point** *spoken* (=used when something seems to have no purpose and be certain to fail): *There's no point in going now – we're already too* *late.* **6** [C] the sharp end of something: *the point of a needle* **7** **good/bad/strong etc points** something about a person or thing that is good, bad etc: *He has his good points.* **8** [C] a unit used for showing the SCORE in a game or competition: *The Rams beat the Giants by 6 points.* **9** [C] the sign (.) used for separating a whole number from the DECIMALS that follow it: *four point seven five percent* (=4.75%) **10** [C] a unit for measuring something on a SCALE: *Stocks were down 12 points today at 5,098.* **11** **boiling/freezing/melting point** the temperature at which something boils, freezes etc **12** **sb has a point** used to say that you think someone is right: *I think he may have a point.* **13** **I (can) see your point** *spoken* used to say that what someone has said seems reasonable and you can understand why they have said it: *She wants him to spend more time with the children, and I can see her point.* **14** **up to a point** partly, but not completely: *He's right up to a point.* **15** [C] one of the marks on a COMPASS that shows direction, especially north, south, east, and west **16** **make a point of doing sth** to be careful to do something, or deliberately do something so that people notice: *Sarah made a point of telling everyone how much the ring had cost.* **17** [C] a very small spot: *a tiny point of light* **18** [C] a long thin piece of land that stretches out into the sea **19** **to the point** mentioning only the most important things, and not mentioning anything else: *Her next letter was short and to the point.* **20** **on the point of doing sth** to be going to do something very soon, when something happens: *I was just on the point of leaving for work when the phone rang.* **21** **to the point of** so much that something almost happens or is almost true: *The bird has been hunted to the point of extinction.* **22** **the point of no return** the time when it becomes impossible to stop something from happening **23** **in point of fact** *formal* used when you mention something important that is connected with what you have just been talking about ➡ see also GUNPOINT, POINT OF VIEW

point² *v* **1** [I] to move your finger in the direction of something in order to show it to someone: + **to/at/towards etc** *John pointed to a chair: "Please, sit down."* | *"That's my car," she said, pointing at a white Ford.* ➡ see colour picture on page 473 **2** [T] to move something so that it is facing in a particular direction, or to be facing in a particular direction: *He pointed a gun at the old man's head.* | *Hold the bat so that your fingers point toward the end.* **3** [T] to show someone which direction to go: *There should be signs pointing the way to her house.* **4** **point the finger at sb** *informal* to blame someone; ACCUSE

point out *phr v* **1** [T point sth ↔ out] to tell someone something that they had not noticed or thought about: *Someone pointed out that Washington hadn't won a game in L.A. since 1980.* **2** [T point sb/sth ↔ out] to show a person or thing to someone by pointing at them: *I'll point him out to you next time we see him.*

point to/toward *sb/sth phr v* [T] to show that something is probably true: *The study points to stress as a cause of heart disease.*

point-blank /ˌ. ˈ. ◂/ *adj,adv* **1** **at point-blank range** shooting at someone from an extremely close position: *The victim was shot dead at point-blank range.* **2** in a very firm and often rude way, without any explanation: *She refused point-blank to help them.*

point·ed /ˈpɔɪntɪd/ *adj* **1** having a point at the end: *cowboy boots with pointed toes* **2** a **pointed question/look/remark etc** a question, look etc that shows clearly that you think something is wrong, or that you are annoyed with someone

point·ed·ly /ˈpɔɪntɪdli/ *adv* in a way that shows clearly that you think something is wrong or that you are annoyed with someone: *Wilton pointedly avoided asking Reiter for advice.*

point·er /ˈpɔɪntə-ər/ *n* [C] **1** a thin ARROW that points to something on a piece of equipment such as a computer etc **2** a helpful piece of advice; TIP: *I can give you some pointers on how to improve your game.* **3** a long stick used for pointing at things on a map, board etc

point·less /ˈpɔɪntləs/ *adj* **1** without any purpose: *pointless violence on TV* **2** not likely to have any effect: *It's pointless trying to talk to him – he won't listen.*

point of view /ˌ. . ˈ. / *n* [C] **1** a way of thinking about or judging a situation: *From a purely practical point of view, this is not a good decision.* **2** what someone thinks about something, especially when this is influenced by the situation they are in: *My parents never seem to be able to see my point of view.*

points /pɔɪnts/ *n* [plural] a part of a railway line that can be moved so that a train can change to another line

point·y /ˈpɔɪnti/ *adj informal* having a point at the end

poise /pɔɪz/ *n* [U] **1** calm, confident behaviour: **recover your poise** (=become calm again): *He struggled to recover his normal poise.* **2** a graceful way of moving or standing: *the poise of a ballet dancer*

poised /pɔɪzd/ *adj* **1** ready to do something or soon going to do it: *The army was poised to attack.* **2** not moving, but ready to move: *runners poised at the start of a race* **3** behaving in a calm confident way

poi·son¹ /ˈpɔɪzən/ *n* [C,U] a substance that can kill or harm you if you eat it, drink it etc: *Poison from the snake can kill very quickly.* | *poison gas*

poison² *v* [T] **1** to kill or harm someone by giving them poison: *He tried to poison his parents.* **2** to add poison to food or drink in order to kill someone **3** to make water, air, land etc dangerous by adding harmful chemicals to it: *The lake has been poisoned by toxic waste from factories.* **4** to spoil something completely: *The quarrel had poisoned their relationship.* **5** **poison sb's mind (against)** to make someone dislike someone or something, especially by telling them things that are not true: *Fagin was trying to poison the young boy's mind.* —**poisoned** *adj* —**poisoner** *n* [C]

poi·son·ing /ˈpɔɪzənɪŋ/ *n* [C,U] an illness that is caused by swallowing, touching, or breathing a poisonous substance: *lead poisoning* ➡ see also FOOD POISONING

poi·son·ous /ˈpɔɪzənəs/ *adj* **1** containing poison: *poisonous chemicals* **2** a poisonous snake, insect etc produces poison which it uses to fight other animals

poke /pəʊk‖poʊk/ v **1** [I,T] to push your finger or something such as a stick into something: *Stop poking me!* | *He poked at the campfire with a stick.* | **poke a hole** (=make a hole using your finger, a stick etc) **2** [T] to push something through a space or out of an opening: **poke sth through/out of/around** etc *David poked his head around the door.* **3** [I] to appear through a hole or opening: **+ up/through/out of** etc *The roots of the trees are poking up through the sidewalk.* **4 poke fun at** to joke about someone in an unkind way: *You shouldn't poke fun at her like that.* —**poke** *n* [C] → see also **stick/poke your nose into sth** (NOSE¹)

pok·er /ˈpəʊkə‖ˈpoʊkər/ *n* **1** [U] a card game that people usually play for money **2** [C] a metal stick used for moving coal or wood in a fire

poker-faced /ˌ.. ˈ.◂/ *adj* showing no signs of interest, amusement, friendliness etc on your face

pok·y, pokey /ˈpəʊki‖ˈpoʊ-/ *adj* **1** too small and not pleasant or comfortable: *a pokey apartment* **2** *AmE* doing things too slowly, especially in an annoying way: *a pokey driver*

po·lar /ˈpəʊlə‖ˈpoʊlər/ *adj* relating to the North or South Pole: *polar ice caps*

polar bear /ˌ.. ˈ.‖ˈ.. ./ *n* [C] a large white bear that lives near the North Pole

po·lar·ize (also **-ise** *BrE*) /ˈpəʊləraɪz‖ˈpoʊ-/ *v* [I,T] *formal* to make people divide into two groups with completely opposite opinions: *The Vietnam War polarized public opinion.* —**polarization** /ˌpəʊləraɪˈzeɪʃən‖-rə-/ *n* [U]

Po·lar·oid /ˈpəʊlərɔɪd‖ˈpoʊ-/ *n* [C,U] *trademark* a camera that uses a special film to produce a photograph very quickly, or a picture taken using this camera

pole /pəʊl‖poʊl/ *n* [C] **1** a long piece of wood or metal: *tent poles* | *a fishing pole* **2 North/South Pole** the most northern and southern point on Earth: *an expedition to the North Pole* **3 be poles apart** to be completely different: *Their political views are poles apart.*

po·lem·ic /pəˈlemɪk/ *n* [C,U] strong arguments that criticize or defend an idea, opinion etc —**polemical** *adj*

pole vault /ˈ. . / *n* [U] a sport in which you jump over a high bar using a special long pole

po·lice¹ /pəˈliːs/ *n* [plural] **the police** the official organization whose job is to catch criminals and make sure that people obey the law: *The police are hunting for the killer of a 14-year-old boy.* | *a police car*

police² *v* [T] to make sure that people obey laws or rules: *new ways of policing the neighborhood* | *an agency that polices the nuclear power industry*

police con·sta·ble /ˌ.. ˈ...◂/ *n* [C] *BrE* a police officer of the lowest rank

police de·part·ment /ˈ. .ˌ../ *n* [C] *AmE* the official police organization in a particular area or city

police force /ˈ. ./ *n* [C] the official police organization in a country or area

po·lice·man /pəˈliːsmən/ *n* [C] a male police officer

police of·fi·cer /ˈ. .ˌ../ *n* [C] a member of the police

police state /ˈ. ./ *n* [C] a country where the government controls people's lives very strictly and people have very little freedom

police sta·tion /ˈ. .ˌ../ *n* [C] a local office of the police

po·lice·wom·an /pəˈliːsˌwʊmən/ *n* [C] a female police officer

pol·i·cy /ˈpɒlɪsi‖ˈpɑː-/ *n* **1** [C,U] a way of doing or dealing with things, especially one that has been officially decided by a political party or organization: *the government's foreign policy* | *The best policy is probably to wait until she calms down.* **2** a written agreement with an insurance company: *a homeowner's policy*

po·li·o /ˈpəʊliəʊ‖ˈpoʊlioʊ/ *n* [C] a serious disease that makes you unable to move your muscles

pol·ish¹ /ˈpɒlɪʃ‖ˈpɑː-/ *v* [T] to make something clean and shiny by rubbing it with a cloth or brush: *Davy spent all morning polishing his car.* —**polisher** *n* [C] —**polishing** *n* [U]

polish sth ↔ off *phr v* [T] *informal* to quickly eat or finish all of something: *The kids polished off the rest of the cake.*

polish sth ↔ up *phr v* [T] to improve something, especially a skill: *I need to polish up my French.*

pol·ish² /ˈpɒlɪʃ‖ˈpɑː-/ *n* **1** [C,U] a liquid, cream etc used for polishing things: *shoe polish* **2** if you give something a polish, you polish it: *I'll just give the table a quick polish.* → see also NAIL POLISH

pol·ished /ˈpɒlɪʃt‖ˈpɑː-/ *adj* **1** shiny because of being rubbed with polish: *polished shoes* **2** [singular] done with great skill and style: *a polished performance*

po·lite /pəˈlaɪt/ *adj* speaking or behaving in a way that is not rude and shows respect for other people: *It's not polite to talk with food in your mouth.* | *polite language* | *He was always very helpful and polite.* —**politely** *adv* —**politeness** *n* [U]

po·lit·i·cal /pəˈlɪtɪkəl/ *adj* **1** relating to the government, politics, and public affairs of a country: *The US has two main political parties.* | *changes to the British political system* **2** interested in or involved in politics: *I'm not really a political person.* —**politically** /-kli/ *adv*

political a·sy·lum /ˌ.... .ˈ../ *n* [U] the right to stay in another country because your political activities have made it too dangerous for you to live in your own country

politically cor·rect /ˌ.... .ˈ./ also **PC** *adj* speaking or behaving in a way that shows you

---

GRAMMAR NOTE: transitive and intransitive (1)
Transitive verbs have an object: *I like your dress.* | *Did you find the key?* These verbs are shown like this: *v* [T]. **Intransitive** verbs do not have an object: *He laughed.* | *I'll wait in the car.* These verbs are shown like this: *v* [I].

are being careful not to offend women, people of a particular race, DISABLED people etc: *It's not politically correct to say 'handicapped' anymore.* —**political correctness** *n* [U]

political pris·on·er /.,... '.../ *n* [C] someone who is put in prison because of political activities or opinions that oppose the government

political sci·ence /.,... '../ *n* [U] the study of politics and government

pol·i·ti·cian /,pɒlɪ'tɪʃən‖,pɑ:-/ *n* [C] someone who works in politics: *Unfortunately politicians are not highly trusted these days.*

po·li·ti·cize (also **-ise** *BrE*) /pə'lɪtɪˌsaɪz/ *v* [T] to make something concerned with politics, or make people interested in politics: *Sport has become much more politicized these days.* —**politicized** *adj*

pol·i·tics /'pɒlɪtɪks‖'pɑ:-/ *n* [U] **1** ideas and activities that are concerned with how a country or area is governed and who has power: *Most young people aren't interested in politics.* **2** the job of being a politician: *He plans to retire from politics before the next election.* **3** when people or groups in a company or organization try to get advantages for themselves: *Colin tries not to get involved in office politics.* **4** someone's political beliefs and opinions: *I'm not sure what Ellen's politics are.*

pol·ka /'pɒlkə, 'pəʊlkə‖'poʊlkə/ *n* [C] a kind of dance, or the music for this dance

polka dot /'.. ./ *adj* have a pattern that consists of many spots on a plain background: *a polka-dot scarf* ➡ see colour picture on page 114

poll¹ /pəʊl‖poʊl/ also **opinion poll** *n* [C] when a lot of people are asked a question in order to find out what most people think about it: *Recent polls show that support for the President is strong.* ➡ see also POLLS

poll² *v* [T] **1** to try to find out what people think about a subject by asking a lot of people the same question: *We polled 600 teachers, asking their opinion about the changes.* **2** to get a particular number of votes at an election: *Clinton polled over 50 percent of the votes.*

pol·len /'pɒlən‖'pɑ:-/ *n* [U] a powder produced by flowers, which is carried by the wind or insects to make other flowers produce seeds

pollen count /'.. ./ *n* [C] a measurement of the amount of pollen in the air

pol·li·nate /'pɒlɪneɪt‖'pɑ:-/ *v* [T] to make a flower or plant produce seeds by giving it POLLEN —**pollination** /,pɒlɪ'neɪʃən‖,pɑ:-/ *n* [U]

polling day /'.. ./ *n* [C] the day when people vote in an election

polling sta·tion /'.. ,../ also **polling place** /'.. ,./ *AmE* — *n* [C] the place where you can go to vote in an election

polls /pəʊlz‖poʊlz/ *n* [plural] **the polls** when people vote in an election: **go to the polls** (=vote): *French voters go to the polls tomorrow.*

poll·ster /'pəʊlstə‖'poʊlstər/ *n* [C] someone who asks questions to find out what most people think about a subject, especially politics

pol·lut·ant /pə'lu:tənt/ *n* [C] a substance that pollutes the air, water etc

pol·lute /pə'lu:t/ *v* [I,T] to make air, water, soil etc dirty or dangerous: *companies that pollute the environment* —**polluter** *n* [C]

pol·lut·ed /pə'lu:tɪd/ *adj* full of pollution: *The rivers are heavily polluted.* (=badly polluted)

pol·lu·tion /pə'lu:ʃən/ *n* [U] damage caused to the environment by harmful chemicals and waste: *Pollution levels are dangerously high in many of our rivers.* ➡ see also NOISE POLLUTION

po·lo /'pəʊləʊ‖'poʊloʊ/ *n* [U] a game played between two teams riding horses, who hit a small ball with long wooden hammers

polo neck /'.. ./ *n* [C] *BrE* a SWEATER with a band that covers most of your neck; TURTLENECK *AmE*

pol·ter·geist /'pɒltəgaɪst‖'poʊltər-/ *n* [C] a spirit that moves objects around and causes strange noises

pol·y·es·ter /'pɒliestə, ,pɒli'estə‖'pɑ:liestər/ *n* [U] an artificial material used for making cloth

po·lyg·a·my /pə'lɪgəmi/ *n* [U] the custom of having more than one wife or husband at the same time —**polygamous** *adj*

pol·y·sty·rene /,pɒli'staɪri:n‖,pɑ:-/ *n* [U] *especially BrE* a light plastic substance, used especially to make containers

pol·y·tech·nic /,pɒli'teknɪk‖,pɑ:-/ *n* [C] a college where you can study practical or technical subjects. In 1992 all polytechnics in Britain became universities.

pol·y·thene /'pɒliθi:n‖'pɑ:-/ *n* [U] *BrE* a type of thin plastic material, used especially for making bags

pom·e·gran·ate /'pɒmɪˌgrænət‖'pɑ:mə-/ *n* [C] a round fruit with thick red skin and many seeds

pomp /pɒmp‖pɑ:mp/ *n* [U] *formal* all the impressive clothes, decorations, music etc at an important official ceremony

pom·pom /'pɒmpɒm‖'pɑ:mpɑ:m/ *n* [C] a ball of wool used as a decoration on clothes

pom·pous /'pɒmpəs‖'pɑ:m-/ *adj* trying to make people think you are important, especially by using a lot of formal words: *a pompous little man* —**pompously** *adv* —**pomposity** /pɒm'pɒsɪti‖pɑ:m'pɑ:-/ *n* [U]

pond /pɒnd‖pɑ:nd/ *n* [C] a small area of water, especially one that is made in a field or garden: *fish swimming in the pond*

pon·der /'pɒndə‖'pɑ:ndər/ *v* [I,T] *literary* to think carefully and seriously about something: *She pondered her answer for a long time.*

pon·der·ous /'pɒndərəs‖'pɑ:n-/ *adj* **1** boring and too serious: *a ponderous style of writing* **2** moving slowly because of being very big: *an elephant's ponderous walk*

pong /pɒŋ‖pɑ:ŋ/ *v* [I] *BrE informal* to have an unpleasant smell: *It really pongs in here.* —**pong** *n* [singular]

pon·tif·i·cate /pɒn'tɪfɪˌkeɪt‖pɑ:n-/ *v* [I] to give your opinion about something in a way that shows you think you are always right: *pontificating about moral values*

po·ny /'pəʊni‖'poʊ-/ *n* [C] a small horse

po·ny·tail /'pəʊniteɪl‖'poʊ-/ *n* [C] hair tied at the back of your head so that it hangs down like a horse's tail ➡ see colour picture on page 244

pony-trekking /'.. ,../ *n* [U] *BrE* the activity of riding through the countryside on ponies

pooch /pu:tʃ/ *n* [C] *informal humorous* a dog

poo·dle /'pu:dl/ *n* [C] a type of dog with thick curly hair

pooh-pooh /ˌpuː ˈpuː/ v [T] *informal* to say that you think an idea, suggestion etc is silly or useless: *He pooh-poohs everything I say.*

pool[1] /puːl/ n **1** [C] a place that has been made for people to swim in: *Does the hotel have a pool?* **2** [U] a game in which you use a long stick to hit numbered balls into holes at the edge of a table **3 a pool of water/oil/light etc** a small area of water, oil etc on a surface: *Creighton lay there in a pool of blood.* **4** [C] a small area of still water in the ground: *A shallow pool had formed among the rocks.* **5** [C] a quantity of money, things, or workers that is shared by several people: *a car pool*

pool[2] v [T] if people pool their money, knowledge etc, they put it all together in order to share it: *a meeting to pool ideas*

pools /puːlz/ n **the pools** a GAMBLING competition in Britain in which people try to win money by guessing the results of football games

poor /pɔː‖pʊr/ adj **1** having very little money and not many possessions: *She comes from a poor family.*|*a poor country* **2 the poor** people who are poor: *a charity that distributes food to the poor* **3** something that is poor is not as good as it should be: *a poor standard of work*|*poor health* **4** [only before noun] *spoken* used to show that you feel sorry for someone: *The poor girl gets blamed for everything that goes wrong.* **5** not good at doing something: *a poor swimmer*

poor·ly[1] /ˈpɔːliː‖ˈpʊrliː/ adv badly: *a poorly paid job*

poorly[2] adj *BrE informal* ill: *Rita was poorly last week.*

pop[1] /pɒp‖pɑːp/ v **-pped, -pping 1 pop in/ out/along etc** *spoken* to go somewhere for a very short time: *Dave's popped out to get some bread.* **2 pop sth in/on/into etc** *BrE spoken* to put something somewhere: *Pop the box in the corner.* **3 pop out/up** to suddenly come out of something: *A tiny chick's head popped out of the egg.* **4** [I,T] to make a sound like a small explosion, or to make something make this sound: *Champagne corks were popping.* **5** also **pop out** [I] if someone's eyes pop, or pop out, they look very surprised **6 pop the question** *informal* to ask someone to marry you

pop up *phr v* [I] *informal* to appear suddenly and unexpectedly: *His face keeps popping up on television.*

pop[2] n **1** [U] modern music that is popular with young people: *a pop singer* **2** [C] a sudden short sound like a small explosion: *The balloon burst with a loud pop.* **3** [U] *informal* a sweet FIZZY drink **4** [singular] *AmE old-fashioned* father

pop·corn /ˈpɒpkɔːn‖ˈpɑːpkɔːrn/ n [U] corn that is heated until it swells. You eat it with salt or sugar.

Pope /pəʊp‖poʊp/ n **the Pope** the leader of the Roman Catholic Church

pop·lar /ˈpɒplə‖ˈpɑːplər/ n [C] a tall thin tree

pop·py /ˈpɒpiː‖ˈpɑː-/ n [C] a bright red flower with small black seeds

pop quiz /ˈ. ./ n [C] *AmE* a short test given to students when they do not expect it

Pop·si·cle /ˈpɒpsɪkəl‖ˈpɑːp-/ n [C] *AmE trademark* a piece of ice, tasting of fruit, that you suck on a stick

pop·u·lace /ˈpɒpjʊləs‖ˈpɑː-/ n [singular] *formal* the ordinary people of a country

pop·u·lar /ˈpɒpjʊlə‖ˈpɑːpjʊlər/ adj **1** liked by a lot of people: *a popular teacher*|+ **with** *The nightclub is popular with tourists.* → opposite UN-POPULAR **2 popular belief/opinion/view etc** a belief etc that a lot of people have **3** for ordinary people: *popular entertainment*|*the popular press*

pop·u·lar·i·ty /ˌpɒpjʊˈlærˌtiː‖ˌpɑː-/ n [U] when a lot of people like someone or something, or the number of people who like someone or something: *The band's popularity has grown steadily in the last five years.*

pop·u·lar·ize (also **-ise** *BrE*) /ˈpɒpjʊləraɪz‖ˈpɑː-/ v [T] to make a lot of people become interested in something or make them know about it and understand it: *Jane Fonda popularized aerobic exercise.*

pop·u·lar·ly /ˈpɒpjʊləliː‖ˈpɑːpjʊlər-/ adv **popularly believed/called/known etc** believed, called etc by many people: *It's popularly believed that people need eight hours sleep a night.*

pop·u·late /ˈpɒpjʊleɪt‖ˈpɑː-/ v [T] **be populated** if an area is populated by a group of people, they live there: *The Central Highlands are populated mainly by peasant farmers.*|**densely populated** (=a lot of people live there)|**sparsely populated** (=very few people live there)

pop·u·la·tion /ˌpɒpjʊˈleɪʃən‖ˌpɑː-/ n **1** [C,U] the number of people living in an area, country etc: *What's the population of Tokyo?*|**population explosion** (=when there is a sudden large increase in population) **2** [C] all of the people who live in an area, or all the people of a particular type: *The whole population came out to welcome us home.*|*30% of the male population suffer from heart disease.*

pop·u·lous /ˈpɒpjʊləs‖ˈpɑː-/ adj *formal* having a large population: *Sichuan is China's most populous province.*

porce·lain /ˈpɔːslˌn‖ˈpɔːrsəlˌn/ n [U] **1** a hard shiny white substance that is used to make expensive plates, cups etc **2** plates, cups etc made of this substance

porch /pɔːtʃ‖pɔːrtʃ/ n [C] **1** an entrance covered by a roof built onto a house or church **2** *AmE* a VERANDA

por·cu·pine /ˈpɔːkjʊpaɪn‖ˈpɔːr-/ n [C] an animal with long needles on its back and sides

pore[1] /pɔː‖pɔːr/ n [C] one of the small holes in your skin that SWEAT can pass through

pore[2] v

pore over sth *phr v* [T] to read or look at something very carefully for a long time: *We spent all day poring over wedding magazines.*

pork /pɔːk‖pɔːrk/ n [U] meat from pigs: *pork chops*

por·nog·ra·phy /pɔːˈnɒɡrəfiː‖pɔːrˈnɑːɡ-/ also **porn** /pɔːn‖pɔːrn/ n [U] magazines, films etc that are intended to make people feel sexually excited — **pornographic** /ˌpɔːnəˈɡræfɪk◂‖ˌpɔːr-/ also **porn** adj: *porn videos*

po·rous /ˈpɔːrəs/ adj allowing liquid, air etc to pass through slowly: *porous rock*

por·poise /ˈpɔːpəs‖ˈpɔːr-/ n [C] a large sea animal similar to a DOLPHIN

por·ridge /ˈpɒrɪdʒ‖ˈpɑː-, ˈpɔː-/ n [U] food made by boiling OATMEAL in milk or water

port /pɔːt‖pɔːrt/ n **1** [C,U] an area or town where ships arrive and leave from: *the port of Dover* | **in port** *The ship was back in port after a week at sea.* **2** [C] a place on the outside of a computer where you can connect another piece of equipment **3** [U] a strong sweet Portuguese wine **4** [U] the left side of a ship or aircraft when you are looking towards the front

por·ta·ble /ˈpɔːtəbəl‖ˈpɔːr-/ adj easy to carry: *a portable television* —**portable** n [C]

por·ter /ˈpɔːtəl‖ˈpɔːrtər/ n [C] someone whose job is to carry bags at airports, stations, hotels etc

port·fo·li·o /pɔːtˈfəʊliəʊ‖pɔːrtˈfəʊlioʊ/ n [C] a set of pictures that an artist, photographer etc uses as examples of his or her work, or the case used for carrying them in

port·hole /ˈpɔːthəʊl‖ˈpɔːrthoʊl/ n [C] a small round window in the side of a ship or plane

por·ti·co /ˈpɔːtɪkəʊ‖ˈpɔːrtɪkoʊ/ n [C] a covered entrance to a building, consisting of a roof supported by PILLARS

por·tion /ˈpɔːʃən‖ˈpɔːr-/ n [C] **1** a part of something: *A large portion of the money has been spent on advertising.* | *Both drivers must bear a portion of the blame.* **2** an amount of food for one person: *A small portion of icecream costs $5.*

port·ly /ˈpɔːtli‖ˈpɔːr-/ adj fairly fat: *a portly gentleman*

por·trait /ˈpɔːtrɪt‖ˈpɔːr-/ n [C] **1** a painting, drawing, or photograph of a person: *a portrait of the queen* **2** a description in a story, film etc of someone or something: *The novel is a portrait of life in Harlem in the 1940s.*

por·tray /pɔːˈtreɪ/ v [T] **1** to describe or show something or someone in a story, film etc: *a film that portrays the life of Charlie Chaplin* | **portray sb/sth as sth** (=show someone or something in a particular way): *Diana is portrayed as the victim of a loveless marriage.* **2** to act the part of a character in a play: *Robin Williams portrayed Peter Pan in the movie.* —**portrayal** n [C,U] *an excellent portrayal of King Arthur*

pose¹ /pəʊz‖poʊz/ v **1** **pose a problem/threat/danger** to cause a problem or danger: *Nuclear waste poses a threat to the environment.* **2** to sit or stand in a particular position in order to be photographed or painted: **+ for** *The astronauts posed for pictures alongside the shuttle.* **3** **pose a question** formal to ask a question that needs to be carefully thought about: *His speech poses a number of interesting questions.* **4** **pose as** to pretend to be someone else: *He obtained the drugs by posing as a doctor.*

pose² n **1** [C] the position that someone stands or sits in while they are being painted or photographed **2** [singular] BrE when someone behaves in a way that is different from their real character and pretends to be a different kind of person: *He's not really the macho type – it's all just a pose.*

posh /pɒʃ‖pɑːʃ/ adj **1** expensive and used by rich people: *a posh restaurant* **2** BrE informal behaving or speaking in a way that is typical of people from a high social class: *a posh voice*

po·si·tion¹ /pəˈzɪʃən/ n **1** [C usually singular] the situation that someone is in: *He's in a difficult position right now.* | *The current financial position is not good.* | **be in a position to**

do sth (=be able to do something): *I'm afraid I'm not in a position to advise you.* **2** the way someone stands or sits, or the direction that an object is pointing in: *He raised himself into an upright sitting position.* | *Make sure the switch is in the 'off' position.* **3** [C] the level of importance that someone has when compared with other people in a society or organization: *the position of women in our society* **4** [C] the opinion or attitude that a government, organization etc has about a subject: **+ on** *What's the party's position on foreign aid?* **5** [C,U] the place where someone or something is, in relation to other things: *the sun's position in the sky* | **in position** (=in the place where something is supposed to be): *the screws that held the shelf in position* **6** [C] formal a job: *He's applied for a position at the bank.* **7** [C] where you play in relation to other players in a team game, such as football: *"What position did Swift play?" "He was goalkeeper."* **8** [C] your place in a race or competition, for example whether you come first, second, or third: *Schumacher has moved into second position.*

position² v [T] to put something or someone in a place: *Police positioned themselves around the bank.*

pos·i·tive /ˈpɒzətɪv‖ˈpɑː-/ adj **1** hopeful and confident: *a positive attitude to life* **2** [not before noun] very sure that something is true: *"Are you sure you don't want a drink?" "Positive."* **3** encouraging someone or supporting an idea: *The response to our proposals has been very positive.* **4** showing clearly and definitely that something is true: *the first positive evidence that life exists on other planets* **5** if a scientific test has a positive result, it shows that a substance or condition is present: *Her pregnancy test was positive.* **6** having a good or useful effect: *Living abroad has been a positive experience.* **7** technical a positive number is higher than zero **8** technical having the type of electrical charge that is carried by PROTONs, shown by a (+) sign → compare NEGATIVE¹

pos·i·tive·ly /ˈpɒzətɪvli‖ˈpɑː-/ adv **1** spoken used to emphasize what you are saying: *Some patients positively enjoy being in hospital.* **2** in a way that shows you agree with something and want it to succeed: *News of the changes was viewed positively by most people.*

pos·sess /pəˈzes/ v [T] **1** formal to own or have something: *The fire destroyed everything he possessed.* | *She possesses a great talent for poetry.* **2** **what possessed you/him etc?** spoken used when someone has done something stupid and you cannot understand why: *What possessed you to sell the car?* —**possessor** n [C]

pos·sessed /pəˈzest/ adj controlled by an evil spirit

pos·ses·sion /pəˈzeʃən/ n **1** [C usually plural] something that you own: *When they left, they had to sell most of their possessions.* **2** [U] formal when you have or own something: **in possession of sth** (=having something): *He was found in possession of stolen goods.* | **have sth in your possession** *I have in my possession a number of secret documents.* | **take possession of sth** (=start to own something, or take something from someone): *When do you actually take possession of the house?*

pos·ses·sive¹ /pəˈzesɪv/ adj **1** wanting all of someone's love and attention for yourself: *I love*

Dave, but he's very possessive. **2** unwilling to let other people use your things —**possessiveness** *n* [U]

possessive² *n* [C] a word such as 'my', 'mine', 'your', or 'their', used to show who something belongs to

pos·si·bil·i·ty /ˌpɒsəˈbɪlətiǁˌpɑː-/ *n* **1** [C,U] something that may happen or may be true: **+ of** *the possibility of an enemy attack* | *There's a real possibility that people will lose their jobs.* **2** [C] one of the things that you could try to do: *Beth decided that she wanted to start her own business, and began to explore the possibilities.*

pos·si·ble /ˈpɒsəbəlǁˈpɑː-/ *adj* **1** if something is possible, it can be done: **it is possible to do sth** *Is it possible to pay by credit card?* | **if possible** (=if it is possible): *I want to get back by 5 o'clock, if possible.* | **as much/soon/quickly etc as possible** (=as much, as soon etc as you can): *We must get her to hospital as quickly as possible.* → opposite IMPOSSIBLE **2** something that is possible may happen or may be true, but is not certain: *They were warned of all the possible risks and dangers.* | **it is possible (that)** *It's possible we might be late.* **3** **the best/worst/greatest etc possible** the best, worst etc that can exist: *She was determined to get the best possible price for her paintings.*

pos·si·bly /ˈpɒsəbliǁˈpɑː-/ *adv* **1** used to say that something may be true, but you are not sure; perhaps: *The journey will take three hours – possibly more.* **2** **can/could possibly** used to emphasize that something is or is not possible: *I couldn't possibly eat all that!* | *We did everything we possibly could to help them.* **3** *spoken* used when you are asking someone something very politely: *I wonder if you could possibly help me?*

post- /pəʊstǁpoʊst/ *prefix* later than; after: *post-war* (=after a war)

post¹ /pəʊstǁpoʊst/ *n* **1** [U] *BrE* the official system for sending letters, packages etc; MAIL: *The cheque's in the post.* | **by post** *He sent it by post.* **2** [U] *BrE* letters or packages that are delivered to your house; MAIL: *Is there any post for me?* **3** [C] an upright wooden or metal pole that is stuck into the ground **4** [C] an important job: *She was offered the post of Sales Manager.* **5** [C] the place where a soldier or guard has to be: *The guards cannot leave their posts.*

post² *v* [T] **1** *BrE* to send a letter or package by putting it in a POSTBOX or taking it to a POST OFFICE; MAIL: *I must post that letter to Clare today.* **2** also **post up** to put a notice about something on a wall or board: *They've posted warning signs on the gate.* **3** to send someone somewhere, especially to a foreign country, to do a job there: *a young diplomat who had been posted to Cairo* **4** **keep sb posted** to regularly tell someone the latest news about something

post·age /ˈpəʊstɪdʒǁˈpoʊs-/ *n* [U] the money charged for sending a letter or package by post

post·al /ˈpəʊstlǁˈpoʊs-/ *adj* [only before noun] connected with the official service that

takes letters from one place to another: *postal workers*

postal or·der /ˈ.. ˌ../ *n* [C] *BrE* an official paper that you buy at a POST OFFICE as a safe way of sending money by post

post·box /ˈpəʊstbɒksǁˈpoʊstbɑːks/ *n* [C] *BrE* a box in a public place where you put letters that you want to send; MAILBOX *AmE*

post·card /ˈpəʊstkɑːdǁˈpoʊstkɑːrd/ *n* [C] a card, often with a picture on the front, that you can send by post without an envelope: *a postcard of Paris* → see picture at CARD

post·code /ˈpəʊstkəʊdǁˈpoʊstkoʊd/ *n* [C] *BrE* a group of letters and numbers that you put at the end of someone's address so that letters can be delivered more quickly; ZIP CODE *AmE*

post·er /ˈpəʊstəǁˈpoʊstər/ *n* [C] a large notice, picture, etc used to advertise something or as a decoration

pos·ter·i·ty /pɒˈsterətiǁpɑː-/ *n* [U] the people who will live after you are dead: **for posterity** *I'm saving these pictures for posterity.*

post·grad·u·ate /ˌpəʊstˈɡrædʒuətǁˌpoʊst-ˈɡrædʒuət/ *n* [C] *BrE* someone who is studying at a university to get a MASTER'S DEGREE or PHD; GRADUATE student *AmE* —**postgraduate** *adj*: *postgraduate students*

post·hu·mous /ˈpɒstjʊməsǁˈpɑːstʃə-/ *adj* happening after someone's death —**posthumously** *adv*: *His last book was published posthumously.*

post·ing /ˈpəʊstɪŋǁˈpoʊs-/ *n* [C] *especially BrE* when someone is sent to another place to do a job

post·man /ˈpəʊstmənǁˈpoʊst-/ *n* [C] *BrE* someone whose job is to collect and deliver letters; MAILMAN *AmE*

post·mark /ˈpəʊstmɑːkǁˈpoʊstmɑːrk/ *n* [C] a mark on an envelope that shows the place and time it was sent —**postmark** *v* [T]

post·mor·tem /ˌpəʊstˈmɔːtəmǁˌpoʊstˈmɔːr-/ *n* [C] an official examination of a dead body to discover why the person died

post·na·tal /ˌpəʊstˈneɪtl◂ǁˌpoʊst-/ *adj* relating to the time after a baby is born: *postnatal care*

post of·fice /ˈ. ˌ../ *n* [C] a place where you can buy stamps, and send letters and packages

post·pone /pəʊsˈpəʊnǁpoʊsˈpoʊn/ *v* [T] to change an event to a later time or date: *The game was postponed because of rain.* —**postponement** *n* [C,U]

post·script /ˈpəʊsˌskrɪptǁˈpoʊs-/ *n* [C] a PS

pos·ture /ˈpɒstʃəǁˈpɑːstʃər/ *n* [C,U] the way that you sit or stand, or the position your body is in: *By maintaining good posture you can avoid back pain.*

po·sy /ˈpəʊziǁˈpoʊ-/ *n* [C] *literary* a small BUNCH of flowers

pot¹ /pɒtǁpɑːt/ *n* **1** [C] a round container, especially one used for cooking or storing food: *pots and pans* | *a pot of honey* | *a plant growing in a pot* **2** [C] a container for pouring hot tea or

---

GRAMMAR NOTE: transitive and **intransitive (2)**
Some verbs can be used **transitive** or **intransitive**. For example: **read** *v* [T,I]
• Transitive: *I can't read your handwriting.*
• Intransitive: *Tom learned to read at the age of four.*

coffee **3 go to pot** *informal* if an organization or a place goes to pot, its condition becomes worse because no one takes care of it: *The business went to pot after George died.* **4** [U] *old-fashioned* MARIJUANA

pots

a teapot

a coffeepot

a pot of paint

a flowerpot

pot² *v* [T] **-tted, -tting** to put a plant in a pot filled with soil

po·ta·to /pəˈteɪtəʊ‖-toʊ/ *n* [C,U], *plural* **potatoes** a round white vegetable with a brown or pale yellow skin, that grows under the ground ➜ see picture at VEGETABLES ➜ see also **hot potato** (HOT¹)

potato chip /.ˈ.. ./ *n* [C] *AmE* one of a quantity of thin hard pieces of potato cooked in oil that are sold in packages; CRISP *BrE*

po·tent /ˈpəʊtənt‖ˈpoʊ-/ *adj* powerful and effective: *potent drugs* —**potency** *n* [U]

po·ten·tial¹ /pəˈtenʃəl/ *adj* [only before noun] a potential problem, advantage, customer etc is not a problem, advantage etc now, but may become one in the future: *a potential danger* | *The salesmen were eager to impress potential customers.* —**potentially** *adv*: *a potentially dangerous situation*

potential² *n* **1** [singular] the possibility that something will happen or develop in a particular way: *There's a potential for conflict in the area.* **2** [U] natural abilities or qualities that may possibly develop and make someone or something very successful or useful: *She was told she had great potential as a singer.*

pot·hole /ˈpɒthəʊl‖ˈpɑːthoʊl/ *n* [C] **1** a hole in the surface of a road **2** a natural hole deep under the ground that leads to CAVEs

pot·hol·ing /ˈpɒtˌhəʊlɪŋ‖ˈpɑːtˌhoʊl-/ *n* [U] the sport of climbing down inside holes under the ground

po·tion /ˈpəʊʃən‖ˈpoʊ-/ *n* [C] *literary* a drink that is intended to have a magic effect: *a love potion*

pot luck /ˌ. ˈ./ *n* **take pot luck** *informal* to take what is offered without having any choice

pot shot /ˈ. ./ *n* **take a pot shot at** *informal* to shoot at something without aiming carefully

pot·ted /ˈpɒtɪd‖ˈpɑː-/ *adj* **1** *BrE* potted meat or fish has been made into a PASTE and can be spread on bread **2** a potted plant is grown in a pot indoors **3 potted history/version etc** *BrE* a short description of something that gives only the main details

pot·ter¹ /ˈpɒtə‖ˈpɑːtər/ also **potter around/about** *v* [I] *BrE* to spend time slowly doing pleasant things: *pottering in the garden*

potter² *n* [C] someone who makes pottery

pot·ter·y /ˈpɒtəri‖ˈpɑː-/ *n* [U] **1** pots, dishes etc made out of baked clay **2** the activity of making objects out of baked clay

pot·ty¹ /ˈpɒti‖ˈpɑːti/ *n* [C] *informal* a plastic pot used by very young children as a toilet

potty² *adj* *BrE informal* crazy or silly: *a potty idea*

pouch /paʊtʃ/ *n* [C] **1** a small leather or cloth bag **2** a pocket of skin that animals such as KANGAROOs keep their babies in ➜ see picture at KANGAROO

poul·try /ˈpəʊltri‖ˈpoʊl-/ *n* [U] chickens, ducks etc that are kept on farms, or the meat from these birds

pounce /paʊns/ *v* [I] to suddenly jump towards a person or animal in order to catch them: *a cat pouncing on a mouse*

pounce on sb/sth *phr v* [T] to immediately criticize something that someone has said: *She would pounce on any grammatical mistakes.*

pound¹ /paʊnd/ *n* [C] **1** written abbreviation **lb**; a unit for measuring weight, equal to 16 OUNCES or 453.6 grams: *a pound of apples* **2** written sign **£**; the standard unit of money in Britain and some other countries **3** a coin or piece of paper worth this amount

pound² *v* **1** [I,T] to hit something hard, many times, making a lot of noise: *We were woken by someone pounding on the door.* | *Enemy guns pounded the city until morning.* **2** [I] if your heart pounds, it beats very quickly **3** [I] to walk or run quickly with heavy steps: *He pounded up the stairs in front of her.* **4** [T] to crush something by hitting it many times

pour /pɔː‖pɔːr/ *v* **1** [T] to make a liquid flow out of or into something: **pour sth into/down etc** *Pour the milk into a jug.* | **pour sb sth** *Why don't you pour yourself another drink?* ➜ see colour picture on page 439 **2** [I] to flow quickly and in large amounts: **+ from/out of etc** *Water was pouring from a crack in the pipe.* **3** [I] to rain heavily: **it's pouring** *It's been pouring down all afternoon.* **4** [I] if people or things pour into or out of a place, a lot of them arrive or leave at the same time: **+ in/out of** *Letters of complaint poured in.*

pour sth ↔ **out** *phr v* [T] to tell someone all your unhappy thoughts or feelings: *Sonia poured out her grief in a letter to her sister.*

pout /paʊt/ *v* [I,T] to push out your lips because you are annoyed, or in order to look sexually attractive —**pout** *n* [C]

pov·er·ty /ˈpɒvəti‖ˈpɑːvərti/ *n* [U] when people have very little money: *She was shocked by the poverty she saw in parts of Africa.* | **in poverty** *families living in extreme poverty*

poverty-strick·en /ˈ... ˌ../ *adj* extremely poor: *a poverty-stricken area*

POW /ˌpiː əʊ ˈdʌbəljuː‖-oʊ-/ *n* [C] the abbreviation of PRISONER OF WAR: *a POW camp*

pow·der¹ /ˈpaʊdə‖-ər/ *n* [C,U] a dry substance in the form of very small grains: *talcum powder*

powder² *v* [T] to put powder on your skin

pow·dered /ˈpaʊdəd‖-ərd/ *adj* produced or sold in the form of powder: *powdered milk*

pow·der·y /ˈpaʊdəri/ *adj* like powder: *powdery snow*

pow·er[1] /ˈpaʊəll paʊr/ *n* **1** [U] control over people or events: *the struggle for power within the union | the immense power of the press | + over The company has too much power over its employees. | be in sb's power* (=be controlled by someone) **2** [U] political control of a country: *be in power The Socialists have been in power since the revolution. | come to power* (=begin to control a country): *De Gaulle came to power in 1958.* **3** [U] energy such as electricity that can be used to make a machine work: *nuclear power | power cut* (= when the electricity supply suddenly stops): *The storm caused a power cut.* **4** [C,U] the legal right or authority to do something: *power to do sth The police have powers to stop and search people.* **5** [C] a country that is very strong and important: *a meeting of world powers* **6** [C] force or physical strength: *the power of the explosion* **7** [C,U] a natural or special ability to do something: *He lost the power of speech after the accident.* **8 do everything in your power** to do everything that you are able to do: *I did everything in my power to save her.* **9 the powers that be** *informal* the people who have positions of authority

power[2] *v* **1** [T] to supply power to a machine: *The camera is powered by a small battery.* **2 battery-powered/nuclear-powered etc** made to work by power from a BATTERY etc

pow·er·ful /ˈpaʊəfəll paʊr-/ *adj* **1** able to control and influence people and events: *a meeting of the world's most powerful leaders* **2** having a lot of physical power, strength, or force: *a powerful engine | the lion's powerful jaws* **3** having a strong effect: *Love is a powerful emotion. | a powerful argument/speech | powerful drugs* —**powerfully** *adv*

pow·er·less /ˈpaʊələsll paʊr-/ *adj* unable to control what happens or prevent something from happening: *The people of Hungary were powerless against the tanks of the Red Army.* —**powerlessness** *n* [U]

power-nap·ping /ˈ.. ,../ *n* [U] when someone sleeps for a short time during the daytime so that they can work more efficiently later in the day —**power-nap** *v,n*

power sta·tion /ˈ.. ,../ also **power plant** /ˈ.. ,./ *AmE* — *n* [C] a building where electricity is made → see colour picture on page 278

power tool /ˈ.. ./ *n* [C] a tool that works by electricity

pp the written abbreviation of PAGES: *Read pp 20–35.*

PR /ˌpiː ˈɑːll ˈɑːr/ *n* [U] PUBLIC RELATIONS

prac·ti·ca·ble /ˈpræktɪkəbəl/ *adj formal* something that is practicable can be done successfully

prac·ti·cal[1] /ˈpræktɪkəl/ *adj* **1** relating to real situations and events rather than ideas: *How much practical experience of classroom teaching have you had?* **2** sensible and good at dealing with problems: *Be practical! We can't afford all these expensive luxuries.* **3** designed to be useful rather than attractive: *I wish you'd choose shoes that were more practical for everyday use.* **4** good at repairing or making things with your hands: *I'm not very practical – I don't know the first thing about cooking.*

practical[2] *n* [C] *BrE* a lesson or test where you do or make something rather than writing: *a chemistry practical*

prac·ti·cal·i·ty /ˌpræktɪˈkælɪti/ *n* **1 practicalities** [plural] the real facts of a situation, rather than ideas about how it might be: *We have to think about practicalities – how much will it cost?* **2** [U] how sensible and possible an idea is: *It's a great idea, but I'm not sure about the practicality of it.*

practical joke /ˌ... ˈ./ *n* [C] a trick that is intended to surprise someone and make other people laugh at them

prac·ti·cal·ly /ˈpræktɪkli/ *adv* **1** *spoken* almost: *The theatre was practically empty.* **2** in a sensible way

prac·tice /ˈpræktɪs/ *n* **1** [U] **a)** regular activity that you do to improve a skill: *It takes a lot of practice to be a good piano player.* **b)** the period of time when you do this: *It's football practice tonight.* **2** [C,U] something that people do often or regularly in a particular way: *dangerous working practices | The use of chemical sprays has become common practice.* **3 in practice** used to say what really happens, instead of what people think may happen: *It looks difficult to make, but in practice it's quite easy.* **4** [C] the work of a doctor or lawyer, or the place where they work: *She has a successful legal practice.* **5 be out of practice** to be unable to do something well because you have not done it for a long time: *I'd like to sing with you, but I'm so out of practice.* **6 put sth into practice** to start using an idea, plan etc: *The new methods will be put into practice next month.*

prac·tise *BrE*, **practice** *AmE* /ˈpræktɪs/ *v* **1** [I,T] to do an activity regularly to improve your skill or ability: *I came to Paris to practise my French. | + for He's practicing for his driving test.* **2** [I,T] to work as a doctor or lawyer: *Bill is practising law in Glasgow now.* **3** [T] to regularly do things according to a custom, religion, or set of rules: *communities where black magic is still practised* **4 practise what you preach** to do what you always say other people should do

prac·tised *BrE*, **practiced** *AmE* /ˈpræktɪst/ *adj* good at doing something because you have done it many times before: *skilful salesmen, practised in the art of persuasion*

prac·tis·ing *BrE*, **practicing** *AmE* /ˈpræktɪsɪŋ/ *adj* **practising Catholic/Jew/ Muslim etc** someone who obeys the rules of a particular religion

prac·ti·tion·er /prækˈtɪʃənəll -ər/ *n* [C] *formal* someone who works as a doctor or lawyer: *a medical practitioner*

prag·mat·ic /prægˈmætɪk/ *adj* dealing with problems in a sensible and practical way rather than following a set of ideas: *a pragmatic approach to education* —**pragmatism** /ˈprægmətɪzəm/ *n* [U] —**pragmatist** *n* [C]

prai·rie /ˈpreərill ˈpreri/ *n* [C] a large area of flat land in North America that is covered in grass

praise[1] /preɪz/ *v* [T] **1** to say that someone has done something well or that you admire them **praise sb for sth** *Mr Lee praised Jill for the quality of her work.* **2** to give thanks to God: *Praise Allah.*

praise[2] *n* [U] things you say to praise someone

or something: **be full of praise for** *Most parents are full of praise for the school.*

praise·wor·thy /ˈpreɪzwɜːðiǁ-ɜːr-/ *adj formal* deserving praise

pram /præm/ *n* [C] *BrE* a thing on wheels that you can put a baby in and push around; BABY CARRIAGE *AmE*

prance /prɑːnsǁpræns/ *v* [I] **1** to walk or dance around proudly, showing yourself to people: *He started prancing around in front of the cameras.* **2** if a horse prances, it moves with high steps

prank /præŋk/ *n* [C] a trick that is intended to make someone look silly: *a childish prank*

prat·tle /ˈprætl/ *v* [I] to talk continuously about silly or unimportant things —**prattle** *n* [U]

prawn /prɔːnǁprɒːn/ *n* [C] a small pink sea animal like a SHRIMP that you can eat

pray /preɪ/ *v* [I,T] **1** to speak to God in order to ask for help or give thanks: + **for** *Let us pray for peace.* **2** to hope for something very strongly: *We're praying for good weather for the wedding.*

prayer /preəǁprer/ *n* **1** [C] words that you say to God: **say your prayers** *The children knelt down to say their prayers.* **2** [U] the activity of praying: *the power of prayer* **3** **prayers** [plural] when people pray together at an arranged time: *morning prayers*

pre- /priː/ *prefix* used at the beginning of some words to mean 'before': *prewar* | *preschool*

preach /priːtʃ/ *v* **1** [I,T] to give a speech about a religious subject, usually in a church: *The pastor preached a sermon on forgiveness.* **2** [T] to try to persuade other people to accept an idea, method etc: *politicians who preach fairness and equality* **3** [I] to give advice in a way that annoys people: *I'm sorry, I didn't mean to preach.*

preach·er /ˈpriːtʃəǁ-ər/ *n* [C] someone who gives talks at religious meetings

pre·am·ble /priˈæmbəlǁˈpriːæmbəl/ *n* [C] *formal* a statement at the beginning of a book or speech, explaining what it is about

pre·car·i·ous /prɪˈkeəriəsǁ-ˈker-/ *adj* **1** a precarious situation is likely to become dangerous or result in failure: *The club is in a precarious financial position.* **2** not held in place firmly and likely to fall —**precariously** *adv*

pre·cau·tion /prɪˈkɔːʃənǁ-ˈkɒː-/ *n* [C] something that you do to prevent something bad or dangerous from happening: *fire precautions* | + **against** *precautions against theft* | **take the precaution** *of I took the precaution of telling the police we were going away.* —**precautionary** *adj*: *Residents were evacuated from the area as a precautionary measure.*

pre·cede /prɪˈsiːd/ *v* [T] *formal* to happen or exist before something else: *The fire was preceded by a loud explosion.* —**preceding** *adj* [only before noun] *an increase of 18% on the preceding year* → compare SUCCEED

pre·ce·dence /ˈpresɪdəns/ *n* **take/have precedence (over)** to be considered more important or urgent than something else: *This project takes precedence over everything else.*

pre·ce·dent /ˈpresɪdənt/ *n* [C,U] an action or official decision that is used as an example for a similar action or decision that is taken in the fu-

ture: **set a precedent** *The trial set a precedent for civil rights.*

pre·cinct /ˈpriːsɪŋkt/ *n* [C] **1** shopping/pedestrian precinct *BrE* an area with shops in a town where cars are not allowed **2** *AmE* a part of a city that has its own police force, local government etc: *the 12th precinct*

pre·cincts /ˈpriːsɪŋkts/ *n* [plural] the area of land around an important building: *in the precincts of the cathedral*

pre·cious¹ /ˈpreʃəs/ *adj* **1** very important to you: *precious memories of my wife* **2** valuable because of being rare: *A number of precious objects were stolen.* | **precious metal** (=a rare and valuable metal such as gold or silver) | **precious stone** (=a rare and valuable jewel, such as a diamond or ruby)

precious² *adv* **precious little/few** *informal* very little or very few: *We had precious little time left.*

pre·ci·pice /ˈpresɪpɪs/ *n* [C] a very steep side of a mountain or cliff

pre·cip·i·tate¹ /prɪˈsɪpɪteɪt/ *v* [T] *formal* to make something happen suddenly: *The President's death precipitated a huge political crisis.*

pre·cip·i·tate² /prɪˈsɪpɪtɪt/ *adj formal* done too quickly, without thinking carefully: *Avoid taking any precipitate action.*

pre·cip·i·ta·tion /prɪˌsɪpɪˈteɪʃən/ *n* [C,U] *technical* rain or snow that falls on the ground, or the amount that falls

pre·cip·i·tous /prɪˈsɪpɪtəs/ *adj formal* dangerously high or steep: *precipitous cliffs*

pré·cis /ˈpreɪsiːǁpreɪˈsiː/ *n* [C], *plural* **précis** /-iːz/ *formal* a piece of writing giving only the main ideas of a longer piece of writing, speech etc

pre·cise /prɪˈsaɪs/ *adj* **1** exact and correct in every detail: *She gave a precise description of her attacker.* **2** **to be precise** used to add exact details about something: *It's 9 o'clock, or 9.02 to be precise.* **3** [only before noun] exactly correct; SPECIFIC: *No one seems to know the precise cause of the illness.*

pre·cise·ly /prɪˈsaɪsli/ *adv* **1** exactly: *That's precisely what I mean.* | *at precisely 4 o'clock* **2** *spoken* used to say that you agree completely with someone: *"So Harris is responsible for the mistake." "Precisely."*

pre·ci·sion /prɪˈsɪʒən/ *n* [U] when something is measured, described etc very exactly: *The atom's weight can be measured with great precision.*

pre·clude /prɪˈkluːd/ *v* [T] *formal* to make it impossible for something to happen: **preclude sb from (doing) sth** *Bad eyesight may preclude you from driving.*

pre·co·cious /prɪˈkəʊʃəsǁ-ˈkoʊ-/ *adj* a precocious child behaves like an adult in some ways, especially by asking difficult or unusually intelligent questions —**precociously** *adv*

pre·con·ceived /ˌpriːkənˈsiːvd/ *adj* preconceived ideas are formed before you know what something is really like: *He has a lot of preconceived ideas about life in America.*

pre·con·cep·tion /ˌpriːkənˈsepʃən/ *n* [C] an idea that is formed before you know what something is really like

pre·con·di·tion /ˌpriːkənˈdɪʃən/ *n* [C] something that must happen before something else can happen: **+ for/of** *An end to the fighting is a precondition for peace negotiations.*

pre·cur·sor /prɪˈkɜːsəll-ˈkɜːrsər/ *n* [C] *formal* something that existed or happened before something else and influenced its development: **+ of** *a machine that was the precursor of the computer*

pre·date /priːˈdeɪt/ *v* [T] to happen or exist before something else: *animals that predate humans.*

pred·a·tor /ˈpredətəll-ər/ *n* [C] an animal that kills and eats other animals

pred·a·to·ry /ˈpredətərill-tɔːri/ *adj* **1** predatory animals kill and eat other animals **2** trying to use someone's weakness to get an advantage for yourself: *Many people see her not as a victim but as a ruthless, predatory woman.*

pre·de·ces·sor /ˈpriːdɪˌsesəll-ˈpredɪˌsesər/ *n* [C] **1** the person who had a job before the person who has it now: *My predecessor worked here for ten years.* **2** a machine, system etc that existed before another one

pre·des·tined /priːˈdestɪnd/ *adj* something that is predestined is certain to happen and cannot be changed

pre·de·ter·mined /ˌpriːdɪˈtɜːmɪndˌ ll-ɜːr-/ *adj formal* already decided or arranged: *Those taking part will meet at a predetermined location.*

pre·dic·a·ment /prɪˈdɪkəmənt/ *n* [C] a difficult situation where you do not know what is the best thing to do

pred·i·cate /ˈpredɪkɪt/ *n* [C] the part of a sentence that gives information about the subject. In the sentence 'He ran out of the house', 'ran out of the house' is the predicate. → compare SUBJECT[1]

pre·dic·a·tive /prɪˈdɪkətɪvll-ˈpredɪkeɪ-/ *adj* a predicative adjective comes after a verb and describes the subject, for example 'sad' in 'She is sad'.

pre·dict /prɪˈdɪkt/ *v* [T] to say that something will happen: *Experts are predicting an easy victory for the Socialists.* **| + (that)** *We predict that student numbers will double in the next ten years.*

pre·dict·a·ble /prɪˈdɪktəbəl/ *adj* behaving or happening in the way that you expect, and not different or interesting: *As the comedian got older his act became repetitive and his jokes predictable.* —**predictably** *adv*: *Predictably, the new TV show was as bad as the old one.* —**predictability** /prɪˌdɪktəˈbɪlɪti/ *n* [U]

pre·dic·tion /prɪˈdɪkʃən/ *n* [C,U] a statement saying what you expect to happen, or when you make this kind of statement: **make a prediction** *It's hard to make a prediction about who'll win the championship this year.*

pre·di·lec·tion /ˌpriːdɪˈlekʃənll,predlˈek-/ *n* [C] *formal* strong liking for something: *a predilection for chocolate*

pre·dis·posed /ˌpriːdɪsˈpəʊzdll-ˈpoʊzd/ *adj* **predisposed to/towards sth** likely to behave in a particular way, or likely to have particular problems: *Some people are predisposed to depression.*

pre·dis·po·si·tion /ˌpriːdɪspəˈzɪʃən/ *n* [C] a tendency to behave in a particular way, or to have particular problems: **+ to/towards** *a predisposition to violence*

pre·dom·i·nance /prɪˈdɒmɪnənsll-ˈdɑː-/ *n* **1** [singular] when there is more of one type of thing or person in a group than of any other type: **+ of** *the predominance of white people in the audience* **2** [U] the person or thing that has predominance in a group or place has the most power or importance: *rival supermarkets fighting to achieve predominance*

pre·dom·i·nant /prɪˈdɒmɪnəntll-ˈdɑː-/ *adj* more powerful or common than other people or things: *The environment is one of the predominant issues of the nineties.*

pre·dom·i·nant·ly /prɪˈdɒmɪnəntlill-ˈdɑː-/ *adv* mostly or mainly: *a college in a predominantly working class area*

pre·dom·i·nate /prɪˈdɒmɪneɪtll-ˈdɑː-/ *v* [I] to have the most importance, or to be the most in number: *areas where industries such as mining predominate*

pre·em·i·nent /priːˈemɪnənt/ *adj* much more important or powerful than other people or things in a group: *a pre-eminent expert in cancer treatment* —**pre-eminence** *n* [U]

pre·empt /priːˈempt/ *v* [T] to make what someone else has planned to do unnecessary or not effective by doing something first: *The company pre-empted the strike by offering workers an immediate pay increase.* —**pre-emptive** *adj*: *a pre-emptive attack on an enemy naval base*

preen /priːn/ *v* **1** **preen yourself** to spend a lot of time making yourself look attractive: *He's always preening himself in the mirror.* **2** [I,T] if a bird preens, or preens itself, it makes its feathers clean and smooth

pre·ex·ist·ing /ˌ. .ˈ..ˌ/ *adj* existing already, or before something else: *a pre-existing arrangement*

pre·fab·ri·cat·ed /priːˈfæbrɪkeɪtɪd/ *adj* a prefabricated building is built using parts which have been made in a factory and fitted together in another place

pref·ace[1] /ˈprefɪs/ *n* [C] an introduction at the beginning of a book

preface[2] *v* [T] *formal* if you preface what you are going to say with something, you say or do this other thing first: *I'd like to preface my speech with an expression of thanks to the organizers.*

pre·fect /ˈpriːfekt/ *n* [C] *BrE* an older student in a school who has special powers and duties

pre·fer /prɪˈfɜːll-ˈfɜːr/ *v* [T] **-rred, -rring** **1** to like someone or something more than someone or something else: *Would you prefer a hot or a cold drink?* **| prefer sb/sth to sb/sth** *She prefers walking to driving.* **| prefer to do sth** *I'd prefer not to talk about it at the moment.* **| prefer doing sth** *Most kids prefer wearing casual clothes.* **2** **I would prefer it if** *spoken* used to tell someone politely not to do something: *I'd prefer it if you didn't smoke in the house.*

GRAMMAR NOTE: the passive (2)

Most transitive verbs can be made **passive**. If you want to say who or what did the action in a passive sentence, use **by**. ACTIVE: *An American millionaire **bought** the picture.* PASSIVE: *The picture was bought by an American millionaire.*

pref·e·ra·ble /ˈprefərəbəl/ adj better or more suitable: **+ to** *Anything is preferable to war.*

pref·e·ra·bly /ˈprefərəbli/ adv used to show which person, thing, place etc would be the best or most suitable: *You'll need some form of identification, preferably a passport.*

pref·e·rence /ˈprefərəns/ n **1** [C,U] when someone likes something more than something else: *She has her own personal preferences and tastes, like everyone else* | **have a preference (for sth)** *There's strawberry or apricot yoghurt – do you have a preference?* | **in preference to** *Many people go by train in preference to driving.* **2** give/show preference to sb to treat someone better or give them an advantage over other people: *Preference will be given to candidates who speak foreign languages.*

pref·e·ren·tial /ˌprefəˈrenʃəl◂/ adj if you are given preferential treatment you are treated better than another person, giving you an advantage over them: *Why should she get preferential treatment?*

pre·fix /ˈpriːfɪks/ n [C] a group of letters added to the beginning of a word to make a new word ➞ compare AFFIX, SUFFIX

preg·nan·cy /ˈpregnənsi/ n [C,U] the condition of being pregnant: *You should try to avoid alcohol during pregnancy.*

preg·nant /ˈpregnənt/ adj **1** having an unborn baby growing in your body: *She's three months pregnant.* | **get pregnant** *I got pregnant when I was only 16.* **2** a pregnant silence/pause a silence or pause which is full of meaning or emotion that everyone feels but is not expressed in words

pre·his·tor·ic /ˌpriːhɪˈstɒrɪk◂ ‖ -ˈstɔː-, -ˈstɑː-/ adj relating to the time a long way in the past before anything was written down: *prehistoric cave drawings*

prej·u·dice¹ /ˈpredʒʊdʒs/ n [C,U] when people do not like or trust someone who is different to you in some way, for example because they belong to a different race, country, or religion: **+ against** *There's still a lot of prejudice against gay men in employment.* | **racial prejudice** (=because of someone's race): *the problem of racial prejudice in the police force*

prejudice² v [T] **1** to influence someone so that they have an unfair opinion about someone or something : **prejudice sb against sth** *I didn't want to say anything that might prejudice him against her.* **2** to have a bad effect on someone's opportunities or chances of success: *Stories in the newspapers are prejudicing their chances of a fair trial.*

prej·u·diced /ˈpredʒʊdʒst/ adj having an unfair attitude towards someone or something, so that you dislike them without any good reason: **+ against** *He's prejudiced against anyone who doesn't have a degree.*

prej·u·di·cial /ˌpredʒʊˈdɪʃəl◂/ adj formal having a bad or harmful effect on someone or something: **+ to** *Lawson is being held on suspicion of carrying out actions prejudicial to national security.*

pre·lim·i·na·ry¹ /prɪˈlɪmɪnəri‖-neri/ adj [only before noun] happening or done at the beginning of a process, especially in order to prepare for what will come later: *European leaders meet tomorrow for preliminary talks.*

preliminary² n [C usually plural] something that is done at the beginning of an activity, event, or process in order to prepare for it: *the preliminaries of the competition*

prel·ude /ˈpreljuːd/ n **1** be a prelude to sth to happen just before something else, often as an introduction to it: *The attack may be a prelude to full-scale war.* **2** [C] a short piece of music that comes before a longer musical piece

pre·mar·i·tal /priːˈmærɪtəl/ adj happening before marriage: *premarital sex*

pre·ma·ture /ˈpremətʃə, -tʃʊə, ˌpreməˈtʃʊəl ˌpriːməˈtʃʊər◂/ adj **1** happening too early or before the usual time: *Smoking is one of the major causes of premature death.* **2** a premature baby is born too early and is small or weak: *The baby was six weeks premature.* — **prematurely** adv: *The sun causes your skin to age prematurely.*

pre·med·i·tat·ed /priːˈmedɪteɪtɪd‖prɪ-/ adj a premeditated attack or crime is planned in advance: *a premeditated murder* — **premeditation** /priːˌmedɪˈteɪʃən‖prɪ-/ n [U]

prem·i·er¹ /ˈpremiə‖prɪˈmɪr/ n [C] the leader of a government — **premiership** n [U] *at the beginning of Clinton's premiership*

premier² adj formal best or most important: *one of Dublin's premier hotels*

prem·i·ere /ˈpremiə‖prɪˈmɪr/ n [C] the first public performance of a film or play: *a movie premiere* — **premiere** v [I,T]

prem·ise /ˈpremɪs/ n [C] formal a statement or idea that you consider to be true and use to develop other ideas: **+ that** *The argument is based on the premise that men and women are equal.*

prem·is·es /ˈpremɪsɪz/ n [plural] the buildings and land that a shop, company etc uses: **off the premises/on the premises** *No smoking is allowed on the premises.*

pre·mi·um /ˈpriːmiəm/ n **1** [C] an amount of money that you pay for insurance: *health-insurance premiums* **2** [C] an additional amount of money above the usual rate or amount: *The shares are being sold at a premium.* **3** be at a premium to be difficult to get because there is only a limited amount available: *Parking space is at a premium in most cities.* **4** put/place a premium on sth to think that one quality or activity is much more important than others: *schools that put a premium on exam results*

pre·mo·ni·tion /ˌpreməˈnɪʃən, ˌpriː-/ n [C] a feeling that something bad is going to happen: *She had a premonition that her daughter was in danger.*

pre·na·tal /ˌpriːˈneɪtl◂/ adj prenatal care is the medical care given to a woman who is going to have a baby; ANTENATAL *BrE* ➞ compare POST-NATAL

pre·oc·cu·pa·tion /priˌɒkjʊˈpeɪʃən‖-ɑːk-/ n [C,U] **1** when you think or worry about something all the time, or something that you think about a lot: *the usual preoccupations of job, money, and family* | **+ with** *the artist's preoccupation with death* **2** [C] something that you think about a lot

pre·oc·cu·pied /priˈɒkjʊpaɪd‖-ˈɑːk-/ adj thinking or worrying about something a lot, so that you do not pay attention to other things: *I was too preoccupied with my own problems to notice.*

pre·oc·cu·py /prɪˈɒkjʊˌpaɪ‖-ˈɑːk-/ v [T] if something preoccupies you, you think or worry about it a lot

prep·a·ra·tion /ˌprepəˈreɪʃən/ n [U] the time and work that is needed to prepare for something: **+ for** *The England team have begun their preparation for next week's game.* | **+ of** *the preparation of the report*

prep·a·ra·tions /ˌprepəˈreɪʃənz/ n [plural] arrangements for something that is going to happen: *wedding preparations* | **make preparations for sth** *Preparations are being made for the President's visit.*

pre·par·a·to·ry /prɪˈpærətəri‖-tɔːri/ adj done in order to get ready for something: *preparatory negotiations*

preparatory school /ˈ..... ./ n a PREP SCHOOL

pre·pare /prɪˈpeə‖-ˈper/ v **1** [T] to make something ready to be used: *Carol was upstairs preparing a room for the guests.* **2** [I,T] to make plans or arrangements for something that will happen soon, or get yourself ready for it: **+ for** *I haven't even begun to prepare for tomorrow's test.* | *Prepare yourself for a shock.* | **prepare to do sth** *Just as we were preparing to leave, the phone rang.* **3** [T] to give someone the training or skills that they need to do something: **prepare sb for sth** *Our job is to prepare these soldiers for war.* **4** [T] to make food ready to eat: *This dish can be prepared the day before.*

USAGE NOTE: prepare and get ready

Use **prepare** to talk about making or producing something so that it is ready to be used: *Edwards only had two days to prepare the report.* | *This dish can be prepared ahead of time.* Use **get ready** to talk about doing the things that you need to do so you are ready for an activity: *You guys still have to get your stuff ready for school.* In spoken or informal English, people usually use **get ready**: *I have to get supper ready now.*

---

pre·pared /prɪˈpeəd‖-ˈperd/ adj **1** ready to deal with a situation: **+ for** *He wasn't really prepared for the interviewer's questions.* **2** **be prepared to do sth** to be willing to do something, especially something difficult or unpleasant: *You'll have to be prepared to work hard if you want to make progress in this job.* **3** [only before noun] already planned, written etc and ready to be used: *Danson's lawyer read out a prepared statement to journalists.* —**preparedness** /prɪˈpeədnɪ̥s, -ˈpeərɪ̥d-‖-ˈperɪ̥d-, -ˈperd-/ n [U] *the country's preparedness for war*

pre·pon·de·rance /prɪˈpɒndərəns‖-ˈpɑːn-/ n [singular] *formal* when there is more of one type of person or thing in a group than any other: **+ of** *There was a preponderance of students in the audience.*

prep·o·si·tion /ˌprepəˈzɪʃən/ n [C] a word or phrase used before a noun or PRONOUN to show place, time, direction etc. 'At', 'with', and 'into' are all prepositions. → see colour picture on page 474

pre·pos·ter·ous /prɪˈpɒstərəs‖-ˈpɑːs-/ adj completely unreasonable or silly; ABSURD: *That's a preposterous suggestion!*

prep school /ˈprep skuːl/ n [C,U] **1** a private school in Britain for children between 8 and 13: *I*

was at prep school in Sussex. **2** a private school in the US that prepares students for college

pre·req·ui·site /priːˈrekwɪ̥zɪ̥t/ n [C] something that is necessary before another thing can happen or be done: **+ for/of/to** *A degree in French is a prerequisite for the job.*

pre·rog·a·tive /prɪˈrɒgətɪv‖-ˈrɑː-/ n [C] *formal* a special right that someone has: *It's my prerogative as his mother to take him out of school.*

pres·age /ˈpresɪdʒ, prɪˈseɪdʒ/ v [T] *literary* to be a sign that something bad is going to happen

pre·school /ˈpriːskuːl/ n [C] *AmE* a school for children between two and five

pre·school /ˌ. ˈ.◂/ adj pre-school activities happen before a child is old enough to go to school: *a pre-school playgroup*

pre·scribe /prɪˈskraɪb/ v [T] **1** to say what medicine or treatment an ill person should have: *The doctor prescribed tranquilizers.* **2** *formal* to state officially what must be done in a situation: *a punishment prescribed by the law*

pre·scrip·tion /prɪˈskrɪpʃən/ n **1** [C] a piece of paper on which a doctor writes what medicine a sick person should have, or the medicine itself: *free prescriptions* **2** **on prescription** a drug that is only available on prescription can only be obtained with a written order from a doctor → compare OVER-THE-COUNTER

pre·scrip·tive /prɪˈskrɪptɪv/ adj saying how something should be done or what someone should do

pres·ence /ˈprezəns/ n **1** [singular] when someone or something is in a particular place at a particular time: *Your presence is requested at Friday's meeting.* | **in sb's presence** (=in the same place as someone): *The document should be signed in the presence of a witness.* **2** [singular] a group of soldiers who have been sent to a place to watch or influence what is happening: *protests against the UN presence in Bosnia.* **3** [U] the ability to make people notice and admire you: *an actor with great stage presence* **4** **presence of mind** the ability to deal with a dangerous or difficult situation quickly and calmly: *Luckily, she had the presence of mind to phone for an ambulance.* **5** **make your presence felt** to have a strong effect on a situation or the people you are with: *Hanley has certainly made his presence felt since joining the company.*

pres·ent¹ /ˈprezənt/ adj **1** **be present** to be in a particular place: *How many people were present at the meeting?* **2** [only before noun] happening or existing now: *He has lived in Montana from 1979 to the present time.* **3** **the present tense** the form of a verb that shows what exists or is happening now → see also PRESENT PARTICIPLE, PRESENT PERFECT

pre·sent² /prɪˈzent/ v [T] **1** to give something to someone, especially at an official occasion: **present sb with sth/present sth to sb** *We will present a cheque for £5000 to the winner.* **2** to give or show information in a particular way: *The evidence was presented to the court by Connor's lawyer.* **3** if something presents a problem, threat etc, it causes a problem, threat etc: *Heavy rain has presented a new difficulty for tournament organisers.* **4** to give a performance in a theatre or cinema, or broadcast a programme on television or radio: *The Lyric Theatre is presenting a brand new production of "Hamlet".*

5 *especially BrE* to introduce a television or radio programme: *Tonight's show will be presented by Jay Williams.* **6** to introduce someone formally to someone else: *May I present my parents, Mr and Mrs Benning.* **7** if an opportunity or situation presents itself, it suddenly starts to exist: *If the opportunity ever presented itself, I'd love to go and work abroad.*

pres·ent³ / 'prezənt/ *n* **1** [C] something that you give to someone, for example at Christmas or to say thank you etc; GIFT: *He got the computer as a birthday present.* **2 the present** the time that is happening now: *Live in the present – don't worry about the past!* **3 at present** at this time; now: *We have no plans at present for closing the factory.*

pre·sen·ta·ble /prɪ'zentəbəl/ *adj* attractive and tidy enough to be seen by other people: *Do I look presentable?*

pre·sen·ta·tion /ˌprezən'teɪʃən||ˌpriːzen-, -zən-/ *n* **1** [C] an event at which a new product or idea is described and explained: **give a presentation** *I've been asked to give a short presentation on the new research project.* **2** [C] when someone gives someone else a prize or present at a formal ceremony: *the presentation of the awards* **3** [U] the way in which something is arranged, shown, explained etc: *The presentation of the food is important.*

pres·ent-day /ˌ.. '.◂/ *adj* existing now: *present-day society*

pre·sent·er /prɪ'zentəll-ər/ *n* [C] someone who introduces a television or radio show

pres·ent·ly / 'prezəntli/ *adv formal* **1** at this time; now: *He's presently working for a computer company in San Jose.* **2** in a short time; soon: *The doctor will be here presently.*

present par·ti·ci·ple /ˌ.. '..../ *n* [C] a PARTICIPLE that is formed by adding "-ing" to a verb

present per·fect /ˌ.. '../ *n* **the present perfect** the tense of a verb that shows a time up to and including the present, and is formed with 'have' and the PAST PARTICIPLE as in 'he has gone'.

pres·er·va·tion /ˌprezə'veɪʃənll-zər-/ *n* [U] when something is kept from changing or ending, from being harmed or damaged: **+ of** *the preservation of human rights | the preservation of the rainforest*

pre·ser·va·tive /prɪ'zɜːvətɪvll-ɜːr-/ *n* [C,U] a chemical substance that stops food or wood from decaying

pre·serve¹ /prɪ'zɜːv||-ɜːrv/ *v* [T] **1** to keep something from being harmed or damaged: *All the old buildings had been very well preserved.* **2** to make a situation or quality continue without changing or ending: *the need to preserve law and order* **3** to add something to food which stops it from decaying: *onions preserved in vinegar*

preserve² *n* **1** [singular] if an activity or place is the preserve of a group of people, only that group is able or allowed to do it or use it: *Politics is no longer the preserve of wealthy white men. | Child-rearing has traditionally been a female preserve.* **2** [C] an area of land or water that is kept for private hunting or fishing: *a wildlife preserve* **3** [C] a sweet food such as JAM made from boiled fruit and sugar

pre·side /prɪ'zaɪd/ *v* [I] to be in charge of a formal meeting, ceremony etc: *Judge Baxter presided at the trial.*

preside over *phr v* [T] to be in charge of a situation or process: *Kohl presided over a period of remarkable economic expansion.*

pres·i·den·cy / 'prezədənsi/ *n* **1** [singular] the job of a president **2** [C] the period of time when someone is a president: *the early days of Clinton's presidency*

pres·i·dent also **President** / 'prezədənt/ *n* [C] **1** the official leader of a country that does not have a king or queen: *President Lincoln* **2** someone who is in charge of a large organization, company, club etc: *the President of Brown University*

pres·i·den·tial /ˌprezə'denʃəl◂/ *adj* **presidential election/campaign/powers etc** relating to the president of a country: *the party's presidential candidate*

press¹ /pres/ *v* **1** [I,T] to push something firmly and steadily: *To send a fax just press the red button. | I pressed the brake pedal but nothing happened. | Press down with your left foot and pull back the lever.* **2** [T] to push something firmly against something else: **press sth against/into sth** *Their faces were pressed against the window.* **3** [I,T] to try very hard to persuade someone to do something: **+ for** *Teachers are pressing for a pay increase. | press sb for sth Blair's interviewer kept pressing him for an answer. | press sb to do sth She pressed them to stay a little longer.* **4** [I] to move in direction by pushing: **+ forward/around** *The crowd pressed forward for a better view.* **5 press a claim/case/point** to try hard to get something accepted **6 press charges** to say officially that someone has done something illegal and must go to a court of law **7** [T] to make clothes smooth, using heat; IRON: *I need to press these trousers for tomorrow.* **8** [T] to use heavy weights to crush something or make something flat, for example to get juice out of fruit: *a machine for pressing grapes*

press on, press ahead, press forward *phr v* [I] to continue doing something in a determined way: **+ with** *The club is pressing on with plans to build a new stadium.*

press² *n* **1 the press** newspapers, magazines etc or the people who work for them: *Members of the press were waiting outside. | Reports of the incident appeared in the national press.* **2 get a good/bad press** to be praised or criticized in the newspapers or on radio or television: *Britain's royal family has had a bad press in recent years.* **3 go to press** if a newspaper or book goes to press, it begins to be printed **4** [C] a piece of equipment used to make something flat or to force liquid out of fruit: *a trouser press* **5** [C] a PRINTING PRESS **6** [singular] an act of pressing something: *I'll just give this skirt a quick press.*

press con·fer·ence /ˈ. ˌ.../ *n* [C] a meeting at which an important or famous person answers questions asked by people from newspapers, television etc

pressed /prest/ *adj* **be pressed for time/money etc** to not have enough time, money etc: *I can't stop now – I'm a bit pressed for time.*

press·ing /ˈpresɪŋ/ adj needing to be dealt with very soon; URGENT: *Unemployment is one of the region's most pressing problems.*

press re·lease /ˈ. ˌ./ n [C] an official statement giving information to newspapers, radio, television etc

press-up /ˈ. ./ n [C] BrE an exercise in which you lie facing the ground and push your body up using your arms; PUSH-UP AmE

pres·sure[1] /ˈpreʃəl-ər/ n **1** [U] attempts to make someone do something by threatening them, arguing with them etc: *growing pressure for change inside the party* | **be/come under pressure to do sth** *NASA has been under political pressure to launch a new space program.* | **put pressure on sb (to do sth)** *Environmental groups are putting pressure on the state to change the smoking laws.* **2** [C,U] conditions in your life that make you anxious: *the pressures of modern life* | **be under pressure** *Jerry's been under a lot of pressure at work recently.* **3** [C,U] the force that a gas or liquid has when it is inside a container or place: *Is there enough pressure in the tyres?* | **high/low pressure** *high blood pressure* **4** [U] the force produced by pressing against something

pressure[2] v especially AmE PRESSURIZE

pressure cook·er /ˈ.. ˌ./ n [C] a tightly covered pot that cooks food very quickly by the pressure of hot steam → see picture at KITCHEN

pressure group /ˈ.. ./ n [C] a group of people who try to influence public opinion and government action

pres·sur·ize (also -ise BrE) /ˈpreʃəraɪz/ v [T] to try to make someone do something by threatening them, arguing with them etc: *I was pressurized into lending him the money.*

pres·sur·ized (also -ised BrE) /ˈpreʃəraɪzd/ adj containing air that has controlled pressure: *pressurized aircraft cabins*

pres·tige /preˈstiːʒ/ n [U] when you are respected and admired because of your social position, your profession, the high standard of your work etc

pres·ti·gious /preˈstɪdʒəsǁ-ˈstiː-, -ˈstɪ-/ adj admired or respected as one of the best and most important: *a prestigious award*

pre·su·ma·bly /prɪˈzjuːməbliǁ-ˈzuː-/ adv used to say that something is probably true: *Presumably, you've heard the news by now.*

pre·sume /prɪˈzjuːmǁ-ˈzuːm/ v **1** [T] to think that something is true, although you are not certain: **+ (that)** *I presume that she'll be coming.* | **be presumed dead/innocent etc** (=to think that someone is dead, innocent etc until this is proved untrue): *a list of soldiers missing, presumed dead* **2** [I] formal to behave rudely by doing something that you have no right to do: **presume to do sth** *I wouldn't presume to interfere.*

pre·sump·tion /prɪˈzʌmpʃən/ n **1** [C] something that you suppose is true because it seems very likely: *the presumption that Evans was*
guilty **2** [U] when someone confidently does something that they have no right to do

pre·sump·tu·ous /prɪˈzʌmptʃuəs/ adj confidently doing or saying something that you have no right to: *It was presumptuous of her to assume she would be invited.*

pre·sup·pose /ˌpriːsəˈpəʊzǁ-ˈpoʊz/ v [T] formal to depend on something that is thought to be true but may not be; ASSUME: **+ (that)** *All these plans presuppose that the bank will be willing to give us the money.* —**presupposition** /ˌpriːsʌpə-ˈzɪʃən/ n [C,U]

pre·tence BrE, **pretense** AmE /prɪˈtensǁ prɪˈtens/ n **1** [C usually singular, U] when you pretend that something is true: **make a pretence of doing sth/make no pretence of doing sth** *Al made no pretence of hiding his surprise.* **2 under false pretences** if you do something under false pretences, you do it by dishonestly pretending that something is true: *They were found guilty of obtaining money under false pretences.*

pre·tend /prɪˈtend/ v [I,T] **1** to behave as if something is true when you know it is not: **+ (that)** *She walked past and pretended she hadn't seen me.* | **pretend to do sth** *The kids were pretending to be asleep.* **2** to imagine that something is true or real as a game: **+ (that)** *Let's pretend we're on the moon!* | **pretend to be sb/sth** *John was pretending to be Batman.*

pre·tense /prɪˈtensǁˈpriːtens/ n the American spelling of PRETENCE

pre·ten·sion /prɪˈtenʃən/ n [C usually plural, U] when someone tries to seem better, more skilful, more important etc than they really are: *a pleasant young man without any pretensions*

pre·ten·tious /prɪˈtenʃəs/ adj trying to seem more important, serious, or clever than you really are: *He was a pretentious young man, given to quoting from little known French poets.*

pre·text /ˈpriːtekst/ n [C] a reason that is given for doing something, which hides the real reason: **on/under the pretext of doing sth** *She went to see James on the pretext of wanting to borrow a book.*

pret·ty[1] /ˈprɪti/ adv **1** spoken fairly, but not completely: *I'm pretty sure she'll say yes.* **2** spoken very: *Dad was pretty angry about it.* **3 pretty much/pretty well** almost completely: *The streets were pretty well deserted by 9 o'clock.*

pretty[2] adj **1** a woman or child who is pretty is attractive: *What a pretty little girl!* **2** a place or thing that is pretty is pleasant to look at or listen to: *a pretty pink dress* **3 not a pretty picture/sight** ugly, upsetting, or worrying: *After a night's drinking, Dan was not a pretty sight!* —**prettily** adv —**prettiness** n [U]

pre·vail /prɪˈveɪl/ v [I] **1** if a belief, opinion, or attitude prevails, it is common among a group of people: **+ in/among** *A belief in magic still prevails in some societies.* **2** formal to win or get control after a struggle or argument: *Justice prevailed in the end.*

P

GRAMMAR NOTE: phrasal verbs (1)
Phrasal verbs are verbs with more than one part. They consist of **verb + adverb** or **verb + preposition** (e.g. *look after, turn out, put off*). Some phrasal verbs have three parts: **verb + adverb + preposition** (e.g. *look forward to, put up with*).

prevail on/upon *phr v* [T] *formal* to persuade someone to do something: *Jennings prevailed upon the committee to reconsider its decision.*

pre·vail·ing /prɪˈveɪlɪŋ/ *adj* **1** [only before noun] most common in a place at a particular time; CURRENT: *Williams' book challenged prevailing views of US history.* **2 a prevailing wind** a wind that blows over a particular area most of the time

prev·a·lent /ˈprevələnt/ *adj* common at a particular time or in a place: **+ in/among** *a disease that is prevalent among young people* — **prevalence** *n* [U]

pre·vent /prɪˈvent/ *v* [T] to stop something from happening, or stop someone from doing something: *Brushing your teeth regularly helps prevent tooth decay.* | **prevent sb from doing sth** *A knee injury prevented Gary from playing in Saturday's game.* — **preventable** *adj*

pre·ven·ta·tive /prɪˈventətɪv/ *adj* PREVENTIVE

pre·ven·tion /prɪˈvenʃən/ *n* [U] when something is prevented: *crime prevention* | **+ of** *the prevention of war*

pre·ven·tive /prɪˈventɪv/ also **preventative** *adj* intended to prevent something bad from happening: *preventive medicine* (=medicine that prevents people from becoming sick)

pre·view /ˈpriːvjuː/ *n* [C] **1** an occasion when you see a film, play etc before it is shown to the public **2** an advertisement for a film or television programme consisting of short parts from it — **preview** *v* [T]

pre·vi·ous /ˈpriːviəs/ *adj* happening or existing at an earlier time: *She has two children from a previous marriage.* | *She said she had seen him the previous day.*

pre·vi·ous·ly /ˈpriːviəsli/ *adv* before a time or event in the past: *She had previously worked for a computer company in Cambridge.*

pre·war /ˌ. ˈ. ◂ / *adj* happening or existing before a war, especially World War II: *the prewar years*

prey¹ /preɪ/ *n* **1** [U] an animal that is hunted and eaten by another animal: *a tiger stalking its prey* **2 a bird/beast of prey** a bird or animal that lives by killing and eating other animals **3 fall prey to sth** to be strongly affected by something bad: *More and more teenagers are falling prey to drugs.*

prey² *v*

prey on sb/sth *phr v* [T] **1** if an animal or bird preys on another creature, it hunts and eats it **2** to get an unfair advantage by deceiving someone who is not as clever, experienced etc as you are: *dishonest salesmen who prey on elderly people* **3 prey on your mind** to worry you a lot: *It wasn't your fault – you mustn't let it prey on your mind.*

price¹ /praɪs/ *n* **1** [C,U] the amount of money you pay to buy something: *House prices have gone up again.* | *Computers have come down in price lately.* | **+ of** *The price of the vacation includes food and accommodation.* | **full/half price** *Children under 14 travel half price.* | **asking price** (=the price someone wants for something): *The asking price was $500, but we got it for $400.* → compare COST¹ **2 at any price** even if something is very difficult: *She was determined to have a child at any price.* **3 at a price**

a) available but expensive: *They sell excellent wine – at a price.* **b)** used to say that something can be achieved, but that it involves something unpleasant: *She finally became company director – but at what price!*

price² *v* [T] to decide or say how much something costs: *a new software package, priced at $49.95*

price·less /ˈpraɪsləs/ *adj* **1** worth a lot of money: *priceless antiques* **2** very important or useful: *The ability to motivate people is a priceless asset.* **3** *informal* very funny or silly: *The look on his face when I walked in the room was priceless!*

pric·ey, pricy /ˈpraɪsi/ *adj informal* expensive: *a pricey restaurant*

prick¹ /prɪk/ *v* **1** [T] to make a small hole in the surface of something, using a sharp point: *Prick the sausages with a fork.* **2** [I,T] to feel an unpleasant stinging on your skin: *Tears pricked her eyes.* **3 prick (up) its ears** if an animal pricks up its ears, it raises them and points them towards a sound **4 prick up your ears** to start listening to what someone is saying because it interests you

prick² *n* [C] a slight pain you feel when something sharp goes into your skin: *You'll feel a slight prick as the needle goes into your arm.*

prick·le¹ /ˈprɪkəl/ *n* [C] a sharp point on the skin of some plants and animals

prickle² *v* [I,T] to feel a stinging pain on your skin or part of your body: *a terrifying sound that make her skin prickle*

prick·ly /ˈprɪkli/ *adj* **1** covered with prickles: *prickly bushes* **2** *informal* easily annoyed or offended: *Bob's in a very prickly mood this morning.*

pric·y /ˈpraɪsi/ *adj* another spelling of PRICEY

pride¹ /praɪd/ *n* [U] **1** the feeling of being proud of something special you have achieved, someone special you are connected with etc: **take pride in sth** *She takes a great pride in her work.* | **with pride** *Tony glanced with pride at his wife.* **2** the feeling that you are better or more important than other people: *He has too much pride to say he's sorry.* **3** when you like and respect yourself and feel that you should be respected by others: **hurt sb's pride** (=make someone feel embarrassed or offended because they feel that other people have less respect for them): *Don't offer her money – you'll hurt her pride.* **4 have/take pride of place** to have the most important position in a group: *A portrait of the Queen took pride of place on the wall.* **5 the pride of** the best or most important person or thing: *The football team is the pride of the whole town.* **6 sb's pride and joy** someone or something that is very important to someone: *Ken's new car is his pride and joy.*

pride² *v* **pride yourself on sth** to be very proud of something that you do well, or of a quality that you have: *Sandy prides herself on her ability to speak four languages.*

priest /priːst/ *n* [C] someone who performs religious duties and ceremonies, for example in the Catholic Church

priest·ess /ˈpriːstes/ *n* [C] a woman with religious duties and responsibilities in some non-Christian religions

priest·hood /ˈpriːsthʊd/ *n* **the priesthood** the job or position of a priest: *enter the priesthood* (=become a priest)

prim /prɪm/ *adj* always behaving very correctly, and easily shocked by anything rude: **prim and proper** *Janet's much too prim and proper to laugh at a joke like that.* —**primly** *adv*

pri·ma·cy /ˈpraɪməsi/ *n* [U] *formal* when someone or something is more important or powerful than anyone or anything else: *the primacy of communist thinking* | *the primacy of practical skill over theoretical knowledge*

prima don·na /ˌpriːmə ˈdɒnəǁ-ˈdɑːnə/ *n* [C] someone who thinks that they are very good at what they do, and expects a lot of admiration and attention from other people

pri·mal /ˈpraɪməl/ *adj formal* primal feelings are basic and seem to come from ancient times when humans lived like animals: *the primal instinct for survival*

pri·ma·ri·ly /ˈpraɪmərəliǁpraɪˈmerəli/ *adv* mainly: *a course aimed primarily at adult students*

pri·ma·ry[1] /ˈpraɪməriǁ-meri/ *adj* most important; main: *Our primary concern is the welfare of the child.*

primary[2] *n* [C] an election in the US when people vote to decide who will be their political party's CANDIDATE for a political position

primary col·our /ˌ... ˈ.../ *n* [C] one of the three colours that you can mix together to make any other colour. These are red, yellow, and blue for paint; red, green, and blue for light

primary school /ˈ... ˌ./ *n* [C] *especially BrE* a school for children between the ages of 5 and 11; ELEMENTARY SCHOOL *AmE*

pri·mate /ˈpraɪmeɪt/ *n* [C] a member of the group of MAMMALS that includes humans and monkeys

prime[1] /praɪm/ *adj* **1** main or most important: *Smoking is one of the prime causes of heart disease.* **2** of the very best quality or kind: *a house in a prime location* **3 a prime example** a very good example of something

prime[2] *n* **be in your prime/be in the prime of life** to be at the time in your life when you are strongest and most active

prime[3] *v* [T] to prepare someone for a situation so that they know what to do: *The senators were primed to ask some tough questions.*

prime min·is·ter, Prime Minister /ˌ. ˈ...◂/ *n* [C] the leader of the government in some countries with a PARLIAMENT

prim·er /ˈpraɪməǁ-ər/ *n* [C,U] a special paint that is spread over wood, metal etc as the first layer before putting normal paint onto it

prime time /ˈ. ˌ./ *n* [U] the time in the evening when the biggest number of people watch television: *a prime-time TV show*

pri·me·val /praɪˈmiːvəl/ *adj* belonging to the earliest period of the Earth's existence: *primeval forests*

prim·i·tive /ˈprɪmɪtɪv/ *adj* **1** belonging to an early stage of the development of humans or animals: *primitive societies* **2** very simple, uncomfortable, or old-fashioned: *primitive living conditions*

prim·rose /ˈprɪmrəʊzǁ-roʊz/ *n* [C] a small wild plant with pale yellow flowers

prince, Prince /prɪns/ *n* [C] **1** the son of a king or queen, or one of their male relations **2 Prince** the title used by a prince: *Prince Charles* **3** the male ruler of some small countries: *Prince Rainier of Monaco*

prince·ly /ˈprɪnsli/ *adj* **princely sum** a large amount of money, usually used when you want to make a joke about how small the amount really is: *He earns the princely sum of £2.50 an hour.*

prin·cess, Princess /ˌprɪnˈsesǁ ˈprɪnsəs/ *n* [C] **1** the daughter of a king or queen, or one of their female relations **2 Princess** the title used by a princess: *Princess Diana* **3** the wife of a prince

prin·ci·pal[1] /ˈprɪnsɪpəl/ *adj* [only before noun] most important; main: *Our principal aim is to provide support for one-parent families.*

principal[2] *n* [C] the person in charge of a school or college

prin·ci·pal·i·ty /ˌprɪnsɪˈpæləti/ *n* [C] a country ruled by a prince

prin·ci·pally /ˈprɪnsɪpli/ *adv* mainly: *a course designed principally for people who have no qualifications*

prin·ci·ple /ˈprɪnsɪpəl/ *n* **1** [C,U] a moral rule or idea that has a strong influence on the way you behave: *It's against my principles to hit a child.* | **on the principle that** *beliefs based on the principle that everyone is equal* | **on principle** (=because of a moral idea): *She doesn't eat meat on principle.* **2** [C] a rule that explains the way something works, especially in science or mathematics: *the principles of geometry* **3 in principle a)** if something is possible in principle, there is no reason why it should not happen: *In principle, you can leave work early on Friday, but it's not always possible.* **b)** if you agree in principle, you agree with the main parts of a plan: *We're hoping the contract will be approved in principle.*

prin·ci·pled /ˈprɪnsɪpəld/ *adj* having strong beliefs about what is morally right and wrong

print[1] /prɪnt/ *v* **1** [T] to produce words or pictures on paper or material, using a machine: *The poster is printed on recycled paper.* | *Can you print on your computer?* **2** [T] to produce copies of a book, newspaper etc: *We're printing 10,000 copies of his new book.* **3** [T] to print a letter, speech etc in a newspaper or magazine: *All the newspapers have printed the president's speech.* **4** [I,T] to write words by hand without joining the letters: *Please print your name in capital letters.*

print sth ↔ **off/out** *phr v* [T] to produce a printed copy of a computer document

print[2] *n* **1** [U] writing that has been printed in books, newspapers etc: *I can't read small print without my glasses.* | **in print** *I wouldn't have believed it if I hadn't seen it in print.* **2 be in print** if a book is in print, it is still being printed and you can buy new copies of it **3 be out of print** if a book is out of print, it is no longer being printed and you cannot buy new copies of it **4** [C] a picture that has been printed, or a copy of a painting **5** [C] a photograph: *You can pick up your prints on Friday.* **6** [C] a mark made on a surface when you press something onto it: *His feet left prints in the snow.* → see also FINGERPRINT, FOOTPRINT

print·er /ˈprɪntəll-ər/ *n* [C] **1** a machine that can copy documents from a computer onto paper **2** someone who works in a printing business → see colour picture on page 80

print·ing /ˈprɪntɪŋ/ *n* [U] the process of making a book, magazine etc using a machine: *a printing error*

printing press /ˈ.. ˌ./ *n* [C] a machine that prints newspapers, books etc

print·out /ˈprɪntˌaʊt/ *n* [C,U] a piece of paper containing information printed from a computer → see colour picture on page 80

pri·or /ˈpraɪəllpraɪr/ *adj formal* **1 prior to** before: *You should not eat anything for six hours prior to your operation.* **2** [only before noun] done, planned, or existing earlier than something else: *We couldn't attend because of a prior commitment.*

pri·o·ri·tize (also **-ise** *BrE*) /praɪˈɒrɪ̯taɪzll-ˈɔːr-/ *v* [I,T] to put several things in order of importance so that you can deal with the most important first: *Try and prioritize your work.* —**prioritization** /praɪˌɒrɪ̯taɪˈzeɪʃənll-ˌɔːrɪ̯tə-/ *n* [U]

pri·or·i·ty /praɪˈɒrɪ̯till-ˈɔːr-/ *n* **1** [C] the thing that you think is most important and should be dealt with first: *Let's decide what our priorities are.* **2 be given/have/take priority** to be considered most important and dealt with first: *The course gives priority to improving spoken English.* |+ **over** *Your family should take priority over your job.*

prise /praɪz/ *v* [T] *BrE* to force something open or away from something else; PRY *AmE*: **prise sth off/open etc** *I prised the lid off the tin.*

pris·m /ˈprɪzəm/ *n* [C] a transparent block of glass with three sides that separates white light into different colours

pris·on /ˈprɪzən/ *n* [C,U] a building where criminals are kept as a punishment: **be in prison** *Her husband's in prison.*

pris·on·er /ˈprɪzənəll-ər/ *n* [C] **1** someone who is kept in a prison **2** someone who is forced to stay somewhere, for example during a war: **be taken/held prisoner** *Hundreds of soldiers were taken prisoner.*

prisoner of war /ˌ... . ./ **P.O.W.** *n* [C] a soldier etc who is caught by an enemy during a war and kept as a prisoner

pris·tine /ˈprɪstiːn/ *adj* extremely clean and looking like new: *a 1973 Volkswagen Beetle in pristine condition*

priv·a·cy /ˈprɪvəsi, ˈpraɪ-llˈpraɪ-/ *n* [U] when you are alone and other people cannot see or hear you: *Joan read the letter in the privacy of her own room.*

pri·vate[1] /ˈpraɪvɪ̯t/ *adj* **1** for use by only one person or group, not for everyone: *Rooms are available for private parties.* **2** private feelings, information etc are secret or personal and not for other people to know about: *You had no right to look at my private letters.* **3** not owned or paid for by the government: *a private school* **4** not connected with your work: *The president will be making a private visit to Mexico.* |**private life** (=your life with your family, friends etc when you are not working) **5** quiet and without other people there: *Is there a private corner where we can talk?* —**privately** *adv*

private[2] *n* **1 in private** without other people listening or watching: *Miss Smith, can I speak to you in private?* **2** [C] also **Private** a soldier who has the lowest rank in the army

private en·ter·prise /ˌ.. ˈ.../ *n* [U] the economic system in which businesses compete, and the government does not control industry

pri·va·tion /praɪˈveɪʃən/ *n* [C,U] *formal* when someone does not have enough food, money etc

pri·vat·ize (also **-ise** *BrE*) /ˈpraɪvətaɪz/ *v* [T] to sell an organization, industry etc that was previously owned by a government —**privatization** /ˌpraɪvətaɪˈzeɪʃənll-tə-/ *n* [U] → opposite NATIONALIZE

priv·i·lege /ˈprɪvɪ̯lɪdʒ/ *n* **1** [C] a special advantage that is given only to one person or group: *Education should be a right, not a privilege.* **2** [U] when someone who is rich or powerful has more advantages or rights than other people: *aristocratic privilege* **3 be a privilege/have the privilege** used to say that you are grateful for something, or to show respect to someone: *It's been a privilege to meet you, sir.* —**privileged** *adj*

priv·y /ˈprɪvi/ *adj formal* **privy to sth** knowing information that had been kept secret from most other people: *Only a few managers had been privy to the deal.*

prize[1] /praɪz/ *n* [C] something that is given to someone who is successful in a competition, race etc: *First prize was a weekend for two in Paris.*

prize[2] *adj* [only before noun] good enough to win a prize or to have won a prize: *prize cattle*

prize[3] *v* [T] to think that someone or something is very important or valuable: *These coins are prized by collectors.* —**prized** *adj*: *Nick's car is his most prized possession.*

pro /prəʊllproʊ/ *n* [C] **1** *informal* someone who earns money because they are good at a particular sport or skill **2 the pros and cons** the advantages and disadvantages of something: *We discussed the pros and cons of starting our own business.*

pro- /prəʊllproʊ/ *prefix* supporting something or approving of something: *pro-government troops* | *a pro-abortion demonstration*

prob·a·bil·i·ty /ˌprɒbəˈbɪlɪ̯till-ˌprɑː-/ *n* **1** [singular, U] how likely it is that something will happen: + **of** *What's the probability of the hostages being released soon?* **2 in all probability** used to say that you think something is very likely to happen or be true: *In all probability the motive for the crime was money.* **3** [C] something that is likely to happen or exist: *War is a real probability now.*

prob·a·ble /ˈprɒbəbəll-ˈprɑː-/ *adj* likely to happen, exist, or be true: *The probable cause of the plane crash was ice on the wings.* |**it is probable (that)** *It is probable that she won't survive.*

prob·a·bly /ˈprɒbəblill-ˈprɑː-/ *adv* likely to happen or be true: *We'll probably go to France next year.*

pro·ba·tion /prəˈbeɪʃənllproʊ-/ *n* [U] **1** a system of keeping an official check on criminals, helping them to behave well instead of sending them to prison: **on probation** *He's on probation for theft.* **2** a period of time when someone starts a new job in which they can show whether or not they are suitable for that job —**pro·bationary** *adj*

probation of·fi·cer /.'. .,.../ *n* [C] someone whose job is to keep an official check on people who are on probation and help them find work etc

probe[1] /prəʊb‖proʊb/ *v* [I,T] **1** to ask questions in order to find things out: + **into** *You have no right to start probing into my personal life.* **2** to look for something or examine something, using a long thin object —**probing** *adj*

probe[2] *n* [C] **1** a long thin tool that doctors and scientists use to examine parts of someone's body **2** a careful and thorough process of getting information by asking a lot of questions

prob·lem /'prɒbləm‖'prɑː-/ *n* [C] **1** a difficult situation that you have to deal with: *Unemployment is the main problem in the area.* | **have a problem (with)** *Since losing my job I've been having financial problems.* | **drug/crime problem** *an area with a huge crime problem* **2** a question that you must solve, connected with numbers or facts: *a mathematical problem* **3 no problem** spoken **a)** used to say that you are very willing to do something: *"Could you drive me to the station?" "Sure, no problem."* **b)** used after someone has thanked you or said they are sorry: *"Thanks for your help." "Oh, no problem."* **4 that's your/his etc problem** used to say that someone else is responsible for dealing with a situation, not you: *If you can't get yourself there on time, that's your problem.*

prob·lem·at·ic /ˌprɒbləˈmætɪk◂ ‖ˌprɑː-/ also **problematical** *adj* full of problems and difficult to deal with: *Our plans for a quiet wedding were becoming ever more problematic.* —**problematically** /-kli/ *adv*

pro·ce·dure /prəˈsiːdʒə‖-ər/ *n* [C,U] the correct or normal way of doing something: + **for** *the procedure for shutting down a computer* —**procedural** *adj*

pro·ceed /prəˈsiːd/ *v* [I] *formal* **1** to continue to do something that has already been started: *Talks are proceeding smoothly.* | + **with** *Protesters made it impossible for him to proceed with his speech.* **2 proceed to do sth** to do something after you have done something else: *She took out a bottle and proceeded to drink the contents.* **3** *formal* to move in a particular direction: *Please proceed to the nearest exit.*

pro·ceed·ings /prəˈsiːdɪŋz/ *n* [plural] **1** an event or things that happen at it: *We watched the proceedings from a third floor window.* **2** legal actions taken in a law court: *divorce proceedings*

pro·ceeds /'prəʊsiːdz‖-proʊ-/ *n* [plural] the money that you get from selling something or from an event: *The proceeds from the concert will go to charity.*

pro·cess[1] /'prəʊses‖'prɑː-/ *n* [C] **1** a series of events or changes that happen naturally: *the ageing process* **2** a series of things you do to achieve a particular result: *The reorganization process will take some time.* **3 be in the process of doing sth** to have started doing something

and not yet be finished: *We're in the process of buying a house.* **4 in the process** while you are doing something else, or while something else is happening: *I ran for the bus and twisted my ankle in the process.*

process[2] *v* [T] **1** to add chemicals to a substance or food to give it colour, keep it fresh etc: *processed cheese* **2** to deal with information by putting it through a system or computer: *Your membership application is still being processed.* **3** to print a photograph or film —**processing** *n* [U]

pro·ces·sion /prəˈseʃən/ *n* [C] **1** a line of people or vehicles moving slowly as part of a ceremony: *a funeral procession* ➡ compare PARADE[1] **2** many people or things of the same kind, appearing or happening one after the other: + **of** *an endless procession of well meaning visitors* —**processional** *adj*

pro·ces·sor /'prəʊsesə‖'prɑːsesər/ *n* [C] the part of a computer that does the processes needed to deal with information ➡ see also FOOD PROCESSOR

pro·claim /prəˈkleɪm‖proʊ-/ *v* [T] *formal* to officially tell people about something or to say that something is true: *Romania was proclaimed a People's Republic in 1947.*

proc·la·ma·tion /ˌprɒkləˈmeɪʃən‖ˌprɑː-/ *n* [C] an official statement that tells people about something important

pro·cras·ti·nate /prəˈkræstɪneɪt/ *v* [I] *formal* to delay doing something that you ought to do: *Though war seemed likely, the government continued to procrastinate.* —**procrastination** /prəˌkræstɪˈneɪʃən/ *n* [U]

pro·cre·ate /'prəʊkrieɪt‖proʊ-/ *v* [I,T] *formal* to produce children or baby animals; REPRODUCE —**procreation** /ˌprəʊkriˈeɪʃən‖proʊ-/ *n* [U]

pro·cure /prəˈkjʊə‖proʊˈkjʊr/ *v* [T] *formal* to get something, especially something that is difficult to get: *Clark was accused of procuring guns for the rebels.* —**procurement** *n* [U]

prod /prɒd‖prɑːd/ *v* [I,T] **-dded, -dding 1** to push someone or something with your finger or a pointed object: *He prodded the dead snake with a stick.* **2** to encourage someone to do something: **prod sb into doing sth** *We had to prod Louis into applying for the job.* —**prod** *n* [singular]

pro·di·gious /prəˈdɪdʒəs/ *adj formal* very large or impressive: *a prodigious amount of money* —**prodigiously** *adv*

prod·i·gy /'prɒdɪdʒi‖'prɑː-/ *n* [C] a young person who is extremely good at doing something: *Mozart was a child prodigy.* ➡ compare GENIUS

pro·duce[1] /prəˈdjuːs‖-ˈduːs/ *v* [T] **1** to grow or make something: *Much of the world's finest wine is produced in France.* | *a snake that produces a deadly poison* **2** to make something happen or develop, or have a particular result or effect: *The drug can produce serious side effects in some people.* **3** to show something so that some-

---

GRAMMAR NOTE: phrasal verbs (1)
Phrasal verbs are verbs with more than one part. They consist of **verb + adverb** or **verb + preposition** (e.g. *look after, turn out, put off*). Some phrasal verbs have three parts: **verb + adverb + preposition** (e.g. *look forward to, put up with*).

one can see it: *He suddenly produced a gun.* **4** to control how a play, film etc is made

prod·uce² /'pɒdjuːs‖'proʊduːs/ *n* [U] food that is grown in large quantities to be sold: *dairy produce*

pro·duc·er /prə'djuːsə‖-'duːsər/ *n* [C] **1** a company or country that makes or grows something: *Scotland is a producer of high quality wool.* **2** someone who controls the making of a play, film etc

prod·uct /'prɒdʌkt‖'prɑː-/ *n* **1** [C] something that is made or grown to be sold: *None of our products are tested on animals.* **2 be the product of sth** to be the result of particular experiences and events: *Criminals are often the product of bad homes.*

pro·duc·tion /prə'dʌkʃən/ *n* **1** [U] the process of making or growing things, or the amount that is produced: *Our production has increased by 35%.* **2** [C] a play or film: *a modern production of Romeo and Juliet*

pro·duc·tive /prə'dʌktɪv/ *adj* producing or achieving a lot: *a very productive meeting* —**productively** *adv*

pro·duc·tiv·i·ty /ˌprɒdʌk'tɪvˌti, -dək-‖ˌprɑː-/ *n* [U] the speed at which goods are produced, and the amount that is produced: *Factory managers want to increase productivity.*

Prof. *n* the written abbreviation of PROFESSOR

pro·fane /prə'feɪn/ *adj* showing disrespect for God or religion, especially by what you say: *profane language* —**profanity** /-'fænˌti/ *n* [C,U]

pro·fess /prə'fes/ *v* [T] *formal* **1** to say that you have something, do something etc, especially when it is not true: *profess to do sth He professes to love his son, although I've never seen any proof.* **2** to express a personal feeling or belief —**professed** *adj*

pro·fes·sion /prə'feʃən/ *n* **1** [C] a job that needs special education and training: **by profession** (=as your job): *He's a lawyer by profession.* **2** [singular] all the people in a profession: *the teaching profession*

pro·fes·sion·al¹ /prə'feʃənəl/ *adj* **1** doing a sport or activity as your job: *a professional tennis player* **2** [only before noun] professional sports are played by people who are paid: *a professional golf championship* **3** [only before noun] relating to a job that needs special knowledge and training: *You should speak to a lawyer for professional advice.* **4** showing that someone has been well trained and is good at their work: *The report looks very professional.* —**professionally** *adv*

professional² *n* [C] **1** someone who works in a job that needs special education and training: *a health care professional* **2** someone who earns money by doing a sport or activity that other people do for enjoyment → compare AMATEUR²

pro·fes·sion·al·is·m /prə'feʃənəlɪzəm/ *n* [U] the skill and high standards of behaviour that a professional person is expected to have

pro·fes·sor /prə'fesə‖-ər/ *n* [C] **1** *BrE* a teacher at the highest level in a university department **2** *AmE* a teacher at a university or college who has a PHD

prof·fer /'prɒfə‖'prɑːfər/ *v* [T] *formal* to offer something to someone

pro·fi·cien·cy /prə'fɪʃənsi/ *n* [U] the ability to do something very skilfully

pro·fi·cient /prə'fɪʃənt/ *adj* able to do something very skilfully: **+ in/at** *Gwen is proficient in three languages.* —**proficiently** *adv*

pro·file¹ /'prəʊfaɪl‖'proʊ-/ *n* [C] **1** a side view of someone's head: **in profile** *a drawing of her in profile* **2** a short description that gives important details about someone's character, work, life etc: **+ of** *a profile of Paul McCartney in a Sunday paper* **3 keep a low profile** to avoid doing things that will make people notice you → see also HIGH-PROFILE

profile² *v* [T] to write or give a short description of someone or something, especially in a newspaper or magazine

prof·it¹ /'prɒfˌt‖'prɑː-/ *n* [C,U] the money you get when you sell something for more than it cost you to make or buy it, especially in business: **make a profit** *Their shop now makes profits of over $1m a year.* | **at a profit** *They sold the company at a huge profit.*

profit² *v* [I,T] *formal* to get something good or useful from a situation: **profit by/from sth** *Only wealthy people will profit from the new tax laws.*

prof·it·a·bil·i·ty /ˌprɒfˌtə'bɪlˌti‖ˌprɑː-/ *n* [U] the amount of profit that a business can or does make

prof·it·a·ble /'prɒfˌtəbəl‖'prɑː-/ *adj* producing a profit or a useful result: *profitable investments* —**profitably** *adv*

prof·i·teer /ˌprɒfˌ'tɪə‖ˌprɑːfˌ'tɪr/ *n* [C] a person or company that makes unfairly large profits —**profiteering** *n* [U]

pro·found /prə'faʊnd/ *adj* **1** affecting someone very strongly: *Her death was a profound shock to all of us.* **2** meant very sincerely: *a profound apology* **3** showing a lot of knowledge and understanding of a subject: *a profound remark* —**profoundly** *adv* —**profundity** /prə'fʌndˌti/ *n* [C,U]

pro·fuse /prə'fjuːs/ *adj* produced in large amounts: *symptoms include a fever and profuse sweating* —**profusely** *adv*: *Keith thanked them profusely.*

pro·fu·sion /prə'fjuːʒən/ *n* [singular, U] a very large amount: **+ of** *a profusion of flowers* | **in profusion** *Wildlife is here in profusion.*

prog·no·sis /prɒg'nəʊsˌs‖prɑː'gnoʊ-/ *n* [C], *plural* **prognoses** /-siːz/ **1** *technical* a doctor's opinion of how an illness or disease will develop: *With some types of cancer the prognosis is good.* **2** the way something seems likely to develop in the future

pro·gram¹ /'prəʊgræm‖'proʊ-/ *n* [C] **1** the American spelling of PROGRAMME **2** a set of instructions given to a computer to make it do something

program² *v* [T] **-mmed, -mming** to give a set of instructions to a computer to make it do something

pro·gramme¹ *BrE*, **program** *AmE* /'prəʊgræm‖'proʊ-/ *n* [C] **1** a show on television or radio: *What's your favourite TV programme?* **2** an important plan to develop or improve something: *the US space program* **3** a set of planned activities: *a fitness programme* **4** a written description you get at a concert, play etc that tells you what will happen, who is performing etc

programme² *BrE,* **program** *AmE — v* [T]
1 **be programmed (to do sth)** to be made to behave or think in a particular way: *Are girls programmed at an early age not to like science?*
2 to give a set of instructions to a machine to make it do something: *I've programmed the VCR to record tonight's movie.* → see also PROGRAM²

pro·gram·mer /ˈprəʊɡræməˈˈprəʊɡræmər/ *n*
[C] someone whose job is to write PROGRAMs for computers — **programming** *n* [U]

pro·gress¹ /ˈprəʊɡresˈˈprɑː-/ *n* [U] **1** the process of getting better at something, or of getting closer to finishing or achieving something: *Millions of people watched the progress of the trial on TV.* | **make progress** *Nick has made a lot of progress since coming to our school.*
2 change towards a better society because of scientific developments or fairer methods of doing things: *technological progress* **3 in progress** *formal* happening now: *Please do not enter while there is a class in progress.*
4 movement towards a place: *The ship's progress was slowed by rough seas.*

pro·gress² /prəˈɡres/ *v* [I] **1** to develop and become better or more complete: *Work on the new building progressed quickly.* **2** to continue slowly: *He got more and more crazy as the years progressed.*

pro·gres·sion /prəˈɡreʃən/ *n* [C,U] a change or development: *career progression | the rapid progression of the disease*

pro·gres·sive¹ /prəˈɡresɪv/ *adj* **1** supporting or using modern ideas and methods: *progressive teaching methods* **2** a progressive change happens gradually and continuously over a period of time: *the progressive decline of the coal industry* — **progressively** *adv*

progressive ² *n* **the progressive** the form of the verb that is used to show that an action is continuing to happen

pro·hib·it /prəˈhɪbɪtˈˈprəʊ-/ *v* [T] *formal* to have a law or rule that stops people doing something: *Smoking is prohibited inside the building.* | **prohibit sb from doing sth** *Shops in Britain are prohibited from selling alcohol to people under 18.* — **prohibition** /ˌprəʊhɪˈbɪʃən/ *n* [U]

pro·hib·i·tive /prəˈhɪbɪtɪvˈˈprəʊ-/ *adj* prohibitive prices are so high that they prevent people from buying or doing something — **prohibitively** *adv*

proj·ect¹ /ˈprɒdʒektˈˈprɑː-/ *n* [C] **1** important work that is planned and organized carefully over a period of time: *the new road project | a project to help the homeless* **2** a piece of school work in which students have to collect information and write about a subject: **+ on** *a project on pollution*

pro·ject² /prəˈdʒekt/ *v* **1** [T] to calculate or plan what will happen in the future, using information you have now: *projected sales for next year* **2** [T] if you project a feeling or quality, you show it in the way you behave: *Jim always projects an image of self-confidence.* **3** [T] to make an image such as a photograph appear on a screen, using light **4** [I,T] *formal* to stick out beyond an edge or surface: **+ over/from etc** *The roof projects over the driveway.* **5 be projected**

to be planned to happen in the future: *A visit by President Clinton is projected for March.*

pro·jec·tile /prəˈdʒektaɪlˈ-tl/ *n* [C] *formal* an object that is thrown or fired from a weapon

pro·jec·tion /prəˈdʒekʃən/ *n* **1** [C] a statement about something you think will happen: *projections of economic growth* **2** [C] something that sticks out beyond an edge or surface **3** [C,U] the use of light to make an image appear on a screen or surface, or the image itself

pro·jec·tor /prəˈdʒektəˈ-ər/ *n* [C] a piece of equipment that uses light to make a film or pictures appear on a screen

pro·lif·e·rate /prəˈlɪfəreɪt/ *v* [I] *formal* to increase very quickly in number: *Projects to clean up the environment are proliferating.*

pro·lif·e·ra·tion /prəˌlɪfəˈreɪʃən/ *n* [singular, U] a fast increase in the amount or number of something: **+ of** *The proliferation of hotels and nightclubs has spoilt the charm of the area.*

pro·lif·ic /prəˈlɪfɪk/ *adj* producing a lot of something: *Agatha Christie was a prolific writer.* — **prolifically** /-kli/ *adv*

pro·logue /ˈprəʊlɒɡˈˈprəʊlɔːɡ, -lɑːɡ/ *n* [C] the introduction to a book, film, or play

pro·long /prəˈlɒŋˈ-ˈlɔːŋ/ *v* [T] to make something continue for longer: *Having your car serviced regularly prolongs its life.*

pro·longed /prəˈlɒŋdˈ-ˈlɔːŋd/ *adj* continuing for a long time: *a prolonged illness*

prom /prɒmˈprɑːm/ *n* [C] a formal dance party for HIGH SCHOOL students in the US

prom·e·nade /ˌprɒməˈnɑːd◂, ˈprɒmənɑːd ˌprɑːməˈneɪd◂/ *n* [C] *BrE* a wide path next to the sea which people walk along for pleasure — **promenade** *v* [I]

prom·i·nence /ˈprɒmɪnənsˈˈprɑː-/ *n* [U] when someone or something is important and well-known: **come/rise to prominence** *Stallone rose to prominence with the movie "Rocky."*

prom·i·nent /ˈprɒmɪnəntˈˈprɑː-/ *adj* **1** famous or important: *prominent politicians* **2** easy to see or notice: *a prominent nose* — **prominently** *adv*

pro·mis·cu·ous /prəˈmɪskjuəs/ *adj* having sex with many different people: *In the study, single men were the most promiscuous group.* — **promiscuity** /ˌprɒmɪˈskjuːˌtiˈˈprɑː-/ *n* [U]

prom·ise¹ /ˈprɒmɪsˈˈprɑː-/ *v* **1** [I,T] to say that you will definitely do something or that something will definitely happen: **+ (that)** *Will you promise me you won't be late?* | **promise to do sth** *Dad's promised to take us to Disneyland.* | **promise sb sth** *I've already promised them free tickets if they win.* **2** [T] if a situation or event promises something, you expect that thing to happen: **promise to be sth** *The game promises to be exciting.*

promise² *n* **1** [C] a statement that you will definitely do something or that something will definitely happen: **make a promise** *He's always making promises that he can't keep.* | **keep a promise** (=do what you said you would do): *Anna kept her promise to be back at 10 o'clock.* | **break a promise** (=not do what you said you would do) **2** [U] something that makes you think someone will be good or successful in the future: **show promise** *He shows a lot of promise as a writer.*

P

prom·is·ing /ˈprɒmɪˌsɪŋ‖ˈprɑː-/ *adj* likely to be successful in the future: *a promising young singer* —**promisingly** *adv*

prom·on·to·ry /ˈprɒməntəriɪ‖ˈprɑːməntɔːri/ *n* [C] a high narrow piece of land that goes out into the sea

pro·mote /prəˈməʊt‖-ˈmoʊt/ *v* [T] **1** to help something develop and be successful: *We aim to promote understanding between cultures.* **2** to advertise a product or event: *The company is spending millions promoting its new software.* **3** to give someone a better, more responsible position at work: **promote sb to sth** *Ted has been promoted to senior sales manager.*

pro·mot·er /prəˈməʊtə‖-ˈmoʊtər/ *n* [C] **1** someone whose job is to arrange large public events **2** someone who tries to make people support an idea or way of doing things: *promoters of organic farming*

pro·mo·tion /prəˈməʊʃən‖-ˈmoʊ-/ *n* **1** [C,U] a move to a better, more responsible position at work: **get promotion** *You only ever get a pay rise if you get promotion.* **2** [C,U] an activity intended to advertise a product or event: *a sales promotion* **3** [singular, U] when you try to make an idea popular: **+ of** *the promotion of equal rights*

pro·mo·tion·al /prəˈməʊʃənəl‖-ˈmoʊ-/ *adj* promotional products and activities are designed to advertise something

prompt¹ /prɒmpt‖prɑːmpt/ *v* **1** [T] to make someone decide to do something, especially something they were already thinking about doing: **prompt sb to do sth** *Bad weather at home has prompted people to go abroad this summer.* | *The accident has prompted an investigation into rail safety.* **2** [I,T] to remind someone, especially an actor, of what they should say next

prompt² *adj* done quickly, immediately, or at the right time: *We request prompt payment of bills.* —**promptly** *adv* —**promptness** *n* [U]

prompt³ *n* [C] a sign on a computer screen that shows the computer is ready for the next command

prone /prəʊn‖proʊn/ *adj* **1** likely to do something, especially something bad, or likely to suffer from something: **+ to** *The narrow river is prone to flooding in winter.* | **prone to do sth** *She's prone to eat too much when she's unhappy.* | **accident prone** (=having a lot of accidents) **2** *formal* lying down flat, especially with the front of your body facing down

prong /prɒŋ‖prɔːŋ/ *n* **1** [C] a thin sharp part of something that has several points, for example a fork **2** **two-pronged/three-pronged** a two-pronged or three-pronged attack is made against two or three parts of something at the same time

pro·noun /ˈprəʊnaʊn‖ˈproʊ-/ *n* [C] *technical* a word that is used instead of a noun or noun phrase, such as 'he' instead of 'Peter' or instead of 'the man'

pro·nounce /prəˈnaʊns/ *v* [T] **1** to make the sound of a letter, word etc: *How do you pronounce your name?* **2** to state something officially and formally: *He was pronounced dead at 11:00 p.m.*

pro·nounced /prəˈnaʊnst/ *adj* very noticeable: *Harold walks with a pronounced limp.*

pro·nounce·ment /prəˈnaʊnsmənt/ *n* [C] *formal* an official statement

pro·nun·ci·a·tion /prəˌnʌnsiˈeɪʃən/ *n* **1** [C,U] the way that a language or word is pronounced: *There are two different pronunciations of the word 'bow'.* **2** [singular, U] the way someone pronounces a word or words: *The cassette helps you check your pronunciation.*

proof /pruːf/ *n* **1** [C,U] facts, documents etc that prove something is true: **+ of** *You need proof of your age to buy cigarettes.* | **+ (that)** *You've got no real proof that he's having an affair.* **2** [C] *technical* a first copy of a printed page that you correct mistakes on **3** [U] a measurement of how much alcohol is in a drink

proof·read /ˈpruːfˌriːd/ *v* [I,T] to read something in order to correct any mistakes in it —**proofreader** *n* [C]

prop¹ /prɒp‖prɑːp/ *v* [T] **-pped, -pping** to support something and make it stay in a particular position: **prop sth against/on** *He propped his bike against the fence.*

prop sth ↔ up *phr v* [T] **1** to prevent something from falling by putting something against it or under it: *Steel poles prop up the crumbling walls.* **2** to help something to continue to exist: *Willis sold stocks to prop up his failing company.*

prop² *n* [C] **1** an object that you put under or against something to make it stay in a particular position **2** an object such as a piece of furniture, a book, a weapon etc that is used in a play or film

prop·a·gan·da /ˌprɒpəˈgændə‖ˌprɑː-/ *n* [U] information, especially false information, that a government or political organization uses to make people agree with them —**propagandist** *n* [C]

prop·a·gate /ˈprɒpəgeɪt‖ˈprɑː-/ *v* *formal* **1** [T] to tell a lot of people your ideas or beliefs in order to make them believe them or support them: *Politicians use the media to propagate their message.* **2** [I,T] to grow or produce new plants, or to make a plant do this —**propagation** /ˌprɒpəˈgeɪʃən‖ˌprɑː-/ *n* [U]

pro·pel /prəˈpel/ *v* [T] **-lled, -lling** **1** if something propels you into an activity or profession, it makes you do it: *The actress's striking good looks helped propel her to stardom.* **2** to move or push something forwards: *old ships propelled by steam*

pro·pel·ler /prəˈpelə‖-ər/ *n* [C] a piece of equipment with blades that spin around making a ship or aircraft move

pro·pen·si·ty /prəˈpensɪti/ *n* [C] *formal* a natural tendency to behave in a particular way: *He has a propensity to smile at every woman he sees.*

prop·er /ˈprɒpə‖ˈprɑːpər/ *adj* **1** [only before noun] correct or suitable for a particular situation: *Put the bread back in its proper place.* | *You have to go through the proper procedures.* **2** [only before noun] *BrE spoken* used to emphasize that someone or something really is that kind of person or thing: *Alex was my first proper boyfriend.* **3** socially correct and acceptable: *I didn't think it was proper to ask for her phone number so soon.* **4** [only after noun] limited to the central or main part of a place or subject: *We no longer live in Dallas proper; we moved to Mesquite.*

prop·er·ly /ˈprɒpəli‖ˈprɑːpərli/ *adv* correctly, in an acceptable way: *I can't see properly without glasses.*| *Did you tidy your room properly?*

proper noun /ˌ‥ ˈ‥/ *also* **proper name** *n* [C] a noun such as 'Mike,' 'Paris,' or 'Easter' that is the name of a person, place, or thing and is spelled with a capital letter

prop·er·ty /ˈprɒpəti‖ˈprɑːpər-/ *n* **1** [U] something that someone owns: *Police recovered some of the stolen property.* **2** [C,U] land or buildings: *Property prices are rising.* **3** [C] a natural quality that something has: *herbs with healing properties*

proph·e·cy /ˈprɒfɪsi‖ˈprɑː-/ *n* [C,U] a statement saying that something will happen in the future —**prophesy** /-fɪsaɪ/ *v* [I,T]

proph·et /ˈprɒfɪtl‖ˈprɑː-/ *n* [C] someone who people believe has been sent by God to teach them the right way to follow their religion

pro·phet·ic /prəˈfetɪk/ *adj* correctly saying what will happen in the future: *The Ambassador's warnings proved prophetic.* —**prophetically** /-kli/ *adv*

pro·pi·tious /prəˈpɪʃəs/ *adj formal* likely to be successful or bring good results: *a propitious time to attack*

pro·po·nent /prəˈpəunənt‖-ˈpou-/ *n* [C] *formal* someone who supports something or persuades people to support something: *a proponent of women's rights* —compare OPPONENT

pro·por·tion /prəˈpɔːʃən‖-ˈpɔːr-/ *n* **1** [C] a part of a larger amount or number: *The proportion of adults who smoke is lower than before.* **2** [C,U] the relationship between the amounts, numbers, or sizes of related things **proportion of sth to sth** *Girls outnumber boys at the school by a proportion of three to one.* **in proportion to sth** *Taxes rise in proportion to the amount you earn.* **3** [U] when the size or shape of the different parts of something look correct in relation to each other: **out of/in proportion** *The porch is out of proportion with the rest of the house.* **4 sense of proportion** the ability to decide what is important and what is not important in a situation **5 get/blow things out of proportion** to react to a situation as if it is worse or more serious than it really is → see also PROPORTIONS

pro·por·tion·al /prəˈpɔːʃənəl‖-ˈpɔːr-/ *also* **proportion·ate** /-ʃənɪt/ *adj* two things that are proportional increase and decrease at the same rate, so the relationship between them stays the same: *The number of Representatives each state has is proportional to its population.*

pro·por·tions /prəˈpɔːʃənz‖-ˈpɔːr-/ *n* [plural] **1** the size or shape of something, especially something large: *The plant can grow to gigantic proportions in the tropics.* **2** the degree to which something is important: *By 1939 the disease had reached epidemic proportions.*

pro·pos·al /prəˈpəʊzəl‖-ˈpou-/ *n* [C] **1** a plan that is suggested officially: **proposal to do sth** *a proposal to build a new road* **2** when you ask someone to marry you: *Did you accept his proposal?*

pro·pose /prəˈpəʊz‖-ˈpouz/ *v* **1** [T] to officially suggest a plan: *They are proposing changes in working hours.*| + **that** *I propose that we close the meeting.* **2** [I] to ask someone to marry you: + **to** *I proposed to my wife in Paris.* **3** [T] *formal* to intend to do something: **propose to do sth** *What do you propose to do about it?* **4** [T] to formally suggest someone for an official position: *Mrs Banks has been proposed for the position of Treasurer.*

prop·o·si·tion¹ /ˌprɒpəˈzɪʃən‖ˌprɑː-/ *n* [C] **1** an offer or suggestion, especially in business or politics: *I've got a business proposition for you.*| *Running my own company is an attractive proposition.* **2** a statement in which you express an idea or opinion

proposition² *v* [T] to ask someone to have sex with you

pro·pri·e·tor /prəˈpraɪətə‖-tər/ *n* [C] *formal* the owner of a shop, hotel, newspaper etc

pro·pri·e·ty /prəˈpraɪəti/ *n* [singular, U] *formal* correct social or moral behaviour

pro·pul·sion /prəˈpʌlʃən/ *n* [U] *technical* the force that moves a vehicle forward: *jet propulsion*

pro ra·ta /ˌprəʊ ˈrɑːtə‖ˌprou- ˈreɪtə/ *adj technical* calculated or paid according to exactly how much of something is used or how much work is done

pro·sa·ic /prəʊˈzeɪ-ɪk, prə-‖prou-, prə-/ *adj formal* boring and ordinary —**prosaically** /-kli/ *adv*

pro·scribe /prəʊˈskraɪb‖prou-/ *v* [T] *formal* to officially say that something is not allowed: *Child labor is proscribed by federal law.* —**proscription** /-ˈskrɪpʃən/ *n* [C,U]

prose /prəʊz‖prouz/ *n* [U] written language in its usual form, not as poetry

pros·e·cute /ˈprɒsɪkjuːt‖ˈprɑː-/ *v* [I,T] to say officially that someone might be guilty of a crime and must be judged by a court of law: **prosecute sb for sth** *He was prosecuted for theft.*

pros·e·cu·tion /ˌprɒsɪˈkjuːʃən‖ˌprɑː-/ *n* **1 the prosecution** the lawyers who try to prove that someone is guilty of a crime in a court of law: *a witness for the prosecution* → compare DEFENCE **2** [C,U] when someone is legally charged with a crime or judged in a court of law

pros·e·cu·tor /ˈprɒsɪkjuːtə‖ˈprɑːsɪkjuːtər/ *n* [C] a lawyer who tries to prove that someone is guilty of a crime in a court of law

pros·pect¹ /ˈprɒspekt‖ˈprɑː-/ *n* **1** [C,U] the chance that something you hope for will happen soon: + **of** *There's little prospect of ending the war.*| + **for** *an economy with good prospects for growth* **2** [singular] something you think will happen in the future and your idea of what it will be like: + **of** *The prospect of making a speech at the wedding fills me with dread.* **3 (sb's) prospects** someone's chances of being successful in the future, especially in their job: *His job prospects are not very good.*

pro·spect² /prəˈspekt‖ˈprɑːspekt/ *v* [I,T] to look

GRAMMAR NOTE: the progressive
You form the **present progressive** by using **be/is/was** + present participle: *They are coming.*
You form the **past progressive** by using **was/were** + present participle: *He was lying.*

for things such as gold or oil in the ground or under the sea —**prospector** n [C]

pro·spec·tive /prəˈspektɪv/ adj [only before noun] **propspective buyer/husband/employer etc** someone who is likely to buy something, become your husband, become your employer etc: *There are only two prospective candidates for the election.*

pro·spec·tus /prəˈspektəs/ n [C] a small book that gives details about a university or company

pros·per /ˈprɒspəˈprɑːspər/ v [I] to be successful, especially financially: *an environment in which small businesses can prosper*

pro·sper·i·ty /prɒˈsperˌtiˈprɑː-/ n [U] when people have money and everything they need for a good life

pros·per·ous /ˈprɒspərəsˈprɑː-/ adj successful and rich: *a prosperous community* —**prosperously** adv

pros·ti·tute /ˈprɒstˌtjuːtˈprɑːstˌtuːt/ n [C] someone who has sex to earn money

pros·ti·tu·tion /ˌprɒstˌtjuːʃənˌprɑːstˌtuːʃən/ n [U] when someone earns money by having sex with people

pros·trate /ˈprɒstreɪtˈprɑː-/ adj lying flat on the ground with your face downwards

pro·tag·o·nist /prəʊˈtægənˌstˈproʊ-/ n [C] *formal* the main character in a play, film, or story

pro·tect /prəˈtekt/ v [T] to prevent someone or something from being harmed or damaged: **protect sb/sth from sth** *New sea defences have been built to protect the town from flooding.* | **protect (sb/sth) against sth** *a cream to protect your skin against sunburn* —**protected** adj: *Owls are a protected species.* —**protector** n [C]

pro·tec·tion /prəˈtekʃən/ n [singular, U] when someone or something is protected, or something that protects you: **give/offer/provide protection** *Heidi's thin coat gave little protection against the cold.* | *The organization provides help and protection for abused teenagers.*

pro·tec·tive /prəˈtektɪv/ adj **1** used to protect someone or something: *protective clothing* **2** wanting to protect someone from danger or harm: *She suddenly felt very protective towards him.*

prot·é·gé /ˈprɒtəʒeɪˈproʊ-/ n [C] a young person who is guided and helped by an older and more experienced person

pro·tein /ˈprəʊtiːnˈproʊ-/ n [C,U] a substance in food such as meat and eggs, which helps your body to grow and be healthy

pro·test[1] /ˈprəʊtestˈproʊ-/ n [C] **1** when a group of people do something to show publicly that they think something is wrong or unfair: *protests against the war* | *protest marches* **2** [C] when you tell someone that they should not do something because it is wrong: *He ignored her protests.* **3 do sth under protest** to do something because you have to, while saying that you do not want to do it

pro·test[2] /prəˈtest/ v **1** [I,T] to do something to show publicly that you think something is wrong or unfair: **+ against** *a group protesting against human rights abuses* | **protest sth** *AmE*: *Students carried signs protesting the war.* **2** [I] to tell someone that what they are saying or doing is wrong or unfair: *"That's not true!" she*

protested angrily. **3 protest your innocence** to say strongly that you are not guilty

Prot·es·tant /ˈprɒtˌstəntˈprɑː-/ n [C] someone who belongs to the part of the Christian religion that separated from the Roman Catholic church in the 16th century —**Protestant** adj —**Protestantism** n [U]

prot·es·ta·tion /ˌprɒtˌsteɪʃən, ˌprəʊ-ˌprɑː-, ˌproʊ-/ n [C] *formal* a strong statement saying that something is true, especially when other people say it is not

pro·test·er, protestor /prəˈtestəˈ-ər/ n [C] someone who takes part in an activity with a large group of people to show publicly that they think something is wrong or unfair: *anti-government protesters*

pro·to·col /ˈprəʊtəkɒlˈproʊtəkɔːl, -kɑːl/ n [U] a system of rules about the correct way to behave on official occasions

pro·ton /ˈprəʊtɒnˈproʊtɑːn/ n [C] *technical* a part of the NUCLEUS of an atom, that carries POSITIVE electricity

pro·to·type /ˈprəʊtətaɪpˈproʊ-/ n [C] the first example of a new car, machine etc, which is used to test the design before it is produced

pro·trac·ted /prəˈtræktˌd/ adj continuing for a long time, usually longer than necessary: *a protracted legal dispute* —**protraction** /-ˈtrækʃən/ n [U]

pro·trac·tor /prəˈtræktəˈproʊˈtræktər/ n [C] a flat object shaped like a half circle, used for measuring and drawing angles

pro·trude /prəˈtruːdˈproʊ-/ v [I] *formal* to stick out from somewhere: *a rock protruding from the water* —**protruding** adj —**protrusion** /-ˈtruː-ʒən/ n [C,U]

proud /praʊd/ adj **1** feeling pleased with your achievements, possessions, family etc because you think they are very good: **+ of** *Her parents are very proud of her.* | **proud to do sth** *I'm proud to receive this award.* **2 be too proud (to do sth)** to feel too embarrassed to do something, especially to ask other people to help you, or to admit you are wrong **3 do sb proud** to make someone feel proud of you by doing something well: *The team did their fans proud and won the game 6-0.* **4** thinking that you are more important, skilful etc than you really are: *He has always been a proud and arrogant man.* —**proudly** adv → see also PRIDE[1]

prove /pruːv/ v proved, proved or proven /ˈpruːvən/ proving **1** [T] to show that something is definitely true: *They have evidence to prove that she is guilty.* **2** [I,T] if someone or something proves to be useful, successful, correct etc, they show that they are useful etc: *The competition has proved to be a great success.* **3 prove yourself** to show that you can do something well: *At seventeen years old, she had yet to prove herself as a player.* —**provable** adj

prov·en[1] /ˈpruːvən, ˈprəʊvənˈproʊvən, ˈpruːvən/ adj shown to be good, effective, or true: *a proven method of learning*

pro·ven[2] /ˈpruːvən/ v a past participle of PROVE

prov·erb /ˈprɒvɜːbˈprɑːvɜːrb/ n [C] a short well-known phrase or sentence, which contains advice about life

pro·ver·bi·al /prəˈvɜːbiəlˈ-ɜːr-/ adj used when you are talking about part of a well-known phrase to describe someone or something: *I was running around like the proverbial headless chicken!* —**proverbially** *adv*

pro·vide /prə'vaɪd/ *v* [T] to give or supply something to someone. especially something that they need: *The EU is providing the money for the project.* | **provide sb with sth** *I was provided with a car and a guide.*

    provide for sb/sth *phr v* [T] **1** to give someone the things that they need, such as money, food, or clothing: *He has to provide for a family of five.* **2** if a plan provides for something, for example something that might happen in the future, it is included in the plan

pro·vid·ed /prə'vaɪdɪd/ also **provided (that)** *linking word* used to say that something will only happen if another thing happens: *The equipment is perfectly safe, provided it is used in the right way.*

prov·i·dence /'prɒvɪdəns‖'prɑː-/ *n* [U] a force that some people believe controls our lives, especially so that good things happen

pro·vid·er /prə'vaɪdər/ *n* [C] a person or company that provides something such as a service: *a health-care provider*

pro·vid·ing /prə'vaɪdɪŋ/ also **providing that** *linking word* PROVIDED

prov·ince /'prɒvɪns‖'prɑː-/ *n* [C] one of the large areas into which some countries are divided: *the Canadian provinces*

pro·vin·cial /prə'vɪnʃəl/ *adj* **1** relating to a PROVINCE: *the provincial capital* **2** someone who is provincial is not modern or fashionable, because they do not live in a large city

pro·vi·sion /prə'vɪʒən/ *n* **1** [C,U] the act of providing something for someone: *the provision of services for the elderly* **2** **make provisions for** to make arrangements to deal with something or take care of someone: *He has made provisions for his wife in his will.* **3** [C] a part of an agreement or law: *the provisions of the treaty*

pro·vi·sion·al /prə'vɪʒənəl/ *adj* existing for only a short time and likely to be changed in the future: *A provisional government was set up after the war.*

pro·vi·sions /prə'vɪʒənz/ *n* [plural] food supplies, especially for a journey: *We had enough provisions for two weeks.*

pro·vi·so /prə'vaɪzəʊ‖-zoʊ/ *n* [C] *formal* when you agree to allow something to happen, but only if something else happens

prov·o·ca·tion /ˌprɒvə'keɪʃən‖ˌprɑː-/ *n* [C,U] something that is likely to make someone angry and want to attack another person: *The police acted calmly, in the face of great provocation.*

pro·voc·a·tive /prə'vɒkətɪv‖-'vɑː-/ *adj* **1** intending to make someone angry or start arguing: *a provocative remark* **2** intending to make someone sexually excited —**provocatively** *adv*: *a provocatively low-cut dress*

pro·voke /prə'vəʊk‖-'voʊk/ *v* [T] **1** to deliberately make someone angry and make them behave in a violent way: *She hit him, but he provoked her into it.* **2** to cause a feeling or reaction: *The article provoked a heated discussion.*

prov·ost /'prɒvəst‖'proʊvoʊst/ *n* [C] an important official at a university

prow /praʊ/ *n* [C] the front part of a ship or boat

prow·ess /'praʊɪs/ *n* [U] *formal* great skill at doing something: *athletic prowess*

prowl¹ /praʊl/ *v* [I,T] to move around an area quietly, especially when hunting: *a tiger prowling through the jungle*

prowl² *n* **be on the prowl** to be moving quietly, hunting for another animal, or looking for someone to attack

prowl·er /'praʊlər/ *n* [C] someone who moves around quietly at night, especially in order to steal things or attack someone

prox·im·i·ty /prɒk'sɪmɪti‖prɑːk-/ *n* [U] *formal* when something is close to something else: *We chose this house because of its proximity to the school.*

prox·y /'prɒksi‖'prɑːksi/ *n* **do sth by proxy** to arrange for someone else to do something for you

prude /pruːd/ *n* [C] someone who is easily shocked by anything relating to sex —**prudish** *adj* —**prudishness, prudery** *n* [U]

pru·dent /'pruːdənt/ *adj* sensible and careful, especially by avoiding risks or not wasting anything: *prudent use of resources* —**prudence** *n* [U]

prune¹ /pruːn/ also **prune back** *v* [T] to cut some of the branches of a tree or bush to make them grow back more strongly or thickly

prune² *n* [C] a dried PLUM

pru·ri·ent /'prʊəriənt‖'prʊr-/ *adj* *formal* showing too much interest in sex —**prurience** *n* [U]

pry /praɪ/ *v* **pried, pried, prying** **1** [I] to try to find out details about someone's private life, especially in a way that seems rude: *a secret honeymoon, away from the prying eyes of the press* **2** [T] to force something to open, or force something to separate from something else; PRISE: **pry sth open/off etc** *I used a screwdriver to pry off the lid.*

PS /ˌpiː 'es/ used when you want to add something at the end of a letter: *PS I love you*

psalm /sɑːm‖sɑːm, sɑːlm/ *n* [C] a song or poem from the Bible praising God

pseudo- /sjuːdəʊ‖suːdoʊ/ *prefix* not real: *pseudoscience*

pseu·do·nym /'sjuːdənɪm‖'suːdənɪm/ *n* [C] a false name used by someone, especially a writer, instead of their real name

psych /saɪk/ *v*

    psych yourself **up** *phr v* [T] *informal* make yourself feel mentally ready to do something difficult, by telling yourself that you can do it —**psyched up** *adj*

psy·che /'saɪki/ *n* [C] someone's mind and their deepest feelings: *the male psyche*

psy·che·del·ic /ˌsaɪkɪ'delɪk◂/ *adj* **1** psychedelic drugs such as LSD have a strong effect on your mind and make you see things that do not really exist **2** psychedelic art, clothing etc has a lot of bright colours and patterns

psy·chi·a·trist /saɪ'kaɪətrɪst‖sə-/ *n* [C] a doctor who treats people who have a mental illness → compare PSYCHOLOGIST

psy·chi·a·try /saɪ'kaɪətri‖sə-/ *n* [U] the study and treatment of mental illness —**psychiatric** /ˌsaɪki'ætrɪk◂/ *adj*: *a psychiatric hospital*

psy·chic¹ /'saɪkɪk/ *adj* **1** relating to strange events that science cannot explain, for example when people see GHOSTS: *psychic phenomena*

2 having strange powers, for example so that you know what will happen in the future, or know what someone is thinking: *How did you know I was coming? You must be psychic!*

psychic² *n* [C] someone who is believed to have strange powers, such as the ability to see into the future

psy·cho /ˈsaɪkəʊ‖-koʊ/ *n* [C] *informal* a crazy person who is likely to behave in a violent way

psy·cho·a·nal·y·sis /ˌsaɪkəʊ-ə'nælɪsɪs‖-koʊ-/ *n* [U] a way of treating someone who is mentally ill by talking to them about their life, feelings etc

psy·cho·an·a·lyst /ˌsaɪkəʊ'ænəl-ɪst‖-koʊ-/ *n* [C] someone who treats people using psycho-analysis

psy·cho·log·i·cal /ˌsaɪkə'lɒdʒɪkəl‖-'lɑː-/ *adj* **1** relating to the way people's minds work and the way this affects their behaviour: *psychological problems* **2** relating to PSYCHOLOGY — **psychologically** /-kli/ *adv*

psy·chol·o·gist /saɪ'kɒlədʒ ɪst‖-'kɑː-/ *n* [C] someone who studies the way people's minds work and how mental problems can be treated → compare PSYCHIATRIST

psy·chol·o·gy /saɪ'kɒlədʒi‖-'kɑː-/ *n* **1** [U] the scientific study of the mind and how it works: *a professor of psychology* **2** [C,U] the way that a particular kind of person thinks and behaves: *the psychology of child killers*

psy·cho·path /ˈsaɪkəpæθ/ *n* [C] someone who has a mental illness that makes them behave in a violent or criminal way — **psychopathic** /ˌsaɪkə'pæθɪk‹/ *adj*

psy·cho·sis /saɪ'kəʊsɪs‖-koʊ-/ *n, plural* **psychoses** /-siːz/ [C,U] a serious mental illness

psy·cho·so·mat·ic /ˌsaɪkəʊsə'mætɪk‹‖-kəsə-/ *adj* a psychosomatic illness is caused by fear or anxiety, rather than by any physical problem

psy·cho·ther·a·py /ˌsaɪkəʊ'θerəpi‖-koʊ-/ *n* [U] the treatment of mental illness by talking to someone and discussing their problems, rather than using drugs or medicine — **psychotherapist** *n* [C]

psy·chot·ic /saɪ'kɒtɪk‖-'kɑː-/ *adj* relating to serious mental illness: *psychotic behaviour*

pt. the written abbreviation of PART and PINT

PTA /ˌpiː tiː 'eɪ/ *n* [C] Parent Teacher Association; an organization of the teachers and parents of children at a school

PTO /ˌpiː tiː 'əʊ‖-'oʊ/ *BrE* please turn over; used at the bottom of a page to tell the reader to look at the next page

pub /pʌb/ *n* [C] a place, especially in Britain and Ireland, where you can buy and drink alcohol; bar

pu·ber·ty /ˈpjuːbəti‖-ər-/ *n* [U] the time when your body changes from being a child to being an adult who is able to have children

pu·bic /ˈpjuːbɪk/ *adj* relating to or near the sex organs: *pubic hair*

pub·lic¹ /ˈpʌblɪk/ *adj* **1** relating to all the ordinary people in a country or area: *Public support for the strike has increased.* | **public opinion** (=the opinion that most ordinary people have): *Public opinion is in favour of the death penalty.* | **in the public interest** (=useful or helpful to ordinary people) **2** provided or available for anyone to use: *a public swimming pool* | *public*

transportation → opposite PRIVATE¹ **3** relating to the government and the services that it provides: *cuts in public spending* | **public office** (=an important government job): *She was elected to public office in 1992.* **4** **make sth public** to tell everyone about something that was secret: *Last night the name of the killer was made public.* **5** done in a place where anyone can see or hear you: *public displays of emotion* — **publicly** *adv*

public² *n* **1** **the public** also **the general public** all the ordinary people in a country or place: *The museum is open to the public five days a week.* | *This product is not for sale to the general public.* **2** **in public** if you do something in public, you do it in a place where anyone can see or hear you: *He was always very nice to her in public.*

public ad·dress sys·tem /ˌ... .'. ˌ../ *n* [C] PA

pub·li·ca·tion /ˌpʌblɪ'keɪʃən/ *n* **1** [U] when a book, magazine etc is printed and made available for people to buy: *The book is ready for publication.* **2** [U] when people are told information about something, for example in a report in a newspaper: *the publication of the test results* **3** [C] *formal* a book, magazine etc that is printed and made available for people to buy: *a monthly publication*

public fig·ure /ˌ.. '../ *n* [C] a well-known person who is often on television, in newspapers and magazines etc

public hol·i·day /ˌ.. '.../ *n* [C] a day when people in a country do not work and the shops are closed; NATIONAL HOLIDAY

public house /ˌ.. './ *n* [C] *BrE formal* a PUB

pub·li·cist /ˈpʌblɪsɪst/ *n* [C] someone whose job is to make sure that people know about a new film, book etc, or about a famous person is doing

pub·lic·i·ty /pʌ'blɪsɪti/ *n* [U] **1** attention that someone or something gets from newspapers, television etc: *a murder trial that received a lot of publicity* **2** the business of making sure that people know about a new film, book etc, or about something that is planned to happen

pub·li·cize (also **-ise** *BrE*) /ˈpʌblɪsaɪz/ *v* [T] to tell people about a new film, book etc, or about something that is planned to happen, in newspapers, on television etc: **well/highly publicized** (=when something is mentioned a lot in newspapers, on television etc): *Camilla's highly publicized relationship with Prince Charles*

public re·la·tions /ˌ.. .'../ **PR** *n* **1** [U] the work of explaining what a company, organization etc does, and making people have a good opinion of them: *the public relations department* **2** [plural] the relationship between an organization and ordinary people: *Organizing events for charity is always good for public relations.*

public school /ˌ.. './ *n* [C] **1** *BrE* an expensive school that parents pay to send their children to: *Many of the people in the British Government went to public schools.* **2** *AmE* a free school that is controlled and paid for by the government

public tel·e·vi·sion /ˌ.. '...., ˌ.. ..'../ *n* [U] a television service in the US that is paid for by the government, large companies, and by ordinary people

pub·lish /ˈpʌblɪʃ/ v **1** [I,T] if a book, magazine etc is published, it is printed and made available for people to buy: *a book that was first published in 1851* **2** [T] if a newspaper, magazine etc publishes a story, photograph etc, they include it so that people can read it or see it: *The article was first published in the Los Angeles Times.* **3** [T] to make official information available for people to read about: *When will the results be published?*

pub·lish·er /ˈpʌblɪʃəll-ər/ n [C] a person or company that produces books, magazines etc and makes them available for people to buy

pub·lish·ing /ˈpʌblɪʃɪŋ/ n [U] the business of producing books, magazines etc and making them available for people to buy

pud·ding /ˈpʊdɪŋ/ n [C,U] **1** a sweet food made with milk, eggs, sugar, flour etc: *chocolate pudding* **2** *BrE* the last part of a meal, when you eat sweet food: *What's for pudding?*

pud·dle /ˈpʌdl/ n [C] a small pool of water on the ground, often left after it rains

pudg·y /ˈpʌdʒi/ adj fat, especially in a way that seems unattractive: *short, pudgy fingers*

pu·er·ile /ˈpjʊəraɪl||ˈpjʊrəl/ adj formal silly and stupid; CHILDISH: *puerile jokes*

puff¹ /pʌf/ v **1** [I] to breathe quickly and with difficulty after running, carrying something heavy etc: *Max was puffing heavily after climbing the stairs.* **2** [I,T] to breathe smoke from a cigarette, pipe etc in and out: + **on** *William sat there puffing on his pipe.*

puff sth ↔ **out** phr v [T] to make part of your body bigger by filling it with air

puff up phr v **1** [T] to make part of your body bigger by filling it with air: *Birds puff up their feathers to stay warm.* **2** if part of your body puffs up, it becomes swollen

puff² n [C] **1** the action of breathing smoke into your mouth and blowing it out again: *He took a puff on his cigar.* **2** a small amount of air, smokes or wind that is suddenly blown somewhere: *puffs of smoke coming from the chimney*

puf·fin /ˈpʌfɪ̩n/ n [C] a sea bird with a black and white body and a large brightly coloured beak

puff·y /ˈpʌfi/ adj if part of your body is puffy, it is swollen: *Her eyes were red and puffy from crying.* —**puffiness** n [U]

pug·na·cious /pʌɡˈneɪʃəs/ adj formal very eager to argue or fight with people

puke /pjuːk/ v [I,T] informal to VOMIT —**puke** n [U]

pull¹ /pʊl/ v **1** [I,T] to hold something firmly and move it towards you, or move it in a particular direction: *Mom, Sara's pulling my hair!* | *Can you help me pull the trunk into the corner?* | *I managed to pull the drawer open.* → see colour picture on page 670 **2** to remove or take something from somewhere, especially suddenly or by using force: **pull sth out/off/ from/away etc** *The dentist pulled out one of my back teeth.* **3** [I,T] if a vehicle or horse pulls something, it makes it move along behind it: *The car was pulling a camper behind it.* **4** **pull a gun/knife on sb** to suddenly take out a gun or knife and threaten someone with it **5** **pull sb's leg** to tell someone something that is not true, as a joke **6** **pull a muscle** to injure a muscle by stretching it too much while exercising **7** **pull your weight** to do your share of the work: *Some men still don't pull their weight when it comes to housework.* **8** **pull strings** to arrange for something to happen by talking to someone you know who has an important job **9** **pull the strings** to secretly control what is happening, especially instead of a much more important person: *Who is really pulling the strings in the White House?* **10** **pull a fast one** spoken to secretly try to trick someone in order to get advantages for yourself **11** **pull out all the stops** to do everything you possibly can to make something happen or succeed → see also **make/pull faces** (FACE¹)

pull sth ↔ **apart** phr v [T] to separate something into two or more pieces or groups: *Loosen the roots and gently pull the plants apart.*

pull away phr v [I] **1** to start to drive away from somewhere: *She watched the car pull away.* **2** to go faster than someone during a race, or get more points than another person or team during a game: *Chicago pulled away in the third quarter to win 107-76.* **3** to move away from someone, especially someone who is holding you: *Jess tried to pull away from him.*

pull sth ↔ **down** phr v [T] to destroy a building, wall etc: *All the old houses are being pulled down.*

pull in phr v **1** [I] to drive to the side of the road and stop: *A police car pulled in behind me.* **2** if a train pulls in, it arrives at a station

pull off phr v **1** [T **pull** sth ↔ **off**] to succeed in doing something difficult: *UCLA pulled off a win in Saturday's game.* **2** [I,T **pull off** sth] to leave a road in order to stop or go into another road

pull out phr v **1** [I] if a car pulls out, it moves out towards the middle of the road: *Someone pulled out in front of me, and we nearly crashed.* **2** [I] If a train pulls out of a station, it starts to move out of the station **3** [I] to not take part in something that you have agreed to do: *Sampras was forced to pull out of the competition.* **4** [I,T] if an army pulls out or is pulled out of a country, they leave it: *US forces pulled out of Somalia.* **5** **pull out all the stops** to do everything you can to achieve something or make something successful

pull over phr v [I,T **pull** sb/sth ↔ **over**] to move to the side of the road and stop, or to order someone to do this: *The police pulled him over for speeding.*

pull through phr v [I] informal to stay alive after a serious injury or illness, or continue to exist in spite of problems: *Do you think she'll pull through?*

pull together phr v **1** [I] to work hard with other people to achieve something: *If we all*

GRAMMAR NOTE: the passive (1)

You use a verb in the **passive** to say that something happens to the subject of the sentence. You form the passive using **be/is/was** and the past participle.

ACTIVE: *They **chose** a new leader.* → PASSIVE: *A new leader **was chosen**.*

pull together, I'm sure we can win. **2 pull yourself together** *informal* to stop being upset or afraid and behave in a calm way: *Pull yourself together, man!*

pull up *phr v* **1** [I] if a car pulls up, it stops: *A red Buick pulled up at the lights.* **2 pull up a chair** to get a chair and sit down near someone **3** [T **pull** sth ↔ **up**] to pull plants out of the ground

pull² *n* **1** [C] the movement you make when you pull something towards you: *Give the rope a pull.* **2** [singular] a strong force such as GRAVITY that makes things move in a particular direction: *the gravitational pull of the moon*

pul·ley /ˈpʊli/ *n* [C] a piece of equipment for lifting things, which consists of a wheel and a rope

pull·out, pull-out /ˈpʊlaʊt/ *n* [C] when an army, organization etc leaves a place: *the pullout of NATO troops*

pull·o·ver /ˈpʊl,əʊvə‖-,ouvər/ *n* [C] a piece of warm clothing usually made of wool, which covers the top half of your body; SWEATER

pul·mo·na·ry /ˈpʊlmənəri, ˈpʌl-/ *adj technical* relating to the lungs: *pulmonary diseases*

pulp /pʌlp/ *n* [U] **1** the soft inside part of a fruit or vegetable **2** a soft substance made by crushing something: *wood pulp*

pul·pit /ˈpʊlpɪt/ *n* [C] the place where a priest speaks from in a church

pul·sate /pʌlˈseɪt‖ˈpʌlseɪt/ *v* [I] to make strong regular sounds or movements: *loud pulsating music* —**pulsation** /pʌlˈseɪʃən/ *n* [C,U]

pulse¹ /pʌls/ *n* **1** [C usually singular] the regular beat made by your heart when it is moving blood around your body: **take sb's pulse** (=check how fast someone's heart is beating): *A nurse came in and took my pulse.* **2** [C usually plural] a seed such as beans and PEAs that you can eat

pulse² *v* [I] to move quickly with a strong regular beat or sound: *blood pulsing through his veins*

pul·ver·ize /ˈpʌlvəraɪz/ *v* [T] **1** to crush something into powder: *a machine that pulverizes rocks* **2** *informal* to defeat someone completely

pum·ice /ˈpʌmɪs/ *n* [C,U] very light rock from a VOLCANO

pum·mel /ˈpʌməl/ *v* [T] to hit someone or something many times with your FISTS (=closed hands)

pump¹ /pʌmp/ *n* [C] **1** a machine that forces liquid or gas into or out of something: *a fuel pump* **2** a type of plain light shoe: *a pair of black pumps*

pump² *v* **1** [I,T] to make liquid or gas flow somewhere continuously: *a machine that pumps water into the fields* **2** [T] *informal* to ask someone a lot of questions about something in order to get information **3 pump money into** to spend a lot of money on something: *Millions of dollars have been pumped into research.*

pump out *phr v* **1** [I,T **pump** sth ↔ **out**] to produce something, or be produced in large amounts: *I heard the music pumping out of the speakers.* **2** [T **pump** sth ↔ **out**] to remove liquid from somewhere using a special machine

pump sth ↔ **up** *phr v* [T **pump** sth ↔ **up**] to fill a tyre, ball etc with air; INFLATE

pum·per·nick·el /ˈpʌmpənɪkəl‖ˈpʌmpər-/ *n* [U] a type of heavy dark brown bread

pump·kin /ˈpʌmpkɪn/ *n* [C,U] a large round orange vegetable that grows on the ground: *pumpkin pie* → see picture at VEGETABLES

pun /pʌn/ *n* [C] a joke that is based on two words that sound the same —**pun** *v* [I]

punch¹ /pʌntʃ/ *v* [T] **1** to hit someone or something hard with your FIST (=closed hand): *He threatened to punch me in the face.* → see colour picture on page 670 **2** to make a hole in something using a metal tool or other sharp object: *The inspector came around and punched our tickets.*

punch² *n* **1** [C] when you hit someone once with your FIST (=closed hand): *a punch in the stomach* **2** [U] a drink made from fruit juice, sugar, water, and often alcohol **3** [C] a metal tool for cutting holes, or for pushing something into a small hole

punch bag /ˈ. ./ *BrE*, **punching bag** /ˈ.. ./ *AmE* — *n* [C] a heavy leather bag that BOXERS hit when they are training

punch·line, punch line /ˈpʌntʃlaɪn/ *n* [C] the last few words of a joke or story, that make it funny or clever

punc·tu·al /ˈpʌŋktʃuəl/ *adj* arriving at exactly the time that has been arranged: *Ted's always very punctual.* —**punctually** *adv* —**punctuality** /,pʌŋktʃuˈæləti/ *n* [U]

punc·tu·ate /ˈpʌŋktʃueɪt/ *v* [T] **1** to divide your writing into sentences, phrases etc using COMMAS [,], FULL STOPS [.] etc **2 be punctuated by/with** used to say that something happens often, or that something is often interrupted by another thing: *The early 70s were punctuated by a series of strikes and demonstrations.*

punc·tu·a·tion /,pʌŋktʃuˈeɪʃən/ *n* [U] the use of COMMAS [,], FULL STOPS [.] etc in a piece of writing

punctuation marks

.	full stop *BrE*/ period *AmE*	? question mark
,	comma	! exclamation mark *BrE*/ exclamation point *AmE*
;	semi-colon	() brackets
:	colon	" " quotation marks

punctuation mark /,..ˈ.. ./ *n* [C] a sign, such as a COMMA [,] or a FULL STOP [.], that is used when you are dividing a piece of writing into sentences, phrases etc

punc·ture¹ /ˈpʌŋktʃə‖-ər/ *n* [C] **1** a small hole made by a sharp point **2** *BrE* a hole in a tyre: *Looks like you've got a puncture.*

puncture² *v* [I,T] if something punctures or is

punctured, a small hole appears in it and air or liquid can get out

puncture

pun·dit /ˈpʌndɪt/ n [C] someone who often appears on television or in newspapers and gives their opinions, especially about political subjects

pun·gent /ˈpʌndʒənt/ adj having a strong taste or smell: *the pungent smell of frying garlic* —**pungency** n [U]

pun·ish /ˈpʌnɪʃ/ v [T] to do something unpleasant to someone, for example put them in prison or make them pay money, because they have done something wrong or illegal: *If he's broken the law he deserves to be punished.*

pun·ish·a·ble /ˈpʌnɪʃəbəl/ adj a crime that is punishable by death, prison etc, is punished in that way

pun·ish·ing /ˈpʌnɪʃɪŋ/ adj very tiring and difficult: *a punishing walk*

pun·ish·ment /ˈpʌnɪʃmənt/ n [C,U] when someone is punished: *tougher punishments for sex offenders | They had to stay late after school as a punishment.* ➞ see also CAPITAL PUNISHMENT

pu·ni·tive /ˈpjuːnɪtɪv/ adj intended as punishment: *punitive action* —**punitively** adv

punk /pʌŋk/ n [U] **1** [U] also **punk rock** /ˌ. ˈ./ a type of loud violent music popular in the late 1970s and early 1980s **2** [C] someone who dresses like people who like punk music, and has brightly-coloured hair, pins and chains and torn clothing **3** *AmE informal* a young man who causes trouble and does not respect other people

pun·net /ˈpʌnɪt/ n [C] a small basket or box in which fruit is sold

punt /pʌnt/ n [C] a long narrow boat, moved by pushing a long pole against the bottom of the river —**punt** v [T]

punt·er /ˈpʌntə-ər/ n [C] *BrE informal* someone who makes a BET, or someone who buys something

pu·ny /ˈpjuːni/ adj small, thin, and weak: *a puny little kid*

pup /pʌp/ n [C] PUPPY

pu·pil /ˈpjuːpəl/ n [C] **1** *especially BrE* a child in a school ➞ see colour picture on page 80 **2** the round black part in the middle of your eye **3** someone who is taught skills by an experienced musician, artist etc: *a pupil of Yehudi Menuhin*

pup·pet /ˈpʌpɪt/ n [C] **1** a MODEL of a person or animal that you can move by pulling wires, or by putting your hand inside it: *a puppet show* **2** a leader or government that is not independent, and is controlled by another more powerful government or organization

pup·pe·teer /ˌpʌpɪˈtɪə-ˈtɪr/ n [C] someone who performs with puppets

pup·py /ˈpʌpi/ n [C] a young dog

puppet

pur·chase¹ /ˈpɜːtʃɪs‖ˈpɜːr-/ v [T] *formal* to buy something: *Sangster recently purchased 10 acres of land in France.*

purchase² n *formal* **1** [C,U] when someone buys something: *money for the purchase of new equipment* **2** [C] something that has been bought: *We deliver your purchases to your door.*

pure /pjʊə‖pjʊr/ adj **1** not mixed with anything else: *pure gold* **2** completely and only – used before a noun to emphasize what you are saying: *It was pure chance that we were there at the same time.* **3** clean and not containing anything harmful or unhealthy: *pure drinking water* **4** pure science is concerned only with ideas and knowledge about a subject, not about the practical use of this knowledge ➞ compare APPLIED **5** *especially literary* not having bad thoughts, and always behaving in a morally good way

pu·ree /ˈpjʊəreɪ‖pjʊˈreɪ/ n [C,U] food that is boiled or crushed until it is almost a liquid: *tomato puree*

pure·ly /ˈpjʊəli‖ˈpjʊrli/ adv completely and only: *He did it for purely selfish reasons.| We met purely by chance.*

pur·ga·to·ry /ˈpɜːgətəri‖ˈpɜːrgətɔːri/ n [U] **1** a place where, according to Roman Catholic beliefs, the souls of dead people must suffer for the bad things they did, until they are allowed to go to HEAVEN **2** a situation that is very unpleasant

purge /pɜːdʒ‖pɜːrdʒ/ v [T] **1** to force people to leave an organization, often by using violence, because they do not agree with your political ideas, will not support you etc **2** *literary or technical* to get rid of bad feelings, or something bad that is in your body —**purge** n [C] *the Stalinist purges of the 1930s*

pu·ri·fy /ˈpjʊərɪfaɪ‖ˈpjʊr-/ v [T] to remove dirty or unwanted parts from something: *purified water* —**purification** /ˌpjʊərɪfɪˈkeɪʃən‖ˌpjʊr-/ n [U]

pur·ist /ˈpjʊərɪst‖ˈpjʊr-/ n [C] someone who has very strict ideas about the correct way to do something

pu·ri·tan·i·cal /ˌpjʊərɪˈtænɪkəl‖ˌpjʊr-/ adj having very strict ideas about how people should behave, especially about things that people enjoy: *Her parents had very puritanical views about sex.* —**puritan** /ˈpjʊərɪtən‖ˈpjʊr-/ n [C]

pu·ri·ty /ˈpjʊərɪti‖ˈpjʊr-/ n [U] the quality of being pure: *the purity of our water | moral purity*

pur·ple /ˈpɜːpəl‖ˈpɜːr-/ n [U] a dark colour made from red mixed with blue ➞ see colour picture on page 114 —**purple** adj

pur·port /pɜːˈpɔːt‖pɜːrˈpɔːrt/ v **purport to be/ be purported to be** *formal* used to say that people say that something is true about something or someone, especially when you doubt this: *The painting is purported to be the work of Monet.*

pur·pose /'pɜːpəs‖'pɜːr-/ *n* **1** [C] what you want to achieve when you do something: *The main purpose of my stay is to visit the museum.* **2 on purpose** deliberately: *I'm sorry I hurt you. I didn't do it on purpose.* **3** [C] what something is used for: *The planes may be used for military purposes.* **4** [U] determination to succeed in what you want to do: *She went back to her work with a new sense of purpose.*

pur·pose·ful /'pɜːpəsfəl‖'pɜːr-/ *adj* behaving in a way that shows you have a definite intention of doing something: *He picked up his toolbox in a purposeful manner.*

pur·pose·ly /'pɜːpəsli‖'pɜːr-/ *adv* deliberately: *They purposely left him out of the discussion.*

purr /pɜː‖pɜːr/ *v* [I] **1** if a cat purrs, it makes a soft, low sound in its throat **2** if an engine purrs, it makes a quiet smooth sound **3** to speak in a soft low voice —**purr** *n* [C]

purse[1] /pɜːs‖pɜːrs/ *n* [C] **1** *BrE* a small container used for carrying money, especially by women **2** *AmE* a bag used by women to carry money and personal things; HANDBAG *BrE* → see picture at BAG

purse[2] *v* [T] **purse your lips** to bring your lips together tightly, especially to show that you disapprove of something

purs·er /'pɜːsə‖'pɜːrsər/ *n* [C] an officer who is responsible for the money on a ship and deals with passengers' problems

pur·sue /pə'sjuː‖pər'suː/ *v* [T] **1** to continue doing something, or to try to achieve something over a long period of time: *He hoped to pursue a career in film-making.* | **pursue the matter** (=continue asking someone about a problem, or ask a court or official person to deal with it) **2** to chase someone or something in order to catch them: *The stolen car was pursued by police for several miles.*

pur·suit /pə'sjuːt‖pər'suːt/ *n* **1** [U] when someone chases another person in order to try to catch them: **in hot pursuit** (=following close behind someone) **2** [U] when someone tries to achieve something or get something: *the pursuit of happiness* **3** pursuits *formal* things that you spend time doing, especially to enjoy yourself: *outdoor pursuits*

pur·vey·or /pə'veɪə‖pɜːr'veɪər/ *n* [C] *formal* a shop or company that sells or provides something: *purveyors of fine cheeses*

pus /pʌs/ *n* [U] yellow liquid produced in an infected part of your body

push[1] /pʊʃ/ *v* **1** [I,T] to make someone or something move away from you by pressing with your hands: *Can you push harder?* | **push sth/sb up/down/into etc** *I helped him push the Volkswagen up the street.* | *Lisa pushed Amy into the pool.* → see colour picture on page 670 → opposite PULL[1] **2** [I,T] to press a button, SWITCH etc: *Someone pushed the wrong button and the machine went into reverse.* **3** [I,T] to move forward by pushing people away from you: *Heather pushed past us without speaking.* | *people trying to push their way to the front* **4** [I,T] to try to make someone do something, especially by asking or telling them many times: **push sb to do/into doing sth** *My parents pushed me into going to college.* | + **for** *They're pushing for*

stricter gun controls. **5** [T] to make someone work very hard: **push yourself** *Michael has been pushing himself too much lately.* **6** [I,T] to make a number, amount, price etc greater or less: **push sth up/down** *The new tax will push up the price of consumer goods.* **7** [T] *informal* to sell illegal drugs **8 be pushed for time** *informal* to have very little time **9 push your luck** *informal* to do something that may be too risky, in the hope that you will continue to have good luck

push ahead *phr v* [I] to continue trying to do something you have planned to do: + **with** *Keating has promised to push ahead with reform.*

push sb around *phr v* [T] *informal* to tell someone what to do in rude or threatening way

push off *phr v* [I] *BrE spoken* used to rudely tell someone to go away

push on *phr v* [I] to continue travelling somewhere or trying to achieve something: *The others stopped for a rest, but I pushed on to the top.*

push sth ↔ through *phr v* [T] to make a parliament or group of people agree to a law or plan, especially when this is not easy

push[2] *n* [C usually singular] **1** when you push someone or something: **give sb a push** (=push them once): *If the door's stuck, just give it a push.* **2** when people try to achieve something using a lot of effort: *the party's final push for victory* **3 give sb the push** *BrE informal* to end a relationship with someone or take away their job: *She gave her boyfriend the push.* **4 at a push** *BrE informal* used to say that something can be done if necessary, but it will be difficult **5 when/if push comes to shove** used to say that you could do something if you really had to do it: *If push comes to shove, I can always rent out the house.*

push·bike /'pʊʃbaɪk/ *n* [C] *BrE informal* a bicycle

push·chair /'pʊʃtʃeə‖-tʃer/ *n* [C] *BrE* a small folding chair on wheels, used for pushing young children in; STROLLER *AmE*

push·er /'pʊʃə‖-ər/ *n* [C] *informal* someone who sells illegal drugs

push·ing /'pʊʃɪŋ/ *prep* **be pushing 40, 50 etc** *informal* to be almost 40, 50 etc years old

push·o·ver /'pʊʃˌəʊvə‖-ˌoʊvər/ *n* **a** pushover *informal* **a)** someone who is easily defeated, or a game in which someone is easily defeated **b)** someone who you can easily persuade to do something

push-up /'. ./ *n* [C] *AmE* an exercise in which you lie on the floor and push yourself up with your arms; PRESS-UP *BrE*

push·y /'pʊʃi/ *adj* determined to get what you want or make other people do what you want, in a way that seems rude: *pushy salespeople*

pussy·cat /'pʊsikæt/ also **puss** /pʊs/, **pus·sy** /'pʊsi/ *BrE* — *n* [C] *informal* a cat – used especially by children

pus·sy·foot /'pʊsifʊt/ *v* [I] *informal* to be too careful and afraid to deal with a situation firmly

pussy wil·low /'.. ˌ../ *n* [C] a tree with long thin branches and soft round flowers that look like fur

put /pʊt/ *v* **put, put, putting** [T] **1** to move something to or into a place or position: **put sth in/on/there etc** *Just put the bags on the table.* | *Where did you put the newspaper?* | *I put* *the letter back in the envelope.* **2** to make arrangements for someone to go to a place and stay there: *I don't want to put my dad into a hospital.*| *You put the kids to bed and I'll make dinner.* **3** to change someone's situation or the way they feel: *The long delay had put us all in a bad mood.* **4** to write or print something: *Put your name at the top of each answer sheet.* **5** to say something in a particular way: *Derek's – how shall I put it – not very attractive.*| *I thought she put her argument over well.* **6 put an end to sth/put a stop to sth** to stop an activity: *a law designed to put an end to discrimination against women* **7 put (your) faith/trust etc in** to trust someone or something: *people who put their trust in God* **8 put sth behind you** to stop thinking about a bad experience or a mistake so that it no longer affects you **9 not put it past sb to do sth** used to say that you think someone might do something unpleasant or dishonest: *I wouldn't put it past him to blackmail them.* → see also **put your mind to it** (MIND)

put sth ↔ **across** *phr v* [T] to explain something so that other people can understand it: *She's good at putting her ideas across.*

put sth ↔ **aside** *phr v* [T] **1** to save money regularly in order to use it later: *We're trying to put some money aside for a new car.* **2** to stop doing an activity, for example reading or working, so that you can do something else: *Charles put his newspaper aside and got up to answer the door.*

put sth ↔ **away** *phr v* [T] to put something in the place where it is usually kept: *Those kids never put anything away!*

put sth ↔ **back** *phr v* [T] **1** to delay something: *The publication date has been put back by three months.* **2 put a clock/a watch back** to make a clock or watch show an earlier time

put sb/sth ↔ **down** *phr v* [T] **1** [**put** sth ↔ **down**] to put something onto a surface such as a table or the floor: *She put down her knitting.* → see colour picture on page 670 **2** [**put** sb ↔ **down**] to criticize someone and make them feel silly or stupid: *I don't like the way she's always putting him down.* **3** [**put** sth ↔ **down**] *BrE* to write something on a piece of paper: *Don't forget to put your name down on the list.* **4** [**put** sth ↔ **down**] to kill an animal because it is old or ill **5 put down a revolution/revolt/rebellion etc** to stop a REVOLUTION by using force

put sth **down to** sth *phr v* [T] to think that something is caused by something else: *She put her illness down to stress.*

put sth ↔ **forward** *phr v* [T] **1** to suggest that someone considers employing a particular person or using a particular plan, idea etc: *Milne has put his name forward as a candidate at the next election.* **2 put a clock/a watch forward** to make a clock or watch show a later time

put sth ↔ **in** *phr v* [T] **1 put in a claim/request** to officially ask for something **2** to spend time or effort doing something: *Doug's been putting in a lot of hours at work recently.*

3 to add or replace equipment in your home: *They're having a new bathroom put in.*

put into *phr v* [T] **put sth into practice/action/effect** to start using something such as an idea or plan: *The college hopes to put the changes into effect by September 1.*

put sb/sth **off** *phr v* [T] **1** to make someone dislike someone or something, or to make them not want to do something: *Don't be put off by the title – it's a really good book.* **2** to delay doing something: *You can't keep putting the decision off.* **3** to tell someone that you cannot do something that you had agreed to do: *I managed to put him off by promising to pay next week.* **4** *BrE* to make it difficult for someone to do something by preventing them from thinking clearly about what they are doing: *Stop laughing – you're putting me off!*

put on/take off

He put on his jumper.

She took off her jumper.

put sth ↔ **on** *phr v* [T] **1** to put clothes on your body: *Put your coat on – it's cold.* **2** to put MAKE-UP or cream on your skin: *I need to put on some more lipstick.* **3** to make a machine or a piece of equipment start working: *Is it all right if I put the fire on?* **4** to put a record, VIDEO etc into a machine and start playing it: *Let's put some music on.* **5 put on weight/2 pounds/2 kg etc** to become fatter **6** to arrange or perform a concert, play etc: *They're putting on a concert to raise money for landmine victims.* **7 put it on** to pretend to feel or believe something that you do not really feel or believe: *Don't take any notice of her – she's just putting it on.*

put sb/sth ↔ **out** *phr v* [T] **1** to stop a fire or cigarette from burning **2** to make an electric light stop working by pressing a button: *Don't forget to put out the lights when you leave.* **3** *AmE* to produce something such as a book, record, film etc: *They're putting out a new album in the fall.* **4 put out your hand/foot/arm** to move your hand, foot, or arm away from your body: *Jack put out his foot and tripped her.* **5** to make extra work or problems for someone: *Will it put you out if I bring an extra guest?* **6 put out information/a warning/statistics etc** to produce information

---

GRAMMAR NOTE: the passive (1)
You use a verb in the **passive** to say that something happens to the subject of the sentence. You form the passive using **be/is/was** and the past participle.
ACTIVE: *They **chose** a new leader.* → PASSIVE: *A new leader **was chosen**.*

for people to read or listen to: *The police put out a warning about car thieves in the area.*

put through *phr v* [T] **1** [**put** sb **through** sth] to make someone experience something unpleasant: *She was put through a lot during her first marriage, so I'm glad she's happy now.* **2** [**put** sb **through**] to connect someone to someone else on the telephone

put sth **to** sb *phr v* [T] **1** explain something such as an idea or an opinion to other people, so that they will consider it: *The proposal will be put to the committee next month.* **2** to ask someone a question

put sth ↔ **together** *phr v* [T] **1** to make a machine or model by joining the different parts: *It took us all day to put the table together.* **2** to prepare or produce something by collecting information, ideas etc: *The band are currently putting a new album together.* **3** **put together** used to talk about the combined total of something: *Italy scored more points than the rest of the group put together.*

put up *phr v* [T] **1** [**put** sth ↔ **up**] to build something such as a wall, or to raise something so that it is upright: *The kids were putting a tent up in the garden.* **2** [**put** sth ↔ **up**] to put a picture, sign etc on a wall so that people can see it: *Posters advertising the concert were put up on all the notice boards.* **3** [**put** sth ↔ **up**] to increase the cost of something: *Our landlord keeps putting the rent up.* **4** **put up money/£500/$3 million etc** to provide the money that is needed to do something: *Firth put up $42,000 in prize money for the contest.* **5** [**put** sb ↔ **up**] to let someone stay in your house for a short time: *Yeah, we can put you up for the night.* **6** **put up resistance/a fight/a struggle** to argue against something or fight against someone in a determined way

put sb **up to** sth *phr v* [T] to encourage someone to do something that is wrong or dangerous: *It's not like Martha to steal – someone must have put her up to it.*

put up with sth *phr v* [T] to accept a bad situation without complaining: *I don't know how you put up with all this noise.*

put-down /ˈ. ./ *n* [C] *informal* something some-

one says that is intended to make you feel stupid

put out /ˌ. ˈ./ *adj* **be/feel put out** to feel upset or offended: *She felt put out at not being invited.*

pu·trid /ˈpjuːtrɪd/ *adj* decayed and smelling extremely bad: *an overpowering and putrid odour*

putt /pʌt/ *v* [I,T] to hit a GOLF ball gently along the ground towards the hole —**putt** *n* [C]

put·ty /ˈpʌti/ *n* [U] a soft substance used for fixing glass into window frames

puz·zle[1] /ˈpʌzəl/ *n* **1** [C] a game or toy that you have to think about carefully in order to solve it: *a crossword puzzle | a jigsaw puzzle* **2** [singular] something that is difficult to understand or explain: *Bergson's reasons for leaving remain something of a puzzle.*

puzzle[2] *v* **1** [T] if something puzzles you, you feel confused because you do not understand it: *What puzzles me is why he never mentioned this before.* **2** **puzzle over** sth to think about something for a long time in order to understand it: *Joe sat puzzling over the map.*

puz·zled /ˈpʌzəld/ *adj* confused and unable to understand something: *Don had a puzzled expression on his face.* → see colour picture on page 277

puz·zling /ˈpʌzlɪŋ/ *adj* difficult to understand or explain: *The results of the survey were a little puzzling.*

py·ja·mas *BrE*, **pajamas** *AmE* /pəˈdʒɑːməz ‖ -ˈdʒæ-, -ˈdʒɑː-/ *n* [plural] light trousers and a shirt that you wear in bed

py·lon /ˈpaɪlən‖-lɑːn, -lən/ *n* [C] a tall metal structure that supports electric wires high above the ground

pyr·a·mid /ˈpɪrəmɪd/ *n* [C] **1** an ancient stone building with four walls shaped like TRIANGLES that slope to a point at the top **2** an object that has this shape → see picture at SHAPES

pyre /paɪə‖paɪr/ *n* [C] a high pile of wood on which a dead body is burned at a funeral ceremony

py·thon /ˈpaɪθən‖-θɑːn, -θən/ *n* [C] a large tropical snake that kills animals for food by crushing them

Qq

Q, q /ˈkjuː/ the letter 'q'

quack¹ /kwæk/ v [I] to make the sound that a duck makes

quack² n [C] **1** the sound a duck makes **2** BrE informal a doctor who is not QUALIFIED **3** BrE a humorous word for a doctor

quad /kwɒd/ also **quadrangle** /ˈkwɒd-ræŋɡəl/ n [C] a square area with buildings all around it in a school or college

quad·ru·ple /ˈkwɒdrupəl, kwɒˈdruː-/ v [I,T] if you quadruple an amount, or if an amount quadruples, it becomes four times as big: *The number of car owners has quadrupled in the last twenty years.*

quag·mire /ˈkwæɡmaɪə, ˈkwɒɡ-/ n [C] **1** a very difficult or complicated situation: *a legal quagmire* **2** an area of soft wet muddy ground that is dangerous to walk on: *Torrential rain turned the site into a quagmire.*

quail¹ /kweɪl/ n [C,U] a small bird that is hunted and shot for food and sport, or this bird as food

quail² v [I] literary to feel afraid: *She quailed at the thought of seeing him again.*

quaint /kweɪnt/ adj unusual and attractive, especially in an old-fashioned way: *quaint narrow streets*

quake¹ /kweɪk/ v [I] formal to shake because you are afraid: **+ with** *Kate stood in the doorway quaking with fear.*

quake² n [C] informal an EARTHQUAKE

Quak·er /ˈkweɪkə/ n [C] a member of the Society of Friends, a Christian religious group that opposes violence and has no religious leaders or ceremonies

qual·i·fi·ca·tion /ˌkwɒlɪfɪˈkeɪʃən, ˌkwɑː-/ n **1** [C usually plural] an examination that you have passed at school or university: *He left school without any qualifications.* **2** [C] a skill or quality that you need to do a job: *Patience is a necessary qualification for this kind of work.* **3** [U] when you achieve the necessary standard to work in a profession, enter a sports competition etc: *Portugal's qualification for the European Championships* **4** [C,U] something that you add to a statement to limit its effect or meaning: *He welcomed the proposal without qualification.*

qual·i·fied /ˈkwɒlɪfaɪd/ adj **1** having passed an examination that shows you have the training, knowledge, or skills to do a job: *a qualified teacher* **2** qualified agreement, approval etc is limited in some way because you do not agree or approve completely

qual·i·fi·er /ˈkwɒlɪfaɪə/ n [C] **1** a game that you have to win to take part in a sports competition: *Norway drew 2-2 with Poland in the World Cup qualifier.* **2** a person or team who achieves the necessary standard to enter a sports competition

qual·i·fy /ˈkwɒlɪfaɪ/ v **1** [I] to pass an examination in order to work in a profession: **+ as** *Sue qualified as a solicitor last year.* **2** [I]

to be successful at one stage of a sports competition and continue to the next stage: **+ for** *The US beat Nigeria to qualify for the finals.* **3** [I,T] to have the right to do something, or to give someone the right to do something: **+ for** *Members qualify for a 20% discount.* **4** [T] to add information to something you have already said, to limit its meaning or effect: *Let me qualify that statement.*

qual·i·ta·tive /ˈkwɒlɪtətɪv/ˈkwɑːlɪˌteɪ-/ adj formal relating to the quality of something rather than its size: *a qualitative study of the health care program* → compare QUANTITATIVE

qual·i·ty¹ /ˈkwɒlɪti/ˈkwɑː-/ n **1** [U] whether the standard of something is good or bad: *the decline in air quality in our cities* | *Good quality shoes last longer.* **2** [U] a high standard: *I've been impressed by the quality of his work.* **3** [C usually plural] a good or bad part of someone's character: *a job that demands the qualities of honesty and integrity* **4** [C] something that is typical of a person or thing: *Atkinson's novels all have a humorous quality.*

quality² adj [only before noun] of a high standard: *We sell quality clothing at a price you can afford.*

qualm /kwɑːm/kwɑːm, kwɑːlm/ n [C] a worry or doubt about whether what you are doing is right: **have no qualms about sth** *She had no qualms whatsoever about firing people.*

quan·da·ry /ˈkwɒndəri/ˈkwɑːn-/ n **be in a quandary (about/over sth)** to be unable to decide what to do about a difficult situation: *Ian's in a quandary about whether to accept their offer.*

quan·ti·fi·er /ˈkwɒntɪfaɪə/ˈkwɑːntɪˌfaɪr/ n [C] a word or phrase such as 'much', 'few', or 'a lot of', which is used with a noun to show a quantity, without showing the exact amount

quan·ti·fy /ˈkwɒntɪfaɪ/ˈkwɑːn-/ v [T] to measure something and express it as a number or amount: *These kinds of improvement are hard to quantify.* —**quantifiable** adj

quan·ti·ta·tive /ˈkwɒntɪtətɪv/ˈkwɑːntɪˌteɪ-/ adj formal relating to amounts: *quantitative estimates* → compare QUALITATIVE

quan·ti·ty /ˈkwɒntɪti/ˈkwɑːn-/ n **1** [C,U] an amount of something that can be measured or counted: **+ of** *Large quantities of drugs were found in their luggage.* | **in quantity** (=in large amounts): *It's cheaper buying goods in quantity.* **2** [U] the amount of something that is produced: *It's quality that's important, not quantity.*

quantum leap /ˌkwɒntəm ˈliːp/ˌkwɑːn-/ n [C usually singular] a big and sudden improvement: *a quantum leap in medical science*

quar·an·tine /ˈkwɒrəntiːn/ˈkwɔː-/ n [U] when a person or animal is kept apart from other people or animals because they may have an infectious disease: **in quarantine** *Animals coming into Britain must be kept in quarantine.* —**quarantine** v [T]

quar·rel¹ /ˈkwɒrəl/ˈkwɔː-, ˈkwɑː-/ n **1** [C] an angry argument: **+ with** *We've had a quarrel with our neighbours.* **2** **have no quarrel with** formal to have no reason to disagree with someone or something: *We have no quarrel with the court's decision.*

quarrel² v [I] **-lled, -lling** BrE, **-led, -ling** AmE to have an angry argument: **+ with** *She's always quarrelling with her sister.*

quar·rel·some /ˈkwɒrəlsəm‖ˈkwɔː-, ˈkwɑː-/ *adj* a quarrelsome person is always quarrelling with other people

quar·ry¹ /ˈkwɒri‖ˈkwɔː-, ˈkwɑː-/ *n* **1** [C] a place where sand or stone is dug out of the ground **2** [singular] an animal or person that is being hunted

quarry² *v* [T] to dig out sand or stone from a quarry

quart /kwɔːt‖kwɔːrt/ written abbreviation **qt** *n* [C] a unit for measuring liquid, equal to 2 pints

quar·ter /ˈkwɔːtəl‖ˈkwɔːr-tər/ *n* [C] **1** one of four equal parts into which something can be divided: **+ of** *A quarter of Canada's population is French-speaking.* **2** one of the four periods of 15 minutes into which each hour can be divided: *Can you be ready in a quarter of an hour?* | **quarter to/ quarter of** *AmE* (=15 minutes before the hour): *It's quarter to five.* | **quarter past** *BrE*/**quarter after** *AmE* (=15 minutes after the hour): *It's quarter past five.* **3** a period of three months, used to talk about bills, wages, and incomes: *Profits increased by 2% in the first quarter.* **4** a coin in the US and Canada worth 25 cents (=¼ of a dollar) **5** *AmE* one of the four periods into which a year at school or college is divided → compare SEMESTER **6** *AmE* one of the four equal periods of time into which some sports games are divided **7** a group of people who all do something or who all share a belief or opinion: *Concern has been expressed in several quarters about the decision.* **8** an area of a town where a particular group of people live: *the student quarter*

quarter

quarter

quar·ter·back /ˈkwɔːtəbæk‖ˈkwɔːrtər-/ *n* [C] the player in American football who directs the ATTACK and throws the ball

quar·ter·fi·nal /ˌkwɔːtəˈfaɪnl‖ˌkwɔːrtər-/ *n* [C] one of four games near the end of a competition. The winners play in the two SEMIFINALS

quar·ter·ly /ˈkwɔːtəli‖ˈkwɔːrtər-/ *adj, adv* produced or happening four times a year: *a quarterly report* | *The magazine is published quarterly.*

quartz /kwɔːts‖kwɔːrts/ *n* [U] a type of hard rock used for making electronic watches and clocks

quash /kwɒʃ‖kwɑːʃ, kwɒʃ/ *v* [T] *formal* **1** to officially say that a judgement or legal decision is no longer legal or correct: *The Court of Appeal quashed Maloney's conviction.* **2** to use force or violence to stop fighting or protests: *Troops loyal to the President quashed the rebellion in just a few hours.*

qua·ver /ˈkweɪvəl-ər/ *v* [I] if your voice quavers, it shakes as you speak because you are nervous or upset

quay /kiː/ *n* [C] a place beside the sea or a river where boats can be tied up, and loaded (LOAD) or unloaded

quea·sy /ˈkwiːzi/ *adj* feeling sick; NAUSEOUS — **queasiness** *n* [U]

queen /kwiːn/ *n* [C] **1** also **Queen** the female ruler of a country, or the wife of a king **2** a playing card with a picture of a queen on it **3** a large female BEE that lays the eggs for a whole group

queen-size /ˈ. ./ *adj especially AmE* bigger than the normal size: *a queen-size bed*

queer¹ /kwɪəl‖kwɪr/ *adj* **1** strange and not normal: *There's something a bit queer about him.* **2** *informal* an offensive word meaning HOMO-SEXUAL

queer² *n* [C] *informal* an offensive word for a HOMOSEXUAL man

quell /kwel/ *v* [T] **1** to stop feelings of doubt, worry, fear etc about something: *Police were trying to quell public fear about the murders.* **2** to end a violent situation: *Troops were called in to quell the riots.*

quench /kwentʃ/ *v* **quench your thirst** to drink enough so that you are no longer thirsty

que·ry¹ /ˈkwɪəri‖ˈkwɪri/ *n* [C] a question asking for more information

query² *v* [T] *formal* **1** to check that something is true or correct by asking questions about it: *Adams kept querying the referee's decisions.* **2** to ask a question

quest /kwest/ *n* [C] *formal* a long and difficult search — **quest** *v* [I]

ques·tion¹ /ˈkwestʃən/ *n* **1** [C] something you say or write when you are asking for information: **ask/answer a question** *Do you mind if I ask you a personal question?* | **+ about** *I have one or two questions about the timetable.* **2** [C] a part of a test: *Some of the questions were really difficult.* **3** [C] a subject that needs to be discussed or a problem that needs to be solved; ISSUE: *European leaders met yesterday to discuss the question of nuclear arms.* **4** [C,U] a feeling of doubt about something: **there's no question about sth** (=there is no doubt): *The Bulls are the best team in the league – there's no question about it.* | **beyond question** (=certain and unable to be doubted): *Her honesty is beyond question.* | **call sth into question** (=make people doubt something): *Recent events have called into question the wisdom of the government's decision.* **5 without question a)** without complaining or asking why: *A good soldier is supposed to follow orders without question.* **b)** used to say that something is definitely true: *Joyce is without question a great writer.* **6 there's no question of** used to say that something will definitely not happen: *There's no question of Shearer leaving the team.* **7 in question** the person or thing that is being discussed: *On the afternoon in question, Myers was seen leaving the building at 3.30.* **8 be out of the question** used to emphasize that something is not possible or not allowed: *Walking home on your own is out of the question.* **9 (that's a) good question!** *spoken* used as a way of saying that you do not know the answer to a question: *"If we don't have enough people to help, how can we finish the job?" "Good question!"*

question² *v* [T] **1** to ask someone questions about something: *A 31 year-old man is being questioned by police in connection with the murder.* **2** to express doubts about something: *Are you questioning my honesty?*

ques·tion·a·ble /ˈkwestʃənəbəl/ *adj* **1** something that is questionable seems likely to be dishonest or morally wrong: *I think her motives are highly questionable.* **2** not certain to be true or correct: *It's questionable whether this kind of research is actually useful.*

ques·tion·ing /ˈkwestʃənɪŋ/ *adj* a questioning look or expression shows that you want more information or an answer to a question —**questioningly** *adv*

question mark /ˈ.. ./ *n* [C] the sign (?), written at the end of a question

ques·tion·naire /ˌkwestʃəˈneə, ˌkes-ll-ˈner/ *n* [C] a set of written questions answered by a large number of people that is used to provide information

question tag /ˈ.. ./ *n* [C] a phrase such as 'isn't it?' or 'does she?' that you add to the end of a sentence to make it a question or check that someone agrees with you.

queue[1] /kjuː/ *n* [C] *BrE* a line of people or vehicles that are waiting for something; LINE *AmE*: *There was a long queue outside the cinema.*

queue[2] also **queue up** *v* [I] *BrE* to wait in a line of people in order to do something; LINE UP *AmE*: *We had to queue for over an hour to get tickets.*

quib·ble /ˈkwɪbəl/ *v* [I] to argue about something that is not very important: + **about/over/ with** *Let's stop quibbling over small details.* —**quibble** *n* [C]

quiche /kiːʃ/ *n* [C,U] a type of food that consists of PASTRY filled with a mixture of eggs, cheese, vegetables etc

quick[1] /kwɪk/ *adj* **1** taking only a very short time: *I'll just have a quick shower first.* | *The journey to Wilmington's much quicker by train.* **2** moving or happening fast: *Have you finished already? That was quick.* **3** able to learn things fast: *Carolyn's a quick learner.* **4** be quick to do sth to do something without any delay, especially react to something someone says or does: *The President was quick to deny the rumours.*

quick[2] *adv informal* quickly: *Come quick! There's been an accident.* → see also QUICKLY

quick·en /ˈkwɪkən/ *v* [I,T] to become quicker, or to make something quicker: *Her heartbeat quickened when she saw him.*

quick·ly /ˈkwɪkli/ *adv* fast, or done in a short amount of time: *I promise I'll do it as quickly as I can.* | *He quickly put the money back in the box.*

quick·sand /ˈkwɪksænd/ *n* [U] wet sand that is dangerous to walk on because you sink into it

quid /kwɪd/ *n* [C] *plural* **quid** *BrE informal* a pound in British money

qui·et[1] /ˈkwaɪət/ *adj* **1** not making a lot of noise: *We'll have to be quiet – we don't want to wake your parents.* | **be quiet** *spoken* (=used to tell someone to stop talking): *Be quiet! I've got a headache.* **2** with little or no noise, or without much activity or things happening: *The shop has been really quiet today.* | *They live in a quiet part of town.* **3** not speaking or not likely to say

much: *Sam's a quiet hardworking boy.* **4 keep (sth) quiet** to not tell other people about something: *Let's keep quiet about this for now.*

quiet[2] *n* [U] when there is little noise or activity: **peace and quiet** *Now Stella's gone, we can have some peace and quiet around here.* **2 on the quiet** secretly

qui·et·en /ˈkwaɪətn/ *BrE*, **quiet** *AmE* — *v* [T] to make someone or something quiet: *His appeal for calm failed to quieten the protesters.*

quieten down *BrE*, **quiet down** *AmE* — *phr v* [I,T] to become quiet, or make someone quiet: *After a while the children quietened down.*

qui·et·ly /ˈkwaɪətli/ *adv* **1** without making much noise: *Ron shut the door quietly.* | "*I'm sorry,*" *he said quietly.* **2** in a way that does not attract attention: *He quietly got on with his work.* **3 quietly confident/optimistic** fairly confident of success, but not talking proudly about it

quill /kwɪl/ *n* [C] a pen made from a large feather, used in the past

quilt /kwɪlt/ *n* [C] a cover for a bed filled with soft warm material

quilt·ed /ˈkwɪltɪd/ *adj* quilted cloth has a thick layer of material sewn into it

quilt

quin·tes·sen·tial /ˌkwɪntɪˈsenʃəl/ *adj* very typical of a particular person or thing: *New York is the quintessential big city.* —**quintessentially** *adv*

quip /kwɪp/ *v* [I,T] **-pped, -pping** to make an amusing remark —**quip** *n* [C]

quirk /kwɜːk‖kwɜːrk/ *n* [C] **1** a strange habit or feature that someone or something has: *one of her annoying little quirks* **2 a quirk of fate** something strange that happens by chance: *By a quirk of fate, I met him again the following day.*

quirk·y /ˈkwɜːki‖-ɜːr-/ *adj* slightly strange or different from normal: *a quirky sense of humour*

quit /kwɪt/ *v* [I,T] **quit, quitting** *informal* **1** to leave your job, school etc permanently: *Barry quit his job in order to travel around the world.* **2** to stop doing something: *I quit smoking three years ago.* **3** to leave a place

quite /kwaɪt/ *adv, quantifier* **1** *BrE* fairly: *She's quite tall for her age.* | *They live quite a long way from the nearest town.* **2** completely: *Although they're sisters, they're quite different.* | *I was quite disgusted at the way they behaved.* **3 not quite** almost, but not completely or not exactly: *I'm not quite sure how the system works.* | *Lewis isn't quite as fast as he used to be.* **4 quite a lot/bit/few** a large number or amount: *They've had quite a bit of snow this year.* | *There were quite a few people at the party.* **5 quite a/quite some** used to emphasize that something is especially good, bad etc: *He certainly made quite an impression on the kids.* | *That's quite some car, where did you buy it?*

quiv·er /ˈkwɪvəll-ər/ *v* [I] to shake slightly, especially because you are angry, upset, or nervous:

+ **with** *His voice was quivering with rage.*
—**quiver** *n* [singular]

quiz[1] /kwɪz/ *n* [C] **1** a competition in which you have to answer questions: *a quiz show on TV* **2** *AmE* a short test that a teacher gives to a class: *a math quiz*

quiz[2] *v* [T] **-zzed, -zzing** to ask someone a lot of questions: *Reporters quizzed Harvey about his plans for the future.*

quiz·zi·cal /'kwɪzɪkəl/ *adj* a quizzical look, smile etc shows that you have a slight doubt about something or are slightly amused by something

quo·rum /'kwɔːrəm/ *n* [singular] the smallest number of people that must be at a meeting in order for official decisions to be made

quo·ta /'kwəʊtəll'kwoʊ-/ *n* [C] a limited or fixed number or amount: *a strict quota on imports*

quo·ta·tion /kwəʊ'teɪʃənllkwoʊ-/ *n* [C] **1** words from a book, poem etc that are re-

peated by someone else: *a quotation from Shakespeare* **2** a written statement showing how much money it will cost to do something: *Get at least three quotations and don't just go for the cheapest.*

quotation mark /.'.. ./ *n* [C usually plural] a sign (", ") used before and after words that are quoted

quote[1] /kwəʊtllkwoʊt/ *v* **1** [I,T] to repeat exactly what someone else has said or written: *The star was quoted as saying that she was disgusted at the way she had been treated.* | + **from** *He quoted extensively from the works of Marx and Lenin.* **2** [T] to give an example of something in order to support or prove what you are saying: *Wilkins quoted several cases where errors had occurred.* **3** [T] to tell a customer the price you will charge them for doing something

quote[2] *n* [C] a QUOTATION

Rr

R, r /ɑːǁɑːr/ *n* [C] the letter 'r'

rab·bi /'ræbaɪ/ *n* [C], *plural* **rabbis** a Jewish religious leader

rab·bit /'ræbɪt/ *n* [C] a common small animal with long ears and soft fur that lives in the ground

rabbit

rab·ble /'ræbəl/ *n* [singular] a noisy crowd of people who are likely to cause trouble

ra·bies /'reɪbiːz/ *n* [U] a very dangerous disease that is passed on when someone is bitten by an infected animal, especially a dog

rac·coon /rə'kuːn, ræ-ǁræ-/ *n* [C] an animal with black fur around its eyes and black and white bands on its tail

race¹ /reɪs/ *n* **1** [C] a competition in which people try to run, drive, ride etc faster than each other: *Hill won the race and Schumacher finished second.* **2** [C,U] one of the main groups into which people are divided according to the colour of their skin and physical appearance: *The law forbids discrimination on the grounds of race or religion.* **3** [C] a group of people with the same language, customs etc **4** [C] a situation in which people or organizations compete with each other for something: *Chirac lost the 1988 presidential race.* **5 a race against time** when you must finish doing something in a short period of time → see also ARMS RACE, HUMAN RACE

race

USAGE NOTE: race, nation, state, and tribe

Use these words to talk about groups of people. The largest group is a **race**, which means people who have the same skin colour, type of hair, and physical features: *The survey was given to people of different races and ages.* A **nation** is a country and its social and political structure, or a group of people with the same history and language: *Leaders of several Western nations are meeting in Paris this week.* Use **state** to talk about the politics or the government of a country: *The state still owns much of the country's media.* A **tribe** is a group of families within a country who are the same race and have the same traditions and the same leader: *The Navajo tribe is the second largest in the US.*

---

race² *v* **1** [I,T] to compete in a race: *She will be racing against some of the world's top athletes.* **2** [T] to ride a horse, drive a car etc in a race **3** [I,T] to go somewhere very quickly, or to move someone or something very quickly: **+ across/back/down** *I raced down the stairs to answer the phone.* | **race sb to/back etc** *The crash victims were raced to Pacific Hospital.*

4 [I] if your heart or mind races, it works more quickly than normal, often because you are frightened or excited

race·course /'reɪs-kɔːsǁ-kɔːrs/ *n* [C] a track that runners, cars, horses etc use in a race

race·horse /'reɪshɔːsǁ-hɔːrs/ *n* [C] a horse that is trained to run in races

race re·la·tions /'. .ˌ../ *n* [plural] the relationships that exist between people of different races who live in the same country, city etc

rac·es /'reɪsɪz/ *n* [C] **the races** an event at which horses race against each other

race·track /'reɪs-træk/ *n* [C] a track that runners, cars, horses etc use in a race

ra·cial /'reɪʃəl/ *adj* relating to someone's race or with the relationships between people of different races: *people from different racial groups* | *a city with a high degree of racial tension* | **racial discrimination** (=unfair treatment of people because of their race) — **racially** *adv*

rac·ing /'reɪsɪŋ/ *n* **horse/motor etc racing** a sport in which there are races between people on horses, in cars etc — **racing** *adj* [only before noun]

ra·cis·m /'reɪsɪzəm/ *n* [U] **1** unfair treatment of people because of their race: *the struggle against racism* **2** the belief that other races are not as good as your own and therefore should not be treated equally: *The author has been accused of extreme racism and sexism.*

rac·ist /'reɪsɪst/ *n* [C] someone who believes that people of their own race are better than others, and who treats people of other races unfairly or violently — **racist** *adj*: *I found his racist remarks quite offensive.*

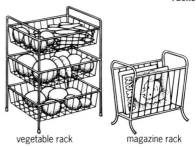
racks

vegetable rack   magazine rack

rack¹ /ræk/ *n* [C] a shelf or frame made of bars, used for holding things: *a luggage rack* | *a wine rack*

rack² *v* [T] **1 rack your brain(s)** to think very hard or for a long time: *I had to rack my brains to remember his name.* **2 be racked with pain/guilt/doubt etc** to feel a lot of pain, shame, doubt etc

rack·et /'rækɪt/ *n* [C] **1** also **racquet** the thing you use for hitting the ball in games such as tennis → see colour picture on page 636 **2** *informal* an illegal or dishonest activity in which a lot of money is made: *a drugs racket* **3** *informal* a loud noise: *Who's making that racket?*

rac·y /'reɪsi/ *adj* speech or writing that is racy

is exciting and amusing, often because it is about sex: *a racy novel*

ra·dar /ˈreɪdɑː‖-ɑːr/ *n* [C,U] a method of finding the position of things such as planes and ships by sending out radio WAVES, or the piece of equipment that does this

ra·di·ance /ˈreɪdiəns/ *n* [U] **1** happiness or energy that shows in someone's appearance: *Her face had a youthful radiance.* **2** a soft light that shines from or onto something

ra·di·ant /ˈreɪdiənt/ *adj* **1** full of happiness or love in a way that shows in your face **2** very bright: *a radiant summer morning* —**radiantly** *adv*

ra·di·ate /ˈreɪdieɪt/ *v* **1** [I,T] to clearly show a quality or feeling in your appearance or behaviour: *She radiated an air of calm and confidence.* + **from** *Intense pleasure radiated from their eyes.* **2** [I,T] to send out light or heat: + **from/out/to etc** *Warmth radiated from the fire.* **3** [I] to go out in all directions from a central point: + **from/out/away etc** *a system of roads radiating from the town centre*

ra·di·a·tion /ˌreɪdiˈeɪʃən/ *n* [U] **1** a form of energy that comes from a NUCLEAR reaction, that can be extremely harmful to living things: *The level of radiation in the area is worrying.* | *radiation sickness* **2** energy in the form of heat or light sent out as beams that you cannot see: *ultraviolet radiation from the sun*

ra·di·a·tor /ˈreɪdieɪtəl-ər/ *n* [C] **1** a piece of equipment that heats a room, consisting of a hollow metal container that fills up with hot water **2** a piece of equipment on a vehicle that stops the engine from getting too hot

rad·i·cal¹ /ˈrædɪkəl/ *adj* **1** a radical change is very big and has important effects: *radical legal reforms* **2** supporting big political and social changes: *radical leftwing MPs* —**radically** /-kli/ *adv*

radical² *n* [C] someone who wants, supports, or works for a lot of social and political change —**radicalism** *n* [U]

ra·di·o¹ /ˈreɪdiəʊ‖-dioʊ/ *n* **1** [C] a piece of electronic equipment that you use to listen to music or programmes that are broadcast: *Do you have a radio in your car?* **2** [U] the system of broadcasting sound: *He works for local radio.* **3** (**on**) **the radio** the programmes that are broadcast and you hear on radio: *I like listening to talk shows on the radio.* **4** [C] a piece of electronic equipment used to send and receive spoken messages: *the ship's radio*

radio² *v* [I,T] to send a message using a radio: *We'll have to radio Chicago for permission to land.*

ra·di·o·ac·tive /ˌreɪdiəʊˈæktɪv‖-dioʊ-/ *adj* containing RADIATION: *radioactive waste*

ra·di·o·ac·tiv·i·ty /ˌreɪdiəʊækˈtɪvɪti‖-dioʊ-/ *n* [U] when a substance sends out RADIATION or produces energy in this way: *High levels of radioactivity have been found in drinking water.*

ra·di·ol·o·gy /ˌreɪdiˈɒlədʒi‖-ˈɑː-/ *n* [U] the study of the use of RADIATION and X-RAYS in medical treatment

ra·di·o·ther·a·py /ˌreɪdiəʊˈθerəpi‖-dioʊ-/ *n* [U] the treatment of illnesses using RADIATION

rad·ish /ˈrædɪʃ/ *n* [C] a small red or white root

that has a slightly hot taste and is eaten RAW → see picture at VEGETABLES

ra·di·us /ˈreɪdiəs/ *n* [C], *plural* **radii** /-diaɪ/ **1** the distance from the centre of a circle to the edge **2** **within a 10 mile/100 metre etc radius** within a distance of 10 miles etc from a place in any direction

raf·fle /ˈræfəl/ *n* [C] a competition in which people buy tickets with numbers on them and win a prize if one of their numbers is chosen: *a raffle ticket* —**raffle** *v* [T]

raft /rɑːft‖ræft/ *n* [C] **1** a flat floating structure made from long pieces of wood tied together **2** a small rubber boat filled with air **3** **a raft of** a lot of

raf·ter /ˈrɑːftə‖ˈræftər/ *n* [C] a piece of wood that supports a roof

rag /ræg/ *n* [C] **1** a piece of old cloth: *She carefully cleaned the lamp with a rag.* **2** **rags** old torn clothes: *beggars dressed in rags* **3** (**go from**) **rags to riches** to become very rich after starting your life very poor

rag·a·muf·fin /ˈrægəˌmʌfɪn/ *n* [C] *literary* a dirty young child wearing torn clothes

rag·bag /ˈrægbæg/ *n* **a ragbag of** a mixture of things that are very different: *a ragbag of ideas*

rage¹ /reɪdʒ/ *n* [C,U] **1** a feeling of extreme anger: *His remarks left her quite speechless with rage.* | **fly into a rage** (=suddenly become very angry): *When I asked him what he was doing there, he flew into a rage.* **2** **all the rage** *informal* very popular and fashionable: *Roller blading is all the rage at the moment.*

rage² *v* [I] **1** to continue happening with a lot of force or violence: *The battle raged on for several days.* **2** to speak or behave in a way that shows you are extremely angry: *She raged at the injustice of the decision.*

rag·ged /ˈrægɪd/ *adj* **1** torn or in bad condition: *a pair of ragged shorts* **2** wearing clothes that are old and torn: *ragged children*

rag·time /ˈrægtaɪm/ *n* [U] a type of JAZZ music with a strong beat, popular in the US in the early 1900s

raid¹ /reɪd/ *n* [C] **1** a short sudden military attack on a place: *an air raid* **2** a sudden visit by the police to find illegal goods or criminals: *drug dealers arrested after a police raid* **3** when thieves enter a bank, shop etc and steal something: *a bank raid*

raid² *v* [T] **1** if the police raid a place, they suddenly arrive there to search for something illegal **2** to make a sudden military attack: *Troops raided the village at dawn.* **3** *informal* to take or steal a lot of things from a place: *The kids always raid the fridge after school.*

rail¹ /reɪl/ *n* [C] **1** a bar along or around something that prevents you from falling: *Tourists stood at the rail taking pictures of the waterfall.* **2** a bar that you use to hang things on: *a bath rail* **3** one of the two long metal tracks that trains move along **4** **by rail** by train: *They sent the parcel by rail.*

rail² *v* [I] *formal* to complain angrily

rail·ing /ˈreɪlɪŋ/ *n* [C usually plural] a fence consisting of upright metal bars: *a little garden with a railing around it*

rail·road /ˈreɪlrəʊd‖-roʊd/ *v* [T] to force or persuade someone to do something without giving them enough time to think about it: *She was railroaded into signing the agreement.*

rail·way /ˈreɪlweɪ/ *BrE,* **railroad** *AmE — n* **1** [C] a track for trains to travel along: *They built a railway to the Pacific Coast.* → see colour picture on page 669 **2 the railway/the railroad** the work and organizations connected with train services

rain¹ /reɪn/ *n* **1** [U] water that falls in small drops from clouds in the sky: *The rain fell throughout the night.|There's been no rain for weeks.|* **heavy rain** (=a lot of rain) **2 the rains** a time of the year when there is heavy rain in tropical ountries

rain² *v* **1 it is raining** if it is raining, drops of water fall from clouds in the sky: *Is it still raining?* **2 be rained off** *BrE/* **be rained out** *AmE* to be stopped because there is too much rain: *Today's tennis final was rained off.*

rain down *phr v* [I] to fall in large quantities: *Falling rocks rained down on cars and houses.*

rain·bow /ˈreɪnbəʊll-boʊ/ *n* [C] a large curve of different colours in the sky that is caused by the sun shining through rain

rain check /ˈ. ./ *n* **I'll take a rain check** *spoken* used to say that you cannot accept an offer or an invitation now but you would like to at a later time: *"Can I buy you a coffee?" "Not right now, but I'll take a rain check!"*

rain·coat /ˈreɪnkəʊtll-koʊt/ *n* [C] a coat that you wear to protect you from the rain

rain·drop /ˈreɪndrɒpll-draːp/ *n* [C] a single drop of rain

rain·fall /ˈreɪnfɔːlll-fɔːl/ *n* [C,U] the amount of rain that falls on an area in a particular period of time: *The northwest has the highest rainfall in England.*

rain for·est /ˈ. ,. ./ *n* [C] tropical forest with tall trees that are very close together, growing in an area where it rains a lot

rain·storm /ˈreɪnstɔːmll-ɔːrm/ *n* [C] a storm with a lot of rain and strong winds

rain·wa·ter /ˈreɪnwɔːtəll-wɒtər, -wɑː-/ *n* [U] water that has fallen as rain

rain·y /ˈreɪni/ *adj* **1 rainy day/afternoon/ weather etc** a day etc when it rains a lot: *a rainy weekend* **2 save sth for a rainy day** to keep something, especially money, until a time when you will need it

raise¹ /reɪz/ *v* [T] **1** to move or lift something to a higher position or into an upright position: *He raised the lid of the box.|Raise your hand if you know the answer.* **2** to increase an amount, number, or level: *a plan to raise taxes* **3** to improve the quality or standard of something: *an attempt to raise standards in primary schools* **4** to look after a child until he or she grows up: *They've raised seven children.* **5** to collect money: *The concert raised over $500,000 for famine relief.* **6** to grow crops or keep animals to sell: *Most of their income is from raising pigs.* **7 raise your voice** to shout at someone **8 raise a subject/question/point etc** to mention something that you want someone else to

consider: *She didn't like to raise the subject of money again.* **9 raise hopes/fears/suspicions etc** to make people feel hopeful, afraid etc **10 raise the alarm** to warn people about danger

raise² *n* [C] *AmE* an increase in the money you earn; RISE *BrE: a raise of $100 a month*

rai·sin /ˈreɪzən/ *n* [C] a dried GRAPE

rake¹ /reɪk/ *n* [C] a gardening tool used for gathering dead leaves etc, that has a row of metal teeth at the end of a long handle → see picture at GARDENING EQUIPMENT

rake² *v* **1** [I,T] to move a rake across a surface in order to make soil level, gather dead leaves etc: **+ up/over** *An old man was raking up leaves in the park.* **2** [I] to search very thoroughly for something: **+ through/around** *I found him raking through the drawers of my desk.*

rake sth ↔ **in** *phr v* [T] *informal spoken* to earn a lot of money: **rake it in** *Since he got that job in Hong Kong he's been raking it in.*

rake sth ↔ **up** *phr v* [T] to talk about something that happened in the past that people would prefer was not mentioned: *Why do you have to rake up the war again?*

ral·ly¹ /ˈræli/ *n* [C] **1** a large public meeting to support a political idea, sports event etc: *a political rally* **2** a car race on public roads

rally² *v* **1** [I,T] to come together or bring people together to support an idea, a political party etc: *The Prime Minister is trying to rally support in rural areas.* **2** [I] to become stronger again: *The price of gold rallied after a slight drop.*

rally around (also **rally round** *BrE*) *phr v* [T **rally around** sb] *informal* if a group of people rally around, they all try to help you in a difficult situation: *Her friends all rallied round when her father died.*

ram¹ /ræm/ *v* [T] **-mmed, -mming 1** to crash into something with a lot of force: *When I stopped, a truck rammed my car from behind.* **2** to push something into something else with a lot of force: *He rammed his clothes into his suitcase and left.* **3 ram sth down sb's throat** *informal* to try to force someone to accept an idea or opinion

ram² *n* [C] a male sheep

RAM *n* [U] *technical* random access memory; the part of a computer that keeps information temporarily so that it can be used immediately → compare ROM

Ram·a·dan /ˈræmədæn, -dɑːn, ˌræməˈdɑːn, -ˈdæn/ *n* [singular] the ninth month of the Muslim year, during which no food may be eaten during the hours of the day when it is light

ram·ble¹ /ˈræmbəl/ *v* [I] **1** to talk in a very confused way, not keeping to one subject: *He's getting old now, and tends to ramble.* **2** to go on a walk for pleasure, especially in the countryside: *We rambled through the woods all afternoon.*

ramble on *phr v* [I] to talk or write for a long time in a confused and boring way: *Kevin was rambling on about his trip to New York.*

GRAMMAR NOTE: a or the (1)

Use **a** or **an** before a noun when you are mentioning a person or thing for the first time, but use **the** when you mention that same person or thing again: **A** man and **a** woman were sitting at the next table. **The** woman was much younger than **the** man.

ramble² *n* [C] a long walk for pleasure

ram·bler /ˈræmblər-ər/ *n* [C] someone who walks in the countryside for pleasure

ram·bling /ˈræmblɪŋ/ *adj* **1** rambling speech or writing is very long and does not seem to have any clear meaning or purpose: *a long, rambling letter* **2** a rambling building has an irregular shape and covers a large area

ram·i·fi·ca·tions /ˌræmɪfɪˈkeɪʃənz/ *n* [plural] additional results of an event or action that were not clearly known about when a decision was first made: *all the political ramifications of the Treaty of Rome*

ramp /ræmp/ *n* [C] **1** a slope that has been built to connect two places that are at different levels: *ramps for wheelchair users* **2** *AmE* a road for driving onto or off a large main road

ram·page¹ /ˈræmpeɪdʒ, ræmˈpeɪdʒ/ *v* [I] to rush around in a group behaving in a noisy or violent way and causing damage: *rioters rampaging through the streets*

rampage² *n* **on the rampage** rushing around in a noisy and violent way: *gangs on the rampage*

ram·pant /ˈræmpənt/ *adj* something bad that is rampant is increasing or spreading quickly and is very difficult to control: *The refugees are facing food shortages and rampant disease.*

ram·part /ˈræmpɑːt‖-ɑːrt/ *n* [C] a wide pile of earth or a stone wall built to protect a castle or city

ram·shack·le /ˈræmˌʃækəl/ *adj* a ramshackle building is in very bad condition and looks as if it may fall down: *a ramshackle farm house*

ran /ræn/ *v* the past tense of RUN

ranch /rɑːntʃ‖ræntʃ/ *n* [C] a very big farm where cattle, horses, or sheep are kept

ranch·er /ˈrɑːntʃə‖ˈræntʃər/ *n* [C] someone who owns or works on a ranch: *a cattle rancher*

ranch house /ˈ. ./ *n* [C] a house built on one level, with a slightly sloping roof

ran·cid /ˈrænsɪd/ *adj* oily or fatty food that is rancid smells or tastes unpleasant because it is no longer fresh: *rancid butter*

ran·cour *BrE*, **rancor** *AmE* /ˈræŋkər-ər/ *n* [U] *formal* an angry feeling towards someone when you hate them and cannot forgive them

ran·dom /ˈrændəm/ *adj* **1** **at random** if you choose something at random, you give each of the things within a group an equal chance of being chosen: *Winning lottery numbers are chosen at random.* **2** happening or chosen without any definite plan or system: *a random survey* **—randomly** *adv*

rang /ræŋ/ *v* the past tense of RING

range¹ /reɪndʒ/ *n* **1** [C] a group of things that are different, but belong to the same general type: **+ of** *books on a wide range of subjects* **2** [C usually singular] the amounts, numbers etc between particular limits: *games for the 8-12 age range* **3** [C usually singular] a set of products of the same type: *a new range of mountain bikes* **4** [singular, U] the distance that something can travel or within which it can be seen, heard, or reached: **+ of** *missiles with a range of over 1000 miles* | **within range** (=near enough to see, hear, or reach): *The ship was within range of enemy radar.* **5** [C] a line of mountains or hills: *a*

mountain range **6** [C] an area where you can practise shooting: *a rifle range*

range² *v* [I] **1** **range from sth to sth a)** to include a lower amount and a higher amount and everything in between: *toys ranging in price from $5 to $25* **b)** to include many different types of things: *weapons ranging from swords to anti-tank missiles* **2** to deal with a large number of subjects in the same speech, piece of writing etc: **+ over** *Her speech ranged over several topics.*

rang·er /ˈreɪndʒər-ər/ *n* [C] someone whose job is to look after a forest or area of public land: *a forest ranger*

rank¹ /ræŋk/ *n* **1** [C,U] the level of importance that someone has in an organization such as the army or police, or in society: *He's just been promoted to the rank of Sergeant.* **2** **the ranks** the ordinary soldiers in an army etc **3** **the ranks of** the people within a particular group or organization: *Priests were usually from the ranks of the middle class.* **4** [C] a line of people or things: *a taxi rank* **5** **the rank and file** the ordinary members of an organization

rank² *v* [I,T] to have a particular position in a list that shows how good or important someone or something is, or to decide someone's or something's position in a list like this: *Woods is ranked number one in the world.* | *I rank London as one of the best cities in the world.*

rank³ *adj* having a very strong and unpleasant smell or taste

rank·ing /ˈræŋkɪŋ/ *n* [C] a position on a list that shows how good someone or something is compared to others

ran·kle /ˈræŋkəl/ *v* [I,T] if something rankles, it continues to make you angry a long time after it happens: *an insult that still rankles*

ran·sack /ˈrænsæk/ *v* [T] **1** to go through a place stealing things and causing damage: *She returned home to find that her house had been ransacked.* **2** to search a place very thoroughly

ran·som /ˈrænsəm/ *n* [C,U] **1** the money paid to free someone who is being kept as a prisoner: *The kidnappers demanded a ransom of $50,000.* **2** **hold sb to ransom a)** to try to force someone to do what you want by threatening to do something that will have a very bad effect if they do not do it **b)** to keep someone as a prisoner until money is paid to you

rant /rænt/ *v* [I] to talk in a loud, excited, or angry way: *My father, as usual, was ranting on about young people.* | **rant and rave** (=talk or complain very loudly and angrily)

rap¹ /ræp/ *n* **1** [C] a quick light hit or knock: *There was a rap at the door.* **2** [C,U] a type of popular music in which the words are spoken not sung **3** [singular] *informal* blame or punishment for a mistake or a crime

rap² *v* **-pped, -pping 1** [I,T] to hit something quickly and lightly: *Someone was rapping on the window.* **2** [T] *informal* to publicly criticize someone: *A film that has been rapped by critics for its excessive violence.*

rap·per /ˈræpər-ər/ *n* [C] someone who sings RAP songs

rape¹ /reɪp/ *v* [T] to force someone to have sex when they do not want to

rape² *n* [C,U] the crime of raping someone: *He is serving a nine-year prison sentence for rape.*

rap·id /'ræpₐd/ *adj* done or happening very quickly: *rapid political changes* —**rapidly** *adv* —**rapidity** /rə'pɪdₐti/ *n* [U]

rap·ids /'ræpₐdz/ *n* [plural] a part of a river where the water looks white because it is moving very fast over rocks

rap·ist /'reɪpₐst/ *n* [C] someone who forces someone else to have sex when they do not want to

rap·port /ræ'pɔːll-ɔːr/ *n* [singular,U] friendly understanding and agreement between people: *She quickly established a rapport with her students.*

rapt /ræpt/ *adj* so interested in something that you do not notice anything else

rap·ture /'ræptʃₐll-ər/ *n* [U] great excitement, pleasure, and happiness: *a look of rapture on her face* —**rapturous** *adj* —**rapturously** *adv*

rare /reₐllrer/ *adj* **1** very unusual or uncommon: *a disease that is very rare among children | Rare plants such as orchids can be found here.* **2** meat that is rare has only been cooked for a short time and is still red

> **USAGE NOTE: rare and scarce**
>
> Use **rare** to talk about something that is valuable and that there is not much of: *Rare coins are usually worth a lot of money.* Use **scarce** to talk about something that is difficult to get at a particular time: *During the war, food and clothing were scarce.*

rare·ly /'reₐllꞌrerli/ *adv* not often: *She rarely goes out after dark.*

rar·ing /'reₐrɪŋll'rer-/ *adj* **raring to go** *informal* very eager to start an activity: *Shelley was now in the job, and raring to go.*

rar·i·ty /'reₐrₐtill'rer-/ *n* **1 be a rarity** to not happen or exist very often: *Old cars in good condition are a rarity.* **2** [U] the quality of being uncommon

ras·cal /'rɑːskₐll'ræs-/ *n* [C] **1** *humorous* a child who behaves badly but whom you still like **2** *old-fashioned* a dishonest man

rash¹ /ræʃ/ *adj* doing something too quickly, without thinking carefully first: *a rash decision* —**rashly** *adv*

rash² *n* **1** [C] a lot of small red spots on someone's skin: *The rash covered the baby's entire body.* **2 a rash of** *informal* a lot of unpleasant things that suddenly start happening: *There has been a rash of unofficial strikes in the past few months.*

rash·er /'ræʃₐll-er/ *n* [C] *BrE* a thin piece of BACON

rasp /rɑːspll ræsp/ *v* [I] to make a rough unpleasant sound: *The hinges rasped as we pushed the gate open.* —**rasp** *n* [singular]

rasp·ber·ry /'rɑːzbₐrill'ræzberi/ *n* [C] a small soft sweet red fruit that grows on bushes

rat¹ /ræt/ *n* [C] **1** an animal like a large mouse with a long tail: *There was a dead rat on the cellar steps.* **2** *informal spoken* someone you trusted who deceives you: *But you promised to help us – you rat!*

rat² *v*

rat on *sb/sth phr v* [T] **1** to tell someone in authority about something wrong that someone else has done **2** to not do something or support someone even though you agreed that you would

rate¹ /reɪt/ *n* [C] **1** the number of times something happens over a period of time, or the number of people it happens to: *a country with a low birth rate | the rising crime rate* **2** the amount of money that is charged or paid according to a system: *Workers are demanding higher rates of pay. | a tax rate of 25%* **3** the speed at which something happens: *Our money was running out at an alarming rate.* (=very quickly) **4 at any rate** *spoken* used when you are stating one good fact in a bad situation or one definite fact in an uncertain situation: *Well, at any rate we won't starve. | They've got technical problems – at any rate that's what they told me.* **5 at this rate** *spoken* used to say what will happen if things continue in the same way: *At this rate, we'll never finish on time.* **6 first-rate/second-rate/third-rate** of good, bad, or very bad quality: *a third-rate movie*

rate² *v* [T] **1** to think that someone or something is good, bad etc: *Johnson is rated one of the best basketball players in the world.* **2** *informal* to deserve something: *You all rate a big thank-you for your work.*

ra·ther /'rɑːðₐll'ræðər/ *adv, predeterminer* **1** *BrE* a little; fairly: *I think she was rather upset last night. | It's a rather difficult problem.* **2 rather than** instead of something else: *We decided to have the wedding in the summer rather than in the spring.* **3 would rather** if you would rather do or have something, you would prefer to do or have it: *I hate sitting doing nothing – I'd rather be working.* **4** *spoken* used to give more correct or exact information about what you have said: *Mr Dewey, or rather his secretary, asked me to come to the meeting.*

rat·i·fy /'rætₐfaɪ/ *v* [T] to make a written agreement official: *Both nations ratified the treaty.* —**ratification** /ˌrætₐfₐ'keɪʃₐn/ *n* [U]

rat·ing /'reɪtɪŋ/ *n* **1** [C] a measurement of how popular, good, important etc someone or something is: *The president's popularity rating has fallen.* **2 the ratings** a list that shows which films, television programmes etc are the most popular: *Her show is at the top of the ratings.*

ra·ti·o /'reɪʃiₐʊ ll'reɪʃoʊ/ *n* [C], *plural* **ratios** a relationship between two amounts written as two numbers that show how much bigger one amount is than the other: **ratio of sth to sth** *a school where the ratio of students to teachers is about 5:1* (=five students for every teacher)

ra·tion¹ /'ræʃₐnll'ræ-, 'reɪ-/ *n* [C] a limited amount of something such as food that you are allowed to have when there is not much available: *the weekly meat ration*

ration² *v* [T] to control the supply of something by allowing people to have only a limited amount of it: *Bread, cheese and eggs were all rationed during the war.* —**rationing** *n* [U]

ra·tion·al /'ræʃₐnₐl/ *adj* **1** based on real facts or scientific knowledge, and not influenced by feelings: *There must be a rational explanation for their disappearance.* **2** able to make decisions based on the facts of a situation, and not influenced too much by feelings: *Let's try to discuss*

R

this like rational human beings. → opposite IRRA-TIONAL —**rationally** *adv*

ra·tio·nale / ˌræʃəˈnɑːlǁ-ˈnæl/ *n* [C,U] the reasons and principles that a decision, plan etc is based on: *What's the rationale behind the President's decision?*

ra·tion·al·ize (also **-ise** *BrE*) /ˈræʃənəlaɪz/ *v* [I,T] **1** to think of reasons to explain your behaviour, especially when you have done something wrong: *He rationalized that his parents would have given him the money anyway, so why not just take it?* **2** [T] to organize a business or system in a more effective way —**rationalization** /ˌræʃənəlaɪˈzeɪʃənǁ-lə-/ *n* [C,U]

rat race /ˈ. ./ *n* **the rat race** *informal* the unpleasant situation, especially at work, in which people have to continuously compete against each other for success

rat·tle[1] /ˈrætl/ *v* **1** [I,T] if something rattles, or if you rattle it, it makes a noise because it keeps shaking and hitting against something else: *The wind was rattling the windows.* → see colour picture on page 635 **2** [T] to make someone lose their confidence and become more nervous: *Keep calm – don't let yourself get rattled.*

rattle sth ↔ **off** *phr v* [T] to say something very quickly and easily from your memory: *She rattled off the names of all the American states.*

rattle[2] *n* **1** [C] a baby's toy that makes a noise when it is shaken **2** [singular] the noise made when something rattles → see colour picture on page 635

rattle·snake /ˈrætlsneɪk/ *n* [C] a poisonous American snake that makes a noise with its tail

rau·cous /ˈrɔːkəsǁˈrɒ:-/ *adj* a raucous voice or noise is very loud and unpleasant

raunch·y /ˈrɔːntʃiǁˈrɒ:-/ *adj informal* intended to make you think about sex: *a raunchy movie*

rav·age /ˈrævɪdʒ/ *v* [T] to destroy, ruin, or damage something very badly: *The forest was ravaged by fire*

rav·ag·es /ˈrævɪdʒ½z/ *n* **the ravages of sth** damage or destruction caused by something such as war, disease, or time

rave[1] /reɪv/ *n* [C] a large party where young people dance to electronic music

rave[2] *v* [I] **1** to talk in an excited way about something because you think it is very good: *Everybody raved about the movie, but I hated it.* **2** to talk in an angry and uncontrolled way → see also **rant and rave** (RANT)

rave[3] *adj* **rave reviews** strong praise for a new film, book, play etc

ra·ven /ˈreɪvən/ *n* [C] a large black bird

rav·e·nous /ˈrævənəs/ *adj* extremely hungry —**ravenously** *adv*

ra·vine /rəˈviːn/ *n* [C] a deep narrow valley with steep sides

rav·ing /ˈreɪvɪŋ/ *adj informal* crazy: *a raving lunatic* —**raving** *adv*

rav·ings /ˈreɪvɪŋz/ *n* [plural] crazy things that someone says

rav·ish·ing /ˈrævɪʃɪŋ/ *adj* very beautiful

raw /rɔː/ *adj* **1** not cooked: *raw onions* **2** raw cotton, sugar etc are still in their natural state: **raw materials** (=natural substances that industrial products are made from): *the export of raw materials such as coal and iron* **3** skin that

is raw is red and sore **4** not trained or experienced: **raw recruit** (=someone who has just joined an army) **5** **hit/touch a raw nerve** to accidentally upset or annoy someone by something you say: *I think I hit a raw nerve by asking him about his wife.* **6** **a raw deal** unfair treatment —**rawness** *n* [U]

ray /reɪ/ *n* [C] **1** a narrow beam of light or energy from the sun, a lamp etc: *the rays of the sun*|*gamma rays* **2** **ray of hope/comfort etc** something that gives you a small amount of hope, happiness etc

ray·on /ˈreɪɒnǁ-ɑːn/ *n* [U] a smooth artificial material like silk used for making clothes

raze /reɪz/ *v* [T] to destroy a city, building etc completely: **raze sth to the ground** *Three buildings had been razed to the ground.*

razors

safety razor

electric razor / electric shaver

ra·zor /ˈreɪzəǁ-ər/ *n* [C] a sharp instrument for removing hair, especially from a man's face

razor blade /ˈ.. ./ *n* [C] a small flat very sharp blade that is put inside a razor

razz /ræz/ *v* [T] *AmE informal* to try to embarrass or annoy someone by making jokes about them; TEASE

Rd., Rd *n* the written abbreviation of 'road', used in addresses: *5007 Rowan Rd.*

re- /riː/ *prefix* again: *remake* (=make something again)|*rethink* (=think about something again)

're /ələr/ the short form of ARE: *We're* (=we are) *ready now.*

reach[1] /riːtʃ/ *v* **1** [T] to arrive at a place: *It took four days for the letter to reach me.* **2** [I,T] to move your hand or arm in order to touch, hold, or pick up something: **+ for** *He threatened me and reached for his knife.* | **+ out** *Mike reached out and took her hand.* **3** **can reach** to be able to touch or take hold of something by stretching your arm: *If I stand on a chair, I can reach the top shelf.* **4** [I,T] to be big enough, long enough etc to get to a particular place: *Will the ladder reach the roof?* **5** [T] to get as far as a particular level, stage or standard: *Temperatures will reach 95° today.*|*a team that reached the World Cup Final in 1962* **6** **reach a decision/agreement etc** to succeed in deciding something, agreeing on something etc **7** [T] to speak to someone, especially by telephone: *I wasn't able to reach him yesterday.* **8** [T] if a message, television programme etc reaches people, they hear it or watch it

reach² n **1** out of (sb's) reach/beyond sb's reach **a)** too far away to pick up or touch when you stretch out your hand: *Gary jumped for the ball, but it was just out of reach.* **b)** beyond the limit of someone's ability, power or influence: *He fled to Paraguay, beyond the reach of the British tax authorities.* **2** within reach **a)** near enough to be touched or picked up when you stretch out your hand: *As soon as she was within reach, he grabbed her wrist.* **b)** within a distance that you can easily travel: + of *We live within easy reach of the shops.*

re·act /ri'ækt/ v [I] **1** to behave in a particular way because of what someone has done or said to you, or because of the situation you are in: *The audience reacted by shouting and booing.* | *How did she react to the news?* **2** if one chemical reacts with another chemical, it changes when it is mixed with the other chemical

react against sth phr v [T] to show that you do not like someone else's rules or ideas by doing the opposite: *Many teenagers reacted against the strict discipline of the school.*

re·ac·tion /ri'ækʃən/ n **1** [C,U] something that you feel or do because of what has happened to you or been said to you: *What was his reaction when you told him you were leaving?* **2** reactions [plural] your ability to move quickly when something dangerous happens suddenly: *In motor racing drivers need to have quick reactions* **3** [C] a bad effect, especially an illness, caused by something you have eaten or drunk: *Some people have a very bad reaction to peanuts.* (=peanuts make them ill) **4** [singular] a change in someone's attitudes, behaviour etc because they do not agree with something that was done in the past: + against *There was a strong public reaction against nuclear tests.* **5** [C,U] a change that happens when two or more chemical substances are mixed together → see also **gut reaction** (GUT¹)

re·ac·tion·a·ry /ri'ækʃənərill-ʃəneri/ adj strongly opposing any social or political change —**reactionary** n

re·ac·tor /ri'æktəll-ər/ n [C] a NUCLEAR REACTOR

read /riːd/ v read /red/, read, reading **1** [I,T] to look at written words or numbers and understand what they mean: *Can Billy read yet?* | *She sat reading a magazine.* | *I'm sorry, I can't read your handwriting.* | + about *I read about the accident in the paper.* | + that *Steve was annoyed to read that his sister had won a prize.* **2** [I,T] to read something so that other people can listen to you reading: read to sb/read sb a story *Our mother used to read to us every evening.* **3** [T] to look at signs or pictures and understand what they mean: *Can you read music?* | map reading **4** read between the lines to guess what someone really feels or what is really happening, even though no one had told you directly **5** [T] if a measuring instrument reads a

particular number, it shows that number: *The thermometer read 100°*

read sth **into** sth phr v [T] to think that a situation, action etc means more than it really does: *You shouldn't read so much into what she says.*

read sth ↔ **out** phr v [T] to say the words you are reading to someone else: *He read out the names on the list.*

read sth ↔ **through/over** phr v [T] to read something carefully from beginning to end: *Read the contract over carefully before you sign it.*

read up on sth phr v [T] to read a lot about something because you will need to know about it: *We need to read up on the new tax laws.*

read·a·ble /'riːdəbəl/ adj **1** interesting and enjoyable to read: *a very readable history of Western Philosophy* **2** writing or print that is readable is clear and very easy to read; LEGIBLE

read·er /'riːdəll-ər/ n [C] **1** someone who reads: *an adventure series for young readers* | *Are you a fast reader?* **2** someone who reads a particular book, newspaper etc: *Many of our readers wrote in to complain about the article.*

read·er·ship /'riːdəʃɪpll-ər-/ n [singular] the people who read a newspaper, magazine etc

read·i·ly /'redⅼli/ adv **1** quickly and easily: *The information is readily available on computer.* **2** willingly and without hesitating or saying that you disagree or have doubts: *He readily agreed to the suggestion.*

read·i·ness /'redⅼnⅼs/ n **1** [U] willingness to do something: *I admire his readiness to help people.* **2** [U] when someone is prepared and ready for something that might happen: in readiness *The army was standing by in readiness for an attack.*

read·ing /'riːdɪŋ/ n **1** [U] the activity of looking at and understanding written words: *I enjoy reading in bed.* **2** [U] the books, articles etc that you read: *Her main reading seems to be romantic novels.* **3** [C] a number or amount shown on a measuring instrument: *a thermometer reading of 40°C* **4** [C] a meeting where something is read to people: *a poetry reading*

re·ad·just /ˌriːə'dʒʌst/ v **1** [I] to get used to a new job, situation, or way of life: *After the war, I needed time to readjust to life at home.* **2** [T] to make a small change to something, or move something to a new position: *She readjusted the microphone and began to sing.* —**readjustment** n [C,U]

read·out /'riːdaʊt/ n [C] information produced by a computer that is shown on a screen or in print

read·y /'redi/ adj **1** [not before noun] prepared for what you are going to do: *Aren't you ready yet?* | + for *I don't think Joey is ready for school yet.* | ready to do sth *We're just about ready to eat.* | get ready (=prepare yourself): *Go and get ready for bed.* **2** prepared and available to be used, eaten etc immediately: *Is supper ready?* | ready to eat/drink/wear etc *These*

GRAMMAR NOTE: a or the (1)

Use **a** or **an** before a noun when you are mentioning a person or thing for the first time, but use **the** when you mention that same person or thing again: *A man and a woman were sitting at the next table. The woman was much younger than the man.*

apples are almost ready to eat. | + **for** *Is every-thing ready for the party?* | **have sth ready** *Have your passport ready for when we go through immigration.* | a **ready answer** (=an answer that you have prepared in case you were asked a question) **3** **ready to do sth** willing or likely to do something: *She's always ready to help in a crisis.* **4** **ready cash/money** money that is available for you to use immediately

ready-made / ̩.. ˈ.. / *adj* already made or provided and ready for you to use: *a ready-made Christmas cake* | *a ready-made excuse*

real[1] / rɪəl/ *adj* **1** actually existing and not just imagined: *The new system has real advantages.* | *Do your kids still think Santa Claus is a real person?* | **in real life** *This kind of thing only happens in films, not in real life.* **2** true and not pretended: *What's the real reason you were late?* | *Jack isn't his real name.* **3** not false or artificial; GENUINE: *real gold* | *real leather* | **the real thing** *I don't want a plastic Christmas tree – I want the real thing.* **4** used to emphasize what you are saying: *It's a real pleasure to meet you.* **5** **get real!** *spoken* used to tell someone that what they are suggesting is not sensible or possible

real[2] *adv AmE spoken* very: *I'm real sorry!*

real es·tate / ˈ. .̩./ *n* [U] *especially AmE* property such as houses or land: *Real estate prices fell again last year.*

real estate a·gent / ˈ. .. ̩../ *n* [C] *AmE* someone whose job is to sell houses or land; ESTATE AGENT *BrE*

rea·lism / ˈrɪəlɪzəm/ *n* [U] **1** when things are shown as they really are in literature, films, on television etc **2** when you accept and deal with a situation as it really is, not as you would like it to be

rea·list / ˈrɪəl̩st/ *n* [C] someone who accepts situations as they really are and realizes which things are possible or impossible

rea·lis·tic / rɪəˈlɪstɪk/ *adj* **1** judging and dealing with situations in a sensible practical way because you realize which things are possible: *It's not realistic to expect my parents to lend us any more money.* **2** showing things as they really are: *a very realistic TV drama* —**realistically** / -kli/ *adv*: *We can't realistically hope for any improvement this year.*

re·al·i·ty / rɪˈælʲti/ *n* **1** [U] the way something really is, not the way you imagine it to be or would like it to be: *He finds it difficult to face up to reality.* **2** **the reality/realities of** what a situation or thing is really like: *the reality of living in a big city* | **the harsh/tough realities** (=unpleasant things that are real): *the harsh realities of life* **3** **in reality** used to say that something is different from what seems to be true: *He said he'd retired, but in reality he was fired.* **4** **become a reality** something that actually happens: *Marilyn's dream of becoming a film star had become a reality.*

re·a·li·za·tion (also **-isation** *BrE*) / ̩rɪəlaɪ-ˈzeɪʃən‖-lə-/ *n* [singular, U] **1** when you begin to understand or realize something that you did not know before: + **that** *She finally came to the realization that Jeff had been lying all the time.* **2** when you achieve something you had planned or hoped to do: + **of** *Climbing Everest was the realization of a lifelong ambition.*

rea·lize (also **-ise** *BrE*) / ˈrɪəlaɪz/ *v* [T] **1** to notice something that you did not notice or understand before: *He obviously didn't realize the dangers involved.* | + **that** *I'm sorry, I didn't realize that it was so late.* **2** **realize an ambition/hope/dream** etc to achieve something you always wanted

real·ly / ˈrɪəli/ *adv* **1** very or very much: *Yeah, he's a really nice guy.* | *I don't really trust her.* **2** used to say that something is true, especially when people think something else is true: *Oliver's not really her cousin.* | *Now tell us what really happened.* **3** **really?** *spoken* used when you are surprised about or interested in what someone has said: *"Jay's getting married." "Really? When?"* **4** **not really** *spoken* used to say no, especially when something is not completely true: *"Is it cold outside?" "Not really."*

realm / relm/ *n* [C] **1** *formal* an area of knowledge, interest, or thought: *new discoveries in the realm of science* **2** *literary* a country ruled over by a king or queen

real·tor / ˈrɪəltə, -tɔː‖-ər, -ɔːr/ *n* [C] *AmE* REAL ESTATE AGENT

reams / riːmz/ *n* [plural] a large amount of writing on paper: *She wrote reams of notes.*

reap / riːp/ *v* [T] **1** to get something good as a result of the effort you have made: **reap the advantages/benefits/rewards** *It will be some time before we'll reap the rewards of the investment.* **2** [I,T] to cut and gather a crop of grain

re·ap·pear / ̩riːəˈpɪəl‖-ˈpɪr/ *v* [I] to appear again after not being seen for some time —**reappearance** *n* [C,U]

re·ap·prais·al / ̩riːəˈpreɪzəl/ *n* [C,U] *formal* careful thought about something to decide whether you should change your opinion of it

rear[1] / rɪəl‖rɪr/ *n* **1** **the rear** [singular] the back part of an object, vehicle, building etc: *There are more seats at the rear of the hall.* **2** **bring up the rear** to be at the back of a line of people or a group of people in a race —**rear** *adj*: *a rear window*

rear[2] *v* **1** [T] to look after a person or animal until they are fully grown: *She reared seven children by herself.* **2** [I] also **rear up** if an animal rears, it rises up on its back legs **3** **rear its ugly head** if a problem or something bad rears its ugly head, it appears or happens: *We must fight racism wherever it rears its ugly head.*

rear-end / ˈ. .̩./ *v* [T] *AmE* if one vehicle rear-ends another, it hits the back of the other vehicle

re·ar·range / ̩riːəˈreɪndʒ/ *v* [T] **1** to change the position or order of things: *He rearranged the papers on his desk.* **2** to change the time of a meeting etc —**rearrangement** *n* [C,U]

rear·ward / ˈrɪəwəd‖ˈrɪrwərd/ *adv AmE* in or towards the back of something: *a rearward facing seat*

rea·son[1] / ˈriːzən/ *n* **1** [C] the fact that explains why something happens or exists: + **for** *Did he give any reason for leaving?* | **why** *He's too old – that's the main reason why he wasn't chosen.* **2** [C,U] a fact that makes it right or fair to do something: *There is no reason to panic.* | *You have every reason to complain.* **3** [U] the ability to think, understand, and make sensible decisions: *a conflict between reason and emotion* **4** [U] sensible ideas or advice: *She just won't* *listen to reason.* **5 within reason** within reason-able limits: *You can go anywhere you want, with-in reason.*

reason² *v* **1** [T] to decide that something is true by thinking carefully about the facts: **+ that** *The jury reasoned that he could not have committed the crimes.* **2** [I] to think about facts clearly and intelligently

reason with sb *phr v* [T] to talk to someone in order to persuade them to be more sensible: *I tried to reason with her, but she wouldn't listen.*

rea·son·a·ble /ˈriːzənəbəl/ *adj* **1** fair and sensible: *a reasonable suggestion | Be reasonable, Barry – it wasn't my fault.* **2** a reasonable amount, number, or price is not too much or too big: *good furniture at reasonable prices* —**reasonableness** *n* [U]

rea·son·a·bly /ˈriːzənəbli/ *adv* **1** fairly but not completely: *I think I did reasonably well on the test.* **2** in a way that is fair or sensible: *You can't reasonably expect people to work for such low wages.*

rea·soned /ˈriːzənd/ *adj* based on careful thought; LOGICAL: *a reasoned argument*

rea·son·ing /ˈriːzənɪŋ/ *n* [U] the process of thinking carefully about something in order to form an opinion or make a decision: *a decision based on sound reasoning* (=good reasoning)

re·as·sur·ance /ˌriːəˈʃʊərəns‖-ˈʃʊr-/ *n* [C,U] something that you say or do to make someone feel less worried: *She's not very confident about her schoolwork – she needs plenty of reassurance.*

re·as·sure /ˌriːəˈʃʊə‖-ˈʃʊr/ *v* [T] to make some-one feel less worried about something: **reassure sb that** *Police have reassured the public that the area is now perfectly safe.*

re·as·sur·ing /ˌriːəˈʃʊərɪŋ‖-ˈʃʊr-/ *adj* making you feel calmer and less worried: *a reassuring smile* —**reassuringly** *adv*

re·bate /ˈriːbeɪt/ *n* [C] an amount of money that is paid back to you when you have paid too much rent, tax etc: *a tax rebate*

reb·el¹ /ˈrebəl/ *n* [C] someone who opposes or fights against people in authority: *Rebels have overthrown the government.*

re·bel² /rɪˈbel/ *v* [I] **-lled, -lling** to oppose or fight against someone who is in authority: **+ against** *the story of a teenager who rebels against his father*

re·bel·lion /rɪˈbeljən/ *n* [C,U] **1** an organized attempt to change the government using vio-lence: *He led an armed rebellion against the government.* **2** opposition to someone in authority: *teenage rebellion*

re·bel·lious /rɪˈbeljəs/ *adj* deliberately dis-obeying or fighting against someone in author-ity: *I was a rebellious child. | rebellious troops*

re·birth /ˌriːˈbɜːθ‖-ˈbɜːrθ/ *n* [singular] a change when something becomes active or popular again: **+ of** *the rebirth of British rock music*

re·bound /rɪˈbaʊnd/ *v* [I] if a ball or other ob-ject rebounds, it moves quickly back after hitting something solid: **+ off** *The ball rebounded off the wall.*

rebound on sb *phr v* [T] if something you do rebounds on you, it has a bad effect on you, especially when you intended this effect for someone else

re·buff /rɪˈbʌf/ *v* [T] *formal* to refuse someone's offer or suggestion in an unfriendly way: *His offer of help was rebuffed.* —**rebuff** *n* [C]

re·build /ˌriːˈbɪld/ *v* **rebuilt** /-ˈbɪlt/, **rebuilt, re-building** [T] **1** to build something again, after it has been damaged or destroyed: *The entire city centre had to be rebuilt.* **2** to make something strong and successful again: *We try to help drug addicts rebuild their lives.*

re·buke /rɪˈbjuːk/ *v* [T] *formal* to criticize someone because they have done something wrong —**rebuke** *n* [C,U]

re·but /rɪˈbʌt/ *v* [T] **-tted, -tting** *formal* to say or prove that a statement is false —**rebuttal** *n* [C]

re·cal·ci·trant /rɪˈkælsɪ̩trənt/ *adj formal* refus-ing to obey rules or orders, even after being punished —**recalcitrance** *n* [U]

re·call /rɪˈkɔːl‖-ˈkɒːl/ *v* [T] **1** to remember something: *I don't recall meeting him.* **2** to arrange for something to be returned or for someone to go back to their previous job —**recall** /ˈriːkɔːl, ˈriːkɔːl‖-ɒːl/ *n* [U]

re·cap /ˈriːkæp/ *n* [C usually singular] when you repeat the main points of something you have just said: *And now for a recap of tonight's news.* —**recap** /ˈriːkæp, riːˈkæp/ *v* [I,T]

re·cap·ture /riːˈkæptʃə‖-ər/ *v* [T] **1** to catch a prisoner or animal that has escaped: *Both men were recaptured by the police.* **2** to make some-one experience or feel something again: *a movie that recaptures the innocence of childhood*

re·cede /rɪˈsiːd/ *v* [I] **1** if something recedes, it gets further away, less strong, or less likely: *The sound receded into the distance. | Hopes for a peaceful solution are receding.* **2** be receding to be losing the hair at the front of your head ➔ see colour picture on page 244

re·ceipt /rɪˈsiːt/ *n* **1** [C] a piece of paper that shows that you have received money or goods: *Remember to keep your receipt in case you want to change the goods.* **2** [U] *formal* the act of receiving something: **on/upon receipt of** (=when something is received)

re·ceive /rɪˈsiːv/ *v* [T] **1** to get or be given something: *He received an award from his old college. | Did you receive my letter? | She had just received some good news.* **2 be on/at the receiving end** to be the person who is affected, usually in an unpleasant way, by what someone else does: **+of** *No-one wanted to be on the receiving end of one of his jokes.* **3** *formal* to accept or welcome someone officially as a guest: *Perez was formally received at the White House.*

re·ceiv·er /rɪˈsiːvə‖-ər/ *n* [C] **1** the part of a telephone that you hold to your ear **2** someone who is officially put in control of a business that is BANKRUPT **3** a piece of electronic equipment that receives television, radio, or other elec-tronic SIGNALs

re·ceiv·er·ship /rɪˈsiːvəʃɪp‖-vər-/ *n* [U] **go into receivership** if a business goes into receiver-ship, control of it is taken by an official receiver because it has too many debts

re·cent /ˈriːsənt/ *adj* having happened or be-gun to exist only a short time ago: *Please attach a recent photo to the form. | A recent survey showed that one in five teenagers had tried drugs.*

re·cent·ly /ˈriːsəntli/ *adv* **1** not long ago: *They recently moved from South Africa.* **2** in the period of time just before now: *I haven't seen him recently.*

re·cep·ta·cle /rɪˈseptəkəl/ *n* [C] *formal* a container

re·cep·tion /rɪˈsepʃən/ *n* **1** [U] the place in a building such as a hotel, company building etc that you go to say you have arrived, get information: *Please leave your keys at reception at the end of your stay.* **2** [C] a big formal party to celebrate something or to welcome someone: *a wedding reception* **3** the way you react to or welcome someone: *She got an enthusiastic reception from the audience.* **4** [U] the quality of the sound on a radio or the picture on a television.

reception class /ˈ.. .,./ *n* [C] *BrE* the first class that children are in when they start school, usually at the age of five

re·cep·tion·ist /rɪˈsepʃənɪst/ *n* [C] someone whose job is to welcome and help people at a hotel, office etc

re·cep·tive /rɪˈseptɪv/ *adj* willing to listen to new ideas or opinions: **+ to** *Ron isn't very receptive to new suggestions.*

re·cess /rɪˈses, ˈriːses‖ˈriːses, rɪˈses/ *n* **1** [C,U] a time when a parliament, a law court etc is not working: **be in recess** *Congress is in recess until January.* **2** [U] *AmE* a short period of free time between classes at school: *Charlie got into a fight during recess.* **3** [C] a space in the wall of a room for shelves, cupboards etc

re·ces·sion /rɪˈseʃən/ *n* [C] a period when there is less business activity, trade etc than usual, and a country's ECONOMY is no longer successful

re·charge /ˌriːˈtʃɑːdʒ‖-ɑːr-/ *v* **1** [T] to put a new supply of electricity into a BATTERY **2** **recharge your batteries** to get back your strength and energy again: *He goes to Florida every summer to recharge his batteries.*

re·charge·a·ble /ˌriːˈtʃɑːdʒəbəl‖-ɑːr-/ *adj* rechargeable batteries can be recharged

re·ci·pe /ˈresɪpi/ *n* **1** [C] a set of instructions that tells you how to cook something: **+ for** *a recipe for chocolate cake* **2** **be a recipe for happiness/trouble/disaster etc** *informal* to be very likely to result in happiness, trouble etc

re·cip·i·ent /rɪˈsɪpiənt/ *n* [C] someone who receives something: **+ of** *the recipient of the 1977 Nobel Peace Prize*

re·cip·ro·cal /rɪˈsɪprəkəl/ *adj* a reciprocal arrangement, relationship etc is one in which two people or groups do or give the same things to each other: *a reciprocal trade agreement* —**reciprocally** *adv*

re·cip·ro·cate /rɪˈsɪprəkeɪt/ *v* [I,T] to do or give something in return for something that has been done or given to you —**reciprocation** /rɪ-ˌsɪprəˈkeɪʃən/ *n* [U]

re·cit·al /rɪˈsaɪtl/ *n* [C] a public performance of a piece of music or poetry: *a piano recital*

re·cite /rɪˈsaɪt/ *v* [I,T] to say something that you know by memory, for example a poem or list of facts: *children reciting French verbs* —**recitation** /ˌresɪˈteɪʃən/ *n* [C,U]

reck·less /ˈrekləs/ *adj* doing something dangerous or stupid without worrying that someone might get hurt: *reckless driving* —**recklessly** *adv* —**recklessness** *n* [U]

reck·on /ˈrekən/ *v* [T] **1** to guess a number, amount etc without calculating it exactly: *He reckons the cost to be about one million dollars.* **2** *spoken* to think or suppose something: *I reckon they'll be late.* ǀ *She is generally reckoned to be one of Hollywood's greatest actors.*

reckon on sth *phr v* [T] to expect something to happen

reckon with sb/sth *phr v* **1** [T usually negative] to think of something as a problem you will have to deal with: *We hadn't reckoned with the possibility it might rain.* **2** **a force to be reckoned with** someone or something that will not be easy to defeat or deal with

reck·on·ing /ˈrekənɪŋ/ *n* [U] a calculation that is not exact: *By my reckoning, they should be there by now.*

re·claim /rɪˈkleɪm/ *v* [T] **1** to ask for something to be given back to you: *Any lost property that is not reclaimed will be destroyed or sold.* **2** to make land suitable to be used for farming, building etc: *Acres of valuable agricultural land have now been reclaimed from the sea.* —**reclamation** /ˌrekləˈmeɪʃən/ *n* [U]

re·cline /rɪˈklaɪn/ *v* **1** [I] *formal* to lie or sit back so that part of your body is supported **2** [I,T] if a seat reclines, or if you recline it, the back of it slopes backwards so that you can lie on it: *a reclining chair*

re·cluse /rɪˈkluːs‖ˈrekluːs/ *n* [C] someone who lives alone and avoids other people —**reclusive** /rɪˈkluːsɪv/ *adj*

rec·og·ni·tion /ˌrekəgˈnɪʃən/ *n* [U] **1** public attention, admiration, or thanks for someone's work or achievements: *The band eventually gained recognition in 1995.* ǀ **in recognition of** (=in order to publicly thank someone for) **2** when you know someone or something because you have seen them before: *He looked past me with no sign of recognition.* **3** when you realize what a situation is really like: **+ of/that** *a growing recognition of the problems of homelessness*

rec·og·nize (also **-ise** *BrE*) /ˈrekəgnaɪz, ˈrekən-/ *v* [T] **1** to know someone or something because you have seen them before: *He's lost so much weight I hardly recognized him!* **2** to accept officially that an organization, government etc is legal: *The UN refused to recognize the new government.* **3** to accept and admit that something is true: **+ that** *I recognize that not everyone will agree with me.* **4** to realize that someone or something is good: *They never recognized her talent until it was too late.* —**recognizable** /ˈrekəgnaɪzəbəl, -kən-, ˌrekəgˈnaɪ-/ *adj* —**recognizably** *adv*

re·coil /rɪˈkɔɪl/ *v* [I] to move back suddenly, especially from something that you do not like or are afraid of: *Emily recoiled at the sight of the snake.*

rec·ol·lect /ˌrekəˈlekt/ *v* [T] to remember something: *I don't recollect her name.*

rec·ol·lec·tion /ˌrekəˈlekʃən/ *n* [C,U] something that you remember: *He has no recollection of the crash.*

rec·om·mend /ˌrekəˈmend/ *v* [T] **1** to advise someone to do something: **recommend sb to do sth** *I'd recommend you to take the train.* ǀ **+ that** *Police are recommending that women should avoid the area at night.* **2** to tell someone that something is good, useful, enjoyable etc: *Can you recommend a local restaurant?*

rec·om·men·da·tion /ˌrekəmen'deɪʃən/ *n*
1 [C] a piece of advice, especially about what to do: **make a recommendation** *The committee was able to make detailed recommendations to the school.* | **+ that** *The department's recommendation was that he should be fired.* **2** [U] when you say that someone or something is good, useful, enjoyable etc: **on sb's recommendation** (=because someone recommended it): *We took the tour on a friend's recommendation.* **3** [C] especially AmE a letter or statement saying that someone is suitable for a job, a course of study etc

rec·om·pense /'rekəmpens/ *v* [T] *formal* to give someone something for trouble or loss that you have caused them —**recompense** *n* [singular, U]

rec·on·cile /'rekənsaɪl/ *v* **1** **be reconciled (with)** to have a good relationship with someone again after arguing with them: *The couple are now reconciled.* **2** [T] to show that two different ideas, situations etc are not opposed to each other: *How can you reconcile being both anti-abortion and in favour of the death penalty?* —**reconciliation** /ˌrekənsɪli'eɪʃən/ *n* [singular, U]

reconcile yourself to sth *phr v* [T] to be able to accept an unpleasant situation: *She never reconciled herself to the death of her son.*

re·con·di·tion /ˌriːkən'dɪʃən/ *v* [T] to repair something so that it works well or looks good again: *a reconditioned sewing machine*

re·con·nais·sance /rɪ'kɒnɪ̩səns‖rɪ'kɑː-/ *n* [U] when aircraft and soldiers are sent out in order to get information about the enemy

re·con·sid·er /ˌriːkən'sɪdər/ *v* [I,T] to think again about something in order to decide whether you should change your opinion: *Won't you reconsider our offer?* —**reconsideration** /ˌriːkənsɪdə'reɪʃən/ *n* [U]

re·con·sti·tute /riː'kɒnstɪ̩tjuːt‖rɪ'kɑːnstɪ̩tuːt/ *v* [T] **1** to change something so that it exists in a different form **2** to add water to dried food so that it goes back to the form it was in before it was dried

re·con·struct /ˌriːkən'strʌkt/ *v* [T] **1** to produce a description or picture of something using the information you have: *Police have reconstructed the events leading up to the crime.* **2** to build or make something again after it has been destroyed

re·con·struc·tion /ˌriːkən'strʌkʃən/ *n* **1** [U] work that is done to build, improve, or make something again after it has been destroyed or damaged: *the reconstruction of the former East Germany* **2** [C] when the police use actors to show what happened in a crime, because they hope it might make people remember more about it

rec·ord¹ /'rekɔːd‖-ərd/ *n* **1** [C,U] information about something that is written down so that it can be looked at in the future: **keep a record** *Keep a record of how much you spend on this*

trip. | **on record** (=that has been recorded): *the highest water levels on record* **2** [C] the fastest speed, longest distance, highest or lowest level etc ever: **break a record** (=be the first to do better than the record): *She broke the record for the 1500 metre run.* | **+ for** *What's the record for the highest number of people to fit into a phone booth?* **3** [C] the known facts about someone's past behaviour and how good or bad it has been: *a criminal record* **4** [C] a round flat piece of plastic that music is stored on: *a record collection* **5** **off the record** not official and not meant to be repeated **6** **for the record** used to tell someone that what you are saying should be remembered: *For the record, my salary has never been anywhere near $1 million!*

re·cord² /rɪ'kɔːd‖-ɔːrd/ *v* **1** [T] to store information so that it can be looked at in the future: *All the data is recorded on computer.* **2** [I,T] to store films, events, music etc on TAPE so that you can watch or listen to them again: *Will you record "The X-Files" for me?* | *The band has just finished recording their third album.* **3** [T] to measure the size, speed, temperature etc of something

record-break·ing /'.. ˌ../ *adj* better, higher, faster etc than anything done before: *a record-breaking $5 billion profit*

re·cord·er /rɪ'kɔːdə‖-'kɔːrdər/ *n* [C] a simple musical instrument shaped like a tube, which you play by blowing into it

re·cord·ing /rɪ'kɔːdɪŋ‖-ɔːr-/ *n* [C] a piece of music, a speech etc that has been recorded: *a recording of Bob Marley live in concert*

record play·er /'.. ˌ../ *n* [C] a piece of equipment that you play records on

re·count¹ /'riːkaʊnt/ *n* [C] a process of counting votes again

re·count² /rɪ'kaʊnt/ *v* [T] **1** *formal* to tell a story or describe events: *a TV film recounting the war years* **2** to count something again

re·coup /rɪ'kuːp/ *v* [T] to get back money that you have lost or spent

re·course /rɪ'kɔːs‖'riːkɔːrs/ *n* [U] *formal* something you can use or do to help you in a difficult situation: **have recourse to** (=be able to use something) | **without recourse to** (=without having to use)

re·cov·er /rɪ'kʌvər/ *v* **1** [I] to get better after an illness, injury, shock etc: **+ from** *My uncle is recovering from a heart attack.* **2** [I] to return to a normal condition after a period of trouble or difficulty: *The economy will take at least three years to recover.* **3** [T] to get back something that was taken from you, spent, or almost destroyed: *The police managed to recover the stolen goods.* **4** [T] to get back control over your feelings, your movements etc: *He never recovered the use of his arm.* —**recovery** *n* [singular, U]

re·cre·ate /ˌriːkri'eɪt/ *v* [T] to make something so that it seems the same as it was somewhere else: *We're trying to recreate the conditions of everyday life in Stone Age times.*

rec·re·a·tion /ˌrekri'eɪʃən/ n [C,U] something you do for pleasure or fun: *It's important that students find time for recreation and leisure.* —**recreational** *adj*

re·crim·i·na·tion /rɪˌkrɪmᵻ'neɪʃən/ n [C usually plural, U] a situation in which people blame each other, or the things they say when they are blaming each other

re·cruit[1] /rɪ'kruːt/ v [I,T] to find new people to work in a company, join an organization, do a job etc: *It's not easy to recruit well-qualified and experienced people.* —**recruitment** n [U]

recruit[2] n [C] someone who has recently joined a company or an organization

rec·tan·gle /'rektæŋgəl/ n [C] a shape with four straight sides, two of which are longer than the other two → see picture at SHAPES —**rectangular** /rek'tæŋgjᵊlər/ adj

rec·ti·fy /'rektᵻfaɪ/ v [T] *formal* to put right something that is wrong: *efforts to rectify the problem*

rec·tor /'rektər/ n [C] **1** a priest in some Christian religions **2** a person in charge of a school or college, especially in Scotland

rec·tum /'rektəm/ n [C] *technical* the lowest part of your BOWEL —**rectal** *adj*

re·cu·pe·rate /rɪ'kjuːpəreɪt, -'kuː-/ v [I] to spend time getting better after an illness, injury etc: *Jan is still recuperating from her operation.* —**recuperation** /rɪˌkjuːpə'reɪʃən, -ˌkuː-/ n [U]

re·cur /rɪ'kɜːll-ɜːr/ v [I] **-rred, -rring** to happen again, or to happen several times: *a recurring dream* —**recurrence** /-'kʌrənsll-'kɜːr-/ n [C,U] —**recurrent** *adj*

re·cy·cle /ˌriː'saɪkəl/ v [I,T] to put used objects or materials through a process so that they can be used again: *Most glass bottles and aluminium cans can be recycled.* —**recyclable** adj: *recyclable plastics* (=that can be recycled) —**recycled** adj: *recycled paper* (=that has been recycled) —**recycling** n [U] → see colour picture on page 278

red[1] /red/ **-dder, -ddest** adj **1** having the colour of blood: *a red dress* → see colour picture on page 114 **2** red hair is an orange-brown colour → see colour picture on page 244 **3** *informal* COMMUNIST **4** **be like a red rag to a bull** *BrE* to be certain to make someone very angry —**redness** n [U]

red[2] n **1** [C,U] a red colour → see colour picture on page 114 **2** **in the red** owing more money than you have → opposite **be in the black** (BLACK[2]) **3** **see red** to become very angry: *The way he was hitting his dog just made me see red.* **4** [C] *informal* a disapproving word for a COMMUNIST

red car·pet /ˌ. '../ n **the red carpet** special treatment that you give someone important who is visiting you: *the red carpet treatment*

red·den /'redn/ v [I,T] to become red, or to make something do this: *Tina's face reddened with embarrassment.*

re·deem /rɪ'diːm/ v [T] **1** to make something less bad: *His performance redeemed what was otherwise a pretty awful movie.* **2** to free someone from the power of evil, used especially in the Christian religion **3** to get back something you have given or lent to someone **4** **redeem yourself** to do something to improve other

people's opinion of you, after you have done something wrong —**redeemable** *adj*

re·demp·tion /rɪ'dempʃən/ n [U] **1** *past/beyond redemption* too bad to be saved or improved **2** when someone is saved from the power of evil, especially according to the Christian religion

re·de·ploy /ˌriːdɪ'plɔɪ/ v [T] to use soldiers, workers, equipment etc in a different place or in a more effective way

re·de·vel·op /ˌriːdɪ'veləp/ v [T] to make an area more modern by putting in new buildings and businesses or improving old ones —**redevelopment** n [C,U]

red-hand·ed /ˌ. '..◂/ adj **catch sb red-handed** *informal* to catch someone at the moment when they are doing something wrong

red·head /'redhed/ n [C] someone who has red hair

red her·ring /ˌ. '../ n [C] a fact or idea that is not important but is introduced in order to take your attention away from something that is important

red-hot /ˌ. '.◂/ adj extremely hot: *red-hot metal*

re·di·rect, re-direct /ˌriːdaɪ'rekt, -dᵻ-/ v [T] to send something in a different direction, or use something for a different purpose: *She needs to redirect her energy into something more useful.*

red-light dis·trict /ˌ. '. ,../ n [C] the area of a city where there is a lot of PROSTITUTION

red meat /ˌ. './ n [U] dark coloured meat such as BEEF

red·neck /'rednek/ n [C] *AmE informal* an uneducated man who lives in a country area, who has strong unreasonable opinions

re·do /riː'duː/ v [T], **redid** /-'dɪd/, **redone** /-'dʌn/, **redoing** to do something again: *You'll have to redo this essay.*

re·dou·ble /ˌriː'dʌbəl/ v **redouble your efforts** to greatly increase your efforts to do something

re·dress /rɪ'dres/ v [T] *formal* to correct something that is wrong, not equal, or unfair —**redress** /rɪ'dresll'riː'dres/ n [U]

red tape /ˌ. './ n [U] official rules that seem unnecessary and prevent things from being done quickly

re·duce /rɪ'djuːsllrɪ'duːs/ v [T] to make something become less in size, amount, price etc: *They're trying to reduce the number of students in the college.* | **reduce sth from ... to** *The jacket was reduced from £75 to £35.*
  reduce sb/sth to sth *phr v* **1** **reduce sb to tears/silence/poverty etc** to make someone cry, be silent, become poor etc: *They were reduced to begging on the streets.* **2** **reduce sth to rubble/ashes/ruins** to destroy something, especially a building or city, completely —**reduction** /rɪ'dʌkʃən/ n [C,U]

re·dun·dant /rɪ'dʌndənt/ adj **1** *BrE* no longer employed by a company because there is not enough work: **make sb redundant** *Over 1000 workers were made redundant.* **2** something that is redundant is no longer needed because something else does the same thing —**redundancy** n [U]

red·wood /'redwʊd/ n [C,U] a very tall tree that grows in parts of the US

reed /riːd/ n [C] **1** a tall plant like grass that grows near water **2** a thin piece of wood in some musical instruments that produces a sound when air is blown over it

reef /riːf/ n [C] a line of sharp rocks or a raised area near the surface of the sea, often made of CORAL

reek /riːk/ v [I] to smell of something unpleasant: *His breath reeked of garlic.* —**reek** n [singular]

reel¹ /riːl/ n [C] a round object that things such as thread or film can be wound onto

reel² v [I] **1** to walk in an unsteady way, almost falling over, as if you are drunk: *A guy came reeling down the hallway.* **2** to feel very shocked or confused: *The party is still reeling from its defeat in the election.*

    reel sth ↔ **off** phr v [T] to repeat a lot of information quickly and easily: *Andy can reel off the names of all the state capitals.*

re-e-lect /ˌriː ɪ'lekt/ v [T] to elect someone again —**re-election** /-ɪ'lekʃən/ n [C,U]

re-en-try /ˌriː'entri/ n [C,U] when someone or something enters a place again: *The shuttle made a successful reentry into the Earth's atmosphere.*

ref /ref/ n [C] *spoken* a referee

re·fer /rɪ'fɜː‖-ɜːr/ v -**rred**, -**rring**
    refer to phr v [T] **1** [**refer to** sb/sth] to mention someone or something: *He referred to her several times.* **2** [**refer to** sth] to look at a book, map, piece of paper etc for information: *Refer to page 14 for instructions.* **3** [**refer** sb/sth to sb/sth] to send someone to another place or person for information, advice etc: *Professor Harris referred me to an article she had written.*

ref·er·ee¹ /ˌrefə'riː/ n [C] **1** someone who makes sure that the rules are followed during a sports game **2** *BrE* someone who writes a letter saying that you are suitable for a job, course etc

---

USAGE NOTE: referee and umpire

Both of these words mean the person who makes sure that the rules are followed in a sports game. Use **referee** with basketball, boxing, football, hockey, and wrestling. Use **umpire** with baseball, cricket, tennis, and volleyball.

---

referee² v [I,T] to be the referee for a game

ref·er·ence /'refərəns/ n **1** [C,U] something you say or write that mentions another person or thing: **make (a) reference to** *In his letter, Sam made no reference to his illness.* **2** [C,U] when you look at something for information, or the place you get information from: *Keep this dictionary on your desk for easy reference.* **3** [C] **a)** a letter saying that someone is suitable for a new job, course etc **b)** the person who writes this letter; REFEREE

reference book /'... ./ n [C] a book, for example a dictionary, that you look at to find information

ref·e·ren·dum /ˌrefə'rendəm/ n [C,U] an election in which people vote on just one thing, rather than on who will govern the country: *the Irish referendum on divorce*

re·fill¹ /ˌriː'fɪl/ v [T] to fill something again: *A waiter refilled our glasses.* —**refillable** adj

re·fill² /'riːfɪl/ n [C] a container filled with a substance that you use to refill something: *refills for a pen*

re·fine /rɪ'faɪn/ v [T] **1** to use an industrial process to make a natural substance more pure: *The sugar is refined and then shipped abroad.* **2** to improve a method, plan, system etc by making small changes to it —**refinement** n [U]

re·fined /rɪ'faɪnd/ adj **1** improved and made more effective **2** made more pure using an industrial process: *refined flour* **3** polite, educated, and interested in art, music, and literature: *the refined world of 19th century Paris*

re·fin·e·ry /rɪ'faɪnəri/ n [C] a factory where something such as oil, sugar, or metal is refined

re·flect /rɪ'flekt/ v

reflect

1 [I,T] if something such as a mirror or water reflects something, you can see the image of that thing in the mirror or water: *She could see the truck behind reflected in her wing mirror.* **2** [T] if a surface reflects heat, light, sound etc, heat, light, and sound are thrown back by it and do not go through it: *White clothes reflect more heat than dark ones.* **3** [T] to show or be the result of something: *Low levels of investment often reflect a lack of confidence in a country's government.* **2** [I] *formal* to think carefully: + **on** *Take some time to reflect on what I've just told you.*

    reflect on sb/sth phr v [T] to influence people's opinion about someone or something, especially in a bad way: *Behaviour like that always reflects very badly on the school.*

re·flec·tion /rɪ'flekʃən/ n **1** [C] an image that is reflected in a mirror or a similar surface: *We looked at our reflections in the pool.* **2** [U] when an image, light, sound etc is reflected **3** [C,U] careful and serious thought: *She paused for a moment's reflection.* **4** [C] something that is a result or sign of another situation: + **of** *That people will accept such low wages is a reflection of how few jobs there are.* **5** [singular] the way a situation or someone's behaviour makes someone else seem, especially in a bad way: + **on** *It's unfair to say that bad student results are always a reflection on the teacher.*

re·flec·tive /rɪ'flektɪv/ adj **1** a reflective surface reflects light **2** thinking quietly: *in a reflective mood*

re·flec·tor /rɪ'flektə‖-ər/ n [C] a piece of plastic that reflects light

re·flex /'riːfleks/ n [C] a quick physical reaction that you have without thinking: *Blinking is an automatic reflex.*

re·flex·ive /rɪ'fleksɪv/ adj a reflexive verb or PRONOUN shows that an action affects the person or thing that does the action. In the sentence 'I enjoyed myself', 'myself' is a reflexive pronoun. —**reflexive** n [C]

re·form¹ /rɪ'fɔːm‖-ɔːrm/ v **1** [T] to change a law, system, or organization so that it is fairer or more effective: *plans to reform the voting system* **2** [I,T] to change your behaviour and become a better person, or to make someone do this: *We should be more concerned with reforming criminals than punishing them.* | **a reformed character** (=someone who has reformed): *Oh no,*

R

he doesn't drink any more – he's a reformed character!

reform² /ˌ/ *n* [C,U] a change that is made to a political or legal system in order to make it fairer or more effective: *the reform of local government*

ref·or·ma·tion /ˌrefəˈmeɪʃən‖-fər-/ *n* [C,U]
1 when someone or something is changed so much that they seem completely different **2 the Reformation** the religious movement in Europe in the 16th century that led to the PROTESTANT churches being established

re·form·er /rɪˈfɔːməl‖-ɔːrmər/ *n* [C] someone who works to improve laws or society

reform school /ˌ. ˈ./ *n* [C] a special school where young people who have broken the law are sent

re·frain /rɪˈfreɪn/ *v* [I] *formal* to stop yourself from doing something: **+ from** *Please refrain from smoking.*

re·fresh /rɪˈfreʃ/ *v* **1** [T] to make someone feel less tired or hot: *A shower will refresh you.* **2 refresh sb's memory** to make someone remember something —**refreshed** *adj*

re·fresh·ing /rɪˈfreʃɪŋ/ *adj* **1** making you feel less tired or less hot: *a refreshing drink* **2** pleasantly different and interesting: *It makes a refreshing change to have someone new working here.* —**refreshingly** *adv*

re·fresh·ment /rɪˈfreʃmənt/ *n* [U] *formal* food and drinks that are provided at a meeting, party, sports event etc: *Refreshments will be served at the interval.*

re·fri·ge·rate /rɪˈfrɪdʒəreɪt/ *v* [T] to make food or drink cold so that is stays fresh for longer: *You should always keep milk refrigerated.* —**refrigeration** /rɪˌfrɪdʒəˈreɪʃən/ *n* [U]

re·fri·ge·rat·ed /rɪˈfrɪdʒəreɪtɪd/ *adj* **1** a refrigerated container, vehicle, ship etc keeps the food it contains cold **2** refrigerated food or drink has been kept cold in a refrigerator

re·fri·ge·ra·tor /rɪˈfrɪdʒəreɪtəl‖-ər/ *also* **fridge** *n* [C] a piece of kitchen equipment like a cupboard that keeps food cold so that it stays fresh for longer → see picture at KITCHEN

re·fuel /ˌriːˈfjuːəl/ *v* [I,T] to fill a vehicle or plane with FUEL again before continuing a journey

ref·uge /ˈrefjuːdʒ/ *n* **1** [U] protection from danger, bad weather, trouble etc **2** [C] a place that provides protection from danger: *a refuge for abused women*

ref·u·gee /ˌrefjʊˈdʒiː/ *n* [C] someone who has been forced to leave their country, especially during a war

re·fund¹ /ˈriːfʌnd/ *n* [C] an amount of money you have paid that is given back to you: **give sb a refund** *If you're not completely satisfied, we'll give you a refund.*

re·fund² /rɪˈfʌnd/ *v* [T] to give back money that has been paid to you

re·fur·bish /ˌriːˈfɜːbɪʃ‖-ɜːr-/ *v* [T] to repair and improve a building —**refurbishment** *n* [C,U]

re·fus·al /rɪˈfjuːzəl/ *n* [C,U] when someone refuses to do, accept, or allow something: **refusal to do sth** *His refusal to pay the fine means he may go to prison.*

re·fuse¹ /rɪˈfjuːz/ *v* **1** [I,T] to say firmly that you will not do or accept something: *I asked her to marry me, but she refused.* | **refuse to do sth** *Cindy refuses to go to school.* **2** [T] to not give

or allow someone something that they want: **refuse sb sth** *We were refused permission to enter the country.*

> **USAGE NOTE: reject, turn down, refuse,** and **decline**
>
> All these words mean 'to not accept something'. If you **reject** something or someone, you say firmly that you will not accept an offer, a suggestion, someone's friendship etc: *They have until December 19 to accept or reject the proposal.* | *Kieran's book got rejected by every publisher.* **Turn down** is a slightly less formal word for **reject**: *You'd be stupid to turn down such a good job offer.* If you **refuse** something, you say no, although someone very much wants you to accept it: *Peggy refused all offers of help.* If you **decline** an offer, you say politely that you cannot or will not accept it: *I'm sorry, but I'll have to decline the invitation.*

ref·use² /ˈrefjuːs/ *n* [U] *formal* waste material; RUBBISH

re·fute /rɪˈfjuːt/ *v* [T] *formal* to prove that a statement or idea is wrong

re·gain /rɪˈgeɪn/ *v* [T] to get something back: *The army has regained control of the area.*

re·gal /ˈriːgəl/ *adj* typical of a king or queen and therefore very impressive: *a regal mansion* —**regally** *adv*

re·gard¹ /rɪˈgɑːd‖-ɑːrd/ *n* **1** [U] respect for someone or something: **have regard for** *She has no regard for other people's feelings.* **2 with/in regard to** *formal* used to say what subject you are talking or writing about: *Several changes have been made with regard to security.*

regard² *v* [T] **1** to think about someone or something in a particular way: **regard sb as sth** *I've always regarded you as my friend.* **2** *formal* to look at someone or something: *She regarded him thoughtfully.*

re·gard·ing /rɪˈgɑːdɪŋ‖-ɑːr-/ *prep formal* a word used especially in business letters to introduce the subject you are writing about: *Regarding your recent inquiry, I've enclosed a copy of our new brochure.*

re·gard·less /rɪˈgɑːdləs‖-ɑːr-/ *adv* **1 regardless of** in spite of: *He'll sign that contract regardless of what anyone says!* **2** without being affected by problems or difficulties: *You get a lot of criticism but you just have to carry on regardless.*

re·gards /rɪˈgɑːdz‖-ɑːrdz/ *n* [plural] a word used in some forms of polite greeting: **give sb your regards** *Give him my regards, won't you?*

re·gat·ta /rɪˈgætə/ *n* [C] a sports event in which there are boat races

re·gen·e·ra·tion /rɪˌdʒenəˈreɪʃən/ *n* [U] something that is done to make something develop, improve, or grow strong again: *inner city regeneration* —**regenerate** /rɪˈdʒenəreɪt/ *v* [T]

reg·gae /ˈregeɪ/ *n* [U] a type of popular music from Jamaica with a strong regular beat

re·gime /reɪˈʒiːm/ *n* [C] a system of government or management, especially one you disapprove of: *the Communist regime*

re·gi·ment /ˈredʒɪmənt/ *n* [C] a large group of soldiers consisting of several BATTALIONS —**regimental** /ˌredʒɪˈmentl‖/ *adj*

re·gi·men·ted /'redʒɪˌmentᵻd/ *adj* strictly controlled —**regiment** *v* [T]

re·gion /'riːdʒən/ *n* [C] **1** a fairly large area within a state, country etc, usually without exact limits: *Snow is expected in mountain regions.* **2** an area of your body: *pain in the lower back region* **3 (somewhere) in the region of** about; APPROXIMATELY: *It will cost in the region of $750.* —**regional** *adj* —**regionally** *adv*

re·gis·ter[1] /'redʒɪstəll-ər/ *n* [C] **1** an official list or record of something: *the National Register of Historic Places* **2** [C,U] a way of speaking or writing that is formal, informal, humorous etc according to the situation you are in → see also CASH REGISTER

register[2] *v* **1** [T] to record names, facts etc on an official list: *The car is registered in my sister's name.* **2** [I,T] to put your name on an official list, for example of people attending a particular school: **+ with/for** *Are you registered with a doctor?* **3** [T] to show a feeling or opinion: *Her face registered surprise and shock.* **4** [I,T] if an instrument registers an amount, or an amount registers on it, the instrument shows that amount: *The thermometer registered 74°F.*

registered mail /ˌ... '. / *n* [U] a postal service in which the post office records when your mail is sent and delivered

re·gis·trar /ˌredʒɪˈstrɑː◂ ‖ 'redʒɪstrɑːr/ *n* [C] **1** someone who is in charge of official records, for example of births and deaths **2** *BrE* a hospital doctor

re·gis·tra·tion /ˌredʒɪˈstreɪʃən/ *n* [U] **1** when names, facts etc are recorded on an official list, or when you add your name to an official list **2** *BrE* a time when school students' names are taken to record that they are in school that day; ROLL CALL *AmE*: *Morning registration is at 9 am.* **3** *BrE* a car's registration number

registration num·ber /ˌ...' ... ˌ.../ *n* [C] *BrE* the numbers and letters on a car's NUMBER PLATE

re·gis·try /'redʒɪstri/ *n* [C] a place where official records are kept

re·gress /rɪˈgres/ *v* [I] *formal* to go back to an earlier, less developed state —**regression** /-ˈgreʃən/ *n* [U] → compare PROGRESS[2]

re·gret[1] /rɪˈgret/ *v* [T] **1** to feel sorry about something you have done and wish you had not done it: **regret doing sth** *We've always regretted selling that car.* **| + (that)** *He regrets that he never went to college.* **2** *formal* to be sorry and sad about a situation: **+ (that)** *Miss Otis regrets she's unable to attend today.*

regret[2] *n* [C,U] sadness that you feel about something because you wish it had not happened or that you had not done it: **+ at** *The company expressed deep regret at the accident.* **| have regrets about** *Carl said he had no regrets about his decision.* —**regretfully** *adv* —**regretful** *adj*

re·gret·ta·ble /rɪˈgretəbəl/ *adj* something regrettable is something you wish had never happened: *a regrettable mistake* —**regrettably** *adv*

reg·u·lar[1] /'regjʊləll-ər/ *adj* **1** repeated, with the same amount of time or space between each thing and the next: *His heartbeat became slow and regular.* **|** *War planes were taking off at regular intervals.* **2** planned for the same time every day, month, year etc: *regular meetings* **3** happening or doing something very often: *He's one of our regular customers.* **4** normal or usual: *She's not our regular babysitter.* **5** of a standard size: *fries and a regular coke* **6** *especially AmE* ordinary and not special or different from other things or people of that type: *I'm just a regular doctor, not a specialist.* **7** evenly shaped with parts or sides of equal size **8** a regular verb or noun changes its forms in the same way as most verbs or nouns. The verb 'walk' is regular, but 'be' is not —**regularity** /ˌregjʊˈlærᵻti/ *n* [U]

regular[2] *n* [C] **1** *informal* a customer who goes to the same shop, restaurant etc very often **2** [U] *AmE* petrol that contains LEAD → compare UNLEADED

reg·u·lar·ly /'regjʊləlɪ‖-ərli/ *adj* **1** often: *He visits the old man regularly.* **2** at regular times, for example every day, week, or month

reg·u·late /'regjʊleɪt/ *v* [T] **1** to control an activity or process, especially by having rules: *laws that regulate what goods can be imported* **2** to keep something at a particular speed, temperature etc

reg·u·la·tion /ˌregjʊˈleɪʃən/ *n* **1** [C] an official rule or order: *safety regulations* **2** [U] when a system or process is controlled: *government regulation of arms sales* —**regulatory** /ˌregjʊˈleɪtəri‖ˈregjʊlətɔːri/ *adj*

re·hab /'riːhæb/ *n* [U] *informal especially AmE* treatment to help someone who takes drugs or drinks too much alcohol: **be in rehab** *Frank's been in rehab for six weeks.*

re·ha·bil·i·tate /ˌriːhəˈbɪlᵻteɪt/ *v* [T] **1** to help someone to live a healthy or useful life again after they have been ill or in prison: *rehabilitating young criminals* **2** to improve a building, business, or area

re·ha·bil·i·ta·tion /ˌriːhəbɪlᵻˈteɪʃən/ *n* [U] treatment to help someone who takes drugs or drinks too much alcohol

re·hash /riːˈhæʃ/ *v* [T] *informal* to use the same ideas again in a way that is not really different or better: *He keeps rehashing the same old speech.* —**rehash** /'riːhæʃ/ *n* [C]

re·hears·al /rɪˈhɜːsəll-ɜːr-/ *n* [C,U] a time when all the people in a play, concert etc practise it before giving a public performance: *She was late for the rehearsal again.*

re·hearse /rɪˈhɜːsll-ɜːrs/ *v* [I,T] to practise or make people practise something such as a play or concert before giving a public performance

re·house /riːˈhaʊz/ *v* [T] to provide someone with a new or better home: *a program to rehouse war refugees*

reign[1] /reɪn/ *n* **1** [C] a period of time during which someone, especially a king or queen, rules a country: *the reign of Queen Anne* **2** [singular] a period of time during which

---

SPELLING NOTE
Words with the sound /r/, may be spelt **wr-**, like **wrong**.

someone is in control of an organization, business etc: *his 4-year reign as team coach* **3 reign of terror** when a government, army etc uses violence and threats to control people

reign² *v* [I] **1** to be the ruler of a country **2 the reigning champion** the most recent winner of a competition **3** *formal* to be the main feature or feeling of a situation: *Confusion reigned among members of the jury this week.*

re·im·burse /ˌriːɪmˈbɜːsǁ-ɜːrs/ *v* [T] *formal* to pay money back to someone: **reimburse sb for sth** *The company will reimburse you for your travel expenses.* **—reimbursement** *n* [U]

rein /reɪn/ *n* **1** [C usually plural] a long narrow band of leather that is fastened around a horse's head in order to control it **2 free rein** complete freedom to say or do things the way you want to: *She was given a free rein to run the department as she thought best.* **3 keep a tight rein on** to strictly control someone or something: *They've promised to keep a tight rein on spending.*

re·in·car·nate /ˌriːɪnˈkɑːneɪtǁ-ɑːr-/ *v* **be re·incarnated** to be born again in another body after you have died

re·in·car·na·tion /ˌriːɪnkɑːˈneɪʃənǁ-ɑːr-/ *n* **1** [U] the belief that people return to life in another body after they have died **2** the person or animal that a reincarnated person becomes

rein·deer /ˈreɪndɪəǁ-dɪr/ *n* [C] a type of DEER with long horns that lives in very cold places

re·in·force /ˌriːɪnˈfɔːsǁ-ˈfɔːrs/ *v* [T] **1** to support an opinion, feeling, system etc and make it stronger: *Parents should try to reinforce the reading skills their children learn at school.* **2** to make something such as a part of a building, a piece of clothing etc stronger: *a wall reinforced with concrete* **—reinforced** *adj*: *reinforced, bullet-proof glass* **—reinforcement** /ˌriːɪnˈfɔːsməntǁ-ˈfɔːrs-/ *n* [C,U]

re·in·force·ments /ˌriːɪnˈfɔːsməntsǁ-ˈfɔːrs-/ *n* [plural] additional soldiers who are sent to help an army

re·in·state /ˌriːɪnˈsteɪt/ *v* [T] to put someone back into a job that they had before: *Two employees who were wrongfully fired will be reinstated.* **—reinstatement** *n* [C,U]

re·invent /ˌriːɪnˈvent/ *v* **1 reinvent yourself** to deliberately change the way you appear to people and what you do so that you seem very different from the way you were before **2 reinvent the wheel** *informal* to waste time trying to find a way of doing something, when someone else has already discovered the best way to do it

re·it·e·rate /riːˈɪtəreɪt/ *v* [T] *formal* to say something more than once so that people take notice of it **—reiteration** /riːˌɪtəˈreɪʃən/ *n* [C,U]

re·ject¹ /rɪˈdʒekt/ *v* [T] **1** to refuse to accept, believe in, or agree with something: *They completely rejected the terms of the peace treaty.* **2** to refuse to accept someone for a job or position: *Yale rejected his application.* **3** to not give someone any love or attention: *She feels rejected by her parents.*

re·ject² /ˈriːdʒekt/ *n* [C] a product that is damaged or not perfect

re·jec·tion /rɪˈdʒekʃən/ *n* **1** [C,U] when someone refuses to accept or agree with something: **+ of** *his total rejection of his parents' way of life*

2 [C] a statement, letter etc that refuses to accept something or someone: *She got a lot of rejections before the book was finally published.* **3** [U] when someone stops giving love or attention to someone who expects it: *I couldn't deal with any more rejection.*

re·joice /rɪˈdʒɔɪs/ *v* [I] to be very happy because something good has happened

re·joic·ing /rɪˈdʒɔɪsɪŋ/ *n* [U] when a lot of people behave in a very happy way because they have good news

re·join /ˌriːˈdʒɔɪn/ *v* [T] to go back to a group or an organization that you were with before: *Alex rejoined his family in Japan.*

re·join·der /rɪˈdʒɔɪndəǁ-ər/ *n* [C] *formal* a quick reply, especially a rude one

re·ju·ve·nate /rɪˈdʒuːvəneɪt/ *v* [T] to make someone feel or look young and strong again: *She felt refreshed and rejuvenated after her holiday.* **—rejuvenation** /rɪˌdʒuːvəˈneɪʃən/ *n* [singular, U]

re·kin·dle /riːˈkɪndl/ *v* [T] to make someone have a feeling, thought etc again after it seemed to be finished : *a chance to rekindle an old romance*

re·lapse /rɪˈlæps/ *n* [C,U] **1** when someone becomes ill again after they were getting better: **have a relapse** *He had a relapse and was taken back into hospital.* **2** when someone or something gets worse again after being better **—relapse** /rɪˈlæpsǁˈriːlæps/ *v* [I]

re·late /rɪˈleɪt/ *v* **1** [I,T] to be connected to or to show that two or more thing are connected: *I don't understand how the two ideas relate.* **2** [T] *formal* to tell a story or talk about something that happened

relate to sb/sth *phr v* [T] **1** to be connected or concerned with something: *This point relates to environmental ideas.* **2** to be able to understand someone's problems, feelings etc: *I find it hard to relate to kids.*

re·lat·ed /rɪˈleɪtɪd/ *adj* **1** connected: **+ to** *diseases related to smoking*| **closely related** *The police believe the murders are closely related.* **2** connected by a family relationship: **be related to sb** *Are you related to Paula?*

re·la·tion /rɪˈleɪʃən/ *n* **1 in relation to** used to compare or show the connection between two things: *The area of land is tiny in relation to the population.* **2** [C,U] a connection between two things: **+ between** *Doctors say there was no relation between the drugs he was taking and his death* **3** [C] a member of your family: RELATIVE: *Joan Bartell, the author, is no relation to Governor Bartell.*

re·la·tions /rɪˈleɪʃənz/ *n* [plural] the way two groups, countries, organizations etc deal with or behave towards each other: *East–West relations*| **+ between** *Relations between the two companies have never been good*

re·la·tion·ship /rɪˈleɪʃənʃɪp/ *n* **1** [C] the way in which two people or groups behave towards each other: **+ with** *The police have a good relationship with the community.* **2** [C] a situation in which two people have sexual or romantic feelings for each other: *My parents had a strong relationship.* **3** [C,U] the way in which two or more things or ideas are connected with each other: **+ between** *the relationship between pay and performance at work*

rel·a·tive[1] /ˈrelətɪv/ n [C] a member of your family: *He's staying with relatives in Manchester.*

relative[2] adj **1** having a particular quality when compared with something else: *The Victorian age was a period of relative peace in England.* **2 relative to sth** compared with something: *Demand for corn is low relative to the supply.*

relative clause /ˌ… ˈ./ n [C] a part of a sentence that has a verb in it and is joined to the rest of the sentence by a relative pronoun such as "which"

rel·a·tive·ly /ˈrelətɪvli/ adv **relatively cheap/small/easy etc** fairly cheap, small, easy etc, especially when compared with other things of the same kind; quite: *My job is relatively well paid.* | *This car is relatively cheap to run.*

relative pro·noun /ˌ… ˈ../ n [C] a PRONOUN such as 'who', 'which', or 'that', which connects a relative clause to the rest of the sentence

rel·a·tiv·i·ty /ˌreləˈtɪvɪti/ n [U] *technical* the relationship in PHYSICS between time, space, and speed: *Einstein's theory of relativity*

re·lax /rɪˈlæks/ v **1** [I,T] to become more calm, comfortable, and less worried, or to make someone do this: *Sit down and relax!* | *The music will help relax you.* **2** [I,T] if a part of your body relaxes, or if you relax it, it become less stiff and tight: *Try to relax your neck.* | *Let your muscles relax.* **3** [T] to make rules, laws etc less strict: *There are no plans to relax the present immigration laws.* —**relaxation** /ˌriːlækˈseɪʃən/ n [U]

relaxed /rɪˈlækst/ adj **1** feeling calm and comfortable and not worried about anything: *Gail was lying in the sun, looking happy and relaxed.* **2** a situation that is relaxed is comfortable and informal: *There was a relaxed atmosphere at the meeting.*

relaxing /rɪˈlæksɪŋ/ adj pleasant and making you feel calm and comfortable: *a nice relaxing week on the beach*

re·lay[1] /ˈriːleɪ‖rɪˈleɪ, ˈriːleɪ/ v [T] **1** to pass a message from one person or place to another **2** to send out a radio or television SIGNAL

re·lay[2] also **relay race** /ˈ.. ˌ./ n [C] a race in which each member of a team runs or swims part of the distance: *the 1000 metre relay*

re·lease[1] /rɪˈliːs/ v [T] **1** to let someone go free after keeping them as a prisoner: *Three hostages were released this morning.* **2** to stop holding something: *He released her arm when she screamed.* **3** to let news or information be known publicly: *Details of the crime have not been released.* **4** to make a film or record available for people to buy or see

release[2] n **1** [singular] when someone is released from prison: *After his release, he intends to train as a carpenter.* **2** [C] a new film or record that is available for people to see or buy: *the singer's latest release* **3** [U] a feeling that you have no worry or pain: *a sense of emotional release* → see also PRESS RELEASE

rel·e·gate /ˈreləɡeɪt/ v [T] to make someone or something less important than before: **+ to** *He's been relegated to the role of assistant.*

re·lent /rɪˈlent/ v [I] to let someone do something that you refused to let them do before: *Park officials relented, and allowed campers to stay.*

re·lent·less /rɪˈlentləs/ adj continuing without getting any less severe or determined —**relentlessly** adv

rel·e·vance /ˈreləvəns/ also **rel·e·van·cy** /-vənsi/ *AmE* — n [U] the degree to which something is connected with a particular subject or problem: **+ to** *a statement with no relevance to the issue*

rel·e·vant /ˈreləvənt/ adj directly relating to the subject or problem being discussed: **+ to** *The question is not relevant to my point.* → opposite IRRELEVANT

re·li·a·ble /rɪˈlaɪəbəl/ adj someone or something that is reliable can be trusted or depended on; DEPENDABLE: *He's not very reliable.* | *a reliable car* —**reliably** adv —**reliability** /rɪˌlaɪəˈbɪlɪti/ n [U] → opposite UNRELIABLE

re·li·ance /rɪˈlaɪəns/ n [U] when something depends on something else: *the country's reliance on imported oil*

re·li·ant /rɪˈlaɪənt/ adj **be reliant on sb/sth** to depend on something or someone: *She's still reliant on her parents for money.*

rel·ic /ˈrelɪk/ n [C] **1** an old custom, idea, or thing that still exists: **+ of** *a relic of ancient times* **2** something that once belonged to a holy person or SAINT

re·lief /rɪˈliːf/ n **1** [singular, U] the feeling you have when you are no longer worried about something: *a tremendous feeling of relief* | **What a relief!** *spoken* (used when you are pleased that something has finished or did not happen): *Exams are finally over. What a relief!* **2** [U] money, food, clothing etc given to people who need them: *famine relief* **3** [U] when pain is made less severe: *a medicine for pain relief* **4 in stark relief** very different from everything around and therefore easy to notice

re·lieve /rɪˈliːv/ v [T] **1** to make pain, a problem, a bad feeling etc less severe: *The county is building a new school to relieve overcrowding.* | *playing cards to relieve the boredom* **2** to replace someone else at a job or duty when they are finished for the day

relieve sb of sth *phr v* [T] *formal* to take something away from someone

re·lieved /rɪˈliːvd/ adj happy because something bad did not happen or you are no longer worried about something: **be relieved to do sth** *I was relieved to be out of the hospital.* | **+ that** *She'll be very relieved that she won't have to go to court.*

re·li·gion /rɪˈlɪdʒən/ n [C,U] a belief in one or more gods, or a particular system of belief in God or gods: *the study of religion* | *the Muslim religion*

re·li·gious /rɪˈlɪdʒəs/ adj **1** relating to religion: *religious beliefs* **2** believing strongly in your religion and obeying its rules: *a very religious woman*

re·li·gious·ly /rɪˈlɪdʒəsli/ adv if you do something religiously, you do it regularly, especially something you feel it is your duty to do: *He phones his mother religiously every evening.*

re·lin·quish /rɪˈlɪŋkwɪʃ/ v [T] *formal* to give your position, power, rights etc to someone else: *The General refuses to relinquish control of the city.*

rel·ish[1] /ˈrelɪʃ/ v [T] to enjoy the thought that something good is going to happen: **not relish the thought/idea** *Jamie didn't relish the idea of getting up so early.*

relish[2] n [U] great enjoyment: *Barry ate with great relish.*

re·live /ˌriːˈlɪv/ v [T] to remember, describe, or show something so clearly that it seems as if it is happening again: *We spent the whole morning reliving our schooldays.*

re·lo·cate /ˌriːləʊˈkeɪt‖riːˈloʊkeɪt/ v [I,T] to move to a new place: **+ to** *Our company relocated to the West Coast.* —**relocation** /ˌriːləʊˈkeɪʃən‖-loʊ-/ n [U]

re·luc·tant /rɪˈlʌktənt/ adj unwilling and therefore slow to do something: **be reluctant to do sth** *She was very reluctant to ask for help.* —**reluctance** n [U] —**reluctantly** adv

re·ly /rɪˈlaɪ/ v

rely on sb/sth phr v [T] to trust or depend on someone or something: *We're relying on him to help.*

re·main /rɪˈmeɪn/ v **1** [I, linking verb] to continue in the same way or condition: *The Communist Party remained in power.*|*She remained silent.* **2** [I] *formal* to stay in the same place or position: *Milly remained at home.* **3** [I] to continue to exist after other people or things have gone or been destroyed: *Only half the statue remains.* **4 it remains to be seen** used to say that what will happen is still uncertain: *It remains to be seen whether the operation will be successful.*

re·main·der /rɪˈmeɪndəﻝ-ər/ n **the remainder (of sth)** what is left after everything else has gone or been dealt with: *Would the remainder of the class please stay behind.*

re·main·ing /rɪˈmeɪnɪŋ/ adj left when other things or people have gone or been dealt with: *The remaining puppies were given away.*

re·mains /rɪˈmeɪnz/ n [plural] **1** the parts of something that are left after the rest has been destroyed: *We visited the remains of the temple.* **2** *formal* someone's body after they have died, especially after a long time

re·make /ˈriːmeɪk/ n [C] a film or song that has the same story or music as one that was made before: *a remake of "The Wizard of Oz"* —**remake** /riːˈmeɪk/ v [T]

re·mand[1] /rɪˈmɑːnd‖rɪˈmænd/ v [T] BrE **be remanded in custody** to be kept in prison until your TRIAL

remand[2] n BrE **1 be on remand** to be in prison waiting for your TRIAL **2 remand prisoner/centre/prison etc** someone who is on remand or a place for people who are on remand

re·mark[1] /rɪˈmɑːk‖-ɑːrk/ n [C] something that you say: **make a remark** *Carl made a sarcastic remark.*

remark[2] v [T] to say something: **+ that** *One woman remarked that he was very handsome.*

remark on/upon sth phr v [T] to notice something and to say something about it: *No-one dared remark upon the fact that the President was two hours late.*

re·mark·a·ble /rɪˈmɑːkəbﻝ-ɑːr-/ adj very unusual or noticeable in a way that deserves admiration: *He called Gorbachev "one of the most remarkable men in history".*

re·mark·a·bly /rɪˈmɑːkəblɪ‖-ɑːr-/ adv in a way that is surprising: *Charlotte and her cousin look remarkably similar.*

re·mar·ry /ˌriːˈmæri/ v [I,T] to marry again: *He's been divorced and remarried several times.* —**remarriage** n [C,U]

re·me·di·al /rɪˈmiːdiəl/ adj **1** intended to help students who are having difficulty learning something **2** *formal* intended to provide a cure or improvement in something

rem·e·dy[1] /ˈremɪdi/ n [C] **1** a medicine that cures pain or illness: *herbal remedies* **2** a successful way of dealing with a problem: **+ for** *There seems to be no remedy for the rising crime rate.*

remedy[2] v [T] to deal successfully with a problem or improve a bad situation: *The hospital is trying to remedy the problem of inexperienced staff.*

re·mem·ber /rɪˈmembəﻝ-ər/ v **1** [I,T] to have in your memory people, places, and events from the past: *Do you remember the first job you ever had?* **2** [I,T] to bring information or facts that you know back into your mind: *I can't remember her name.*|**+ (that)** *She suddenly remembered that she had to go to the dentist.* **3** [I,T] to not forget to do something: **remember to do sth** *Did you remember to phone Nicky?* → compare REMIND **4** [T] to think about someone who has died with special respect

---

USAGE NOTE: remember and remind

If you **remember** something, a fact or event from the past, or something you earlier decided to do, comes back into your mind: *Do you remember that guy we met at the party?* | *I can't remember how much I paid for it.* | *He suddenly remembered he had to go to the bank.* If someone **reminds** you to do something, or something **reminds** you of something, they make you remember it: *This song always reminds me of when I was at college.* | *Remind me to call him later today.*

---

re·mem·brance /rɪˈmembrəns/ n [U] the act of remembering and showing respect for someone who has died: **in remembrance of** *She planted a tree in remembrance of her husband.*

re·mind /rɪˈmaɪnd/ v [T] **1** to make someone remember something that they must do: **remind sb to do sth** *Remind me to go to the post office.* **2 remind sb of** to be similar to another person, thing, place etc, so that you think of that person, thing, place etc: *She reminds me of Dawn French.*

re·mind·er /rɪˈmaɪndəﻝ-ər/ n [C] something that makes you notice or remember something else: **+ of** *The photos were a painful reminder of his first wife.*

rem·i·nisce /ˌremɪˈnɪs/ v [I] to talk or think about pleasant events in your past: **+ about** *She sat reminiscing about the old days.* —**reminiscence** n [C,U]

rem·i·nis·cent /ˌremɪˈnɪsənt/ adj **reminiscent of** making you think of someone or something similar: *The scene was reminiscent of a Hollywood gangster movie.*

re·mis·sion /rɪˈmɪʃən/ n [C,U] a period of time when an illness improves: **be in remission** *Her cancer is in remission.*

re·mit /rɪ'mɪt/ n [singular] *BrE* an area of work that someone is responsible for

re·mit·tance /rɪ'mɪtəns/ n [C,U] *formal* an amount of money that is paid

rem·nant /'remnənt/ n [C] a small part of something that remains after the rest no longer exists: + **of** *the remnants of the defeated army*

re·mod·el /ˌriː'mɒdl‖ˌriː'mɑːdl/ v [T] to change the shape, purpose, or appearance of something: *The house was remodelled in 1764 by Robert Adams.*

rem·on·strate /'remənstreɪt‖rɪ'mɑːn-/ v [I] *formal* to tell someone that you strongly disapprove of what they have done

re·morse /rɪ'mɔːs‖-ɔːrs/ n [U] a feeling of being sorry for something bad that you have done: *Keating showed no remorse for his crime.* —**remorseful** *adj* —**remorsefully** *adv*

re·morse·less /rɪ'mɔːsləs‖-ɔːr-/ *adj* **1** continuing without stopping **2** cruel and determined —**remorselessly** *adv*

re·mote /rɪ'məʊt‖-'moʊt/ *adj* **1** far away in distance or time: *a remote planet* | *the remote past* **2** very slight or small: *There's a remote possibility that the operation will not work.* —**remotely** *adv*: *The two situations aren't remotely similar.* —**remoteness** n [U]

remote con·trol /ˌ.ˌ .'./ n **1** [U] the use of radio waves to control something such as a television from a distance **2** [C] also **remote** a piece of equipment that you use to control something such as a television from a distance ➡ see colour picture on page 474 —**remote-controlled** *adj*

re·mov·a·ble /rɪ'muːvəbəl/ *adj* something that is removable can be removed: *a coat with a removable hood*

re·move /rɪ'muːv/ v [T] **1** to take something away: *The police will remove any illegally parked cars.* **2** to get rid of a problem, law, system etc: *There are several obstacles still to be removed.* **3** be **(far) removed from sth** to be very different from something else: *His millionaire lifestyle is far removed from the poverty of his childhood.* —**removal** n [C,U]

re·mov·er /rɪ'muːvəl-ər/ n [C,U] **paint/stain/ nail polish etc remover** a substance that removes paint or other substances from something

re·mu·ne·rate /rɪ'mjuːnəreɪt/ v [T] *formal* to pay someone for something they have done —**remuneration** /rɪˌmjuːnə'reɪʃən/ n [C,U]

Re·nais·sance /rɪ'neɪsəns‖'renəˌsɑːns/ n **the Renaissance** the time in Europe between the 14th and 17th centuries when the art, literature, and ideas of ancient Greece were discovered again and developed

re·name /ˌriː'neɪm/ v [T] to change the name of something: *St Petersburg was renamed Leningrad.*

ren·der /'rendəl-ər/ v *formal* **1 render sth useless/unsafe/harmless etc** to make something useless, unsafe etc: *He twisted the man's arm, rendering him incapable of moving.*

2 render an apology/an explanation/a service etc to say sorry, explain something etc to someone

ren·der·ing /'rendərɪŋ/ n [C] the way a poem, play, piece of music etc is performed

ren·dez·vous /'rɒndʲvuː, -deɪ-‖'rɑːndeɪ-/ n [C] an arrangement to meet someone at a particular time and place, or the place where you meet: *a midnight rendezvous* —**rendezvous** v [I]

ren·di·tion /ren'dɪʃən/ n [C] the way that a play, piece of music etc is performed or produced

ren·e·gade /'renɪgeɪd/ n [C] someone who changes to the opposing side in a war, political organization etc —**renegade** *adj*: *renegade soldiers*

re·nege /rɪ'niːg, rɪ'neɪg‖rɪ'nɪg, rɪ'niːg/ v [I] **renege on a promise/agreement/deal etc** to not do something that you promised to do

re·new /rɪ'njuː‖rɪ'nuː/ v [T] **1** to arrange for a contract, official agreement etc to continue: *When does the car insurance need renewing?* **2** to begin to do something again: *Congress renewed its demand for tax cuts.* **3** to put something new in the place of something old or broken —**renewal** n [C,U]

re·new·a·ble /rɪ'njuːəbəl‖rɪ'nuː-/ *adj* **1** something that is renewable can be replaced at the same speed that it is used up: *a renewable energy source* **2** a renewable contract, ticket etc can be made to continue after the time limit on it has been reached

re·newed /rɪ'njuːd‖-'nuːd/ *adj* increasing or getting stronger again: *renewed efforts to tackle poverty*

re·nounce /rɪ'naʊns/ v [T] **1** to say publicly that you no longer have a right to something **2** to say publicly that you do not believe in or support an idea, a religion, a political party etc: *The IRA have been repeatedly urged to renounce violence.* —**renunciation** /rɪˌnʌnsi'eɪʃən/ n [U]

ren·o·vate /'renəveɪt/ v [T] to repair something, especially a building, so that it is in good condition again —**renovation** /ˌrenə'veɪʃən/ n [C,U]

re·nown /rɪ'naʊn/ n [U] *informal* when someone is famous for something they do

re·nowned /rɪ'naʊnd/ *adj* famous: **be renowned for sth** *The hotel is renowned for its excellent service.*

rent[1] /rent/ v **1** [I,T] to pay money regularly to live in a place that belongs to someone else: *They're renting an apartment near the beach.* **2** [T] to pay money for the use of something for a short period of time; **HIRE** *BrE*: *Did you rent a car while you were in Europe?* **3** [T] also **rent** sth ↔ **out** to let someone live in a place that you own in return for money: *They've rented out their house for the summer.* —**renter** n [C] *AmE*

rent[2] n [C,U] the amount of money you pay for the use of a house, room, car etc that belongs to someone else: *Rents are very high around here.* | **for rent** (=available to be rented)

GRAMMAR NOTE: the present perfect (2)
You use the **present perfect**: **1** to talk about something that happened in the past, but which still affects the situation now: *I've lost my passport.* **2** to talk about something that happened in the past, and continues to happen now: *I have lived in London for many years.* (=I still live there now).

rent·al /ˈrentl/ n [C,U] **1** an arrangement to rent something: *a video rental store* **2** the money that you pay to rent something: *Ski rental is $14.* —**rental** adj

re·or·gan·ize (also **-ise** BrE) /riːˈɔːɡənaɪz‖ -ˈɔːr-/ v [I,T] to organize something in a new and better way: *The filing system needs to be reorganized.* —**reorganization** /riːˌɔːɡənaɪˈzeɪʃən‖ -ˌɔːrɡənə-/ n [U]

rep /rep/ n [C] informal someone who sells products for a company: *a sales rep*

re·paid /rɪˈpeɪd/ the past tense and past participle of REPAY

re·pair¹ /rɪˈpeə‖-ˈper/ v [T] **1** to fix something that is broken or damaged: **get sth repaired** (=arrange for someone to fix it) **2** to put something right that is wrong: *The two governments are trying to repair the damage done to the peace process.*

repair² n **1** [C,U] something you do to fix something that is broken or damaged: *They're doing repairs on the bridge.* **2** **in good/bad repair** in good or bad condition: *The roads are in pretty good repair.*

re·pair·man /rɪˈpeəmæn‖-ˈper-/ n [C] someone whose job is to fix things: *a TV repairman*

rep·a·ra·tion /ˌrepəˈreɪʃən/ n [C,U] formal payment made to someone for damage, injury etc that you have caused

re·pat·ri·ate /riːˈpætrieɪt‖riːˈpeɪ-/ v [T] to send someone or something back to the country they came from —**repatriation** /riːˌpætriˈeɪʃən‖riː-ˌpeɪ-/ n [U]

re·pay /rɪˈpeɪ/ v [T] **1** to pay back money that you have borrowed: *How long will it take to repay the loan?* **2** to reward someone for helping you: *How can I ever repay you?* —**repayment** n [C,U]

re·peal /rɪˈpiːl/ v [T] to officially end a law: *plans to repeal anti-immigration laws* —**repeal** n [U]

re·peat¹ /rɪˈpiːt/ v [T] **1** to say or do something again: *Sally kept repeating, "It wasn't me, it wasn't me."* | *You'll have to repeat the course.* **2** to say something that you have heard someone else say: **repeat sth to sb** *Please don't repeat this to anyone.*

repeat² n **1** [singular] a situation or event that has happened before: **+ of** *Are you expecting a repeat of last year's trouble?* | **a repeat victory/performance/operation etc** (=one that is repeated) **2** [C] especially BrE a television or radio programme that has been shown before; RERUN AmE

re·peat·ed /rɪˈpiːtɪd/ adj done or happening several times: *Repeated attempts to fix the satellite have failed.* —**repeatedly** adv

re·pel /rɪˈpel/ v **-lled, -lling** **1** [T] to force someone to go away or to stop attacking you: *Tear gas was used to repel the rioters.* **2** **repel sb** if something repels you, you dislike it very much **3** [I,T] technical to push something away with an electrical force

re·pel·lent¹ /rɪˈpelənt/ n [C,U] a substance that keeps something, especially insects, away: *mosquito repellent*

repellent² adj extremely unpleasant: *She'd always found her cousin quite repellent.*

re·pent /rɪˈpent/ v [I,T] formal to be sorry for something bad that you have done —**repentance** n [U]

re·pen·tant /rɪˈpentənt/ adj feeling sorry because of something bad that you have done

re·per·cus·sion /ˌriːpəˈkʌʃən‖-pər-/ n [C usually plural] the result of something that happens, especially when this affects things for a long time afterwards: *The fall of Communism has had worldwide repercussions.*

rep·er·toire /ˈrepətwɑː‖-pərtwɑːr/ n [C] the plays, songs, jokes etc that a performer performs

rep·e·ti·tion /ˌrepɪˈtɪʃən/ n [C,U] when something happens again or is done again many times: **+ of** *his boring repetition of the same old facts*

re·pet·i·tive /rɪˈpetɪtɪv/ also **repetitious** /ˌrepɪˈtɪʃəs/ adj doing or saying the same thing many times in a way that seems boring: *repetitive exercises* —**repetitively** adv

re·phrase /ˌriːˈfreɪz/ v [T] to say or write something in different words so that its meaning is clearer: *OK, let me rephrase the question.*

re·place /rɪˈpleɪs/ v [T] **1 a)** to start using a different person or thing instead of the one you use now: **replace sb/sth with** *They later replaced the coach with a younger man.* **b)** to start being used instead of someone or something else: *The new software package replaces the old one.* **2** to put something back in its correct place: *Please replace the books when you are finished.* **3** to get something new because the old one has been lost, stolen, damaged etc

re·place·ment /rɪˈpleɪsmənt/ n **1** [C] someone or something that replaces another person or thing: *We're waiting for Mr. Dunley's replacement.* **2** [U] when something is replaced

re·play /ˈriːpleɪ/ n **1** [C,U] something that happens in a sports game on television that is immediately shown again **2** [C] BrE a sports game that is played again: *The replay will be on Thursday.* —**replay** /ˌriːˈpleɪ/ v [T]

re·plen·ish /rɪˈplenɪʃ/ v [T] formal to make something full or complete again —**replenishment** n [U]

re·plete /rɪˈpliːt/ adj formal full of something or containing a lot of it

rep·li·ca /ˈreplɪkə/ n [C] an almost exact copy of something: *replica guns*

rep·li·cate /ˈreplɪkeɪt/ v [T] formal to do or make something again, in exactly the same way —**replication** /ˌreplɪˈkeɪʃən/ n [C,U]

re·ply¹ /rɪˈplaɪ/ v [I,T] to answer: *"Of course," she replied.* | **reply to sth** *I haven't replied to his letter yet.*

reply² n [C,U] something that you say, write, or do as an answer: **+ to** *There have been no replies to our ad.* | **do sth in reply** (=as a reply): *Marcy said nothing in reply.*

re·port¹ /rɪˈpɔːt‖-ɔːrt/ n [C] **1** a written or spoken description of a situation or event: *a police report on the accident* | *a weather report* **2** also **school report** BrE a written statement about a child's progress at school **3** formal the noise of an explosion or gun shot

report² v **1** [I,T] to tell people about something, especially in newspapers, on television, or on the radio: **+ on** *She was sent to report on the floods in Bangladesh.* | **+ that** *The newspaper* *wrongly reported that he had died.* **2** [T] to tell someone in authority that a crime or accident has happened: *Who reported the fire?* **3** [T] to officially complain about someone: *Somebody reported Kyle for smoking in school.* **4** [I] to go somewhere and say that you have arrived or are ready to do something: *Visitors must report to the main reception desk.*

report card /.'. ./ *n* [C] *AmE* a written statement giving a school student's GRADES

re·port·ed·ly /rɪ'pɔːtɪdlɪ‖-ɔːr-/ *adv* according to what people say: *She's reportedly one of the richest women in Europe.*

reported speech /.,.. './ *n* [U] the style of speech or writing that is used for reporting what someone says, without repeating the actual words

re·port·er /rɪ'pɔːtəl‖-'pɔːrtər/ *n* [C] someone whose job is to find out about news stories and write or tell people about them in newspapers, on television etc

re·pos·sess /,riːpə'zes/ *v* [T] to take back something that someone has partly paid for, because they cannot pay the rest of the money they owe —**repossession** /-'zeʃən/ *n* [C,U]

rep·re·hen·si·ble /,reprɪ'hensɪbəl/ *adj formal* reprehensible behaviour is very bad

rep·re·sent /,reprɪ'zent/ *v* [T] **1** to speak and do things for someone else because they have asked you to: *Craig hired a lawyer to represent him.* **2** if you represent a country, school etc in a competition, you compete in it for the country, school etc **3** to be a sign for something: *The green triangles on the map represent campgrounds.* **4** be the same as: *This figure represents a 25% increase in wages.* **5** to describe or show someone in a particular way

rep·re·sen·ta·tion /,reprɪzen'teɪʃən/ *n* **1** [U] when someone represents someone else, for example in government: *Children get no representation in most countries.* **2** the way something is described or shown: *the negative representation of black people in movies*

rep·re·sen·ta·tive¹ /,reprɪ'zentətɪv/ *n* [C] someone who is chosen to do things, speak, vote etc for someone else

representative² *adj* typical of the people or things in a particular group: **+ of** *I don't claim to be representative of the majority of young people.*

re·press /rɪ'pres/ *v* [T] **1** to stop yourself from expressing what you really feel: *It's not healthy to repress your emotions.* **2** to control people by force —**repression** /-'preʃən/ *n* [U]

re·pressed /rɪ'prest/ *adj* having feelings or needs that you do not express: *repressed feelings of hatred for her mother*

re·pres·sive /rɪ'presɪv/ *adj* cruel and very strict: *a repressive political system*

re·prieve /rɪ'priːv/ *n* [C] **1** an official order stopping a prisoner from being killed as a punishment **2** when something happens to stop a bad situation continuing —**reprieve** *v* [T]

rep·ri·mand /'reprɪmɑːnd‖-mænd/ *v* [T] to tell someone officially that they have done something wrong: *He was formally reprimanded and ordered to pay a £500 fine.* —**reprimand** *n* [C]

re·pri·sal /rɪ'praɪzəl/ *n* [C,U] something that is done to punish an enemy: *He's afraid to help the police for fear of reprisals against his family.*

re·proach¹ /rɪ'prəʊtʃ‖-'prəʊtʃ/ *n* [C,U] **1** blame or criticism, or something you say to blame or criticize someone: *His mother gave him a look of reproach.* **2** **above/beyond reproach** impossible to criticize: *The police should be above reproach.* —**reproachful** *adj* —**reproachfully** *adv*

reproach² *v* [T] to blame someone and try to make them sorry for something they have done

re·pro·duce /,riːprə'djuːs‖-'duːs/ *v* **1** [T] to make a copy of something or do it again in the same way: *an attempt by scientists to reproduce conditions on Mars* **2** [I] to produce young plants, humans, or animals: *Most birds and fish reproduce by laying eggs.*

re·pro·duc·tion /,riːprə'dʌkʃən/ *n* **1** [U] the process of producing young plants or animals: *human reproduction* **2** [C] a copy of something, especially a work of art or piece of expensive furniture

re·pro·duc·tive /,riːprə'dʌktɪv/ *adj* relating to reproduction: *the reproductive organs*

re·prove /rɪ'pruːv/ *v* [T] *formal* to angrily criticize someone for doing something bad —**reproof** /rɪ'pruːf/ *n* [C,U]

rep·tile /'reptaɪl‖'reptl/ *n* [C] an animal such as a snake or LIZARD that lays eggs, and whose blood changes temperature with the temperature around it —**reptilian** /rep'tɪlɪən/ *adj*

re·pub·lic /rɪ'pʌblɪk/ *n* [C] a country that has an elected government, and does not have a king or queen ➙ compare MONARCHY

re·pub·li·can /rɪ'pʌblɪkən/ *adj* relating to a REPUBLIC: *the spread of republican ideas in the 17th century* —**republican** *n* [C]

Republican *adj* relating to or supporting the US Republican Party: *a Republican candidate for the Senate* —**Republican** *n* [C]

Republican Par·ty /.'... ,../ *n* **the Republican Party** one of the two main political parties of the US

re·pu·di·ate /rɪ'pjuːdieɪt/ *v* [T] *formal* to completely refuse to accept or agree with something: *He repudiated any suggestion that he had bribed his opponents.* —**repudiation** /rɪ,pjuːdi'eɪʃən/ *n* [U]

re·pug·nance /rɪ'pʌgnəns/ *n* [U] *formal* a feeling of disliking something very much; DISGUST

re·pug·nant /rɪ'pʌgnənt/ *adj formal* very unpleasant and offensive: *behaviour that is morally repugnant*

re·pulse /rɪ'pʌls/ *v* [T] **1** to make someone feel very shocked, upset, and angry: *The whole nation was repulsed by the crime.* **2** to defeat a military attack: *Enemy forces were repulsed with the help of French troops.*

re·pul·sion /rɪ'pʌlʃən/ *n* [U] **1** a feeling of disliking something very much **2** *technical* the MAGNETIC force by which one object pushes another away from it

re·pul·sive /rɪ'pʌlsɪv/ *adj* extremely unpleasant: *What a repulsive man!*

rep·u·ta·ble /'repjʊtəbəl/ *adj* respected for being honest and doing good work: *a reputable company*

rep·u·ta·tion /,repjʊ'teɪʃən/ *n* [C] the opinion that people have of a person, product, company etc: *The neighbourhood used to have a very bad* *reputation.* | + **for** *a man with a reputation for honesty*

re·pute /rɪ'pjuːt/ *n* of good/bad etc repute *formal* having a good, bad etc reputation

re·put·ed /rɪ'pjuːtɪd/ *adj formal* according to what most people think or say: **reputed to be sth** *He is reputed to be a millionaire.* —**reputedly** *adv*

re·quest[1] /rɪ'kwest/ *n* **1** [C,U] when someone politely or formally asks for something: **make a request** *We've made a request for new equipment.* | **on request** (=if you ask): *Drinks are available on request.* **2** [C] a piece of music that someone asks to be played

request[2] *v* [T] to ask for something officially or formally: *The pilot requested permission to land.* | + **that** *We request that everyone remain quiet.*

req·ui·em /'rekwiəm, 'rekwiem/ *n* [C,U] a Christian ceremony of prayers for someone who has died, or music written for this ceremony

re·quire /rɪ'kwaɪə‖-'kwaɪr/ *v* [T] **1** to need something: *Pets require a lot of care.* **2** *formal* to officially demand that someone does something: **require sb to do sth** *All passengers are required to show their tickets.*

re·quire·ment /rɪ'kwaɪəmənt‖-'kwaɪr-/ *n* [C] something that is needed or asked for: *Whatever your requirements, we can supply them.*

req·ui·site /'rekwɪzɪt/ *adj formal* needed for a particular purpose

req·ui·si·tion /ˌrekwɪ'zɪʃən/ *n* [C,U] *formal* an official demand to be given something, usually made by an army —**requisition** *v* [T]

re·route /ˌriː'ruːt‖-'ruːt, -'raʊt/ *v* [T] to make vehicles, runners etc go a different way from the way they normally go

re·run /'riːrʌn/ *n* [C] *especially AmE* a television programme that is shown again; REPEAT *BrE* —**rerun** /riː'rʌn/ *v* [T]

res·cue[1] /'reskjuː/ *v* [T] to save someone from harm or danger: *He rescued two people from the fire.* —**rescuer** *n* [C]

rescue[2] *n* [C,U] when someone is saved from harm or danger: *a daring rescue from a sinking ship.* | **come to the rescue** (=rescue someone)

re·search[1] /rɪ'sɜːtʃ, 'riːsɜːtʃ‖-ɜːr-/ *n* [U] serious and detailed study of a subject in order to find out new information: + **on/into** *scientific research into heart disease* | **do research** *He is doing research for a book on the Middle Ages.*

research[2] *v* [I,T] to study a subject in detail so you can discover new facts about it: *Conner spent eight years researching the history of the group.* —**researcher** *n* [C]

re·sem·blance /rɪ'zembləns/ *n* [C,U] a similarity between two people or things: + **between** *There's a slight resemblance between Mike and his cousin.*

re·sem·ble /rɪ'zembəl/ *v* [T] to be similar to someone or something: *She resembles her mother in many ways.*

re·sent /rɪ'zent/ *v* [T] to feel angry and upset about something that someone has done to you: *I've always resented my father for leaving the family.*

re·sent·ful /rɪ'zentfəl/ *adj* angry and upset about something that someone has done: *a resentful look* —**resentfully** *adv*

re·sent·ment /rɪ'zentmənt/ *n* [U] a feeling of anger about something that someone has done to you

res·er·va·tion /ˌrezə'veɪʃən‖-zər-/ *n* **1** [C] an arrangement you make so that a place in a hotel, on a plane etc is kept for you to use: **make a reservation** *Have you made reservations at the restaurant yet?* **2** [C,U] a feeling of doubt because you do not completely agree with a plan, idea etc: **have reservations** *I still have reservations about promoting her.*

re·serve[1] /rɪ'zɜːv‖-ɜːrv/ *v* [T] **1** to arrange for a place in a hotel, on a plane etc to be kept for you to use: *I'd like to reserve a table for 8:00.* **2** to keep something separate so that it can be used for a particular purpose: + **for** *a parking space reserved for the disabled*

reserve[2] *n* **1** [C] a supply of something that is kept to be used at a time when it is needed: *Water reserves are dangerously low.* **2** [U] when someone does not show or talk about their thoughts and feelings: *His natural reserve made it difficult to know what he really thought.* **3** [C] an area of land where wild animals, plants etc are protected: *a nature reserve*

re·served /rɪ'zɜːvd‖-ɜːr-/ *adj* unwilling to show or talk about your thoughts and feelings: *a cool, reserved young man*

res·er·voir /'rezəvwɑː‖-ərvwɑːr, -vɔːr/ *n* [C] **1** an artificial lake where water is stored before it is supplied to people's houses **2** a supply of something that can be used if it is needed: *a reservoir of oil beneath the desert*

re·shuf·fle /ˌriː'ʃʌfəl/ *v* [T] to change the jobs of people who work in an organization —**reshuffle** /'riːʃʌfəl, ˌriːʃʌfəl/ *n* [C]

re·side /rɪ'zaɪd/ *v* [I] *formal* to live somewhere

res·i·dence /'rezɪdəns/ *n formal* **1** [C] a house, apartment etc where someone lives: *a private residence* **2** [U] when someone lives in a particular place: **take up residence** (=start to live somewhere) **3** **in residence** living or working in a place: *Mr. Moreau is our artist in residence.*

res·i·dent /'rezɪdənt/ *n* [C] **1** someone who lives in a house, apartment, area etc: *a park for local residents* **2** *AmE* a doctor working at a hospital where he or she is being trained —**resident** *adj*

res·i·den·tial /ˌrezɪ'denʃəl◂/ *adj* a residential area consists of houses, not offices or factories

re·sid·u·al /rɪ'zɪdʒuəl/ *adj* remaining after a process, event etc has finished: *the residual effects of radiation exposure*

res·i·due /'rezɪdjuː‖-duː/ *n* [C] a substance that remains after something else has disappeared or been removed: *an oily residue*

re·sign /rɪ'zaɪn/ *v* [I,T] **1** to officially tell your employer that you are going to leave your job: + **from** *Burton resigned from the company yesterday.* **2** **resign yourself to (doing) sth** to accept a situation that you do not like but cannot change: *I've resigned myself to living in the city for a while.*

res·ig·na·tion /ˌrezɪg'neɪʃən/ *n* **1** [C,U] when someone officially tells their employer that they are going to leave their job: **hand in your resignation** (=resign) **2** [U] when you accept a situation that you cannot change although you do not like it

re·signed /rɪ'zaɪnd/ *adj* willing to accept a situation, even if you do not like it

re·sil·i·ent /rɪ'zɪliənt/ *adj* **1** strong enough to get better quickly after problems, illness, damage etc: *Small babies can be remarkably resilient.* **2** a resilient substance will not break or get damaged easily — **resilience** *n* [U]

res·in /'rezɪn/ *n* **1** [U] a thick sticky liquid produced by some trees **2** [C] a substance used in making plastics

re·sist /rɪ'zɪst/ *v* [I,T] **1** to try to prevent yourself from being forced to do something: *Residents were ordered to leave the area, but they resisted.* **2** to oppose or fight against someone or something: *British troops could not resist the attack any longer.* **3** to try to prevent yourself from doing something that you should not do, even though you want to: **resist doing sth** *I couldn't resist trying to see who the letter was from.*

re·sist·ance /rɪ'zɪstəns/ *n* **1** [U] when people disagree with new ideas, changes etc and do not want them to happen: **+ to** *There is strong public resistance to the new taxes.* **2** [U] fighting against someone or something that is attacking you: **put up resistance** (=fight): *The rebels put up fierce resistance against the army.* **3 the resistance** an organized group who fight against an army that has taken control of their country: *the French resistance* **4** [U] *technical* the degree to which a substance can stop electricity flowing through it

re·sis·tant /rɪ'zɪstənt/ *adj* **1** not easily harmed or damaged by something: *a fire-resistant cover* **2** unwilling to accept new ideas or changes: *people who are resistant to change*

re·sit /,riː'sɪt/ *v* [T] *especially BrE* to take a test or examination again — **resit** /'riːsɪt/ *n* [C]

res·o·lute /'rezəluːt/ *adj formal* determined not to change what you are doing because you are sure that you are right — **resolutely** *adv*

res·o·lu·tion /,rezə'luːʃən/ *n* **1** [C] an official decision by a group or organization, especially after a vote: *a United Nations resolution* **2** [singular, U] the final solution to a problem: *a peaceful resolution to the crisis* **3** [C] a promise that you make to yourself to do something: *I made a New Year's resolution to stop smoking.* **4** [U] *formal* determination

re·solve[1] /rɪ'zɒlv‖rɪ'zɑːlv, rɪ'zɔːlv/ *v* **1** [T] to find a way of dealing with a problem or of ending a disagreement: *efforts to resolve the conflict in the Middle East* **2** [I,T] *formal* to make a definite decision to do something: *He resolved to leave the country as soon as possible.*

resolve[2] *n* [U] *formal* strong determination to succeed in doing something

res·o·nant /'rezənənt/ *adj* having a loud, pleasant, strong sound: *a resonant voice* — **resonance** *n* [U]

res·o·nate /'rezəneɪt/ *v* [I] to make a loud strong sound

re·sort[1] /rɪ'zɔːt‖-ɔːrt/ *n* **1** [C] a place where a lot of people go for a holiday: *a beach resort* **2 as a last resort** if everything else fails: *I could borrow the money off my parents, but only as a last resort.*

resort[2] *v* **resort to sth** *phr v* [T] to do something that you do not want to do, in order to try to achieve something: *They may have to resort to court action.*

re·sound /rɪ'zaʊnd/ *v* [I] to make a loud sound, or be full of a loud sound: *His voice resounded throughout the house.*

re·sound·ing /rɪ'zaʊndɪŋ/ *adj* **1** a resounding success/victory/defeat etc a great success, victory etc **2** very loud: *a resounding crash*

re·source /rɪ'zɔːs, -'sɔːs‖'riːsɔːrs/ *n* [C usually plural] something that a country, organization, person etc has which they can use: *South Africa's vast natural resources*

re·source·ful /rɪ'zɔːsfəl, -'sɔːs-‖-ɔːr-/ *adj* good at finding ways to deal with problems effectively — **resourcefulness** *n* [U]

re·spect[1] /rɪ'spekt/ *n* **1** [U] admiration for someone because of their knowledge, skill etc: **+ for** *I have great respect for her as a writer.* **2** [U] when you treat someone in a polite way, especially because they are older or more important than you: **+ for** *He ought to show more respect for authority.* (=for his parents, teachers, managers etc) → opposite DISRESPECT **3** [U] when you show by your behaviour that you think something is important: *countries where there is no respect for basic human rights* **4** in one respect/in many respects etc used to say that something is true about one part of something, about many parts of it etc: *In some respects, José is right.* **5 with (all due) respect** *spoken formal* used before you say something to disagree with someone: *With all due respect, that is not the point.* **6 with respect to/in respect of** *formal* concerning a particular thing; REGARDING: *With respect to your question about jobs, all our positions are filled.* → see also RESPECTS, SELF-RESPECT

re·spect[2] *v* [T] **1** to admire someone because of their knowledge, skill etc: *The students like and respect him.* **2** if you respect someone's wishes, rights, customs etc, you are careful not to do anything that they do not want, or that they think is wrong **3** if you respect the law or the rules, you do what they say

re·spec·ta·ble /rɪ'spektəbəl/ *adj* **1** behaving in a way that people think is socially acceptable or morally right: *a respectable middle-class family* **2** neatly dressed and not dirty or untidy: *Do I look respectable?* **3** good enough; satisfactory: *a respectable score* — **respectably** *adv* — **respectability** /rɪ,spektə'bɪlɪti/ *n* [U]

re·spect·ed /rɪ'spektɪd/ *adj* admired by many people because of your achievements, skills etc: *a highly respected political leader*

re·spect·ful /rɪ'spektfəl/ *adj* showing respect for someone or something → opposite DISRESPECTFUL — **respectfully** *adv*

GRAMMAR NOTE: a or the (2)
Use **the** before a thing or person when it is clear which one you are talking about: *the old man who lives next door.* Use **a** or **an** to talk about a person or thing when it is not important to say which one: *I went out to buy **a** newspaper.* | **A** girl in my class told me about it.

re·spec·tive /rɪ'spektɪv/ adj used to talk about each of a group of people or things: two sisters and their respective husbands —**respectively** adv:: The dollar and yen rose by 2% and 3% respectively.

re·spects /rɪ'spekts/ n [plural] **1 pay your (last) respects** to go to someone's funeral **2 pay your respects** formal to visit someone or go to talk to them

res·pi·ra·tion /ˌresp‚'reɪʃən/ n [U] technical the process of breathing and using oxygen in the body → see also ARTIFICIAL RESPIRATION

res·pi·ra·tor /'resp‚reɪtəll-ər/ n [C] a piece of equipment that helps you to breathe

res·pi·ra·to·ry /rɪ'spɪrətəri, 'resp‚reɪtəri, rɪ-'spaɪərə-ll'respərətɔːri, rɪ'spaɪrə-/ adj technical relating to breathing and the use of oxygen in the body: the respiratory system

res·pite /'respɪt, -paɪtll-pɪt/ n [singular, U] a short period when something unpleasant stops happening: + **from** The Northwest should have a brief respite from the rain today.

re·splen·dent /rɪ'splendənt/ adj formal having a very impressive appearance, in a way that looks expensive: + **in** Lady Frances, resplendent in a sea-green dress

re·spond /rɪ'spɒndllrɪ'spɑːnd/ v [I] **1** to behave in a particular way after something has happened or someone has done something: The US responded by sending in food and medical supplies. **2** to say or write something as a reply: How did he respond to your question? **3** to improve as a result of a particular treatment: She is responding well to the drugs.

re·sponse /rɪ'spɒnsllrɪ'spɑːns/ n [C,U] something that is done or said as a reaction or reply to something else: There was still no response from him.| **in response to** I am writing in response to your advertisement.

re·spon·si·bil·i·ty /rɪˌspɒns‚'bɪl‚tillrɪˌspɑːn-/ n **1** [C,U] if something is your responsibility, it is your duty to make sure that it is done: Parents have a responsibility to see that their children attend school.| She wanted a job with more responsibility. (=with more things that she was in charge of) **2 take/accept responsibility for sth** to say that you are responsible for something that has happened, especially something bad: The company has refused to take responsibility for the accident.

re·spon·si·ble /rɪ'spɒns‚bəllrɪ'spɑːn-/ adj **1** if you are responsible for something that has happened, you caused it, or you are the person who should be blamed: + **for** the man responsible for the Oklahoma bombing **2** in charge of something: + **for** She's responsible for the day-to-day running of the department. **3** a responsible job is important because other people depend on you and you have to make important decisions **4** sensible and able to be trusted: a responsible young man

re·spon·si·bly /rɪ'spɒns‚blillrɪ'spɑːn-/ adv in a sensible way, so that other people trust you: Can I trust you to behave responsibly while I'm gone?

re·spon·sive /rɪ'spɒnsɪvllrɪ'spɑːn-/ adj **1** paying attention to what people want, and trying to help them: We try to be responsive to the needs of the customer. **2** willing to talk and show your feelings: Teenagers are often shy and not very responsive. —**responsiveness** n [U] —**responsively** adv

rest[1] /rest/ n **1 the rest** the other part of something, or the other people or things: What shall I do with the rest of the pizza?| Most of the tourists were German. The rest were American or Japanese. **2** [C,U] a period of time when you can relax or sleep: I need to get some rest. **3 put/set sb's mind at rest** to stop someone from feeling worried **4 come to rest** to stop moving: A truck went off the road and came to rest at the bottom of the hill. **5 lay/put sth to rest** to show that an idea or story is not true, and stop people believing it: The book puts to rest some of the myths surrounding Picasso's life. **6 at rest** formal not moving

rest[2] v **1** [I] to stop doing something and relax or sleep for a period of time: Can I rest for a few minutes? I'm feeling tired. **2 rest your feet/legs/eyes etc** to stop using part of your body for a period of time because it is tired or painful **3** [T] to support an object or part of your body by putting it on or against something: The baby rested its head on my shoulder. **4 rest assured (that)** formal used to tell someone not to worry because you are sure that something will happen or someone will do something **5 rest on your laurels** to be satisfied with your achievements, and not try hard to succeed any more **6 let sth rest** to stop talking about something, especially if it annoys or upsets someone

rest on/upon sth phr v [T] formal to depend on something or be based on something: The whole case rests on his evidence.

rest with sb phr v [T] formal if a decision rests with someone, they must make it: The final decision rests with you.

re·state /ˌriː'steɪt/ v [T] **1** to say something again in a different way **2** to say officially that you still believe something —**restatement** n [C,U]

res·tau·rant /'restərɒntll-rənt, -rɑːnt/ n [C] a place where you can buy and eat a meal: They had dinner in an Italian restaurant in Soho.

rest·ful /'restfəl/ adj peaceful and quiet, and making you feel relaxed: a restful weekend

rest home /'. ./ n [C] a NURSING HOME

res·ti·tu·tion /ˌrest‚'tjuːʃənll-'tuː-/ n [U] formal when someone is given back something that was stolen from them, or money that is owed to them

res·tive /'restɪv/ adj formal restless

rest·less /'restləs/ adj **1** unable to keep still, especially because you are impatient, anxious, or bored: The children are getting restless. **2** not satisfied and wanting new experiences: After eight years in the same job you start to get restless. —**restlessly** adv —**restlessness** n [U]

re·store /rɪ'stɔːll-ɔːr/ v [T] **1** to repair something so that it is in its original condition: He likes restoring old cars. **2** to make something exist again, or make someone have the same feeling again: The game helped restore his confidence.| **restore order/peace** (=make people stop fighting or causing trouble) **3** formal to give back to someone something that was lost or stolen: The jewels were restored to their rightful owners. —**restoration** /ˌrestə'reɪʃən/ n [C,U] the restoration of a 15th century church

re·strain /rɪ'streɪn/ v [T] **1** to prevent someone from doing something: He had to be physically restrained by the other players. **2** to control something: efforts to restrain inflation

re·strained /rɪ'streɪnd/ *adj* **1** calm and not excited, angry etc: *a typically restrained performance* **2** not brightly coloured

re·straint /rɪ'streɪnt/ *n* **1** [U] when someone reacts in a calm way, without becoming angry or excited: *The police showed great restraint.* **2** [C,U] something that limits what you can do: *financial restraints*

re·strict /rɪ'strɪkt/ *v* [T] **1** to limit something: *new laws to restrict the sale of guns* **2** **restrict yourself to sth** to only do a particular thing, or only have a particular amount of something: *Can you restrict yourself to discussing the main topic?*

re·strict·ed /rɪ'strɪktᵻd/ *adj* **1** if something is restricted to a particular group of people, only they can have it, use it etc: **+ to** *The sale of alcohol is restricted to people over the age of 21.* | **restricted area** (=one that you need special permission to enter) **2** if something is restricted, there is only a small amount of it, or it includes only a few types of things: *a restricted diet*

re·stric·tion /rɪ'strɪkʃən/ *n* [C,U] a rule or law that limits what you are allowed to do: **+ on** *There's no restriction on how many tickets you can buy.* | **without restriction** *freedom to travel without restriction*

re·stric·tive /rɪ'strɪktɪv/ *adj* if something is restrictive, it limits too much what people can do: *restrictive trade policies*

rest·room /'restrʊm, -ruːm/ *n* [C] *AmE* a room with a toilet, in a place such as a restaurant or theatre

re·struc·ture /ˌriː'strʌktʃəll-ər/ *v* [T] to change the way in which a company, system etc is organized, often by getting rid of workers —**restructuring** *n* [U]

re·sult¹ /rɪ'zʌlt/ *n* **1** [C,U] something that happens or exists because of something else: **as a result (of)** (=because of something): *She feels much better as a result of the treatment.* | **with the result (that)** *We arrived a few minutes late, with the result that we missed our train.* | **be the result of** *His death was the result of years of drug abuse.* **2** [C] the final number of points, votes etc at the end of a game, competition, election etc: *What was the result of the England–Italy game?* | *a disastrous result for the Republicans* **3** [C] the information found in a scientific study or test: *When will I have the results of my blood test?* **4** [C] *especially BrE* a number or letter which shows how successful someone has been in a test or examination; SCORE *AmE*: *The results come out in August.* **5** [C,U] if you get a result, you succeed in doing something

result² *v* [I] to happen or exist because of something: *changes in society that have resulted from the use of computers*
　　result in sth *phr v* [T] to make something happen: *a fire that resulted in the death of two children*

re·sul·tant /rɪ'zʌltənt/ *adj formal* happening or existing because of something else: *resultant damage*

re·sume /rɪ'zjuːmllrɪ'zuːm/ *v* [I,T] *formal* to start doing something again after a pause: *She hopes to resume her duties soon.* —**resumption** /rɪ'zʌmpʃən/ *n* [singular, U]

rés·u·mé /'rezjʊmeɪ, 'reɪ-ll,rezʊ'meɪ/ *n* [C] *especially AmE* a short description of your education and your previous jobs, which you send to companies and organizations when you are looking for a job; CV *BrE*

re·sur·face /ˌriː'sɜːfᵻsll-ɜːr-/ *v* **1** [I] to appear again: *Old arguments began to resurface.* **2** [T] to put a new surface on a road **3** [I] to come back up to the surface of water

re·sur·gence /rɪ'sɜːdʒənsll-ɜːr-/ *n* [singular, U] when something starts to happen a lot again, or a lot of people have the same feeling again: *a resurgence of racial violence* —**resurgent** *adj*

res·ur·rect /ˌrezə'rekt/ *v* [T] to start using something again after it has not been used for a long time, or make something exist again: *Designers have resurrected the styles of the 1960s.*

res·ur·rec·tion /ˌrezə'rekʃən/ *n* **1** **the Resurrection** when Jesus Christ started to live again after his death, which is one of the main beliefs of the Christian religion **2** [U] when something starts to be used again or exist again: *the resurrection of the British film industry*

re·sus·ci·tate /rɪ'sʌsᵻteɪt/ *v* [T] to make someone start breathing again —**resuscitation** /rɪ-ˌsʌsᵻ'teɪʃən/ *n* [U]

re·tail¹ /'riːteɪl/ *n* [U] the activity or business of selling goods to people in shops: *Retail profits went up by over 50%.* ➞ compare WHOLESALE

re·tail² /rɪ'teɪl/ *v* [I] to be sold for a particular price in shops: *The Toshiba KT3301S retails at around $600.*

re·tail·er /'riːteɪləll-ər/ *n* [C] a person or company that sells goods to people

re·tain /rɪ'teɪn/ *v* [T] to keep something and not lose it, give it away etc: *The town had retained much of its old charm.* —**retention** /-'tenʃən/ *n* [U]

re·tain·er /rɪ'teɪnəll-ər/ *n* [C] **1** an amount of money that you pay regularly to someone, so that they will continue to work for you **2** *AmE* something that you wear inside your mouth to make your teeth stay straight; BRACE *BrE*

re·take /ˌriː'teɪk/ *v* [T] **1** to use military force to get control of a place again: *Government forces have retaken the city.* **2** *BrE* to take an examination again

re·tal·i·ate /rɪ'tælieɪt/ *v* [I] to do something unpleasant to someone because they have done something unpleasant to you: *The police retaliated by firing tear gas grenades.* —**retaliation** /rɪˌtæli'eɪʃən/ *n* [U] —**retaliatory** /rɪ'tæliətərill -tɔːri/ *adj: retaliatory action*

re·tard /rɪ'tɑːdll-ɑːrd/ *v* [T] *formal* to delay something or make it happen more slowly, or in a less successful way: *Drugs given to the mother retarded the baby's growth.* —**retardation** /ˌriːtɑː'deɪʃənll-ɑːr-/ *n* [U]

re·tard·ed /rɪ'tɑːdᵻdll-ɑːr-/ *adj* less mentally developed than other people. Many people consider this word to be offensive.

retch /retʃ/ *v* [I] to almost VOMIT

re·think /ˌriː'θɪŋk/ *v* [I,T] to think about a plan or idea again and decide what changes should be made —**rethink** /'riːθɪŋk/ *n* [singular] *We're calling for a complete rethink of the government's transport policy.*

ret·i·cent /'retᵻsənt/ *adj* not wanting to talk about what you know or how you feel: *Bryn is* *reticent about his part in the war.* —**reticence** *n* [U]

ret·i·na /ˈretɪnə/ *n* [C] the area at the back of your eye that receives images and sends them to your brain

ret·i·nue /ˈretɪnjuː‖-nuː/ *n* [C] a group of helpers or supporters who travel with a famous person: *the rock star's retinue*

re·tire /rɪˈtaɪə‖-ˈtaɪr/ *v* **1** [I] to stop working, usually because of old age: *Barney wants to retire next year.* **2** [I] *formal* to go away to a quiet place, or go to bed: *He retired to his room at about 10 o'clock.*

re·tired /rɪˈtaɪəd‖-ˈtaɪrd/ *adj* retired people have stopped working, usually because of their age: *a retired police officer*

re·tire·ment /rɪˈtaɪəmənt‖-ˈtaɪr-/ *n* **1** [C,U] when someone leaves their job and stops working completely, especially because they are old: *a party for Bill's retirement* **2** [singular, U] the period of your life after you have stopped working completely: *a long and happy retirement*

re·tir·ing /rɪˈtaɪərɪŋ‖-ˈtaɪrɪŋ/ *adj* shy and not wanting to be with other people

re·tort /rɪˈtɔːt‖-ɔːrt/ *v* [T] to reply quickly in an angry or humorous way: *"It's easy for you to say that !" he retorted.* —**retort** *n* [C]

re·trace /rɪˈtreɪs, riː-/ *v* [T] **1** to go back the way you came: *She retraced her steps to try to find her ring.* **2** to repeat the same journey that someone else has made: *They are retracing the route taken by Captain Cook.*

re·tract /rɪˈtrækt/ *v* [T] to make an official statement saying that something you said earlier is not true: *He later retracted his confession.* —**retraction** /-ˈtrækʃən/ *n* [C,U]

re·tract·a·ble /rɪˈtræktəbəl/ *adj* part of something that is retractable can be pulled back into the main part: *a knife with a retractable blade*

re·train·ing /riːˈtreɪnɪŋ/ *n* [U] when someone is trained to do a different job

re·treat[1] /rɪˈtriːt/ *v* [I] **1** if an army retreats, it moves back, especially to avoid fighting: *The British retreated to the beaches of Dunkirk.* **2** to move back and go to a safe or quiet place: *She treated into the kitchen at the first sign of an argument.*

retreat[2] *n* **1** [C,U] when an army moves back, especially to avoid fighting: *Napoleon's retreat from Moscow* **2** [singular, U] when someone moves back, especially because they are afraid, embarrassed etc: **beat a retreat** *They beat a hasty retreat back to the house.* (=They went back there quickly) **3** [C] a place where you can go to that is quiet or safe: *a weekend retreat* **4** [C,U] when you change your mind about a promise or plan, because it seems too difficult: *a retreat from the government's earlier promises*

re·tri·al /ˌriːˈtraɪəl, ˈriːtraɪəl‖ˌriːˈtraɪəl/ *n* [C] a second TRIAL of the same person or crime in a court of law: *My lawyer demanded a retrial.*

ret·ri·bu·tion /ˌretrɪˈbjuːʃən/ *n* [singular, U] when someone is punished for what they have done

re·trieve /rɪˈtriːv/ *v* [T] to find something and bring it back: *I retrieved my suitcase from the hall cupboard.* —**retrieval** *n* [U] —**retrievable** *adj*

re·triev·er /rɪˈtriːvə‖-ər/ *n* [C] a type of dog

ret·ro·spect /ˈretrəspekt/ *n* **in retrospect** when you think about something that happened in the past, and know more about it than was known then: *In retrospect, it was the wrong time to leave my job.*

ret·ro·spec·tive[1] /ˌretrəˈspektɪv◂/ *adj* a law or decision that is retrospective is effective from a particular date in the past

retrospective[2] *n* [C] a show of the past work of an artist

re·turn[1] /rɪˈtɜːn‖-ɜːrn/ *v* **1** [I] to come back or go back to a place: *Caesar returned to Rome.* | *She didn't return until after 8 o'clock.* **2** [I] to start to happen again, or become the same as before: *Next morning, the pain had returned.* | **return to normal** *Everything will soon return to normal.* **3** [T] to give, put, send, or take something back: *The letter was returned unopened.* **4** [I] to start doing something again, or start talking about something again: *Does Kate plan to return to work after the baby is born?* **5** [T] to do something to someone, after they have done the same thing to you: **return sb's call** (=telephone someone after they have tried to telephone you) **6 return a verdict** if a JURY returns their VERDICT, they say whether someone is guilty or not

return[2] *n* **1** [singular] when someone comes back or goes back to a place: **on sb's return** *On his return to Japan, he began work on his first novel.* **2** [singular] when something is given back, put back etc: *a reward for the return of the stolen necklace* **3** [singular] when something starts to happen or exist again: *the return of the death penalty* **4** [singular] when someone starts doing something again: *Allen's return to film-making* **5** [C,U] the amount of profit that you get from an INVESTMENT: *He expects a big return on his shares.* **6** [U] a button that you press on a computer or TYPEWRITER after you have finished writing the line you are writing **7** [C] *BrE* a ticket for a journey to a place and back again; ROUND TRIP *AmE* **8 in return (for)** because someone has given you something or done something for you: *She drives me to work, and in return I pay for her lunches.* **9 many happy returns** *BrE* used to wish someone a happy BIRTHDAY

return vis·it /ˌ.. ˈ../ *n* [C] when you visit someone who visited you before, or you go back to a place that you visited before

re·u·ni·fi·ca·tion /ˌriːˌjuːnɪfɪˈkeɪʃən/ *n* [U] when two or more parts of a country, are joined together again and become one nation: *German reunification*

re·u·nion /riːˈjuːnjən/ *n* [C,U] a meeting of people who have not met for a long time: *a college reunion*

re·u·nite /ˌriːjuːˈnaɪt/ *v* [I,T] to be together again, or bring people or things together again: *He was at last reunited with his children.*

rev /rev/ also **rev up** *v* [I,T] **-ved, -vving** if you rev an engine, or if it revs, it works faster

Rev. the written abbreviation of REVEREND

re·vamp /riːˈvæmp/ *v* [T] to change something in order to try to improve it: *an attempt to revamp the city's image*

re·veal /rɪˈviːl/ *v* [T] **1** to make something known that was previously secret or not known: *Their affair was first revealed in a Sunday news-*

paper. **2** to show something that was previously hidden: *The curtains went back to reveal the stage.*

re·veal·ing /rɪ'viːlɪŋ/ *adj* **1** showing what someone or something is really like, or what someone really feels: *Some of her comments were very revealing.* **2** revealing clothes show parts of your body that are usually kept covered: *a revealing nightdress*

rev·el /'revəl/ *v*
revel in sth *phr v* [T] to enjoy something very much: *He was secretly revelling in his new fame.*

rev·e·la·tion /ˌrevə'leɪʃən/ *n* **1** [C,U] when people are told about a surprising fact, which was previously secret: *revelations about Charles and Diana's marriage* **2** **be a revelation** to be surprisingly good: *The blackberry gateau was a revelation.*

rev·ell·er *BrE,* **reveler** *AmE* /'revələ‖-lər/ *n* [C] someone who is enjoying himself or herself by drinking alcohol, dancing, singing etc

rev·el·ry /'revəlri/ *n* [C,U] wild noisy dancing, eating, drinking etc

revenge¹ /rɪ'vendʒ/ *n* [U] something you do in order to punish someone who has harmed you: **get/take/have your revenge** *When she found out that he had been unfaithful, she was determined to get her revenge.* —**revengeful** *adj*

revenge² *v* [T] **revenge yourself on sb** to do something to punish someone who has harmed you → see also AVENGE

rev·e·nue /'revɪnjuː‖-nuː/ *n* [U] also **revenues** [plural] money that is earned by a company or money that the government receives from tax

re·ver·be·rate /rɪ'vɜːbəreɪt‖-ɜːr-/ *v* [I] **1** if a loud sound reverberates, it is heard many times as it is sent back from different surfaces: *Her voice reverberated around the empty warehouse.* **2** to have a an important effect which continues for a long time —**reverberation** /rɪˌvɜːbə'reɪʃən‖-ɜːr-/ *n* [C,U]

re·vere /rɪ'vɪə‖-'vɪr/ *v* [T] *formal* to respect and admire someone or something very much —**revered** *adj: Ireland's most revered poet*

rev·e·rence /'revərəns/ *n* [U] *formal* great respect and admiration

Rev·e·rend /'revərənd/ used in the title of a Christian priest: *Reverend Larson*

rev·e·rent /'revərənt/ also **rev·e·ren·tial** /ˌrevə'renʃəl/ *adj formal* showing respect and admiration —**reverently, reverentially** *adv*

rev·e·rie /'revəri/ *n* [C,U] *literary* when someone thinks about and imagines pleasant things

re·vers·al /rɪ'vɜːsəl‖-ɜːr-/ *n* **1** [C,U] when something changes and becomes the opposite of what it was before: *a reversal of the previous policy* **2** [C] *formal* a failure or problem that prevents you from doing what you want

re·verse¹ /rɪ'vɜːs‖-ɜːrs/ *v* **1** [I,T] if a car or other vehicle reverses, it moves backwards: *Someone reversed into the back of my car.* **2** [T] to change something, such as a decision or way of doing something so that it is the opposite of

what it was before: *The judge reversed his original decision.* **3** **reverse the charges** *BrE* if you reverse the charges, the person who you are telephoning pays for the call; **CALL COLLECT** *AmE* —**reversible** *adj: a reversible coat*

reverse² *n* **1** [U] also **reverse gear** if a car is in reverse, it is in the GEAR that makes it go backwards: *Put the car in reverse.* **2** **the reverse** the opposite: *In fact, the reverse is true.* **3** **in reverse** done in the opposite way, or having the opposite effect: *They're taking the same route, but in reverse.*

reverse³ *adj* happening in the opposite way to what usually happens, or to the way you have just mentioned: *The names were read out in reverse order*

re·vers·i·ble /rɪ'vɜːsɪbəl‖-ɜːr-/ *adj* **1** something that is reversible can be changed back to how it was before: *This decision may be reversible in the future.* **2** if a coat, SWEATER etc is reversible, the inside part can be worn on the outside

re·vert /rɪ'vɜːt‖-ɜːrt/ *v* **revert to sth** if something reverts to how it was before, it changes back to how it was before: *Leningrad reverted to its former name of St Petersburg.* —**reversion** /rɪ'vɜːʃən‖-'vɜːrʒən/ *n* [singular, U]

review¹ /rɪ'vjuː/ *n* **1** [C,U] when something is examined and considered in order to decide what changes need to be made: *an urgent review of safety procedures* | **under review** (=being examined and considered): *Our salaries are currently under review.* **2** [C] a report in a newspaper, on television etc, in which someone says their opinion about a new book, film etc: *The Water People has already received a lot of good reviews.* **3** [C] a television programme, article, report etc remembering and considering things that have happened in the past year, week etc: *The BBC Review of the Year will be at 10 pm on January 31st.*

review² *v* **1** [T] to examine and consider something, in order to decide what changes need to be made: *The state is reviewing its education policy.* **2** [I,T] to give your opinion in a newspaper report, on television etc about a new book, film etc **3** [I,T] *AmE* to prepare for a test by studying books, notes from your classes etc; **REVISE** *BrE*

re·view·er /rɪ'vjuːə‖-ər/ *n* [C] someone who writes in newspapers or speaks on television and gives their opinion about new books, films etc

re·vile /rɪ'vaɪl/ *v* **be reviled** *formal* to be hated

re·vise /rɪ'vaɪz/ *v* **1** [T] to change something to improve it or make it more correct or suitable: *They were forced to revise their plans.* | *the revised edition of the book* **2** [I] *BrE* to prepare for a test by studying books, notes from your lessons etc; **REVIEW** *AmE*

re·vi·sion /rɪ'vɪʒən/ *n* **1** [C,U] when something is changed in order to improve it or make it more correct **2** [U] *BrE* when you prepare

---

for a test by studying books, notes from your lessons etc

re·vi·tal·ize (also **-ise** BrE) /riː'vaɪtəlaɪz/ v [T] to make a place, organization, etc strong and active again: *attempts to revitalize the economy* —**revitalization** /riːˌvaɪtəlaɪ'zeɪʃən‖-tl-ə-/ n [U]

re·vi·val /rɪ'vaɪvəl/ n 1 [C,U] when something becomes stronger, more active, or more popular again: *the revival of interest in sixties music* | *hopes for an economic revival* 2 [C] a new performance of a play, song etc that has not been performed for a long time: *a revival of 'Oklahoma!'*

re·vive /rɪ'vaɪv/ v [I,T] 1 [T] to make something become popular again, or make something exist again: *Old customs are being revived.* 2 [T] to make someone become conscious again: *The doctors were unable to revive him.* 3 [I,T] to make someone or something stronger or healthier again, or to become stronger or healthier again: *She came back from her trip feeling revived.*

re·voke /rɪ'vəʊk‖-'voʊk/ v [T] *formal* to officially end a law or agreement, or change an official decision

re·volt¹ /rɪ'vəʊlt‖-'voʊlt/ v 1 [I] to refuse to obey the government and try to change it, often in a violent way, or refuse to do what someone in authority tells you to do: **+ against** *In 1986 the people revolted against the government of President Marcos.* 2 [T] if you are revolted by something, you feel shocked because it is very unpleasant: *I was revolted by what I saw.*

revolt² n [C,U] when people try to change the government, often by using violence, or refuse to do what someone in authority tells them to do: *the Paris student revolt of May 1968*

re·volt·ing /rɪ'vəʊltɪŋ‖-'voʊl-/ adj extremely unpleasant: *What a revolting meal!*

rev·o·lu·tion /ˌrevə'luːʃən/ n 1 [C,U] when the people of a country get rid of the government and change the political system completely, especially by using force: *the Russian Revolution* 2 [singular] a complete change in the way people do something, or in the ideas that people have about a subject: *a revolution in scientific thinking* | *the Industrial Revolution* 3 [C,U] one complete circular movement around a central point: *a wheel turning at a speed of 100 revolutions per minute*

rev·o·lu·tion·a·ry¹ /ˌrevə'luːʃənəri‖-'ʃoʊneri/ adj 1 completely new and different: *a revolutionary new treatment for cancer* 2 connected with a political revolution: *a revolutionary army*

revolutionary² n [C] someone who takes part in or supports a political revolution

rev·o·lu·tion·ize (also **-ise** BrE) /ˌrevə'luːʃənaɪz/ v [T] to completely change the way people think or do things: *The Internet has revolutionized the way people work.*

re·volve /rɪ'vɒlv‖rɪ'vɑːlv/ v [I] to move in a circle around a central point: *The wheels began to revolve slowly.* —**revolving** adj: *a revolving door*

revolve around sb/sth phr v [T] to have something as the most important part: *Her life seems to revolve around her job.*

re·volv·er /rɪ'vɒlvə‖rɪ'vɑːlvər/ n [C] a type of small gun

re·vue /rɪ'vjuː/ n [C] a show in a theatre that includes singing, dancing, and jokes

re·vul·sion /rɪ'vʌlʃən/ n [U] the feeling you have when you are very shocked by something unpleasant

re·ward¹ /rɪ'wɔːd‖-'wɔːrd/ n [C,U] something, especially money, that is given to someone for doing something good, providing information etc: *A $25,000 reward is being offered for information leading to the arrest of the robbers.* → compare AWARD²

reward² v [T] if you are rewarded for what you have done, you get something or are given something: *He was finally rewarded for all his hard work.*

re·ward·ing /rɪ'wɔːdɪŋ‖-ɔːr-/ adj making you feel happy and satisfied: *a rewarding job*

re·wind /riː'waɪnd/ v [I,T] to make a TAPE go back to the beginning

re·work /ˌriː'wɜːk‖-'wɜːrk/ v [T] to change or improve a plan, piece of music, story etc

re·write /ˌriː'raɪt/ v [T] to write something again in a different way in order to improve it —**rewrite** /'riːraɪt/ n [C]

rhap·so·dy /'ræpsədi/ n [C] a type of music

rhet·o·ric /'retərɪk/ n [U] 1 when someone uses words that sound impressive, but are not sincere, especially in a political speech: *Despite all the rhetoric, very little has been done to help the poor.* 2 the skill of using words effectively to persuade people, especially in a political speech —**rhetorical** /rɪ'tɒrɪkəl‖-'tɔː-, -'tɑː-/ adj —**rhetorically** /-kli/ adv

rhetorical ques·tion /.ˌ.. '../ n [C] a question that you ask as a way of making a statement, without expecting an answer

rheu·ma·tis·m /'ruːmətɪzəm/ n [U] a disease that makes muscles and joints painful and stiff

rhine·stone /'raɪnstəʊn‖-stoʊn/ n [C,U] a jewel made from glass or a rock that is intended to look like a DIAMOND

rhi·no·ce·ros /raɪ'nɒsərəs‖-'nɑː-/, also **rhi·no** /'raɪnəʊ-noʊ/ n [C] a large heavy animal with thick skin and a horn on its nose

rho·do·den·dron /ˌrəʊdə'dendrən‖ˌroʊ-/ n [C] a large bush with groups of red, purple, or white flowers

rhu·barb /'ruːbɑːb‖-ɑːrb/ n [U] a plant with red stems that are cooked and eaten as a fruit

rhyme¹ /raɪm/ v 1 [I] if two words or lines of poetry rhyme, they end with the same sound: *'House' rhymes with 'mouse'.* 2 [T] to put two or more words together to make them rhyme: *You can't rhyme 'box' with 'backs'.*

rhyme² n 1 [C] a short poem or song, using words that rhyme → see also NURSERY RHYME 2 [C] a word that ends with the same sound as another word, used at the end of a line in poetry: *I can't find a rhyme for 'donkey'.* 3 [U] the use of words that rhyme in poetry, especially at the ends of lines

rhythm /'rɪðəm/ n [C,U] a regular repeated pattern of sounds in music, speech etc —**rhythmic** /'rɪðmɪk/ adj

rib /rɪb/ n [C] one of the pairs of curved bones in your chest → see picture at SKELETON

rib·ald /'rɪbəld/ adj ribald humour is about sex in a rude way

ribbed /rɪbd/ *adj* having a pattern of raised lines: *a ribbed sweater*

rib·bon /ˈrɪbən/ *n* **1** [C,U] a long narrow piece of cloth, used especially for tying things or as a decoration: *She had a red ribbon in her hair.* **2** a long narrow piece of cloth with ink on it that is used in a TYPEWRITER

rib cage /ˈ. ./ *n* [C] the structure of RIBS protecting your lungs and heart

rice /raɪs/ *n* [U] food that consists of small white or brown grains that are boiled

rice pud·ding /ˌ. ˈ../ *n* [C] a sweet food made from rice, sugar, and milk

rich /rɪtʃ/ *adj* **1** having a lot of money or things that are worth a lot of money: *a very rich man | a rich and powerful nation* **2** rich foods contain a lot of butter, cream, sugar, or eggs, and make you feel full very quickly: *a rich chocolate cake* **3** containing a lot of something, especially something good or useful: *a rich source of ideas | + in a tiny island rich in wildlife* **4** the **rich** people who have a lot of money or valuable possessions **5** a rich colour, sound, or smell is very deep and strong: *a rich dark blue | the rich tone of a cello* **6** rich soil is good for growing plants in — **richness** *n* [U]

rich·es /ˈrɪtʃɪz/ *n* [plural] *literary* a lot of money, or a lot of valuable things

rich·ly /ˈrɪtʃli/ *adv* **1** in a beautiful or expensive way: *The walls were richly decorated with marble.* **2** richly coloured/scented etc having a pleasant deep colour, a pleasantly strong taste etc **3** richly deserve sth to deserve something very much: *They got the punishment they so richly deserved.*

rick·et·y /ˈrɪkɪti/ *adj* a rickety chair, gate etc is in bad condition and is likely to break

rick·shaw /ˈrɪkʃɔː-ʃɒː/ *n* [C] a small vehicle used in Asia for carrying one or two passengers, that is pulled by someone walking or riding a bicycle

ric·o·chet /ˈrɪkəʃeɪ/ *v* [I] if a bullet, rock etc ricochets off a surface, it hits the surface and BOUNCES off it in a different direction — **ricochet** *n* [C]

rid¹ /rɪd/ *adj* **1** get rid of **a)** if you get rid of something that you do not want, you throw it away, sell it etc so that you do not have it any longer: *Do you want to get rid of these old shirts?* **b)** to make something that is unpleasant go away, stop happening, or stop existing: *I can't get rid of this cold.* **c)** to make someone leave because they are annoying you, or causing problems: *She's worried that they want to get rid of her.* **2** be rid of to have got rid of someone who annoys you, or something that is unpleasant: *To be honest, I'm glad to be rid of him.*

rid² *v* rid *or* ridded, rid, ridding
 rid sb/sth **of** sth *phr v* [T] **1** to remove something bad or harmful from a place, organization etc: *efforts to rid the government of corruption* **2** rid yourself of sth to stop having a feeling, thought, or problem that was causing you trouble

rid·dance /ˈrɪdns/ *n* good riddance *spoken* used to say that you are glad that an annoying person or thing has gone away

rid·dle /ˈrɪdl/ *n* [C] **1** a mysterious situation or event which you cannot understand or explain: *the riddle of Elise's death* **2** a difficult and amusing question that you must guess the answer to

rid·dled /ˈrɪdld/ *adj* riddled with containing a lot of something, especially something bad: *His argument is riddled with contradictions.*

ride¹ /raɪd/ *v* [I,T] rode /rəʊd‖roʊd/, ridden /ˈrɪdn/, riding **1** to sit on and control the movement of a horse, or bicycle: *Fiona rides every weekend. | Can you ride a bike?* **2** *AmE* to travel in a car, train, or other vehicle: *Fred rides the subway to work every day.*
 ride on sth *phr v* [T] to depend on something, especially on whether or not something is successful: *There's a lot riding on this film.*
 ride sth ↔ **out** *phr v* [T] to come out of a difficult situation without being badly affected by it: *The company managed to ride out the scandal.*

ride² *n* [C] **1** a trip in a car, train, or other vehicle: *Mick gave me a ride to work.* **2** a large machine that people ride on for pleasure at a FAIR or AMUSEMENT PARK: *Have you been on the new ride at Disneyland?* **3** a trip on a horse or bicycle

rid·er /ˈraɪdə‖-ər/ *n* [C] someone who rides a horse, bicycle etc

ridge /rɪdʒ/ *n* [C] **1** a long narrow area of high land, especially along the top of a mountain: *the ridge along the Virginia–Kentucky border* **2** a raised line on a surface: *the ridges on the soles of her shoes*

rid·i·cule¹ /ˈrɪdɪkjuːl/ *n* [U] when people laugh at someone or something and say unkind things about them: *She became an object of ridicule.* (=people laughed at her and said unkind things)

ridicule² *v* [T] to laugh at someone or something and say unkind things about them: *Darwin's theories were ridiculed.*

ri·dic·u·lous /rɪˈdɪkjɒləs/ *adj* very silly, especially in a way that seems surprising; ABSURD: *What a ridiculous suggestion!* — **ridiculously** *adv* — **ridiculousness** *n* [U]

rid·ing /ˈraɪdɪŋ/ *n* [U] the sport of riding horses

rife /raɪf/ *adj* if something bad is rife, it is very common: *Corruption is rife.*

riff-raff /ˈrɪf ræf/ *n* [U] *often humorous* people who you do not approve of, especially because they belong to a lower social class

ri·fle¹ /ˈraɪfəl/ *n* [C] a gun with a long BARREL (=tube-shaped part) that you hold up to your shoulder to shoot

rifle² *v* [I,T] to search a place and steal things from it: *Somebody has been rifling through my desk.*

rift /rɪft/ *n* [C] **1** a serious disagreement: *a growing rift between the two countries* **2** a crack in a large rock

rig¹ /rɪg/ *v* [T] -gged, -gging to dishonestly influence the result of an election, competition etc: *The newspapers claimed that the election was rigged.*
 rig sth ↔ **up** *phr v* [T] *informal* to make something using materials that you can find quickly and easily: *We rigged up a shelter using a piece of plastic sheeting.*

rig² *n* [C] **1** a large structure used for getting oil or gas from under the bottom of the sea **2** *informal, especially AmE* a large TRUCK

rig·ging /'rɪgɪŋ/ *n* [U] the ropes, sails etc on a ship

right[1] /raɪt/ *adj* **1** correct or true: *Did you get the right answer?* | *Yes, you're right – that's Bev's car in the driveway.* | **be right about** (=have the right opinion): *You were right about the party – it was awful.* **2** [only before noun] your right side is towards your right hand, which is the hand most people write with: *Make a right turn after the gas station.* | *Raise your right arm.* **3** best or most suitable for a particular situation or purpose: *We all agree that Carey is the right person for the job.* **4** fair, reasonable, or morally good: *Do you think I was right to report them to the police?* | *I hope we've made the right decision.* **5** **put/set sth right** to deal with a problem successfully: *If anything goes wrong, the technicians are here to put it right.* **6** **that's right** spoken used to say that you agree with what someone has said, or to answer "yes" to a question: *"Your mother's a teacher isn't she?" "Yes, that's right."* **7** *spoken* used to ask if what you have said was correct: *You wanted to go to the show, right?* **8** *BrE spoken* used to emphasize how bad someone or something is: *He made me feel a right idiot.* **9** **right as rain** *informal* completely healthy, especially after an illness → see also ALL RIGHT[1]

right[2] *adv* **1** exactly in a particular place or at a particular time: *He was standing right in front of our car.* | *The show started right on time.* **2** **right now/away** immediately: *I'll find the address for you right away.* **3** **right now** spoken at this time: *I'm sorry, I can't talk to you right now.* **4** correctly: *They didn't spell my name right.* **5** towards the direction or side that is on the right: *Turn right at the lights.* **6** all the way to something, through something etc: *Go right to the end of the road.* | *The bullet went right through the car door.* **7** *BrE spoken* used to get someone's attention or to tell them to be ready to do something: *Right! Open your books at page 16.*

right[3] *n* **1** [C] if you have the right to do something, you are legally or morally allowed to do it: *Women didn't have the right to vote until 1920.* | **+ to** **have no right to** do sth *You have no right to interfere.* **2** [singular] the side of your body where you have the hand that most people write with, or the direction towards this side: *Our house is on the right.* **3** [U] behaviour that is morally correct: *You're old enough to know the difference between right and wrong.* **4** **in his/her/its own right** without depending on anyone or anything else: *San Jose is a city in its own right, not just a suburb of San Francisco.* **5** **have a right to be angry/upset etc** to have a good reason to be angry, upset etc: *He has every right to be suspicious of him.* **6** **the right** political parties that support CAPITALISM and oppose SOCIALISM → see also RIGHTS

right[4] *v* [T] **1** to put something back in an upright position: *We finally managed to right the canoe.* **2** **right a wrong** to do something to stop an unfair situation from continuing

right an·gle /'. ,./ *n* [C] an angle of 90°, like the angles at the corners of a square —**right-angled** *adj*

righ·teous /'raɪtʃəs/ *adj* **1** **righteous indignation/anger etc** strong feelings of anger when you think something is not morally right

or fair **2** *literary* morally good and fair —**righteously** *adv* —**righteousness** *n* [U]

right·ful /'raɪtfəl/ *adj* according to what is legally and morally correct: *the property's rightful owner* —**rightfully** *adv*: *Money that should rightfully be yours.*

right-hand /'. ./ *adj* **1** on or to your right side: *on the right-hand side* | *Make a right-hand turn.* **2** **right-hand man** the person who supports and helps you the most, especially in your job

right-hand·ed /,. '...'/ *adj* using your right hand rather than your left hand to do most things

Chrissie is right-handed.

right·ly /'raɪtli/ *adv* correctly or for a good reason: *His opponents point out, quite rightly, that government money is taxpayers' money.*

right-mind·ed /,. '...'/ *adj* having good sensible attitudes and opinions: *a decision that will be welcomed by all right-minded people*

right of way /,. . './ *n* **1** [U] the right to drive into or across a road before other vehicles **2** [C] a path across someone's land that people have the legal right to use

rights /raɪts/ *n* [plural] **1** the political and social freedom that everyone in a country should have: *laws that have gradually taken away workers' rights* | **equal rights** (=the right of everyone to be treated equally): *equal rights for women* **2** legal permission to print or use a story, film etc: *Several studios are bidding for the rights to Crichton's last book.* → see also HUMAN RIGHTS, CIVIL RIGHTS

right-wing /,. '. / *adj* supporting the political aims of CAPITALISM rather than SOCIALISM: *a right-wing newspaper* —**right-winger** *n* [C] —**right wing** *n* [singular]

ri·gid /'rɪdʒɪd/ *adj* **1** rigid methods, systems etc are very strict and difficult to change: *the rigid discipline of army life* **2** very unwilling to change your ideas **3** stiff and not moving or bending: *a tent supported on a rigid frame* —**rigidly** *adv*: *The laws were rigidly enforced.* —**rigidity** /rɪ'dʒɪdʒti/ *n* [U]

rig·ma·role /'rɪgmərəʊl‖-roʊl/ *n* [singular, U] a long complicated process or set of actions that seems silly: *the rigmarole of filling out all these forms*

rig·or·ous /'rɪgərəs/ *adj* careful and thorough: *rigorous safety checks* —**rigorously** *adv*

rig·our *BrE*, **rigor** *AmE* /'rɪgə‖-ər/ *n* [U] strictness and thoroughness in making sure that something is correct: *the rigour of scientific methods*

rig·ours *BrE*, **rigors** *AmE* /'rɪgəz‖-ərz/ *n* [plural] the unpleasant conditions of a difficult situation: *the rigors of a Canadian winter*

rile /raɪl/ also **rile up** *AmE* — *v* [T] *informal* to make someone very angry: *It really riled her to think that Henry was lying.*

rim /rɪm/ *n* **1** [C] the outside edge of something circular, such as a glass or a wheel **2** **steel-rimmed/red-rimmed etc** with a particular type of rim: *gold-rimmed glasses*

rind /raɪnd/ n [C,U] the thick skin on the outside of some foods or fruits

ring¹ /rɪŋ/ n [C] **1** a piece of jewellery that you wear on your finger: *a wedding ring* → see picture at JEWELLERY **2** a line in the shape of a circle, especially a circle of people or things surrounding something: *The cottage was surrounded by a ring of trees.* **3** an object in the shape of a circle: *a key ring* **4** a group of people who illegally control a business or criminal activity: *a drug ring* **5** the sound made by a bell: *a ring at the door* → see colour picture on page 635 **6** **give sb a ring** *BrE* to telephone someone **7** a square or circular area surrounded by seats where BOXING or a CIRCUS takes place: *a boxing ring*

ring² v **rang** /ræŋ/, **rung** /rʌŋ/, **ringing** **1** [I,T] to make a bell make a sound: *I rang the bell but there was no answer.* → see colour picture on page 635 **2** [I] if a bell rings, it makes a noise: *The telephone's ringing.* **3** [I,T] *BrE* to telephone someone; CALL *AmE*: *I rang you yesterday, but you weren't in.* **4** [I] to be filled with a continuous sound: *We walked home from the disco with our ears still ringing.* **5** **ring a bell** *informal* if something rings a bell, you think you have heard it before: *Her name rings a bell, but I can't remember her face.* **6** **not ring true** to sound untrue: *His excuse didn't really ring true.*

ring back *phr v* [I,T **ring sb back**] *BrE* to telephone someone again; CALL BACK *AmE*: *I'm busy just now. Could you ring back in an hour?*

ring off *phr v* [I] *BrE* to end a telephone conversation: *I'd better ring off now. There's someone at the door.*

ring out *phr v* [I] to make a loud and clear sound: *The sound of a shot rang out.*

ring up *phr v* [I,T **ring sb ↔ up**] to telephone someone; CALL UP *AmE*: *I'll ring him up and ask him.*

ring³ v [T] **ringed, ringed, ringing** **1** to surround something: *The police ringed the building.* **2** to draw a circular mark around something: *My teacher ringed every mistake in red.*

ring·lead·er /ˈrɪŋˌliːdəʳ-ər/ n [C] someone who leads a group that is doing something illegal or wrong: *Police arrested the two ringleaders last night.*

ring·let /ˈrɪŋlət/ n [C] a long curl of hair

ring road /ˈ. ./ n [C] *BrE* a road that goes around a large town so that traffic does not have to go through the centre

rink /rɪŋk/ n [C] a specially prepared indoor area where you can ICE SKATE or ROLLER SKATE

rinse¹ /rɪns/ v [T] to wash something in clean water in order to remove dirt, soap etc: *Rinse the lettuce in cold water.* | **rinse out sth** (=rinse the inside of it): *He rinsed out a glass and poured himself a whisky.*

rinse² n **1** **give sth a rinse** to rinse something: *I'll just give this shirt a quick rinse.* **2** [C,U] a product used for slightly changing the colour of hair: *a blond rinse*

ri·ot¹ /ˈraɪət/ n **1** [C] when a crowd of people behaves violently in a public place: *Rises in food prices caused riots and strikes.* **2** **run riot** to become impossible to control: *parents who let their children run riot*

riot² v [I] if a lot of people riot, they behave violently in a public place — **rioter** n [C] *Police fired on rioters.*

ri·ot·ing /ˈraɪətɪŋ/ n [U] when a crowd riots: *Rioting broke out in the city late last night.*

ri·ot·ous /ˈraɪətəs/ adj **1** noisy and excited: *riotous celebrations* **2** behaving violently, without any control: *riotous crowds*

rip¹ /rɪp/ v **-pped, -pping 1** [I,T] to tear something, or be torn, quickly and violently: *Oh, no! I've just ripped my sleeve.* | *Don't pull the curtain too hard – it'll rip.* | **rip sth open** (=open something by tearing it): *Impatiently, Sue ripped the letter open.* **2** [T] to remove something by pulling it away quickly and violently: *He ripped off his clothes and jumped into the pool.*

rip sb off *phr v* [T] *spoken informal* to charge someone too much money for something: *That taxi driver tried to rip me off!*

rip sth ↔ up *phr v* [T] to tear something violently into several pieces: *Angrily, Fran ripped up her contract.*

rip² n [C] a long tear or cut: *a rip in the tyre*

ripe /raɪp/ adj **1** fruit or corn that is ripe is ready to eat: *Those peaches don't look ripe yet.* **2** **be ripe for** to be in the right condition for something: *a region that is ripe for industrial development* **3** **the time is ripe (for)** used to say that it is the right time for something to happen: *The time is ripe for trade talks.* **4** **live to a ripe old age** to live until you are very old — **ripeness** n [U]

rip·en /ˈraɪpən/ v [I,T] if food or crops ripen, or if the sun ripens them, they become ripe: *Corn ripens quickly in the summer sun.*

rip-off /ˈ. ./ n [C] *spoken informal* something that is unreasonably expensive: *The drinks in the hotel bar are a ripoff!*

rip·ple¹ /ˈrɪpəl/ v [I,T] to move in small waves, or to make something move in this way: *a flag rippling in the wind*

ripple² n [C] **1** a small low wave on the surface of a liquid: *A gentle breeze made ripples on the lake.* **2** a feeling or sound that spreads through a person or group: *A ripple of laughter ran through the audience.*

ripple

ripple

rise¹ /raɪz/ v [I] **rose** /rəʊz‖roʊz/, **risen** /ˈrɪzən/, **rising 1** to increase: *World oil prices are rising.* | *The population has risen steadily since the 1950s.* | **rise by 10%/£500 etc** *Salaries rose by 10% last year.* → opposite FALL¹ **2** to go up: *Smoke rose from the chimney.* | *Flood waters are still rising in parts of Missouri.* **3** to stand up: *Thornton rose to his feet and turned to speak to them.* **4** to become important, powerful, successful, or rich: **+ to** *the story of how Marilyn Monroe rose to stardom* **5** to become stronger or louder: *You could feel the excitement rising as we waited.* **6** if the sun or moon rises, it appears in the sky: *The sun rises at around 6 am.* → opposite SET[1] **7** to be taller than anything else around: *Then they could see Mount Shasta rising in the distance.* **8 rise to the occasion/challenge** to deal with a difficult situation successfully **9** *literary* to get out of bed in the morning **10** *literary* also **rise up** to start to fight against the government of your country: *In 1917 the Russian people rose against the Czar.*

rise above sth *phr v* [T] to not let a bad situation affect you: *She was able to rise above her family's foolish quarrels.*

USAGE NOTE: rise and raise

Rise is an intransitive verb meaning 'to move to a higher position': *The curtain rose and the play began.* **Raise** is a transitive verb, and means 'to move someone or something to a higher position': *They raised the curtain and the play began.*

---

rise² *n* **1** [C] an increase: *a tax rise* | **+ in** *a sudden rise in temperature* **2** [singular] when someone or something becomes more important, more successful, or more powerful: **rise to power/fame etc** *Stalin's rise to power* **3 give rise to** to cause something: *The president's absence gave rise to rumours about his health.* **4** [C] an upward slope: *a slight rise in the road* **5** [C] *BrE* an increase in wages; RAISE *AmE*: *We got a 4% rise last year.*

ris·er /ˈraɪzə‖-ər/ *n* **early/late riser** someone who usually gets out of bed very early or very late

risk¹ /rɪsk/ *n* **1** [C,U] the possibility that something bad may happen: *risks involved in starting a small business* | **+ of** *the risk of serious injury* | **+ that** *There is always the risk that someone may press the wrong button.* **2 take a risk/ run the risk** to do something even though there is a possibility that something bad will happen: *You'll be running the risk of getting caught.* **3 at risk** likely to be harmed: **+ from** *people at risk from AIDS* **4 at your own risk** if you do something at your own risk, no one else is responsible if something bad happens: *Customers may park here at their own risk.* **5** [C] something or someone that is likely to be dangerous: **health/fire/security risk** *The tire dump is a major fire risk.* | **+ to** *Polluted water supplies are a risk to public health.*

risk² *v* [T] **1** to put something in a situation in which it could be lost, destroyed, or harmed: *I'm not going to risk my life to save a cat!* **2** to do something that you know may have bad results: **risk doing sth** *I daren't risk leaving the children alone.* **3 risk death/punishment/defeat etc** to do something which could result in your being killed, punished etc: *risking death or imprisonment to escape from Vietnam*

risk·y /ˈrɪski/ *adj* involving a risk that something bad will happen: *a risky financial investment* — **riskiness** *n* [U]

ris·qué /ˈrɪskeɪ‖rɪˈskeɪ/ *adj* a joke, remark etc that is risqué is slightly shocking because it is about sex

rite /raɪt/ *n* [C] a traditional ceremony that is always performed in the same way, especially for a religious purpose: *funeral rites*

rit·u·al¹ /ˈrɪtʃuəl/ *n* [C,U] a ceremony or set of actions that is always done in the same way: *church rituals* | *The children performed the bedtime ritual of washing and brushing their teeth.*

ritual² *adj* done as part of a rite or ritual: *ritual dancing* — **ritually** *adv*

ritz·y /ˈrɪtsi/ *adj informal* fashionable and expensive: *a ritzy neighborhood*

ri·val¹ /ˈraɪvəl/ *n* [C] a person, team, or company that you compete with: *The two teams had always been rivals.* — **rival** *adj*: *rival gangs*

rival² *v* [T] to be as good as someone or something else: *The college has sports facilities that rival those of Yale or Harvard.*

ri·val·ry /ˈraɪvəlri/ *n* [C,U] when people, teams, companies etc try to do better than each other: *There has always been a kind of friendly rivalry between the two teams.*

riv·er /ˈrɪvəl-ər/ *n* [C] a natural and continuous flow of water in a long line that goes into a sea: *the River Nile* | *Let's go for a swim in the river.* → see colour picture on page 243

riv·er·side /ˈrɪvəsaɪd‖-ər-/ *n* [singular] the land along the sides of a river: *riverside apartments*

riv·et¹ /ˈrɪvɪt/ *v* **be riveted** if you are riveted by something, you cannot stop looking at it or listening to it: *People sat riveted to their TVs during the trial.*

rivet² *n* [C] a metal pin for fastening flat pieces of metal together

riv·et·ing /ˈrɪvɪtɪŋ/ *adj* extremely interesting: *a riveting movie*

roach /rəʊtʃ‖roʊtʃ/ *n* [C] *AmE* a COCKROACH

road /rəʊd‖roʊd/ *n* **1** [C,U] a specially prepared hard surface for vehicles to travel on: *They're building a new road around the city centre.* | *Her address is 25 Park Road.* | **along/up/down the road** *The boys go to the school down the road.* | **across/over the road** (=on the other side of the road): *Who lives in that house across the road?* | **main road** (=a large road with a lot of traffic) | **by road** (=travelling in a vehicle): *the transportation of goods by road* → see colour picture on page 79 **2 on the road** travelling for a long distance, especially in a car: *We've been on the road since 7:00 a.m.* **3 on the road to success/recovery etc** developing in a way that will result in success, better health etc

road·block /ˈrəʊdblɒk‖ˈroʊdblɑːk/ *n* [C] **1** a place where the police or army have blocked the road to stop traffic: *Two dangerous prisoners have escaped and the police are setting up roadblocks.* **2** *AmE* a problem that stops you from achieving something: *Lack of training is regarded as the main roadblock to success.*

road·house /ˈrəʊdhaʊs‖ˈroʊd-/ *n* [C] *AmE* a restaurant or bar on a road outside a city

road rage /ˈ. ./ *n* [U] when drivers suddenly become angry and start shouting or attacking other drivers, especially because there is too much traffic and they feel STRESSED: *As the volume of traffic has increased, road rage incidents have become more and more common.*

road·side /ˈrəʊdsaɪd‖ˈroʊd-/ *n* [singular] the edge of a road: *a roadside café*

road·works /'rəʊdwɜːks‖'roʊdwɜːrks/ n [plural] BrE work that is being done to repair a road

road·wor·thy /'rəʊd‚wɜːði‖'roʊd‚wɜːr-/ adj if a car is roadworthy, it is in a good enough condition to drive

roam /rəʊm‖roʊm/ v [I,T] to walk or travel with no definite purpose: Teenage gangs roamed the streets. | + around/through etc bears roaming through the forest

roar¹ /rɔː‖rɔːr/ v 1 [I] to make a deep very loud noise: We heard a lion roar in the distance. 2 [I] to travel very fast, making a loud noise: There was a cloud of dust as a truck roared past. 3 [I,T] to shout with a deep loud voice: "Get out of here now!" he roared.

roar² n [C] a deep loud continuous sound: a roar of laughter

roar·ing /'rɔːrɪŋ/ adj 1 making a deep, very loud continuous noise: roaring floodwaters 2 roaring fire a fire that burns with a lot of flames and heat 3 do a roaring trade (in) BrE informal to sell a lot of something very quickly: At weekends the souvenir shops do a roaring trade.

roast¹ /rəʊst‖roʊst/ v [I,T] to cook something in an OVEN or over a fire

roast² n [C] 1 a large piece of roasted meat 2 AmE an outdoor party where you cook food on an open fire: a hot dog roast

roast³ adj [only before noun] cooked in an oven or on a fire: roast beef

rob /rɒb‖rɑːb/ v [T] 1 to steal money or property from a person, bank, shop etc: The two men were jailed for robbing a jeweller's. 2 rob sb of sth to take away something important from someone: a failure that robbed him of his self-confidence

---

USAGE NOTE: rob and steal

Both these words are about taking things that do not belong to you. **Rob** means 'to take money or property from a person or place': Someone robbed the bank last night. | We don't carry cash because we're afraid we'll get robbed. Don't say "someone stole a bank" or "we're afraid we'll get stolen". **Steal** is used to talk about the actual things that are taken: Matt's bike was stolen. | They caught him trying to steal some cigarettes. Don't say "Matt's bike was robbed" or "rob some cigarettes".

---

rob·ber /'rɒbə‖'rɑːbər/ n [C] someone who steals money or property from banks, shops etc: a bank robber

rob·ber·y /'rɒbəri‖'rɑː-/ n [C,U] the crime of stealing money or property from a bank, shop etc: armed robbery (=robbery with a gun): They're in prison for armed robbery.

robe /rəʊb‖roʊb/ n [C] 1 a long loose piece of clothing, especially worn for ceremonies: a judge's robe 2 AmE a long loose coat that you wear over your night clothes; DRESSING GOWN BrE

rob·in /'rɒbən‖'rɑː-/ n [C] a common wild bird with a red chest and brown back

ro·bot /'rəʊbɒt‖'roʊbɑːt, -bət/ n [C] a machine controlled by a computer, that can move and do jobs that humans usually do: industrial robots —**robotic** /rəʊ'bɒtɪk‖roʊ'bɑː-/ adj

ro·bust /rə'bʌst, 'rəʊbʌst‖rə'bʌst, 'roʊ-/ adj 1 strong or healthy: a surprisingly robust 70-year-old | a robust structure 2 determined and confident: a robust defence of the government's economic policy

rock¹ /rɒk‖rɑːk/ n 1 [U] the hard substance in the Earth's surface that consists of any type of stone: a tunnel cut through solid rock 2 [C] a large piece or solid mass of stone: Their ship was driven onto the rocks by the storm. → see colour picture on page 243 3 [U] a type of popular modern music with a strong loud beat → see also ROCKS

rock² v 1 [I,T] to move gently backwards and forwards or from side to side, or to make something do this: Jane sat rocking the baby. | Waves were making the boat rock. 2 [T] to make the people in a place feel very shocked or surprised: a city rocked by violence 3 rock the boat informal to spoil a situation that everyone else is satisfied with

rock and roll /‚. . '. / n [U] ROCK 'N' ROLL

rock bot·tom /‚. '. ‹ / n hit/reach rock bottom informal to become as bad as something can possibly be: By June, their marriage had hit rock bottom.

rock-bottom adj rock-bottom prices are as low as they can possibly be

rock·er /'rɒkə‖'rɑːkər/ n [C] 1 AmE a ROCKING CHAIR 2 be off your rocker spoken to be crazy

rock·e·ry /'rɒkəri‖'rɑː-/ n [C] a part of a garden where there are rocks with plants growing among them

rock·et¹ /'rɒkət‖'rɑː-/ n [C] 1 a tube-shaped vehicle that carries people or scientific equipment into space: a Soviet space rocket 2 a tube-shaped weapon that carries a bomb and is fired from a plane, ship etc: anti-tank rockets 3 a FIREWORK that goes high into the air and explodes

rocket² v [I] 1 to increase very quickly: The price of coffee has rocketed. 2 to quickly become successful: + to a song that has rocketed to number one in the charts

rock·ing chair /'.. ./ n [C] a chair that has two curved pieces of wood under it, so that it moves backwards and forwards → see picture at CHAIR

rocking horse /'... / n [C] a toy horse for children to ride on

rock 'n' roll /‚rɒk ən 'rəʊl‖‚rɑːk ən 'roʊl/ n [U] a type of popular dance music with a strong loud beat

rocks /rɒks‖rɑːks/ n be on the rocks if a marriage or business is on the rocks, there are a lot of problems and it is likely to fail

rock·y /'rɒki‖'rɑːki/ adj covered with rocks or made of rock: the rocky coast of Maine

rod /rɒd‖rɑːd/ n [C] a long thin pole or stick: a fishing rod

rode /rəʊd‖roʊd/ v the past tense of RIDE

ro·dent /'rəʊdənt‖'roʊ-/ n [C] an animal such as a rat or a rabbit that has long sharp front teeth

ro·de·o /'rəʊdiəʊ, rəʊ'deɪ-əʊ‖'roʊdioʊ, roʊ-'deɪ-oʊ/ n [C] a show in which COWBOYS ride wild horses and catch cattle with ropes

roe /rəʊ‖roʊ/ n [C,U] fish eggs

rogue /rəʊg‖roʊg/ n [C] old-fashioned a man or boy who behaves badly or is dishonest

role /rəʊl‖roʊl/ n [C] **1** the position that someone or something has in a situation or activity: **+ as** *the importance of her role as mother of the family* | **play a major/key role in** (=be important in): *companies that play a major role in the world's economy* **2** the character played by an actor in a play: *Brendan will play the role of Romeo.*

role mod·el /'. ,../ n [C] someone that you try to copy because you admire them

role-play /'. ./ n [C,U] a training activity in which you try to behave in the way that someone else would behave in a particular situation

roll[1] /rəʊl‖roʊl/ v **1** [I,T] to move by turning over and over, or to make something move this way: *The ball rolled across the lawn.* **2** [I] to move steadily and smoothly: *Tears rolled down his cheeks.* | *The van was starting to roll backward.* **3** also **roll over** [I] to turn your body over once or many times: *Beth's dog had been rolling in the mud.* | *He rolled over onto his stomach.* **4** [T] to curl or wind something into the shape of a tube or ball: *Bob rolled another cigarette.* **5** [I] to swing from side to side: *The ship was starting to roll.* **6** also **roll out** [T] to make something flat by moving a round and heavy object over it: *Roll the pastry out.* **7** **(all) rolled into one** if something or someone is several different things all rolled into one, they include qualities of all those things

roll in *phr v* [I] *informal* to arrive in large numbers or quantities: *The money soon came rolling in.* → see also **rolling in it** (ROLLING)

roll up *phr v* **1** [T **roll** sth ↔ **up**] to curl or fold cloth, paper etc around several times: *Roll up your sleeves.* | *a rolled-up newspaper* **2** [I] *informal* to arrive, usually late: *David rolled up after everyone else had left.*

roll[2] n [C] **1** a piece of paper, film, or other material that has been curled into the shape of a tube: *a roll of toilet paper* **2** a small round LOAF of bread for one person **3** an official list of names: *the union membership roll* **4** **be on a roll** *informal* to be having a lot of success with what you are doing **5** a long deep sound: *a roll of thunder*

roll call /'. ./ n [C,U] when someone reads out all the names on an official list to check who is at a meeting or in a class

roll·er /'rəʊlə‖'roʊlər/ n [C] **1** a tube-shaped piece of wood, metal etc that can be rolled over and over **2** one of several tubes that women wind their hair around to make it curl

Rol·ler·blade /'rəʊləbleɪd‖'roʊlər-/ n [C] *trademark* a special boot with a single row of wheels fixed under it → compare ROLLER SKATE

roller coast·er /'.. ,../ n [C] **1** a track with sudden steep slopes and curves, that people ride on in special vehicles for fun at FAIRS **2** a situation that is impossible to control because it keeps changing very quickly: *the story of two women's lives riding a rollercoaster of love, revenge and murder*

roller skate /'.. ./ n [C] a special boot with four wheels fixed under it —**roller skate** v [I] —**roller skating** n [U]

roll·ing /'rəʊlɪŋ‖'roʊ-/ adj **1** rolling hills have a lot of long slopes **2** **rolling in it** *informal* very rich

rolling pin /'.. ./ n [C] a long tube-shaped piece of wood used for making PASTRY flat before you cook it

ROM /rɒm‖rɑːm/ n [U] *technical* read-only memory; the part of a computer where permanent instructions and information are stored → compare RAM

Ro·man[1] /'rəʊmən‖'roʊ-/ adj relating to ancient Rome: *the Roman Empire*

Roman[2] n [C] a citizen of the ancient empire or city of Rome

Roman Cath·o·lic /,.. '...◂/ adj belonging to the part of the Christian religion whose leader is the Pope —**Roman Catholic** n [C] —**Roman Catholicism** /,.. '..../ n [U]

ro·mance /rəʊ'mæns, 'rəʊmæns‖roʊ'mæns, 'roʊ-/ n **1** [C,U] an exciting short relationship between two people who love each other: *a summer romance* **2** [C] a story about love between two people **3** [U] the feeling of excitement and adventure that is connected with a particular place, activity etc: *the romance of travelling to distant places*

Roman nu·me·ral /,.. '...◂/ n [C] a number in a system that was used in ancient Rome, for example I, II, III, IV etc instead of 1, 2, 3, 4 etc

ro·man·tic[1] /rəʊ'mæntɪk, rə-‖roʊ-, rə-/ adj **1** treating the person you love in a very special way: *"Paul always sends me roses on my birthday." "How romantic!"* **2** involving or describing feelings of love between two people: *She enjoys romantic movies.* **3** based too much on the way you would like things to be, rather than on the way they really are: *her romantic dreams of becoming a famous writer* —**romantically** /-kli/ adv

romantic[2] n [C] someone who bases their ideas about the world on how they imagine and want it to be, rather than on how it really is: *an incurable romantic*

ro·man·ti·cize (also **-ise** BrE) /rəʊ'mæntɪˌsaɪz, rə-‖roʊ-, rə-/ v [I,T] to talk or think about things in a way that makes them seem more attractive than they really are: *a romanticized idea of country life*

roof /ruːf‖ruːf, rʊf/ n [C], *plural* **roofs** /ruːfs, ruːvz‖ruːfs, ruːvz, rʊfs, rʊvz/ **1** the top part of a building or vehicle, that covers it: *The storm ripped the roof off our house.* → see colour picture on page 79 **2** the top of a PASSAGE under the ground: *The roof of the tunnel suddenly collapsed.* **3** **a roof over your head** a place to live in: *I can go and live with my sister, so at least I'll have a roof over my head.* **4** the top part of the inside of your mouth **5** **hit the roof** BrE *spoken informal* to become very angry **6** **under one roof/under the same roof** in one building or house: *several families living under the same roof*

roof·ing /'ruːfɪŋ‖'ruːf-, 'rʊf-/ n [U] material for making or covering roofs

roof·top /'ruːftɒp‖'ruːftɑːp, 'rʊf-/ n [C] the top surface of a roof: *Beyond the rooftops she could see the bay.*

rook /rʊk/ n [C] a large black bird

rook·ie /'rʊki/ n [C] *especially AmE* someone who has just started doing a job or playing a sport: *rookie cops*

room[1] /ruːm, rʊm/ *n* **1** [C] a part of the inside of a building that has its own walls, floor, and ceiling: *My brother was sleeping in the next room.: the living room* **2** [U] enough space for something or someone: **+ for** *Is there room for my camera in your bag?* | **room to do sth** *There isn't much room to move around.* | **make room for** (=move so that there is enough space): *Would you please move along and make room for Jerry.* | **leg room/head room** (=the amount of space in front of you, or above you in a vehicle) **3** **there's room for improvement** used to say that someone's work needs to be improved

room[2] *v* **room with sb** *AmE* to share the room that you live in with someone, for example at college

room·mate /ˈruːmmeɪt, ˈrʊm-/ *n* [C] **1** someone that you share a room with, especially at college **2** *AmE* someone that you share a room, apartment, or house with

room ser·vice /ˈ. ˌ../ *n* [U] a service provided by a hotel, by which food, drinks etc can be brought to your room

room·y /ˈruːmi/ *adj* with plenty of space inside: *a roomy car*

roost /ruːst/ *n* [C] a place where birds rest and sleep —**roost** *v* [I]

roost·er /ˈruːstəl-ər/ *n* [C] a male chicken

root[1] /ruːt/ *n* [C] **1** the part of a plant or tree that grows under the ground and takes water from the soil: *When you plant a rose bush, be careful not to damage the roots.* **2** the basic cause of a problem: **be/lie at the root of** *religious differences which lie at the root of the conflict* | **root cause** *the root cause of the problem* **3** the part of a tooth, hair etc that is under the skin **4** **take root** if an idea takes root, people begin to accept or believe it: *helping democracy take root* ➡ see also ROOTS, SQUARE ROOT

root[2] *v* [I] to search for something by moving things around: **+ around/through/among etc** *I waited while she rooted around in her bag for a pen.*
root for sb *phr v* [T] *informal* to support and encourage someone: *Good luck – I'll be rooting for you!*
root sth ↔ **out** *phr v* [T] to find out where a problem exists and get rid of it: *We are doing all we can to root out violence in schools.*

root·ed /ˈruːtɪd/ *adj* **1** **be rooted in** to have developed from something and be strongly influenced by it: *attitudes that are deeply rooted in religious tradition* **2** **be rooted to the spot** to be unable to move: *He was so terrified – he stood there, rooted to the spot.*

roots /ruːts/ *n* [plural] **1** the origins of something: *Jazz has its roots in African music.* **2** **sb's roots** someone's connection with a place because they were born there or their family lived there: *the Kennedy family's Irish roots* **3** **put down roots** to start to live in a place as your permanent home

rope[1] /rəʊpllrʊp/ *n* [C,U] very strong thick string, made by twisting together many threads: *They tied a rope around the dog's neck.*

rope[2] *v* [T] to tie things or people together, using rope: *The climbers were roped together for safety.*
rope sb ↔ **in** *phr v* [T] *informal* to persuade someone to help you: *I've been roped in to help with the entertainment.*
rope sth ↔ **off** *phr v* [T] to put ropes around an area to keep people out: *Police roped off the area where the bomb was found.*

ropes /rəʊpsllrʊps/ *n* **1** **know the ropes** to know how to do all the parts of a job **2** **show sb the ropes** to show someone how to do a job

rop·ey, ropy /ˈrəʊpillrʊp-/ *adj BrE informal* in a bad condition or of bad quality

ro·sa·ry /ˈrəʊzərillrʊp-/ *n* [C] a string of BEADS used especially by Roman Catholics for counting prayers

rose[1] /rəʊzllrʊz/ *n* **1** [C] a common sweet-smelling garden flower that grows on a bush that has THORNS **2** [U] a pink colour

rose[2] *v* the past tense of RISE

ro·sé /ˈrəʊzeillrʊʊˈzeɪ/ *n* [U] pink wine

ro·sette /rəʊˈzetllrʊʊ-/ *n* [C] a circular BADGE made of coloured silk that is given as a prize or worn during elections in Britain

ros·ter /ˈrɒstəllˈruːstər/ *n* [C] a list of people's names showing the jobs they must do and when they must do them

ros·trum /ˈrɒstrəmllˈrɑː-/ *n* [C] a small PLATFORM (=raised area) that someone stands on to make a speech or to CONDUCT a group of musicians

ros·y /ˈrəʊzillrʊp-/ *adj* **1** pink: *rosy cheeks* **2** seeming to offer hope of success or happiness: *a rosier future*

rot[1] /rɒtllrɑːt/ *v* [I,T] to decay or to make something decay: *The vegetables were left to rot.* | *Too much sugar rots your teeth.*

rot[2] *n* **1** [U] the natural process of decaying, or the part of something that has decayed: *a tree full of rot* **2** **the rot** *informal* a bad situation that is getting worse: *how to stop the rot* | **the rot set in** *As the rot set in, she publicly showed her loathing of her husband's family.*

ro·ta /ˈrəʊtəllrʊp-/ *n* [C] *BrE* a list of people's names showing the jobs they must do and when they must do them; ROSTER *AmE*

ro·ta·ry /ˈrəʊtərillrʊp-/ *adj* turning in a circle around a fixed point: *the rotary movement of helicopter blades*

ro·tate /rəʊˈteɪtllˈrʊʊteɪt/ *v* [I,T] **1** to turn around a fixed point, or to make something do this: *The Earth rotates every 24 hours.* | *Rotate the handle to the right.* **2** if a job or the use of something rotates, or if someone rotates it, different people do the job or different things are used in a regular order: *the EU's rotating presidency*

ro·ta·tion /rəʊˈteɪʃənllrʊp-/ *n* **1** [C,U] the action of turning around a fixed point, or one complete turn: *the rotation of the Earth on its axis* **2** **in rotation** if people do something in rotation, first one person does it, then another, then the first person etc: *We work in rotation.*

R

GRAMMAR NOTE: for and **since**
Use **for** with periods of time: *I've been waiting here for 25 minutes.* | *We've lived here for 6 years.*
Use **since** with the date or time when something started: *I've been waiting here since 7 o'clock.* | *We've lived here since 1992.*

rote /rəʊt‖roʊt/ *n* [U] **learn sth by rote** to learn something by repeating it until you remember it

ro·tor /ˈrəʊtə‖ˈroʊtər/ *n* [C] a part of a machine that turns around on a fixed point especially on a HELICOPTER

rot·ten /ˈrɒtn‖ˈrɑːtn/ *adj* **1** food, wood etc that is rotten has been spoiled or is in bad condition because it is old; DECAYED: *rotten apples* **2** *informal* unkind or unfair: *What a rotten thing to do!* **3** *informal* very bad at doing something: *Betty is a rotten cook.*

rott·wei·ler /ˈrɒtvaɪlə, -waɪlə‖ˈrɑːtwaɪlər/ *n* [C] a type of strong dangerous dog

ro·tund /rəʊˈtʌnd‖roʊ-/ *adj* having a fat round body

rouge /ruːʒ/ *n* [U] *old-fashioned* a pink powder or cream used by women to give colour to their cheeks

rough[1] /rʌf/ *adj* **1** having an uneven surface: *Our jeep's good for travelling over rough ground.* **2** not exact or not containing many details: *Can you give us a rough idea of the cost?|a rough draft of an essay* **3** using too much force or violence: *You mustn't be too rough with her.|Ice hockey is a rough sport.* **4** a rough area has a lot of violence and crime: *a rough part of the town* **5** a rough situation or period of time is difficult and unpleasant: *She's had a rough couple of weeks at work.* **6** **have a rough night** to sleep badly **7** a rough sea has large waves because of strong winds or storms **8** **feel rough** to feel ill —**roughness** *n* [U]

rough[2] *n* **1** **take the rough with the smooth** to accept the bad things in life as well as the good ones **2** **in rough** *BrE* if you work or draw something in rough, you do it quickly and without making it exact or detailed

rough[3] *v* **rough it** to live in conditions that are not as comfortable as the ones you usually live in: *We're going to rough it in the mountains for a few days.*
rough sb ↔ **up** *phr v* [T] *informal* to attack someone by hitting them

rough[4] *adv* **sleep rough** *BrE* to sleep outdoors because you have no home

rough·age /ˈrʌfɪdʒ/ *n* [U] a substance in some foods that helps your BOWELS to work; FIBRE

rough-and-tum·ble /ˌ.. ..ˈ../ *n* [U] **1** noisy and violent play, especially by children **2** the usual busy noisy way in which an activity takes place: *the rough-and-tumble of politics*

rough·en /ˈrʌfən/ *v* [I,T] to make a surface uneven or feel rough: *The wind can roughen your skin.*

rough·ly /ˈrʌfli/ *adv* **1** not exactly; about: *Roughly 100 people came.|I worked out roughly how much it would cost.* **2** not gently or carefully: *She pushed him away roughly.*

rough·shod /ˈrʌfʃɒd‖-ʃɑːd/ *adv* **ride roughshod over sb/sth** to take no notice of other people's feelings or opinions

rou·lette /ruːˈlet/ *n* [U] a game played for money in which people try to guess which hole a small ball will fall into when a wheel is spun

round[1] /raʊnd/ *adj* **1** shaped like a circle, a ball, or the letter "o": *a round table|her little round face* **2** **in round figures/numbers** not expressed as an exact number but as the nearest 10, 100, 1000 etc —**roundness** *n* [U]

round[2] *especially BrE also* **around** *adv, prep* **1** in a circle or on all sides of something: *The wheel is still spinning round.|We sat round the fire.|The children gathered round to watch the magician.* ➔ see colour picture on page 518 **2** moving to face the opposite direction: *I looked round to see who had come into the room.|Turn your chair round the other way.* **3** **round and round** turning many times in a circle: *We drove round and round but couldn't find the place.* **4** going from one place to another: *A guide showed us round.* **5** from one person to another: *Pass round the chocolates, please!* **6** to a particular place or to someone's house: *I'll come round about 7 o'clock.* **7** in or from a particular area of a city, country etc: *I don't live round here.|Round this part of Wales, they don't speak much English.* **8** **round about sth** nearly but not exactly: *I'm expecting them round about 10 o'clock.* **9** **round about** near a place: *There are lots of nice pubs round about.* ➔ see also AROUND

round[3] *n* [C] **1** a set of events that are connected: *the latest round of peace talks* **2** a regular set of visits that someone makes as part of their job: *The doctor is out on her rounds.|The postman starts his round at 6 am.* **3** **round of applause** when people CLAP to show that they enjoyed a performance **4** alcoholic drinks bought for all the people in a group, usually by one person: *I'll buy the first round of drinks.* **5** one of the parts of a sports competition or game that you have to finish before you can go to the next part: *Graf has made it to the third round.* **6** a complete game of GOLF **7** a bullet or several bullets fired from a gun: *He let off a round of ammunition.*

round[4] *v* [T] to go around something such as a bend or the corner of a building: *The car rounded the bend at 75 mph.*
round sth ↔ **down** *phr v* [T] to change an exact figure to the nearest whole lower number: *round it down to £20*
round sth ↔ **off** *phr v* [T] to end something in a pleasant or suitable way: *The evening was rounded off with carols around the Christmas tree.*
round sb/sth ↔ **up** *phr v* [T] to find and bring together a group of people: *Police rounded up 20 people for questioning.*
round sth **up** *phr v* [T] to change an exact figure to the nearest whole higher number

round·a·bout[1] /ˈraʊndəbaʊt/ *adj* not done in the shortest or most direct way: *a roundabout route to avoid heavy traffic*

roundabout[2] *n* [C] *BrE* **1** a circular area where several roads meet, which you have to drive around until you reach the road you want; TRAFFIC CIRCLE *AmE*: *Turn left at the next roundabout.* ➔ see colour picture on page 669 **2** a circular structure that children play on by sitting on it and making it spin around

round·ed /ˈraʊndɪd/ *adj* curved, not pointed or sharp: *a knife with a rounded end*

roun·ders /ˈraʊndəz‖-ərz/ *n* [U] a British ball game in which players hit the ball and then run around the edge of an area

round-the-clock /ˌ. .ˈ.◂/ *adj* all the time, both day and night: *round-the-clock hospital care*

round trip /ˌ. './ n [C] a journey to a place and back again —**round-trip** adj AmE: a round-trip ticket

round-up /'. ./ n [C] **1** when a lot of people or animals are brought together, often by force: a roundup of criminal suspects **2** a short description of the most important pieces of news

rouse /raʊz/ v [T] **1** formal to wake someone up: We were roused from a deep sleep. **2** to make someone become excited or angry enough to start doing something: The speech roused King's supporters to action.

rous·ing /'raʊzɪŋ/ adj making people feel excited and eager to do something: a rousing speech

rout /raʊt/ v [T] to defeat someone completely in a battle, competition, election etc —**rout** n [singular]

route[1] /ruːt‖ruːt, raʊt/ n [C] **1** the way from one place to another: What is the shortest route from here to the station? | local bus routes → see also EN ROUTE **2** a way of achieving something: Getting lots of money is not necessarily a route to happiness.

route[2] v [T] to send something or someone by a particular route: Flights are being routed through Paris because of the war.

rou·tine[1] /ruː'tiːn/ n **1** [C,U] the usual way in which you do things: Harry doesn't like any change in his daily routine. **2** [C] a set of dance steps, jokes, actions etc learned by a dancer or other performer: a dance routine

rou·tine[2] /ˌruː'tiːnˌ/ adj **1** regular and usual: a routine medical test | a few routine questions **2** ordinary and boring: routine jobs around the house —**routinely** adv

rov·ing /'raʊvɪŋ‖'roʊvɪŋ/ adj [only before noun] travelling or moving from one place to another: a roving reporter

row

There are two empty seats in the front row.

row[1] /raʊ‖roʊ/ n **1** [C] a line of things or people next to each other: a row of houses **2** **three/four etc in a row** three times, four times etc, one after the other: We've lost four games in a row. **3** [C] a line of seats in a theatre, cinema etc: I sat in the front row.

row[2] v [I,T] to make a boat move through water using OARS: Slowly she rowed across the lake. —**rowing** n [U]

row[3] /raʊ/ n [C] BrE **1** an angry argument, especially between people who know each other well: **have a row** Anna and her boyfriend are always having rows. **2** [C] a situation in which people disagree strongly about important public affairs: **+ over** the row over government plans to cut benefit payments to single mothers

3 [singular] an annoying loud noise: I wish they'd stop that row!

row·dy /'raʊdi/ adj behaving in a noisy and uncontrolled way: a group of rowdy children —**rowdiness** n [U]

row house /'raʊ haʊs‖'roʊ-/ n [C] AmE a house that is part of a line of houses that are joined together; TERRACED HOUSE BrE

rowing boat /'raʊɪŋ bəʊt‖'roʊɪŋ boʊt/ BrE, **row·boat** /'raʊbəʊt‖'roʊboʊt/ AmE — n [C] a small boat that you move through water using OARS → see colour picture on page 669

roy·al[1] /'rɔɪəl/ adj relating to or belonging to a king or queen: the royal family | a royal palace

royal blue /ˌ. '.ˌ/ adj a strong bright blue colour

roy·al·ist /'rɔɪəlɪst/ n [C] someone who believes that their country should be ruled by a king or queen

roy·al·ties /'rɔɪəltiz/ n [plural] payments made to the writer of a book or piece of music

roy·al·ty /'rɔɪəlti/ n [U] members of a royal family

RSVP /ˌɑːr es viː' piː/ an abbreviation that is written on invitations to ask someone to reply

rub[1] /rʌb/ v -bbed, -bbing **1** [I,T] to move your hand, a cloth etc over a surface while pressing against it: The stain should come out if you rub harder. | She woke up and rubbed her eyes. | **rub sth into/onto/over etc** (=put cream, liquid etc on a surface by pressing it with your hand or a cloth and moving it around): Can you rub some lotion on my back, please? **2** [I,T] to press against a surface while moving it backwards and forwards, especially in a way that is painful or causes damage: My shoes are rubbing my heels. **3** **rub it in** informal to make someone remember something that they want to forget, especially because they are embarrassed about it: OK, there's no need to rub it in! **4** **rub shoulders with sb** informal to spend time with important or famous people **5** **rub sb up the wrong way** informal to annoy someone by the way you talk or behave towards them **6** **rub salt into the wound** to make someone feel worse about a situation which is already bad

rub sb/sth↔**down** phr v [T] to make something dry or smooth by rubbing it with a cloth: Rub yourself down with a towel. | She rubbed the door down before painting it.

rub off phr v **1** [I,T **rub** sth ↔ **off**] to remove something from a surface by rubbing it: These pen marks won't rub off. **2** **rub off on sb** if a feeling, habit etc rubs off on someone, they start to have it because the person they are with has it: Her positive attitude seemed to rub off on everyone.

rub sth ↔ **out** phr v [T] to remove pencil marks using a piece of rubber; ERASE: I'll have to rub it out and start again.

rub[2] n [C, usually singular] an act of rubbing something: Could you give my back a rub?

rub·ber[1] /'rʌbə‖-ər/ n **1** [U] a substance used for making tyres, boots etc that is made from chemicals or the juice of tropical trees: The tyres were smooth where the rubber had completely worn away. **2** [C] BrE a thing you use to remove pencil marks from paper; ERASER especially AmE **3** [C] AmE informal a CONDOM

rub·ber[2] adj made of rubber: rubber gloves

rubber band /ˌ.. './ *n* [C] a thin circular piece of rubber used for holding things together; ELASTIC BAND

rubber boots /'... ./ *n* [C] boots made of rubber that you wear to walk on wet or muddy ground; WELLINGTONS, WELLIES *BrE*

rubber-stamp /ˌ.. './ *v* [T] to give official approval to something without considering it carefully

rub·ber·y /'rʌbəri/ *adj* looking or feeling like rubber: *a rubbery steak*

rub·bish /'rʌbɪʃ/ *n* [U] *especially BrE* **1** food, paper etc that you no longer need and that is thrown away; GARBAGE *AmE*: *Put the rubbish in the bin.* **2** *informal* something you think is silly, wrong, or bad: **a load of rubbish** *That programme was a load of rubbish.*

rub·ble /'rʌbəl/ *n* [U] broken stones or bricks from a building that has been destroyed: *a pile of rubble*

ru·bel·la /ruː'belə/ *n* [U] *technical* GERMAN MEASLES (=a common illness among children)

ru·by /'ruːbi/ *n* [C,U] a valuable dark red jewel —**ruby** *adj*

ruck·sack /'rʌksæk/ *n* [C] *BrE* a bag you carry on your back ➔ see picture at BAG

rud·der /'rʌdəll-ər/ *n* [C] a flat part at the back of a boat or plane that is turned in order to change the direction in which the boat or plane moves

rud·dy /'rʌdi/ *adj* a ruddy face looks pink and healthy

rude /ruːd/ *adj* **1** speaking or behaving in a way that is not polite: *a rude remark* | *Don't be so rude to your mother!* **2** rude words, jokes, songs etc are about sex or using the toilet, especially in a way that may be offensive to some people: *a rude joke* **3** **a rude awakening** a situation in which someone suddenly realizes that something unpleasant is true —**rudely** *adv* —**rudeness** *n* [U]

ru·di·men·ta·ry /ˌruːdɪ'mentəri◄/ *adj formal* very simple and basic: *a rudimentary knowledge of Chinese*

ru·di·ments /'ruːdɪmənts/ *n* [plural] *formal* the most basic parts of a subject: *They know the rudiments of grammar.*

rue·ful /'ruːfəl/ *adj* showing that you wish something had not happened but that you accept it: *a rueful smile* —**ruefully** *adv*

ruf·fle[1] /'rʌfəl/ *v* [T] **1** to make something that was smooth and neat uneven or untidy: *The wind ruffled his hair.* **2** [usually passive] to offend, annoy, or upset someone: *Don't let yourself get ruffled.*

ruffle[2] *n* [C] cloth sewn in folds as a decoration around the edges of a shirt, skirt etc

rug /rʌg/ *n* [C] **1** a piece of thick cloth or wool that is put on the floor as a decoration ➔ see colour picture on page 474 ➔ compare CARPET **2** *BrE* a type of BLANKET that is used especially to sit on outdoors

rug·by /'rʌgbi/ *n* [U] a game in which two teams carry, kick, or throw an OVAL ball ➔ see colour picture on page 636

rug·ged /'rʌgɪd/ *adj.* **1** rough and uneven and with many large rocks: *a rugged coastline* **2** if a man has a rugged appearance, he is good-looking with strong features: *a rugged face*

3 strongly built: *a rugged vehicle* —**ruggedly** *adv*

ru·in[1] /'ruːɪn/ *v* [T] **1** to spoil or destroy something completely: *Her behaviour ruined the party.* | *On no! My dress is completely ruined.* **2** to make someone lose all their money: *He had been ruined in the Depression of the '30s.*

ruin[2] *n* **1** [U] a situation in which something is damaged, spoiled, or destroyed: **fall into ruin** (=become in a very bad condition): *The old barn has fallen into ruin.* **2** **be in ruins** to be badly damaged: *The country's economy is in ruins.* **3** [U] a situation in which someone loses their social position or money, especially because of a business failure: *financial ruin* **4** [C] also **ruins** [plural] the part of a building that is left after the rest has been destroyed: *the ruins of the Artemis temple*

ru·in·ous /'ruːɪnəs/ *adj* **1** costing much more money that you can afford: *a ruinous court case* **2** extremely damaging: *a ruinous decision*

rule[1] /ruːl/ *n* **1** [C] an instruction that says how something should be done or what is allowed: *Do you know the rules of the game?* | **break a rule** (=disobey a rule): *Well, that's what happens if you break the school rules.* | **be against the rules** *It's against the rules to pick up the ball.* **2** [U] the government or control of a country: *At that time Vietnam was under French rule.* (=was controlled and governed by France) **3** [C] a statement of the correct way of doing something: *the rules of grammar* **4** **the rule** the way things usually are: *Not having a television is the exception rather than the rule.* **5** **as a (general) rule** usually: *As a rule, I try to drink a litre of mineral water a day.* **6** **bend/stretch the rules** to allow something to happen even if it is against the rules: *Can't we bend the rules just this once?* **7** **a rule of thumb** a general principle or method: *As a rule of thumb, a chicken should cook 15 minutes for each pound in weight.*

rule[2] *v* **1** [I,T] to have the official power to control a country: *The King ruled for 30 years.* **2** [I,T] to make an official decision about something such as a legal problem: **+ that** *The judge ruled that the baby should live with his father.* **3** [T] if a feeling or desire rules someone, it has a powerful influence in their life: *Don't let your job rule your life.*

rule sth/sb ↔ out *phr v* [T] to decide that something or someone is not possible or suitable: *We can't rule out the possibility that he may have left the country.*

ruled /ruːld/ *adj* ruled paper has lines printed across it for you to write on

rul·er /'ruːləll-ər/ *n* [C] **1** someone such as a king who has official power over a country **2** a flat narrow piece of plastic, wood, or metal with straight edges that you use for measuring things and drawing straight lines

rul·ing[1] /'ruːlɪŋ/ *n* [C] an official decision, especially one made by a law court: *the Supreme Court's ruling on the case*

ruling[2] *adj* having the most power within a country or organization: *the ruling class*

rum /rʌm/ *n* [C,U] a strong alcoholic drink made from sugar

rum·ble /'rʌmbəl/ *v* [I] to make a continuous low sound: *Thunder rumbled in the distance.* | *My* *stomach was rumbling, I was so hungry.* —**rumble** *n* [singular]

rum·bling /'rʌmblɪŋ/ *n* [C] **1** a long low sound **2** a sign that people are starting to become annoyed or that a difficult situation is developing: +**of** *rumblings of discontent*

ru·mi·nate /'ruːmɪ̹neɪt/ *v* [I] *formal* to think about something carefully

rum·mage /'rʌmɪdʒ/ *v* [I] to search for something by moving things around: *Kerry was rummaging through a drawer looking for a pen.*

rummage sale /'.. ./ *n* [C] *AmE* an event at which old clothes, furniture, toys etc are sold; JUMBLE SALE *BrE*

ru·mour *BrE*, **rumor** *AmE* /'ruːməll-ər/ *n* [C,U] information that is passed from one person to another and may not be true: *There are rumours that the President may have to resign.* | *At the moment, the reports are nothing more than rumour.*

ru·moured *BrE*, **rumored** *AmE* /'ruːmədll-ərd/ *adj* if something is rumoured to be true, people are saying that it may be true but no one is sure: *It was rumoured that a magazine offered £10,000 for her story.*

rump /rʌmp/ *n* [C,U] the part of an animal that is just above its back legs

run[1] /rʌn/ *v* **ran** /ræn/, **run**, **running 1** [I] to move very quickly, moving your legs faster than when you walk: *Some kids were running down the street.* | *If we run, we can still catch the bus.* | *Duncan's running in the marathon.* (=he is taking part in that race) ➡ see colour picture on page 670 **2** [T] to control, organize, or operate a business, organization, activity etc: *My parents run their own business.* | *They run full-time and part-time courses of study.* **3** [I] to move somewhere quickly: *A car ran off the road right here.* **4** [T] to move your fingers or an object through or over something: *She ran her fingers through her hair.* | *Run the highlighter over the chosen text.* **5** [I,T] if a machine, engine, or other piece of equipment runs, or if someone runs it, it is working: *Dad left the engine running.* | **run on coal/petrol/batteries etc** (=use coal, petrol etc to work) **6** [I,T] to go in a particular direction: *The road runs along the coast.* **7** [I,T] to flow or to make water flow: *Tears ran down her face.* | *Who left the water running?* | *I'm just running a bath.* (=filling it with water) | **sb's nose is running** (=liquid is coming out and it needs wiping) **8** [T] to start or use a computer PROGRAM: *You can run this software on any PC.* **9** [I,T] to print or broadcast a story, piece of news etc, or to be printed or broadcast: *They ran the item on the 6 o'clock news.* **10 run smoothly/run according to plan** to happen in the way that you want or expect: *The tour guide helps to keep things running smoothly.* **11** [I] to try to get elected: +**for** *He is running for President.* **12** [I] to go from one place to another at regular times: *Subway trains run every 7 minutes.* **13 run late/on time etc** to do something late, at the right time etc: *Sorry you had to wait – I've been running late all day.* **14** [I] to conti-

nue to be performed or used for a period of time: +**for** *The play ran for two years.* **15** [T] to use and pay for something: *I can't afford to run a car.* **16** [T] to drive someone somewhere: *I'll run you home if you like.* **17** [I] if a colour runs, it spreads to other parts of a piece of material when it is washed **18 be running short/low** to have very little of something left: *I'm running short of money.* **19 run in the family** if something such as a quality, disease, or skill runs in the family, many people in that family have it **20 be running at** to be at a particular level: *Inflation was running at 20% a year.*

run across sb/sth *phr v* [T] to meet or find someone or something by chance: *I ran across my old school photos the other day.*

run after sb/sth *phr v* [T] to chase someone or something: *She started to leave, but Smith ran after her.*

run away *phr v* [I] to leave a place in order to escape from someone or something: *Kathy ran away from home at the age of 16.*

run by sb *phr v* [T] *informal* to ask or tell someone about something in order to find out their opinion about it: *Can you run that by me again?*

run down *phr v* **1** [T **run** sb ↔ **down**] to hit a person or animal with a car: *A man was arrested for attempting to run down a police officer.* **2** [I,T **run** sth ↔ **down**] to gradually lose power, or to make something do this: *Don't leave it switched on – you'll run down the batteries.* **3** [T **run** sb ↔ **down**] to criticize someone or something: *Her boyfriend's always running her down.*

run into *phr v* [T] **1** [**run into** sb] *informal* to meet someone by chance: *I run into her sometimes on campus.* **2 run into trouble/ problems/debt etc** to begin to have trouble, problems etc: *She ran into trouble when she couldn't get a work permit.* **3** [**run into** sb/sth] to hit someone or something with a car: *He lost control and ran into another car.*

run off *phr v* [I] to leave a place or person when you should not: *Our dog keeps running off.*

run off with *phr v* [T] **1** [**run off with** sb] to go away with someone that you are having a sexual relationship with: *Her husband ran off with his secretary.* **2** [**run off with** sth] to take or steal something: *Looters smashed windows and ran off with TVs and videos.*

run out *phr v* [I] **1** to use all of something, so that there is none left: +**of** *We've run out of sugar.* | *I'm running out of ideas.* **2** to come to an end, or no longer be useful or acceptable: *Time is running out.* | *My membership runs out in September.*

run sb/sth ↔ **over** *phr v* [T] to hit someone or something with your car, and drive over them: *I think you just ran over some broken glass.*

run through sth *phr v* [T] **1** to read, check, or practise something quickly: *I'd like to run through the questions again before you start.*

SPELLING NOTE

Words with the sound /r/, may be spelt **wr-**, like **wrong**.

2 to exist in many parts of something: *the prejudices that run through society*

run up sth *phr v* [T] to make a debt, cost etc increase: *We ran up a huge phone bill.*

run up against sth *phr v* [T] to suddenly have to deal with something difficult: *The team ran up against tough opposition.*

run[2] *n* **1** [C] when someone runs, or the distance that someone runs: *He usually goes for a run before breakfast.* | *a five-mile run* **2** [C] a point in a game such as BASEBALL or CRICKET **3** **in the short/long run** in the near future, or later in the future: *Wood is more expensive, but in the long run it's better value.* **4** [C] a period of time during which a play, film, or television show is shown or performed regularly: *The play starts an 8-week run on Friday.* **5** **be on the run** to be trying to escape from someone, especially the police **6** **a run on** sth when a lot of people suddenly buy something at the same time: *a run on swimwear in hot weather* **7** **a run of good luck/bad luck etc** a period when you are lucky or unlucky many times: *She has had a run of bad luck recently.* **8** [C] an area or track: *a chicken run* | *a ski run* **9** **make a run for it** to try to escape by suddenly running away **10** [C] *AmE* a line where TIGHTS, STOCKINGS etc are torn; LADDER *BrE* → see also **RUNS**

run·a·way[1] /ˈrʌnəweɪ/ *adj* [only before noun] **1** moving fast and out of control: *a runaway train* **2** happening quickly and suddenly: *a runaway success*

runaway[2] *n* [C] someone, especially a child, who has left home, school etc

run·down /ˈrʌndaʊn/ *n* [C] a quick report or explanation: *Can you give me a rundown on what happened while I was away?*

run-down /ˌ. ˈ.◂/ *adj* **1** in very bad condition: *a run-down apartment block in Brooklyn* **2** feeling tired and ill: *He's been feeling run-down lately.*

rung[1] /rʌŋ/ *v* the past participle of RING

rung[2] *n* [C] **1** one of the steps of a LADDER **2** *informal* a particular level or position in an organization: *I started on the bottom rung in the company.*

run-in /ˈ. ./ *n* [C] an argument with someone in authority: *He was fired after he had a run-in with his boss.*

run·ner /ˈrʌnəll-ər/ *n* [C] **1** someone who runs as a sport: *a long-distance runner* **2** a long thin piece of wood or metal on the bottom of something such as a SLEDGE that helps it move more easily **3** **gun/drug runner** someone who illegally takes guns or drugs from one country to another

runner bean /ˌ.. ˈ./ *n* [C] a type of long green bean

runner-up /ˌ.. ˈ./ *n* [C], *plural* **runners-up** the person or team that finishes second in a competition

run·ning[1] /ˈrʌnɪŋ/ *n* [U] **1** the activity of running: *a running track* | **go running** *Do you want to go running?* **2** **be in the running/out of the running** to have some chance or no chance of winning or being successful: *Is Sam still in the running for the swimming team?*

running[2] *adj* **1** **running water** water that flows from a TAP: *hot and cold running water* **2** a **running battle/argument** an argument that continues or is repeated over a long period of time: *I'm having a running battle with my dad about how often I can go out.* **3** **a running commentary** a spoken description of an event while it is happening **4** **a running total** a total that gets bigger as new amounts are added to it

running[3] *adv* **three years/five times etc running** for three years, five times etc without a change: *This is the fourth day running that it has rained.*

running costs /ˈ.. ./ *n* [plural] the amount of money you have to pay to operate something

run·ny /ˈrʌni/ *adj informal* **1** a **runny** nose or runny eyes have liquid coming out of them because you are ill **2** something that is runny has become too liquid or contains too much liquid: *The sauce is far too runny.*

run-of-the-mill /ˌ. . . ˈ.◂/ *adj* not special or interesting; ORDINARY: *a run-of-the-mill Hollywood movie*

runs /rʌnz/ *n* **the runs** *informal* DIARRHOEA

run-up /ˈ. ./ *n* **the run-up to** the period just before an important event: *the run-up to the election*

run·way /ˈrʌnweɪ/ *n* [C] a long wide road that planes land on and take off from → see colour picture on page 669

rup·ture /ˈrʌptʃəll-ər/ *v* [I,T] to break open violently: *An oil pipeline ruptured early this morning.* —**rupture** *n* [C,U]

ru·ral /ˈrʊərəlll-ˈrʊr-/ *adj* relating to or happening in the country rather than in the city: *a peaceful rural setting* | *scenes from rural life* → compare URBAN

ruse /ruːzllruːs, ruːz/ *n* [C] a clever trick

rush[1] /rʌʃ/ *v* **1** [I] to move or go somewhere quickly; HURRY: *There's no need to rush – we have plenty of time.* | **rush into/along/from etc** *David rushed into the bathroom.* **2** **rush to do** sth to do something eagerly and without delay: *Everyone was rushing to buy the new album.* **3** [I,T] to do something quickly; HURRY: *Don't rush your food.* **4** [T] to take or send a person or thing somewhere very quickly: **rush sb/sth to/away etc** *We had to rush Helen to the hospital.* **5** [T] to try to make someone hurry to do something more quickly than they want to: *Don't rush me – let me think.*

rush around *phr v* [I] to try to go to a lot of places or do a lot of things in a short period of time

rush into sth *phr v* [T] to get involved in something, without thinking carefully enough about it first: *He's asked me to marry him, but I don't want to rush into it.* | **rush sb into** sth (=make someone rush into something): *Don't let your parents rush you into doing a course that you don't really like.*

rush[2] *n* **1** [singular] a sudden fast movement, especially by a crowd: **make a rush for** sth *We all made a rush for the seats at the front.* **2** [singular, U] a situation in which you need to hurry: *We have plenty of time. There's no rush.* | **be in a rush** *I can't stop – I'm in a rush.* | **a rush to do** sth *There's a big rush to get tickets.* **3** **the rush** the time when a lot of people are doing something, for example travelling or shopping: *the Christmas rush* **4** [C usually plural] a tall grass or plant that grows near a river and is used to make baskets etc

rushed /rʌʃt/ *adj* **1** done too quickly and without enough care: *Your work always looks rushed and badly presented.* **2 rushed off your feet** extremely busy and therefore having to hurry

rush hour /'. ./ *n* [C,U] the time of day when there is a lot of traffic because people are going to and from work

rust¹ /rʌst/ *n* [U] the reddish-brown substance that forms on iron, steel etc when it gets wet

rust² *v* [I,T] to become covered with rust, or to make rust form on something: *The lock on the door had rusted.*

rus·tic /'rʌstɪk/ *adj* simple and old-fashioned in a way that is attractive and typical of the country: *a rustic mountain cabin*

rus·tle /'rʌsəl/ *v* [I,T] if papers, dry leaves etc rustle, or if you rustle them, they make a soft noise as they move against each other: *the sound of kids rustling ice-cream wrappers* ➡ see colour picture on page 635 —**rustle** *n* [singular]

rustle sth ↔ **up** *phr v* [T] *informal* to make something quickly, especially food for a meal

rust·y /'rʌsti/ *adj* **1** covered with rust: *rusty nails* **2** if a skill someone has is rusty, it is not as good as it once was because they have not used it for a long time: *My tennis is a little rusty.*

rut /rʌt/ *n* **1 in a rut** *informal* living or working in a boring situation that you cannot easily change: *Margaret felt she was stuck in a rut.* **2** [C] a deep narrow track left in the ground by a wheel

ru·ta·ba·ga /ˌruːtə'beɪgə/ *n* [C,U] *AmE* a round yellow vegetable that grows under the ground; SWEDE *BrE*

ruth·less /'ruːθləs/ *adj* cruel, and not caring if you harm other people in order to get what you want: *a ruthless dictator* —**ruthlessly** *adv* —**ruthlessness** *n* [U]

rye /raɪ/ *n* [U] a type of grain that is used for making bread and WHISKY

R

Ss

S, s /es/ the letter 's'

S the written abbreviation of SOUTH or SOUTHERN

-'s /z, s/ **1** the short form of 'is' or 'has': *What's that?|He's gone out.* **2** used to show the POSSESSIVE form of nouns: *Bill is one of Jason's friends.* **3** the short form of 'us', used only with 'let's': *Let's go!*

USAGE NOTE: 's and s'

Use **'s** at the end of a word to show that something belongs to a particular person: *Mary's book | His mother's car.* Use **s'** when the plural noun ends in 's': *our parents' house | the dogs' food.* Use **'s** after a person's name, even if it ends in 's': *Ms Collins's office | Kris's new boyfriend.*

Sab·bath /ˈsæbəθ/ *n* **the Sabbath** the day of the week that Jews and Christians have as a day for resting and praying. The Sabbath is on Sunday for Christians, and on Saturday for Jews.

sab·bat·i·cal /səˈbætɪkəl/ *n* [C,U] a period when someone, especially a university teacher, stops doing their usual work to travel or study: **on sabbatical** *The professor is on sabbatical for two months.*

sab·o·tage /ˈsæbətɑːʒ/ *v* [T] **1** to secretly damage or destroy something so that an enemy cannot use it: *The plane had been sabotaged and it exploded in mid-air.* **2** to secretly spoil someone's plans or spoil what they are doing because you do not want them to succeed: *Mr Trimble denied he was trying to sabotage the talks.* —**sabotage** *n* [U] *deliberate acts of sabotage*

sa·bre *BrE,* **saber** *AmE* /ˈseɪbəll-ər/ *n* [C] a military sword

sac /sæk/ *n* [C] *technical* a small bag inside a plant or animal that contains air or liquid

sac·cha·rin /ˈsækərɪn/ *n* [U] a chemical that tastes very sweet and is used in food instead of sugar

sach·et /ˈsæʃeɪllsæˈʃeɪ/ *n* [C] a small bag containing a liquid or powder: *a sachet of shampoo* → see picture at CONTAINER

sack[1] /sæk/ *n* **1** [C] a large bag made of strong cloth, plastic, or paper in which you carry or store things: *a sack of potatoes* **2 get the sack/give sb the sack** *BrE* to be told to leave your job or to tell someone to leave **3 hit the sack** *spoken* to go to bed

sack[2] *v* [T] **1** *BrE* to tell someone to leave their job; FIRE: *Campbell was sacked for coming in drunk.* **2** if an army sacks a place, the soldiers go through it, destroying and stealing things

sac·ra·ment /ˈsækrəmənt/ *n* [C] an important Christian ceremony such as marriage or COMMUNION

sa·cred /ˈseɪkrɪd/ *adj* relating to a god or religion, and believed to be holy or extremely important: *In India the cow is a sacred animal.*

sac·ri·fice[1] /ˈsækrɪfaɪs/ *n* [C,U] **1** when you give up something important or valuable in order to get something that is more important:

make a sacrifice *Her parents made a lot of sacrifices to give her a good education.* **2** when something is offered to God in a ceremony, especially an animal that is killed —**sacrificial** /ˌsækrɪˈfɪʃəl/ *adj*

sacrifice[2] *v* **1** [T] to give up something important or valuable in order to get something: **sacrifice sth for sth** *It's not worth sacrificing your health for your job.* **2** [I,T] to offer something, especially an animal, to a god in a ceremony, often by killing it

sac·ri·lege /ˈsækrɪlɪdʒ/ *n* [C,U] when something holy or important is treated in a way that does not show respect: *It would be sacrilege to demolish such a beautiful building.* —**sacrilegious** /ˌsækrɪˈlɪdʒəs/ *adj*

sac·ro·sanct /ˈsækrəʊsæŋktll-krəʊ-/ *adj* too important to be changed or criticized in any way: *Though a busy politician, his time with his family is sacrosanct.*

sad /sæd/ *adj* **1** unhappy or making you feel unhappy: *Linda looks very sad today.|What a sad story!* **+ that** *It was sad that Jane couldn't come with us.* **be sad to do sth** *I liked my school, and I was sad to leave.* → see colour picture on page 277 → opposite HAPPY **2** very bad or unacceptable: *It's a sad state of affairs when a person isn't safe in her own home.* **3** *spoken informal* boring and not popular or fashionable: *It's a bit sad staying home on Saturday night isn't it?|What a sad guy!* —**sadness** *n* [U]

sad·den /ˈsædn/ *v* [T] *formal* to make someone feel sad or disappointed: *They were shocked and saddened by his death.*

sad·dle[1] /ˈsædl/ *n* [C] **1** a seat made of leather that is put on a horse's back so that you can ride it **2** a seat on a bicycle or a MOTORCYCLE

saddle[2] also **saddle up** *v* [I,T] to put a saddle on a horse

saddle sb with sth *phr v* [T] to make someone have to deal with a difficult or boring job, or pay a lot of money: *In the '70s many African countries became saddled with huge debts.*

sa·dis·m /ˈseɪdɪzəm/ *n* [U] when someone gets enjoyment or sexual pleasure from being cruel or violent: *a sadistic boss* —**sadist** *n* [C] —**sadistic** /səˈdɪstɪk/ *adj* → compare MASOCHISM

sad·ly /ˈsædli/ *adv* **1** in a sad way: *Jimmy nodded sadly.* **2** unfortunately: *Sadly, the concert was cancelled.* **3** in a way that seems wrong or bad: *Politeness is sadly lacking these days.|You're sadly mistaken if you think Anne will help.*

sae /ˌes eɪ ˈiː/ *n* [C] *BrE* stamped addressed envelope; an envelope that you put your name and address and a stamp on, so that someone can send you something in it

sa·fa·ri /səˈfɑːri/ *n* [C,U] a trip through the country areas of Africa in order to watch wild animals: **on safari** *a vacation on safari in Kenya*

safe[1] /seɪf/ *adj* **1** not in danger of being harmed: *I won't feel safe until the plane lands.|Have a safe trip!* **+ from** *The city is now safe from further attack.* **2** not harmed or damaged: **safe and sound** (=not harmed or damaged in any way): *Both children were found safe and sound.* **3** not likely to injure or harm anyone: *She's one of the safest drivers I know.|* **safe to do sth** *Is it safe to swim here?* **4** a safe place is one where something is not likely to be stolen or lost: *Keep your passport in a safe place.* **5** not likely to be wrong or to fail: *Gold is a safe investment.* | *I think it's a safe bet that he'll remember.* **6 just to be safe/to be on the safe side** to be careful and not take any risks: *Take some extra money with you, just to be on the safe side.* **7 in safe hands** with someone who will look after you well —**safely** *adv*: *Drive safely!* | *Did the package arrive safely?*

safe² *n* [C] a strong metal box or cupboard with a lock on it, where you keep money and valuable things

safe·guard /'seɪfgɑːd‖-gɑːrd/ *n* [C] a law, agreement etc that protects someone or something: *Copy the data as a safeguard against loss or damage.* —**safeguard** *v* [T] *laws to safeguard endangered animals*

safe ha·ven /ˌ. '../ *n* [C] a place where someone can go to escape from danger

safe·keep·ing /ˌseɪfˈkiːpɪŋ/ *n* **for safekeeping** if you put something somewhere for safekeeping, you put it in a place where it will not get damaged, lost, or stolen

safe·ty /'seɪfti/ *n* [U] **1** when people are safe from danger or harm: *Hundreds of people were led to safety after the explosion.* | *road safety* **2** how safe someone or something is: *There are fears for the safety of the hostages.*

safety belt /'.. ./ *n* [C] a SEAT BELT

safety net /'.. ./ *n* [C] **1** a system that helps people when they are too ill, poor etc to help themselves: *the safety net of unemployment pay and pensions* **2** a large net used for catching someone if they fall from a high place

safety pin /'.. ./ *n* [C] a wire pin with a cover that its point fits into

safety valve /'.. ./ *n* [C] **1** something that prevents a dangerous situation developing **2** a part of a machine that allows gas, steam etc to be let out when the pressure is too high

sag /sæg/ *v* [I] **-gged, -gging** to sink or bend down: *The branches sagged under the weight of the snow.*

sa·ga /'sɑːgə/ *n* [C] a long story or a description of a long series of events

sage¹ /seɪdʒ/ *n* **1** [U] a plant used to give flavour to food **2** [C] *literary* someone who is very wise

sage² *adj literary* very wise, especially as a result of age and experience —**sagely** *adv*

Sa·git·tar·i·us /ˌsædʒ‖'teəriəs‖-'ter-/ *n* [C,U] the sign of the Zodiac of people who are born between November 22nd and December 21st, or someone who belongs to this sign

said¹ /sed/ *v* the past tense and past participle of SAY

said² *adj formal* used to give more information about something that has just been mentioned: *The said weapon was later found in the defendant's home.*

sail¹ /seɪl/ *v* **1** [I] to travel across water in a boat or ship: *We sailed along the coast of Alaska.* **2** [I,T] to control the movement of a boat or

ship: *The captain sailed the ship safely past the rocks.* | *I'd like to learn how to sail.* **3** [I] to start a trip by boat or ship: *What time do we sail?* **4** [I] to move quickly and gracefully, especially through the air: *The ball sailed past the goalkeeper into the back of the net.*

sail² *n* **1** [C] a large piece of strong cloth fixed onto a boat, so that the wind will push the boat along: *a yacht with white sails* **2 set sail** to begin a trip by boat or ship: *The ship set sail at dawn.*

sail boat /'. ./ *n* [C] a small boat with one or more sails

sail·ing /'seɪlɪŋ/ *n* [U] the activity of sailing in boats

sail·or /'seɪlə‖-ər/ *n* [C] **1** someone who sails on boats or ships, especially as a job → compare SEAMAN **2** someone who is in a navy

saint /seɪnt/ *n* [C] **1** someone who is considered to be very special and holy, especially by the Catholic Church **2** *spoken* someone who is very good, kind, or patient: *You're a real saint to help us like this.* —**sainthood** *n* [U]

saint·ly /'seɪntli/ *adj* very good, kind, and patient

sake /seɪk/ *n* **1 for the sake of** in order to help or improve a situation: *Both sides are willing to take risks for the sake of peace.* **2 for sb's sake** in order to help or please someone: *She only stays with her husband for the children's sake.* **3 for goodness'/Pete's/heaven's etc sake** *spoken* used when you are annoyed or impatient with someone: *Why didn't you tell me, for heaven's sake?*

sal·a·ble, saleable /'seɪləbəl/ *adj* something that is salable can be sold, or is easy to sell: *salable products*

sal·ad /'sæləd/ *n* [C,U] **1** a mixture of vegetables eaten cold and usually RAW: *a salad of lettuce, tomatoes and cucumber* | *a large mixed salad* **2** RAW or cooked food cut into small pieces and served cold: *potato salad*

sal·a·man·der /'sæləmændə‖-ər/ *n* [C] a small animal similar to a LIZARD, that can live in water and on land

sa·la·mi /sə'lɑːmi/ *n* [C,U] a large SAUSAGE with a strong taste which is cut into thin pieces before being eaten

sal·a·ried /'sælərid/ *adj* receiving a salary: *salaried workers*

sal·a·ry /'sæləri/ *n* [C,U] money that you receive every month as payment from the organization you work for: *She earns a good salary.*

sale /seɪl/ *n* **1** [C,U] an act of selling something, or when something is sold: *The sale of alcohol to under-18s is forbidden.* | **make a sale** (=sell something) **2 for sale** available to be bought: *Is this table for sale?* | **put sth up for sale** (=make something): *They had to put their home up for sale.* **3** [C] a time when a shop sells its goods at lower prices than usual: *There's a great sale on at Macy's now.* **4 on sale** available to be bought in a shop, or available for a lower price

---

SPELLING NOTE
Words with the sound /s/, may be spelt c-, like **city**, or ps-, like **psychology**.

S

than usual: *Don's found a really good CD player on sale.*

sales /seɪlz/ n **1** [plural] the total amount of something that is sold, or the money made from it: *Company sales were down 15% last year.* (=they were 15% lower) **2** [U] the part of a company that deals with selling products: *Sally got a job as sales manager.*

sales as·sis·tant /ˈ. .ˌ.../, **sales clerk** /ˈ. ./ *AmE* n [C] someone who sells things in a shop; SHOP ASSISTANT *BrE*

sales·man /ˈseɪlzmən/ n [C] a man whose job is to sell things: *a car salesman*

sales·per·son /ˈseɪlzpɜːsən‖-ɜːr-/ n [C] someone whose job is to sell things

sales rep·re·sen·ta·tive /ˈ. ...ˌ.../ also **sales rep** /ˈ. ./ n [C] someone who travels around an area selling their company's products

sales slip /ˈ. ./ n [C] *especially AmE* a small piece of paper that you are given in a shop when you buy something; RECEIPT

sales·wom·an /ˈseɪlzˌwʊmən/ n [C] a woman whose job is selling things

sa·li·ent /ˈseɪliənt/ adj *formal* the salient points or features of something are the most noticeable or important ones — **salience** n [U]

sa·line /ˈseɪlaɪn/ adj containing salt: *a saline solution* (=liquid with salt in it)

sa·li·va /səˈlaɪvə/ n [U] the liquid that is produced naturally in your mouth

sal·i·vate /ˈsælɪveɪt/ v [I] to produce more saliva in your mouth than usual, especially because you see or smell food

sal·low /ˈsæləʊ‖-loʊ/ adj sallow skin looks slightly yellow and unhealthy

salm·on /ˈsæmən/ n [C,U] a large fish with silver skin and pink flesh: *smoked salmon | a salmon river*

sal·on /ˈsælɒn‖səˈlɑːn/ n [C] a place where you can get your hair cut, have BEAUTY TREATMENTs etc: *a beauty salon*

sa·loon /səˈluːn/ n [C] **1** a place where alcoholic drinks were sold and drunk in the US in the 19th century **2** *BrE* a car that has a separate enclosed space for bags, cases etc; SEDAN *AmE*: *a four-door saloon* **3** **saloon bar** *BrE* a comfortable room in a PUB

sal·sa /ˈsælsə‖ˈsɑːl-/ n [U] **1** a hot-tasting SAUCE **2** a type of Latin American dance music

salt¹ /sɔːlt‖sɒlt/ n [U] **1** a natural white mineral that is added to food to make it taste better: *Add a pinch of salt to the mixture.* (=a small amount) | *Could you pass me the salt, please.* ➡ see colour picture on page 440 **2** **take sth with a pinch/grain of salt** to not completely believe what someone tells you because you have reason to think that it might not be true **3** *technical* a type of chemical formed by combining an acid with another substance

salt² v [T] to add salt to food — **salted** adj: *salted peanuts*

salt³ adj **1** preserved by salt: *salt pork* **2** containing salt: *salt lake | salt water*

salt cel·lar /ˈ. ˌ../ *BrE*, **salt shak·er** /ˈ. ˌ../ *AmE* n [C] a small container for salt

salt·wa·ter /ˈsɔːlt,wɔːtə‖-,wɒːtər, -,wɑː-/ adj living in salty water: *saltwater fish*

salt·y /ˈsɔːlti‖ˈsɒlti/ adj tasting of or containing salt — **saltiness** n [U]

sa·lute¹ /səˈluːt/ v [I,T] to move your right hand to your head to show respect to an officer in the army, navy etc

salute² n [C] **1** when someone salutes another person of higher rank, for example an officer in the army, navy etc **2** when guns are fired into the air as part of a military ceremony: *a 21-gun salute*

sal·vage¹ /ˈsælvɪdʒ/ v [T] to save something from a situation in which other things have already been damaged, destroyed, or lost: *Farmers are trying to salvage their wheat after the heavy rains.*

salvage² n [U] **1** when things are saved from being destroyed, damaged, or lost: *a salvage operation* **2** the things that are saved from being destroyed, damaged, or lost

sal·va·tion /sælˈveɪʃən/ n [U] **1** the state of being saved from evil by God, according to the Christian religion **2** something that prevents danger, loss, or failure: *Donations of food and clothing have been the salvation of the refugees.*

Salvation Ar·my /.ˌ.. ˈ../ n **the Salvation Army** a Christian organization that tries to help poor people

salve¹ /sælv, sɑːv‖sæv/ n [C,U] a substance that you put on sore skin to make it less painful: *lip salve*

salve² v [T] **salve your conscience** to make yourself feel less guilty about something you have done wrong

same /seɪm/ adj, pron **1** **the same** not changed or different: *They go to the same place for their vacation every summer.* | *Kim's birthday and Roger's are on the same day.* **2** **the same** used to say that two people or things are exactly like each other: **the same ... as** *She does the same job as I do, but in a bigger company.* | **look/sound/taste etc the same** *Classical music all sounds the same to me.* **3** **at the same time** if two things happen at the same time they happen together: *How can you type and talk at the same time?* **4** **the same old story/excuse etc** *informal* something that you have heard many times before: *It's the same old story – his wife didn't understand him.* **5** **be in the same boat** to be in the same difficult situation that someone else is in **6** **same here** *spoken* used in order to say that you feel the same way as someone else: *"I hate shopping malls." "Same here."*

same·ness /ˈseɪmnɪs/ n [U] when everything is the same and is therefore boring

sam·ple¹ /ˈsɑːmpəl‖ˈsæm-/ n [C] a small part or amount of something that is examined or tried to find out what the rest is like: *Do you have a sample of your work? | free samples of a new shampoo | We asked a sample of 500 college students whether they had ever taken drugs.*

sample² v [T] **1** to taste food or drink to see what it is like: *We sampled several local cheeses.* **2** to do something for the first time to see what it is like: *Win a chance to sample the exotic nightlife of Paris!*

san·a·to·ri·um /ˌsænəˈtɔːriəm/ also **sani·tarium** n [C] a hospital for people who are getting better but still need rest and care

sanc·ti·fy /ˈsæŋktɪfaɪ/ v [T] **1** to say that something is socially and morally acceptable:

sarcasm

The law as it is seems to sanctify the use of violence against children. **2** to make something holy

sanc·ti·mo·ni·ous /ˌsæŋktɪˈməʊniəs◂ ‖-ˈmoʊ-/ *adj* behaving as if you were morally better than other people: *a long and sanctimonious speech* —**sanctimoniously** *adv*

sanc·tion¹ /ˈsæŋkʃən/ *n* **1** [U] official permission or approval: *The protest march was held without government sanction.* **2** [C] something such as a punishment that makes people obey a rule or law: *severe sanctions against those who avoid paying taxes* → see also SANCTIONS

sanction² *v* [T] *formal* to officially approve of or allow something: *The UN refused to sanction the use of force.*

sanc·tions /ˈsæŋkʃənz/ *n* [plural] official action taken by a government making trade with another country illegal, as a way of forcing its leaders to make political changes: *a call for sanctions against countries that use torture*

sanc·ti·ty /ˈsæŋktɪ̩ti/ *n* **the sanctity of sth** the quality that makes something so important that it must be respected and preserved: *the sanctity of marriage*

sanc·tu·a·ry /ˈsæŋktʃuəri, -tʃərɪ‖-tʃueri/ *n* **1** [C,U] a peaceful place that is safe and provides protection, especially for people who are in danger: *The rebel leader took sanctuary in the French embassy.* **2** [C] an area for birds or animals where they are protected and cannot be hunted

sanc·tum /ˈsæŋktəm/ *n* **1 the inner sanctum** *often humorous* a place that only a few important people are allowed to enter: *We were only allowed into the director's inner sanctum for a few minutes.* **2** [C] a holy place inside a TEMPLE

sand¹ /sænd/ *n* [U] the substance that forms deserts and BEACHes, which consists of many small grains or rocks or minerals → see colour picture on page 243

sand² *v* [T] to make a surface smooth by rubbing it with SANDPAPER

san·dal /ˈsændl/ *n* [C] a light open shoe that you wear in warm weather: *a pair of leather sandals* → see picture at SHOE

sand·bag¹ /ˈsændbæg/ *n* [C] a bag filled with sand, used for protection against floods, explosions etc

sandbag² *v* [I,T] **-gged, -gging** *AmE* to deliberately do something to prevent a process from being successful, especially in politics: *Senator Murphy has been accused of sandbagging the investigation.*

sand·bank /ˈsændbæŋk/ *n* [C] a raised area of sand in a river, sea etc

sand·box /ˈsændbɒks‖-bɑːks/ *n* [C] *AmE* a sandpit

sand·cas·tle /ˈsænd,kɑːsəl‖-,kæ-/ *n* [C] a small MODEL of a castle made out of sand, usually by children on a BEACH

sand dune /ˈ. ./ *n* [C] a DUNE

sand·pa·per /ˈsændpeɪpə‖-ər/ *n* [U] strong paper covered with a rough substance, used for rubbing wood in order to make it smooth —**sandpaper** *v* [T]

sand·pit /ˈsænd,pɪt/ *BrE*, **sandbox** *AmE* — *n* [C] an enclosed area of sand for children to play in

sand·stone /ˈsændstəʊn‖-stoʊn/ *n* [U] a type of rock formed from sand

sand·storm /ˈsændstɔːm‖-ɔːrm/ *n* [C] a storm in a desert in which sand is blown around by strong wind

sand·trap /ˈsændtræp/ *n* [C] *AmE* a wide hole on a GOLF COURSE filled with sand; BUNKER *BrE*

sand·wich¹ /ˈsænwɪdʒ‖ˈsændwɪtʃ, ˈsænwɪtʃ/ *n* [C] two pieces of bread with cheese, meat, egg etc between them: *chicken sandwiches*

sandwich² *v* [T] **be sandwiched between** to be in a very small space between two other things: *a motorcycle sandwiched between two vans*

sand·y /ˈsændi/ *adj* covered with or containing sand: *a sandy beach* | *sandy soil*

sane /seɪn/ *adj* **1** able to think in a normal and reasonable way → opposite INSANE **2** reasonable and based on sensible thinking: *a sane solution to a difficult problem*

sang /sæŋ/ *v* the past tense of SING

san·i·tar·i·um /ˌsænɪˈteəriəm‖-ˈter-/ *n* [C] a SANATORIUM

san·i·ta·ry /ˈsænɪtərɪ‖-teri/ *adj* **1** relating to health, especially to the removal of dirt, infection, or human waste: *Workers complained about sanitary arrangements at the factory.* **2** clean and not involving any danger to your health: *All food is stored under sanitary conditions.*

sanitary tow·el *BrE* /ˈ.... ,../, **sanitary napkin** *AmE* — *n* [C] a piece of soft material that a woman wears when she has her PERIOD, to take up the blood

san·i·ta·tion /ˌsænɪˈteɪʃən/ *n* [U] the protection of public health by removing and treating waste, dirty water etc

san·i·tize (also **-ise** *BrE*) /ˈsænɪtaɪz/ *v* [T] to make news, literature etc less offensive or shocking by taking out anything unpleasant

san·i·ty /ˈsænɪti/ *n* [U] **1** the ability to think in a normal and reasonable way: *I went away for the weekend to try and keep my sanity.* **2** the condition of being mentally healthy: *He lost his sanity after his children were killed.*

sank /sæŋk/ *v* the past tense of SINK

San·ta Claus /ˈsæntə klɔːz‖ˈsænti klɔːz, ˈsæntə-/ also **Santa** /ˈsæntə/ *n* [singular] an old man with red clothes and a long white BEARD, who children believe brings them presents at Christmas; FATHER CHRISTMAS *BrE*

sap¹ /sæp/ *n* **1** [U] the liquid that carries food through a plant **2** [C] *informal* a stupid person who is easy to deceive or treat badly

sap² *v* [T] to gradually make something weaker or destroy it: *The illness sapped her strength.*

sap·ling /ˈsæplɪŋ/ *n* [C] a young tree

sap·phire /ˈsæfaɪə‖-faɪr/ *n* [C,U] a transparent bright blue jewel

sap·py /ˈsæpi/ *adj* *AmE* expressing love and emotions in a way that seems silly: *a sappy love song*

Sa·ran Wrap /səˈræn ræp/ *n* [U] *AmE* trademark thin transparent plastic used for wrapping food; CLINGFILM *BrE*

sar·cas·m /ˈsɑːkæzəm‖ˈsɑːr-/ *n* [U] a way of speaking or writing in which you say the opposite of what you mean in order to make an unkind joke or to show that you are annoyed: *"I'm* *glad you could make it," said Jim, with heavy sarcasm.*

sar·cas·tic /saːˈkæstɪkǁsaːr-/ *adj* using sarcasm: *Do you have to be so sarcastic?* —**sarcastically** /-kli/ *adv*

sar·dine /saːˈdiːnǁsaːr-/ *n* [C,U] **1** a small silver-coloured fish, often sold in cans **2 be packed like sardines** to be in a group of people or things that are placed tightly together in a small space

sar·don·ic /saːˈdɒnɪkǁsaːrˈdɑː-/ *adj* speaking or smiling in an unpleasant way that shows you have no respect for someone or something

sa·ri /ˈsaːri/ *n* [C] a type of loose dress worn especially by Indian women ➔ see colour picture on page 113

sash /sæʃ/ *n* [C] **1** a long piece of cloth that is worn around your waist: *a white dress with a blue sash* **2** a long piece of cloth that is worn over one shoulder and across the chest, especially during a ceremony **3** a frame that has a sheet of glass fixed into it to form part of a window

sass /sæs/ *v* [T] *AmE spoken informal* to talk in a rude way to someone you should respect: *Stop sassing me young lady!*

sas·sy /ˈsæsi/ *adj AmE informal* rude to someone you should respect: *a sassy child*

sat /sæt/ *v* the past tense and past participle of SIT

Sa·tan /ˈseɪtn/ *n* [singular] the DEVIL

sa·tan·ic /səˈtænɪk/ *adj* **1** relating to practices that treat the Devil like a god: *satanic rites* **2** extremely cruel or evil: *satanic laughter*

Sat·an·is·m /ˈseɪtənɪzəm/ *n* [U] the practice of treating the Devil like a god —**satanist** *n* [C]

satch·el /ˈsætʃəl/ *n* [C] a leather bag that you carry over your shoulder, used especially in the past by children for carrying their books to school ➔ see picture at BAG

sat·el·lite /ˈsætəlaɪt/ *n* [C] **1** a machine that is sent into space and travels around the Earth, moon etc, used especially for radio or television communication: *a broadcast coming in live by satellite from South Africa* **2** a moon that moves around a PLANET **3** a country, town, or organization that is controlled by or is part of a larger one

satellite dish /ˈ... ./ *n* [C] a large circular piece of metal that receives the SIGNALs for satellite television ➔ see colour picture on page 79

satellite tel·e·vi·sion /ˌ... ˈ...., ˌ... ..ˈ../ also **satellite TV** /ˌ...ˈ./ *n* [U] television programmes that are broadcast using SATELLITEs in space

sat·in /ˈsætn̩ǁˈsætn/ *n* [U] a type of cloth that is very smooth and shiny

sat·ire /ˈsætaɪəǁ-taɪr/ *n* **1** [U] an amusing way of talking or writing about someone or something, especially so that people see their faults: *political satire* **2** [C] a play, story etc written in this way —**satirical** /səˈtɪrɪkəl/ *adj* —**satirically** /-kli/ *adv*

sat·ir·ize (also **-ise** *BrE*) /ˈsætɪraɪz/ *v* [T] to use SATIRE to make people see someone or something's faults: *a movie satirizing the fashion industry*

sat·is·fac·tion /ˌsætɪsˈfækʃən/ *n* **1** [C,U] a feeling of happiness or pleasure because you have achieved something or got what you

wanted: *He looked around the room with satisfaction.* | *Both leaders expressed satisfaction with the talks.* **2 to sb's satisfaction** as well or completely as someone wants: *I'm not sure I can answer that question to your satisfaction.*

sat·is·fac·to·ry /ˌsætɪsˈfæktəri/ *adj* **1** good enough: *The students are not making satisfactory progress.* **2** making you feel pleased: *a satisfactory result* —**satisfactorily** *adv*

sat·is·fied /ˈsætɪsfaɪd/ *adj* **1** pleased because something has happened in the way that you want, or because you have achieved something: **+ with** *Most of our customers are satisfied with the food we provide.* **2** feeling sure that something is right or true: **+ (that)** *I'm satisfied (that) he's telling the truth.*

sat·is·fy /ˈsætɪsfaɪ/ *v* [T] **1** to make someone happy by providing what they want or need: *She doesn't feel she works hard enough to satisfy her boss.* **2** to provide someone with enough information to show that something is true or has been done correctly: **satisfy sb that** *The evidence isn't enough to satisfy us that he's innocent.* **3** to have achieved a high enough standard: *I'm afraid you haven't satisfied the college entrance requirements.*

sat·is·fy·ing /ˈsætɪsfaɪ-ɪŋ/ *adj* making you feel pleased and happy, especially because you have got what you wanted: *a satisfying career*

sat·u·rate /ˈsætʃəreɪt/ *v* [T] **1** to make something completely wet: *The rain saturated the soil.* **2 be saturated with** to have too much of a particular type of thing, so there is no space for any more —**saturation** /ˌsætʃəˈreɪʃən/ *n* [U] *The number of tourists has now reached saturation point.* (=there is not enough space for any more)

saturated fat /ˌ.... ˈ./ *n* [C,U] a kind of fat from meat and milk products

Sat·ur·day /ˈsætədiǁ-ər-/ written abbreviation **Sat** *n* [C,U] the day of the week between Friday and Sunday ➔ see Usage Note at DAY

Sat·urn /ˈsætən̩ǁ-ərn/ *n* [singular] the second largest PLANET, sixth from the sun

sauce /sɔːsǁsɒːs/ *n* [C,U] a thick cooked liquid that is served with food: *spaghetti with tomato sauce*

sauce·pan /ˈsɔːspæn, -pənǁˈsɒːs-/ *n* [C] a deep round metal container with a handle, used for cooking

sau·cer /ˈsɔːsəǁ-ər/ *n* [C] a small round plate that you put a cup on

sauc·y /ˈsɔːsiǁˈsɒːsi/ *adj* slightly rude, in a way that is amusing: *a saucy look*

sau·er·kraut /ˈsaʊəkraʊtǁ-ər-/ *n* [U] a salty German food made of CABBAGE

sau·na /ˈsaʊnə, ˈsɔːnəǁˈsaʊnə/ *n* [C] **1** a room that is made very hot with steam, where people sit because it is considered healthy **2** the time you spend in a room this this: *It's nice to have a sauna after swimming.*

saun·ter /ˈsɔːntəǁˈsɒːntər/ *v* [I] to walk in a slow and confident way: *He sauntered up to her and grinned.*

saus·age /ˈsɒsɪdʒǁˈsɒː-/ *n* [C,U] a tube-shaped mixture of meat and SPICEs, eaten hot or cold: *beef sausages*

sausage roll /ˌ.. ˈ./ *n* [C] a small quantity of sausage meat wrapped in PASTRY, eaten as a SNACK

sau·té /ˈsəʊteɪ‖soʊˈteɪ/ v [T] to cook something in hot oil or fat

sav·age[1] /ˈsævɪdʒ/ adj **1** very cruel and violent: *savage fighting* **2** criticizing someone or something very severely: *a savage attack on the newspaper industry* **3** very severe and harmful: *savage measures to control begging* —**savagely** adv

savage[2] n [C] *old-fashioned* an insulting word for someone from a country where the way of living is simple and undeveloped

savage[3] v [T] **1** to attack someone violently, causing serious injuries: *The little girl was savaged by the family dog.* **2** to criticize someone or something very severely: *a movie savaged by the critics*

sav·age·ry /ˈsævɪdʒəri/ n [U] extremely cruel and violent behaviour

save[1] /seɪv/ v **1** [T] to make someone or something safe from danger, harm, or destruction: *The new speed limit should save more lives.* | **save sb/sth from** *Only three people were saved from the fire.* **2** [I,T] also **save up** to keep money so that you can use it later: *I'm saving up to buy a car.* | *Brian's saved $6,000 to put towards a new house.* **3** [T] to use less time, money, energy etc, so that you do not waste any: *We'll save time if we take a taxi.* **4** [T] to keep something so that you can use or enjoy it in the future: *Let's save the rest of the pie for later.* **5** [T] to help someone by making it unnecessary for them to do something unpleasant or inconvenient: *If you could pick up the medicine, it would save me a trip to the pharmacy.* **6** [T] also **save** sth ↔ **up** to keep all the objects of a particular kind that you can find, so that they can be used for a particular purpose: *She's saving foreign coins for her son's collection.* **7** [T] to stop people from using something, so that it is available for someone else: *We'll save you a seat in the theatre.* **8** [I,T] to make a computer keep the work that you have done on it **9** [T] to stop someone getting a GOAL in games such as football or HOCKEY → see also **lose/save face** (FACE[1])

save on sth *phr v* [T] to avoid wasting something by using as little of it as possible: *We turn the heat off at night to save on electricity.*

save[2] n [C] an action by the GOALKEEPER in football, HOCKEY etc that prevents the other team from getting a GOAL

sav·er /ˈseɪvəl-ər/ n [C] someone who saves money in a bank

sav·ing /ˈseɪvɪŋ/ n **1 savings** [plural] all the money that you have saved: *He has savings of over $150,000.* | *a savings account* **2** [C, usually singular] an amount of something that you have not used or do not have to spend: **+ on** *Enjoy a 25% saving on prices.*

saving grace /ˌ.. ˈ./ n [C] a good quality that makes something not completely bad: *The movie's only saving grace is its beautiful scenery.*

savings and loan as·so·ci·a·tion /ˌ.. ˈ. ... ˌ.-/ n [C] *AmE* a type of bank where you can save money or borrow money to buy a house; BUILDING SOCIETY *BrE*

sa·viour *BrE*, **savior** *AmE* /ˈseɪvjəl-ər/ n **1** [C] someone or something that saves you from a difficult or dangerous situation: *The country is searching for some kind of economic saviour.* **2** **the/our Saviour** another name for Jesus Christ, used in the Christian religion

sa·vour *BrE*, **savor** *AmE* /ˈseɪvəl-ər/ v [T] to make an activity or experience last as long as you can, because you are enjoying every moment of it: *Drink it slowly and savour every drop.*

sa·vour·y *BrE*, **savory** *AmE* /ˈseɪvəri/ adj having a pleasant but not sweet taste: *a savoury snack* → see also UNSAVOURY

saw[1] /sɔː‖sɒː/ v the past tense of SEE

saw[2] n [C] a tool that has a flat blade with a row of sharp points, used for cutting wood → see picture at TOOLS

saw[3] v [I,T] **sawed, sawed** or **sawn** /sɔːn‖sɒːn/ **sawing** to cut something using a saw: *Dad was outside sawing logs.* | **+ off** *We decided to saw off the lower branches of the apple tree.*

saw·dust /ˈsɔːdʌst‖ˈsɒː-/ n [U] very small pieces of wood that are left when you cut wood with a saw

saw·mill /ˈsɔːmɪl‖ˈsɒː-/ n [C] a factory where trees are cut into boards

sax /sæks/ n [C] *informal* a saxophone

sax·o·phone /ˈsæksəfəʊn‖-foʊn/ n [C] a metal musical instrument that you play by blowing into it and pressing buttons, used especially in JAZZ music

say[1] /seɪ/ v **said** /sed/, **said, saying** *3rd person singular, present tense* **says** /sez/ **1** [T] to speak words: *Tell her I said hi.* | *I'm sorry, I didn't hear what you said.* | **+ that** *He said he'd call back.* **2** [I,T] to express a thought, feeling, opinion etc in words: *He didn't seem to understand anything I said.* | *Did she say what time to come?* | **+ (that)** *The doctor says that I can't go home yet.* | **a nice/nasty etc thing to say** *That's a pretty mean thing to say.* **3** [I,T] to express something without using words: *His expression seems to say he's not at all pleased.* **4** [T] to give information in writing, pictures, or numbers: *The clock said nine thirty.* | *What do the instructions say?* **5** **to say the least** used when what you have said could have been stated much more strongly: *They weren't very friendly, to say the least.* **6** **go without saying** used to say that the thing you have just mentioned is so clear that it really did not need to be said: *It goes without saying it will be a very difficult job.* **7** **having said that** used before saying something that makes the opinion you have given seem less strong: *This isn't really a brilliant movie, but having said that, the kids should enjoy it.* **8** **say to yourself** *spoken* to think something: *I was worried about it, but I said to myself, "You can do this."* **9** [T] *spoken* to suggest or suppose something: *Say you were going to an interview. What would you wear?* **10** **say when** used when you are pouring a drink for someone and

---

SPELLING NOTE
Words with the sound /s/, may be spelt **c**-, like **city**, or **ps**-, like **psychology**.

you want them to tell you when there is enough in their glass **11 you don't say!** *spoken* used to say that you are not at all surprised by what someone has told you

say² *n* [singular, U] **1** the right to help decide something: *Members felt that they had no say in the proposed changes.* | **the final say** (=the final decision): *Who has the final say?* **2 have your say** to give your opinion on something: *You'll all have the chance to have your say.*

say·ing /'seɪ-ɪŋ/ *n* [C] a well-known wise statement; PROVERB

scab /skæb/ *n* [C] **1** a hard layer of dried blood that forms over a cut or wound **2** *informal* an insulting word for someone who goes to work when the other workers are on STRIKE

scaf·fold /'skæfəld, -fəʊld‖-fəld, -foʊld/ *n* [C] **1** a temporary structure built next to a building or high wall, for people to stand on while they work on the building or wall **2** a structure with a raised stage, used in the past for legally executing (EXECUTE) criminals

scaf·fold·ing /'skæfəldɪŋ/ *n* [U] poles and boards that are made into a structure for people to stand on when they are working on a high wall or the outside of a building

scald /skɔːld‖skɒːld/ *v* [T] to burn someone or something with hot liquid or steam: *The coffee scalded his tongue. | She was badly scalded as a child.* —**scald** *n* [C]

scald·ing /'skɔːldɪŋ‖'skɒːl-/ *adj* extremely hot: *scalding hot water*

scales

scale¹ /skeɪl/ *n* **1** [singular, U] the size or level of something, compared to what is usual: **large-/small-scale** *a large-/small-scale project* | **on a grand scale** (=very big and impressive): *They have built their new house on a grand scale.* **2** [C usually singular] a system for measuring the force, speed, amount etc of something, or of comparing it with something else: *What scale do they use for measuring wind speed? | the Richter scale | On a scale from 1 to 10, I'd give it an 8.* **3** [C usually plural] a piece of

equipment for weighing people or objects: *kitchen scales | bathroom scales* (=for weighing people) → see picture at KITCHEN **4** [C] a set of marks with regular spaces between them on a measuring instrument: *a ruler with a metric scale* **5** [C,U] the relationship between the size of a map, drawing, or MODEL and the actual size of the place or thing that it shows: *a scale of 1 inch to the mile* **6** [C] a series of musical notes that have a fixed order and become gradually higher or lower **7** [C usually plural] one of the small flat pieces of hard skin that cover the bodies of fish, snakes etc

scale² *v* [T] to climb to the top of something that is high: *They scaled a 40-foot wall and escaped.*
scale sth ↔ **back/down** *phr v* [T] to reduce the size or effectiveness of something: *a plan to scale down military operations in the area*

scal·lop /'skæləp‖'skɑ:-/ *n* [C] a small sea animal that has a hard flat shell, and is eaten as food

scal·loped /'skæləpt‖'skɑ:-/ *adj* scalloped edges are cut in a series of small curves as a decoration

scalp¹ /skælp/ *n* [C] the skin on the top of your head, where your hair grows

scalp² *v* [T] **1** to cut off a dead enemy's scalp as a sign of victory **2** *especially AmE informal* to buy tickets for an event and sell them again at a much higher price

scal·pel /'skælpəl/ *n* [C] a small and very sharp knife used by doctors during operations

scal·y /'skeɪli/ *adj* **1** an animal that is scaly is covered with small flat pieces of hard skin **2** scaly skin is dry and rough

scam /skæm/ *n* [C] *slang* a dishonest plan, usually to get money

scam·per /'skæmpə‖-ər/ *v* [I] to run with short quick steps, like a child or small animal: **+ in/out/off etc** *A mouse scampered into its hole.*

scam·pi /'skæmpi/ *n* [C] *BrE* PRAWNS covered in flour and cooked in oil: *scampi and chips*

scan /skæn/ *v* **-nned, -nning 1** [I,T] also **scan through** to read something quickly in order to understand its main meaning or to find a particular piece of information: *I had a chance to scan through the report on the plane.* **2** [T] to examine an area carefully, because you are looking for a particular person or thing: *Lookouts were scanning the sky for enemy planes.* **3** [T] if a machine scans an object or a part of your body, it produces a picture of what is inside it: *All luggage has to be scanned at the airport.* —**scan** *n* [C] → see also SCANNER

scan·dal /'skændl/ *n* [C,U] something that happens that people think is immoral or shocking: *a scandal involving several important politicians | Reporters are always looking for scandal and gossip.*

scan·dal·ize (also **-ise** *BrE*) /'skændəl-aɪz/ *v* [T] to do something that shocks people very much: *a crime that has scandalized the entire city*

scan·dal·ous /'skændələs/ *adj* completely immoral and shocking: *scandalous behaviour*

scan·ner /'skænə‖-ər/ *n* [C] **1** a machine that passes electronic waves through something in order to produce a picture of what is inside it **2** a piece of computer equipment that copies an image from paper onto the computer

scant /skænt/ *adj* very little and not enough: *After two weeks, they had made scant progress.*

scant·y /'skænti/ *adj* very small and often not big enough: *a scanty bikini* —**scantily** *adv*: *scantily dressed* (=wearing only a few clothes and showing a lot of your body)

scape·goat /'skeɪpgəʊt‖-goʊt/ *n* [C] someone who is blamed for something bad that happens, even if it is not their fault —**scapegoat** *v* [T]

scar¹ /skɑː‖skɑːr/ *n* **1** [C] a permanent mark on someone's skin from a cut or wound **2** [C usually plural] a permanent emotional problem caused by a bad experience

scar² *v* [T] **-rred, -rring 1 be scarred** to have or be given a permanent mark on your skin from a cut or wound: **be scarred for life** (=for ever): *The fire had left him scarred for life.* **2** to have or get permanent emotional or mental problems because of a bad experience: **scar sb for life** (=for ever): *Something like that would scar a kid for life.*

scarce /skeəs‖skers/ *adj* if food, clothing, water etc is scarce, there is not enough of it available

scarce·ly /'skeəsli‖'sker-/ *adv* **1** almost not at all, or almost none at all: *Their teaching methods have scarcely changed in the last 100 years.* **2** definitely not, or almost certainly not: *Owen is really angry, and you can scarcely blame him.*

scar·ci·ty /'skeəsˌtil‖'sker-/ *n* [C,U] when there is not enough of something: **+ of** *a scarcity of clean water and medical supplies*

scare¹ /skeə‖sker/ *v informal* [T] to make someone feel frightened: *I didn't see you there – you scared me!*

scare sb/sth ↔ off/away *phr v* [T] **1** to make someone or something go away by frightening them: *They lit fires to scare away the wild animals.* **2** to make someone uncertain or worried, so that they do not do something they were going to do

scare² *n* **1** [singular] a sudden feeling of fear: **give sb a scare** *She once gave her parents a big scare by going off with a stranger.* **2** [C] a situation in which many people become frightened about something: *a bomb scare*

scare·crow /'skeəkrəʊl‖'skerkroʊ/ *n* [C] an object made to look like a person that is put in a field to frighten birds away from crops

scared /skeəd‖skerd/ *adj* frightened or nervous about something: **+ (that)** *We were scared that something terrible might happen.* **+ of** *She's always been scared of flying.* **scared stiff/scared to death** (=very frightened): *There was one teacher all the kids were scared stiff of.* ➞ see colour picture on page 277

scarf /skɑːf‖skɑːrf/ *n* [C], *plural* **scarves** /skɑːvz‖skɑːrvz/ *or* **scarfs** a piece of material that you wear around your neck, head, or shoulders ➞ see colour picture on page 113

scar·let /'skɑːlət‖-ɑːr-/ *n* [U] a bright red colour —**scarlet** *adj*

scar·y /'skeəri‖'skeri/ *adj informal* frightening: *a scary movie*

scath·ing /'skeɪðɪŋ/ *adj* criticizing someone or something very strongly: *Mr Dewar launched a scathing attack on the Government's plans.*

scat·ter /'skætə‖-ər/ *v* **1** [T] to throw or drop things all over an area: *He scatters his dirty clothes all over the bedroom floor!* **2** [I,T] if a group of people or animals scatters, or something scatters them, they suddenly run away in different directions, usually to escape danger: *Guns started firing, and the crowd scattered in terror.*

scat·tered /'skætəd‖-ərd/ *adj* spread over a wide area or over a long period of time: *books scattered all over the room | The weather forecast is for scattered showers.*

scav·enge /'skævˌndʒ/ *v* [I,T] to search for food or things to use among unwanted food or waste objects: *wild dogs scavenging for food* —**scavenger** *n* [C]

sce·na·ri·o /sˌ'nɑːriəʊ‖-'næ-, -'ne-/ *n* [C] a situation that could happen but has not happened yet: *The worst scenario would be if the college had to close.*

scene /siːn/ *n* [C] **1** a short part of a play or film, when the events happen in one place: *She comes on in Act 2, Scene 3. | a love scene* **2** a view or picture of a place: *a peaceful country scene* **3** the place where an accident or crime happened: *Firefighters arrived at the scene within minutes. | the scene of the crime* **4 the music/fashion/political etc scene** a set of activities and the people who are involved in them: *Exciting things have been happening on the London music scene.* **5** [usually singular] a loud angry argument in a public place: *Sit down and stop making a scene.* **6 behind the scenes** if preparations, discussions etc take place behind the scenes, they do not happen publicly and most people do not see them or know about them: *You have no idea what goes on behind the scenes.* **7 set the scene a)** to provide the conditions in which an event can happen: *an invention that set the scene for dramatic changes in all our lives* **b)** to describe the situation before you tell a story

sce·ne·ry /'siːnəri/ *n* [U] **1** the natural features of a place, such as the mountains, forests etc, especially when these are beautiful: *You should visit Norway – the scenery is magnificent!* **2** the painted background of a theatre stage

sce·nic /'siːnɪk/ *adj* a scenic place or road has beautiful views of the countryside: *If you have time, take the scenic coastal route.*

scent /sent/ *n* **1** [C] a pleasant smell: *the scent of roses* **2** [C,U] the smell left behind by an animal or person: *The fox had disappeared, but the dogs soon picked up the scent.* **3** [C,U] a liquid with a pleasant smell that you put on your skin; PERFUME

scent·ed /'sentˌd/ *adj* something that is scented has a pleasant smell: *scented bath oil*

scep·tic *BrE,* **skeptic** *AmE* /'skeptɪk/ *n* [C] someone who has doubts about whether something is true or right

scep·ti·cal *BrE,* **skeptical** *AmE* /'skeptɪkəl/ *adj* doubting whether something is true or right: **+ about/of** *Many scientists remain sceptical about the value of this research.*

scep·ti·cis·m *BrE,* **skepticism** *AmE* /'skeptˌsɪzəm/ *n* [U] doubts about whether something is true or right: *scepticism about claims that there may be life on one of Saturn's moons*

sched·ule¹ /'ʃedjuːl‖'skedʒʊl, -dʒəl/ *n* **1** [C,U] a plan of what someone is going to do and when they will do it, or a plan of when work is to be done: *I have a very busy schedule this week.* | *We're on schedule to finish in May.* (=we will finish by the planned date) **2** [C] *especially AmE* a list that shows the times that buses, trains etc leave or arrive; TIMETABLE *BrE* **3** [C] a formal written list: *a schedule of postal charges*

schedule² *v* [T] to plan that something will happen at a particular time: *The meeting has been scheduled for Friday.*

scheme¹ /skiːm/ *n* [C] **1** *BrE* a system arranged by a government or organization to help people or to achieve something: *a government training scheme for young people* | *a road improvement scheme* **2** an idea or plan that someone has, especially a slightly dishonest or stupid one: *another of his crazy schemes for making money*

scheme² *v* [I] to secretly make plans to get or achieve something, often dishonestly; PLOT: *politicians scheming to win votes* — **schemer** *n* [C]

schiz·o·phre·ni·a /ˌskɪtsəʊˈfriːniə, -sə-ǁ-soʊ-, -sə-/ *n* [U] a mental illness in which someone's thoughts become separated from what is really happening around them — **schizophrenic** /-ˈfrenɪk◄/ *adj, n* [C]

schol·ar /ˈskɒləǁˈskɑːlər/ *n* [C] **1** someone who studies a subject and knows a lot about it: *a Latin scholar* **2** someone who has been given a scholarship to study at a school or college

schol·ar·ly /ˈskɒləliǁˈskɑːlərli/ *adj* **1** involving a serious study of a subject: *a scholarly journal* **2** a scholarly person spends a lot of time studying, and knows a lot about a subject

schol·ar·ship /ˈskɒləʃɪpǁˈskɑːlər-/ *n* [C] **1** an amount of money given to someone by an organization to help pay for their education **2** [U] the knowledge, work, or methods used in serious studying

scho·las·tic /skəˈlæstɪk/ *adj* relating to schools or teaching: *an excellent scholastic record*

school /skuːl/ *n* **1** [C] a place where children are taught: *Which school do you go to?* | *There are several good schools in the area.* | *a school trip to the Science Museum* **2** [U] the time spent at school: *What are you doing after school?* | *We won't be moving house while the kids are still at school.* | *She started school when she was four.* **3** [singular] the students and teachers at a school: *The whole school was sorry when she left.* **4** [C] **riding/driving/language school** a place where a subject or skill is taught: *an art school* | *the Amwell School of Motoring* **5** [C] a department that teaches a particular subject at a university: *She's a lecturer in the school of English.* **6** [C,U] *AmE* a university, or the time when you study there: *If I pass my exams, I'll go to medical school.* | *Are your boys still in school?* **7** [C] a group of painters or writers whose work is similar: *the Dutch school of painting* **8** **school of thought** an opinion that is shared by a group of people: *One school of thought says that red wine is good for you.* **9** [C] a school of fish is a large group of fish swimming together: *a school of dolphins*

school·boy /ˈskuːlbɔɪ/ *n* [C] *especially BrE* a boy who goes to school

school·child /ˈskuːltʃaɪld/ *n* [C], *plural* **schoolchildren** a child who goes to school

school·days /ˈskuːldeɪz/ *n* [plural] the time of your life when you go to school

school·girl /ˈskuːlɡɜːlǁ-ɡɜːrl/ *n* [C] *especially BrE* a girl who goes to school

school·ing /ˈskuːlɪŋ/ *n* [U] education at school

school leav·er /ˈ. ˌ../ *n* [C] *BrE* someone who leaves school, especially someone who is looking for work: *a shortage of jobs for school leavers*

school·mas·ter /ˈskuːlˌmɑːstəǁ-ˌmæstər/ *n* [C] *old-fashioned* a male teacher

school·mis·tress /ˈskuːlˌmɪstrɪs/ *n* [C] *old-fashioned* a female teacher

school·teach·er /ˈskuːlˌtiːtʃəǁ-ər/ *n* [C] a teacher in a school

sci·ence /ˈsaɪəns/ *n* **1** [U] knowledge that is based on testing and proving facts, or the study that produces this knowledge: *developments in science and technology* **2** [C] an area of science, such as BIOLOGY or chemistry, or a subject that is studied like a science

science fic·tion /ˌ.. ˈ../ *n* [U] books and stories about life in the future

sci·en·tif·ic /ˌsaɪənˈtɪfɪk◄/ *adj* **1** scientific work is about science or is done using the methods of science: *scientific discoveries* | *a scientific experiment* **2** done very carefully, using an organized system: *We do keep records, but we're not very scientific about it.* — **scientifically** /-kli/ *adv*

sci·en·tist /ˈsaɪəntɪst/ *n* [C] someone who works in science

sci-fi /ˌsaɪ ˈfaɪ◄/ *n* [U] *informal* science fiction

scin·til·lat·ing /ˈsɪntɪleɪtɪŋ/ *adj* very interesting and exciting: *a scintillating speech*

scis·sors /ˈsɪzəzǁ-ərz/ *n* [plural] a tool for cutting paper, with two sharp blades that are joined together and have handles with holes for your fingers: *a pair of scissors* ➠ see colour picture on page 80

scoff /skɒfǁskɔːf, skɑːf/ *v* [I] to criticize and make fun of a person or idea that you think is stupid: *He scoffed at my suggestions for improving the system.*

scold /skəʊldǁskoʊld/ *v* [I,T] to tell someone in an angry way that they have done something wrong: *My grandmother was always scolding me for getting my clothes dirty.* — **scolding** *n* [C,U]

scone /skɒn, skəʊnǁskoʊn, skɑːn/ *n* [C] a small round soft cake that you eat covered with butter or cream and JAM

scoop¹ /skuːp/ *n* [C] **1** a deep spoon for picking up or serving food: *an ice-cream scoop* **2** also **scoopful** /-fʊl/ the amount that a scoop will hold: *two scoops of sugar* **3** an important news story that is printed in one newspaper before any of the others know about it

scoop² *v* [T] to push something up with a scoop, a spoon, or with your curved hand: *Cut the melon in half and scoop out the seeds.*

scoot /skuːt/ *v* [I] *informal* to leave a place quickly: *You kids, get out of here – scoot!*

scoot·er /ˈskuːtəǁ-ər/ *n* [C] a small two-wheeled vehicle like a bicycle with an engine

scope /skəʊpǁskoʊp/ *n* **1** [singular] the scope of a book, discussion etc is the RANGE of subjects that it deals with: *Environmental issues are beyond the scope of this inquiry.* **2** [U] the opportunity to do or develop something: *an* *attractive old house with a lot of scope for improvement*

scorch[1] /skɔːtʃ‖skɔːrtʃ/ *v* [I,T] if you scorch something, or if it scorches, its surface burns slightly and leaves a brown mark: *He scorched my favourite shirt with the iron!* —**scorched** *adj*: *scorched brown grass*

scorch[2] *n* [C] a brown mark made on something where its surface has been burned

scorch·er /'skɔːtʃəl‖'skɔːrtʃər/ *n* [C] *informal* an extremely hot day: *It's going to be a real scorcher.*

scorch·ing /'skɔːtʃɪŋ‖'skɔːr-/ *adj informal* if the weather is scorching, it is very hot: *the scorching heat of an Australian summer*

score[1] /skɔː‖skɔːr/ *n* [C] **1** the number of points earned in a game or competition: *The final score was 35 to 17.* | *What's the score?* **2** the printed copy of a piece of music **3 know the score** *informal* to know the real facts of a situation, including any unpleasant ones: *He knew the score when he decided to get involved.* **4 settle a score** to do something to punish someone who has harmed you in the past: *Jack came back after five years to settle some old scores.* **5 on that score** *spoken* concerning the thing you have just mentioned: *We've got plenty of money, so don't worry on that score.*

score[2] *v* **1** [I,T] to win points in a game or competition: *Dallas scored in the final minute of the game.* | *How many goals has he scored this year?* **2** [I,T] *informal* to be successful or succeed in getting something you want: *Barnes has scored again with another popular book.* **3** [T] to mark a line on a piece of paper, wood etc with something sharp → see also SCORES

score·board /'skɔːbɔːd‖'skɔːrbɔːrd/ *n* [C] a large sign on which the score of a game is shown

scor·er /'skɔːrəl‖-ər/ *n* [C] **1** someone who scores a goal, point etc in a game **2** also **score-keeper** someone who officially records the number of points won in a game

scores /skɔːz‖skɔːrz/ *n* [plural] a large number: *Scores of children ran and screamed in the playground.*

scorn[1] /skɔːn‖skɔːrn/ *n* [U] an opinion or attitude that someone or something is stupid or not very good: *Scientists treated the findings with scorn.* —**scornful** *adj*

scorn[2] *v* [T] *formal* to show that you think that a person, idea, or suggestion is stupid or not worth considering: *young people who scorn the attitudes of their parents*

Scor·pi·o /'skɔːpiəʊ‖'skɔːrpioʊ/ *n* [C,U] the sign of the Zodiac of people who are born between October 23rd and November 21st, or someone who belongs to this sign

scor·pi·on /'skɔːpiən‖'skɔːr-/ *n* [C] a creature like a large insect with a curved tail that has a poisonous sting

Scotch /skɒtʃ‖skɑːtʃ/ *n* [C,U] a strong alcoholic drink made in Scotland, or a glass of this drink; WHISKY

Scotch tape /ˌ. './, '. ./ *n* [U] *AmE trademark* thin clear TAPE used for sticking things together; SELLOTAPE *BrE*

scoun·drel /'skaʊndrəl/ *n* [C] *old-fashioned* a bad or dishonest person

scour /skaʊəl‖skaʊr/ *v* [T] **1** to search for something very carefully: *Archie scoured the town for more yellow roses.* | *I've scoured the newspapers, but I can't find any mention of it.* **2** to clean something thoroughly by rubbing it with something rough: *Do you have something I can scour the pan with?*

scourge /skɜːdʒ‖skɜːrdʒ/ *n* [C] *formal* something that causes a lot of harm or suffering: *the scourge of war*

scout[1] /skaʊt/ *n* [C] **1** also **boy scout, girl scout** a member of an organization that teaches young people practical skills such as camping, and teaches them to be good members of society: *He joined the Scouts when he was eleven.* **2 the Scouts** an organization that teaches young people practical skills such as camping, and teaches them to be good members of society **3** a soldier who is sent to search an area in front of an army and get information **4** someone whose job is to look for good sports players, musicians etc in order to employ them: *a talent scout*

scout[2] *v* [I] also **scout around** to look for something in an area: **+ for** *I'm going to scout around for a place to eat.*

scowl /skaʊl/ *v* [I] to look at someone in an angry way: **+ at** *What are you scowling at?* —**scowl** *n* [C]

scrab·ble /'skræbəl/ *v* [I] **scrabble about/ around** to quickly feel around with your fingers in order to look for something: *I was scrabbling around in the bottom of my bag for some money.*

scram·ble[1] /'skræmbəl/ *v* [I] **1** to climb up or over something quickly, using your hands to help you: *We scrambled up a rocky slope.* **2** to struggle and compete with other people in order to get or reach something: **+ for** *people scrambling for shelter*

scramble[2] *n* [singular] **1** a difficult climb where you have to use your hands: *a rough scramble over loose rocks* **2** when people struggle and compete with each other to get or do something: *a scramble for the best seats*

scrambled eggs /ˌ.. './ *n* [plural] eggs which are mixed together and cooked

scrap[1] /skræp/ *n* **1** [C] a small piece or amount of something: *If you've got a scrap of paper, I'll write down my address.* | *There's not a scrap of evidence to connect him with the murder.* **2** [U] old cars and other machines that are no longer useful but have parts or metal that can be used again: *The car's not worth fixing – we'll have to sell it for scrap.* **3** [C] *informal* a short fight or argument: *He had a scrap with one of the boys at school.* ➡ see also SCRAPS

scrap[2] *v* [T] **-pped, -pping 1** *informal* to decide not to do or use something: *We've decided to*

GRAMMAR NOTE: countable and uncountable (2)
Some nouns can be **countable** or **uncountable**. For example: **chicken** *n* [C,U].
• Countable: *A fox had killed some of the chickens.* (=birds)
• Uncountable: *chicken cooked in red wine* (=meat)

scrapbook

scrap the whole idea of renting a car. **2** to get rid of an old machine or vehicle

scrap·book /'skræpbʊk/ *n* [C] a book with empty pages where you can stick pictures, newspaper articles, or other things you want to keep

scrape[1] /skreɪp/ *v* **1** [T] to remove something from a surface, using the edge of a knife, stick etc: *Scrape some of the mud off your boots.* **2** [T] to damage something slightly by rubbing it against a rough surface: *She fell over and scraped her knee.* | *Careful! You nearly scraped the side of the car!* **3** [I,T] to rub against or rub something against a surface, making an unpleasant noise: *Her fingernails scraped down the blackboard.*

scrape by *phr v* [I] to have just enough money to live: *They just manage to scrape by on her tiny salary.*

scrape through *phr v* [I,T] to only just succeed: *He just managed to scrape through his degree course.*

scrape sth ↔ **together/up** *phr v* [T] to get enough money for something with difficulty: *We're trying to scrape together enough money for a vacation.*

scrape² *n* [C] **1** slight damage caused by rubbing against a rough surface: *She wasn't seriously hurt – only a few cuts and scrapes.* **2** *informal* a difficult or dangerous situation that you have caused yourself: *He got into all sorts of scrapes as a boy.*

scrap·heap /'skræphiːp/ *n* **on the scrapheap** no longer wanted or considered useful: *When I lost my job at fifty, I felt I'd been thrown on the scrapheap.*

scrap met·al /'. ,../ *n* [U] metal from old cars and other machines which can be melted and used again to make other things

scrap·py /'skræpi/ *adj* **1** untidy or badly organized: *a scrappy, badly written report* | *a scrappy piece of paper* **2** *AmE informal* always wanting to argue or fight

scraps /skræps/ *n* [plural] pieces of food that are left after you have finished eating: *Save the scraps for the dog.*

scratch¹ /skrætʃ/ *v* [I,T] **1** to rub your skin with your nails to stop it itching: *Try not to scratch those mosquito bites.* ➡ see colour picture on page 473 **2** to make a long thin cut or mark on something with a sharp object: *Ow! I've scratched my hand on a thorn.* | *Does the cat scratch?* **3** to rub a surface with something hard or sharp: *My dog scratches at the door when it wants to come in.*

scratch² *n* **1** [C] a long thin cut or mark on something: *Where did this scratch on the car come from?* **2 from scratch** if you do something from scratch, you start it without using anything that was prepared before: *I deleted the file from the computer by mistake so I had to start again from scratch.* **3 not come/be up to scratch** *informal* to not be good enough: *Your work hasn't really been up to scratch lately.* **4** [singular] if you have a scratch, you rub your skin with your nails: *My back needs a good scratch.*

scratch·y /'skrætʃi/ *adj* scratchy clothes or materials have a rough surface and are uncomfortable to wear: *a scratchy pair of wool socks*

scrawl /skrɔːl‖skrɒːl/ *v* [T] to write something in a careless or untidy way: *a telephone number scrawled on the bathroom wall* **—scrawl** *n* [C,U] *The notebook was covered in a large black scrawl.*

scraw·ny /'skrɔːni‖'skrɒːni/ *adj* someone who is scrawny looks thin, weak, and unattractive: *a scrawny little kid*

scream[1] /skriːm/ *v* [I,T] to make a loud high noise with your voice, or shout something loudly because you are hurt, frightened, or angry: *There was a huge bang and people started screaming.* | *Suddenly she screamed, "Look out!"*

scream² *n* [C] **1** a loud high noise that you make when you are hurt, frightened, or angry: *a scream of terror* **2** a very loud high sound: *the scream of the jet engines* **3 be a scream** *informal* to be very funny: *We all dressed up as animals – it was a real scream!*

screech /skriːtʃ/ *v* **1** [I,T] to make a very high loud unpleasant sound: *The police came flying round the corner, tyres screeching and sirens wailing.* | *"Get out of my way!" she screeched.* **2 screech to a halt/stop/standstill** if a vehicle screeches to a halt, it stops very suddenly, with its BRAKES making an unpleasant high sound **—screech** *n* [C]

screen[1] /skriːn/ *n* **1** [C] the flat glass part of a television or a computer: *The sunlight was reflecting off the screen.* ➡ see colour picture on page 80 **2 on screen** on or using a computer: *Ted doesn't like working on screen.* **3** [C] a large flat white surface that a film is shown on in a cinema **4** [singular,U] films or the cinema generally: *stars of the silver screen* | *He hates watching himself on screen.* **5** [C] a wire net covering a door or window to keep insects out **6** [C] a piece of material on a frame that can be moved, used for dividing one part of a room from another

screen² *v* [T] **1** to do medical tests on people to find out whether they have an illness: *Women over the age of 50 are screened for breast cancer.* **2** to find out things about someone's personal life, political activities etc in order to decide whether they are suitable for a particular job: *People wanting to work with children should be thoroughly screened before a job offer is made.* **3** also **screen off** to hide or protect something by putting something in front of it: *You can't see anything – the police have screened off the area.* | *The garden is screened by tall hedges.* **4** to show a film or programme at the cinema or on television

screen·play /'skriːnpleɪ/ *n* [C] a story written for film or television

screen·writ·er /'skriːn,raɪtə‖-ər/ *n* [C] someone who writes stories for film or television

screw[1] /skruː/ *n* [C] a thin pointed piece of metal that you push and turn to fasten pieces of wood, metal etc together

screw² *v* **1** [T] to fasten one thing to another, using a screw: *Screw the socket onto the wall.* **2** [I,T] if something screws somewhere, or if you screw something somewhere, you fasten it by twisting it around until it is tight: *Don't forget to screw the top of the jar back on.* **3** also **screw up** [T] to twist or crush a piece of paper: *Furiously she screwed the letter into a ball and flung it in the bin.* **4** [I,T] *spoken informal* a rude word meaning to have sex with someone

screw up phr v **1** screw up your eyes/face to make the muscles in your face tight so that your eyes become narrow **2** [I,T **screw** sth ↔ **up**] informal to spoil something or do something stupid: I broke my ankle, so that really screwed up our holiday plans!

screw·driv·er /'skru:,draɪvəl-ər/ n [C] a tool with a long thin metal end, used for turning screws → see picture at TOOLS

screwed up /ˌ '.◂/ adj informal very unhappy or anxious, or having mental problems, because you have had a lot of bad experiences: He's not a bad guy, but he's really screwed up.

scrib·ble /'skrɪbəl/ v [I,T] **1** to write something quickly in an untidy way: I scribbled his address on the back of an envelope. **2** to draw marks that do not mean anything — **scribble** n [U]

script /skrɪpt/ n **1** [C] the written form of a speech, play, film etc: Bring your script to rehearsal. **2** [C,U] the letters used in writing a language; ALPHABET: Arabic script

script·ed /'skrɪptⁱd/ adj a scripted speech or broadcast has been planned and written down before it is read

scrip·ture /'skrɪptʃəl-ər/ n [U] also the **Scriptures** n [plural] [C,U] the holy books of a religion, for example the Bible

script·writ·er /'skrɪpt,raɪtəl-ər/ n [C] someone who writes the words for films, or for radio and television programmes

scroll[1] /skrəʊlǁskroʊl/ n [C] a long document that is rolled up, used especially in past times instead of separate flat sheets of paper

scroll[2] v [I,T] to move information up or down a computer screen so that you can read it

scrooge /skru:dʒ/ n [C] informal someone who hates spending money

scrounge /skraʊndʒ/ v [T] informal to get something you want by asking someone for it instead of paying for it yourself: I'll try to scrounge some money off my dad.

scrub[1] /skrʌb/ v [I,T] to clean something by rubbing it hard with a brush or rough cloth: Scrub the board clean. | Tom scrubbed at the stain, but it wouldn't come out.

scrub[2] n **1** [U] low bushes and trees growing in a dry place **2** [singular] if you give something a scrub, you clean it by rubbing it hard

scrub

scruff /skrʌf/ n **by the scruff of the neck** if you hold an animal or person by the scruff of the neck, you hold the back of their neck

scruf·fy /'skrʌfi/ adj dirty and untidy: a scruffy kid | a scruffy old pair of jeans

scrum /skrʌm/ n [C] when players in a RUGBY game form a group and push against each other to try and get the ball

scrunch /skrʌntʃ/ v **scrunch** sth ↔ **up** phr v [T] to twist or crush something into a small shape: Scrunch up the paper and pack it round the pots.

scru·ple /'skru:pəl/ n [C usually plural] a belief about what is right and wrong that prevents you from doing something bad: a ruthless criminal with no scruples

scru·pu·lous /'skru:pj‚ləs/ adj **1** done very carefully so that every detail is correct: scrupulous attention to detail **2** always careful to be honest and fair: A less scrupulous person might have been tempted to accept the bribe. → opposite UNSCRUPULOUS — **scrupulously** adv

scru·ti·nize (also **-ise** BrE) /'skru:t‚naɪz/ v [T] to examine someone or something very carefully and thoroughly: Inspectors scrutinize every aspect of the laboratories' activities.

scru·ti·ny /'skru:t‚ni/ n [U] a careful and thorough examination of something: Close scrutiny of the document showed it to be a forgery. | Famous people have to live their lives under constant public scrutiny.

scu·ba div·ing /'sku:bə ˌdaɪvɪŋ/ n [U] the sport of swimming under water while breathing from a container of air on your back

scuff /skʌf/ v [I,T] if you scuff your shoes, or if they scuff, you accidentally rub them against something rough, leaving a mark on them **2** [T] if you scuff your feet, you walk in a lazy way, rubbing your feet along the ground

scuf·fle /'skʌfəl/ n [C] a short fight that is not very serious: A policeman was injured in a scuffle with demonstrators yesterday. — **scuffle** v [I]

sculp·tor /'skʌlptəl-ər/ n [C] someone who makes sculptures

sculp·ture /'skʌlptʃəl-ər/ n **1** [C,U] a work of art made from stone, wood, clay etc: a bronze sculpture by Peter Helzer | an exhibition of modern sculpture **2** [U] the art of making these objects: a talent for sculpture | a sculpture class — **sculptured** adj

scum /skʌm/ n **1** [singular, U] an unpleasant thick substance that forms on the surface of a liquid: Green scum covered the old pond. **2** [U] someone who you hate and disapprove of very much

scur·ri·lous /'skʌr‚ləsǁ'skɜːr-/ adj a scurrilous remark, article etc contains damaging and untrue statements about someone

scur·ry /'skʌriǁ'skɜːri/ v [I] to move very quickly with small steps: + along/past/across etc a beetle scurried across the path

scut·tle /'skʌtl/ v **1** [I] to move quickly with small steps: across/away/off etc crabs scuttling along the beach **2** [T] to sink a ship, especially to prevent it being used by an enemy

scythe /saɪð/ n [C] a tool with a long curved blade, used for cutting grass or other tall crops

SE the written abbreviation of SOUTHEAST

sea /si:/ n [C,U] **1** also **Sea** a large area of salty water; OCEAN: the Mediterranean Sea | The boat was heading out to sea. (=travelling away from land) | **at sea** (=sailing on the sea): We spent the next six weeks at sea. | **by sea** (=on a ship): It takes longer to send goods by sea, but it's cheaper. → see colour picture on page 243 **2** **a sea of** a large number or amount of something: The speaker stared at the sea of faces in front of him.

sea·bed also **sea bed** /'si:bed/ n [singular] the land at the bottom of the sea: a wrecked ship lying on the seabed

sea·far·ing /'si:ˌfeərɪŋǁ-ˌfer-/ adj connected

with or working with ships and the sea: *a seafaring nation*

sea·food /'siːfuːd/ *n* [U] animals from the sea that you can eat, especially creatures with shells

sea·front /'siːfrʌnt/ *n* [C usually singular] a part of a town next to the sea: *a hotel on the seafront*

sea·gull /'siːgʌl/ also **gull** *n* [C] a common grey and white bird that lives near the sea

sea·horse /'siːhɔːs‖-hɔːrs/ *n* [C] a small sea fish with a head and neck that look like those of a horse

seal¹ /siːl/ *n* [C] **1** an animal that has smooth fur, eats fish and lives by the sea in cold areas **2** a piece of paper or plastic that you break to open a container: *Do not use this product if the seal on the bottle is broken.* **3** a piece of WAX, paper, or metal with an official mark that is put on documents to prove that they are legal or official: *The letter had the seal of the Department of Justice at the top.* **4** a piece of rubber or plastic on a pipe, machine or container that prevents liquid or air going into or out of it

seal² *v* [T] **1** also **seal up** to close an entrance or container with something that stops air or liquid getting into or out of it: *Many of the tombs have remained sealed since the 16th century.* **2** to close an envelope or package using something sticky to fasten the edges in place **3 seal a deal/agreement etc** to make a deal, agreement etc official

seal sth ↔ **in** *phr v* [T] to stop something getting out of the thing it is contained in: *Fry the meat quickly to seal in the flavour.*

seal sth ↔ **off** *phr v* [T] to stop people entering an area or building, especially because it is dangerous: *Following a bomb warning, police have sealed off the city centre.*

sealed /siːld/ *adj* something that is sealed is closed, especially in a way that prevents liquid or air from getting in or out: *Medical dressings are supplied in sealed sterile packs.* | *a sealed envelope*

sea lev·el /'. ˌ../ *n* [U] the average level of the sea, used as a standard for measuring the height of an area of land: *The village is 200 feet above sea level.*

sea li·on /'. ˌ../ *n* [C] a large type of SEAL

seam /siːm/ *n* [C] **1** the line where two pieces of cloth have been sewn together: *The seam on my jeans has split.* **2** a layer of coal under the ground

sea·man /'siːmən/ *n* [C] a SAILOR who belongs to one of the lowest ranks

seam·less /'siːmləs/ *adj* done or made so well that you do not notice where one part ends and another part begins: *The show is a seamless blend of song, dance, and storytelling.*

seam·y /'siːmi/ *adj* involving bad things such as crime, violence, or POVERTY

se·ance /'seɪɑːns, -ɒns‖'seɪɑːns/ *n* [C] a meeting where people try to talk to the spirits of dead people, or receive messages from them

sear /sɪə‖sɪr/ *v* [T] to burn something with a sudden powerful heat: *The food should be hot, but not enough to sear your mouth.* —**seared** *adj* → see also SEARING

search¹ /sɜːtʃ‖sɜːrtʃ/ *n* **1** [C usually singular] an attempt to find someone or something: *Hundreds of local people are helping in the search for the missing girl.* | **in search of** (=looking for): *We set off in search of somewhere to eat.* | **call off a search** (=stop looking for someone): *After three days, rescue workers have called off the search for survivors.* **2** [singular] an attempt to find the explanation of a difficult problem: *the search for the meaning of life*

search² *v* **1** [I,T] to look carefully for someone or something: *I searched all over the house, but I couldn't find them anywhere.* | *animals searching for food* **2** [T] if the police search someone, they look in their clothes or bags for weapons, drugs etc: *We were all searched at the airport.* **3** [I] to try to find an answer or explanation for a difficult problem: **+ for** *Scientists have spent years searching for a solution.*

search·ing /'sɜːtʃɪŋ‖'sɜːr-/ *adj* intended to discover as much as possible about someone or something: *She asked several searching questions about his past.*

search·light /'sɜːtʃlaɪt‖'sɜːrtʃ-/ *n* [C] a large bright light used for finding people, planes etc at night

search par·ty /'. ˌ../ *n* [C] a group of people organized to look for someone who is lost

search war·rant /'. ˌ../ *n* [C] a legal document that officially allows the police to search a building

sear·ing /'sɪərɪŋ‖'sɪr-/ *adj* **1** searing heat is very hot **2** searing pain is very painful **3** searing criticism criticizes someone very strongly

sea·shell /'siːʃel/ *n* [C] the shell of some types of sea animals

sea·shore /'siːʃɔː‖-ʃɔːr/ *n* **the seashore** the land, rocks, and sand along the edge of the sea → compare BEACH, SEASIDE

sea·sick /'siːˌsɪk/ *adj* feeling ill because of the movement of a boat or ship —**seasickness** *n* [U]

sea·side /'siːsaɪd/ *n* **the seaside** an area or town next to the sea, especially where you go to enjoy yourself: *a day at the seaside* | **seaside resort** (=where a lot of people go for their holidays)

sea·son¹ /'siːzən/ *n* [C] **1** one of the four main periods in the year; winter, spring, summer, or autumn **2** a period of time in a year when something happens most often or when something is usually done: *the holiday season* | **the rainy/wet/dry season** *The rainy season usually starts in May.* | **the football/baseball etc season** *I hardly ever see him during the cricket season!* **3 be in season a)** if vegetables or fruit are in season, it is the time of year when they are ready to eat **b)** if a female animal is in season, she is ready to MATE **4 out of season a)** if vegetables or fruit are out of season, it is not the time of year when they are normally ready to eat or normally available **b)** if you go somewhere out of season, you go when there are not many people there on holiday

sea·son² *v* [T] to add salt, pepper etc to something you are cooking to make it taste better: *Season the soup just before serving.*

sea·son·al /'siːzənəl/ *adj* only happening, available, or needed during a particular season: *seasonal jobs in the tourist industry*

sea·soned /'siːzənd/ *adj* having a lot of experience of doing something: *Even seasoned travellers are advised to avoid the area.*

sea·son·ing /ˈsiːzənɪŋ/ *n* [C,U] salt, pepper, SPICEs etc that you add to food to make it taste better

season tick·et /ˈ.. ˌ..ǁˌ.. ˈ../ *n* [C] a ticket for several journeys, performances, games etc that continues for a fixed period of time

seat[1] /siːt/ *n* [C] **1** something that you can sit on, for example a chair: *the front seat of the car* | *I've reserved two seats for Saturday night's performance.* | *a 150-seat airliner* | **take/have a seat** (=to sit down): *Please take a seat, Ms. Carson.* **2** the part of a chair, bicycle etc that you sit on **3** a position as a member of a government or an official group: **win/lose a seat** *She lost her seat at the last election.*

seat[2] *v* [T] **1 be seated a)** to be sitting down: *The chairman and senior officials were seated on the platform.* **b)** *spoken formal* used to politely ask someone to sit down: *Would everyone please be seated.* **2** *formal* if you seat yourself somewhere, you sit there: *Seating himself on a nearby chair, he asked, "So how can I help?"* **3** if a room, vehicle, theatre etc seats a particular number of people, it has enough seats for that number: *The new Olympic stadium seats over 70,000.*

seat belt /ˈ. ./ *n* [C] a strong belt fastened to the seat of a car or plane, that stops you being thrown from your seat if you have an accident; SAFETY BELT

seat·ing /ˈsiːtɪŋ/ *n* [U] the seats in a theatre, restaurant, plane etc or the way that they are arranged: *a comfortable modern ferry with seating for 3,000 passengers.*

sea·weed /ˈsiːwiːd/ *n* [U] a common plant that grows in the sea and is often found on beaches

sec /sek/ *n* [C] *spoken* a very short time: *Wait a sec – I'm coming too!*

se·cede /sɪˈsiːd/ *v* [I] *formal* to formally leave an organization, especially because of disagreement about its aims, principles etc: *The southern states wanted to secede from the US in the 1850s.* **— secession** /-ˈseʃən/ *n* [singular, U]

se·clud·ed /sɪˈkluːdɪd/ *adj* a secluded place is very quiet and private: *a relaxing vacation on a secluded island*

se·clu·sion /sɪˈkluːʒən/ *n* [U] when someone lives or is kept alone and away from other people: *He lives in seclusion inside an old castle.*

sec·ond[1] /ˈsekənd/ *number, pron, adj* **1** the person, thing, or event that is after the first one; 2nd: *He's just scored his second goal.* | *Joanna's in her second year at university.* | **come/finish second** (=be the one after the winner): *She was disappointed to only come second.* **2 be second to none** used to emphasize that someone or something is better than anyone or anything else: *The service in our hotel is second to none.* **3 your second wind** if you get your second wind, you feel less tired and feel you have more energy to do something than before **4 have second thoughts** to have doubts about whether you have made the right decision about something: *Denise said she wanted them to get*

married, *but now she's having second thoughts.* **5 on second thoughts** *spoken* used when you want to change what you have just said or want to do; what you have just suggested etc: *I'll have the apple pie...on second thoughts I think I'll have an ice cream instead.* **6 without (giving it) a second thought** without thinking carefully about whether you should do something: *I used to stay out all night without giving it a second thought.*

second[2] *n* [C] **1** a period of time equal to 1/60 of a minute: *It takes about 30 seconds for the computer to start up.* **2** *spoken* a very short period of time: *Just wait a second and I'll come and help.* | *It'll only take a few seconds.* **3 seconds** goods that are sold cheaply because they have something slightly wrong with them

second[3] *v* [T] to formally support a suggestion made by another person at a meeting: **second a motion/proposal/amendment** *Sarah has proposed this motion – do we have someone who will second it?*

se·cond[4] /sɪˈkɒndǁ-ˈkɑːnd/ *v* [T] *BrE* to send someone to do another job for a short time: *Jill's been seconded to the marketing department while David's away.*

sec·ond·a·ry /ˈsekəndəriǁ-deri/ *adj* **1** secondary education/schooling/teaching etc the education of children between 11 and 18 **2** not as important as something else: *She regards getting married as being of secondary importance.* **3** developing from something of the same type, especially a disease: *a secondary infection*

secondary school /ˈ.... ˌ./ *n* [C] *especially BrE* a school for children between the ages of 11 and 18

second best /ˌ.. ˈ.◂/ *adj* not as good as the best thing of the same type: *Hunt has the second best scoring record at the club.* **— second best** *n* [U]

second class /ˌ.. ˈ./ *n* **1** [U] a way of travelling that is cheaper but not as comfortable as FIRST CLASS **2** [singular] a level of a university degree in Britain that is below the top level

second-class /ˌ.. ˈ.◂/ *adj* **1** second-class seat/ticket/carriage etc costing less than FIRST-CLASS travel, but not so comfortable **2** less important than other people or things: *They treated us like second-class citizens.* **3** second-class/post/stamp etc a system of sending letters in Britain, which costs less than FIRST-CLASS post, but takes longer to arrive

second-guess /ˌ.. ˈ./ *v* [T] **1** to try to guess what will happen, or to say what someone will do before they do it: *You have to try to second-guess the other team's moves.* **2** *AmE* to criticize something after it has already happened: *There's no point in second-guessing what should have been done.*

sec·ond·hand /ˌsekəndˈhænd◂/ *adj* secondhand clothes, furniture, books etc have already been owned by someone else: *We bought a cheap secondhand car.* **— secondhand** *adv*

S

GRAMMAR NOTE: much and many
You can only use **much**, **how much** and **a little** with <u>uncountable</u> nouns: *How much information do you have?* You can only use **many**, **how many** and **a few** with plural <u>countable</u> nouns: *How many people are coming to the party?* | *I've invited a few friends.*

sec·ond lan·guage /ˌ.. '../ n [C] a language that you speak in addition to the language that you learned as a child

sec·ond·ly /'sekəndli/ adv used to introduce the second fact, reason etc that you want to talk about: *And secondly, a large number of her poems deal with love.*

second na·ture /ˌ.. '../ n [U] something you have done so often that you do it almost without thinking: *Wearing a seatbelt is second nature to most drivers.*

second per·son /ˌ.. '../ n **the second person** a form of a verb that you use with 'you' → compare FIRST PERSON, THIRD PERSON

second-rate /ˌ.. '.◂/ adj not very good: *second-rate hospital care for poor people*

se·cre·cy /'siːkrəsi/ n [U] when something is kept secret: *The operation was carried out in total secrecy.*

se·cret¹ /'siːkrɪt/ adj **1** known about by only a few people: *a secret plan* | *Don't tell anyone your number – keep it secret.* **2** [only before noun] doing something that you do not want anyone to find out about: *a secret admirer* — **secretly** adv

secret² n **1** [C] something that you do not tell other people or only tell a few people: *I can't tell you his name. It's a secret.* | **keep a secret** *Can you keep a secret?* **2** **the secret of** an explanation for something that only a few people know or understand: *What's the secret of your success?* **3** **in secret** without any other people knowing: *Negotiations are being conducted in secret.*

secret a·gent /ˌ.. '../ n [C] a SPY

sec·re·ta·ry /'sekrɪˌtəri‖-teri/ n [C] **1** someone whose job is to TYPE letters, arrange meetings, answer telephone calls etc in an office: *The secretary will make an appointment for you.* **2** also **Secretary** an official who is in charge of a large government department: *the Secretary of Education* — **secretarial** /ˌsekrɪˈteəriəl ‖-ˈter-/ adj: *secretarial skills*

se·crete /sɪˈkriːt/ v [T] **1** if part of a plant or animal secretes a substance, it produces that substance: *a hormone that is secreted into the bloodstream* **2** *formal* to hide something — **secretion** /-ˈkriːʃən/ n [C,U]

se·cre·tive /'siːkrɪtɪv, sɪˈkriːtɪv/ adj unwilling to tell people about what you are doing or what you know about something: *Why are you being so secretive about your new girlfriend?* — **secretively** adv

secret ser·vice /ˌ.. '../ n [singular] **1** *BrE* a government department that tries to find out secret information **2** a US government department whose main purpose is to protect the President

sect /sekt/ n [C] a group of people with its own set of beliefs or religious practices that separate it from a larger group

sec·tar·i·an /sekˈteəriən‖-ˈter-/ adj relating to the differences and strong feelings between religious groups: *sectarian violence*

sec·tion /'sekʃən/ n [C] **1** one of the parts that an object, group, place etc is divided into: *the sports section of the newspaper* | *The rocket is built in sections.* (=in parts that are then fitted together) **2** a view of something that shows what it would look like if it were cut from top to bottom and looked at from the side: *a section of a volcano* — **sectional** adj

sec·tor /'sektəl-ər/ n [C] **1** a part of an economic system, such as a business or industry: *the public sector* (=businesses controlled by the government) | *the private sector* (=businesses controlled by private companies) **2** one of the parts that an area or large group of people is divided into: *the former eastern sector of Berlin*

sec·u·lar /'sekjˈlə‖-ər/ adj not religious or not controlled by a religious authority: *secular education*

se·cure¹ /sɪˈkjʊə‖-ˈkjʊr/ adj **1** not likely to change or become a risk: *a secure job* **2** safe and protected from danger: *The garage isn't a very secure place.* **3** firmly fastened and therefore not likely to fall: *That mirror doesn't look very secure.* — **securely** adv

secure² v [T] **1** to get something important, especially after a lot of effort: *a treaty that will secure peace* **2** to fasten or tie something firmly: *We secured the boat with a rope.* **3** to make something safe from being attacked or harmed

se·cu·ri·ty /sɪˈkjʊərˌti‖-ˈkjʊr-/ n [U] **1** the state of being safe, or the things you do to keep someone or something safe: *airport security checks* | *Tight security surrounded the President's visit.* **2** protection from change, risks, or bad situations: *financial security* **3** a feeling of being safe and protected: *Rules can give a child a sense of security.* **4** something of value such as property that you promise to give to someone if you fail to pay back money you have borrowed: *She had to put up her house as security for the loan.*

se·dan /sɪˈdæn/ n [C] *AmE* a large car that has a separate enclosed space for bags, cases etc; SALOON *BrE*

se·date¹ /sɪˈdeɪt/ adj moving in a slow, formal way

sedate² v [T] to give someone a drug to make them feel sleepy and calm — **sedated** adj — **sedation** /-ˈdeɪʃən/ n [U]

sed·a·tive /'sedətɪv/ n [C] a drug used to make someone sleepy or calm

sed·en·ta·ry /'sedəntəri‖-teri/ adj a sedentary job involves sitting down and not being physically active

sed·i·ment /'sedɪmənt/ n [singular, U] small pieces of a solid substance that form a layer at the bottom of a liquid — **sedimentary** /ˌsedɪˈmentəri◂/ adj

se·di·tion /sɪˈdɪʃən/ n [U] *formal* speeches, writing, activities etc that are intended to encourage people to disobey a government — **seditious** adj

se·duce /sɪˈdjuːs‖-ˈduːs/ v [T] to persuade someone to have sex with you, especially someone younger or with less experience than you — **seduction** /-ˈdʌkʃən/ n [C,U]

se·duc·tive /sɪˈdʌktɪv/ adj **1** sexually attractive **2** making something very attractive and interesting to you: *highly seductive advertising*

see /siː/ v **saw** /sɔː‖sɒː/, **seen** /siːn/, **seeing** **1** [I,T] to use your eyes to look at and notice people or things: *I can't see without my glasses.* | *It was too dark to see anything.* | *I saw a* *man take the bag and run off.* **2** [I,T] to understand or realize something: *Do you see how it works?| I can't see that Pat will agree to that.| "Just press the red button." "Oh, I see."* (=I understand) *| I can't see the point of* (=understand the reason for) *waiting any longer.| Do you see what I mean about the camera being broken?* **3** [T] to watch a film, television programme etc: *What movie shall we go and see?| Did you see that concert on TV last night?* **4** [T] to visit or meet someone: *I saw her in the park yesterday.| You ought to see a doctor.* **5** [T] to find out information or a fact: *Plug it in and see if it's working.| I'll see what time the train leaves.* **6** [T] to think about someone or something in a particular way: *Fighting on TV can make children see violence as normal.* **7** [T] to have experience of something: *The judge said he had never seen a case like this before.* **8** [T] to be the time when or the place where something happens: *The 20th century saw huge social changes.* **9** [I,T] to think something, especially about what is going to happen in the future: *We are supposed to move house in May, but I don't see that happening.* **10** [T] to make sure that something is done correctly: *Please see that everything is put back in the right place.* **11** [T] to go with someone or take them to a particular place, usually to make sure they get there safely: *Just wait a minute and I'll see you home.* **12 see eye to eye (with sb)** to agree with someone: *Ros and her mother don't always see eye to eye.* **13 see you** used to say goodbye to someone you will meet again: *Okay, I'll see you later.| See you, Ben.* **14 let's see/let me see** used when you are trying to remember something or are thinking about something: *Let's see. When did you send it?* **15 I'll/we'll see** used when you do not want to make a decision immediately: *"Can we go to Disney World this year?" "We'll see."*

---

see

Karen was blindfolded so she couldn't see.

They looked at the paintings.

Dad's watching TV.

see about sth *phr v* [T] to make arrangements or deal with something: *Fran went to see about her passport.*

see sb ↔ **off** *phr v* [T] to go to an airport, train station etc to say goodbye to someone who is leaving: *We saw her off from Stansted Airport.*

see sb **out** *phr v* [T] to go with someone to the door when they leave: *No, that's okay, I'll see myself out.* (=go by myself to the door)

see through *phr v* [T] **1** [**see through** sb/sth] to be able to know what the truth is when someone is not being honest with you: *Can't you see through his lies?* **2** [**see** sb/sth **through**] to continue doing something difficult until it is finished, or to help someone until the end of a difficult time: *Miller is determined to see the project through.*

see to sth *phr v* [T] to deal with something or make sure that it happens: *We'll see to it that he gets there safely,*

> **USAGE NOTE: see, look at, and watch**
>
> If you **see** something, you notice it with your eyes, whether or not you want to: *I saw some terrible things during the war.* When you **look at** something, you deliberately turn your eyes towards it: *Look at that rainbow!* **Watch** means that you look at something that is happening or moving for a period of time: *He was watching TV. | They're going to watch the game.*

seed[1] /siːd/ *n* seed or seeds **1** [C,U] a small hard thing produced by plants that a new plant will grow from: *Sow* (=plant) *the seeds one inch deep in the soil.* **2 (the) seeds of sth** the beginning of something that will grow and develop: *From the start, the jury had seeds of doubt in their minds.*

seed[2] *v* [T] to plant seeds in the ground

seed·less /'siːdləs/ *adj* without any seeds: *seedless grapes*

seed·ling /'siːdlɪŋ/ *n* [C] a young plant grown from a seed

seed·y /'siːdi/ *adj informal* looking dirty or poor, and often connected with illegal or immoral activity: *the seedy side of town*

seeing eye dog /ˌ.. ˈ. ˌ./ *n* [C] *AmE* a dog that is trained to guide blind people; GUIDE DOG *BrE*

seek /siːk/ *v* sought /sɔːt‖sɒːt/, sought, seek·ing *formal* **1** [I,T] to try to find or get something: *The UN is seeking a political solution.| You should seek advice from a lawyer.* **2** [T] to try to achieve or do something: *The Governor will not say whether he will seek re-election next year.| seek to do sth We are seeking to stop such cruelty to farm animals.*

seem /siːm/ *v* [linking verb] **1** to appear to be a particular thing or to have a particular quality or feeling: *Henry seems a bit upset today.| seems to be There seems to be a problem with the brakes.* **2** to appear to exist or be true: *We seem to have taken the wrong road.| it seems to sb It seems to me that it's a complete waste of time.*

seem·ing·ly /'siːmɪŋli/ *adv* in a way that seems to be true, but usually is not: *A seemingly innocent young girl, she is in fact a brutal murderer.*

seen /siːn/ *v* the past participle of SEE

seep /siːp/ v [I] to flow slowly through small holes or cracks: *Water was seeping through the ceiling.*

see·saw[1] /'siːsɔː‖-sɒ-/ n [C] a long board on which children play, that is balanced in the middle so that when one end goes up the other end goes down

seesaw[2] v [I] to move suddenly from one state or condition to another and back again

seethe /siːð/ v [I] to be very angry, but not show it openly: *He walked out of the house, seething with anger.* —**seething** adj

seg·ment /'segmənt/ n [C] one of the parts that something can be divided into: *a large segment of the population* | *orange segments* ➝ see colour picture on page 440

seg·ment·ed /seg'mentɪd/ adj divided into separate parts

seg·re·gate /'segrɪgeɪt/ v [T] to separate one group of people from others, especially because of race, sex, religion etc: *Black and white people were segregated both at home and at work.* —**segregation** /ˌsegrɪ'geɪʃən/ n [U] *racial segregation*

seg·re·gat·ed /'segrɪgeɪtɪd/ adj segregated buildings, organizations, areas etc can only be used by members of one particular race, sex, religion etc

seis·mic /'saɪzmɪk/ adj technical relating to or caused by EARTHQUAKES

seize /siːz/ v [T] **1** to take hold of something quickly and with a lot of force: *Ron seized the child's arm and lifted her to safety.* **2** **seize control/power** to take control of a place suddenly, using military force: *Rebel soldiers seized control of the embassy.* **3** to take away something such as illegal guns, drugs etc: *Police seized 10 kilos of cocaine.*

seize on/upon phr v [T] to accept something eagerly when you have the chance: *She seized on the opportunity to study overseas.*

seize up phr v [I] **a)** if a machine seizes up, it stops working, for example because of lack of oil **b)** if part of your body seizes up, you cannot move it and it is very painful

sei·zure /'siːʒə‖-ər/ n **1** [U] when something is suddenly taken, or when someone suddenly takes control of a country, government etc: *The police say this is their biggest ever seizure of illegal guns.* **2** [C] a sudden attack of an illness: *a heart seizure*

sel·dom /'seldəm/ adv very rarely: *Glen seldom eats breakfast.*

se·lect[1] /sɪ'lekt/ v [T] to choose something or someone: *He was not selected for the team.*

select[2] adj formal consisting of or used by a small group of specially chosen people: *a select club* | *Only a select few have been invited.*

se·lec·tion /sɪ'lekʃən/ n **1** [U] when something or someone is chosen from among a bigger group: *Selection of candidates for the job will take place next week.* **2** [C] someone or something that has been chosen from a group of people or things: *a selection of songs from the show* **3** [C] a group of things that have been gathered together, especially things for sale: *The store has a wide selection of children's books.*

se·lec·tive /sɪ'lektɪv/ adj **1** careful about what you choose to do, buy etc: *She's very selec-tive about her clothes.* **2** affecting or involving only a few specially chosen people or things: *the selective breeding of animals*

self /self/ n [C,U], plural **selves** /selvz/ your feeling of who you are, including your character, abilities etc: *He's starting to feel like his old self again.* (=feel normal again) | *a child's sense of self*

self-as·sured /ˌ. .'.◂/ adj confident about what you are doing —**self-assurance** n [U]

self-cen·tred BrE, **self-centered** AmE /ˌ.'..◂/ adj interested only in yourself and not caring about other people; SELFISH

self-con·fi·dent /ˌ. '.../ adj feeling sure about your ability to be successful, look attractive etc, and not shy or nervous with other people —**self-confidence** n [U]

self-con·scious /ˌ. '..◂/ adj worried and embarrassed about what you look like or what other people think of you: *She feels self-conscious about wearing glasses.* —**self-consciously** adv —**self-consciousness** n [U]

self-con·tained /ˌ. .'.◂/ adj **1** something that is self-contained is complete in itself and does not need other things to make it work: *a self-contained computer package* **2** BrE a self-contained FLAT has its own kitchen, bathroom, and entrance

self-con·trol /ˌ. .'./ n [U] the ability to control your feelings and behaviour even when you are angry, excited, or upset

self-de·fence BrE, **self-defense** AmE /ˌ. .'./ n [U] the use of force to protect yourself from attack: *She shot the man in self-defence.*

self-de·struc·tive /ˌ. .'..◂/ adj self-destructive actions are likely to harm or kill the person who is doing them

self-dis·ci·pline /ˌ. '.../ n [U] the ability to make yourself do the things that you should do —**self-disciplined** adj

self-em·ployed /ˌ. .'.◂/ adj working for yourself rather than for a company

self-es·teem /ˌ. .'./ n [U] the confident feeling that you deserve to be liked and respected

self-ev·i·dent /ˌ. '.../ adj clearly true and not needing any proof; OBVIOUS

self-ex·plan·a·to·ry /ˌ. .'....◂/ adj clear and easy to understand, with no need for explanation

self-help /ˌ. './ n [U] the use of your own efforts to deal with your problems, instead of depending on other people

self-im·age /ˌ. '..◂/ n [singular] the idea that you have of your own abilities, appearance, and character

self-im·posed /ˌ. .'.◂/ adj self-imposed rules, conditions, limits etc are ones that you make yourself keep to, and no one else has asked you to accept

self-in·dul·gent /ˌ. .'.◂/ adj allowing yourself to have or enjoy something that you do not need —**self-indulgence** n [C,U]

self-in·flict·ed /ˌ. .'..◂/ adj a self-inflicted injury, problem etc is one that you have caused yourself

self-in·terest /ˌ. '../ n [U] concern for what is best for you, rather than for other people

self·ish /'selfɪʃ/ adj caring only about yourself rather than about other people: *Why are you*

being so selfish? | *He's a mean and selfish old man.*
— **selfishness** *n* [U] — **selfishly** *adv* → opposite
UNSELFISH

self·less /ˈselfləs/ *adj* caring and thinking about other people more than about yourself

self-made /ˌ. ˈ.◂/ *adj* successful and having a lot of money because of your own efforts: *a self-made millionaire*

self-pit·y /ˌ. ˈ../ *n* [U] a feeling of being too sorry for yourself

self-por·trait /ˌ. ˈ../ *n* [C] a picture that you make of yourself

self-pos·sessed /ˌ. .ˈ.◂/ *adj* calm and confident, because you are in control of your feelings

self-re·li·ant /ˌ. .ˈ.◂/ *adj* able to make decisions by yourself without depending on other people

self-re·spect /ˌ. .ˈ./ *n* [U] a feeling of confidence and pride in your abilities, ideas, and character — **self-respecting** *adj*: *No self-respecting trade union would give up its right to strike.*

self-right·eous /ˌ. ˈ.◂/ *adj* too sure that your beliefs, attitudes etc are right, in a way that annoys other people

self-sac·ri·fice /ˌ. ˈ../ *n* [U] when you give up what you need or want in order to help someone else — **self-sacrificing** *adj*

self-sat·is·fied /ˌ. ˈ.../ *adj* too pleased with yourself

self-serv·ice /ˌ. ˈ.◂/ *adj* used to describe places where you get things for yourself, rather than being served by the people who work there: *a self-service restaurant*

self-suf·fi·cient /ˌ. .ˈ. ◂/ *adj* able to provide for all your own needs without help from other people: *a country that is self-sufficient in food* — **self-sufficiency** *n* [U]

sell /sel/ *v* sold /səʊld‖soʊld/, sold, selling
1 [I,T] to give something to someone in exchange for money: **sell sth for** *We sold the car for $5000.* | **sell sth to sb** *Scott sold his CD player to a kid at school.* | **sell sb sth** *Sally's going to sell me her bike.* → compare BUY[1] **2** [T] to offer something for people to buy: *Do you sell stamps?* | **sell at/for** (=to be offered for sale at a particular price): *The T-shirts sell at £10 each.* **3** [T] to make someone want to buy something: *Bad news sells newspapers.* **4** [I,T] to be bought or sold in large numbers or amounts: *Toys based on the movie are really selling.* | *The CD sold over a million copies in a week.* **5** [T] to try to persuade someone to accept a new plan, idea etc: *Now we have to try to sell the idea to the viewers.* **6 be sold on sth** to think something is a very good idea and want to do it: *I suggested she should come to stay with us, and she was completely sold on the idea.* **7 sell yourself short** *informal* to not have the confidence in your abilities that you should have

sell sth ↔ off *phr v* [T] to sell things quickly and cheaply: *The shop is closing and selling everything off at half price.*

sell out *phr v* **1** [I] to sell all of something so that there is none left: **have/be sold out** *I'm sorry, but the tickets are all sold out.* | **sell out of** *They've sold out of newspapers.* **2** [I,T] *informal* to do something that is against your beliefs or principles, in order to get power or money

sell up *phr v* [I] to sell everything you have when you move to another place, change your life etc: *The Martins sold up and moved to Florida.*

sell-by date /ˈ. . ˌ./ *n* [C] *BrE* **1** the date printed on a food product after which it should not be sold **2 be past its sell-by date** *informal* to no longer be interesting, useful etc

sell·er /ˈseləʳ‖-ər/ *n* [C] **1** a person or company that sells something: *the largest seller of household equipment* → compare BUYER **2** a product that a company sells: *The multi-CD player is our biggest seller.* (=a lot of them are sold) → see also BESTSELLER

Sel·lo·tape /ˈseləteɪp, -loʊ-‖-lə-, -loʊ-/ *n* [U] *BrE* trademark thin clear TAPE used for sticking things together: SCOTCH TAPE *AmE*

sell-out /ˈselaʊt/ *n* [singular] **1** a performance, sports event etc for which all the tickets have been sold **2** *informal* when someone does something that is against their principles, especially in order to get power or money

selves /selvz/ *n* the plural of SELF

sem·blance /ˈsembləns/ *n* [singular, U] a condition or quality that is slightly like another one: **+ of** *I'm just trying to create some semblance of order here.*

se·men /ˈsiːmən/ *n* [U] the liquid that is produced by the male sex organs, that contains SPERM

se·mes·ter /sᵻˈmestəʳ‖-ər/ *n* [C] *especially AmE* one of two periods into which the school or college year is divided → compare QUARTER

semi- /ˈsemi/ *prefix* **1** used at the beginning of some words to mean 'exactly half': *a semicircle* **2** used at the beginning of some words to mean 'partly but not completely': *semidarkness* | *semiliterate*

sem·i·cir·cle /ˈsemiˌsɜːkəl‖-ɜːr-/ *n* [C] **1** half a circle **2** a group arranged in a curved line: *Could everyone please sit in a semicircle?* → see picture at SHAPES

sem·i·co·lon /ˌsemiˈkəʊlən‖ˈsemiˌkoʊlən/ *n* [C] the mark (;) used in writing to separate different parts of a sentence or list

semi-de·tached /ˌ. .ˈ.◂/ *adj BrE* a semi-detached house is joined to another house by one shared wall → see colour picture on page 79

sem·i·fi·nal /ˌsemiˈfaɪnl◂/ *n* [C] one of the two sports games whose winners then play each other to decide who wins the whole competition

sem·i·nar /ˈsemᵻnɑː‖-ɑːr/ *n* [C] a class in which a small group of students meet to study or talk about a subject

sem·i·na·ry /ˈsemᵻnəri‖-neri/ *n* [C] a college for training priests

---

SPELLING NOTE
Words with the sound /s/, may be spelt **c-**, like **city**, or **ps-**, like **psychology**.

sem·i·pre·cious /ˌsemiˈpreʃəs◂/ adj a semi-precious jewel or stone is valuable, but not as valuable as a PRECIOUS stone

Se·mit·ic /sɪˈmɪtɪk/ adj **1** belonging to the race of people that includes Jews, Arabs, and other ancient peoples from the Middle East **2** Jewish

sen·ate /ˈsenɪt/ n **the Senate** the smaller of the two parts of government in countries such as the US and Australia → compare HOUSE OF REPRE-SENTATIVES

sen·a·tor, Senator /ˈsenətəll-tər/ n [C] a member of a senate: Senator Kennedy

send /send/ v [T] **sent** /sent/, **sent, sending 1** to arrange for something to go or be taken to another place, especially by mail: I sent the letter last week. | **send sb sth** I forgot to send Dad a birthday card. | **send sth back** She sent back the form immediately. **2** to make someone go some-where: The UN is sending troops to the region. **3** to make someone do or feel something: Sitting in the library usually sends me to sleep.

send for sb/sth phr v [T] **1** to send a message asking someone to come to you: She sent for the doctor. **2** also **send off/away for** to ask or write for something to be sent to you by mail: Send now for your free catalogue.

send in phr v [T] **1** [send sth ↔ in] to send something, usually by mail, to a place where it can be dealt with: Did you send in your applica-tion? **2** [send sb ↔ in] to send soldiers, police etc somewhere to deal with a dangerous situa-tion: Finally, the mayor had to send in the po-lice.

send off phr v [T] **1** [send sth ↔ off] to send something somewhere by post: Have you sent the cheque off yet? **2** [send sb ↔ off] to make someone go somewhere: We got sent off to camp every summer. **3** [send sb ↔ off] BrE to order a sports player to leave the game because of bad behaviour

send out phr v [T] **1** [send sb/sth ↔ out] to send something or someone from a central point to various other places: The wedding in-vitations were sent out weeks ago. **2** [send sth ↔ out] to broadcast something, or to produce light, sound etc: The ship sent out an SOS message.

send up phr v [T **send** sb/sth **up**] BrE informal to make someone or something look silly by copying them in a funny way

send-off /ˈ. ./ n [C] informal an occasion when people gather together to say goodbye to some-one who is leaving: The team got a great send-off at the airport.

se·nile /ˈsiːnaɪl/ adj mentally confused or be-having strangely, because of old age — **senility** /sɪˈnɪlɪti/ n [U]

se·ni·or /ˈsiːniəll-ər/ adj **1** having an important or more important job, position, or rank: a senior officer in the Navy | She's senior to you. (=She has a more important job, position, or rank) **2** older: Senior pupils get special privi-leges. → compare JUNIOR[1]

senior² n **1** be two/five/ten etc years sb's se-nior to be two, five, ten etc years older than someone **2** [C] AmE a student in the last year of HIGH SCHOOL or college → compare JUNIOR[2] **3** [C] AmE a senior citizen

senior cit·i·zen /ˌ... ˈ.../ n [C] an old person, especially one over the age of 65

senior high school /ˌ... ˈ. ./ n [C] HIGH SCHOOL

se·ni·or·i·ty /ˌsiːniˈɒrɪtill-ˈɔːr-, -ˈɑː-/ n [U] the state of being older or having a higher position than someone else: Her seniority earned her the promotion.

sen·sa·tion /senˈseɪʃən/ n **1** [C,U] the ability to feel, or a feeling that you get from one of your five senses: Matt had a burning sensation in his arm. | Ian had no sensation in his legs after the accident. **2** [C] a feeling or experience that is hard to describe: I had the strangest sensation that everything was happening very slowly. **3** [singular] extreme excitement or interest, or someone or something that causes this: The announcement caused a sensation.

sen·sa·tion·al /senˈseɪʃənəl/ adj **1** reporting events in a way that is intended to make people shocked or excited, rather than give them ser-ious news: a sensational news report of the murder **2** very interesting or exciting: a sensa-tional finish to the race

sen·sa·tion·al·is·m /senˈseɪʃənəlɪzəm/ n [U] a way of reporting events or stories that is in-tended to make people shocked or excited

sense¹ /sens/ n **1** [U] good understanding and judgement, especially about practical things: Earl had the sense not to move the injured man. → compare COMMON SENSE **2** [singular] a feeling about something: She felt a strong sense of loyalty to him. **3** make sense a) to have a clear meaning that is easy to understand: Do these instructions make any sense to you? b) to have a good reason or explanation: Why did she go off alone? It just doesn't make sense. c) to be a sensible thing to do: It makes sense to take care of your health while you're young. **4** make sense of to understand something, especially something difficult or complicated **5** [C] one of the five natural powers of sight, hearing, touch, taste, and smell: Dogs have a very sensitive sense of smell. **6** [singular] a natural ability or skill: She has excellent business sense. | Bullfighters need to have an excellent sense of timing. **7** sense of humour BrE, humor AmE the abil-ity to understand and enjoy things that are funny, or to make people laugh: Laura has a great sense of humour. **8** [C] the meaning of a word, phrase, sentence etc: Many words have more than one sense. **9** come to your senses to realize that you should do something because it is the most sensible thing to do: I'm glad that Lisa finally came to her senses and went to college. **10** in a sense/in some senses in one way, but without thinking about all the facts: In one sense he's right, but things are more compli-cated than that.

sense² v [T] to feel or know something without being told or having proof: Sandy sensed that David wanted to be alone.

sense·less /ˈsensləs/ adj **1** happening or done for no good reason or with no purpose: a senseless killing **2** not conscious: The ball hit him on the head, and knocked him senseless.

sen·si·bil·i·ty /ˌsensɪˈbɪlɪti/ n [C,U] formal someone's feelings, or the ability to understand people's feelings: The movie was said to upset the sensibilities of the black community.

sen·si·ble /ˈsensɪbəl/ adj **1** showing good judgement: a sensible decision **2** suitable for a particular purpose, especially a practical one: sensible clothes —**sensibly** adv

sen·si·tive /ˈsensɪtɪv/ adj **1** able to understand other people's feelings and problems: a sensitive and caring person|A good teacher is sensitive to their students' needs → opposite IN-SENSITIVE **2** easily offended or hurt by the things that other people do or say: Chrissy is very sensitive to comments about her weight. **3** easily affected by physical things: sensitive skin **4** a sensitive situation or subject needs to be dealt with very carefully because it may offend people: The interviewer avoided asking questions on sensitive issues. **5** sensitive equipment can measure or record very small changes —**sensitively** adv —**sensitivity** /ˌsensɪˈtɪvɪti/ n [U]

sen·sor /ˈsensəll-ər/ n [C] a piece of equipment that finds heat, light, sound etc, even in very small amounts

sen·so·ry /ˈsensəri/ adj relating to your senses of sight, hearing, smell, taste, or touch

sen·su·al /ˈsenʃuəl/ adj relating to or enjoying physical pleasure, especially sexual pleasure: sensual music —**sensuality** /ˌsenʃuˈælɪti/ n [U]

sen·su·ous /ˈsenʃuəs/ adj making you feel physical pleasure: the sensuous feel of silk

sent /sent/ v the past tense and past participle of SEND

sen·tence[1] /ˈsentəns/ n [C] **1** in grammar, a group of words that expresses a complete idea and usually contains a subject and a verb. A sentence begins with a capital letter and ends with a FULL STOP. **2** a punishment that a judge gives to someone who is guilty of a crime: a ten-year sentence for robbery

sentence[2] v [T] to give a legal punishment to someone who is guilty of a crime: He was sentenced to six years in prison.

sen·ti·ment /ˈsentɪmənt/ n **1** [C,U] formal an opinion that comes from your feelings about something: Pacifist sentiment was strong among the demonstrators. | "Anderson ought to be fired." "My sentiments exactly." (=I completely agree) **2** [U] feelings such as pity, love, or sadness that are considered to be too strong: There's no room for sentiment in business.

sen·ti·men·tal /ˌsentɪˈmentl/ adj **1** showing emotions such as love, PITY, and sadness too strongly or in a silly way: sentimental love songs | Laurie still gets sentimental about our old house. **2** based on feelings, happy memories etc, rather than being worth a lot of money: The watch had great sentimental value. —**sentimentality** /ˌsentɪmenˈtælɪti/ n [U]

sen·try /ˈsentri/ n [C] a soldier standing outside a building as a guard

sep·a·ra·ble /ˈsepərəbəl/ adj able to be separated from something else → opposite INSEPARABLE

sep·a·rate[1] /ˈsepərɪt/ adj **1** not joined or touching another thing: Always keep cooked and raw food separate. **2** not connected to or affecting anything else: + from He keeps his professional life separate from his private life. **3** different or not shared: The kids have separate bedrooms. —**separately** adv

sep·a·rate[2] /ˈsepəreɪt/ v **1** [I,T] to divide or split something into two or more parts, or to make something do this: + into Ms. Barker separated the class into four groups. | + from Separate the egg yolk from the white. **2** [T] to be between two things so that they cannot touch each other or communicate with each other: A screen separates the dining area from the kitchen. **3** [I,T] to move apart, or make people move apart: Police moved in to separate the crowd. **4** [I] to start to live apart from your husband, wife, or sexual partner: When did Lyle and Jan separate?

sep·a·rat·ed /ˈsepəreɪtɪd/ adj not living with your husband, wife, or sexual partner any more: Her parents are separated.

sep·a·ra·tion /ˌsepəˈreɪʃən/ n **1** [U] the act of separating or the state of being separate: the separation of powers between Congress and the President **2** [C,U] a period of time when people live apart from each other: Separation from their parents is very hard on children. **3** [C] a legal agreement between a husband and wife to live apart from each other

Sep·tem·ber /sepˈtembəll-ər/ written abbreviation **Sept** n [C,U] the ninth month of the year → see usage note at MONTH

sep·tic /ˈseptɪk/ adj infected by disease

sep·ul·chre /ˈsepəlkəll-kər/ n [C] literary a large TOMB

se·quel /ˈsiːkwəl/ n [C] a film, book etc that continues the story of an earlier one

se·quence /ˈsiːkwəns/ n **1** [C] a series of events or actions that have a particular order: the sequence of events that led to the war **2** [C,U] the order in which things are arranged or should happen: Two of the pages were out of sequence. (=not in order)

se·quin /ˈsiːkwɪn/ n [C] a small round piece of shiny metal that is sewn on clothes for decoration

ser·e·nade /ˌserɪˈneɪd/ n [C] a song, especially a love song —**serenade** v [T]

se·rene /sɪˈriːn/ adj **1** someone who is serene is very calm **2** a place that is serene is peaceful and quiet —**serenity** /sɪˈrenɪti/ n [U]

ser·geant /ˈsɑːdʒəntll-ɑːr-/ n [C] an officer of fairly low rank in the army or police

se·ri·al[1] /ˈsɪəriəlll-ˈsɪr-/ n [C] a story that is broadcast or printed in several separate parts on television, in a magazine etc

serial[2] adj arranged or happening one after the other in the correct order: serial processing on a computer

serial ki·ller /ˈ... ˌ.../ n [C] someone who has murdered several people one after the other

se·ries /ˈsɪəriːzll-ˈsɪr-/ n [C], plural **series** **1** several events or actions of the same kind that happen one after the other: There has been a series of accidents along this road. **2** a set of television or radio programmes with the same characters or on the same subject: a new comedy series

se·ri·ous /ˈsɪəriəsll-ˈsɪr-/ adj **1** a serious problem, situation etc is bad and worrying: a serious illness **2 be serious** to be sincere about what you say or do: John's serious about becoming an actor. **3** a serious person is always quiet and sensible and does not often laugh —**seriousness** *n* [U]

se·ri·ous·ly /ˈsɪəriəsliǁˈsɪr-/ *adv* **1** in a serious way: *I'm seriously worried about Ben. | You should think seriously about what I've said.* **2 take sb/sth seriously** to believe that someone or something is important and worth paying attention to: *You shouldn't take everything he says so seriously.* **3** *spoken* used to show that the next thing you say is true or not a joke: *Seriously, he's going out with Sara.*

ser·mon /ˈsɜːmənǁˈsɜːr-/ *n* [C] **1** a religious talk given at a church **2** *informal* a talk in which someone gives you unwanted moral advice ➔ see also PREACH

ser·pent /ˈsɜːpəntǁˈsɜːr-/ *n* [C] *literary* a snake

ser·rat·ed /sɪˈreɪtɪd, se-/ *adj* a serrated knife has a sharp blade made from a series of connected V shapes

se·rum /ˈsɪərəmǁˈsɪr-/ *n* [C,U] *technical* a liquid containing substances that fight infection ➔ compare VACCINE

ser·vant /ˈsɜːvəntǁˈsɜːr-/ *n* [C] someone whose job is to live in another person's house and do jobs such as cleaning and cooking, especially in past times

serve[1] /sɜːvǁsɜːrv/ *v* **1** [I,T] to give someone food or drinks as part of a meal: *Dinner is served at eight.* **2** [I,T] to work in the army or in an organization doing a useful and helpful job: *Kelly served in the army for three years. | She serves on the student committee.* **3** [T] to provide someone with something that is useful or necessary: *The new airport will serve several large cities in the north.* **4** [I,T] to give help, bring things etc to a customer in a shop: *Are you being served, Sir?* **5** [T] to spend time in prison: *Baxter served a five-year sentence for theft.* **6** [I,T] to be useful or suitable for a particular purpose: *The sofa can also serve as a bed.* **7** [I,T] to start playing a game such as TENNIS etc by throwing the ball into the air and hitting it to your opponent **8 it serves sb right** *spoken* used to say that someone deserves something unpleasant, because they have done something stupid or unkind: *I'm sorry Eddie crashed his car, but it serves him right for driving so fast!*

serve[2] *n* [C] the action in a game such as tennis in which you throw the ball into the air and hit it to your opponent

serv·er /ˈsɜːvəǁ-ər/ *n* [C] the main computer on a NETWORK that controls all the others

ser·vice[1] /ˈsɜːvɪsǁˈsɜːr-/ *n* **1** [U] the help that people who work in a restaurant, hotel, shop etc give you: *The food is terrific but the service is very slow. | the customer service department* **2** [C] a place such as a hospital, school etc that is provided for the public to use: *People want good public services. | the National Health Service* **3** [C,U] the work that you do for a person or organization: *He retired after 20 years of service.* **4** [C] a business that provides help or does jobs for people, rather than producing things: *regular bus services | We offer a free information service.* **5 the services** a country's military forces **6** [C] an organization that works for a government: *the diplomatic service* **7** [C] a formal religious ceremony, especially in a church: *the evening service at St Marks* **8** [C] an act of hitting the ball to your opponent to start a game of tennis etc **9 be in service/out of service** to be available or not available for people to use: *Sorry, this bus is out of service.* **10** [C] the regular examination of a machine or vehicle to make sure it works correctly: *The car is in the garage for a service.* **11 services** *BrE* a place where you can stop to buy petrol, food etc on a MOTORWAY

service[2] *v* [T] to examine a machine or vehicle and fix it if necessary: *When did you last have the car serviced?*

service charge /ˈ.. ./ *n* [C] *BrE* an amount of money that is added to a bill to pay for additional services

ser·vice·man /ˈsɜːvɪsmənǁˈsɜːr-/ *n* [C] a man who serves in the army, navy, AIRFORCE etc

service sta·tion /ˈ.. ../ *n* [C] a place that sells petrol, food etc

ser·vice·wom·an /ˈsɜːvɪsˌwʊmənǁˈsɜːr-/ *n* [C] a woman who serves in the army, navy, AIRFORCE etc

ser·vi·ette /ˌsɜːviˈetǁˌsɜːr-/ *n* [C] *BrE* a small piece of cloth or paper used for protecting your clothes and cleaning your hands when you are eating; NAPKIN

ser·vile /ˈsɜːvaɪlǁˈsɜːrvəl, -vaɪl/ *adj* too eager to obey someone and do whatever they tell you to

serv·ing /ˈsɜːvɪŋǁˈsɜːr-/ *n* [C] an amount of food that is enough for one person; HELPING

ses·sion /ˈseʃən/ *n* [C] **1** a period of time used for a particular purpose, especially by a group of people: *a question-and-answer session* **2** a formal meeting, especially of a court of law or government organization: *The State Court is now in session.*

set[1] /set/ *v* **set, set, setting 1** [T] to decide what something should be: *Have they set a date for the wedding? | The target that was set was much too high.* **2** [T] to put the control on a machine or piece of equipment in a particular position, or make it ready to be used: *Set the oven to 180°. | Do you know how to set the videorecorder?* **3** [T] if a story, film etc is set in a place or at a particular time, it happens there or at that time: *Clavell's novel is set in 17th century Japan.* **4 set fire to sth/set light to sth** to make something start burning: *Vandals set fire to the school.* **5** [T] to give someone some school work, a test, or an examination: *Did he set you any homework?* **6** [T] to put something somewhere: **set sth down/set down sth** *She set the tray down on the bed.* **7** [I] if a liquid mixture sets, it becomes hard and solid: *The concrete will set within two hours.* **8** [I] when the sun sets, it moves lower in the sky until it can no longer be seen **9 set a record** to do something quicker or better than anyone has ever done it before: *Lewis set a new world record in the 100 metres.* **10 set an example** to behave in a good way to show other people how they should behave: *It's up to parents to set an example to their children.* **11 set the table** to arrange plates, knives etc on a table so that it is ready for people to eat a meal **12 set sb free/loose** to allow a person or animal to leave a prison or cage, or untie them **13 set foot in** to go into a place, especially for the first time: *Stella had never set foot in a church before.* **14 set your sights on sth** to decide that you want to achieve or get something: *She's set her sights on* *winning the world championship.* **15 set a trap** to make a trap to catch someone, or put down a trap to catch an animal **16 set your heart on sth** to want something very much **17 set (sb) to work** to start doing something, or make someone start doing something: *He set to work clearing up all the mess.* **18 set sail** to start sailing somewhere **19 set sth in motion** to make something start happening: *Once the process is set in motion, we cannot stop it.* **20 set great store by sth** to believe that something is very important or useful **21** [I,T] if a broken bone sets, or someone sets it, it becomes joined together again **22** [T] if a jewel is set in gold, silver etc, it is surrounded by gold, silver etc → see also **set/start the ball rolling** (BALL), **put/set sb's mind at rest** (REST¹)

set about sth *phr v* [T] **set about doing sth** to start doing something, especially something that will take a long time: *Johnny set about improving his Spanish.*

set sb **against** sb *phr v* [T] to make someone start to argue or fight with someone else: *a bitter civil war that set brother against brother*

set sth ↔ **apart** *phr v* [T] to make someone or something different from other similar people or things: *There was something about her that set her apart from the other women.*

set sth ↔ **aside** *phr v* [T] **1** to save something for a special purpose: *I set aside a little money every week.* **2 set aside your differences** to agree to stop arguing

set back *phr v* [T] **1** [**set** sb/sth ↔ **back**] to delay something: *The accident could set back the Russian space programme by several months.* **2** [**set** sb **back**] to cost someone a lot of money: *Dinner set us back $300.*

set sth ↔ **down** *phr v* [T] to write something, especially in an official document

set forth sth *phr v* [T] *literary* to start a journey

set in *phr v* [I] if something sets in, especially something unpleasant, it begins and is likely to continue: *Winter was setting in.*

set off *phr v* **1** [I] to leave and start going somewhere: *We'd better set off now before it gets dark.* **2** [T **set** sth ↔ **off**] to make something explode or make a loud noise: *Some kids were setting off fireworks.* **3** [T **set** sth ↔ **off**] to make something start happening, or make people suddenly start doing something: *The killings set off a storm of protest.*

set out *phr v* **1 set out to do sth** to start trying to do something, or to deliberately intend to do something: *The four men set out to prove their innocence.* **2** [I] to leave a place and start a long journey: *The couple set out for Fresno the next day.* **3** [T **set out** sth] to write or talk about something in a clear and organized way: *You'll find the terms and conditions set out in the agreement.*

set up *phr v* **1** [I,T **set** sth ↔ **up**] to start a company or organization: *In 1976, he set up his own import-export business.* | **set up shop** (=start a business somewhere): *Ernest set up*

shop as a photographer. **2** [T **set** sth ↔ **up**] to make arrangements for something to happen: *Do you want me to set up a meeting?* **3** [T **set** sth ↔ **up**] to put something somewhere, or make equipment ready to be used: *The police set up roadblocks to try to catch the terrorists.* **4** [T **set** sb ↔ **up**] to deliberately make other people think that someone has done something wrong: *Hudson accused his partners of setting him up.*

set² *n* [C] **1** a group of things that belong together or are used together: *a set of dishes* | *a chess set* **2** a television or radio: *a TV set* **3** a place where a film or programme is filmed, or the things that are used on stage in a play to show where it happens: *OK everybody, quiet on the set!* **4** one part of a game of tennis: *Sampras leads by two sets to one.*

set³ *adj* **1** fixed and not changing: *We meet at a set time each week.* **2** *informal* ready to do something: **all set** *spoken* (=completely ready): *If everyone is all set, we'll start the meeting.* **3 be set to do sth** used to say that something is likely to happen: *The band's success story looks set to continue.* **4 set on/upon sth** *informal* determined to do something **5 set against sth** strongly opposed to something: *My parents seemed set against the idea.* **6 be set in your ways** to be used to doing things in the same way and not want to change **7** to be in a particular place: *The palace is set on an island in the middle of the lake.*

set·back /ˈsetbæk/ *n* [C] a problem that happens that stops you from making progress: *Today's result was a setback, but we can still win the championship.*

set·tee /seˈtiː/ *n* [C] *BrE* a comfortable seat for two or three people; SOFA

set·ting /ˈsetɪŋ/ *n* [C usually singular] **1** the place or time in which something happens, especially a book or film: *London is the setting for his most recent novel.* **2** the place where something is and the things that surround it: *a mansion in a beautiful parkland setting* **3** one of the positions that the controls on a machine can be turned to: *Turn the oven to its highest setting.*

set·tle /ˈsetl/ *v* **1** [I,T] to end an argument or disagreement: *They asked me to settle the argument.* **2** [I,T] to move into a comfortable position: *Dave settled back and turned on the TV.* **3** [T] to decide or arrange the details of something: *We need to get everything settled as soon as possible.* **4** [I] to start living in a place where you intend to live for a long time: *My family finally settled in Los Angeles.* **5** [I] to come or fall to the ground or bottom of something and stay there **6** [T] if you settle a bill, debt etc, you pay the money that you owe **7 settle a score** to do something bad to someone because they have done something bad to you

settle down *phr v* [I] **1** to start living in one place, and get married or get a permanent job: *My parents want me to settle down and have children.* **2** to stop moving around and give your attention to doing something: *Settle down kids, and eat your dinner.*

settle for sth *phr v* [T] to accept something that is less than what you wanted: *We had to settle for the cheapest apartment.*

settle in *phr v* [I] to start to feel happy after moving to a new house, job, or school: *Adam seems to have settled in at his new school.*

settle on/upon sth *phr v* [T] to choose something after thinking about a lot of different possibilities: *They haven't settled on a name for the baby yet.*

settle up *phr v* [I] *informal* to pay money that you owe for something

set·tled /ˈsetld/ *adj* **1 feel/be settled** to start to feel happy in your new house, job, or school **2** not changing, or not likely to change: *The weather should be more settled over the weekend.* → compare UNSETTLED

set·tle·ment /ˈsetlmənt/ *n* [C] **1** an official agreement that ends an argument or fighting: *efforts to find a political settlement to the conflict* **2** a place where a group of people live: *a Stone Age settlement*

set·tler /ˈsetlə‖-ər/ *n* [C] someone who goes to live in an area where not many people have lived before: *the early settlers in the American West*

set·up /ˈ.. ./ *n* [C usually singular] *informal* **1** the situation that exists because of the way that something is organized: *What do you think of the new set-up at work?* **2** a dishonest plan that is intended to trick someone: *I knew immediately that the whole thing was a set-up.*

sev·en /ˈsevən/ *number* 7

sev·en·teen /ˌsevənˈtiːn‹/ *number* 17 —**seventeenth** *number*

sev·enth[1] /ˈsevənθ/ *number* 7th

seventh[2] *n* [C] one of the seven equal parts of something; 1/7

sev·en·ty /ˈsevənti/ *number* **1** 70 **2 the seventies a)** the years between 1970 and 1979 **b)** the numbers between 70 and 79 **3 be in your seventies** to be aged between 70 and 79 —**seventieth** *number: her seventieth birthday*

sev·er /ˈsevə‖-ər/ *v* [T] *formal* **1** to cut through something completely: *His finger was severed in the accident.* **2** to completely end a relationship or agreement with someone: *The US severed all ties with Iraq.* —**severance** *n* [U]

sev·er·al /ˈsevərəl/ *quantifier* more than a few, but not a lot: *I called her several times on the phone.* | **+ of** *I've talked to several of my students about this.* → compare FEW

se·vere /sɪˈvɪə‖-ˈvɪr/ *adj* **1** very bad: *severe head injuries* | *severe problems* **2** a severe punishment or criticism is when someone is criticized or punished a lot: *Drug smugglers face severe punishment.* **3** someone who looks severe seems angry or strict —**severity** /sɪˈverɪ̯ti/ *n* [C,U]

se·vere·ly /sɪˈvɪəli‖-ˈvɪr-/ *adv* **1** very badly: *Many houses were severely damaged by the storm.* **2** if someone is severely criticized or punished, they are criticized or punished a lot **3** in a strict way

sew /səʊ‖soʊ/ *v* [I,T] **sewed, sewn** /səʊn‖soʊn/ *or* **sewed, sewing** to use a needle and thread to join pieces of cloth together or fasten something to a piece of cloth: *Can you sew a button on this shirt for me?*

sew

sew sth ↔ **up** *phr v* [T] **1** to close or repair something by sewing it: *I need to sew up this hole in my jeans.* **2 have sth sewn up** *informal* if you have something sewn up, you are certain to succeed

sew·age /ˈsjuːɪdʒ,ˈsuː-‖-ˈsuː-/ *n* [U] waste material that is carried away from homes and factories through pipes

sew·er /ˈsjuːə, ˈsuːəl‖suːər/ *n* [C] a pipe under the ground that carries away sewage

sew·ing /ˈsəʊɪŋ‖ˈsoʊ-/ *n* [U] **1** the activity of sewing **2** something that you have been sewing

sewing ma·chine /ˈ.. .,./ *n* [C] a machine for sewing cloth or clothes together

sewn /səʊn‖soʊn/ *v* a past participle of SEW

sex /seks/ *n* **1** [U] when two people take part in sexual activities with each other: **have sex (with sb)** *How old were you when you first had sex?* **2** [U] whether someone is male or female: *I don't care what sex the baby is.* **3** [C] one of the two groups of people or animals, male and female: **the opposite sex** (=people who are a different sex from you): *She finds it difficult to talk to members of the opposite sex.*

sex·is·m /ˈseksɪzəm/ *n* [U] when someone is treated in an unfair way because of the sex that they are

sex·ist /ˈseksɪ̯st/ *adj* treating someone in an unfair way because of their sex: *I get a lot of sexist comments at work.* —**sexist** *n* [C]

sex sym·bol /ˈ. ,../ *n* [C] a famous person who a lot of people think is very attractive

sex·u·al /ˈsekʃuəl/ *adj* **1** relating to sex: *sexual abuse* **2** relating to men and women: *sexual stereotypes* —**sexually** *adv*

sexual har·ass·ment /ˌ... ˈ...,ˌ... .ˈ../ *n* [U] when someone, especially someone you work with, says things about sex to you or touches you when you do not want them to

sexual in·ter·course /ˌ... ˈ.../ *n* [U] *formal* when two people have sex with each other

sex·u·al·i·ty /ˌsekʃuˈælɪ̯ti/ *n* [U] someone's sexual activities and feelings about sex

sex·y /ˈseksi/ *adj* sexually attractive or exciting: *A lot of women find him sexy.* | *sexy underwear*

Sgt *n* the written abbreviation of SERGEANT

sh, shh /ʃ/ *interjection* used to tell someone to be quiet

shab·by /ˈʃæbi/ *adj* **1** old and in bad condition: *a shabby old jacket* **2** unfair or slightly dishonest: *shabby treatment* —**shabbily** *adv* —**shabbiness** *n* [U]

shack[1] /ʃæk/ *n* [C] a small building that has not been built very well

shack[2] *v*

shack up *phr v* [I] *informal* to start living with someone in a sexual relationship

shack·le[1] /ˈʃækəl/ *n* [C] one of a pair of metal rings joined by a chain, used to keep a prisoner's hands or feet together

shackle² *v* [T] **be shackled by sth** to be prevented from doing what you want to do by something: *a company shackled by debts*

shade¹ /ʃeɪd/ *n* **1** [U] an area that is less warm and darker because the light of the sun cannot reach it: *They sat in the shade of an oak tree.* **2** [C] something that keeps out light or reduces light: *a lamp shade* **3** [C] a particular type of colour: *a rather unattractive shade of green* **4** **a shade** very slightly: *His brother is a shade taller.* **5** [C] a slight difference between two opinions or meanings: *shades of meaning* **6** **put sth in the shade** *informal* to be much better than something else

---

USAGE NOTE: shade and shadow

Shade is an area where there is no sunlight: *It's too hot here – let's find some shade.* A **shadow** is a dark shape you see on a surface that is caused by something blocking the light: *As the sun set, the shadows became longer.* | *She could see the shadow of a man in the doorway.*

---

shade

shade

shadow

shade² *v* [T] to cover something to protect it from light or heat: *She used her hand to shade her eyes.*

shades /ʃeɪdz/ *n* [plural] *informal* SUNGLASSES

shad·ow¹ /ˈʃædəʊ‖-doʊ/ *n* **1** [C] a dark shape that appears on the surface behind an object when a light shines on it → see picture at SHADE **2** [U] a part of an area that is dark, because light cannot reach it: *Most of the room was in shadow.* **3** **without/beyond a shadow of a doubt** used when you are completely sure about something: *He's guilty beyond any shadow of a doubt.*

shadow² *v* [T] to follow someone closely in order to watch what they are doing

shad·ow·y /ˈʃædəʊi‖-doʊi/ *adj* **1** a shadowy person or thing is mysterious and not much is known about them: *a shadowy figure from his past* **2** dark and full of shadows or difficult to see: *a shadowy corner*

shad·y /ˈʃeɪdi/ *adj* **1** protected from the sun: *a shady spot for a picnic* **2** *informal* not honest or legal: *a shady business deal*

shaft /ʃɑːft‖ʃæft/ *n* [C] **1** a long hole that goes up through a building, or down into the ground: *an elevator shaft* **2** a long handle on a tool, SPEAR etc **3** a narrow beam of light

shag·gy /ˈʃægi/ *adj* shaggy hair or fur is long and not neat

shake¹ /ʃeɪk/ *v* **shook** /ʃʊk/, **shaken** /ˈʃeɪkən/, **shaking** **1** [I,T] to move up and down or from side to side with quick movements, or to make something do this: *His hands were shaking.* | *Shake the bottle to mix the contents.* **2** **shake your head** to move your head from side to side as a way of saying no → see picture at NOD → compare NOD **3** **shake hands (with sb)** to hold someone's hand and move it up and down, as a greeting or when you have made an agreement: *We shook hands and said goodbye.* **4** [I] if your voice is shaking, it sounds nervous and unsteady: *I couldn't stop my voice from shaking.* **5** [T] if you are shaken by something, it makes you feel frightened, shocked, or upset: *Mark was clearly shaken by the news.* **6** **shake sb's confidence/faith/belief** to make someone feel less confident, or less sure about their beliefs

shake sb **down** *phr v* [T] *AmE informal* to get money from someone by using threats → see also SHAKEDOWN

shake off *phr v* **1** [T **shake** sth ↔ **off**] to get rid of an illness or problem: *I can't seem to shake off this cold.* **2** [T **shake** sb ↔ **off**] to escape from someone who is chasing you

shake sth ↔ **out** *phr v* [T] to shake something so that small pieces of dirt, dust etc come off it

shake sb/sth ↔ **up** *phr v* [T] to make someone feel shocked or upset: *She was really shaken up by the accident.* → see also SHAKE-UP

shake² *n* [C] **1** when someone shakes something **2** a MILKSHAKE

shake·down /ˈʃeɪkdaʊn/ *n* [C] *AmE informal* when someone gets money from another person by using threats

shak·en /ˈʃeɪkən/ *v* the past participle of SHAKE

shake-up /ˈ. ./ *n* [C] when big changes are made to the way something is organized

shak·y /ˈʃeɪki/ *adj* **1** weak and unsteady because you are ill, old, or have had a shock: *a shaky voice* **2** not likely to last a long time or be successful: *a shaky marriage* **3** not held firmly, and likely to move: *a shaky ladder*

shall /ʃəl; *strong* ʃæl/ *modal verb especially BrE* **1** **I/we shall** used to say what you are going to do: *We shall be on holiday next week.* **2** **shall I/we?** used to make a suggestion or offer, or to ask someone about what to do: *Shall I turn on the radio?* | *Where shall we meet?*

USAGE NOTE: shall and will

Shall and **will** can mean the same thing, but **will** or the short form **'ll** is usually used in ordinary speech. **Shall** is most often used to politely offer to do something: *Shall I open the window?*

---

shal·low /ˈʃæləʊ‖-loʊ/ *adj* **1** not deep: *a shallow pool* **2** not showing any serious or careful thought: *a shallow argument* → see picture at DEEP

shal·lows /ˈʃæləʊz‖-loʊz/ *n* **the shallows** a part of a river, lake etc that is not deep

sham /ʃæm/ *n* [singular] something that has been carefully planned to deceive people

sham·bles /ˈʃæmbəlz/ *n* [singular] **be a shambles** *informal* if something is a shambles, it is badly organized or very untidy: *The whole evening was a complete shambles.*

shame¹ /ʃeɪm/ *n* **1** [U] the feeling that you have when you know that you have behaved badly or that you have lost other people's respect: *He hung his head in shame.* → see also ASHAMED **2 it's a shame/what a shame** *spoken* used to say that a situation is disappointing and you wish that it was different: *It's a shame you can't come with us.* **3 Shame on you!** *spoken* used to tell someone that they should not have done something, and they should feel ashamed **4 put sb/sth to shame** to be much better than someone or something else

shame² *v* [T] to make someone feel ashamed

shame·faced /ˌʃeɪmˈfeɪst◂/ *adj* looking ashamed or embarrassed

shame·ful /ˈʃeɪmfəl/ *adj* so bad that someone should be ashamed: *a shameful waste of money* —**shamefully** *adv*

shame·less /ˈʃeɪmləs/ *adj* behaving badly and not caring whether other people disapprove: *a shameless piece of hypocrisy* —**shamelessly** *adv*

sham·poo¹ /ʃæmˈpuː/ *n* [C,U] liquid soap used for washing your hair

shampoo² *v* [T] to wash something with shampoo

shan·dy /ˈʃændi/ *n* [C] a drink made from BEER mixed with LEMONADE

shan't /ʃɑːnt‖ʃænt/ *BrE* the short form of 'shall not'

shan·ty town /ˈʃænti taʊn/ *n* [C] an area of badly built temporary buildings where very poor people live

shapes

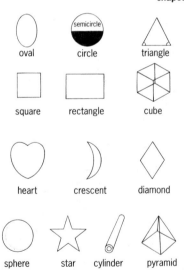

oval   circle *semicircle*   triangle

square   rectangle   cube

heart   crescent   diamond

sphere   star   cylinder   pyramid

shape¹ /ʃeɪp/ *n* **1** [C,U] the form made by the outside edge of something, for example whether it is curved, round, square etc: *a card in the shape of a heart* **2** [C] a particular kind of form such as a circle, square, or a TRIANGLE **3 in good/bad/poor shape** in good, bad etc condition or health: *His voice is still in good shape.* **4 in shape** fit and healthy because you do a lot of exercise: *What do you do to keep in shape?* **5 out of shape** unfit and unhealthy because

you do not do enough exercise **6 take shape** if something takes shape, it develops and becomes clear and definite: *A plan was beginning to take shape in his mind.*

shape² *v* [T] **1** to influence something such as a belief or opinion and make it develop in a particular way: *the power of parents to shape a child's personality* **2** to make something have a particular shape: *Shape the clay into small balls.*
  shape up *phr v* [I] *informal* used to say what a situation is like, or to say how well someone is doing something: *How's she shaping up in her new job?*

shaped /ʃeɪpt/ *adj* having a particular shape: *The alien's head was egg-shaped.*

shape·less /ˈʃeɪpləs/ *adj* something that is shapeless does not have a clear or attractive shape

shape·ly /ˈʃeɪpli/ *adj* having an attractive shape: *her long shapely legs*

share¹ /ʃeə‖ʃer/ *v* **1** [I,T] if you share something with another person, you both have it or use it: *I shared a room with her when I was at college.* **2** also **share out** [I,T] to divide something between two or more people: *We shared the cake between four of us.* **3** [T] to have the same interests, opinion etc as someone else: *She didn't share my point of view.* **4** [I,T] to tell someone else about an idea, secret, problem etc: *share your problems with someone*

share² *n* **1** [singular] a part of something which has been divided between two or more people: *I paid my share of the bill and left.* **2** [C] one of the equal parts into which the OWNERSHIP of a company is divided, which are bought and sold: **+ in** *Shares in Avon Rubber rose by almost 50%.* → compare STOCK¹ **3 have had your (fair) share of sth** if you have had your share of something, it has happened to you a lot: *I've had my share of bad luck this year.*

shark /ʃɑːk‖ʃɑːrk/ *n* [C] a large sea fish with very sharp teeth

sharp

sharp

blunt

sharp¹ /ʃɑːp‖ʃɑːrp/ *adj* **1** something that is sharp has a very thin edge or narrow point and can cut things easily: *a sharp knife* | *razor sharp* (=very sharp) → opposite BLUNT¹ **2** a sharp turn, bend, corner etc changes direction very suddenly: *a sharp turn in the road* **3** able to think and understand things very quickly, or good at noticing small details: *a sharp lawyer* **4** criticizing someone or something a lot, especially in an angry or unkind way: *Blair had to face some sharp criticism from the press.* **5** a sharp pain is very sudden and very bad: *He felt a* *sharp pain in his chest.* **6** a sharp increase, decrease etc is big and very easy to notice: *a sharp rise in profits* **7** *AmE* wearing clothes that look neat and attractive; SMART *BrE* **8** a sharp image is clear and you can see all the details in it **9** a sharp taste is strong and a little sour **10** loud, short, and sudden: *a sharp cry* **11** **have a sharp tongue** someone who has a sharp tongue criticizes people in an unkind way and often upsets them **12** **F sharp/C sharp etc** the musical note that is halfway between F, C etc and the note above **13** a musical note that is sharp is played or sung slightly higher than it should be → compare FLAT¹ —**sharply** *adv* —**sharpness** *n* [U]

sharp² *adv* at **8 o'clock/two-thirty etc sharp** at exactly 8:00, 2:30 etc: *I expect you to be here at 10:30 sharp.*

sharp³ *n* [C] a musical note that is one SEMITONE higher than a particular note, shown by the sign (♯) in written music → compare FLAT¹

sharp·en /ˈʃɑːpən‖ˈʃɑːr-/ *v* [I,T] to make something sharp: *She sharpened all her pencils.*

sharp·en·er /ˈʃɑːpənə, ˈʃɑːpnəl‖ˈʃɑːrpənər, ˈʃɑːrpnər/ *n* [C] a thing you use for making pencils, knives etc sharp → see colour picture on page 80

sharp-eyed /ˌ. ˈ.◂/ *adj* good at noticing things

shat·ter /ˈʃætə‖-ər/ *v* **1** [I,T] to break suddenly into very small pieces, or to make something do this: *The mirror shattered into a thousand pieces.* **2** [T] to completely destroy something, especially someone's hopes or beliefs: *An injury shattered his hopes of a baseball career.*

shat·tered /ˈʃætəd‖-ərd/ *adj* **1** very shocked and upset **2** *BrE informal* very tired

shat·ter·ing /ˈʃætərɪŋ/ *adj* very shocking or having a great effect: *shattering news*

shave¹ /ʃeɪv/ *v* **1** [I,T] to cut off hair from the skin on your face, legs etc **2** [T] to remove very thin pieces from the surface of something using a sharp tool → see also CLEAN-SHAVEN

shave² *n* **1** [C usually singular] if a man has a shave, he shaves the hair growing on his face **2** **a close shave** a situation in which you only just avoid an accident or something bad

shav·er /ˈʃeɪvə‖-ər/ *n* [C] a small piece of electrical equipment used for shaving → see also RAZOR

shav·ings /ˈʃeɪvɪŋz/ *n* [plural] very thin pieces of something such as wood that have been cut from a surface

shawl /ʃɔːl‖ʃɒːl/ *n* [C] a large piece of cloth that a woman wears around her shoulders or head

she /ʃi; *strong* ʃiː/ *pron* used to talk about a female person or animal who has already been mentioned: *"I saw Suzy today." "Oh really, how is she?"*

sheaf /ʃiːf/ *n* [C], *plural* **sheaves** /ʃiːvz/ **1** several pieces of paper that are held or tied together **2** wheat, corn etc that is tied together after it has been cut

shear /ʃɪə‖ʃɪr/ *v* [T] **sheared, sheared** *or* **shorn** /ʃɔːn‖ʃɔːrn/, **shearing** to cut the wool off a sheep

shears /ʃɪəz‖ʃɪrz/ *n* [plural] a tool like a large pair of scissors → see picture at GARDENING EQUIPMENT

sheath /ʃiːθ/ *n* [C] a cover for the blade of a knife or sword

shed¹ /ʃed/ *n* [C] a small building used especially for storing things: *a tool shed*

shed² *v* [T] **shed, shedding 1 a)** when a tree sheds its leaves, the leaves drop off **b)** when a snake sheds its skin, the old skin drops off **2** to get rid of something that you do not want: *He needs to shed some weight.* **3** **shed light on sth** to make something easier to understand by giving people information about it **4** **shed tears** cry about something

she'd /ʃid; *strong* ʃiːd/ the short form of 'she had' or 'she would': *She'd forgotten to close the door. | Paula said she'd love to come.*

sheen /ʃiːn/ *n* [singular, U] a smooth shiny appearance that makes something look attractive

sheep /ʃiːp/ *n* [C], *plural* **sheep** a farm animal that is kept for its wool and meat → compare LAMB

sheep·ish /ˈʃiːpɪʃ/ *adj* a little embarrassed, especially because you have done something silly or wrong: *Ernie gave a sheepish grin.* —**sheepishly** *adv*

sheer /ʃɪə‖ʃɪr/ *adj* [only before noun] **1** a word meaning complete or only, used when you want to emphasize what you are saying: *I think I won by sheer luck!* **2** used when you want to emphasize how big something is, or how many of something there are: *The impressive thing about Alaska is its sheer size.* **3** extremely steep: *a sheer drop*

sheet /ʃiːt/ *n* [C] **1** a large piece of thin cloth that you put on a bed to lie on or under: *Have you changed the sheets?* (=put clean sheets on the bed) **2** a thin flat piece of metal, glass etc: *a sheet of paper*

sheik, sheikh /ʃeɪk‖ʃiːk/ *n* [C] an Arab leader or prince

shelf /ʃelf/ *n* [C], *plural* **shelves** /ʃelvz/ a long flat board fixed to a wall or in a cupboard, that you use for storing things on: *two shelves for books* → see colour picture on page 474

shell¹ /ʃel/ *n* [C] **1 a)** the hard outside part of a nut, egg, or seed **b)** the hard outside part that covers some animals, for example SNAILs and CRABs: *The turtle put its head into its shell.* → see picture at SLUG **2** a metal container filled with explosive material, which is fired from a large gun

shell² *v* [T] to fire shells at something
shell out *phr v* [T] *informal* to pay a lot of money for something

she'll /ʃil; *strong* ʃiːl/ the short form of 'she will': *She'll be here soon.*

GRAMMAR NOTE: comparatives and superlatives
For short adjectives of one syllable, add **-er** or **-est** to the word: e.g. *old - older - oldest.* (Sometimes you must double the last letter: e.g. *big - bigger - biggest).* For long adjectives put **more** or **the most** before the word: e.g. *more comfortable - the most interesting.*

shell·fish /'ʃel.fɪʃ/ n [C,U], plural **shellfish** a small animal that lives under the water, has a shell, and is eaten as food

shel·ter¹ /'ʃeltəl-ər/ n **1** [C] a small building or covered place that protects you from bad weather or from attack: *an air-raid shelter* **2** [U] protection from bad weather or danger: **take shelter** (=go somewhere for protection): *They took shelter under a tree.*

shelter² v **1** [I] to go somewhere in order to be protected from bad weather or danger: *People were sheltering from the rain in doorways.* **2** [T] to give someone a place to stay where they can hide from people who are trying to catch or hurt them: *familes who sheltered Jews from the Nazis*

shel·tered /'ʃeltədll-ərd/ adj **1** if someone has had a sheltered life, there are many things that they have not experienced: *Gina had a sheltered childhood.* **2** protected from strong wind and bad weather: *a sheltered beach*

shelve /ʃelv/ v [T] to decide not to continue with a plan, although you might continue with it later: *The project has been shelved due to lack of funding.*

shelves /ʃelvz/ n the plural of SHELF

shelv·ing /'ʃelvɪŋ/ n [U] a set of shelves, or the material used for making them

shep·herd¹ /'ʃepədll-ərd/ n [C] someone whose job is to take care of sheep

shepherd² v [T] to go with someone and make sure that they go somewhere: *We were shepherded into the dining room by Mrs Clark.*

sher·iff /'ʃerɪf/ n [C] an elected chief police officer in the US

sher·ry /'ʃeri/ n [C,U] a strong Spanish wine

she's /ʃiz; strong ʃiːz/ spoken the short form of 'she is' or 'she has': *She's my little sister.* | *She's invited us all.*

shh /ʃ/ interjection SH

shield¹ /ʃiːld/ n [C] **1** something that protects someone or something from being hurt or damaged: *police carrying riot shields* **2** a piece of metal used in the past by soldiers to protect themselves in a battle, or something that has this shape

shield² v [T] to protect someone or something from being hurt, damaged, or affected badly by something: *The hat shields your eyes from the sun.*

shift¹ /ʃɪft/ n [C] **1** a change in the way most people think about something, or in the way something is done: **+ in** *There's been a big shift in public opinion.* **2** one of the periods during each day and night when workers in a factory, hospital etc do their work: *the night shift* **3** AmE a GEAR STICK

shift² v **1** [T] to move something from one place to another: *Can you help me shift this table?* **2** [I] to move your body into a different position: *Jan shifted uncomfortably in her seat.* **3** [I,T] to change your opinion or attitude: *Washington's policy appears to have shifted.* **4** **shift the blame/responsibility** to make someone else get the blame or the responsibility for something

shift·y /'ʃɪfti/ adj someone who is shifty looks as if they cannot be trusted

shil·ling /'ʃɪlɪŋ/ n [C] a unit of money, used in the past in Britain

shim·mer /'ʃɪməl-ər/ v [I] to shine with a soft light that seems to shake slightly: *a lake shimmering in the moonlight*

shin /ʃɪn/ n [C] the front part of your leg between your knee and your foot

shine¹ /ʃaɪn/ v **shone** /ʃɒnllʃoʊn/, **shone**, **shining** **1** [I] to produce light: *The sun shone brightly.* **2** [I] to look bright and smooth: *Dan polished the car until it shone.* **3** [T] to point a light in a particular direction: *Shine the flashlight over here.* **4** [I] if your eyes shine, they are very bright, especially because you are happy or excited **5** [I] to do something very well: *She shone at English.*

shine² n [singular, U] **1** the brightness that something has when light shines on it: *hair with lots of shine* **2** **take a shine to sb** informal to like someone who they have just met

shin·gle /'ʃɪŋgəl/ n [U] small pieces of stone and shells on a beach

shin·y /'ʃaɪni/ adj something that is shiny has a smooth bright surface, especially because it has been POLISHed or cleaned: *shiny leather boots*

ship¹ /ʃɪp/ n [C] **1** a large boat used for carrying people and things: *a cruise ship* ➡ see colour picture on page 669 **2** a SPACECRAFT: *a rocket ship*

ship² v [T] **-pped, -pping** to send goods somewhere so that people can buy or use them: *The wine is shipped all over the world.*

ship·ment /'ʃɪpmənt/ n **1** [C] goods that are sent somewhere: *The first shipment of UN aid arrived yesterday.* **2** [U] when goods are sent somewhere: *the high cost of shipment*

ship·ping /'ʃɪpɪŋ/ n [U] ships considered as a group: *The canal has been closed to shipping.*

ship·wreck¹ /'ʃɪp-rek/ n [C,U] an accident in which a ship is destroyed at sea: *survivors of a shipwreck*

shipwreck² v **be shipwrecked** if you are shipwrecked, the ship you are travelling on is destroyed in an accident at sea

ship·yard /'ʃɪp-jɑːdll-jɑːrd/ n [C] a place where ships are built or repaired

shirk /ʃɜːkllʃɜːrk/ v [I,T] to deliberately avoid doing something you should do, because you are lazy: *They accused him of shirking his duties.* —**shirker** n [C]

shirt /ʃɜːtllʃɜːrt/ n [C] a piece of clothing that covers the upper part of your body, and has a collar and buttons down the front ➡ see colour picture on page 113 ➡ see also T-SHIRT ➡ compare BLOUSE

shirt·sleeves /'ʃɜːtsliːvzll'ʃɜːrt-/ n **in your shirtsleeves** wearing a shirt but no JACKET

shit¹ /ʃɪt/ interjection a rude word used when you are annoyed about something, for example when you realize that you have made a mistake or have forgotten something

shit² n [U] a rude word for the solid waste that comes out of your body

shiv·er /'ʃɪvəl-ər/ v [I] to shake slightly because you are cold or frightened —**shiver** n [C] *A shiver ran down my spine.* (=I felt afraid) —**shivery** adj

shoal /ʃəʊllʃoʊl/ n [C] a large group of fish that swim together

shock¹ /ʃɒkllʃɑːk/ n **1** [C] when something

very bad happens which you did not expect, or the feeling you have when this happens: **have/get a shock** *He'll have a shock when he sees the bill.* | **come as a shock (to sb)** (=be a shock to someone): *Rob's death came as a complete shock to us.* **2** also **electric shock** [C] a sudden strong pain you feel when electricity suddenly flows through your body: *I got a shock off the toaster this morning.* **3** [U] if someone is in shock after an accident, their body is very weak, especially because they have been injured or have seen something terrible happen: *The victims are being treated for shock.* **4** [C] a

shiver

sudden violent movement caused by something: *the shock of the earthquake*

shock² *v* [I,T] to make someone feel very surprised and upset or offended: *The shooting has shocked the entire community.* | *Visitors were shocked by the terrible conditions in the prison.* | *The language in the film may shock some people.* —**shocked** *adj*

shock·ing /ˈʃɒkɪŋ‖ˈʃɑː-/ *adj* very upsetting, wrong, or immoral: *a shocking crime*

shod¹ /ʃɒd‖ʃɑːd/ *adj literary* wearing shoes

shod² *v* the past tense and past participle of SHOE²

shod·dy /ˈʃɒdi‖ˈʃɑː-/ *adj* **1** done or made badly or using materials that are of bad quality: *Whoever fixed the roof did a shoddy job.* **2** unfair and dishonest: *a shoddy trick* —**shoddily** *adv*

shoe¹ /ʃuː/ *n* [C] **1** something that you wear to cover your feet, which is made of leather or some other strong material: *a pair of shoes* | *tennis shoes* → see colour picture on page 113 **2 be in sb's shoes** to be in the situation that someone else is in: *I'm glad I'm not in his shoes, with all those debts to pay.*

shoe² *v* [T] **shod** /ʃɒd‖ʃɑːd/, **shod, shoeing** to put shoes on a horse

shoe·horn /ˈʃuːhɔːn‖-hɔːrn/ *n* [C] an object that you use to help you put a shoe on easily

shoe·lace /ˈʃuːleɪs/ *n* [C] a thin piece of string or leather that you use to tie your shoes

shoe·string /ˈʃuːˌstrɪŋ/ *n* [C] **on a shoestring** done or made without spending much money: *a movie made on a shoestring*

shone /ʃɒn‖ʃoʊn/ *v* the past tense and past participle of SHINE

shoo /ʃuː/ *interjection* used in order to tell an annoying child or animal to go away —**shoo** *v* [T] *Aunt Betty shooed us out of the kitchen.*

shook /ʃʊk/ *v* the past tense of SHAKE

shoot¹ /ʃuːt/ *v* **shot** /ʃɒt‖ʃɑːt/, **shot, shooting** **1** [T] to kill or injure someone with a gun: *She pulled out a gun and shot him.* | *One police officer was shot dead in the incident.* **2** [I,T] to fire a weapon at someone or something, or to make a weapon fire: *Please don't shoot!* | *He learned to shoot when he was only three.* **3** [I,T] to move quickly in a particular direction, or to make something move in this way: *She shot down the stairs.* | *A severe pain shot through his chest.* **4** [I,T] to make a film or take photographs: *Spielberg is shooting on location.* **5** [I,T] to throw, kick, or hit a ball towards the place in a sports game where you can make points **6** [I] *AmE spoken* used to tell someone you are ready to listen: *"I've got a question." "Okay, shoot."* **7 shoot the breeze** *AmE informal* to have a friendly conversation about unimportant things

shoot ↔ **sb/sth down** *phr v* [T] **1** to destroy an enemy plane while it is flying: *Tim's plane was shot down over enemy territory.* **2 shoot sb down** also **shoot sb down in flames** *BrE* to say that what someone has suggested is wrong or stupid: *When she tried to ask them to consider another point of view, she was simply shot down in flames.*

shoot up *phr v* [I] to increase very quickly: *Oil prices have shot up.*

shoes

heel · lace · toe · sole

stiletto · clog

sandals · slipper

boots

trainer *BrE*/ sneaker *AmE*

Wellington boot *BrE*/ rubber boot *AmE*

S

shoot² n [C] **1** an occasion when someone takes photographs or makes a film: *a fashion shoot* **2** a new part of a plant

shoot³ *interjection AmE* used when you are annoyed, disappointed, or surprised: *Oh shoot, I forgot to call up Danny.*

shoot·ing /ˈʃuːtɪŋ/ n **1** [C] a situation in which someone is killed or injured by a gun: *Two teenagers were killed in a drive-by shooting.* **2** [U] the sport of killing animals and birds with guns

shooting star /ˌ.. ˈ./ n [C] a piece of rock or metal from space that burns brightly as it falls towards the Earth; METEOR

shop¹ /ʃɒp‖ʃɑːp/ n **1** [C] *especially BrE* a building or room in a building where you can buy things; STORE *especially AmE: a clothes shop* **2** [C] a place that sells one type of goods: *a card shop* **3** [U] *AmE* a subject taught in school, in which students use tools and machinery to make things out of wood and metal → see also **talk shop** (TALK)

shop² v [I] to go to a shop or shops to buy things: + **for** *I'm shopping for a new television.* | **go shopping** *Let's go shopping on Saturday.* —**shopper** n [C]

shop around *phr v* [I] to compare the price and quality of different things before you decide which to buy: *It's a good idea to shop around before buying a laptop.*

shop as·sis·tant /ˈ. .ˌ../ n [C] *BrE* someone who works in a shop selling things and helping customers; SALES ASSISTANT; SALES CLERK *AmE*

shop floor /ˌ. ˈ. ◂/ n [singular] the part of a factory where goods are made, or the ordinary people who work there and are not managers

shop·keep·er /ˈʃɒpˌkiːpə‖ˈʃɑːpˌkiːpər/ n [C] *especially BrE* someone who owns or is in charge of a small shop; STOREKEEPER *AmE*

shop·lift·ing /ˈʃɒpˌlɪftɪŋ‖ˈʃɑːp-/ n [U] the crime of taking things from shops without paying for them —**shoplifter** n [C] —**shoplift** v [I]

shop·ping /ˈʃɒpɪŋ‖ˈʃɑː-/ n [U] the activity of going to shops to buy things: *Christmas shopping*

shopping cen·tre *BrE*, **shopping center** *AmE* /ˈ.. ˌ../ n [C] a group of shops built together in one area

shopping mall /ˈ.. ./ n [C] a MALL

shore¹ /ʃɔː‖ʃɔːr/ n [C,U] the land along the edge of a large area of water: *a house on the eastern shore of the bay*

hotels, shops, restaurants etc, where you go to enjoy yourself.

shore² v

shore sth up *phr v* [T] **1** to support a wall with pieces of wood, metal etc to stop it from falling down **2** to help or support something that is likely to fail or is not working well: *The coal industry has been shored up with government money.*

shorn /ʃɔːn‖ʃɔːrn/ v the past participle of SHEAR

short¹ /ʃɔːt‖ʃɔːrt/ *adj* **1** happening for only a little time or for less time than usual: *I'm afraid there might be a short delay.* | *She was here a short time ago.* **2** not long in distance or length: *Sophie's got short blond hair.* | *It's only a short distance from here to the river.* → see colour picture on page 244 **3** not as tall as average height: *a short fat man with glasses* → see colour picture on page 244 **4** not having enough of something you need: + **of** *I'm a bit short of cash at the moment.* | **sth is in short supply** (=there is not enough of it available): *Fresh fruit and vegetables were in short supply.* **5** **be short for** to be a shorter way of saying a name: *Her name's Becky, short for Rebecca.* **6** **for short** as a shorter way of saying a name: *It's called the Message Handling System – MHS for short.* **7** **at short notice** *BrE*, **on short notice** *AmE* with very little warning that something is going to happen: *Sorry, we can't come on such short notice.* **8** **in the short term/run** during a short period of time after the present and no longer: *These policies will only help us in the short term – in 10 years things will change.* **9** **be short with sb** to speak to someone in a rude or unfriendly way: *Sorry I was so short with you on the phone.* **10** **have a short temper** someone who has a short temper becomes angry very easily **11** **be short of breath** if you are short of breath, you have difficulty breathing —**shortness** n [U]

short² *adv* short of doing sth except for doing something: *They've done everything short of cancelling the project.* → see also **cut sth short** (CUT¹), **fall short of** (FALL¹), **run short** (RUN), **stop short** (STOP)

short³ n **1** **in short** used when you want to say the most important point in a few words: *In short, I don't think we can do it.* **2** [C] *BrE* a strong alcoholic drink such as WHISKY or GIN **3** [C] *informal* a SHORT CIRCUIT

short·age /ˈʃɔːtɪdʒ‖ˈʃɔːrt-/ n [C,U] a situation in which there is not enough of something that people need: *food shortages* | + **of** *a shortage of medicine*

short·bread /ˈʃɔːtbred‖ˈʃɔːrt-/ n [U] a hard sweet type of BISCUIT

short-change /ˌ. ˈ./ v [T] **1** to treat someone unfairly by not giving them what they deserve: *Older people looking for work feel they have been short-changed.* **2** to give back too little money to someone who has paid for something

short cir·cuit /ˌ. ˈ../ n [C] a bad electrical connection that makes a machine stop working properly —**short circuit** v [I,T]

short·com·ing /ˈʃɔːtˌkʌmɪŋ‖ˈʃɔːrt-/ n [C usually plural] a fault in someone's character, or in a product, system etc: *shortcomings in the public health system*

short cut /ˌ. ˈ., ˈ. .‖ˈ. ./ n [C] **1** a quicker, more direct way of going somewhere: *Let's take a short* cut across the park. **2** a quicker way of doing something: *There are no short cuts to becoming an actor.*

short·en /ˈʃɔːtn‖ˈʃɔːrtn/ v [I,T] to become shorter or make something shorter: *Can you help me shorten this skirt?*

short·fall /ˈʃɔːtfɔːl‖ˈʃɔːrtfɒːl/ n [C] the difference between the amount you have and the amount you need or expect: *shortfalls in the city's budget*

short·hand /ˈʃɔːthænd‖ˈʃɔːrt-/ n [U] a fast method of writing down what people say using special signs instead of letters, words, and phrases

short list¹ /ˈ. ./ n [C] BrE a list of people or things that have been chosen, for example for a job or prize

short-list² /ˈʃɔːtlɪst‖ˈʃɔːrt-/ v **be short-listed** BrE to be put on a short list

short-lived /ˌʃɔːtˈlɪvd‖ˌʃɔːrt ˈlaɪvd◂/ adj continuing only a short time: *a short-lived fashion*

short·ly /ˈʃɔːtli‖ˈʃɔːrt-/ adv **1** very soon: *I expect him home shortly.* | **shortly before/after** (=a short time before or after): *The President left for Washington shortly before noon.* **2** speaking impatiently: *"Yes, yes, I understand," he said shortly.*

short-range /ˌ. ˈ.◂/ adj designed to travel or operate only within a short distance: *short-range nuclear weapons*

shorts /ʃɔːts‖ʃɔːrts/ n [plural] **1** short trousers: *a pair of tennis shorts* → see colour picture on page 113 **2** AmE men's UNDERPANTS

short·sight·ed, short-sighted /ˌʃɔːtˈsaɪtɪd◂ ‖ˌʃɔːrt-/ adj **1** unable to see very far without GLASSES **2** not considering the future effects of something: *short-sighted planning*

short sto·ry /ˌ. ˈ../ n [C] a short written story

short-term /ˌ. ˈ.◂/ adj continuing for only a short time: *short-term benefits*

short wave /ˈ. ./ n [U] a system of radio broadcasting used for broadcasting programmes around the world

shot¹ /ʃɒt‖ʃɑːt/ n [C] **1** when someone fires a gun, or the sound that this makes: *Troops fired a warning shot.* | *the sound of a gun shot* **2** *informal* when a doctor puts medicine into your body using a needle; INJECTION: *Have you had your flu shot?* **3** a photograph, or a picture of something in a film: *a beautiful shot of the countryside around Prague* **4** *informal* an attempt to do something: **take/have a shot at sth** (=try to do it): *Marty always wanted to take a shot at acting.* **5** a small amount of a strong alcoholic drink **6** an attempt to throw, kick, or hit the ball towards the place in a sports game where you can get a point: *Nice shot!* **7** **a shot in the arm** something that makes you more confident or successful: *Winning the scholarship was a real shot in the arm for Mike.* **8** **like a shot** very quickly: *He jumped up like a shot and ran to the door.* → see also BIG SHOT, LONG SHOT, **call the shots** (CALL)

shot² v the past tense and participle of SHOOT

shot·gun /ˈʃɒtɡʌn‖ˈʃɑːt-/ n [C] a long gun, used especially for shooting animals and birds

shot put /ˈ. ./ n [singular] a sport in which you throw a heavy metal ball as far as you can —**shot putter** n [C]

should /ʃəd; *strong* ʃʊd/ *modal verb* **1** used to say that you expect something to happen or be true: *Yvonne should be back by eight.* | *He's a good cook, so there should be good food.* **2** used to give or ask for advice or an opinion: *You should see a doctor.* | *They should have called the police.* | *Should I wear my black dress?* **3** *formal* used to talk about a situation that might happen: *Should you decide to accept the offer, please return the enclosed form.* (=if you decide to accept)

shoul·der¹ /ˈʃəʊldə‖ˈʃoʊldər/ n [C] **1** one of the two parts of the body at each side of the neck where the arm is connected: *Andy put his arm around his wife's shoulder.* | *When we asked him what was wrong, he just shrugged his shoulders.* (=raised them to show that he did not know or care) **2** the part of a piece of clothing that covers your shoulders **3** **a shoulder to cry on** someone who gives you sympathy: *Jan's always there when I need a shoulder to cry on.* **4** AmE an area of ground beside a road where drivers can stop their cars if they are having trouble

shoulder² v [T] **1** **shoulder a responsibility/the blame etc** to accept a difficult or unpleasant responsibility, the blame for something etc: *You can't expect me to shoulder the blame for everything.* **2** to lift something onto your shoulder to carry it

shoulder bag /ˈ.. ./ n [C] a bag that hangs from your shoulder

shoulder blade /ˈ.. ./ n [C] one of the two flat bones just below your shoulders on your back → see picture at SKELETON

should·n't /ˈʃʊdnt/ v the short form of 'should not': *You shouldn't work so hard.*

should've /ˈʃʊdəv/ v the short form of 'should have': *I should've stayed at home.*

shout¹ /ʃaʊt/ v [I,T] to say something very loudly: *Someone shouted, "She's over here!"* | *Two women were shouting at each other outside the supermarket.*

shout sb ↔ down *phr v* [T] to shout in order to prevent someone from being heard: *The mayor was shouted down at the meeting.*

shout² n [C] something that someone says very loudly: *She heard a shout and looked up.* | *There were shouts of "More!" from the crowd.*

shove /ʃʌv/ v **1** [I,T] to push someone or something in a rough or careless way: *She shoved him out of the door into the street.* **2** [T] *informal* to put something somewhere without thinking carefully about where you should put it: *Just shove those papers into the drawer for now.* —**shove** n [C]

shov·el¹ /ˈʃʌvəl/ n [C] a tool with a long handle used for digging or moving earth, stones etc → see picture at GARDENING EQUIPMENT

SPELLING NOTE
Words with the sound /ʃ/, may be spelt **ch-**, like **chauffeur**.

shovel² v [I,T] **-lled, lling** BrE, **-led, -ling** AmE
1 to dig or move earth, stones etc with a SHOVEL **2 shovel sth into/onto sth** to put large amounts of something into a place quickly: *He sat shovelling his dinner into his mouth.*

show¹ /ʃəʊ‖ʃoʊ/ v **showed, shown** /ʃəʊn‖ ʃoʊn/, **showing 1** [T] to make it clear that something is true or exists by providing facts or information: *The report shows a rise in employment.* | **+ (that)** *Their receipt showed that they had already paid.* | **+ how/what** *The article shows how attitudes have changed in the past few years.*
2 [T] to let someone see something: *All student passes must be shown.* | **show sb sth** *Karen showed us her wedding pictures.* | **show sth to sb** *Is that his letter? Show it to me!* **3** [T] if you show your feelings, other people can see how you feel because of your expression, your behaviour etc: *Her face showed her disappointment.* | *Even after a long hike he showed no signs of being tired.* **4** [T] if a film, picture, map etc shows something, you can see it on the film, picture, map etc: *The advertisement shows a couple eating ice cream together.* **5** [T] to tell someone how to do something or where something is: **show sb where/how/what** *Show the guests where to put their coats.* | *Can you show me what I should do?* **6** [T] to go with someone and guide them to a place: *Mrs O'Shea showed us to our rooms.* **7** [I,T] if something shows, it can be seen or noticed: *His muscles showed beneath his shirt.* | *This shirt really shows the dirt.* **8 have something/nothing to show for** to have achieved something or nothing after trying: *I've been practising so hard, and I still have nothing to show for it.* **9** [I,T] if a film or programme is showing at a cinema or on television, people are able to see it: *What's showing at the Carlton?*
10 show a profit/loss if a business shows a profit or loss, its accounts show that it made a profit or a loss

show sb ↔ around (sth) phr v [T] to go with someone around a place and show them what is important, interesting etc: *Kim will show you around the museum.*

show off phr v **1** [I] to try to make people admire you and think you are attractive, clever, funny etc: *Jason's showing off in front of the girls.* **2** [T **show** sth ↔ **off**] to show something to someone because you are very proud of it: *The Wilsons are having a party to show off their new house.*

show up phr v **1** [I] informal to arrive somewhere: *The coach was mad because Bill showed up late for the game.* **2** [I] to be easy to see or notice: *The doctor said that the bacteria didn't show up at first under the microscope.* **3** [T **show** sb ↔ **up**] to do something in order to embarrass someone or make them seem stupid when other people are there: *Why did you have to show me up in front of the whole class?*

show² n **1** [C] a performance in a theatre or on radio or television: *a new show opening on Broadway* | *a popular TV show* **2** [C] a group of things for the public to look at: *the Chelsea flower show* **3 be on show** to be shown to the public: *The photographs will be on show until the end of the month.* **4** [singular, U] something that you do to pretend to other people that something is true or to IMPRESS them: **for show** *He bought her lots of expensive presents, but she*

knew they were just for show. **5 a show of temper/strength/force etc** something that shows you that someone is angry, strong etc: *The army marched through the town in a show of force.* **6 let's get this show on the road** spoken said when you want to tell people it is time to start working or start a trip

show busi·ness /'. ˌ../ also **show biz** /'ʃəʊ bɪz‖ 'ʃoʊ-/ informal — n [U] the entertainment industry, for example films, television, dancing etc: *She started in show business as a child.*

show·case /'ʃəʊkeɪs‖'ʃoʊ-/ n [C] something that is designed to show the good qualities of a person, organization etc: *Clapton's new album is a showcase for his talents.*

show·down /'ʃəʊdaʊn‖'ʃoʊ-/ n [C] **1** a big argument or fight that is intended to end a disagreement or fight that has continued for a long time: *a showdown between the top two teams in the league* **2** an important game in which two teams or players play against each other to find out who is the best team or player

show·er¹ /'ʃaʊəll-ər/ n [C] **1** a thing that you stand under to wash your whole body: **be in the shower** *The phone always rings when I'm in the shower.* **2** when you wash your body under the shower: *Hurry up! I want to take a shower.* **3** a short period of rain: *Showers are expected later today.* **4** a lot of small things in the air or falling through the air: *a shower of sparks* **5** especially AmE a party at which presents are given to a woman who is going to get married or have a baby

shower² v **1** [I] to wash your whole body while standing under a shower **2** [T] to generously give someone a lot of things: **shower sb with sth** *My mother used to shower the kids with toys and gifts.*

show·er·y /'ʃaʊəri/ adj raining frequently for short periods: *a showery day*

show·ing /'ʃəʊɪŋ‖'ʃoʊ-/ n [C] **1** when a film, programme, art show etc can be seen or looked at: *a special showing of Georgia O'Keefe's paintings* **2** something that shows how well or badly you are doing: *The Senator made a strong showing at the polls.*

show·man /'ʃoʊmən‖'ʃoʊ-/ n [C] someone who is good at entertaining people and getting a lot of public attention — **showmanship** n [U]

shown /ʃəʊn‖ʃoʊn/ v the past participle of SHOW

show-off /'. ./ n [C] someone who always tries to show how attractive, clever, funny etc they are so that other people will admire them: *Don't be such a show-off!*

show·piece /'ʃəʊpiːs‖'ʃoʊ-/ n [C] something that an organization wants people to see because it is a successful example of what they are doing

show·room /'ʃəʊrʊm, -ruːm‖'ʃoʊ-/ n [C] a large room where you can look at things that are for sale: *a car showroom*

show·y /'ʃəʊi‖'ʃoʊi/ adj very big, expensive, brightly coloured etc in a way that attracts people's attention: *showy clothes*

shrank /ʃræŋk/ v the past tense of SHRINK

shrap·nel /'ʃræpnəl/ n [U] small pieces of metal from a bomb, bullet etc that are scattered when it explodes

shred¹ /ʃred/ n **1** [C usually plural] a small thin piece that is torn or cut roughly from some-

thing: *The kitten had ripped the toy to shreds.*
2 not a shred not even a small amount: *There's not a shred of evidence to prove he's guilty.*

shred² *v* [T] **-dded, -dding 1** to cut or tear something into small pieces **2** to put a document into a shredder

shred·der /ˈʃredəll-ər/ *n* [C] a machine that cuts documents into small pieces so that no one can read them

shrewd /ʃruːd/ *adj* good at judging what people or situations are really like, especially in a way that makes you successful: *a shrewd business-woman*

shriek /ʃriːk/ *v* [I,T] to suddenly SCREAM in a high voice, for example because you are frightened, excited, or angry: *"Stop it!" she shrieked.* —**shriek** *n* [C]

shrill /ʃrɪl/ *adj* a shrill sound is very high and unpleasant: *shrill voices*

shrimp /ʃrɪmp/ *n* [C,U] a small pink sea animal that has ten legs and a soft shell, that you can eat; PRAWN *BrE*

shrine /ʃraɪn/ *n* [C] **1** a place that is connected with a holy event or holy person, which people visit to pray **2** a place that people visit and respect because it is connected with a famous person: *Elvis Presley's home has become a shrine for thousands of fans.*

shrink¹ /ʃrɪŋk/ *v* [I,T] **shrank** /ʃræŋk/, **shrunk** /ʃrʌŋk/ **shrinking 1** to become smaller or to make something smaller: *My sweater shrank in the wash. | The economy has shrunk by 20% in the last two years.* **2 shrink back/away etc** to move away from someone or something because you are very frightened

    shrink from sth *phr v* [T] to avoid doing something difficult or unpleasant: *She never shrank from doing her duty.*

shrink² *n* [C] *informal humorous* a PSYCHOANALYST or PSYCHIATRIST

shrink·age /ˈʃrɪŋkɪdʒ/ *n* [U] when something shrinks, or the amount that something shrinks

shrink-wrapped /ˌ.ˈ.◄/ *adj* goods that are shrink-wrapped are wrapped tightly in plastic

shriv·el /ˈʃrɪvəl/ also **shrivel up** *v* [I,T] **-lled, -lling** *BrE*, **-led, -ling** *AmE* if something shrivels or is shrivelled, it becomes smaller and its surface is covered in lines because it is dry or old: *The flowers had all shrivelled up.* —**shrivelled** *adj*

shroud¹ /ʃraʊd/ *n* [C] **1** a cloth that is wrapped around a dead person's body before it is buried **2** something that hides or covers another object or area

shroud² *v* **be shrouded in mist/smoke etc** to be *covered and hidden by mist, smoke etc: The mountains were shrouded in clouds.*

shrub /ʃrʌb/ *n* [C] a small bush

shrub·be·ry /ˈʃrʌbəri/ *n* [C] an area where shrubs are planted close together

shrug /ʃrʌg/ *v* [I,T] **-gged, -gging** to raise and then lower your shoulders in order to show that you do not know something or do

not care about something: *Dan shrugged and went back to what he was doing.* —**shrug** *n* [C]

    shrug sth ↔ **off** *phr v* [T] to treat something as unimportant and not worry about it: *Marge tried to shrug off the boss's criticism.*

shrunk /ʃrʌŋk/ *v* the past participle of SHRINK

shrunk·en /ˈʃrʌŋkən/ *adj* seeming to have become smaller or having been made smaller: *a shrunken old woman*

shuck /ʃʌk/ *v* [T] *AmE* to remove the outside part of a vegetable such as corn or PEAS

shucks /ʃʌks/ *interjection AmE old-fashioned* used to show you are disappointed about something

shud·der /ˈʃʌdəll-ər/ *v* [I] **1** to shake because you are frightened or cold, or because you think something is very unpleasant: *Gwen shuddered as she described the man who had attacked her.*
2 if a vehicle or machine shudders, it shakes suddenly —**shudder** *n* [C]

shuf·fle /ˈʃʌfəl/ *v* **1** [I] to walk slowly and noisily, without lifting your feet off the ground: *The old man shuffled across the room.* **2** [T] to move something such as papers or cards into a different position or order: *Ginny shuffled the papers on her desk.* **3** [I,T] to move your body around when sitting down or to move your feet slightly because you are bored or embarrassed: *Ernie looked nervous and shuffled his feet.* **4** [I,T] to mix PLAYING CARDS into a different order before playing a game: *It's Jo's turn to shuffle.* —**shuffle** *n* [C,U]

shun /ʃʌn/ *v* [T] to deliberately avoid someone or something

shunt /ʃʌnt/ *v* [T] to move someone or something somewhere, especially in a way that is inconvenient or unfair: *She was tired of being shunted from place to place.*

shush /ʃʊʃ/ *interjection* **shush!** *spoken* used to tell someone to be quiet: *"Shush!" said Tim. "Don't talk so loud."*

shut¹ /ʃʌt/ *v* **shut, shut, shutting 1** [I,T] to close something, or to become closed: *Do you want me to shut the window? | I heard the back door shut. | She leaned back and shut her eyes.* **2** [I,T] *especially BrE* if a shop, bank, or other public place shuts, it stops being open to the public: *The park shuts at 5.30.* **3** [T] to close something such as a door against something, accidentally catching or trapping it **4 shut your mouth/trap/face!** *spoken* used to rudely and angrily tell someone to stop talking

    shut sb/sth ↔ **away** *phr v* [T] to put someone or something in a place where other people cannot see them

    shut sb/sth ↔ **down** *phr v* [I,T] if a company, factory or a large machine shuts down or is shut down, it stops operating: *Three nuclear generators were shut down for safety reasons. | The factory will shut down for two weeks this month.*

    shut sb/sth ↔ **off** *phr v* [I,T] if a machine or the supply of something shuts off, or you shut it off, it stops operating or flowing: *We shut the engine off when it overheated. | The heat shuts off automatically.*

    shut sb/sth ↔ **out** *phr v* [T] **1** to prevent someone or something from going into a place: *The curtains help to shut out the traffic noise.*
2 to stop yourself from seeing, hearing, or

S

shrug

thinking about something: *I tried to shut her out of my mind.*

shut sb/sth **up** phr v **1 shut up!** *spoken* used to rudely tell someone to stop talking: *Just shut up! I'm trying to think.* **2** [I,T **shut** sb **up**] to stop talking or make someone stop talking: *Will someone shut that kid up!*

shut[2] *adj* [not before noun] closed: *Is the door shut?*

shut·down /'ʃʌtdaʊn/ *n* [C] when a factory or business closes, or a machine stops operating

shut-in /'. ./ *n* [C] *AmE* someone who is ill or DISABLED and has to stay indoors

shut·ter /'ʃʌtəll-ər/ *n* [C] **1** [usually plural] a wooden or metal cover in front of a window → see colour picture on page 79 **2** a part of a camera that opens to let light onto the film

shut·tle[1] /'ʃʌtl/ *n* [C] **1** a plane, bus, or train that makes regular short trips between two places: *the Washington–New York shuttle* **2** a SPACECRAFT that can travel into space and return to Earth more than once: *the launch of the space shuttle*

shuttle[2] *v* [I,T] to move or to move people between one place and another: *Passengers are shuttled to and from the hotel by bus.*

shut·tle·cock /'ʃʌtlkɒkll-kɑːk/ *n* [C] a small light object with feathers that you hit across a net in BADMINTON; BIRDIE *AmE*

shy[1] /ʃaɪ/ *adj* **1** nervous and embarrassed about talking to other people: *Cal's painfully shy.* → see colour picture on page 277 **2** unwilling to do something or get involved in something: **+ about** *He's not shy about showing off his wealth.* —**shyly** *adv* —**shyness** *n* [U]

shy[2] *v* [I] if a horse shies, it makes a sudden movement away from something because it is frightened

shy away from sth phr v [T] to avoid something you do not like or do not want to do: *He shies away from contact with women.*

shys·ter /'ʃaɪstəll-ər/ *n* [C] *AmE informal* a dishonest person, especially a lawyer or politician

sib·ling /'sɪblɪŋ/ *n* [C] *formal* a brother or sister

sic /sɪk/ *adv written* (**sic**) used after a written word that you have copied in order to show that you know it was not spelled or used correctly

sick[1] /sɪk/ *adj* **1** suffering from a disease or illness; ill: *Jan's not coming in today – she's sick.* | *a sick child* **2 be sick** to make food come up from your stomach through your mouth; VOMIT: *Uh oh, the dog's going to be sick!* **3 feel sick** to feel as if you are going to VOMIT: *I felt really sick after eating all that popcorn.* **4 be sick (and tired) of sth** also **be sick to death of sth** to be annoyed and bored with a situation that has gone on for too long: *I'm sick to death of all this arguing.* **5 sth makes me sick** *spoken* used to say that something makes you very angry: *When I hear about people being cruel to animals, it makes me sick.* **6** someone who is sick does things that are strange and cruel: *The murders are obviously the work of a sick mind.* **7** sick stories, jokes etc deal with death and suffering in a cruel and unpleasant way **8** *formal or literary* **the sick** people who are ill: *nurses taking care of the sick and wounded*

sick[2] *n* [U] *BrE informal* food or drink that has come out of someone's mouth from their stomach; VOMIT

sick·en /'sɪkən/ *v* [T] to make someone feel very shocked and angry: *Many of the protesters were men who were sickened by what they experienced during the war.*

sick·en·ing /'sɪkənɪŋ, 'sɪknɪŋ/ *adj* very unpleasant, especially in a way that makes you shocked or angry: *It's sickening to see so many poor people in such a wealthy country.* | *His head hit the floor with a sickening crack.*

sick·le /'sɪkəl/ *n* [C] a tool with a blade in the shape of a hook, used especially for cutting wheat

sick·ly /'sɪkli/ *adj* **1** weak and unhealthy: *a sickly child* **2** a sickly smell, taste etc is very unpleasant and makes you feel a little sick

sick·ness /'sɪknɪs/ *n* **1** [U] the condition of being ill; ILLNESS: *soldiers suffering from hunger and sickness* **2** [C] an illness

side[1] /saɪd/ *n* [C] **1** one of the two areas left or right of an imaginary line down the middle of something: *the left side of the brain* | *The right side of his face was covered in blood.* | *Jim grew up on Detroit's east side.* **2** the place or area directly next to someone or something: *I could hear voices coming from the other side of the wall.* | **by the side of** (=next to): *She lives by the side of a big lake.* | **by/at sb's side** (=next to someone or with them, especially to help them or show that you care about them): *His wife was by his side at all times.* **3 side by side** next to each other: *They walked together side by side.* **4** the part of an object or area that is furthest from the middle; the edge: *A man was standing at the side of the road.* **5** a surface of something that is not its front, back, top, or bottom: *A truck ran into the left side of the bus.* **6** a flat surface of an object: *A cube has six sides.* **7** one of the two surfaces of a thin flat object: *You can write on both sides of the paper.* **8 from side to side** moving continuously from right to left: *They sang and danced, swaying from side to side.* **9 from all sides** from every direction: *enemy gunfire coming from all sides* **10** one part of a subject, problem, or situation: *I'd like to hear her side of the story.* | *We need to look at the issue from all sides.* **11** one of the people, groups, teams etc opposing each other in an argument, sports game, fight etc: *Neither side is willing to compromise.* **12 take sides** to say that you support one person, group etc in an argument or fight **13 be on sb's side** to be supporting someone in an argument, fight, or war: *Don't worry, I'm on your side.* **14 on the side** in addition to your regular job: *He runs a little business on the side.* **15** the part of your body from your shoulder to the top of your leg: *She was wounded in her right side.* **16** the part of your family that consists of the parents, grandparents etc of your mother or father: *Her father's side of the family is German.* **17** one of the sloping areas of a hill, valley etc **18** *BrE informal* a television station; CHANNEL: *Is there anything on the other side?* **19 on the high/big/heavy etc side** *spoken* a little too high, big etc **20 put/leave/set sth to one side** to leave or save something so that you can deal with it or use it later **21 get on the right/wrong side of sb** *informal* to make someone pleased or angry with you

side[2] *adj* **1** in or on the side of something: *You can leave by the side door.* | *side pockets* **2 side street/road** a small street or road that is near a main street: *She lives in a comfortable apartment in a quiet side street.* **3** from the side of something: *a side view of the statue*

side[3] *v* [I]

side with sb (**against** sb) *phr v* [T] to support a particular person, group, or country in an argument, fight, election etc

side·board /ˈsaɪdbɔːdǁ-bɔːrd/ *n* [C] a long low piece of furniture that you store dishes and glasses in

side·burns /ˈsaɪdbɜːnzǁ-bɜːrns/ *n* [plural] hair that grows down the sides of a man's face

side·car /ˈsaɪdkɑːǁ-kɑːr/ *n* [C] an enclosed seat that is joined to the side of a MOTORCYCLE

side dish /ˈ. ./ *n* [C] a separate dish that is served with the main food at a meal

side ef·fect /ˈ. .ˌ./ *n* [C] **1** an effect, usually a bad effect, that a drug has on your body in addition to curing illness or pain: *The most common side effect is a slight fever.* **2** an unexpected result of an activity, situation, or event

side·kick /ˈsaɪdˌkɪk/ *n* [C] *informal* a friend or helper of someone who is more important: *Batman's sidekick, Robin*

side·line[1] /ˈsaɪdlaɪn/ *n* **1** [C] something that you do to earn money in addition to your regular job: *Mark does translation work as a sideline.* **2 on the sidelines** not taking part in an activity that other people are involved in: *There are still buyers on the sidelines waiting to get stocks.* **3 the sidelines** the area around the edges of a sports field

side·line[2] *v* [T] **be sidelined** to not be included in an activity or event, especially a sports game: *Their quarterback was sidelined with a knee injury.*

side·long /ˈsaɪdlɒŋǁ-lɔːŋ/ *adj* **sidelong look/ glance** a way of looking at someone by moving your eyes to the side, done secretly or when you are nervous

side·show /ˈsaɪdʃəʊǁ-ʃoʊ/ *n* [C] **1** a separate small part of a CIRCUS or FAIR **2** an event that is much less important or serious than another similar one

side·step /ˈsaɪdstep/ *v* [T] to avoid talking about or dealing with a difficult or unpleasant question or problem: *Congressman Howell sidestepped questions about his involvement in the affair.*

side·swipe /ˈsaɪdswaɪp/ *v* [T] to hit the side of a car or other vehicle with your car

side·track /ˈsaɪdtræk/ *v* [T] to make someone stop talking about or dealing with the main subject or problem by making them interested in something else that is less important: *I think we're getting sidetracked from the main issue here.*

side·walk /ˈsaɪdwɔːkǁ-wɒːk/ *n* [C] *AmE* a hard surface or path for people to walk on along the side of a street; PAVEMENT *BrE* → see colour picture on page 79

side·ways /ˈsaɪdweɪz/ *adj* towards one side, or with the side facing forwards: *Mel's car slid sideways across the icy road.*

sid·ing /ˈsaɪdɪŋ/ *n* [C] *BrE* a short railway track next to a main track where trains are kept when they are not being used

si·dle /ˈsaɪdl/ *v* [I] to walk towards someone or something slowly, as if you do not want to be noticed: **+ up/over etc** *Tom sidled up to me with an embarrassed look.*

siege /siːdʒ/ *n* [C,U] **1** a military operation in which an army surrounds a place and stops supplies of food, weapons etc from getting to it: *the siege of Vienna* | *a city under siege* (=surrounded by an army) **2** when a building is surrounded by a group of people, and the people inside cannot get out: **be under siege** *Mellor's apartment was soon under siege from newspaper and TV reporters.*

si·es·ta /siˈestə/ *n* [C] a short period of sleep or rest taken in the afternoon by people who live in hot countries

sieve /sɪv/ *n* [C] a piece of kitchen equipment that looks like a wire net, used for separating solid things from liquids or small pieces from large pieces — **sieve** *v* [T]

sift /sɪft/ *v* [T] **1** to put flour, sugar etc through a sieve in order to remove large pieces **2** also **sift through** to examine something very carefully in order to find something: *Police investigators are still sifting through the evidence.*

sigh /saɪ/ *v* [I] to breathe out heavily, especially when you are tired, annoyed, bored etc: *The police inspector sighed and shook his head.* —**sigh** *n* [C] *a sigh of relief*

sight[1] /saɪt/ *n* **1** [singular, U] when you see something: **the sight of** *I can't stand the sight of blood.* | **catch sight of** (=see someone or something for a very short time): *We caught sight of Henry as we turned the corner.* **2** [U] the ability to see: *My grandmother is losing her sight.* **3** [C] something you can see, especially something beautiful or unusual: **the sights** (=the most famous and interesting places in an area, which many people visit): *The Wrigley Building is one of the most famous sights in Chicago.* **4 in/ within sight a)** in the area that you can see: *There was nobody in sight.* | *We camped within sight of the beach.* **b)** likely to happen soon: *Peace is in sight.* **5 out of sight** outside the area that you can see: *The police parked down the road, out of sight of the house.* **6 lose sight of** to be so concerned with unimportant details that you forget to think about the most important thing: *I think the party has lost sight of its ideals.* **7 set your sights on sth** to decide that you definitely want to achieve something **8 sights** [plural] the part of a gun that you use for aiming → see also **at first glance/sight** (FIRST[1])

sight[2] *v* [T] to see something, especially something you have been looking for, or something

---

GRAMMAR NOTE: transitive and intransitive (2)
Some verbs can be used **transitive** or **intransitive**. For example: **read** v [T,I]
● Transitive: *I can't read your handwriting.*
● Intransitive: *Tom learned to read at the age of four.*

that is rare or difficult to see: *The missing child was sighted in central Manchester.*

sight·ed /'saɪtɪd/ *adj* able to see and not blind

sight·ing /'saɪtɪŋ/ *n* [C] an occasion when something is seen, especially something unusual or rare: *UFO sightings*

sight·less /'saɪtləs/ *adj literary* blind

sight·see·ing /'saɪt,siːɪŋ/ *n* [U] the activity of visiting famous or interesting places, especially as a tourist: *a sightseeing tour of Berlin* — **sightseer** *n* [C]

sign[1] /saɪn/ *n* [C] **1** a set of words or shapes in a public place that gives information, for example directions or the name of a town: *He ignored the 'No Smoking' sign.* | *Just follow the road signs.* **2** an event, fact etc that shows that something exists or is starting to happen: **+ that** *There were signs that someone had been there earlier.* | **+ of** *Tiredness can be a sign of illness.* **3** a picture or shape that has a particular meaning: *the dollar sign* **4** a movement that you make in order to tell someone something: *He made a sign for me to follow him.* → see also STAR SIGN

sign

sign[2] *v* **1** [I,T] to write your name on a letter or document to show that you wrote it or agree with it: *I forgot to sign the cheque.* **2** also **sign up** [T] to agree to give someone a job, for example in a sports team or musical group: *He's been signed by United.*

sign sth ↔ **away** *phr v* [T] to give something you have to someone else by signing an official document, especially when this does not seem a sensible thing to do

sign for sth *phr v* [T] to write your name on a document to prove that you have received something

sign in *phr v* [I] to write your name in a book when you enter an office building, club etc

sign on *phr v* [I] **1** to put your name on a list because you want to do a course: **+ for** *I've signed on for a French course.* **2** *BrE* to get money from the government by signing (SIGN) a document to officially say you do not have a job

sign out *phr v* [I] to write your name in a book when you leave an office building, club etc

sign sth ↔ **over** *phr v* [T] to give something you own to someone else by signing an official document

sign up *phr v* **1** [T **sign** sb ↔ **up**] to agree to give someone a job, for example in a sports team or musical group: *The Yankees signed him up when he finished college.* **2** [I] to put your name on a list because you want to do something: **+ for** *Twenty people signed up for the trip to Paris.*

sig·nal[1] /'sɪgnəl/ *n* [C] **1** a sound, action, or event that gives information or tells someone to do something: *Wait for my signal.* | *The result is a clear signal that voters are not happy.* **2** a series of light waves, sound waves etc that carry information to a radio, television etc: *broadcasting signals* **3** a piece of equipment that tells a train driver whether to go or stop

signal[2] *v* **-lled, -lling** *BrE*, **-led, -ling** *AmE* **1** [I,T] to move your hand, head etc as a way of telling someone something: *Max pushed his plate away and signalled for coffee.* **2** [T] to be a sign or proof of something: *The elections signalled the end of a nine-year civil war.* **3** [T] to make something clear by what you say or do: *Carter has signalled his intention to resign.*

sig·na·to·ry /'sɪgnət₃riǁ-tɔːri/ *n* [C] *formal* a person or country that signs a formal agreement

sig·na·ture /'sɪgnətʃəl-ər/ *n* [C] your name written the way you usually write it, for example on a cheque

sig·nif·i·cance /sɪg'nɪfɪkəns/ *n* [U] the importance of something, especially something that might affect you in the future: *What was the significance of that last remark?* | *a political agreement of some significance* (=it is important)

sig·nif·i·cant /sɪg'nɪfɪkənt/ *adj* **1** noticeable or important: *There has been a significant change in people's attitudes since the 1950s.* **2** having a special meaning: *Anna and Tom exchanged significant looks.* — **significantly** *adv* → opposite INSIGNIFICANT

sig·ni·fy /'sɪgnɪfaɪ/ *v* [T] **1** to be a sign of something: *Does this signify a change in policy?* **2** to show what you think, want etc by doing something: *Everyone nodded to signify their agreement.*

sign lan·guage /'. ,../ *n* [C,U] a language that uses hand movements, used by people who cannot hear

sign·post[1] /'saɪnpəʊstǁ-poʊst/ *n* [C] a sign on a road that shows directions and distances

signpost[2] *v BrE* **be signposted** to have signposts showing you which way to go: *The zoo is signposted from the town centre.*

Sikh /siːk/ *n* [C] a member of an Indian religious group that developed from Hinduism — **Sikh** *adj*

si·lence[1] /'saɪləns/ *n* **1** [C,U] when there is no sound: *There was a long silence before he answered.* | **in silence** (=not saying anything): *The two men sat in silence.* **2** [U] when someone refuses to talk about something: *So far, he has maintained his silence on the subject.*

silence[2] *v* [T] **1** to make someone stop criticizing or giving their opinions: *Critics of the system were quickly silenced.* **2** to stop someone from talking, or to stop something from making a noise

si·lenc·er /'saɪlənsəl-sər/ *n* [C] **1** a thing that is put on the end of a gun so that it makes less noise **2** *BrE* a piece of equipment that makes an engine quieter; MUFFLER *AmE*

si·lent /'saɪlənt/ *adj* **1** not saying anything or making any sound: *Simon was silent for a moment.* | **fall silent** (=become silent): *The whole room fell silent.* **2** refusing to talk about something: *John remained silent when asked about the money.* — **silently** *adv*

sil·hou·ette /ˌsɪlu'et/ *n* [C] a dark shape or shadow, seen against a light background — **silhouetted** *adj*: *tall chimneys silhouetted against the sunset*

sil·i·con /'sɪlɪkən/ *n* [U] an ELEMENT that is used for making glass, bricks, and computer parts

silk /sɪlk/ *n* [C,U] soft cloth made from the threads produced by a silkworm: *a silk shirt*

silk·en /ˈsɪlkən/ adj literary soft and smooth like silk, or made of silk: her silken hair

silk·worm /ˈsɪlkwɜːm‖-wɜːrm/ n [C] a type of CATERPILLAR that produces threads which can be made into silk

silk·y /ˈsɪlki/ adj soft and smooth like silk: silky fur

sill /sɪl/ n [C] a WINDOWSILL

sil·ly /ˈsɪli/ adj stupid or not sensible: Don't be silly; we can't afford a new car. —**silliness** n [U]

si·lo /ˈsaɪləʊ‖-loʊ/ n [C] a building used for storing grain and food for farm animals

silt /sɪlt/ n [U] sand or mud in a river

sil·ver[1] /ˈsɪlvər/ n [U] **1** a valuable shiny white metal, used for making jewellery, spoons etc **2** things that are made of silver: polishing the silver

silver[2] adj **1** made of silver: a silver spoon **2** with the colour of silver: a shimmering silver dress

silver med·al /ˌ.. ˈ../ n [C] a prize given to someone who finishes second in a race or competition

sil·ver·ware /ˈsɪlvəweə‖-vərwer/ n [U] **1** things that are made of silver **2** AmE metal knives, forks and spoons

silver wed·ding an·ni·ver·sa·ry /ˌ.. ˈ.. ..ˌ../ n [C] the date that is exactly 25 years after the date of a wedding

sil·ver·y /ˈsɪlvəri/ adj like silver in colour or appearance

sim·i·lar /ˈsɪmələ, ˈsɪmɪlə‖-ər/ adj almost the same but not exactly the same: They came from similar backgrounds. | + to Your shoes are similar to mine.

sim·i·lar·i·ty /ˌsɪmɪˈlærɪti/ n [C,U] when people or things are similar, or a way in which they are similar: + between There is some similarity between the styles of the two authors. | + with/to English has many similarities with German.

sim·i·lar·ly /ˈsɪmɪləli‖-ərli/ adv in a similar way

sim·i·le /ˈsɪmɪli/ n [C] an expression that describes something by comparing it with something else using the word 'like' or 'as', for example 'as red as blood'

sim·mer /ˈsɪmə‖-ər/ v [I,T] to cook food in liquid that is boiling very gently: Let the soup simmer for 5 minutes.

sim·per /ˈsɪmpə‖-ər/ v [I] to smile in a way that is silly and annoying

sim·ple /ˈsɪmpəl/ adj **1** not difficult or complicated: The instructions are very simple. **2** without a lot of unnecessary decorations or additions: a simple white dress **3** used to emphasize that something is the only reason, fact etc that is important: The simple truth is that he wasn't good enough. **4** ordinary and not special in any way: a simple country existence **5** not very intelligent **6** simple past/present/future a tense of a verb in English that is formed without using a PARTICIPLE that ends in "-ing" → compare CONTINUOUS

sim·pli·ci·ty /sɪmˈplɪsɪti/ n [U] **1** when something does not have a lot of unnecessary decorations or additions: The church is beautiful in its simplicity. **2** when something is easy to do or understand

sim·pli·fy /ˈsɪmplɪfaɪ/ v [T] to make something easier to do or understand: an attempt to simplify the tax system —**simplification** /ˌsɪmplɪfɪˈkeɪʃən/ n [U]

sim·plis·tic /sɪmˈplɪstɪk/ adj making something seem less complicated than it really is: a rather simplistic view of life

sim·ply /ˈsɪmpli/ adv **1** only, used especially when explaining the reason for something, when saying what something is: Some students lose marks simply because they don't read the question properly. **2** used to emphasize what you are saying: But that simply isn't true! **3** in a way that is easy to understand: **to put it simply** (=used when explaining something in a simple way): To put it simply, the bank won't lend us the money. **4** in a plain and ordinary way: a simply decorated room

sim·u·late /ˈsɪmjʊleɪt/ v [T] to make or do something that seems like the real thing but is not: an experiment to simulate the effects of being weightless —**simulator** n [C] a flight simulator —**simulated** adj

sim·u·la·tion /ˌsɪmjʊˈleɪʃən/ n [C,U] something you do in order to practise what you would do in a real situation: The course includes a computer simulation of an emergency landing.

sim·ul·ta·ne·ous /ˌsɪməlˈteɪniəs‖ˌsaɪ-/ adj happening or done at the same time as something else: a simultaneous broadcast on TV and radio —**simultaneously** adv

sin[1] /sɪn/ n **1** [C,U] something that religious laws do not allow: the sin of greed **2** [singular] informal something that you do not approve of: It's a sin to waste good food.

sin[2] v [I] **-nned, -nning** to do something that religious laws do not allow —**sinner** n [C] He believes that all sinners will go to Hell.

since[1] /sɪns/ linking word **1** from a particular time in the past, or during a period that began after another time or event: I haven't seen him since we left school. | Jim's been working at Citibank since he finished college. **2** used to give a reason or explanation for something; as: I'll do it myself since you're obviously not going to help.

since[2] prep, adv **1** from a particular time in the past, or during a period that began after another time or event: So much has changed since the war. | I've been living here since February. | He left yesterday – I haven't seen him since. **2 since when** spoken used to show that you feel annoyed or surprised about something: Since when does it cost £200 to put a new tyre on the car?

sin·cere /sɪnˈsɪə‖-ˈsɪr/ adj honest and really meaning what you say: a sincere and loyal friend | a sincere apology → opposite INSINCERE —**sincerity** /sɪnˈserɪti/ n [U]

sin·cere·ly /sɪnˈsɪəli‖-ˈsɪrli/ adv **1** in a sincere way: I sincerely hope we meet again. **2 Yours sincerely** BrE/**Sincerely (yours)** AmE something you write at the end of a formal letter before you sign your name

sin·ew·y /ˈsɪnjuːi/ adj having strong muscles: sinewy arms

sin·ful /ˈsɪnfəl/ adj morally bad or wrong

sing /sɪŋ/ v [I,T] **sang** /sæŋ/, **sung** /sʌŋ/, **sing·ing** to produce songs or musical sounds with your voice: *Sophie sings in a choir.* | *They sang a beautiful song.* —**singing** *n* [U]

sing. the written abbreviation of SINGULAR

singe /sɪndʒ/ *v* [T] to burn something slightly on its surface or edge: *I singed my hair on a candle.*

sing·er /'sɪŋəⁱr/ *n* [C] someone who sings, especially as a job: *an opera singer*

sin·gle[1] /'sɪŋgəl/ *adj* **1** [only before noun] only one: *We lost the game by a single point.* **2** not married: *Terry is 34 and still single.* **3** [only before noun] intended to be used by only one person: *a single bed* → see picture at BED **4 every single** used to emphasize that something happens every day, week etc, or that something is true about every one of a group of things: *My dad has every single Beatles album.* **5** used to emphasize that you are talking about the biggest, greatest etc thing of its kind: **the single biggest/greatest etc** *The single biggest problem is lack of money.* **6** *BrE* a single ticket is for a trip from one place to another but not back again; ONE-WAY

single[2] *n* [C] **1** a musical record with one song on each side: *Michael Jackson's new single* **2** *BrE* a ticket to go from one place to another but not back again: *a single to Liverpool* → compare RETURN[2] → see also SINGLES

single[3] *v*

single sb/sth ↔ **out** *phr v* [T] to choose someone or something from a group, especially in order to praise or criticize them: *The school was singled out for its excellent academic results.*

single file /ˌ.. './ *n* [U] **in single file** in a line with one person behind the other

single-hand·ed·ly /ˌ.. '../ , **single-hand·ed** /ˌ.. '../ *adv* done by one person with no help from anyone else: *She's brought up four kids, single-handedly.* —**single-handed** *adj* [only before noun] *his single-handed voyage across the Atlantic*

single-mind·ed /ˌ.. '../ *adj* having one aim and working hard to achieve it: *a single-minded determination to succeed.* —**single-mindedness** *n* [U]

single par·ent /ˌ.. '../ *n* [C] a mother or father who looks after her or his children alone

singles /'sɪŋgəlz/ *n* **1** [U] a game, especially tennis, played by one person against another person **2 singles bar/club/night etc** a bar, club etc for people who are not married

sin·gly /'sɪŋgli/ *adv* separately or one at a time: *The animals live singly or in small groups.*

sing-song[1] /'. ./ *n* [C] *BrE* when people sing songs together for fun, for example at a party

sing-song[2] *adj* a sing-song voice rises and falls a lot

sin·gu·lar[1] /'sɪŋgjʊləⁱr/ *adj* **1** the singular form of a word is used when you are talking or writing about one person or thing → compare PLURAL **2** *formal* very great or noticeable: *singular beauty*

singular[2] *n* **the singular** the form of a word that you use when you are talking or writing about one person or thing

sin·gu·lar·ly /'sɪŋgjʊləⁱlɪ-lərli/ *adv formal* very noticeably: *a singularly unattractive building*

sin·is·ter /'sɪnˌstəⁱr/ *adj* seeming to be bad or evil: *There's something sinister about the whole thing.*

sink[1] /sɪŋk/ *v* **sank** /sæŋk/ *or* **sunk** /sʌŋk/, **sunk, sinking 1** [I,T] to go down, or make something go down, below the surface of water: *The boat sank after hitting a rock.* | **+ to** *He watched his keys sink to the bottom of the river.* **2** [I] **a)** to move down into a chair, onto the floor etc because you are weak or tired: **+ into/down etc** *Lee sank into a chair and went to sleep.* **b)** to move to a lower level: *The sun sank beneath the horizon.* | *House prices in the area are sinking fast.* **3 your heart sinks/your spirits sink** if your heart or your spirits sink, you suddenly become unhappy or annoyed, especially because you know you will have to do something boring or difficult → see also SINKING

sink in *phr v* [I] if information, news etc sinks in, you finally realize the effect it will have: *Her mother died last week but it's only just starting to sink in.*

sink into *phr v* **1** [T **sink into**] to gradually get into a worse state: *She could see him sinking into depression.* **2** [T **sink sth into** sth] to spend a lot of money on a business, in order to make more money: *They had sunk thousands into the business.* **3 sink your teeth/a knife etc into sth** to put your teeth or something sharp into someone's flesh, into food etc: *The dog sank its teeth into her arm.*

sink[2] *n* [C] the thing in a kitchen or bathroom that you fill with water to wash dishes, your hands etc → see picture at KITCHEN

sink·ing /'sɪŋkɪŋ/ *adj* **a sinking feeling** a feeling you get when you realize that something bad is going to happen

si·nus /'saɪnəs/ *n* [C] one of the two hollow spaces behind your nose

sip /sɪp/ *v* [I,T] **-pped, -pping** to drink something slowly, taking only small amounts: *She sipped her tea.* —**sip** *n* [C] *He took a sip of coffee.*

si·phon[1] *also* **syphon** /'saɪfən/ *n* [C] a tube that you use to take liquid out of a container

siphon[2] *also* **syphon** *v* [T] **1** to remove liquid from a container using a siphon **2** to secretly take money from an organization over a period of time: **siphon sth off/from** *He had been steadily siphoning money from his employer's account.*

sir /sə; *strong* sɜːⁱlsər; *strong* sɜːr/ *n* **1** *spoken* a polite way of addressing a man, for example a customer in a shop: *Can I help you, sir?* **2** *AmE spoken* used to get the attention of a man whose name you do not know: *Sir! You dropped your wallet!* **3 Dear Sir** used at the beginning of a business letter to a man whom you do not know his name **4 Sir** used before the name of a KNIGHT: *Sir James*

si·ren /'saɪərən|'saɪr-/ *n* [C] a piece of equipment that makes loud warning sounds, used on police cars, fire engines etc

sis·sy /'sɪsɪ/ *n* [C] *informal* a boy that other boys do not like because he does things that girls do —**sissy** *adj*

sis·ter /'sɪstəⁱr/ *n* [C] **1** a girl or woman who has the same parents as you: *I've got two sisters.* → see picture at FAMILY **2** a woman who belongs to the same race, religion, or organization as you **3 Sister** a title given to a NUN: *Sister Frances* **4** *BrE* **Sister** a nurse who is in charge of a hospital WARD **5 sister company/ organization/ship** etc a company, ship etc that belongs to the same group or organization —**sisterly** adv → compare BROTHER

sister-in-law /'.. ../ n [C] **1** the sister of your husband or wife **2** the wife of your brother → see picture at FAMILY

sit /sɪt/ v **sat** /sæt/, **sat, sitting 1** [I] **a)** to be on a chair, on the ground etc with the top half of your body upright and your weight resting on your bottom: + **on/in/by** etc The children were sitting on the floor. → see colour picture on page 670 **b)** also **sit down** to move to a sitting position after you have been standing: + **by/beside** etc Come and sit by me. **2** [I] to be in a particular position: + **on/in** etc A number of old books sat on the shelf. **3** [I] to stay in one place for a long time doing nothing useful: I spent half the morning sitting in a traffic jam. **4** [T] to make someone sit somewhere: **sit sb in/on** etc She sat the boy in the corner. **5 sit tight** to stay in the same place or situation and not do anything: Investors should sit tight and see what happens in a few days. **6 sit still** to sit and not move: Sit still and let me fix your hair. **7** [T] BrE to take an examination: Anna's sitting her GCSEs this year. **8** [I] if a committee, court, or parliament sits, it does its work in an official meeting: The court sits once a month. **9 sit on the fence** to avoid saying which side of an argument you support or what you think is the best thing to do

    sit around (also **sit about** BrE) phr v [I] to sit and not do very much: Dan just sits around watching TV all day.

    sit back phr v [I] to let someone else do something or let something happen, without taking any action yourself

    sit down phr v [I] to move into a sitting position after you have been standing: Come over here and sit down.

    sit in phr v **1 sit in for sb** to do a job, go to a meeting etc instead of the person who usually does it **2 sit in on sth** to watch a meeting or activity but not get involved in it: Do you mind if I sit in on your class?

    sit sth ↔ **out** phr v [T] to stay where you are until something finishes and not get involved in it: I'll sit this dance out.

    sit through phr v [T] to stay until a meeting, performance etc finishes, even if it is very long or boring: We had to sit through a three-hour class this morning.

    sit up phr v [I] **1** to move to a sitting position after you have been lying down: He sat up and rubbed his eyes. **2** to stay awake and not go to bed: We sat up all night talking.

sit·com /'sɪtkɒm‖-kɑːm/ n [C,U] a funny television programme that has the same characters every week in a different story

site[1] /saɪt/ n [C] **1** a place where something important or interesting happened: an archaeological site | the site of the battle **2** an area where something is being built or will be built: a construction site

site[2] v **be sited** formal to be put or built in a particular place: The castle is superbly sited above the valley.

sit-in /'.. ./ n [C] a protest in which people refuse to leave a place until they get what they want

sit·ter /'sɪtə‖-ər/ n [C] spoken, especially AmE a BABYSITTER

sit·ting /'sɪtɪŋ/ n [C] one of the times when a meal is served when it is not possible for everyone to eat at the same time

sitting room /'.. ./ n [C] BrE a LIVING ROOM

sit·u·at·ed /'sɪtʃueɪtɪd/ adj **be situated** formal to be in a particular place: The hotel is situated on the lakeside.

sit·u·a·tion /ˌsɪtʃu'eɪʃən/ n [C] **1** the combination of all the things that are happening and all the conditions that exist at a particular time and place: She's in a very difficult situation. **2** formal the position of a building or a town

sit-up /'. ./ n [C usually plural] an exercise in which you sit up from a lying position while keeping your feet on the floor

six /sɪks/ number **1** 6 **2 be hit/knocked for six** BrE to be suddenly and badly affected by something that happens

six·teen /ˌsɪks'tiːn◂/ number 16 —**sixteenth** number

sixth[1] /sɪksθ/ number 6th: his sixth birthday

sixth[2] n [C] one of the six equal parts of something

sixth form /'. ./ n [C] the classes of school students between the ages of 16 and 18 in Britain —**sixth former** /ˌ. '../

sixth sense /ˌ. './ n [singular] a special ability to know something without using any of your five usual senses such as hearing or sight: Some sixth sense told her that she was in danger.

six·ties /'sɪkstiz/ n **1 the sixties** the years between 1960 and 1969 **2 be in your sixties** to be between the ages of 60 and 69

six·ty /'sɪksti/ number 60 —**sixtieth** number

siz·a·ble /'saɪzəbəl/ adj another spelling of SIZEABLE

size[1] /saɪz/ n **1** [C,U] how big or small something is: A diamond's value depends on its size. | Their house is twice the size of ours. **2** [U] the fact of being very big: Look at the size of that ship! **3** [C] a measurement for clothes, shoes etc: What size shoes do you take? | a size 14 dress **4 large-sized/medium-sized** etc large etc in size: a medium-sized car

size[2] v

    size sb/sth ↔ **up** phr v [T] informal to think carefully about a situation or person so that you can decide how to react: Julie had an ability to size people up quickly.

size·a·ble also **sizable** /'saɪzəbəl/ adj fairly large: a sizeable amount of money

siz·zle /'sɪzəl/ v [I] to make a sound like water falling on hot metal: bacon sizzling in the pan → see colour picture on page 635

S

GRAMMAR NOTE: 'if' clauses (1)
Use the simple present to talk about the future in clauses beginning **if...** : I will hit you **if** you **do** that again. not 'if you will do that again'. **If** you **take** a taxi, you'll be OK. not 'if you will take a taxi...'
Use 'will' in the other part of the sentence.

skate[1] /skeɪt/ n **1** [C] an ICE SKATE **2** [C] a ROLLER SKATE **3** [C,U] a large flat sea fish **4 get your skates on** *BrE informal* used to tell someone to hurry

skate[2] v [I] to move on skates: *I never learned how to skate.* —**skating** n [U] —**skater** n [C]

skate·board /'skeɪtbɔːd‖-bɔːrd/ n [C] a short board with wheels that you stand and ride on —**skateboarding** n [U]

skeleton

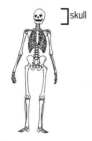

]skull

skel·e·ton /'skelᵻtən/ n [C] **1** the structure consisting of all the bones in a human or animal body: *the human skeleton* **2 have a skeleton in the closet/cupboard** to have a secret about something embarrassing or unpleasant that happened to you in the past **3 skeleton staff/ crew/service** only just enough people to keep an organization working: *a skeleton bus service on Christmas Day* —**skeletal** adj

skep·tic /'skeptɪk/ the American spelling of SCEPTIC

skep·ti·cal /'skeptɪkəl/ the American spelling of SCEPTICAL

skep·ti·ci·sm /'skeptᵻsɪzəm/ the American spelling of SCEPTICISM

sketch[1] /sketʃ/ n [C] **1** a drawing that you do quickly and without a lot of details: *a pencil sketch of a bird* **2** a short humorous scene that is part of a larger performance: *a comic sketch* **3** a short written or spoken description

sketch[2] v [I,T] to draw a sketch of something
sketch in sth *phr v* [T] to add more information or details: *I'll try to sketch in the historical background.*
sketch sth ↔ **out** *phr v* [T] to describe something giving only the basic details: *Barry sketched out a plan for next year's campaign.*

sketch·y /'sketʃi/ adj including only a few details or pieces of information, and not showing exactly or completely what something is like: *I made a few sketchy notes.*

skew·er /'skjuːə‖-ər/ n [C] a metal or wooden stick that you put through pieces of food that you want to cook —**skewer** v [T]

ski[1] /skiː/ n [C], *plural* **skis** one of a pair of long narrow pieces of wood or plastic that you fasten to boots so you can move easily on snow → see colour picture on page 636

ski[2] v [I] **skied, skied, skiing** to move over snow on skis: *Can you ski?* → see colour picture on page 636 —**skiing** n [U] *We're going skiing this winter.* —**skier** n [C]

skid /skɪd/ v [I] **-dded, -dding** if a vehicle skids,

it suddenly slides sideways and you cannot control it: *The car skidded on ice.* —**skid** n [C]

skies /skaɪz/ n [plural] the sky – used especially to describe the weather: *Tomorrow there will be clear skies and some sunshine.*

skil·ful *BrE*, **skillful** *AmE* /'skɪlfəl/ adj **1** good at doing something: *a skilful photographer* **2** made or done very well: *a skilful performance* —**skilfully** adv

skill /skɪl/ n [C,U] an ability to do something well, especially because you have practised it: *basic computer skills* | *As a footballer he shows great skill.*

skilled /skɪld/ adj **1** having the training and experience needed to do something well: **highly skilled** *a highly skilled workforce* **2** skilled work needs people who have special training to do it → opposite UNSKILLED

skil·let /'skɪlᵻt/ n [C] a heavy cooking pan made of iron

skillful /'skɪlfəl/ adj the American spelling of SKILFUL

skim /skɪm/ v [T] **-mmed, -mming 1** to remove something that is floating on the surface of a liquid: **skim sth off/from** *Skim the fat off the soup.* **2** also **skim through** to read something quickly to find the main facts or ideas in it: *She skimmed through that morning's headlines.* **3** to move along quickly, nearly touching the surface of something: *a plane skimming the tops of the trees*

skimmed milk *BrE*, **skim milk** *AmE* /ˌ. './ n [U] milk that has had most of the fat removed from it

skimp /skɪmp/ v [I] to not spend enough money or time on something so it is unsuccessful or of bad quality: **+ on** *They try to save money by skimping on staff.*

skimp·y /'skɪmpi/ adj skimpy clothes do not cover much of your body: *a skimpy little dress*

skin[1] /skɪn/ n [C,U] **1** the outside part of a human's or animal's body: *The sheets felt cool against her skin.* | *a skin disease* **2** the skin of an animal used as leather, fur etc: *a tiger skin rug* **3** the natural outside part of many fruits and vegetables: *banana skins* **4** a thin solid layer that forms on top of a liquid, especially when it gets cold **5 dark-skinned/smooth-skinned etc** having skin that is dark, smooth etc **6** a thin solid layer that forms on the top of a liquid **7 do sth by the skin of your teeth** *informal* to only just succeed in doing something: *He escaped by the skin of his teeth.* **8 have thick skin** to not care if people criticize you

skin[2] v [T] **-nned, -nning** to remove the skin from an animal, fruit, or vegetable

skin·head /'skɪnhed/ n [C] a man who cuts his hair very short, especially one who behaves violently towards people of other races

skin·ny /'skɪni/ adj a skinny person is too thin

skint /skɪnt/ adj [not before noun] *BrE informal* having no money: *I'm skint at the moment.*

skip[1] /skɪp/ v **-pped, -pping 1** [I] to move forwards with quick jumps from one foot to the other: **+ down/along etc** *children skipping down the street* → see colour picture on page 670 **2** [I] also **skip rope** *AmE* to jump over a rope as you move it under your feet, as an exercise or as a game **3** [T] to not do something that you would usually do or that you should do: *You shouldn't skip breakfast.* **4** [I,T] to deliberately miss something that would usually come next when you are reading or talking: *Let's skip the next question.* | **+ over** *I'll skip over the details.*

skip² *n* [C] **1** when you skip **2** *BrE* a large container where you put waste such as bricks and broken furniture

skip·per /ˈskɪpəl-ər/ *n* [C] *informal* a CAPTAIN of a ship, sports team etc

skir·mish /ˈskɜːmɪʃ‖ˈskɜːr-/ *n* [C] a fight between small groups of soldiers

skirt¹ /skɜːt‖skɜːrt/ *n* [C] a piece of clothing for girls and women that fits around the waist and hangs down like a dress → see colour picture on page 113

skirt² also **skirt around** *v* [T] **1** to go around the outside edge of a place: *The train skirted around the lake.* **2** to avoid talking directly about a problem, subject etc: *We cannot skirt around the issues of poverty and inequality.*

skit·tle /ˈskɪtl/ *n* **1** **skittles** [U] a British game in which you roll a ball to try to knock down objects shaped like bottles **2** [C] one of the objects you roll the ball at in skittles

skive /skaɪv/ also **skive off** *v* [I] *BrE informal* to not go to school or work when you should do: *He skived off work and went fishing.* — **skiver** *n* [C]

skulk /skʌlk/ *v* [I] to hide or move around quietly because you do not want people to see you: **+ in/behind etc** *Two men were skulking in the shadows.*

skull /skʌl/ *n* [C] the bones of a person's or animal's head → see picture at SKELETON

skull·cap /ˈskʌlkæp/ *n* [C] a small men's hat that members of some religions wear

skunk /skʌŋk/ *n* [C] a small black and white animal that produces an unpleasant smell if it is attacked

sky /skaɪ/ *n* [singular, U] **1** the space above the earth where the sun, clouds, and stars are: *a clear blue sky* **2** **the sky's the limit** *spoken* used to say that there is no limit to what someone can achieve, spend etc → see also SKIES

sky·div·ing /ˈskaɪˌdaɪvɪŋ/ *n* [U] the sport of jumping from a plane with a PARACHUTE

sky·light /ˈskaɪlaɪt/ *n* [C] a window in the roof of a building

sky·line /ˈskaɪlaɪn/ *n* [C] the shape made by tall buildings or hills against the sky

sky·scrap·er /ˈskaɪˌskreɪpəl-ər/ *n* [C] a very tall building in a city → see colour picture on page 79

slab /slæb/ *n* [C] a thick flat piece of something hard such as stone: *a concrete slab*

slack¹ /slæk/ *adj* **1** loose and not pulled tight: *a slack rope* **2** with less business activity than usual: *Trade is slack at the moment.* **3** not taking enough care to do things correctly: *slack safety procedures* | *I've been slack about getting this work done.*

slack² also **slack off** *v* [I] to not work as quickly as you should: *Don't let me see you slacking off!* — **slacker** *n* [C]

slack·en /ˈslækən/ *v* [I,T] **1** to gradually become slower, weaker, or less active, or to make something do this: *He slackened his speed so I could catch up.* **2** to make something looser, or to become looser: *Slacken the screw a little.*

slacks /slæks/ *n* [plural] *old-fashioned* trousers

slag¹ /slæg/ *n* **1** [U] waste material that is left when metal has been taken from rock **2** [C] *BrE spoken informal* an offensive word for a woman

slag² *v*

slag sb ↔ off *phr v* [T] *BrE spoken informal* to criticize someone, especially unfairly

slain /sleɪn/ *v* the past participle of SLAY

slake /sleɪk/ *v literary* **slake your thirst** to drink so that you are not THIRSTY

slam¹ /slæm/ *v* **-mmed, -mming** **1** [I,T] if a door, gate etc slams, or someone slams it, it shuts quickly and loudly: *Baxter left the room, slamming the door.* **2** [T] to put something somewhere, quickly and violently: **slam sth onto/down etc** *Andy slammed the phone down.*

slam² *n* [C usually singular] the action of hitting or closing something noisily or violently: *She shut the door with a slam.*

slan·der /ˈslɑːndəl‖ˈslændər/ *n* [C,U] the illegal action of saying bad and untrue things about someone — **slander** *v* [T] — **slanderous** *adj* → compare LIBEL

slang /slæŋ/ *n* [U] informal language with its own set of words, expressions, and meanings, often used only by people who belong to a particular group: *army slang* — **slangy** *adj*

slant¹ /slɑːnt‖slænt/ *v* [I] to slope, or move in a sloping line

slant² *n* [C singular] **1** a sloping position or angle: **at/on a slant** *The pole was set at a slant.* **2** a way of writing about a subject that shows support for a particular set of ideas: *a feminist slant on the subject*

slap¹ /slæp/ *v* [T] **-pped, -pping** to hit someone with the flat part of your hand: *She slapped him across the face.*

slap sth ↔ on *phr v* [T] to put or spread something quickly on a surface: *Just slap some paint on and it'll look a bit better.*

slap² *n* **1** [C] a quick hit with the flat part of your hand **2** **a slap in the face** something someone does that makes you feel very shocked and offended

slap·dash /ˈslæpdæʃ/ *adj* done quickly and carelessly: *a slapdash job of painting the house*

slap·per /ˈslæpəl-ər/ *n* [C] *BrE informal, often humorous* an insulting word for a woman who has sexual relationships with a lot of men

slap·stick /ˈslæpˌstɪk/ *n* [U] humorous acting in which the actors fall over, throw things at each other, get wet etc

slap-up /ˈ. ./ *adj* **slap-up meal/dinner etc** *BrE informal* a big and good meal

slash¹ /slæʃ/ *v* [T] **1** to cut something violently, making a long deep cut: *He tried to kill himself by slashing his wrists.* **2** *informal* to reduce something by a lot: *Many companies are slashing jobs.*

slash² *n* [C] **1** a long deep cut **2** also **slash mark** a line (/) used in writing to separate words, numbers etc

slate¹ /sleɪt/ *n* **1** [U] a dark grey rock that can be easily split into thin flat pieces **2** [C] a small piece of flat grey rock used as a roof covering → see also **a clean slate** (CLEAN)

slate² *v* **1** *AmE* **be slated** to be going to do or be something, or to have had something arranged to be done to you: *Manley is slated to become the next principal.* **2** [T] *BrE* to criticize someone or something severely: *Leconte's latest film has been slated by the critics.*

slaugh·ter /'slɔːtəll'slɔːtər/ *v* [T] **1** to kill an animal for its meat **2** to kill a lot of people in a violent way: *Over 500 men, women and children were slaughtered.* **3** *informal* to defeat an opponent easily: *Italy were slaughtered by Brazil.* —**slaughter** *n* [U]

slaugh·ter·house /'slɔːtəhaʊsll'slɔːtər-/ *n* [C] a building where animals are killed for their meat

slave[1] /sleɪv/ *n* [C] **1** someone who is owned by another person and must work for them without any pay **2** **be a slave to/of sth** to be completely influenced or controlled by something: *She's a slave to fashion.*

slave[2] *v* [I] to work very hard: *Michael's been slaving away in the kitchen all day.*

slave la·bour *BrE*, **slave labor** *AmE* /ˌ. '../ *n* [U] **1** *informal* work for which you are very badly paid: *£2.00 an hour? That's slave labour!* **2** work done by slaves, or the slaves that do this work

sla·ve·ry /'sleɪvəri/ *n* [U] the system of using slaves or the condition of being a slave: *Slavery was abolished after the Civil War.*

slav·ish /'sleɪvɪʃ/ *adj* too willing to obey someone, or to behave like them: *slavish devotion to duty*

slay /sleɪ/ *v* [T] **slew** /sluː/, **slain** /sleɪn/, **slaying** *literary* to kill someone violently —**slaying** *n* [C]

sleaze /sliːz/ *n* [U] dishonest or immoral activities, especially by politicians or business men: *He has recently been plagued by allegations of sleaze.*

slea·zy /'sliːzi/ *adj* **1** a sleazy place is dirty and unpleasant: *a sleazy nightclub* **2** dishonest or morally wrong: *sleazy political scandals*

sledge /sledʒ/ *BrE*, **sled** /sled/ *especially AmE* — *n* [C] a vehicle used for travelling on snow —**sledge** *BrE v* [I]

sledge ham·mer /'. ,../ *n* [C] a large heavy hammer

sleek /sliːk/ *adj* **1** sleek hair or fur is smooth and shiny **2** attractive and expensive: *a sleek white sports car*

sleep[1] /sliːp/ *v* **slept** /slept/, **slept**, **sleeping** **1** [I] to have your eyes closed and be resting in a state of unconsciousness: **sleep well/soundly/badly etc** *I didn't sleep very well last night.* | **sleep in/on/with etc** *You'll have to sleep on the air bed.* | **be sleeping** *Be quiet — the baby's sleeping.* | **not sleep a wink** (=not sleep at all): *She hardly slept a wink last night.* **2** [T] if a room, building, or tent sleeps ten, five, two etc, there are enough beds in it for ten, five etc people **3** **sleep on it** to not make a decision about something important until the next day: *Sleep on it, and we'll discuss it tomorrow.* **4** **sleep rough** *BrE* to sleep outdoors because you have no home

sleep around *phr v* [I] *informal* to have sex with a lot of different people

sleep in *phr v* [I] to wake up later than usual in the morning: *I slept in till 10:00 on Saturday.*

sleep sth ↔ **off** *phr v* [T] to sleep until you do not feel ill or drunk any more

sleep through sth *phr v* [T] to continue to sleep while something is happening: *How could you have slept through the storm?*

sleep together *phr v* [I] *informal* if two people, especially people who are not married to each other, sleep together, they regularly have sex with each other

sleep with sb *phr v* [T] *informal* to have sex with someone: *When did you first find out that she was sleeping with your husband?*

sleep[2] *n* **1** [singular, U] when you are sleeping: *Lack of sleep can make you bad-tempered.* | **in your sleep** *Ed sometimes talks in his sleep.* | **get some sleep** *We didn't get much sleep last night.* | **a good night's sleep** (=a long sleep at night): *What you need is a good night's sleep.* **2** **go to sleep a)** to start sleeping: *Be quiet and go to sleep!* **b)** if a part of your body goes to sleep, you cannot feel it for a short time, because it has not been getting enough blood → compare **fall asleep** (ASLEEP) **3** **not lose (any) sleep over sth** to not worry about something **4** **be put to sleep** if an animal is put to sleep, it is killed by a VET because it is old or ill

sleep·er /'sliːpəll-ər/ *n* [C] **1** a light/heavy sleeper someone who wakes up easily or does not wake up easily from sleep **2** *BrE* a train with beds for passengers to sleep on, or a bed on this kind of train **3** *BrE* a piece of wood or CONCRETE that supports a railway track

sleeping bag /'.. ../ *n* [C] a large warm bag for sleeping in

sleeping pill /'.. ../ *n* [C] a drug that helps you to sleep

sleep·less /'sliːpləs/ *adj* unable to sleep: *I lay sleepless on my lumpy mattress.* | **a sleepless night** (=a night when you do not sleep): *He spent a sleepless night worrying about what to do.* —**sleeplessness** *n* [U]

sleep·walk /'sliːp,wɔːkll-,wɔːk/ *v* [I] to get out of bed and walk somewhere while you are asleep —**sleepwalker** *n* [C]

sleep·y /'sliːpi/ *adj* **1** tired and ready to sleep: *I felt really sleepy after lunch.* **2** quiet and without much activity: *a sleepy little town* —**sleepily** *adv* —**sleepiness** *n* [U]

sleet /sliːt/ *n* [U] a mixture of rain and snow —**sleet** *v* [I]

sleeve[1] /sliːv/ *n* **1** [C] the part of a piece of clothing that covers your arm: *a blouse with short sleeves* **2** **-sleeved** having a particular type of sleeve: *a long-sleeved sweater* **3** **have sth up your sleeve** *informal* to have a secret plan that you are going to use later: *Jansen usually has a few surprises up his sleeve.* **4** [C] *BrE* a cover for a record; JACKET *AmE*

sleeve·less /'sliːvləs/ *adj* without sleeves: *a sleeveless dress*

sleigh /sleɪ/ *n* [C] a large vehicle that is pulled by animals, used for travelling on snow

sleight of hand /ˌslaɪt əv 'hænd/ *n* [U] when you do something skilful or slightly dishonest to achieve something

slen·der /'slendəll-ər/ *adj* thin in an attractive way: *long slender fingers*

slept /slept/ *v* the past tense and past participle of SLEEP

sleuth /sluːθ/ *n* [C] *old-fashioned* a DETECTIVE

slew[1] /sluː/ n AmE informal **a slew of** a large number: a slew of new TV programs

slew[2] v the past tense and past participle of SLAY

slice[1] /slaɪs/ n [C] **1** a flat piece of bread, meat etc cut from a larger piece: Cut the tomato into thin slices. → see colour picture on page 440 **2 a slice of sth** a share of something: Everyone wants a slice of the profits.

slice[2] v **1** also **slice up** [T] to cut meat, bread etc into thin flat pieces: Could you slice the bread? → see colour picture on page 439 **2** [I,T] to cut through or into something with a knife or other sharp object: She sliced off the top of her finger with a bread knife.

slice sth ↔ **up** phr v [T] to cut meat, bread etc into thin flat pieces

slick[1] /slɪk/ adj **1** clever or attractive, but often in a way that seems insincere or dishonest: a slick salesman **2** done or performed very skilfully and confidently: The band gave a very slick performance.

slick[2] n [C] an OIL SLICK

slick[3] v

slick sth ↔ **back/down** phr v [T] to make your hair smooth and shiny using oil or water

slide[1] /slaɪd/ v [I,T] **slid** /slɪd/, **slid, sliding 1** to move somewhere smoothly and quietly, or to move something smoothly and quietly: **+ into/out of** She slid out of bed. | **slide sth into/around etc** Jones slid a hand into his pocket and took out a gun. **2** to move smoothly across a surface, or to make something do this: **+ along/around/down** The children were all sliding around on the ice.

slide[2] n **1** [C] a small piece of film in a frame that you shine light through to show a picture **2** [C] a large structure for children to slide down when they are playing **3** [singular] a decrease in the price, level, standard etc of something: a slide in profits **4** [C] a piece of thin glass used for holding something under a MICROSCOPE

sliding scale /ˌ.. ˈ./ n [C] a system for paying taxes, wages etc in which the amount that you pay changes when conditions change

slight[1] /slaɪt/ adj **1** small and not very important or noticeable: There has been a slight change of plan. **2** a slight person is thin and delicate: a small slight old lady

slight[2] n [C] a remark or action that offends someone: I consider her comments a slight on my work.

slight·ed /ˈslaɪtɪd/ adj offended because you feel as though someone has treated you as if you are not important: Meg felt slighted at not being invited to the party.

slight·est /ˈslaɪtɪst/ adj **1 the slightest difference/change/amount etc** used to emphasize that something is as small as it can be: It doesn't make the slightest difference to me. **2 not in the slightest** not at all: "You're not worried are you?" "Not in the slightest."

slight·ly /ˈslaɪtli/ adv **1** a little: She's slightly older than I am. **2 slightly-built** having a thin and delicate body

slim[1] /slɪm/ adj **1** thin in an attractive way: You're looking a lot slimmer – have you lost weight? → see colour picture on page 244 **2** very small: Doctors said she had only a slim hope of recovery.

slim[2] v [I] **-mmed, -mming** to become thinner by eating less or by exercising: delicious slimming recipes

slim down phr v [I,T **slim** sth ↔ **down**] to reduce the size or number of something: Apex Co. is slimming down its workforce to cut costs.

slime /slaɪm/ n [U] a thick liquid that looks or smells unpleasant

slim·y /ˈslaɪmi/ adj **1** covered with slime: slimy rocks **2** informal friendly in a way that is not sincere

sling[1] /slɪŋ/ v [T] **slung** /slʌŋ/, **slung, slinging 1** to put one thing over or across another so that it hangs there loosely: Mark slung his jacket over his shoulder. **2** to throw something somewhere carelessly

sling[2] n [C] **1** a piece of cloth tied around your neck to support your arm or hand when you have injured it **2** ropes or strong pieces of cloth used for lifting or carrying heavy objects: a baby sling

sling·shot /ˈslɪŋʃɒtǁ-ʃɑːt/ n [C] AmE a thing used by children to shoot stones, which consists of a stick in the shape of a Y with a band of rubber fastened to it; CATAPULT BrE

slink /slɪŋk/ v [I] **slunk** /slʌŋk/, **slunk, slinking** to move somewhere quietly and secretly: The cat slunk behind the chair.

slip[1] /slɪp/ v **1** [I] to accidentally slide so that you fall or almost fall: Joan slipped on the wet floor and broke her ankle. **2** [I] to go somewhere quickly and quietly: **+ out of/away/through etc** Brad slipped out of the back door while no one was looking. **3** [T] to put something somewhere or give someone something quietly or secretly: **slip sth into/around etc sth** He slipped his arm around her waist and kissed her. **4** [I] to slide out of the correct position or out of your hand: The hammer slipped and hit his fingers. **5** [I] to become worse than before: Standards in our schools have been slipping. **6 slip your mind** if something slips your mind, you forget to do it **7 let sth slip** to say something that is supposed to be a secret without intending to: Don't let it slip that I'm in town.

slip into sth phr v [T] to put on a piece of clothing, quickly and easily: I'll just slip into something more comfortable.

slip sth ↔ **off** phr v [T] to take off a piece of clothing, quickly and easily: He slipped off his coat and went upstairs.

slip sth ↔ **on** phr v [T] to put on an item of clothing, quickly and easily: Could you just slip on this gown?

slip out phr v [I] if something slips out, you say it without intending to: Sorry, I shouldn't have said that – it just slipped out.

SPELLING NOTE

Words with the sound /s/, may be spelt **c-**, like **city**, or **ps-**, like **psychology**.

slip out of sth *phr v* [T] to take off clothes or shoes quickly and easily: *Ken slipped out of his shoes and put on his slippers.*

slip up *phr v* [I] to make a mistake: *Every time you slip up, it costs me money.*

slip² *n* [C] **1** a small piece of paper: *He wrote his address down on a slip of paper.* **2** *especially BrE* a small mistake **3** a piece of clothing worn by women under a dress or skirt **4** an act of sliding accidentally so that you fall or almost fall **5 a slip of the tongue** something that you say when you meant to say something else **6 give sb the slip** *informal* to escape from someone: *Palmer gave them the slip in the hotel lobby.*

slipped disc /ˌ. ˈ./ *n* [C] an injury caused when one of the bones in your SPINE moves out of position

slip·per /ˈslɪpəll-ər/ *n* [C usually plural] a light soft shoe that you wear indoors ➡ see picture at SHOE

slip·per·y /ˈslɪpəri/ *adj* **1** smooth or wet and difficult to hold, walk on etc: *a slippery mountain path* **2** *informal* unable to be trusted: *Al's a slippery character.* **3 be on the slippery slope** *BrE* to have started a process or habit that will develop into something dangerous or harmful

slip road /ˈ. ./ *n* [C] *BrE* a road used when you drive onto or off a MOTORWAY

slip·shod /ˈslɪpʃɒdll-ʃɑːd/ *adj* done carelessly and too quickly: *slipshod work*

slit¹ /slɪt/ *n* [C] a straight narrow cut or opening: *a slit in the curtains*

slit² *v* [T] to make a straight narrow cut in something: *He killed the sheep by slitting its throat.*

slith·er /ˈslɪðəll-ər/ *v* [I] to move by twisting and sliding like a snake

sliv·er /ˈslɪvəll-ər/ *n* [C] a small thin pointed piece that has been cut or broken off something: *a sliver of glass* ➡ see colour picture on page 440

slob /slɒbllslɑːb/ *n* [C] *informal* someone who is lazy, dirty, or untidy: *The guy is a total slob.*

slog¹ /slɒgllslɑːg/ *v* [I] *informal* **1** to walk somewhere with difficulty: *We had to slog through mud and dirt to get to the farm.* **2** (also **slog away**) to work very hard without stopping: *I don't want to slog away in a factory for the rest of my life.*

slog² *n* [singular, U] *BrE informal* a long period of hard work, or a long difficult journey: *It was a hard slog to the top of the hill.*

slo·gan /ˈsləʊgənllˈsloʊ-/ *n* [C] a short clever phrase used especially in advertising and politics

slop¹ /slɒpllslɑːp/ *v* [I,T] if liquid slops, or if you slop it, it moves around or over the edge of a container: *Water was slopping over the side of the bath.*

slop² *n* [U] waste from food, that is used for feeding animals

slope¹ /sləʊpllsloʊp/ *n* [C] a piece of ground or a surface that is higher at one end than the other: *a ski slope*

slope² *v* [I] to be higher at one end than at the other: *a narrow road sloping gently upwards*

slop·py /ˈslɒpillˈslɑː-/ *adj* **1** not neat, careful, or thorough: *I will not tolerate sloppy work!* **2** sloppy clothes are large, loose, and not neat: *a sloppy sweater* **3** expressing romantic feelings in a silly way: *sloppy love songs* — **sloppily** *adv* — **sloppiness** *n* [U]

slosh /slɒʃllslɑːʃ/ *v* [I] if liquid in a container sloshes, it moves against or over the sides of the container: *Water was sloshing around in the bottom of the boat.*

sloshed /slɒʃtllslɑːʃt/ *adj informal* drunk

slot

slot¹ /slɒtllslɑːt/ *n* [C] **1** a long narrow hole made in something, especially for putting coins in: *Put 20p in the slot and see how much you weigh.* **2** a time, or position in a SCHEDULE: *I was offered a slot on a local radio station.*

slot² *v* [I,T] to put something into a slot, or to go in a slot: *The cassette slots in here.* | *The instructions tell you how to slot the shelf together.*

slot in *phr v* [I,T **slot** sb/sth ↔ **in**] to find a time or a place for someone or something in a plan, organization etc: *Can you slot me in today?*

sloth /sləʊθllsloʊθ/ *n* **1** [C] a slow-moving animal from Central and South America **2** [U] *literary* laziness

slot ma·chine /ˈ. .ˌ./ *n* [C] a machine that you put coins into to try to win more money

slouch¹ /slaʊtʃ/ *v* [I] to stand, sit, or walk with your shoulders bent forward: *Don't slouch – stand up straight!*

slouch² *n* **1** [singular] the position of your body when you slouch **2 be no slouch (at)** *informal* to be very good or skilful at something: *He's no slouch at football.*

slov·en·ly /ˈslʌvənli/ *adj* dirty, untidy, and careless: *Where did you pick up such slovenly habits?*

slow¹ /sləʊllsloʊ/ *adj* **1** not moving, being done, or happening quickly: *The slowest runners started at the back.* | *It's a very slow process.* **2 slow to do sth/be slow in doing sth** to delay before you do something: *We were slow to realize what was happening.* **3** a clock that is slow shows a time earlier than the true time: *My watch is a few minutes slow.* **4** if business is slow, there are not many customers **5** not quick at understanding things: *The school gives extra help for slower students.*

slow² *v* [I,T] also **slow down** to become slower or make something slower: *The traffic slowed to a crawl.*

slow down *phr v* [I,T **slow** sth ↔ **down**] to become slower or make something slower: *The car slowed down as it approached the store.*

slow³ *adv* SLOWLY — some people consider this usage to be incorrect. Don't use it in written English

slow·coach /ˈsləʊkəʊtʃllˈsloʊkoʊtʃ/ *n* [C] *BrE informal* someone who moves or does something too slowly: *Hurry up, slowcoach!;* SLOWPOKE *AmE*

slow·down /ˈsləʊdaʊn‖ˈsloʊ-/ *n* [C] when an activity takes place more slowly than it did before: *a slowdown in the tourist trade*

slow·ly /ˈsləʊli‖ˈsloʊ-/ *adv* at a slow speed or rate: *White clouds drifted slowly across the sky.*

slow mo·tion /ˌ. ˈ../ *n* [U] something that is shown in a film or television picture at a much slower speed than the speed at which it happened: *a replay of the goal shown in slow motion*

slow·poke /ˈsləʊpəʊk‖ˈsloʊpoʊk/ *n* [C] *AmE informal* someone who moves or does something too slowly; SLOWCOACH *BrE*

sludge /slʌdʒ/ *n* [U] a soft thick unpleasant substance

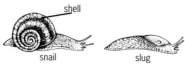

slug

shell

snail   slug

slug¹ /slʌg/ *n* [C] **1** a small soft creature, like a SNAIL but with no shell **2** *AmE* a bullet **3** *AmE* a small quantity of a drink, especially alcohol: *a slug of whisky.*

slug² *v* [T] **-gged, -gging 1** *informal* to hit someone hard with your closed hand: *I stood up and he slugged me again.* **2 slug it out** to argue or fight until someone wins: *The two sides are slugging it out in court.*

slug·gish /ˈslʌgɪʃ/ *adj* moving, working, or reacting more slowly than usual: *The traffic was sluggish that morning.*

sluice¹ /sluːs/ *n* [C] a PASSAGE for water to flow through, with a gate that can stop the water if necessary

sluice² *v* [T] to wash something with a lot of water

slum /slʌm/ *n* [C] an area of a city with old buildings in very bad condition, where many poor people live: *She grew up in the slums of São Paolo.*

slum·ber /ˈslʌmbə‖-ər/ *n* [U] also **slumbers** *n* [plural] *literary* sleep: *She awoke from her slumbers.* —**slumber** *v* [I]

slump /slʌmp/ *v* [I] **1** to suddenly go down in amount, price, or value: *Car sales have slumped recently.* **2 be slumped** to be sitting with your body bent forwards, as if you were unconscious: *He was found slumped over the steering wheel of his car.* —**slump** *n* [C] *a slump in profits*

slung /slʌŋ/ *v* the past tense and past participle of SLING

slunk /slʌŋk/ *v* the past tense and past participle of SLINK

slur¹ /sləː‖slɜːr/ *v* [I,T] **-rred, -rring** to speak in an unclear way without separating words or sounds: *After a few drinks, he started to slur his words.*

slur² *n* [C] an unfair criticism: *a serious slur on his character*

slurp /slɜːp‖slɜːrp/ *v* [I,T] *informal* to drink noisily: *Stop slurping your soup!* —**slurp** *n* [C]

slush /slʌʃ/ *n* [U] partly melted snow

slut /slʌt/ *n* [C] an offensive word for a woman who has sex with a lot of different people

sly /slaɪ/ *adj* **slyer** *or* **slier, slyest** *or* **sliest 1** using tricks and dishonest methods to get what you want: *He's sly and greedy.* **2** showing that you know something that others do not know: *a sly smile* **3 on the sly** *informal* secretly doing something you are not supposed to be doing: *He's been smoking on the sly.* —**slyly** *adv*

smack¹ /smæk/ *v* [T] **1** to hit someone or something, especially with your open hand: *She smacked him hard across the face.* **2 smack your lips** to make a short loud noise with your lips, especially because something tastes good

smack of sth *phr v* [T] to seem to have a particular quality, especially a bad one: *a policy that smacks of sex discrimination*

smack² *n* **1** [C] a hit with your open hand, or a sound like this: *a smack on the head* **2** [U] *informal* the drug HEROIN

smack³ *adv informal* **1** exactly or directly in, on, or through something: *an old building smack in the middle of campus* **2** with a lot of force: *The van ran smack into a wall.*

small¹ /smɔːl‖smɒːl/ *adj* **1** not big: *Rhode Island is the smallest state in the US.|a small group of protesters* ➧ see colour picture on page 244 **2** unimportant or easy to deal with: *a small problem* **3** a small child is young: *She has two small children.* **4 feel/look small** to feel or look silly: *She was always trying to make me look small.* **5 a small fortune** a lot of money: *That house must have cost him a small fortune.* **6 the small hours** the early morning hours, between about one and four o'clock: *We stayed up talking into the small hours.*

small² *adv* in a small size: *He writes so small I can hardly read his letters.*

small change /ˌ. ˈ./ *n* [U] money in coins of low value

small fry /ˈ. ./ *n* [U] *informal* **1** unimportant people or things: *They're small fry compared to the real criminals.* **2** *AmE* children

small-mind·ed /ˌ. ˈ..◂/ *adj* only interested in things that affect you, and too willing to criticize people according to your own opinions: *greedy, small-minded people*

small·pox /ˈsmɔːlpɒks‖ˈsmɒːlpɑːks/ *n* [U] a serious disease that killed a lot of people in past times

small print /ˈ. ./ also **fine print** *n* [U] the parts of a legal document or agreement that contain details that you sometimes do not notice: *Make sure you read the small print before you sign anything.*

small-scale /ˌ. ˈ.◂/ *adj* not very big, or not involving a lot of people: *small-scale enterprises*

small talk /ˈ. ./ *n* [U] polite friendly conversation about unimportant subjects: *He's not very good at making small talk.*

small-time /ˌ. ˈ.◂/ *adj* not important or successful: *a small-time gangster*

smart¹ /smɑːt‖smɑːrt/ *adj* **1** intelligent and sensible: *Jill's a smart kid.* **2** smart machines, weapons etc use computers or the latest methods to work **3** saying funny or clever things in a way that is rude and does not show respect towards someone: *Don't get smart with me, young lady!* **4** *especially BrE* if you look smart or your* clothes are smart, you are dressed in an attractive way and you look very neat; SHARP *AmE*: *You look smart. Are you going anywhere special?* **5** a smart movement is done quickly and with force: *a smart blow on the head* —**smartly** *adv*

smart² *v* [I] **1** to be upset because someone has offended you: *He's still smarting from the insult.* **2** if a part of your body smarts, it hurts with a stinging pain

smash¹ /smæʃ/ *v* **1** [I,T] to break into a lot of small pieces with a loud noise, or to make something do this: *The plates smashed on the floor.* | *Rioters smashed store windows.* **2** [I,T] to hit an object or surface violently, or to make something do this: *Murray smashed his fist against the wall.* **3** [T] to destroy something such as a political system or criminal organization: *Police have smashed a drug smuggling ring.*
smash sth ↔ **in** *phr v* [T] to hit something so violently that you damage it: *Pete's window was smashed in by another driver.*
smash sth ↔ **up** *phr v* [T] to damage or destroy something: *She smashed up the truck in an accident.*

smash², also **smash hit** /ˌ. ˈ./ *n* [C] a very successful new song, film, play etc: *This song's definitely going to be a smash hit.*

smashed /smæʃt/ *adj informal* drunk

smash·ing /ˈsmæʃɪŋ/ *adj BrE old-fashioned* extremely good: *We had a smashing holiday.*

smat·ter·ing /ˈsmætərɪŋ/ *n* [singular] a small amount of something: **+ of** *a smattering of applause*

smear¹ /smɪəllsmɪr/ *v* **1** [I,T] to spread a liquid or soft substance on a surface, or to become spread on a surface: *Jill smeared lotion on Rick's back.* **2** [T] to spread an untrue story about someone in order to harm them, especially in politics

smear² *n* [C] **1** a dirty mark that is left when a substance is spread on a surface: *a dirty smear* **2** an untrue story about someone that is meant to harm them

smell¹ /smel/ *v* **smelled** *or* **smelt** /smelt/, **smelled** *or* **smelling 1** [I] to have a particular smell: **smell of/like** *This wine smells like strawberries.* **2** [I] to have an unpleasant smell; STINK: *Something in the refrigerator smells.* **3** [T] to notice or recognize a smell: *I can smell something burning!* **4** [T] to put your nose near something and breathe in, to discover what kind of smell it has: *Come and smell these roses.* **5** [I] to have the ability to notice and recognize smells: *I've got a cold and I can't smell anything.*

smell² *n* **1** [C] the quality by which you know what things are, using your nose: *What a lovely smell!* | **+ of** *the smell of fresh bread* **2** [C] an unpleasant smell; STINK **3** [U] the ability to notice or recognize smells: *Dogs have an excellent sense of smell.*

USAGE NOTE: smell, odour, scent, fragrance, and **aroma**

Use **smell** in a general way to talk about something that you notice or recognize using your nose: *the smell of rotten eggs* | *There are some wonderful smells coming from the kitchen.* An **odour** is an unpleasant smell: *The odour of stale*

---

cigarette smoke was in the air. A **scent** is what something smells like, especially something that smells pleasant: *a cleaning liquid with a pine scent.* A **fragrance** is an extremely pleasant scent: *the deliciously sweet fragrance of flowers.* An **aroma** is a pleasant smell from food or drinks: *The aroma of fresh coffee filled the house.*

---

smell·y /ˈsmeli/ *adj* having an unpleasant smell: *smelly socks*

smelt /smelt/ *v* [T] to melt a rock that contains metal in order to remove the metal

smid·gen /ˈsmɪdʒən/, also **smidge** /smɪdʒ/ *n* [singular] *informal* a small amount of something: *"Want some more wine?" "Just a smidgen."*

smile¹ /smaɪl/ *v* **1** [I] to have a happy expression on your face in which your mouth curves: *Her baby's always smiling.* | **+ at** *Keith smiled at me.* **2** [T] to say or express something with a smile: *"Thanks very much," she smiled.*

smile² *n* [C] the expression you have when you smile: *She came in with a broad smile on her face.*

smirk /smɜːkllsmɜːrk/ *v* [I] to smile in a satisfied and annoying way: *Both officers smirked when he mentioned who his father was.* —**smirk** *n* [C]

smith·e·reens /ˌsmɪðəˈriːnz/ *n* **blown/smashed etc to smithereens** *informal* broken into a lot of small pieces

smit·ten /ˈsmɪtn/ *adj* loving someone or something very much: **be smitten with sb/sth** *He's absolutely smitten with that new girl.*

smock /smɒkllsmɑːk/ *n* [C] a loose piece of clothing like a long shirt, worn to protect your clothes

smog /smɒgllsmɑːg, smɔːg/ *n* [U] unhealthy air in cities that is a mixture of smoke, gases, and chemicals —**smoggy** *adj*

smoke¹ /sməʊkllsmoʊk/ *n* **1** [U] the white, grey, or black gas that is produced by something burning **2 go up in smoke** *informal* if your plans go up in smoke, you cannot do what you intended to do

smoke² *v* **1** [I,T] to breathe in smoke from a cigarette or pipe: *Do you mind if I smoke?* **2** [I] to send out smoke: *a smoking chimney* **3** [T] to give fish or meat a special taste by hanging it in smoke —**smoking** *n* [U]

smok·er /ˈsməʊkəllˈsmoʊkər/ *n* [C] someone who smokes → opposite NONSMOKER

smok·y /ˈsməʊkillˈsmoʊ-/ *adj* **1** filled with smoke: *a smoky room* **2** producing a lot of smoke: *a smoky fire* **3** having the taste, smell, or appearance of smoke: *smoky cheese*

smol·der /ˈsməʊldəllˈsmoʊldər/ the American spelling of SMOULDER

smooch /smuːtʃ/ *v* [I] *informal* to kiss someone in a romantic way —**smooch** *n* [singular]

smooth¹ /smuːð/ *adj* **1** having an even surface: *a smooth road* | *smooth skin* **2** a substance that is smooth has no big pieces in it: *smooth peanut butter* **3** graceful with no sudden changes: *Swing the racket in one smooth motion.* **4** happening or continuing without problems: *a smooth transition from school to university* **5** polite and confident in a way that people do not trust: *a smooth talker* —**smoothly** *adv* —**smoothness** *n* [U]

smooth² *v* [T] **1** to make something flat by moving your hands across it: *Tanya sat down, smoothing her skirt.* **2** to take away the roughness from a surface: *a face cream that smooths your skin*

    smooth sth ↔ **over** *phr v* [T] to make problems or difficulties seem less important: *He depended on Nancy to smooth over any troubles.*

smoth·er /ˈsmʌðəll-ər/ *v* [T] **1** to kill someone by putting something over their face so that they cannot breathe **2** to put a large amount of a substance onto something: **smother sth with/in sth** *a cake smothered with chocolate* **3** to express your feelings for someone so strongly that your relationship cannot develop normally: *He's a nice guy, but he tries to completely smother me.* **4** to hide your feelings: *She tried hard to smother her anger.* **5** to make a fire stop burning by preventing air from reaching it

smoul·der *BrE*, **smolder** *AmE* /ˈsməʊldəll ˈsmoʊldər/ *v* [I] **1** to burn slowly, with smoke but without flames: *The factory is still smouldering after last night's blaze.* **2** to have strong feelings but not express them: + **with** *Nick left Judy smouldering with anger.*

smudge

smudge¹ /smʌdʒ/ *n* [C] a dirty spot or area caused by touching or rubbing something wet or soft — **smudgy** *adj*

smudge² *v* [I,T] if a substance such as ink or paint smudges, or if it is smudged, it becomes unclear because someone has rubbed it, especially accidentally: *Now look! You've smudged my drawing!*

smug /smʌg/ *adj* **-gger, -ggest** too satisfied with how lucky or good you are: *a smug smile* — **smugly** *adv*

smug·gle /ˈsmʌgəl/ *v* [T] to take something illegally from one place to another: *cocaine smuggled from South America* — **smuggler** *n* [C] — **smuggling** *n* [U]

smut /smʌt/ *n* [U] writing, pictures, or remarks that are about sex in an unpleasant or silly way — **smutty** *adj*: *a smutty seaside postcard*

snack /snæk/ *n* [C] a small amount of food eaten between meals or instead of a meal

snack bar /ˈ. ./ *n* [C] a place where you can buy snacks

snag¹ /snæg/ *n* [C] **1** *informal* a difficulty or problem: *The only snag is, I don't have enough money.* **2** a thread that has been accidentally pulled out of a piece of cloth

snag² *v* [I,T] **-gged, -gging** to become stuck on something, or to make something do this: *Marty's fishing line snagged on a tree branch.*

snail /sneɪl/ *n* **1** [C] a small creature with a long soft body and no legs that has a round shell on its back **2** **at a snail's pace** extremely slowly → see picture at SLUG

snake¹ /sneɪk/ *n* [C] a long thin animal that slides across the ground

snake

snake² *v* [I] to move in long twisting curves: *The train snaked its way through the hills.*

snap¹ /snæp/ *v* **-pped, -pping** **1** [I,T] if something long and thin snaps, or if you snap it, it breaks with a short loud noise: *Dry branches snapped under their feet.* | *He snapped the chalk in two.* (=into two pieces) **2** [I,T] to move into a particular position with a short loud noise, or to make something move like this: + **together/ open/shut etc** *She snapped her briefcase shut.* **3** [I] to speak suddenly in an angry way: *There's no need to snap.* | + **at** *I'm sorry I snapped at you.* **4** [I] if an animal such as a dog snaps, it tries to bite you **5** **snap your fingers** to make a short loud noise with a finger and thumb of the same hand **6** [I] to be suddenly unable to control a strong feeling such as anger or worry: *I don't know what happened – I guess I just snapped.* **7** [T] to take a photograph of something

    snap out of sth *phr v* [T] *informal* to stop being sad, tired, upset etc: *It's time you snapped out of this bad mood.*

    snap sb/sth ↔ **up** *phr v* [T] to eagerly take an opportunity to buy something, have someone on your team etc: *They're such a bargain they'll be snapped up in no time.*

snap² *n* **1** [singular] a sudden short loud noise, especially of something breaking or closing: *I heard a snap and then the tree just fell over.* **2** **be a snap** *AmE informal* to be very easy to do: *Making pie crust is a snap.* **3** also **snapshot** [C] a photograph, especially one that you take quickly without thinking carefully: *my holiday snaps.* **4** [U] a card game in which players say "snap" when there are two cards the same

snap³ *adj* **snap judgement/decision** a judgement or decision made too quickly

snap·drag·on /ˈsnæpˌdrægən/ *n* [C] a white, yellow, or red garden flower

snap·per /ˈsnæpəll-ər/ *n* [C,U] a common fish that lives in warm seas, or this fish as food

snap·py /ˈsnæpi/ *adj* **1** **make it snappy** *spoken* used to tell someone to hurry **2** spoken or written in a short, clear, and often funny way: *a snappy answer*

snap·shot /ˈsnæpʃɒtll-ʃɑːt/ *n* [C] a photograph, especially one that you take quickly without thinking carefully; SNAP

S

GRAMMAR NOTE: 'if' clauses (2)

When you imagine a present situation that is not real, or a future situation that is very unlikely, use **if** + **simple past**: *If he really loved you, he wouldn't treat you like this.* (=he does not love you). | *If I won a million dollars on the lottery, I would buy a yacht.* Use **would** in the other part of the sentence.

snare[1] /sneə‖sner/ n [C] a trap for catching birds or small animals

snare[2] v [T] **1** to catch an animal using a snare **2** to catch someone, especially by tricking them: *Ships patrol the coast to snare drug dealers.*

snarl /snɑ:l‖snɑ:rl/ v **1** [I,T] to speak or say something in an angry way: *"Shut up!" he snarled.* **2** [I] if an animal snarls it makes a low angry sound and shows its teeth — **snarl** n [C]

snatch[1] /snætʃ/ v [T] **1** to take something from someone with a quick, sudden movement: *The boy snatched her purse and ran.* **2** to quickly do something when you have a short amount of time available: *I managed to snatch an hour's sleep on the train.*

snatch[2] n a snatch of conversation/song etc a short part of something that you hear

sneak[1] /sni:k/ v **sneaked** or **snuck** /snʌk/, **sneaked** or **snuck, sneaking 1** [I] to go somewhere quietly and secretly: *We managed to sneak past the guard.* **2** [T] to take something somewhere secretly: *I'll sneak some beer up to my room.* **3 sneak a look/glance at** to look at something quickly and secretly: *She sneaked a look at the open diary.*

  sneak up phr v [I] to come close to someone very quietly, so that they do not notice you: **+ on/behind** *Don't sneak up on me like that!*

sneak[2] n [C] BrE informal a child who is disliked because they tell adults when other children have done something wrong

sneak·er /'sni:kə‖-ər/ n [C] especially AmE a light soft sports shoe → see picture at SHOE and colour picture on page 113

sneak·ing /'sni:kɪŋ/ adj **1 have a sneaking suspicion/feeling (that)** to think you know something without being sure: *I've a sneaking feeling that this isn't going to work.* **2 have a sneaking admiration/affection for sb** to like someone secretly, perhaps without wanting to

sneak·y /'sni:ki/ adj doing things in a secret and clever but unfair way

sneer /snɪə‖snɪr/ v [I] to smile or speak about someone or something in a way that shows you have no respect for them: *Ned always sneered at the type of people who went to the opera.* — **sneer** n [C]

sneeze /sni:z/ v [I] when you sneeze, air suddenly comes out of your nose and mouth in a noisy and uncontrollable way: *The dust is making me sneeze!* — **sneeze** n [C]

snick·er /'snɪkə‖-ər/ v [I] AmE to laugh quietly in an unkind way; SNIGGER BrE — **snicker** n [C]

snide /snaɪd/ adj a snide remark criticizes someone in an unkind and unpleasant way

sniff /snɪf/ v [I,T] to breathe air into your nose with a short noisy breaths to clear your nose or to smell something: *"What's this?" he asked, sniffing it suspiciously.* | *The girl sitting behind me was coughing and sniffing.* — **sniff** n [C]

snif·fle /'snɪfəl/ v [I] to sniff a lot, especially when you are crying or ill

snig·ger /'snɪgə‖-ər/ v [I] BrE to laugh quietly in an unkind way; SNICKER AmE

snip[1] /snɪp/ v [I,T] **-pped, -pping** to cut something with quick small cuts, using scissors

snip[2] n [C] **1** a quick small cut with scissors **2 be a snip** BrE informal to be surprisingly cheap

snipe /snaɪp/ v [I] **1** to criticize someone in an unkind way: *I wish you two would stop sniping at each other.* **2** to shoot at people from a hidden position — **sniping** n [U]

snip·er /'snaɪpə‖-ər/ n [C] someone who shoots at people from a hidden position

snip·pet /'snɪpət/ n [C] **snippet of information/news etc** a small piece of information etc

sniv·el /'snɪvəl/ v [I] **-lled, -lling** BrE, **-led, -ling** AmE to cry and behave in a weak complaining way — **snivelling** adj: *a snivelling little brat*

snob /snɒb‖snɑ:b/ n [C] **1** someone who thinks they are better than people from a lower social position **2 music/wine etc snob** someone who knows a lot about music, wine etc and thinks their opinions are better than other people's

snob·be·ry /'snɒbəri‖'snɑ:-/ n [U] the attitudes and behaviour of snobs

snob·bish /'snɒbɪʃ‖'snɑ:-/ **snob·by** /'snɒbi‖'snɑ:bi/ adj a snobbish person thinks and behaves like a snob

snoo·ker /'snu:kə‖'snʊkər/ n [U] a game played on a table with a green cover and holes round the edge, in which you use long sticks to hit coloured balls into the holes

snoop /snu:p/ v [I] to try to find out about someone's activities by secretly looking at their things: *I caught her snooping around in my office.* — **snoop** n [singular] — **snooper** n [C]

snoot·y /'snu:ti/ adj someone who is snooty is rude and unfriendly because they think they are better than other people: *snooty neighbours*

snooze /snu:z/ v [I] informal to sleep for a short time: *Dad was snoozing in a deckchair.* — **snooze** n [C] *I'm going to have a little snooze.*

snore /snɔ:‖snɔ:r/ v [I] to make a loud noise each time you breathe while you are asleep — **snore** n [C]

snor·kel[1] /'snɔ:kəl‖'snɔ:r-/ n [C] a tube that makes it possible for a swimmer to breathe air while his or her face is under water

snorkel[2] v [I] **-lled, -lling** BrE, **-led, -ling** AmE to swim using a snorkel — **snorkelling** n [U]

snort /snɔ:t‖snɔ:rt/ v [I,T] to make a noise by forcing air out through your nose, especially to express impatience or amusement: *"Don't be so ridiculous!" he snorted.* — **snort** n [C]

snot /snɒt‖snɑ:t/ n [U] informal an impolite word for the thick liquid that is produced in your nose

snot·ty /'snɒti‖'snɑ:ti/ adj informal **1** a snotty person thinks they are better than other people and is rude and unfriendly; SNOBBISH **2** an impolite word meaning wet and dirty with the thick liquid that is produced in your nose

snout /snaʊt/ n [C] the long nose of some animals, such as pigs

snow[1] /snəʊ‖snoʊ/ n [U] soft white pieces of frozen water that fall like rain in cold weather

snow[2] v **1 it snows** when it snows, snow falls from the sky: *Look, it's snowing!* | *It snowed throughout the night.* **2 be snowed in** to be unable to leave a place because so much snow has fallen: *We were snowed in for a week.* **3 be snowed under (with sth)** to have too much work to do: *I'd love to come, but I'm totally snowed under.*

snow·ball[1] /ˈsnəʊbɔːl‖ˈsnoʊbɔːl/ *n* [C] a ball made out of snow that children throw at each other as a game

snowball[2] *v* [I] if a problem or situation snowballs, it gets bigger at a faster and faster rate

snow·board·ing /ˈsnəʊˌbɔːdɪŋ‖ˈsnoʊˌbɔːr-/ *n* [U] a sport in which you move over the snow on a long wide board — **snowboarder** *n* [C] — **snowboard** *n* [C]

snow·bound /ˈsnəʊbaʊnd‖ˈsnoʊ-/ *adj* unable to leave a place because there is too much snow

snow·drift /ˈsnəʊdrɪft‖ˈsnoʊ-/ *n* [C] a deep mass of snow, which the wind has blown

snow·drop /ˈsnəʊdrɒp‖ˈsnoʊdrɑːp/ *n* [C] a plant with a small white flower that appears in early spring

snow·fall /ˈsnəʊfɔːl‖ˈsnoʊfɒːl/ *n* [C,U] when snow falls, or the amount that falls in a period of time: *Their average annual snowfall is 24 inches.*

snow·flake /ˈsnəʊfleɪk‖ˈsnoʊ-/ *n* [C] a small soft white piece of falling snow

snow·man /ˈsnəʊmæn‖ˈsnoʊ-/ *n* [C], *plural* **snowmen** /-men/ a figure of a person made out of snow

snow·plough *BrE*, **snowplow** *AmE* /ˈsnəʊplaʊ‖ˈsnoʊ-/ *n* [C] a vehicle for pushing snow off roads or railways

snow·shoe /ˈsnəʊʃuː‖ˈsnoʊ-/ *n* [C usually plural] snowshoes are wide flat frames that you fasten to your shoes so that you can walk in deep snow

snow·storm /ˈsnəʊstɔːm‖ˈsnoʊstɔːrm/ *n* [C] a storm with a lot of snow

snow·y /ˈsnəʊi‖ˈsnoʊi/ *adj* if it is snowy, the ground is covered with snow or snow is falling: *a dazzling snowy landscape*

snub /snʌb/ *v* [T] **-bbed, -bbing** to be rude to someone, especially by ignoring them: *I saw Clare today and she completely snubbed me.* — **snub** *n* [C]

snuck /snʌk/ *v* a past tense and past participle of SNEAK

snuff[1] /snʌf/ *v*
snuff sth ↔ **out** *phr v* [T] to put out a CANDLE flame by covering it or pressing the burning part with your fingers

snuff[2] *n* [U] tobacco made into a powder, which people breathe in through their noses

snuf·fle /ˈsnʌfəl/ *v* [T] to breathe noisily in and out through your nose: *pigs snuffling around*

snug /snʌg/ *adj* **1** warm and comfortable: *a snug little room* **2** clothes that are snug fit tightly but comfortably — **snugly** *adv*

snug·gle /ˈsnʌgəl/ *v* [I] to get into a warm comfortable position: *We snuggled up together on the sofa and watched TV.*

so[1] /səʊ‖soʊ/ *adv* **1** **so big/good/many etc** used to emphasize what you are saying: *It was so embarrassing – everyone was looking at us!* | *She drives so fast!* | **so much/many** *I've never seen so many people in one place before!* **2** **so tall/big etc (that)** used to emphasize something and explain that this is the reason for something else: *He was so fat that he couldn't get through the door.* **3** used when you are giving a short answer to a question: *"Will I need my coat?" "I*

don't think so." | *Are you going into town? If so, can I come?* **4** **I told you so/I said so** *spoken* used to say that something has happened in the way you said it would **5** **so do I/so is he/so is mine etc** used to say that another person also does the same thing, or that the same thing is true about someone or something else: *If you're going to have a drink then so will I.* **6** used to get someone's attention, for example when you are going to ask a question or start talking about something different: *So, what do you think of your new school?* **7** used with a movement of your hand to show how big, tall etc something or someone is, or how to do something: *It was about so big.* | *Then you fold the paper like so.* **8** **or so** used when you cannot be exact about a number, amount, or period of time: *He left week or so ago.* **9** **and so on/forth** used after a list to show that there are other similar things that could be mentioned: *a room full of old furniture, paintings, and so forth* **10** **so as (not) to do sth** in order to do or not do something: *Try to remain calm so as not to alarm anyone.* **11** **so?/so what?** used to say that you do not think that something is important, especially in a way that seems impolite: *Yes, I'm late. So what?* **12** **only so much/many** used to say that there is a limit to something and it is not very large: *The museum is tiny and only so many people are allowed in at one time.*

so[2] *linking word* **1** used when you are explaining that something made something else happen: *I heard a noise so I got out of bed.* **2** **so (that)** in order to make something happen, or to make something possible: *I put your keys in the drawer so they wouldn't get lost.*

so[3] *adj* **be so** to be true or correct: *The newspapers claim that the exams are getting easier, but it just isn't so!*

soak /səʊk‖soʊk/ *v* [I,T] **1** if you soak something or let it soak, you cover it with liquid for a period of time: *Leave that dish in the sink to soak.* | *Soak the beans overnight.* **2** if water soaks somewhere or soaks something, it makes something completely wet: *The rain had soaked through her jacket.*
soak sth ↔ **up** *phr v* [T] if something soaks up a liquid, it takes the liquid into itself; ABSORB: *When you pour the milk into the dish, the bread will soak it up.*

soaked /səʊkt‖soʊkt/ *adj* very wet: *I'm absolutely soaked.*

soak·ing /ˈsəʊkɪŋ‖ˈsoʊ-/ also **soaking wet** /ˌ.. ˈ. ◂/ *adj* completely wet: *You're soaking! Come in and dry off.*

so-and-so /ˈ. . ˌ./ *n* **1** [U] used to talk about someone or a type of person, without saying their name: *They're always gossiping about so-and-so having an affair with so-and-so.* **2** [C] *informal* someone who is unpleasant or has behaved badly: *He's a miserable old so-and-so.*

soap[1] /səʊp‖soʊp/ *n* **1** [U] a substance that you use to wash yourself with: *a bar of soap* **2** [C] *informal* a soap opera

soap[2] *v* [T] to rub soap on someone or something

soap·box /ˈsəʊpbɒks‖ˈsoʊpbɑːks/ *n* **be/get on your soapbox** *informal* to start talking about your opinions and continue for a long time, especially in a way that is boring and annoying for other people to listen to: *Don't mention politics or Dan will be back on his soapbox again!*

soap op·e·ra /ˈ. ˌ.../ n [C] a television or radio story about the ordinary lives of the same group of people, which is broadcast very frequently

soap·y /ˈsəupi‖ˈsoupi/ adj containing soap: *soapy water*

soar /sɔː‖sɔːr/ v [I] **1** to increase quickly to a high level: *The temperature soared to 97°.* **2** to fly smoothly and fast or high up into the air: *birds soaring overhead* **3** to look very tall and impressive: *The cliffs soar 500 feet above the sea.* —**soaring** adj

sob /sɒb‖sɑːb/ v [I] **-bbed, -bbing** to cry noisily and breathe quickly and noisily at the same time —**sob** n [C]

so·ber¹ /ˈsəubə‖ˈsoubər/ adj **1** not drunk **2** a sober person is sensible, quiet, and thinks a lot: *a sober and intelligent young man* **3** plain and not brightly coloured: *a sober grey suit* —**soberly** adv

so·ber² v

sober sb ↔ **up** phr v [I,T] to gradually become or make someone become less drunk: *Some black coffee might sober you up.*

so·ber·ing /ˈsəubərɪŋ‖ˈsou-/ adj a sobering thought or experience makes you feel very serious: *The same could happen to you – it's a sobering thought.*

sob sto·ry /ˈ. ˌ../ n [C] informal a story that someone tells you to make you feel sorry for them

so-called /ˌ. ˈ.◂/ adj [only before noun] used to show that you think the word used to describe something is wrong: *The so-called expert turned out to be a research student.*

soc·cer /ˈsɒkə‖ˈsɑːkər/ n [U] a game in which two teams try to kick a ball between two posts at either end of a field; football BrE ➔ see colour picture on page 636

so·cia·ble /ˈsəuʃəbəl‖ˈsou-/ adj someone who is sociable is friendly and likes to be with other people ➔ opposite UNSOCIABLE

so·cial /ˈsəuʃəl‖ˈsou-/ adj **1** relating to human society and its organization, or the quality of people's lives: *social issues such as unemployment and homelessness | people from different social backgrounds* **2** social activities are the things that you do with other people for enjoyment: *social events for employees | social life College is great – the social life's brilliant!* —**socially** adv

so·cial·is·m /ˈsəuʃəl-ɪzəm‖ˈsou-/ n [U] a political system that tries to give equal opportunities to all people, and in which many industries belong to the government —**socialist** n [C] adj ➔ compare CAPITALISM, COMMUNISM

so·cial·ite /ˈsəuʃəl-aɪt‖ˈsou-/ n [C] someone who goes to many fashionable parties

so·cial·ize (also **-ise** BrE) /ˈsəuʃəl-aɪz‖ˈsou-/ v [I] to spend time with other people in a friendly way: *We're colleagues, but I don't socialize with him.*

social sci·ence /ˌ.. ˈ../ n [C,U] the study of people in society, which includes history, politics, ECONOMICS, and SOCIOLOGY , or any one of these subjects

social se·cu·ri·ty /ˌ.. .ˈ.../ n [U] **1** BrE money paid by the government to people who are very poor, not working, ill etc: **be on social security** (=be receiving it) **2** AmE a system run by the government to provide money for people when they are old, ill, or cannot work; WELFARE AmE

social stud·ies /ˈ.. ˌ../ n [plural]SOCIAL SCIENCE

social work·er /ˈ.. ˌ../ n [C] someone who is trained to help people with social problems, because, for example, they live in bad conditions, are very ill, or have difficulties with their families —**social work** n [U]

so·ci·e·ty /səˈsaɪəti/ n **1** [C,U] a large group of people who live in the same country or area and share the same laws, ways of doing things, religion etc: *Britain is a multi-racial society.| problems affecting modern Western society* **2** [C] an organization or club with members who have similar interests: *I joined the school film society.* **3** [U] the group of rich, fashionable people within a country: *a society wedding*

so·ci·o·ec·o·nom·ic /ˌsəusiəuekəˈnɒmɪk, ˌsəuʃiəu-, -iːkə-‖ˌsousiouekəˈnɑː-, ˌsouʃiou-, -iːkə-/ adj relating to both social and economic conditions

so·ci·ol·o·gy /ˌsəusiˈɒlədʒi, ˌsəuʃi-‖ˌsousiˈɑːl-, ˌsouʃi-/ n [U] the study of society and relationships between the different classes and groups in society —**sociologist** n [C]

sock¹ /sɒk‖sɑːk/ n [C usually plural] a piece of clothing that you wear on your foot inside your shoe: *a pair of socks* ➔ see colour picture on page 113

sock² v [T] informal to hit someone hard: *Somebody socked him in the mouth.*

sock·et /ˈsɒkɪt‖ˈsɑː-/ n [C] **1** the place in a wall where you can connect electrical equipment to the supply of electricity **2** the hollow part of something, into which another part fits: *He nearly pulled my arm out of its socket!*

so·da /ˈsəudə‖ˈsou-/ n [C,U] also **soda water** water that contains BUBBLES, added to alcoholic drinks or fruit juice

sod·den /ˈsɒdn‖ˈsɑːdn/ adj very wet: *sodden clothing*

so·di·um /ˈsəudiəm‖ˈsou-/ n [U] a silver-white metal that is an ELEMENT that produces salt when mixed with CHLORINE

so·fa /ˈsəufə‖ˈsoufə/ n [C] a comfortable seat with arms and a back, wide enough for two or three people ➔ see colour picture on page 474

soft /sɒft‖sɔːft/ adj **1** not hard, firm, or stiff, but easy to press: *a soft pillow* **2** smooth and pleasant to touch: *soft skin* **3** soft sounds are quiet **4** soft colours or lights are not too bright: *Soft lighting is much more romantic.* **5** soft drugs are considered to be less harmful and not as strong as hard drugs **6** informal a soft job, life etc does not involve hard work or difficulties: **soft option** *The computer course is not a soft option.* **7** informal someone who is soft does not treat people severely enough when they have done something wrong: *The Governor does not want to seem soft on crime.* **8** soft water does not contain a lot of minerals and makes a lot of BUBBLES when you use soap **9** **have a soft spot for sb** to like someone: *She's always had a soft spot for Grant.* **10** **a soft touch** informal someone who you can easily persuade to give you money, because they are kind or easy to deceive —**softness** n [U]

soft·ball /'sɒftbɔːl‖'sɒːftbɔːl/ n [C,U] an outdoor game similar to BASEBALL but played with a larger and softer ball, or the ball used in this game

soft-boiled /ˌ. '.◂/ adj a soft-boiled egg has been boiled until the white part is solid, but the yellow part is still liquid

soft drink /'. ./ n [C] a cold drink that does not contain alcohol: *We serve cola and a range of other soft drinks.*

soft·en /'sɒfən‖'sɒː-/ v [I,T] **1** to become softer, or to make something do this: *Cook the onion until it has softened.* **2** to become less severe and more gentle, or to make something do this: *The police seem to be softening their attitude towards drug users.* → opposite HARDEN

soften sb ↔ **up** phr v [T] informal to be nice to someone so that they will do something for you

soft·heart·ed /ˌsɒft'hɑːtɪd◂‖ˌsɒːft'hɑːr-/ adj kind and sympathetic

soft·ly /'sɒftli‖'sɒː-/ adv quietly or gently: *She spoke softly, so that the baby did not wake.* | *He softly stroked her hands.*

soft-ped·al /ˌ. '../ v [I,T] -lled, -lling BrE, -led, -ling AmE — informal to make something seem less important and spend less time trying to achieve it: *The government has decided to soft-pedal on welfare reform for a while.*

soft sell /ˌ. '.◂/ n [singular] a way of selling something that involves gently persuading someone in a friendly way → compare HARD SELL

soft-spok·en /ˌ. '..◂/ adj a soft-spoken person has a quiet pleasant voice

software /'sɒftweə‖'sɒːftwer/ n [U] the PROGRAMS (=sets of instructions) that you can put into a computer so that you can use it to do different jobs: *word processing software* → compare HARDWARE

soft·y /'sɒfti‖'sɒː-/ n [C] informal someone who is very kind and sympathetic, or is easily persuaded: *He looks like a thug, but he's just a big softy.*

sog·gy /'sɒgi‖'sɑːgi/ adj wet, soft, and unpleasant: *The bottom of the pie has gone all soggy.*

soil /sɔɪl/ n [C,U] the top layer of the earth in which plants grow: *plants that grow in sandy soil*

soil² v [T] formal to make something dirty — **soiled** adj

sol·ace /'sɒlɪs‖'sɑː-/ n [U] formal comfort or happiness after you have been very sad or upset: *Mary was a great solace to me after Arthur died.*

so·lar /'səʊlə‖'soʊlər/ adj **1** happening to or involving the sun: *a solar eclipse* **2** solar power is obtained using heat and light from the sun: *solar energy*

solar pan·el /ˌ.. '../ n [C] a piece of equipment that changes the sun's light into electricity → see colour picture on page 278

solar sys·tem /'.. ../ n **the solar system** the sun and all the PLANETS that move around it

sold /səʊld‖soʊld/ v the past tense and past participle of SELL

sol·der¹ /'sɒldə, 'səʊl-‖'sɑːdər/ v [T] to join metal surfaces together using melted metal

solder² n [U] the metal used to solder something

sol·dier /'səʊldʒə‖'soʊldʒər/ n [C] a member of the army, especially someone who is not an officer

sold-out /ˌ. '.◂/ adj if a concert, film etc is sold out, all the tickets have been sold

sole¹ /səʊl‖soʊl/ adj **1** the sole person, thing etc is the only one: *the sole survivor of the plane crash* **2** not sharing a right, responsibility, duty etc with anyone else: *sole ownership of the company*

sole² n **1** [C] the sole of your foot is the bottom of it **2** [C] the bottom part of a shoe, not including the heel → see picture at SHOE **3** [C,U] a flat fish that you can eat

sole·ly /'səʊl-li‖'soʊl-/ adv not involving anyone or anything else; only: *Grants are awarded solely on the basis of need.*

sol·emn /'sɒləm‖'sɑː-/ adj **1** very serious or sad: *a solemn expression* | *solemn music* **2** **solemn promise/sb's solemn word** a promise that you will definitely keep — **solemnly** adv — **solemnity** /sə'lemnɪti/ n [U]

so·li·cit /sə'lɪsɪt/ v **1** [T] to ask someone for money, help, or information: *We solicited the views of all our members.* **2** [I] to offer to have sex with someone for money, especially in a public place — **soliciting** n [U] *She was arrested for soliciting.* — **solicitation** /sə,lɪsɪ'teɪʃən/ n [C,U]

so·lic·i·tor /sə'lɪsɪtə‖-ər/ n [C] a lawyer in Britain who gives legal advice, deals with the buying and selling of houses, and works in the lower courts of law

so·lic·i·tous /sə'lɪsɪtəs/ adj formal careful to make someone feel happy or comfortable: *Our tour guide was extremely solicitous.*

solid¹ /'sɒlɪd‖'sɑː-/ adj **1** firm and usually hard, without spaces or holes, and not liquid or gas: *solid rock* | *The milk was frozen solid.* **2** strong and well-made: *a good, solid chair* **3** **solid gold/silver/oak etc** completely made of gold etc: *a solid gold necklace* **4** continuously, without any pauses: *She didn't talk to me for three solid weeks.* **5** [only before noun] solid information or EVIDENCE is based on facts and is definitely correct: *Suspicions are no good – we need solid evidence.* **6** someone who is solid is honest and can be trusted to do the right thing: *a firm with a solid reputation* — **solidly** adv — **solidity** /sə'lɪdɪti/ n [U]

solid² n [C] **1** an object or substance that has a firm shape and is not a gas or liquid **2** technical a shape that has length, width and height, not something flat → see also SOLIDS

sol·i·dar·i·ty /ˌsɒlɪ'dærɪti‖ˌsɑː-/ n [U] support and agreement among a group of people that share the same aim or opinions: *We are striking to show solidarity with the nurses.*

so·lid·i·fy /sə'lɪdɪfaɪ/ v [I] if a liquid solidifies it becomes solid: *The oil solidifies as it cools.*

S

GRAMMAR NOTE: the passive (1)

You use a verb in the **passive** to say that something happens to the subject of the sentence. You form the passive using **be/is/was** and the past participle.

ACTIVE: *They **chose** a new leader.* → PASSIVE: *A new leader **was chosen**.*

sol·ids /ˈsɒlɪdz‖ˈsɑː-/ n [plural] food that is not liquid: *The doctor says I can't eat solids for another week.*

so·lil·o·quy /səˈlɪləkwi/ n [C] a long speech in a play said by one person, and not to the other characters in the play

sol·i·taire /ˌsɒlɪˈteə‖ˌsɑːlɪˈter/ n [U] **1** *AmE* a card game for one player; PATIENCE *BrE* **2** **solitaire diamond/ring** a piece of jewellery with only one jewel in it

sol·i·ta·ry /ˈsɒlətəri‖ˈsɑːteri/ adj **1** a solitary person or thing is the only one in a place: *A solitary tree grew on the hilltop.* **2** a solitary activity is something that you do alone: *a long solitary walk* **3** a solitary person chooses to spend a lot of time alone

solitary con·fine·ment /ˌ.... ..ˈ../ n [U] a punishment in which a prisoner is kept alone

sol·i·tude /ˈsɒlɪtjuːd‖ˈsɑːlɪtuːd/ n [U] when you are alone: *She spent the last years of her life living in solitude.*

so·lo[1] /ˈsəʊləʊ‖ˈsoʊloʊ/ adj done alone, without anyone else helping you: *his first solo flight* —**solo** adv

solo[2] n [C], *plural* **solos** a piece of music for one performer

so·lo·ist /ˈsəʊləʊɪst‖ˈsoʊloʊ-/ n [C] a musician who performs a solo

sol·stice /ˈsɒlstɪs‖ˈsɑːl-/ n [C] the longest or the shortest day of the year: *the summer solstice*

sol·u·ble /ˈsɒljʊbəl‖ˈsɑːl-/ adj a soluble substance becomes part of a liquid when it is mixed with it

so·lu·tion /səˈluːʃən/ n [C] **1** a solution to a problem or PUZZLE is a way of dealing with it or an answer: *The only solution was to move into a quieter apartment.* | *The solution to the puzzle is on p.14.* **2** a liquid mixed with a solid or a gas

solve /sɒlv‖sɑːlv/ v [T] to find an answer to a problem: *The tax may be the only way to solve the city's budget crisis.* | **solve a crime/mystery/case** *one of the many cases that the police have been unable to solve* —**solvable** adj

sol·vent[1] /ˈsɒlvənt‖ˈsɑːl-/ adj someone who is solvent has enough money to pay their debts —**solvency** n [U] → opposite INSOLVENT

solvent[2] n [C,U] a liquid that can change a solid substance into liquid

solvent a·buse /ˈ.. .../ n [U] the illegal and dangerous activity of breathing in gases from glue or similar substances; GLUE-SNIFFING

som·bre *BrE*, **somber** *AmE* /ˈsɒmbə‖ˈsɑːmbər/ adj **1** sad and serious; GRAVE: *a sombre mood* **2** dark and without any bright colours: *a somber room* —**sombrely** adv

some[1] /səm; *strong* sʌm/ quantifier **1** an amount or number of something when the exact amount is not stated: *Do you want some coffee?* | *I need to buy some new socks.* **2** a few people or things, or part of an amount, but not all: *Some guys at work have tickets to the Superbowl.* | *Some days, I just can't get out of bed.* **3** *informal* used to talk about a person or thing when you do not know or remember their name or exact details: *I read about it in some magazine.* **4** **some time/days etc** rather a long time: *It was some time before the police finally arrived.*

USAGE NOTE: some, somebody, any, and anybody

Use **some** and **somebody** in questions when you think that the answer will be 'yes': *Is there still some pizza in the fridge?* | *Can somebody help me with this box?* Use **any** and **anybody** in questions when you do not know what the answer will be: *Is there any mail for me?* | *Did anybody call while I was out?*

some[2] pron **1** an amount or number of something when the exact amount is not stated: *I've made a cake; would you like some?* **2** a few people or things, or part of an amount but not all: *Some of the roads were closed because of snow.*

some[3] adv **1** **some 10 people/some 50%/some $600** about 10 people, about 50% etc: *Some 700 homes were damaged by the storm.* **2** **some more** an additional number or amount of something: *Would you like some more cake?* **3** *AmE spoken* a little: *"Are you feeling better today?" "Some, I guess."*

some·bod·y /ˈsʌmbədi, -bədi‖-bɑːdi, -bədi/ SOMEONE

some·day /ˈsʌmdeɪ/ adv at an unknown time in the future: *Maybe someday I'll be rich!*

some·how /ˈsʌmhaʊ/ adv **1** in some way although you do not know how: *We'll get the money back somehow.* | **somehow or other** *Maybe we could glue it together somehow or other.* **2** for some reason, but you are not sure why: *Somehow I don't trust him.*

some·one /ˈsʌmwʌn/ pron used to mention a person without saying who the person is: *Be careful! Someone could get hurt.* | **someone else** (=a different person): *"Does Mike still live here?" "No someone else is renting it now."*

some·place /ˈsʌmpleɪs/ adv *AmE* SOMEWHERE

som·er·sault /ˈsʌməsɔːlt‖-ərsɒːlt/ n [C] a movement when you roll or jump forwards until your feet go over your head and touch the ground again —**somersault** v [I]

some·thing /ˈsʌmθɪŋ/ pron **1** used to mention a particular thing without saying its name or exactly what it is: *There's something in my eye.* | *Would you like something to drink?* | *Sarah said something about a party.* | **something else** (=something different) | **do something (about)** *Can't you do something about that noise?* **2** **something like 100/£40 etc** used when you cannot be exact about a number or amount: *There is something like 3,000 homeless people in this city.* **3** **have/be something to do with** to be connected with a person, thing, or activity in a way that you are not sure about: *High-fat diets may have something to do with the disease.* **4** **or something...** said when you cannot remember or cannot be sure: *Maybe I cooked it too long or something.* | *She works in sales or something like that.* **5** **there's something in** used to admit that a suggestion or idea is good and worth considering: *There's something in what you say.* **6** **that's something** *spoken* used to say that there is one thing that you should be glad about, even if everything else is wrong: *At least we've got some money left – that's something.* **7** **be (really) something** used when something is impressive or unusual: *It's really something to see all those jets taking off together.*

some·time /ˈsʌmtaɪm/ *adv* at an unknown time in the past or future: *I'll call you sometime next week.*

some·times /ˈsʌmtaɪmz/ *adv* on some occasions, but not always: *Sometimes I don't get home until 9:00 at night.*

some·what /ˈsʌmwɒt‖-wɑːt/ *adv* more than a little, but not very: *I was somewhat annoyed.*

some·where /ˈsʌmweə‖-wer/ also **some-place** *AmE* — *adv* **1** in or to a place although you do not say exactly where: *I think he wants you to drive him somewhere.* | *Let's find somewhere to eat.* | **somewhere else** (=somewhere different): *Go and play somewhere else – I'm trying to work.* **2 somewhere around/between etc** a little more or a little less than a particular number or amount: *A good CD player costs somewhere around $500.* **3 be getting somewhere** to be starting to succeed or achieve what you wanted: *That's one problem solved – now we're getting somewhere!* **4 somewhere along the line/the way** at some time, although you do not know exactly when or it is not important when: *Somewhere along the line they began to lose interest in each other.*

son /sʌn/ *n* **1** [C] your male child: *Her son Sean was born in 1990.* → see picture at FAMILY **2** [singular] used by an older person when they are speaking to a boy in a friendly way: *What's your name, son?*

so·na·ta /səˈnɑːtə/ *n* [C] a piece of music written for a piano or for another instrument with a piano

song /sɒŋ‖sɔːŋ/ *n* **1** [C] a short piece of music with words: *Turn up the radio, this is my favourite song.* **2** [C,U] a bird's song is the musical sound it makes **3** [U] the art of singing or writing songs

song·writ·er /ˈsɒŋˌraɪtə‖ˈsɔːŋˌraɪtər/ *n* [C] a person who writes songs: *Paul Simon is one of pop music's finest living songwriters.*

son·ic /ˈsɒnɪk‖ˈsɑː-/ *adj technical* relating to sound

sonic boom /ˌ‥ ˈ‥/ *n* [C] the loud sound that a plane makes when it reaches the speed of sound

son-in-law /ˈ‥ . ‚ ‚/ *n* [C] your daughter's husband → see picture at FAMILY

son·net /ˈsɒnᵻt‖ˈsɑː-/ *n* [C] a poem with fourteen lines that RHYME with each other in a fixed pattern

so·nor·ous /ˈsɒnərəs, səˈnɔːrəs‖səˈnɔːrəs, ˈsɑːnərəs/ *adj* a sonorous voice is deep and pleasantly loud

soon /suːn/ *adv* **1** in a short time from now, or a short time after something else happens: *It will be dark soon.* | *They soon realized their mistake.* | **as soon as possible** (=as quickly as possible): *I'll get it fixed as soon as possible.* | **how soon** *How soon can you get here?* **2 as soon as** immediately after something has happened: *I came as soon as I heard the news.* **3 sooner or later** used to say that something will definitely happen but you are not sure when: *He's bound to find out sooner or later.* **4 no sooner had ... than** used to say that something happened almost immediately after something else: *No sooner had I stepped in the shower than the phone rang.* **5 I would sooner/I would just as soon (do sth)** used when you are saying what you

would like to happen: *I'd just as soon stay in and watch TV.*

soot /sʊt/ *n* [U] black powder that is produced when something burns — **sooty** *adj*

soothe /suːð/ *v* [T] **1** to make someone feel calmer and less worried or upset: *School officials were trying to soothe anxious parents.* **2** to make something less painful: *a gel that soothes aching muscles* — **soothing** *adj*: *gentle soothing music*

so·phis·ti·cat·ed /səˈfɪstᵻkeɪtᵻd/ *adj* **1** a sophisticated person is well educated and has a lot of experience of modern fashionable life: *a play that appeals to a sophisticated audience* **2** a sophisticated machine or system is designed in a very clever way: *highly sophisticated weapons systems* — **sophistication** /səˌfɪstᵻˈkeɪʃən/ *n* [U] → opposite UNSOPHISTICATED

sop·o·rif·ic /ˌsɒpəˈrɪfɪk‖ˌsɑː-/ *adj formal* making you feel ready to sleep

sop·ping /ˈsɒpɪŋ‖ˈsɑː-/ also **sopping wet** /ˌ‥ ˈ‥/ *adj* very wet: *By the time I got home, I was sopping wet.*

sop·py /ˈsɒpi‖ˈsɑːpi/ *adj BrE informal* expressing sadness or love in a way that seems silly; SAPPY *AmE*: *a soppy film*

so·pra·no /səˈprɑːnəʊ‖-ˈprænoʊ/ *n* [C,U] a woman, girl, or young boy singer with a very high voice

sor·bet /ˈsɔːbeɪ‖ˈsɔːrbᵻt/ *n* [C,U] a sweet frozen food made from fruit juice, sugar, and water

sor·cer·er /ˈsɔːsərə‖ˈsɔːrsərər/ *n* [C] a person in stories who uses magic; WIZARD

sor·cer·y /ˈsɔːsəri‖ˈsɔːr-/ *n* [U] magic, especially evil magic

sor·did /ˈsɔːdᵻd‖ˈsɔːr-/ *adj* sordid behaviour is unacceptable and unpleasant, or dishonest: *all the sordid details of the scandal*

sore¹ /sɔː‖sɔːr/ *adj* **1** a part of your body that is sore is painful because of an illness or injury: *I've got a sore throat.* **2 sore point/spot** something that is likely to make someone upset or angry if you talk about it: *Don't mention marriage – it's a sore point with him.* — **soreness** *n* [U]

sore² *n* [C] a painful place on your body where your skin or a cut is infected

sore·ly /ˈsɔːli‖ˈsɔːrli/ *adv* very much: *He was so rude, I was sorely tempted to hit him.*

sor·row /ˈsɒrəʊ‖ˈsɑːroʊ, ˈsɔː-/ *n* [C,U] a feeling of great sadness, or an event that makes you feel very sad: *the joys and sorrows of family life* — **sorrowful** *adj*

sor·ry /ˈsɒri‖ˈsɑːri, ˈsɔːri/ *adj* **1 sorry/I'm sorry** *spoken* **a)** used to apologize for something you have done: *I'm sorry, I didn't mean to be rude.* | *Sorry, did I step on your foot?* | **+ about/for** *Sorry about all the mess!* | **+ (that)** *He's sorry that he couldn't come to your party.* | **sorry to do sth** *I'm sorry to bother you, but there's a call for you.* **b)** used to say "no" or disagree with someone politely: *"Can I borrow the car?" "Sorry, I'm using it myself."* | *I'm sorry, I think you're wrong.* **2 be/feel sorry for sb** to feel sadness and sympathy for someone who has problems: *It's no use feeling sorry for yourself – it's your own fault!* **3** [not before noun] feeling disappointed about a situation: *Dad's still sorry that he never joined the army.* **4** [only before noun] in a bad condition: **a sorry state** *The cottage hadn't been lived in for years and was in a sorry state.* **5 sorry?** *especially BrE* used to ask someone to repeat something because you have not heard properly; **PARDON**

sort[1] /sɔːt‖sɔːrt/ *n* **1** [C] a group of things considered to be a type of something because they all have the same features or qualities; kind: **+ of** *"What sort of flowers do you like best?"* *"Roses, I think."* | *On expeditions of this sort you have to be prepared for trouble.* | **all sorts of** (=a lot of different types of): *They sell all sorts of things.* **2 sort of** used when what is said does not describe the situation exactly: *"Were you disappointed?"* *"Well, sort of, but it didn't matter really."* | *He got a sort of special degree from the university.* **3** [singular] if a computer does a sort, it arranges a list of things in the right order

sort[2] *v* [T] **1** to put things in the right order, or to arrange them in groups according to size, type etc: *All the letters have to be sorted and delivered by Friday.* **2 be sorted** *BrE spoken* a problem that is sorted is dealt with successfully: *"We'll have to explain this to your mum." "It's OK, I'll get it sorted."*

sort sth ↔ **out** *phr v* [T] **1** to organize something that is untidy or in the wrong order: *This office is a mess – I must sort it out!* **2** if you sort out a problem, you deal with it: *There's been a mistake – I'll sort it out and phone you back.*

sort through sth *phr v* [T] to look at a lot of similar things, especially documents and

stored information: *We had to sort through all his papers after he died.*

sor·tie /'sɔːtiǁ'sɔːrti/ *n* [C] a short trip to find out what a place is like or to make an attack: *Our first sortie from our hotel was a disaster.*

SOS /ˌes əʊ 'es/ *n* [singular] used as a **SIGNAL** to call for help when a ship, plane, or person is in danger

so-so /'. ./ *adj, adv spoken* not very good: *"How was the meal?" "So-so."*

souf·flé /'suːfleɪǁsuː'fleɪ/ *n* [C,U] a baked dish that is very light and made from the white part of an egg

sought /sɔːt‖sɒːt/ *v* the past tense and past participle of **SEEK**

sought-af·ter /'. ../ *adj* wanted by a lot of people, but difficult to get: *Her paintings are highly sought-after nowadays.*

soul /səʊlǁsoʊl/ *n* **1** [C] the part of a person that contains their deepest thoughts and feelings and which many people believe continues to exist after death **2** [C] a person: *Don't tell a soul!* **3** also **soul music** [U] a type of popular music, which often expresses deep emotions, usually performed by Black singers and musicians

soul·ful /'səʊlfəlǁ'soʊl-/ *adj* expressing deep sad emotions: *a soulful cry*

soul·less /'səʊl-ləsǁ'soʊl-/ *adj* a soulless place has no interesting or attractive qualities: *a soulless city of concrete and steel* —**soullessly** *adv*

soul-search·ing /'. ˌ../ *n* [U] careful thought about your feelings when you are not sure what

---

Sounds

Exercise 1

Look at the pictures. Complete this text about the detective.

The message said 'Go to the old house at 11

o'clock tonight.'

The detective walked towards the old dark

house. It was autumn and dead leaves were on

the path. She heard the rustle[1] of the leaves

as she stepped on them. The big dark door

was shut. There was a rope beside the door.

She pulled the rope. Far away, inside the

house, she heard a bell _____ing[2]. The

detective waited for a moment and listened.

The house was silent. Then she heard a mouse

_____[3] in the garden. The old door

_____ed[4] as she opened it.

The detective waited inside the house and

listened. She heard a big old clock

_____ing[5] in the hall. Then she heard a

_____[6], like someone eating an apple.

Then she heard a short _____[7]. Was

someone opening a bottle? What was that

noise? Then she heard a soft _____[8]

as someone switched on all the lights in the

house. The detective looked around and saw

all her friends. They had cakes and fruit and

bottles of drink. 'Happy Birthday!' they shouted.

ring

tick

crash

squeak

creak

bang

splash

rustle

buzz

click

rattle

crunch

crackle

sizzle

fizz

hiss

American football *BrE*/ **football** *AmE*
helmet

athletics *BrE*/ **track & field** *AmE*
bat
track

baseball

backboard
basketball
bas

boxing
boxing glove

rugby

cycling

cricket

golf
club

horse-riding *BrE*/ **horseback riding** *AmE*
rider
saddle

ice hockey
puck

ba

ice skating
skate

football *BrE*/ **soccer** *AmE*
goal

tennis
racket
net

swimming
cap
goggles

skiing
pole
ski
ski boot

glo

snowboard
snowboard

is the right thing to do: *After much soul-searching, I decided to resign.*

sound¹ /saʊnd/ *n* **1** [C,U] something that you hear, or something that can be heard: *the sound of breaking glass* | *Turn the sound up on the TV.* **2** **by the sound of it/things** *spoken* used when you are giving your opinion based on what you have heard or read: *By the sound of it, he's being forced out of his job.* **3** **not like the sound of** to be worried about something that you have heard or read: *I don't like the sound of this. How long has she been missing?*

sound² *v* **1** [linking verb] used to say that someone or something seems good, strange, interesting etc when you are told about them: + **(like)** *Your friend sounds like a nice guy.* **2** [linking verb] to show a particular quality or emotion in your voice: *You sound upset. Are you OK?* **3** [I,T] to produce a noise, or to make something do this: *The whistle sounded.*

  sound off *phr v* [I] to complain angrily about something: + **about** *We were told not to sound off about our problems to the press.*
  sound out *phr v* [T] [**sound sb/sth ↔ out**] to talk to someone in order to find out what they think about a plan or idea: *We've found a way of sounding out public opinion on the issue.*

sound³ *adj* **1** based on good judgement, and likely to produce good results: *Our helpline offers sound advice to new parents.* **a sound investment* **2** in good condition: *The roof leaks, but the floors are sound.* **3** **of sound mind** *law* not mentally ill → opposite UNSOUND → see also SOUNDLY

sound⁴ *adv* **sound asleep** completely asleep

sound bar·ri·er /ˈ. ˌ.../ *n* **the sound barrier** the point when an aircraft reaches the speed of sound

sound bite /ˈ. ./ *n* [C] a short clever phrase used especially by a politician

sound ef·fects /ˈ. .ˌ/ *n* [plural] the sounds produced artificially for a film, radio programme etc

sound·ly /ˈsaʊndli/ *adv* **1** **sleep soundly** to sleep well, without waking up or dreaming **2** completely or severely: **soundly beaten/ defeated** *Washington was soundly defeated in the final match.* **3** in a way that is strong and unlikely to break: *The building is soundly designed.*

sound·proof¹ /ˈsaʊndpruːf/ *adj* a soundproof wall, room etc is one that sound cannot go through or go out of

soundproof² *v* [T] to make something soundproof

sound·track /ˈsaʊndtræk/ *n* [C] the recorded music from a film

soup¹ /suːp/ *n* [C,U] a hot liquid food that usually has pieces of meat or vegetables in it: *chicken noodle soup*

soup² *v*
  soup sth ↔ up *phr v* [T] to improve something such as a car by making it more powerful or exciting — **souped-up** *adj*

soup kitch·en /ˈ. ˌ../ *n* [C] a place where free food is given to poor people with no homes

S

Sports

Exercise 1

Look at the picture. Underline the sports below you can enjoy alone – without any other people.

American football, track and field, baseball, basketball, boxing, cricket, cycling, soccer, golf, horse-riding, ice hockey, ice skating, rugby, skiing, snowboarding, swimming, tennis.

Exercise 2

Look at the pictures. Read the definitions of the sports in the dictionary. Which sports are these people playing?

1 Peter bowled the ball. Neil hit it with his bat and started to run towards the other wicket. **cricket**

2 Antonio kicked the ball in the air and Enrico headed the ball into the net. It was a goal!
   _____

3 Mary dived into the water and started to move towards the other end of the pool.
   _____

4 Maurice hit the ball with the bat and ran towards the first base. _____

5 Helen hit the ball with her racket over the net to Linda on the other side of the court
   _____ .

6 Henry punched Frank in the face. Frank fell to ground and the referee started counting: one, two, three… _____

7 Christine took a club out of her bag and hit the ball towards the hole on the green.
   _____

8 Richie jumped up and threw the ball into the net. _____

Exercise 3

Which of the sports in the picture have you enjoyed? Tell your friends about where and when you played.

sour /sauə‖saur/ adj **1** having an acid taste, like the taste of a LEMON: *sour green apples* **2** milk or other food that is sour is not fresh and has an unpleasant taste and smell: **go sour** *The milk has gone sour.* **3** looking unfriendly and angry: *a sour expression* **4** **go/turn sour** *informal* to stop being enjoyable or pleasant, or SATISFACTORY, especially because people feel annoyed or disappointed: *By that time, their relationship had turned sour.* **5 sour grapes** when someone pretends to dislike something that they really want, because they cannot have it —**sour** v [I,T]

source /sɔːs‖sɔːrs/ n [C] **1** the thing, place, or person that you get something from: **+ of** *Tourism is the city's greatest source of income.* | *sources of energy* **2** the cause of a problem, or the place where it starts: *Engineers have found the source of the trouble.* **3** a person, book, or document that you get information from: *Reliable sources say the company is going bankrupt.* **4** the place where a stream or river starts

south[1], **South** /sauθ/ n [singular, U] **1** the direction towards the bottom of a map of the world, or to the right of you if you are facing the rising sun: *Which way is south?* | *White sandy beaches lie to the south.* **2** the south the southern part of a country or area: *The south is much poorer than the north.* | *My uncle lives in the south of France.*

south[2] adj **1** in the south or facing south: *the south wall of the building* **2** **south wind** a wind that comes from the south

south[3] adv **1** towards the south: *Go 5 miles south on the freeway.* **2** **down south** in the south or to the south: *They live down south, somewhere near Brighton.*

south·bound /ˈsauθbaund/ adj travelling or leading towards the south: *southbound traffic*

south·east[1], **Southeast** /ˌsauθˈiːst◂/ n [singular, U] **1** the direction that is between the south and the east **2** the southeast the southeast part of a country, state etc —**southeastern** adj

southeast[2], **Southeast** adj, adv in, from, or towards the southeast: *flying southeast* | *a southeast wind*

south·er·ly /ˈsʌðəli‖-ərli/ adj **1** towards the south or in the south: *a ship on a southerly course* **2** a southerly wind comes from the south

south·ern, **Southern** /ˈsʌðən‖-ərn/ adj in or from the south part of a country or area: *southern New Mexico*

south·ern·er, **Southerner** /ˈsʌðənə‖-ərnər/ n [C] someone who comes from the south part of a country

south·ern·most /ˈsʌðənməust‖-ərnmoust/ adj furthest south of the south part: *the southernmost tip of the island*

South Pole /ˌ. ˈ./ n the South Pole the most southern point of the Earth, or the land around it

south·ward /ˈsauθwəd‖-wərd/ also **southwards** /-wədz‖-wərdz/ towards the south —**southward** adj

south·west[1], **Southwest** /ˌsauθˈwest◂/ n [singular, U] **1** the direction that is between the south and the west **2** the southwest the southwest part of a country, state etc —**southwestern** adj

southwest[2], **Southwest** adj, adv in, from, or towards the southwest: *driving southwest* | *a southwest wind*

sou·ve·nir /ˌsuːvəˈnɪə, ˈsuːvənɪə‖-ɪr/ n [C] an object that you keep to remind yourself of a special occasion or place that you have visited: **+ of** *a souvenir of New York*

sove·reign[1] /ˈsɒvrɪn‖ˈsɑːv-/ adj **1** a sovereign country is independent and governs itself **2** having the highest power or authority in a country —**sovereignty** n [U]

sovereign[2] n [C] **1** *formal* a king or queen **2** a gold coin used in Britain in past times

So·vi·et /ˈsəuviət, ˈsɒv-‖ˈsou-, ˈsɑː-/ adj relating to or coming from the former Soviet Union

sow[1] /səu‖sou/ v [I,T] **sowed**, **sown** /səun‖soun/ or **sowed**, **sowing** to plant or scatter seeds: *We sow the corn in the early spring.*

sow[2] /sau/ n [C] a female pig

soy·a bean /ˈsɔɪə biːn/ also **soy·bean** /ˈsɔɪbiːn/ n [C] a bean that is eaten and is used in making many other foods

spa /spɑː/ n [C] a place that people go to in order to improve their health, especially because the water there has special minerals in it

space[1] /speɪs/ n **1** [U] the amount of an area, room, container etc that is empty or available to be used: *Is there any more space in the basement?* | *There's not enough space in the computer's memory.* **2** [C,U] an empty area that is used for a particular purpose: *parking spaces* | *6,900 square feet of office space* **3** [C] an empty area between two things; GAP: *There's a space for it there – between the books.* **4** [U] the area outside the Earth's air where the stars and PLANETS are: *space exploration* **5** **in/during/within the space of** within a particular period of time: *In the space of a few seconds it was done.* **6** [C,U] land that does not have anything built on it: *a fight to save the city's open spaces*

space[2] v [T] to arrange objects, events etc so that they have an equal amount of space or time between them: *Space the plants four feet apart.* —**spacing** n [U]

space·ship /ˈspeɪsˌʃɪp/ also **spacecraft** /ˈspeɪsˌkrɑːft‖-kræft/ n [C] a vehicle that can travel to space

space shut·tle /ˈ. ˌ./ n [C] a SPACESHIP that can travel into space and return to Earth more than once

spa·cious /ˈspeɪʃəs/ adj having a lot of space in which you can move around

spade /speɪd/ n [C] **1** a tool with a long handle and a wide flat part at the end used for digging ➙ see picture at GARDENING EQUIPMENT **2** **spades** a group of playing cards with one or more black shapes like pointed leaves printed on them **3** **in spades** *spoken* in large amounts

spa·ghet·ti /spəˈgeti/ n [U] long thin pieces of PASTA that look like strings

span[1] /spæn/ n [C] **1** the amount of time during which something exists or happens: *Most children have a short attention span.* | *The mayfly has a two-day life span.* **2** a period of time between two dates or events: *Over a span of five years, they planted 10,000 new trees.* **3** the distance from one side of something to the other: *a wing span of three feet*

span[2] *v* [T] **-nned, -nning 1** to include all of a period of time: *Mariani's career spanned 45 years.* **2** to go from one side of something to the other: *a bridge spanning the river*

span·gle /'spæŋgəl/ *n* [C] *AmE* a SEQUIN —**spangled** *adj*

span·iel /'spænjəl/ *n* [C] a dog with long hair and long ears

spank /spæŋk/ *v* [T] to hit a child on the bottom with your open hand —**spanking** *n* [C,U]

span·ner /'spænəll-ər/ *n* [C] *BrE* a tool used for making NUTS tighter or for undoing them; WRENCH *AmE* → see picture at TOOLS

spar /spɑːllspɑːr/ *v* [I] **-rred, -rring** to practise BOXING with someone

spare[1] /speəllsper/ *adj* **1** **spare key/tyre etc** a key, tyre etc that you have in addition to the one you usually use so that it is available if it is needed **2** not being used by anyone and therefore available: *a spare bedroom* **3** **spare time** time when you are not working: *I play tennis in my spare time.*

spare[2] *v* [T] **1** to let someone have or use something, because you do not need it: *Can you spare any change?* **2** to prevent someone from having to do something difficult or unpleasant: **spare sb sth** *I was trying to spare you unnecessary work.* **3** **to spare** if you have time, money etc to spare, you have plenty or enough of it: *helpers with a few hours to spare each week* **4** **Could you spare (me) ...?** *spoken* used to ask someone if they will lend or give you something, or if they have time to talk to you: *Could you spare me twenty minutes of your time?* **5** **spare no expense** to spend a lot of money on something: *We will spare no expense in buying new equipment.* **6** to not damage or harm someone or something: *The children's lives were spared.*

spare[3] *n* [C] an additional key, tyre etc that you keep so that it is available if it is needed: *I've lost my key. Do you have a spare?*

spar·ing·ly /'speərɪŋlill'sper-/ *adv* if you use something sparingly, you use only a little of it —**sparing** *adj*

spark[1] /spɑːkllspɑːrk/ *n* [C] **1** a very small piece of brightly burning material that comes from a fire or is produced by hitting two hard objects together **2** a flash of light caused by electricity passing across a small space **3** **spark of interest/intelligence/humour etc** a small amount of interest, intelligence etc that you see in someone's expression or behaviour: *She saw a spark of hope in the little girl's eyes.*

spark[2] *v* **1** [T] also **spark off** to make something start happening: *The speech sparked off riots throughout the city.* **2** [I] to produce sparks

spar·kle /'spɑːkəll'spɑːr-/ *v* [I] to shine with small bright flashes: *diamonds sparkling in the light* —**sparkle** *n* [C,U]

spar·kler /'spɑːkləll-ər/ *n* [C] a type of thin FIREWORK that you hold

spark plug /'. ./ *n* [C] a part in a car engine that produces the SPARK to make the petrol mixture start burning

spar·row /'spærəull-rou/ *n* [C] a common small brown or grey bird

sparse /spɑːsllspɑːrs/ *adj* existing only in small amounts, and often spread over a large area: *sparse vegetation* —**sparsely** *adv*

spar·tan /'spɑːtnll-ɑːr-/ *adj* very simple and often uncomfortable: *spartan living conditions*

spas·m /'spæzəm/ *n* [C,U] an uncontrollable movement in which your muscles become suddenly and painfully tight: *back spasms*

spas·mod·ic /spæz'mɒdɪkll-'mɑː-/ *adj* happening for short periods of time but not regularly or continuously: *my spasmodic efforts to stop smoking* —**spasmodically** /-kli/ *adv*

spas·tic /'spæstɪk/ *adj* old-fashioned suffering from CEREBRAL PALSY

spat /spæt/ *v* the past tense and past participle of SPIT

spate /speɪt/ *n* **a spate of sth** a large number of similar, especially bad, events that happen within a short period of time: *a spate of burglaries*

spa·tial /'speɪʃəl/ *adj* technical relating to the position, size, or shape of things

spat·ter /'spætəll-ər/ *v* [I,T] if a liquid spatters or you spatter it, drops of it fall onto a surface: *Rain began to spatter on the steps.*

spawn[1] /spɔːnllspɒːn/ *v* **1** [T] if something spawns other, similar things, they start to happen or exist: *The book 'Dracula' has spawned a number of movies.* **2** [I,T] if a fish or FROG spawns, it lays a lot of eggs

spawn[2] *n* [U] the eggs of a fish or FROG

speak /spiːk/ *v* **spoke** /spəʊkllspouk/, **spoken** /'spəʊkənll'spou-/, **speaking 1** [I] to talk to someone about something or have a conversation: **speak to sb** also **speak with sb** *especially AmE*: *Hello, can I speak to Mr. Sherwood please?* **+ about** *Have you spoken to Michael about this?* **2** [I] to use your voice to say words: *For a minute she was too frightened to speak.* **3** [T] to be able to talk in a particular language: *My brother speaks English.* **4** [I] to make a formal speech: *I get so nervous if I have to speak in public.* **5** [I] to tell someone about a particular subject or person: **+of/about** *He spoke about his love of acting.* **6** [I] *informal* to be friendly with someone, especially after an argument: *I'm surprised she's still speaking to you after all you've done.* **7** **be on speaking terms** to be friendly with someone, especially after an argument: *He hasn't been on speaking terms with his father for years.* **8** **generally/technically etc speaking** used to say that you are expressing a general opinion, technical opinion etc: *Generally speaking, I agree with you.* **9** **so to speak** *spoken* used to say that the expression you have used does not have its usual meaning: *He found the problem in his own back yard, so to speak.* **10** **speaking of ...** *spoken* used when you want to say more about someone or something that has just been mentioned: *Speaking of Jody, how is she?* **11** **speak your mind** to say exactly what

S

---

you think **12 none/nothing to speak of** nothing important enough to mention: *"Did you get any snow last week?" "None to speak of."*

speak for sb/sth *phr v* [T] **1** to express the feelings, thoughts etc of another person or group: *I'm speaking for all of us in wishing you the best of luck.* **2 sth speaks for itself** to show something so clearly that no further explanation is necessary: *Our profits speak for themselves.* **3 be spoken for** to be promised to someone else: *The puppies are already spoken for.*

speak out *phr v* [I] to say publicly what you think about something, especially as a protest: **+ against** *people speaking out against human rights abuses*

speak up *phr v* [I] **1** *spoken* used to ask someone to speak more loudly: *Could you speak up please, I can't hear you.* **2** to say publicly what you think about something: *If we don't speak up nobody can help us.*

speak·er /'spiːkəll-ər/ *n* [C] **1** someone who makes a speech: *Our speaker this evening is Professor Gill.* **2 English speaker/French speaker** etc someone who speaks English, French etc **3** the part of a radio, CD PLAYER etc where the sound comes out → see colour picture on page 474

spear[1] /spɪəllspɪr/ *n* [C] a pole with a sharp pointed blade at one end, used as a weapon

spear[2] *v* [T] **1** to push a pointed object such as a fork into something so you can pick it up **2** to push or throw a spear into something

spear·head /'spɪəhedll'spɪr-/ *v* [T] to lead an attack or an organized action: *a strike spearheaded by textile workers*

spear·mint /'spɪəmɪntll'spɪr-/ *n* [U] a kind of MINT plant often used to give its taste to other foods

spe·cial[1] /'speʃəl/ *adj* **1** better, more important, or deserving more love and attention than ordinary things, events, or people: *I want to go somewhere special for our anniversary.* | *a special friend* **2** different from, and usually better than, what is usual: *special facilities for language learners* **3 special care/attention etc** more care, attention etc than is usual: *We try to give special care to the youngest patients.*

special[2] *n* [C] **1** something that is not ordinary or usual, but is made or done for a particular purpose: *a two-hour TV special on the election* **2** a meal, dish, or cheaper price that a restaurant offers for one day only: *today's sandwich special*

special ef·fects /ˌ.. '. ./ *n* [plural] images and sounds produced for a film or television programme that make something that does not really happen or exist seem real

spe·cial·ist /'speʃəlɪst/ *n* [C] someone who knows a lot about a particular subject or has a lot of skill in it: *a heart specialist*

spe·ci·al·i·ty /ˌspeʃiˈæləti/ *BrE*, **spe·cial·ty** /'speʃəlti/ *especially AmE* — *n* [C] **1** a subject that you know a lot about, or a skill that you have: *His speciality is mid-19th century literature.* **2** a food or product that is very good, especially one produced in a particular restaurant, area etc: *The grilled fish is their speciality.*

spe·cial·ize (also **-ise** *BrE*) /'speʃəlaɪz/ *v* [I] to limit most of your study, business etc to a

particular subject or activity: **+ in** *a lawyer who specializes in divorce* — **specialization** /ˌspeʃəlaɪˈzeɪʃənll-lə-/ *n* [C,U]

spe·cial·ized (also **-ised** *BrE*) /'speʃəlaɪzd/ *adj* trained, designed, or developed for a particular purpose: *a job that requires specialized knowledge*

spe·cial·ly /'speʃəli/ *adv* **1** for one particular purpose or person, especially: *The plane is specially designed for speed.* | *I bought it specially for you.* **2** *spoken* much more than usual, or much more then other people or things; especially: *a specially gifted child* | *All the prices have been specially reduced.*

spe·cial·ty /'speʃəlti/ *n* [C] *AmE* SPECIALITY

spe·cies /'spiːʃiːz/ *n* [C], *plural* **species** a group of animals or plants of the same kind

spe·cif·ic /spɪˈsɪfɪk/ *adj* **1** used to talk about a particular thing, person, time etc: *There are three specific types of treatment.* | *specific issues to discuss* **2** detailed and exact: *Can you be more specific?*

spe·cif·ic·ally /spɪˈsɪfɪkli/ *adv* **1** for a particular type of person or thing: *a book written specifically for teenagers* **2** in a detailed or exact way: *I was told specifically to arrive ten minutes early.*

spe·ci·fi·ca·tion /ˌspesɪfɪˈkeɪʃən/ *n* [C usually plural] a detailed instruction about how something should be done, made etc: *a rocket built to exact specifications*

spe·cif·ics /spɪˈsɪfɪks/ *n* [plural] exact details: *We can discuss the specifics of the deal later.*

spe·ci·fy /'spesɪfaɪ/ *v* [T] to state something in an exact and detailed way: *The plan didn't specify how the money should be spent.*

spe·ci·men /'spesɪmən/ *n* [C] **1** blood, skin, etc that is taken from your body to be tested or examined: *a blood specimen* **2** a single example of something from a larger group of similar things: *This specimen was found in northwestern China.*

speck /spek/ *n* [C] a very small spot or piece of something: **+ of** *a speck of dirt*

speck·led /'spekəld/ *adj* covered with a lot of small spots or marks: *speckled bird's eggs*

specs /speks/ *n* [plural] *informal* GLASSES

spec·ta·cle /'spektəkəl/ *n* [C] **1** an unusual or strange thing or situation that you see: *a fascinating spectacle.* **2** an impressive public scene or show: *the spectacle of the annual Thanksgiving parade*

spec·ta·cles /'spektəkəlz/ *n* [plural] *formal* GLASSES

spec·tac·u·lar[1] /spekˈtækjʊləll-ər/ *adj* very impressive or exciting: *a spectacular view of the Grand Canyon* — **spectacularly** *adv*

spectacular[2] *n* [C] a big and impressive event or performance

spec·ta·tor /spekˈteɪtəll'spekteɪtər/ *n* [C] someone who watches an event, game etc: *Over 50,000 spectators saw the final game.*

spec·tre *BrE*, **specter** *AmE* /'spektəll-ər/ *n* **1 the spectre of sth** something frightening that might happen: *The spectre of war lingered over the talks.* **2** [C] *literary* a GHOST

spec·trum /'spektrəm/ *n* [C] **1** the set of different colours that light can be separated into: *the full spectrum of colours of the rainbow* **2** a wide RANGE of different opinions, ideas, situations etc: *The officials represent a wide spectrum of political opinion.*

spec·u·late /'spekjǝleɪt/ *v* **1** [I,T] to guess why something happened or what will happen next without knowing all the facts: **+ on/about** *Police refuse to speculate on the murderer's motives.* **2** [I] to buy SHARES, goods, property etc, intending to make a large profit when you sell them —**speculator** *n* [C] —**speculation** /ˌspekjǝ'leɪʃǝn/ *n* [C,U] —**speculative** /'spekjǝlǝtɪv‖ -leɪtɪv/ *adj*

sped /sped/ *v* the past tense and past participle of SPEED

speech /spiːtʃ/ *n* **1** [C] a talk, especially a formal one given to a group of people: **give a speech** *The President gave a speech in Congress on the state of the nation.* | **make a speech** *My dad will make a short speech at the wedding.* **2** [U] the ability to speak **3** [U] the way someone speaks: *Her speech was slow and distinct.* **4** [U] spoken language rather than written language **5 freedom of speech/free speech** the right to say or print whatever you want

speech·less /'spiːtʃlǝs/ *adj* unable to speak because you are angry, shocked, upset etc: *Barry's answer left her speechless.*

speech marks /'. ./ *n* [plural] the marks (" ") or (' ') that you use in writing to show when someone starts and stops speaking

speed[1] /spiːd/ *n* **1** [C,U] how fast something moves or travels: *The cyclists were riding at a speed of 35 mph.* | **at high speed** (=very quickly): *a car travelling at high speed* **2** [U] the rate at which something happens or is done: *the speed at which computers have changed modern life* **3** [U] *informal* an illegal drug that makes you very active

speed[2] *v* **sped** /sped/ *or* **speeded, speeding 1** [I] to move or happen quickly: *The train sped along.* **2 be speeding** to be driving faster than the legal limit

   speed up *phr v* [I,T] to move or happen faster, or make something do this: *an attempt to speed up production at the factory*

speed·boat /'spiːdbǝʊt‖-bǝʊt/ *n* [C] a small fast boat with a powerful engine → see colour picture on page 669

speed·ing /'spiːdɪŋ/ *n* [U] the crime of driving faster than you are legally allowed to: *I got a ticket for speeding.*

speed lim·it /'. ˌ../ *n* [C] the fastest speed that you are legally allowed to drive at: *a 40 mph speed limit*

speed·om·e·ter /spɪ'dɒmǝtǝl‖-'dɑːmǝtǝr/ *n* [C] an instrument in a car that shows how fast it is going

speed·y /'spiːdi/ *adj* happening or done quickly, or working quickly: *We hope you make a speedy recovery.* | *a speedy little car* —**speedily** *adv*

spell[1] /spel/ *v* **spelled** *or* **spelt** /spelt/ *BrE*, **spelling 1** [I,T] to form a word by writing or saying the letters in the correct order: *My last name is Haines, spelled H-A-I-N-E-S.* **2 spell trouble/defeat/danger etc** if a situation spells trouble etc, it makes you expect trouble: *The latest setback may spell defeat for the Democrats.*

3 [T] if letters spell a word, they form it

   spell sth ↔ **out** *phr v* [T] to explain something clearly and in detail: *Do I have to spell it out for you? John's seeing another girl.*

spell[2] *n* [C] **1** a piece of magic, or the special words or ceremonies used in making magic happen: **cast a spell** *The witches cast a spell on the young prince.* | **put a spell on sb** *A spell was put on her that made her sleep for 100 years.* **2** a short period of time: *He once spent a short spell in jail.*

spell·bound /'spelbaʊnd/ *adj, adv* extremely interested in something you are listening to: *The children listened spellbound to his story.*

spell·ing /'spelɪŋ/ *n* **1** [U] the ability to spell words correctly: *His spelling has improved.* **2** [C] the way that a word is spelled: *There are two different spellings for this word.*

spelt /spelt/ *v especially BrE* the past tense and past participle of SPELL

spend /spend/ *v* **spent** /spent/, **spent, spending 1** [I,T] to use your money to buy or pay for something: *How much do you want to spend?* | **+ on** *I spent $40 on these shoes.* **2** [T] to use time doing a particular activity: *We spent the whole morning by the pool.* | *I need to spend more time with my family.*

spend·ing /'spendɪŋ/ *n* [U] the amount of money spent on something, especially by a government: *a cut in public spending*

spend·thrift /'spendˌθrɪft/ *n* [C] someone who spends a lot of money in a careless way

spent[1] /spent/ *v* the past tense and past participle of SPEND

spent[2] *adj* **1** already used and now empty or useless: *spent cartridges* **2** extremely tired

sperm /spɜːm‖spɜːrm/ *n* **1** [C], *plural* **sperm** a cell produced by the male sex organ that joins with an egg to produce new life **2** [U] SEMEN

spew /spjuː/ *v* [I,T] **1** also **spew out** to flow out of something in large quantities, or to make something do this: *Smoke and gas were spewing out of the volcano.* **2** also **spew up** *BrE informal* to VOMIT

sphere /sfɪǝ‖sfɪr/ *n* [C] **1** the shape of a ball: *The Earth is a sphere.* → see picture at SHAPES **2** an area of work, interest, knowledge etc: *He works in the sphere of international banking.*

spher·i·cal /'sferɪkǝl/ *adj* having a round shape like a ball

sphinx /sfɪŋks/ *n* [C] an ancient Egyptian image of a lion with a human head

spice[1] /spaɪs/ *n* **1** [C,U] a part of a plant, for example the seeds, that is put into food to give it a special taste: *herbs and spices* **2** [singular, U] interest or excitement that is added to something: *Variety is the spice of life!* —**spiced** *adj*

spice[2] also **spice up** *v* [T] **1** to add interest or excitement to something: *I need a few jokes to spice up my speech.* **2** to add spice to food

spick-and-span /ˌspɪk ǝn 'spæn/ *adj* very clean and neat

spicy 642

spic·y /ˈspaɪsi/ *adj* spicy food contains a lot of spices: *spicy meatballs*

spi·der /ˈspaɪdəⁱ-əⁱ/ *n* [C] a small creature with eight legs that makes nets of sticky threads to catch insects: *a spider's web*

spider
web

spi·der·y /ˈspaɪdəri/ *adj* spidery writing is untidy with a lot of long thin lines

spiel /ʃpiːl, spiːl/ *n* [C] *informal* a long explanation of something, often used to try to persuade someone that something is good or true

spike¹ /spaɪk/ *n* [C] a long thin object with a sharp point, especially a piece of metal — **spiky** *adj* → see colour picture on page 244

spike² *v* [T] **spike sb's drink** to add alcohol or a drug to someone's drink

spill¹ /spɪl/ *v* **spilled, spilled** *or* **spilt** /spɪlt/ *BrE*, **spilling 1** [I,T] if a liquid spills or you spill it, it flows over the edge of a container by accident: *I spilled coffee on my shirt.* **2** **spill the beans** *informal* to tell something that other people wanted you to keep secret

spill over *phr v* [I] if a problem or bad situation spills over, it begins to affect other places, people etc: *There's a danger that the fighting will spill over into other countries.*

spill² *n* [C] an act of spilling something or the amount that is spilled: *a huge oil spill in the Atlantic*

spilt /spɪlt/ *v especially BrE* the past tense and past participle of SPILL

spin¹ /spɪn/ *v* **spun** /spʌn/, **spun, spinning 1** [I,T] to turn around and around very quickly, or to make something do this: *skaters spinning on the ice* **2** [I,T] to make cotton, wool etc into thread by twisting it together **3** [T] to get water out of wet clothes by turning it around and around very quickly in a washing machine **4** [T] if an insect spins a WEB or a COCOON, it produces the thread to make it — **spinning** *n* [U] *the cotton spinning industry*

spin sth ↔ **out** *phr v* [T] to make something last longer than is necessary

spin² *n* **1** [C] an act of turning around quickly: *The truck went into a spin.* **2** [C] *informal* a short trip in a car for pleasure: *Would you like to go for a spin?* **3** [singular, U] a way of giving information, especially so that a situation, product, political party etc seems better than it really is

spin

spin·ach /ˈspɪnɪdʒ, -ɪtʃ/ *n* [U] a vegetable with large dark green leaves

spin·al /ˈspaɪnl/ *adj* relating to or affecting the SPINE: *a spinal injury*

spinal cord /ˌ.. ˈ./ *n* [C] the long string of NERVES that goes from your brain to the bottom of your back

spin·dly /ˈspɪndli/ *adj* long, thin, and not strong: *spindly legs*

spin doc·tor /ˈ. ˌ../ *n* [C] *informal* someone whose job is to give information to the public in a way that makes a politician or organization seem very good

spin dry·er /ˌ. ˈ./ *n* [C] *especially BrE* a machine that removes water from wet clothes by spinning them around very fast

spine /spaɪn/ *n* [C] **1** *also* **spinal col·umn** /ˈ.. ˌ../ the long row of bones down the centre of your back → see picture at SKELETON **2** a stiff sharp point on an animal or plant: *cactus spines* **3** the part of a book that the pages are joined to

spine·less /ˈspaɪnləs/ *adj* lacking courage and determination: *He's too spineless to speak for himself.* — **spinelessly** *adv*

spinning wheel /ˈ.. ./ *n* [C] a machine used in past times to make cotton, wool etc into thread

spin-off /ˈ. ./ *n* [C] a useful product that develops from something else in an unexpected way

spin·ster /ˈspɪnstəⁱ-əⁱ/ *n* [C] *old-fashioned* an unmarried woman

spi·ral¹ /ˈspaɪərəlǁˈspaɪr-/ *n* [C] a curve in the form of a line that winds around a central point — **spiral** *adj*: *a spiral staircase*

spiral² *v* [I] **-lled, -lling** *BrE*, **-led, -ling** *AmE* to move up or down in the shape of a spiral: *a leaf spiralling to the ground*

spire /spaɪəⁱspaɪr/ *n* [C] a tower that rises steeply to a point, especially on a church

spir·it¹ /ˈspɪrɪt/ *n* **1** [C,U] a person's mind, including their attitudes, thoughts, and feelings: *I'm 85, but I still feel young in spirit.* **2** [C] a living thing without a physical body such as a GHOST or ANGEL **3** [U] courage and determination: *I don't agree with her, but I admire her spirit.* **4** [singular] the attitude that you have towards something: *There's a real spirit of cooperation between the two clubs.* **5** **team/community/public etc spirit** the strong feeling that you belong to a particular group and you want to help them **6** [C usually plural] a strong alcoholic drink such as VODKA **7** **the spirit of the law/an agreement/a plan etc** the main purpose of a law, agreement etc, although it may be possible to consider it or use it in different ways

spirit² *v*

spirit sb/sth ↔ **away** *phr v* [T] to remove someone or something from a place in a secret or mysterious way: *After the concert the band was spirited away in a cab.*

spir·it·ed /ˈspɪrɪtɪd/ *adj* having a lot of courage and determination: *She made a spirited defense of the plan.*

spir·its /ˈspɪrɪts/ *n* [plural] the way someone feels at a particular time: **be in high spirits** (=be happy and excited): *The children were in high spirits.* | **sb's spirits rise** (=they become happier)

spir·i·tu·al /ˈspɪrɪtʃuəl/ *adj* **1** relating to someone's mind and their deepest thoughts and feelings, rather than things such as possessions, money etc: *spiritual health and well-being* **2** relating to religion: *spiritual songs* — **spiritually** *adv*

spir·i·tual·is·m /ˈspɪrɪtʃʊlɪzəm/ *n* [C] the belief that dead people send messages to living people, often through a MEDIUM —**spiritualist** *n* [C]

spit¹ /spɪt/ *v* **spat** /spæt/ *or* **spit** *AmE*, **spat**, **spitting 1** [I,T] to force a small amount of liquid, blood, food etc from your mouth: *He spat on the ground.* | **spit sth out** *He tasted the wine and then spat it out.* **2 spit it out** *spoken* used to tell someone to say something they do not want to say: *Tell me what you did – come on, spit it out.* **3 it is spitting** it is raining very lightly **4 be the spitting image of sb** to look exactly like another person

spit² *n* **1** [U] the liquid that is produced in your mouth; SALIVA **2** [C] a long thin stick that you put through meat to cook it over a fire

spite¹ /spaɪt/ *n* **1 in spite of** although; DE-SPITE: *She loved him in spite of the fact that he drank too much.* **2** [U] a feeling of wanting to hurt, annoy, or upset someone: *Lola refused out of spite.* (=because of spite)

spite² *v* [T] to annoy or upset someone deliberately: *He's doing this just to spite me!*

spite·ful /ˈspaɪtfəl/ *adj* deliberately intending to annoy or upset someone —**spitefully** *adv* —**spitefulness** *n* [U]

splash¹ /splæʃ/ *v* [I,T] **1** if a liquid splashes or you make it splash, it falls on something or hits against it: *He splashed some cold water on his face.* **2** to make water go up into the air by hitting it or moving around in it: *children splashing around in puddles*

splash² *n* [C] **1** the sound of splashing: *Jerry jumped into the water with a loud splash.* → see colour picture on page 635 **2** a small amount of a liquid splashing onto something, or a mark made by this: *splashes of paint on the floorboards* **3 a splash of colour** colour that you add to something to make it brighter

splat·ter /ˈsplætəll-ər/ *v* [I,T] if a liquid splatters, it hits against a surface: *rain splattering against the window*

splay /spleɪ/ *also* **splay out** *v* [I,T] to spread something such as your fingers apart

splen·did /ˈsplendɪd/ *adj* very good: *a splendid vacation* —**spendidly** *adv*

splen·dour *BrE*, **splendor** *AmE* /ˈsplendəll-ər/ *n* [U] impressive beauty: *the splendor of Yosemite Valley*

splice /splaɪs/ *v* [T] to join the ends of two pieces of film, rope etc so they form one continuous piece

splint /splɪnt/ *n* [C] a flat piece of wood, metal etc that is used to prevent a broken bone from moving while it becomes healthy again

splin·ter¹ /ˈsplɪntəll-ər/ *n* **1** [C] a small sharp piece of wood, glass, or metal that has broken off a larger piece: *splinters of glass* **2 splinter group/organization** a group of people who separate from a larger organization because they have different ideas

splinter² *v* [I,T] to break into thin sharp pieces, or to make something do this

split¹ /splɪt/ *v* **split, split, splitting 1** [I,T] *also* **split up** to divide or make something divide into two or more groups, parts etc: *We'll split up into three work groups.* | *a row that split the Catholic Church* (=made two or more opposing groups) **2** [I,T] to tear or break something along a straight line, or to be torn or broken in this way: *His coat had split down the back.* **3** [T] to divide something among two or more people in equal parts: *We decided to split the money between us.* **4** [I] *informal* to leave quickly **5 split hairs** to argue about small unimportant details

split up *phr v* [I] to end a marriage or a relationship: *Eve's parents split up when she was three.*

split² *n* [C] **1** a long straight hole caused when something breaks or tears: *a split in the seam of her skirt* **2** a serious disagreement that divides an organization or group of people: *a split in the Republican Party*

split-lev·el /ˌ. ˈ..◂/ *adj* a split-level house has a ground floor that is on two different levels

split sec·ond /ˌ. ˈ..◂/ *n* [C] a split second an extremely short period of time: *I only had a split second to decide.* —**split-second** *adj*

split·ting /ˈsplɪtɪŋ/ *adj* **splitting headache** a very painful HEADACHE

spoil /spɔɪl/ *v* **spoiled** *or* **spoilt** /spɔɪlt/, **spoiling 1** [T] to ruin something by making it less attractive, enjoyable, useful etc: *Don't let his bad mood spoil your evening.* **2** [T] to let a child have or do whatever they want, with the result that they behave badly **3** [I] to start to decay: *The meat has spoiled.* **4** [T] to treat someone very generously and kindly

spoiled /spɔɪld/ *also* **spoilt** /spɔɪlt/ *BrE —adj* a child who is spoiled is rude and behaves badly because they are always given what they want: *a spoiled brat*

spoils /spɔɪlz/ *n* [plural] *formal* things taken by an army from a defeated enemy, or things taken by thieves

spoil·sport /ˈspɔɪlspɔːtll-spɔːrt/ *n* [C] *informal* someone who spoils other people's fun: *Come on and play, don't be a spoilsport.*

spoke¹ /spəʊkllspoʊk/ *v* the past tense of SPEAK

spoke² *n* [C] one of the thin metal bars which connect the ring around the outside of a wheel to the centre

spok·en¹ /ˈspəʊkənllˈspoʊ-/ *v* the past participle of SPEAK

spoken² *adj* **1 spoken English/language** the form of language that you speak rather than write **2 soft-spoken/well-spoken etc** speaking quietly, in an educated way etc

spokes·per·son /ˈspəʊks,pɜːsənllˈspoʊks-/ **spokesman** /ˈspəʊksmənllˈspoʊks-/ **spokeswoman** /ˈspəʊks,wʊmənllˈspoʊks-/ *n* [C] someone who has been chosen to speak officially for a group, organization, government etc

---

GRAMMAR NOTE: the passive (2)
Most transitive verbs can be made **passive**. If you want to say who or what did the action in a passive sentence, use **by**. ACTIVE: *An American millionaire **bought** the picture.* PASSIVE: *The picture **was bought by** an American millionaire.*

sponge[1] /spʌndʒ/ n **1** [C,U] a piece of a light substance which is full of small holes and is used for washing things **2** [C] a sea animal with a soft body from which sponges are made

sponge[2] v **1** [T] also **sponge down** to wash something with a wet sponge **2** [T] to remove liquid from a surface using a sponge **3** [I] *informal* to get money, food etc from someone without working for it: **+ off** *He's been sponging off his friends for years.*

sponge bag /'. ./ n [C] *BrE* a small bag for carrying the things that you need to wash with

sponge cake /'. ./ n [C,U] a soft light cake

spong·y /'spʌndʒi/ adj soft and full of holes like a SPONGE: *spongy wet earth*

spon·sor[1] /'sppnsə‖'spɑ:nsər/ v [T] **1** to provide some of the money for an event, television programme etc so that you can advertise something at the event or on the programme: *The tournament is sponsored by a tobacco company.* **2** to agree to give someone money for a CHARITY if they walk, swim etc a particular distance: **sponsored walk/swim etc** (=when you walk, swim etc to get money for a charity) — **sponsorship** n [U]

sponsor[2] n [C] a person or company that provides some of the money for an event, competition etc

spon·ta·ne·ous /sppn'teiniəs‖spɑ:n-/ adj something that is spontaneous is done because you suddenly want to do it, not because you planned to do it: *a spontaneous decision* — **spontaneously** adv — **spontaneity** /,sppntə'ni:ɪ̥ti, -'neɪ̥ti‖,spɑ:n-/ n [U]

spoof /spu:f/ n [C] a funny book, film etc that humorously copies a serious one: *a spoof on one of Shakespeare's plays* — **spoof** v [T]

spook·y /'spu:ki/ adj *informal* strange and frightening: *a spooky old house*

spool /spu:l/ n [C] an object like a small wheel that you wind thread, camera film etc around

spoon[1] /spu:n/ n [C] a thing used for eating and serving food, shaped like a small bowl with a long handle → see picture at CUTLERY

spoon[2] v [T] to move food with a spoon: *Spoon the sauce over the fish.*

spoon-feed /'. ./ v [T] to help someone too much so that they do not learn anything: *Spoon-feeding students does not help them remember things.*

spoon·ful /'spu:nful/ n [C] the amount that a spoon can hold: *a spoonful of sugar*

spo·rad·ic /spə'rædɪk/ adj not happening regularly, or happening only in a few places: *sporadic outbreaks of fighting* — **sporadically** /-kli/ adv

sport[1] /spɔ:t‖spɔ:rt/ n **1** [C] a physical activity in which people compete against each other: *Tennis is my favourite sport.* → see colour picture on page 636 **2** [U] *BrE* sports in general: *Why is there so much sport on television?* **3** a sport also a good sport someone who does not get angry about losing a game or being joked about

---

USAGE NOTE: sport, recreation, game, and match

Use **sport** to talk about an activity that uses physical effort and skill, has rules, and in which people compete to win: *Her favourite sport is basketball.* | *I'm no good at sports.* Use **recreation** to talk about all the activities that people do in order to relax: *the city's Parks and Recreation Department.* A **game** is an occasion on which people meet to compete or play in a sports activity: *Let's have a game of football.* | *a game of tennis.* **Match** is a word used especially in British English meaning a public or organized sports game: *Tottenham have lost nearly all their matches this season.* | *a tennis match*

---

sport[2] v **be sporting sth** to be wearing something, especially something unusual or something that you seem proud of: *He walked in sporting an orange bow tie.*

sport·ing /'spɔ:tɪŋ‖'spɔ:r-/ adj [only before noun] relating to sports: *sporting events*

sports /spɔ:ts‖spɔ:rts/ adj [only before noun] relating to sports or used for sports: *a sports reporter* | *a sports club*

sports car /'. ./ n [C] a fast car with only two seats

sports·cast /'spɔ:tskɑ:st‖spɔ:rtskæst/ n [C] *AmE* a television programme of a sports game

sports cen·tre /'. ,../ n [C] *BrE* a place where you can do different sports

sports·man /'spɔ:tsmən‖'spɔ:rts-/ n [C] a man who plays sports

sports·man·like /'spɔ:tsmənlaɪk‖'spɔ:rts-/ adj behaving fairly and honestly in a game or competition

sports·man·ship /'spɔ:tsmənʃɪp‖'spɔ:rts-/ n [U] behaviour that is fair and honest in a game or competition

sports·wom·an /'spɔ:ts,wumən‖'spɔ:rts-/ n [C] a woman who plays sports

sport·y /'spɔ:ti‖'spɔ:rti/ adj **1** a sporty car is designed to look fast **2** *BrE* good at sport: *I'm not very sporty.*

spot[1] /sppt‖spɑ:t/ n [C] **1** a small round area on a surface, that is a different colour from the rest: *a white dog with black spots* **2** a place: *a great spot for a picnic* | *This is the spot where the accident happened.* **3** a dirty mark on something: *grease spots* **4** *BrE* a small red mark on someone's skin: *Most teenagers get spots.* **5 on the spot a)** immediately: *Kim was offered the job on the spot.* **b)** at the place where something is happening: *Our reporter is on the spot.* **6 put sb on the spot** to force someone to make a decision or answer a question without giving them time to think: *Don't put me on the spot like that.* **7** a short time that is available for something on television, radio etc: *an advertising spot* **8** a SPOTLIGHT **9** a spot of sth *BrE spoken* a small amount of something: *a spot of bother* (=a little trouble) → see also SPOT ON

spot[2] v [T] **-tted, -tting** to notice or see something: *A helicopter pilot spotted the wreckage.* | *His talent was spotted at an early age.*

spot check /,. '.‖'. ,./ n [C] when someone checks a few things without warning, to see whether everything is legal or being done correctly: *Police are making spot checks on cars.*

spot·less /'spptləs‖'spɑ:t-/ adj completely clean: *The kitchen was spotless.* — **spotlessly** adv: *Her house is always spotlessly clean.*

spot·light /'spɒtlaɪt‖'spɑːt-/ n **1** [C] a very powerful light that you can point at different things **2** **be in/out of the spotlight** to get a lot of attention from newspapers, television etc, or to stop getting this attention: *She's never out of the media spotlight for long.* —**spotlight** v [T] *In today's programme we're spotlighting the problem of racism in schools.*

spot on /ˌ. './ adj [not before noun] BrE exactly right: *Your calculations were spot on.*

spot·ted /'spɒtɪd‖'spɑː-/ adj covered in small round marks, especially in a way that forms a pattern: *a red and white spotted dress* ➔ see colour picture on page 114

spot·ty /'spɒti‖'spɑː-/ adj **1** BrE having a lot of spots on your face: *a spotty young man* **2** AmE good in some parts but not in others; PATCHY BrE **3** covered in small round marks, especially in a way that forms a pattern: *a spotty dog*

spouse /spaʊs, spaʊz/ n [C] formal someone's husband or wife

spout¹ /spaʊt/ n [C] a tube on a container that you pour out liquid through: *a teapot with a chipped spout*

spout² v [I,T] **1** if a liquid spouts, or something spouts in, it comes out of a narrow place with a lot of force: *Blood spouted from her leg.* | *a whale spouting water* **2** informal also **spout off** to talk a lot in a boring way: *He's always spouting off about politics.*

sprain /spreɪn/ v [T] to injure your wrist, knee etc by suddenly twisting it: *Amy fell and sprained her ankle.* —**sprain** n [C] *a bad sprain*

sprang /spræŋ/ v the past tense of SPRING

sprawl /sprɔːl‖sprɒːl/ v [I] **1** also **sprawl out** to lie or sit with your arms or legs stretched out: + **in/on** etc *Ian was sprawled on the sofa.* **2** if a building or town sprawls, it spreads out over a wide area —**sprawl** n [singular, U] *urban sprawl*

spray

aerosol

spray¹ /spreɪ/ v **1** [T] to make liquid come out of a container in a stream of very small drops: *She sprayed some perfume on her wrists.* **2** [I] to be scattered in small drops or pieces through the air: *The glass shattered and pieces sprayed everywhere.*

spray² n **1** [C,U] liquid in a special container that is forced out in very small drops through the air: *hair spray* **2** [U] water in very small drops from the sea or from a wet surface that is blown through the air **3** [C] leaves and flowers arranged as a decoration: *a spray of violets*

spread¹ /spred/ v spread, spread, spreading **1** [T] also **spread out** to open something so that it lies flat across a surface, or to arrange things

so that they cover a large area: *Tracy spread the map on the floor.* | **spread sth over/across sth** *His books and papers were spread all over the table.* **2** [I,T] to affect a larger area or more people, or to make something do this: *Rain will spread throughout the area tonight.* | *Rats often spread disease.* **3** [T] to put a soft substance onto a surface in order to cover it: *Spread the remaining cream over the top of the cake.* ➔ see colour picture on page 439 **4** [I,T] to tell a lot of people about something, or to become known by a lot of people: *She's been spreading lies about me.* | *News of her arrest spread quickly.* **5** [T] also **spread out** to push your arms, legs, or fingers wide apart: *He spread his arms wide.* **6** [T] also **spread out** to do something in stages over a period of time: **spread sth over sth** *You can spread the payments over a year.*

spread out phr v [I] if a group of people spread out, they move apart from each other: *They spread out to search the forest.*

spread² n **1** [singular] when something spreads: + **of** *the spread of disease* **2** [C,U] a soft food that you put on bread: *cheese spread* **3** [C] an article or advertisement in a newspaper or magazine: *a two-page spread about Jamaica* **4** [singular] a set of things which includes ones that are very different from each other: *the wide spread of ages in the class*

spread·sheet /'spredʃiːt/ n [C] a type of computer programme that shows and calculates financial information

spree /spriː/ n [C] a short period of time when you do a lot of something you enjoy: *a shopping spree*

sprig /sprɪg/ n [C] a small stem with leaves or flowers on it: *a sprig of parsley*

spright·ly /'spraɪtli/ adj an old person who is sprightly still has a lot of energy

spring¹ /sprɪŋ/ v sprang /spræŋ/, sprung /sprʌŋ/ springing **1** [I] to move or jump suddenly and quickly: + **out/at/back** etc *He turned off the alarm and sprang out of bed.* | **spring open/shut** (=to open or shut suddenly) **2** **spring to mind** if something springs to mind, you immediately think of it: *Pam's name springs to mind as someone who could do the job.* **3** **spring a leak** if a boat or a container springs a leak, it begins to let liquid in or out through a hole

spring from sth phr v [T] to be caused by something: *problems springing from childhood experiences*

spring sth **on** sb phr v [T] informal to tell someone news that they were not expecting: *I'm sorry to spring this on you, but my mother's coming tomorrow.*

spring up phr v [I] to suddenly appear or start to exist: *New houses sprang up along the river.*

spring² n **1** [C,U] the season between winter and summer: *spring flowers* **2** [C] a place where water comes up naturally from the ground: *hot springs* **3** [C] a piece of metal wire twisted into a series of rings: *bed springs* **4** [C] a sudden quick movement or jump

spring·board /'sprɪŋbɔːd‖-bɔːrd/ n [C] **1** something that helps you start a new activity: *His TV appearance was a springboard to success.* **2** a strong board that bends, used to help you jump high, for example into water

spring-clean /ˌ. '.‹ / v [T] to clean a place thoroughly: *I'm going to spring-clean the house.* —**spring-cleaning** n [U]

spring on·ion /ˌ. '../ n [C] BrE an onion with a small white round part and a long green stem; GREEN ONION AmE

spring·time /'sprɪŋtaɪm/ n [U] the time of year when it is spring

spring·y /'sprɪŋi/ adj something that is springy goes back to its original shape after you have pressed it

sprin·kle /'sprɪŋkəl/ v **1** [T] to scatter small drops of liquid or small pieces of something onto something else: *spaghetti sprinkled with parmesan cheese* **2** [I] AmE to rain a little: *It was sprinkling when we left.* —**sprinkle** n [C]

sprin·kler /'sprɪŋklər/ n [C] a piece of equipment used for scattering drops of water → see picture at GARDENING EQUIPMENT

sprint /sprɪnt/ v [I] to run very fast for a short distance: *He sprinted after the bus.* —**sprinter** n [C] —**sprint** n [C]

sprout¹ /spraʊt/ v [I,T] to start to grow or produce new flowers, leaves etc
  sprout up phr v [I] to appear suddenly and quickly: *new homes sprouting up in the suburbs*

sprout² n [C] **1** a new stem, leaf etc that is starting to grow on a plant **2** also **brussels sprout** a green vegetable like a very small CABBAGE → see picture at VEGETABLES

spruce¹ /spruːs/ n [C,U] a tree with short leaves shaped like needles

spruce² v
  spruce up phr v [I,T **spruce** sb/sth **up**] informal to make yourself or a place look cleaner and neater: *I want to spruce up before dinner.*

sprung /sprʌŋ/ v the past participle of SPRING

spry /spraɪ/ adj an old person who is spry is active and cheerful

spud /spʌd/ n [C] informal a POTATO

spun /spʌn/ v the past tense and past participle of SPIN

spur¹ /spɜː‖spɜːr/ n **1** [C] a sharp pointed object on the heel of a rider's boot **2 do sth on the spur of the moment** to do something suddenly without planning it: *We decided to go to Paris on the spur of the moment.*

spur² v [T] **-rred, -rring 1** to make an improvement or change happen faster: *The growth of the city was spurred by cheap housing.* **2** also **spur on** to encourage someone to try harder: *Her sister's success spurred her on to practise harder.*

spu·ri·ous /'spjʊəriəs‖'spjʊr-/ adj formal based on incorrect facts and reasons: *spurious arguments*

spurn /spɜːn‖spɜːrn/ v [T] literary to refuse an offer or someone's love: *a spurned lover*

spurt¹ /spɜːt‖spɜːrt/ v [I] to flow out suddenly with a lot of force: + **from/out of etc** *Blood spurted from his arm.*

spurt² n [C] **1** a stream of liquid that comes out suddenly: *Water was coming out in spurts.* (=quickly for short periods) **2** a short sudden increase in activity, effort, or speed: *a growth spurt*

sput·ter /'spʌtər/ v **1** [I] to make several quick soft sounds: *The engine sputtered and died.* **2** [I,T] to say something with difficulty, speaking in quick short phrases, especially because you are angry: *"Don't be so stupid," he sputtered.*

spy¹ /spaɪ/ v **1** [I] to secretly get information or watch people for a government or company **2** [T] literary to suddenly see someone or something: *Ellen spied her friend in the crowd.* **3 spy on sb** to secretly watch people: *He's always spying on the neighbours.*

spy² n [C] someone whose job is to find out secret information about a country or organization

sq the written abbreviation of 'square'

squab·ble /'skwɒbəl‖'skwɑː-/ v [I] to argue about something that is not important: + **about/over** *What are you two squabbling about now?* —**squabble** n [C]

squad /skwɒd‖skwɑːd/ n [C] **1** a team of people who do a job that needs special skills: *soldiers in the bomb squad* **2** BrE the group of people that a sports team is chosen from

squad car /'. ./ n [C] a car used by police

squad·ron /'skwɒdrən‖'skwɑː-/ n [C] a military group consisting of planes or ships

squal·id /'skwɒlɪd‖'skwɑː-/ adj **1** extremely dirty and unhealthy: *squalid living conditions* **2** dishonest or morally bad: *a squalid love affair*

squall /skwɔːl‖skwɒːl/ n [C] a sudden strong wind that brings rain or snow

squal·or /'skwɒlə‖'skwɒːlər, 'skwɑː-/ n [U] extremely dirty and unhealthy conditions: *people living in squalor*

squan·der /'skwɒndə‖'skwɑːndər/ v [T] to waste your time or money: **squander sth on sth** *He squanders most of his wages on drink.*

square¹ /skweə‖skwer/ adj **1** having four straight equal sides and four angles of 90 degrees: *a square window* **2 square inch/metre etc** a measurement of an area equal to a square with sides an inch, metre etc long: *two square acres of land* **3** like a square in shape: *a square jaw* **4 a square deal** honest and fair treatment from someone: *a car dealer that gives customers a square deal* **5 a square meal** a big healthy meal **6 be square** if two people are square, they do not owe each other any money: *Here's your $20, so now we're square.*

square² n [C] **1** a shape with four straight equal sides and four angles of 90 degrees → see picture at SHAPES and colour picture on page 440 **2** an open area with buildings around it in the middle of a town: *Trafalgar Square* **3 be back to square one** to be back in exactly the same situation that you started from **4** the result of multiplying a number by itself: *The square of 5 is 25.*

square³ v [T] technical to multiply a number by itself: *Three squared is nine.*
  square up phr v [I] to pay money that you owe: *I'll get the drinks, and we can square up later.*
  square with phr v **1 square with sth** to seem true when compared with other statements or with facts: *evidence that doesn't square with the facts* **2 square sth with sb** to check that someone accepts or allows something: *You can stay out till midnight – I've squared it with your dad.*

square·ly /'skweəli‖'skwer-/ adv **1** exactly or completely: *The report puts the blame squarely* *on senior managers.* **2** also **square** directly: *He looked her squarely in the eye.*

square root /ˌ. ˈ./ *n* [C] the number that produces another number when multiplied by itself: *The square root of nine is three.*

squash[1] /skwɒʃ‖skwɑːʃ, skwɔːʃ/ *v* **1** [T] to press something into a flat shape so that it is damaged: *My hat got squashed on the flight.*
2 [I,T] to push yourself or something into a space that is too small: + **into** *Seven of us squashed into the car.*

squash[2] *n* **1** [U] a game played by two people who hit a small rubber ball against the four walls of a court **2 it's a squash** *spoken* used to say that there is not enough space for everyone to fit comfortably in **3** [C,U] a type of big hard fruit, such as a PUMPKIN, that you cook and eat as a vegetable **4** [U] *BrE* a drink that has the taste of sweet fruit, for example orange or LEMON

squat[1] /skwɒt‖skwɑːt/ *v* [I] **-tted, -tting 1** also **squat down** to balance on your feet with your knees bent: *He squatted down next to the child.*
2 to live somewhere without permission and without paying rent

squat[2] *adj* short and thick, or low and wide: *small squat houses*

squat[3] *n* [singular] *BrE* a home that people are living in without permission and without paying rent

squat·ter /ˈskwɒtə‖ˈskwɑːtər/ *n* [C] someone who is living in a place without permission and without paying rent

squawk /skwɔːk‖skwɑːk/ *v* [I] if a bird squawks, it makes a loud angry cry — **squawk** *n* [C]

squeak /skwiːk/ *v* [I] to make a very high sound: *Is that your chair squeaking?* — **squeak** *n* [C] → see colour picture on page 635

squeak·y /ˈskwiːki/ *adj* **1** making a very high sound: *a squeaky voice* **2 squeaky clean** *informal* never having done anything morally wrong

squeal /skwiːl/ *v* [I] to make a long loud high sound: + **with** *children squealing with excitement* — **squeal** *n* [C] *squeals of delight*

squeam·ish /ˈskwiːmɪʃ/ *adj* easily upset by seeing unpleasant things: *I couldn't be a nurse – I'm too squeamish.*

squeeze[1] /skwiːz/ *v* **1** [T] to press something firmly: *She squeezed Jim's arm affectionately.* → see colour picture on page 473 **2** [T] to twist or press something in order to get liquid out of it: *Squeeze some lemon juice onto the salad.* → see colour picture on page 439 **3** [I,T] to try to get into a small space or try to make a person or thing fit into a small space: + **in/into/through** etc *Can you squeeze in next to Rick?*

squeeze[2] *n* **1 it's a (tight) squeeze** *spoken* used to say that there is only just enough room for a group of people or things: *It'll be a tight squeeze with 14 of us at the table.* **2** [C] when you press something firmly with your hand: *Laurie gave his hand a little squeeze.*

squelch /skweltʃ/ *v* [I] to make a sucking sound by moving through something soft and wet, such as mud

squid /skwɪd/ *n* [C] a sea creature with a long soft body and ten TENTACLES (=arms)

squig·gle /ˈskwɪɡəl/ *n* [C] a short written line that curls and twists — **squiggly** *adj*

squint[1] /skwɪnt/ *v* [I] **1** to look at something with your eyes partly closed in order to see better: *He looked at me, squinting in the sun.*
2 to have a condition in which each of your eyes looks in a different direction

squint[2] *n* [singular] a condition that makes each eye look in a different direction: *a child with a squint*

squire /skwaɪə‖skwaɪr/ *n* [C] a man who, in the past, owned most of the land around a village

squirm /skwɜːm‖skwɜːrm/ *v* [I] to twist your body from side to side because you are uncomfortable or nervous: *Stop squirming so I can comb your hair!*

squir·rel /ˈskwɪrəl‖ˈskwɜːrəl/ *n* [C] a small animal with a long FURRY tail that lives in trees and eats nuts

squirt /skwɜːt‖skwɜːrt/ *v* [I,T] if you squirt liquid or it squirts, it is forced out of a narrow hole in a thin fast stream: *You need to squirt some oil onto the lock.* | **squirt sb/sth with sth** *He squirted me with water.* — **squirt** *n* [C]

squish /skwɪʃ/ *v* [I,T] *informal* SQUASH

squish·y /ˈskwɪʃi/ *adj* something that is squishy feels soft and often wet when you press it: *squishy clay*

St., St 1 the written abbreviation of STREET: *Oxford St.* **2** the written abbreviation of SAINT: *St. John's church*

stab[1] /stæb/ *v* [T] **-bbed, -bbing 1** to push a knife into someone **stab sb in the arm/chest etc** *The man had been stabbed several times in the stomach.* **2 stab sb in the back** *informal* to do something bad to someone who likes and trusts you

stab[2] *n* **1** [C] when someone is stabbed: *The victim had four stab wounds.* **2 have a stab at (doing) sth** *informal* to try to do something that is difficult or that you have never done before: *Anna encouraged me to have a stab at modelling.*
3 a stab of pain/guilt/regret etc *literary* a sudden feeling of pain etc: *Monique felt a stab of regret.*

stab·bing[1] /ˈstæbɪŋ/ *n* [C] a crime in which someone is stabbed

stabbing[2] *adj* [only before noun] a stabbing pain is very sudden and strong

sta·bil·i·ty /stəˈbɪləti/ *n* [U] when a situation or condition is steady and does not change: *a long period of political stability* → opposite INSTABILITY

sta·bil·ize (also **-ise** *BrE*) /ˈsteɪbəlaɪz/ *v* [I,T] to stop changing and to become steady, or to make something do this: *The financial markets are finally stabilizing.* — **stabilization** /ˌsteɪbəlaɪˈzeɪʃən‖-lə-/ *n* [U] → opposite DESTABILIZE

S

GRAMMAR NOTE: direct and indirect speech
There are two ways of reporting what someone said:
DIRECT SPEECH (using "..."): *"**I forgot** to phone you," she said, "**I am** really sorry."*
INDIRECT SPEECH: *She said that she **had forgotten** to phone me and she **was** really sorry.*

sta·ble[1] /ˈsteɪbəl/ *adj* **1** strong and not likely to move or change: *a stable marriage* | *The chair isn't stable.* **2** calm, reasonable, and not easily upset: *mentally stable* → opposite UNSTABLE

stable[2] *n* [C] a building where horses are kept

stack[1] /stæk/ *n* [C] **1** a neat pile of things: *a stack of magazines* → see picture at PILE **2 stacks of sth** *BrE informal* a lot of something: *I've got stacks of work to do.*

stack[2] *v* **1** [I,T] also **stack up** to make a neat pile: *Just stack the dishes in the sink.* | *chairs designed to stack easily* **2** [T] to put piles of things on or in a place: *Al has a job stacking shelves in the supermarket.*

sta·di·um /ˈsteɪdiəm/ *n* [C] a large area for playing sports, surrounded by a building that has rows of seats: *a football stadium*

staff[1] /stɑːf ‖ stæf/ *n* [singular, U] the group of people who work for an organization: *The hotel staff were on strike.* | **member of staff** *Lisa's the only female member of staff.*

staff[2] *v* [T] to provide the workers for an organization: *a hospital staffed by experienced nurses* — **staffing** *n* [U] *staffing cuts*

staf·fer /ˈstɑːfə ‖ ˈstæfər/ *n* [C] *AmE* one of the people who works for an organization: *a Mercury News staffer*

stag /stæg/ *n* [C] an adult male DEER → see also STAG NIGHT

stage[1] /steɪdʒ/ *n* **1** [C] a state or level that someone or something reaches in a process: *Children go through various stages of development.* | *At this stage, I'm not sure what the result will be.* **2** [C,U] the raised floor in a theatre where actors perform a play: **on stage** *I get very nervous before I go on stage.* **3 the stage** the profession of acting: *Larry's always wanted to go on the stage.* (=become an actor)

stage[2] *v* [T] to organize an event or performance: *They're staging a rock concert in the park.* — **staging** *n* [C,U] *a staging of 'Hamlet'*

stage·coach /ˈsteɪdʒkəʊtʃ ‖ -koʊtʃ/ *n* [C] a vehicle pulled by horses that was used in the past to carry passengers

stage fright /ˈ. ./ *n* [U] the nervous feeling some people have before they perform in front of a lot of people

stage man·ag·er /ˈ. ˌ.../ *n* [C] a person in charge of what happens on stage during a performance

stag·ger /ˈstægə ‖ -ər/ *v* **1** [I] to walk or move in an unsteady way: + **along/down etc** *Tom staggered drunkenly into the kitchen.* **2** [T] to make someone feel very surprised or shocked **3** [T] to arrange the time things happen so that they do not all happen at the same time: *Student registration will be staggered to avoid delays.*

stag·gered /ˈstægəd ‖ -ərd/ *adj* [not before noun] very shocked or surprised: *I was staggered by the size of the phone bill.*

stag·ger·ing /ˈstægərɪŋ/ *adj* very surprising or shocking, and hard to believe: *She spent a staggering £2000 on a new dress.*

stag·nant /ˈstægnənt/ *adj* **1** stagnant water or air does not move and often smells bad **2** not changing or improving: *Steel production has remained stagnant.*

stag·nate /stægˈneɪt ‖ ˈstægneɪt/ *v* [I] to stop developing or improving: *a stagnating economy* — **stagnation** /stægˈneɪʃən/ *n* [U]

stag night /ˈ. ./ *n* [C] a social occasion when a man goes out with his male friends just before his wedding

staid /steɪd/ *adj* serious, old-fashioned, and boring: *a staid old bachelor*

stain[1] /steɪn/ *v* **1** [I,T] to accidentally make a mark on something, especially one that is difficult to remove, or to be marked in this way: *The carpet stains easily.* | + **with** *a tablecloth stained with wine* **2** [T] to paint wood with a stain

stain[2] *n* **1** [C] a mark that is difficult to remove: *coffee stains* **2** [C,U] thin paint used to protect wood and make it darker

stained glass /ˌ. ˈ. ◂/ *n* [U] coloured glass used to make pictures and patterns in windows

stainless steel /ˌ. ˈ. / *n* [U] a type of steel that does not RUST

stair /steə ‖ ster/ *n* [C] one of the steps in a set of stairs: *Jane sat on the bottom stair.*

stair·case /ˈsteəkeɪs ‖ ster-/ also **stair·way** /ˈsteəweɪ ‖ ster-/ *n* [C] a set of stairs inside a building, and the structure that supports it

stairs /steəz ‖ sterz/ *n* [plural] a set of steps that you use to go from one level of a building to another: **up/down the stairs** *Kim ran up the stairs.* | **a flight of stairs** *The office is up two flights of stairs.* → see also DOWNSTAIRS, UPSTAIRS

stair·way /ˈsteəweɪ ‖ ster-/ *n* [C] a staircase, especially a large or impressive one

stake[1] /steɪk/ *n* **1** [C] a long sharp piece of wood, metal etc that you push into the ground to mark something or to support a plant **2 be at stake** if something is at stake, you will lose it if a plan or action is not successful: *We need this contract – hundreds of jobs are at stake.* **3 a stake in sth** a part or share in a business, plan etc: *She has a 5% stake in the company.* **4** [C] money risked on the result of a game, race etc; BET: *a £10 stake*

stake[2] *v* [T] **1** to risk something on the result of a game, race etc, or on the result of a plan or action: **stake sth on sth** *The President is staking his reputation on the peace plan.* **2 stake a claim** to say that you think you have a right to have something

stake sth ↔ **out** *phr v* [T] *informal* to watch a place secretly and continuously: *The police have been staking out the club for weeks.* — **stakeout** *n* [C]

stakes /steɪks/ *n* [plural] the things you could lose in a game or uncertain situation: *I don't think you should get involved – the stakes are too high.*

stale /steɪl/ *adj* **1** no longer fresh: *stale bread* **2** no longer interesting: *stale news* **3** someone who is stale has no new ideas or interest because they have been doing something for too long: *I was getting stale in my old job.*

stale·mate /ˈsteɪlmeɪt/ *n* [C,U] the situation when neither side in an argument, battle etc can make progress or win

stalk[1] /stɔːk ‖ stɒːk/ *n* [C] the main stem of a plant

stalk[2] *v* **1** [T] to follow a person or animal in order to watch or attack them **2** [I,T] to walk in a stiff, proud, or angry way: *They say a ghost* *stalks the castle at night.* | + **about/out** etc *She rose from her chair and stalked out of the room.*

stalk·er /'stɔːkəl'stɔːkər/ *n* [C] a person who follows and watches someone for a long time in a way that annoys or harms them —**stalking** *n* [U]

stall[1] /stɔːl‖stɔːl/ *n* [C] **1** a large table on which you put things you want to sell: *a market stall* **2** *AmE* a small enclosed area for washing or using the toilet: *a shower stall*

stall[2] *v* [I,T] **1** if an engine stalls or you stall it, it suddenly stops working: *The car stalled at the junction.* **2** *informal* to deliberately delay doing something, or to make someone else do this: *Quit stalling and answer my question!*

stal·lion /'stæljən/ *n* [C] an adult male horse

stalls /stɔːlz‖stɔːlz/ *n* [plural] **the stalls** the seats nearest to the stage in a theatre

stal·wart /'stɔːlwət‖'stɔːlwərt/ *n* [C] someone who is very loyal in their support for an organization: *Conservative party stalwarts* —**stalwart** *adj*

stam·i·na /'stæmɪnə/ *n* [U] physical or mental strength that lets you continue doing something for a long time

stam·mer /'stæməl-ər/ *v* [I,T] to repeat the first sound of a word when you speak because you have a speech problem, or because you are nervous: *He stammered an excuse.* —**stammer** *n* [singular] *She has a bad stammer.*

stamp[1] /stæmp/ *n* [C] **1** a small piece of paper that you buy and stick on a letter before you post it **2 a)** an official mark that has been printed on a document using a small block covered with ink: *a stamp in my passport* **b)** the small block with a handle that is used to make this mark, by pressing it onto the paper **3** **have/bear the stamp of sth** to clearly have a particular quality: *a speech that definitely bore the stamp of authority*

stamp[2] *v* **1** [I,T] to put your foot down very hard on the ground, or to walk in this way: *Tony stamped upstairs.* | **stamp your feet** *She was stamping her feet to keep warm.* **2** [T] to print an official mark on a document by pressing a small block covered with ink onto it: *The date was stamped on the letter.*

stamp sth ↔ **out** *phr v* [T] to prevent something bad continuing: *efforts to stamp out drug abuse*

stam·pede /stæm'piːd/ *n* [C] **1** when a large number of animals suddenly start running together **2** when a lot of people suddenly want to do the same thing or go to the same place: *a stampede to buy gold* —**stampede** *v* [I,T]

stance /stɑːns‖stæns/ *n* [C] **1** an opinion that someone states publicly: + **on** *Senator, what is your stance on nuclear tests?* **2** *formal* a way of standing: *a wide-legged stance*

stanch /stɑːntʃ‖stɔːntʃ, stɑːntʃ/ an American spelling of STAUNCH[2]

stand[1] /stænd/ *v* **stood** /stʊd/, **stood, standing** **1** [I] to be on your feet in an upright position: *Anna was standing in front of me.* | *Hundreds of people stood watching.* | **stand still** (=stand without moving): *Jo stood still and listened.* | **stand back/aside** (=move back or to the side): *A policeman told everyone to stand back.* **2** also **stand up** [I] to move into a stand-

ing position after you have been sitting, bending, or lying down: *Everybody stood up to applaud.* **3** [I,T] to be in an upright position somewhere, or to put something in an upright position: *We stood the lamp in the corner.* | *Few houses were left standing after the explosion.* **4** [I] to be in a particular place or position: *Their house stood on a corner near the park.* **5** **can't stand** *spoken* to hate someone or something: *Dave can't stand dogs.* | **can't stand (sb) doing sth** *I can't stand being late.* **6** [T] to be able to accept or deal with something unpleasant or difficult: *She couldn't stand the pain any longer.* | **stand (sb) doing sth** *How can she stand him treating her like that?* **7** **stand trial** if you stand trial for a crime, people try to prove that you are guilty of the crime in a court of law **8** [I] to be at a particular level or amount: + **at** *The unemployment rate stands at 8%.* **9** **stand to do sth** to be likely to get something: *They stand to make more than £12 million on the deal.* **10** [I] to remain unchanged: *My offer of a place to stay still stands.* | **as sth stands** *Your proposal, as it stands, is not acceptable.* **11** **stand 50 m/35 feet etc tall/high** *written* to have a height of 50 metres etc: *The Eiffel Tower stands 300 metres high.* **12** **stand a chance (of doing sth)** to be likely to succeed in doing something: *You don't stand a chance of going out with her.* **13** [T] to be good or strong enough not to be damaged or destroyed by something: *jeans that can stand the rough wear kids give them* | **stand the test of time** (=stay strong): *Their marriage has certainly stood the test of time.* **14** **stand in the way/ stand in sb's way** to prevent someone from doing something, or prevent something from happening: *There are a few problems that stand in the way of the merger.* **15** **where/how you stand (on sth)** what your opinion about something is: *Where do you stand on the issue of immigration?* **16** **know where you stand** to know what someone's feelings or intentions towards you are: *You never know where you stand with Debbie.* **17** **stand on your own two feet** to be independent and not need help from other people: *It's about time you learned to stand on your own two feet.* **18** [I] to try to become elected: *He stood for parliament in 1959.* **19** **it stands to reason** used to say that something is clearly true: *It stands to reason that children will want to do what their friends do.* **20** **stand sb a drink/meal etc** *spoken* to pay for someone's drink, meal etc → see also **stand guard** (GUARD[1])

stand around *phr v* [I] to stand somewhere and not do anything: *Everybody was just standing around waiting.*

stand by *phr v* **1** [T **stand by** sth] if you stand by something you believe or something you have said, you do not change it: *I stand by what I said earlier.* **2** [T **stand by** sb] to stay loyal to someone and support them in a difficult situation: *Matt's parents have stood by him throughout his drug treatments.* **3** [I] to be ready to do something: *Fire crews are now standing by.* **4** [I] to allow something bad to happen by doing nothing: *People just stood by and watched him being attacked.*

stand down *phr v* [I] to leave an important job or position: *The chairman stood down last month.*

stand for sth *phr v* [T] **1** to be a short form of a word, phrase, or idea: *Jr. stands for 'junior'.*
2 not stand for sth to not allow something to happen or continue: *I won't stand for this behaviour.* **3** to support an idea, principle etc: *I don't like her, or what she stands for.*

stand in *phr v* [I] to do someone else's job while they are away: **+ for** *Lyn stood in for me while I was ill.*

stand out *phr v* [I] **1** to be clearly better than other things or people: *Morrison stands out as the most experienced candidate.* **2** to be very easy to see or notice: *She really stood out in her bright green dress.*

stand up *phr v* **1** [I] to be proved to be true, useful, or strong when tested: *The accusations will never stand up in court.* **2** [T **stand** sb **up**] to not meet someone when you have promised to meet them: *Tom stood me up last night.*

stand up for sb/sth *phr v* [T] to defend a person or idea when they are being criticized: *Why didn't you stand up for me?*

stand up to sb *phr v* [T] to be brave and refuse to do what someone is trying to make you do: *He became a hero for standing up to the local gangs.*

stand² *n* [C] **1** a piece of furniture or equipment for supporting something: *a music stand* **2** a table or small structure used for selling or showing things: *a hotdog stand* **3** an opinion that you state publicly: **take a stand** (=state your opinion firmly): *The prime minister took a firm stand on the issue of import controls.* **4 the stand** *AmE* the place in a court of law where someone sits when the lawyer asks them questions **5** [C] a building where people sit or stand to watch a game in a sports STADIUM **6 make a stand** to make a strong attempt to defend yourself or stop an enemy: *The retreating army made a last stand at Yorktown.*

stan·dard¹ /ˈstændəd‖-ərd/ *n* [C] **1** a level of quality, skill, or ability, especially a high level: *They don't seem to care much about standards.* | **high/low standard** *a high standard of service* | **meet/reach a standard** *This work does not meet the standard required.* | **set a standard** (=decide what level is acceptable): *Mr Arnison sets very high standards for his students.* **2** the ideas of what is good or normal that you use to compare things: **by sb's standards** *By today's standards, I earned very little.*

standard² *adj* normal or usual: *Security checks are now standard procedure.*

stan·dard·ize (also **-ise** *BrE*) /ˈstændədaɪz‖-ər-/ *v* [T] to make all the things of one type the same as each other: *standardized tests* —**standardization** /ˌstændədaɪˈzeɪʃən‖-dərdə-/ *n* [U]

standard of liv·ing /ˌ.. ˈ../ *n* [C] the amount of money that people have to spend, and how comfortable their life is: *Japan has a very high standard of living.*

stand·by /ˈstændbaɪ/ *n* **1** [C] something that is ready to be used if needed: *a standby generator* **2 on standby a)** ready to be used if needed: *The police have been kept on standby in case of trouble.* **b)** if you are on standby for a plane ticket, you will be allowed to travel if there are any seats that are not being used.

stand-in /ˈ. ./ *n* [C] someone who does another

person's job or does something instead of them for a short time

stand·ing¹ /ˈstændɪŋ/ *n* [U] the opinion that people have about someone, and how good and important they are: *the president's standing in the opinion polls*

standing² *adj* **1 a standing invitation** when someone has invited you to come whenever you want **2 give sb a standing ovation** when people stand to clap after a performance because they think it is very good **3 a standing joke** something that happens often and that people make jokes about

standing army /ˌ.. ˈ../ *n* [C] a permanent army, rather than one that has been formed for a war

standing or·der /ˌ.. ˈ../ *n* [C] when you ask your bank to pay money regularly to someone

stand-off, stand·off /ˈstændɒf‖-ɒːf/ *n* [C] a situation in which neither person or group in a fight or battle can get an advantage, so neither of them does anything

stand·out /ˈstændaʊt/ *n* [C] *AmE* someone who is much better at doing something than other people in a group —**standout** *adj*

stand·point /ˈstændpɔɪnt/ *n* [C] someone's particular way of thinking about a problem or subject; POINT OF VIEW

stand·still /ˈstænd‚stɪl/ *n* [singular] a situation in which something is not moving, or no one is doing anything: *The whole city came to a complete standstill on the day of the funeral.*

stand-up /ˈ. ./ *adj* a stand-up COMEDIAN stands alone in front of a group of people and tells jokes —**stand-up** *n* [C]

stank /stæŋk/ *v* the past tense of STINK

stan·za /ˈstænzə/ *n* [C] a group of lines that forms part of a poem; VERSE

sta·ple¹ /ˈsteɪpəl/ *n* [C] a small thin piece of metal used to fasten pieces of paper together —**staple** *v* [T]

staple² *adj* a staple food is one of the main foods that people eat —**staple** *n* [C]

sta·pler /ˈsteɪplə‖-ər/ *n* [C] a machine used for putting staples through paper ➡ see colour picture on page 80

star¹ /stɑː‖stɑːr/ *n* [C] **1** a very large ball of burning gases in space, which looks like a point of light in the sky at night: *The stars were shining brightly.* **2** a famous actor, singer, sports player etc: *a movie star* | *pop stars* **3** a shape with five or six points sticking out of it: *the star at the top of the Christmas tree* ➡ see picture at SHAPES **4 two-star/four-star etc** used to show how good the quality of something is, especially a hotel or restaurant **5** the best of a group of players, performers etc: *Jim is definitely our star player.* **6 the stars/sb's stars** the power that some people believe that the stars have to affect our lives

star² *v* [I,T] **-rred, -rring** if a film, play etc stars someone or if someone stars in a film, play etc, they are the main character in it: *a movie starring Bruce Willis*

star·board /ˈstɑːbəd‖ˈstɑːrbərd/ *n* [U] the right side of a ship or plane when you are facing the front

starch¹ /stɑːtʃ‖stɑːrtʃ/ *n* **1** [C,U] a substance

in foods such as bread, rice, and potatoes **2** [U] a substance used for making cloth stiff

starch·y /ˈstɑːtʃi‖ˈstɑːr-/ adj containing a lot of starch: *starchy foods*

star·dom /ˈstɑːdəm‖ˈstɑːr-/ n [U] when someone is very famous as an actor, singer, sports player etc

stare /steə‖ster/ v [I] to look at someone or something for a long time without moving your eyes: **+ at** *Stop staring at me!* —**stare** n [C] *She gave him a long hard stare.*

star·fish /ˈstɑːfɪʃ‖ˈstɑːr-/ n [C] a sea animal that is shaped like a star

stark[1] /stɑːk‖stɑːrk/ adj **1** very simple and plain looking: *the stark beauty of the desert* **2** unpleasantly clear and impossible to avoid: *the stark realities of drug addiction* —**starkly** adv

stark[2] adv **stark naked** not wearing any clothes

star·ling /ˈstɑːlɪŋ‖ˈstɑːr-/ n [C] a common black European bird

star·lit /ˈstɑːlɪt‖ˈstɑːr-/ adj made bright by the light of the stars: *a starlit night*

star·ry /ˈstɑːri/ adj a starry sky or night is one in which you can see many stars

starry-eyed /ˌ.ˈ..◂/ adj hopeful about things in a way that is silly or unreasonable, especially because you are young: *a starry-eyed teenager*

Stars and Stripes /ˌ. . ˈ./ **the Stars and Stripes** the national flag of the US

star sign /ˈ. ./ n [C] a sign which is based on the time of the year when you were born, which some people believe shows what kind of person you are: *"What star sign are you?" "I'm a Leo."*

star-stud·ded /ˈ. ˌ../ adj including many famous performers: *a star-studded cast*

start[1] /stɑːt‖stɑːrt/ v **1** [I,T] to begin doing something: **start doing sth** *Have you started making dinner?* | **start to do sth** *It's starting to rain.* | **start sth** *When does she start college?* **2** [I] to begin happening: *The race starts in ten minutes.* | **+ from** *Starting from tomorrow, we all have to be at work by 8.30.* **3** [T] to make something begin happening: *The fire was started by a loose wire.* **4** [T] also **start up** to make a company, organization etc begin to exist: *In 1996 the band started their own record company.* **5** [I,T] also **start up** if you start a car or engine, or if it starts, it begins to work: *It's often difficult to start the car when it's wet.* **6** [I] if prices start at or from a particular amount, that is the lowest amount that you can pay to buy something **7** [I] if a road, river etc starts somewhere, it begins in that place: *The Red River starts in New Mexico.* **8** [I] to move suddenly because you are surprised or afraid **9 to start with** *spoken* **a)** used to emphasize the first of a list of things you want to mention: *"Why aren't you happy in your job?" "Well, to start with, I don't get enough money."* **b)** used to talk about the beginning of a situation, which later changes: *I was nervous to start with, but later on I was fine.*

start off phr v **1** [I] to begin an activity by doing something: *Let's start off by reviewing what we did last week.* **2** [T **start** sb/sth ↔ **off**] to make someone start doing something, or make something start happening: *What first started off your interest in the theatre?*

start on sth phr v [T] to begin doing something: *I'd better start on the housework.*

start out phr v [I] to begin your CAREER or your life in a particular way: *She started out as a nightclub singer.*

start over phr v [I] *AmE* to start doing something again from the beginning: *Coming back home was like a chance to start over.*

USAGE NOTE: start and begin

Usually, these words mean the same thing. However **start** has some special meanings for which **begin** cannot be used. Use **start** to talk about making a machine work: *Bob couldn't start the car.* You should also use **start** to talk about making something begin to exist: *Starting a new business is hard work.*

---

start[2] n **1** [C] the beginning of something, or the way something begins: *Hurry, or we'll miss the start of the show.* | **from the start** *They've had problems from the start.* | **from start to finish** *It was a close race from start to finish.* | **get off to a good/bad start** *The year got off to a good start.* **2** **it's a start** used to say that something may not be impressive, but it shows you are beginning to achieve what you want: *We only have $92 million of the $600 million needed, but it's a start.* **3** **for a start** *spoken* used to emphasize the first of several reasons or other things you want to mention: *I don't think she'll get the job. She's too young, for a start.* **4** [C usually singular] an advantage you have when you start something before other people, especially in a race: *He had a 50 metre start on the other boys.* **5** **the start** the place where a race or game begins **6** [singular] a sudden movement, caused especially by fear or surprise: *Ed woke up with a start.* → see also **make a fresh start** (FRESH)

start·er /ˈstɑːtə‖ˈstɑːrtər/ n [C] **1** *BrE* the first part of a meal **2** someone who gives the SIGNAL for a race to begin

star·tle /ˈstɑːtl‖ˈstɑːrtl/ v [T] to suddenly surprise or slightly shock someone, especially by appearing when they did not know you were there: *Sorry, I didn't mean to startle you.* —**startled** adj: *a startled expression* —**startling** adj

start-up /ˈ. ./ adj start-up costs are connected with starting a new business

starv·a·tion /stɑːˈveɪʃən‖stɑːr-/ n [U] when someone becomes ill or dies because they do not have enough to eat

starve /stɑːv‖stɑːrv/ v [I,T] to become ill or die because you do not have enough to eat, or to make someone do this: *Thousands of people could starve to death.* | *starving refugees*

---

starved /stɑːvdǁstɑːrvd/ *adj* **1 be starved of** also **be starved for** *AmE* to not get enough of something that you need very much: *The public health system has been starved of money.* **2** *AmE spoken* very hungry; STARVING

starv·ing /ˈstɑːvɪŋǁˈstɑːr-/ *adj* **1** someone who is starving has not had enough food for a long time and will die soon if they do not eat: *starving children* **2** *spoken* also **starved** *AmE* very hungry: *Can we stop for lunch now? I'm absolutely starving.*

stash[1] /stæʃ/ *v* [T] *informal* to keep something in a secret place: *The money is stashed away in a Swiss bank.*

stash[2] *n* [C] *informal* an amount of something that is kept in a secret place

state[1] /steɪt/ *n* **1** [C] the condition that someone or something is in: *The economy is in a terrible state.* | *The driver was still in a state of shock.* **2** [C] also **State** one of the parts that the US and some other countries are divided into, which each have their own government: *the state of Oklahoma* **3** [singular, U] the government of a country: *the power of the state* **4 state visit/ ceremony/opening etc** an important official visit, ceremony etc involving a leader or members of the government: *the President's state visit to Moscow* **5** [C,U] also **State** a country that has its own government: *France and other European states* | **head of state** (=the leader of a country): *a meeting between heads of state* **6 in/into a state** *informal* very nervous or upset ➡ see also POLICE STATE, STATE OF AFFAIRS, STATE OF MIND

state[2] *v* [T] *formal* to say something publicly or officially: **+ (that)** *The rules state that smoking is not allowed in any part of the building.*

state·ly /ˈsteɪtli/ *adj* big and impressive: *a stately mansion*

stately home /ˌ.. ˈ./ *n* [C] a very large old house in the countryside in Britain

state·ment /ˈsteɪtmənt/ *n* [C] **1** something that someone says or writes publicly or officially: *The company will make a statement about the accident later today.* **2** also **bank statement** a list showing amounts of money paid into or from a bank account

state of af·fairs /ˌ. .. ˈ./ *n* a situation

state of mind /ˌ. .. ˈ./ *n* someone's mental condition, especially when this affects their actions

state-of-the-art /ˌ. .. ˈ.◂ / *adj* using the newest methods, materials, or knowledge: *state-of-the-art technology*

States /steɪts/ *n* **the States** *spoken* the US

state school /ˈ. ˌ./ *n* [C] *BrE* a school which provides free education and is paid for by the government

states·man /ˈsteɪtsmən/ *n* [C] a political leader, especially one who people respect and admire —**statesmanlike** *adj* —**statesmanship** *n* [U]

stat·ic[1] /ˈstætɪk/ *adj* not changing, or moving: *Prices have been fairly static.*

static[2] *n* [U] **1** also **static electricity** electricity caused when two surfaces rub together, which can give you a small electric shock **2** noise caused by electricity in the air, which spoils the sound on the radio or television

sta·tion[1] /ˈsteɪʃən/ *n* [C] **1** a building where trains or buses stop so that passengers can get on and off, or where they begin or end their journey: *I'll meet you at the station.* ➡ see colour picture on page 669 **2** a company that broadcasts on radio or television: *a country music station* **3** a building where a service or activity is based: *a space station* | *a police station*

station[2] *v* [T] if someone, especially a soldier, is stationed in a place, he or she has been sent there: *He was stationed in Germany.*

sta·tion·a·ry /ˈsteɪʃənəriǁ-neri/ *adj* not moving: *a stationary vehicle*

sta·tion·er's /ˈsteɪʃənəzǁ-ərz/ *n* [C] *BrE* a shop that sells things that you use for writing, for example pens and paper

sta·tion·e·ry /ˈsteɪʃənəriǁ-neri/ *n* [U] things such as paper or pens that you use for writing

station wag·on /ˈ.. ˌ../ *n* [C] *AmE* a large car with space for boxes, cases etc at the back; ESTATE CAR *BrE*

stat·is·ti·cian /ˌstætɪˈstɪʃən/ *n* [C] someone who works with statistics

sta·tis·tics /stəˈtɪstɪks/ *n* **1** [plural] a set of numbers that have been collected to show information about something: *the latest crime statistics* **2** [U] the science which involves collecting and studying numbers that show information about something —**statistical** *adj*: *statistical analysis* —**statistically** /-kli/ *adv*

stat·ue /ˈstætʃuː/ *n* [C] a stone, metal etc object that has been made to look like a person or animal: *the Statue of Liberty*

stat·ure /ˈstætʃəl-ər/ *n* [U] *formal* **1** the importance that someone has because of their work or achievements: *a musician of great stature* **2** someone's height

sta·tus /ˈsteɪtəsǁˈsteɪtəs, ˈstæ-/ *n* **1** [U] the position that someone or something has, compared to other people or things, or according to the law: *the status of women* | **marital status** (=whether or not you are married) **2** [singular, U] special importance that someone has because of their job, achievements, or social position: *Teachers used to have a lot more status in those days.*

status quo /ˌsteɪtəs ˈkwəʊǁˌsteɪtəs ˈkwoʊ, ˌstæ-/ *n* **the status quo** the situation that exists at a particular time

status sym·bol /ˈ.. ˌ../ *n* [C] something that someone owns that shows that they have a lot of money, an important job etc

stat·ute /ˈstætʃuːt/ *n* [C] *formal* a law or rule

stat·u·to·ry /ˈstætʃʊtəriǁ-tɔːri/ *adj* *formal* fixed or controlled by law: *statutory rights*

staunch[1] /stɔːntʃǁstɒːntʃ, stɑːntʃ/ *adj* very loyal: *a staunch supporter* —**staunchly** *adv*

staunch[2] (also **stanch** *AmE*) *v* [T] to stop a flow of a liquid, especially blood

stave /steɪv/ *v*
stave sth ↔ off *phr v* [T] to stop something unpleasant from happening to you now, although it is likely to happen soon: *The government managed to stave off economic disaster.*

stay[1] /steɪ/ *v* **1** [I] to continue to be in the same place, job, school etc, and not leave: *Can you stay here and look after my bags for me?* | *She's decided to stay in her present job.* **2** [T] to continue to be the same as before and not change: *I tried to stay calm and not lose my temper.* **3** [I,T] to spend a short period of time in a place, especially on holiday, on a business trip etc: *How long are you staying in New York?* | **+ at** *They're staying at the Hilton.* | **stay with sb** *We've got some friends staying with us this weekend.* **4 stay put** *informal* to continue to be in the same place and not move

stay away from sb/sth *phr v* [T] to not go near someone or something: *Stay away from my husband!*

stay behind *phr v* [I] to stay in a place after the other people have left: *I had to stay behind after school.*

stay in *phr v* [I] to stay in your home and not go out: *Why don't we stay in and watch TV?*

stay on *phr v* [I] to continue to do a job or to study after the time when people can leave: *Rachel is staying on for a fifth year in college.*

stay out *phr v* [I] to stay outside at night and not go back to your home: *She lets her children stay out till midnight.*

stay out of sth *phr v* [T] to not become involved in something such as an argument: *You stay out of this, Campbell!*

stay up *phr v* [I] to not go to bed: *We stayed up to watch the late-night movie.*

stay² *n* [C] a period of time that you spend somewhere: *Did you enjoy your stay in Mexico?*

stead /sted/ *n* **stand sb in good stead** to be very useful for someone in the future

stead·fast /'stedfɑːst‖-fæst/ *adj literary* refusing to change your beliefs or what you are doing, or refusing to change your support for someone

stead·y¹ /'stedi/ *adj* **1** not moving or shaking: *Keep the ladder steady.* **2** continuing to happen in a gradual regular way: *a steady improvement* **3** not changing: *a steady speed of 50 mph* **4 a steady job** a job you get paid regularly for, and is likely to continue for a long time **5** a steady girlfriend or boyfriend is one that you have had a relationship with for a long time: **go steady** (=become boyfriend and girlfriend) —**steadily** *adv* —**steadiness** *n* [U]

steady² *v* [T] **1** to stop someone from falling, or stop something from shaking: *He put out his hand to steady himself.* **2 steady your nerves** to make yourself feel calm and less nervous

steak /steɪk/ *n* [C,U] a thick flat piece of meat or fish

steal /stiːl/ *v* **stole** /stəʊl‖stoʊl/, **stolen** /'stəʊlən‖stoʊ-/, **stealing 1** [I,T] to take something that does not belong to you: *Someone stole my passport.* | *a stolen car* **2** [I] to move secretly and quietly

stealth /stelθ/ *n* [U] when someone deliberately does something secretly or quietly —**stealthily** *adv: moving stealthily* —**stealthy** *adj*

steam¹ /stiːm/ *n* **1** [U] the gas that water produces when it is boiled: **steam engine/boat/train etc** (=that uses power from steam) **2 let/work off steam** to get rid of your anger, excitement etc by shouting, doing sports etc **3 run out of steam** to no longer have the energy or support you need to continue doing something

steam² *v* **1** [T] to use steam to cook something: *Steam the vegetables for five minutes.* **2** [I] to produce steam: *a cup of steaming coffee*

steamed up /ˌ. '.◂/ *adj* **1** covered with steam or liquid from the air: *My glasses were all steamed up.* **2** *informal* angry or worried about something

steam·er /'stiːməǁ-ər/ *n* [C] a ship that uses steam power

steam·roll·er¹ /'stiːmˌrəʊləǁ-ˌroʊlər/ also **steam·roll** /'stiːmrəʊlǁ-roʊl/ *v* [T] *informal* to defeat someone or force someone to do something by using all your power

steamroller² *n* [C] a heavy vehicle used for making road surfaces flat

steam·y /'stiːmi/ *adj* **1** very hot and full of steam, or hot wet air: *the steamy heat of New York* **2** sexually exciting: *a steamy love scene*

steed /stiːd/ *n* [C] *literary* a horse

steel¹ /stiːl/ *n* [U] **1** a strong hard metal used for making knives, cars etc **2 nerves of steel** the ability to be very brave and calm in a dangerous or difficult situation

steel² *v* [T] **steel yourself** to prepare yourself to do something that you know will be unpleasant

steel·works /'stiːlwɜːksǁ-wɜːrks/ *n* [C] a factory where steel is made —**steelworker** *n* [C]

steel·y /'stiːli/ *adj* extremely strong and determined: *a steely expression*

steep¹ /stiːp/ *adj* **1** a steep road, hill etc goes down or up at a sharp angle **2** a steep increase or fall in something is large and happens quickly **3** *informal* very expensive —**steeply** *adv* —**steepness** *n* [U]

steep² *v* [T] **1** to put something in a liquid and leave it there **2 be steeped in history/tradition etc** to have existed for a long time and have a long history, a lot of TRADITIONS etc

stee·ple /'stiːpəl/ *n* [C] a tall pointed tower on a church

steer¹ /stɪəǁstɪr/ *v* **1** [I,T] to control the direction of a vehicle you are driving: *I steered the boat out to sea.* **2** [T] to influence someone's behaviour or the way a situation develops: *Helen tried to steer the conversation away from school.* **3** [T] to take someone somewhere, especially by holding them: *Bobby took my arm and steered me into the next room.* **4 steer clear of** *informal* to try to avoid someone or something that is unpleasant

steer² *n* [C] a young male cow

steer·ing /'stɪərɪŋǁ'stɪr-/ *n* [U] the parts of a vehicle used for controlling its direction

steering wheel /'.. ./ *n* [C] a wheel that you turn to control the direction of a vehicle

stem¹ /stem/ *n* [C] **1** the long thin part of a plant, from which leaves or flowers grow **2** the thin part of a wine glass, between the base and the wide top

stem² *v* [T] **-mmed, -mming** to stop something from spreading or growing

stem from sth *phr v* [T] to develop as a result of something

stench /stentʃ/ *n* [C] a very strong unpleasant smell

sten·cil /'stensəl/ *n* [C] a piece of paper, plastic etc, that has holes in the shape of letters or patterns in it, which you use for painting letters or patterns onto a surface —**stencil** *v* [T]

step¹ /step/ *n* [C] **1** a movement when you are walking when you put one foot down in front of the other: **take a step** (=walk one step): *He took a few steps forward and then stopped.* **2** one of a series of things that you do in order to deal with a problem or achieve something: *an important first step toward peace* | **take steps** (=do things to deal with or achieve something): *We must take steps to make sure it never happens again.* **3** the surfaces that you walk on when you are going up or down stairs: *Jenny waited on the church steps.* **4** one of the movements you make with your feet when you are doing a dance **5 watch your step** *spoken* to be careful about what you say, how you behave, or where you walk **6 in step/out of step** moving your feet at the same time as the other people in a group, or not at the same time **7 be one step ahead of sb** to have done something or thought of something before someone else → see also FOOTSTEP, STEP-BY-STEP

step[2] *v* [I] **-pped, -pping 1** to move somewhere by putting one foot down in front of the other: **+ back/forward** *We all stepped back to let the doctor through.* **2** to put your foot on or in something: *Sorry, I didn't mean to step on your foot.* **3 step out of line** to break the rules, or not do what you have been told to do **4 step on sb's toes** to offend or upset someone, especially by trying to do their work

step down/aside *phr v* [I] to leave an important job or official position

step forward *phr v* [I] to come and offer help: *Several volunteers have kindly stepped forward.*

step in *phr v* [I] to become involved in a situation, for example to help someone or stop people fighting: *The referee stepped in and stopped the fight.*

step out *phr v* [I] to go out for a short time

step sth ↔ up *phr v* [T] to increase something or spend more effort trying to do something: *Airlines are stepping up security checks.*

step·broth·er /ˈstepˌbrʌðəll-ər/ *n* [C] a boy or man whose father or mother has married your mother or father

step-by-step /ˌ. . ˈ.◂/ *adj* a step-by-step plan, method etc deals with things carefully and in a fixed order

step·child /ˈsteptʃaɪld/ *n* [C] a child that your husband or wife has from a previous marriage

step·daugh·ter /ˈstepˌdɔːtəll-ˌdɔːtər/ *n* [C] a daughter that your husband or wife has from a previous marriage

step·fa·ther /ˈstepˌfɑːðəll-ər/ *n* [C] a man who is married to your mother, but who is not your father

step·lad·der /ˈstepˌlædəll-ər/ *n* [C] a LADDER with two sloping parts that are joined at the top so that it can stand without support

step·moth·er /ˈstepˌmʌðəll-ər/ *n* [C] a woman who is married to your father, but who is not your mother

step·ping-stone /ˈ...ˈ/ *n* [C] **1** something that will help you to achieve something else: *a stepping-stone to a better job* **2** one of a row of stones that you walk on to go across a stream

step·sis·ter /ˈstepˌsɪstəll-ər/ *n* [C] a girl or woman whose father or mother has married your mother or father

step·son /ˈstepsʌn/ *n* [C] a son that your husband or wife has from a previous marriage

ster·e·o /ˈsteriəʊ,ˈstɪər-ll-ˈster-, ˈstɪr-/ *n* [C] **1** a machine for playing records, CDs etc that produces sound from two SPEAKERS → see colour picture on page 474 **2 in stereo** if a record, film, programme etc is in stereo, it is intended to be heard through two SPEAKERS

ster·e·o·type /ˈsteriətaɪp, ˈstɪər-ll-ˈster-, ˈstɪr-/ *n* [C] an idea of what a type of person is that many people have, especially one which is wrong or unfair —**stereotype** *v* [T] —**stereotypical** /ˌsteriəʊˈtɪpɪkəl◂, ˌstɪər-ll-ˌster-, ˌstɪr-/ *adj*: *the stereotypical Englishman*

ster·ile /ˈsteraɪll-rəl/ *adj* **1** completely clean and not containing any BACTERIA: *a sterile bandage* **2** lacking any new ideas or anything exciting: *sterile argument* **3** unable to have children —**sterility** /stəˈrɪlɪti/ *n* [U]

ster·il·ize (also **-ise** *BrE*) /ˈsterɪlaɪz/ *v* [T] **1** to make something completely clean and kill any BACTERIA in it: *a sterilized needle* **2** to make someone unable to have children by a medical operation —**sterilization** /ˌsterɪlaɪˈzeɪʃənll-lə-/ *n* [C,U]

ster·ling /ˈstɜːlɪŋll-ˈstɜːr-/ *n* [U] the standard unit of money in the United Kingdom; the pound

stern[1] /stɜːnll-stɜːrn/ *adj* very strict and severe: *a stern expression* | *He was fined and given a stern warning.* —**sternly** *adv*

stern[2] *n* [C] the back part of a ship

ste·roid /ˈstɪərɔɪd, ˈste-ll-ˈstɪr-/ *n* [C] a drug used for treating injuries that people sometimes use illegally in sport to get bigger muscles

steth·o·scope /ˈsteθəskəʊpll-skoʊp/ *n* [C] a piece of equipment that doctors use to listen to someone's heart or breathing

stew[1] /stjuːllstuː/ *n* [C,U] a food made of meat, vegetables etc cooked together

stew[2] *v* [T] to cook something slowly in liquid: *stewed apples*

stew·ard /ˈstjuːədllˈstuːərd/ *n* [C] **1** a man who serves food and drinks to people on a ship etc; a FLIGHT ATTENDANT **2** *BrE* someone who helps to organize a race

stew·ard·ess /ˈstjuːədɪsllˈstuːərd-/ *n* [C] a woman who serves food and drinks to people on a plane, ship etc; a FLIGHT ATTENDANT

stick[1] /stɪk/ *v* **stuck** /stʌk/, **stuck, sticking 1** [I,T] to join something to something else using a substance such as glue, or to become joined to something: *Did you remember to stick a stamp on the envelope?* | *The pages were all stuck together.* **2** [T] *informal* to put something somewhere: *Just stick your coat on that chair.* **3** [T] to push a pointed object into something: *The nurse stuck a needle in my arm.* **4** [I] if a pointed object sticks into something, it goes into it **5** [I,T] if something sticks, it becomes fixed in one position and is difficult to move: *The door had stuck.* **6 stick in your mind** if something sticks in your mind, you remember it well because it was surprising, interesting etc **7 stick your neck out** *informal* to take the risk of saying or doing something that may be wrong, or that other people may disagree with **8 can't stick** *informal* if you can't stick an unpleasant situation, it seems so unpleasant that you feel you cannot deal with it any more: *I can't stick ironing.*

stick around *phr v* [I] *informal* to stay somewhere

stick at sth *phr v* [T] to continue working hard to do something

stick by sb/sth *phr v* [T] *informal* **1** to help and support someone who is in a difficult situation: *Laura has always stuck by me.* **2** to not change what you have decided to do, or not change what you have said: *The paper is sticking by its original story.*

stick out *phr v* **1** [I] if a part of something sticks out, it comes out much further than the rest of a surface and is very easy to notice: *He's not very good-looking. His front teeth stick out.* **2** [T **stick** sth ↔ **out**] to deliberately make something come forward or out: *Don't stick your tongue out at me!* **3** **stick out (like a sore thumb)** *informal* to be easily noticed because of looking very different from everyone or everything else **4** **stick it out** *informal* to continue doing something that is difficult, boring etc

stick to sth *phr v* [T] **1** to not change what you are doing, or not change what you have said, decided, or promised: *We decided to stick to our original plan.* **2** **stick to your guns** to behave in a determined way and refuse to change what you are doing, even though other people say that you are wrong **3** to keep doing or using one particular thing and not change to anything else: *If you're driving you'd better stick to soft drinks.*

stick together *phr v* [I] *informal* if people stick together, they stay together and help each other

stick up *phr v* [I] if a part of something sticks up, it is pointing up above a surface

stick up for sb *phr v* [T] *informal* to defend someone who is being criticized

stick with sb/sth *phr v* [T] to continue doing something or supporting someone: *Let's just stick with the original plan.*

stick² *n* [C] **1** a long thin piece of wood, especially one that has fallen from a tree **2** a long thin piece of something: *a stick of chewing gum* → see also **get (hold of) the wrong end of the stick** (WRONG¹)

stick·er /ˈstɪkəll-ər/ *n* [C] a small piece of paper or plastic with a picture or writing on it, that you can put onto something → see also BUMPER STICKER

stick·ler /ˈstɪkləll-ər/ *n* [C] someone who is very strict about rules or small details

sticks /stɪks/ *n* **out in the sticks** in a place that is a long way from a town or city

stick shift /ˈ. ./ *n* [C] *AmE* a piece of equipment in a car that you move with your hand to control its GEARS → opposite AUTOMATIC²

stick·y /ˈstɪki/ *adj* **1** made of or covered with a substance like glue that sticks to surfaces: *sticky candy* | *Your hands are all sticky.* **2** if the weather is sticky, the air feels hot and wet **3** *informal* difficult to deal with: *a sticky situation* — **stickiness** *n* [U]

stiff¹ /stɪf/ *adj* **1** hard and difficult to bend or move: *stiff cardboard* **2** if a part of your body is stiff, your muscles hurt and it is difficult to

move **3** very strict, severe, or difficult: *a stiff penalty* | *They had to face stiff competition from the Russian team.* **4** behaving in a formal and not very friendly way: *a stiff smile* **5** **a stiff wind/breeze** a fairly strong wind or BREEZE **6** **a stiff drink** a large amount of a strong alcoholic drink — **stiffly** *adv* — **stiffness** *n* [U]

stiff² *adv* **bored/worried/scared stiff** *informal* extremely bored, worried, frightened etc

stiff·en /ˈstɪfən/ *v* [I] to suddenly stop moving, especially because you are frightened or worried: *Harold stiffened, sensing danger.*

sti·fle /ˈstaɪfəl/ *v* [T] to stop something from happening or developing: *He tried to stifle a yawn.* | *Annette felt college was stifling her creativity.*

stif·ling /ˈstaɪflɪŋ/ *adj* very hot, so that you feel uncomfortable: *the stifling heat*

stig·ma /ˈstɪgmə/ *n* [singular, U] a strong feeling in society that something should be disapproved of, even when this is unreasonable: *the stigma attached to mental illness* — **stigmatize** *v* [T]

stile /staɪl/ *n* [C] a part of a fence that is specially designed so that you can climb over it

sti·let·to /stɪˈletəʊll-toʊ/ *n* [C] a woman's shoe with a high pointed heel, or the heel of this kind of shoe → see picture at SHOE

still¹ /stɪl/ *adv* **1** used to say that something continues to happen, or someone continues to do something: *Andy was still asleep.* | *I went back to my old school, and it still looks the same.* **2** used to say that something continues to be possible: *We could still catch the bus if we hurry.* **3** in spite of what someone has said or something that happened: *He injured his leg in practice, but he still won the race.* | *It hasn't been a very good day. Still, it could have been a lot worse.* **4** **colder/harder/better etc still** even colder, harder etc than something else: *The first question was difficult, but the next one was harder still.* **5** **be still going strong** to continue to be active or successful, even after a long time: *Edith's over 80, but she's still going strong.*

still² *adj* **1** not moving: **keep/stay/stand still** *The children wouldn't keep still.* **2** if a place is still, it is quiet and nothing is moving: *At that time of day, the forest was completely still.* **3** a still drink is not FIZZY: *still lemonade* —**stillness** *n* [U]

still[3] *n* [C] a piece of equipment for making strong alcoholic drinks out of grain or potatoes

still-born /ˈstɪlbɔːn, stɪlˈbɔːn‖-ɔːrn/ *adj* born dead

still life /ˌ. ˈ.◂/ *n* [C,U] *plural* **still lifes** a picture of objects, especially flowers or fruit

stilt-ed /ˈstɪltɪd/ *adj* writing or speaking in a way that is formal and unnatural

stilts /stɪlts/ *n* [plural] a pair of poles you can stand on, used for walking high above the ground

stim-u-lant /ˈstɪmjˠlənt/ *n* [C] a drug or substance that makes you more active: *Caffeine is a stimulant.*

stim-u-late /ˈstɪmjˠleɪt/ *v* [T] **1** to encourage something to grow and develop, or happen more: *The drug stimulates the flow of blood to the brain.* **2** to make someone interested and excited —**stimulation** /ˌstɪmjˠˈleɪʃən/ *n* [U]

stim-u-lat-ing /ˈstɪmjˠleɪtɪŋ/ *adj* interesting and enjoyable, and giving you new ideas to think about: *a stimulating conversation*

stim-u-lus /ˈstɪmjˠləs/ *n, plural* **stimuli** /-laɪ/ **1** [singular, U] something that encourages another thing to grow and develop, or happen more: *a stimulus to industrial development* **2** [C] something that makes you or your body react: *visual stimuli*

sting[1] /stɪŋ/ *v* **stung** /stʌŋ/, **stung, stinging** **1** [T] if an insect, animal, or plant stings you, it hurts you by putting poison into your skin: *Jamie was stung by a bee.* **2** [I,T] to feel a pain in your eyes or skin, or to make someone feel this: *It stings if you get soap in your eyes.* **3** **be stung by** to be very shocked and upset by what someone has said: *She felt stung by his reply.*

sting[2] *n* [C] **1** a wound made when an insect, animal, plant etc stings you: *a bee sting* **2** [singular] a pain that you feel in your eyes, throat, or on your skin **3** a trick used to catch someone who is doing something illegal

sting-ing /ˈstɪŋɪŋ/ *adj* criticizing someone very severely: *a stinging attack*

stin-gy /ˈstɪndʒi/ *adj* not generous with your money, even though you are not poor —**stinginess** *n* [U]

stink[1] /stɪŋk/ *v* [I] **stank** /stæŋk/, **stunk** /stʌŋk/, **stinking** **1** to have a very strong and unpleasant smell: *The room stank of cigar smoke.* **2** *sth stinks! spoken informal* to be very bad, unpleasant, or unfair: *If you ask me, the whole thing stinks.*

stink[2] *n* [singular] **1** **make/cause/raise a stink** complain about something so much that a lot of people notice you **2** a very unpleasant smell

stint /stɪnt/ *n* [C] a period of time that you spend doing something somewhere: *a five-year stint teaching English in Korea*

stip-u-late /ˈstɪpjˠleɪt/ *v* [T] *formal* to say that something must be done: *the terms stipulated under the agreement* —**stipulation** /ˌstɪpjˠ-ˈleɪʃən/ *n* [C]

stir[1] /stɜː‖stɜːr/ *v* **-rred, -rring** **1** [T] to mix a liquid or food by moving a spoon around in it: *Add milk, then stir for 5 minutes.* **2** [I,T] to move slightly, or to make someone or something do this: *Rachel stirred in her sleep.* **3** [T] to make someone feel an emotion: *The music stirred memories of his childhood.*

stir sth ↔ **up** *phr v* [T] to try to cause trouble by making people argue with each other

stir

stir[2] *n* [singular]
1 **create/cause a stir** to make people very excited, angry, or surprised: *The movie caused quite a stir when it was first shown.* **2** when you stir a liquid or food

stir-fry /ˈ. ./ *v* [T] to quickly cook vegetables or meat in a little hot oil —**stir-fry** *n* [C]

stir-ring /ˈstɜːrɪŋ/ *adj* making people feel very excited, proud etc: *a stirring speech*

stir-rup /ˈstɪrəp‖ˈstɜː-/ *n* [C] one of the two metal things that you put your feet in when you are riding a horse

stitch[1] /stɪtʃ/ *n* **1** [C] a line of thread that has been sewn in a piece of cloth: *a white tablecloth with blue stitches around the edges* **2** [C] a piece of thread that a doctor uses to sew together a cut or wound: *Tony needed five stitches to his face.* **3** [C] one of the small circles of wool that you KNIT when you are making a SWEATER **4** [singular] a pain in your chest that you get from exercising too much **5** **in stitches** laughing so much that you cannot stop: *Nancy kept us in stitches all evening.* **6** **not have a stitch on** to not be wearing any clothes at all

stitch[2] *v* [I,T] to sew two things together, or to sew something onto a piece of cloth: *He had a scout badge stitched to his shirt.* —**stitching** *n* [U]

stitch sth ↔ **up** *phr v* [T] to sew together the edges of a wound or two pieces of cloth

stock[1] /stɒk‖stɑːk/ *n* **1** [C] also **stocks** [plural] a supply of something that is to be used later: *How long will the country's coal stocks last?* |+ **of** *She kept a stock of candles in the cupboard.* **2** [U] also **stocks** [plural] the goods available to be sold in a shop: *Hurry – buy now while stocks last!* | **be in stock** (=available to be sold): *Their new album is now in stock.* **3** [C,U] a SHARE or SHARES in a company **4** [U] a liquid made from boiling meat, bones, or vegetables, used in cooking: *chicken stock* **5** **take stock (of sth)** to think carefully about a situation so that you can decide what to do next: *We need to slow down a little and take stock.* **6** **the stocks** a wooden structure in a public place in which criminals were fastened in past times as a punishment

stock[2] *v* [T] **1** to have something available for people to buy: *Do you stock camping equipment?* **2** **well-stocked** containing large quantities of food, drink, or things you need: *a well-stocked cocktail cabinet*

stock up *phr v* [I] to buy a lot of something to use when you need to: *The supermarket was full of people stocking up for the holidays.*

stock[3] *adj* **stock** answers, phrases etc are things that people usually say, but which are not interesting, helpful or original

stock-ade /stɒˈkeɪd‖stɑː-/ *n* [C] a wall or fence built to defend a place, made from large upright pieces of wood

stock-brok-er /ˈstɒkˌbrəʊkə‖-ˌbrəʊkər/ *n* [C] someone whose job is to buy and sell SHARES,

STOCKs, and BONDs for other people —**stock·broking** n [U]

stock ex·change /'. ·ˌ·/ n **1 the stock exchange** the business of buying and selling STOCKs and SHARES **2 the New York/London/Tokyo etc stock exchange** a place where this happens

stock·ing /'stɒkɪŋ‖'staː-/ n [C] a very thin piece of clothing that fits closely over a woman's foot and leg: *a pair of silk stockings*

stock mar·ket /'. ·ˌ·/ n [singular] **1** the stock exchange **2** the average value of STOCKs sold in the stock exchange

stock·pile /'stɒkpaɪl‖'staːk-/ v [T] to collect a large supply of something to use in the future: *Rebel troops have been stockpiling food and weapons.* —**stockpile** n [C]

stocktaking /'stɒk,teɪkɪŋ‖'staː-/ n [U] BrE when people in a shop or business check what goods they have

stock·y /'stɒki‖'staːki/ adj having a short, heavy, strong-looking body: *a stocky man*

stodg·y /'stɒdʒi‖'staː-/ adj **1** BrE stodgy food is heavy and makes you feel full very quickly: *a stodgy rice pudding* **2** a stodgy person is boring and old-fashioned: *a stodgy old professor*

sto·ic /'stəʊɪk‖'stoʊɪk/, also **sto·ic·al** /'stəʊɪkəl‖ 'stoʊ-/ adj formal patient and not complaining even when something bad happens to you: *a look of stoic resignation* —**stoicism** /-sɪzəm/ n [U] —**stoically** /-kli/ adv

stoke /stəʊk‖stoʊk/ v [T] **1** to add more coal, wood etc to a fire **2** also **stoke up** to make a bad feeling such as anger even stronger

stole[1] /stəʊl‖stoʊl/ v the past tense of STEAL

stole[2] n [C] a long straight piece of cloth or fur that is worn over the shoulders

sto·len /'stəʊlən‖'stoʊ-/ v the past participle of STEAL

stol·id /'stɒlɪd‖'staː-/ adj not showing your emotions or becoming excited easily —**stolidly** adv

stom·ach[1] /'stʌmək/ n [C] **1** the part of your body where food is DIGESTed: *My stomach hurts.* **2** the front part of your body, below your chest: *She had a long scar across her stomach.* **3 on an empty stomach** without having eaten: *It was a long walk, especially on an empty stomach.* **4 have no stomach for sth** to not be able to deal with something unpleasant

stomach[2] v [T] **can't stomach sth** to be unable to watch, listen to, or accept something because it seems very unpleasant: *He couldn't stomach the sight of blood.*

stom·ach·ache /'stʌmək-eɪk/ n [C] a pain in your stomach

stomp /stɒmp‖staːmp/ v [I] to walk with heavy steps, especially because you are angry: *Henry was stomping around like an elephant.*

stone[1] /stəʊn‖stoʊn/ n **1** [C] a small rock or piece of rock **2** [U] rock, or a hard mineral substance: *stone benches* | *a wall made of stone* **3** [C] a jewel: *a gold-plated necklace with fake stones* **4** [C], plural **stone** or **stones** a measurement of weight used in Britain that is equal to 14 lbs or 6.35 kg: *His weight dropped to six stone.* **5** [C] BrE a large hard single seed in the centre of a fruit; PIT AmE: *cherry stones* ➝ see picture at

FRUIT **6 stone cold** very cold: *This coffee's stone cold!*

stone[2] v [T] to kill or hurt someone by throwing stones at them

Stone Age /'. ./ n **the Stone Age** the earliest period in human history, when tools and equipment were made from stone: *Stone Age man*

stoned /stəʊnd‖stoʊnd/ adj informal **1** very relaxed or excited because of taking an illegal drug: *His friends just sit around and get stoned all day.* **2** very drunk

stone·ma·son /'stəʊn,meɪsən‖'stoʊn-/ n [C] someone whose job is cutting and shaping stone to be used for buildings etc

stone·work /'stəʊnwɜːk‖'stoʊnwɜːrk/ n [U] the parts of a building made of or decorated with stone

ston·y /'stəʊni‖'stoʊni/ adj **1** covered with stones or containing stones: *a stony path* **2** unfriendly, especially because someone feels angry: *a stony silence*

stony-faced /ˌ.. '.◂/ adj showing no sympathy or emotion

stood /stʊd/ v the past tense and past participle of STAND

stool /stuːl/ n [C] **1** a chair without a support for your back: *a bar stool* | *a piano stool* ➝ see picture at CHAIR and KITCHEN **2** [usually plural] technical a piece of solid waste from the body

stoop /stuːp/ v [I] to bend your body forward and down, especially your head and shoulders: *The teacher stooped to pick up a pencil.* —**stoop** n [singular]

stoop to sth phr v [T] to do something dishonest or immoral that people would normally not do: *I wouldn't stoop to taking money from a little kid.*

stop[1] /stɒp‖staːp/ v **-pped, -pping 1** [I,T] to no longer continue to do something, or no longer continue to happen: *The baby's been crying all morning – I wish he'd stop!* | *Has the rain stopped yet?* | **stop doing sth** *Everyone stopped talking as soon as she came into the room.* | **stop it/that** spoken (=used to tell someone to stop doing something, especially something annoying or painful): *Stop it! You're hurting me!* **2** [I] to no longer continue to move or operate: *The car stopped outside a big hotel.* | *My watch has stopped.* **3** [I] to pause for a short time when you are doing something or travelling somewhere: *What time do you want to stop?* | **stop to do sth** (=stop in order to do something): *We stopped to get some gas in Louisville.* **4** [I] if a train, bus etc stops somewhere, you can get on or off it there: **+ at** *Does this train stop at Broxbourne?* **5** [T] to make something end: *The referee stopped the fight in the second round.* **6** [T] to prevent someone from doing something, or prevent something from happening: *efforts to stop the spread of AIDS* | **stop sth (from) doing sth** *She can't stop me from leaving!* **7** [T] to make a vehicle or machine no longer continue to move or operate: *Stop the car. I want to be sick!* | *How do you stop the motor?* **8** [T] to prevent someone from continuing to move or travel somewhere: *A man stopped me in the street and asked for a light.* | **the police stop sb** (=because they think that person has done something illegal): *He's been stopped twice by the police for speeding.* **9 stop short of sth** to not do something, although you almost do it: *Tom stopped short of calling her a liar.* **10 sb will stop at nothing** used to say that someone will do anything, even things that are illegal, cruel, or dangerous, in order to get what they want **11 stop a cheque** to tell your bank not to pay money to someone after you have written them a CHEQUE

stop by *phr v* [I] to make a short, unplanned visit to a friend: *It was nice of Judy to stop by.*

stop off *phr v* [I] to make a short visit to a place when you are going somewhere else: **+ at/in** *We stopped off at the supermarket on the way home.*

stop sth ↔ up *phr v* [T] to block a hole in something: *I need something to stop up the sink.*

stop² *n* **1** [C] a place where a bus or train regularly stops for its passengers: *I get off at the next stop.* **2** [C] a place where you stop during a trip, or the short period you spend there: *Our first stop is Brussels, and then we're going to Paris.* **3 come to a stop** stop moving: *The taxi came to a stop outside his house.* **4 put a stop to sth** make something stop: *Mrs Drayton put a stop to the gossip.* → see also **pull out all the stops** (PULL¹)

stop·gap /ˈstɒpgæp‖ˈstɑːp-/ *n* [C] something you use or do for a short time until you have something better: *a stopgap measure to deal with the parking problem*

stop·light /ˈstɒplaɪt‖ˈstɑːp-/ *n* [C] *AmE* a set of red, yellow, and green lights used for controlling traffic; TRAFFIC LIGHT

stop·o·ver /ˈstɒpəʊvə‖ˈstɑːpoʊvər/ *n* [C] a short stop between parts of a journey, especially a long plane journey: *a three-hour stopover in Atlanta*

stop·page /ˈstɒpɪdʒ‖ˈstɑː-/ *n* [C] when people stop working as a protest

stop·per /ˈstɒpə‖ˈstɑːpər/ *n* [C] a piece of plastic, CORK etc that you put in the top of a bottle to close it

stop·watch /ˈstɒpwɒtʃ‖ˈstɑːpwɑːtʃ, -wɔːtʃ/ *n* [C] a watch used for measuring the exact time it takes to do something, especially a race or sports activity

stor·age /ˈstɔːrɪdʒ/ *n* [U] when things are kept somewhere until they are needed: *There's plenty of storage space in the garage.* | **be in storage** (=being stored in a place): *The furniture is in storage until we find a new house.*

store¹ /stɔː‖stɔːr/ *n* [C] **1** *especially AmE* a building or part of a building where goods are sold to the public; a shop. In American English, 'store' is used to mean any kind of shop. In British English, 'store' is used especially about large shops that sell a variety of goods: *a book store* | *I'm going to the store to get some milk.* | *She works in a clothes store.* → see also CHAIN STORE, DEPARTMENT STORE **2** a supply of something, especially something that you can use later: **+ of** *secret stores of weapons* **3 be in store** to be going to happen to someone in the future: *There's a surprise in store for you tomorrow!* **4 set great store by sth** to think that something is very important or useful

store² *v* [T] **1** also **store away** to put things away and keep them there until you need them: *All my old clothes are stored in the loft.* **2** to

keep facts or information in a computer: *You can store your files on this disk.*

store·keep·er /ˈstɔːˌkiːpə‖ˈstɔːr,kiːpər/ *n* [C] *AmE* someone who owns or is in charge of a shop; SHOPKEEPER *BrE*

store·room /ˈstɔːrʊm, -ruːm/ *n* [C] a room where goods are stored

sto·rey *BrE*, **story** *AmE* /ˈstɔːri/ *n* [C] a level of a building: *a five-storey house*

stork /stɔːk‖stɔːrk/ *n* [C] a tall white water bird with long legs and a long beak

storm¹ /stɔːm‖stɔːrm/ *n* **1** [C] very bad weather in which there is a lot of wind, rain, snow etc: *a snow storm* **2 a storm of protest/criticism/disapproval etc** when people disagree very strongly with something and react to it in an angry and excited way: *The mayor's speech caused a storm of protest among local people.* **3 take sth by storm** to suddenly become extremely successful and admired by a lot of people: *a new show that's taking Broadway by storm*

storm² *v* **1** [T] to attack a place and enter it with a lot of people, soldiers etc: *Enemy troops stormed the city.* **2** to walk somewhere in a way that shows you are very angry: **+ out of/off** *She stormed out of the meeting.*

storm·y /ˈstɔːmi‖ˈstɔːr-/ *adj* **1** when there is a lot of rain, or snow etc: *stormy weather* | *a stormy day* **2** a stormy relationship or situation is one in which people argue a lot with each other and have strong feelings

sto·ry /ˈstɔːri/ *n* [C] **1** a description of a series of real or imaginary events, which is told or written to entertain people: *a book of short stories* | *the story of Cinderella* | *a ghost story* | **tell/read sb a story** *Grandma used to tell us stories every night.* **2** a report in a newspaper or news programme about something that has happened: *a front-page story in the New York Times* **3 it's a long story** *spoken* used to say that something will take too long to explain: *It's a long story – I'll tell you later.* **4 to cut a long story short** *spoken* when you want to finish explaining something quickly: *To cut a long story short, she's leaving him.* **5** an explanation about something that happened, which may be untrue: *Do you believe his story?*

sto·ry·tell·er /ˈstɔːriˌtelə‖-ər/ *n* [C] someone who tells stories

stout¹ /staʊt/ *adj* **1** rather fat: *a stout middle-aged man* **2** stout shoes, branches etc are strong and thick **3** brave and determined: *a stout defence*

stout² *n* [U] a strong dark beer

stove /stəʊv‖stoʊv/ *n* [C] **1** a piece of kitchen equipment that you cook on; COOKER *BrE*: *She left a pan of milk on the stove and it boiled over.* → see picture at KITCHEN **2** a piece of equipment used for heating a room, which burns gas, wood, coal etc

stow /stəʊ‖stoʊ/ also **stow** sth ↔ **away** *v* [T] to put something away in a place until it is needed: *Please stow all your bags under your seat.*

stow·a·way /ˈstəʊəweɪ‖ˈstoʊ-/ *n* [C] someone who hides on a ship or plane in order to travel without paying

strad·dle /ˈstrædl/ *v* [T] **1** to sit or stand with your legs on either side of something: *He sat* *straddling the fence.* **2** to be on either side of a place: *The town straddles the River Oder.*

strag·gle /ˈstrægəl/ *v* [I] **1** to move much more slowly than the other members of a group, so that you remain behind them: *Runners were still straggling in hours after the winners had finished.* **2** to move, grow, or spread out in an untidy way in different directions: *thin black straggling hair*

strag·gly /ˈstrægəli/ *adj* growing or spreading out in an untidy, uneven way: *a straggly moustache*

a straight road across the desert

straight[1] /streɪt/ *adj* **1** not bent or curved: *a straight line* | *My sister has straight hair.* (=without curls) → see colour picture on page 244 **2** level or upright, and not bent or leaning: *Is this sign straight?* | *straight teeth* **3** honest and direct: *I wish you'd give me a straight answer.* **4** one after the other: *The Australian team won three straight victories.* **5 get straight A's** to get the GRADE 'A' in all of your school subjects **6** *informal* a straight person behaves in a way that a lot of people think is normal, but that you think is boring **7** if you drink an alcoholic drink straight, you drink it without any ice, water etc: *a straight Scotch* **8 get sth straight** *spoken* to make sure that you completely understand the true facts about a situation: *Let's get this straight. You don't want us to get married?* **9 put/set the record straight** to correct what has been said to show the true facts about a situation **10 to keep a straight face** to continue to have a serious expression on your face even though you want to laugh or smile: *How did you manage to keep a straight face?* **11** *informal* not HOMOSEXUAL

straight[2] *adv* **1** in a straight line: **+ down/in front of/out etc** *The truck was coming straight towards me.* | *She kept staring straight ahead.* **2** also **straight away** immediately or without delay: *Why didn't you go straight to the police?* | *Come home straight after school.* **3 sit up/stand up straight** to sit or stand with your body in an upright position **4 go straight** to stop being a criminal **5 tell sb straight/ straight out** to tell someone something clearly and honestly: *I told him straight what I thought of him.* **6 not see/think straight** to be unable to see or think clearly: *It was so noisy I could hardly think straight.*

straight·en /ˈstreɪtn/ *v* **1** [I,T] also **straighten out** to make something straight, or become straight: *He straightened his tie.* **2** [T] *especially AmE* also **straighten up** to clean a room that is untidy

   straighten out *phr v* **1** [T **straighten** sth ↔ **out**] to deal with a problem or difficult situation: *I'll talk to him and see if I can straighten things out.* **2** [I,T **straighten** sth ↔ **out**] to become straight or make something straight: *The path straightened out.*

   straighten up *phr v* [I] to stand with your back straight

straight·for·ward /ˌstreɪtˈfɔːwəd◂ ǁ-ˈfɔːrwərd◂/ *adj* **1** simple to do or easy to understand: *The questions are fairly straightforward.* **2** honest and not hiding what you think: *Is he being straightforward?*

straight·jack·et /ˈstreɪtˌdʒækɪt/ *n* [C] a STRAITJACKET

strain[1] /streɪn/ *n* **1** [C,U] when you feel worried because you are always too busy or always dealing with problems: *He couldn't cope with the strain of being a teacher.* **2** [C usually singular] a difficult situation in which a person or organization does not have enough time, money, workers etc to do something: **put a strain on sb/sth** (=make them be in a difficult situation): *The new taxation system has put a huge strain on small businesses.* **3** [U] when something is pulled or stretched very tightly or has to carry a lot of weight: *The rope snapped under the strain.* (=because of the strain) **4** [C,U] an injury caused by stretching a muscle or using part of your body too much: *eye strain* **5** [C] one of the different types of a disease or plant: *a new strain of the virus*

strain[2] *v* **1** [T] to injure part of your body by stretching it too much: *Kevin strained a muscle in his neck.* **2** [I,T] to try hard to do something, especially to hear or see something: **strain to do sth** *She moved closer, straining to hear what they said.* **3** [T] to make a situation or relationship more difficult: *It's one of the issues that is straining relations between the countries.* **4** [T] to separate solid things from a liquid by pouring the mixture through a strainer or cloth **5** [T] to make a person, country etc have to use too much of the money or other things that they have available, and cause problems: *The refugee crisis is straining the country's limited financial resources.*

strained /streɪnd/ *adj* **1** making you feel a little uncomfortable or nervous: *a strained conversation* **2** if relations between two people, countries etc are strained, they feel they cannot trust or be friendly to each other because of something that has happened **3** worried and tired: *Alex looks strained.*

strain·er /ˈstreɪnəǁ-ər/ *n* [C] a kitchen tool used for separating solid food from a liquid

strait /streɪt/ *n* [C usually plural] a narrow area of water that joins two larger areas of water: *the Straits of Gibraltar*

GRAMMAR NOTE: a or the (2)

Use **the** before a thing or person when it is clear which one you are talking about: *the old man who lives next door.* Use **a** or **an** to talk about a person or thing when it is not important to say which one: *I went out to buy a newspaper.* | *A girl in my class told me about it.*

strait·jack·et /'streɪt,dʒækɪ̯t/ *n* [C] a special piece of clothing for violent or mentally ill people that prevents them from moving their arms

straits /streɪts/ *n* **in dire/desperate straits** in an extremely difficult situation, for example because of not having enough money

strand /strænd/ *n* [C] **1** a single thin piece of thread, hair, wire etc **2** one part of a story, problem, idea etc

strand·ed /'strændɪd/ *adj* unable to get away from a place: *I was stranded at the airport without any money.*

strange /streɪndʒ/ *adj* **1** unusual, surprising, or difficult to understand: *I had a strange dream last night.* | **+ that** *It's strange that Brad isn't here yet.* | **that's strange** *That's strange – I thought I left my keys on the table.* **2** unusual in a way that makes you feel frightened or nervous: *There was something strange about him.* **3** not familiar: *I was all alone in a strange country.* —**strangely** *adv*: *She was looking at me very strangely.* —**strangeness** *n* [U]

strang·er /'streɪndʒəll-ər/ *n* [C] **1** someone you do not know: *Mom told us never to talk to strangers.* **2** someone in a new and unfamiliar place or situation: *a stranger to New York*

stran·gle /'stræŋgəl/ *v* [T] **1** to kill someone by tightly pressing their throat with your hands, a rope etc **2** to completely prevent something from developing —**strangulation** /ˌstræŋgjʊ̩-'leɪʃən/ *n* [U]

stran·gle·hold /'stræŋgəlhəʊldll-hoʊld/ *n* [C] complete control over something so that it cannot develop or people cannot do what they want: **+ on** *The government had a stranglehold on the media.*

strap[1] /stræp/ *n* [C] a strong band of cloth or leather used to fasten something onto another thing or to carry something: *a watch-strap* | *The strap on her bag had broken.*

strap[2] *v* [T] **-pped, -pping** to fasten to a place using one or more straps: *Make sure your backpack is strapped on tightly.*

strapped /stræpt/ *adj* **strapped (for cash)** *informal* having very little money to spend

stra·ta /'strɑːtəll'streɪtə/ *n* the plural of STRATUM

strat·a·gem /'strætədʒəm/ *n* [C] a trick or plan used for deceiving an enemy or getting an advantage

stra·te·gic /strə'tiːdʒɪk/ *adj* **1** done as part of a military, business, or political plan: *The takeover is being seen as a strategic move by Microsoft.* **2** connected with fighting wars against other countries: *strategic weapons* (=powerful weapons used for attacking other countries) **3** a strategic position or place is very effective or useful for doing something: *He placed himself in a strategic position next to the door.* —**strategically** /-kli/ *adv*

strat·e·gy /'strætɪdʒi/ *n* **1** [C] a set of plans used to achieve something or to help you be successful: *the President's long-term economic strategy* **2** [U] the skill of making plans so that you are successful, especially in a war: *an expert in military strategy* —**strategist** *n* [C]

strat·os·phere /'strætsfɪəll-sfɪr/ *n* **the stratosphere** the part of the Earth's ATMOSPHERE that starts about 6 miles above the Earth

stra·tum /'strɑːtəmll'streɪ-/ *n* [C], *plural* **strata** /-tə/ *formal* **1** a layer of rock or soil **2** a social class in society

straw /strɔːllstrɒː/ *n* **1** [U] dried stems of wheat or similar plants, used for animals to sleep on or for making things such as baskets: *a straw hat* **2** [C] a thin dried stem of wheat, rice etc **3** a thin tube of plastic used for sucking a drink from a bottle or cup **4** **the last/final straw** the last problem in a series of problems that makes you finally give up or become angry

straw·ber·ry /'strɔːbərill'strɒːberi, -bəri/ *n* [C] a small red juicy fruit that grows on plants near the ground: *strawberries and cream*

stray[1] /streɪ/ *v* [I] to move away from a safe or familiar area without intending to: *The kitten had strayed from its mother.*

stray[2] *adj* **1** a stray animal is lost or has no home: *a stray dog* **2** a stray piece of something has become separated from the rest of it: *a few stray hairs*

stray[3] *n* [C] an animal that is lost or has no home

streak[1] /striːk/ *n* [C] **1** a thin coloured line or thin mark: *a few grey streaks in her hair* **2** a quality that seems different from the rest of your character: *Richard has a wild streak in him.* **3** **a winning/losing streak** a period when you are always successful or always unsuccessful: *Our team was on a winning streak.* —**streaky** *adj*

streak[2] *v* **1** [I] to move or run very quickly: *A fighter jet streaked across the sky.* **2** **be streaked with sth** to be covered with thin lines of a particular colour or substance: *Marcia's face was streaked with sweat.*

stream[1] /striːm/ *n* [C] **1** a very small river: *a mountain stream* ➡ see colour picture on page 243 **2** a long continuous series of people or vehicles: *a stream of traffic* **3** a series of things of the same kind that happen one after the other: *a stream of questions* | *a stream of ideas* **4** an area of moving liquid, gas, smoke etc: *a stream of warm air*

stream[2] *v* [I] to move or flow quickly and continuously in one direction, especially in large amounts: *Tears were streaming down his cheeks.* | *People streamed through the gates.*

stream·er /'striːməll-ər/ *n* [C] a long narrow flag or piece of coloured paper used as a decoration at a party or celebration

stream·line /'striːmlaɪn/ *v* [T] **1** to make something such as a business or process become simple and effective: *The hospital has streamlined the paperwork for doctors.* **2** to make something have a smooth shape so that it moves easily through the air or water —**streamlined** *adj*: *streamlined trains*

street /striːt/ *n* [C] **1** a road in a town or city with houses, shops etc on one or both sides: *What street do you live on?* | *the corner of Main Street and 4th Avenue* **2** **streets ahead** *BrE informal* much better than someone or something else: *The Scandinavian countries are streets ahead when it comes to welfare services.* **3** **be right up your street** *informal* to be the kind of subject that you are very interested in, or the kind of job that you are very suitable for ➡ see also **the man in the street** (MAN[1])

street·car /'striːtkɑːǁ-kɑːr/ *n* [C] *especially AmE* an electric bus that moves along metal tracks in the road; TRAM *BrE*

street light, **street·light** /'striːtlaɪt/ *n* [C] a light on a long pole that stands next to a street → see colour picture on page 79

strength /streŋθ, streŋθ/ *n* **1** [U] physical power and energy: *I didn't have the strength to get up. | They pushed with all their strength.* **2** [U] the power of an organization, country, or system: *US military strength* **3** [U] how strong a feeling, belief, or relationship is: **strength of feeling** *The president was wrong to ignore the strength of feeling in the country over this issue.* **4** [C] a quality or ability that makes someone or something successful and effective: *His ambition is both a strength and a weakness.* **5** [U] the quality of being brave or determined in dealing with difficult situations: *moral strength* | **strength of character** (=ability to deal well with difficult situations) **6** [C,U] how strong a liquid such as an alcoholic drink, medicine etc is: *high-strength beers* **7** [U] the value of a type of money compared to others: *the strength of the dollar* **8** **go from strength to strength** become more and more successful: *In the last decade, his career has gone from strength to strength.* **9** **on the strength of sth** because of information that you have or because of someone's advice **10** **at full strength/below strength** having all the people, good players etc that you need or usually have, or having less than this: *The French team are at full strength.* → compare WEAKNESS

strength·en /'streŋθən, 'streŋθən/ *v* [I,T] to make something stronger or become stronger: *an exercise to strengthen your arms | Extra supports were needed to strengthen the bridge. | The new laws strengthened the position of women in the workplace.* → opposite WEAKEN

stren·u·ous /'strenjuəs/ *adj* using a lot of effort or strength: *strenuous exercise | He made strenuous efforts to persuade them to change their minds.* — **strenuously** *adv*

stress[1] /stres/ *n* **1** [C,U] continuous feelings of worry about your work or personal life that prevent you from relaxing: *Headaches are often caused by stress.* | **be under stress** *She's been under a lot of stress at work lately.* | **stresses and strains** *the stresses and strains of modern life* **2** [U] special attention or importance given to something; EMPHASIS: **lay stress on** *In his report, he laid stress on the need for more training.* **3** [C,U] physical force or pressure on something: *rocks subjected to stress and high temperatures* **4** [C,U] the force or loudness with which you say a part of a word, play a note of music etc: *The stress is on the last syllable.*

stress[2] *v* [T] **1** to emphasize a statement, fact, or idea: *She stressed the need for more money for the programme.* **2** [T] to say a word or part of a word more loudly or with more force than the

other words **3** [I] *AmE spoken* to become stressed: *Terry's stressing about her interview tomorrow.*

stressed /strest/ also **stressed out** /ˌ ·ˈ· / *adj* so worried and tired that you cannot relax: *You look really stressed out. What's the matter?*

stress·ful /'stresfəl/ *adj* making you very worried and unable to relax: *a stressful job | Teaching can be very stressful.*

stretch[1] /stretʃ/ *v* **1** [I,T] to become bigger or looser as a result of being pulled, or make something do this by pulling it: *Don't worry if the shoes feel a bit tight, they'll soon stretch. | Stretch the canvas so that it covers the whole frame* **2** [I,T] to straighten your arms, legs, or body to full length: *He stretched out his arms to try and reach the branch. | If I stretch up I can touch the ceiling.* → see colour picture on page 670 **3** [I] to spread out over a large area: *The desert stretched to the horizon.* **4** [I] to continue for a long period: *The project will probably stretch into next year.* **5** [T] to pull something so it is tight: *We can stretch a rope between two trees.* **6** **stretch sth to the limit** to use as much of a supply of something as is available, without having enough for anything else: *Our resources are already stretched to the limit.* **7** **stretch your legs** *informal* to go for a walk

stretch out *phr v* **1** [I] *informal* to lie down so you can rest or sleep: *I think I'll stretch out on the couch for a while.* **2** [T] to put out your hand, foot etc in order to reach something

stretch[2] *n* [C] **1** an area of land or water: *a dangerous stretch of road* **2** a continuous period of time: **at a stretch** (=without stopping): *During the summer we worked twelve hours at a stretch.* **3** the action of stretching part of your body **4** **not by any stretch (of the imagination)** *spoken* used to say that something is definitely not true: *She isn't fat, not by any stretch of the imagination.*

stretch·er /'stretʃəǁ-ər/ *n* [C] a covered frame on which you carry someone who is too injured or ill to walk

strew /struː/ *v* [T] **strewed**, **strewn** /struːn/ *or* **strewed**, **strewing** to throw or drop a lot of things over an area in an untidy way: *Papers were strewn all over the floor.*

strick·en /'strɪkən/ *adj formal* suffering the bad effects of trouble, illness, sadness etc: *a patient suddenly stricken with flu* → see also POVERTY-STRICKEN

strict /strɪkt/ *adj* **1** a strict person makes sure that people always obey rules and do exactly what they say, and does not let people behave badly: *Her parents are very strict.* **2** a strict rule, order etc must be obeyed completely: *I have strict instructions not to let you leave the building.* **3** always behaving according to a particular set of: *a strict vegetarian* **4** very exact and correct: *It's not a restaurant in the strictest sense of the word – it's more like a cafe.*

strict·ly /'strɪktli/ *adv* **1** exactly and correctly: *That is not strictly true.* | **strictly speaking** (=used when you are explaining something in a very exact or correct way): *Strictly speaking, a spider is not an insect.* **2** used to emphasize that something is only done for a particular purpose or by a particular person etc: *She says she drinks wine strictly for health reasons.* **3** **strictly**

prohibited/forbidden used to emphasize that something is definitely not allowed: *Smoking is strictly forbidden throughout the building.* **4** in a strict way: *The children were brought up very strictly.*

stride[1] /straɪd/ *v* [I] **strode** /strəʊd‖stroʊd/, **stridden** /'strɪdn/, **striding** to walk with quick long steps: *He strode across the room.*

stride[2] *n* [C] **1** a long step that you take when you walk **2 make great strides** to develop or make progress quickly: *The city has made great strides in cleaning up its streets.* **3 take sth in your stride** to deal with a problem calmly without becoming annoyed or upset

stri·dent /'straɪdənt/ *adj* **1** expressing opinions in a very determined and noticeable way, especially in a way that other people disapprove of: *a strident critic of the reforms* **2** loud and unpleasant: *the teacher's strident voice* — **stridently** *adv*

strife /straɪf/ *n* [U] *formal* trouble or disagreement between two people or groups; CONFLICT

strike[1] /straɪk/ *v* **struck** /strʌk/ **struck, striking 1** [T] to hit someone or something: *He was struck on the head by a falling rock.* | *The car struck a tree.* | *She struck him across the face.* | *Lightning rarely strikes the same place twice.* **2** [T] if a thought or idea strikes you, you suddenly realize it or think of it: **it strikes sb (that)** *It suddenly struck me that he might be lying.* | **be struck by sth** (=something seems surprising, noticeable, interesting etc to you): *I was struck by her honesty.* **3** to seem to someone to have a particular quality: **strike sb as sth** *He strikes me as being very intelligent.* **4** [I] to stop working for a period of time because you want better pay, better working conditions etc: **+ for** *They're striking for a shorter working week.* **5** [I] to attack quickly and suddenly: *The police are waiting for the killer to strike again.* **6** [T] if something very bad strikes someone or something, it affects them: *The town was struck by an earthquake.* **7 strike a balance** to give the correct amount of attention or importance to two different things: *It's never easy to strike a balance between work and family.* **8 strike a deal** to agree to do something if someone else does something for you: *The dispute ended when the company struck a deal with the union.* **9 strike a match** to make a match start burning **10 strike oil/gold etc** to discover oil, gold etc under the ground **11** [I,T] if a clock strikes, its bell makes a number of sounds to show the time: *The clock struck four.* (=it showed the time was four o'clock) **12 strike a chord with sb** to make people agree or feel sympathy with you **13 within striking distance** very close to something or near to achieving something

strike back *phr v* [I] to attack someone or something after they have attacked you

strike out *phr v* **1** [T **strike** sth ↔ **out**] to remove part of a piece of writing by drawing a line through it **2** [I] to try to reach somewhere: **+ for** *They struck out for the coast.* **3 strike out on your own** to start doing something new without other people's help **4** [I] to try to hit someone: **+ at** *She suddenly struck out at him for no reason.* **5** [I,T] if you are struck out in BASEBALL, you are not allowed to continue because you have already had three attempts to hit the ball

strike up *phr v* [T] **1 strike up a conversation/friendship etc** to begin a conversation, friendship etc with someone **2** [T] to begin to play or sing something: *The band struck up an Irish tune.*

strike[2] *n* [C] **1** when a group of workers stop working for a period of time in order to get better pay, better working conditions etc: **go on strike** *The union decided to go on strike.* **2** a military attack: *threats of an air strike* **3** an attempt to hit or throw the ball in BASEBALL that fails

strik·er /'straɪkəll-ər/ *n* [C] **1** someone who is not at work because they are on STRIKE **2** a football player whose main job is to try to get GOALS

strik·ing /'straɪkɪŋ/ *adj* **1** unusual and noticeable: *There's a striking similarity between the two girls.* **2** very attractive, often in an unusual way: *a man with striking good looks*

string[1] /strɪŋ/ *n* **1** [C,U] a thin rope made of several threads twisted together, used for tying things: *The package was tied up with string.* **2** [C] a set of things connected together on a thread: *a string of onions* | *a string of beads* **3 a string of sth** a number of similar things or events that happen one after the other: *The police asked me a string of questions.* **4** [C] one of the long thin pieces of wire that is stretched across a musical instrument to produce sound **5 (with) no strings attached** with no special conditions or limits: *He asked me to go to Vegas with him — with no strings attached.* ➔ see also STRINGS, **pull strings** (PULL[1])

string[2] *v* [T] **strung** /strʌŋ/, **strung, stringing** to join things together using string, or hang up decorations in this way: *Dad was busy stringing up the Christmas lights.* ➔ see also STRUNG-OUT

string sb **along** *phr v* [T] *informal* to continue to promise to do something that you do not intend to do: *Jerry's been stringing her along for years — he'll never marry her.*

string out *phr v* **be strung out** to be spread out in a long line

string sth ↔ **together** *phr v* [T] to put words or sentences together and speak sensibly

stringed in·stru·ment /ˌ. '.../ *n* [C] a musical instrument that produces sound from strings, for example a VIOLIN

strin·gent /'strɪndʒənt/ *adj* **stringent** rules, laws, conditions etc are very strict or severe: *stringent laboratory conditions*

strings /strɪŋz/ *n* **the strings** [plural] the people in an ORCHESTRA who play instruments such as the VIOLIN or the CELLO

strip[1] /strɪp/ *v* **-pped, -pping 1** [I,T] also **strip off** to take off your clothes, or take someone else's clothes off: *He stripped and got into the shower.* **2** [T] also **strip off** to remove something that is covering the surface of something else: *It took all day to strip the paint off the walls.* **3 strip sb of sth** to take something important away from someone, especially their possessions, rank, or property

strip[2] *n* [C] **1** a long narrow piece of cloth, paper etc: *Tear the paper into one-inch strips.* **2** a long narrow area of land or water: *a strip of sand*

stripe /straɪp/ *n* [C] a long narrow area of colour: *a shirt with blue and red stripes*

striped /straɪpt/ adj having a pattern of stripes: *a blue and white striped shirt* → see colour picture on page 114

strip·ey /ˈstraɪpi/ adj STRIPY

strip·per /ˈstrɪpəl-ər/ n [C] someone who is paid to take off their clothes in a sexually exciting way

strip·tease /ˈstrɪptiːz, ˌstrɪpˈtiːz/ n [C,U] a performance in which someone takes off their clothes in a sexually exciting way

strip·y, stripey /ˈstraɪpi/ adj having a pattern of stripes: *stripy socks*

strive /straɪv/ v [I] **strove** /strəʊvǁstroʊv/, **striven** /ˈstrɪvən/, **striving** formal to try very hard to get or do something: **+ for** *Ross is constantly striving for perfection.*

strode /strəʊdǁstroʊd/ v the past tense of STRIDE

stroke[1] /strəʊkǁstroʊk/ n **1** [C] a sudden illness in which an ARTERY in your brain BURSTS or becomes blocked, and which often makes you unable to move part of your body: **have a stroke** *Since Tom had a stroke he's had trouble talking.* **2** [C,U] a way of swimming: *back stroke* **3** **stroke of luck** something lucky that happens to you: *By some stroke of luck, we got the last hotel room.* **4** [C] a single movement of a pen or brush, or a line made by doing this **5** **not do a stroke (of work)** informal to not do any work at all **6** **at a stroke/at one stroke** with a single sudden action: *The problem was solved at a stroke.*

stroke[2] v [T] to move your hand gently over something: *She stroked the baby's face.* → see colour picture on page 473   **stroke**

stroll /strəʊlǁstroʊl/ v [I] to walk in a slow relaxed way: *We strolled along the beach.* —**stroll** n [C]

stroll·er /ˈstrəʊləl ˈstroʊlər/ n [C] AmE a chair on wheels in which a small child sits and is pushed along; BUGGY BrE

strong /strɒŋǁstrɔːŋ/ adj **1** someone who is strong has big muscles and is able to lift heavy things, do hard physical work etc: *It took four strong men to lift the piano.|strong hands* **2** not easily broken or damaged: *a strong rope|The bags are made of strong black plastic.* **3** having a lot of power, or using your power firmly to control what happens: *strong leadership|a strong army* **4** strong feelings, beliefs or opinions are ones that affect you a lot of that you think are very important: *Lewis had a strong belief in God.|a strong temptation* **5** a strong taste or smell is one that you notice easily: *strong coffee|a strong smell of gas* **6** containing a lot of alcohol: *strong liquor* **7** strong reasons, evidence etc show clearly that something is true: *There's strong evidence to suggest Bentley was innocent.* **8** a strong friendship or relationship is likely to last a long time: *A strong bond devel-*

oped between the two men. **9** able to deal with problems without becoming too upset or worried by them: *Do you think he's strong enough to cope with living abroad on his own?* **10** if there is a strong chance or possibility of something happening, it is very likely to happen: *There's a strong possibility that the US will attack.* **11** strong winds, currents etc have a powerful effect and move quickly **12** **strong language** rude words that some people may find offensive **13** **strong point** something that someone is good at, or a good quality that someone has: *Tact was never her strong point.* **14** **500/10,000 etc strong** having 500, 10,000 etc people: *By now the crowd was over 100,000 strong.* **15** **be still going strong** to continue to be active or successful, even after a long time: *The Rolling Stones are still going strong.* → see also STRENGTH

strong·hold /ˈstrɒŋhəʊldǁˈstrɔːŋhoʊld/ n [C] **1** an area where there is a lot of support for a particular political party, attitude etc: *a Republican Party stronghold* **2** an area that is strongly defended: *a rebel stronghold*

strong·ly /ˈstrɒŋliǁˈstrɔːŋ-/ adv **1** if you believe something strongly, you think it is important or care a lot about it **2** tasting or smelling of something very noticeable: *The house smelled strongly of gas.* **3** used to emphasize that someone should seriously consider what you are saying to them: *I strongly advise you to get more facts before deciding.*

strong-willed /ˌ. ˈ.◂ / adj determined to do what you want, even though other people tell you not to do it: *a strong-willed child*

strop·py /ˈstrɒpiǁˈstrɑːpi/ adj BrE informal angry or easily annoyed —**stroppily** adv

strove /strəʊvǁstroʊv/ v the past tense of STRIVE

struck /strʌk/ v the past tense of STRIKE

struc·tur·al /ˈstrʌktʃərəl/ adj relating to the structure of something: *structural damage to the aircraft*

struc·ture[1] /ˈstrʌktʃəl-ər/ n **1** [C,U] the way in which the parts of something are organized and are related to each other: *the structure of society|molecular structure* **2** [C] something that has been built: *a huge steel structure*

structure[2] v [T] to arrange something carefully in an organized way: *Students learn how to structure their essays.*

strug·gle[1] /ˈstrʌɡəl/ v [I] **1** to try very hard to achieve something that is difficult to do: **struggle to do sth** *After Hal lost his job we had to struggle to pay the bills.* **2** to fight someone who is attacking or holding you: **+ with** *She struggled with the man and screamed for help.* **3** to move somewhere with a lot of difficulty: *He struggled up the stairs with the luggage.*

struggle on phr v [I] to continue doing something, even though it is difficult

struggle[2] n [C] **1** when someone tries hard for a long time to achieve something: *Nelson Mandela's struggle for freedom* **2** a fight between two people

strum /strʌm/ *v* [I,T] **-mmed, -mming** to play an instrument such as a GUITAR by moving your fingers across the strings

strung /strʌŋ/ *v* the past tense and past participle of STRING

strung-out /ˌ. '. ◂ / *adj informal* badly affected by a drug so that you cannot think or behave normally

strut[1] /strʌt/ *v* [I] **-tted, -tting** to walk in a proud way that annoys other people

strut[2] *n* [C] a long thin piece of metal or wood used for supporting a part of a bridge, the wing of an aircraft etc

stub[1] /stʌb/ *n* [C] the part of a cigarette or pencil that is left after the rest has been used

stub[2] *v* **stub your toe** to hurt your toe by hitting it against something
stub sth ↔ **out** *phr v* [T] to stop a cigarette burning by pressing it against something

stub·ble /ˈstʌbəl/ *n* [U] **1** the very short hairs on a man's face when he has not shaved (SHAVE) → see colour picture on page 244 **2** short pieces of corn, wheat etc left in a field after it has been cut — **stubbly** *adj*

stub·born /ˈstʌbən‖-bərn/ *adj* refusing to change your opinions, beliefs etc because you are sure you are right: *a stubborn woman* — **stubbornly** *adv* — **stubbornness** *n* [U]

stub·by /ˈstʌbi/ *adj* short and thick or fat: *stubby fingers*

stuck[1] /stʌk/ *v* the past tense and past participle of STICK

stuck[2] *adj* [not before noun] **1** not able to move: **get stuck** *Our car got stuck in the mud.* **2** not able to continue with work because it is too difficult: *Can you help me with this? I'm stuck.* **3** not able to get away from a boring or unpleasant situation: *It's horrible being stuck in a classroom when the weather's so nice.*

stud /stʌd/ *n* **1** [C] a small round piece of metal stuck into the surface of something as a decoration, or onto the bottom of a shoe to stop you from sliding: *a leather jacket with silver studs* **2** [C] a small round EARRING **3** [C,U] a number of horses or other animals kept for breeding (BREED): *a stud farm*

stud·ded /ˈstʌdɪd/ *adj* decorated with a lot of studs or jewels: *a bracelet studded with diamonds* → see also STAR-STUDDED

stu·dent /ˈstjuːdənt‖ˈstuː-/ *n* [C] someone who studies at a school, university etc: *a medical student* | *She has 30 students in her class.* → see colour picture on page 80

stu·di·o /ˈstjuːdiəʊ‖ˈstuːdioʊ/ *n* [C] **1** a room where a painter or photographer works: *an art studio* **2** a room where television and radio programmes are made **3** a film company, or the place where films are made: *the big Hollywood studios*

stu·di·ous /ˈstjuːdiəs‖ˈstuː-/ *adj* spending a lot of time reading and studying

stu·di·ous·ly /ˈstjuːdiəsli‖ˈstuː-/ *adv* carefully making sure that you do something

stud·y[1] /ˈstʌdi/ *n* **1** [C] a piece of work that someone does to find out more about something: **+ of** *a study of teenagers' language* **2** [U] when you study something: *a period of study* **3** **studies** [plural] **a)** the subjects that you study: *a degree in Business Studies* **b)** the work

you do as a student: *He went on to continue his studies at Harvard.* **4** [C] a room in your house where you read, write or study

study[2] *v* **1** [I,T] to spend time learning about a subject: *Her son's at university studying medicine.* **2** [T] to look at something carefully to find out more about it: *He studied the document carefully.*

stuff[1] /stʌf/ *n* [U] *informal* **1** a substance or material of any sort: *What's this stuff on the floor?* **2** several different things, used when you want to talk about them in general: *I need a place to store my stuff for a while.* | *Have you got a lot of stuff to do this weekend?*

stuff[2] *v* [T] **1** to push things into a small space quickly: **stuff** sth **into/behind etc** *She stuffed some clothes into a bag and left.* **2** to fill something with a soft material until it is full: *a pillow stuffed with feathers* **3** **stuff yourself** *informal* to eat a lot of food: *The kids have been stuffing themselves all afternoon.* **4** to fill a chicken, vegetable etc with a mixture of food before cooking it **5** to fill the body of a dead animal with a special substance in order to preserve it and make it look alive

stuff·ing /ˈstʌfɪŋ/ *n* [U] **1** a mixture of food that you put inside a chicken etc before cooking it **2** material that is used to fill something such as a PILLOW

stuff·y /ˈstʌfi/ *adj* **1** a room or building that is stuffy does not have enough fresh air in it **2** boring and old-fashioned: *Rob's family is really stuffy.*

stum·ble /ˈstʌmbəl/ *v* [I] **1** to almost fall while you are walking: *She stumbled and grabbed hold of the handrail.* **2** to stop or make a mistake when you are making a speech, reading to people etc: **+ over** *He continued his speech nervously, hesitating and stumbling over the words.*
stumble on/across sb/sth *phr v* [T] to find something or someone that you did not expect to find: *Clearing out a cupboard that evening, she stumbled across one of her old diaries.*

stumbling block /ˈ.. ˌ./ *n* [C] a problem that stops you achieving something: *The question of disarmament is still the main stumbling block to peace.*

stump[1] /stʌmp/ *n* [C] the part of something that is left when the rest has been cut off: *an old tree stump*

stump[2] *v* **1** [I] to walk with very firm heavy steps: **+ along/down etc** *He turned and stumped back into the house.* **2** [T] to ask someone a question that they are unable to answer: *Many students were stumped by questions on the written paper.*
stump up *phr v* [I,T] *BrE informal* to pay money, especially when you do not want to: *I'm not stumping up £1000 just to join a golf club!*

stun /stʌn/ *v* [T] **-nned, -nning** **1** to surprise or shock someone so much that they do not react: *Everyone was stunned by Betty's answer.* **2** to make someone unconscious for a short time by hitting them on the head

stung /stʌŋ/ *v* the past tense and past participle of STING

stunk /stʌŋk/ *v* the past participle of STINK

stun·ning /ˈstʌnɪŋ/ *adj* **1** extremely attractive or beautiful: *You look stunning in that dress.* **2** very surprising or shocking: *stunning news*

stunt¹ /stʌnt/ *n* [C] **1** a dangerous action that someone does to entertain people, especially in a film **2** something that is done to get people's attention: *a publicity stunt*

stunt² *v* [T] to stop something or someone from growing or developing properly: *The plant's growth was stunted by lack of light.*

stu·pe·fied /ˈstjuːpɪˌfaɪd‖ˈstuː-/ *adj* so surprised or bored that you cannot think clearly — **stupefy** *v* [T] — **stupefying** *adj*

stu·pen·dous /stjuːˈpendəs‖stuː-/ *adj* extremely large or impressive: *a stupendous achievement*

stu·pid /ˈstjuːpɪd‖ˈstuː-/ *adj* **1** not intelligent or sensible: *How could you be so stupid?* | *a stupid mistake* **2** *spoken* used to talk about something that annoys you: *I can't get this stupid door open!* — **stupidity** /stjuːˈpɪdɪti‖stuː-/ *n* [C,U]

stu·por /ˈstjuːpə‖ˈstuːpər/ *n* [C,U] when you are almost unconscious and cannot think clearly, especially because you are drunk: *a drunken stupor*

stur·dy /ˈstɜːdi‖ˈstɜːr-/ *adj* strong and not likely to break or be hurt: *sturdy shoes* | *a sturdy woman* — **sturdily** *adv*

stut·ter /ˈstʌtə‖-ər/ *v* [I,T] to have difficulty speaking so that you repeat the first sound of a word: *"I w-w-want to g-g-go too," he stuttered.* — **stutter** *n* [singular]

sty /staɪ/ *n* [C] **1** a PIGSTY **2** also **stye** an infection at the edge of your EYELID

style¹ /staɪl/ *n* **1** [C] a way of doing or making something that is typical of a particular person, group, or period: *He's trying to copy Picasso's style of painting.* | *architecture in the Gothic style* | *Mandela's style of leadership* | *'70s styles are coming back into fashion* **2** [C,U] the fashion or design of something, especially clothes, hair, or furniture: *Shoes are available in several styles.* | *His hair was cut in a very strange style.* **3** [U] a quality that people admire or think is attractive: **have style** *You may not like him, but you have to admit that he has style.*

style² *v* [T] **1** to cut someone's hair in a particular way **2** **be styled** to be designed or made in a particular way

styl·ish /ˈstaɪlɪʃ/ *adj* attractive in a fashionable way: *a very stylish woman* | *stylish clothes* — **stylishly** *adv*

styl·is·tic /staɪˈlɪstɪk/ *adj* relating to the style of a piece of writing, music, or art: *I've made a few stylistic changes to your report.*

sty·lized (also **-ised** *BrE*) /ˈstaɪlaɪzd/ *adj* done in a style that is not natural or like real life: *stylized paintings*

suave /swɑːv/ *adj* polite, attractive, and confident, especially in a way that is not sincere

sub /sʌb/ *n* [C] **1** a SUBMARINE **2** a SUBSTITUTE **3** *AmE* a large long SANDWICH

sub- /sʌb/ *prefix* **1** used at the beginning of some words to mean 'under' or 'below': *subzero temperatures* **2** used at the beginning of some words to mean 'less important', or 'part of a larger thing': *subcommittee*

sub·con·scious¹ /sʌbˈkɒnʃəs‖-ˈkɑːn-/ *adj* subconscious feelings affect your behaviour although you do not realize that they exist: *a subconscious fear of failure* — **subconsciously** *adv*

subconscious² *n* [singular] the part of your mind that has thoughts and feelings that you do not realize exist, but which influence your behaviour

sub·con·ti·nent /sʌbˈkɒntɪˌnənt‖-ˈkɑːn-/ *n* [C] a large area of land that forms part of a CONTINENT: *the Indian subcontinent*

sub·cul·ture /ˈsʌbˌkʌltʃə‖-ər/ *n* [C] the behaviour, beliefs, activities etc of a group of people that are different from the rest of the society: *the drug subculture*

sub·di·vide /ˌsʌbdɪˈvaɪd/ *v* [T] to divide something into smaller parts — **subdivision** /-ˈvɪʒən/ *n* [C,U]

sub·due /səbˈdjuː‖-ˈduː-/ *v* [T] to stop someone from behaving violently, especially by using force: *The nurses were trying to subdue a violent patient.*

sub·dued /səbˈdjuːd‖-ˈduːd/ *adj* **1** someone who is subdued is quiet because they are sad or worried: *Lawrie's been very subdued all week.* **2** not as bright or loud as usual: *subdued lighting* | *subdued colours*

sub·ject¹ /ˈsʌbdʒɪkt/ *n* [C] **1** something that you are talking or writing about: *She's written several books on the subject.* | **change the subject** (=talk about something else): *Stop trying to change the subject!* **2** something that you study at a school or university: *"What's your favourite subject?" "Science."* **3** the word that usually comes before the verb in a sentence and shows who is doing the action of the verb. In the sentence 'Jean loves cats', 'Jean' is the subject. **4** a person or animal that is used in a test or EXPERIMENT **5** someone who is from a country that has a king or queen

subject² *adj* **subject to sth a)** likely to be affected by something: *All prices are subject to change.* **b)** only happening if something else happens: *We're going to build a garage, subject to planning permission.*

sub·ject³ /səbˈdʒekt/ *v*
subject sb/sth to sth *phr v* [T] to make someone or something experience something unpleasant: *The victim was subjected to a terrifying ordeal.*

sub·jec·tive /səbˈdʒektɪv/ *adj* influenced by your own opinions and feelings rather than facts → compare OBJECTIVE²

subject mat·ter /ˈ.. ˌ../ *n* [U] the things that are being written about, talked about, or shown in a book, speech, film etc

sub·ju·gate /ˈsʌbdʒʊɡeɪt/ *v* [T] *formal* to force a person or group to obey you — **subjugation** /ˌsʌbdʒʊˈɡeɪʃən/ *n* [U]

sub·junc·tive /səbˈdʒʌŋktɪv/ *n* [singular] a verb form used to express doubt, wish or possibility. In the sentence 'He suggested we leave early', 'leave' is the subjunctive

sub·let /sʌbˈlet/ *v* [I,T] **-tted, -tting** to take rent from someone for a room, house etc that you rent from someone else: *I'm subletting the room for the summer.*

sub·lime /səˈblaɪm/ *adj* excellent and making you feel very happy: *a sublime view of the mountains*

S

sub·ma·rine /ˈsʌbməriːn, ˌsʌbməˈriːn/ *n* [C] a ship that can travel under water

sub·merge /səbˈmɜːdʒ‖-ˈmɜːrdʒ/ *v* [I,T] to go or put something below the surface of water: *Whole villages were submerged by the flood.* —**submerged** *adj* —**submersion** /-ˈmɜːʃən‖-ˈmɜːr-ʒən/ *n* [U]

sub·mis·sion /səbˈmɪʃən/ *n* **1** [U] when you accept that someone else has power over you: *The prisoners were starved into submission.* **2** [C,U] when you give a document such as a legal contract to someone so that they can consider or approve it, or the document itself

sub·mis·sive /səbˈmɪsɪv/ *adj* someone who is submissive always does what they are told to do

sub·mit /səbˈmɪt/ *v* **-tted, -tting 1** [T] to formally send something in writing to someone for them to consider: *They submitted a report calling for changes in the law.* **2** [I,T] to do what someone else tells you to, especially because you have no choice: **+ to** *They were forced to submit to the kidnappers' demands.* | **submit yourself to** *John submitted himself to the first of many body searches.*

sub·or·di·nate[1] /səˈbɔːdɪnət‖-ˈbɔːr-/ *n* [C] *formal* someone who has a less important job than someone else in an organization

subordinate[2] *adj formal* less important than something else, or having a lower rank or less authority: *a subordinate position*

sub·or·di·nate[3] /səˈbɔːdɪneɪt‖-ˈbɔːr-/ *v* [T] *formal* to put someone or something in a subordinate position —**subordination** /səˌbɔːdɪˈneɪʃən‖ˌbɔːr-/ *n* [U]

sub·poe·na /səˈpiːnə, səb-/ *n* [C] *law* a legal document that orders someone to attend a TRIAL in a law court

sub·scribe /səbˈskraɪb/ *v* [I] to pay money so that a newspaper or magazine is regularly sent to you: **+ to** *What magazines do you subscribe to?* —**subscriber** *n* [C]

subscribe to sth *phr v* [T] to agree with or support an idea, opinion etc

sub·scrip·tion /səbˈskrɪpʃən/ *n* [C] an amount of money that you pay to regularly get a newspaper or magazine, or to belong to an organization

sub·se·quent /ˈsʌbsɪkwənt/ *adj* [only before a noun] *formal* coming after something else: *The accident had a subsequent effect on his long-term health.* —**subsequently** *adv*

sub·ser·vi·ent /səbˈsɜːviənt‖-ˈsɜːr-/ *adj* too willing to do what other people want you to do —**subservience** *n* [U]

sub·side /səbˈsaɪd/ *v* [I] to become less strong: *The storm subsided around dawn.*

sub·sid·ence /səbˈsaɪdəns, ˈsʌbsɪdəns/ *n* [C,U] when the ground sinks to a lower level, especially when this causes damage to buildings

sub·sid·i·a·ry[1] /səbˈsɪdiəri‖-dieri/ *n* [C] a company that is owned or controlled by another company

subsidiary[2] *adj* relating to something but less important than it

sub·si·dize (also **-ise** *BrE*) /ˈsʌbsɪdaɪz/ *v* [T] to pay part of the cost of something: *housing that is subsidized by the government*

sub·si·dy /ˈsʌbsɪdi/ *n* [C] money that a govern-

ment or organization pays to help with the cost of something

sub·sist /səbˈsɪst/ *v* [I] *formal* to stay alive using only small amounts of food or money: **+ on** *The prisoners subsisted on rice and water.* —**subsistence** *n* [U]

sub·stance /ˈsʌbstəns/ *n* **1** [C] a type of solid or liquid, for example a chemical or natural material: *The bag was covered with a sticky substance.* | *poisonous substances* | **illegal substances** (=drugs) **2** [singular, U] the most important ideas in a speech, report etc: **the substance of** *The news report said little about the substance of the peace talks.* **3** [U] *formal* facts that are true and important: *There's no substance to the rumour.*

sub·stan·dard /ˌsʌbˈstændəd‖-dərd/ *adj* something that is substandard is not as good as it should be, or not as good as it usually is: *substandard health care*

sub·stan·tial /səbˈstænʃəl/ *adj* **1** large in amount: *She earns a substantial amount of money.* **2** big and strong: *a substantial piece of furniture*

sub·stan·tial·ly /səbˈstænʃəli/ *adv* by a large amount or degree: *Prices have increased substantially.*

sub·stan·ti·ate /səbˈstænʃieɪt/ *v* [T] *formal* to prove that something someone has said is true: *Can he substantiate his claims?*

sub·sti·tute[1] /ˈsʌbstɪtjuːt‖-tuːt/ *n* [C] **1** someone who does someone else's job for a short time: *a substitute teacher* **2** something new or different that you use instead of something else: *a sugar substitute*

substitute[2] *v* **1** [T] to use something new or different instead of something else: **substitute sth for sth** *You can substitute olive oil for butter in the recipe.* **2** [I] to do someone's job for a short time until they are able to do it again: **+ for** *I substituted for John when he was sick.* —**substitution** /ˌsʌbstɪˈtjuːʃən‖-ˈtuː-/ *n* [C,U]

sub·ter·fuge /ˈsʌbtəfjuːdʒ‖-ər-/ *n* [C,U] *formal* a trick or dishonest way of doing something, or when someone does this

sub·ter·ra·ne·an /ˌsʌbtəˈreɪniən/ *adj formal* under the surface of the earth: *a subterranean lake*

sub·ti·tles /ˈsʌbˌtaɪtlz/ *n* [plural] words on a film or television screen that translate what the actors are saying, or show the words that are spoken —**subtitled** *adj*

sub·tle /ˈsʌtl/ *adj* **1** not easy to notice: *subtle changes in climate* | *subtle humour* **2** a subtle taste, smell, sound, or colour is pleasant and delicate: *the subtle scent of mint in the air* **3** a subtle person skilfully hides what they intend to do or achieve **4** a subtle plan is clever, especially in a way that deceives people —**subtly** *adv*

sub·tle·ty /ˈsʌtlti/ *n* [C,U] the quality of being subtle, or something that is subtle: *The subtleties of the story do not translate well.*

sub·tract /səbˈtrækt/ *v* [T] to take one number away from another number: **subtract sth from sth** *If you subtract 15 from 25 you get 10.* —**subtraction** /-ˈtrækʃən/ *n* [C,U] ➡ compare ADD

sub·urb /'sʌbɜːb‖-ɜːrb/ *n* [C] an area where people live which is away from the centre of a city: **+ of** *a suburb of Chicago*

sub·ur·ban /sə'bɜːbən‖-'bɜːr-/ *adj* **1** relating to a suburb **2** boring and ordinary: *suburban attitudes*

sub·ur·bi·a /sə'bɜːbiə‖-'bɜːr-/ *n* [U] suburbs in general

sub·ver·sive /səb'vɜːsɪv‖-'vɜːr-/ *adj* intending to destroy or damage a government, society, religion etc: *a subversive speech* —**subversive** *n* [C]

sub·vert /səb'vɜːt‖-'vɜːrt/ *v* [T] *formal* to try to destroy or damage a government, system of doing things etc

sub·way /'sʌbweɪ/ *n* [C] **1** *BrE* a path for people to walk under a road or railway; UNDER-PASS **2** *AmE* a railway that runs under the ground; UNDERGROUND *BrE*

suc·ceed /sək'siːd/ *v* **1** [I] to do what you have tried to do: **+ in** *Did you succeed in finding a place to stay?* **2** [I] to reach a high position in something such as your job: **+ as** *She gave herself one year to succeed as a writer.* **3** [I] to have the result or effect that was intended: *The negotiations are unlikely to succeed.* **4** [I,T] to take a position or do a job after someone else: **succeed sb as sth** *Mr. Harvey will succeed Mrs. Lincoln as chairman.* ➝ compare FAIL[1]

suc·ceed·ing /sək'siːdɪŋ/ *adj* coming after something else: *Sales improved in succeeding years.*

suc·cess /sək'ses/ *n* **1** [U] when you achieve what you have been trying to do: *Her success is due to hard work.* | *I've been trying to contact Ann all day, without success.* **2** [C] something that has the result or effect that you wanted it to have: *The party was a great success.* ➝ opposite FAILURE

suc·cess·ful /sək'sesfəl/ *adj* **1** having the result or effect that was wanted: *a successful attempt to sail around the world* **2** someone who is successful reaches a high position in their job or profession: *a successful business-woman* **3** something that is successful is popular and makes a lot of money: *a hugely successful film* ➝ opposite UNSUCCESSFUL —**successfully** *adv*

suc·ces·sion /sək'seʃən/ *n* **1** [singular, U] happening one after the other: **+ of** *She's had a succession of failed marriages.* | **in succession** *United have won four championships in succession.* **2** [U] when someone takes a position or job after someone else

suc·ces·sive /sək'sesɪv/ *adj* happening or existing one after the other: *The concerts took place on three successive days.* —**successively** *adv*

suc·ces·sor /sək'sesə‖-ər/ *n* [C] someone's successor is the person who has their job after they leave: *No one was certain who Mao's successor would be.*

suc·cinct /sək'sɪŋkt/ *adj* clearly expressed in a few words —**succinctly** *adv*

suc·cour *BrE*, **succor** *AmE* /'sʌkə‖-ər/ *n* [U] *literary* help for people who are suffering —**succour** *BrE v* [T]

suc·cu·lent /'sʌkjʊ̯lənt/ *adj* succulent food has a lot of juice and tastes very good: *a succulent steak* —**succulence** *n* [U]

suc·cumb /sə'kʌm/ *v* [I] *formal* **1** to be unable to stop yourself from being influenced by someone or from wanting something: **+ to** *Eventually, she succumbed to his charms.* **2** to get an illness or die from one

such /sʌtʃ/ *determiner, pron* **1** used to talk about a person or thing of the same type as the one that you have just mentioned: *Such behavior is not acceptable here.* | *What would you do in such a situation?* **2** **such as** used to give an example of something: *big cities such as New York* **3** **such a kind man/such cold weather** etc used to emphasize how kind a man is, how cold the weather is etc: *He's such an idiot* **4** **not ... as such** *spoken* used to say that something is not a very exact description: *He doesn't have a degree as such, just a lot of business qualifications.* **5** **there's no such thing/person** used to say that something or someone does not exist: *There's no such thing as a perfect marriage.* **6** **such ... that** used to say what the result of something is: *The animal was such a nuisance that we had to get rid of it.*

USAGE NOTE: such and **so**

Use **such** and **so** to emphasize a quality that a person or thng has. Use **so** just before an adjective: *Your dress is so pretty.* | *Some people are so rude.* However, if the adjective is used before a noun, use **such**: *She has such pretty eyes.* | *Mark is such a good swimmer.* You can also use **so** to emphasize an adverb: *He always sings so loudly.*

---

such-and-such /'. ./ *determiner spoken* used instead of the name of something: *They kept arguing about whether they should do such-and-such a thing.* | *She kept mentioning such-and-such a movie that she knows.*

suck /sʌk/ *v* [I,T] **1** to hold something in your mouth and pull on it with your tongue and lips: *Don't suck your thumb, Katie.* | **+ on** *Barry was sucking on a candy bar.* **2** to take liquid into your mouth, through a STRAW etc **3** to pull someone or something with a lot of force: **+ down/under etc** *A man almost got sucked under the water by the current.* **4** **be sucked into (doing) sth** to become involved in something unpleasant: *He was quickly sucked into a life of crime.*

suck·er /'sʌkə‖-ər/ *n* [C] *spoken* someone who is easily tricked: *Ellen always was a sucker.*

suc·tion /'sʌkʃən/ *n* [U] when air or liquid is removed from a container or space so that another substance can be pulled in

sud·den /'sʌdn/ *adj* **1** done or happening unexpectedly: *We've had a sudden change of plan.* | *His death was very sudden.* **2** **all of a**

GRAMMAR NOTE: countable and **uncountable (2)**

Some nouns can be **countable** or **uncountable**. For example: **chicken** *n* [C,U].
• Countable: *A fox had killed some of the chickens.* (=birds)
• Uncountable: *chicken cooked in red wine* (=meat)

sudden suddenly: *All of a sudden, the lights went out.* —**suddenness** n [U]

sud·den·ly /'sʌdnli/ adv quickly and unexpectedly: *I suddenly remembered that it was Jim's birthday.*

suds /sʌdz/ n [plural] the BUBBLEs produced when soap and water are mixed together

sue /sjuː‖suː/ v [I,T] to start a legal process to get money from someone who has harmed you in some way: *She plans to sue the company for $1 million.*

suede /sweɪd/ n [U] soft leather with a slightly rough surface

suf·fer /'sʌfəll-ər/ v **1** [I,T] to experience physical or emotional pain: *My mother still suffers a lot of pain in her leg.* | *Children always suffer when parents divorce.* **2** [I,T] to be affected by a bad situation: *Small businesses suffered financially because of the crisis.* **3 suffer a loss/defeat/injury etc** to lose something: *The President suffered a massive defeat in the election.* **4** [I] to become worse because of a bad situation: *He started to drink a lot and his work suffered.* —**sufferer** n [C] —**suffering** n [C,U]

suffer from sth phr v [T] to have an illness or health problem: *Has he ever suffered from any mental illness?*

suf·fice /sə'faɪs/ v [I] *formal* to be enough: *A light lunch will suffice.*

suf·fi·cien·cy /sə'fɪʃənsi/ n [singular, U] when you have all that you need of something

suf·fi·cient /sə'fɪʃənt/ adj as much as you need for a particular purpose; ENOUGH: *The police have sufficient evidence to charge him with murder.* —**sufficiently** adv

suf·fix /'sʌfɪks/ n [C] a letter or letters added to the end of a word to make a new word, for example 'ness' at the end of 'kindness' → compare PREFIX

suf·fo·cate /'sʌfəkeɪt/ v [I,T] to die because there is not enough air, or to kill someone by preventing them from breathing —**suffocation** /ˌsʌfə'keɪʃən/ n [U]

suf·frage /'sʌfrɪdʒ/ n [U] *formal* the right to vote

sug·ar /'ʃʊgəll-ər/ n **1** [U] a sweet substance obtained from plants and used for making food and drinks sweet: *Do you take sugar in your tea?* → see colour picture on page 440 **2** [C] the amount of sugar that a small spoon can hold: *How many sugars do you want in your coffee?* —**sugar** v [T]

sug·gest /sə'dʒest‖səg'dʒest/ v [T] **1** to tell someone your ideas about what should be done: *My doctor suggested a week off work.* | + **(that)** *Don suggested that we should go to Japan next year.* **2** to say that someone or something would be suitable for a particular purpose: **suggest sb for** *Gina Reed's name has been suggested for the job.* **3** to make someone think that something might be true: + **(that)** *All the evidence seems to suggest that he is guilty.*

sug·ges·tion /sə'dʒestʃən‖səg-/ n *singular* **1** [C] an idea or plan that someone suggests:

Transport

Exercise 1

Read the descriptions below. Write how they will travel.

1 Rebecca and Frank are moving from their old apartment to a new house. They are taking all their furniture. van, lorry/ truck

2 Fifty-two children and four teachers are travelling a hundred kilometres to a museum in Sao Paolo. _____

3 Pierre is a French artist. He has made a very big statue of President Kennedy. It is ten metres high. Pierre is taking it to America. _____

4 Sven Johansen is taking 55,000 packets of frozen fish from Oslo to Bratislava. _____

5 Sam is carrying an important letter from South London to North London. There is a lot of traffic but he must travel very quickly. _____

6 Belinda Frost is very rich. She is flying from the roof of her office to the airport. _____

7 Jenny Connor is flying from Melbourne to Bangkok. _____

8 Karen is going to the mall and then to Heartfield Elementary School. She is getting her children, Mandy, Lisa and Daniel. _____

9 Lim Swee Peng is at Gare du Nord in Paris. He wants to go to a hotel in Rue de la Paix but he doesn't know how to get there. He has three large suitcases. _____

10 Svetlana Turayeva is sleeping. She is going from St Petersberg to Moscow. She will arrive in Moscow at 8 o'clock tomorrow morning. _____

Exercise 2

Where can you find these means of transport? Match the vehicle and the place.

1 train	a airport
2 taxi	b harbour
3 aeroplane	c bus stop
4 ferry	d railway station
5 bus	e taxi rank

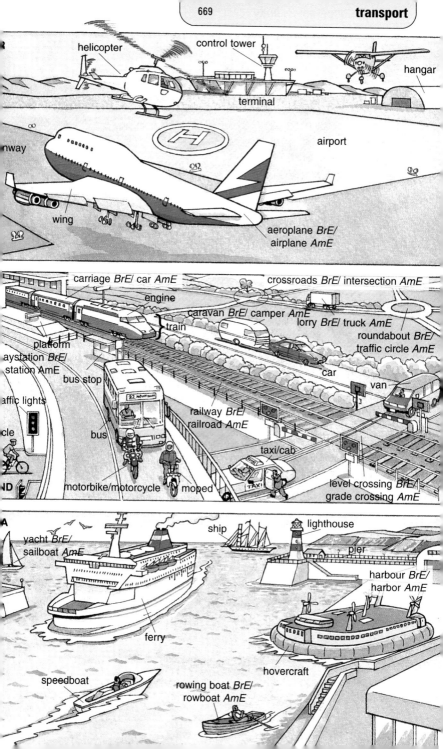

helicopter

control tower

hangar

terminal

airport

nway

wing

aeroplane *BrE*/ airplane *AmE*

carriage *BrE*/ car *AmE*

crossroads *BrE*/ intersection *AmE*

engine

caravan *BrE*/ camper *AmE*

lorry *BrE*/ truck *AmE*

train

roundabout *BrE*/ traffic circle *AmE*

platform

aystation *BrE*/ station *AmE*

bus stop

car

van

railway *BrE*/ railroad *AmE*

affic lights

cle

bus

taxi/cab

motorbike/motorcycle

moped

level crossing *BrE*/ grade crossing *AmE*

ND

yacht *BrE*/ sailboat *AmE*

ship

lighthouse

pier

harbour *BrE*/ harbor *AmE*

ferry

hovercraft

speedboat

rowing boat *BrE*/ rowboat *AmE*

hold

stretch

bend

put down

carry

pick up

lift

squat

hop

skip

kneel

crouch

jump

drop

drag

push

pull

climb

fall

jog

walk

march

sit

crawl

tiptoe

run

throw

hit

punch

cat

kick

have a suggestion *Do you have any suggestions about what we can do in London?*| **make a suggestion** *Can I make a suggestion?* **2** [singular, U] when you tell someone your idea about what should be done: **at sb's suggestion/at the suggestion of sb** (=because someone suggested something): *He came to London at my suggestion.* **3 a suggestion of** a slight sign of something: *There was a suggestion of a smile on her face.* **4 suggestion that/of** a possibility that something might be true: *The police said that there was no suggestion of murder.*

sug·ges·tive /sə'dʒestɪv‖səg-/ *adj* **1** making you think of sex: *a suggestive remark* **2 suggestive of sth** making you think of something: *a spotted rug, suggestive of a leopard skin*

su·i·cid·al /ˌsuːɪ'saɪdl◂, ˌsjuː-‖ˌsuː-/ *adj* **1** wanting to kill yourself: *She admits that she sometimes had suicidal thoughts.* **2** very dangerous or likely to have a very bad result: *It would be suicidal to attack in daylight.*

su·i·cide /'suːɪˌsaɪd, 'sjuː-‖'suː-/ *n* **1** [C,U] when someone deliberately kills himself or herself: *There's been a rise in the number of suicides among young men.*| **commit suicide** (=kill yourself): *Her brother committed suicide last year.* **2** [U] when someone does something that will have an extremely bad effect on their posi-

tion and make them fail completely: *It would be political suicide to hold an election now.*

suit[1] /suːt, sjuːt‖suːt/ *n* [C] **1** a JACKET and trousers or a skirt that are made of the same material and are worn together: *an expensive Armani suit* → see colour picture on page 113 **2** a piece of clothing or a set of clothes that you wear for a particular activity: *a ski suit* **3** a LAWSUIT **4** one of the four types of playing cards in a set of playing cards

suit[2] *v* [T] **1** to be acceptable or right for someone: *It's difficult to find a date that suits everyone.* **2** to make someone look attractive: *Short hair really suits you.* **3 be well/ideally/best suited** to have the right qualities to do something: *Lucy's ideally suited for the job.*

suit·a·ble /'suːtəbəl, 'sjuː-‖'suː-/ *adj* right or acceptable for a particular purpose or situation: **+ for** *The film isn't suitable for young children.* —**suitably** *adv* —**suitability** /ˌsuːtə'bɪlɪti, ˌsjuː-‖ˌsuː-/ *n* [U]

suit·case /'suːtkeɪs, 'sjuːt-‖'suːt-/ *n* [C] a case with a handle, used for carrying clothes etc when you travel

suite /swiːt/ *n* [C] **1** a set of expensive rooms in a hotel: *the honeymoon suite* **2** a set of furniture for a room that is all covered in simi-

Verbs of Movement 2 – Body

S

Exercise 1

Complete the passage with verbs from the illustration.

Harry and his friends, Joe and Sue, were in the living room of their apartment in London. Their pet, a beautiful green and yellow bird, had escaped from its cage. It was flying around the room. They were trying to catch it.

'Look it's on the curtain above the window,' said Harry. 'Can you catch it Joe?' Joe *jumped*[1] up and tried to c _ _ _ _[2] the bird in his hands.

'Don't do that!' said Harry, 't_ _ _ _[3] your coat over it.'

The bird flew down from the curtain and landed on the floor. It h _ _ _ _ _[4] behind the sofa.

'Sue, k _ _ _ _[5] down beside the sofa,' said Harry, 'can you see it?'

'Yes,' said Sue 'it's at the back. I can see it but I can't touch it.'

'S _ _ _ _ _ _[6] your arm under the sofa. Can you catch it now?' asked Harry.

The bird ran from under the sofa towards Joe.

'Quick Joe. D _ _ _[7] your coat over it' shouted Harry.

Joe dropped his coat but he didn't catch the bird. It ran behind the television.

'Now, we must all be very quiet,' said Harry.

'Sue, t _ _ _ _ _[8] to the television. Good. Now b _ _ _[9] down. Can you get the budgie?'

'Yes, I've got it!' said Sue. She was h _ _ _-_ _ _[10] the bird in her hands. She w _ _ _-_ _[11] to the cage and put the bird inside.

lar material: *a living-room suite* **3** a piece of music made up of several short parts: *the Nutcracker Suite*

sui·tor /ˈsuːtə, ˈsjuː-‖ˈsuːtər/ *n* [C] *old-fashioned* a man who wants to marry a particular woman

sul·fur /ˈsʌlfəl-ər/ *n* [U] an American spelling of SULPHUR

sulk /sʌlk/ *v* [I] to show that you are annoyed by being silent and looking unhappy: *Stop sulking – you can go out and play later.* —**sulk** *n* [C] —**sulky** *adj*

sul·len /ˈsʌlən/ *adj* being in a bad temper but not saying anything: *a sullen expression* —**sullenly** *adv*

sul·phur especially BrE, **sulfur** AmE /ˈsʌlfəl-fər/ *n* [U] a yellow chemical powder that smells unpleasant —**sulphurous** *adj*

sul·tan /ˈsʌltən/ *n* [C] a ruler in some Muslim countries

sul·ta·na /sʌlˈtɑːnəl-ˈtænə/ *n* [C] BrE a dried white GRAPE, used in cooking

sul·try /ˈsʌltri/ *adj* **1** sultry weather is hot with no wind **2** a woman who deliberately behaves in a way that makes her sexually attractive

sum[1] /sʌm/ *n* [C] **1** an amount of money: *The city has spent a large sum of money on parks.* **2** BrE a simple CALCULATION such as adding or dividing numbers **3** **the sum of** the total when you add two or more numbers together: *The sum of 4 and 5 is 9.*

sum[2] *v*

sum up *phr v* **1** [I,T **sum** sth ↔ **up**] to end a discussion or speech by giving the main information about it in a short statement: *So, to sum up, we need to organize our time better.* **2** [T **sum** sth/sb ↔ **up**] to form an opinion about someone or something: *Pat summed up the situation at a glance.*

sum·mar·ize (also **-ise** BrE) /ˈsʌməraɪz/ *v* [I,T] to give only the main information about something without the details

sum·ma·ry[1] /ˈsʌməri/ *n* [C] a short statement that gives the main information about something: *Read the article and write a summary of it.*

summary[2] *adj* [only before noun] *formal* done immediately following the usual processes or rules: *the powers of summary arrest*

sum·mer /ˈsʌməl-ər/ *n* [C,U] the season between spring and autumn, when the weather is hottest: *Are you going away this summer?*

sum·mer·house /ˈsʌməhaʊsl-ər-/ *n* [C] a small building in a garden where you sit in warm weather

sum·mer·time /ˈsʌmətaɪml-ər-/ *n* [U] the time of year when it is summer

sum·mit /ˈsʌmɪt/ *n* [C] **1** a meeting between the leaders of several governments: *an economic summit* **2** the top of a mountain ➔ see colour picture on page 243

sum·mon /ˈsʌmən/ *v* [T] *formal* **1** to officially order someone to come to a particular place **summon sb to sth** *I was summoned to the principal's office.* **2** also **summon up** if you summon your courage, strength etc, you try to be brave, strong etc even though it is difficult: *Tom summoned up his courage to ask Kay for a date.*

sum·mons /ˈsʌmənz/ *n* [C], *plural* summonses an official letter that says you must go to a court of law —**summons** *v* [T]

sump·tu·ous /ˈsʌmptʃuəs/ *adj* very impressive and expensive: *a sumptuous meal* —**sumptuously** *adv*

sun[1] /sʌn/ *n* **1** [singular] the large bright object in the sky that gives us light and heat, and which the Earth moves around **2** [singular, U] the heat and light that come from the sun: **in the sun** *Val lay in the sun, reading a book.* **3** [C] any star that PLANETs move around ➔ see also **catch the sun** (CATCH[1])

sun[2] *v* **sun yourself** to sit or lie outside when the sun is shining

Sun. the written abbreviation of SUNDAY

sun·bathe /ˈsʌnbeɪð/ *v* [I] to sit or lie outside in the sun in order to become brown —**sunbathing** *n* [U]

sun·beam /ˈsʌnbiːm/ *n* [C] a line of light shining down from the sun

sun·burn /ˈsʌnbɜːnl-bɜːrn/ *n* [U] when your skin is burnt from spending too much time in the sun —**sunburned**, **sunburnt** *adj*

sun cream /ˈ. ./ *n* [C,U] SUNSCREEN

sun·dae /ˈsʌndeɪl-di/ *n* [C] a dish made with ICE CREAM, fruit, nuts etc

Sun·day /ˈsʌndi/ written abbreviation **Sun** *n* [C,U] the day of the week between Saturday and Monday ➔ see Usage Note at DAY

sun·dial /ˈsʌndaɪəl/ *n* [C] an object that shows the time by using the shadow made on it by the sun

sun·down /ˈsʌndaʊn/ *n* [U] SUNSET

sun·dry /ˈsʌndri/ *adj* *formal* **1** [only before noun] not simple enough to consider as a group; VARIOUS **2** **all and sundry** everyone, not just a few people who you think should be allowed to do something: *I don't want all and sundry coming into our garden.*

sun·flow·er /ˈsʌnflaʊəl-ər/ *n* [C] a tall plant with a large yellow flower and seeds that you can eat

sung /sʌŋ/ *v* the past participle of SING

sun·glass·es /ˈsʌnˌɡlɑːsɪzl-ˌɡlæ-/ *n* [plural] dark glasses that you wear to protect your eyes from the sun

sunk /sʌŋk/ *v* the past tense and past participle of SINK

sunk·en /ˈsʌŋkən/ *adj* [only before noun] **1** built or put at a lower level than the surrounding area: *a sunken garden* **2** having fallen to the bottom of the sea: *sunken treasure* **3** sunken cheeks or eyes curve inwards, making you look ill

sun·light /ˈsʌnlaɪt/ *n* [U] natural light that comes from the sun: *He stepped out into the strong sunlight*

sun·lit /ˈsʌnlɪt/ *adj* made brighter by light from the sun: *a sunlit kitchen*

sun·ny /ˈsʌni/ *adj* **1** full of light from the sun: *a sunny day | a sunny garden* **2** cheerful and happy: *a sunny personality*

sun·rise /ˈsʌnraɪz/ *n* **1** [U] when the sun first appears in the morning **2** [C] the light and colours that you see in the sky when the sun first appears

sun·screen /ˈsʌnskriːn/ also **sun cream** BrE — *n* [C,U] a skin cream to stop the sun from burning you

sun·set /ˈsʌnset/ *n* **1** [U] when the sun disappears and night begins **2** [C] the light and colours you see in the sky when the sun disappears

sun·shine /ˈsʌnʃaɪn/ *n* [singular, U] the light and heat that comes from the sun: *Let's go out and enjoy the sunshine.*

sun·stroke /ˈsʌnstrəʊkǁ-stroʊk/ *n* [U] an illness caused by being in the sun too long

sun·tan /ˈsʌntæn/ also **tan** *n* [C] when your skin goes brown from being in the sun — **suntanned** *adj*

su·per[1] /ˈsuːpə, ˈsjuː-ǁˈsuːpər/ *adj informal* extremely good: *a super idea*

super[2] *adv, prefix spoken* extremely: *a super expensive restaurant* | *a super-efficient secretary*

su·perb /sjuːˈpɜːb, suː-ǁsʊˈpɜːrb/ *adj* very good: *a superb cook* — **superbly** *adv*

su·per·fi·cial /ˌsuːpəˈfɪʃəl◂, ˌsjuː-ǁ-ˌsuːpər-/ *adj*
1 based only on the first or most noticeable things you see, not because you have examined or studied something carefully: *a superficial knowledge of the subject* | *There are superficial similarities between animal and human behaviour.* **2** superficial damage, injury etc only affects the skin or surface and is not serious: *superficial cuts* **3** someone who is superficial does not think about things that are serious or important — **superficially** *adv*

su·per·flu·ous /suːˈpɜːfluəs, sjuː-ǁsuːˈpɜːr-/ *adj formal* not necessary, or more than is needed: *superfluous details*

su·per·hu·man /ˌsuːpəˈhjuːmən◂, ˌsjuː-ǁˌsuːpər-ˈhjuː-, -ˈjuː-/ *adj* using powers that are much greater than those of ordinary people: *Finishing the marathon race required superhuman effort.*

su·per·im·pose /ˌsuːpərɪmˈpəʊz, ˌsjuː-ǁˌsuːpərɪmˈpoʊz/ *v* [T] to put a picture, photograph etc on top of another one so that both of them can be seen

su·per·in·tend·ent /ˌsuːpərɪnˈtendənt, ˌsjuː-ǁˌsuːpər-/ *n* [C] **1** someone who is officially responsible for a place, job, or activity **2** a British police officer who has a fairly high rank

su·pe·ri·or[1] /suːˈpɪəriə, sjuː-ǁsʊˈpɪriər/ *adj*
1 better than something or someone else: **+ to** *a new design that is superior to anything the Americans have produced* **2** of a very good quality: *superior wines* **3** showing that you think you are better than other people: *a superior attitude* → opposite INFERIOR[1]

superior[2] *n* [C] someone who has a higher position than you at work: *I'll have to discuss this with my superiors.*

su·per·i·or·i·ty /suːˌpɪəriˈɒrɪti, sjuː-ǁsʊˌpɪriˈɔːr-, -ˈɑːr-/ *n* [U] **1** the quality of being better than other things: *We are confident of the superiority of our new computer system.* **2** when you show that you think you are better than other people: *Janet always spoke with an air of superiority.*

su·per·la·tive[1] /suːˈpɜːlətɪv, sjuː-ǁsʊˈpɜːr-/ *adj* extremely good: *a superlative actor*

superlative[2] *n* **the superlative** the form of an adjective or adverb that you use when saying that someone or something is the biggest, best, worst etc. For example 'fastest' is the superlative of 'fast', and 'most expensive' is the superlative of 'expensive' → compare COMPARATIVE[2]

su·per·mar·ket /ˈsuːpəˌmɑːkɪt, ˈsjuː-ǁˈsuːpərˌmɑːr-/ *n* [C] a large shop that sells food, drink, products for cleaning the house etc

su·per·mod·el /ˈsuːpəˌmɒdl, ˈsjuː-ǁˈsuːpərˌmɑː-/ *n* [C] a very famous fashion MODEL

su·per·nat·u·ral /ˌsuːpəˈnætʃərəl◂, ˌsjuː-ǁˌsuːpər-/ *n* **the supernatural** events, powers, or creatures that are impossible to explain by science or natural causes — **supernatural** *adj*: *supernatural powers*

su·per·pow·er /ˈsuːpəˌpaʊə, ˈsjuː-ǁˈsuːpərˌpaʊr/ *n* [C] a country that has a lot of military and political power

su·per·sede /ˌsuːpəˈsiːd, ˌsjuː-ǁˌsuːpər-/ *v* [T] if a new product, method etc supersedes another one, people start to use the new one instead of the other one: *TV had superseded radio by the 1960s.*

su·per·son·ic /ˌsuːpəˈsɒnɪk◂, ˌsjuː-ǁˌsuːpərˈsɑː-/ *adj* faster than the speed of sound: *supersonic jets*

su·per·star /ˈsuːpəstɑː, ˈsjuː-ǁˈsuːpərstɑːr/ *n* [C] an extremely famous actor, singer etc

su·per·sti·tion /ˌsuːpəˈstɪʃən, ˌsjuː-ǁˌsuːpər-/ *n* [C,U] a belief that some objects or actions are lucky and some are unlucky: *the old superstition that the number 13 is unlucky*

su·per·sti·tious /ˌsuːpəˈstɪʃəs◂, ˌsjuː-ǁˌsuːpər-/ *adj* believing that some objects or actions are lucky or unlucky: *Are you superstitious?*

super·store /ˈsuːpəstɔː, ˈsjuː-ǁˈsuːpərstɔːr/ *n* [C] *BrE* a very large shop that sells many different types of goods, usually just outside a town

su·per·vise /ˈsuːpəvaɪz, ˈsjuː-ǁˈsuːpər-/ *v* [I,T] to make sure someone is doing their work or behaving correctly, especially by watching them: *My job is to supervise school children at lunchtime.* — **supervisor** *n* [C] *I'll have to ask my supervisor.* — **supervisory** /ˌsuːpəˈvaɪzəri◂, ˌsjuː-ǁˌsuːpər-/ *adj*: *a supervisory role*

su·per·vi·sion /ˌsuːpəˈvɪʒən, ˌsjuː-ǁˌsuːpər-/ *n* [U] when you supervise someone or something

sup·per /ˈsʌpəǁ-ər/ *n* [C] a meal that you eat in the evening

sup·plant /səˈplɑːntǁ-ˈplænt/ *v* [T] *formal* to take the place of another person or thing: *The old factories have all been supplanted by new high-tech industries.*

sup·ple /ˈsʌpəl/ *adj* able to bend and move easily: *supple leather*

sup·ple·ment /ˈsʌpl̩mənt/ *n* [C] something that you add to something else to improve it: *You may need vitamin supplements.* — **supplement** /ˈsʌpl̩ment/ *v* [T] *I supplement my income by teaching Italian at weekends.*

sup·ple·men·ta·ry /ˌsʌpl̩ˈmentəri◂/ also **sup·ple·men·tal** /-ˈmentl◂/ *AmE* — *adj* added to something, or provided as well as something; additional: *supplementary vitamins* | *supplementary teaching materials*

sup·pli·er /səˈplaɪəǁ-ər/ *n* [C] a company that provides goods for shops and businesses: *medical suppliers*

sup·plies /səˈplaɪz/ *n* [plural] food, clothes, and other necessary things, especially those you take with you or use for a limited period of time: *supplies for a camping trip*

sup·ply[1] /səˈplaɪ/ *n* **1** [C,U] an amount of something that can be used, or the process of

S

providing this: *the supply of oxygen to the brain* | **be in short supply** (=there is very little of something available) **2** [C] a system of providing gas, water etc: *We've had problems with the water supply lately.*

supply² *v* [T] to provide people with something that they need, especially regularly over a period of time: **supply sb with** *Drivers are supplied with a uniform.* | **supply sth to sb** *We supply books to schools.*

sup·port¹ /səˈpɔːt‖-ˈpɔːrt/ *v* [T] **1** to say that you agree with an idea, group, or person and want them to succeed: *I don't support any one political party.* **2** to hold the weight of something to prevent it from falling: *The bridge is supported by two stone columns.* **3** to help and encourage someone or something: *My parents have always supported my decision to be an actor.* **4** to provide someone with enough money for food, clothes and other things they need: *How can Brad support a family on his salary?* **5** to help to show that something is true: *There is little evidence to support the theory.* **6** especially BrE to like a particular sports team and want them to win: *Which football team do you support?*

support² *n* **1** [U] help and encouragement that you give to a person or group of people: *Thanks for all your support.* | *Teachers don't always have the support of parents.* **2** [U] money that provides food, clothes and help for people: *financial support for families on low incomes* **3 in support of** showing your approval of someone or something: *a demonstration in support of animal rights* **4** [C,U] an object that carries the weight of something else: *supports for the roof*

sup·port·er /səˈpɔːtə‖-ˈpɔːrtər/ *n* [C] **1** someone who supports a person, group, or plan **2** especially BrE someone who likes a particular team and wants them to win: *Manchester United supporters*

sup·por·tive /səˈpɔːtɪv‖-ˈpɔːr-/ *adj* giving help or encouragement: *Mark and Sally are very supportive of each other.*

sup·pose¹ /səˈpəʊz‖-ˈpoʊz/ *v* [T] **1 be supposed** **a)** used when saying what is expected or intended to happen, especially when it fails to happen: *There's supposed to be a bus at half past four.* | *I thought this was supposed to be a holiday!* **b)** used when saying what someone should or should not do, according to rules or what someone has said should happen: *You're not supposed to smoke in here.* **c)** if something is supposed to be true, many people believe it is true: *This is supposed to be the oldest theater in New York.* **2** to think that something is probably true, based on what you know: + **(that)** *She usually finished work at 6, so I suppose she's gone home.* **3 I suppose a)** used when saying that something is probably true, although you are not sure about it: *"How old is she?" "She's about 50, I suppose."* **b)** used when agreeing to let someone do something, especially when you do not want to: **I suppose so** *"Can I borrow your car?" "I suppose so, if you're careful with it."* **c)** used when you are angry with someone: + **(that)** *I suppose you thought that was funny!* | *I don't suppose you care, do you?*

suppose² also **supposing** *linking word spoken* **1** used to ask what might happen: *Suppose*

Mom found out? She'd go crazy! **2** used to suggest something: *Suppose we try to finish this part first?*

sup·posed /səˈpəʊzd, səˈpəʊzɪd‖-ˈpoʊzd, -ˈpoʊzɪd/ *adj* [only before noun] used to say that what you are talking about is believed to be true, but that you do not believe or agree with it yourself: *the supposed link between violent movies and crime*

sup·pos·ed·ly /səˈpəʊzɪdli‖-ˈpoʊ-/ *adv* used to say that you do not believe what you are saying about the thing or person you are describing, even though other people think it is true: *supposedly environmentally-friendly products* | *Supposedly, he doesn't have any money.*

sup·pos·ing /səˈpəʊzɪŋ‖-ˈpoʊ-/ *linking word* SUPPOSE²

sup·po·si·tion /ˌsʌpəˈzɪʃən/ *n* [C,U] *formal* something that someone believes is true even though they cannot prove it

sup·press /səˈpres/ *v* [T] **1** to stop people from opposing the government, especially by using force: *The army was called in to suppress the revolt.* **2** to control a feeling, so that you do not show it or it does not affect you: *Andy could barely suppress his anger.* **3** to prevent important opinions or opinions from becoming known: *His lawyer illegally suppressed evidence.* —**suppression** /-ˈpreʃən/ *n* [U]

su·prem·a·cy /səˈpreməsi/ *n* [U] when a group, team, country etc is much more powerful, successful, or ADVANCED than anyone else

su·preme /suːˈpriːm, sjuː-, səˈ‖sə-, suː-/ *adj* **1** having the highest position of power or importance: *the Supreme Commander of the UN forces* **2** the greatest possible: *a question of supreme importance* —**supremely** *adv*

Supreme Court /ˌ. ˈ./ *n* [singular] the law court with the most authority in the US

sur·charge /ˈsɜːtʃɑːdʒ‖ˈsɜːrtʃɑːrdʒ/ *n* [C] money that you have to pay in addition to the basic price of something

sure¹ /ʃɔː‖ʃʊr/ *adj* **1** [not before noun] certain about something: + **(that)** *Are you sure you've met him before?* | + **about** *Are you quite sure about this?* | + **what/where/why etc** *I'm not sure how many people are coming to the party.* **2 make sure a)** to check that something is true or that something has been done: *"Did you lock the front door?" "I think so, but I'd better make sure."* | + **(that)** *He called to make sure we got home okay.* **b)** to do something so that something will definitely happen: *Make sure you get there early.* **3** certain to happen or be true: *a sure winner* | *a sure sign of rain* | **sure to do sth** *Jan is sure to call while I'm out.* **4 be sure of sth** to be certain to get something or certain that something will happen: *You're sure of a warm welcome at Liz's.* **5 sure of yourself** confident about your own abilities and opinions **6 be sure to do sth** *spoken* used to tell someone to remember to do something: *Be sure to write!* **7 sure thing** *AmE spoken* used to agree to something: *"See you Friday." "Yeah, sure thing."*

sure² *adv* **1 for sure** *informal* if you know something for sure, you are certain about it: *I think Jack's married, but I don't know for sure.* **2 that's for sure** used to emphasize that something is true: *It's a lot better than it was, that's for sure.* **3** *spoken* used to say yes to someone:

"Can I read your paper?" "Sure." **4 sure enough** *informal* used to say that something happened that you expected to happen: *Sure enough, the car broke down on the way.* **5** *informal* used to admit that something is true, before you say something very different: *Sure, he's attractive, but I'm not interested.* **6** *AmE informal* used to emphasize what you are saying: *This bad weather sure doesn't make my job any easier.*

sure-fire /ˈ. .ˌ/ *adj informal* certain to succeed: *a sure-fire way to make money*

sure·ly /ˈʃɔːli‖ˈʃʊrli/ *adv* **1** used to show that you are surprised at something: *Surely you're not leaving so soon?* **2** used to show that you think something must be true: *This will surely result in more people losing their jobs.*

surf[1] /sɜːf‖sɜːrf/ *v* [I] **1** to ride on ocean waves standing on a special board: **go surfing** *Matt goes surfing every day.* **2 surf the net** to look for information on the INTERNET —**surfer** *n* [C] —**surfing** *n* [U]

surf[2] *n* [U] the white part that forms on the top of waves

sur·face[1] /ˈsɜːfɪs‖ˈsɜːr-/ *n* **1** [C] the outside or top layer of something: *a cleaner for all kitchen surfaces* | *the Earth's surface* **2** [C usually singular] the top of an area of water: *The diver swam to the surface.* **3** [singular] the way that someone or something seems to be until you find out more about what they are really like: **on the surface** *On the surface she seems happy enough.* | **below/beneath/under the surface** *Under the surface, it's not as peaceful a society as people imagine.*

surface[2] *v* **1** [I] to rise from under water to its surface: *Whales were surfacing near our boat.* **2** [I] to appear again or become known after being hidden: *A few problems started to surface in their relationship.* **3** [T] to cover a road with a hard surface

surface mail /ˈ.. ˌ./ *n* [U] letters and packages that are carried by road, railway, or boat, not by plane

surf·board /ˈsɜːfbɔːd‖ˈsɜːrfbɔːrd/ *n* [C] a long piece of plastic or wood that you stand on to ride on ocean waves

sur·feit /ˈsɜːfɪt‖ˈsɜːr-/ *n* [singular] too much of something

surge[1] /sɜːdʒ‖sɜːrdʒ/ *v* [I] **1** if a crowd of people surges, it suddenly moves forward quickly **2** also **surge up** if an emotion such as anger surges, you suddenly begin to feel it very strongly: *Rage surged up inside her.*

surge[2] *n* [C] **1** a sudden large increase in something: **+ of/in** *a surge of excitement* | *a surge in oil prices* **2** a sudden movement of a lot of people: *There was a surge forward as the band came on stage.*

sur·geon /ˈsɜːdʒən‖ˈsɜːr-/ *n* [C] a doctor who does operations in a hospital

sur·ge·ry /ˈsɜːdʒəri‖ˈsɜːr-/ *n* **1** [U] medical treatment in which a doctor cuts open your body to repair or remove something inside: *heart*

surgery 2 [C] *BrE* a place where you go to see a doctor or DENTIST, or where you go to someone for advice

sur·gi·cal /ˈsɜːdʒɪkəl‖ˈsɜːr-/ *adj* relating to or used for medical operations: *surgical gloves* —**surgically** /-kli/ *adv*

sur·ly /ˈsɜːli‖ˈsɜːrli/ *adj* unfriendly, bad-tempered, and rude: *surly waitress*

sur·mise /səˈmaɪz‖sər-/ *v* [T] *formal* to guess that something is true using information you have: *We can only surmise what happened.*

sur·mount /səˈmaʊnt‖sər-/ *v* [T] *formal* to succeed in dealing with a problem or difficulty

sur·name /ˈsɜːneɪm‖ˈsɜːr-/ *n* [C] your family name → compare FIRST NAME

sur·pass /səˈpɑːs‖sərˈpæs/ *v* [T] *formal* to be better than someone or something else: *The results surpassed my expectations.*

sur·plus[1] /ˈsɜːpləs‖ˈsɜːr-/ *n* [C,U] more of something than is needed or used: *The country produces a huge surplus of grain.*

surplus[2] *adj* more than what is needed or used: *surplus land*

sur·prise[1] /səˈpraɪz‖sər-/ *n* **1** [C,U] something that is unexpected or unusual: *What a surprise to see you here!* | *I've got a surprise for you!* | **come as no surprise** (=not be surprising): *It came as no surprise when Jeff left.* **2** [U] the feeling you have when something unexpected or unusual happens: *Imagine our surprise when we heard the news.* | **to my surprise** *To my surprise, Ann agreed.* **3 take/catch sb by surprise** to happen in an unexpected way: *The heavy snowfall caught everyone by surprise.*

surprise[2] *v* [T] **1** to make someone feel surprise: *Her reaction surprised me.* **2** to find, catch, or attack someone when they do not expect it: *A security guard surprised the robber.*

sur·prised /səˈpraɪzd‖sər-/ *adj* if you are surprised by something, you do not expect it and it seems strange or unusual: **+ (that)** *We were surprised David wasn't invited.* | **+ at** *She was surprised at how much it cost.* | **surprised to hear/see/find sth** *I'm surprised to hear you say that.* → see colour picture on page 277

sur·pris·ing /səˈpraɪzɪŋ‖sər-/ *adj* unusual or unexpected and making you feel surprised: *surprising news* | *It's hardly surprising that they lost the game.* —**surprisingly** *adv*: *The test was surprisingly easy.*

sur·real /səˈrɪəl/ also **sur·re·a·lis·tic** /səˌrɪəˈlɪstɪk◂/ *adj* very strange, like something from a dream

sur·ren·der /səˈrendə‖-ər/ *v* **1** [I] to officially announce that you are stopping fighting because you know that you cannot win: *They were determined never to surrender.* | *The rebel forces have surrendered.* **2** [T] *formal* to give something to someone in authority, for example weapons or official documents: *They had to surrender their passports.* —**surrender** *n* [U]

sur·rep·ti·tious /ˌsʌrəpˈtɪʃəs◂ ‖ˌsɜː-/ *adj* done

GRAMMAR NOTE: much and many
You can only use **much**, **how much** and **a little** with <u>uncountable</u> nouns: *How much information do you have?* You can only use **many**, **how many** and **a few** with plural <u>countable</u> nouns: *How many people are coming to the party?* | *I've invited a few friends.*

secretly so that other people do not notice
— **surreptitiously** adv

sur·ro·gate /ˈsʌrəgeɪt, -gɪt‖ˈsɜː-/ adj [only before noun] taking the place of someone or something else: a surrogate mother (=a woman who has a baby for another woman who cannot have children) — **surrogate** n [C]

sur·round /səˈraʊnd/ v **1** [T] to be or go all around someone or something: a lake surrounded by trees | The police surrounded the house. **2** [T] to be closely connected with a situation or event: The President's visit was surrounded in secrecy. **3 be surrounded by sb/sth** to have a lot of people or things near you: She is surrounded by friends. — **surrounding** adj: the surrounding countryside

sur·round·ings /səˈraʊndɪŋz/ n [plural] the place where you are and all the things in it: It took me a few weeks to get used to my new surroundings.

sur·veil·lance /səˈveɪləns‖sər-/ n [U] when someone such as the police or army carefully watches a person or place: **under surveillance** Police have the man under surveillance.

sur·vey¹ /ˈsɜːveɪ‖ˈsɜːr-/ n [C] **1** a set of questions that you ask a lot of people in order to find out information about their general opinions or behaviour: a survey of people's eating habits **2** a careful examination of an area, used for making a map of it **3** an examination of a building that tells you if it is in good condition

sur·vey² /səˈveɪ‖sər-/ v [T] **1** to ask a lot of people a set of questions in order to find out about their opinions or behaviour: More than 50% of the students surveyed take regular exercise. **2** to look at someone or something carefully: I surveyed the damage to my car. **3** to examine and measure an area of land in order to make a map

sur·vey·or /səˈveɪə‖sərˈveɪər/ n [C] someone whose job is to examine and measure land or buildings

sur·viv·al /səˈvaɪvəl‖sər-/ n [U] when someone continues to live or exist, especially after a difficult or dangerous situation: The operation will increase his chances of survival.

sur·vive /səˈvaɪv‖sər-/ v [I,T] **1** to continue to live after an accident, illness etc: Only one person survived the crash. **2** to continue to exist after a difficult or dangerous situation or event: Most of the cathedral survived the earthquake. | "How was the interview?" "Well, I survived!"

sur·vi·vor /səˈvaɪvə‖sərˈvaɪvər/ n [C] someone who continues to live after an accident, illness etc: No survivors of the plane crash were found.

sus·cep·ti·ble /səˈseptɪbəl/ adj likely to be affected by a particular illness or problem: **susceptible to sth** I've always been very susceptible to colds.

sus·pect¹ /ˈsʌspekt/ n [C] someone who may be guilty of a crime

sus·pect² /səˈspekt/ v [T] **1** to think that someone may be guilty of a crime: **suspect sb of sth** She is suspected of murder. **2** to think that something is true or may happen: **+ that** I suspected that Suki had been lying. **3** to doubt that you can trust someone or believe something: Do you have reason to suspect his motives?

sus·pect³ /ˈsʌspekt/ adj difficult to believe or trust: Her explanation seems suspect.

sus·pend /səˈspend/ v [T] **1** to officially stop or delay something for a short time: The match was suspended because of rain. | His prison sentence was suspended for two years. (=he will not go to prison unless he commits another crime within two years) **2** to hang something from a high place: **suspend sth from sth** a chandelier suspended from the ceiling **3** to officially stop someone from working, going to school etc for a fixed period, because they have broken the rules: **suspend sb from sth** Joe was suspended from school.

sus·pen·ders /səˈspendəz‖-ərz/ n [plural] **1** BrE two short STRAPS fastened to a belt that hold up a woman's STOCKINGS **2** AmE two STRAPS that go over your shoulders and are fastened to your trousers to hold them up; BRACES BrE ➝ see colour picture on page 113

sus·pense /səˈspens/ n [U] the feeling you have when waiting for something exciting to happen: **keep sb in suspense** (=make someone have this feeling): Don't keep us in suspense. What happened?

sus·pen·sion /səˈspenʃən/ n **1** [U] when someone stops or delays something for a period of time **2** [C,U] when someone is removed from a school or job for a short time as a punishment: a three-day suspension for cheating **3** [U] equipment fixed to the wheels of a vehicle to make it comfortable to ride in

sus·pi·cion /səˈspɪʃən/ n **1** [C,U] a feeling that someone has done something wrong: He was arrested on suspicion of robbery. | Nobody saw who did it, but I have my suspicions. | **under suspicion** (=thought to have done something wrong): A number of people are under suspicion for the murder. **2** [C] a feeling that something may be true: She had a suspicion that Steve might be right.

sus·pi·cious /səˈspɪʃəs/ adj **1** making you think that something bad or illegal is happening or that someone has done something wrong: Passengers should report any bags that seem suspicious. | suspicious circumstances **2** a feeling that you do not trust someone: He has a suspicious mind. | **+ of** I'm suspicious of her intentions. — **suspiciously** adv: Two youths were having suspiciously outside the shop.

sus·tain /səˈsteɪn/ v [T] **1** to make something continue to exist: He couldn't sustain his interest in learning the violin. **2** to keep someone strong or healthy: A good breakfast will sustain you through the morning. **3 sustain injuries/damage/losses** formal to be injured, damaged etc: Two people sustained minor injuries in the fire.

sus·tained /səˈsteɪnd/ adj continuing without becoming weaker: A sustained effort is needed to fight drug abuse. | sustained economic growth

svelte /svelt/ adj thin and graceful

SW the written abbreviation of southwest

swab /swɒb‖swɑːb/ n [C] a small piece of material, used to clean wounds or do medical tests

swag·ger /ˈswægə‖-ər/ v [I] to walk with a swinging movement, in a way that seems too proud and confident — **swagger** n [singular]

swal·low¹ /ˈswɒləʊ‖ˈswɑːloʊ/ v **1** [T] to make food or drink go down your throat: If you drink

some water it'll make the pills easier to swallow.
2 [I] to make a movement in your throat, especially because you are nervous: *He swallowed anxiously before answering.* **3** [T] *informal* to believe that something is true or right, especially when it seems very unlikely or is intended to deceive you: *You didn't swallow that story about Harry, did you?* **4** **swallow your pride** to do something that seems necessary even though you feel embarrassed or ashamed

swallow sth ↔ **up** *phr v* [T] to make something disappear, especially into something larger or stronger: *Most of my money is swallowed up by rent.*

swallow[2] *n* [C] **1** when you make food or drink go down your throat **2** a common small bird with pointed wings and a tail with two points

swam /swæm/ *v* the past tense of SWIM

swamp[1] /swɒmp‖swɑːmp/ *n* [C,U] land that is always very wet or covered with water

swamp[2] *v* [T] **1** *informal* to suddenly give someone more work, problems etc than they can deal with: *We've been swamped with phone calls about the article.* **2** to suddenly cover something with a lot of water: *High waves swamped the boat.*

swan /swɒn‖swɑːn/ *n* [C] a large white bird with a long neck, that lives on lakes and rivers

swank·y /'swæŋki/ *adj informal* very fashionable or expensive: *a swanky hotel*

swap also **swop** /swɒp‖swɑːp/ *v* [I,T] **-pped, -pping** to exchange something you have for something that someone else has: **swap (sth) with sb** *Can I swap seats with you?* | **swap sth for sth** *I'll swap my red T-shirt for your green one.* —**swap** *n* [C] *Shall we do a swap?*

swarm[1] /swɔːm‖swɔːrm/ *v* [I] to move in a large uncontrolled crowd: *Tourists swarmed around the museum.*

swarm with sth *phr v* [T] to be full of a moving crowd of people, birds, or insects: *The beach was swarming with people.*

swarm[2] *n* [C] a large group of insects that move together: *a swarm of bees*

swar·thy /'swɔːði‖'swɔːr-/ *adj* having dark skin. Some people consider this word to be offensive.

swat /swɒt‖swɑːt/ *v* [T] **-tted, -tting** to hit an insect to try to kill it

sway /sweɪ/ *v* **1** [I] to move slowly from one side to another: *trees swaying in the breeze* **2** [T] to try to influence someone to change their opinion about something: *Nothing you say will sway her.*

swear /sweə‖swer/ *v* **swore** /swɔː‖swɔːr/, **sworn** /swɔːn‖swɔːrn/, **swearing** **1** [I] to use rude or offensive language: *She doesn't smoke, drink, or swear.* | **+ at** *He was fired for swearing at his boss.* **2** [I,T] to make a very serious promise: *Do you swear to tell the truth?* | *I swear I'll never leave you.* **3** [T] *spoken* used to emphasize something or to say that you are certain about something: *I swear I'll kill him!* | *I could have sworn* (=I was certain) *I put the ticket in my pocket.*

swear by sth *phr v* [T] *informal* to strongly believe that something is effective: *Heidi swears by acupuncture.*

swear sb ↔ **in** *phr v* [T] to make someone formally promise that they will tell the truth for a

court of law, or be loyal to a country when they start to do an important public job: *She was sworn in as president just two weeks ago.*

swear word /'. ./ *n* [C] a word that is considered to be rude or shocking by most people

sweat[1] /swet/ *v* **1** [I] to have liquid coming out through your skin, especially when you are hot or nervous; PERSPIRE: *As he approached the customs post he began to sweat.* **2** [I] *informal* to work hard: *I sweated all night to get the report finished.*

sweat sth ↔ **out** *phr v* [T] to continue in an unpleasant situation and wait anxiously for it to end: *We had to sweat it out until they arrived.*

sweat[2] *n* **1** [U] liquid that comes out through your skin, especially when you are hot or nervous; PERSPIRATION: *Sweat was running down her face.* **2** [singular] when you sweat: **break into a sweat** (=start to sweat): *He broke into a sweat as soon as he went on stage.* **3** **no sweat** *spoken* used to say that you can do something easily: *"Can you give Kara a ride home?" "Yeah, no sweat!"*

sweat·er /'swetə‖-ər/ *n* [C] a piece of warm woollen clothing for the top half of your body ➔ see colour picture on page 113

sweats /swets/ *n* [plural] *informal AmE* clothes made of thick soft cotton, usually worn for playing sports ➔ see colour picture on page 113

sweat·shirt /'swet-ʃɜːt‖-ʃɜːrt/ *n* [C] a thick soft cotton shirt with long SLEEVES and no buttons down the front ➔ see colour picture on page 113

sweat·shop /'swet-ʃɒp‖-ʃɑːp/ *n* [C] a factory where people work hard in bad conditions for very little money

sweat·y /'sweti/ *adj* covered with SWEAT, or smelling of sweat: *I was hot and sweaty from working in the sun.*

swede /swiːd/ *n* [C,U] *BrE* a round yellow vegetable that grows under the ground; RUTABAGA *AmE*

sweep[1] /swiːp/ *v* **1** [I,T] **swept** /swept/, **swept, sweeping** also **sweep up** to clean the dirt from the floor or ground by brushing: *I've just swept the kitchen floor.* | *Could you sweep up the leaves?* **2** [I,T] to move quickly or spread, often with a lot of force: **through/across etc** *A storm swept across the country.* | **sweep the country/nation** *a fashion that is sweeping the nation* **3** [I] to move quickly in a way that shows you are very confident or annoyed, or think that you are important: *She swept into the meeting and demanded to know why she hadn't been invited.* **4** [T] to push or move something in a particular direction with a brushing movement: *He swept his hair away from his face.*

sweep

sweep sth ↔ **away** *phr v* [T] to completely destroy something or make something disappear: *Many houses were swept away by the floods.*

sweep² n [C] **1** [usually singular] a long, swinging movement: *She spoke with a sweep of her arm.* **2** a long curved line or area of land: *the sweep of the bay* **3** also **chimney sweep** a child whose job was to clean CHIMNEYs in past times

sweep·ing /'swiːpɪŋ/ adj **1** affecting many things, or affecting one thing very much: *sweeping changes* **2 sweeping statement/generalization** a statement that is unfair because it includes all the people in a group, all the parts of a situation etc without saying that some may be different: *Women tend to be more sensitive than men – but of course that's a sweeping generalization.*

sweep·stake /'swiːpsteɪk/ n [C] a type of gambling (GAMBLE) in which the winner gets all the money

sweet¹ /swiːt/ adj **1** having a taste like sugar: *Is your coffee too sweet?* | *a sweet, sticky chocolate cake* **2** having a pleasant smell or sound: *a sweet-smelling rose* | *the sweet sounds of the cello* **3** kind, gentle, and friendly: *It was sweet of you to help.* **4** pretty and pleasant – used when you are talking about children or small things: *Her baby is so sweet!* **5 have a sweet tooth** to like to eat sweet foods —**sweetly** adv —**sweetness** n [U]

sweet² n [C] *BrE* a small piece of sweet food made of sugar or chocolate; CANDY *AmE: Try not to eat too many sweets, crisps and biscuits.*

sweet·corn /'swiːtkɔːn‖-kɔːrn/ n [U] *BrE* soft yellow seeds from MAIZE that are cooked and eaten as a vegetable; CORN *AmE*

sweet·en /'swiːtn/ v **1** [I,T] to make something sweeter or to become sweeter: *Sweeten the mixture with honey.* **2** also **sweeten sb up** to do nice things for someone or give them presents, in order to persuade them to do something: *They tried to sweeten him up with compliments before asking for more money.*

sweet·ener /'swiːtnə‖-ər/ n **1** [C,U] a substance used instead of sugar to make food or drinks taste sweeter **2** [C] *informal* something that you give to someone to persuade them to do something: *The tax cut is just a sweetener before the election.*

sweet·heart /'swiːthɑːt‖-hɑːrt/ n [C] someone who you love – used especially when talking to the person who you love: *Good night, sweetheart.*

sweet po·ta·to /ˌ. .'.., '. .ˌ../ n [C] a root that looks like a long red potato, cooked and eaten as a vegetable

swell¹ /swel/ v **swelled, swollen** /'swəʊlən‖ 'swoʊ-/ **swelling 1** [I] also **swell up** to increase in size: *My ankle swelled up like a balloon.* **2** [I,T] to increase to a much bigger amount or number: *The city's population has swollen to 2 million.*

swell² n [singular] the way the sea moves up and down

swell³ adj *AmE old-fashioned* very good: *a swell party*

swell·ing /'swelɪŋ/ n [C,U] an area on your body that becomes bigger than usual because of injury or illness: *a swelling on the knee*

swel·ter·ing /'sweltərɪŋ/ adj unpleasantly hot

swept /swept/ v the past tense and past participle of SWEEP

swerve /swɜːv‖swɜːrv/ v [I] to turn suddenly while you are driving or flying: *Mark swerved to avoid hitting a dog.*

swift /swɪft/ adj happening or moving very quickly and smoothly: *a swift reply* —**swiftly** adv: *a swiftly flowing river*

swig /swɪg/ v [T] **-gged, -gging** *informal* to drink something quickly, taking a large amount in your mouth each time you drink —**swig** n [C] *a swig of brandy*

swill¹ /swɪl/ n [U] food for pigs

swill² v [T] **1** also **swill out** to wash something by pouring a lot of water over or through it: *Get a bucket of water and swill the yard down.* **2** to drink a lot of something, especially alcohol: *men swilling beer*

swim¹ /swɪm/ v **swam** /swæm/, **swum** /swʌm/, **swimming 1** [I,T] to move through water using your arms, legs etc: *Can Lucy swim?* | *fish swimming up the stream* | *She swims 20 lengths every day.* → see colour picture on page 636 **2** [I] if your head is swimming, you feel confused and DIZZY **3** [I] if objects are swimming, they seem to be moving, because you are ill or have been looking at them for too long: *The screen was swimming in front of me.* —**swimming** n [U] *Let's go swimming.* —**swimmer** n [C]

swim² n [C] a time when you swim: **go for a swim** *I went for a swim after school.*

swimming cos·tume /'.. ..ˌ../ n [C] *BrE* a piece of clothing worn for swimming

swimming pool /'.. ./ also **pool** n [C] a place where you can swim

swimming trunks /'.. ./ also **trunks** n [plural] a piece of clothing that boys and men wear for swimming

swim·suit /'swɪmsuːt, -sjuːt‖-suːt/ n [C] a piece of clothing that girls and women wear for swimming

swin·dle /'swɪndl/ v [T] to get money from someone by tricking them —**swindle** n [C] *victims of a swindle* —**swindler** n [C]

swine /swaɪn/ n [C], *plural* **swine 1** *old-fashioned* a pig **2** *informal* someone who behaves very badly

swing¹ /swɪŋ/ v **swung** /swʌŋ/, **swung**, **swinging 1** [I,T] to move backwards and forwards while hanging, or to make something do this: *a sign swinging in the wind* | *They walked along, swinging their arms.* **2** [I,T] to move smoothly in a curved direction, or to make something move this way: *The gate swung open.* **3** [I] if opinions or feelings swing, they change a lot: *Her mood can swing from sadness to happiness quite suddenly.*

swing around phr v [I] to turn around quickly: *Mike swung around to look at me.*

swing at sb/sth phr v [T] to try to hit someone or something: *He swung at me and missed.*

swing² n [C] **1** a hanging seat that swings, that children play on **2** an attempt to hit someone or something: *The guy took a swing at me.* **3** a change from one feeling, opinion etc to another: **+ in** *a big swing in public opinion* **4 be in full swing** if a party, event etc is in full swing, it has reached a stage where there is a lot of activity

swipe /swaɪp/ v [T] **1** *informal* to steal something: *Somebody swiped my wallet.* **2** also **swipe**

at to hit or try to hit someone or something by swinging your arm at them — **swipe** n [C]

swipe·card /'swaɪpkɑːd‖-kɑːrd/ n [C] a small plastic card that operates electronic equipment, for example electronically controlled doors or CASH REGISTERS

swirl /swɜːl‖swɜːrl/ v [I,T] to turn around and around, or to make something do this: *leaves swirling around on the ground*

swish /swɪʃ/ v [I,T] to move through the air with a soft sound, or to make something do this: *a cow swishing its tail* — **swish** n [C]

switch¹ /swɪtʃ/ v [I,T] **1** to change from doing or using one thing to doing or using something else: *Switch channels and see if there's a movie on.* | **switch (sth) to sth** *He studied biology before switching to law.* **2** to exchange a thing, job, or position with someone else: *We must have switched jackets by accident.* | **switch (sth) with sb** *Will you switch places with me?*
   switch off phr v **1** [I,T **switch** sth ↔ **off**] to turn off a machine, light etc with a switch: *Don't forget to switch off the TV when you go to bed.* **2** [I] *informal* to stop listening or paying attention: *He just switches off when he's tired.*
   switch sth ↔ **on** phr v [T] to turn on a machine, radio, light etc with a switch: *Switch on the light, please.*
   switch over phr v [I] to change to a different television CHANNEL

switch² n [C] **1** the part that you press up or down on a machine, light etc so that it starts or stops operating: *a light switch* **2** a change from doing or using one thing to doing or using something else: *The switch to the new computer system has been difficult.*

switch·board /'swɪtʃbɔːd‖-bɔːrd/ n [C] a piece of equipment that directs all the telephone calls made to or from a business, hotel etc

swiv·el /'swɪvəl/ also **swivel around** v [I,T] to turn around while staying in the same place, or to make something do this: *a chair that swivels*

swol·len¹ /'swəʊlən‖swoʊ-/ v the past participle of SWELL

swollen² adj **1** a part of your body that is swollen is bigger than usual, especially because it is injured **2** a swollen river has more water in it than usual

swoop /swuːp/ v **1** [I] to suddenly and quickly move through the air, especially to attack something: + **down/through** etc *The hawk hovered for a moment in the air and then swooped down.* **2** to make an unexpected attack: + **on/in** *Police swooped on the house and made several arrests.* — **swoop** n [C]

swop /swɒp‖swɑːp/ another spelling of SWAP

sword /sɔːd‖sɔːrd/ n [C] a weapon with a long sharp blade and a handle

sword·fish /'sɔːd,fɪʃ‖'sɔːrd-/ n [C] a large fish with a long pointed upper jaw shaped like a sword

swore /swɔː‖swɔːr/ v the past tense of SWEAR

sworn¹ /swɔːn‖swɔːrn/ v the past participle of SWEAR

sworn² adj **1 sworn statement/testimony** something you say or write that you have officially promised is the truth **2 sworn enemies** two people or groups who hate each other

swot¹ /swɒt/ n [C] *BrE informal* someone who studies too hard

swot² *BrE informal* to study hard

swum /swʌm/ v the past participle of SWIM

swung /swʌŋ/ v the past tense and past participle of SWING

syc·a·more /'sɪkəmɔː‖-mɔːr/ n [C,U] a tree with broad leaves, or the wood from this tree

syc·o·phant /'sɪkəfənt/ n [C] *formal* someone who tries too hard to please important people in order to get something from them — **sycophantic** adj

syl·la·ble /'sɪləbəl/ n [C] a part of a word that contains a single vowel sound. 'Cat' has one syllable, and 'butter' has two.

syl·la·bus /'sɪləbəs/ n [C], *plural* **syllabuses** or **syllabi** /-baɪ/ a list of what is studied for a particular course or subject

sym·bol /'sɪmbəl/ n [C] **1** a picture, object etc that is the sign of a particular quality, idea, or organization: *the five-ring symbol of the Olympic Games* | *a symbol of hope* **2** a letter, number, or sign that is used instead of a sound, amount, chemical substance etc: *What's the chemical symbol for oxygen?*

sym·bol·ic /sɪm'bɒlɪk‖-'bɑː-/ adj if something is symbolic of something else, it means something else: *Water in dreams is symbolic of emotions.* — **symbolically** /-kli/ adv

sym·bol·is·m /'sɪmbəlɪzəm/ n [U] the use of ideas, images etc to explain something else: *religious symbolism*

sym·bol·ize (also **-ise** *BrE*) /'sɪmbəlaɪz/ v [T] to be used or seen as a symbol of something: *A wedding ring symbolizes a couple's vows to each other.*

sym·met·ri·cal /sɪ'metrɪkəl/ also **sym·met·ric** /sɪ'metrɪk/ adj having halves or sides that are exactly the same size and shape → opposite ASYMMETRICAL

sym·me·try /'sɪmɪtri/ n [U] when both halves or sides of something are exactly the same size and shape

sym·pa·thet·ic /ˌsɪmpə'θetɪk◂/ adj **1** showing that you understand how sad, hurt etc someone feels: *a sympathetic nurse* **2** willing to support someone's ideas, opinions or actions: *He was quite sympathetic to my plan.* — **sympathetically** /-kli/ adv → opposite UNSYMPATHETIC

sym·pa·thize (also **-ise** *BrE*) /'sɪmpəθaɪz/ v [I] **1** to understand how sad, hurt etc someone feels: + **with** *I sympathize with her husband.* **2** to support someone's ideas, opinions or actions: + **with** *Not many people sympathize with his political views.*

sym·pa·thiz·er (also **-iser** *BrE*) /'sɪmpəθaɪzə‖-ər/ n [C] someone who supports a political

---

SPELLING NOTE

Words with the sound /s/, may be spelt **c-**, like **city**, or **ps-**, like **psychology**.

party but does not belong to it, especially one that you disapprove of

sym·pa·thy /'sɪmpəθi/ n [C,U] **1** the feeling you have when you feel sorry for someone who is having problems, and you understand how they feel: **+ with/for** *My sympathies are with the victims' families.* | *I have no sympathy for Joan – it's her own fault.* **2** support for someone's ideas, opinions or actions: **in sympathy with** (=in order to show support): *Students marched in sympathy with the strikers.*

sym·pho·ny /'sɪmfəni/ n [C] a long piece of music written for an ORCHESTRA: *Beethoven's Fifth Symphony*

symp·tom /'sɪmptəm/ n [C] **1** a physical condition that shows you may have a particular disease: *The symptoms are a fever, sore throat and headache.* **2** a sign that a serious problem exists: *The rise in the crime rate is another symptom of widespread poverty.* —**symptomatic** /ˌsɪmptəˈmætɪk◂/ adj

syn·a·gogue /'sɪnəgɒgǁ-gɑːg/ n [C] a building where Jewish people meet for religious services

sync /sɪŋk/ informal **1 in sync** two or more things that are in sync are happening at the same time: *The band wasn't in sync with the drummer.* **2 out of sync** two or more things that are out of sync are not happening at the same time

syn·chro·nize (also **-ise** BrE) /'sɪŋkrənaɪz/ v [T] **1** to make two or more things happen at the same time: *The soldiers synchronized their steps as they marched.* **2** to make two or more watches or clocks show exactly the same time —**synchronization** /ˌsɪŋkrənaɪˈzeɪʃənǁ-nə-/ n [U]

syn·di·cate /'sɪndɪkət/ n [C] a group of people, companies etc that have joined together to achieve the same aim: *a drugs syndicate*

syn·drome /'sɪndrəʊmǁ-droʊm/ n [C] a set of problems, features, events etc that go with a particular situation or medical condition: *Sudden Infant Death Syndrome*

syn·o·nym /'sɪnənɪm/ n [C] a word with the same meaning as another word in the same language: *'Shut' and 'close' are synonyms.*
→ opposite ANTONYM

sy·non·y·mous /sɪ'nɒnɪməsǁ-'nɑː-/ adj **1** very closely connected with or always involving another situation, condition etc: *Success is not necessarily synonymous with happiness.* **2** having the same meaning as another word

sy·nop·sis /sɪ'nɒpsɪsǁ-'nɑːp-/ n [C], plural **synopses** /-siːz/ a short description of the main parts of a story

syn·tax /'sɪntæks/ n [U] technical the way words are arranged to form sentences or phrases

syn·the·sis /'sɪnθəsɪs/ n [C,U] formal when several things are combined to form a single unit

syn·the·size (also **-ise** BrE) /'sɪnθəsaɪz/ v [T] to combine several ideas, styles, substances etc in order to produce something: *Plants can synthesize energy from sunlight and water.*

syn·the·siz·er (also **-iser** BrE) /'sɪnθəsaɪzəǁ-ər/ n [C] an electronic musical instrument that can sound like many different musical instruments

syn·thet·ic /sɪn'θetɪk/ adj made from artificial substances, not natural ones: *synthetic fabrics like acrylic* —**synthetically** /-kli/ adv

syph·i·lis /'sɪfəlɪs/ n [U] a very serious disease that can be passed from one person to another during sex

sy·ringe /sɪ'rɪndʒ/ n [C] a hollow tube and needle used for removing blood from your body, or for putting medicine or drugs into it

syr·up /'sɪrəpǁ'sɜː-, 'sɪ-/ n [U] thick sticky liquid made from sugar —**syrupy** adj

sys·tem /'sɪstəm/ n **1** [C] an organized way of doing something: *the public transport system* | *a system for measuring liquids* | *Oregon's school system* **2** parts of your body, such as bones or organs, that work together: *the nervous system* **3 the system** informal the rules, TRADITIONS, government etc in a society: *You can't fight the system.* **4 get sth out of your system** informal to do something that helps you stop feeling angry, annoyed, or upset

sys·te·mat·ic /ˌsɪstɪ'mætɪk◂/ adj using an organized plan or process; THOROUGH: *a systematic search* —**systematically** /-kli/ adv

Tt

T, t /tiː/ the letter 't'

T **to a T/to a tee** *informal* exactly or perfectly: *The dress fits her to a T.*

tab /tæb/ n **1** [C] *especially AmE* the amount you owe for a restaurant meal or a service; BILL *BrE*: **pick up the tab** (=pay): *Jeff picked up the tab for lunch.* **2** **keep tabs on sb/sth** *informal* to carefully watch what someone or something is doing: *The police are keeping close tabs on her.* **3** [C] a small piece of metal, plastic, paper, or cloth that is fixed to something and gives information about it or can be used to open it

tab·by /'tæbi/ n [C] a cat with different coloured marks on its fur, usually grey and brown and white or orange

ta·ble[1] /'teɪbəl/ n [C] **1** a piece of furniture with a flat top supported by legs: *They all sat around the kitchen table.* | *I've booked a table for 8 o'clock* (=in a restaurant). → see colour picture on page 474 **2** a list of numbers or set of facts arranged in rows across and down a page: *The report is full of tables and statistics.* | **the table of contents** (=a list of the parts of a book and what page they are on) **3** **set the table** also **lay the table** *BrE* to put knives, forks, dishes etc on a table before a meal **4** **turn the tables on sb** to change a situation completely so that you are no longer in a weak position and someone else is no longer in a strong one

table[2] v [T] **1** **table a proposal/question etc** *BrE* to formally suggest something to be discussed at a meeting **2** **table an offer/idea etc** *AmE* to decide to deal with an offer, idea, etc later

ta·ble·cloth /'teɪbəlklɒθ‖-klɔːθ/ n [C] a cloth used for covering a table

ta·ble·spoon /'teɪbəlspuːn/ n [C] **1** a large spoon used for measuring or serving food **2** also **tablespoonful** /-fʊl/ the amount that this spoon holds

tab·let[1] /'tæblɪt/ n [C] **1** a small round hard thing that you swallow, which contains medicine; PILL: *sleeping tablets* **2** a piece of clay or stone that has words cut into it

table ten·nis /'.. ,../ n [U] a game played on a table, in which people hit a small ball to each other across a low net; PING-PONG

tab·loid /'tæblɔɪd/ n [C] a newspaper that has small pages, short simple reports, and usually not much serious news

ta·boo /tə'buː, tæ'buː/ n [C,U] something that you must not do or talk about, because people think that it is morally wrong or embarrassing —**taboo** adj: *Sex is a taboo subject in many homes.*

tab·u·late /'tæbjʊleɪt/ v [T] to arrange information together in lists or rows —**tabulation** /ˌtæbjʊ'leɪʃən/ n [U]

ta·cit /'tæsɪt/ adj tacit agreement, approval, or support is given without being stated or officially agreed —**tacitly** adv

ta·ci·turn /'tæsɪtɜːn‖-ɜːrn/ adj a taciturn person does not talk a lot, and seems unfriendly

tack[1] /tæk/ v [T] to fasten something to a wall, board etc using a small nail

tack sth ↔ on *phr v* [T] *informal* to add something to another thing: *Joan tacked a few words on the end of my letter.*

tack[2] n [singular] **1** a way of dealing with a problem, a difficult situation etc: *If polite requests don't work, you'll have to try a different tack.* **2** [C] *AmE* a THUMBTACK **3** [C] a small nail with a sharp point and a flat top: *carpet tacks*

tack·le[1] /'tækəl/ v [T] **1** to make a determined effort to deal with a difficult problem: *a new attempt to tackle the problem of homelessness* **2** to try to take the ball away from someone in a game such as football or RUGBY

tackle[2] n **1** [C] when someone tries to take the ball away from another player in a game such as football or RUGBY: *a dangerous tackle* **2** [U] the equipment used in some sports such as FISHING

tack·y /'tæki/ adj *informal* looking cheap and of bad quality: *tacky furniture* **2** slightly sticky, and not quiet dry —**tackiness** n [U]

ta·co /'tɑːkəʊ‖-koʊ/ n [C] a Mexican-American food made from a round flat corn bread, that is folded and filled with meat, beans etc

tact /tækt/ n [U] the ability to say or do things carefully and politely so that you do not embarrass or upset someone

tact·ful /'tæktfəl/ adj careful not to say or do something that will upset or embarrass someone —**tactfully** adv

tac·tic /'tæktɪk/ n [C usually plural] a method that you use to achieve what you want, especially in a game, competition, or battle: *aggressive business tactics*

tac·tic·al /'tæktɪkəl/ adj **1** done to achieve what you want: *a tactical move to avoid criticism* **2** connected with tactics: *a serious tactical error* —**tactically** /-kli/ adv

tact·less /'tæktləs/ adj not careful to avoid doing or saying something that will upset or embarrass someone → opposite TACTFUL

tad /tæd/ n **a tad** *spoken* a small amount

tad·pole /'tædpəʊl‖-poʊl/ n [C] a small creature that will become a FROG or TOAD

taf·fe·ta /'tæfɪtə/ n [U] a shiny stiff cloth made from silk or NYLON: *a taffeta dress*

tag[1] /tæg/ n [C] a small piece of paper, plastic etc that is fastened to something to show information about it: *I can't find the price tag on these jeans.* → see also QUESTION TAG

tag[2] v [T] **-gged, -gging** to fasten a tag onto something

tag along *phr v* [I] *informal* to go somewhere with someone: *Is it all right if I tag along?*

tail[1] /teɪl/ n [C] **1** the long thin part at the back of the body of a dog, cat, fish etc: *The dog was wagging its tail.* **2** the back part of a plane, or of something long and thin: *the tail of a comet* → see picture at AIRCRAFT **3** **the tail end of** the last part of something: *the tail end of the century* → see also TAILS

tail[2] v [T] *informal* to secretly follow someone who you think is doing something wrong

tail off *phr v* [I] to gradually become quieter, smaller, less etc: *His voice tailed off as he saw his father approaching.*

tail·back /ˈteɪlbæk/ n [C] a long line of cars that have stopped or are moving slowly, caused by an accident, repairs to the road etc

tail·coat /teɪlˈkəʊt, ˈteɪlkəʊt‖-koʊt/ n [C] TAILS

tail·gate /ˈteɪlɡeɪt/ v [I,T] to drive too closely behind another vehicle —**tailgating** n [U]

tail-light, tail light /ˈ. ./ n [C] one of the two red lights at the back of a car → see picture at CAR

tai·lor¹ /ˈteɪlə‖-ər/ n [C] someone whose job is to make clothes, especially men's clothes that are measured to fit each customer

tailor² v [T] to make something so that it is exactly what someone wants or needs: *Courses are specially tailored to the needs of each student.*

tai·lor·ing /ˈteɪlərɪŋ/ n [U] the way that clothes are made, or the job of making them

tailor-made /ˌ.. ˈ. ◂/ adj **1** very suitable for someone or something: *The job seems tailor-made for him.* **2** made by a tailor: *a tailor-made silk suit*

tail·pipe /ˈteɪlpaɪp/ n [C] AmE an EXHAUST PIPE

tails /teɪlz/ n **1** [U] the side of a coin that does not have a picture of someone's head on it **2** [plural] a man's suit coat with two long parts that hang down the back, worn to formal events

taint /teɪnt/ v [T] **1** be tainted (by/with) to be connected with something illegal or dishonest, so that people are less likely to approve of you: *The previous government had been tainted by accusations of corruption.* | *tainted money* **2** food or other things that are tainted have been spoiled or have something harmful in them: *tainted blood products* —**taint** n [singular]

take¹ /teɪk/ v [T] took /tʊk/, taken /ˈteɪkən/, taking **1** to move someone or something from one place to another: *He took some money out of his pocket.* | *Merritt was taken by ambulance to the nearest hospital.* **2** to carry or have something with you somewhere: *Don't forget to take your car keys!* **3** to steal something or borrow it without permission: *Someone's taken my wallet!* **4** to put your hand around something and hold it: *Let me take your coat.* | *She took his arm.* **5** to go with someone to a place: *I'm taking her to an Italian restaurant.* | *They took us downstairs.* **6** used with some nouns, to say that someone does something, or that something happens: *Here, take a look.* | *Let me just take a quick shower first.* | **take action** (=do something to deal with a problem) **7** if something takes a period of time, you need that amount of time to do it: *It takes about three days to drive up there.* **8** if something takes courage, skill, effort, money etc, you need courage etc to do it: *Looking after children takes a lot of hard work.* **9** to accept or receive something: *Are you going to take the job?* | *Take my advice and go see a doctor.* | **take credit cards/a cheque etc** (=accept them as a way of paying): *Do you take American Express?* **10 take a picture/photograph** to photograph something **11 take a holiday/break/rest etc** to have a holiday etc **12 take a test/exam** to do a test or examination: *I'm taking my driving test next week.* **13** to swallow or use a medicine or drug: *Why don't you take an aspirin or something?* | **take drugs** (=take illegal drugs): *A lot of kids start taking drugs when they're 14 or 15.* **14** to use a car, bus, train etc to go somewhere, or to travel using a particular road: *I'll take the subway*

home. **15** to accept an unpleasant situation: *can't take She couldn't take the pressure of teaching.* **16** to have a particular feeling about something: **take pleasure/pride/an interest etc** *She seems to take pleasure in hurting people.* | **take sth seriously** (=think that it is important): *Alan takes his job very seriously.* **17** to have enough space for a particular number of people or things: *Our car can take up to six people.* **18** to choose to buy something: **I'll take it** *spoken: "It's $50." "OK, I'll take it."* **19** to wear a particular size of clothes: *What size shoes do you take?* **20 take milk/sugar etc** to have milk, sugar etc in your coffee, tea etc **21** to understand that someone means a particular thing, or that something shows that another thing is true: *I shall take that as a compliment.* **22 take a lot out of sb** to make someone very tired **23 take some doing/a lot of doing** to be very difficult to do **24 take it from me** *spoken* used to persuade someone that what you are saying is true **25 I take it that** *spoken* used to check with someone that something is true or has been done **26 take a message** to listen to or write down what someone says, so that you can tell it to another person later: *He's not here right now; can I take a message?* **27** to test or measure something: *The doctor took her blood pressure.* **28** to get control of something by using military force: *Rebel forces have taken the airport.* **29 take it upon yourself** to decide to do something, even though no one has asked you to do it: *Parents have taken it upon themselves to raise extra cash for the school.* → see also **be taken aback** (ABACK), **take care** (CARE²), **take care of** (CARE²), **take part** (PART¹), **take place** (PLACE¹), **take sides** (SIDE¹)

take after sb phr v [T] to look or behave like another member of your family: *Jenny takes after her dad.*

take sth ↔ apart phr v [T] to separate something into pieces: *Jim took apart the faucet and put in a new washer.*

take away phr v **1** [T take sth ↔ away] to remove something from someone or somewhere: *They took away his licence.* **2** [take sb ↔ away] to take someone to a prison or hospital: *Hyde was taken away in handcuffs.*

take sth ↔ back phr v [T] **1** to return something to the shop where you bought it **2** to admit that something you said was wrong: *All right, I'm sorry, I take it back.*

take sth ↔ down phr v [T] **1** to remove something from the place where it was: *We take down the Christmas tree on January 6.* → opposite **put up** (PUT) **2** to write information on a piece of paper: *The receptionist took down his name.*

take in phr v [T] **1** [take sth ↔ in] to understand what you see, read, or hear: *There was so much happening in the film, it was difficult to take it all in.* **2 be taken in** to be deceived by someone or something: *The bank had been taken in by the forged receipts.* **3** [take sb/sth ↔ in] to let someone stay with you because they have nowhere else to stay: *The Humane Society took in almost 38,000 cats and dogs last year.* **4** [take in sth] to go to see a film, play etc **5** [take in sth] to make a piece of clothing narrower, so that it fits you

take off _phr v_ **1** [T **take** sth ↔ **off**] to remove something: _Your name has been taken off the list._|_He took off his shoes._ **2** [I] if a plane takes off, it goes up into the air **3 take some time/a day/a week off** to not go to work for a period of time **4** [I] _informal_ to leave somewhere quickly and suddenly: _We packed everything in the car and took off._ **5** [I] to suddenly become successful: _Her career took off as soon as she moved to Hollywood._

take on _phr v_ [T] **1** [**take** sb ↔ **on**] to compete or fight against someone: _The winner of this game will take on Houston._ **2** [**take on** sth] to start to seem different in some way: _Once we had children, Christmas took on a different sort of importance._ **3** [**take** sth ↔ **on**] to start doing some work or start being responsible for something: _I've taken on far too much work lately._ **4** [**take** sb **on**] to start to employ someone: _The team has taken on a new coach._

take out _phr v_ [T] **1** [**take** sth ↔ **out**] to remove something: _The dentist says she may have to take out one of my back teeth._ **2** [**take** sb **out**] to go out with someone to a restaurant, film, party etc, and pay for them: _I'm taking Helen out for dinner next week._ **3** [**take** sth ↔ **out**] to arrange to get something from a bank, court etc: _The couple took out a £20,000 loan._

take sth ↔ **out on** sb _phr v_ [T] to behave angrily towards someone because you are upset or angry about something, even though it is not their fault

take over _phr v_ [I,T **take** sth ↔ **over**] to get control of something, or get responsibility for something: _His son will take over the business._

take to _phr v_ [T] **1** [**take to** sb/sth] to start to like someone or something: _The two women took to each other right away._ **2 take to doing** sth to begin doing something regularly: _Sandra has taken to getting up early to go jogging._

take up sth _phr v_ [T] **1** to begin doing a job or activity: _I've just taken up golf._ **2** to use an amount of time or space: _The program takes up a lot of memory on the hard drive._

take sb **up on** sth _phr v_ [T] to accept an offer, invitation etc: _Thanks for the offer. I might take you up on it._

take sth **up with** sb _phr v_ [T] to discuss something with someone, especially a complaint or problem: _You should take it up with the union._

take² _n_ **1** [C] an attempt to film a scene for a film or television programme: _Cut! Take 2!_ **2** [singular] _informal_ TAKINGS

take·a·way /ˈteɪkəweɪ/ _n_ [C] _BrE_ a meal that you buy from a restaurant to eat somewhere else, or a restaurant that sells this food; TAKEOUT _AmE_ —**takeaway** _adj_

take-off, takeoff /ˈteɪkɒf‖-ɔːf/ _n_ **1** [C,U] when a plane moves off the ground into the air **2** [C] a funny performance that copies the style of a particular show, film, or performer: _'Spaceball' is supposed to be a take-off of 'Star Wars'._

take·out /ˈteɪkaʊt/ _n_ [C] _AmE_ a TAKEAWAY — **take-out** _adj_

take·o·ver /ˈteɪkˌəʊvəˈ-ˌoʊvər/ _n_ [C] when a company gets control of another company, or a political group or a country gets control of another country: _the union's fears about job losses after the takeover_

tak·ings /ˈteɪkɪŋz/ _n_ [plural] the amount of money that a shop, bar etc gets from selling things: _the day's takings_

tal·cum pow·der /ˈtælkəm ˌpaʊdəˈ-dər/ also **talc** /tælk/ _n_ [U] a fine powder that you put on your skin to keep it dry

tale /teɪl/ _n_ [C] a story about imaginary events: _a book of fairy tales_

tal·ent /ˈtælənt/ _n_ [C,U] a natural ability to do something well: _She has a talent for painting._

tal·ent·ed /ˈtæləntˌd/ _adj_ having the natural ability to do something well: _talented young players_

tal·is·man /ˈtælˌzmən/ _n_ [C] a magic object that people think can protect them or bring them good luck

talk¹ /tɔːk‖tɒːk/ _v_ **1** [I] to say things to someone: _How old was your baby when she started to talk?_|**talk to sb** also **talk with sb** _AmE Who's he talking to on the phone?_|**+ about** _Grandpa never talks much about the war._ **2** [I,T] to discuss something with someone: **talk to sb** also **talk with sb** _AmE I'd like to talk with you in private._|**+ about** _It always helps to talk about your problems._ **3** [I] to tell someone secret information because you are forced to: _They threatened to shoot him, but he still refused to talk._ **4 talk your way out of sth** _informal_ to avoid an unpleasant situation by talking and giving explanations: _He usually manages to talk his way out of trouble._ **5 what are you talking about?** _spoken_ used when someone has said something stupid or annoying: _Aliens? UFOs? What are you talking about?_ **6 talk about** _spoken informal_ used to emphasize what you are saying: _Talk about lucky!_ **7 talk sense** to say things that are sensible and true **8 talk (some) sense into sb** to talk to someone and make them start behaving in a sensible way, or make them change their decision to a more sensible one **9 talking of** _spoken_ used when you mention something that is connected with what you have just been talking about: _Talking of food, isn't it time for lunch?_ **10 talk shop** _informal_ to talk about things that are connected with your work when you are not at the place where you work, in a way that is boring for other people: _The trouble with teachers is that they're always talking shop._

talk back _phr v_ [I] to answer someone rudely: _Don't talk back to your father!_

talk down to sb _phr v_ [T] to speak to someone in a way that shows you think they are less important, less intelligent than you

talk sb **into** sth _phr v_ [T] to persuade someone to do something, especially something that they do not want to do: _I didn't want to go, but my friends talked me into it._

talk sb **out of** sth _phr v_ [T] to persuade someone not to do something

---

GRAMMAR NOTE: transitive and intransitive (2)
Some verbs can be used **transitive** or **intransitive**. For example: **read** _v_ [T,I]
• Transitive: _I can't read your handwriting._
• Intransitive: _Tom learned to read at the age of four._

talk sth ↔ **over** *phr v* [T] to discuss all the details of something before making a decision about it

talk[2] *n* **1** [C] a conversation about something: *Steve and I had a long talk last night.* **2** [C] a speech or LECTURE: *Professor Mason will be giving a talk on the Civil War.* **3** [U] when people say that something may be true or may happen: *There was talk of the factory closing down.* **4** **it's just talk/it's all talk** *spoken* used to say that you do not think someone will really do what they say, or that something will really happen → see also SMALL TALK, TALKS

talk·a·tive /ˈtɔːkətɪvǁˈtɔːk-/ *adj* someone who is talkative talks a lot

talk·er /ˈtɔːkəǁˈtɔːkər/ *n* [C] *informal* used to say how often someone talks, how good they are at talking etc: *He's a great talker.* (=he talks a lot)

talks /tɔːksǁtɔːks/ *n* [plural] *formal* discussions between two governments, organizations etc: *the latest trade talks*

talk show /ˈ. ./ *n* [C] *AmE* a television or radio show in which people answer questions about themselves or discuss important subjects; CHAT SHOW *BrE*

tall /tɔːlǁtɔːl/ *adj* **1** having a greater than average height: *the tallest boy in the class | tall buildings* → see colour picture on page 244 and picture at HIGH **2** used to talk about someone's height: *My brother's almost 6 feet tall. | How tall are you?* **3** **be a tall order** *spoken* used to say that something will be extremely difficult to do **4** **a tall tale** *AmE*, **a tall story** *BrE* a story about something that has happened that makes it seem much more exciting, dangerous etc than it really is

tal·low /ˈtæləʊǁ-loʊ/ *n* [U] animal fat used for making CANDLES and soap

tal·ly[1] /ˈtæli/ *n* [C] a record of how much you have won, spent, used etc so far

tally[2] *v* **1** [I] if two numbers or statements tally, they match each other: *The witnesses' statements didn't tally.* **2** [T] also **tally up** to calculate the total number of something: *Can you tally up the scores?*

tal·on /ˈtælən/ *n* [C] one of the sharp curved CLAWS on the feet of some birds, which they use for hunting

tam·bou·rine /ˌtæmbəˈriːn/ *n* [C] a round musical instrument with small pieces of metal around the edge that you play by hitting or shaking

tame[1] /teɪm/ *adj* **1** a tame animal is not afraid of people and does not want to attack people **2** not as exciting or interesting as you had expected: *"How was the movie?" "Pretty tame."*

tame[2] *v* [T] to train a wild animal to obey people and not be afraid of them

tam·per /ˈtæmpəǁ-ər/ *v*
tamper with sth *phr v* [T] to change something without permission, especially in order to damage it: *Several bottles of aspirin had been tampered with.*

tam·pon /ˈtæmpɒnǁ-pɑːn/ *n* [C] a tube-shaped piece of cotton that a woman puts into her body during her PERIOD to collect the blood

tan[1] /tæn/ *n* [C] **1** when someone's skin becomes a darker colour because they have spent a lot of time in the sun; SUNTAN **2** [U] a pale yellow-brown colour

tan[2] *adj* **1** having a pale yellow-brown colour: *light tan shoes* **2** *AmE* having darker skin after spending a lot of time in the sun; TANNED: *Your face is really tan.*

tan[3] *v* [I,T] to get darker skin by spending time in the sun: *I don't tan easily.*

tan·dem /ˈtændəm/ *n* [C] a bicycle for two people

tan·gent /ˈtændʒənt/ *n* [C] **1** **go off on a tangent** to suddenly start talking or thinking about a completely different subject **2** *technical* a straight line that touches the edge of a curve but does not go through it

tan·ge·rine /ˌtændʒəˈriːnǁˈtændʒəriːn/ *n* [C] a small sweet orange

tan·gi·ble /ˈtændʒɪbəl/ *adj* clear and definite: *tangible proof* → opposite INTANGIBLE

tan·gle[1] /ˈtæŋɡəl/ *n* [C] a mass of hair, wires, branches etc that have become twisted together

tangle[2] *v* [I,T] to become twisted together, or to make something twisted together
tangle with sb *phr v* [T] *informal* to argue or fight with someone

tan·gled /ˈtæŋɡəld/ also **tangled up** *adj* **1** twisted together: *tangled blonde hair* **2** complicated and confusing: *tangled emotions*

tan·go /ˈtæŋɡəʊǁ-ɡoʊ/ *n* **the tango** a LIVELY dance from South America, or the music for this dance

tang·y /ˈtæŋi/ *adj* having a pleasant slightly sour taste, or a pleasantly strong smell: *a tangy lemon sauce* — **tang** *n* [singular]

tank[1] /tæŋk/ *n* [C] **1** a large container for holding liquid or gas: *the hot water tank | petrol tank BrE/gas tank AmE* (=a tank in a car for petrol) **2** a heavy military vehicle with a large gun, which moves on special belts that are turned by several wheels

tank[2] *v*
tank sth ↔ **up** *phr v* [I,T] *AmE* to fill a car's tank with petrol

tan·kard /ˈtæŋkədǁ-ərd/ *n* [C] a large metal cup, used for drinking beer

tank·er /ˈtæŋkəǁ-ər/ *n* [C] a ship or vehicle used for carrying liquid or gas: *an oil tanker*

tanned /tænd/ *adj* having a darker skin colour because you have spent a long time in the sun

tan·noy /ˈtænɔɪ/ *n* [singular] *BrE trademark* a system of LOUDSPEAKERS, used for announcing things in public places

tan·ta·liz·ing (also **-ising** *BrE*) /ˈtæntəl-aɪzɪŋ/ *adj* making you want something very much, especially something that you cannot have: *tantalizing smells from the kitchen* — **tantalizingly** *adv*: *Liverpool came tantalizingly close to victory.* (=they almost won)

tan·ta·mount /ˈtæntəmaʊnt/ *adj* **be tantamount to** to be almost the same thing as something else, especially something bad: *His refusal to speak was tantamount to admitting he was guilty.*

tan·trum /ˈtæntrəm/ *n* [C] when someone, especially a child, suddenly becomes very angry: *Some kid threw a tantrum in the store.*

tap[1] /tæp/ v **-pped, -pping 1** [I,T] to gently hit your finger or foot against something: *Someone was tapping on the window outside.* | *Caroline tapped her feet in time to the music.* **2** [I,T] to use or take things from a large supply of something: *tapping the country's natural resources* | **+ into** *With the Internet you can tap into information from around the world.* **3** [T] to secretly listen to someone's telephone conversations, using special equipment

tap[2] n [C] **1** *especially BrE* something that you turn on or off in order to control the flow of water from a pipe; FAUCET *AmE*: *I turned on the cold water tap.* **2** when you hit something gently, especially to get someone's attention: *Suddenly I felt a tap on my shoulder.* **3 on tap** available to be used: *unlimited data on tap*

tap danc·ing /'. ,../ n [U] dancing in which you make a noise with special shoes that have metal pieces on the bottom —**tap dancer** n [C]

tape[1] /teɪp/ n **1** [C,U] a thin narrow band of plastic material used for recording sounds, VIDEO pictures, or computer information: *Did you get the interview on tape?* (=recorded on tape) → see also VIDEOTAPE[1] **2** [C] a flat plastic case that contains this type of tape: *Can I borrow your old Beatles tape?* **3** [U] a band of sticky material used for fastening things together or covering things, such as paper or packages **4** [C,U] a flat narrow piece of material used in sewing, for tying things together etc

tape[2] v [I,T] **1** to record sounds or pictures on a tape → see also VIDEOTAPE[2] **2** to fasten something to a surface, using tape: *He has lots of postcards taped to his wall.*

tape deck /'. ./ n [C] the part of a STEREO used for recording and playing tapes

tape mea·sure /'. ,../ n [C] a long band of cloth or metal with inches, CENTIMETRES etc marked on it, used for measuring things → see picture at MEASURE

ta·per /'teɪpəll-ər/ v [I,T] to become gradually narrower towards one end —**tapered** *adj*: *pants with tapered legs*

taper off *phr* v [I] to decrease gradually: *The rain finally tapered off in the afternoon.*

tape re·cord·er /'. .,../ n [C] a piece of electronic equipment used for recording and playing sounds on a TAPE

tape re·cord·ing /'. .,../ n [C] something that has been recorded on TAPE

tap·es·try /'tæpɪstri/ n [C,U] heavy cloth with coloured threads woven into it to make a picture, or a large piece of this cloth

tap wa·ter /'. ,../ n [U] water from a TAP

tar[1] /tɑːlltɑːr/ n [U] **1** a black sticky substance used to cover roads, roofs etc **2** a black sticky substance that forms when tobacco is burned

tar[2] v [T] **-rred, -rring** to cover something with tar

ta·ran·tu·la /təˈræntjʊləll-tʃələ/ n [C] a large poisonous SPIDER

tar·get[1] /'tɑːgɪtll'tɑːr-/ n [C] **1** a person, place etc that is chosen to be attacked: *a military target* | *Tourists are an easy target for thieves.* **2** a result that you are trying to achieve: *He set himself a target of learning 20 new words each week.* **3** something that you practice shooting

at: *Pete missed the target by two inches.* **4** someone or something that is being criticized or blamed for something **5 be on target a)** to be likely to reach the result you are aiming for **b)** if a weapon or bomb is on target, it hits or is moving directly towards its target

target[2] v [T] **1** to aim something at someone or something: *The missiles were targeted at major US cities.* **2** to try to make something have an effect on a particular group of people: *welfare programmes targeted at the unemployed* **3** to carefully choose which person, place etc you are going to attack or harm: *Smaller banks with less security have been targeted.*

tar·iff /'tærɪf/ n [C] a tax on goods that are brought into a country

tar·mac /'tɑːmækll'tɑːr-/ n **1 the tarmac** surface used by planes at an airport, or the surface of a road **2** [U] *BrE* a material used for making road surfaces; BLACKTOP *AmE*

tar·nish /'tɑːnɪʃll'tɑːr-/ v **1** [T] if an event or fact tarnishes the opinion people have about someone or something, it makes it worse: *the violence that tarnished Miami's reputation* **2** [I] if a metal tarnishes, it becomes darker and less shiny

tar·ot /'tærəʊll-roʊ/ n [singular,U] a set of cards that some people believe can be used to find out what will happen to someone in the future

tar·pau·lin /tɑːˈpɔːlɪnlltɑːrˈpɒː-/ n [C,U] a thick cloth that water cannot go through, used for protecting things from the rain

tar·ry /'tæri/ v [I] *literary* to stay in a place too long, or delay going somewhere

tart[1] /tɑːtlltɑːrt/ n [C] **1** a small PIE without a top, usually containing fruit **2** *BrE* an offensive word for a woman who has sex with a lot of men

tart[2] *adj* having a sour taste: *tart green apples*

tar·tan /'tɑːtnll'tɑːrtn/ n [C,U] a traditional Scottish pattern with coloured squares and STRIPEs, or cloth with this pattern → see colour picture on page 114

task /tɑːsklltæsk/ n **1** [C] a piece of work that someone has to do, especially one that is difficult or unpleasant: *Finding the killer is not going to be an easy task.* **2 take sb to task** to angrily criticize someone for doing something wrong

task force /'. ./ n [C] a group that is formed to deal with a problem, or a group of soldiers who are sent somewhere for a particular purpose

tas·sel /'tæsəl/ n [C] a group of threads tied together at one end and hung as a decoration on curtains, clothes etc

taste[1] /teɪst/ n **1** [C,U] the feeling that something you eat or drink produces in your mouth: *I don't like the taste of garlic.* | *a bitter taste* **2** [C,U] the kind of things or people that someone likes: **+ in** *We both have the same taste in music.* **3** [U] the ability to judge what things are of good quality, are attractive, are suitable etc: **have good taste** (=be good at choosing which things are attractive): *Emma always wears nice clothes. She's got good taste.* **4** [singular] if you get the taste for something, you start to like it and want to do it or have it a lot: *Greene never lost his taste for travel.* **5 a taste** a small amount of a food or drink that you have in order to find out what it is like: *Here, have a taste and*

T

tell me what you think. **6** [singular] when you experience something for a short time, and find out what it is like: *a taste of life in Japan* **7 be in bad/poor etc taste** to be unpleasant or offensive, and not suitable for a particular occasion: *That joke was in very bad taste.* **8 be in good taste** to be suitable and not likely to seem offensive or unpleasant

taste² *v* **1** [linking verb] to have a particular taste: *This milk tastes a little sour.* | **taste of sth** *The wine tastes a little of strawberries.* **2** [T] to eat or drink a little of something, to find out what it is like: *She tasted the casserole, then added a few more herbs.* **3 can taste sth** if you can taste something, you can feel its taste in your mouth: *You can really taste the spices in this curry.*

taste·ful /ˈteɪstfəl/ *adj* chosen, decorated, or made in a way that is attractive and of good quality: *The room was painted in a tasteful shade of green.* —**tastefully** *adv*: *a tastefully furnished apartment*

taste·less /ˈteɪstləs/ *adj* **1** not attractive, and showing that the person who chose it does not know what is good or bad: *tasteless ornaments* **2** likely to offend people: *tasteless jokes* **3** not having any taste: *tasteless food*

tast·er /ˈteɪstəl-ər/ *n* [C] someone whose job is to test the quality of a food or drink by tasting it: *wine tasters*

tast·y /ˈteɪsti/ *adj* food that is tasty has a very good taste

tat·tered /ˈtætədl-ərd/ *adj* old and torn: *tattered curtains*

tat·ters /ˈtætəzl-ərz/ *n* [plural] **in tatters a)** clothes that are in tatters are old and torn **b)** very badly damaged or spoiled: *Her self-confidence was in tatters.*

tat·too /təˈtuː, tæˈtuː/ *n* [C] a picture or design that is put permanently onto someone's skin using a needle and ink —**tattooed** *adj* —**tattoo** *v* [T]

tat·ty /ˈtæti/ *adj BrE informal* in bad condition: *Max was wearing dirty jeans and a tatty old jumper.*

taught /tɔːtlltɔːt/ *v* the past tense and past participle of TEACH

taunt /tɔːntlltɔːnt/ *v* [T] to keep saying unkind things to someone to try to make them angry or unhappy: *The other kids taunted him about his weight.* —**taunt** *n* [C]

Tau·rus /ˈtɔːrəs/ *n* [C,U] the sign of the Zodiac of people who are born between April 20th and May 20th, or someone who belongs to this sign

taut /tɔːtlltɔːt/ *adj* stretched tight: *a taut rope* —**tautly** *adv*

tav·ern /ˈtævənll-ərn/ *n* [C] *old-fashioned* a PUB

taw·dry /ˈtɔːdriːlltɔː-/ *adj* **1** unpleasant and involving immoral behaviour: *Wolfe's tawdry tale of life on Wall Street* **2** cheap and of bad quality: *a tawdry imitation* —**tawdriness** *n* [U]

taw·ny /ˈtɔːniːlltɔː-/ *adj* having a light gold-brown colour: *tawny fur*

tax¹ /tæks/ *n* [C,U] money that you have to pay to the government from your wages, when you buy something etc: *Taxes on alcohol and cigarettes have gone up again.* | *She earns about $50,000 a year, after tax.* (=after she has paid tax)

tax² *v* [T] **1** to make someone have to pay tax: *Incomes of under $30,000 are taxed at 15%.* **2 tax sb's patience/strength etc** to use almost all of someone's patience, strength etc

tax·a·tion /tækˈseɪʃən/ *n* [U] the system of charging taxes, or the money collected from taxes

tax-free /ˌ. ˈ.◂/ *adj* if something is tax-free, you do not pay tax on it

tax·i¹ /ˈtæksi/ also **tax·i·cab** /ˈtæksikæb/ *n* [C] a car with a driver that you pay to drive you somewhere: *We took a taxi home.* | *a taxi driver* → see colour picture on page 669

taxi² *v* [I] if a plane taxis along the ground, it is driven on the ground, moving on its wheels

tax·ing /ˈtæksɪŋ/ *adj* making you feel very tired, weak, or annoyed: *a taxing job*

taxi rank *BrE*, **taxi-stand** *AmE* /ˈ.. ./ *n* [C] a place where taxis wait for passengers

tax·pay·er /ˈtæksˌpeɪəl-ər/ *n* [C] someone who pays taxes

tax re·turn /ˈ. .ˌ./ *n* [C] an official piece of paper on which you write details of what you have earned, so that the government can calculate how much tax you should pay

TB /ˌtiː ˈbiː/ *n* [U] the abbreviation of TUBERCULOSIS

tea /tiː/ *n* [C,U] **1** a drink made by pouring boiling water onto dried leaves, or the leaves that are used to make this drink: *a cup of tea* | *herbal teas* **2** *BrE* A small afternoon meal of tea with SANDWICHes or cakes **3** *BrE informal* a meal you eat in the evening; DINNER

tea bag, tea·bag /ˈtiːbæg/ *n* [C] a small paper bag with dried leaves in it, used for making tea

teach /tiːtʃ/ *v* **taught** /tɔːtlltɔːt/, **taught, teaching 1** [I,T] to give lessons in a subject at a school or college: *Mr Rochet has been teaching for 17 years.* | *She teaches science at the local school.* **2** [T] to show someone how to do something: *My dad taught me how to swim.* **3 teach sb a lesson** *informal* to punish someone and make them never want to do something again

teach·er /ˈtiːtʃəl-ər/ *n* [C] someone whose job is to teach: *Mr Paulin is my history teacher.* → see colour picture on page 80

teacher's pet /ˌ.. ˈ./ *n* [singular] *informal often humorous* a child who everyone thinks is the teacher's favourite student and is therefore disliked by the other students

teach·ing /ˈtiːtʃɪŋ/ *n* **1** [U] the work or job of being a teacher: *I'd like to go into teaching when I finish college.* (=I want to become a teacher) **2 teachings** the ideas, especially about religion or politics, of a famous religious leader, philosopher, or writer: *the teachings of Karl Marx*

tea co·sy *BrE*, **tea cozy** *AmE* /ˈ. ˌ../ *n* [C] a thick cover that you put over a TEAPOT to keep the tea hot

tea·cup /ˈtiːkʌp/ *n* [C] a cup that you drink tea out of

teak /tiːk/ *n* [C,U] an expensive hard wood used for making furniture

team¹ /tiːm/ *n* [C] **1** a group of people who play a sport or game together against another group: *Which is your favourite baseball team?* **2** a group of people who work together to do a particular job: *a team of doctors* **3** a group of dogs, horses etc, used for pulling a vehicle

team[2] *v*

team up *phr v* [I] to join another person, company etc in order to work together: *The band teamed up with other leading artists to produce the single.*

team·mate /'tiːm-meɪt/ *n* [C] someone who is in the same team as you

team·ster /'tiːmstəll-ər/ *n* [C] *AmE* someone whose job is to drive a TRUCK

team·work /'tiːmwɜːkll-wɜːrk/ *n* [U] the ability of a group to work well together

tea·pot /'tiːpɒtll-pɑːt/ *n* [C] a container used for making and serving tea, which has a handle and a SPOUT ➝ see picture at POT

tear

tear out   tear up

tear[1] /teəllter/ *tore* /tɔːlltɔːr/, *torn* /tɔːnll tɔːrn/, *tearing* *v* **1 a)** [T] to pull paper or cloth into pieces, or accidentally make a hole in it: *He tore the envelope open.* | *Oh no, I've torn a hole in my jeans.* **b)** [I] to become damaged in this way: *When paper is wet, it tears easily.* **2** [I] *informal* to move very quickly, often in a dangerous or careless way: **+ around/into/out of etc** *Two kids came tearing around the corner.* **3** [T] to remove something by pulling it violently: *Protestors began tearing down the fence.*

tear apart *phr v* [T] **1** [**tear sth ↔ apart**] to make the people in a family, organization, country etc argue or fight with each other: *Yugoslavia was torn apart by a bloody civil war.* **2** [**tear sb/sth ↔ apart**] to destroy something or someone **3** [**tear sb apart**] to make someone extremely unhappy or upset: *It tears me apart to see Linda cry.*

tear sth ↔ **down** *phr v* [T] to deliberately destroy something completely, especially if a building: *The school was torn down to make way for a car park.*

tear into sb *phr v* [T] *informal* to strongly criticize someone

tear sth ↔ **off** *phr v* [T] to remove your clothes very quickly: *He tore off his sweater.*

tear sth ↔ **up** *phr v* [T] to tear paper into a lot of little pieces: *He tore up all of Linda's old letters.*

tear[2] /tɪəlltɪr/ *n* [C] a drop of liquid that flows from your eyes when you cry: *When she looked round, there were tears in her eyes.* | **burst into tears** (=suddenly start crying): *Suddenly Brian*

burst into tears. | **be in tears** (=be crying): *Most of the audience were in tears.*

tear[3] /teəllter/ *n* [C] a hole in a piece of paper, cloth etc where it has been torn

tear·drop /'tɪədrɒpll'tɪrdrɑːp/ *n* [C] a large drop of liquid that flows from your eyes when you cry

tear·ful /'tɪəfəlll'tɪr-/ *adj* crying or almost crying: *They said a tearful goodbye at the airport.* —**tearfully** *adv*

tear·gas /'tɪəgæsll'tɪr-/ *n* [U] a gas that makes people's eyes hurt so that they cannot see, used by the police against violent crowds

tease /tiːz/ *v* [I,T] **1** to gently make fun of someone, in a way that shows you like them: *Don't worry, I was just teasing.* **2** to say unkind things to someone and laugh at them so that they become angry or upset: *The other boys all teased him because he was overweight.*

tea·spoon /'tiːspuːn/ *n* [C] **1** a small spoon used for measuring small amounts of food or for putting sugar into tea, coffee etc ➝ see picture at CUTLERY **2** also **teaspoonful** /-fʊl/ the amount this spoon can hold

teat /tiːt/ *n* [C] **1** the part of a female animal which baby animals suck to get milk; NIPPLE **2** the soft rubber part of a baby's bottle that a baby sucks

tea tow·el /'. ,../ *n* [C] *BrE* a small TOWEL used for drying cups, plates etc; DISH TOWEL *AmE* ➝ see picture at KITCHEN

tech·ni·cal /'teknɪkəl/ *adj* **1** relating to the practical skills, knowledge, and methods used in science or industry: *technical experts* **2** relating to the knowledge and methods of a particular subject or profession: *a legal document full of technical terms*

tech·ni·cal·i·ty /ˌteknɪ'kælɪti/ *n* **1** **technicalities** [plural] the details of a system or process that you need special knowledge to understand **2** [C] a small detail in a law or rule

tech·ni·cally /'teknɪkli/ *adv* according to the exact details of a rule or law: *Technically he's responsible for fixing all the damage.*

tech·ni·cian /tek'nɪʃən/ *n* [C] someone who does practical work connected with science or technology, for example someone who uses scientific equipment or makes sure that complicated machines work properly: *a laboratory technician*

tech·nique /tek'niːk/ *n* [C,U] a special skill or way of doing something: *pencil drawing techniques*

tech·nol·o·gy /tek'nɒlədʒɪll-'nɑː-/ *n* [C,U] a combination of all the knowledge, equipment, methods etc that are used in scientific or industrial work: *the achievements of modern technology* —**technological** /ˌteknə'lɒdʒɪkəlll -'lɑː-/ *adj*: *technological advances*

teddy bear

GRAMMAR NOTE: transitive and intransitive (2)

Some verbs can be used **transitive** or **intransitive**. For example: *read* v [T,I]

• Transitive: *I can't read your handwriting.*
• Intransitive: *Tom learned to read at the age of four.*

ted·dy bear /ˈtedi beə ‖-ber/ also **teddy** /ˈtedi/ *BrE* — *n* [C] a soft toy shaped like a bear

te·di·ous /ˈtiːdiəs/ *adj* boring, and continuing for a long time: *a tedious discussion* —**tediously** *adv*

tee /tiː/ *n* [C] a small object used for holding a GOLF ball

teem /tiːm/ *v*
  teem with sth/sb *phr v* [T] to be full of people or animals that are all moving around **be teeming with** *The lake was teeming with fish.* —**teeming** *adj*: *the teeming streets of Cairo*

teen /tiːn/ *n* [C] *AmE informal* a teenager

teen·age /ˈtiːneɪdʒ/ *adj* [only before noun] aged between 13 and 19, or suitable for people between 13 and 19: *She's got two teenage sons.* | *a teenage club*

teen·ag·er /ˈtiːneɪdʒəll-ər/ *n* [C] someone who is between 13 and 19 years old

teens /tiːnz/ *n* [plural] the period in your life when you are aged between 13 and 19 **be in your teens** *She got married when she was still in her teens*

tee·ny /ˈtiːni/ also **teeny-wee·ny** /ˌtiːni ˈwiːni/ *adj spoken* very small: *He's had a teeny bit too much wine.*

tee shirt /ˈ. ˌ./ *n* [C] a T-SHIRT

tee·ter /ˈtiːtəll-ər/ *v* **1** [I] to move or stand in a way that looks as though you are going to fall over: *Ann was teetering about in high-heeled shoes.* **2 be teetering on the brink/edge of** to be close to a very bad situation: *a country teetering on the brink of war*

teeth /tiːθ/ *n* the plural of TOOTH

teethe /tiːð/ *v* [I] **1** if a baby is teething, his or her teeth are starting to grow **2 teething troubles/problems** *BrE* problems with something new when it is first starting or first being used

tee·to·tal·ler *BrE*, **teetotaler** *AmE* /tiːˈtəʊtələ ‖-ˈtoʊtələr/ *n* [C] someone who never drinks alcohol —**teetotal** *adj*

tel·e·com·mu·ni·ca·tions /ˌtelikəmjuːnɪˈkeɪʃənz/ *n* [plural] the process or business of sending and receiving messages by telephone, radio, SATELLITE etc

tel·e·gram /ˈtelɪɡræm/ *n* [C] a message sent by telegraph

tel·e·graph /ˈtelɪɡrɑːf‖-ɡræf/ *n* [U] an old-fashioned way of sending messages using electrical SIGNALS

te·lep·a·thy /tɪˈlepəθi/ *n* [U] the ability to communicate thoughts directly to someone else's mind without speaking or writing —**telepathic** /ˌtelɪˈpæθɪk◄/ *adj*

tel·e·phone¹ /ˈtelɪfəʊn‖-foʊn/ also **phone** *n* [C] a piece of equipment you use to speak to someone who is in another place: *I was on the telephone.* | *a telephone call*

USAGE NOTE: telephone, phone, call, ring

These are all verbs meaning 'to communicate with someone by telephone'. **Phone** is the most usual word in British English, and **call** is the most usual in American English: *Chris phoned to say he'd be late.* | *What time did he call?* British English speakers also use **ring**: *I'm just ringing to see how you are.* **Telephone** is used only in fair-

---

ly formal English: *Our staff will telephone for a taxi for you.*

telephone² *v* [I,T] *formal* to use a telephone to talk to someone; phone CALL

telephone di·rec·to·ry /ˈ... ˌ.../ *n* [C] a book containing the names, addresses, and telephone numbers of people in an area: PHONE BOOK

telephone ex·change /ˈ... ˌ./ also **exchange** *n* [C] a place where telephone calls are connected to each other

tel·e·scope /ˈtelɪskəʊp‖-skoʊp/ *n* [C] a piece of equipment like a tube, that makes things that are far away seem closer and larger

tel·e·vise /ˈtelɪvaɪz/ *v* [T] to broadcast something on television: *Is the game going to be televised?*

tel·e·vi·sion /ˈtelɪˌvɪʒən, ˌtelɪˈvɪʒən/ *n* **1** also **television set** [C] a thing shaped like a box with a screen, that you use to watch programmes ➝ see colour picture on page 474 **2** [U] the programmes that you can watch on a television **watch television** *He's been watching television all day.* **on television** *Have you ever been on television?* **3** [U] the system of broadcasting pictures and sound: *Who invented television?* **4** [U] the activity of making and broadcasting programmes for television: *a job in television*

tell off

tell /tel/ *v* told /təʊld‖toʊld/, told, telling **1** [T] to give someone facts or information about something: **tell sb about sth** *Have you told John about the party?* | **tell sb (that)** *She told me she can't come on Friday.* | **tell sb how/where etc** *Could you tell me where the post office is, please?* **2 can tell** to be able to know that something is true about someone or something: **can tell (that)** *I could tell that Jo was in a bad mood.* | **can tell the difference** (=be able to know that two things are different): *Use yoghurt instead of cream – you can't tell the difference.* **3** [T] to say that someone should or must do something: **tell sb to do sth** *He told me to come in and sit down.* | **tell yourself** *I keep telling myself not to worry.* **4** [T] to give information in a way that does not use speech or writing: *The machine's red light tells you it's recording.* **5 tell the time** *BrE*/**tell time** *AmE* to be able to know what time it is by looking at a clock **6 there's no telling what/how/whether etc** *spoken* used to say that it is impossible to know what will happen: *There's just no telling what he'll say next.* **7** [I,T] *spoken informal* to tell a teacher, parent etc about something wrong that someone else has done: **tell on sb** *Please don't tell on me!* **8 (I'll) tell you what** used to suggest something: *Tell you what, call me on Friday.* **9 I tell you/I'm telling you** *spoken* used to emphasize something: *I'm telling you, the food was unbelievable!* **10 I told you (so)** *spoken* used when someone does something they have warned them not to do, and it has had a bad result: *I told you so – I told you it wouldn't work.* **11 you never can tell/you can never tell** *spoken* used to say that you can never be certain about what will happen in the future: *They're not likely to win, but you never can tell.* → see also **all told** (ALL[1])

tell sb/sth apart *phr v* [T] to be able to see the difference between two people or things, even though they are similar: *It's difficult to tell them apart.*

tell sb ↔ off *phr v* [T] *informal* to talk angrily to someone because they have done something wrong: **be/get told off** *Sean's always getting told off at school.*

tell·er /ˈtelə‖-ər/ *n* [C] *especially AmE* someone whose job is to take and pay out money in a bank

tell·ing /ˈtelɪŋ/ *adj* showing what someone really thinks or what a situation is really like: *a telling remark*

tell·tale /ˈtelteɪl/ *adj* clearly showing something that is unpleasant or supposed to be secret: **telltale sign** *the telltale sign of drug addiction*

tel·ly /ˈteli/ *n* [C] *BrE informal* television

temp[1] /temp/ *n* [C] someone who works in an office for a short time: *We're getting a temp in while Jane's away.*

temp[2] *v* [I] to work as a temp: *Anne's temping until she can find another job.*

tem·per /ˈtempə‖-ər/ *n* **1** [C,U] a tendency to become suddenly angry: *Mark needs to learn to control his temper.* **2** [singular, U] the angry or happy way that you feel: **be in a bad/foul/good temper** *You're certainly in a foul temper this morning.* **3 be in a temper** to be very angry and unable to control your behaviour for a short time **4 lose your temper** to suddenly become very angry: *I lost my temper and slammed the door.* **5 keep your temper** to stay calm and not to become angry: *As a teacher, you must be able to keep your temper.* → see also **BAD-TEMPERED**

tem·pe·ra·ment /ˈtempərəmənt/ *n* [C,U] the part of your character that makes you likely to be happy, angry, sad etc: *a baby with a sweet temperament*

tem·pe·ra·men·tal /ˌtempərəˈmentl‖/ *adj* becoming angry, excited etc very easily

tem·pe·rate /ˈtempərɪt/ *adj* having neither very hot nor very cold weather: *Britain has a temperate climate.*

tem·pe·ra·ture /ˈtempərətʃə‖-ər/ *n* **1** [C,U] how hot or cold something is: **+ of** *Water boils at a temperature of 100°C.* **2 sb's temperature** the temperature of your body, used as a sign of whether you are ill: **take sb's temperature** (=measure it) **3 have/run a temperature** to be hot because you are ill

tem·pest /ˈtempɪst/ *n* [C] *literary* a violent storm

tem·pes·tu·ous /temˈpestʃuəs/ *adj* full of strong emotions: *a tempestuous relationship*

tem·plate /ˈtempleɪt, -plɪt/ *n* [C] **1** a piece of paper, plastic etc that you use to help you cut other materials in the same shape **2** a system for arranging information on a computer screen

tem·ple /ˈtempəl/ *n* [C] **1** a building where people in some religions go to pray, sing etc **2** the area on the side of your head, between your eye and your ear

tem·po /ˈtempəʊ‖-poʊ/ *n* [C, U] **1** the speed at which music is played **2** the speed at which something happens: *the tempo of city life*

tem·po·ra·ry /ˈtempərəri, -pərɪl-pəreri/ *adj* existing or happening for a limited period of time: *Temporary jobs are becoming more common.* —**temporarily** /ˈtempərər‖lil, tempə-ˈrer‖li/ *adv*: *The library is temporarily closed.* → compare **PERMANENT**

tempt /tempt/ *v* **1** [T] to attract someone and make them want to have or do something, even though it may be wrong or they may not need it: *he was tempted by the big profits of the drugs trade.* **tempt sb to do sth** *They're offering free gifts to tempt people to join.* **2 be tempted to do sth** to feel you would like to do something: *I was tempted to tell him what his girlfriend had been saying about him.* —**tempting** *adj*: *a tempting offer*

temp·ta·tion /tempˈteɪʃən/ *n* **1** [C,U] a strong feeling that you want to do something, although you know you should not: **resist (the) temptation** *I really had to resist the temptation to slap him.* **give in to temptation** (=do something although you know you should not) **2** [C] something that makes you have this feeling: *Having chocolate in the house is a great temptation!*

ten /ten/ *number* 10 → see also **TENTH**[1]

te·na·cious /t‖ˈneɪʃəs/ *adj* very determined to do something, and unwilling to stop trying —**tenaciously** *adv* —**tenacity** /təˈnæs‖ti/ *n* [U]

ten·an·cy /ˈtenənsi/ *n* [C,U] the period of time when someone rents a house, room etc, or their right to use the house etc

ten·ant /ˈtenənt/ *n* [C] someone who lives in a house, room etc and pays rent to the person who owns it

tend /tend/ *v* **1 tend to do sth** to be likely to do a particular thing: *It tends to be very wet at this time of year.* **2** *also* **tend to** [T] *formal* to take care of someone or something: *Rescue teams were tending to the survivors.*

ten·den·cy /ˈtendənsi/ *n* [C] **1** a part of your character that makes you likely to develop, think, or behave in a particular way **+towards** *Some people may inherit a tendency towards alcoholism.* **have a tendency to do sth** *He has a tendency to talk too much.* **2** something that people usually do, or a changing situation that makes them more likely to do it **+ for** *There's a tendency for men to marry younger women.*

ten·der[1] /ˈtendə‖-ər/ *adj* **1** tender meat or vegetables are soft and easy to cut and eat → opposite **TOUGH** **2** a tender part of your body is painful if someone touches it **3** gentle in a way that shows love: *a tender look* **4 at a tender age** *literary* young and without much experience of life: *He lost his father at the tender age of seven.* —**tenderly** *adv* —**tenderness** *n* [U]

ten·der[2] *v* **1** [I] to make a formal offer to do a job or provide goods and services **2** [T] *formal* to formally offer something such as a suggestion or idea: **tender your resignation** (=formally say you will leave your job)

tender-heart·ed /ˌ.. ˈ..◂/ adj very kind and gentle

ten·don /ˈtendən/ n [C] a thick strong part of your body that connects a muscle to a bone

ten·e·ment /ˈtenɪmənt/ n [C] a large building divided into apartments, especially in a poor area of a city

ten·et /ˈtenɪt/ n [C] a principle or belief: *the tenets of Buddhism*

ten·ner /ˈtenə-ər/ n [C] *BrE spoken* £10 or a ten pound note: *Can you lend me a tenner?*

ten·nis /ˈtenɪs/ n [U] a game in which two or four people use RACKETS to hit a ball to each other over a net ➡ see colour picture on page 636

ten·or /ˈtenəll-ər/ n **1** [C] a male singer with a high voice **2** **the tenor of** *formal* the general meaning or attitude behind something: *the tenor of an argument*

tense¹ /tens/ adj **1** nervous and anxious: *You seem really tense – what's wrong?| a tense situation* **2** muscles that are tense feel tight and stiff: *Massage helps to relax tense neck muscles.*

tense² also **tense up** v [I,T] to become tight and stiff, or to make your muscles do this

tense³ n [C,U] one of the forms of a verb that shows whether something happens in the past, now, or in the future. For example, 'he studied' is in the past tense, 'he studies' is in the present tense etc

ten·sion /ˈtenʃən/ n **1** [C,U] the feeling that exists when people do not trust each other and may suddenly attack each other: *efforts to calm racial tensions* **2** [U] a nervous and anxious feeling: *The tension as we waited for the news was unbearable.* **3** [U] tightness or stiffness in a wire, rope, muscle etc: *You can increase the tension by turning this screw.*

tent /tent/ n [C] a temporary structure used for camping, which is made of cloth or plastic and is supported by poles and ropes: **put up a tent** (=put the poles and sheets in position so that a tent is ready to use)

tent

ten·ta·cle /ˈtentɪkəl/ n [C] one of the long parts like arms of a sea creature such as an OCTOPUS

ten·ta·tive /ˈtentətɪv/ adj **1** not definite or certain: *tentative plans* **2** done as though you are not sure what you are doing: *a tentative smile* —**tentatively** adv

tenth¹ /tenθ/ number 10th

tenth² n [C] one of ten equal parts in something

ten·u·ous /ˈtenjuəs/ adj **tenuous link/ relationship etc** a connection, relationship etc that seems weak or uncertain —**tenuously** adv

ten·ure /ˈtenjə, -juəll-jər/ n [U] **1** the legal right to use land or buildings for a period of time **2** the period of time when someone has an important job: *his tenure as major*

te·pee /ˈtiːpiː/ n [C] a round tent used by some Native Americans

tep·id /ˈtepɪd/ adj tepid liquid is slightly warm

te·qui·la /tɪˈkiːlə/ n [U] a strong alcoholic drink made in Mexico

term¹ /tɜːmlltɜːrm/ n [C] **1** a word or phrase that has a particular meaning, especially in a technical or scientific subject: *I don't understand all the legal terms.* **2** *BrE* one of the periods of time that a school or university year is divided into **3** a fixed period of time that someone does an important political job: *The President hopes to be elected for a second term.* **4** **in the long/short term** during a long or short period from now: *Things don't look good in the short term.* ➡ see also **TERMS**

term² v [T] *formal* to use a particular word to describe something **be termed sth** *The meeting could hardly be termed a success.*

ter·mi·nal¹ /ˈtɜːmɪnəlllˈtɜːr-/ n [C] **1** a building where you get onto planes, buses, or ships: *They're building a new terminal at the airport.* ➡ see colour picture on page 669 **2** a KEYBOARD and screen connected to a computer

terminal² adj a terminal disease cannot be cured, and causes death: *terminal cancer* —**terminally** adv: *Her mother is terminally ill.*

ter·mi·nate /ˈtɜːmɪneɪtllˈtɜːr-/ v [I,T] *formal* if something terminates, or if you terminate it, it ends —**termination** /ˌtɜːmɪˈneɪʃən/ n [C,U]

ter·mi·nol·o·gy /ˌtɜːmɪˈnɒlədʒillˌtɜːrmɪˈnɑː-/ n [C,U] the technical words that are used in a subject: *scientific terminology*

ter·mi·nus /ˈtɜːmɪnəsllˈtɜːr-/ n [C] the place at the end of a railway line or bus service

ter·mite /ˈtɜːmaɪtllˈtɜːr-/ n [C] an insect like a large ANT that eats wood and often causes damage to buildings etc

terms /tɜːmzlltɜːrmz/ n [plural] **1** the parts of an agreement, legal document etc: *Sign here to say you agree to the terms and conditions.* **2** **in terms of** used to explain which part of something you are talking about: *In terms of sales, the book hasn't been very successful.| in financial/ artistic etc terms** (=considering something in a financial etc way): *A million years isn't a very long time in geological terms.* **3** **come to terms with** to understand and deal with a difficult situation: *It was hard to come to terms with Marie's death.* **4** **in no uncertain terms** in a clear and usually angry way: *He told me in no uncertain terms not to come back.* **5** **be on good/ bad/friendly etc terms** to have a good, bad, friendly etc relationship with someone: *We're on good terms with most of the people who live here.* **6** **be on speaking terms** to be able to talk to someone and have a friendly relationship with them: *We're barely on speaking terms now.* ➡ see also **on equal terms** (EQUAL¹)

ter·race /ˈterɪs/ n [C] **1** a flat area next to a building or on a roof, where you can sit **2** *BrE* a row of houses that are joined to each other

terraced house /ˌ.. ˈ./ n [C] *BrE* a house that is one of a row of houses joined together ➡ see colour picture on page 79

ter·ra·cot·ta /ˌterəˈkɒtə◂ ll-ˈkɑː-/ n [U] hard red-brown baked clay: *a terracotta pot*

ter·rain /teˈreɪn, tɪ-/ n [C,U] land: *mountainous terrain*

ter·res·tri·al /tɪˈrestriəl/ adj *technical* **1** relating to the earth rather than space **2** living on or relating to land rather than water

ter·ri·ble /ˈterɪbəl/ adj very bad or unpleasant: *The food at the hotel was terrible.*

ter·ri·bly /ˈterɪbli/ adv **1** very badly: *We played terribly, and that's why we lost.* **2** *BrE* extremely: *I'm terribly sorry, but the answer is no.*

ter·ri·er /'teriə-ər/ *n* [C] a small type of dog

ter·rif·ic /tə'rıfık/ *adj informal* **1** very good: *There was a terrific view from the top of the hill.* **2** very big or very much: *Losing his job was a terrific shock.* —**terrifically** /-klı/ *adv*

ter·ri·fied /'terjfaɪd/ *adj* very frightened: **+ of** *I'm absolutely terrified of spiders.*

ter·ri·fy /'terjfaɪ/ *v* [T] to make someone extremely frightened: *The thought of giving a speech terrified her.* —**terrifying** *adj*

ter·ri·to·ri·al /,terj'tɔːriəl/ *adj* relating to land that is owned or controlled by a particular country: *US territorial waters*

ter·ri·to·ry /'terjtɔrill-tɔːri/ *n* **1** [C,U] land that a particular country owns and controls: *Canadian territory* **2** [C,U] the area that a person or animal thinks is his or her own **3** [U] an area of business, experience, or knowledge: *We are moving into unfamiliar territory with the new software.*

ter·ror /'terəll-ər/ *n* [C,U] a feeling of extreme fear, or something that causes this: **in terror** *She screamed in terror.*

ter·ror·is·m /'terərızəm/ *n* [U] the use of violence to achieve political aims, especially against a legally elected government and its people

ter·ror·ist /'terərjst/ *n* [C] someone who uses violent actions to achieve political aims, for example by putting bombs in public places, especially against a legally elected government and its people → compare FREEDOM FIGHTER

ter·ror·ize (also **-ise** *BrE*) /'terəraɪz/ *v* [T] to deliberately frighten people by threatening them with violence: *Gangs have been terrorizing the community.*

terse /tɜːslltɜːrs/ *adj* using very few words, especially in a way that shows that you are annoyed: *a terse answer* —**tersely** *adv*

test[1] /test/ *n* [C] **1** a set of questions or exercises to measure someone's skill or knowledge: *I've got a history test tomorrow.* | **pass/fail a test** *I failed my driving test twice.* | **do/take a test** *The children are doing a French test at the moment.* **2** a short medical check on part of your body: *an eye test* | *the results of blood tests* **3** a process used to find out whether something works, whether it is safe etc: *safety tests on diving equipment* **4** a situation that shows how good, bad etc something is: **+ of** *Today's race is a real test of skill.*

test[2] *v* [T] **1** to measure someone's skill or knowledge by giving them questions or activities to do: **test sb on sth** *We're being tested on grammar tomorrow.* **2** to use or check something to find out whether it works, whether it is safe etc: *testing nuclear weapons* **3** to do a medical check on part of someone's body: *You need to get your eyes tested.* **4** to show how good or strong something is: *The next six months will test her powers of leadership.*

tes·ta·ment /'testəmənt/ *n* **a testament to sth** *formal* something that shows or proves something else very clearly: *His latest CD is a testament to his growing musical abilities.* → see also NEW TESTAMENT, OLD TESTAMENT

test case /'. ./ *n* [C] a legal CASE that makes a principle of law clear and is used to judge future cases

tes·ti·cle /'testɪkəl/ *n* [C], *plural* **testicles**, *or* **testes** /-tiːz/ one of the two round organs below a man's PENIS that produce SPERM

tes·ti·fy /'testjfaɪ/ *v* [I,T] to formally say what you know in a law court: **+ that** *Two men testified that they saw you outside the bank.*

tes·ti·mo·ni·al /,testj'məʊniəll-'moʊ-/ *n* [C] a formal written statement about someone's character and abilities

tes·ti·mo·ny /'testjmənill-moʊni/ *n* [C,U] **1** a formal statement of what is true, especially one made in a law court **2** something that shows or proves something else : **+ to** *His achievement is a testimony to his hard work*

test tube /'. ./ *n* [C] a small glass container shaped like a tube that is used in scientific tests

tes·ty /'testi/ *adj* impatient and easily annoyed: *a testy old man* —**testily** *adv*

tet·a·nus /'tetənəs/ *n* [U] a serious disease that makes your muscles stiff and is caused by an infection in a wound

teth·er /'teðəll-ər/ *n* [C] **1 be at the end of your tether** *BrE* to be so worried and tired because of your problems that you feel you cannot deal with them any more **2** a rope or chain used to tie an animal to something —**tether** *v* [T] *a dog tethered to a post*

text /tekst/ *n* **1** [C,U] the writing in a book, magazine etc rather than the pictures **2** **the text of sth** the exact words of something: *The text of the speech was printed in the newspaper.*

text·book[1] /'tekstbʊk/ *n* [C] a book about a subject, used by students: *a history textbook* → see colour picture on page 80

textbook[2] *adj* **a textbook example/case (of sth)** a very clear and typical example of how something happens or is done

tex·tile /'tekstaɪl/ *n* [C] any material or cloth that is made by weaving

tex·ture /'tekstʃəll-ər/ *n* [C,U] the way that a surface, material etc feels when you touch it: *fabric with a coarse texture*

tex·tured /'tekstʃədll-ərd/ *adj* having a surface that is not smooth: *a wall with a textured surface*

than /ðən; *strong* ðæn/ *linking word, prep* used to compare two things, amounts etc that are different: *Jean's taller than Stella.* | *I can swim better than you.* | *He earns more than I do.* → see also **rather than** (RATHER)

thank /θæŋk/ *v* **1** [T] to tell someone that you are pleased and grateful for something that they have given you or done for you: **thank sb for sth** *We'd like to thank everyone for all the wedding presents.* **2** **thank God/goodness/heavens** *spo-*

GRAMMAR NOTE: the passive (2)
Most transitive verbs can be made **passive**. If you want to say who or what did the action in a passive sentence, use **by**. ACTIVE: *An American millionaire* **bought** *the picture.* PASSIVE: *The picture* **was bought by** *an American millionaire.*

ken used to say that you are very glad about something: *Thank God no one was hurt!*

thank·ful /ˈθæŋkfəl/ *adj* glad and grateful that something good has happened: **+ for** *I was thankful for the chance to sit down at last.* | **+ (that)** *We're thankful that the accident wasn't more serious.* —**thankfully** *adv*: *Thankfully, everything turned out all right.*

thank·less /ˈθæŋkləs/ *adj* a thankless job is difficult and you do not get much praise for doing it

thanks¹ /θæŋks/ *interjection* **1** thank you: *Can I borrow your pen? Thanks very much.* | **+ for** *Thanks for ironing my shirt.* **2 thanks/no thanks** used to accept or refuse something that someone is offering you: *"Would you like a drink?" "No, thanks."*

thanks² *n* [plural] **1** things you say or do to show that you are grateful to someone: *He left without a word of thanks.* **2 thanks to** because of: *We're late, thanks to you.*

Thanks·giv·ing /ˌθæŋksˈgɪvɪŋ◂/ *n* [U] a holiday in the US and Canada in autumn, when families have a large meal together

thank you /ˈ. ./ *interj* **1** used to tell someone that you are grateful for something they have given you or done for you : *"Here's the book you wanted, Katy." "Oh, thank you."* | **+ for** *Thank you for coming to the party.* **2 thank you/no thank you** used to accept or refuse something that someone is offering you: *"Would you like another piece of cake?" "No, thank you."*

thank-you /ˈ. ./ *n* [C] something that you say or do to thank someone for something: *a special thank-you for all your help*

that¹ /ðæt/ *determiner, pron, plural* **those** /ðəʊzǁðoʊz/ **1** used to talk about someone or something that is a distance away from you: *Look at that pink car!* compare THIS¹ **2** used to talk about someone or something that has already been mentioned or is already known about: *We met for coffee later that day.* | *How much is that hat in the window?* | *Who told you that?* **3 that is (to say)** used to correct something you have said or give more exact information about something: *Everyong passed the test – everyone, that is, except Janet, who was ill.* **4 that's it/that's that** *spoken* used when something is completely finished or when a decision will not be changed: *You're not going and that's that!* **5 that's all there is to it** *spoken* used to emphasize that something is simple to do, explain etc : *We lost because we didn't play well. That's all there is to it.*

USAGE NOTE: that, who, and which

You should only leave out the pronoun **that** when it is the object of a verb: *She's the woman (that) I love.* Only use **that** instead of **who** or **which** when the meaning of the noun is limited to show which one(s) you mean: *This is the man* **who/that** *told the police.* Do not use **that** instead of **who** or **which** when you are simply adding information: *This is my father,* **who** *lives in Dublin.* | *She owns an old Rolls Royce, which she bought in 1954.* In spoken English, **that** is usually left out before a noun clause, especially after verbs about saying or thinking: *She said (that) it wasn't true.* | *I think (that) you're right.*

---

that² /ðət; *strong* ðæt/ *linking word* **1** used after some verbs, adjectives and nouns to start a new CLAUSE: *She claims that she wasn't there.* | *Is it true that you're leaving?* **2** used as a RELATIVE PRONOUN instead of 'which' or 'who': *Did you get the books that I sent you.* ➝ see also **so...that** (SO²) **such...that** (SUCH)

that³ /ðæt/ *adv* **1 that long/much/big etc** used when you are showing or talking about the size or amount of something: *The fish he caught was that big.* **2 not (all) that much/long/big etc** not very much, long etc: *I'm not that tired considering I didn't sleep.* | *I didn't expect her to be that tall!*

thatch /θætʃ/ *n* [C,U] dried STRAW used for making roofs —**thatched** *adj*: *a thatched cottage*

thaw¹ /θɔːǁθɒː/ *v* **1** also **thaw out** [I,T] if frozen food thaws or is thawed, it becomes soft so it is ready to be cooked **2** also **thaw out** [I] if ice or snow thaws, it becomes warmer and turns into water **3** [I] to become more friendly or less formal: *Relations between the two countries are beginning to thaw.* ➝ compare MELT

thaw² *n* **1** [C] a period of warm weather when snow and ice melt: *the spring thaw* **2** [singular] a time when people become friendly again after they have been unfriendly

the /ðə; *before vowels* ði; *strong* ðiː/ *determiner* **1** used before nouns to show that you are talking about a particular person or thing that has already been mentioned or is already known about, or that is the only one: *I need to go to the bank.* | *That's the woman I saw.* | *Whose is the red jacket?* ➝ compare A **2** used as part of some names: *the United States* | *the Nile* **3** used before an adjective to make it into a noun: *They provide services for the blind.* **4** used before a singular noun to show that you are talking about that thing in general: *The computer has changed the way people work.* **5** each or every: *He's paid by the hour.* | *There are 9 francs to the pound.* **6** used before the names of musical instruments: *Kira's learning to play the piano.* **7** used to talk about a part of the body : *The ball hit him right in the eye!* **8** used before dates or periods of time: *Tuesday the thirteenth of April* | *in the late 1800s* **9 the ... the ...** used to show that two things happen together and depend on each other: *The more you practise, the better you'll play.*

thea·tre *BrE*, **theater** *AmE* /ˈθɪətəǁ-ər/ *n* **1** [C] a building or stage where plays are performed: *the Apollo Theater* **2** [U] plays as entertainment: *a study of modern Russian theatre* **3** [U] the work of acting in, writing, or organizing plays: *She's been working in theatre for many years.* **4** [C] also **movie theater** *AmE* a building where you go to see films **5** [C,U] the room in a hospital where doctors do operations: *The patient is in theatre now.*

the·at·ri·cal /θiˈætrɪkəl/ *adj* **1** relating to the theatre: *a theatrical production* **2** behaving in a way that is intended to make people notice you: *a theatrical gesture*

theft /θeft/ *n* [C,U] the crime of stealing something: *Car theft is on the increase.*

their /ðə; *strong* ðeəǁðər; *strong* ðer/ *adj* **1** relating to or belonging to the people or things that have already been mentioned: *The children closed their eyes.* | *Their daughter is a* *teacher.* **2** used instead of 'his' or 'her' after words such as someone, anyone etc: *Everybody brought their own wine to the party.*

theirs /ðeəz‖ðerz/ *pron* **1** relating to or belonging to the people or things that have already been mentioned: *Some friends of theirs are staying with them.* | *When our computer broke Tom and Sue let us use theirs.* **2** used instead of 'his' or 'hers' after words such as someone, anyone etc: *There's a coat left. Someone must have forgotten theirs.*

them /ðəm; *strong* ðem/ *pron* **1** the object form of 'they' – the people, animals, or things that have already been mentioned: *Has anybody seen my keys? I can't find them.* | *My friends want me to go out with them tonight.* **2** the object form of 'they' – used instead of 'him' or 'her': *If anyone phones, can you tell them to call back later?*

theme /θi:m/ *n* [C] **1** the main subject or idea in a book, film etc: *Love is the theme of several of his poems.* **2** **theme music/song/tune** music that is always played with a particular television or radio programme

theme park /'. ./ *n* [C] an AMUSEMENT PARK that is based on one subject such as water or space travel

themselves /ðəm'selvz/ *pron* **1** the REFLEXIVE form of "they": *People usually like to talk about themselves.* **2** a plural used to emphasize subject or object of a sentence: *Doctors themselves admit that the treatment does not always work.* **3** **(all) by themselves a)** alone: *Many old people live by themselves.* **b)** without help: *The kids made the cake all by themselves.*

then[1] /ðen/ *adv* **1** at a particular time in the past or future: *He's coming at eight, but I'll have left by then.* | *My family lived in New York then.* **2** after something has happened; next: *We had lunch and then went shopping.* **3** *spoken* used to show that what you are saying is related in some way to what has been said before: *"He can't come on Friday." "Then how about Saturday?"* | *So you're going into nursing then?* **4** used in sentences with 'if' to show the result of a possible situation.: *If Bobby wants to go, then I'll go too.* **5** **now/OK/right then** *spoken* used to introduce a new subject or idea: *Right then, who wants to come swimming?* **6** used to add something to what you have just said: *He's really busy at work, and then there's the new baby, too!* **7** **then and there/there and then** immediately, after something has happened: *I would have given up then and there if my parents hadn't encouraged me.* → see also **but then (again)...** (BUT[1]), **(every) now and then** (NOW[1])

then[2] *adj* at that time in the past: *George Bush, the then president of the US*

thence /ðens/ *adv* old-fashioned formal from that place: *They travelled to Paris, and thence by train to Calais.*

the·ol·o·gy /θi'ɒlədʒi‖θi'ɑ:-/ *n* [U] the study of religion —**theological** /ˌθi:ə'lɒdʒɪkəl‖-'lɑ:-/ *adj*

theo·rem /'θɪərəm‖'θi:ə-/ *n* [C] technical a statement that you can prove is true, especially in mathematics

theo·ret·i·cal /θɪə'retɪkəl‖ˌθi:ə-/ *adj* **1** relating to theories: *theoretical physics* **2** a theoretical situation or condition could exist but does not yet exist —**theoretically** /-kli/ *adv: Theoretic-*

ally, there's no reason why you can't clone humans.

theo·rist /'θɪərɪst‖'θi:ə-/ also **theo·re·ti·cian** /ˌθɪərə'tɪʃən‖ˌθi:ə-/ *n* [C] someone who develops ideas that explain why particular things happen or are true

theo·rize (also **-ise** BrE) /'θɪəraɪz‖'θi:ə-/ *v* [I,T] to think of a possible explanation or reason for an event, fact etc: *Doctors theorize that the infection is passed from animals to humans.*

theo·ry /'θɪəri‖'θi:əri/ *n* **1** [C] an explanation for something that has not yet been proved to be true: *Darwin's theory of evolution* **2** **in theory** something that is true in theory should be true, but may not be: *In theory, the crime rate should decrease as employment increases.* **3** [U] general principles of a subject such as science or music: *studying music theory*

ther·a·peu·tic /ˌθerə'pju:tɪk‹/ *adj* **1** relating to the treatment or cure of a disease: *therapeutic drugs* **2** making you feel calm and relaxed: *Long walks can be therapeutic.*

ther·a·pist /'θerəpɪst/ *n* [C] someone whose job is to do a particular type of therapy: *a speech therapist*

ther·a·py /'θerəpi/ *n* [C,U] the treatment of mental or physical illness, especially without using drugs or operations : *He's having therapy to help with alcohol addiction.*

there[1] /ðeə, ðə‖ðer, ðər/ *pron* used as the subject of a sentence to say that something exists or happens: *There were several people hurt in the accident.* | *Suddenly, there was a loud crash.* | *Are there any questions?*

there[2] *adv* **1** in or to a particular place that is not where you are or near you: *Would you hand me that glass over there?* | *I don't know what happened – I wasn't there.* | **get there** (=arrive somewhere): *If we leave now, we'll get there for lunch.* → compare HERE **2** at a particular point in time, in a story etc: *I'll read this chapter and stop there.* **3** **there you are** *spoken* **a)** used when you are giving something to someone or when you have done something for them: *I'll just get you the key – there you are.* **b)** used when something proves that you were right: *There you are – I knew their relationship wouldn't last.* **4** **there** *spoken* used when you have finished something: *There, that's the last piece of the puzzle.* **5** *spoken* available or ready to help: *The money's always there if you need it.* **6** **there's...** *spoken* used to make someone look at someone or something: *Oh, look, there's a robin.* **7** **there and then** also **then and there** immediately: *They offered my the job there and then.* → see also **here and there** (HERE)

there·a·bouts /ˌðeərə'baʊts‖ˌðer-/ *adv* somewhere near a particular number, amount, time etc: *We'll aim to arrive at 10 o'clock, or thereabouts.*

there·af·ter /ðeər'ɑ:ftə‖ðer'æftər/ *adv* formal after a particular event or time; AFTERWARDS: *He became ill in May and died shortly thereafter .*

there·by /ðeə'baɪ, 'ðeəbaɪ‖ðer'baɪ, 'ðer-/ *adv* formal with the result that: *Expenses were cut 12%, thereby increasing efficiency.*

therefore /'ðeəfɔ:‖'ðerfɔ:r/ *adv* formal for the reason that has just been mentioned: *The car is smaller and therefore cheaper to run.*

there·in /ðeər'ɪnǁðer-/ *adv formal* **1** in that place, or in that piece of writing: *the contract and all the rules therein* **2** **therein lies** used in order to say what the cause of something is: *He speaks the truth, and therein lies his power.*

there·of /ðeər'ɒvǁðer'ɑːv/ *adv formal* relating to something that has just been mentioned : *insurance for the home and the contents thereof*

there·up·on /ˌðeərə'pɒn, 'ðeərəpɒnǁˌðerə'pɒːn, -'pɑːn, 'ðerə-/ *adv formal* immediately after something happens and as a result of it : *Thereupon the whole audience stood up and cheered.*

ther·mal /'θɜːməlǁ'θɜːr-/ *adj* **1** relating to or caused by heat: *thermal energy* **2** thermal clothes are designed to keep you warm

ther·mom·e·ter /θə'mɒmɪtəǁθər'mɑːmɪtər/ *n* [C] a piece of equipment that measures the temperature of the air, your body etc

ther·mo·nu·cle·ar /ˌθɜːməʊ'njuːkliə◂ ǁˌθɜːrmoʊ'nuːkliər◂/ *adj* relating to a NUCLEAR reaction involving extremely high temperatures

Ther·mos /'θɜːmɒsǁ'θɜːr-/ also **Thermos flask** /'.. ./ *n* [C] *trademark* a container like a bottle that keeps drinks hot or cold

ther·mo·stat /'θɜːməstætǁ'θɜːr-/ *n* [C] a piece of equipment that controls the temperature of a room, machine etc

the·sau·rus /θɪ'sɔːrəs/ *n* [C] a book in which words are put into groups with other words that have a similar meaning: *Roget's Thesaurus*

these /ðiːz/ *determiner, pronoun* the plural form of THIS

the·sis /'θiːsɪsǁs/ *n* [C], *plural* **theses** /-siːz/ **1** a long piece of writing that you do for a university degree: *She's writing her thesis on women criminals.* **2** *formal* an idea or statement that tries to explain why something happens

they /ðeɪ/ *pron* **1** the people, animals, or things that have already been mentioned or that are already known about: *Ken gave me some flowers, aren't they beautiful?| I went to Ann and Ed's place, but they weren't there.* **2** a particular group or organization, or the people involved in it: *They're going to build a new road.* **3** used to say what people in general think, say etc: *They say it's bad luck to spill salt.* **4** used instead of 'he' or 'she' after words such as someone, everyone etc: *Someone at work said they saw you at the party.*

they'd /ðeɪd/ **1** the short form of 'they had': *They'd had a lot to drink.* **2** the short form of they would': *They'd like to visit us.*

they'll /ðeɪl/ the short form of 'they will': *They'll have to wait.*

they're /ðə; *strong* ðeə, deɪəǁðer; *strong* ðer, ðeɪər/ the short form of 'they are': *They're very nice people.*

they've /ðeɪv/ the short form of 'they have': *They've been here before.*

thick /θɪk/ *adj* **1** if something is thick, there is more than usual between its opposite surfaces: *a nice thick piece of bread* → opposite THIN¹ **2** **5cm/1m etc thick** used to say exactly how thick something is: *The walls are 30cm thick.* **3** a thick liquid does not have much water in it and does not flow easily: *thick soup* **4** thick smoke, cloud, or FOG is difficult to see through

5 growing very close together with not much space in between: *a thick forest| He has thick black hair.* **6** *BrE informal* stupid: *Don't be so thick!.* —**thickly** *adv*

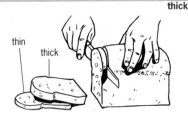

thin

thick

thick

thick² *n* **1** **be in the thick of sth** to be involved in the most active, dangerous, etc part of a situation: *US troops are right in the thick of the action.* **2** **through thick and thin** in spite of any difficulties or problems: *The brothers have always stuck with each other (=supported each other) through thick and thin.*

thick·en /'θɪkən/ *v* [I,T] to become thick, or make something thick: *The fog had thickened.| Thicken the soup with flour.*

thick·et /'θɪkɪt/ *n* [C] a group of bushes or small trees that are very close together

thick·ness /'θɪknɪs/ *n* [C,U] **1** how thick something is: *Look at the thickness of that wall.* **2** [C] a layer of something

thick-skinned /ˌ. '.◂/ *adj* not easily upset by criticism or insults

thief /θiːf/ *n* [C], *plural* **thieves** /θiːvz/ someone who steals things: *a car thief*

thigh /θaɪ/ *n* [C] the top part of your leg above your knee

thim·ble /'θɪmbəl/ *n* [C] a small hard cap that you put over the end of your finger to protect it when you are sewing

thin /θɪn/ *adj* **1** if something is thin, there is very little between its opposite surfaces: *a thin slice of bread| She was wearing a thin summer jacket.* → see picture at THICK → opposite THICK¹ **2** having very little fat on your body → see colour picture on page 244 → opposite FAT¹ → compare SLIM¹ **3** a liquid that is thin is watery and flows very easily: *thin soup* **4** **vanish/disappear into thin air** to suddenly disappear completely in a mysterious way **5** **be thin on the ground** *informal* to be very few **6** air that is thin is difficult to breathe be-

cause there is little OXYGEN —**thinness** *n* [U]
➡ see also THINLY

Thin is a general word that describes people
who do not have much fat on their bodies: *a tall,
thin man* If someone is thin in a way that is
attractive, use **slim** or **slender**: *You're looking
slim! Have you lost weight?* | *an elegant slender
figure.* **Skinny** is an informal word that means
that someone is too thin: *I was a small skinny kid.*
Underweight means that someone does not
weigh enough, and is often used by doctors or
people who are worried about their weight:
*Doctors found that the children were seriously
underweight.* **Emaciated** means that someone is
extremely thin in a way that is dangerous to their
health: *photographs of emaciated prisoners of
war*

thin² *v* [T] **-nned, -nning** to make a liquid weaker
by adding water, oil etc ➡ see also THINNING
  thin out *phr v* [I] if a crowd thins out, people
  gradually leave until there are not many
  people left

thing /θɪŋ/ *n* **1** [C] used to talk about something without saying its name, for example an
object, or event, or something that someone says
or does: *What's that thing on the kitchen table?* | *A
funny thing happened last week.* | *That was a
terrible thing to say.* **2** **things** [plural] *especially
spoken* the situation that exists, and how it
affects your life: *Things have improved a lot since
I last saw you.* | *How are things?* **3** **sb's things**
your possessions, clothes, or equipment: *Pack
your things – we have to leave right now.* **4** **not
know/feel/see etc a thing** to not know, feel, see
etc anything: *I don't know a thing about opera.*
5 **be seeing/hearing things** to imagine that
you are seeing or hearing something that is not
really there **6** **for one thing** *spoken* used to give
one of the reasons why you think something is
true or will happen: *I don't think she'll get the
job – for one thing she can't drive!* **7** **the thing is**
spoken used to explain what a particular
problem is: *I'd like to come, but the thing is, I promised to see Jim tonight.* **8** **the last thing sb
wants/expects/needs etc** used to say that
someone definitely does not want, expect etc
something: *The last thing we wanted was to start
a fight.* **9** **first thing/last thing** *spoken* at the beginning of the day or at the end of the day: *I'll
call you first thing tomorrow, OK?* **10** **(just) the
thing** something that is very suitable or desirable: *a handy little cool box that's just the thing
for summer picnics* **11** **it's (just) one thing after
another** used to say that a lot of unpleasant
things have happened to you **12** **do your own
thing** *informal* to do what you want, and not what
other people tell you to do **13** **have a thing about
sb/sth** *informal* to like or dislike someone or something very much ➡ see also **it's a good thing/job**
(GOOD¹), **there's no such thing/person** (SUCH)

think¹ /θɪŋk/ *v* **thought** /θɔːt‖θɒːt/ **thought,
thinking** **1** [I] to use your mind to decide or remember something or solve a problem: +
about/of *Have you thought about which subjects
you want to study at university?* | *I was thinking
of all the happy times we'd spent together.* | **think
hard** (=think a lot): *Think hard before you make
your final decision.* **2** [T] to have a particular
opinion about someone or something: *What do
you think of my new hairstyle?* | + **(that)** *I didn't
think the concert was very good.* | *She thinks I'm
crazy.* | **think well/highly of** (=have a good opi-
nion of someone or something): *His teachers
seem to think highly of him* | **not think much of**
(=think something or someone is not very good)
*spoken: The hotel was okay but I didn't think
much of the food.* **3** to believe that something is
true, although you are not sure: *I think he may
have gone home, but I could be wrong.* | *"Are we
late?" "I don't think so."* **4** **I think I'll/I thought
I'd** *spoken* used to tell someone what you have
decided to do: *I thought I'd go jogging today.*
5 **think of/about doing sth** to consider the idea
of doing something: *We are thinking of moving to
the countryside.* **6** **I can't think what/why/who
etc** *spoken* used to say that you cannot understand or remember something: *I can't think why
she married him.* **7** **think twice** to think carefully before deciding to do something that may
cause problems for you: *I'd think twice before
getting involved with a married man if I were
you.* **8** **think nothing of doing sth** to do something often or easily, even though other people
think it is very difficult: *Purdey thinks nothing
of driving two hours to work every day.* **9** **think
better of it** to decide not to do something that
you had intended to do: *He reached for a cigar,
but then thought better of it.* **10** **think the world
of sb** to love or admire someone very much
  think back *phr v* [I] to remember something from
  the past: *She thought back to her childhood.*
  think of sth/sb *phr v* [T] **1** to produce a new
  idea, suggestion etc by thinking: *Can you think
  of any way of solving the problem?* **2** to remember a name or a fact: *I can't think of his
  name right now.* **3** to care about someone's
  happiness, comfort etc: *He never thinks of other
  people – only of himself.*
  think sth ↔ **out** *phr v* [T] to plan all the details
  of something very carefully: *Everything has
  been really well thought out.*
  think sth ↔ **over** *phr v* [T] to consider something carefully before making a decision: *Take
  a few days to think over our offer.*
  think sth ↔ **through** *phr v* [T] to think carefully about the possible results of doing something
  think sth ↔ **up** *phr v* [T] to produce a new idea,
  plan, explanation etc: *It's a great idea. I wonder
  who first thought it up.*

think² *n* **have a think** to think carefully about
something: *I need to have a think about this.*

think·er /ˈθɪŋkəll-ər/ *n* [C] someone who uses
their mind to produce new ideas about life and
the world

GRAMMAR NOTE: phrasal verbs (1)
Phrasal verbs are verbs with more than one part. They consist of **verb + adverb** or **verb +
preposition** (e.g. *look after, turn out, put off*). Some phrasal verbs have three parts: **verb + adverb
+ preposition** (e.g. *look forward to, put up with*).

think·ing /ˈθɪŋkɪŋ/ *n* [U] **1** someone's opinions and ideas about a subject: *modern scientific thinking on the origins of the universe* **2** when you use your mind to think about something: *a situation that requires careful thinking* → see also WISHFUL THINKING

thin·ly /ˈθɪnli/ *adv* **1 thinly sliced** cut into thin pieces: *a thinly sliced onion* **2** when there are few people or things in a large area: *thinly populated*

thin·ning /ˈθɪnɪŋ/ *adj* if your hair is thinning, some of it has fallen out: *a middle-aged man with thinning brown hair*

third¹ /θɜːd‖ˈθɜːrd/ *number* 3rd

third² *n* [C] one of the three equal parts of something; 1/3

third·ly /ˈθɜːdli‖ˈθɜːr-/ *adv* used when you are talking about the third fact or reason in a series

third par·ty /ˌ. ˈ..◂/ *n* [singular] someone who is not one of the two main people or groups that are involved in something

third per·son /ˌ. ˈ..◂/ *n* **the third person** a form of a verb that you use with 'he', 'she', 'it', or 'they' → compare FIRST PERSON, SECOND PERSON

third-rate /ˌ. ˈ.◂/ *adj* of very bad quality

Third World /ˌ. ˈ.◂/ *n* **the Third World** the poorer countries of the world that do not have well developed industries — **Third World** *adj*

thirst /θɜːst‖θɜːrst/ *n* **1** [singular, U] the feeling you have when you need a drink very much: *These children are dying of thirst.* | **quench your thirst** (=make yourself stop feeling thirsty by drinking something) **2 a thirst for knowledge/power etc** a desire for knowledge, power etc

thirst·y /ˈθɜːsti‖ˈθɜːr-/ *adj* feeling that you want to drink something: *I'm thirsty – let's get some beer.* | *thirsty work* (=making you feel thirsty) — **thirstily** *adv*

thir·teen /ˌθɜːˈtiːn◂‖ˌθɜːr-/ *number* 13 — **thirteenth** *number*

thir·ty /ˈθɜːti‖ˈθɜːrti/ *number* **1** 30 **2 the thirties a)** the years from 1930 to 1939 **b)** the numbers between 30 and 39 **3 be in your thirties** to be aged between 30 and 39 — **thirtieth** *number*

this¹ /ðɪs/ *determiner, pron, plural* **these** /ðiːz/ **1** used to talk about something or someone that is near to you: *My mother gave me this necklace.* | *Where did you get this from?* | *My name's Elaine, and this is my sister, Nancy.* **2** used to talk about the present time or a time that is close to the present: *What are you doing this week?* **3** used to talk about something that has just been mentioned or that has just happened: *I'm going to make sure this doesn't happen again.* **4 this and that** various different things: *"What did you talk about?" "Oh, this and that."*

this² *adv* as much as this: *I've never stayed up this late before.*

this·tle /ˈθɪsəl/ *n* [C] a wild plant with leaves that have sharp points and purple flowers

thong /θɒŋ‖θɒːŋ/ *n* [C] *AmE* a FLIP-FLOP

thorn /θɔːn‖θɔːrn/ *n* [C] a sharp pointed part on the stem of a plant such as a rose

thorn·y /ˈθɔːni‖ˈθɔːrni/ *adj* **1 thorny question/problem/issue etc** a difficult question, problem etc **2** having a lot of thorns

thor·ough /ˈθʌrə‖ˈθʌroʊ, ˈθʌrə/ *adj* careful to check every part of something, or doing something carefully so that you do not make mistakes: *The police carried out a thorough search of the house.* | *As a scientist, Madison is methodical and thorough.* — **thoroughness** *n* [U]

thor·ough·bred /ˈθʌrəbred‖ˈθʌroʊ-, ˈθʌrə-/ *n* [C] a horse that has parents of the same very good BREED

thor·ough·fare /ˈθʌrəfeə‖ˈθʌroʊfer, ˈθʌrə-/ *n* [C] a main road through a city

thor·ough·ly /ˈθʌrəli‖ˈθʌroʊli, ˈθʌrə-/ *adv* **1** very or very much: *Thanks for the meal. I thoroughly enjoyed it.* **2** carefully and completely: *Rinse the vegetables thoroughly.*

those /ðəʊz‖ðoʊz/ *determiner, pron* the plural of THAT

thou /ðaʊ/ *pron* a word meaning 'you', which was used in the past

though¹ /ðəʊ‖ðoʊ/ *conjunction* **1** also **even though** in spite of the fact that something is true; although: *Though Beattie is almost 40, she still plans to compete.* | *I seem to keep gaining weight, even though I'm exercising regularly.* **2** but: *I don't really like classical music, though I did enjoy the Pavarotti concert.* | *I think she's Swiss, I'm not sure though.* **3 as though** used to say how something seems; as if: *She was staring at me as though she knew me.* | *It looks as though we're lost.*

though² *adv spoken* in spite of the fact that you have just mentioned: *You should pass your test. It won't be easy though.*

thought¹ /θɔːt/ *v* the past tense and past participle of THINK

thought² *n* **1** [C] something that you think of, for example an idea or opinion: *I've just had a thought. Why don't we ask Terry if he wants to come?* | *What are your thoughts on the subject?* **2** [U] when you think about something: *I've been giving your proposal some thought* (=thinking about it). | **lost/deep in thought** (=thinking so much about something that you do not notice what is happening): *She was staring out of the window, lost in thought.* **3** [singular,U] when someone shows that they care about someone or something: *He acted without any thought for his own safety.* | *Thank you for the flowers – it was a kind thought.* **4** [U] the ideas that people have about a subject: *Newton's influence on modern scientific thought.*

thought·ful /ˈθɔːtfəl‖ˈθɔːt-/ *adj* **1** serious and quiet because you are thinking about something: *a thoughtful expression on his face* **2** kind and always thinking of things you can do to make other people happy: *It was very thoughtful of you to come and visit me.* — **thoughtfully** *adv* — **thoughtfulness** *n* [U]

thought·less /ˈθɔːtləs‖ˈθɔːt-/ *adj* not thinking about other people or how your actions or words will affect them: *a thoughtless remark* — **thoughtlessly** *adv* — **thoughtlessness** *n* [U]

thou·sand /ˈθaʊzənd/ *number* **1** 1000 **2 thousands** *informal* a lot: *Steve's had thousands of girlfriends.* — **thousandth** *adj*

thrash /θræʃ/ *v* **1** [T] to hit someone violently, usually as a punishment **2** [I] to move violently from side to side: *a fish thrashing around in the net* **3** [T] *informal* to easily win a game against someone — **thrashing** *n* [C,U]

thrash sth ↔ **out** *phr v* [T] to discuss something thoroughly until you reach an agreement: *Officials are still trying to thrash out an agreement.*

thread[1] /θred/ *n* **1** [C,U] a long thin string of cotton, silk etc,, used to sew cloth: *a needle and thread* **2** [C] the connection between different parts of a story, explanation etc: **lose the thread** (=no longer understand how events or ideas are connected): *Halfway through the film I started to lose the thread.* **3** [C] a raised line of metal that goes around a screw

thread[2] *v* [T] **1** to put thread, string etc through a hole: *Will you thread the needle for me?* **2** **thread your way through/along etc** to move through a place by carefully going around things and people: *He threaded his way through the traffic.*

thread·bare /'θredbeə‖-ber/ *adj* threadbare clothes, CARPETS etc are thin and in bad condition because they have been used a lot

threat /θret/ *n* [C] **1** when you tell someone that you will hurt them or cause problems for them if they do not do what you want: *Threats were made against his life.* **2** [usually singular] someone or something that may cause damage or harm to another person or thing: *pollution that is a major threat to the environment* **3** [usually singular] the possibility that something bad will happen: *the threat of famine*

threat·en /'θretn/ *v* **1** [T] to tell someone that you will hurt them or cause serious problems for them if they do not do what you want: **threaten to do sth** *The hijackers threatened to shoot him.* | **threaten sb with sth** *I was threatened with jail if I published the story.* **2** [T] to be likely to harm or destroy something: *Illegal hunting threatens the survival of the white rhino.* **3** [I,T] if something unpleasant threatens to cause an unpleasant situation, it seems likely to cause it: *The fighting threatens to turn into a major civil war.* —**threatening** *adj*: *a threatening letter* —**threateningly** *adv*

three /θriː/ *number* 3

three-di·men·sion·al /ˌ. .'...◂/ also **3-D** /ˌθriː 'diː◂/ *adj* having or seeming to have length, depth, and height: *a 3-D movie*

thresh·old /'θreʃhəʊld, -ʃəʊld‖-ould/ *n* **1** **on the threshold of sth** at the beginning of a new and important event or period: *We're on the threshold of a new era in telecommunications.* **2** [C] the lowest level at which something starts: *the tax threshold* **3** [C] the floor of the entrance to a room or building

threw /θruː/ *v* the past tense of THROW

thrift /θrɪft/ *n* [U] wise and careful use of money —**thrifty** *adj*: *thrifty shoppers*

thrift shop /'. ./ *n* [C] *AmE* a shop that sells used things, especially clothes, at a cheap price, in order to make money for a charity, a church etc; CHARITY SHOP *BrE*

thrill[1] /θrɪl/ *n* [C] a strong feeling of excitement and pleasure, or something that makes you feel this: *the thrill of driving a fast car*

thrill[2] *v* [T] to make someone very excited and pleased: *The magic of his music continues to thrill audiences.*

thrilled /θrɪld/ *adj* very excited, pleased, or happy: *She'll be thrilled when she hears the news.*

thrill·er /'θrɪlə‖-ər/ *n* [C] an exciting film or book about murder or a crime

thril·ling /'θrɪlɪŋ/ *adj* very exciting: *a thrilling end to the game*

thrive /θraɪv/ *v* [I] to become very successful and very strong and healthy: *a plant that is able to thrive in dry conditions*

thri·ving /'θraɪvɪŋ/ *adj* very successful: *a thriving business*

throat /θrəʊt‖θroʊt/ *n* [C] **1** the back part of your mouth and the tubes that go down the inside of your neck: *I have a sore throat.* **2** the front of your neck: *His attacker held him by the throat.* → see picture at HEAD → see also **clear your throat** (CLEAR[2])

throat·y /'θrəʊti‖'θroʊ-/ *adj* making a low rough sound when you speak or sing: *a throaty whisper*

throb[1] /θrɒb‖θrɑːb/ *v* [I] **-bbed, -bbing 1** if a part of your body throbs, you get a regular feeling of pain in it: *My head was throbbing.* **2** to beat strongly and regularly: *the throbbing sound of the engines*

throb[2] *n* [C] a strong regular sound or movement: *the low throb of distant war drums*

throes /θrəʊz‖θroʊz/ *n* **in the throes of** experiencing something unpleasant or painful, or doing something very difficult: *Nigeria was in the throes of a bloody civil war.*

throne /θrəʊn‖θroʊn/ *n* **1** [C] the chair that a king or queen sits on **2** **the throne** the position and power of being king or queen

throng[1] /θrɒŋ‖θrɔːŋ/ *n* [C] *literary* a crowd of people

throng[2] *v* [I,T] *literary* if people throng a place, they go there in large numbers: *crowds thronging St. Peter's Square*

throt·tle[1] /'θrɒtl‖'θrɑːtl/ *v* [T] to hold someone's throat tightly, stopping them from breathing; STRANGLE

throttle[2] *n* [C] a part of a vehicle or machine that controls the amount of FUEL going into the engine and therefore controls the speed

through[1] /θruː/ *prep* **1** from one side or end of something to the other: *The train went through the tunnel.* | *I pushed my way through the crowd.* | *They drove through Switzerland.* | *Someone had been watching us through the window.* → see colour picture on page 474 **2** because of something or with the help of something or someone: *She succeeded through sheer hard work.* | *I got the job through an employment agency.* **3** from the beginning to the end, including all parts of something: *She slept through the film.* | *I've searched through all the papers but I can't find your certificate.* **4** **Friday through Sunday/March through May etc** *AmE* from Friday until the end of Sunday, from March until the end of May etc

through[2] *adv* **1** from one side or end of something to the other: *We found a gap in the fence and climbed through.* **2** **read/think etc sth through** to read, think etc about something very carefully from beginning to end: *Make sure to read it through before you sign it.* **3** **through and through** completely: *a typical Englishman through and through* **4** *BrE* if you get through to someone on the telephone, you are able to talk to them: **put sb through** (=connect someone by telephone to another person): *"I'd like to speak to Mr Smith, please." "I'm putting you through."*

through³ *adj* **1 be through with sth** *informal* to have finished using something, doing something etc.: *Can I borrow the book when you're through with it?* **2 be through (with sb)** to no longer have a relationship: *That's it. Steve and I are through!* **3 through train/road** a train or road that goes all the way to another place

through·out /θru:'aʊt/ *adv, prep* **1** in every part of a place: *Thanksgiving is celebrated throughout the US.* **2** during all of an event or a period of time: *She was calm throughout the interview.*

throw away

throw   throw away

throw¹ /θrəʊ‖θroʊ/ *v* [T] **threw** /θru:/ **thrown** /θrəʊn‖θroʊn/ **throwing** **1** to make something fly through the air by letting it go from your hand with a quick movement of your arm: **throw sth to/at** *Cromartie throws the ball back to the pitcher.* | *Demonstrators began throwing rocks at the police.* | **throw sb sth** *Throw me a towel, would you.* ➡ see colour picture on page 670 **2** to put something somewhere quickly and carelessly: *Just throw your coat on the bed.* **3** to push someone or something suddenly and violently, or make them fall down: *They were thrown to the ground by the force of the explosion.* **4** to suddenly move your body or part of your body: *She threw her arms around him.* | **throw yourself down/onto/into etc** *When he got home, he threw himself into an armchair.* **5 throw sb in jail/prison** to put someone in prison **6 throw yourself into sth** to start doing an activity eagerly **7 throw a party** to organize a party **8 throw your weight around** to use your authority in an unreasonable way **9** to make someone feel confused or shocked: *Her sudden question threw me completely for a moment.* | *Everyone was thrown into confusion by this news.* **10** to make shadows or light fall on something: *Where trees threw long shadows across the lawn.*

throw sth ↔ **away** *phr v* [T] **1** to get rid of something that you do not want or need: *Do you still want the newspaper, or can I throw it away?* **2** to waste a chance or advantage etc: *He had everything – a good job, a beautiful wife – but he threw it all away.*

throw sth ↔ **in** *phr v* [T] to add something to what you are selling, without increasing the price: *The computer is going for only £900 with a free software package thrown in.*

throw sth ↔ **on** *phr v* [T] to quickly put on a piece of clothing

throw sth/sb **out** *phr v* [T] **1** to get rid of something: *The meat smells bad – you'd better*

throw it out. **2** to make someone leave: *Jim got thrown out of the Navy for taking drugs.* **3** to refuse to accept a suggestion or idea

throw up *phr v* **1** [I] *informal* to make food come out of your mouth from your stomach because you are ill; VOMIT **2** [T **throw** sth ↔ **up**] to make something fly up into the air: *Passing trucks threw up clouds of dust.*

throw² *n* [C] when you throw something such as a ball: *a long throw*

throw·back /'θrəʊbæk‖'θroʊ-/ *n* [C] something that is like another thing that existed in the past: *His music is a throwback to the 1970s.*

thrown /θrəʊn‖θroʊn/ *v* the past participle of THROW

thru /θru:/ *adj, adv, prep, nonstandard, especially AmE* another spelling of THROUGH sometimes used in notes, written signs etc

thrush /θrʌʃ/ *n* [C] a brown bird with spots on its front

thrust¹ /θrʌst/ *v* [T] **thrust, thrust, thrusting** to push something somewhere suddenly or with a lot of force: *Dean thrust his hands in his pockets.*

thrust² *n* **1** [C,U] when something is pushed forward with force or the power used to push something forward **2 the thrust of sth** the main meaning of what someone says or does: *What was the main thrust of his argument?*

thru·way /'θru:weɪ/ *n* [C] *AmE* a wide road for fast traffic

thud /θʌd/ *n* [C] the low sound made when something heavy falls or hits another thing: *He hit the floor with a thud.* —**thud** *v* [I]

thug /θʌg/ *n* [C] a violent person who may attack people

thumb¹ /θʌm/ *n* [C] **1** the short thick finger on the side of your hand which helps you to hold things **2 be under sb's thumb** if you are under someone's thumb, they control everything you do **3 give sth the thumbs up/down** to say you approve or disapprove of something

thumb² *v*

thumb through sth *phr v* [T] to quickly look at each page of a book, magazine etc

thumb·tack /'θʌmtæk/ *n* [C] *AmE* a short pin with a wide flat top, used for fastening notices to walls; DRAWING PIN *BrE*

thump /θʌmp/ *v* **1** [T] *informal* to hit someone or something hard with your hand closed: *I'm going to thump you if you don't shut up!* **2** [I,T] to make a repeated low sound by beating or by hitting a surface: *I could hear my heart thumping.* | *the dog's tail thumping against the floor.* —**thump** *n* [C]

thun·der¹ /'θʌndə‖-ər/ *n* [U] the loud noise that you hear during a storm after a flash of LIGHTNING —**thundery** *adj*

thunder² *v* **1 it thunders** if it thunders, a loud noise comes from the sky after LIGHTNING **2** [I] to make a very deep loud sound: *The guns thundered in the distance.*

thun·der·bolt /'θʌndəbəʊlt‖-dərboʊlt/ *n* [C] a flash of LIGHTNING that hits something

thun·der·ous /'θʌndərəs/ *adj* extremely loud: *thunderous applause*

thun·der·storm /'θʌndəstɔ:m‖-dərstɔ:rm/ *n* [C] a storm with THUNDER and LIGHTNING

Thurs·day /'θɜːzdi‖'θɜːr-/ written abbreviation **Thurs** n [C,U] the day of the week between Wednesday and Friday → see Usage Note at DAY

thus /ðʌs/ adv formal **1** as a result of something that you have just mentioned; so: *Traffic will become heavier, thus increasing pollution.* **2** in this way or like this: *Thus began one of the darkest periods in the country's history.*

thwart /θwɔːt‖θwɔːrt/ v [T] to prevent someone from doing what they are trying to do

thy /ðaɪ/ determiner a word meaning 'your', which was used in the past

thyme /taɪm/ n [U] a plant used for giving a special taste to food

ti·a·ra /ti'ɑːrə/ n [C] a piece of jewellery like a small CROWN

tic /tɪk/ n [C] a sudden uncontrolled movement of a muscle in your face

tick¹ /tɪk/ n [C] **1** the sound that a clock or watch makes every second → see colour picture on page 635 **2** BrE a mark (✓) used to show that something is correct or has been done; CHECK AmE **3** BrE spoken a moment: *I'll be back in a tick.* **4** a small creature that sticks to animals and sucks their blood

tick² v **1** [I] if a clock or watch ticks, it makes a short sound every second **2** [T] BrE to mark something with a tick **3 what makes sb tick** informal the reasons that make them behave in a particular way: *I can't figure out what makes him tick.*

    tick away/by phr v [I] if time ticks away or by, it passes

    tick sb/sth ↔ **off** phr v [T] **1** BrE informal to angrily tell someone that they should not have done something **2** AmE informal to annoy someone **3** BrE to put a tick next to something on a list to show that it has been done

    tick over phr v [I] BrE to continue working at a slow steady rate without producing much: *We kept the business just ticking over until new orders arrived.*

tick·et /'tɪkɪt/ n [C] **1** a printed piece of paper that shows that you have paid to do something, for example to travel on a train or watch a film: *Have you bought your plane tickets yet?* **2 speeding/parking ticket** an official piece of paper that orders you to pay money because you have parked your car illegally, or driven too fast

tick·le /'tɪkəl/ v **1** [T] to gently touch part of someone's body with your fingers in order to make them laugh → see colour picture on page 473 **2** [I,T] if something touching your body tickles, it makes you feel uncomfortable so that you want to rub your body **3** [T] to amuse someone: *I was tickled by her remarks.* —**tickle** n [C]

tidal wave /'.. ./ n [C] a large wave that flows over the land and destroys things

tid·bit /'tɪd,bɪt/ n [C] AmE a TITBIT

tide¹ /taɪd/ n **1** [C] the regular movement of the level of the sea up and down the SHORE: *The tide is coming in* (=towards the shore). | **high/low tide** (=when the level of the sea is high or low)

2 [singular] the way that events or people's opinions are developing: *the rising tide of unemployment* —**tidal** adj

tide² v

    tide sb **over** phr v [T] to lend someone money while they are waiting for money from another person etc: *Could you lend me $50 to tide me over until payday?*

ti·dy¹ /'taɪdi/ adj **1** a tidy place looks nice because everything is neatly arranged and in the right place: *Her desk is always very tidy.* **2** especially BrE a tidy person always keeps their things neatly arranged and in the right place; NEAT AmE —**tidily** adv —**tidiness** n [U]

tidy² also **tidy up** v [I,T] BrE to make a place look tidy: *Make sure you tidy up after you've finished.*

    tidy sth ↔ **away** phr v [T] BrE to put things back in the place where they should be

tie¹ /taɪ/ v **1** [T] to fasten something with string, rope etc: **tie sth to/around/together etc** *She tied a scarf around her head.* | *Tie this label to your suitcase.* **2** [T] to make a knot in a rope, string etc: *Can you tie your shoelaces yet?* **3** also [I] **be tied** to have the same number of points in a competition: *San Diego tied with the Denver Broncos for second place.*

    tie sb **down** phr v [T] to stop someone from being free to do what they want to do: *Neil doesn't like feeling tied down.*

    tie in with sth phr v [I] if one things ties in with another, it is connected with the other thing, for example because it contains the same information: *His evidence doesn't really tie in with hers.*

    tie up phr v [T] **1** [**tie** sb ↔ **up**] to tie someone's arms, legs etc so that they cannot move **2** [**tie** sth ↔ **up**] to fasten something together by using string or rope **3 be tied up a)** to be very busy: *Mr Baker can't see you now. He's tied up in a meeting.* **b)** if your money is tied up in something, you cannot use it for anything else: *Our money's tied up in a long-term savings plan.*

tie² n [C] **1** a long narrow piece of cloth that you wear around your neck with a shirt → see colour picture on page 113 **2** [usually plural] a relationship between two people, groups, or countries: *close family ties* **3** when a game, competition, or election ends with two people or teams getting the same number of points, votes etc: *There was a tie for first place.*

tier /tɪə‖tɪr/ n [C] **1** a row of seats that has other rows above or below it **2** one of several levels in an organization or system: *a company with four tiers of management*

tiff /tɪf/ n [C] a slight argument between two people: *a lovers' tiff*

ti·ger /'taɪɡə‖-ər/ n [C] a large wild cat with yellow and black lines on its fur

tight¹ /taɪt/ adj **1** fitting part of your body very closely: *tight jeans* | *These shoes feel too tight.* **2** firm and difficult to move: *Make sure the screws are tight.* | *He kept a tight grip on her* *arm.* → opposite LOOSE[1] **3** strictly controlled: *Security is tight for the President's visit.* **4** material, string etc that is tight has been pulled or stretched so that it is straight: *If the straps aren't tight enough, the saddle will slip.* → opposite LOOSE[1] **5** with hardly enough time, space, or money: *It's a tight schedule, but we can manage.* | *It was a tight squeeze, but somehow we all got in the car.* | **be on a tight budget** (=not have much money to spend) **6** *informal* drunk **7** **in a tight spot** *informal* in a difficult situation —**tightly** *adv*

tight[2] *adv* firmly or closely: *Hold tight and don't let go of my hand.* | *Put the lid on tight.*

tight·en /ˈtaɪtn/ *v* [I,T] to become tighter, or to make something tighter: *Richard's grip tightened on her arm.* | *How do I tighten my seat belt?* **2** **tighten your belt** *informal* to try to spend less money than you used to spend

tighten sth ↔ **up** also **tighten up on** sth *phr v* [T] to make a rule, law, or system stricter: *They're tightening up the laws on immigration.*

tight·rope /ˈtaɪt-rəʊp‖-roʊp/ *n* [C] **1** a rope or wire high above the ground that a performer walks along in a CIRCUS **2** **walk a tightrope** to be in a difficult situation in which you have to be careful about what you say or do

tights /taɪts/ *n* [plural] a piece of girls' or women's clothing that fits closely around the feet and legs and up to the waist → see colour picture on page 113

tight·wad /ˈtaɪtwɒd‖-wɑːd/ *n* [C] *AmE informal* someone who hates to spend or give money

tile /taɪl/ *n* [C] one of the thin square pieces of clay or other material that are used for covering roofs, walls, or floors —**tile** *v* [T]

till[1] /tɪl, tl/ *prep, linking word* until: *Let's wait till tomorrow.*

till[2] /tɪl/ *n* [C] a machine used in a shop to keep money in and show how much customers have to pay; CASH REGISTER

tilt /tɪlt/ *v* [I,T] to move or make something move into a position where one side is higher than the other: *She tilted her head.* —**tilt** *n* [C]

tim·ber /ˈtɪmbə‖-ər/ *n* **1** [U] *BrE* wood used for building or making things; LUMBER **2** [C] a large piece of wood used for building or making something: *the timbers that hold up the roof*

time[1] /taɪm/ *n* **1** [U] what we measure in minutes, hours, years etc: *Time goes by* (=passes) *so quickly these days.* **2** [C,U] a particular minute or hour of the day: *a list giving the dates and times of the exams* | *What time do you go to bed?* | **what time is it?**/**do you have the time?** *"Excuse me, do you have the time?" "It's five o'clock."* **3** [C] an occasion when something happens or when you do something: *How many times have you been to Paris before?* | **last/next time** *I'll pay you back next time I see you.* **4** [singular, U] an amount of time: *The meeting lasted a long time.* | *It all happened a very long time ago.* | **take time** (=take a long time): *Learning a language takes time.* **5** [C] a period of time or history: *The play is set in the time of Alexander the Great.* | *My time at university was the happiest time of my life.* | **at the time**/**at that time** (=a time in the past when something happened): *I was living in Mexico at the time.* | **at one time** (=in the past): *At one time the island belonged to France.* | **before your time** (=before you

were born) **6** **it's time** used to say that something should happen now: *Come on, kids. It's time to go home.* **7** **by the time** when: *By the time you get this letter, I'll be in Canada.* **8** **all the time** **a)** continuously or during the whole of a period of time: *I don't have to wear my glasses all the time.* **b)** very often: *It happens all the time.* **9** **most of the time**/**some of the time** usually or sometimes **10** **on time** at the correct time or the time that was arranged: *In Japan the trains are always on time.* **11** **in (good) time** early or at the right time: *They arrived in time for dinner.* **12** **in a week's/three months' etc time** a week, three months etc from now: *We'll meet again in a months time.* **13** **in no time** very soon or quickly: *We'll be there in no time.* **14** **good/right/bad etc time** a suitable or unsuitable time to do something, or for something to happen: *This isn't the right time to ask for more money.* **15** **have a good/great time** to enjoy yourself **16** **have (the) time** to have enough time to do something: *I'm sorry, I don't have time to talk now.* **17** **take your time** to do something carefully, without hurrying: *Take your time – you don't have to rush.* **18** **at times** sometimes: *The work can be very stressful at times.* **19** **from time to time** sometimes, but not often: *We still see each other from time to time.* **20** **time after time** again and again **21** **one/two etc at a time** one, two etc at the same time: *You can borrow three books at a time from the library.* **22** **five/ten/many etc times** used to compare things, to say how much bigger, better one thing is than something else: *She earns three times as much as I do.* **23** **(it's) about time** *spoken* used to say that something should already have happened: *It's about time you got a job!* **24** **for the time being** for a short time but not permanently: *They'll let us live here for the time being.* **25** **have no time for** to not like or respect someone or something: *She's always complaining – I've no time for people like that.* **26** **behind the times** not modern; old-fashioned **27** **in time (to the music)** if you do something in time to a piece of music, you do it using the same RHYTHM and speed as the music **28** [C] the amount of time taken by someone in a race: *The winner's time was 2 hours and 6 minutes.* **29** [U] the time in a particular part of the world: *The train finally left Prague at 5.30 local time.* → see also **at the same time** (SAME)

USAGE NOTE: time

Compare **spend time, pass time,** and **waste time**. If you **spend time** on something, you use time sensibly, or in a way that is neither good nor bad: *He spends a lot of time studying.* If you have too much time that you need to fill in, you might **pass the time**: *We passed the time playing cards.* If you use your time badly or without any success, you **waste time**: *I wasted nearly an hour trying to find a parking space!*

---

time[2] *v* [T] **1** to arrange that something will happen at a particular time: *The bomb was timed to go off at 5:00.* | **well/badly timed** (=arranged to happen at a suitable or unsuitable time: *The announcement was badly timed.* **2** to measure how quickly someone does something or how long something takes to happen: *We timed our journey – it took two and a half hours.*

time bomb /'. ./ *n* [C] **1** a situation that is likely to become a very serious problem: *the population time bomb* **2** a bomb that is set to explode at a particular time

time-con·sum·ing /'. .,../ *adj* needing a long time to do: *a time-consuming process*

time-hon·oured *BrE*, **time-honored** *AmE* /'. ,../ *adj* used to say that something has always been done in the same way for a long time: *time-honoured customs*

time·keep·er /'taɪm,kiːpəll-ər/ *n* [C] someone who officially records the times taken to do something, especially at a sports event

time·less /'taɪmləs/ *adj* always remaining beautiful, attractive etc: *the timeless beauty of Venice*

time·ly /'taɪmli/ *adj* done or happening at a very suitable time: *a timely decision*

time off /,. './ *n* [U] time when you are officially allowed not to be at work or studying

time out /,. './ *n* **1 take time out** to rest or do something different from your usual job or activities **2** [C] a short period during a game of BASKETBALL, ICE HOCKEY etc, when the teams can rest

tim·er /'taɪməll-ər/ *n* [C] a piece of equipment used for measuring time, or for making a machine operate for a particular amount of time

times /taɪmz/ *prep* multiplied by: *two times two equals four*

time·ta·ble /'taɪm,teɪbəl/ *n* [C] **1** a list of times and dates when things are planned to happen: *the school timetable* ➔ see colour picture on page 80 **2** *BrE* a list of the times of buses, trains etc; SCHEDULE *AmE* —**timetable** *v* [T]

time zone /'. ./ *n* [C] one of the 24 areas that the world is divided into, each of which has its own time

tim·id /'tɪmɪ̰d/ *adj* shy and not confident, or easily frightened: *a timid child* —**timidly** *adv* —**timidity** /tɪ'mɪdɪ̰ti/ *n* [U]

tim·ing /'taɪmɪŋ/ *n* [U] **1** the time, day etc when someone does something or when something happens – used especially when you are considering how suitable this is: *the timing of the election* **2** someone's ability to choose the most suitable time to do something: *Good comedy depends on timing.*

tin /tɪn/ *n* **1** [C] *BrE* a small metal container in which food is sold; CAN: *a tin of sardines* ➔ see picture at CONTAINER **2** [U] a soft light metal that is often mixed with other metals: *a tin can*

tin·foil /'tɪnfɔɪl/ *n* [U] a thin sheet of shiny metal that bends like paper, used especially for covering food

tinge /tɪndʒ/ *n* [C] a very small amount of a feeling or colour: *There was a tinge of sadness in her voice.* —**tinged** *adj*: *His hair was black, tinged with grey.*

tin·gle /'tɪŋgəl/ *v* [I] if your skin tingles, it feels uncomfortable and you feel short slight pains in it: *My fingers tingled with the cold.* —**tingle** *n* [C]

tin·ker /'tɪŋkəll-ər/ *v* [I] *informal* to make small changes to something to improve it or make it work better, often in a way that causes problems

tin·kle /'tɪŋkəl/ *v* [I] to make a gentle high ringing sound —**tinkle** *n* [C] *the tinkle of distant cowbells*

tinned /tɪnd/ *adj BrE* tinned food is sold in small metal containers; CANNED: *tinned tomatoes*

tin·ny /'tɪni/ *adj* a tinny sound is unpleasant to listen to, like small pieces of metal hitting each other: *tinny music*

tin o·pen·er /'. ,.../ *n* [C] *BrE* a tool for opening TINS; CAN OPENER ➔ see picture at KITCHEN

tin·sel /'tɪnsəl/ *n* [U] thin pieces of shiny silver paper, used especially as Christmas decorations

tint¹ /tɪnt/ *n* [C] a particular kind of colour: *The sky had a pink tint.*

tint² *v* [T] to change parts of your hair to a slightly different colour, in order to make it look more attractive

tint·ed /'tɪntɪ̰d/ *adj* tinted glass is coloured, so that less light can go through it

ti·ny /'taɪni/ *adj* extremely small: *thousands of tiny fish*

tip¹ /tɪp/ *n* [C] **1** the narrow or pointed end of something: *the tip of your nose* **2** an additional amount of money that you give to someone such as a WAITER or taxi driver: *Did you leave a tip?* **3** a simple but useful piece of advice about how to do something: *He gave me some useful tips on how to take good pictures.* **4** *BrE* an area where unwanted waste is taken and left; DUMP: *a rubbish tip* **5** *BrE informal* a very dirty or untidy place **6 be on the tip of your tongue** if a word, name etc is on the tip of your tongue, you know it but you cannot remember it immediately **7 the tip of the iceberg** a small sign of a much larger problem

tip² *v* **-pped, -pping** **1** [I,T] to move something so that one side is higher than the other, or to move in this way: *He tipped his seat back and stared at the ceiling.* **2** [T] to pour something out of a container: *Edward tipped the last of the wine into their glasses.* **3** [I,T] to give a small additional amount of money to a WAITER, taxi driver etc **4 be tipped to do sth** if someone is tipped to win something, get an important job etc, many people say this will happen: *Tom Cruise is tipped to win an Oscar.*

tip sb ↔ off *phr v* [T] *informal* to tell someone, especially the police, that someone has secretly planned to do something: *The police must have been tipped off about the robbery.*

tip over *phr v* [I,T **tip sth ↔ over**] to fall or turn over, or make something do this: *A can of paint had tipped over in the back of the van.*

tip·sy /'tɪpsi/ *adj* slightly drunk

tip·toe /'tɪptəʊll-toʊ/ *n* **on tiptoe** standing on your toes, with the rest of your feet above the ground —**tiptoe** *v* [I] *They tiptoed past the door.* ➔ see colour picture on page 670

ti·rade /taɪ'reɪd, tɪ̰-ll'taɪreɪd, tɪ̰'reɪd/ *n* [C] a long angry speech criticizing someone or something

tire¹ /taɪəll taɪr/ *n* [C] *AmE* a thick round piece of rubber filled with air, that fits around the wheel of a car, bicycle etc; TYRE *BrE*: **flat tire** (=one that has no air in it) ➔ see picture at CAR

tire² *v* **1 tire of sth** to become bored with something: *Luke soon tired of his new toy.* **2** [I,T] to make someone feel tired, or to become tired: *Even short walks tire her.*

tire sb ↔ out *phr v* [T] to make someone very tired: *Those kids have tired me out.*

tired /taɪədll taɪrd/ *adj* **1** feeling that you want to sleep or rest: *You look tired. Do you want to lie* *down?* | **tired out** (=very tired): *It had been a long hard day, and they were all tired out.* → see colour picture on page 277 **2 tired of sth** bored or annoyed with something: *I'm tired of her stupid comments.*

tire·less /ˈtaɪələs‖ˈtaɪr-/ *adj* working very hard to do something and not stopping or becoming tired: *a tireless campaigner for women's rights* —**tirelessly** *adv*

tire·some /ˈtaɪəsəm‖ˈtaɪr-/ *adj* annoying or boring: *a tiresome younger sister*

tir·ing /ˈtaɪərɪŋ‖ˈtaɪr-/ *adj* making you feel tired: *a long and tiring journey*

tis·sue /ˈtɪʃuː, -sjuː‖-ʃuː/ *n* **1** [C] soft thin paper, used for cleaning your nose **2** [U] also **tissue paper** soft thin paper used to wrap things in order to prevent them from being damaged **3** [U] the material that animals and plants consist of, which contains groups of cells

tit /tɪt/ *n* [C] **1** a small European bird **2** *informal* an offensive word for a woman's breast

ti·ta·ni·um /taɪˈteɪniəm/ *n* [C] a very strong light white metal

tit·bit /ˈtɪtˌbɪt/ *n* [C] *BrE* a small piece of food or interesting information; TIDBIT *AmE*

tit-for-tat /ˌtɪt fə ˈtæt‖-fər-/ *adj informal* when someone does something unpleasant to another person, because the other person has done something unpleasant to them

tit·il·late /ˈtɪtɪleɪt/ *v* [T] to make someone feel excited or interested, especially sexually: *a story to titillate the readers*

ti·tle[1] /ˈtaɪtl/ *n* [C] **1** the name given to a book, painting, play etc: *What's the title of his latest novel?* **2** the position of being the best person in a sport, which someone gets after winning a very important game or competition: *Schumacher looks likely to win the world title.* **3** the official name of someone's job: *Her official title is editorial manager.* **4** a word such as Mr, Mrs, Dr, or Lord, that is used before someone's name

title[2] *v* [T] to give a book, film etc a particular name

ti·tled /ˈtaɪtld/ *adj* have a title such as LORD, DUKE, EARL etc

title-hold·er /ˈ.. ˌ../ *n* [C] someone who has won an important sports competition

title role /ˈ.. ./ *n* [C] the main character in a film or play, after which the film or play is named

tit·ter /ˈtɪtə‖-ər/ *v* [I] to laugh quietly, especially in a nervous way —**titter** *n* [C]

T-junc·tion /ˈtiː ˌdʒʌŋkʃən/ *n* [C] *BrE* a place where two roads meet and form the shape of the letter T

TNT /ˌtiː en ˈtiː/ *n* [U] a powerful explosive

to[1] /tə, *before vowels* tʊ; *strong* tuː/ **1** used with the basic form of the verb to make the INFINITIVE: *I want to go home.* | *They decided to wait.* | *Can you show me how to use the fax machine?* **2** used to say the purpose of doing something; IN ORDER TO: *Helen went there to see some old friends.*

to[2] *prep* **1** going somewhere: *He's gone to Australia.* | *She stood up and walked to the door.* | *the road to the airport* → see colour picture on page 474 **2** used to say that someone gives someone

something, tells someone something etc: *Martha always says "hello" to me.* | *He handed his ticket to the inspector.* **3** **from ... to ...** **a)** used when you are talking about the period between two times or the distance between two places: *The banks are open from 9.30 to 3.00.* | *It's 30 miles from here to Toronto.* **b)** used to say what something includes: **from ... to ...** *They have books on everything from cooking to camping.* **4** touching or facing something: *He had his back to the door.* | **to the south/east etc** *The town lies 50 miles to the south of Indianapolis.* **5** used to mean 'before' when you are saying what time it is: *It's ten to four.* **6** used to say what someone's opinion or feeling was about something: *Tickets cost £20, and to some people that's a lot of money.* **7** **to sb's surprise/amazement/relief etc** used to say that someone is surprised etc by something: *To her surprise, they offered her the job.* **8** used to say that something is part of something else, or is connected with them: *the key to the front door* **9** used to compare two things or numbers: *I prefer Japanese food to French food.* | *The Bears won 27 to 10.* **10** **to yourself** for yourself and no one else: *I had a room to myself.*

to[3] /tuː/ *adv* **1** **to and fro** moving in one direction and then back again: *walking to and fro* **2** if you pull or push a door to, you close it

toad /təʊd‖toʊd/ *n* [C] an animal like a large FROG, which has a brownish colour

toad·stool /ˈtəʊdstuːl‖ˈtoʊd-/ *n* [C] a wild plant that looks like a MUSHROOM, but is often poisonous

toast[1] /təʊst‖toʊst/ *n* **1** [U] bread that has been heated until it is brown: *cheese on toast* **2** [C] when a group of people lift up their glasses and drink to thank someone, wish them good luck etc: *I'd like to propose a toast to the happy couple.* **3** **be the toast of Broadway/Hollywood etc** to be very popular and praised by a lot of people in a place

toast[2] *v* [T] **1** to ask people to drink something with you in order to thank someone, wish someone luck etc **2** to make bread turn brown by heating it

toast·er /ˈtəʊstə‖ˈtoʊstər/ *n* [C] a machine used for making toast → see picture at KITCHEN

to·bac·co /təˈbækəʊ‖-koʊ/ *n* [U] dried brown leaves used for making cigarettes, CIGARS etc

to·bac·co·nist /təˈbækənɪst/ *n* [C] **1** also **to·bacconist's** a small shop that sells tobacco, cigarettes etc **2** someone who owns or works in a small shop that sells tobacco, cigarettes etc

to·bog·gan /təˈbɒɡən‖-ˈbɑː-/ *n* [C] a wooden board that curves up at the front, used for going down a hill over snow —**tobagganing** *n* [U]

to·day /təˈdeɪ/ *n* [U] , *adv* **1** the day that is happening now, or on this day: *Today is Wednesday.* | *Can we go to the park today?* **2** the period of time that is happening now, or during this period: *today's athletic superstars* | *Today more and more girls are taking up smoking.*

tod·dle /ˈtɒdl‖ˈtɑːdl/ *v* [I] *informal* to go somewhere

tod·dler /ˈtɒdlə‖ˈtɑːdlər/ *n* [C] a young child who has just learned to walk

to-do /tə ˈduː/ *n* [singular] *informal* unnecessary excitement or angry feelings about something; FUSS

toe[1] /təʊ‖toʊ/ *n* [C] **1** one of the five parts like fingers at the end of your foot: *I hurt my big toe.* (=largest toe) **2 on your toes** ready for anything that might happen

toe[2] *v* **toe the line** to do what you are told to do by people in authority

toe·nail /'təʊneɪl‖'toʊ-/ *n* [C] the hard flat part that covers the top end of your toe

toff /tɒf‖tɑːf/ *n* [C] *BrE old-fashioned* someone who is rich or has a high social position

tof·fee /'tɒfi‖'tɑːfi/ *n* [C,U] a sticky brown sweet food made from sugar and butter

to·ga /'təʊgə‖'toʊ-/ *n* [C] a long loose piece of clothing worn by people in ancient Greece and Rome

to·geth·er[1] /tə'geðə‖-ər/ *adv* **1** with each other: *Kevin and I went to school together.* **2** used to say that things are joined, mixed, used etc with each other: *Mix the flour and the sugar together.* **3** used to say that people or things are with each other in the same place: *The children were all sitting together in a group.* **4** at the same time: *Why do all the bills seem to come together?* | **together with** *Bring it back to the store together with your receipt.*

together[2] *adj informal* someone who is together is good at organizing his or her life: *Carla seems really together.*

to·geth·er·ness /tə'geðən̩s‖-ðər-/ *n* [U] a feeling of having a close relationship with other people

tog·gle /'tɒgəl‖'tɑː-/ *n* [C] a small piece of wood or plastic that is used like a button to fasten coats, bags etc ➔ see picture at FASTENERS

toil /tɔɪl/ *v* [I] *literary* to work very hard for a long period of time —**toil** *n* [U]

toi·let /'tɔɪlɪ̩t/ *n* [C] **1** a large bowl that you sit on to get rid of waste substances from your body **2** *BrE* a room with a toilet: *the men's toilet* **3 go to the toilet** *BrE* to make liquid or solid waste go out of your body

toilet bag /'.. ./ *n* [C] a bag in which you keep things such as soap, TOOTHPASTE etc when travelling; SPONGE BAG *BrE*

toilet pa·per /'.. ,../ *n* [U] soft thin paper used for cleaning yourself after you have used the toilet

toi·let·ries /'tɔɪlɪ̩triz/ *n* [plural] things such as soap and TOOTHPASTE that you use for washing yourself, brushing your teeth etc

toilet roll /'.. ,./ *n* [C] toilet paper that is wound around a small tube

to·ken[1] /'təʊkən‖'toʊ-/ *n* [C] **1** *formal* something that is intended to show your intentions or feelings: *He had given her the ring as a token of his love.* **2** a piece of metal or plastic, that you use instead of money **3 book/record/gift token** *BrE* a piece of paper that you can exchange for a book, record etc in a shop, given to someone as a present; GIFT CERTIFICATE *AmE*

token[2] *adj* **1 token woman/black person etc** someone who is chosen by an organization in order to make people think that the organization cares about including more women, black people etc, although this is not really true **2** a token payment or action is not very big or important, but shows your intentions or feelings —**token·ism** *n* [U]

told /təʊld‖toʊld/ *v* the past tense and past participle of TELL

tol·e·ra·ble /'tɒlərəbəl‖'tɑː-/ *adj* something that is tolerable is acceptable, although it is not very pleasant or good: *tolerable levels of pollution* —**tolerably** *adv*

tol·e·rance /'tɒlərəns‖'tɑː-/ *n* [U] when people allow other people to do or believe what they want, without criticizing or punishing them: *greater religious tolerance* ➔ opposite INTOLERANCE

tol·e·rant /'tɒlərənt‖'tɑː-/ *adj* allowing other people to do or say what they want, even though you may not approve of what they are doing: *My parents were very tolerant when I was a teenager.*

tol·e·rate /'tɒləreɪt‖'tɑː-/ *v* [T] **1** to accept or allow something, especially something that you do not like or approve of: *He said he refused to tolerate this sort of behaviour in his house.* **2** to not be harmed by something: *plants that will tolerate all kinds of weather conditions* —**toleration** /ˌtɒlə'reɪʃən‖ˌtɑː-/ *n* [U]

toll[1] /təʊl‖toʊl/ *n* **1** [singular] the number of people killed or injured by something: *The death toll has risen to 83.* **2 take its toll (on)** to have a bad effect on someone or something over a long period of time: *Years of smoking has taken its toll on his health.* **3** [C] money you pay to use a road, bridge etc: *a toll bridge* (=one you have to pay to use)

toll[2] *v* [I,T] if a bell tolls, or someone tolls it, it rings slowly, especially because someone has died

to·ma·to /tə'mɑːtəʊ‖-'meɪtoʊ/ *n* [C], *plural* **tomatoes** a soft round red fruit, eaten especially in SALADS ➔ see picture at VEGETABLES

tomb /tuːm/ *n* [C] a grave, especially a large one

tom·boy /'tɒmbɔɪ‖'tɑːm-/ *n* [C] a girl who likes to play the same games as boys

tomb·stone /'tuːmstəʊn‖-stoʊn/ *n* [C] a stone on a grave that shows the name of the dead person

tom·cat /'tɒmkæt‖'tɑːm-/ *n* [C] a male cat

tome /təʊm‖toʊm/ *n* [C] *formal* a large heavy book

to·mor·row /tə'mɒrəʊ‖-'mɔːroʊ, -'mɑː-/ *adv, n* [U] **1** the day after today, on this day: *Tomorrow is Thursday.* | *What are you doing tomorrow?* **2** the future, or in the future: *the world of tomorrow*

tom-tom /'tɒm tɒm‖'tɑːm tɑːm/ *n* [C] a drum you play with your hands

ton /tʌn/ *n* [C] **1** a unit for measuring weight, equal to 2240 pounds or 1016 kilos in Britain, and 2000 pounds in the US **2 tons of** *informal* a lot: *tons of letters* **3 weigh a ton** *informal* to be very heavy

---

GRAMMAR NOTE: the present (2)

Use the **simple present** to talk about things that are true in general: *Carlos lives in Madrid.* | *She works in a bank.* | *Water boils at 100°C.* But use the **present progressive** to talk about what you are studying: *I'm learning English.* | *She's studying history.*

tools

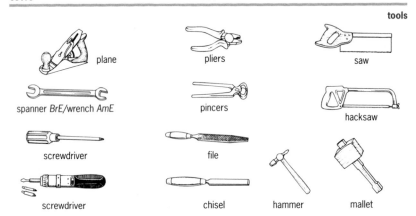

plane

pliers

saw

spanner *BrE*/wrench *AmE*

pincers

hacksaw

screwdriver

file

screwdriver

chisel

hammer

mallet

tone[1] /təʊnǁtoʊn/ *n* **1** [C,U] the quality of a sound, especially the way in which someone says something, which shows how they are feeling: *tone of voice* *He spoke in a rather threatening tone of voice.* **2** [singular, U] the general feeling or attitude that something seems to have: *The whole tone of her letter was rather formal and unfriendly.* **3** [C] a sound made by a piece of electronic equipment, especially a telephone: *Please leave a message after the tone.* **4** [C] a particular kind of colour —**tonal** *adj*

tone[2], **tone up** *v* [T] to make your muscles or skin feel firmer, healthier etc: *I'm trying to tone up my stomach.*
tone sth ↔ down *phr v* [T] to change the words of something so that it is less likely to offend someone, or is less exciting: *They toned down the words to the song so it could be played on the radio.*

tone-deaf /ˌ. ˈ.◂/ *adj* unable to hear the difference between different musical notes, and unable to sing

ton·er /ˈtəʊnəǁˈtoʊnər/ *n* [C,U] a type of ink used in computer PRINTERS, PHOTOCOPIERS etc

tongs /tɒŋzǁtɑːŋz, tɔːŋz/ *n* [plural] a tool for picking things up, which consists of two moveable bars that are joined together at one end

tongue /tʌŋ/ *n* **1** [C] the soft moveable part in your mouth that you use for tasting and speaking **2** **hold your tongue** to stop speaking, or not say anything about something **3** [C] a language: **mother/native tongue** (=the first language you learned as a child) **4** [C,U] the tongue of a cow or sheep eaten as food → see also **on the tip of your tongue** (TIP[1]), **slip of the tongue** (SLIP[2]), **have a sharp tongue** (SHARP[1])

tongue-in-cheek /ˌ. . ˈ.◂/ *adv* said or done as a joke, although you pretend to be serious: *The show was done in a tongue-in-cheek style.*

tongue-tied /ˈ. ./ *adj* unable to speak because you are nervous

tongue-twist·er /ˈ. ˌ../ *n* [C] a phrase or sentence with many similar sounds, which is difficult to say quickly

ton·ic /ˈtɒnɪkǁˈtɑː-/ *n* **1** [C,U] also **tonic water** a drink with BUBBLES that tastes slightly BITTER, that is added to some alcoholic drinks, for

example GIN **2** [singular] something that makes you healthier, happier, or have more energy

to·night /təˈnaɪt/ *adv, n* [U] the evening or night of today, or on this evening or night: *Tonight is a very special occasion.* | *Do you want to go out tonight?*

ton·nage /ˈtʌnɪdʒ/ *n* [U] the total weight or amount of something, measured in TONS

tonne /tʌn/ *n* [C] a unit for measuring weight, equal to 1000 kilograms

ton·sil /ˈtɒnsəlǁˈtɑːn-/ *n* [C] one of the two small things in your throat near the back of your tongue

ton·sil·li·tis /ˌtɒnsɪˈlaɪtɪsǁˌtɑːn-/ *n* [U] an infection of the tonsils

too /tuː/ *adv* **1** more than is right or necessary, or more than you want: *He was driving too fast.* | *This dress is much too small for me.* | *It's too cold to swim.* | **too much/many** *$200 for a room? That's far too much.* **2** also: *Sheila wants to come too.* | *"I'm really hungry." "Me too!"* **3** **not too** not very: *He wasn't too pleased when I told him I was leaving.* **4** **all too/only too** used to emphasize that something happens too easily, too often, too much etc: *This kind of attack happens all too often these days.*

USAGE NOTE: too and very

Compare **too** and **very**. **Too** is usually used about something bad or unacceptable: *It's too cold today.* | *I can't buy that – it's too expensive.* Use **very** about something that is neither good nor bad, to emphasize something about it: *It's very cold today.* | *Our vacation was very expensive, but it was worth it.* Use **too** before adjectives on their own: *This coffee is too sweet.* However, do not use **too** before an adjective followed by a noun. Don't say 'too sweet coffee'.

---

took /tʊk/ *v* the past tense of TAKE

tool /tuːl/ *n* [C] **1** something such as a hammer or a SCREWDRIVER which you use to make or repair things: *a tool kit* (=a set of tools) **2** something that can be used for a particular purpose: *Home computers can be used as a tool for learning.*

toot /tuːt/ *v* [I,T] if you toot your horn, or if it toots, it makes a short sound —**toot** *n* [C]

tooth /tuːθ/ *n* [C], *plural* **teeth** /tiːθ/ **1** one of the hard white things in your mouth, used for biting food: *Did you remember to brush your teeth?* **2** one of the pointed parts that sticks out from a comb, SAW etc ➙ see also **have a sweet tooth** (SWEET¹)

tooth·ache /ˈtuːθ-eɪk/ *n* [C] a pain in a tooth

tooth·brush /ˈtuːθbrʌʃ/ *n* [C] a small brush for cleaning your teeth ➙ see picture at BRUSH

tooth·paste /ˈtuːθpeɪst/ *n* [U] a substance used for cleaning your teeth

tooth·pick /ˈtuːθˌpɪk/ *n* [C] a small pointed piece of wood used for removing pieces of food from between your teeth

top¹ /tɒp‖taːp/ *n* **1** [C] the highest part of something: *Write your name at the top of the page.* | **on top (of)** *They stood together on top of Mount Everest.* | *a house with a chimney on top* ➙ opposite BOTTOM¹ **2** [C] the flat upper surface of an object: *The table has a glass top.* | *the top of my desk* ➙ opposite BOTTOM¹ **3 on top of a)** in addition to something: *On top of everything else, I need $700 to fix my car!* **b)** completely able to deal with a job or situation: *Don't worry I'm back on top of things now.* **c)** *spoken* unpleasantly or dangerously close to something or someone: *The truck was almost on top of us.* **4 the top** the best, most successful, or most important position in a company, group, competition etc: *United are at the top of the league.* **5 on top** winning: *The Australians were on top throughout the game.* **6** [C] a cover for a pen, container etc, especially something that you push or turn: *Can you help me get the top off this jar?* **7** [C] a piece of clothing that you wear on the upper part of your body: *She was wearing a yellow top.* **8 off the top of your head** *informal* when you give an answer or opinion immediately, without checking that you are right: *Off the top of my head I'd say there were about 50.* **9 at the top of your voice** shouting or singing as loudly as you can **10** [C] a toy that spins and balances on its point **11 on top of the world** *informal* extremely happy **12 from top to bottom** completely and thoroughly: *They searched the house from top to bottom.* **13 get on top of sb** if something gets on top of you, it makes you feel very unhappy, because you have too many problems to deal with **14 over the top** too extreme and therefore unacceptable ➙ see also **blow your top** (BLOW¹)

top² *adj* **1** best or most successful: *the world's top tennis players* **2** at the top; highest: *the top button of my shirt* | *the top drawer* ➙ opposite BOTTOM² **3** the top level of something is the highest level: *The new Jaguar has a top speed of 155 mph.* **4 top dog** *informal* the person who has the most power or the most important position

top³ *v* [T] **-pped, -pping 1** to be more than something or better than something: *Their profits have topped $9 million this year.* **2** if something is topped with another thing, it is covered with it: *ice cream topped with maple syrup*

top sth ↔ **off** *phr v* [T] *informal* to do one final thing to finish something: *We topped off the evening with a visit to a local bar.*

top up *phr v* [T] to fill something that is partly empty: *Do you want me to top up your glass?*

top hat /ˌ. ˈ./ *n* [C] a tall hat with a flat top, worn by men in past times

top-heav·y /ˌ. ˈ..◂/ *adj* too heavy at the top and therefore likely to fall over

top·ic /ˈtɒpɪk‖ˈtaː-/ *n* [C] a subject that people talk or write about: *Jackie's engagement was the main topic of conversation.*

top·ic·al /ˈtɒpɪkəl‖ˈtaː-/ *adj* relating to something that is important at the present time: *a new TV show dealing with topical issues*

top·less /ˈtɒpləs‖ˈtaːp-/ *adj* not wearing any clothes on the upper part of the body

top·most /ˈtɒpməʊst‖ˈtaːpmoʊst/ *adj* highest: *the topmost branches*

top-notch /ˌ. ˈ.◂/ *adj informal* having the highest quality or standard: *top-notch equipment*

to·pog·ra·phy /təˈpɒɡrəfi‖-ˈpaː-/ *n* [U] the shape of an area of land and the things that are on it, including its hills, valleys etc —**topographical** /ˌtɒpəˈɡræfɪkəl◂‖ˌtaː-, ˌtoʊ-/ *adj*

top·ping /ˈtɒpɪŋ‖ˈtaː-/ *n* [C,U] food that you put on top of other food to make it taste or look better: *a pizza with five toppings*

top·ple /ˈtɒpəl‖ˈtaː-/ *v* **1** [I] to fall over: **+ over** *Several trees toppled over in the storm.* **2** [T] to take power away from a leader or government: *The scandal could topple the government.*

top-se·cret /ˌ. ˈ..◂/ *adj* top secret documents or information must be kept completely secret: *top-secret information*

top·sy-tur·vy /ˌtɒpsi ˈtɜːvi ‖ˌtaːpsi ˈtɜːrvi / *adj* very confused, or completely the opposite of what normally happens

torch¹ /tɔːtʃ‖tɔːrtʃ/ *n* [C] **1** *BrE* a small electric lamp that you carry in your hand; FLASHLIGHT ➙ see picture at LIGHT **2** a long stick that you burn at one end for light or as a SYMBOL: *the Olympic torch*

torch² *v* [T] *informal* to start a fire deliberately in order to destroy something: *Someone had torched the car.*

tore /tɔː‖tɔːr/ *v* the past tense of TEAR

tor·ment¹ /tɔːˈment‖tɔːr-/ *v* [T] **1** if you are tormented by something, it makes you feel very worried and unhappy: *He was tormented by feelings of guilt.* **2** to treat someone very cruelly —**tormentor** *n* [C]

tor·ment² /ˈtɔːment‖ˈtɔːr-/ *n* [C,U] great pain and suffering, or something that causes this

torn /tɔːn‖tɔːrn/ *v* the past participle of TEAR

tor·na·do /tɔːˈneɪdəʊ‖tɔːrˈneɪdoʊ/ *n* [C], *plural* **tornadoes** a very violent storm with air that spins very quickly in the shape of a FUNNEL

tor·pe·do /tɔːˈpiːdəʊ‖tɔːrˈpiːdoʊ/ *n* [C], *plural* **torpedoes** a weapon that is fired under the surface of the sea from one ship at another —**torpedo** *v* [T]

tor·rent /ˈtɒrənt‖ˈtɔː-, ˈtaː-/ *n* **1** [singular] a **torrent of sth** a lot of something: **+ of** *a torrent of abuse* **2** [C] a large amount of water moving very quickly in a particular direction —**torrential** /təˈrenʃəl/ *adj*: *torrential rain*

tor·so /ˈtɔːsəʊ‖ˈtɔːrsoʊ/ *n* [C], *plural* **torsos** the main part of your body, not including your arms, legs, or head

T

tor·toise /ˈtɔːtəs‖ˈtɔːr-/ *n* [C] a slow moving land animal that can put its head and legs into the shell that covers its body

tor·tu·ous /ˈtɔːtʃuəs‖ˈtɔːr-/ *adj* **1** very long, complicated and difficult: *a tortuous process* **2** a tortuous road has a lot of turns and is very difficult to travel along

tor·ture¹ /ˈtɔːtʃə‖ˈtɔːrtʃər/ *v* [T] to deliberately cause someone a lot of pain over a long period of time, especially in order to punish them or make them give you information: *Resistance leaders were tortured to death in prison.* —**torturer** *n* [C]

torture² *n* [C,U] **1** when someone is tortured: *the torture of innocent civilians* **2** an extremely unpleasant or painful experience: *The last year of their marriage was absolute torture.*

To·ry /ˈtɔːri/ *n* [C] someone who belongs to or votes for the Conservative Party in Britain

toss¹ /tɒs‖tɔːs/ *v* **1** [T] to throw something, especially in a careless way: *He tossed his jacket on the bed.* **2** also **toss up** [I,T] *especially BrE* to throw a coin up and make it spin, then see which side it lands on as a way of deciding something: *Let's toss up to see who goes first.* **3** **toss and turn** to change your position a lot in bed because you cannot sleep **4** **toss your head (back)** to move your head back quickly

toss² *n* **1** **a toss of a coin** if you decide something by a toss of a coin, you decide what should happen by throwing up a coin into the air and seeing which side faces upwards **2** **a toss of his/her head** when someone moves their head backwards quickly and suddenly

tot /tɒt‖tɑːt/ *n* [C] *informal* **1** a small child **2** *especially BrE* a small amount of an alcoholic drink

to·tal¹ /ˈtəʊtl‖ˈtoʊ-/ *adj* **1** including everything: *His farm has a total area of 100 acres. | The total cost of the building will be $6 million.* **2** complete – used to emphasize what you are saying: *The meeting was a total waste of time.*

total² *n* [C] the final number or amount of something after everything has been included or all the parts have been added together: *The city spent a total of two million dollars on the library. |* **in total** (=including everything): *In total, the journey took about 8 hours.*

total³ *v* [T] **-lled, -lling** *BrE*, **-led, -ling** *AmE* **1** to add up to a particular amount: *Sales totalled nearly $700,000 last year.* **2** *AmE informal* to damage a car so badly that it cannot be repaired

to·tal·i·tar·i·an /ˌtəʊˌtælɪˈteəriən‖toʊˌtælɪˈter-/ *adj* based on a political system in which people are completely controlled by the government —**totalitarianism** *n* [U]

to·tal·i·ty /təʊˈtælɪti‖toʊ-/ *n* [U] *formal* the whole of something

to·tal·ly /ˈtəʊtl-i‖ˈtoʊ-/ *adv* completely: *I totally agree with you. | The whole thing was totally unfair.*

tote bag /ˈtəʊt bæg‖ˈtoʊt-/ *n* [C] *AmE* a large bag in which you carry things

tot·ter /ˈtɒtə‖ˈtɑːtər/ *v* [I] to walk or move in an unsteady way: *a woman tottering around in high heels*

tou·can /ˈtuːkən, -kæn/ *n* [C] a tropical bird with a very large brightly coloured beak

touch¹ /tʌtʃ/ *v* **1** [T] to put your hand or finger on something: *Don't touch the paint – it's still wet! | She touched his forehead gently.* **2** [I,T] if two things are touching, there is no space in between them: *Make sure the wires aren't touching.* **3** **not touch sth** **a)** to not use, eat, or drink something: *He never touches a drop of alcohol.* **b)** to not deal with or become involved in something: *Clancy said he wouldn't touch the case.* **4** **not touch sb/sth** to not hurt someone or damage something: *I swear I didn't touch him!* **5** [T] to affect someone's emotions, especially by making them feel pity or sympathy: *Chaplin's films touched the hearts of millions.* **6** **touch base** *AmE* to talk to someone for a short time, especially about something you are both working on **7** **no one to touch sb/ nothing to touch sth** *spoken* used to say that someone or something is the best: *A brilliant player! There's no one to touch her.* **8** **touch wood** *BrE spoken* something you say when you do not want your good luck to end; KNOCK ON WOOD *AmE* → see also TOUCHED

touch down *phr v* [I] if a plane touches down, it lands on the ground at an airport

touch sth ↔ **off** *phr v* [T] to make people start arguing or fighting with each other: *The report touched off a fierce debate.*

touch on/upon sth *phr v* [T] to mention something when you are talking or writing

touch sth ↔ **up** *phr v* [T] to improve something by making small changes to it

touch² *n* **1** [singular] when you put your hand, finger etc on someone or something: *Rita felt the touch of his hand on her arm.* **2** **get in touch (with sb)** to write to someone or telephone them: *I've been trying to get in touch for days.* **3** **keep/stay in touch** to speak or write to someone, when you can no longer meet them as often as before **4** **lose touch (with sb)** to no longer speak or write to someone, because they do not live near you or work with you any more: *I've lost touch with most of my high school friends.* **5** **in touch/out of touch (with sth)** knowing or not knowing the latest things that have happened, or what people think about a subject: *The government is out of touch with public opinion on this issue.* **6** **a touch of sth** a very small amount of something: *There was a touch of sadness in her voice.* **7** [C] a small detail or change that improves something: *Becky put the finishing touches on the cake.* **8** [U] someone's ability to do something well: *I must be losing my touch* **9** [U] the sense that you use in order to feel things, especially by putting your finger, hand etc on something: *The reptile's skin was cold to the touch.* → see also SOFT TOUCH

touch-and-go /ˌ. . ˈ./ *adj informal* if a situation is touch-and-go, there is a risk that something bad could happen

touch·down /ˈtʌtʃdaʊn/ *n* [C] **1** when a team in RUGBY or American football gets points by taking the ball over the other team's line **2** when a plane or space vehicle lands on the ground

touched /tʌtʃt/ *adj* feeling pleased, grateful, sad etc because of something that someone has done, something you have seen etc: *She was touched by his kindness.*

touch·ing /ˈtʌtʃɪŋ/ *adj* making you feel sympathy, PITY, sadness etc: *a touching story*

touch·stone /'tʌtʃstəʊn‖-stoʊn/ *n* [singular] a standard used for measuring how good something is

touch·y /'tʌtʃi/ *adj* **1** easily offended or annoyed: *You've been very touchy lately – what's wrong?* **2 touchy subject/question etc** something that you have to be careful talking about, because you may offend someone

tough /tʌf/ *adj* **1** difficult: *It's going to be a tough job.* | *They asked some tough questions.* | *a tough choice* **2** physically strong and not easily frightened: *Clint Eastwood plays the part of a tough cop.* **3** determined to get what you want and able to deal with difficult situations and people: *a tough businesswoman* **4** very strict: *tough anti-smoking laws* **5** not easily broken, cut, or damaged: *a tough waterproof material* | *This steak is really tough.* **6** unfortunate in a way that is unfair: *It's always tough on the children when a family breaks up.* **7** a tough area is one where there is a lot of violence and crime —**toughness** *n* [U]

tough·en /'tʌfən/ *also* **toughen up** *v* [I,T] to become stronger, or to make someone or something stronger

tou·pee /'tuːpeɪ‖tuːˈpeɪ/ *n* [C] artificial hair that a man can wear when he has no hair on part of his head

tour[1] /tʊə‖tʊr/ *n* **1** [C,U] a journey in which you visit several different places in a country, area etc: *a 14-day tour of Egypt.* | **on tour** (=when a group of musicians, actors etc travel to several different places to give concerts, plays etc) **2** [C] a short trip through a place in order to see the things in it: *We had a guided tour of the museum.*

tour[2] *v* [I,T] to travel around an area, visiting or performing at different places there

tour·is·m /'tʊərɪzəm‖'tʊr-/ *n* [U] when people travel to a place for pleasure on their holidays, or the business of providing them with places to stay, things to do etc: *The island depends on tourism for most of its income.*

tour·ist /'tʊərɪst‖'tʊr-/ *n* [C] someone who visits a place for pleasure: *Oxford is full of tourists in the summer.*

tour·na·ment /'tʊənəmənt, 'tɔː-‖'tɜːr-, 'tʊr-/ *n* [C] a competition in which many players compete against each other until there is one winner

tour·ni·quet /'tʊənɪkeɪ, 'tɔː-‖'tɜːrnɪkɪt, 'tʊr-/ *n* [C] a band of cloth that you twist tightly around an injured arm or leg to make it stop bleeding (BLEED)

tou·sled /'taʊzəld/ *adj* tousled hair looks untidy —**tousle** *v* [T]

tow[1] /təʊ‖toʊ/ *v* [T] to pull a vehicle or ship: *Our car had to be towed away.*

tow[2] *n* **1** [singular, U] when a vehicle or ship is pulled by another vehicle or ship **2 in tow** following closely behind someone or something: *Mattie arrived with all her children in tow.*

to·wards *especially BrE* /təˈwɔːdz‖ˈtɔːrdz, twɔːrdz/, **toward** *especially AmE* /təˈwɔːrd, twɔːrd/ *prep* **1** moving, facing, or pointing in a particular direction: *I saw a man coming towards me.* → see colour picture on page 474 **2** your feeling towards something is how you feel about it: *Attitudes towards divorce have changed.* **3** in order to help pay for the cost of something: *My parents gave us some money towards the cost of the apartment.* **4** near a time or place: *I often feel tired towards the end of the day.* | *It was cooler towards the coast.*

tow·el /'taʊəl/ *n* [C] a piece of cloth used for drying something: *a bath towel* (=for drying yourself after a bath)

tow·er[1] /'taʊəl-ər/ *n* [C] **1** a tall narrow building, or a tall narrow part of a castle, church etc: *the Eiffel Tower* **2 a tower of strength** someone who gives you a lot of help, sympathy etc when you are in a difficult and worrying situation

tower[2] *v* [I] to be much taller than someone or something that is next to you: **+ over/above** *The teacher towered above him.* —**towering** *adj*

tower block /'.. ./ *n* [C] *BrE* a tall building that contains offices or apartments

town /taʊn/ *n* **1** [C,U] a place where people live and work, which is smaller than a city: *a little town on the coast* | **go into town** (=go into the part of a town where all the shops, offices etc are): *I need to go into town this morning.* **2** [singular] all the people who live in a town: *The whole town got involved in the celebrations.* **3 go to town (on sth)** *informal* to spend a lot of time, effort, or money doing something **4 on the town** *informal* if you go out on the town, you go to a restaurant, bar, theatre etc and drink and enjoy yourself

town hall /ˌ. './ *n* [C] a public building used for a town's local government

towns·peo·ple /'taʊnz,piːpəl/ *also* **towns·folk** /-fəʊk‖-foʊk/ *n* [plural] all the people who live in a town

tox·ic /'tɒksɪk‖'tɑːk-/ *adj* poisonous, or containing poison: *toxic chemicals* | **toxic waste** (=waste products from industry that are very harmful to people and the environment) —**toxicity** /tɒkˈsɪsɪti‖tɑːk-/ *n* [U]

tox·in /'tɒksɪn‖'tɑːk-/ *n* [C] *technical* a poisonous substance

toy[1] /tɔɪ/ *n* [C] a thing for children to play with: *her favourite toys* | *a toy gun*

toy[2] *v*

toy with sb/sth *phr v* [T] **1** to think for a short time about doing something, although you do not really intend to do it: *She had toyed with the idea of becoming an actress.* **2** to move something around, without thinking about what you are doing: *Roy toyed with his pen before he spoke.*

trace[1] /treɪs/ *v* [T] **1** to find someone or something that has disappeared by searching carefully for them: *Police are still trying to trace her husband.* **2** to find the origins of something

T

and find out how it has developed: *He traced his family history back to the 17th century.* **3** to copy something by putting paper over it and drawing the lines that you can see through the paper **4** to find out where a telephone call is coming from using electronic equipment

trace² *n* **1** [C,U] a small sign that someone or something has been in a place: *We found no trace of them on the island.* |**disappear/vanish without trace** (=disappear completely) **2** [C] a very small amount of something, which is difficult to notice: *There was a trace of sadness in his voice.*

track¹ /træk/ *n* **1** [C] a narrow road or path with a rough surface: *a dirt track through the woods* ➝ see colour picture on page 243 **2 keep track of sth** to know what is happening, where things are etc, when there are a lot of different things involved: *It's hard to keep track of everyone's birthdays.* **3 lose track of sth** to not know what is happening, where things are etc any more **4 be on the right/wrong track** to be doing something in a way that is likely to be successful or unsuccessful: *Keep going, you're on the right track* **5** [C] one of the songs or pieces of music on a record: *the best track on the album* **6** [C] the two metal lines that a train travels on **7** [C] a special path or road used for races: *the fastest man on the track* ➝ see colour picture on page 636 **8** [U] *especially AmE* the sport of running on a track: *track events* **9 tracks** marks on the ground made by an animal, person, or vehicle

track² *v* [T] to follow someone or something by checking for signs of where they have been, or by using special electronic equipment: *The whales were tracked across the Atlantic.*
track sb/sth ↔ down *phr v* [T] to find someone or something by searching for a long time in different places: *They finally succeeded in tracking down their daughter.*

track and field /ˌ. ˈ. ./ *n* [U] *especially AmE* all sports that involve running races, jumping, and throwing things ➝ see colour picture on page 636

track rec·ord /ˈ. ˌ../ *n* [singular] the things that a person, country, organization etc has done in the past, which show how good they are at doing something: *The company has an excellent track record on environmental issues.*

track·suit /ˈtræksuːt, -sjuːt/ *n* [C] *BrE* loose clothes that consist of trousers and a JACKET or SWEATER, worn especially for sport ➝ see colour picture on page 113

tract /trækt/ *n* [C] **1 respiratory/digestive etc tract** the part of your body that you use for breathing etc, which consists of a system of tubes **2** a large area of land: *vast tracts of virgin rainforest*

trac·tor /ˈtræktəl-ər/ *n* [C] a strong vehicle with large wheels, used for pulling farm equipment

trade¹ /treɪd/ *n* **1** [U] the activity of buying and selling large quantities of goods, especially between one country and another **2 banking/retail/tourist etc trade** business done by banks, shops, hotels etc **3** [C] the kind of job that someone does, especially one in which they work with their hands: **by trade** *Jerry's a plumber by trade.* (=that is his job)

trade² *v* [I,T] **1** to buy or sell large quantities of goods, especially between one country and another: *Our company has a lot of experience of trading in Asia.* **2** *AmE* to give something to someone in exchange for something else: *I love your pink sneakers. Do you want to trade?*
trade sth ↔ in *phr v* [T] to give something old that you own as part of the payment when you buy something new: *I traded my Chevy in for a Honda.*

trade·mark /ˈtreɪdmɑːkǁ-mɑːrk/ *n* [C] a special name, mark, or word on a product that shows it is made by a particular company

trade-off /ˈ. ./ *n* [C] an acceptable balance between two very different things: *the trade-off between the benefits and the risks involved*

trad·er /ˈtreɪdəl-ər/ *n* [C] someone whose job is buying and selling things, especially STOCKs and SHARES

trades·man /ˈtreɪdzmən/ *n* [C] *BrE, plural* **tradesmen** /-mən/ someone who brings goods to people's houses, or has a shop

trade u·nion /ˌ. ˈ../ *n* [C] *BrE* an organization of workers who do the same kind of job; UNION —**trade unionist** *n* [C] —**trade unionism** *n* [U]

tra·di·tion /trəˈdɪʃən/ *n* [C,U] a custom, belief, or way of doing something that has existed for a long time: *an old Jewish tradition*

tra·di·tion·al /trəˈdɪʃənəl/ *adj* **1** relating to the TRADITIONs of a country, group of people etc: *traditional Irish music* **2** having ideas or using methods that have existed for a long time, and not using modern ideas or methods: *My father has very traditional ideas about marriage.* —**traditionally** *adv*

tra·di·tion·al·ist /trəˈdɪʃənəl਼st/ *n* [C] someone who likes traditional ideas and methods and does not like modern ones

traf·fic /ˈtræfɪk/ *n* [U] **1** the vehicles travelling on a road: **heavy traffic** (=a lot of traffic): *There was heavy traffic on the roads this morning.* **2** the movement of planes, ships etc from one place to another **3** the movement of illegal drugs, weapons etc from one place to another

traffic cir·cle /ˈ. ˌ../ *n* [C] *AmE* a circular area where several roads meet, which you have to drive around until you reach the road you want; ROUNDABOUT *BrE*

traffic jam /ˈ. ˌ./ *n* [C] a long line of vehicles on the road that cannot move, or that move very slowly: *We were stuck in a traffic jam for two hours.* ➝ see colour picture on page 278

traf·fick·ing /ˈtræfɪkɪŋ/ *n* **drug/arms trafficking** the activity of buying and selling illegal drugs or weapons —**traffic** *v* [T] —**trafficker** *n* [C]

traffic light /ˈ. ./ *also* **traffic sig·nal** /ˈ. ˌ../ *n* [C] a set of coloured lights where two roads meet, which tell cars when to stop ➝ see colour picture on page 669

traffic war·den /ˈ. ˌ../ *n* [C] *BrE* someone who checks that cars are not parked illegally

trag·e·dy /ˈtrædʒ਼di/ *n* [C,U] **1** an extremely sad event, in which something very bad happens: *They never recovered from the tragedy of their son's death.* **2** a serious play or book that ends sadly, usually with the death of the main character, or this kind of play or book in general: *Shakespeare's tragedies*

tra·gic /ˈtrædʒɪk/ *adj* **1** something that is tragic is very sad because something very bad happens, for example someone dies: *The Princess was killed in a tragic car accident in Paris.* **2** relating to a serious play or book that ends sadly usually with the death of the main character: *the tragic hero in 'A Tale of Two Cities'* —**tragically** /-kli/ *adv*

trail¹ /treɪl/ *n* [C] **1** a rough path across the countryside, through a forest etc: *a hiking trail in the mountains* **2** a series of marks or signs that are left behind by someone or something as they move along: *a trail of blood | The storm left a trail of destruction across southern England.* **3** **be on sb/sth's trail** to be following someone and trying to catch them, or to be trying to find out information about something: *The FBI were hot on his trail.* (=very close to catching him)

trail² *v* **1** [T] to follow someone, for example a criminal, in order to try to catch them **2** [I,T] to be losing a game, competition, election etc: *The Cowboys are trailing 21-14 in the third quarter.* **3** [I,T] if you trail something or it trails behind you, it gets pulled behind you as you move along: *She wore a long dress, which trailed along the ground behind her.* **4** [I] to hang down or be lying across something: *a trailing plant | You shouldn't leave wires trailing across the floor.* **5** [I] to walk slowly behind someone: *The two mothers walked along with their kids trailing behind them.*

trail away/off *phr v* [I] if someone's voice trails away or trails off, it becomes quieter until it cannot be heard

trail·er /ˈtreɪlə-ər/ *n* [C] **1** a vehicle that can be pulled behind a car, used for living in on holiday, or for carrying things **2** the part of a big TRUCK that is used for carrying things, which can be separated from the part that has the engine **3** a short part of a film or television programme, which is shown to advertise it

trailer park /ˈ.. ./ *n* [C] *AmE* an area where trailers are parked and used as people's homes

train¹ /treɪn/ *n* [C] **1** a line of carriages pulled by an ENGINE, which travels along a railway and carries people or goods: *What time's the next train to Birmingham?* → see colour picture on page 669 **2** **train of thought** a series of connected ideas that you have when you are thinking about or discussing something **3** a long line of moving people or animals: *a camel train*

train² *v* **1** [I] to study how to do a job: *She trained as a nurse for four years.* **2** [T] to teach someone how to do something, especially the practical skills they need to do a job: *Staff are trained in how to deal with difficult customers.* **3** [I,T] to prepare for a sports event by exercising and practising, or to help someone to prepare by improving their skills: *He's training for the Olympics.* —**trained** *adj*: *highly trained riot police*

train·ee /ˌtreɪˈniː/ *n* [C] someone who is being trained for a job: *a trainee teacher*

train·er /ˈtreɪnə-ər/ *n* [C] **1** someone whose job is to train people how to do something **2** *BrE* a kind of shoe worn for sports such as running → see colour picture on page 113 and picture at SHOE

train·ing /ˈtreɪnɪŋ/ *n* [U] **1** when someone is taught the skills they need to do something: *a training course* **2** physical exercises that you do to stay healthy or prepare for a sports event: *She injured her knee in training.*

trait /treɪ, treɪt/ *n* [C] a quality that is part of someone's character; CHARACTERISTIC: *His jealousy is one of his worst traits.*

trai·tor /ˈtreɪtə-ər/ *n* [C] someone who is not loyal to their country, friends etc

tra·jec·to·ry /trəˈdʒektəri/ *n* [C] *technical* the direction or line along which something moves when it goes through the air

tram /træm/ *n* [C] *especially BrE* an electric vehicle for carrying passengers, which moves along the street on metal tracks; STREETCAR *AmE*

tramp¹ /træmp/ *n* [C] someone who has no home or job and moves from place to place

tramp² *v* [I,T] to walk slowly with heavy steps: *They tramped through the snow.*

tram·ple /ˈtræmpəl/ *v* [I,T] **1** to step heavily on something and crush it with your feet: *One woman was trampled to death by the crowd.* **2** to behave in a way that shows you do not care about someone's rights, feelings etc

tram·po·line /ˈtræmpəliːn‖ˌtræmpəˈliːn/ *n* [C] a piece of sports equipment that you jump up and down on, made of a sheet of material tightly stretched across a large frame

trance /trɑːns‖træns/ *n* [C] if you are in a trance, you seem to be asleep, but you are still able to hear and understand what is said to you

tran·quil /ˈtræŋkwɪl/ *adj* pleasantly calm, quiet, and peaceful: *a tranquil little town* —**tranquility, tranquillity** /træŋˈkwɪləti/ *n* [U]

tran·qui·liz·er (also **-iser** *BrE*) /ˈtræŋkwɪlaɪzə ‖-ər/ *n* [C] a drug used to make someone calm or unconscious —**tranquilize** *v* [T]

trans- /træns, trænz/ *prefix* used at the beginning of some words to mean 'across' or 'between': *transatlantic | transcontinental*

trans·ac·tion /trænˈzækʃən/ *n* [C] *formal* an occasion when a company buys or sells something, or provides a service for someone: *financial transactions*

trans·at·lan·tic /ˌtrænzətˈlæntɪk◂/ *adj* crossing the Atlantic Ocean, or involving people on both sides of the Atlantic: *a transatlantic flight*

tran·scend /trænˈsend/ *v* [T] *formal* to go beyond the limits of something: *Mandela's ability to transcend political boundaries* —**transcendence** *n* [U]

trans·con·ti·nen·tal /ˌtrænzkɒntɪˈnentl, ˌtræns-‖-kɑːn-/ *adj* crossing a CONTINENT: *the first transcontinental railroad*

tran·scribe /trænˈskraɪb/ *v* [T] to write down the words that someone has said, or write down the notes of a piece of music —**transcription** /-ˈskrɪpʃən/ *n* [C,U]

tran·script /ˈtrænskrɪpt/ *n* [C] an exact written copy of what has been said: *a transcript of the witness's testimony*

trans·fer¹ /trænsˈfɜː‖-ˈfɜːr/ *v* **-rred, -rring** **1** [T] to move someone or something from one place, part of an organization to another: *She's been transferred to head office. | I'd like to transfer some money into my savings account.* **2** [I] to change to a different job, course, team etc —**transferable** *adj*

T

trans·fer[2] /ˈtrænsfɜː‖-ɜːr/ n [C,U] when someone or something is transferred: *the transfer of power*

trans·fixed /trænsˈfɪkst/ adj so shocked, interested, frightened etc by something that you cannot move: *She stood transfixed, unable to look away.*

trans·form /trænsˈfɔːm‖-ˈfɔːrm/ v [T] to change something or someone completely, especially in a way that improves them: *discoveries that have transformed the world we live in* —**transformation** /ˌtrænsfəˈmeɪʃən‖-fər-/ n [C,U] *The city has undergone a total transformation.* (=it has changed completely)

trans·form·er /trænsˈfɔːmə‖-ˈfɔːrmər/ n [C] a piece of electrical equipment that changes electricity from one VOLTAGE to another

trans·fu·sion /trænsˈfjuːʒən/ n [C,U] if you have a blood transfusion, doctors put blood into your body, for example after an accident

trans·gress /trænzˈgres‖træns-/ v [I,T] formal to do something that is against the rules —**transgression** /-ˈgreʃən/ n [C,U]

tran·si·ent[1] /ˈtrænziənt‖ˈtrænʃənt/ adj formal **1** continuing or existing only for a short time: *a transient phenomenon* **2** staying in a place only for a short time and then moving to a different place

transient[2] n [C] someone who has no home or job and moves from place to place; TRAMP

tran·sis·tor /trænˈzɪstə‖-ˈsɪstəl-ər/ n [C] a small piece of electronic equipment used in radios, televisions etc

tran·sit /ˈtrænsɪt, -zɪt/ n [U] when people, goods etc are moved from one place to another: **in transit** *Goods often get lost in transit.*

tran·si·tion /trænˈzɪʃən, -ˈsɪ-/ n [C,U] formal the process of changing from one system, method, situation etc to another: *the transition from dictatorship to democracy* —**transitional** adj: *a two year transitional period*

tran·si·tive /ˈtrænsɪtɪv -zɪ-/ n [C] a transitive verb has an object. In the sentence 'She makes her own clothes', 'makes' is a transitive verb ➡ compare INTRANSITIVE

tran·si·to·ry /ˈtrænzɪtəri‖-tɔːri/ adj formal existing only for a short time

trans·late /trænsˈleɪt, trænz-/ v [I,T] **1** to change speech or writing from one language to another: *The book has been translated into several European languages.* **2** formal to produce a particular result, or make something produce a particular result: **+ into** *This should translate into lower production costs.*

trans·la·tion /trænsˈleɪʃən, trænz-/ n [C,U] something that has been translated into a different language, or the process of translating something into a different language

trans·la·tor /trænsˈleɪtə, trænz-‖-ər/ n [C] someone whose job is to change writing or speech into a different language

trans·lu·cent /trænzˈluːsənt‖træns-/ adj clear enough for some light to pass through, especially in a way that seems attractive —**translucence** n [U]

trans·mis·sion /trænzˈmɪʃən‖træns-/ n **1** [C,U] the process of broadcasting radio or television programmes, or a television or radio programme **2** [C,U] the system of GEARS in a car: *automatic transmission* **3** [U] formal the process of sending or passing something from

one place, person etc to another: *the transmission of diseases*

trans·mit /trænzˈmɪt‖træns-/ v [T] **-tted, -tting 1** to send out electronic SIGNALs for radio or television or messages, especially so that radio or television programmes can be shown **2** informal to send or pass something from one place, person etc to another: *The virus is transmitted through sexual contact.*

trans·mit·ter /trænzˈmɪtə‖træns·ˈmɪtər/ n [C] a piece of equipment that sends out radio or television SIGNALs

trans·par·en·cy /trænˈspærənsi, -ˈspeər-‖-ˈspær-, -ˈsper-/ n [C,U] a type of photograph that you look at by shining light through it onto a large screen; SLIDE

trans·par·ent /trænˈspærənt, -ˈspeər-‖-ˈspær-, -ˈsper-/ adj **1** clear and able to be seen through: *transparent plastic* **2** easy to notice; OBVIOUS: *a transparent lie* —**transparently** adv

tran·spire /trænˈspaɪə‖-ˈspaɪr/ v [T] formal to happen

trans·plant[1] /ˈtrænsplɑːnt‖-plænt/ n [C,U] a medical operation in which part of someone's body is put into the body of another person: *a heart transplant*

trans·plant[2] /trænsˈplɑːnt‖-ˈplænt/ v [T] **1** to remove part of someone's body and put it into the body of another person **2** to move something to another place

trans·port[1] /ˈtrænspɔːt‖-ɔːrt/ n [U] BrE **1** a kind of vehicle, or a system of buses, trains etc, that you use for going from one place to another: *Do you have your own transport?* (=do you have your own car?)| *Buses are the main form of public transport.* ➡ see colour picture on page 669 **2** when people, goods etc are moved from one place to another; TRANSPORTATION: *the transport of live animals*

USAGE NOTE: transport

Transport is the usual British English word. The usual American English word is **transportation**. For most methods of transport, use **by** to talk about how someone gets to a place: *I came by car/plane/train* etc. However, when someone walks, use **on foot**: *I came on foot.* When you are talking about something that happens while you are using a form of public transport, use **on**: *I met Jim on the train/bus/plane* etc.

---

trans·port[2] /trænˈspɔːt‖-ɔːrt/ v [T] to move goods, people etc from one place to another in a vehicle

trans·por·ta·tion /ˌtrænspɔːˈteɪʃən‖-spər-/ n [U] especially AmE **1** a kind of vehicle, or a system of buses, trains etc, that you use for going from one place to another; TRANSPORT BrE: *the city's transportation system* ➡ see colour picture on page 669 **2** when people, goods etc are moved from one place to another; also TRANSPORT BrE: *transportation costs*

trans·ves·tite /trænzˈvestaɪt‖træns-/ n [C] someone who enjoys dressing like a person of the opposite sex

trap[1] /træp/ n **1** [C] a piece of equipment for catching animals: *a mouse trap* **2** [singular] an unpleasant situation from which it is difficult to escape: *the deadly trap of drug and alcohol addic-*

tion **3** [singular] a trick that is intended to catch someone or make them do something that they do not want to do

trap² *v* [T] **-pped, -pping 1 be trapped** if you are trapped in a dangerous place or an unpleasant situation, you cannot escape from it: *The children were trapped in a burning building* | *She felt trapped in a loveless marriage.* **2** to catch an animal in a trap **3** to trick someone in order to catch them, or to make them do or say something that they do not want to: *a series of questions intended to trap him* **4** to keep a liquid, substance etc in one place and prevent it from moving to another place: *They put a bucket underneath, to trap the water.*

trap·door / ˈtræpdɔːllˈdɔːr/ *n* [C] a small door that covers an opening in a floor or roof

tra·peze / trəˈpiːz/ *n* [C] a short bar hanging from two ropes high above the ground, used by ACROBATS

trap·pings / ˈtræpɪŋz/ *n* [plural] the things that someone gets because of their position, especially because they are rich, famous, successful etc: *the trappings of stardom*

trash¹ / træʃ/ *n* [U] **1** *AmE* waste material such as old food or paper that is thrown away; RUBBISH *BrE* **2** *informal* something that is of very poor quality: *There's so much trash on TV these days.*

trash² *v* [T] *informal* to destroy something completely

trash·can / ˈtræʃkæn/ *n* [C] *AmE* a container for keeping waste material in

trash·y / ˈtræʃi/ *adj* of extremely bad quality: *trashy novels*

trau·ma / ˈtrɔːmə, ˈtraʊməllˈtraʊmə, ˈtrɔː-/ *n* [C] [U] the shock caused by an unpleasant and upsetting experience, or an experience that causes this feeling: *Children often have trouble coping with the trauma of divorce.*

trau·mat·ic / trɔːˈmætɪklltrɔː-/ *adj* very shocking and upsetting: *a traumatic experience*

trau·ma·tized (also **-ised** *BrE*) / ˈtrɔːmətaɪzd, ˈtraʊ-llˈtraʊ-, ˈtrɔː-/ so badly shocked by something that you cannot forget it or have a normal life

trav·el¹ / ˈtrævəl/ *v* **-lled, -lling** *BrE*, **-led, -ling** *AmE* **1** [I,T] to make a journey from one place to another: *Jack spent the summer travelling around Europe.* | *I usually travel to work by car.* | *They travelled over 400 miles on the first day.* **2** [I] to move from one place or person to another: *News travels fast in a small town like this.*

travel² *n* [U] the activity of travelling: *Heavy rain is making road travel difficult.*

USAGE NOTE: travel, travels, journey, voyage, and trip

Travel is the general activity of moving from place to place: *He returned after years of foreign travel.* Use **travels** when someone goes to different places over a period of time: *Did you go to LA during your travels around the US?* Use

---

journey especially to talk about the time spent or distance travelled going from one place to another: *a 60-hour journey by train.* A **voyage** is a journey by sea: *the voyage from England to Australia.* A **trip** is used especially about a short journey, or when you spend only a short time in another place: *a week-long trip to Barcelona* | *I hope you enjoy your trip.*

travel a·gen·cy / ˈ.. ˌ../ also **travel a·gent's** / ˈ.. ˌ../ *n* [C] a shop or company that makes arrangements for people to travel or have holidays

travel a·gent / ˈ.. ˌ../ *n* [C] someone who works in a travel agency

trav·el·ler *BrE*, **traveler** *AmE* / ˈtrævələllˈ-ər/ *n* [C] someone who is on a journey or who travels a lot

traveller's cheque *BrE*, **traveler's check** *AmE* / ˈ... ˌ./ *n* [C] a special cheque that can be exchanged for the money of a foreign country

tra·verse / ˈtrævɜːsllträ'vɜːrs/ *v* [T] *formal* to go across or over something

trav·es·ty / ˈtrævɪ̣sti/ *n* [singular] if something is a travesty of another thing, it is very badly done or unfair, and is a very bad example of that kind of thing: *The trial was a travesty of justice.*

trawl / trɔːllträːl/ *v*
trawl through sth *phr v* [T] to search through something in order to find something —**trawl** *n* [C]

trawl·er / ˈtrɔːləllˈträːlər/ *n* [C] a large fishing boat that pulls a big net along the sea bottom

tray / treɪ/ *n* [C] a flat piece of plastic, wood etc with raised edges, used for carrying plates, food etc

tray

treach·e·rous / ˈtretʃə-rəs/ *adj* **1** extremely dangerous because you cannot see the dangers: *Black ice on the roads is making driving treacherous.* **2** someone who is treacherous cannot be trusted because they secretly intend to harm you: *his treacherous colleagues*

treach·e·ry / ˈtretʃəri/ *n* [U] actions that are not loyal to someone who trusts you

trea·cle / ˈtriːkəl/ *n* [U] *BrE* a dark sweet sticky liquid made from sugar plants; MOLASSES *AmE*

tread¹ / tred/ *v* **trod** / trɒdlltrɑːd/, **trodden** / ˈtrɒdnllˈtrɑːdn/, **treading 1** [I,T] *especially BrE* to put your foot on something: **+ on/in** *Sorry. Did I tread on your foot?* | **tread sth down/into** (=push something down with your foot) **2 tread carefully** to be very careful about what you say or do **3 tread water** to stay floating upright by moving your legs

tread² *n* **1** [C,U] the pattern of deep lines on the surface of a tyre **2** [singular] the sound that someone makes when they walk: *a heavy tread*

tread·mill / ˈtred,mɪl/ *n* [singular] a job or situation that seems very boring because you always have to do the same things

---

GRAMMAR NOTE: the present perfect (2)

You use the **present perfect 1** to talk about something that happened in the past, but which still affects the situation now: *I've lost my passport.* **2** to talk about something that happened in the past, and continues to happen now: *I have lived in London for many years.* (=I still live there now).

trea·son /ˈtriːzən/ *n* [U] the crime of doing something that could cause great harm to your country or government, especially by helping its enemies

trea·sure[1] /ˈtreʒəll-ər/ *n* **1** [U] a collection of gold, silver, jewels etc, especially one that has been hidden: *a story about buried treasure* **2** [C] a very valuable and important object, for example an old painting: *the treasures of the Louvre*

treasure[2] *v* [T] if you treasure something, you think it is very special or important: *one of his most treasured memories*

trea·sur·er /ˈtreʒərəll-ər/ *n* [C] someone who takes care of the money for an organization

trea·su·ry /ˈtreʒəri/ *n* **the Treasury** the government department that controls a country's money

treat[1] /triːt/ *v* [T] **1** to behave towards someone in a particular way: *Why do you always treat me like a child?| Tracy felt she had been badly treated.* **2** to consider something in a particular way: **treat sth as sth** *He treats everything I say as some kind of joke.* **3** to give someone medical treatment for an illness or injury: *Eleven people were treated for minor injuries.* **4** to buy or arrange something special for someone: *We're treating Jill to dinner for her birthday.| treat yourself (to sth)* *I thought I'd treat myself to a new haircut.* **5** to put a special substance on something or use a chemical process, in order to protect it or clean it: *The metal has been treated against rust.*

treat[2] *n* **1** [C] something special that you give someone or do for them because you know they will enjoy it: *Stephen took his son to Disneyland as a birthday treat.* **2** [singular] an unexpected event that gives you a lot of pleasure: *Getting your letter was a real treat.* **3** **my treat** *spoken* used to tell someone that you will pay for something, especially a meal

trea·tise /ˈtriːtᵻs, -tᵻz/ *n* [C] a serious book or article about a subject: *a treatise on political philosophy*

treat·ment /ˈtriːtmənt/ *n* **1** [C,U] something that doctors, nurses etc do to try to cure an illness or injury, for example giving someone drugs or an operation: *a new treatment for cancer* **2** [U] a way of behaving towards someone or of dealing with them: *complaints about the treatment of political prisoners*

treat·y /ˈtriːti/ *n* [C] a formal written agreement between two or more countries: *a peace treaty*

tre·ble /ˈtrebəl/ *v* [I,T] to become three times as much, or to make something do this; TRIPLE

tree /triː/ *n* [C] a tall plant that has a TRUNK, branches, and leaves: *an apple tree*

trek /trek/ *v* [I] **-kked, -kking** to make a long and difficult journey on foot: *We're planning to go trekking in Nepal.* —**trek** *n* [C] *a three hour trek back to camp*

trel·lis /ˈtrelᵻs/ *n* [C] a wooden frame for supporting climbing plants

trem·ble /ˈtrembəl/ *v* [I] to shake because you are afraid, worried, or excited: *His voice trembled as he spoke.*

tre·men·dous /trɪˈmendəs/ *adj* **1** very great or very large: *I have tremendous respect for her.* **2** very good or impressive: *The police did a tremendous job.*

trem·or /ˈtremɒll-ər/ *n* [C] **1** a small EARTHQUAKE **2** a slight shaking movement that you cannot control

trench /trentʃ/ *n* [C] a long narrow hole that is dug along the ground

tren·chant /ˈtrentʃənt/ *adj* saying your opinions in a very firm and clear way: *a trenchant critic of big business*

trench·coat /ˈtrentʃkəʊtll-koʊt/ *n* [C] a type of RAINCOAT that is similar to a military coat, with pockets and a belt

trend /trend/ *n* [C] **1** the way a situation is generally developing or changing: *There's a trend toward more part-time employment.| the latest fashion trends* **2** **set the trend** to start doing something that other people copy

trend·y /ˈtrendi/ *adj* modern and fashionable: *a trendy bar*

trep·i·da·tion /ˌtrepᵻˈdeɪʃən/ *n* [U] *formal* anxiety or fear about something that is going to happen

tres·pass /ˈtrespəsll-pəs, -pæs/ *v* [I] to go onto someone's land without permission —**trespasser** *n* [C]

tres·tle /ˈtresəl/ *n* [C] a wooden support under a table or bridge

tri- /traɪ/ *prefix* used at the beginning of some words to mean 'three' or 'three times': *trilingual* (=speaking three languages)

tri·al /ˈtraɪəl/ *n* **1** [C,U] a legal process in which a court of law decides whether or not someone is guilty of a crime: *a murder trail| be on trial/stand trial* (=when a court tries to decide if someone is guilty of a crime): *The two men are on trial for armed robbery.* **2** [C,U] when something or someone is tested to find out how good, effective etc they are: *clinical trials of a new drug* **3** **trial and error** when you test different methods or answers in order to find the most suitable one: *Students learn through a process of trial and error.* ➞ see also TRIALS

trial run /ˌ. ˈ./ *n* [C] when something new is tested to see if it works

tri·als /ˈtraɪəlz/ *n* [plural] **1** a sports competition that tests a player's ability **2** also **trials and tribulations** difficult experiences and troubles: *the trials and tribulations of being a teenager*

tri·an·gle /ˈtraɪæŋɡəl/ *n* [C] **1** a flat shape with three straight sides and three angles ➞ see picture at SHAPES **2** a small musical instrument shaped like a triangle, that you play by hitting it with a small metal bar —**triangular** /traɪˈæŋɡjᵿləll-ər/ *adj*

tribe /traɪb/ *n* [C] a group of people who have the same race, language, and customs, and who live together in the same area, for example in the countryside or forests of America or Africa —**tribal** *adj*: *tribal art*

trib·u·la·tion /ˌtrɪbjᵿˈleɪʃən/ *n* [C,U] ➞ see TRIALS

tri·bu·nal /traɪˈbjuːnl/ *n* [C] a type of court that

has official authority to deal with a particular situation or problem: *a war crimes tribunal*

trib·u·ta·ry /ˈtrɪbjɪ̯t̬ərɪ‖-teri/ *n* [C] a river or stream that flows into a larger river

trib·ute /ˈtrɪbjuːt/ *n* **1** [C,U] something that you say or do to show how much you admire and respect someone: *The concert was held as a tribute to Bob Dylan.* | **pay tribute to sb** (=praise and thank someone publicly) **2** **be a tribute to** to be a sign of how good, effective etc someone or something is

trick¹ /trɪk/ *n* [C] **1** something you do in order to deceive someone: *The phone call was just a trick to get him out of the office.* | **play a trick on sb** (=do something to deceive or surprise someone, especially as a joke): *a naughty boy who was always playing tricks on his parents* **2** **do the trick** *spoken* if something does the trick, it helps you to succeed in doing what you want: *A little salt should do the trick.* **3** a clever and effective way of doing something: *There's a trick to getting the audience's attention.* **4** when someone does something that seems like magic in order to entertain people: *Do you know any good card tricks?*

trick² *v* [T] to deceive someone in order to get something from them, or to make them do something: *They tricked her out of all her money.*

trick·e·ry /ˈtrɪkəri/ *n* [U] the use of tricks to deceive or cheat people

trick·le¹ /ˈtrɪkəl/ *v* [I] **1** if liquid trickles somewhere, it flows slowly in drops or in a thin stream: *Sweat trickled down his face.* **2** if people or things trickle somewhere, they move there slowly in small groups or amounts

trickle² *n* [C] when a small amount of something moves somewhere: *a tiny trickle of blood*

trick or treat /ˌ. . ˈ./ **go trick or treating** if children go trick or treating, they go to people's houses on HALLOWEEN (October 31st) and say 'trick or treat' in order to get sweets and other small presents

trick·ster /ˈtrɪkstəll-ər/ *n* [C] someone who deceives or cheats people

trick·y /ˈtrɪki/ *adj* difficult to do or deal with: *It was a tricky decision.*

tri·cy·cle /ˈtraɪsɪkəl/ *n* [C] a bicycle with three wheels

tried¹ /traɪd/ *v* the past tense and past participle of TRY

tried² *adj* **tried and tested/trusted** used successfully many times: *tried and tested methods*

tri·fle /ˈtraɪfəl/ *n* **1** **a trifle** slightly: *He looked a trifle unhappy.* **2** something that has little value or importance: *a mere trifle*

trig·ger¹ /ˈtrɪgəll-ər/ *n* [C] the part of a gun that you pull with your finger to fire it: *He pointed the gun and pulled the trigger.*

trig·ger² also **trigger off** *v* [T] to make something start to happen: *Heavy rain may trigger mudslides.*

trigger hap·py /ˈ.. ˌ../ *adj* too willing to shoot at people

tril·lion /ˈtrɪljən/ *number* 1,000,000,000,000

tril·o·gy /ˈtrɪlədʒi/ *n* [C] a series of three books, plays, films etc, which have the same subject or characters

trim¹ /trɪm/ *v* **-mmed, -mming** **1** [I,T] to cut a small amount off something to make it look neat-

er: *My hair needs trimming.* **2** [T] to reduce the size or amount of something: *plans to trim the city's budget* **3** **be trimmed with sth** to be decorated around the edges with something: *The sleeves were trimmed with velvet.*

trim² *adj* **1** thin and healthy looking: *a trim figure* **2** neat and attractive

trim³ *n* **1** [singular] when something is cut to make it look neater: *Your beard needs a trim.* **2** [singular, U] the decoration on something such as a piece of clothing **3** **in trim** in good physical condition

tri·mes·ter /trɪˈmestəll traɪˈmestər/ *n* [C] *especially AmE* one of three periods that a year at school or college is divided into

trim·ming /ˈtrɪmɪŋ/ *n* **1** [C,U] decoration on the edge of a piece of clothing **2** **with all the trimmings** with all the other types of food that are traditionally served with the main dish of a meal: *a turkey dinner with all the trimmings*

trin·i·ty /ˈtrɪnɪti/ *n* **the Trinity** the three forms of God in the Christian religion, which are the Father, the Son, and the Holy Spirit

trin·ket /ˈtrɪŋkɪ̯t/ *n* [C] a piece of jewellery or a small pretty object that is not worth much money

tri·o /ˈtriːəʊ‖ˈtriːoʊ/ *n* [C] a group of three people, especially a group of three musicians who play together

trip/slip

trip   slip

trip¹ /trɪp/ *n* [C] a journey in which you go to a place for a short time and come back: *We're taking a trip to Florida.* | *a business trip*

trip² *v* **-pped, -pping** **1** [I] to hit something with your foot while you are walking or running so that you fall or almost fall: **+ on/over** *I tripped over a chair.* **2** [T] also **trip up** to make someone fall by putting your foot in front of them

trip (sb) up *phr v* [I,T] to make a mistake, or make someone make a mistake: *The others were all waiting for her to trip up.*

tripe /traɪp/ *n* [U] the stomach of a cow or pig, used as food

trip·le¹ /ˈtrɪpəl/ *adj* consisting of three things or parts of the same kind, or doing something three times: *a triple gold medal winner*

triple² *v* [I,T] to become three times as big or as many, or to make something do this: *The population may triple in 20 years.*

trip·let /ˈtrɪplɪ̯t/ *n* [C] one of three children born at the same time to the same mother

tri·pod /ˈtraɪpɒdll-paːd/ *n* [C] a piece of equipment with three legs, used for holding a camera in position

trite / traɪt / *adj* something that is trite seems boring or not sincere, because it has been said before too often or is too simple

tri·umph[1] / ˈtraɪəmf / *n* **1** [C] an important success or victory, especially after a difficult struggle: *San Francisco's triumph over Cincinnati in the Super Bowl* **2** [U] the feeling you have when you have won or succeeded in doing something: *He raised his arms in triumph.* —**triumphal** / traɪˈʌmfəl / *adj*: *a triumphal march*

triumph[2] *v* [I] to win a victory or be successful, especially after a difficult struggle

tri·um·phant / traɪˈʌmfənt / *adj* feeling very pleased because you have succeeded or won: *a triumphant army*

triv·i·a / ˈtrɪviə / *n* [plural] unimportant details or facts

triv·i·al / ˈtrɪviəl / *adj* unimportant and not serious: *a trivial matter*

triv·i·al·ize (also **-ise** *BrE*) / ˈtrɪviəlaɪz / *v* [T] to make something important and serious seem much less important than it really is

trod / trɒd‖trɑːd / *v* the past tense of TREAD

trod·den / ˈtrɒdn‖ˈtrɑːdn / *v* the past participle of TREAD

trol·ley / ˈtrɒli‖ˈtrɑːli / *n* [C] *BrE* a metal basket or frame with wheels, that you use for carrying things, for example in a SUPERMARKET; CART *AmE*

trom·bone / trɒmˈbəʊn‖trɑːmˈboʊn / *n* [C] a metal musical instrument, that you play by blowing into it and moving a long sliding tube

troop[1] / truːp / *n* [C] **1** **troops** soldiers, especially organized groups of soldiers: *Troops were sent in to stop the riots.* **2** a large group of people or animals

troop[2] *v* [I] *informal* to walk somewhere in a group: *+ into/out of etc The children all trooped into the dining-room and sat down.*

troop·er / ˈtruːpə‖-ər / *n* [C] **1** a soldier **2** a member of a state police force in the US

tro·phy / ˈtrəʊfi‖ˈtroʊ- / *n* [C] a prize for winning a competition or race, especially a silver cup

trop·i·cal / ˈtrɒpɪkəl‖ˈtrɑː- / *adj* in or from the hottest parts of the world: *tropical countries | tropical fish*

trop·ics / ˈtrɒpɪks‖ˈtrɑː- / *n* **the tropics** the hottest parts of the world, which are near the EQUATOR

trot / trɒt‖trɑːt / *v* [I] **-tted, -tting** to walk or run with quick short steps: *A group of horses trotted past. | Jimmy trotted along behind his parents.* —**trot** *n* [singular]
trot sth ↔ out *phr v* [T] *informal* to give opinions, reasons etc, especially ones that have been used too often before and do not seem sincere: *They always trot out the same old excuses.*

trou·ba·dour / ˈtruːbədɔː, -dʊə‖-dɔːr, -dʊr / *n* [C] a singer and poet who travelled around in past times

troub·le[1] / ˈtrʌbəl / *n* **1** [C,U] problems that make a situation difficult for you, especially ones that make you feel worried, unhappy, or annoyed: *She's been having some kind of trouble with her boyfriend. | It's good to be able to talk to someone about your troubles. | **the trouble is** spoken (=used to talk about something that causes*

problems or prevents you from doing what you want): *I'd love to go with you. The trouble is, I don't have enough money.* **2** [U] a problem that stops a machine, car, system etc from working: *engine trouble | What seems to be the trouble?* **3** **in trouble a)** in a difficult situation and having a lot of problems: *The company was in serious trouble financially.* **b)** if you are in trouble, you are likely to be punished because you have done something that you should not do: *Joe's in trouble with the police again. | **get into trouble** He was always getting into trouble at school.* **4** [U] when someone has to use a lot of time and effort to do something: **take a lot of trouble/go to a lot of trouble** *It was a fantastic meal. They'd obviously gone to a lot of trouble over it. | **take the trouble to do sth** He'd taken the trouble to learn all our names.* **5** [C,U] a situation in which people fight or argue with each other: **cause/create trouble** *English fans have a reputation for causing trouble.* **6** [U] a problem with your health that affects part of your body: *back trouble* **7** **the trouble with sb/sth** *spoken* used to say what you think is wrong with someone or something: *The trouble with Tom is he never listens to what other people say.* **8** **sb is asking for trouble** *informal* used to say that what someone is doing is likely to cause problems for them and they should not do it

trouble[2] *v* [T] **1** if something is troubling you, it makes you feel worried or causes problems for you: *I tried to find out what's troubling her.* **2** *formal* to ask someone to do something for you when it is difficult for them – used especially when asking someone politely to help you: *I'm sorry to trouble you, but could you open the door for me?*

troub·led / ˈtrʌbəld / *adj* having a lot of problems and worries: *a deeply troubled man*

troub·le·mak·er / ˈtrʌbəlˌmeɪkə‖-ər / *n* [C] someone who deliberately causes problems

troub·le·shoot·er / ˈtrʌbəlˌʃuːtə‖-ər / *n* [C] someone whose job is to deal with serious problems in a company or organization —**troubleshooting** *n* [U]

troub·le·some / ˈtrʌbəlsəm / *adj* causing a lot of trouble or problems: *a troublesome employee*

trouble·spot / ˈ... . / *n* [C] a place where there is likely to be fighting or trouble: *Tourists have been warned to stay away from troublespots.*

trough / trɒf‖trɒːf / *n* [C] a long container for animals to drink from

trounce / traʊns / *v* [T] to defeat someone completely: *Colorado trounced Minnesota 58-7.*

troupe / truːp / *n* [C] a group of singers, actors, dancers etc who work together

trou·sers[ ] / ˈtraʊzəz‖-ərz / *n* [plural] a piece of clothing that covers the lower part of your body, with a separate part covering each leg; PANTS *AmE* → see colour picture on page 113

trouser suit / ˈ... . / *n* [C] *BrE* a suit for women, which consists of a JACKET and trousers: PANT-SUIT *AmE*

trout / traʊt / *n* [C,U] a common river fish

trow·el / ˈtraʊəl / *n* [C] **1** a small garden tool used for digging small holes for plants, removing WEEDS etc **2** a small tool used for spreading CEMENT on bricks

tru·ant / ˈtruːənt / *n* [C] a student who stays away from school without permission: **play**

truant *BrE* (=stay away from school without permission) —**truancy** *n* [U]

truce /truːs/ *n* [C] an agreement between two enemies to stop fighting or arguing for a short time: *The two sides have declared a truce.*

truck /trʌk/ *n* [C] a large road vehicle used for carrying heavy loads ➡ see colour picture on page 669 —**truck** *v* [T]

truck·er /ˈtrʌkəll-ər/ *n* [C] *especially AmE* someone whose job is to drive a truck

truck·ing /ˈtrʌkɪŋ/ *n* [U] *especially AmE* the business of taking goods from one place to another by truck

truck·load /ˈtrʌkləʊdll-loʊd/ *n* [C] the amount of something a truck can carry

truc·u·lent /ˈtrʌkjʊlənt/ *adj formal* bad-tempered and often arguing with people

trudge /trʌdʒ/ *v* [I] to walk with slow heavy steps, especially because you are tired: *He trudged up the stairs.*

true /truː/ *adj* **1** based on facts and not imagined or invented: *Believe me, it's a true story.* | **is true (that)** *Is it true that you're moving to Denver?* ➡ opposite FALSE **2** real and having all the qualities that this kind of thing or person should have: *a true friend* | *true love* **3** **come true** if dreams or wishes come true, they really happen: *Their dream of owning a house in the mountains had finally come true.* **4** *spoken* used to admit that something is a fact: *True, he has a college degree, but he doesn't have enough job experience.* **5** **true to sb/sth** faithful and loyal to someone, or doing what you have promised to do: *He was true to his word.* (=he did what he promised) **6** **hold true** *formal* to be true in a particular situation

true-life /ˌ. ˈ. ◂/ *adj* based on what really happened, and not something that someone has imagined: *a true-life adventure*

truf·fle /ˈtrʌfəl/ *n* [C] **1** a piece of soft sweet food made with chocolate **2** a FUNGUS you can eat that grows under the ground

tru·is·m /ˈtruːɪzəm/ *n* [C] a statement that is clearly true, so that there is no need to say it ➡ compare CLICHÉ

tru·ly /ˈtruːli/ *adv* **1** used to emphasize your description of something: *a truly amazing story* | **well and truly** (=completely): *By now we were well and truly lost.* **2** used to emphasize that something is really true about someone or something in every way: *a truly democratic country* | *She truly loved him.* ➡ see also **yours (truly)** (YOURS)

trump /trʌmp/ *n* [C] a kind of playing card that has a higher value than the other cards in some card games, for example BRIDGE

trump card /ˈ. ./ *n* [C] a special advantage that you have kept secret until now, that will help you get what you want

trumped-up /ˌ. ˈ. ◂/ *adj* **trumped-up charges/ evidence etc** when people try to make someone seem guilty of a crime using false information

trum·pet /ˈtrʌmpɪt/ *n* [C] a musical instrument that you blow into, that consists of a metal tube that is wide at one end, often used in JAZZ —**trumpeter** *n* [C]

trun·cat·ed /trʌŋˈkeɪtɪdllˈtrʌŋkeɪtɪd/ *adj* made shorter: *a truncated version of the report*

trun·cheon /ˈtrʌnʃən/ *n* [C] *BrE* a short stick that police officers carry as a weapon

trun·dle /ˈtrʌndl/ *v* [I,T] to move slowly on wheels, or to make something do this by pushing it or pulling it

trunk /trʌŋk/ *n* [C] **1** the thick main part of a tree which the branches grow from ➡ see picture at TREE **2** *AmE* the space at the back of a car where you can put large bags, tools etc; BOOT *BrE* ➡ see picture at CAR **3** the very long nose of an ELEPHANT **4** a large box used for storing or carrying clothes, books etc **5** *technical* the main part of your body, not including your head, arms, or legs

trunk road /ˈ. ./ *n* [C] *BrE* a main road used for travelling long distances

trunks /trʌŋks/ *n* [plural] a piece of clothing that men wear when swimming

trust¹ /trʌst/ *v* [T] **1** to believe that someone is honest and will not lie to you or harm you: *David is one of my oldest friends, I trust him completely.* **2** to believe that you can depend on someone to do something, or that something is right: *I'm not sure if I trust his judgement.* | **trust sb with sth** (=allow someone to look after or deal with something, because you think you can trust them): *Do you think we can trust her with the children?* **3** **I trust (that)** *spoken formal* used to say that you hope something is true: *I trust that you had a successful trip.*

trust in sb/sth *phr v* [T] *formal* to believe that you can depend on someone or something

trust² *n* **1** [U] the belief that you can trust someone: *the lack of trust between local people and the police* | **a position of trust** (=a job or position in which people have to trust that you are honest or will not harm anyone) ➡ opposite DISTRUST¹ **2** [C] an organization that has control over how a large amount of money is used: *an investment trust* **3** [U] an arrangement in which someone legally controls your money or property, usually until you are old enough to have it: *$100,000 is being held in trust for his daughter.*

trust·ee /ˌtrʌsˈtiː◂/ *n* [C] a person or company that legally controls someone else's property or money

trust·ing /ˈtrʌstɪŋ/ *adj* always believing that other people are good and honest and will not try to cheat or harm you: *Sarah's trusting nature led her to believe all of Tony's lies.*

trust·wor·thy /ˈtrʌstˌwɜːðill-ɜːr-/ *adj* able to be trusted or depended on

trust·y /ˈtrʌsti/ *adj humorous* a trusty weapon, horse etc is one you can depend on

truth /truːθ/ *n* **1** **the truth** the true facts about something: *I'm sure she's telling the truth.* **2** [U] the quality of being true: *Do you think there's*

GRAMMAR NOTE: the present perfect progressive
You use the **present perfect progressive** to say how long you have been doing something: *I **have been learning** English for two years.* Remember that some verbs are not usually used in the progressive: *I **have known** Richard for 4 years.* not *I have been knowing Richard for 4 years.*

any truth in these accusations? (=do you think they may be true) **3** [C] *formal* an important fact or idea that is accepted as being true: *scientific truths* **4 to tell (you) the truth** *spoken* used to say what you really think about something: *To tell you the truth, I've never really liked him.*

truth·ful /ˈtruːθfəl/ *adj* honest and not telling lies, or giving the true facts about something: *a truthful little boy | a truthful account* —**truthfully** *adv*

try[1] /traɪ/ *v* **tried, tried, trying** **1** [I,T] to attempt to do something: *Tim tried to get another job, but he had no luck. | I tried not to laugh.* | **try the door/window** (=try to open it) **2** [T] to do, use, or taste something in order to find out if it works or is good: *You must try some of this cake! | She tried all kinds of diets, but none of them seemed to work.* **3** [T] if you are tried for a crime, a court examines all the facts and decides if you are guilty: *Three men were tried for murder.*

> **try** sth ↔ **on** *phr v* [T] to put on a piece of clothing to find out if it fits or if you like it: *Would you like to try these jeans on?*

> **try** sth ↔ **out** *phr v* [T] to use something to find out if it works or is good: *I can't wait to try out my new camera.*

USAGE NOTE: try

You can make **try** stronger by using **hard**: *I tried hard to persuade him to stay.* Compare **try to do** something and **try doing** something. If you **try to do** something, you make an effort to do something but do not succeed: *I tried to finish the work, but didn't have enough time.* If you **try doing** something, you do it in order to see what will happen: *If the machine doesn't work, try giving it a kick.*

---

try[2] *n* **1** [C] an attempt to do something: *He succeeded on his first try.* **2 give sth a try** to do or use something in order to find out if it works or is good: *I've never skated before, but I'll give it a try.* **3** [C] when a team gets points in RUGBY by putting the ball down behind the other team's goal line

try·ing /ˈtraɪ-ɪŋ/ *adj* difficult and making you feel annoyed or impatient: *It's been a trying time for us all.*

try·out /ˈtraɪaʊt/ *n* [C] *especially AmE* when someone is tested to find out whether they are good enough to be on a sports team

tsar, tzar, czar /zɑː, tsɑː‖zɑːr, tsɑːr/ *n* [C] a ruler of Russia before 1917

T-shirt /ˈtiː ʃɜːt‖-ʃɜːrt/ *n* [C] a cotton shirt with short SLEEVES and no collar → see colour picture on page 113

tsp. *n* [C] the written abbreviation of TEASPOON

tub /tʌb/ *n* [C] **1** a container with a lid in which food is sold: *a tub of ice cream* **2** a large round container for washing or storing things in → see picture at CONTAINER **3** *AmE* a container that you fill with water and sit and wash yourself in; a bath

tu·ba /ˈtjuːbə‖ˈtuːbə/ *n* [C] a large metal musical instrument with a wide opening that points upwards, which you play by blowing

tub·by /ˈtʌbi/ *adj informal* rather fat

tube /tjuːb‖tuːb/ *n* **1** [C] a pipe made of glass, rubber, metal etc, especially one that liquids or gases go through: *She was lying in a hospital bed with tubes coming out of her mouth.* **2** [C] **a)** a container for a soft substance, that you SQUEEZE to make the substance come out → see picture at CONTAINERS: *a tube of toothpaste* **b)** a container shaped like a short pipe, usually made of CARD-BOARD or plastic → see picture at CONTAINER **3 the Tube** the railway system under the ground in London

tu·ber·cu·lo·sis /tjuːˌbɜːkjʊˈləʊsɪs‖tuːˌbɜːrkjʊˈloʊ-/ *n* [U] a serious infectious disease that affects the lungs; TB

tub·ing /ˈtjuːbɪŋ‖ˈtuː-/ *n* [U] tubes, usually connected together in a system: *copper tubing*

tu·bu·lar /ˈtjuːbjʊlə‖ˈtuːbjʊlər/ *adj* made of tubes or shaped like a tube

tuck /tʌk/ *v* [T] **1** to push the end of a shirt, sheet etc under something so that it looks neat: *You've forgotten to tuck your shirt into your trousers!* **2** to put something in a small space, especially so that it is safe or comfortable: *She tucked the money into her pocket. | The duck had its head tucked under its wing.*

> **tuck** sth ↔ **away** *phr v* [T] **1** to store something in a safe place: *He tucked the letter away in a drawer.* **2 be tucked away** to be in a place that is far away or difficult to find: *a little village tucked away in the mountains*

> **tuck in/into** *phr v* **1** [T] [**tuck** sb **in**] to make someone comfortable in bed by pressing the sheets under them **2** [I,T **tuck into** sth] *BrE informal* to start eating something

> **tuck** sb **up** *phr v* [T] **be tucked up (in bed)** to be sitting or lying in a comfortable warm bed

Tu·dor /ˈtjuːdə‖ˈtuːdər/ *adj* connected with the period of British history between 1485 and 1603

Tues·day /ˈtjuːzdi‖ˈtuːz-/ written abbreviation **Tues** *n* [C,U] the day of the week between Monday and Wednesday → see Usage Note at DAY

tuft /tʌft/ *n* [C] a short thick group of hairs, feathers, grass etc: *a tuft of hair* —**tufted** *adj*

tug[1] /tʌɡ/ *v* [I,T] **-gged, -gging** to pull something suddenly and hard: *Alice tugged at my hand.*

tug[2] *n* [C] **1** also **tug boat** a boat used for pulling ships **2** a sudden strong pull

tug-of-war /ˌ.. . ˈ./ *n* [singular] a competition in which two teams pull on the opposite ends of a rope

tu·i·tion /tjuːˈɪʃən‖tuː-/ *n* [U] **1** when someone teaches a subject to one student or a small group of students: *private tuition* **2** *AmE* the money you pay for being taught: *Tuition went up to $3000 last semester.*

tu·lip /ˈtjuːlɪp‖ˈtuː-/ *n* [C] a garden flower that grows from a BULB in spring, and is grown especially in Holland

tum·ble /ˈtʌmbəl/ *v* [I] **1** to suddenly fall or move somewhere: *She tumbled out of bed.* **2** if prices tumble, they suddenly become lower: *Share prices tumbled on the New York Stock Exchange.* —**tumble** *n* [C]

tumble dry·er /ˌ.. ˈ../ *n* [C] *BrE* a machine for drying clothes

tum·bler /ˈtʌmblə‖-ər/ *n* [C] a glass for drinking out of, which has a flat bottom and no handle

tum·my /ˈtʌmi/ n [C] informal stomach

tu·mour BrE, **tumor** AmE /ˈtjuːməll-ər/ n [C] a group of diseased cells in the body that grow too quickly: a brain tumor

tu·mult /ˈtjuːmʌltllˈtuː-/ n [singular,U] formal a situation in which there is a lot of noise, confusion, or excitement: the tumult of the civil war

tu·mul·tu·ous /tjuːˈmʌltʃuəslltu-/ adj very noisy because people are very excited: They received a tumultuous welcome from the crowd.

tu·na /ˈtjuːnəllˈtuːnə/ n [C,U] a large sea fish, or the meat from this fish, usually sold in cans

tun·dra /ˈtʌndrə/ n [U] large flat areas of land in the northern part of the world, where it is very cold and there are no trees

tune[1] /ˈtjuːnlltuːn/ n **1** [C] a series of musical notes that are nice to listen to: Jill was humming a little tune to herself. **2 in tune** playing or singing the correct musical notes **3 out of tune** playing or singing notes that are too high or low: My guitar's completely out of tune. **4 change your tune** to suddenly have a different opinion about something

tune[2] v [T] **1** to make changes to a musical instrument so that it plays the correct musical notes: The piano needs tuning. **2** to make a television or radio receive broadcasts from a particular television or radio company: **stay tuned** (=continue watching or listening to the same programme or the same television or radio company): Stay tuned for more great music on KHPI, the city's best rock station. **3** also **tune up** to make small changes to a car engine so that it works better

tune in phr v [I] to watch or listen to a television or radio programme: + to Over 3 million viewers tune in to our show daily.

tune up phr v **1** [I,T **tune sth ↔ up**] if a group of musicians tune up, they make their instruments play the same notes so that they are ready to play **2** [T **tune sth ↔ up**] to make small changes to a car engine so that it works better

tung·sten /ˈtʌŋstən/ n [U] a greyish white metal, used for making lights

tu·nic /ˈtjuːnɪkllˈtuː-/ n [C] a long loose piece of clothing with SLEEVES, often worn with a belt

tun·nel[1] /ˈtʌnl/ n [C] a long hole that has been dug under the ground or through a mountain, for example for cars or trains to go through

tunnel[2] v [I,T] to dig a tunnel

tur·ban /ˈtɜːbənllˈtɜːr-/ n [C] a kind of hat that consists of a long piece of cloth that is twisted around the top of your head → see colour picture on page 113

tur·bine /ˈtɜːbaɪnllˈtɜːrbᵊn, -baɪn/ n [C] an engine or motor in which the pressure of steam, gas, liquid etc moves a special wheel around → see also WIND TURBINE

tur·bu·lent /ˈtɜːbjʊləntllˈtɜːr-/ adj **1** a turbulent period, situation etc, is one in which there are a lot of sudden changes, and often wars or violence: a turbulent period in Russian history **2** turbulent air or water moves suddenly and violently —**turbulence** n [U] There was a lot of turbulence during the flight.

tu·reen /tjʊˈriːnlltəˈriːn/ n [C] a large dish with a lid, used especially for serving soup

turf[1] /ˈtɜːfllˈtɜːrf/ n [U] **1** thick short grass and the soil under it **2** informal someone's turf is the area that they control or that they know well: They didn't want another gang invading their turf.

turf[2] v

turf sb ↔ out phr v [T] BrE informal to force someone to leave a place or organization

tur·gid /ˈtɜːdʒɪdllˈtɜːr-/ adj boring and difficult to understand: turgid prose

tur·key /ˈtɜːkillˈtɜːrki/ n [C,U] a bird similar to a chicken but larger, or the meat from this bird → see also COLD TURKEY

tur·moil /ˈtɜːmɔɪllˈtɜːr-/ n [singular, U] a situation in which there is a lot of trouble or confusion: **in turmoil** In 1968 the country was in turmoil.

turn off/turn on

turn on

turn off

turn[1] /ˈtɜːnllˈtɜːrn/ v **1** [I] to move your body so that you are looking in a different direction: Alison turned towards us.|He turned to look behind him. **2** [T] to move something round so that it is in a different position: She turned the key in the lock. **3** [I,T] to go in a new direction when you are walking, driving etc: The car turned a corner.|Turn right at the next stop light. **4** [I,T] if something such as a wheel turns or you turn it, it moves around: The wheels turned slowly. **5 turn green/violent/hotter etc** to become green, violent, hotter etc: Helen turned bright red.|The weather will turn colder. **6 turn 30/midnight etc** to reach a particular age or time: She's just turned 40. **7** [T] to move a page in a book or magazine so that you can see the next one **8 turn your back on** to refuse to help or be connected with someone or something: She turned her back on all her old friends. **9 turn your nose up at sth** to refuse to accept something because you do not think it is good enough for you **10 turn over a new leaf** to decide that you will change your behaviour to make it better: I'm going to turn over a new leaf and start exercising. **11 turn back the clock** to try to do things the way they were done in the past **12 turn a blind eye** to pretend not to notice that someone is doing something illegal **13 turn the tables (on sb)** to change the situation completely so that you are in a much better position than your opponent: The team managed to turn the tables in the second half of the game.

14 turn sb/sth loose to allow a person or animal to be free **15 sb's thoughts turn to sth** if your thoughts turn to something, you start to think about it

turn against sb/sth *phr v* [T] to make someone stop liking or agreeing with someone or something: *His experiences in Vietnam turned him against the war.*

turn sth ↔ **around** *phr v* [T] to make a company, business etc become successful again

turn sb ↔ **away** *phr v* [T] to refuse to allow someone to go into a place, or refuse to help them

turn back *phr v* [I,T **turn** sb ↔ **back**] to go in the opposite direction, or tell someone to do this: *They had to turn back because of the snow.* | *Journalists are being turned back at the border.*

turn down *phr v* [T] **1** [**turn** sth ↔ **down**] to make a machine such as a television, OVEN etc produce less sound, heat etc: *Can you turn down your radio? I'm trying to work.* **2** [**turn** sb/sth ↔ **down**] to refuse an offer, REQUEST, or invitation: *She got an offer of a job at Microsoft, but she turned it down.*

turn in *phr v* [T] **1** [**turn** sth ↔ **in**] to give something to the police or some other person in authority, especially something you have found or a weapon: *Luckily someone had turned my purse in.* **2** [**turn** sb **in**] to tell the police where a criminal is **3** [I] *informal* to go to bed: *I think I'll turn in.* **4** [T **turn** sth **in**] *especially AmE* to give work that you have done to a teacher: *Has everyone turned in last night's homework?*

turn into *phr v* [T] **1** [**turn into** sb/sth] to change and become a completely different type of person, substance, situation etc: *The argument turned into a fight* **2** [**turn** sb/sth **into** sb/sth] to make someone or something change and become completely different: *They want to turn the country into some kind of police state.*

turn off *phr v* **1** [T **turn** sth ↔ **off**] to make a machine, light etc stop working or stop the supply of water, electricity etc: *Turn off the television – it's dinner time.* **2** [I,T **turn off** sth] to leave one road and drive onto another

turn on *phr v* [T] **1** [**turn** sth ↔ **on**] to make a machine, light etc start working, or make water, electricity etc start flowing: *Could you turn on the TV?* **2** [**turn on** sb] to suddenly attack or criticize someone: *The dog turned on him and bit him.*

turn out *phr v* **1** [I] to happen in a particular way, or have a particular result: *Joanna wished things had turned out differently.* | it **turned out that** (=used to say that something surprising happened): *It turned out that he was married to someone else!* **2** [T **turn** sth ↔ **out**] to make a light stop working by pressing a SWITCH: *Don't forget to turn out the lights when you leave.* **3** [I] if people turn out to see something, they go to see it: *Only about 30 people turned out for the show.* ➡ see also TURNOUT **4** [T **turn** sth ↔ **out**] to produce or make something: *Why do our high schools turn out students who can't read?*

turn over *phr v* [T] **1** [T **turn** sth ↔ **over to** sb] to bring a criminal to the police or another official organization: *Benson was turned over to the FBI yesterday.* **2** [I,T] *BrE* to change to a

different television CHANNEL **3** [I **turn** sth **over**] if you turn something over in your mind, you think about it carefully **4** [T **turn** sth ↔ **over to** sb] to give something to someone else, especially the right to own or be responsible for something: *The industry is being turned over to private ownership.*

turn to *phr v* [T] **1** [**turn to** sb/sth] to ask someone to help or advise you: *He still turns to us for advice.* **2** [**turn to** sth] to go to a page in a book, magazine etc: *Turn to page 45 in your history book.* **3 turn to drugs/crime/drink etc** to start doing something that you should not do, for example taking illegal drugs, taking part in criminal activities, or drinking too much alcohol: *There's very little work, and a lot of young people turn to crime.*

turn up *phr v* **1** [T **turn** sth ↔ **up**] to make a television, radio, HEATER etc produce more sound, heat etc: *Turn up the radio – I love this song.* **2** [I] if something turns up after you have been looking for it, you suddenly find it: *We looked for the ring for weeks, and then it turned up in my pocket.* **3** [I] to arrive: *Danny turned up late as usual.*

turn[2] *n* **1** [C usually singular] if it is your turn to do something, it is the time when you can or should do it, after or before the other people who are also doing it: *You'll just have to wait your turn.* **2 take turns** also **take it in turns** *BrE* if a group of people take turns doing something, first one person does it, then another: *We took it in turns to do the driving.* **3 in turn** one after another: *He spoke to each of the students in turn.* **4** [C] a change in the direction you are moving in: **left/right turn** *The car made a left turn at the lights.* **5** a bend or corner in a road, river etc: *Take the next turn.* **6** [C] if you give something a turn, you move it round: *Give the wheel another turn.* **7 the turn of the century** the beginning of a century **8 take a turn for the better/worse** to suddenly become better or worse: *Her health took a turn for the worse.* **9 turn of events** an unexpected change in a situation: *By some unfortunate turn of events, the documents were lost.* **10 do sb a good turn** to help someone

turn·a·round /ˈtɜːnəraʊnd‖ˈtɜːrn-/ *n* [C] a complete change from a bad situation to a good one: *a turnaround in the team's fortunes*

turning point /ˈ.. ./ *n* [C] the time when an important change starts to happen: *The film marks a turning point in Kubrick's career.*

tur·nip /ˈtɜːnɪp‖ˈtɜːr-/ *n* [C,U] a vegetable that consists of a large round pale yellow or white root

turn-off /ˈ. ./ *n* [C] a place where you can leave a big road to go onto another one

turn·out /ˈtɜːnaʊt‖ˈtɜːrn-/ *n* [singular] the number of people who go to an event such as a party, meeting, or election

turn·o·ver /ˈtɜːn,əʊvə‖ˈtɜːrn,oʊvər/ *n* **1** [singular] the amount of money a business earns in a period of time: *an annual turnover of $35 million* **2** [U] the rate at which people leave an organization and are replaced by others: *The company has a high turnover of staff.* **3** [C] a small fruit PIE: *an apple turnover*

turn·pike /ˈtɜːnpaɪk‖ˈtɜːrn-/ *n* [C] a main road that you have to pay to use

turn·round /ˈtɜːnraʊndǁˈtɜːrn-/ n [C] BrE a TURNAROUND

turn sig·nal /ˈ. ˌ../ n [C] AmE one of the lights on a car which show which way it is going to turn; INDICATOR BrE

turn·stile /ˈtɜːnstaɪlǁˈtɜːrn-/ n [C] a gate that only lets one person through at a time

turn·ta·ble /ˈtɜːnˌteɪbəlǁˈtɜːrn-/ n [C] a piece of equipment used for playing RECORDS

tur·pen·tine /ˈtɜːpəntaɪnǁˈtɜːr-/ also **turps** / tɜːpsǁtɜːrps/ BrE — n [U] a strong-smelling liquid used for removing paint

tur·quoise /ˈtɜːkwɔɪz, -kwɑːzǁˈtɜːrkwɔɪz/ n [U] a bright blue-green colour —**turquoise** adj

tur·ret /ˈtʌrɪ̆t/ n [C] a small tower on a large building, especially a CASTLE

tur·tle /ˈtɜːtlǁˈtɜːrtl/ n [C] an animal that lives mainly in water, which has four legs and a hard shell

tur·tle·neck /ˈtɜːtlnekǁˈtɜːr-/ n [C] AmE a type of SWEATER with a band that covers most of your neck; POLO NECK BrE: wearing a tweed skirt and a turtleneck sweater

tusk /tʌsk/ n [C] one of the two very long teeth that stick out of an animal's mouth, especially an ELEPHANT

tus·sle /ˈtʌsəl/ n [C] a struggle or fight —**tussle** v [I]

tut /tʌt/ also **tut-tut** /ˌ. ˈ./ interjection often humorous a sound you make to show that you disapprove of something

tu·tor /ˈtjuːtəǁˈtuːtər/ n [C] **1** someone who teaches one person or a small group of people **2** someone who teaches small groups of students at a British university and advises them about their studies —**tutor** v [T] —**tutorial** / tjuːˈtɔːriəlǁtuː-/ adj

tu·to·ri·al /tjuːˈtɔːriəlǁtuː-/ n [C] a class, especially at a British university, in which a small group of students discuss a subject with their tutor

tux·e·do /tʌkˈsiːdəʊǁ-doʊ/ also **tux** /tʌks/ informal n [C] a black or white JACKET that is worn by men at formal occasions

TV /ˌtiː ˈviː◂/ n [C,U] television: What's on TV? | Sue just bought a new TV. → see colour picture on page 474

TV din·ner /ˌ. ˈ../ n [C] a frozen prepared meal that you buy from a shop and heat up at home

twad·dle /ˈtwɒdlǁˈtwɑːdl/ n [U] informal nonsense

twang /twæŋ/ n [C] **1** a short sound like the one made by quickly pulling a tight string **2** a way of speaking in which the sound seems to come from your nose as well as your mouth —**twang** v [I,T]

twas /twɒzǁtwɑːz/ literary a word meaning 'it was', used in past times

tweak /twiːk/ v [T] **1** to quickly pull or twist something: Grandpa tweaked my nose and laughed. **2** to make small changes to something in order to improve it —**tweak** n [C]

tweed /twiːd/ n [U] a rough wool cloth used especially for making JACKETS

twee·zers /ˈtwiːzəzǁ-ərz/ n [plural] a small tool consisting of two thin pieces of metal joined at one end, used for pulling out hairs or picking up small things

twelfth /twelfθ/ number **1** 12th **2** 1/12

twelve /twelv/ number **1** 12 **2** twelve o'clock: I'm going to lunch at twelve.

twen·ty[1] /ˈtwenti/ number **1** 20 **2** the twenties **a)** the years between 1920 and 1929 **b)** the numbers between 20 and 29 —**twentieth** number

twenty[2] n [C] a piece of paper money worth $20

twice /twaɪs/ adv two times: I've seen that movie twice already.

twid·dle /ˈtwɪdl/ v [I,T] to move your fingers around, or to turn something around many times, usually because you are bored

twig /twɪg/ n [C] a very thin branch that grows on a larger branch of a tree

twi·light /ˈtwaɪlaɪt/ n [U] the time between day and night when the sky starts to become dark, or the pale light at this time

twin[1] /twɪn/ n [C] one of two children who are born at the same time to the same mother: her twin brother

twin[2] adj used to talk about two things of the same kind that are considered together as a pair: twin doors → see picture at BED

twine[1] /twaɪn/ n [U] thick strong string

twine[2] v [I,T] to twist something around something else, or to become twisted around something: The plant had twined itself around the fence.

twinge /twɪndʒ/ n [C] **1** a sudden slight pain **2** a sudden feeling of sadness, sympathy, GUILT etc

twin·kle /ˈtwɪŋkəl/ v [I] **1** if a star or light twinkles, it shines and changes quickly from being bright to dark **2** if someone's eyes twinkle, they look happy —**twinkle** n [C]

twin room /ˌ. ˈ./ n [C] a room for two people, which has two separate beds

twirl /twɜːlǁtwɜːrl/ v [I,T] to turn quickly, or to make something do this: a twirling ballet dancer —**twirl** n [C]

twist[1] /twɪst/ v **1** [T] to turn something around quickly and firmly using your hand: Can you twist the top off this bottle for me? **2** [T] to bend something several times and change its shape: Her hair was twisted in a bun. **3** [I,T] to turn a part of your body around, or change your position by turning: He twisted around in order to get a better look. | twist your knee/ankle etc (=hurt your knee etc by suddenly turning it) **4** [T] if someone twists the meaning of what you say, they change it unfairly and pretend that you intended to say something different: They twisted the story around and said we tried to cheat them. **5** [I] if a road, river etc twists, it has a lot of curves in it **6** twist sb's arm in-

---

formal to force or persuade someone to do something that they do not want to do

twist² *n* [C] **1** a shape made by twisting something, such as paper, rope, or hair: *pasta twists* **2** a sudden unexpected change in a story or situation: *Her disappearance added a new twist to the story.* **3** a part of something that has become twisted: *twists in the wire* **4** a bend in a road, river etc

twist·ed /ˈtwɪstɪd/ *adj* **1** something that is twisted is bent many times from its normal shape: *a twisted piece of metal* **2** strange and slightly cruel: *a twisted joke*

twist·er /ˈtwɪstəl-ər/ *n* [C] *AmE informal* a TORNADO

twit /twɪt/ *n* [C] *informal* a stupid or silly person

twitch /twɪtʃ/ *v* [I] if a part of your body twitches, it makes sudden small uncontrolled movements: *Her fingers twitched nervously.* —**twitch** *n* [C]

twit·ter /ˈtwɪtəl-ər/ *v* [I] if a bird twitters, it makes a lot of short high sounds —**twitter** *n* [singular]

two /tuː/ *number* **1** 2 **2** two o'clock: *The game begins at two.* **3** **in two** if something breaks or divides in two, it breaks or divides into two pieces

two-bit /ˈ. ./ *adj AmE informal* not very good or important: *a two-bit actor*

two-di·men·sion·al /ˌ. .ˈ...◂/ *adj* **1** showing something as a flat picture, not as a solid object: *a two-dimensional drawing* **2** a two-dimensional character in a book, film etc does not seem real

two-faced /ˌ. ˈ.◂/ *adj* saying very different things about something to different people, in a way that is not honest or sincere

two-piece /ˌ. ˈ.◂/ *adj* a two-piece suit has a JACKET and trousers that are made of the same material

two·some /ˈtuːsəm/ *n* [C] a group of two people

two-time /ˈ. ./ *v* [T] *informal* if you two-time your girlfriend, boyfriend etc, you secretly have a sexual relationship with someone else

two-tone /ˈ. ./ *adj* having two colours: *two-tone shoes*

two-way /ˌ. ˈ.◂/ *adj* **1** moving or allowing movement in two opposite directions: *two-way traffic* **2** a two-way radio sends and receives messages

ty·coon /taɪˈkuːn/ *n* [C] someone who is very successful in business and has a lot of money: *an oil tycoon*

ty·ing /ˈtaɪ-ɪŋ/ *v* the present participle of TIE

type¹ /taɪp/ *n* **1** [C] a kind of person or thing, or a group of people or things that have similar features or qualities: *You need to use a special type of paper | Accidents of this type are very* common. **2** [C] a kind of person, especially one who has a particular kind of appearance, likes doing a particular kind of thing etc: *He's not really the athletic type.* **3** **not be sb's type** *informal* to not be the kind of person that someone is attracted to: *Alex is OK – but he's not really my type.* **4** [U] printed letters: *italic type*

type² *v* [I,T] to write something using a computer or typewriter

type·cast /ˈtaɪpkɑːstǁ-kæst/ *v* **be typecast** if an actor is typecast, he or she is always given the same kind of characters to play: *He became typecast as the bad guy.*

type·face /ˈtaɪpfeɪs/ *n* [C] a group of letters, numbers etc of the same style and size, used in printing

type·writ·er /ˈtaɪpˌraɪtəl-ər/ *n* [C] a machine that prints letters, numbers etc onto paper, that you operate by pressing buttons with the letters and numbers on

type·writ·ten /ˈtaɪpˌrɪtn/ *adj* written using a typewriter

ty·phoid /ˈtaɪfɔɪd/ **typhoid fe·ver** /ˌ.. ˈ../ *n* [U] a serious infectious disease

ty·phoon /ˌtaɪˈfuːn◂/ *n* [C] a violent tropical storm in which there are very strong winds

ty·phus /ˈtaɪfəs/ *n* [U] a serious infectious disease

typ·i·cal /ˈtɪpɪkəl/ *adj* having the usual features or qualities of a particular thing, person, or group: *a typical working class family | + of This painting is typical of his early work.*

typ·i·cal·ly /ˈtɪpɪkli/ *adv* **1** used before an adjective to say that something is typical of a country or a kind of person or thing: *a typically Japanese dish* **2** used to say that something usually happens in a particular way: *prices typically start at around $600*

typ·i·fy /ˈtɪpɪˌfaɪ/ *v* [T] to be a typical example or feature of something

typ·ing /ˈtaɪpɪŋ/ *n* [U] the activity of writing using a TYPEWRITER, or something that is printed using a TYPEWRITER

typ·ist /ˈtaɪpɪst/ *n* [C] someone who uses a TYPEWRITER, especially as a job

tyr·an·ny /ˈtɪrəni/ *n* [U] when a government, leader etc uses their power in a cruel and unfair way —**tyrannical** /tɪˈrænɪkəl/ *adj*

ty·rant /ˈtaɪərəntǁˈtaɪr-/ *n* [C] someone who uses their power in a cruel and unfair way: *Her father was a tyrant.*

tyre *BrE,* **tire** *AmE* /taɪəǁtaɪr/ *n* [C] a round piece of rubber filled with air that fits around the wheel of a car, bicycle etc: **a flat tyre** (=one that has no air in it) → see picture at CAR

tzar /zɑː, tsɑːǁzɑːr, tsɑːr/ another spelling of TSAR

Uu

U, u /juː/ the letter 'u'

u·biq·ui·tous /juːˈbɪkwɪ̩təs/ *adj formal* seeming to be everywhere: *the ubiquitous microchip*

ud·der /ˈʌdəl-ər/ *n* [C] the part of a cow, goat etc that hangs below its body and produces milk

UFO /ˈjuːfəʊ, ˌjuː ef ˈəʊ‖-foʊ, -ˈoʊ/ *n* [C] an Unidentified Flying Object; a mysterious object in the sky, especially one that could be carrying creatures from another part of the universe

ugh /ʊx, ʌɡ/ *interjection* used to show that you dislike something very much: *Ugh! This tastes foul!*

ug·ly /ˈʌɡli/ *adj* **1** very unattractive or unpleasant to look at: *ugly modern buildings* **2** unpleasant and violent: *There were ugly scenes at the England – Italy game.* —**ugliness** *n* [U]

ul·cer /ˈʌlsəl-ər/ *n* [C] a sore area on or inside your body, that may BLEED: *a stomach ulcer*

ul·te·ri·or /ʌlˈtɪəriəl-ˈtɪriər/ *adj* **ulterior motive/reason** a secret reason for doing something

ul·ti·mate¹ /ˈʌltɪ̩mɪ̩t/ *adj* **1** used to say that something is the best, greatest, or worst of its kind: *A Rolls Royce is the ultimate symbol of wealth.* | *the ultimate disgrace* **2** used to say that something is the final or most important thing: *their ultimate objective*

ultimate² *n* **the ultimate in sth** the best example or highest level of something: *The Orient-Express is the ultimate in luxury.*

ul·ti·mate·ly /ˈʌltɪ̩mɪ̩tli/ *adv* **1** finally, after many other things have happened: *Their efforts ultimately resulted in his release from prison.* **2** used to emphasize the most important or basic part of a situation: *Ultimately it's your decision.*

ul·ti·ma·tum /ˌʌltɪ̩ˈmeɪtəm/ *n* [C] a warning that if someone does not do something, you will do something that will have a bad effect on them: **issue/give an ultimatum** *The government issued an ultimatum to the rebels to surrender.*

ul·tra /ˈʌltrə/ *prefix* used at the beginning of words to mean 'extremely': *an ultramodern design*

ul·tra·son·ic /ˌʌltrəˈsɒnɪk‖-ˈsɑː-/ *adj technical* ultrasonic sounds are too high for humans to hear

ul·tra·vi·o·let /ˌʌltrəˈvaɪəlɪ̩t‖/ *adj* ultraviolet light is beyond the RANGE of colours that humans can see, and can make people's skin become darker ➔ see also INFRARED

um·bil·i·cal cord /ʌmˌbɪlɪkəl ˈkɔːd‖-ˈkɔːrd/ *n* [C] a tube of flesh that joins an unborn baby to its mother

um·brage /ˈʌmbrɪdʒ/ *n* **take umbrage** *old-fashioned* to be offended

um·brel·la /ʌmˈbrelə/ *n* [C] **1** a thing that you hold above your head to protect yourself from the rain **2** umbrella

umbrella

organization/group etc an organization that includes several smaller organizations, groups etc

um·pire /ˈʌmpaɪə‖-paɪr/ *n* [C] the person in a sports game who makes sure that the players obey the rules —**umpire** *v* [I,T]

ump·teen /ˌʌmpˈtiːn‹/ *quantifier informal* very many – used when you want to emphasize what you are saying: *umpteen reasons* —**umpteenth** /ˌʌmpˈtiːnθ‹/ *adj: for the umpteenth time*

UN /ˌjuː ˈen/ *n* [U] the United Nations

un- /ʌn-/ *prefix* **1** used at the beginning of words to mean 'not': *unhappy* | *unexpected* **2** used at the beginning of some verbs, meaning to do the opposite of the meaning of the verb, especially when talking about removing things: *undress* (=take off your clothes) | *unfasten*

un·a·bat·ed /ˌʌnəˈbeɪtɪ̩d‹/ *adj* if something continues unabated, it does not stop or become weaker: *The storm continued unabated.*

un·a·ble /ʌnˈeɪbəl/ *adj* not able to do something: *Many people were unable to leave their homes.*

un·a·bridged /ˌʌnəˈbrɪdʒd‹/ *adj* a book, play etc that is unabridged has not been made shorter or had anything taken out

un·ac·cept·a·ble /ˌʌnəkˈseptəbəl‹/ *adj* something that is unacceptable is wrong or bad and should not be allowed to continue: *Your behaviour is totally unacceptable.* —**unacceptably** *adv*

un·ac·com·pa·nied /ˌʌnəˈkʌmpənid‹/ *adj* if you go somewhere unaccompanied, you go there without anyone with you

un·ac·count·a·ble /ˌʌnəˈkaʊntəbəl‹/ *adj* **1** not having to explain your actions or decisions to anyone else **2** very surprising and difficult to explain: *For some unaccountable reason he's moving to New York.* —**unaccountably** *adv*

un·a·dul·te·rat·ed /ˌʌnəˈdʌltəreɪtɪ̩d‹/ *adj* complete or pure: *sheer unadulterated pleasure*

un·af·fect·ed /ˌʌnəˈfektɪ̩d‹/ *adj* not changed or harmed by something: *Parts of the city remained unaffected by the fire.*

un·aid·ed /ʌnˈeɪdɪ̩d/ *adj* without help: *She managed to climb the stairs unaided.*

u·nan·i·mous /juːˈnænɪ̩məs/ *adj* a unanimous decision, vote etc is one in which everyone agrees —**unanimously** *adv* —**unanimity** /ˌjuːnəˈnɪmɪ̩ti/ *n* [U]

un·an·nounced /ˌʌnəˈnaʊnst‹/ *adj* if you arrive somewhere or do something unannounced, you arrive or do it without telling anyone

un·an·swered /ʌnˈɑːnsəd‖-ˈænsərd/ *adj* an unanswered letter, question etc has not been answered

un·ap·proach·a·ble /ˌʌnəˈprəʊtʃəbəl‹-ˈprəʊ-/ *adj* not friendly and not easy to talk to

un·armed /ʌnˈɑːmd‖-ˈɑːrmd/ *adj* not carrying any weapons

un·a·sham·ed·ly /ˌʌnəˈʃeɪmɪ̩dli/ *adv* in a way that shows you are not embarrassed or worried that other people will disapprove of what you are doing: *Their latest record is unashamedly commercial.* —**unashamed** /-ˈʃeɪmd‹/ *adj*

un·as·sum·ing /ˌʌnəˈsjuːmɪŋ‹, -ˈsuː-‖-ˈsuː-/ *adj* quiet and not trying to make people notice you, or not attracting attention; MODEST: *a quiet un-assuming man*

un·at·tached /ˌʌnəˈtætʃt◂/ *adj* not involved in a romantic relationship

un·at·tend·ed /ˌʌnəˈtendɪd◂/ *adj* left alone without being watched or looked after: *Passengers should not leave their bags unattended.*

un·au·tho·rized (also **-ised** *BrE*) /ʌnˈɔːθəraɪzd‖-ˈɒː-/ *adj* done without official permission: *an unauthorized biography*

un·a·vail·a·ble /ˌʌnəˈveɪləbəl/ *adj* 1 not able to meet someone or do something, especially because you are too busy: *I'm afraid she's unavailable at the moment.* 2 not able to be bought or obtained: *an album previously unavailable on CD*

un·a·void·a·ble /ˌʌnəˈvɔɪdəbəl/ *adj* if something is unavoidable, nothing can be done to prevent it: *an unavoidable delay*

un·a·ware /ˌʌnəˈweə‖-ˈwer/ *adj* not noticing or knowing about something: **+ of** *She seemed completely unaware of what was happening.*

un·a·wares /ˌʌnəˈweəz‖-ˈwerz/ *adv* **catch/take sb unawares** if something catches you unawares, it happens when you are not expecting it: *The enemy had been caught unawares.*

un·bal·anced /ʌnˈbælənst/ *adj* 1 slightly crazy: *He's obviously mentally unbalanced.* 2 unfair or unequal: *unbalanced reporting*

un·bear·a·ble /ʌnˈbeərəbəl‖-ˈber-/ *adj* too painful, unpleasant etc for you to accept or deal with; INTOLERABLE: *The pain was unbearable.* —**unbearably** *adv*

un·beat·a·ble /ʌnˈbiːtəbəl/ *adj* much better than any other people or things of the same kind: *Their prices are unbeatable.*

un·be·liev·a·ble /ˌʌnbɪˈliːvəbəl◂/ *adj* 1 extremely bad, impressive, or surprising: *The noise was unbelievable.* 2 if something is unbelievable, you cannot believe that it is true: *His story sounded completely unbelievable.* —**unbelievably** *adv*

un·born /ʌnˈbɔːn◂‖-ɔːrn◂/ *adj* not yet born: *an unborn child*

un·bro·ken /ʌnˈbrəʊkən‖-ˈbroʊ-/ *adj* continuing without stopping: *unbroken silence*

un·but·ton /ʌnˈbʌtn/ *v* [T] to unfasten the buttons on a piece of clothing

un·called for /ʌnˈkɔːld fɔː‖-ˈkɔːld fɔːr/ *adj* if something that someone says or does is uncalled for, it is unsuitable, unkind, or rude

un·can·ny /ʌnˈkæni/ *adj* very strange and difficult to explain —**uncannily** *adv*

un·car·ing /ʌnˈkeərɪŋ‖-ˈker-/ *adj* not caring about other people's feelings: *his cold and uncaring manner*

un·cer·tain /ʌnˈsɜːtn‖-ɜːr-/ *adj* 1 not sure or having doubts about something: *I was uncertain about what to do next.* 2 not known or not definite: *His future with the company is uncertain.* —**uncertainty** *n* [C,U] —**uncertainly** *adv*

un·changed /ˌʌnˈtʃeɪndʒd◂/ *adj* remaining the same and not changed

un·char·ac·ter·is·tic /ʌnˌkærəktəˈrɪstɪk◂/ *adj* not typical of someone or something —**uncharacteristically** /-kli/ *adv*

un·chart·ed /ʌnˈtʃɑːtɪd‖-ɑːr-/ *adj* **uncharted territory/waters** a situation or activity that you have never experienced before

un·checked /ˌʌnˈtʃekt◂/ *adj* if something bad continues unchecked, it is allowed to continue

un·cle /ˈʌŋkəl/ *n* [C] the brother of your mother or father, or the husband of your AUNT → see picture at FAMILY

un·clean /ˌʌnˈkliːn◂/ *adj* not considered pure or morally good according to the rules of religion

un·clear /ʌnˈklɪə‖-ˈklɪr◂/ *adj* 1 difficult to understand or be sure about: *The law is unclear on this issue.* 2 if you are unclear about something, you are not sure about it or do not understand it: *I'm a little unclear about what they mean.*

un·com·fort·a·ble /ʌnˈkʌmftəbəl, -ˈkʌmfət-‖-ˈkʌmfərt-, -ˈkʌmft-/ *adj* 1 not feeling physically relaxed, or not making someone feel physically relaxed: *an uncomfortable chair | The heat made her feel uncomfortable.* 2 unable to relax because you are embarrassed or worried, or making you feel embarrassed and worried: *There was an uncomfortable silence.* —**uncomfortably** *adv*

un·com·mon /ʌnˈkɒmən‖-ˈkɑː-/ *adj* rare or unusual: *It is not uncommon for patients to have to wait five hours to see a doctor.* —**uncommonly** *adv*

un·com·pro·mis·ing /ʌnˈkɒmprəmaɪzɪŋ‖-ˈkɑːm-/ *adj* very determined and not willing to change your ideas or what you are doing: *his uncompromising attitude towards winning*

un·con·cerned /ˌʌnkənˈsɜːnd‖-ɜːrnd/ *adj* not worried about or interested in something: *Her parents seemed unconcerned by her absence.*

un·con·di·tion·al /ˌʌnkənˈdɪʃənəl◂/ *adj* agreeing to do something, especially officially, without any conditions or limits: *unconditional surrender* —**unconditionally** *adv*

un·con·firmed /ˌʌnkənˈfɜːmd‖-ˈfɜːrmd/ *adj* if a report or story is unconfirmed, there is no definite proof that it is true

un·con·nect·ed /ˌʌnkəˈnektɪd◂/ *adj* not related in any way

un·con·scious[1] /ʌnˈkɒnʃəs‖-ˈkɑːn-/ *adj* 1 unable to see, move, feel etc, especially because you have had an accident, been given drugs etc: *The driver was knocked unconscious.* 2 an unconscious feeling is one that you do not realize that you have: *an unconscious desire* —**unconsciously** *adv* —**unconsciousness** *n* [U]

unconscious[2] *n* [singular] the part of your mind that contains thoughts and feelings that you do not realize that you have, which can affect your behaviour

un·con·sti·tu·tion·al /ˌʌnkɒnstɪˈtjuːʃənəl‖-kɑːnstɪˈtuː-/ *adj* not allowed by the rules that govern a country or organization

un·con·trol·la·ble /ˌʌnkənˈtrəʊləbəl‖-ˈtroʊl-/ *adj* something that is uncontrollable cannot be controlled or stopped: *uncontrollable rage*

un·con·ven·tion·al /ˌʌnkənˈvenʃənəl◂/ *adj* behaving in a way that is very different from the way people usually behave or do things: *unconventional teaching methods*

un·count·a·ble /ʌnˈkaʊntəbəl/ *adj* an uncountable noun has no plural form, for example 'water', 'gold', or 'furniture'

un·couth /ʌnˈkuːθ/ adj behaving or speaking in a rude, rough way

un·cov·er /ʌnˈkʌvəll-ər/ v [T] **1** to discover something: *They uncovered a plot to kill the president.* **2** to remove the cover from something

un·daunt·ed /ʌnˈdɔːntɪdll-ˈdɔːn-/ adj not afraid to continue doing something, in spite of difficulties or danger: *Fisher was undaunted by their opposition.*

un·de·cid·ed /ˌʌndɪˈsaɪdɪd/ adj if you are undecided about something, you have not made a decision about it: *Many people are still undecided about how they will vote.*

un·de·ni·a·ble /ˌʌndɪˈnaɪəbəl/ adj definitely true or certain —**undeniably** adv

un·der[1] /ˈʌndəll-ər/ prep **1** directly below something or covered by it: *The cat was asleep under a chair.| She kept her head under the blankets.| We sailed under the Golden Gate Bridge.* → see colour picture on page 474 **2** below the surface of something: *She dived under the water.* **3** less than or younger than: *You can buy a good computer for under $1,000.| children under 18* **4** controlled or governed by a particular leader, government etc: *a country under Marxist rule* **5** **be under discussion/construction/attack etc** being discussed, built etc: *The tunnel is still under construction.* **6** **under way** if something is under way, it is being done or happening: *Important changes are now under way.* **7** used to say that someone is affected by something: *She performs well under pressure.* **8** if you are under someone, they are in charge of you: *She has a team of researchers under her.* **9** according to a law, agreement, system etc: *Under strict new laws smoking is banned in all public places.* **10** in a part of a list, book, library etc that has a particular title: *You'll find her books under 'Modern Fiction'.* **11** using a particular name: *He writes under the name of Taki.*

under[2] adv **1** under or below the surface of something: *He dived into the water and stayed under for over a minute.* **2** less than the age, number, or amount that is mentioned: *children aged nine and under*

under- prefix **1** used at the beginning of words to mean 'not enough': *underestimate | underpaid.* **2** used at the beginning of words to mean 'having a lower position or rank': *undergrowth | underclass*

under-age /ˌ... ˈ.◂/ adj too young to legally buy alcohol, drive a car etc: *under-age drinking*

un·der·class /ˈʌndəklɑːsll-dərklæs/ n [singular] a group of people in society who are very poor, and cannot change the situation they are in

un·der·clothes /ˈʌndəkləʊðz, -kləʊz-ll-dərkləʊðz, -kləʊz/ n [plural] old-fashioned clothes that you wear next to your body, under your other clothes

un·der·cov·er /ˌʌndəˈkʌvə◂ ll-dərˈkʌvər◂/ adj, adv working secretly in order to find out in-

formation for the government or the police: *an undercover agent*

un·der·cur·rent /ˈʌndə.kʌrəntll-dər.kɜːr-/ n [C] a feeling or attitude that people do not talk about, but which affects their behaviour: *an undercurrent of racism*

un·der·cut /ˌʌndəˈkʌtll-ər-/ v [T] to sell something more cheaply than someone else: *We've undercut our competitors by 15%.*

un·der·dog /ˈʌndədɒgll-ʌndərdɔːg/ n **the underdog** the person, team etc in a game or competition that is not expected to win

un·der·es·ti·mate /ˌʌndərˈestɪ̣meɪt/ v **1** [I,T] to think that something is smaller, less expensive, or less important than it really is: *They underestimated the size of the problem.* **2** [T] to think that someone is less skilful, intelligent etc than they really are: *Never underestimate your opponent.* —**underestimate** /-mɪ̣t/ n [C] → opposite OVERESTIMATE

un·der·foot /ˌʌndəˈfʊtll-ər-/ adv under your feet when you are walking

un·der·go /ˌʌndəˈgəʊll-dərˈgoʊ/ v [T] **underwent** /-ˈwent/, **undergone** /-ˈgɒnll-ˈgɔːn/, **undergoing** if you undergo something such as medical treatment or a change, it happens to you or is done to you: *He had to undergo major heart surgery.*

un·der·grad·u·ate /ˌʌndəˈgrædʒụɪ̣t ll-ər-/ n [C] a student who is doing his or her first degree at university —**undergraduate** adj

un·der·ground[1] /ˈʌndəgraʊndll-ər-/ adj **1** under the earth's surface: *underground streams* —**underground** /ˌʌndəˈgraʊndll-ər-/ adv: *creatures that live underground* **2** an underground political organization is secret and illegal: *an underground resistance movement*

un·der·ground[2] /ˈʌndəgraʊndll-ər-/ n [singular] *BrE* a railway system under a city; SUBWAY *AmE*: *the London Underground*

un·der·growth /ˈʌndəgrəʊθll-dərgroʊθ/ n [U] bushes and plants that grow around bigger trees

un·der·hand /ˌʌndəˈhænd◂ ll-ʌndərhænd/ **un·der·hand·ed** /ˌʌndəˈhændɪ̣d◂ ll-ʌndər-hændɪ̣d/ adj a disapproving word meaning using secret and often dishonest methods: *underhand tactics*

un·der·line /ˌʌndəˈlaɪnll-ər-/ v [T] **1** to draw a line under a word **2** to show or emphasize that something is important: *This latest accident underlines the need for an urgent review of safety procedures.*

un·der·ly·ing /ˌʌndəˈlaɪ-ɪŋ ll-ər-/ adj an underlying reason, cause, problem etc has an important effect but is not easy to notice

un·der·mine /ˌʌndəˈmaɪnll-ər-/ v [T] to gradually make someone less confident or make something less strong or effective: *She totally undermined his self-confidence.*

un·der·neath[1] /ˌʌndəˈniːθll-ər-/ prep, adv directly under something: *I found the keys underneath a cushion.| He got out of the car and looked underneath.*

GRAMMAR NOTE: the past perfect
You form the **past perfect** using **had** and the past participle. Use the past perfect to talk about something that happened in the past before another past action: *Kay stayed behind after everyone else **had gone** home. | She told me what she **had done**.*

underneath[2] *n* **the underneath** the bottom part of something

un·der·paid /ˌʌndəˈpeɪd◂ ‖-ər-/ *adj* earning less money than you should

un·der·pants /ˈʌndəpænts‖-ər-/ *n* [plural] a short piece of underwear worn on the lower part of the body

un·der·pass /ˈʌndəpɑːs‖ˈʌndərpæs/ *n* [C] a road or path that goes under another road or a railway

un·der·priv·i·leged /ˌʌndəˈprɪvˈlɪdʒd◂ ‖-dər-/ *adj* poor and not having the advantages of most other people in society: *underprivileged children*

un·der·rat·ed /ˌʌndəˈreɪtˈd◂/ *adj* if someone or something is underrated, people do not think they are as good, effective etc as they really are: *an underrated player* —**underrate** *v* [T]

un·der·score /ˌʌndəˈskɔː‖-dərˈskɔːr/ *v* [T] *especially AmE* to emphasize that something is important; UNDERLINE

un·der·shirt /ˈʌndəʃɜːt‖ˈʌndərʃɜːrt/ *n* [C] a piece of underwear worn under a shirt

un·der·side /ˈʌndəsaɪd‖-ər-/ *n* **the underside** the bottom side or surface of something: *white spots on the underside of the leaves*

un·der·staffed /ˌʌndəˈstɑːft◂ ‖ˌʌndərˈstæft◂/ *adj* not having enough workers

un·der·stand /ˌʌndəˈstænd‖-ər-/ *v* [I,T] **understood** /-ˈstʊd/, **understood**, **understanding** **1** to know the meaning of what someone says, or the meaning of the words of a language: *She spoke clearly, so that everyone could understand.|Most people there understand English.* **2** to know how someone feels and why they behave in the way they do, and feel sympathy for them: *Believe me, John – I understand how you feel.* **3** to know how something works, or why something happens: *Scientists still don't really understand this phenomenon.* **4** **make yourself understood** to explain or say something in a way that people find easy to understand **5** **I understand (that)** *spoken formal* used to say politely that someone has told you something: *I understand that you want to buy a painting.*

un·der·stand·a·ble /ˌʌndəˈstændəbəl‖ˌʌndər-/ *adj* understandable behaviour etc seems reasonable because of the situation: *Of course she's upset. It's a perfectly understandable reaction.*

un·der·stand·ing[1] /ˌʌndəˈstændɪŋ‖-ər-/ *n* **1** [U] knowledge about something and what makes it work, why it is how it is etc: *advances in our understanding of the brain* **2** [U] the ability to think or learn about something: *a concept beyond the understanding of a four-year-old* **3** [singular] an informal private agreement about something, which is not written down and which you do not tell other people about: *I thought we had an understanding about the price.* **4** [U] sympathy towards someone: *Harry thanked us for our understanding.*

understanding[2] *adj* showing sympathy towards someone who has problems: *an understanding boss*

un·der·stat·ed /ˌʌndəˈsteɪtˈd◂ ‖-ər-/ *adj* done in a simple style in a way that seems attractive: *understated elegance*

un·der·state·ment /ˌʌndəˈsteɪtmənt‖-dər-/ *n* [C,U] when you say that someone or something is much less good, bad, big etc than they really

are: *To say I'm pleased would be an understatement.*

un·der·stood /ˌʌndəˈstʊd‖-ər-/ *v* the past tense and past participle of UNDERSTAND

un·der·stud·y /ˈʌndəˌstʌdi‖-ər-/ *n* [C] an actor who learns the words of a character in a play so that they can perform it if the usual actor is ill

un·der·take /ˌʌndəˈteɪk‖-ər-/ *v* [T] **undertook** /-ˈtʊk/, **undertaken** /-ˈteɪkən/, **undertaking** *formal* **1** to start to do a piece of work, especially one that is long and difficult: *Baker undertook the task of writing the report.* **2** **undertake to do sth** to promise officially to do something

un·der·tak·er /ˈʌndəteɪkə‖-dərteɪkər/ *n* [C] someone whose job is to arrange funerals

un·der·tak·ing /ˌʌndəˈteɪkɪŋ‖ˈʌndərteɪ-/ *n* [C usually singular] **1** an important or difficult piece of work: *Setting up the Summer Olympics was a massive undertaking.* **2** a formal legal promise to do something

un·der·tone /ˈʌndətəʊn‖-dərtoʊn/ *n* [C] **1** a feeling or quality that you notice: *the political undertones of Sartre's work* **2** **in an undertone** in a low quiet voice

un·der·took /ˌʌndəˈtʊk‖-ər-/ *v* the past tense of UNDERTAKE

un·der·val·ued /ˌʌndəˈvæljuːd◂ ‖-ər-/ *adj* if someone or something is undervalued, people think they are less important or valuable than they really are

un·der·wa·ter /ˌʌndə-ˈwɔːtə◂ ‖ˌʌndərˈwɔːtər◂, -ˈwɑː-/ *adj* below the surface of the water: *underwater photography* —**underwater** *adv*

underwater

un·der·way /ˌʌndəˈweɪ‖-ər-/ *adj* if something is underway, it has started happening

un·der·wear /ˈʌndəweə‖-dərwer/ *n* [U] clothes that you wear next to your body under your other clothes

un·der·weight /ˌʌndəˈweɪt◂ ‖-ər-/ *adj* below the normal weight: *an underweight baby* → opposite OVERWEIGHT

un·der·went /ˌʌndəˈwent‖-ər-/ *v* the past tense of UNDERGO

un·der·world /ˈʌndəwɜːld‖ˈʌndərwɜːrld/ *n* [singular] **1** the criminals in a place and the activities they are involved in: *the London underworld of the 1960s* **2** the place where the spirits of the dead live in ancient Greek stories

un·de·sir·a·ble /ˌʌndɪˈzaɪərəbəl◂ ‖-ˈzaɪr-/ *adj* *formal* something that is undesirable is not wanted because it may have a bad effect: *The treatment has no undesirable side-effects.*

un·de·vel·oped /ˌʌndɪˈveləpt◂/ *adj* undeveloped land has not been built on or used for anything

un·did /ʌnˈdɪd/ *v* the past tense of UNDO

un·dis·closed /ˌʌndɪsˈkləʊzd◂ ‖-ˈkloʊzd◂/ *adj* if official information is undisclosed, people have not been told about it: *They bought the company for an undisclosed sum.*

un·dis·guised /ˌʌndɪsˈɡaɪzd◂/ *adj* clearly shown and not hidden: *She looked at him with undisguised admiration.*

un·di·sput·ed /ˌʌndɪˈspjuːtɪd◂/ *adj* **undisputed leader/champion/master etc** someone who everyone agrees is the leader etc

un·dis·turbed /ˌʌndɪˈstɜːbd‖-ɜːr-/ *adj* not interrupted, moved, or changed: *I was able to work undisturbed.*

un·di·vid·ed /ˌʌndɪˈvaɪdɪd◂/ *adj* **undivided attention/loyalty** complete attention, loyalty etc: *I need your undivided attention.*

un·do /ʌnˈduː/ *v* [T] **undid** /-ˈdɪd/, **undone** /-ˈdʌn/, **undoing** **1** to untie or unfasten something that is tied or fastened: *He undid his shoelaces.*|*Have you undone all the screws?* **2** to get rid of all the effects of something: *There's no way of undoing the damage done to his reputation.*

un·do·ing /ʌnˈduːɪŋ/ *n* **be sb's undoing** to make someone be unsuccessful: *His overconfidence proved to be his undoing.*

un·done /ˌʌnˈdʌn◂/ *adj* **1** not tied or fastened: *Your shirt button has come undone.* **2** not finished or completed: *Much of the repair work has been left undone.*

un·doubt·ed·ly /ʌnˈdaʊtɪdli/ *adv* used to emphasize that something is definitely true: *Amis is undoubtedly one of the best writers of his generation.* —**undoubted** *adj*

un·dress /ʌnˈdres/ *v* [I,T] to take off your clothes, or take off someone else's clothes —**undressed** *adj*: *The doctor told me to get undressed.*

un·due /ˌʌnˈdjuː◂‖-ˈduː◂/ *adj formal* more than is reasonable or necessary

un·du·lat·ing /ˈʌndjʊleɪtɪŋ‖-dʒə-/ *adj* having gentle slopes or curves, or gently moving up and down: *undulating countryside* —**undulation** /ˌʌndjʊˈleɪʃən‖-dʒə-/ *n* [C]

un·du·ly /ʌnˈdjuːli‖-ˈduː-/ *adv formal* too much: *Helen didn't seem unduly worried.*

un·dy·ing /ʌnˈdaɪ-ɪŋ/ *adj* continuing for ever: *undying love*

un·earth /ʌnˈɜːθ‖-ˈɜːrθ/ *v* [T] **1** to find something that was buried in the ground: *They unearthed a collection of Roman coins.* **2** to find something after searching for a long time, for example secret information: *The newspapers had succeeded in unearthing details of an affair he'd had 6 years ago.*

un·earth·ly /ʌnˈɜːθli‖-ˈɜːr-/ *adj* very strange and not seeming natural: *an unearthly cry*

un·ease /ʌnˈiːz/ *n* [U] the feeling you have when you feel nervous and worried because you think something bad may happen

un·eas·y /ʌnˈiːzi/ *adj* worried because you think something bad may happen: *We felt uneasy about his decision.* —**uneasiness** *n* [U] —**uneasily** *adv*

un·e·co·nom·ic·al /ˌʌniːkəˈnɒmɪkəl, ˌʌnekə-‖-ˈnɑː-/ *adj* using too much petrol, money, effort etc

un·em·ployed /ˌʌnɪmˈplɔɪd◂/ *adj* **1** without a job: *an unemployed teacher* **2** **the unemployed** people who do not have jobs

un·em·ploy·ment /ˌʌnɪmˈplɔɪmənt/ *n* [U] when someone does not have a job, or the number of people who do not have a job: *areas of high unemployment*

un·e·qual /ʌnˈiːkwəl/ *adj* **1** not the same in size, amount, value etc **2** unfair because people are treated differently and do not have the same

rights: *unequal treatment of men and women* **3** an unequal situation or competition is one in which people do not have the same power, skills, or advantages: *an unequal contest* —**unequally** *adv*

un·e·quiv·o·cal /ˌʌnɪˈkwɪvəkəl◂/ *adj formal* completely clear and definite: *unequivocal proof* —**unequivocally** /-kli/ *adv*

un·er·ring /ʌnˈɜːrɪŋ/ *adj* completely right or always right: *He hit the target with unerring accuracy.*

un·eth·i·cal /ʌnˈeθɪkəl/ *adj* morally wrong —**unethically** /-kli/ *adv*

un·e·ven /ʌnˈiːvən/ *adj* **1** not flat, smooth, or level: *uneven ground* **2** good in some parts and bad in others: *The film is very uneven.* **3** not equal, balanced, or regular: *Her breathing became slow and uneven.* —**unevenly** *adv*

un·ex·pect·ed /ˌʌnɪkˈspektɪd◂/ *adj* something that is unexpected is surprising because you did not expect it to happen: *the unexpected death of his father* —**unexpectedly** *adv*

un·fail·ing /ʌnˈfeɪlɪŋ/ *adj* **unfailing support/ loyalty/kindness etc** when someone always continues to give their support, always behaves in a kind way etc —**unfailingly** *adv*

un·fair /ˌʌnˈfeə◂‖-ˈfer◂/ *adj* **1** not treating people equally: *She gets much more money than I do. It's so unfair!* **2** not reasonable or right: *unfair dismissal* —**unfairly** *adv* —**unfairness** *n* [U]

un·faith·ful /ʌnˈfeɪθfəl/ *adj* someone who is unfaithful has sex with someone who is not their wife, husband, BOYFRIEND etc —**unfaithfully** *adv*

un·fa·mil·i·ar /ˌʌnfəˈmɪliə◂‖-ər/ *adj* if someone or something is unfamiliar to you, or you are unfamiliar with them, you have never seen, heard, or experienced them before: *an unfamiliar face*|*I am unfamiliar with his work.* —**unfamiliarity** /ˌʌnfəmɪliˈærɪti/ *n* [U]

un·fash·ion·a·ble /ʌnˈfæʃənəbəl/ *adj* not popular or fashionable: *In Blair's new Britain the term 'socialist' has become rather unfashionable.*

un·fas·ten /ʌnˈfɑːsn‖-ˈfæsn/ *v* [T] to open the two sides of a piece of clothing, bag, belt etc

un·fa·vour·a·ble *BrE*, **unfavorable** *AmE* ʌnˈfeɪvərəbəl/ *adj* **1** criticizing someone or something, or showing that you do not like them: *The play received unfavourable reviews.* **2** not good and not suitable for doing something: *unfavorable weather conditions*

un·feel·ing /ʌnˈfiːlɪŋ/ *adj* not showing sympathy or PITY for others

un·fin·ished /ʌnˈfɪnɪʃt/ *adj* not finished

un·fit /ʌnˈfɪt/ *adj* not suitable or good enough to do something or be used for something: *meat that is unfit for human consumption*

un·fold /ʌnˈfəʊld‖-ˈfoʊld/ *v* **1** [I] if a story, event etc unfolds, it starts to happen and you find out more about it: *the dramatic events that were unfolding in Eastern Europe* **2** [T] to open something that is folded: *She unfolded the map.*

un·fore·seen /ˌʌnfɔːˈsiːn◂‖-fɔːr-/ *adj* an unforeseen situation is one that you did not expect to happen: *unforeseen problems*

un·for·get·ta·ble /ˌʌnfəˈɡetəbəl◂‖-fər-/ *adj* something that is unforgettable is extremely good, exciting etc and you will remember it for a

U

long time: *Climbing in Nepal was an unforgettable experience.*

un·for·tu·nate /ʌnˈfɔːtʃənɟtll-ˈfɔːr-/ *adj* **1** used to say that you wish something had not happened or was not true: *It was just an unfortunate accident, that's all.* **2** if you are unfortunate, you are unlucky because something bad happens to you: *One unfortunate driver was hit by a falling tree.*

un·for·tu·nate·ly /ʌnˈfɔːtʃənɟtlll-ˈfɔːr-/ *adv* used to say that you wish that something had not happened or was not true: *Unfortunately the show had to be cancelled.*

un·found·ed /ʌnˈfaʊndɟd/ *adj* not true and not based on fact: *unfounded allegations*

un·friend·ly /ʌnˈfrendli/ *adj* not friendly and often unkind: *The local people seemed cold and unfriendly.* **—unfriendliness** *n* [U]

un·furl /ʌnˈfɜːlll-ɜːrl/ *v* [I,T] *literary* if you unfurl a flag, UMBRELLA etc or it unfurls, you open or unroll it

un·gain·ly /ʌnˈɡeɪnli/ *adj* moving in a way that is not graceful: *an ungainly teenager*

un·gra·cious /ʌnˈɡreɪʃəs/ *adj* not polite or friendly **—ungraciously** *adv*

un·gram·mat·i·cal /ˌʌnɡrəˈmætɪkəl/ *adj* wrong according to the rules of grammar

un·grate·ful /ʌnˈɡreɪtfəl/ *adj* not thanking someone for something they have given to you or done for you **—ungratefully** *adv*

un·hap·py /ʌnˈhæpi/ *adj* **1** not happy: *an unhappy childhood* **+ about** *Pauline seemed deeply unhappy about something.* **2** not pleased or satisfied with something: **+ with/about** *O'Neill was unhappy with his team's performance.* **—unhappiness** *n* [U] **—unhappily** *adv*

un·harmed /ʌnˈhɑːmdll-ɑːr-/ *adj* not hurt or damaged after an accident or attack

un·health·y /ʌnˈhelθi/ *adj* **1** likely to make you ill or less healthy: *an unhealthy diet* **2** not healthy: *a rather unhealthy looking child* **3** not normal or natural and likely to be harmful: *an unhealthy obsession with sex*

un·heard-of /ʌnˈhɜːd ɒvll-ˈhɜːrd ɑːv/ *adj* something that is unheard-of has never happened before and seems surprising: *Women airline pilots were practically unheard-of twenty years ago.*

un·help·ful /ʌnˈhelpfəl/ *adj* **1** not willing to help someone, in a way that seems rude and unfriendly: *The staff were unfriendly and unhelpful.* **2** having a bad effect and making it more difficult for you to do something: *unhelpful interference*

un·hurt /ʌnˈhɜːtll-ɜːrt/ *adj* not injured

u·ni·corn /ˈjuːnɟkɔːnll-ɔːrn/ *n* [C] an imaginary animal like a white horse with a long straight horn on its head

un·i·den·ti·fied /ˌʌnaɪˈdentɟfaɪd/ *adj* an unidentified person or thing is one that you do not recognize or know the name of **→** see also UFO

u·ni·fi·ca·tion /ˌjuːnɟfɟˈkeɪʃən/ *n* [U] when two or more countries or groups are joined together to form a single group or country: *the unification of Germany*

u·ni·form[1] /ˈjuːnɟfɔːmll-ɔːrm/ *n* [C,U] a type of clothing worn by all the members of an organization, or all the children at a school: *school uniform* | *The policeman was in uniform.* (=wearing his uniform) **—uniformed** *adj*

uniform[2] *adj* things that are uniform are all the same size, shape etc **—uniformly** *adv* **—uniformity** /ˌjuːnɟˈfɔːmɟtill-ɔːr-/ *n* [U]

u·ni·fy /ˈjuːnɟfaɪ/ *v* [T] **1** to join the parts of a country, organization etc together to make a single country, organization etc: *Spain was unified in the 16th century.* **2** to change a group of things so that they are all the same **→** see also UNIFICATION **—unified** *adj*

u·ni·lat·er·al /ˌjuːnɟˈlætərəl/ *adj* a unilateral decision, action etc is taken or done by one country, group etc, without waiting for other countries or groups to do the same: *a unilateral ceasefire* **—unilaterally** *adv*

un·i·ma·gin·a·ble /ˌʌnɪˈmædʒɟnəbəl/ *adj* impossible to imagine or extremely big, bad etc: *The heat was unimaginable.*

un·im·por·tant /ˌʌnɪmˈpɔːtəntll-ɔːr-/ *adj* not important

un·in·hab·it·a·ble /ˌʌnɪnˈhæbɟtəbəl/ *adj* a place that is uninhabitable is impossible to live in

un·in·hab·it·ed /ˌʌnɪnˈhæbɟtɟd/ *adj* a place that is uninhabited has no one living there

un·in·hib·it·ed /ˌʌnɪnˈhɪbɟtɟd/ *adj* feeling free to behave how you want, without worrying about what other people think

un·in·tel·li·gi·ble /ˌʌnɪnˈtelɟdʒɟbəl/ *adj* impossible to understand

un·in·terest·ed /ʌnˈɪntrɟstɟd/ *adj* not interested **→** compare DISINTERESTED

un·in·ter·rupt·ed /ˌʌnɪntəˈrʌptɟd/ *adj* continuing without stopping or being interrupted: *an uninterrupted view of the mountains*

u·nion /ˈjuːnjən/ *n* **1** [C] an organization that is formed by workers in order to protect their rights: *the auto workers' union* **2** [singular, U] when two or more countries, groups etc are joined together: *the union of East and West Germany*

Union Jack /ˌ.. ˈ./ *n* [C] the national flag of the United Kingdom (=Great Britain and Northern Ireland)

u·nique /juːˈniːk/ *adj* something that is unique is the only one of its kind, and is often very good or special: *a unique opportunity* | *Each person's fingerprint is unique.* | **be unique to** (=only existing in a particular place, group etc): *animals that are unique to Australia* **—uniquely** *adv* **—uniqueness** *n* [U]

u·ni·sex /ˈjuːnɪseks/ *adj* intended for both men and women: *a unisex jacket*

u·ni·son /ˈjuːnɟsən, -zən/ *n* **in unison** if a group of people do something in unison, they all do it at the same time

u·nit /ˈjuːnɟt/ *n* [C] **1** something that is one whole part of a larger thing: *The apartment building is divided into eight units.* **2** a part of an organization, especially one that has a particular purpose: *the emergency unit at the hospital* **3** an amount or quantity of something that is used as a standard of measurement: **+ of** *The dollar is the basic unit of money in the US.* **4** a machine that has a particular purpose, especially one that is part of a larger piece of equipment: *The cooling unit is broken.* **5** one of the parts that a course or schoolbook is divided into **6** a piece of furniture, especially one that can be fitted to others of the same type: *a storage unit*

u·nite /juːˈnaɪt/ *v* [I,T] to join together as a group, or to make people join together: *Congress united behind the President.* | *Germany was united in 1990.*

u·nit·ed /juːˈnaɪtɪd/ *adj* **1** if a group of people, countries etc is united, they all want to stay together, or they all agree with each other: *the Democrats are united on this issue* **2** a united country has been formed by two or more countries or states joining together: *a united Europe*

United Na·tions /ˌ..ˈ../ abbreviation **UN** *n* [singular] the international organization that most countries belong to, which tries to find peaceful solutions to world problems

u·ni·ty /ˈjuːnɪti/ *n* [singular, U] when everyone in a group, country etc wants to stay together, or they all agree with each other: *party unity*

u·ni·ver·sal /ˌjuːnɪˈvɜːsəl ‖ -ɜːr-/ *adj* **1** by or concerning everyone in the world, or everyone in a group: *a universal ban on nuclear weapons* | *There was almost universal agreement.* **2** a universal truth, principle etc is always true in every situation or affects everything —**universally** *adv*

u·ni·verse /ˈjuːnɪvɜːs‖-ɜːrs/ *n* **the universe** all the stars and PLANETs and all of space

u·ni·ver·si·ty /ˌjuːnɪˈvɜːsɪti ‖ -ɜːr-/ *n* [C,U] a place where students study a subject at a high level in order to get DEGREEs: *Which university did you go to?* | *a university professor* | *My sister's at Leeds University.*

un·just /ˌʌnˈdʒʌst◂/ *adj* not fair or reasonable: *unjust laws* —**unjustly** *adv*

un·jus·ti·fied /ʌnˈdʒʌstɪfaɪd/ *adj* done without any good reason: *unjustified spending cuts*

un·kempt /ˌʌnˈkempt◂/ *adj* not neat or tidy: *His hair looked dirty and unkempt.*

un·kind /ˌʌnˈkaɪnd◂/ *adj* behaving in an unpleasant or unfriendly way to someone, which will make them unhappy: *an unkind remark* —**unkindly** *adv* —**unkindness** *n* [U]

un·know·ing·ly /ʌnˈnəʊɪŋli‖-ˈnoʊ-/ *adv* without realizing what you are doing or what is happening —**unknowing** *adj*

un·known¹ /ˌʌnˈnəʊn◂ ‖-ˈnoʊn◂/ *adj* **1** not known: *The number of people injured is still unknown.* **2** not famous: *an unknown actor*

unknown² *n* **1** **the unknown** things that you know nothing about and have never experienced before: *a fear of the unknown* **2** [C] someone who is not famous

un·law·ful /ʌnˈlɔːfəl‖-ˈlɒː-/ *adj formal* not legal: *unlawful killing* —**unlawfully** *adv*

un·lead·ed /ʌnˈledɪd/ *adj* unleaded petrol does not contain any LEAD

un·leash /ʌnˈliːʃ/ *v* [T] to suddenly make something start happening which has a great effect: *The decision unleashed a storm of protest.*

un·less /ʌnˈles, ən-/ *linking word* used to say that something will not happen or be true except

if something else happens or is true: *He won't go to sleep unless you tell him a story.*

un·like /ˌʌnˈlaɪk◂/ *prep* **1** completely different from another person or thing: *Unlike me, she's very intelligent.* **2** not typical of the way someone usually behaves: *It's unlike Judy to leave without telling anyone.*

un·like·ly /ʌnˈlaɪkli/ *adj* something that is unlikely will probably not happen or is probably not true: *It's very unlikely that they'll win.* —**unlikelihood** *n* [U]

un·lim·it·ed /ʌnˈlɪmɪtɪd/ *adj* without a fixed limit: *unlimited freedom*

un·lit /ˌʌnˈlɪt◂/ *adj* dark because there are no lights

un·load /ʌnˈləʊd‖-ˈloʊd/ *v* **1** [T] to remove things from a vehicle or large container: *They unloaded the car.* **2** [I,T] to take film out of a camera or bullets out of a gun **3** [I] if a ship, plane etc unloads, goods are taken off it

un·lock /ʌnˈlɒk‖-ˈlɑːk/ *v* [T] to unfasten the lock on a door, box etc

un·luck·y /ʌnˈlʌki/ *adj* **1** having bad luck: *We were unlucky with the weather this weekend.* **2** happening because of bad luck: *an unlucky accident* **3** something that is unlucky is believed to make you have bad luck: *13 is an unlucky number* —**unluckily** *adv*

un·marked /ˌʌnˈmɑːkt◂‖-ˈmɑːrkt◂/ *adj* something that is unmarked has no words or signs on it to show what it is: *an unmarked police car*

un·mar·ried /ˌʌnˈmærɪd◂/ *adj* not married; SINGLE

un·mis·tak·a·ble /ˌʌnmɪˈsteɪkəbəl◂/ *adj* if something is unmistakable, you know immediately what it is: *the unmistakable taste of garlic*

un·mit·i·gat·ed /ʌnˈmɪtɪɡeɪtɪd/ *adj* used to emphasize how bad something is: *an unmitigated disaster*

un·moved /ʌnˈmuːvd/ *adj* not feeling any sympathy, excitement, worry etc because of something

un·named /ˌʌnˈneɪmd◂/ *adj* an unnamed person or thing is one whose name is not mentioned: *a report from an unnamed source*

un·nat·u·ral /ʌnˈnætʃərəl/ *adj* different from normal, in a way that seems strange or wrong: *It's unnatural for a child to spend so much time alone.* —**unnaturally** *adv*

un·ne·ces·sa·ry /ʌnˈnesəsərɪ‖-seri/ *adj* **1** something that is unnecessary is not needed, or does not have to be done: *the unnecessary use of drugs* **2** unkind or unreasonable: *a rather unnecessary remark* —**unnecessarily** /ʌnˈnesəsərɪli‖ʌnˌnesəˈserɪli/ *adv*

un·nerve /ʌnˈnɜːv‖-ˈnɜːrv/ *v* [T] to make someone very frightened or nervous, so that they cannot behave normally: *Dave was completely unnerved by the accident.* —**unnerving** *adj*

un·no·ticed /ʌnˈnəʊtɪst‖-ˈnoʊ-/ *adj* if someone or something is unnoticed, people do not see or notice them: *She sat unnoticed at the back of the room.*

U

GRAMMAR NOTE: the past perfect
You form the **past perfect** using **had** and the past participle. Use the past perfect to talk about something that happened in the past before another past action: *Kay stayed behind after everyone else **had gone** home.* | *She told me what she **had done**.*

un·ob·served /ˌʌnəb'zɜːvd‖-ɜːrvd/ *adj, adv* without being seen

un·ob·tru·sive /ˌʌnəb'truːsɪv◂/ *adj* not attracting attention and not likely to be noticed —**unobtrusively** *adv*

un·oc·cu·pied /ʌn'ɒkjᵿpaɪd‖-'ɑːk-/ *adj* a seat, house, room etc that is unoccupied has no one in it

un·of·fi·cial /ˌʌnə'fɪʃəl◂/ *adj* **1** not approved or done by someone in authority: *Unofficial reports say about 25 people are dead.* **2** not done as part of someone's official duties: *The Senator is in Berlin on an unofficial visit.* —**unofficially** *adv*

un·or·tho·dox /ʌn'ɔːθədɒks‖ʌn'ɔːrθədɑːks/ *adj* unusual and different from most people's ideas or ways of doing things: *her unorthodox lifestyle*

un·pack /ʌn'pæk/ *v* [I,T] to take everything out of a box or SUITCASE

un·paid /ˌʌn'peɪd◂/ *adj* **1** an unpaid bill or debt has not been paid **2** working without receiving any money: *unpaid workers* | *unpaid work*

un·pal·at·a·ble /ʌn'pælətəbəl/ *adj formal* unpleasant and difficult to accept: *the unpalatable truth*

un·par·al·leled /ʌn'pærəleld/ *adj formal* much greater or better than anything else: *an unparalleled success*

un·pick /ʌn'pɪk/ *v* [T] to remove stitches from a piece of sewing

un·pleas·ant /ʌn'plezənt/ **1** not pleasant or enjoyable: *an unpleasant surprise* **2** unkind or rude: *She was rather unpleasant to me on the phone.* —**unpleasantly** *adv*

un·plug /ʌn'plʌg/ *v* [T] **-gged, -gging** to disconnect a piece of electrical equipment by taking its PLUG out of a SOCKET

un·pop·u·lar /ʌn'pɒpjᵿlə‖-'pɑːpjᵿlər/ *adj* not liked by most people: *an unpopular decision* —**unpopularity** /ˌʌn,pɒpjᵿ'lærᵻti‖-pɑːp-/ *n* [U]

un·pre·ce·dent·ed /ʌn'presᵻdentᵻd/ *adj* something that is unprecedented has never happened before: *an unprecedented achievement*

un·pre·dict·a·ble /ˌʌnprɪ'dɪktəbəl◂/ *adj* changing so much that you do not know what to expect: *unpredictable weather*

un·pro·fes·sion·al /ˌʌnprə'feʃənəl◂/ *adj* not behaving in the way that people in a particular job should behave: *unprofessional conduct*

un·pro·voked /ˌʌnprə'vəʊkt◂‖-'voʊkt◂/ *adj* an unprovoked attack is one in which the person who is attacked has done nothing to make the other person attack them

un·qual·i·fied /ʌn'kwɒlᵻfaɪd‖-'kwɑː-/ *adj* **1** not having the right knowledge, experience, or QUALIFICATIONS to do something: *She was totally unqualified for her new job.* **2** completely and in every way: **unqualified success/disaster** *The festival was an unqualified success.*

un·ques·tion·a·bly /ʌn'kwestʃənəbli/ *adv* if something is unquestionably true, it is definitely true and there are no doubts about it: *He is unquestionably the world's greatest living composer.* —**unquestionable** *adj*

un·rav·el /ʌn'rævəl/ *v* **-lled, -lling** *BrE*, **-led, -ling** *AmE* [I,T] **1** if you unravel a complicated situation or it unravels, it becomes clear and you start to understand it: *Detectives are trying*

to unravel the mystery surrounding his death. **2** if you unravel threads, STRING etc or they unravel, they stop being twisted together

un·real /ˌʌn'rɪəl◂/ *adj* something that is unreal seems so strange that you think you must be imagining it: *The whole situation was completely unreal.* —**unreality** /ˌʌnrɪ'ælᵻti/ *n* [U]

un·rea·lis·tic /ˌʌnrɪə'lɪstɪk◂/ *adj* not basing your ideas on what is really likely to happen or what someone is really able to do: *A lot of women have unrealistic expectations about marriage.*

un·rea·son·a·ble /ʌn'riːzənəbəl/ *adj* **1** behaving in a way that is not fair or sensible, for example by asking someone to do too much: *unreasonable demands* | *Do you think I'm being unreasonable?* **2** unreasonable charges or prices are much too high —**unreasonably** *adv*

un·rec·og·niz·a·ble (also **-isable** *BrE*) /ʌn-'rekəgnaɪzəbəl, -'rekə-, ˌʌn,rekəg'naɪzəbəl/ *adj* someone or something that is unrecognizable has changed or been damaged so much that they seem completely different

un·re·lat·ed /ˌʌnrɪ'leɪtᵻd◂/ *adj* two things that are unrelated have no connection with each other: *unrelated events*

un·re·lent·ing /ˌʌnrɪ'lentɪŋ◂/ *adj formal* continuing for a long time, especially in a difficult, unpleasant, or determined way : *a bitter unrelenting struggle*

un·re·li·a·ble /ˌʌnrɪ'laɪəbəl◂/ *adj* if someone or something is unreliable, you cannot trust or depend on them: *The old machines were notoriously unreliable and slow.*

un·re·mit·ting /ˌʌnrɪ'mɪtɪŋ◂/ *adj formal* something that is unremitting continues for a long time and seems unlikely to stop or become less severe: *a year of unremitting economic gloom*

un·re·pent·ant /ˌʌnrɪ'pentənt◂/ *adj* not feeling ashamed of what you have done or of your beliefs

un·re·quit·ed /ˌʌnrɪ'kwaɪtᵻd◂/ *adj* **unrequited** *love especially literary* when you love someone, but they do not love you

un·res·erv·ed·ly /ˌʌnrɪ'zɜːvᵻdli‖-ɜːr-/ *adv* completely: *He apologized unreservedly.* —**unreserved** *adj*

un·re·solved /ˌʌnrɪ'zɒlvd◂‖-'zɑːlvd◂, -'zɔːlvd◂/ *adj* if a problem, question etc is unresolved, no solution has been found

un·res·pon·sive /ˌʌnrɪ'spɒnsɪv‖-'spɑːn-/ *adj* **1** not reacting to something or not affected by it: *illnesses that are unresponsive to conventional medical treatment* **2** not reacting to what people say to you: *Her manner was cold and unresponsive.*

un·rest /ʌn'rest/ *n* [U] when a lot of people in a country feel angry or not satisfied with the situation and protest about it, often violently: *growing political unrest in Algeria*

un·re·strained /ˌʌnrɪ'streɪnd◂/ *adj* not controlled or limited: *unrestrained economic growth*

un·ri·valled *BrE*, **unrivaled** *AmE* /ʌn'raɪvəld/ *adj* better than anyone or anything else: *an unrivaled collection of 19th century art*

un·roll /ʌn'rəʊl‖-'roʊl/ *v* [T] to open something and make it flat: *He unrolled his sleeping bag.*

un·ruf·fled /ʌn'rʌfəld/ *adj* surprisingly calm and not upset by something that has happened

un·ru·ly /ʌnˈruːli/ *adj* behaving in an uncontrolled or violent way: *unruly schoolchildren*

un·safe /ˌʌnˈseɪf◂/ *adj* a machine, building, place etc that is unsafe is dangerous: *The streets are unsafe for people to walk alone at night.*

un·said /ʌnˈsed/ *adj* **be left unsaid** if something is left unsaid, you do not say it although you think it: *Some things are better left unsaid.*

un·sat·is·fac·to·ry /ˌʌnsætɪsˈfæktəri/ *adj* something that is unsatisfactory is not as good as it should be and is not acceptable: *The present system is completely unsatisfactory.*

un·sa·vour·y *BrE*, **unsavory** *AmE* /ʌnˈseɪvəri/ *adj* unpleasant or morally unacceptable: *The bar was full of all kinds of unsavoury characters.*

un·scathed /ʌnˈskeɪðd/ *adj* not injured or harmed: *The driver emerged from the crash unscathed.*

un·screw /ʌnˈskruː/ *v* [T] to twist something in order to remove it or unfasten it: *She unscrewed the light bulb.*

un·scru·pu·lous /ʌnˈskruːpjələs/ *adj* an unscrupulous person behaves in an unfair or dishonest way in order to get what they want: *unscrupulous employers*

un·seat /ʌnˈsiːt/ *v* [T] to remove someone from a position of power: *Two candidates are trying to unseat the mayor.*

un·seem·ly /ʌnˈsiːmli/ *adj formal* unseemly behaviour is not polite or not suitable for the situation you are in: *an unseemly argument over money*

un·seen /ˌʌnˈsiːn◂/ *adj, adv formal* not noticed or seen: *She left the building unseen.*

un·self·ish /ʌnˈselfɪʃ/ *adj* behaving in a way that shows you care more about other people than about yourself: *an unselfish and generous man who risks his life for his friend*

un·set·tled /ʌnˈsetld/ *adj* **1** feeling worried or nervous because of something that has happened or that might happen: *Children often feel unsettled by divorce.* **2** if an argument or problem is unsettled, people have not agreed to end it or found a solution to it: *The issue remains unsettled.* **3** if a situation is unsettled, people are unsure about what will happen: *These are difficult and unsettled times.* **4** if the weather is unsettled, it keeps changing and often rains —**unsettle** *v* [T]

un·set·tling /ʌnˈsetlɪŋ/ *adj* making you feel worried or nervous: *Going to your first interview can be an unsettling experience.*

un·shav·en /ʌnˈʃeɪvən/ *adj* a man who is unshaven has short hairs growing on his face because he has not shaved (SHAVE)

un·sight·ly /ʌnˈsaɪtli/ *adj* unpleasant to look at: *unsightly modern office buildings*

un·skilled /ˌʌnˈskɪld◂/ *adj* **1** unskilled workers have not had any special training to do a job **2** unskilled work does not need special skills or training

un·so·cial /ˌʌnˈsəʊʃəlǁ-ˈsəʊ-/, /ˌʌnˈsəʊʃəbəlǁ-ˈsoʊ-/ *adj* **unsocial hours** when someone has to work very late at night or early in the morning, when other people do not have to work

un·so·li·cit·ed /ˌʌnsəˈlɪsɪtɪd◂/ *adj formal* something that is unsolicited is given or sent without being asked for, and is often not wanted: *unsolicited mail*

un·so·phis·ti·cat·ed /ˌʌnsəˈfɪstɪkeɪtɪd◂/ *adj* **1** someone who is unsophisticated knows little about modern ideas and fashions: *unsophisticated audiences* **2** unsophisticated equipment, methods etc are very simple

un·sound /ˌʌnˈsaʊnd◂/ *adj* **1** based on ideas or reasons that are wrong **2** in bad condition and likely to fall down

un·speak·a·ble /ʌnˈspiːkəbəl/ *adj* extremely unpleasant or bad: *unspeakable crimes* —**unspeakably** *adv*

un·spe·ci·fied /ʌnˈspesɪfaɪd/ *adj* if something is unspecified, people do not say what it is: *The painting was sold for an unspecified amount of money.*

un·spoiled /ˌʌnˈspɔɪld◂/ *adj especially BrE* a place that is unspoiled is beautiful because it has not been changed and has not had roads, modern buildings etc built on it: *unspoiled countryside*

un·spok·en /ʌnˈspəʊkənǁ-ˈspoʊ-/ *adj* if something is unspoken, you do not speak about it: *unspoken fears* | *an unspoken agreement*

un·sta·ble /ʌnˈsteɪbəl/ *adj* **1** likely to change suddenly and become worse: *The political situation is very unstable at the moment.* **2** someone who is unstable is likely to suddenly become violent, angry etc, especially because there is something mentally wrong with them **3** likely to fall over: *an unstable wall*

un·stead·y /ʌnˈstedi/ *adj* **1** shaking when you try to walk or hold something or when you speak: *I felt unsteady on my feet.* **2** an object that is unsteady does not stand firmly in one position and is likely to move or fall down: *an unsteady ladder*

un·stop·pa·ble /ʌnˈstɒpəbəlǁ-ˈstɑːp-/ *adj* unable to be stopped or beaten: *The team seems unstoppable this year.*

un·stuck /ˌʌnˈstʌk◂/ *adj* **come unstuck a)** *BrE* to fail or start to go wrong: *Our plans came unstuck* **b)** if something comes unstuck, it separates from the surface that it is glued or fastened to

un·sub·stan·ti·at·ed /ˌʌnsəbˈstænʃieɪtɪd/ *adj* unsubstantiated reports, stories, statements etc have not been proved to be true: *an unsubstantiated rumour*

un·suc·cess·ful /ˌʌnsəkˈsesfəl◂/ *adj* not achieving what you wanted to achieve: *an unsuccessful experiment* —**unsuccessfully** *adv*

un·suit·a·ble /ʌnˈsuːtəbəl, ʌnˈsjuː-ǁ-ˈsuː-/ *adj* not having the right qualities for a particular purpose, situation, person etc: *This movie is unsuitable for young children.*

un·sung /ˌʌnˈsʌŋ◂/ *adj* not praised or famous for something you have done, although you deserve to be: *unsung heroes*

un·sure /ˌʌnˈʃʊə◂ǁ-ˈʃʊr◂/ *adj* **1** not certain about something or about what you have to do: *At first, he was unsure about accepting the job.* **2 unsure of yourself** lacking confidence: *Clara seemed shy and unsure of herself.*

un·sur·passed /ˌʌnsəˈpɑːst◂ǁ-sərˈpæst◂/ *adj* better than anyone or anything else

un·sus·pect·ing /ˌʌnsəˈspektɪŋ◂/ *adj* not knowing that something bad is about to happen: *her unsuspecting victim*

U

un·swerv·ing /ʌnˈswɜːvɪŋǁ-ɜːr-/ adj never changing in spite of difficulties: *unswerving loyalty*

un·sym·pa·thet·ic /ˌʌnsɪmpəˈθetɪk/ adj **1** behaving in a way that shows you do not care about someone's problems or feelings, and seems unkind: *Her father was cold and unsympathetic.* **2** not supporting or approving of someone or something **3** an unsympathetic character in a book, film etc seems rather unpleasant and difficult to like

un·tan·gle /ˌʌnˈtæŋgəl/ v [T] to make things no longer be twisted together or connected with each other: *conditioner that helps untangle your hair*

un·tapped /ˌʌnˈtæpt◂/ adj an untapped supply of something has not been used: *untapped oil reserves*

un·ten·a·ble /ʌnˈtenəbəl/ adj formal impossible to defend against criticism

un·think·a·ble /ʌnˈθɪŋkəbəl/ adj impossible to imagine or accept: *It seemed unthinkable that a woman would run for President.*

un·ti·dy /ʌnˈtaɪdi/ adj especially BrE **1** not neatly arranged; MESSY: *Why's your desk always so untidy?* **2** an untidy person does not keep their house, clothes, hair etc neatly arranged

un·tie /ʌnˈtaɪ/ v [T] to unfasten the knots in something or unfasten something that has been tied: *Mommy, can you untie my shoelaces?*

un·til /ʌnˈtɪl, ən-/ also **till** prep, linking word **1** if something happens until a time, it continues and then stops at that time: *The banks are open until 3.30.* | *Debbie's on vacation until Monday.* **2** not until used to say that something will not happen before a particular time: *The movie doesn't start until 8.*

un·time·ly /ʌnˈtaɪmli/ adj happening too soon: *her untimely death*

un·told /ˌʌnˈtəʊldǁ-ˈtoʊld◂/ adj used to emphasize how bad something is, or how much of something there is: *The floods caused untold damage.*

un·touched /ˌʌnˈtʌtʃt◂/ adj **1** not affected or damaged by something: *an area untouched by the war* **2** food or drink that is untouched has not been eaten or drunk

un·to·ward /ˌʌntəˈwɔːdǁˌʌnˈtɔːrd/ adj unexpected and unpleasant: *Nothing untoward happened.*

un·trained /ˌʌnˈtreɪnd◂/ adj **1** not trained **2** to the untrained eye/ear to someone who does not know a lot about something: *To the untrained eye, the painting looks like a Van Gogh.*

un·tried /ˌʌnˈtraɪd◂/ adj new and not tested by being used

un·true /ʌnˈtruː/ adj not true: *Their story was completely untrue.*

un·truth /ʌnˈtruːθ, ˈʌntruːθ/ n [C] formal something that is not true; a lie

un·truth·ful /ʌnˈtruːθfəl/ adj dishonest or not true

un·used[1] /ˌʌnˈjuːzd◂/ adj something that is unused has not been used, or is not being used at the moment: *unused land*

un·used[2] /ʌnˈjuːst/ adj unused to if you are unused to something, you have not done it before or experienced it before: *She's unused to driving at night.*

un·u·su·al /ʌnˈjuːʒuəl, -ʒəl/ adj different from what usually happens, or different from the ordinary kind: *It's very unusual to have snow in April.* | *a rather unusual taste*

un·u·su·ally /ʌnˈjuːʒuəli, -ʒəli/ adv **1** unusually hot/big etc hotter, bigger etc than is usual **2** in a way that is different from usual: *Unusually for Michael, he arrived on time.*

un·veil /ʌnˈveɪl/ v [T] **1** to officially show or tell people something that was a secret: *The mayor will unveil plans for a new park.* **2** to remove the cover from something as part of an official ceremony

un·want·ed /ʌnˈwɒntɪdǁ-ˈwɒnt-, -ˈwɑːnt-/ adj not wanted or needed: *an unwanted gift*

un·war·rant·ed /ʌnˈwɒrəntɪdǁ-ˈwɔː-, -ˈwɑː-/ adj formal if something is unwarranted, there is no good reason for doing it, and people should not do it: *unwarranted interference*

un·wa·ry /ʌnˈweəriǁ-ˈweri/ adj not having any experience of doing something and therefore likely to be harmed or deceived: *unwary tourists*

un·wel·come /ʌnˈwelkəm/ adj **1** something that is unwelcome is not wanted, especially because it might cause embarrassment or problems: *unwelcome publicity* **2** if someone is unwelcome, you do not want them to be with you: *an unwelcome visitor*

un·well /ʌnˈwel/ adj formal ill

un·wiel·dy /ʌnˈwiːldi/ adj big and heavy, and difficult to move or carry: *The first clocks were large and unwieldy.*

un·will·ing /ʌnˈwɪlɪŋ/ adj if you are unwilling to do something, you do not want to do it: *He's unwilling to admit he was wrong.* —**unwillingly** adv —**unwillingness** n [U]

un·wind /ʌnˈwaɪnd/ v unwound /-ˈwaʊnd/, unwound, unwinding **1** [I] to relax and stop thinking about your work, your problems etc: *Swimming helps me unwind.* **2** [I,T] to undo something, or to stop being wrapped around something else: *He unwound the rope.*

un·wise /ʌnˈwaɪz/ adj something that is unwise is not sensible and is likely to have a bad result: *an unwise decision* —**unwisely** adv

un·wit·ting·ly /ʌnˈwɪtɪŋli/ adv without knowing or realizing something: *Several employees unwittingly became involved in illegal activities.* —**unwitting** adj

un·work·a·ble /ʌnˈwɜːkəbəlǁ-ɜːr-/ adj a plan, idea, system etc that is unworkable cannot succeed

un·wound /ʌnˈwaʊnd/ v the past tense and past participle of UNWIND

un·wrap /ʌnˈræp/ v [T] to remove the paper that is covering something

un·writ·ten /ʌnˈrɪtn/ adj known about and understood by everyone but not written down: *an unwritten rule*

un·yield·ing /ʌnˈjiːldɪŋ/ adj **1** refusing to change what you are doing or change what you say: *The terrorists were unyielding in their demands.* **2** very hard and firm

un·zip /ˌʌnˈzɪp/ v [T] -pped, -pping to unfasten the ZIP on a piece of clothing, bag etc

up[1] /ʌp/ adv, prep **1** towards a higher position or in a higher position: *They began walking up the hill.* | *Can you move the picture up a little higher?* | *"Where's Dave?" "He's up in his room."*

(=in a higher part of the building where you are now) → see colour picture on page 474 **2** if you get up or stand up, you move into an upright position: *They all stood up to sing.* **3** used to say that something increases, becomes louder, hotter etc: *Can you turn up the TV?* **4** used to emphasize that someone does something completely or finishes all of something: *He's eaten up all his food.* | *They soon used up all their money.* **5** not in bed: *Are you still up?* | *They stayed up all night to watch the game.* **6** if the amount of something is up, it has increased: *Profits were up by 4% this year.* **7** *spoken* if a period of time is up, it has finished **8** in or towards the north: *His relatives all live up in Scotland.* **9 up the street/road/river etc** further along the street, road etc: *She lives just up the street.* **10 up to a)** used to say how large a number or amount can be: *Up to 10 people are allowed in the elevator at one time.* **b)** as good as a particular level or standard: *The band's latest record isn't up to their usual high standard.* **11 walk/go/come etc up to** to walk etc towards someone or something until you are next to them: *A man came up to me and asked for a light.* **12 up to/up until** until a particular date or time: *The offer is valid up to December 15.* **13 it's up to sb** *spoken* used to say that someone should decide about something: *"Do you think I should get the dress?" "It's up to you."* **14 be/feel up to sth** to feel healthy enough or strong enough to do something: *Do you feel up to a walk today?* **15 be up to something** to be doing something secretly, especially something that you should not do: *He keeps looking behind him. I'm sure he's up to something.* **16 be up against sth** to have to compete against a very difficult opponent, or deal with a very difficult situation: *We're up against some of the biggest companies in the world.* **17 up for sale/discussion etc** being sold, discussed etc: *Their house is up for sale.* **18 be up and running** if something is up and running, it is working: *The system should be up and running early next year.* → see also UPS AND DOWNS, **what's up** (WHAT)

Up² *v* [T] to increase the amount or level of something: *They've upped her salary by $2500!*

up-and-com·ing /ˌ. .ˈ. ◂/ *adj* likely to be successful: *an up-and-coming actor*

up·beat /ˈʌpbiːt/ *adj* cheerful and feeling that good things will happen: *a movie with an upbeat ending*

up·bring·ing /ˈʌpˌbrɪŋɪŋ/ *n* [singular] the way that a child is treated and taught to behave by his or her parents: *He had a strict upbringing.*

up·com·ing /ˈʌpˌkʌmɪŋ/ *adj* happening soon: *the upcoming elections*

up·date¹ /ʌpˈdeɪt/ *v* [T] **1** to add the most recent information to something: *The files need to be updated.* **2** to make something more modern in the way it looks or operates

up·date² /ˈʌpdeɪt/ *n* [C] the most recent news about something: *an update on the earthquake*

up·front¹ /ˌʌpˈfrʌnt/ *adv* if you pay someone upfront, you pay them before they do something

upfront² *adj spoken* speaking honestly about something and not trying to keep anything secret

up·grade /ˌʌpˈɡreɪd/ *v* [T] to improve something, or exchange something for something better: *We need to upgrade our computer.* —**upgrade** /ˈʌpɡreɪd/ *n* [C]

up·heav·al /ʌpˈhiːvəl/ *n* [C,U] a very big change that causes a lot of problems: *an enormous political upheaval*

up·hill /ˌʌpˈhɪl◂/ *adj, adv* **1** towards the top of a hill: *an uphill climb* → opposite DOWNHILL **2** difficult and needing a lot of effort: *It's going to be an uphill struggle.*

up·hold /ˌʌpˈhəʊldǁ-ˈhoʊld/ *v* [T] **upheld** /-ˈheld/, **upheld, upholding 1** to make sure that laws are obeyed or that a system, right etc continues to exist: *The job of the police is to uphold law and order.* **2** if a court upholds a decision made by another court, it says officially that the decision was correct

up·hol·ster·y /ʌpˈhəʊlstəriǁ-ˈhoʊl-/ *n* [U] material that chairs are covered with: *leather upholstery*

up·keep /ˈʌpkiːp/ *n* [U] the things that must be done when taking care of children, animals, or a building, and the money needed to pay for this

up·lands /ˈʌpləndz/ *n* [plural] high areas of land —**upland** *adj*

up·lift·ing /ʌpˈlɪftɪŋ/ *adj* making you feel cheerful and happy: *an uplifting experience*

up·mar·ket /ˌʌpˈmɑːkɪt◂/ *adj BrE* used by people who are rich or have a high social position; UPSCALE *AmE*: *an upmarket restaurant*

up·on /əˈpɒnǁəˈpɔːn, əˈpɑːn/ *prep formal* on: *countries that are dependent upon the West for aid*

up·per /ˈʌpəǁ-ər/ *adj* **1** in a higher position than the other part or parts of something: *the upper jaw* | *the upper floors of the building* → opposite LOWER¹ **2** more important or having a higher position: *the upper levels of society* **3 have/get the upper hand** to have or get more power than someone else, so that you are able to control a situation: *Government forces now have the upper hand.* **4 the upper limit** the highest limit

upper case /ˌ.. ˈ. ◂/ *n* [U] letters written in CAPITALS (A, B, C) → compare LOWER CASE

upper class /ˌ.. ˈ. ◂/ *n* **the upper class** the group of people who belong to the highest social class

up·per·most /ˈʌpəməʊstǁ-pərmoʊst/ *adj* **1 be uppermost in sb's mind** to be the most important thing to you, or the thing that you are most worried about **2** highest: *the uppermost branches of the tree*

up·right /ˈʌp-raɪt/ *adj* **1** standing or pointing straight up: *Make sure that your seat is in an upright position.* **2** *formal* always behaving in

U

GRAMMAR NOTE: the future

To talk about the **future** you can use: 1. **will** + basic form of verb: *I'll* (=I will) *see you tomorrow.* 2. **be going to** (used to say that something will happen soon): *I think it's going to rain.* 3. the **present progressive** (used to say what is planned or intended): *We're having a party on Saturday.*

an honest and morally right way: *upright citizens* —**upright** *adv*

up·ris·ing /ˈʌpˌraɪzɪŋ/ *n* [C] when a large group of people fight against the people who have power in their country, especially in order to try to change the government: *the Hungarian uprising of 1956*

up·riv·er /ˌʌpˈrɪvəl-ər/ *adv* in the opposite direction to the way the river water is flowing

up·roar /ˈʌp-rɔːll-rɔːr/ *n* [singular, U] **1** when people protest angrily about something that has just been announced **2** when there is a lot of shouting and noise

up·root /ˌʌpˈruːt/ *v* [T] **1** to pull a plant and its roots out of the ground **2** to make someone have to leave their home and move to a new place: *If I took the job it would mean uprooting the whole family.*

ups and downs /ˌ. . ˈ./ *n* [plural] the good and bad things that happen in a particular situation: *Every marriage has its ups and downs.*

up·scale /ˈʌpskeɪl/ *adj AmE* used by people who are rich or have a high social position; **UPMARKET** *BrE*: *upscale housing*

up·set[1] /ʌpˈset/ *adj* **1** unhappy because something unpleasant has happened, so that you feel shocked or want to cry: *She's still very upset about her dad.* | **get upset** *When I told him he'd failed, he got very upset.* **2** an upset stomach/tummy when your stomach feels slightly ill

upset[2] *v* [T] **1** to make someone feel unhappy or worried, especially by saying or doing something that shocks them: *Kopp's comments upset many of his listeners.* **2** to spoil something and cause a lot of problems: *I hope I haven't upset all your plans.* **3** upset your stomach to make you feel sick **4** to make something fall over: *He upset the table and everything on it.*

up·set[3] /ˈʌpset/ *n* [C] **1** when a player or team unexpectedly wins: *There's been a big upset at Wimbledon.* **2** an unexpected problem or difficulty: *We've had one or two minor upsets.* **3** a stomach upset when your stomach feels slightly ill

up·set·ting /ʌpˈsetɪŋ/ *adj* making you feel shocked and unhappy or worried: *an upsetting experience*

up·shot /ˈʌpʃɒtll-ʃɑːt/ *n* the upshot the final result of a situation: *The upshot is that she's decided to take the job.*

up·side down /ˌʌpsaɪd ˈdaʊn◂/ *adj, adv* **1** with the top at the bottom and the bottom at the top: *Isn't that picture upside down?* **2** turn sth upside down **a)** to move a lot of things and make a place untidy because you are looking for something: *The police turned the place upside down.* **b)** to change something completely: *Her whole world was turned upside down when Charles asked her to marry him.*

up·stage /ˌʌpˈsteɪdʒ/ *v* [T] to do something that takes people's attention away from a more important person or event

up·stairs /ˌʌpˈsteəz◂ll-ˈsterz◂/ *adv* on or going towards a higher floor of a building: *Her office is upstairs on your right.* —**upstairs** *adj*: *the upstairs bathroom* → opposite DOWNSTAIRS

up·start /ˈʌpstɑːtll-ɑːrt/ *n* [C] someone who is new in their job and thinks they are more important or better at doing it than they really are

up·state /ˈʌpsteɪt/ *adj, adv AmE* in or towards the northern part of a state: *She lives upstate.*

up·stream /ˌʌpˈstriːm◂/ *adv* along a river in the opposite direction from the way the river is flowing

up·surge /ˈʌpsɜːdʒll-ɜːr-/ *n* [C] a sudden increase: *the recent upsurge in crime*

up·take /ˈʌpteɪk/ *n* **be slow/quick on the uptake** *informal* to be slow or fast at understanding or learning things

up·tight /ˈʌptaɪt, ʌpˈtaɪt/ *adj informal* nervous and worried, and often easily becoming annoyed: *You shouldn't get so uptight about it.*

up-to-date /ˌ. . ˈ.◂/ *adj* **1** up-to-date equipment, methods, books etc are modern and use all the newest knowledge and information **2** up-to-date information is the most recent information about what has happened

up-to-the-min·ute /ˌ. . . ˈ.◂/ *adj* including the most recent information, details etc: *a service that provides up-to-the-minute information on share prices*

up·town /ˌʌpˈtaʊn◂/ *adv AmE* to or in the northern area of a city or town, or the area where the richer people live: *The Parkers live uptown.* —**uptown** *adj* → compare DOWNTOWN

up·turn /ˈʌptɜːnll-ɜːrn/ *n* [C] when economic conditions improve and business activity increases: *an upturn in the economy*

up·turned /ˌʌpˈtɜːnd◂ll-ɜːr-/ *adj* **1** turning upwards at the end: *an upturned nose* **2** turned so that the bottom is facing upwards: *upturned boxes*

upward /ˈʌpwədll-wərd/ *adj* [only before noun] **1** moving or pointing towards a higher position: *an upward movement of his hand* **2** increasing to a higher level: *the recent upward trend in house prices* → opposite DOWNWARD

up·wards /ˈʌpwədzll-wərdz/ also **upward** *especially AmE adv* **1** moving or pointing towards a higher position: *Billy pointed upward at the clouds.* **2** increasing to a higher level: *Salaries have been moving steadily upwards.* → opposite DOWNWARDS **3** upwards of more than: *Thieves stole paintings valued at upwards of $100 million.*

u·ra·ni·um /jʊˈreɪniəm/ *n* [U] a RADIOACTIVE metal used to produce NUCLEAR power and weapons

U·ra·nus /ˈjʊərənəs, jʊˈreɪnəsll-ˈjʊr-, jʊˈreɪ-/ *n* [singular] the seventh PLANET from the sun

ur·ban /ˈɜːbənll-ɜːr-/ *adj* in or relating to a town or city: *urban areas* → compare RURAL

ur·bane /ɜːˈbeɪnll-ɜːr-/ *adj* behaving in a relaxed and confident way in social situations: *He was a wealthy banker – urbane, sophisticated, charming.*

ur·chin /ˈɜːtʃɪnll-ɜːr-/ *n* [C] *old-fashioned* a small dirty child

urge[1] /ɜːdʒll-ɜːr-/ *v* [T] to strongly advise someone to do something: *Her friends urged her to go* *to France.* | *The banks are urging caution.* (=they are advising people to be careful)

urge sb ↔ **on** *phr v* [T] to encourage someone to try harder, go faster etc: *Urged on by the crowd, he scored two more goals.*

urge² *n* [C] a strong wish or need: *sexual urges* | *I felt a sudden urge to hit him.*

ur·gent /'ɜːdʒənt‖'ɜːr-/ *adj* if something is urgent, it needs to be done or dealt with immediately because it is very important: *an urgent message* | *She's in urgent need of medical attention.* —**urgency** *n* [U] —**urgently** *adv*

u·ri·nal /'jʊərɪnəl, jʊˈraɪ-‖'jʊr-/ *n* [C] a toilet where men urinate

u·ri·nate /'jʊərɪneɪt‖'jʊr-/ *v* [I] technical to make urine flow out of your body

u·rine /'jʊərɪn‖'jʊr-/ *n* [U] liquid waste that comes out of your body when you go to the toilet

urn /ɜːn‖ɜːrn/ *n* [C] **1** a large container for hot coffee or tea **2** a decorated container, especially one that is used for holding the ASHes of a dead person

us /əs, s; *strong* ʌs/ *pron* the object form of 'we': *I'm sure he didn't see us.*

us·a·ble /'juːsəbəl/ *adj* something that is usable is in a good enough condition to be used

us·age /'juːsɪdʒ, 'juːzɪdʒ/ *n* **1** [C,U] the way that words are used in a language: *a book on modern English usage* **2** [U] the way in which something is used, or the amount of it that is used: *Car usage has increased dramatically.*

use¹ /juːz/ *v* [T] **1** if you use something, you do something with it for a particular purpose: *Can I use your phone?* | *Use a food processor to grate the vegetables.* **2** to need an amount of electricity, petrol etc in order to work; CONSUME: *These light bulbs use less electricity.* | *Our car's using too much oil.* **3** to treat someone in an unkind and unfair way by deceiving them in order to get something that you want: *I thought he loved me, but in fact he was just using me.* **4** to say or write a particular word or phrase: *Why did you use the word 'if'?*

use sth ↔ **up** *phr v* [T] to use all of something: *Who used up the toothpaste?*

use² /juːs/ *n* **1** [U] when people use something to do something: *Are you in favour of the use of animals for research?* | *the use of American airpower* **2** [C] a purpose for which something can be used: *The drug has many uses.* **3** [U] if you have the use of something, you are able to use it or someone has allowed you to use it: *Joe's given me the use of his office.* | *She lost the use of both legs.* **4** **make use of** to use something that is available: *I wanted to make use of all the hotel facilities.* **5** **be of no use (to sb)** to not be useful to someone: *The ticket's of no use to me now.* **6** **it's no use/what's the use** *spoken* used to say that doing something will not have any effect, and you should not do it: *It's no use arguing with her. She just won't listen.* **7** **put sth to good use** to use your knowledge, skills etc well: *a chance to put your medical training to good use* **8** **have no/little use for** to not think someone or something is useful or effective, and not use them: *Meisner has little use for rules about acting.* **9** **in use** being used: *The meeting room is in use all morning.* **10** [C] a way in which a word or phrase is used, so that it has a particular meaning: *an interesting use of the word 'brave'*

used¹ /juːst/ *adj* **be used to (doing) sth** if you are used to something, you have done it or experienced it many times before and it no longer seems surprising, difficult etc: *Are you used to getting up so early?* | **get used to sth** *I soon got used to the Japanese way of life.*

used² /juːzd/ *adj* used cars, clothes etc have already been owned by someone and are then sold; SECONDHAND

used to /'juːst tuː/ *modal verb* if something used to happen, it happened often or regularly in the past but does not happen now: *We used to go to the movies every week.* | *didn't sb use/used to "Didn't you used to smoke?" "Yes, but I quit."*

> **USAGE NOTE: used to, be used to** and **get used to**
>
> Use **used to** to talk about something that someone did regularly in the past: *I used to play tennis twice a week, but I don't have time now.* Use **be used to** and **get used to** to talk about being or becoming more comfortable with a situation or activity, so that it does not seem strange or difficult: *Are you used to the cold winters yet?* | *I can't get used to living in a big city.*

use·ful /'juːsfəl/ *adj* something that is useful makes it easier for you to do something or get something: *a useful book for travellers* | **come in useful** (=be useful and help you to do something): *His knowledge of Italian was to come in useful later on.* —**usefully** *adv* —**usefulness** *n* [U]

use·less /'juːsləs/ *adj* **1** not useful at all: *These scissors are completely useless.* | *useless information* **2** if it is useless doing something, it does not help you achieve anything: *It's useless trying to talk to her.* **3** *informal* very bad at doing something: *I'm useless at golf.*

us·er /'juːzə‖-ər/ *n* [C] someone who uses a product, service etc: *computer users*

user-friend·ly /ˌ... '..◂/ *adj* something that is user-friendly is designed so that it is easy to use

ush·er¹ /'ʌʃə‖-ər/ *v* [T] to take someone into or out of a room or building: *His secretary ushered us into his office.*

usher in sth *phr v* [T] to make something new start happening: *Gorbachev ushered in a new era of reform.*

ush·er² *n* [C] someone who shows people to their seats in a theatre, at a wedding etc

ush·er·ette /ˌʌʃəˈret/ *n* [C] *BrE* a woman who shows people where to sit in a cinema or theatre

u·su·al /'juːʒuəl, 'juːʒəl/ *adj* **1** the same as what happens most of the time or in most situations: *Let's meet at the usual place.* | *It's warmer than usual for March.* **2** **as usual** in the way that happens or exists most of the time: *They were late, as usual.*

u·su·al·ly /'juːʒuəli, 'juːʒəli/ *adv* used to say what happens on most occasions or in most situations: *We usually go out for dinner on Saturday.*

u·surp /juːˈzɜːp‖-ɜːrp/ *v* [T] *formal* to take someone else's power, position, or job

u·ten·sil /juːˈtensəl/ *n* [C] a tool or object that you use for doing something, especially for cooking: *kitchen utensils*

U

u·te·rus /ˈjuːtərəs/ n [C] technical the part of a woman or female MAMMAL where babies develop; WOMB

u·til·i·ties /juːˈtɪlɪtiz/ n [C] services such as gas or electricity that are provided for people to use: Does the rent include utilities?

u·til·ize (also **-ise** BrE) /ˈjuːtɪˌlaɪz/ v [T] formal to use something —**utilization** /ˌjuːtɪlaɪˈzeɪʃən‖ -tələ-/ n [U]

ut·most¹ /ˈʌtməʊst‖-moʊst/ adj **the utmost importance/care etc** the greatest possible importance, care etc: a matter of the utmost importance

utmost² n [singular] **1 do your utmost** to try as hard as you can in order to do something **2 to the utmost** to the highest limit, amount, degree etc possible: The course challenges drivers to the utmost.

u·to·pi·a /juːˈtəʊpiə‖-ˈtoʊ-/ n [C,U] an imaginary perfect world where everyone is happy

ut·ter¹ /ˈʌtəll-ər/ adj complete or extreme: We watched in utter amazement. —**utterly** adv

utter² v [T] especially literary to say something: No one uttered a word. —**utterance** n [C]

U-turn /ˈjuː tɜːn‖-tɜːrn/ n [C] **1** when you turn your car around in the road and go back in the direction you came from **2** when a government, company etc changes a previous decision and does something completely different

U

Vv

V, v /viː/ the letter 'v'

V having a shape like the letter V: *a dress with a V neck*

v *BrE* an abbreviation of versus; used to say that one team or player is playing against another: *England v Australia*

va·can·cy /'veɪkənsi/ *n* [C] **1** a room that is available in a hotel: *The sign said "no vacancies".* **2** a job that is available for someone to start doing: *Are there any vacancies for cooks?*

va·cant /'veɪkənt/ *adj* **1** empty and available for someone to use: *vacant apartments* **2** a vacant job is available for someone to start doing **3** a vacant expression shows that someone is not thinking about anything or they are not at all interested in something —**vacantly** *adv*

va·cate /və'keɪt, veɪ-‖'veɪkeɪt/ *v* [T] *formal* to leave a seat, room etc so that someone else can use it: *Guests must vacate their rooms by noon.*

va·ca·tion /və'keɪʃən‖veɪ-/ *n* [C,U] **1** especially *AmE* a period of time when you do not have to work or go to school: *HOLIDAY BrE*: *the summer vacation* | **on vacation** *They're on vacation for the next two weeks.* **2** *AmE* a period of time that you spend in another place or country for enjoyment; *HOLIDAY BrE*: **take a vacation** *We're thinking of taking a vacation in the Virgin Islands.* | **on vacation** *I went there once on vacation.* —**vacation** *v* [I]

> **USAGE NOTE: vacation and holiday**
>
> **Vacation** is the usual American English word for a period of time you spend away from school or work, or when you travel to another place during this time: *Where are you going on vacation this summer?* | *a two-week vacation.* The usual British English word is **holiday** or **holidays**: *the summer holidays* | *We went to Ireland for our holiday last year.* However, **holiday** is used in both British and American English to talk about a day when no one officially has to go to work or school: *Christmas Day is a holiday in most Western countries.* | *a national holiday*

vac·cin·ation /ˌvæksɪ'neɪʃən/ *n* [C,U] when someone is given a vaccine to protect them from a disease: *Have you been vaccinated against measles?* —**vaccinate** /'væksɪneɪt/ *v* [T]

vac·cine /'væksiːn‖væk'siːn/ *n* [C,U] a substance used to protect people against a disease, which contains the VIRUS that causes the disease: *polio vaccine*

vac·il·late /'væsɪleɪt/ *v* [I] *formal* to be unsure and keep changing your opinions, ideas etc because you cannot decide between two choices

vac·u·um¹ /'vækjuəm, -kjum/ *n* **1** [C] a vacuum cleaner **2** [C] a space that is completely empty of all air or gas **3** [singular] a situation in which someone or something is missing or lacking: *His death left a vacuum in her life.*

vacuum² *v* [I,T] to clean a place using a vacuum cleaner

vacuum clean·er /'... ˌ../
n [C] a machine that cleans floors by sucking up the dirt from them

vacuum cleaner

va·gi·na /və'dʒaɪnə/ *n* [C] the PASSAGE from a woman's outer sexual organs to her UTERUS —**vaginal** *adj*

va·grant /'veɪgrənt/ *n* [C] *formal* someone who has no home or work

vague /veɪg/ *adj* **1** not clear or definite: *She's been a bit vague about her plans for the summer.* | *I had only a vague idea where the house was.* | *Looking closely, he could just see the vague outline of her face.* **2** in a way that shows you are not thinking about what you are doing: *The professor looked at me in a rather vague way.*

vague·ly /'veɪgli/ *adv* **1** slightly: *The woman's face looked vaguely familiar.* **2** in a way that shows you are not thinking about what you are doing: *He smiled vaguely.* **3** in a way that is not clear or definite: *a vaguely worded statement*

vain /veɪn/ *adj* **1** **in vain** without success: *Doctors tried in vain to save his life.* **2** **vain attempt/hope** a vain hope or attempt is not successful or does not happen in the way that you want **3** having too much pride in yourself, your appearance, and your abilities: *Men are so vain.* —**vainly** *adv*

Val·en·tine also **Valentine's card** /'væləntaɪn/ *n* [C] a card sent to someone on Valentine's Day

Valentine's Day /'... ˌ./ *n* [C,U] a day (February 14th) when people give special cards, chocolates, flowers etc to people they love

val·et /'vælɪt, 'væleɪ‖væ'leɪ/ *n* [C] **1** a male servant who takes care of a man's clothes, serves his meals etc **2** *AmE* someone whose job is to park your car for you at a hotel or restaurant

val·i·ant /'væliənt/ *adj formal* very brave: *a valiant rescue attempt* —**valiantly** *adv*

val·id /'vælɪd/ *adj* **1** a valid ticket, document, or agreement can be used legally and is officially acceptable: *a valid passport* **2** something that is valid seems right and reasonable because it is based on strong reasons or facts: *valid criticism* —**validity** /və'lɪdɪti/ *n* [U]

val·i·date /'vælɪdeɪt/ *v* [T] *formal* to prove that something is true or correct

val·ley /'væli/ *n* [C] an area of lower land between two lines of hills or mountains → see colour picture on page 243

val·our *BrE*, **valor** *AmE* /'vælə-ər/ *n* [U] *literary* great courage, especially in war

val·u·a·ble /'væljuəbəl, -jʊbəl‖'væljʊbəl/ *adj* **1** worth a lot of money: *a valuable ring*

> **GRAMMAR NOTE: 'if' clauses (1)**
> Use the simple present to talk about the future in clauses beginning **if...** : *I will hit you* **if** *you* **do** *that again*. *not* 'if you will do that again'. **If** *you* **take** *a taxi, you'll be OK*. *not* 'if you will take a taxi...'
> Use 'will' in the other part of the sentence.

2 help, advice etc that is valuable is very useful → compare INVALUABLE

val·u·a·bles /'væljuəbəlz, -jʊˈbəlz‖-jʊˈbəlz/ *n* [plural] things that you own that are worth a lot of money, such as jewellery or cameras

val·u·a·tion /ˌvæljuˈeɪʃən/ *n* [C,U] when people decide how much something is worth

val·ue[1] /'vælju:/ *n* [U] **1** [C,U] the amount of money that something is worth: *The value of the house has gone up.* | *Did the thieves take anything of value?* (=anything that was worth much money) **2** [U] the importance or usefulness of something: *the value of direct personal experience* | **be of great/little value** *His research was of great value to doctors working with the disease.* **3 be good/excellent value (for money)** *BrE* used to say that you get a lot of something or that its quality is good, considering the amount you pay for it

value[2] *v* [T] **1** to think that something is important to you: *I always value your advice.* **2** to say how much something is worth: *a painting valued at $5 million*

val·ues /'vælju:z/ *n* [plural] your moral beliefs about what is right and wrong, or your ideas about what is important in life: *traditional family values*

valve /vælv/ *n* [C] a part of a tube or pipe that opens and closes to control the flow of liquid, gas, air etc passing through: *the valves of the heart*

vam·pire /'væmpaɪə‖-paɪr/ *n* [C] a person in stories who bites people's necks and sucks their blood

van /væn/ *n* [C] a vehicle used for carrying goods which is covered and has metal sides, and is smaller than a TRUCK → see colour picture on page 669

van·dal /'vændl/ *n* [C] someone who deliberately damages things, especially public property

van·dal·is·m /'vændəl-ɪzəm/ *n* [U] the crime of deliberately damaging things, especially public property

van·dal·ize (also **-ise** *BrE*) /'vændəl-aɪz/ *v* [T] to deliberately damage or destroy things, especially public property

van·guard /'vænɡɑːd‖-ɡɑːrd/ *n* **in the vanguard** in the most ADVANCED position concerning new ideas, changes etc: *a group in the vanguard of political reform*

va·nil·la /vəˈnɪlə/ *n* [U] a substance with a slightly sweet taste, used in ICE CREAM and other foods

van·ish /'vænɪʃ/ *v* [I] to disappear suddenly, especially in a way that cannot be easily explained: *When I looked again, he'd vanished.* | *The ship vanished without trace.* (=it disappeared completely, leaving no sign of what had happened to it) —**vanishing** *adj*

van·i·ty /'vænɪti/ *n* [U] when someone is too proud or too concerned about their appearance, their abilities etc

van·quish /'væŋkwɪʃ/ *v* [T] *literary* to defeat someone or something completely

van·tage point /'vɑːntɪdʒ pɔɪnt‖'væn-/ *n* [C] **1** a position from which you can look at something **2** a way of thinking about things that comes from your own situation

va·por·ize (also **-ise** *BrE*) /'veɪpəraɪz/ *v* [I,T] to be changed into a vapour, or change a liquid into a vapour

va·pour *BrE*, **vapor** *AmE* /'veɪpəl-ər/ *n* [C,U] many small drops of liquid that float in the air: *water vapour*

var·i·a·ble[1] /'veəriəbəl‖-ver-/ *adj* likely to change often or be different in different situations: *the variable nature of the weather* —**variability** /ˌveəriəˈbɪlɪti‖ˌver-/ *n* [U]

variable[2] *n* [C] something that may be different in different situations: *economic variables*

var·i·ance /'veəriəns‖-ver-/ *n* **be at variance with** *formal* to be completely different or contain very different information from something else, especially in a way that seems wrong or unusual: *The two reports seemed to be at variance with each other on several points.*

var·i·ant /'veəriənt‖-ver-/ *n* [C] something that is slightly different from the usual form of something: *a spelling variant* —**variant** *adj*

var·i·a·tion /ˌveəriˈeɪʃən‖ˌver-/ *n* **1** [C,U] a difference or change from the usual amount or form of something: + **in** *variations in price from store to store* **2** [C] something that is slightly different from the usual form of something, especially because it is done in a slightly different way: *This is the traditional way of making Christmas pudding, but of course there are many variations.*

var·i·cose veins /ˌværɪˈkəʊs ˈveɪnz‖-koʊs-/ *n* [plural] a medical condition in which the VEINS in your leg become swollen and painful

var·ied /'veərid‖-ver-/ *adj* consisting of many different types of things or people: *a varied diet*

va·ri·e·ty /vəˈraɪəti/ *n* **1 a variety of** a lot of different types of things or people: *The college offers a wide variety of language courses.* **2** [U] when something consists of many different types of things or people, and seems interesting because of this: *I wanted a job with plenty of variety.* **3** [C] a type of something: *different varieties of lettuce*

var·i·ous /'veəriəs‖-ver-/ *adj* several different: *The coats are available in various colours.*

var·i·ous·ly /'veəriəsli‖-ver-/ *adv* in many different ways: *He's been variously called a genius and a madman.*

var·nish[1] /'vɑːnɪʃ‖'vɑːr-/ *n* [C,U] a clear liquid that is painted onto wood to protect it and give it a shiny surface → see also NAIL VARNISH

varnish[2] *v* [T] to paint something with VARNISH or NAIL POLISH

var·y /'veəri‖'veri/ *v* **1** [I] if things of the same type vary, they are all different from each other: *Prices vary from store to store.* | *The windows varied in size and shape.* **2** [I] to change: *His moods seem to vary a lot.* **3** [T] to regularly change what you do or the way that you do it: *You need to vary your diet.* —**varying** *adj*: *varying degrees of success*

vase /vɑːz‖veɪs, veɪz/ *n* [C] a container used for putting flowers in or as a decoration → see colour picture on page 474 and picture at CONTAINERS

va·sec·to·my /vəˈsektəmi/ *n* [C] a medical operation to prevent a man from having children

V

vast /vɑːst‖væst/ adj **1** extremely large: *vast deserts* **2 the vast majority** almost all of a group of people or things

vast·ly /'vɑːstli‖'væstli/ adv very greatly: *vastly improved performance*

vat /væt/ n [C] a very large container for keeping liquids in

VAT /ˌviː eɪ 'tiː, væt/ n [U] value added tax; a tax on goods and services in Britain and Europe

vault¹ /vɔːlt‖vɒːlt/ n [C] **1** a room in a bank with thick walls and a strong door, used for keeping money, jewels etc **2** a room where people from the same family are buried

vault², **vault over** v [T] to jump over something in one movement, using your hands or a pole to help you: *He vaulted over the fence and ran off.*

vault·ed /'vɔːltɪd‖'vɒːl-/ adj a vaulted ceiling, roof etc has ARCH*es* in it

VCR /ˌviː siː 'ɑː‖-'ɑːr/ n [C] *especially AmE* a video cassette recorder; a machine used for recording television programmes or playing VIDEO-TAPE*s*

VD /ˌviː 'diː/ n [U] venereal disease; a disease that is passed from one person to another during sex

VDU /ˌviː diː 'juː/ n [C] visual display unit; a machine like a television that shows the information from a computer

've /v, əv/ the short form of 'have': *We've finished.*

veal /viːl/ n [U] meat from a CALF (=a young cow)

veer /vɪə‖vɪr/ v [I] to change direction suddenly: *The car veered sharply to the left.*

veg /vedʒ/ v

   veg out *phr v* [I] *informal* to relax and not do anything

ve·gan /'viːgən‖'viːdʒən/ n [C] someone who does not eat meat, fish, eggs, or milk products

vege·ta·ble /'vedʒtəbəl/ n [C] a plant such as a CARROT, CABBAGE or potato, which is grown in order to be eaten

veg·e·tar·i·an /ˌvedʒ'teəriən‖-'ter-/ n [C] someone who does not eat meat or fish —**vegetarian** adj: *More and more people are becoming vegetarian.*

veg·e·ta·tion /ˌvedʒ'teɪʃən/ n [U] the plants, flowers, trees etc that grow in a particular area: *dense vegetation*

veg·gie /'vedʒi/ n [C] *BrE informal* a vegetarian —**veggie** adj

veg·gies /'vedʒiz/ n [plural] *AmE informal* vegetables

ve·he·ment /'viːəmənt/ adj having very strong feelings or opinions about something: *vehement opposition* —**vehemently** adv

ve·hi·cle /'viːɪkəl/ n [C] **1** a thing such as a car or bus that is used for carrying people or things from one place to another **2 a vehicle for (doing) sth** something that you use as a way of spreading ideas, opinions etc

veil

veil /veɪl/ n **1** [C] a thin piece of material that women wear to cover their faces: *a bridal veil* **2 a veil of secrecy/silence etc**

something that stops you finding out the truth about something: *A veil of mystery surrounded Gomez's death.* **3 a veil of mist/darkness etc** MIST, darkness etc that surrounds something and makes it difficult to see

veiled /veɪld/ adj veiled criticisms, threats etc are not said directly

vegetables

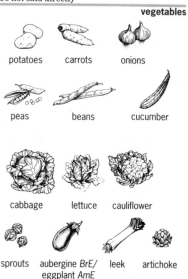

potatoes   carrots   onions

peas   beans   cucumber

cabbage   lettuce   cauliflower

sprouts   aubergine *BrE*/ eggplant *AmE*   leek   artichoke

pepper   tomatoes   celery   radishes

courgettes *BrE*/ zucchini *AmE*   marrow *BrE*/ squash *AmE*   pumpkin

vein /veɪn/ n [C] **1** one of the tubes through which blood flows to your heart from other parts of your body → compare ARTERY **2** one of the thin lines on a leaf or on the wing of an insect **3** a thin layer of coal, gold etc in rock **4** *literary* a particular style of speaking or writing about something: *She went on in the same vein for several minutes.*

Vel·cro /'velkrəʊ‖-kroʊ/ n [U] *trademark* a material used for fastening shoes, clothes etc, made from two special pieces of cloth that stick to each other

ve·lo·ci·ty /vɪ'lɒsɪti‖-'lɑː-/ n [C,U] *technical* the speed at which something moves in a particular direction: *the velocity of light*

ve·lour /və'lʊə‖-'lʊr/ n [U] heavy cloth that has a soft surface like VELVET

V

vel·vet /'velvₜt/ *n* [U] cloth with a soft surface on one side, used for making JACKETS, curtains etc

vel·vet·y /'velvₜti/ *adj* pleasantly smooth and soft: *a velvety voice*

ven·det·ta /ven'detə/ *n* [C] a QUARREL that continues for a long time in which one group or person tries to harm another because they feel angry about something that happened in the past

vend·ing ma·chine /'vendɪŋ mə,ʃiːn/ *n* [C] a machine that sells cigarettes, drinks etc

vend·or /'vendəll-ər/ *n* [C] someone who sells something, especially in the street: *street vendors*

ve·neer /vₐ'nɪəll-'nɪr/ *n* **1** [C,U] a thin layer of good quality wood that covers the outside of a piece of furniture that is made of a cheaper material: *rosewood veneer* **2 a veneer of** *formal* behaviour that hides someone's real feelings or character: *a veneer of politeness*

ven·e·ra·ble /'venₐrəbəl/ *adj formal* a venerable person or organization is very old and respected: *venerable institutions*

ven·e·rate /'venəreɪt/ *v* [T] *formal* to treat someone or something with great respect, especially because they are old: *The Chinese venerate their ancestors.*

ve·ne·re·al dis·ease /vₐ'nɪərɪəl dɪ,ziːzll-'nɪr-/ *n* [C,U] VD

ve·ne·tian blind /vₐ,niːʃən 'blaɪnd/ *n* [C] a set of long flat bars used for covering a window, which can be raised or lowered to let in light

ven·geance /'vendʒəns/ *n* **1** [U] when you do something violent or harmful to someone in order to punish them for hurting you or doing something bad to you: *a desire for vengeance* **2 with a vengeance** used to say that someone does something or something happens a lot, especially much more than before: *The hot weather is back with a vengeance.*

venge·ful /'vendʒfₐl/ *adj literary* wanting to punish someone who has hurt you

ven·i·son /'venₜzən, -sən/ *n* [U] the meat of a DEER

ven·om /'venəm/ *n* [U] **1** poison produced by some snakes, insects etc **2** great anger or hatred: *a speech full of venom* **—venomous** *adj*: *a venomous snake*

vent¹ /vent/ *n* [C] **1** a special hole through which smoke or smells can go out, or air can come in: *an air vent* **2 give vent to sth** *formal* to do something that shows how angry, annoyed etc you feel about something

vent² *v* [T] if you vent your anger or other strong feelings, you do something that shows how angry etc you feel

ven·ti·late /'ventₜleɪtll-tl-eɪt/ *v* [T] to allow air to come into and go out of a room, building etc **—ventilated** *adj* **—ventilation** /,ventₜ'leɪʃənll-tl-eɪ-/ *n* [U] *the ventilation system*

ven·ti·la·tor /'ventₜleɪtəll-tl-eɪtər/ *n* [C] a piece of equipment that pumps air into and out of someone's lungs so that they can breathe

ven·tril·o·quist /ven'trɪləkwₜst/ *n* [C] someone who speaks without moving their lips, in a way that makes the sound seem to come from somewhere else, especially from a PUPPET **—ventriloquism** *n* [U]

ven·ture¹ /'ventʃəll-ər/ *n* [C] a new activity that involves taking risks, especially in business: *The new venture was not a success.* → see also JOINT VENTURE

venture² *v formal* **1** [I] to go somewhere or do something new that may involve risks because you are not sure what will happen: *Kate rarely ventured beyond her nearest town.* | *He was the first member of his family to venture into politics.* **2** [T] to say something, especially when you are afraid of how other people may react to it: *No-one else ventured an opinion.*

ven·ue /'venjuː/ *n* [C] a place where a concert, sports game etc takes place: *a popular jazz venue*

Ve·nus /'viːnəs/ *n* [singular] the second PLANET from the sun

ve·ra·ci·ty /vₐ'ræsₜti/ *n* [U] *formal* the quality of being true

ve·ran·da, verandah /vₐ'rændə/ *n* [C] an open area with a floor and a roof, that is built on the side of a house

verb /vɜːbllvɜːrb/ *n* [C] a word or group of words used to say that someone does something or that something happens, for example 'go', 'eat', or 'finish'

verb·al /'vɜːbₐllvɜːr-/ *adj* **1** spoken: *a verbal agreement* **2** relating to words or using words: *verbal skills* **—verbally** *adv*

ver·ba·tim /vɜː'beɪtₜmllvɜːr-/ *adj, adv* repeating the actual words that were spoken or written

ver·bose /vɜː'bəʊsllvɜːr'boʊs/ *adj formal* using too many words

ver·dict /'vɜːdɪktllvɜːr-/ *n* [C] **1** an official decision in a court of law about whether someone is guilty: *Has the jury reached a verdict?* (=made a decision) **2** someone's opinion about something, after thinking about it or discussing it: *The general verdict was that the film wasn't very good.*

verge¹ /vɜːdʒllvɜːrdʒ/ *n* **be on the verge of** to be about to do something: *Helen was on the verge of tears.*

verge² *v*

verge on/upon sth *phr v* [T] to be very close to being something bad, stupid, crazy etc: *Their behaviour sometimes verged on insanity.*

ver·i·fy /'verₜfaɪ/ *v* [T] to check or prove that something is true or correct: *There's no way of verifying his story.* **—verification** /,verₜfₜ'keɪʃən/ *n* [U]

ver·i·ta·ble /'verₜtəbəl/ *adj formal* used to emphasize your description of someone or something: *a veritable masterpiece*

ver·min /'vɜːmₜnllvɜːr-/ *n* [plural] small animals such as rats that spread disease, damage crops etc, which people think should be killed

ver·nac·u·lar /vₐ'nækjₜləllvₐr'nækjₜlər/ *n* [singular] the language or DIALECT that the ordinary people in a country or area speak

ver·sa·tile /'vɜːsətaɪllvɜːrsətl/ *adj* **1** good at doing a lot of different things and able to learn new skills quickly and easily: *a versatile actor* **2** having many different uses: *a versatile computer system* **—versatility** /,vɜːsə'tɪlₜtill ,vɜːr-/ *n* [U]

verse /vɜːsllvɜːrs/ *n* [C] **1** a set of lines of words that forms one part of a poem or song: *the last verse of the poem* **2** [U] words arranged in the form of poetry: *a book of verse* **3** [C] a numbered sentence or group of sentences in the Bible

versed / vɜːst‖vɜːrst / *adj* **be (well) versed in** *formal* to know a lot about a subject or be skilled in doing something: *lawyers who are well-versed in these matters*

ver·sion / 'vɜːʃən‖'vɜːrʒən/ *n* [C] **1** a form of something that is different from other forms: *the original version of the film 'Gone with the Wind'* | *a new version of the Beatles 'Hey Jude'* **2** someone's description of what happened: *The newspapers all gave different versions of the story.*

ver·sus / 'vɜːsəs‖'vɜːr-/ written abbreviation **vs** *prep* **1** used to say that two people or teams are playing against each other in a game or fighting a court case: *Connors versus McEnroe* **2** used to compare two different things or ideas, and deciding which one is more important, better etc: *quantity versus quality*

ver·te·bra / 'vɜːtɪbrə‖'vɜːr-/ *n* [C], *plural* **vertebrae** /-briː, -breɪ/ one of the small hollow bones down the centre of your back

ver·ti·cal / 'vɜːtɪkəl‖'vɜːr-/ *adj* pointing straight up at an angle of 90 degrees from the ground or from another line: *a vertical rock face* —**vertically** /-kli/ *adv* ➔ compare HORIZONTAL

ver·ti·go / 'vɜːtɪɡəʊ‖'vɜːrtɪɡoʊ/ *n* [U] when someone feels very uncomfortable and sick because of looking down from a very high place

verve / vɜːv‖vɜːrv/ *n* [U] *formal* if you do something with verve, they do it in an exciting and cheerful way with a lot of energy

ve·ry¹ / 'veri/ *adv* **1** used to emphasize an adjective or adverb: *It's a very good book.* | *John gets embarrassed very easily.* | *I miss her very much.* **2** **not very good/difficult/happy etc** not good, difficult, pleased etc: *I'm not very good at spelling.* | *"Was the game exciting?" "Not very."* **3** **very well** *spoken* used when you are agreeing to do something or allow something, especially when you do not want to: *"Are you coming?" "Oh, very well, if I must."*

USAGE NOTE: very

Don't use **very** with adjectives and adverbs that already have a strong meaning, such as **huge**, **terrible** or **starving**: *By the time I got home I was exhausted.* (not 'very exhausted'). Use **much** not **very**, to make the comparative form of an adjective. You can say 'very big' or 'the very biggest', but not 'very bigger'. The correct way of saying this is **much bigger**.

---

very² *adj* used to emphasize a noun in certain phrases: **the very beginning/end** *Start again from the very beginning.*

ves·sel / 'vesəl/ *n* [C] **1** *formal* a ship or large boat **2** a container for keeping liquids in ➔ see also BLOOD VESSEL

vest / vest/ *n* [C] **1** *BrE* a piece of underwear without SLEEVES that you wear under a shirt **2** *AmE* a piece of clothing without SLEEVES that has buttons down the front, worn over a shirt, especially as part of a suit; WAISTCOAT *BrE* ➔ see colour picture on page 113

vested in·ter·est / ˌvestɪd 'ɪntrɪst / *n* [C] if you have a vested interest in something happening, you have a strong reason for wanting it to happen because you will get money or advantages from it

ves·ti·bule / 'vestɪbjuːl/ *n* [C] *formal* a wide PASSAGE or small room inside the front door of a public building

ves·tige / 'vestɪdʒ/ *n* [C] a small part or amount of something that still remains, when most of it no longer exists: *the last vestiges of the British Empire*

vet /vet/ *n* [C] **1** someone who is trained to give medical care and treatment to sick animals: *We had to take our cat to the vet.* **2** *informal* someone who was a soldier, sailor etc in a war: *Vietnam vets*

vet·er·an / 'vetərən/ *n* [C] **1** someone who was a soldier, sailor etc in a war **2** someone who has had a lot of experience of doing something: *veteran Hollywood entertainer Bob Hope*

vet·er·i·na·ri·an / ˌvetərɪ'neəriən‖-'ner-/ *n* [C] *AmE* a VET

vet·er·i·na·ry / 'vetərɪˌnərɪ‖-neri/ *adj* *technical* relating to the medical care and treatment of sick animals

ve·to¹ / 'viːtəʊ‖-toʊ/ *v* [T] to officially refuse to allow something to happen, especially something that other people or organizations have agreed: *Britain and the US vetoed the proposal.*

veto² *n* [C,U], *plural* **vetos** when someone officially refuses to allow something to happen: *France has threatened to use its veto.*

vex / veks/ *v* [T] *old-fashioned* to make someone feel annoyed or worried

vexed / vekst/ *adj* **1** **vexed question/issue/problem** a question or problem that is difficult to deal with and causes a lot of problems or discussion **2** *old-fashioned* worried or annoyed

vi·a / 'vaɪə,'viːə/ *prep* **1** travelling through or stopping at a place when you are going to another place: *We're flying to Denver via Chicago.* **2** using a particular machine, system, person etc to send or broadcast something: *The concert was broadcast around the world via satellite.*

vi·a·ble / 'vaɪəbəl/ *adj* something that is viable is able to succeed or do what it is intended to do without any problems: *a viable alternative to the petrol engine* —**viability** / ˌvaɪə'bɪlɪti/ *n* [U]

vi·a·duct / 'vaɪədʌkt / *n* [C] a long high bridge across a valley

vibe / vaɪb/ *n* [C usually plural] *informal* the feelings that you get from a person, group, situation etc

vi·brant / 'vaɪbrənt/ *adj* **1** full of excitement, energy, and ENTHUSIASM: *a vibrant personality* **2** a vibrant colour is very bright and looks very attractive

---

GRAMMAR NOTE: 'if' clauses (2)
When you imagine a present situation that is not real, or a future situation that is very unlikely, use **if** + **simple past**: *If he really loved you, he wouldn't treat you like this.* (=he does not love you). | *If I won a million dollars on the lottery, I would buy a yacht.* Use **would** in the other part of the sentence.

vi·brate /vaɪˈbreɪt‖ˈvaɪbreɪt/ v [I,T] to shake or make something shake with small fast movements: *The vocal chords vibrate as air passes over them.*

vi·bra·tion /vaɪˈbreɪʃən/ n [C,U] a continuous slight shaking movement: *vibration caused by passing traffic*

vic·ar /ˈvɪkəl-ər/ n [C] a priest in the Church of England

vic·ar·age /ˈvɪkərɪdʒ/ n [C] the house where a vicar lives

vi·car·i·ous /vɪˈkeəriəs‖vaɪˈker-/ adj vicarious feelings are feelings that you get by watching or reading about someone else doing something —**vicariousness** n [U] —**vicariously** adv

vice /vaɪs/ n **1** [C] a bad habit or a bad part of someone's character: *Smoking is my only vice.* **2** [U] criminal activities that involve sex or drugs **3** [C] *BrE* a tool used to hold something firmly while you do work on it; VISE *AmE*

vice pres·i·dent /ˌ. ˈ.../ n [C] **1** the person who is next in rank to the president of a country **2** *AmE* someone who is responsible for a particular part of a company: *the vice president of marketing*

vice ver·sa /ˌvaɪs ˈvɜːsə, ˌvaɪsi-‖-ɜːr-/ adv used to talk about the opposite of a situation you have just described: *It is socially acceptable for older men to marry younger women, but not vice versa.*

vi·cin·i·ty /vɪˈsɪnɪti/ n in the vicinity (of) *formal* in the area around a place; near: *The car was found in the vicinity of the bus station.*

vi·cious /ˈvɪʃəs/ adj **1** violent and dangerous, and likely to hurt someone: *a vicious attack* **2** cruel and deliberately trying to upset someone or make other people have a very bad opinion of them: *a vicious rumour* —**viciously** adv —**viciousness** n [U]

vicious cir·cle /ˌ.. ˈ../ n [singular] a situation in which one problem causes another problem which then causes the first problem again

vic·tim /ˈvɪktɪm/ n [C] someone who has been hurt or killed by someone or something: *victims of the earthquake | He terrorized his victims.*

vic·tim·ize (also **-ise** *BrE*) /ˈvɪktɪmaɪz/ v [T] to deliberately treat someone unfairly: *People with AIDS have been victimized and abused at work.* —**victimization** /ˌvɪktɪmaɪˈzeɪʃən‖-mə-/ n [U]

vic·tor /ˈvɪktəl-ər/ n [C] *formal* the winner of a battle or competition

Vic·to·ri·an /vɪkˈtɔːriən/ adj connected with the period in British history between 1837 and 1901: *Victorian buildings* —**Victorian** n [C]

vic·to·ri·ous /vɪkˈtɔːriəs/ adj successful in a battle or competition

vic·to·ry /ˈvɪktəri/ n [C,U] when a player, team, party etc wins a game, election, battle etc: *Napoleon's armies won a great victory | the Lakers' victory over the Celtics* → opposite DEFEAT²

vid·e·o¹ /ˈvɪdiəʊ‖-dioʊ/ n **1** [C,U] a TAPE of a film or television programme, or a TAPE that you can use for recording films, programmes etc: *Do you want to watch a video tonight? | The movie is now available on video.* → see colour picture on page 474 **2** [C] *BrE* a video cassette recorder → see colour picture on page 474 **3** [U] when people use video equipment and cameras to record what is happening or to play VIDEOTAPES: *Many teachers now use video in the classroom.*

video² v [T] to record something using a video cassette recorder or a camera

video cas·sette re·cord·er /ˌ... .ˈ. ˌ..‖video re·cord·er** /ˈ... ˌ../ **VCR** n [C] a machine used for recording television programmes or playing videotapes → see colour picture on page 474

video game /ˈ... ˌ./ n [C] a game in which you move images on a screen by pressing electronic controls

vid·e·o·tape¹ /ˈvɪdiəʊˌteɪp‖-dioʊ-/ n [C] a long narrow band of MAGNETIC material in a plastic container, on which films, television programmes etc can be recorded

videotape² v [T] to record something using a video cassette recorder or a camera

vie /vaɪ/ v [I] **vied**, **vying** to compete with another person, company etc in order to get something: *The brothers vied for her attention.*

view¹ /vjuː/ n **1** [C] your opinion about something, especially about a serious or important subject: *the view that sex before marriage is wrong | people with different political views | in my/her/John's etc view* (=used when giving someone's opinion): *The judge said that in his view the trial should never have taken place.* **2** [C] everything that you can see from a place: *There was a beautiful view of the mountains from our hotel room.* **3** [singular] how well you can see something: *They had a really good view of the stage.* **4** [C] a photograph or picture that shows a beautiful or interesting place: *postcards showing views of New York* **5** [U] a position in which something can be seen: **be in/come into view** *The harbour lights came into view.* **6** **in full view** of happening where people can clearly see: *She began screaming and hitting him, in full view of all the other guests.* **7** **be on view** if something is on view, it is being shown, especially as part of an EXHIBITION **8** **in view of** *formal* used when you are mentioning a reason or something important that affects your decision: *In view of your previous good behaviour we have decided not to take any further action.*

USAGE NOTE: view, scenery, scene, and **landscape**

View is countable, and is used to talk about all the things you can see at a distance from a particular place: *a magnificent view of the harbour.* **Scenery** is uncountable, and is used to talk about all the mountains, rivers, forests etc that you see around you, especially when they are beautiful: *We stopped to admire the scenery.* **Scene** is uncountable, and is what you can see either close up or at a distance, and might include people and movement: *a happy scene of children playing.* A **landscape** is all the land you can see around you, either in the country or the city, with its hills, buildings, fields etc: *a typical desert landscape | a depressing industrial landscape.*

---

view² v [T] *formal* **1** to think of someone or something in a particular way: *Women were viewed as sex objects.* **2** to look at or watch something: *The scenery was spectacular, especially when viewed from high ground.*

view·er /ˈvjuːəl-ər/ n [C] someone who watches a television programme: *The series is watched by millions of viewers.*

vig·il /'vɪdʒɪl/ *n* [C,U] when people stand or sit quietly somewhere, especially in order to protest about something or to stay with someone who is ill: *A crowd of people held a vigil outside the embassy.*

vig·i·lant /'vɪdʒɪlənt/ *adj* watching carefully and paying attention, so that you notice anything dangerous or illegal: *People should remain vigilant at all times and report any suspicious packages to the police.* —**vigilance** *n* [C]

vig·i·lan·te /,vɪdʒɪ'lænti/ *n* [C] a member of an unofficial group of people who join together to catch and punish criminals

vig·or /'vɪgər/ *n* the American spelling of vigour

vig·o·rous /'vɪgərəs/ *adj* **1** using a lot of effort and energy: *vigorous exercise* **2** saying your opinions very strongly and trying hard to persuade people that you are right: *a vigorous campaigner for women's rights*

vig·our *BrE*, **vigor** *AmE* /'vɪgər/ *n* [U] when people use a lot of effort and energy to try to do something

vile /vaɪl/ *adj* very unpleasant: *The food tasted vile.*

vil·i·fy /'vɪlɪfaɪ/ *v* [T] *formal* to say bad things about someone in order to make other people have a bad opinion of them: *He was vilified by the press.*

vil·la /'vɪlə/ *n* [C] a house with a garden in the countryside or near the sea, used especially for holidays

vil·lage /'vɪlɪdʒ/ *n* [C] a place where there is a group of houses with a church, shop, school etc in the countryside, which is smaller than a town: *She was born in the village of Arkesden in Essex.*

vil·lag·er /'vɪlɪdʒər/ *n* [C] someone who lives in a village

vil·lain /'vɪlən/ *n* [C] **1** a bad character in a story, film etc **2** *BrE informal* a criminal

vin·di·cate /'vɪndɪkeɪt/ *v* [T] *formal* if you are vindicated, you are proved to be right after other people have said you were wrong —**vindication** /,vɪndɪ'keɪʃən/ *n* [singular, U]

vin·dic·tive /vɪn'dɪktɪv/ *adj* deliberately cruel and unfair —**vindictively** *adv* —**vindictiveness** *n* [U]

vine /vaɪn/ *n* [C] a climbing plant, especially one that produces GRAPES

vin·e·gar /'vɪnɪgər/ *n* [U] a liquid with a strong sour taste, used for preserving vegetables and made from sour wine or MALT

vine·yard /'vɪnjəd, -jɑːd/ *n* [C] an area of land where GRAPES are grown to make wine

vin·tage¹ /'vɪntɪdʒ/ *adj* **1** vintage wine is good quality wine that is made in a particular year **2** a vintage car was made in the early part of the twentieth century **3** used to emphasize that something is one of the best of its kind: *vintage recordings*

vintage² *n* [C] a particular year in which a wine is made

vi·nyl /'vaɪnɪl/ *n* [U] a type of strong plastic

vi·o·la /vi'əʊlə/ *n* [C] a wooden musical instrument shaped like a VIOLIN but larger and with a lower sound

vi·o·late /'vaɪəleɪt/ *v* [T] *formal* **1** to disobey a law, agreement etc **2** if someone's rights have been violated, they have been ignored **3** to treat something without respect and damage or spoil it —**violation** /,vaɪə'leɪʃən/ *n* [C,U] *human rights violations*

vi·o·lence /'vaɪələns/ *n* [U] **1** when people use force to attack other people and try to hurt or kill them: *There's too much violence on TV these days.* **2** when something happens suddenly with a lot of force: *the violence of the storm* **3** when someone has very strong feelings, and is very angry, hates another person very much etc: *the violence of their emotions*

vi·o·lent /'vaɪələnt/ *adj* **1** attacking people and trying to hurt or kill them: *violent criminals* | *a violent attack on a defenceless old woman* **2** a violent film, play etc is one that shows people trying to hurt or kill each other **3** having very strong and often angry feelings about someone or something: *a violent argument* **4** a violent storm, EARTHQUAKE etc happens with a lot of force and often causes a lot of damage **5** violent pains are very severe —**violently** *adv*

vi·o·let /'vaɪələt/ *n* **1** [C] a small sweet-smelling dark purple flower **2** [U] a bluish-purple colour —**violet** *adj*

vi·o·lin /,vaɪə'lɪn/ *n* [C] a musical instrument that you play by pulling a special stick across the strings, while holding it under your chin

VIP /,viː aɪ 'piː/ *n* [C] a very important person; someone who is famous or powerful and receives special treatment

vi·per /'vaɪpər/ *n* [C] a small poisonous snake

vir·gin¹ /'vɜːdʒɪn, 'vɜːr-/ *n* [C] someone who has never had sex

virgin² *adj* virgin land, forest etc is still in its natural condition and has not been used or spoiled by people

vir·gin·i·ty /vɜː'dʒɪnɪti, vɜːr-/ *n* **lose your virginity** to have sex for the first time

Vir·go /'vɜːgəʊ, 'vɜːrgoʊ/ *n* [C,U] the sign of the ZODIAC of people who are born between August 23rd and September 22nd, or someone who belongs to this sign

vir·ile /'vɪraɪl, 'vɪrəl/ *adj* a man who is virile is strong in a sexually attractive way —**virility** /vɪ'rɪlɪti/ *n* [U]

vir·tu·al /'vɜːtʃuəl, 'vɜːr-/ *adj* **1** used to say that something is almost true: *He became a virtual prisoner in his own home.* **2** using virtual reality: *a virtual library*

vir·tu·al·ly /'vɜːtʃuəli, 'vɜːr-/ *adv* almost completely: *The town was virtually destroyed.*

virtual re·al·i·ty /,... .'.../ *n* [U] when a computer makes you feel as though you are in a real situation by showing images and sounds

vir·tue /'vɜːtʃuː, 'vɜːr-/ *n* **1** [C,U] an advantage that makes something better or more useful than other things: *the virtues of a non-meat diet* **2** [C] a good quality in someone's character: *Stella has many virtues.* **3** **by virtue of** *formal* because of: *people who get promoted by virtue of their age* **4** [U] *formal* morally good behaviour: *a life of virtue*

vir·tu·o·so /,vɜːtʃu'əʊsəʊ, vɜːrtʃu'oʊsoʊ/ *n* [C] someone who is extremely skilful at doing something, especially at playing a musical instrument: *a piano virtuoso* —**virtuoso** *adj*: *a virtuoso performance*

vir·tu·ous /ˈvɜːtʃuəs‖ˈvɜːr-/ *adj* behaving in a way that is morally good

vir·u·lent /ˈvɪrˤlənt/ *adj* **1** *formal* hating someone or something very much, or criticizing them very severely: *a virulent critic of Thatcherism* **2** a virulent poison or disease is very dangerous and affects people very quickly

vi·rus /ˈvaɪərəs‖ˈvaɪrəs/ *n* [C] **1** a very small living thing that causes diseases, or an illness caused by this: *the common cold virus* **2** a set of instructions secretly put into a computer, that can destroy information stored in the computer

vi·sa /ˈviːzə/ *n* [C] an official mark that is put on your PASSPORT, that allows you to enter or leave another country: *She's here on a student visa.*

vis-à-vis /ˌviːz ɑː ˈviː, ˌviːz ə ˈviː/ *prep formal* concerning or compared with: *Where do we stand vis-à-vis last week's change in the law.*

vis·cous /ˈvɪskəs/ *adj technical* a viscous liquid is thick and does not flow easily —**viscosity** / vɪsˈkɒsˤtiǁ-ˈkɑː-/ *n* [U]

vise /vaɪs/ *n* [C] *AmE* a tool that holds an object firmly so that you can work on it using both hands; VICE *BrE*

vis·i·bil·i·ty /ˌvɪzˤˈbɪlˤti/ *n* [U] the distance that you can see, especially when this is affected by the weather conditions: *There is poor visibility on many roads due to heavy fog.*

vis·i·ble /ˈvɪzˤbəl/ *adj* something that is visible can be seen or noticed: *The lights of the city were clearly visible below them.| a visible change in her attitude* → opposite INVISIBLE —**visibly** *adv*: *She was visibly shaken.*

vi·sion /ˈvɪʒən/ *n* **1** [C] an idea or picture in your mind of what a future situation could be like: *Martin Luther King's vision of a better world* **2** [U] the ability to see: *Will the operation improve my vision?* **3** [U] the ability to imagine what the future could be like and how important changes can be achieved: *We need a leader with vision.* **4** [C] something you see in a dream as part of a religious experience

vi·sion·a·ry /ˈvɪʒənərɪǁ-neri/ *adj* having great ideas of how the world can be in the future, especially how it can be improved —**visionary** *n* [C]

vis·it[1] /ˈvɪzˤt/ *v* **1** [I,T] to go and spend time with someone: *My aunt is coming to visit us next week.* **2** [I,T] to go to a place and spend a short period of time there: *The Chinese Foreign Minister is visiting Moscow this week.* **3** [I] *AmE informal* to have a conversation with someone: **+ with** *We watched TV while Mom visited with Mrs. Levison.*

visit[2] *n* **1** [C] when someone visits a place or person **pay a visit** (=visit somewhere) **2** [singular] *AmE informal* a conversation with someone: *Barbara and I had a nice long visit.*

vis·it·or /ˈvɪzˤtəlˤ-ər/ *n* [C] someone who visits a place or person: *a guidebook for visitors to Mexico City*

vi·sor /ˈvaɪzəlˤ-ər/ *n* [C] **1** the part of a HELMET (=a kind of hard hat) that can be lowered to protect your face **2** the curved part of a hat or HELMET that sticks out above your eyes, or a special hat that consists only of this **3** a flat piece of material in the front window of a car

that you pull down to keep the sun out of your eyes

vis·ta /ˈvɪstə/ *n* [C] *literary* a view, especially over a large area of land

vi·su·al /ˈvɪʒuəl/ *adj* relating to seeing or your ability to see: *The movie has a strong visual impact.| the visual arts* (=arts such as painting, not music or literature) —**visually** *adv*

visual aid /ˌ... '. './ *n* [C] something such as a picture, film etc that is used to help people learn

vi·su·al·ize (also **-ise** *BrE*) /ˈvɪʒuəlaɪz/ *v* [T] to form a picture of someone or something in your mind; imagine: *I tried to visualize the house as she had described it.* —**visualization** /ˌvɪʒuəlaɪˈzeɪʃənǁ-lə-/ *n* [U]

vi·tal /ˈvaɪtl/ *adj* **1** extremely important or necessary: *His evidence was vital to the defence case.| It is absolutely vital that you do as I say.* **2** having a lot of energy, in a way that seems attractive

vi·tal·i·ty /vaɪˈtælˤti/ *n* [U] energy and cheerfulness: *Even though she's in her 80s, she's still full of vitality.*

vi·tal·ly /ˈvaɪtl-i/ *adv* **vitally important** extremely important or necessary

vit·a·min /ˈvɪtəmˤn, ˈvaɪ-ǁˈvaɪ-/ *n* [C] a chemical substance found in food that is necessary for good health: *The doctor told me to get more vitamin A and vitamin C.*

vit·ri·ol·ic /ˌvɪtriˈɒlɪkǁ-ˈɑːlɪk/ *adj formal* criticizing someone or something very strongly and often cruelly: *a vitriolic attack*

vi·va·cious /vˤˈveɪʃəs/ *adj* someone, especially a woman, who is vivacious has a lot of energy and a happy attractive way of behaving

viv·id /ˈvɪvˤd/ *adj* **1** vivid descriptions, memories, dreams etc are so clear that they seem real: *a vivid description of her childhood in Cornwall* **2** vivid colours are very bright —**vividly** *adv*

viv·i·sec·tion /ˌvɪvˤˈsekʃən/ *n* [U] when scientists operate on living animals in order to do scientific tests

vix·en /ˈvɪksən/ *n* [C] a female FOX

vo·cab·u·la·ry /vəˈkæbjˤləri, vəʊ-ǁ-leri, voʊ-/ *n* **1** [C,U] all the words that someone knows or uses: *Reading is a good way to increase your vocabulary.* **2** [singular] all the words in a language or all the words that are used in a type of language: *new words coming into the English vocabulary| business vocabulary* **3** [singular] a list of words with explanations of what they mean, at the back of a book for learning a foreign language

vo·cal /ˈvəʊkəlǁˈvoʊ-/ *adj* **1** speaking publicly about your opinions in a way that makes a lot of people notice you: *Environmental groups have become increasingly vocal.* **2** relating to the human voice, especially in singing: *vocal music* —**vocally** *adv*

vocal cords /ˈ... ., ,... './ *n* [plural] thin pieces of muscle in your throat that produce sound when you speak or sing

vo·cal·ist /ˈvəʊkəlˤstǁˈvoʊ-/ *n* [C] someone who sings, especially with a group of people who play POP songs

vo·cals /ˈvəʊkəlzǁˈvoʊ-/ *n* [plural] the part of a piece of music that is sung rather than played on an instrument: *The song features Elton John on vocals.*

vo·ca·tion /vəʊˈkeɪʃənǁvoʊ-/ *n* [C,U] the feeling that the purpose of your life is to do a particular kind of work, or a job that gives you this feeling: *Teaching isn't just a job to her – it's her vocation.*

vo·ca·tion·al /vəʊˈkeɪʃənəlǁvoʊ-/ *adj* concerned with teaching or learning the skills needed to do a job: *vocational training*

vo·cif·er·ous /vəˈsɪfərəs, vəʊ-ǁvoʊ-/ *adj formal* saying your opinions publicly in a way that makes a lot of people notice you: *Professor Black is one of his most vociferous critics.* — **vociferously** *adv*

vod·ka /ˈvɒdkəǁˈvɑːdkə/ *n* [U] a strong alcoholic drink from Russia

vogue /vəʊgǁvoʊg/ *n* [singular,U] when something is fashionable and popular: **be in vogue** (=be fashionable): *Japanese food is very much in vogue these days.*

voice¹ /vɔɪs/ *n* **1** [C,U] the sound you make when you speak or sing: *I could hear Jo's voice outside my window.* | *Pavarotti has an amazing voice.* | **lose your voice** (=become unable to speak): *She'd been shouting so much she'd almost lost her voice.* | **raise your voice** (=speak louder, often because you are angry): *There's no need to raise your voice. I can hear you perfectly well.* | **sb's voice breaks** (=a boy's voice changes and becomes deeper like a man's) **2** [singular] a person, organization, newspaper etc that says publicly what a group of people think or want: *By the early 1960s, King had become the voice of the Civil Rights Movement.* **3** [C,U] someone's opinion about what should happen or be done: **have a voice in sth** (=be able to give your opinion and take part in deciding what should be done): *Parents should have a voice in deciding how their children are educated.* **4 the voice of reason/experience etc** when someone speaks in a way that seems sensible, that shows they have had a lot of experience of doing something etc **5 keep your voice down** *spoken* used to tell someone to be quiet because other people will hear them

voice² *v* [T] *formal* to tell people your opinions or feelings about something

voice·mail /ˈvɔɪsˌmeɪl/ *n* [U] a system that records telephone calls so that you can listen to them later

void¹ /vɔɪd/ *adj* **1** an agreement, result, or ticket that is void is not legally or officially acceptable → see also NULL AND VOID **2 be void of** *especially literary* to be completely without something: *Her eyes were void of all expression.*

void² *n* [singular] **1** a feeling that you no longer have something you need that is important to you: *Their son's death left a void in their lives.* **2** an empty space where nothing exists

vol·a·tile /ˈvɒlətaɪlǁˈvɑːlətl/ *adj* **1** a volatile situation is likely to change suddenly **2** a volatile person is someone whose MOODS change suddenly and who quickly becomes angry — **volatility** /ˌvɒləˈtɪlɪtiǁˌvɑː-/ *n* [U]

vol·ca·no /vɒlˈkeɪnəʊǁvɑːlˈkeɪnoʊ/ *n* [C], *plural* **volcanoes**, *or* **volcanos** a mountain that sometimes explodes and makes smoke and hot melted rock come out of the top: *The island has several active volcanoes.* — **volcanic** /-ˈkænɪk/ *adj*: *volcanic rocks*

vole /vəʊlǁvoʊl/ *n* [C] a small animal like a mouse that lives in fields and near rivers

vo·li·tion /vəˈlɪʃənǁvoʊ-, və-/ *n* [U] *formal* **of your own volition** because you want to do something and not because you are forced to do it: *She left the company of her own volition.*

vol·ley /ˈvɒliǁˈvɑːli/ *n* [C] **1** a large number of bullets, rocks etc fired or thrown at the same time: *a volley of shots* **2** **a volley of questions/abuse etc** a lot of questions, INSULTS etc that are all said together one after the other **3** when someone hits or kicks a ball before it touches the ground

vol·ley·ball /ˈvɒlibɔːlǁˈvɑːlibɑːl/ *n* [U] a game in which two teams hit a ball to each other across a net with their hands and try not to let it touch the ground

volt /vəʊltǁvoʊlt/ *n* [C] a unit for measuring the force of an electric current

volt·age /ˈvəʊltɪdʒǁˈvoʊl-/ *n* [C,U] the force of an electric current measured in volts

vol·ume /ˈvɒljuːmǁˈvɑːljəm/ *n* **1** [U] the amount of sound produced by a television, radio etc: *Can you turn down the volume on the TV?* **2** [C,U] the total amount of something: *an increase in the volume of traffic* **3** [C] a book, especially one that is part of a series of books: *a 12 volume set of poetry* **4** [U] the amount of space that an object contains or that a substance fills

vo·lu·mi·nous /vəˈluːmɪnəs, vəˈljuː-ǁvəˈluː-/ *adj formal* very large: *a voluminous skirt*

vol·un·ta·ry /ˈvɒləntəriǁˈvɑːlənteri/ *adj* **1** working without being paid, especially to help people: *voluntary work* | *voluntary organizations* **2** something that is voluntary is done because you want to do it, not because someone says you must do it: *voluntary contributions* — **voluntarily** /ˈvɒləntərɪli, ˌvɒlənˈterɪliǁˌvɑːlənˈterɪli/ *adv*

vol·un·teer¹ /ˌvɒlənˈtɪəǁˌvɑːlənˈtɪr/ *v* **1** [I,T] to offer to do something without being told that you must do it: *Ernie volunteered to wash the dishes.* **2** [I] to join the army, navy etc, without being told that you must join: *When the war began, my brother immediately volunteered.* **3** [T] *formal* to tell someone about something without being asked: *None of them was willing to volunteer an opinion.*

volunteer² *n* [C] **1** someone who does work without being paid: *The helplines are manned by volunteers.* **2** someone who offers to do something without being told that they must do it: *I need someone to help me with the barbecue. Any volunteers?*

vo·lup·tu·ous /vəˈlʌptʃuəs/ *adj* a voluptuous woman has large breasts and an attractively curved body

V

GRAMMAR NOTE: 'if' clauses (3)
When you imagine a past situation that did not really happen, use **if + past perfect**: *If they had offered me the job, I would have taken it.* (=but they did not offer me it). Use **would have + past participle** in the other part of the sentence.

vom·it[1] /'vɒmɪt‖'vɑː-/ v [I,T] *formal* if you vomit, food comes up from your stomach and comes out of your mouth

vomit[2] n [U] the food or drink that comes out of your mouth when you vomit

voo·doo /'vuːduː/ n [U] magical beliefs and practices used as a form of religion, especially in parts of Africa and the Caribbean

vo·ra·cious /və'reɪʃəs, vɒ-‖vɔː-, və-/ adj *formal* wanting to eat a lot or do something a lot, in a way that seems surprising: *He had a voracious appetite.* —**voracity** /-'ræsɪti/ n [U]

vote[1] /vəʊt‖voʊt/ n [C] **1** when someone shows that they support a particular person, party, plan etc by making a mark on a piece of paper, raising their hands etc: *The Communist Party came third with 421,775 votes.* | *The bill was passed by 319 votes to 316.* **2** when a group of people votes so that a decision can be made about something: *next month's vote on constitutional reform* | **take a vote** (=decide about something by voting) **3 the vote a)** the total number of votes or people who can vote: *The Nationalists won 25% of the vote.* **b)** the right to vote: *In France, women didn't get the vote until 1945.*

vote[2] v [I,T] to show which person you want to elect, which plan you support, who you want to win a particular prize etc by making a mark on a piece of paper, raising your hand etc: **vote for/against** *70% of the population voted for independence.* | **vote to do sth** *Congress voted to increase taxes.*

vot·er /'vəʊtə‖'voʊtər/ n [C] someone who votes or has the right to vote

vouch /vaʊtʃ/ v

vouch for sb/sth *phr v* [T] to say something is definitely true or good, or that someone is honest and will behave properly

vouch·er /'vaʊtʃə‖-ər/ n [C] a kind of ticket that can be used instead of money to pay for things

vow[1] /vaʊ/ v [T] to make a serious promise that you will definitely do something or not do something: *I vowed that I would never drink again.*

vow[2] n [C] a serious promise: *marriage vows* | *She made a vow to herself that she would never go back.*

vow·el /'vaʊəl/ n [C] the sounds shown by letters a, e, i, o, or u, and sometimes y

voy·age /'vɔɪɪdʒ/ n [C] a long trip, especially in a ship or space vehicle: *The voyage from England to America took several weeks.*

voy·eur /vwɑː'jɜː‖-'jɜːr/ n [C] someone who gets sexual pleasure from secretly watching other people's sexual activities —**voyeurism** n [U] —**voyeuristic** /ˌvwɑːjə'rɪstɪk◂/ adj

vs the written abbreviation of VERSUS

vul·gar /'vʌlgə‖-ər/ adj **1** behaving in a way that is not polite, especially by talking in a rude way: *vulgar jokes* **2** *especially BrE* not showing good judgement about what is attractive or suitable: *Some of the ornaments looked rather vulgar.* —**vulgarity** /vʌl'gærɪti/ n [U]

vul·ne·ra·ble /'vʌlnərəbəl/ adj easily harmed, hurt, or attacked: *The army was in a vulnerable position.* | *She looked so young and vulnerable.* —**vulnerability** /ˌvʌlnərə'bɪlɪti/ n [U]

vul·ture /'vʌltʃə‖-ər/ n [C] a large wild bird that eats dead animals

vy·ing /'vaɪ-ɪŋ/ v the present participle of VIE

V

Ww

W, w the letter 'w'

W /ˈdʌbəlju:/ **1** the written abbreviation of WEST or WESTERN **2** the written abbreviation of WATT

wack·y /ˈwæki/ *adj informal* silly in an amusing way

wad /wɒd‖wɑːd/ *n* [C] **1** a thick pile of thin sheets of something, especially money: *a wad of dollar bills* **2** a thick soft mass of material that has been pressed together: *a wad of cotton*

wad·dle /ˈwɒdl‖ˈwɑːdl/ *v* [I] if short fat people or ducks waddle, they walk with short steps, swinging their body from one side to the other

wade /weɪd/ *v* [I,T] to walk through water: *We waded across the stream.*
  wade through sth *phr v* [T] to read something that is very long and boring

wa·fer /ˈweɪfə‖-ər/ *n* [C] a very thin BISCUIT

waf·fle¹ /ˈwɒfəl‖ˈwɑː-/ *n* **1** [C] a flat cake with a pattern of holes in it, often eaten for breakfast in the US **2** [U] *informal* when someone talks or writes about something using a lot of words without saying anything important

waffle² *v* [I] *informal* to talk or write using a lot of words without saying anything important: *What's he waffling about now?*

waft /wɑːft, wɒft‖wɑːft, wæft/ *v* [I,T] to move gently through the air: *The smell of bacon wafted up from the kitchen.*

wag /wæg/ *v* [I,T] **-gged, -gging 1** if a dog wags it tail, it shakes its tail from one side to another **2** to shake your finger forwards and backwards, especially in order to tell someone not to do something

wage¹ /weɪdʒ/ *n* [singular] also **wages** [plural] the amount of money that someone is paid every week by their employer, especially someone who works in a factory or a shop: *Wages keep going up.* | *wage demands* | *the average weekly wage* —compare SALARY

wage² *v* [T] to fight a war or battle against someone, or take part in a CAMPAIGN to do something: *The rebels have been waging a nine-year war against the government.*

wa·ger /ˈweɪdʒə‖-ər/ *n* [C] *old-fashioned* when you try to win money by guessing the result of a race, game etc; a BET —**wager** *v* [T]

wag·gle /ˈwægəl/ *v* [I,T] to move something quickly from side to side or up and down

wag·on /ˈwægən/ *n* [C] **1** a strong vehicle with four wheels, especially pulled by horses **2** *BrE* a vehicle used for carrying goods, which is pulled by a train; FREIGHT CAR *AmE* **3 be on the wagon** *informal* if someone is on the wagon, they have stopped drinking alcohol

waif /weɪf/ *n* [C] *literary* someone, especially a child, who is small and thin, and needs looking after because they have no home

wail /weɪl/ *v* [I] **1** to cry loudly because you are very sad, or in pain: *"I want my Daddy!" she wailed.* **2** if a SIREN wails, it makes a long high sound —**wail** *n* [C]

waist /weɪst/ *n* [C] **1** the part around the middle of your body just above your HIPS: *She has a slim waist.* **2** the part of a piece of clothing that goes around your waist

waist·coat /ˈweɪskəʊt, ˈweskət‖ˈweskət/ *n* [C] *BrE* a piece of clothing without SLEEVES that has buttons down the front, worn over a shirt, especially as part of a suit; VEST *AmE* → see colour picture on page 113

waist·line /ˈweɪstlaɪn/ *n* [C, usually singular] **1** the measurement around your waist **2** the part of a piece of clothing that fits around the waist

wait¹ /weɪt/ *v* [I] **1** to sit or stand somewhere or not do something until something else happens, someone arrives etc: *Hurry up! Everyone's waiting.* **| + for** *We had to wait 45 minutes for a bus.* | **wait to do sth** *Are you waiting to use the phone?* **2 can't wait** *especially spoken* if you can't wait to do something, you want to do it very much and are very excited about it: *Roz can't wait to see Angelo again.* **3** [I] if something is waiting for you, it is ready for you to use, eat, collect etc: *My meal was waiting for me on the table when I got home.* **4 wait and see** to wait and find out what will happen **5 it can wait** *spoken* used to say that you do not need to do something immediately **6 (just) you wait** *spoken* used to warn or threaten someone **7 wait tables** *AmE* to serve food to people at their table in a restaurant

  wait around (also **wait about** *BrE*) *phr v* [I] to do nothing while you are waiting for something to happen, someone to arrive etc: *The people at the embassy kept us waiting around for hours.*

  wait on sb *phr v* [T] to serve food to someone at their table, especially in a restaurant

  wait up *phr v* [I] **1** to wait for someone to come back home before you go to bed: *Please don't wait up for me.* **2** to wait for someone: *Hey, wait up. I'm coming.*

USAGE NOTE: wait and expect

Use **wait** to talk about staying somewhere until someone comes or something happens: *Please wait until Mr Feltcher arrives.* | *She's been waiting all day for that phone to ring.* Use **expect** to say that you think something will probably happen, arrive etc, whether you want it to or not: *I didn't expect her to be so angry.* | *Were you expecting a phone call?*

---

wait² *n* [singular] a period of time when you wait for something to happen, someone to arrive etc: *We had a three-hour wait for our flight.* → see also **lie in wait** (LIE¹)

wait·er /ˈweɪtə‖-ər/ *n* [C] a man who serves food in a restaurant

wait·ing list /ˈ.. ./ *n* [C] a list of people who want to buy or do something but who must wait for other people who are on the list before them: *waiting lists for operations*

waiting room /ˈ.. ./ *n* [C] a room for people to wait in, for example to see a doctor

wait·ress /ˈweɪtr‹s/ *n* [C] a woman who serves food in a restaurant

waive /weɪv/ *v* [T] **1** to say officially that someone does not have to obey a rule, pay for something etc: *The judge waived the fine.* **2** if you waive your right to do something, you say officially that you do not want to use it: *She waived her right to a lawyer.*

wake[1] /weɪk/ v [I,T] **woke** /wəʊk‖woʊk/, **woken** /ˈwəʊkən‖ˈwoʊ-/, **waking** also **wake up** to stop sleeping, or make someone stop sleeping: *I woke up at 5.00 this morning.* | *Try not to wake the baby.*

wake up to sth *phr v* [T] to start to realize and understand that something important is true or is happening: *People are now waking up to the fact that cars cause more problems than they are worth.*

wake[2] *n* **1 in the wake of sth** happening after something, especially as a result of it: *Five members of the city council resigned in the wake of the scandal.* **2** [C] the waves and moving water that a ship leaves behind as it moves along **3** [C] the time before a funeral when people meet to remember the dead person

wak·en /ˈweɪkən/ v [I,T] *formal* to wake up, or make someone wake up

wak·ing /ˈweɪkɪŋ/ *adj* **waking hours/moments** all the time, when you are awake: *He spends every waking moment in front of his computer.*

walk[1] /wɔːk‖wɒːk/ v **1** [I,T] to move forwards by putting one foot in front of the other: *We must have walked ten miles today.* | *She walked up to him and kissed him.* → see colour picture on page 670 **2** [T] to walk somewhere with someone: *It's late – I'll walk you home.* | *Tamara usually walks the dogs twice a day.* (=she takes them outside for a walk) **3 walk all over sb** *informal* to treat someone very badly: *She lets those kids walk all over her.*

walk away *phr v* [I] to leave a situation without caring what happens: *You can't just walk away from 8 years of marriage!*

walk away with sth *phr v* [T] to win something easily: *Carrie walked away with the prize.*

walk into sth *phr v* [T] **1** if you walk into a job, you get it easily and without any effort **2** to be easily deceived by something, especially in a way that makes you seem silly: *You walked straight into that one!*

walk off with sth *phr v* [T] **1** to take something that does not belong to you: *Someone walked off with my new jacket!* **2** to win something easily

walk out *phr v* [I] to stop working as a protest

walk out on sb *phr v* [T] to leave your husband, wife etc suddenly: *Mary just walked out on him one day.*

walk[2] *n* [C] **1** a journey that you make by walking: **go for a walk** (=walk for pleasure or exercise): *Would you like to go for a walk?* | a **long/short/ten-minute etc walk** (=used to say how long it takes to walk somewhere): *It's only a short walk to the beach.* **2** a path or ROUTE that people can walk along for pleasure: *popular walks in Yellowstone National Park* **3** (people) **from all walks of life** people who have very different jobs or positions in society —**walker** *n* [C]

walk·ie-talk·ie /ˌwɔːki ˈtɔːki‖ˌwɒːki ˈtɒːki/ *n* [C] a small radio that you can carry and use to speak to other people who have the same kind of radio

walking stick /ˈ.. ./ *n* [C] a long thin stick, used to help support you when you walk

walk·way /ˈwɔːkweɪ‖ˈwɒːk-/ *n* [C] a path, often above the ground, that connects two parts of a building or two buildings

wall[1] /wɔːl‖wɒːl/ *n* [C] **1** one of the sides of a room or building: *We've decided to paint the walls blue.* | *the picture on the wall* → see colour picture on page 79 /**2** an upright structure made of stone or brick, that divides one area from another: *The garden is surrounded by a high wall.* **3 drive sb up the wall** *informal* to make someone very annoyed —**walled** *adj* → see also **have your back to the wall** (BACK[1])

wal·let /ˈwɒlᵻt‖ˈwɑː-/ *n* [C] a small flat container usually made of leather, for putting paper money and CREDIT CARDS in, which you carry in your pocket

wal·lop /ˈwɒləp‖ˈwɑː-/ *v* [T] *informal* to hit someone or something very hard —**wallop** *n*

wal·low /ˈwɒləʊ‖ˈwɑːloʊ/ *v* [I] **1** if someone wallows in an unpleasant feeling or situation, they seem to enjoy it and want to be unhappy: *She accused him of wallowing in self-pity.* **2** to lie or roll around in mud, water etc for pleasure

wall·pa·per /ˈwɔːlˌpeɪpə‖ˈwɒːlˌpeɪpər/ *n* [U] paper that you stick onto the walls of a room in order to decorate it —**wallpaper** *v* [T]

Wall Street /ˈ. ./ *n* [singular] the New York City STOCK EXCHANGE

wall-to-wall /ˌ. ˈ. ◂/ *adj* covering the whole floor: *wall-to-wall carpeting*

wal·ly /ˈwɒli‖ˈwɑː-/ *n* [C] *BrE informal* a stupid person

wal·nut /ˈwɔːlnʌt‖ˈwɒːl-/ *n* **1** [C] a nut that looks like a brain, which has a large light brown shell **2** [U] the dark brown wood of the tree on which this nut grows

wal·rus /ˈwɔːlrəs‖ˈwɒːl-, ˈwɑːl-/ *n* [C] a large sea animal similar to a SEAL, which has two very long thick teeth

waltz[1] /wɔːls‖wɒːlts/ *n* [C] a fairly slow dance with a RHYTHM consisting of patterns of 3 beats, or the music for this dance

waltz[2] *v* [I] **1** to dance a waltz **2** *informal* to walk somewhere calmly and confidently: **+ up/past etc** *Jeff waltzed up to the bar and poured himself a drink.*

wan /wɒn‖wɑːn/ *adj* looking pale, weak, or tired: *a wan smile*

wand /wɒnd‖wɑːnd/ *n* [C] a thin stick you hold in your hand to do magic tricks

wan·der /ˈwɒndə‖ˈwɑːndər/ *v* **1** [I,T] to walk somewhere without hurrying and without going in a particular direction or having a fixed purpose: *We spent the morning wandering around the old part of the city.* **2** [I] also **wander off** to move away from the place where you are supposed to stay: *Don't let the children wander off.* **3** [I] if your mind or your thoughts wander, you stop paying attention to something and start thinking about other things: *She's getting old, and sometimes her mind wanders.* **4** [I] to start to talk or write about something not connected with the main subject: *I wish he'd stop wandering off the subject.* —**wander** *n* [singular] —**wanderer** *n* [C]

wane[1] /weɪn/ *v* [I] if someone's power, interest, support etc wanes, it gradually becomes weaker or less: *After a while his enthusiasm for the sport began to wane.*

wane² *n* **on the wane** becoming weaker or less: *The president's popularity seems to be on the wane.*

wan·gle /'wæŋɡəl/ *v* [T] *informal* to succeed in getting something that is difficult to get, especially by using clever or slightly dishonest methods: *"I've got two tickets to the Wimbledon finals." "How did you wangle that?"*

wan·na /'wɒnə‖'wɑː-/ *nonstandard informal* a way of saying or writing 'want to' or 'want a'

wan·na·be /'wɒnəbi‖'wɑː-/ *n* [C] *informal* someone who tries to look or behave like a famous or popular person: *Tom Cruise wannabes*

want¹ /wɒnt‖wɒːnt, wɑːnt/ *v* [T] **1** to have a desire or need for something: *What do you want for your birthday?* | **want to do sth** *I want to go home.* | **want sb to do sth** *Her parents want her to find a rich husband.* **2** used to say that something needs doing: *The car wants a good clean.* **3** *informal* used to tell someone what they should do; OUGHT TO: *You want to be more careful next time.*

want² *n* **1** **for want of** because there is nothing else available or because there is nothing else you can do: *We watched television, for want of anything better to do.* **2** [singular, U] a lack of something important → see also WANTS

want·ed /'wɒntɪd‖'wɒn-, 'wɑːn-/ *adj* someone who is wanted is being looked for by the police, because they are thought to be guilty of a crime: *He is wanted for murder.*

want·ing /'wɒntɪŋ‖'wɒn-, 'wɑːn-/ *adj* **be found wanting** *formal* if something is found wanting, it has been shown to be not good enough: *Traditional solutions had been tried and found wanting.*

wan·ton /'wɒntən‖'wɒn-, 'wɑːn-/ *adj formal* deliberately causing damage or harm for no reason: *the wanton destruction of the rainforests*

wants /wɒnts‖wɒːnts, wɑːnts/ *n* [plural] someone's wants are things they want or need to have

war /wɔː‖wɔːr/ *n* **1** [C,U] a long period of fighting between the armies of two or more countries in many different places: *the Vietnam War* | *the war years* | **be at war** (=be fighting a war with another country): *In 1793 England was at war with France.* | **go to war** (=start fighting a war) **2** [C,U] when two countries, companies etc compete with each other and try to win against each other: *a trade war* **3** [singular] when people try to stop something bad or illegal from happening: **+ against/on** *the war against drugs* → see also CIVIL WAR, PRISONER OF WAR, WARRING

war crime /'. ./ *n* [C] an illegal and cruel act done during a war —**war criminal** *n* [C]

ward¹ /wɔːd‖wɔːrd/ *n* [C] a part of a hospital where people stay, especially people who need a particular kind of medical treatment: *the maternity ward*

ward² *v*

ward sth ↔ off *phr v* [T] to prevent something from affecting you or attacking you: *a spray to ward off insects*

war·den /'wɔːdn‖'wɔːrdn/ *n* [C] *AmE* the person in charge of a prison; GOVERNOR *BrE* → see also TRAFFIC WARDEN

ward·er /'wɔːdə‖'wɔːrdər/ *n* [C] *BrE* a prison guard

ward·robe /'wɔːdrəʊb‖'wɔːrdroʊb/ *n* **1** [C] *BrE* a piece of furniture like a large cupboard, which you hang clothes in; CLOSET *AmE* **2** [singular] the clothes that someone has: *the latest addition to her wardrobe*

ware·house /'weəhaʊs‖'wer-/ *n* [C] a large building for storing large quantities of goods

wares /weəz‖werz/ *n* [plural] *literary* the things that someone is selling, usually not in a shop

war·fare /'wɔːfeə‖'wɔːrfer/ *n* [U] the activity of fighting in a war, especially a particular kind of fighting: *chemical warfare*

war game /'. ,./ *n* [C] when people pretend to fight battles, especially to test military plans

war·head /'wɔːhed‖'wɔːr-/ *n* [C] the explosive part at the front of a MISSILE

war·like /'wɔːlaɪk‖'wɔːr-/ *adj* warlike countries or people are eager to fight wars or often fight wars: *a warlike race*

war·lock /'wɔːlɒk‖'wɔːrlɑːk/ *n* [C] a man who is supposed to have magic powers, especially to do bad things

war·lord /'wɔːlɔːd‖'wɔːrlɔːrd/ *n* [C] the leader of a group of people who fight against other groups in a country, especially a country where the government has lost control

warm¹ /wɔːm‖wɔːrm/ *adj* **1** slightly hot, especially in a way that is pleasant: *a nice warm bath* | *The weather was lovely and warm.* | **keep/ stay warm** (=stop yourself from feeling cold) **2** warm clothes and BLANKETS stop you from feeling cold **3** friendly: *a warm welcome* —**warmly** *adv*

warm² *v* [T] to make something warm, especially part of your body: *I warmed my hands over the fire.*

warm to sb/sth *phr v* [T] to start to like someone or something: *They soon warmed to the idea.*

warm up *phr v* **1** [I,T] to become warm or hot, or to make something warm or hot: *The weather's starting to warm up.* **2** [I,T] to do gentle exercises to prepare your body before doing a sport, dancing etc: *The athletes were warming up for the race.* **3** [I] if a machine warms up, it becomes ready to work properly

warmed o·ver /,. '..◂/ *adj AmE* **1** warmed over ideas or arguments have been used before and are not interesting or useful any more **2** food that is warmed over has been cooked before and then heated again for eating

warm-heart·ed /,. '..◂/ *adj* friendly and kind: *a warm-hearted old lady*

war·mon·ger /'wɔː,mʌŋɡə‖'wɔːr,mɑːŋɡər, -,mʌŋ-/ *n* [C] someone who is eager to start a war —**warmongering** *n* [U]

warmth /wɔːmθ‖wɔːrmθ/ *n* [U] **1** the heat that something produces, especially when this gives

W

GRAMMAR NOTE: a or the (1)

Use **a** or **an** before a noun when you are mentioning a person or thing for the first time, but use **the** when you mention that same person or thing again: *A man and a woman were sitting at the next table. The woman was much younger than the man.*

you a pleasant feeling: *the warmth of the sun* **2** friendliness: *the warmth of her smile*

warm-up /ˈ. ./ *n* [C] a set of gentle exercises you do to prepare your body before doing a sport, dancing etc

warn /wɔːn‖wɔːrn/ *v* [T] to tell someone that something bad or dangerous may happen, so that they can avoid it or prevent it: *We tried to warn her, but she wouldn't listen.* | **warn sb (that)** *Allen warned him that he might be killed if he stayed in Beirut.* | **warn sb not to do sth** (=tell someone they should not do something, because it is dangerous): *Police are warning drivers not to go out on the roads unless their journey is really necessary.*

warn·ing /ˈwɔːnɪŋ‖ˈwɔːrn-/ *n* [C,U] something that tells you that something bad or dangerous may happen: *The planes attacked without warning.* | *The referee gave him a warning* (=told him that if he behaved badly again, he would be punished).

warp /wɔːp‖wɔːrp/ *v* **1** [I,T] to become bent or twisted, especially because of the effect of heat or water, or to make something do this: *The wood had warped in the heat.* **2** [T] if something warps your mind, it makes you think or behave in a strange way

war·path /ˈwɔːpæθ‖ˈwɔːrpæθ/ *n* **be on the warpath** *often humorous* to be angry about something and want to punish someone for it

warped /wɔːpt‖wɔːrpt/ *adj* **1** thinking or behaving in a way that most people think is not normal and is often unpleasant: *a warped sense of humour* **2** bent or twisted into the wrong shape: *The boards had become warped.*

war·rant[1] /ˈwɒrənt‖ˈwɔː-, ˈwɑː-/ *n* [C] an official document that allows the police to search inside someone's house, ARREST someone etc: *A warrant has been issued for his arrest.*

warrant[2] *v* [T] *formal* to be a good enough reason for something to happen or be done: *The story doesn't really warrant the attention it's been given in the press.* → compare UNWARRANTED

war·ran·ty /ˈwɒrəntɪ‖ˈwɔː-, ˈwɑː-/ *n* [C,U] a written promise that a company will repair something or give you another thing of the same kind if it breaks after you have bought it; GUARANTEE: *The TV comes with a 3-year warranty.*

war·ren /ˈwɒrən‖ˈwɔː-, ˈwɑː-/ *n* [C] **1** a group of holes under the ground used by rabbits **2** a lot of narrow PASSAGEs in a building or between buildings: *a warren of alleyways*

war·ring /ˈwɔːrɪŋ/ *adj* warring groups fight or argue with each other: *warring factions within the party*

war·ri·or /ˈwɒriə‖ˈwɔːriər, ˈwɑː-/ *n* [C] *literary* someone who fought in battles in past times, especially someone who was very brave

war·ship /ˈwɔːˌʃɪp‖ˈwɔːr-/ *n* [C] a ship with guns, used in wars

wart /wɔːt‖wɔːrt/ *n* [C] a small hard raised spot on your skin

war·time /ˈwɔːtaɪm‖ˈwɔːr-/ *n* [U] the time when a war is happening: *a book about his wartime experiences*

war-torn /ˈ. ./ *adj* badly affected by a war

war·y /ˈweərɪ‖ˈweri/ *adj* careful because you are worried that someone or something may be

harmful or cause problems: **+ of** *She was a bit wary of him at first.* —**warily** *adv*

was /wəz; *strong* wɒz‖wəz; *strong* wɑːz/ *v* the past tense of the verb BE in the first and third person singular

wash[1] /wɒʃ‖wɒ:ʃ, wɑːʃ/ *v* **1** [T] to clean something with water and often soap: *He spent the morning washing the car.* | *These jeans need to be washed.* **2** [I] to clean your body with soap and water: *Go upstairs and wash your hands.* | **get washed** *He got washed and had his breakfast.* **3** [I,T] to flow somewhere: *The waves washed softly against the shore.* **4** [T] if something is washed somewhere, the sea or a river carries it there: *The body was washed out to sea.* **5 wash your hands of** to refuse to be responsible for something or someone

wash sth **away** *phr v* [T] if water washes something away, it makes it disappear

wash sth↔**down** *phr v* [T] to drink something with food or medicine, for example in order to help you swallow it: *a big plate of pasta washed down with a bottle of red wine*

wash off *phr v* [I] if a substance washes off, you can remove it from the surface of something by washing: *"I've spilt coffee all over the carpet." "Don't worry. It'll wash off."*

wash out *phr v* [I,T **wash** sth ↔ **out**] to remove dirt, a spot etc from something by washing it, or to be removed in this way

wash up *phr v* [I] **1** [I,T **wash** sth↔**up**] *BrE* to wash the plates, dishes etc after a meal **2** [I] *AmE* to wash your hands: *Go wash up for supper.* **3** [I,T] if something washes up or is washed up, it is moved onto the SHORE by the sea or a river

wash[2] *n* [singular] **1** a **wash** when you wash something, or wash yourself using soap and water: **have a wash** (=wash yourself): *I'm just going to have a wash.* | **give sth a wash** (=wash it) **2** in the **wash** if clothes are in the wash, they are being washed

wash·a·ble /ˈwɒʃəbəl‖ˈwɒ:-, ˈwɑː-/ *adj* able to be washed without being damaged: *a machine washable sweater*

wash·ba·sin /ˈwɒʃˌbeɪsən‖ˈwɒ:ʃ-, ˈwɑːʃ-/ *n* [C] *especially BrE* a container like a small SINK, used for washing your hands and face

washed-out /ˌ. ˈ.◂/ *adj* very tired or pale: *washed out colours* | *She looked washed out.*

wash·er /ˈwɒʃə‖ˈwɒːʃər, ˈwɑːʃər/ *n* [C] a small ring of plastic or metal that you put between a NUT and a BOLT, or between two pipes, to make them fit together tightly

wash·ing /ˈwɒʃɪŋ‖ˈwɒ:-, ˈwɑː-/ *n* [U] clothes, TOWELs etc that need to be washed or have just been washed: **do the washing** *BrE* (=wash the clothes, towels etc)

washing ma·chine /ˈ.. .ˌ./ *n* [C] a machine that washes clothes → see picture at KITCHEN

washing-up /ˌ.. ˈ./ *n* do the washing-up *BrE* to wash all the plates, dishes etc that have been used for a meal

wash·out /ˈwɒʃ-aʊt‖ˈwɒ:ʃ-, ˈwɑːʃ-/ *n* [singular] *informal* if something is a washout, it is very unsuccessful: *The party was a complete washout.*

wash·room /ˈwɒʃrʊm, -ruːm‖ˈwɒ:ʃ-, ˈwɑːʃ-/ *n* [C] *old-fashioned* a room where there are toilets and where you can wash your hands

was·n't /'wɒzənt‖'wɑː-/ the short form of 'was not': *He wasn't there.*

wasp /wɒsp‖wɑːsp, wɔːsp/ *n* [C] a black and yellow flying insect similar to a BEE, but with a thinner body, which can sting you

wast·age /'weɪstɪdʒ/ *n* [U] when something is wasted: *the huge wastage of resources*

waste¹ /weɪst/ *n* **1** [singular, U] when something is used in a way that is not useful or sensible, or when you use more of something than is necessary: **be a waste of time/money/effort** *My father thought college would be a complete waste of time.* **2** [C,U] materials that are left after you have used something, which you want to get rid of because you no longer need them: *radio-active waste from nuclear power stations | recycling household waste* **3 go to waste** if something goes to waste, it is not used and is wasted: *A lot of the food ended up going to waste.* → see also WASTES

waste² *v* [T] **1** to use something in a way that is not sensible or useful, or use more of it than you should: **waste time/money etc** *They wasted a lot of time trying to fix the computer themselves.* **2 waste no time/not waste any time** to do something as quickly as you can because you know it will be useful to you **3 be wasted** if someone is wasted in their job, they have many skills that are not used, and they should get a different job

  waste away *phr v* [I] to gradually become thinner and weaker, especially because you are ill

waste³ *adj* [only before noun] waste paper, waste products etc are things that people want to get rid of because they do not need them, for example because they have already used them

waste·bas·ket /'weɪst,bɑːskɪt‖-,bæs-/ *n* [C] *especially AmE* a WASTEPAPER BASKET → see colour picture on page 80

wast·ed /'weɪstɪd/ *adj* not having any useful result: *It was a wasted trip because there were no CDs left.*

waste·ful /'weɪstfəl/ *adj* using much more of something than you should, or using something in a way that is not sensible or useful

waste·land /'weɪstlænd, -lənd/ *n* [C,U] an area of land that cannot be used for any useful purpose, especially one that looks very unattractive: *When I first came here, this place was just a wasteland.*

waste·pa·per bas·ket /,weɪst'peɪpə ,bɑːskɪt, 'weɪst,peɪpə-‖'weɪst,peɪpər,bæ-/ *n* [C] *especially BrE* a container into which you put paper and other small things that you do not need and want to get rid of; WASTEBASKET *AmE* → see colour picture on page 80

wastes /weɪsts/ *[plural] literary* a large empty area of land: *the icy wastes of Antarctica*

watch¹ /wɒtʃ‖wɑːtʃ, wɔːtʃ/ *v* **1** [I,T] to look at and pay attention to something that is happening or changing: *Harry was watching the game on TV. | watch sb do(ing) sth She watched him drive away.* **2** [T] to be careful about something: *I need to watch my weight.* **3 watch it** *spoken informal* used to warn someone to be careful: *Hey, watch it – you nearly hit that truck!* **4 watch your step** be careful what you do, because you may make someone angry with you: *The boss is back tomorrow, so you'd better watch*

your step. **5** [T] to take care of someone or something for a short time and make sure they are safe: *Can you watch my bags for me?*

  watch out *phr v* [I] to be careful and pay attention, because something unpleasant might happen: *Watch out! You might cut yourself. | + for You can ride your bike here, but watch out for cars.*

  watch over sb/sth *phr v* [T] to take care of someone or something and make sure that nothing bad happens to them: *His mother was there to watch over him.*

watch² *n* **1** [C] a small clock you wear on your wrist or carry in your pocket: *My watch has stopped.* **2 keep a (close) watch on** to carefully watch or pay attention to something, so that you always know what is happening and are ready to deal with it: *The United Nations Security Council is keeping a close watch on the situation in Iraq.* **3 keep watch** to look around a place so that you can warn people if there is any danger: *Douglas kept watch while the others slept.*

watch·dog /'wɒtʃdɒg‖'wɑːtʃdɔːg, 'wɔːtʃ-/ *n* [C] a person or organization that checks to make sure that large companies and organizations obey the rules, and protects the rights of ordinary people: *a US Department of Energy watchdog committee*

watch·ful /'wɒtʃfəl‖'wɑːtʃ-, 'wɔːtʃ-/ *adj* careful to notice what is happening: *She kept a watchful eye on the children.* (=she watched them carefully)

watch·mak·er /'wɒtʃ,meɪkə‖'wɑːtʃ,meɪkər, 'wɔːtʃ-/ *n* [C] someone who makes and repairs watches and clocks

watch·man /'wɒtʃmən‖'wɑːtʃ-, 'wɔːtʃ-/ *n* [C] someone whose job is to guard a building: *the night watchman*

watch·word /'wɒtʃwɜːd‖'wɑːtʃwɜːrd, 'wɔːtʃ-/ *n* [singular] the most important principle or rule in a particular situation: *Caution is still the watchword.*

water¹ /'wɔːtəl‖wɒtər, 'wɑː-/ *n* **1** [U] the clear liquid in rivers, seas, rain etc: *Can I have a drink of water?* **2** [U] also **waters** an area of water in a sea, lake or river: *The ship ran aground in shallow water. | the cool clear waters of the lake* **3 in hot/deep water** in a very difficult situation in which you have a lot of trouble → see also **keep your head above water** (HEAD¹)

water² *v* **1** [T] to pour water on a plant to help it to grow **2** [I] if your eyes water, they fill with water because they hurt: *The onions are making my eyes water.* **3** [I] if food makes your mouth water, it looks as if it has a very good taste and makes you want to eat it → see also MOUTH-WATERING

  water sth ↔ **down** *phr v* [T] **1** to change a statement, plan etc in a way that makes it less effective, weaker etc: *The proposals have been watered down.* **2** to make alcoholic drinks weaker by adding water, in order to deceive people: *The whisky had been watered down.*

wa·ter·col·our *BrE*, **watercolor** *AmE* /'wɔːtə-,kʌlə‖'wɔːtər,kʌlər, 'wɑː-/ *n* [C,U] a kind of paint that you mix with water, or a painting using this kind of paint

wa·ter·cress /'wɔːtəkres‖'wɒtər-, 'wɑː-/ *n* [C]

W

a small plant with strong-tasting green leaves, used in SALADS

wa·ter·fall /ˈwɔːtəfɔːl‖ˈwɒtərfɔːl, ˈwɑː-/ n [C] a place where water flows down over a rock or from a high place ➝ see colour picture on page 243

wa·ter·front /ˈwɔːtəfrʌnt‖ˈwɒtər-, ˈwɑː-/ n [C] a part of a town or area of land that is next to a lake, river, sea etc

wa·ter·hole /ˈwɔːtəhəʊl‖ˈwɒtərhoʊl, ˈwɑː-/ n [C] a small area of water in a dry country, where wild animals go to drink

water·ing can /ˈ... ./ n [C] a container used for pouring water on plants ➝ see picture at GARDENING EQUIPMENT

wa·ter·logged /ˈwɔːtəlɒgd‖ˈwɒtərlɔːgd, ˈwɑː-, -lɑːgd/ adj land that is waterlogged is very wet or covered with water: *The pitch was waterlogged.*

wa·ter·mark /ˈwɔːtəmɑːk‖ˈwɒtərmɑːrk, ˈwɑː-/ n [C] a special design on a piece of paper, especially on money, that you can only see when it is held up to the light

wa·ter·mel·on /ˈwɔːtəˌmelən‖ˈwɒtər-, ˈwɑː-/ n [C] a large round fruit with a thick green skin which is red inside and has a lot of black seeds

water po·lo /ˈ.. ˌ../ n [U] a game played in a swimming pool, in which two teams of players try to throw a ball into their opponents' GOAL

wa·ter·proof /ˈwɔːtəpruːf‖ˈwɒtər-, ˈwɑː-/ adj waterproof clothing or material does not let water go through: *waterproof boots*

wa·ters /ˈwɔːtəz‖ˈwɒtərz, ˈwɑː-/ n [plural] an area of water in a sea, lake, or river: *British waters* (=that belong to Britain)|*the point where the waters of the Amazon flow into the sea*

wa·ter·shed /ˈwɔːtəʃed‖ˈwɒtər-, ˈwɑː-/ n [singular] an event or time when very important changes happen in the history of something: *The election marked a watershed in American politics.*

water-ski·ing /ˈ.. ˌ../ n [U] a sport in which someone wearing SKIs is pulled over water by a boat —**water-ski** v [I] —**water skier** n [C]

wa·ter·tight /ˈwɔːtətaɪt‖ˈwɒtər-, ˈwɑː-/ adj **1** a watertight argument, agreement etc does not contain any mistakes or weaknesses which people can criticize: *The police thought they had a watertight case.* **2** not allowing any water to get in or out: *a watertight container*

wa·ter·way /ˈwɔːtəweɪ‖ˈwɒtər-, ˈwɑː-/ n [C] a river, CANAL etc that boats or ships can travel along

wa·ter·y /ˈwɔːtəri‖ˈwɒ-, ˈwɑː-/ adj **1** containing too much water: *watery soup* **2** if your eyes are watery, they have water in them, especially because you feel sad and want to cry **3** a watery light is very pale or weak

watt /wɒt‖wɑːt/ n [C] a unit for measuring electrical power: *a 100 watt light bulb*

wave[1] /weɪv/ v **waved, waving 1** [I,T] to move your hand, or something you hold in your hand, as a SIGNAL or greeting: *Her parents stood in the doorway and waved goodbye.*|*He started shouting and waving his arms.*|*The crowd were waving flags and cheering.*|**wave sb through/away** (=tell them they should go through, away etc by waving your hand): *The customs inspector waved us through.* ➝ see colour picture on page

473 **2** [I] if something such as a flag waves, it moves gently with the wind

wave sth↔ **aside** phr v [T] to refuse to pay attention to what someone has said, because you do not think it is important

wave[2] n [C] **1** a raised line of water that moves across the surface of a large area of water, especially the sea: *Huge waves were crashing into the sides of the boat.* ➝ see colour picture on page 243 **2** when something suddenly starts happening a lot: *the crime wave*|*a wave of strikes* **3** the movement you make when you wave your hand: *The Governor gave a wave to the crowd.* **4** when someone suddenly feels a particular feeling very strongly: *Harriet was overcome by a wave of homesickness.* **5** the form in which some types of energy move, for example light and sound: *radio waves* ➝ see also HEAT WAVE

wave·length /ˈweɪvleŋθ/ n [C] **1** the size of radio wave used by a radio company to broadcast its programmes **2 be on the same wavelength** to think in the same way about something as someone else does **3** the distance between two waves of energy such as sound or light

wa·ver /ˈweɪvəl-ər/ v [I] **1** to be unsure and HESITATE before making a decision, or to be unsure about whether you should support someone: *While the West wavered about taking military action, thousands of people were killed.* **2** to shake and be unsteady: *His hand wavered for a moment.*

wav·y /ˈweɪvi/ adj wavy hair or lines are not straight and have curves in them ➝ see colour picture on page 244

wax[1] /wæks/ n [U] a thick substance made of fats or oils, used for making things such as CANDLES or for POLISHing things

wax[2] v [T] to put wax on something, especially in order to POLISH it

wax·y /ˈwæksi/ adj having a soft smooth surface like wax: *waxy leaves*

way[1] /weɪ/ n **1** [C] the road, path etc that you have to follow in order to go to a place: *Could you tell me the way to the station?*|*The usual road was blocked, so we came back a different way.*|**lose your way** *They lost their way coming down off the mountain.* **2** [C] a particular direction or position: *Which way is north?*|*Face this way, please.*|*Is this picture the right way up?*|**way around** (=the order or position that something is in): *You've got the letters the wrong way around* **3** [C] a method of doing something: *The best way to learn a language is to go and live in the country where it is spoken.*|*OK, let's do it your way.* (=using your method) **4** [C] how someone behaves, talks, feels etc: *We both think the same way about a lot of things.*|*I knew by the way he was looking at me that he was annoyed.* **5** [singular] the distance between two places, or the period between two times: *We're a long way from home.*|*It's still a long way to go till Christmas.* **6 half way/most of the way/all the way** etc used to say how much of something has happened, or how much you have done: *The other team scored half way through the game.* **7 by the way** spoken used when you want to tell someone about something that you have just remembered: *Oh, by the way, I saw Marie yester-*

day. **8 no way!** *spoken* used to say that you will definitely not do or allow something: *"Dad, can I have the car tonight?" "No way!"* **9 in a way/in some ways** used to say that something is true about some parts of something: *In a way, I'm glad it's all over.* **10 in the way/in sb's way** if something is in the way, it is in front of you and prevents you from going somewhere or seeing something: *When we tried to turn down the next street we found a big truck in the way.* **11 get in the way of sth** to prevent someone from being able to do something that they want to do: *Don't let your social life get in the way of your studying.* **12 make way a)** to move to one side so that someone or something can pass **b)** if one thing makes way for something else, this other thing replaces it: *Several houses were torn down to make way for a new fire station.* **13 make your way** to move towards something, especially when this takes a long time: *They started to make their way towards the exit.* **14 know/find your way around** to know or find out where something in a place is: *It takes a few weeks to find your way around.* **15 on my/your way etc** while you are going somewhere: *Could you get some milk on your way back home from work?* **16 be on its/his etc way** to be arriving soon: *The taxi is on its way.* **17 have/get your (own) way** to do what you want even if someone else wants something different: *They always let that kid get his own way.* **18 go out of your way to do sth** to make a special effort to do something, especially to help someone or be kind to them: *Ben went out of his way to help us.* **19 keep/ stay out of sb's way** to avoid someone: *She's in a funny mood today – I'd stay out of her way.* **20 be out of the way** if something is out of the way, it is finished or you have dealt with it **21 you can't have it both ways** *spoken* used to say that someone cannot have the advantages of two opposite things and must choose one **22 sth has come a long way** if something has come a long way, it has developed and improved a lot: *Psychiatry has come a long way since the 1920s.* **23 in a big way/in a small way** used to say how much something happens or how important an effect something has: *He helped in a big way.* → see also OUT-OF-THE-WAY, **give way** (GIVE), **know your way around** (KNOW¹), **be set in your ways** (SET¹), **under way** (UNDER¹), WAY OF LIFE

USAGE NOTE: way, road, path, and track

Don't use **way** when you are thinking about a particular **road**, **path**, or **track**: *a muddy path through the forest* | *We walked to the village along a narrow track instead of taking the main road.*

way² *adv usually spoken* used to emphasize that something is a lot, a large amount, a long time etc: **way too** (=much too): *The film was way too long.* | **way above/beyond etc** (=a lot above, beyond etc): *The temperature's way above normal.*

way·lay /ˈweɪleɪ/ *v* [T] *literary* to stop someone in order to talk to them, or to harm or steal things from them

way of life /ˌ. . ˈ./ *n* [C] the way someone lives, especially the people in a particular country: *the American way of life*

way out /ˌ. ˈ./ *n* [C] *BrE* **1** a door or PASSAGE through which you can leave a building; EXIT **2** a way of getting away from a difficult or unpleasant situation

way-out /ˌ. ˈ.◄/ *adj spoken* something that is way-out seems very strange, especially because it is very modern: *I like jazz, but not the way-out stuff.*

way·side /ˈweɪsaɪd/ *n* **fall/go by the wayside** to stop being successful: *Many of our best players are falling by the wayside.*

way·ward /ˈweɪwəd‖-wərd/ *adj literary* behaving in a way that is different from other people and that causes problems: *the Minister's wayward son*

WC /ˌdʌbəlju: ˈsi:/ *n* [C] *BrE* the abbreviation for water closet; toilet — used especially on signs

we /wi; *strong* wi:/ *pron* **1** the person who is speaking and one or more other people: *We ordered our meal.* **2** people in general: *Today we know much more about what causes the disease.*

weak /wi:k/ *adj* **1** not having much strength or energy: *Jerry's still weak after his operation.* | *Her knees felt weak.* **2** not powerful: *a weak government* **3** not having a strong character and easily persuaded to do things by other people: *a weak and indecisive man* **4** not having much ability or skill at doing something: *His spelling was weak.* | *one of the weaker students in the class* **5** a weak argument or excuse is not good enough or believable enough to persuade people: *a weak excuse* **6** having very little taste or containing too much water: *weak tea* **7** difficult to see or hear: *a weak light* **8** unable to support a lot of weight and likely to break: *a weak bridge* —**weakly** *adv*

weak·en /ˈwi:kən/ *v* [I,T] **1** to become less powerful or physically strong, or to make someone or something do this: *a country weakened by war* **2** to become less determined about something, or to make someone less determined: *Nothing could weaken her resolve.*

weak·ling /ˈwi:klɪŋ/ *n* [C] a disapproving word for someone who is not physically strong

weak·ness /ˈwi:knɪs/ *n* **1** [U] when someone or something is not powerful or determined, or not physically strong: *the weakness of the previous administration* | *a sign of weakness* **2** [C] a problem that makes someone or something less likely to be successful, or that can be easily attacked or criticized: *What are your main strengths and weaknesses?* | *I've found a weakness in their argument.* **3** a weakness for sth if you have a weakness for something, you like it very much, even though it may not be good for you: *She's always had a weakness for chocolate.*

W

GRAMMAR NOTE: a or the (1)

Use **a** or **an** before a noun when you are mentioning a person or thing for the first time, but use **the** when you mention that same person or thing again: *A man and a woman were sitting at the next table. The woman was much younger than the man.*

wealth /welθ/ n **1** [U] the large amount of money and possessions that a rich person has: *a family of great wealth* **2** **a wealth of sth** a large amount of something that is available: *the wealth of information on the Internet*

wealth·y /'welθi/ adj **1** having a lot of money, land, or valuable possessions, especially when you or your family have owned them for a long time: *wealthy landowners* **2** **the wealthy** people who have a lot of money or valuable possessions

wean /wiːn/ v [I] to gradually stop feeding a baby on his or her mother's milk and start giving him or her ordinary food
wean sb off sth phr v [T] to make someone gradually stop doing something, especially something that is bad for them: *Dr Rossdale tried to wean her off the sleeping tablets.*

weap·on /'wepən/ n [C] something that you use to fight with, especially a knife or gun —**weaponry** n [U]

wear[1] /weə‖wer/ v **wore** /wɔː‖wɔːr/, **worn** /wɔːn‖wɔːrn/, **wearing** **1** [T] to have clothes, shoes, glasses, jewellery etc on your body: *Dad was wearing his best suit.* | *She doesn't usually wear a lot of make-up.* **2** [T] to have your hair in a particular style: *Fay wore her hair in a bun.* **3** [T] to have a particular expression on your face: *He came out wearing a big grin on his face.* **4** [I,T] to become thin or damaged because of being held or rubbed a lot: *The carpet was starting to wear at the edges.* | **wear a hole in sth** (=make a hole in it by using it, rubbing it etc) **5** **wear well/badly** to stay/not stay in good condition after being used **6** **wear thin** if an excuse, joke etc is wearing thin, it has been used so often that is it no longer believable, funny, or effective: *That joke is wearing a bit thin.*
wear sth↔ **away** phr v [I,T] if something wears away or is worn away, it gradually becomes thinner and disappears because it has been rubbed or used a lot: *rocks worn away by the sea*
wear down phr v **1** [T **wear** sb↔ **down**] to make someone weaker or less determined, especially by attacking them or trying to persuade them: *Lewis gradually wore down his opponent and knocked him out in the eighth round.* **2** [I,T **wear** sth↔ **down**] if you wear something down or it wears down, it becomes flatter or smaller because it has been rubbed or used a lot: *My shoes have worn down at the heel.*
wear off phr v [I] if a feeling or the effect of something wears off, it gradually stops: *The drug was starting to wear off.*
wear on phr v [I] **as the day/evening etc wore on** used to say that something happened gradually during a particular day, evening etc: *It became hotter as the day wore on.*
wear out phr v **1** [I,T **wear** sth↔ **out**] if something wears out, or you wear it out, it becomes damaged and useless because it has been used so much: *After only a month Terry had worn out the soles of his shoes, and we had to buy some new ones.* **2** [T **wear** sb↔ **out**] to make someone feel very tired: *The kids are wearing me out.* → see also WEAR OUT

wear[2] n [U] **1** **children's/women's/casual etc wear** a particular kind of clothes worn by children, women, for informal occasions etc

2 damage caused when something is used over a long period: *The carpets are showing signs of wear.* | **wear and tear** (=damage caused by normal use) → see also **the worse for wear** (WORSE[1])

wear·ing /'weərɪŋ‖'wer-/ adj making you feel tired or annoyed: *He can be a bit wearing at times.*

wear·i·some /'wɪərɪsəm‖'wɪr-/ adj formal making you feel tired or annoyed: *a wearisome task*

wear·y /'wɪəri‖'wɪri/ adj especially literary **1** very tired: *a weary smile* **2** **weary of sth** wanting something to stop because you feel it has continued for too long: *The people were growing weary of the war.* —**wearily** adv —**weariness** n [U]

wea·sel /'wiːzəl/ n [C] an animal that lives in the countryside and looks like a long thin rat

weath·er[1] /'weðə‖-ər/ n **1** [singular, U] the temperature and other conditions such as sun, rain, and wind in a place at a particular time: *What was the weather like on your vacation?* | *The game was cancelled due to bad weather.* **2** **under the weather** spoken slightly ill

weather[2] v **1** [T] also **weather the storm** to succeed in continuing, in spite of being affected by a bad situation: *companies that have managed to weather the recession* **2** [I,T] if an object is weathered by the rain, wind etc, its colour and shape have been changed: *a weathered statue*

weather-beat·en /'.. ,../ adj made rough and red or dark by the wind and the sun: *the sailor's weather-beaten face*

weather fore·cast /'.. ,../ n [C] a report on the television or radio that says what the weather is expected to be like

weather fore·cast·er /'.. ,../ also **weatherman, weathergirl** n [C] a man or woman on the television or radio whose job is to say what the weather will be like

weather vane /'.. ./ n [C] a metal object usually on the top of a building, that moves to show the direction the wind is blowing

weave /wiːv/ v **wove** /wəʊv‖woʊv/ or **weaved**, **woven** /'wəʊvən‖'woʊ-/ or **weaved**, **weaving** **1** [I,T] to make cloth by crossing threads under and over each other using a special machine: *a beautifully woven carpet* **2** [T] to make something by twisting pieces of wood, string etc together: *basket-weaving* **3** [I,T] to move somewhere by turning and changing direction a lot: *The snake was weaving its way across the grass towards us.* —**weaver** n [C]

web /web/ n **1** [C] a net of thin threads made by a SPIDER to catch insects → see picture at SPIDER **2** **the Web** the WORLD WIDE WEB; a system that connects computers around the world together so that people can use and find information on the Internet **3** a set of things that are connected with each other in a complicated and confusing way: *a web of lies*

webbed /webd/ adj webbed feet have skin between the toes

web·site /'websaɪt/ n [C] a place on the Internet where you can go to find out information about a company, person, subject etc

wed /wed/ v [I,T] literary to marry

we'd /wid; *strong* wiːd/ the short form of 'we had' or 'we would': *We'd better go now. | We'd like some more coffee.*

wed·ding /'wedɪŋ/ *n* [C] a marriage ceremony, especially one with a meal and a party after it: *Have you been invited to their wedding? | a lovely silk wedding dress*

wedding ring /'... ./ *n* [C] a ring worn to show that you are married

wedge[1] /wedʒ/ *n* [C] a piece of something, which is thin and pointed at one end and thick at the other end: *a wedge of chocolate cake*

wedge[2] *v* [T] **1** to force something firmly into a narrow space: *She kept her hands wedged between her knees.* **2 wedge sth open/shut** to put something under a door, window etc to make it stay open or shut

Wednes·day /'wenzdi/ written abbreviation **Wed** *n* [C,U] the day of the week between Tuesday and Thursday → see Usage Note at DAY

wee[1] /wiː/ *adj* very small – used especially in Scotland: *a wee child*

wee[2] *v* [I] *BrE spoken* a word meaning to URINATE (=make liquid waste flow out of your body), used by children — **wee** *n* [U]

weed[1] /wiːd/ *n* [C] a wild plant that grows where you do not want it to grow

weed[2] *v* [I,T] to remove weeds from a place
weed sb/sth↔ out *phr v* [T] to get rid of people or things that are not very good or that you do not want

weed·y /'wiːdi/ *adj BrE informal* weak and not having a strong body or a strong character

week /wiːk/ *n* [C] **1** a period of seven days, which begins on Monday and ends on Sunday in Britain, and begins on Sunday and ends on Saturday in the US: *The movie starts this week. | They spent a couple of weeks in India.* **2** the part of the week between Monday and Friday, when people are working or studying: *I don't see the kids much during the week.*

week·day /'wiːkdeɪ/ *n* [C] any day of the week except Saturday and Sunday

week·end /ˌwiːk'endˌ, 'wiːkendǁ'wiːkend/ *n* [C] Saturday and Sunday: *What are you doing this weekend? | **at the weekend** BrE/**on the weekend** AmE I like to play golf at the weekend.*

week·ly /'wiːkli/ *adj* happening or done every week: *a weekly newspaper* —**weekly** *adv*

weep /wiːp/ *v* [I,T] **wept** /wept/, **wept, weeping** *especially literary* to cry: *She wept at the news.*

weigh /weɪ/ *v* **1** [linking verb] to have a particular weight: *The baby weighs 12 pounds. | How much do you weigh?* **2** [T] to use a machine to find out what something or someone weighs: *Have you weighed yourself lately?* **3** [T] also **weigh sth↔ up** to consider something carefully before making a decision: **weigh sth against sth** (=consider whether one thing is more important, better etc than another): *You have to weigh the benefits against the extra costs.* **4 weigh against sb/sth** to be considered an important disadvantage of someone or something: *Her age weighs against her.* **5 weigh on sb's mind** to make someone feel worried
weigh down *phr v* [T] **1** if you are weighed down by heavy things that you are carrying, they stop you from moving easily **2** if you are

weighed down by your problems and responsibilities, you worry a lot about them
weigh sth↔ out *phr v* [T] to measure an amount of something by weighing it: *Could you weigh out half a pound of flour for me?*
weigh up *phr v* [T] **1** [**weigh sth↔ up**] to consider something carefully: *She weighed up the options before giving her decision.* **2** [**weigh sb up**] to think carefully about what someone is like and form an opinion about them

weight[1] /weɪt/ *n* **1** [C,U] the amount that someone or something weighs: *Your weight is about right. | **put on/lose weight** (=become heavier or lighter): She's been trying to lose weight for months. | **the weight of sth** The roof collapsed under the weight of the snow.* **2** [singular, U] something that makes you feel worried: *the weight of responsibility | **be a weight off your mind/shoulders** (=used to say that you are glad that you no longer have to worry about something)* **3 weights** [plural] heavy pieces of metal, usually fixed to a metal bar, that people lift to make their muscles bigger **4** [C] a piece of metal weighing a particular amount that is balanced against something else to measure how much it weighs **5** [C] a heavy object: *Avoid lifting heavy weights.* → see also **carry weight** (CARRY), **pull your weight** (PULL[1]), **throw your weight around** (THROW[1])

weight[2]
weight sth↔ down *phr v* [T] to put something heavy on or in something so that it does not move: *The nets are weighted down with lead.*

weight·ed /'weɪtɪd/ *adj* **be weighted in favour of sb/against sb** if a system is weighted in favour of or against a group of people, it gives them advantages or disadvantages

weight·less /'weɪtləs/ *adj* having no weight, especially when you are floating in space —**weightlessness** *n* [U]

weight·lift·ing /'weɪtˌlɪftɪŋ/ *n* [U] the sport of lifting weights attached to the ends of a bar —**weight-lifter** *n* [C]

weight·y /'weɪti/ *adj* important and serious: *a weighty problem*

weir /wɪəǁwɪr/ *n* [C] a wall or fence built across a river to control or stop the flow of water

weird /wɪədǁwɪrd/ *adj informal* unusual and strange: *I've just had a really weird phonecall from Michael.* —**weirdly** *adv*

weird·o /'wɪədəʊǁ'wɪrdoʊ/ *n* [C] *informal* someone who seems very strange and behaves in a very strange way

wel·come[1] /'welkəm/ *interjection* used to greet someone who has just arrived: *Welcome to Chicago!*

welcome[2] *adj* **1 you're welcome!** *spoken, especially AmE* used to reply politely to someone who has just thanked you for something: *"Thanks for the coffee." "You're welcome."* **2** if you are welcome in a place, the other people want you to be there and are friendly to you: *I had the feeling I wasn't welcome. | **make sb welcome** They all did their best to make me feel welcome.* **3** if something is welcome, people are pleased that it has happened, because it is useful, pleasant etc: *a welcome suggestion | a welcome breeze* **4 be welcome to do sth** used to say that someone can do something if they want to: *You're welcome to stay for lunch.* **5 sb is wel-**

W

come to sth used to say that someone can have something if they want it, because you definitely do not want it: *If Rob wants that job he's welcome to it!*

welcome³ *v* [T] **1** to say hello in a friendly way to someone who has just arrived: *Jill was welcoming the guests at the door.* **2** if you welcome something, you approve of it and want it to happen: *We would welcome a change in the law.*

welcome⁴ *n* [singular] **1** the way in which people greet someone and behave towards them when they arrive somewhere: **give sb a warm welcome** (=treat someone in a very friendly way which shows you are pleased to see them) **2 outstay your welcome** to stay too long with someone, so that they wish you would leave

weld /weld/ *v* [T] to join metal objects to each other by heating them and pressing them together when they are hot —**welder** *n* [C]

wel·fare /'welfeəll-fer/ *n* [U] **1** whether or not someone has the things they need to be healthy, comfortable, and happy: *We're only concerned with your welfare.* **2** *AmE* also **Welfare** money paid by the government to people who are very poor, not working, ill etc: **be on welfare** (=be receiving it)

well¹ /wel/ *adv* **better** /'betəll-ər/ **best** /best/ **1** in a good, successful, or a satisfactory way: *Did you sleep well?* | **do well** (=be successful): *The business is doing well.* | **go well** (=happen in a successful way): *I hope the party goes well.* **2** thoroughly or completely: *Shake well before opening.* | *I don't know her very well.* | **well and truly** *especially spoken* (=completely or definitely): *Summer is now well and truly over.* **3 as well as** in addition to something else: *He's learning French as well as Italian.* | **as well** also: *My sister's going as well.* **5 well done** used to tell someone that you are pleased about their success: *"I got an 'A' in Spanish." "Well done!"* **6 may/might/could well** used to say that something is likely to happen or is likely to be true: *There may well be another earthquake very soon.* **7 may/might as well do sth** used to say that you think you should do something although you may not want to, for example because there is nothing else you can do: *We may as well get started.* **8** very much: **well after/ before etc** *By the time they finished it was well after midnight.* **9 can't/couldn't very well** *spoken* used to say that it does not seem sensible or fair to do something: *We can't very well just leave her on her own.* → see also **mean well** (MEAN¹)

well² *adj* **better, best 1** healthy and not ill: *You look well!* | *His mother's not very well.* | **very well thanks** (=used when answering someone's greeting): *"How are you?" "Very well thank you."* **2 it's just as well (that)** *spoken* used to say that it is lucky or good that things have happened in the way they have done: *It's just as well we didn't wait any longer, because the bus never came.* **3 it's/that's all very well** *spoken* used to say that you are not happy or satisfied with something: *It's all very well for you to say you're sorry, but I've been waiting here for two hours!*

well³ *interjection* **1** used when you want to pause before saying something, for example because you are not sure what to say or you feel doubtful: *"What do you think of pale pink for the bedroom?" "Well, it's a nice colour, but I'm not so*

sure." **2** also **well, well** used when you are surprised about something: *"She's just got a job with CNN." "Well, well."* **3** also **oh well** used to say that you accept a situation, even though it is not a very good one: *Oh well, at least you did your best.* **4** used when you want to start telling someone more about someone or something that you have just mentioned: *You know that guy I was telling you about? Well, he's been arrested!* → see also **very well** (VERY¹)

well⁴ *n* [C] a deep hole in the ground from which water or oil is taken

well⁵ *v*

well up *phr v* [I] *literary* **1** if tears well up in your eyes, they come into your eyes and you want to cry **2** if feelings well up, they start to get stronger: *Anger welled up inside him.*

we'll /wil; *strong* wiːl/ the short form of 'we will': *We'll have to leave soon.*

well-ad·vised /ˌ. .'. / *adj formal* **you would be well-advised to do sth** used to strongly advise someone to do something: *You would be well-advised to see a lawyer.*

well-bal·anced /ˌ. '.. / *adj* **1** a well-balanced person is sensible and does not suddenly become angry, upset etc **2** a well-balanced meal or DIET contains all the things you need to stay healthy

well-be·haved /ˌ. .'. / *adj* a well-behaved child behaves in the way he or she should

well-be·ing /ˌ. '.., '. ,../ *n* [U] a feeling of being comfortable, healthy, and happy

well-brought-up /ˌ. . '. / *adj* a well-brought-up child has been taught to be polite and behave well

well-built /ˌ. '. / *adj* someone who is well-built is big and strong

well-done /ˌ. '. / *adj* meat that is well-done has been cooked thoroughly: *He likes his steak well-done.*

well-dressed /ˌ. '. / *adj* wearing good clothes

well-earned /ˌ. '. / *adj* a well-earned rest, holiday etc is one that you deserve a lot, especially because you have been working hard

well-es·tab·lished /ˌ. .'.. / *adj* a well-established company, or organization has existed for a long time and people respect it

well-fed /ˌ. '. / *adj* someone who is well-fed gets plenty of good food to eat

well-heeled /ˌ. '. / *adj informal* rich

wel·lies /'weliz/ *n* [plural] *BrE informal* rubber boots that you wear to walk on wet or muddy ground; WELLINGTONS, RUBBER BOOTS *especially AmE* → see picture at SHOE

well-in·formed /ˌ. .'. / *adj* someone who is well-informed knows a lot about a subject or different subjects

wel·ling·tons /'welɪŋtənz/ also **wellington boots** /ˌ... '. / *n* [plural] *BrE* WELLIES; RUBBER BOOTS *especially AmE*

well-in·ten·tioned /ˌ. .'.. / *adj* well-meaning

well-kept /ˌ. '. / *adj* **1** looked after carefully and neat and tidy **2** a well-kept secret is one that few people know about

well-known /ˌ. '. / *adj* known by a lot of people: *a well-known artist and writer*

well-mean·ing /ˌ. '.. / *adj* intending to be helpful, but often not being helpful and making the situation worse: *well-meaning advice*

well-off /ˌ. '.◂ / *adj* having enough money to have a comfortable life and do the things that you want to do: *Her family are quite well-off.*

well-paid /ˌ. '.◂ / *adj* someone who is well-paid receives a lot of money for their work

well-read /ˌwel 'red◂ / *adj* someone who is well-read has read many books and knows a lot about different subjects

well-re·spect·ed /ˌ. .'.◂ / *adj* respected a lot by many people

well-timed /ˌ. '.◂ / *adj* said or done at a very suitable moment: *My arrival wasn't very well-timed.*

well-to-do /ˌ. . '.◂ / *adj* rich and having a high position in society: *a well-to-do family*

well-wish·er /'. ˌ.◂ / *n* [C] someone who does something to show that they want another person to succeed, become healthy again etc: *She received hundreds of cards from well-wishers.*

wel·ter /'weltəll-ər/ *n* **a welter of** *formal* a large and confusing number of different details or feelings: *a welter of information*

went /went/ *v* the past tense of GO

wept /wept/ *v* the past tense and past participle of WEEP

were /wə; *strong* wɜːllwər; *strong* wɜːr/ *v* the past tense of BE

we're /wɪəllwɪr/ the short form of 'we are': *We're going home.*

weren't /wɜːntllwɜːrnt/ the short form of 'were not': *His parents weren't very pleased when they found out.*

were·wolf /'weəwolf, 'wɪə-ll'wer-, 'wɪr-/ *n* [C] a person in stories who changes into a WOLF

west[1], **West** /west/ *n* [singular, U] **1** the direction towards the place where the sun goes down: *Which way is west?* **2 the west** the western part of a country or area: *Rain will spread to the west later today.* **3 the West a)** the countries in North America and the western part of Europe **b)** the part of the US west of the Mississippi River

west[2], **West** *adj* **1** in the west or facing west: *the west coast of the island* **2 west wind** a wind that comes from the west

west[3] *adv* towards the west: *The window faces west.* | *four miles west of Toronto*

west·bound /'westbaʊnd/ *adj* travelling or leading towards the west: *an accident on the westbound side of the freeway*

west·er·ly /'westəlill-ərli/ *adj* **1** towards the west or in the west: *sailing in a westerly direction* **2** westerly winds come from the west

west·ern[1], **Western** /'westənll-ərn/ *adj* **1** in or from the west of a country or area: *the largest city in western Iowa* **2 Western** in or from the countries in North America and the Western part of Europe: *Western technology*

western[2], **Western** *n* [C] a film about life in the 19th century in the American West, especially about COWBOYS

west·ern·er, Westerner /'westənəll-tərnər/ *n* [C] someone who comes from a country in North America or the western part of Europe

west·ern·ize (also **-ise** *BrE*) /'westənaɪzll-ər-/ *v* [T] if a country becomes westernized, it becomes like countries in North America and Western Europe ‘—**westernization** /ˌwestənaɪ'zeɪʃənll-tərnə-/ *n* [U]

west·ern·most /'westənməʊstll-tərnmoʊst/ *adj* furthest west: *the westernmost part of the island*

west·ward /'westwədll-wərd/ also **west·wards** /-wədzll-wərdz/ *adv* going or facing towards the west —**westward** *adj*

wet[1] /wet/ *adj* **1** covered in water or another liquid: *wet clothes* | *I didn't want to get my hair wet.* | **wet through** (=completely wet): *My jeans are wet through.* **2** rainy: *wet weather* | **the wet** (=the wet weather): *Come in out of the wet.* **3** not yet dry: *wet paint* —**wetness** *n* [U]

wet[2] *v* [T] **wet,** *or* **wetted, wet, wetting 1** to make something wet: *Wet this cloth and put it on her forehead.* **2 wet the bed/your pants etc** to make your bed etc wet because you URINATE by accident

wet blan·ket /ˌ. '..ll'. ˌ../ *n* [singular] *informal* someone who spoils other people's enjoyment by not taking part in an activity

wet suit /'. ./ *n* [C] rubber clothing that people wear to keep warm when swimming under water

we've /wiv; *strong* wiːv/ the short form of 'we have': *We've got to leave soon.*

whack /wæk/ *v* [T] *informal* to hit someone or something hard: *He whacked me with a stick.* —**whack** *n* [C]

whacked /wækt/ also **whacked out** /ˌ. '.◂/ *adj* *spoken* **1** very tired **2** *AmE* behaving in a very strange way

whale

whale /weɪl/ *n* **1** [C] a very large animal that swims in the sea and breathes through a hole on the top of its head **2 have a whale of a time** *informal* to enjoy yourself very much

whal·er /'weɪləll-ər/ *n* [C] someone who hunts whales, or a boat used for hunting whales

whal·ing /'weɪlɪŋ/ *n* [U] the activity of hunting whales

wham /wæm/ *n* [singular] the sound made when something hits another thing very hard

wharf /wɔːfllwɔːrf/ *n* [C], *plural* **wharves** a PLATFORM that is built out into the water so that boats can stop next to it and goods can be taken on and off; PIER

what /wɒtllwɑːt, wʌt/ *determiner, pron* **1** *especially spoken* used in questions to ask for information about something: *What are you doing?* | *What did Ellen say?* | *What kind of dog is*

GRAMMAR NOTE: a or the (1)

Use **a** or **an** before a noun when you are mentioning a person or thing for the first time, but use **the** when you mention that same person or thing again: *A man and **a** woman were sitting at the next table.* **The** woman was much younger than **the** man.

that? **2** used to talk about the things that someone asks, that someone is sure or not sure about etc: *I'm not sure what you can do.* | *She asked them what they wanted for lunch.* | *Father showed us what he'd made.* **3** used to say which things someone does, says, thinks etc: *I told him what to do.* **4** used at the beginning of a sentence to emphasize what you are saying, especially when you are very surprised, excited, annoyed etc: *What an idiot!* | *What a nice day!* **5** *spoken informal* used when you have not heard something that someone said. This use is often considered slightly rude: *"Do you want a fried egg?" "What?"* **6** used to ask what someone wants when they call your name: *"Anita?" "What?" "Can you come here for a minute?"* **7** **what's up?/what's happening?** *informal, especially AmE* used to say hello to someone you know well: *"Hey Chris! What's up?"* **8** **what's up (with sb/sth)** used to ask what is wrong with someone or something: *What's up with Denise?* **9** **what if...?** *spoken* **a)** used to talk about something that might happen, especially something bad or frightening: *What if he got lost?* **b)** used to make a suggestion: *What if I took you there in my car?* **10** **what with** *spoken* used when you are giving the reasons for something, especially a bad situation: *I can't afford to run a car, what with petrol, insurance and everything.* **11** **what's more** *spoken* used to add another thing to what you have just said, especially something interesting or surprising **12** **have what it takes** to have the ability or courage to do something: *Whitman doesn't have what it takes to do the job.* ➡ see also **guess what?** (GUESS[1]), **so?/so what?** (SO[1])

USAGE NOTE: what

When you are talking to someone and you do not understand what they say or you do not hear them clearly, it is polite to say, "I'm sorry, I didn't hear you" or "I'm sorry, I don't understand." It is not polite to just say "What?"

---

what·ev·er[1] / wɒt'evə‖wɑːt'evər, wʌt-/ *determiner, pron* **1** any or all of a group of things: *Just take whatever you need.* | **or whatever** *spoken* (=or any other similar thing): *You can go swimming, scuba diving, or whatever.* **2** used to say that it is not important what happens, what you do, what someone says etc, because the result will be the same in every case: *Whatever I say, she always disagrees.* **3** *spoken* used when you are surprised or annoyed: *Whatever are you talking about?*

whatever[2] *adj* of any possible kind: *He needs whatever help he can get.*

whatever[3], also **what·so·ev·er** /ˌwɒtsəʊ'evə‖ˌwɑːtsoʊ'evər, ˌwʌt-/ *adv* used to emphasize a negative statement: *She had no money whatsoever.*

wheat / wiːt / *n* [U] a plant that produces grain used for making flour, or grain that is used for making flour

whee·dle / 'wiːdl / *v* [I,T] to persuade someone to do something or give you something, especially by saying things that you do not really mean: *She managed to wheedle some money out of her parents.*

wheel[1] / wiːl / *n* [C] **1** one of the round things under a car, bicycle etc that turns on the surface of the ground when it moves **2** a round object joined to a ROD in a machine, which turns when the machine operates: *a gear wheel* **3** a STEERING WHEEL **4** **be at the wheel** to be driving a car

wheel[2] *v* **1** [T] to move something that has wheels: *She wheeled her bike into the garage.* **2** [I] to turn around suddenly: **+ around** *Anita wheeled around and started yelling at us.* ➡ see also WHEELING AND DEALING

wheel·bar·row / 'wiːl-ˌbærəʊ‖-roʊ / *n* [C] a small CART with one wheel in the front and two long handles for pushing, which you use outdoors to carry things, for example in a garden

wheelbarrow

wheel·chair / 'wiːltʃeə‖-tʃer / *n* [C] a chair with wheels, used by people who cannot walk ➡ see picture at CHAIR

wheel·ing and deal·ing /ˌ... '../ *n* [U] when someone uses complicated, secret and often dishonest methods to get what they want in business or politics

wheeze / wiːz / *v* [I] to breathe with difficulty and make a whistling sound in your chest —**wheezy** *adj*

when / wen / *adv, linking word* **1** at what time: *When are we leaving?* | *When did you notice he was gone?* **2** at or during a particular time: *I found some old letters when I was clearing out my desk.* | *When she was a little girl she wanted to be an actress.* **3** used to say when something happens: *Monday is the day when I visit my mother.* **4** even though something else is true: *Why do you want a new camera when your old one's perfectly good?* ➡ see also **since when** (SINCE)

when·ev·er / wen'evə‖-'evər / *adv, linking word* **1** every time: *Whenever we come here we always see someone we know.* **2** at any time: *Come over whenever you want.*

where / weə‖wer / *adv, linking word* **1** in or to which place: *Where do you live?* | *I think I know where he's gone.* **2** used to talk about a part of a process or situation: *It had reached the point where both of us wanted a divorce.* **3** **where possible** at all times when it is possible

where·a·bouts[1] / ˌweərə'baʊts‖'werabaʊts/ *adv spoken* used to ask where something is: *Whereabouts do you live?*

where·a·bouts[2] / 'weərəbaʊts‖'wer-/ *n* [U] the place where someone or something is: *His whereabouts are a mystery.*

where·as / weər'æz‖wer-/ *linking word* used to compare two situations, things, people etc and say how they are different from each other: *Nowadays the journey takes 6 hours, whereas then it took several weeks.*

where·by / weə'baɪ‖wer-/ *adv formal* by or according to which: *a law whereby all children could receive free education*

where·in / weər'ɪn‖wer-/ *adv, linking word formal* in which

where·u·pon / ˌweərə'pɒn‖'werəpɑːn, -pɒn/ *linking word formal* after which: *One of them called the other a liar, whereupon a fight broke out.*

wher·ev·er /weərˈevəllwerˈevər/ *adv* **1** in or to any place: *I always have her picture with me wherever I go.* **2 wherever possible** every time when it is possible to do something: *We try to use locally produced food wherever possible.* **3** *spoken* used at the beginning of a question to show surprise: *Wherever did you find that old thing?*

where·with·al /ˈweəwɪðɔːlllˈwerwɪðɒːl/ *n* the **wherewithal to do sth** the money, skills, or equipment you need in order to do something

whet /wet/ *v* **whet sb's appetite** to make someone want more of something, especially by giving or showing them a little of it

weth·er /ˈweðəl-ər/ *linking word* **1** used to talk about a choice between different possibilities: *He asked her whether she was coming.* | *I couldn't decide whether or not I wanted to go.* **2** used to say that something definitely will or will not happen, in spite of what someone wants or what the situation is: *Whether you like it or not, you have to take that test.*

whew /hjuː/ *interjection* PHEW

which /wɪtʃ/ *determiner, pron* **1** used in questions to ask about the thing or things you mean, when there are two or more of them: *Which of these books is yours?* **2** used to talk about a choice between two or more things: *I wondered which dress to buy.* | *It doesn't matter which school he goes to.* **3** used to say what kind of thing you are talking about, or to give more information about something: *I want a car which doesn't use too much petrol.* | *The house, which was built in the 16th century, is estimated to be worth several million pounds.* **4** *especially spoken* used to relate something that has just been mentioned to what you are going to say: *Which reminds me. Isn't it time we had lunch?*

USAGE NOTE: which and what

Use these words to ask a question about a choice you need to make. Use **what** when you make a choice from an unknown number or things or people: *What colour would you like your room to be painted?* Use **which** when you make a choice from a limited number of things or people: *Which colour would you like – blue or yellow?* **Which** can be followed by **of**, but **what** cannot: *Which of the colours do you like best?*

---

which·ev·er /wɪtʃˈevəl-ˈevər/ *determiner, pron* **1** any of a group of things or people: *You can choose whichever one you like.* **2** used to say that it is not important how you do something because the result will be the same in every case: *Whichever way you look at it he's guilty.*

whiff /wɪf/ *n* [C] a slight smell of something: *As she walked past, I caught a whiff of her perfume.* (=I could smell it)

while¹ /waɪl/ *linking word* **1** during the time that something is happening or someone is doing something: *They arrived while we were having dinner.* | *While you're here, can you help me with a little problem?* **2** in spite of the fact that; although: *While there was no conclusive evidence, most people thought he was guilty.* **3** used to say that although something is true of one thing, it is not true of another; WHEREAS: *The Tate Gallery has mostly modern art, while*

the National Gallery contains a lot of classical paintings.

while² *n* **a while** a period of time, especially a short one: *He'll be back in a little while.* → see also **(every) once in a while** (ONCE¹) **be worth (your) while** (WORTH¹)

while³ *v* **while away the hours/evening/days** etc to spend time in a pleasant and lazy way: *We whiled away the evenings playing cards.*

whilst /waɪlst/ *linking word especially BrE* while

whim /wɪm/ *n* [C] a sudden desire to do or have something, especially when there is no good reason for it: *I went to visit her on a whim.* (=because of a whim)

whim·per /ˈwɪmpəl-ər/ *v* [I] to make low crying sounds, because you are in pain or very sad: *The dog ran off whimpering.* —**whimper** *n* [C]

whim·si·cal /ˈwɪmzɪkəl/ *adj* doing something in a slightly unusual way for fun: *He had a rather whimsical sense of humour.*

whine /waɪn/ *v* [I] **1** to complain in an annoying way about something in a sad voice: *Stop whining and do your homework!* **2** to make a long high sound, which seems sad or unpleasant: *The baby was whining next door.* —**whine** *n* [C]

whinge /wɪndʒ/ *v* [I] *BrE* to complain in an annoying way about something unimportant —**whinge** *n* [C]

whin·ny /ˈwɪni/ *v* [I] if a horse whinnies, it makes a high but not very loud sound

whip¹ /wɪp/ *n* [C] a long thin piece of leather or rope with a handle, used for making animals move faster or for hitting people as a punishment

whip

whip² *v* **-pped, -pping** **1** [T] to hit a person or animal with a whip **2** [T] also **whip up** to mix something such as cream or an egg very quickly until it becomes thicker or more solid **3** [I,T] *informal* to move or take something with a quick sudden movement: *The wind whipped across the plain.* | *He whipped out a gun.* **4** **whip sb/sth into** shape *informal* to make a system, group of people etc start to work in an organized way **5** [T] *informal, especially AmE* to defeat someone easily: *The Hawks whipped the Huskies 42-3.*

whip up *phr v* [T] **1** to make people have a particular feeling, for example to make them hate or support something **2** [whip sth↔ up] *informal* to quickly make something to eat: *I could whip up a salad.*

whip-round /ˈ. ./ *n* **have a whip-round** *BrE informal* if a group of people have a whip-round, they all give some money so that they can buy something for one of the group

whir /wɜː‖wɜːr/ *v* the usual American spelling of WHIRR

whirl¹ /wɜːl‖wɜːrl/ *v* [I,T] to turn around very quickly, or to make something do this: *The leaves whirled around in the wind.*

whirl² *n* [singular] **1** when a lot of things happen in an exciting or confusing way: *Her life was a whirl of parties and dinner dates.* **2** when someone or something turns around very quickly: *a whirl of dust* | *the whirl of the dancers*

W

3 give sth a whirl *informal* to do something or use something once to find out if it works or if you like it **4 be in a whirl** to feel very excited or confused about something: *Debbie's head was all in a whirl.*

whirl·pool /ˈwɜːlpuːl‖ˈwɜːrl-/ *n* [C] a powerful current of water that turns around very quickly and pulls things down into it

whirl·wind /ˈwɜːl,wɪnd‖ˈwɜːrl-/ *n* **1 a whirlwind romance/tour etc** a ROMANCE etc that happens extremely quickly **2** [C] an extremely strong wind that moves quickly with a circular movement, causing a lot of damage **3 a whirlwind of activity/emotions etc** a situation in which there is a lot of activity or you experience a lot of different emotions

whirr *BrE*, **whir** *AmE* /wɜː‖wɜːr/ *v* [I] if something, especially a machine, whirrs, it makes a continuous low sound: *the whirring of the fax machine* —**whirr** *n* [singular]

whisk¹ /wɪsk/ *v* [T] **1** to move eggs, cream etc round very quickly using a fork or a special kitchen tool, so that air is mixed in: *Whisk the yolks in a bowl.* **2** to quickly take someone or something somewhere: *The band was whisked off to their hotel in a big limousine.*

whisk² *n* [C] a small kitchen tool made of curved pieces of wire, used for whisking eggs, cream etc

whis·ker /ˈwɪskə‖-ər/ *n* [C] one of the long, stiff hairs that grow near the mouth of a cat, mouse etc

whis·kers /ˈwɪskəz‖-ərz/ *n* [plural] the hair that grows on a man's face

whis·key /ˈwɪski/ *n* [C,U] whisky made in Ireland or the United States

whis·ky /ˈwɪski/ *n* [C, U] a strong alcoholic drink made from grain and produced especially in Scotland

whis·per¹ /ˈwɪspə‖-ər/ *v* **1** [I,T] to say something very quietly to someone, so that other people cannot hear: *She whispered something in my ear.* **2** [I] *literary* to make a soft sound like a whisper: *The wind whispered in the trees.*

whisper² *n* [C] **1** a very quiet voice: *He spoke in a whisper.* **2** *literary* a soft sound: *the whisper of the wind in the trees*

whis·tle¹ /ˈwɪsəl/ *v* **1** [I,T] to make a high sound or tune by blowing air out through your lips: *Adam whistled softly to himself as he walked down the street.* **2** [I] to move quickly with a high sound: *Bullets were whistling through the air.* **3** [I] to make a high sound when air or steam is forced through a small hole: *a whistling kettle*

whistle² *n* [C] **1** a small object that produces a high sound when you blow into it: *The referee blew his whistle.* **2** a high sound made by blowing air through a whistle, your lips etc

whistle

white¹ /waɪt/ *adj* **1** having the colour of milk, snow, or salt: *white paint* ➡ see colour picture on page 114 **2** someone who is white has pale skin: *Most of the students in this class are white.* | **go white** (=become very pale, especially because you are very frightened or shocked): *Her face went white.* **3** *BrE* white coffee has milk or cream in it **4** white wine is a clear pale yellow or pale green colour — **whiteness** *n* [U]

white² *n* **1** [U] a white colour ➡ see colour picture on page 114 **2** [C] also **White** someone who has pale skin **3** [C,U] the clear part of the inside of an egg, that surrounds the yellow part

white·board /ˈwaɪtbɔːd‖-bɔːrd/ *n* [C] a large white board used for writing on in classrooms

white-col·lar /ˌ. ˈ..◂/ *adj* white collar workers do jobs in offices, banks etc ➡ compare BLUE-COLLAR

white el·e·phant /ˌ. ˈ.../ *n* [C] something that is not at all useful, especially something that has cost a lot of money

White House /ˈ. ./ *n* [singular] the president of the US and the people who advise him or her —**White House** *adj*: *a White House spokesperson*

white lie /ˌ. ˈ./ *n* [C] a small lie, especially one that you tell in order to avoid upsetting someone or making them angry

whit·en /ˈwaɪtn/ *v* [I,T] to make something white or become white

white·wash /ˈwaɪtwɒʃ‖-wɒːʃ, -wɑːʃ/ *n* **1** [C usually singular] when a government or official organization tries to hide the true facts about a situation and make it seem much less serious than it really is: *The newspapers are calling the report a whitewash.* **2** [U] a white liquid used for painting walls —**whitewash** *v* [T]

whit·tle /ˈwɪtl/ *v* [I,T] to cut a piece of wood into a particular shape by cutting off small pieces

whittle away *phr v* [I,T] to gradually make something smaller or less effective: *His power has been slowly whittled away.*

whittle sth↔down *phr v* [T] to gradually reduce the number or amount of something by taking parts away: *I've whittled down the list of guests from 30 to 16.*

whizz¹, **whiz** *especially AmE* /wɪz/ *v* [I] *informal* to move very quickly: *Marty whizzed past us on his motorbike.*

whizz² also **whiz** *especially AmE* — *n* [singular] *informal* someone who is very good or quick at doing something

whizz·kid /ˈwɪzkɪd/ *n* [C] someone who is young and very successful or very good at doing something: *high-tech whizzkids in Silicon Valley*

who /huː/ *pron* **1** used in questions to ask the name of a person or group of people: *"Who is that?" "That's Amy's brother." | "Who told you about the fire?" "Mr Garcia."* **2** used to say that a person or group of people does something: *I know who sent you that card.* **3** used to say which person you mean, or to add more information about someone: *That's the woman who owns the house. | She asked their English teacher, who had studied at Oxford.* ➡ see also WHOM

who'd /huːd/ the short form of 'who had': *a young girl who'd been attacked*

who·dun·it, whodunnit /ˌhuːˈdʌnɪt/ *n* [C] a book, film etc about a murder, in which you do not find out who the killer is until the end

who·ev·er /huːˈevə‖-ˈevər/ *pron* **1** used to talk about someone when you do not know who he or she is: *Whoever did this is in big trouble.* **2** used to say that it is not important which person does something or which person is chosen: *Whoever gets there first can find a table.*

W

whole[1] /həʊl‖hoʊl/ adj **1** all of something; ENTIRE: *She drank a whole bottle of wine.| Barney spent the whole day in bed.* **2** complete and not divided or broken into parts: *The bird opened its mouth and swallowed the fish whole.*

whole[2] n **1** **the whole of** all of something: *The whole of Southern England is covered in cloud.* **2** **on the whole** used to say that something is generally true: *On the whole, life was much quieter after John left.* **3** **as a whole** used to say that all the parts of something are being considered: *We must look at our educational system as a whole.*

whole·food /'həʊlfuːd‖'hoʊl-/ n [U] food that does not contain harmful chemicals and artificial things, and is as natural as possible

whole·heart·ed /ˌ. '..◂/ adj **wholehearted support/agreement/approval etc** when someone supports or agrees with something completely —**wholeheartedly** adv

whole·meal /'həʊlmiːl‖'hoʊl-/ adj BrE wholemeal flour or bread uses all of the grain, including all of the outside layer; WHOLE WHEAT AmE

whole·sale /'həʊlseɪl‖'hoʊl-/ adj **1** connected with the sale of goods in large quantities, usually at low prices: *wholesale prices* **2** very great and affecting large areas, numbers of people etc, and usually having a very bad effect: *the wholesale destruction of the rainforest* —**wholesale** adv

whole·sal·er /'həʊlˌseɪlə‖'hoʊl,seɪlər/ n [C] a person or company that buys goods in large quantities and sells them to shops, usually at low prices

whole·some /'həʊlsəm‖'hoʊl-/ adj **1** good for your health: *a good wholesome breakfast* **2** morally good, or having a good moral effect: *a nice clean wholesome kid | wholesome family entertainment*

whole wheat /'. ./ adj AmE whole wheat flour or bread uses all of the grain, including the outside layer; WHOLEMEAL BrE

who'll /huːl/ the short form of 'who will': *This is Denise, who'll be your guide today.*

whol·ly /'həʊl-li‖'hoʊl-/ adv formal completely: *The rumours are wholly untrue.*

whom /huːm/ pron the object form of 'who', used especially in formal speech or writing: *The club has 200 members, most of whom are men.*

whoop /wuːp, huːp/ v [I] to shout loudly and happily —**whoop** n [C]

whooping cough /'huːpɪŋ kɒf/ n [U] a serious disease in which you make a loud noise after you cough, which affects mostly children

whoops /wʊps/ interjection used when you make a small mistake, drop something, or fall

whop·per /'wɒpə‖'wɑːpər/ n [C] informal something that is unusually large

whore /hɔː‖hɔːr/ n [C] an offensive word for a PROSTITUTE

who're /'huːə-ər/ the short form of 'who are': *Who're those two guys?*

who's /huːz/ the short form of 'who is' or 'who has': *Who's sitting next to Reggie?| That's Karl, the guy who's come over from Germany.*

whose /huːz/ determiner, possessive pron **1** used to ask who something belongs to or is connected with: *Whose jacket is this?* **2** used to say that something belongs to someone, or that something or someone is connected with another person: *families whose relatives have been killed*

who've /huːv/ the short form of 'who have': *people who've been in prison*

why /waɪ/ adv, linking word **1** for what reason: *Why are these books so cheap?| I think I know why I didn't get the job.* **2** **why don't you/why not ... etc** spoken used to make a suggestion: *Why don't you try this one?* **3** **why not?** spoken used to agree with someone's suggestion: "*Do you want to come along?" "Yeah, why not?"*

wick /wɪk/ n [C] the string that burns in a CANDLE or in an oil lamp

wick·ed /'wɪkɪd/ adj **1** behaving in a way that is morally very bad; evil: *the wicked stepmother in 'Cinderella'* **2** behaving badly in a way that is amusing MISCHIEVOUS: *a wicked grin* **3** informal very good: "*How was the concert?" "Wicked!"* —**wickedness** n [U] — **wickedly** adv

wick·er /'wɪkə-ər/ n [U] a material made from thin dry branches or CANES woven together: *a white wicker chair*

wick·et /'wɪkɪt/ n [C] one of the sets of sticks that the BOWLER tries to hit with the ball in CRICKET

wide[1] /waɪd/ adj **1** measuring a large distance from one side to another: *a wide street | a wide mouth | The earthquake was felt over a wide area.* → see picture at NARROW **2** measuring a particular distance from one side to the other: *The bathtub's three feet wide.* **3** including a large variety of different people, things etc: *We offer a wide range of vegetarian dishes.* **4** **wide difference/gap etc** a large and noticeable difference, GAP etc: *wide differences of opinion* **5** fully open: *Their eyes were wide.| a wide grin* **6** **wider** wider problems, questions, or parts of a situation are more general and often more important: *The trial also raises a much wider issue.*

wide[2] adv **1** **wide open/apart** open as far as possible, or as far as possible apart: *Somebody left the door wide open.| He stood with his legs wide apart.* **2** **wide awake** completely awake **3** away from the point that you were aiming at: *His shot went wide.*

wide-eyed /ˌ. '.◂/ adj **1** with your eyes wide open, especially because you are surprised or frightened: *a look of wide-eyed amazement* **2** too willing to believe, accept, or admire things because you do not have much experience of life: *wide-eyed innocence* —**wide-eyed** adv

wide·ly /'waɪdli/ adv **1** in a lot of different places or by a lot of people: *products that are*

W

GRAMMAR NOTE: countable and uncountable (1)
If you can put numbers in front of a noun (*one horse, two tickets* etc) and make it plural, that noun is **countable**: n [C]. A substance (e.g. *butter, air*), or an idea or quality (e.g. *beauty, information*) cannot be made plural or used with **a** or **an**. These are **uncountable**: n [U].

widely available | a widely read newspaper **2** to a large degree; a lot: *Taxes vary widely from state to state.*

wid·en /ˈwaɪdn/ v [I,T] **1** to become wider or to make something wider: *They're widening the road.* **2** to become greater or larger, or to make something do this: *The gap between rich and poor began to widen.*

wide-rang·ing /ˌ. ˈ.../ adv affecting or including a lot of different things, people etc: *a wide-ranging discussion*

wide·spread /ˈwaɪdspred/ adj happening in many places, among many people, or in many situations: *the widespread use of illegal drugs*

wid·ow /ˈwɪdəʊ‖-doʊ/ n [C] a woman whose husband has died, who has not married again

wid·owed /ˈwɪdəʊd‖-doʊd/ adj if someone is widowed, their husband or wife dies

wid·ow·er /ˈwɪdəʊə‖-doʊər/ n [C] a man whose wife has died, who has not married again

width /wɪdθ/ n [C,U] the distance from one side of something to the other: *the width of the window* | *a width of 10 inches* ➙ see picture at HEIGHT

wield /wiːld/ v [T] **1** **wield power/influence/authority etc** to have a lot of power, influence etc and be able to use it: *the influence wielded by the church* **2** to hold a weapon or tool and use it

wie·ner /ˈwiːnəl-ər/ n [C] *AmE* a FRANKFURTER

wife /waɪf/ n [C], *plural* **wives** /waɪvz/ the woman that a man is married to: *This is my wife, Elaine.*

wig /wɪg/ n [C] artificial hair that you wear on your head: *a blond wig*

wig·gle /ˈwɪgəl/ v [I,T] to make small movements from side to side or up and down, or to make something move this way: *Can you wiggle your toes?* —**wiggle** n [C]

wig·wam /ˈwɪgwæm‖-wɑːm/ n [C] a type of tent that was used by Native Americans

wild¹ /waɪld/ adj **1** wild animals and plants live or grow in natural conditions, and are not looked after by people on farms, in gardens etc: *wild horses* | *wild flowers* **2** a wild area of land is in a completely natural state and does not have farms, towns etc on it: *some of the wildest and most beautiful parts of Pakistan* **3** very excited, angry, or happy and unable to control your feelings: *A wild look came into her eyes.* | **go wild** (=become very excited or angry): *When the band came back on stage the crowd went wild.* **4** stormy and windy: *It was a wild night.* **5** done or said without thinking carefully or without knowing all the facts, with the result that you may be completely wrong: *a wild guess* | *wild accusations* **6** **be wild about** *spoken* to like someone or something very much: *I'm not too wild about his movies.* **7** **run wild** to behave in an uncontrolled way because people do not try to control you and tell you what you should do: *She lets her children run wild.* —**wildly** adv

wild² n **1** **in the wild** in an area outside a farm or a zoo, where animals can live freely and naturally: *animals that live in the wild* **2** **the wilds** areas that are very far from towns and cities, where very few people live: *the wilds of Tibet*

wil·der·ness /ˈwɪldənəs‖-dər-/ n [singular,U] a large natural area of land that has never had farms, buildings etc on it: *the Alaskan wilderness*

wild·fire /ˈwaɪldfaɪəl-faɪr/ n **spread like wildfire** to spread very quickly

wild goose chase /ˌ. ˈ. ./ n [singular] a situation in which you waste a lot of time looking for something that cannot be found

wild·life /ˈwaɪldlaɪf/ n [U] animals and plants that live in natural conditions: *the wildlife of Crete*

wiles /waɪlz/ n [plural] things you say or tricks you use in order to persuade someone to do what you want, especially in a secret and slightly dishonest way

wil·ful *especially BrE*, **willful** *AmE* /ˈwɪlfəl/ adj doing what you want even though people tell you not to: *a wilful child* —**wilfully** adv

will¹ /wɪl/ *modal verb* **1** used to talk about the future, especially to say what you think or hope will happen, or to say what you have decided to do: *I'm sure everything will be OK.* | *I'll* (=I will) *tell you later.* | *What time will she get here?* **2** used to say that you are willing to do something, or that something can do something: *I'll do whatever you say.* | *Vern said he won't* (=will not) *work for Joe.* | *My computer won't come on.* **3** used to ask someone to do something or offer something to someone: *Will you do me a favour?* | *Won't you have another glass of wine?* **4** used in CONDITIONAL sentences that use the present tense in the 'if' clause: *If it rains, we'll have the barbecue in the clubhouse.* **5** used to say what always happens or what is generally true: *Prices will always go up.* **6** used to say that someone often does something which you find annoying: *He will keep talking about himself all the time.* **7** **that/it will be** *spoken* used to say who someone is or what something is: *"There's someone at the front door." "That'll be Nick."*

will² n **1** [C,U] the determination to do something: *the will to succeed* | *He's lost his will to live.* **2** [C] a legal document in which you say who you want to give your money and property to after you die: *Grandma Stacy left me $7,000 in her will.* **3** [singular] what someone wants to happen: *the will of the people* | **against your will** (=when you are forced to do something that you do not want to do): *No one can make you stay here against your will.* | **of your own free will** (=because you want to do something, not because you are forced to do it): *She left of her own free will.* **4** **at will** whenever you want, without any difficulty or opposition: *The England defence was weak, and their opponents were able to score almost at will.*

will³ v [T] to try to make something happen by thinking about it very hard: *The crowd were all willing her to win.*

will·ful /ˈwɪlfəl/ the usual American spelling of WILFUL

will·ing /ˈwɪlɪŋ/ adj **1** **be willing to do sth** if you are willing to do something, you will agree to do it if someone asks you to do it: *How much are they willing to pay?* **2** eager and wanting to do something very much: *willing helpers* —**willingly** adv —**willingness** n [U] ➙ opposite UNWILLING

wil·low /ˈwɪləʊ‖-loʊ/ n [C] a tree with very long thin branches that grows near water

wil·low·y /ˈwɪləʊiǁ-loʊi/ *adj* tall, thin, and graceful

will·pow·er /ˈwɪlˌpaʊəǁ-ˌpaʊr/ *n* [U] determination and the ability to control your thoughts and actions so that you can achieve something: *I'd love to give up smoking, but I don't have the willpower.*

wilt /wɪlt/ *v* [I] if a plant or flower wilts, it bends and becomes weak because it needs water, is old etc

wil·y /ˈwaɪli/ *adj* good at using tricks to get what you want: *a wily politician*

wimp /wɪmp/ *n* [C] *informal often humorous* a disapproving word for someone who is too afraid to do something because they think it is difficult or unpleasant: *Don't be such a wimp!* —**wimpy** *adj*

win[1] /wɪn/ *v* **won** /wʌn/ **won, winning** **1** [I,T] to get the most points or votes in a competition, game, election etc: *Who do you think will win the Superbowl?* | *Dad won at chess again.* | *Marcy's team is winning by 3 points.* **2** [I,T] to be successful in a war, fight, or argument against another country, person etc: *The English army won a great victory.* **3** [T] to get a prize in a competition or game: *I won $200 playing poker.* **4** [T] to get something good because of your effort, skill etc: *Dr Lee's work won her the admiration of scientists worldwide.* **5 you can't win** *spoken* used to say that whatever you do in a situation, someone will be annoyed, or you will be unsuccessful in some way → opposite LOSE

win sb↔ **over** *phr v* [T] to persuade someone to support you, agree with you, or like you: *Clinton managed to win over his critics.*

win[2] *n* [C] when a team or player wins in a sport or competition: *a record of 7 wins and 6 losses*

wince /wɪns/ *v* [I] to suddenly change the expression on your face when you see or remember something painful or embarrassing: *She winced when she saw the needle going into her arm.*

winch /wɪntʃ/ *n* [C] a machine with a rope or chain used for lifting heavy objects —**winch** *v* [T]

wind[1] /wɪnd/ *n* **1** [C,U] a moving current of air near the ground: *We walked home through the wind and the rain.* | *A strong wind was blowing.* **2 get wind of sth** to accidentally find out about something that has been secretly planned **3** [U] if you get wind, you have air or gas in your stomach and it feels uncomfortable **4 get your wind (back)** to breathe regularly and easily again → see also SECOND WIND

wind[2] /waɪnd/ *v* **wound** /waʊnd/ **wound, winding** **1** [I,T] to turn or twist something long and thin several times: *She wound the bandage around his arm.* → opposite UNWIND **2** [T] also **wind up** to make a machine, toy, clock etc work by turning a small handle around several times: *I forgot to wind my watch.* **3** [I] if a road, river etc winds, it curves or bends many times

wind down *phr v* **1** [I,T **wind** sth↔ **down**] to gradually end, or make something end: *The party started winding down after midnight.* **2** [I] to rest and relax

wind up *phr v* **1** [I] to go somewhere or do something without intending to: *We always wind up doing what she wants to do.* | *Most of them wound up in prison.* **2** [I,T **wind** sth↔ **up**] to end an activity, meeting etc: *It's almost 5:00 — we'd better wind things up.* **3** [T **wind** sb↔ **up**] *BrE informal* to deliberately say something to annoy someone as a joke

wind[3] /wɪnd/ *v* [T] to make someone have difficulty breathing

wind·chill fac·tor /ˈwɪndtʃɪl ˌfæktəlǁ-ər/ *n* [U] the combination of cold weather and strong winds, which makes the temperature seem colder

wind·ed /ˈwɪndɪd/ *adj* if you are winded, you cannot breathe for a few seconds because you have been running or have been hit in the stomach

wind·fall /ˈwɪndfɔːlǁ-fɒːl/ *n* [C] an amount of money that you get unexpectedly

wind farm /ˈ. ./ *n* [C] a group of WINDMILLs that are used to produce electricity

wind·ing /ˈwaɪndɪŋ/ *adj* curving or bending many times: *a long, winding river*

wind in·stru·ment /ˈwɪnd ˌɪnstrᵿmənt/ *n* [C] a musical instrument such as a FLUTE which you play by blowing into it

wind·mill /ˈwɪndˌmɪl/ *n* [C] a building with parts that turn with the wind, which is used to make power, for example to crush grain

win·dow /ˈwɪndəʊǁ-doʊ/ *n* [C] **1** a space with glass across it in the wall of a building, car etc, used for letting in light and seeing out of: *Can I open the window?* → see colour picture on page 79 **2** one of the areas on a computer screen where you can do different types of work

window box /ˈ.. ./ *n* [C] a long narrow container used for growing plants outside your window

win·dow·pane /ˈwɪndəʊpeɪnǁ-doʊ-/ *n* [C] a piece of glass used in a window

window shop·ping /ˈ.. ˌ../ *n* [U] when you look at goods in shops, without intending to buy them

win·dow·sill /ˈwɪndəʊˌsɪlǁ-doʊ-/ *n* [C] a shelf at the bottom of a window → see colour picture on page 79

wind·pipe /ˈwɪndpaɪp/ *n* [C] the tube through which air passes from your throat to your lungs

wind·screen /ˈwɪndskriːn/ *BrE*, **wind·shield** /-ʃiːld/ *AmE* — *n* [C] the large window at the front of a car, bus etc → see picture at CAR

windscreen wip·er *BrE*, **windshield wiper** /ˈ.. ˌ../ *AmE n* [C] a long piece of metal with rubber on it that moves across a car windscreen to remove the rain → see picture at CAR

wind·surf·ing /ˈwɪndˌsɜːfɪŋǁ-ɜːr-/ *n* [U] the sport of sailing across water by standing on a special board and holding onto a large sail —**windsurfer** *n* [C]

wind·swept /ˈwɪndswept/ *adj* a place that is windswept has few trees, buildings etc and is often very windy

wind tur·bine /ˈwɪnd ˌtɜːbaɪnǁ-ˌtɜːr-/ *n* [C] a tall structure with parts that are turned by the wind, used for making electricity

wind·y /ˈwɪndi/ *adj* if the weather is windy, there is a lot of wind: *It's been windy all day.*

wine /waɪn/ *n* [C,U] an alcoholic drink made from GRAPES or other fruit: *a glass of red wine* | *a fine selection of German wines*

wing /wɪŋ/ *n* [C] **1** one of the two parts of a bird's or insect's body that it uses for flying:

ducks *flapping their wings* **2** one of the two flat parts that stick out of a plane's sides and help it stay in the air **3** one of the parts that a large building is divided into: *the east wing of the library* **4** one of the groups that a political party is divided into, based on the members' opinions: *the conservative wing of the Democrats* → see also LEFT-WING RIGHT-WING **5 take sb under your wing** to give help and advice to someone who is younger or less experienced than you **6** *BrE* one of the parts of a car that covers the wheels; FENDER *AmE* → see picture at CAR **7** a player who attacks along one side of the field, in games such as football

winged / wɪŋd / *adj* having wings: *winged insects*

wings / wɪŋz / *n* [plural] **1 the wings** the side parts of a stage where actors are hidden from people watching the play **2 waiting in the wings** ready to be used or ready to do something

wing·span / ˈwɪŋspæn / *n* [C] the distance from the end of one wing to the end of the other

wing·tip / ˈwɪŋtɪp / *n* [C] the end of a wing

wink / wɪŋk / *v* [I] to close and open one eye quickly, especially to show that you are joking or being friendly: *"Don't tell dad," he said, winking at her.* —**wink** *n* [C] → see also **not sleep a wink** (SLEEP[1])

wink

win·ner / ˈwɪnəl-ər / *n* [C] the person who wins a competition, game, election etc: *the winner of the poetry contest*

win·nings / ˈwɪnɪŋz / *n* [plural] money that you win in a game or competition

wi·no / ˈwaɪnəʊll-noʊ / *n* [C] *informal* someone who drinks a lot of alcohol and lives on the streets

win·ter / ˈwɪntəl-ər / *n* [C,U] the season between autumn and spring, when the weather is coldest: *I hope it snows this winter.* | *cold winter evenings*

win·try / ˈwɪntri / *adj* typical of winter, especially because it is cold or snowing: *wintry weather*

wipe / waɪp / *v* **1** [I,T] to clean something by rubbing it with a cloth or a soft surface: *Could you wipe the table for me?* | *Wipe your feet before you come in.* **2** [I,T] to remove dirt, water etc from something with a cloth or your hand: *He wiped the sweat from his face.* | *wiping away her tears* **3** [T] to remove all the information that is stored on a TAPE, VIDEO, or computer DISK —**wipe** *n* [C]

wipe

wipe out *phr v* [T **wipe** sb/sth↔ **out**] to destroy something completely: *Whole towns were wiped out.*

wipe sth↔ **up** *phr v* [T] to remove liquid from a surface using a cloth: *Wipe up this mess!*

wip·er / ˈwaɪpəl-ər / *n* [C usually plural] a WINDSCREEN WIPER

wire[1] / waɪəll waɪr / *n* **1** [C,U] metal that is shaped like thick thread, used in fences and for fastening things together: *a wire fence* **2** [C] a piece of metal like a thick thread, used for carry-

ing electricity: *Have you connected up all the wires?* | *a telephone wire* **3** [C] *AmE* a TELEGRAM

wire[2] *v* [T] **1** also **wire up** to connect the wires so that a piece of electrical equipment can work, or so that electricity can flow to different parts of a building: *I've almost finished wiring up the alarm.* **2** to fasten two or more things together using wire: *Lila had to have her jaw wired.* **3** to send money electronically from one bank to another **4** *AmE* to send a TELEGRAM

wired / waɪədll waɪrd / *adj AmE informal* feeling very active, excited, and awake

wire·less / ˈwaɪələsll waɪr- / *n* [C,U] *old-fashioned* a radio

wir·ing / ˈwaɪərɪŋ ll waɪr- / *n* [U] the system of wires that carries electricity to the rooms in a building

wir·y / ˈwaɪəri ll waɪri / *adj* **1** someone who is wiry is thin but strong **2** wiry hair is stiff and curly

wis·dom / ˈwɪzdəm / *n* **1** [U] knowledge or the ability to make good decisions because you have had a lot of experience **2 the wisdom of sth** whether something is sensible and based on good judgement: *Some people doubted the wisdom of his decision.*

wisdom tooth / ˈ. . / *n* [C] one of the four large teeth at the back of your mouth that do not grow until you are an adult

wise[1] / waɪz / *adj* **1** a wise decision or action is sensible: *I think you've made a wise decision.* | *It would be wise to leave early.* → opposite UNWISE **2** a wise person is able to make good decisions and give good advice because they have had a lot of experience: *a wise leader* **3 be none the wiser** to not understand something any better after someone has tried to explain it to you: *They sent me on a training course, but I'm still none the wiser.* **4 price-wise/time-wise etc** *spoken* when considering prices, time etc: *Price-wise the house seems OK, but I'm not sure it's big enough.* —**wisely** *adv*

wise[2] *v*

wise up *phr v* [I] *informal* to realize that something important is true: *Companies are starting to wise up to the fact that it's cheaper to employ people who work from home.*

wise·crack / ˈwaɪzkræk / *n* [C] *informal* a quick, funny, and often slightly unkind remark

wise guy / ˈ. . / *n* [C] *informal, especially AmE* an annoying person who thinks that they know more than other people

wish[1] / wɪʃ / *v* **1** [I,T] to want something to happen even though it is very unlikely, or you cannot control what will happen: **+ (that)** *I wish I had a car like that.* | *Beth wished she could stay there forever.* | **wish sb/sth would do sth** *I wish they would turn that music down.* | **for** *the best birthday present I could ever have wished for* **2** [I,T] *formal* to want to do something: *I wish to make a complaint.* **3** [T] to say that you hope someone will be happy, successful, lucky etc: *Wish me luck!* **4 I/you wish!** *spoken* used to say that you are sure something is not true, even though someone wants it to be true: *"I think she wants to go out with me." "You wish!"*

wish[2] *n* **1** [C] something that you want to happen: **make a wish** (=secretly say to yourself that you hope that something happens): *Close your eyes and make a wish!* | **have no wish to do sth**

(=definitely not want to do something): *I had no wish to see him again.* **2 best wishes** a friendly phrase written in cards or at the end of letters

wish·ful think·ing /ˌ·· '··/ *n* [U] when someone thinks that something good might happen, even though it is completely impossible

wish·y-wash·y /'wɪʃi ˌwɒʃi‖-ˌwɒːʃi, -ˌwɑːʃi/ *adj* informal not having clear and definite ideas about what you want to do or what you think should happen: *a bunch of wishy-washy liberals*

wisp /wɪsp/ *n* [C] **1** a small thin amount of hair that is separate from the rest **2** a small thin line of smoke, cloud etc that rises upwards —**wispy** *adj*

wist·ful /'wɪstfəl/ *adj* a little sad because you know that you cannot have something you want: *a wistful expression* —**wistfully** *adv*

wit /wɪt/ *n* [U] the ability to say things that are clever and amusing: *Wilde was famous for his wit.* ➡ see also WITS

witch /wɪtʃ/ *n* [C] a woman who is believed to have magic powers, especially to do bad things

witch·craft /'wɪtʃkrɑːft‖-kræft/ *n* [U] the use of magic to make strange things happen

witch doc·tor /'· ˌ··/ *n* [C] a man who is believed to be able to cure people using magic, especially in some parts of Africa

witch hunt /'· ·/ *n* [C] when a government or organization tries to find and punish people whose opinions are believed to be wrong or dangerous, in a way that seems very unfair

with /wɪð, wɪθ/ *prep* **1** used to say that two or more people or things are together or near each other: *She's staying with some friends.* | *Put this bag with the others.* | *eggs mixed with milk* **2** used to say that someone or something has something, or includes something: *a boy with a broken arm* | *a house with a garden* | *Do you want your coffee with or without sugar?* **3** if two or more people do something with each other, for example play, argue, or fight, they do it together or against each other: *Neal and Tracy were always arguing with each other.* | *I agree with you.* **4** used to describe the way in which someone does something: *The other team played with great skill and determination.* **5** using something: *Don't eat with your fingers!* **6** because of something: *The room was bright with sunlight.* | *Her face glowed with pride.* **7** used to say what covers or fills something: *His hands were covered with blood.* **8** concerning something or someone: *What's wrong with the radio?* | *She's in love with you.* **9** used to describe the sound that something makes: *The door closed with a loud bang.* **10** used to describe the position of someone's body: *He was standing with his hands in his pockets.* **11 be with me/you** *spoken* to understand what someone is saying: *Are you with me?*

with·draw /wɪð'drɔː, wɪθ-‖-'drɔː/ *v* **withdrew** /-'druː/, **withdrawn** /-'drɔːn‖-'drɒːn/, **withdrawing 1** [T] to take something from somewhere, especially to take money out of a bank account: *He withdrew $200 from his savings account.*

2 [T] to stop giving something support, money etc: *Congress threatened to withdraw support for the space project.* **3** [I,T] to not take part in a race, competition etc that you have arranged to take part in, or leave an organization: *Decker was forced to withdraw from the race because of a knee injury.* **4** [I,T] if an army withdraws or is withdrawn, it leaves a place and moves back to where it was before **5** [T] *formal* if you withdraw something you have said, you admit that it was untrue

with·draw·al /wɪð'drɔːəl, wɪθ-‖-'drɔːəl/ *n* **1** [C,U] when someone takes money out of a bank account: *I'd like to make a withdrawal, please.* **2** [C,U] when military forces are moved out of an area: *the withdrawal of NATO forces from Bosnia* **3** [C,U] when someone stops doing something, for example helping someone: *the withdrawal of government aid* **4** [U] the set of unpleasant physical and mental feelings that an ADDICT gets when he or she tries to stop taking a drug: **withdrawal symptoms** (=the things that happen)

with·drawn /wɪð'drɔːn, wɪθ-‖-'drɔːn/ *adj* quiet and not wanting to talk to people

with·er /'wɪðə‖-ər/ *v* [I] **1** also **wither away** if a plant withers, its leaves become dry and it starts to die **2** to become weaker and stop existing

with·er·ing /'wɪðərɪŋ/ *adj* a withering look, attack etc shows that you strongly disapprove of someone or something

with·hold /wɪð'həʊld, wɪθ-‖-'hoʊld/ *v* [T] to refuse to give information, money etc to someone: *His name was withheld for legal reasons.*

with·in /wɪð'ɪn‖wɪð'ɪn, wɪθ'ɪn/ *adv, prep* **1** after only a short time, or before a period of time has ended: *The police arrived within minutes.* | *Within a year he was dead.* **2** inside a group, organization, or area, or inside someone: *critics within the party* **3** less than a distance, amount, or limit: *The hotel is within a mile of the airport.* **4 within the rules/the law/your rights etc** allowed according to the rules or the law

with·out /wɪð'aʊt‖wɪð'aʊt, wɪθ'aʊt/ *adv, prep* **1** when you do not have something, use something, or do something: *I can't see anything without my glasses.* | *He left without saying goodbye.* **2** when someone is not with you or does not help you: *We can't finish this job without him.* **3 do without/go without** to not have something that you want or need: *They went without food and water for 2 days.*

with·stand /wɪð'stænd, wɪθ-‖ *v* [T] to be strong enough not to be harmed by something: *material that can withstand high temperatures*

wit·ness¹ /'wɪtnʲs/ *n* [C] **1** someone who appears in a court of law and says what they have seen or what they know: *He asked the witness how well she knew the defendant.* **2** someone who sees an accident or a crime and can describe what happened: *Police are appealing for witnesses after the accident.* ➡ see also EYEWITNESS **3** someone who watches another

---

person sign an official document, and then signs it also to prove this

witness² /v [T] **1** to see something happen, especially an accident or a crime: *a girl who witnessed a murder* **2** to watch someone sign an official document, and then also sign it to prove this

witness box *BrE*, **witness stand** *AmE* /'.. ./ *n* [C] the place where a WITNESS stands or sits when they are being asked questions in a court of law

wits /wɪts/ *n* [plural] **1** someone's ability to think quickly and decide the right thing to do in a difficult situation: **keep/have your wits about you** (=be ready to think quickly so that you can deal with any problems) **2 scare sb out of their wits** to frighten someone very much **3 be at your wits' end** to feel very worried because you cannot think of any way of dealing with a difficult situation

wit·ter /'wɪtəll-ər/ also **witter on** *v* [I] *BrE informal* to talk about silly and unimportant things in an annoying way

wit·ti·cis·m /'wɪtɪˌsɪzəm/ *n* [C] something clever and amusing that someone says or writes

wit·ty /'wɪti/ *adj* using words in a funny, intelligent, and interesting way: *a witty response*

wives /waɪvz/ *n* the plural of WIFE

wiz·ard /'wɪzədll-ərd/ *n* [C] **1** a man who is believed to have special magic powers **2** also **wiz** *informal* someone who is very good at doing something: *a financial wizard*

wiz·ened /'wɪzənd/ *adj* old and having dry skin with a lot of WRINKLES (=lines)

wk *n* the written abbreviation of WEEK

wob·ble /'wɒbəll'wɑː-/ *v* [I] to move from one side to the other in an unsteady way — **wobbly** *adj*: *a wobbly chair* — **wobble** *n* [C]

woe /wəʊllwoʊ/ *n* [U] *literary* great sadness

woe·ful·ly /'wəʊfəlill'woʊ-/ *adv* **1** used to emphasize that something is not good enough, is very disappointing etc: *The hospital facilities are woefully inadequate.* **2** in a very sad way: *He sighed and looked woefully around the room.* — **woeful** *adj*

woes /wəʊzllwoʊz/ *n* [plural] *literary* serious problems or difficulties

wok /wɒkllwɑːk/ *n* [C] a large round pan for FRYing Chinese food

woke /wəʊkllwoʊk/ *v* the past tense of WAKE

wok·en /'wəʊkənll'woʊ-/ *v* the past participle of WAKE

wolf¹ /wʊlf/ *n* [C], *plural* **wolves** /wʊlvz/ a wild animal similar to a large dog

wolf² *v* [T] also **wolf down** *informal* to eat something very quickly: *She wolfed down her breakfast.*

wom·an /'wʊmən/ *n* [C], *plural* **women** /'wɪmɪn/ an adult female person: *the women I work with | a woman doctor*

wom·an·hood /'wʊmənhʊd/ *n* [U] the state of being a woman, or the time when someone is a woman

wom·an·iz·er (also **-iser** *BrE*) /'wʊmənaɪzəll-ər/ *n* [C] a man who has sexual relationships with a lot of women

wom·an·kind /'wʊmənkaɪnd/ *n* [U] women considered together as a group

wom·an·ly /'wʊmənli/ *adj* typical of a woman

womb /wuːm/ *n* [C] the part of a woman's body where a baby grows before it is born

wom·en /'wɪmɪn/ *n* the plural of WOMAN

won /wʌn/ *v* the past tense and past participle of WIN

won·der¹ /'wʌndəll-ər/ *v* [I,T] **1** to think about something and want to know why it is true, what happened etc: *I sometimes wonder why I married her. | We wondered where you'd gone.* **2 I was wondering if/whether** *spoken* used to politely ask someone something: *I was wondering if I could use your phone. | We were wondering if you wanted to come over for a meal.* **3** to be surprised by something, especially by how good something is: + **at** *Ellie was still wondering at her good luck.*

wonder² *n* **1** [U] a feeling of admiration and surprise: **in wonder** *They listened to Lisa's story in wonder.* **2 no wonder** *spoken* used to say that something is not surprising, because something else is true: *No wonder you feel sick if you ate the whole pizza!* **3 it is a wonder (that)** used to say that something is surprising: *It's a wonder that he can still stand up.* **4** [C] something that is very impressive: *the wonders of modern technology*

wonder³ *adj* [only before noun] extremely good or effective: *a new wonder drug*

won·der·ful /'wʌndəfəlll-dər-/ *adj* extremely good: *Congratulations! That's wonderful news!* — **wonderfully** *adv*

won·ky /'wɒŋkill'wɑːŋki/ *adj* *BrE informal* not straight, not steady, or not working properly

wont¹ /wəʊntllwɒːnt/ *adv* *formal* **be wont to do sth** to have the habit of doing something

wont² *n* *formal* **as is sb's wont** used to say that it is someone's habit to do something

won't /wəʊntllwoʊnt/ the short form of 'will not': *Dad won't like it.*

woo /wuː/ *v* [T] **1** to try to persuade someone to support you or vote for you: *Politicians were busy wooing voters.* **2** *old-fashioned* if a man woos a woman, he spends time with her, hoping to persuade her to marry him

wood /wʊd/ *n* **1** [C,U] a material made from trees: *The statue is carved out of a single piece of wood.* **2** [C] also **woods** a small forest → see colour picture on page 243

wood·ed /'wʊdɪd/ *adj* covered with trees

wood·en /'wʊdn/ *adj* made from wood: *a wooden box*

wood·land /'wʊdlənd, -lænd/ *n* [C,U] an area of land that is covered with trees

wood·peck·er /'wʊdˌpekəll-ər/ *n* [C] a bird with a long beak that makes holes in trees

wood·wind /'wʊdˌwɪnd/ *n* [U] musical instruments that you blow into

wood·work /'wʊdwɜːkll-wɜːrk/ *n* [U] **1** the activity of making wooden objects **2** the parts of a building that are made of wood, usually for decoration

wood·worm /'wʊdwɜːmll-wɜːrm/ *n* [C,U] an insect that makes holes in wood, or the damage caused by this insect

wood·y /'wʊdi/ *adj* woody plants have thick hard stems

woof /wʊf/ *n* [singular] the sound that a dog makes

wool /wʊl/ n [U] **1** the soft thick hair of a sheep **2** the soft thick thread or cloth that is made from the hair of sheep: *a ball of wool | a mixture of wool and cotton*

wool·len BrE, **woolen** AmE /'wʊlən/ adj made from wool: *a warm woollen blanket*

wool·lens BrE, **woolens** AmE /'wʊlənz/ n [plural] clothes that are made from wool

wool·ly BrE, **wooly** AmE /'wʊli/ adj made of wool or a material that looks like wool: *a woolly hat*

woo·zy /'wuːzi/ adj informal feeling weak and unable to think clearly; DIZZY

word[1] /wɜːd‖wɜːrd/ n **1** [C] a sound or letter or a group of sounds or letters that are used together and have a particular meaning: *'Casa' is the Spanish word for 'house'. | We had to write a 500-word essay about our holidays.* **2 words** the things that someone said: *Those were his last words.* | **in sb's words** (=used to report what someone said): *In Kennedy's words: "Ask not what your country can do for you".* **3 have a word with sb** to talk to someone about something, especially to advise them, talk about a problem etc **4 not say/understand/believe/hear a word** to not say, understand etc anything **5 a word of advice/warning/encouragement etc** something that you say to advise someone, warn them etc **6** [singular] a promise: **give sb your word** *I give you my word: we'll take good care of him* **7 in other words** used when you are explaining what something means in a simpler, more direct way **8 in your own words** if you describe something in your own words, you say what you think without repeating what other people have said **9 word for word** using exactly the same words that someone else used **10 take sb's word for it** to believe what someone says even though you have no proof **11 by word of mouth** used to say that you hear news about something because someone tells you, not because it is reported in a newspaper, on television etc **12 put in a (good) word for sb** to say good things about someone to an important person: *Could you put in a good word for me with your boss?* **13 give/say the word** to tell someone to start doing something: *Don't move until I give the word.* **14 not in so many words** spoken used to say that someone did not say something directly, but you think that is what they intended to say: *"So Dad said he'd pay for it?" "Not in so many words."* **15 the word** is spoken used to tell someone what other people have said will probably happen: *The word is they're going to get married.* **16 cannot get a word in edgeways** to be unable to say anything in a conversation because someone else is talking all the time **17 my word!** old-fashioned spoken used when you are very surprised: *My word! Isn't he tall!*

word[2] v [T] to carefully choose the words you use when you are saying or writing something: *He worded his request very carefully.*

word·ing /'wɜːdɪŋ‖'wɜːr-/ n [U] the words and phrases used in a piece of writing or speech

word pro·ces·sor /ˌ. ˌ.../ n [C] a small computer or a computer programme that you use for writing letters — **word processing** n [U]

word·y /'wɜːdi‖'wɜːrdi/ adj using too many words: *a long wordy explanation*

wore /wɔː‖wɔːr/ v the past tense of WEAR

work[1] /wɜːk‖wɜːrk/ v **1** [I] to do a job, especially in order to earn money: *Heidi works for a law firm in Toronto. | I used to work at Burger King. | Joe worked as a builder for 5 years.* **2** [I] if a machine or piece of equipment works, it does what it is designed to do: *The CD player isn't working.* **3** [T] to use a complicated machine or piece of equipment: *Does anybody know how to work the printer?* **4** [I] if something works, it is effective and gives you the results that you want: *Most diets don't work.* **5** [I,T] to do something that needs a lot of time and effort, or to make someone do this: *Rescuers worked to free the passengers from the wreckage. | Our coach has been working us really hard lately.* **6 work your way** to move somewhere or achieve something gradually and with effort: *Dave worked his way to the top of the firm.* **7** [I,T] to move into a position slowly with many small movements, or to make something do this: *The screw must have worked loose.* **8 work against sb** to prevent someone from being successful: *Unfortunately her bad grades worked against her.* **9 work in sb's favour** BrE/**favor** AmE to help someone be successful **10 work up an appetite/sweat** to do so much exercise that you become very hungry or SWEATY **11 work the land** to grow crops

work on sth phr v [T] to try to make, repair, or improve something: *Dad's still working on the car. | You need to work on your pronunciation.*

work out phr v **1** [T **work** sth ↔ **out**] to calculate an amount, price, or value: *Have you worked out how much we owe them?* **2** [I] to cost a particular amount: **+ at** *The hotel works out at about $50 a night.* **3** [T **work** sth↔**out**] to find a solution to a problem or make a decision after thinking carefully about it: *He still hasn't worked out which college he's going to.* **4** [I] if a problem works out, it gradually stops being a problem: *Don't worry. I'm sure everything will work out fine.* **5** [I] to do exercises regularly: *Sue works out in the gym twice a week.*

work up to sth phr v [T] to gradually prepare yourself to do something difficult: *I'm working up to being able to do 20 laps.*

work[2] n **1** [U] the use of physical or mental effort to do something: *Looking after two children can be hard work.* (=a lot of work) | *The house looks fantastic – it must have taken a lot of work.* **2** [U] something that you do in order to earn money: *My dad started work when he was 14. | Jo's hoping to find work in television.* **3** [U] the place where you do your job: *She met her future husband at work.* **4** [U] the period of time during the day when you are working: *Do you want to go out to dinner after work?* **5** [U] something that you have to do in your job, at school, or when you are trying to achieve something: *I've got so much work to do today.* **piece of work** The teacher said it was an excellent piece of work. **6** [U] something that you have written or produced for your job, or when studying a subject: *We're pleased with your work. | Einstein's work on nuclear physics* **7** [C,U] a book, picture, or piece of music etc by a writer, artist, or musician: *great works of art | I prefer his early work.* **8 be in work/be out of work** to have or not have a job **9 at work** doing a job or an

W

activity: *Crews were at work repairing the roads.*
→ see also HOMEWORK, HOUSEWORK, WORKS

work·a·ble /ˈwɜːkəbəl‖ˈwɜːr-/ *adj* a workable plan, system, idea etc can be used or done effectively: *a workable solution*

work·a·hol·ic /ˌwɜːkəˈhɒlɪk‖ˌwɜːrkəˈhɔː-/ *n* [C] *informal* someone who spends a lot of time working and has little time to do anything else

worked up /ˌ. ˈ./ *adj informal* very upset or excited about something: *There's no need to get so worked up about it.*

work·er /ˈwɜːkə‖ˈwɜːrkər/ *n* [C] **1** someone who works for a company or other organization, but is not a manager: *Fifty workers lost their jobs.* | *factory workers* **2** **a good/hard/quick etc worker** someone who works well etc

work·force /ˈwɜːkfɔːs‖ˈwɜːrkfɔːrs/ *n* [singular] all the people who work in a country or company

work·ing /ˈwɜːkɪŋ‖ˈwɜːr-/ *adj* [only before noun] **1** having a job: *working parents* **2** relating to work: *bad working conditions* **3** **be in (good) working order** to be working well and not broken: *My father's watch is still in good working order.* **4** **a working knowledge** of enough practical knowledge about something to use it effectively: *a working knowledge of Spanish*

working class /ˌ. ˈ. ◂/ *n* **the working class** the social class that includes people who do not have much money or power and who usually do physical work —**working-class** *adj*

work·ings /ˈwɜːkɪŋz‖ˈwɜːr-/ *n* [plural] the ways in which something works: *the workings of government departments*

work·load /ˈwɜːkləʊd‖ˈwɜːrkloʊd/ *n* [C] the amount of work that a person or machine is expected to do: *Teachers often have a heavy workload.* (=they have to do a lot of work)

work·man /ˈwɜːkmən‖ˈwɜːrk-/ *n* [C] someone who does physical work such as building

work·man·like /ˈwɜːkmənlaɪk‖ˈwɜːrk-/ *adj* skilfully and carefully done

work·man·ship /ˈwɜːkmənʃɪp‖ˈwɜːrk-/ *n* [U] the skill with which something has been made

work·out /ˈwɜːkaʊt‖ˈwɜːrk-/ *n* [C] a period of exercise that you do in a GYM or class

works /wɜːks‖wɜːrks/ *n* **1** [plural] all of the writing, paintings etc that a writer or artist has done: *the complete works of Shakespeare* **2** **the works** *spoken informal* everything that it is possible to have: *We were special guests, so we got the works – champagne, caviar, and a huge steak.* **3** *old-fashioned* a factory or industrial building: *the gas works*

work·sheet /ˈwɜːkʃiːt‖ˈwɜːrk-/ *n* [C] a piece of paper with questions, exercises etc for students to practise what they have learned

work·shop /ˈwɜːkʃɒp‖ˈwɜːrkʃɑːp/ *n* [C] **1** a room or building where tools and machines are used to make or repair things **2** a meeting at which people try to improve their skills by discussing their experiences and doing practical exercises

work·sta·tion /ˈwɜːkˌsteɪʃən‖ˈwɜːrk-/ *n* [C] the part of an office where you work, including your desk, computer etc

work·top /ˈwɜːktɒp‖ˈwɜːrktɑːp/ *also* **work·sur·face** /ˈ. ˌ../ *n* [C] a flat surface in a kitchen, used especially when preparing food, drinks etc
→ see picture at KITCHEN

world¹ /wɜːld‖wɜːrld/ *n* **1** **the world** the PLANET we live on, including all of the people, countries etc on it; the Earth: *Athletes came from all over the world to compete in the Games.* | *the longest river in the world* **2** [C usually singular] all the things and people that are connected with a particular subject or activity: *the world of baseball* | *the music world* **3** **in the world** *spoken* used to emphasize something you are saying: *You're the best dad in the world.* **4** [singular] a part of the world: *the Western World* | *the industrialized world* **5** [C] your world is your life and the things that you do, the people that you know etc: *Dean's world was filled with music and laughter.* **6** **the animal/plant/insect world** animals etc considered as a group **7** [C] a PLANET other than the Earth: *creatures from another world* **8** **the whole world** everybody **9** **the outside world** the people, places, and things that are happening in the area outside where you live: *Japan was cut off from the outside world.* **10** **do sb a world of good** *informal* to make someone feel a lot better: *A vacation would do you a world of good.* **11** **be out of this world** to be extremely good: *Have you tried their ice cream? It's out of this world!* **12** **be on top of the world** to be extremely happy **13** **mean the world to sb** to be the person or thing that someone cares about most **14** **move/go up in the world** to get a better job or a more important social position **15** **have the best of both worlds** to have the advantages of two completely different things

world² *adj* [only before noun] in or of all the world: *the search for world peace* | *world champion Michael Schumacher*

world-class /ˌ. ˈ. ◂/ *adj* among the best in the world: *a world-class tennis player*

world-famous /ˌ. ˈ.. ◂/ *adj* known about by people all over the world: *a world-famous singer*

world·ly /ˈwɜːldli‖ˈwɜːrld-/ *adj* **1** **sb's worldly goods/possessions** everything someone owns **2** having a lot of knowledge and experience about life

world pow·er /ˌ. ˈ../ *n* [C] one of the few most powerful countries in the world

world·wide /ˌwɜːldˈwaɪd ◂‖ˌwɜːrld-/ *adj, adv* in every part of the world: *The company employs 2000 people worldwide.*

World Wide Web /ˌ. . ˈ./ written abbreviation **WWW** *n* [singular] a system that connects together information and pictures from computers in many parts of the world, so that people can find them on the INTERNET

worm¹ /wɜːm‖wɜːrm/ *n* [C] a small creature with a long soft body and no legs, which lives in the ground → see also **a (whole) can of worms** (CAN²)

worm² *v* **1** **worm your way a)** to gradually make someone trust and like you by deceiving them, in order to get what you want: **+ into** *She managed to worm her way into his affections.* **b)** to move somewhere slowly and with difficulty, especially through a place where there are many people or that is very narrow **2** **worm sth out of sb** to get information from someone who does not want to give it

worn /wɔːn‖wɔːrn/ *v* the past participle of WEAR

worn out, worn-out /ˌ. ˈ.◂/ adj **1** very tired, especially because you have been working too much: *I'm all worn out.* **2** too old or damaged to use any more: *worn-out shoes*

wor·ried /ˈwʌrid‖ˈwɜːrid/ adj not feeling happy or relaxed, because you keep thinking about a problem or something that might happen: **+ that** *Doctors are worried that the drug may have serious side-effects.* → see colour picture on page 277

wor·ry[1] /ˈwʌri‖ˈwɜːri/ v **1** [I] to keep thinking about a problem or about something bad that might happen, so that you cannot relax or feel happy: **+ about** *She's always worrying about her weight.* | **+ that** *I sometimes worry that he doesn't love me anymore.* **2** [T] to make someone feel worried: **it worries sb that** *it worries me that she hasn't called yet.* **3 don't worry** *spoken* used to tell someone that they do not have to do something: *Don't worry about the kids – I can drive them to school.*

worry[2] n **1** [C] something that makes you worried: *money worries* **2** [U] the feeling of being worried about something: *He was up all night with worry.*

wor·ry·ing /ˈwʌri-ɪŋ‖ˈwɜː-/ adj making you feel worried: *I've just had a rather worrying phonecall from Emma.*

worse[1] /wɜːs‖wɜːrs/ adj [the comparative of 'bad'] **1** not as good as something else that is also bad: **+ than** *The next song was even worse than the first one.* | **get worse** *The traffic always gets worse after 4:30.* **2** more ill: *On Tuesday I felt worse, and I decided to go to see the doctor.* **3 the worse for wear** in bad condition, or very tired, or drunk: *He arrived home at 5 am, looking somewhat the worse for wear.*

worse[2] n [U] something worse: *Worse was yet to come.*

worse[3] adv **1** in a more severe or serious way than before: *The pain hurts worse than it did yesterday.* **2** not as well: *Jan sings even worse than I do!*

wors·en /ˈwɜːsən‖ˈwɜːr-/ v [I,T] to become worse, or to make something become worse: *If the weather worsens, the flight will have to be cancelled.*

worse off /ˌ. ˈ.◂/ adj poorer, less successful, or having fewer advantages than you did before: *We're actually worse off than I thought.*

wor·ship[1] /ˈwɜːʃɪp‖ˈwɜːr-/ v **-pped, -pping** *BrE*, **-ped, -ping** *AmE* **1** [I,T] to show respect and love for God, especially by praying in a church, TEMPLE etc **2** [T] to love and admire someone very much: *She absolutely worships her Grandpa!* —**worship** n [U] *places of worship* (=where people can pray) —**worshipper** n [C]

worst[1] /wɜːst‖wɜːrst/ adj [the superlative of 'bad'] worse than anything or anyone else of the same type: *the worst movie I've ever seen*

worst[2] n **1 the worst** someone or something that is worse than every other person, thing, situation etc: *This is the worst I've ever done on a test.* | *They've written a lot of bad songs, but this one is definitely the worst.* **2 at worst** used to say what the worst possible situation or result

could be, especially when it is not very bad: *At worst the repairs will cost you around $700.* **3 if the worst comes to the worst** used to say what you will do if the worst possible situation happens: *If the worst comes to the worst, we'll have to sell the house.*

worst[3] adv in the worst way or most severely: *the cities that were worst affected by the war*

worth[1] /wɜːθ‖wɜːrθ/ adj **1 be worth sth** to have a particular value: *Our house is worth about $350,000.* | *Each question is worth 4 points.* **2** used to say that doing something is useful, helpful, or enjoyable, especially when you are advising someone to do it: **be worth doing/seeing** etc *The film is definitely worth seeing.* | **it's worth it/it's not worth it** *Don't try arguing with her – it's just not worth it.* | **be worth (your) while** (=be useful, helpful, or enjoyable): *"Do you think I should check with my lawyer?" "It might be worth your while."*

worth[2] n **1 a) $10/£500 etc worth** an amount of something that is worth $10, £500 etc: *They came home with $300 worth of food.* **b) a day's/10 years' etc worth** something that takes a day, 10 years etc to do, use, or happen: *There's at least a week's worth of work to do.* **2 sb's worth** how good someone is at doing something, or how important they are to someone: *a chance for Paul to show his true worth*

worth·less /ˈwɜːθləs‖ˈwɜːrθ-/ adj **1** not worth any money: *Are you saying that the shares are worthless?* **2** not useful or important: *worthless qualifications* **3** a worthless person has no good qualities or useful skills: *She made him feel completely worthless.*

worth·while /ˌwɜːθˈwaɪl◂‖ˌwɜːrθ-/ adj useful or enjoyable, even though you have to spend a lot of time, effort, or money doing it: *The job they do is very worthwhile.*

wor·thy /ˈwɜːði‖ˈwɜːrði/ adj **1** good enough to deserve respect, admiration, or attention: *a worthy opponent* | *worthy achievements* **2 be worthy of** *formal* to deserve something: *a leader who is worthy of our trust*

would /wʊd/ *modal verb* **1** used to say what someone has said or thought: *He said he would call back later.* | *Her doctors seemed to think that everything would be alright.* **2** used to talk about what might happen, if something else happened: *Dad would be really angry if he knew.* **3** used to say that you expected something to happen or be true, especially when it did not happen or was not true: *I thought Caroline would be happy, but instead she was really upset.* **4 would like/would love** used to say that you want something: *I would love to see your new house.* **5 would** *spoken* used to politely ask someone if they want something, or to politely ask someone to do something: *Would you hold the door open for me?* | *Would you like some coffee?* **6 (if I were you) I would/I wouldn't** *spoken* used to give advice: *I wouldn't leave the car unlocked, if I were you.* **7 I would think/imagine/guess** used to say what you think is probably true: *I would think she's gone back*

GRAMMAR NOTE: much and many

You can only use **much, how much** and **a little** with <u>uncountable</u> nouns: *How much information do you have?* You can only use **many, how many** and **a few** with plural <u>countable</u> nouns: *How many people are coming to the party?* | *I've invited a few friends.*

home. **8 would not/wouldn't** used to say that someone refused to do something or that something did not happen in spite of your efforts: *Blair wouldn't answer the question.* **9** used after 'wish': *I wish they would stop making the noise.* **10** used to say that something happened often in the past: *Sometimes, Eva would come over and make dinner.* **11** used when you are annoyed about what someone has said or done, because it is typical of them: *You would say that wouldn't you!* → see also ·D **would rather** (RATHER)

would-be /'. ./ *adj* a would-be actor, customer, writer etc is someone who wants to be or may be an actor, customer, writer etc

would·n't /'wʊdnt/ the short form of 'would not': *She wouldn't answer.*

would've /'wʊdəv/ the short form of 'would have': *I would've gone to the party, but I felt too tired.*

wound[1] /wuːnd/ *n* [C] an injury, especially a deep cut made in your skin by a knife or bullet: *gunshot wounds*

wound[2] /wuːnd/ *v* [T] **1** to injure someone, especially with a knife or gun: *Two officers were badly wounded.* **2 wound sb's pride** to upset someone by criticizing them —**wounded** *adj*

> **USAGE NOTE: wounded, injured, and hurt**
>
> Use **wounded** when a part of the body is damaged by a weapon: *a wounded soldier.* Use **injured** when someone has been hurt in an accident or in an event such as an explosion: *One passenger was killed and four were injured.* Use **hurt** to say that a part of your body feels pain: *My neck hurts.*

wound[3] /waʊnd/ *v* the past tense and past participle of WIND

wound up /ˌwaʊnd 'ʌp/ *adj* very angry, nervous, or excited: *He got so wound up he couldn't sleep.*

wove /wəʊv‖woʊv/ *v* the past tense of WEAVE

wov·en /'wəʊvən‖'woʊ-/ *v* the past participle of WEAVE

wow /waʊ/ *interjection* used when you think something is very impressive or surprising: *Wow! You look great!*

wran·gle /'ræŋgəl/ *v* [I] to argue with someone angrily for a long time

W

wrap up

wrap[1] /ræp/ *v* [T] **-pped, -pping 1** to fold cloth, paper etc around something to cover it: *I haven't wrapped her present yet.| Wrap this blanket around you.* **2** to hold someone or something by putting your arms, legs, fingers etc around them: *Mary sat with her arms wrapped around her legs.* **3 have sb wrapped around**

your (little) finger to be able to persuade someone to do whatever you want

wrap sth ↔ **up** *phr v* **1** [T] to completely cover something by folding paper, cloth etc around it: *sandwiches wrapped up in foil* **2** [T] to finish something, for example a piece of work or a meeting: *We should have the project wrapped up in a month.* **3 be wrapped up in sth** to spend so much time thinking about someone or something, that you forget about other people or things **4** [I] also **wrap yourself up** to put on warm clothes: *Make sure you wrap up warm.*

wrap[2] *n* [C] *old-fashioned* a SHAWL

wrap·per /'ræpə‖-ər/ *n* [C] the paper or plastic that covers something you buy, especially food

wrap·ping /'ræpɪŋ/ *n* [C,U] paper, cloth, etc that is wrapped around something to protect it

wrapping pa·per /'.. ,./ *n* [C,U] coloured paper used for wrapping presents

wrath /rɒθ‖ræθ/ *n* [U] *formal* very great anger

wreak /riːk/ *v* **wreak havoc** to cause a lot of damage or problems

wreath /riːθ/ *n* [C] a decoration made from flowers and leaves arranged in a circle

wreathed /riːðd/ *adj literary* **be wreathed in** to be surrounded by or covered in something: *The valley was wreathed in mist.*

wreck[1] /rek/ *v* [T] *informal* to completely destroy or spoil something: *The Opera House was wrecked by a huge explosion.| a serious injury that nearly wrecked his career*

wreck[2] *n* [C] **1** a car, plane, or ship that is so badly damaged it cannot be repaired **2** [usually singular] *informal* someone who is very tired, unhealthy, or worried: *I was a wreck by the time I got home.* **3** *AmE* a bad accident involving cars or planes; CRASH *BrE: Only one person survived the wreck.*

wreck·age /'rekɪdʒ/ *n* [U] the broken parts of something that has been destroyed in an accident: *Ambulance crews removed a man from the wreckage.*

wren /ren/ *n* [C] a very small brown bird

wrench[1] /rentʃ/ *v* **1** [T] to injure part of your body by twisting it suddenly: *Sam wrenched his back lifting furniture.* **2** [T] to twist and pull something from somewhere, using force: *Prisoners had even wrenched doors off their hinges.* **3** [I,T] if you wrench yourself away from someone who is holding you, you move away from them using force

wrench[2] *n* **1** [C] *especially AmE* a metal tool with a round end, used for turning NUTS; SPANNER *BrE* → see picture at TOOLS **2 be a wrench** if it is a wrench to leave someone or something, it makes you feel very sad: *It was a wrench to leave LA.*

wrest /rest/ *v* [T] *formal* to take something from someone, especially by using force

wres·tle /'resəl/ *v* **1** [I,T] to fight by holding someone and trying to push them to the ground **2** [I] to try to deal with a difficult problem or feeling: *For weeks he wrestled with his guilt.*

wres·tling /'reslɪŋ/ *n* [U] a sport in which you try to throw your opponent onto the ground and hold them there —**wrestler** *n* [C]

wretch /retʃ/ *n* [C] *old-fashioned* someone who is unhappy, unlucky, poor etc

wretch·ed /ˈretʃˌɪd/ *adj* **1** very unhappy, unlucky etc **2** [only before noun] used when you do not like someone or something, or when they make you angry: *I wish that wretched man would shut up!*

wrig·gle /ˈrɪɡəl/ *v* [I,T] to twist from side to side with small quick movements, or to move part of your body this way: *a worm wriggling through the mud* —**wriggle** *n* [C]

wring /rɪŋ/ *v* [T] **wrung** /rʌŋ/, **wrung, wringing** **1** also **wring out** to tightly twist wet clothes, sheets etc to remove water from them **2 wring sth's neck** to kill something, especially a bird, by twisting its neck

wrin·kle /ˈrɪŋkəl/ *n* [C] **1** a small line on the skin on your face that you get when you are old **2** a small line in cloth caused by crushing it or accidentally folding it —**wrinkled** *adj*: *Her face was old and wrinkled.* —**wrinkle** *v* [I,T]

wrist /rɪst/ *n* [C] the joint between your hand and your arm

wrist·watch /ˈrɪstwɒtʃ, -wɔːtʃ/ *n* [C] a watch that you wear on your wrist

writ /rɪt/ *n* [C] a legal document that orders someone to do something or not do something

write /raɪt/ *v* **wrote** /rəʊt‖roʊt/, **written** /ˈrɪtn/, **writing** **1** [I,T] to produce a new book, story, song etc: *a poem written by Walt Whitman* | *Proust wrote about life in Paris in the early part of this century.* **2** [I,T] to make words, letters, or numbers: *Tony could read and write when he was six.* | *The sign was written in Spanish.* **3** [I,T] to write a letter to someone: *Have you written to Mom yet?* | *He finally wrote me a letter.* **4** [T] also **write out** to write information on a cheque, form etc: *She calmly wrote out a cheque for the full £5,000.*

    write back *phr v* [I] to answer someone's letter by sending them a letter: *Write back soon!*

    write sth↔**down** *phr v* [T] to write something on a piece of paper, especially so that you do not forget it: *Why didn't you write down her address?*

    write in *phr v* [I] to send a letter about something to an organization

    write off *phr v* **1** [I] to send a letter to an organization, especially to ask them to send you something **2** [T **write** sth↔**off**] to accept that you will never be paid back an amount of money that someone owes you **3** [T **write** sb/sth↔**off**] to decide that someone or something will never be successful or will never get any better: *The critics had all written him off.*

    write sth↔**up** *phr v* [T] to write something based on notes you made earlier: *I need to write up my talk for tomorrow.*

write-off /ˈ. ./ *n* [C] *BrE* if a vehicle is a write-off, it is so badly damaged in an accident that it is not worth repairing

writ·er /ˈraɪtə‖-ər/ *n* [C] someone who writes books, stories etc

write-up /ˈ. ./ *n* [C] a piece of writing in a newspaper, magazine etc, in which someone gives their opinion about a new book, film etc: *The album got a good write-up in DJ magazine.*

writhe /raɪð/ *v* [I] to twist your body, especially because you have a lot of pain: *writhing in agony*

writ·ing /ˈraɪtɪŋ/ *n* [U] **1** words that are written or printed, or the way someone writes: *the writing on the label* | *I can't read her writing.*

2 in writing an agreement etc that is in writing has been written down, proving that it is official **3** books, stories, and poems in general: *We're studying European writing from the 1930s.* **4** the activity or job of writing books, stories etc: *creative writing*

wri·tings /ˈraɪtɪŋz/ *n* [plural] the books, stories, poems etc that someone has written: *the writings of Mark Twain*

writ·ten /ˈrɪtn/ *v* the past participle of WRITE

wrong[1] /rɒŋ‖rɔːŋ/ *adj* **1** not correct – used to say that someone has made a mistake: *Paul's wrong: Hilary's 17, not 18.* | *You must have dialled the wrong number.* → opposite RIGHT[1] **2** not morally right – used to say that someone should not do something: *Most people think that hunting is wrong.* **3** not suitable: *It's the wrong time of year to go skiing.* **4 what's wrong? spoken a)** used to ask someone why they are unhappy, what is making them ill: *"What's wrong, Jenny?"* *"I miss Daddy."* | *What's wrong with your shoulder?* **b)** used to ask why something is not working: + **with** *What's wrong with the phone?* **5 get (hold of) the wrong end of the stick** *informal* to understand a completely different meaning from what someone had intended **6 get on the wrong side of sb** to make someone angry with you

wrong[2] *adv* **1** not in the correct way: *You spelled my name wrong.* → opposite CORRECTLY **2 go wrong** if something goes wrong, it starts to have problems or it is unsuccessful: *If anything goes wrong with your car, we'll fix it for free.* **3 get sth wrong** to make a mistake when you are doing, understanding, or remembering something: *I got the answer wrong.* **4 don't get me wrong** *spoken* used when you are worried that someone will not understand you, and think that you do not like someone or something

wrong[3] *n* **1** [U] behaviour that is not morally correct: *He doesn't know the difference between right and wrong.* **2** [C] a situation in which someone is treated badly or unfairly: *the wrongs they have suffered in the past* **3 be in the wrong** to have made a mistake or deserve the blame for something bad that has happened **4 sb can do no wrong** used to say that someone thinks that another person is perfect, especially when you know that they are not perfect

wrong[4] *v* [T] *formal* to treat someone unfairly

wrong·do·ing /ˈrɒŋˌduːɪŋ‖ˌrɔːŋˈduːɪŋ/ *n* [C,U] *formal* when someone does something illegal or wrong —**wrongdoer** *n* [C]

wrong·ful /ˈrɒŋfəl‖ˈrɔːŋ-/ *adj* treating someone unfairly or illegally, especially by punishing them for something they have not done: *wrongful arrest* —**wrongfully** *adv*

wrote /rəʊt‖roʊt/ *v* the past tense of WRITE

wrought i·ron /ˌrɔːt ˈaɪən‖ˌrɔːt ˈaɪərn/ *n* [U] long, thin pieces of iron formed into shapes: *a wrought iron gate*

wrung /rʌŋ/ *v* the past tense and past participle of WRING

wry /raɪ/ *adj* showing a mixture of amusement and disappointment: *a wry smile*

WWW *n* the written abbreviation of WORLD WIDE WEB

X, x

X, x /eks/ the letter 'x'

X 1 used at the end of a letter to give someone a kiss **2** used instead of someone's name, because you want to keep it secret, or you do not know their name: *Miss X* **3** used to show that an answer is wrong

xen·o·pho·bi·a /ˌzenəˈfəʊbiə‖-ˈfoʊ-/ *n* [U] hatred or fear of people from other countries —**xenophobic** *adj*

xe·rox, Xerox /ˈzɪərɒks, ˈze-‖ˈzɪrɑːks, ˈziː-/ *n* [C] *trademark* a copy of a piece of paper made using a special machine; a PHOTOCOPY —**xerox** *v* [T]

X·mas /ˈkrɪsməs, ˈeksməs/ *n* [C,U] *informal* Christmas – mainly used in writing, for example on shop signs and Christmas cards: *Happy Xmas*

X-ray¹ /ˈeks reɪ/ *n* [C] **1** a beam of RADIATION that can go through solid objects and is used for photographing the inside of the body **2** a photograph of the inside of someone's body, taken using RADIATION

x-ray² *v* [T] to photograph the inside of someone's body using RADIATION

xy·lo·phone /ˈzaɪləfəʊn‖-foʊn/ *n* [C] a musical instrument with flat metal bars, that you play by hitting the bars with a stick

Y, y

Y, y /waɪ/ the letter 'y'

ya /jə/ *pron spoken nonstandard* you: *See ya!*

yacht /jɒt‖jɑːt/ *n* [C] **1** a boat with sails used for races or sailing for pleasure: *the round-the-world yacht race* →see colour picture on page 669 **2** a large expensive boat, used for travelling for pleasure: *the royal yacht*

yachts·man /ˈjɒtsmən‖ˈjɑːts-/ *n* [C] a man who sails a yacht

yachts·wom·an /ˈjɒtswʊmən‖ˈjɔːts-/ *n* [C] a woman who sails a yacht

yak¹ /jæk/ *n* [C] a type of long-haired cow that lives in high parts of Asia

yak² *v* [I] *spoken informal* to talk a lot about unimportant things

y'all /jɔːl‖jɒːl/ *pron AmE spoken* a word meaning 'you' or 'all of you', used mainly in the southern US

yam /jæm/ *n* [C,U] a SWEET POTATO

yank /jæŋk/ *v* [I,T] to suddenly pull something hard, using a lot of force: *He yanked the door open.*

Yank *n* [C] *informal* someone from the US – some people consider this word to be offensive

yap /jæp/ *v* [I] **-pped, -pping** if a small dog yaps, it BARKS in an excited way —**yap** *n* [C]

yard /jɑːd‖jɑːrd/ *n* [C] **1** written abbreviation **yd**; a unit for measuring length, equal to 3 feet or 0.9144 metres **2** *AmE* an area of land next to a house, usually covered with grass; garden *BrE*: *Somebody kicked a ball into our front yard.* →see colour picture on page 79 **3** an area of land with a wall around it, next to a building: *I waited in the yard outside the police station.* **4** an area of land used for a particular purpose: *a builder's yard* →see also BACKYARD

yard·stick /ˈjɑːdˌstɪk‖ˈjɑːrd-/ *n* [C] something that you compare another thing with, to show how good it is: *He used Jill's career as a yardstick for his own achievements.*

yarn /jɑːn‖jɑːrn/ *n* **1** [U] woollen thread used for knitting (KNIT) **2** [C] *informal* a long story that is not completely true

yawn¹ /jɔːn‖jɒːn/ *v* [I] to open your mouth wide and breathe very deeply, usually because you are tired or bored: *He looked at his watch and yawned.*

yawn

yawn² *n* [C] when someone yawns: *"I'm tired," she said with a yawn.*

yawn·ing /ˈjɔːnɪŋ‖ˈjɒː-/ *adj* a yawning GAP or hole is very wide or deep

yd *n* [C] the written abbreviation of YARD

ye /jiː/ *old-fashioned* you

yeah /jeə/ *adv spoken informal* yes

year /jɪə, jɜː‖jɪr/ *n* [C] **1** a period of time equal to 365 or 366 days, or 12 months: *Jenny is five years old.* | *She's been teaching for six years.* | *a top executive earning $100,000 a year* **2** also **calendar year** the period from January 1 to December 31: *this year Where are you spending Christmas this year?* | *next year They're getting married next year.* **3 years** *informal* a long time: *It's been years since I last saw him.* **4 school/financial/college etc year** a period of 12 months in a school, in which taxes are calculated etc: *The tax year begins on April 1st.* **5 first year/third year/final year etc** *BrE* used for saying what class someone is in a school or college, according to their age or how long they have been there **6 seven/twenty/three etc years old** used to say how old someone is: *She's 18 years old today!* **7 a seven/twenty/three etc year old** someone who is seven, twenty, three etc years old **8 all year round** during the whole year: *It's sunny there all year round.*

year·book /ˈjɪəbʊk, ˈjɜː-‖ˈjɪr-/ *n* [C] a book that an organization or school produces every year, giving information about its activities

year·ly /ˈjɪəli, ˈjɜː-‖ˈjɪrli/ *adj, adv* happening every year or once a year: *The meeting is held twice yearly.* (=twice every year)

yearn /jɜːn‖jɜːrn/ *v* [I] *formal* to want something very much, especially something difficult or impossible to get: **+ for** *the child she had yearned for* —**yearning** *n* [U]

yeast /jiːst/ *n* [U] a substance used for making bread rise and for producing alcohol in beer, wine etc

yell /jel/ *v* [I,T] also **yell out** to shout or say something very loudly: *He yelled at her to stop.* —**yell** *n* [C]

yel·low¹ /ˈjeləʊ‖-loʊ/ *adj* having the same colour as LEMONS or BANANAS: *bright yellow curtains* →see colour picture on page 114

yellow[2] *n* [U] a yellow colour —**yellow** *v* [I,T] *the yellowing pages of an old book* →see colour picture on page 114

yellow line /ˌ.. ˈ./ *n* [C] *BrE* a line on the side of a road that shows that you must not park there

Yellow Pag·es /ˌ.. ˈ../ *trademark* the Yellow Pages a book with the telephone numbers and addresses of the shops, companies etc in an area

yelp /jelp/ *v* [I] if a dog yelps, it makes a short high sound because it is in pain or excited —**yelp** *n* [C]

yep /jep/ *adv spoken informal* yes

yes[1] /jes/ *adv* **1** used as an answer to say that you want something, that something is true, that you will do something, or allow something etc: *"Do you want some more pie?" "Yes, please."* | *Why don't you ask Dad? I'm sure he'll say yes.* | *"You look tired today." "Yes – I didn't sleep much last night."* **2** used to say that a negative statement is not true: *"John doesn't love me anymore." "Yes he does!"* **3** *spoken* used to show that you have heard someone or that you are paying attention to them: *"Linda!" "Yes?"* **4** *spoken* used when you are very happy or excited: *Yes! I got the job!* →opposite NO

yes[2] *n* [C] an answer, decision, or vote that agrees with or supports something

yes·ter·day /ˈjestədi‖-ər-/ *adv, n* [U] **1** the day before today: *Yesterday was their tenth anniversary.* | *Did you go to the game yesterday?* **2** the past, especially the recent past: *yesterday's fashions*

yet[1] /jet/ *adv* **1** used in negative sentences and questions to say that something has not happened, although you expect it to happen: *Have you heard their new song yet?* | *Just a moment! I haven't finished yet.* | **as yet** (=until now): *As yet there is still no news.* **2** used in negative sentences to say that something should not happen now: *You don't have to leave yet.* **3** at some time in the future: *She may yet change her mind.* **4** **best/fastest etc yet** best, fastest etc until and including now: *This is their best record yet.* **5** **yet another/yet more/yet again** used to emphasize that there is more of something or something happens again, especially when this is surprising or annoying: *I've just spotted yet another mistake.* | *I'm sorry to ask for help yet again.* **6** used to emphasize that something could still happen, or there is still time left to do something: *There's still plenty of time yet to enter the competition.* **7** but or in spite of something: *a quiet yet powerful leader*

yet[2] *linking word* used to add something that is surprising after what you have just said: *The story's unbelievable, yet supposedly it's all true.*

yew /juː/ *n* [C] a tree with dark green leaves

y-fronts /ˈwaɪ frʌnts/ *n* [plural] *BrE* a kind of underwear for men

Yid·dish /ˈjɪdɪʃ/ *n* [U] a modern Jewish language based on German

yield[1] /jiːld/ *v* **1** [T] to produce something, especially an amount of money or a quantity of

something: *investments that yield high rates of profit* **2** [I,T] to be forced to agree to do something: *The government yielded to demands to get rid of the tax.* **3** [I] *AmE* to allow the traffic on a bigger road to go first; GIVE WAY *BrE* **4** [I] to move, bend, or break because of physical force or pressure **5** [I] *literary* to stop fighting and admit you have lost **6** [T] to allow someone else to have power or control over something

yield[2] *n* [C] the amount of money or the quantity of something that another thing produces: *investments with high yields*

yikes /jaɪks/ *interjection informal* used when you suddenly notice or realize something: *Yikes! I'm late!*

yip·pee /jɪˈpiː‖ˈjɪpi/ *interjection informal* used when you are very happy or excited about something

YMCA /ˌwaɪ em siː ˈeɪ/ *n* the YMCA Young Men's Christian Association; an organization that provides places to stay for young people in large cities

yo /jəʊ‖joʊ/ *interjection informal, especially AmE* used to say hello to someone or get their attention

yob /jɒb‖jɑːb/ *n* [C] *BrE* a rude and often violent young man: *a gang of yobs*

yo·del /ˈjəʊdl‖ˈjoʊdl/ *v* [I] to sing by continually changing between your natural voice and a very high voice, which was traditionally done in the mountains of Switzerland and Austria

yo·ga /ˈjəʊgə‖ˈjoʊgə/ *n* [U] a system of exercises which helps you to relax your body and mind

yog·hurt, yogurt /ˈjɒgət‖ˈjoʊgərt/ *n* [C,U] a thick liquid food made from milk

yoke /jəʊk‖joʊk/ *n* [C] **1** a wooden bar used for joining together two animals, especially cattle, in order to pull heavy loads **2** **the yoke of** *literary* something that prevents people from being free: *the yoke of colonial rule*

yo·kel /ˈjəʊkəl‖ˈjoʊ-/ *n* [C] *humorous* someone who lives in the countryside and knows very little about city life

yolk /jəʊk‖joʊk, jelk/ *n* [C,U] the yellow part of an egg

yon·der /ˈjɒndə‖ˈjɑːndər/ *adv, determiner literary* in or towards a place not far from where you are now

you /jə, jʊ; *strong* juː/ *pron* [used as a subject or object] **1** the person or people that someone is speaking or writing to: *Do you want a cigarette?* | *I can't hear you.* **2** people in general: *As you get older you tend to forget things.* →compare ONE[2] **3** used with nouns or phrases when you are talking to or calling someone: *You idiot!*

you'd /jəd, jʊd; *strong* juːd/ **1** the short form of 'you would': *I didn't think you'd mind.* **2** the short form of 'you had': *You'd better do what he says.*

you'll /jəl, jʊl; *strong* juːl/ the short form of 'you will': *You'll have to speak louder.*

GRAMMAR NOTE: comparatives and **superlatives**
For short adjectives of one syllable, add **-er** or **-est** to the word: e.g. *old - older - oldest*. (Sometimes you must double the last letter: e.g. *big - bigger - biggest*). For long adjectives put **more** or **the most** before the word: e.g. *more comfortable - the most interesting*.

young¹ /jʌŋ/ adj **1** someone who is young has not lived for a long time: *young children | I used to ski when I was young. | She's much younger than he is.* (=much less old) **2 young at heart** feeling or behaving like a young person, even though you are not young any more **3** intended for young people: *Is this dress too young for me?* **4** a young country or company has not existed for a long time

young² n [plural] **1 the young** young people considered as a group **2** young animals: *a turtle and her young*

young·ster /'jʌŋstəl-ər/ n [C] a young person

your /jə; strong jɔːlljər; strong jɔːr/ determiner **1** belonging to you or relating to you: *Is that your mother? | Don't worry, it's not your fault.* **2** belonging to or relating to anyone – used when talking about people in general: *When times are bad you know you can rely on your friends.*

you're /jə; strong jɔːlljər; strong jʊr, jɔːr/ the short form of 'you are': *You're too old.*

yours /jɔːzlljʊrz, jɔːrz/ pron **1** something that belongs to you or is connected with you: *Yours is the nicest car. | That bag is yours, isn't it? | of yours* (=belonging to you or connected with you): *Is he a friend of yours?* **2 yours truly/yours faithfully** used at the end of a letter before you sign your name **3 yours truly a)** humorous used instead of 'I': *Yes, yours truly finally quit smoking.*

your·self /jə'selflljər-/ pron, plural **yourselves** /-'selvz/ **1** the REFLEXIVE form of 'you': *Did you hurt yourself?* **2** the strong form of 'you', used to emphasize the subject or object of a sentence: *Why don't you do it yourself?* **3 (all) by yourself** alone or without anyone else: *You're going to Ecuador by yourself?* **4 have sth (all) to yourself** to be the only person in a place and able to do what you want: *You've got the house all to yourself this weekend.* **5 you don't look yourself** spoken used to say that someone looks ill or worried

youth /juːθ/ n **1** [U] the period of time when someone is young, or the quality of being young: *During his youth he lived in France.* **2** [C] a boy or young man, especially a TEENAGER: *Three youths were arrested for stealing.* **3** [U] young people in general: *the youth of today*

youth club /'. . / n [C] a place where young people can meet, play games, dance etc

youth·ful /'juːθfəl/ adj **1** seeming younger than you really are: *a youthful 50-year-old* **2** typical of young people: *youthful enthusiasm*

youth hos·tel /'. ,../ n [C] a place where people can stay cheaply when they are travelling

you've /jəv; strong juːv/ the short form of 'you have': *You've got to take care of yourself.*

yo-yo /'jəʊ jəʊll'joʊ joʊ/ n [C] a toy that moves up and down a string when you lift your hand up and down

yr n the written abbreviation of YEAR

yuck /jʌk/ interjection informal used to say that you think something is unpleasant: *Yuck! This stuff tastes disgusting!*

yucky /'jʌki/ adj informal something that is yucky looks or tastes unpleasant

yule·tide /'juːltaɪd/ n [U] literary the period m just before Christmas until just after it

yum /jʌm/ interjection used to say that you think something tastes good: *Yum! Apple pie!*

yum·my /'jʌmi/ adj spoken informal food that is yummy tastes very good

yup·pie /'jʌpi/ n [C] a young person who earns a lot of money and buys expensive things

YWCA /ˌwaɪ dʌbəljuː siː 'eɪ/ n **the YWCA** Young Women's Christian Association; an organization that provides places to stay for young women in large cities

Zz

Z, z /zedllziː/ the last letter of the English alphabet

za·ny /'zeɪni/ adj unusual and funny: *a zany new TV comedy*

zap /zæp/ v [T] informal to kill or attack something very quickly

zap·per /'zæpəl-ər/ n [C] AmE informal a television REMOTE CONTROL

zeal /ziːl/ n [U] great interest in something and eagerness to do it: *political zeal*

zeal·ous /'zeləs/ adj extremely eager to do something because you believe strongly that it should be done — **zealously** adv

ze·bra /'ziːbrə, 'ze-ll'ziːbrə/ n [C] a black and white striped (STRIPE) African animal like a horse

zebra

zebra cros·sing /ˌ.. '../ n [C] BrE a place with black and white lines where people can cross a road safely; CROSSWALK AmE

zen·ith /'zenɪθll'ziː-/ n [singular] the time when something is most successful: *The Moghul Empire had reached its zenith.*

ze·ro /'zɪərəʊll'ziːroʊ/ number **1** 0: *zero degrees Fahrenheit* **2** the temperature in Celsius at which water freezes: *20°C below zero | sub-zero temperatures*

zero² v

zero in on sth phr v [T] **1** to aim or move towards something: *The missile zeroed in on its target.* **2** to pay special attention to something: *He immediately zeroed in on Turner's lack of political experience.*

zest /zest/ n [U] a feeling of eagerness, excitement, and enjoyment: *a zest for life*

zig·zag¹ /'zɪgzæg/ n [C] a line that looks like a row of w's joined together

zigzag

zigzag² v [I] **-gged, -gging** to move forward by going to the left at an angle, then to the right, then to the left etc: *The path zigzags up the mountain*

zilch /zɪltʃ/ n [U] informal nothing

zil·lion /'zɪljən/ number informal an extremely large number or amount: *She asked a zillion questions.*

zinc /zɪŋk/ *n* [U] a metal used to produce or cover other metals

zip[1] /zɪp/ *v* **-pped, -pping** **1** [T] also **zip up** to close or fasten something using a zip: *Zip up your coat.* → opposite UNZIP **2** [I] to go somewhere or do something very quickly: *A few cars zipped past us.*

zip[2] *n* **1** [C] *BrE* a thing you use for fastening clothes, bags etc, which consists of two lines of small pieces of metal or plastic that join together; ZIPPER *AmE* → see picture at FASTENERS **2** [C] *AmE spoken* ZIP CODE **3** [U] *AmE spoken informal* none; zero

zip code /'. ./ *n* [C] *AmE* a number you write below an address on an envelope, that helps the post office deliver the letter more quickly; POST CODE *BrE*

zip·per /'zɪpəǁ-ər/ *n* [C] *AmE* a zip → see picture at FASTENERS

zit /zɪt/ *n* [C] *informal* a small round raised part on your face; a SPOT

zo·di·ac /'zəʊdiækǁ'zoʊ-/ *n* **the signs of the zodiac** the 12 signs used in ASTROLOGY, based on the position of the stars and PLANETs, which some people believe affect what type of person you are and what will happen to you

zom·bie /'zɒmbiǁ'zɑːm-/ *n* [C] **1** like a **zombie** moving very slowly and unable to think clearly, especially because you are very tired **2** a dead body that is made to move by magic

zone /zəʊnǁzoʊn/ *n* [C] an area where a particular thing happens or where there are particular rules: *a no-parking zone* | *a war zone* → see also TIME ZONE

zoo /zuː/ *n* [C] a place where a lot of different types of wild animals are kept so that people can see or study them

zoo·keep·er /'zuːˌkiːpəǁ-ər/ *n* [C] someone who looks after animals in a zoo

zo·ol·o·gy /zuːˈɒlədʒi, zəʊˈɒ-ǁzoʊˈɑːl-/ *n* [U] the scientific study of animals and their behaviour —**zoologist** *n* [C] —**zoological** /ˌzuːəˈlɒdʒɪkəl◂, ˌzəʊ-ǁˌzoʊəˈlɑː-/ *adj*

zoom[1] /zuːm/ *v* [I] *informal* to travel very quickly: + **down/along/off etc** *We zoomed down the highway.*

zoom in *phr v* [I] if a camera zooms in, it makes the object it is photographing seem much closer and bigger

zoom[2] *n* [singular] the sound made by a car, plane etc moving very quickly

zoom lens /'. ˌ./ *n* [C] a camera LENS that can make the object being photographed look bigger or smaller

Zs /ziːz/ *n* [plural] *AmE informal* **catch/get some Zs** to sleep

zuc·chi·ni /zʊˈkiːni/ *n* [C,U] *AmE* a long vegetable with dark green skin; COURGETTE *BrE* → see picture at VEGETABLES

ZZZ, zzz used in CARTOONs to show that someone is sleeping

Z

COUNTABLE AND UNCOUNTABLE NOUNS

Countable Nouns

Apple and **chair** are both COUNTABLE nouns, because they are things you can count – there can be more than one of them:

 an apple

 three apples

 a chair

 two chairs

These nouns can be used in the plural, and can be used with **a** or **an** when they are singular. In this dictionary, countable nouns are shown like this: [C].

Uncountable Nouns

Sand and **water** are UNCOUNTABLE NOUNS, because they are substances which cannot be counted:

 sand

 water

These nouns are not usually used in the plural. There are some nouns, like **love** and **beauty** (abstract nouns) which cannot be counted because they are not physical things like apples and chairs. These are uncountable nouns too. Note also that **information, news, advice** and **money** are uncountable. In this dictionary, uncountable nouns are shown like this: [U].

Nouns that are both Countable and Uncountable

Some nouns, like **light** and **coffee**, can be countable in one meaning and uncountable in another. When they are countable, they can be made plural. When they are uncountable, they cannot be made plural. For example:

light

the light of the sun – [U]

Turn on the lights. [C]

coffee

a jar of coffee – [U]   a pot of coffee – [U]

Three coffees, please. – [C]

Plural and Singular Nouns

Some nouns, for example **scissors**, are used only in the plural and take a plural verb. These nouns are marked [plural] in the dictionary.

scis·sors /ˈsɪzəz‖-ərz/ *n* [plural] a tool for cutting paper, with two sharp blades that are joined together and have handles with holes for your fingers: *a pair of scissors* → see colour picture on page 80

Some nouns, for example **rush**, are usually used only in the singular. these nouns are used with a and an, and are marked [singular] in the dictionary:

rush[2] *n* **1** [singular] a sudden fast movement, especially by a crowd: **make a rush for sth** *We all made a rush for the seats at the front.* **2** [singular, U] a situation in which you need to hurry: *We have plenty of time.   There's no rush.* | **be in a rush** *I can't stop – I'm in a rush.* | **a rush to do sth** *There's a big rush to get tickets.* **3 the rush** the time when a lot of people are doing something, for example travelling or shopping: *the Christmas rush* **4** [C usually plural] a tall grass or plant that grows near a river and is used to make baskets etc

more and less

The list below shows you which words to use with [C] and [U] nouns to show quantity. They answer questions like *How many?* and *How much?*

all

How many
(use with [C] nouns)

every, all
*Every student came to the meeting/
All the students came to the meeting.*

most
Most of my friends came to the party.

many, a lot of
Many people can't afford private health insurance.

some, several
*Some of the games had to be cancelled.
Several people were injured in the accident.*

not many, only a few
*There aren't many tickets left.
There are only a few tickets left.*

not...any, no, none
*He couldn't answer any of the questions.
There are no serious problems.
None of her friends came.*

none

How much
(use with [U] nouns)

all
Someone had drunk all the wine.

most
Her baby spends most of the time sleeping.

much, a lot of, a great deal of
*Much of what he says is true.
I gave the matter a lot of thought.
There is a great deal of work to be done.*

some
There's some bread in the cupboard.

Little, not much
*There's only a little room left.
There's not much room left.*

not...any, no, none
*He didn't give me any help.
There's no milk in the fridge,
none at all.*

some and any

Any is usually used instead of **some** in questions and sentences with not.
Have you got any change/stamps?
No, I haven't got any change/stamps.
It is also possible to use some in a question, especially when you expect the answer to be yes:
Could you spare some stamps/change?
Would you like some more coffee?

Some common mistakes with uncountable nouns

If a noun is marked [U] do NOT use it in the plural. If a particular meaning of a noun is marked [U] do not use it in the plural with that meaning: *We need some more information.* | *They've just bought a lot of new furniture.* | *I must wash my hair tonight.*
If a noun, or a meaning of a noun, is marked [U] do NOT use it with a or an in sentences like these: *The hotel is surrounded by beautiful scenery.* | *We are having really fine weather at the moment.* | *She gave me very good advice.* Remember that uncountable nouns are used WITHOUT an article in statements like these: *Crime is a problem in most big cities.* (Don't say: 'the crime is a problem') | *She wrote an article about the role of women in society.* (Don't say: 'in the society') *He is studying medicine.* (Don't say: 'the medicine')

TRANSITIVE AND INTRANSITIVE VERBS

Transitive verbs [T]

Find, hit, enjoy, and **expect** are all transitive verbs. This means that they must be followed by a noun or noun phrase that is the direct object. If you take away the direct object, the sentence no longer makes sense.

subject	verb	object
I	found	your keys.
Becker	hit	the ball.
Sue	enjoys	swimming.
No one	thought	that it would rain.

NOTE: the object can be a clause with *that*.

Some transitive verbs can take two objects, a direct object and an indirect object for example: **give, tell, send**

subj	vb	indirect obj.	direct obj.
I	gave	him	$10.
He	told	them	a story.

Transitive verbs can be made passive:
The dog chased the cat. →
The cat was chased by the dog
In this dictionary transitive verbs are shown like this: [T]

en·joy /ɪnˈdʒɔɪ/ *v* [T] **1** to get pleasure from something: *Did you enjoy the movie?* | **enjoy doing sth** *My wife really enjoys playing golf.* **2 enjoy yourself** to be happy and have fun: *It was a wonderful party, and we all enjoyed ourselves enormously.* **3** to have something good, such as success or a particular right or advantage: *The team enjoyed unexpected success this season.* —**enjoyment** *n* [U] *We hope the bad weather didn't spoil your enjoyment.*

Intransitive verbs [I]

Fall, laugh, rise, and **arrive** are all intransitive verbs. This means that they never take a direct object and their meaning ís complete without a direct object.

subject	verb
David	had fallen.
The children	laughed.
The sun	was rising.
A taxi	arrived.

NOTE: that you can add another phrase after the verb, eg *David had fallen off his bike.* but the noun *bike* in this sentence is not the direct object.

Intransitive verbs cannot be made passive.

In the dictionary intransitive verbs are shown like this: [I]

laugh[1] /lɑːf‖læf/ *v* [I] to make a sound with your voice when you think something is funny: *Why are you laughing?* | **+ at** *No one ever laughs at my jokes!* | **burst out laughing** (=suddenly start laughing)
laugh at sb/sth *phr v* [T] to say unkind things about someone or something and make jokes about them: *Mommy, all the kids at school were laughing at me!*
laugh sth ↔ **off** *phr v* [T] to pretend that something is not very serious or important by joking about it: *He laughed off suggestions that he was planning to resign.*

Verbs which can be both transitive and intransitive [I,T]

A lot of verbs such as **see** and **speak** can be used in a transitive or an intransitive way:

Cats can see in the dark. [I]	Have you seen my pen anywhere? [T]
Try to speak more clearly. [I]	The Pope speaks several languages. [T]

In this dictionary these verbs are shown like this: [I,T]

see /siː/ *v* **saw** /sɔː‖sɒː/, **seen** /siːn/, **seeing** **1** [I,T] to use your eyes to look at and notice people or things: *I can't see without my glasses.* | *It was too dark to see anything.* | *I saw a man take the bag and run off.*

Linking verbs

Some verbs such as **be, become,** and **seem,** are not marked [I] or [T]. These verbs are followed by a complement, which may be a noun or noun phrase, or an adjective or adjective phrase:
The weather was becoming warmer. | *She seems happy in her new job.*
In this dictionary linking verbs are shown like this: [linking verb]

be·come /bɪkʌm/ *v* **became** /bɪˈkeɪm/, **become, becoming 1** [linking verb] if something becomes warmer, harder etc it was not warm in the past but now it is: *The weather had become warmer.* | *Kennedy became the first Catholic president.* | *It is becoming harder to find good staff.*

MODAL VERBS

Modal verbs are used with other verbs to add another part to their meaning. The nine main modal verbs are: **must, can, will, shall, may, could, would, should, might**

Special grammar of modal verbs

- they are followed by the basic form of a verb (the infinitive without **to**): *I can swim.* | *You must wait.*
- the third person singular of the simple present tense does not end in **-s**
- they form questions without using **do** or **did**; the subject comes after the main verb: *Can Larry swim?* | *Should we wait ?*
- they form negatives by adding **not** or **n't** but <u>without</u> using **do** or **did**; the negative of **can** is **cannot** or **can't**; the short form negatives of **will** and **shall** are **won't** and **shan't**: *We must not waste time.* | *I can't swim.* | *It won't rain*

Semi-modals

ought to, used to, and **need** are partly used like modal verbs:

	statement	question	negative
ought to	He ought to come.	Ought he to come?	He oughtn't to come.
used to	She used to live here.	Did she use to live here?	She didn't use to live here.
need	They need to wait.	Do they need to wait?	They needn't wait.

Uses of modals

SAYING WHETHER SOMEONE IS ABLE TO DO SOMETHING: **can, could**
present tense: *Can you guess the answer?*
past tense: *I couldn't read your handwriting.*

SAYING WHETHER SOMEONE IS WILLING TO DO SOMETHING: **will, would**
present tense: *I will help you if no one else will.*
past tense: *No one would lend me the money.*

ASKING FOR AND GIVING PERMISSION: **can, could, may, might**
Can I go home now? | *You can borrow my bike, if you want.*
polite: *Could I use your phone please?*
formal: *May I ask a question?* | *Students may borrow up to six books.*

ASKING SOMEONE TO DO SOMETHING: **will, would, could, can**

Will you hold this rope for a moment? | *Can you help me lift this box?*
polite: *Would you close the door, please?* | *Could you all please face the camera?*

SAYING THAT SOMETHING IS NECESSARY: **must, need to, have to**
We must go now – it's getting late. | *We need to buy some more potatoes.*| *Do we have to take our passports with us?*

SAYING THAT SOMETHING IS NOT NECESSARY: **need not/not need to/ needn't, not have to**
We needn't lock the car – it's safe here. | *You don't need to tell Sandy – she already knows.* | *You don't have to go if you don't want to.*

GIVING COMMANDS OR INSTRUCTIONS: **must, should**
Now, you must all listen carefully. | *All passengers must wear seat belts.* | *Accidents should be reported to the Health and Safety Officer.*

SAYING WHAT IS THE RIGHT THING TO DO: **should, ought to, must**
I think you should tell her the truth.| *I shouldn't have shouted at you.* | *You ought to apologize for being so rude.* | *They ought not to use animals for their experiments.* | *We must all do our best.*

SAYING THAT SOMETHING IS POSSIBLE: **may, might, could**
Hundreds of workers may lose their jobs if the strike continues. | *Take your umbrella – it might rain.* | *I'm not sure – you could be right.*

SAYING THAT SOMETHING SEEMS CERTAIN OR IMPOSSIBLE: **must, cannot/can't**
Someone must have made a mistake. (=it seems certain) | *It can't be true* (=it seems impossible).

SAYING THAT SOMETHING SEEMS PROBABLE: **should, ought to**
They should be home by now.| *He's a good player – he ought to win easily.*

TALKING ABOUT THE FUTURE: **will, won't, would, shall, shan't**
(In British English **shall** and **shan't** are sometimes used instead of **will** and **won't** in the first person)
Kathy will be there tomorrow. | *He won't be home until eight.* | *The weatherman said it would rain.* | *I shall see you all next week.*

TALKING ABOUT THE PAST: **used to**
I used to live on a farm before I came to London. | *Did you use to play football, when you were a student?*

PHRASAL VERBS

Verbs like **get up**, **deal with**, and **put up with** are very common in English. They are called <u>phrasal verbs</u>. A phrasal verb consists of two or three parts. The first part is a verb. It is followed by an adverb or a preposition, or by both. The meaning of a phrasal verb is often very different from the meaning of the verb on its own. For example, **look up** (=find information in a book) and **look after** (=take care of) have completely separate meanings.

How to find a phrasal verb in this dictionary

Phrasal verbs are listed in alphabetical order below the entry for the main verb. They are marked *phr v*.

In this entry **cheer on** and **cheer up** are listed under the main verb **cheer:**

cheer¹ /tʃɪəlltʃɪr/ *v* [I,T] to shout approval, encouragement etc: *The audience cheered as the band began to play.*
  cheer sb/sth ↔ **on** *phr v* [T] to encourage a person or a team by cheering for them: *Highbury Stadium was packed with fans cheering on their home team.*
  cheer sb **up** *phr v* [I,T] to become happier, or to make someone feel happier: *She took him out to dinner to cheer him up.*

Sometimes the main verb in a phrasal verb is not used alone. This entry shows that the verb **keel** is always used with the adverb **over**, so it is only ever used as part of a phrasal verb.

keel² *v*
  keel over *phr v* [I] to fall over

Transitive or Intransitive?

Phrasal verbs, like all verbs, are either transitive or intransitive or both. In this dictionary they are marked [I], [T], or [I,T].

These entries show that **grow out of** is a transitive verb and **grow up** is an intransitive verb.

grow out of *phr v* [T] **1** if children grow out of clothes, they become too big to wear them **2** to stop doing something as you get older: *Sarah still sucks her thumb, but she'll grow out of it.*

grow up *phr v* [T] **1** to develop from being a child to being an adult: *I grew up in Glasgow.* **2** to start to exist and become bigger: *Villages grew up along the river.*

Some phrasal verbs can be used both transitively and intransitively, sometimes with a similar meaning, for example **get back:**

get back *phr v* **1** [I] to return, especially to the place where you live: *What time do you think you'll get back?* **2** [T **get** sth **back**] to have something that you had lent or lost returned to you: *Did you get your purse back?*

Sometimes the meaning completely changes according to whether it is transitive or intransitive, for example **get around:**

get around (also **get round** *BrE*) *phr v* **1** [T **get around** sth] to find a way of dealing with a problem, usually by avoiding it: *Businesses are looking for ways to get around the tax laws.* **2** [I] to be able to move or travel to different places

Position of the Direct Object

When a phrasal verb is transitive [T], the dictionary tells you where to put the direct object. You should look at the beginning of the entry to see how the verb is written.

This entry shows you that the direct object of pick on always comes at the end of the phrasal verb:

pick on *phr v* [T] to repeatedly criticize or upset someone unfairly: *Greg, stop picking on your sister!*

Sometimes, for example in **take sb out** the object must always come between the two parts of the phrasal verb, although this does not happen very often:

take out *phr v* [T] **1** [**take** sth ↔ **out**] to remove something: *The dentist says she may have to take out one of my back teeth.* **2** [**take** sb **out**] to go with someone to a restaurant, film, party etc, and pay for them: *I'm taking Helen out for dinner next week.* **3** [**take** sth ↔ **out**] to arrange to get something from a bank, court, etc: *The couple took out a £20,000 loan.*

With many phrasal verbs, however, the object can appear in either position. This is shown in this dictionary by the symbol ↔ :

---

hand sth ↔ **in** *phr v* [T] to give something to someone in a position of authority: *Please hand in your application by September 30.*

This shows that you can either say 'hand sth in' or 'hand in sth': *Please hand in your books at the end of the class. / Please hand your books in at the end of the class.* Note however that with verbs of this type when the object is a pronoun, it must come between the two parts of the phrasal verb: *Hand in your books. /Hand them in.* (NEVER "hand in them").

Phrasal verbs with two objects

Some transitive phrasal verbs have two objects. The dictionary will show you where to put these objects.

This entry shows that **put down to** has two objects. The first goes after **put** and the second goes after **to**:

---

put sth **down to** sth *phr v* [T] to think that something is caused by something else: *She put her illness down to stress.*

WORD CLASSES or PARTS OF SPEECH

In order to use a word correctly you need to know what word class (or 'part of speech') it belongs to. Is it a noun, a verb, an adjective etc?

All the words in this dictionary have a label which tells you which word class they belong to. You will find a list of these labels at the front of the book. Now look at the notes and examples below:

NOUN **n** A noun is a word such as **child, house, Africa**, or **beauty**. It has as its meaning a person, a thing, a place, or an idea. In the following sentence the nouns are underlined:

There was no evidence that Williams had been in the park on the night when the murder was committed.

VERB **v** A verb is a word or group of words such as **go, make, become**, or **be born**. It is used to say that a person or thing does something, that something happens to them, or that they are in a particular state. In the following sentence the verbs are underlined:

The police arrested Williams because they believed that he was guilty, and they took him to the police station, where he was kept until his lawyer arrived.

PREPOSITION **prep** A preposition is a word such as **of, in, at,** or **about**, that is used before a noun or pronoun to show a connection with another word or phrase. In the following sentences the prepositions are underlined:

If someone is arrested by the police and charged with a crime, they have to go to court. The trial takes place in a courtroom, where the details of the charge are presented.

ADJECTIVE **adj** An adjective is a word such as **big, happy,** or **British** that describes a noun. In the following sentences the adjectives are underlined:

Williams was lucky enough to find a good

lawyer. She told him about his legal rights, and during the long trial she put forward strong arguments to prove that he was innocent.

ADVERB **adv** An adverb is a word that describes or adds to the meaning of a verb, eg **slowly, often, everywhere** or describes an adjective or another adverb, eg **very** good, **completely** wrong. In the following sentences the adverbs are underlined:

Eventually, Williams was officially told that he must stand trial. He had always insisted that he was completely innocent. His defence lawyer argued his case very forcefully. and it seemed almost certain that they would win.

linking word A linking word is a word such as **but, and,** or **while,** that connects phrases, clauses, or parts of a sentence. In the following sentence the linking words are underlined:

The jury listened to all the evidence and considered their verdict, but at first they could not agree because some of them thought that Williams was innocent, whereas others were not sure.

PRONOUN **pron** A pronoun is a word such as **she, they, it,** or **who,** that is used instead of a noun. In the following sentences the pronouns are underlined:

The judge asked the foreman of the jury, "Have you reached a verdict?" "Yes, we have." "And what is it?" "Not guilty," he answered. Williams, who was very relieved, turned to his lawyer and thanked her.

ADJECTIVE WORD ORDER

When you use more than one adjective before a noun, the adjectives are usually in the following order:

	1	2	3	4	5	6	7	noun
	your opinion about sb/sth	size	age	shape/colour	where sb/ sth is from	what sth is made of	specific type	
a	nice		new			woollen		sweater
his				blue			naval	uniform
a	serious						medical	problem
a	lovely	big			American			car
that		tall	young		French			woman
a	strange			triangular		stone		building
her	silly	little	teenage					brother

Therefore say   *a little old man*   **NOT**   *an old little man*
                 strange new ideas   **NOT**   *new strange ideas*

NOTE: **same, whole, entire, only, next, last**
If one of these adjectives comes in a series of adjectives before a noun, it should always come first, immediately after the determiner: *the same stupid old jokes* | *the only serious problem* | *his next big political speech.*

COMPARATIVE AND SUPERLATIVE OF ADJECTIVES

Use the *comparative* form of an adjective (e.g. **bigger, more interesting**) when you are comparing two things. Use the *superlative* (e.g. **biggest, most interesting**) to say that something is bigger, more interesting etc than all the others in a particular group.

Comparatives and superlatives are formed in various ways.

The girls are all quite **tall**. Meg is **taller** than Gill. Sue is the **tallest** of the three.

These rings are **expensive**. The gold ring is **more expensive** than the silver one. The diamond ring is the **most expensive** of all.

1. Adjectives of one syllable

Form the comparative and superlative by adding **-er** or **-est** to the end of the word;

tall   taller   tallest
rich   richer   richest

If the adjective already ends in **-e** you only need to add **-r** or **-st**

nice   nicer   nicest
rare   rarer   rarest

Sometimes, when the adjective ends in a single consonant, you need to double the final consonant before forming the comparative and superlative.

big   bigger   biggest
fat   fatter   fattest

2. Adjectives of two syllables

If the word ends in **-y**, change the **-y** to **-i** and then add **-er** or **-est**.

heavy   heavier   heaviest
happy   happier   happiest

If the adjective does NOT end in **-y**, then form the comparative and superlative using **more** and **most**:

useful   more useful   most useful
famous   more famous   most famous

3. Adjectives of three syllables or more

Form the comparative and superlative using more and most

expensive   more expensive   most expensive
comfortable more comfortable most comfortable

4. 'Irregular' Comparatives and Superlatives

Some adjectives use a completely different word for the comparative and superlative forms.

good   better   best
bad   worse   worst

NOTE: For adjectives which are formed from a verb and end in **-ed** or **-ing**, always use **more** and **most** for the comparative and superlative:

bored   more bored   most bored
boring   more boring   most boring

Adjectives which start with the negative prefix **un-** can use **-er** and **-est** even if they have three syllables:

unhappy   unhappier   unhappiest

5. Comparisons using 'less' and 'least'

You can make comparisons in the opposite way by using **less** and **least,** instead of **more** and **most,** before adjectives of two or more syllables:

The gold ring is less expensive than the diamond ring. The silver ring is the least expensive of all.

With one syllable adjectives use **not as...as** for this kind of comparison.

Boston is not as big as New York. = New York is bigger than Boston.

BRITISH AND AMERICAN ENGLISH

Although English is generally the same all over the world, there are several differences between British and American English.

Spelling

Sometimes American and British English users spell things differently. Some of the main differences are:

British words end in	American words end in
-our	**-or**
colour, labour, humour	color, labor, humor
-tre	**-ter**
theatre, centre, metre	theater, center, meter
-nce	**-nse**
defence, offence, licence	defense, offense, license
-elled, -elling	**-eled, elled**
travelled, cancelling	traveled, canceling

In British English, words that end in **-ize** or **-ization** can often also be spelled **-ise** or **-isation,** for example both **organization** and **organisation** are correct in British English, but the letter **z** is the correct American spelling. However, the word **advertise** is always spelt with an **s**.

Vocabulary

Some words for the same things are different in British and American English. Here are some examples:

British	American
tap	**faucet**
cooker	**stove**
petrol	**gas**
toilet	**bathroom**
trousers	**pants**
railway	**railroad**
wash up	**do the dishes**
wash your hands	**wash up**
jug	**pitcher**
campsite	**campground**

Sometimes words are neither specifically British or American, but a British or American speaker is more likely to use one word than another. For example, the word **angry** is correct in British and American English, but Americans usually use the word **mad.** The phrase **a bit** is also acceptable in both, but Americans are more likely to say **a little.** Similarly, British speakers are more likely to use the noun and verb **post** instead of **mail,** although **mail** is correct in both British and American English.

Grammar

There are also some grammatical differences between British and American English, for example when you are choosing the correct preposition to use. Here are some examples:

British	American
You can phone us **on** 0800 123123.	You can phone us **at** 01 800 555.
He looked **round** the corner.	He looked **around** the corner.
Her accent is different **from/to** mine.	Her accent is different **from/than** mine.

Sometimes, Americans can miss out a preposition when British people would always use one, for example with the verb **protest.** British speakers would always use the preposition **about:** Some students were protesting about the war, but the preposition can be missed out in American English: Some students were protesting the war.

SENTENCE CONNECTORS

When you are writing, it is important that your reader understands *the connection* between the things that you are saying.

What is the connection between these two sentences?

There has been a big rise in food prices this year.
The price of meat has almost doubled.

The second sentence gives an example of the idea in the first sentence.

You can help people to understand what you are saying by showing how one idea is connected to another. To show connections, you can use words and phrases such as **for example, therefore,** and **however.**

Position of connectors

Connectors can go in various places in a sentence. They can go at the beginning of a sentence:

*We had no oil resources. **Therefore** we had to import oil from the Middle East.*

in the middle of a sentence:

*Their plans were almost complete. There were, **however,** a number of unsolved problems still remaining.*

at the end of a sentence:

*There are lots of things you could do to earn some money. You could help in the shop, **for instance.***

Types of connectors

1. *ALSO connectors*
Use these when you are adding another fact or idea to what you have just said.

also/either
*Bernstein was certainly a great conductor. He was **also** the composer of 'West Side Story'.*
If you want to connect two negative sentences, use **either**: *Nadia doesn't smoke. She doesn't drink **either.***

too/as well
Use these at the end of a sentence when you are adding something to a list of things you have already mentioned: *This car's fast and comfortable. It's economical, **too**. | Are you coming to Sasha's party **as well**?*

moreover/furthermore
Use **moreover** or **furthermore** in formal written English to add a more important fact than the one you mentioned in the previous sentence: *Local people would like a new road. **Moreover** there are good economic reasons for building one. | The drug has powerful side-effects. **Furthermore,** it may be addictive.*

besides
Use **besides** especially in spoken English at the beginning of a sentence, when you have given one reason for something and you are adding another.
*I don't really need a new car. **Besides,** I can't afford one.*

2. *BUT connectors*
Use these connectors when you are adding a sentence that gives facts or ideas that you would not have expected from the previous sentence.

but
But is not usually used at the beginning of a sentence.
*He never did much studying, **but** he always got the highest grades in the exams.*

however/nevertheless
Use **however** and **nevertheless** especially in written English: *Tourists are enjoying the dry sunny weather. The farmers, **however,** are praying for rain. | It was a terrible accident. **Nevertheless,** air travel is still the safest form of transport.*

3. *FOR EXAMPLE connectors*
Use these connectors when you are giving an example of the fact or idea that was stated in the previous sentence.

for example/for instance

Car prices vary a lot. **For example**, *in Belgium a VW Golf costs £1000 less than in Britain.* | *The Romans developed some advanced technology. They had underfloor central heating,* **for instance**.

4. THEREFORE connectors

Use these connectors to connect a result in one sentence with the reason given in the previous sentence.

so

Use **so** in spoken English or informal written English: *John's sick,* **so** *won't be able to come tonight.*

therefore

Use **therefore** in more formal or written English: *I would like to spend more time with my family. I have* **therefore** *decided to resign as chairman.*

5. Summarising connectors

Use these connectors when you have already said something and you want to say it again in a simpler or shorter way.

in other words

Use **in other words** when you want to explain something again in a different way, or to explain the result of what you have said: *The company has to reduce labour costs.* **In other words** *some of us are going to lose our jobs.*

in short

Use **in short** when you want to say something again in a shorter or simpler way: *The truth doesn't come into Jake's reasoning – he'll tell you whatever he thinks you want to hear.* **In short**, *he's a liar.*

CAPITALIZATION

1. The first word of every sentence begins with a capital letter: *How are you today?*

2. Proper names begin with capital letters, including:

    • names of people, places, organizations, and events: *Robin* | *London* | *Japan* | *the Red Cross* | *World War II*

    • words that have developed from proper names, such as names of languages, nationalities, religions: *French* | *American* | *Christian*

    • things that are trademarks: *Pepsi Cola* | *Ferrari*

    • names of days of the week and months of the year (but not seasons): *Sunday* | *July*

    • titles and ranks used with people's names: *Mr Jones* | *Professor Leech* | *Colonel Blimp*
    NOTE: *I'm going to see the doctor.* **BUT** *I'm going to see Dr Taylor / Doctor Taylor.*

    • titles of books, films, essays etc: *'The Merchant of Venice'* | *'Gone with the Wind'*
    NOTE: In the titles of books, films etc, capitalize the first word, the last word, and other important words. Do not capitalize prepositions (*of, with, for* etc), determiners (*a, an, the, his* etc) or linking words such as *and* in the middle of a title.

3. Initials – groups of letters which are the first letters of the name of something – are written as capitals: *NATO* | *AIDS*

INTENSIFIERS

Adverbs such as **very** and **extremely** can be used to give a stronger meaning to adjectives and other adverbs. Adverbs such as **slightly** and **fairly** can be used to make the meaning less strong. In the list of adverbs below, the words get stronger as you move from top to bottom:

WORD GROUP	MEANING	EXAMPLES
***slightly** ***a little/a little bit** ***a bit** (BrE informal)	a little	a slightly sweet taste Life in England is a little different from what I expected. The news is a bit depressing, isn't it?
fairly **rather** **reasonably** **pretty** (spoken) **quite**	less than 'very', but more than a little	Both their children are fairly intelligent. I was rather surprised at her remarks. We can be reasonably certain that there is no risk. The food here is pretty good. I thought the movie was quite good.
very **really** (spoken) **highly**	very	The test was very difficult. It's really nice to be home again. a team of highly skilled engineers
extremely **very very** (spoken) **terribly/awfully** (spoken)	more than 'very'	I am extremely grateful for all your help. What I have to tell you is very very important. I'm terribly sorry, but there are no tickets left.
incredibly **amazingly**	much more than you expected	I have been incredibly lucky in my career. an amazingly generous offer
completely **totally** **absolutely**	as much as possible	By Friday I'm completely exhausted. We're all totally confused. The weather was absolutely terrible.

*NOTE: **slightly, a little,** and **a bit** are mainly used with adjectives and adverbs in their comparative forms: slightly better, a little stronger, a bit worse.

WORD FORMATION

A lot of English words are formed from two or more different parts.

In some words a <u>prefix</u> has been added at the beginning, before the main part of the word, and this changes its meaning. For example the word **semicircle** is made up of two parts – the prefix **semi-** (meaning 'half') and the word **circle**; so a **semicircle** is a half-circle.

In some words a <u>suffix</u> has been added at the end, after the main part of the word. For example, the word **painless** is made up of the word **pain** and the suffix **-less** (meaning 'without'); so **painless** means 'without pain'. There are also words that have a prefix at the beginning as well as a suffix at the end. For example **unrecognizable** is made up of the prefix **un-** (meaning 'not'), the word **recognize** and the suffix **-able** (used to say that something can be done to the subject); so something that is **unrecognizable** cannot be recognized.

If you know what the parts of a word mean, you can often guess its meaning. The list of prefixes and suffixes on Page789 will help you. Notice that a prefix or a suffix may have two meanings. For example **sub-** can mean 1) under (as in **subway**) or 2) less than (as in **sub-zero**).

Prefixes

Several prefixes have the effect of making a word negative:

prefixes meaning NOT	examples
un-	*unfair, unfortunate*
in-, im-, il-, ir-	*inconvenient, impossible, illegal, irregular*
non-	*non-violent*

Some prefixes tell you how many things are involved:

<u>number prefixes</u>

mono- (one)	*monosyllable* (a word with one syllable)
bi- (two)	*bicycle* (two wheels), *biennial* (every two years)
tri- (three)	*triangle* (three angles), *tripod* (three legs)
multi-, poly- (many)	*multicoloured, polygon* (a shape with many sides)

A lot of prefixes tell you about position, direction, and time:

<u>position/direction prefixes</u>

sub-, under-	*submarine* (under the sea), *underground*
trans- (across)	*transatlantic*
pre- (before)	*pre-war, pre-school*

Suffixes

Suffixes are added to the end of words. A suffix has the effect of changing a word and making it a different part of speech. For example the suffix **-ly** can be added to an adjective to make it an adverb.

quick + ly ➡ quickly.

<u>suffixes that produce verbs:</u>
-fy (make or become)
solidify (make sth solid or become solid)
-ize/ise (make)
popularize (make sth popular)

<u>suffixes that produce nouns:</u>
-er (someone who does an activity):
singer, hunter
-ness (the quality of being…)
goodness, brightness

<u>suffixes that produce adjectives:</u>
-able, -ible
washable (which can be washed)
-less (without)
powerless (without any power)

WORD BUILDING
Word beginnings

anti- /'ænti ‖ 'æntaɪ, 'ænti/ **1** opposed to: **antinuclear** opposed to the use of nuclear weapons and power —compare **pro- 2** used to prevent something: **antifreeze** a liquid put into water in a car to stop it from freezing **3** opposite to: **anticlockwise** in the opposite direction to the movement of the hands of a clock

auto- /'ɔːtəʊ, 'ɔːtə/ **1** relating to a machine, computer, or system that can operate or move without being controlled by humans: **autopilot** a computer that operates the controls of a plane **2** about or by yourself: **autobiography** a book about your life that you write yourself

bi- /baɪ/ two or twice: **biplane** a plane with two wings ‖ **bilingual** able to speak two languages equally well ‖ **bimonthly** twice a month or once every two months

bio- /'baɪəʊ/ relating to life and living things: **bio-chemistry** the scientific study of the chemistry of living things

centi- /sentị/ also **cent** /'sent/ **1** 100: **Centigrade** a scale of temperature in which water boils at 100° **2** 100th: **centimetre** 0.01 metres

co- /kəʊ/ with or together: **co-worker** a person who works with you

contra- /'kɒntrə ‖ 'kɑːn-/ opposite or against: **contradict** to say the opposite of a statement, opinion etc

cross- /krɒs ‖ krɔːs/ going across or between: **cross-Channel** going across the Channel ‖ **cross-cultural** going between two or more cultures

de- /diː, dɪ/ **1** to remove something: **decaffeinated coffee** coffee that has had the CAFFEINE removed **2** to reduce something: **devalue** to reduce the value of a country's money compared to other countries' money

dis- /dɪs/ **1** not: **discontented** not satisfied with the situation you are in ‖ **disagree** to not agree **2** to remove something: **disconnect** to make something no longer be connected to the supply of electricity, water, gas etc

eco- /iːkəʊ ‖ iːkoʊ/ relating to the environment: **eco-friendly** not likely to harm the environment

ex- /eks/ former: **ex-husband** a man who was a woman's husband, but who is now DIVORCE*d* from her ‖ **ex-prime minister** former prime minister

extra- /'ekstrə/ beyond or outside, or not included in something: **extracurricular** not part of your usual schoolwork

in- /ɪn/ **1** also **il-** /ɪl/, **im-** /ɪm/, **ir-** /ɪr/ not: **inexact** not exact **2** in or into: **input** ideas, advice, money etc that you put into something or give to someone in order to help them succeed

> **USAGE NOTE**
> **in-** meaning "not" usually changes to **il-** before *l*: **illegal** not legal; **im-** before *b, m,* or *p*: **imbalance** lack of balance ‖ **immobile** not moving ‖ **impatient** not patient; **ir-** before *r*: **irregular** not regular or even; not usual

inter- /'ɪntər/ between or among: **international** involving many countries ‖ **intermarriage** marriage between members of different groups, families etc

kilo- /'kɪlə/ 1,000: **kilogram** 1,000 grams ‖ **kilometre** 1,000 metres

micro- /'maɪkrəʊ/ relating to very small things: **microcomputer** a very small computer

mid- /mɪd/ middle: **midpoint** a point at or near the centre or middle ‖ **midway** halfway or in a middle position

milli- /'mɪlị/ a thousandth of: **milligram** 1,000th (=0.001) of a gram ‖ **millimetre** 1,000th (=0.001) of a metre

mini- /'mɪni/ *infml* very small: **minibreak** a short holiday

mis- /mɪs/ **1** bad or wrong: **misspelling** a wrong spelling ‖ **misjudge** to have a wrong opinion of **2** the opposite of: **mistrust** to not trust someone or something

mono- /'mɒnəʊ, mɒnə ‖ mɑː-/ consisting of only one: **monorail** a railway with only one rail ‖ **monopoly** a situation where only one company or country produces or sells something

multi- /'mʌltʲ/ many: **multicoloured** having many colours ǀ **multistorey** (**carpark**) a CARPARK that has many levels

non- /nɒn ǁ nɑːn/ not: **nonstop** without stopping ǀ **nonpayment** when someone does not pay something

out- /aʊt/ **1** outside: **outdoors** outside homes or buildings **2** more than or beyond: **outgrow** to grow too big for something

over- /'əʊvəʳ/ **1** too much: **overexcited** too excited ǀ **overpopulation** when there are too many people in a country or place **2** across or above: **overland** across or by land ǀ **overhead** in the air above people's heads

post- /pəʊst/ after or later than: **postwar** belonging to the time after a war ǀ **postpone** to decide to do something at a later time

pre- /priː/ before: **prewar** before a war ǀ **preschool** relating to children who are too young to go to school

pro- /prəʊ/ in favour of: **pro-abortion** in favour of ABORTION –compare **anti**

psycho- /'saɪkəʊ/ relating to the mind: **psychology** the study of the mind and how this affects people's behaviour

re- /riː, rɪ/ again: **remake** to make something again, especially a film ǀ **rethink** to think about something again

self- /self/ of or by yourself: **self-control** the ability to control your feelings and emotions ǀ **self-employed**

working for yourself, not a company

semi- /'semɪ/ **1** partly: **semi-skilled** semi-skilled jobs do not need a lot of skill or training ǀ **semi-detached** a semi-detached house is partly joined to another house by one shared wall **2** half: **semicircle** half a circle

sub- /sʌb/ **1** under: **submarine** a ship that can travel under water **2** less important or powerful than another person or thing: **sublieutenant** a rank that is just below LIEUTENANT **3** a smaller part of: **subsection** a small part of a document or piece of writing

super- /'suːpəʳ, 'sjuː- ǁ 'suː/ much greater, bigger, or more than others of the same kind: **supertanker** a very large ship, used especially for carrying oil ǀ **superstar** a very famous and popular performer

trans- /træns, trænz/ **1** across or on the other side of an area of land or sea: **transatlantic** across, on the other side of, or concerning countries on both sides of the Atlantic **2** used in verbs that mean to change something: **transform** to change something completely

tri- /traɪ/ three: **triangle** a flat shape with three straight sides

ultra- /'ʌltrə/ **1** extremely: **ultramodern** very modern **2** beyond: **ultrasonic** ultrasonic sound waves are beyond the range of human hearing

un- /ʌn/ **1** (*makes adjectives and **adverbs***) not: **uncomfortable** not

comfortable ǀ **unhappy** not happy ǀ **unwashed** not washed **2** (*makes adverbs*) to remove or unfasten something: **undress** to take off your clothes ǀ **unlock** to unfasten a lock on something ǀ **untie** to undo a knot or something that has been tied

Word endings

-ability, -ibility /ə'bɪlʲti/ (*makes nouns from adjectives ending in* -able, -ible): **reliability** when someone or something is reliable (=able to be trusted or depended upon) ǀ **flexibility** when someone or something is flexible (=willing to change what they are doing, or easy to bend)

-able, -ible /əbəl/ **1** (*makes adjectives from verbs*) able to be ...ed: **washable** able to be washed ǀ **drinkable** that you can drink **2** having a particular quality: **knowledgeable** having a lot of knowledge ǀ **reasonable** based on reason

-al /əl/ *also* **-ial 1** (*makes adjectives from nouns*) relating to something: **political** relating to politics **2** (*makes nouns from verbs*) used to say that someone does something or something happens: **arrival** when someone or something arrives ǀ **refusal** when someone refuses to do something

-an /ən/ *also* **-ian** (*makes adjectives and nouns from names of places, people, or subjects*) relating to a particular place, person, or subject: **American** someone from America ǀ **Christian** someone who believes in the teachings of Jesus Christ | **historian** someone who studies or writes about history

-ation /eɪʃən/ (*makes nouns from verbs*) used to say that someone does something or something happens: **declaration** when someone declares that something is true | **hesitation** when someone hesitates | **exploration** when someone explores a place

-ator /eʊtər/ (*makes nouns from verbs*) a person or thing that does something: **narrator** a person who NARRATES (=tells a story) | **generator** a machine that GENERATES (=makes) energy, especially electricity

-cy /sɪ/ (*makes nouns from adjectives*) used in the names of qualities: **accuracy** the quality of being ACCURATE (=exact and correct) | **fluency** the quality of being FLUENT (=speaking a language perfectly)

-ed, -d /d, ɪd, t/ (*makes adjectives*) having a particular thing: **bearded** having a beard

-en /ən/ **1** (*makes adjectives*) made of: **golden** made of gold or looking like gold | **wooden** made of wood **2** (*makes verbs*) to become or make something become: **darken** to make or become dark: *The sky darkened after sunset.* | **soften** to make or become soft

-er¹, -r /ər/ (*makes the comparative of short adjectives and adverbs*) **hotter** more hot | **safer** more safe

-er², -ar, -or, -r /ər/ (*makes nouns*) **1** a person who does an activity: **footballer** a person

who plays football | **teacher** a person who teaches | **liar** a person who tells lies | **actor** a person who acts | **writer** a person who writes **2** a person who lives in a place: **Londoner** a person who lives in London | **villager** a person who lives in a village **3** a thing that does something: **cooker** a machine for cooking food | **heater** a machine for heating air, water, etc

-est, -st /ɪst/ (*makes the superlative of many short adjectives and adverbs*) **highest** higher than any others: **hottest** hotter than any others

-ette /et/ (*makes nouns*) used in words that mean a small kind of a particular thing: **kitchenette** a small kitchen

-ful¹ /fəl/ (*makes adjectives from nouns*) having a particular quality: **delightful** very pleasant | **painful** causing pain

-ful² /fʊl/ (*makes nouns*) the amount that a container holds: **cupful** the amount held by a cup | **spoonful** the amount held by a spoon

-ish /ɪʃ/ (*makes adjectives*) **1** relating to a country, its language, or its people: **British** from or about Britain | **Swedish** from or about Sweden **2** like or typical of: **childish** behaving like a child, in a way that seems silly and that you disapprove of **3** rather or slightly: **reddish** slightly red | **smallish** rather small **4** approximately: **fortyish** about forty | **sixish** at about 6 o'clock

-ism /izəm/ (*makes nouns*) **1** used in the names of political and religious beliefs or sets of ideas: **communism** | **socialism** | **Buddhism** a religion based on the teachings of the Buddha

-ist /ɪst/ **1** (*makes nouns and adjectives*) someone who supports a particular set of ideas or beliefs: **socialist** someone who supports the ideas of SOCIALISM **2** (*makes nouns*) someone who plays a particular musical instrument, who does a particular type of writing or study, or who does a particular type of work: **guitarist** someone who plays the guitar | **pianist** someone who plays the piano | **novelist** someone who writes NOVELS

-ity /ɪti/ *also* **-ty** (*makes nouns from adjectives*) used in the names of types of behaviour or qualities: **stupidity** stupid behaviour | **cruelty** cruel behaviour

-ive /ɪv/ (*makes adjectives from verbs*) used to say that someone or something does something or can do something: **creative** (good at) creating new ideas and things | **descriptive** describing something | **explosive** that can explode

-ize, -ise /aɪz/ (*makes verbs especially from adjectives*) to make something become, or to become: **popularize** to make something popular | **legalize** to make something legal USAGE Both **-ize** and **-ise** are used in British English, but only **-ize** is generally used in American English

-less /ləs/ (*makes adjectives*

from nouns) without: **hopeless** without hope | **painless** causing you no pain | **careless** done without taking care | **powerless** without power or strength

-let /lɪt/ used in words that mean a small kind of thing: **booklet** a small book, usually with paper covers | **piglet** a young pig

-like /laɪk/ (*makes adjectives*) like or typical of: **childlike** like or typical of a child

-ly /li/ **1** (*makes adverbs from adjectives*) in a particular way: **carefully** | **slowly** | **easily** **2** (*makes adjectives and adverbs*) happening regularly: **hourly** happening every hour | **daily** happening every day **3** (*makes adjectives*) behaving in a way that is typical of a particular kind of person: **motherly** | **brotherly**

-ment /mənt/ (*makes nouns from verbs*) used to talk about an activity or method of doing something: **development** when something develops | **bombardment** when people BOMBARD a place (=attack it with bombs and guns)

-most /məʊst/ (*makes the superlative of some adjectives and adverbs*) most: **topmost** nearest the top | **northernmost** furthest north

-ness /nəs/ (*makes nouns from adjectives*) used in the names of qualities: **goodness** the quality of being good | **loudness** the quality of being loud

-ology /ɒlədʒi/ (*makes nouns*) the science or study of: **geology** the study of the materials which make up the earth | **sociology** the scientific study of societies and human groups

-ous /əs/ (*makes adjectives from nouns*) having a particular quality: **dangerous** likely to harm or kill someone | **spacious** having a lot of space

-ship /ʃip/ (*makes nouns*) **1** used in words that mean a situation in which people, organizations etc have a particular kind of relationship or connection with each other: **friendship** a relationship between friends | **partnership** when two or more people, organizations etc are partners **2** used in words that mean a skill or ability to do something well: **workmanship** skill in making things | **musicianship** skill in performing or judging music

-th /θ/ (*makes adjectives from numbers, except for those ending in 1, 2, or 3*) used to talk about the order of something: **sixth** | **hundredth** | **fortieth**

-ward /wəd ‖ wərd/ *also -wards* /wədz ‖ wərdz/ (*makes adjectives and adverbs*) in a particular direction: **northwards** towards the north | **forward** towards a place that is in front of you

-ware /weər/ (*makes nouns*) used in the names of particular kinds of goods: **hardware** metal goods for the home and garden, such as pans, tools, etc | **ironware** goods made from iron

-y /i/ **1** (*makes adjectives from nouns*) covered in something, having a lot of something, or having a particular quality: **cloudy** | **noisy** | **dirty** **2** (*makes nouns*) used in the names of feelings or types of behaviour: **jealousy** | **sympathy** **3** (*makes nouns*) used in names for animals, especially by small children: **doggy** a dog

ANSWER KEY

Workbook Exercises

Exercise 1
1. actor
2. celebrate
3. hour
4. job
5. quick
6. world

Exercise 2
1. weight
2. where
3. which
4. white
5. wife
6. wrong

Exercise 3
1. camera
2. cycle
3. general
4. question
5. knife
6. physical

Exercise 4
1. abdicate
2. brutal
3. carnivore
4. disseminate
5. explicit
6. fantastic

Exercise 5
1. tyre
2. centre
3. travelled
4. millimetre
5. defence
6. catalogue
7. theatre
8. manoeuvre
9. honour

Exercise 6
1. adapt
2. amusing
3. baffle
4. banking
5. closing
6. convict

Exercise 7
1. come from
2. looking after
3. fill up
4. look out for
5. filled in
6. cut off

Exercise 8
a. 6
b. 5
c. 2
d. 3
e. 1
f. 4

Exercise 9
1. sundial
2. suntan
3. sunbathe, sunburn, sunscreen
4. sunlight
5. sunrise, sunset
6. sunlit

Exercise 10
1. aspirin
2. laughter
3. survey, instructions, orders
4. shoulder
5. songs and stories
6. If you drink too much coffee.

Exercise 11
1. 2
2. 9
3. 6
4. 4
5. 11
6. 1
7. 5
8. 7
9. 8
10. 3

Exercise 12
1. 2
2. 1
3. 2
4. 3
5. 1

Exercise 13
1. knives
2. sheep
3. teeth
4. men
5. children
6. feet

Exercise 14
go, went, gone, going
make, made, made, making
drive, drove, driven, driving
give, gave, given, giving
take, took, taken, taking
write, wrote, written, writing
teach, taught, taught, teaching

Exercise 15
1. clean^1 *adj*, clean^2 *v*, clean^3 *adv*
2. jump^1 *v*, jump^2 *n*
3. murder^1 *n*, murder^2 *v*
4. photograph^1 *n*, photograph^2 *v*
5. exercise^1 *n*, exercise^2 *v*
6. heat^1 *n*, heat^2 *v*

Exercise 16
1. C
2. U
3. U
4. U
5. U
6. C

Exercise 17
1. ✗
2. ✓
3. ✓
4. ✗
5. ✗
6. ✓

Exercise 18
1. commit
2. made
3. reach
4. took
5. having
6. strike

Exercise 19
1. affect
2. effects
3. a
4. an
5. notorious
6. famous
7. price
8. cost
9. electrical
10. electric

Exercise 20
1. aBOVE
2. proFUSE
3. BIcycle
4. comPARison
5. ecoNOMic
6. iMAGination

Exercise 21
1. inCREASE
2. INcrease
3. PERmit
4. perMIT

Exercise 22
1. arm
2. foot
3. head
4. hair
5. face
6. knee
7. leg
8. mouth
9. shoulder

Exercise 23
1. syllable: cheek, coin
2. syllables: children, chocolate
3. syllables: cinema, chemistry

Illustration exercises

1 Buildings

Exercise 1
1. balcony
2. patio
3. basement
4. attic
5. drain
6. chimney
7. fence
8. letterbox
9. garage
10. pavement
11. satellite dish
12. skyscraper

Exercise 2
Open answers

2 Classroom

Exercise 1
Open answers

Exercise 2
1. desk
2. blackboard
3. disk drive
4. pencil sharpener
5. whiteboard
6. printout
7. teacher
8. mouse

Exercise 3
1. pen
2. keyboard
3. chalk
4. marker
5. pencil

3 Clothes

head: cap, turban
chest: sweater, blouse, shirt, jacket, sweatshirt
feet: shoes, trainers, boots, socks
legs: trousers, jeans, skirt, leggings, tights
whole body: suit, sari, dress, coveralls, tracksuit
accessories: gloves, tie, bow tie, belt, scarf,

4 Colours and Patterns

Exercise 1
1. beige
2. grey
3. khaki
4. yellow
5. red
6. brown
7. black
8. blue

Exercise 2
1. e
2. a
3. b
4. c
5. d

Exercise 3
Open answers

5 Countryside

Exercise 1 (suggested responses)
pick up: pebble, sand, grass,
enter: waterfall, stream, beach, sea, wave, river, cottage, valley, forest
grow: hedge, grass, bush, forest
move: waterfall, stream, sea, wave, river
hear: waterfall, stream, beach, sea, wave, river
smell: stream, beach, sea, wave, grass, river, bush, forest

Exercise 2
Open answers

6 Describing People

Exercise 1
a. 4
b. 2
c. 7
d. 10
e. 8
f. 1
g. 6
h. 3
i. 5
j. 9

Exercise 2
Open answers

7 Feelings

1. embarrassed
2. angry
3. bored
4. furious
5. shy
6. surprised
7. worried
8. happy
9. tired
10. sad
11. frightened
12. confused

8 The Environment

Exercise 1

pollution ✗, solar panel ✓, bottle bank ✓,
recycled paper ✓, bicycle ✓, effluent ✗,
acid rain ✗, traffic jam ✗, exhaust fumes ✗,
public transport ✓, harmful gases ✗, wind
turbine ✓, litter ✗, global warming ✗

Exercise 2
1. acid rain
2. solar power
3. dropping litter
4. recycling
5. traffic congestion
6. global warming

9 Food – Verbs

Exercise 1
chop 7
pour 5
grate 4
slice 1
mash 8
spread 2
peel 6
squeeze 3

Exercise 2 (suggested responses)
chop: apple, potato, tomato
grate: apple, cheese, potato, tomato
mash: potato
peel: apple, potato, tomato
pour: milk, water
slice: apple, bread, cheese, potato, tomato
spread: cheese, jam
squeeze: apple, bread, cheese, tomato

10 Food – Pieces

Exercise 1
1. lumps
2. bar, squares
3. bunch
4. lump
5. chunk
6. crumbs
7. pinch
8. hunk, sliver
9. segment
10. slice

Exercise 2
1. bananas, grapes, oranges
2. cheese, butter
3. bread, biscuits, cake
4. ham, meat
5. sugar, chocolate

11 Verbs of Movement 1 – Hands

Exercise 1
1. flick
2. clap
3. knock
4. pinch
5. point

6. scratch
7. squeeze
8. stroke
9. shake
10. tickle

Exercise 2
knocked, holding, stroking, shook, waved,
pointed, scratched, squeeze

12 Prepositions

Exercise 1
1. in
2. in front of
3. below
4. against
5. on top of
6. outside
7. inside
8. under
9. between

Exercise 2
1. off
2. into
3. to/towards
4. down
5. into

13 Sounds

1. rustle
2. ringing
3. squeak
4. creaked
5. tick
6. crunch
7. fizz
8. click

14 Sports

Exercise 1
track and field, cycling, golf, horse-riding, ice
skating, skiing, snowboarding, swimming

Exercise 2
1. cricket
2. football/soccer
3. swimming
4. baseball
5. tennis

6. boxing
7. golf
8. basketball

Exercise 3
Open answers

15 Transport

Exercise 1
1. van, lorry/truck
2. bus
3. ship
4. lorry/truck
5. motorbike
6. helicopter
7. aeroplane/airplane
8. car
9. taxi/cab
10. train

Exercise 2
1. d
2. e
3. a
4. b
5. c

16 Verbs of Movement 2 – Body

1. jumped
2. catch
3. throw
4. hopped
5. kneel
6. stretch
7. drop
8. tiptoe
9. bend
10. holding
11. walked